Praise for *Men of War*

"Yet *another* set of old battle stories whipped together into a book by a writer-journalist, you say? Hardly. *Men of War* is a strikingly vivid, well-observed, and compulsively readable exploration of combat—of its sounds, smells, feel, of the explosive emotions it engenders, of its beauty and its terror—and a book that has a great deal of interesting things to say about the place of major battles, and the ordinary men (and, more lately, women) who fight them, in the collective American consciousness. . . . *Men of War* transports us to scores of frightful and desperate scenes of combat with shockingly evocative narrative reconstructions and penetrating, precise analysis. . . . *Men of War* is a *tour de force*."
—*The Daily Beast*

"Alexander Rose's *Men of War* is a worthy successor to *The Face of Battle*, telling the stories of three famous American battles that were fought in three very different technological eras. . . . Rose recounts the horror of Iwo Jima with gut-wrenching prose, offering up vivid scenes from the fighting. . . . This is indeed war up-close, as those who fought and lived it—and survived it if they could. *Men of War* is deeply researched, beautifully written. It is military history at its best."
—*The Wall Street Journal*

"The fact is that *Men of War* moves and educates, with the reader finding something interesting and intriguing on virtually every page."
—*National Review*

"A brilliant, riveting, unique book: *Men of War* does for the American soldier what *The Face of Battle* did for the British soldier. Using three iconic battles—Bunker Hill, Gettysburg, and Iwo Jima—Alexander Rose takes us into the ranks and helps us understand the experiences of those fighting on the ground. He captures vividly the emotions and

conditions of combat—the terror and the boredom, the barbarity and the magnanimity—helping readers understand the realities known to those who have earned membership in that most treasured of fraternities, the brotherhood of the close fight. *Men of War* will be a classic."
—GENERAL DAVID H. PETRAEUS, U.S. ARMY (RETIRED)

"A welcome perspective in an era where most people have no military experience to speak of." —*The Washington Times*

"Rose poignantly captures the terror and confusion of hand-to-hand combat during the battle, as well as the ghastly damage caused by large-caliber bullets and the primitive state of medical care."
—*The Dallas Morning News*

"History lovers and veterans of modern wars have here a book that does not glamorize conflict. Those new to military writing may be shocked. What separates *Men of War* from other works on these three battles is Rose's ability to mix extensive strategic and cultural knowledge of these wars with descriptive, often excruciating first-person accounts. Rose's expertise as a researcher and historian serves him well on this topic. Rose's most descriptive stories bring these distant conflicts into a vivid and painful reality on the page."
—*The Washington Free Beacon*

"A highly recommended addition to the literature of military history . . . Rose builds up a detailed picture of each of these battles, sparing few gritty details and romanticizing almost nothing. He writes vividly and memorably, with a good eye for the telling detail or anecdote as well as big-picture perspectives."
—*Kirkus Reviews* (starred review)

"Rose's grim, unadorned, yet immensely readable look at battle is a dose of what real war is like, and a good balance to the more common sanitized military fare." —*Publishers Weekly*

"*Men of War* is extraordinary for its research, vivid scenes, and penetrating insights. Required reading for all who face battle or are interested in what actually occurs in face-to-face fighting."

—BING WEST, author of *One Million Steps: A Marine Platoon at War*

"Honor, fear, cowardice, leadership, anxiety, compulsion, elation, doubt, misinformation, cruelty, violence, self-sacrifice, and compassion: this book covers everything in a brilliant analysis of the phenomenon of men in battle. Rose has written the best book on the subject since John Keegan's *The Face of Battle* four decades ago."

—ANDREW ROBERTS, author of *Napoleon: A Life* and *The Storm of War: A New History of the Second World War*

"On the model of John Keegan's *The Face of Battle*, Alexander Rose has applied the same technique of description and analysis to three iconic battles in American history. The overwhelming experience of combat for frontline soldiers who lived to write about it, and through their eyes those who did not, comes through with stark realism. If you want to know the meaning of war at the sharp end, this is the book to read."

—JAMES McPHERSON, author of *The War That Forged a Nation: Why the Civil War Still Matters*

"An American sequel to *The Face of Battle*. Like Keegan, Alexander Rose tells us about war from the perspective of those who fought it, capturing a myriad of combat details to weave a gripping tapestry of three of the most iconic battles in U.S. history—Bunker Hill, Gettysburg, and Iwo Jima."

—ROBERT L. O'CONNELL, author of *Fierce Patriot: The Tangled Lives of William Tecumseh Sherman*

MEN OF WAR

The American Soldier

in Combat at Bunker Hill,

Gettysburg, and Iwo Jima

MEN
OF
WAR

ALEXANDER ROSE

RANDOM HOUSE

NEW YORK

2016 Random House Trade Paperback Edition

Copyright © 2015 by Rosewriter, Inc.
Maps copyright © 2015 by David Lindroth, Inc.

Published in the United States by Random House, an imprint and division of
Penguin Random House LLC, New York.

RANDOM HOUSE and the HOUSE colophon are registered trademarks of
Penguin Random House LLC.

Originally published in hardcover in the United States by Random House,
an imprint and division of Penguin Random House LLC, in 2015.

LIBRARY OF CONGRESS CATALOGING-IN-PUBLICATION DATA
Rose, Alexander
Men of war: the American soldier in combat at Bunker Hill,
Gettysburg, and Iwo Jima. / by Alexander Rose.
Pages cm.
Includes bibliographical references and index.
ISBN 978-0-553-38439-0—ISBN 978-0-8129-9686-9 (eBook)
1. Battles—United States. 2. Combat—Psychological aspects—History.
3. Soldiers—United States—History. 4. United States—
History, Military—Case studies. I. Title.
E181.R77 2015
355.00973—dc23
2014030958

Printed in the United States of America on acid-free paper

randomhousebooks.com

2 4 6 8 9 7 5 3 1

Title page image: © iStock.com / LifeJourneys
Bunker Hill image: © iStock.com / Duncan Walker
Gettysburg image: © iStock.com / Constance McGuire
Iwo Jima photo by Lt. James T. Dockery, 4TH MAR. DIV.

*To Rebecca, without whom this book could not
have been written, and to Edmund (aged five),
without whom it might have been written faster.*

Contents

MEN OF WAR

Introduction

"The Lord is a man of war."
—Exodus 15:3

A single question lies at the heart of this book: What's it like being in a battle?

It's one I've been asking myself since I was an undergraduate, when I discovered, in the university bookstore, a copy of John Keegan's *The Face of Battle,* a book published just a few years after I was born. I still have it, nearly a quarter of a century later. Cheaply bound and badly printed, the old paperback sits on a shelf in my study, but such are the times that I now also own a digital version that is duplicated on a variety of electronic devices as well as a Folio Society limited edition. I can legitimately say that, as priests and Puritans once did their Bibles, I carry my Keegan with me everywhere.

To those unfamiliar with *The Face of Battle,* let me explain. Keegan, who died in 2012, investigated the experience of the common British soldier—what he felt, heard, and saw—in three epic battles: Agincourt in 1415, Waterloo in 1815, and the Somme in 1916. Keegan also discussed the mechanics of fighting—for instance, the means by which King Henry V's longbowmen demolished the French cavalry—as well as the historiography of warfare (how we write about battles over time). His book can justly lay claim to being one of the finest works of history, military or otherwise, of the twentieth century.

Keegan was an inspiration to me as a historian, and *The Face of Battle* is the inspiration for this book. While Keegan restricted himself to English/British battles, I found that there was no American version based on American battles fought by American soldiers.

Writing one was easier said than done. The great majority of military books focus not on the combat experience of the regular soldier but on history from the bird's-eye perspective.[1] Popular historians still tend to accord top billing to what quaintly used to be called the Great Captains—the Caesars, the Pattons, the Lees and Grants, the Hannibals of history. Napoleon, like many an Immortal a monster of conceit, himself believed that "it was not the Roman army which conquered Gaul, but Caesar; it was not the Carthaginian army which, at the gates of Rome, made the Eternal City tremble, but Hannibal; it was not the Macedonian army which marched as far as the Indus, but Alexander."[2] To which he did not feel the need to add, it was not the million men of the *Grande Armée* that shook Europe, but myself.

Consequently, innumerable volumes have been written about the generalship of various commanders, their leadership skills, and how they won (or lost) their battles at the operational level, but relatively few about the lowly soldiers who served under them. Bertolt Brecht, the German playwright, alluded to this curious blind spot when he asked—*contra* Napoleon:

> The young Alexander conquered India.
> Was he alone?
> Caesar beat the Gauls.
> Did he not have even a cook with him?
> Philip of Spain wept when his armada
> Went down. Was he the only one to weep?
> Frederick [the Great] won the Seven Years' War. Who
> Else won it?[3]

To be sure, commanders are important in their own right, but I was more intrigued by the overlooked and the ordinary, the men whose names are catalogued in muster rolls and inscribed on gravestones, the men who are otherwise forgotten. We know what the general on his horse thought, but what of the corporal and private at the sharp end?

What was combat like for them? I was certainly not the first to wonder. As Tolstoy once put it, "War always interested me: not war in the sense of maneuvers devised by great generals—my imagination refused to follow such immense movements, I did not understand them—but the reality of war, the actual killing."[4]

Unlike that Russian novelist, who served in the artillery during the Crimean War, I could not seek answers within the realm of my own experience. I have never heard a shot fired in anger. Like Keegan, I am not a "flesh-witness" to war.

Instead, I—following Keegan's lead—exploited my status as an impartial observer to listen to, read about, and report on what veterans thought, felt, and did. There is a surprisingly large trove of raw information available if one, say, excavates the now-forgotten volumes of regimental histories published after the Civil War. These books were written by soldiers for soldiers and in them they speak with surprising frankness of their shared experiences. Then there is the Niagara of letters, memoirs, diaries, interviews, and newspaper accounts of various soldiers over the centuries; these often contain the unvarnished sentiments of vanished ages.

Selecting three properly representative battles from the legions of firsthand sources available was critical. So allow me to explain the thinking behind my decisions to include Bunker Hill in 1775, Gettysburg in 1863, and Iwo Jima in 1945. First, this trio is not supposed to represent necessarily the most *important* clashes; none of them, for example, were, to use a dated Victorian expression, "decisive battles."[5] Instead, I settled on finding the most *iconic* battles in American history, the major battles that everyone has heard of. Even so, of course, some readers may query my choices. Why Iwo Jima, for example, and not the Battle of the Bulge? To which I can only reply, well, I thought the European theater has already been treated more comprehensively than its Pacific counterpart. That's really all there was to it. All right, then, if that's the case and we restrict ourselves to the Pacific, why Iwo and not Okinawa or Peleliu? In this instance, I would argue that I am interested in a *typical* soldier's *typical* combat experience, not the details of a particular person's response to a specific battle. In other words, the experiences of a Marine at Iwo Jima are generally applicable to, or illustrative of, those of comrades fighting on other islands. In some respects, the battles, I guess you could say, don't matter that much. I felt that Bunker Hill, Gettysburg, and Iwo Jima presented fascinating case studies of combat up close, and the fact that copious primary and secondary resources were available for each clash was an additional, and most valuable, advantage.

Certainly, a few other factors swung the final decisions one way or another. For instance, I weighted the scale in favor of actions that involved American troops within a limited area in order to exclude the additional complications engendered by the presence of allies and the sister arms of land forces. Thus, Yorktown in 1783 was rejected owing to the significant contribution of the French navy to victory over the British. This is not to diminish French valor or to bang the jingoistic drum, but *Men of War* is a book about *American* soldiers. From this perspective, then, Bunker Hill seems more optimal: It took place on a small peninsula, lasted less than a day, and involved only American militiamen and British regulars; furthermore, naval participation was peripheral. Additionally, I attempt to remain as close to the killing ground as possible. Hence, for Gettysburg I devote little space to the cavalry actions since the overwhelming brunt of combat fell on the poor bloody infantry, and in the Iwo Jima chapter you will look in vain for material on airpower, important as it was.

You may notice, as well, that by starting with the Revolutionary War and jumping to the Civil War and thence to World War II, I've omitted several rather major conflicts: the War of 1812, for example, and World War I. But this is neither an exhaustive history of American warfare nor a general overview of U.S. military history. *Men of War* is instead a collection of snapshots of American soldiers in combat, one that draws hard distinctions and highlights continuities between the evolving forms and varieties of fighting over time.

So this is, you might have gathered, an unconventional book. It is a book about battles that is not about battles. As I am concerned almost exclusively with the combat experience of soldiers, I allocate only the minimum time necessary to discussing the *course* of the battles I've chosen. I have instead included summaries of what happened and other pertinent details at the beginning of each chapter so that you can follow the action, but my focus is on what the soldiers went through. For precisely the same reason, I devote much more space to wounds, their treatment, and the psychological effects of combat than on strategy, logistics, and politics.

The battles are distinct, and each chapter has a particular structure and essential theme. That of Bunker Hill takes perhaps the most traditional approach, but its intention is more radical: It argues that, notwithstanding the zealous attempts of historians to impose an orderly interpretation on the course of Bunker Hill (dividing it into phases, stages, and so forth), this is an intellectual artifice that would be wholly unintelligible to the actual participants. There is, in other words, no single authoritative sequence of events or narrative for the battle. Even for so seemingly basic a fact as the location of many units, there are multiple possibilities.

Bunker Hill is not unique in that respect: Combat, in any battle, is inherently chaotic, and most of the time the soldiers fighting on the ground have little or no idea what is happening even fifty yards away. On Iwo Jima, to take one example, very few Marines knew what time it was, let alone the day or where they were. (Many of their watches had broken by the fourth or fifth day, and the lack of sleep confused them still further.) To take another, at Gettysburg, the ambit of one's knowledge of the battlefield extended to the men on either side, a few ahead of you, the color-bearer, and, if you were lucky, the officer on his horse behind. No one knew what was going on, and much of the time battles are decided not by clever war games or brilliant generalship but by accident, initiative, chance, and such other intangibles as morale, background, culture, ideology, and experience.

For the Gettysburg section, my intention was to reconstruct for modern readers how a Civil War infantry action worked—the ways in which the defenders and the attackers acted and felt during a typical episode. How was a charge organized? What was the best way to defeat an assault? Why did officers wear swords and soldiers wield bayonets when they inflicted hardly any casualties? How did men withstand a preliminary artillery bombardment? What did the first few minutes of a fight feel like?

To most of us, upon learning the mechanics and ethos of nineteenth-century infantry tactics, they seem quite bizarre, even rather stupid. Why did soldiers line up, advance shoulder-to-shoulder toward the enemy, and then tolerate their own slaughter? It makes no *sense*. The chapter argues that while combat on the personal level is chaotic, in fact there is a logic, grammar, and vocabulary to it that shifts over time. In the case of the Civil War, massing troops together and using their combined momentum to advance was the key to victory, not a cause of failure. To that end, the defenders would try to atomize the attacking force into its component parts and thus retard its momentum. Today, in contrast, soldiers keep their distance from each other and move forward as they think fit.

Neither should we omit the nineteenth century's emphasis on *enduring* casualties to achieve battlefield objectives. Casualty aversion, in other words, is a more modern yardstick of effectiveness, often wrongly retrofitted to past eras. Indeed, a willingness to suffer, rather than inflict, high casualties was, at that time, considered evidence of a proudly masculine and divinely suffused will to win, not a worrying signal of lunacy or incompetence. Central, then, to the Gettysburg chapter is the principle that there exists no "universal soldier," in the sense that the internal motivations and beliefs—and the external culture enveloping them—of a past generation of soldiers are not necessarily applicable to a future one.[6] That is, a warrior of ancient Greece will have a profoundly different worldview, outlook, or mentality from one of the American Civil War. Military affairs and organizations are not, therefore, static and unchanging but typified instead by diversity, variety, and evolution (hopefully forward, but sometimes backward; often random, but occasionally punctuated). Battles, it should be obvious, need to be examined in their rightful context, and their participants, too, in order to understand why and how they fought, as well as to grasp what they experienced.

As for Iwo Jima, this chapter demonstrates the ways in which soldiers learn through combat how both to survive and to become more lethal as they intersect with the enemy, who also adapts his behavior in response. The conduct of warfare, then, is always dynamic, even—perhaps especially—at the level of the private soldier. This section of the book is structured in such a way as to delineate the kind of learning curves that any army must climb to reach maximum productivity and effectiveness, the awful irony being that acquiring such knowledge entails, as the poet Auden averred, the "necessary murder" of friendly troops—the very ones who would most profit from that knowledge. This is the true pity, and tragedy, of war, which is why a good number of military historians and professional soldiers tend to be more cautious and pacific than one might perhaps expect.

It is fitting that Iwo took place at the end of a long war, by which time Americans had gained bitter experience of the Japanese and had developed new techniques to combat them, whereas Gettysburg occurs at the Civil War's midpoint and Bunker Hill at the very outset of the War of Independence. At Bunker Hill, the Americans relied on their own older, culturally specific methods; at Gettysburg, Union and Confederate forces alike employed the same contemporary tactics; but at Iwo, U.S. Marines forged new ways to defeat the defenders, even in the midst of battle.

Their willingness to adapt to circumstances so rapidly was governed by practicality: Marines found that their traditional countermeasures against the Japanese did not work on Iwo owing to the singular nature of the island's geography and their discovery that the Japanese had updated their own defensive tactics. For that matter, American perceptions of the Japanese soldier's fighting abilities had also shifted drastically since Pearl Harbor. It would have been a very foolish Marine who landed on the beach still believing that the Japanese were a verminous race of miniature, bespectacled cowards, as contemporary racist propaganda suggested. In short, despite modern assertions to the contrary, American (and Japanese) racism played little role in how the battle of Iwo Jima was fought. Culture, in this case, came a very distant second to common sense. Marines quickly learned to treat combat as a job, admittedly foul, but one that had to be executed with grim efficiency. There was nothing romantic or cinematic about their task, no glorious uniforms or glittering medals, but instead there prevailed merely the imperative to process live humans into dead ones. Yet, so affected are we by Joe Rosenthal's emotionally evocative photograph of the Marines raising the American flag atop Mount Suribachi that we tend to overlook the industrialized nature of this Pacific battle and the toll it exacted.

Terrible as it may be, it seems war has its attractions. That flag fluttering high above Iwo marks a proud patriotic achievement, and there must, after all, be other reasons for war's historically universal presence and continuing global popularity. Notwithstanding the philosophical and abstract objections to the contrary, for a significant proportion of the young, war can be fantastic fun, at least in the beginning and before disillusionment sets in. It was George Washington, fresh from his first firefight during the French and Indian War, who excitedly related to his brother that "I heard the bullets whistle, and, believe me, there is something charming in the sound."[7] (Upon hearing of this upstart's braggadocio, King George II, a more bloodied old warhorse, wryly commented, "He would not say so, if he had been used to hear many.")[8]

Quite apart from the whiff of danger acting as a stimulant, combat can be narcotically attractive in other ways. For those away from home for the first time, war is a unique chance to see exotic, astonishing, and extraordinary things beyond imagination. Not only can the sight of fine uniforms, dressed lines, and blades glinting in the sun be beautiful, the titanic destructiveness of weaponry is also spectacular.[9] Participants can easily lose themselves in the enthralling majesty of it all. General John Burgoyne, who watched the battle of Bunker Hill from Boston, rapturously captured the sensory bounty unveiled before him in a letter to his nephew:

And now ensued one of the greatest scenes of war that can be conceived; if we look to the height, Howe's corps, ascending the hill in the face of entrenchments, and in a very disadvantageous ground, was much engaged; to the left the enemy pouring in fresh troops by the thousands, over the land; and in the arm of the sea our ships and floating batteries cannonading them; straight before us a large

and noble town in one great blaze—the church steeples, being timber, were great pyramids of fire above the rest; . . . The roar of cannon, mortars and musketry; the crash of churches, ships upon
stocks, and whole streets falling together, to fill the ear; the storm
of the redoubts, with the objects above described, to fill the eye;
and the reflection that, perhaps, a defeat was a final loss to the British Empire in America, to fill the mind.[10]

War, then, is vile, but experiencing combat is not necessarily all to
the bad—even if we may not envy those given (voluntarily or not) the
opportunity to fight—for no other activity allows individuals to sample
the extremes of what it means to be human. Combat encompasses un-
adulterated terror and grinding boredom, unstinting comradeship and
man being wolf to man, callous randomness and coolly calculated risk,
barbarism and unexpected virtue.

If we can take anything from this book, it would be that there is not
one "Face of Battle" but many, and therein lies the root of my, and
perhaps your, fascination with the experience of combat.

BUNKER HILL
1775

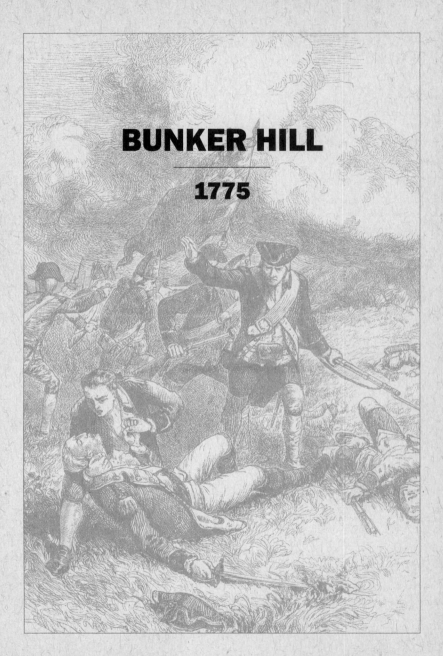

1. Introduction

The most curious thing about Bunker Hill is that, despite its iconic status in American history, it was in some respects quite a minor affair. Anywhere between 1,500 and 3,500 American militiamen—their strength varied over the course of the day, as men left and reinforcements arrived—fought roughly 2,400 to 3,000 British soldiers over the course of a few hours one pleasant afternoon on June 17, 1775, on a small peninsula across from Boston. By way of contrast, a more typical conflict of the era was the War of the Bavarian Succession between Austria and Prussia. In 1778—contemporaneous with the struggle in the American colonies—Prussia, the least populous and the poorest of the European powers, fielded no fewer than 160,000 troops.[1]

Yet these dry statistics belie Bunker Hill's consequence. As the *Annual Register* would briskly conclude near the end of the Revolution, "Most of these actions would in other wars be considered but as skirmishes of little account [though] it is by such skirmishes that the fate of America must be necessarily decided. They are therefore as important as battles in which an hundred thousand men are drawn up on each side."[2]

To its participants the battle certainly did not feel like a "skirmish": Bunker Hill holds the wretched distinction of being the bloodiest clash of the War of Independence. "I can only say from the oldest soldiers here," wrote the newly arrived Lieutenant William Feilding, "that it was the hottest fire they ever saw."[3] By day's end, almost half the British troops engaged would be dead or wounded. "Tho' Masters of the Field of Battle," one contemporary grimly judged, "the King's Troops are much the greatest Sufferers."[4] Another determined that the British army could now be divided into three: "The first company is under ground; the second is above ground; the third is in the hospital."[5] American losses were relatively small.

Before Bunker Hill, few believed that part-time militiamen could stand, face, and fight a professional army. Yet they did, and by acquitting themselves so magnificently demonstrated that the American cause was a viable and worthy enterprise. Which means we must ask: Who were they? How did they do it? And what was it like to fight at Bunker Hill?

2. The Battle

First, a summary of what happened. Late at night on June 16, 1775, a detachment of American militiamen commanded by General Israel Putnam sneakily took possession of Bunker Hill, a modest rise on the Charlestown peninsula. This triangular piece of land was attached to the Massachusetts mainland by a narrow strip called Charlestown Neck, and it jutted out between the Mystic and Charles Rivers to face Boston, where the British were holed up. Early the next morning, the British realized that these Americans were so close to Boston that they could bombard the city with cannon, but far worse, that Colonel William Prescott's men were now building an earthen "Redoubt" (a type of small fort) atop *Breed's* Hill, which was nearer even than Bunker. Once their work was done, the Americans would be so securely ensconced that it would be exceedingly difficult to dislodge them. Accordingly, British troops under General Sir William Howe were transported across the bay to the peninsula, where they prepared to assault the enemy before time ran out. Additionally, after the Americans had been put to the sword, Howe intended to advance on Cambridge, where the main American forces under General Artemas Ward were stationed. If all went well, the rebellion would be over by close of play, either that day or the next.

Meanwhile, fresh American militia units under Colonel John Stark had arrived to support Prescott, now grievously exposed at Breed's Hill. Instead of reinforcing him directly, however, they marched to *Bunker*

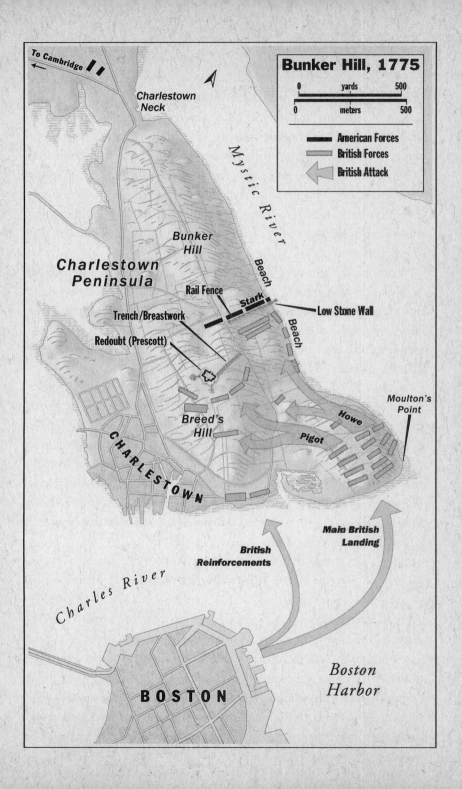

Bunker Hill, 1775

| 0 | yards | 500 |
| 0 | meters | 500 |

American Forces
British Forces
British Attack

To Cambridge

Charlestown Neck

Mystic River

Bunker Hill

Charlestown Peninsula

Rail Fence

Beach

Stark

Low Stone Wall

Trench/Breastwork

Beach

Redoubt (Prescott)

Moulton's Point

Breed's Hill

Howe

CHARLESTOWN

Pigot

Main British Landing

British Reinforcements

Charles River

Boston Harbor

BOSTON

Hill, which guarded the vulnerable Neck against a British attack from the rear. At the foot of Bunker Hill they hurriedly assembled a long defensive structure termed the "Rail Fence," which faced the spot where the British were assembling in preparation for the imminent clash. On the "Beach" directly below and perpendicular to his position, Stark built a low stone wall to prevent a surprise flank attack. Despite these precautions, Prescott had by this time realized the danger he was in and ordered his men to dig a trench, or breastwork, extending from the redoubt's walls to cover a weak spot between his position and that of Stark.

The British were now confronted by firmly entrenched defenders, making nonsense of their original plan. Even so, come what may, the Americans had to be destroyed. Howe divided his force into two divisions, the right under him, the left under Robert Pigot. Howe would attack the rail fence and the beach while Pigot assaulted Prescott's redoubt at Breed's Hill.

Following a series of bloody attacks, Howe's wing stalled but Pigot's managed to break through Prescott's defenses. A vicious bout of hand-to-hand combat sent the militiamen fleeing for the safety of Bunker Hill. Their positions lost, the Americans retreated across the Neck and set up defensive positions on the mainland. Some of the British gamely tried to pursue the enemy, but physical exhaustion and the sheer scale of Howe's losses convinced him to halt for the night. The battle of Bunker Hill was over, but the War of Independence had only just begun.

3. The Redoubt, Part One

The militiamen came garbed for battle as they did for work—as farmers and artisans.[1] Some even had on the same leather aprons they wore in their shops.[2] For the most part, the New England militia units reflected their respectable rural environments. In Captain Hutchins's company, two-thirds listed their occupations as "husbandmen"—that is, farmers—with most of the rest making a decent living as carpenters, cobblers, tailors, millers, and the like.[3] Many outfits also had within their ranks former slaves, maybe a couple of itinerants, the odd Native American perhaps, but the militiamen who fought at Bunker Hill for the most part owned property of some sort—an average-sized farm, say—and most of those who did not were the sons of men who did.

Many wore homespun shirts, sometimes made of canvas but of linen or flax in the summer, that were "a kind of loose frock, reaching half way down the thighs, with large sleeves, open before, and so wide as to lap over a foot or more when belted."[4] Their gaiters or stockings were tanned a dead-leaf color in vats, and their feet were clad in "cowhide shoes ornamented by large buckles, while not a pair of boots graced the company," as one octogenarian recollected decades later. Many had on weatherbeaten broad-brimmed hats often turned up on three sides to form a sloppy tricorne, sometimes complemented by a sprig of green or a homemade cockade; around their necks they tied an off-colored neckerchief or stock.[5]

It was hard, perhaps impossible, to distinguish the men sartorially from their officers—a profound difference to European military custom. Of the ten richest men in Lexington, for example, no fewer than eight were content to sign on as privates, and they dressed accordingly; rare indeed was the officer who took pains to get "above himself" and stand out from the crowd.

Typical was Experience Storrs of Mansfield, Connecticut, a prosperous farmer "portly in figure" who, when not tending his sick wife ("troubled with Histeruk Colluk Pains"), hewed wood, attended church, cleaned drains, worried about his colds, and mended stone walls—all while serving as his regiment's lieutenant colonel (an almost regal rank far beyond a man of Storrs's socioeconomic background in Europe). In March 1775 he agreed, with his friends Colonel Jedediah Elderkin and Major Thomas Brown, "to dress in a plain manner."[6] Similarly, at the redoubt Colonel Prescott wore a simple linen coat: British soldiers were later convinced that their foe was commanded by a "farmer dressed in his frock."[7] Even starchy Colonel John Stark, a man "always mindful of his rank," as his biographer had it, was "never a stickler for dress," restricting the peacockery to a waistcoat and some kind of "insignia."[8]

If the militiamen's outfits added up to a drab uniformity, their assortment of weapons was motley, to say the least. One veteran of the battle remembered, "Here an old soldier carried a heavy Queen's arm, with which he had done service at the conquest of Canada twenty years previous, while by his side walked a stripling boy, with a Spanish fuzee not half its weight or calibre, which his grandfather may have taken at the Havana [1762], while not a few had old French pieces, that dated back to the reduction of Louisburg [1758]."[9] Ezekiel Worthen of Kensington, New Hampshire, shouldered a French musket, made in 1752, that had been taken from the enemy, taken again by Indians, and retaken by Worthen during a skirmish. He also brought along a newer accessory: a cartridge box engraved with "Liberty or Death."[10] (Some weapons were newer acquisitions: Nathaniel Rice of East Sudbury proudly carried "a musket I took from the British at Concord.")[11]

The antiquity of most of the militiamen's pieces should not obscure their lethality. These were working, effective firearms. In an era when guns were expensive and manufacturing them was a painstaking business, it was common for even regular soldiers to use hand-me-downs. The British, for instance, were using Brown Bess muskets—still perfectly serviceable—purchased as far back as 1730.[12] By that standard, the Americans' arms, most of which dated from the French and Indian War, were relatively new and almost certainly better maintained.

Virtually every man at Bunker Hill brought his own firearm. Ascertaining exact figures for gun ownership in 1775 is extremely difficult. However, an analysis of the returns of thirty New England militia companies finds that the overall rate of private ownership was at least 75 percent and probably much higher. A keen company commander, such as Timothy Pickering of Salem, Massachusetts, ensured that 100 percent of his men were armed. Likewise, at the end of May 1775 all of the 509 men in Colonel Moses Little's Ipswich, Massachusetts, regiment were, boasted a Provincial Congress report, "armed with good effective firelocks." Meanwhile, "only" two-thirds of the fishermen from maritime Cape Cod owned their own weapons, no doubt because there was less call for them in their line of work.[13] Ultimately, those who fought at Bunker Hill would either bring their own musket, use ones illicitly stockpiled by their local militias, or, in a pinch, borrow them from stay-at-home neighbors.[14]

Like Colonel Abijah Pierce, who touted a fearsome walking cane at Lexington, the militias also lugged along a formidable, if ragged, collection of hand and edged weapons.[15] Many were repurposed from agricultural uses: At least one man was seen bearing a grain flail, numerous others with pitchforks, and a few with shillelaghs (wooden cudgels or clubs).[16]

Some armed themselves more traditionally. Cutlasses—short, machete-like hacking swords—could be wielded handily by beginners. Before he left for Boston, Israel Litchfield took the precaution of buying one, despite his complete lack of training.[17] During the battle his compatriot Israel Potter thought himself fortunate to be armed so: "Although without an edge and much rust-eaten, I found [the cutlass] of infinite more service to me than my musket" when a British officer swiped at his head with a sword. "With one well-directed stroke I deprived him of the power of very soon again measuring swords with 'a Yankee rebel.'"[18]

Nearly every American sword "had been made by our Province blacksmiths, perhaps from some farming utensil; they looked serviceable, but heavy and uncouth," remembered one veteran.[19] The country metalworkers had tried their best, but in style these weapons looked decidedly dated, as if they had been excavated from some century-old time capsule buried during the English Civil War (1642–1651). Aside from the cutlasses, American swords tended to be simple-hilted straight rapiers for thrusting.[20] For their part, recent immigrants fighting alongside the colonials tended to wield weapons from the Old Country: On the night before Bunker Hill the militant cleric John Martin girded himself with his trusty "Irish long sword," with which he soon slew one unfortunate Briton "by letting out his bowels" and another "by a stroke on the neck."[21]

What the Americans lacked and the British enjoyed in abundance were bayonets, but this would not prove a critical omission. While Captain Henry Dearborn alleged that among all the Americans there were only fifty bayonets available—and in his company just one—

bayonets were in fact rarely used in combat, their effect being primarily psychological rather than practical.[22] The bayonet, it was thought, made soldiers *feel* more aggressive when assaulting an already nervous enemy, who was liable to panic and run before a well-officered attack actually connected. But if the two sides came to blows at close quarters, a grain flail, cutlass, or pitchfork was almost certainly as dangerous as a bayonet, and probably more so. At Bunker Hill, it was only near the end, by which time the redoubt's defenders had been severely weakened by casualties and were out of ammunition, that bayonets—wielded by reinvigorated and reinforced British troops surging forward—helped to provoke flight.

For now, though—the night of June 16—the militiamen were bearing shovels, axes, and any other tools they could scrounge that could be used for entrenching.[23] Said fourteen-year-old Isaac Glynney, who was substituting for his sick father on militia duty, "I was firnishd with A Shuvel & orderd to March[.] I was Marchd on to Bunker hill [and] here I was Orderd to go to Useing [the shovel] to throw up A Brest work."[24]

Like many other participants, Glynney got Bunker and Breed's Hills confused. It was at Breed's Hill—a rise closer to Boston—that Glynney and the rest of Colonel Prescott's detachment stacked their muskets and began digging sometime between 11 P.M. and midnight. Accompanying them was Colonel Richard Gridley, a military engineer whose experience extended back to even before the French and Indian War.[25]

Gridley staked out an outline of what was to be called the "redoubt." This small fort was roughly 132 feet square, or rather, slightly rectangular, oriented northeastward.[26] Because Prescott insisted that the redoubt's walls be as complete and as high as possible, each man was detailed to labor for a one-hour shift, then to stand on watch for the next to rest, alternating through the night.[27] Gridley and Prescott both knew that when the British began shelling their position, the men, if they weren't protected, would break. The colonels agreed on six-foot-high earthen walls with a wooden and dirt platform running along the inner perimeter for the militiamen to stand on. Then, only their heads (and muskets) would be visible from outside.[28] Given the time constraints, it is unlikely that the walls to the rear were as lofty or as sturdy as those in front, but they would nevertheless afford a measure of protection. A break in the rear wall would serve as a passage for reinforcements and supplies—or a retreat.

The existing literature on the battle pays no attention to the design of this fort atop Breed's Hill, a consequence of assuming that Gridley improvised the fortifications and that they were nothing more than a few dirt walls, hastily dug. That the fort was quickly constructed—and left unfinished—is certainly true, but haste should not obscure the degree of knowledge and skill that Gridley applied to the task. Prescott's fort was in fact a scaled-down version of a European-style fortification. Indeed, at the time the name "redoubt" had a specific meaning: "a detached work, enclosed on all sides."[29] It was no ordinary rectangle, either, for as contemporary maps highlight, from the center of its southeastern wall (known as the *enceinte*, or main perimeter) jutted, prow-like, a hybrid of a ravelin and a bastion. Technically speaking, ravelins—a triangular structure described by the Marquis de Vauban (1633–1707), the French master of the lethal geometry of fortifications whose works were undoubtedly familiar to Gridley, as "beyond all doubt the best and most excellent of all outworks"—were freestanding, while bastions were four-sided edifices (two angled faces with two flanks) that looked like sharpened, angular spearheads and were attached to a wall.[30]

Ravelins and bastions enabled the defenders of a fortress to fire backward to either side to thwart attacks on the main wall while promoting greater depth of defense. Gridley's dirt-and-wood redoubt would not hold out for long against a concentrated artillery barrage or a sustained siege, but we should remember that he had had but a night to build it, that it was intended as a temporary defense, and above all that, thanks to its ravelin/bastion protrusion, inner platform, and good sightlines, it presented a formidable obstacle to British assaults.[31]

It would not be the only one. Later in the morning, Prescott would realize that he had left his northern, Mystic River–facing flank exposed, and so directed his men to dig a sixty-foot-long, four-foot-wide trench with a rudimentary breastwork made out of the excavated dirt. Connected to the redoubt, the breastwork was not much, but it would have to do.[32]

At about 4 A.M., when a lookout awoke him with news that the Americans seemed to be building a fort on the peninsula, Captain Thomas Bishop of HMS *Lively,* a twenty-gun sloop patrolling the bay, wasted no time beating to quarters and opening fire on the redoubt.[33] His guns soon began to take their toll, psychologically as well as physically.

No other class of weaponry inspired as much trepidation and fear in infantry as artillery. "A young soldier is much more alarmed at a nine-pounder shot passing within four yards of his head than he is of a bullet at a distance of as many inches," the British officer George Hennell later observed, "although one would settle him as effectively as the other."[34] Understandably so, for the feeling of powerlessness that came of being under fire from afar was then and still is among soldiering's greatest terrors. "The standing to be cannonaded, and having nothing else to do, is about the most unpleasant thing that can happen to soldiers in an engagement," said one veteran.[35] "To be exposed to fire without being able to return it," wrote another, was like "receiving a personal insult, and not having the power to resent it."[36] Unlike frontier fighting or close-quarters combat, where one's judgment, experience, and initiative could reduce the physical dangers, artillery fire rendered all such virtues irrelevant. A cannonball knew no distinction between veterans and rookies, but killed seemingly indiscriminately, randomly, instantly.

The good news was that once they accepted that their lives were in the hands of blind Fate, divine Providence, or dumb Luck (and had survived intact a fusillade or two), most soldiers tamed their instinct to panic. At Bunker Hill, Captain John Chester said, only his "new recruits" were "terribly frightened" by the cannon shot "buzz[ing] around us like hail."[37] In these moments, to calm their fears, officers made sure to inform them that relatively few fatalities were actually caused by cannon fire. "It frightens more than it hurts," as one French marshal used to assure his understandably skeptical troops.[38]

He was right, up to a point: In the eighteenth century, artillery accounted for just over 20 percent of all casualties.[39] A great deal, however, hinged upon whether the incoming fire was concentrated and
aimed—which was more lethal—or merely an occasional barrage—
which was much less so, owing to its random distribution.[40] Whether
the defending troops were formed up in the open or scattered around
under cover also made a great difference. At Bunker Hill in both cases,
the latter form at this stage was typical, leading to relatively low American casualties.

Those who grasped the principle that a cannon's bark was worse
than its bite often proceeded on their merry way, even as shells fell
around them. Dr. James Thacher later saw American troops attending
church who manifested "little or no fear of the consequences" and kept
singing when a few cannonballs crashed through a wall or the roof.[41] In
every case, officers were expected to affect a languid manner no matter
how "hot" the shot. Near the redoubt, old General Putnam—who had
seen it all before—"appeared unintimidated, as if they had not fired a
gun," according to John Dexter, who watched him stride back and
forth.[42] William Low thought that "Putnam was as cool as ever a man
was."[43] Another veteran who remained unfazed was a man named Hill,
a British deserter, who, said a grateful Amos Foster, "watched [the]
British [guns], and, when they were about to fire, [he warned us and]
we all laid down."[44] Having a few such men around to assuage the wor-
ries of others made an enormous difference.

Nevertheless, when artillery bit, its bite hurt. Direct hits were invariably fatal. At Bunker Hill, Major Andrew McClary, a New Hampshire tavernkeeper, would be torn apart when "a random shot . . .
passed directly through his body."[45] And the head of a Dr. Dole outside
Boston would be carried off by a cannonball with such force that a
passing sergeant saw nothing but "a piece of the skin of his head with
the hair on it, which was of a light brown beginning to be sprinkled
with white hairs."[46]

Cannon fire, though, often affected more than just a single individual. A solid, round iron ball, launched into the side of a rank of
men—known as "firing in enfilade"—would kill the first few and might

grievously wound the next several.[47] During the battle, Private Peter Brown saw a British cannonball fired in enfilade that "cut off three men in two"—in other words, sever them in half.[48] Sergeant Elisha Bostwick described another that "first took the head of Smith, a stout heavy man & dash't it open, then it took off Chilson's arm which was amputated & he recovered it, then took Taylor [through] the bowels, it then struck Sergt. Garret of our company on the hip [and] took off the point of the hip bone." (Smith, Taylor, and Garret died.)[49]

Even so, shot that hit troops directly was not as panic-inducing as that which landed a distance off and bounced toward them at thigh height—perfect for crippling.[50] Though less immediately lethal than a direct hit, these balls that "grazed" the ground were particularly effective against dense formations. One contemporary soldier noticed that "balls which the troops perceive striking the ground about 100 or more paces in front of them, and approaching them with short bounds, cause much unsteadiness, waving, pressing, and confusion in the ranks, as everyone endeavours to get out of their way." Perhaps worse, whereas a soldier could sometimes see the dark sphere of a cannonball looming larger in the sky as it descended and plan to be elsewhere when it landed, one caroming off rough ground could be deflected in almost any direction. Nowhere was safe.[51]

Wounds caused by artillery were more terrible than ones inflicted by musket balls. Cannonballs, when they collided at full speed with an abdomen or chest, tore a hole corresponding to their size—a 12-pound round had about a 4.5-inch diameter—and splattered viscera outward. Hitting a leg or arm resulted in a stump left behind with a nearly smooth, darkly bruised layer of pulpified tissue with the bone sticking out.[52] A round, by way of comparison, might require a surgical amputation but never could remove an entire limb at a stroke.

Injuries to other parts of the body amply demonstrated the difference between the two types of ammunition. While the American surgeon Dr. Thacher tended one young soldier who had "received a musket ball through his cheeks, cutting its way through the teeth on each side, and the substance of his tongue," the victim later began "to articulate tolerably well." Another of his patients, however, "had the whole side of his face torn off by a cannon ball, laying his mouth and throat open to view."[53] He would have died soon afterward.

From relatively short ranges, mysteriously, a cannonball could kill or wound without even making contact. Captain Ebenezer Bancroft was standing near the redoubt when "a ball from the *Somerset* passed within a few inches of my head, which seriously affected my left eye so that it finally became totally blind."[54] Later, John Martin felt a cannonball hurtling past his chest "without touching." He was knocked briefly unconscious and upon wakening "vomited or raised much blood." Alive but "still in pain at his breast" and concussed, Martin could fight no more that day.[55]

Owing to the kinetic violence of an artillery hit, surgeons occasionally found parts of other men lodged in a comrade. One discovered a piece of jaw wedged in another man's palate, the item belonging to a friend whose head had disintegrated. Eyes, owing to their gelatinousness, made a prime site for foreign objects: There was a soldier whose eyeball contained someone else's tooth and another with a skull fragment lodged underneath his eyelid. In one wounded soldier's thigh, a doctor found three coins, none of which had originally belonged to the fellow in question.[56]

More common, at least among those new to war, were dreadful wounds to the feet and ankles caused by expended balls rolling sluggishly along. Asa Prince, for instance, had his ankle dislocated by one such as he crossed the Neck on his way to Bunker Hill. Luckily, he had only to crack it back into its socket and continue onward.[57] Others, not so fortunate, "lost their feet" when they "were crushed by the weight of the rolling shot" as they tried to stop them. After that, the more experienced men cautioned youngsters "against touching a ball, until it was entirely at rest," according to John Trumbull.[58]

At the redoubt, Private Asa Pollard of Billerica, a scout during the French and Indian War, knew enough to refrain from trying to stop cannonballs but became the battle of Bunker Hill's first victim when he sat down on the dirt embankment to devour a few leftover scraps of food.[59] Working nearby, Amos Foster saw how the fatal ball "struck the ground and hopped along before it struck him," evidently from behind. The cannon shot tore off Pollard's head.[60] Now that the *Lively's* guns had found their range, casualties began to mount. Soon, Aaron Barr of Captain Maxwell's company was struck by another cannonball that sheared off his leg. He was trundled back to Cambridge but died later in the day.[61]

Pollard's death and Barr's hideous cries scared the rest of the men, especially the younger ones. Colonel Prescott urgently needed to put a stop to the murmurings and reinspire confidence before their fears led them to put down their tools and retreat, or desert, back across the Neck. As it was, said a witness, "a number of the men [had already gone] and never returned."[62] William French of Dunstable, more bluntly, said that "some slunk off" at this time.[63]

Thus, when a subaltern asked what to do about Pollard, the colonel curtly ordered, "Bury him." "What? Without prayers!" replied the shocked lieutenant. Prescott conceded that a service could be held later. Unmollified, the men continued to congregate around the corpse, prompting Prescott's demand that Pollard's body be thrown into a trench and immediately covered with soil. The sooner Pollard disappeared, the sooner his troops would forget their fears. The colonel only reluctantly consented to a quick service then and there when a minister noisily insisted on a Christian burial, which was attended, under fire, by Pollard's company. After that, Prescott told them to get back to digging.

In ordering Pollard's funeral and distracting the men's minds with work, Prescott hoped to prevent them becoming maudlin about the loss of their comrade, but they clearly needed an additional dose of encouragement. Leaping onto the parapet, he leisurely walked back and forth, here encouraging the men, there entertaining them with a joke. He neither ducked nor flinched as the cannonballs flew over. Every man could see him, and Prescott was soon joined by other captains. By dint of such leadership, "the men soon became indifferent to the fire of the artillery" even after several more of them were killed—and just as rapidly removed from sight. (After the battle, the British found near the redoubt a mass grave, about two feet deep, containing a number of corpses, probably including Pollard's, of men killed in the artillery barrage.)[64]

For the moment, Prescott's actions successfully calmed the urge to run. As the sun rose and the day proceeded, however, the instinct for self-preservation would grow more pronounced. By late morning, his men could witness for themselves the forces gathering for the coming assault—as well as discover how vulnerable they were in their half-finished dirt fort. "We saw our danger being against ships of the line and all Boston fortified against us," wrote Peter Brown. "The danger we were in made us think there was treachery, and that we were brought there to be all slain."[65]

Brown was right to be alarmed. The militiamen had to sustain themselves on only a bite of bread and a nip of rum (the British had landed a lucky shot that blew up their two hogsheads of water). Having labored since midnight, they were exhausted. There were no reinforcements expected, no rescue anticipated. The arrival of three or four heavily armed boats—floating batteries—allowed the British to continue their bombardment. Joined by the *Lively*—and later the *Falcon* and the *Somerset* as well as the *Glasgow* and the *Symmetry*—they made any further work on the entrenchments too dangerous, even for the jaunty Colonel Prescott.[66] Now the redoubt's sole line of communication and retreat lay across the Neck, easily swept by naval fire. Prescott's Last Stand beckoned.

As the militiamen hunkered down, they could see the British forming their attack units on the Boston wharves.[67] British regiments at the time generally had attached two elite, or "flank," companies—one Grenadier, the other Light—which could be split off from the ordinary battalion, or line, companies for special operations. Grenadiers, chosen from their regiment's beefiest, tallest, and most aggressive men, represented brute force and served as heavy shock troops. The average height of the Grenadiers in the 4th Regiment, for instance, was five feet eleven inches—counted as gigantic at the time—while that of the hatmen (normal battalion troops) was five feet eight inches.[68]

The Lights were a recent innovation, one dating from the French

and Indian War and a particular specialty of General Howe, commanding the nascent expeditionary force. In rocky, hilly, or forested terrain,
a regiment's most agile and sure-footed soldiers were used as scouts and
sweeping flankers. They traveled fast, too, jogging several miles at a
time to catch the enemy unawares. Howe believed his Lights would
play a critical role in the battle to come, for, as a British military writer
of the time judged, they were especially useful for "seiz[ing] upon elevated positions and important posts, with a rapidity peculiar to themselves."[69]

At this early stage, the British plan appears to have been to land the
main Grenadier/Light formation plus two regiments (the 5th and the
38th) at Moulton's Point. Once ashore, the Grenadiers, supported by
the battalion companies, would assault the redoubt while the Lights
nosed toward the Neck. The latter's tasks would be to reconnoiter
ahead for American positions, to harry and trap soldiers fleeing the redoubt, and to shield the Neck and Bunker Hill from enemy counterattack. Meanwhile, the transports would return to Boston and convey a
second wave of regiments—the 43rd and the 52nd—to the peninsula.
Once Prescott had surrendered, the 1st Marines and the 47th Regiment would land, after which the remaining British forces in Boston
would be ferried over. That night, or perhaps the next morning, the
main army would move on Cambridge to destroy whatever was left of
the Americans.

Given the commotion on the Boston shorefront, it is not surprising
that when General Putnam arrived after midday and asked Prescott to
send a party back to Cambridge with the tools, the colonel retorted
that "not one of them would return." Nonsense, cried Putnam patri-
otically, "They shall every man return."[70] Prescott, knowing that the
tools were more valuable than the men, let his people go. Captain Bancroft, who witnessed the exchange, discreetly remarked that "an order
was never obeyed with more readiness." A group of volunteers enthusiastically picked up a shovel or two and "hurried over the hills." Few
would return.[71]

With the British assault imminent, it was again critical to buttress
the faltering confidence of those left behind at the redoubt. Prescott

and Putnam rallied the men with one of the most vivid and memorable exhortations in American history: "Don't fire until you see the whites of their eyes." What is less well known is that that cry was not conceived in 1775, but some time before, during Frederick the Great's wars in Europe. The first recorded instance of its use occurred on May 22, 1745, when Prince Charles Alexander directed his Austrians awaiting Prussia's strike to be "silent, till you see the whites of their eyes."[72] The phrase seems to have taken off, and by 1757, at the battle of Prague, it was sufficiently familiar to be included in the General Orders to the Prussian infantry: "By push of bayonets; no firing till you see the whites of their eyes."[73]

In America, older soldiers had picked up the catchphrase in the intervening decades. At Bunker Hill, it seems to have been not Prescott but General Putnam who first used it. Israel Potter in the redoubt wrote that at about noon the general "charged us to be cool and to reserve our fire until the enemy approached so near as to enable us to see the whites of their eyes."[74]

Yet there were more men who did *not* hear Putnam at all but were nevertheless familiar with the rally. For instance, Elijah Jordan recalled that "while we were waiting . . . orders were given to us not to fire till we could see the whites of their eyes; and this order, I was then told, came from Gen. Putnam; but I did not hear it from him."[75]

So, who said what when? The confusion highlights the problem of the mechanics of what is technically known as a "harangue": brief pep talks intended to buttress and burnish the confidence of soldiers.[76] Generally speaking, the shorter, more informal, and less complicated a harangue, the more effective it is, particularly when the commander is trusted and respected by his men. The Duke of Wellington, for one, never bothered with long speeches, high-minded sentiment, or impressive grammar. What was the point, he asked, "since you cannot conveniently make it heard by more than a thousand men standing about you?"[77]

To spread the word as far and as rapidly as possible, there were two methods of delivery. First, the commander paced up and down the line successively addressing units with a selection of rousing apothegms until all had heard at least one.[78] Second, he could declaim once, and his subordinates would pass the message down to their respective units.

What probably happened in the American lines, then, is that Putnam visited the redoubt before the fighting began. He did not give just one speech to everyone at once but toured the defenses bucking up the men here and there with the catchy exhortation not to shoot until they could see the whites of the enemy's eyes. Once the general had left, the mantra was repeated and emphasized by Prescott and his subordinates. The colonel, for instance, was remembered as imploring his paladins to "wait till you see the whites of their eyes"—but added, as a soundly thrifty New England militia chief would, "waste no powder."[79]

By 1 P.M., Prescott had also sent a 200-strong Connecticut detachment under Captain Thomas Knowlton to stake out Moulton's Point and give the British a warm welcome as they landed. But on his way there Knowlton was likely prevailed upon by General Putnam—who may, despite his brave words, have been having second thoughts as to the wisdom of a knockdown fight at the redoubt—to withdraw to Bunker Hill and establish a strong defense there to forestall a British rush for the Neck and keep an escape route open for Prescott's men. Once the British attack began in earnest, the Connecticuters could fire off a few volleys at the enemy before themselves wriggling free from Howe's noose and withdrawing. There would be neither a "battle of Bunker Hill" nor a capitulation, merely another Lexington writ larger.

Meanwhile, on the coast, as his scarlet-clad soldiers formed into three orderly lines, Howe paused. There in the distance, toward Bunker Hill, he could see thickening clouds of men where there were supposed to be none—as well as a defended position, also not there just an hour or two before. Suddenly, his first wave of 1,550 redcoats—a force he had assumed would be more than sufficient to cow Prescott or, if need be, take the redoubt and race ahead to the Neck—looked too few for the job.

What Howe was witnessing were Colonels John Stark and James Reed's New Hampshire regiments taking their place alongside Knowlton at a place commonly dubbed the "rail fence." Soon, even more men would arrive in response to the alarms being sounded throughout the

American camps. "Turn out! The enemy's all landed at Charlestown," Stephen Jenkins of Captain John Noyes's company remembered crying.[80] What had happened was that General Ward, informed of Howe's arrival, had finally decided that he must hold the British at the peninsula rather than passively wait for them in Cambridge and had directed every available man to speed to Charlestown. There was going to be a battle, after all.

Reacting to the American change of plan, Howe improvised. It was now critical to amputate the peninsula from the Neck without delay. As it was, Americans were already streaming over Bunker Hill.[81] No longer could the redoubt be the primary objective and seizing the Neck the secondary; now, rail fence and redoubt were of equal importance. *Both* needed to fall in order to conquer the peninsula. To that end, once the second wave of troops arrived, Howe split his forces more or less in half.

He would command the right division, comprising the nippy Light infantry (about 350 men), the ponderous Grenadier spearhead (about the same), and 500 to 600 line troops of the 5th and 52nd Regiments. He assigned the left division to Brigadier General Robert Pigot. That wing, of 600 to 750 line troops drawn mostly from the 38th and 43rd Regiments, would eventually be joined by the 47th Regiment and the 1st Marines under Major Thomas Pitcairn, adding another 600 to its number. Remaining behind in Boston as reserve but already preparing to leave were 140 men of the Light and Grenadier companies of the 63rd Regiment and the 2nd Marines.[82]

Howe's men were entrusted with the task of breaking the rail fence and thence rushing to block Charlestown Neck. In the meantime, Pigot's men would assault the redoubt and then swing rearward to flank the rail fence, should it still be standing. It was a tall order, but Howe expected a quick victory thanks to his excellent land artillery. After all, no fewer than six 6-pounders, two 12-pounders, and two 5.5-inch howitzers would soften up the defenders before the attacks even began.[83] Probably begged by Pigot for extra support, Howe shifted several of his guns to the center to help enfilade the breastwork shoring up Prescott's redoubt. This would ultimately prove to be a wise decision.

Howe's artillery alone might have been sufficient to cleanse the peninsula of militiamen but for a disastrous problem with his ammunition supply. Possibly due to the incompetence, or inattention, of his colonel of artillery, Samuel Cleaveland, who, it was widely rumored, "spends his whole time in dallying with the schoolmaster's daughters," Howe brought over crates of twelve-pound balls but no six-pounders, rendering most of his guns useless.[84] Perhaps, but it is also possible that the soldiers detailed to lug the ammunition simply brought the larger ones by mistake. Alternatively, young Benjamin Lovell, the clerk of artillery stores, *might* have been prevailed upon by his brother, James Lovell—a future member of the Continental Congress—to send the wrong ammunition deliberately. (The "schoolmaster" referred to above, perhaps not uncoincidentally, was their father, a Loyalist later judged to be insane.)[85] Whatever the reason for the mix-up, it meant that Howe would have to rely much more on his infantry than he had originally intended.

For maximum effect, the dual attacks on redoubt and rail fence were to take place simultaneously—a tough proposition owing to the hilly terrain between Howe and Pigot that obscured their sightlines and left them unable to communicate in a timely manner. The upshot was that the two wings would have to work autonomously, each commander hoping that his counterpart was keeping both pace and to the plan.

Within minutes at the beach, this optimistic scheme would come to grief.

4. The Beach

As ten companies of Howe's Grenadiers, backed up by the 5th and 52nd Regiments, splayed across the field, eleven companies of Light infantry formed below in a narrow but long column on the peninsula's "beach"—in actuality a muddy, stony shelf several yards wide at low tide. The intention was to launch a sneak flank attack while the heavy and regular troops diverted the attention of the rail-fence defenders with a frontal advance.

Within minutes of arriving at the rail fence, Colonel Stark, however, had perceived the danger and sent one of his best companies under Captain John Moore—a wily veteran of the French and Indian War—to clamber down the bank and build a low stone wall, behind which they were now crouched in a triple row. Owing to the curvature of the shoreline, the Lights and the Americans could not see each other.[1]

The British had not thought to scout ahead, and the leading company of the Lights—that of the 23rd Regiment, better known as the Royal Welch Fusiliers—advanced confidently to its doom, four men abreast in eight rows.[2] Not until they were 100 to 150 yards away from the stone wall did it begin to dawn on the Lights that the Americans had anticipated their move. When they finally saw Moore and his militiamen, the British probably halted around the curve to consult urgently with Howe via messenger.

Howe ordered forward the Lights. It was the worst possible plan of attack, but he desperately needed to coordinate their advance with that of his Grenadiers against the rail fence. The 23rd Regiment's Lights began to pick up speed; once they were between 50 and 80 yards from the American position, Moore's Yankee accent could be heard bawling for his men to open fire. When the first volley smashed into the 23rd, the front rows immediately toppled over, and the men behind them, suddenly stopping short, began tripping over their fallen comrades as those farther back collided with those in front of them. The slippery mud, the ankle-twisting rocks, and the tide's lapping waves only compounded the confusion. The officers desperately tried to rally their men into some sort of order as incessant sheets of fire roiled the ranks. It did no good. Within a minute, at least a third of the company was down. Miraculously, not a single man was killed instantly—testament to the Americans' lack of murderous accuracy, which had been sacrificed for rapidity—though over the coming months two corporals, a drummer, and six privates would die of their injuries; a sergeant and four privates remained disabled, probably permanently.[3] To the Americans, no other battle action "exhibit[ed] equal scenes of blood in so short a time from so few men engaged."[4] Abigail Adams informed her husband, John, two days later that "our enemies were cut down like grass before the scythe."[5]

The remaining men of the 23rd naturally recoiled backward to escape the furious slaughter. As they could not run sideways, there was nowhere for them to go but to barge, pushing and brawling, into the ranks of the unit behind them—the Lights of the 4th Regiment—instigating further derangement as companies successively collapsed under continuing American fusillades.

This phenomenon of panic rippling through the ranks is a relatively common one. A Prussian named Küster who fought at the battle of Hochkirch in 1758 recalled what it felt like to be unexpectedly gripped by panic: "All of a sudden I was overtaken by a fear which deprived me of all my courage, and a terror which set my limbs a-trembling. A little child could have pushed me over."[6] Then came the relentlessly insistent urge to run.

Panic rarely breaks out simultaneously among an entire group. Instead, flight involves at first only a few individuals—like the survivors of the 23rd or Küster—whose behavior then adversely influences those nearby. Once it begins, the effect of "panic upon a multitude," said an officer who saw troops fall to pieces in 1780, is "like sympathy, it is irresistible where it touches."[7] The astounding rapidity with which the cantagion spreads "can only be fully realized by those who have witnessed a false alarm on a dark night with an army in the field," warned Viscount Wolseley, a nineteenth-century general. "When under the influence of panic, men for the moment are mad, and act without reason. Whilst the fit lasts, they are capable of the most idiotic actions [and] nothing but some violent shock . . . or some chance and often trifling occurrence brings them back to the grave realities of their position."[8]

At the bloody beach, there was no such "violent shock" to bring the Lights back to their senses. Instead, the situation only worsened when the rear units—which had suffered no casualties—took fright as the forward companies came scrambling pell-mell around the curve. The men at the back had not yet seen what was happening up front. They had heard the cries of pain and the crash of muskets, they smelled the smoke, they felt the anxiety wafting in the air, but this excess of sensory stimuli went unmatched by hard information. In the absence of data on what lay around the fatal bend—ultimately, just a company of militiamen, greatly outnumbered—they could not make rational assessments of risks and probabilities. So they imagined instead the fearful and awful things awaiting them: a battery of artillery, perhaps, or American cavalry, or thousands of reinforcements. Dread of the unknown turned these otherwise disciplined infantrymen into a stampeding horde, proving the old military rule of thumb that it is always the troops in the least immediate danger who turn and run first.[9]

According to Peter Thacher, who was watching the debacle from across the Mystic River, the entire column of Lights "retreated in very great disorder down to the point where they [had] landed, and there some of them even [scrambled] into their boats." Their officers, chasing them, used "the most passionate gestures and even push[ed] forward the men with their swords." After a time, they successfully managed to prod some of the men back onto the beach, but when they suffered another of Moore's broadsides, the remnant of the Lights again fled to Moulton's Point and the safety of their landing craft.[10] Howe's flanking gambit had failed disastrously.

Worse, some of the shaken and shuddering remnants of the Lights scrambled up to the field above, where the Grenadiers had started their advance toward the rail fence, and opened fire. They were, in the words of an officer writing in the *Edinburgh Advertiser,* "in such consternation that they fired at random, and unfortunately killed several of [the Grenadier] officers." For a more precise account of what happened, we must rely on a private letter written by Lieutenant Colonel James Abercrombie, who was commanding the Grenadier companies. The Lights, said Abercrombie, "gave me a plumper [army slang for volley] and killed two officers and three privates." Perhaps another twenty men were wounded. Abercrombie himself was shot in the middle of his right thigh and would die of an infection five days later, but not before understatedly mentioning that the Lights "must be drilled before they are carried to action again."[11]

Abercrombie's comment highlights a deeper truth regarding the beach assault. The real cause of the collapse on the beach was not the tactical situation—had the British surged ahead, Moore's defenders would have been overrun—but the Lights' unreadiness for combat. They were, in other words, susceptible to disintegration even before Moore unleashed his volleys. Historically, when a unit with a large proportion of battle-seasoned veterans panics, the underlying reason is often administrative incompetence: excessive demands on already combat-stressed men or retention at the battlefront past their peak effectiveness.[12] Raw or inexperienced soldiers, in contrast, tend to run when unpleasantly shocked by enemy action or the novelty of combat. Lacking the bonds of unit pride and loyalty to comrades, which require substantial spells of training and service to develop, individuals have little to lose if they forbear sacrificing themselves for the greater good of the outfit or their friends.[13] Even so, the presence of a respected leader can often induce them to return to their positions either by appeals to remember their duty or by a violent act (such as shooting "cowards").[14]

On that beach, not only were there few such respected leaders, either because they were dead or too new to their positions (Captain Thomas Mecan had taken over the 23rd Lights only that morning) to have earned sufficient trust, but British morale, experience, and training were also quite poor to begin with.

There is a long-standing idea that the British army was at the time the finest in the world.[15] Perhaps it was, but even so, the regiments stationed in Boston in 1775 could not be said to be the cream of the crop. Too often forgotten is that before the running skirmish at Lexington and excepting a minor war against the Caribs, the British had not seen real combat since the battles of Minden and the Plains of Abraham (both times against the French) in 1759. Back then, more than half of British soldiers had been older than thirty, with a fair deal of fighting under their belts. By Bunker Hill, that cohort of now-gray-haired veterans had mostly retired. Though there were still a few "Old Soldiers" around—such as John Henderson, a veteran of Culloden in 1746 and a soldier under Wolfe at Quebec—who could keep order among the younger men when the lead started flying, they had their work cut out for them.[16] The army as a whole in Boston contained a significant proportion of soldiers who had served several years in uniform, but very few had any combat experience at all; they were accustomed only to peacetime duty.[17]

Junior officers tended to be unblooded, green, often new to the army. On June 9—not even ten days before Bunker Hill—General Thomas Gage ordered that because "there are many young officers who have lately joined their Corps, [their superiors] will take care that they are instructed in their duty, and not put on out-guards or posts of consequences till they are well informed, and have a knowledge of what they are to do." He was not amused to discover a week later that these selfsame young officers had been sending their troops out on exercises while they luxuriated in their quarters.[18]

In a telling indication that the raw officers and soldiers ignorant of battle conditions at the Boston garrison desperately needed practice, on June 14—only three days before the battle—Gage urgently directed that every regiment "will drill the recruits and drafts without a day's delay . . . beginning with the platoon exercise, and teaching them to fire ball. Proper marksmen to instruct them in taking aim and the position in which they ought to stand in firing. And to do this man by man before they are offered to fire together."[19]

To understand the import of Gage's words, it is crucial to know that five stages of drill were taught. Following a course in the fundamentals of marching, the first was the "manual exercise," in which the recruit learned the tedious sequence of movements allowing him to load and fire his musket and to use a bayonet. The second was the "platoon exercise," a step that showed soldiers how to fire in volley as quickly as possible. After this came the advanced exercises, such as "evolutions" (about-turns, left-turns, closing files, and the like), "firings" (an elaborate system designed to perfect firing when advancing, retreating, and standing by section), and, finally, "manoeuvres" (a fiendishly complex repertoire of battlefield deployments).[20] Gage's *specific* instruction to begin training with the "platoon exercise" indicates that many of his Boston regiments had completed only the most basic training. Their lack of fire control and tactical coordination would exact a dreadful toll during the coming battle.

Gage also mentioned the men known as "drafts," a reference to the custom wherein soldiers serving in various regiments at home and abroad could be transferred away from their friends and family to fill slots where needed. In early 1775, America was clearly the next battle-ground, and drafts were dispatched as reinforcements. The official size of each regiment in or bound for the Colonies was increased from 380 privates to 560, though in actuality their strengths varied.[21] To take a more specific example, roughly a quarter of the men in the Grenadier companies of the 4th, 52nd, and 59th Regiments were fresh drafts. These newcomers lacked the opportunity to meld and assimilate with the old-timers, to learn their rhythms and habits, and it was perhaps no coincidence that these units would suffer among the highest casualties on June 17.[22]

As late as June 12, the Grenadiers were still bringing in unfamiliar men who had never trained for a heavy-infantry, first-strike role. The Grenadiers were capable soldiers individually, but at the company level they sorely needed more time to integrate their disparate elements and increase their military effectiveness and esprit de corps.[23] More broadly, the various Grenadier companies were unaccustomed to working jointly, and there had been virtually no collective training. Indeed, they had formed together for exercises just once (on June 4) after Lexington.

The baleful state of a significant portion of British regiments at the time can be quantified using the example of the three companies of the 18th Regiment, which were sent to Boston in October 1774 and spliced together with two companies of the 65th. It's possible that this composite battalion stood out to contemporaries as a particular handful—we have no explicit data either way for any other regiment in Boston at the time—but what is certain is that immediately afterward, the number of disciplinary problems rocketed. Between October 1774 and May 1775, no fewer than a third of the composite battalion's strength of 218 men were punished, one third of those multiple times. Drunkenness was cited most of the time, as well as the kind of disor-derly behavior (insolence, fighting, and causing disturbances) that was no doubt often exacerbated by booze. About four in ten men had been sentenced to receive one hundred lashes.[24]

Gage's measures before Bunker Hill were too little, too late. Bad habits among the regulars could be broken only by proper training, purges of troublesome officers and men, the evolution of cohesion, and the annealment of combat, which is why Lieutenant Richard Williams concluded that "it requires one campaign at least, to make a good soldier."[25] Some musketry practice here and there, in other words, could not compensate for the hard hand of war, competent leadership, and unit pride.

Unfortunately for the British, age, experience, cohesion, and perhaps even training were all on the American side. During the French and Indian War, the provincial militias had been much younger than their British-regular counterparts. In 1756, volunteers from Massachusetts had a mean average age of twenty-six, with more than half aged between fourteen and twenty-four years old.[26] At the war's beginning, unlike the older British, these youths were mostly unblooded, but over its course they acquired an enormous amount of combat experience. That experience, moreover, was not restricted to a small band of veterans, but encompassed an entire, exceedingly martial society. The population of Massachusetts, for instance, would grow from about 205,000 to 255,000 between 1755 and 1763, during which period there were approximately 34,000 males who fell within the prime age range of sixteen to twenty-nine years. Of that group, between 15,000 and 20,000 would serve in the provincials at some point (or multiple times) during the French and Indian War. Thus, *an absolute minimum of 30 percent and probably closer to 40 percent* of all Massachusetts males aged between sixteen and twenty-nine enlisted for military service.[27] In some towns, the proportion was still higher: In Lexington, up to 60 percent of eligible men went to war.[28] Perhaps it was little wonder that everybody, it seemed, had a relative away with the militias at one time or another. Nathaniel Hawthorne was not exaggerating when he later wrote that during the war "every man was a soldier, or the father or brother of a soldier; and the whole land literally echoed with the roll of the drum, either beating up for recruits among the towns and villages, or striking the march towards the frontiers. . . . The country has never known a period of such excitement and warlike life, except during the Revolution."[29]

Flitting forward twenty years, to 1775, we find that those relatively young males had matured into men in the thirty-to-forty-nine age bracket. Nearly 40 percent of the militiamen Peterborough, New Hampshire, dispatched to Boston that summer were in that band. This pattern is found elsewhere. The youngest Lexington militiaman was aged sixteen, the oldest sixty-six. Half were between thirty and forty-nine, and about a quarter were in their twenties, giving a mean and median age average of thirty-two years—about the same as for Peterborough.[30] And in Captain Hutchins's company of sixty-three Derryfield men, just nine were not yet nineteen.[31] Judging by these statistics, we can safely assert that there were more older brothers than younger, more fathers than sons, more uncles than nephews fighting in 1775.

Indeed, the character of these militia units resembled nothing less than a family enterprise. A representative case at Bunker Hill was Captain "Short Bill" Scott's Peterborough company, consisting of twenty-six men.[32]

Capt. William "Short Bill" Scott
Lieutenant William "Long Bill" Scott
Sergeant Randall McAlister
Corporal Charles White
George McLeod
James Hockley
John Graham
David Scott
James Scott
Thomas Scott
David Robbe
John Taggart
Samuel Mitchell
Thomas Morison
David Alld
Thomas Greene
Joseph Henderson
Richard Gilchrist

William Scott
Joseph Greene
Dudley (or James) Taggart
William Gilchrist
William White
James McKean
Joseph Taylor
William Graham

A not overly interesting catalogue of names, it may seem at first, but if you run your eye down the list, certain surnames recur. Among these twenty-six individuals there are six Scotts, for instance, along with two Whites, two Grahams, two Taggarts, two Greenes, and two Gilchrists. In other companies throughout the region, we see the same incidence. Thus, in Captain John Parker's Lexington militia there were sixteen Munroes, thirteen Harringtons, eleven Smiths, eight Reeds, four Hadleys, four Muzzys, four Hastings, four Tidds, three Simonds, three Wellingtons, three Winships, and many pairs. Out of 141 names on the total roster, only 27 had a unique surname. More than a quarter of his men were directly related to Parker himself.[33] In New Salem, Connecticut, Captain William Meacham was killed at Bunker Hill, but in his fifty-three-man company, three of his brothers (all privates) and his brother-in-law served alongside no fewer than seventeen of his kinsmen.[34] In Captain Benjamin Ames's Andover company, his deputy, Lieutenant David Chandler, was aided by Sergeant William Chandler and marched off to war to the beat of drummer James Chandler alongside a further five relatives, privates all.[35]

Generally, the senior men of a local dynasty—the older fellows, the better established, the veterans of the French and Indian War—occupied a company's top slots (captain, lieutenant, sergeant, and corporal) while their younger relatives served as privates or drummers. So in Concord, Massachusetts, Colonel Thomas Barrett's son and son-in-law were both captains under his command, and they in turn relied on two more of the colonel's sons serving as ensigns, who in turn passed orders down to yet another of the colonel's sons and a nephew acting as corporals, and they in turn told still more nephews in the ranks what to do.[36] War as a family business was not, in short, anything out of the ordinary.

As rural America was a close-knit society—two-thirds of marriages were between partners born in the same small town and half of all families were "re-related" to each other via wedded cousins or siblings—even unrelated individuals would nevertheless be connected to their militia brethren through local business relationships, childhood friendships, political affiliations, and religious ties. The bonds between the militiamen magnified their fighting power, particularly when the chips were down and the enemy threatened to break them. In battle, the reluctance to appear a coward in front of one's comrades is an age-old phenomenon, one only intensified by the men's familiarity with one another. The shame of running away would be terrible and result in disinheritance or loss of commercial, property, and marriage opportunities while forming an inextinguishable source of malicious town gossip for a lifetime. In an era when personal mobility was limited, gaining such a reputation would be devastating, as the afflicted could rarely move away to start their lives afresh.[37]

Often forgotten is the relatively high degree to which blacks were integrated within the militia companies—not until after World War II would so many again serve alongside whites in the military. None, of course, were officers—tolerance went only so far—but at least thirty-three blacks would fight at Bunker Hill. Fifteen of these were free, the balance enslaved.[38]

This number might not sound very high, but there were relatively few blacks living in rural New England in the eighteenth century. Boston's population in 1760 was 15,631, of whom 14,390 were white and 1,241 black, or about 8 percent, but as one traveled farther inland, away from the coastal fisheries, ports, and trading vessels that employed large numbers of seafaring blacks, it became increasingly rare to see African-Americans. In Concord, according to the 1754 census, there were just fifteen; in Lexington, twenty-four. Even by 1790 the total black population of the five New England states would amount to a mere 16,822, or 1.5 percent of the more than a million people living there.[39]

The number of blacks who fought at Bunker Hill was broadly proportionate to their presence in the white population.[40] That slaves participated in combat at all was a quirk of the Puritan outlook. Those in, for instance, Massachusetts, were treated differently than in the South. Slaves were considered not quite property—though they were—but as "servants for life"; they sat at the family's table, worked alongside their masters, and wore similar clothes. Blacks could also testify in court, even against their owners. On the other hand, as "servants for life," their children were considered, as one observer remarked in 1795, "an incumbrance in a family; and when weaned, were given away like puppies."

Reflecting this ambiguous status, blacks were forbidden to participate in militia training but, in spite of the fear of a slave insurrection on the part of whites, there was no prohibition on their using firearms. This loophole was a relic of the days when Indian raids and French attacks were distinct dangers and every man was needed in an emergency. Consequently, on May 20, 1775, the Massachusetts Committee of Safety banned slaves, but not free blacks, from serving in the militia forces outside Boston. The Provincial Congress, however, ignored the resolution, so there were both slaves and freemen at Bunker Hill. Even so, there was no obligation for a slave to fight; indeed, one reason for them to volunteer was the possibility of earning their freedom.[41]

Blacks' familiarity with weapons, if not militia drill, helps explain the presence of one carrying a musket in John Trumbull's famous 1786 picture *The Death of General Warren at the Battle of Bunker's Hill, June 17, 1775*. There is every evidence, too, that blacks were not relegated to auxiliary or support roles but participated fully in the fighting. Salem Poor of Andover, for instance, had purchased his freedom in 1769 and was enlisted in Colonel James Frye's regiment. He helped dig the redoubt's defenses on the night of June 16. Six months after the battle, on December 5, Poor received an extraordinary, perhaps unique, accolade: No fewer than two colonels (including Prescott), one lieutenant colonel, and three lieutenants testified to the General Court of Massachusetts that he had "behaved like an experienced officer as well as an excellent soldier" during the battle.[42]

The family and community bonds that connected the militiamen meant that the Americans could generally trust their leaders to an extent that the British regiments at Bunker Hill could never match. Those in charge of the militia units had neither purchased their commissions nor risen thanks to backroom politicking. They were, after all, elected. What counted among the militiamen was experience, which is why when they voted for their officers they generally chose men who had learned their business in the French and Indian War. For instance, in 1755, one Lieutenant William Prescott of Massachusetts enlisted twenty-five men to fight the French in Nova Scotia. In 1775, more than half his original company joined him—now a colonel—at Bunker Hill, to live or die alongside their clan chief at the redoubt.[43] Similarly, Captain Isaac Baldwin of Hillsborough, New Hampshire, could bring to bear the experience garnered from participating in fully twenty firefights alongside John Stark—now also a colonel, but holding the rail fence—during the French and Indian War. So attractive was his résumé that of Hillsborough's forty-three eligible residents, nearly half signed on to his company, and many more living in nearby towns rushed to volunteer.[44]

Militiamen refused to serve under officers who had not proven their credentials. Just before Bunker Hill, four Massachusetts companies decided that they disliked their commanding officer, Colonel Samuel Gerrish, so they ousted him and elected Captain Moses Little in his place. Having raised 509 men, nearly all armed with good muskets, Captain Little had, after all, more amply demonstrated his abilities as a warrior than his hapless superior. Meanwhile, another three companies voted to depart from Colonel John Nixon's regiment and align themselves with ones more to their liking.[45] The administrative havoc these changes caused within the American high command was offset by an increase in unit morale and cohesion as men picked which of their kinsmen and comrades they wished to fight alongside.

Despite not having been to war for two decades, the militias were not out of practice. More than half a year before Bunker Hill, many militia companies had secretly begun to train together. As a result, not only did the French and Indian War veterans become accustomed to working with the younger, greener men but the latter also learned to heed their elders.

In the winter of 1774, the Provincial Congress strongly recommended that since "the improvement of the militias in general in the art military has been therefore thought necessary," each town should provide drill and target practice "three times a week, and oftener as opportunity may offer."[46] Now, thrice may have been somewhat ambitious, but twice was common. To that end, Captain Isaac Davis, a gunsmith and farmer from Acton, set up a firing range that his men used at least two days a week between November 1774 and April 1775.[47]

Israel Litchfield, a twenty-two-year-old shoemaker from Scituate, Massachusetts, left a record of what it was like to be a militiaman in those heady days.[48] One afternoon, he and his friends went to Foster's tavern, where his new company had arranged to meet for their first training session. More than sixty local men turned up.[49] Between November 1774 and April 1775, they followed the Provincial Congress's drill recommendations, no matter how harsh the weather. Unlike the British in Boston, they made sure to exercise with other local militia companies to improve their coordination. On April 13, 1775, with that in mind, the Scituate outfit congregated with Captain Turner's "company of Rangers" and Captain John Clapp's "company of minute men" at a Liberty Tree, after which "the three companies drew up in battalion and were exercised by Major Jacobs."[50]

They, like most others, used the Norfolk Exercise, a system of training developed in England in 1757 specifically for militias and helpfully reprinted in abridged cut-out-and-keep form in the *Massachusetts Gazette* of October 6, 1774 (and thereafter given wide circulation).[51] The authors of the quick-to-learn Norfolk Exercise boasted that it would teach an officer the essentials of drill and turn citizens into "half soldiers" within a week.[52] Perfect, then, for your average militiaman, like Israel Litchfield, who knew his way around a rifle but less so a parade ground.

At the time the British army was using the official 1764 manual for its drill, but the Provincial Congress considered it too perplexing for militiamen to use.[53] The main objection was not that militiamen were too ignorant to be able to follow its rules but that the manual obsessed over minor ceremonial details and added dozens of superfluous steps and exercises. Just as their sartorial philosophy went back to basics, so did the militia leadership insist on a simpler way of fighting, one more fluid and more flexible than that generally taught to redcoats. While the European tactics of the day required officers to maneuver large bodies of men in column and line precisely around the battlefield—a process requiring intense drill practice and harsh punishments for errors—Americans had little need for such iron discipline, given how loosely organized their militia companies were.

In this respect, the British enjoyed, in their own eyes, the significant advantages of a clear hierarchy, a robust organizational structure, and a sound system of discipline—the hallmarks of a professional army. They were right. At Bunker Hill, American operations would be hampered by personal dislikes and local rivalries. From the beginning, no one was quite sure who was in command of the peninsula and who was to take orders from whom. General Israel Putnam of Connecticut claimed paramountcy, but Prescott at the redoubt was a Massachusetts colonel who owed no fealty to him and could, if he wished, ignore his directives. As John Adams later wrote, because "Massachusetts had her army, Connecticut her army, New Hampshire her army, and Rhode Island her army," in practice this meant that despite their differences in rank Putnam and Prescott regarded each other as equals and (usually) worked by consensus while retaining their own authority.[54]

At least Putnam and Prescott managed to get along. Colonel John Stark at the rail fence, on the other hand, loathed Putnam, a dislike, according to a Dr. Snow, apparently stemming from "Putnam's [earlier] interference with the irregularities of the N.[ew] H.[ampshire] troops, particularly some violence committed by Stark and his regiment against

Col. Hobart, the [New Hampshire] paymaster." The "violence," pro-voked by Hobart's reluctance to issue pay or supplies, probably involved some roughhousing and hurtful remarks about his parentage. What-ever the issue was, the court-martial subsequently pursued by Putnam had "reported unfavorably" concerning Stark, a man in whom it is said that New England cantankerousness combined with Scots-Irish con-tentiousness. He was never easy to get along with, and there was also much "rivalry and jealousy" between him and his fellow New Hamp-shireman at the rail fence, Colonel James Reed.[55] One of the reasons that Stark did not join Prescott in defending the redoubt may lie in the official list drawn up of each regiment's seniority within the American forces—a ranking that depended on a number of factors including when the regiment was raised and its commander promoted. In it, Stark's was ranked seventh and Prescott's tenth, and the prideful Stark might have bristled at subsuming himself under Prescott, so he plumped for the rail fence and stayed out of Prescott's ambit. In the end, this proved the correct decision, but we can speculate that it was more spite than brilliance that prompted it.[56]

The *amour propre* of the various militia commanders and their re-luctance to recognize anyone's authority but their own added substance to the spreading suspicion in Congress that the militia was an obsolete institution, one that had once been useful for combating Indian raids but was no match for a professional force like the British army. Chal-lenged by the redcoats, the members of Congress predicted, the militia-men would break and run. Their revolutionary enthusiasm might be commendable, but the harsh reality was that when militias were "op-posed to troops regularly trained, disciplined, and appointed, superior in knowledge, and superior in arms," as George Washington declared, they turned "timid, and ready to fly from their own shadow."[57]

To that end, Nathanael Greene, who would rise to become one of Washington's finest commanders, was so exasperated with the motley collection of militia companies at Cambridge that he asserted that "we have no occasion for them. We have here as many of the Province mi-litia as we know what to do with." He—as did Washington—preferred establishing a *real* army, based on British lines, to fight the coming war.[58] Indeed, only three days before the battle, the Continental Congress authorized just such a thing, the Continental Army, and placed Washington in charge.

Putnam was aware that Bunker Hill looked to be the militias' last, defiant gasp before the business of war was handed over to the experts. It was absolutely true that no militia could withstand an aggressive assault by the British across an open field, but Putnam understood a key distinction the critics had overlooked: Militia units were immensely robust if wielded properly in battle yet brittle and easily cracked if not. Wise commanders were aware of this characteristic, wiser ones took it into account in their campaign planning, and the wisest did not place militias in untenable positions in the first place.

The heart of the matter was that a militia's weaknesses emerged only if its members were expected to behave and perform as regulars: American militias were short-term citizen soldiers, not long-service professional troops, and had to be treated as such. This entailed insisting, first, that battles had to be fought on American terms, not British ones, to benefit fully from the militias' strengths; second, that they were best at manning defensible positions, not overcoming them; and, third, that their task was to stave off an enemy's easy triumph, not to defeat him.

His militiamen "were not afraid of their heads," the general shrewdly remarked, "though very much afraid of their legs; if you cover these, they will fight forever."[59] And so they were. By providing protection for their men's legs behind wall and fence, Putnam and the other commanders at Bunker Hill ensured that they would stand and fight. Moreover, the defensive posture played to their strengths, for, as the militia officer Timothy Pickering believed, the provincial companies needed "no other discipline" than "being good marksmen and dexterous in skulking behind trees and bushes."[60] In other words, to Americans "discipline" meant *self*-discipline based on experience, prudence, and independence. It was not a synonym for authority imposed from above.

This was a critical distinction between the worldviews of American militiamen and their British antagonists. To outsiders, the militias circa 1775 did look "undisciplined"—as indeed they were, judged by conventional European yardsticks—but to derive, as the British did, from that uncomplimentary description the idea that they accordingly lacked combat effectiveness was an ultimately fatal category error. At the rail fence, where Stark's men were waiting for the Grenadiers to come at them after the debacle on the beach, this harsh lesson would soon be driven home.

5. The Rail Fence

With their flank on the beach secured, the militiamen behind the rail fence at Bunker Hill watched the orderly lines of Grenadiers and regulars begin their frontal assault. For the Americans, the choice of ground was inspired. When the Connecticut detachment under Captain Knowlton had first arrived there, they had found "a fence half of stone and two rails of wood. Here nature had formed something of a breastwork, or else there had been a ditch many years gone. [The Connecticut detachment] grounded arms, and went to a neighboring parallel fence, and brought [its] rails" back.[1] The original fence had demarcated the boundary of a farmer's land; now it was fortified by the extra wood, and any gaps between the rails were packed with hay, grass, earth, and bushes.[2] Opinions vary on the extent of protection it provided: The American Captain Chester believed the barrier "made a slight fortification against musket-ball," but General Howe—who attacked it—felt that it "effectually secured those behind it from musketry," and still another soldier, that it was "ball-proof."[3] Another militia officer discreetly remarked that it didn't really matter, "for if it did not stop the balls, the men would think that it would, and that would give them confidence."[4]

Despite its admirable location, the rail fence was severely undermanned until Colonels Stark and Reed reinforced Knowlton's Nutmeggers. That captain had too few troops to protect the length of the fence, leaving its left-hand side (which ran north to the Charles River) almost undefended. Since British practice was to place the most elite troops on the right—a place of honor since the Middle Ages—when the attack came, it was certain that the defenders' left would come under heavy pressure. With Knowlton graciously acknowledging his help, Stark accordingly strung out his regiment along that section, with Colonel Reed's men taking their place between Stark and Knowlton.

Ahead of them stretched roughly 700 yards of open fields. At that range, one soldier could see only another's head as a small "round ball" and the rest of him, very hazily, only if he was wearing bright white cross-belts and breeches. Not until 600 yards would our soldier be able to see "upper and lower parts of the body," while at 500 yards "the face may be observed as a light coloured spot; the head, body, arms, and their movements, as well as the uniform, and the firelocks (when bright barrels) can be made out." Only when the British reached a distance of between 200 and 250 yards would "all parts of the body [become] clearly visible, the details of the uniform . . . tolerably clear, and the officers . . . distinguished from the men."[5]

In short, not for some time would there have been any visible target worth pointing a musket at, let alone being able to see the whites of their eyes—especially since those waiting behind the rail fence were amazed at the enemy's "very slow march" and their "slow step."[6] Their lethargy was considered quite curious. After all, the British army was taught to move at three different speeds: the "ordinary" or common step of 75 paces per minute, each pace measuring 30 inches (covering roughly 60 yards of ground per minute); the "quick" step of 108 30-inch paces per minute to seize ground rapidly (90 yards); and a still quicker rate for wheeling motions.[7]

By the standards of the day, the British generally marched at a smart clip.[8] During the coming war, for instance, whenever German mercenaries (whose cadence topped out at 72 paces per minute) served alongside British soldiers, they would complain—in between deep gulps of air—whenever the drums began beating the quick step. Captain Georg Pausch grumbled that such rapidity was appropriate only in the winter "in the chase, with fast horses and good dogs!"[9] The American militias advanced more slowly still. Their common step, the default march in the field, was to a 24-inch pace at a rate of 60 per minute.[10] From the American point of view, then, when they recalled that the British were approaching with a "very slow march," we can assume that the red-coats' pace was less than between 60 and 75 paces per minute.

The question is why. The usual reason given for their nonchalance is that the British were weighed down by heavy packs and equipment. According to Charles Stedman, who in 1794 wrote one of the first narratives of the battle—and in so doing created one of its enduring myths—the Grenadiers were "encumbered with three days' provisions, their knapsacks on their backs, which, together with cartouche-box, ammunition, and firelock, may be estimated at one hundred and twenty-five pounds weight."[11]

A more careful measurement, however, finds that a redcoat bearing this load would in fact be carrying about fifty, perhaps up to sixty pounds—less than a French Foreign Legionnaire of the 1830s (100 pounds) or a British Chindit guerrilla of World War II (86 pounds), but about the same as a modern American soldier's kit in urban combat.[12] It doesn't really matter, though, because the Grenadiers were not lugging much more than their muskets, some ammunition, and their bayonets. The rest of their baggage and packs had been left in Boston, whence they would be ferried to Moulton's Point following their inevitable victory.[13]

Heavy knapsacks were not, therefore, the reason for the languid pace. At bottom, Howe was faced at Bunker Hill with a terrible and irreconcilable dilemma. It is often forgotten that Howe, despite his later reputation as a ditherer, had long been in the progressive vanguard of British tacticians, his particular specialty being the then-innovative Light troops and their fast, flexible formations (known as "open order").[14] Howe recognized more than anyone that speed and suppleness were of the essence, then, if one wanted to attack a fixed entrenchment like the rail fence. But Howe had wasted his skilled Lights at the beach, and the rest of his line troops lacked their abilities, leaving him in the unenviable position of having to march his forces slowly toward Stark's expectant guns.

Tactically speaking, conventional eighteenth-century armies relied on long, straight lines marching steadily forward to gain momentum and menace as they methodically, remorselessly, imperturbably rolled toward wavering defenders, who would often break and flee before the mass onslaught. There was no better way to lose battles than for soldiers to become higgledy-piggledy. Tacticians therefore devoted much thought to the deceptively complex task of keeping lines uniform and even. The key to success was for every man to march in precise lockstep, "without tottering, and with perfect steadiness," according to one British manual.[15]

For well-drilled troops, this ideal could be realized, but at Bunker Hill the redcoats' lack of training and coordination bedeviled them from the outset. Howe was accordingly forced to rely on rather dated, if relatively simple, tactics to chivy the various regiments' troops into a straight line and get them marching toward the rail fence—if at a slow place, to maintain their cohesion. Twenty years earlier, during the Seven Years' War in Europe, marching three ranks in "close order" had been the accepted standard. Such a formation crammed as much firepower into as compact a space as possible, intensifying the damage inflicted by each volley. Yet a slimmer two-rank system in which the men were relatively spread out had temporarily gained a toehold during the French and Indian War in North America, a land where free-ranging forest firefights were common.[16]

Through the start of June, however, in Boston the British units were *still* drilling in three ranks, in close order. Only on June 3, just two weeks before Bunker Hill and probably prompted by Howe, did Gage order his troops to start "draw[ing] up two deep on their regimental parades as well as on the general parade."[17] Such a change caused much confusion among men and officers alike, requiring as it did major alterations in marching order and firing procedures. Sergeants, corporals, lieutenants, and captains all had to stand in different places, unlearn their memorized training, and try to accustom themselves to maneuvering these much longer, but only slightly thinner, formations. Now, just wheeling the line to reorient which direction it faced required immense concentration from everyone involved.

A turning movement resembled the hub and spoke of a wagon wheel. The men on the hub had only to swivel at a relatively slow pace to turn, say, forty-five degrees, while those on the outer end of the spoke would have to march with sufficient speed to ensure that they arrived at the same time. If the varying speeds were not precisely timed and carved into the men's muscle memory, the once-rigid line would end up looking like a tangled piece of string. Another eternal problem was, as a French specialist remarked in 1772, "once the battalion begins to move at any speed, the second and third ranks fall into inevitable disorder, the formation wavers on the march, the files get in each others' way, and the direction of fire loses its proper alignment."[18]

It would not have been possible for the Boston regiments to hone these skills in a fortnight. As it was, none, apart from the Lights, appeared to have even attempted to practice expanding their files—an advanced technique that would have caused untold chaos without first having perfected the basic two-rank formation. So it was that at Bunker Hill Howe was encumbered with troops who could neither be reliably maneuvered nor permitted to spread themselves out. In his mind, then, it was imperative to get them lined up nice and straight at Moulton's Point and then, as he ordered, to start "moving slowly and frequently halting" so that the Grenadiers and the regulars could shuffle back into place.[19] The result, as his colleague General Henry Clinton observed, was "one long straggling line two deep."[20] Hence the bemusing sight of the British troops advancing far more slowly than expected.

Making matters worse was the topography. As a Prussian soldier of the time cautioned, "a ploughed field or a churned up meadow" would inevitably reduce "harmony to dissonance."[21] Since the hay growing in the fields between Moulton's Point and the rail fence had not been cut in some time, it was now waist-high. Worse, the hay hid the deep furrows left behind by plowing the rocky dirt. Twisted ankles and stumbles were a certainty. The crop also obscured the ten or twelve fences of "strong posts and close railing, very high, and which could not be broken readily" (as Howe admitted), that divided one field from another.[22] Over each of these "great obstruction[s]," remarked Lieutenant Williams, the Grenadiers would have to clamber, not only further throwing off their pace but turning them into targets as they scaled the top and were backdropped by the sky behind.[23] Captain Thomas Stanley, who visited the site a few months later, heard that "the men were obliged to ground their arms to get over them."[24] Once on the other side, they had to waste still more time hauling the muskets over.

It's important to realize that these problems did not affect every British soldier in the same way at the same time, just as not every company in the army was overwhelmed by raw recruits and unable to fire effectively. Otherwise, none of Howe's regiments could have conjured themselves up out of bed that morning, let alone begun to mount an assault. These liabilities, in other words, were less cumulative than piecemeal, in the sense that each bore an impact on individual units differently and to a greater or lesser extent. A Grenadier company, for instance, comprising men with five to fifteen years' experience would not have found advancing in two lines onerous—unless it was also confronted by disadvantageous terrain or held up by a green and poorly officered unit nearby. Taken together, however, the various challenges severely depreciated the entire army's combat effectiveness.

This was before taking into account the pitiful vulnerability of the British to the defensive advantages enjoyed by their opponents. Chief among the latter was the volume of fire emanating from the rail fence, which was, according to Lieutenant Thomas Page (who mapped the battlefield), 900 feet long.[25] Records suggest roughly 1,595 militiamen (1,395 New Hampshiremen and 200 Connecticuters) awaited the British behind the fence—or one man for every half a foot.[26]

This, clearly, is an impossible figure, even if they stood sideways rather than frontally. British manuals generally allocated 22 inches—1.83 feet—to each man when calculating ranks (as the Marine Corps does today), but they needed more space to reload and fire.[27] The Americans, more loosely organized, probably required more elbow room, so let us say they were allotted 2.5 feet (or 30 inches) per man.

Simple arithmetic indicates that there must have been *four* ranks of men along the greater part of the fence. Even assuming (because the right-hand side was farther from the heaviest fighting) that each of the men in the Connecticut detachment occupied just two feet and was "double-parked" (so covering 200 instead of 400 feet of fence if standing in single line), that would still leave only 700 feet available for the

1,395 New Hampshiremen. Using the 2.5-foot measure, 700 feet would fit just 280 men in a single rank, or 560 in two, 1,120 in three, and 1,400—almost exactly our 1,395 calculation—in four.

How, then, did they all shoot? The most probable explanation is that during the battle the front row fired, then stepped back several feet so that the man behind him could take his place while he reloaded. This was done repeatedly so that all four men waiting their turn had a chance to shoot. Owing to the strong familial structure of New England companies, most militiamen would have chosen their trio of "teammates," so while there no doubt would have been some jostling, ribbing, and elbowing if someone took his own sweet time to fire, the cycle probably worked quite smoothly and allowed plenty of opportunity for each man to load and prime his firearm carefully. With three other men eager to take their shots, those needing a few minutes to clean their barrels, measure their powder, or change the flint had ample time to do so. In contrast, a leading complaint among professional soldiers was that the synchronized volleys common in Europe forced men to prepare their muskets for the next round with excessive haste, thereby causing innumerable misfires and wasted shots.

At the rail fence, after Stark "harangued his regiment in a short but animated address; then directed them to give three cheers" (according to Henry Dearborn), he encouraged his militiamen to take their shots as they wished and at whatever range they judged effective.[28] This was a slap in the face of General Putnam, who had earlier visited the position. Then, recalled Reuben Kemp (of Stark's regiment), Putnam had "charged the men not to fire till the enemy came close to the works; and then to take good aim, and make every shot kill a man. But there were a few pieces discharged before the order was given to fire. General Putnam appeared very angry and passed along the lines quickly, with his sword drawn, and threatened to stab any man that fired without order."[29]

That the New Hampshire colonel and his men ignored Putnam so defiantly illustrates the division between the old-school officers like him and such stiff-necked soldiers as Stark, who preferred to do things their own way, the French and Indian way. Putnam's whites-of-the-eyes insistence on the troops withholding their fire until they could unleash at close range a synchronized blast was based on European practice. But for Stark, the British made an attractive target *now,* his men were keen as mustard, and some three or four ranks impatiently wanted their turn. He understood, as well, the folly of trying to keep the boys reined in. Any "attempt to control them by uniformity and system," according to the rail-fence veteran Henry Dearborn, was doomed to failure, because "each [man had] his peculiar manner of loading and firing, which had been practised upon for years, with the same gun."[30]

The importance of knowing every inch of a weapon to maximize combat effectiveness cannot be overestimated. The advent of machined, interchangeable parts and standardized production lay far in the future, and this was an age when every single piece of a firearm was hand-made.[31] The quality of construction, the type of wood and robustness of the iron, the length of the barrel, the placement of the sights, the tightness of the screws, the strength of the firing mechanism, the pull of the trigger, the weight of the weapon, all varied widely from weapon to weapon. Neither should we forget the idiosyncrasies introduced by deviations in the ammunition itself, such as the ball being unsymmetrical through faulty casting (air pockets in the lead, for instance), improper measuring, mixed granulation, dampness, and indifferent ramming of the gunpowder.

As hunters and farmers, the militiamen relied on their guns to sustain and defend themselves, and since they had generally used the same firearms for much of their lives, they knew exactly what their peculiar tics were and compensated accordingly. For instance, Israel Litchfield, from Scituate, was quite typical in devoting a great deal of time to maintaining his weapon and its accoutrements in the lead-up to Bunker Hill. According to his diary, on November 16, 1774, he "worked upon [his] gun." In February 1775 he "made [. . .] a cartridge-box, [. . .] covered it with a coltskin. It will carry 19 rounds." Then he helped his captain, Samuel Stockbridge, make some cartridge-boxes for the other men in the company. On March 10, he "scoured up [his] gun" to clear away the fouling in the barrel caused by unburned gunpowder residue before taking it the following day to Hezekiah Hutson, the gunsmith, to "put in a new main-spring into [his] lock."[32]

On March 20—about a month before the fight at Lexington—
Litchfield (now a sergeant) proudly brandished his refurbished firearm
at target practice, where "we fired three volleys. Capt. Stockbridge shot
at a mark about 12 or 14 rods [70 yards or so] and hit it exactly within
an inch."[33] The next day, Litchfield busily fine-tuned his musket and,
more specifically, made sure that he was using exactly the right amount
of gunpowder to guarantee a successful firing with sufficient energy
propelling the ball to kill at a hundred yards:

> I spent the whole day a-scouring her and cleaning the lock and fix-
> ing her. After I had cleaned and oiled the lock I put in a good flint
> and tried her to burn three corns [grains] of powder. I cocked her
> and snapped and she burned them. I told out just three corns and
> tried her again and she burned it so I tried her eleven times success-
> fully and she burnt three corns of powder every time and did not
> miss. The 12th time she missed them but I overhauled and cocked
> her and she burnt them the next time. Then I tried her to burn a
> single corn of powder and she catched a single corn four time suc-
> cessively after that: the fifth time she missed a single corn, but I
> overhauled her again and she burnt it the next time.[34]

It is unknown at precisely what range Stark's men began firing in
earnest: The cross-straps marking white Xs on the Grenadiers' chests
certainly made an attractive target at 200 to 250 yards, though some of
the defenders (as Reuben Kemp mentioned) loosed a few rounds before
they reached that point. The latter would have inflicted little or no
physical effect, for, owing to their ballistic and aerodynamic inefficien-
cies, lead balls decelerate quickly as they travel toward the target. On
flat ground, a .69-caliber ball (a common one at the time) powered by
a normal load of 482 grains of gunpowder will exit the muzzle at about
1,500 feet per second; at 100 yards that velocity will have dropped by
nearly a third, to 1,029 fps.[35] Thereafter, it will fall at a still greater rate
and drag its kinetic energy down with it, meaning that if a soldier was
a few hundred yards away a bullet striking him would essentially
bounce off him as if he were Superman. Many accordingly ended up

with such splendid war souvenirs as dented watches and snuff boxes that had deflected bullets. Dick Mather was especially fortunate. A musket ball that hit him directly in the forehead was "flattened . . . like a bullet of clay when it has been thrown against a stone wall." A friend suggested he donate both his head and the squashed ball to the Royal Society in London as Wonders of Science.[36]

At about 200 yards, the Grenadiers and regulars would have started suffering casualties, though few outright fatalities. While the great majority of shots would have missed, a steadily increasing proportion would have told—and that number would only rise as the British narrowed the distance. "The generality of the Americans were good marksmen," later judged Sergeant Roger Lamb of the Fusiliers, a talent he attributed to their fondness for "hunting, and the ordinary amusements of sportsmen. The dexterity which by long habit they had acquired in hitting beasts, birds, and marks, was fatally applied."[37] Stark also markedly enhanced his men's aim by ordering them to rest their muskets on the fence rather than shoot from the shoulder.[38]

Such precision was not particularly important at this stage, in any case, since the volume of fire emanating from Stark's position offset any missed shots, especially when the enemy paused to negotiate fences. The morning after the battle, ominously reported the *London Chronicle*, their wooden rails "were found studded with bullets, not a hand's breadth from each other."[39]

The moment when the British reached a range of around 100 yards would help decide the engagement. Among professional military men, that was judged the optimal distance to balance accuracy against hitting power. At that range, a standard musket firing a nearly one-ounce ball would leave a bloody cavity in a man's flesh measuring 9.5 cubic inches—more than enough to take him out of action and probably necessitating a limb's amputation if the bullet hit a bone.[40] From there, the extent of trauma rose sharply. At 75 yards, a typical round created an entry wound nearly two inches in diameter, then tunneled through the flesh and juiced tissue to leave an exit wound more than three inches wide.[41] A range of between 25 and 60 yards seems to have been the ideal killing distance, as musket balls had not yet lost most of their kinetic energy, and neither had they sheared too far off their intended vectors, thus almost allowing the defending musketman to count on hitting what he was aiming at.[42] The militiaman Needham Maynard, describing the "thundering noise" of the fusillade along the length of the rail fence, estimated that at a range of 55 yards (or thereabouts) the British "fell in heaps—actually in heaps. They kept falling. . . . The bodies lay there very thick."[43] Generally, the last chance a defending soldier would have to fire a round at the enemy would occur between ten and twenty yards. If it hit, the bullet would scoop out nearly 23 cubic inches of tissue, muscle, and flesh, but if it did not, the enemy would be imminently within bayonet's reach and the defending line seconds away from collapse and panic.[44]

The object of any attacking force was obviously to reach that crucial stage in as whole a condition as possible and with the greatest possible momentum, while that of the defenders was to break the oncoming mass down into small pieces and slow its advance. Accordingly, the first step was to destroy the enemy leaders and those accomplices who helped keep the formations together. "Our men were intent on cutting down every officer they could distinguish in the British line," said Dearborn. "When any of them discovered one he would instantly exclaim, 'there,' 'see that officer,' 'let us have a shot at him,' when two or three would fire at the same moment; and as our soldiers were excellent marksmen and rested their muskets over the fence, they were sure of their object."[45] After the battle, it was noticed by the British that among their hit officers "few had less than three or four wounds," indicating that they were the unfortunate objects of several Americans' interest.[46]

General Howe, who led from the front, naturally received special attention. He was, to put it mildly, conspicuous on the battlefield, not only for his fine uniform and a servant named Evans, who showed the proper feudal spirit under fire by valiantly bearing a bottle of wine "for refreshment," but for the twelve staff officers accompanying him. The group attracted such intense fire that of that dozen, eleven were seriously wounded and the twelfth killed in action.[47] Howe, either through the grace of God or because his escorts painfully shielded him from the bullets, escaped from the carnage with little more than a bruised ankle caused by a ricocheting ball, though his uniform was soggy with his aides' splashed, spurting blood. (The faithful Evans was shot in the arm but was more upset about the demise of the wine bottle.)[48]

In Europe, officers were generally ruled out of bounds for such targeting, for they were the social superiors of those they commanded, and to the British a pungent whiff of dishonor surrounded the baleful colonial practice of remaining hidden and aiming at one's betters. The American way of fighting would later reduce the British to purplish, sputtering rage as the full horror sank in of Bunker Hill's butcher's bill. One typical rant went, "Dastardly, hypocritical cowards, who . . . do not feel bold enough to dare to look a soldier in the face!" They were nothing better than "skulking assassins, who can only fire at a distance, from behind stone-walls and hedges!"[49]

This American trick was particularly unsettling for Enlightenment-era officers because it challenged their rational interpretation of war. In the words of Captain Robert Donkin, "The cowardliness of the rebels [makes them] delight more in murdering from woods, walls, and houses, than in showing any genius or science in the art military."[50] Smart shooting, in other words, was proof of an inability to fight well. An odd position to take, at least to our modern sensibilities, but one that helps us glean the essentially alien nature of eighteenth-century warfare.

On the heels of the attritional losses of officers, the attacking companies began to falter but kept plowing onward. It is here that one Lieutenant James Dana enters the story. An officer serving with Knowlton's Connecticut contingent, he claimed to have fired the shot that finally provoked the British into throwing away their remaining ace in the hole: the "First Fire."[51]

As muskets were charged with a single ball and reloading was time-consuming, conventional eighteenth-century actions were based on the principle of "first fire," according to which the attackers reserved their precious musket blast until they were well within point-blank range, after which they could finish off the job with a rapid bayonet assault. It was "a received maxim," according to the foremost military writer of the day, "that those who preserve their fire the longest, will be sure to conquer."[52]

Forbearance was key. The attacking troops were expected to absorb the enemy's first fire and march indomitably on until they could shock the empty-musketed defenders with their counter-volley. Against undertrained or unprepared troops, the technique was often devastatingly effective. Lord Percy bragged to a friend that during the battle of New York—a fiasco for General Washington—the redcoats were ordered to "receive the rebels' first fire, and then rush on them before they had recovered their arms, with their bayonets." The tactic "threw the [Americans] into the utmost disorder and confusion, they being unacquainted with such a manoeuvre."[53]

At Bunker Hill, it was expected that the Grenadiers and regulars would keep forging ahead after the Americans had loosed their first fire. Howe's plan, therefore, hinged on maintaining strict fire control among his troops, but Stark's militiamen obliterated such assumptions. For one thing, they were not guided by the same military manuals. In other words, they ignored the traditional stress on first fire and indulged instead in free fire—from relatively long range and with sufficient accuracy to test the redcoats' patience to the breaking point. Further, owing to the four ranks of militiamen cyclically laying down fire, there was no "first" volley to endure. The incoming shots were incessant.

And the relative greenness of the British troops played, yet again, an adverse role in the battle. Even at Lexington, their lack of forbearance had been noticed. One report concluded that when the soldiers returned the rebels' fire, they did so "with too much eagerness, so that at first most of it was thrown away for want of that coolness and steadiness which distinguishes troops who have been inured to service." After criticizing the lieutenants and captains who had not prevented this "improper conduct," the report conceded that "most of them were young soldiers who had never been in action, and had been taught that every thing was to be effected by a quick firing. This ineffectual fire gave the rebels more confidence [as] they suffered but little from it."[54] There is little reason to believe that matters had greatly improved in the two-month interval between Lexington and Bunker Hill. Lieutenant Frederick Mackenzie of the 23rd complained after the first fight that "our men threw away their fire very inconsiderately . . . and without being certain of its effect."[55] Of their performance at Bunker Hill another officer of the same regiment, Lieutenant Richard Williams, would write privately that the men "foolishly imagine[d] that when danger is feared they [should] secure themselves by discharging their muskets, with or without aim."[56]

Now under, in Howe's words to a confidant, "a heavy fire, well kept up by the rebels" and checked by yet another of the infernal fences, a good number of aggrieved Grenadiers paused to exchange shots. They had hitherto executed the advance, continued he, "with a laudable perseverance, but not with the greatest share of discipline" and now Howe's line became jumbled by some raising their muskets to their shoulders while others continued to march forward. More and more shots rang out as the rest of the Grenadiers stopped to fire, "and by crowding fell into disorder, and in this state the 2nd line mixed with them."[57]

Hardly a round went unwasted. The British could point their muskets only at the Americans' exposed heads—a difficult shot at the best of times, and particularly treacherous when under pressure—and nearly all of their fire sailed skyward. "I should presume that forty-nine balls out of fifty passed from one to six feet over our head," recalled Henry Dearborn, "for I noticed an apple tree, some paces in the rear, which had scarcely a ball in it from the . . . ground as high as a man's head, while the trunk and branches above were literally cut to pieces."[58] Needham Maynard added, "there was hardly one of us hit [even while] their officers were shot down; there seemed to be nobody to command 'em."[59]

Among the militias on the receiving end, the sound of bullets, even if flying harmlessly overhead, was at first alarming—especially if one was new to battle. But warriors often steadied the worriers, said Roger Lamb, by assuring them that "there is no danger if you hear the sound of the bullet which is fired against you, you are safe."[60] This was something of a comforting fib, or perhaps an old soldier's tale, because at any distance immediately beyond the muzzle from which they exited, projectiles traveled at less than the speed of sound, meaning that their subsonic approach, passage, and departure could be easily heard from several feet away. They made a kind of distinctive "whistling noise not very agreeable to the ear," in the words of one man, to which another added that it sounded like "hissing" and "whining."[61] Amos Farnsworth, soon to fight at Bunker Hill, wrote in his diary on May 27 that during a recent skirmish "the bauls sung like bees round our heds."[62] Indeed, soldiers of the era might remark at the relative quietness of today's firefights, wherein bullets fly as fast as 4,000 feet per second. The loud, sharp "whip-crack" noise characteristic of a modern round is owed to its breaking of the sound barrier. As the bullet is traveling faster than the shock wave it generates, a person downrange cannot hear a supersonic bullet approaching—only after it has passed, as indicated by the "crack" left in its wake. In that case, it is certainly good news, because it means that you are not dead, so Lamb was prematurely right after all.[63]

Still worse than being left with empty barrels and nothing to show for it was the "disorder," as Howe put it, into which the British companies had descended. Once a unified formation atomized into small, scared groups scurrying for cover, it marked the death knell of any assault. It was now, Howe confided to a friend, that he experienced "a moment that I never felt before."[64] For an officer of proven valiance, one raised in the most tightly coiled, tight-lipped eighteenth-century martial tradition, to admit to even a tincture of alarm or a scintilla of doubt is remarkable, and one of only a few such instances extant.[65] Honor was virtually synonymous with displaying courage and maintaining one's reputation for steadiness under fire.[66] For that reason, Monsieur de Lamont, a leading French military intellectual whose works were popular in America, advised every officer that he "must never turn his back, [no matter] how great soever the loss is on his side; for if a man is once suspected of cowardice, he is past all hopes."[67] (It was no shame to lack natural courage if one wasn't an officer, he conceded with a slight but detectible sniff, but those sorts of people became churchmen and lawyers.)[68]

No matter his inclination and notwithstanding his losses, Howe had little choice therefore but to continue the attack. It was almost immaterial now whether he failed, but it was critical that he do so honor-, ably. Fortunately for the general, his career, and his reputation, the surviving officers managed to chivy the Grenadiers back into a rough line, but not before, in the words of the militiaman Captain Chester, they had "partly brok[e and re]treated."[69]

Collecting his wits, Howe made two decisions. He sent a message back to Boston urgently ordering the reserves, still waiting on the wharf, to sail for the peninsula. These reserves comprised the 47th Regiment and the 1st Battalion of Marines. Second, he instructed the Light infantry to salvage their honor by attacking the rail fence directly and immediately on the right. With the reserves still some time away, Howe needed to keep up the pressure on the enemy by using his Lights as regular infantry.

What happened next is bitterly described by an anonymous British officer:

> As we approached, an incessant stream of fire poured from the rebel lines: it seemed a continued sheet of fire for near thirty minutes. Our light infantry were served up in companies against the grass [i.e., rail] fence, without being able to penetrate; indeed, how could we penetrate? Most of our Grenadiers and Light Infantry, the moment of presenting themselves lost three-fourths, and many nine-tenths, of their men. Some had only eight or nine men a company left; some only three, four, and five.

"I have lost some of those I most valued," he continued. "This madness or ignorance nothing can excuse. The brave men's lives were wantonly thrown away. Our conductor [Howe] as much murdered them as if he had cut their throats himself on Boston common. Had he fallen, ought we have to have regretted him?"[70]

The folly of continuing an assault with disrupted soldiers against a fixed entrenchment was borne out by the devastating casualties sustained by the Grenadiers, the Lights, and the regulars at this stage of the action. Truly, as Stark remarked a year later when he toured the battlefield, before his rail fence the British "dead lay as thick as sheep in a foal."[71] The devastating results can be gleaned from the British muster rolls compiled after the battle. Take the Light company of the 35th. At breakfast that morning of June 17, the company consisted of one captain (Drewe), two lieutenants (Bard and Massey), one volunteer gentleman (Madden), two sergeants (Knowles and Poulton), one corporal (Nodder), one drummer (Russ), and thirty privates—making a total of 38. By dinner, just three privates were left unharmed. *Everybody* else was dead, dying, or wounded. Ten were killed in the field, and they were joined within the next two weeks by five others, followed by still more dying of their injuries and infection over the coming months.[72] In sum, when Captain Drewe (himself hit several times) compiled his report at month's end, nearly 40 percent of his command was dead, about 53 percent wounded, and 7 percent left unhit—a casualty rate of 93 percent incurred within just a few minutes.

Losses among the Grenadiers were equally terrible. A day after the battle, Captain Walter Sloan Laurie of the 43rd's Light infantry was detailed to bury the dead, now lying where they fell. Laurie had missed the action, being relegated to Boston duty, so as one of the few of his regiment's officers still in one piece, he sailed to the peninsula to supervise the grisly task. His party buried no fewer than ninety comrades (ten sergeants, seven corporals, and seventy-three privates) belonging to thirteen regiments. Of the total, one sergeant and eleven privates were shown to have been Grenadiers of the 43rd. Over the next few days, five more Grenadier corpses were discovered. If we assume that the 43rd's Grenadier company numbered, as did the others, between thirty-eight and forty men, then on June 17 alone it lost nearly half its strength. By August, another four privates and a sergeant would die of their wounds.[73] And of course the line troops also suffered grievously. Even marching behind the Grenadier vanguard, by day's end the battalions of the 5th and 52nd had lost (killed and wounded) a major, eight captains, five lieutenants, four ensigns, seventeen sergeants, and 225 privates.[74]

Imagine the scene. Before the militiamen lie hundreds of contorted British corpses. Hundreds more are desperately crawling toward a fence, a rock, or a ditch to find shelter before dying. The rounds that kill instantly elicit a loud shrill cry on impact, noticed soldiers of the time, while those that will eventually be fatal cause rapid unconsciousness. With the others, the wounded soldiers will experience pain, shock, and primary hemorrhage.

The degree of pain hinged on where and in what context he was hit. If the soldier was passionately engaged in fighting at the time, he may not even have realized he had been shot until dizziness, tiredness, and nausea (from loss of blood) overcame him—or if a concerned comrade pointed to the wound. More commonly, of course, the victim was aware that he was wounded. Survivors described the pain on being struck by a musket ball as being "like a flash of fire," "the sharp stinging pain from a sudden smart stroke of a cane," or the "shock of a heavy, intense blow." The latter sensation appeared most often in connection with a bullet hitting flesh or muscle but avoiding bone. That was a good thing, for the shattering of bone nearly always meant amputation. Because spherical bullets, universal at the time, entered relatively cleanly but tore flesh and tissue as they left at reduced velocities, generally little pain was felt at the entrance wound but much more at the exit—which is why there are several instances of soldiers shot through the outer neck or the thigh who turned around angrily to the rank behind to berate the poor man there of being careless with his bayonet.[75]

The intensity of the pain was not a reliable indicator of wound severity. A very serious injury could well be less agonizing than a minor one owing to loss of sensation and function as well as the advent of shocked stupefaction. The agony, in most cases, soon faded and was replaced by numbness. Then came, as John Malcolm recalled, the "burning thirst, universally felt after gunshot wounds."[76] On a hot June day, the desire to drink would have become maddeningly intense.

Dr. Grant, a surgeon in Boston who tended the injured after the battle, bitterly wrote, "Many of the wounded are daily dying, and many must have both legs amputated," adding that most of the casualties he had seen had been shot in the lower extremities.[77] Relatively few could have saved themselves by walking away from the combat zone, then, but would have had to wait until after the Americans had left to be transported to the hospital. Many would not last so long; they died where they had fallen before the rail fence.

Dr. Grant's remark also sheds additional light on the lethal mechanics of Stark's defense. Whereas the British had shot over the Americans' heads, the militiamen had "under-elevated" their muskets by aiming at the enemy's abdomens (in the redoubt, for instance, Prescott was heard shouting, "aim as low as the waistband" and "aim at their hips") to benefit from their shots ricocheting upward even if they fell short and hit the ground ahead of the enemy.[78] Such a bullet, thanks to the shallow angle at which it hit, would theoretically deflect at a similar or slightly more acute one, thus placing the groin, thighs, knees, shins, ankles, and feet at risk. A crippling hit in those places would render a man *hors de combat*—almost as good as a kill.[79] Hence Putnam's insistence that if you protected their legs, the militias would hold.

Dr. Grant, however, also mentioned that he had never seen such severe trauma caused by musket balls and accused the Americans of charging their guns with "old nails and angular pieces of iron" to enhance their deadliness. If true, then at close range these makeshift projectiles would have exacted injuries far more horrific than those meted out by the more ballistically efficient regular bullets. Their irregular shapes, propensity to fragment, and erratic yawing would have shredded more tissue and flesh, as well as have left larger, more jagged entry and exit holes, than regulation round balls.

But what were these "angular pieces of iron" and "iron nails"? A musket was a highly adaptable weapon in the sense that any object, so long as there was gunpowder in the chamber, could be blasted from its muzzle. It was not uncommon, for instance, to see ramrods—left inside the barrel by forgetful soldiers—flying out, and neither was it unheard of to load small bits of scrap metal along with the ball to make a primitive shotgun. Alternatively, a few individuals might have scored a deep cross into the lead balls, turning them into rudimentary dumdum bullets, which burst or mushroomed and shredded meat rather as "angular pieces of iron" would. Just as likely, perhaps, is that a number of defenders, having run low on ammunition, borrowed rounds from their neighbors that were too large a caliber to fit their barrels and improvised hammers to bash them into a usable size. Hitting a round ball naturally contorts it into a cylindrical shape; such an object tumbles rather than spins, causing greater damage to flesh, tissue, and organs. And lastly, it is not altogether improbable that some militiamen had customized their rounds by molding the lead around a broken-off piece of nail or thick wire. It was a nasty, if lethal, trick akin to inserting a stone into a snowball; later in the war, commanders on both sides stamped it out whenever it was detected. Howe, for instance, complained to Washington in September 1777 that his soldiers had found bullets "cut and fixed to the end of a nail" in an "encampment quitted by your troops." Washington replied that though this was "the first of the kind I ever saw or heard of[,] you may depend the contrivance is highly abhorred by me" and assured his counterpart that this "wicked and infamous" practice would cease.[80]

But that effort to humanize combat would come later; for now, over at the redoubt, the savagery was about to peak.

6. The Redoubt, Part Two

There are two contemporary maps of the battle of Bunker Hill, one drawn by Lieutenant Henry de Berniere and the other by Lieutenant Page, British officers both. On them, one notices rigidly straight lines of advance and retreat, symmetrically precise formations, neatly dotted vectors of artillery fire. Just as a highway map cannot convey the actual feeling of driving, their sketches are an abstraction of the battle. In a manner typical of Enlightenment military science—not art—they depict an idealized and rational vision of what happened, not the gritty, addled reality. During battle itself, similarly, soldiers are rarely sure what happened. Blurriness, scattered memories, tunnel vision, and fuzziness are almost universal among veterans. That both Berniere and Page mistakenly transposed Breed's Hill with Bunker Hill—and that no one noticed—is only further evidence of their maps' illusory qualities.

Superimposing ex post facto a neat, easily comprehensible pattern on the tumult and bedlam of battle, any battle, is ultimately an exercise in futility, albeit a necessary one—for how else could we construct a coherent account of their course? In this respect Bunker Hill suffers

from a defect common to every clash in history: No man was everywhere at once. Each individual present had his own restricted view of
how the fighting progressed. Those in the redoubt, for instance, could
barely see their comrades behind the rail fence, and vice versa. For that
reason, in his account Colonel Prescott vaguely mentions "a party of
Hampshire, in conjunction with some other forces, lined a fence at
the distance of three score rods [330 yards] back of the Fort"—the
redoubt—and never again refers to the events that happened there.[1]
Mirroring Prescott's confined perspective, Captain Charles Stuart, who
watched the battle from Boston with his brother-in-law, Lord Percy,
talks only of an attack on the "Fort" and had no idea what was happening at the rail fence, which he could not see from his position.[2] Likewise, Colonel Stark would have been as cut off from the redoubt as
Howe, who could not have known in any timely manner how Pigot
was faring against Prescott's defenses. Consequently, envisaging the battle, as traditional narratives do, as a sequence of coordinated, planned
actions and reactions is wrongheaded from the outset. Each commander instead worked autonomously and tried to make sense of what
was happening only in his immediate area.

Within the lower ranks, similarly, every memoir, diary, account,
and letter tends to capture only a snippet of the broader battle; their
takes are microscopic and subjective, not panoramic and objective. In
scientific terms, combat is anisotropic, in the sense that its properties
and characteristics vary according to the changing perspectives of observers and participants.

There are, in other words, *many* Bunker Hills, or rather, multiple
facets of the same battle. Every soldier, in short, focused solely on what
was happening directly before his eyes to the exclusion of all else. He
could not help but do otherwise. When engaged in a battle, soldiers
pay virtually no heed to the precise topographical names or characteristics of where they are: They classify terrain not as map coordinates but
as, say, a useful hill from which to hold off the enemy or a bit of woodland with good cover or a difficult field to traverse. It is only afterward,
sometimes long afterward, when they consult maps and photos or talk
to former comrades or read a history of the battle that they begin to

work out, piece by piece, where they were and what happened. By that time, "official" names have been bestowed upon various geographical features or famous episodes, and the old soldiers naturally adopt them to help make sense of their experiences.[3]

Even then, owing to the cunning of memory, their recollections of what happened are inevitably jerky and disordered. Of combat, vivid details seem real yet may be false, uncontestable facts become uncertain, and the conventional linear progression from past to present to future dissolves into a half-remembered sludge periodically interrupted by disturbing flashbacks, out-of-order sequences, and fragmented recollections. These disconcerting effects are not a product of passing time and increasing age but set in immediately after combat.

At Bunker Hill, for that reason, nobody seems even able to give a universally accepted answer to the basic question of how long the fighting lasted. Participants and spectators variously estimated the time between the first exchanges of musketry and the militias' withdrawal at "ten or fifteen minutes," "about an hour," "battle began about 3, and retreat about 5," "thirty-five minutes," "above an hour," "three quarters of an hour," "about three hours," "four hours," "an hour and a half," and "half an hour," to list just a few.[4] The disparities are partly owing to the companies' different arrival times and the subjective reliance on tracking the sun's passage across the sky to estimate the time of day, as well as the extent of their heavy combat involvement, but the faulty memories that attend combat are generally caused, or at least exacerbated, by underlying psychological and physiological factors.

Under conditions of high stress and extreme excitement, such as during a gunfight, the way in which individuals process incoming sensory information alters. They think less rationally, their deliberative and analytical skills rapidly deteriorating as their cortexes filter or tune out stimuli unessential to survival. Actions become automatic, instinctive—a type of cognition known as "experiential." A common symptom of operating in such mode is that sensory perceptions undergo severe distortion.

Studies have found at least half of participants will experience the event in slow motion, a fifth in faster-than-normal time; two-thirds will hear at "diminished volume," meaning that the sound of nearby gunshots is greatly muffled, and a fifth at amplified levels; about half will see what is happening with tunnel vision and black out everything not directly ahead and the other half with amazingly heightened clarity. Most individuals will suffer memory loss, while others will "remember" events that never occurred. These symptoms nearly always overlap. So someone with tunnel vision may see objects in startling, swollen detail—such as shell casings apparently the size of beer cans—swimming within their narrow field of vision while being oblivious to all else.[5]

Weirdly, too, combat can turn men into supermen, or so they think. More than half of respondents to a detailed questionnaire on their physical changes during shooting events said they experienced a sense of increased strength or a potent adrenaline rush.[6] Some, as a result, become impervious to pain. At Bunker Hill, the British captain Edward Drewe was so enraged by fighting that he was shot three times (thigh, foot, and shoulder), dislocated his shoulder, and received two serious contusions before he finally fell—but he survived.[7] Others may not even realize they've been wounded. Abel Potter, for instance, was bayoneted in the leg but was shocked to discover later that his "boot was filled with blood."[8] David Holbrook of Massachusetts was not only bayoneted (also in the leg) but "thump[ed] on the head" by a musket and yet felt fine until he almost lost consciousness through loss of blood.[9] Interestingly, it was only some time after they had left combat that these men noticed the flow of their own blood. In high-stress environments, the body restricts the blood supply to the extremities in order to ensure the core functionality of the heart, lungs, and other major organs. Owing to vasoconstriction, then, a soldier may be wounded in the arm or leg without bleeding much; ironically, once the external danger recedes, the risk to life increases as the wound reopens.[10]

Even when they remain unscathed, soldiers experience a host of powerful physiological effects in combat. Whereas a normal resting heart rate is between 60 and 80 beats per minute, hormonal or fear-induced pulse spikes allow individuals to reach their optimal combat-performance level—complex motor skills, visual reaction times, and cognitive reaction times hit their peak, though fine motor skills have deteriorated—between 115 and 145 bpm. They may feel as if they are gods.

Nevertheless, if stress levels continue to rise, so do heart rates. Between about 150 and 175 bpm, mental and physical abilities begin to deteriorate and their ability to process cognitive information and to use logical reasoning to act quickly, effectively, and decisively on that data plummets. Researchers have found that the deficits on performance at this stage are greater than for major alcohol intoxication, drug sedation, or clinical hypoglycemia (low blood glucose). Understandably, for many soldiers the heady combination of elevated heart rates, adrenaline surges, and a euphoric sense of invulnerability makes war feel great. For some, the experience becomes narcotically addictive, as any hallucinogenic, dreamlike state would be.

Above 175 bpm, however, individuals regress to infantilism or animal instinct. Soldiers engage in submissive behavior and lose control over their bowels or bladders. They will tend to freeze, torn between the desires to fight and flee. Headlong, unstoppable, unthinking flight frequently results but if they plunge ahead, their gross motor skills— used in charging or running—are at their zenith and may cause them to carry a position, though this condition renders soldiers useless for any task other than overwhelming an enemy.[11]

The ambiguity, fragmentation, and distortion that come with combat should raise suspicions about the "official version" of what happened during any given battle. It certainly does for Bunker Hill, where accounts continue to insist that at the redoubt, the British were repulsed twice by the Americans before launching a third successful assault that swept away the defenders.[12] We first read of this interpretation in a missive from the Massachusetts Provincial Congress to the Continental Congress dated June 20—just three days after the battle.[13] Accordingly, the Committee of Safety's official report—the one communicated to His Majesty's Government in London five weeks later, on July 25—observed that there were two failed assaults followed by a third, triumphant attack.[14] In Britain, the press followed this line in their reports of the battle—a remarkable instance of newspapers printing a story essentially dictated by the enemy, one that has proved amazingly resilient over the centuries. Small wonder, perhaps: The battle of Bunker Hill, seen this way, appears to have been a rationally organized, straightforward affair with discernible lines, precise movements, and three meticulous attacks.

Yet it was not nearly so clear and easily comprehensible to those who participated in it. Militiamen and soldiers alike were much vaguer on what happened. Said Sergeant Thomas Boynton, who was in the redoubt, after the enemy "came within gun shot we fired, and then ensued a very hot engagement. After a number of shots passed, the enemy retreated, and we ceased our fire for a few minutes. They advanced again, and we began a hot fire for a short time."[15] His chief, Prescott, told John Adams that "the enemy advanced and fired very hotly on the fort, and meeting with a warm reception, there was a very smart firing on both sides. After a considerable time, finding our ammunition was almost spent, I commanded a cessation till the enemy advanced within thirty yards, when we gave them such a hot fire that they were obliged to retire nearly one hundred and fifty yards before they could rally and come again to the attack."[16] On the other side, Captain Charles Stuart observed that "our men, astonished at the heat of their fire, retreated from the Fort, but were rallied by the courage and intrepidity of their officers, and renewed the charge *again and again* till they conquered."[17]

These recollections all describe intervals of waiting interrupted sporadically by "hot" or "smart" bouts of firing comprising "a number" of shots back and forth. Prescott at one point managed to orchestrate a volley when the British were thirty yards away, but aside from an initial organized line advance, there does not appear to be a succession of distinct attacks and retreats in formation, only multiple bursts of piecemeal rallies and advances in, as we shall see, various locations.

The "charges" alluded to by Captain Stuart were made in fact by small knots of men gamely attempting to keep the line but failing. Some took cover, others opportunistically rushed ahead ten yards while the defenders were reloading, and still more stumbled backward before recovering and moving forward again. The soldiers did not uniformly move as one but followed a ragged, ad hoc combination of keeping up, keeping down, keeping back, and above all, keeping moving. This is the reality of close combat with small arms, then as now.

The nitty-gritty details of Pigot's assault emerge more clearly if we ignore the official version and focus instead on the random snippets of what participants saw and experienced. Thus, once the British landed and began forming up for the initial attack, Prescott—a more conventional commander than Stark—followed Putnam's directions and ordered his defenders to reserve their first fire. He even became "indignant" when a few miscreants did not toe the line. Prescott "threatened to shoot any man who disobeyed; his lieutenant-colonel, Robinson, sprang upon the top of the works and knocked up the leveled muskets."[18]

In the meantime, the 1st Marines and the 47th, 38th, and 43rd Regiments had found that the upwardly sloping ground before them, like that stretching ahead of Howe's Grenadiers, was covered with "rails, hedges, and stone walls," according to Lieutenant John Waller. Here, however, they were at least told to "shelter ourselves by laying on the grass" as they waited to climb the obstacles.[19] Still, once they surmounted them they persisted in marching "rather slowly, but with a confident, imposing air."[20]

This attitude did not last long. The problem of fire control yet again proved the Achilles heel of the British. According to Isaac Glynney, the British first formed up and "marchd on towards us [and] as soon as they Came within gun Shot they Begun to fire upon us." We should assume that "within gun shot" range means roughly 100 yards away—way too far to have inflicted any significant hits on the protected militiamen. In some places, conversely, Prescott's threats held true. Referring to his company commanders, "our officers," said Glynney, "thinking it more Proper to Reserve our fire we with Held till they Came within four or five Rods [between 22 and 27.5 yards, or 66–82 feet] of us[. T]hen we were Orderd to fire which we Did."[21] But in many other spots along the wall, the militiamen opened up as they wished, as Prescott acknowledged in his letter to Adams. He was not altogether happy about it, noting archly that "after a considerable time . . . our ammunition was almost spent," thanks to all the enthusiastic free firing.

Part of the problem, of course, was that Prescott could not be everywhere at once, especially as the attacks occurred at unpredictable times and varying speeds on opposite sides of the redoubt. To the south, the 1st Marines and the three battered regular regiments were already struggling, but to the north, Howe inadvertently came to Pigot's rescue when elements of the Grenadiers, the 5th, and the 52nd swerved to avoid the rail-fence fire and ran toward the rough breastwork that was connected to the redoubt. Prescott was now under attack on two flanks.[22]

Only now, belatedly, did the British artillery come into its own. Mired in mud, too distant to threaten the rail fence, and low on suitable ammunition, these cannon were coincidentally close to the outlying American defenses. Dragged at great cost into position—two captains, one lieutenant, a sergeant, and eight privates were wounded in the process—the guns raked the breastwork with grapeshot to open a path for the beleaguered Grenadiers and their support.[23] The Americans stationed outside the redoubt's walls now began to incur heavy losses as they fled the breastwork. Of Lieutenant Thomas Grosvenor's "own immediate command of thirty men and one subaltern, there were eleven killed and wounded; among the latter was myself, though not so severely as to prevent my retiring."[24]

It was the first British success of the day. Seizing upon it, Howe adapted his plan. No longer was the rail fence his primary objective. Instead, he ordered the Lights to continue to hold their ground there as a feint to draw off militia fire while the Grenadiers, 5th, and 52nd exploited their position. According to a rather surprised Henry Dearborn, who had been expecting a renewed assault at the fence, "only a few small detached parties again advanced, which kept up a distant, ineffectual, scattering fire."[25] All the action now switched to the redoubt.

Howe was also optimistic that reinforcements from Boston would soon arrive. General Clinton, who had been impatiently cooling his heels in the city, had taken the opportunity to "embark 2 marines [2nd Marines] and another batt[alio]n"—the 63rd—and ordered them to sail to the peninsula as quickly as possible. Clinton himself did not wait for the 63rd and the 2nd Marines to finish boarding; he raced for the battlefield in his own boat and "landed under fire" on the beach near the redoubt. Once there, Clinton roused "all the guards and such wounded men as could follow which to their honour were many and advanced in column."[26]

As best we can make out, to the south the British were creeping forward and had made it to around 30 yards from the redoubt. As Clinton indicates, the redcoats were no longer in a hidebound line formation but had organized into much more mobile columns that were surging closer and closer. Prescott husbanded his men on the wall and urged them to hold fire. When he gave the word, as Isaac Glynney wrote, "we Shoed [showed] them yankey Play & Drove them Back again[.]"[27] There was probably another volley of sorts a little later, when the British reached a distance of ten yards. By now, wrote Prescott, "the ground in front of the [redoubt was] covered with dead and wounded, some lying within a few yards."[28] A man inside the redoubt noted that "it was surprising how they would step over their dead bodies, as though they had been logs of wood."[29] As losses mounted, the British columns naturally dissolved into small groups of men spread out and taking cover where they could.

It was becoming evident that this was the beginning of the end. Prescott was now so short of ammunition that he ordered any remaining shells for his cannon broken open and their precious grains of powder distributed.[30] More alarmingly still, his little army was shriveling, not through death or dismemberment but by desertion. Scores of militiamen had made themselves discreetly scarce by means of the gap, or exit, at the northwestern side of the redoubt. Prescott's force by now may have amounted to just 150 men.[31]

The only good news was that the reinforcements General Ward had sent from Cambridge had by now arrived at the Neck or were standing atop Bunker Hill. Yet some were balking from entering the fray. Amos Farnsworth in the redoubt was annoyed to see "a great body of men near by" who were doing nothing to help.[32] Others, noticed Captain Chester, were being *too* helpful: "Frequently twenty men round a wounded man, retreating, when not more than three or four could touch him to advantage."[33] Colonel Gerrish's regiment, for instance, was not budging from its safe spot, but his deputy, a Dane named Christian Febiger, roused enough men to form a useful detachment and led them into battle.[34] While heading toward the redoubt with his unit, Chester met "with a considerable company, who was going off rank and file"; he "ordered my men to make ready. They immediately cocked, and declared that if I ordered would fire. Upon that [the other company] stopped short, tried to excuse themselves," and complied with Chester's instruction to follow him to the redoubt.[35] Thanks to the influx of fresh men (and the not entirely voluntary additions commandeered by Chester), Prescott's outpost was able to hold out for some time longer.

Inside, nevertheless, the situation was growing ever more precarious. The British, too, had received reinforcements and were obviously girding themselves for a renewed attack. The militiamen were each grappling with the dilemma of staying or going. Wrote Captain Bancroft, "Our men turned their heads every minute to look on the one side for their fellow soldiers . . . and on the other to see a sight to most of them new, a veteran enemy marching on firmly to the attack, *directly in their front*. It was an awful moment."[36]

Their spirits remained halfheartedly hearty ("We are ready for the redcoats again!" they cheered, with one eye on the exit). In preparation for the final struggle, Prescott "directed the few [of his men] who had bayonets to be stationed at the points most likely to be scaled" around the redoubt.[37] Then came, remembered Bancroft, "the very crisis of the day, the moment on which every thing depended." As more and more of the men decided to sneak toward the rear, he accompanied Prescott to harangue them. Prescott's unflappable assurance and his towering reputation momentarily held them in check. He did not *order* the defenders to stay—that was no way to motivate a militiaman—but he earnestly pleaded with them to hold fast the line for a short time, if only for the sake of honor, before promising to allow the faithful to go in peace.

Bancroft, who was convinced nothing could be done to stem the rising panic, was so amazed by the speech he claimed to recall it verbatim nearly half a century later. Prescott entreated his listeners "that they must *not go off,* that if *they* did *all* would go; that it would disgrace us to leave at the bare *sight* of the enemy the work we had been all night throwing up, that we had no expectation of being able to hold our ground, but we wanted to give them *a warm reception, and retreat.*[38]

Reassured that they were not expected to sacrifice themselves as a futile gesture to salvage American honor, the men returned to their posts—Amos Farnsworth proudly recorded that subsequently "I did not leave the intrenchment until the enemy got in"—after which Prescott told all to hoard their ammunition and prepare for one last point-blank broadside before they could escape to the rear.[39]

In the meantime, according to Abel Parker, the colonel "ordered the men from one side to the other, in order to defend that part which was pressed hardest by the enemy," while bellowing (added Bancroft) that they were "to take particular notice of the fine coats and to aim as low as the waistband, and not to fire till ordered."[40]

Given the contradictions in the various accounts, which side of the redoubt was being "pressed hardest" at that moment is hard to say. What is incontrovertible is that the British now had the bit between their teeth and were pressing hard on both flanks.

To the south and under "a very heavy and severe fire," Lieutenant John Waller of the 1st Marines and his men were "checked . . . but did not retreat an inch" as they approached the redoubt's walls.[41] Nearby, however, the situation was fast unraveling. The Marine commander, Major John Pitcairn, was shot and severely wounded while "rallying the dispersed British troops" (according to the Rev. Dr. Jeremy Belknap in 1787), who were, in Waller's words, "jumbled" and "in confusion" and "half mad" near the foot of the redoubt's earthen walls.[42] Since Pitcairn (claimed the Rev. Dr. John Eliot) "received four balls in his body," his shooting was a collective one by diverse hands.[43] Pitcairn, no doubt wearing a "fine coat," would certainly have made a tempting target for any of the militiamen guarding the walls, but the number of wounds he suffered gives some indication of the ferocity of the fighting taking place.[44] (Major John Tupper of the 2nd Marines would report to the Admiralty that Pitcairn "died about two or three hours later," after being transported to Boston.)[45]

With Pitcairn incapacitated, Captain Stephen Ellis assumed command of the remnants of the 1st Marines near the wall. It was do or die. "Had we stopped there much longer, the enemy would have picked us all off," Lieutenant Waller told his brother, so he rushed to form "the two companies on our right" while begging "Colonel Nesbitt, of the 47th, to form on our left, in order that we might advance with our bayonets to the parapet. I ran from right to left, and stopped our men from firing; while this was doing, and when we had got in tolerable order, we rushed on, leaped the ditch, and climbed the parapet, under a most sore and heavy fire."[46]

On the opposite side, the Grenadiers, the 5th, and the 52nd were mounting their own push toward the redoubt wall and were also making headway despite heavy losses among their officers. Among them was Major Williams of the 52nd, who after being wounded was left to lie there bleeding out because his juniors, said Ensign Martin Hunter, refused to leave cover for fear of being shot. Perhaps he might still have done the right thing, Hunter admitted, but Williams "was not a very great favorite [with me], as he had obliged me to sell a pony that I had bought for seven and sixpence." (The major would die in a Boston hospital of his wound.)[47]

Captain George Harris was more fortunate. Upon his being shot in the head, Lieutenant Francis Rawdon ordered four men to rush Harris to safety despite the captain's murmuring, "For God's sake, let me die in peace." So hot was the American fire—perhaps the sight of a killable officer attracted it—that two of his escorts were wounded and a third killed (thus bearing out Hunter's reluctance to lend aid).[48] Meanwhile, as his men roared, "Push on, push on," Rawdon was impressed that the Americans kept up their shooting until "we were within ten yards of them." Indeed, "there are few instances of regular troops defending a redoubt till the enemy were in the very ditch of it," but Rawdon saw "several [Americans] pop their heads up [over the wall] and fire even after some of our men were upon them."[49]

The British paused at the foot of the walls, fearful that the defenders were reserving their main broadside for a point-blank massacre. But then, said one American, "one of our people imprudently spoke aloud that their powder was all gone, which being heard by some of the regular officers, they encouraged their men to march up [the parapet] with fixed bayonets."[50]

It may have been a sergeant of the 63rd's Grenadiers, or perhaps a Lieutenant Richardson, who was the first to mount the parapet and shout "Victory!"[51] Elsewhere, Lieutenant Waller clambered to the top while a captain and lieutenant fell next to him. It was now, he mourned to a friend, that "poor Ellis," "Archy Campbell," and "Shea" were killed and "Chudleigh, Ragg, and Dyer" wounded. Across from him, he saw that "three captains of the 52nd"—Nicholas Addison, William Davison, and George Smith—"were killed on the parapet," as well as "others I knew nothing of."[52]

Even as their chances of turning back the assault were inexorably declining, the Americans were giving as good as they got. When "a British officer mounted the embankment, and cried out to his soldiers to 'rush on, as the fort was their own,'" Phinehas Whitney shouted "'let him have it,' and he fell into the entrenchment."[53] Ensign Studholme Brownrigg of the 38th was so astounded by the tenacity of the defenders that he thought there were 3,000 of them.[54] Another officer told his friend in England that at this point he honestly believed that he and his men would end up as nothing more than "food for gunpowder."[55] "They advanced towards us in order to swallow us up," the redoubt's young Peter Brown later proudly told his mother, "but they found a choaky mouthful of us."[56]

Finally, noticing that the British were placing their muskets on top of the wall as they scrambled on top, Prescott bawled, "Take their guns away—twitch 'em away! And you that can handle stones, seize 'em and knock about!" Isaac Glynney picked up a few and pelted the invaders while others fired at whoever was in front of them. Ebenezer Bancroft "was loading my gun the last time, just withdrawing the ramrod," when "an officer sprang over the breastwork in front of me and presented his piece. I threw away the rammer which was in my hand, and instantly placed the muzzle of my gun against his right shoulder, a little below the collar-bone, and fired, and he fell into the trench."[57]

Prescott later maintained that he could have held the position "with the handful of men under his command, if he had been supplied with ammunition." He believed the enemy "would not have rallied, if they had been again repulsed" by a good couple of volleys.[58] Perhaps so, but this is immaterial, given that by now the militiamen were almost out of ammunition. Though the conventional narrative of the battle, in order to magnify for patriotic and cultural reasons the disparity between the modest yeomen-militia and the superior, tyrannical foe they faced, has emphasized that the Americans had been short from the very start, in fact most men were initially more than adequately equipped.[59] Or more precisely, they had sufficient ammunition for an *ordinary* firefight, but they exhausted their supplies when Bunker Hill proved an *extra*ordinary one.[60]

"Each individual was furnished with one quarter of a pound of powder in a horn, one flint, and lead sufficient to make fifteen charges either of ball or buck shot," attested James Wilkinson.[61] It has naturally been assumed that these officially distributed fifteen rounds were all that was obtainable, yet in fact the amount of available ammunition was highly variable by province. Thus, the troops in some Connecticut regiments received eighteen rounds apiece even as Lieutenant Thomas Grosvenor's company enjoyed no less than "one pound of gunpowder and forty-eight balls" per man.[62] On the other hand, Colonel Brewer's Massachusetts regiment initially had to make do with just five rounds.[63]

Moreover, the ammunition supply was not static. The walking wounded were employed to hurriedly pare and scrape dead men's ammunition down to roughly compatible sizes for the varying barrel calibers and hand them out so that none went to waste.[64] And ammunition could be pooled: Aaron Smith later said that "a man at his side, a negro, [was] so crippled by a shot in the leg that he could not rise up to discharge his gun, but could load and re-load, which he continued to do, both Smith's and his own, and then hand them to Smith to fire, until their ammunition was expended."[65]

Even so, let us assume that on average each militiaman arrived on the field with fifteen rounds. Few before Bunker Hill had imagined that men could blaze through so much ammunition in a single brief encounter: That number was judged by American commanders as more than sufficient and at the time was counted as a needlessly lavish distribution. George Washington, for his part, believed that between twelve and fifteen rounds per man could last for an entire months-long *campaign,* while the British, less parsimonious, regarded sixty as enough for a season of several battles—but they expected a lot to be left over for the following year.[66]

In the event, Jesse Lukens reckoned that at Bunker Hill alone he and his comrades had each fired about *sixty rounds,* and Josiah Cleaveland remembered that he "fired 40 cartridges; borrowed 3 more." Another Bunker Hill soldier boasted that "he discharged his piece more than thirty times," while Nathaniel Rice of East Sudbury claimed that he fired his musket twenty-six times and another militiaman "seventeen times at our unnatural enemies."[67] Still others "fired at the enemy twenty times, some thirty, and some till their guns were so heated, that they dared not to charge them any more."[68] Even accounting for the men's exaggerations and erroneous recollections, judging by the amount of ammunition used relative to the smallness of the battlefield, the brevity of the battle, and the limited number of participants, Bunker Hill featured perhaps the heaviest, fiercest combat of the eighteenth century.

But finally run out of rounds the militias did—heralding the inevitable collapse of the redoubt. Throughout the battle, the Americans had wisely avoided close-quarters combat in favor of shooting from afar, but during the struggles for fixed defenses bayonets came into their own.[69] This was a British specialty, and the opportunity they had panged for all day. As General Burgoyne advised, against enemies who placed "their whole dependence in intrenchments and [firearms,] it will be our glory, and our preservation to storm when possible."[70] When confronted by such obstacles as walls and breastworks, he was implying, it was more sensible to risk one's life charging them than to lose it waiting to be picked off by distant musketry.

After the battle, angry participants would allege that it was "barbarous to let men be obliged to oppose bayonets with only gun barrels."[71] In an enclosed area, like the redoubt, soldiers thrusting bayonets forward would herd defenders toward a wall or corner by impaling or pricking them with the steel points. The writhing and flailing bodies could then be used as a kind of bulldozer to push deeper into the crowd of other defenders and cram them into a still more constricted space for easier killing.

For their part, the militiamen "began to knock the guns [with bayonets] aside—to spring on 'em with stones—to give 'em heavy punches, feeling that they must sell their lives there," said Maynard. The Americans tore muskets away from their British owners and "for a moment we had a pretty good time: We hit 'em . . . with their own guns. We took about 30 of their guns, I should think."[72] One of Lieutenant Webb's militiamen, Edward Brown, "sprang, seized a regular's gun, took it from him and killed him on the spot."[73]

Nevertheless, the weight of the British had the advantage, and the Americans fell back. For Waller, "nothing could be more shocking than the carnage that followed the storming of this work. We tumbled over the dead to get at the living, who were crowding out of the gorge of the redoubt."[74] The "gorge" to which he referred was the exit that Prescott had prudently left clear. Acknowledging that his militiamen had done all they could, he sounded a general retreat. Most gratefully took up the offer. There was nothing dishonorable in their decision; these men were exhausted. Unlike the British, who had enjoyed a sound night's sleep and a hot breakfast, Prescott's defenders had been awake since early Friday morning, nearly thirty-six hours before. After a busy day in camp, they had marched to the peninsula and spent the night building the redoubt with barely a morsel or gulp to sustain them. In the morning they had been under prolonged artillery fire and, of course, for most of Saturday afternoon, they were fighting for their lives. Ravenous, thirsty, disoriented, scared, dusty, outnumbered, the Americans could hold out no longer.

For his part, Peter Brown "jumped over the walls and ran half a mile, where balls flew like hailstones and cannon roared like thunder," while David How remembered that after his friend was shot right next to him, he grabbed his musket, "let fly" at a looming redcoat, and fled for the rear.[75] Meanwhile, to cover them, Prescott and a band of die-hards heroically defended the gateway to Bunker Hill, the Neck, and safety.

The scene became one heaving, bloody bedlam amid the swirling dust and smoke—so thick and dark that men had to feel their way to an exit.[76] With bayonets bent and muzzles dipped in gore, the British thrust ahead, delayed only by Prescott's paladins, who swung their cut-lasses and employed muskets as makeshift poles to parry the enemy's bayonets. Another particularly effective method was to "club" a mus-ket: holding it by the muzzle and swinging it with force at a head or face, often shivering to pieces their wooden stocks.[77] In general during such melees, men do not tackle each other individually but instead lunge or swing at, hit or cut anyone nearby not instantly recognizable as an ally. When two men do come to blows, the resulting fight is rarely a thing of choreographed beauty; it is all flailing fists and clumsy re-buffs and desperate slashes.

Understandably, then, for this stage in an infantry action, that of hand-to-hand combat, it is rare to find coherent or authoritative ac-counts of what happened. As it is probably the most exhilarating, ter-rifying, animalistic, anarchic, primitive experience of all, this mode of fighting is more prone to memory blackouts, disjointed recollections, and sensory kaleidoscoping than even conventional combat. Descrip-tions of what happened are accordingly sparse, but we are fortunate in possessing a few vivid snapshots of what the final moments in the re-doubt were like.

Israel Potter and some comrades had "to fight our way through a very considerable body of the enemy, with clubbed muskets," in order to escape. Fortunately, Potter had brought a cutlass, with which he par-ried a sword slash at his head by an officer. The point of the latter's blade cut his right arm near the elbow, but Potter managed to make "one well-directed stroke" that almost severed the other's arm.[78] Cap-tain Bancroft, meanwhile, had "a severe struggle to escape out of the fort." Holding "my gun broadwise before my face," he "rushed upon" the redcoats in the way "and at first bore some of them down, but I soon lost my gun." Now disarmed, he "leaped upon the heads of the throng in the gateway and fortunately struck my head upon the head of a soldier, who settled down under me, so that I came with my feet to the ground." Immediately, "a blow was aimed at me, with the butt of a gun, which missed my head but gave me a severe contusion on the right shoulder. Numbers were trying to seize me by the arms but I broke from them, and with my elbows and knees cleared the way so that at length I got through the crowd." There was now just one man standing between Bancroft and life, "and the thought struck me that he might kill me after I had passed him." So, "as I ran by him I struck him a blow across the throat with the side of my hand. I saw his mouth open, and I have not seen him since."[79]

Once the majority of militiamen had fled, the ground, said Lieutenant Waller of the Marines, was "streaming with blood and strewed with dead and dying men." At least thirty Americans had been bayoneted or killed in the fort during the fighting, but now "the soldiers [were] stabbing some and dashing out the brains of others." It "was a sight too dreadful for me to dwell any longer on."[80]

As many of the wounded as possible had been borne away by their friends, but some thirty-six or thirty-seven were left behind, including Colonel Parker and two or three other officers.[81] Some of these, if we rely on Waller, were later murdered in the redoubt. We can be quite sure, as well, that all the victims were Americans, for killing takes time and possession of the field, and the fleeing militiamen had neither.

Such is the savagery of hand-to-hand combat that it is hard to leash one's intense emotions, particularly in the immediate aftermath of the fighting. It is then that the overwhelming majority of slayings occur of prisoners and the wounded, not days or even hours later, when passions have cooled. At Bunker Hill, the British repeatedly bashed in the skulls of the wounded—or the already dead—with the butts of the muskets and ran them through multiple times with bayonets. We see this kind of frenzied "overkill" erupting among victors in any number of past battles. To take one example, in England, at Towton in 1461, there was a fierce clash between the Lancastrian and Yorkist forces during the Wars of the Roses. Recently excavated skeletons reveal that out of twenty-eight skulls, fully twenty-seven bore multiple wounds—nearly all inflicted *after* the killing stroke on the first or second blow. Some men had been hit up to thirteen times. One typical victim received five strokes from a bladed weapon to the left front side of his head, followed by another powerful down-to-up slash from behind that left a wide horizontal gash. With the corpse lying face up, one of the soldiers then delivered a massive blow with a heavy sword that cleaved open his face diagonally from the left eye to the right jaw, severing most of his throat at the same time. As at Bunker Hill, not only did these manic attacks occur once the victim was already dead but also after the main fighting was over and the perpetrators were no longer in danger.[82]

Had the British found Prescott among the wounded, there can be little doubt of his awful fate. However, quite astoundingly—almost as much so as Howe's miraculous survival—the colonel escaped from the maelstrom with nothing worse than a coat rent by several bayonet slashes and a ripped waistcoat. One of his men remembered that Prescott "did not run, but stepped long, with his sword up" throughout.[83] One can only speculate that the British did not focus all their energies upon killing him because Prescott was dressed as an ordinary farmer and did not stand out.

The refugees from the redoubt had exchanged one hell for another. As they ran toward Bunker Hill, the British followed and shot at them from behind. A large number of men who had escaped relatively unscathed from the melee now fell, more severely wounded. Israel Potter, for instance, who had so far received only that "slight cut" from an officer's sword, now suffered two hits, one in the hip and the other in his left ankle.[84]

The retreat could easily have turned into a rout had a mixed bag of companies and a few packets of militiamen not rapidly set up a rough line to cover those men streaming their way. Captain Chester's Nutmeggers, as well as the units headed by James Clark and William Coit, plus a hodgepodge of companies from Colonel Moses Little's and Colonel Thomas Gardner's regiments banded together on the south slope of Bunker Hill, looking toward Breed's. They took positions "just by a poor stone fence, two or three feet high, and very thin, so that the bullets came through." "Here we lost our regularity," wrote Chester, with "every man loading and firing as fast as he could. As near as I could guess, we fought standing about six minutes." His lieutenant affirmed that that they held back the British with "a brisk fire from our small-arms."[85]

General Clinton appealed to Howe, who was still shaken by the debacle at the rail fence, to let him chase and catch the militiamen before they could exit the peninsula. He would have only minutes to regain the initiative. "All was in confusion," Clinton noted. "Officers told me that they could not command their men and I never saw so great a want of order."[86] Howe allowed him to take whatever troops he could round up and try to flank the troops on Bunker Hill—a plan that held out the possibility of severing the disrupted Americans from the Neck. Clinton ran with his men to the abandoned fort, ordered Lieutenant Colonel John Gunning to "remain in the redoubt with 100 with positive orders to keep it, and took with me all the rest" toward the thin American line.[87]

Clinton's boldness might have paid off had the militias utterly collapsed in panic, but on Bunker Hill the initial chaos was instead subsiding into an orderly withdrawal across the Neck. Small groups of militiamen paused to shoot at Clinton's troops to cover others moving to the rear, until they in turn were relieved and fell back. Lieutenant Rawdon acknowledged that the Americans maintained "a running fight from one fence, or wall, to another, till we entirely drove them off the peninsula."[88] General Burgoyne agreed, saying "the retreat was no flight; it was even covered with bravery and military skill."[89]

It was a hard fight. Colonel Gardner was mortally wounded and, according to a neighbor, Colonel Little "narrowly escaped with his life, as two men were killed one on each side of him, and he came to the camp all bespattered with blood." And of Captain Nathaniel Warner's twenty-three-man company, no fewer than seventeen were killed and wounded.[90] Robert Steele, a drummer boy, was told to go fetch two quarts of rum and a pail of water to succor the twice-hit Major Willard Moore and other injured militiamen. The beverages, perhaps unsurprisingly, "went very quick," he wrote.[91]

The British could see wounded men being carried from the field under fire. Among those who made it across the Neck was a Peterborough, New Hampshire, sergeant named McAlister—a Scotsman who had deserted the British army some years before; he had been shot "in the face and side of the neck, the ball having entered the mouth, and coming out one-half in the back of the neck and the other half in the mouth." He was rescued by a comrade who, knowing his fate as a deserter should he be captured, threw him across his back and brought him to safety.[92] Another man, John Barker, saw his friend Captain Benjamin Farnum fall wounded. Ignoring the oncoming British, Barker hauled Farnum across his shoulders, told him to hold on for dear life, and ran to safety, mumbling to himself, "The Regulars sha'n't have Ben."[93] In 1829, aged eighty-three, Farnum had the honor of becoming the last captain at Bunker Hill still alive, though he was somewhat lamed by the two musket balls in his thigh.[94]

Thanks to the American refusal to abandon their comrades, only thirty-one prisoners were eventually taken by the British, many of whom were severely injured. Most lay in the redoubt, but others would have fallen along the line of retreat. None were treated with much gentleness. Hit in the hip, a Mr. Frost had "crept in among the British wounded," presumably for warmth, companionship, or in hopes that someone would take pity on him and help him. Unfortunately, when he was found, the soldiers threatened to run him through if he did not get up. "But I was too stiff to move," so "they hauled me about till I became more limber," and he was taken to Boston.[95] Bill Scott suffered a fractured leg early in the fighting and would be shot another four times over the next few hours. Waking from unconsciousness and bleeding from "nine orifices" (entry and exit wounds, presumably), he discovered a British soldier looming over him. The redcoat demanded to know why he should not execute him, to which Bill, now beyond caring, replied, "I am in your power and you can do with me as you please." The soldier was pleased to but a passing officer stopped him and took Scott prisoner. Left out overnight, the militiaman was trundled onto a wagon and transported to Boston for treatment the following day. Like Frost, he was later evacuated to Halifax in Canada (and, like Frost, escaped a year later).[96] They were the lucky ones: By September, just ten of the wounded prisoners were still alive.[97]

There were even some uninjured Americans trapped on the peninsula, who hid as best they could, but by the early evening they were emerging—armed, scared, and dangerous, as Lieutenant John Dutton of the 38th would find out. Suffering from gout, he had left his company to change his stockings and was warned by his orderly that two men were approaching. The orderly thought it prudent to fall back, but Dutton laughed off the suggestion, supposing that "they were coming to surrender and give up their arms." But "his incredulity proved fatal to him [when] they lodged the contents of their muskets in the bodies of the hard-fated lieutenant and servant, notwithstanding that the King's Troops were within fifty yards of him when he lost his life, and some of the Light Infantry quite close to him." The Americans were killed a few minutes later.[98] Dutton and his luckless servant were the last British casualties of the bloody day.

Meanwhile, noticing that knots of militiamen were holed up in some houses on the Neck, Clinton urgently requested Howe to permit him to take some game Light and Grenadier companies to pursue them once they were flushed out by artillery. "I knew it would be a complete finishing to a great though *dear bought victory*"—another such, he admitted, "would have ruined us"—but, he sadly noted, "my scheme was not approved."[99]

Howe was probably right. There was no point in continuing the battle. It was getting dark, and his soldiers would have found it impossible to force their way across the Neck, let alone to continue on to face Ward's forces in Cambridge. It would have been hard attritional fighting every step of the way, for, as Burgoyne reported, all the Americans had done was proceed "no farther than to the next hill [Winter Hill], where a new post was taken, new intrenchments instantly begun."[100]

The British troops, also, were exhausted, a result of the typical crash after a lengthy bout of combat. The burn-off of adrenaline causes soldiers intense fatigue and helps explain why even victorious commanders can find it difficult to execute a knockout blow against a weakened opponent in the closing moments of an engagement. At Bunker Hill, officers often spoke of their men, even in victory and no matter how high their spirits before the battle, to be "weak and outdone," "very dull," "confused," and "discouraged and beat out" immediately following it.[101]

Soldiers who have not yet fully purged adrenaline from their system tend to suffer from jitters—a hallmark of insomnia.[102] As the sky darkened over the peninsula, any number of men found themselves unable to sleep. One such was Martin Hunter of the 52nd, who never could forget "the night of the 17th of June" as he vainly sought restfulness. "The cries of the wounded of the enemy . . . and the recollection of the loss of so many friends was a very trying scene for so young a soldier."[103] On the other side, John Trumbull felt "that night was a fearful breaking in for [the] young soldiers" surrounded by such a scene "of military magnificence and ruin."[104]

For most of those present that day, the battle of Bunker Hill was over. For the wounded, it was as if it had never ended.

7. The Wounded and the Dead

Those militiamen borne by their comrades to safety were, by the standards of the day, well cared for. Losses had not been overwhelming, and among the American forces there was a laudable number of doctors—a general rubric that at the time included barbers, apothecaries, butchers, and enterprising clergymen turning their hand to succoring the travails of the body rather than of the soul.[1] At Bunker Hill alone, twenty-nine physicians fought, and Americans as a whole were looked after by a young and credentialed lot. Of the forty-three doctors who attended during the siege of Boston, about 85 percent were in their twenties and thirties, half had attended college, all had been trained as medical apprentices—a rarity—and two even possessed medical degrees.[2]

Though they were short of medical supplies and new to battlefield surgery, many of these local and country practitioners were accustomed to dealing with gunshot wounds incurred during hunting as well as deep cuts—agricultural tools caused many injuries. Nevertheless, as in any war, the variety and severity of wounds inflicted by weaponry were really quite remarkable: Men could be hacked, shot, fractured, bludgeoned, pierced, exploded.

Sword slashes, for instance, which would have occurred in the redoubt, were particularly damaging to the face and head. At the battle of Waxhaws (May 29, 1780), the American lieutenant Pearson's "nose and lip were bisected obliquely, several of his teeth were broken out in the upper jaw, and the under completely divided on each side" after he was attacked with one.[3] Another time, Jonathan Nickerson was "struck down to the ground, his skull fractured, and cut through the bone for four inches or more and, while lying on the ground, was . . . struck four strokes to the head and several in the body with a cutlass."[4] Curiously, such injuries were not usually fatal, and many similar victims lived without major surgical intervention.[5]

Bayonet wounds, unless they were in the abdomen, were usually quite simple to treat, the weapon itself being a sharp instrument that penetrated without introducing foreign objects that would infect the wound. Abdominal injuries, which could lead to peritonitis—caused by food leaking through a perforated intestine—would not kill instantly, but often surely. A surgeon would poke inside the gut with a probe tipped with lint. If it came out dirty and smelly, the patient was fated to die. Otherwise, he did the best he could to suture the wound while pushing an escaping intestine back into place with two forefingers.

Gunshot cases were more troublesome, as there were any number of places a soldier could be hit. Lieutenant Mackenzie compiled a list of wounded officers at Lexington while usefully noting the locations of most of their injuries. On that baleful day, Lieutenants Gould, Baker, and Hawkstone ("said to be the greatest beauty of the British army") were hit in, respectively, the foot, hand, and cheeks, while Lieutenants Cox and Kelly and Ensign Lister were wounded in the arm, Lieutenant Colonels Smith and Bernard and Captain Souter in the leg, Lieutenants Sutherland and McLeod in the breast, and Lieutenant Baldwin in the throat. Lieutenants Knight and Hull died of serious trauma. Hull was hit at least three times but survived until May 2, while Knight, who died the next day, was likely the victim of a head shot.[6] Worse, bullets inflicted a wide variety of wounds, ranging from compound fractures and loss of soft tissue to injured ligaments, burst vessels, and joint trauma.

Nor was there a concept of triage—of separating the less severely wounded from those with greater need and then focusing on the cases with a higher possibility of survival.[7] (For those with obviously inoperable wounds, wrote a doctor, "a few words of consolation, or perhaps a little opium, was all that could be done or recommended . . . for prudence equally forbids the rash interposition of unavailing art, and the useless indulgence of delusive hope.")[8] Officers on both sides received premium treatment, of course—but everyone nonetheless suffered from a lack of litters and ambulancemen in an era before the advent of an institutionalized system of hospitals and a professional body of military surgeons—so the regular ranks waited their turn, notwithstanding the extent of their injuries.

Accordingly, especially when confronted by hundreds of casualties, doctors simplified their techniques to a few one-size-fits-all basics in order to expedite treatment for the most men possible.

Amputation was the accepted method of treatment for bullet wounds, and few doctors devoted much time to debating alternative avenues of treatment. Medical textbooks were firm on the issue, stating forthrightly that "if the bone is smashed, the limb has to be removed" or "if the joint is injured, the appendage has to be amputated."[9] Given a sharp blade and a steady hand, most skilled surgeons could whip off a leg in twenty minutes—a handful could do it in fewer than five.[10] The good news for the wounded was that the first cut and dealing with the loose arteries hurt by far the most—"all thought that [a] red-hot iron was applied to them when the arteries were taken up," said one observer—while the rest of the operation passed indifferently and apparently (almost) painlessly, thanks to opium, alcohol, and general stupefaction.[11]

Contemporary surgeons were brisk and businesslike. Dr. Thacher, after describing the "mutilated bodies, mangled limbs, and bleeding, incurable wounds . . . covered with putrefied blood [and] filled with maggots," nonchalantly remarked that "amputating limbs, trepanning fractured skulls, and dressing the most formidable wounds, have familiarized my mind to scenes of woe."[12] To their minds, the more rapid and decisive an action, the greater the easing of pain and suffering. The calculus was very simple: Forgoing surgery would lead to septicemia and gangrene, while even waiting to see if the body healed itself often led to secondary hemorrhaging and tetanus. In either case, death was certain. If, on the other hand, the surgeon operated immediately to excise traumatized flesh, at least the patient would enjoy a modest chance of survival. The aggressive policy to amputate as soon as possible stemmed not from callousness but from the humanistic, if utilitarian, conviction that severing the injured limb would aid the greater good of the body.[13]

Speed was of the essence. The official necrology reported to London a week after the battle by a chastened General Gage were 226 British killed and 828 wounded.[14] At first glance, the battlefield ratio of killed to wounded—one fatality for every 3.6 men wounded—appears quite "good" by eighteenth-century standards in the sense that there were relatively few deaths. At four major European battles of that era (Blenheim, Ramillies, Belgrade, and Kunnersdorf), by way of comparison, the average ratio was 1:2.[15]

Read another way, however, the figures from Bunker Hill reveal a staggeringly high number of wounded. As noted earlier, the Americans had aimed "below the waistbands" of the British at fairly close range, a practice that resulted in severe injuries to the legs. Many redcoats, as Dr. Grant observed, needed to have *both* amputated; it is worth bearing in mind that about half to two-thirds of soldiers whose legs were removed at mid-thigh died soon afterward, mostly owing to traumatic hemorrhaging.[16] Indeed, the volume of severe lower-limb wounds and the concomitant rise in deaths sparked a rumor in Boston that the militiamen had played a dirty trick. Dr. Jackson Hall, an American physician, was outraged to hear from a Boston customs collector named George Messerve "that all the balls fired by our people were poisoned, they were (he said) first dipped in some glutinous matter then rolled in white arsenic and dried, that he himself saw a box containing 60 pounds weight thus poisoned taken from off Bunker's Hill" as the militiamen retreated. It was, of course, an "infamous and damnable false representation," reported Hall, but "this story is believed here by the Government party." (For their part, the Americans would charge that when the British eventually evacuated Boston, they mixed arsenic in with bottles of medicine to kill *their* unwitting wounded.)[17]

The myth that one side was poisoning its rounds stretched back to the sixteenth century, when firearms were first making their appearance on the battlefield and physicians struggled to explain their frighteningly high fatality rate. After William Clowes, the finest surgeon of the Elizabethan era, suggested that musket balls secretly coated with poison were the reason, there was a spate of executions of prisoners by captors outraged that their dead comrades had been murdered by means most foul. (Not for another century after Bunker Hill would the actual cause of so many deaths be shown to be simple infection.)[18]

Ultimately, many of the wounded would die over the coming weeks and months—a fact cunningly omitted from Gage's report, which had an interest in obfuscating the figures he sent to London so as to avoid ignominy. Judged Dr. Ezra Stiles, the future president of Yale who took it upon himself to investigate Gage's fudged numbers, the British commanders were indulging in "designed concealment" of the facts by means of "insidious stratagems and delusions" to confuse outsiders.[19] Take the 23rd's Grenadier company, originally of thirty privates plus noncommissioned officers. On June 17 itself, not a single of its members was killed in action—which would have "improved" Gage's totals—yet between that date and September 24, no fewer than two sergeants, two corporals, a drummer, and five privates died of their injuries, and another nine privates were still listed as "wounded." Given the time span, we can assume that those wounds were permanently debilitating.[20]

Similar attrition, covered up, can also be detected among General Howe's staff of twelve aides-de-camp who accompanied him during the attack on the rail fence. Of this dozen, just one (Captain Sherwin) was killed in action that day, but all the rest were wounded. Gage's report noted this, but it would not be until January 1776—when interest and fury had long since subsided—that the dire truth about these "wounded" officers emerged. That month, the *London Chronicle* noted in passing that "a few days ago arrived in town, from Boston, Lieutenant Page, of His Majesty's Corps of Engineers, on account of the wounds he received the 17th of June, in the action at Charlestown. This gentleman is the only one now living of those who acted as aides-de-camp to General Howe." Over the intervening months, it seems, all but he had died. (Page had lost his leg.)[21]

Regarding American casualties, George Washington, the incoming commander of the Continental Army, told his brother on July 27 that there were 138 killed, 276 wounded, and 36 missing (really, captured, perhaps including a few who took the opportunity to "disappear" to escape creditors or wives), or 414 killed and wounded.[22] This makes for a killed-to-wounded ratio of 1:2—the typical rate, as already noted, for a contemporary battle.

Unfortunately, it is quite impossible to deduce the American wound-lethality rate. All I can say is that in all the documents I have consulted, I cannot recall citations of large numbers of men subsequently dying, and there are grounds to believe that that figure was significantly lower than that of the British.

First, there might have been a qualitative difference between British and American wounds. The most fearsome British injuries were sustained at fairly close range in the lower limbs, increasing the likelihood of damaging arteries and rapid blood loss, whereas relatively few Americans were shot at that distance. During the retreat from the redoubt, when many Americans were hit, they were some distance away from the advancing British, thereby lessening the bullets' potency. American anecdotes suggest that men were either killed outright or they limped away. Israel Potter, sprinting for Bunker Hill, was hit in the hip and the left ankle but made his way to safety "without any assistance." Though in much pain from his leg injury—"the bone was badly fractured and several pieces were extracted by the surgeon"—he rejoined his regiment six weeks later.[23] Amos Farnsworth was between 55 and 80 yards away from the redoubt when he was shot in the right arm, "the bawl gowing through a little below my elbow breaking the little shel bone." He was also hit by a ball in the back, "taking off a piece of skin about as big as a penny but I got to Cambridge that night." Considering that a British silver penny of the time measured .47 inches in diameter and the standard British musket caliber was .75, Farnsworth's entry wound was a small one, probably the consequence of a ricochet or grazing shot. Not overly serious, in short.[24]

Second, Farnsworth's elbow injury raises the possibility that American doctors treated their wounded patients differently than did British doctors. The British were following established custom, and they had no time, as we've seen, for pausing to allow wounds to heal themselves. Had Farnsworth been wearing a red coat, his arm would have been off in short order, increasing the chances of infection and death. American doctors, on the other hand, enjoyed a measure of discretion. On the frontier or in rural areas, where most of them practiced, patients with gunshot wounds were brought home for treatment, not consigned to a rough hospital where disease ran rampant. Since the loss of a limb in an agricultural society would adversely affect a family's sustenance and means of survival, amputation would not be the immediate, unquestioning first resort of a doctor rushing to get to the next victim. He would instead treat and dress the wound with traditional poultices and ointments and wait to see what happened. If, after a few days, the patient's condition appeared to be worsening, he would perform the necessary operation; if, conversely, the patient seemed stable, he would postpone the surgery, perhaps forever. Thomas Greene, for instance, received "a bad wound from the enemy by a musket ball which passed quite through the shoulder, thereby making a compound fracture of the scapula and socket of the humerus." He, "in a fainting and almost expiring state, was saved by his friend [Richard] Gilchrist, who transported him on his back from Bunker Hill to Medford." In Boston, such a wound would have naturally resulted in an amputation, but as it was, the doctor decided to keep him whole. Greene survived the war, though he was painfully troubled by his shoulder wound for many years afterward and eventually received a pension for being "unsound and unable to do but little" work.[25]

Third, and lastly, unlike the British the Americans were not over-whelmed with casualties, which meant that there was not an intermi-nable line of patients needing treatment by exhausted, shorthanded doctors. Each of the distressed could be given more time and attention by one of the no fewer than eight physicians plus associated staff avail-able in the hospitals—the governor's house and a minister's home, quite hygienic places both—set up for them.[26] (By way of comparison, the British could initially call on three surgeons, with a few support staff, and casualties were crammed onto the docks, the almshouse, and the poorhouse—whose occupants were expelled.)[27] The militiaman Is-rael Potter certainly did not complain about the quality of care. He was "conveyed to the hospital in Cambridge, where my wounds were dressed and the bullet extracted from my hip by one of the surgeons. The house was nearly filled with the poor fellows who, like myself, had received wounds in the late engagement, and presented a melancholy spectacle."[28] Melancholy it might have been, but it is probable that far fewer wounded militiamen subsequently died than their British coun-terparts. (The ones who did were interred in the garden.)

British officers who died were buried in Boston "in a private man-ner, in the different churches and churchyards there." Bunker Hill was an anomaly in this respect. Because Boston was so close, the corpses could be properly entombed. More commonly, battles were fought well away from cities, and officers were laid to rest in individual, though anonymous, graves on the field. Enlisted men were deposited in com-munal pits, and on Sunday, the day after the battle, burial parties ar-rived on the peninsula to begin that grisly chore.

So it was that Captain Walter Sloan Laurie, supervising one such burial party, put Prescott's breastwork to good use by dragging at least ninety bodies into it and ordering his men to shovel the excavated earth on top.[29] At least then he could be sure that the grave was sufficiently deep so that if there was a heavy rain, the "heads, legs, and arms" of the dead would not, as often happened elsewhere, emerge from the ground, causing, in the words of one veteran, "a most dreadful smell."[30]

Laurie additionally interred sixty-eight corpses described as "reb-els." (They included the former president of Congress, Joseph Warren, who had joined Prescott in the redoubt. As Laurie boasted, "I found [him] among the slain, and stuffed the scoundrel with another rebel, into one hole, and there he, and his seditious principles may remain.")[31] Clearly, whether the militiamen were due the honors of war was not among his foremost concerns. Hygiene, however, was. In the words of General Howe, "a pestilence from the infection of the putrified bodies might reach the Camp," and so they had to be properly buried whether Laurie liked it or not.[32]

Another officer assigned to burial duty, Lieutenant Robert Dupont, discreetly alluded to a historically endemic problem of war: the looting of corpses. On Monday, June 19, his detail buried sixty-nine privates from "regiments not distinguishable being stript of uniforms." By that not only did he mean such regimental insignia as metal buttons, epaulettes, and decorations but indeed, anything portable. Some of the dead would have been stripped of their shoes, shirt, coat, gaiters, belt, and hat. There being no militiamen present and the peninsula clear of local residents, who often were responsible for such desecration, the culprits were certainly British troops. In many cases, cash was, of course, the object. William Crawford of the 20th forthrightly bragged that during his time in the army he retained a prayer book (despite possessing "no religion in my heart") because he "found [it] a safe depositary for my money, which I won in battle by rifling the dead and wounded."[33] In mid-July, so many off-duty soldiers were "opening the tombs or graves in the burying ground in Charlestown" that Howe announced that anyone caught doing so would be "severely punished."[34]

For their part, soldiers felt that plundering the dead helped make up for the privations they suffered and the risks they ran for distinctly modest wages. What harm was there, as one wrote, in taking an officer's good shoes? Another declared that "exchange is no robbery" when he swapped his old equipment for better kit belonging to a dead comrade. On the other hand, Sergeant Cooper was not ashamed to admit that there was once a soldier whose belt he coveted, and "though he was not quite dead I stripped him of it."[35] The sergeant did not bother to help him—he was beyond help—but it was certainly not unheard of to kill even a moderately wounded man for his belongings. Since Dupont was working on Monday, the initial round of looting would have taken place over the course of Saturday night or the Sabbath, and we can be quite sure that at least a few of those sixty-nine privates had survived the battle only to be murdered by their own side when it was over.

There was generally very little ceremony, respect, or solemnness allotted to the task of burial and memory. "The frequency of danger made us regard death as one of the most common occurrences of life," wrote one British officer, who clarified that if a man was wounded he received every commiseration, but if he died, his fellows showed an "indifference . . . which manifested in them a stoical disregard of existence." Another attested that "there was no real grief for any [officer] beyond a week or two—all a shadow that passed away. Their effects were sold by auction. We bought their clothes and wore them, and they were sold again perhaps in a month, being once more part of the kit of deceased officers killed in action." Even over their graves, there was rarely a funeral oration; instead, as happened with the late Major Jervoise, visitors "cut indecent jokes, laughing and jeering at the memory of a man whose heart was good and whose soul was brave."[36] Junior officers tended to be the most jovial, for the death of a luckless superior meant preferment.[37] Lieutenant William Gordon of the 52nd excitedly wrote home that thanks to the battle "I got five steps, which brings me within three of being the eldest lieutenant: I am in great spirits, and expectations, of getting a company [i.e., reach the rank of captain] before matters [in America] can possibly be concluded."[38]

Though the number of physically wounded was simple to tabulate, the extent and degree of mental trauma incurred by Bunker Hill veterans is more of a challenge. It is likely that profound psychological problems were, relative to their modern incidence, somewhat uncommon. For one, militia and civilian life existed along a continuum; among the Americans, "tours of duty" lasted only a few months, so there was no perceived need for men to readjust to home life as the stressful absences from home were relatively brief. Within the militia companies, moreover, many men worked alongside their kinsmen and friends, further reducing the incidences of isolation, depression, alienation, or anxiety upon their return home.

Just as important, there was no inkling of combat stress, shell shock, or what would later be called post-traumatic stress disorder (PTSD), since eighteenth-century soldiers lacked much of what we might term psychiatric self-awareness. Sigmund Freud would not be born for another three-quarters of a century, and such familiar (to us) mental concepts as the unconscious and neuroses were unheard of. Though the word *psychology* had been coined in the sixteenth century, it had long been the province not of doctors but of Protestant theologians concerned with the mysterious origins of the soul, or more precisely, whether its attributes were created by God or transmitted by parents. By the time of the War of Independence, philosophers had begun applying the notion to the great questions of free will and responsibility, but it was very far from being understood in the modern sense or being applied to ordinary people, let alone soldiers and their experience of combat.[39]

In other words, troops simply did not understand what happened to them in war in the same way as those born in later centuries. Though they might have behaved oddly and suffered from psychological problems after a battle like Bunker Hill, it was difficult to express their inner thoughts and emotions in terms meaningful to us—even if they had wished to. Unable to comprehend that future generations might find his memoirs fascinating, for instance, Amos Foster, a veteran of Bunker Hill, instead tantalizingly wrote, "I saw a good deal, and remember a good deal, but it is not worth writing that I know of."[40] We know of just eleven autobiographical accounts left behind by British common soldiers who were stationed in America between 1770 and 1783, yet nearly fifty thousand men served in the infantry during the War of Independence. Of the British redcoat or the American militiaman—as a thinking, feeling individual—we know very little, to put it mildly.[41]

Much of what we can gather from their diaries and letters, British and American alike, is an uncomplaining acceptance of death, hardship, and scarcity—not surprising given their routine experiences of cold, hunger, pain, sickness, and cruelty even during peacetime. Jarring to today's sensibilities is the soldiers' propensity to list in the most matter-of-fact way the whereabouts and number of their wounds while remaining silent as to the suffering that accompanied them. The pension applications that they submitted many decades later accordingly restrict themselves to citing, say, an elbow or knee that has been "troublesome" since the battle or a shoulder injury that has prevented them from working. There is never a hint of self-pity, only a surfeit of understatement masking the physical and psychic pain many must have experienced. For those accustomed to the graphic, introspective modern version of the genre, accordingly, the writings of those who fought at Bunker Hill come across as sparse, unfeeling, and chilly, strangely obsessed by the names of regimental colonels, the time they went to church, and the weather. Occasionally, a classical allusion to a hero of Troy, Athens, or Rome enlivens the text.

Of paramount importance to them, then, was not inner experience but external behavior. It was critical that one's actions be seen by peers, superiors, and kin as honorable, noble, and valiant, and that meant remaining mum even in the face of terror and hurt. Hence artists of the era avoided depicting soldiers in contemporary uniforms, preferring instead the robes and togas of the ancients—for they represented the timeless aristocratic virtues of heroism, honor, and sacrifice. King George III dismissed Benjamin West's 1770 painting of the 1759 death of General Wolfe at the Plains of Abraham specifically because he had portrayed some redcoats "in coats, breeches, and cock'd hats."[42] By the time of Bunker Hill there was a movement toward greater historical realism—West was eventually encouraged to depict the late Wolfe in what he actually wore—but the painter nevertheless continued to insist that in his picture "Wolfe must not die like a common soldier under a bush."[43] Wolfe could not be shown to be suffering or to be acting dishonorably, for fear of being "common"—and no one at Bunker Hill, be he humble farmer or modest artisan, desired to be tarred with that form of indignity.

Even so, there can be no doubt that some Bunker Hill veterans had fitful dreams, reacted to certain triggers, or experienced violent episodes, even if—for the reasons given above—we can glean only sparse hints, not absolute proof, of the phenomenon. One comes from a diary kept by the British lieutenant John Barker. In his entry for September 13, 1775, he wrote that "Captn. [Charles] Chandless of the Marines cut his throat." Three weeks later, another officer clarified to Lord Denbigh that Chandless had "in a violent fever cut his own throat."[44] General Gage's casualty report to London does not cite Chandless as having been wounded in action, so an injury was not the instigating factor. The reason for his suicide therefore remains a mystery. It is possible he was simply delusional owing to sickness or that he suffered from preexisting mental problems—but it might be that he was scarred by what he had seen during the battle and could not stand to live any longer. There may have been more sufferers among the relatively high number of officers who sold their commissions and resigned from the army in the weeks and months following the battle.[45]

More anecdotal evidence of disturbance may be found in the American painter John Trumbull's memoirs, where he says that on June 18 he met:

> my favorite sister, the wife of Colonel, afterwards General Huntington, whose regiment was on its march to join the army. The novelty of military scenes excited great curiosity through the country, and my sister was one of a party of young friends who were attracted to visit the army before Boston. She was a woman of deep and affectionate sensibility, and the moment of her visit was most unfortunate. She found herself surrounded, not by the "pomp and circumstance of glorious war," but in the midst of all its horrible realities. She saw too clearly the life of danger and hardship upon which her husband and her favorite brother had entered, and it overcame her strong, but too sensitive mind. She became deranged, and died the following November, in Dedham.[46]

Then there is the Rev. David Osgood, once the brimstone-spewing chaplain of a New Hampshire regiment, who was long tormented by what he saw and experienced that sunny June 17. Years later he could not forget, "nor can I ever forget while consciousness abides with me, my own mental sufferings" caused by battle. His heart "sickened with pain and anguish, [which] seemed without end, a burden lay upon my spirits, by day and by night, almost too heavy for frail mortality." When he tried to sleep, "visions of horror rose in my imagination." Nothing, not "the delightful vicissitudes of day and night, the cheery rotation of the seasons," could bring him the "accustomed pleasure" they once had.[47] Yet he retained his unshakeable faith that "on our part it was necessary" to fight for liberty in this needful hell, and he eventually emerged into the light and found peace.

8. Aftermath

In this period, generally speaking, the side that enjoyed numerical superiority on the field beat its opponent. At Bunker Hill, the Americans outnumbered their foes at most points during the battle, yet they quit the battleground, and in this conventional sense may be said to have lost. British victory hinged not on numbers, then, but on applying, accidentally, the most force at the critical point. When the Americans at the redoubt were weak, the British managed to storm the works, thereby sparking the retreat. Many of the latter were under no illusions how close a call it was. "Had we been defeated on the 17th of June," Lieutenant Rawdon wrote to his powerful uncle, the Earl of Huntingdon, "it was over with the British empire in America, and I can assure you at one time the chance was against us."[1]

But could their possession of the peninsula at sunset really be declared a victory? Howe had established his paramountcy there, but that was cold comfort while General Frederick Haldimand, who had served as Gage's second-in-command until he departed Boston the day before the battle, could comment in his diary that the British commanders had, he hoped, learned enough to never again try to "buy another hill at the same price."[2]

The terrible losses the British incurred certainly cast some doubt on their triumph, mostly because winners at this time tended to suffer fewer casualties (expressed as a percentage of total forces engaged) than did losers. Let us compare Bunker Hill with other battles of the era in Europe and America. There had been little fighting since the Seven

Years' War/French and Indian War, and so all of our examples date between 1756 and 1760, well within living memory. The average percentage of casualties among winners was 15 percent; among losers, 24 percent.[3] At Bunker Hill, conversely, British casualties amounted to 44 percent; American casualties 16.5 percent (assuming an elastic average of 2,500 men present—and 414 casualties). The American figure, clearly, approximates the general average among the winners, whereas the British was almost twice that of the usual *losers'* percentage.

On a more abstract level, we should also take into account the impact on morale and strategy caused by the fight at Bunker Hill. A week later, a shaken General Gage confidentially informed the Earl of Dartmouth that "the trials we have had show that the rebels are not the despicable rabble too many have supposed them to be, and I find it owing to a military spirit . . . joined with an uncommon degree of zeal and enthusiasm."[4] The body blow inflicted by a seeming hodgepodge of militiamen to its prestige and hubris was felt throughout the British army. One officer conceded to a friend that "the Americans are not those poltroons I myself was once taught to believe them to be; they are men of liberal and noble sentiments; their very characteristic is the love of liberty; and though I am an officer under the King of Great Britain, I tacitly admire their resolution and perserverance, against the present oppressive measures of the British Government."[5] Another ruefully confessed the day after the battle that "we have indeed learnt one melancholy truth, which is, that the Americans, if they are equally well commanded, are full as good soldiers as ours."[6]

By yardsticks such as these, the Americans were the victors, despite an inconsequential and temporary loss of territory that would be regained nine months later to the day, when, as a consequence of George Washington continuing the siege of Boston, the British evacuated that untenable city and left for Canada. In the summer of 1776, they would return, not to Boston—forever lost—but to a new base, New York, and continue the war from there.

The militiamen would not fight that war, but they made it possible. Whereas their mutinous stand at Lexington and Concord two months before on April 19, 1775, could have been otherwise dismissed as a one-off incident, a single act of cheeky defiance before inevitable submission, an annoying little gunfight in some country village, the sheer effrontery and stiff-necked stubbornness of the militias at Bunker Hill bloodily demonstrated that the rebellion was a potent, viable threat to His Majesty's interests—and one that would not be so easily vanquished as expected.

That June 17, the militias guaranteed their place in history while exiting from it. Militiamen there would still be, but even before the battle Congress had decided to establish a professional Continental Army to fight the protracted war rendered likely by their valor. Bunker Hill was thus both the last silver-trumpeted blast of the old colonial order and the herald of a new age of independence.

And so, when speaking of these obstreperous clan-like companies, these little platoons raised in the backwoods and the farmlands, we should reflect upon the pithy words of the Revolutionary soldier Colonel William Grayson (paraphrasing the poet Matthew Prior): "In short, at this time of day, we must say of them, as [of the] price of a wife: Be to their faults a little blind, And to their virtues very kind."[7]

GETTYSBURG

1863

1. Introduction

In early July 1938, some 1,800 veterans of the Civil War gathered for the last time at Gettysburg. Their average age was ninety-four, and each passing year was thinning their spindly ranks. To the other 75,000 visitors to the battlefield on that seventy-fifth anniversary of the great clash, the old men were the last remaining representatives of an America long vanished. Their accents, their clothes, their manners, everything about them bespoke an era fast receding from living memory. Since their youth, the country had transformed from a sleepy rural society where no one could travel faster than a horse into a gleamingly modern superpower of cities and corporations, movies and electricity, machines and factories.

The old men, many with empty trouser legs pinned up or sleeves tucked neatly into coat pockets, sat sheltered from the sultry heat under canvas tents set up on the field where Pickett had launched his terrible Charge, arguably the most glorious, and the most misbegotten, episode in American military history. Some reminisced fondly of the cannon fire and rifle volleys; others mutely remembered the carnage. Then, from above, a strange hum was heard, growing louder by the second. Looking up into the beautiful blue sky, the soldiers saw eighteen fighter planes soaring overhead that suddenly spiraled down like angry hornets to escort six new B-17 Flying Fortress bombers—the same aircraft that would soon desolate and incinerate Nazi Germany. If that sight was not astounding enough, a billowing cloud of yellow dust heralded the approach of thirty-one tanks that in turn performed maneuvers in the very same field where 12,500 doughty Confederates had once marched forward in flawless lines for nearly a mile under heavy Union fire.[1]

The clank of armor and the buzz of propellers aweing and alarming the wizened survivors of the Civil War vividly demonstrated to all the gulf between the old nineteenth-century warfare of glinting bayonets and unfurled banners and the new, mechanized, industrialized version. Nevertheless, the Civil War is today too often counted as the first of a trilogy of great *modern* and *total* wars of annihilation, the mighty clash from which would spring the demonic struggle of the First World War and its still more incarnadined successor two decades later.[2]

Popular as it is, this view of the Civil War is wrongheaded. To begin with, to describe the fighting from 1861 to 1865 as a "total war" is to retrofit a French term only confected in 1917. Adopted and adapted by the Nazis in the 1930s, it was cleansed of its dubious antecedents after 1945 by American military writers, who likened the recent bombing campaigns against Germany and Japan to Sherman's March to the Sea.[3] Total war, in other words, was a singularly twentieth-century form of warfare that considered the enemy population, industry, and infrastructure as legitimate and as important a military target as combatants in the field—a concept and means of warfare quite alien to those living in the nineteenth century, when generals thought almost exclusively in terms of defeating the enemy in a decisive battle, at least at the interstate level of army versus army.

If it was not total, neither was the Civil War "modern," though it can appear more contemporary than it actually was because some of its technology bears a distinct family resemblance to that of a later era.[4] The Civil War witnessed the use of railroad transport, rapid-firing guns, electric-telegraph wires, mortars, barbed wire, land mines, hand grenades, submarines, torpedoes, ironclad warships, gas shells, explosive bullets, telescopic-sighted sniper rifles—all put to bloody work in the next century and in some cases still used today. But very few of these technological marvels exerted a meaningful impact on the war's conduct or outcome, and virtually all of them had already been used in European wars.

If anything, the Civil War was characterized not by its gleamingly advanced technology but by a reliance on traditional tools, methods, and aesthetics. Nearly all movement was conducted on foot and by beast, and the vast majority of soldiers used guns similar to those owned by their grandfathers. As had long been the case, for much of the Civil War battlefields were compact, engagements generally lasted a few days rather than months or years, and senior commanders led personally from the front. Even the dress affected by generals and colonels alike recalled an earlier era. Their formal uniforms drooping under the weight of colossal, tasseled epaulettes and groaning with gold buttons, their swords proudly clattering in their scabbards and their boots polished to a gleam, American officers still followed the fashion dictates of Napoleon's marshals.

For much of its duration, the Civil War was thus a standard-issue late-nineteenth-century conflict with more in common with the Crimean War, the Napoleonic Wars, and even the War of Independence than World Wars I and II. If the Civil War was typical of its era, then so, too, was Gettysburg. Despite the attention it has subsequently attracted from historians, filmmakers, and the public, Gettysburg was neither extraordinary nor even that "important" in the grand scheme of the Civil War (the fall of Vicksburg on July 4, for instance, was of far greater import). It is Gettysburg's *conventionality*, not its uniqueness, that makes it such an interesting case study in the American soldier's experience of combat.

2. Combat in the Civil War

The style of fighting at Gettysburg was reminiscent of, if not identical to, that of Bunker Hill nearly a century earlier. The typical infantry engagement involved three crisis points. The first was located at the hundred-yard mark, the median range for Civil War firefights.[1] There are reports of shots being taken at 220 yards and upward, but most soldiers soon realized that long-distance fire was pointless: One rarely hit anything.[2] Instead, in order to improve its lethality, defending officers often tried to avoid firing the first volley until the enemy was fifty yards away—the second crisis point, for it was here that the attacking side collectively decided whether to continue on or to retreat. The final crisis point was at around thirty yards, when it was the defenders' turn to weigh whether to hold the line or to withdraw.[3] If they stood their ground, hand-to-hand combat would soon ensue.

The default tactic of Civil War combat was the straightforward frontal assault. To modern observers, these blunt force attacks and their colossal casualty lists seem astoundingly bloody, and, not to mince words, astonishingly stupid. Over time, their repeated use burned through manpower to a remarkable degree. For instance, a fairly typical unit that fought at Gettysburg, Company E of the 20th North Carolina, began its war on April 16, 1861, with 107 men. Over the next four years, twenty-six of these would die in battle and fourteen of disease, leaving sixty-seven living at war's end. Of the survivors, fifteen were permanently disabled with wounds, and sixteen had been wounded but recovered fully (at least physically, if perhaps not psychologically), thus leaving thirty-six unharmed (or one-third of the original recruits). Nineteen of these, however, had never been in combat, as they were detailed for other duties, so really only seventeen (16 percent of combat veterans) emerged from the war unscathed.[4] Another example is provided by the 137th New York regiment, which mustered 1,007 men on September 27, 1862. Of these, a third—323—would be killed and wounded during the war, and another 171 would perish of disease, accidents, and other noncombat causes.[5]

Despite these unencouraging figures, to those living at the time assaults made sense and few complained about them. To understand why, one must bear in mind two factors. First, the widespread acceptance of high losses was partly due to the belief that the primary intent of battle was not to kill the enemy while minimizing your own casualties—this is a byproduct of a very twentieth-century reliance on kill ratios, body counts, and casualty aversion as yardsticks of military effectiveness—but to *endure* startling (to us) casualties in order to achieve victory. A willingness to suffer, rather than inflict, high casualties was considered evidence of a muscularly Christian and heroically masculine will to win, not of lamentably poor command, bad planning, flawed execution, and idiotic decision-making, as we might assume today. In our eyes, attacking an entrenched position manned by thrice one's number might be regarded as insane and criminally wasteful rather than as bold and brave, but to Civil War contemporaries a man's internal "moral" power could conquer any such "physical" obstacles as fieldworks, artillery, and rifle fire.

Soldiers of the era were fascinated by the mysteries of this intangible inner spirit. There was a religious aspect to it, undoubtedly, but they were also profoundly influenced by the Romantic movement, originally an artistic and philosophical endeavor that exalted the dramatic, celebrated the intense, cheered the wondrous, and venerated the sublime. Since armed forces are as swayed by trends and fashions as any other sector of society, it is also important to factor in what might be called militarily correct thinking when it comes to organizing for war. For instance, in line with the Enlightenment fascination with mechanisms, tidiness, and rules, the characteristic metaphor of conventional eighteenth-century warfare had been that of the clock: a system of cogs, springs, and shafts precisely calibrated, eminently predictable, and dutifully subject to known principles that ticked in perfect time. Generals played the role of lordly watchmakers, elegantly maneuvering their magnificently drilled units across a given space and occupying such recommended terrain features and power centers as hills, bridges, and cities to gain the advantage of a positional fait accompli over the enemy. Theoretically, once realizing he had lost freedom of movement or action, the enemy would honorably capitulate without a fight. Thereafter, the victor would extract from him a duchy or two, purely as compensation for time and trouble. If he played the game well, said Maurice de Saxe (1696–1750), who gloried in the title of Marshal General of All the Armies of France, a truly successful commander might end his career without a battle honor to his name.[6] (As we've seen, reality was much messier; at Bunker Hill the American militias did not follow the rules.)

By the early nineteenth century, the martial world's orderly "clock" had been smashed by Napoleon, hero of the Romantics and guiding light for generations of commanders. American generals in particular enthusiastically succumbed to the Napoleonic fantasia.[7] Thomas Jackson, soon to be famed as "Stonewall," spent several days touring Waterloo in 1856. "In listening to Jackson talking of Napoleon Bonaparte, as I often did," recalled Dr. Hunter McGuire, "I was struck with the fact that he regarded him as the greatest general that ever lived."[8]

What the new breed of soldier thought of eighteenth-century generalship was perfectly captured by Napoleon in his dismissive notes, scribbled in the margins of the *Military Memoirs* of Henry Lloyd (c.1718–1783), once the echt and ur of Enlightenment military intellectuals who wanted to learn how to war. In response to the ousted master's impeccably Enlightened precepts, he wrote: "Ignorance," "Ignorance," "Ignorance," "Absurde," "Absurde," "Absurde," "Impossible," "Impossible," "Faux." This was all just in the first four pages.[9]

The clock was replaced by the steam engine—a new invention that generated its own motion.[10] Its thermodynamic process *transformed* energy from one source into another, unlike a clock, which merely transmitted it. As the engine converted lumpen coal into power, a lumpen man in combat, animated by his impulses, imagination, and ideology, could achieve the impossible.

No more was the heady blood-red wine of battle to be avoided; it, not skillful choreography, was to be embraced instead as the supreme test. A standard textbook studied by West Pointers just before the Civil War emphasized that whereas the fuddy-duddy Enlightenment style of warfare "looked only to the capture of one or two places, or to the occupation of a petty adjacent province," the secret of Napoleon's exciting success was "to burst, with the rapidity of lightning, upon the centre of this [enemy] army [or] to outflank it, to cut it off, to break it up, to pursue it to the utmost, forcing it in divergent directions; finally, quitting it only after having annihilated or dispersed it."[11] Indeed, a few days before Gettysburg, Robert E. Lee echoed the sentiment: "I shall throw an overwhelming force on their advance, crush it, follow up the success, drive one corps back upon another, and by successive repulses and surprises, before they can concentrate, create a panic and virtually destroy the army."[12] Later, Ulysses Grant would agree, albeit in typically blunter terms, that "the art of war is simple enough. Find out where your enemy is. Get at him as soon as you can. Strike at him as hard as you can, and keep moving on."[13]

In this light—the quest for decisive battle to demonstrate vigor and virility—losses in the tens of thousands were obviously peripheral. "Troops are made to let themselves be killed," Napoleon averred, proving his point by losing fully 863,000 of them.[14] It mattered not, because soldiers were nothing but coals to be cast into the furnace of war, their cindered remains testament to the energy their bodies had supplied for victory.

As Lee, Grant, and a host of other generals would find, the "spirit of the offensive" did not, nevertheless, radiate naturally from the souls of most men, especially at the outset of a real-world assault. "There is no romance in making one of these charges," as John Dooley of the 1st Virginia put it, for "when you rise to your feet . . . I tell you the enthu-siasm of ardent breasts in many cases *ain't there,* and instead of burning to avenge the insults to our country, families and altars and firesides, the thought is most frequently, *Oh,* if I could just come out of this charge safely how thankful *would I be*!"[15] That was not quite the right attitude, needless to say, and hence the reliance on morale-boosting bayonets to inspire men during attacks.

Bayonets are perhaps the most misunderstood weapon of them all. They were virtually useless in combat, except in very specific circumstances—as at the redoubt at Bunker Hill, when the British could poke and prod the exhausted militiamen into flight. Subsequent generations have laughed them off as ridiculously quaint, as passé as the halberd, the lance, and the crossbow.[16] As evidence of their archa-ism, critics point to the manifold uses to which Civil War soldiers put them: skewers, tent stakes, and, in the memorable case of the chaplain of the Irish Brigade, a candelabrum, to hold the burning taper while he read his daily office.[17] So impotent were they that between May 8 and May 21, 1864—a period encompassing the battle of Spotsylvania, which featured some of the most intense combat of the war—the Army of the Potomac recorded a mere 14 bayonet wounds, compared to 749 caused by artillery fire and 8,218 by bullets.[18] Indeed, when someone actually died of a bayonet wound, it excited comment: Ignoring the other 185 casualties suffered by his regiment, Oscar Ladley of the 75th Ohio marveled to his family that a man "was killed by a rebel bayonet thrust in the groin."[19]

Yet soldiers of the time considered the weapon indispensable. The Union commander General George B. McClellan—in a sentiment echoed by his Confederate counterparts—instructed the troops in 1862 to "above all things rely upon the bayonet."[20] *Scientific American,* a publication never hesitant to rap the knuckles of what it regarded as reactionary military types, commented approvingly that, at least when it came to bayonets, McClellan "understands his business."[21] Stonewall Jackson, meanwhile, demanded a super-sized version for his men that was "six or more inches longer than the musket with the bayonet on, so that when we teach our troops to rely upon the bayonet they may feel that they have the superiority of arm resulting from its length." He wanted more cold steel, in other words, not more hot lead. General Lee, it should be added, approved the request.[22]

Leading soldiers understood that bayonets, when employed during an assault, symbolized for their bearers the aggressive necessity of coming to grips with the enemy—even if they were not used to kill. As Ambrose Bierce, the writer who fought at Shiloh (and several other battles), pointed out, while the bayonet was "a useless weapon for slaughter," this was irrelevant since "its purpose is a moral one."[23] Civilians like Sidney Fisher, who mentioned to a veteran "that a confused melee of furious men armed with [bayonets], stabbing each other & fighting hand to hand in a mass of hundreds, was something shocking even to think of," were invariably surprised when old soldiers clarified that while they had participated in many bayonet *assaults,* they had never been involved in any bayonet *fights.*[24] The Confederate officer Heros von Borcke went so far as to dismiss any accounts of bayonet-fighting as "exist[ing] only in the imagination."[25] By the time soldiers reached the enemy position, either the other side had run away or there was the usual melee of clubbed muskets, stones, and fists.

Thanks to their bayonets, their faith in the spirit of the offensive, and the detonation of their internal dynamos, soldiers spoke of becoming possessed by a "great magnificent passion" that "sublime[d] every sense and faculty" as they charged.[26] A man of the 19th Maine inexplicably "found myself rushing with all our crowd upon the enemy with an impetuosity that was irresistible."[27] By the time they reached the objective, said Benjamin Urban of the 30th Pennsylvania, troops typically "screamed in the mad delirium of battle, the fury of hell seemed to have entered into every breast, and the insane desire to kill dominated every other passion."[28] Achieving such an exalted state was the pinnacle of Civil War combat.

The second factor contributing to the enduring popularity of the frontal assault becomes clearer when we consider the real-world dilemmas facing a captain or colonel needing to make an urgent tactical decision about how to tackle a nearby enemy. He could choose from only a limited menu of options.

He could deploy in a defensive line and await the attack. This was the safest response, but would gain him neither ground nor glory. If his men did fend off the enemy, they would still be expected to mount a rapid counterattack.

Alternatively, he could order an immediate, full-throated, bayonets-fixed frontal assault. Many would die in the attack, but if successful it would break the enemy line and put them to flight.

Third, he could request a neighboring unit to create a diversion to one side while he organized an attack on the enemy front. On a smoky battlefield where communications were poor, however, coordinating and synchronizing such a complex plan was beyond the abilities of many officers. Again, too, success still required a frontal attack.

The final option was to mount a flank attack of his own. This high-status maneuver was a potentially decisive stroke, but the associated risks were enormous. Thus, Colonel Wheelock G. Veazey, commanding 16th Vermont, "moved [his forces] about 15 rods by marching by the left flank and filing to the left, so as to gain upon the enemy and bring my front facing obliquely to his left flank. When this position was gained I received permission to charge. The result of this charge was a very large number of prisoners, and, in the two movements, three stand of colors, the colors being stripped from one standard."[29] Veazey's gamble succeeded, but more often a commander had to split his force, with one smaller section holding the enemy's attention from the front as the larger discreetly circled to the side, which left his weakened center vulnerable to an enemy charge if the flankers were spotted, as they usually were. Even if the enemy did not take the opportunity to charge, they could swiftly change direction to face the oncoming flank attack—thereby unexpectedly turning it into a frontal attack, but now one where our luckless commander was outnumbered.[30]

Given the unappetizing choices available and the painful costs of failure, it becomes obvious why Civil War officers often relied on a conventional frontal attack in line formation. The most realistic option, as well as the easiest to arrange and the fastest to execute, it was also, paradoxically, far likelier to succeed than more creative tactics. And tempting as they may have been, these "cleverer" tactics were generally beyond the abilities of Union and Confederate officers. Few of these men, after all, were professional soldiers, and the majority had been civilians just a short time before. They were urged to keep it simple, not least by Henry Halleck, the general-in-chief of the Union armies at the time of Gettysburg, whose manual *Elements of Military Art and Science* was first printed in 1846 and republished each year until the end of the war. In it, he prescribed twelve fundamental "orders of battle" for units on the battlefield. Of these, fully eleven recommended plain linear deployments.[31] Similarly, Southerners, said General P. T. Beauregard, "always attack in *line* of battle" to get the job done.[32]

3. The Machine Breaks Down: The Reality of Combat

The stress on basic frontal line assaults stands in stark contrast to what a first-class commander aided by trusted subordinates and equipped with an excellent army could achieve. The acknowledged master in this respect had been, of course, Napoleon. The late emperor had instilled within his marshals an appreciation of the fluid concepts of versatility, surprise, and swiftness, and his corps and divisions maneuvered along multiple axes to exploit an opponent's weakness, phased their attacks to place him under unrelenting pressure, mixed infantry with cavalry to form rudimentary combined-operations arms, switched rapidly between columns and lines as needed, and swiveled freely to seize unexpected opportunities. Even a regular line was broken into components capable of autonomous articulation: One section could turn to face an oncoming threat while the others kept still or advanced.[1]

These were exceedingly difficult tricks to pull off. Which is why Civil War officers stuck to the basic rules they had learned from their manuals. As a result, when they tried to maneuver bodies of enthusiastic but often semi-trained volunteers to the right place at the right time, their attacks were generally clumsy, ill coordinated, asynchronous, and unimaginative, almost invariably following a binary structure of either holding position or advancing along a single axis directly at the enemy.

This absence of martial dexterity played a major, if unacknowledged, role at Gettysburg and during the war as a whole. One can easily see why frontal attacks took so many casualties when we consider that, for instance, just four of the 124th New York's thirty-nine field, staff, and company officers had any military experience whatsoever, and yet they were expected to handle a raw regiment in battle.[2] More alarmingly, during XI Corps's approach to Gettysburg on July 1, news arrived of Major General John Reynolds's death. Its senior officers were thus instantly promoted a notch to positions for which they lacked any training or background. And so, in one historian's words, "minutes before engaging the enemy, the oncoming troops would be thrust into mortal combat led by a general who had never before commanded a corps in action, another who had never before commanded a division in combat, a colonel who had never maneuvered a brigade in action, and a lieutenant colonel who had never led a regiment in combat."[3] Such challenges have humbled even history's greatest soldiers, let alone those recently drawn from the towns and farms of New England and the Mississippi Valley.

We should also bear in mind the rotten state of field communications. Superiors habitually issued unclear, contradictory, confusing, or taskless orders to their subordinates: V Corps was once directed to advance in four different directions at the same time.[4] Perhaps worse, field officers would receive orders long after they were pertinent or necessary—unsurprising, as it required nearly two hours for a message to wend its way from army headquarters down to even a brigade commander.[5] Subordinates, for their part, could cause chaos by issuing foolish or foolhardy commands without referring to their superiors. On the cusp of taking a battery of Union guns, for instance, South Carolinian regiments immediately obeyed an abstruse instruction (one participant, Private John Coxe of the 2nd South Carolina, called it "an insane order") to "'move by the right flank,' by some unauthorized person," allowing the fleeing Union gunners to return to their guns and unleash close-range fire upon the hapless attackers. General Joseph B. Kershaw later lamented that "hundreds of the bravest and best men of Carolina fell, victims of this fatal blunder."[6]

Meanwhile, brigade and regimental commanders, let alone company officers like captains and lieutenants, rarely enjoyed knowledge of broader goals, the purpose of their unit's movements, what was happening elsewhere—or even where they were.[7] For that reason, Brigadier General John Geary of XII Corps was left to stumble around in the dark at Gettysburg, wondering what to do and never knowing what was expected. He reported that when his 2nd Division was ordered to leave its entrenchments, "I received no specific instructions as to the object of the move, the direction to be taken, or the point to be reached, beyond the order to move, by the right flank and to follow the First Division."[8] Likewise, Brigadier General Alpheus Williams, commanding the XII's 1st Division, confessed that he too was "wholly ignorant of the topography of the country, I had seen no map of the localities around Gettysburg."[9]

Civil War battlefields were therefore often haphazard affairs, with regiments bumping into one another, waiting impotently while under heavy fire, wandering aimlessly to and fro, or attacking the nearest enemy who came to hand with no support and a complete lack of coordination. John Dooley, 1st Virginia, complained mightily of some North Carolinian regiments, which "should have charged simultaneously or immediately following us, thus overlapping our flank (right), and preventing our force from being surrounded in that direction. Unfortunately, owing to bad management . . . they were of no assistance to us in the charge; and, advancing either in the wrong direction or when too late, two thousand of them fell into the enemy's hands."[10]

When they were not directly engaged in the chaos, soldiers often lingered around uselessly before moving somewhere else and lingering there instead. Captain William Danforth told his wife that after arriving at Gettysburg on July 2 "we lay under a cross fire for three or four hours. It was hard. Then we marched under fire to another position. We marched by the flank 4 men abreast, for more than ½ mile then we changed to the front & marched in line of battle about a 100 rods [a third of a mile] and then lay behind a wall some time. We could not do much with our muskets, but lay in 3d line of battle until about dark. Then we went into the front line and lay in line until morning."[11] At no point did Danforth have any idea where he was, whether he could be helping an ailing unit, or what he was otherwise supposed to be doing.

Too much opprobrium should not be heaped on participants' heads; most officers tried the best they could but soon realized that the tactical movements so cleanly delineated in their manuals bore little resemblance to the messy reality unfolding before them. "The idea almost everyone forms of a battle is something like a vast chessboard," warned Thomas Evans of the 12th U.S. Infantry, "on which the masses of infantry are pawns, the cavalry, light artillery, and commanding officers the pieces, and the commanding generals the players," but naïfs were quickly disabused of that notion.[12] "To the book-soldier all order seems destroyed, months of drill apparently going for nothing in a few minutes" once the guns started firing, wrote D. L. Thompson of the 9th New York.[13]

War was entropy, they learned. Under battle conditions, the structure of even a well-trained company or regiment, perfectly formed up and pointed in the correct direction at a clear objective, would begin to disintegrate the minute it began moving forward. Frontal assaults relied on a combination of mass and momentum to sweep them forward swiftly enough to retain a semblance of cohesion. And so any attack that dissolved into scattered groups of men was almost certainly doomed to costly failure. Some scared soldiers would instinctually fire their weapons, prompting their comrades to stop, seek cover, and take their individual shots. The enemy thus gained time to recharge his artillery pieces and fire extra rifle volleys. Withdrawal—a euphemism for flight—accompanied by heavy casualties was inevitable unless officers could get their men back into line and moving again at a rapid clip, a highly rare occurrence.[14]

If the engine driving Civil War combat was the frontal assault, then in order to understand how one worked in practice, we need to disassemble it and study each piece. So, following a brief interlude to outline the background and main events of the battle, I'll examine what happened and what soldiers experienced by breaking down a generic infantry action in which one side is attacking the other's defending position. By such means, the genuine face of Gettysburg can be revealed in all its glory—or horror.

4. The Battle

In late June 1863, during his invasion of the North, General Robert E. Lee ordered his Army of Northern Virginia to converge near the Pennsylvania town of Gettysburg, as did the recently appointed chief of the Army of the Potomac, Major General George G. Meade. Both expected a major clash sometime in the first week of July, yet both were surprised when it actually occurred. On June 30, Confederate advance troops under Brigadier General J. Johnston Pettigrew were approaching Gettysburg when they witnessed a body of Union cavalry commanded by Brigadier General John Buford closing in from the south. Without engaging, Pettigrew returned to headquarters and reported his discovery. Early the next morning, his superior, division commander Major General Henry Heth, sent two brigades to reconnaissance in force. . . .

July 1. Day One, *Morning:* The heavily outnumbered Buford, in the meantime, had deployed defensively across three successive ridges to the west of Gettysburg: Herr Ridge (the most westerly), McPherson Ridge, and Seminary Ridge (the most easterly). His intention was to delay the Confederate advance long enough to permit the main Union forces to establish a position on the heights—Cemetery Hill, Cemetery

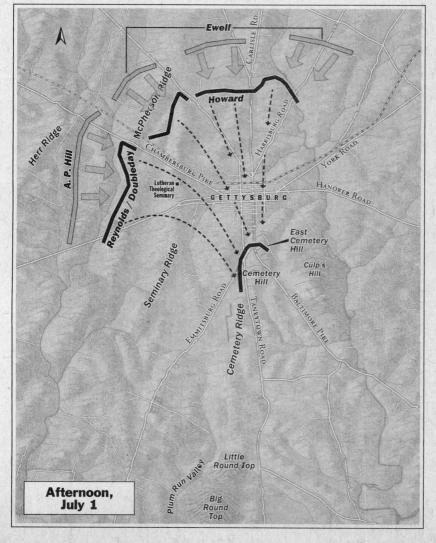

Morning, July 1

UNFINISHED RAIL LINE

Herr Ridge

Heth's Division

McPherson Ridge

CARLISLE RD.

HARRISBURG RD.

CHAMBERSBURG PIKE

Buford

RAILROAD

Lutheran Theological Seminary

G E T T Y S B U R G

Afternoon, July 1

Ewell

CARLISLE RD.

McPherson Ridge

Howard

HARRISBURG ROAD

Herr Ridge

A. P. Hill

CHAMBERSBURG PIKE

Lutheran Theological Seminary

YORK ROAD

G E T T Y S B U R G

HANOVER ROAD

Reynolds / Doubleday

Seminary Ridge

East Cemetery Hill

Culp's Hill

Cemetery Hill

EMMITSBURG ROAD

Cemetery Ridge

TANEYTOWN ROAD

BALTIMORE PIKE

Plum Run Valley

Little Round Top

Big Round Top

Ridge, and Culp's Hill—south of Gettysburg. At about 7:30 A.M., the two Southern brigades marching eastward along the Chambersburg Pike encountered Buford's forward outposts. It was here that the first shots were fired. By 10:30, the Confederate brigades had pushed Buford's men back to McPherson Ridge. Fortunately for the Union Forces, the vanguard of Major General John Reynolds's I Corps had arrived (Union corps are designated with Roman numerals, Confederate with Arabic) and would soon be followed by reinforcements. Reynolds was killed early in the fighting, with Major General Abner Doubleday assuming command of his corps. The Southern brigades, meanwhile, were heavily engaged with mixed success until midday, when they paused to await the other two brigades of Heth's division and another division to arrive.

July 1. Day One, *Afternoon:* The fighting recommenced, this time more advantageously for the Confederates as their Union opponents fell back to Seminary Ridge, thence to the Lutheran Theological Seminary and subsequently to Cemetery Hill to the east. To the north, meanwhile, Lieutenant General Richard Ewell's 2nd Corps had proceeded along the Harrisburg and Carlisle roads as Major General Oliver Howard's XI Corps hastened to block it by setting up a semicircular defensive line arcing from west of Gettysburg to the northeast. Howard, however, had tried to cover too much ground with too few troops. At about 2 P.M., two full Confederate divisions crashed into the Union positions, which quickly disintegrated. Howard retreated south past Gettysburg to Cemetery Hill, an immensely strong position. Grasping that Union forces would be difficult to dislodge if they were given an opportunity to entrench, Lee ordered Ewell to take the Hill "if practicable"—a dangerous caveat—while the Northern troops were still reeling from the onslaught. Ewell eventually decided against an all-out assault, giving his foe critical time to recover.

July 2. Day Two, *Morning:* By mid-morning, the rest of the two armies had arrived. Overnight, the Union soldiers had worked hard to solidify their position. Most of XII Corps had been sent to Culp's Hill, and the

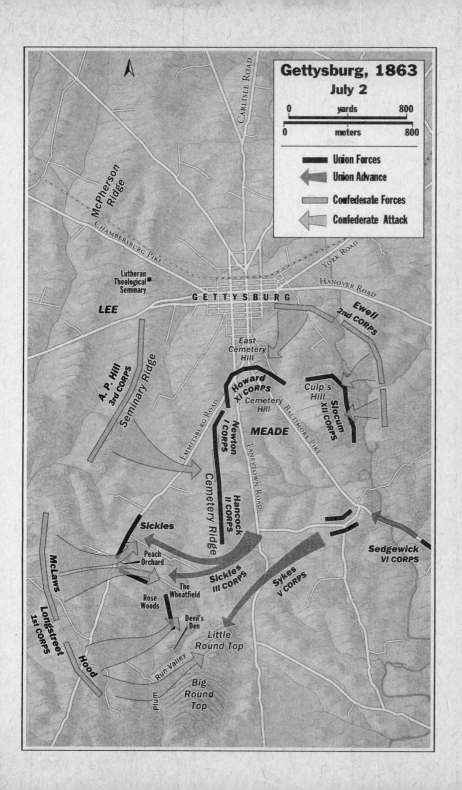

Gettysburg, 1863
July 2

0   yards   800

0   meters   800

■■■ Union Forces

◄■ Union Advance

▭ Confederate Forces

◄ Confederate Attack

CARLISLE ROAD

McPherson Ridge

CHAMBERSBURG PIKE

YORK ROAD

Lutheran Theological Seminary

HANOVER ROAD

G E T T Y S B U R G

LEE

Ewell 2nd CORPS

A. P. Hill 3rd CORPS

Seminary Ridge

East Cemetery Hill

Howard XI CORPS

Cemetery Hill

Culp's Hill

Slocum XII CORPS

EMMITSBURG ROAD

Newton I CORPS

MEADE

BALTIMORE PIKE

TANEYTOWN ROAD

Cemetery Ridge

Hancock II CORPS

Sickles

Sedgewick VI CORPS

Peach Orchard

McLaws

Sickles III CORPS

Sykes V CORPS

Rose Woods

The Wheatfield

Longstreet 1st CORPS

Hood

Devil's Den

Little Round Top

Plum Run Valley

Big Round Top

line from there circled northwest to Cemetery Hill (I and XI Corps), then straight south, spine-like, for nearly two miles along Cemetery Ridge (II and III Corps), ending just north of a prominence named Little Round Top. From above, the Union defenses resembled an upside-down fishhook. The Confederate 3rd Corps was centered on Seminary Ridge, about a mile west of Cemetery Ridge, while more soldiers occupied Gettysburg and staked out a curved line mirroring that of their opponents, terminating opposite Culp's Hill. The Confederate line was considerably longer than the Union's, and worse, there were fewer men to hold it. The Union commanders, on the other hand, could easily shuttle units back and forth if a weak spot developed. Lee's trump card was Lieutenant General James Longstreet's 1st Corps, which had stealthily moved south along the Emmitsburg Road, beyond the Union's farthermost flank. Lee planned for his 2nd Corps divisions to mount a diversionary expedition against Culp's Hill as the 3rd Corps attacked Cemetery Hill. At the same time, Longstreet's two divisions (under Major Generals John Bell Hood and Lafayette McLaws) would hit the Union left. If all went well, Meade's advantage of interior lines would be negated as his troops were pinned down and flanked, but success hinged on a rapid and well-coordinated general attack taking place. Unbeknownst to Lee, however, Major General Daniel Sickles's III Corps had left its original position at the southern end of Cemetery Ridge to move forward to the Emmitsburg Road. The Union line now ran from the boulder-strewn Devil's Den northwest to the Peach Orchard and then northeast along Emmitsburg Road. The position, which Sickles had selected without bothering to wait for Meade's approval, was fundamentally untenable in the face of superior Confederate numbers, but instead of Longstreet being able to outflank the Union left, McLaws's division, much to its surprise, would now need to undertake a direct frontal assault.

July 2. Day Two, *Afternoon:* Worse, owing to delays, Longstreet's attack did not begin until 4 P.M. Meade immediately sent in his reserves, comprising V Corps, most of XII Corps, a division of II Corps, and a portion of VI Corps. Meanwhile, Hood's division had deviated east from

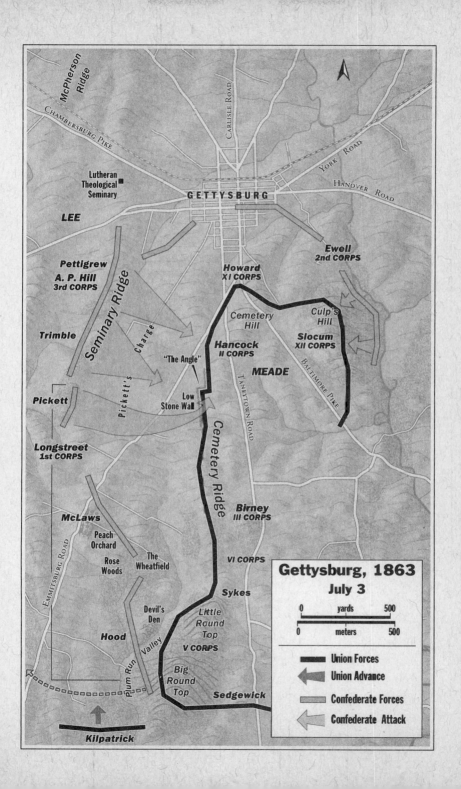

McPherson Ridge

CHAMBERSBURG PIKE

CARLISLE ROAD

YORK ROAD

HANOVER ROAD

Lutheran
Theological
Seminary

GETTYSBURG

LEE

Pettigrew

A. P. Hill
3rd CORPS

Ewell
2nd CORPS

Howard
XI CORPS

Seminary Ridge

Cemetery
Hill

Culp's
Hill

Trimble

Charge

Hancock
II CORPS

Slocum
XII CORPS

"The Angle"

MEADE

BALTIMORE PIKE

Pickett's

Low
Stone Wall

Pickett

TANEYTOWN ROAD

Cemetery Ridge

Longstreet
1st CORPS

McLaws

Birney
III CORPS

Peach
Orchard

EMMITSBURG ROAD

Rose
Woods

The
Wheatfield

VI CORPS

Sykes

Devil's
Den

Hood

Plum Run Valley

Little
Round
Top

V CORPS

Big
Round
Top

Sedgewick

Gettysburg, 1863

July 3

0   yards   500

0   meters   500

Union Forces

Union Advance

Confederate Forces

Confederate Attack

Kilpatrick

its assigned course and was engaged in heavy fighting at Devil's Den, Plum Run Valley, and Little Round Top as it swung north. At the latter, a key strategic point, a small brigade held out against multiple Confederate assaults by men of Hood's division, culminating in a famous bayonet charge against the disheartened Southerners. McLaws had been held back during Hood's action, and only at 5 P.M. could he unleash his brigades at III Corps. His initial target was the twenty-acre Wheatfield and Rose Woods, and it was here that some of the bloodiest combat occurred as Union and Confederate forces mounted a welter of attacks and counterattacks. To their northwest, two Confederate brigades eventually pushed through the Peach Orchard as Sickles's men broke. By that point, III Corps was essentially destroyed. To the northeast, however, a Confederate attack under Major General Richard Anderson that began at 6 P.M. against the remnants of III Corps initially won some success but eventually petered out. Despite enormous losses, the Union left still stood. On Meade's right, the Confederate 2nd Corps did not begin its attack on Culp's Hill until 7 P.M. Owing to the failure to synchronize Confederate movements, Meade had benefited from being able to shunt most of his XII Corps from Culp's Hill to the left, leaving but a single New York brigade and some reinforcements to defend his right. The New Yorkers, however, were strongly entrenched, and the Confederate attack was fended off. The XI Corps troops on East Cemetery Hill likewise held out against a determined, if unsupported, assault that evening.

July 3. Day Three, *Morning:* The piecemeal attacks on the Union left and right had failed, but Meade's center remained relatively unscathed. It was toward this position on Cemetery Ridge—defended primarily by the II Corps—that Lee now directed his attention. He intended to coordinate a major attack there with a smaller one at Culp's Hill. A breakthrough in the center would provoke a Union collapse as Meade's left and right lost contact with one another, leaving them prey to Confederate flank attacks. To soften up the Union defenders, there would be a colossal artillery bombardment before the infantry advanced. Meade, however, did not permit Lee the luxury of completing his dispositions. At dawn, the Union batteries on Culp's Hill fired on the Confederate brigades below, prompting a futile succession of three Southern infantry assaults on the hill, each ending in failure and ultimately disrupting Lee's plan to harmonize the twin attacks.

July 3. Day Three, *Afternoon:* Despite the setback, at approximately 1 P.M. the Confederate guns thunderously opened up against Cemetery Ridge. A quarter of an hour later, their Union counterparts returned fire. Low on ammunition and poorly coordinated, the South's artillery did not inflict significant damage on the defenders—though gunners mistakenly believed otherwise—and at about 3 P.M. firing virtually ceased and 12,500 soldiers began their advance across three-quarters of a mile of mostly open ground. This mile-wide grand infantry assault would come to be known as Pickett's Charge after Major General George Pickett. Casualties quickly mounted as flanking artillery fire raked their ranks, followed by shells and canister from the guns in the Union center. The Confederates marched indomitably on. There was a near-breakthrough at a salient in a low stone wall called the Angle, but inrushing reinforcements repulsed the attackers, and they were unable to exploit the temporary breach. The Confederates fell back to their own lines in disarray, but half never returned. The battle was over.

Aftermath: That night, Lee established a strong defensive position on Seminary Ridge, vainly hoping that Meade would take the bait and attack. After collecting as many of the dead and wounded as he could on July 4, Lee evacuated and began the long and difficult retreat to Virginia. Meade would shadowbox with his opponent along the way but failed to exterminate the Army of Northern Virginia, leaving Lee free to fight another day.

5. Marching to Gettysburg

Every single soldier at Gettysburg was tired, thirsty, and hot. Regiments, bundled into brigades, had been ordered to rush to the area once it was known that a major battle was in the offing. Even for troops accustomed to long marches along dusty or muddy roads, the hurried advance to Gettysburg was reckoned especially onerous.

"They marched us like dogs," complained Private Daniel Handy of the 2nd Rhode Island. A companion, Charles Nichols, told his sister that by the end his "feet [were] all blistered, and every bone [was] aching. As for me I could scarcely move a foot" when he actually arrived at the battlefield. Their regiment had tramped thirty-five miles overnight and for much of the following day with just three five-minute halts.[1] Blisters the size of quarters were the least of it. After the 5th Wisconsin marched twenty-six miles in a day, Richard Carter's right leg was as "swollen as full as the skin can hold + so full that the skin is discolored."[2]

Sheer exhaustion would affect performance during the battle. Despite having tramped twenty-eight miles in eleven hours, Law's Alabama Brigade was upon its arrival almost immediately ordered forward to storm Devil's Den and Little Round Top—an assignment difficult even for fresh troops and close to impossible for tired ones.[3] During the colossal artillery duel on the third day, Colonel Wheelock Veazey saw "the most astonishing thing I ever witnessed in any battle" along his section of the Union line. Most of the men of his 16th Vermont, having lain down to take cover from the shell and shot screaming overhead, actually "fell asleep, and it was with the greatest effort only that I could keep awake myself."[4]

The Alabamians' failure to take Little Round Top was also caused partly, said one, by parchedness: Lack of water combined with fatigue rendered men helpless when the Union counterattacked.[5] In suffering from dehydration, the Alabamians were not alone. Few soldiers in either army had consumed much more than the barest amount of water required to function. While there was plenty available, the liquid was believed harmful to drink straight on hot days thanks in part to a well-known *New York Times* letter to the editor—much clipped out and sent on by parents and spouses eager to help their favorite recruit as he marched off to war—that had advised soldiers to consume as little as possible.[6]

Sunstroke, exacerbated by dehydration, predictably afflicted both armies on the way to Gettysburg. Artilleryman Robert Carter said that Colonel Gleason of the 25th New York and seventeen men in his division all died of it within a day.[7] The Texas Brigade recorded no fewer than two hundred cases of fainting, severe muscle cramps, body-temperature spikes, and blinding headaches in a single day.[8]

Not every unit suffered equally. In regiments whose officers ignored conventional wisdom and told their men to drink freely when they were thirsty, sunstroke was a minor problem. Just four men of the 5th Maine's 340 troops, for instance, went down with it, a rate of 1.2 percent. The officers of the 124th New York and the 17th U.S. Regulars, on the other hand, actively prevented their men from refilling their canteens at roadside wells and pumps—and suffered grievously as a result. More than half the New Yorkers were rendered useless, while a third of the Regulars were too weak to stand by the time they were needed to launch an important attack at the Wheatfield.[9]

Since there was little contemporary comprehension of the link between adequate hydration and heat-related illness, there was generally little sympathy expended on sufferers, for "sunstroke" was an excuse commonly offered by malingerers. If the afflicted were lucky, as was Captain McKee of the 155th Pennsylvania when he fainted near Gettysburg, they could rest and return to their regiment once they recovered.[10] More often, they were ordered to march until they dropped; even then, officers would sometimes beat the semiconscious with the flat of their swords as punishment for their cowardice.[11]

But the oppressive heat was most often cited by soldiers as their abiding memory of those July days. Michael Jacobs, a resident of Gettysburg, kept meticulous observations of the weather conditions during the battle. The first day was cloudy, with a barely discernible breeze—smoke sometimes rose vertically—and temperatures in the mid-seventies by 2 P.M. July 2 was just as calm and cloudy, but the sun emerged after lunch and the temperature hit 81 degrees in the early afternoon. The final day was much brighter by 2 P.M., though a "massive thunder-cloud of summer" threateningly rolled in that afternoon. Wind speed was again very gentle, but the mercury had risen to 87 degrees by the time of Pickett's Charge.[12] Despite the otherwise tolerable temperatures, exceptionally high humidity made wool-clad, parched soldiers feel as if it was in the high nineties at least. Even on the morning of July 1, when it was a very pleasant 72 degrees, the humidity was so pervasive that thirty men of the 150th Pennsylvania simply passed out or stopped marching.[13]

For much of the battle, the sun looked, fittingly, like Mars—both the god of war and his planet: Suspended high in the heavens and glowering down upon these mortals, it resembled nothing less than "a big ball of blood," in the words of Thomas Day of the 3rd Indiana Cavalry.[14]

As soldiers neared the field, they forgot their woes as the "deep-toned booming" of the artillery grew louder. The sound, wrote a captain, was easily mistaken by raw troops for fireworks or drums.[15] The young lieutenant Lloyd Harris assumed that the silly residents of Gettysburg were celebrating July 4 early. His veterans, who had run the gauntlet at Antietam, Fredericksburg, and Chancellorsville, knew better.[16] As they marched closer, they would begin to feel the ground trembling and quaking beneath their feet. Billy Bayly, who lived near Gettysburg, heard the Union batteries firing in unison and likened the barrage to "the roar of a continuous thunderstorm and the sharp angry crashes of the thunderbolt." The "reverberation from [the] discharges shook the windows in the house," which itself shuddered.[17]

The first sight soldiers would have of the field were the black and gray clouds of smoke the artillery was belching out. It was hard to see what lay ahead. Sometimes emerging from the enshrouding fug were the panicked and blackened figures of their fellow soldiers, lately bested by the enemy. The spectacle threatened to unman them. George Squier of Indiana confessed that the sight of ragged troops streaming back missing fingers or hands "rather daunted my fervor and for the first time I doubted my courage."[18] It certainly did not help that as the survivors passed, they cried, " 'Don't go out there' 'You'll catch hell' 'We are all cut to pieces' 'We are whipped.' "[19]

Benjamin Thompson soon found it "difficult to keep a line in the face of these squads of flying men" pushing through his brigade's ranks and between its files.[20] Some soldiers tried their best to help by grabbing hold of these broken and maddened men, said Alfred Carpenter of 1st Minnesota, but "at last gave it up entirely, believing they were more injury than help to us."[21] A few tried more direct means, such as a Corporal Plunkett who swore "like a pirate," seized "a big tin coffee pot," and "smash[ed] it over the head of one of the frightened boys. . . . The blow broke in the bottom but the fellow kept running."[22]

It would soon be their turn to enter the maelstrom. They kept on marching.

6. Skirmishing

As the regiments reached their positions and settled in to prepare for an action, a number of men were selected for skirmish work. Skirmishing was a relatively new development, dating from the Napoleonic Wars. Because so many aristocrats had been executed or exiled in the early years of the French Revolution, the new republic's generals had been hard-pressed to find sufficient officers to lead and train their enthusiastic but inexperienced armies. Until they reconstituted their officer corps, French commanders adapted an eighteenth-century practice of sending small numbers of *piquets* ("pickets" in English) forward to guard outlying approaches. They also released swarms of men ahead of the main body to harass the enemy. The British, meanwhile, were relying ever more heavily on their highly trained Light units to snipe at and scout the foe. In short order, the once-distinct roles of *piquets,* harassers, and Light troops had merged into a single form of fighting known as skirmishing.

American military manuals from 1812 onward attached increasing importance to skirmishing, and by the Civil War it was standard practice to send detachments forward to anywhere between fifty and four hundred yards of the enemy's positions. There, they would perform the same role as an insect's antennae: to feel out the foe's whereabouts and numbers, to sense when dangerous movement was afoot, and to brush against over-territorial rivals. The heavy work of combat, meanwhile, would be left to the jaws and pincers of the line troops and artillery waiting behind.

A company or two per regiment would be assigned skirmishing duty whenever the enemy was in the vicinity. More were ordered when hostile forces were close enough at hand to launch an attack—either surprise or counter. For that reason, the worried commander of the 16th Vermont sent up three companies (about a third of the regiment) on the night of July 2; that of the 47th Alabama did the same before the assault on Big Round Top; but fully four companies of the 19th Maine (almost half the regiment) were dispatched on July 3.[1] When Davis's Brigade came under fire early on July 1 by Buford's cavalrymen, for instance, the former immediately threw forward three lines of skirmishers to keep the Northerners busy while the rest of his troops readied themselves.[2] The folly of neglecting one's skirmish line was borne out disastrously by Brigadier General Alfred Iverson, commanding the 5th, 12th, 20th, and 23rd North Carolina, when he sent his brigade across a field without an advance screen. It walked straight into a Union line that had been crouching behind a wall and instantly opened up with a devastating volley, killing and wounding hundreds.[3]

Having been selected, each skirmisher would slither forward a few hundred yards, seek out a modicum of cover to wait out his time, and keep an adequate distance from his comrades.[4] It was lonely work, especially for soldiers accustomed to the main battle line's elbow-to-elbow familiarity, and when it wasn't boring it was exceedingly dangerous. Since a skirmisher was expected to shoot at his counterpart whenever possible, he was constantly under threat of assassination by an unseen foe. The 25th Ohio lost fourteen men by such means in a twenty-hour stint on the skirmish line, while the 136th New York suffered 106 casualties over two days.[5] During the bitter tussle over the Bliss Farm, a key tactical point, twenty-eight skirmishers of the 39th New York were killed and wounded in four hours.[6]

During a charge, of course, such high casualties would be incurred within minutes, but the slow attrition and the constant stress of skirmishing ground agonizingly on men's nerves. Small wonder that soldiers almost universally hated it.[7] For Benjamin Thompson, "line fighting is barbarous, but skirmishing is savage—nay, devilish. To juke and hide and skulk for men and deliberately aim at and murder them one by one is far too bloodthirsty for Christian men."[8] George Yost of the 126th New York told his father that "I would do anything rather than skirmish with those fellows. I never want to do it again. I will charge and repel charges but don't put me in that place again."[9]

It was the silence, not just the solitude, that was unsettling. In regular combat, the pervasive, encompassing cacophony of noise allowed a soldier to reassure, or delude, himself that the enemy had not noticed him in particular; out skirmishing, however, it was painfully obvious when he was being specifically targeted. An incoming bullet was disconcertingly distinct amid the quiet of the skirmish line: The sound of one passing nearby was described as a "sharp *zip*—p-i-n-g-g-g," while another soldier likened it to "a very small circular saw cutting through thin strips of wood." One musician's ear was so finely attuned that he could define the noise as "a swell from E flat to F, and as it retrograded in the distance receded to D—a very pretty change."[10]

Even if one was hidden, merely firing one's rifle immediately attracted unwelcome attention when its revealing puff of smoke floated upward. An enemy bullet or two often followed, catnip for daredevils but heart-stoppingly terrifying for ordinary men.[11] Understandably, many skirmishers ignored their orders to shoot the enemy whenever possible in order to keep themselves safely hidden until they could be relieved. They hoped the favor would be returned, but not everyone played by the unwritten rules. Corporal Samuel Huxham of Company B, 14th Connecticut, was out on the skirmish line on July 3 in front of Cemetery Ridge. His company had crawled two hundred yards through a wheat field before arriving at a rail fence where they could secrete themselves among its posts and lower rails. After some time lying prone and motionless, Huxham needed to stretch and began to kneel. Several minutes later, Private Hiram Fox quietly called to him but received no answer. Wriggling his way over, Fox found Huxham dead with a bullet hole in his head.[12]

Poor Huxham was evidently the victim of a marksman prowling the dangerous no-man's-land of the skirmish lines. Some of these were simply regular soldiers with a hunting background who happened to be on skirmishing duty, but there were other fine shots formally designated as sharpshooters and often collated into specialist units. A scattered few were renowned as the elite of the elite: former national or state shooting champions, or those capable of competing at that level, who owned a customized target rifle equipped with advanced optical sights and a tripod.[13]

Sharpshooters were an effective defense against skirmishers. Soldiers often spoke of snipers "annoying" or "galling" them, and they were truly a nuisance. For the most part, sharpshooters served to hold up forward movements, as happened when several hidden marksmen pinned down Louisiana Brigade skirmishers below Cemetery Ridge on July 2. "We had to remain there—more than five hundred yards in advance of Ewell's main line of battle—hugging the ground behind a very low ridge," wrote Captain William Seymour. "It was almost certain death for a man to stand upright and we lost during the day forty-five men in killed and wounded from the fire of the enemy's sharpshooters, who were armed with long-ranged Whitworth rifles."[14]

In difficult terrain, sharpshooters came into their own. At Gettysburg the boulder-strewn, crevice-filled landscape of Devil's Den was a marksman's paradise. Eight men of Company E of 3rd Arkansas were found shot precisely in the head, while, as A. P. Case of the 146th New York noted, "behind one short low ridge of rock lay a row of eighteen dead who had been tallied out one by one by our sharpshooters."[15] As Captain R. K. Beechan explained, Confederate sharpshooters exacted their own heavy toll against Union soldiers standing backlit against the setting sun.[16] They lost so many men that, according to the 30th Pennsyvania's Benjamin Urban, "strict orders were given to keep down."[17]

Sharpshooters, being detested for their trade, were not taken prisoner. Said the 2nd Pennsylvania's E. M. Woodward, "the boys never showed [them] any mercy" if they surrendered.[18] When some Union soldiers charged into Devil's Den and captured twenty Confederate snipers, "they were much alarmed at being caught, because as sharpshooters they expected no quarter, and begged lustily for their lives." When Sergeant Richard Tyler assured them that they would be treated fairly, they refused to believe him until they discovered that their captors were members of a sharpshooter company themselves. Only then did their "dejected spirit" suddenly transform to "one of undisguised happiness."[19]

Since there was no need to capture sharpshooters alive, soldiers invented several invariably lethal ways to flush out an irritant. One effective method was to flank him. A few men of Urban's regiment "crept out through the grass as far as possible without being seen," circling to the left and right of the tree branches where they suspected their tormentor was hiding. "Then several men in the center deliberately stood up . . . to draw his fire and compel him to reveal his exact location, which he promptly did, and as promptly was he riddled by the deadly fire of the concealed Bucktails. It was afterwards seen that he had tied himself to the tree so that he could not fall down."[20]

Alternatively, overwhelming firepower could accomplish wonders. When the 40th Virginia was being harassed by sharpshooters "concealed in a large wooden building on our left," Captain Wayland Dunaway ordered his entire company to stand up and "fire a volley into the house and that put a stop to the murderous villainy."[21] In standing up en masse like that, however, the company had to be wary of being suckered into exposing an entire unit to deadly counterfire from other marksmen hidden nearby. The 22nd Massachusetts fell hook, line, and sinker when they rose up and poured a lively broadside into what they thought was a nest of sharpshooters from the 3rd Arkansas. Remembered one of those fooled, "we soon learned that our fire had been drawn by the old, well-known Yankee trick of displaying hats upon sticks or ramrods."[22] A related gambit was the bait-and-switch. While on skirmish duty, Private Charles Comstock of the 13th Massachusetts was plagued by a Confederate directly ahead of him who sent a shot whizzing past whenever Comstock fired. He loaded a gun left behind by some wounded unfortunate, set it alongside his own, and pulled its trigger. The rebel's head popped up and Comstock removed it with a follow-up shot from his own gun.[23]

Finally, if all else failed, one could set a thief to catch a thief. Bedeviled by Confederate sharpshooters firing "from two openings in the second [story]" of a barn, Richard Thompson of the 12th New Jersey called upon a detachment of Captain William Plumer's Massachusetts snipers who carried their own "very heavy, long-range telescope rifles, with a sort of tripod rest." After Plumer's men hit a few of them, the Confederates understandably turned more cautious. Now, whenever they saw a muzzle flash they vanished from the openings until the bullet hit wood, then returned fire and ducked back down.

The frustrated Union snipers countered by forming "themselves into squads or partnerships of three." The first man would fire, the rebels would vanish, then the two others would count to three, see the Confederates reappear at the pair of openings, and each would fire at his appointed target. The trouble from these miscreants soon ceased. "Alas! How little we thought human life was the stake for which this game was being played," exclaimed Thompson, who was nonetheless relieved at their being put out of his misery.[24]

While sharpshooters roamed in the daylight, night possessed its own terrors for skirmishers. Push too far forward into the unrelenting darkness and a skirmish line would run smack into one coming the other way or even the main force itself, provoking a firefight at close quarters.[25] Lieutenant Milton Daniels, Sergeant Patrick Wade, and ten privates of the 17th Connecticut had a fearfully close call when, before dawn, they unwittingly crept into a field whose "trampled grass" and scattered "bits of cracker and bread" meant only one thing: A brigade at the very least had recently camped there. In the end, it turned out well, for this was the morn of July 4, and Lee's army had retreated an hour before.[26]

Being kidnapped was also a danger. Four men of the 14th Connecticut vanished one night, snatched by Confederates when they accidentally ventured too far beyond their lines. Thomas Galwey, of the

8th Ohio, had been stalking an orderly searching for General Stephen Ramseur's brigade and was just about to pounce when a comrade named Private "Bucktown" Brown cocked his gun and "alarmed our bird, and he turned and fled."[27]

That orderly was remarkably lucky: Out on the forward lines, the wounded often died alone. There were times, however, when someone took pity on an ailing man and tried to help. Thomas Galwey, the Ohioan, was skirmishing on July 3 when "about the middle of the forenoon, a cry of, 'Don't fire, Yanks!' rang out [and] a [Confederate emerged from hiding behind a tree to] give a drink to one of our wounded who lay there beyond us. Of course we cheered the Reb, and someone shouted, 'Bully for you Johnny!' " After Union and Confederate alike stood to cheer, the sharpshooter turned around and went back to the tree, and then at the top of his voice shouted, 'Down Yanks, we're going to fire.' And down we lay again."[28] Such admirable demonstrations of chivalry were few and far between, despite mawkish tales told after the war in the spirit of brotherly reconciliation. Less edifying were instances of outright sadism, such as that witnessed by a 14th Connecticut soldier named Stevens. He watched a Union sharpshooter entertain himself by hunting a wounded skirmisher "unable to stand, who was trying, by a series of flops, to drag his body up the slope to the shelter of his own lines." Said Stevens, the unsporting gentleman "fired at him for several minutes as frequently as he could load and take aim; but we confess[ed] to a feeling of relief and gladness . . . when the man let up on the poor fellow and had failed to hit him."[29]

A skirmisher was not safe even at the end of his shift. The palpable relief gained from repairing rearward was tempered by the "lively popping all along the line of their opponents as long as a man was in sight," remembered one with a shudder.[30] Those returning were only too keen to see the enemy paid back in kind. Some men of Battery D, 5th U.S. Artillery were preparing their guns for the next phase of combat when a skirmisher of III Corps limped toward them holding his eyeball, still attached to its cord. The victim of a sharpshooter, he told the artillerists, "See what they gave me. Give them [Hell] and I will support you."[31]

7. Artillery Versus Artillery

As skirmishers and sharpshooters hunted each other, the men in the main line were preparing either to advance or to dig in. For them, the period before an imminent action contained its own terror, one that those assigned forward duty were thankful to escape: coming under artillery fire.

The primary task of artillery was, depending on the side, either to hinder an infantry attack or to ease its path. Before turning its unwelcome attention to the waiting soldiery, however, the enemy artillery would seek first to suppress any nearby guns. Neutralizing the opposing batteries was counted, said Captain James Smith, as the supreme "trial of skill between artillerists."[1] Indeed, Colonel Benjamin Scribner of the 38th Indiana noticed of artillerymen that "cannon against cannon they appear to delight in; they seem to feel complimented when the enemy turns his guns upon them."[2] One Vermont soldier likened the sight of rival batteries menacing each other to "grim bulldogs" facing off before a fight.[3]

It was best, if possible, to fire on batteries still trundling into position, when they were most vulnerable—as well as most visible, since smoke had yet to obscure their whereabouts. It was likely, too, that the guns' limbers and caissons—two-wheeled wagons that bore the battery's ammunition chests, spare parts, and tools—would be close at hand, increasing the chances of destroying something vital with each shot.[4]

If such an opportunity did not arise, an artillery commander would try to situate his guns at an oblique angle to those opposite. While the enemy lost valuable time reorienting his cannons to face the new threat directly, the other's guns would be firing at the lengthy profiles of the wheels and carriage rather than the slimmer silhouette presented by their muzzles. Both sides always sought a slight hill to hide behind. A rise of even just two feet meant that low-trajectory cannonballs would hit the ridge and bounce over their heads. Additionally, because artillerists watched for a puff of dust and dirt to see where their shot had landed, a reverse slope obscured those telltale signs and made it harder for the enemy to adjust his aim.[5]

It was tempting to allow each crew to select its own target, but experienced commanders ordered their battery to concentrate all fire on a single gun.[6] Converging upon one target from multiple angles increased the likelihood of destroying it, and a completely wrecked gun was not only worth more than several lightly damaged, and quickly repaired, ones, but often unnerved neighboring gunners and reduced their accuracy.[7] "The moral effect produced by such a result [is] still more terrible than the physical," advised one of the leading American artillery experts, John Gibbon, for all knew then that the enemy had found his range and would be searching for a new victim.[8]

Even at the best of times, artillerymen were rarely sure whether their shots were causing damage. During a duel between the 9th and 5th Massachusetts batteries and Captain James Reilly's and Captain A. C. Latham's North Carolina guns southeast of Seminary Ridge, Sergeant Baker of the 9th admitted that "what effect our firing had on them we do not know; but their fire seemed to slacken somewhat."[9] His captain claimed that two rebel limbers were destroyed, whereas none were—but since Latham and Reilly did lose a howitzer and a six-pounder gun, the Bay Staters' fire was actually more effective than they thought.[10]

That uncertainty could be exploited. As one colonel warned his general, "I will only be able to judge the effect of our fire on the enemy by his return fire," so to deceive an aggressor into believing that he had inflicted more damage than he had, defending guns might play dead amid the darkening smoke.[11] When Colonel H. C. Cabell's Confederate position fell suddenly silent, for instance, his opponent reported that he had either silenced the Southerners or compelled them to withdraw.[12] When the unwitting attacker turned his guns toward another target, he would be left prey to accurate counterfire from the "destroyed" cannons.

Adding to the problem, too, was that artillery fire could be virtually impotent—even when accurate. Shoddy manufacturing, incompatible fuses, and defective primers sabotaged a surprisingly large amount of

ammunition. Owing to production problems and diminishing resources, Confederate shells malfunctioned more frequently than that of
the Union. One Northern newspaper reported in August 1863 that
"the ground occupied by our forces is literally strewn with unexploded
rebel shells, while along the Confederate fortifications very few can be
found," adding, "not one-sixth of the shells thrown by the rebels exploded."[13] This was probably an exaggeration but, even so, artillerists
low on ammunition made do with whatever they could scrounge, even
failed shells. On July 3, William Jenvey of Hill's battery (1st West Virginia Artillery) "fired back a few of the Rebel shells, hot as they were,
literally paying them back in their own coin."[14]

Part of the inherent confusion and wastage of artillery battle was
owed to distance—ranges of 1,200 to 1,600 yards were not uncommon, making targets difficult to see and leading to unreliable damage
assessments—but the lion's share may be attributed to the sheer volume
of smoke that rapidly accumulated. A 1st Rhode Island battery was
enveloped so murkily, said a witness, that "objects could not be seen at
a distance of four rods [66 feet]."[15] Artillerymen therefore sought to
find and destroy their target in the short window between commencing
firing and total blackout.

There were various ad hoc methods of acquiring a bead quickly.
Augustus Hesse, manning the 9th Massachusetts's rightmost gun,
would drop flat to the ground after each shot so that he could see its
effect beneath the billowing curtain of smoke. Meanwhile, Captain
James Smith would run out beyond the smoke cloud, peer into the
distance, and observe "the position and proximity of the enemy," then
"rush back, seize the trail of a gun, slew it around for the purpose of
directing the fire a little to the right or left."[16] Inevitably, however, the
deepening fug left gunners working blind. Captain John Bigelow said
that Confederate firing (as did his own, presumably) eventually became
"so wild, that not one of their shots was conspicuously effective."[17]

Unsurprisingly, given the speed with which gunners had to work
and the randomness of the shells and shot landing hither and yon, artillery duels were most unpleasant for not only anyone involved but also
those close by. The thudding, shaking, and din caused by a heavy or

direct cannonade, for instance, disoriented gunners and those around them. In the midst of one such bombardment, said Sergeant Frederick Fuger of the 4th U.S. Artillery, "the hills and woods [around him] seemed to reel like a drunken man."[18] Another soldier noticed that as the enemy shot hurtled overhead, he and his comrades' "nerves were strung to the highest pitch; water ran from every pore in the skin like squeezing a wet sponge, and our clothes were wringing wet. It was nature's provision for our safety, as it prevented a total collapse of the nervous system, and the mind from going out in darkness."[19]

The harm was not just psychological. Artillerists, especially those assigned spots near the muzzle, frequently ruptured their tympana, which caused blood to stream out of their ears; severe hearing loss would be the bane of many gunners' lives. Thomas Fisher, who was sixteen and attached to the 9th Massachusetts, for instance, lived to eighty-eight, but for him the world would be permanently silent.[20] After battles, men were so hard of hearing that they often had to shout at one another for a week or more. And one could always recognize the postwar reunions of artillerymen by all the shouting into ear trumpets.[21]

Among infantrymen, one of the least desired duties was guarding the batteries from a surprise attack by cavalry. Detachments were usually placed either to the side or just behind the guns but sometimes were told to stay in front and keep their heads down. Wherever they were, however, it was awful. Lieutenant L. A. Smith, 136th New York, recalled that "if you laid down on the ground and put your fingers in your ears you got, in addition to the crash in the air, the full effect of the earth's tremor and its additional force as a conductor. One of our men found afterwards that his teeth were loose and within a few days nearly all of them dropped out."[22]

Above, he continued, the sky was "fairly black with missiles exploding continually and sending their broken fragments in every direction" and when, if one dared to glance around, "you saw long fiery tongues leaping toward you, thick clouds of sulphurous smoke settle down around you, blackening the countenance almost beyond recognition."[23] The effect was nauseating, said the 14th Connecticut's Sergeant Hincks:

With every discharge, a gun directly behind him "threw the gravel over me, and I could not only see and smell the thick cloud of burning powder but could *taste* it also."[24]

Perhaps the worst part of guard duty was its danger, much grumbled about by unprotected soldiers, who became collateral damage as they passively endured a bombardment. The 108th New York was obliged, for instance, to lose around 50 percent of its engaged strength to enemy cannon fire while stoically protecting the 1st U.S. Artillery.[25] Artillerymen were not wholly sympathetic to their complaints. For gunners, the duel with their opposites was extraordinarily hazardous, and they were sacrificing themselves for the good of the infantry. However, being in the artillery was generally less risky than infantry service—in the Army of Northern Virginia, four in ten foot soldiers were killed and wounded in the war, compared to one in five gunners, and at Gettysburg the Union and Confederate artillery suffered an average of 11.5 percent casualties as against a general infantry loss of 30 percent—up to 80 percent of all artillery casualties were incurred during these intense shoot-outs.[26]

This was because while most artillery shots missed, when they did hit they were truly devastating. Surveying the aftermath of the duel between the Confederate batteries and the Union artillery massed on Cemetery Hill and Culp's Hill, Robert Stiles of the Richmond Howitzers wrote that "never, before or after, did I see fifteen or twenty guns in such a condition of wreck and destruction as this battalion was. It had been hurled backward, as it were, by the very weight and impact of the metal from the position it had occupied on the crest of a little ridge into the saucer-shaped depression behind it." All around he could see nothing but "guns dismounted and disabled, carriages splintered and crushed, ammunition chests exploded, [and] limbers upset."[27]

Exploding ammunition-laden caissons or limbers, each bearing hundreds of pounds of shot, shell, and canister, were the most impressive sights to onlookers. When a shot struck home, it provoked "a thundering report" (in the words of a Vermont veteran) and, wrote Alanson Nelson of the 57th Pennsylvania, made "the ground tremble something like an earthquake." Then came a swirling pillar of smoke that ascended several hundred feet "carrying fragments of timber, wheels, clothing and bodies high in the air," as one sergeant described it.[28] Sometimes one could see "frightened horses, one or two missing a leg," dashing wildly from the smoke as the enemy's cheers rang out.[29]

There was usually nothing left of those who manned the wagons. After a limber belonging to Battery B, 4th U.S. Artillery, was blown up, a gunner held up a blackened piece of jacket to Captain James Stewart and said, "Sir, this is all I can find of Smith, the driver." (In this very rare instance, there was an agreeably happy ending. Stewart discovered a month later that Smith was actually in a Detroit hospital, having lost nothing more than his eyes and limbs.)[30] Passing infantry, unless warned away, were blissfully ignorant of the risks they ran by marching too closely to the ammunition stockpile. One such explosion on July 3 killed several sergeants and corporals of the 14th Vermont.[31]

The artillerists actually operating the guns may rarely have fallen victim to exploding limbers and caissons, which were stationed well away from the battery once the fighting started, but they were still vulnerable to incoming shell and shot. The key to keeping casualties low was to keep the crews some distance apart. For this reason, it was optimal to spread out one's guns a minimum of twelve yards from each other—thirty was better, advised Colonel Charles Wainwright.[32] Responsible siting explained why, according to an analysis of eighteen documented solid-shot hits, only one man was killed or wounded in fully fourteen of them, with two men killed in the other four.[33]

In an understandable if misdirected instinct, the men sometimes gathered around a stricken friend to try to help. Not only did their well-meant intentions hinder the gun's firing, but their clustering exposed everyone to grave risk. Captain Bigelow, wondering why a gun had gone silent, pushed his way through a small crowd of new recruits and saw Henry Fenn lying on the ground with much of his skull torn off by a shell fragment. The artillerymen "asked me, seemingly regardless of the shells exploding about themselves, if they could not take him to the rear. The poor fellow, however, was unconscious and dying; I saw there was no hope and answered them 'No! but back to your guns and give as good as you have received.'" The men did so but were "horrified at my heartlessness."[34]

Veterans, on the other hand, knew only too well what could happen if they clumped together. Private Cyrus Boyd was alerted to the dangers when he came across "five dead Confederates all killed by one [small] six pound solid shot." They had been sitting in a row when the shot raked them from the side. "One of them had his head taken off. One had been struck at the right shoulder and his chest lay open. One had been cut in two at the bowels and nothing held his carcass together but the spine. One had been hit at the thighs and the legs were torn from the body. The fifth and last one was piled up into a mass of skull, arms, some toes, and the remains of a [uniform]. Just a few feet from where they lay the cannon ball had struck a large tree and lodged."[35]

From this interesting description we can reconstruct the path of the lethal object. Fired from some distance away, the shot descended along its parabolic arc—it sequentially hit a head, a shoulder, an abdomen, and the pelvis or thighs—but such was its kinetic force that it did not, despite the many bony obstacles, deviate from its trajectory. The odd man out is the final victim, who ended up as a "mass" of gore. It is likely that the cannonball hit him in the feet as he crouched, ricocheted off the ground directly upward through the groin and abdomen, and violently exited through his upper torso, thereby separating his arms and shattering his head.

As the official medical history of the war would equably remark, cannonballs "virtually encounter no resistance from a single human body."[36] Being hit by one generally entailed death. The Mississippian private Jeremiah Gage lost only his left arm, but when the hospital surgeon encouragingly remarked that he looked likely to survive, he replied, "'Why, Doctor, that is nothing; here is where I am really hurt,' and he laid back the blanket and exposed the lower abdomen torn from left to right by a cannon shot, largely carrying away the bladder, much intestine, and a third of the right half of the pelvis; but in both wounds so grinding and twisting the tissues that there was no hemorrhage."[37]

There was usually no need for a hospital. On one occasion Edward

Ripley was standing behind a gun when he was suddenly "dashed in the face with a hot steaming mass of something horrible" that spattered shut his eyes and seeped into his mouth and nose. Thinking, perhaps irrationally, that his own head had exploded, Ripley was grateful for the attentions of a nearby officer who cleaned away the "mass of brains, skull, hair, and blood" from his face and chest. "As I opened my eyes the headless trunk of the artillery man lay between my feet with the blood gurgling out."[38] Though mercifully quick, decapitation by cannonball was extremely violent. Corpses did not slowly fall to their knees and fall over, as one tends to see in movies; rather, as Lieutenant Frederick Hitchcock observed upon seeing a Confederate major die, "his poor body went down as though some giant had picked it up and furiously slammed it on the ground."[39]

Solid shot's dire effects on animals disturbed even hardened soldiers. One witness saw dead horses littering the field—Cushing's battery alone lost sixty-three of its eighty-four horses on July 3—"some torn almost asunder by cannon balls, some pierced in the side . . . and others with their legs completely shot away."[40] A stricken artillery horse, meanwhile, was a dangerous beast—Robert Stiles of the Richmond Howitzers saw not a few "plunging and kicking, dashing out the brains of men tangled in the harness"—but these at least could be put down, as happened when "cannoneers with pistols [crawled] through the wreck shooting the struggling horses to save the lives of the wounded men."[41]

More unnerving were the horses that cried. The Pennsylvanian Benjamin Urban noticed that while nearly all horses perished silently, there was an occasional exception. After being "struck fairly in the back by a cannon ball, and his spine shattered and broken," there was one who kept "rising on his front feet and trying to drag his paralyzed body, and when he could not, he gave that awful cry which I pray I may never hear again. It was the most dreadful thing I ever heard, and sent the cold chills down every man's back that heard it. One of the men quickly crept up, and pressing a revolver against his head, sent a merciful bullet crashing through his brain."[42]

There were wickeder things in the offing, not least of which was the surviving artillery's imminent bombardment of the hitherto untouched infantry. It was when the guns went conspicuously silent that everyone knew their crews were loading them with shell in preparation for the storm to come.

8. Artillery Versus Infantry

Shell was a hollow projectile of cast iron containing a bursting charge. This was intended either to explode some way above troops' heads, sending spinning, sharp metal fragments downward, or to plunge into the ground and burst upward. A related weapon was spherical case-shot, whose interior was packed with small iron or lead balls suspended in a sulfur or tar-pitch mixture that would detonate outward in a cone-shaped pattern.

There was an unnervingly diabolical aspect to shellfire. One soldier wrote that as shells flew over and detonated, "such a shrieking, hissing, seething I never dreamed was imaginable, it seemed as though it must be the work of the very devil himself."[1] The 136th New York's J. W. Hand employed similar Miltonic language when recalling how the shards hurtling through the air gave "forth the whole infernal gamut of unmusical high notes, the key depending on the velocity."[2] Most horrid to Benjamin Thompson, meanwhile, were "the stifling fumes of burning sulphur from exploding shrapnel"—a sign, surely, of Lucifer's malevolent presence.[3]

Shells, unlike solid shot, were designedly anti-personnel forms of ammunition and as such were feared and detested more fervently. To give some idea of the disparity in effectiveness, between May and July 1864 the Army of the Potomac recorded 88 wounds caused by cannonballs—but 2,112 by shells.[4] Before Pickett's Charge, Major Thomas Osborn of the Union XI Corps artillery on Cemetery Hill could see the enemy formation in plain view. While each of his solid shot "which struck either line cut out two men," when "a shell exploded immediately in front of either line it cut out four, six, eight, or even more men, making a wide open gap in their line."[5]

Those on the receiving end of shellfire bitterly understood Major Osborn's point. When one found its mark it exacted a heavy toll. Franklin Sawyer of the 8th Ohio watched as a Virginian brigade came under accurate Union fire: "They were at once enveloped in a dense cloud of smoke and dust. Arms, heads, blankets, guns, and knapsacks were thrown and tossed into the clear air."[6] A South Carolinian named W. A. Johnson was with Kershaw's Brigade in the Peach Orchard as "shells were cutting off the arms, legs and heads of our men, cutting them in two and exploding in their bodies, tearing them into mincemeat."[7] Similarly, when a Confederate shell hit Company C, 150th Pennsylvania, six men were killed—it alone was responsible for 11 percent of the regiment's deaths at Gettysburg.[8] The men of 2nd North Carolina were on the edge of the woods crowning Oak Hill when a shell burst among them, killing and wounding nine.[9] George Benedict was hurrying past the 13th Vermont when a shell killed a private and sergeant outright, halved another man (a leg, "bared of all but the shoe and stocking [was] thrown several feet from the body"), and knocked out the lieutenant colonel.[10]

William Peel of the 11th Mississippi "heard a shell strike in the right of the reg't, &, turning over, as I lay on my back, I looked just in time to witness the most appalling scene that perhaps ever greeted the human eye. Lt. Daniel Featherston, of Co. F, from Noxubee County, was the unfortunate victim. He was a large man—would have weighed perhaps two hundred pounds. He was lying on his face, when the shell struck the ground near his head, &, in the ricochet, entered his breast, exploding about the same time & knocking him at least ten feet high, & not less than twenty feet from where he was lying."[11] Even when they failed to explode, they were dangerous: What was apparently a twenty-pound Parrott shell, wrote Colonel Wainwright in his diary, "struck in the center of a line of infantry who were lying down behind the wall. Taking the line lengthwise, it literally ploughed up two or three yards of men, killing and wounding a dozen men or more. Fortunately, it did not burst."[12]

The single deadliest shell fired at Gettysburg seems to have been the one that inflicted twenty-seven casualties on the 55th Ohio, but we should bear in mind Colonel Goode Bryan of the 16th Georgia's claim of thirty killed and wounded among a company that was left with just seven men and an officer.[13]

It was one thing to be shelled by the enemy, quite another by one's own side, as could happen when artillerymen carelessly shortened their fuses so that shells exploded either too soon or too low.[14] At Culp's Hill, where about half XII Corps's casualties were caused by friendly fire, the 123rd New York's Robert Cruikshanks explained to his wife that "the battery had to throw their shells close to our heads and for some cause some of [them exploded behind] us which killed and wounded some of the men in the 46th Penn. Vols."[15]

As artillerists plainly could not see what they were hitting, shouting and gesticulating did little good. Lieutenant John Callis "raised my sabre above my head waving it, and at the top of my voice ordering the Capt. of the battery to cease firing. But amid the roar of musketry, and screeching of shot and shell through the air, he seemed not to hear me."[16] The only sure way of telling errant guns to cease fire was to send a runner (as did the 145th New York, only to be told "not to fret," right before three further casualties), or, better still, for a livid commander to go back and chew out the miscreant himself.[17] After one such incident, said Robert Cruikshanks, "there were no more shell exploded behind us after the Colonel had seen the officer."[18]

The best protection, such as it was, against shell, no matter from which side it originated, was to lie down and not move. Understandably, every soldier was desperate to present the smallest possible target. Winfield Scott of 126th New York "wished to be made thin, thinner than hard-tack, yea as thin as a wafer," and the 15th Massachusetts's Private Roland Bowen "thinned myself down to an old five-cent piece, crowding my nose into the sand, out of sight." Meanwhile, William Johnson, 2nd South Carolina hunkered down in a depression and watched Union artillerists preparing to pull the lanyard that would discharge the gun. When they did, he instinctively "stopped still and turned my thin edge to the fire."[19]

Whereas solid shot was often instantaneously fatal, shell fragments ripped off extremities, snapped bones, punctured organs, pulped tissue, and gashed flesh, leaving many alive but in urgent need of aid, which they rarely received. At Antietam, Dr. G. J. Fischer calculated that of fifty-seven amputations he had performed, only about 10 percent were due to shell fragments whereas three-quarters stemmed from bullets.[20] The relatively low number of the former was due not to the ineffectiveness of artillery but to the unlikelihood of the victims' reaching a hospital in time.

Survivors of shell attack, even if they did not lose limbs, suffered from a variety of mental and physical symptoms, some of which would later come to be associated with combat stress disorders. Intrigued by the phenomenon, the Union's medical authorities compiled records on such cases during the war, eventually providing an analysis of 130 such nonfatal casualties. Of these, seventy-one returned to duty a short time later after suffering from temporary deafness, blindness, muteness, or grinding headaches. More than thirty also returned to their units following a bombardment, but their symptoms could not be ascertained. Some twenty-three, however, were discharged from the army for a variety or combination of often euphemistic reasons, including permanent deafness, meningitis, paralysis, optical nerve palsy, insanity, and "spinal affliction and nervous prostration"—that is, they cringed, shook, and whimpered almost incessantly.[21]

There were some extraordinary instances of survival against the odds. Luther White, 20th Massachusetts, was unconscious for three days after being struck by a shell fragment that tore away much of his jaw, throat, and one of his ears, awakening only when he was about to be buried.[22] A man named Hubbard, 7th Indiana, saw a member of the 66th Ohio hit in the face by a fragment and "thought it the ugliest sight I witnessed during my three years of service. As he was led along it seemed to me that his face would clap together, and the blood would gush out, making a sickening sight. I have learned that man got well and lived after the war."[23] And on July 3 Abe Goldstein of the 6th Carolina witnessed a Georgia sergeant nearby "tumble headlong to the earth." The man eventually rose and curious observers could see where "a fragment of a shell . . . had taken his right ear off close to his head, as clean as though it had been cut off with a Surgeon's knife." Asked what the sensations were, the sergeant "said he felt as though he had been overtaken by a cyclone and that a six-storey building had fallen upon him. The noise of the passing fragment of a shell on the drum of his ear sounded like the sudden explosion of a thunderbolt." He then coolly bit off the end of a cartridge and prepared to charge with Pickett.[24]

The sergeant had it right. Since, as Captain Edward Bowen of the 114th Pennsylvania advised, no duty called "for such bravery and endurance, as . . . remaining passive under an enemy's artillery fire that has got an accurate range, and from which there is no protection," there really was just one viable defense against the torment.[25] And that was to attack as soon as possible.

9. Infantry Versus Infantry—The Attack

The longer a unit dawdled at its start line, the higher its casualties as artillerists improved their aim. Time was blood. Whereas the 2nd South Carolina, which was kept waiting, incurred two-thirds of its casualties from artillery fire and the rest from musketry, the 13th Mississippi, which promptly left its position and mounted a shock assault, suffered just two casualties (of 62 known wounded, or 3.2 percent) from shell-fire and the balance (96.8 percent) from infantry fire.[1]

Soldiers were keen to go, for the "howling, shrieking story of shot and shell was more trying to the nerves than to be engaged in close action with the enemy," wrote E. C. Strouss of the 57th Pennsylvania, which waited in a field as a Confederate cannonade rained down upon them.[2] Officers knew they had only a limited window to order an assault before a unit began to disintegrate and the men's courage to flag. As it was, in the minutes leading up to a charge, soldiers turned uncharacteristically silent, a sure sign that they were brooding on what was to come. Captain William Seymour of the Louisiana Brigade, whose men were about to storm Cemetery Hill on July 2, looked around and saw, not fear, but only their "quiet, solemn mien" that (he rather subtly added) "fully appreciated the desperate character of the undertaking."[3]

Some men softly murmured prayers, some gazed on photographs of their loved ones, others read letters from them, a few composed suitably heroic last words in their heads.[4] Anyone who did, smoked—vigorously.[5] Those who did not tore the tough brown paper from a cartridge and chewed it mixed with a few grains of gunpowder.[6]

The pervasive quiet masked a knot of tension growing within each soldier. Illinoisan Lucius Barber recalled that he, and every man, experienced a creeping sense of "involuntary awe and dread" in the lead-up to action.[7] As it spread, said the Confederate Edmund Patterson, this sense turned into "a painful nervous anxiety" that, in him at least, manifested itself as "a dull feeling about the chest that made breathing painful."[8] No one, no matter how tried and tested in battle, ever escaped this gnawing unease before a fight. The 1st Virginia's John Dooley concluded that "soldiers generally do not fear death less because of their repeated escape from its jaws," for in each battle they saw so many frightful and novel forms of mutilation and death, and were so thankful for their deliverance from those fates, that they dreaded for their lives anew every time.[9]

Yet surprisingly, few men actually broke and fled to the rear. Several factors probably account for their remarkable fortitude. First, they understood that according to contemporary opinion, combat itself was not the only test of manhood—so was waiting for it. Abner Small, who fought in many of the war's major battles, believed that what counted was how men coped with "dread" when their unit was on the cusp of a fight, where they were "near enough to feel its fierce pulsations and get an occasional shock of its power."[10] If they could just control their mounting fear and hold fast, this would all soon be over.

The most common way of staying put was to look side to side at one's friends and be reassured that they, too, were intent on keeping the line. No man wanted to be the coward, hereafter reviled and shunned in equal measure. Officers, too, played an important role in stiffening sinews. In a citizen army soldiers were impressed by raw charismatic courage, not necessarily competency—an attribute stressed more by modern professionals—and leaders were expected to exhibit absolute coolness and unyielding fearlessness under fire. At Seminary Ridge on

July 3, the 2nd Vermont came under, in George Benedict's words, heavy artillery bombardment "from direct point-blank" and then "an enfilading fire, from a battery of Whitworth guns far to the right, which sent their six-sided bolts screaming by, parallel to our lines." But, never minding the deadly maelstrom, "the general, staff, and field officers alone, *as their duties required*," stood erect even as everyone else kept their heads down.[11] Sergeant Isaac Barnes told a friend that seeing his higher-ups so calm "cured my fears in a great measure."[12]

Sometimes, the desire to demonstrate an almost preternatural imperturbability to those around them reached comic levels of one-upmanship, such as the time Captain Wadsworth rode up to Major Thomas Osborn at the height of an incoming bombardment. Both men sat astride beautiful horses which they deliberately stood broadside to the enemy fire to increase their vulnerability. "While we were talking," recalled Osborn, "a percussion shell struck the ground directly under the horses and exploded. The momentum of the shell carried the fragments along so that neither horse was struck nor did either horse move. When the shell exploded, I was in complete control of my nerves and did not move a muscle of my body or my face. Neither did Wadsworth, but I dropped my eyes to the ground where the shell exploded, and Wadsworth did not. I never quite forgave myself for looking down to the ground when that shell exploded under us."[13]

Officers' conspicuous heedlessness of danger steadied the line and buttressed morale—but at great cost to their own lives. In the Army of Northern Virginia, for instance, officers were 2.25 times more likely to be killed in action than enlisted men. At Gettysburg, more than a quarter of Union officers were killed and wounded, compared to a fifth of enlisted men; fully a third of Lee's generals became casualties.[14] In some hard-fighting units, the proportion was higher still: After the battle, Lieutenant Oscar Ladley of the 75th Ohio informed his mother and sisters that "15 out of 18 [officers] are gone."[15] And on July 2, in less than a quarter of an hour the 11th New Jersey lost no fewer than five commanding officers, some of them in charge for a minute or two at most.[16]

To further ease tension as the minutes ticked by, officers encouraged their men to make noise—and lots of it. Northerners awaiting an onslaught were often disquieted to hear "jerky, canine cries" issuing from the Confederate lines.[17] This psychologically intimidating sound, redolent of the war cries of Indian tribes or the booming yelps of Scottish Highlanders, was the infamous Rebel Yell—a frightful thing to hear, even for veterans. The men of Company A, 6th Wisconsin, had first encountered it at Gainesville, but at Gettysburg they still shuddered whenever it echoed toward them. "There is nothing like it this side of the infernal region," they said, recalling with horror "the peculiar corkscrew sensation that it sends down your backbone."[18]

According to an enthusiastic practitioner, W. H. Morgan, the yell was "one continuous shout of mingled voices, without any intermission, unisonance or time. Each man just opened his mouth as wide as he could, strained his voice to the highest pitch and yelled as long as his breath lasted, then refilling the lungs, repeated it again and again. It was a commingling of shrill, loud sounds, that rent the air and could be heard for a distance of two miles or more, often carrying terror to the enemy."[19]

To counter its effects, Union officers encouraged their men to remain composed by crying, as Morgan remembered, "hip, hip, huzza, huzza, huzza" in "unison and in time." To him, it may have sounded "coarse and harsh to the ear," but to Yankees the clipped syllables and indomitable rhythm betokened masculine control over themselves and their environment in the final moments before all hell broke loose. For the men of the 22nd Massachusetts and others, "our solid, defiant cheers" (in contrapuntal reply to the "discordant screeches" and "womanlike scream[s]" of the rebels) did more than anything else to steady the nerves.[20]

At this point, it was best for the attacking side to get their men up and out—even if such a move appeared to make little obvious sense. Hence the colonel, lieutenant colonel, and major of the 7th New Jersey, which was pinned down by Confederate guns, recognized that soon "it would be impossible to hold the men together inactive" and ordered them to "Fix bayonets; forward, double-quick, charge!" toward the Southern lines, which they could not even see. Over a third of the regiment became casualties within a few minutes—including its colonel and lieutenant colonel.[21] Despite these fiascos, it was rarely hard to persuade soldiers to begin to advance at a good clip. If anything, as Private Boland, 13th Alabama, admitted, "we moved somewhat faster, attempting to run from under the shells, which were just falling behind us."[22]

Once they began to move, soldiers felt the violent release of their pent-up tensions. Rice Bull, a soldier of the 123rd New York, wrote in his diary that until jumping off, one's "nerves are almost at the breaking point," but "then the strain relaxes and the fear and nervousness passes away."[23] W. L. Goss had been suffering from a "sickening feeling and a cold perspiration" and "a sort of faintness and lack of strength in the joints of my legs, as if they would sink from under me," but as soon as he began marching forward, "my knees recovered from their unpleasant limpness, and my mind gradually regained its balance and composure."[24]

Initially, they exulted in the feeling of liberation. Andrew Humphreys "felt like a young girl of sixteen at her first ball; I felt more like a god than a man; I now understand what Charles XII meant when he said, 'Let the whistling of the bullets hereafter be my music.' "[25] For his part, Sam Watkins from Tennessee "had been feeling mean all the morning as if I had stolen a sheep, but [now] I felt happier than a fellow does when he professes religion at a big Methodist camp-meeting. I shouted. It was fun then. Everybody looked happy."[26]

That palpable sense of joy was soon followed by the unpleasant realization that one was participating in a very serious pastime. Watkins said that for a time "it all seemed to me a dream" and that "I seemed to be in a sort of haze," but he was brought abruptly short when "siz, siz, siz, the minnie balls from the Yankee line began to whistle around our ears," and he surmised (correctly) that "sure enough, those fellows are shooting bullets!"[27] Henry Stanley, the future explorer of Africa, served in the 6th Arkansas and remembered that while at first "my ears tingled, my pulses beat double-quick, my heart throbbed loudly," he began to look around and saw that his comrades were shedding their excitability and turning "pale, solemn, and absorbed."[28]

As well they might. Within the first minute or two of an advance the attackers would begin taking casualties, as would the defenders (at a much slower rate and depending on whether shell was still falling or there was enfilading fire). For the men on both sides, it became critical to maintain, as one Lieutenant Wheeler advised, "a perfect indifference to circumstances" to avoid falling prey to paralyzing fear and shock at seeing one's comrades come to grief.[29] For the sake of personal survival, then, Charles Benton of the 150th New York quickly hardened himself to seeing "men killed in numbers . . . without any . . . emotions of dread or horror" so that his mind was able to "[devote] itself to whatever work it may have [had] at hand."[30] Charles Wainwright, in his first battle, immediately grasped this harsh but vital truth, confiding that to his surprise "I had no feeling but one of perfect indifference" to "seeing men shot, dead or dying." Indeed, "when Lieutenant Eakin fell against me, and cried out that he was 'a dead man,' I had no more feeling for him, than if he had tripped over a stump and fallen; nor do I think it would have been different had he been my brother."[31] Many soldiers followed Wainwright's example in suppressing their normal "civilian" emotions, like that of empathy. John Campbell, 5th Iowa, conceded that despite the dead and dying strewn around "there was a strange, unaccountable lack of *feeling* with me." He clarified why: "Out of battle and in a battle, I find myself two different beings."[32]

As these men understood, the best way to get an unpleasant and dangerous job over with was to switch off, keep plugging forward, and look nowhere but straight ahead—to treat the bloody affair, as Benton said, strictly as "work." When on July 2 eight companies of the 1st Minnesota formed up and marched on the double through concentrated fire toward the Alabama Brigade—they were outnumbered five to one and the charge was regarded as suicidal—Matthew Marvin remembered that "it seemed as if every step was over some fallen comrade. Yet no man wavers, every gap is closed up. . . . Bringing down their bayonets, the boys press forward in unbroken line. Men stumbled and fell. Some stayed down but others got up and continued." Another Minnesotan, Alfred Carpenter, added, "Bullets whistled past us; shells screeched over us; canister . . . fell among us; comrade after comrade dropped from the ranks; but on the line went. No one took a second look at his fallen companion. We had no time to weep."[33] Of the 262 men who took part in the assault, 215 became casualties within five minutes. Despite losses of 82 percent, the Minnesotans achieved their objective of protecting Cemetery Ridge.

The example of the 1st Minnesota was perhaps a statistical outlier, but a constant in every infantry advance was maintaining command and control over formations whose neatness began to decay from the moment they set off. Holding a straight line through rough terrain, over uneven ground, up and down even moderate slopes, past fences and around hedges was almost always harder than anticipated. A clump of trees in the path of the oncoming line, for instance, would force some sections to skew around it and then rush to catch up to the others. Negotiating the side of a shallow ditch would cause some to lag while others jumped across; when all reached the other side they would have to risk pausing to re-form the line, often under fire. On broken terrain, like that of Devil's Den, where "the ground [was] covered with large boulders, from the size of a wash pot to that of a wagon bed," preserving "anything like line of battle [was] impossible" but, as 5th Texas's Private John Stevens pledged, "we do the best we can."[34]

To understand the scale of the problem, consider that a company at full strength occupied a 27-yard-long front, a regiment of ten similarly endowed companies needed 300 yards (with three yards between each company), and a brigade of four regiments spread out over 1,300 yards, or nearly three-quarters of a mile.[35] At the beginning of its advance, a formation, rifles nursed against right shoulders, would march at the "double"—140 steps per minute, or 109 yards every sixty seconds, for up to 300 yards—meaning that any butterfly effect precipitated by an obstacle would ripple through the ranks.[36] And ripple quickly: Private Coxe, 2nd South Carolina, was charging at Union guns in a hitherto successful assault when a foolish order halted the advance, causing havoc where there had been none. "In a few moments," Coxe annoyedly wrote, "the whole brigade was jumbled up in a space less than a regiment behind a rocky, heavily wooded bluff. . . . We were truly 'in a box,' liable to be captured or annihilated at any moment."[37]

It was a badge of pride when officers, aided by sergeants and corporals, succeeded in maintaining their troops' orderliness. When Kershaw's Brigade attacked the Union positions it was, for instance, universally regarded as fine work, prompting a colonel to boast, "For four hundred yards our line moved forward not wavering nor hesitating in the slightest degree."[38] During Pickett's Charge, the gray waves were so immaculate that General Lewis Armistead took the time to ask General James Kemper, "Did you ever see a more perfect line than that on dress parade?"[39]

One textbook method of promoting good line formations was borrowed from seventeenth- and eighteenth-century European practice. In order of battle a regiment's companies were arranged in a specific configuration based on the seniority of their captains. Thus, from right to left the order was generally 1st, 6th, 4th, 9th, 3rd, 8th, 5th, 7th, and 2nd companies. (In American regiments, companies were named alphabetically, but the principle was the same.) The most experienced captain led the extreme right, the second most senior the extreme left, the third-most in the center, and so forth. By interspersing veteran commanders with raw ones a colonel could keep his lines long, strong, and hopefully disentangled by not placing too many newly commissioned officers at one end.[40]

Music had once helped regulate the rhythm of the march, but those days were long gone, even if the romantic visions remained. The young Charles Benton, for instance, was disappointed not to find "bands and drum corps march[ing] ahead of the soldiers and play[ing] sweet music to drown the groans of the dying and cheer the living on to victory and glory. Had I not seen more than one brave picture of our revered ancestral patriots being led to the fray in that poetic manner? But in real service I never heard a note of music [apart from an occasional bugle] during a battle."[41] This was partly because musicians were seconded as medical orderlies to fetch and carry the wounded from the battlefield, and in any case, the roar of artillery and crackle of musketry would have drowned out their drums and fifes.[42]

In the absence of instruments, officers fell back on their swords to maintain formation and pace. Major Edward Pye, 95th New York, employed his to lead the regiment forward by waving it above his head while crying, "Guide Right! Forward, Charge!"[43] They occasionally came in handy, too, for thwacking recalcitrant men across the shoulders or rear. Lieutenant Oscar D. Ladley boasted to his family that when a few soldiers of his regiment faltered, "my sword was out and if I didn't welt them with it my name ain't O.D.L. It was the only good service it has done me yet."[44]

The widespread ownership of swords can bemuse modern audiences. To be sure, they were worthless in combat. In desperate firefights, wrote Lieutenant Colonel Philip Work of the 1st Texas at Houck's Ridge and Devil's Den, "many of the officers threw aside their swords, seized a rifle, and, going into the ranks, fought bravely and nobly."[45]

Yet these mostly ceremonial implements were treated reverently by contemporary soldiers, for being useless did not make them pointless. At the outset of the Civil War, high birth bought high rank—despite lacking any military qualifications, Philippe Regis Denis de Keredern de Trobriand, who inherited a French title, was appointed colonel of the 55th New York, while Captain Joseph Davis (nephew of CSA President Jefferson Davis) made general in about a year. But by Gettysburg, any man's neighbor, no matter how mean or modest, could, either through merit, attrition, luck, conniving, or favoritism, be promoted and outrank him.[46] An increasing number of humble men had been raised from the dust to positions once reserved for the American nobility. The recent immigrants and lowly artisans who joined as privates and later received commissions to lieutenant or captain could not expect, as if by *dieu et mon droit,* to be followed by their former peers, especially those who in civilian life had been their social or economic superiors. A sword—ancient token of rightful command—therefore served as a marker of traditional authority for men who lacked it. Even if they did not acknowledge an officer's hereditary legitimacy to lead them, enlisted men were obliged to respect the emblem of his power. This realization dawned on one young officer when he noticed that the Pennsylvanians were breaking under the Confederate onslaught at the

Angle. Drawing his sword and successfully ordering them to "halt" and "face about," it was only then that he understood that this implement, which "had always hung idle by my side, the sign of rank only," had transformed, when wielded "bright and gleaming" at the critical moment, into "the symbol of command."[47]

Swords were undoubtedly handy for rousing the men to follow their appointed, if not anointed, leader, as well as for directing soldiers back into line, but they were hard to see once the assault began in earnest. Troops were accordingly told to keep their eye on the regimental and state colors—large flags, descended from heraldic and Napoleonic banners, borne aloft in the center of the line and easily discernible against a smoke-darkened background. Amid the coming tumult, any man, no matter how disoriented or scared or alone, could count on finding his regiment (or what was left of it) wheresoever were its colors. The colors were life, a sign that its heart pulsated and throbbed still.

On a broader level, colors represented group pride and identification, the implication being that even if a soldier was reluctant to acknowledge "swordly" authority, he would nevertheless strive to maintain the high regard and favorable opinion of his friends by marching forward together. More practically, officers used the colors as a mobile rallying point, a center of alignment, and a directional indicator. During the 6th Wisconsin's advance it soon devolved into a V-shaped wedge, with the colors "moving firmly and hurriedly forward," according to Colonel Rufus Dawes, "while the whole field behind [began] streaming with men who had been shot, and who [were] struggling to the rear or sinking in death upon the ground." Dawes bawled, "Align on the colors! Close up on that color! Close up on that color!" arresting the regiment's dissolution and "hold[ing] the body together."[48] On the Confederate side, when the colors belonging to the 42nd Mississippi drooped during an attack on the 147th New York, J. V. Pierce on the Union side watched as "an officer in front of the [42nd's] centre corrected the alignment as if passing in review. It was the finest exhibition of discipline and drill I ever saw, before or since, on a battlefield."[49]

10. Infantry Versus Infantry—The Defense

Across the swath of deadly ground separating the antagonists, the defenders were steeling themselves for the onslaught. Whenever possible, they would line up behind a low stone wall, a wooden fence, some hastily erected breastworks, a slight ridge, even a hedge—anything that might serve to shield their bodies. There were times when soldiers had to fight in the open, but once they had enjoyed the benefits of digging in, few preferred it otherwise. Said Harry Dean of the 7th Ohio, which fought for the first time "behind breastworks or fortifications" at Culp's Hill, "all agree that it is a pretty good way to fight."[1]

Once ensconced, their eyes focused most immediately on the faraway flutterings and snappings of the various flags calling their flocks to congregate, but they kept their ears pitched for the jangling and rattling of metal equipment—the most telltale sign of movement en masse. Officers and NCOs kept a particularly beady eye open for men who looked less preoccupied than unoccupied. To keep them busy, they would stalk back and forth ordering soldiers to double- and triple-check their weapons or repeatedly run through the manual of arms—the series of motions by which soldiers loaded, fired, and recharged their rifles. The 18th Massachusetts performed precisely this exercise over and over again as they awaited the Confederates during Pickett's Charge.[2] Among the several benefits of the practice, its sheer mindlessness took the men's thoughts off the imminent melee.

Some soldiers were also dispatched to harvest as many guns as they could find. Fortunately, there were usually plenty lying around, especially if the ground had already been fought over. Once they were brought back, they too were cleaned and loaded and, as the 1st Delaware did when the grand Confederate assault began to coalesce on July 3, were "distributed along the line . . . thus forming an embryo arsenal," according to J. L. Brady.[3] "Some of the men were so energetic as to have four loaded muskets, it was very common for men to have two," wrote Captain David Shields.[4]

They would need them. Each time a soldier fired, unburnt powder residue was blasted down the barrel; after heavy use the accumulated fouling made the gun prone to malfunction and increasingly difficult to reload. That was why George Bowen, 12th New Jersey, in the process of firing thirty or forty shots over the course of a day, had to use "several guns to do it as they got so full [with residue] that [I] could not get a load down them."[5] At one critical moment during a firefight, the gun belonging to Private Valerius Giles of the 5th Texas became so clogged that his ramrod got stuck midway in the barrel and he had to bang it on a rock to drive it down.[6] Once the weapons had been divvied up, defenders methodically inventoried their ammunition. As cartridges and the percussion caps needed to ignite the gunpowder were fiddly things at the best of times, it was only sensible, as the 12th New Jersey did while awaiting a Confederate attack, to empty their cartridge boxes and arrange the ammunition on top of a wall or, as Private Robert Carter of the 22nd Massachusetts noticed, to make a little pile on the ground.[7]

Only then did they have a chance to watch the spectacle unfolding before them. The first sight of approaching troops was one of initial grandeur tinctured with mounting horror. The New Yorker Winfield Scott enjoyed a close-up view of Pickett's Charge, waxing that "the movement of such a force over such a field, in such perfect order, to such a destiny, was grand beyond expression"; Scott's "heart was thrilled at the sight. I was so absorbed with the beauty and grandeur of the scene that I became oblivious to the shells that were bursting about us. This passage of scripture came to my mind, and I repeated it aloud: 'Fair as the moon, bright as the sun, and terrible as an army with banners.'" (He was referencing the Song of Solomon 6:10.)[8] Edwin Southard of the 119th New York was similarly mesmerized by the first appearance of Early's Division on July 1—until he realized that the "beautiful" long gray line rolling forward "in excellent array, the sunlight flashing from their fixed bayonets and unsheathed swords" was in fact an "appalling spectacle, for it rendered our line untenable and defenseless."[9] According to Oscar Jackson, the scariest sight of all was a mass of men advancing "with a firm, slow, steady step"; he later "stood a bayonet charge when the enemy came at us on the double-quick with a yell and it was not so trying on the nerves as that steady, solemn advance."[10]

The attacking side only marched that slowly when it was out of effective rifle range—as the more excitable defenders soon learned. Warren Olney's regiment could see the enemy forming up about four hundred yards away and so "without word of command," took some potshots at them. "After three or four rounds, the absurdity of firing at the enemy at that distance with our guns dawned upon us, and we stopped. As the smoke cleared up we saw the enemy still there, not having budged or fired a shot in return."[11]

When the enemy approached the two-hundred-yard mark and began to pick up the pace, defending officers would cry, "Up men! They are coming! Fall in—fall in!" as Private David Ballinger, 12th New Jersey, recalled, and pace up and down the line, issuing a reassuring word here and adjusting a poorly placed rifle there.[12] Alonzo Hill, 8th Pennsylvania, saw his friend Jake Archibald raise his rifle to a 45-degree angle, only for an officer to bellow, "Not so high! You're not firing a salute," as he used his sword to press the offending piece down horizontally.[13]

As the enemy colors hove nearer and one could become hopeful or crestfallen by counting the number of battle honors stitched into the flags—the more there were, the more hardboiled the regiment—the defenders took beads on the most prominent targets. Officers, of course, were always eminently selectable, but others were equally popular. Distinctively tall or stout men, for instance, would attract unwelcome attention. Worried that he might otherwise miss, the 116th Pennsylvania's Daniel Chisholm jotted down in his notebook that he "picked out the very largest man I could see & took sight."[14] Color-bearers always came in for more than their fair share of bullets, as demonstrated by the ragged state of their flags at the end of a hard fight: that of the 149th New York was perforated by eighty-one bullet holes at Gettysburg.[15] Private John Vautier, 88th Pennsylvania, was behind a wall with his friends when Iverson's Brigade (5th, 12th, 20th, and 23rd North Carolina) appeared. "A color-bearer making himself very conspicuous by defiantly flaunting his flag in plain view [caused Sergeant

Evans to remark], as he brought his piece to his shoulder, . . . 'I will give those colors a whack.'"[16]

Then they waited. And waited. And waited.

The officers' most important task was to remind the men not to jump the gun and start firing willy-nilly. They must await the command to pull the trigger in order to maximize the devastation inflicted by a synchronized first volley. Over at the 14th Connecticut's position, "Major Ellis emphasized this order, Adjutant Doten went forth and back along the line repeating it, and Sergeant Major Hincks and the line officers reiterated it—and so our men, with aim well taken and finger on trigger, submissively waited."[17]

Finally, the order would come to fire: "Give it to them!" would shout the colonel, and the men (in this case, the 19th Maine) "sent a sudden volley into the teeth of the advancing enemy."[18] The first broadside, as a correspondent for *Scientific American* described it, was "a rattle and roll, which sounds like a falling of a building, just as some of you have heard the bricks tumble at a great fire."[19] Leander Stillwell, a country boy like so many others, employed more rural imagery in likening the roar down the line to "the sweep of a thunder-storm in summer-time over the hard ground of a stubble-field"—only, he added, "a million times louder."[20]

The efficacy of this initial volley varied proportionally to the distance between defenders and attackers, and accounting for that differential was part, but just one part, of the dismal mathematics of Civil War combat. It was widely reckoned that a unified force approaching at the double-quick traversed a hundred yards per minute.[21] Another rule of thumb was that a defending unit could fire in combat an average of once per minute (estimates range from once every two minutes to twice a minute).[22] Therefore, if the enemy had reached the hundred-yard mark, the defenders had time for only a single volley before its line was breached. But these were merely theoretical averages, not real-world ones. Skill and judgment were needed to adjust one's particular circumstances to fit the developing situation. For instance, marching one hundred yards under fire and over hard terrain would slow down any attacking force, leaving it vulnerable to extra shots from the defenders. On the other hand, not only did the terrain—hillocks, barns, and ditches, for example—reduce incoming fire by obscuring the defenders' sightlines but the attackers also naturally accelerated into a run upon reaching the thirty-yard mark, thereby leaving the defenders with even less time to get off another shot. Another example: Some units fired more often than others. Thus, one of the fastest times recorded was a round every thirty seconds (at Antietam, by the 52nd New York) and the slowest every 4.6 minutes (at Stones River, by the 3rd Kentucky).[23] And, as we've seen, many soldiers stockpiled between two and four guns before a fight; not having to reload between each shot, or at least being able to switch rifles when their barrels began to foul or overheat, multiplied the number of times they could fire. Jeremiah Hoffman, 142nd Pennsylvania, said that during one clash he and the others simply dropped their guns when they became too hot to handle and grabbed the ones waiting next to them.[24] Even when they ran out of spares, a New Yorker recalled, a man could throw away his gun and bid "those beside him to be careful where they fired, rush forward and pick up, in place of it, one that had fallen from the hands [of] a dead or wounded comrade."[25] When all these factors are taken into consideration, it becomes more evident how at Gettysburg the 154th New York, facing two Confederate brigades (Louisianans and North Carolinians) managed to expend between six and nine shots per man in the limited time available. Even if that figure was a statistical outlier, it is perfectly reasonable to presume that the defending side could fire between two and four shots if they began the cycle when the enemy began its assault at the hundred-yard point.

As at Bunker Hill, that range was used as the benchmark because it balanced hitting power against accuracy. In 1775, the militiamen had been good shots but the technological limitations of their weapons and ammunition had restricted their lethality at more than one hundred yards. By Gettysburg, conversely, bullets and firearms alike had greatly improved but marksmanship had declined so precipitously that one hundred yards, more or less, was still the point where defenders could begin to inflict any damage.[26]

In the 1850s, the U.S. Army had given shooting practice short shrift. Given the compressed training of Civil War regiments, little better could be expected. When Captain George Wingate first tested his New York company, for example, he found that hardly anyone could hit a barrel lid at a hundred yards.[27] Then there was the 5th Connecticut, a prestigious unit that held a shooting contest to entertain its members in August 1861. Forty men lined up and took aim at the side of a barn twenty feet long and fifteen feet high. Less entertainingly, at a range of one hundred yards, just one of the forty rounds hit the wood lower than the average height of a soldier. Put another way, had this result been replicated in battle, 97.5 percent of the shots unleashed by this fearsome, company-strong volley would have missed the approaching enemy. "And these soldiers were probably a fair average of New England troops in this respect," commented an embarrassed Captain Edwin Marvin.[28]

Troops new to war were often surprised by how few of them were hit even at such a moderate range. Leander Stillwell, for instance, was puzzled to hear "an incessant humming sound away up above our heads, like the flight of a swarm of bees." He and his comrades eventually surmised that the sound was caused by bullets sailing harmlessly anywhere from twenty to a hundred feet overhead.[29] Private Robert Carter observed that "the green leaves and twigs overhead fell in a constant shower, as they were clipped by the singing bullets."[30] As he and his fellows advanced in the face of a Union broadside, George Neese assumed that they would all die, yet "the regiments appeared as complete as they were before the fight."[31] Of this phenomenon, the authoritative *Army and Navy Journal* concluded that "the escape of so large a majority of the men, amid such storms sweeping and yelling around their ears, has always been the greatest mystery."[32]

Since one hundred yards was something of a crapshoot, it was generally preferable, if more nerve-racking, to reserve the first fire until the enemy was fifty yards away (some excellent regiments, such as the 19th Maine, sometimes held their volley until as little as thirty-five yards separated the two sides).[33] At that range, hits were almost guaranteed. Sergeant John Freer was at Brinkerhoff's Ridge when "twenty-five or thirty rebs came almost straight for the place we occupied [behind a rail fence]" as "another party, of about the same number, [headed] toward the cross-fence to our left. The boys were restless and wanted to open the ball, but I ordered them to hold their fire. When the rebs were within eight or ten rods [about fifty yards] I gave the order to . . . Give 'em hell!"[34]

At this crisis point, without any room for error if the defenders blew their opportunity to devastate the enemy, officers and sergeants prowled up and down the line, repeating the admonition, as George Grant of the 88th Pennsylvania recorded, "to await command and aim low" when the Confederates reached the fifty-yard mark.[35] At the Angle on July 3, the Union troops could see Pickett's Confederates moving forward and their fingers instinctively tightened on the triggers. "Do not hurry, men, and fire too fast," their own Brigadier General John Gibbon reassuringly counseled as he rode to and fro. "Let them come up close before you fire, and then aim low, and steadily."[36]

"Low" was defined as the knees or shins.[37] As at Bunker Hill, aiming low helped counteract soldiers' fatal tendency to over-elevate their rifles while exploiting the principle that a leg wound neutralized a combatant almost as effectively as a head shot. Crippling attackers en masse was the surest means of slowing a formation's momentum and atomizing its mass. Another advantage was that as the smoke rose, the enemy's lower limbs became the first visible target. At Devil's Den, for instance, when Benjamin Urban heard someone cry, "Look under the smoke, boys!" he and the others "depressed our pieces and sent a volley into the mass of 'men in grey' struggling up the hill, some on their hands and knees, sending them flying down the slope broken and demoralized."[38]

If performed correctly at close range, the first volley or two would mow down the oncoming tide of men. Private John Vautier was a member of the 88th Pennsylvania, part of a group of regiments determined to fend off Iverson's Brigade of Tar Heels: He described seeing "the field in front . . . swarming with Confederates, who came sweeping on in magnificent order, with perfect alignment, guns at right shoulder and colors to the front." At the word, there was a simultaneous crash of rifles, and a sheet of flame and smoke "flar[ed] full in the faces of the advancing troops, the ground being quickly covered with their killed and wounded as the balls hissed and cut through the exposed line."[39]

A Confederate artilleryman named Robin Berkeley walked the same contested ground that night and counted "79 North Carolinians laying dead in a straight line. I stood on their right and looked down their line. It was perfectly dressed. Three had fallen to the front, the rest had fallen backward; yet the feet of all these dead men were in a perfectly straight line" thanks to a single "volley of musketry."[40]

Generally speaking, however, the aftermath of an infantry charge was messier than that: One broadside rarely ended the action. It was hard to stop troops when their blood was up. Edmund Patterson, 9th Alabama, described how his regiment "met such a perfect storm of lead right in our faces that the whole brigade literally *staggered* backward several paces as though pushed by a tornado," and yet after the officers cried "Forward, Alabamians,—Forward!" the remaining men "swept forward with wild cheers."[41] According to Private Roland Bowen (15th Massachusetts), infantry formations that had received a blow would momentarily seem "to be suspicious or in doubt as if they had lost their confidence. They hesitated, they reeled, they staggered, and wavered slightly, yet there was no panic."[42] The gored attacking line—even when "gappy, hesitating, incoherent, and sensitive," according to Henry Stanley—would pull itself together as officers urgently began "waving their swords and telling them to stand fast and not break or run," as Chauncey Harris of the 108th New York related to his father.[43]

After successive charges on a position, one could sometimes tell just by looking at the ebb and flow of corpses where the line had been dammed, fallen back, and renewed the attack.[44] The Pennsylvanian Amos Judson recounted of the Confederate assault on his position at Little Round Top that, following the initial volley, "which made the enemy reel and stagger, and fall back in confusion," the Southerners rallied and advanced, hundreds approaching "even within fifteen yards of our line, but they approached only to be shot down or hurled back covered with gaping wounds." Later, Judson counted "over forty dead bodies within a circle of fifty feet in circumference. They laid in every conceivable position among the rocks in that low swampy ground, some crouched behind rocks as if about to fire, some lying upon their faces, and some stretched upon their backs."[45] A circle with a fifty-foot circumference has a diameter of nearly sixteen feet and an area of just under two hundred square feet. Fitting more than forty bodies in such a space implies that a significant number overlapped or were entangled— telltale evidence that multiple fusillades had been fired at troops who had refused to cede the day to the defenders.

Once soldiers began firing, they did not cease. At first, depending on how they had been trained, either every rifleman fired a single volley simultaneously, or the soldiers would cycle through front and rear ranks to create an almost continuous hail, or they fired serially either by file or company to create a ripple effect from right to left.[46] The simplest and most reliable method of keeping control for the longest possible time was the second option: shooting by rank. At Culp's Hill, said S. R. Norris of the 7th Ohio, they reserved "our fire until the first line of battle was well up the slope and in easy range, when the command, 'Front rank—Ready—Aim low—Fire!' was given and executed, and immediately the rear rank the same, and kept up as long as the line remained unbroken."[47] A common, if minor, complaint among defenders was that the frontmost rank was often deafened or scorched by the one behind. Tactical manuals may have emphasized that the rear men should always jut their muzzles to "reach as much beyond the front rank as possible," but even when George Bowen, 12th New Jersey, carefully followed this instruction, every time he fired those ahead of him "looked back and told me I would shoot them, swearing about it."[48]

There was always a lot of swearing in a defensive line, especially once fire synchronization began to disintegrate after a few volleys. As the need for self-control evaporated, loud cursing spread through the ranks from top to bottom. Captain John DeForest remembered that "the swearing mania [became] irrepressible."[49] Hitherto genteel officers and docile privates suddenly erupted into every "extremity of language." Remembered Theodore Dodge, there were unending cries of "Give 'em ____, boys!" and "Rake ____ out of 'em, boys!" while Private Henry Meyer (148th Pennsylvania) found it peculiar that "some of the boys swore energetically, who never before were heard to utter an oath."[50] Benjamin Winger said that the men liked it when their officers burst into "a lot of good, hard swearing" because "they thought if the officers could swear till a blue streak went up, they [too] could afford to be brave."[51] As Victorian curse words were less sexual or scatological than blasphemous (as Dodge clarified, the "familiar synonym for heat"—Hell—was incessant), a captain's willingness to utter ungodly oaths was a confident and heartening sign that he did not expect to be justifying himself before Saint Peter anytime soon.

11. The Attack Continues

The defense often concentrated its fire on the color company (the unit entrusted with the regimental standards or flags), which accordingly incurred higher losses than any other.[1] But it was the color-bearer and color-guard themselves, rather than the whole company, who were the true loci of attention. Aiming at them was not mere sport; if the colors fell, the entire attacking force could collapse as its command structure unraveled, lines stopped moving, and units became ensnarled. The object, then, was to eliminate bearer and guards as rapidly as possible. For that reason, every guard escorting William Murphy, who carried the colors of the 2nd Mississippi, was "killed and wounded in less than five minutes."[2]

Murphy was extraordinarily lucky to survive; more often, when assaults went wrong, color-bearers were massacred. The record number of losses at Gettysburg was set by the 26th North Carolina, with seventeen color-bearers killed and wounded. The hideous comedy of the 26th began with color-bearer Sergeant J. B. Mansfield, who was stationed with his guards six paces ahead of the regimental line. As the North Carolinians advanced toward the 24th Michigan, Mansfield was shot in the foot (no doubt by a Union man aiming low) and then handed the colors to Sergeant Hiram Johnson. Less than a dozen yards later, he, too, was shot, and the banner was taken by Private John

Stamper. The line remained dressed until the 26th reached a ravine covered in reeds and underbrush. The formation began to break up as the men scrambled to cross the stream. Stamper was shot at that point. Private George Washington Kelly next took the flag but was hit in the ankle within a minute by another low-flying round. His successor, Private Larkin Thomas, was hit before he could take more than a few steps. The flag then fell to Private John Vinson, who fared still worse than Thomas, he being shot but a second or two later. Two more, Privates John Marley and William Ingram, grabbed it but both were killed within a few minutes. Thankfully, Captain W. W. McCreery took the banner and waved it aloft to encourage the men, some of whose spirits may have been sagging by this point. For his pains, he was shot through the heart and fell on top of the flag. Next, Lieutenant George Wilcox pulled it out from under McCreery, but within two steps he was shot twice in the chest. Now Colonel Henry Burgwyn himself seized the flag, bawling "Dress on the colors" and handing them to Private Frank Honeycutt just before he was shot through both lungs. Honeycutt, as he reached over, was shot through the head. Lieutenant Colonel John Lane cried, "It is my time to take them now! Twenty-sixth, follow me." But he was shot in the neck, jaw, and mouth about thirty paces from the enemy line. Lane nevertheless managed to entrust the colors to Captain W. S. Brewer, who carried them to victory. By the end of the battle, four more men (including Brewer) would become casualties. Unfortunately, when the last, wounded bearer, Private Daniel Thomas, finally reached the enemy's works, he was obliged to surrender because hardly anyone from his regiment was left to help him fight. (The 26th suffered 89 percent casualties, or 743 men out of 839.)[3]

The sometimes suicidal requirements of the color-bearer's task may prompt us to ask why anyone would volunteer for the job. For the sake of regimental honor is the traditional reason given, but while this factor may have influenced some men's decisions to abide by the flag come what may, it is too general, romantic, and convenient a motivation to explain the phenomenon fully.

There were several other competing reasons why soldiers undertook color service. First and foremost, surprisingly, much of the time nothing happened to you. As the new color-bearer of the 28th Massachusetts, Sergeant Peter Welsh, assured his worried wife before Gettysburg, "this regiment has been in seven battles and has had but one color bearer killed [and] two men wounded."[4] It certainly helped that the other soldiers "swarmed around [the color-bearer] as bees cover their queen" during an advance, wrote another veteran, further reducing the likelihood of getting hit.[5]

But the chances of survival improved still more because color units often included the more experienced soldiers, were supervised by senior commanders, and were the least likely to be lethally enfiladed thanks to their central position in the line. There were also sound personal motives for accepting an ostensibly higher level of risk. As color-bearer, crowed Sergeant Welsh, he was excused general picket and guard duty, did not have to carry a musket or ammunition when marching, nor would he be ordered to skirmish, for the colors always remained safely behind the forward screen. Bravely bearing the colors, too, brought a man to the attention of his major and colonel, and it was upon their good offices that a sergeant could be commissioned. The best part of becoming a lieutenant, Welsh brightly reminded his wife, was that one could then resign and return home. (Though he survived Gettysburg, Welsh would be mortally wounded carrying the colors in May 1864 at Spotsylvania.)[6] Then, too, for men with a checkered service record, volunteering offered the possibility of redemption: Private Vinson of the 26th North Carolina, who, as noted, was shot after (briefly) seizing the colors, had been tried for desertion a month before the battle, and on June 30 was given the choice of color duty or execution.[7]

No matter where men were in the line, however, for every yard they gained, comrades on either side, in front and behind, were shot in increasing numbers. Oddly, the sounds rather than the sights stuck more in their memories. The 74th Pennsylvania's Louis Fischer long remembered the "dull thud" of bullets striking his nearby friend, Lieutenant Roth.[8] Roth had evidently been hit in a soft spot: Soldiers like Thomas Evans, 12th U.S. Infantry, soon learned to distinguish between "the grating sound a ball makes when it hits a bone" and "the heavy thud when it strikes flesh."[9] John DeForest knew that the man next to him was as good as dead when he heard "a sharp crack of broken bone, followed by a loud 'Oh' of pain and horror." Looking around for confirmation, he saw the victim "fall slowly backward, with blood spurting from his mouth and a stare of woeful amazement in his eyes. A bullet had shattered his front teeth and come out behind his left jaw."[10]

Almost every old soldier could later tell a story of his or a friend's astounding escape from the jaws of death thanks to a lucky object that stopped an otherwise fatal bullet. Salmon Beardsley, 154th New York, recalled "a ball [that] went through my canteen and bruised my hip a little . . . but [I] soon found that I was only scared by the water running down from my *wounded* canteen instead of blood from my body."[11] John Roberts of the 17th Maine, said Private John Haley, was "wounded in the Testament which had stopped the bullet on the way to his heart," though for others "packs of cards had played the same part several times."[12]

The vast majority of bullet wounds, however, *were* serious. The sensation of being shot varied with the distance between muzzle and flesh as well as the location and nature of the wound, but generally there was little prolonged agony. Soldiers described a brief pang of pain when first hit—Alfred Lee, 82nd Ohio, "felt the sting of a bullet"—and spoke of a dull feeling of "shock, without discomfort" (A. B. Isham, 7th Michigan Cavalry) or of being struck by "something blunt" (Vincent Osborne, 2nd Kansas), similar to a "blow as from a stone" (Confederate Major Henry Kyd Douglas).

Shortly afterward came "slight dizziness" (Osborne) and "a peculiar tingling as though a slight electrical current was playing about the site of injury" (Isham) or extending down the affected limb, on the heels of which numbness and paralysis quickly set in. One's breathing would then turn "hard and labored, with a croup-like sound" (Ebenezer Hannaford), and the victim would feel as if the wind "had been thumped out" of him (Douglas).

By this stage, the soldier would be experiencing a "metamorphosis from strength and vigor to utter helplessness" (Lee) and a spreading "powerlessness" that forced him to drop his gun (Hannaford), presaging "a sinking sensation to the earth; and, falling, all things growing dark" (Private Ward, 4th Alabama).[13] Observers would see the wounded man, said Alonzo Hill of 8th Pennsylvania, "convulsively clasp his hand to his breast—perhaps brow—a moment stand, then stagger, reel, and fall to the earth gasping for breath—the hot blood gushing from his wound."[14]

Breathless and fading from shock, when soldiers tried to cry out for help, often nothing but pathetic groans or hoarse pleas would emerge. As Samuel Wing of the 3rd Maine explained, "The first effect of a [serious] wound is numbness, and the wounded seldom speak above a whisper."[15] If the soldier was dying, even a whisper was beyond his abilities. When a comrade was shot in the head, all that Robert Carter of the 22nd Massachusetts could hear was him "gasping in that peculiar, almost indescribable way that a mortally wounded man has. I shall never forget the pleading expression, speechless, yet imploring."[16] In either case, we can dispense with the usual sentimental tales of soldiers' clearly enunciated last words and worthy declarations of how fortunate they were to die doing their duty. Most just blubbered incomprehensibly for their mothers or tormentedly contemplated their final moments.

A few men who were surprised to survive their wounds left behind vivid accounts of what it felt like to die. Temporarily blinded and paralyzed, Sam Emerson of the 3rd Arkansas had been left lying at Devil's Den, where "occasionally the rattle of musketry and the roar of cannon came rushing over my lacerated brain like traces of fire. In vain did I attempt to calm my feelings. . . . I doubted the reality of all around me, and strove to shake it off as a horrible dream. . . . I was mad with terror and anguish. . . . By and by the storm of battle passed away. The distant mutterings of the cannons soon ceased to fall upon my ear. Then again all was dark. . . . I felt as if eternity had begun its reign. . . . Oblivion had stretched her pall over me."[17]

12. The Critical Moment

During every assault there arrived a moment—generally around the fifty-yard crisis point—when soldiers either fought or fled. An attacking force that had sustained overwhelming casualties, experienced a drastic loss of momentum, or received an unexpected enfilade was by far the most liable to retreat. In these circumstances, a false alarm, the death of a beloved commander, or a misheard order could produce immediate panic. The slightest equivocation could result in collapse. On the other hand, advised Colonel Scribner, "victory is often achieved by the troops that hold out even for a moment after both sides have become impressed with the idea that they all will be killed and must fly to safety."[1] At this stage, as Charles Benton (150th New York) observed, the relationship between attackers and defenders was liable to turn into "a resolute test of endurance; a grim determination to fight to a finish; a primordial test of blood and nerve; a trying of which [side] could longest bear being killed. It was a death grapple."[2]

There was no universally applicable determination of when or if an attack would fail. The timing and outcome of the matter hinged on several varying factors, such as the rate and severity of the attackers' losses, the experience of the unit involved, the quality of leadership, and the distance to their objective. Thus, when the 6th Wisconsin rushed the Confederates in the railway cut on July 1, it started with 420 men but ended with 240. Normally, such rapid casualty accumulation might induce retreat, but the 6th was a first-class regiment under sound and able command that knew it had to cross the deadly zone or be annihilated.[3]

At this tipping point, the bravest, or most reckless, men of the unit played an important role. Even as their comrades were contemplating withdrawal, some soldiers would propel themselves forward to the "dead-line"—an imaginary frontier beyond which no man could survive unless his fellows followed en masse. If they hesitated, he was doomed. At Pickett's Mill in May 1864, for instance, Ambrose Bierce noticed a "well-defined edge of corpses" at the dead-line, with not a single man managing to get closer to the Confederate position. Behind them, "man by man, the survivors withdrew at will."[4]

Once a retreat was in the offing, it tended to take one of three forms. First, as Bierce noted, individuals would peel off and scurry away "man by man" until hardly anyone was left. A few would fire their weapons before taking cover or going mysteriously "missing" in some nearby woods. Soldiers who had stayed on the field then became targets for the defenders, who now had time to reload at leisure.

Alternatively, there might be a steady and dignified withdrawal as the attack petered out. As an Indianan colonel pointed out, veteran soldiers would yield ground but "keep together as if attracted to each other by a sort of moral gravitation." He likened the sight of old troops "unconsciously reform[ing] their ranks" as they retreated to that of cavalry horses, which instinctively closed up in formation when their riders were absent.[5] Even under pressure, said Berry Benson of South Carolina, veterans "dressed upon the colors in some rough fashion."[6] Order and bulk were to be found wheresoever the flag was—command and mass being the most critical factors in making it out alive. No matter the devastation, a regiment needed to stay together to dissuade a counter-charge and pursuit by the defenders, an act that invariably ended in an easy slaughter. An excellent example of grace under fire was the withdrawal of the 2nd Division of III Corps on July 2. Watching the drama, Alfred Carpenter wrote that "back over the plain they came, slowly, not faster than a walk, loading as they came and every now and then turning and pouring a deadly volley into the pursuing foe. The Rebs came in two splendid lines, firing as they advanced," but were hesitant to risk coming in closer for the kill.[7]

More often, however, a check during an assault rapidly descended into collective headlong flight. In these cases, the fastest runners, said Corporal George Mason of the 154th New York, would be the lucky ones who got away.[8] To lighten the load, those fleeing "threw away everything—cartridge boxes, waistbelts, and haversacks—in their stampede," wrote the 8th Ohio's Thomas Galwey of a Virginia brigade's retreat after Pickett's Charge. "The ground was covered with flying Confederates. They all seemed to extend their arms in their flight, as if to assist their speed."[9]

The slow were soon left behind. When the 143rd Pennsylvania hurriedly departed the Seminary, said Avery Harris of Company B, there was no "semblance of military order with every man for himself and the Rebs take the hindmost."[10] George Bowen of the 12th New Jersey cheerfully admitted to competing against the rest of his company to return to safety. "Seeing the men all running for the rear I took after them, soon catching up with Lieut. Col. Harris of the 1st Del. who was getting to the rear as fast as he could, he swung his sword around, called me a hard name, telling me to go back, this I did not do but made a detour around him and got across that three-quarters of a mile in record time to the rear."[11]

The wounded and the lame were also abandoned. The 8th Florida's William Penn Pigman was retreating from the Wheatfield and Peach Orchard on July 2 and confessed that "there is no time to stop for friends who are hurt during the heat of an engagement." Others were more circumspect but equally clear-eyed. William Warren, 17th Connecticut, heard a dear friend cry, "O Dear, Help me, Help me" when he was shot, but "it was not time for me to stop," he confided to his journal, "so I kept on."[12] Those forsaken may have given "beseeching looks"—as Captain James Stewart remembered—but received only, in the words of the 143rd Pennsylvania's John Musser, "a parting glance of sympathy" from those who remained mobile.[13] Decades later, J. V. Pierce could still hear the mortally wounded Edwin Aylesworth's piteous appeal, "Don't leave me, boys," though they had.[14]

All knew their fates. Following a fight in the Wheatfield, W. H. Sanderson (2nd U.S. Infantry) recalled many years later, "out of that squad of 17 we left seven of our comrades in the wheat. All were wounded, and I think one or two killed. We never saw any of them again, and so concluded they all died of their wounds in some Southern prison-pen, as they fell into the hands of the rebels."[15] He was probably right: The fatality rate among POWs on both sides was astonishingly high. To take a typical instance, the 154th New York went to Gettysburg with 265 officers and men, of whom 173 were taken prisoner. More than a third (63) would die in captivity. At least another eight would die soon after coming home, and many more would suffer terribly in later years as the scarring left behind by dietary deficiencies, disease, and stress exacted its price in the form of poor mental and physical health.[16]

13. Holding the Line

Assuming that the attacking infantry absorbed the blow at the fifty-yard mark and plowed on, the defending side would soon face the choice of whether to stay or run. Unless they were greatly outnumbered or out of ammunition, it was generally better for defenders to try to hold their position, for while the attackers were in the midst of a furious, unthinking rage that spurred them to suicidal extremes, the defenders now found their most intense focus. During the fighting at Culp's Hill, "I was struck by the cool and matter-of-fact way in which our men were loading and firing," said Charles Benton of the 150th New York. "And yet it was but yesterday the same men had paled at the sight of a wounded man."[1] In a fierce firefight near the Lutheran Seminary, Nathan Cooper of the 151st Pennsylvania, meanwhile, was amazed to find himself "just as cool and composed as I ever was butchering hogs."[2]

If they could muster themselves into a volley line, the defenders might even unleash one final broadside that would put paid to the attack once and for all. During their advance on the seminary, the men of Company K, 14th South Carolina, came so close that they heard the enemy's lieutenants "distinctly encouraging their men to hold their fire, until the command to fire was given. They obeyed their command implicitly, and rose to their feet and took deliberate aim as if they were on dress parade, and to show you how accurate their aim was, 34 out of our 39 men fell."[3]

The defenders also had one lethal trick left up their sleeve: Artillery would blast canister to scythe down the attacking infantry. Canister essentially converted a cannon into a giant shotgun peppering dozens of iron balls at high speed into the approaching ranks at essentially point-blank range (less than fifty yards). Not only could a cannon fire roughly three times a minute and be aimed low to exploit ricochets, but crews would also double- or even triple-shot their piece for short periods to increase lethality.[4] During Pickett's Charge, for instance, Sergeant Fuger of Cushing's Battery opened up with overcharged canister, punching two fifty-foot-wide holes in the Confederate line.[5] If the enemy came still nearer, artillerists urgently set about "cutting the fuses . . . so that they would explode near the muzzles of [their] guns."[6]

Against a few rounds of well-directed canister, human beings were distressingly vulnerable.[7] A single gun blast against Lieutenant William Johnson's company in the 2nd South Carolina killed Captain George McDowell and Privates R. Elmore Chaney and William Lomax, mangled Private John Fooshe's leg (he died a few weeks later), ripped off Private James Casson's skull above the eye, and shoved Private George McKenzie's rifle across his chest with such force that he was almost killed. The rest of the 2nd South Carolina fared just as poorly. According to Lieutenant Colonel Gaillard, "I saw half a dozen at a time knocked up and flung to the ground like trifles. There were familiar forms and faces with parts of their heads shot away, legs shattered, arms tore off." Between a third and a half of the regiment would be recorded as dead or wounded. All Private John Coxe could or wished to recall of the experience was "the awful deathly surging sounds of those little black balls as they flew by."[8]

Those "little black balls" inflicted graver wounds than any bullet. Lewis Crandell of 125th New York told his parents that "my pants were stiff with dark clotted blood, one man by me [was] shot with grape [canister] in the head the hot blood flew in my face nearly blinding me."[9] After he was hit, South Carolinian J. R. Boyle of the 12th watched his shoe (with ankle and calf attached) soar away.[10] A day after the battle, Robert Carter found a man with "as many as twenty canister or case shots through different parts of his body, though none through a vital organ, and he was still gasping and twitching with a slight motion of the muscles and vibrations of the pulse, although utterly unconscious of approaching death."[11]

For those not yet hit, the single avenue of escape from death or disfigurement lay in reaching the defensive line and storming the artillery. If they had made it this far, attacking soldiers had overcome any desire to retreat and were in a state of combat narcosis—a combination of stoicism and fury that propelled them inexorably forward. According to a rattled Northern gunner during Pickett's Charge, the Confederates swarming toward him were aware of the muzzles of the guns pointing directly at them but did not care: "The poor wretches knew what it meant—it meant death within the next three seconds to many of them, and they knew it. I remember distinctly that they pulled their caps down over their eyes and bowed their heads as men do in walking against a hail storm. They knew what was coming."[12] But they also knew that there was no stopping them now that their blood was up. "We were mad and fully determined to take and silence those batteries at once," wrote Coxe.[13]

14. At Close Quarters

Once the attackers reached the thirty-yard crisis point *and* showed no sign of slowing down, then the tactical advantage shifted to the aggressors. By this time, defensive fire was beginning to slacken and sputter out: Adrenaline surges could only spur on attackers and hurt defenders because they complicated coordination, degraded dexterity, and reduced fine motor control—precisely the skills needed to load and fire a weapon with any accuracy.

"It is not an uncommon thing for a soldier amidst the excitement of battle, to load his gun, shut his eyes and fire in the air straight over his head," complained Adjutant John Schoonover of the 11th New Jersey.[1] Much of the time, actually, these panicking defenders were not, despite repeatedly pulling the trigger, even firing at all. After the battle Union officials collected twenty-four thousand loaded guns that had been left abandoned on the field. Now, some of these had been discarded in favor of better rifles—every man of the 15th New Jersey was ordered to leave behind his Enfield and pick up an "excellent Springfield musket"—but at least half of them were charged with two loads, and another quarter with between three and ten. One specimen was packed with no fewer than twenty-three charges. In most cases, soldiers under pressure had either crammed down the cartridge without first breaking it or had inserted it the wrong way up (so that ball preceded powder).[2] A German military expert named Hohenlohe confirmed in 1866 that during his tours of various European battlefields he too had "found muzzle-loading rifles loaded with ten successive cartridges, of which the first was put in hind before (a proof that the soldier had not noticed that the first shot had missed fire, and had therefore kept putting in fresh cartridges one over the other)."[3]

Anyone, no matter how green or veteran, could overcharge his firearm as the attackers rapidly narrowed the gap. Scared and new to battle, Josiah Wolf of the 143rd Pennsylvania thought he had rammed home two cartridges by mistake and was loath to fire his gun during a firefight with the 2nd North Carolina. Corporal Simon Hubler took it upon himself to do it for him and painfully discovered that "the recoil was terrific. . . . I am of the opinion that he had five or six charges in instead of two."[4] Leander Stillwell, conversely, was a highly experienced and competent soldier, accustomed to guns since his boyhood days of squirrel-hunting, and yet the pervasive "confusion and uproar" around him caused even him to unwittingly double-load and fire, suffering for his error "a deafening explosion, and a kick that sent me a-sprawling on my back!"[5]

While this was all happening, the attack wave would be breaking into a run and readying a vengeful blast to stagger the defenders and give them time to storm the entrenchments before the defenders recovered. The 1st Minnesota did just that when, after a purposeful march forward in perfect alignment, they loosed a volley at thirty yards before their colonel shouted "Charge" and the regiment surged forward with leveled bayonets.[6]

The defenders now had roughly twenty seconds, if that, to react before the wave hit. Sometimes they evacuated. An orderly withdrawal would force the attackers to pay a heavy price for the ground gained, as when the 1st Texas assaulted the 124th New York at Houck's Ridge. "The enemy stood their ground bravely, until we were close on them, but did not await the bayonet," recalled Private James Bradfield. "They broke away from the rock fence as we closed in with a rush and a wild rebel yell, and fell back to the top of the ridge, where they halted and formed on their second line. Having passed the rock fence, and as we were moving on up the hill, an order came to halt." No doubt some diligent officers of the 1st Texas wanted to re-form their lines for a final push, but "it cost us dearly, for as we lay in close range of their now double lines, the enemy poured a hail of bullets on us, and in a few minutes a number of our men were killed and wounded."[7] A panicked retreat, on the other hand, led inevitably to disaster. As Sam Watkins fondly remembered, when the enemy ahead of him wavered and fled "we were jubilant; we were triumphant. Officers could not curb the men to keep in line. Discharge after discharge was poured into the retreating line. The Federal dead and wounded covered the ground."[8]

When the defenders stayed put, however, the fighting instantly reached its ferocious climax. "If men ever became devils," wrote William Harmon, it was when they finally collided. "We were crazy with the excitement of the fight. We just rushed in like beasts. Men swore and cussed and struggled and fought, grappled in hand-to-hand fight, threw stones, clubbed their muskets, kicked, yelled, and hurrahed."[9] Similarly, when the 19th Maine was thrown into the melee, according to John Smith, "for ten or fifteen minutes the contending forces, in some places within rifle length of each other and in other places hopelessly mingled, fought with desperation. Those in front used the butt ends of their rifles, and those in the rear of the crowd of Union soldiers fired over the heads of those in front, and some of them hurled stones at the heads of the Confederates."[10] But Edward Hill put it most vividly when he characterized the 16th Michigan's struggle at Little Round Top as follows: "guns clubbed, stones hurled with barbaric strength, death welcomed in a teeth-a-set and hand to throat embrace, mercy vainly asked."[11]

Seizing the enemy colors was the primary objective; once they had fallen, it was the end. Men were promised the most wonderful reward—a trip home—if they managed to take them. Spurred on by that prospect, a Confederate of the Phillips Legion, having shot one man and bludgeoned five others, "was in the act of reaching for the flag when a fellow named Smith jumped in ahead of me and grabbed it. I came very near clubbing him, but he put up such a pitiful mouth about having a family of small children that he wanted to see so bad, I let him have it so he could get a furlough."[12]

Owing to the value of the big guns, both as trophies and as assets, storming them was of almost equal importance, but artillerymen were notorious for being tough hand-to-hand fighters. They were well equipped with tools that could be turned smartly into dangerous weapons. Sergeant Frederick Fuger of Cushing's Battery, for instance, told his men to fight off the oncoming Confederates with their trail hand-spikes. These were heavy metal or wooden poles about four and a half feet long originally intended to lever the cannon left and right, but they made, explained Fuger, "the finest weapons for close contact."[13] They did, indeed. One Sergeant Darveau of Pettit's Battery, confronted by a Confederate officer, "seized a trail hand-spike, and struck him full across the forehead, killing him on the spot."[14] Another favored option was the rammer, a lengthy wooden staff that pushed powder and ammunition down the barrel. When their battery was overrun by the 21st Mississippi, for instance, Corporal Adams watched the 9th Massachusetts's Private John Ligal "[save] himself by braining a Confederate with his rammer head."[15]

If they managed to hold off the attackers, the artillerymen would hasten to disable their guns.[16] They could break the wheels, shove several cannonballs down the muzzle, dent the barrel by smashing it with sledgehammers, or spike it—anything to prevent the victors from turning the guns around and firing them at retreating troops.[17] Alternatively, they could try to limber up their guns to horses to haul them to a safer place. To stop their escaping, attackers slew the animals, as happened when the 2nd Mississippi overran Captain James Hall's 2nd Maine battery. First, they shot the horses and only then, said W. B. Murphy, did they stop to pour "such a deadly fire into [the hapless gunners] that they left their [last] piece and ran for life."[18]

The most popular method of claiming a gun was to jump on it. Colonel Humphrey of the 21st Mississippi remembered how "Lt. George Kempton [straddled] a gun [of the 9th Massachusetts] waving his sword and exclaiming, 'Colonel, I claim this gun for Company I.'

Lieutenant W. P. McNeily was astraddle of another, claiming it for Company E."[19] One had to perform this ritual in a sober and sensible way to avoid misfortune. Mounting a gun, for instance, promptly turned a man into the foremost target of everyone around him. When the Louisiana Brigade broke through the Union lines at East Cemetery Hill, Major Harry Gilmor "saw one of our color-bearers jump on a gun and display his flag. He was instantly killed. But the flag was seized by an Irishman, who, with a wild shout, sprang upon the gun, and he too was shot down. Then a little bit of a fellow, a captain, seized the staff and mounted the same gun; but, as he raised the flag, a ball broke the arm which held it. He dropped his sword, and caught the staff with his right before it fell, waved it over his head with a cheer, indifferent to the pain of his shattered limb and the whizzing balls around him. His third cheer was just heard, when he tottered and fell, pierced through the lungs." (The captain survived.)[20]

15. Surrender

Once the guns were taken and the colors lowered, surrender was nigh. There were few instances in the Civil War of massacres after an action, so long as the act of capitulation was performed properly. By and large, officers would not throw away the lives of their men on useless last stands but instead surrender on their behalf once it was evident that the opposing side had the advantage, either in position, numbers, or initiative. In return for throwing in the towel early and behaving in a knightly manner, an officer was accorded due dignity, not least of which included the right to surrender his sword to another. During the struggle at the railway cut, for instance, Colonel Rufus Dawes sensibly adhered to protocol by addressing only Major J. R. Blair, 2nd Mississippi, who "replied not a word, but promptly handed me his sword, and his men . . . threw down their muskets."[1]

If no officers were present, men began "wav[ing] hats, handkerchiefs, newspaper or whatever they had to surrender," according to a Union soldier accepting the submissions of Confederates when Pickett's Charge collapsed.[2] V. A. Tapscott, 56th Virginia, saw those around him surrendering "some with hands up, some with feet up, some with black clothes, some one color and some another, most of them shedding hats and caps."[3]

Soldiers could be shot out of hand, however, if they abused their privileges. The 30th Pennsylvania, after an uphill charge, received the surrenders of twenty Confederates, among whom was, said Benjamin Urban, "one big fellow [who thought] he could kill one Yankee yet, raised his gun again and fired it in the faces of the men not ten feet in front of him, and then threw it down. A fatal mistake for him, for one of the Bucktails, who had just barely dodged the bullet, with a 'No you don't; you _____,' shot him through the body."[4]

In movies, soldiers are frequently shown cheering after a hardfought victory. There was little of that in reality. Instead, recalled Major John D. Musser, 143rd Pennsylvania, "officers and men shook hands in silence, great tear drops standing in their undaunted eyes."[5] Inside, as the wrath and rage of the assault burned out as rapidly as once they had flared, soldiers, according to Abner Small of the 16th Maine, "felt a strange exaltation" because they were "horribly glad to be alive and unhurt."[6]

In any case, the survivors were in no fit state for celebration. The immediate physical toll exacted by combat is often overlooked, but it would help explain the oddly pacific aftermath to the bloody, broken *mise en scène* surrounding them. Soldiers had, wrote Colonel Włodzimierz Krzyżanowski, "bloodshot eyes" and "were sweaty, blackened by the gunpowder, and they looked more like animals than human beings [with an] animal-like eagerness for blood."[7] The 9th Alabama's Edmund Patterson "was almost too weak to stand, and my cheeks as hollow as though emaciated by a long spell of sickness."[8] "Think you of a gang of coal-heavers who have just finished putting in a winter's supply ordered by some provident householder in midsummer, and you get a fair impression of troops at the end of a day's fighting," attested Allen Redwood, 55th Virginia, while a veteran told *Scientific American* that "at the end of a battle I always found that I had perspired so profusely as to wet through all my clothes. I was as sore as if I had been beaten all over with a club."[9] Frank Haskell claimed that he too was "drenched with sweat," but his skin had turned a "burning red" color, and he resembled nothing less than a "boiled man."[10]

16. The Return to Normal

The sun and lack of water at Gettysburg would have compounded the soldiers' exhaustion significantly; it was a wise officer who sought billets for his men in the hours following a clash. Every soldier longed for sleep, though some, like Thomas Evans of the 12th U.S. Infantry, could not get even that. "After the heat and excitement of the day were over I lay down and tried to sleep," he said. "But the din of the engagement was still in my ears, and kept up a perpetual buzzing that I could not drive away. I had a bad headache, my throat was parched, my eyes were aching. I could not sleep."[1]

As they eventually drifted off one by one, false alarms remained a menace. At around 1 A.M., reported Colonel Dawes of the 6th Wisconsin, "a man in the Seventh Indiana Regiment, next on our right, cried so loudly in his sleep that he aroused all the troops in the vicinity. Springing up, half bewildered, I ordered my regiment to 'fall in,' and a heavy fire of musketry broke out from along the whole line of fire."[2]

But when soldiers did drift away, it was wonderful. The Confederate artilleryman E. P. Alexander ruminated that "in ten seconds I was . . . sounder asleep than I had ever been before, or ever before even realized it was possible to be. For there is a sort of higher power of sleep, with qualities as entirely different from the ordinary as light is from heat. . . . I have never been able to obtain it except in connection with the excitement attendant on a battle & not more than three or four times even then." It felt as if he had let himself "sink under a dense fluid which penetrated alike eyes & ears & pores until it pervaded the very bones bringing with it, instantly, everywhere a trance of delicious rest & freedom even from dreams."[3]

By the following day and night, soldiers were returning to their normal selves. "Sad as were the memories of the previous evening, as much as we missed the comrades who fell in that desperate charge," recalled one New Yorker, "yet soldiers and officers sat and chatted and joked, even as if nothing had happened."[4] David Hunter Strother witnessed, sitting amidst the carrion of 300 slain Confederates at Antietam, Union troops "cooking, eating, jabbering, and smoking," even sleeping among the corpses, with nary a second thought.[5]

Strother's account affirms that following the massive adrenaline surge-and-dump of combat and a good night's sleep, the extraordinary became the ordinary. Thus, when Benjamin Urban saw men "playing a quiet game of cards on the bloody stretchers they had been carrying" he was briefly irritated but "soon began to think differently, for I saw that behind the simple act there was absolutely no sense of its incongruity."[6] A Union soldier accordingly thought it entirely unexceptional to eat his dinner

within six paces of a rebel in four pieces. Both legs were blown off. His pelvis was the third piece, and his head and chest were the fourth piece. Those four pieces occupied a space of twelve feet square. I saw five dead rebels in a row, with their heads knocked off by a round shot. Myself and other amateur anatomists, when the regiment was resting temporarily on arms, would leave to examine the internal structure of man. We would examine brains, heart, stomach, layers of muscles, structure of bones, &c., for there was every form of mutilation. At home I used to wince at the sight of a wound or of a corpse; but here, in one day, I learned to be among the scenes I am describing without emotion.[7]

A protective sense of imperturbability seemingly radiated from participants, as if nothing remarkable had recently occurred. Rufus Dawes told his wife that just a few days after he had lost half his regiment, the entire "terrible ordeal" seemed "more like a fearful, horrible dream than reality."[8] When George Bowen of the 12th New Jersey settled down for a well-earned dinner, a stray cannonball flew over and, glancing off a nearby tree, narrowly missed him but smashed into the chest of the man sitting alongside. Bowen was coated with his neighbor's blood, flesh, and shattered bones, but he barely noticed; he just slowly shook the residue from his hand, wiped the stuff from his face, and scraped off his rations before tucking in.[9]

Veterans like Cyrus Boyd, however, were less convinced that Bowen and those like him could keep their minds and emotions switched off after combat so easily. He had seen "pieces of clothing and strings of flesh hang on the limbs of trees," and he believed that something untoward did change within men who experienced intense combat. "War is *hell* broke *loose* and benumbs all the tender feelings of men and makes of them *brutes*," he confided in his diary. The pity of war was not that killing happened but that indifference to killing became normal. Still, combat retained its attractions, even for Boyd, partly explaining why soldiers kept soldiering: "I do not want to see any more such scenes and yet I would not have missed this for any consideration."[10]

17. Sights, Sounds, Smells

What first struck soldiers as they emerged from their post-combat fog was the mess war leaves behind. Robert Carter, 22nd Massachusetts, described the "debris of battle" as comprising "haversacks, canteens, hats, caps, sombreros, blankets of every shade and hue, bayonets, cartridge boxes—every conceivable part of the equipment of a soldier."[1] A nurse witnessed a landscape of "artillery wagons crushed, broken muskets scattered in every direction, unused cartridges in immense numbers, balls of all kinds, ramrods and bayonets, bits of clothing, belts, gloves, knapsacks, letters in great quantities, all lying promiscuously on the field."[2]

Then the bodies—dead and still alive—swam into focus. They were everywhere.[3] At Gettysburg, both armies lost around twenty-three thousand men (including killed, wounded, missing, and captured), with Lee expending a third of his force and Meade a comparatively impressive quarter. The ten worst-hit Confederate regiments lost an average of three-quarters of their troops, which alone accounted for 2,651 of Lee's casualties.[4] On the Union side, the once-two-hundred strong 141st Pennsylvania suffered so many losses that for three months afterward the regiment could muster no more than forty men at any one time.[5] Private William Smith of the 116th Pennsylvania told his family a week after Gettysburg that there were just nine men left in his company, 108 in the entire regiment.[6] The 116th, which was weak to begin with, was not even one of the hardest-hit regiments, losing merely a third of its strength.[7] In comparison, some fifty-four Union and thirty-four Confederate regiments—between them, an average of one in five infantry regiments engaged—suffered losses of greater than 50 percent.[8]

These dry statistics euphemistically disguise what "casualties" and "losses" actually looked like. Robert Carter saw how Kershaw's and Wofford's brigades had marched right up to the muzzles of the Union artillery at the Rose Farm. The guns, double-shotted with one-second fuses, had left behind "arms, legs, heads, and parts of dismembered bodies . . . scattered all about, and sticking among the rocks, and against the trunks of trees, hair, brains, entrails, and shreds of human flesh still hung, a disgusting, sickening, heartrending spectacle."[9] Try as he might, John Haley from Maine could not adequately depict the carnage or make it seem real to outsiders; all he could see before him was a wasteland of "men's heads blown off or split open; horrible gashes cut; some split from the top of the head to the extremities, as butchers split beef."[10] Walking around Culp's Hill, Nurse Sophronia Bucklin saw "boots, with a foot and leg putrifying within, l[ying] beside the pathway, and ghastly heads, too—over the exposed skulls of which insects crawled—while great worms bored through the rotting eyeballs. Astride a tree sat a bloody horror, with head and limbs severed by shells, the birds having banqueted on it."[11] Another man saw a pair of "booted and stockinged feet, still standing in their place." Their owner had crawled away, leaving behind a sloppy red stain, as from a snail.[12]

Robert Stiles happened across "several human or unhuman corpses s[itting] upright against a fence, with arms extended in the air and faces hideous with something very much like a fixed leer."[13] Private Robin Berkeley of the Confederate artillery "saw the body of a Yankee, which had been cut in two. The head, arms, and about one-half of his ribs had been thrown against a fence, and remained with his heart and entrails sticking to the top rail, while some 10 feet off the lower part of the body had been thrown into a mud hole in the road."[14] Over at Culp's Hill, Philo Buckingham saw "some [soldiers] sitting up against trees or rocks stark dead with their eyes wide open staring at you as if they were still alive—others with their heads blown off with shell or round shot[,] others shot through the head with musket bullets. Some struck by a shell in the breast or abdomen and blown almost to pieces, others with their hands up as if to fend of[f] the bullets we fired upon them, others laying against a stump or stone with a testament in their hand or a likeness of a friend, as if wounded and had lived for some time."[15]

As Buckingham inferred, not everyone had enjoyed the good fortune of dying quickly. In the days following the battle, untold numbers of wounded were left in the field, a great many expiring before they could be found or rescued. One of the casualties, George Metcalf of the 136th New York, recalled that at first the air around him "was filled with groans, moans, shrieks, and yells. Prayers were offered and curses pronounced. Piteous appeals were made for water, for help, for death." But as time went on, this cacophony slowly grew "fainter and more indistinct until lost in one constant low, faraway moaning sound." Over the next night or so, even the moans evaporated, and you would only occasionally see "a dark form rise from the ground as some poor wretch by a superhuman effort would attempt to rise, and then it would disappear."[16]

For those left behind who survived, the experience was, to put it mildly, a memorable one. Decades later, Metcalf could still see the afflicted "when my eyes are shut, and hear the sounds I cannot describe whenever I let my mind dwell upon that night of all nights, as I lay among the dead and dying on the night of July 3rd on the battlefield of Gettysburg."[17] Elsewhere, a wounded Lieutenant Inman, 118th Pennsylvania, was abandoned behind enemy lines and left alone among the dead. "That night a number of stray hogs came to where I lay and commenced rooting and tearing at the dead men around me," he wrote. "Finally one fellow that in the darkness looked of enormous size approached and attempted to poke me—grunting loudly the while. Several others also came up, when, waiting my chance, I jammed my sword into his belly, which made him set up a prolonged, sharp cry. By constant vigilance and keeping from sleeping I contrived to fight the monsters off till daylight."[18] The New Hampshireman Charles Drake was not so fortunate: His right leg had been mangled by canister, and he could only watch helplessly as the hogs gnawed the flesh from its bones.[19]

Man was wolf to man, of course. Sergeant J. A. Bosworth of the 141st Pennsylvania was lying with a leg wound behind Confederate lines and had hid himself behind a stone wall. A group of Southerners came along in time, and "I asked one of them for a drink of water; he gave it to me, but while I was drinking he was loading his gun. He said he hated our men, then went off about eight rods [44 yards] and shot at me." Bosworth managed to plunge deeper into the bushes, and after several rounds the sadist got bored and left.[20]

Fortunately, soldiers essayed out each night to scout for their wounded friends. A group from the 6th New Jersey was picking its way through some woods when a man tripped and tumbled over. One of his hands landed on a cold, dead head, while "my feet rested on another body, and my lantern was out. I felt for a match. I had none. But presently some of the men came up; the lantern was relighted, and the glare revealed a sight which I pray God my eyes may never look upon again. The body upon which my hand had fallen was that of a corporal; both legs were blown completely off. That over which I had stumbled was the body of a private with one arm severed, not entirely off, at the shoulder." With the lantern illuminating a circle of twenty feet, the soldiers glanced around and slowly realized that surrounding them lay seventeen slaughtered bodies.[21]

As early as July 4, said Sergeant Thomas Meyer, "the dead were already in a terrific state of putrefaction. Faces black as charcoal and bloated out of all human semblance; eyes, cheeks, forehead, and nose all one general level of putrid swelling, twice the normal size . . . while the bodies were bloated to the full capacity of the uniforms that enclosed them."[22] George Benedict of the 12th Vermont specified that the dead's faces exhibited "a deep bluish *black*, giving to a corpse with black hair the appearance of a negro, and to one with light or red hair and whiskers a strange and revolting aspect."[23] Staring into their faces, one could see, said Edmund Brown of the 27th Indiana, "their lips as thick as one's hand, their eyes wide open with glossy, glaring eyeballs, unspeakably hideous and revolting."[24]

Robert Stiles, a Confederate artilleryman, observed corpses that had "burst asunder with the pressure of foul gases and vapors."[25] The horses were worse, wrote Alanson Haines, 15th New Jersey, because they "swelled to elephantine proportions."[26] A chaplain added the curious detail that as horses bloated, their "uppermost hind leg[s] lifted into the air."[27]

There were even worse ways to die than by shot and shell. A soldier of the 77th New York visited Sherfy's barn, used as a hospital before shellfire set it ablaze with the wounded trapped inside. "The crisped and blackened limbs, heads and other portions of bodies lying half consumed among the heaps of ruins and ashes" were among the "most ghastly pictures" he ever witnessed.[28] There were, as on any battlefield, the remains of those who died in strange and tantalizing circumstances. William Livermore and his comrades in the 20th Maine entered a house near the Peach Orchard on July 6 and found "some [dead] Rebels with there [*sic*] hands tied but did not know what it was for unless they tried to desert. One we found with a handkerchief tied over his mouth. He was wound[ed] mortally and they did it to keep him from hollaring."[29]

If the sights were awful, worse perhaps, and certainly more lingering, was the smell. "The stench on the battlefield was something indescribable, it would come up as if in waves and when at its worst the breath would stop in the throat; the lungs could not take it in, and a sense of suffocation would be experienced. We would cover our faces tightly with our hands and turn the back towards the breeze and retch and gasp for breath," was how Sergeant Meyer put it afterward.[30] Late into the night, "the fearful odors I had inhaled," wrote Stiles, the Confederate gunner, "remained with me and made me loathe myself as if an already rotting corpse."[31]

18. The Dead

For the still-living, being found by their friends did not necessarily entail rescue. Soldiers followed an ad hoc system of triage: Men suffering from serious abdominal, head, or chest wounds were left where they were in order to concentrate on bringing those with a chance of surviving to the hospital.[1] Shooting the mortally wounded to put them out of their misery does not seem to have occurred regularly, and there were too many people looking to bayonet them discreetly, but suicides did happen with some frequency. After the Confederate charge at Culp's Hill, the 147th Pennsylvania's A. M. Eby saw a Confederate soldier of the 1st Maryland Battalion with a stomach wound flopping about in agony. He and his fellows watched as the man diligently loaded his musket, placed the muzzle under his chin, and pulled the trigger with the ramrod.[2] When Private Arsenal Griffin, an artilleryman, was disemboweled by an exploding shell, he cried out for this comrades to finish him. When none did it, he drew his revolver, said "Goodbye, boys," and blew his brains out.[3]

For those unable or unwilling to kill themselves, soldiers instead waited respectfully for the inevitable before burying their remains. Thus, on Sunday, two days after the battle ended, George Bowen (12th New Jersey) watched a Confederate, "who had been wounded in a dozen places, still breathing, one shot had gone clean through his head, striking the temple on one side and coming out at the other temple, he laid there just breathing, he would gradually stretch out his hand, feel around till he got something between his fingers, whether grass or dirt it did not matter, then he would gradually raise his hand to his head and try to poke the stuff into the wound." Bowen and his friends assumed he would "die at any moment, so dug a grave for him," but were summoned away before he expired.[4]

It was normal practice to loot dead men. Sergeant Thomas Meyer of 148th Pennsylvania observed that "it was a rare occurrence to find one [a corpse] who not been robbed by the battlefield bandit or robber of the dead. Generally the pockets were cut open and rifled through the incision." The guilty "were well known by the large amounts of money they had, and the watches, pocketbooks, pocket knives, and other valuable trinkets they had for sale after the battle. All regiments had them."[5] A Vermont man noticed how many of the dead had their jackets and shirts torn or thrown open in the front, exposing their chests and stomachs, presumably by "human jackal[s] searching for money."[6]

The wounded were by no means inviolate, and it was always sensible to cooperate when your turn came for frisking for fear of being silenced. Private Robert Wadding of the 148th Pennsylvania, shot in the groin on July 1 and disabled for life, was lying stricken in a field but remained quiescent when a pair of looters searched his knapsack and belongings. They otherwise left him alone before moving on to their next victim.[7]

Union troops profited greatly from their victory. Left in possession of the field, they had ample opportunity to loot both Confederate *and* Union corpses. The pickings could be good. William Livermore of the 20th Maine found one Confederate carrying forty-three sheets of expensive writing paper (originally taken from a Union soldier) as well as "30 or 40 envelopes in the same, nice stockings & shirts that never was put on."[8] Others struck pay dirt when they came across Southerners who had not yet spent the cash from their last payday at the end of June, just a few days earlier. One such scavenger found $30.60 (nearly three months' wages) on a single corpse, which made for a most welcome surprise.[9] Dead officers of either side were highly sought after because they had more money and nicer things. The body of the late Captain Lucius Larrabee (44th New York) was recovered with $90 missing from his pockets, while Lieutenant Willis Babcock (64th New York) was stripped of his sword, watch, memorandum book, and purse.[10] Lieutenant Colonel Morgan recalled that by the morning of July 4, "our men" had plundered every dead Confederate who had participated in Pickett's Charge. "I saw a Federal trying unsuccessfully to pull a ring from the finger of one of the bodies. As I rode away I heard the Federal's companion say, 'Oh Damn it, cut the finger off.'"[11]

So comprehensively would the dead be liberated from their earthly possessions that when civilians sneaked onto the battlefield a few days later to see what they could steal, there was annoyingly little left but worthless love letters and such unsellable trash as locks of some child's hair.

After the civilians came, a small team of doctors arrived from Washington, D.C. Their mission was a sensitive one, one they preferred to keep secret. They were content to let witnesses assume that they were there to help set up the hospitals to take care of the long-term wounded.

In fact, they had been sent by Dr. John Brinton, chief of the army's new Medical Museum, to collect specimens. Resident Jenny Jacobs recollected seeing several "medical students . . . preparing skeletons, and in a cauldron [they were] boiling the remains of heroes." She could learn nothing more of this mysterious activity, but it is evident that the doctors were reducing the fleshy bits of corpses to bones for more efficient storage in the kegs they had brought with them. Private Phillip Pindell, 1st Maryland Battalion, (involuntarily) aided the interests of science by having his face and hair boiled away. Nevertheless, the haul—just thirty-eight—from Gettysburg would be surprisingly small considering the bounteous supply of possible specimens lying around, but that was mostly owed to the rapid work of the burial details.[12]

If the dead were lucky, their comrades took good care of their remains. Sergeant William Howe of the 134th New York wrote home that "all our men killed were buried where they fell, and in a nice place, too, by the fence in the pasture. . . . Our boys are all buried by one another."[13] When they could, they added headboards with their names, ranks, and regiments, but identification tags were rare (soldiers could buy their own from sutlers or stores in the cities if they wanted), so it was often difficult to recognize a man, even a familiar one, if he was dismembered or decomposed. Looting, too, had stripped many of belongings that might otherwise have helped identify them. Today, around 1,600 of the 3,512 Union troops buried at Soldiers' National Cemetery remain unknown.[14] Confederates fared still worse. Frank Haskell saw "patches of fresh earth, raised a foot or so above the surrounding ground," with signs nearby on which was scrawled in red chalk, "75 Rebils berid hear" or, next to an arrow, "54 Rebs there."[15] As often happens in war, the occasional bizarre anomaly provoked every man's curiosity, such as the discovery of a female dressed in a Confederate uniform who was buried by soldiers of II Corps.[16]

Most often, burial parties dug long, shallow trenches near concentrations of corpses and indiscriminately let them "[tumble] in just as they fell, with not a prayer, eulogy, or tear," wrote Robert Carter. Up to ninety would be squeezed into a single mass grave.[17] At other times, as the men of the 17th Maine did, they bent their bayonets into hooks to drag the dead to the pits, but this method was not always satisfactory.[18] When two gravediggers came across a soldier "all bloated up, seated leaning against a tree," they found it "impossible to handle the man to get him there [to the pit], he was so decayed like, and we hitched his belt to his legs and dragged him along, and no sooner did we start with him than his scalp slipped right off. We just turned him in on his side and covered him with earth" instead of taking him any farther.[19] Bodies that had been hit by shell fragments were particularly prone to falling to pieces. Better than dragging was to jerry-rig a stretcher out of two poles with a canvas strip attached between. Two men handled the stretcher while a third used another, shorter pole to roll the body onto it. Still, as Private John Parker of the 22nd Massachusetts said of his work on July 5, often the carcasses were so badly decomposed and flayed that they tended to "slide off" into the grave.[20]

Unfortunately, once they were in there, the corpses' limbs were all askew, wrote Cyrus Boyd, so soldiers would jump "on top of the dead straightening out their legs and arms and tramping them down so as to make the hole contain as many as possible."[21] The 12th New Jersey's George Bowen "saw one man who had died with his arm in such position that it stuck up when put in the hole," so "a man took his shovel struck it a blow breaking his arm so that it fell, this was done to save having so much dirt to throw."[22]

Horses were harder to bury than humans, and soldiers soon gave up trying. Instead, they either left them to rot or dragged them to a pyre for burning. John Foster, who was helping the wounded, saw "here and there great girdles of fire blazon[ing] the slopes, telling of slaughtered animals slowly consuming."[23] Since some 4,400 were killed at Gettysburg, it took a long time to burn them all.[24]

19. The Wounded

Given the limitations of care in the field, soldiers brought to a hospital had generally suffered only wounds optimistically considered surviv- able. It was usually the subsequent infection that killed them, for while it was understood that cleanliness was an important part of treatment, the way in which germs were transmitted was unknown. Decades later, Dr. W. W. Keen asked God to

> forgive us our sins of ignorance. We operated in old blood-stained and often pus-stained coats, the veterans of a hundred fights. . . . We used undisinfected instruments from undisinfected plush- lined cases, and still worse, used marine sponges which had been used in prior pus cases and had been only washed in tap water. If a sponge or an instrument fell on the floor it was washed and squeezed in a basin of tap water and used as if it were clean. Our silk to tie blood vessels [and sew up wounds] was undisinfected. . . . If there was any difficulty in threading the needle we moistened it with (as we now know) bacteria-laden saliva, and rolled it between bacteria-infected fingers. We dressed the wounds with clean but undisinfected sheets, shirts, tablecloths, or other old soft linen res- cued from the family ragbag. We had no sterilized gauze dressing, no gauze sponges.[1]

Keen's words should be borne in mind when, using modern stan- dards as a yardstick, Civil War surgeons are belittled for their seeming incompetence and cruelty. Most former civilian physicians were in fact scrupulous and well-meaning but had to learn on the job owing to a lack of resources at the beginning of the war. In 1860, for example, the entire sixteen-thousand-man U.S. Army employed all of thirty sur- geons and eighty-three assistant surgeons—of whom twenty-four joined the Confederacy—and the Medical Department's budget was $90,000. From there, military medicine made enormous strides, an achievement obscured by an emphasis on judging progress by anachronistic standards of care, training, and knowledge. Indeed, by 1865 more than 12,000 doctors had served with the Union armies and 3,236 in those of the Confederacy. The North's medical budget, meanwhile, had risen to $11,594,000 by around the time of Gettysburg—a 12,882 percent increase in three years.[2]

Though there were a few fools—such as a Dr. Bailey of the 12th South Carolina who was so drunk that he botched Lieutenant J. R. Boyle's leg amputation not just the first time, but also when he redid it—most doctors at Gettysburg were dedicated and hardworking men who had to perform untold numbers of operations under extraordinarily trying circumstances.[3] Dr. John Billings wrote to his wife on July 6 that he was "utterly exhausted mentally and physically, have been operating night and day and am still hard at work." Even three days later, he was "covered with blood and . . . tired out almost completely," the only good news being that he had "got the chief part of the butchering done in a satisfactory manner." It was only on July 10 that he managed to get someone to scrub "all the blood out of my hair with Castile soap and bay-rum and my scalp feels as though a steam plough had been passed through it."[4] Others were not so lucky: One surgeon complained that his feet were so swollen after working almost nonstop for four days and two nights that he could barely stand. Rest was out of the question because he had another hundred amputations scheduled.[5]

The onerousness of their task was magnified by the relative scarcity of ambulances, orderlies, and supplies caused by the unexpected number of casualties, Lee's desire to travel light (the Confederates had four hundred ambulances, to the Army of the Potomac's thousand), and Meade's decision to move his extra wagons (carrying tents, stretchers, blankets, and food) to the rear in case he needed to retreat. Additionally, when the Union general pursued Lee on July 6 and 7, he took with him most of the medical personnel, leaving just 106 medical officers to deal with some 21,000 wounded men. Granted, most of the required surgeries had already been performed, but post-operative care was often minimal.[6] Whereas his leg had been removed on July 3, Charles Fuller of the 61st New York had to wait another six days "before a doctor could be found to look at my stump."[7] Nevertheless, it is difficult to find many complaints about the quality of medical treatment by injured soldiers. That the experience was awful should be taken as a given, but as J. W. Hand of the 136th New York put it many years later, "the care of the wounded was all that could be desired."[8]

Even the enemy wounded were often given proper attention. The 4th Texas's splendidly named Captain Decimus et Ultimus Barziza (he was the tenth and, his parents presumably hoped, last child) was shot in the leg and taken to a hospital where he and his fellow wounded were placed "side by side with the enemy's."[9] Suffering from a serious lung wound, Lieutenant Samuel Davis was told by a "very diminutive surgeon of Teutonic persuasion" that "I dink the probability is you die," but he recovered after being taken to a fine hospital in Chester, Pennsylvania. (Indeed, he fared so well that on the night of August 16 he escaped back to Richmond.)[10] On the other hand, Barziza and Davis were officers. Enlisted Confederates and Union men were generally treated decently but received second-class care. Few seemed to regard this as beyond the pale: As H. S. Peltz, a nurse at one Union hospital pointed out, the Confederates were housed in a nearby barn, and "while the soldiers of the North were dying for lack of care it was not strange that these poor creatures were left in an even worse condition."[11]

Whosoever they were, doctors tended to ease the exits of those who stood little chance of making it. For euthanistic purposes, Dr. Joseph Holt always carried a handy "two ounce bottle of black drop—a concentrated solution of opium, much stronger than laudanum" that ensured the mortally wounded never woke up.[12] If any man had been hit in the abdomen, said one surgeon, "one need not amuse oneself by hunting" for any bullets lost in there; he was as good as dead, and it was best to put him out of his misery quickly.[13]

Those left over might be placed in temporarily converted schools, houses, barns, and churches but were often kept outdoors. An orderly urged readers to put out of their minds any "thoughts of a long room, with cots having white sheets" when they heard the word *hospital*.[14] Instead, as Lieutenant Beath of the 88th Pennsylvania saw at McPherson's Barn, there were rows of "helpless soldiers, torn and mangled, [whose] lacerated limbs were frightfully swollen and, turning black, had begun to decompose; the blood flowing from gaping wounds had glued some of the sufferers to the floor."[15] In another field hospital, according to J. W. Stuckenberg, the patients were "writhing in pain, and deeply moaning and groaning and calling for relief which cannot be afforded them. The finest forms are horribly disfigured & mutilated."[16]

Any number of soldiers went almost mad waiting their turn for treatment—little surprise considering the conditions. John Dooley, a Confederate taken in by a Union hospital, said of his first night that all he heard were "groans and shrieks and maniacal ravings; bitter sobs, and heavy sighs, piteous cries; horrid oaths; despair." One man of his regiment lapsed into delirium, shouting "frantically a hundred times at least the words, 'I'm proud I belong to the 1st Va. Regiment!' "[17]

When Charles Weygant visited III Corps hospital, "a man I was about stepping over, sprang to his feet, shook in front of me a bloody bandage he had just torn from a dreadful gaping wound in his breast, and uttered a hideous, laughing shriek which sent the hot blood spurting from his wound into my very face; at which he threw up his arms as if a bullet had just entered his heart, and fell heavily backward across a poor mangled fellow, whose piercing wails of anguish were heart-rending beyond description."[18] The screams emanating from one place were so distressing that, as Fannie Buehler remembered, "the Regimental Bands . . . came every afternoon and played patriotic airs in front of the hospital" to muffle their sound.[19]

In the days following the battle, the primary duty of hospitals was not to make patients comfortable but to amputate in order to save lives. A common sight was "the surgeons, with sleeves rolled up and bloody to the elbows, [who] were continually employed in amputating limbs. The red, human blood ran in streams from under the operating tables, and [there were] huge piles of arms and legs, withered and horrible to behold."[20] These discarded bits and pieces of people accumulated frighteningly quickly. J. W. Muffly of the 148th Pennsylvania saw a "pile of hands, arms, feet, and legs . . . which had now reached the window sill."[21] Nellie Aughinbaugh of Gettysburg remembered watching surgeons throwing "arms and legs out the windows into the yard to lay there in the sweltering sun of that hot July."[22] Corporal George Wilson of the 150th New York gained still more direct experience when, after being hit in the head with a spent bullet and knocked unconscious, he was taken to the hospital and then mistakenly laid outside among the dead. The next morning he "awoke to find himself partly covered with the arms and legs the surgeons had amputated and thrown near him."

But there was little doctors could do with severed limbs but get rid of them as quickly as possible. They were working not only against the unending procession of casualties but the clock as well. According to the best contemporary medical opinion, the optimum time for amputation—that is, the window in which mortality was lowest—was roughly within twenty-four hours of receiving the injury, though it was far better to operate within half a day, before inflammation or contamination set in as shock wore off. From that point on, the fatality rate rose to more than a third of patients if the surgeons delayed longer than forty-eight hours from time of injury. If they did not operate at all, however, half of all men would die, and half the remainder would be left forever unfit for civilian employment.[23]

In this respect, the very fact that there were so many amputees in, for instance, Mississippi in 1865 that the state was obliged to spend one fifth of its revenue on prosthetic limbs can be counted as a positive consequence of the belief that it was better to err and amputate unnecessarily than to be overly cautious. If an infection or gangrene developed because a surgeon had delayed, he would need to wield the knife higher up the limb than he otherwise would have—making an already risky operation markedly more so. A Confederate soldier in Lee's army at this time enjoyed a 97 percent survival rate if his foot was taken off in reasonable time, but only a 62 percent chance if his leg was severed at the thigh. With good reason, then, amputations were a surgeon's first choice, not his last resort.[24]

In any case, very few soldiers opted to postpone or avoid amputation in the hopes of recovering naturally. At least proceeding to the operating table promised a rapid relief from pain thanks to the recent introduction of the miracle drug chloroform. The first reported clinical use of it as a stupefacient was by the Scot James Simpson on January 19, 1847, at his obstetrical practice, after which its use in wartime rocketed.[25] We should bear in mind that chloroform was a new technology, and as such, some doctors resisted its application—also that given the choice, some soldiers preferred to grit their teeth rather than take the newfangled drug. Private C. L. F. Worley of 5th Alabama, for instance, said, "Cut off the leg, Doc, but leave off the chloroform; if you can stand it I can."[26]

Their behavior was motivated more by fear about their manliness than by any concern about safety. Death from a chloroform overdose or adverse reaction was very rare—there would be just thirty-seven such deaths during the Civil War—but a minority of physicians regarded anesthetic as appropriate only for women and children.[27] Virile, vigorous males, counseled one Dr. White, a Union surgeon with a Massachusetts regiment, should avoid the stuff. When White brusquely asked Private James Winchell whether he was going to have his arm taken off, or "are you going to lie here and let the maggots eat you up," Winchell opted for the chloroform, to which request White replied, " 'No, and I have no time to dillydally with you.' " Finally, a humiliated Winchell agreed to the operation, set his teeth together, and had his arm cut off, proudly relating that afterward "Surgeon White praised my spunk, as he called it, and treated me to a half gill of brandy."[28]

White was an aberration in this respect. More representative of the profession was Dr. John Chisolm of South Carolina, who rued the tendency of old-school sawbones to "moralize upon the duty of suffering," to laud "the lusty bawling of the wounded from the smart of the knife," and to "characterize the cries of the patient as music to the ear."[29] Like most other doctors, Chisolm saw the introduction of chloroform as a divine blessing, for, as F. E. Daniel, another Confederate surgeon, put it, the patient "slept all through the ordeal. A minute seems not to have elapsed since the first whiff of the chloroform; he felt nothing, knew nothing. He wakes to find his leg gone."[30]

For the soldier who chose chloroform, the process was swift and straightforward. When it was the 61st New York's Charles Fuller's turn to have a leg sawn off, he was lifted onto the table and "a napkin was formed into a tunnel shape, a liberal supply of chloroform poured into it, and the thing placed over my nose and mouth. I was told to take in long breaths. To me it seemed a long time before the effect came, probably it was a short time, but at last my head seemed to grow big and spin around." When he awoke, he was given morphine, which presently "produced a happy state of mind and body."[31]

That is not to say that chloroform could not lead to some frightening moments. After Sergeant Francis Strickland of the 154th New York was shot in the right elbow, Dr. Van Aernam administered the anesthetic but did not dose him sufficiently. Strickland awoke halfway through the procedure and blurrily watched with horror as the surgeon tied his slippery arteries and sewed his flapping skin over the stump to cover it. Then he saw an orderly throw his arm and clothes through an open window and onto a big, sloppy pile of severed limbs.[32]

There were cases, too, of Lovecraftian hallucinations under the drug's influence. Adoniram Warner "fancied that I was wafting at an inconceivable velocity over space through regions of every degree of darkness and of light now in one and now in another and whirled round and round at a rate so horrible that I shudder to think of it and still I thought there was no end to this and that these wild pangs that I felt would last forever." At one moment, "all would be light and glorious—the universe radiant all over with rainbow light and then in a moment, as it seemed to me, all was black and dark and the universe seemed filled with all loathsome things—serpents, lizards . . . crockodiles—monstrous beasts of all shapes mixing their slime in their gnashing for me and sounds that no letters will spell greeted my ears."[33]

But thankfully, these horrible instances were few and far between. They would, in any case, pale against the long-term aftereffects of battle. Most obviously, the wounded would continue to die for days, weeks, months afterward, sometimes even a year later. The 62nd Pennsylvanian offers a typical timeline. Private Cyrus Plummer was shot in the groin on July 2 and lasted a day before succumbing. That same day, Private Charles Gibbs was shot in the left lung but held on until July 6. Sergeant Jacob Myers, who was hit in the forehead, died on July 9, with Lieutenant Patrick Morrise dying two days later from a bullet taking off much of his skull. Corporal Joseph Sherran died on July 27 from two leg wounds, one in each. Captain James Brown died July 28 from injuries. Finally, Corporal Jacob Funk made it to a hospital in Philadelphia but died from his wounds on May 24, 1864.[34]

Then there were injuries that may have appeared minor or superficial but never healed. Private William Goodell was admitted to a hospital after a shell exploded a few feet behind him. He exhibited no physical wounds, but it was known at the time that shells or shot landing nearby could cause partial or complete paralysis, deafness, blindness, loss of voice, rupturing of blood vessels, and profound mental confusion—all without leaving a mark. Goodell was apparently struck deaf and dumb. He had electricity applied to his misbehaving tongue but still, within six months he was suffering paralysis in his left leg and the right-hand side of his face drooped. There were also occasional, half-hour-long convulsions and severe head pains. He undertook some "trifling mechanical work," in the words of his doctors, but by January 1876 his spine had curved severely rightward, his hands and feet had partially lost sensation, and he was totally incapacitated. An attendant was needed to tend to his daily wants and needs. By September 4, 1877, a doctor reported that Goodell was now "quite lame and gets about with difficulty." Unfortunately, the story ends there, but it is likely that he died soon afterward.[35]

The prevalence and virulence of long-term wounds contributed heavily to the explosion in morphine and opium use after the war. A large number of veterans became addicted to these painkillers during their hospital treatments. In 1868, Horace Day estimated that addicts numbered in the tens of thousands; by 1870, state officials were actively worrying about the profusion of homegrown opium, particularly in Vermont, New Hampshire, and Connecticut. There were also crops being raised in Florida, Louisiana, California, and Arizona. As late as 1902, investigators were still finding chronic drug abuse in old soldiers' homes.[36]

There was intense psychic scarring as well, but we should bear in mind that, as with the Bunker Hill veterans, confidently assigning diagnoses of PTSD to Civil War veterans is fraught with difficulty owing to changing standards and definitions based on historical and current samples.[37]

A common error is to elide temporary cases of acute stress disorder or combat stress reaction (immediate but usually recoverable reactions to trauma that include paralysis, weeping, muteness, curling fetally, and screaming) with deeper post-traumatic stress disorder (resulting from long-term exposure to extreme psychological pressure, with symptoms that may include irritability, anxiety, flashbacks, nausea, insomnia, paranoia, delusions, memory problems, violent behavior, and headaches). The gloom exhibited by Corporal Augustus Hesse of the 9th Massachusetts Battery is a case in point. At Gettysburg, his battery, which lost three of its four officers, six of eight sergeants, and nineteen enlisted men, was "cut up so terable[.] oh I feel so bad that I could cry."[38] He wrote this on July 7. But we cannot assume that he never recovered from the initial shock of losing so many comrades; it is possible that his was a temporary reaction. Indeed, Hesse (who was wounded in the arm) returned to the army and mustered out in June 1865 as a sergeant. His letters subsequent to the battle come across as quite cheery.[39] Another example is that of Lieutenant Colonel David Thomson of the 82nd Ohio, whose adjutant, Lieutenant Stowell Burnham, was mortally wounded on July 1. On July 16, Thomson wrote to his daughter saying, "Oh! How I miss Burnham," and on August 11 added, "How much I miss Burnham. Glorious good fellow was he, and most generously did he live." A little more than a week later, on August 19, Thomson wrote again: "I miss Burnham more and more. It was too bad that he was killed. Yet he died nobly and bravely. He and I were companions. I had none more so. Now I am alone." A close reading of the lines seems to indicate that Thomson was slowly coming to terms with his grief, had begun to console himself that his friend had lived well and had died "nobly and bravely," and was in the process of accepting that he must soldier on, even if it must be alone. It cannot be definitively proven, but it does seem likely that Thomson's incapacitating sorrow was not debilitatingly permanent.[40]

Similarly, many examples of men running away owing to "cowardice"—evidence, at the time, of low moral character—can be ascribed to simple combat stress reaction, while any number of men registered as "missing" were in fact soldiers who had succumbed to stress sometime during the fight and would make their way back to their units once they had recovered their composure. When Captain Francis Jones of the 149th Pennsylvania was wounded and lying in the McPherson Barn, he spotted a German of his company named Private Frederick Heiner "looking in the stable door. I called to him to inquire how he was wounded. He replied that he was not wounded at all, but he said, 'Captain, I was so terribly frightened on the first of July, I crawled under a hay stack as we passed it.'" His panic having subsided, Heiner redeemed himself by staying to help Jones.[41]

There were many others, like the wounded Jesse Morgan of the 7th New Jersey, who ran the gauntlet at Gettysburg and mused thereafter on the cruelty and waste of war, only to be back with their regiments within a few months.[42] Indeed, every Civil War army depended on the willingness of men to return to fight for their ideals (for union, for independence, for freedom, for slavery, for money, for pride, for fun), even if they suffered for them. Benjamin Thompson was a captain of the 111th New York at Gettysburg who in the immediate aftermath of Pickett's Charge "could not long endure the gory, ghastly spectacle." He "found my head reeling, the tears flowing and my stomach sick at the sight" of "the men [lying] in heaps, the wounded wriggling and groaning under the weight of the dead among whom they were entangled." For "months the spectre haunted my dreams, and even after forty seven years it comes back as the most horrible vision I have ever conceived."[43] Thompson was a troubled man, yet he continued with his regiment until March 1864, when he volunteered to transfer to the 32nd United States Colored Regiment—proof of his steadfast abolitionist beliefs—and stayed in harness until the end of the war, finishing it as lieutenant colonel. During Reconstruction he served at Fort Pulaski in Georgia as provost marshal and later moved to Minneapolis to become a successful tea merchant with a "large circle of friends" and an elder in the First Presbyterian Church.[44]

Thompson overcame his short-term combat stress and, while disturbed occasionally thereafter by nightmares, does not appear to have been actively disabled by full-blown PTSD over the subsequent decades. Compare his case with that of Colonel William Lee, beloved commander of the 20th Massachusetts at the battle of Antietam, where almost half his regiment was lost. A lieutenant, Henry Abbott, wrote to his father two months after the clash that Lee had come undone: "After the battle he was completely distraught. He didn't give any orders. He wouldn't do anything. The next morning he mounted his horse, and without any leave of absence, without letting any body [know] where he was going, he set out alone." He vanished for an entire month until Lieutenant George Macy, "who was bringing up some recruits, met him about ten miles away from the regt. Without a cent in his pocket, without any thing to eat or drink, without having changed his clothes for 4 weeks, during all which times he had this terrible diarrhea. . . . Macy gave him a drink and some money and got him into a house, put him to bed stark naked, and got his wits more settled, and then came on. When the poor old man came back to the regt. they thought he been on an awful [drinking] spree, he was so livid and shaky. Macy says he was just like a little child wandering away from home." Even now, he "is undoubtedly very much shaken in his intellects." Lee would resign his commission on December 17, though in actuality his duties had long been relinquished to subordinates.[45] He died thirty years later, forgotten and alone. The only people who remembered him at his funeral in a near-empty church, said one of his former officers, were some immediate relatives and "the few grey heads who stood for the men of the Twentieth."[46] It seems quite clear that Lee never recovered from his mental breakdown.

We also cannot know for certain the extent and depth of short-term stress and long-term PTSD in Civil War veterans, partly because so many likely cases were euphemized out of the record to preserve their subjects' dignity. In Colonel Lee's case, for instance, the official regimental history confined itself to stating delicately that after Antietam he "suffered a great deal from the various illnesses of camp brought on by exposure to wet and cold [and became] dangerously sick [and] left for Boston on [October] 29th on leave of absence for his health."[47]

Not least, too, given the rudimentary psychiatric knowledge of the era, it is often hard to distinguish between genuine PTSD symptoms and hereditary or genetic ailments. An ambiguous case was that of John Corns, who had shown no signs of disability before the war. Over the course of his service, however, he became pale, emaciated, and estranged from his relatives at home. After mustering out of his unit, he returned to Indiana but could not hold on to jobs and turned progressively more unstable. He would "look wild and excited and being evidently in great mental commotion," then shout "there is some one after me" and "do you see them coming over the hill, we will all be lost and destroyed." He said that his head hurt and would cover it with his hands and cry out. At other times, he would imagine that he was drilling troops or that he was an aide to a famous general. Corns was later sent to a poorhouse, where he was chained up. The question is whether these symptoms were manifestations of developing mental illness or part of a combat-induced disorder—or a combination of both.

Corns was not alone in this respect. A study of sixty-nine Union soldiers committed to the Indiana Hospital for the Insane between 1860 and 1871 reported the following symptoms: "raves—talks about the war and the Bible," "tears clothing," "was exposed in Army. Has not been well since," "has suffered great lack of sleep . . . Is troubled in sleep with persons [unintelligible] his life . . . and threatens to do these imaginary persons harm," "tried to stab his father and himself," "loses consciousness but does not fall down," "has had fear of being killed by [unintelligible] and others," and "became insane at Battle of Pea Ridge."[48]

As with Corns, these are all strongly positive indicators of delayed stress reactions, but at the time as many as a quarter of these cases were deemed hereditary and presumed to have relatively little to do with their Civil War service. Perhaps that is so, though only 14.5 percent of the patients had previously demonstrated signs of insanity, a hint that the physicians might have been conveniently classifying combat-related cases as "inherited" ones.

Even taking into account all these cautionary factors, we can say with some certitude that many Civil War soldiers were traumatized and afflicted, either in the immediate or the longer term, by their battle experiences. Thus, a sophisticated statistical analysis of the postwar medical records of 17,700 veterans found a very strong correlation between the percentage of regimental company killed and increased incidence of postwar gastrointestinal and cardiac problems, nervous disease, and depression. In this instance, the number of a man's friends killed stands as an index for such traumatic stressors as combat intensity, handling corpses, witnessing death and dismemberment, killing others, and realizing the imminence of one's death.[49]

The harder and more gallantly he struggled for cause, country, and comrades, then, the more likely that a soldier would be wretched with sickness and racked with pain, that he would be tormented by fears that he was neither useful nor ornamental to the world, when he attended those old men's reunions celebrating that great fight near the town of Gettysburg.

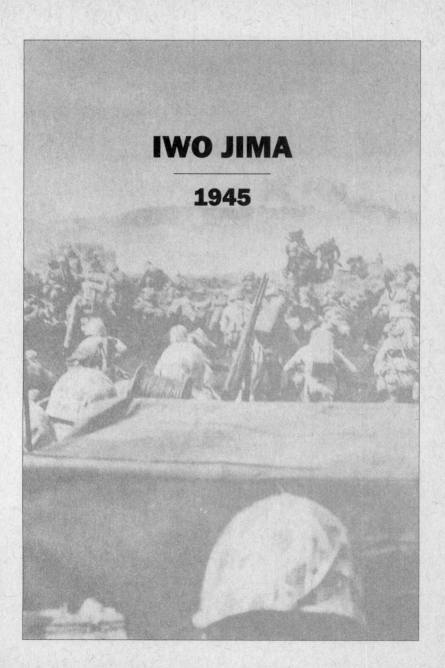

IWO JIMA

1945

1. Introduction

Of all the Pacific battles fought by the Marines—among them Guadalcanal, Peleliu, Saipan, Tarawa, Okinawa—Iwo Jima is the most iconic,
the most famous. It is the Gettysburg of World War II. As the subject
of bestselling books (*Flags of Our Fathers*) and popular movies (*Sands of
Iwo Jima, Letters from Iwo Jima*), as well as the location of "The
Photo"—Joe Rosenthal's immortal shot of five Marines and a U.S.
Navy corpsman raising a flag atop Mount Suribachi—Iwo Jima overshadows any other amphibious Pacific battle in the American public's
imagination, emotions, and memory.

In World War II, the Marine Corps was expressly designed for one
thing: to hurl itself with the greatest possible violence toward a hostile
beach, destroy the enemy at close quarters, and seize control of an island.[1] Part of the fascination with the battle on Iwo Jima stems from its
legendary ferocity and annihilatory nature—the consequences of the
American republic's bloodied sword arm meeting the Japanese empire's
obstinate shield. Nearly two and a half times as many Marines would
die at Iwo Jima—a speck just a third of the size of Manhattan—in five
weeks as in the entirety of World War I (about eighteen months). Indeed, of all the Marines killed during the Second World War, a third
would die at Iwo Jima. It is the only battle in which Marine casualties
exceeded those of the Japanese.

Objectively and strategically speaking, however, Iwo neither formed
a "turning point" in the war nor was "decisive" in the sense of deciding
outcomes. By 1945, the Japanese Empire as a whole was doomed, and
the Americans were everywhere triumphant. In Washington, the only
issues were how long it would take to conquer Tokyo and how many

corpses would there be along the way. Likewise, the Marines had won the battle of Iwo Jima from the moment they splashed ashore; it was just a matter of time, multiplied by force.

The battle, moreover, may not even have been so very important. The reasons for which it was ostensibly fought—to provide a base for bombing operations against Japan and an unsinkable aircraft carrier for damaged B-29s that would otherwise have ditched into the sea and drowned their crews—have lately been questioned as justifications *ex post facto* for the blood-price paid by the Marine Corps. Such assertions, understandably and predictably, remain extremely controversial among veterans as well as the public at large.[2]

Be that as it may, Iwo Jima is the focus of this chapter because it presents a case study in how armies solve problems and learn to fight. The Marines quickly invented new techniques and adapted their tactics after landing on Iwo Jima and discovering that their best-laid plans had come undone against unexpectedly dense Japanese defenses. Iwo Jima, then, *is* important, just perhaps not for the reasons traditionally suggested.

The Marines' rapid adaptation to circumstances undermines the popular suppositions that the war in the Pacific was racially based and that the "barbaric savagery" against the Japanese (and vice versa) was motivated by biological hatred. A close study of the actions of the Marines on Iwo Jima highlights instead that American responses to the Japanese were instrumentalist, not ideological, in nature. That is, Japanese were killed by the most effective methods and weaponry available because, in the face of unyielding resistance amid difficult terrain, this was the only way to win. This very practical aspect has been omitted from most accounts of Iwo Jima but will be discussed in detail here.

2. The Nature of the Battle

First, a brief account of the general course of the battle, which will, unavoidably, be vague. Unlike Bunker Hill or Gettysburg, where units' movements can be more or less tracked for the duration of the fighting, to the ordinary Marine on Iwo each day and night was just like the previous and the next. The battle was less one of structured stages than of dull, unvarying routines. Each and every day was consumed by advancing painfully slowly, taking cover, avoiding snipers, destroying pillboxes and bunkers, helping wounded comrades, killing Japanese, and killing more Japanese. Then trying, and failing, to get some sleep. The next day, it started all over again, and so on until there was literally no more island left to conquer. As their severely attrited squads, platoons, and companies dissolved and re-formed, Marines lost track of time, location, and unit. Their memories of what happened where and when and with whom are uniformly hazy, making it difficult to construct a solid timeline or map of their movements.

The structure of this chapter necessarily differs from the earlier two. Whereas for Bunker Hill, we could deduce a militiaman's experience of combat depending on his location (redoubt, beach, rail fence) and for Gettysburg we could do the same by deconstructing the era's formal templates (artillery bombardment, attack, defense), for Iwo Jima I'll mostly examine combat method—that is, how Marines first confronted obstacles and then surmounted them by watching, doing, adapting, and learning. The Marines on Iwo Jima would discover that by adhering to the method they could make sense out of madness, even vanquish it.

3. The Strategy

The Pacific War was predicated on the twin principles of acquiring advanced bases and island-hopping, both accomplished through amphibious assaults. Westward across the central Pacific the Marines would drive toward the Japanese home islands.[1]

To hold them up, the Japanese had established a defense-in-depth strategy of zones and rings, each tiny island chain supporting the others as a base of operations. The Marines, in turn, would assault a given stronghold, subdue it, and move out and onward to allow fresh troops room to garrison it. The island would thereafter be turned into a staging point for the next assault as Seabees—naval construction engineers —built airfields and harbors. Aircraft would begin to use the island as a secure base, supplies would be stockpiled in vast quantities, and the Navy could find safe anchorage for refitting and repair. An offshoot of island-hopping was leapfrogging, in which certain Japanese strongholds on an island chain would be bypassed and isolated from reinforcements using airpower and submarines. The Pacific strategy was an updating of Frederick the Great's eighteenth-century wars of geography, in which possession of certain fortresses, towns, and roads would eventually constrict the opponent's freedom of movement until he either surrendered or, alternately, fought at a disadvantage—and then surrendered. The major difference was that the Japanese were not princes and lords of the Enlightenment: They did not surrender but fought—to the very end.

Adhering to the set strategy, between November 1943 and November the following year the Marines successively seized advanced bases in the Gilbert, Marshall, Mariana, and Palau chains of islands and atolls, each hop bringing them closer to Japan. Guarding what Tokyo called its "Inner Vital Defense Zone" was Iwo Jima, described by one Japanese officer as the "doorkeeper to the Imperial capital" itself. Once Iwo Jima was taken, the next stop would be Okinawa (340 miles from mainland Japan), where the Marines advancing westward from the Central Pacific would join up with the Army divisions that had driven northward from the South Pacific. Together, they would invade Japan— but the dropping of the atomic bombs and the Soviet conquest of Manchuria ended the Pacific War before that inevitable cataclysm could take place.

From the Japanese perspective, Iwo Jima was admirably located to harass the B-29 Superfortress bombers raiding Nippon on their way both in and out. Iwo served also as a two-hour early warning system that could alert the mainland of incoming sorties while its complement of prowling fighters forced Allied bombers to fly more circuitous routes to their targets, making it necessary to carry extra fuel at the expense of their bomb payloads. On the way back, damaged planes were easy prey for the waiting fighters. In addition, Iwo's own complement of bombers had staged raids on U.S. bases at Saipan and Tinian. By the fall of 1944, more B-29s had been lost on the ground than in the sky.

Originally, the assault on Iwo Jima had been scheduled for October 1944, but unexpected delays caused by the Mariana and Palau invasions forced a postponement until the new year. The five-month wait proved expensive, as the Japanese, now commanded by the extraordinarily able Lieutenant General Tadamichi Kuribayashi, a fifth-generation soldier who would fight the Americans here for the first and last time, worked feverishly to reinforce the island's garrison (it ballooned from around fifteen hundred to roughly twenty thousand) and to strengthen its fortifications. The Marines would pay the price in blood.

The Americans themselves had done their utmost to frustrate the Japanese preparations in the hopes of making their assault easier. Beginning in August 1944, the Seventh Army Air Force dispatched regular bombing raids on Iwo. From December 8, as the Marines ramped up to invade, Iwo was subjected to daily attack. Near the end of January 1945, aircraft pummeled Iwo remorselessly, day and night, for two weeks. Heavy cruisers bombarded it five times in December and January alone. In total, the softening-up stage was the heaviest cumulative bombardment of the Pacific War, with 6,800 tons of bombs and 22,000 naval shells slamming into a piece of earth 5.5 miles long, 2.5 miles broad at its widest point, and comprising about eight square miles.

Three days before D-Day—the day of the invasion of Iwo Jima, February 19, 1945—the Navy hit Iwo with still more intense ferocity to blast away any remaining opposition before the Marines landed. The Japanese by then were too deeply entrenched, too hardened, for the bombardment to have any chance of succeeding. Waiting offshore, nonetheless, were the 3rd, 4th, and 5th Marine Divisions (together making up the V Amphibious Corps), the largest force of Marines ever committed to a single battle.

4. The Battle

At 0645 on February 19, the order went out: "Land the landing force." With the 3rd Division held in reserve, the 5th was to storm the 2.5-mile-long beach just north of 548-foot-high Mount Suribachi as the 4th landed on its right flank, overlooked by the Rock Quarry perched on the bluffs dominating the beach.

After the first wave of Marines landed at approximately 0900, they rapidly advanced inland, receiving fire from concealed Japanese machine-gun positions, pillboxes, and mortar teams. Shortly after 10 A.M., Kuribayashi unmasked his heavy guns, hidden in the interior, and attacked the assault troops now crowding the beachhead. Horizontal-firing anti-aircraft guns on either side of the bight supplemented the deadly crossfire. Barrages were expertly rolled up and down the beach, slaying Marines by the score. The assault came close to stalling as panicked Marines remained frozen on the beach, their only cover the craters left behind by Japanese artillery—which, of course, had now registered their locations. Over the next hour U.S. commanders on the ships received radio messages similar to the following one, sent at 1046 by a 28th Marines unit: "Taking heavy fire and forward movement stopped. Machine gun and artillery fire heaviest ever seen." Aircraft urgently swooped in to drop napalm while the naval guns blasted whatever they could see. Slowly the Japanese fire tailed off and, with the aid of tank and mobile-artillery support, the Marines managed to restore their momentum and get off the beach.

By the end of the day, the Marines had daringly hacked their way seven hundred yards across the neck of the island, severing Suribachi from reinforcement and establishing a line of control across to the western coast. Some thirty thousand Marines had landed (with another forty thousand or so to come as the battle ground on), along with artillery units and many tanks. At one point there would be sixty thousand men crammed into an area of 3.5 square miles—or 17,143 per square mile, about the same density as the crowded city of San Francisco.

On the right flank, the struggle for the Rock Quarry continued.

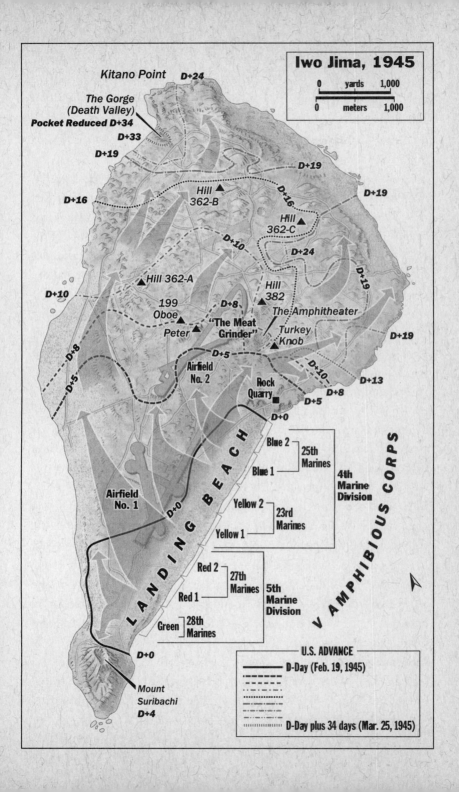

Iwo Jima, 1945

Kitano Point

The Gorge
(Death Valley)
Pocket Reduced D+34

D+24

D+33

D+19

D+19

D+16

Hill
362-B

D+16

D+19

Hill
362-C

D+19

D+10

D+24

Hill 362-A

Hill
382

D+10

D+8

The Amphitheater

199
Oboe

"The Meat
Grinder"

Turkey
Knob

Peter

D+8

D+5

D+19

Airfield
No. 2

D+10

D+5

Rock
Quarry

D+13

D+8

D+8

D+5

D+0

LANDING BEACH

Blue 2

25th
Marines

Blue 1

4th
Marine
Division

Airfield
No. 1

Yellow 2

23rd
Marines

V AMPHIBIOUS CORPS

D+0

Yellow 1

Red 2

27th
Marines

5th
Marine
Division

Red 1

Green

28th
Marines

D+0

Mount
Suribachi
D+4

U.S. ADVANCE

—— D-Day (Feb. 19, 1945)

·········· D-Day plus 34 days (Mar. 25, 1945)

The 3rd Battalion, 25th Marines, would clamber the cliffs by nightfall, sacrificing five hundred men and twenty-two officers in the process. The Marines on the first day suffered total losses of 2,420 men, about 8 percent of their strength and a casualty rate impossible to sustain for more than a few days without general collapse.

That night, the Marines settled down and prepared for the expected mass banzai charge—but none came. Instead, there was just indirect fire from the island's interior and small probes by what Kuribayashi called "prowling wolves" (infiltrators and scouts). On the second day, Marines attacked Suribachi. Scores of concrete blockhouses guarded the approach and lower elevations. All of them would need to be destroyed. It took three more days, but on February 23 (D+4), they did it and famously raised the flags to flutter over Iwo Jima. Hard fighting continued, however, even past the Rock Quarry. There was no cover from enemy fire, and pillboxes exacted a heavy toll. Marines in that sector were able to advance perhaps a couple of hundred yards a day with disproportionate casualties.

Moreover, the Japanese defenses in the north of the island remained defiant and were, if anything, more thickly studded and deeply implanted than those in the south. On February 24 (D+5), the Marines turned their attention to pushing up the island and penetrating Kuribayashi's double-tiered main defensive belt. They were initially organized into a pleasingly straight (in terms of military aesthetics) line crossing the island east to west, but over the coming weeks the battle would degenerate into a random staccato of small-unit actions as the Marines struggled against the impregnable defenses. On the left (west) side, Hills 362-A and -B would prove particularly difficult, and on the right (east) side, Hill 382, Turkey Knob, and the Amphitheater—a complex collectively dubbed "the Meat Grinder"—would kill and maim thousands of Marines. Taking just two small hills (Peter and 199 Oboe) alone required three days of intense close-quarters combat.

The American advance continually bogged down amid the tortuous terrain and stubborn resistance. In nine days' fighting, for instance, V Amphibious Corps advanced four thousand yards in exchange for seven thousand casualties—a loss equivalent to a third of an entire division. Despite the severe losses, Marine prowess and mission effectiveness began to rise sharply about two weeks into the battle as they integrated the myriad of combat lessons acquired since D-Day. They had, in a very real sense, learned on the job. Soon afterward, Kuribayashi's main line was forced, and he moved back to a command blockhouse in the far north. The Marines plowed forward, proceeding ever farther into the northern badlands of narrow, twisting gorges and dark caves. On March 9 (D+18) a patrol finally reached the northern coast, its squad leader sending back to headquarters a canteen filled with seawater, accompanied by a note reading, "For inspection—not consumption."

On March 16 (D+25), Iwo Jima was officially declared "secured" (to much unofficial laughter) when the Americans controlled 90 percent of the island. The remaining 10 percent was the real trouble. Kuribayashi's stronghold at Kitano Point remained defiant, and scores of caves, spider traps, and pillboxes still had to be cleared. Fighting moved on to the Gorge (sometimes known as Death Valley), an eight-hundred-yard pocket honeycombed with man-made and natural defenses, followed by more than a week of relentless cave-by-cave, rock-by-rock assaults.

Kuribayashi died, perhaps leading a final banzai charge on the night of March 25. Or he may have committed suicide on March 23. His body has never been found. On the evening of March 25 (D+34), the Marines flushed out what was evidently the very last cave, and the next day the battle was declared over.

5. The Landing

Like lambs being fattened up for the kill, or so they joked, Marines always feasted on steak and eggs before landing on hostile shores.[1] As the traditional sacrament of D-Days, it made a nice change from the usual beans and coffee, even if the Navy's largesse turned out to be the last rite of many.[2] A few were too nervous to eat; their mates wolfed down their leavings.[3] Francis Cockrel, for his part, derived no little reassurance from the no-expenses-spared breakfast upgrade: The appearance of expensive steak and real eggs "made us feel the government was being pretty big about the thing."[4]

There certainly had been no stinting on the Iwo Jima operation. The task force assembled to assault Guadalcanal back in August 1942 had numbered fifty-one ships; for the task of wresting Iwo Jima from the grip of its Japanese occupants, the American armada grew to ten times that size.[5] No fewer than twelve aircraft carriers, six colossal battleships, nineteen cruisers, and forty-four destroyers were present, aided by hundreds of assorted patrol, escort, and support vessels.

Their holds contained the raw sinews of war: 4,100,000 barrels of black oil, 595,000 barrels of diesel oil, 33,775,000 gallons of aviation gasoline, 6,703,000 gallons of motor gas; 38 tons of clothing; 10,000 tons of fleet freight; 7,000 tons of ship supplies (rope, canvas, fenders, cleaning gear, hardware); 1,000 tons of candy; and 14,500 tons of fresh, frozen, and dry provisions. The 5th Division alone was accompanied by 100 million cigarettes.

Ammunition, the currency of combat, arrived in similarly stupendous quantities. In little over a month of fighting, the Navy and Marines would together expend 2,400 rounds of 16-inch shells; 5,700 rounds of 14-inch; 1,400 rounds of 12-inch; 11,700 rounds of 8-inch high-capacity; 8,400 rounds of 6-inch high-capacity; 17,700 rounds of 5-inch star; 12,000 rounds of 5-inch; 10,000 rounds of 4-inch; 70,000 rounds of 4.2-inch mortar; and some 28,000 tons of infantry cartridges—the combined weight of 237 Boeing 747s.[6] One can understand the necessity of amassing such stockpiles: During the recent battle for Peleliu (September–November 1944), the Marines had expended a statistical average of 1,590 rounds of heavy and light ammunition to kill each Japanese on the island. This figure included 1,330 standard rifle rounds and ten grenades.[7]

By way of comparison, the Japanese on Iwo had stockpiled 20 million rifle and machine-gun cartridges for their 20,000-odd small arms. At first glance, a thousand rounds per man seems sufficient, but since the Japanese had forecast that the battle would last two months (their prediction was more accurate than that of the Americans, who forecast a couple of weeks at most), it worked out to seventeen cartridges per day per man over sixty days—including machine guns, which guzzled ammunition at a prodigious rate. A Marine who fired just two eight-round magazines from his M1 Garand rifle—which he might every few minutes during a firefight—would have almost equaled his Japanese counterpart's entire allotment for the whole day.[8] Unlike the Marines, too, the Japanese could not resupply. With a single exception, they had to fight with what they had. (That exception: One time, a lone plane got through the American air screen and dropped a cargo of bamboo spears for the beleaguered garrison.)[9]

For three days the Navy had bombarded Iwo Jima to soften up its defenders for the amphibious assault to come. Even now, as H-Hour approached, pilots were assailing Japanese defenses and emplacements, swooping low to strafe targets with their machine guns. Now, while the Japanese had their heads down, it was time for the Marines to go. They formed up on deck in preparation for disembarking to the landing craft assigned to their units.

There was the usual rush for the lavatories. The line at one head, recalled Allen Matthews, "was as long as a beer line back in camp," and many of the men, like Dan Levin, had already urinated multiple times.[10] Others, among them Captain Bertram Yaffe, simply vomited over the side as often as they needed to.[11]

In a well-meaning effort to take the men's minds off what fates awaited them, the bandsmen of the 3rd Division struck up a selection of toe-tapping symphonic melodies, and (often unwilling) listeners had to guess what they were. Most were unfamiliar with both composer and work, but there were a few experts among the crowd. Alvin Josephy watched a burly Marine listen to a Tchaikovsky piece and exclaim jubilantly, "Christ! That's the *Moon Song*. Tommy Dorsey, ain't it?"[12]

As at Bunker Hill and Gettysburg, equipment checks were obsessively repeated to stave off attacks of nerves. Pfc. Robert Snodgrass busied himself reconfirming that every piece of the company's machine guns was locked into place and scrounged an impressive number of spare parts "so you can save your ass once the thing actually gets going."[13] Allen Matthews ran through his checklist over and over:

"Canteen tops tightly screwed, yes; grenade pins bent sufficiently to keep them from being pulled accidentally but not enough to hamper my pulling them when I needed to, yes; chamber and operating rod of my rifle free of dust, yes; oil and thong case and combination tool in my rifle butt." And, of course, "extra cigarettes were in the gas mask carrier."[14]

A gas mask was, perhaps surprisingly, considered absolutely necessary by Marine planners, for at this late stage in the war the Japanese were assumed to be sufficiently desperate to use chemical weapons. At Peleliu just a few short months earlier, small stockpiles of grenade-sized glass spheres filled with hydrocyanic acid, a volatile nerve agent, had been discovered.[15] (On Iwo, nothing similar would be found, though one day a thick green vapor wafted past Sergeant Ray Miller. The mysterious cloud turned out to be caused by the detonation of picric acid, used in some older Japanese artillery shells.)[16] While a few of the more nervous Marines, like Pfc. Fred Schribert, hurriedly slipped on masks as soon as they saw even a wisp of white smoke, others soon "repurposed" theirs. James Vedder, a battalion surgeon with the 27th Marines, used his to store six apples and oranges he'd liberated from the ship's mess that morning.[17] Most men, though, threw them away as soon as they landed.

Disposal of a mask barely lightened the considerable load Marines carried. Depending upon his specialty, each bore anywhere between 50 pounds (for a corpsman or surgeon) and 122 pounds (for mortarmen) of gear during the landing.[18] Because it was critical to get as much equipment ashore as rapidly as possible, the earlier waves of Marines were treated as temporary packhorses and had to lug an extra burden, such as a five-gallon can of water, a couple of mines, or a box of machine-gun ammunition. All these encumbrances were inevitably dumped the second their boots touched sand for the sake of reaching cover in short order.[19] Aside from their packs, which included a poncho, canteens, an entrenching tool, socks, rations, a first-aid kit, and the like, Marines made sure that they were adequately armed. Gerald Averill, for example, carried a .45 pistol, a Thompson submachine gun, two 30-round magazines taped end to end, and four more in canvas carriers on his belt.[20] Jay Rebstock hauled a Browning Automatic Rifle (known as a BAR, it was essentially a light-machine gun), a .45 pistol, 240 rounds of BAR ammunition, a bandolier containing even more ammo around his chest, and a bunch of grenades.[21] Allen Matthews was typical in bringing "a dangerously sharpened bayonet," his combat knife, four grenades, and a cartridge belt with no fewer than ten magazines.[22]

As time went on, Marines would ruthlessly dispense with any frippery. Within the week, Richard Wheeler was down to just his "helmet, rifle, bayonet, two fragmentation grenades, one thermite grenade, a cartridge belt, a knife, two canteens, and a first aid kit—still a good 25-pound load."[23] By the end of the battle, men often carried nothing but a spare bandage, a rifle, some ammo, a canteen, and a few grenades—not even a helmet, which they had discovered was better at deflecting shrapnel than rifle bullets, the only type of ammunition the Japanese had left by then. They preferred to wear soft hats, which were in any case "less trouble when you had to run," said Howard McLaughlin.[24]

For the moment, nevertheless, they were clean and eminently presentable in their fresh dungarees, which had been dunked in a soapy mixture and impregnated with insect repellent. The evening before, they had all shaved, not merely for cosmetic reasons but because doctors insisted that if you were shot in the face, at least your dirty whiskers could not infect the wound and complicate recovery. It was thoughtful advice considering that the campaign was expected to last less than a fortnight.[25] But it would be soon forgotten. While in Rosenthal's photograph, the flag-raisers' uniforms still look relatively clean, if lived-in, by the battle's dire finale, the Marines' clothes had disintegrated: There were deep rips in the knees and elbows, and most looked like hoboes. Nearly everyone wound up with athlete's foot and, from lack of washing, red, raw "creeping crud" or body fungus under the arms and in the crotch that required painful fungicidal treatment to eradicate.[26]

For the moment, those assigned to LVTs (Landing Vehicle Tracked, often called *amtracs,* short for "amphibious tractor") descended ladders into the dark, deep bowels of the Landing Ship, Tanks (LST, sometimes known scornfully as a "Large Slow Target"), where their conveyances awaited.[27] The noise of the engines was deafening, and the cavernous space was soon filled with noxious, thick exhaust fumes. Some men put on their gas masks, but these merely filtered, not freshened, the poisonous air. Nausea and dizziness spread quickly. Irritated men jostled each other in the crowded vehicles. They stood where they were for up to half an hour.[28]

Then, unexpectedly, the colossal jaws of the ship clanked open and the Marines craned their necks to see the emerald sea and azure sky that lay before them. Blessedly clean, 70-degree air rushed in. Ahead, the first of the tractors beetled forward, followed one by one by the rest. Then it was Allen Matthews's turn:

> The roar of the motors increased, the treads screeched against the steel deck, and we jerked forward a few feet, swerved awkwardly to the center of the tank deck and moved towards the bow doors and the fumes of the tanks preceding us brought tears to our eyes. . . . Each of us held to the side of the tractor for support . . . and the huge machine thrust its nose into the air suddenly, climbed laboriously, leveled off momentarily, and then plunged sickeningly into the water. . . . The spray flew back over us, but we did not know it until the tank righted in the water, rolled heavily, then gently, and our treads churned at the water and we too moved to the starboard.[29]

Those selected for boat transport avoided nausea but had their own troubles. They were expected to clamber down almost fifty feet on cargo nets into a moving, unstable, barge-like vessel—a Landing Craft, Vehicle, Personnel (LCVP), better known as a Higgins boat—while balancing their packs and loads.[30] One misstep, worried Corporal Hershel "Woody" Williams, and an equipment-laden Marine would tumble into the vasty deep, sinking instantly.[31] Their trainers had emphasized that good timing was key to a successful descent, for the most dangerous moment was when a Marine had to leap from the bottom of the cargo net into the boat below. If the gap between troop transport and landing craft was too wide, he might easily slip through into the water, but assuming the coxswain was keeping his craft sufficiently close, the soldier needed to make sure that he let go just as the boat reached the crest of a swell. Timed correctly, the Marine had to fall only a couple of feet. But if he jumped too early and the boat rose suddenly, shattered ankles, concussions, and fractured spines would be the result. Too late, and the poor Marine would plummet between five and twelve feet into a boat lurching downward.[32] Since a Marine often waited for three or four waves to time his leap of faith just right, disembarkations of thousands of men were prolonged affairs that annoyed those trapped in the amtracs paddling nearby.

The landing boats joined the packs of amtracs already formed into circles, endlessly trailing each other's wakes as they waited for the order to draw up in line abreast and pause at the "Line of Departure"—the invisible boundary two miles offshore running parallel to the beach—to prepare for the charge toward Iwo Jima. It was only now that Sergeant Henry Weaver noticed that his boat's coxswain had painted "TOO LATE TO WORRY" on the inside bow ramp.[33] It was.

Marines at least could take comfort from the massive barrage hitting the beach to ease their landing. A Japanese military report had estimated that a single American battleship possessed firepower equivalent to five full-strength Japanese infantry divisions.[34] At Iwo Jima, the Navy put on a show that impressed even the most jaded Marines. Corporal James "Salty" Hathaway was an amtrac crew chief circling his vessel below a battleship firing into the rock and sand of Iwo: "You could actually see a sixteen-inch shell come out of the muzzle of those ships." As it soared overhead, sounding like a freight train rushing by, the shock waves lifted the amtrac out of the water, and Hathaway heard its tracks speed up as they urgently sought purchase in the air. Meanwhile, as each thundering broadside was loosed, the battleship rocked back twelve feet to absorb the titanic recoil of her guns. It was as if the vessel had reared up like a horse.[35] A man on board likened the concussive feeling to having your chest "pushed by invisible hands" each time a gun went off.[36]

Surrounding the island like hunters warily circling a wounded, and still dangerous, animal, the *Tennessee, Nevada, New York,* and *California* had concentrated their fire on the coastal guns and beach defenses—blockhouses, pillboxes, and anti-aircraft batteries, mostly—picked out by low-flying aerial spotters. Intelligence analysts concluded, not entirely accurately, that 17 coastal guns, 16 out of 20 blockhouses, and 50 of 100 or so pillboxes—some of which turned out to be dummies—had already been destroyed in the landing zone. That left a significant number of mobile mortars, rocket launchers, mines, and artillery pieces as well as the remaining strongholds for the Marines to handle. To help, a screen of destroyers and assault vessels was currently engaged off the beach, laying down curtains of heavy suppressive fire on targets overlooked by their larger kin. In the half hour before the first wave began its run in, no fewer than eight thousand shells of various sizes slammed into Iwo Jima.[37] Like many others awed by the intensity and ferocity of the bombardment being inflicted on the island, Robert Sherrod could not help thinking, "Nobody can live through this." The landing would surely be a cakewalk, as the more optimistic souls were already predicting. But as a veteran of several harrowing amphibious assaults, Sherrod reminded himself privately, "I know better."[38]

In the meantime, the armada of landing craft formed up abreast at the Line of Departure. A control vessel was stationed at either end, and smaller ships placed along the Line marked a grid-like layout of lanes and rows. The more exalted ranks—brigadier generals and above—visited the Line to ensure that all was in order, sailing here and there, as Civil War commanders had once traveled on their horses, to exchange pleasantries with the officers and reassure the men. By 0815, the first three waves were ready. Flags snapped in the breeze. All was eerily still. The sky was bright and clear. Thanks to the unlimited visibility, Marines could see to their left the thick, wartlike, mustard-yellow volcano of Mount Suribachi and to their right the looming bluffs of the Motoyama Plateau. Iwo's "silhouette was like a sea monster with the little dead volcano for the head, and the beach area for the neck, and all the rest of it with its scrubby, brown cliffs for the body," wrote John Marquand, a *Harper's* correspondent.[39]

This sea monster seemed alive. There were menacing shrouds of grayish-black smoke clinging to its silhouette, left behind by the on-slaught of liquid fire and high explosives. Those around him, remem-bered Sergeant T. Grady Gallant, could see "that the island itself was strange, stripped bare and standing in the cold waters of the sea, its face ghostly and smeared with tans and yellows and grays and dull black."[40]

The Marines' sandy destination lay betwixt volcano and bluff, as per the preferred practice of landing midway on an island, advancing rapidly crosswise to sever it and its garrison in two, then mopping up the forces isolated at either end.[41]

At precisely 0830, the command vessel dipped its pennant. Nearly seventy armored LVTs gunned their engines and crossed the Line. As they plowed steadily through the waves, braving the whistling shells that suddenly emanated from the island, from the air they resembled water bugs trailing white-plumed wakes. Their job was to form the vanguard of the subsequent infantry waves by firing their powerful 75mm howitzers and machine guns at close range into the landing area as a *coup de grace* to the naval and air attacks that were tailing off. Then came the first infantry assault wave, transporting some 1,360 Marines. Every five minutes, so as to leave sufficient room between them, a successive wave would begin its journey. Within forty-five minutes, planners expected, nine thousand Marines would have landed in an expanding, unstoppable torrent upon the sands of Iwo Jima. Ulti-mately, there would be nearly a score of waves of flesh and steel, most carrying soldiers but others bringing heavy equipment, headquarters staff, and supplies. On their return journeys, they would ferry casual-ties.

Those involved might have been surprised to learn that, despite its modernity, Marine amphibious warfare bore distinct resemblances to nineteenth-century land tactics. The men at Iwo Jima were not so very different from their ancestors at Gettysburg, themselves similar to those who had fought at Bunker Hill. Off that tiny Pacific island in 1945, the artillery (naval gunfire and aerial strafing) softened up the enemy in preparation for the primary charge to come; then skirmishers (the first amtracs) were thrown forward to screen the main assault, probe the defenses, and disrupt the opposing line; and finally, the regiments (Marines in landing craft, organized into waves) advanced in orderly, inexorable fashion to achieve their objectives and break the enemy's will.

Marine Patrick Caruso "gazed at the others in the craft; their faces reflected the appearance of purpose, determination, seriousness, and an occasional smile. There was a definite air of exhilaration among the men. Morale was high and contagious. The feeling can best be described as that of an impatient football player sitting on the bench and eagerly waiting to be called by the coach to get into the game. Our anxiety to 'get into the game' supplanted any sense of fear. Yes, certainly there was apprehension about not knowing what to expect, but there definitely was not fear at this point—that came later."[42] There were some lighter moments to pass the time. George Wahlen and his friends watched the Corsair fighters swoop overhead and scored their pilots' prowess by how closely they approached Suribachi's slopes. When they dived daringly deeply to hit a camouflaged gun, they shouted out, "Single!" and if they pulled out gingerly to avoid counterfire, "Married!"[43]

On Dan Levin's boat, things were more muted. His "trip in was a thing of profound resignation, congealed thought, emotion searing and intense." Most enlisted men crouched, occasionally glancing over the side, while the sergeants preferred to stand up. One of the latter, Frank Krywicki, saw the craft next to theirs get hit by incoming fire but said nothing to his men.[44]

His discretion was probably for the best. When a Japanese gunner zeroed in a boat, there were rarely survivors. Sergeant John Thurman watched a landing craft to his right receive a direct hit. Blown upward, it splashed down, "taking its men with her as the amtrac disappeared below the water and leaving a whirlpool like effect. I saw what looked like a back pack and then a helmet liner spinning around in the bloody water. That's all that was left."[45] Machinist's Mate 3rd Class Albert D'Amico was horrified to see "a boat take a direct hit, thirty-six Marines plus two sailors. You didn't even see a toothpick [left] in the water." But, as at Gettysburg, there could be no stopping an advance once it started. "I kept going, and a shell would land here, a shell would land there, all around you, you didn't know where, you just kept going to the beach. You get hit, you got hit, that's all."[46]

On the Japanese side, their spirits had run high since the arrival of the fleet—despite the immense, dazing bombardment they had endured. At 0630 on February 19, antitank officer Lieutenant Sugihara Kinryu spotted American landing craft circling about two thousand yards offshore. "So, the real landing has come at last!" he exulted in his diary, with palpable relief. As part of a purification ritual to prepare for death, he changed into new underwear the army had thoughtfully provided, cleansed himself, and issued to his men the new socks and towels that had arrived the night before.[47] Other men donned the *senninbari,* a thousand-stitch cloth band that was wrapped around the stomach as a spiritual charm for good luck. Intended to ward off bullets, they did not always work.[48]

The first Marines ashore landed at 0903, three minutes past their scheduled arrival time. Nothing more than some sporadic small-arms fire and some light mortars greeted them. The Marines waiting their turn at the Line of Departure speculated that the Japanese had already evacuated, or, better still, had committed mass suicide. *This would be easy,* thought some. By 10 A.M., an entire assault battalion had landed. "On shipboard, listening to the optimistic reports, we relaxed," Alvin Josephy reported. "Then the Japs came to life."[49] They had initially held their fire to lure more troops onto the beach, which they intended to turn into a slaughterhouse. Machine guns, mortars, and artillery, everything they had, opened up mercilessly on the surprised Marines. It didn't matter: The attack must continue, come what may.

So, not long after Sugihara had steeled himself to meet death and Josephy had breathed a sigh of relief, Dan Levin "heard an abrupt violent howl and the boat lifted, then rammed forward grating and stopped with a shock. We were all hurled off our feet." They had hit the beach. Then the metal bow ramp cranked suddenly down. "A smell I imagined—but I smelled it!—of roasted and burning flesh swept into my nostrils. I leaped ashore on a new and fearful world."[50] Soon afterward, A. J. Benard, a Seabee in charge of a bulldozer being shipped in, realized that "there were so many dead men in front of the ship that there was no way for me to unload [the vehicle] without crushing their bodies. . . . I had no choice but to go over them."[51]

6. The Beach

Marines experienced the first minute or so of their time on Iwo Jima as a chaotic, vivid melee of images. Few were as fortunate as the last man out of Gerald Averill's boat, who "caught a mortar fragment in the calf of his leg before he reached the ramp. He tumbled backward into the boat, the ramp came up and was secured, the boat backed off and headed seaward. A Purple Heart, a battle star on the Asiatic-Pacific ribbon, and a free ride to the hospital ship without ever setting foot on Iwo." A million-dollar wound if ever there was one.[1]

The experience of the 27th Marines' Mike Vinich was more typical. "The ramp went down, and honest to God, the bullets came in. Many of the men were machine-gunned to death as they were exiting. I was pulling bodies of my men aside as I tried to make my way out. Blood was everywhere. It was very similar to the opening scene in *Saving Private Ryan,* but I think the fire was more concentrated at Iwo."[2]

When their amtrac disgorged, Corporal William McConnell saw the other squad leader, Corporal Paul Langford, break the rules by leading his men out to the left. Their training had emphasized alternating left and right for each man, precisely to avoid what happened next. A Japanese machine gunner merely traversed his barking weapon at chest level and every Marine but one was killed. But for this minor error, their military careers might have lasted longer than five seconds. McConnell's squad, which he had been forced to take right to avoid getting entangled with Langford's, lost no one.[3]

As they exited, Marines caught brief, brilliant flashes of extreme horror. Sergeant Gallant saw a Marine with blond, close-cropped hair who from the shoulder down had been severed precisely along his spine, leaving behind a kind of half-man. The left side was entirely gone, but its opposite was still dressed in dungarees with a complete head and neck, arm, and leg. Strung out from his remaining torso was a seemingly endless length of grayish-white intestine stretched out like a snake and coiling at Gallant's feet. When his eyes tracked its course, Gallant found the man's left chest, albeit lacking its arm and leg, lying several yards away. Marines were jumping over it as they exited their own craft.[4]

Dan Levin sought cover as rapidly as possible. He plunged through the ankle-deep water, found his footing in the sand, and "then fell forward into it, in a depression scooped out by some shell. I burrowed my body into the sand but kept glaring around, still startled and unbelieving." He realized, despite having urinated several times before leaving the troop transport, that he'd wet himself. Next to him, he was startled to discover, was a "Marine with a beautiful face and shoulders and all below the shoulders a viscous, red-shot, and dragging mess of rag." Nearby, his fellow Marines were wildly piling mangled legs and severed heads around them to use as barricades against the bullets.[5]

When Gallant looked to either side and behind him, all his overwhelmed mind could take in was a snapshot of "broken amphibious tractors, wrecked and riddled with holes, some overturned and smoking, others flooded and listing with waves breaking against them, splashing them and then running back into the deep. Out to sea were clusters of boats milling about in twos and threes, and mostly heading out to sea, though some craft were adrift, tossed by the waves and dead in the water. In these wallowing boats and amphibious tractors, sailors bailed with helmets or prepared to abandon ship as the crippled vessels shipped water and slowly sank in the swells."[6]

Despite the messy and unpleasant reality from the individual or personal perspective, on the grander scale all was proceeding according to plan. The Marine amphibious-warfare theorizing of the prewar years was being played out, almost to the minute, in what by any definition could be counted as a highly successful landing operation on a distinctly hostile shore.

Key to its continuing success was to move inland en masse to seize airfields and ground while the Japanese were still in disarray and reeling from the onslaught. Every man knew, and had been told repeatedly, to get off the beach as quickly as possible. The beach was death, to be sure, and they had to make room for the constant stream of new arrivals. Ultimately, a bare minimum of five hundred yards' depth would be required on the beachhead to squeeze in vehicle parking areas, roads, mess kitchens, supply centers, aid stations, evacuation areas, command and headquarters posts, anti-aircraft guns, reserves meeting zones, and ammunition dumps—everything needed to keep the Marines fighting elsewhere on the island.[7] In the words of one combat correspondent, "imagine a city the size of Sioux City, Iowa; Saginaw, Michigan; or Stockton, Calif., springing up in a few days and dependent for its food, water, clothing supplies (to say nothing of tons and tons of ammunition, which a city would not require) on sources entirely outside it."[8] Unfortunately, the beach itself ranged from just 150 to 500 feet deep, so it was clearly imperative that combat units move out while they still could.

Space would become a growing problem over the next few days. The more crowded the beach became, the more Marines would need to cluster together, leading to spiraling casualties as the enemy artillerymen found their marks. Allen Matthews found himself mentally repeating his trainer's warnings: *Run run run get off the beach get off the beach don't ever hole up on the beach unless it's absolutely necessary because they are sighting on the beach and they'll get you sure as hell get off the beach.*[9]

Easier said than done. Two factors militated against "getting off the beach." The first was the terrain. The "sand" of Iwo Jima was not normal beach sand; instead it was soft, black volcanic ash into which men sunk up to their calves. They moved, seemingly in slow motion, amid the bone-dry cinders; it was like trying to plod through a shifting, slippery mountain of dry beans. But at least men could move. Vehicles quickly bogged down, rendering their crews vulnerable to artillery fire and leaving the infantry without support. Robert Neiman, commanding a company of tanks, was held until the fourth wave to allow a few scouts to check whether their planned landing place could bear the weight of the machines. Hearing nothing even as the fifth wave passed by, Neiman ordered the skipper of his landing craft to head in, telling

him to beach very gently so that they could test the ground and retract
the boat if necessary. Despite his best efforts, the craft became stuck,
and Neiman drove his lead tank ("Ill Wind") down the ramp. Within
seconds, it was trapped in the ash. He and Gunnery Sergeant Johnston
got out and dug around the tracks while the driver vainly tried reversing. They had to abandon Ill Wind on the beach and reboard. After
landing somewhere else, they again had to retract. Finally, one of the
scouts, Corporal Charles Jewell, appeared and shouted that he had
found a spot where the sand would hold firm. Only there, after much
time and far from their assigned zone, could they and two other tank
units finally land and blast a way past the beach.[10]

Further hampering the Marines' progress, ahead of them about
forty feet from the surf line, lay the first of a succession of unusual
wave-cut "terraces," each ranging from 10 to 15 feet high. These provided some cover from machine-gun fire but none whatsoever from
trajectory projectiles like mortars. Worse, scaling them took the wind
out of men, already lumbered down with their heavy loads. Francis
Cockrel sprinted twenty yards off the boat to the first terrace, climbed
it, and sank, spent. "I was exhausted. Not tired; just utterly limp and
useless. It was that sand, as loose as sugar. I lay there five minutes before
I had energy to run another twenty yards and hit the stuff again."[11]

Every second that a Marine stayed in the open catching his breath,
he was under bombardment from the Japanese gunners. Sergeant Gallant likened this unenviable situation to standing on what was, in effect, a two-mile-wide street "bounded on the left by a height
comparable to a 55-story building [Mount Suribachi], and on the right
by a rise comparable to a 35-story building [Motoyama Plateau]."[12]
Their residents fired almost nonstop on the pedestrians below. Many of
the shots were not random: Allan Mortenson saw enigmatic "narrow
boards with Japanese characters on them driven vertically into the
ground" near him. It would later emerge that these were markers used
by hidden forward observers to determine accurate ranges for the gunners above.[13]

The second factor hampering rapid transit from the beach inland
was the natural temptation to stay prone, preferably in one of the hun-

dreds of holes left behind by exploding shells and mortars. In moments of mortal danger, most people tend to freeze, their minds unable to encompass the magnitude of the existing risks; it requires a deliberate, cool decision to take quick action, in this case to leave cover and move forward under fire. Doing the latter was on the face of it the more dangerous option, which made staying put even more attractive—only, however, on the face of it.

Indeed, passively sheltering on the beach was by far the most lethal thing one could do. Hunkering down by yourself in a shell hole was bad enough; charitably allowing others to share it was worse, for then a well-placed shot would kill several occupants rather than just one. Japanese observers would wait for a hole to fill up before directing fire into it to maximize casualties. Thus, John McMahon made the mistake of clustering in a shell hole with twelve others. Inevitably, a shell arrived. McMahon was the sole survivor—escaping with only a broken ankle.[14]

The baleful results were everywhere evident. Jim Craig passed a shell hole six or seven yards across in which were scattered the torsos and limbs of eight Marines. A single mortar had landed directly on them.[15] Shortly afterward, Robert Sherrod walked along the beach tallying up the bodies that had died with hideous violence: "In one shell hole there were 12 dead, in another eight, in another seven. Four corpsmen, their stretcher beside them, had perished not far from the water line."[16]

Direct hits left little behind. When Colonel Chandler Johnson was killed, "the biggest piece we could find," said Rolla Perry, "was his rib cage." Art Stanton found his collar, weirdly bloodless. Another Marine found a hand and wrist with watch attached. The watch still worked.[17] Of a Marine Jim Craig stumbled across whose hole had been hit by a mortar, "all that was left was a shoe with a foot and part of a leg still in it. The [hole] was pink and white around the sides with blood and tissue mixed in with the black volcanic ash."[18]

Whatever pieces could be found were scattered far and wide. Sherrod saw plenty of "legs and arms [lying] fifty feet away from any body."[19] Likewise, while digging a hole, Frank Walker pulled up someone's leg. His friend Tom Nichols was four feet away doing the same and excavated much of the fellow's intestines.[20] There was a lieutenant who ducked as a mortar landed nearby. When he opened his eyes, a severed finger was lying placidly beside him. Immediately, "he looked at his own hands, then examined the hands of the two men crouched beside him. All were intact. The finger belonged to one of three men in the hole fifteen yards away, whom the mortar had struck and torn into three bloody rags."[21] Some strikes resulted in utter obliteration. Of the 5,931 Marine deaths at Iwo Jima, 117 remain unaccounted for. Some of these had left absolutely no trace of their existence after artillery or mortar hits.[22] Their coffins would later be shipped home empty, with grieving relatives sensitively left none the wiser.[23]

The shrapnel flung off by indirect hits was almost as devastating. One surgeon analyzed the composition of the shrapnel he was rapidly learning about: "The smaller fragments buzzed by like swarms of angry bees. The medium-sized pieces sounded like a flock of purple grackles moving from one clump of trees to another. Some of the largest chunks were the size of dinner plates and make a soft sighing sound as they passed by. They were also clearly visible as they floated close by overhead. These large fragments could readily cut a man in half if he were to get in their way."[24] They could certainly decapitate you. When Patrick Caruso jumped into a shell crater he found a headless Marine sitting there with "a cigarette still burning between two of his fingers and a rifle in his other hand."[25] Another Marine recalled that he had just given a man a cracker when he was killed. The fragment "cut the top of his head off right above the eyes, all the way to the back of his neck, and the piece was hanging from his collar like a bucket lid."[26]

A near-miss by an explosion or shrapnel was always a shaking occurrence. Howard McLaughlin vividly recorded his experience of the last few seconds before a shell landed inches from his left foot. Amid the cacophony of battle, "everything went totally silent and there was no sound but the air passing around the shell as it fell toward me. I didn't hear the explosion till long after it hit, but I could hear the shell breaking apart from the explosion as it hit the sand. There was total silence for what seemed like two or three minutes and then I heard the crash of thunder inside my helmet, along with the wave of air and heat of the concussion."[27] After taking cover on the beach, recalled Howard Baxter, "big hunks of shrapnel were falling all over the place. I had a piece . . . that landed along the side of my shell hole. It was molten red hot—just sizzling. It just missed the whole frame of my body by about six inches. It burned itself in the sand. It was steaming, and you could almost see through it, it was so hot."[28] Allen Matthews was nearly as lucky when he was thumped by a large piece of shrapnel that was completing the end of its arc. "I felt a blow on my back, my knees buckled and I sprawled forward." He later found it lying on the ground and kept it as a souvenir, this thing that "had struck me with the force of a hard-thrown baseball."[29]

When shrapnel did not kill immediately, it left injuries that at best rendered Marines unable to serve and at worst killed them later. Two quite typical casualties were treated by the surgeon James Vedder. The first was left with a shattered face and could barely suck in a breath. Vedder cleared his airway by plunging a rat-toothed forceps down what was left of his throat and pulling out a large piece of jawbone. He wondered "how our plastic surgeons would ever restore this man's identity." The second "was sprawled on his back in a deep coma with several square inches of bone missing from the side of his head, leaving the brain covered only by the dura membranes. Another piece of shrapnel had sliced off all the upper muscles of his left shoulder." The best Vedder could do was tend him with sterile dressings, infuse plasma, and get him ready for evacuation.[30] It is unlikely that he made it home alive.

Shrapnel was not the only danger: The Japanese interspersed phosphorus shells among their high-explosive barrages. According to Howard McLaughlin, the former, exploding two hundred feet above, admittedly "looked pretty from a distance" when they "went off like big multi-legged white spiders in a Fourth of July fireworks display."[31] But then hurtling down came the shards of bright-white phosphorus, burning at a temperature that ate through clothing, skin, flesh, even bone. Exposure to air accelerated oxidation and resulted in hideous burns. Water did nothing but exacerbate the trauma, a lesson well-meaning friends often learned too late. The only way of rescuing the victim was to brush off particles using dry gauze or cotton (or to dig

them out using the point of a combat knife), then apply an oily oint-
ment like Vaseline and bandages to prevent air from further inflaming
the phosphorus.[32]

During an attack, luck determined whether one would vanish from
the earth, lose several limbs, or emerge unscathed. When the hit came,
survivors were momentarily confounded by what had just occurred.
Glen Lougee, a corpsman, was tending to Leon Justice, whose leg had
been blown off, helped by Gilman Horgan. A mortar round landed
nearby. Lougee remembered "we both turned and looked. As I turned
back, I stared into Horgan's eyes for just an instant. Then it happened.
Another mortar shell exploded close to Horgan. He disappeared, just
like that. Everything went black for me." When he returned to consciousness a few minutes later, Justice was still in a stupor but otherwise
all right. "Pieces of meat were sticking to my uniform. It wasn't mine,
nor was the blood which ran into my mouth. Leon started moaning.
Part of Horgan's trunk, a section of his disintegrated body, lay across
Leon's chest. I lifted my hands to remove it, and realized his entrails
were lashed across my arms. Feces oozed from an open end of one of
the pieces. A sharp piece of bone stuck outward from my belt. Very
slowly it dawned on me that Horgan took a direct hit from the shell."[33]

The randomness of the hits disconcerted even veterans. John
Thompson had landed at Saipan and Tinian, but the sustained mortar
barrage on Iwo was unlike anything he had previously experienced: "It
gave me the most helpless feeling in the world. The artillery shelling
was bad enough, but at least you felt you could get a fix on their shells.
Not those mortars. It was impossible to figure out where they were
coming from or going to, simply impossible."[34] Was it better to stay
where you were? Or scuttle to a new hole? Or find one that had already
been hit? Which of these was the place of greatest safety?

Much of the time, despite their training, soldiers just stayed put, for
the storm of steel and high explosives breaking over their heads on the
beach was numbing. While the mortars "whistled like ghouls just overhead," recalled Dan Levin, beneath Alvin Josephy the ground literally
shook: "It was as if a man were lying on a bouncing beach."[35] In just
one minute, Robert Sherrod counted a furious tattoo of no fewer than

twenty explosions within fifty yards of him.[36] Such was their elevated stress that men unconsciously ground their teeth, clamping down especially hard whenever a shell exploded. They were left to wonder hours later why their teeth hurt so much.[37] Adrenaline- and fear-triggered thirst afflicted everyone. Allen Matthews was possessed by a "compelling desire for a drink of water, for my mouth was so dry that gum which I had been chewing suddenly adhered to my teeth and to my gums and to my tongue and to my lips." Soon his blood was pumping so hard "that I could feel my temples expand and contract within the fatigue cap which I wore under my helmet."[38]

An overwhelming onslaught of potent sensory stimulants paralyzed men into inaction. "Surrounded by a crescendo of whistling mortars, artillery shells, and whirring rockets, all followed by thundering blasts," Bertram Yaffe simply froze. It took the screams that followed to startle him into motion.[39] Any number of others, however, remained stunned and subjugated into submission. Some men sat, said Yaffe, "with haunting, vacant stares—the hollow men, rigid in the benumbed silence of combat fatigue. They don't bother to dive for cover. I touch a shoulder, open a canteen, help light a cigarette, but I don't linger. I want to get on with my job. It's easier that way."[40] He knew that they were sitting ducks, but everyone had been ordered not to stop to help wounded or helpless men. Lending a hand slowed the assault's momentum, tied up riflemen of greater utility in the front lines, hampered the medics, and, as a practical matter, caused the kind of "bunching up" or clustering that Japanese observers were keeping a keen eye out for.[41] Helping a lost soul, in other words, could not help but lose more.

Others exhibited more extreme symptoms. Two hours after the first wave had landed, ships began receiving the first psychiatric casualties. Robert Sherrod saw one "screaming at the top of his voice and twisting violently in his stretcher."[42] A man, already lying wounded, was sent into hysteria when a shell burst nearby, observed Sergeant Gallant. "Then he opened his mouth as wide as he could. His eyes were staring and fixed upon the sky, his forehead deeply furrowed and his eyebrows lifted, pulling at his eyelids, almost. He sat this way—taut and stiff and straining every muscle of his body. He sat, his mouth wide open, stretched white at the sides . . . and screamed . . . and screamed . . . and screamed."[43]

The nightmarish quality of the beach in the initial hours was exacerbated by the unexpected number of wounded. Planners had forecast a high casualty rate, but not as steep as this. For the entire battle, planners had predicted an 18 percent casualty rate.[44] Yet on D-Day alone, *a single day,* fully 8 percent (2,420) of the thirty thousand men who landed would be killed or wounded. The potential implications of a *months*-long battle on the cumulative casualty total were horrifying.[45] As it was, the hospital ships and transports were overwhelmed. Len Maffioli was aboard the USS *Sanborn,* and there were "at least a dozen landing craft circling our ship and requesting that we take their wounded. We couldn't help them because our sick bay was already full. The tables in the officers' wardroom were being used as operating tables, and the wardroom and passageways were jammed with casualties on stretchers."[46]

On the beach, corpsmen hurriedly patched up wounded Marines as best they could and, if they could walk, directed them toward the water, hoping that someone would help them back to a ship. Otherwise, they were on their own. When Edward Jones came across a Marine with his right eye hanging from its socket, he pushed it back in as best he could, shot him with morphine, scrawled a large red M on his forehead (to prevent accidental overdoses), pointed out where he should go, and moved on to the next patient.[47]

Slowly, inexorably, nevertheless, the Marines inched forward. Hole by hole, they advanced closer and closer to and then over the terraces. Movement began for two related reasons. The first was that senior officers, as they had done at Bunker Hill and Gettysburg, visibly behaved as if everything was under control and remained resolutely imperturbable. When Greeley Wells landed, he followed everyone else in leaping into a shell hole and staying put. But then he saw Colonel Harry B. Liversedge and Lieutenant Colonel Robert H. Williams striding up the beach "as if they were in the middle of a parade." One had a riding crop, "which he was slapping on the side of his leg, and both of them were urging us on, saying, 'Get up! Get off the damn beach!' It was an amazing thing. They walked the length of that doggone beach yelling at the men, and the Marines just did it—they got right up and started to move. Of course it jarred me as well, and I got up, and we got over the high ground."[48] Francis Cockrel later saw Liversedge acting so coolly that "I thought that things couldn't be very bad. I guess the sight of him helped a lot of other guys too."[49]

The stirring sight of colonels and the like acting as if everything was proceeding precisely according to schedule convinced the worried, panicked Marines that the chaos was surmountable, that there was "a Plan," that if they followed orders, adhered to their training, and paid attention to their superiors, all would be well. There was a logic to the madness enveloping them, it seemed. As a result, the initial kinetic and sensory shock began to wear off, psychiatric stress decreased, and experience kicked in.[50]

Booze helped, too. Though alcohol was not widely available, medical personnel had access to extraordinarily potent medicinal brandy. One Marine, feeling increasingly nervous, downed a refreshing two-ounce bottle a friendly doctor had given him and felt much better.[51] Corpsman Edward Jones had been entrusted by a Dr. Collins with a duffel bag containing fifty such servings. While under shellfire he drank one. "It smoothed everything out for me. It calmed anxiety and restored reason."[52]

Critical to survival was learning how to sense when shelling was least likely and to move in tandem with its ebbs. Mortars were not quite so random as originally imagined. Like anyone else, their Japanese operators followed predictable rhythms and routines. John Lardner estimated that "it seems to take about twenty minutes under shellfire to adjust your nerves and evolve a working formula by which you can make progress and gauge, very roughly, the nearness of hits and the pattern of fire." Once you had mastered this trick, you realized the folly and danger of "wishful pinned-down thinking" (Lardner's term for staying in a hole and hoping you were safe).[53]

To that end, Bertram Yaffe had learned at Bougainville and Guam how to tell when "the whistling is headed in my direction. I dive under a disabled tank or hug a revetment. If the interval between bursts shortens, I move on quickly. It means they have zeroed in on that spot."[54] Similarly, another Marine veteran knew that if a shell was low and about to hit the earth, it made a "tearing sound"; if it was high but descending quickly, it had a "rushing, ghostly cry"; and if "it is absolutely safe, very high and very fast, it [left] behind it a *whish-whish-whishing* sound."[55] Ray Miller, a neophyte, was nevertheless fortunate enough to land in the same shell hole as Gunnery Sergeant Joe Whalen, who had survived several battles. He advised Miller to watch the planes overhead. They would come in to strafe and when they dropped napalm on gun emplacements the firing would let up for between ten and fifteen seconds. That was the cue to run to the next shell hole.[56]

When they finally surmounted the terraces, Marines were subjected to withering fire from the myriad of blockhouses, bunkers, and pillboxes waiting for them. For Stanley Dobrowski, "everything fell apart. It was just mass confusion. The thing I noticed immediately was the tremendous amount of noise, concussion, small-arms fire, explosions of artillery and mortar shells." "That's when the Japs opened up with everything they had," recalled Ray Jacobs. "I mean everything. The din of all those different-caliber weapons, the blasts of the shells, it was just incredible."[57]

Once they got their bearings, though, the slog was easier than on the beach. There was now little risk of being pushed back into the sea, and the way forward to their objectives was clear. Taking an active role in demolishing pillboxes and other Japanese emplacements, no matter how dangerous, was better than waiting passively for a mortar round to kill you. Whereas on the beach units had instantly atomized into individuals desperately scrabbling for a hole in the ground, once they were over the terraces Marines began to find their comrades and crystallized back into distinct squads and platoons reporting to a familiar chain of command.

On the plains above the beach, even the artillery bombardments seemed more "rational," if still terrifying. Marines could look up and watch, as at a tennis match, the naval and Japanese gunners exchanging fire. Both sides used coherent rolling artillery barrages, the kind recognized by Robert Leader, who had never experienced one before but was sharing a crater with a sergeant who had, "as a work of devilish crafts-manship. It was so well executed that the sergeant could predict the arrival and impact point of each shell as the gunners moved the barrage back and forth and up and down over our position."[58] Rolling barrages were easily survivable—even enjoyable to an extent, because they re-stored a sense of predictability to the battlefield after the chaotic ran-domness of the beach—unless you happened to be directly underneath one. Lieutenant Jim Craig was in a hole with his men about 75 yards inland when he saw a telltale series of explosions 200 yards ahead. The next salvo came 100 yards closer. Then the third landed in front of them but hurt no one. The next was behind them. It was over.[59] They had nothing to fear from the American retort, which began its own "heavy steps inland, two hundred yards at a stride, crashing and thun-dering and tearing with burning, metallic hands" as it advanced toward the Japanese defenders.[60]

Very few Marines had actually seen a Japanese. There had been some expendable troops on the beach, lucklessly assigned to manning anti-aircraft guns, machine guns, and the like, who had been rapidly eliminated. Early on, for instance, Jay Rebstock had scrambled from his LVT to find, sited twenty feet directly in front of him, a fire pit. His comrades soon clubbed the occupants to death with their rifles.[61] Dan Levin even found one of the sacrificed enemy in an embrace of sorts with a dead Marine. "Each had been torn away except for the head and some entrails—the Japanese boy by our shelling, the American boy later by Japanese shell or mortar fire. The two helmeted heads lay fac-ing each other, with such pained and soulful expressions on the two faces that I could hardly bear to look. Their entrails curled around and their ends met, twining about each other."[62]

These doomed beach defenders would be the last Japanese most Marines would see for some time. Over the next while, for instance, Rebstock would encounter precisely one of the enemy, a lone soldier who suddenly charged him at full pelt from out of nowhere. He mowed him down with his trusty BAR.[63]

Frustration at this invisible enemy, the one hammering them with impunity, sometimes boiled over. When a Japanese soldier was briefly glimpsed in the distance, said Howard McLaughlin, men would "stand up, holler and shout like kids at a football game, with everybody firing at him as if he was a duck in the shooting gallery at a county fair."[64]

The most curious, if discomfiting, thing about the Japanese was not their invisibility during combat—their tactic of holing up in bunkers, pillboxes, and tunnels was well known—but the lack of dead bodies. It seemed to Marines that, despite their best efforts, the immense fire-power at their command, and the liberal, even wanton, shedding of their own blood, hardly any Japanese were being killed. When Guy Rowe landed in the evening of D-Day and strode inland, he saw stacks of piled bodies. He was cheered that "we sure killed a lot of Japanese"— until he realized they were wearing Marine dungarees.[65] No enemy uniforms were to be seen. Richard Nummer, a corporal, estimated that "for every dead Jap, I seen twenty-five dead marines easy."[66]

On the larger scale, Jim Craig's battalion would suffer 20 percent casualties over the course of the first three days, for instance, but inflicted, *at least as it appeared,* none, since resistance remained unvacillating.[67] They felt as if they were fighting a phantom war. Indeed, by the third day, as a whole the Marines had suffered 5,300 casualties and yet could account for just 600 Japanese.[68] Air observers overhead reported the strange phenomenon of seeing thousands of moving figures in one half of the battlefield and none on the other.[69]

Understandably, morale among Marines fell quite precipitously in the days following the landing, particularly once they began noticing the Meat Wagons. Combat reporters did not send dispatches home about these gruesome vehicles for fear, as one put it, that relating "total battlefield truth could injure morale" among the civilian population.[70] But every Marine was familiar with them. Operated by Graves Registration units, these vehicles picked up the dead and transported them back to the collection points and cemeteries already sprouting up.

No one spoke when they were near. Frank Crowe watched as the Graves people, wearing heavy rubber gloves reaching to their armpits as well as black rubber aprons, stopped their trucks and carefully laid the slain on the flatbeds. "Of course, there was also a detached arm or leg here, a head there, and half a torso somewhere else. These, too, were gathered and placed in the truck."[71] Ernest Moreau noted that "this one dead Marine . . . was just like a baked potato. Two men went to pick him up, and the bones came right out of his arms. Just like a chicken that's overdone."[72] Stanley Bryan recalled the body fluids that were "oozing out and sometimes you'd see gorgeous blond hair on this black face of some 18-year-old kid—and millions of flies, billions of flies."[73] When Pfc. John Thurman saw a convoy of three trucks trundle slowly across the broken terrain, he could see "five layers of dead Marines laying crosswise over each other; it was hard to tell how many Marines there were. There were bodies that were badly torn up with legs and arms missing, or half of a body left and the smell was suffocating." The first two trucks bore bodies and the last "the legs and arms, but [they were] chunks of meat and flesh you could not make out and these parts were stacked and mixed in a pile not knowing who they belong to."[74]

Given the depressing one-sidedness of the casualty count, Marines naturally began to wonder whether Iwo Jima was a defeat in the making. The words of Tokyo Rose, broadcast to much mockery on the voyage out, came back to Ken Cosbey and now seemed more tragic than comic: "Good morning, 4th Division, I understand you are headed for Iwo Jima. The week after you land you can hold your roll call in a phone booth."[75]

The decline in morale proved short-lived, as the mystery of the absent bodies was soon solved. The Japanese, it emerged, had been venturing out, usually at night, and hauling their dead back to their bolt-holes. Investigating one site of a recent firefight, where he knew there would be corpses, John Thurman found only Japanese shoe prints and drag marks.[76] The mass dumping grounds would eventually be found once Marines, said Anthony Visconti, "got into the caves" pockmarking the island. "You've never smelled anything like it. There were hundreds of decaying corpses."[77] Soon after landing, for instance, Len Maffioli and his friend John "Hook" Grant noticed a cave entrance and decided, rather foolishly, to explore it. The cave opened up into a large room carved out of sandstone. In a corner a ramp led down to another room the same size, ten feet below. Then another ramp led down about fifty feet into another large space, this one packed with the bloated, stinking carcasses of Japanese soldiers. They left in a hurry after hearing voices wafting up from a still lower level.[78] Since the secret to the Japanese vanishing act was now known, there was no attempt to catalogue the dead or tote a body count. Instead, the cave was rapidly "sealed" with explosive, trapping all, alive and dead, within. The Japanese efforts to hide their dead lasted less than a week, for by that time they were on the run. From then on, corpses were simply left behind to rot in the sun.

Some of these "corpses" were not, however, dead. They were wounded men feigning death and holding grenades to kill unwary Marines or to blow up a vehicle. Saturo Omagari was one such, along with three or four comrades who sliced open their own slain, daubed themselves in the congealing blood, and stuffed their uniforms with unraveled intestines. Omagari, who miraculously survived the battle, hoped to gain glory by destroying a Sherman tank and had to try "hard to remain calm, clenching my teeth to avoid nausea" as he lay among the bodies.[79] Elsewhere, remembered Corporal Richard Nummer, when you were on burial duty you had "to watch out there wasn't a Jap among 'em waiting for us, with a rifle or grenade, whatever they could find."[80] (The trick sometimes backfired: Ray Crowder saw two dead Japanese dressed in Marine uniforms who had shot each other by accident.)[81]

Despite Kuribayashi's assurance to Imperial Headquarters that such sacrifices caused "great damage to American tanks and forces," the truth is that, like hiding bodies, this tactic succeeded only for a short time before Marines began taking effective countermeasures.[82] In this case, the solution was brutally straightforward: "Shoot their dead to be sure they were," as Robert Leader put it. While he "found this *coup de grace* repulsive," it had to be done.[83] Every time corpses were discovered, either in overrun pillboxes or simply lying around, what was known as a "possum patrol" would shoot each one several times. "It was cheap insurance—a bullet only costs a dime," as one Marine explained.[84]

In his entire time on Iwo, George Nations could recall seeing just one dead Japanese with but a single bullet hole in him.[85]

7. The Nights

The Marines' conquest of Iwo Jima was executed strictly by day; the night they yielded to the Japanese. Every dusk, then, the Marines ceased operations and hunkered down along the line in their foxholes.

Of central concern to American units was "tying in" to the ones on either side of them in order to form a straight line across their assigned area. This desire to close gaps in the defensive perimeter and to link up with neighbors began at the division level and continued down successively through the regiment, battalion, company, platoon, squad, and finally, individual foxhole level. There was nothing more dangerous than being left too far forward of the line at nightfall, if, or rather when, the Japanese attacked.

In previous operations, the Japanese had mounted mass banzai charges on the first night of an invasion, and on Iwo Marines accordingly prepared for one—only to be left bewildered when the enemy never appeared, as bewildered, indeed, as when the first wave to hit the beach had encountered paltry counterfire. The actions of the Japanese on Iwo Jima were becoming ever more enigmatic. On other islands, they had emphasized the banzai frontal assault to break through a weak spot on a nascent Marine line. Over the coming weeks on *this* island, such attacks would be exceptionally rare. Instead, Marines would cope with small-scale "cutting-in attacks," as the Japanese dubbed them, by infiltrators hoping to create a sense of insecurity behind the lines by sniping opportunistically at random soldiers and sabotaging arms dumps. One remarkably successful effort resulted in a huge explosion at a 4th Division dump as two boatloads of flamethrower fuel, gas, and ammunition went up.

The nocturnal spate of cutting-in attacks wore on Marines to a greater degree than a single, all-out banzai assault at the beginning of an operation. Although banzais were initially terrifying, any satisfactorily tied-in unit could deal with them easily enough: Coordinated machine guns squirting bullets at close range would leave hundreds of Japanese dead and wounded in short order. On Iwo, there were a few attempts to organize banzais, but these were minor piecemeal threats, quickly extinguished. Thus, when Howard Snyder and his squad were facing a trench containing a number of Japanese they could hear were becoming more excited, as if whipping themselves up into a fury before launching a final, diehard bid for glory, he and Harold Keller merely lobbed in grenade after grenade while James Robeson and Louie Adrian used their BARs to cut down anyone who emerged. Eventually, all went silent and that was the end of that.[1]

This is not to say that infiltration tactics were of much use, however. Kuribayashi was forced to report to Tokyo by the beginning of March that "the look-out American forces became very strict and it is difficult to pass through their guarded line. Don't overestimate the value of cutting-in attacks," he advised.[2] As Kuribayashi indicated, because Marines actively learned from experience and improved their defensive methods, over the course of the battle these stealth attacks dramatically declined in frequency, skill, and scale. A battalion of the 28th Marines, for instance, counted seventy-five bodies lying outside its perimeter very early on, but in coming weeks there would be just a handful.[3] The introduction of star shells, which brightly illuminated the deep Pacific dark, was particularly advantageous: One Marine, frustratedly trying to fight off invisible Japanese, was saved when a star shell went up and outlined a dozen of them running through a ravine. "They looked like little devils running through the gates of Hell," he said. "All they needed were pitchforks."[4] Another important factor was the sheer magnitude of Marine firepower that could be rapidly applied in an emergency. On March 9 (D+18), for instance, the Japanese launched a powerful attack on the joint tying in two regiments. A single company there lavishly burned through 500 grenades, 200 rounds of 60mm mortars, and 20,000 rifle and machine-gun rounds in exterminating the enemy. Within twenty-four hours, much of the ordnance had been replaced.[5]

Marine defensive proficiency reached such a pitch that some Americans, like Allen Matthews, began to prefer night actions to daylight operations. When the sun was up, he argued, the enemy vanished and Marines were "charged with routing him out of emplacements we seldom saw until we were fired on." When the moon was up, conversely, the Japanese had to come to them, and Marines quickly understood "that the enemy was not superhuman, that he possessed no special faculties for night vision, and that consequently when we were alert we almost always saw him before he saw us."[6]

As Matthews conceded, one had to stay frosty to keep winning. Despite their improving abilities, Marines did not, or could not, relax their guard, for, no matter how infrequent, when an infiltration was attempted, it happened without warning and could be very messy. For this reason, without fail the very first things Marines did when the sun began its descent was to check the immediate area for anyone, as Frank Caldwell put it, who might "give us some trouble at night." They would peer into holes and investigate suspicious terrain to make sure no one was hiding there. They took no chances—with good reason. When Caldwell and some others noticed a pile of rocks lying against a six-foot rise they threw a phosphorus grenade among them. "All of a sudden those rocks parted, and out comes a Japanese soldier just reeking with smoke. His uniform was on fire. Tears were coming out of his eyes. I could even see that, I was so close to him. He had one of those Japanese grenades in his hand. He was in the process of throwing that as a last resort right amongst us. He got it away, but we dodged it, and we proceeded to mow him down." Curious about him, Caldwell removed his helmet and found a family photo tucked inside featuring his wife and six "cute-looking little children." He was otherwise anonymous.[7]

Afterward, Marines dug a line of foxholes, each about ten yards from each other. A regulation foxhole was designed to accommodate two men—three at a pinch—and was six feet long, three deep, and four wide.[8] The dimensions varied depending on soil and laziness, but a foxhole either too deep or shallow was asking for trouble. Once done, the next step was to site the machine guns properly. Squads and platoons could call on a few water-cooled heavy machine guns and several lighter air-cooled ones that needed setting up to interlock their fields of fire "in a solid wall right down the line," according to Corporal Glenn Buzzard.[9]

Specialist machine gunners escorted the heavies, which weighed 98 pounds and were transported by Jeep but could fire their powerful .50-caliber ammunition almost ceaselessly thanks to a large water tank that prevented the mechanism and barrel from overheating. Regular Marines handled the .30-caliber lights and were ordered to hold their fire until they saw at least five Japanese attacking. Any fewer than that and riflemen could do the job. It was an order honored more in the breach than the observance, for every Marine detailed to man a light machine gun immediately inserted an ammo belt and cocked twice to ready it to fire at the touch of a finger.[10]

Nevertheless, all realized the importance of not wantonly revealing one's positions, so gunners assiduously devoted themselves to stripping out every tracer bullet from their freshly issued ammunition belts.[11] The Marine Corps had considerately made every fifth bullet in a belt a tracer that tore bright streaks in the night to allow men to see where they were firing. Unfortunately, the Japanese could then also see where they were firing from. In the event, the most useful weapon was not a gun at all but a grenade. Since a muzzle flash of any kind served as a homing beacon for the enemy directly to your foxhole, it was far better to toss grenades and avoid revealing their source.

Trip wires, noisemakers, and barbed wire were set up beyond the defensive line as early warning signals. Much of the time these did not work as well as a few dozen pairs of eyes and ears nervously scanning for anything out of the ordinary, as the Japanese were dab hands at crawling silently, avoiding silhouettes, and camouflaging themselves against blackened backdrops. Bayonets were wrapped in rags to prevent their glinting; likewise boot soles to muffle footfalls. Barbed wire, in any case, was easily dug under using a scoop, though in one instance some enterprising Marines neutralized the problem by sprinkling grenades around to "go off like booby traps" if the wire was disturbed. "Blew hell out of the Japs," grunted their sergeant.[12] Another relatively effective technique was to string a length of cord between the holes so that if a sentry saw a Japanese soldier, or even thought he saw one, he would "jerk it five times or more—just pull like hell—to let them know what's up" along the rest of the line while noiselessly safeguarding one's location.[13] It was, however, rather more common to start firing to let everyone know as unmistakably as possible that an attack was in the offing.

With these basics completed, the men settled down into their foxholes and started their nightly routine. First things first: Weapons needed cleaning. Iwo's powdery sand fouled and clogged guns at a frightening rate, a systematic problem that military planners had failed to predict. In Dave Davenport's platoon, rifles regularly misfired and machine guns often loosed just a single round before jamming. Before setting off on a mission, everyone would snap off a few shots to make sure their rifles were working.[14] A malfunctioning gun was, of course, no minor issue: Corporal Bill Faulkner described one action against a bunker that almost led to the deaths of several comrades. Led by Lieutenant Wesley Bates, the patrol had damaged the structure when "some wounded Japs came charging around the bunker. We tried to fire but our weapons were jammed with sand. I finally got off a round. The Japs turned and ran right into a machine gun we had set up to cover the attack. We moved around to the front of the bunker and found several Japs, all wounded but jabbering and trying to pull the pins of grenades. Bates tried his Japanese on them, asking them to surrender, but no luck. Five or six guys tried to shoot them, but all [their] rifles were jammed. Finally a rifle began to work, and the job was done."[15]

When they could, Marines prudently threw away useless weapons and picked up new ones as they came along. Corporal Frank Walker was probably quite typical in that in four days he went through ten carbines, five or six Garands, and several flamethrowers.[16] There were pickings galore if the troops were either in the field (where they could grab guns left behind by the dead and wounded) or visiting an arms collection area (where they were issued recycled ones collated from the same source). Marines preparing to spend the night in their foxholes, however, had to make do. A man's most valuable possession in that instance was a toothbrush—not for its intended use but for scouring sand out of his rifle.[17]

Personal care came next. Since Iwo lacked fresh water (as Japanese supplies diminished they became increasingly desperate to steal it), barrels were shipped from Hawaii, and it inevitably tasted metallic. Stale, too, as their initial supply had been canned seven weeks before, and there would be times when gasoline cans had been reused, lending the contents a distinctive taste. If they were lucky, Marines were given a packet of hot-chocolate powder that they could stir in using their combat knives (which served also as spoons and forks). More often, there was coffee powder, and Marines were justly envious of those in the demolitions squad or the combat engineers, as their perks included free access to C2 explosives. They would find three fist-sized rocks on which to balance an upturned helmet discarded by someone less fortunate, pour in a pint of water with the coffee, and place a golf-ball–sized chunk of C2 underneath. Burning at white heat, the C2 boiled the water in less than twenty seconds.[18] The king of beverages on Iwo Jima, however, was pineapple juice, a rare taste of the tropics that arrived in a four-gallon can issued at the behest of a quartermaster—sometimes with the aid of a bribe. It was invariably guzzled immediately.[19]

While the Japanese soldiery survived on occasional handfuls of rice, the Marine diet was sufficient to keep immediate hunger at bay and to provide scientifically determined minimums of nutrition, even if it was later found that there were not sufficient calories in each meal to sustain a combat soldier for more than five days (hence the dramatic weight loss among Marines on Iwo; William Hurza, for instance, weighed 180 pounds on D-Day and 145 a month later.)[20] There was just enough variety in the official K-ration to avoid complete monotony. Foxhole-bound Marines opening the waxed cardboard box would find two packages of hard biscuits, a small metal container holding one of three types of "spread" (some kind of repulsive eggy concoction, cheese, or minced meat), some sweets, coffee or powdered grape "juice," and a pack of four cigarettes. The rations were hardly luxurious, but they were better, as Sergeant Ray Miller pointed out, than what a lot of the men were used to at home, including himself. Sometimes "there was maybe enough time for a piece of candy, some coffee . . . , and a pleasant after-dinner cigarette," he enthused. "Boy, this was livin'!"[21]

Given their diet, Marines were constipated for most of their time on Iwo. Howard McLaughlin was typical in defecating just once a week or every ten days. Part of the popularity of the Marine Corps pineapple juice was that it acted as an instant, if quite violent, laxative. After weeks of K-rations, Ray Miller was ecstatic when a pal gave him some. "This was delicious," he exclaimed. "How good to taste fruit again; such refreshing sweetness." And very soon afterward, with an unfortunate degree of bad timing, his insides began to churn just as a Japanese barrage began. But he had no choice: He "pulled 'em down fast, and added my own contribution to the chorus of artillery. . . . I ate no pineapple again for forty years."[22]

Contributing to the endemic bowel blockage was that, once ensconced in their foxholes, Marines were loath to risk exiting them. If there was any daylight remaining, they could come under sniper fire as they squatted; if Japanese mortars were falling, leaving the safety of a foxhole was madness; and if one simply had to do one's business outside at night, the others did not say, "We'll see you" or "Take it easy," but "Keep a tight asshole."[23] At night, too, it was easy to get lost trying to find your way around. One Marine became disoriented in the pitch black and ended up walking in front of his own line; he was mistaken for an infiltrator and killed by an alert sentry.[24] Provided one's foxholemate was amenable, of course, it was preferable to dig a deep hole at one end and "cover [it] like a cat," remembered Gerald Averill.[25] But it would be you who had to sleep on top of it.[26] As for urinating, that, too, was dealt with by digging a sump hole and filling it with earth. But to avoid being shot in the head by a sniper, you never stood up to do it; you lay on your side and aimed as best you could.[27]

When night fell, the two-man teams in each foxhole divvied up sentry duty. Each Marine took one hour on, one hour off, and so on until the next morning. Until lights out, the men would chat back and forth, about mostly innocuous matters. If, as they say, there were no atheists in foxholes—though this cliché is quite inaccurate; on Iwo there were plenty—neither was there much deep philosophizing or many spiritual crises to overcome. A journalist, walking the line of foxholes, wrote down the snippets of conversation he overheard. They included: "Huh! I got seven letters today . . . and an ad from a roller-skating rink in L.A."; "Reckon they'll banzai tonight. 'Bout time for a big one"; "Had some coffee today. Feel like a million now"; "My wife's birthday comes this month . . . she's eighteen"; "You shoulda heard those Nips yelling last night. When they sealed up that cave, they hollered and squealed all night"; and "Let's hit the sack. It's seven o'clock."[28]

At about 7 o'clock, then, one man would bunk down as best he could at the far end of the foxhole. Because it was cold, he wrapped a poncho around himself (usually over his head, as well), which provided the additional benefit of creating a "tent" for having a cigarette. The exuded smoke was believed to keep you warm.[29] His rifle stood next to him—upright, of course, to reduce the risk of dirt entering the mechanism and barrel.[30] Grenades were always within easy reach, and often he grasped a combat knife. Many men kept a .45-caliber pistol handy as well. The rifle and grenades were for fending off a sneak attack; the knife and pistol were for hand-to-hand fighting in the foxhole.

As the one dozed, the other set up his position. Several grenades were lined up on a dug-out "shelf" below the parapet, each primed for instant use by pulling the safety pin halfway free. A knife was stuck into the sand. Several ammunition magazines were carefully lined up next to the grenades. And then came night.

Sentry duty was generally tedious. Smoking at least relieved the boredom and provided a way of keeping awake, even if officers issued severe reprimands if they saw or heard a cigarette being lit. Dave Davenport used to check whether the coast was clear of superiors, spread out his poncho, and wait for a flare or star shell to go up. Then he used a Zippo to light up underneath the poncho. "If the lighted cigarette is cupped carefully and the smoker bends below ground level to puff, using the light of a newly opened flare it is safe enough. Perhaps not safe and sound—but anyway safe." Everyone did it.[31]

Another method to keep one's eyes open until the end of the shift was to think about a succession of almost random things. Patrick Caruso, for instance, speculated about what his brothers were doing (both were fighting in other theaters) and how his sister was. He mused over how before Iwo going on dates, making the football team, and doing well in exams had been so important but now seemed merely quaint relics of a previous life. For those who found such reminders of home and peace too maudlin, a well-known trick was to "focus on a trivial thought or perform an exercise." In Caruso's case, he would compile a list of the various possible functions of his helmet: as a bucket to wash clothes, a pail to catch rainfall, a bowl for shaving, a basin for washing, a spade to dig a foxhole, a seat, a pot over a fire, and even protection from bullets.[32]

Generally through sheer fatigue, a sentry would sometimes fall asleep. This was the greatest crime conceivable on Iwo Jima, for the man who drifted off was placing not just his and his foxhole mate's lives but the lives of the entire line at risk. Sentries accordingly glanced to their left and right to make sure they could see a bobbing or moving helmet, indicating wakefulness, in the neighboring foxholes, but it was often difficult to tell in the dark.[33] Once, Corporal William McConnell was shaken by his friend Tipton, who told him that Malotte next door was asleep. McConnell looked over and said he wasn't. Both men checked several times, not quite able to decide. It eventually turned out that Malotte had fallen asleep kneeling against the wall with his head and torso perfectly upright.[34]

Such miscreants were roundly abused, humiliated, and insulted. When a foxhole pal of Allen Matthews passed the word along to the next hole along that a counterattack was imminent but received no acknowledgment, he rightly suspected that its occupants were asleep. He strode angrily across and bawled them out, brandishing the grenade that he swore he would throw in there the next time it happened.[35] Punishment was not restricted to harsh words and threats. No one wanted to share a foxhole with a man who had fallen asleep, and each night offenders from up and down the line were forced to hole in together until they had redeemed themselves.[36]

The primary role of the sentry was, of course, to watch for possible infiltrators and the warning signs of a banzai. Theoretically, anyone moving in front of the line was an enemy and must be shot immediately, but sentries enjoyed a little discretion, particularly if it was still a little light outside and the wounded still needed bringing in. Passwords were used without fail to weed out Japanese infiltrators. They changed nightly. Sometimes they were states and capitals; at other times, American automobile makers; and at still others, cities. The presumption was that the Japanese might conceivably know one or two examples offhand but certainly not five recited rapidly in a row. Thus, all along the line you would hear repeated cries of "Chicago, Louisville, Atlanta, New Orleans, San Diego" or "Buicks, Studebakers, Fords, Chevrolets, Chryslers" as corpsmen and litter-bearers came in from the cold.[37]

Depending on the unit, there were variations on the theme. In Richard Wheeler's, the sentry would challenge with one car make and expect to hear another in return.[38] In another, the sentry would cry "President" and the visitor had to reply with the name of one.[39] Being clever and answering with one of the more obscure occupants of the Oval Office was asking for trouble. Abe Levine of Brooklyn, evidently a man not overly conversant with antebellum history, nearly shot a Marine who supplied "Fillmore." Levine's rule of thumb was that "when you give me the password, you give me Roosevelt, Washington, or Lincoln. Them's the only presidents I remember."[40]

The Japanese soon learned most of these simple-to-guess passwords (or eavesdropped from close by), and some—much to the surprise of many Marines—were quite proficient in mimicking an American accent. Some overcame the shibbolethic inability to pronounce "r" and "l," though this was very rare, and failed attempts resulted in death. Marines like Pfc. Thomas Farkas adapted by demanding two car makes, for example, in quick demand-and-response succession (one of which had to be "Chevrolet," which usefully contained both an "r" and an "l") or resorted to passwords like "lemon," "lanolin," and "yellow."[41] After several corpsmen were murdered going to the aid of wounded men—who turned out to be Japanese ambushers—crying "Corpsman, corpsman," medics like Milton Gertz advised Marines to call for them using the code word "Tallulah."[42] More securely still, a Marine would shout "rotten" and want to hear "lemons" back. Only a natural English speaker could match the proper adjective-noun combination and pronounce it properly.[43]

As the Marines advanced up the island, the use of passwords on the front line would decline precipitously.[44] There, because no one was sufficiently mad to patrol too far ahead and risk being left isolated at night in the badlands, any moving object was assumed to be Japanese. Corporal Al Abbatiello laid out the simple principle: On the line, "nobody got out of that hole after dark. If there was anybody walking around, and it was dark, you shot him. That's the way it went."[45]

The pressures of sentry duty often caused one's sight and hearing to play tricks. One Marine recalled that there inevitably came a moment when you realized that all noise had ceased: "Suddenly you can hear movement and scraping sounds from every depression and rock pile around you. Nights like that can take hundreds of hours to end." Sometimes, simply to break the silence, a sentry would fire a few rounds or lob a grenade in order to spook others into action.[46]

More often, jittery sentries began firing at phantom infiltrators because their eyes told them that they were lurking amongst the shrubs, behind the rocks, and under the wire ahead of them. (They well could have been: Japanese soldiers were trained to scout to within thirty yards of enemy positions without being detected.)[47] Allen Matthews was absolutely convinced that an innocent bush concealed "the form of a squatting man" and that nearby tufts of grass were crawling with Japanese. The steam rising from the sulfurous rocks conjured up visions of murderous figures emerging from the penumbra. Abbatiello confided that "I shot more steam than I did anything else" at night on Iwo Jima.[48]

Adding to the confusion were the startling, blinding shifts from dark to light. The Marines' world was either an inky, impenetrable black or suddenly filled with eerie greenish or sickly yellow light when a star shell or flare burst. At first, it was as if a flashbulb had gone off directly in your eyes, and sentries had to adjust quickly. Suspended from parachutes, the shells rocked back and forth as they floated languidly to earth, "making the shadows around the rocks and debris ahead of you constantly change shape and size. Is that the silhouette of a man you see along the side of that pile of rocks? You look away to the side for a second to clear your vision and now that 'man' had moved." The only way to keep one's bearings was to not concentrate on a fixed spot as the light descended, but at the same time, not to allow the eyes to move too much. Otherwise, your imagination would run wild and convince you that the Japanese were sneaking forward to slit your throat. Better, instead, to rely on peripheral vision to detect movement.

The optimum method, Marines learned, was to "turn your whole head slowly from side to side to side, starting with the ground closest to you and working outward till the flare goes out."[49]

No matter who was asleep and who on guard, everyone was permanently on edge. Land crabs, one of the island's few native specimens of fauna, caused numerous false alarms. A dozing John Thurman jumped out of his skin when something heavy landed on his chest. Assuming that the enemy was about to bayonet him, he frantically grabbed for a weapon but saw only a large crab scuttling away. He stabbed it and threw it out of the foxhole.[50] When Bernard Dobbins did the same, he heard shouts of "Grenade!" and two Marines came rocketing out of the next hole over.[51]

Not every infiltrator was a phantom or impertinent crab, of course. The threat was very real. When a surprise attack did happen, it happened very quickly and at unsettlingly close range. Joe Simms was wide awake at 0130, finger on the trigger, ready to detect twigs snapping or a shadowy figure briefly glimpsed. Then "suddenly, in rapid succession," he heard cushioned footsteps, "blinked as a bright parachute flare flashed . . . and heard a rifle crack from the neighboring foxhole. He swung his BAR around as a second shot rang out." Just ten yards away from his foxhole lay sprawled two Japanese. They were perhaps dead—but only perhaps—so he fired his BAR into their bodies to make sure.[52]

As a last resort, there were always grenades. A Marine in the 3rd Battalion, 9th Marines, liked to simulate them by rolling stones down the slope outside his foxhole to worry any approaching Japanese.[53] But much of the time close-quarters grenade fights were a matter of timing and judgment, for there were critical differences between American and Japanese grenades. Japanese ones supplied a more powerful explosion than their American counterparts, but the latter were better designed and manufactured. Japanese grenades fragmented into metal shards much smaller and finer than the chunks flung off by American ones.[54] All things equal, fewer casualties on average were incurred by Americans than Japanese during grenade fights. There was no equivalent on the defenders' side, for instance, to a prolonged duel on the third day near Mount Suribachi in which apparently seventy-seven Japanese in one area were killed by American grenades.[55]

If a direct hit was scored by a Japanese grenade, the victim generally died. Thus, Allen Matthews observed several Japanese who had died tightly clutching grenades (owing either to faulty fuses or to suicidal impulses). One corpse he examined "lay on his back and his arms were flung wide. Both hands were gone and what had been his chest was now a gaping hole with small bits of ribs sticking out of the torn flesh"; another's "arms were mutilated and his hands missing but the cavity in his body from the blast of his grenade was lower—across his belly so that portions of his intestines hung over his legs."[56]

But if a Marine had dived to the ground, had taken even minimum cover, or was a few yards away, he had a decent chance of being left either lightly wounded or unscathed (if shaken).[57] John Thompson, for example, was lying in a shell hole when a Japanese grenade blew up behind him. "If it had been an American grenade I would have been killed, but as it was my pack absorbed a good deal of the blast."[58]

Jack Lucas was one of those who survived a Japanese grenade. During a grenade exchange, he leaped on one to save his comrades (an act for which he won the Medal of Honor) and described the experience when it exploded:

> The blast was deafening. One moment I was prostrate on the ground, and the next, I was floating upward. With eyes wide open, I watched as my body rose above the trench floor. . . . After the initial blast, silence filled my universe. The peace and tranquility was euphoric and calming. There was no noise, no pain, no battle, and no real time, only total and absolute peace. I never lost consciousness. The force propelled me into the air, rotating my body 180 degrees. When the momentum had spent itself, I dropped to the earth, landing on my back. My ears began to ring as though I had received a near-knockout punch. . . . My mind struggled to process the muffled noises but everything sounded as though I were underwater. . . . Except for an intense tingling sensation, I had no feeling. I was numb all over. I had suffered over 250 en-

trance wounds. . . . As feeling gradually returned to my body, the initial unpleasantness of pain made its presence known, and soon accelerated to an excruciating level finally enveloping me completely in an unrelenting grip of agony.[59]

Japanese grenades differed also in that whereas American ones could be prepared earlier by leaving the safety pin halfway out, the former was first armed by screwing the firing pin down and pulling the safety pin (a kind of fork attached to a short length of string, cord, or rope), and only then was the fuse ignited by a sharp blow to a hard object, such as a helmet or rock. That final step, that distinctive click of metal against stone or steel, served as the fatal giveaway in the silence of the night, said John Lyttle.[60] Once a Marine heard it, he knew he had between four and five seconds (the same delay as an American grenade) before it exploded. If that was not enough, he could also see the streak of its red arc as the grenade flew toward him.

The handful of seconds between ignition and detonation was, pointed out one Marine, "a surprisingly long time. It was possible to throw a grenade at a Jap, have him pick it up and throw it back at you, and still have enough time for you to scoop the grenade up and get it away from you before the explosion."[61] That was a dangerous game: Tibor Torok avoided playing it by each night filling with dirt an empty sandbag he always carried so that with it he could smother any grenade that fell in to his foxhole.[62]

If grenades and close-range fire failed to stop an attack, the infiltrators would jump into the nearest foxhole and attempt to slay the occupants. Nighttime hand-to-hand combat in such a confined space can probably be counted as the ne plus ultra of raw savagery on Iwo, pitting as it did men of equal skill and ruthlessness against each other in a lethal duel. There were no rules, no quarter, no surrender. Such melees were inevitably chaotic, with each participant's version differing slightly from the others, but the sequence of events (from his own perspective) were etched vividly in the memory.[63]

Corporal William Byrd and his foxhole mate fought off two Japanese in a "struggle [that] lasted an eternity. I had one of them in a viselike grip around the neck. I remember how he smelled. He probably didn't think I smelled very good either. My buddy . . . was cut on his hand and arm, but he was still fighting. I was hit with a rifle butt under my left eye. It was the hardest blow I ever received in my life. I still have the scar. I vaguely remember another Marine coming to help. One of the Japanese was stabbed to death, the other was shot. I remember blood running into my mouth."[64]

There was neither rhyme nor reason in foxhole fighting. There was no doctrine or approved method. One used whatever weapon came to hand—a pistol, a knife, a clubbed rifle, a grenade. Such apparently antiquated arms as swords and bayonets were surprisingly common. Near Mount Suribachi, a Japanese officer lunged with his sword at a Marine, who caught the blade in his hands, wrenched it away, and slew its owner.[65] Indeed, bayonets were used for actual *fighting* far more frequently than in the Civil or Revolutionary War. When Alfred Stone, for instance, was rushed by a soldier, "I raised my rifle up and watched him impale himself on my bayonet in the midsection of his body. He fell to his left, and I could not get the bayonet out of his body. I had to fire a round into his body to loosen the bayonet." He then shot another Japanese trying to work the bolt of his rifle.[66] The Japanese preference for bayonets—they were taught that it exemplified the "spirit" of the offensive—may have, paradoxically, saved Marines' lives. In the confines of a foxhole, their technique of the single "long thrust" was of little utility whereas Marines were taught to rely on short, violent movements with their bayonets.[67] Worse, their instructors had directed them never to club their rifles, an American tradition since at least the time of Bunker Hill, and one of which the Marines took full advantage.[68]

Still, Americans would experience a remarkable variety of attempts to kill them. Sergeant Bill Harrell and Pfc. Andrew Jackson Carter were sharing a foxhole when Harrell, asleep, heard Carter's M1 bark several times. Instantly alert, he saw four Japanese lying before them and heard a bubbly groan emanating from one of them. They shot at the lump a few times to guarantee he was dead before Carter's rifle jammed due to the sand and he headed back to the command post for a replacement.

In the meantime, a grenade landed next to Harrell from an overlooked infiltrator. Flung backward by the blast, Harrell was left with a numbed body but could feel a "peculiar" sensation, as if strange fingers were scratching at his left forearm. Wondering what it was, he looked down and saw his "left hand was off at the wrist and hung by shreds of tendon down along his forearm." Carter, luckily, returned and Harrell pulled out his .45 with his good right hand. Two Japanese scrambled from some nearby foliage, one swinging a sword. Carter fired his new rifle, which jammed (the damn sand, again), but grabbed an enemy one they had recently found lying around and were saving as a souvenir. As one Japanese piled into Carter, who ran him through with the souvenir gun's bayonet, the swordsman lunged, deeply slashing Carter's left wrist, but Harrell's .45 roared and killed him. Meanwhile, the bayoneted Japanese was gurgling and coughing his life out. After he was dealt with, Harrell ordered Carter to go get help. The sergeant had no illusions that he would die before Carter returned, but as he settled down and made his peace with the Lord, a panting figure landed next to him. Harrell stirred and swiveled his head only to meet the gaze of a Japanese next to him, their heads a foot apart as the enemy checked whether he was dead. His unwelcome new acquaintance chattered to someone else, crouching nearby. Then the first very deliberately and slowly took a grenade—making sure Harrell could see it—cracked it on his helmet, and shoved it under the Marine's chin. As he prepared to leap from the hole, Harrell shot him with his invaluable .45 and coaxed the grenade loose. At the opposite end of the foxhole, the other Japanese tried to scramble out in a panic as Harrell tossed the grenade, now a second or two from exploding, at him. Harrell would lose his other hand when it went off, but the Japanese lost his life. The next morning, even hardened Marines were astounded by what was being called Harrell's and Carter's "pocket Alamo" (they were Texan): No fewer than twelve Japanese lay dead in and around their foxhole. (Harrell became a rancher after the war.)[69]

Despite the heroics, the survivors of such deadly, adrenaline-powered encounters were left shaking and disturbed. Frequently, dead Japanese were shot, stabbed, and beaten by Marines exorcising their aggression

in a frenzied manner reminiscent of the British following their conquest of the redoubt at Bunker Hill. When Ray Hansen frantically used
his entrenching tool to hit a Japanese who had grabbed his leg and foot,
he cried to Les Murrah to shoot him. Murrah did so by standing on the
man's head and firing directly into it. Afterward, Hansen began to
pummel the corpse and when Murrah asked why, he replied, "I'm killing him." "But I've already killed him," pointed out a quizzical Murrah. "I know it, Les," said Hansen, but "I'm killing him again before he
kills one of us." When he had finished, there was little left of the Japanese apart from some flayed flesh and a red mess. Murrah found that
his own hands would not stop shaking for a long time.[70] Quite a few
Marines, understandably, were worse affected, though generally only
temporarily. Russell Boydston, for instance, had to be evacuated to a
ship to recover from hearing the screams and seeing what his friend Bill
Terrill had done to the Japanese soldier who had tried to kill him.[71]

All that can be said is that if the nights were bad, the days were
worse.

8. The Madness in the Method

During the day, every day, Iwo Jima was Pandemonium, the High Capital of Satan, its blasted plains, pyres of ruins, and cave-pocked ridges
luring Marines ever closer to a City of Dis. Nothing, at least at first,
made sense on Iwo: It was a Golgothic madhouse, a place where men
did nothing but die. Fittingly, the place even looked, as someone
quipped to Alvin Josephy, "like Hell with the fire out."[1]

But Iwo had never been pretty. In 1891, a naturalist named Henry
Seebohm had received a "box of birds' skins and eggs from Sulphur
Island," or Iwo Jima, sent by a Mr. Holst, a recent visitor. Seebohm
would inform readers of *The Ibis,* an ornithological journal, that its
"centre is very barren, principally black sand and grey clay, with a few
dried-up tufts of grass, and an occasional hardy bush. Everywhere are
scattered stones and rocks, especially to the north-east." There was also

"a plain of what seemed to be pure sulphur, which was boiling furiously in three or four holes when visited by Mr. Holst. Close to the north shore are some hot springs. There are a few large trees on the island, and both in the north-east and in the south-east is dense low scrub, bound together with climbers."[2]

By the time the Marines were hurled headlong firing from the ethereal sea toward the damnable island, the terrain was more malefic still. Its twisted gullies, its narrow blind alleys and dark crevices, its jutting rocks and threatening boulders, its (few) gnarled trees and clumps of dead brown grass combined to bestow on the island a diabolical aspect. "Looking around" as he waited out a bombardment, John Lardner noted, "I had the leisure for the first time to think what a miserable piece of real estate Iwo Jima is. Later, when I had seen nearly all the island, I knew that there were no extenuating features." This fiendish place "has no water, few birds, no butterflies, no discernible animal life—nothing but sand and clay, humpbacked hills, stunted trees, knife-edged kuna grass in which mites who carry scrub typhus live, and a steady, dusty wind."[3] Dave Davenport, slogging it out across the barren landscape, was somewhat curter in his description: "This fucking bloody bastard of an island."[4]

Naval and artillery fire tore deeply into the heart and guts of the island, leaving behind a wasteland that lay, as Bertram Yaffe put it, "perforated by bomb craters and eerie geysers of sulfurous mist—an expanse broken by the silhouettes of derelict tanks and places and bodies half-rising as they stiffen grotesquely."[5] It was the sulfur, the reeking, Luciferian sulfur that made the ground hot to the touch, so hot you could warm rations in the dirt, that caused the bodies to "half-rise."[6]

When corpses lay on the earth for days, absorbing the gas, they puffed up, and Marines heard a mysterious sound "like letting the air out of a bicycle tire, loud at first, then gradually becoming softer, until it stopped." The culprits were dead soldiers whose bloated bodies had burst, releasing noxious effusions of sulfuric stench.[7] Whenever a stray bullet or piece of shrapnel rent a hole in one's torso, which was quite often, "the smell would become almost suffocating," recalled John

Thurman.[8] Bored Marines accordingly played pranks, according to George Gentile, by throwing stones at gassy Japanese corpses to "pop" them and annoy passersby.[9]

When a body expanded, *everything* did. John Lyttle noticed "one guy [who] looked like he was ready to float down the streets of New York in the Macy's Thanksgiving Day Parade. This bloating was not limited to the stomach, but every arm, leg and finger as well. Even his head was swollen." A Marine fetched out his wallet, and the men gawked at a photo of the man and his smiling bride on their wedding day.[10]

Lyttle was too delicate to mention one specific part of the anatomy that also grew. Howard McLaughlin saw a naked Japanese soldier whose "seemingly intact corpse saluted each passing Marine with an erection, swollen somehow by the violence of his death to monstrous size."[11] Finding another similarly affected, Ernest Moreau and his friends lay down and began "shooting at that thing for target practice."[12]

Some Marines began to indulge in extreme behavior. There was, as always, an enthusiasm for souvenirs, but, as the Japanese commonly booby-trapped corpses, it was generally tempered by an appreciation for the risks involved. Most booby traps consisted of eight ounces of explosives packed into a container the size of a large tuna can. In its center there was a small round plunger that, when ejected by a spring, would detonate the contents. A U-shaped safety clip held the spring in place, and after perching a bait object on top the operator would pull out the safety, arming the trap. If the bait was removed it would go off instantly.[13] When they came across a suspicious body, then, Marines would loop a length of rope around a hand or foot, retreat a safe distance, and tug hard enough to move the corpse some distance.[14] Not just bodies were booby-trapped: Anything known to attract Marines' magpieish attention could be wired. Helmets, saki bottles, pistols, and the pièce de résistance, officers' "samurai swords," were often found ready to harm unwary Marines. When the Japanese had time, even dead Marines were used as bait to kill those collecting them.[15]

Every Marine knew the dangers.[16] One time, John Thurman saw a dead Japanese officer lying twenty feet away in the entrance to a pillbox knocked out by artillery. There was a nice pistol in his holster, a lovely souvenir. He had obviously, however, been killed some time ago, which meant that he was almost certainly rigged to explode. And so he was: As Thurman peered more closely, he caught "the remaining sunlight reflecting off of a very fine hair wire that was tied to the pistol."[17]

Still, there were those willing to take a risk to pick up some prime souvenirs. Fred Schribert, who later conceded that what he and two friends had done was "stupid," once ducked into a cave and emerged with a valuable trove that included a flag, a sword, a pistol, a fountain pen, combat ribbons, and even some family photos, which they kept.[18] The trick, of course, was to scavenge only very recently killed Japanese; particularly popular were their wristwatches.[19] Flags, too, preferably bloodstained and bullet-holed. For those with more elevated tastes, such as James Vedder, an intact porcelain cup embossed with the symbol of the Imperial Japanese Army and a working phonograph provided much-missed elements of refinement.[20]

The Japanese, in contrast, did not loot as thoroughly as Marines. This was for several reasons, including a lack of opportunity. Neither did the Marines carry much that might interest a beleaguered garrison. On Iwo, Allen Matthews's worldly possessions consisted of two penknives, an empty wallet, eleven cents in change, a rifle-cleaning brush, a few photographs of his family, an inkless fountain pen, and a package of rifle-cleaning patches.[21] Tibor Torok, like many others, left behind on the ship his money, photos, letters, jewelry, and any identification save his dog tags, which were wrapped with tape so they did not clink or reflect the sun's rays.[22] The Japanese wanted only food and water, so if they were lucky, they might have managed to acquire from the slain a half-empty canteen and some crackers.[23]

These material objects aside, in some quarters there was a penchant for the removal of body parts. In a practice unheard of at Bunker Hill and Gettysburg, where the enemy was generally regarded as civilized (if wrong-headed) and combat was not zero-sum, one could see, said Jack Lucas, Marines severing the little fingers of the enemy dead, packing them in salt bags, and sending them home as good-luck charms.[24] Ears, too, were sometimes sliced off.[25] It is unlikely, simply because of the fear of booby traps, that collecting bodily bric-a-brac was inordinately widespread among Marines. More probably, the hobby was restricted to a very small number of Americans who actively amassed these treasures—and they, in turn, were seen as perverse by their peers, who were nonetheless reluctant to snitch on them.

A subtle distinction, perhaps, but a significant proportion of body souvenirs were acquired not for thrills but for immediate commercial gain. Gerald Copeland once found a group of Marines standing around a fifty-gallon oil drum in which they were boiling skulls, after having first "popped the eyes out." Copeland "thought that was interesting" and asked why they were doing it. They replied that "we make a lot of money at this" and related further that sailors aboard the ships were buying Japanese skulls in a frenzy.[26] Then there was the quartermaster back at the beach who offered Ernest Moreau and his clique a lavish supply of K-rations in exchange for a Japanese head. After acquiring one (details are patchy), they "boiled the skull to kill all the maggots, and knocked all the gold teeth out." It turned out that the quartermaster, a former dentist, was overjoyed at their otherwise toothful gift, so it worked out profitably for all concerned.[27] The instigators of skull-boiling were, it seems, rear-echelon and ship-based personnel, the ones who rarely got a chance to go up front and experience combat first-hand.[28]

Gold teeth were another matter, as Moreau indicated. The Japanese were famed for their fillings, and more than one Marine supplemented his assets with Nippon gold. George Nations and a friend were most annoyed when they searched near the front lines (getting sniped at for their pains) only to find nothing but heads with missing teeth.[29] Many decades after the war, a mild-mannered former teacher and school administrator named Warren Peters confided that he had been one of those who collected a "sackful" of gold teeth on Iwo Jima. "That's a gruesome thing," he explained, "but I think that's an indication of how ruthless you let yourself become and how you don't care, you don't really consider them as humans. It's a hard thing to explain. I couldn't do that, I don't think if I were a mortician I could do that at the present time."[30]

Taking body parts of any kind for fun or profit was officially frowned upon, and overly zealous indulgence in the practice was widely regarded as an incipient sign that a Marine was perhaps overdue for a rest. A clearly traumatized Peters, for instance, seems to have begun to descend into a moral haze after his best friend, Charles Chapman, was killed by a sniper while standing next to him. Similarly, George Gentile remembered one fellow who everyone knew had "started to go wacko, and he had a pouch hanging from his cartridge belt and a pair of pliers." He went "around extracting the teeth out of the Japs' mouths and put them in his pouch just as if it were an everyday thing."[31]

There were other warnings that Iwo Jima was getting to a Marine. The least serious affliction manifested itself as disorientation, temporary amnesia, deafness, vomiting, and headaches and was caused primarily by concussion blasts emanating from shells and mortars landing nearby. Their explosions created intense waves of compressed air that disrupted or blocked the brain's nervous electrotransmissions, inflicted blunt trauma damage, or caused severe internal injuries. A passing pressure wave could, for instance, rapidly inflate the victim's stomach with air before emptying it so violently that his intestines were torn apart, his lungs collapsed, and his brain knocked the inside of his skull. It was possible to die instantly if the round fell close, and many men remarked—as they also had at Bunker Hill and Gettysburg—on the placid, statuelike corpses they found, many with no obvious bleeding. The extent of the concussive effects varied upon the size of the round and the locations of the victims. Inside one concrete blockhouse, for instance, Captain Fred Haynes saw eight or ten corpses. Some of them, killed by concussive waves and evidently protected from the primary explosive blast by walls or doors, "looked almost peaceful," while the unluckier ones had their "intestines and arms and legs scattered around."[32] The power of a 16-inch naval shell was colossal, however, no matter where you were. Thomas Brown saw three motionless Japanese lying intact fifty feet away from a huge, fifty-foot-wide crater. Fifty feet from the opposite side—150 feet distant from the first group, in other words—lay another five.[33]

There were considerable numbers of temporarily shocked Marines, especially after a prolonged barrage, and their strange and befuddled behavior prompted many to believe that they had entered a surreal world. Most of the time, the symptoms evaporated shortly after, even if the headaches sometimes took weeks or even months to dissipate. One such was Corporal Glenn Buzzard, who was in a shell hole with Otis Boxx when a shell struck. Nothing remained of Boxx but his lower jaw, while Buzzard, miraculously, received only slight shrapnel wounds. "I was shocked, no question about it . . . my mind was gone," said Buzzard. He couldn't hear, and his vision was blurry. He passed out and came to later in a hospital ship; he later returned to his unit.[34]

More seriously, a man's comrades had to watch for subsequent indications of what was variously known as the Asiatic stare, the bulkhead stare, or, perhaps most famously, the thousand-yard stare (sometimes two-thousand-yard stare)—a phrase coined during the Peleliu campaign a few months earlier and popularized by *Life* magazine.[35] This affliction was caused neither by trauma nor by the fall of artillery, but by day after grinding day of bone-tiredness, nervous exhaustion, poor diet, and exposure to extreme danger. The most obvious symptom was, predictably enough, "a vacant, faraway stare," as James Vedder described the condition, characterized by wide-open, bloodshot eyes, whites showing all around the pupils, wrinkled forehead, and raised eyebrows. Irritability, extreme reaction to noise, and obsessive behavior about minor things usually went hand in hand.[36] Thereafter, victims would begin to act strangely and erratically. As a doctor explained, Marines' reflexes slowed considerably, and they were unable to make conscious decisions, ultimately entering a stupefied, dreamlike state. It was "a way the brain tried to keep you from going crazy," the doctor thought.[37]

The "stare" could infect not just individuals but also entire units, or whatever was left of them. At one point, Odell Arnold's thirteen-man squad had lost three killed and four wounded while the rest suffered from combat-fatigue symptoms.[38] When Alvin Josephy encountered two companies of combat-hardened Marines, they

looked as if they had just come out of a hard-fought football game. They leaned against the sides of their foxholes, exhausted and breathing heavily. Their eyes were wide open and staring, as if they could not forget the terrible sights they had seen. I recognized many friends and tried talking to them, but it was useless: They looked through me, their answers made no sense, their minds wandered. One man tried to ask me how the battle was going. He couldn't get his question out. He finished half the sentence, then repeated the last words, over and over, like a man falling asleep. But he wasn't drowsing; his mind just wouldn't function.[39]

Some men would cry and purge the condition temporarily from their system. After a bloody attack on a pillbox, Howard Baxter's platoon sergeant "pulled us back and broke down and cried. He lost one of his best friends. He reached a point and had a good bawl for about five minutes, and then he was all right."[40] Others, like Baxter himself, felt the same but predicted that "if I let myself go, I'd be gone. I just jammed it down inside. I think a lot of us did."[41] But as Raymond Mik warned, those who continued to stare "off into space, those were the ones who gave you a lot of trouble." They were perched precariously on a mental ledge. Keith Renstrom suspected that his lieutenant, hitherto "a solid officer," was entering dangerous territory when he ordered Renstrom to fetch barbed wire from the beach when none was needed. Speaking in an unsettling tone of voice, the lieutenant kept weirdly repeating, "Wire, wire, go get lots of wire." By the time Renstrom returned, he had cracked up—"who knows what pushed him over"—and was being evacuated.[42]

Renstrom had observed a phenomenon that commonly occurred during one of these states. Quite often men would snap, usually after a relatively minor incident. As Sergeant Gallant clarified, the "Gooney Bird Stare did not come all at once. A Marine did not suddenly have it. It came by slow, subtle changes over a period of time." At first, he became inattentive and unaware or uncaring of what was happening around him. Then he would fixate on something inconsequential but seemingly very important, such as fried eggs—how he missed them, how he liked them cooked, how outrageous it was that there were none—and slowly work himself up into a lather. Shortly after, his reddening eyes would grow ever wider and his movements increasingly robotic. It was still possible to return to a normal state from that point, but some men were too far gone.[43] They would plunge into a fit of madness and might begin to mutilate the dead, launch a suicidal one-man assault against a machine-gun nest, or see hordes of invisible Japanese trying to kill them. Corporal Willard Burroughs, for instance, stunned his friends on March 9 when, in the midst of intense sniper fire, he suddenly and inexplicably stood up in full view of the enemy, shouted insults at the Japanese soldiers nearby, and was shot in the heart.[44] Added Raymond Mik, "At night, if that happened in the line, you had to be sure that they got off the ones who were screaming. I never reached that point, but I was probably close to losing it."[45] Another man, witnessed by Robert Allen, did lose it when he "reached down and picked up an object protruding from the sand. The sight of a detached hand destroyed the last of his fragile sanity. . . . Screaming, he began to tear the clothing from his body, and he disappeared."[46]

The most alarming incidents occurred when the victim relived, amplified, or perhaps imagined the event that had provoked him. Dr. Vedder described one private who arrived at the aid station: "His eyes were rolling about wildly. His facial muscles ran through the gamut of contortions that alternately depicted fear, hate, and rage as he shouted incoherently. He was swinging a large samurai sword about indiscriminately. If anyone tried to approach him, he would make half-hearted lunges with his recently captured weapon. From his disjointed remarks, we learned that we were the enemy and he was surrounded. Before he died, he planned to kill as many Nips as possible." Generally, the only way to calm men in this condition was to knock them down and out; in this case, an assistant crept behind the private and decked him with a shovel between his shoulder blades. He was quickly disarmed, heavily sedated, and evacuated to a hospital ship.[47]

The good news was that a few days away after a breakdown was generally sufficient to restore normality. Ideally, though, officers would notice men "starting to crack, who'd had too much," said William Doran, and "let them go back and get supplies, get away from the front action."[48] Afterward, if there remained lingering doubts as to the soldier's mental stability, they would be assigned to a beachmaster like Sergeant James Boyle, who used them to carry equipment and ammunition until they could return to their units.[49] Even a minor respite from the immediate front line could be enough to restore a man. Frank Caldwell, a company commander, was asked by one of his Marines to send him back because he was liable to crack. Caldwell proposed letting him join the mortar section for a time. The mortarmen were located just twenty yards to the rear, but that was far enough away to bring the Marine back from the edge. He later rejoined his squad.[50]

George Wahlen, a corpsman, first noticed significant and rapidly escalating numbers of combat-fatigued troops on the fifth day of the campaign, or February 24 (D+5).[51] Another corpsman, Ray Crowder, who had just arrived, confirmed that on February 25 "the majority" of his patients were suffering from "shell shock, combat fatigue, and blast concussion."[52] There had been psychological casualties, of course, on the very first day, even the very first hour, but the quality of the trauma had shifted. At first, men psychologically more disposed to breakdown—owing to existing mental disturbance, family background, insufficient screening during recruitment, genetic factors, their particular experience upon landing, or a combination of these elements—had tended to collapse. Socioeconomic status, age, and education, too, were correlated with elevated anxiety and stress; by far the highest rates (77 percent) were seen among rural or poor urban soldiers over thirty years old with but a grade-school education (this was at a time when college attendance was a rarity and mostly confined to officers), and the lowest (40 percent) among high-school graduates aged under twenty-five, who were believed to be more adaptable to circumstances.[53]

From D+5 onward, however, combat fatigue began to afflict everyone, regardless of background, genes, and prior experience. No one could count himself immune. Aside from a lack of proper food and protracted exposure to fire, a prime cause was that by that time hardly any Marines had snatched more than a few hours' sleep on each of the preceding four nights. The random crash of nighttime artillery and the whirring of missiles and flares above denied men the luxury of deep sleep; all they could do was "doze." The clamor, said Alvin Josephy, invaded their "fitful dreams" so that it "sounded like someone banging doors in a house in which we were trying to sleep. The doors were all around us, upstairs and downstairs, in the same room and on the other side of the house."[54] That was only if they managed to nod off, of course. Most of the men digging in, he noticed, "seemed too groggy and dazed to sleep. It was as if they were afraid something else might happen to them if they relaxed their guard and closed their eyes."[55]

Sleep deprivation combined with stress was clearly exacting a severe toll by D+5. Indeed, by the end of that day, total Marine casualties amounted to 7,758, of which 558 were listed as cases of combat fatigue.[56] As the Marine Corps lagged behind the Army in acknowledging and treating neuropsychiatric casualties, instead choosing to classify them euphemistically as resulting from such external factors as "blast concussions" or "severe dehydration" (just as "sunstroke" had been used during the Civil War), the official figure of 558 is certainly a grave underestimate.[57] Alice Goudreau, a nurse at a naval hospital that treated Iwo Jima casualties, wrote soon afterward (in November 1945, before the issue could be hushed up) that "the majority of our ambulatory admissions" were men suffering from "war neuroses." They arrived, she said, "by the hundreds" and "were in such a severe state of shock that they had to be led by the hand from the planes and ambulances." An air-raid siren, a blackout, even "the sharp slam of a screen door" would "send them scurrying into corners and under their beds in quivering, stuttering huddles."[58] Many more men remained on the island, never diagnosed, staring listlessly and moving like zombies until either the end came or they were wounded.

It was on D+5, and this was no coincidence, that Marines first noticeably began losing track of time and place. George Nations wrote that after that date "events are no longer separated in my mind as to the day they happened. All the days and events seem to run together."[59] Tibor Torok suffered "about two weeks of memory loss" from about D+5 onward.[60] It did not help that their watches were easily lost or stopped working owing to sand, saltwater, and shock. Frank Walker misplaced his "watch early on" and that belonging to John Thurman broke on the fourth day.[61] Foxhole mates Ernest Moreau, who had lost his watch, and Tony Steltzer, whose broke, were forced to time their hour-long sentry shifts by using a rosary to recite a given number of Hail Marys.[62] The disorienting loss of chronology affected the Japanese as well. Seaman First Class Koizumi Tadayoshi stated that after the first few nights "I lost track of what the date was or even the day was."[63] Even when their watches still worked, Marines like Howard McLaughlin descended into a haze, their sense of continuity inexorably vanishing as time went on: He rued that he had "no guide posts, no references to tie remembered events to. Between running off one landing craft on D-Day and staggering aboard another one 36 days later, I am sure that there are many days that I have no recollection of at all."[64]

Unlike set-piece battles like Bunker Hill or Gettysburg, which were conducted over a limited time span, on Iwo Jima days and nights, mornings and afternoons elided. All became permanent penumbra, the grayish, shadowy place between light and darkness. The raising of the flag atop Mount Suribachi on the fourth day is quite often the last distinct memory men had of the battle's progress; after that, it descended into a series of repetitive, automatic small-unit and individual actions hardly distinguishable from one another. For one corporal, "each day and night was filled with points of contact with a determined enemy. Blockhouse after blockhouse contained Japanese soldiers determined to kill us."[65] Robert Maiden spent entire days "snooping and pooping and running and hitting the deck and running" between bunkers. He never had any idea where he was, nor was he interested.[66] For another Marine, Iwo Jima's problem was "that there are too many damned ridges. You take one ridge and then you got to take another. There's always another ridge."[67] The next was just like the last, and the one before, and the one after the next. That was all Iwo Jima was—a grinding, repetitive slog that had to be endured until it ended.

Later on, veterans could relate precisely *what* happened during particularly vivid events but not *when* or *where* they occurred. Gerald Averill described the jarring moment when normal continuity disappeared as resembling "when a smoothly moving film on the screen change[s] to a series of color slides, some of them painfully acute. Slide on. Slide off. Click. Click. Nothing in between."[68] In combat, which was near constant, one man recalled that "time seemed to take on a surrealistic quality. Everything happened in slow motion. Small sounds were amplified, and the din of battle was silence. Your eyes saw everything. Your mind noted and remembered it all in minute detail. Time will never dull these scenes, nor will I ever be able to erase them from my mind's eye."[69] And yet, as Liberato G. Riccio put it, "I still don't know for sure where I was at any point on the island, even when I read about it later and started retracing my steps. I sort of recognize certain locations, like when we were under a mortar attack."[70]

A sense of powerlessness, too, set in. Marines quickly realized that they stood very little chance of making it off Iwo in one piece, let alone alive. As far as they were concerned, no matter the fine doctrine and intricate planning of the Marine Corps, they had been sent there to die.

In the beginning, Marines were optimistic rationalists: Men calculated the odds of dying but "were convinced it wouldn't happen" to them, observed Corporal John Thompson.[71] Before every landing, Dave Davenport "always looked at the other guys. I never figured it would be me. I always kind of measured the thickness of a buddy, or buddies, near me during a shelling or a pin-down by small arms fire. Will their bodies stop shrapnel or a bullet and shield me? I knew others looked at me the same way. We talked about it. It was always the other guy not you."[72] Believers tempered their rationalism with a faith that God would see them through, but secular and religious alike always pictured themselves, said Allen Matthews, "as grieving over the loss of friends, for never could we picture our friends grieving over us. Thus does ignorance protect the sanity of the untutored mind."[73]

For most battles, such mental tactics were adequate preparation. But not on Iwo, where, "after a few days" of combat "a funny thing occurred," according to Thompson. "You started to realize the chances of not only your buddy getting hit but of you getting clobbered were extremely high. It became a matter of would you be killed or just wounded?"[74] Fred McDiarmid confidently began his time on Iwo by assuming, "They can't hurt me," but after seeing how many others were being hit, started saying to himself, "I hope they don't hurt me," until finally the best he could hold out for was, "I hope I don't get killed."[75]

His pessimism was fully merited by the remarkable attrition rates on Iwo Jima. Very, very few men lasted the entire battle unscathed. The casualty figures, moreover, are untainted by the incidence of disease, that historical bane of armies but almost nonexistent on Iwo Jima. (When "sickness" or "illness" was mentioned as a reason for evacuation, it really meant mental breakdown.)

The staggering churn of casualties began at the regimental level. The 26th Marines, for instance, began D-Day with 146 officers and 3,110 enlisted men. Even after receiving 882 replacements during the battle, its strength at the end was 80 officers and 1,388 men. At the battalion level, the figures turn starker still. The average battalion size at the beginning was 36 officers and 885 enlisted men, but by mid-March these had fallen to 16 and 300 (including hundreds of replacements)—not much larger than a peacetime company.[76] Frank Walker was a corporal in 2nd Battalion, 28th Marines, which happened to start with 1,680 men, of which 1,571 (including replacements) would be killed or wounded. Only 109 made it off Iwo safe and sound.[77] Perhaps most vividly, whereas a battalion's complement of sergeants on paper was 69, at the end one sergeant major sadly mused to an enquirer of his, "Well, I got six now."[78]

Lower down, company after company reported numbing losses. Just over a month after D-Day, the strength of the companies comprising the 2nd Battalion, 28th Marines, had plummeted from an average of 250 men each to between 45 and 85, over half of them replacements.[79] Gerald Averill's company in the 26th Marines landed with 242 men, and a week later half were gone; even after influxes of replacements, just 80 Marines from his outfit would leave Iwo at the end of the battle.[80] Other companies' losses were even severer: Company F, 1st Battalion, 26th Marines, was left with 45 men; Howard Baxter's company in 2nd Battalion, 27th Marines, declined from more than 200 to 27; Robert Maiden's Company D, 2nd Battalion, 26th Marines, dropped from 224 to 24; K Company, 3rd Battalion, 9th Marines landed a few days after D-Day, but of its 252 officers and enlisted plus replacements, only 12 would be left standing at battle's end.[81] The most rapid depletion appears to have been suffered by Company C, 1st Battalion, 21st Marines, which landed with 279 men two days after D-Day and could roll call, according to Corporal Woody Williams, just 17 Marines on March 5—not even two weeks later.[82] The skeletal nature of many companies by the end becomes more shockingly apparent when the replacement Marines are removed from consideration: Seventeen days into the battle, of the more than 200 in one company that had landed on D-Day, there were just three original members left.[83]

Losses among platoons and squads were accordingly horrendous: The 28th Marines' first platoon in C Company was diminished by 95.5 percent, with just one Marine (Pvt. Antoine Chiasson) remaining alive and unwounded among its original three squads, each of twelve or thirteen men.[84] If that was not extraordinary enough, a significant number of platoons and squads experienced a hitherto unthinkable casualty rate of greater than 100 percent. In these units, no original members remained, and even their replacements, and *their* replacements, had been burned through.

The turnover of junior officers and noncommissioned officers was so rapid that there was little point in introducing oneself. Pfc. Keith Neilson's company went through three commanders in two days, while Captain David Severance's new lieutenant was shot fifteen minutes after arriving.[85] That was, admittedly, an extreme case: The more usual life expectancy of a junior officer was roughly forty-eight to seventy-two hours—an ominous milestone considering that in World War II the rule of thumb was that if you could make it past the first seventy-two hours in the field, your chances of dying declined to 1 percent.[86] By that time, you could expect to have learned the necessary fundamentals of staying alive; on Iwo, officers died before they could learn how not to. Corporal Richard Lowe used to see Sergeant Vince Varzevicius showing their fresh-faced lieutenant around the platoon's lines and positions. Then he would do it again a couple of days later for the anonymous new guy, and then again.[87]

In Lieutenant Patrick Caruso's case, his fellow officers did not enjoy even those few days in harness. When he landed on February 23, of the company's seven officers he was sixth in seniority. By the following evening, he was informed by Sergeant Moore, "Lieutenant, you're in charge of K Company." (The seventh in seniority, due to be Caruso's replacement when it was his turn to die, himself died a day later. And all three sergeants who served under him would die, too. And every officer of I and L companies to boot.)[88]

The "official" toll exacted by the fighting on Iwo Jima is complicated by these sour facts. Whereas on paper, total Marine casualties amounted to roughly 35 percent (25,851 casualties of 75,000 Marine and Navy personnel)—itself an extremely high figure—a significant proportion of those were men from support units (motor transport, cooks, and so forth) roped in later on as hapless replacements. In certain units, as well, such as the heavy machine-gun detachments that were generally located just behind the front line to provide emergency backup, attrition was less severe. Corporal William McConnell's machine-gun squad saw major action and yet suffered just one man killed and several more lightly wounded (none were evacuated).[89] Among the frontline combat infantrymen, however, a more accurate overall casualty rate has been estimated at 80 percent.[90]

Worse, as they advanced up the island and Japanese resistance turned ever more ferocious, the risks increased for frontline Marines. In the later stages of the battle, the Marines' desire to end the fighting as quickly as possible, combined with their exhaustion, the influx of inexperienced replacements, and the harsh terrain's imposing a need for ruthless close-quarters engagements, resulted in many, perhaps preventable, casualties.

There were frequent cases of carelessness—in the twin senses of making errors and not caring—in the final weeks. According to Fred Haynes, by that point

> many men fought in a murky half-awake state, too tired to remain attuned to their surroundings. This was a grave problem, because on Iwo Jima, vigilance could not guarantee survival, but its absence all but ensured death or serious wounding. Among the frontline

veterans, one often saw men who had lost a great deal of weight. Their eye sockets appeared hollow, and there was a strange disjunction between the movement of the head and the eyes. Many very tough Marines were approaching the point where we officers could not expect them to continue fighting indefinitely.

Indeed, instances of falling asleep on sentry duty rose at this time, even when every Marine knew it jeopardized lives.[91]

We also begin to see an increasing incidence of acts of brave foolhardiness intended to win the battle faster and go home. In the northern cliffs, Patrick Caruso and his company became "cocky and brash . . . because we sensed the end was actually within reach." Caruso, who should have known better, took to running in open terrain to take a message rather than zigzagging and jumping between foxholes to avoid the snipers. (For his recklessness, he was soon shot in the leg and evacuated to Guam.)[92] Similarly, Captain Carl Bachman led an unnecessary raid of sixty volunteers, which was caught in the open and massacred by mortars and machine-gun fire. Among the few who returned was Bachman, who, said Fred Haynes, from then on "led his company with total disregard for his own life." He was soon killed.[93]

Only in the last days did Marine behavior become overtly, maybe sometimes overly, cautious—for the understandable reason that no one wanted to be the final casualty of Iwo Jima, the guy who died just hours before his unit returned to the ship. Jim Doyle almost became that guy when, after having come through the entire battle without a scratch, he lost two fingers to a grenade-armed infiltrator.[94] A typical reaction was recorded by Bernard Dobbins. He and his squad were actually heading to the beach to depart when an officer ordered them to pick up any unexploded shells they happened to come across. They refused, telling the lieutenant, "You want to pick up duds, you go do it," and kept walking.[95] Likewise, on Richard Lowe's last day, he "was extra careful walking back to the beach." As his company filed up the ship's ramp, "I could hear a machine gun rattling away in the distance [but] I didn't look back. I just kept walking."[96]

From the first few days onward, then, a sense of fatalistic randomness replaced that of optimistic rationalization among Marines. No longer did they believe the quaint notion, inculcated during their training, that they were monarchs of their own fates, never slaves to chance, and could rely on their Marine-taught skills, judgment, and prowess to control the future. Instead, as Howard McLaughlin put it, pretty soon everyone realized that the best outcome was to be wounded.[97] Mused McLaughlin, the men directly engaged with the Japanese were better off accepting what was coming. It was a revelation born of "realizing that [a soldier] has no control over whether he lives or dies, and relying on some higher authority to determine when it's his time."[98]

Whereas McLaughlin harked back to the conventional Calvinistic assumption that God determined a man's exit from life, drawing succor from its corollary that he could therefore fight unhindered by any sense of foreboding, its secular variant—increasingly popular in World War II—was the "your number on it" theory of being hit. It was a credo among the older, more experienced men, such as the sergeant sharing Jim Doyle's shell hole. Doyle was lugging a heavy radio set, and the sergeant pulled the long aerial over the top of the hole's rim, alarming Doyle, who feared being marked by the Japanese gunners. His mate just laughed, telling him to "take it easy on your first cruise, son. If you're going to get it, you're going to get it; that's all there is to it."[99]

In this respect these Marines echoed their Civil War ancestors, who were equally intrigued by the interplay of uncaring Fate, blind Chance, and divine protection in battle. Back then, after several actions William Ketcham of the 13th Indiana "knew perfectly well that if a cannon ball struck in the right place, it would kill or maim [and] I knew it was always liable to strike somebody and therefore liable to strike me, but I always went where I was ordered to go and the others went, and when I was ordered to run and the others ran, I ran."[100] As the more pious J. W. Hand of the 136th New York added, one should treat the "concentrated fire of a hundred cannons" as one did the "destructive forces of nature—the lightning, the tornado, the earthquake": Do your best to avoid them, but do not attempt to "resist." After all, who were you to resist the will of the Lord?[101]

On Iwo, likewise, William Doran saw men on either side of him in a foxhole blown up by a mortar, and others shot seconds after he had been talking to them, but he himself was never wounded. It was "a perfect example of how you have no control over what's going to happen" in war. "There's no rhyme or reason for it, just count your blessings."[102] Fred Haynes and Colonel Harry Liversedge were standing a couple of feet from Daniel McCarthy, the regimental surgeon, when a mortar round landed. "A small fragment of shrapnel killed him [McCarthy] instantly," said Haynes. "Neither the colonel nor I suffered even so much as a scratch. It was just plain luck. There is no way to explain who was hit and who wasn't."[103]

Belief and atheism alike left men equally mystified why they were saved. Glenn Buzzard confessed that "when I stop to think about it, I have no idea. I'm a Christian. I believe in God. I believe in the hereafter. But why me? I was no better or no worse than [his friends] Cooksey or Elmer Neff or Bowman or any of those guys. But yet they took it, you know what I mean? They're gone. Why, I don't know. I can't answer it. I didn't do anything any better than they did. I wasn't a better scholar, I wasn't a better . . . anything. . . . I have no idea. I cannot answer it."[104] Craig Leman, on the other hand, reasoned that "it's not going to make a damn difference if I pray or not. If it's going to hit me it's going to hit me. I'm not going to pray and see what happens. That's what I did and I never got hit." In fact, "I saw people get shot while they were praying."[105] To that end, Robin Barrett, who landed on five Pacific islands and yet was never wounded—his Civil War equivalent would have been one Private John Haley, who made it through twenty-eight battles and skirmishes from August 1862 until June 1865 and emerged without a scratch—concluded that the best way to handle the subject was not to "question why somebody else got killed or somebody else got injured or whatever it is, just be thankful that you didn't. And it's the only way you can survive. Otherwise, you'd go completely off your rocker." Ultimately, the best way to get by, then, was just not to think either too deeply or too hard about one's chances in a lethal environment. Private Haley, for example, was content to attribute his own remarkable record to having "achieved successful mediocrity" in all things.[106]

Despite assertions or convictions to the contrary, whether one was hit on Iwo was not entirely a matter of chance or destiny but was, in the end, partly conditioned by choices, skill, and experience. There were, in other words, ways to rig the game, if only slightly—as Marines would gradually realize over the course of the battle. Of course, it was still depressingly possible to do everything "right" and die, but the odds were slightly shortened in your favor if you learned some tricks.

Some were as simple as remembering never to walk fully upright or in a straight line. To present a slightly smaller target for shrapnel and sniper alike, the men on Iwo would crouch, hunch, or crawl, except when they ran, and then they made sure to zigzag and corkscrew as they jumped in and out of cover.[107] Allen Matthews described the method, mastered only through experience, by which one painstakingly moved forward: When shelling subsided, "I rose to my knees, looked quickly about to try to locate my squad [and] headed out toward my direct front. My eye glimpsed two holes either of which could serve as the next possible haven." He saw there was a dead Marine in one, which meant it had already been zeroed in by the enemy mortars. So "I veered immediately to the left and entered the second crater." After a few minutes, he "peered over the lip of the hole to determine the next avenue of advance. A small hole lay to the left about 20 yards away but I could see the helmets of other men already there. To my direct front was a large crater, and although it appeared about 50 yards away, an inordinately long distance, I decided to run for it."[108]

Another rule was that you never, ever repeated your movements. If you went right last time around a rock, go left next time. If you paused last time, don't wait this time, advised Howard McLaughlin.[109] Likewise, never pop your head up to look around more than once in the same place. Snipers were everywhere, and they searched for such behavioral predictability. Even when in their "own" territory, said Bertrand Yaffe, wise Marines kept to the rules and habitually took an hour to traverse less than a mile.[110]

Other tricks were practical in nature, allowing a Marine to get the best out of his equipment, regardless of what his training had taught him. Within a few days every Marine learned to undo the chinstrap on his helmet, despite having scrupulously tightened it during the landing. This counterintuitive act, which seemingly placed the wearer at greater risk of head injuries, actually helped prevent them. First, if you were shot in the head (as many were, by snipers), a fastened chinstrap hampered the corpsman from getting your helmet off. Second, it was better to let a concussion blast knock a helmet off and send it flying rather than let your head absorb the full impact—*and* have your neck snapped by the tight chinstrap for good measure.[111] When, for instance, Pfc. Fred Schribert was on watch at 0530 and a shell fell nearby, "my helmet took off and went about twenty-five yards. Lucky I didn't have it buttoned. That thing took off and I thought for sure my head was in it."[112] Hence the frequent and seemingly inexplicable sight of Marines running with one hand grasping a rifle while holding their helmets down with the other, their otherwise easily secured chinstraps flapping freely.

More important than anything else, though, was the ability of a new arrival to learn quickly and to adopt best practices by watching and listening to the "old men"—defined as Marines who had survived, miraculously, all of ten days on Iwo Jima, and who, as Alvin Josephy put it, "were bearded and hunched over. Their clothes were dirty and torn, their eyes watery and distant, their hair matted, their lips puffed and black; and their mouths were open as if they were having trouble breathing."[113] Perhaps so, but they were still alive.

Replacements, of which there were two types, were "cannon fodder, that was it," according to Frank Caldwell. "A lot of them didn't know what end the bullet came out of. We had to really get them up to speed [and did] the best we could."[114] Caldwell was not exaggerating: One replacement threw a dozen grenades at the Japanese, just as he had seen in the movies, before someone helpfully mentioned that he needed to pull the pin first.[115]

The first type of replacement, sometimes called "infantillery" because they were sent into whatever branch had the most urgent call, was drawn from clerks, stevedores, liaisons, cooks, and other rear-echelon units, who were often less than enthusiastic about their new assignment because they had seen and heard enough of the battle to want to avoid it.[116] Thus, when Captain Jack Downer was asked to raise fifty volunteers from a headquarters and service company, just ten men stepped forward. The other forty were chosen by lot.[117]

The second type, by far the more common, were young draftees who were intended as shipborne reserves to be fed into battle as required. Such was the Marines' insatiable need for manpower to offset losses that these received poor, almost useless training before being dispatched to the battlefield. One large draftee group at Iwo Jima had received just six weeks' training and another unit four.[118] This was perhaps enough time to break in their boots, but by any measure it was murderously inadequate preparation for combat. Line troops, in contrast, benefited from an extra six months of exercises to impart skills in weapons handling and field tactics.[119] The extra time and practice made a critical difference in surviving Iwo, as everyone but the replacements was aware. On March 8, when Marines were being ground up and minced into the ground at a prodigious rate, Major Robert Kreindler, a personnel officer of Third Division, commented sadly to a combat journalist that "so many of these casualty reports indicate what green troops we are having to use. They get killed the day they go into battle as brand-new replacements. Seventeen years old . . . and they are dead."[120] The only people worse off than replacement infantry were replacement litter-bearers, teenagers who on average enjoyed the shortest life expectancy of anyone on Iwo. Dr. James Vedder was once assigned sixteen of them: None knew anything about setting up perimeters or firing automatic weapons, but all had just turned eighteen and had surnames starting with B. For all the fine talk of valor, patriotism, and sacrifice, Vedder's assignees had been selected in a block and hurriedly sent to be killed. On Iwo, four litter-bearers were sent out to recover a wounded Marine, but typically only two or three came back. A replacement litter-bearer would embark on multiple runs each day until the inevitable happened.[121] Those sixteen would not last long.

Replacements of any kind were instantly recognizable by their appearance, among other things. Robert Donahoo, for instance, joined a company on his first day ashore. A veteran described him as clean-shaven and wearing "fresh, immaculate clothing." Before he had even reached the front line or unhitched his rifle from his shoulder he was dead, killed in a rocket attack before two hours had passed.[122] Apart from a lack of whiskers, the instant giveaway—to friend and foe alike—of a replacement was his uniform. The smarter ones quickly realized that the Japanese took an especial interest in their clean dungarees. Bernard Dobbins saw one new, and clearly astute, guy remove his helmet, pour water and sand into it to make mud, and then rub it all over his face and clothes.[123]

Key to staying alive on Iwo was camouflage: Never stand out from the crowd, as that enterprising replacement demonstrated. On the island, it was a kind of sartorial race to the bottom, with junior officers leading the effort to blend in with the men. They sometimes succeeded only too well, exceeding the enlisted Marines in slovenliness, bedraggledness, and general dirtiness in order to avoid being targeted by snipers. The first things lieutenants and captains did was tear off their bars and other identifying insignia, ditch their carbines and .45 pistols for Garands, and ban anyone from saluting them.[124] Soon, the only way to distinguish an officer from an enlisted man on Iwo was by checking a small stenciled number and rank marker on his jacket.[125] Sergeants and corporals, too, faded into the background as best they could. As Colonel Thomas Wornham pointed out, "The Japanese were just sitting back, and anybody who looked as though he was giving an order, why they'd pick him off."[126] Officers and NCOs alike curtailed non-urgent visits to their foxholes and ordered radiomen and messengers to stay away after it was realized that the activity attracted Japanese fire.[127] Any orders that had to be given were, according to Ted Salisbury, "whispered."[128] The same necessity to avoid sticking out applied to others, of course. Because the Japanese actively targeted physicians, battalion surgeons always traveled between aid stations by shouldering stretchers and dressing as regular litter-bearers.[129] They would still be shot at, but at least not singled out.

Replacements were easily killed because they unwittingly broke every rule until they wised up. As they walked they naturally clustered together, said Guy Rowe, whereas standard procedure was to move in single file, each man anywhere from fifteen to forty-five feet from the other in order to mitigate the risk of a mortar killing them all at once.[130] When carrying a box of grenades or rations, replacements had not yet learned to heave it, as the more grizzled men did, onto whichever shoulder was facing known sniper territory. The heavy wooden box performed a satisfactory job of protecting one's head from a bullet, re- called George Gentile, once a replacement himself.[131]

Worse, they had no idea how to act when the firing started. After four officers and ninety-nine enlisted men arrived as reinforcements and came under fire on March 1, the subsequent report drily observed that "from their actions and movements it was apparent that they had not been in the front lines before." As rockets landed "and the more experienced Marines scattered for foxholes, the replacements stood around wondering at the commotion."[132] Frederick Karch remembered the time when he and several other veterans sixth-sensed an incoming shell and hit the deck even as a newly arrived officer, Captain Jules Blaustein, "was still standing up when the round landed. He was carry- ing his carbine across his chest, and a piece of shrapnel went through the carbine's stock, and left him holding two pieces, and the shell burst impact was such that it knocked him backwards and he fell into a shell hole." (Now inducted into the mysterious ways of combat, he soon got "on with the war.")[133]

Whenever a replacement, like Blaustein, was standing when he should have been prone, or crawling when he should have been run- ning, it was known as being "out of phase," and one unpleasant experi- ence was usually enough to shock anyone into synchronizing with everyone else.[134] As Pfc. Gentile confirmed, "The first time you heard that whine [of mortars], you didn't know enough to move [but] after that first time, boy, you hit the ground faster before the mortar did or else you were dead." Replacements "started to learn survival techniques real early," or they didn't survive, and so they quickly became alert to what their senses were telling them.[135] The silence that descended after a heavy firefight, for instance, was interpreted by beginners to mean the coast was clear, whereas, said one Marine, "most times it meant a pa- tient, well dug in, and hidden enemy was waiting. Waiting for the right moment for them. This, of course, meant it was the wrong moment for you. Too many times, this wrong moment became the last moment for some."[136]

The good news, according to another, was "the infantryman's basic trade, staying alive, is either learned or not learned in one day on the lines."[137] Survival, however, was not simply a matter of picking up practical tips and tricks; it was just as much reliant upon a profound mental adjustment to the demented environment.

9. Understanding Hearts and Minds

Despite the risk, the astounding casualties, and the knowledge that they were liable to die at any moment, Marines kept going. There are any number of possible reasons for this doggedly irrational behavior. A sense of comradeship with others in the unit, love of country, a desire to test one's mettle, of course, but on Iwo the grinding, lengthy nature of the battle argues against any of these as a primary cause. A more profitable avenue to explore is Marines' conquest of fear and their related discovery that, notwithstanding its hellish, thrilling, or grotesque aspects, war is best treated as a job, one that needs to get done to get home. Once a Marine grasped that war is work—unpleasant, unfair, and unwelcome work, but work nonetheless—he could begin to adapt, rather than succumb, to Iwo's idiosyncratic battlefield conditions and accept its necessarily harsh realities.

Everyone was always scared on Iwo, but fear subsisted for the most part as a constant, cumulative, corrosive feeling that bred a "bad memory, inability to concentrate, a demanding appetite for liquor, a short temper, a body that tires quickly, a weary, soul-deep resignation." Men learned to tamp it down and could outwardly appear calm, controlled, and mentally alert—yet the unceasing, low-grade sense of fear chewed "into your body and into your mind like a cancer beyond cure," as one Marine put it.[1]

There was no shame on Iwo at being scared. Indeed, as Francis Cockrel wrote, "It was a familiar, almost a friendly topic; it was the stuff guys bragged about to each other—how full of it they were, this time or that."[2] Everyone knew that a breakdown could happen to anyone. On Iwo, it was a "constant inner battle," said a Marine who had fought at Tarawa, Saipan, and Tinian, "to maintain some semblance of sanity, clarity of mind, and power of speech. Everyone tells me they felt as I did."[3]

But when fear finally hit full on, there was no mistaking it. Left beyond the lines and believing that he had been forgotten about, Allen Matthews "shivered violently and the shivering was different from anything I had ever experienced at night for I shook not only with the muscles in my legs and arms and fingers and neck but I trembled violently internally, too, and my stomach at the base of my ribs felt as if it were suffering from a great tic; it was caught first in a mighty hand which squeezed so violently that my breath caught and then the spasms eased off gradually, only to clutch me angrily again."[4]

The first time a soldier experienced this type of deep fear, he tended to freeze. There were several ways in which a soldier could break the paralysis. First, he could relax and then will himself into action. At one point, Jay Rebstock suddenly stopped and became unbearably thirsty. "Scared shitless," he "could not move, and I drank almost an entire canteen of water, and only then did my legs move forward."[5] To prevent freezing in the first place, when he detected the clammy claw of fear Bertrand Yaffe would repeat, "If I can just get though the next ten minutes, I'll be all right. Just a few minutes!" while Jim Craig confirmed every couple of seconds that "I'm still alive and okay."[6] On Iwo, as at Bunker Hill and Gettysburg, stopping meant death.

Alternately, a paralyzed man could be chivvied or embarrassed into action. When Gerald Averill found a sergeant prostrate in the sand, he managed to break fear's narcotic spell "with a little sweet talk, and some more with considerable sting to it."[7] This technique did not always work. When another sergeant visited Averill's foxhole and confided that he was liable to crack, he tried to console the man by telling him he "must do his duty," but the effect was only temporary. The ruined sergeant was evacuated two days later.[8]

Or third, he could think of home and his earnest desire to return to it. Matthews recovered his mental footing only after he "thought of my family and that was painful. I tried to put the thought aside but could not and they were with me as clearly as if they sat there in the flesh. I knew then more keenly than I'd ever felt before that I did not want to die."[9]

As their forebears had similarly discovered in 1775 and 1863, the best way to keep fear in its box was to keep yourself engaged in your immediate task. William Doran advised that when "you're so busy, and things are happening so fast, you're disconnected from the fear."[10] For Woody Williams, "I had a job to do, and I suppose I got so wrapped up in it I didn't have time to think."[11] Charles Chandler, a corpsman, controlled his nerves by "detach[ing] myself and focus[ing] on what I was doing and then when I was through with that something else would come up and I would pass on to that. Later you start thinking about it, but at the time you don't have the luxury of doing that."[12] Conversely, Francis Cockrel's worst moments on Iwo came when "I had to lie still for a time, and shells were landing not very far off. I had time to think then: 'Maybe the next one will come here.'" But he managed to fight off mounting apprehensions by occupying his mind trying to work out how to storm a nearby pillbox. Thinking through the problem, Cockrel said, ate up the "time to think about what might happen to you. When known risk is involved, you balance it against the . . . importance of the pillbox; but you don't paw it around with your emotions."[13]

It was best to focus solely on what needed to be done, not on what might happen. Thanks to his training, Wayne Bellamy already knew what was required to achieve his unit's objectives for the day, so he just "automatically" went ahead with his task.[14] It was often easier, or rather simpler, than even that. "Whatever they wanted you just did," remembered Domenick Tutalo, a replacement who was initially terrified but succeeding in controlling himself.[15] Likewise, Al Abbatiello was scared but "did what I was told to do, and I did it when I was told to do it."[16]

When everyone "did what they were told to do" or "did what they were trained to do," order arose from chaos, persuading scared waverers that events were under control, madness had not triumphed, and death not imminent. Fred Haynes observed that by mid-afternoon of the first day, for instance, even the beach landing zone had slowly begun to transform into a sane place. Marines "were adapting, finding ways to put together fire teams, taking care of the wounded and dead. . . . In general, we were sorting ourselves out and getting on with the business at hand. Somehow, amid the mayhem, little pockets of order and purpose emerged."[17]

Indeed, the key to taming fear, the solution to achieving victory, was to realize, individually and collectively, that fighting is a job. To keep your balance you cannot cast your mind back and wonder why you volunteered, complain that others get to stay at home, or question whether you should have left your family. "You see, you can't live in that world, at home," explained Joseph Kropf. "Don't ever live in that world. You've got to live in the world of 'This is my job.' "[18] A soldier should never confuse war with "heroics and dramatics, of dash and spectacle," advised Francis Cockrel. While there are "periods of urgency, certainly, demanding the right decision, made instantly, and split-second timing and desperate effort," they are but parts of a whole "and the whole is no more or less than dangerous drudgery—mean, exhausting work at which men get shot and blown apart."[19]

The "work" had to be executed as efficiently and as effectively as possible to reduce casualties and shorten the time needed to conquer the island. As David Severance put it, "We knew that as soon as we covered all the real estate, they were gonna pull us out. It was just a matter of pushing, trying to get up to the north end."[20] Marines quickly adapted to the necessity of fighting a ruthless battle of annihilation against an equally ruthless enemy. In short order, they waged a war where no quarter was given, asked, or expected.

No act was ruled out of bounds so long as it brought the Marine Corps closer to victory. William Doran, for instance, was amused when a raw lieutenant rebuked him for fashioning dum-dum bullets for his .45 pistol. They were forbidden by the Geneva Conventions, he admonished. Doran, a veteran of several Pacific landings, promised the officer that "we'll have a little discussion about the Geneva Convention[s] and what's right and what's wrong in a war. Well, we never had that discussion."[21]

Emotions were fatally tangential to achievement of the objective.

Like many others, Patrick Caruso occasionally came eye to eye with a Japanese trying to kill him, and "you [would] freeze for a brief moment, then the adrenaline flows and you quickly try to get him before he gets you. This soon becomes instinctive."[22] When Joseph Kropf found a wounded Japanese soldier, his lieutenant directed him to execute the man. "So I had to bayonet him. And that's not a nice feeling. You know how you have to bayonet. It's cruel, and you see the blood gushing out, and you see the eyes. That's when you say, That could be me."

In these situations, Marines distinguished between the code of "kill or be killed," which was eminently rational, and "the lust to kill," which was a dangerous sign of mental turmoil.[23] The relative lack of primeval emotion or outright hate or bloodthirsty desire for revenge on Iwo is striking. Marines spoke instead of "numbing" themselves in order to perform their job of taking the island. Luther Crabtree was surprised to find that "I didn't have any anger throughout that entire battle; I was numb. As I look back on that, I think I was so well trained that I just did my job." (Crabtree's calmness is all the more remarkable considering that on February 26 he came across the corpse of his brother, shot in the head by a sniper.)[24] Within only a few days of landing, Charles Lindberg discovered that "I didn't have any feelings. You'd burn them because they'd do it to us. . . . I was numb; just doing my job."[25] Howard Baxter, similarly, thought that the best way of staying alive was to "shut down your emotional system," quash any feelings you might have, and "get the job done."[26]

American behavior on Iwo, among other places, has nevertheless been attributed to individual and institutional racism against the Japanese: The Pacific enemy was treated far more barbarically than his Atlantic counterpart, because Germans (and Italians) were white and the Japanese were not.[27] Certainly, there was endemic and casual racism among American troops and society (particularly toward blacks), but one could say the same of virtually any country or nation at the time, at least by modern standards, and the American version of racism, despite its noxiousness, was a far cry from the annihilationist style practiced elsewhere. In any case, that one race or another was intellectually, physically, and aesthetically superior to others was an evident and universal "truth" taken for granted before 1945 among even the most enlightened citizens of the world. It was a vestige of the "scientific" racism of the nineteenth and early twentieth centuries, and we should not be surprised to find it subsisting among members of the United States Marine Corps. Wartime propaganda depicting the Japanese as termites, bats, rats, monkeys, and the like can be dismissed as just that; how seriously it was taken is open to question.

The free use of flamethrowers, the implacable liquidation of Japanese forces, the mass machine-gunnings, the burial of live men in caves—the exterminationist acts so frequently invoked to demonstrate that Pacific combat was allegedly motivated by a racist urge to rid the world of the Nipponese pestilence—were in fact arguably practical, or instrumental, reactions to the particular conditions pertaining on Iwo Jima. Flamethrowers were used because they were found to work spectacularly well, not because the Japanese were ideologically regarded as a lower race than the white Germans.

Indeed, in the 1930s, American military analysts had not treated the Imperial Japanese Army (IJA) as an "alien" menace whose personnel existed outside the conventional laws of war and thus could be exterminated like vermin. They instead assumed that the IJA was part of a shared, "civilized" military culture and so naturally dissected its capabilities along the same lines as they did its German and Italian equivalents. By those conventional measures, the IJA fell particularly short. It possessed few tanks, aircraft, artillery pieces, and heavy machine guns—then considered the weapons of the future—and lacked any discernible skill in combined air-sea-land operations—then considered the epitome of martial progress. It was a generation, if not more, behind and something of a joke force, much as the Habsburg Austrian army had existed in the nineteenth century only to be beaten.[28] Even Japan's soldiers were ridiculed as being better suited to some medieval peasant army. In the U.S. armed forces, beards were forbidden and shaving compulsory; boots were polished; uniforms starched. In the peacetime IJA, in contrast, except when they donned dress uniforms for ceremonial duties, men and officers alike went unshaven for days, had dull buttons, dirty boots, ill-fitting trousers, and patched elbows.[29] Any number of military analysts confused their relaxed slovenliness with lack of discipline and absence of ability.[30]

Where the IJA crucially erred, all agreed, was in relying so heavily on infantry, the stodgy combat arm effortlessly overshadowed by the silvery glamour of air forces and the globe-spanning might of navies. It was assumed that Japan, if it came to war, would quickly collapse once the Marines took the outlying Pacific islands and the U.S. Navy sunk its fleet. Any lingering apprehensions of the Japanese army were laid to rest in 1939 at the battle of Nomonhan (sometimes known as Khalkhin Gol).

Unlike Britain, the United States, France, and Germany, which had advanced along a steep learning curve on the Western Front between 1914 and 1918, Japan had never fought a first-rank power, only Tsarist Russia and Imperial China. At Nomonhan, that lack of experience became obvious when the IJA was crushed by the Soviet army, itself a force accorded little credit by Western military experts. Put bluntly, regarding Japan's performance at Nomonhan, it is difficult to think of a battle more incompetently fought, of operations more disastrously executed, of plans more obtusely pursued, of armies more ineptly commanded. Japanese generals displayed, for instance, a bizarre obsession with protecting their regimental colors, a necessity in the nineteenth century to ensure unit cohesion and coordination but an affectation in an era of camouflage, radio communication, and integrated armored, air, artillery, and logistics arms.[31] Worryingly, it was not as if Nomonhan was a fluke, a onetime failure by an otherwise sterling force. Throughout Japan's campaigns in China during the 1930s, foreign observers reported that despite winning in the end the IJA consistently struggled against its much weaker opponent.[32]

Informing many of these analyses, of course, was an implicit assumption that an Asian army could not possibly compete with a white Western one. One observer reassured readers that "Japanese officers are technically less sound than ours" and that while they possessed "magnificent 'nerve' and fighting ardor," there was little to worry about. After all, a Japanese's "weakness consists of his failing to remain master of combat," for "his courage and conception of honor are far more in-spired by . . . passion than by a real and realistic understanding of the necessities of the craft of arms." American and European officers, in contrast, were rational, masculine, and disciplined—making them more than a match, if it came down to it, for any Japanese soldier, whose "feminine and emotional quality" typically made them "lose control of their nerves."[33] One should not forget either the curious image many Americans had of the Japanese physique before the war. Bucktoothed, compact, and bespectacled—on top of being feminine and emotional—the Imperial Japanese Army simply was impossible to take seriously.

To reiterate, despite these patronizing remarks (typical of the time as regards foreigners of various creeds and hues), the role that outright rac-ism played in American and European evaluations of the IJA was never-theless minor. The dismissal of Japanese capabilities before the war was partly due to a more prosaic combination of a lack of analysts trained in Japanese—before 1941 there were at most a dozen U.S. Army and Navy intelligence officers capable of making informed evaluations—as well as to Tokyo's habitual secrecy and its impressively effective security police.[34] But the real reason Japan was judged, disastrously, not to be a potentially formidable antagonist in the Pacific is that in order to fill the gaps in their knowledge, American analysts had erred in assessing Japan on the basis of their *own* yardsticks of progress—a terrible blunder when Japan had already shed its once-shared military culture.

To Americans, Japan's unmodern reliance on infantry was *ipso facto* a deplorable weakness, but to the Japanese, it was a strength. Mass-producing modern armaments required a powerful industrial economy, which they lacked, whereas men would be trained along the mystical lines of such martial values as *bushidō*—the warrior's code emphasizing loyalty, duty, sacrifice, courage, and strength—to multiply their strik-ing force, aggression, and speed. If the entire Japanese economy could produce just 47,900 motor vehicles of all classes in 1941—its peak—and the United States that same year manufactured 3.5 million cars, well, then, the Japanese could excel in lightning-fast surprise infantry attacks executed at night with a suicidally "offensive spirit." The Americans might enjoy overwhelming logistical superiority, matchless heavy weaponry, and advanced technology, but the IJA played to its strengths by marching on a bowl of rice a day, traveling with nothing more burdensome than light machine guns, grenades, and portable mortars, and being second to none in unconventional hand-to-hand combat.[35]

Japanese propaganda trumpeted the superiority of the spiritual approach to warfare. Soldiers and the civilian population alike were taught that *bushido* was an ancient tradition unique to Nippon, as was worship of the emperor and the glory of self-sacrifice for the greater good of the nation. But really none of this was true: *Bushido* dated from the seventeenth century—hardly "ancient"—and in most respects was almost indistinguishable from traditional Western, even universal, military or chivalric ideals. In any case, the code had long been in abeyance and only in the mid-1920s was it revived, debased, and radicalized for nationalist and imperialist purposes. Conscripts and officers were brainwashed through harsh discipline and rigorous indoctrination into believing that surrender was disgraceful, that lesser breeds must be brutalized, and that fighting to the death was idyllic.

The sea change in cultural attitudes manifested itself most forcefully in the treatment of prisoners of war. In contrast to their despicable behavior in World War II, before the 1930s Japanese soldiers had treated the prisoners they had taken well. Indeed, they used to themselves surrender with nary a complaint, yet by the end of that decade we find nothing but adulation for a Major Kuga Nobura, who had been taken by the Chinese at Shanghai after being wounded. When he was released from captivity, he immediately returned to the battlefield site of his ignominious and unwilling surrender and committed suicide to erase the shame. For this act, all seven Japanese movie companies produced stirring films about his death.[36]

Just as Americans underestimated (or perhaps, "misestimated") Japanese skills before the war, in the months following the surprise walloping at Pearl Harbor in December 1941 they swung wildly to the opposite extreme as they watched a mere eleven Japanese divisions conquer Southeast Asia. Hong Kong, Malaya, Singapore, the Philippines, the Dutch East Indies, and Burma—all were subdued by their invincible armies. Allied troops, repeatedly surprised and outflanked by the nimble Japanese, conjured up for the public a pessimistic image of the enemy as fanatical "supermen" brilliantly adept at jungle and island warfare—and seemingly unstoppable, thanks to the very same intangible and "ancient" martial qualities once considered quaintly premodern.[37] Thankfully, the reverses at Guadalcanal and New Guinea by the start of 1943 tempered this depressing reaction, and a more realistic evaluation of the enemy ensued.

Analysts began taking a harder and closer look at the Imperial Army's inflated reputation for invincibility. As a February 1943 intelligence report reminded readers, "With more than a year of war behind us and with experience gained in fighting . . . we can begin to see how much we have misunderstood the [Japanese]."[38]

Before the war, the Japanese had been dismissed; after Pearl Harbor, feared. Now, arrogance and terror were replaced by a practical determination to understand this savage and curious foe properly. The acquisition of solid intelligence on IJA doctrine, tactics, and soldiers thus became of prime concern. Rather fortunately, as the Americans assaulted the outer rim of Japan's empire in 1943 they stumbled upon troves of material. Since every Marine and soldier was instructed to bring in any letter, diary, map, or order they found during the fighting (all of which was passed diligently to intelligence specialists), more than 350,000 documents would fall into American hands by the end of the war. Much of the material was invaluable, a result of Japanese High Command's blithe belief that the Americans still lacked translators combined with the IJA's obsession with recording everything in writing and officers' oddly optimistic reluctance to empty their pockets of sensitive memoranda before embarking on suicidal banzai missions.[39]

Over the course of 1943 and 1944, thanks to regular bulletins put out by various intelligence bodies summarizing the latest Japanese techniques and a wholesale reorientation of the training system to take account of these findings, American troops became remarkably familiar with Japanese tactics, habits, and tricks. It is important to remember that this transformation was happening at precisely the same time as "race war" rhetoric was heating up among the American public as once-classified news of Japanese atrocities (such as the execution of captured Doolittle Raid fliers, the Bataan Death March, and the famous photograph of an Australian, Leonard Siffleet, being beheaded by a Japanese officer) was released by Allied governments.[40] While the latter resulted in a lot of chest-puffing at home about mercilessly terminating the Japanese, soldiers—the ones who had actually been in combat—ignored all the brave talk in favor of practical, concrete, and efficient methods of killing the enemy.

Once so feared, Japanese jungle-warfare tactics, for instance, were revealed as being essentially the same as those printed in the U.S. Army's basic manual on the subject. Another crucial finding was that Japanese officers were instilled with a credo of blind obedience, remained inflexible, lacked initiative, and consistently underrated their American opponents. If they were killed, sergeants and corporals were reluctant to assume command, and their units tended to collapse into an unthinking mass defaulting to an all-out banzai charge to exhibit the appropriate degree of self-sacrificing spiritual firmness. The enemy, in other words, was discovered to be *predictable,* the Achilles heel of any armed force.[41]

In response, the Americans adapted their tactics to counter those of the Japanese. The purpose of many small-scale infiltration attacks, it was discovered, was actually to send individuals to probe the strength and location of American defenses before the main force attacked en masse. Whereas the Americans had been employing the traditional method of establishing isolated lookout posts far ahead to sound the alarm, these were always bypassed by the infiltrators. So the practice was soon abandoned in favor of a perimeter line of mutually supporting foxholes, which was much more resistant to both infiltration and banzai attacks (as the Marines on Iwo Jima would gratefully attest). Once tied-in foxholes became the norm, Japanese charges became, as a late 1944 intelligence report commented, "determined but unoriginal" and hence defeatable.[42]

American offensive tactics also evolved to offset the Japanese expertise in siting their defensive entrenchments to best exploit the terrain. Soldiers were actively encouraged to try new tactics and report the results.[43] As data accumulated, it would become standard practice to employ .30-caliber light machine guns for suppressive fire at a distance and to use BARs, once reserved as a support weapon for riflemen, as anti-personnel weapons in their own right. These reforms were originally not top-down instructions outlined in manuals but on-the-ground findings discovered through trial and error by ordinary enlisted men and young officers that were disseminated *because they worked.*

Another example, soon to be of great importance on Iwo, stemmed from soldiers encountering cave defenses at Biak in May/June 1944. Aerial attacks against these fortified rocks were of little avail, and they were situated in places that were hard for naval gunfire to hit. Troops began to clear them out by pouring gasoline into the entrances and igniting by grenade. Pacific-wide intelligence bulletins noted the method's success and suggested increasing the use of flamethrowers in subsequent island battles.[44]

These lessons translated into concrete changes in weaponry. In July 1942, for instance, a regular Marine division had no portable flamethrowers, but by May 1944, no fewer than 243 were standard issue (plus several terrifying flamethrower tanks). At Iwo Jima, a battalion commander would report that "the portable flame thrower was the one indispensable infantry weapon." In the same period, the number of BARs rose from 513 to 853 and rose from there almost every month until the end of the war. Reflecting the Japanese propensity for hand-to-hand combat, shotguns—which served admirably as close-range weapons—were also distributed; their number accordingly increased from zero to 306.[45]

It seems evident, then, that the use of flamethrowers was not predetermined by racial animosity but was instead a situational, instrumental response to the facts on the ground. Consider that flamethrowers, until very late in the war, had been regarded as, at best, marginal weapons. First used against the French by the Germans in 1915, they were but rarely employed afterward, and even then whatever limited success they enjoyed was psychological rather than practical. Firing a brief burst of flame (an igniter lit a mixture of light and heavy fuels, propelled by nitrogen) up to just twenty yards—a suicidal distance from the enemy line for any lone attacker—they were sometimes given to condemned criminals to operate. In 1921, General Amos Fries, the head of the U.S. Chemical Warfare Service, the very man charged with developing the weapon, publicly disparaged flamethrowers as virtually useless.

Only in 1940, when it was reported that German and Italian flamethrowers had been used, did the United States attempt to develop a one-man portable version. In mid-1944, following several unremarkable models, the M2-2 Portable Flame Thrower was belatedly approved. The two factors that rendered it a viable weapon that would quickly be adopted for Pacific use were its new type of fuel and the development of tactical doctrine governing its use.

The earlier, low-viscosity mixture of heavy and light fuels had produced a "bushy" billowing blast of flame accompanied by heavy black smoke—which was fine for the Army, interested as it was in burning away jungle vegetation from defensive emplacements and using the smoke to provide good cover for the follow-up attack. The Marines, however, had different needs. They had found that the prevailing mixture may have provided a roaring blaze outside of a concrete bunker but that it did not kill its occupants. Their preferred method to deal with the problem was to squirt the lit fuel as a stream inside a bunker's narrow openings from longer range.

Fastening on a new technique in which adding a substance dubbed napalm ("na" from aluminum napthenate and "palm" from the coconut fatty acids used to make it) thickened the fuel mixture, the Marines demanded almost three times as much napalm added to their flamethrowers as did the Army in order to create the desired stream effect at up to forty yards with relatively little smoke. It was this new, high-viscosity combination of gasoline, diesel fuel, and napalm that they took to Iwo.

At the same time, Marines were issued new instructions for the tactical employment of flamethrowers to maximize their effectiveness against Japanese combatants. In mid-December 1944, the Marines conceived specialist assault platoons of about twenty men trained in the use and maintenance of flamethrowers, demolitions, and rocket launchers. They would operate in conjunction with and under the protection of riflemen. Less than two months later on Iwo, as we shall see, these assault platoons would prove deadly against their adversaries.[46]

The new technology interacted dynamically with the improved methods, organizational changes, and the fresh insights into Japanese thinking to produce lethally effective tactical countermeasures and an *ahumanized* attitude toward their use. On Iwo Jima Americans approached their task with all the emotional investment of exterminators hired to kill some termites, or as a creditor views a debtor—as red numbers on a spreadsheet that need tidying up.[47] There was, after all, no existential threat to the continental United States by the Japanese Empire, nor was there significant historical enmity between the two countries, nor was there the ideological-racial witches' brew characteristic of the Eastern Front fighting between the Nazis and the Soviets.[48] Instead, beating the Japanese on Iwo was a job that just needed doing, and they used whatever tools worked most satisfactorily. By the end, the task of slaughtering Japanese was known unemotionally as "processing," as in a meat factory, and relied implicitly on machinery, engineers, and chemical products for its success.[49]

Finding the men who could do that job proved simple enough, for the men of the Marines of 1945 were not the same as those who had served earlier. Before the outbreak of war, the Marines had been highly selective, so selective that in 1939, 1940, and 1941 the Corps had accepted just 38,080 volunteers from 205,000 first-time applications—a percentage approaching that of an Ivy League college. Many of the successful inductees, most from poor rural or tough urban backgrounds, had signed up for financial reasons ($21 per month was a lot for a youth otherwise relegated to pumping gas or working in the mines), for adventure, for an escape from Depression-era unemployment, for evading the law after some indiscretions. That all changed on December 7, 1941—Pearl Harbor. What would become known as the "High School Class of '42" rushed to join the colors. Hordes of seniors, wrathful at Japanese perfidy and filled with righteous idealism, quit school and rushed to the recruitment office. According to Roger Doskocill, "we became Marines by choice, and nobody was going to mess around with us or our country." Bearing him out are the numbers: In November

1941, the month before Pearl Harbor, the Marines had inducted 1,978 men; in December 1941, that figure soared to 10,224; and in January 1942 alone, 22,686 men volunteered to fight.

Within a couple of years, a very large proportion of them would be dead or crippled, the result of unexpectedly heavy American losses. By the end of 1942, the Marine Corps was having trouble meeting its recruitment goals using increasingly less gung-ho volunteers. After lowering its physical and moral standards that April to make up numbers, it would soon come to rely on a third type of Marine recruit to fill the ranks. In January 1943, the government eradicated purely volunteer enlistments in one's chosen military service. Henceforth, Selective Service would assign draftees to whichever arm most urgently required manpower. There was one exception—the Marine Corps, which forcefully argued for its traditionally exclusive role—in the sense that a man who received his draft notification could opt to "prefer" the Corps over the Navy and the Army. If there was room in the quota and he passed the qualification procedures, he would become a Marine "enlistee" rather than a conscript. Additional numbers—desperately needed for the increasingly bloody Pacific campaigns—were acquired by targeting seventeen-year-olds (Selective Service covered only men aged 18–36), who would sign up and be activated for duty on their next birthdays. The Corps also, not entirely enthusiastically, took its first women and blacks after realizing that they could fill rear-area and support positions, thereby releasing young white males for frontline combat duty.[50]

Marines of the 1943–45 period, therefore, were not career Marines, nor were they naive—the bloom had come off that rose at Tarawa, Saipan, and Peleliu—let alone idealistic, though they were natively patriotic. A vivid example of their apathy at the time, as opposed to idealized postwar recollections, can be drawn from their knowledge of the Four Freedoms. In the January 1941 State of the Union address intended to serve as a rallying cry for public support of a possible, or likely, war against Germany and Japan, President Roosevelt had listed the "four freedoms" that everyone, everywhere ought to enjoy. These were Freedom of Speech, Freedom of Worship, Freedom from Want, and Freedom from Fear. After Pearl Harbor, the Four Freedoms became increasingly central to the war effort against fascism and imperialism. In February and March 1943, the most popular artist in the country, Norman Rockwell, contributed four paintings to the *Saturday Evening Post*, which were accompanied by widely publicized essays explaining their importance and meaning, while the Postal Service issued a special one-cent stamp. Yet in July 1943 a substantial survey of enlisted men found that *nearly half* had never heard of the Four Freedoms, that the same proportion had heard of them but could name only one or perhaps two (almost certainly the freedoms of speech and of worship, which were familiar from, and perhaps confused with, those enumerated in the Bill of Rights), and that just 13 percent could name at least three. More than 80 percent—four-fifths—of American soldiers, in other words, were unaware of, unclear on, or uninterested in what they were apparently fighting for midway through the war. That situation was unlikely to change: Two-thirds of the soldiers felt that even understanding what America's war aims were was of "medium, low, or no importance" and just 4 percent said that they would "like to know more about" the reasons "why we are fighting the war." Rather, as the researchers concluded, they "were satisfied to regard the war as an unavoidable fact—a fact because it was presented to them as fait accompli, and unavoidable because their love of country required that foreign aggression [e.g., at Pearl Harbor] be opposed."[51]

In the Pacific in 1945, few cared about a grand mission to win the war for democracy. They just wanted to do the job they had been handed as quickly as possible so they could go home. While they were young, highly aggressive, justly proud of the Corps, and aware of their elite status as shock troops, no air of romance suffused their task. On Iwo, there was no place for such inefficient martial virtues as valor or honor, marksmanship or sportsmanship. Those quaint relics had been left behind long ago at Bunker Hill and Gettysburg. These Marines were products of a machine age and trained specifically for industrialized slaughter.

The Japanese, for their part, only obliged the foe by their stubborn adherence to spiritual values as the key to overcoming doctrinal and material deficiencies. The mystical dominated the logistical at every stage. On the small-unit tactical level, *bushidō* could admittedly bring victory against unprepared enemies but not against properly trained and lavishly equipped forces. Individual heroics could achieve only so much (or so little) against an industrialized army, and it is sobering to be reminded that in 1945 alone the United States manufactured sixty-one times as much organic high explosive as Japan did even as (the late) First Lieutenant Sadakaji was still being lauded as a national hero for attacking a tank with a sword at Nomonhan.[52]

By hook or by crook, the Japanese were destined to lose at Iwo Jima. Like a drowning man cursing the sea, they could only rage impotently against the tremendous might of steel and iron, brass and oil, that pressed upon them as they shed their blood. Marines, meanwhile, sustained heavy casualties but whatever they lost numerically in combat effectiveness they more than made up for in improving their mission effectiveness—the ability to execute their tasks and objectives. The reason was that every hour, every day, they spent on Iwo permitted them to enhance their techniques and hone their skills at liquidation. The cost in blood was accordingly high, but despite initial impressions, all was not hopeless and crazy on Iwo: There were ways, it seems, to make Pandemonium more bearable, even beatable.

10. The Method in the Madness

In the lead-up to Iwo Jima, the Marines benefited immensely from sustained intelligence analysis of Japanese tactics, tics, procedures, and routines while avidly pursuing a course of military adaptation in response to their combat experience. As a result, the Corps had successfully evolved to suit the peculiar realities of the Pacific theater, and adversaries once regarded as fierce and strange had ceased to be either—even if they remained formidable and dangerous.

One manifestation of this trend was the development of a new structure of fire team–based rifle squads (each four-man fire team, led by a corporal, was centered on a BAR and supported by two riflemen). They moved in a diamond formation, with the corporal in front, the

BARman and a rifleman five yards behind, and the other rifleman five yards in the rear. There were three fire teams to a squad—twelve men plus a sergeant to command—and a squad in turn advanced in a triangular shape: two fire teams abreast in the front with the third centered in the rear to provide cover. Three squads comprised a platoon of about forty, which was led by a lieutenant. A basic company was made up of three platoons, which again formed into a triangle covering an area of 150 yards. Added in were special-weapons platoons, squads, and teams, all armed with a selection of heavy and light machine guns, mortars, bazookas, explosives, and flamethrowers.[1]

Unlike the traditional line-and-column formations of previous eras, which required precise coordination and experienced command to avoid entropy, the "rule of three" structure was designed for maximum dispersion, flexibility, and adaptability combined with heavy firepower on call. Whereas his forebears at Bunker Hill and Gettysburg had relied on direct sight and close proximity to comrades to maintain cohesion, on Iwo Jima Pfc. Joe Simms kept his eye on only one man, his squad leader, as a "reference point." His squad was usually spread out about thirty-five yards apart and up to twenty yards deep. "Some were down while others were up and running," and Simms "rarely saw all the other twelve men at the same time."[2] Had a Civil War soldier respawned on a battlefield of World War II, he would have been discomfited by its emptiness.

Nor was there any pretense to maintain strict order in combat to preserve forward momentum. When men were told to move out, said Pfc. Don Traub, you were expected to "run forward like hell in a zigzag pattern, then hit the deck while rolling away from the spot where you landed and find some sort of cover."[3] When a platoon as a whole advanced, each Marine "moved from hole to hole, rock to rock," taking turns to cover and be covered by his mates as he rushed forward in a tactic known as "snoopin' and poopin'."[4]

A critical development was the emphasis on cross-training; that is, a regular Marine rifleman was taught how to operate a broad variety of weapons and so, if necessity called, could serve in any capacity.[5] In combat, Marines switched jobs as casually as required. "Anybody who was close, that's who did the shooting [of the light machine gun] and then got out of the way," said Bernard Dobbins. He himself was a machine gunner, but he fetched ammunition, threw grenades, brought water, took point, or picked up a rifle without hesitation.[6] Weapons nonspecialization and a lack of territoriality allowed units to re-form and divide freely to recover from losses and absorb fresh arrivals. Following heavy casualties, the carcass of Dean Voight's platoon, for instance, was left with a mixture of machine gunners and raw replacements but was easily regenerated by an influx of mortar men to form a regular, capable unit.[7]

Marine vertical hierarchies were as fluid as their horizontal organization. If a platoon or squad leader was disabled, said Alfred Stone, everyone knew that "the next man in rank assumes leadership of the unit."[8] The burden of command was shouldered willingly, if with a degree of apprehension. When Dobbins was bumped to squad leader, he confided to his sergeant that he didn't know what to do. Never fear, came the helpful reply, "your first mistake will be your last." There would always be someone to take your place.[9]

For Dave Davenport such instant promotions were key to units remaining organized, self-sufficient, and on the move. "The attack goes on. The [original] plan is carried out or a new plan worked out," he explained. "The fallen leaders are replaced by a natural move up. When Ludvick was killed I was elevated to squad leader. Mueller and Carson became squad leaders the same way. If we fall someone will replace us."[10]

Hence the astonishing ability of American squads, platoons, and companies to continue functioning and fighting despite Iwo's staggering casualty rates. On Iwo, it was common to see junior lieutenants or sergeants in charge of companies and privates overseeing platoons and squads. Thus, Robert Maiden's company went through seven commanders, two of them NCOs.[11] One platoon in the 28th Marines remained viable even after its leadership changed no fewer than eleven times. (Its final commander was Private Dale Cassell, who lasted for three days before being killed on March 14, D+23.)[12]

The Japanese, in contrast, had emphasized officer-led command,

and it was often remarked that once one of their lieutenants or captains was incapacitated his unit collapsed. According to Dave Davenport, the men "milled around in total confusion if they were not in holes. They didn't have instant leadership come to the front. They didn't seem to have any contingency plan. No alternatives were put into effect by anyone. Their inability to adapt and adjust was woeful." So the Marine response was to target the officers. Rather like at Bunker Hill against the British, the Americans cried, "Pick off the leaders. . . . Drop that Nip waving his sword or his arms."[13]

On Iwo itself, the Marines modified equipment, exploited their unit structures, conceived new methods, and finessed existing techniques to enhance performance and to counter unexpected Japanese behavior. During the fighting itself, senior commanders demanded none of these ad hoc improvements, which were instead passed from man to man, squad to squad, by hearsay, observation, and experience at the ground level.

There were three types of self-guided military improvements. First, material changes. For instance, in Europe, whereas American tanks had to contend with powerful antitank guns, *Panzerfausts,* and heavy Tiger tanks, in the Pacific the Japanese relied on direct human attacks using satchel charges, magnetic mines, regular mines, and in many cases, explosives strapped directly to soldiers' bodies. Thus in the Pacific the Sherman tanks were adequate protection against individual Japanese attacks once some singular field modifications were added.[14]

A typical Japanese attack would involve one man blinding the tank with smoke grenades, the next forcing the crew to close the hatches by throwing fragmentation grenades, a third fixing a mine on a track to immobilize it, and a fourth to place a charge on the hull or turret to blow it apart. To "mod" the Shermans, therefore, sandbags were layered over engine covers to dull the explosions. Spare track blocks were wrapped around the turret side armor for the same reason. Sometimes, tankers welded long nails, pointed end up, to turrets and hatches to impale suicidal Japanese who insisted on holding on to their charges. More effective than nails were "birdcages," two-inch-high domes of heavy-duty wire mesh spanning the turret and hull hatches that prevented the enemy from placing explosives directly on top. Each side of a tank was protected by a thick curtain consisting of wooden planks that left four inches of open space between it and the metal skin. Into the void, the crews sometimes poured a secondary wall of reinforced concrete. The concrete diffused explosions; the wood defeated magnetic mines. As an additional measure, as tanks advanced they were surrounded by a screen of riflemen whose job it was to spot hidden. threats and to kill suicide runners.[15]

Taken together, these countermeasures and field modifications drastically reduced tank losses in everyday combat.[16] Seaman First Class Koizumi Tadayoshi was a member of an attack team and later recorded his surprise that he was not able to destroy any tanks. After creeping behind enemy lines, for instance, he watched a Sherman for a time before realizing that there was simply no way to get to it. He found a tree branch and eventually pushed a mine toward one of its tracks but was spotted and shot at by the riflemen. They missed, but as he ran away the tank fired its flamethrower (another expedient improvement created by engineers, who added compressed-air cylinders to propel a stream of napalm over a hundred yards) and burned his legs.[17] His team was finished, as was he, but the tank remained as dangerous as ever. Indeed, on March 9 (D+18), when Saturo Omagari and a few others sliced open their own dead, stuffed their uniforms with the intestines they'd cut out, and then played dead intending to destroy a Sherman, they managed to attack "the tanks, but it was without avail."[18]

11. The Japanese Defensive System

On Iwo, much to their surprise, Marines were confronted by the deep, thick defensive system established by Kuribayashi in the final frantic months before they landed. Their planners had not adequately anticipated its scale. The lesson: If the Americans learned from experience and adapted to changing battlefield conditions, then so too did the Japanese, though at a slower pace. By Iwo they had shifted from an exclusively offensive orientation toward a defensive position designed to delay and frustrate the enemy with high casualties in the (vain) hopes of impeding a probable invasion of Japan.

In the early part of the war, Japanese anti-landing doctrine had directed commanders to destroy the enemy at the "water's edge"—the beach—when he was at his most vulnerable. A thin but potent strip of fortifications on the beach itself would decisively defeat enemy forces as they approached and attempted to disembark. When they landed on Tarawa in November 1943 during the Gilberts campaign, the Marines, as a result, were forced to contend with anti-personnel mines, antitank mines, concrete obstacles studded with iron rails, double-apron barbed-wire fencing, and a hearty coconut-log seawall, from behind which impervious gun emplacements made of reinforced concrete and coral sand blasted their tanks. By nightfall on the first day, twelve out of fourteen tanks had been knocked out, and the Marines were perched precariously on the beach. Had the Japanese vigorously counterattacked that night, when Marine commanders were tremulously reporting that the "issue remains in doubt," it is possible the landing would have been pushed back into the sea.[1]

By January/February 1944, when American forces landed in the Marshalls to conquer Roi-Namur and Eniwetok, Japanese defensive doctrine had not changed. The Marines, meanwhile, had learned to focus on heavier and more prolonged supporting naval gunfire to scour the beach fortifications, equipped themselves with armored vehicles and rocket craft, and were sending underwater demolition teams to reconnoiter beaches before the attack.[2]

In April of that year, Imperial General Headquarters in Tokyo issued a manual called *Explanation of the Combat Guidance for Garrison on Islands,* which continued to stipulate the increasingly discredited water's-edge strategy. Island defenders, headquarters staff insisted, were to fight and die on the beach.[3] When the Americans came to Saipan during the Marianas campaign in June/July 1944, however, the Japanese could not follow Tokyo's dictates because enemy submarines had prevented much of their defensive materiel from arriving. They had hardly any mines or obstacles, while concrete gun positions were unfinished, and there were dozens of artillery pieces left parked in the open awaiting emplacement when the Americans landed. The general in charge of the island was forced to ignore the manual's orders: He left just a third of his force to defend the beach and took the rest inland to prepare to counterattack. His forty-eight tanks were kept away from the landing zone and were poised to launch a major assault once the Americans broke past the waterline. In the end, the Japanese counterattacks were beaten back with heavy losses, and the island was taken, but the creation of a "mobile ground defense" located in the interior impressed a beleaguered Imperial Army staff with its ability to extract American blood while buying time.

A hastily revised manual, *Essentials of Island Defense,* that circulated in August 1944 stressed constant counterattacks supplemented by a series of resistance zones, delaying actions, and defense in depth to offset the advantage of the Americans' devastating naval gunnery. There would be no more efforts to mount a decisive engagement at the waterline during a landing. The new policy was dubbed *fukkaku*—an "endurance engagement" that would bleed the Americans white.[4] Over the coming battle at Peleliu between September and November 1944, Japanese commanders adopted and adapted the new manual's instructions. Following a failed counterattack, Colonel Kunio Nakagawa ended the practice of banzai attacks, instituted "passive infiltration" (defenders hid and attacked the Americans from the rear), and ordered his men to set up honeycombed, fortified positions in caves, ridges, hills, and tunnels.

It was at this point, as the Japanese had successfully transitioned from a beach-deployment doctrine to an inland-deployment one, that American strategists made a terrible error.[5] They had begun planning the Iwo Jima invasion in the summer of 1944, when Saipan-style "human wave" counterattacks on the first night and a "mobile ground defense" later on were au courant.

Had the landing occurred then, Iwo Jima would today be a lesser example of Pacific warfare—an easy victory. Thus, on April 6, 1944, General Hideyoshi Obata, the 31st Army commander, had inspected Iwo and determined that it required a then-recommended waterline defense. But on May 29 Kuribayashi arrived, when Japanese attention was shifting away from the water's edge. He stopped construction of beach defenses and started banking on a modish counterattack followed by defense in depth. But by February 1945, when the actual landing took place, Kuribayashi had updated his tactics, and a dangerous *fukkaku*-style defense instead awaited the Americans.

The United States, in short, had failed to keep up with their enemy. For this mistake, they can be forgiven: The virtually unknown Lieutenant General Tadamichi Kuribayashi was a starchy cavalryman with a solid combat record distinguished primarily by its conservatism. Unexpectedly handed command of Iwo Jima, he would in fact prove to be an innovative, imaginative foe, the one regarded after the war by his Marine antagonists as the most redoubtable and skilled of any Japanese general. Kuribayashi's risky decision to favor a variant of the *fukkaku* endurance engagement amply demonstrates the extent to which the Marines were tangling with a very canny unknown quantity. On Iwo, Kuribayashi created *Shukketsu-Jikyu* (or *Shukketsu and Jikyu Senjutsu—*"bloodletting and delay"), a passive-defense system based on interlinked fortifications inland designed to prolong the operation, reduce the will to fight, and impose maximum enemy casualties.[6]

Hence the Marines' surprise when they first landed on D-Day on Iwo and there was barely any resistance on the beach itself. The consensus among commanders was that Kuribayashi had, according to the journalist John Marquand, "clearly concluded to wait and take his punishment, to keep his men and weapons under cover, until our assault waves were on the beach. Then he would do his best to drive them off."[7] The consensus was wrong. Kuribayashi was all too pleased to let the assault waves land and *not* to drive them off.

What resistance there was had in fact been foisted upon Kuribayashi by his naval counterpart, who insisted on building gun emplacements and pillboxes there. Virtually all of these concrete extravagances were destroyed on the first day: twenty-three of twenty-four naval gun positions were knocked out before the first Marines even landed, as Kuribayashi had predicted, and the Marines overran every single pillbox, all 135 of them, within the first three hours. Nor, despite an intense effort to "button up" Marine positions before the expected banzai charges, were there organized counterattacks to speak of on the first few nights.[8] Very occasionally, one of his more zealous and desperate officers would disobey Kuribayashi's orders and mount a useless banzai charge, mostly for the sake of good form, but their rarity demonstrates only the general's commitment to passive defense. Indeed, the heavy shelling of the beach began only after the Marines had landed in numbers sufficient to justify winnowing them out.

12. Adapt or Die

Despite the initial success of the landing and the establishment of a beachhead, the first two weeks or so of the Iwo Jima operation were characterized by the Marines' desperate struggle to comprehend the newly altered nature of island combat. As a result, when they headed inland, Marines bogged down. Plans that should have worked, or that had worked before, simply did not, owing to the masterpiece of military defensive science that confronted them.

In the space of several short months and with a minimum of resources, Kuribayashi had created the alpha and omega of island strongholds. With the aid of military engineers imported from Japan, he had fortified his Pacific redoubt to near perfection. Later observers, it was noted, "who had inspected German fortified areas in both world wars testified that never had they seen a position so thoroughly defended as was Iwo Jima."[1]

Every square inch of land was exploited to matchless degree. Every position covered its neighbors with interlocking fields of crossfire. In some places they were clustered so thickly that a machine-gun nest would be sited just yards to the rear or flank of its neighbor—and there were tiers of such defenses stacked in the bluffs. In many places, Marines could not tell where bullets or mortars were coming from, or they received more incoming fire from behind and the sides than from the front. According to Sergeant Alfred Edwards, "One of our machine gunners got shot through the mouth. We thought we saw where the bullets came from. We looked over there, and another guy got shot from the opposite direction."[2] Colonel Thomas Wornham likened the situation to being "just like shooting fish in a barrel, and you were the fish."[3]

Worse, each position was connected by underground tunnels (one, for instance, was eight hundred yards long with 214 exits), so that the defenders of a destroyed post could emerge minutes later through an undetected one.[4] There were sixteen miles of tunnels on Iwo Jima. According to Thomas Williams, "The Japs weren't *on* Iwo Jima; they were *in* Iwo Jima," and Robert Leader likened their winding, branching subterranean fortifications "to the ant farms we had as children."[5] Each and every hidden position had to be found and demolished before an area could be secured.

It was not just the absolute number of positions that hindered progress but their sheer density. In one area 2,500 yards long and 1,000 wide, the 4th Marine Division had to contend with no fewer than ten reinforced-concrete blockhouses, seven covered artillery positions, and eighty pillboxes that together contained fourteen 120mm guns of various models, a 90mm dual-purpose gun, one 70mm battalion howitzer, six 47mm antitank/antiboat guns, three 37mm antitank/antiboat guns, nineteen 25mm twin-mount machine guns, and a 13mm machine gun. These were just the armaments and positions that were identified; many others were destroyed before they could be catalogued.[6] In a single map grid alone of 1,000 yards square, air observers spotted twenty-nine pillboxes, eleven machine-gun nests, and fifteen anti-aircraft guns—averaging roughly one position every 135 yards—interspersed with antitank traps, barbed wire, and fire trenches. And the defenses better camouflaged would have been missed.[7] Indeed, an otherwise detailed military map of the time notes ominously in its legend: "Thousands of caves used for defensive purposes, personnel, and storage have not been plotted."[8] Iwo, in short, was a place where, as a report of the time noted, a single company of combat engineers "knocked out more than 165 concrete pillboxes and blockhouses; they blasted 15 strong bunkers and naval gun positions, and dug up or exploded 1,000 mines and booby traps, filled in 200 caves with bulldozers, trapping more than 100 Japs in one cave alone. Some of the caves were three stories high and blocked by high reinforced steel doors."[9]

Such willpower and effort did not come cheaply. As casualties mounted, a disadvantage of the Marine credo of having the next man in line immediately take the place of the one above him became apparent. As junior-ranking officers unused to handling large formations were promoted to fill "vacated" spots, they resorted to dull, unimaginative, officially sanctioned tactics (the same thing had happened during the Civil War) as they sought to overcome the mare's nest of Japanese fortifications. For instance, when a company of the 23rd Marines lined up to storm an airfield two hundred yards away, Arthur Rodriguez could only think, as they got the order to "fix bayonets," that "this is crazy, just like the Civil War. But at least we won't be bunched up." When they set off, "we all started to charge and yell. To me this was like a Banzai charge, so that's what I was yelling. I heard some Rebel Yells."[10] Again, as at Gettysburg, "orders that came down usually w[ere] very elaborate," recalled Ted Salisbury, "but we'd end up going straight ahead as far ahead as you could go. Sometimes it was yards, sometimes it was more, until you [piled up] casualties so hard that you just had to stop. And then they'd reevaluate the situation."[11] Daily progress up the island slowed to increments of fifty or perhaps a hundred yards, every yard yielding a bloody harvest of Marine corpses, as each morning's attack predictably began after the inevitable artillery or naval barrage—following which the enemy, just as inevitably, emerged unfazed from their dugouts. Every attack defaulted to a boring frontal assault, and instead of concentrating their efforts on weak points to force a breakthrough or flank the enemy, commanders parceled out their assets equally and strove to advance in a single, steady line spanning the entire island to prevent Japanese infiltrators. According to Robert Hogaboom, the 3rd Division's chief of staff, at Iwo at first "the Corps appeared to wish to hold hands and to keep the lines dressed abreast, keep the Divisions abreast of each other. This meant that the Division on the left and the Divisions on the right had much more difficult terrain to pass than we did. They had to cross over the ravines and attack across the deep declivities that were across there and I personally believe it slowed up the operation."[12]

One can sympathize with commanders' apprehensions, but the extreme caution might have lost more lives than it saved, as Hogaboom implied. As a result, on many occasions a unit, after sustaining heavy casualties, would return to its original starting point, only to repeat the mistake twenty-four hours later. The official history of the battle noted drily of one such failed assault that the rebuffed unit "continued the attack [the next day] with no change in formation or plan."[13]

It took Marines between two and three weeks to reject what had worked in the past, climb the learning curve, rethink their tactics, and adjust their techniques. It was only then that enemy resistance truly began to collapse. Sometimes, even a minor change could shift the advantage to the American side.

March 5 and March 6 (D+14 and 15) were key dates in this respect. Until then, Marines had been attacking the center strongholds of the island to little avail. Each morning at 0730—the Japanese could set their watches by the bombardment ordered to precede the day's attack—they set out on their assault. And each morning they were halted after a few dozen yards by a "steel wall of Jap mortar and small-arms fire." On March 5, now exasperated and bleeding heavily from their losses, the Marines hoped to break the enemy by organizing "the greatest artillery barrage of the campaign. Three artillery regiments, massed with V Amphibious Corps artillery, fired approximately 45,000 rounds into the concentrated Jap positions among the rocks." No one could possibly have lived through such torment, yet by day's end the Marines had advanced, a report grimly noted, just one hundred yards.[14]

But then on March 6, one general, who was ordered to jump off the next morning at the usual time, instead surprised the enemy by forgoing any artillery and attacking at 0500. Hundreds of yards were gained at little cost.[15] Word of his success spread rapidly. The very next day, Ray Crowder and his company were ordered to launch a surprise attack at 0500 in order to take a ridge that had thus far defied every attempt. Again, there was to be no opening artillery barrage. No one knew whether it would succeed; some of the men grumbled that everyone would be massacred, but in the event they met little resistance. The second platoon encountered some Japanese, but they were asleep, while the first platoon reached its objective without firing a shot.[16] It would not always be so easy, especially once the Japanese adjusted their schedules, but still, the Marines had broken free of their straitjacket. As Corporal William McConnell remembered, he received "an unusual order" around this time: "Units that could advance were to do so even if it meant leaving the flanks open and unprotected. This was new to me." That day, they conquered three hundred yards, a "major" achievement.[17] From then on, it was difficult to go back to the old ways.

We can see adaptation in action by reading the official after-action reports of 2nd Battalion, 26th Marines. On February 21 (D+2), as per approved procedure, their patrols attacked active pillboxes and caves bypassed by preceding units. It took another five days (until February 26, D+7) to establish conclusively that rifles were of course useful in this respect, but only hand grenades and antitank guns could be counted as "indispensable weapons in attacking pillboxes and caves." Corporals Folsom and Trentham of Company F proved the point by using them to destroy five pillboxes. By March 2 and 3 (D+11, 12), grenades had become the weapon of choice against caves because Marines had learned that "flat trajectory weapons [e.g., rifles] were useless except for direct targets of opportunity." Two days later, as they reached the two-week point on Iwo, the battalion was employing tanks, personally directed by infantrymen, to blow apart pillboxes and seal caves. It was a method that "proved more satisfactory" even than relying on grenades. Unfortunately, by March 10 (D+19) the tanks were coming under heavy attack from Japanese artillery and were highly vulnerable in the craggy terrain. After two days of losses, on March 12 "it was decided that new tactics must be used. Artillery, mortar, and small-arms fire was ineffective, and the terrain unsuitable for air bombardment," so combat engineers were brought up to clear the tanks' path of mines while an armored bulldozer leveled a road "through the rocks to the front lines . . . and tanks were immediately brought up to fire to the front." Within a day (March 13, D+22), "the infantry-engineer-tank coordination proved to be the solution to breaking the unusual and particularly strong lines of resistance." As tanks blasted camouflaged positions, infantrymen spread out and "used sniper tactics, firing at all movement to the front." Then "the assault squad was combined with engineer personnel under Sgt. John Potter, of Co. D, and was used very effectively in close fighting, sealing caves and knocking out pillboxes" that the tanks had not quite finished off.

On March 14 (D+23), all the hard work and deadly schooling paid off. The battalion advanced no fewer than four hundred yards in difficult terrain "in spite of low morale, fatigue, and an average strength of 70 men per company." That night, a final infiltration attack was beaten back. It was an unmistakable sign that resistance had broken and that the Japanese were at their wits' end. Two days later the battalion was relieved and departed Iwo Jima on March 27.[18]

On the other side of the hill, we witness the gradual breakdown of the Japanese as the Marines battered them day by day. In the beginning, the Marines were not facing (despite superficial appearances and movie clichés) a ragtag bunch of fanatics scattered haphazardly about. There was, in fact, a professional, balanced, organized order of battle. Not only did Kuribayashi have such distinct elements as machine-gun battalions, engineer companies, infantry regiments, and military police, but he could also call on expert well-digger, disease prevention, and radar/communications components (plus a "special weather unit").[19]

Yet as early as February 23 Japanese organization was falling to pieces under the onslaught by Marines learning and adapting as they went. An official report stated that the plans to stop the enemy advance had "become hopeless," their fixed defenses "useless" against "the air-sea-land cooperation of the enemy." By that date, a third of the island was in U.S. hands.

Under incessant attack, units, or what was left of them, were rapidly cut off from communications and left by themselves to work out what to do. Telephone wires had been severed by artillery; since there was no way to repair them, messengers had to be sent—a time-consuming, unpredictable, and dangerous process. In order to deliver and receive a simple order from his command post just a couple of hundred yards away, a Lieutenant Sugihara had to take three runners with him in the hope that one of them at least would get through. The trip took nearly an hour and a half.[20] By March 10, according to First Lieutenant Musashino Kikuzo, "during the daytime we hid in caves, and at night we wandered in the battlefields, aimlessly, without hope."[21] Adding to the confusion, most of the defenders had no idea where they were on the island, were sealed off from any knowledge of the outside world (including the neighboring bunker), and were kept in the dark as to Kuribayashi's plans (aside from a vague admonition to die gloriously) or their degree of success.

A significant proportion of the "fanatical" fighting in the bunkers, blockhouses, pillboxes, and caves after the first few weeks but before the very end, then, we can ascribe to their defenders' not having an inkling of what was happening or who was winning. In their minds, it was perfectly possible that the Americans were being beaten, so it was rational to keep fighting. As early as dusk of D-Day, Lieutenant Sugihara could gain heart from his estimate that the Americans had failed to land more than two thousand men on Iwo—an easily defeatable force, but one, alas, that Sugihara had drastically undercounted. In fact, V Amphibious Force had brought ashore thirty thousand Marines.[22] He was not alone in his fictions. After all, among the defenders it was common knowledge that Japanese "Special Attack Units" had already sunk "six carriers, two battleships, two cruisers, possibl[y] four destroyers," a belief that, if accurate, would have meant that the U.S. Navy lost more materiel at Iwo Jima than at the battles of the Coral Sea, Midway, the Philippine Sea, and Leyte Gulf combined.[23] Senior commanders knew, of course, that the situation was hopeless—and told Tokyo so—but their subordinates' ignorance was bliss, for then there could be no surrender to the Americans.

13. Minefields and Antitank Weapons

From the bloodless official reports and scarce diary entries of Americans and Japanese alike, we cannot extract much impression of what the learning curve actually entailed, in terms of flesh, for Marines (or Japanese). There were four primary types of defenses the average Marine would encounter on Iwo Jima, so to rectify this we'll examine each of these in turn to discover how they were surmounted.

Of the quartet, minefields were the most easily dealt with, although, as John Thurman pointed out, because the Japanese did not deign to mark their presence, the first inkling of being in one came when somebody suddenly burst apart.[1] When that happened, everyone immediately halted but did not drop deckward (as they would if a mortar had landed). Corpsman Jerry Cunningham was with a squad under Sergeant Smallwood, who ordered the men to freeze one hundred feet along a path. "It seemed like hours, but it was probably a matter of several minutes that we stood there afraid to move," he remembered. Each Marine then precisely and painstakingly, and of course unhurriedly, retraced his footsteps to exit the minefield.[2]

If retreat was impossible, the alternative was to plug on and hope for no more casualties. Sharp eyesight and a light tread became critical. Cecil Downey, an assistant machine gunner lumbered down with a 21-pound box of ammunition in each hand, scanned obsessively for any sign of freshly turned dirt (indicating that the Japanese had planted a mine there) and walked on tiptoes. The man directly ahead of him exploded, and two more soon after. But there was no going back. Then it was Downey's turn: After stepping on a particularly well-hidden mine, he felt himself lifted skyward and hurled back to the ground, "breathless inside a clanging bell of concussion. He couldn't breathe. His lungs fought for air and it wouldn't come. He was conscious of the hot surge of blood rushing out of him." Downey was severely wounded but survived thanks to nearby medics.[3]

The next step was to call in the engineers for mine-clearing. As the Japanese used non-magnetic materials in their mines, they were invisible to mine detectors, so the job needed to be done by hand. Like many others, Howard McLaughlin learned to "crawl along the rows on your belly, probing the ground ahead of you very carefully with your bayonet." He slid it gingerly at a 45-degree angle into any suspicious area; if he met the slightest resistance, then he stopped pushing, for some Japanese mines were set to explode with as little as five pounds of pressure applied. The engineer then gently swept away as much of the sand covering the object as he could and planted a flag, either white (for possible mines) or red (for confirmed ones).[4] White meant that you could cross your fingers and take your chances walking there; red entailed death. If there was time to spare, he would unspool a length of cord with mini-charges attached so that it touched every flag. Ignited, the cord would destroy an entire minefield all at once.[5]

More often, however, engineers did not have time to spare. Mortars sometimes rained in, and slow-moving mineclearers always made tempting targets for snipers. They took shortcuts. "There's acid inside [a common type of mine], and when you break it, a battery is activated, and that sets off the charge," explained Al Abbatiello. "But you could grab them by the handle and set them to the side, so everybody could go around them."[6] In these cases, as they cleared the way through the field, the engineers would mark a narrow safe path with white tape to help the infantrymen following behind. When their squad moved up, Robert Maiden told Lonnie Corrazine, a new machine gunner from Texas, to do "double time across, [and] stay on the white tape. If you should receive fire, hit the deck on the tape." But when the Japanese opened up, Corrazine panicked and strayed outside. "All I saw after the explosion was the upper half of his body about twenty feet in the air," Maiden sadly recalled.[7] It was an iron rule: Stay on the tape. Transgressors would learn their lesson, as happened when Ernest Moreau and his squad were picking their way through a partially cleared minefield. A replacement, seeing an officer's body with a sword, wandered off to pick it up—a foolish thing to do even when one was not in the middle of a minefield—and promptly stepped on a mine. Despite the man's hollering for help, their sergeant ordered the rest of the squad to leave him there and walk on. A corpsman would (possibly) come along once engineers had checked out the mines.[8]

No rifleman liked minefields, but they were a relatively minor threat that engineers, once they had learned their location, could clear without too much trouble. Tanks and other vehicles, however, were particularly menaced by the Japanese practice of burying aerial bombs and torpedoes in places where armor was likeliest to pass. The explosions were often spectacular. Alvin Josephy saw a halftrack moving along a runway when "there was a burst of earth beneath [it], followed by a sharp crash. The vehicle rose slowly and turned over, settling in a cloud of dust and sand." Everyone nearby threw himself to the ground to avoid the flying debris. "Five burned bodies lay among the twisted wreckage."[9] When Robert Neiman's tank company ran into an antitank minefield, losses quickly mounted. "The third tank to my right blew up with a tremendous flash and cloud of dust," followed by at least two more tanks. From one of them, the entire "turret [flew] through the air, led by the flying figure of Gy.Sgt. Joe Bruno" (who miraculously survived).[10]

More dangerous still for their crews was when their advance faltered as they warily slowed or halted after mines had gone off. Their hesitation left them vulnerable to the Japanese antitank gunners hidden nearby. As Gerald Averill watched a Sherman "rising slowly, lazily into the air, turning on its side as it fell back, coming [to] rest, turret down" after it had rolled over a torpedo, the enemy was already "reaching for the [other] Shermans" with their "wicked 47mm antitank rounds." Mortars and artillery finished off any tankers who escaped their burning, shattered vehicles.[11]

While Shermans were impervious to mere bullets, a single Japanese armor-piercing antitank round could destroy them.[12] Sergeant T. Grady Gallant saw a round hit a Sherman's turret, leaving in its wake a hole "remarkably smooth, clean, and efficient, as if it had been made by a punch, but larger—about the circumference of a banana, and very straight." Inside, the round whirled around, bouncing off the sides, and after hitting the stack of high-explosive ammunition "acted like a beater in a mixing bowl of eggs, spinning and mixing the contents, splashing the wall of the bowl with whites and yolks until they are no longer recognizable as eggs at all, but are a jellied, liquefied mass blended into a viscoidal, sticky fluid." A few minutes later another Marine opened the hatch—the metal was still hot to the touch—and "looked at the floor of the tank, into the interior of the big machine, where the crew had been. And he vomited. Vomited over the places where the crew had sat."[13]

More often, the round would explode inside the turret, sending shrapnel flying within the tank's confined space. Pfc. Claude Livingston was a nineteen-year-old gunner in the 5th Tank Battalion whose groin was shredded by metal shards; the shrapnel also sliced through his bladder and colon and tore off his coccyx. Shortly afterward, a wounded Richard Wheeler was lying on the bottom bunk on a plane bound for Hawaii when he smelled something awful emanating from "the man whose body sagged the canvas stretcher bottom eight inches above my nose." It was Livingston. "They had him full of rubber tubes which dripped urine, fecal matter, and pus steadily into a glass jug beside me on the deck. He was in such agony that his face . . . was a twisted knot of pain. . . . A succession of sobs fought their way out through his clenched teeth." Even the morphine did not work. Against the odds (he'd been wounded on February 10), Livingston survived until July 17.[14]

The majority of tank hits occurred in the earlier weeks of the battle, when the Japanese had both substantial numbers of buried mines to create opportunities for the antitank gunners and sufficient antitank guns to take advantage of those opportunities. But as Marines learned on the job such opportunities became ever rarer. By the battle's later stages, tanks traveled in small groups of three or four at the most and were invariably preceded by teams of engineers to clear their way and flanked by infantry detailed with shooting suicidal "Satchel Charlies" before they came anywhere near. At the end, there was no defense left against the Shermans. As a flamethrower tank approached a cave, remembered Frank Caldwell, a group of its hapless defenders emerged and launched one final, impotent bid for glory. "One was an officer and he had his sword pulled, and he charged the tank at maximum range. The range of the flamethrower was about seventy-five feet. This tank guy didn't do a damn thing—he just sat there. That officer was pissed off; he charged this tank out of desperation. He had his sword up high, and . . . the tank gave him a blast with the flamethrower, hit the officer right in the crotch, and he jumped up high—still had his sword up high—and then he fell forward flaming, jamming his sword in the ground."[15]

14. Spider Traps and Snipers

"Spider traps" and snipers were other threats that diminished in direct proportion to the Americans' gradual accumulation of experience, territory, and expertise. A spider trap was a peculiarly Japanese innovation, generally consisting of a modified fifty-five-gallon metal barrel (once used to ship cement) that could fit—tightly—a soldier, a canteen, a gun, and a few rations. Buried, they became a one-man foxhole with a camouflaged steel lid.[1] The occupant could lift the lid to either take a shot or to emerge from hiding to stage an infiltration; when closed, it was as if he had simply vanished. Some spider traps were placed adjacent to a tunnel network, allowing the soldier to shoot from one, travel underground, and pop out somewhere else to shoot again.

As was typical on Iwo, the Japanese did not operate individually but instead covered each other. So, even when one was lucky enough to witness, as Bill Faulkner did, a Japanese opening the lid (and, being just as surprised as Faulkner, quickly dropping it and descending), one had to remain alert. When Faulkner ran over and was about to drop a grenade inside, Conrad Shanker stopped him so that he could explore what turned out to the entrance to a tunnel. A few minutes later, he emerged with blood dripping from his knife only to be shot in the head by a hidden sniper.[2]

Even if spider traps exacted relatively few deaths (at least compared to mortars), they were persistent irritants. In the very center of Gerald Averill's company there was one stay-behind lurking in a spider trap who "would raise his Nambu light machine gun over his head and, with the selector set on full automatic, would twist the gun in a half-circle over his head and then reverse it, filling the air with lead right at head and neck level as we squatted in the foxholes, keeping us ducking. Then he'd slip through a tunnel into another firing position. He was still putting on his act days later, when we were able to move out of position. No one ever saw him, just heard that gun whacking away, the rustle of its bullets passing close overhead."[3] According to Fred Haynes, other Japanese would take a single shot to poach a victim and then wait a few hours before firing again. That was plenty of time for the original unit to have moved out and an unsuspecting one to have moved up—and to lose another man.[4]

If the attritional rate was moderate, the ability of snipers to target individuals nonetheless magnified their impact. Being shot by one was never a pleasant experience, of course, and every Marine detested the feeling of being marked out specifically for attention. Dave Davenport was hit in the back "with paralyzing force. I was on the ground, knocked kicking. The pain was spreading over my torso in eddying whirlpools of agony. . . . I found I couldn't move. The intense pain was beginning to numb my lower body. There was absolutely no strength in my legs to push my body forward. . . . I did experience a noticeable stiffening of my body as I flinched, expecting momentarily another shot."[5]

It did not come, most likely because Davenport was actually serving as bait. It was common practice to wing a Marine and wait for the litter-bearers and corpsmen—the real targets of value; 827 corpsmen would be killed or wounded on Iwo—to arrive.[6] Alvin Josephy watched a four-man stretcher team carrying a wounded man as it came under sniper fire. One bearer was hit in the leg but the rest of the team managed to get under cover before they were killed. The wounded man died before they could get back to him.[7] Marked ambulances attracted many a sniper's eye, as did the medical personnel accompanying the wounded.

Marines tried a variety of ad hoc methods to flush out spider traps. Alfred Stone and a friend worked out one way when they were fired upon and Stone fell, pretending to be wounded. Fortunately, he had spotted the telltale muzzle flash and lay all but motionless for fifteen minutes as he surreptitiously sighted his rifle on the hole. Just after dark the star shells came out and the lid lifted. "The Jap put his head up and was looking at the rocky area where the Marines had gone. Then he began bringing his rifle out to fire, but as he did, I fired twice. Both of the rounds hit him in the head, which exploded. That took care of this problem."[8]

In this instance, Stone was successful, but success was costly in terms of time and effort. A better way eventually became standard practice. When a spider trap was discovered, the leader of a four-man fire team stayed back to provide covering fire if necessary while a rifleman sneaked up to within six yards. The two others moved to either side of the lid and waited. Then the first rifleman pulled the pin on a grenade and signaled for them to raise the lid about 45 degrees. The grenade was tossed in, the men dropped the lid, and it exploded before the surprised occupant had any chance of escaping or throwing the grenade back out.[9]

There was always grim satisfaction when a sniper was killed. After John Thurman and some buddies blew apart a long-troublesome one they took the time to go over and study their late antagonist. "His body was ripped and torn in half," said Thurman. "His head and chest were lying with his hips and legs about ten feet away. It was still very early in the morning and it was just getting light out . . . it was chilly. We could see steam coming off his insides. His heart was hanging just below the ribs of his chest in the sand—his heart was still beating."[10]

As time passed, that satisfaction became not quite so satisfying. Spider traps were rapidly diminishing in number and, perhaps more important, the snipers manning them were declining in expertise. A "sniper" at the beginning of the battle was far more skilled than one so designated by its end, when a sniper could be defined as anyone brandishing a rifle.

Thus, in the first several weeks there are many stories of their pinpoint accuracy, a large number involving shots to the head—the most difficult shots to make. As they were leaving the beach, especially, Marines were subjected to expert sharpshooting; there were many times, as Thomas Williams found, when one would jump into a shell hole and say hello to the other occupant, only to discover that he had already been precisely assassinated.[11] Gerald Averill later came across "a heavy machine gun team, the gunner, feet planted firmly in the sand on either side of the tripod, head low against the rear sight, aiming in on an unknown target. To his left, his assistant gunner lay alongside the gun, his hand on the half-empty belt, just short of the feedway. Both of them had been shot exactly between the eyes."[12] When Jay Rebstock dived into a foxhole the two men there stood up to make room. One was instantly shot in the middle of the forehead and the other had a bullet pierce his helmet and come out the other side. Obviously, snipers had been watching that hole closely.[13]

As U.S. forces advanced up the island, snipers began to miss more often, not only because the Japanese had lost their best-trained marksmen but because the Marines had grown wise to their tricks. For instance, Keith Neilson was running a telephone wire back to a command post when a bullet hit the sand twenty-five feet away. Instead of freezing, as a newbie would do, he immediately jumped into a shell hole. The sniper continued to take shots as he tried to get a bead on the Marine. His next bullet landed fifteen feet away, and the next, ten, and the next, five. Neilson saw that they were landing in a straight line—a rookie mistake—and followed their path with his eyes until he spotted the sniper's hiding spot. Knowing that the sniper now had him targeted, Neilson broke cover and ran off as the sniper vainly tried to hit him. Once a sniper's bolt-hole had been found like that, it was not long until a machine gun or tank eliminated it.[14]

15. Pillboxes, Bunkers, Blockhouses

Pillboxes, bunkers, and other emplacements like blockhouses were altogether a different story. (Marines often used the terms almost interchangeably. Technically speaking, a pillbox is a small concrete guard post equipped with apertures from which to fire a machine gun; a bunker is generally a larger structure, mostly underground; and a blockhouse is a thick-walled, aboveground variant of the bunker.) Even after the Marines had reached their highest level of lethal proficiency, every single one of these continued to form a dangerous obstacle.

In the face of scarcity, the Japanese were nothing if not enterprising. Volcanic sand was mixed with imported cement and seawater and reinforced with low-grade steel bars to form decent concrete—it was no-where near as good as American-made, as there were plenty of air pockets and visible seams, but it was sufficient nonetheless to ward off a limited number of direct hits with artillery and tank guns. Wooden ammunition crates were broken apart and their nails reused to provide additional fortification. Sandbags could be fashioned from the burlap or rice-straw bags used to hold food; a two-deep layer provided adequate protection against small-arms fire. Loose sand piled up and shaped around the walls and roof provided not only camouflage but absorbed projectiles and shell fragments.[1]

Incredibly, the Japanese managed to build at least fifteen hundred pillboxes on Iwo Jima. They tended to fit two or three men and had walls up to a foot thick. Robert Sherrod found a particularly well-protected one that had an additional ten feet of sand covering its sides.[2] Well hidden they were, too: Patrick Caruso received an unpleasant shock when he sat down to rest on a convenient ledge that turned out to be a (thankfully inactive) heavily disguised pillbox.[3] Owing to the inland pillboxes' prevalence and cunning placement, it was hard to knock them out with naval fire. Marines had to tackle each one—one by one.

In those situations, tanks were undoubtedly useful. When Mike Ladich's company was pinned down by a camouflaged pillbox, a tank rumbled up, the hatch opened, and its commander asked him to point out its location. A burst of machine-gun fire that ricocheted off the tank answered the question. The tank's machine gun poured fire into the pillbox's six-by-eighteen-inch aperture, followed by three or four rounds from its powerful 75mm gun. "When the shells exploded inside, the pillbox literally rose up from the ground and shuddered."[4]

Unfortunately, tanks also attracted unwelcome attention. Their presence could be counted on to prompt a rain of mortars and shells on any infantry nearby. Despite trying to help some beleaguered infantry, one commander was angrily told in no uncertain words to "park those fuckin' tanks someplace else" by some disgruntled recipients of his largesse.[5] Even absent any contribution from the enemy, tanks could be dangerous to be around in their own right. For many reasons, including avoiding hours of deafness when a nearby tank opened fire, Marines quickly learned to stay well to their side or rear. "If the tank fired the 75mm gun while a Marine was lying on the ground in front of the tank, the muzzle blast could hurl a person five or ten feet through the air," said Alfred Stone.[6]

Behind them they also left behind a trail of squashed corpses, unpleasant for everybody. Frank Walker was three feet away from a tank that "chewed up a Marine just underneath the surface. . . . The blood and body fluids sprayed onto me and I carried that on my clothes for the remainder of the 36 days."[7] Jim Craig was trying to crawl back to a command post when he came across a group of Japanese infiltrators run over by tanks. "They had lain all day in the warm sun and some were so badly crushed from the tank treads that their exposed intestines lay like coiled snakes. Others were grossly bloated. A swarm of blue flies buzzed in clusters in their gaping mouths and eyes."[8] If the corpses had been there for some time, they deflated and rotted and looked "perfectly flat just like a paper doll."[9] But the smell was nauseating. Richard Lowe accidentally sat on one while resting and soon "moved upwind about 10 feet [and] faced the other way."[10] George Nations, meanwhile, was trying to cook some rations but could "not enjoy my lunch" thanks to the stench.[11]

Tanks, in any case, were of limited use against defensive structures other than pillboxes. A fairly standard blockhouse, for instance, had forty-inch-thick concrete walls, measured ten by twenty feet, and had a five-foot ceiling. Inside were three rooms separated by foot-thick concrete walls, and the doorways between those rooms were narrow, to contain blasts. Even a major explosion in one room would leave the occupants of the other two unscathed and still fighting. Blockhouses, too, were protected by a network of pillboxes and were designed to deflect not merely tank guns but high-caliber naval fire. Even by Iwo Jima standards, Kuribayashi's command blockhouse in the island's north was gargantuan. About 150 feet long and 70 feet wide with five-foot-thick walls and ten feet of reinforced concrete forming the roof, engineers would need 8,500 pounds of explosives in five separate charges to destroy it. Wes Plummer remembered that "when they blew up that blockhouse, I thought the world had come to an end. I'd been in the midst of heavy fighting since D-Day and it was the loudest damned explosion I'd ever heard."[12]

Bunkers, because only their entrances were visible, were also almost impervious to tank fire or artillery. Direct hits with bazookas or a tank gun could blast off chunks of exposed concrete, but infantry needed to perform the "wet work" and the mopping up.[13] Early on, grenades were used plentifully. Throw enough in, and sooner or later the occupants would cease fighting. But they always proved stubborn—and dangerous, too, for the Japanese had their own supply of grenades. For every handful of grenades Captain LaVerne Wagner and his men tossed into one bunker, at least a dozen were thrown out. They persisted until none returned. When they finally entered the structure, they found parts of three corpses and seventy-five fresh grenades, neatly lined up.[14]

It was, in any case, quite simple for the Japanese to mitigate the effects of grenades, as Marines bitterly discovered. Adding a right angle to a rear-entrance passage and using small, slanted apertures hindered grenades from being tossed directly in; a drainpipe-sized ditch scooped in front caught them if they tried to roll them; interior walls reduced concussion and shrapnel; and a deep, narrow "well" at the defenders' feet allowed them to kick live grenades out of harm's way.[15]

The essential problem with using grenades or relying on tank fire was that not every defender was killed instantly. They took time to work, and in the interim if even one Japanese was left alive he was a threat. Outside one bunker, related Bill Faulkner, despite several large explosions, a shower of grenades emanated from the shaken defenders. Then some wounded Japanese charged out and made straight for the Marines, whose rifles had jammed. Fortunately, they "ran right into a machine gun we had set up to cover the attack. We moved around to the front of the bunker and found several Japs, all wounded but jabbering and trying to pull the pins of grenades. [Lieutenant Wesley] Bates tried his Japanese on them, asking them to surrender, but no luck." They had to shoot them one by one.[16]

A new alternative technique developed on Iwo to save time and effort was for a Marine to scramble to the top of a structure while his comrades diverted the defenders by firing into the apertures. Richard Wheeler watched one man scrape away the covering sand and plant an explosive charge directly on the roof. After he bounded to safety, there was a loud blast and a hole opened up in the concrete. Another accompanying Marine now thrust thermite grenades through the fissure to create enough heat and smoke to force the occupants outside. As they shoved open the steel door, Marines rushed forward and opened fire, emptying their magazines into the writhing bodies. Three Japanese managed to make it outside "and fell to the ground. One made a feeble attempt to rise, and Ruhl hurried forward to finish the job with his bayonet."[17]

Only one weapon was judged capable of annihilating Japanese with certainty, celerity, and economy: the flamethrower. The problem was that their operators were highly vulnerable to hostile fire. They had among the shortest life expectancies of any Marine, according to Robert Lanehart: The lifespan of "a flamethrower man [was counted] in seconds, twenty seconds or something like that, when you're in combat. Which I can believe. You make a good target. You can't duck too well with a flamethrower on your back."[18] Flamethrowers were always the largest men physically, as they needed to bear the seventy-two-pound heft of their equipment.[19] Husky or hulking replacements, proudly if innocently believing they were being selected for a signal honor, were often chosen to act as expendable operators by their grizzled, and suspiciously friendly, new comrades.[20] Whoever they were, they rarely lasted long. During a single attack on a pillbox, said Jay Rebstock, his platoon lost no fewer than three flamethrower men in quick succession.[21] Indeed, it was a rare thing to see, as Alvin Josephy did, a wounded one. As he was stretchered to the rear, this remarkably fortunate individual propped himself up on his elbows and giddily exclaimed to everyone he passed: "So long, everybody! I'm going back to the States. I been wounded. I'm saying goodbye to you all. I been wounded!"[22]

A lone flamethrower operator was a dead flamethrower operator. His weapon worked only at fairly close range and had a short duration (about eight seconds per tank), and so he needed sufficient protection to approach the target safely. Following guidelines set in mid-December 1944, Marines began to send escorts of several riflemen and BARmen along with their flamethrower operator; demolitions specialists also accompanied the team.[23]

On Iwo Jima, the Marines gradually evolved a three-stage process for destroying emplacements using these new units. First, the BARmen and riflemen would circle to either side of the structure to cover the flamethrower operator. They would fire into the aperture or apertures to give cover and to provide enough time for the flamethrower man to run up and shoot a stream of fuel inside before igniting it with "a metallic click, a whoosh, and a low-keyed roar" to annihilate the occupants.[24] It was hitting the aperture that required training and experience. According to Woody Williams, who knocked out seven pillboxes in a single day (killing twenty-one Japanese in the process), "if you fired the thing into the air and you had any air blowing toward you, it'd burn all the hair off your arms and eyebrows. It would kick back at you, so we fired it in two- or three-second bursts and rolled the flame on the ground. It would roll across the ground, twenty to twenty-five yards depending on terrain, and right into a pillbox."[25]

At which point began the second stage. Much of the twenty-foot-wide fireball would blow clear outside, "but a lot would penetrate the aperture," Williams added, giving the demolitions men "time to get up there and throw a satchel charge" inside to finish the job and help render the structure unusable.[26] Satchel charges weighed between eight and twenty pounds and contained C2 plastic explosive blocks. As their name indicates, they were canvas bags with a shoulder strap, which made their carriers look like overgrown schoolboys.[27]

Wise Marines stayed well back from the explosion, which sent chunks of concrete and metal fragments flying outward. Incredibly, too, there were some Japanese who had the presence of mind to hurl the satchel charge back outside. Sergeant Krywicki was covering a demolitions man who threw in the charge, only to have it land right back next to him. He vanished while Krywicki was spun around twice and knocked flat. All the buttons had been blown off his shirt, and he was deafened. (One ear would never regain much hearing.) His late colleague's scalp, "with all the hair still on it, flopped like a mop beside him," recalled Dan Levin.[28]

Finally, any survivors had to be killed. For obvious reasons, they were few and far between, as a flamethrower instantly turned a confined space into a super-heated furnace that sucked the oxygen out of the air and lungs. Those inside died of rapid and intense suffocation. (Some Japanese soldiers, ignorant that it was not the temperature but the lack of air that was lethal, hung blankets from the ceilings to reduce the heat.) For occupants not in the immediate vicinity (in the larger structures), their clothes and flesh would catch on fire; if they were able to make it outside, they would either die or be killed in short order. Near Kitano Point, for instance, a Japanese, aflame with napalm oozing over his skin, erupted from an exit holding a grenade in either hand. He threw them both, harmlessly, before expiring. Another time, a few soldiers emerged and "ran straight into the fire from my flamethrower," said Woody Williams. "As if in slow motion they just fell down."[29] The more veteran flamethrower men, like Williams, kept their igniters permanently lit to deal with the running-survivor problem. Thus, when two soldiers surprised Alfred Stone and began firing, he was fortunate to have a flamethrower man about twenty-five feet away who "calmly pulled the trigger on his flamethrower and covered them both with burning napalm. . . . The two Japanese were frozen in position when the burning napalm hit them and died instantly."[30]

While flamethrower operators rarely, if ever, saw the effects of their weapon on those Japanese trapped in pillboxes and bunkers (though they could hear screams and smell the seared flesh), the soldiers killed outside provided vivid evidence of their effectiveness.[31] It was particularly noticeable how men's heads glowed so brightly, like matches, after being deluged with fuel and set alight. It was their skins that blackened and split apart as liquefied fat burst through. A large fatty bubble often emerged from their rectums. As the flames diminished, the bubble did as well, but it never popped, prompting much curious commentary from passersby.[32] If anyone poked his head inside the structure, all he would see would be some "flamethrower-charred and bloodstained concrete walls," along with a few crispy bodies here and there.[33]

In Europe, prisoners were habitually taken before or after flame ac-tions.[34] There, flamethrowers enjoyed a degree of psychological value in the sense that defenders would be frightened or demoralized into sur-rendering upon seeing them. In the Pacific, however, while Japanese soldiers were terrified by these fearsome weapons, they still did not surrender. They kept on fighting to the end, necessitating total annihi-lation.

So ruthlessly deadly was the combination flamethrower/demolition method that there appears to have been just a single prisoner taken on Iwo following its application, though this was more by accident than design. A captain once brought in to the Division Intelligence Section—which was desperately seeking prisoners to interrogate—a small, wiry Japanese who had been burned by a flamethrower. Said a surgeon, "His eyelids were swollen closed. The lips were also cracked and swollen and pouted outwards in a grotesque fashion. The upper teeth could just be seen deep in the tunnel of recently cooked flesh. Shreds of skin were peeling from the ears, nose, and cheeks. The man reeked with the pun-gent odor of burned flesh."[35] Even if little was gained from him, flame actions provided practical intelligence of a different nature. For Patrick Caruso, it was useful indeed to see the smoke billowing out from the emplacement's interconnected exits dozens and scores of yards away, now suddenly revealed. They would form the next targets—and so on and on until the Marines reached the caves of Iwo Jima.[36]

16. The Caves

Encountering cave defenses on Mount Suribachi in the first week of the battle, Marines had attacked them with grenades and flamethrowers in an ad hoc manner.[1] In those innocent days, some Marines had even entered cave systems to search for souvenirs. Howard Snyder and Chick Robeson actually dug their way into a cave that had been sealed a few days before. Inside, the "stench that met us was so foul we had to put on gas masks. We went in with a small flashlight and found the cave to have sections. Dead Japs lay all about, so thick we had to tread on some." The good news was that "we found souvenirs galore. I came out with several rifles, a canteen, and a bag full of smaller stuff, including a wristwatch. We also found some maps and other papers we turned over to Schrier. But we really caught hell for being so stupid, and the cave was blown shut a second time, so completely that no darned fools could try such a trick again."[2]

As they moved north, Marines found the Japanese defenders ever more firmly entrenched in ever more numerous, ever larger caves. Over the weeks of fighting, an eerie sound—"not unlike someone banging on the radiator in the apartment below," wrote Robert Sherrod—could be heard when shellfire died down and Marines placed their ears to the ground. It was the faint sound of metal pickaxes striking soft volcanic rocks as the Japanese burrowed deeper into the heart of the island.[3]

By that time, the process of killing Japanese had become wholly mechanical. For the smaller caves, Marines adapted the now-trusted pillbox method. Squad riflemen and BARmen circled left and right (avoiding the narrow fire lanes of cave-bound machine guns) and fired inside as best they could.[4] In the meantime, two demolitions men, having dispensed with their helmets, cartridge belts, and anything else that might clink or hinder them, would sneak to either side, dragging their satchel charges behind them with one hand grasping a .45 pistol (just in case) and a grenade or two in separate pockets. Once stationed on the cave entrance's lip, they set the thirty-second delay fuses, counted down, and tossed them in at the same moment. The thinking was that even if the defenders managed to throw one back, there would not be enough time to return the other.[5]

The resulting explosions shattered, disoriented, and shook those inside but did not generally bring down the roof or seal the cave's entrance with rubble and dirt. Finishing off the defenders was the task of the flamethrower man, who now rushed up and suffocated anyone still alive. Only then did the demolitions men place another charge above the cave entrance and direct its explosive force downward by piling heavy stones on top of it.[6] It was this step that finally plugged a cave. The last horrible thing that survivors—men toiling deeper down, away from the blasts and flames, as well as wounded men lying in lower chambers—saw before infinite darkness arrived was, in the flickering light of their lamps and candles, a wall of dirt and smashed rocks blocking their exit. A few might escape by groping their way to another undiscovered entrance, and some you could hear, according to Al Abbatiello, "digging at night, trying to get out," but most eventually committed suicide.[7] The muffled explosions Marines typically heard emanating afterward from sealed caves was the sound of Japanese soldiers holding grenades to their stomachs.[8] In one memorable instance, at exactly midnight a colossal explosion rocked an entire ridge, throwing up boulders, temporarily burying wondering Marines in their foxholes, and sending concrete blocks and dirt showering down. Inside a sealed cave system, the defenders had set off their supply of land mines and 125-pound aerial bombs to end their lives in spectacular fashion.[9]

Those trapped in the caves had long had a miserable existence. For weeks before their deaths they had been crammed inside what many suspected would become their charnel-house. The corpses they had dragged in to hide their true losses from the Marines had long since decayed, and the wounded's injuries were turning gangrenous. The air was filled with a sickening, fetid stench of pus, blood, and rot, the water reeked of sulfur, the temperature hit 120 degrees, and the humidity level rose to 98 percent. If any of the wounded "groaned with pain, they were told to shut up or strangled," said Saturo Omagari.[10] Men had fought for light and scraps of food as they succumbed to insanity and incoherence, overcome by fear of the coming flamethrowers and the prospect of being buried alive. Now that the nightmare had been rendered real by the Marine Corps, dying by grenade was their last, blessed choice, a final ray of rationality beaming through the murk of madness that had tormented them as they powerlessly awaited processing.

An archaeological team that opened and explored one such sealed cave in 2010 found that even after seventy years there was "a pervading odour of decomposition, a scent which clung to the team's clothes, skin, and hair." Lying scattered around were cooking utensils, rice cookers, opened food cans, mess kits, and bowls as well as personal items like wallets, spectacles, toothbrushes, and even hair pomade.

Bones were found embedded in the ceiling, implanted by the blast preceding the flames that had instantly boiled and steamed the contents of torn-apart water canteens. There was a gas mask—they were worn to try to filter the foul air—melted into the wall at head height.[11]

For the larger cave mouths, terrain permitting, tanks were used in place of infantry. Near the end, recalled Robert Maiden, two tanks armed with the standard 75mm gun were accompanied by a "Zippo tank" equipped with a flamethrower far more powerful than the portable versions. It could spew flame up to 150 yards for about a minute. Near Kitano Point, he added, there was a huge pit at the bottom of which were three caves with openings you could drive a truck through. The tanks descended until they could get a clear shot. Then two 75mm rounds were fired into each mouth followed by a "hot shot" from the Zippo tank.[12] In these instances, Japanese soldiers, all alight, would often bolt outside where the tanks' machine guns were waiting to cut them down. So automatic had become the Marines' actions by this stage of the battle that even this impressive sight was counted, said Bertrand Yaffe, as "merely a momentary diversion" by those already moving on to the next obstacle.[13]

There were exceptions to the rule, generally when tanks were unable to assist, a prisoner or two was available, or an experienced demolitions team was sufficiently confident to cut a few corners. Known as the most "cold-blooded, methodical, tobacco-chewing Jap annihilators" in the Pacific, a team comprising G. E. Barber and L. J. Byfield (ably assisted by S. Bencich and E. A. Bennett) "had a system that never failed," according to William Huie, a Seabee who saw them in action. Barber and Byfield, both Texans, were forty years old, veteran potash miners, and graduates of the Navy's Mine and Demolition School. Whenever they sallied forth to handle the big caves, they brought along a couple of prisoners. As they covered the entrance with their Tommy guns, a captive, waving a strip of toilet paper (white flags were in such short supply that each demolitions team was equipped with a roll of toilet paper for the purpose) was sent in to ask whether the defenders wished to surrender. If he did not emerge in ten minutes, they assumed he was dead and heaved a huge dynamite charge into the cave's mouth.

Any Japanese who then came running out were machine-gunned before Barber and his mates entered the cave to deal with the rest. In one, he said, "I never seen such a mess o' Japs. That blast had smashed their backbones, their jawbones, and some o' their skulls. One of 'em threw a grenade at me, so I finished killing 'em."

If the prisoner emerged, however, and reported no Japanese inside, they sealed the cave anyway—just in case he was lying. If, on the other hand, he said they refused to surrender Barber and Byfield sent in a second prisoner. "I like to give the little bastards two chances," the sporting Barber told Huie, "but it makes no difference whether they come out or not."

On the rare occasions when the defenders decided to come out peacefully, they were told to first remove their clothes, grab a piece of toilet paper, and walk out slowly with their hands up. Once outside, they had to turn around to show that nothing was being concealed. Then the original prisoner went in, retrieved the clothing, shook it out, and brought it all to Barber, who rechecked it. The prisoners could then get dressed and were escorted under heavy guard to a holding area.[14]

17. Surrendering and Prisoners

Barber and Byfield captured twenty or so prisoners—quite a haul for Iwo Jima—but their caution regarding surrenders was justified. There were many cases of Japanese ostensibly trying to surrender only to play murderous tricks on unwary Marines. Corpsman Jerry Cunningham was helping a Sergeant Holmes to coax Japanese out of a cave when two came running out next to each other. As Holmes shouted, "Hit the deck!" the pair suddenly parted ways, triggering a grenade tied between them on a string.[1] Another squad was approached by three Japanese with their hands raised. As they came closer, "the enemy soldier in the middle went down on all fours and became a human machine-gun tripod—a Nambu light machine gun had been strapped to his back, and one of his comrades fired off half a belt of ammunition, wounding several of the Marines before he was killed, along with his two comrades."[2] It became common practice to order potential captives to strip, even in chilly weather, to confirm that they were not concealing grenades.[3]

Just as often, Japanese committed suicide—the more public the better, in order to demonstrate the full measure of their commitment to the emperor. Once, a dozen Japanese walked out of a cave holding grenades to their heads. There was no attempt to kill the surprised Marines, only a defiant desire to take the honorable way out.[4] Near the end of the battle, Austin Montgomery and Dick Tilghman were awed to "see at least five of the enemy dive head first off the cliffs on the other side of the [Death] Valley, and down to their deaths on the rocks below."[5]

Even severely wounded Japanese proved hard to take prisoner. After exterminating a group who ignored their call to surrender, Marines found one still alive, injured and almost completely buried in the sand. A few inches from his right hand was a grenade. Detected, he hesitated as the Marines readied their guns and, thinking better of it, signaled instead for a cigarette before surrendering.[6] Marines habitually kept a close eye on "dead" soldiers lying with weapons suspiciously close to hand. Bill Faulkner and Robert Wells saw one such in a crater. They skirted the edge, watching him all the time. Suddenly Faulkner whirled and shot him. Asked why, he answered: "His eyes followed us around the crater."[7]

There were, however, times where Japanese soldiers did earnestly try to surrender. Master Sergeant Taizo Sakai, Kuribayashi's chief code clerk, was more than happy to put his hands up, asserting that he was not one of the "fanatics." He proved his worth by helping to induce others to surrender, warning when a banzai was likely to erupt from a cave, and providing much useful intelligence on enemy defenses.[8] John Lyttle was once startled by a Japanese shouting, in perfect English, "I don't go for this hari-kiri shit," and entreating him to accept his submission. It turned out he was from Chicago and had been visiting Japan before Pearl Harbor and found himself conscripted.[9]

But in a pattern replicated across the Pacific theater as a whole, such cases were isolated ones. Whereas in August 1944, some fifty thousand

German prisoners were arriving in the United States each month, just 1,990 Japanese had been captured since Pearl Harbor, two and a half years earlier. A year later, the war over, the U.S. Army held 1,538,837 German POWs and 24,138 Japanese.[10] Accordingly, of Iwo Jima's twenty-thousand-odd (estimates range from 18,060 to 25,000) defenders, every one but 216 died there. Of these, 59 were suborned Korean laborers expected to die with their masters but who had elected instead to disappoint them. Eleven of the prisoners died of their injuries, and 85 percent of the rest had been wounded by the time they fell into American hands.[11] Many of them had been unconscious when they were taken in, so they were hardly voluntary captives. So ashamed were they that when they awoke they gave false names and begged for their families not to be notified.[12]

When Japanese soldiers were captured, because they were indoctrinated to believe that the Americans tortured, beheaded, boiled in oil, and ate their prisoners, they were surprised to find themselves treated to cigarettes, perfunctory questioning, and medical treatment equal to that given to Americans.[13] One man, who asked Patrick Caruso not to torture him but to execute him immediately, was taken aback upon learning that neither would happen.[14] But that was only if they made it back to headquarters or a hospital ship; not all did. After two immobilized casualties were shot "while trying to escape" from a jeep ambulance by their Marine guards, Dr. James Vedder began ordering a corpsman to accompany POWs on their way to the rear to avoid similar incidents in future.[15]

By the final stages on Iwo Jima, however, it was easier, safer, faster, more practical, and more fulfilling to kill potential prisoners. One Japanese who had charged William Smith was wounded and lay at his feet. "So I finished him off. I don't think they could have done anything for him. Wasn't intentional or nothing, you know what I mean. We hardly took any prisoners, let's put it that way."[16] According to Ernest Moreau, after a lieutenant spent fifteen minutes coaxing the defenders from a cave by assuring them they would be treated decently and three Japanese emerged, they were immediately machine-gunned by a waiting Marine. No one but the lieutenant cared.[17]

Marines' responses to taking prisoners were a cross between calm matter-of-factness and vengeful anger. George Nations related an incident involving the latter:

> As our tank maneuvered around a large boulder we saw a Jap sitting down with no clothes on, he appears to be blind and is crying. We fire a burst from the machine gun at him [but] just as we do our tank turns slightly to the right. The burst misses his chest and takes his left arm off at the elbow. His life's blood is now leaping out in great spurts and in rhythm with his heart beat. Our next burst hits him in the chest and his body slams back against the ground with a great invisible force. I'm not proud of this, but it happened forty years ago. We had a different outlook on these things. We had lost so many young Marines we couldn't let a Jap live even when trying to surrender. [18]

Rage at Japanese treatment of American captives helped provoke these harsh reactions. As no American voluntarily surrendered to the Japanese this late in the war, anyone who ended up in their hands had been taken while wounded or, as likely, kidnapped. Lieutenant Herbert Smith, for instance, had vanished without a trace one day as he walked back from battalion headquarters to his company. It is possible that infiltrators dragged him back to the caves.[19]

If so, his fate was unenviable. No Marine survived a Japanese interrogation. First Lieutenant Yamakazi Takeshi wrote that during a visit to regimental headquarters one day he noticed that a "Lieutenant Otani [killed in action shortly after] was then in the process of interrogating an American prisoner of war" and left it at that. As Takeshi was too circumspect to later mention, this POW was being tortured to death.[20]

Dean Winters knew a man who was captured "and pulled into a cave where they tortured him by splitting his finger webs up to his wrists. He was screaming uncontrollably. Our lieutenant got so angry he went in after him and was killed in the process." It is unlikely that the occupants of this cave were taken alive afterward.[21] Other Marines were found with all their fingers broken or their heads smashed open with rifle butts; one was discovered hanging nude by his ankles from the roof of a cave.[22] A pile of cigarette butts lay on the floor under his head. The skin all over his body was pitted by cigarette burns. Some were large, some small, some shallow, some deep.[23] (Regarding cigarettes, any Japanese caught carrying Lucky Strikes or the like was destined for the high jump. As Barber, the Texan demolitions man, put it: "It always makes me want to kill 'em when I find 'em with American cigarettes. I know that they got those cigarettes off'a dead Marines." He would not have been the only one to hold this view.)[24]

While brutal or callous or banal, these are not the words and actions of avowed racists but of men who had reached the end of their emotional and psychological tethers. Unstinting Japanese resistance and culturally shocking deceitfulness, weeks of unrelenting stress and anguish, rising casualty rolls and the loss of friends, the onset of dehumanization and the evolution of processing methods, the overwhelming desire to "just get it over with" and overpowering rage at Japanese atrocities, drove Marines onward to the very end.

18. After the Battle

Even after the virtual extinction of the Japanese garrison, the battle of Iwo Jima was not quite over. More survivors than anyone suspected still remained on the island. The official American tally was 2,469. Most of them (1,602) were quickly hunted down and liquidated. On April 19, for instance, when Marines discovered a group of 220 haggard Japanese in a cave, they squirted aviation fuel inside and ignited it with a flame-thrower, killing 150 within minutes.

The rest (867) were taken prisoner one or two at a time. By early May, the Japanese were spending their days hiding in "the grass, near the bottom of trees, or in the crevices of rocks, and at night they became thieves and burglars, stealing from American supplies," said Lieutenant Musahino Kikuzo. Occasionally, a couple of fellow survivors would bump into one another and each would talk "about his own hard life" before setting out to "start again on his hopeless wandering." Musahino himself camped with a friend named Lieutenant Taki, and they knew these chance meetings were becoming ever rarer. After running into Lieutenant Soma and a companion—survival seemed to hinge on banding together in pairs—they never saw them again. Soma and the other fellow were buried alive in a cave soon after.

On the night of June 8–9, Taki and Musahino found a cave complex "filled with corpses. Hundreds of dead bodies still kept their shape, in a variety of poses." It had once been a field hospital, and everyone in it had been abandoned by their comrades. "So the wounded died of hunger right where they had been left. Black hair was still growing from some of the dead. . . . There were thousands of big black flies. Every time you drew a breath, several would fly into your mouth." Still, it was safe enough, so they stayed there for three days, but a machine gun eventually got Taki.

On June 12 Musahino made his way to the eastern coast to commit suicide by starvation—his sword was long gone, as were his grenades. He fainted and lay beneath a rock, waking a few days later with six or seven soldiers pointing rifles at him. They wrapped him in blankets and brought him to a hospital, where he was given nutritious food, injections, and medical treatment.[1]

There remained a few holdouts, who came in occasionally over the next several months. The very last survivors surrendered to a rather surprised pair of Air Force corporals driving a Jeep around the island on January 6, 1949—three and a half years after Japan's capitulation. According to their immediate superior, Sergeant Donald Cook, they had picked up two pedestrians standing by the side of the road "dressed in army fatigues and wearing army field jackets about two sizes larger than necessary." Originally mistaking them for visiting Chinese personnel (there were Chinese ships offshore removing wartime debris), they drove them to the motor pool and left them waiting while they went inside to the office. Upon the corporals' return, the hitchhikers had disappeared. Soon afterward, a staff sergeant found them gazing wonderingly at an American flag fluttering in the wind. He recognized them as Japanese and took them prisoner. Under questioning, they revealed the location of their hideout cave and solved the long-standing mysteries of the vanished canned ham that the Air Force men never got to eat the Christmas before and the ongoing disappearance of flashlight batteries. The two men, Matsudo Linsoki and Yamakage Kufuku, both machine gunners and former farmers, had learned, it seems, of the end of the war after stealing a copy of *Stars and Stripes* featuring a photo of General MacArthur and Emperor Hirohito standing together in Tokyo. As MacArthur was not bowing in the divine presence, they had begun to suspect that the war's outcome had developed not necessarily to Japan's advantage.[2]

In the meantime, the Americans had buried their dead. Unlike at Gettysburg, the procedure was by now well-established and -executed. The Marine Corps had stockpiled thousands of premade crosses and Stars of David, directed personnel to bury by unit rather than by date of death, and had already marked out the location of the planned cemeteries long before D-Day.[3] Five days after landing, with at least five hundred bodies collected, the first permanent internments began.

At the beginning of the process, a team harvested the dead's helmets, webbing, and weapons, which were driven to salvage depots to be either reissued or destroyed, and then three or four men sorted through the personal effects to establish identities and package whatever would be sent home to relatives. "There were some things that were taken out of the wallets, because we [understood] all the wallets were going back to the families," said Gage Hotaling, a chaplain. "So if we found some pornographic literature, that was immediately removed. . . . There were pictures of Marines with gook girls and so on, in all kinds of poses, and those were always removed."[4]

As at Gettysburg, most of the burial details were black units. Black Marines, the first of whom were recruited by the Marine Corps as late as mid-1942, were segregated from combat roles and otherwise restricted to unloading ammunition, operating transport vehicles, guard duty, road construction, lifting the wounded, and moving supplies. Nearly all, nonetheless, would come under fire, given that Iwo was a small island with a lot of artillery action and that they drove supply trucks to the frontline troops.[5] The details used bulldozers to plow trenches eight feet wide and between four and six feet deep. The bodies, enshrouded in ponchos, were interred two feet apart. As each was laid to rest, Graves Registration personnel removed one dog tag and left the other with the corpse.[6] Sometimes, there was just an unidentified arm or leg left to bury.[7]

A registrar then walked the length of each trench to confirm that the bodies were in the correct order. The burial men would call out the name, rank, and serial number of each corpse, and the registrar would repeat the details and write them down. A chaplain followed two bodies behind the registrar uttering the appropriate benediction for a Protestant, Catholic, or Jew. When all had reached the end of the trench, it would be filled in. A cross or star was planted and the dog tag removed earlier would be strung around it with the serial number, name, and service emblem stenciled on the headstone to allow careful cross-referencing later.[8] A body count of a hundred would have been registered as a light day, while March 2, with 247 burials, appears to have been the worst, according to Hotaling's records.[9]

A year later, relatives were given the choice whether to exhume a loved one and have him sent home for reburial or to leave him among his comrades. Most selected the latter. Unbeknownst to them, and kept a secret, the warm volcanic pumice had in the meantime wicked the moisture and fluids out of the bodies, leaving them as mummies.[10] The letters of condolence they received, as well, were models of discretion in certain matters.

Frank Caldwell, a company commander, devoted days to writing to the families of those killed, each letter comprising "three pages per casualty in longhand, in triplicate." His job was "to tell next of kin how we knew this fellow. Some of them I had to lie a little bit because I didn't know everybody or how they got killed."[11] Sometimes it was not good enough. A Captain Fields, having informed a boy's mother of his valorous death in the face of danger—he had stepped on a mine after disobeying instructions to stay within the safety zone—continued to receive querying letters from her for many months afterward. She refused to believe that her son was dead.[12] Other families angrily accused officers of causing their loved one's death through their incompetence and callousness. After Robert Neiman's tank company was hit by mortars and Sergeant Russell Lippert was killed, Neiman wrote to Lippert's wife describing the terrible magnitude of his loss to all his comrades. "She wrote a scathing reply," he recalled. "She was understandably upset, but she accused me of putting her husband in an untenable position and getting him killed." (The story has a curious postscript. When Joe Rosenthal, the photographer who shot the raising of the flag on Mount Suribachi, lost his helmet, some Marines told him to pick one from a pile collected from the dead. "He wrote that he had often wondered about the man whose helmet he had. The name written on it was Lippert.")[13]

There were, of course, enormous numbers of wounded and debilitated veterans of Iwo Jima. Whether a wounded man survived or not, or suffered more than he ought, largely depended on enjoying a modicum of good fortune in the hours after getting hit. The Marines' experience of the initial trauma period varied enormously. Thus, Richard Wheeler was shot in the neck and was incredibly lucky, first, that the bullet missed his carotid artery and jugular vein; second, that there was a fine surgeon in the next foxhole with the necessary clamps; third, that there was plasma immediately available; and fourth, that he was taken urgently to the beach and evacuated. Within two hours of being wounded he was lying in a clean bunk aboard a modern hospital ship, tended to by competent nurses and doctors.[14]

Not so fortunate was Lieutenant John Noe (who died in 1997). When a bullet collided with his lower jaw, it fractured his left mandible and passed out his right cheek. En route it shattered his right mandible, broke his right upper jaw, and ripped out most of the teeth on that side. Bone fragments and bullet shrapnel tore apart and gashed the cheeks up to his eyes. Bereft of a convenient corpsman, he had to walk to the rear holding the shattered parts of his face together while blood gushing into his throat came close to suffocating him. A hundred yards on, a Japanese sniper hit him in the right calf. Upon finally making it to the battalion aid station, where he was at last given morphine, it took several more hours for him to be evacuated to the beach. Even then, as a cold rain fell his litter was placed in the open hold of a landing craft with forty-five others. Their cries rebounded off the metal walls and, with no corpsman aboard, no drugs could be dispensed. Late at night the vessel clanged against the sides of a ship, and he heard shouting. But there was evidently no room, and they had to try several more times elsewhere before space could be found—nine and a half hours after his being wounded. By then, eight of the forty-six men aboard were dead, and another seven died soon after. Thus, fully a third of the casualties became fatalities on their way to what was not even a hospital ship but a transport ship hurriedly converted to emergency care. It took another six days for Noe to be flown out.[15]

The most serious casualties stayed in hospitals for months, or years, afterward. Keith Wheeler, who visited them in Hawaii, was sure that while Iwo Jima produced no instance of a "living basket case"—men who had lost all their limbs—there were plenty who had lost both of one set.[16] Wheeler had himself been wounded during the battle, and on the evacuation flight he met Chuck, who tossed and turned because he could not position his legs comfortably—despite their having been left somewhere on Iwo.[17] Among the worst cases, said a nurse, were those with gunshot and shrapnel wounds to the chest. Many others were paralyzed (and so lacked bladder and bowel control) by hits to the spine, and still more had lost much of their abdominal cavity, necessitating frequent colostomy dressings. Nearly all required oxygen, and casual observers to the ward could be forgiven for thinking that the men were held "together with rubber tubes" resembling "experiments à la Frankenstein."[18]

In the hospital visited by Wheeler, there was a place called the "quiet room" where there were no mirrors or reflective surfaces. Wheeler saw a youth lying in bed with no face from his nose downward; there was merely a flaring scarlet hole with his tongue lolling across his neck. He would die soon, everyone expected. Until then, it was considered advisable to hide the truth from him.[19]

Private Harold Lumbert, a former mechanic, was the most disfigured surviving veteran of Iwo. A piece of shrapnel had hit his face, and he had "lost the front of his skull from beneath his eyes down to the lower jaw. His lower jaw was fractured in five places. His nose was gone. There was a red gulch where it had been. Without bony support his whole face sagged and lost its human character. His lower eyelids were pulled down. The cheeks drooped. The unsupported upper lip hung like a rag. The broken jaw sagged so that his mouth lay open and drooled constantly." Surgeons sewed the remaining flaps of skin together, though when they burst open the wound "gapped open between sutures like a fat man's shirt." Cartilage was taken from a "recently killed human cadaver" (Wheeler is vague as to its former owner) and used to build a new nose. Surgeons then bolted an aluminum, face-shaped scaffolding to his skull and anchored with orthodontic bands to the two remaining molars on each side of his mouth a massive prosthetic plate to cover the face and replace his upper jaw and palate. That was just the beginning. After that, Lumbert endured an unending series of operations to tuck, fit, stitch, stretch, compress, and adjust his skin and fascia muscles, followed by years of rehabilitation. In late 1961, *Life* published Wheeler's follow-up story detailing a visit to see Lumbert. Wheeler described his return to civilian life and his succor in the arms of a loving family. It was lavishly replete with photographs— all shot from behind. Lumbert died a few years later, still in pain.[20]

Lumbert's long suffering is a reminder that Iwo left deep scars. Psychological, not just physical, trauma afflicted veterans for years afterward. A lot of men suffered from "the shakes" in the immediate aftermath of the battle. Alvin Josephy noticed that many soldiers' handwriting "looked like the jerky scrawl of a drunken man," and Victor Kleber went so far as to apologize to his family for his poor penmanship.[21] "I find it extremely difficult to sit down and write," he explained, "let alone concentrate my thoughts. This, I am told, is the normal reaction to sustained combat."[22]

Most of the time, as with combat fatigue, the shakes subsided after a few days of being away from the battlefield and a couple of good nights' sleep. Other men, especially if they had been grievously wounded, never quite recovered, and there were significant numbers of suicides after the war. These cases went unacknowledged, unrecognized, or unrecorded, but most Marines would have known, or known of, a comrade who had killed himself. One such was Lou Balog, a flamethrower man whose friend, Joe Czerniawski, was badly hit. He was "completely emasculated by shrapnel from that shell and was injured in one leg so it was shorter than the other. Later he went to California, where he committed suicide."[23]

Even after the initial shakes had gone, horrific visions and nightmares continued, though they could long lie dormant. For Dr. Thomas Brown, famed as the most composed man on Iwo, the first inkling that something was wrong came in the winter of 1949, following a long shift at the hospital. Stretched out on the sofa at home while his wife prepared dinner, he listened to a radio program called *Columbia Was There*, a documentary about the Normandy landings. He heard recordings of dive bombers, screeching shells, and bullets hissing by. All of a sudden, Brown "disintegrated emotionally," and began shivering and crying uncontrollably.[24]

Others, like Mike Vinich, were haunted by graphic memories of Japanese soldiers they had killed close-up. There was one youth in particular he had shot, that he "didn't think too much [of] then, but I've thought about it ever since. His face is in my eyes. I see him when I go to sleep at night."[25] The triggering incidents are unknown and unknowable. For Howard McLaughlin, writing only a couple of years ago, at least the visions are "not as bad at night now as it was when I first came home. It was especially bad on Helen when we were first married." Then she was the victim of

> nightmares in which I was trying to get out of the way of a fired sniper round, or to reach some kind of cover as the mortar shells started dropping. In these—to me—very real happenings, my actions were brought on by reflexes learned in combat. In real time if you were lying down, you were always [in] a sort of a crouch, with one foot pulled up for leverage. Then when an emergency arose you were able to instantly jump or throw yourself up and over into another nearby hole for cover. Now, in the middle of the night, I would react to this dreamed threat in the same manner. If Helen was lucky, I went out of the bed on my side, onto the floor. But sometime I tried to jump towards her side of the bed. . . . At other times I would wildly throw an arm back for some reason and hit

her in the face or chest. After all these years sometimes I still have these flashbacks, just as vivid to me as ever. They eventually stopped causing physical damage to Helen, but in some ways they're worse for me these days. Now they seem to run in a pattern in which I'm unable to do something either to help someone else or to save myself from some impending catastrophe. There is still terror in these dreams, but now much frustration also.[26]

Even on Iwo, psychiatric casualties could be divided between the "bulkhead stare" type of fatigue and patients suffering from genuine, terrified hysteria. The surgeon James Vedder was nonplussed when one such Marine was brought in to his aid station with no recognizable wounds. Neither was he obviously combat-fatigued, a condition familiar to Vedder since he saw it so often. Instead, the man's "eyes were rolled upward so only the white sclera were visible. The jaws were so tightly clenched that I could not examine his throat or tongue. Both his arms and legs were held in a rigidly extended position. The elbows could not be bent, and the fingers were so tightly doubled over that the nails were gouging the skin on both palms. His knees were held as stiffly as the elbows, there was no way I could flex them even slightly. In addition, the hips were held rigidly immobile. It was impossible to rotate them in any direction." Yet his breathing was normal and his bladder was functioning (there was an increasingly large wet spot). Overnight, said the corpsman who brought him, he had "stiffened out like a plank." Nothing had "happened" to him. Vedder immediately evacuated him.[27]

Other cases were often taken to base hospitals, their release dates uncertain. Their "disturbed wing," warned attending corpsmen, was a place where "you never dared turn your back on a patient. They'd climb you without warning." Hardly a day passed without their having to subdue somebody forcibly. The patients' symptoms generally conformed: strong and uncontrollable spastic tremors; shoulders, trunk, leg, hands, and neck jerking ceaselessly; anguished expressions on their faces owing, evidently, to physical and mental pain. When they spoke, if they could, they often repeated each word a dozen times, endlessly.

Otherwise, they seemed mute or deaf. Amnesia was common, not only of what happened on Iwo but of their lives before the battle. Each night was filled with terror, the victims quivering and cringing, eyes wide with fear, and they would often slip back into childlike poses.

A common treatment at the time was to administer heavy "hypnotic" doses of sodium amytal, a sedative that temporarily quieted the worst physical symptoms. During these periods of lucidity, a psychiatrist would attempt to tease out childhood events and psychological accelerants, with everything said being recorded by a stenographer. Afterward, a nurse would repeat to the patient all the things he had revealed under sedation. "Pounded long enough, insistently enough, with spoken evidence of his past," wrote a witness to these sessions, he would sometimes begin to recover his memory and speech. "Eventually, usually with surprise, he becomes aware of his strange surroundings" and calms down.

Three months before Iwo, a newer form of treatment for particularly disturbed patients was developed by Lieutenant Commander Ernst Schmidhofer. He hypnotized men until they ceased twitching and jerking, then, talking calmly and monotonously, he asked them to relax by closing their eyes, emptying their minds, focusing on their exhalation and inhalation. He directed them to repeat a line like, "My mind is a blank" or to repeat the letters of the alphabet. Essentially, Schmidhofer was teaching the men to meditate.

An initially skeptical Keith Wheeler watched him treat six patients: two Navy men and six Marines back from Iwo Jima and Okinawa. None had been treated previously, and when they were brought into the room they were trembling, yammering, and contorting so violently that they had to be lifted out of their stretchers. One slumped and cried, "Don't send me back; don't send me back." To Wheeler's surprise, Schmidhofer helped quiet them, but when he woke them up from the trance, their symptoms returned. "The six were like the writhing of the tentacles of an octopus," he said—but the writhing was less severe than it had been at the beginning. Each day they got a little better as they practiced exhalations and relaxation exercises until Schmidhofer announced that henceforth they could do it without his help.[28]

For them and many thousands of other veterans, the battle of Iwo Jima would never really end, but they could still take pride in what the Marine Corps had achieved as they sought to survive and thrive in the new world for which they had fought.

In 1968, the island was returned to Japan.

The Great Red God

I wrote this book to answer the seemingly straightforward question I posed in the introduction: What's it like being in battle? I thought it would be a lot easier, to tell you the truth, and this volume rather shorter. I've learned much over the course of researching the subject for the past X years—it's been such a long time I can't even remember when exactly I started working on *Men of War,* though my son, Edmund, is nearly six and I know that I was reading about Bunker Hill before he was born—but I remain stumped. Every time I think I've got a handle on the topic, that I have finally grasped the experience of combat, it slips infuriatingly away. Fortunately, I'm not the only one. Among old soldiers there exists the discombobulating sensation that war was simultaneously exhilarating and horrifying, terrifying and boring, cruel and kind, tragic and farcical. Mars demands much of his congregants.

Attempting to get to the heart of the problem, I've approached, or at least tried to approach, the subject from the perspective of that of an impartial historian; that is, I've dissected the combat experience from the perspective of an arbiter unweighted by preconceived notions and unhampered by any desire to hammer some political point home. I came, in other words, to the subject deliberately cold. Perhaps too cold, some might say. There are, I grant you, lengthy passages where I may seem detached and clinical—a particularly disturbing habit when discussing such sensitive and painful topics as dead sons, grievous trauma, and vicious suffering. My defense against the charge of hard-heartedness is that there are far too many books about war that sentimentalize, glamorize, or euphemize what happens during combat. If we are to seek the truth, as honest historians should, we must be determined to tell the truths that we find, no matter how discomfiting. But ultimately, I cleave with the poet Robert Southey (1774–1843) to an ironic sensibility on the subject of martial glory. In "The Battle of Blenheim," Southey cast a beady eye on the Duke of Marlborough's defeat of the French and Bavarians in 1704:

> They said it was a shocking sight
> After the field was won;
> For many thousand bodies here
> Lay rotting in the sun;
> But things like that, you know, must be
> After a famous victory.

I should add that my descriptions of the rotting bodies at Bunker Hill, Gettysburg, and Iwo Jima imply neither prescription nor proscription, though I shall admit that over the course of my research I've become somewhat more cautious when it comes to listening to drums beaten by amateurs rousing nations to war with one another. In this I follow Sir John Keegan, who, I recall reading, once observed that professional military historians—perhaps counterintuitively, considering their bloodthirsty interests—tend to be more pacific, if not pacifist, than the population at large because they keenly understand the costs, price, and tolls of war. In other words, they are more aware than most that embarking on war is like entering a dark room—one where monsters lurk and unexpected obstacles lie, where one can only stumble blindly about hoping for the best. In that dark room, even the simplest thing becomes very hard, and no matter what transpires or how incandescent the cause, men will be murdered, often mistakenly or accidentally, and sometimes pointlessly. In the end, no war has ever achieved what it set out to do. That does not mean that war is always unnecessary or never justified, but one must pick one's battles (so to speak) and be realistic as to balancing often incommensurate ends and means, knowns and unknowns.

Some might nevertheless cavil that a person cannot truly write of war until he or she has experienced its bite—which I haven't—but the flesh-witnessing of combat, while allowing an individual to be "blooded" in the mysteries of battle, to join the elite fraternity of veterans who have "seen the elephant" (as the Civil War phrase has it), comes fraught with an important but rarely discussed liability: One naturally tends to assume that one's own experience is automatically applicable to soldiers of times past. In this way, a Marine or army veteran of Fallujah during the latest Iraq War can define himself as the direct spiritual descendant of a Bunker Hill militiaman or perhaps even the latest embodiment in a long line of warriors representing what has been called the "Western way of war," a tradition that, some have argued, stretches back to the Greek hoplites who thwarted the ambitions of the eastern Persians. Hence the myth of the "universal soldier," the ultimately fallacious belief that the phenomenon of combat, and how it is experienced and conceived, is eternal and immutable.

On a superficial basis, this observation is accurate in the sense that men of war have shared certain experiences since the first glimmerings of recorded history. During the battle of Fallujah—regarded by some as a modern Gettysburg—American soldiers echoed their martial forebears in a variety of ways.[1] The sights, noted previously by General Burgoyne at Bunker Hill, were similarly spectacular: Lance Corporal Justin Boswood was in a firefight and "the whole house was shaking with 5.56mm rounds . . . SAWs going off with a two-hundred-round burst and the M-16s firing just as fast as you could pull the trigger. It was just awesome."[2] In place of drums sounding the advance, percussive heavy metal blared.[3] There was the habitual pre-combat accumulation and checking of equipment and weaponry, as documented repeatedly since the time of Homer. Whereas in the *Iliad*, we find loving lists of the helmets, greaves, armor, shields, swords, and spears borne by Greek and Trojan warriors alike, in Fallujah Sergeant David Bellavia's outfit "[threw] on our full battle rattle, which include[d]: ballistic-proof eye protection, smoke grenades for concealment, reinforced knee pads any skateboarder would envy, a five-quart CamelBak reservoir of water[,] thirty-five pound Interceptor Ballistic Armor fully loaded, two-and-a-half-pound Kevlar helmet, night vision, grenades, weapon, and ammunition."[4]

And, as ever, all were filthy. While George Orwell commented that "the men who fought at Verdun, at Waterloo, at Flodden, at Senlac, at Thermopylae—every one of them had lice crawling over his testicles," at Fallujah soldiers like Corporal Jason Howell "lathered Lamasil over their chafed waists, crotches, and feet. . . . Rubbed raw from the constant movement of combat, the young Marines used the cream to soothe the red splotches of peeling skin, blistering feet, and pus-stained sores that had developed on their bodies."[5] Near the end, everyone's uniforms, according to Bellavia, "were covered in dried gore, blood, grime, concrete dust, and smoke stains. All of us have brown slicks of diarrhea pasting our pants to our backsides. We're so sick that some of us can hardly walk. . . . We look like bedraggled castaways with whiskers and wild, red-rimmed eyes."[6]

Physiologically, too, the body's reactions to combat have not changed: Homer's heroes, God's Israelites, Caesar's Romans, Charlemagne's knights, all experienced the same dramatic increases in heart rate, loss of fine motor control, rising stress levels, and post-battle exhaustion following the typical adrenaline high that U.S. soldiers have in Iraq. King Henry V's words at Agincourt (at least as dramatized by Shakespeare) still splendidly describe every man of war's physical reaction to close-quarters combat:

> Then imitate the action of the tiger:
> Stiffen the sinews, summon up the blood,
> Disguise fair nature with hard-favored rage;
> Then lend the eye a terrible aspect: . . .
>
> Now set the teeth and stretch the nostril wide,
> Hold hard the breath and bend every spirit
> To his full height. (*Henry V,* act 3, scene 1, lines 6–17)

Despite these similarities, the assumption undergirding the "universal soldier" concept is fundamentally flawed. Its default position is that battle is statically isotropic: in other words, that the fighting experience has basically remained the same throughout history and can be viewed and understood from a single, unchanging perspective. But it is not. Combat, in fact, is dynamically anisotropic: War is felt, heard, tasted, seen, perceived, interpreted, in a shifting, subjective myriad of ways depending on context and culture. Rightly speaking, then, there is not one eternal experience of combat, but many *experiences* of combat that alter over time and space. Warfare, in short, has been typified not by stasis and continuity, but by diversity and variety, contradiction and change.

Even within the relatively compact American context, which extends only from 1775 until the present, there are gaping differences in how soldiers have understood war. Take, for example, the trope of the "Baptism of Fire," a staple of war literature. As Sergeant Bellavia remarks, "Combat distilled to its purest human form is a test of manhood [and] what a man finds there defines how he measures himself for the rest of his life. I embrace the battle. I welcome it into my soul."[7] To us, as moderns, it seems natural to assume that a person's time in combat is a momentous and life-altering event, and by extension the militiamen at Bunker Hill must have been transformed by their exposure to the British assault. But there is no evidence that they underwent any such form of self-realization. Instead, the older ones saw war as an inescapable part of everyday existence and combat as an interlude between day-to-day hardships, and so followed the biblical Job (7:1) in assuming that "the life of man upon earth is a warfare, and his days are like the days of a hireling." Youths may have been excited about being away from home and chores as they participated in their War Mitzvah (as it were), but their time with the colors was always temporary. During the Revolution, sixteen-year-old Peter Pond, for instance, was chafing under his parents' stricture that he should not leave despite his "Strong Desire to be a Solge" (as he wrote in his diary), but one evening at the tavern the drums and "Instraments of Musick were all Imployed to that Degrea that thay Charmed me" and Pond signed on along with "Miney lads of my Aquantans." Indulging in forbidden gingerbread and beer with his bounty, he completely forgot "that I had left my Parans who were Exceedingly trubled in Minde for my wellfair."[8] There was no more to it than having a lark before coming back to the farm.

It would not be for several more decades and the rise of the Romantic movement, with its focus on introspection, the self, and emotions, that soldiers would begin to believe that everything they had achieved in civilian life up until that moment, the challenges they had faced, and all their book-learning were worthless and empty when measured against a single instant of combat. An early example of this new outlook is provided by John Malcolm, a young, callow officer in 1813–14 who on the eve of his first battle was advised by his comrades that "in less than twenty-four hours hence, I might be wiser than all the sages and philosophers that ever wrote."[9] While Bellavia might certainly agree with that sentiment, such convictions are alien to the militiamen of Bunker Hill, and they must accordingly be understood on their own terms, not those of ours.

By the time of the Civil War, soldiers understood battle as a quest for self-fulfillment that could better the soul and were thus fascinated by their own feelings and passions toward the phenomenon of combat. To them, imagination, impulse, intuition, and the irrational were key to war. The dramatic was exalted, the intense celebrated, horror described, the sublime marveled at. In tones that would have been incomprehensible to those at Bunker Hill, John C. West, a Texas private, devoted no fewer than three letters (to his four-year-old son, his wife, and his brother) detailing at great length his own baptism of fire and what he had experienced at Gettysburg, a transcendent event.[10]

Much of this efflorescent enthusiasm would be killed off, quite literally, in the slaughterhouses of Antietam and the Wilderness. Certainly, by World War II there was little residue of the Romantic attitude that, as the Roman poet Horace had written, it was sweet and fitting to die for one's country. Whereas some very old veterans still saw their war through a gauzy veil of sentiment, few followed their example. In 1900, for instance, C. D. Westbrook, remembering his service with the 120th New York nearly forty years earlier, could assert that his Civil War comrades had "marched with unfaltering step . . . into the very jaws of death" to prove the Roman's maxim, but such a view was seen as noxiously anachronistic even before the end of the Great War.[11] (The poet

Wilfred Owen would devastatingly condemn Horace's famous line as "the old Lie.")

In its place was a regard for combat as a matter of managerial competency. The origins of this conception lay in the Victorian ideology of Positivism, a reaction against Romanticism that stressed a beetle-browed obsession with quantifying, standardizing, listing, and categorizing things, all things, from vertebrate species to human intelligence to economic statistics. Positivists devoured facts and figures, amassed tables and charts, because they believed that the path to illuminating empirical Truth lay in the systematic extrapolation of rational causes and effects from the chaos of the natural world. Charles Darwin, for instance, deduced the theory of evolution only after decades' worth of patient observation and the accumulation of vast amounts of data. In the military sphere, there was a new and keen interest in the science of ballistics, a compiling of intricate tables meticulously comparing the merits and flaws of different small arms, and a fascination with the historical typology of battles and their almost infinite complexity and splendor. Through the application of what was being called "military science," soldiers would fight their future battles based on rules and principles derived from primary facts and their painstaking application.[12]

The Marine Corps, generally seen as an exemplar of the blood-and-guts school of combat, was in fact a leader in this bloodless-and-brains field in the 1930s. At the time, an amphibious operation—the landing of a seaborne force on a defended hostile shore—was regarded among the global military intelligentsia as virtually impossible, a lethal folly.[13] Attacking troops were doomed in the face of beaches and bluffs hardened with machine guns and artillery, mines and barbed wire, entrenchments and emplacements. Proof of the pudding for all to see had been provided in World War I, during the campaign commonly abbreviated to "Gallipoli." In April 1915, the Mediterranean Expeditionary Force undertook a series of assaults against several beaches in the Dardanelles as part of an effort to knock the Turks out of the war. Losses were dreadful: At V Beach, just 21 of the first 200 men to disembark made it ashore; at W Beach, the Lancashire Fusiliers lost 600 out of 1,000 men before even hitting land.

In 1933, the Marines, alarmed at the likelihood of Japanese expansion into the Pacific and the consequent need to storm their conquered islands, took on the role of management consultants when they revisited the subject. The Marine Corps Schools (MCS) at Quantico—where the most promising officers were trained for high command—created an exclusive course in which each student was handed a copy of the official British history of Gallipoli and directed to dissect the operation ruthlessly to discover what had gone wrong. As they dug deeper into the mountain of reports, orders, and correspondence, they found that the Allied landings had collapsed owing not to the inherently risky nature of an amphibious assault but by ignorance, incompetence, bad luck, and gross underpreparation.[14]

With that analysis in hand, the Marine Corps later that year temporarily discontinued all other classes at the MCS so that the fifty-two students and their instructors could devote all their efforts to preparing a manual on amphibious warfare that would serve as the standard how-to guide to launching an assault on a defended Pacific island.[15] They eventually produced the *Tentative Manual for Landing Operations* (June 13, 1934), which would be continually revised until it provided an infallible step-by-step guide to success.[16] The Marines who landed at Iwo Jima (as well as other islands, and, of course, the Allied forces during the Normandy landings) would be its ultimate beneficiaries.

For our purposes, the *Tentative Manual* is most important for understanding the general perspective of the Marines of the Pacific theater. It exemplifies the managerial approach to combat and encapsulates the assumption that industrialized warfare was at heart a logistical issue based on colossal manufacturing capacity applied intelligently and according to "scientific" principles of efficiency. War should be run along business lines, in short.[17] A by-product of this ethos was the transformation of the combat experience into something little more than a technically proficient factory job: The Marines on Iwo Jima, for instance, considered themselves to be working on a lethal production line spewing out corpses. To apply their worldview to that of the Union and

Confederate men at Gettysburg, let alone their ancestors at Bunker Hill, would seem a major historical category error.

The same can be said of their descendants in Iraq and Afghanistan. Given the nature of the continuing shifts in American society and culture, the transformation of its armed forces from mass organizations into professional bodies of specialists, as well as the emphasis on technology and intelligence, perhaps in coming years future historians of combat experiences will similarly distinguish from even their most recent forebears the current generation of soldiers—men, and women, of war alike.

And here I end my investigation, more knowledgeable and maybe a little wiser. But even now, I still do not know for certain whether, at the supreme moment of crisis in combat, I would stand and fight alongside the grim-serried ranks of my comrades, or if I would flee. No one does—not until that dread moment arrives. Perhaps it's better that way.

Acknowledgments

Over the course of writing *Men of War*, I have accumulated a significant number of debts, and so I am glad to be able, at long last, to repay them—partially, at least.

For providing me with hard-to-find articles and essays, I thank John Heiser, historian at Gettysburg National Military Park; Erik Goldstein, curator of mechanical arts & numismatics at Colonial Williamsburg; Kathy O. Jackson of the Medical Society of Delaware; Col. Joseph H. Alexander, USMC (Ret.); and Alan Hawk of the National Museum of Health and Medicine. Matthew A. Boal and Scott N. Hendrix sent copies of their dissertations, both of which proved invaluable. Samuel Fore of the marvelous Harlan Crow Library in Dallas, Texas, very kindly supplied the unpublished transcript of Isaac Glynney's Bunker Hill diary.

I must also thank, profusely, Dr. Earl J. Hess of Lincoln Memorial University for reading an early and ungainly draft of the Bunker Hill chapter, as well as Richard Brookhiser and Michael Stephenson for braving the howling wilderness of the first-draft version of Gettysburg. Don N. Hagist, one of the foremost historians of the British Army during the War of Independence, dissected my arguments in the relevant sections of Bunker Hill and (tried to) set me right when I erred. It should go without saying, though I shall say it, that any remaining inaccuracies or misinterpretations are entirely my own.

The Frederick Lewis Allen Room at the New York Public Library is a haven for every writer, and I was fortunate indeed to benefit from its sanctuary for an unconscionably prolonged time owing to Jay Barksdale, its guardian. I'm also grateful to the librarians and staff of the Irma and Paul Milstein Division of United States History, Local History, and Genealogy for uncomplainingly hauling scores of heavy old books to my desk. Not only am I immensely thankful for the unparalleled resources of the grand old NYPL, but also for the wondrous holdings of the Butler Library at Columbia University: Time and time again they remind me that we all are beholden to the antiquarians, archivists, librarians, and scholars of ages past and present. Without their dedication and diligence, our preserved knowledge of history would be paltry indeed.

Producing and publishing a book requires an enormous investment of skill, time, money, persistence, and patience. Random House has neither stinted in its support nor swayed in its conviction that *Men of War* was a worthwhile project. For their aid and advice, I must thank my editors, Jonathan Jao and Will Murphy, as well as assistant editor Molly Turpin, who supervised the Herculean process of turning an idea into a book with seemingly effortless (though it wasn't) aplomb. Martin Schneider, the copy editor; Loren Noveck, my production editor; and Jenn Backe and Richard Elman, the production managers, devoted untold hours to making sure my prose was relatively coherent, my bibliography tidily arranged, and my pages neatly bound. David Lindroth did a splendid job of composing the maps armed with only the vaguest of instructions. My agent, Eric Lupfer of William Morris Endeavor, is a font of sound advice and shrewd judgment; it was he who so expertly midwifed, nurtured, and raised *Men of War* into the form it is today.

My father, Professor Paul Lawrence Rose, one of the finest and most penetrating of historians, died during my final stages of editing this book. He taught me an enormous amount about practicing history, and I think that he would have enjoyed reading (and commenting on) *Men of War,* as would my late grandfather, Professor Jack Rose (French Army, 1939–40, and the Queen's Own Royal West Kent Regiment until the war's end). My mother, Susan, as well as my siblings—Olivia, Zoë, and Ari—have been immoveable rocks of support throughout the writing process, as have Stephen and Craig. Accolades, too, must be bestowed upon Erna Olafson, David and Carolyn Hellerstein, Chad and Elizabeth, and Ben and Jamie. Mustn't forget, of course, Sabrina and Romy, and Kyla and Iliana.

And finally, I arrive at the dedicatees, my wife, Rebecca, and Edmund, our son. I cannot even begin to describe how wonderful they are, and how beloved. It was a long and difficult trek to finish *Men of War*, and they were unstintingly there every step of the way. To them, I owe everything still.

Notes

INTRODUCTION

1. Regarding the historiography of military history, see R. M. Citino's important essay, "Military Histories Old and New: A Reintroduction," *American Historical Review* 112, no. 4 (2007): 1070–90.
2. Quoted in H. H. Sargent, *Napoleon Bonaparte's First Campaign* (Chicago: A. C. McClurg and Co., 1895), 173.
3. B. Brecht, *Fragen eines lesenden Arbeiters* ("Questions from a worker who reads"), trans. M. Hamburger, in *Bertolt Brecht: Poems, 1913–1956*, ed. J. Willett and R. Manheim (London: Methuen, 1987), 252–53.
4. L. Tolstoy, "The Raid," trans. L. and A. Maude, in *Tales of Army Life* (London: Oxford University Press, 1932), 3.
5. On this issue, see my review, "How the Battle Was Won, If Not Yet the War," *Wall Street Journal*, July 16, 2011.
6. On the errors of the universal soldier thesis, see Lynn, *Battle: A History of Combat and Culture*, xiv–xvii.
7. Letter, Washington to John Augustine Washington, May 31, 1754, in *The Writings of George Washington*, ed. W. C. Ford (New York: G. P. Putnam's Sons, 1889–1893), 1:90.
8. As recorded by Horace Walpole, *Memoirs of the Reign of King George the Second*, 2nd ed. (London: Henry Colburn, 1847), 1:400.
9. See J. Glenn Gray, *The Warriors: Reflections on Men in Battle* (New York: Bison Books, 1998 edn.), 29–30; see also W. Broyles Jr., "Why Men Love War," in *The Vietnam Reader*, ed. W. Capps (New York: Routledge, 1991), 71.
10. Printed in Hatch, "New Hampshire at Bunker Hill," 218.

BUNKER HILL

1. Introduction

1. Paret, "The Relationship Between the American Revolutionary War and European Military Thought and Practice," in Paret, *Understanding War*, 37.
2. The entry may have been written by Edmund Burke. See *The Annual Register*, 83.
3. Letter, Feilding to Denbigh, July 18, 1775, in Balderston and Syrett (eds.), *The Lost War*. The Americans agreed, with Lieutenant Samuel Webb telling Silas Deane that "Major Bruce, who served two years in Portugal with General Lee, told my brother Joe

at the lines, that it was the hottest engagement he ever knew. Even, says he, the Battle of Minden did not equal it." Letter, Webb to Deane, July 11, 1775, in Webb (ed.), *Reminiscences of General Samuel B. Webb*, 11.

4. Letter, I. Seagrove to J. Blackburn, July 2, 1775, quoted in Flavell, "Government Interception of Letters from America and the Quest for Colonial Opinion in 1775," 414.

5. In the *Constitutional Gazette* of October 11, 1775, printed in Moore (ed.), *Diary of the American Revolution*, 1:116.

3. The Redoubt, Part One

1. A "large majority" of the New England militia, according to Dr. Thacher, arrived "carrying ordinary firearms, unprovided with bayonets, and habited in the style of country laborers." Thacher, *Military Journal*, 27. See also "An Account of the Battle of Bunker's Hill, by Major General Henry Dearborn, Published 1818," in which he claims that "not an officer or soldier of the continental troops engaged was in uniform, but were in the plain and ordinary dress of citizens." See Coffin (ed.), *Battle of Breed's Hill*, 23.

2. Swett, *History of Bunker Hill Battle*, 13.

3. Moore, *Life of General John Stark of New Hampshire*, 181. On the militiamen's occupations and wealth, see Fischer, *Paul Revere's Ride*, "Appendix O: The Lexington Militia: Quantitative Research," 319–20; tax list of Derryfield, December 24, 1775, printed in Potter, *History of Manchester*, 418–19.

4. Doddridge, *Notes on the Settlement and Indian Wars of the Western Parts of Virginia and Pennsylvania*, 91.

5. Kidder, *History of New Ipswich*, 95; Bolton, *Private Soldier under Washington*, 91–92; Fischer, *Paul Revere's Ride*, 159; Stephenson, *Patriot Battles*, 151.

6. Hagelin and Brown, "Connecticut Farmers at Bunker Hill."

7. According to G. E. Ellis, Prescott was wearing a linen coat; Swett agrees, calling it a "simple calico frock." R. Frothingham says that he wore a "blue coat and a three-cornered hat." Ellis, *Sketches of Bunker Hill Battle and Monument*, 29; Swett, *History of Bunker Hill Battle*, 19; Frothingham, *Siege of Boston*, 122.

8. Moore, *Life of General John Stark*, 134.

9. Kidder, *History of New Ipswich*, 95; see also Smith, *History of the Town of Peterborough*, 85.

10. Frothingham, "Address," 22.

11. Testimony of Nathaniel Rice, in Swett, *Notes to His Sketch*, 13.

12. Some authorities state 1742 as the oldest Besses in service, but G. Neumann notes that Long Land Pattern 1730s were stockpiled at the beginning of the war. See Stephenson, *Patriot Battles*, 121; Neumann, "Redcoats' Brown Bess." At the beginning of the Revolution, many active units were equipped with the superior—but still not gleamingly new—Pattern 1756 (.75-caliber, 46-inch-long barrel, 17-inch-long triangular socket bayonet, and steel ramrod), but over the course of the war a shortened version called the Short Land Musket Pattern 1769 was issued. See Bohy and Troiani, "'We Meant to Be Free Always,'" 49–51, 58. On cost, see Bolton, *Private Soldier under Washington*, 107. According to Houlding, "It was . . . fairly common to find a regiment of foot armed with old and worn-out firearms." Houlding, *Fit for Service*, 146.

13. Churchill, "Gun Ownership in Early America," esp. 625 and table 1, "Extant Returns and Petitions Reporting Militia Armament, 1775–1776." On Colonel Little's regiment, see Wade and Lively, *This Glorious Cause*, 15.

14. There were, in short, more than enough guns to go around. So it was that Captain Charles Stuart, a Grenadiers officer, commented that General Gage was "foolish" to order that "no townsman [could] carry more than one firelock at a time." The New Englanders instead went to their illicit meetings armed with the single stipulated musket and then cheekily walked to and fro "eight or ten times a day, conveying each time [a different] one" until they had their stockpile. Letter, C. Stuart to Lord Bute, July 24, 1775, in Wortley (ed.), *Prime Minister and His Son*, 67.

15. Fischer, *Paul Revere's Ride*, 161.

16. Smith, *Peterborough, New Hampshire*, 85.

17. Entry for February 27, 1755, in Johnson (ed.), "Diary of Israel Litchfield," part 2, 255.

18. Potter, "Life and Remarkable Adventures," 15.

19. Kidder, *History of New Ipswich*, 95.

20. Fischer, *Paul Revere's Ride*, 161.

21. "Another Account of the Late Action at Bunker's Hill," *Rivington's Gazetteer*, August 3, 1775, printed in Dawson (ed.), "Bunker's Hill," 393.

22. Dearborn, "An Account of the Battle of Bunker's Hill," in Coffin (ed.), *Battle of Breed's Hill*, 19. One result of Bunker Hill was that when they returned home, the New Hampshire men lobbied fiercely for the issuing of bayonets. They told their Committee of Safety that it is "barbarous to let men be obliged to oppose bayonets with only gun barrels." *New Hampshire State Papers*, VI, 526, quoted in Elting, *Bunker's Hill*, 40.

23. Swett, *History of Bunker Hill Battle*, 20.

24. Isaac Glynney diary (unpublished), kindly provided by the Harlan Crow Library, Dallas, Texas.

25. On Gridley's background, see Huntoon, *History of the Town of Canton*, 360–79.

26. There is some debate on the length of the walls. The most authoritative accounts, however, concur that the redoubt was "about eight rods square." Provincial Congress of Massachusetts report, July 25, 1775, in Dawson (ed.), "Bunker's Hill," 388; P. Brown says it was about ten rods by eight. Brown, "Officer's Story of Bunker Hill."

27. Frothingham, *Siege of Boston*, 124.

28. The height of the walls is unclear. Henry Dearborn claimed they were "6 or 7 feet" high, but Lord Percy said the Americans were "intrenched up to their chins," or about four or five feet. Neither man saw the walls up close, with Dearborn fighting at the rail fence while Percy was stationed in Boston. Most accounts tend to support Dearborn, but if the men were standing on platforms it would have looked as if the walls came up only to their chins. Dearborn, "An Account of the Battle of Bunker's Hill," in Coffin (ed.), *Battle of Breed's Hill*, 16; Elting, *Bunker's Hill*, 23. On the platform, see Frothingham, *Siege of Boston*, 125.

29. As defined by Duffy, *Fire and Stone*, 225.

30. Quoted in Duffy, *Fire and Stone*, 72. A solid introduction to Vauban is H. Guerlac's essay, "Vauban: The Impact of Science on War," in *Makers of Modern Strategy*, ed. P. Paret, 64–90. J. Langins challenges Guerlac on several points; see Langins, "Eighteenth-Century French Fortification Theory after Vauban: The Case for Montalembert," in *The Heirs of Archimedes*, ed. B. D. Steele and T. Dorland, 333–59. On Americans' familiarity with Vauban's technical volumes, see Powers, "Studying the Art of War," 783.

31. Later that year, John Montrésor of the royal army composed a map of the area, "A survey of the peninsula of Charles Town shewing the three posts now garrison'd by His Majesty's troops for the winter," December 10, 1775; it is kept in the Henry Clinton Papers at the Clements Library at the University of Michigan. Its chief interest lies in

the new fortification built to cover the Neck from invasion, but Montrésor also shows a small fort on Breed's Hill, calling it the "redout on rebel hill." Its main defensive wall has been reoriented away from Boston toward the approach to the Neck from the mainland, as might be expected given British possession of the city. An online version can be seen at the online presentation of the "The Geometry of War: Fortification Plans from 18th-Century America" exhibition at the William L. Clements Library, University of Michigan, available at www.clements.umich.edu/exhibits/online/ geometry_of_war/geometry10.php, accessed February 7, 2014.

32. French, *First Year,* 216; Fisher, "Objective at Bunker Hill," 48.

33. Elting, *Bunker's Hill,* 21; Van Arsdale (ed.), *Discord And Civil Wars,* 17; letter, Barnard to an unidentified recipient, August 10, 1775, printed in Barnard, "Letter of Rev. Thomas Barnard," 35–41.

34. Hennell, *Gentleman Volunteer,* 91–92.

35. Leeke, *History of Lord Seaton's Regiment,* 1:32.

36. Quoted in Muir, *Tactics and the Experience of Battle,* 47.

37. Letter, Chester to Fish, July 22, 1775, in Dawson (ed.), "Bunker's Hill," 386.

38. Blaise de Lasseran-Massencôme, seigneur de Montluc, quoted in Nosworthy, *Anatomy of Victory,* 13. This almost benign view would change over the coming centuries. During the Second World War, analysts found that whereas just one in five new arrivals to the battlefront listed artillery as the most "fearful" weapon compared to one in two who believed that air attack was worse, with a month's hard combat under their belts these same men reversed their opinions exactly. Stouffer et al. (eds.), *American Soldier,* 2:236, Chart 8, "Ratings of the fearfulness of two enemy weapons in relation to length of time in combat."

39. Duffy, *Military Experience,* 245; Muir, *Tactics and the Experience of Battle,* 46.

40. On this distinction, see Dinter, *Hero or Coward,* 34–35.

41. Thacher, *Military Journal,* 30.

42. Testimony of John Dexter, in Swett, *Notes to His Sketch,* 6.

43. Testimony of William Low, in Swett, *Notes to His Sketch,* 12.

44. Testimony of Amos Foster, in Swett, *Notes to His Sketch,* 14.

45. Dearborn, "An Account of the Battle of Bunker's Hill," in Coffin (ed.), *Battle of Breed's Hill,* 19; Elting, *Bunker's Hill,* 27.

46. Powell, "Connecticut Soldier under Washington," 99.

47. B. P. Hughes, *Firepower,* 29.

48. Brown, "Officer's Story of Bunker Hill."

49. Powell, "Connecticut Soldier under Washington," 101.

50. Hughes, *Firepower,* 32–33.

51. Tielke, *Account of Some of the Most Remarkable Events,* 1:196. William Leeke observed, at Waterloo, that it was much easier to see round-shot from your own side soar over-head than it was to "catch sight of one coming through the air towards you." Leeke, *History of Lord Seaton's Regiment,* 32.

52. Longmore, *Treatise on Gunshot Wounds,* 38–39.

53. Diary entry, October 24, 1777, in Thacher, *Military Journal,* 113.

54. Bancroft's narrative, in Hill (ed.), *Bi-Centennial of Old Dunstable,* 59.

55. Murdock, *Bunker Hill,* 107. In his essay on Martin (99–117), Murdock is skeptical about some of his claims, but in my opinion, this one is very capable of being true.

56. Longmore, *Treatise on Gunshot Wounds,* 31; on the coins, see Longmore, *Gunshot Injuries,* 227–28.

57. Brown, *Beside Old Hearth-Stones,* 221.

58. Trumbull, *Autobiography, Reminiscences, and Letters,* 19. Edward Elley related that a cannonball "came bounding along the ground, and a youngster put his heel against it and was thrown into lockjaw and expired in a short time." Quoted in Dann, *Revolution Remembered,* 237. On "spent" cannon shot and amputated feet, see Longmore, *Treatise on Gunshot Wounds,* 24. Some English soldiers during the wars in Europe seventy years earlier took extraordinary risks by seeking their own side's expired cannonballs near the enemy so as to sell them back to their original owners. Travers, "Development of British Military Historical Writing and Thought from the Eighteenth Century to the Present," in *Military History and the Military Profession,* ed. D. A. Charters, M. Milner, and J. B. Wilson, 25. The error of placing one's feet in the way of a rolling cannonball was not confined to the eighteenth century: At Gettysburg in 1863, a Wisconsin soldier stuck out his heel to stop one such ball and had his leg torn off. He "cried like a child" to think that he had lost his limb in so inglorious a manner and mourned, "I shall always be ashamed to say how I lost it." Davis, Jr., *Three Years in the Army,* 226.

59. For the shot that killed Pollard, see diary entry of June 16 (*sic*) in Green (ed.), "Thomas Boynton's Journal," 255. For the anecdotes about Pollard's French and Indian War service as well as his final moments, see Brown, *Beside Old Hearth-Stones,* 329–33. James Stevens, an Andover man, heard that "they shot won of our men, won polerd of Bilrica." Entry of June 17, 1775, printed in Bailey, *Historical Sketches of Andover,* 336.

60. Letter, Amos Foster, August 3, 1825, printed in Sumner, "Reminiscences," 122. Brown notes that the shot took off his head. Brown, *Beside Old Hearth-Stones,* 332.

61. Holland, *History of Western Massachusetts,* 2:420.

62. Swett, *History of Bunker Hill Battle,* 22.

63. Testimony of William French, in Swett, *Notes to His Sketch,* 11.

64. On ordering the body thrown into the trench, see Dawson (ed.), "Bunker's Hill," 437n.; on the cleric, see Swett, *Notes to His Sketch,* 24 (note H); see also Swett, *History of Bunker Hill Battle,* 22; Frothingham, *Siege of Boston,* 126; "Prescott Manuscript," in Frothingham, *Battle-Field of Bunker Hill,* 19–20. C. Butler adds that Prescott consented to hold a burial after the battle. Butler, *History of the Town of Groton,* 338n5. On the next day's discovery of the grave, see Clarke, "Impartial and Authentic Narrative," 256.

65. Brown, "Officer's Story of Bunker Hill."

66. Brown, "Officer's Story of Bunker Hill"; Elting, *Bunker's Hill,* 25; Bancroft's narrative, in Hill (ed.), *Bi-Centennial of Old Dunstable,* 58. Interestingly, the granddaughter of Captain John Linzee of the *Falcon* later married Prescott's grandson. Brown, *Beside Old Hearth-Stones,* 27.

67. General Morning Orders, June 17, 1775, in Stevens (ed.), *General Sir William Howe's Orderly Book,* 1–2; French, *First Year,* 734–35 (appendix 15), 741 (appendix 20).

68. Spring, *With Zeal,* 60.

69. Cooper, *Practical Guide for the Light Infantry Officer,* xvi.

70. Heath, *Heath's Memoirs of the American War,* 28.

71. Bancroft's narrative, in Hill (ed.), *Bi-Centennial of Old Dunstable,* 59.

72. Winsor (ed.), *Memorial History of Boston,* 3:85n1. See also Bryant and Gay, *Popular History of the United States,* 3:403. A second instance: In June 1746, during the battle of Dettingen, Sir Andrew Agnew steeled his Scots Fusiliers for an oncoming onslaught of French cuirassiers by ordering them to open their ranks and let the cavalry pass through. "Dinna fire till ye can see the whites of their e'en," he cried, adding for good

measure, "If ye dinna kill them they'll kill you." ("So, Sir Andrew, I hear the cuirassiers rode through your regiment today," laconically observed King George II afterward. "Ou, ay, yer Majestee," replied this paragon of Highland sangfroid, "but they didna get oot again.") See Anderson, *Scottish Nation*, 2:679–80; and Agnew, "General Sir Andrew Agnew of Lochnaw," 37–38.

73. Winsor (ed.), *Memorial History of Boston*, 3:85n1.

74. Potter, "Life and Remarkable Adventures," 14.

75. Testimony of Jordan, printed in Swett, *Notes to His Sketch*, 15. Similarly, Isaac Bassett, stationed in the redoubt, "did not, myself, hear the order given; but it was often said by the soldiers of our regiment, that General Putnam ordered them 'not to fire on the enemy till they should see the color of their eyes, and then for every man to make sure of his mark.'" Testimony of Isaac Bassett, printed in Dawson (ed.), "Bunker's Hill," 429.

76. K. Yellin compiles a catalogue of the most common tropes. Yellin, *Battle Exhortation*, 71–72.

77. Quoted in Stanhope, *Notes of Conversations with the Duke of Wellington*, 13.

78. Hansen, "Battle Exhortation in Ancient Historiography," 169.

79. Quoted in Brown, *Beside Old Hearth-Stones*, 35.

80. Testimony of Simeon Noyes, in Swett, *Notes to His Sketch*, 13.

81. Testimony of Captain James Clark of Putnam's regiment, commanding 100 men, who arrived at the rail fence ten minutes after the firing began, in Swett, *Notes to His Sketch*, 7.

82. The deployments and precise numbers of some of the various companies and regiments are ambiguous, not helped by confusion among many writers as to the distinctions separating light infantry, grenadier, flank, and battalion/line troops. This summary is based on several sources, including Murdock, *Bunker Hill*, 14–18; Frothingham, *Siege of Boston*, 140–41; Morrissey, *Boston 1775*, 60; French, *First Year*, 232–34, 741 (appendix 20). Don N. Hagist helped enormously with figures and definitions in this respect.

83. The number of artillery pieces present is not entirely certain. Originally, Howe intended to bring four 6-pounders, four 12-pounders, and four 5.5-inch howitzers, but according to a letter to Lord Harvey, June 22 and June 24, 1775, he had "six field pieces, two light 12 pounders and two howitzers." Elting, *Bunker's Hill*, 23; Fortescue (ed.), *Correspondence of King George the Third*, 3:221.

84. "Letter from Boston, July 5th, 1775," printed in House of Commons, *The Detail and Conduct of the American War*, 14. After the battle, Cleaveland defended himself by testifying that he "sent 66 rounds to each gun, not more than half was fired," adding primly that "a commanding officer of artillery cannot be in every place." Disingenuously, Cleaveland omitted to state precisely which *caliber* these rounds were. Quoted in French, *First Year*, 749 (appendix 24).

85. F. Mackenzie's diary entry for April 22, 1775, notes that five sergeants, five corporals, and one hundred privates were "to do duty with the Royal Artillery." See French (ed.), *British Fusilier*, 73. Regarding the Lovells, who were on the pro-British side of the clan, see Jones, *Loyalists of Massachusetts*, 201–3. It is mentioned in an annotation to Washington's Revolutionary War Expense Accounts that James Lovell "was active in securing intelligence through spies; but how many and who were employed during the siege of Boston is not known." See note for July 15, 1775, in the George Washington Papers, Library of Congress.

4. The Beach

1. Wilkinson, "A Rapid Sketch of the Battle of Breed's Hill," in Coffin (ed.), *Battle of Breed's Hill,* 9–11 (James Wilkinson toured the site with Stark a year later); Moore, *Life of General John Stark,* 161; Potter, *History of Manchester,* 315, 433.
2. For contemporary descriptions of the Fusiliers, see Murdock, *Bunker Hill,* 137–39. Despite the Welch Fusiliers' storied reputation as, in the words of later American accounts, the "flower of the army" stationed in the Colonies, its Light component had been in a terrible mess for some time. At Lexington and Concord two months before, it had retreated in the face of the militia's shots and was only stopped when its officers scrambled to form a small line ahead of them "and presented their bayonets, and told the men that if they advanced they should die." On their performance at Lexington, see H. de Berniere, "General Gage's Instructions with a Curious Narrative of Occurrences" (1779), reprinted in Hudson, *History of the Town of Lexington,* 1:126–27n3; also informative is Urban, *Fusiliers,* 1–49.
3. Based on a compilation of muster-roll figures from WO 12 (National Archives, U.K.) by Don N. Hagist, "Bunker Hill Flank Company Casualties," which he sent to me on April 14, 2014. Another list, dated from about a week after the battle, differs in a few minor respects, and, it should be noted, includes both the 23rd's Light and Grenadier casualties but does not separate them. Thus, "Captain Blakeney, Lieutenant Beckwith, Lieutenant Cochrane, Lieutenant Lenthall, wounded; two sergeants, one drummer, eleven rank and file, killed; two sergeants, one drummer and fifer, thirty-five rank and file, wounded." See Gage, "Return of the Officers," printed in Force (ed.), *American Archives,* 4th ser., vol. 2, cols. 1098–99.
4. "Extracts of Letters Received in Philadelphia from a Gentleman in the Army, Dated Camp at Cambridge, June 27, 1775," printed in Force (ed.), *American Archives,* 4th ser., vol. 2, col. 1119.
5. Letter, Abigail Adams to John Adams, June 27, 1775, in Adams (ed.), *Familiar Letters of John Adams and His Wife Abigail Adams,* 71.
6. Quoted in Duffy, *Military Experience,* 253.
7. Colonel O. Williams, "A Narrative of the Campaign of 1780," Appendix B in Johnson, *Sketches of the Life and Correspondence of Nathanael Greene,* 1:496; Fischer, *Paul Revere's Ride,* 209.
8. Wolseley, *Story of a Soldier's Life,* 1:368–69. M. Hastings notes that "no U.S. or British regimental war diary that I have ever seen explicitly admits that soldiers fled in panic, as of course they sometimes do." Hastings, "Drawing the Wrong Lesson."
9. See Daddis, "Understanding Fear's Effect on Unit Effectiveness," 23.
10. "Rev. Peter Thacher's Narration," in Dawson (ed.), "Bunker's Hill," 383. See also J. Belknap's and E. Hazard's correspondence, August 8 to September 19, 1789, printed in Frothingham et al. (eds.), "Letter of Edward Everett," 96–99.
11. Hagist, "Shedding Light on Friendly Fire," 4–10. I am indebted to Mr. Hagist for kindly sending me the text of Abercrombie's letter to Sir Jeffrey Amherst, June 20, 1775. For surveys of this subject, see Shrader, "Friendly Fire: The Inevitable Price," 29–44; and Steinweg, "Dealing Realistically with Fratricide," 4–29.
12. "Combat stress" is the most common instigator of flight among veteran troops. Sir John Fortescue, historian of the British army, believed that "even the bravest man cannot endure to be under fire for more than a certain number of consecutive days, even if the fire be not very heavy." Letter, Fortescue to Lord Southborough, no date, printed

in *Report of the War Office Committee of Enquiry into "Shell-Shock,"* 9. In the Second World War, army psychiatrists John Appel and Gilbert Beebe concluded that the average soldier reached his peak of fighting effectiveness in the first three months of combat and thereafter was gradually worn down until, at the 180-day mark, he was rendered almost useless until he was rotated to the rear for at least a few days' rest. "Just as an average truck wears out after a certain number of miles, it appears that the doughboy wore out, either developing an acute incapacitating neurosis or else becoming hypersensitive to shell fire, so overly cautious and jittery that he was ineffective and demoralizing to the newer men." See Appel and Beebe, "Preventive Psychiatry," 169–75; Wanke, "American Military Psychiatry," 133–34. The quotation regarding the "average truck" appears in Shephard, *War of Nerves,* 245.

13. For a discussion of this subject, see Stouffer et al. (eds.), *American Soldier,* 2:137–40, 118–27.

14. See L'Etang, "Some Thoughts on Panic in War," 278–85; and Ondishko, Jr., "View of Anxiety, Fear, and Panic," 58–60.

15. See, for instance, Thacher, *Military Journal,* 27. See also Samuel Drake's comment that "the regiments now serving in Boston were the choicest troops that army could muster." Drake (ed.), *Bunker Hill,* 13. Another nineteenth-century authority concurs by alleging that "every man preparing to attack the undisciplined provincials was a drilled soldier, and quite perfect in the art of war." Lossing, *Pictorial Field-Book,* 1:542. Henry Dearborn, a veteran of Bunker Hill, noted that at the battle General Howe "commanded a body of chosen troops, inured to discipline, and nearly double in number to his foe; possessed of artillery in abundance, prepared in the best manner; with an army at hand ready to re-inforce him, and led by officers, many of whom had seen service, all of whom had been bred to arms." "Reflections on the Campaigns of Sir William Howe ... with an Incidental Account of the Battle of Bunker's Hill, Extracted from Major-General Henry Lee's *Memoirs of the War in the Southern Department of the United States,* Published 1812," printed in Coffin (ed.), *Battle of Breed's Hill,* 6–7.

16. On European averages, Fann, "On the Infantryman's Age," 165. On Henderson and others, see Palmer, "Longevity," 434–40. Henderson would die aged 105 in 1836.

17. Regarding the number of new recruits and length of service in America, I'm indebted to Don N. Hagist, who has analyzed the muster rolls for the 4th, 10th, 23rd, 35th, 38th, 43rd, 47th, 52nd, 59th, 63rd, and 64th Regiments, in WO 12 (Commissary General of Musters Office), National Archives (United Kingdom). Private communication, April 13, 2014.

18. Field, *Britain's Sea-Soldiers,* 1:153.

19. Ibid.

20. Houlding, *Fit for Service,* 160–62.

21. On drafting, see Houlding, *Fit for Service,* 120–25, and Hagist, *British Soldiers, American War,* 52–53; see also Spring, *With Zeal,* 105, 107.

22. An observation based on figures provided by Hagist, private communication, April 14, 2014.

23. Hagist, "Shedding Light on Friendly Fire," 7.

24. This section on the 18th/65th is based on the excellent article by Steven Baule and Don Hagist, "The Regimental Punishment Book of the Boston Detachments of the Royal Irish Regiment and 65th Regiment, 1774–1775," published in the *Journal of the Society for Army Research.* Mr. Hagist was kind enough to supply me with an advance copy.

25. Diary entry, June 25, 1775, printed in Van Arsdale (ed.), *Discord and Civil Wars,* 22.

26. Anderson, "People's Army: Provincial Military Service in Massachusetts," 505.

27. Fred Anderson's detailed estimates are used here. See Anderson, *People's Army,* 58–60, esp. n83.

28. Between 1755 and 1763, roughly 140 (but probably more) men signed up out of a total town population in 1760 of almost 760 people. That would mean there were about 380 white males living in Lexington, and we also find that 54 percent of them were older than 16. So let us say there were 205 eligible men. Even taking into account that some volunteers went more than once, that some came home early, and various other mitigating factors, it is hard to avoid concluding that between 50 percent and 60 percent of Lexington's eligible males went to war. See Hudson, *History of the Town of Lexington,* 1:413–16 (for rosters of volunteers) and 477 (for population).

29. Hawthorne, "Old News," in *Snow Image and Other Twice-Told Tales,* 130–31.

30. Data taken from Fischer, *Paul Revere's Ride,* Appendix O: "The Lexington Militia: Quantitative Research," 319–20.

31. Moore, *Life of General John Stark,* 181.

32. This list is based on Smith, *History of the Town of Peterborough,* 157–58, but supplemented by other sources. Some estimates of Peterborough's contribution range as low as sixteen and others, as high as forty or fifty, but twenty-six seems to be the most authoritative number. Resch, *Suffering Soldiers,* 23; Smith, *Peterborough, New Hampshire,* 92, 202–3, 370, 239–40, 176–78, 287, 264–70; Higginbotham, *War of American Independence,* 74.

33. Fischer, *Paul Revere's Ride,* Appendix O, "The Lexington Militia: Quantitative Research," 320.

34. Willcox, "Captain William Meacham at Bunker Hill," 203–7.

35. Roster, "Captain Benjamin Ames's Company (Presumably) at Bunker Hill," in Bailey, *Historical Sketches of Andover,* 319.

36. Gross, *Minutemen and Their World,* 71.

37. Fischer, *Paul Revere's Ride,* 158; Norton, "Marital Migration in Essex County, Massachusetts," 411; Waters, "Family, Inheritance, and Migration in Colonial New England," 65–66; Adams and Kasakoff, "Wealth and Migration in Massachusetts and Maine," 367.

38. See Quintal, Jr., *Patriots of Color,* and Alfred F. Young's preface, reproduced at http://www.nps.gov/archive/bost/patriotsofcolor/preface.htm. See also J. Lee Malcolm's article, "Slavery in Massachusetts and the American Revolution," *Journal of the Historical Society* 10, vol. (2010), 428.

39. Malcolm, "Slavery in Massachusetts," 417; on Boston's population, Greene and Harrington, *American Population,* 22.

40. The number of Americans ranged from 1,500 to 3,500 over the course of the day. If we take the average (2,500) and assume there were 33 blacks, we arrive at a figure of 1.32 percent representation, though there were almost certainly more than that bare minimum.

41. Malcolm, "Slavery in Massachusetts," 419–20, 427.

42. Bailey, *Historical Sketches of Andover,* 324.

43. Green, "Colonel William Prescott, 93.

44. Browne, *History of Hillsborough, New Hampshire,* 1:105–8, 111, esp. the list cataloguing Baldwin's company at Bunker Hill and the town's 1776 tax list. Whitcher, "Relation of New Hampshire Men to the Siege of Boston," 71.

45. Elting, *Bunker's Hill,* 11.

46. Lincoln (ed.), *Journals of Each Provincial Congress of Massachusetts,* entry of December 10, 1774, p. 71.

47. Fischer, *Paul Revere's Ride,* 155.

48. Johnson (ed.), "Diary of Israel Litchfield," 1:151.
49. Diary entry, November 14, 1774, in Johnson (ed.), "Diary of Israel Litchfield," 1:152.
50. Diary entry, April 13, 1775, in Johnson (ed.), "Diary of Israel Litchfield," 2:261.
51. Thus, on November 17, 1774, "in the afternoon 12 of us met . . . and exercised. We used what they call the Norfolk Exercise." Johnson (ed.), "Diary of Israel Litchfield," 1:152–3. See also Wright, "Some Notes on the Continental Army," 84–85.
52. Windham and Townshend, *Plan of Discipline,* iii, v–vi.
53. Anon., "Military Books of the Revolution," 60–61; Pickering, *Life of Timothy Pickering,* 1:18–19.
54. Letter, Adams to George Brinley, June 19, 1818, quoted in Dawson (ed.), "Bunker's Hill," 332n. An unwarrantedly long and mostly unwholesome controversy raged for decades in the nineteenth century over whether Putnam was even present at the battle. I shall spare readers the details, but the affair began with Henry Dearborn's somewhat meretricious accusations implying that Putnam was a grandstanding coward who had usurped Prescott's laurels. The general's defenders proved the case in Putnam's favor by producing dozens of eyewitness testimonies. The tale can be followed in, among other, Coffin (ed.), *Battle of Breed's Hill;* Swett, *Notes to His Sketch;* A. P. Putnam, *General Israel Putnam and the Battle of Bunker Hill: A Critique, Not a History* (Salem, MA: Putnam, 1901); Putnam, *Colonel Daniel Putnam's Letter Relative to the Battle of Bunker Hill and General Israel Putnam* (Hartford: Connecticut Historical Society, 1860); Drake, *General Israel Putnam: The Commander at Bunker Hill* (Boston: Nichols and Hall, 1875); F. J. Parker, *Colonel William Prescott, the Commander in the Battle of Bunker's Hill* (Boston: A. Williams, 1875).
55. Testimony of Dr. Snow, in Swett, *Notes to His Sketch,* 9. For a complaint about Stark's insubordination, General Nathaniel Folsom's letter to the Committee of Safety, June 23, 1775, in Force (ed.), *American Archives,* 4th ser., vol. 2, col. 1069. See also Swett, *Notes to His Sketch,* 26 (note M). On Stark as part–New Englander, part–Scots-Irish, see Elting, *Bunker's Hill,* 12. A fuller narrative of the Stark-Hobart affair is given in Potter, *History of Manchester,* 435–36.
56. "Rank of the Regiments of Foot in the Service of the United Colonies," September 26, 1775, printed in Henshaw, "Orderly Book of Col. William Henshaw," 160.
57. Letter, Washington to Continental Congress, September 24, 1776. Washington Papers.
58. Letter, Greene to Nicholas Cooke, June 18, 1775, in R. K. Showman (ed.), *The Papers of General Nathanael Greene* (Chapel Hill: University of North Carolina Press, 13 vols., 1976–2005), 1:87; and letter, Greene to Samuel Ward, January 4, 1776, p. 176.
59. Quoted in Frothingham, *Siege of Boston,* 116.
60. Pickering, *Life of Thomas Pickering,* 1:19.

5. The Rail Fence

1. Letter, Chester to Fish, July 22, 1775, printed in Dawson (ed.), "Bunker's Hill," 386.
2. "Extract of a Letter From Boston to Gentleman in Scotland, Dated June 25, 1775," in Force (ed.), *American Archives,* 4th ser., vol. 2, cols. 1093–94; Butler, *History of the Town of Groton,* 339n6. On the color of the hay, Moore, *Life of General John Stark,* 159.
3. Letter, Chester to Fish, July 22, 1775, in Dawson (ed.), "Bunker's Hill," 386; Letter, Howe to Harvey, in Fortescue (ed.), *Correspondence of George the Third,* 3:221; "Extract of a Letter From Boston to Gentleman in Scotland, Dated June 25, 1775," in Force (ed.), *American Archives,* 4th ser., vol. 2, cols. 1093–94.

4. "Maynard's Account," in Temple, *History of Framingham*, 289.
5. This is based on a combination of two references: Gibbon, *Artillerist's Manual*, 227, and Griffiths, *Artillerist's Manual*, 371.
6. As noted in the narrative of the Committee of Safety, July 25, 1775, "Account of the Late Battle of Charlestown," in Force (ed.), *American Archives*, 4th ser., vol. 2, col. 1374; extract from letter, Robert Steele to William Sumner, July 10, 1825, in Scheer and Rankin, *Rebels and Redcoats*, 59; Heath, "An Account of the Battle of Bunker's or Breed's Hill," in Coffin (ed.), *Battle of Breed's Hill*, 3.
7. There are several slightly different definitions of these steps. I have used the version given in *Rules and Regulations for the Formations, Field Exercise, and Movements*, 1:11, 22–5, but see also Spring, *With Zeal*, 144–45.
8. Over time, the speed at which armies can move has greatly increased. Today's Marine Corps "normal" cadence is between 112 and 120 30-inch steps per minute, while "double time" consists of 180 36-inch paces. *Marine Corps Drill and Ceremonies Manual* (2003), Sections 1–8, 1–6.
9. Stone (ed.), *Journal of Captain Pausch*, 108.
10. Windham and Townsend, *Plan of Discipline*, 60.
11. Stedman, *History of the Origin, Progress, and Termination of the American War*, 1:128. For similar claims, see Moore, *Life of General John Stark*, 168; Ward, *War of the Revolution*, 1:89; Ketchum, *The Battle for Bunker Hill*, 96; French, *First Year*, 237.
12. See Elting, *Bunker's Hill*, 23. For the Foreign Legion and Chindit figures, see Terraine, *Smoke and the Fire*, 143–47; on what grunts tended to carry during the Fallujah battle, see Camp, *Operation Phantom Fury*, 390. The usual patrol weight "doubles when soldiers must be away from base for days in the unforgiving mountains, valleys and deserts of Afghanistan." T. Shanker, "Army Ends Delays on Lightweight Armor," *New York Times*, April 25, 2009. Thus, during the fighting in Marja in Afghanistan of February 2010, the Marines of Company K, Third Battalion, Sixth Marines, serving as vanguard, "had been told that ground reinforcements and fresh supplies might not reach them for three days. This meant they had to carry everything they would need during that time: water, ammunition, food, first-aid equipment, bedrolls, clothes and spare batteries for radios and night-vision devices. As they jogged forward, the men grunted and swore under their burdens, which in many cases weighed 100 pounds or more." C. J. Chivers, "Afghan Attack Gives Marines a Taste of War," *New York Times*, February 13, 2010.
13. Quoted in Kidder, *History of New Ipswich*, 77.
14. Spring, *With Zeal*, 139. See also Brumwell, *Redcoats*, 254–55. In 1750, during his first campaign, a young Howe was promoted to a captaincy in the 20th Foot, commanded by Lieutenant Colonel Wolfe. Eight years later, Howe gallantly led the 60th at the siege of Louisburg under the watchful eye of Wolfe, now a general. In a letter home, the latter praised "our old comrade" who "is at the head of the best-trained battalion in America, and his conduct in the campaign corresponded with the opinion we had formed of him." Given command of the Light Infantry, Howe distinguished himself at Quebec in 1759 by undertaking a dangerous mission, entrusted to him personally by Wolfe, to scale the Heights of Abraham with a small force and capture the French outpost at the top. Fisher, "Objective at Bunker Hill," 133. For Wolfe's advice, see "Instructions for the 20th Regiment (in Case the French Land) Given by Lieutenant-Colonel Wolfe at Canterbury," December 15, 1755, printed in Wolfe, *Instructions to Young Officers*, 51. The essay was well known in America at this time. See French, *First Year*, 235.

15. War Office, *Rules and Regulations,* 1:11.
16. D. J. Beattie, "The Adaptation of the British Army to Wilderness Warfare, 1755–1763," in *Adapting to Conditions,* ed. M. Ultee, 78. See also Russell, "Redcoats in the Wilderness," 629–52. Three ranks was common but not universal. France opted for four ranks in order to enhance their lines' shock value while the British by the time of Waterloo preferred two, to emphasize firepower. See Lynn, "Linear Warfare: Images and Ideals of Combat in the Age of Enlightenment," in his *Battle,* 120–21.
17. Spring, *With Zeal,* 140.
18. Quoted in Duffy, *Army of Frederick the Great,* 88.
19. General Howe to Lord Howe, June 22, 1775, printed in Fisher, "Objective at Bunker Hill," 120.
20. Letter, Clinton to William Phillips, December 5, 1775, quoted in French, *First Year,* 235. On the two-line formation, see Howe's letter to Lord Harvey, June 22 and 24, 1775, printed in Fortescue (ed.), *Correspondence of King George the Third,* 3:221.
21. Quoted in Duffy, *Army of Frederick the Great,* 88.
22. Letter, General Howe to Lord Howe, June 22, 1775, printed in Fisher, "Objective at Bunker Hill," 120.
23. Diary entry, June 17, 1775, in Van Arsdale (ed.), *Discord and Civil Wars,* 18.
24. Quoted in Spring, *With Zeal,* 140.
25. On the length of the fence, see Frothingham, *Battle-Field of Bunker Hill,* 10, and Moore, *Life of General John Stark,* 159. Howe, in his letter to Lord Harvey, June 22 and 24, 1775, says "this breastwork [was] about 300 yards in extent." Fortescue (ed.), *Correspondence of King George the Third,* 3:221.
26. See figures in Morrissey, *Boston 1775,* 61; and Murdock, *Bunker Hill,* 77n.
27. War Office, *Rules and Regulations,* 3:1. See *Marine Corps Drill and Ceremonies Manual* (May 5, 2003), Section 1–6.
28. Dearborn, "An Account of the Battle of Bunker's Hill," 15–23, published in Coffin (ed.), *Battle of Breed's Hill,* 17.
29. Dawson (ed.), "Bunker's Hill," 428–29.
30. Dearborn, "An Account of the Battle of Bunker's Hill," in Coffin (ed.), *Battle of Breed's Hill,* 23.
31. On this point, see Rose, *American Rifle,* esp. ch. 3.
32. Diary entries, November 16, 1774, February 14, 1775, March 10, March 11, in Johnson (ed.), "Diary of Israel Litchfield," 1:152, 2:253–54, 256–57.
33. Diary entries, March 20 and January 23, 1775, in Johnson (ed.), "Diary of Israel Litchfield," 2:257; 1:163.
34. Diary entry, March 21, 1775, in Johnson (ed.), "Diary of Israel Litchfield," 2:257–58.
35. See table in Harrington, "Roundball Ballistics in the Revolutionary War," 12.
36. Brumwell, *Redcoats,* 250.
37. Lamb, *Original and Authentic Journal of Occurrences,* 32. Dr. William Gordon, who described the battle in a missive from Roxbury (August 15, 1775), noted that the militia "have only common muskets, nor are these in general furnished with bayonets; but then they are almost all marksmen, being accustomed to sporting of one kind or other from their youth." Gordon, *History of the Rise, Progress, and Establishment,* 1:52.
38. Wilkinson, "A Rapid Sketch of the Battle of Breed's Hill," in Coffin (ed.), *Battle of Breed's Hill,* 11.
39. The *Chronicle*'s item of August 3, 1779, is reprinted in appendix 9 of Frothingham, *Siege of Boston,* 398–401. Israel Mauduit, in a hostile tract of 1781, uses identical lan-

guage. Clearly, he was the original author. Mauduit, *Three Letters to Lord Viscount Howe.*

40. This figure derived from Krenn, Kalaus, and Hall, "Material Culture and Military History," 103.
41. N. A. Roberts, J. W. Brown, B. Hammett, and P. D. F. Kingston, "A Detailed Study of the Effectiveness and Capabilities of 18th Century Musketry on the Battlefield," in *Bastions and Barbwire,* ed. T. Pollard and I. Banks, 1–21.
42. James, "Britain's Brown Bess."
43. "Maynard's Account," in Temple, *History of Framingham,* 290.
44. Krenn, Kalaus, and Hall, "Material Culture and Military History," 103.
45. Dearborn, "An Account of the Battle of Bunker's Hill," in Coffin (ed.), *Battle of Breed's Hill,* 20–21.
46. Letter, C. Stuart to Lord Bute, July 24, 1775, in Wortley (ed.), *Prime Minister and His Son,* 69.
47. The *London Chronicle* of January 11, 1776, quoted in Frothingham, *Siege of Boston,* 196n1.
48. Frothingham discovered this vignette in a contemporary British newspaper, which he left unnamed. *Siege of Boston,* 199.
49. Anon., "Observations on the Government's Account of the Late Action Near Charlestown," August 1, 1775, printed in Force (ed.), *American Archives,* 4th ser., vol. 2, col. 1099.
50. Donkin, *Military Collections and Remarks,* 223.
51. Letter, Chester to Fish, July 22, 1775, printed in Dawson (ed.), "Bunker's Hill," 386.
52. Bland, *Treatise of Military Discipline,* 134.
53. Letter, Percy to a "gentleman in London," September 4, 1776, printed in Force (ed.), *American Archives,* 5th ser., vol. 2, col. 168.
54. "Account of the Action of the 19th of April, by an Officer of One of the Flank Companies," printed in French (ed.), *British Fusilier,* 65–66.
55. Diary entry, April 19, 1775, in French (ed.), *British Fusilier,* 56.
56. Diary entry, June 25, 1775, in Van Arsdale (ed.), *Discord and Civil Wars,* 21–22.
57. Letter, Howe to Lord Harvey, June 22 and 24, 1775, printed in Fortescue (ed.), *Correspondence of King George the Third,* 3:221.
58. Dearborn, "An Account," printed in Coffin (ed.), *Battle of Breed's Hill,* 20–21.
59. "Maynard's Account," in Temple, *History of Framingham,* 290.
60. Entry of June 8, 1776, in Lamb, *Original and Authentic Journal of Occurrences,* 107.
61. Quoted in Muir, *Tactics and the Experience of Battle,* 25.
62. Diary entry, May 27, 1775, in Green (ed.), "Amos Farnsworth's Diary," 81. The same simile was recently used by an American sniper in Afghanistan who "noticed that the smaller rounds coming in were not snapping by his ears but buzzing like bumblebees as they passed—air resistance over distance having slowed them to less than the speed of sound." Cited in W. Langewiesche, "Distant Executioner," *Vanity Fair,* February 2010.
63. On the differences over time, see L. C. Haag's definitive article on the subject, "The Sound of Bullets."
64. Letter, Howe to Lord Harvey, June 22 and 24, 1775, printed in Fortescue (ed.), *Correspondence of King George the Third,* 3:221.
65. So rare, in fact, that French claims that Howe "never revealed any emotion or anxiety, even to his brother." *First Year,* 259.

66. On this subject, see Hendrix, *Spirit of the Corps*, 68–100. I am grateful to Dr. Hendrix for supplying me with a copy of his invaluable thesis.

67. Lamont, *Art of War*, 75–76.

68. Lamont, *Art of War*, 71.

69. Letter, Chester to Fish, July 22, 1775, printed in Dawson (ed.), "Bunker's Hill," 386.

70. "Letter from Boston, July 5th, 1775," printed in House of Commons, *Detail and Conduct of the American War*, 13–15. Howe would not be the only one blamed by his subordinates for the debacle. Thomas Gage, for marrying an American woman, was also despised. Conway, "British Army, 'Military Europe,' and the American War of Independence," 69–100, esp. note 15.

71. Quoted in Wilkinson, "Rapid Sketch of the Battle of Breed's Hill," printed in Coffin (ed.), *Battle of Breed's Hill*, 12n.

72. Drewe, *Case of Edward Drewe*, 85 (appendix); on Drewe's career, see 28–29.

73. Goldstein, "British Grenadier's Button," 70–78. I am indebted to Mr. Goldstein for sending me a copy of this important article. For the August tallies, see Gage's "Return of the Officers," printed in Force (ed.), *American Archives*, 4th ser., vol. 2, cols. 1098–99.

74. Gage, "Return of the Officers," printed in Force (ed.), *American Archives*, 4th ser., vol. 2, cols. 1098–99.

75. Longmore, *Gunshot Injuries*, 197–203.

76. J. Malcolm, "Reminiscences of a Campaign in the Pyrenees and South of France in 1814," in Anon. (ed.), *Memorials of the Late War*, 1:298.

77. "Extract of Letter From Doctor Grant, One of the Surgeons of the British Military Hospital in Boston, to a Friend in Westminster," June 23, 1775, printed in Dawson (ed.), "Bunker's Hill," 361.

78. Bancroft's narrative, in Hill (ed.), *Bi-Centennial of Old Dunstable*, 61; "Judge Prescott's Account of the Battle of Bunker Hill," printed in Frothingham, *Battle-Field of Bunker Hill*, 20.

79. On ricochets, see Gibbon, *Artillerist's Manual*, 254–56.

80. Quoted in D. M. Sivilich, "What the Musket Ball Can Tell: Monmouth Battlefield State Park, New Jersey," in *Fields of Conflict*, ed. D. Scott, L. Babits, and C. Haecker, 96.

6. The Redoubt, Part Two

1. Letter, Prescott to John Adams, August 25, 1775, printed in Dawson (ed.), "Bunker's Hill," 390–91.

2. Letter, Stuart to Lord Bute, July 24, 1775, in Wortley (ed.), *Prime Minister and His Son*, 69.

3. On this point, see the Address of Major Edwin B. Wight, printed in Curtis, *History of the Twenty-Fourth Michigan of the Iron Brigade*, 424. An extremely valuable contribution is Reardon, "Writing Battle History," 252–63.

4. See Murdock, *Bunker Hill*, 71–72n; Dearborn, "An Account of the Battle of Bunker's Hill," in Coffin (ed.), *Battle of Breed's Hill*, 18; Swett, *Notes to His Sketch*, 22 (note E); Paul Lunt's diary entry of June 17, printed in Green (ed.), "Paul Lunt's Book," 194; "Extract of a Letter From Boston to Gentleman in Scotland, Dated June 25, 1775," in Force (ed.), *American Archives*, 4th ser., vol. 2, col. 1093; "Rev. Peter Thacher's Narrative," June 1775, printed in Dawson (ed.), "Bunker's Hill," 384; Anon. (ed.), "Journals of Lieut.-Col. Stephen Kemble," entry of June 12, 1775, 44.

5. This material is based on Artwohl, "Perceptual and Memory Distortion," 18–24; Klinger, *Police Responses*.

6. Klinger, *Police Responses*, 19.
7. "The Thirty-fifth, Royal Sussex, Infantry," extracted from *Case of Edward Drewe*, published in Dawson (ed.), "Bunker's Hill," 368–69.
8. Quoted in Dann, *Revolution Remembered*, 25.
9. Quoted in Dann, *Revolution Remembered*, 91.
10. Fontenot, "Fear God and Dreadnought," 23.
11. Grossman, *On Combat*, 31. For the research into performance deficits, see Lieberman et al., "Fog of War," section II, C7–C14.
12. See "Account of the Late Battle of Charlestown," Committee of Safety Report, July 25, 1775, in Force (ed.), *American Archives*, 4th ser., vol. 2, col. 1374.
13. Printed in Dawson (ed.), "Bunker's Hill," 371.
14. "Statement Prepared by Order of the Provincial Congress of Massachusetts, for Transmission to Great Britain," July 25, 1775, in Force (ed.), *American Archives*, 4th ser., vol. 2, cols. 1373–76. Thacher's influential narrative of the battle, upon which the Committee of Safety drew, had also outlined the two-attack scheme. See "Rev. Peter Thacher's Narration," June 1775, printed in Dawson (ed.), "Bunker's Hill," 383.
15. Diary entry, June 16 [*sic*], 1775, in Green (ed.), "Thomas Boynton's Journal," 255.
16. Letter, Prescott to Adams, August 25, 1775, in Dawson (ed.), "Bunker's Hill," 391.
17. Letter, Stuart to Lord Bute, July 24, 1775, in Wortley (ed.), *Prime Minister and His Son*, 69. Emphasis added.
18. Scudder, "Battle of Bunker Hill," 88.
19. Letter, J. Waller to unidentified recipient, June 21, 1775, held by the Massachusetts Historical Society.
20. "Judge Prescott's Account of the Battle of Bunker Hill," printed in Frothingham et al. (eds.), "Letter of Edward Everett," 70.
21. Isaac Glynney diary (unpublished).
22. Page's map remarks that the breastwork "was first forced by Grenadiers and regiments immediately opposite to it, which had for some time before formed one line in order to return the enemy's fire." Quoted in French, *First Year*, 242n29.
23. Gage, "Return of the Officers" (see figures for the Royal Regiment of Artillery), in Force (ed.), *American Archives*, 4th ser., vol. 2, col. 1098; French, *First Year*, 241.
24. Quoted in Webster, "Account of the Battle of Bunker Hill," 20.
25. Dearborn, "An Account of the Battle of Bunker's Hill," in Coffin (ed.), *Battle of Breed's Hill*, 13.
26. Quoted in French, *First Year*, 242–43.
27. Isaac Glynney diary (unpublished).
28. "Judge Prescott's Account of the Battle of Bunker Hill," in Frothingham et al. (eds.), "Letter of Edward Everett," 71.
29. "Another Account of the Late Action at Bunker's Hill," printed in *Rivington's Gazeteer*, August 3, 1775, in Dawson (ed.), "Bunker's Hill," 389–90.
30. "Judge Prescott's Account of the Battle of Bunker Hill," in Frothingham et al. (eds.), "Letter of Edward Everett," 71.
31. Letter, Prescott to Adams, August 25, 1775, in Dawson (ed.), "Bunker's Hill," 391. Peter Brown thought that at about 2:30 P.M. there had been as many as 700 men in the redoubt. Brown, "Officer's Story of Bunker Hill."
32. Diary entry, June 17, 1775, in Green (ed.), "Amos Farnsworth's Diary," 83.
33. Letter, Chester to Fish, July 22, 1775, printed in Dawson (ed.), "Bunker's Hill," 386–87.
34. Frothingham, *Centennial*, 56.
35. Letter, Chester to Fish, July 22, 1775, printed in Dawson (ed.), "Bunker's Hill," 386–87.

36. Bancroft's narrative, in Hill (ed.), *Bi-Centennial of Old Dunstable*, 60. Bancroft's emphasis.

37. Frothingham, *Centennial*, 57. "Maynard's Account," in Temple, *History of Framingham*, 291.

38. Bancroft's narrative, in Hill (ed.), *Bi-Centennial of Old Dunstable*, 61. Emphasis in original.

39. Frothingham (ed.), "Judge Prescott's Account of the Battle of Bunker Hill," in *Proceedings of the Massachusetts Historical Society*, 71. For Farnsworth, see his diary entry of June 17, 1775, in Green (ed.), "Amos Farnsworth's Diary," 83.

40. "A Letter From Abel Parker, Esq., Judge of Probate," May 27, 1818, printed in Dawson (ed.), "Bunker's Hill," 421; Bancroft's narrative, in Hill (ed.), *Bi-Centennial of Old Dunstable*, 61.

41. Letter, J. Waller to unidentified recipient, June 21, 1775, held by the Massachusetts Historical Society.

42. Entry of August 24, 1787, "A Groton Man Shot Pitcairn," in Green (ed.), *Collection of Papers*, 259–60, originally published as "Extracts from Dr. Belknap's Note-books," *Proceedings of the Massachusetts Historical Society*, 93. See also Murphy, " 'We Have All Lost a Father,' " 20–24.

43. Quoted in Frothingham, *Centennial*, 111.

44. J. L. Bell, "Who Killed Major John Pitcairn?" in Andrlik, Harrington, and Hagist (eds.), *Journal of the American Revolution*, 38–43.

45. On Tupper, see Murdock, *Bunker Hill*, 19n; on Gage's report confirming same, see Frothingham, *Siege of Boston*, 195n3.

46. Letter, John Waller to Jacob Waller, June 22, 1775, printed in Drake (ed.), *Bunker Hill*, 29–30.

47. M. Hunter, *The Journal of General Sir Martin Hunter* (Edinburgh, 1894), quoted in French, *First Year*, 248; Gage, "Return of the Officers," in Force (ed.), *American Archives*, 4th ser., vol. 2, col. 1098.

48. Lushington, *Life and Services of General Lord Harris*, 42.

49. Letters, Rawdon to the Earl of Huntingdon, June 20 and August 3, 1775, in Bickley (ed.), *Historical Manuscripts Commission*, 3:155, 157.

50. Letter from a Rhode Island gentleman to a friend in New York, June 29, 1775, *Rivington's Gazetteer*, printed in Moore (ed.), *Diary of the American Revolution*, 1:99n1.

51. Frothingham, *Siege of Boston*, 150n1; Clarke, "Impartial and Authentic Narrative," 22. Neither source has impeccable authority.

52. Letter, John Waller to Jacob Waller, June 22, 1775, printed in Drake (ed.), *Bunker Hill*, 29–30. For the names of Waller's friends, see letter, J. Waller to unidentified recipient, June 21, 1775, held by the Massachusetts Historical Society. For the probable captains, see Clarke, "Impartial and Authentic Narrative" and "General Gage's Despatch to the Home Government," printed in Dawson (ed.), "Bunker's Hill," 260, 361–63.

53. Noyes, *History of Norway*, 44.

54. Report of Ensign Studholme Brownrigg, June 21, 1775, to Lt-Gen Hodgson, in Hart, "Echoes of Bunker Hill," 39.

55. "Extract of a Letter From an Officer of the Army, in Boston, to His Friend in England," June 25, 1775, in Force (ed.), *American Archives*, 4th ser., vol. 2, cols. 1092–93.

56. Peter Brown letter, "Officer's Story of Bunker Hill."

57. "Maynard's Account," in Temple, *History of Framingham*, 291. Isaac Glynney, in his

unpublished diary, confirmed that in the final moments he threw stones. Bancroft's narrative, in Hill (ed.), *Bi-Centennial of Old Dunstable*, 61–62.

58. Butler, *History of the Town of Groton*, 340.

59. A letter from Charles Chauncy to Richard Price, July 18, 1775, observes that the Americans "came out well stocked with" ammunition. Printed in Ashburner (ed.), "Richard Price Letters," 299.

60. Some months before the battle, the Americans had made valiant, if unsuccessful, efforts to secure a plentiful reserve of ammunition for the war to come. On March 18, British lieutenant Mackenzie noted in his diary that a "country man was stopped at the lines, going out of town [Boston] with 19,000 ball cartridges, which were taken from him. When liberated, he had the insolence to go to headquarters to demand the redelivery of them. When asked who they were for, he said they were for his own use." They were not returned. French (ed.), *British Fusilier*, 42. This story was confirmed by Lieutenant Williams of the 23rd Regiment, in Van Arsdale (ed.), *Discord and Civil Wars*, 9.

61. Wilkinson (having heard it from one of the American colonels present), "Rapid Sketch of the Battle of Breed's Hill," printed in Coffin (ed.), *Battle of Breed's Hill*, 11n.

62. Entry for June 14, "Extracts From an Orderly Book, Supposed to Be Capt. Chester's," printed in Frothingham, *Battle-Field of Bunker Hill*, 39; Grosvenor quoted in Webster, "Account of the Battle of Bunker Hill."

63. "Maynard's Account," in Temple, *History of Framingham*, 284.

64. Hatch, "New Hampshire at Bunker Hill," 215; Smith, *Peterborough, New Hampshire*, 325.

65. As told to Ward, *History of the Town of Shrewsbury*, 56.

66. See his letter to Continental Congress, January 30, 1776, in George Washington Papers, Library of Congress.

67. Letter, Jesse Lukens, September 1775, quoted in Frothingham, *Siege of Boston*, 192, with further details cited in Bolton, *Private Soldier Under Washington*, 121; testimonies of Josiah Cleaveland and Nathaniel Rice, in Swett, *Notes to His Sketch*, 13; Frothingham, *Siege of Boston*, 192. On British estimates of their ammunition needs, see Washington's letter to Continental Congress, January 30, 1776, in George Washington Papers.

68. Letter, Chauncy to Price, July 18, 1775, in Ashburner (ed.), "Richard Price Letters," 299.

69. Brumwell, *Redcoats*, 246.

70. Hadden, *Hadden's Journal and Orderly Books*, 74.

71. *New Hampshire State Papers* VI, 526, quoted in Elting, *Bunker's Hill*, 40.

72. "Maynard's Account," in Temple, *History of Framingham*, 291.

73. Letter, Samuel Webb to Silas Deane, July 11, 1775, in Frothingham et al. (eds.), "Letter of Edward Everett," 83.

74. Letter, Waller to Waller, June 22, 1775, in Drake (ed.), *Bunker Hill*, 28.

75. Brown, "Officer's Story of Bunker Hill"; Chase and Dawson (eds.), *Diary of David How*, ix.

76. "Another Account of the Late Action at Bunker's Hill," *Rivington's Gazeteer*, August 3, 1775, printed in Dawson (ed.), "Bunker's Hill," 389–90.

77. Lossing, *Pictorial Field-Book*, 546.

78. Potter, "Life and Remarkable Adventures," 15.

79. Bancroft's narrative, in Hill (ed.), *Bi-Centennial of Old Dunstable*, 62.

80. Letter, J. Waller to unidentified recipient, June 21, 1775, held by the Massachusetts Historical Society.

81. Dearborn, "An Account of the Battle of Bunker's Hill," in Coffin (ed.), *Battle of Breed's Hill*, 19.
82. "Nasty, Brutish and Not That Short," *The Economist*, December 16, 2010. I'm grateful to Mark Lee for this reference.
83. Quoted in Frothingham, *Siege of Boston*, 150; Elting, *Bunker's Hill*, 35.
84. Potter, "Life and Remarkable Adventures," 15.
85. Elting, *Bunker's Hill*, 36; Letter, Chester to Fish, July 22, 1775, in Dawson (ed.), "Bunker's Hill," 387; Letter, Chester and Webb to Webb, June 19, 1775, in Frothingham, *Siege of Boston*, 416.
86. French, *First Year*, 251.
87. French, *First Year*, 252.
88. Letter, Rawdon to the Earl of Huntingdon, June 20, 1775, in Bickley (ed.), *Historical Manuscripts Commission*, 3:155.
89. Letter, Burgoyne to Lord Rochfort, in Fonblanque, *Political and Military Episodes*, 147.
90. Wade and Lively, *This Glorious Cause*, 21.
91. Letter, Steele to W. Sumner, July 10, 1825, printed in Scheer and Rankin, *Rebels and Redcoats*, 59–60.
92. Smith, *Peterborough, New Hampshire*, 232–35.
93. Quoted in Bailey, *Historical Sketches of Andover*, 323.
94. As reported by the *Essex Gazette*, June 1829, printed in Bailey, *Historical Sketches of Andover*, 327.
95. Swett, *Notes to His Sketch*, 25 (note L).
96. Smith, *Peterborough, New Hampshire*, 323–25; Resch, *Suffering Soldiers*, 23.
97. On the number of prisoners taken, their experiences, and survivors, see French, *First Year*, 252; Leach, "Journal Kept by John Leach," 255–63; Green, "American Prisoners Taken at the Battle of Bunker Hill," 168–69. Also, *Rivington's Gazetteer*, July 13, 1775, reported a similar number; see Moore, *Diary of the American Revolution*, 1:103.
98. Clarke, "Impartial and Authentic Narrative," 255–56.
99. Quoted in French, *First Year*, 253–54. Clinton's emphasis.
100. Letter, Burgoyne to Lord Rochfort, in Fonblanque, *Political and Military Episodes*, 147.
101. Lieutenant Archelaus Fuller, Joseph Nichols, and John Cleaveland, quoted in Anderson, *People's Army*, 143–44.
102. Klinger, "Police Responses," 92 (table 10); Grossman, *On Combat*, 14–16.
103. Quoted in French, *First Year*, 255.
104. Trumbull, *Autobiography, Reminiscences, and Letters*, 22.

7. The Wounded and the Dead

1. Norwood, "Medicine in the Era of the American Revolution," 395; Gilman, "Medical Surgery," 493.
2. Allen, "Medicine in the American Revolution," 426. On the breakdown of doctors attached to the American troops, see Estes, "'Disagreeable and Dangerous Employment,'" 290.
3. Stephenson, *Patriot Battles*, 164.
4. Dann, *Revolution Remembered*, 81.
5. Manring et al., "Treatment of War Wounds," 2176.
6. "Return of the Killed, Wounded, and Missing in the Action of the 19th of April, 1775," printed in French (ed.), *British Fusilier*, 61. On Hawkstone, letter from Joseph Thaxter, November 30, 1824, *The United States Literary Gazette* 1 (1824–1825), 264.

7. On triage, see Manring et al., "Treatment of War Wounds," 2169.

8. Neale, *Letters From Portugal and Spain*, 17.

9. Wooden, "Wounds and Weapons of the Revolutionary War," 61. I am indebted to Kathy O. Jackson of the Medical Society of Delaware for supplying me with a copy of this article. See also Cantlie, *History of the Army Medical Department*, 344. On conservative approaches, see Manring et al., "Treatment of War Wounds," 2177.

10. Phalen, "Surgeon James Mann's Observations on Battlefield Amputations," 463–66; diary of Dr. Charles Gilman, quoted in Gilman, "Medical Surgery," 493–94. On Dr. Guthrie, famed as the man who could amputate in five minutes, see Cantlie, *History of the Army Medical Department*, 344.

11. Grattan, *Adventures with the Connaught Rangers*, 77.

12. Diary entry, October 24, 1777, in Thacher, *Military Journal*, 113.

13. See, for instance, Balingall, *Introductory Lectures to a Course of Military Surgery*, Lecture 1, p. 35. In the words of a group of modern researchers, amputation "transformed a complex wound into a simple wound with a better chance of recovery." Manring et al., "Treatment of War Wounds," 2176.

14. Appendix, "Official Account of General Gage, Published in the *London Gazette*," compiled June 25, 1775, supplemented by the "Return of the Officers," in Force (ed.), *American Archives*, 4th ser., vol. 2, cols. 1098–99.

15. I have used the detailed tables in Longmore, *Gunshot Injuries*, 700–2.

16. On the mid-thigh mortality rate, see Gillett, *Army Medical Department*, 18.

17. Letter, J. Hall to Elbridge Gerry, June 27, 1775, published in Henkels (ed.), *Letters and Papers of Elbridge Gerry*, 86.

18. Pruitt, Jr., "Combat Casualty Care and Surgical Progress," 715–18.

19. Diary entry, August 17, 1775, in "Extracts from President Stiles's Diary," in Dawson (ed.), "Bunker's Hill," 397–98.

20. Based on muster-roll information provided by Don N. Hagist, "Bunker Hill Flank Company Casualties," private communication, April 14, 2014.

21. *London Chronicle*, January 11, 1776, quoted in Frothingham, *Siege of Boston*, 196n1. On Page's leg, see French, *First Year*, 747–48 (appendix 23).

22. Letter, Washington to John Augustine Washington, July 27, 1775, in Washington Papers. There are several other tallies, which do not significantly alter these numbers. See Frothingham, *Siege of Boston*, 193; Seybolt, "Note on the Casualties of April 19, and June 17, 1775," 525–28; Murdock, *Bunker Hill*, 75.

23. Potter, "Life and Remarkable Adventures," 15–16.

24. Diary entry, June 17, 1775, in Green (ed.), "Diary of Amos Farnsworth," 83–84.

25. Smith, *History of the Town of Peterborough*, 157; Smith, *Peterborough, New Hampshire*, 199–200, 205–7.

26. Frothingham, *Siege of Boston*, 194. The doctors' names were Thomas Kittredge, William Eustis, Walter Hastings, Thomas Walsh, Isaac Foster, Col. Bricket, David Townsend, and John Hart.

27. Cantlie, *History of the Army Medical Department*, 139. On the takeover of the almshouse and poorhouse, letter dated July 22, 1775, from Chauncy to Richard Price, printed in Ashburner (ed.), "Richard Price Letters," 298; see also Frothingham, *Siege of Boston*, 194.

28. Potter, "Life and Remarkable Adventures," 15–16.

29. Goldstein, "British Grenadier's Button," 70–78.

30. Stephenson, *Patriot Battles*, 167; Clarke, "Impartial and Authentic Narrative," 264.

31. Letter, Laurie to J. Roebuck, June 23, 1775, quoted in Conway, "British Army Officers and the American War for Independence," 271.

32. Orders of July 17, printed in Stevens (ed.), *General Sir William Howe's Orderly Book*, 44.
33. "A Narrative of the Life and Character of William Crawford," reprinted in Hagist, *British Soldiers, American War*, 67. Crawford, aged seventy-three and a cantankerous alcoholic, would be hanged in 1823 for murdering his son.
34. Orders of July 17, printed in Stevens (ed.), *General Sir William Howe's Orderly Book*, 44. Looting has a long history.
35. Muir, *Tactics and the Experience of Battle*, 251–52.
36. Muir, *Tactics and the Experience of Battle*, 221–22.
37. Gage, in letter to Lord Barrington, June 25, 1775, mentions that he is submitting a list of men recommended for promotion "occasioned by the loss of officers on the 17th instant." Carter (ed.), *Correspondence of General Thomas Gage*, 2:685.
38. Letter, Gordon to Dorothea, Lady Fife, July 9, 1775, quoted in Conway, "British Army Officers and the American War for Independence," 276. Some, for political reasons, received still more accelerated promotions. Lieutenant William Pitcairn, whose father, the major, was killed in the battle, had been commissioned on March 2, 1773, making him 109th in seniority among first lieutenants in the Marines. Yet he was elevated to captain lieutenant on July 27, thereby vaulting him over the heads of 108 of his peers, some of whom (such as William Feilding, commissioned January 22, 1764, and ranked 58th) had more than a decade's worth of experience over him. Lieutenant Pitcairn had fought bravely at Bunker Hill, but there was a "sympathy" vote additionally weighing in his favor that led to much envy among those not so fortunate as to lose a famous father. Lord Sandwich comforted Feilding, who was "not a little mortif[ied]" at hearing of Pitcairn's meteoric rise, that the latter's case "is not to be looked upon as a precedent." See letters, Lord Denbigh to Feilding, August 8, 1775, and Feilding to Denbigh, October 8, 1775, in Balderston and Syrett (eds.), *Lost War*, 35–36, 45–47.
39. R. Brown, "Psychology," in *An Oxford Companion to the Romantic Age: British Culture, 1776–1832*, ed. I. McCalman, 361–69; Vidal, "Psychology in the 18th Century," 89–119.
40. Letter, Amos Foster, August 3, 1825, printed in Sumner, "Reminiscences," 122.
41. Hagist, *British Soldiers, American War*, x–xi.
42. Quoted in Paret, *Imagined Battles*, 48.
43. Quoted in Erffa and Staley, *Paintings of Benjamin West*, 222.
44. Barker, *British in Boston*, 64; Letter, Feilding to Denbigh, October 8, 1775, in Balderston and Syrett (eds.), *Lost War*, 45–47. See also "Organization of the Royal Marines, 1775," printed in Drake (ed.), *Bunker Hill*, 74.
45. On the resignations, see Lt. Gordon's letter of July 7, 1775, cited in Conway, "British Army Officers and the American War for Independence," 267.
46. Trumbull, *Autobiography, Reminiscences, and Letters*, 22.
47. Quoted in Bailey, *Historical Sketches of Andover*, 328–29.

8. Aftermath

1. Letter, Rawdon to the Earl of Huntingdon, August 3, 1775, in Bickley (ed.), *Historical Manuscripts Commission*, 3:159.
2. Quoted in French, "General Haldimand in Boston," 94.
3. G. Raudzens, "In Search of Better Quantification for War History," 1–30. I have used Raudzens's compilations for the battles of Lobositz, Leuthen, Prague, Plassy, Kolin, Rossbach, Hochkirch, Zorndorf, the Plains of Abraham, Kunersdorf, Minden, Liegnitz, and Torgau.

4. Letter, Thomas Gage to Dartmouth, June 25, 1775, in Carter (ed.), *Correspondence of General Thomas Gage*, 1:407.
5. "Extract of a Letter From an Officer on Board One of the King's Ships at Boston, to His Friend in London," June 23, 1775, in Force (ed.), *American Archives*, 4th ser., vol. 2, cols. 1067–68.
6. Letter, Anon. to Francis Downman, June 18, 1775, printed in Whinyates (ed.), *Services of Lieut.-Colonel Francis Downman*, 23.
7. Colonel W. Grayson to General Weedon, June 26, 1781, printed in Reed, *Life and Correspondence of Joseph Reed*, 2:355.

GETTYSBURG

1. Introduction

1. Based on the report by MacDonald, "Gettysburg Holds Greatest Fourth."
2. According to Drew Gilpin Faust, for instance, the Civil War "attained a scale that shocks and horrifies—a scale of drama and scale of death that prefigured the slaughter of the century that followed." Indeed, the charnel-houses of Antietam and Chickamauga, Chancellorsville and Gettysburg would "presage the slaughter of World War I's Western Front and the global carnage of the twentieth century." Her lecture, originally given to the National Endowment for the Humanities and titled "The Civil War and the Meaning of Life," was published as "Telling War Stories," 19–25; quotation 20; Faust, "Civil War Soldier and the Art of Dying," 3. For a critical view of the 1865–1945 master narrative, see Chickering, "Total War," in *Anticipating Total War*, 13–28.
3. See Ferro, *Great War*, 199. On interwar Franco-British views, Strachan, "On Total War and Modern War," 348; Baumann and Segesser, "Shadows of Total War," in *Shadows of Total War*, ed. R. Chickering and S. Förster. For German interpretations, see Jünger, "Total Mobilization," in *Heidegger Controversy*, ed. R. Wolin; Ludendorff, *Nation at War*, 169. H. Speier's 1941 essay, "Ludendorff: The German Concept of Total War," in *Makers of Modern Strategy*, ed. E. M. Earle, is a sound source on the general's thoughts, such as they were. See also Kutz, "Fantasy, Reality, and Modes of Perception," in Chickering, Förster, and Grenier (eds.), *World at Total War*, 189–206. On postwar American revisionism, see Walters, "General William T. Sherman and Total War," 447–80; Walters, *Merchant of Terror*, xiii, xviii. This book reproduces and enlarges upon his 1948 argument but was written in the shadow of the My Lai massacre in Vietnam—the consequence, says Walter, of "Sherman's philosophy." R. F. Weigley felt that Lincoln's orders for Sherman to attack Southern resources "held the germ of the total wars of the twentieth century, and of the bomb at Hiroshima." Weigley, *Towards an American Army*, 86–87.
4. A recent example of this modernist view is provided by White, "Born in the USA."

2. Combat in the Civil War

1. This figure excludes shots taken by the cavalry, skirmishers, sharpshooters, or the more excitable soldiers, which would skew the results, and treats only soldiers in attack formation or behind entrenchments. Trinque, "Rifle-Musket in the Civil War," 62–64. Trinque based his finding on some 386 reports in which yardage was mentioned.
2. It is today a commonplace to declare that the new generation of rifle-muskets "changed

the course of the war" owing to their ability to shoot at long range. This technologically teleological view is severely flawed in that it does not take into account real-world battle factors, nor does it include the difference between theoretical capabilities and actual use. The idea seems to have originated with A. L. Wagner's influential book *Organization and Tactics,* in which he says that the new rifles' 1,000-yard range made "infantry fire . . . so deadly as to effect marked changes in tactical formations" and practice. For works based on this theory, see for instance, Linderman, *Embattled Courage,* 135–36; and Catton, *Reflections on the Civil War,* 126–31.

3. These statements are based on painstaking detective work in the official records; see Griffith, *Battle Tactics,* 146–50; Hess, *Rifle Musket in Civil War Combat,* 108, 109–13, table 4.3.

4. Oliver, Hicks, and Carr, *History of Company E,* 23.

5. Anon. (eds.), *Union Army,* 2:148.

6. M. de Saxe, *My Reveries Upon the Art of War,* 298.

7. For background, see M. A. Bonura, "A French Army in America: The U.S. Army's Adoption of a French Way of Warfare From 1814 to 1835," a paper pre-circulated as part of the Transatlantic Currents in Military Theory Session, held at the Society for Military History Annual Meeting, May 2012.

8. E. S. Riley (ed.), *"Stonewall Jackson": A Thesaurus of Anecdotes and Incidents in the Life of Lieut.-General Thomas Jonathan Jackson, C.S.A.* (Annapolis: E. S. Riley, 1920), 101.

9. A. Ducaunnès-Duval (ed.), *Notes inédites de l'Empereur Napoléon Ier sur les mémoires militaires du Général Lloyd* (Bordeaux: G. Gounouilhou, 1901). On Lloyd, see P. J. Speelman, *Henry Lloyd and the Military Enlightenment of Eighteenth-Century Europe* (Westport, CT: Greenwood Press, 2002); and T. Travers, "The Development of British Military Historical Writing and Thought From the Eighteenth Century to the Present," in *Military History and the Military Profession,* ed. D. A. Charters, M. Milner, and J. B. Wilson (Westport, CT: Praeger, 1992), 25–27.

10. Bousquet, *Scientific Way of Warfare,* esp. ch. three, "Thermodynamic Warfare and the Science of Energy."

11. A. H. Jomini (trans. O. F. Winship and E. E. McLean), *Summary of the Art of War, or, a New Analytical Compend of the Principal Combinations of Strategy, of Grand Tactics and of Military Policy* (New York: G. P. Putnam and Co., 1854), 101. D. Chandler discusses Napoleon's tricks in more detail in "Napoleon: Classical Military Theory and the Jominian Legacy," in his *On the Napoleonic Wars,* 245–46. According to R. Von Caemmerer, for Jomini, as for Napoleon, "annihilation of the hostile army in battle and pursuit is the only guiding star for all his military thinking." R. Von Caemmerer (trans. K. Von Donat), *The Development of Strategical Science During the Nineteenth Century* (London: Hugh Rees, 1905), 28; see also 109.

12. To Isaac Trimble, quoted in Freeman, *R. E. Lee: A Biography* (New York: Charles Scribner's Sons, 4 vols., 1934–35), 3:58.

13. L. A. Coolidge, *Ulysses S. Grant* (Boston: Houghton Mifflin, 2 vols., 1924), 54.

14. Fully one in five French men (some claim four in ten) born between 1790 and 1795 died in Napoleon's wars. J. Lynn, "The Sun of Austerlitz: Romantic Visions of Decisive Battle in Nineteenth-Century Europe," in his *Battle,* 397n56, citing J. Houdaille, "Pertes de l'armeé de terre sous le Prémier Empire," *Population,* January–February 1972. Being conscripted in 1812 proved the shortest straw: 70 percent of French youths aged twenty were killed. See J. France, *Perilous Glory: The Rise of Western Military Power* (New Haven: Yale University Press, 2011), 213.

15. Durkin (ed.), *John Dooley, Confederate Soldier,* 104–5.
16. The British military theorist J. F. C. Fuller believed that the bayonet in the Civil War was as obsolete as the pike, a weapon last seen sometime in the seventeenth or early eighteenth century. Fuller, *Grant and Lee,* 47.
17. J. Buechler, "'Give 'Em the Bayonet,'" in J. T. Hubbell (ed.), *Battles Lost and Won,* 135. (Buechler is one of the critics.)
18. "Consolidated Statement of Wounds, &C., for the Battles Around Spotsylvania Court-House, Va., From May 8, 1864 to May 21, 1864," *The War of the Rebellion,* 1st ser., 36, pt. 1, p. 237. Hereafter *Official Records.*
19. Letter, O. Ladley to mother and sisters, July 6, 1863, printed in Becker and Thomas (eds.), *Hearth and Knapsack,* 143. Oscar Jackson wrote that the death of a Confederate by Corporal Selby's bayonet was "a remarkable thing in a battle and was spoken of in the official report." Jackson (ed.), *Colonel's Diary,* 74. On the 75th's casualties, see Busey and Martin (eds.), *Regimental Strengths and Losses at Gettysburg,* 253.
20. General Orders No. 128, May 25, 1862, in *Official Records,* 1st ser., 11, 3:192.
21. *Scientific American,* June 14, 1862, 371.
22. McWhiney and Jamieson, *Attack and Die,* 161; Letter, Jackson to S. Bassett French, March 31, 1862, in *Official Records,* 1st ser., 12, 3:842.
23. Bierce, "Crime at Pickett's Mill," in *Devil's Dictionary, Tales, and Memoirs,* 691.
24. Diary entry, August 31, 1862, in Wainwright (ed.), *Philadelphia Perspective,* 436.
25. Borcke, *Memoirs of the Confederate War for Independence,* 44.
26. Byrne and Weaver (eds.), *Haskell of Gettysburg,* 162.
27. Anon., *Reunions of the Nineteenth Maine Regiment Association,* 13.
28. Excerpt from Urban, "Dreaming on the Conestoga," printed in Felton (ed.), "In Their Words," 95.
29. "Report of Colonel Wheelock G. Veazey, Sixteenth Vermont Infantry," July 17, 1863, in *Official Records,* 1st ser., 27, 1:1042.
30. Castel, "Mars and the Reverend Longstreet," 103–14.
31. Nosworthy, *Bloody Crucible of Courage,* 411–12.
32. Quoted in McWhiney and Jamieson, *Attack and Die,* 153.

3. The Machine Breaks Down: The Reality of Combat

1. Nosworthy, *Bloody Crucible of Courage,* 412–14.
2. Weygant, *History of the One Hundred and Twenty-Fourth Regiment,* 17, 29.
3. Pula, "Fifth German Rifles at Gettysburg," 53.
4. Chamberlain, *Passing of the Armies,* 98.
5. Guelzo, "Unturned Corners of the Battle of Gettysburg," 109n10, citing Cole, *Command and Communications Frictions,* 80.
6. "Report of Brig. Gen. J. B. Kershaw, C.S. Army," October 1, 1863, *Official Records,* 1st ser., 27, 2:368; J. B. Kershaw, "Kershaw's Brigade at Gettysburg," in *Battles and Leaders of the Civil War,* ed. R. U. Johnson and C. C. Buell, 3:335–36; Coxe, "Battle of Gettysburg," 433–36, on 434.
7. In fact, said adjutant Theodore Dodge, the only people who knew "the why and the wherefore, the cause and the effect of the marchings and countermarchings of a large army" were those at Army headquarters. Everyone else was completely at sea. Dodge, "Left Wounded," 317.
8. "Report of Brig. Gen. John W. Geary, U.S. Army, Commanding Second Division," July 29, 1863, *Official Records,* 1st ser., 27, 1:826.

9. Letter, A. S. Williams to J. B. Bachelder, November 10, 1885, in Ladd and Ladd (eds.), *Bachelder Papers*, 1:216.
10. Durkin (ed.), *John Dooley, Confederate Soldier,* 102–3.
11. Quoted in Hutchinson, "To Gettysburg and Beyond," 88.
12. Evans, " 'All Was Complete Chaos,' " 37.
13. D. L. Thompson, "With Burnside at Antietam," in *Battles and Leaders,* ed. Johnson and Buell, 2:660.
14. Colonel Adrian Root, 94th New York, was one of the few who succeeded in rebooting a stalled attack. During the assault against the Confederate positions on Marye's Heights at Fredericksburg on December 13, 1862, "the fire of the enemy became so incessant and galling and so many of my men fell killed or wounded that the front line of the brigade slackened its pace, and the men, without orders, commenced firing. A halt seemed imminent, and a halt in the face of the terrific fire to which the brigade was exposed would have been death; or worse, a disastrous repulse." Root requested that Colonel Bates, leading the 12th Massachusetts, unite his regiment with the brigade and mount a joint bayonet charge. "By the strenuous exertions of the regimental commanders and other officers, the firing was nearly discontinued. The brigade resumed its advance, and as the men recognized the enemy their movement increased in rapidity until, with a shout and a run, the brigade leaped the ditches, charged across the railway, and occupied the wood beyond, driving the enemy from their position, killing a number with the bayonet, and capturing upwards of 200 prisoners." See "Report of Col. Adrian R. Root, Ninety-Fourth New York Infantry, Commanding First Brigade," December 23, 1862, *Official Records,* 1st ser., 21, p. 487.

5. Marching to Gettysburg

1. Grandchamp, "2nd Rhode Island Volunteers," 73, 77.
2. Ward, " 'Sedgwick's Foot Cavalry,' " 58.
3. Longstreet, *From Manassas to Appomattox,* 365.
4. Benedict, *Vermont at Gettysburg,* 14. Charles Benton, 150th New York, suggested an alternative reason: "Heavy cannonading has a tendency to produce sleepiness in some persons." A friend of his "casually remarked, 'That always makes me sleepy. Wake me up if my regiment starts, will you?' and despite the fact that shells were dropping and exploding here and there in our immediate vicinity, or ripping through the trees above us, he was soon sleeping soundly on the grass." Benton, *As Seen From the Ranks,* 39–40.
5. Oates, *War Between the Union and the Confederacy,* 212.
6. Letter, "Suggestions From an Old Soldier," *New York Times,* April 24, 1861, 2. Some of his other advice was actually rather sound and sensible.
7. R. Carter, "Reminiscences of the Campaign and Battle of Gettysburg," in *The Gettysburg Papers,* ed. K. Bandy and F. Freeland, 2:707.
8. Laney, "Wasted Gallantry," 30.
9. Elmore, "Meteorological and Astronomical Chronology of the Gettysburg Campaign," 19.
10. Sword, "Capt. Mckee's Revolver and Capt. Sellers' Sword," 50.
11. For an example, see Elmore, "Meteorological and Astronomical Chronology of the Gettysburg Campaign," 12–13.
12. Anon., "Gettysburg Weather Reports," 23.
13. Elmore, "Meteorological and Astronomical Chronology of the Gettysburg Campaign," 10.

14. Letter, July 30, 1903, printed in Sauers (ed.), *Fighting Them Over*, 448.
15. Bigelow, *Peach Orchard*, 54.
16. Herdegen, "Old Soldiers and War Talk," 17.
17. Quoted in Wheeler, *Witness to Gettysburg*, 221.
18. Doyle, Smith, and McMurry (eds.), *This Wilderness of War*, 10–11.
19. Diary entry, April 6, 1862, in Boyd, *Civil War Diary*, 29.
20. Campbell, "'Remember Harper's Ferry,'" 65.
21. Meinhard, "First Minnesota at Gettysburg," 80–81.
22. Address by A. Cowan, in New York Monuments Commission, *In Memoriam, Alexander Stewart Webb, 1835–1911*, 67.

6. Skirmishing

1. Benedict, *Vermont at Gettysburg*, 8–9; Oates, *War Between the Union and the Confederacy*, 211; Smith, *History of the Nineteenth Regiment*, 79.
2. Winschel, "Heavy Was Their Loss," 8.
3. Patterson, "Death of Iverson's Brigade," 15.
4. Stevens, *Souvenir of Excursion to Battlefields*, 16.
5. Culp, *25th Ohio Veteran Volunteer Infantry*, 78; and New York State Monuments Commission (ed.), *Final Report on the Battlefield of Gettysburg*, 2:932.
6. Letter, C. A. Richardson to J. B. Bachelder, August 18, 1869, in Ladd and Ladd (eds.), *Bachelder Papers*, 1:314–15; "Reports of Lieut. Col. James M. Bull, 126th New York Infantry, Commanding Third Brigade," July 8, 1863, *Official Records*, 1st ser., 27, 1:472.
7. There was an occasional exception, such as John De Forest, who wrote that "skirmishing is not nearly so trying as charging or line fighting. In the first place, you generally have cover; in the second, if you are shot at you can also shoot." Even so, De Forest later changed his mind when he spent more than a month on skirmishing duty and fifty or sixty of his regiment were killed. De Forest, *Volunteer's Adventures*, 111, 116.
8. Wert, *Gettysburg*, 155.
9. Quoted in Hartwig, "Unwilling Witness," 46.
10. See R. Carter, "Reminiscences of the Campaign and Battle of Gettysburg," in *Gettysburg Papers*, ed. K. Bandy and F. Freeland, 2:726; Livermore, *Days and Events*, 67. For the musician's comment, Hunter, "High Private's Sketch of Sharpsburg," 16.
11. Page, *History of the Fourteenth Regiment*, 142–43.
12. Page, *History of the Fourteenth Regiment*, 143.
13. Yee, "Sharpshooting at Gettysburg," 45.
14. Diary entry, July 2, 1863, in Jones (ed.), *Civil War Memoirs of Captain William J. Seymour*, 73.
15. Norton, *Attack and Defense of Little Round Top*, 301.
16. Norton, *Attack and Defense of Little Round Top*, 73.
17. Excerpt from Urban, "Dreaming on the Conestoga," printed in Felton (ed.), "In Their Words," 98.
18. Woodward, *Our Campaigns*, 271.
19. Stevens, *Berdan's United States Sharpshooters*, 340.
20. Urban, "Dreaming on the Conestoga," printed in Felton (ed.), "In Their Words," 98.
21. Dunaway, *Reminiscences of a Rebel*, 87.
22. Parker, *Henry Wilson's Regiment*, 340–41.
23. Stearns, *Three Years with Company K*, 207, 325.

24. R. Thompson, "A Scrap of Gettysburg," in *Gettysburg Papers*, ed. K. Bandy and F. Freeland, 2:955–56. Thompson claims that the Union marksmen were from Berdan's unit, but they were in fact from 1st Company, Massachusetts Sharpshooters (1st Andrew Sharpshooters).
25. Elmore, "Skirmishers," 11.
26. Wade, "Untold History Recited at a Meeting of the Regiment," 1.
27. Stevens, *Souvenir of Excursion to Battlefields*, 15; Galwey, *Valiant Hours*, 107.
28. Galwey, *Valiant Hours*, 110–11.
29. Stevens, *Souvenir of Excursion to Battlefields*, 11.
30. Stevens, *Souvenir of Excursion to Battlefields*, 16.
31. Quoted in Adelman, "Hazlett's Battery at Gettysburg," 69.

7. Artillery Versus Artillery

1. Smith, *Famous Battery and Its Campaigns*, 102.
2. Scribner, *How Soldiers Were Made*, 294.
3. Letter, July 4, 1863, printed in Benedict, *Army Life in Virginia*, 166.
4. Murray, "Artillery Duel in the Peach Orchard," 79.
5. Nosworthy, *Bloody Crucible of Courage*, 421–22; Gibbon, *Artillerist's Manual*, 357.
6. "Report of Lieut. Col. Freeman McGilvery, First Main Light Artillery, Commanding First Volunteer Brigade," no date, *Official Records*, 1st ser., 27, 1:881.
7. Nevins (ed.), *Diary of Battle*, 242–43.
8. Gibbon, *Artillerist's Manual*, 358.
9. Baker, *History of the Ninth Mass. Battery*, 59.
10. Campbell, "Baptism of Fire," 59n53.
11. Alexander, *Military Memoirs of a Confederate*, 421.
12. Murray, "Artillery Duel in the Peach Orchard," 83.
13. Anon., "Visit to the Gettysburg Battlefield," 2.
14. Andrews (ed.), *History of Marietta and Washington County*, 626.
15. Elmore, "Grand Cannonade," 107.
16. Letter, William Johnston to Smith, no date, printed in Smith, *Famous Battery and Its Campaigns*, 143.
17. Bigelow, *Peach Orchard*, 55.
18. Fuger, "Cushing's Battery at Gettysburg," 407.
19. Address by Smith, 136th New York, read May 3, 1894, in Bandy and Freeland (eds.), *Gettysburg Papers*, 1:345.
20. Campbell, "Baptism of Fire," 59n52.
21. Elmore, "Grand Cannonade," 105n15; Meyer, "Pioneer's Story," in Muffly (ed.), *Story of Our Regiment*, 467.
22. Address by Smith, in Bandy and Freeland (eds.), *Gettysburg Papers*, 1:345.
23. Address by Smith, in Bandy and Freeland (eds.), *Gettysburg Papers*, 1:345–46.
24. Stevens, *Souvenir of Excursion to Battlefields*, 25.
25. Diary of Lieutenant Parsons, printed in Washburn, *Complete Military History and Record of the 108th Regiment N.Y. Vols.*, 49–51; Busey and Martin (eds.), *Regimental Strengths and Losses at Gettysburg*, 244.
26. On relative infantry and artillery casualties, Glatthaar, *Soldiering in the Army of Northern Virginia*, 54. On artillery casualties specifically, E. P. Alexander stated that his command of twenty-six guns sustained losses of 147 men and 116 horses; four-fifths of the

human casualties were caused by artillery. Letter, E. P. Alexander, "Causes of Lee's Defeat at Gettysburg," 106; see also Griffith, *Battle Tactics*, 174.

27. Stiles, *Four Years Under Marse Robert*, 217–18.

28. The Vermonter was an anonymous man of the 13th Vermont, whose letter was printed in the *National Tribune*, August 30, 1894, in Sauers (ed.), *Fighting Them Over*, 435; Nelson, *Battles of Chancellorsville and Gettysburg*, 163–64; for the sergeant, see Meinhard, "First Minnesota at Gettysburg," 85. During the artillery fighting on July 2 when Early's guns opened up on Cemetery Hill, Captain William Seymour wrote that "ever and anon an ammunition chest would explode, sending a bright column of smoke far up towards the heavens." See Jones (ed.), *Civil War Memoirs of William J. Seymour*, 74.

29. Letter, July 4, 1863, printed in Benedict, *Army Life in Virginia*, 176.

30. Lecture by James Stewart, "Battery B, Fourth U.S. Artillery at Gettysburg," read April 5, 1893, in Bandy and Freeland (eds.), *Gettysburg Papers*, 1:375.

31. Benedict, *Vermont at Gettysburg*, 10.

32. Nevins (ed.), *Diary of Battle*, 242–43.

33. Elmore, "Grand Cannonade," 102.

34. J. Bigelow, "Account of the Engagement of the 9th Mass. Battery by Capt. Bigelow," no date, printed in Ladd and Ladd (eds.), *Bachelder Papers*, 1:178.

35. Diary entry, April 7, 1862, in Boyd, *Civil War Diary*, 37.

36. Barnes, Otis, and Huntington (eds.), *Medical and Surgical History of the War of the Rebellion*, Part 3, 2:704.

37. On Beary, see Long, "Surgeon's Handiwork," 83–84. On Gage, Dr. Joseph Holt's memoirs, printed in Brown, *University Greys*, 38.

38. Quoted in Hess, *Union Soldier in Battle*, 28–29.

39. Hitchcock, *War from the Inside*, 60.

40. Patriot Daughters of Lancaster, *Hospital Scenes*, 11. On Cushing's battery, see Benedict, *Vermont at Gettysburg*, 15.

41. Stiles, *Four Years Under Marse Robert*, 218.

42. Excerpt from Urban, "Dreaming on the Conestoga," printed in Felton (ed.), "In Their Words," 89–90.

8. Artillery Versus Infantry

1. Campbell, "Baptism of Fire," 59.

2. Letter, J. W. Hand, July 24, 1890, printed in Sauers (ed.), *Fighting Them Over*, 221–22.

3. Campbell, "'Remember Harper's Ferry,'" 104.

4. Nosworthy, "Rifle Musket and Associated Tactics," 35.

5. Crumb (ed.), *Eleventh Corps Artillery at Gettysburg*, 76, 77.

6. Sawyer, *Military History of the 8th Regiment Ohio Vol. Inf'y*, 131.

7. Hartwig, "'I Have Never Been in a Hotter Place,'" 67.

8. Kieffer, *Recollections of a Drummer-Boy*, 112. See Busey and Martin (eds.), *Regimental Strengths and Losses at Gettysburg*, 241.

9. Elmore, "Effects of Artillery Fire on Infantry at Gettysburg," 117.

10. Letter, July 14, 1863, printed in Benedict, *Army Life in Virginia*, 186.

11. Winschel, "Gettysburg Diary of Lieutenant William Peel," 105, quoted in Long, "Confederate Prisoners of Gettysburg," 103.

12. Shultz, "Benner's Hill," 80.

13. On the 55th Ohio, Howard, *Autobiography of Oliver Otis Howard*, 1:436; on the 16th

Georgia, Jorgensen, "Wofford Sweeps the Wheatfield," 37. J. Bigelow reports General Humphries saying that thirty out of thirty-five men in a single company were killed and disabled by a lone shell. Bigelow, *Peach Orchard,* 55.

14. Gottfried, "'Friendly' Fire at Gettysburg," 78–84; Elmore, "Effects of Artillery Fire on Infantry at Gettysburg," 117–22.

15. Letter, Robert Cruikshanks to Mary, July 3, 1863, at "Civil War Letters 1863," available at http://www.salem-ny.com/1863letters.html, accessed September 21, 2011.

16. "'The Iron Brigade' 7th Wisconsin Infantry at Gettysburg, Pa.: report by Lt. Col. John Callis," in Ladd and Ladd (eds.), *Bachelder Papers,* 1:142.

17. "Report of E. Livingston Price, One Hundred and Forty-Fifth New York Infantry," July 23, 1863, *Official Records,* 1st ser., 27, 1:801. The offending officer claimed that Price had been overexcited and that defective shells and improper fuses had been at fault. "Report of Col. Archibald L. MacDougall, One Hundred and Twenty-Third New York Infantry, Commanding First Brigade," July 26, 1863, *Official Records,* 1st ser., 27, 1:784.

18. Letter, Robert Cruikshanks to Mary, July 3, 1863, at "Civil War Letters 1863," available at http://www.salem-ny.com/1863letters.html, accessed September 21, 2011.

19. Talk by Winfield Scott, "Pickett's Charge as Seen From the Front Line," read February 8, 1888, in Bandy and Freeland (eds.), *Gettysburg Papers,* 2:905; Bowen, "From Round Top to Richmond," 2; Wyckoff, "Kershaw's Brigade at Gettysburg," 41.

20. Dougherty, "Wartime Amputations," 756.

21. Barnes, Otis, and Huntington (eds.), *Medical and Surgical History of the War of the Rebellion,* Part 3, 2:707n3.

22. Holstein, *Three Years in the Field Hospitals,* 42.

23. Letter, Hubbard, March 15, 1915, printed in Sauers (ed.), *Fighting Them Over,* 360.

24. Letter, Goldstein, July 19, 1906, printed in Sauers (ed.), *Fighting Them Over,* 412.

25. Address by Bowen, November 11, 1888, in Nicholson (ed.), *Pennsylvania at Gettysburg,* 2:605.

9. Infantry Versus Infantry—The Attack

1. Elmore, "Casualty Analysis of the Gettysburg Battle," 98–99.

2. Martin et al. (eds.), *History of the Fifty-Seventh Regiment,* 88.

3. Diary entry, July 2, 1863, in Jones (ed.), *Civil War Memoirs of Captain William J. Seymour,* 75.

4. Winschel, "Posey's Brigade at Gettysburg," 92. Regarding various reactions, a man of the 14th Connecticut observed his fellows awaiting the Confederate assault on their line: "It was, indeed, an anxious moment. One you can see is looking at the far off home he will never see again. Another is looking at his little ones. . . . Others are communing with Him before whom so many will shortly have to appear." Page, *History of the Fourteenth Regiment,* 152.

5. Campbell, "'Remember Harper's Ferry,'" 1:60.

6. Hess, *Union Soldier in Battle,* 147.

7. Barber, *Army Memoirs,* 52–53.

8. Barrett (ed.), *Yankee Rebel,* 19.

9. Durkin (ed.), *John Dooley, Confederate Soldier,* 99.

10. Small, *Road to Richmond,* 185.

11. Benedict, *Vermont at Gettysburg,* 14. Emphasis added.

12. Sword, "Union Sgt. Isaac W. Barnes," 127.

13. Quoted in Rollins (ed.), *Pickett's Charge*, 131.
14. Glatthaar, *Soldiering in the Army of Northern Virginia*, 174; Fox, *Regimental Losses*, 38; Glatthaar, *General Lee's Army*, 282.
15. Letter, O. Ladley to mother and sisters, July 16, 1863, in Becker and Thomas (eds.), *Hearth and Knapsack*, 147.
16. Marbaker, *History of the Eleventh New Jersey Volunteers*, 98–99, 104.
17. Quoted in Davis, "Music and Gallantry in Combat During the American Civil War," 149.
18. Cheek and Pointon, *History of the Sauk County Riflemen*, 39.
19. Morgan, *Personal Reminiscences of the War of 1861–1865*, 70.
20. Parker, *Henry Wilson's Regiment*, 334. The phrase "womanlike scream" was used by Daniel Chisholm, 116th Pennsylvania, at a later date: See his diary entry of August 25, 1864, in Menke and Shimrak (eds.), *Civil War Notebook of Daniel Chisholm*, 35.
21. Toombs, *New Jersey Troops in the Gettysburg Campaign*, 223–25; Busey and Martin (eds.), *Regimental Strengths and Losses at Gettysburg*, 247.
22. Storch and Storch, " 'What a Deadly Trap We Were in,' " 20.
23. Bauer (ed.), *Soldiering*, 117; Watkins, *"Co. Aytch,"* 34.
24. Goss, *Recollections of a Private*, 39.
25. Letter, Andrew Humphreys to friend, December 1862, in Humphreys, *Andrew Atkinson Humphreys*, 180.
26. Anon., *Reunions of the Nineteenth Maine Regiment Association*, 13.
27. Watkins, *"Co. Aytch,"* 34.
28. Stanley, *Autobiography*, 189–90.
29. Quoted in Hess, *Union Soldier in Battle*, 92.
30. Benton, *As Seen From the Ranks*, 47–48.
31. Nevins (ed.), *Diary of Battle*, 56.
32. Diary entry, September 20, 1862, in Grimsley and Miller (eds.), *Union Must Stand*, 60.
33. Meinhard, "First Minnesota at Gettysburg," 82.
34. Stevens, *Reminiscences of the Civil War*, 114.
35. Nosworthy, *Bloody Crucible of Courage*, 63.
36. On double-quick time, see Pula, "26th Wisconsin Volunteer Infantry at Gettysburg," 78. The 1st Minnesota, a first-class veteran unit, advanced at this pace on July 2. See Meinhard, "First Minnesota at Gettysburg," 82.
37. Coxe, "Battle of Gettysburg," 434.
38. Hartwig, " 'I Have Never Been in a Hotter Place,' " 67.
39. Quoted in Coco, "Rawley W. Martin Story," 34.
40. Nosworthy, *Bloody Crucible of Courage*, 138.
41. Benton, *As Seen From the Ranks*, 161.
42. Wing, *Soldier's Story*, 69. In general, see Davis, "Music and Gallantry in Combat During the American Civil War," 141–72.
43. Sword, "Pye's Sword at the Rail Cut," 29–32.
44. Letter, O. Ladley to mother and sisters, July 16, 1863, in Becker and Thomas (eds.), *Hearth and Knapsack*, 147.
45. "Report of Lieut. Col. P. A. Work, First Texas Infantry," July 9, 1863, *Official Records*, 1st ser., 27, 2:410.
46. See O'Brien, " 'Hold Them with the Bayonet,' " 74; on Davis, see Winschel, "Heavy Was Their Loss," 5–10.
47. Byrne and Weaver (eds.), *Haskell of Gettysburg*, 162.
48. Paper by R. Dawes, "With the Sixth Wisconsin at Gettysburg," (1890), in Bandy and Freeland (eds.), *Gettysburg Papers*, 1:219.

49. Address by J. V. Pierce, 147th New York, July 1, 1888, in New York Monuments Commission, *Final Report on the Battlefield of Gettysburg,* 3:992.

10. Infantry Versus Infantry—The Defense

1. O'Brien, " 'Perfect Roar of Musketry,' " 90.
2. Nosworthy, *Bloody Crucible of Courage,* 256.
3. Letter, J. L. Brady to J. B. Bachelder, May 24, 1886, in Ladd and Ladd (eds.), *Bachelder Papers,* 3:1398.
4. Letter, David Shields to J. B. Bachelder, August 27, 1884, in Ladd and Ladd (eds.), *Bachelder Papers,* 2:1068. To the suggestion that the rear rank loaded and passed up rifles to the front rank, Shields retorted that "it sounds very militia like to me."
5. Bowen, "Diary of Captain George D. Bowen," 133.
6. Adkin, *Gettysburg Companion,* 109.
7. Lader, "Personal Journey of Pvt. David Ballinger," 94; Toombs, *New Jersey Troops in the Gettysburg Campaign,* 290; Carter, *Four Brothers in Blue,* 308. See also Bowen, "From Round Top to Richmond," 3.
8. Address by W. Scott, 126th New York, "Pickett's Charge as Seen From the Front Line," read February 8, 1888, in Bandy and Freeland (eds.), *Gettysburg Papers,* 2:906–7.
9. Letter, E. Southard, August 19, 1897, printed in Sauers (ed.), *Fighting Them Over,* 231.
10. Jackson (ed.), *Colonel's Diary,* 71.
11. Olney, "Battle of Shiloh," 577–89, on 583.
12. Lader, "Personal Journey of Pvt. David Ballinger," 91.
13. Hill, *Our Boys,* 306.
14. Diary entry, August 25, 1864, in Menke and Shimrak (eds.), *Civil War Notebook of Daniel Chisholm,* 36.
15. Saxton, *Regiment Remembered,* 82.
16. Vautier, *History of the 88th Pennsylvania Volunteers,* 106–7.
17. Stevens, *Souvenir of Excursion to Battlefields,* 29.
18. Anon., *Reunions of the Nineteenth Maine Regiment Association,* 11.
19. Anon., "How They Fire in Battle," 279.
20. Stillwell, *Story of a Common Soldier,* 44.
21. Gibbon, *Artillerist's Manual,* 356; Nosworthy, *Bloody Crucible of Courage,* 306, 432.
22. Hess finds two minutes, but Adkin suggests every thirty seconds. I've averaged it out for illustrative purposes. Hess, *Rifle Musket in Civil War Combat,* 100–4; Adkin, *Gettysburg Companion,* 97.
23. Hess, *Rifle Musket in Civil War Combat,* 100–4.
24. Warren, *Declaration of Independence and War History,* 30.
25. Weygant, *History of the One Hundred and Twenty-Fourth Regiment,* 179–80.
26. On the accuracy at Bunker Hill, see Rose, "Marksmanship in 1775," 44–47, 70.
27. See Rose, *American Rifle,* 190–91. On wartime training, or the lack of it, Bilby, *Small Arms at Gettysburg,* 76–80.
28. Marvin, *Fifth Regiment Connecticut Volunteers,* 16.
29. Stillwell, *Story of a Common Soldier,* 55–56.
30. Carter, *Four Brothers in Blue,* 309; Joseph Cogswell noticed the same thing. Cogswell, "The Battle of Gettysburg," in *The 'Dutchess County Regiment' in the Civil War,* ed. S. G. Cook and C. E. Benton, 32.
31. Neese, *Three Years in the Confederate Horse Artillery,* 35–36.
32. Quoted in Nosworthy, *Roll Call to Destiny,* 83.

33. Sergeant Silas Adams, cited in Smith, *History of the Nineteenth Regiment*, 71.
34. Preston, *History of the Tenth Regiment of Cavalry, New York State Volunteers*, 112.
35. Memoir by George Grant, read May 10, 1898, in Bandy and Freeland (eds.), *Gettysburg Papers*, 1:261.
36. Byrne and Weaver (eds.), *Haskell of Gettysburg*, 159.
37. On shins, see letter, W. S. Rosecrans to General McNeil, September 27, 1864, *Official Records*, 1st ser., 41, 3:412; on knees, see Orders of Major General T. C. Hindman, Trans-Mississippi Army; December 4, 1862, 1st ser., 22, 1:83. Report of Lieut. Col. Walton Dwight, September 12, 1863, in *Official Records*, 1st ser., 27, 1:342.
38. Excerpt from Urban, "Dreaming on the Conestoga," printed in Felton (ed.), "In Their Words," 95.
39. Vautier, *History of the 88th Pennsylvania Volunteers*, 106; see also the recollections of Lieutenant Colonel A. J. Sellers (90th Pennsylvania), in Nicholson (ed.), *Pennsylvania at Gettysburg*, 1:484.
40. Diary entry, July 2, 1863, in Runge (ed.), *Four Years in the Confederate Artillery*, 50.
41. Diary entry, June 28, 1862, in Barrett (ed.), *Yankee Rebel*, 32.
42. Bowen, "From Round Top to Richmond," 3.
43. Stanley, *Autobiography*, 190; letter, C. L. Harris to father, July 4, 1863, in Washburn, *Complete Military History and Record of the 108th Regiment N.Y. Vols.*, 52.
44. Nosworthy, *Bloody Crucible of Courage*, 230; Blackford, *War Years with Jeb Stuart*, 123–24.
45. Judson, *History of the Eighty-Third Regiment Pennsylvania Volunteers*, 67, 69–70.
46. For an outline, Adkin, *Gettysburg Companion*, 108.
47. O'Brien, "'Perfect Roar of Musketry,'" 90.
48. Hardee, *Rifle and Light Infantry Tactics*, 58; Bowen, "Diary of Captain George D. Bowen," 133.
49. Quoted in Hess, *Union Soldier in Battle*, 112.
50. Dodge, "Left Wounded," 321.
51. Ward, *History of the Second Pennsylvania Veteran Heavy Artillery*, 66; Meyer, "Private's Story and Story of Company A," in Muffly (ed.), *Story of Our Regiment*, 537.

11. The Attack Continues

1. See Appendix, in Lader, "7th New Jersey in the Gettysburg Campaign," 65–67. In Union regiments the designated company was usually Company K, and a breakdown of the 7th New Jersey's numbers finds that whereas the average number of casualties per company (excluding killed) was about ten, Company K suffered seventeen.
2. Winschel, "Heavy Was Their Loss," 11, 170; Winschel, "Colors Are Shrouded in Mystery," 79–80.
3. Underwood, *History of the Twenty-Sixth Regiment of the North Carolina Troops*, 50–52, 72; Hadden, "Deadly Embrace," 20, 27–33. On casualties, see Smith, Jr., *For the Good of the Old North State*, 4.
4. Letter, P. Welsh to M. Welsh, March 31, 1863, in Kohl and Richard (eds.), *Irish Green and Union Blue*, 81.
5. Dreese, "Ordeal in the Lutheran Theological Seminary," 104.
6. Letter, P. Welsh to M. Welsh, March 31, 1863, in Kohl and Richard (eds.), *Irish Green and Union Blue*, 82, 156–57.
7. Underwood, *History of the Twenty-Sixth Regiment of the North Carolina Troops*, 99.
8. Keller, "Pennsylvania's German-Americans," in *Damn Dutch*, ed. D. L. Valuska and C. B. Keller, 138.

9. Evans, "Cries of the Wounded Were Piercing and Horrible," 35.
10. Quoted in Hess, *Union Soldier in Battle,* 28.
11. Dunkelman, "Additional Notes on the 154th New York at Gettysburg," 74.
12. Jorgensen, "John Haley's Personal Recollection of the Battle of the Wheatfield," 75.
13. This section is based on accounts by Lee, "Reminiscences of the Gettysburg Battle," 54–60, on 56; Isham, "Story of a Gunshot Wound," in Chamberlin, *Sketches of War History, 1861–1865,* 4:430; Farlow and Barry (eds.), "Vincent B. Osborne's Civil War Experiences," 108–33, on 120; (Douglas) Letter, August 5, 1863, in Long, "Confederate Prisoners of Gettysburg," 98; Ward, "Incidents and Personal Experiences on the Battlefield at Gettysburg," 345–49, on 347.
14. Hill, *Our Boys,* 306.
15. Wing, *Soldier's Story,* 69.
16. Carter, *Four Brothers in Blue,* 234.
17. Anon. (ed.), *Biographical and Historical Memoirs,* 337–38.

12. The Critical Moment

1. Scribner, *How Soldiers Were Made,* 273–74.
2. Benton, *As Seen From the Ranks,* 35.
3. Lecture by Dawes, "With the Sixth Wisconsin at Gettysburg," in Bandy and Freeland (eds.), *Gettysburg Papers,* 1:219.
4. Bierce, "Crime at Pickett's Mill," in *Devil's Dictionary,* 690–91.
5. Scribner, *How Soldiers Were Made,* 259.
6. Benson (ed.), *Berry Benson's Civil War Book,* 22.
7. Meinhard, "First Minnesota at Gettysburg," 80–81.
8. Dunkelman and Winey, "Hardtack Regiment in the Brickyard Fight," 22.
9. Galwey, *Valiant Hours,* 118.
10. Diary entry, in Tomasak (ed.), *One Hundred Forty-Third Pennsylvania Volunteer Regiment,* 64–65.
11. Bowen, "Diary of Captain George D. Bowen," 129.
12. Quoted in Hartwig, "11th Army Corps," 33–49.
13. Talk by Stewart, "Battery B, Fourth U.S. Artillery at Gettysburg," in *Gettysburg Papers,* ed. Bandy and Freeland, 1:370–71; Tomasak, "143rd Pennsylvania Volunteer Regiment," 53.
14. Address by Pierce, in New York Monuments Commission, *Final Report on the Battlefield of Gettysburg,* 3:992.
15. Letter, April 2, 1891, in Sauers (ed.), *Fighting Them Over,* 282.
16. Dunkelman, " 'We Were Compelled to Cut Our Way Through Them,' " 34–56. See also the important analysis of Costa, "Scarring and Mortality Selection Among Civil War POWs." On Confederate prisoners and their fates, see Mulligan, "Death of a Secessionist Regiment," 94–110.

13. Holding the Line

1. Benton, *As Seen From the Ranks,* 35. So green had been the regiment that when the first shell screeched over their heads, recalled Thomas Vassar, it provoked "an exhibition of fluttering coat-tails" as scared men sprinted in all directions. T. Vassar, "Reminiscences," in Cook and Benton (eds.), *'Dutchess County Regiment' in the Civil War,* 190.
2. Quoted in Dreese, "151st Pennsylvania Volunteers at Gettysburg," 60.

3. Tompkins and Tompkins, *Company K,* 20.
4. Nosworthy, *Bloody Crucible of Courage,* 436; Gibbon, *Artillerist's Manual,* 359.
5. Fuger, "Cushing's Battery at Gettysburg," 408; Cooksey, "Union Artillery at Gettysburg on July 3," 101.
6. Address by John Bigelow, printed in Baker, *History of the Ninth Mass. Battery,* 214–15.
7. Bigelow, "Account of the Engagement," in Ladd and Ladd (eds.), *Bachelder Papers,* 1:177: "Usually in an engagement a few rounds of canister will repel a charge."
8. Wyckoff, "Kershaw's Brigade at Gettysburg," 42; Coxe, "Battle of Gettysburg," 434.
9. Quoted in Campbell, "Voices of Gettysburg," 19.
10. Miller, "Perrin's Brigade on July 1, 1863," 27.
11. Carter, *Four Brothers in Blue,* 325.
12. Davis, "Death and Burials of General Richard Brooke Garnett," 112–13.
13. Coxe, "Battle of Gettysburg," 434.

14. At Close Quarters

1. Marbaker, *History of the Eleventh New Jersey Volunteers,* 175; see also Dodge, "Left Wounded," 321.
2. Laidley, "Breech-Loading Musket," 67. The official tally is "Report by Lieut. John R. Edie, Acting Chief Ordnance Officer, Army of the Potomac," no date, in *Official Records,* 1st ser., 27, 1:225–26, which differs in minor respects. The total number is close enough to make no difference. The number of guns left behind has been remarked upon several times, generally owing to the misapprehension that the high proportion of overloaded pieces proves that soldiers were reluctant to fire their weapons at the enemy. This is an argument evidently based on S. L. A. Marshall's influential—if now discredited—contention in his *Men Against Fire: The Problem of Battle Command,* that not more than 15 percent of American combat soldiers fired their weapons in World War II. On Marshall's controversial assertion, see Rose, *American Rifle,* 339–41; on replacement arms, see Haines, *History of the Fifteenth Regiment New Jersey Volunteers,* 94.
3. Hohenlohe-Ingelflingen, *Letters on Infantry,* 34.
4. Simon Hubler account, "Just the Plain, Unvarnished Story," 4.
5. Stillwell, *Story of a Common Soldier,* 252.
6. Meinhard, "First Minnesota at Gettysburg," 82, 84.
7. Polley, *Hood's Texas Brigade,* 169.
8. Watkins, *"Co. Aytch,"* 34.
9. Meinhard, "First Minnesota at Gettysburg," 87.
10. Smith, *History of the Nineteenth Regiment,* 82.
11. "Address of Col. Edward Hill," in Trowbridge and Farnsworth (eds.), *Michigan at Gettysburg,* 108–9.
12. Coffman, "Vital Unit," 44.
13. Fuger, "Cushing's Battery at Gettysburg," 409.
14. Address by W. O. Beauchamp, 1st New York Light Artillery, July 3, 1888, in New York Monuments Commission, *Final Report on the Battlefield of Gettysburg,* 3:1184.
15. Baker, *History of the Ninth Mass. Battery,* 81.
16. Smith, *Famous Battery and Its Campaigns,* 104.
17. Nosworthy, *Bloody Crucible of Courage,* 446–47.
18. Winschel, "Heavy Was Their Loss," 11.
19. Campbell, "Baptism of Fire," 74.

20. Gilmor, *Four Years in the Saddle,* 99. One wonders whence this tradition derived. Possibly, it could be Irish in origin. The Louisiana Brigade was heavily Irish, and a year earlier Richard Taylor had seen the same brigade's Irishmen going "mad with cheering," among them a "huge fellow, with one eye closed and half his whiskers burned by powder" who was "riding cock-horse on a gun" at Port Republic. Taylor, *Destruction and Reconstruction,* 93.

15. Surrender

1. Dawes, *Service with the Sixth Wisconsin Volunteers,* 168–69.
2. Campbell, " 'Remember Harper's Ferry,' " 2:106.
3. Letter, December 10, 1909, printed in Sauers (ed.), *Fighting Them Over,* 414.
4. Excerpt from Urban, "Dreaming on the Conestoga," printed in Felton (ed.), "In Their Words," 101.
5. Dougherty, " 'We Have Come to Stay!,' " 53.
6. Small, *Road to Richmond,* 68.
7. Pula (ed.), *Memoirs of Wladimir Krzyżanowski,* 49.
8. Diary entry, June 28, 1862, in Barrett (ed.), *Yankee Rebel,* 34.
9. Redwood, "Confederate in the Field," in *Photographic History of the Civil War,* 8:174; Anon., "Fighting," 339.
10. Byrne and Weaver (eds.), *Haskell of Gettysburg,* 189.

16. The Return to Normal

1. Quoted in Hess, *Union Soldier in Battle,* 1.
2. Talk by Dawes, "With the Sixth Wisconsin at Gettysburg," in Bandy and Freeland (eds.), *Gettysburg Papers,* 1:234.
3. Alexander (ed. G. W. Gallagher), *Fighting for the Confederacy,* 208.
4. Oration by C. D. MacDougall, 111th New York, in New York Monuments Commission, *Final Report on the Battlefield of Gettysburg,* 2:800–1.
5. Eby (ed.), *Virginia Yankee in the Civil War,* 113.
6. Excerpt from Urban, "Dreaming on the Conestoga," in Felton (ed.), "In Their Words," 89.
7. Anonymous Union soldier at Shiloh, quoted in Moore (ed.), *Civil War in Song and Story, 1860–1865,* 64–65.
8. Quoted in Campbell, "Voices of Gettysburg," 16.
9. Lader, "Personal Journey of Pvt. David Ballinger," 88–89.
10. Diary entry, April 8, 1862, in Boyd, *Civil War Diary,* 42.

17. Sights, Sounds, Smells

1. Carter, *Four Brothers in Blue,* 324.
2. Patriot Daughters of Lancaster, *Hospital Scenes,* 11.
3. In the Army of Northern Virginia, one in eight men was killed in action during the war; about the same died of disease. Adding in other causes of noncombat fatalities (e.g., executions, accidents), brings the total to one in four dying while in military service. Another 25 percent were wounded at least once. By adding together the figures of killed, wounded, captured, died of disease, and discharged for disability, three out of every four soldiers who served under Lee became victims. Glatthaar, *Soldiering in the Army of Northern Virginia,* 16–17. A typical unit that fought at Gettysburg, Company

E of the 20th North Carolina, began its war on April 16, 1861, with 107 men. Over the next four years, twenty-six of these would be killed or mortally wounded in battle and fourteen would die of disease, leaving sixty-seven living at war's end. Of the survivors, fifteen were permanently disabled with wounds and sixteen had been wounded but recovered fully, so leaving thirty-six unharmed (or one-third of the original recruits). Nineteen of these, however, had never been in combat as they were detailed for other duties, so really only seventeen (16 percent) emerged from the war unscathed.

4. Adkin, *Gettysburg Companion*, 508.
5. Cited in Lash, " 'Pathetic Story,' " 77.
6. Campbell, "Voices of Gettysburg," 16.
7. Busey and Martin (eds.), *Regimental Strengths and Losses at Gettysburg*, 242 (chart 6.1, "Union Regimental Losses").
8. Busey and Martin (eds.), *Regimental Strengths and Losses at Gettysburg*, 262–63 (chart 6.2, "Union Regiments with Losses Greater Than Fifty Percent"), 298 (chart 7.2, "Confederate Regiments with Losses Greater Than Fifty Percent"), 230 (chart 5.1, "Average Regimental Engaged Strengths").
9. Carter, *Four Brothers in Blue*, 325.
10. Quoted in Coco, *Strange and Blighted Land*, 56.
11. Bucklin, *In Hospital and Camp*, 188.
12. Quoted in Hess, *Union Soldier in Battle*, 38.
13. Stiles, *Four Years Under Marse Robert*, 220.
14. Diary entry, July 2, 1863, in Runge (ed.), *Four Years in the Confederate Artillery*, 50–51.
15. Quoted in Pfanz, *Gettysburg*, 369.
16. Quoted in Hess, *Union Soldier in Battle*, 22.
17. Hess, *Union Soldier in Battle*, 22.
18. Survivors' Association, *History of the 118th Pennsylvania Volunteers*, 249.
19. Musgrove, *Autobiography*, 94, 92. According to John Wert, "swine were found revelling in the remains [of a corpse] in a manner horrible to contemplate." See Wert, *Complete Hand-Book*, 163.
20. Craft, *History of the Hundred Forty-First Regiment*, 128.
21. Anon., "Scenes and Incidents at Gettysburg," 39.
22. Meyer, "Pioneer's Story," in Muffly (ed.), *Story of Our Regiment*, 465; see also Marbaker, *History of the Eleventh New Jersey Volunteers*, 109.
23. Letter, July 14, 1863, printed in Benedict, *Army Life in Virginia*, 190.
24. Brown, *Twenty-Seventh Indiana Volunteer Infantry*, 394.
25. Stiles, *Four Years Under Marse Robert*, 220.
26. Haines, *History of the Fifteenth Regiment New Jersey Volunteers*, 96.
27. Campbell, "Aftermath and Recovery of Gettysburg," 110.
28. Stevens, *Three Years in the Sixth Corps*, 254.
29. Coco, *Strange and Blighted Land*, 51.
30. Meyer, "Pioneer's Story," in Muffly (ed.), *Story of Our Regiment*, 466.
31. Stiles, *Four Years Under Marse Robert*, 220.

18. The Dead

1. Musto, "Treatment of the Wounded at Gettysburg," 123.
2. Letter, A. M. Eby to J. B. Bachelder, October 20, 1885, in Ladd and Ladd (eds.), *Bachelder Papers*, 2:1131. This story is reproduced with a few contrasting details in J. A. Moore's address, in Nicholson (ed.), *Pennsylvania at Gettysburg*, 2:706. According to

Moore (707), the soldier had only been shot in the leg, "by no means fatally," possibly making the reason for his suicide a fear of being captured, but Eby was adamant that his abdominal injury "would beyond doubt have proved mortal."

3. Fulks, "Another Irony of Gettysburg," 62.
4. Bowen, "Diary of Captain George D. Bowen," 135–36.
5. Meyer, "Pioneer's Story," in Muffly (ed.), *Story of Our Regiment,* 465.
6. Letter, July 14, 1863, in Benedict, *Army Life in Virginia,* 190.
7. Wadding, "Story of Company I," in Muffly (ed.), *Story of Our Regiment,* 780.
8. Quoted in Coco, *Strange and Blighted Land,* 50.
9. Elmore, "Less Than Brave," 127.
10. Letter, O. C. Brown to A. Dunham, July 6, 1863, printed in Nash, *History of the Forty-Fourth New York Regiment Volunteer Infantry,* 295; Hutchinson, "Bringing Home a Fallen Son," 68.
11. "Report of Lt. Col. Charles H. Morgan," in Ladd and Ladd (eds.), *Bachelder Papers,* 3:1367.
12. Coco, *Strange and Blighted Land,* 76, and his *On the Bloodstained Field,* 41; Lamb, *History of the United States Army Medical Museum,* 19, 146.
13. Conklin, "Long March to Stevens Run," 54–55.
14. On identification and tags, see Gross, "Grave Situation," 119–23; Stahl, "Pvt. George Matthews," 98–99; Stahl, "Pvt. John Wright," 56–58. In 1906 the War Department approved General Order Number 204 authorizing the universal issuing of dog tags.
15. Byrne and Weaver (eds.), *Haskell of Gettysburg,* 195.
16. Letter, W. Hays to S. Williams, July 17, 1863, in *Official Records,* 1st ser., 27, 1:378, remarking that "one female (private) in rebel uniform" was buried. There was at least one woman captured at Gettysburg. The hospitalized Thomas Read of 5th Michigan excitedly notified his parents that "i must tel you we have got a female secesh here, she was wounded at gettiburg but our doctors soon found her out. i have not seen her but the[y] say she is very good looking. the poor girl [h]as lost a leg; it is a great pity she did not stay at home with her mother." Quoted in Coco, *Strange and Blighted Land,* 152. These enigmatic women may have sneaked into the army to accompany their husbands or fiancés. At Chickamauga, a captured Northern female was purportedly sent back to her lines under a flag of truce and "a message to the effect that, 'As the Confederates do not use women in war, this woman, wounded in battle, is returned to you.'" The original source for this anecdote appears to be Young, *Women and the Crisis,* 97. It has been widely quoted, but generally without the important qualifier "to the effect."
17. Carter, *Four Brothers in Blue,* 325.
18. Jordan, Jr., "Gettysburg and the Seventeenth Maine," 52.
19. Quoted in Johnson, *Battleground Adventures,* 174–75.
20. Parker, *Henry Wilson's Regiment,* 345.
21. Diary entry, April 8, 1862, printed in Boyd, *Civil War Diary,* 41.
22. Bowen, "Diary of Captain George D. Bowen," 135.
23. Foster, "Four Days at Gettysburg," 382. On rotting, see McLean, "Days of Terror in 1863," 2.
24. Adkin, *Gettysburg Companion,* 186.

19. The Wounded

1. Keen, "Military Surgery in 1861 and in 1918," printed in *Rehabilitation of the Wounded,* 11–22 (on 14).

2. Coco, *Strange and Blighted Land,* 154–55.
3. At the end of 1861 the Sanitary Commission had surveyed the medical personnel of 200 regiments and concluded that 2 percent were incompetent and another 13 percent were of doubtful competence. Nevertheless, two-thirds were performing their duties "with creditable energy and earnestness," and the number would rise over the course of the war. Hall, "Lessons of the War Between the States," 412. On Bailey, see Miller, "Perrin's Brigade on July 1, 1863," 31.
4. Letters, July 6, 9, and 10, 1863, in Garrison, *John Shaw Billings,* 64–66.
5. Hall, "Lessons of the War Between the States," 419.
6. "Report of Surg. Jonathan Letterman, U.S. Army, Medical Director, Army of the Potomac," October 3, 1863, in *Official Records,* 1st ser., 27, 1:196.
7. Fuller, *Personal Recollections,* 102.
8. Letter, July 24, 1890, in Sauers (ed.), *Fighting Them Over,* 221.
9. Barziza, *Adventures of a Prisoner of War,* 54.
10. Davis, *Escape of a Confederate Officer From Prison,* 5–6.
11. Peltz, "Two Brass Buttons," 1.
12. See Holt's memoir, in Brown, *University Greys,* 39.
13. Quoted in Adkin, *Gettysburg Companion,* 233.
14. Benton, *As Seen From the Ranks,* 31.
15. Vautier, *History of the 88th Pennsylvania Volunteers,* 109.
16. Campbell, "Aftermath and Recovery of Gettysburg," 114.
17. Durkin (ed.), *John Dooley, Confederate Soldier,* 111, 114.
18. Weygant, *History of the One Hundred and Twenty-Fourth Regiment,* 183.
19. Buehler, *Recollections of the Rebel Invasion,* 26.
20. Barziza, *Adventures of a Prisoner of War,* 54.
21. Muffly, "Adjutant's Story," in Muffly (ed.), *Story of Our Regiment,* 245.
22. Martz, "It Was Not a Happy Time," 121.
23. Dougherty, "Wartime Amputations," 755–63; Diffenbaugh, "Military Surgery in the Civil War," 492; Manring et al., "Treatment of War Wounds," 2177.
24. E. Foner, *Reconstruction,* 125; A. J. Bollet, "Amputations in the Civil War," in *Years of Change and Suffering,* ed. J. M. Schmidt and G. R. Hasegawa, 57–67.
25. Albin, "Use of Anesthetics During the Civil War," 99–100, 106; Connor, "Chloroform and the Civil War."
26. Quoted in Coco, *On the Bloodstained Field,* 7.
27. On deaths, see Albin, "Use of Anesthetics During the Civil War, 1861–1865," 111.
28. Stevens, *Berdan's United States Sharpshooter,* 521–23.
29. Chisolm, *Manual of Military Surgery for the Use of Surgeons in the Confederate Army,* 380–81.
30. Daniel, *Recollections of a Rebel Surgeon,* 205.
31. Fuller, *Personal Recollections,* 101–2.
32. Dunkelman and Winey, "The Hardtack Regiment in the Brickyard Fight," 27–28.
33. Casey (ed.), "Ordeal of Adoniram Judson Warner," 234.
34. Spisak, "62nd Pennsylvania Volunteer Infantry," 92.
35. Barnes, Otis, and Huntington (eds.), *Medical and Surgical History of the War of the Rebellion,* Part 3, 2:707–8.
36. Quinones, "Drug Abuse During the Civil War," 1007–20.
37. For a cautious explanation, see Hyman, Wignall, and Roswell, "War Syndromes and Their Evaluation," 398–99.
38. Quoted in Campbell, "Voices of Gettysburg," 16.

39. A selection is reproduced at http://home.comcast.net/~9thmassbattery/AHesse.html. Accessed September 21, 2014.
40. These letters are quoted in Campbell, "Voices of Gettysburg," 19.
41. Quoted in Dougherty, "History of the McPherson Farm at Gettysburg," 28. On cowardice, see Gordon, " 'I Never Was a Coward.' "
42. Lader, "7th New Jersey in the Gettysburg Campaign," 65.
43. Quoted in Hess, *Pickett's Charge*, 338.
44. On Thompson's career, see his obituary in the *Orange County Times-Press*, December 3, 1918, p. 6; and entry for "Thirty-Second Colored Troops Regiment," in *History of Pennsylvania Volunteers, 1861–5*, ed. S. P. Bates, 5:1047–48.
45. Letter, November 20, 1862, in Scott (ed.), *Fallen Leaves*, 143.
46. The officer in question was Oliver Wendell Holmes. See "The Soldier's Faith," May 30, 1895, in Holmes (ed.), *Speeches by Oliver Wendell Holmes*, 65.
47. Bruce, *Twentieth Regiment of Massachusetts Volunteer Infantry*, 177–79.
48. Dean, Jr., " 'We Will All Be Lost and Destroyed,' " 150–51.
49. Pizarro, Silver, and Prause, "Physical and Mental Health Costs,". 193–200. See also J. Andersen, " 'Haunted Minds': The Impact of Combat Exposure on the Mental and Physical Health of Civil War Veterans," in *Years of Change and Suffering*, ed. Schmidt and Hasegawa, 143–58.

IWO JIMA

1. Introduction

1. Clifford, *Progress and Purpose*, 22; Moy, *War Machines*, 126–28; Isely and Crowl, *U.S. Marines and Amphibious War*, 34; Gordon, "Thomas Holcomb," in Millett and Shulimson (eds.), *Commandants of the Marine Corps*, 255.
2. See, for instance, Burrell, "Breaking the Cycle of Iwo Jima Mythology," 1143–86.

3. The Strategy

1. On the long evolution of this strategy, see Cosmas and Shulimson, "Culebra Maneuver," 121–32; Shulimson and Cosmas, "Teddy Roosevelt and the Corps' Sea-Going Mission," in *Crucibles*, ed. R. S. Burrell, 97–107; Turk, "United States Navy and the 'Taking' of Panama, 1901–03," 92–96; Grenville and Young, *Politics, Strategy, and American Diplomacy*, 305–7; and Herwig and Trask, "Naval Operations Plans Between Germany and the U.S.A., 1898–1913," 56–58; Lorelli, *To Foreign Shores*, 10; Ellis, "Advanced Base Operations in Micronesia," esp. 1, 5, 15–16, 18–23; Ballendorf and Bartlett, *Pete Ellis*; J. J. Reber, "Pete Ellis: Amphibious Warfare Prophet," in *Crucibles*, ed. R. S. Burrell, 175–89. For a comparative view, A. R. Millett, "Assault From the Sea: The Development of Amphibious Warfare Between the Wars: The American, British, and Japanese Experiences," in *Military Innovation in the Interwar Period*, ed. W. Murray and Millett, 72. An excellent survey is Smith, *Development of Amphibious Tactics in the U.S. Navy*, 19.

5. The Landing

1. Recollections of Sgt. Frank Juszli, in Kessler and Bart (eds.), *Never in Doubt*, 121.
2. Recollections of Pfc. Fred Schribert, in Kessler and Bart (eds.), *Never in Doubt*, 40.
3. Averill, *Mustang*, 121.
4. Cockrel, "How It Was on Iwo," in O'Sheel and Cook (eds.), *Semper Fidelis*, 100.
5. Dyer, *Amphibians Came to Conquer*, 2:1005.
6. Carter, *Beans, Bullets, and Black Oil*, 289, 291. On cigarette supplies, see "Death Valley, Iwo Jima, February 25, 1945: Pfc. Jay Rebstock, USMC (E Co., 2nd Bn., 27th Marines)," in Drez (ed.), *Twenty-Five Yards of War*, 228.
7. McMillan, *Old Breed*, 342–43.
8. On Japanese supplies and expectations, see Eldridge and Tatum (eds.), *Fighting Spirit*, 88.
9. Alexander, *Storm Landings*, 146.
10. Matthews, *Assault*, 25–26; Levin, *From the Battlefield*, 64.
11. Yaffe, *Fragments of War*, 82, 83.
12. Josephy, *Long and the Short and the Tall*, 160.
13. Quoted in Haynes and Warren, *Lions of Iwo Jima*, 64.
14. Matthews, *Assault*, 26–27.
15. Price and Knecht, "Peleliu 1944," 21.
16. Recollections of Miller, in McLaughlin and Miller, *From the Volcano to the Gorge*, 274–75.
17. Vedder, *Surgeon on Iwo*, 23.
18. Richard Newcomb, "Invasion," in Smith (ed.), *United States Marine Corps in World War II*, 717; Stone, *Marine Remembers Iwo Jima*, 22; Vedder, *Surgeon on Iwo*, 28. Equipped with a fifty-pound bag filled with medical instruments and supplies, Vedder had to drag it up a 70-degree embankment twelve feet high by attaching a rope, climbing to the top, and then pulling the bag after him while under fire.
19. Interview, Rebstock, in Drez (ed.), *Twenty-Five Yards of War*, 230.
20. Averill, *Mustang*, 123.
21. Interview, Rebstock, in Drez (ed.), *Twenty-Five Yards of War*, 234.
22. Matthews, *Assault*, 20.
23. Wheeler, "'Those Sons-of-Bitches Killed My Buddy!,'" in Smith (ed.), *United States Marine Corps in World War II*, 755.
24. McLaughlin and Miller, *From the Volcano to the Gorge*, 100–2, 183.
25. McLaughlin, in McLaughlin and Miller, *From the Volcano to the Gorge*, 119.
26. McLaughlin, in McLaughlin and Miller, *From the Volcano to the Gorge*, 165.
27. On the development and employment of LVTs, see Roan, "Roebling's Amphibian"; Bailey, *Alligators, Buffaloes, and Bushmasters*, 34–41; Hough, Ludwig, and Shaw, *Pearl Harbor to Guadalcanal*, 1:32–33; Anon., "Roebling's 'Alligator' for Florida Rescues."
28. Wheeler, *Iwo*, 73; interview, Rebstock, in Drez (ed.), *Twenty-Five Yards of War*, 231.
29. Matthews, *Assault*, 29.
30. On the LCVP, Heitmann, "Man Who Won the War," 35–50; Mountcastle, "From Bayou to Beachhead," 20–29.
31. Interview, Williams, in Smith (ed.), *Iwo Jima*, 65.
32. Vedder, *Surgeon on Iwo*, 7.
33. Weaver, "D Day," in O'Sheel and Cook (eds.), *Semper Fidelis*, 106.
34. Kuzuhara, "Operations on Iwo Jima," 35.
35. Interview, Hathaway, in Smith (ed.), *Iwo Jima*, 35.
36. Marquand, "Iwo Jima Before H-hour," 495.

37. Weller, "Development of Naval Gunfire Support in World War Two," in *Assault From the Sea*, ed. M. L. Bartlett, 279–81; Haynes and Warren, *Lions of Iwo Jima*, 65.
38. Sherrod, *On to Westward*, 169.
39. Marquand, "Iwo Jima Before H-hour," 499.
40. Gallant, *Friendly Dead*, 28–30.
41. Rottman and Dennis, *U.S. World War II Amphibious Tactics*, 52.
42. Caruso, *Nightmare on Iwo*, 27–28.
43. Toyn, *Quiet Hero*, 79.
44. Levin, *From the Battlefield*, 64–67.
45. Thurman, *We Were in the First Waves*, loc. 254.
46. Interview, D'Amico, in Kessler and Bart (eds.), *Never in Doubt*, 187.
47. Lofgren (ed.), "Diary of First Lieutenant Sugihara Kinryu," 124.
48. Wheeler, *Iwo*, 40.
49. Josephy, *Long and the Short and the Tall*, 156–57.
50. Levin, *From the Battlefield*, 64–67.
51. Quoted in Huie, *From Omaha to Okinawa*, 46.

6. The Beach

1. Averill, *Mustang*, 123–24.
2. Quoted in O'Donnell, *Into the Rising Sun*, 228.
3. McConnell, "How One Squad Fared."
4. Gallant, *Friendly Dead*, 31–33.
5. Levin, *From the Battlefield*, 66–67, 73.
6. Gallant, *Friendly Dead*, 35.
7. Rottman and Dennis, *U.S. World War II Amphibious Tactics*, 53.
8. R. Henri, "Logistics Afloat," in Smith (ed.), *United States Marine Corps in World War II*, 769–71.
9. Matthews, *Assault*, 36.
10. Neiman and Estes, *Tanks on the Beaches*, 121–22.
11. Cockrel, "How It Was on Iwo," in O'Sheel and Cook (eds.), *Semper Fidelis*, 101.
12. Gallant, *Friendly Dead*, 13.
13. Brown, *Battle Wounds of Iwo Jima*, 26; Report by Intelligence Staffs of CINCPAC-CINCPOA, Fleet Marine Force, V Amphibious Corps, 3rd, 4th, and 5th Marine Divisions, *Defense Installations on Iwo Jima*, Bulletin 136–45, June 10, 1945, p. 5.
14. Wheeler, *We Are the Wounded*, 207.
15. Shiveley, *Last Lieutenant*, 49.
16. Sherrod, *On to Westward*, 180.
17. Wheeler, *Iwo*, 196.
18. Shiveley, *Last Lieutenant*, 53.
19. Sherrod, *On to Westward*, 180.
20. Walker and White, *Preparing for the Rain on Iwo Jima Isle*, 104.
21. Levin, *From the Battlefield*, 94.
22. "Patrick Mooney and the Graves: Deputy Director, Combat Veterans of Iwo Jima; Director, National Museum of the Marine Corps, Docent and Visitors' Services," in Smith (ed.), *Iwo Jima*, 308.
23. Shiveley, *Last Lieutenant*, 63.
24. Vedder, *Surgeon on Iwo*, 35.

25. Caruso, *Nightmare on Iwo*, 29.
26. Wheeler, *Iwo*, 195–96.
27. McLaughlin and Miller, *From the Volcano to the Gorge*, 46.
28. Interview, Baxter, in O'Donnell, *Into the Rising Sun*, 248.
29. Matthews, *Assault*, 139.
30. Vedder, *Surgeon on Iwo*, 36–37.
31. McLaughlin and Miller, *From the Volcano to the Gorge*, 45.
32. Brown, *Battle Wounds of Iwo Jima*, 119.
33. Brown, *Battle Wounds of Iwo Jima*, 125–26.
34. Berry (ed.), *Semper Fi, Mac*, 309.
35. Levin, *From the Battlefield*, 77; Josephy, *Long and the Short and the Tall*, 158.
36. Sherrod, *On to Westward*, 178.
37. Interview, Sergeant William Smith, in Kessler and Bart (eds.), *Never in Doubt*, 47.
38. Kelly, *Battlefire!*, 202; Matthews, *Assault*, 36, 40.
39. Yaffe, *Fragments of War*, 96.
40. Yaffe, *Fragments of War*, 96.
41. McLaughlin and Miller, *From the Volcano to the Gorge*, 25.
42. Sherrod, *On to Westward*, 171, 173.
43. Gallant, *Friendly Dead*, 57.
44. Lorelli, *To Foreign Shores*, 283.
45. Bartley, *Iwo Jima*, 68, also note 24.
46. Norton and Maffioli, *Grown Gray in War*, 43.
47. Brown, *Battle Wounds of Iwo Jima*, 57.
48. Quoted in Haynes and Warren, *Lions of Iwo Jima*, 73.
49. Cockrel, "How It Was on Iwo," in O'Sheel and Cook (eds.), *Semper Fidelis*, 102. In keeping with his mythic reputation, when Liversedge came down with stomach pains and was quietly sedated, Williams discreetly took over until his superior was feeling better. The changeover had to be kept secret, otherwise it "would have been a cataclysmic blow to morale." Haynes and Warren, *Lions of Iwo Jima*, 170.
50. On this subject, Hamner, *Enduring Battle*, 15–16. See also my review, "Where They Got Their Grit," *Wall Street Journal*, May 14, 2011.
51. Sherrod, *On to Westward*, 179.
52. Brown, *Battle Wounds of Iwo Jima*, 57–58.
53. J. Lardner, "A Correspondent at the Battle," in Smith (ed.), *United States Marine Corps in World War II*, 726.
54. Yaffe, *Fragments of War*, 96.
55. Gallant, *On Valor's Side*, 335.
56. McLaughlin and Miller, *From the Volcano to the Gorge*, 226.
57. Haynes and Warren, *Lions of Iwo Jima*, 73–74.
58. Leader, "Killing Fields of Sulfur Island."
59. Shiveley, *Last Lieutenant*, 50.
60. Gallant, *Friendly Dead*, 18.
61. Interview, Rebstock, in Drez (ed.), *Twenty-Five Yards of War*, 233–34.
62. Levin, *From the Battlefield*, 68.
63. Interview, Rebstock, in Drez (ed.), *Twenty-Five Yards of War*, 235.
64. McLaughlin and Miller, *From the Volcano to the Gorge*, 135.
65. Rowe, "Memories."
66. Interview, Nummer, in Smith (ed.), *Iwo Jima*, 10.

67. Shiveley, *Last Lieutenant,* 53.
68. Toyn, *Quiet Hero,* 99.
69. Alexander, *Closing In,* 31.
70. Levin, *From the Battlefield,* 97.
71. Wheeler, *Iwo,* 185.
72. Interview, Moreau, in Kessler and Bart (eds.), *Never in Doubt,* 100.
73. Interview, Bryan, in *Iwo Jima—36 Days of Hell.*
74. Thurman, *We Were in the First Waves,* loc. 794.
75. Berry (ed.), *Semper Fi, Mac,* 92.
76. Thurman, *We Were in the First Waves,* loc. 932–47.
77. Haynes and Warren, *Lions of Iwo Jima,* 95.
78. Norton and Maffioli, *Grown Gray in War,* 46.
79. Quoted in Haynes and Warren, *Lions of Iwo Jima,* 144–45.
80. Interview, Nummer, in Smith, *Iwo Jima,* 10.
81. Crowder, *Iwo Jima Corpsman!,* 86. A similar story is mentioned in Henri et al., *U.S. Marines on Iwo Jima,* 297.
82. For Kuribayashi's bulletin, see Eldridge and Tatum (eds.), *Fighting Spirit,* 92.
83. Leader, "Killing Fields of Sulfur Island."
84. McLaughlin and Miller, *From the Volcano to the Gorge,* 129.
85. Nations, "Iwo Jima—One Man Remembers."

7. The Nights

1. Wheeler, *Iwo,* 136.
2. Y. Horie, "Explanation of Japanese Defense Plan and the Battle of Iwo Jima, Chichi Jima, January 25, 1946," appendix 2, in Eldridge and Tatum (eds.), *Fighting Spirit,* 187.
3. Haynes and Warren, *Lions of Iwo Jima,* 109.
4. Quoted in Haynes and Warren, *Lions of Iwo Jima,* 142–43.
5. Stone, *Marine Remembers Iwo Jima,* 125.
6. Matthews, *Assault,* 173.
7. O'Donnell, *Into the Rising Sun,* 250–51.
8. Toyn, *Quiet Hero,* 85.
9. Interview, Buzzard, in Smith (ed.), *Iwo Jima,* 83.
10. Matthews, *Assault,* 122.
11. McLaughlin and Miller, *From the Volcano to the Gorge,* 109.
12. Eldridge and Tatum (eds.), *Fighting Spirit,* 112; Sherrod, *On to Westward,* 197.
13. Matthews, *Assault,* 67.
14. Davenport, *D-Plus Forever,* 61–62.
15. Wheeler, *Iwo,* 126.
16. Walker and White, *Preparing for the Rain on Iwo Jima Isle,* 97.
17. McLaughlin and Miller, *From the Volcano to the Gorge,* 122.
18. McLaughlin and Miller, *From the Volcano to the Gorge,* 112, 245.
19. Stone, *Marine Remembers Iwo Jima,* 61.
20. Simpson, "Iwo Jima: A Surgeon's Story."
21. McLaughlin and Miller, *From the Volcano to the Gorge,* 240; Matthews, *Assault,* 121.
22. McLaughlin and Miller, *From the Volcano to the Gorge,* 259–60; see also Stone, *Marine Remembers Iwo Jima,* 61, for the bowel-moving benefits of pineapple juice.

23. McLaughlin and Miller, *From the Volcano to the Gorge*, 119–21.
24. Shiveley, *Last Lieutenant*, 65.
25. Averill, *Mustang*, 132.
26. Matthews, *Assault*, 142–43.
27. Torok, *Stepping Stones Across the Pacific*, 70.
28. Dashiell, "Words They Spoke," in O'Sheel and Cook (eds.), *Semper Fidelis*, 217–18.
29. Matthews, *Assault*, 68.
30. Davenport, *D-Plus Forever*, 163.
31. Davenport, *D-Plus Forever*, 164.
32. Caruso, *Nightmare on Iwo*, 68–69.
33. Matthews, *Assault*, 70.
34. McConnell, "How One Squad Fared."
35. Matthews, *Assault*, 124.
36. McLaughlin, and Miller, *From the Volcano to the Gorge*, 66.
37. Vedder, *Surgeon on Iwo*, 38–60.
38. Wheeler, "'Those Sons-of-Bitches Killed My Buddy!,'" in Smith (ed.), *United States Marine Corps in World War II*, 762, 765.
39. Interview, Nummer, in Smith, *Iwo Jima*, 10–11.
40. Huie, *From Omaha to Okinawa*, 48–49.
41. Maiden, *Return to Iwo Jima + 50*, 55.
42. Haynes and Warren, *Lions of Iwo Jima*, 171.
43. Caruso, *Nightmare on Iwo*, 156.
44. McLaughlin and Miller, *From the Volcano to the Gorge*, 65.
45. Interview, Abbatiello, in Smith (ed.), *Iwo Jima*, 150.
46. McLaughlin and Miller, *From the Volcano to the Gorge*, 65.
47. Daugherty, *Fighting Techniques of a Japanese Infantryman*, 32.
48. Matthews, *Assault*, 137; interview, Abbatiello, in Smith (ed.), *Iwo Jima*, 151.
49. McLaughlin and Miller, *From the Volcano to the Gorge*, 86.
50. Thurman, *We Were in the First Waves*, loc. 975.
51. Interview, Dobbins, in Kessler and Bart (eds.), *Never in Doubt*, 33–34.
52. Interview, Simms, in Kelly, *Battlefire!*, 201.
53. Caruso, *Nightmare on Iwo*, 53.
54. Yaffe, *Fragments of War*, 48.
55. Henri et al., *U.S. Marines on Iwo Jima*, 100.
56. Matthews, *Assault*, 75, 88.
57. See, for instance, Matthews, *Assault*, 91.
58. In Berry (ed.), *Semper Fi, Mac*, 306.
59. Lucas with Drum, *Indestructible*, 99–103.
60. Haynes and Warren, *Lions of Iwo Jima*, 214.
61. McLaughlin and Miller, *From the Volcano to the Gorge*, 89–90.
62. Torok, *Stepping Stones Across the Pacific*, 30.
63. Brown's book contains three independent accounts—which differ from each other in several fairly unimportant respects—of a deadly scuffle in a foxhole, an illustration of the degree of confusion attending these occurrences. Brown, *Battle Wounds of Iwo Jima*, 71.
64. Haynes and Warren, *Lions of Iwo Jima*, 180.
65. Wheeler, *Iwo*, 149.
66. Stone, *Marine Remembers Iwo Jima*, 66–67.
67. See Daugherty, *Fighting Techniques of a U.S. Marine*, 69.

68. Daugherty, *Fighting Techniques of a Japanese Infantryman*, 29.
69. Wheeler, *We Are the Wounded*, 120–23, 208; Haynes and Warren, *Lions of Iwo Jima*, 187.
70. Brown, *Battle Wounds of Iwo Jima*, 71. I've integrated a few accounts that differ in minor ways.
71. Caruso, *Nightmare on Iwo*, 79.

8. The Madness in the Method

1. Josephy, *Long and the Short and the Tall*, 179.
2. Seebohm, "On the Birds of the Volcano Islands," 189–92.
3. J. Lardner, "A Correspondent at the Battle," in Smith (ed.), *United States Marine Corps in World War II*, 728.
4. Davenport, *D-Plus Forever*, 175.
5. Yaffe, *Fragments of War*, 96–97.
6. See, for example, Josephy, *Long and the Short and the Tall*, 190; O'Donnell, *Into the Rising Sun*, 247; Maiden, *Return to Iwo Jima + 50*, 46; Renzi and Roehrs, *Never Look Back*, 167.
7. Walker and White, *Preparing for the Rain on Iwo Jima Isle*, 104.
8. Thurman, *We Were in the First Waves*, loc. 863.
9. Interview, Gentile, in Kessler and Bart (eds.), *Never in Doubt*, 97.
10. Haynes and Warren, *Lions of Iwo Jima*, 220.
11. McLaughlin and Miller, *From the Volcano to the Gorge*, 32.
12. Interview, Moreau, in Kessler and Bart (eds.), *Never in Doubt*, 102.
13. McLaughlin and Miller, *From the Volcano to the Gorge*, 75.
14. Vedder, *Surgeon on Iwo*, 77.
15. Stone, *Marine Remembers Iwo Jima*, 50, 123.
16. Crowder, *Iwo Jima Corpsman!*, 23.
17. Thurman, *We Were in the First Waves*, loc. 477.
18. Interview, Schribert, in Kessler and Bart (eds.), *Never in Doubt*, 44.
19. Interview, Pvt. Liberato G. Riccio, in Kessler and Bart (eds.), *Never in Doubt*, 20.
20. Vedder, *Surgeon on Iwo*, 119.
21. Matthews, *Assault*, 2–3.
22. Torok, *Stepping Stones Across the Pacific*, 43–44.
23. One wounded man who was accidentally left behind overnight said that Japanese soldiers searched nearby bodies for food, though his watch was also taken. See Crowder, *Iwo Jima Corpsman!*, 79–80.
24. Lucas with Drum, *Indestructible*, 96.
25. Interview, Pfc. Domenick Tutalo, in Smith (ed.), *Iwo Jima*, 107.
26. Interview, Copeland, in *Iwo Jima—36 Days of Hell*.
27. Interview, Moreau, in Kessler and Bart (eds.), *Never in Doubt*, 102.
28. The most infamous case of skull-taking was publicized in *Life* magazine (May 22, 1944), which reproduced a photograph of a twenty-year-old "war worker" in Phoenix, Arizona, admiring a skull her beau had sent. Revealingly, the boyfriend was a "big, handsome Navy lieutenant" who had "picked [it] up on the New Guinea beach." The officer in question would be reprimanded after the outcry, but we should bear in mind that he was hardly a frontline combat soldier. It seems not unduly unrealistic to speculate that this officer had purchased it from someone on the beach and had not simply stumbled across a cleanly boiled skull. On this case, see Weingartner, "Trophies of War," 53–67.

29. Nations, "Iwo Jima—One Man Remembers." For additional background, see S. Harrison, "Skull Trophies of the Pacific War," 817–36.

30. Interview, Peters, in *Iwo Jima: Red Blood, Black Sand.* An article reporting on Peters's talk to a school class noted that "Peters kept mementos of his time on Iwo Jima that he shared with the class—a small Japanese flag he found in an abandoned sniper's [lair], a money bag from a fallen soldier and a sword surrendered by a Japanese officer." There was no mention of the gold teeth. Faller, "War Memories Still Fresh." Mr. Peters died peacefully on May 27, 2013.

31. Interview, Gentile, in Kessler and Bart (eds.), *Never in Doubt,* 97.

32. Haynes and Warren, *Lions of Iwo Jima,* 86.

33. Brown, *Battle Wounds of Iwo Jima,* 66.

34. Interview, Buzzard, in Smith, *Iwo Jima,* 88–89.

35. Price and Knecht, "Peleliu 1944," 12. The term "Asiatic stare" evolved from a prewar phrase used to "describe the eccentric pattern of behavior characteristic of those who had been too long in Far East stations." See McMillan, *Old Breed,* 230.

36. Vedder, *Surgeon on Iwo,* 113–14; Gallant, *On Valor's Side,* 349–51.

37. McLaughlin and Miller, *From the Volcano to the Gorge,* 190.

38. Jones, *Gyrene,* 217.

39. Josephy, *Long and the Short and the Tall,* 177.

40. Interview, Baxter, in O'Donnell, *Into the Rising Sun,* 249.

41. O'Donnell, *Into the Rising Sun,* 249.

42. Berry (ed.), *Semper Fi, Mac,* 215.

43. Gallant, *On Valor's Side,* 349–50.

44. Allen, *First Battalion of the 28th Marines,* 180.

45. Interview, Mik, in Kessler and Bart (eds.), *Never in Doubt,* 158.

46. Allen, *First Battalion of the 28th Marines,* 165n10.

47. Vedder, *Surgeon on Iwo,* 75–76.

48. Interview, Doran, in Kessler and Bart (eds.), *Never in Doubt,* 175.

49. Interview, Boyle, in Kessler and Bart (eds.), *Never in Doubt,* 117.

50. Jones, *Gyrene,* 209–10.

51. Toyn, *Quiet Hero,* 114.

52. Crowder, *Iwo Jima Corpsman!,* 25.

53. Stouffer et al. (eds.), *American Soldier,* 2:443, Table 12, "Incidence of Anxiety Symptoms Among Overseas Troops, Europe and Pacific Compared."

54. Josephy, *Long and the Short and the Tall,* 178.

55. Josephy, *Long and the Short and the Tall,* 169.

56. Wheeler, *Iwo,* 173.

57. Cameron, *American Samurai,* 157, 159, 162.

58. Goudreau, "Nursing at an Advance Naval Base Hospital," 885–86.

59. For instance, Nations, "Iwo Jima—One Man Remembers."

60. Torok, *Stepping Stones Across the Pacific,* 76.

61. See, for instance, Walker and White, *Preparing for the Rain on Iwo Jima Isle,* 100; and Thurman, *We Were in the First Waves,* loc. 546.

62. Interview, Moreau, in Kessler and Bart (eds.), *Never in Doubt,* 101.

63. Quoted in Eldridge and Tatum (eds.), *Fighting Spirit,* 135.

64. McLaughlin and Miller, *From the Volcano to the Gorge,* 70–72.

65. Walker and White, *Preparing for the Rain on Iwo Jima Isle,* 97.

66. O'Donnell, *Into the Rising Sun,* 231–32.

67. Henri et al., *U.S. Marines on Iwo Jima,* 209.

68. Averill, *Mustang,* 132.
69. McLaughlin and Miller, *From the Volcano to the Gorge,* 23.
70. Interview, Riccio, in Kessler and Bart (eds.), *Never in Doubt,* 19.
71. Berry (ed.), *Semper Fi, Mac,* 309.
72. Davenport, *D-Plus Forever,* 82.
73. Matthews, *Assault,* 33.
74. Berry (ed.), *Semper Fi, Mac,* 309.
75. Interview, McDiarmid, in *Iwo Jima—36 Days of Hell.*
76. Wheeler, *Iwo,* 227.
77. Walker and White, *Preparing for the Rain on Iwo Jima Isle,* 105.
78. Quoted in Cockrel, "How It Was on Iwo," in O'Sheel and Cook (eds.), *Semper Fidelis,* 105.
79. Wheeler, *Iwo,* 227.
80. Averill, *Mustang,* 137, 144.
81. Interviews, Caldwell and Baxter, in O'Donnell, *Into the Rising Sun,* 243–44, 247; Maiden, *Return to Iwo Jima + 50,* 51; Caruso, *Nightmare on Iwo,* 25. See also Alexander, *Closing In,* 47.
82. Interview, Williams, in Smith (ed.), *Iwo Jima,* 66.
83. Josephy, *Long and the Short and the Tall,* 193.
84. Allen, *First Battalion of the 28th Marines,* appendix II, "Unit Rolls for 19 February 1945," esp. 267–68.
85. Interview, Neilson, in *Iwo Jima—36 Days of Hell;* interview, Severance, in O'Donnell, *Into the Rising Sun,* 253.
86. Wheeler, *We Are the Wounded,* 52.
87. Lowe, "Assault on Iwo Jima."
88. Caruso, *Nightmare on Iwo,* 35, 46–47, 96, 123.
89. McConnell, "How One Squad Fared."
90. Kessler and Bart (eds.), *Never in Doubt,* 9–10.
91. Matthews, *Assault,* 70.
92. Caruso, *Nightmare on Iwo,* 103.
93. Haynes and Warren, *Lions of Iwo Jima,* 198–99.
94. Berry (ed.), *Semper Fi, Mac,* 266.
95. Interview, Dobbins, in Kessler and Bart (eds.), *Never in Doubt,* 38.
96. Lowe, "Assault on Iwo Jima."
97. McLaughlin, in McLaughlin and Miller, *From the Volcano to the Gorge,* 86. See, for example, the identical sentiments—"Please make it a wound when it comes, not my death"—expressed by Thompson in Berry (ed.), *Semper Fi, Mac,* 309.
98. McLaughlin and Miller, *From the Volcano to the Gorge,* 96.
99. Interview, Berry (ed.), *Semper Fi, Mac,* 264.
100. Quoted in Hess, *Union Soldier in Battle,* 94.
101. Letter, J. W. Hand, 136th New York, July 24, 1890, printed in in Sauers (ed.), *Fighting Them Over,* 222.
102. Interview, Doran, in Kessler and Bart (eds.), *Never in Doubt,* 174–75.
103. Haynes and Warren, *Lions of Iwo Jima,* 122–23.
104. Interview, Buzzard, in Smith, *Iwo Jima,* 91–92.
105. Interview, Leman, in *Iwo Jima—36 Days of Hell.*
106. Interview, Barrett, in *Iwo Jima—36 Days of Hell.* On Haley, see Jorgensen, "John Haley's Personal Recollection of the Battle of the Wheatfield," 65.

107. Interview, Rebstock, in Drez (ed.), *Twenty-Five Yards of War*, 234; Josephy, *Long and the Short and the Tall*, 176; and Maiden, *Return to Iwo Jima + 50*, 38.
108. Matthews, *Assault*, 52–53.
109. McLaughlin and Miller, *From the Volcano to the Gorge*, 147.
110. Yaffe, *Fragments of War*, 98–99.
111. Interview, Dobbins, in Kessler and Bart (eds.), *Never in Doubt*, 35.
112. Interview, Schribert, in Kessler and Bart (eds.), *Never in Doubt*, 42.
113. Matthews, *Assault*, 202; Wheeler, *Iwo*, 183.
114. Interview, Caldwell, in O'Donnell, *Into the Rising Sun*, 244.
115. Transcript, interview with Wornham 88 (Marine Corps Oral History Program, Columbia University ORHO).
116. On "infantillery," see Cameron, *American Samurai*, 86.
117. Haynes and Warren, *Lions of Iwo Jima*, 202.
118. Cameron, *American Samurai*, 87n105.
119. McLaughlin and Miller, *From the Volcano to the Gorge*, 93.
120. Sherrod, *On to Westward*, 212.
121. Alphabetical selection was common. Replacement rifleman Russell Werts, for instance, was placed with "Wade, Wegman, Wenzel, Westmoreland and White" and ordered to go into combat with a squad, "half of whom I had never met." Vedder, *Surgeon on Iwo*, 5–6, 112. On Werts, see Jones, *Gyrene*, 63.
122. Caruso, *Nightmare on Iwo*, 59.
123. Interview, Dobbins, in Kessler and Bart (eds.), *Never in Doubt*, 34.
124. Shiveley, *Last Lieutenant*, 62; interview, Chandler, in *Iwo Jima—36 Days of Hell*.
125. This insignia system was first tried out on Iwo. Each man had a four-digit identifier: The first number clarified rank (1 for private, up to 9 for general, so anyone higher than 4 was an officer), the second regiment, the third battalion, and the fourth company. They were also color-coded (blue for infantry, yellow for engineers, red for artillery, tanks, and mortars) and surmounted by a division symbol (a rectangle for the 5th, a half-moon for the 4th, and a triangle for the 3rd). For explanations, see Torok, *Stepping Stones Across the Pacific*, 29; interview, Abbatiello, in Smith, *Iwo Jima*, 150; and McLaughlin, in McLaughlin and Miller, *From the Volcano to the Gorge*, 28, 98–99.
126. Transcript, interview with Wornham, 87 (Marine Corps Oral History Program, Columbia University ORHO).
127. Caruso, *Nightmare on Iwo*, 83.
128. Interview, Salisbury, in *Iwo Jima: Red Blood, Black Sand*.
129. Vedder, *Surgeon on Iwo*, 62.
130. Rowe, "Memories." On distance, see also Crowder, *Iwo Jima Corpsman!*, 22.
131. Interview, Gentile, in Kessler and Bart (eds.), *Never in Doubt*, 92–96.
132. Maiden, *Return to Iwo Jima + 50*, 60.
133. Transcript, interview with Karch, 30–31 (Marine Corps Oral History Program, Columbia University ORHO).
134. McMillan, *Old Breed*, 407.
135. Interview, Gentile, in Kessler and Bart (eds.), *Never in Doubt*, 92.
136. Davenport, *D-Plus Forever*, 178.
137. McLaughlin and Miller, *From the Volcano to the Gorge*, 95.

9. Understanding Hearts and Minds

1. Matthews, *Assault,* 18–19.
2. Cockrel, "How It Was on Iwo," in O'Sheel and Cook (eds.), *Semper Fidelis,* 102.
3. Quoted in Zurlinden, Josephy, Dempsey, Levin, and Smith, "Iwo: The Red-Hot Rock," in O'Sheel and Cook (eds.), *Semper Fidelis,* 90.
4. Matthews, *Assault,* 161.
5. Interview, Rebstock, in Drez (ed.), *Twenty-Five Yards of War,* 242.
6. Yaffe, *Fragments of War,* 113; Shiveley, *Last Lieutenant,* 62.
7. Averill, *Mustang,* 127.
8. Averill, *Mustang,* 133.
9. Matthews, *Assault,* 161.
10. Interview, Doran, in Kessler and Bart (eds.), *Never in Doubt,* 243.
11. Interview, Williams, in Smith (ed.), *Iwo Jima,* 66.
12. Interview, Chandler, in *Iwo Jima—36 Days of Hell.*
13. Cockrel, "How It Was on Iwo," in O'Sheel and Cook (eds.), *Semper Fidelis,* 102.
14. Haynes and Warren, *Lions of Iwo Jima,* 91.
15. Interview, Tutalo, in Smith, *Iwo Jima,* 106.
16. Interview, Abbatiello, in Smith, *Iwo Jima,* 154.
17. Haynes and Warren, *Lions of Iwo Jima,* 91.
18. Interview, Kropf, in Kessler and Bart (eds.), *Never in Doubt,* 244.
19. Cockrel, "How It Was on Iwo," in O'Sheel and Cook (eds.), *Semper Fidelis,* 104.
20. Quoted in O'Donnell, *Into the Rising Sun,* 253.
21. Interview, Doran, in Kessler and Bart (eds.), *Never in Doubt,* 171.
22. Caruso, *Nightmare on Iwo,* 66–67.
23. Interview, Kropf, in Kessler and Bart (eds.), *Never in Doubt,* 244.
24. Quoted in O'Donnell, *Into the Rising Sun,* 241.
25. Quoted in O'Donnell, *Into the Rising Sun,* 236–37.
26. Quoted in O'Donnell, *Into the Rising Sun,* 247.
27. On this matter, see Dower's innovative *War Without Mercy,* 9, 11.
28. Ford, " 'Best Equipped Army in Asia?,' " 88, 96, 99–101.
29. Coox, "Effectiveness of the Japanese Military Establishment in the Second World War," in Millett and Murray (eds.), *Military Effectiveness,* 2.
30. See, for example, Kennedy, *Military Side of Japanese Life,* 81.
31. H. Tsuyoshi, review of "Nomonhan: Japan against Russia, 1939, by Alvin D. Coox," 481, 485; for an in-depth analysis of Japanese performance, see Drea, "Nomonhan"; and Goldman, *Nomonhan 1939.*
32. Ford, " 'Best Equipped Army in Asia?,' " 104.
33. Thompson, "Behind the Fog of War: A Glance at the History and Organization of the Jap Army," quoting Robert Leurquin, in Thompson et al., (eds.), *How the Jap Army Fights,* 23–24.
34. Coox, "Effectiveness of the Japanese Military Establishment in the Second World War," in Millett and Murray (eds.), *Military Effectiveness,* 1.
35. Coox, "Effectiveness of the Japanese Military Establishment in the Second World War," in Millett and Murray (eds.), *Military Effectiveness,* 6; on U.S. figures, see "U.S. Automobile Production Figures," Wikipedia.com, available at http://en.wikipedia.org/wiki/U.S._Automobile_Production_Figures, accessed September 16, 2014.
36. Trefalt, "Fanaticism, Japanese Soldiers, and the Pacific War, 1937–45," in *Fanaticism and Conflict in the Modern Age,* ed. M. Hughes and G. Johnson, 39–40; Young, "Ide-

ologies of Difference and the Turn to Atrocity: Japan's War on China," in *World at Total War*, ed. R. Chickering, S. Förster, and B. Greiner, 349–50. On Japanese barracks, discipline, and indoctrination as well as the history of surrendering and treatment of POWs, see Drea, "Trained in the Hardest School," in his *In the Service of the Emperor*, 75–90; and Drea, *Japan's Imperial Army*. On POWs, see also Linderman, *World Within War*, 144–46.

37. Ford, "Dismantling the 'Lesser Men' and 'Supermen' Myths," 544–45; Clifford, *Progress and Purpose*, 269.

38. Ford, "U.S. Assessments of Japanese Ground Warfare Tactics," 325.

39. Ford, "U.S. Perceptions of Military Culture," 77. On passing on documents, which otherwise would have made "very good souvenir[s]," see Crowder, *Iwo Jima Corpsman!*, 61.

40. On the release and impact of these items of news, see Dower, *War Without Mercy*, 48–52. On Siffleet, see "Leonard Siffleet," Wikipedia.com, available at http://en.wikipedia.org/wiki/Leonard_Siffleet, accessed September 16, 2014.

41. Ford, "Dismantling the 'Lesser Men' and 'Supermen' Myths," 547, 553; Ford, "U.S. Assessments of Japanese Ground Warfare Tactics," 326, 329; Ford, "U.S. Perceptions of Military Culture," 90.

42. Ford, "U.S. Assessments of Japanese Ground Warfare Tactics," 344–46.

43. Ford, "Dismantling the 'Lesser Men' and 'Supermen' Myths," 570.

44. Ford, "U.S. Assessments of Japanese Ground Warfare Tactics," 355, 347–50.

45. Alexander, *Storm Landings*, 100–1. The Iwo battalion commander is quoted in McKinney, *Portable Flame Thrower Operations in World War II*, 225.

46. See McKinney, *Portable Flame Thrower Operations in World War II*, 8–16, 34–36, 46–47, 158.

47. Showalter, "War to the Knife," 98. Dower disagrees, remarking that Allies and Japanese dehumanized each other. Dower, *War Without Mercy*, 11.

48. Bergerud, "No Quarter: The Pacific Battlefield," 5, 8–9.

49. Cameron, "Fanaticism and the Barbarisation of the Pacific War, 1941–5," in *Fanaticism and Conflict in the Modern Age*, ed. Hughes and Johnson, 52.

50. This section drawn from Jones, *Gyrene*, 13, 15, 19, 20–21, 26, 40; Cameron, *American Samurai*, 52–57, 60–62 (Table 2, "Monthly Inductions Into the Marine Corps, Volunteer and Selective Service, February 1941–July 1945"); and Millett, *Semper Fidelis*, 373–75.

51. Stouffer et al. (eds.), *American Soldier*, I, Table 4, "Proportion of Men Saying They Are 'Not So Clear' or 'Not Clear at All' About Why We Are Fighting This War, Classified by Their Evaluation of the Importance of Such Understanding and Their Knowledge of the Four Freedoms," 439–40 (and see footnote 2, 433–34), and Table 3, "Topics Chosen by Enlisted Men as Those They Would Most Like to Know More About," 438.

52. On production, see Coox, "Effectiveness of the Japanese Military Establishment in the Second World War," in Millett and Murray (eds.), *Military Effectiveness*, 21; on Sadakaji, see Drea, "Nomonhan," 90.

10. The Method in the Madness

1. Stone, *Marine Remembers Iwo Jima*, 4–5; Interview, Oullette, in *Never in Doubt*, ed. Kessler and Bart, 10. On Marine organizational reforms, see Gordon, "Thomas Holcomb," in *Commandants of the Marine Corps*, ed. Millett and Shulimson, 266.

2. Kelly, *Battlefire!*, 198.

3. Haynes and Warren, *Lions of Iwo Jima*, 217–18.

4. Davenport, *D-Plus Forever,* 75.
5. Interview, Gentile, in Kessler and Bart (eds.), *Never in Doubt,* 96; Maiden, *Return to Iwo Jima + 50,* 53.
6. Interview, Dobbins, in Kessler and Bart (eds.), *Never in Doubt,* 33.
7. Interview, Voight, in O'Donnell, *Into the Rising Sun,* 242.
8. Stone, *Marine Remembers Iwo Jima,* 5.
9. Interview, Dobbins, in Kessler and Bart (eds.), *Never in Doubt,* 37.
10. Davenport, *D-Plus Forever,* 184.
11. Maiden, *Return to Iwo Jima + 50,* 37; interview, Caldwell, in O'Donnell, *Into the Rising Sun,* 250; Wheeler, *Iwo,* 220.
12. Sherrod, *On to Westward,* 215.
13. Davenport, *D-Plus Forever,* 184.
14. Boal, "Field Expedient Armor Modifications to U.S. Armored Vehicles," 21–25.
15. Neiman and Estes, *Tanks on the Beaches,* 94, 119.
16. About two other threats, tankers could do nothing. For the first several days, Japanese artillery fire scored deadly hits and their bottom hulls, always a weak spot, were vulnerable to huge naval and torpedo mines buried in the sand. Nevertheless, as the fighting continued and the Japanese lost ground and equipment, these twin dangers declined.
17. Eldridge and Tatum (eds.), *Fighting Spirit,* 135.
18. Haynes and Warren, *Lions of Iwo Jima,* 144–45.

11. The Japanese Defensive System

1. Gatchel, *At the Water's Edge,* 122–24, 128.
2. Gatchel, *At the Water's Edge,* 131.
3. On the factional politics at Imperial Headquarters, see, for instance, Kuzuhara, "Operations on Iwo Jima," 34.
4. Alexander, *Storm Landings,* 110; Hayashi, *Kogun,* 115–16; Kuzuhara, "Operations on Iwo Jima," 28–29.
5. It is important to realize that the evolutionary process of Japanese defensive strategy was neither predetermined nor upwardly unidirectional. The U.S. Army, for example, had encountered at Attu Island as early as May 1943 a deserted beach while 2,500 defenders under Colonel Yasuyo Yamasaki hid in the hills. As the army advanced inland, fire erupted from three sides of the valley surrounding them. There would be just 29 Japanese taken alive, but the defenders would inflict 1,750 casualties out of a force of 15,000. Likewise, at Biak Island in May 1944, Colonel Naoyuki Kuzume's garrison of 11,400 abandoned the beach and retreated to a spider's web of fortified positions, foxholes, pillboxes, tunnels, AA guns, observation posts, and bunkers located in the caves and along ridgelines. It took the 41st Infantry Division nearly a month to take the island. Denfield, *Japanese World War II Fortifications,* 10–12.
6. Kuzuhara, "Operations on Iwo Jima," 37.
7. Marquand, "Iwo Jima Before H-hour," 498.
8. Transcript, interview with Rogers, 84–85 (Marine Corps Oral History Program, Columbia University ORHO). On the pillboxes, Alexander, *Storm Landings,* 132.

12. Adapt or Die

1. Isely and Crowl, *U.S. Marines and Amphibious War,* 485–86.
2. Henri et al., *U.S. Marines on Iwo Jima,* 275.

3. Transcript, interview with Wornham, 82 (Marine Corps Oral History Program, Columbia University ORHO).
4. Report, "Defense Installations on Iwo Jima," 3–4.
5. Interview, Williams, in *Iwo Jima—36 Days of Hell;* Leader, "Killing Fields of Sulfur Island."
6. Gallant, *Friendly Dead,* 85–86.
7. See frontispiece in Gallant, *Friendly Dead.* Author's calculation.
8. "Iwo Jima operation, February–March 1945," prepared for Joint Intelligence Center, Pacific Ocean Area (JICPOA), Map NH-104136, available at www.history.navy.mil/photos/events/wwii-pac/iwojima/iwo-0.htm, accessed January 29, 2014.
9. Interview, Abbatiello, in Smith, *Iwo Jima,* 156.
10. Rodriguez, "Battle for Iwo Jima."
11. Interview, Salisbury, in *Iwo Jima: Red Blood, Black Sand.*
12. Transcript, interview with Hogaboom, 226 (Marine Corps Oral History Program, Columbia University ORHO).
13. Hoffman, "Legacy and Lessons of Iwo Jima," 75–76.
14. Henri et al., *U.S. Marines on Iwo Jima,* 146–47.
15. Interview, Bain, in Kessler and Bart (eds.), *Never in Doubt,* 26n.
16. Crowder, *Iwo Jima Corpsman!,* 67–68.
17. McConnell, "How One Squad Fared."
18. See the reports in Maiden, *Return to Iwo Jima + 50,* 54–65.
19. Eldridge and Tatum (eds.), *Fighting Spirit,* 85–86.
20. Diary entry, February 21, 1945, in Lofgren (ed.), "Diary of First Lieutenant Sugihara Kinryu," 126–27.
21. Eldridge and Tatum (eds.), *Fighting Spirit,* 113.
22. Cited in Alexander, *Storm Landings,* 140.
23. Diary entry, February 23, 1945, in Lofgren (ed.), "Diary of First Lieutenant Sugihara Kinryu," 130.

13. Minefields and Antitank Weapons

1. Thurman, *We Were in the First Waves,* loc. 588.
2. Brown, *Battle Wounds of Iwo Jima,* 61.
3. Wheeler, *We Are the Wounded,* 113–15.
4. McLaughlin and Miller, *From the Volcano to the Gorge,* 74–75.
5. McLaughlin and Miller, *From the Volcano to the Gorge,* 74–75.
6. Interview, Abbatiello, in Smith (ed.), *Iwo Jima,* 151.
7. Interview, Maiden, in O'Donnell, *Into the Rising Sun,* 245–46.
8. Interview, Moreau, in Kessler and Bart (eds.), *Never in Doubt,* 103.
9. Josephy, *Long and the Short and the Tall,* 174.
10. Neiman and Estes, *Tanks on the Beaches,* 127–29.
11. Averill, *Mustang,* 133.
12. Stone, *Marine Remembers Iwo Jima,* 121.
13. Gallant, *Friendly Dead,* 81–82.
14. Wheeler, *We Are the Wounded,* 91, 171–75.
15. Interview, Caldwell, in O'Donnell, *Into the Rising Sun,* 249–50. The phrase "Satchel Charlies" comes from McLaughlin and Miller, *From the Volcano to the Gorge,* 63.

14. Spider Traps and Snipers

1. Shiveley, *Last Lieutenant*, 66; Toyn, *Quiet Hero*, 95.
2. Wheeler, *Iwo*, 89–90.
3. Averill, *Mustang*, 132–33.
4. Haynes and Warren, *Lions of Iwo Jima*, 200.
5. Davenport, *D-Plus Forever*, 227–28.
6. On corpsmen casualties, see Alexander, *Closing In*, 38–39.
7. Josephy, *Long and the Short and the Tall*, 183.
8. Stone, *Marine Remembers Iwo Jima*, 113.
9. Stone, *Marine Remembers Iwo Jima*, 18–19.
10. Thurman, *We Were in the First Waves*, loc. 1018.
11. Interview, Williams, in *Iwo Jima—36 Days of Hell*. See also interviews with Herb Hammond and Craig Leman.
12. Averill, *Mustang*, 135.
13. Interview, Rebstock, in Drez (ed.), *Twenty-Five Yards of War*, 242.
14. Brown, *Battle Wounds of Iwo Jima*, 29.

15. Pillboxes, Bunkers, Blockhouses

1. Rottman and Palmer, *Japanese Pacific Island Defenses*, 25–26, 30.
2. Sherrod, *On to Westward*, 193.
3. Caruso, *Nightmare on Iwo*, 74.
4. Brown, *Battle Wounds of Iwo Jima*, 25–26.
5. Yaffe, *Fragments of War*, 99–100.
6. Stone, *Marine Remembers Iwo Jima*, 6; see also Pfc. Jack Russell in Toyn, *Quiet Hero*, 131.
7. Walker and White, *Preparing for the Rain on Iwo Jima Isle*, 93.
8. Shiveley, *Last Lieutenant*, 83.
9. Nations, "Iwo Jima—One Man Remembers."
10. Lowe, "Assault on Iwo Jima."
11. Nations, "Iwo Jima—One Man Remembers."
12. Haynes and Warren, *Lions of Iwo Jima*, 223.
13. Wheeler, *Iwo*, 142. According to artillery officer William Buchanan, "At the time we didn't have an effective method of either destroying or neutralizing the defenders in a very restricted area so that it fell to the job of the thin green line to get in there and dig them out in hand to hand combat." See transcript of interview with Buchanan, 81 (Marine Corps Oral History Program, Columbia University ORHO).
14. Wheeler, *Iwo*, 102.
15. Rottman and Palmer, *Japanese Pacific Island Defenses, 1941–45*, 25.
16. Wheeler, Iwo, 126.
17. Wheeler, "'Those Sons-of-Bitches Killed My Buddy!,'" in Smith (ed.), *United States Marine Corps in World War II*, 760.
18. Interview, Lanehart, in Kessler and Bart (eds.), *Never in Doubt*, 83.
19. See Pfc. Bernard Link, in Haynes and Warren, *Lions of Iwo Jima*, 118; and Thompson, in Berry (ed.), *Semper Fi, Mac*, 302.
20. Gallant, *Friendly Dead*, 76.
21. Interview, Rebstock, in Drez (ed.), *Twenty-Five Yards of War*, 241.
22. Josephy, *Long and the Short and the Tall*, 194.

23. See McKinney, *Portable Flame Thrower Operations in World War II,* appendix 17, Training Order, 3rd Marine Division HQ, "Tactical Employment of Flame Throwers," 19 December 1944, 307–11.
24. On the description of a flamethrower's sound, Wheeler, *Iwo,* 148–49.
25. Interview, Williams, in Smith (ed.), *Iwo Jima,* 67–69.
26. Interview, Williams, in Smith (ed.), *Iwo Jima,* 67–69; see also interview with Luther Crabtree, a demolitions man, in O'Donnell, *Into the Rising Sun,* 239–40.
27. Shiveley, *Last Lieutenant,* 68; interview, Williams, in Smith (ed.), *Iwo Jima,* 70.
28. Levin, *From the Battlefield,* 102.
29. Interview, Williams, in Smith (ed.), *Iwo Jima,* 67–69; interview, Lindberg, in O'Donnell, *Into the Rising Sun,* 236–37; Wheeler, *Iwo,* 192, 216.
30. Stone, *Marine Remembers Iwo Jima,* 82.
31. Interview, Lanehart, in Kessler and Bart (eds.), *Never in Doubt,* 84; interview, Lindberg, in O'Donnell, *Into the Rising Sun,* 236–37.
32. Gallant, *Friendly Dead,* 75.
33. Yaffe, *Fragments of War,* 112.
34. McKinney, *Portable Flame Thrower Operations in World War II,* 223–24.
35. Vedder, *Surgeon on Iwo,* 87–88.
36. Caruso, *Nightmare on Iwo,* 94–95.

16. The Caves

1. Wheeler, *Iwo,* 143.
2. Wheeler, *Iwo,* 177.
3. Sherrod, *On to Westward,* 183; Vedder, *Surgeon on Iwo,* 133.
4. Shiveley, *Last Lieutenant,* 70.
5. McLaughlin and Miller, *From the Volcano to the Gorge,* 79.
6. McLaughlin and Miller, *From the Volcano to the Gorge,* 105.
7. Interview, Abbatiello, in Smith (ed.), *Iwo Jima,* 151.
8. Wheeler, *Iwo,* 167.
9. Josephy, *Long and the Short and the Tall,* 187; Stone, *Marine Remembers Iwo Jima,* 98; Crowder, *Iwo Jima Corpsman!,* 53, all referring to the same incident.
10. Haynes and Warren, *Lions of Iwo Jima,* 144–45.
11. Price and Knecht, "Peleliu 1944," 33–34.
12. Interview, Maiden, in O'Donnell, *Into the Rising Sun,* 252.
13. Yaffe, *Fragments of War,* 139.
14. Huie, *From Omaha to Okinawa,* 53–55.

17. Surrendering and Prisoners

1. Brown, *Battle Wounds of Iwo Jima,* 60.
2. Haynes and Warren, *Lions of Iwo Jima,* 147.
3. Vedder, *Surgeon on Iwo,* 191.
4. Shiveley, *Last Lieutenant,* 91–92.
5. Brown, *Battle Wounds of Iwo Jima,* 34.
6. Wheeler, *Iwo,* 150.
7. Wheeler, *Iwo,* 150.
8. Haynes and Warren, *Lions of Iwo Jima,* 224.
9. Haynes and Warren, *Lions of Iwo Jima,* 226.

10. Laurie, "Ultimate Dilemma of Psychological Warfare in the Pacific," 117, 120 (appendix, "Place of Custody of Enemy POWs").
11. Gallant, *Friendly Dead*, 92.
12. Renzi and Roehrs, *Never Look Back*, 97.
13. Laurie, "Ultimate Dilemma of Psychological Warfare in the Pacific," 109.
14. Caruso, *Nightmare on Iwo*, 87.
15. Vedder, *Surgeon on Iwo*, 217.
16. Interview, Smith, in Kessler and Bart (eds.), *Never in Doubt*, 48.
17. Interview, Moreau, in Kessler and Bart (eds.), *Never in Doubt*, 103.
18. Nations, "Iwo Jima—One Man Remembers."
19. Caruso, *Nightmare on Iwo*, 92–93.
20. Quoted in Eldridge and Tatum (eds.), *Fighting Spirit*, 122.
21. Interview, Winters, in O'Donnell, *Into the Rising Sun*, 238–39.
22. Haynes and Warren, *Lions of Iwo Jima*, 146.
23. Brown, *Battle Wounds of Iwo Jima*, 151–52.
24. Huie, *From Omaha to Okinawa*, 53–55.

18. After the Battle

1. His story is included in Eldridge and Tatum (eds.), *Fighting Spirit*, 113–20. See also Straus, *Anguish of Surrender*, 57–59.
2. See "Matsudo Linsoki," available at www.wanpela.com/holdouts/profiles/linsoki.html, accessed February 5, 2014; see also the brief AP story in *New York Times*, January 9, 1949, 22; and Smith (ed.), *Iwo Jima*, xxi.
3. "Patrick Mooney and the Graves," in Smith (ed.), *Iwo Jima*, 308–9.
4. Interview, Hotaling, in Kessler and Bart (eds.), *Never in Doubt*, 112–13.
5. See Willie, *African American Voices from Iwo Jima*, esp. chapter 5, "Taking the Island."
6. "Patrick Mooney and the Graves," in Smith (ed.), *Iwo Jima*, 309–10.
7. According to Rebstock, in Drez (ed.), *Twenty-Five Yards of War*, 245.
8. "Patrick Mooney and the Graves," in Smith (ed.), *Iwo Jima*, 311–12.
9. Interview, Hotaling, in Kessler and Bart (eds.), *Never in Doubt*, 113.
10. "Patrick Mooney and the Graves," in Smith (ed.), *Iwo Jima*, 312–13.
11. Interview, Caldwell, in O'Donnell, *Into the Rising Sun*, 244.
12. Interview, Maiden, in O'Donnell, *Into the Rising Sun*, 45–46.
13. Neiman and Estes, *Tanks on the Beaches*, 131.
14. Wheeler, *We Are the Wounded*, 38.
15. Wheeler, *We Are the Wounded*, 39–42.
16. Wheeler, *We Are the Wounded*, 110.
17. Wheeler, *We Are the Wounded*, 92.
18. Goudreau, "Nursing at an Advance Naval Base Hospital," 886.
19. Wheeler, *We Are the Wounded*, 203.
20. Wheeler, *We Are the Wounded*, 193; Wheeler, "The Story of a Man's Face," 90–115.
21. Josephy, *Long and the Short and the Tall*, 174–75.
22. Haynes and Warren, *Lions of Iwo Jima*, 235–36.
23. Brown, *Battle Wounds of Iwo Jima*, 36.
24. Brown, *Battle Wounds of Iwo Jima*, 157–58.
25. Interview, Vinich, in O'Donnell, *Into the Rising Sun*, 238.
26. McLaughlin and Miller, *From the Volcano to the Gorge*, 196–98.

27. Vedder, *Surgeon on Iwo*, 65.
28. Wheeler, *We Are the Wounded*, 140–53.

The Great Red God

1. Thus, the colonel of the 2nd Brigade, 10th Mountain Division: "Fallujah will be the Gettysburg of this war." Quoted in P. K. O'Donnell, *We Were One: Shoulder to Shoulder with the Marines Who Took Fallujah* (Philadelphia: Da Capo Press, 2006), 221.
2. Quoted in D. Camp, *Operation Phantom Fury: The Assault and Capture of Fallujah, Iraq* (Minneapolis: Zenith Press, 2009), 267.
3. D. Bellavia and J. R. Bruning, *House to House: A Soldier's Memoir* (New York: Free Press, 2008), 69. For an extended examination, see J. Pieslak, *Sound Targets: American Soldiers and Music in the Iraq War* (Bloomington: University of Indiana Press, 2009).
4. Bellavia and Bruning, *House to House*, 71.
5. G. Orwell, *Homage to Catalonia* (New York: Harcourt, 1980 [1938]), 76; D. J. Danelo, *Blood Stripes: The Grunt's View of the War in Iraq* (Mechanicsburg, PA: Stackpole Books, 2006), 149. J. C. McManus observes that "the skin of the grunts was peppered with nicks and cuts. Their eyes were rimmed with dark circles. They stank of dust, cordite, stale MRE crumbs, body odor, and soiled underwear. The sweaty T-shirts that hugged their irritated skin had given many of them prickly heat." McManus, *Grunts: Inside the American Infantry Combat Experience, World War II Through Iraq* (New York: NAL Caliber, 2010), 379.
6. Bellavia, *House to House*, 273.
7. Bellavia, *House to House*, 112–13.
8. N. G. Pond (ed.), "Experiences in Early Wars in America: Life Story of an Ambitious American Youth Who at Sixteen Years of Age Was Fired with the Spirit of Patriotism and Against the Will of His Parents Marched to the Battle-Line in Defense of His Country," *Journal of American History* 1 (1907): 89–93.
9. J. Malcolm, "Reminiscences of a Campaign in the Pyrenees and South of France in 1814," in *Memorials of the Late War*, ed. Anon. (Edinburgh: Constable & Co., 1831), 1:247–48.
10. See Letters No. 8, July 8, 1863; No. 9, July 9; and No. 10, July 27, in J. C. West, *A Texan in Search of a Fight: Being the Diary and Letters of a Private Soldier in Hood's Texas Brigade* (Waco, TX: J. S. Hill and Co., 1901), 84–97.
11. Letter, Westbrook, September 20, 1900, printed in R. A. Sauers (ed.), *Fighting Them Over: How the Veterans Remembered Gettysburg in the Pages of the National Tribune* (Baltimore: Butternut and Blue, 1998), 316.
12. For instance, E. B. Hamley, *The Operations of War Explained and Illustrated* (Edinburgh and London: William Blackwood and Sons, 1878), 472.
13. See, for depressing summaries of the situation, H. W. Wilson, *Battleships in Action* (Boston: Little Brown, and Company, 1926), 2:286; and B. Liddell Hart, *The Defence of Britain* (New York: Random House, 1939), 130.
14. See J. A. Isely and P. A. Crowl, *The U.S. Marines and Amphibious War: Its Theory, and Its Practice in the Pacific* (Princeton, NJ: Princeton University Press, 1951), 18–20; H. M. Smith, *The Development of Amphibious Tactics in the U.S. Navy* (Washington, DC: History and Museums Division Headquarters, U.S. Marine Corps, 1992), 19; T. A. Gibson, "Gallipoli, 1915," and D. M. Weller, "The Development of Naval Gunfire Support in World War Two," in *Assault From the Sea: Essays on the History of Am-*

phibious Warfare, ed. M. L. Bartlett (Annapolis, MD: Naval Institute Press, 1983), 142–53, 262–64.

15. K. J. Clifford, *Progress and Purpose: A Developmental History of the United States Marine Corps, 1900–1970* (Washington, DC: History and Museums Division Headquarters, United States Marine Corps, 1973), 139–40 (appendix F, "Outline of the Development of the Landing Operations Manual"), 141–42 (appendix G, "Students and Instructors Who Were Assigned to MCS During Preparation of *Tentative Landing Operations Manual*—November 1933 Through May 1934").

16. T. Moy, *War Machines: Transforming Technologies in the U.S. Military, 1920–1940* (College Station: Texas A&M University Press, 2001), 134–37; Clifford, *Progress and Purpose,* 45–46.

17. On this subject, see Rose, *American Rifle* (New York: Delacorte Press, 2008), ch. 8, "Roosevelt's Rifle."

Bibliography

BUNKER HILL

Adams, C. F. (ed.). *Familiar Letters of John Adams and His Wife Abigail Adams, During the Revolution.* New York: Hurd and Houghton, 1876.

Adams, J. W., and A. B. Kasakoff. "Wealth and Migration in Massachusetts and Maine, 1771–1798." *Journal of Economic History* 45 (1985).

Agnew, C. "General Sir Andrew Agnew of Lochnaw, Bt—28 Years a Fusilier." *Journal of the Royal Highland Fusiliers* 24, no. 2 (2000).

Allen, V. "Medicine in the American Revolution." Part 2. *Journal of the Oklahoma State Medical Association* 63, no. 11 (1970).

Anderson, F. *A People's Army: Massachusetts Soldiers and Society in the Seven Years' War.* Chapel Hill: Institute of Early American History and Culture/University of North Carolina Press, 1984.

————. "A People's Army: Provincial Military Service in Massachusetts During the Seven Years' War." *William and Mary Quarterly* 40, no. 4 (1983).

Anderson, W. *The Scottish Nation: Or, the Surnames, Families, Literature, Honours, and Biographical History of the People of Scotland.* 3 vols. Edinburgh: A. Fullarton and Co., 1864.

Andrlik, T., H. T. Harrington, and D. N. Hagist (eds.). *Journal of the American Revolution.* Yellow Springs, OH: Ertel Publishing, 2013.

Anon. *The Annual Register, or a View of the History, Politics, and Literature for the Year 1781.* London: J. Dodsley, 1782.

Anon. (ed.). "Journals of Lieut.-Col. Stephen Kemble, 1773–1789." *Collections of the New-York Historical Society* 16 (1883).

Anon. (ed.). *Memorials of the Late War.* 2 vols. Edinburgh: Constable and Co., 1831.

Anon. "Military Books of the Revolution." *The Historical Magazine and Notes and Queries Concerning the Antiquities, History, and Biography of America*, vol. 1 (1857).

Appel, J. W., and G. W. Beebe. "Preventive Psychiatry: An Epidemiologic Approach." *Journal of the American Medical Association* 131 (1946). August 13.

Artwohl, A. "Perceptual and Memory Distortion During Officer-Involved Shootings." *FBI Law Enforcement Bulletin* 71, no. 10 (2002).

Ashburner, W. (ed.). "Richard Price Letters, 1767–1790." *Proceedings of the Massachusetts Historical Society* 17 (1903).

Bailey, S. L. *Historical Sketches of Andover (Comprising the Present Towns of North Andover and Andover), Massachusetts.* Boston: Houghton, Mifflin and Company, 1880.

Balderston, M., and D. Syrett (eds.). *The Lost War: Letters From British Officers During the American Revolution.* New York: Horizon Press, 1975.

Balingall, G. *Introductory Lectures to a Course of Military Surgery, Delivered in the University of Edinburgh.* Edinburgh: Adam Black, 1830.

Barker, J. *The British in Boston: Being the Diary of Lieutenant John Barker of the King's Own Regiment From November 15, 1774 to May 31, 1776.* Edited by E. E. Dana. Cambridge, MA: Harvard University Press, 1924.

Barnard, T. "Letter of Rev. Thomas Barnard." *Proceedings of the Bunker Hill Monument Association,* 1902.

Bickley, F. (ed.). *Historical Manuscripts Commission: Report on the Manuscripts of the Late Reginald Rawdon Hastings, Esq., of the Manor House, Ashby de la Zouch.* 4 vols. London: His Majesty's Stationery Office, 1928–47.

Bland, H. *A Treatise of Military Discipline; in Which Is Laid Down and Explained the Duty of the Officer and Soldier, Through the Several Branches of the Service.* 6th ed. London: J. and P. Knapton, S. Birt, T. Longman, and T. Shewell, 1746.

Bohy, J., and D. Troiani. "'We Meant to Be Free Always': The Guns of April 19, 1775." *American Rifleman,* July 2010.

Bolton, C. K. *The Private Soldier Under Washington.* New York: Charles Scribner's Sons, 1902.

Brown, A. E. *Beside Old Hearth-Stones.* Boston: Lee and Shepard, 1897.

Brown, P. "Officer's Story of Bunker Hill." *New York Times,* June 21, 1896.

Browne, G. W. *The History of Hillsborough, New Hampshire, 1735–1921.* 2 vols. Manchester, NH: John B. Clarke Company, 1921.

Brumwell, S. *Redcoats: The British Soldier and War in the Americas, 1755–1763.* Cambridge, U.K.: Cambridge University Press, 2002.

Bryant, W. B., and S. H. Gay. *A Popular History of the United States, From the First Discovery of the Western Hemisphere by the Northmen, to the End of the Civil War.* 5 vols. New York: Charles Scribner's Sons, 1896.

Butler, C. *History of the Town of Groton, Including Pepperell and Shirley, From the First Grant of Groton Plantation in 1655.* Boston: T. R. Marvin, 1848.

Camp, D. *Operation Phantom Fury: The Assault and Capture of Fallujah, Iraq.* Minneapolis: Zenith Press, 2009.

Cantlie, N. *The History of the Army Medical Department.* 2 vols. London: Churchill Livingstone, 1974.

Carter, C. E. (ed.). *The Correspondence of General Thomas Gage, 1763–1775.* 2 vols. New Haven: Yale University Press, 1931–33.

Charters, D. A., M. Milner, and J. B. Wilson (eds.). *Military History and the Military Profession.* Westport, CT: Praeger, 1992.

Chase, G. W., and H. B. Dawson (eds.). *Diary of David How, a Private in Colonel Paul Dudley Sargent's Regiment of the Massachusetts Line, in the Army of the American Revolution.* New York: Morrisania, 1865.

Churchill, R. H. "Gun Ownership in Early America: A Survey of Manuscript Militia Returns." *William and Mary Quarterly* 60, no. 3 (2003).

Clarke, J. "An Impartial and Authentic Narrative of the Battle Fought on the 17th of June, 1775, Between His Britannic Majesty's Troops and the American Provincial Army on Bunker's Hill Near Charles Town in New England." *Magazine of History with Notes and Queries, Extra Numbers 5–8* (1909).

Coffin, C. (ed.). *History of the Battle of Breed's Hill.* Portland, ME: D.C. Colesworthy, 1835.

Conway, S. "The British Army, 'Military Europe,' and the American War of Independence." *William and Mary Quarterly* 67, no. 1 (2010).

———. "British Army Officers and the American War for Independence." *William and Mary Quarterly* 41, no. 2 (1984).

Cooper, T. H. *A Practical Guide for the Light Infantry Officer: Comprising Valuable Extracts From All the Most Popular Works on the Subject, with Further Valuable Information.* London: Robert Wilks, 1806.

Curtis, O. B. *History of the Twenty-Fourth Michigan of the Iron Brigade, Known as the Detroit and Wayne County Regiment.* Detroit: Winn and Hammond, 1891.

Daddis, G. A. "Understanding Fear's Effect on Unit Effectiveness." *Military Review* 84, no. 4 (2004).

Dann, J. C. (ed.), *The Revolution Remembered: Eyewitness Accounts of the War for Independence.* Chicago: University of Chicago, 1980.

Davis, Jr., C. E. *Three Years in the Army: The Story of the 13th Massachusetts Volunteers From July 16, 1861 to August 1, 1864.* Boston: Rockwell and Churchill, 1893.

Dawson, C. B. (ed.). "Bunker's Hill." *Historical Magazine* 3, no. 6 (1868).

Dinter, E. *Hero or Coward: Pressures Facing the Soldier in Battle.* London: Frank Cass, 1985.

Doddridge, J. *Notes on the Settlement and Indian Wars of the Western Parts of Virginia and Pennsylvania From 1763 to 1783, Inclusive, Together with a Review of the State of Society and Manners of the First Settlers of the Western Country.* Pittsburgh: J. S. Ritenour and W. T. Lindsey, 1912 [1824].

Donkin, R. *Military Collections and Remarks.* New York: H. Gaine, 1777.

Drake, S. A. (ed.). *Bunker Hill: The Story Told in Letters From the Battlefield by British Officers Engaged.* Boston: Nichols and Hall, 1875.

Drewe, E. *The Case of Edward Drewe, Late Major of the Thirty-Fifth Regiment of Foot.* Exeter, U.K.: B. Thorn and Son, 1782.

Duffy, C. *The Army of Frederick the Great.* Newton Abbot, U.K.: David and Charles, 1974.

———. *Fire and Stone: The Science of Fortress Warfare, 1660–1860.* 2nd ed. Mechanicsburg, PA: Stackpole Books, 1996.

———. *Military Experience in the Age of Reason.* London: Routledge and Kegan Paul, 1987.

Ellis, G. E. *Sketches of Bunker Hill Battle and Monument: With Illustrative Documents.* Charlestown, MA: C. P. Emmons, 1851.

Elting, J. *Battle of Bunker's Hill.* Monmouth Beach, NJ: Phillip Freneau Press, 1975.

Erffa, H. von, and A. Staley. *The Paintings of Benjamin West.* New Haven and London: Yale University Press, 1986.

Estes, J. W. "'A Disagreeable and Dangerous Employment': Medical Letters From the Siege of Boston, 1775." *Journal of the History of Medicine and Allied Sciences* 31 (1976).

Fann, W. R. "On the Infantryman's Age in Eighteenth-Century Prussia." *Military Affairs* 41, no. 4 (1977).

Field, C. *Britain's Sea-Soldiers: A History of the Royal Marines and Their Predecessors and of Their Services in Action, Ashore and Afloat.* 2 vols. Liverpool: Lyceum Press, 1924.

Fischer, D. H. *Paul Revere's Ride.* New York: Oxford University Press, 1994.

Fisher, H. "The Objective at Bunker Hill." *Proceedings of the Bunker Hill Memorial Association* (1907).

Flavell, J. M. "Government Interception of Letters From America and the Quest for Colonial Opinion in 1775." *William and Mary Quarterly* 58, no. 2 (2001).

Fonblanque, E. B. *Political and Military Episodes in the Latter Half of the Eighteenth Century Derived From the Life and Correspondence of the Right Hon. J. Burgoyne, General, Statesman, Dramatist.* 2 vols. London: Macmillan and Co., 1876.

Fontenot, G. "Fear God and Dreadnought: Preparing a Unit for Confronting Fear." *Military Review* 75, no. 4 (1995).

Force, P. (ed.). *American Archives: Consisting of a Collection of Authentick Records, State Papers, Debates, and Letters and Other Notices of Publick Affairs, the Whole Forming a Documentary History of the Origin and Progress of the North American Colonies; of the Causes and Accomplishment of the American Revolution; and of the Constitution of the Government of the United States.* 9 vols. Washington, DC: M. St. Claire Clarke and P. Force, 1837–53.

Fortescue, J. (ed.). *The Correspondence of King George the Third.* 6 vols. London: Macmillan and Co., 1927–28.

French, A. (ed.). *A British Fusilier in Revolutionary Boston; Being the Diary of Lieutenant Frederick Mackenzie, Adjutant of the Royal Welch Fusiliers, January 5–April 30, 1775, with a Letter Describing His Voyage to America.* Cambridge, MA: Harvard University Press, 1926.

———. *The First Year of the American Revolution.* New York: Houghton Mifflin, 1934.

———. "General Haldimand in Boston, 1774–1775." *Proceedings of the Massachusetts Historical Society* 66 (1936–1941).

Frothingham, R. "Address." *Proceedings of the Bunker Hill Monument Association,* 1876.

———. *The Battle-Field of Bunker Hill: With a Relation of the Action by William Prescott, and Illustrative Documents.* Boston: R. Frothingham, 1876.

———. *The Centennial: Battle of Bunker Hill, with a View of Charlestown in 1775, Page's Plan of the Action, Romane's Exact View of the Battle, and Other Illustrations.* Boston: Little, Brown, and Co., 1875.

———. *History of the Siege of Boston, and of the Battles of Lexington, Concord, and Bunker Hill, Also, an Account of the Bunker Hill Monument, with Illustrative Documents.* 6th ed. Boston: Little, Brown, and Co., 1903.

Frothingham, R., M. Tuttle, T. C. Amory, D. Hoppin, M. Foote, and S. A. Green. "Letter of Edward Everett; Account of the Battle of Bunker Hill; Letter of James Warren; Letter of Samuel B. Webb; Diary of Lieutenant-Colonel Storrs; Extracts From an Orderly Book; Letter of Brigadier-General Jones; Note-Books of Jeremy Belknap." *Proceedings of the Massachusetts Historical Society* 14 (1875).

Gibbon, J. *The Artillerist's Manual, Compiled From Various Sources, and Adapted to the Service of the United States.* 2nd ed. New York: D. Van Nostrand, 1863.

Gillett, M. C. *The Army Medical Department, 1775–1918.* Washington, DC: Center of Military History, 1981.

Gilman, C. M. "Medical Surgery in the American Revolution." *Journal of the Medical Society of New Jersey* 57, no. 8 (1960).

Glynney, I. *Diary* (unpublished). Harlan Crow Library, Dallas, TX.

Goldstein, E. "A British Grenadier's Button From a Bunker Hill Grave." *Military Collector and Historian* 60, no. 1 (2008).

Gordon, W. *The History of the Rise, Progress, and Establishment of the Independence of the United States of America: Including an Account of the Late War and of the Thirteen Colonies, From Their Origin to That Period.* 3 vols. New York: Samuel Campbell, 1794.

Grattan, W. *Adventures with the Connaught Rangers, 1809–1814.* Edited by C. Oman. London: Edward Arnold, 1902 [1847].

Green, S. A. "American Prisoners Taken at the Battle of Bunker Hill." *New England Historical and Genealogical Register* 42 (1888).

———. (ed.). "Amos Farnsworth's Diary." *Proceedings of the Massachusetts Historical Society* 12 (1897–99).

———. (ed.). *A Collection of Papers Relating to the History of the Town of Groton, Massachusetts.* Cambridge, MA: John Wilson and Son, 1899.

———. "Colonel William Prescott, and Groton Soldiers at the Battle of Bunker Hill." *Proceedings of the Massachusetts Historical Society* 43 (1909–1910).

———. (ed.). "Paul Lunt's Book." *Proceedings of the Massachusetts Historical Society* 12 (1871–73).

———. (ed.). "Thomas Boynton's Journal." *Proceedings of the Massachusetts Historical Society* 15 (1876–77).

Greene, E. B., and V. D. Harrington. *American Population Before the Federal Census of 1790.* New York: Columbia University Press, 1932.

Griffiths, F. A. *The Artillerist's Manual, and British Soldier's Compendium.* 9th ed. London: Parker and Son, 1862.

Gross, R. A. *The Minutemen and Their World.* New York: Hill and Wang, 1976.

Grossman, D. *On Combat: The Psychology and Physiology of Deadly Conflict in War and in Peace.* 3rd ed. Millstadt, IL: Warrior Science Publications, 2008.

Haag, L. C. "The Sound of Bullets." *AFTE Journal* 34 (2002).

Hadden, J. M. *Hadden's Journal and Orderly Books: A Journal Kept in Canada and Upon Burgoyne's Campaign in 1776 and 1777.* Albany, NY: Joel Munsell's Sons, 1884.

Hagelin, W., and R. A. Brown. "Connecticut Farmers at Bunker Hill: The Diary of Colonel Experience Storrs." *New England Quarterly* 28, no. 1 (1955).

Hagist, D. N. *British Soldiers, American War: Voices of the American Revolution.* Yardley, PA: Westholme Publishing, 2012.

———. "Shedding Light on Friendly Fire at Bunker Hill." *American Revolution* 1, no. 3 (2009).

Hansen, M. H. "Battle Exhortation in Ancient Historiography: Fact or Fiction?" *Historia* 42, no. 2 (1993).

Harrington, H. T. "Roundball Ballistics in the Revolutionary War: What Caused Rifle Shots to Go Over the Heads of the Enemy." *Southern Campaigns of the American Revolution* 3, no. 5 (2006).

Hart, A. B. "Echoes of Bunker Hill." *Proceedings of the Bunker Hill Monument Association* (1911).

Hastings, M. "Drawing the Wrong Lesson." *New York Review of Books,* March 11, 2010.

Hatch, R. M. "New Hampshire at Bunker Hill." *Historic New Hampshire* 30, no. 4 (1975).

Hawthorne, N. *The Snow Image and Other Twice-Told Tales.* New York: Thomas Y. Crowell and Co., 1902.

Heath, W. *Heath's Memoirs of the American War.* New York: A. Wessels Co., 1904.

Hendrix, S. *The Spirit of the Corps: The British Army and the Pre-National Pan-European Military World and the Origins of American Martial Culture, 1754–1783.* PhD. diss., University of Pittsburgh, 2005.

Henkels, S. V. (ed.). *The Letters and Papers of Elbridge Gerry, Catalogue No. 1005 for an Auction Held December 6, 1909* (1909).

Hennell, G. *A Gentleman Volunteer: The Letters of George Hennell From the Peninsular War, 1812–13.* Edited by M. Glover. London: Heinemann, 1979.

Henshaw, W. "Orderly Book of Col. William Henshaw." *Proceedings of the Massachusetts Historical Society* 15 (1876–77).

Higginbotham, D. *The War of American Independence: Military Attitudes, Policies, and Politics, 1763–1789.* New York: Macmillan, 1971.

Hill, J. B. (ed.). *Bi-Centennial of Old Dunstable, Address by Hon. S. T. Worcester, October 27, 1873, Also Colonel Bancroft's Personal Narrative of the Battle of Bunker Hill.* Nashua, NH: E. H. Spalding, 1878.

Holland, J. G. *History of Western Massachusetts: The Counties of Hampden, Hampshire, Frank-lin, and Berkshire.* 2 vols. Springfield, MA: Samuel Bowles and Co., 1855.

Houlding, J. A. *Fit for Service: The Training of the British Army, 1715–1795.* Oxford, U.K.: Oxford University Press, 1981.

House of Commons. *The Detail and Conduct of the American War, Under Generals Gage, Howe, Burgoyne, and Vice Admiral Lord Howe: With a Very Full and Correct State of the Whole of the Evidence, as Given Before a Committee of the House of Commons; and the Celebrated Fugitive Pieces, Which Are Said to Have Given Rise to That Important Enquiry, the Whole Exhibiting a Circumstantial, Connected, and Complete History of the Real Causes, Rise, Progress, and Present State of the American Rebellion.* 3rd ed. London: Richardson and Urquhart, 1780.

Hudson, C. *History of the Town of Lexington, Middlesex County, Massachusetts, From Its First Settlement to 1868.* 2 vols. New York and Boston: Houghton Mifflin, 1913.

Hughes, B. P. *Firepower: Weapons Effectiveness on the Battlefield, 1630–1850.* New York: Sarpedon, 1997.

Huntoon, D. T. V. *History of the Town of Canton, Norfolk County, Massachusetts.* Cambridge, MA: John Wilson and Son, 1893.

James, G. "Britain's Brown Bess." *Petersen's Rifle Shooter,* September 23, 2010. Available at www.rifleshootermag.com/rifles/featured_rifles_bess_092407/, accessed September 15, 2014.

Johnson, R. B. (ed.). "Diary of Israel Litchfield." Parts 1 and 2. *New England Historical and Genealogical Register* 129 (1975).

Johnson, W. *Sketches of the Life and Correspondence of Nathanael Greene, Major General of the Armies of the United States, in the War of the Revolution.* 2 vols. Charleston, SC: A. E. Miller, 1822.

Jones, E. A. *The Loyalists of Massachusetts: Their Memorials, Petitions, and Claims.* London: St. Catherine Press, 1930.

Ketchum, R. M. *The Battle for Bunker Hill.* New York: Doubleday, 1962.

Kidder, F. *The History of New Ipswich: From Its First Grant in 1736, to the Present Time: with Genealogical Notices of the Principal Families, and Also the Proceedings of the Centennial Celebration, September 11, 1850.* Boston: Gould and Lincoln, 1852.

Klinger, D. *Police Responses to Officer-Involved Shootings.* Department of Justice report, NCJ 192286 (2006).

Krenn, P., P. Kalaus, and B. Hall. "Material Culture and Military History: Test-Firing Early Modern Small Arms." *Material History Review* 42 (1995).

Lamb, R. *An Original and Authentic Journal of Occurrences During the Late American War From Its Commencement to the Year 1783.* Dublin: Wilkinson & Courtney, 1809.

Lamont, M. de. *The Art of War, Containing the Duties of All Military Officers in Actual Service; Including Necessary Instructions, in Many Capital Matters, by the Knowledge of Which, a Man May Soon Become an Ornament to the Profession of Arms.* Philadelphia: Robert Bell, 1776.

Leach, J. "A Journal Kept by John Leach, During His Confinement by the British, in Boston Gaol, in 1775." *New England Historical and Genealogical Register* 19, no. 3 (1865).

Lee Malcolm, J. "Slavery in Massachusetts and the American Revolution." *Journal of the Historical Society* 10, no. 4 (2010).

Leeke, W. *The History of Lord Seaton's Regiment (the 52nd Light Infantry) at the Battle of Waterloo.* 2 vols. London: Hatchard and Co., 1866.

L'Etang, H. "Some Thoughts on Panic in War." *Brassey's Annual* 77 (1966).

Lieberman, H. R., G. P. Bathalon, C. M. Falco, C. A. Morgan III, P. J. Niro, and W. J. Tharion. "The Fog of War: Decrements in Cognitive Performance and Mood Associated with Combat-Like Stress." Section 2. *Aviation, Space, and Environmental Medicine* 76, no. 7 (2005).

Lincoln, W. (ed.). *The Journals of Each Provincial Congress of Massachusetts in 1774 and 1775, and of the Committee of Safety.* Boston: Dutton and Wentworth, 1838.

Longmore, T. *Gunshot Injuries: Their History, Characteristic Features, Complications, and General Treatment, with Statistics Concerning Them as They Have Been Met with in Warfare.* 2nd ed. London: Longmans, Green and Co., 1895.

———. *A Treatise on Gunshot Wounds.* Philadelphia: J. B. Lippincott and Co., 1862.

Lossing, B. J. *The Pictorial Field-Book of the Revolution.* 2 vols. New York: Harper and Brothers, 1851.

Lushington, S. R. *The Life and Services of General Lord Harris, G. C. B. During His Campaigns in America, the West Indies, and India.* 2nd ed. London: J. W. Parker, 1845.

Lynn, J. A. *Battle: A History of Combat and Culture.* Cambridge, MA: Westview, 2003.

Manring, M. M., A. Hawk, J. H. Calhoun, and R. C. Andersen. "Treatment of War Wounds: A Historical Review." *Clinical Orthopaedics and Related Research* 467 (2009).

Mauduit, I. *Three Letters to Lord Viscount Howe, with Remarks on the Attack at Bunker's Hill, to Which Is Added, a Comparative View of the Conduct of Lord Cornwallis and General Howe.* London: G. Wilkie, 1781.

McCalman, I. *An Oxford Companion to the Romantic Age: British Culture, 1776–1832.* Oxford: Oxford University Press, 1999.

Moore, F. (ed.). *Diary of the American Revolution: From Newspapers and Original Documents.* 2 vols. New York: Charles Scribner, 1860.

Moore, H. P. *A Life of General John Stark of New Hampshire.* New York: No publisher, 1949.

Morrissey, B. *Boston 1775: The Shot Heard Around the World.* London: Osprey, 1995.

Muir, R. *Tactics and the Experience of Battle in the Age of Napoleon.* New Haven and London: Yale University Press, 2000 edn.

Murdock, H. *Bunker Hill: Notes and Queries on a Famous Battle.* Boston: Houghton Mifflin, 1927.

Murphy, J. F. "We Have All Lost a Father." *Naval History* 16, no. 5 (2002).

Neale, A. *Letters From Portugal and Spain; Comprising the Account of the Operations of the Armies Under Their Excellences Sir Arthur Wellesley and Sir John Moore, From the Landing of the Troops at Mondego Bay to the Battle at Corunna.* London: Richard Phillips, 1809.

Neumann, G. "The Redcoats' Brown Bess." *American Rifleman,* December 9, 2009. Available at www.americanrifleman.org/article.php?id=14722&cat=3&sub=11, accessed September 15, 2014.

Norton, S. L. "Marital Migration in Essex County, Massachusetts, in the Colonial and Early Federal Periods." *Journal of Marriage and the Family* 35, no. 3 (1973).

Norwood, W. F. "Medicine in the Era of the American Revolution." Part 2. *International Record of Medicine* 171, no. 7 (1958).

Nosworthy, B. *The Anatomy of Victory: Battle Tactics, 1689–1763.* New York: Hippocrene Books, 1990.

Noyes, D. *The History of Norway: Comprising a Minute Account of Its First Settlement, Town Officers, the Annual Expenditures of the Town, with Other Statistical Matters; Interspersed with Historical Sketches, Narrative and Anecdote, and Occasional Remarks of the Author.* Norway, ME: D. Noyes, 1852.

Ondishko, Jr., J. J. "A View of Anxiety, Fear, and Panic." *Military Affairs* 36, no. 2 (1972).

Palmer, J. "Longevity." *Proceedings of the Massachusetts Historical Society* 8 (1866).

Paret, P. *Imagined Battles: Reflections of War in European Art*. Chapel Hill: University of North Carolina Press, 1997.

———. (ed.). *Makers of Modern Strategy: From Machiavelli to the Nuclear Age*. Princeton, NJ: Princeton University Press, 1986.

———. *Understanding War: Essays on Clausewitz and the History of Military Power*. Princeton, NJ: Princeton University Press, 1992.

Phalen, J. "Surgeon James Mann's Observations on Battlefield Amputations." *Military Surgeon* 87 (1940).

Pickering, O. *The Life of Timothy Pickering*. 4 vols. Boston: Little, Brown, and Co., 1867–73.

Pollard, T., and I. Banks (eds.). *Bastions and Barbwire*. Leiden, The Netherlands: Brill, 2008.

Potter, C. E. *The History of Manchester, Formerly Derryfield, in New Hampshire; Including That of Ancient Amoskeag, of the Middle Merrimack Valley*. Manchester, NH: C. E. Potter, 1856.

Potter, I. R. "The Life and Remarkable Adventures of Israel Ralph Potter." *Magazine of History with Notes and Queries, Extra Numbers 13–16* (1911).

Powell, W. S. "A Connecticut Soldier Under Washington: Elisha Bostwick's Memoirs of the First Years of the Revolution." *William and Mary Quarterly* 6, no. 1 (1949).

Powers, S. L. "Studying the Art of War: Military Books Known to American Officers and Their French Counterparts During the Second Half of the Eighteenth Century." *Journal of Military History* 70, no. 3 (2006).

Pruitt, Jr., B. A. "Combat Casualty Care and Surgical Progress." *Annals of Surgery* 243, no. 6 (2006).

Quintal, Jr., G. *Patriots of Color: 'A Peculiar Beauty and Merit;' African Americans and Native Americans at Battle Road and Bunker Hill*. Boston: National Historical Park, 2002.

Raudzens, G. "In Search of Better Quantification for War History: Numerical Superiority and Casualty Rates in Early Modern Europe." *War and Society* 15, no. 1 (1997).

Reardon, C. "Writing Battle History: The Challenge of Memory." *Civil War History* 53, no. 3 (2007).

Reed, W. B. *The Life and Correspondence of Joseph Reed*. 2 vols. Philadelphia: Lindsay and Blakiston, 1847.

Report of the War Office Committee of Enquiry into 'Shell-Shock.' London: Imperial War Museum, 2004 [1922].

Resch, J. P. *Suffering Soldiers: Revolutionary War Veterans, Moral Sentiment, and Political Culture in the Early Republic*. Amherst: University of Massachusetts Press, 1999.

Rose, A. *American Rifle: A Biography*. New York: Delacorte Press, 2008.

Russell, P. E. "Redcoats in the Wilderness: British Officers and Irregular Warfare in Europe and America, 1740 to 1760." *William and Mary Quarterly* 35, no. 4 (1978).

Scheer, G. F., and H. F. Rankin. *Rebels and Redcoats: The American Revolution Through the Eyes of Those Who Fought and Lived It*. New York: World Publishing Company, 1957.

Scott, D., L. Babits, and C. Haecker (eds.). *Fields of Conflict: Battlefield Archaeology from the Roman Empire to the Korean War*. Washington, DC: Potomac Books, 2009.

Scudder, H. N. "The Battle of Bunker Hill." *Atlantic Monthly* 36 (1875).

Seybolt, R. F. "Note on the Casualties of April 19, and June 17, 1775." *New England Quarterly* 4, no. 3 (1931).

Shephard, B. *A War of Nerves: Soldiers and Psychiatrists in the Twentieth Century*. Cambridge, MA: Harvard University Press, 2003.

Showman, R. K. (ed.). *The Papers of General Nathanael Greene*. 13 vols. Chapel Hill: University of North Carolina Press, 1976–2005.

Shrader, C. R. "Friendly Fire: The Inevitable Price." *Parameters* 22 (1992).

Smith, A. *History of the Town of Peterborough, Hillsborough County, New Hampshire: With the Report of the Proceedings at the Centennial Celebration in 1839; an Appendix Containing the Records of the Original Proprietors; and a Genealogical and Historical Register.* Boston: George H. Ellis Co., 1876.

Smith, J. *Peterborough, New Hampshire, in the American Revolution.* Peterborough, NH: Peterborough Historical Society, 1913.

Spring, M. *With Zeal and with Bayonets Only: The British Army on Campaign in North America, 1775–1783.* Norman: University of Oklahoma Press, 2008.

Stanhope, P. H. *Notes of Conversations with the Duke of Wellington, 1831–1851.* New York: Longmans, Green, and Co., 1888.

Stedman, C. *The History of the Origin, Progress, and Termination of the American War.* 2 vols. London: C. Stedman, 1794.

Steele, B. D., and T. Dorland (eds.). *The Heirs of Archimedes: Science and the Art of War Through the Age of Enlightenment.* Cambridge, MA: MIT Press, 2005.

Steinweg, K. K. "Dealing Realistically with Fratricide." *Parameters* 25 (1995).

Stephenson, M. *Patriot Battles: How the War of Independence Was Fought.* New York: Harper-Collins, 2007.

Stevens, B. F. (ed.). *General Sir William Howe's Orderly Book at Charlestown, Boston, and Halifax, June 17, 1775 to May 26, 1776.* London: Benjamin Franklin Stevens, 1890.

Stone, W. L. (ed.). *Journal of Captain Pausch, Chief of the Hanau Artillery During the Burgoyne Campaign.* Albany, NY: Joel Munsell's Sons, 1886.

Stouffer, R., A. A. Lumsdaine, M. H. Lumsdaine, R. M. Williams, Jr., M. B. Smith, I. L. Janis, S. A. Star, and L. S. Cottrell, Jr. (eds.). *The American Soldier: Studies in Social Psychology in World War II.* 4 vols. Princeton, NJ: Princeton University Press, 1949–50.

Sumner, W. H. "Reminiscences Relating to General Warren and Bunker Hill." *New England Genealogical and Historical Register* 12 (1858).

Swett, S. *History of Bunker Hill Battle: With a Plan.* Boston: Munroe and Francis, 1826.

———. *Notes to His Sketch of Bunker Hill Battle.* Boston: Munroe and Francis, 1825.

Temple, J. H. *History of Framingham, Massachusetts, Early Known as Danforth's Farms, 1640–1880, with a Genealogical Register.* Framingham, MA: Town of Framingham, 1887.

Terraine, J. *The Smoke and the Fire: Myths and Anti-Myths of War, 1861–1945.* London: Sidgwick & Jackson, 1980.

Thacher, J. *A Military Journal During the American Revolution, from the Commencement to the Disbanding of the American Army.* Hartford, CT: Hurlbut, Williams, and Co., 1862.

Tielke, J. G. von (trans. C. and R. Craufurd). *An Account of Some of the Most Remarkable Events of the War Between the Prussians, Austrians, and Russians, From 1756 to 1763; and a Treatise on Several Branches of the Military Art.* 2 vols. London: C. and R. Craufurd, 1787–88.

Trumbull, J. *Autobiography, Reminiscences, and Letters of John Trumbull, from 1756 to 1841.* New York: Wiley and Putnam, 1841.

Ultee, M. (ed.). *Adapting to Conditions: War and Society in the Eighteenth Century.* Tuscaloosa: University of Alabama Press, 1986.

Urban, M. *Fusiliers: The Saga of a British Redcoat Regiment in the American Revolution.* New York: Walker and Co., 2007.

Van Arsdale, J. (ed.). *Discord and Civil Wars, Being a Portion of the Journal Kept by Lieutenant Williams of His Majesty's Twenty-Third Regiment While Stationed in British North America During the Time of the Revolution.* Buffalo, NY: Salisbury Club, 1954.

Vidal, F. "Psychology in the 18th Century: A View from Encyclopedias." *History of the Human Sciences* 6, no. 1 (1993).

Wade, H. T., and R. A. Lively. *This Glorious Cause: The Adventures of Two Company Officers in Washington's Army.* Princeton, NJ: Princeton University Press, 1958.

Wanke, P. "American Military Psychiatry and Its Role Among Ground Forces in World War II." *Journal of Military History* 63, no. 1 (1999).

War Office. *Rules and Regulations for the Formations, Field Exercise, and Movements of His Majesty's Forces.* London: J. Walter for the War Office, 1792.

Ward, A. H. *History of the Town of Shrewsbury, Massachusetts: From Its Settlement in 1717 to 1829, with Other Matter Relating Thereto Before Not Published, Including an Extensive Family Register.* Shrewsbury: S. G. Drake, 1847.

Ward, C. *The War of the Revolution.* 2 vols. New York: Macmillan, 1952.

Waters, J. J. "Family, Inheritance, and Migration in Colonial New England: The Evidence from Guilford, Connecticut." *William and Mary Quarterly* 39, no. 1 (1982).

Webb, J. W. (ed.). *Reminiscences of General Samuel B. Webb of the Revolutionary Army.* New York: Globe Stationery and Printing Co., 1882.

Webster, D. "An Account of the Battle of Bunker Hill." *North American Review* 7 (1818).

Whinyates, F. A. (ed.). *The Services of Lieut.-Colonel Francis Downman, R.A., in France, North America, and the West Indies, Between the Years 1758 and 1784.* Woolwich, U.K.: Royal Artillery Institution, 1898.

Whitcher, W. "The Relation of New Hampshire Men to the Siege of Boston." *Magazine of History with Notes and Queries* 6 (1907).

Willcox, E. S. "Captain William Meacham at Bunker Hill." *New England Historical and Genealogical Register* 49 (1895).

Windham, W., and G. Townshend. *A Plan of Discipline Composed for the Use of the Militia of the County of Norfolk.* London: J. Shuckburgh, 1760.

Winsor, J. (ed.). *The Memorial History of Boston, Including Suffolk County, Massachusetts, 1630–1880.* 4 vols. Boston: James R. Osgood and Co., 1882.

Wolfe, J. *Instructions to Young Officers.* 2nd ed. Edinburgh, 1780.

Wolseley, G. J. *The Story of a Soldier's Life.* 2 vols. New York: Charles Scribner's Sons, 1904.

Wooden, A. C. "The Wounds and Weapons of the Revolutionary War from 1775 to 1783." *Delaware Medical Journal* 44, no. 3 (1972).

Wortley, J. (ed.). *A Prime Minister and His Son: From the Correspondence of the 3rd Earl of Bute and of Lt.-General the Hon. Sir Charles Stuart, K.B.* London: John Murray, 1925.

Wright, J. W. "Some Notes on the Continental Army." *William and Mary Quarterly* 11, no. 2 (1931).

Yellin, K. *Battle Exhortation: The Rhetoric of Combat Leadership.* Columbia: University of South Carolina Press, 2008.

GETTYSBURG

Adelman, G. E. "Hazlett's Battery at Gettysburg." *Gettysburg Magazine* 21 (1999).

Adkin, M. *The Gettysburg Companion: The Complete Guide to America's Most Famous Battle.* Mechanicsburg, PA: Stackpole Books, 2008.

Albin, M. A. "The Use of Anesthetics During the Civil War, 1861–1865." *Pharmacy in History* 42, nos. 3 and 4 (2000).

Alexander, E. P. "Causes of Lee's Defeat at Gettysburg." *Southern Historical Society Papers* 4, no. 3 (1877).

———. *Fighting for the Confederacy: The Personal Recollections of General Edward Porter Alexander.* Edited by G. W. Gallagher. Chapel Hill: University of North Carolina Press, 1989.

————. *Military Memoirs of a Confederate: A Critical Narrative.* New York: Charles Scribner's Sons, 1907.

Andrews, M. R. (ed.). *History of Marietta and Washington County, Ohio and Representative Citizens.* Chicago: Biographical Publishing Company, 1902.

Anon. (ed.). *Biographical and Historical Memoirs of Pulaski, Jefferson, Lonoke, Faulkner, Grant, Saline, Perry, Garland, and Hot Spring Counties, Arkansas.* Chicago: Goodspeed Publishing Company, 1889.

Anon. "Fighting." *Scientific American* 7, no. 22, Nov. 29, 1862.

Anon. "Gettysburg Weather Reports." *Blue and Gray Magazine* 5, no. 2 (1987).

Anon. "How They Fire in Battle." *Scientific American* 7, no. 18, Nov. 1, 1862.

Anon. *Reunions of the Nineteenth Maine Regiment Association, at Portland, Bath, Belfast, Augusta and Richmond.* Augusta, ME: Sprague, Owen, and Nash, 1878.

Anon. "Scenes and Incidents at Gettysburg." *Harper's Weekly* 8, no. 368, Jan. 16, 1864.

Anon. "Suggestions From an Old Soldier." *New York Times,* April 24, 1861.

Anon. (eds.). *The Union Army: A History of Military Affairs in the Loyal States, 1861–1865— Records of the Regiments in the Union Army—Cyclopedia of Battles—Memoirs of Commanders and Soldiers.* 8 vols. Madison, WI: Federal Publishing Co., 1908.

Anon. "A Visit to the Gettysburg Battlefield." *Brooklyn Daily Eagle,* August 1, 1863.

Baker, L. W. *History of the Ninth Mass. Battery: Recruited July, 1862; Mustered in Aug. 10, 1862; Mustered Out June 9, 1865, at the Close of the Rebellion.* South Framingham, MA: Lakeview Press, 1888.

Bandy, K., and F. Freeland (eds.). *The Gettysburg Papers.* 2 vols. Dayton, OH: Morningside Press, 1978.

Barber, L. W. *Army Memoirs.* Chicago: J. M. W. Jones Stationery and Printing Co., 1894.

Barnes, J. K., G. A. Otis, and D. L. Huntington (eds.). *The Medical and Surgical History of the War of the Rebellion.* Washington, DC: Government Printing Office, 1883.

Barrett, J. G. (ed.). *Yankee Rebel: The Civil War Journal of Edmund Dewitt Patterson.* Knoxville: University of Tennessee Press, 2004.

Barziza, D. et U. *The Adventures of a Prisoner of War, 1863–1864.* Edited by R. H. Shuffler. Austin: University of Texas Press, 1964.

Bates, S. P. (ed.). *History of Pennsylvania Volunteers, 1861–5: Prepared in Compliance with Acts of the Legislature.* 5 vols. Harrisburg, PA: B. Singerly, 1869–1871.

Bauer, K. J. (ed.). *Soldiering: The Civil War Diary of Rice C. Bull, 123rd New York Volunteer Infantry.* San Rafael, CA: Presidio Press, 1977.

Baumann, T., and D. M. Segesser. "Shadows of Total War in French and British Military Journals, 1918–1939." In *The Shadows of Total War: Europe, East Asia, and the United States, 1919–1939,* edited by R. Chickering and S. Förster. New York: Cambridge University Press, 2003.

Becker, C. M., and R. Thomas (eds.). *Hearth and Knapsack: The Ladley Letters, 1857–1880.* Athens: Ohio University Press, 1988.

Benedict, G. G. *Army Life in Virginia: Letters From the Twelfth Vermont Regiment and Personal Experiences of Volunteer Service in the War for the Union, 1862–63.* Burlington, VT: Free Press Association, 1895.

————. *Vermont at Gettysburg: A Sketch of the Part Taken by the Vermont Troops in the Battle for Gettysburgh.* Burlington, VT: Free Press Association, 1870.

Benson, S. W. (ed.). *Berry Benson's Civil War Book: Memoirs of a Confederate Scout and Sharpshooter.* Athens: University of Georgia Press, 2007.

Benton, C. E. *As Seen From the Ranks: A Boy in the Civil War.* New York: G. P. Putnam's Sons, 1902.

Bierce, A. "The Crime at Pickett's Mill." In *The Devil's Dictionary, Tales, and Memoirs*, edited by S. T. Joshi. New York: Library of America, 2011.

Bigelow, J. *The Peach Orchard: Gettysburg, July 2, 1863*. Minneapolis: Kimball-Storer Co., 1910.

Bilby, J. G. *Small Arms at Gettysburg: Infantry and Cavalry Weapons in America's Greatest Battle*. Yardley, PA: Westholme, 2008.

Blackford, W. W. *War Years with Jeb Stuart*. New York: Charles Scribner's Sons, 1946.

Blake, H. N. *Three Years in the Army of the Potomac*. Boston: Lee and Shepard, 1865.

Borcke, H. von. *Memoirs of the Confederate War for Independence*. Philadelphia: J. B. Lippincott and Co., 1867.

Bousquet, A. *The Scientific Way of Warfare: Order and Chaos on the Battlefields of Modernity*. New York: Columbia University Press, 2009.

Bowen, G. A. "The Diary of Captain George D. Bowen, 12th Regiment New Jersey Volunteers." *Valley Forge Journal* 2, no. 2 (1984).

Bowen, R. E. "From Round Top to Richmond." *The Old Guard* 4, no. 1 (1889).

Boyd, C. F. (ed. M. Throne). *The Civil War Diary of Cyrus R. Boyd, Fifteenth Iowa Infantry, 1861–1863*. Baton Rouge: Louisiana State University Press, 1998.

Brown, E. *The Twenty-Seventh Indiana Volunteer Infantry in the War of the Rebellion, 1861 to 1865: First Division, 12th and 20th Corps: a History of Its Recruiting, Organization, Camp Life, Marches, and Battles*. Monticello, IN: R. E. Brown, 1899.

Brown, M. M. *The University Greys: Company A, Eleventh Mississippi Regiment, Army of Northern Virginia, 1861–1865*. Richmond, VA: Garrett and Massie, 1940.

Browne, Jr., E. C. "Battery H, 1st Ohio Light Artillery: Controversy in the Cemetery." *Gettysburg Magazine* 26 (2002).

Bruce, G. A. *The Twentieth Regiment of Massachusetts Volunteer Infantry, 1861–1865*. Boston and New York: Houghton, Mifflin, and Co., 1906.

Bucklin, S. *In Hospital and Camp: A Woman's Record of Thrilling Incidents Among the Wounded in the Late War*. Philadelphia: John E. Potter and Co., 1869.

Buechler, J. "'Give 'Em the Bayonet'—a Note on Civil War Mythology." In *Battles Lost and Won: Essays From Civil War History*, edited by J. T. Hubbell. Westport, CT: Greenwood Press, 1975.

Buehler, F. J. *Recollections of the Rebel Invasion and One Woman's Experience During the Battle of Gettysburg*. Gettysburg, PA: Star and Sentinel Printing, 1900.

Busey, J. P., and D. G. Martin (eds.). *Regimental Strengths and Losses at Gettysburg*. Hightstown, NJ: Longstreet House, 1994.

Byrne, F. L., and A. T. Weaver (eds.). *Haskell of Gettysburg: His Life and Civil War Papers*. Kent, OH: Kent State University Press, 1989.

Campbell, E. "The Aftermath and Recovery of Gettysburg." Part 1. *Gettysburg Magazine* 11 (1994).

———. "Baptism of Fire: The Ninth Massachusetts Battery at Gettysburg, July 2, 1863." *Gettysburg Magazine* 5 (1991).

———. "'Remember Harper's Ferry': The Degradation, Humiliation, and Redemption of Col. George L. Willard's Brigade, Part 1." *Gettysburg Magazine* 7 (1992).

———. "'Remember Harper's Ferry': The Degradation, Humiliation, and Redemption of Col. George L. Willard's Brigade, Part 2." *Gettysburg Magazine* 8 (1993).

———. "Voices of Gettysburg: How the Army of the Potomac Viewed the Campaign." *North and South* 7 (2004).

Carter, R. G. *Four Brothers in Blue, or Sunshine and Shadows of the War of the Rebellion: A Story of the Great Civil War From Bull Run to Appomattox*. Washington, DC: Gibson Bros., 1913.

Casey, J. B. (ed.). "The Ordeal of Adoniram Judson Warner: His Minutes of South Mountain and Antietam." *Civil War History* 28, no. 3 (1982).

Castel, A. "Mars and the Reverend Longstreet: Or, Attacking and Dying in the Civil War." *Civil War History* 33, no. 2 (1987).

Catton, B. *Reflections on the Civil War.* Edited by J. Leekley. Garden City, NY: Doubleday & Co., 1981.

Chamberlain, J. L. *The Passing of the Armies: An Account of the Final Campaign of the Army of the Potomac, Based Upon Personal Reminiscences of the Fifth Army Corps.* New York: G. P. Putnam's Sons, 1915.

Chandler, D. G. *On the Napoleonic Wars: Collected Essays.* Mechanicsburg, PA: Stackpole Books, 1999 edn.

Cheek, P., and M. Pointon. *History of the Sauk County Riflemen, Known as Company 'A,' Sixth Wisconsin Veteran Volunteer Infantry, 1861–1865.* Madison, WI: Democrat Printing Company, 1909.

Chickering, R. "Total War: The Use and Abuse of a Concept." In *Anticipating Total War: The German and American Experiences, 1871–1914,* edited by M. F. Boemeke, R. Chickering, and S. Förster. Cambridge, U.K.: Cambridge University Press, 1999.

Chisolm, J. J. *Manual of Military Surgery for the Use of Surgeons in the Confederate Army; with an Appendix of the Rules and Regulations of the Medical Department of the Confederate Army.* Charleston, SC: Evans and Cogswell, 1861.

Coco, G. A. *On the Bloodstained Field: 130 Human Interest Stories of the Campaign and Battle of Gettysburg.* Gettysburg, PA: Thomas Publications, 1987.

———. "The Rawley W. Martin Story." *Gettysburg Magazine* 33 (2005).

———. *A Strange and Blighted Land: Gettysburg: the Aftermath of a Battle.* Gettysburg, PA: Thomas Publications, 1995.

Coffman, R. "A Vital Unit." *Civil War Times Illustrated* 20 (June 1982).

Cole, P. M. *Command and Communications Frictions in the Gettysburg Campaign.* Orrtanna, PA: Colecraft Industries, 2006.

Conklin, G. W. "The Long March to Stevens-Run: The 134th New York Volunteer Infantry at Gettysburg." *Gettysburg Magazine* 21 (1999).

Connor, J. T. H. "Chloroform and the Civil War." *Military Medicine* 169 (Feb. 2004).

Cook, S. G., and C. E. Benton (eds.). *The 'Dutchess County Regiment' in the Civil War: Its Story as Told by Its Members.* Danbury, CT: Danbury Medical Printing Co., 1907.

Cooksey, P. C. "The Union Artillery at Gettysburg on July 3." *Gettysburg Magazine* 38 (2008).

Costa, D. L. "Scarring and Mortality Selection Among Civil War Pows: A Long-Term Mortality, Morbidity, and Socioeconomic Follow-Up." California Center for Population Research On-Line Working Paper Series PWP-CCPR-2010–035, November 29, 2010.

Coxe, J. "The Battle of Gettysburg." *Confederate Veteran* 21, no. 9 (September 1913).

Craft, D. *History of the Hundred Forty-First Regiment, Pennsylvania Volunteers, 1862–1865.* Towanda, PA: Reporter-Journal Printing Company, 1885.

Crumb, H. S. (ed.). *The Eleventh Corps Artillery at Gettysburg: The Papers of Major Thomas Ward Osborn, Chief of Artillery.* Hamilton, NY: Edmonston Publishing, Inc., 1991.

Culp, E. C. *The 25th Ohio Veteran Volunteer Infantry in the War of the Union.* Topeka, KS: George W. Crane & Co., 1885.

Daniel, F. E. *Recollections of a Rebel Surgeon (and Other Sketches), or, in the Doctor's Sappy Days.* Chicago: Clinic Publishing Co., 1901.

Davis, J. A. "Music and Gallantry in Combat During the American Civil War." *American Music* 28, no. 2 (2010).

Davis, S. "The Death and Burials of General Richard Brooke Garnett." *Gettysburg Magazine* 5 (1991).

Davis, S. B. *Escape of a Confederate Officer From Prison: What He Saw at Andersonville: How He Was Sentenced to Death and Saved by the Interposition of Abraham Lincoln.* Norfolk, VA: Landmark Publishing Company, 1892.

Dawes, R. R. *Service with the Sixth Wisconsin Volunteers.* Marietta, OH: E. R. Alderman, 1890.

Dean, Jr., E. T. "'We Will All Be Lost and Destroyed': Post-Traumatic Stress Disorder and the Civil War." *Civil War History* 37 (1991).

De Forest, J. *A Volunteer's Adventures: A Union Captain's Record of the Civil War.* Edited by J. H. Croushore. New Haven: Yale University Press, 1946.

De Saxe, M. "My Reveries upon the Art of War." In *Roots of Strategy: A Collection of Military Classics.* Edited by Maj. T. R. Philips. Mechanicsburg, PA: Stackpole Books, 2002.

Diffenbaugh, W. G. "Military Surgery in the Civil War." *Military Medicine* 130 (May 1965).

Dodge, T. A. "Left Wounded on the Field." *Putnam's Monthly Magazine* 14, no. 21 (September 1869).

Dougherty, J. J. "A History of the Mcpherson Farm at Gettysburg." *Gettysburg Magazine* 26 (2002).

———. "'We Have Come to Stay!': The 143rd Regiment Pennsylvania Volunteer Infantry and the Fight for Mcpherson's Ridge, July 1, 1863." *Gettysburg Magazine* 24 (2001).

Dougherty, P. J. "Wartime Amputations." *Military Medicine* 158 (December 1993).

Doyle, J. A., J. D. Smith, and R. M. McMurry (eds.). *This Wilderness of War: The Civil War Letters of George W. Squier, Hoosier Volunteer.* Knoxville: University of Tennessee Press, 1998.

Dreese, M. A. "The 151st Pennsylvania Volunteers at Gettysburg: July 1, 1863." *Gettysburg Magazine* 23 (2000).

———. "Ordeal in the Lutheran Theological Seminary: The Recollections of First Lt. Jeremiah Hoffman, 142nd Pennsylvania Volunteers." *Gettysburg Magazine* 23 (2000).

Dunaway, W. F. *Reminiscences of a Rebel.* New York: Neale Publishing Company, 1913.

———. "Additional Notes on the 154th New York at Gettysburg." *Gettysburg Magazine* 29 (2003).

Dunkelman, M. H. "'We Were Compelled to Cut Our Way Through Them, and in Doing So Our Losses Were Heavy': Gettysburg Casualties of the 154th New York Volunteers." *Gettysburg Magazine* 18 (1998).

Dunkelman, M. H., and M. J. Winey. "The Hardtack Regiment in the Brickyard Fight." *Gettysburg Magazine* 8 (1993).

Durkin, J. T. (ed.). *John Dooley, Confederate Soldier: His War Journal.* Washington, DC: Georgetown University Press, 1945.

Eby, C. D. (ed.). *A Virginia Yankee in the Civil War: The Diaries of David Hunter Strother.* Chapel Hill: University of North Carolina Press, 1961.

Elmore, T. L. "Casualty Analysis of the Gettysburg Battle." *Gettysburg Magazine* 35 (2006).

———. "The Effects of Artillery Fire on Infantry at Gettysburg." *Gettysburg Magazine* 5 (1991).

———. "The Grand Cannonade: A Confederate Perspective." *Gettysburg Magazine* 19 (1999).

———. "Less Than Brave: Shirkers, Stragglers, and Scavengers in the Army of Northern Virginia." *Gettysburg Magazine* 31 (2004).

———. "A Meteorological and Astronomical Chronology of the Gettysburg Campaign." *Gettysburg Magazine* 13 (1995).

————. "Skirmishers." *Gettysburg Magazine* 6 (1992).

Evans, T. "'All Was Complete Chaos': As a Federal Regular Saw Second Manassas." *Civil War Times Illustrated* 6, no. 9 (January 1968).

————. "The Cries of the Wounded Were Piercing and Horrible." *Civil War Times Illustrated* 7, no. 4 (July 1968).

Farlow, J., and L. Barry (eds.). "Vincent B. Osborne's Civil War Experiences." *Kansas Historical Quarterly* 20 (May 1952).

Faust, D. G. "The Civil War Soldier and the Art of Dying." *Journal of Southern History* 67, no. 1 (2001).

————. "Telling War Stories." *New Republic,* June 30, 2011.

Ferro, M. *The Great War, 1914–1918.* London: Routledge, 1991 [1969].

Foner, E. *Reconstruction: America's Unfinished Revolution, 1863–1877.* New York: Harper Perennial, 2002.

Foster, J. Y. "Four Days at Gettysburg." *Harper's New Monthly Magazine* 28, no. 165 (Feb. 1864).

Fox, W. F. *Regimental Losses in the American Civil War, 1861–1865.* 4th ed. Albany, NY: Albany Publishing Company, 1898.

Fuger, F. "Cushing's Battery at Gettysburg." *Journal of the Military Service Institution of the United States* 41 (1907).

Fulks, S. "Another Irony of Gettysburg." *Gettysburg Magazine* 44 (2011).

Fuller, C. A. *Personal Recollections of the War of 1861 as Private, Sergeant, and Lieutenant in the Sixty-First Regiment, New York Volunteer Infantry.* Sherburne, NY: News Job Publishing House, 1906.

Fuller, J. F. C. *Grant and Lee: A Study in Personality and Generalship.* Bloomington: Indiana University Press, 1957.

Galwey, T. F. *The Valiant Hours: Narrative of 'Captain Brevet,' an Irish-American in the Army of the Potomac.* Edited by W. S. Nye. Harrisburg, PA: Stackpole Company, 1961.

Garrison, F. H. *John Shaw Billings: A Memoir.* New York: G. P. Putnam's Sons, 1915.

Gibbon, J. *The Artillerist's Manual, Compiled From Various Sources, and Adapted to the Service of the United States.* 2nd ed. New York: D. Van Nostrand, 1863.

Gilmor, H. *Four Years in the Saddle.* New York: Harper and Brothers, 1866.

Glatthaar, J. T. *General Lee's Army: From Victory to Collapse.* New York: Free Press, 2008.

————. *Soldiering in the Army of Northern Virginia: A Statistical Portrait of the Troops Who Served Under Robert E. Lee.* Chapel Hill: University of North Carolina Press, 2011.

Gordon, L. J. "'I Never Was a Coward': Questions of Bravery in a Civil War Regiment." Frank L. Klement Lecture No. 14. Milwaukee: Marquette University Press, 2005.

Goss, W. L. *Recollections of a Private: A Story of the Army of the Potomac.* New York: Thomas Y. Crowell and Co., 1890.

Gottfried, B. M. "'Friendly' Fire at Gettysburg." *Gettysburg Magazine* 27 (2002).

Grandchamp, R. "The 2nd Rhode Island Volunteers in the Gettysburg Campaign." *Gettysburg Magazine* 42 (2010).

Griffith, P. *Battle Tactics in the Civil War.* New Haven: Yale University Press, 2001.

Grimsley, M., and T. D. Miller (eds.). *The Union Must Stand: The Civil War Diary of John Quincy Adams Campbell, Fifth Iowa Volunteer Infantry.* Knoxville: University of Tennessee Press, 2000.

Gross, J. "A Grave Situation: Privately Purchased Identification Devices with Gettysburg Association." *Gettysburg Magazine* 42 (2010).

Guelzo, A. C. "The Unturned Corners of the Battle of Gettysburg: Tactics, Geography, and Politics." *Gettysburg Magazine* 45 (2011).

Hadden, R. L. "The Deadly Embrace: The Meeting of the Twenty-Fourth Regiment, Michigan Infantry and the Twenty-Sixth Regiment of North Carolina Troops at Mcpherson's Woods, Gettysburg, Pennsylvania, July 1, 1863." *Gettysburg Magazine* 5 (1991).

Haines, A. *History of the Fifteenth Regiment New Jersey Volunteers.* New York: Jenkins and Thomas, 1883.

Hall, C. R. "The Lessons of the War Between the States." *International Record of Medicine* 171, no. 7 (July 1958).

Hardee, W. J. *Rifle and Light Infantry Tactics; for the Exercise and Manoeuvres of Troops When Acting as Light Infantry or Riflemen.* Philadelphia: Lippincott, Grambo, and Co., 1855.

Hartwig, D. S. "The 11th Army Corps on July 1, 1863." *Gettysburg Magazine* 2 (1990).

———. "'I Have Never Been in a Hotter Place': Brigade Command at Gettysburg." *Gettysburg Magazine* 25 (2001).

———. "Unwilling Witness to the Rage of Gettysburg." In *The Most Shocking Battle I Have Ever Witnessed: The Second Day at Gettysburg.* Papers of the 2006 Gettysburg National Military Park Seminar. National Park Service, 2008.

Herdegen, L. J. "Old Soldiers and War Talk: The Controversy Over the Opening Infantry Fight at Gettysburg." *Gettysburg Magazine* 2 (1990).

Hess, E. J. *Pickett's Charge: The Last Attack at Gettysburg.* Chapel Hill and London: University of North Carolina Press, 2001.

———. *The Rifle Musket in Civil War Combat: Reality and Myth.* Lawrence: University Press of Kansas, 2008.

———. *The Union Soldier in Battle: Enduring the Ordeal of Combat.* Lawrence: University Press of Kansas, 1997.

Hill, A. F. *Our Boys: The Personal Experiences of a Soldier in the Army of the Potomac.* Philadelphia: John E. Potter, 1864.

Hitchcock, F. L. *War from the Inside, or Personal Experiences, Impressions, and Reminiscences of One of the 'Boys' in the War of the Rebellion.* Philadelphia: J. B. Lippincott, 1904.

Hohenlohe-Ingelfingen, K. zu. *Letters on Infantry.* Translated by N. L. Walford. 2nd ed. London: Edward Stanford, 1892.

Holmes, O. W. (ed.). *Speeches by Oliver Wendell Holmes.* Boston: Little, Brown, and Co., 1900.

Holstein, A. M. E. *Three Years in the Field Hospitals of the Army of the Potomac.* Philadelphia: J. B. Lippincott, 1867.

Howard, O. O. *Autobiography of Oliver Otis Howard.* 2 vols. New York: Baker and Taylor Co., 1907.

Hubler, S. "Just the Plain, Unvarnished Story of a Soldier in the Ranks." *New York Times,* June 29, 1913.

Humphreys, H. H. *Andrew Atkinson Humphreys: A Biography.* Philadelphia: John C. Winston Co., 1924.

Hunter, A. "A High Private's Sketch of Sharpsburg." *Southern Historical Society Papers* 11 (1883).

Hutchinson, M. W. "Bringing Home a Fallen Son: The Story of Lt. Willis G. Babcock, 64th New York Volunteer Infantry." *Gettysburg Magazine* 30 (2004).

———. "To Gettysburg and Beyond: A Vermont Captain's Letters to His Wife." *Gettysburg Magazine* 25 (2001).

Hyman, K. C., S. Wignall, and R. Roswell, "War Syndromes and Their Evaluation: From the U.S. Civil War to the Persian Gulf War." *Annals of Internal Medicine* 125, no. 5 (1996).

Isham, A. B. "The Story of a Gunshot Wound." In *Sketches of War History, 1861–1865: Papers Prepared for the Ohio Commandery of the Military Order of the Loyal Legion of the*

United States, 1890–1896. Edited by W. H. Chamberlin. Cincinnati: Robert Clarke Company, 1896.

Jackson, D. P. (ed.). *The Colonel's Diary: Journals Kept Before and During the Civil War by the Late Colonel Oscar L. Jackson of New Castle, Pennsylvania, Sometime Commander of the 63rd Regiment O.V.I.* Sharon, PA: David P. Jackson, 1922.

Johnson, C. *Battleground Adventures: The Stories of Dwellers on the Scenes of Conflict in Some of the Most Notable Battles of the Civil War.* Boston: Houghton Mifflin, 1915.

Johnson, R. U., and C. C. Buell (eds.). *Battles and Leaders of the Civil War.* 4 vols. New York: Century Company, 1884–88.

Jones, T. L. (ed.). *The Civil War Memoirs of Captain William J. Seymour: Reminiscences of a Louisiana Tiger.* Baton Rouge: Louisiana State University Press, 1991.

Jordan, Jr., W. B. "Gettysburg and the Seventeenth Maine." *Gettysburg Magazine* 8 (1993).

Jorgensen, J. "John Haley's Personal Recollection of the Battle of the Wheatfield." *Gettysburg Magazine* 27 (2002).

———. "Wofford Sweeps the Wheatfield." *Gettysburg Magazine* 22 (2000).

Judson, A. M. *History of the Eighty-Third Regiment Pennsylvania Volunteers.* Erie, PA: B. F. H. Lynn, 1865.

Jünger, E. "Total Mobilization." In *The Heidegger Controversy: A Critical Reader,* edited by R. Wolin, translated by J. Golb and R. Wolin. New York: Columbia University Press, 1991.

Keen, W. W. "Military Surgery in 1861 and in 1918." *Rehabilitation of the Wounded: Annals of the American Academy of Political and Social Science* 80 (1918).

Keller, C. B. "Pennsylvania's German-Americans, a Popular Myth, and the Importance of Perception." In *Damn Dutch: Pennsylvania Germans at Gettysburg,* edited by D. L. Valuska and C. B. Keller. Mechanicsburg, PA: Stackpole Books, 2004.

Kernek, C. B. "Civil War Surgery: Gettysburg, Summer of 1863." *Indiana Medicine* 84, no. 12 (Dec. 1991).

Kieffer, H. M. *The Recollections of a Drummer-Boy.* 6th ed. Boston: Ticknor and Co., 1889.

Kohl, L. F., and M. C. Richard (eds.). *Irish Green and Union Blue: The Civil War Letters of Peter Welsh, Color Sergeant, 28th Regiment Massachusetts Volunteers.* New York: Fordham University Press, 1986.

Kutz, M. "Fantasy, Reality, and Modes of Perception in Ludendorff's and Goebbels's Concepts of 'Total War.'" In *A World at Total War: Global Conflict and the Politics of Destruction, 1937–1945,* edited by R. Chickering, S. Förster, and B. Grenier. Cambridge, U.K.: Cambridge University Press, 2005.

Ladd, D. L., and A. J. Ladd (eds.). *The Bachelder Papers: Gettysburg in Their Own Words.* 3 vols. Dayton, OH: Morningside Press, 1994.

Lader, P. J. "The 7th New Jersey in the Gettysburg Campaign." *Gettysburg Magazine* 16 (1997).

———. "The Personal Journey of Pvt. David Ballinger, Company H, 12th New Jersey Volunteers." *Gettysburg Magazine* 24 (2001).

Laidley, T. T. S. "Breech-Loading Musket." *United States Service Magazine* 3 (1865).

Lamb, D. A. *A History of the United States Army Medical Museum, 1862–1917, Compiled From the Official Records.* Unpublished manuscript, 1917.

Laney, D. M. "Wasted Gallantry: Hood's Texas Brigade at Gettysburg." *Gettysburg Magazine* 16 (1997).

Lash, G. G. "'A Pathetic Story': The 141st Pennsylvania (Graham's Brigade) at Gettysburg," *Gettysburg Magazine* 14 (1996).

Lee, A. "Reminiscences of the Gettysburg Battle." *Lippincott's Magazine of Popular Literature and Science* 6 (1883).

Linderman, G. F. *Embattled Courage: The Experience of Combat in the American Civil War.* New York: Free Press, 1989.

Linn, J. B. "A Tourist at Gettysburg." *Civil War Times Illustrated* 29, no. 4 (Sept./Oct. 1990).

Livermore, T. L. *Days and Events, 1860–1866.* Boston: Houghton Mifflin, 1920.

Long, R. "The Confederate Prisoners of Gettysburg." *Gettysburg Magazine* 2 (1990).

———. "A Gettysburg Encounter." *Gettysburg Magazine* 7 (1992).

———. "A Surgeon's Handiwork." *Gettysburg Magazine* 12 (1995).

Longstreet, J. *From Manassas to Appomattox: Memoirs of the Civil War in America.* Philadelphia: J. B. Lippincott, 1896.

Ludendorff, E. *The Nation at War.* Translated by A. S. Rappoport. London: Hutchinson and Co., 1936.

Lynn, J. A. *Battle: A History of Combat and Culture.* Cambridge, MA: Westview, 2003.

MacDonald, W. A. "Gettysburg Holds Greatest Fourth." *New York Times,* July 5, 1938.

Manring, M. M., A. Hawk, J. H. Calhoun, and R. C. Andersen, "Treatment of War Wounds: A Historical Review." *Clinical Orthopaedics and Related Research* 467 (2009).

Marbaker, T. D. *History of the Eleventh New Jersey Volunteers From Its Organization to Appomattox, to Which Is Added Experiences of Prison Life and Sketches of Individual Members.* Trenton, NJ: MacCrellish and Quigley, 1898.

Marshall, S. L. A. *Men Against Fire: The Problem of Battle Command.* Norman: University of Oklahoma Press, 2000 [1947].

Martin, J. M., E. C. Strouss, R. G. Madge, R. I. Campbell, and M. C. Zahniser (eds.). *History of the Fifty-Seventh Regiment, Pennsylvania Veteran Volunteer Infantry.* Meadville, PA: McCoy and Calvin, 1904.

Martz, J. A. "It Was Not a Happy Time: What the Civilians of Gettysburg Saw and Heard During the Battle." *Gettysburg Magazine* 18 (1998).

Marvin, E. E. *The Fifth Regiment Connecticut Volunteers: A History Compiled From Diaries and Official Reports.* Hartford, CT: Wiley, Waterman, and Eaton, 1889.

McLean, W. "The Days of Terror in 1863." *Gettysburg Compiler,* July 1, 1908.

McWhiney, G., and P. D. Jamieson. *Attack and Die: Civil War Military Tactics and the Southern Heritage.* Tuscaloosa: University of Alabama Press, 1982.

Meinhard, R. W. "The First Minnesota at Gettysburg." *Gettysburg Magazine* 5 (1991).

Menke, W. S., and J. A. Shimrak (eds.). *The Civil War Notebook of Daniel Chisholm: A Chronicle of Daily Life in the Union Army, 1864–1865.* New York: Orion Books, 1989.

Miller, J. M. "Perrin's Brigade on July 1, 1863." *Gettysburg Magazine* 13 (1995).

Moore, F. (ed.). *The Civil War in Song and Story, 1860–1865.* New York: P. F. Collier, 1889.

Morgan, W. H. *Personal Reminiscences of the War of 1861–1865.* Lynchburg, VA: J. P. Bell Co., 1911.

Muffly, J. W. (ed.). *The Story of Our Regiment: A History of the 148th Pennsylvania Vols., Written by the Comrades.* Des Moines, IA: Kenyon Printing and Manufacturing Company, 1904.

Mulligan, T. P. "Death of a Secessionist Regiment: The Losses of the 1st Tennessee at Gettysburg." *Gettysburg Magazine* 40 (2009).

Murray, R. L. "The Artillery Duel in the Peach Orchard, July 2, 1863." *Gettysburg Magazine* 36 (2007).

Musgrove, R. W. *Autobiography of Captain Richard W. Musgrove.* 1921.

Musto, R. J. "The Treatment of the Wounded at Gettysburg: Jonathan Letterman: the Father of Modern Battlefield Medicine." *Gettysburg Magazine* 37 (2007).

Nash, E. A. *A History of the Forty-Fourth New York Regiment Volunteer Infantry in the Civil War, 1861–1865.* Chicago: R. R. Donnelley and Sons, 1911.

Neese, G. M. *Three Years in the Confederate Horse Artillery.* New York: Neale Publishing Company, 1911.

Nelson, A. H. *The Battles of Chancellorsville and Gettysburg.* Minneapolis: A. H. Nelson, 1899.

Nevins, A. (ed.). *A Diary of Battle: The Personal Journals of Colonel Charles S. Wainwright, 1861–1865.* New York: Da Capo Press, 1998.

New York Monuments Commission (ed.). *In Memoriam, Alexander Stewart Webb, 1835–1911.* Albany: J. B. Lyon, 1916.

New York State Monuments Commission (ed.). *Final Report on the Battlefield of Gettysburg.* 3 vols. Albany, NY: J. B. Lyon, 1900.

Nicholson, J. P. (ed.). *Pennsylvania at Gettysburg: Ceremonies at the Dedication of the Monuments Erected by the Commonwealth of Pennsylvania to Mark the Positions of the Pennsylvania Commands Engaged in the Battle.* 2 vols. Harrisburg, PA: E. K. Meyers, 1893.

Norton, O. W. *The Attack and Defense of Little Round Top, Gettysburg, July 2, 1863.* New York: Neale Publishing Company, 1913.

Nosworthy, B. *The Bloody Crucible of Courage: Fighting Methods and Combat Experience of the Civil War.* New York: Carroll and Graf, 2003.

———. "The Rifle Musket and Associated Tactics." *North and South* 7, no. 1 (2004).

———. *Roll Call to Destiny: The Soldier's Eye View of Civil War Battles.* New York: Carroll and Graf, 2008.

Oates, W. C. *The War Between the Union and the Confederacy and Its Lost Opportunities, with a History of the 15th Alabama Regiment and the Forty-Eight Battles in Which It Was Engaged.* New York and Washington, DC: Neale Publishing Company, 1905.

O'Brien, K. E. "'A Perfect Roar of Musketry': Candy's Brigade in the Fight for Culp's Hill." *Gettysburg Magazine* 9 (1993).

———. "'To Unflinchingly Face Danger and Death': Carr's Brigade Defends Emmitsburg Road." *Gettysburg Magazine* 12 (1995).

———. "'Hold Them with the Bayonet': De Trobriand's Brigade Defends the Wheatfield." *Gettysburg Magazine* 21 (1999).

Olds, F. A. "Brave Carolinian Who Fell at Gettysburg: How Colonel Henry King Burgwyn Lost His Life." *Southern Historical Society Papers* 36 (1908).

Oliver, J. B., E. F. Hicks, and B. B. Carr. *History of Company E, 20th N.C. Regiment, 1861–'65.* Goldsboro, NC: Nash Brothers, 1905.

Olney, W. "The Battle of Shiloh, with Some Personal Reminiscences." *Overland Monthly* 5 (1885).

Page, C. D. *History of the Fourteenth Regiment, Connecticut Volunteer Infantry.* Meriden, CT: Horton Printing Company, 1906.

Parker, J. L. *Henry Wilson's Regiment: The History of the Twenty-Second Massachusetts Infantry, the Second Company Sharpshooters, and the Third Light Battery, in the War of the Rebellion.* Boston: Regimental Association, 1887.

Patriot Daughters of Lancaster. *Hospital Scenes After the Battle of Gettysburg, July 1863.* Lancaster, PA: Daily Inquirer Steam Job Print, 1864.

Patterson, G. A. "The Death of Iverson's Brigade." *Gettysburg Magazine* 5 (1991).

Peltz, H. S. "Two Brass Buttons." *Gettysburg Compiler,* March 15, 1887.

Pfanz, H. *Gettysburg: Culp's Hill and Cemetery Hill.* Chapel Hill: University of North Carolina Press, 1993.

Pizarro, J., R. C. Silver, and J. Prause. "Physical and Mental Health Costs of Traumatic War Experiences Among Civil War Veterans." *Archives of General Psychiatry* 63 (2006).

Polley, J. B. *Hood's Texas Brigade: Its Marches, Its Battles, Its Achievements*. New York: Neale Publishing Company, 1910.

Preston, N. D. *History of the Tenth Regiment of Cavalry, New York State Volunteers: August, 1861, to August, 1865*. New York: D. Appleton and Co., 1892.

Pula, J. S. "The 26th Wisconsin Volunteer Infantry at Gettysburg." *Gettysburg Magazine* 23 (2000).

———. "The Fifth German Rifles at Gettysburg." *Gettysburg Magazine* 37 (2007).

———. (ed.). *The Memoirs of Wladimir Krzyżanowski*. San Francisco: R & E Research Associates, 1978.

Quinones, M. A. "Drug Abuse During the Civil War (1861–1865)." *International Journal of the Addictions* 10, no. 6 (1975).

Redwood, A. C. "The Confederate in the Field." In *The Photographic History of the Civil War*. 10 vols. New York: Review of Reviews Co., 1911.

Rollins, R. (ed.). *Pickett's Charge: Eyewitness Accounts at the Battle of Gettysburg*. Mechanicsburg, PA: Stackpole Books, 2005.

Rose, A. *American Rifle: A Biography*. New York: Delacorte Press, 2008.

———. "Marksmanship in 1775: Myth or Reality?" *American Rifleman*, July 2010.

Runge, W. H. (ed.). *Four Years in the Confederate Artillery: The Diary of Private Henry Robinson Berkeley*. Chapel Hill: University of North Carolina Press, 1961.

Sauers, R. A. (ed.). *Fighting Them Over: How the Veterans Remembered Gettysburg in the Pages of the National Tribune*. Baltimore: Butternut and Blue, 1998.

Sawyer, F. *A Military History of the 8th Regiment Ohio Vol. Inf'y: Its Battles, Marches, and Army Movements*. Cleveland: Fairbanks and Co., 1881.

Saxton, W. *A Regiment Remembered: The 157th New York Volunteers: From the Diary of Capt. William Saxton*. Cortland, NY: Cortland County Historical Society, 1996.

Schmidt, J. M., and G. R. Hasegawa (eds.). *Years of Change and Suffering: Modern Perspectives on Civil War Medicine*. Roseville, MN: Edinborough Press, 2009.

Scott, R. G. (ed.). *Fallen Leaves: The Civil War Letters of Major Henry Livermore Abbott*. Kent, OH: Kent State University Press, 1991.

Scribner, B. F. *How Soldiers Were Made, or, the War as I Saw It Under Buell, Rosecrans, Thomas, Grant and Sherman*. New Albany, IN: Donohoe and Henneberry, 1887.

Shotwell, M., and C. G. Samito. "An Irish-American at Gettysburg: Capt. James F. McGunnigle and the Ninth Massachusetts Volunteer Infantry." *Gettysburg Magazine* 21 (1999).

Shultz, D. "Benner's Hill: What Value? Andrews' Artillery Battalion and the Heights East of Town." *Gettysburg Magazine* 44 (2011).

Small, A. R. *The Road to Richmond: The Civil War Letters of Major Abner R. Small of the Sixteenth Maine Volunteers*. Edited by H. A. Small. New York: Fordham University Press, 2000.

Smith, J. D. *The History of the Nineteenth Regiment of Maine Volunteer Infantry, 1862–1865*. Minneapolis: Great Western Printing Co., 1909.

Smith, J. E. *A Famous Battery and Its Campaigns, 1861–'64*. Washington, DC: W. H. Lowdermilk and Co., 1892.

Smith, Jr., L. W. *For the Good of the Old North State: A Statistical Study of North Carolina and Army of Northern Virginia at the Battle of Gettysburg*. Society for the Preservation of the 26th Regiment North Carolina Troops, 2005.

Speier, H. "Ludendorff: The German Concept of Total War." In *Makers of Modern Strategy: Military Thought From Machiavelli to Hitler*, edited by E. M. Earle. New York: Atheneum, 1966.

Spisak, E. D. "The 62nd Pennsylvania Volunteer Infantry: A Forgotten Regiment of Distinction." *Gettysburg Magazine* 26 (2002).

Stahl, J. "Pvt. George Matthews of the 87th and 40th New York State Volunteers." *Gettysburg Magazine* 33 (2005).

————. "Pvt. John Wright of the 61st Ohio Infantry." *Gettysburg Magazine* 38 (2008).

Stanley, H. M. *The Autobiography of Sir Henry Morton Stanley.* New York: Houghton Mifflin, 1909.

Stearns, A. C. *Three Years with Company K.* Edited by A. A. Kent. Cranbury, NJ: Associated University Presses, 1976.

Stevens, C. M. *Berdan's United States Sharpshooters in the Army of the Potomac, 1861–1865.* St. Paul, MN: Price-McGill Company, 1892.

Stevens, G. T. *Three Years in the Sixth Corps: A Concise Narrative of Events in the Army of the Potomac, From 1861 to the Close of the Rebellion, April, 1865.* Albany, NY: S. R. Gray, 1866.

Stevens, H. S. *Souvenir of Excursion to Battlefields by the Society of the Fourteenth Connecticut Regiment and Reunion at Antietam, September 1891.* Washington, DC: Gibson, 1893.

Stevens, J. W. *Reminiscences of the Civil War: A Soldier in Hood's Texas Brigade, Army of Northern Virginia.* Hillsboro, TX: Hillsboro Mirror Print, 1902.

Stiles, R. *Four Years Under Marse Robert.* New York: Neale Publishing Co., 1910.

Stillwell, L. *The Story of a Common Soldier; or, Army Life in the Civil War, 1861–1865.* 2nd ed. Kansas City, MO: Franklin Hudson Publishing Co., 1920.

Storch, M., and B. Storch. "'What a Deadly Trap We Were in': Archer's Brigade on July 1, 1863." *Gettysburg Magazine* 6 (1992).

Strachan, H. "On Total War and Modern War." *International History Review* 22, no. 2 (2000).

Survivors' Association. *History of the 118th Pennsylvania Volunteers (Corn Exchange Regiment), From Their First Engagement at Antietam to Appomattox.* Philadelphia: J. L. Smith, 1905.

Sword, W. "Capt. Mckee's Revolver and Capt. Sellers' Sword with Weed's Brigade on Little Round Top." *Gettysburg Magazine* 9 (1993).

————. "An Iron Brigade Captain's Revolver in the Fight on Mcpherson's Ridge." *Gettysburg Magazine* 7 (1992).

————. "Pye's Sword at the Rail Cut." *Gettysburg Magazine* 6 (1992).

————. "Roll of the Dice: Two 24th Michigan Officers Test Their Luck in the Gettysburg Campaign." *Gettysburg Magazine* 21 (1999).

————. "Union Sgt. Isaac W. Barnes: Company E, 125th New York Volunteer Infantry Describes in Vivid Detail the Fighting at Plum Run on July 2, and 'Pickett's Charge' on July 3." *Gettysburg Magazine* 29 (2003).

Taylor, R. *Destruction and Reconstruction: Personal Experiences of the Late War in the United States.* Edinburgh and London: William Blackwood and Sons, 1879.

Taylor, W. H. "Some Experiences of a Confederate Assistant Surgeon." *Transactions of the College of Physicians of Philadelphia* 28 (1906).

Tomasak, P. (ed.). *One Hundred Forty-Third Pennsylvania Volunteer Regiment: Avery Harris Civil War Journal.* Luzerne, PA: Luzerne National Bank, 2000.

————. "The 143rd Pennsylvania Volunteer Regiment in Hell's Firestorm on July 1 at Gettysburg." *Gettysburg Magazine* 38 (2008).

Tompkins, D. A., and A. S. Tompkins, *Company K, Fourteenth South Carolina Volunteers.* Charlotte, NC: Observer Printing and Publishing House, 1897.

446 | BIBLIOGRAPHY

Toombs, S. *New Jersey Troops in the Gettysburg Campaign, June 5 to July 31, 1863.* Orange, NJ: Evening Mail Publishing House, 1888.

Trinque, B. "The Rifle-Musket in the Civil War." *North and South* 11, no. 3 (2009).

Trowbridge, L. S., and F. E. Farnsworth (eds.). *Michigan at Gettysburg: Proceedings Incident to the Dedication of the Michigan Monuments Upon the Battlefield of Gettysburg, June 12th, 1889, Together with a Full Report of the Monument Commission.* Detroit: Winn & Hammond, 1889.

Underwood, G. C. *History of the Twenty-Sixth Regiment of the North Carolina Troops, in the Great War, 1861–'65.* Wilmington, NC: Broadfoot Publishing Company, 1999 [1901].

Urban, B. F. W. "Dreaming on the Conestoga." In "In Their Words: Dreaming on the Conestoga," edited by S. Felton. *Gettysburg Magazine* 37 (2007).

Vautier, J. D. *History of the 88th Pennsylvania Volunteers in the War for the Union, 1861–1865.* Philadelphia: J. B. Lippincott, 1894.

Wade, P. "Untold History Recited at a Meeting of the Regiment in Bridgeport, Conn." *Gettysburg Compiler,* September 22, 1896.

Wagner, A. L. *Organization and Tactics.* 2nd ed. Kansas City, MO: Hudson-Kimberly, 1897.

Wainwright, N. B. (ed.). *A Philadelphia Perspective: The Diary of Sidney George Fisher Covering the Years 1834–1871.* Philadelphia: Historical Society of Pennsylvania, 1967.

Walters, J. B. "General William T. Sherman and Total War." *Journal of Southern History* 14, no. 3 (1948).

———. *Merchant of Terror: General Sherman and Total War.* New York: Bobbs-Merrill Co., 1973.

The War of the Rebellion: A Compilation of the Official Records of the Union and Confederate Armies. 70 vols. in 128 parts. Washington, DC: Government Printing Office, 1880–1901.

Ward, D. A. " 'Sedgwick's Foot Cavalry': The March of the Sixth Corps to Gettysburg." *Gettysburg Magazine* 22 (2000).

Ward, G. W. *History of the Second Pennsylvania Veteran Heavy Artillery (112th Regiment Pennsylvania Volunteers), from 1861 to 1866, including the Provisional Second Penn'a Heavy Artillery.* 2nd ed. Philadelphia: Geo. W. Ward, 1904.

Ward, W. C. "Incidents and Personal Experiences on the Battlefield at Gettysburg." *Confederate Veteran* 8, no. 8 (August 1900).

Warren, H. N. *The Declaration of Independence and War History: Bull Run to the Appomattox.* Buffalo, NY: Courier Co., 1894.

Washburn, G. H. *A Complete Military History and Record of the 108th Regiment N.Y. Vols. From 1862 to 1864, Together with Roster, Letters, Rebel Oaths of Allegiance, Rebel Passes, Reminiscences, Life Sketches, Photographs, Etc., Etc.* Rochester, NY: No publisher, 1894.

Watkins, S. R. *"Co. Aytch," Maury Grays, First Tennessee Regiment; or, a Side Show of the Big Show.* Nashville: Cumberland Presbyterian Publishing House, 1882.

Weigley, R. F. *Towards an American Army: Military Thought From Washington to Marshall.* New York: Columbia University Press, 1962.

Wert, J. D. *Gettysburg: Day Three.* New York: Simon and Schuster, 2001.

Wert, J. H. *A Complete Hand-Book of the Monuments and Indications and Guide to the Positions on the Gettysburg Battlefield.* Harrisburg, PA: R. M. Sturgeon, 1886.

Weygant, C. H. *History of the One Hundred and Twenty-Fourth Regiment, N.Y.S.V.* Newburgh, NY: Journal Printing House, 1877.

Wheeler, R. *Witness to Gettysburg: Inside the Battle That Changed the Course of the Civil War.* Mechanicsburg, PA: Stackpole Books, 2006.

White, D. "Born in the USA: A New World of War." *History Today* 60, no. 6 (June 2010).

Wing, S. *The Soldier's Story: A Personal Narrative of the Life, Army Experiences, and Marvelous Sufferings Since the War of Samuel B. Wing.* Phillips, ME: Phonograph Steam Book and Job Printing, 1898.

Winschel, T. J. "The Colors Are Shrowded in Mystery." *Gettysburg Magazine* 6 (1992).

———. "The Gettysburg Diary of Lieutenant William Peel." *Gettysburg Magazine* 9 (1993).

———. "Heavy Was Their Loss: Joe Davis's Brigade at Gettysburg." *Gettysburg Magazine* 2 (1990).

———. "Posey's Brigade at Gettysburg." *Gettysburg Magazine* 5 (1991).

Woodward, E. M. *Our Campaigns; or, the Marches, Bivouacs, Battles, Incidents of Camp Life and History of Our Regiment During Its Three Years Term of Service.* Philadelphia: John E. Potter, 1865.

Wyckoff, M. "Kershaw's Brigade at Gettysburg." *Gettysburg Magazine* 5 (1991).

Yee, G. "Sharpshooting at Gettysburg." *Gettysburg Magazine* 39 (2008).

Young, A. *The Women and the Crisis: Women of the North in the Civil War.* New York: McDowell, Obolensky, 1959.

IWO JIMA

Alexander, J. H. *Closing In: Marines in the Seizure of Iwo Jima.* Washington, DC: Marine Corps Historical Center, 1994.

———. *Storm Landings: Epic Amphibious Battles in the Central Pacific.* Annapolis, MD: Naval Institute Press, 1997.

Allen, R. E. *The First Battalion of the 28th Marines on Iwo Jima: A Day-by-Day History From Personal Accounts and Official Reports, with Complete Muster Rolls.* Jefferson, NC: McFarland & Co., 1999.

Anon. "Roebling's 'Alligator' for Florida Rescues." *Life,* October 4, 1937.

Averill, G. P. *Mustang: A Combat Marine.* Novato, CA: Presidio Press, 1987.

Bailey, A. W. *Alligators, Buffaloes, and Bushmasters: The History of the Development of the LVT Through World War II.* Washington, DC: History and Museums Division, Headquarters, U.S. Marine Corps, 1986.

Ballendorf, D. A., and M. L. Bartlett. *Pete Ellis: An Amphibious Warfare Prophet, 1880–1923.* Annapolis, MD: Naval Institute Press, 1997.

Bartlett, M. L. (ed.). *Assault From the Sea: Essays on the History of Amphibious Warfare.* Annapolis, MD: Naval Institute Press, 1983.

Bartley, W. S. *Iwo Jima: Amphibious Epic.* Historical Section, Division of Public Information Headquarters, U.S. Marine Corps, 1954.

Bergerud, E. "No Quarter: The Pacific Battlefield." *Historically Speaking* 3, no. 5 (2002).

Berry, H. (ed.). *Semper Fi, Mac: Living Memories of the U.S. Marines in World War II.* New York: Arbor House, 1982.

Boal, M. A. "Field Expedient Armor Modifications to U.S. Armored Vehicles." Unpublished MA thesis. U.S. Army Command and General Staff College, Fort Leavenworth, Kansas, 2006.

Brown, T. M. *Battle Wounds of Iwo Jima.* New York: Vantage Press, 2002.

Burrell, R. S. "Breaking the Cycle of Iwo Jima Mythology: A Strategic Study of Operation Detachment." *Journal of Military History* 68, no. 4 (2004).

———. (ed.). *Crucibles: Selected Readings in U.S. Marine Corps History.* 2nd ed. Bel Air, MD: Academx Publishing Services, 2004.

Cameron, C. M. *American Samurai: Myth, Imagination, and the Conduct of Battle in the First Marine Division, 1941–1951.* Cambridge, U.K.: Cambridge University Press, 1994.

Carter, W. R. *Beans, Bullets, and Black Oil: The Story of Fleet Logistics Afloat in the Pacific During World War II.* Newport, RI: Naval War College Press, 1998 [1953].

Caruso, P. F. *Nightmare on Iwo.* Annapolis, MD: Naval Institute Press, 2001.

Chickering, R., S. Förster, and B. Greiner (eds.). *A World at Total War: Global Conflict and the Politics of Destruction, 1937–1945.* Cambridge, U.K.: Cambridge University Press, 2005.

Clifford, K. J. *Progress and Purpose: A Developmental History of the United States Marine Corps, 1900–1970.* Washington, DC: History and Museums Division Headquarters, United States Marine Corps, 1973.

Cosmas, G. A., and J. Shulimson. "The Culebra Maneuver and the Formation of the U.S. Marine Corps' Advance Base Force, 1913–14." In *Assault From the Sea: Essays on the History of Amphibious Warfare,* edited by M. L. Bartlett. Annapolis, MD: Naval Institute Press, 1983.

Crowder, R. *Iwo Jima Corpsman!: The Bloodiest Battle of the Marine Corps, Written by a Navy Corpsman Attached to the Third Marine Division, 1945.* Tuscaloosa, AL: SEVGO Press, 1988.

Daugherty III, L. J. *Fighting Techniques of a Japanese Infantryman, 1941–1945: Training, Techniques, and Weapons.* St. Paul, MN: MBI Publishing Co., 2002.

———. *Fighting Techniques of a U.S. Marine, 1941–1945: Training, Techniques, and Weapons.* Osceola, WI: MBI Publishing Co., 2000.

Davenport, D. *D-Plus Forever.* New York: Rivercross Publishing, 1993.

Denfield, D. C. *Japanese World War II Fortifications and Other Military Structures in the Central Pacific.* Edited by S. Russell. 3rd ed. Saipan: Northern Mariana Islands Division of Historic Preservation, 2002.

Dower, J. *War Without Mercy: Race and Power in the Pacific War.* New York: Pantheon Books, 1986.

Drea, E. J. *In the Service of the Emperor: Essays on the Imperial Japanese Army.* Lincoln: University of Nebraska, 1998.

———. *Japan's Imperial Army: Its Rise and Fall, 1853–1945.* Lincoln: University of Nebraska, 2009.

———. "Nomonhan: Japanese-Soviet Tactical Combat, 1939." Leavenworth Papers No. 2, Combat Studies Institute, U.S. Army Command and General Staff College, Fort Leavenworth, Kansas, January 1981.

Drez, R. J. (ed.). *Twenty-Five Yards of War: The Extraordinary Courage of Ordinary Men in World War II.* New York: Hyperion, 2001.

Dyer, G. C. *The Amphibians Came to Conquer: The Story of Admiral Richmond Kelly Turner.* 2 vols. Washington, DC: U.S. Government Printing Office, 1972.

Eldridge, R. E., and C. W. Tatum (eds.). *Fighting Spirit: The Memoirs of Major Yoshitaka Horie and the Battle of Iwo Jima.* Annapolis, MD: Naval Institute Press, 2011.

Ellis, E. H. "Advanced Base Operations in Micronesia." Report 712J, Intelligence Section, Division of Operations and Training, U.S. Marine Corps, 1921.

Faller, A. "War Memories Still Fresh." *Effingham Daily News,* March 27, 2009.

Ford, D. " 'The Best Equipped Army in Asia?': U.S. Military Intelligence and the Imperial Japanese Army Before the Pacific War, 1919–41." *International Journal of Intelligence and CounterIntelligence* 21, no. 1 (2007).

———. "Dismantling the 'Lesser Men' and 'Supermen' Myths: U.S. Intelligence on the Imperial Japanese Army After the Fall of the Philippines, Winter 1942 to Spring 1943." *International Journal of Intelligence and CounterIntelligence* 24, no. 4 (2009).

———. "U.S. Assessments of Japanese Ground Warfare Tactics and the Army's Campaigns in the Pacific Theatres, 1943–1945: Lessons Learned and Methods Applied." *War in History* 16, no. 3 (2009).

———. "U.S. Perceptions of Military Culture and the Japanese Army's Performance During the Pacific War." *War and Society* 29, no. 1 (2010).

Gallant, T. G. *The Friendly Dead.* Garden City, NY: Doubleday & Co., 1964.

———. *On Valor's Side.* Garden City, NY: Doubleday & Co., 1963.

Gatchel, T. L. *At the Water's Edge: Defending Against the Modern Amphibious Assault.* Annapolis, MD: Naval Institute Press, 1996.

Goldman, S. D. *Nomonhan 1939: The Red Army's Victory That Shaped World War II.* Annapolis, MD: Naval Institute Press, 2012.

Gordon, J. W. "Thomas Holcomb." In *Commandants of the Marine Corps,* edited by A. R. Millett and J. Shulimson. Annapolis, MD: Naval Institute Press, 2004.

Goudreau, A. A. "Nursing at an Advance Naval Base Hospital During the Iwo Jima Campaign." *American Journal of Nursing* 45, no. 11 (1945).

Grenville, J. A. S., and G. B. Young. *Politics, Strategy, and American Diplomacy: Studies in Foreign Policy, 1873–1917.* New Haven: Yale University Press, 1966.

Hamner, C. H. *Enduring Battle: American Soldiers in Three Wars, 1776–1945.* Lawrence: Kansas University Press, 2011.

Harrison, S. "Skull Trophies of the Pacific War: Transgressive Objects of Remembrance." *Journal of the Royal Anthropological Institute* 12 (2006).

Hayashi, S. *Kogun: The Japanese Army in the Pacific War.* Edited by A. D. Coox. Quantico, VA: Marine Corps Association, 1959 [1951].

Haynes, F., and J. A. Warren, *The Lions of Iwo Jima.* New York: Henry Holt and Co., 2008.

Heitmann, J. A. "The Man Who Won the War: Andrew Jackson Higgins." *Louisiana History* 34, no. 1 (1993).

Henri, R., J. G. Lucas, W. Keyes Breech, D. K. Dempsey, and A. M. Josephy, Jr. *The U.S. Marines on Iwo Jima: By Five Official Marine Combat Writers.* Washington, DC: Infantry Journal, 1945.

Herwig, H. H., and D. F. Trask. "Naval Operations Plans Between Germany and the U.S.A., 1898–1913." In *The War Plans of the Great Powers, 1880–1914,* edited by P. Kennedy. Boston: Allen & Unwin, 1985.

Hess, E. J. *The Union Soldier in Battle: Enduring the Ordeal of Combat.* Lawrence: University Press of Kansas, 1997.

Hoffman, J. T. "The Legacy and Lessons of Iwo Jima." *Marine Corps Gazette* 79, no. 2 (1995).

Hough, F. O., V. E. Ludwig, and H. I. Shaw, Jr. *Pearl Harbor to Guadalcanal: History of U.S. Marine Corps Operations in World War II.* Historical Branch, G-3 Division, U.S. Marine Corps, Washington, DC, 1958.

Hughes, M., and G. Johnson (eds.). *Fanaticism and Conflict in the Modern Age.* New York and London: Frank Cass, 2005.

Huie, W. B. *From Omaha to Okinawa: The Story of the Seabees.* New York: E. P. Dutton & Co., 1945.

Isely, J. A., and P. A. Crowl, *The U.S. Marines and Amphibious War: Its Theory, and Its Practice in the Pacific.* Princeton, NJ: Princeton University Press, 1951.

Jones, Jr., W. D. *Gyrene: The World War II United States Marine.* Shippensburg, PA: White Mane Books, 1998.

Jorgenson, J. "John Haley's Personal Recollection of the Battle of the Wheatfield." *Gettysburg Magazine* 27 (2002).

Josephy, Jr., A. M. *The Long and the Short and the Tall.* Short Hills, NJ: Burford Books, 2000 [1946].

Kelly, A. L. *Battlefire! Combat Stories From World War II*. Lexington: University Press of Kentucky, 1997.

Kennedy, A. D. *The Military Side of Japanese Life*. London, 1924.

Kennedy, P. (ed.). *The War Plans of the Great Powers, 1880–1914*. Boston: Allen & Unwin, 1985.

Kessler, L. S., and E. B. Bart (eds.). *Never in Doubt: Remembering Iwo Jima*. Annapolis, MD: Naval Institute Press, 1999.

Kuzuhara, K. "Operations on Iwo Jima: Utility of Combat Lessons Learned." Paper presented to USA-Japanese Ground Self-Defense Force Military History Exchange, U.S. Army Command and General Staff College, Fort Leavenworth, September 1990.

Laurie, C. D. "The Ultimate Dilemma of Psychological Warfare in the Pacific: Enemies Who Don't Surrender, and GIs Who Don't Take Prisoners." *War and Society* 14, no. 1 (1996).

Leader, R. A. "The Killing Fields of Sulfur Island." *Notre Dame Magazine*, Winter 2002–03.

Levin, D. *From the Battlefield: Dispatches of a World War II Marine*. Annapolis, MD: Naval Institute Press, 1995.

Linderman, G. F. *The World Within War: America's Combat Experience in World War II*. New York: Free Press, 1997.

Lofgren, J. F., (ed.). "Diary of First Lieutenant Sugihara Kinryu: Iwo Jima, January-February 1945." *Journal of Military History* 59, no. 1 (1995).

Lorelli, J. A. *To Foreign Shores: U.S. Amphibious Operations in World War II*. Annapolis, MD: Naval Institute Press, 1995.

Lowe, R. "The Assault on Iwo Jima: Memories." "Company C, 1st Battalion, 23rd Marines" website. Available at www.c123rd.com/our-wwii-marines/lowe-richard/memories, accessed September 14, 2014.

Lucas, J. F., with D. K. Drum. *Indestructible: The Unforgettable Story of a Marine Hero at the Battle of Iwo Jima*. New York: Da Capo Press, 2006.

Maiden, R. F. *Return to Iwo Jima + 50*. Xlibris, 2000.

Marquand, J. P. "Iwo Jima Before H-hour." *Harper's Magazine*, May 1945.

Matthews, A. R. *The Assault*. New York: Simon and Schuster, 1947.

McConnell, W. W. "How One Squad Fared on Iwo Jima." *Marine Corps Gazette* 93, no. 2 (Feb. 2009). Online version.

McKinney, L. L. *Portable Flame Thrower Operations in World War II*. Washington, DC: Historical Office, Chemical Corps, 1949.

McLaughlin, Jr., H. N., and R. C. Miller. *From the Volcano to the Gorge: Getting the Job Done on Iwo Jima*. Kindle edition. Standish, ME: Tower Publishing, 2010.

McMillan, G. *The Old Breed: A History of the First Marine Division in World War II*. Washington, DC: Infantry Journal Press, 1949.

Millett, A. R. *Semper Fidelis: The History of the United States Marine Corps*. New York: Free Press, 1991.

Millett, A. R., and W. Murray (eds.). *Military Effectiveness: The Second World War*. Cambridge, U.K.: Cambridge University Press, 2010.

Millett, A. R., and J. Shulimson (eds.). *Commandants of the Marine Corps*. Annapolis, MD: Naval Institute Press, 2004.

Mountcastle, J. W. "From Bayou to Beachhead: The Marines and Mr. Higgins." *Military Review* 60, no. 3 (1980).

Moy, T. *War Machines: Transforming Technologies in the U.S. Military, 1920–1940*. College Station: Texas A&M University Press, 2001.

Murray, W., and A. R. Millett (eds.). *Military Innovation in the Interwar Period.* Cambridge, U.K.: Cambridge University Press, 1996.

Nations, G. W. "Iwo Jima—One Man Remembers." Available at www.iwojima-onemanremembers.com/Iwo_Jima-One_Man_Remembers.htm, accessed September 16, 2015.

Neiman, R. M., and K. W. Estes. *Tanks on the Beaches: A Marine Tanker in the Pacific War.* College Station: Texas A&M University Press, 2003.

Norton, B. N., and L. Maffioli. *Grown Gray in War: The Len Maffioli Story.* Annapolis, MD: Naval Institute Press, 1997.

O'Donnell, P. K. *Into the Rising Sun: In Their Own Words, World War II's Pacific Veterans Reveal the Heart of Combat.* New York: Free Press, 2002.

O'Sheel, P., and G. Cook (eds.). *Semper Fidelis: The U.S. Marines in the Pacific, 1942–1945.* New York: William Sloane Associates, 1947.

Price, N., and R. Knecht. "Peleliu 1944: The Archaeology of a South Pacific D-Day." *Journal of Conflict Archaeology* 7, no. 1 (2012).

Renzi, W. A., and M. D. Roehrs. *Never Look Back: A History of World War II in the Pacific.* Armonk, NY: M. E. Sharpe, 1991.

Report by Intelligence Staffs of CINCPAC-CINCPOA, Fleet Marine Force, V Amphibious Corps, 3rd, 4th, and 5th Marine Divisions. *Defense Installations on Iwo Jima.* Bulletin 136–45, June 10, 1945.

Report by Joint Intelligence Center, Pacific Ocean Area. "Iwo Jima Operation, February–March 1945." Map NH-104136, March 1945.

Roan, R. W. "Roebling's Amphibian: The Origin of the Assault Amphibian." Command and Staff College Education Center, Marine Corps Development and Education Command, Quantico, VA, 1987.

Rodriguez, A. W. "The Battle for Iwo Jima." "Company C, 1st Battalion, 23rd Marines" website. Available at www.c123rd.com/our-wwii-marines/rodriguez-arthur-w-rod/the-battle-for-iwo-jima, accessed September 14, 2014.

Rottman, G. L., and P. Dennis. *U.S. World War II Amphibious Tactics: Army and Marine Corps, Pacific Theater.* New York: Osprey Publishing, 2004.

Rottman, G. L., and I. Palmer. *Japanese Pacific Island Defenses, 1941–45.* Oxford, U.K.: Osprey Publishing, 2003.

Rowe, G. "Memories." "Company C, 1st Battalion, 23rd Marines" website. Available at www.c123rd.com/our-wwii-marines/rowe-guy/memories, accessed September 14, 2014.

Sauers, K. A. (ed.) *Fighting Them Over: How the Veterans Remembered Gettysburg in the Pages of the National Tribune.* Baltimore: Butternut and Blue, 1998.

Seebohm, H. "On the Birds of the Volcano Islands." *The Ibis* 3, no. 10 (1891).

Sherrod, R. *On to Westward: War in the Central Pacific.* New York: Duell, Sloan, and Pearce, 1945.

Shiveley, J. C. *The Last Lieutenant: A Foxhole View of the Epic Battle for Iwo Jima.* Bloomington and Indianapolis: Indiana University Press, 2006.

Showalter, D. "War to the Knife: The U.S. in the Pacific, 1941–1945." Address to the National Institute for Defense Studies, Tenth Forum, "The Pacific War as Total War," 2011.

Shulimson, J., and G. A. Cosmas. "Teddy Roosevelt and the Corps' Sea-Going Mission." In *Crucibles: Selected Readings in U.S. Marine Corps History,* edited by R. S. Burrell. 2nd ed. Bel Air, MD: Academx Publishing Services, 2004.

Simpson, R. W. "Iwo Jima: A Surgeon's Story." *Leatherneck,* February 1990. Online version.

Smith, H. M. *The Development of Amphibious Tactics in the U.S. Navy.* History and Museums Division Headquarters, U.S. Marine Corps, Washington, DC, 1992.

Smith, L. (ed.). *Iwo Jima: World War II Veterans Remember the Greatest Battle of the Pacific.* New York: W. W. Norton & Co., 2008.

Smith, S. E. (ed.). *The United States Marine Corps in World War II: The One-Volume History, From Wake to Tsingtao—by the Men Who Fought in the Pacific, and by Distinguished Marine Experts, Authors, and Newspapermen.* New York: Random House, 1969.

Stone, A. R. *A Marine Remembers Iwo Jima: Dog Company, 2nd Battalion, 27th Marines, Fifth Marine Division.* Austin, TX: Eakin Press, 2000.

Stouffer, R. A., A. A. Lumsdaine, M. H. Lumsdaine, R. M. Williams, Jr., M. B. Smith, I. L. Janis, S. A. Star, and L. S. Cottrell, Jr. (eds.). *The American Soldier: Studies in Social Psychology in World War II.* 4 vols. Princeton, NJ: Princeton University Press, 1949–50.

Straus, U. *The Anguish of Surrender: Japanese POWs of World War II.* Seattle: University of Washington Press, 2003.

Thompson, P. W., H. Doud, J. Scofield, and M. A. Hill (eds.). *How the Jap Army Fights.* New York and London: Penguin Books, 1942.

Thurman, J. R. *We Were in the First Waves of Steel Amtracs Who Landed on Iwo Jima.* Kindle edition. Bloomington, IN: AuthorHouse, 2009.

Torok, T. *Stepping Stones Across the Pacific: A Collection of Short Stories from the Pacific War.* CreateSpace, 1999; no pub., 2011 edition.

Toyn, G. W. *The Quiet Hero: The Untold Medal of Honor Story of George E. Wahlen at the Battle for Iwo Jima.* Clearfield, UT: American Legacy Media, 2006.

Tsuyoshi, H. Review of "Nomonhan: Japan Against Russia, 1939, by Alvin D. Coox." *Journal of Japanese Studies* 13, no. 2 (1987).

Turk, R. W. "The United States Navy and the 'Taking' of Panama, 1901–03." *Military Affairs* 38, no. 3 (1974).

Vedder, J. S. *Surgeon on Iwo: Up Front with the 27th Marines.* Novato, CA: Presidio Press, 1984.

Walker, M. F., and B. White. *Preparing for the Rain on Iwo Jima Isle: The True Story of the Battle of Iwo Jima Survivor, Marion Frank Walker, Corporal, United States Marine Corps.* Kindle edition. Bloomington, IN: AuthorHouse, 2009.

Weingartner, J. J. "Trophies of War: U.S. Troops and the Mutilation of Japanese War Dead, 1941–1945." *Pacific Historical Review* 61, no. 1 (1992).

Wheeler, K. "The Story of a Man's Face." *Life,* December 8, 1961.

———. *We Are the Wounded.* New York: E. P. Dutton & Co., 1945.

Wheeler, R. *Iwo.* New York: Lippincott & Crowell, 1980.

Willie, C. E. *African American Voices from Iwo Jima.* Jefferson, NC: McFarland & Co., 2010.

Yaffe, B. A. *Fragments of War: A Marine's Personal Journey.* Annapolis, MD: Naval Institute Press, 1999.

Video

Iwo Jima: Red Blood, Black Sand. Spectrum Films, 1995.

Iwo Jima—36 Days of Hell. Timeless Media Group Production, 2006.

Transcripts

Interview with Brigadier General W. W. Buchanan, by B. M. Frank, June 11 and 16, 1969.

Interview with General R. E. Hogaboom, by B. M. Frank, April 1–3 and 8, 1970, no. 813.

Interview with Brigadier General F. Karch, by J. Ringler, January 15, 1972, no. 1072.

Interview with Brigadier General W. W. Rogers, by L. E. Tatem, June 15, 22, and 24, 1969, no. 740.

Interview with Lieut. General T. Wornham, by B. M. Frank, February 23, 1967 and April 2, 1968, no. 717.

All transcripts available at the Marine Corps Oral History Program, Columbia University Oral History Research Office (ORHO), Columbia University, New York City.

Index

trail hand-spikes, 186
  trembling ground from, 134, 144–45,
    146–47
artillery at Iwo Jima
  barrage compared to Saipan and Tinian,
    241
  clustering of men and casualties, 236,
    238
  confirmed destruction by U.S., 230
  Japanese, 220, 222, 237, 245–46, 314,
    315, 316, 318, 322, 329
  Japanese range markers, 237
  random nature of hits, 241
  rolling barrages, 245–46
  sounds and shock waves, 229, 239–40
  trembling of the ground, 241–42
  U.S. Marine Corps, 220, 317
  U.S. Navy bombardment, 219, 225,
    229–30, 231, 245–46, 316, 317
Attu Island, battle of, 418n5
Auden, D. H., 9
Aughinbaugh, Nellie, 203
Averill, Gerald, 226–27, 234, 256, 277–78,
  279, 291, 325, 327–28
Aylesworth, Edwin, 180

B-29 Superfortress, 218–19
Babcock, Lt. Willis, 197
Bachman, Cpt. Carl, 282
Bailey, Dr., 201
Baker, Sgt., 143
Baldwin, Cpt. Isaac, 46
Ballinger, Pvt. David, 166
Balog, Lou, 349–50
Bancroft, Cpt. Ebenezer, 27, 79–80, 82,
  86–87
Barber, G. E., 338, 339, 343
Barber, Lucius, 155
Barker, John, 90, 103–4
Barnes, Sgt. Isaac, 156
Barr, Aaron, 28
Barrett, Robin, 284
Barrett, Col. Thomas, 43–44
Barziza, Cpt. Decimus et Ultimus, 202
Bassett, Isaac, 374n75
Bates, Lt. Wesley, 254, 331
battle, 292
  accounts, variations in, 71–77, 359
  as addictive, 74

adrenaline and, 73, 74, 91, 183, 190,
  242, 265, 294
alcohol and, 244
behavior before a charge, 154–55, 157,
  164, 396n4
being "out of phase," 289
Civil War beliefs about, 283
combat as anisotropic, 71, 359
combat narcosis, 182–83
critical moment (fight or flight), 177–80
"dead-line," 178
debris left by, 191
defecating and urinating during, 255–56
fatigue following, 91–92, 188, 189
filthy body and clothes, 286, 288, 358,
  423n5
freezing under fire, 74, 238, 242, 291,
  294, 328
grace under fire, 179
heroics, 264–65, 306
inexperienced men, 288–90
Iwo Jima, nightly routine, 254
Iwo Jima, replacements and, 286–90
limited perceptions of, 71
loss of orientation and time, 276–78
luck and, 241
maps' illusory qualities and, 70
memory loss and, 276–77
music and, 161
"official version," 74–75
paintings of, 103
pre-combat checking of equipment, 164,
  225–26, 357
psychiatric damage from, 101–5, 153,
  207–12, 265–66, 272–77, 291, 349–
  54
psychological and physiological responses
  to, 72–74, 91–92, 145–46, 188–89,
  242–43, 265–66, 271, 286, 291, 358,
  392n4
reality of close combat, 75–76
recklessness and brave foolhardiness,
  282
return to normal following, 189–91
sensory distortions and, 72–73, 278
smoking cigarettes and, 257
soldiers lack of clarity about, 70
sounds of, 161, 164, 167, 175, 182,
  241–42, 245

PHOTO: © REBECCA ROSE

Alexander Rose is the author of *Washington's Spies: The Story of America's First Spy Ring*, upon which the AMC drama series *Turn* is based, as well as *American Rifle: A Biography*.

www.alexrose.com
www.facebook.com/Alex.Rose.Writer
@AlexRoseWriter

About the Type

This book was set in Garamond, a typeface originally designed by the Parisian type cutter Claude Garamond (c. 1500–61). This version of Garamond was modeled on a 1592 specimen sheet from the Egenolff-Berner foundry, which was produced from types assumed to have been brought to Frankfurt by the punch cutter Jacques Sabon (c. 1520–80).

Claude Garamond's distinguished romans and italics first appeared in *Opera Ciceronis* in 1543–44. The Garamond types are clear, open, and elegant.

THE MODERN LIBRARY
of the World's Best Books

JOHN KEATS

PERCY BYSSHE SHELLEY

>>>

>>>

JOHN KEATS
AND
PERCY BYSSHE SHELLEY
COMPLETE POETICAL WORKS

>>>

WITH THE EXPLANATORY NOTES
OF SHELLEY'S POEMS BY MRS. SHELLEY

>>>

BENNETT A. CERF · DONALD S. KLOPFER
THE MODERN LIBRARY
NEW YORK

THE MODERN LIBRARY

IS PUBLISHED BY

RANDOM HOUSE, INC.

BENNETT A. CERF • DONALD S. KLOPFER • ROBERT K. HAAS

Manufactured in the United States of America
Printed by Parkway Printing Company   *Bound by H. Wolff*

CONTENTS

▼

POEMS
PUBLISHED IN 1817

DEDICATION

TO LEIGH HUNT, ESQ.

GLORY and loveliness have pass'd away;
    For if we wander out in early morn,
    No wreathed incense do we see upborne
Into the east, to meet the smiling day:
No crowd of nymphs soft voic'd and young, and gay,   5
    In woven baskets bringing ears of corn,
    Roses, and pinks, and violets, to adorn
The shrine of Flora in her early May.
But there are left delights as high as these,
    And I shall ever bless my destiny,
That in a time, when under pleasant trees
    Pan is no longer sought, I feel a free,
A leafy luxury, seeing I could please
    With these poor offerings, a man like thee.

POEMS

"Places of nestling green for Poets made."
Story of Rimini.

I STOOD tip-toe upon a little hill,
The air was cooling, and so very still,
That the sweet buds which with a modest pride
Pull droopingly, in slanting curve aside,
Their scantly leav'd, and finely tapering stems,
Had not yet lost those starry diadems
Caught from the early sobbing of the morn.
The clouds were pure and white as flocks new shorn,
And fresh from the clear brook; sweetly they slept
On the blue fields of heaven, and then there crept   10
A little noiseless noise among the leaves,
Born of the very sigh that silence heaves:
For not the faintest motion could be seen
Of all the shades that slanted o'er the green.
There was wide wand'ring for the greediest eye,
To peer about upon variety;
Far round the horizon's crystal air to skim,
And trace the dwindled edgings of its brim;
To picture out the quaint, and curious bending
Of a fresh woodland alley, never ending;   20
Or by the bowery clefts, and leafy shelves,
Guess where the jaunty streams refresh themselves.
I gazed awhile, and felt as light, and free
As though the fanning wings of Mercury
Had play'd upon my heels: I was light-hearted,
And many pleasures to my vision started;
So I straightway began to pluck a posey
Of luxuries bright, milky, soft and rosy.

A bush of May flowers with the bees about them;
Ah, sure no tasteful nook would be without them;   30
And let a lush laburnum oversweep them,
And let long grass grow round the roots to keep them
Moist, cool and green; and shade the violets,
That they may bind the moss in leafy nets.
A filbert hedge with wild briar overtwined,
And clumps of woodbine taking the soft wind

Upon their summer thrones; there too should be
The frequent chequer of a youngling tree,
That with a score of light green brethren shoots
From the quaint mossiness of aged roots: 40
Round which is heard a spring-head of clear waters
Babbling so wildly of its lovely daughters
The spreading blue-bells: it may haply mourn
That such fair clusters should be rudely torn
From their fresh beds, and scattered thoughtlessly
By infant hands, left on the path to die.

Open afresh your round of starry folds,
Ye ardent marigolds!
Dry up the moisture from your golden lids,
For great Apollo bids   50
That in these days your praises should be sung
On many harps, which he has lately strung;
And when again your dewiness he kisses,
Tell him, I have you in my world of blisses:
So haply when I rove in some far vale,
His mighty voice may come upon the gale.

Here are sweet peas, on tip-toe for a flight:
With wings of gentle flush o'er delicate white,
And taper fingers catching at all things,
To bind them all about with tiny rings.   60

Linger awhile upon some bending planks
That lean against a streamlet's rushy banks,
And watch intently Nature's gentle doings:
They will be found softer than ring-dove's cooings.
How silent comes the water round that bend;
Not the minutest whisper does it send
To the o'erhanging sallows: blades of grass
Slowly across the chequer'd shadows pass.

Why, you might read two sonnets, ere they reach
To where the hurrying freshnesses aye preach   70
A natural sermon o'er their pebbly beds;
Where swarms of minnows show their little heads,
Staying their wavy bodies 'gainst the streams,
To taste the luxury of sunny beams
Temper'd with coolness. How they ever wrestle
With their own sweet delight, and ever nestle
Their silver bellies on the pebbly sand.
If you but scantily hold out the hand,
That very instant not one will remain;

But turn your eye, and they are there again.   80
The ripples seem right glad to reach those cresses,
And cool themselves among the em'rald tresses;
The while they cool themselves, they freshness give,
And moisture, that the bowery green may live:
So keeping up an interchange of favours,
Like good men in the truth of their behaviours.
Sometimes goldfinches one by one will drop
From low hung branches; little space they stop;
But sip, and twitter, and their feathers sleek;
Then off at once, as in a wanton freak: 90
Or perhaps, to show their black, and golden wings,
Pausing upon their yellow flutterings.
Were I in such a place, I sure should pray
That naught less sweet, might call my thoughts away,
Than the soft rustle of a maiden's gown
Fanning away the dandelion's down;
Than the light music of her nimble toes
Patting against the sorrel as she goes.
How she would start, and blush, thus to be caught
Playing in all her innocence of thought.   100
O let me lead her gently o'er the brook,
Watch her half-smiling lips, and downward look;
O let me for one moment touch her wrist;
Let me one moment to her breathing list;
And as she leaves me may she often turn
Her fair eyes looking through her locks auburne.
What next? A tuft of evening primroses,
O'er which the mind may hover till it dozes;
O'er which it well might take a pleasant sleep,
But that 'tis ever startled by the leap   110
Of buds into ripe flowers; or by the flitting
Of diverse moths, that aye their rest are quitting;
Or by the moon lifting her silver rim
Above a cloud, and with a gradual swim
Coming into the blue with all her light.
O Maker of sweet poets, dear delight
Of this fair world, and all its gentle livers;
Spangler of clouds, halo of crystal rivers,
Mingler with leaves, and dew and tumbling streams,
Closer of lovely eyes to lovely dreams,   120
Lover of loneliness, and wandering,
Of upcast eye, and tender pondering!
Thee must I praise above all other glories
That smile us on to tell delightful stories.
For what has made the sage or poet write
But the fair paradise of Nature's light?

In the calm grandeur of a sober line,
We see the waving of the mountain pine;
And when a tale is beautifully staid,
We feel the safety of a hawthorn glade: 130
When it is moving on luxurious wings,
The soul is lost in pleasant smotherings:
Fair dewy roses brush against our faces,
And flowering laurels spring from diamond vases;
O'er head we see the jasmine and sweet briar,
And bloomy grapes laughing from green attire;
While at our feet, the voice of crystal bubbles
Charms us at once away from all our troubles:
So that we feel uplifted from the world,
Walking upon the white clouds wreath'd and curl'd.
So felt he, who first told, how Psyche went   141
On the smooth wind to realms of wonderment;
What Psyche felt, and Love, when their full lips
First touch'd; what amorous, and fondling nips
They gave each other's cheeks; with all their sighs,
And how they kist each other's tremulous eyes:
The silver lamp,—the ravishment,—the wonder—
The darkness,—loneliness,—the fearful thunder;
Their woes gone by, and both to heaven upflown,
To bow for gratitude before Jove's throne.   150
So did he feel, who pull'd the boughs aside,
That we might look into a forest wide,
To catch a glimpse of Fauns, and Dryades
Coming with softest rustle through the trees;
And garlands woven of flowers wild, and sweet,
Upheld on ivory wrists, or sporting feet:
Telling us how fair, trembling Syrinx fled
Arcadian Pan, with such a fearful dread.
Poor nymph,—poor Pan,—how he did weep to find,
Naught but a lovely sighing of the wind   160
Along the reedy stream; a half-heard strain,
Full of sweet desolation—balmy pain.

What first inspired a bard of old to sing
Narcissus pining o'er the untainted spring?
In some delicious ramble, he had found
A little space, with boughs all woven round;
And in the midst of all, a clearer pool
Than e'er reflected in its pleasant cool,
The blue sky here, and there, serenely peeping
Through tendril wreaths fantastically creeping.   170
And on the bank a lonely flower he spied,
A meek and forlorn flower, with naught of pride,

Drooping its beauty o'er the watery clearness,
To woo its own sad image into nearness:
Deaf to light Zephyrus it would not move;
But still would seem to droop, to pine, to love.
So while the poet stood in this sweet spot,
Some fainter gleamings o'er his fancy shot;
Nor was it long ere he had told the tale
Of young Narcissus, and sad Echo's bale.   180

Where had he been, from whose warm head out-flew
That sweetest of all songs, that ever new,
That aye refreshing, pure deliciousness,
Coming ever to bless
The wanderer by moonlight? to him bringing
Shapes from the invisible world, unearthly singing
From out the middle air, from flowery nests,
And from the pillowy silkiness that rests
Full in the speculation of the stars.
Ah! surely he had burst our mortal bars;   190
Into some wond'rous region he had gone,
To search for thee, divine Endymion!

He was a Poet, sure a lover too,
Who stood on Latmus' top, what time there blew
Soft breezes from the myrtle vale below;
And brought in faintness solemn, sweet, and slow
A hymn from Dian's temple; while upswelling,
The incense went to her own starry dwelling.
But though her face was clear as infant's eyes,
Though she stood smiling o'er the sacrifice,   200
The Poet wept at her so piteous fate,
Wept that such beauty should be desolate:
So in fine wrath some golden sounds he won,
And gave meek Cynthia her Endymion.

Queen of the wide air; thou most lovely queen
Of all the brightness that mine eyes have seen!
As thou exceedest all things in thy shine,
So every tale, does this sweet tale of thine.
O for three words of honey, that I might
Tell but one wonder of thy bridal night!   210

Where distant ships do seem to show their keels,
Phoebus awhile delay'd his mighty wheels,
And turn'd to smile upon thy bashful eyes,
Ere he his unseen pomp would solemnize.
The evening weather was so bright, and clear,

That men of health were of unusual cheer;
Stepping like Homer at the trumpet's call,
Or young Apollo on the pedestal:
And lovely women were as fair and warm,
As Venus looking sideways in alarm.   220
The breezes were ethereal, and pure,
And crept through half-closed lattices to cure
The languid sick; it cool'd their fever'd sleep,
And soothed them into slumbers full and deep.
Soon they awoke clear eyed: nor burnt with thirsting,
Nor with hot fingers, nor with temples bursting:
And springing up, they met the wond'ring sight
Of their dear friends, nigh foolish with delight;
Who feel their arms, and breasts, and kiss and stare,
And on their placid foreheads part the hair.   230
Young men, and maidens at each other gaz'd
With hands held back, and motionless, amaz'd
To see the brightness in each other's eyes;
And so they stood, fill'd with a sweet surprise,
Until their tongues were loos'd in poesy.
Therefore no lover did of anguish die:
But the soft numbers, in that moment spoken,
Made silken ties, that never may be broken.
Cynthia! I cannot tell the greater blisses,
That follow'd thine, and thy dear shepherd's kisses: 240
Was there a poet born?—but now no more,
My wand'ring spirit must no further soar.—

SPECIMEN OF AN INDUCTION TO A POEM

Lo! I must tell a tale of chivalry;
For large white plumes are dancing in mine eye.
Not like the formal crest of latter days:
But bending in a thousand graceful ways;
So graceful, that it seems no mortal hand,
Or e'en the touch of Archimago's wand,
Could charm them into such an attitude.
We must think rather, that in playful mood,
Some mountain breeze had turn'd its chief delight,
To show this wonder of its gentle might.   10
Lo! I must tell a tale of chivalry;
For while I muse, the lance points slantingly
Athwart the morning air: some lady sweet,
Who cannot feel for cold her tender feet,
From the worn top of some old battlement
Hails it with tears, her stout defender sent:

And from her own pure self no joy dissembling,
Wraps round her ample robe with happy trembling.
Sometimes, when the good Knight his rest would take,
It is reflected, clearly, in a lake,   20
With the young ashen boughs, 'gainst which it rests,
And th' half seen mossiness of linnets' nests.
Ah! shall I ever tell its cruelty,
When the fire flashes from a warrior's eye,
And his tremendous hand is grasping it,
And his dark brow for very wrath is knit?
Or when his spirit, with more calm intent,
Leaps to the honors of a tournament,
And makes the gazers round about the ring
Stare at the grandeur of the ballancing?   30
No, no! this is far off:—then how shall I
Revive the dying tones of minstrelsy,
Which linger yet about long gothic arches,
In dark green ivy, and among wild larches?
How sing the splendour of the revelries,
When butts of wine are drunk off to the lees?
And that bright lance, against the fretted wall,
Beneath the shade of stately banneral,
Is slung with shining cuirass, sword, and shield?
Where ye may see a spur in bloody field.   40
Light-footed damsels move with gentle paces
Round the wide hall, and show their happy faces;
Or stand in courtly talk by fives and sevens:
Like those fair stars that twinkle in the heavens.
Yet must I tell a tale of chivalry:
Or wherefore comes that steed so proudly by?
Wherefore more proudly does the gentle knight,
Rein in the swelling of his ample might?

Spenser! thy brows are arched, open, kind,
And come like a clear sun-rise to my mind;   50
And always does my heart with pleasure dance,
When I think on thy noble countenance:
Where never yet was aught more earthly seen
Than the pure freshness of thy laurels green.
Therefore, great bard, I not so fearfully
Call on thy gentle spirit to hover nigh
My daring steps: or if thy tender care,
Thus startled unaware,
Be jealous that the foot of other wight
Should madly follow that bright path of light   60
Trac'd by thy lov'd Libertas; he will speak,
And tell thee that my prayer is very meek;

That I will follow with due reverence,
And start with awe at mine own strange pretence.
Him thou wilt hear; so I will rest in hope
To see wide plains, fair trees and lawny slope:
The morn, the eve, the light, the shade, the flowers;
Clear streams, smooth lakes, and overlooking towers.

CALIDORE

A FRAGMENT

YOUNG Calidore is paddling o'er the lake;
His healthful spirit eager and awake
To feel the beauty of a silent eve,
Which seem'd full loth this happy world to leave;
The light dwelt o'er the scene so lingeringly.
He bares his forehead to the cool blue sky,
And smiles at the far clearness all around,
Until his heart is well nigh over wound,
And turns for calmness to the pleasant green
Of easy slopes, and shadowy trees that lean   10
So elegantly o'er the waters' brim
And show their blossoms trim.
Scarce can his clear and nimble eye-sight follow
The freaks, and dartings of the black-wing'd swallow,
Delighting much, to see it half at rest,
Dip so refreshingly its wings, and breast
'Gainst the smooth surface, and to mark anon,
The widening circles into nothing gone.

And now the sharp keel of his little boat
Comes up with ripple, and with easy float,   20
And glides into a bed of water lillies:
Broad leav'd are they and their white canopies
Are upward turn'd to catch the heavens' dew.
Near to a little island's point they grew;
Whence Calidore might have the goodliest view
Of this sweet spot of earth. The bowery shore
Went off in gentle windings to the hoar
And light blue mountains: but no breathing man
With a warm heart, and eye prepared to scan
Nature's clear beauty, could pass lightly by   30
Objects that look'd out so invitingly
On either side. These, gentle Calidore
Greeted, as he had known them long before.
The sidelong view of swelling leafiness,

Which the glad setting sun, in gold doth dress;
Whence ever, and anon the jay outsprings,
And scales upon the beauty of its wings.
The lonely turret, shatter'd, and outworn,
Stands venerably proud; too proud to mourn
Its long lost grandeur: fir trees grow around,   40
Aye dropping their hard fruit upon the ground.
The little chapel with the cross above
Upholding wreaths of ivy; the white dove,
That on the window spreads his feathers light,
And seems from purple clouds to wing its flight.
Green tufted islands casting their soft shades
Across the lake; sequester'd leafy glades,
That through the dimness of their twilight show
Large dock leaves, spiral foxgloves, or the glow
Of the wild cat's eyes, or the silvery stems   50
Of delicate birch trees, or long grass which hems
A little brook. The youth had long been viewing
These pleasant things, and heaven was bedewing
The mountain flowers, when his glad senses caught
A trumpet's silver voice. Ah! it was fraught
With many joys for him: the warder's ken
Had found white coursers prancing in the glen:
Friends very dear to him he soon will see;
So pushes off his boat most eagerly,
And soon upon the lake he skims along,   60
Deaf to the nightingale's first under-song;
Nor minds he the white swans that dream so sweetly:
His spirit flies before him so completely.

And now he turns a jutting point of land,
Whence may be seen the castle gloomy, and grand:
Nor will a bee buzz round two swelling peaches,
Before the point of his light shallop reaches
Those marble steps that through the water dip:
Now over them he goes with hasty trip,
And scarcely stays to ope the folding doors: 70
Anon he leaps along the oaken floors
Of halls and corridors.
Delicious sounds! those little bright-eyed things
That float about the air on azure wings,
Had been less heartfelt by him than the clang
Of clattering hoofs; into the court he sprang,
Just as two noble steeds, and palfreys twain,
Were slanting out their necks with loosened rein;
While from beneath the threat'ning portcullis
They brought their happy burthens. What a kiss,   80

What gentle squeeze he gave each lady's hand!
How tremblingly their delicate ankles spann'd!
Into how sweet a trance his soul was gone,
While whisperings of affection
Made him delay to let their tender feet
Come to the earth; with an incline so sweet
From their low palfreys o'er his neck they bent:
And whether there were tears of languishment,
Or that the evening dew had pearl'd their tresses
He feels a moisture on his cheek, and blesses   90
With lips that tremble, and with glistening eye,
All the soft luxury
That nestled in his arms. A dimpled hand,
Fair as some wonder out of fairy land,
Hung from his shoulder like the drooping flowers
Of whitest Cassia, fresh from summer showers:
And this he fondled with his happy cheek
As if for joy he would no further seek;
When the kind voice of good Sir Clerimond
Came to his ear, like something from beyond   100
His present being; so he gently drew
His warm arms, thrilling now with pulses new,
From their sweet thrall, and forward meekly bending,
Thank'd heaven that his joy was never ending;
While 'gainst his forehead he devoutly press'd
A hand heaven made to succour the distress'd:
A hand that from the world's bleak promontory
Had lifted Calidore for deeds of Glory.

Amid the pages, and the torches' glare,
There stood a knight, patting the flowing hair   110
Of his proud horse's mane: he was withal
A man of elegance, and stature tall:
So that the waving of his plumes would be
High as the berries of a wild ash tree,
Or as the winged cap of Mercury.
His armour was so dexterously wrought
In shape, that sure no living man had thought
It hard, and heavy steel: but that indeed
It was some glorious form, some splendid weed,
In which a spirit new come from the skies   120
Might live, and show itself to human eyes.
'Tis the far-fam'd, the brave Sir Gondibert,
Said the good man to Calidore alert;
While the young warrior with a step of grace
Came up,—a courtly smile upon his face,
And mailed hand held out, ready to greet

The large-eyed wonder, and ambitious heat
Of the aspiring boy; who as he led
Those smiling ladies, often turn'd his head
To admire the visor arch'd so gracefully   130
Over a knightly brow; while they went by
The lamps that from the high roof'd hall were pendent,
And gave the steel a shining quite transcendent.

Soon in a pleasant chamber they are seated;
The sweet-lipp'd ladies have already greeted
All the green leaves that round the window clamber,
To show their purple stars, and bells of amber.
Sir Gondibert has doff'd his shining steel,
Gladdening in the free, and airy feel
Of a light mantle; and while Clerimond   140
Is looking round about him with a fond,
And placid eye, young Calidore is burning
To hear of knightly deeds, and gallant spurning
Of all unworthiness; and how the strong of arm
Kept off dismay, and terror, and alarm
From lovely women: while brimful of this,
He gave each damsel's hand so warm a kiss,
And had such manly ardour in his eye,
That each at other look'd half staringly;
And then their features started into smiles   150
Sweet as blue heavens o'er enchanted isles.

Softly the breezes from the forest came,
Softly they blew aside the taper's flame;
Clear was the song from Philomel's far bower;
Grateful the incense from the lime-tree flower;
Mysterious, wild, the far heard trumpet's tone;
Lovely the moon in ether, all alone:
Sweet too the converse of these happy mortals,
As that of busy spirits when the portals
Are closing in the west; or that soft humming   160
We hear around when Hesperus is coming.
Sweet be their sleep. * * * * * * * * *

TO SOME LADIES

WHAT though while the wonders of nature exploring,
    I cannot your light, mazy footsteps attend;
Nor listen to accents, that almost adoring,
    Bless Cynthia's face. the enthusiast's friend:

Yet over the steep, whence the mountain stream rushes,
  With you, kindest friends, in idea I muse;
Mark the clear tumbling crystal, its passionate gushes,
  In spray that the wild flower kindly bedews.

Why linger you so, the wild labyrinth strolling?
  Why breathless, unable your bliss to declare?   10
Ah! you list to the nightingale's tender condoling,
  Responsive to sylphs, in the moon-beamy air.

'Tis morn, and the flowers with dew are yet drooping,
  I see you are treading the verge of the sea:
And now! ah, I see it—you just now are stooping
  To pick up the keep-sake intended for me.

If a cherub, on pinions of silver descending,
  Had brought me a gem from the fret-work of heaven;
And smiles, with his star-cheering voice sweetly blending,
  The blessings of Tighe had melodiously given;   20

It had not created a warmer emotion
  Than the present, fair nymphs, I was blest with from you,
Than the shell, from the bright golden sands of the ocean
  Which the emerald waves at your feet gladly threw.

For, indeed, 'tis a sweet and peculiar pleasure
  (And blissful is he who such happiness finds),
To possess but a span of the hour of leisure,
  In elegant, pure, and aerial minds.

ON RECEIVING A CURIOUS SHELL, AND A COPY OF VERSES,

FROM THE SAME LADIES

HAST thou from the caves of Golconda, a gem
  Pure as the ice-drop that froze on the mountain?
Bright as the humming-bird's green diadem,
  When it flutters in sun-beams that shine through a fountain?

Hast thou a goblet for dark sparkling wine?
  That goblet right heavy, and massy, and gold?
And splendidly mark'd with the story divine
  Of Armida the fair, and Rinaldo the bold?

Hast thou a steed with a mane richly flowing?
   Hast thou a sword that thine enemy's smart is?   10
Hast thou a trumpet rich melodies blowing?
   And wear'st thou the shield of the fam'd Britomartis?

What is it that hangs from thy shoulder, so brave,
   Embroider'd with many a spring peering flower?
Is it a scarf that thy fair lady gave?
   And hastest thou now to that fair lady's bower?

Ah! courteous Sir Knight, with large joy thou art crown'd;
   Full many the glories that brighten thy youth!
I will tell thee my blisses, which richly abound
   In magical powers to bless, and to sooth.   20

On this scroll thou seest written in characters fair
   A sun-beamy tale of a wreath, and a chain;
And, warrior, it nurtures the property rare
   Of charming my mind from the trammels of pain.

This canopy mark: 'tis the work of a fay;
   Beneath its rich shade did King Oberon languish,
When lovely Titania was far, far away,
   And cruelly left him to sorrow, and anguish.

There, oft would he bring from his soft sighing lute
   Wild strains to which, spell-bound, the nightingales listen'd;   30
The wondering spirits of heaven were mute,
   And tears 'mong the dewdrops of morning oft glisten'd.

In this little dome, all those melodies strange,
   Soft, plaintive, and melting, for ever will sigh;
Nor e'er will the notes from their tenderness change;
   Nor e'er will the music of Oberon die.

So, when I am in a voluptuous vein,
   I pillow my head on the sweets of the rose,
And list to the tale of the wreath, and the chain,
   Till its echoes depart; then I sink to repose.   40

Adieu, valiant Eric! with joy thou art crown'd;
   Full many the glories that brighten thy youth,
I too have my blisses, which richly abound
   In magical powers, to bless and to sooth.

TO * * * *

[Georgiana Augusta Wylie, afterwards Mrs. George Keats]

Hadst thou liv'd in days of old,
O what wonders had been told
Of thy lively countenance,
And thy humid eyes that dance
In the midst of their own brightness;
In the very fane of lightness.
Over which thine eyebrows, leaning,
Picture out each lovely meaning:
In a dainty bend they lie,
Like to streaks across the sky,   10
Or the feathers from a crow,
Fallen on a bed of snow.
Of thy dark hair that extends
Into many graceful bends:
As the leaves of Hellebore
Turn to whence they sprung before
And behind each ample curl
Peeps the richness of a pearl.
Downward too flows many a tress
With a glossy waviness;   20
Full, and round like globes that rise
From the censer to the skies
Through sunny air. Add too, the sweetness
Of thy honey'd voice; the neatness
Of thine ankle lightly turn'd:
With those beauties, scarce discern'd,
Kept with such sweet privacy,
That they seldom meet the eye
Of the little loves that fly
Round about with eager pry.   30
Saving when, with freshening lave,
Thou dipp'st them in the taintless wave;
Like twin water lillies, born
In the coolness of the morn.
O, if thou hadst breathed then,
Now the Muses had been ten.
Couldst thou wish for lineage higher
Than twin sister of Thalia?
At least for ever, evermore,
Will I call the Graces four.   40

Hadst thou liv'd when chivalry
Lifted up her lance on high,
Tell me what thou wouldst have been?
Ah! I see the silver sheen
Of thy broider'd, floating vest
Cov'ring half thine ivory breast;
Which, O heavens! I should see,
But that cruel destiny
Has placed a golden cuirass there;
Keeping secret what is fair. 50
Like sunbeams in a cloudlet nested
Thy locks in knightly casque are rested:
O'er which bend four milky plumes
Like the gentle lilly's blooms
Springing from a costly vase.
See with what a stately pace
Comes thine alabaster steed;
Servant of heroic deed!
O'er his loins, his trappings glow
Like the northern lights on snow. 60
Mount his back! thy sword unsheath!
Sign of the enchanter's death;
Bane of every wicked spell;
Silencer of dragon's yell.
Alas! thou this wilt never do:
Thou art an enchantress too,
And wilt surely never spill
Blood of these whose eyes can kill.

TO HOPE

When by my solitary hearth I sit,
  And hateful thoughts enwrap my soul in gloom;
When no fair dreams before my 'mind's eye' flit,
  And the bare heath of life presents no bloom;
    Sweet Hope, ethereal balm upon me shed,
    And wave thy silver pinions o'er my head.

Whene'er I wander, at the fall of night,
  Where woven boughs shut out the moon's bright ray,
Should sad Despondency my musings fright,
  And frown, to drive fair Cheerfulness away, 10
    Peep with the moon-beams through the leafy roof
    And keep that fiend Despondence far aloof.

Should Disappointment, parent of Despair,
  Strive for her son to seize my careless heart;
When, like a cloud, he sits upon the air,
  Preparing on his spell-bound prey to dart:
    Chace him away, sweet Hope, with visage bright,
    And fright him as the morning frightens night!

Whene'er the fate of those I hold most dear
  Tells to my fearful breast a tale of sorrow,   20
O bright-eyed Hope, my morbid fancy cheer;
  Let me awhile thy sweetest comforts borrow:
    Thy heaven-born radiance around me shed,
    And wave thy silver pinions o'er my head!

Should e'er unhappy love my bosom pain,
  From cruel parents, or relentless fair;
O let me think it is not quite in vain
  To sigh out sonnets to the midnight air!
    Sweet Hope, ethereal balm upon me shed,
    And wave thy silver pinions o'er my head!   30

In the long vista of the years to roll,
  Let me not see our country's honour fade:
O let me see our land retain her soul,
  Her pride, her freedom; and not freedom's shade.
    From thy bright eyes unusual brightness shed—
    Beneath thy pinions canopy my head!

Let me not see the patriot's high bequest,
  Great Liberty! how great in plain attire!
With the base purple of a court oppress'd,
  Bowing her head, and ready to expire: 40
    But let me see thee stoop from heaven on wings
    That fill the skies with silver glitterings!

And as, in sparkling majesty, a star
  Gilds the bright summit of some gloomy cloud;
Brightening the half veil'd face of heaven afar:
  So. when dark thoughts my boding spirit shroud,
    Sweet Hope, celestial influence round me shed,
    Waving thy silver pinions o'er my head.
  February, 1815.

IMITATION OF SPENSER

* * * * * * *

Now Morning from her orient chamber came,
And her first footsteps touch'd a verdant hill;
Crowning its lawny crest with amber flame,
Silv'ring the untainted gushes of its rill;
Which, pure from mossy beds, did down distill,
And after parting beds of simple flowers,
By many streams a little lake did fill,
Which round its marge reflected woven bowers,
And, in its middle space, a sky that never lowers.

There the king-fisher saw his plumage bright   10
Vieing with fish of brilliant dye below;
Whose silken fins, and golden scales' light
Cast upward, through the waves, a ruby glow:
There saw the swan his neck of arched snow,
And oar'd himself along with majesty;
Sparkled his jetty eyes; his feet did show
Beneath the waves like Afric's ebony,
And on his back a fay reclined voluptuously.

Ah! could I tell the wonders of an isle
That in that fairest lake had placed been,   20
I could e'en Dido of her grief beguile;
Or rob from aged Lear his bitter teen:
For sure so fair a place was never seen,
Of all that ever charm'd romantic eye:
It seem'd an emerald in the silver sheen
Of the bright waters; or as when on high,
Through clouds of fleecy white, laughs the cœrulean sky.

And all around it dipp'd luxuriously
Slopings of verdure through the glossy tide,
Which, as it were in gentle amity,   30
Rippled delighted up the flowery side;
As if to glean the ruddy tears, it tried,
Which fell profusely from the rose-tree stem!
Haply it was the workings of its pride,
In strife to throw upon the shore a gem
Outvieing all the buds in Flora's diadem.

* * * * * * *

[EDMONTON.]

WOMAN! when I behold thee flippant, vain,
  Inconstant, childish, proud, and full of fancies;
  Without that modest softening that enhances
The downcast eye, repentant of the pain
That its mild light creates to heal again:
  E'en then, elate, my spirit leaps, and prances,
  E'en then my soul with exultation dances

For that to love, so long, I've dormant lain:
But when I see thee meek, and kind, and tender,
  Heavens! how desperately do I adore   **10**
Thy winning graces;—to be thy defender
  I hotly burn—to be a Calidore—
A very Red Cross Knight—a stout Leander—
  Might I be loved by thee like these of yore.

Light feet, dark violet eyes, and parted hair;
  Soft dimpled hands, white neck, and creamy breast,
  Are things on which the dazzled senses rest
Till the fond, fixed eyes, forget they stare.
From such fine pictures, heavens! I cannot dare
  To turn my admiration, though unpossess'd   **20**
  They be of what is worthy,—though not drest
In lovely modesty, and virtues rare.
Yet these I leave as thoughtless as a lark;
  These lures I straight forget,—e'en ere I dine,
Or thrice my palate moisten: but when I mark
  Such charms with mild intelligences shine,
My ear is open like a greedy shark,
  To catch the tunings of a voice divine.

Ah! who can e'er forget so fair a being?
  Who can forget her half retiring sweets?   **30**
  God! she is like a milk-white lamb that bleats
For man's protection. Surely the All-seeing,
Who joys to see us with his gifts agreeing,
  Will never give him pinions, who intreats
  Such innocence to ruin,—who vilely cheats
A dove-like bosom. In truth there is no freeing
One's thoughts from such a beauty; when I hear
  A lay that once I saw her hand awake,
Her form seems floating palpable, and near;
  Had I e'er seen her from an arbour take   **40**
A dewy flower, oft would that hand appear,
  And o'er my eyes the trembling moisture shake.

EPISTLES

TO GEORGE FELTON MATHEW

SWEET are the pleasures that to verse belong,
And doubly sweet a brotherhood in song;
Nor can remembrance, Mathew! bring to view
A fate more pleasing, a delight more true
Than that in which the brother Poets joy'd,
Who with combined powers, their wit employ'd
To raise a trophy to the drama's muses.
The thought of this great partnership diffuses
Over the genius loving heart, a feeling
Of all that's high, and great, and good, and healing.

Too partial friend! fain would I follow thee   11
Past each horizon of fine poesy;
Fain would I echo back each pleasant note
As o'er Sicilian seas, clear anthems float
'Mong the light skimming gondolas far parted,
Just when the sun his farewell beam has darted:
But 'tis impossible; far different cares
Beckon me sternly from soft 'Lydian airs,'
And hold my faculties so long in thrall,
That I am oft in doubt whether at all   20
I shall again see Phœbus in the morning:
Or flush'd Aurora in the roseate dawning!
Or a white Naiad in a rippling stream;
Or a rapt seraph in a moonlight beam;
Or again witness what with thee I've seen,
The dew by fairy feet swept from the green,
After a night of some quaint jubilee
Which every elf and fay had come to see:
When bright processions took their airy march
Beneath the curved moon's triumphal arch.   30
But might I now each passing moment give
To the coy muse, with me she would not live
In this dark city, nor would condescend
'Mid contradictions her delights to lend.
Should e'er the fine-eyed maid to me be kind,
Ah! surely it must be whene'er I find
Some flowery spot, sequester'd, wild, romantic,
That often must have seen a poet frantic;
Where oaks, that erst the Druid knew, are growing,

And flowers, the glory of one day, are blowing;   40
Where the dark-leav'd laburnum's drooping clusters
Reflect athwart the stream their yellow lustres,
And intertwined the cassia's arms unite,
With its own drooping buds, but very white.
Where on one side are covert branches hung,
'Mong which the nightingales have always sung
In leafy quiet: where to pry, aloof,
Atween the pillars of the sylvan roof,
Would be to find where violet beds were nestling,
And where the bee with cowslip bells was wrestling.
There must be too a ruin dark, and gloomy,   ·   51
To say 'joy not too much in all that's bloomy.'

Yet this is vain—O Mathew lend thy aid
To find a place where I may greet the maid—
Where we may soft humanity put on,
And sit, and rhyme and think on Chatterton;
And that warm-hearted Shakespeare sent to meet him
Four laurell'd spirits, heaven-ward to intreat him.
With reverence would we speak of all the sages   59
Who have left streaks of light athwart their ages:
And thou shouldst moralize on Milton's blindness,
And mourn the fearful dearth of human kindness
To those who strove with the bright golden wing
Of genius, to flap away each sting
Thrown by the pitiless world. We next could tell
Of those who in the cause of freedom fell;
Of our own Alfred, of Helvetian Tell;
Of him whose name to ev'ry heart's a solace,
High-minded and unbending William Wallace.
While to the rugged north our musing turns   70
We well might drop a tear for him, and Burns.
Felton! without incitements such as these,
How vain for me the niggard Muse to tease:
For thee, she will thy every dwelling grace,
And make 'a sun-shine in a shady place:'
For thou wast once a flowret blooming wild,
Close to the source, bright, pure, and undefil'd,
Whence gush the streams of song: in happy hour
Came chaste Diana from her shady bower,
Just as the sun was from the east uprising;   80
And, as for him some gift she was devising,
Beheld thee, pluck'd thee, cast thee in the stream
To meet her glorious brother's greeting beam.
I marvel much that thou hast never told
How, from a flower, into a fish of gold

The sage will mingle with each moral theme
My happy thoughts sententious; he will teem
With lofty periods when my verses fire him,
And then I'll stoop from heaven to inspire him.   80
Lays have I left of such a dear delight
That maids will sing them on their bridal night.
Gay villagers, upon a morn of May,
When they have tired their gentle limbs with play,
And form'd a snowy circle on the grass,
And plac'd in midst of all that lovely lass
Who chosen is their queen,—with her fine head
Crowned with flowers purple, white, and red:
For there the lilly, and the musk-rose, sighing,
Are emblems true of hapless lovers dying: 90
Between her breasts, that never yet felt trouble,
A bunch of violets full blown, and double,
Serenely sleep:—she from a casket takes
A little book,—and then a joy awakes
About each youthful heart,—with stifled cries,
And rubbing of white hands, and sparkling eyes:
For she's to read a tale of hopes, and fears;
One that I foster'd in my youthful years:
The pearls, that on each glist'ning circlet sleep,
Gush ever and anon with silent creep,   100
Lured by the innocent dimples. To sweet rest
Shall the dear babe, upon its mother's breast,
Be lull'd with songs of mine. Fair world, adieu!
Thy dales, and hills, are fading from my view:
Swiftly I mount, upon wide spreading pinions,
Far from the narrow bounds of thy dominions.
Full joy I feel, while thus I cleave the air,
That my soft verse will charm thy daughters fair,
And warm thy sons!" Ah, my dear friend and brother,
Could I, at once, my mad ambition smother,   110
For tasting joys like these, sure I should be
Happier, and dearer to society.
At times, 'tis true, I've felt relief from pain
When some bright thought has darted through my brain;
Through all that day I've felt a greater pleasure
Than if I'd brought to light a hidden treasure.
As to my sonnets, though none else should heed them,
I feel delighted, still, that you should read them.
Of late, too, I have had much calm enjoyment,   119
Stretch'd on the grass at my best lov'd employment
Of scribbling lines for you. These things I thought
While, in my face, the freshest breeze I caught.

E'en now I'm pillow'd on a bed of flowers
That crowns a lofty clift, which proudly towers
Above the ocean-waves. The stalks, and blades,
Chequer my tablet with their quivering shades.
On one side is a field of drooping oats,
Through which the poppies show their scarlet coats;
So pert and useless, that they bring to mind
The scarlet coats that pester human-kind.   130
And on the other side, outspread, is seen
Ocean's blue mantle streak'd with purple, and green.
Now 'tis I see a canvass'd ship, and now
Mark the bright silver curling round her prow.
I see the lark down-dropping to his nest,
And the broad winged sea-gull never at rest;
For when no more he spreads his feathers free,
His breast is dancing on the restless sea.
Now I direct my eyes into the west,
Which at this moment is in sun-beams drest: 140
Why westward turn? 'Twas but to say adieu!
'Twas but to kiss my hand, dear George, to you!
    [MARGATE] *August, 1816.*

TO CHARLES COWDEN CLARKE

OFT have you seen a swan superbly frowning,
And with proud breast his own white shadow crowning;
He slants his neck beneath the waters bright
So silently, it seems a beam of light
Come from the galaxy: anon he sports,—
With outspread wings the Naiad Zephyr courts,
Or ruffles all the surface of the lake
In striving from its crystal face to take
Some diamond water drops, and them to treasure
In milky nest, and sip them off at leisure.   10
But not a moment can he there insure them,
Nor to such downy rest can he allure them;
For down they rush as though they would be free,
And drop like hours into eternity.
Just like that bird am I in loss of time,
Whene'er I venture on the stream of rhyme;
With shatter'd boat, oar snapt, and canvass rent
I slowly sail, scarce knowing my intent;
Still scooping up the water with my fingers,
In which a trembling diamond never lingers.   20
By this, friend Charles, you may full plainly see
Why I have never penn'd a line to thee:

Because my thoughts were never free, and clear,
And little fit to please a classic ear;
Because my wine was of too poor a savour
For one whose palate gladdens in the flavour
Of sparkling Helicon:—small good it were
To take him to a desert rude, and bare,
Who had on Baiæ's shore reclin'd at ease,
While Tasso's page was floating in a breeze   30
That gave soft music from Armida's bowers,
Mingled with fragrance from her rarest flowers:
Small good to one who had by Mulla's stream
Fondled the maidens with the breasts of cream;
Who had beheld Belphœbe in a brook,
And lovely Una in a leafy nook,
And Archimago leaning o'er his book:
Who had of all that's sweet tasted, and seen,
From silv'ry ripple, up to beauty's queen;
From the sequester'd haunts of gay Titania,   40
To the blue dwelling of divine Urania:
One, who, of late, had ta'en sweet forest walks
With him who elegantly chats and talks—
The wrong'd Libertas,—who has told you stories
Of laurel chaplets, and Apollo's glories;
Of troops chivalrous prancing through a city,
And tearful ladies made for love, and pity:
With many else which I have never known.
Thus have I thought; and days on days have flown
Slowly, or rapidly—unwilling still   50
For you to try my dull, unlearned quill.
Nor should I now, but that I've known you long;
That you first taught me all the sweets of song:
The grand, the sweet, the terse, the free, the fine;
What swell'd with pathos, and what right divine:
Spenserian vowels that elope with ease,
And float along like birds o'er summer seas;
Miltonian storms, and more, Miltonian tenderness;
Michael in arms, and more, meek Eve's fair slenderness.
Who read for me the sonnet swelling loudly   60
Up to its climax and then dying proudly?
Who found for me the grandeur of the ode,
Growing, like Atlas, stronger from its load?
Who let me taste that more than cordial dram,
The sharp, the rapier-pointed epigram?
Show'd me that epic was of all the king,
Round, vast, and spanning all like Saturn's ring?
You too upheld the veil from Clio's beauty,
And pointed out the patriot's stern duty;

The might of Alfred, and the shaft of Tell;
The hand of Brutus, that so grandly fell
Upon a tyrant's head. Ah! had I never seen,
Or known your kindness, what might I have been?
What my enjoyments in my youthful years,
Bereft of all that now my life endears?
And can I e'er these benefits forget?
And can I e'er repay the friendly debt?
No, doubly no;—yet should these rhymings please,
I shall roll on the grass with two-fold ease:
For I have long time been my fancy feeding   80
With hopes that you would one day think the reading
Of my rough verses not an hour misspent;
Should it e'er be so, what a rich content!
Some weeks have pass'd since last I saw the spires
In lucent Thames reflected:—warm desires
To see the sun o'erpeep the eastern dimness,
And morning shadows streaking into slimness
Across the lawny fields, and pebbly water;
To mark the time as they grow broad, and shorter;
To feel the air that plays about the hills,   90
And sips its freshness from the little rills;
To see high, golden corn wave in the light
When Cynthia smiles upon a summer's night,
And peers among the cloudlets jet and white,
As though she were reclining in a bed
Of bean blossoms, in heaven freshly shed.
No sooner had I stepp'd into these pleasures
Than I began to think of rhymes and measures:
The air that floated by me seem'd to say
"Write! thou wilt never have a better day."   100
And so I did. When many lines I'd written,
Though with their grace I was not oversmitten,
Yet, as my hand was warm, I thought I'd better
Trust to my feelings, and write you a letter.
Such an attempt required an inspiration
Of a peculiar sort,—a consummation;—
Which, had I felt, these scribblings might have been
Verses from which the soul would never wean:
But many days have passed since last my heart
Was warm'd luxuriously by divine Mozart;   110
By Arne delighted, or by Handel madden'd;
Or by the song of Erin pierc'd and sadden'd:
What time you were before the music sitting,
And the rich notes to each sensation fitting.
Since I have walk'd with you through shady lanes
That freshly terminate in open plains,

And revel'd in a chat that ceased not
When at night-fall among your books we got:
No, nor when supper came, nor after that,—
Nor when reluctantly I took my hat;   120
No, nor till cordially you shook my hand
Mid-way between our homes:—your accents bland
Still sounded in my ears, when I no more
Could hear your footsteps touch the grav'ly floor.
Sometimes I lost them, and then found again;
You chang'd the footpath for the grassy plain.
In those still moments I have wish'd you joys
That well you know to honour:—"Life's very toys
"With him," said I, "will take a pleasant charm;
"It cannot be that aught will work him harm."   130
These thoughts now come o'er me with all their might:—
Again I shake your hand,—friend Charles, good night.

    September, 1816.

SONNETS

I

TO MY BROTHER GEORGE

MANY the wonders I this day have seen:
  The sun, when first he kist away the tears
  That fill'd the eyes of morn;—the laurell'd peers
Who from the feathery gold of evening lean;—
The ocean with its vastness, its blue green,
  Its ships, its rocks, its caves, its hopes, its fears,—
  Its voice mysterious, which whoso hears
Must think on what will be, and what has been.
E'en now, dear George, while this for you I write,
  Cynthia is from her silken curtains peeping   10
So scantly, that it seems her bridal night,
  And she her half-discover'd revels keeping.
But what, without the social thought of thee,
Would be the wonders of the sky and sea?

II

TO * * * * * *

HAD I a man's fair form, then might my sighs
  Be echoed swiftly through that ivory shell
  Thine ear, and find thy gentle heart; so well
Would passion arm me for the enterprise:
But ah! I am no knight whose foeman dies;
  No cuirass glistens on my bosom's swell;
  I am no happy shepherd of the dell
Whose lips have trembled with a maiden's eyes.
Yet must I dote upon thee,—call thee sweet,
  Sweeter by far than Hybla's honied roses   10
    When steep'd in dew rich to intoxication.
Ah! I will taste that dew, for me 'tis meet,
  And when the moon her pallid face discloses,
    I'll gather some by spells, and incantation.

III

WRITTEN ON THE DAY THAT MR. LEIGH HUNT LEFT PRISON

WHAT though, for showing truth to flatter'd state,
  Kind Hunt was shut in prison, yet has he,
  In his immortal spirit, been as free

28

As the sky-searching lark, and as elate.
Minion of grandeur! think you he did wait?
  Think you he naught but prison walls did see,
  Till, so unwilling, thou unturn'dst the key?
Ah, no! far happier, nobler was his fate!
In Spenser's halls he stray'd, and bowers fair,
  Culling enchanted flowers; and he flew   10
With daring Milton through the fields of air:
  To regions of his own his genius true
Took happy flights. Who shall his fame impair
  When thou art dead, and all thy wretched crew?

IV

How many bards gild the lapses of time!
  A few of them have ever been the food
  Of my delighted fancy,—I could brood
Over their beauties, earthly, or sublime:
And often, when I sit me down to rhyme,
  These will in throngs before my mind intrude:
  But no confusion, no disturbance rude
Do they occasion; 'tis a pleasing chime.
So the unnumber'd sounds that evening store;   9
The songs of birds—the whisp'ring of the leaves—
  The voice of waters—the great bell that heaves
With solemn sound,—and thousand others more,
  That distance of recognizance bereaves,
Make pleasing music, and not wild uproar.

V

TO A FRIEND WHO SENT ME SOME ROSES

As late I rambled in the happy fields,
  What time the sky-lark shakes the tremulous dew
  From his lush clover covert;—when anew
Adventurous knights take up their dinted shields:
I saw the sweetest flower wild nature yields,
  A fresh-blown musk-rose; 'twas the first that threw
  Its sweets upon the summer: graceful it grew
As is the wand that queen Titania wields.
And, as I feasted on its fragrancy,
  I thought the garden-rose it far excell'd: 10
But when, O Wells! thy roses came to me
  My sense with their deliciousness was spell'd:
Soft voices had they, that with tender plea
  Whisper'd of peace, and truth, and friendliness unquell'd.
    June 29, 1816.

VI

TO G. A. W.

[Georgiana Augusta Wylie]

Nymph of the downward smile and sidelong glance,
    In what diviner moments of the day
    Art thou most lovely?—when gone far astray
Into the labyrinths of sweet utterance,
Or when serenely wand'ring in a trance
    Of sober thought?—or when starting away
    With careless robe to meet the morning ray
Thou spar'st the flowers in thy mazy dance?
Haply 'tis when thy ruby lips part sweetly,
    And so remain, because thou listenest: 10
But thou to please wert nurtured so completely
    That I can never tell what mood is best.
I shall as soon pronounce which Grace more neatly
    Trips it before Apollo than the rest.

VII

O Solitude! if I must with thee dwell,
    Let it not be among the jumbled heap
    Of murky buildings; climb with me the steep,—
Nature's observatory—whence the dell,
Its flowery slopes, its river's crystal swell,
    May seem a span; let me thy vigils keep
    'Mongst boughs pavillion'd, where the deer's swift leap
Startles the wild bee from the fox-glove bell.
But though I'll gladly trace these scenes with thee,
    Yet the sweet converse of an innocent mind,   10
    Whose words are images of thoughts refin'd,
Is my soul's pleasure; and it sure must be
    Almost the highest bliss of human-kind,
When to thy haunts two kindred spirits flee.

VIII

TO MY BROTHERS

Small, busy flames play through the fresh laid coals,
    And their faint cracklings o'er our silence creep
    Like whispers of the household gods that keep
A gentle empire o'er fraternal souls.
And while, for rhymes, I search around the poles,

Your eyes are fix'd, as in poetic sleep,
Upon the lore so voluble and deep,
That aye at fall of night our care condoles.
This is your birth-day Tom, and I rejoice
    That thus it passes smoothly, quietly.   10
Many such eves of gently whisp'ring noise
    May we together pass, and calmly try
What are this world's true joys,—ere the great voice,
    From its fair face, shall bid our spirits fly.
November 18, 1816.

IX

KEEN, fitful gusts are whisp'ring here and there
    Among the bushes half leafless, and dry;
    The stars look very cold about the sky,
And I have many miles on foot to fare.
Yet feel I little of the cool bleak air,
    Or of the dead leaves rustling drearily,
    Or of those silver lamps that burn on high,
Or of the distance from home's pleasant lair:
For I am brimfull of the friendliness
    That in a little cottage I have found;   10
Of fair-hair'd Milton's eloquent distress,
    And all his love for gentle Lycid drown'd;
Of lovely Laura in her light green dress,
    And faithful Petrarch gloriously crown'd.

X

To one who has been long in city pent,
    'Tis very sweet to look into the fair
    And open face of heaven,—to breathe a prayer
Full in the smile of the blue firmament.
Who is more happy, when, with heart's content,
    Fatigued he sinks into some pleasant lair
    Of wavy grass, and reads a debonair
And gentle tale of love and languishment?
Returning home at evening, with an ear
    Catching the notes of Philomel,—an eye   10
Watching the sailing cloudlet's bright career,
    He mourns that day so soon has glided by:
E'en like the passage of an angel's tear
    That falls through the clear ether silently.

XI

ON FIRST LOOKING INTO CHAPMAN'S HOMER

MUCH have I travell'd in the realms of gold,
    And many goodly states and kingdoms seen;
    Round many western islands have I been
Which bards in fealty to Apollo hold.
Oft of one wide expanse had I been told
    That deep-brow'd Homer ruled as his demesne;
    Yet did I never breathe its pure serene
Till I heard Chapman speak out loud and bold:
Then felt I like some watcher of the skies
    When a new planet swims into his ken;   10
Or like stout Cortez when with eagle eyes
    He star'd at the Pacific—and all his men
Look'd at each other with a wild surmise—
    Silent, upon a peak in Darien.

XII

ON LEAVING SOME FRIENDS AT AN EARLY HOUR

GIVE me a golden pen, and let me lean
    On heap'd up flowers, in regions clear, and far;
    Bring me a tablet whiter than a star,
Or hand of hymning angel, when 'tis seen
The silver strings of heavenly harp atween:
    And let there glide by many a pearly car,
    Pink robes, and wavy hair, and diamond jar,
And half discovered wings, and glances keen.
The while let music wander round my ears,
    And as it reaches each delicious ending,   10
        Let me write down a line of glorious tone,
And full of many wonders of the spheres:
    For what a height my spirit is contending!
        'Tis not content so soon to be alone.

XIII

ADDRESSED TO HAYDON

HIGHMINDEDNESS, a jealousy for good,
    A loving-kindness for the great man's fame,
    Dwells here and there with people of no name,
In noisome alley, and in pathless wood:
And where we think the truth least understood,

Oft may be found a "singleness of aim,"
That ought to frighten into hooded shame
A money-mong'ring, pitiable brood.
How glorious this affection for the cause
  Of stedfast genius, toiling gallantly!   10
What when a stout unbending champion awes
  Envy, and Malice to their native sty?
Unnumber'd souls breathe out a still applause,
  Proud to behold him in his country's eye.

XIV

ADDRESSED TO THE SAME

GREAT spirits now on earth are sojourning;
  He of the cloud, the cataract, the lake,
  Who on Helvellyn's summit, wide awake,
Catches his freshness from Archangel's wing:
He of the rose, the violet, the spring,
  The social smile, the chain for Freedom's sake:
  And lo!—whose stedfastness would never take
A meaner sound than Raphael's whispering.
And other spirits there are standing apart
  Upon the forehead of the age to come;   10
These, these will give the world another heart,
  And other pulses. Hear ye not the hum
Of mighty workings?——
  Listen awhile, ye nations, and be dumb.

XV

ON THE GRASSHOPPER AND CRICKET

THE poetry of earth is never dead:
  When all the birds are faint with the hot sun,
  And hide in cooling trees, a voice will run
From hedge to hedge about the new-mown mead;
That is the Grasshopper's—he takes the lead
  In summer luxury,—he has never done
  With his delights; for when tired out with fun
He rests at ease beneath some pleasant weed.
The poetry of earth is ceasing never:
  On a lone winter evening, when the frost   10
    Has wrought a silence, from the stove there shrills
The Cricket's song, in warmth increasing ever,
  And seems to one in drowsiness half lost,
    The Grasshopper's among some grassy hills.
December 30, 1816.

XVI

TO KOSCIUSKO

Good Kosciusko, thy great name alone
 Is a full harvest whence to reap high feeling;
 It comes upon us like the glorious pealing
Of the wide spheres—an everlasting tone.
And now it tells me, that in worlds unknown,
 The names of heroes; burst from clouds concealing,
 And change to harmonies, for ever stealing
Through cloudless blue, and round each silver throne.
It tells me too, that on a happy day,
 When some good spirit walks upon the earth,   10
  Thy name with Alfred's, and the great of yore
 Gently commingling, gives tremendous birth
To a loud hymn, that sounds far, far away
  To where the great God lives for evermore.
 December, 1816.

XVII

Happy is England! I could be content
 To see no other verdure than its own;
 To feel no other breezes than are blown
Through its tall woods with high romances blent:
Yet do I sometimes feel a languishment
 For skies Italian, and an inward groan
 To sit upon an Alp as on a throne,
And half forget what world or worldling meant.
Happy is England, sweet her artless daughters;
 Enough their simple loveliness for me,   10
  Enough their whitest arms in silence clinging:
 Yet do I often warmly burn to see
  Beauties of deeper glance, and hear their singing,
And float with them about the summer waters.

SLEEP AND POETRY

WHAT is more gentle than a wind in summer?
What is more soothing than the pretty hummer
That stays one moment in an open flower,
And buzzes cheerily from bower to bower?
What is more tranquil than a musk-rose blowing
In a green island, far from all men's knowing?
More healthful than the leafiness of dales?
More secret than a nest of nightingales?
More serene than Cordelia's countenance?
More full of visions than a high romance?   10
What, but thee Sleep? Soft closer of our eyes!
Low murmurer of tender lullabies!
Light hoverer around our happy pillows!
Wreather of poppy buds, and weeping willows!
Silent entangler of a beauty's tresses!
Most happy listener! when the morning blesses
Thee for enlivening all the cheerful eyes
That glance so brightly at the new sun-rise.

But what is higher beyond thought than thee?
Fresher than berries of a mountain tree?   20
More strange, more beautiful, more smooth, more regal,
Than wings of swans, than doves, than dim-seen eagle?
What is it? And to what shall I compare it?
It has a glory, and naught else can share it:
The thought thereof is awful, sweet, and holy,
Chasing away all worldliness and folly;
Coming sometimes like fearful claps of thunder,
Or the low rumblings earth's regions under;
And sometimes like a gentle whispering
Of all the secrets of some wond'rous thing   30
That breathes about us in the vacant air;
So that we look around with prying stare,
Perhaps to see shapes of light, aerial limning,
And catch soft floatings from a faint-heard hymning;
To see the laurel wreath, on high suspended,
That is to crown our name when life is ended.

Sometimes it gives a glory to the voice,
And from the heart up-springs, rejoice! rejoice!
Sounds which will reach the Framer of all things,
And die away in ardent mutterings.   40

No one who once the glorious sun has seen,
And all the clouds, and felt his bosom clean
For his great Maker's presence, but must know
What 'tis I mean, and feel his being glow:
Therefore no insult will I give his spirit,
By telling what he sees from native merit.

O Poesy! for thee I hold my pen
That am not yet a glorious denizen
Of thy wide heaven—Should I rather kneel
Upon some mountain-top until I feel   50
A glowing splendour round about me hung,
And echo back the voice of thine own tongue?
O Poesy! for thee I grasp my pen
That am not yet a glorious denizen
Of thy wide heaven; yet, to my ardent prayer,
Yield from thy sanctuary some clear air,
Smooth'd for intoxication by the breath
Of flowering bays, that I may die a death
Of luxury, and my young spirit follow
The morning sun-beams to the great Apollo   60
Like a fresh sacrifice; or, if I can bear
The o'erwhelming sweets, 'twill bring to me the fair
Visions of all places: a bowery nook
Will be elysium—an eternal book
Whence I may copy many a lovely saying
About the leaves, and flowers—about the playing
Of nymphs in woods, and fountains; and the shade
Keeping a silence round a sleeping maid;
And many a verse from so strange influence
That we must ever wonder how, and whence   70
It came. Also imaginings will hover
Round my fire-side, and haply there discover
Vistas of solemn beauty, where I'd wander
In happy silence, like the clear Meander
Through its lone vales; and where I found a spot
Of awfuller shade, or an enchanted grot,
Or a green hill o'erspread with chequer'd dress
Of flowers, and fearful from its loveliness,
Write on my tablets all that was permitted,
All that was for our human senses fitted.   80

Then the events of this wide world I'd seize
Like a strong giant, and my spirit teaze
Till at its shoulders it should proudly see
Wings to find out an immortality.

Stop and consider! life is but a day;
A fragile dew-drop on its perilous way
From a tree's summit; a poor Indian's sleep
While his boat hastens to the monstrous steep
Of Montmorenci. Why so sad a moan?
Life is the rose's hope while yet unblown;   90
The reading of an ever-changing tale;
The light uplifting of a maiden's veil;
A pigeon tumbling in clear summer air;
A laughing school-boy, without grief or care,
Riding the springy branches of an elm.

O for ten years, that I may overwhelm
Myself in poesy; so I may do the deed
That my own soul has to itself decreed.
Then will I pass the countries that I see
In long perspective, and continually   100
Taste their pure fountains. First the realm I'll pass
Of Flora, and old Pan: sleep in the grass,
Feed upon apples red, and strawberries,
And choose each pleasure that my fancy sees;
Catch the white-handed nymphs in shady places,
To woo sweet kisses from averted faces,—
Play with their fingers, touch their shoulders white
Into a pretty shrinking with a bite
As hard as lips can make it: till agreed,
A lovely tale of human life we'll read.   110
And one will teach a tame dove how it best
May fan the cool air gently o'er my rest;
Another, bending o'er her nimble tread,
Will set a green robe floating round her head,
And still will dance with ever varied ease,
Smiling upon the flowers and the trees:
Another will entice me on, and on
Through almond blossoms and rich cinnamon;
Till in the bosom of a leafy world
We rest in silence, like two gems upcurl'd   120
In the recesses of a pearly shell.

And can I ever bid these joys farewell?
Yes, I must pass them for a nobler life,
Where I may find the agonies, the strife

Of human hearts: for lo! I see afar,
O'ersailing the blue cragginess, a car
And steeds with streamy manes—the charioteer
Looks out upon the winds with glorious fear:
And now the numerous tramplings quiver lightly
Along a huge cloud's ridge; and now with sprightly
Wheel downward come they into fresher skies,   131
Tipt round with silver from the sun's bright eyes.
Still downward with capacious whirl they glide;
And now I see them on the green-hill's side
In breezy rest among the nodding stalks.
The charioteer with wond'rous gesture talks
To the trees and mountains; and there soon appear
Shapes of delight, of mystery, and fear,
Passing along before a dusky space
Made by some mighty oaks: as they would chace   140
Some ever-fleeting music on they sweep.
Lo! how they murmur, laugh, and smile, and weep:
Some with upholden hand and mouth severe;
Some with their faces muffled to the ear
Between their arms; some, clear in youthful bloom,
Go glad and smilingly athwart the gloom;
Some looking back, and some with upward gaze;
Yes, thousands in a thousand different ways
Flit onward—now a lovely wreath of girls
Dancing their sleek hair into tangled curls;   150
And now broad wings. Most awfully intent
The driver of those steeds is forward bent,
And seems to listen: O that I might know
All that he writes with such a hurrying glow.

The visions all are fled—the car is fled
Into the light of heaven, and in their stead
A sense of real things comes doubly strong,
And, like a muddy stream, would bear along
My soul to nothingness: but I will strive
Against all doubtings, and will keep alive   160
The thought of that same chariot, and the strange
Journey it went.

                    Is there so small a range
In the present strength of mankind, that the high
Imagination cannot freely fly
As she was wont of old? prepare her steeds,
Paw up against the light, and do strange deeds
Upon the clouds? Has she not shown us all?
From the clear space of ether, to the small

Breath of new buds unfolding? From the meaning
Of Jove's large eye-brow, to the tender greening   170
Of April meadows? Here her altar shone,
E'en in this isle; and who could paragon
The fervid choir that lifted up a noise
Of harmony, to where it aye will poise
Its mighty self of convoluting sound,
Huge as a planet, and like that roll round,
Eternally around a dizzy void?
Ay, in those days the Muses were nigh cloy'd
With honours; nor had any other care
Than to sing out and soothe their wavy hair.   180

Could all this be forgotten? Yes, a schism
Nurtured by foppery and barbarism,
Made great Apollo blush for this his land.
Men were thought wise who could not understand
His glories: with a puling infant's force
They sway'd about upon a rocking horse,
And thought it Pegasus. Ah dismal soul'd!
The winds of heaven blew, the ocean roll'd
Its gathering waves—ye felt it not. The blue
Bared its eternal bosom, and the dew   190
Of summer nights collected still to make
The morning precious: beauty was awake!
Why were ye not awake? But ye were dead
To things ye knew not of,—were closely wed
To musty laws lined out with wretched rule
And compass vile: so that ye taught a school
Of dolts to smooth, inlay, and clip, and fit,
Till, like the certain wands of Jacob's wit,
Their verses tallied. Easy was the task:
A thousand handicraftsmen wore the mask   200
Of Poesy. Ill-fated, impious race!
That blasphemed the bright Lyrist to his face,
And did not know it,—no, they went about,
Holding a poor, decrepid standard out
Mark'd with most flimsy mottos, and in large
The name of one Boileau!

                              O ye whose charge
It is to hover round our pleasant hills!
Whose congregated majesty so fills
My boundly reverence, that I cannot trace
Your hallowed names, in this unholy place,   210
So near those common folk; did not their shames
Affright you? Did our old lamenting Thames

Delight you? Did ye never cluster round
Delicious Avon, with a mournful sound,
And weep? Or did ye wholly bid adieu
To regions where no more the laurel grew?
Or did ye stay to give a welcoming
To some lone spirits who could proudly sing
Their youth away, and die? 'Twas even so:
But let me think away those times of woe: 220
Now 'tis a fairer season; ye have breathed
Rich benedictions o'er us; ye have wreathed
Fresh garlands: for sweet music has been heard
In many places;—some has been upstirr'd
From out its crystal dwelling in a lake,
By a swan's ebon bill; from a thick brake,
Nested and quiet in a valley mild,
Bubbles a pipe; fine sounds are floating wild
About the earth: happy are ye and glad.   229

These things are doubtless: yet in truth we've had
Strange thunders from the potency of song;
Mingled indeed with what is sweet and strong,
From majesty: but in clear truth the themes
Are ugly clubs, the Poets' Polyphemes
Disturbing the grand sea. A drainless shower
Of light is poesy; 'tis the supreme of power;
'Tis might half slumb'ring on its own right arm.
The very archings of her eye-lids charm
A thousand willing agents to obey,
And still she governs with the mildest sway: 240
But strength alone though of the Muses born
Is like a fallen angel: trees uptorn,
Darkness, and worms, and shrouds, and sepulchres
Delight it; for it feeds upon the burrs,
And thorns of life; forgetting the great end
Of poesy, that it should be a friend
To soothe the cares, and lift the thoughts of man.

     Yet I rejoice: a myrtle fairer than
E'er grew in Paphos, from the bitter weeds
Lifts its sweet head into the air, and feeds   250
A silent space with ever sprouting green.
All tenderest birds there find a pleasant screen,
Creep through the shade with jaunty fluttering,
Nibble the little cupped flowers and sing.
Then let us clear away the choking thorns
From round its gentle stem; let the young fawns,

Yeaned in after times, when we are flown,
Find a fresh sward beneath it, overgrown
With simple flowers: let there nothing be
More boisterous than a lover's bended knee;   260
Nought more ungentle than the placid look
Of one who leans upon a closed book;
Nought more untranquil than the grassy slopes
Between two hills. All hail delightful hopes!
As she was wont, th' imagination
Into most lovely labyrinths will be gone,
And they shall be accounted poet kings
Who simply tell the most heart-easing things.
O may these joys be ripe before I die.

Will not some say that I presumptuously   270
Have spoken? that from hastening disgrace
'Twere better far to hide my foolish face?
That whining boyhood should with reverence bow
Ere the dread thunderbolt could reach? How!
If I do hide myself, it sure shall be
In the very fane, the light of Poesy:
If I do fall, at least I will be laid
Beneath the silence of a poplar shade;
And over me the grass shall be smooth shaven;
And there shall be a kind memorial graven.   280
But off Despondence! miserable bane!
They should not know thee, who athirst to gain
A noble end, are thirsty every hour.
What though I am not wealthy in the dower
Of spanning wisdom; though I do not know
The shiftings of the mighty winds that blow
Hither and thither all the changing thoughts
Of man: though no great minist'ring reason sorts
Out the dark mysteries of human souls
To clear conceiving: yet there ever rolls   290
A vast idea before me, and I glean
Therefrom my liberty; thence too I've seen
The end and aim of Poesy. 'Tis clear
As anything most true; as that the year
Is made of the four seasons—manifest
As a large cross, some old cathedral's crest,
Lifted to the white clouds. Therefore should I
Be but the essence of deformity,
A coward, did my very eye-lids wink
At speaking out what I have dared to think.   300
Ah! rather let me like a madman run
Over some precipice; let the hot sun

Melt my Dedalian wings, and drive me down
Convuls'd and headlong! Stay! an inward frown
Of conscience bids me be more calm awhile.
An ocean dim, sprinkled with many an isle,
Spreads awfully before me. How much toil!
How many days! what desperate turmoil!
Ere I can have explored its widenesses.
Ah, what a task! upon my bended knees,   310
I could unsay those—no, impossible!
Impossible!

       For sweet relief I'll dwell
On humbler thoughts, and let this strange assay
Begun in gentleness die so away.
E'en now all tumult from my bosom fades:
I turn full hearted to the friendly aids
That smooth the path of honour; brotherhood,
And friendliness the nurse of mutual good.
The hearty grasp that sends a pleasant sonnet
Into the brain ere one can think upon it;   320
The silence when some rhymes are coming out;
And when they're come, the very pleasant rout:
The message certain to be done to-morrow.
'Tis perhaps as well that it should be to borrow
Some precious book from out its snug retreat,
To cluster round it when we next shall meet.
Scarce can I scribble on; for lovely airs
Are fluttering round the room like doves in pairs;
Many delights of that glad day recalling,
When first my senses caught their tender falling.   330
And with these airs come forms of elegance
Stooping their shoulders o'er a horse's prance,
Careless, and grand—fingers soft and round
Parting luxuriant curls;—and the swift bound
Of Bacchus from his chariot, when his eye
Made Ariadne's cheek look blushingly.
Thus I remember all the pleasant flow
Of words at opening a portfolio.

Things such as these are ever harbingers
To trains of peaceful images: the stirs   340
Of a swan's neck unseen among the rushes:
A linnet starting all about the bushes:
A butterfly, with golden wings broad parted,
Nestling a rose, convuls'd as though it smarted
With over pleasure—many, many more,
Might I indulge at large in all my store

Of luxuries: yet I must not forget
Sleep, quiet with his poppy coronet:
For what there may be worthy in these rhymes
I partly owe to him: and thus, the chimes   350
Of friendly voices had just given place
To as sweet a silence, when I 'gan retrace
The pleasant day, upon a couch at ease.
It was a poet's house who keeps the keys
Of pleasure's temple. Round about were hung
The glorious features of the bards who sung
In other ages—cold and sacred busts
Smiled at each other. Happy he who trusts
To clear Futurity his darling fame!
Then there were fauns and satyrs taking aim   360
At swelling apples with a frisky leap
And reaching fingers, 'mid a luscious heap
Of vine-leaves. Then there rose to view a fane
Of liny marble, and thereto a train
Of nymphs approaching fairly o'er the sward:
One, loveliest, holding her white hand toward
The dazzling sun-rise: two sisters sweet
Bending their graceful figures till they meet
Over the trippings of a little child:
And some are hearing, eagerly, the wild   370
Thrilling liquidity of dewy piping.
See, in another picture, nymphs are wiping
Cherishingly Diana's timorous limbs;—
A fold of lawny mantle dabbling swims
At the bath's edge, and keeps a gentle motion
With the subsiding crystal: as when ocean
Heaves calmly its broad swelling smoothness o'er
Its rocky marge, and balances once more
The patient weeds; that now unshent by foam
Feel all about their undulating home.   380

Sappho's meek head was there half smiling down
At nothing; just as though the earnest frown
Of over thinking had that moment gone
From off her brow, and left her all alone.
Great Alfred's too, with anxious, pitying eyes,
As if he always listened to the sighs
Of the goaded world; and Kosciusko's worn
By horrid suffrance—mightily forlorn.
Petrarch, outstepping from the shady green,
Starts at the sight of Laura; nor can wean   390
His eyes from her sweet face. Most happy they!
For over them was seen a free display

Of out-spread wings, and from between them shone
The face of Poesy: from off her throne
She overlook'd things that I scarce could tell.
The very sense of where I was might well
Keep Sleep aloof: but more than that there came
Thought after thought to nourish up the flame
Within my breast; so that the morning light
Surprised me even from a sleepless night;   400
And up I rose refresh'd, and glad, and gay,
Resolving to begin that very day
These lines; and howsoever they be done,
I leave them as a father does his son.

ENDYMION

A POETIC ROMANCE

INSCRIBED

TO THE MEMORY

OF

THOMAS CHATTERTON

1818

PREFACE

KNOWING within myself the manner in which this Poem has been produced, it is not without a feeling of regret that I make it public. What manner I mean, will be quite clear to the reader, who must soon perceive great inexperience, immaturity, and every error denoting a feverish attempt, rather than a deed accomplished. The two first books, and indeed the two last, I feel sensible are not of such completion as to warrant their passing the press; nor should they if I thought a year's castigation would do them any good;—it will not: the foundations are too sandy. It is just that this youngster should die away: a sad thought for me, if I had not some hope that while it is dwindling I may be plotting, and fitting myself for verses fit to live.

This may be speaking too presumptuously, and may deserve a punishment: but no feeling man will be forward to inflict it: he will leave me alone, with the conviction that there is not a fiercer hell than the failure in a great object. This is not written with the least atom of purpose to forestall criticisms of course, but from the desire I have to conciliate men who are competent to look, and who do look with a zealous eye, to the honour of English literature.

The imagination of a boy is healthy, and the mature imagination of a man is healthy; but there is a space of life between, in which the soul is in a ferment, the character undecided, the way of life uncertain, the ambition thick-sighted: thence proceeds mawkishness, and all the thousand bitters which those men I speak of must necessarily taste in going over the following pages.

I hope I have not in too late a day touched the beautiful mythology of Greece, and dulled its brightness: for I wish to try once more, before I bid it farewell.

[TEIGNMOUTH] April 10, 1818.

ENDYMION:

BOOK I

A THING of beauty is a joy for ever:
Its loveliness increases; it will never
Pass into nothingness; but still will keep
A bower quiet for us, and a sleep
Full of sweet dreams, and health, and quiet breathing.
Therefore, on every morrow, are we wreathing
A flowery band to bind us to the earth,
Spite of despondence, of the inhuman dearth
Of noble natures, of the gloomy days,
Of all the unhealthy and o'er-darkened ways   10
Made for our searching: yes, in spite of all,
Some shape of beauty moves away the pall
From our dark spirits. Such the sun, the moon,
Trees old, and young, sprouting a shady boon
For simple sheep; and such are daffodils
With the green world they live in; and clear rills
That for themselves a cooling covert make
'Gainst the hot season; the mid forest brake,
Rich with a sprinkling of fair musk-rose blooms:
And such too is the grandeur of the dooms   20
We have imagined for the mighty dead;
All lovely tales that we have heard or read:
An endless fountain of immortal drink,
Pouring unto us from the heaven's brink.

Nor do we merely feel these essences
For one short hour; no, even as the trees
That whisper round a temple become soon
Dear as the temple's self, so does the moon,
The passion poesy, glories infinite,
Haunt us till they become a cheering light   30
Unto our souls, and bound to us so fast,
That, whether there be shine, or gloom o'ercast,
They always must be with us, or we die.

Therefore, 'tis with full happiness that I
Will trace the story of Endymion.
The very music of the name has gone

Into my being, and each pleasant scene
Is growing fresh before me as the green
Of our own vallies: so I will begin
Now while I cannot hear the city's din;   40
Now while the early budders are just new,
And run in mazes of the youngest hue
About old forests; while the willow trails ·
Its delicate amber; and the dairy pails
Bring home increase of milk. And, as the year
Grows lush in juicy stalks, I'll smoothly steer
My little boat, for many quiet hours,
With streams that deepen freshly into bowers.
Many and many a verse I hope to write,
Before the daisies, vermeil rimm'd and white,   50
Hide in deep herbage; and ere yet the bees
Hum about globes of clover and sweet peas,
I must be near the middle of my story.
O may no wintry season, bare and hoary,
See it half finish'd: but let Autumn bold,
With universal tinge of sober gold,
Be all about me when I make an end.
And now at once, adventuresome, I send
My herald thought into a wilderness:
There let its trumpet blow, and quickly dress   60
My uncertain path with green, that I may speed
Easily onward, thorough flowers and weed.

    Upon the sides of Latmos was outspread
A mighty forest; for the moist earth fed
So plenteously all weed-hidden roots
Into o'er-hanging boughs, and precious fruits.
And it had gloomy shades, sequestered deep,
Where no man went; and if from shepherd's keep
A lamb stray'd far a-down those inmost glens,
Never again saw he the happy pens   70
Whither his brethren, bleating with content,
Over the hills at every nightfall went.
Among the shepherds, 'twas believed ever,
That not one fleecy lamb which thus did sever
From the white flock, but pass'd unworried
By angry wolf, or pard with prying head,
Until it came to some unfooted plains
Where fed the herds of Pan: aye great his gains
Who thus one lamb did lose. Paths there were many,
Winding through palmy fern, and rushes fenny,   80
And ivy banks; all leading pleasantly
To a wide lawn, whence one could only see

Stems thronging all around between the swell
Of turf and slanting branches: who could tell
The freshness of the space of heaven above,
Edg'd round with dark tree tops? through which a dove
Would often beat its wings, and often too
A little cloud would move across the blue.

Full in the middle of this pleasantness
There stood a marble altar, with a tress   90
Of flowers budded newly; and the dew
Had taken fairy phantasies to strew
Daisies upon the sacred sward last eve,
And so the dawned light in pomp receive.
For 'twas the morn: Apollo's upward fire
Made every eastern cloud a silvery pyre
Of brightness so unsullied, that therein
A melancholy spirit well might win
Oblivion, and melt out his essence fine
Into the winds: rain-scented eglantine   100
Gave temperate sweets to that well-wooing sun;
The lark was lost in him; cold springs had run
To warm their chilliest bubbles in the grass;
Man's voice was on the mountains; and the mass
Of nature's lives and wonders puls'd tenfold,
To feel this sun-rise and its glories old.

Now while the silent workings of the dawn
Were busiest, into that self-same lawn
All suddenly, with joyful cries, there sped
A troop of little children garlanded;   110
Who gathering round the altar, seem'd to pry
Earnestly round as wishing to espy
Some folk of holiday: nor had they waited
For many moments, ere their ears were sated
With a faint breath of music, which ev'n then
Fill'd out its voice, and died away again.
Within a little space again it gave
Its airy swellings, with a gentle wave,
To light-hung leaves, in smoothest echoes breaking
Through copse-clad vallies,—ere their death, o'ertaking
The surgy murmurs of the lonely sea.   121

And now, as deep into the wood as we
Might mark a lynx's eye, there glimmered light
Fair faces and a rush of garments white,
Plainer and plainer showing, till at last
Into the widest alley they all past,

Making directly for the woodland altar.
O kindly muse! let not my weak tongue faulter
In telling of this goodly company,
Of their old piety, and of their glee: 130
But let a portion of ethereal dew
Fall on my head, and presently unmew
My soul; that I may dare, in wayfaring,
To stammer where old Chaucer us'd to sing.

Leading the way, young damsels danced along,
Bearing the burden of a shepherd song;
Each having a white wicker over brimm'd
With April's tender younglings: next, well trimm'd,
A crowd of shepherds with as sunburnt looks
As may be read of in Arcadian books;   140
Such as sat listening round Apollo's pipe,
When the great deity, for earth too ripe,
Let his divinity o'erflowing die
In music, through the vales of Thessaly:
Some idly trail'd their sheep-hooks on the ground,
And some kept up a shrilly mellow sound
With ebon-tipped flutes: close after these,
Now coming from beneath the forest trees,
A venerable priest full soberly,
Begirt with ministring looks: alway his eye   150
Stedfast upon the matted turf he kept,
And after him his sacred vestments swept.
From his right hand there swung a vase, milk-white,
Of mingled wine, out-sparkling generous light;
And in his left he held a basket full
Of all sweet herbs that searching eye could cull:
Wild thyme, and valley-lillies whiter still
Than Leda's love, and cresses from the rill.
His aged head, crowned with beechen wreath,
Seem'd like a poll of ivy in the teeth   160
Of winter hoar. Then came another crowd
Of shepherds, lifting in due time aloud
Their share of the ditty. After them appear'd,
Up-followed by a multitude that rear'd
Their voices to the clouds, a fair wrought car
Easily rolling so as scarce to mar
The freedom of three steeds of dapple brown:
Who stood therein did seem of great renown
Among the throng. His youth was fully blown,
Showing like Ganymede to manhood grown;   170
And, for those simple times, his garments were
A chieftain king's: beneath his breast, half bare,

Was hung a silver bugle, and between
His nervy knees there lay a boar-spear keen.
A smile was on his countenance; he seem'd,
To common lookers on, like one who dream'd
Of idleness in groves Elysian:
But there were some who feelingly could scan
A lurking trouble in his nether lip,
And see that oftentimes the reins would slip   180
Through his forgotten hands: then would they sigh,
And think of yellow leaves, of owlets' cry,
Of logs piled solemnly.—Ah, well-a-day,
Why should our young Endymion pine away!

  Soon the assembly, in a circle rang'd,
Stood silent round the shrine: each look was chang'd
To sudden veneration: women meek
Beckon'd their sons to silence; while each cheek
Of virgin bloom paled gently for slight fear.
Endymion too, without a forest peer,   190
Stood, wan, and pale, and with an awed face,
Among his brothers of the mountain chace.
In midst of all, the venerable priest
Eyed them with joy from greatest to the least,
And, after lifting up his aged hands,
Thus spake he: "Men of Latmos! shepherd bands!
Whose care it is to guard a thousand flocks:
Whether descended from beneath the rocks
That overtop your mountains; whether come
From vallies where the pipe is never dumb;   200
Or from your swelling downs, where sweet air stirs
Blue hare-bells lightly, and where prickly furze
Buds lavish gold; or ye, whose precious charge
Nibble their fill at ocean's very marge,
Whose mellow reeds are touch'd with sounds forlorn
By the dim echoes of Old Triton's horn:
Mothers and wives! who day by day prepare
The scrip, with needments, for the mountain air;
And all ye gentle girls who foster up
Udderless lambs, and in a little cup   210
Will put choice honey for a favoured youth:
Yea, every one attend! for in good truth
Our vows are wanting to our great god Pan.
Are not our lowing heifers sleeker than
Night-swollen mushrooms? Are not our wide plains
Speckled with countless fleeces? Have not rains
Green'd over April's lap? No howling sad
Sickens our fearful ewes; and we have had

Great bounty from Endymion our lord.
The earth is glad: the merry lark has pour'd   220
His early song against yon breezy sky,
That spreads so clear o'er our solemnity."

Thus ending, on the shrine he heap'd a spire
Of teeming sweets, enkindling sacred fire;
Anon he stain'd the thick and spongy sod
With wine, in honour of the shepherd-god.
Now while the earth was drinking it, and while
Bay leaves were crackling in the fragrant pile,
And gummy frankincense was sparkling bright
'Neath smothering parsley, and a hazy light   230
Spread greyly eastward, thus a chorus sang:

"O THOU, whose mighty palace roof doth hang
From jagged trunks, and overshadoweth
Eternal whispers, glooms, the birth, life, death ·
Of unseen flowers in heavy peacefulness;
Who lov'st to see the hamadryads dress
Their ruffled locks where meeting hazels darken;
And through whole solemn hours dost sit, and hearken
The dreary melody of bedded reeds—
In desolate places, where dank moisture breeds   240
The pipy hemlock to strange overgrowth;
Bethinking thee, how melancholy loth
Thou wast to lose fair Syrinx—do thou now,
By thy love's milky brow!
By all the trembling mazes that she ran,
Hear us, great Pan!

"O thou, for whose soul-soothing quiet, turtles
Passion their voices cooingly 'mong myrtles,
What time thou wanderest at eventide
Through sunny meadows, that outskirt the side   250
Of thine enmossed realms: O thou, to whom
Broad leaved fig trees even now foredoom
Their ripen'd fruitage; yellow girted bees
Their golden honeycombs; our village leas
Their fairest blossom'd beans and poppied corn;
The chuckling linnet its five young unborn,
To sing for thee; low creeping strawberries
Their summer coolness; pent up butterflies
Their freckled wings; yea, the fresh budding year
All its completions—be quickly near,   260
By every wind that nods the mountain pine,
O forester divine!

"Thou, to whom every faun and satyr flies
For willing service; whether to surprise
The squatted hare while in half sleeping fit;
Or upward ragged precipices flit
To save poor lambkins from the eagle's maw;
Or by mysterious enticement draw
Bewildered shepherds to their path again;
Or to tread breathless round the frothy main,   270
And gather up all fancifullest shells
For thee to tumble into Naiads' cells,
And, being hidden, laugh at their out-peeping;
Or to delight thee with fantastic leaping,
The while they pelt each other on the crown
With silvery oak apples, and fir cones brown—
By all the echoes that about thee ring,
Hear us, O satyr king!

"O Hearkener to the loud clapping shears
While ever and anon to his shorn peers   280
A ram goes bleating: Winder of the horn,
When snouted wild-boars routing tender corn
Anger our huntsmen: Breather round our farms,
To keep off mildews, and all weather harms:
Strange ministrant of undescribed sounds,
That come a swooning over hollow grounds,
And wither drearily on barren moors:
Dread opener of the mysterious doors
Leading to universal knowledge—see,
Great son of Dryope,   290
The many that are come to pay their vows
With leaves about their brows!

"Be still the unimaginable lodge
For solitary thinkings; such as dodge
Conception to the very bourne of heaven,
Then leave the naked brain: be still the leaven,
That spreading in this dull and clodded earth
Gives it a touch ethereal—a new birth:
Be still a symbol of immensity;
A firmament reflected in a sea;   300
An element filling the space between;
An unknown—but no more: we humbly screen
With uplift hands our foreheads, lowly bending,
And giving out a shout most heaven rending,
Conjure thee to receive our humble Pæan,
Upon thy Mount Lycean!"

Even while they brought the burden to a close,
A shout from the whole multitude arose,
That lingered in the air like dying rolls
Of abrupt thunder, when Ionian shoals   310
Of dolphins bob their noses through the brine.
Meantime, on shady levels, mossy fine,
Young companies nimbly began dancing
To the swift treble pipe, and humming string.
Aye, those fair living forms swam heavily
To tunes forgotten—out of memory:
Fair creatures! whose young children's children bred
Thermopylæ its heroes—not yet dead,
But in old marbles ever beautiful.
High genitors, unconscious did they cull   320
Time's sweet first-fruits—they danc'd to weariness,
And then in quiet circles did they press
The hillock turf, and caught the latter end
Of some strange history, potent to send
A young mind from its bodily tenement.
Or they might watch the quoit-pitchers, intent
On either side; pitying the sad death
Of Hyacinthus, when the cruel breath
Of Zephyr slew him,—Zephyr penitent,
Who now, ere Phœbus mounts the firmament,   330
Fondles the flower amid the sobbing rain.
The archers too, upon a wider plain,
Beside the feathery whizzing of the shaft,
And the dull twanging bowstring, and the raft
Branch down sweeping from a tall ash top,
Call'd up a thousand thoughts to envelope
Those who would watch. Perhaps, the trembling knee
And frantic gape of lonely Niobe,
Poor, lonely Niobe! when her lovely young
Were dead and gone, and her caressing tongue   340
Lay a lost thing upon her paly lip,
And very, very deadliness did nip
Her motherly cheeks. Arous'd from this sad mood
By one, who at a distance loud halloo'd,
Uplifting his strong bow into the air,
Many might after brighter visions stare:
After the Argonauts, in blind amaze
Tossing about on Neptune's restless ways,
Until, from the horizon's vaulted side,
There shot a golden splendour far and wide,   350
Spangling those million poutings of the brine
With quivering ore: 'twas even an awful shine

From the exaltation of Apollo's bow;
A heavenly beacon in their dreary woe.
Who thus were ripe for high contemplating,
Might turn their steps towards the sober ring
Where sat Endymion and the aged priest
'Mong shepherds gone in eld, whose looks increas'd
The silvery setting of their mortal star.
There they discours'd upon the fragile bar   360
That keeps us from our homes ethereal;
And what our duties there: to nightly call
Vesper, the beauty-crest of summer weather;
To summon all the downiest clouds together
For the sun's purple couch; to emulate
In minist'ring the potent rule of fate
With speed of fire-tail'd exhalations;
To tint her pallid cheek with bloom, who cons
Sweet poesy by moonlight: besides these,
A world of other unguess'd offices.   370
Anon they wander'd, by divine converse,
Into Elysium; vieing to rehearse
Each one his own anticipated bliss.
One felt heart-certain that he could not miss
His quick gone love, among fair blossom'd boughs,
Where every zephyr-sigh pouts, and endows
Her lips with music for the welcoming.
Another wish'd, mid that eternal spring,
To meet his rosy child, with feathery sails,
Sweeping, eye-earnestly, through almond vales: 380
Who, suddenly, should stoop through the smooth wind,
And with the balmiest leaves his temples bind;
And, ever after, through those regions be
His messenger, his little Mercury.
Some were athirst in soul to see again
Their fellow huntsmen o'er the wide champaign
In times long past; to sit with them, and talk
Of all the chances in their earthly walk;
Comparing, joyfully, their plenteous stores
Of happiness, to when upon the moors,   390
Benighted, close they huddled from the cold,
And shar'd their famish'd scrips. Thus all out-told
Their fond imaginations,—saving him
Whose eyelids curtain'd up their jewels dim,
Endymion: yet hourly had he striven
To hide the cankering venom, that had riven
His fainting recollections. Now indeed
His senses had swoon'd off: he did not heed

The sudden silence, or the whispers low,
Or the old eyes dissolving at his woe,   400
Or anxious calls, or close of trembling palms,
Or maiden's sigh, that grief itself embalms:
But in the self-same fixed trance he kept,
Like one who on the earth had never stept.
Aye, even as dead-still as a marble man,
Frozen in that old tale Arabian.

    Who whispers him so pantingly and close?
Peona, his sweet sister: of all those,
His friends, the dearest. Hushing signs she made,
And breath'd a sister's sorrow to persuade   410
A yielding up, a cradling on her care.
Her eloquence did breathe away the curse:
She led him, like some midnight spirit nurse
Of happy changes in emphatic dreams,
Along a path between two little streams,—
Guarding his forehead, with her round elbow,
From low-grown branches, and his footsteps slow
From stumbling over stumps and hillocks small;
Until they came to where these streamlets fall,
With mingled bubblings and a gentle rush,   420
Into a river, clear, brimful, and flush
With crystal mocking of the trees and sky.
A little shallop, floating there hard by,
Pointed its beak over the fringed bank;
And soon it lightly dipt, and rose, and sank,
And dipt again, with the young couple's weight,—
Peona guiding, through the water straight,
Towards a bowery island opposite;
Which gaining presently, she steered light
Into a shady, fresh, and ripply cove,   430
Where nested was an arbour, overwove
By many a summer's silent fingering;
To whose cool bosom she was used to bring
Her playmates, with their needle broidery,
And minstrel memories of times gone by.

    So she was gently glad to see him laid
Under her favourite bower's quiet shade,
On her own couch, new made of flower leaves,
Dried carefully on the cooler side of sheaves
When last the sun his autumn tresses shook,   440
And the tann'd harvesters rich armfuls took.
Soon was he quieted to slumbrous rest:
But, ere it crept upon him, he had prest

Peona's busy hand against his lips,
And still, a sleeping, held her finger-tips
In tender pressure. And as a willow keeps
A patient watch over the stream that creeps
Windingly by it, so the quiet maid
Held her in peace: so that a whispering blade
Of grass, a wailful gnat, a bee bustling   450
Down in the blue-bells, or a wren light rustling
Among sere leaves and twigs, might all be heard.

   O magic sleep! O comfortable bird,
That broodest o'er the troubled sea of the mind
Till it is hush'd and smooth! O unconfin'd
Restraint! imprisoned liberty! great key
To golden palaces, strange minstrelsy,
Fountains grotesque, new trees, bespangled caves,
Echoing grottos, full of tumbling waves
And moonlight; aye, to all the mazy world   460
Of silvery enchantment!—who, upfurl'd
Beneath thy drowsy wing a triple hour,
But renovates and lives?—Thus, in the bower,
Endymion was calm'd to life again.
Opening his eyelids with a healthier brain,
He said: "I feel this thine endearing love
All through my bosom: thou art as a dove
Trembling its closed eyes and sleeked wings
About me; and the pearliest dew not brings
Such morning incense from the fields of May,   470
As do those brighter drops that twinkling stray
From those kind eyes,—the very home and haunt
Of sisterly affection. Can I want
Aught else, aught nearer heaven, than such tears?
Yet dry them up, in bidding hence all fears
That, any longer, I will pass my days
Alone and sad. No, I will once more raise
My voice upon the mountain-heights; once more
Make my horn parley from their foreheads hoar:
Again my trooping hounds their tongues shall loll   480
Around the breathed boar: again I'll poll
The fair-grown yew tree, for a chosen bow:
And, when the pleasant sun is getting low,
Again I'll linger in a sloping mead
To hear the speckled thrushes, and see feed
Our idle sheep. So be thou cheered sweet,
And, if thy lute is here, softly intreat
My soul to keep in its resolved course."

Hereat Peona, in their silver source,
Shut her pure sorrow drops with glad exclaim,   490
And took a lute, from which there pulsing came
A lively prelude, fashioning the way
In which her voice should wander. 'Twas a lay
More subtle cadenced, more forest wild
Than Dryope's lone lulling of her child;
And nothing since has floated in the air
So mournful strange. Surely some influence rare
Went, spiritual, through the damsel's hand;
For still, with Delphic emphasis, she spann'd
The quick invisible strings, even though she saw   500
Endymion's spirit melt away and thaw
Before the deep intoxication.
But soon she came, with sudden burst, upon
Her self-possession—swung the lute aside,
And earnestly said: "Brother, 'tis vain to hide
That thou dost know of things mysterious,
Immortal, starry; such alone could thus
Weigh down thy nature. Hast thou sinn'd in aught
Offensive to the heavenly powers? Caught
A Paphian dove upon a message sent?   510
Thy deathful bow against some deer-herd bent
Sacred to Dian? Haply, thou hast seen
Her naked limbs among the alders green;
And that, alas, is death. No, I can trace
Something more high perplexing in thy face!"

Endymion look'd at her, and press'd her hand,
And said, "Art thou so pale, who wast so bland
And merry in our meadows? How is this?
Tell me thine ailment: tell me all amiss!—
Ah! thou hast been unhappy at the change   520
Wrought suddenly in me. What indeed more strange?
Or more complete to overwhelm surmise?
Ambition is so sluggard: 'tis no prize,
That toiling years would put within my grasp,
That I have sighed for: with so deadly gasp
No man e'er panted for a mortal love.
So all have set my heavier grief above
These things which happen. Rightly have they done:
I, who still saw the horizontal sun
Heave his broad shoulder o'er the edge of the world,
Out-facing Lucifer, and then had hurl'd   531
My spear aloft, as signal for the chace—
I, who, for very sport of heart, would race

With my own steed from Araby; pluck down
A vulture from his towery perching; frown
A lion into growling, loth retire—
To lose, at once, all my toil-breeding fire,
And sing thus low! but I will ease my breast
Of secret grief, here in this bowery nest.

"This river does not see the naked sky,   540
Till it begins to progress silverly
Around the western border of the wood,
Whence, from a certain spot, its winding flood
Seems at the distance like a crescent moon:
And in that nook, the very pride of June,
Had I been used to pass my weary eves;
The rather for the sun unwilling leaves
So dear a picture of his sovereign power,
And I could witness his most kingly hour,
When he doth tighten up the golden reins,   550
And paces leisurely down amber plains
His snorting four. Now when his chariot last
Its beams against the zodiac-lion cast,
There blossom'd suddenly a magic bed
Of sacred ditamy, and poppies red:
At which I wondered greatly, knowing well
That but one night had wrought this flowery spell;
And, sitting down close by, began to muse
What it might mean. Perhaps, thought I, Morpheus,
In passing here, his owlet pinions shook;   560
Or, it may be, ere matron Night uptook
Her ebon urn, young Mercury, by stealth,
Had dipt his rod in it: such garland wealth
Came not by common growth. Thus on I thought,
Until my head was dizzy and distraught.
Moreover, through the dancing poppies stole
A breeze, most softly lulling to my soul;
And shaping visions all about my sight
Of colours, wings, and bursts of spangly light;
The which became more strange, and strange, and dim,
And then were gulph'd in a tumultuous swim: 571
And then I fell asleep. Ah, can I tell
The enchantment that afterwards befel?
Yet it was but a dream: yet such a dream
That never tongue, although it overteem
With mellow utterance, like a cavern spring,
Could figure out and to conception bring
All I beheld and felt. Methought I lay
Watching the zenith, where the milky way

Among the stars in virgin splendour pours;
And travelling my eye, until the doors
Of heaven appear'd to open for my flight,
I became loth and fearful to alight
From such high soaring by a downward glance:
So kept me stedfast in that airy trance,
Spreading imaginary pinions wide.
When, presently, the stars began to glide,
And faint away, before my eager view:
At which I sigh'd that I could not pursue,   590
And dropt my vision to the horizon's verge;
And lo! from opening clouds, I saw emerge
The loveliest moon, that ever silver'd o'er
A shell for Neptune's goblet: she did soar
So passionately bright, my dazzled soul
Commingling with her argent spheres did roll
Through clear and cloudy, even when she went
At last into a dark and vapoury tent—
Whereat, methought, the lidless-eyed train
Of planets all were in the blue again.   600
To commune with those orbs, once more I rais'd
My sight right upward: but it was quite dazed
By a bright something, sailing down apace,
Making me quickly veil my eyes and face:
Again I look'd, and, O ye deities,
Who from Olympus watch our destinies!
Whence that completed form of all completeness?
Whence came that high perfection of all sweetness?
Speak, stubborn earth, and tell me where, O where
Hast thou a symbol of her golden hair?   610
Not oat-sheaves drooping in the western sun;
Not—thy soft hand, fair sister! let me shun
Such follying before thee—yet she had,
Indeed, locks bright enough to make me mad;
And they were simply gordian'd up and braided,
Leaving, in naked comeliness, unshaded,
Her pearl round ears, white neck, and orbed brow;
The which were blended in, I know not how,
With such a paradise of lips and eyes,
Blush-tinted cheeks, half smiles, and faintest sighs,   620
That, when I think thereon, my spirit clings
And plays about its fancy, till the stings
Of human neighbourhood envenom all.
Unto what awful power shall I call?
To what high fane?—Ah! see her hovering feet,
More bluely vein'd, more soft, more whitely sweet

Than those of sea-born Venus, when she rose
From out her cradle shell. The wind out-blows
Her scarf into a fluttering pavillion;
'Tis blue, and over-spangled with a million
Of little eyes, as though thou wert to shed,   630
Over the darkest, lushest blue-bell bed,
Handfuls of daisies."—"Endymion, how strange!
Dream within dream!"—"She took an airy range,
And then, towards me, like a very maid,
Came blushing, waning, willing, and afraid,
And press'd me by the hand: Ah! 'twas too much;
Methought I fainted at the charmed touch,
Yet held my recollection, even as one
Who dives three fathoms where the waters run
Gurgling in beds of coral: for anon,   640
I felt upmounted in that region
Where falling stars dart their artillery forth,
And eagles struggle with the buffeting north
That ballances the heavy meteor-stone;—
Felt too, I was not fearful, nor alone,
But lapp'd and lull'd along the dangerous sky.
Soon, as it seem'd, we left our journeying high,
And straightway into frightful eddies swoop'd;
Such as aye muster where grey time has scoop'd
Huge dens and caverns in a mountain's side: 650
There hollow sounds arous'd me, and I sigh'd
To faint once more by looking on my bliss—
I was distracted; madly did I kiss
The wooing arms which held me, and did give
My eyes at once to death: but 'twas to live,
To take in draughts of life from the gold fount
Of kind and passionate looks; to count, and count
The moments, by some greedy help that seem'd
A second self, that each might be redeem'd
And plunder'd of its load of blessedness.   660
Ah, desperate mortal! I e'en dar'd to press
Her very cheek against my crowned lip,
And, at that moment, felt my body dip
Into a warmer air: a moment more,
Our feet were soft in flowers. There was store
Of newest joys upon that alp. Sometimes
A scent of violets, and blossoming limes,
Loiter'd around us; then of honey cells,
Made delicate from all white-flower bells;
And once, above the edges of our nest,   670
An arch face peep'd,—an Oread as I guess'd.

"Why did I dream that sleep o'er-power'd me
In midst of all this heaven? Why not see,
Far off, the shadows of his pinions dark,
And stare them from me? But no, like a spark
That needs must die, although its little beam
Reflects upon a diamond, my sweet dream
Fell into nothing—into stupid sleep.
And so it was, until a gentle creep,
A careful moving caught my waking ears,   680
And up I started: Ah! my sighs, my tears,
My clenched hands;—for lo! the poppies hung
Dew-dabbled on their stalks, the ouzel sung
A heavy ditty, and the sullen day
Had chidden herald Hesperus away,
With leaden looks: the solitary breeze
Bluster'd, and slept, and its wild self did teaze
With wayward melancholy; and I thought,
Mark me, Peona! that sometimes it brought
Faint fare-thee-wells, and sigh-shrilled adieus!—   690
Away I wander'd—all the pleasant hues
Of heaven and earth had faded: deepest shades
Were deepest dungeons: heaths and sunny glades
Were full of pestilent light; our taintless rills
Seem'd sooty, and o'er-spread with upturn'd gills
Of dying fish; the vermeil rose had blown
In frightful scarlet, and its thorns out-grown
Like spiked aloe. If an innocent bird
Before my heedless footsteps stirr'd, and stirr'd   700
In little journeys, I beheld in it
A disguis'd demon, missioned to knit
My soul with under darkness; to entice
My stumblings down some monstrous precipice:
Therefore I eager followed, and did curse
The disappointment. Time, that aged nurse,
Rock'd me to patience. Now, thank gentle heaven!
These things, with all their comfortings, are given
To my down-sunken hours, and with thee,
Sweet sister, help to stem the ebbing sea
Of weary life."
            Thus ended he, and both   710
Sat silent: for the maid was very loth
To answer; feeling well that breathed words
Would all be lost, unheard, and vain as swords
Against the enchased crocodile, or leaps
Of grasshoppers against the sun. She weeps,
And wonders; struggles to devise some blame;
To put on such a look as would say, *Shame*

On this poor weakness! but, for all her strife,
She could as soon have crush'd away the life   719
From a sick dove. At length, to break the pause,
She said with trembling chance: "Is this the cause?
This all? Yet it is strange, and sad, alas!
That one who through this middle earth should pass
Most like a sojourning demi-god, and leave
His name upon the harp-string, should achieve
No higher bard than simple maidenhood,
Singing alone, and fearfully,—how the blood
Left his young cheek; and how he used to stray
He knew not where; and how he would say, *nay,*
If any said 'twas love: and yet 'twas love;   730
What could it be but love? How a ring-dove
Let fall a sprig of yew tree in his path;
And how he died: and then, that love doth scathe,
The gentle heart, as northern blasts do roses;
And then the ballad of his sad life closes
With sighs, and an alas!—Endymion!
Be rather in the trumpet's mouth,—anon
Among the winds at large—that all may hearken!
Although, before the crystal heavens darken,
I watch and dote upon the silver lakes   740
Pictur'd in western cloudiness, that takes
The semblance of gold rocks and bright gold sands,
Islands, and creeks, and amber-fretted strands
With horses prancing o'er them, palaces
And towers of amethyst,—would I so teaze
My pleasant days, because I could not mount
Into those regions? The Morphean fount
Of that fine element that visions, dreams,
And fitful whims of sleep are made of, streams
Into its airy channels with so subtle,   750
So thin a breathing, not the spider's shuttle,
Circled a million times within the space
Of a swallow's nest-door, could delay a trace,
A tinting of its quality: how light
Must dreams themselves be; seeing they're more slight
Than the mere nothing that engenders them!
Then wherefore sully the entrusted gem
Of high and noble life with thoughts so sick?
Why pierce high-fronted honour to the quick
For nothing but a dream?" Hereat the youth   760
Look'd up: a conflicting of shame and ruth
Was in his plaited brow: yet, his eyelids
Widened a little, as when Zephyr bids

A little breeze to creep between the fans
Of careless butterflies: amid his pains
He seemed to taste a drop of manna-dew,
Full palatable; and a colour grew
Upon his cheek, while thus he lifeful spake.

"Peona! ever have I long'd to slake
My thirst for the world's praises: nothing base,   770
No merely slumberous phantasm, could unlace
The stubborn canvas for my voyage prepar'd—
Though now 'tis tatter'd; leaving my bark bar'd
And sullenly drifting: yet my higher hope
Is of too wide, too rainbow-large a scope,
To fret at myriads of earthly wrecks.
Wherein lies happiness? In that which becks
Our ready minds to fellowship divine,
A fellowship with essence; till we shine,
Full alchemiz'd, and free of space. Behold   780
The clear religion of heaven! Fold
A rose leaf round thy finger's taperness,
And soothe thy lips: hist, when the airy stress
Of music's kiss impregnates the free winds,
And with a sympathetic touch unbinds
Æolian magic from their lucid wombs:
Then old songs waken from enclouded tombs;
Old ditties sigh above their father's grave;
Ghosts of melodious prophecyings rave
Round every spot where trod Apollo's foot;   790
Bronze clarions awake, and faintly bruit,
Where long ago a giant battle was;
And, from the turf, a lullaby doth pass
In every place where infant Orpheus slept.
Feel we these things?—that moment have we stept
Into a sort of oneness, and our state
Is like a floating spirit's. But there are
Richer entanglements, enthralments far
More self-destroying, leading, by degrees,
To the chief intensity: the crown of these   800
Is made of love and friendship, and sits high
Upon the forehead of humanity.
All its more ponderous and bulky worth
Is friendship, whence there ever issues forth
A steady splendour; but at the tip-top,
There hangs by unseen film, an orbed drop
Of light, and that is love: its influence,
Thrown in our eyes, genders a novel sense,

At which we start and fret; till in the end,
Melting into its radiance, we blend,   810
Mingle, and so become a part of it,—
Nor with aught else can our souls interknit
So wingedly: when we combine therewith,
Life's self is nourish'd by its proper pith,
And we are nurtured like a pelican brood.
Aye, so delicious is the unsating food,
That men, who might have tower'd in the van
Of all the congregated world, to fan
And winnow from the coming step of time
All chaff of custom, wipe away all slime   820
Left by men-slugs and human serpentry,
Have been content to let occasion die,
Whilst they did sleep in love's elysium.
And, truly, I would rather be struck dumb,
Than speak against this ardent listlessness:
For I have ever thought that it might bless
The world with benefits unknowingly;
As does the nightingale, upperched high,
And cloister'd among cool and bunched leaves—
She sings but to her love, nor e'er conceives   830
How tiptoe Night holds back her dark-grey hood.
Just so may love, although 'tis understood
The mere commingling of passionate breath,
Produce more than our searching witnesseth:
What I know not: but who, of men, can tell
That flowers would bloom, or that green fruit would swell
To melting pulp, that fish would have bright mail,
The earth its dower of river, wood, and vale,
The meadows runnels, runnels pebble-stones,
The seed its harvest, or the lute its tones,   840
Tones ravishment, or ravishment its sweet
If human souls did never kiss and greet?

   "Now, if this earthly love has power to make
Men's being mortal, immortal; to shake
Ambition from their memories, and brim
Their measure of content: what merest whim,
Seems all this poor endeavour after fame,
To one, who keeps within his stedfast aim
A love immortal, an immortal too.
Look not so wilder'd; for these things are true,   850
And never can be born of atomies
That buzz about our slumbers, like brain-flies,
Leaving us fancy-sick. No, no, I'm sure,
My restless spirit never could endure

To breed so long upon one luxury,
Unless it did, though fearfully, espy
A hope beyond the shadow of a dream.
My sayings will the less obscured seem,
When I have told thee how my waking sight
Has made me scruple whether that same night   860
Was pass'd in dreaming. Hearken, sweet Peona!
Beyond the matron-temple of Latona,
Which we should see but for these darkening boughs,
Lies a deep hollow, from whose ragged brows
Bushes and trees do lean all round athwart
And meet so nearly, that with wings outraught,
And spreaded tail, a vulture could not glide
Past them, but he must brush on every side.
Some moulder'd steps lead into this cool cell,
Far as the slabbed margin of a well,   870
Whose patient level peeps its crystal eye
Right upward, through the bushes, to the sky.
Oft have I brought thee flowers, on their stalks set
Like vestal primroses, but dark velvet
Edges them round, and they have golden pits:
'Twas there I got them, from the gaps and slits
In a mossy stone, that sometimes was my seat,
When all above was faint with mid-day heat.
And there in strife no burning thoughts to heed,
I'd bubble up the water through a reed;   880
So reaching back to boy-hood: make me ships
Of moulted feathers, touchwood, alder chips,
With leaves stuck in them; and the Neptune be
Of their petty ocean. Oftener, heavily,
When love-lorn hours had left me less a child,
I sat contemplating the figures wild
Of o'er-head clouds melting the mirror through.
Upon a day, while thus I watch'd, by flew
A cloudy Cupid, with his bow and quiver;
So plainly character'd, no breeze would shiver   890
The happy chance: so happy, I was fain
To follow it upon the open plain,
And, therefore, was just going; when, behold!
A wonder, fair as any I have told—
The same bright face I tasted in my sleep,
Smiling in the clear well. My heart did leap
Through the cool depth.—It moved as if to flee—
I started up, when lo! refreshfully,
There came upon my face in plenteous showers   899
Dew-drops, and dewy buds, and leaves, and flowers,

Wrapping all objects from my smothered sight,
Bathing my spirit in a new delight.
Aye, such a breathless honey-feel of bliss
Alone preserved me from the drear abyss
Of death, for the fair form had gone again.
Pleasure is oft a visitant; but pain
Clings cruelly to us, like the gnawing sloth
On the deer's tender haunches: late, and loth,
'Tis scar'd away by slow returning pleasure.
How sickening, how dark the dreadful leisure   910
Of weary days, made deeper exquisite,
By a fore-knowledge of unslumbrous night!
Like sorrow came upon me, heavier still,
Than when I wander'd from the poppy hill:
And a whole age of lingering moments crept
Sluggishly by, ere more contentment swept
Away at once the deadly yellow spleen.
Yes, thrice have I this fair enchantment seen;
Once more been tortured with renewed life.
When last the wintry gusts gave over strife   920
With the conquering sun of spring, and left the skies
Warm and serene, but yet with moistened eyes
In pity of the shatter'd infant buds,—
That time thou didst adorn, with amber studs,
My hunting cap, because I laugh'd and smil'd,
Chatted with thee, and many days exil'd
All torment from my breast;—'twas even then,
Straying about, yet, coop'd up in the den
Of helpless discontent,—hurling my lance
From place to place, and following at chance,   930
At last, by hap, through some young trees it struck,
And, plashing among bedded pebbles, stuck
In the middle of a brook,—whose silver ramble
Down twenty little falls, through reeds and bramble,
Tracing along, it brought me to a cave,
Whence it ran brightly forth, and white did lave
The nether sides of mossy stones and rock,—
'Mong which it gurgled blythe adieus, to mock
its own sweet grief at parting. Overhead,   939
Hung a lush screen of drooping weeds, and spread
Thick, as to curtain up some wood-nymph's home.
"Ah! impious mortal, whither do I roam?"
Said I, low voic'd: "Ah, whither! 'Tis the grot
"Of Proserpine, when Hell, obscure and hot,
"Doth her resign; and where her tender hands
"She dabbles, on the cool and sluicy sands:

"Or 'tis the cell of Echo, where she sits,
"And babbles thorough silence, till her wits
"Are gone in tender madness, and anon,
"Faints into sleep, with many a dying tone   950
"Of sadness. O that she would take my vows,
"And breathe them sighingly among the boughs,
"To sue her gentle ears for whose fair head,
"Daily, I pluck sweet flowerets from their bed,
"And weave them dyingly—send honey-whispers
"Round every leaf, that all those gentle lispers
"May sigh my love unto her pitying!
"O charitable Echo! hear, and sing
"This ditty to her!—tell her"—so I stay'd
My foolish tongue, and listening, half afraid,   960
Stood stupefied with my own empty folly,
And blushing for the freaks of melancholy.
Salt tears were coming, when I heard my name
Most fondly lipp'd, and then these accents came:
"Endymion! the cave is secreter
"Than the isle of Delos. Echo hence shall stir
"No sighs but sigh-warm kisses, or light noise
"Of thy combing hand, the while it travelling cloys
"And trembles through my labyrinthine hair."
At that oppress'd I hurried in.—Ah! where   970
Are those swift moments? Whither are they fled?
I'll smile no more, Peona; nor will wed
Sorrow the way to death; but patiently
Bear up against it: so farewell, sad sigh;
And come instead demurest meditation,
To occupy me wholly, and to fashion
My pilgrimage for the world's dusky brink.
No more will I count over, link by link,
My chain of grief: no longer strive to find
A half-forgetfulness in mountain wind   980
Blustering about my ears: aye, thou shalt see,
Dearest of sisters, what my life shall be;
What a calm round of hours shall make my days.
There is a paly flame of hope that plays
Where'er I look: but yet, I'll say 'tis naught—
And here I bid it die. Have not I caught,
Already, a more healthy countenance?
By this the sun is setting; we may chance
Meet some of our near-dwellers with my car."

This said, he rose, faint-smiling like a star   990
Through autumn mists, and took Peona's hand:
They stept into the boat, and launch'd from land.

BOOK II

O SOVEREIGN power of love! O grief! O balm!
All records, saving thine, come cool, and calm,
And shadowy, through the mist of passed years:
For others, good or bad, hatred and tears
Have become indolent; but touching thine,
One sigh doth echo, one poor sob doth pine,
One kiss brings honey-dew from buried days.
The woes of Troy, towers smothering o'er their blaze,
Stiff-holden shields, far-piercing spears, keen blades,
Struggling, and blood, and shrieks—all dimly fades
Into some backward corner of the brain;   11
Yet, in our very souls, we feel amain
The close of Troilus and Cressid sweet.
Hence, pageant history! hence, gilded cheat!
Swart planet in the universe of deeds!
Wide sea, that one continuous murmur breeds
Along the pebbled shore of memory!
Many old rotten-timber'd boats there be
Upon thy vaporous bosom, magnified
To goodly vessels; many a sail of pride,   20
And golden keel'd, is left unlaunch'd and dry.
But wherefore this? What care, though owl did fly
About the great Athenian admiral's mast?
What care, though striding Alexander past
The Indus with his Macedonian numbers?
Though old Ulysses tortured from his slumbers
The glutted Cyclops, what care?—Juliet leaning
Amid her window-flowers,—sighing,—weaning
Tenderly her fancy from its maiden snow,
Doth more avail than these: the silver flow   30
Of Hero's tears, the swoon of Imogen,
Fair Pastorella in the bandit's den,
Are things to brood on with more ardency
Than the death-day of empires. Fearfully
Must such conviction come upon his head,
Who, thus far, discontent, has dared to tread,
Without one muse's smile, or kind behest,
The path of love and poesy. But rest,
In chaffing restlessness, is yet more drear
Than to be crush'd, in striving to uprear   40
Love's standard on the battlements of song.
So once more days and nights aid me along,
Like legion'd soldiers.

Brain-sick shepherd prince,
What promise hast thou faithful guarded since
The day of sacrifice? Or, have new sorrows
Come with the constant dawn upon thy morrows?
Alas! 'tis his old grief. For many days,
Has he been wandering in uncertain ways:
Through wilderness, and woods of mossed oaks;
Counting his woe-worn minutes, by the strokes   50
Of the lone woodcutter; and listening still,
Hour after hour, to each lush-leav'd rill.
Now he is sitting by a shady spring,
And elbow-deep with feverous fingering
Stems the upbursting cold: a wild rose tree
Pavillions him in bloom, and he doth see
A bud which snares his fancy: lo! but now
He plucks it, dips its stalk in the water: how!
It swells, it buds, it flowers beneath his sight;
And, in the middle, there is softly pight   60
A golden butterfly; upon whose wings
There must be surely character'd strange things,
For with wide eye he wonders, and smiles oft.

Lightly this little herald flew aloft,
Follow'd by glad Endymion's clasped hands:
Onward it flies. From languor's sullen bands
His limbs are loos'd, and eager, on he hies
Dazzled to trace it in the sunny skies.
It seem'd he flew, the way so easy was;
And like a new-born spirit did he pass   70
Through the green evening quiet in the sun,
O'er many a heath, through many a woodland dun,
Through buried paths, where sleepy twilight dreams
The summer time away. One track unseams
A wooded cleft, and, far away, the blue
Of ocean fades upon him; then, anew,
He sinks adown a solitary glen,
Where there was never sound of mortal men,
Saving, perhaps, some snow-light cadences
Melting to silence, when upon the breeze   80
Some holy bark let forth an anthem sweet,
To cheer itself to Delphi. Still his feet
Went swift beneath the merry-winged guide,
Until it reach'd a splashing fountain's side
That, near a cavern's mouth, for ever pour'd
Unto the temperate air: then high it soar'd,
And, downward, suddenly began to dip,
As if, athirst with so much toil, 'twould sip

The crystal spout-head: so it did, with touch
Most delicate, as though afraid to smutch   90
Even with mealy gold the waters clear.
But, at that very touch, to disappear
So fairy-quick, was strange! Bewildered,
Endymion sought around, and shook each bed
Of covert flowers in vain; and then he flung
Himself along the grass. What gentle tongue,
What whisperer disturb'd his gloomy rest?
It was a nymph uprisen to the breast
In the fountain's pebbly margin, and she stood
'Mong lillies, like the youngest of the brood.   100
To him her dripping hand she softly kist,
And anxiously began to plait and twist
Her ringlets round her fingers, saying: "Youth!
Too long, alas, hast thou starv'd on the ruth,
The bitterness of love: too long indeed,
Seeing thou art so gentle. Could I weed
Thy soul of care, by heavens, I would offer
All the bright riches of my crystal coffer
To Amphitrite; all my clear-eyed fish,
Golden, or rainbow-sided, or purplish,   110
Vermilion-tail'd, or finn'd with silvery gauze;
Yea, or my veined pebble-floor, that draws
A virgin light to the deep; my grotto-sands
Tawny and gold, ooz'd slowly from far lands
By my diligent springs; my level lillies, shells,
My charming rod, my potent river spells;
Yes, every thing, even to the pearly cup
Meander gave me,—for I bubbled up
To fainting creatures in a desert wild.
But woe is me, I am but as a child   120
To gladden thee; and all I dare to say,
Is, that I pity thee; that on this day
I've been thy guide; that thou must wander far
In other regions, past the scanty bar
To mortal steps, before thou can'st be ta'en
From every wasting sigh, from every pain,
Into the gentle bosom of thy love.
Why it is thus, one knows in heaven above:
But, a poor Naiad, I guess not. Farewell!
I have a ditty for my hollow cell."   130

Hereat, she vanished from Endymion's gaze,
Who brooded o'er the water in amaze:
The dashing fount pour'd on, and where its pool
Lay, half asleep, in grass and rushes cool,

Quick waterflies and gnats were sporting still,
And fish were dimpling, as if good nor ill
Had fallen out that hour. The wanderer,
Holding his forehead, to keep off the burr
Of smothering fancies, patiently sat down;
And, while beneath the evening's sleepy frown   140
Glow-worms began to trim their starry lamps,
Thus breath'd he to himself: "Whoso encamps
To take a fancied city of delight,
O what a wretch is he! and when 'tis his,
After long toil and travelling, to miss
The kernel of his hopes, how more than vile:
Yet, for him there's refreshment even in toil;
Another city doth he set about,
Free from the smallest pebble-bead of doubt
That he will seize on trickling honey-combs: 150
Alas, he finds them dry; and then he foams,
And onward to another city speeds.
But this is human life: the war, the deeds,
The disappointment, the anxiety,
Imagination's struggles, far and nigh,
All human; bearing in themselves this good,
That they are still the air, the subtle food,
To make us feel existence, and to show
How quiet death is. Where soil is men grow,
Whether to weeds or flowers; but for me,   160
There is no depth to strike in: I can see
Naught earthly worth my compassing; so stand
Upon a misty, jutting head of land—
Alone? No, no; and by the Orphean lute,
When mad Eurydice is listening to't;
I'd rather stand upon this misty peak,
With not a thing to sigh for, or to seek,
But the soft shadow of my thrice-seen love,
Than be—I care not what. O meekest dove
Of heaven! O Cynthia, ten-times bright and fair!
From thy blue throne, now filling all the air,   171
Glance but one little beam of temper'd light
Into my bosom, that the dreadful might
And tyranny of love be somewhat scar'd!
Yet do not so, sweet queen; one torment spar'd,
Would give a pang to jealous misery,
Worse than the torment's self: but rather tie
Large wings upon my shoulders, and point out
My love's far dwelling. Though the playful rout
Of Cupids shun thee, too divine art thou,   180
Too keen in beauty, for thy silver prow

Not to have dipp'd in love's most gentle stream,
O be propitious, nor severely deem
My madness impious; for, by all the stars
That tend thy bidding, I do think the bars
That kept my spirit in are burst—that I
Am sailing with thee through the dizzy sky!
How beautiful thou art! The world how deep!
How tremulous-dazzlingly the wheels sweep
Around their axle! Then these gleaming reins,   190
How lithe! When this thy chariot attains
Its airy goal, haply some bower veils
Those twilight eyes? Those eyes!—my spirit fails—
Dear goddess, help! or the wide-gaping air
Will gulph me—help!"—At this with madden'd stare,
And lifted hands, and trembling lips he stood;
Like old Deucalion mountain'd o'er the flood,
Or blind Orion hungry for the morn.
And, but from the deep cavern there was borne
A voice, he had been froze to senseless stone;   200
Nor sigh of his, nor plaint, nor passion'd moan
Had more been heard. Thus swell'd it forth: "Descend,
Young mountaineer! descend where alleys bend
Into the sparry hollows of the world!
Oft hast thou seen bolts of the thunder hurl'd
As from thy threshold; day by day hast been
A little lower than the chilly sheen
Of icy pinnacles, and dipp'dst thine arms
Into the deadening ether that still charms
Their marble being: now, as deep profound   210
As those are high, descend! He ne'er is crown'd
With immortality, who fears to follow
Where airy voices lead: so through the hollow,
The silent mysteries of earth, descend!"

He heard but the last words, nor could contend
One moment in reflection: for he fled
Into the fearful deep, to hide his head
From the clear moon, the trees, and coming madness.

'Twas far too strange, and wonderful for sadness;
Sharpening, by degrees, his appetite   220
To dive into the deepest. Dark, nor light,
The region; nor bright, nor sombre wholly,
But mingled up; a gleaming melancholy;
A dusky empire and its diadems;
One faint eternal eventide of gems.

Aye, millions sparkled on a vein of gold,
Along whose track the prince quick footsteps told,
With all its lines abrupt and angular:
Out-shooting sometimes, like a meteor-star,
Through a vast antre; then the metal woof,   230
Like Vulcan's rainbow, with some monstrous roof
Curves hugely: now, far in the deep abyss,
It seems an angry lightning, and doth hiss
Fancy into belief: anon it leads
Through winding passages, where sameness breeds
Vexing conceptions of some sudden change;
Whether to silver grots, or giant range
Of sapphire columns, or fantastic bridge
Athwart a flood of crystal. On a ridge
Now fareth he, that o'er the vast beneath   240
Towers like an ocean-cliff, and whence he seeth
A hundred waterfalls, whose voices come
But as the murmuring surge. Chilly and numb
His bosom grew, when first he, far away
Descried an orbed diamond, set to fray
Old darkness from his throne: 'twas like the sun
Uprisen o'er chaos: and with such a stun
Came the amazement, that, absorb'd in it,
He saw not fiercer wonders—past the wit
Of any spirit to tell, but one of those   250
Who, when this planet's sphering time doth close,
Will be its high remembrancers: who they?
The mighty ones who have made eternal day
For Greece and England. While astonishment
With deep-drawn sighs was quieting, he went
Into a marble gallery, passing through
A mimic temple, so complete and true
In sacred custom, that he well nigh fear'd
To search it inwards; whence far off appear'd,
Through a long pillar'd vista, a fair shrine,   260
And just beyond, on light tiptoe divine,
A quiver'd Dian. Stepping awfully,
The youth approach'd; oft turning his veil'd eye
Down sidelong aisles, and into niches old.
And when, more near against the marble cold
He had touch'd his forehead, he began to thread
All courts and passages, where silence dead
Rous'd by his whispering footsteps murmured faint:
And long he travers'd to and fro, to acquaint
Himself with every mystery, and awe;   270
Till, weary, he sat down before the maw

Of a wide outlet, fathomless and dim,
To wild uncertainty and shadows grim.
There, when new wonders ceas'd to float before,
And thoughts of self came on, how crude and sore
The journey homeward to habitual self!
A mad-pursuing of the fog-born elf,
Whose flitting lantern, through rude nettle-briar,
Cheats us into a swamp, into a fire,
Into the bosom of a hated thing.   280

What misery most drowningly doth sing
In lone Endymion's ear, now he has raught
The goal of consciousness? Ah, 'tis the thought,
The deadly feel of solitude: for lo!
He cannot see the heavens, nor the flow
Of rivers, nor hill-flowers running wild
In pink and purple chequer, nor, up-pil'd,
The cloudy rack slow journeying in the west,
Like herded elephants; nor felt, nor prest
Cool grass, nor tasted the fresh slumberous air;   290
But far from such companionship to wear
An unknown time, surcharg'd with grief, away,
Was now his lot. And must he patient stay,
Tracing fantastic figures with his spear?
"No!" exclaim'd he, "why should I tarry here?"
No! loudly echoed times innumerable.
At which he straightway started, and 'gan tell
His paces back into the temple's chief;
Warming and glowing strong in the belief
Of help from Dian: so that when again   300
He caught her airy form, thus did he plain,
Moving more near the while: "O Haunter chaste
Of river sides, and woods, and heathy waste,
Where with thy silver bow and arrows keen
Art thou now forested? O woodland Queen,
What smoothest air thy smoother forehead woos?
Where dost thou listen to the wide halloos
Of thy disparted nymphs? Through what dark tree
Glimmers thy crescent? Wheresoe'er it be,
'Tis in the breath of heaven: thou dost taste   310
Freedom as none can taste it, nor dost waste
Thy loveliness in dismal elements;
But, finding in our green earth sweet contents,
There livest blissfully. Ah, if to thee
It feels Elysian, how rich to me,
An exil'd mortal, sounds its pleasant name!
Within my breast there lives a choking flame—

O let me cool't the zephyr-boughs among!
A homeward fever parches up my tongue—
O let me slake it at the running springs!   320
Upon my ear a noisy nothing rings—
O let me once more hear the linnet's note!
Before mine eyes thick films and shadows float—
O let me 'noint them with the heaven's light!
Dost thou now lave thy feet and ankles white?
O think how sweet to me the freshening sluice!
Dost thou now please thy thirst with berry-juice?
O think how this dry palate would rejoice!
If in soft slumber thou dost hear my voice,
O think how I should love a bed of flowers!—   330
Young goddess! let me see my native bowers!
Deliver me from this rapacious deep!"

     Thus ending loudly, as he would o'erleap
His destiny, alert he stood: but when
Obstinate silence came heavily again,
Feeling about for its old couch of space
And airy cradle, lowly bow'd his face
Desponding, o'er the marble floor's cold thrill.
But 'twas not long; for, sweeter than the rill
To its old channel, or a swollen tide   340
To margin sallows, were the leaves he spied,
And flowers, and wreaths, and ready myrtle crowns
Up heaping through the slab: refreshment drowns
Itself, and strives its own delights to hide—
Nor in one spot alone; the floral pride
In a long whispering birth enchanted grew
Before his footsteps; as when heav'd anew
Old ocean rolls a lengthened wave to the shore,
Down whose green back the short-liv'd foam, all hoar,
Bursts gradual, with a wayward indolence.   350

     Increasing still in heart, and pleasant sense,
Upon his fairy journey on he hastes;
So anxious for the end, he scarcely wastes
One moment with his hand among the sweets:
Onward he goes—he stops—his bosom beats
As plainly in his ear, as the faint charm
Of which the throbs were born. This still alarm,
This sleepy music, forc'd him walk tiptoe:
For it came more softly than the east could blow
Arion's magic to the Atlantic isles;   360
Or than the west, made jealous by the smiles

Of thron'd Apollo, could breathe back the lyre
To seas Ionian and Tyrian.

O did he ever live, that lonely man,
Who lov'd—and music slew not? 'Tis the pest
Of love, that fairest joys give most unrest;
That things of delicate and tenderest worth
Are swallow'd all, and made a seared dearth,
By one consuming flame: it doth immerse
And suffocate true blessings in a curse. 370
Half-happy, by comparison of bliss,
Is miserable. 'Twas even so with this
Dew-dropping melody, in the Carian's ear;
First heaven, then hell, and then forgotten clear,
Vanish'd in elemental passion.

And down some swart abysm he had gone,
Had not a heavenly guide benignant led
To where thick myrtle branches, 'gainst his head
Brushing, awakened: then the sounds again
Went noiseless as a passing noontide rain 380
Over a bower, where little space he stood;
For as the sunset peeps into a wood
So saw he panting light, and towards it went
Through winding alleys; and lo, wonderment!
Upon soft verdure saw, one here, one there,
Cupids a slumbering on their pinions fair.

After a thousand mazes overgone,
At last, with sudden step, he came upon
A chamber, myrtle wall'd, embowered high,
Full of light, incense, tender minstrelsy, 390
And more of beautiful and strange beside:
For on a silken couch of rosy pride,
In midst of all, there lay a sleeping youth
Of fondest beauty; fonder, in fair sooth,
Than sighs could fathom, or contentment reach:
And coverlids gold-tinted like the peach,
Or ripe October's faded marigolds,
Fell sleek about him in a thousand folds—
Not hiding up an Apollonian curve
Of neck and shoulder, nor the tenting swerve 400
Of knee from knee, nor ankles pointing light;
But rather, giving them to the filled sight
Officiously. Sideway his face repos'd
On one white arm, and tenderly unclos'd,

By tenderest pressure, a faint damask mouth
To slumbery pout; just as the morning south
Disparts a dew-lipp'd rose. Above his head,
Four lilly stalks did their white honours wed
To make a coronal; and round him grew
All tendrils green, of every bloom and hue,   410
Together intertwin'd and trammell'd fresh:
The vine of glossy sprout; the ivy mesh,
Shading its Ethiop berries; and woodbine,
Of velvet leaves and bugle-blooms divine;
Convolvulus in streaked vases flush;
The creeper, mellowing for an autumn blush;
And virgin's bower, trailing airily;
With others of the sisterhood. Hard by,
Stood serene Cupids watching silently.
One, kneeling to a lyre, touch'd the strings,   420
Muffling to death the pathos with his wings;
And, ever and anon, uprose to look
At the youth's slumber; while another took
A willow-bough, distilling odorous dew,
And shook it on his hair; another flew
In through the woven roof, and fluttering-wise
Rain'd violets upon his sleeping eyes.

     At these enchantments, and yet many more,
The breathless Latmian wonder'd o'er and o'er;
Until, impatient in embarrassment,   430
He forthright pass'd, and lightly treading went
To that same feather'd lyrist, who straightway,
Smiling, thus whisper'd: "Though from upper day
Thou art a wanderer, and thy presence here
Might seem unholy, be of happy cheer!
For 'tis the nicest touch of human honour,
When some ethereal and high-favouring donor
Presents immortal bowers to mortal sense;
As now 'tis done to thee, Endymion. Hence
Was I in no wise startled. So recline   440
Upon these living flowers. Here is wine,
Alive with sparkles—never, I aver,
Since Ariadne was a vintager,
So cool a purple: taste these juicy pears,
Sent me by sad Vertumnus, when his fears
Were high about Pomona: here is cream,
Deepening to richness from a snowy gleam;
Sweeter than that nurse Amalthea skimm'd
For the boy Jupiter: and here, undimm'd

By any touch, a bunch of blooming plums
Ready to melt between an infant's gums:
And here is manna pick'd from Syrian trees,
In starlight, by the three Hesperides.
Feast on, and meanwhile I will let thee know
Of all these things around us." He did so,
Still brooding o'er the cadence of his lyre;
And thus: "I need not any hearing tire
By telling how the sea-born goddess pin'd
For a mortal youth, and how she strove to bind   460
Him all in all unto her doting self,
Who would not be so prison'd? but, fond elf,
He was content to let her amorous plea
Faint through his careless arms; content to see
An unseiz'd heaven dying at his feet;
Content, O fool! to make a cold retreat,
When on the pleasant grass such love, lovelorn,
Lay sorrowing; when every tear was born
Of diverse passion; when her lips and eyes
Were clos'd in sullen moisture, and quick sighs
Came vex'd and pettish through her nostrils small.
Hush! no exclaim—yet, justly mightst thou call   472
Curses upon his head.—I was half glad
But my poor mistress went distract and mad,
When the boar tusk'd him: so away she flew
To Jove's high throne, and by her plainings drew
Immortal tear-drops down the thunderer's beard;
Whereon, it was decreed he should be rear'd
Each summer time to life. Lo! this is he,
That same Adonis, safe in the privacy   480
Of this still region all his winter-sleep.
Aye, sleep; for when our love-sick queen did weep
Over his waned corse, the tremulous shower
Heal'd up the wound, and, with a balmy power,
Medicined death to a lengthened drowsiness:
The which she fills with visions, and doth dress
In all this quiet luxury; and hath set
Us young immortals, without any let,
To watch his slumber through. 'Tis well nigh pass'd,
Even to a moment's filling up, and fast
She scuds with summer breezes, to pant through   490
The first long kiss, warm firstling, to renew
Embower'd sports in Cytherea's isle.
Look! how those winged listeners all this while
Stand anxious: see! behold!"—This clamant word
Broke through the careful silence; for they heard

A rustling noise of leaves, and out there flutter'd
Pigeons and doves: Adonis something mutter'd
The while one hand, that erst upon his thigh
Lay dormant, mov'd convuls'd and gradually
Up to his forehead. Then there was a hum   500
Of sudden voices, echoing, "Come! come!
Arise! awake! Clear summer has forth walk'd
Unto the clover-sward, and she has talk'd
Full soothingly to every nested finch:
Rise, Cupids! or we'll give the blue-bell pinch
To your dimpled arms. Once more sweet life begin!"
At this, from every side they hurried in,
Rubbing their sleepy eyes with lazy wrists,
And doubling over head their little fists
In backward yawns. But all were soon alive: 510
For as delicious wine doth, sparkling, dive
In nectar'd clouds and curls through water fair,
So from the arbour roof down swell'd an air
Odorous and enlivening; making all
To laugh, and play, and sing, and loudly call
For their sweet queen: when lo! the wreathed green
Disparted, and far upward could be seen
Blue heaven, and a silver car, air-borne,
Whose silent wheels, fresh wet from clouds of morn,
Spun off a drizzling dew,—which falling chill   520
On soft Adonis' shoulders, made him still
Nestle and turn uneasily about.
Soon were the white doves plain, with neck stretch'd out,
And silken traces lighten'd in descent;
And soon, returning from love's banishment,
Queen Venus leaning downward open arm'd:
Her shadow fell upon his breast, and charm'd
A tumult to his heart, and a new life
Into his eyes. Ah, miserable strife,
But for her comforting! unhappy sight,   530
But meeting her blue orbs! Who, who can write
Of these first minutes? The unchariest muse
To embracements warm as theirs makes coy excuse.

    O it has ruffled every spirit there,
Saving Love's self, who stands superb to share
The general gladness: awfully he stands;
A sovereign quell is in his waving hands;
No sight can bear the lightning of his bow;
His quiver is mysterious, none can know   539
What themselves think of it; from forth his eyes
There darts strange light of varied hues and dies:

A scowl is sometimes on his brow, but who
Look full upon it feel anon the blue
Of his fair eyes run liquid through their souls.
Endymion feels it, and no more controls
The burning prayer within him; so, bent low,
He had begun a plaining of his woe.
But Venus, bending forward, said: "My child,
Favour this gentle youth; his days are wild
With love—he—but alas! too well I see   550
Thou know'st the deepness of his misery.
Ah, smile not so, my son: I tell thee true,
That when through heavy hours I used to rue
The endless sleep of this new-born Adon',
This stranger aye I pitied. For upon
A dreary morning once I fled away
Into the breezy clouds, to weep and pray
For this my love: for vexing Mars had teaz'd
Me even to tears: thence, when a little eas'd,
Down-looking, vacant, through a hazy wood,   560
I saw this youth as he despairing stood:
Those same dark curls blown vagrant in the wind;
Those same full fringed lids a constant blind
Over his sullen eyes: I saw him throw
Himself on wither'd leaves, even as though
Death had come sudden; for no jot he mov'd,
Yet mutter'd wildly. I could hear he lov'd
Some fair immortal, and that his embrace
Had zoned her through the night. There is no trace
Of this in heaven: I have mark'd each cheek,   570
And find it is the vainest thing to seek;
And that of all things 'tis kept secretest.
Endymion! one day thou wilt be blest:
So still obey the guiding hand that fends
Thee safely through these wonders for sweet ends.
'Tis a concealment needful in extreme;
And if I guess'd not so, the sunny beam
Thou shouldst mount up to with me. Now adieu!
Here must we leave thee."—At these words upflew
The impatient doves, uprose the floating car,   580
Up went the hum celestial. High afar
The Latmian saw them minish into naught;
And, when all were clear vanish'd, still he caught
A vivid lightning from that dreadful bow.
When all was darkened, with Ætnean throe
The earth clos'd—gave a solitary moan—
And left him once again in twilight lone.

He did not rave, he did not stare aghast,
For all those visions were o'ergone, and past,
And he in loneliness: he felt assur'd   590
Of happy times, when all he had endur'd
Would seem a feather to the mighty prize.
So, with unusual gladness, on he hies
Through caves, and palaces of mottled ore,
Gold dome, and crystal wall, and turquoise floor,
Black polish'd porticos of awful shade,
And, at the last, a diamond balustrade,
Leading afar past wild magnificence,
Spiral through ruggedest loopholes, and thence
Stretching across a void, then guiding o'er   600
Enormous chasms, where, all foam and roar,
Streams subterranean teaze their granite beds;
Then heighten'd just above the silvery heads
Of a thousand fountains, so that he could dash
The waters with his spear; but at the splash,
Done heedlessly, those spouting columns rose
Sudden a poplar's height, and 'gan to enclose
His diamond path with fretwork, streaming round
Alive, and dazzling cool, and with a sound,
Haply, like dolphin tumults, when sweet shells   610
Welcome the float of Thetis. Long he dwells
On this delight; for, every minute's space,
The streams with changed magic interlace:
Sometimes like delicatest lattices,
Cover'd with crystal vines; then weeping trees.
Moving about as in a gentle wind,
Which, in a wink, to watery gauze refin'd,
Pour'd into shapes of curtain'd canopies,
Spangled, and rich with liquid broideries
Of flowers, peacocks, swans, and naiads fair.   620
Swifter than lightning went these wonders rare;
And then the water, into stubborn streams
Collecting, mimick'd the wrought oaken beams,
Pillars, and frieze, and high fantastic roof,
Of those dusk places in times far aloof
Cathedrals call'd. He bade a loth farewell
To these founts Protean, passing gulph, and dell,
And torrent, and ten thousand jutting shapes,
Half seen through deepest gloom, and grisly gapes,
Blackening on every side, and overhead   630
A vaulted dome like Heaven's, far bespread
With starlight gems: aye, all so huge and strange,
The solitary felt a hurried change

Working within him into something dreary,—
Vex'd like a morning eagle, lost, and weary,
And purblind amid foggy, midnight wolds.
But he revives at once: for who beholds
New sudden things, nor casts his mental slough?
Forth from a rugged arch, in the dusk below,
Came mother Cybele! alone—alone—   640
In sombre chariot; dark foldings thrown
About her majesty, and front death-pale,
With turrets crown'd. Four maned lions hale
The sluggish wheels; solemn their toothed maws,
Their surly eyes brow-hidden, heavy paws
Uplifted drowsily, and nervy tails
Cowering their tawny brushes. Silent sails
This shadowy queen athwart, and faints away
In another gloomy arch.

     Wherefore delay,
Young traveller, in such a mournful place?   650
Art thou wayworn, or canst not further trace
The diamond path? And does it indeed end
Abrupt in middle air? Yet earthward bend
Thy forehead, and to Jupiter cloud-borne
Call ardently! He was indeed wayworn;
Abrupt, in middle air, his way was lost;
To cloud-borne Jove he bowed, and there crost
Towards him a large eagle, 'twixt whose wings,
Without one impious word, himself he flings,
Committed to the darkness and the gloom: 660
Down, down, uncertain to what pleasant doom,
Swift as a fathoming plummet down he fell
Through unknown things; till exhaled asphodel,
And rose, with spicy fannings interbreath'd,
Came swelling forth where little caves were wreath'd
So thick with leaves and mosses, that they seem'd
Large honeycombs of green, and freshly teem'd
With airs delicious. In the greenest nook
The eagle landed him, and farewell took.

  It was a jasmine bower, all bestrown   670
With golden moss. His every sense had grown
Ethereal for pleasure; 'bove his head
Flew a delight half-graspable; his tread
Was Hesperean; to his capable ears
Silence was music from the holy spheres;
A dewy luxury was in his eyes;
The little flowers felt his pleasant sighs

And stirr'd them faintly. Verdant cave and cell
He wander'd through, oft wondering at such swell
Of sudden exaltation: but, "Alas!"　　　　　　　　680
Said he, "will all this gush of feeling pass
Away in solitude? And must they wane,
Like melodies upon a sandy plain,
Without an echo? Then shall I be left
So sad, so melancholy, so bereft!
Yet still I feel immortal! O my love,
My breath of life, where art thou? High above,
Dancing before the morning gates of heaven?
Or keeping watch among those starry seven,
Old Atlas' children? Art a maid of the waters,　　690
One of shell-winding Triton's bright-hair'd daughters?
Or art, impossible! a nymph of Dian's,
Weaving a coronal of tender scions
For very idleness? Where'er thou art,
Methinks it now is at my will to start
Into thine arms; to scare Aurora's train,
And snatch thee from the morning; o'er the main
To scud like a wild bird, and take thee off
From thy sea-foamy cradle; or to doff
Thy shepherd vest, and woo thee mid fresh leaves.　700
No, no, too eagerly my soul deceives
Its powerless self: I know this cannot be.
O let me then by some sweet dreaming flee
To her entrancements: hither sleep awhile!
Hither most gentle sleep! and soothing foil
For some few hours the coming solitude."

　　Thus spake he, and that moment felt endued
With power to dream deliciously; so wound
Through a dim passage, searching till he found
The smoothest mossy bed and deepest, where　　710
He threw himself, and just into the air
Stretching his indolent arms, he took, O bliss!
A naked waist: "Fair Cupid, whence is this?"
A well-known voice sigh'd, "Sweetest, here am I!"
At which soft ravishment, with doting cry
They trembled to each other.—Helicon!
O fountain'd hill! Old Homer's Helicon!
That thou wouldst spout a little streamlet o'er
These sorry pages; then the verse would soar
And sing above this gentle pair, like lark　　720
Over his nested young: but all is dark
Around thine aged top, and thy clear fount
Exhales in mists to heaven. Aye, the count

Of mighty Poets is made up; the scroll
Is folded by the Muses; the bright roll
Is in Apollo's hand: our dazed eyes
Have seen a new tinge in the western skies:
The world has done its duty. Yet, oh yet,
Although the sun of poesy is set,
These lovers did embrace, and we must weep   730
That there is no old power left to steep
A quill immortal in their joyous tears.
Long time ere silence did their anxious fears
Question that thus it was; long time they lay
Fondling and kissing every doubt away;
Long time ere soft caressing sobs began
To mellow into words, and then there ran
Two bubbling springs of talk from their sweet lips.
"O known Unknown! from whom my being sips
Such darling essence, wherefore may I not   740
Be ever in these arms? in this sweet spot
Pillow my chin for ever? ever press
These toying hands and kiss their smooth excess?
Why not for ever and for ever feel.
That breath about my eyes? Ah, thou wilt steal
Away from me again, indeed, indeed—
Thou wilt be gone away, and wilt not heed
My lonely madness. Speak, delicious fair!
Is—is it to be so? No! Who will dare
To pluck thee from me? And, of thine own will,   750
Full well I feel thou wouldst not leave me. Still
Let me entwine thee surer, surer—now
How can we part? Elysium! who art thou?
Who, that thou canst not be for ever here,
Or lift me with thee to some starry sphere?
Enchantress! tell me by this soft embrace,
By the most soft completion of thy face,
Those lips, O slippery blisses, twinkling eyes,
And by these tenderest, milky sovereignties—
These tenderest, and by the nectar-wine,   760
The passion"———"O dov'd Ida the divine!
Endymion! dearest! Ah, unhappy me!
His soul will 'scape us—O felicity!
How he does love me! His poor temples beat
To the very tune of love—how sweet, sweet, sweet.
Revive, dear youth, or I shall faint and die;
Revive, or these soft hours will hurry by
In tranced dulness; speak, and let that spell
Affright this lethargy! I cannot quell

Its heavy pressure, and will press at least   770
My lips to thine, that they may richly feast
Until we taste the life of love again.
What! dost thou move? dost kiss? O bliss! O pain!
I love thee, youth, more than I can conceive;
And so long absence from thee doth bereave
My soul of any rest: yet must I hence:
Yet, can I not to starry eminence
Uplift thee; nor for very shame can own
Myself to thee: Ah, dearest, do not groan
Or thou wilt force me from this secrecy,   780
And I must blush in heaven. O that I
Had done 't already; that the dreadful smiles
At my lost brightness, my impassion'd wiles,
Had waned from Olympus' solemn height,
And from all serious Gods; that our delight
Was quite forgotten, save of us alone!
And wherefore so ashamed? 'Tis but to atone
For endless pleasure, by some coward blushes:
Yet must I be a coward!—Horror rushes
Too palpable before me—the sad look   790
Of Jove—Minerva's start—no bosom shook
With awe of purity—no Cupid pinion
In reverence vailed—my crystalline dominion
Half lost, and all old hymns made nullity!
But what is this to love? O I could fly
With thee into the ken of heavenly powers,
So thou wouldst thus, for many sequent hours,
Press me so sweetly. Now I swear at once
That I am wise, that Pallas is a dunce—
Perhaps her love like mine is but unknown—   800
O I do think that I have been alone
In chastity: yes, Pallas has been sighing,
While every eve saw me my hair uptying
With fingers cool as aspen leaves. Sweet love,
I was as vague as solitary dove,
Nor knew that nests were built. Now a soft kiss—
Aye, by that kiss, I vow an endless bliss,
An immortality of passion's thine:
Ere long I will exalt thee to the shine
Of heaven ambrosial; and we will shade   810
Ourselves whole summers by a river glade;
And I will tell thee stories of the sky,
And breathe thee whispers of its minstrelsy.
My happy love will overwing all bounds!
O let me melt into thee; let the sounds

Of our close voices marry at their birth;
Let us entwine hoveringly—O dearth
Of human words! roughness of mortal speech!
Lispings empyrean will I sometime teach
Thine honied tongue—lute-breathings, which I gasp
To have thee understand, now while I clasp   821
Thee thus, and weep for fondness—I am pain'd,
Endymion: woe! woe! is grief contain'd
In the very deeps of pleasure, my sole life?"—
Hereat, with many sobs, her gentle strife
Melted into a languor. He return'd
Entranced vows and tears.

                 Ye who have yearn'd
With too much passion, will here stay and pity,
For the mere sake of truth; as 'tis a ditty
Not of these days, but long ago 'twas told   830
By a cavern wind unto a forest old;
And then the forest told it in a dream
To a sleeping lake, whose cool and level gleam
A poet caught as he was journeying
To Phœbus' shrine; and in it he did fling
His weary limbs, bathing an hour's space,
And after, straight in that inspired place
He sang the story up into the air,
Giving it universal freedom. There
Has it been ever sounding for those ears   840
Whose tips are glowing hot. The legend cheers
Yon centinel stars; and he who listens to it
Must surely be self-doom'd or he will rue it:
For quenchless burnings come upon the heart,
Made fiercer by a fear lest any part
Should be engulphed in the eddying wind.
As much as here is penn'd doth always find
A resting place, thus much comes clear and plain;
Anon the strange voice is upon the wane—
And 'tis but echo'd from departing sound,   850
That the fair visitant at last unwound
Her gentle limbs, and left the youth asleep.—
Thus the tradition of the gusty deep.

   Now turn we to our former chroniclers.—
Endymion awoke, that grief of hers
Sweet paining on his ear: he sickly guess'd
How lone he was once more, and sadly press'd
His empty arms together, hung his head,
And most forlorn upon that widow'd bed

Sat silently. Love's madness he had known:
Often with more than tortured lion's groan
Moanings had burst from him; but now that rage
Had pass'd away: no longer did he wage
A rough-voic'd war against the dooming stars.
No, he had felt too much for such harsh jars:
The lyre of his soul Æolian tun'd
Forgot all violence, and but commun'd
With melancholy thought: O he had swoon'd
Drunken from pleasure's nipple; and his love
Henceforth was dove-like.—Loth was he to move   870
From the imprinted couch, and when he did,
'Twas with slow, languid paces, and face hid
In muffling hands. So temper'd, out he stray'd
Half seeing visions that might have dismay'd
Alecto's serpents; ravishments more keen
Than Hermes' pipe, when anxious he did lean
Over eclipsing eyes: and at the last
It was a sounding grotto, vaulted, vast,
O'er studded with a thousand, thousand pearls,
And crimson mouthed shells with stubborn curls,   880
Of every shape and size, even to the bulk
In which whales arbour close, to brood and sulk
Against an endless storm. Moreover too,
Fish-semblances, of green and azure hue,
Ready to snort their streams. In this cool wonder
Endymion sat down, and 'gan to ponder
On all his life: his youth, up to the day
When 'mid acclaim, and feasts, and garlands gay,
He stept upon his shepherd throne: the look
Of his white palace in wild forest nook,   890
And all the revels he had lorded there:
Each tender maiden whom he once thought fair,
With every friend and fellow-woodlander—
Pass'd like a dream before him. Then the spur
Of the old bards to mighty deeds: his plans
To nurse the golden age 'mong shepherd clans:
That wondrous night: the great Pan-festival:
His sister's sorrow; and his wanderings all,
Until into the earth's deep maw he rush'd:
Then all its buried magic, till it flush'd   900
High with excessive love. "And now," thought he,
"How long must I remain in jeopardy
Of blank amazements that amaze no more?
Now I have tasted her sweet soul to the core
All other depths are shallow: essences,
Once spiritual, are like muddy lees,

Meant but to fertilize my earthly root,
And make my branches lift a golden fruit
Into the bloom of heaven: other light,
Though it be quick and sharp enough to blight   910
The Olympian eagle's vision, is dark,
Dark as the parentage of chaos. Hark!
My silent thoughts are echoing from these shells;
Or they are but the ghosts, the dying swells
Of noises far away?—list!"—Hereupon
He kept an anxious ear. The humming tone
Came louder, and behold, there as he lay,
On either side outgush'd, with misty spray,
A copious spring; and both together dash'd
Swift, mad, fantastic round the rocks, and lash'd   920
Among the conchs and shells of the lofty grot,
Leaving a trickling-dew. At last they shot
Down from the ceiling's height, pouring a noise
As of some breathless racers whose hopes poize
Upon the last few steps, and with spent force
Along the ground they took a winding course.
Endymion follow'd—for it seem'd that one
Ever pursued, the other strove to shun—
Follow'd their languid mazes, till well nigh
He had left thinking of the mystery,—   930
And was now rapt in tender hoverings
Over the vanish'd bliss. Ah! what is it sings
His dream away? What melodies are these?
They sound as through the whispering of trees,
Not native in such barren vaults. Give ear!

"O Arethusa, peerless nymph! why fear
Such tenderness as mine? Great Dian, why,
Why didst thou hear her prayer? O that I
Were rippling round her dainty fairness now,
Circling about her waist, and striving how   940
To entice her to a dive! then stealing in
Between her luscious lips and eyelids thin.
O that her shining hair was in the sun,
And I distilling from it thence to run
In amorous rillets down her shrinking form!
To linger on her lilly shoulders, warm
Between her kissing breasts, and every charm
Touch raptur'd!—See how painfully I flow:
Fair maid, be pitiful to my great woe.
Stay, stay thy weary course, and let me lead   950
A happy wooer, to the flowery mead

Where all that beauty snar'd me."—"Cruel god,
Desist! or my offended mistress' nod
Will stagnate all thy fountains:—teaze me not
With syren words—Ah, have I really got
Such power to madden thee? And is it true—
Away, away, or I shall dearly rue
My very thoughts: in mercy then away,
Kindest Alpheus, for should I obey
My own dear will, 'twould be a deadly bane.   960
O, Oread-Queen! would that thou hadst a pain
Like this of mine, then would I fearless turn
And be a criminal. Alas, I burn,
I shudder—gentle river, get thee hence.
Alpheus! thou enchanter! every sense
Of mine was once made perfect in these woods.
Fresh breezes, bowery lawns, and innocent floods,
Ripe fruits, and lonely couch, contentment gave;
But ever since I heedlessly did lave
In thy deceitful stream, a panting glow   970
Grew strong within me: wherefore serve me so,
And call it love? Alas, 'twas cruelty.
Not once more did I close my happy eye
Amid the thrushes' song. Away! Avaunt!
O 'twas a cruel thing."—"Now thou dost taunt
So softly, Arethusa, that I think
If thou wast playing on my shady brink,
Thou wouldst bathe once again. Innocent maid!
Stifle thine heart no more; nor be afraid
Of angry powers: there are deities   980
Will shade us with their wings. Those fitful sighs
'Tis almost death to hear: O let me pour
A dewy balm upon them!—fear no more,
Sweet Arethusa! Dian's self must feel
Sometime these very pangs. Dear maiden, steal
Blushing into my soul, and let us fly
These dreary caverns for the open sky.
I will delight thee all my winding course,
From the green sea up to my hidden source
About Arcadian forests; and will show   990
The channels where my coolest waters flow
Through mossy rocks; where, 'mid exuberant green,
I roam in pleasant darkness, more unseen
Than Saturn in his exile; where I brim
Round flowery islands, and take thence a skim
Of mealy sweets, which myriads of bees
Buzz from their honey'd wings: and thou shouldst please

Thyself to choose the richest, where we might
Be incense-pillow'd every summer night.
Doff all sad fears, thou white deliciousness,   1000
And let us be thus comforted; unless
Thou couldst rejoice to see my hopeless stream
Hurry distracted from Sol's temperate beam,
And pour to death along some hungry sands."—
"What can I do, Alpheus? Dian stands
Severe before me: persecuting fate!
Unhappy Arethusa! thou wast late
A huntress free in"—At this, sudden fell
Those two sad streams adown a fearful dell.
The Latmian listen'd, but he heard no more,   1010
Save echo, faint repeating o'er and o'er
The name of Arethusa. On the verge
Of that dark gulph he wept, and said: "I urge
Thee, gentle Goddess of my pilgrimage,
By our eternal hopes, to soothe, to assuage,
If thou art powerful, these lovers' pains;
And make them happy in some happy plains."

He turn'd—there was a whelming sound—he slept,
There was a cooler light; and so he kept
Towards it by a sandy path, and lo!   1020
More suddenly than doth a moment go,
The visions of the earth were gone and fled—
He saw the giant sea above his head.

BOOK III

THERE are who lord it o'er their fellow-men
With most prevailing tinsel: who unpen
Their baaing vanities, to browse away
The comfortable green and juicy hay
From human pastures; or, O torturing fact!
Who, through an idiot blink, will see unpack'd
Fire-branded foxes to sear up and singe
Our gold and ripe-ear'd hopes. With not one tinge
Of sanctuary splendour, not a sight
Able to face an owl's, they still are dight   10
By the blear-eyed nations in empurpled vests,
And crowns, and turbans. With unladen breasts,
Save of blown self-applause, they proudly mount
To their spirit's perch, their being's high account,
Their tiptop nothings, their dull skies, their thrones—
Amid the fierce intoxicating tones

Of trumpets, shoutings, and belabour'd drums,
And sudden cannon. Ah! how all this hums,
In wakeful ears, like uproar past and gone—
Like thunder clouds that spake to Babylon,   20
And set those old Chaldeans to their tasks.—
Are then regalities all gilded masks?
No, there are thronèd seats unscalable
But by a patient wing, a constant spell,
Or by ethereal things that, unconfin'd,
Can make a ladder of the eternal wind,
And poize about in cloudy thunder-tents
To watch the abysm-birth of elements.
Aye, 'bove the withering of old-lipp'd Fate
A thousand Powers keep religious state,   30
In water, fiery realm, and airy bourne;
And, silent as a consecrated urn,
Hold sphery sessions for a season due.
Yet few of these far majesties, ah, few!
Have bared their operations to this globe—
Few, who with gorgeous pageantry enrobe
Our piece of heaven—whose benevolence
Shakes hand with our own Ceres; every sense
Filling with spiritual sweets to plenitude,
As bees gorge full their cells. And, by the feud   40
'Twixt Nothing and Creation, I here swear,
Eterne Apollo! that thy Sister fair
Is of all these the gentlier-mightiest.
When thy gold breath is misting in the west,
She unobserved steals unto her throne,
And there she sits most meek and most alone;
As if she had not pomp subservient;
As if thine eye, high Poet! was not bent
Towards her with the Muses in thine heart;
As if the ministring stars kept not apart,   50
Waiting for silver-footed messages.
O Moon! the oldest shades 'mong oldest trees
Feel palpitations when thou lookest in:
O Moon! old boughs lisp forth a holier din
The while they feel thine airy fellowship.
Thou dost bless every where, with silver lip
Kissing dead things to life. The sleeping kine,
Couch'd in thy brightness, dream of fields divine:
Innumerable mountains rise, and rise,
Ambitious for the hallowing of thine eyes;   60
And yet thy benediction passeth not
One obscure hiding-place, one little spot

Where pleasure may be sent: the nested wren
Has thy fair face within its tranquil ken,
And from beneath a sheltering ivy leaf
Takes glimpses of thee; thou art a relief
To the poor patient oyster, where it sleeps
Within its pearly house.—The mighty deeps,
The monstrous sea is thine—the myriad sea!
O Moon! far-spooming Ocean bows to thee,   70
And Tellus feels his forehead's cumbrous load.

    Cynthia! where art thou now? What far abode
Of green or silvery bower doth enshrine
Such utmost beauty? Alas, thou dost pine
For one as sorrowful: thy cheek is pale
For one whose cheek is pale: thou dost bewail
His tears, who weeps for thee. Where dost thou sigh?
Ah! surely that light peeps from Vesper's eye,
Or what a thing is love! 'Tis She, but lo!
How chang'd, how full of ache, how gone in woe!   80
She dies at the thinnest cloud; her loveliness
Is wan on Neptune's blue: yet there's a stress
Of love-spangles, just off yon cape of trees,
Dancing upon the waves, as if to please
The curly foam with amorous influence.
O, not so idle: for down-glancing thence
She fathoms eddies, and runs wild about
O'erwhelming water-courses; scaring out
The thorny sharks from hiding-holes, and fright'ning
Their savage eyes with unaccustom'd lightning.   90
Where will the splendour be content to reach?
O love! how potent hast thou been to teach
Strange journeyings! Wherever beauty dwells,
In gulph or aerie, mountains or deep dells,
In light, in gloom, in star or blazing sun,
Thou pointest out the way, and straight 'tis won.
Amid his toil thou gav'st Leander breath;
Thou leddest Orpheus through the gleams of death;
Thou madest Pluto bear thin element;
And now, O winged Chieftain! thou hast sent   100
A moon-beam to the deep, deep water-world,
To find Endymion.

           On gold sand impearl'd
With lilly shells, and pebbles milky white,
Poor Cynthia greeted him, and sooth'd her light
Against his pallid face: he felt the charm
To breathlessness, and suddenly a warm

Of his heart's blood: 'twas very sweet; he stay'd
His wandering steps, and half-entranced laid
His head upon a tuft of straggling weeds,
To taste the gentle moon, and freshening beads,   110
Lash'd from the crystal roof by fishes' tails.
And so he kept, until the rosy veils
Mantling the east, by Aurora's peering hand
Were lifted from the water's breast, and fann'd
Into sweet air; and sober'd morning came
Meekly through billows:—when like taper-flame
Left sudden by a dallying breath of air,
He rose in silence, and once more 'gan fare
Along his fated way.

               Far had he roam'd,
With nothing save the hollow vast, that foam'd,   120
Above, around, and at his feet; save things
More dead than Morpheus' imaginings:
Old rusted anchors, helmets, breast-plates large
Of gone sea-warriors; brazen beaks and targe;
Rudders that for a hundred years had lost
The sway of human hand; gold vase emboss'd
With long-forgotten story, and wherein
No reveller had ever dipp'd a chin
But those of Saturn's vintage; mouldering scrolls,
Writ in the tongue of heaven, by those souls   130
Who first were on the earth; and sculptures rude
In ponderous stone, developing the mood
Of ancient Nox;—then skeletons of man,
Of beast, behemoth, and leviathan,
And elephant, and eagle, and huge jaw
Of nameless monster. A cold leaden awe
These secrets struck into him; and unless
Dian had chaced away that heaviness,
He might have died: but now, with cheered feel,
He onward kept; wooing these thoughts to steal   140
About the labyrinth in his soul of love.

   "What is there in thee, Moon! that thou shouldst move
My heart so potently? When yet a child
I oft have dried my tears when thou hast smil'd.
Thou seem'dst my sister: hand in hand we went
From eve to morn across the firmament.
No apples would I gather from the tree,
Till thou hadst cool'd their cheeks deliciously:
No tumbling water ever spake romance,
But when my eyes with thine thereon could dance: 150

No woods were green enough, no bower divine,
Until thou liftedst up thine eyelids fine:
In sowing time ne'er would I dibble take,
Or drop a seed, till thou wast wide awake;
And, in the summer tide of blossoming,
No one but thee hath heard me blythly sing
And mesh my dewy flowers all the night.
No melody was like a passing spright
If it went not to solemnize thy reign.
Yes, in my boyhood, every joy and pain   160
By thee were fashion'd to the self-same end;
And as I grew in years, still didst thou blend
With all my ardours: thou wast the deep glen;
Thou wast the mountain-top—the sage's pen—
The poet's harp—the voice of friends—the sun;
Thou wast the river—thou wast glory won;
Thou wast my clarion's blast—thou wast my steed—
My goblet full of wine—my topmost deed:—
Thou wast the charm of women, lovely Moon!
O what a wild and harmonized tune   170
My spirit struck from all the beautiful!
On some bright essence could I lean, and lull
Myself to immortality: I prest
Nature's soft pillow in a wakeful rest.
But, gentle Orb! there came a nearer bliss—
My strange love came—Felicity's abyss!
She came, and thou didst fade, and fade away—
Yet not entirely; no, thy starry sway
Has been an under-passion to this hour.
Now I begin to feel thine orby power   180
Is coming fresh upon me: O be kind,
Keep back thine influence, and do not blind
My sovereign vision.—Dearest love, forgive
That I can think away from thee and live!—
Pardon me, airy planet, that I prize
One thought beyond thine argent luxuries!
How far beyond!" At this a surpris'd start
Frosted the springing verdure of his heart;
For as he lifted up his eyes to swear
How his own goddess was past all things fair,   190
He saw far in the concave green of the sea
An old man sitting calm and peacefully.
Upon a weeded rock this old man sat,
And his white hair was awful, and a mat
Of weeds were cold beneath his cold thin feet;
And, ample as the largest winding-sheet,

A cloak of blue wrapp'd up his aged bones,
O'erwrought with symbols by the deepest groans
Of ambitious magic: every ocean-form
Was woven in with black distinctness; storm,   200
And calm, and whispering, and hideous roar,
Quicksand, and whirlpool, and deserted shore,
Were emblem'd in the woof; with every shape
That skims, or dives, or sleeps, 'twixt cape and cape.
The gulphing whale was like a dot in the spell,
Yet look upon it, and 'twould size and swell
To its huge self; and the minutest fish
Would pass the very hardest gazer's wish,
And show his little eye's anatomy.
Then there was pictur'd the regality   210
Of Neptune; and the sea nymphs round his state,
In beauteous vassalage, look up and wait.
Beside this old man lay a pearly wand,
And in his lap a book, the which he conn'd
So stedfastly, that the new denizen
Had time to keep him in amazed ken,
To mark these shadowings, and stand in awe.

The old man rais'd his hoary head and saw
The wilder'd stranger—seeming not to see,
His features were so lifeless. Suddenly   220
He woke as from a trance; his snow-white brows
Went arching up, and like two magic ploughs
Furrow'd deep wrinkles in his forehead large,
Which kept as fixedly as rocky marge,
Till round his wither'd lips had gone a smile.
Then up he rose, like one whose tedious toil
Had watch'd for years in forlorn hermitage,
Who had not from mid-life to utmost age
Eas'd in one accent his o'er-burden'd soul,
Even to the trees. He rose: he grasp'd his stole,
With convuls'd clenches waving it abroad,   231
And in a voice of solemn joy, that aw'd
Echo into oblivion, he said:—

"Thou art the man! Now shall I lay my head
In peace upon my watery pillow: now
Sleep will come smoothly to my weary brow.
O Jove! I shall be young again, be young!
O shell-borne Neptune, I am pierc'd and stung
With new-born life! What shall I do? Where go,
When I have cast this serpent-skin of woe?—   240

I'll swim to the syrens, and one moment listen
Their melodies, and see their long hair glisten;
Anon upon that giant's arm I'll be,
That writhes about the roots of Sicily:
To northern seas I'll in a twinkling sail,
And mount upon the snortings of a whale
To some black cloud; thence down I'll madly sweep
On forked lightning, to the deepest deep,
Where through some sucking pool I will be hurl'd
With rapture to the other side of the world!   250
O, I am full of gladness! Sisters three,
I bow full hearted to your old decree!
Yes, every god be thank'd, and power benign,
For I no more shall wither, droop, and pine.
Thou art the man!" Endymion started back
Dismay'd; and, like a wretch from whom the rack
Tortures hot breath, and speech of agony,
Mutter'd: "What lonely death am I to die
In this cold region? Will he let me freeze,
And float my brittle limbs o'er polar seas?   260
Or will he touch me with his searing hand,
And leave a black memorial on the sand?
Or tear me piece-meal with a bony saw,
And keep me as a chosen food to draw
His magian fish through hated fire and flame?
O misery of hell! resistless, tame,
Am I to be burnt up? No, I will shout,
Until the gods through heaven's blue look out!——
O Tartarus! but some few days agone
Her soft arms were entwining me, and on   270
Her voice I hung like fruit among green leaves:
Her lips were all my own, and—ah, ripe sheaves
Of happiness! ye on the stubble droop,
But never may be garner'd. I must stoop
My head, and kiss death's foot. Love! love, farewell!
Is there no hope from thee? This horrid spell
Would melt at thy sweet breath.—By Dian's hind
Feeding from her white fingers, on the wind
I see thy streaming hair! and now, by Pan,
I care not for this old mysterious man!"   280

    He spoke, and walking to that aged form,
Look'd high defiance. Lo! his heart 'gan warm
With pity, for the grey-hair'd creature wept.
Had he then wrong'd a heart where sorrow kept?
Had he, though blindly contumelious, brought
Rheum to kind eyes, a sting to humane thought,

Convulsion to a mouth of many years?
He had in truth; and he was ripe for tears.
The penitent shower fell, as down he knelt
Before that care-worn sage, who trembling felt   290
About his large dark locks, and faultering spake:

"Arise, good youth, for sacred Phœbus' sake!
I know thine inmost bosom, and I feel
A very brother's yearning for thee steal
Into mine own: for why? thou openest
The prison gates that have so long opprest
My weary watching. Though thou know'st it not,
Thou art commission'd to this fated spot
For great enfranchisement. O weep no more;
I am a friend to love, to loves of yore: 300
Aye, hadst thou never lov'd an unknown power,
I had been grieving at this joyous hour.
But even now most miserable old,
I saw thee, and my blood no longer cold
Gave mighty pulses: in this tottering case
Grew a new heart, which at this moment plays
As dancingly as thine. Be not afraid,
For thou shalt hear this secret all display'd,
Now as we speed towards our joyous task."

So saying, this young soul in age's mask   310
Went forward with the Carian side by side:
Resuming quickly thus; while ocean's tide
Hung swollen at their backs, and jewel'd sands
Took silently their foot-prints.
                          "My soul stands
Now past the midway from mortality,
And so I can prepare without a sigh
To tell thee briefly all my joy and pain.
I was a fisher once, upon this main,
And my boat danc'd in every creek and bay;
Rough billows were my home by night and day,—
The sea-gulls not more constant; for I had   321
No housing from the storm and tempests mad,
But hollow rocks,—and they were palaces
Of silent happiness, of slumberous ease:
Long years of misery have told me so.
Aye, thus it was one thousand years ago.
One thousand years!—Is it then possible
To look so plainly through them? to dispel
A thousand years with backward glance sublime?
To breathe away as 'twere all scummy slime   330

From off a crystal pool, to see its deep,
And one's own image from the bottom peep?
Yes: now I am no longer wretched thrall,
My long captivity and moanings all
Are but a slime, a thin-pervading scum,
The which I breathe away, and thronging come
Like things of yesterday my youthful pleasures.

"I touch'd no lute, I sang not, trod no measures:
I was a lonely youth on desert shores.
My sports were lonely, 'mid continuous roars,   340
And craggy isles, and sea-mew's plaintive cry
Plaining discrepant between sea and sky.
Dolphins were still my playmates; shapes unseen
Would let me feel their scales of gold and green,
Nor be my desolation; and, full oft,
When a dread waterspout had rear'd aloft
Its hungry hugeness, seeming ready ripe
To burst with hoarsest thunderings, and wipe
My life away like a vast sponge of fate,
Some friendly monster, pitying my sad state,   350
Has dived to its foundations, gulph'd it down,
And left me tossing safely. But the crown
Of all my life was utmost quietude:
More did I love to lie in cavern rude,
Keeping in wait whole days for Neptune's voice,
And if it came at last, hark, and rejoice!
There blush'd no summer eve but I would steer
My skiff along green shelving coasts, to hear
The shepherd's pipe come clear from aery steep,
Mingled with ceaseless bleatings of his sheep: 360
And never was a day of summer shine,
But I beheld its birth upon the brine:
For I would watch all night to see unfold
Heaven's gates, and Æthon snort his morning gold
Wide o'er the swelling streams: and constantly
At brim of day-tide, on some grassy lea,
My nets would be spread out, and I at rest.
The poor folk of the sea-country I blest
With daily boon of fish most delicate:
They knew not whence this bounty, and elate   370
Would strew sweet flowers on a sterile beach.

"Why was I not contented? Wherefore reach
At things which, but for thee, O Latmian!
Had been my dreary death? Fool! I began

To feel distemper'd longings: to desire
The utmost privilege that ocean's sire
Could grant in benediction: to be free
Of all his kingdom. Long in misery
I wasted, ere in one extremest fit
I plung'd for life or death. To interknit   380
One's senses with so dense a breathing stuff
Might seem a work of pain; so not enough
Can I admire how crystal-smooth it felt,
And buoyant round my limbs. At first I dwelt
Whole days and days in sheer astonishment;
Forgetful utterly of self-intent;
Moving but with the mighty ebb and flow.
Then, like a new fledg'd bird that first doth show
His spreaded feathers to the morrow chill,
I tried in fear the pinions of my will.   390
'Twas freedom! and at once I visited
The ceaseless wonders of this ocean-bed.
No need to tell thee of them, for I see
That thou hast been a witness—it must be—
For these I know thou canst not feel a drouth,
By the melancholy corners of that mouth.
So I will in my story straightway pass
To more immediate matter. Woe, alas!
That love should be my bane! Ah, Scylla fair!
Why did poor Glaucus ever—ever dare   400
To sue thee to his heart? Kind stranger-youth!
I lov'd her to the very white of truth,
And she would not conceive it. Timid thing!
She fled me swift as sea-bird on the wing,
Round every isle, and point, and promontory,
From where large Hercules wound up his story
Far as Egyptian Nile. My passion grew
The more, the more I saw her dainty hue
Gleam delicately through the azure clear:
Until 'twas too fierce agony to bear;   410
And in that agony, across my grief
It flash'd, that Circe might find some relief—
Cruel enchantress! So above the water
I rear'd my head, and look'd for Phœbus' daughter.
Æœa's isle was wondering at the moon:—
It seem'd to whirl around me, and a swoon
Left me dead-drifting to that fatal power.

"When I awoke, 'twas in a twilight bower;
Just when the light of morn, with hum of bees,
Stole through its verdurous matting of fresh trees.

How sweet, and sweeter; for I heard a lyre,   421
And over it a sighing voice expire.
It ceased—I caught light footsteps; and anon
The fairest face that morn e'er look'd upon
Push'd through a screen of roses. Starry Jove!
With tears, and smiles, and honey-words she wove
A net whose thraldom was more bliss than all
The range of flower'd Elysium. Thus did fall
The dew of her rich speech: "Ah! Art awake?
"O let me hear thee speak, for Cupid's sake!   430
"I am so oppress'd with joy! Why, I have shed
"An urn of tears, as though thou wert cold dead;
"And now I find thee living, I will pour
"From these devoted eyes their silver store,
"Until exhausted of the latest drop,
"So it will pleasure thee, and force thee stop
"Here, that I too may live: but if beyond
"Such cool and sorrowful offerings, thou art fond
"Of soothing warmth, of dalliance supreme;
"If thou art ripe to taste a long love dream;   440
"If smiles, if dimples, tongues for ardour mute,
"Hang in thy vision like a tempting fruit,
"O let me pluck it for thee." Thus she link'd
Her charming syllables, till indistinct
Their music came to my o'er-sweeten'd soul;
And then she hover'd over me, and stole
So near, that if no nearer it had been
This furrow'd visage thou hadst never seen.

      "Young man of Latmos! thus particular
Am I, that thou may'st plainly see how far   450
This fierce temptation went: and thou may'st not
Exclaim, How then, was Scylla quite forgot?

      "Who could resist? Who in this universe?
She did so breathe ambrosia; so immerse
My fine existence in a golden clime.
She took me like a child of suckling time,
And cradled me in roses. Thus condemn'd,
The current of my former life was stemm'd,
And to this arbitrary queen of sense
I bow'd a tranced vassal: nor would thence   460
Have mov'd, even though Amphion's harp had woo'd
Me back to Scylla o'er the billows rude.
For as Apollo each eve doth devise
A new appareling for western skies;

So every eve, nay every spendthrift hour
Shed balmy consciousness within that bower.
And I was free of haunts umbrageous;
Could wander in the mazy forest-house
Of squirrels, foxes shy, and antler'd deer,
And birds from coverts innermost and drear   470
Warbling for very joy melliflous sorrow—
To me new born delights!   •
                        "Now let me borrow,
For moments, few, a temperament as stern
As Pluto's sceptre, that my words not burn
These uttering lips, while I in calm speech tell
How specious heaven was changed to real hell.

"One morn she left me sleeping: half awake
I sought for her smooth arms and lips, to slake
My greedy thirst with nectarous camel-draughts;
But she was gone. Whereat the barbed shafts   480
Of disappointment stuck in me so sore,
That out I ran and search'd the forest o'er.
Wandering about in pine and cedar gloom
Damp awe assail'd me; for there 'gan to boom
A sound of moan, an agony of sound,
Sepulchral from the distance all around.
Then came a conquering earth-thunder, and rumbled
That fierce complain to silence: while I stúmbled
Down a precipitous path, as if impell'd.
I came to a dark valley.—Groanings swell'd   490
Poisonous about my ears, and louder grew,
The nearer I approach'd a flame's gaunt blue,
That glar'd before me through a thorny brake.
This fire, like the eye of gordian snake,   •
Bewitch'd me towards; and I soon was near
A sight too fearful for the feel of fear:
In thicket hid I curs'd the haggard scene—
The banquet of my arms, my arbour queen,
Seated upon an uptorn forest root;
And all around her shapes, wizard and brute,   500
Laughing and wailing, groveling, serpenting,
Showing tooth, tusk, and venom-bag, and sting!
O such deformities! Old Charon's self,
Should he give up awhile his penny pelf,
And take a dream 'mong rushes Stygian,
It could not be so phantasied. Fierce, wan,
And tyrannizing was the lady's look,
As over them a gnarled staff she shook.

Oft-times upon the sudden she laugh'd out,
And from a basket emptied to the rout   510
Clusters of grapes, the which they raven'd quick
And roar'd for more; with many a hungry lick
About their shaggy jaws. Avenging, slow,
Anon she took a branch of mistletoe,
And emptied on't a black dull-gurgling phial:
Groan'd one and all, as if some piercing trial
Was sharpening for their pitiable bones.
She lifted up the charm: appealing groans
From their poor breasts went sueing to her ear
In vain; remorseless as an infant's bier   520
She whisk'd against their eyes the sooty oil.
Whereat was heard a noise of painful toil,
Increasing gradual to a tempest rage,
Shrieks, yells, and groans of torture-pilgrimage;
Until their grieved bodies 'gan to bloat
And puff from the tail's end to stifled throat:
Then was appalling silence: then a sight
More wildering than all that hoarse affright;
For the whole herd, as by a whirlwind writhen,
Went through the dismal air like one huge Python
Antagonizing Boreas,—and so vanish'd.   531
Yet there was not a breath of wind: she banish'd
These phantoms with a nod. Lo! from the dark
Came waggish fauns, and nymphs, and satyrs stark,
With dancing and loud revelry,—and went
Swifter than centaurs after rapine bent.—
Sighing an elephant appear'd and bow'd
Before the fierce witch, speaking thus aloud
In human accent: "Potent goddess! chief
"Of pains resistless! make my being brief,   540
"Or let me from this heavy prison fly:
"Or give me to the air, or let me die!
"I sue not for my happy crown again;
"I sue not for my phalanx on the plain;
"I sue not for my lone, my widow'd wife;
"I sue not for my ruddy drops of life,
"My children fair, my lovely girls and boys!
"I will forget them; I will pass these joys;
"Ask nought so heavenward, so too—too high:
"Only I pray, as fairest boon, to die,   550
"Or be deliver'd from this cumbrous flesh,
"From this gross, detestable, filthy mesh,
"And merely given to the cold bleak air.
"Have mercy, Goddess! Circe, feel my prayer!"

"That curst magician's name fell icy numb
Upon my wild conjecturing: truth had come
Naked and sabre-like against my heart.
I saw a fury whetting a death-dart;
And my slain spirit, overwrought with fright,
Fainted away in that dark lair of night.   560
Think, my deliverer, how desolate
My waking must have been! disgust, and hate,
And terrors manifold divided me
A spoil amongst them. I prepar'd to flee
Into the dungeon core of that wild wood:
I fled three days—when lo! before me stood
Glaring the angry witch. O Dis, even now,
A clammy dew is beading on my brow,
At mere remembering her pale laugh, and curse.
"Ha! ha! Sir Dainty! there must be a nurse   570
"Made of rose leaves and thistledown, express,
"To cradle thee my sweet, and lull thee: yes,
"I am too flinty-hard for thy nice touch:
"My tenderest squeeze is but a giant's clutch.
"So, fairy-thing, it shall have lullabies
"Unheard of yet: and it shall still its cries
"Upon some breast more lilly-feminine.
"Oh, no—it shall not pine, and pine, and pine
"More than one pretty, trifling thousand years;
"And then 'twere pity, but fate's gentle shears   580
"Cut short its immortality. Sea-flirt!
"Young dove of the waters! truly I'll not hurt
"One hair of thine: see how I weep and sigh,
"That our heart-broken parting is so nigh.
"And must we part? Ah, yes, it must be so.
"Yet ere thou leavest me in utter woe,
"Let me sob over thee my last adieus,
"And speak a blessing: Mark me! Thou hast thews
"Immortal, for thou art of heavenly race:
"But such a love is mine, that here I chace   590
"Eternally away from thee all bloom
"Of youth, and destine thee towards a tomb.
"Hence shalt thou quickly to the watery vast;
"And there, ere many days be overpast,
"Disabled age shall seize thee; and even then
"Thou shalt not go the way of aged men;
"But live and wither, cripple and still breathe
"Ten hundred years: which gone, I then bequeath
"Thy fragile bones to unknown burial.
"Adieu, sweet love, adieu!"—As shot stars fall,

She fled ere I could groan for mercy. Stung   601
And poison'd was my spirit: despair sung
A war-song of defiance 'gainst all hell.
A hand was at my shoulder to compel
My sullen steps; another 'fore my eyes
Moved on with pointed finger. In this guise
Enforced, at the last by ocean's foam
I found me; by my fresh, my native home.
Its tempering coolness, to my life akin,
Came salutary as I waded in;   610
And, with a blind voluptuous rage, I gave
Battle to the swollen billow-ridge, and drave
Large froth before me, while there yet remain'd
Hale strength, nor from my bones all marrow drain'd.

   "Young lover, I must weep—such hellish spite
With dry cheek who can tell? While thus my might
Proving upon this element, dismay'd,
Upon a dead thing's face my hand I laid;
I look'd—'twas Scylla! Cursed, cursed Circe!
O vulture-witch, hast never heard of mercy?   620
Could not thy harshest vengeance be content,
But thou must nip this tender innocent
Because I lov'd her?—Cold, O cold indeed
Were her fair limbs, and like a common weed
The sea-swell took her hair. Dead as she was
I clung about her waist, nor ceas'd to pass
Fleet as an arrow through unfathom'd brine,
Until there shone a fabric crystalline,
Ribb'd and inlaid with coral, pebble, and pearl.
Headlong I darted; at one eager swirl   630
Gain'd its bright portal, enter'd, and behold!
'Twas vast, and desolate, and icy-cold;
And all around—But wherefore this to thee
Who in few minutes more thyself shalt see?—
I left poor Scylla in a niche and fled.
My fever'd parchings up, my scathing dread
Met palsy half way: soon these limbs became
Gaunt, wither'd, sapless, feeble, cramp'd, and lame.

   "Now let me pass a cruel, cruel space,
Without one hope, without one faintest trace   640
Of mitigation, or redeeming bubble
Of colour'd phantasy; for I fear 'twould trouble
Thy brain to loss of reason: and next tell
How a restoring chance came down to quell
One half of the witch in me.

　　　　　　　　　　　　　　"On a day,
Sitting upon a rock above the spray,
I saw grow up from the horizon's brink
A gallant vessel: soon she seem'd to sink
Away from me again, as though her course
Had been resum'd in spite of hindering force——　　650
So vanish'd: and not long, before arose
Dark clouds, and muttering of winds morose.
Old Æolus would stifle his mad spleen,
But could not: therefore all the billows green
Toss'd up the silver spume against the clouds.
The tempest came: I saw that vessel's shrouds
In perilous bustle; while upon the deck
Stood trembling creatures. I beheld the wreck;
The final gulphing; the poor struggling souls:
I heard their cries amid loud thunder-rolls.　　　660
O they had all been sav'd but crazed eld
Annull'd my vigorous cravings: and thus quell'd
And curb'd, think on't, O Latmian! did I sit
Writhing with pity, and a cursing fit
Against that hell-born Circe. The crew had gone,
By one and one, to pale oblivion;
And I was gazing on the surges prone,
With many a scalding tear and many a groan,
When at my feet emerg'd an old man's hand,
Grasping this scroll, and this same slender wand.　　670
I knelt with pain—reach'd out my hand—had grasp'd
These treasures—touch'd the knuckles—they unclasp'd—
I caught a finger: but the downward weight
O'erpowered me—it sank. Then 'gan abate
The storm, and through chill aguish gloom outburst
The comfortable sun. I was athirst
To search the book, and in the warming air
Parted its dripping leaves with eager care.
Strange matters did it treat of, and drew on
My soul page after page, till well-nigh won　　　680
Into forgetfulness; when, stupefied,
I read these words, and read again, and tried
My eyes against the heavens, and read again.
O what a load of misery and pain
Each Atlas-line bore off!—a shine of hope
Came gold around me, cheering me to cope
Strenuous with hellish tyranny. Attend!
For thou hast brought their promise to an end.

　　"*In wide sea there lives a forlorn wretch,*
Doom'd with enfeebled carcase to outstretch　　690

His loath'd existence through ten centuries,
And then to die alone. Who can devise
A total opposition? No one. So
One million times ocean must ebb and flow,
And he oppressed. Yet he shall not die,
These things accomplish'd:—If he utterly
Scans all the depths of magic, and expounds
The meanings of all motions, shapes and sounds;
If he explores all forms and substances
Straight homeward to their symbol-essences;   700
He shall not die. Moreover, and in chief,
He must pursue this task of joy and grief
Most piously;—all lovers tempest-tost,
And in the savage overwhelming lost,
He shall deposit side by side, until
Time's creeping shall the dreary space fulfil:
Which done, and all these labours ripened,
A youth, by heavenly power lov'd and led,
Shall stand before him; whom he shall direct
How to consummate all. The youth elect   710
Must do the thing, or both will be destroy'd."—

"Then," cried the young Endymion, overjoy'd,
"We are twin brothers in this destiny!
Say, I intreat thee, what achievement high
Is, in this restless world, for me reserv'd.
What! if from thee my wandering feet had swerv'd,
Had we both perish'd?"—"Look!" the sage replied,
"Dost thou not mark a gleaming through the tide,
Of diverse brilliances? 'tis the edifice
I told thee of, where lovely Scylla lies;   720
And where I have enshrined piously
All lovers, whom fell storms have doom'd to die
Throughout my bondage." Thus discoursing, on
They went till unobscur'd the porches shone;
Which hurrying they gain'd, and enter'd straight.
Sure never since king Neptune held his state
Was seen such wonder underneath the stars.
Turn to some level plain where haughty Mars
Has legion'd all his battle; and behold
How every soldier, with firm foot, doth hold   730
His even breast: see, many steeled squares,
And rigid ranks of iron—whence who dares
One step? Imagine further, line by line,
These warrior thousands on the field supine:—
So in that crystal place, in silent rows,
Poor lovers lay at rest from joys and woes.—

The stranger from the mountains, breathless, trac'd
Such thousands of shut eyes in order plac'd;
Such ranges of white feet, and patient lips
All ruddy,—for here death no blossom nips.   740
He mark'd their brows and foreheads; saw their hair
Put sleekly on one side with nicest care;
And each one's gentle wrists, with reverence,
Put cross-wise to its heart.
                              "Let us commence,"
Whisper'd the guide, stuttering with joy, "even now."
He spake, and, trembling like an aspen-bough,
Began to tear his scroll in pieces small,
Uttering the while some mumblings funeral.
He tore it into pieces small as snow
That drifts unfeather'd when bleak northerns blow;
And having done it, took his dark blue cloak   751
And bound it round Endymion: then struck
His wand against the empty air times nine.—
"What more there is to do, young man, is thine:
But first a little patience; first undo
This tangled thread, and wind it to a clue.
Ah, gentle! 'tis as weak as spider's skein;
And shouldst thou break it—What, is it done so clean?
A power overshadows thee! O, brave!
The spite of hell is tumbling to its grave.   760
Here is a shell; 'tis pearly blank to me,
Nor mark'd with any sign or charactery—
Canst thou read aught? O read for pity's sake!
Olympus! we are safe! Now, Carian, break
This wand against yon lyre on the pedestal."

    'Twas done: and straight with sudden swell and fall
Sweet music breath'd her soul away, and sigh'd
A lullaby to silence.—"Youth! now strew
These minced leaves on me, and passing through
Those files of dead, scatter the same around,   770
And thou wilt see the issue."—'Mid the sound
Of flutes and viols, ravishing his heart,
Endymion from Glaucus stood apart,
And scatter'd in his face some fragments light.
How lightning-swift the change! a youthful wight
Smiling beneath a coral diadem,
Out-sparkling sudden like an upturn'd gem,
Appear'd, and, stepping to a beauteous corse,
Kneel'd down beside it, and with tenderest force
Press'd its cold hand, and wept,—and Scylla sigh'd!
Endymion, with quick hand, the charm applied—   781

The nymph arose: he left them to their joy,
And onward went upon his high employ,
Showering those powerful fragments on the dead.
And, as he pass'd, each lifted up his head,
As doth a flower at Apollo's touch.
Death felt it to his inwards: 'twas too much:
Death fell a weeping in his charnel-house.
The Latmian persever'd along, and thus
All were re-animated. There arose   790
A noise of harmony, pulses and throes
Of gladness in the air—-while many, who
Had died in mutual arms devout and true,
Sprang to each other madly; and the rest
Felt a high certainty of being blest.
They gaz'd upon Endymion. Enchantment
Grew drunken, and would have its head and bent.
Delicious symphonies, like airy flowers,
Budded, and swell'd, and, full-blown, shed full showers
Of light, soft, unseen leaves of sounds divine.   800
The two deliverers tasted a pure wine
Of happiness, from fairy-press ooz'd out.
Speechless they eyed each other, and about
The fair assembly wander'd to and fro,
Distracted with the richest overflow
Of joy that ever pour'd from heaven.

                                    ——"Away!"
Shouted the new born god; "Follow, and pay
Our piety to Neptunus supreme!"—-
Then Scylla, blushing sweetly from her dream,
They led on first, bent to her meek surprise,   810
Through portal columns of a giant size,
Into the vaulted, boundless emerald.
Joyous all follow'd as the leader call'd,
Down marble steps; pouring as easily
As hour-glass sand,—and fast, as you might see
Swallows obeying the south summer's call,
Or swans upon a gentle waterfall.

  Thus went that beautiful multitude, nor far,
Ere from among some rocks of glittering spar,
Just within ken, they saw descending thick   820
Another multitude. Whereat more quick
Moved either host. On a wide sand they met,
And of those numbers every eye was wet;
For each their old love found. A murmuring rose,
Like what was never heard in all the throes

Of wind and waters: 'tis past human wit
To tell; 'tis dizziness to think of it.

This mighty consummation made, the host
Mov'd on for many a league; and gain'd, and lost
Huge sea-marks; vanward swelling in array,   830
And from the rear diminishing away,—
Till a faint dawn surpris'd them. Glaucus cried,
"Behold! behold, the palace of his pride!
God Neptune's palaces!" With noise increas'd,
They shoulder'd on towards that brightening east.
At every onward step proud domes arose
In prospect,—diamond gleams, and golden glows
Of amber 'gainst their faces levelling.
Joyous, and many as the leaves in spring,
Still onward; still the splendour gradual swell'd.   840
Rich opal domes were seen, on high upheld
By jasper pillars, letting through their shafts
A blush of coral. Copious wonder-draughts
Each gazer drank; and deeper drank more near:
For what poor mortals fragment up, as mere
As marble was there lavish, to the vast
Of one fair palace, that far far surpass'd,
Even for common bulk, those olden three,
Memphis, and Babylon, and Nineveh.

As large, as bright, as colour'd as the bow   850
Of Iris, when unfading it doth show
Beyond a silvery shower, was the arch
Through which this Paphian army took its march,
Into the outer courts of Neptune's state:
Whence could be seen, direct, a golden gate,
To which the leaders sped; but not half raught
Ere it burst open swift as fairy thought,
And made those dazzled thousands veil their eyes
Like callow eagles at the first sunrise.
Soon with an eagle nativeness their gaze   860
Ripe from hue-golden swoons took all the blaze,
And then, behold! large Neptune on his throne
Of emerald deep: yet not exalt alone;
At his right hand stood winged Love, and on
His left sat smiling Beauty's paragon.

Far as the mariner on highest mast
Can see all round upon the calmed vast,
So wide was Neptune's hall: and as the blue
Doth vault the waters, so the waters drew

Their doming curtains, high, magnificent,   870
Aw'd from the throne aloof;—and when storm-rent
Disclos'd the thunder-gloomings in Jove's air;
But sooth'd as now, flash'd sudden everywhere,
Noiseless, sub-marine cloudlets, glittering
Death to a human eye: for there did spring
From natural west, and east, and south, and north,
A light as of four sunsets, blazing forth
A gold-green zenith 'bove the Sea-God's head.
Of lucid depth the floor, and far outspread
As breezeless lake, on which the slim canoe   880
Of feather'd Indian darts about, as through
The delicatest air: air verily,
But for the portraiture of clouds and sky:
This palace floor breath-air,—but for the amaze
Of deep-seen wonders motionless,—and blaze
Of the dome pomp, reflected in extremes,
Globing a golden sphere.

                         They stood in dreams
Till Triton blew his horn. The palace rang;
The Nereids danc'd; the Syrens faintly sang;
And the great Sea-King bow'd his dripping head.   890
Then Love took wing, and from his pinions shed
On all the multitude a nectarous dew.
The ooze-born Goddess beckoned and drew
Fair Scylla and her guides to conference;
And when they reach'd the throned eminence
She kist the sea-nymph's cheek,—who sat her down
A toying with the doves. Then,—"Mighty crown
And sceptre of this kingdom!" Venus said,
"Thy vows were on a time to Nais paid:
Behold!"— Two copious tear-drops instant fell   900
From the God's large eyes; he smil'd delectable,
And over Glaucus held his blessing hands.—
"Endymion! Ah! still wandering in the bands
Of love? Now this is cruel. Since the hour
I met thee in earth's bosom, all my power
Have I put forth to serve thee. What, not yet
Escap'd from dull mortality's harsh net?
A little patience, youth! 'twill not be long,
Or I am skilless quite: an idle tongue,
A humid eye, and steps luxurious,   910
Where these are new and strange, are ominous.
Aye, I have seen these signs in one of heaven,
When others were all blind: and were I given

To utter secrets, haply I might say
Some pleasant words:—but Love will have his day.
So wait awhile expectant. Pr'ythee soon,
Even in the passing of thine honey-moon,
Visit thou my Cythera: thou wilt find
Cupid well-natured, my Adonis kind;
And pray persuade with thee—Ah, I have done,
All blisses be upon thee, my sweet son!"—   921
Thus the fair goddess: While Endymion
Knelt to receive those accents halcyon.

Meantime a glorious revelry began
Before the Water-Monarch. Nectar ran
In courteous fountains to all cups outreaeh'd;
And plunder'd vines, teeming exhaustless, pleach'd
New growth about each shell and pendent lyre;
The which, in disentangling for their fire,
Pull'd down fresh foliage and coverture   930
For dainty toying. Cupid, empire-sure,
Flutter'd and laugh'd, and oft-times through the throng
Made a delighted way. Then dance, and song,
And garlanding grew wild; and pleasure reign'd.
In harmless tendril they each other chain'd,
And strove who should be smother'd deepest in
Fresh crush of leaves.

O 'tis a very sin
For one so weak to venture his poor verse
In such a place as this. O do not curse,
High Muses! let him hurry to the ending.   940

All suddenly were silent. A soft blending
Of dulcet instruments came charmingly;
And then a hymn.

"KING of the stormy sea!
Brother of Jove, and co-inheritor
Of elements! Eternally before
Thee the waves awful bow. Fast, stubborn rock,
At thy fear'd trident shrinking, doth unlock
Its deep foundations, hissing into foam.
All mountain-rivers, lost in the wide home
Of thy capacious bosom, ever flow.   950
Thou frownest, and old Æolus thy foe
Skulks to his cavern, 'mid the gruff complaint
Of all his rebel tempests. Dark clouds faint

When, from thy diadem, a silver gleam
Slants over blue dominion. Thy bright team
Gulphs in the morning light, and scuds along
To bring thee nearer to that golden song
Apollo singeth, while his chariot
Waits at the doors of heaven. Thou art not
For scenes like this: an empire stern hast thou;   960
And it hath furrow'd that large front: yet now,
As newly come of heaven, dost thou sit
To blend and interknit
Subdued majesty with this glad time.
O shell-borne King sublime!
We lay our hearts before thee evermore—
We sing, and we adore!

　　"Breathe softly, flutes;
Be tender of your strings, ye soothing lutes;
Nor be the trumpet heard! O vain, O vain;   970
Not flowers budding in an April rain,
Nor breath of sleeping dove, nor river's flow,—
No, nor the Æolian twang of Love's own bow,
Can mingle music fit for the soft ear
Of goddess Cytherea!
Yet deign, white Queen of Beauty, thy fair eyes
On our souls' sacrifice.

　　"Bright-winged Child!
Who has another care when thou hast smil'd?
Unfortunates on earth, we see at last   980
All death-shadows, and glooms that overcast
Our spirits, fann'd away by thy light pinions.
O sweetest essence! sweetest of all minions!
God of warm pulses, and dishevell'd hair,
And panting bosoms bare!
Dear unseen light in darkness! eclipser
Of light in light! delicious poisoner!
Thy venom'd goblet will we quaff until
We fill—we fill!
And by thy Mother's lips———"

　　　　　　　　Was heard no more   990
For clamour, when the golden palace door
Opened again, and from without, in shone
A new magnificence. On oozy throne
Smooth-moving came Oceanus the old,
To take a latest glimpse at his sheep-fold,
Before he went into his quiet cave
To muse for ever—Then a lucid wave,

Scoop'd from its trembling sisters of mid-sea,
Afloat, and pillowing up the majesty
Of Doris, and the Ægean seer, her spouse—   1000
Next, on a dolphin, clad in laurel boughs,
Theban Amphion leaning on his lute:
His fingers went across it—All were mute
To gaze on Amphitrite, queen of pearls,
And Thetis pearly too.—

                The palace whirls
Around giddy Endymion; seeing he
Was there far strayed from mortality.
He could not bear it—shut his eyes in vain;
Imagination gave a dizzier pain.
"O I shall die! sweet Venus, be my stay!   1010
Where is my lovely mistress? Well-away!
I die—I hear her voice—I feel my wing—"
At Neptune's feet he sank. A sudden ring
Of Nereids were about him, in kind strife
To usher back his spirit into life:
But still he slept. At last they interwove
Their cradling arms, and purpos'd to convey
Towards a crystal bower far away.

    Lo! while slow carried through the pitying crowd,
To his inward senses these words spake aloud;   1020
Written in star-light on the dark above:
Dearest Endymion! my entire love!
How have I dwelt in fear of fate: 'tis done—
Immortal bliss for me too hast thou won.
Arise then! for the hen-dove shall not hatch
Her ready eggs, before I'll kissing snatch
Thee into endless heaven. Awake! awake!

    The youth at once arose: a placid lake
Came quiet to his eyes; and forest green,
Cooler than all the wonders he had seen,   1030
Lull'd with its simple song his fluttering breast.
How happy once again in grassy nest!

BOOK IV

Muse of my native land! loftiest Muse!
O first-born on the mountains! by the hues
Of heaven on the spiritual air begot:
Long didst thou sit alone in northern grot,

While yet our England was a wolfish den;
Before our forests heard the talk of men;
Before the first of Druids was a child;—
Long didst thou sit amid our regions wild
Rapt in a deep prophetic solitude.
There came an eastern voice of solemn mood:—   10
Yet wast thou patient. Then sang forth the Nine,
Apollo's garland:—yet didst thou divine
Such home-bred glory, that they cry'd in vain,
"Come hither, Sister of the Island!" Plain
Spake fair Ausonia; and once more she spake
A higher summons:—still didst thou betake
Thee to thy native hopes. O thou hast won
A full accomplishment! The thing is done,
Which undone, these our latter days had risen
On barren souls. Great Muse, thou know'st what prison,
Of flesh and bone, curbs, and confines, and frets   21
Our spirit's wings: despondency besets
Our pillows; and the fresh to-morrow morn
Seems to give forth its light in very scorn
Of our dull, uninspired, snail-paced lives.
Long have I said, how happy he who shrives
To thee! But then I thought on poets gone,
And could not pray:—nor could I now—so on
I move to the end in lowliness of heart.——

"Ah, woe is me! that I should fondly part   30
From my dear native land! Ah, foolish maid!
Glad was the hour, when, with thee, myriads bade
Adieu to Ganges and their pleasant fields!
To one so friendless the clear freshet yields
A bitter coolness; the ripe grape is sour:
Yet I would have, great gods! but one short hour
Of native air—let me but die at home."

Endymion to heaven's airy dome
Was offering up a hecatomb of vows,
When these words reach'd him. Whereupon he bows
His head through thorny-green entanglement   41
Of underwood, and to the sound is bent,
Anxious as hind towards her hidden fawn.

"Is no one near to help me? No fair dawn
Of life from charitable voice? No sweet saying
To set my dull and sadden'd spirit playing?

No hand to toy with mine? No lips so sweet
That I may worship them? No eyelids meet
To twinkle on my bosom? No one dies
Before me, till from these enslaving eyes   50
Redemption sparkles!—I am sad and lost."

    Thou, Carian lord, hadst better have been tost
Into a whirlpool. Vanish into air,
Warm mountaineer! for canst thou only bear
A woman's sigh alone and in distress?
See not her charms! Is Phœbe passionless?
Phœbe is fairer far—O gaze no more:—
Yet if thou wilt behold all beauty's store,
Behold her panting in the forest grass!
Do not those curls of glossy jet surpass   60
For tenderness the arms so idly lain
Amongst them? Feelest not a kindred pain,
To see such lovely eyes in swimming search
After some warm delight, that seems to perch
Dovelike in the dim cell lying beyond
Their upper lids?—Hist!

                    "O for Hermes' wand,
To touch this flower into human shape!
That woodland Hyacinthus could escape
From his green prison, and here kneeling down
Call me his queen, his second life's fair crown!   70
Ah me, how I could love!—My soul doth melt
For the unhappy youth—Love! I have felt
So faint a kindness, such a meek surrender
To what my own full thoughts had made too **tender,**
That but for tears my life had fled away!—
Ye deaf and senseless minutes of the day,
And thou, old forest, hold ye this for true,
There is no lightning, no authentic dew
But in the eye of love: there's not a sound,
Melodious howsoever, can confound   80
The heavens and earth in one to such a death
As doth the voice of love: there's not a breath
Will mingle kindly with the meadow air,
Till it has panted round, and stolen a share
Of passion from the heart!"—

                    Upon a bough
He leant, wretched. He surely cannot now
Thirst for another love: O impious,
That he can ever dream upon it thus!—

Thought he, "Why am I not as are the dead,
Since to a woe like this I have been led   90
Through the dark earth, and through the wondrous sea?
Goddess! I love thee not the less: from thee
By Juno's smile I turn not—no, no, no—
While the great waters are at ebb and flow.—
I have a triple soul! O fond pretence—
For both, for both my love is so immense,
I feel my heart is cut for them in twain."

  And so he groan'd, as one by beauty slain.
The lady's heart beat quick, and he could see
Her gentle bosom heave tumultuously.   100
He sprang from his green covert: there she lay,
Sweet as a muskrose upon new-made hay;
With all her limbs on tremble, and her eyes
Shut softly up alive. To speak he tries.
"Fair damsel, pity me! forgive that I
Thus violate thy bower's sanctity!
O pardon me, for I am full of grief—
Grief born of thee, young angel! fairest thief!
Who stolen hast away the wings wherewith
I was to top the heavens. Dear maid, sith   110
Thou art my executioner, and I feel
Loving and hatred, misery and weal,
Will in a few short hours be nothing to me,
And all my story that much passion slew me;
Do smile upon the evening of my days:
And, for my tortur'd brain begins to craze,
Be thou my nurse; and let me understand
How dying I shall kiss that lilly hand.—
Dost weep for me? Then should I be content.
Scowl on, ye fates! until the firmament   120
Outblackens Erebus, and the full-cavern'd earth
Crumbles into itself. By the cloud girth
Of Jove, those tears have given me a thirst
To meet oblivion."—As her heart would burst
The maiden sobb'd awhile, and then replied:
"Why must such desolation betide
As that thou speak'st of? Are not these green nooks
Empty of all misfortune? Do the brooks
Utter a gorgon voice? Does yonder thrush,
Schooling its half-fledg'd little ones to brush   130
About the dewy forest, whisper tales?—
Speak not of grief, young stranger, or cold snails

Will slime the rose to night. Though if thou wilt,
Methinks 'twould be a guilt—a very guilt—
Not to companion thee, and sigh away
The light—the dusk—the dark—till break of day!"
"Dear lady," said Endymion, " 'tis past:
I love thee! and my days can never last.
That I may pass in patience still speak:
Let me have music dying, and I seek   140
No more delight—I bid adieu to all.
Didst thou not after other climates call,
And murmur about Indian streams?"—Then she,
Sitting beneath the midmost forest tree,
For pity sang this roundelay———

      "O Sorrow,
      Why dost borrow
The natural hue of health, from vermeil lips?—
      To give maiden blushes
      To the white rose bushes?   150
Or is't thy dewy hand the daisy tips?

      "O Sorrow,
      Why dost borrow
The lustrous passion from a falcon-eye?—
      To give the glow-worm light?
      Or, on a moonless night,
To tinge, on syren shores, the salt sea-spry?

      "O Sorrow,
      Why dost borrow
The mellow ditties from a mourning tongue?—   160
      To give at evening pale
      Unto the nightingale,
That thou mayst listen the cold dews among?

      "O Sorrow,
      Why dost borrow
Heart's lightness from the merriment of May?—
      A lover would not tread
      A cowslip on the head,
Though he should dance from eve till peep of day—
      Nor any drooping flower   170
      Held sacred for thy bower,
Wherever he may sport himself and play.

"To Sorrow,
I bade good-morrow,
And thought to leave her far away behind;
But cheerly, cheerly,
She loves me dearly;
She is so constant to me, and so kind:
I would deceive her
And so leave her,   180
But ah! she is so constant and so kind.

"Beneath my palm trees, by the river side,
I sat a weeping: in the whole world wide
There was no one to ask me why I wept,—
And so I kept
Brimming the water-lilly cups with tears
Cold as my fears.

"Beneath my palm trees, by the river side,
I sat a weeping: what enamour'd bride,
Cheated by shadowy wooer from the clouds,   190
But hides and shrouds
Beneath dark palm trees by a river side?

"And as I sat, over the light blue hills
There came a noise of revellers: the rills
Into the wide stream came of purple hue—
'Twas Bacchus and his crew!
The earnest trumpet spake, and silver thrills
From kissing cymbals made a merry din—
'Twas Bacchus and his kin!
Like to a moving vintage down they came,   200
Crown'd with green leaves, and faces all on flame;
All madly dancing through the pleasant valley,
To scare thee, Melancholy!
O then, O then, thou wast a simple name!
And I forgot thee, as the berried holly
By shepherds is forgotten, when, in June,
Tall chestnuts keep away the sun and moon: —
I rush'd into the folly!

"Within his car, aloft, young Bacchus stood,
Trifling his ivy-dart, in dancing mood,   210
With sidelong laughing;
And little rills of crimson wine imbrued
His plump white arms, and shoulders, enough white
For Venus' pearly bite:

And near him rode Silenus on his ass,
Pelted with flowers as he on did pass
      Tipsily quaffing.

"Whence came ye, merry Damsels! whence came ye!
So many, and so many, and such glee?
Why have ye left your bowers desolate,   220
      Your lutes, and gentler fate?—
'We follow Bacchus! Bacchus on the wing,
      A conquering!
Bacchus, young Bacchus! good or ill betide,
We dance before him thorough kingdoms wide:—
Come hither, lady fair, and joined be
      To our wild minstrelsy!'

"Whence came ye, jolly Satyrs! whence came ye!
So many, and so many, and such glee?
Why have ye left your forest haunts, why left   230
      Your nuts in oak-tree cleft?—
'For wine, for wine we left our kernel tree;
For wine we left our heath, and yellow brooms,
      And cold mushrooms;
For wine we follow Bacchus through the earth;
Great God of breathless cups and chirping mirth!—
Come hither, lady fair, and joined be
      To our mad minstrelsy!'

"Over wide streams and mountains great we went,
And, save when Bacchus kept his ivy tent,   240
Onward the tiger and the leopard pants,
      With Asian elephants:
Onward these myriads—with song and dance,
With zebras striped, and sleek Arabians' prance,
Web-footed alligators, crocodiles,
Bearing upon their scaly backs, in files,
Plump infant laughers mimicking the coil
Of seamen, and stout galley-rowers' toil:
With toying oars and silken sails they glide,
      Nor care for wind and tide.   250

"Mounted on panthers' furs and lions' manes,
From rear to van they scour about the plains;
A three days' journey in a moment done:
And always, at the rising of the sun,
About the wilds they hunt with spear and horn,
      On spleenful unicorn.

"I saw Osirian Egypt kneel adown
        Before the vine-wreath crown!
I saw parch'd Abyssinia rouse and sing
        To the silver cymbals' ring!   260
I saw the whelming vintage hotly pierce
        Old Tartary the fierce!
The kings of Inde their jewel-sceptres vail,
And from their treasures scatter pearled hail;
Great Brahma from his mystic heaven groans,
        And all his priesthood moans;
Before young Bacchus' eye-wink turning pale.—
Into these regions came I following him,
Sick hearted, weary—so I took a whim
To stray away into these forests drear   270
        Alone, without a peer:
And I have told thee all thou mayest hear.

        "Young stranger!
        I've been a ranger
In search of pleasure throughout every clime:
        Alas, 'tis not for me!
        Bewitch'd I sure must be,
To lose in grieving all my maiden prime.

        "Come then, Sorrow!
        Sweetest Sorrow!   280
Like an own babe I nurse thee on my breast:
        I thought to leave thee
        And deceive thee,
But now of all the world I love thee best.

        "There is not one,
        No, no, not one
But thee to comfort a poor lonely maid:
        Thou art her mother,
        And her brother,
Her playmate, and her wooer in the shade."   290

    O what a sigh she gave in finishing,
And look, quite dead to every worldly thing!
Endymion could not speak, but gazed on her;
And listened to the wind that now did stir
About the crisped oaks full drearily,
Yet with as sweet a softness as might be
Remember'd from its velvet summer song.
At last he said: "Poor lady, how thus long

Have I been able to endure that voice?
Fair Melody! kind Syren! I've no choice;   300
I must be thy sad servant evermore:
I cannot choose but kneel here and adore.
Alas, I must not think—by Phœbe, no!
Let me not think, soft Angel! shall it be so?
Say, beautifullest, shall I never think?
O thou could'st foster me beyond the brink
Of recollection! make my watchful care
Close up its bloodshot eyes, nor see despair!
Do gently murder half my soul, and I
Shall feel the other half so utterly!—   310
I'm giddy at that cheek so fair and smooth;
O let it blush so ever! let it soothe
My madness! let it mantle rosy-warm
With the tinge of love, panting in safe alarm.—
This cannot be thy hand, and yet it is;
And this is sure thine other softling—this
Thine own fair bosom, and I am so near!
Wilt fall asleep? O let me sip that tear!
And whisper one sweet word that I may know
This is this world—sweet dewy blossom!"—*Woe!*   320
Woe! Woe to that Endymion! Where is he?—
Even these words went echoing dismally
Through the wide forest—a most fearful tone,
Like one repenting in his latest moan;
And while it died away a shade pass'd by,
As of a thunder cloud. When arrows fly
Through the thick branches, poor ring-doves sleek forth
Their timid necks and tremble; so these both
Leant to each other trembling, and sat so
Waiting for some destruction—when lo,   330
Foot-feather'd Mercury appear'd sublime
Beyond the tall tree tops; and in less time
Than shoots the slanted hail-storm, down he dropt
Towards the ground; but rested not, nor stopt
One moment from his home: only the sward
He with his wand light touch'd, and heavenward
Swifter than sight was gone—even before
The teeming earth a sudden witness bore
Of his swift magic. Diving swans appear
Above the crystal circlings white and clear;   340
And catch the cheated eye in wide surprise,
How they can dive in sight and unseen rise—
So from the turf outsprang two steeds jet-black,
Each with large dark blue wings upon his back.

The youth of Caria plac'd the lovely dame
On one, and felt himself in spleen to tame
The other's fierceness. Through the air they flew,
High as the eagles. Like two drops of dew
Exhal'd to Phœbus' lips, away they are gone,
Far from the earth away—unseen, alone,   350
Among cool clouds and winds, but that the free,
The buoyant life of song can floating be
Above their heads, and follow them untir'd.—
Muse of my native land, am I inspir'd?
This is the giddy air, and I must spread
Wide pinions to keep here; nor do I dread
Or height, or depth, or width, or any chance
Precipitous: I have beneath my glance
Those towering horses and their mournful freight.
Could I thus sail, and see, and thus await   360
Fearless for power of thought, without thine aid?—

     There is a sleepy dusk, an odorous shade
From some approaching wonder, and behold
Those winged steeds, with snorting nostrils bold
Snuff at its faint extreme, and seem to tire,
Dying to embers from their native fire!

     There curl'd a purple mist around them; soon,
It seem'd as when around the pale new moon
Sad Zephyr droops the clouds like weeping willow:
'Twas Sleep slow journeying with head on pillow.   370
For the first time, since he came nigh dead born
From the old womb of night, his cave forlorn
Had he left more forlorn; for the first time,
He felt aloof the day and morning's prime—
Because into his depth Cimmerian
There came a dream, showing how a young man,
Ere a lean bat could plump its wintery skin,
Would at high Jove's empyreal footstool win
An immortality, and how espouse
Jove's daughter, and be reckon'd of his house.   380
Now was he slumbering towards heaven's gate,
That he might at the threshold one hour wait
To hear the marriage melodies, and then
Sink downward to his dusky cave again.
His litter of smooth semilucent mist,
Diversely ting'd with rose and amethyst,
Puzzled those eyes that for the centre sought;
And scarcely for one moment could be caught

His sluggish form reposing motionless.
Those two on winged steeds, with all the stress   390
Of vision search'd for him, as one would look
Athwart the sallows of a river nook
To catch a glance at silver-throated eels,—
Or from old Skiddaw's top, when fog conceals
His rugged forehead in a mantle pale,
With an eye-guess towards some pleasant vale
Descry a favourite hamlet faint and far.

These raven horses, though they foster'd are
Of earth's splenetic fire, dully drop
Their full-vein'd ears, nostrils blood wide, and stop;   400
Upon the spiritless mist have they outspread
Their ample feathers, are in slumber dead,—
And on those pinions, level in mid air,
Endymion sleepeth and the lady fair.
Slowly they sail, slowly as icy isle
Upon a calm sea drifting: and meanwhile
The mournful wanderer dreams. Behold! he walks
On heaven's pavement; brotherly he talks
To divine powers: from his hand full fain
Juno's proud birds are pecking pearly grain: 410
He tries the nerve of Phœbus' golden bow,
And asketh where the golden apples grow:
Upon his arm he braces Pallas' shield,
And strives in vain to unsettle and wield
A Jovian thunderbolt: arch Hebe brings
A full-brimm'd goblet, dances lightly, sings
And tantalizes long; at last he drinks,
And lost in pleasure at her feet he sinks,
Touching with dazzled lips her starlight hand.
He blows a bugle,—an ethereal band   420
Are visible above: the Seasons four,—
Green-kyrtled Spring, flush Summer, golden store
In Autumn's sickle, Winter frosty hoar,
Join dance with shadowy Hours; while still the blast,
In swells unmitigated, still doth last
To sway their floating morris. "Whose is this?
Whose bugle?" he inquires; they smile—"O Dis!
Why is this mortal here? Dost thou not know
Its mistress' lips? Not thou?—'Tis Dian's: lo!
She rises crescented!" He looks, 'tis she,   430
His very goddess: good-bye earth, and sea,
And air, and pains, and care, and suffering;
Good-bye to all but love! Then doth he spring

Towards her, and awakes—and, strange, o'erhead,
Of those same fragrant exhalations bred,
Beheld awake his very dream: the gods
Stood smiling; merry Hebe laughs and nods;
And Phœbe bends towards him crescented.
O state perplexing! On the pinion bed,
Too well awake, he feels the panting side   440
Of his delicious lady. He who died
For soaring too audacious in the sun,
When that same treacherous wax began to run,
Felt not more tongue-tied than Endymion.
His heart leapt up as to its rightful throne,
To that fair shadow'd passion puls'd its way—
Ah, what perplexity! Ah, well a day!
So fond, so beauteous was his bed-fellow,
He could not help but kiss her: then he grew
Awhile forgetful of all beauty save   450
Young Phœbe's, golden hair'd; and so 'gan crave
Forgiveness: yet he turn'd once more to look
At the sweet sleeper,—all his soul was shook,—
She press'd his hand in slumber; so once more
He could not help but kiss her and adore.
At this the shadow wept, melting away.
The Latmian started up: "Bright goddess, stay!
Search my most hidden breast! By truth's own tongue,
I have no dædale heart: why is it wrung
To desperation? Is there nought for me,   460
Upon the bourne of bliss, but misery?"

These words awoke the stranger of dark tresses:
Her dawning love-look rapt Endymion blesses
With 'haviour soft. Sleep yawn'd from underneath.
"Thou swan of Ganges, let us no more breathe
This murky phantasm! thou contented seem'st
Pillow'd in lovely idleness, nor dream'st
What horrors may discomfort thee and me.
Ah, shouldst thou die from my heart-treachery!—
Yet did she merely weep—her gentle soul   470
Hath no revenge in it: as it is whole
In tenderness, would I were whole in love!
Can I prize thee, fair maid, all price above,
Even when I feel as true as innocence?
I do, I do.—What is this soul then? Whence
Came it? It does not seem my own, and I
Have no self-passion or identity.
Some fearful end must be: where, where is it?
By Nemesis, I see my spirit flit

Alone about the dark—Forgive me, sweet: 480
Shall we away?" He rous'd the steeds: they beat
Their wings chivalrous into the clear air,
Leaving old Sleep within his vapoury lair.

The good-night blush of eve was waning slow,
And Vesper, risen star, began to throe
In the dusk heavens silverly, when they
Thus sprang direct towards the Galaxy.
Nor did speed hinder converse soft and strange—
Eternal oaths and vows they interchange,   490
In such wise, in such temper, so aloof
Up in the winds, beneath a starry roof,
So witless of their doom, that verily
'Tis well nigh past man's search their hearts to see;
Whether they wept, or laugh'd, or griev'd, or toy'd—
Most like with joy gone mad, with sorrow cloy'd.

Full facing their swift flight, from ebon streak,
The moon put forth a little diamond peak,
No bigger than an unobserved star,
Or tiny point of fairy scymetar;   500
Bright signal that she only stoop'd to tie
Her silver sandals, ere deliciously
She bow'd into the heavens her timid head.
Slowly she rose, as though she would have fled,
While to his lady meek the Carian turn'd,
To mark if her dark eyes had yet discern'd
This beauty in its birth—Despair! despair!
He saw her body fading gaunt and spare
In the cold moonshine. Straight he seiz'd her wrist;
It melted from his grasp: her hand he kiss'd,   510
And, horror! kiss'd his own—he was alone.
Her steed a little higher soar'd, and then
Dropt hawkwise to the earth.
                         There lies a den,
Beyond the seeming confines of the space
Made for the soul to wander in and trace
Its own existence, of remotest glooms.
Dark regions are around it, where the tombs
Of buried griefs the spirit sees, but scarce
One hour doth linger weeping, for the pierce
Of new-born woe it feels more inly smart:
And in these regions many a venom'd dart   520
At random flies; they are the proper home
Of every ill: the man is yet to come

Who hath not journeyed in this native hell.
But few have ever felt how calm and well
Sleep may be had in that deep den of all.
There anguish does not sting; nor pleasure pall:
Woe-hurricanes beat ever at the gate,
Yet all is still within and desolate.
Beset with plainful gusts, within ye hear
No sound so loud as when on curtain'd bier   530
The death-watch tick is stifled. Enter none
Who strive therefore on the sudden it is won.
Just when the sufferer begins to burn,
Then it is free to him; and from an urn,
Still fed by melting ice, he takes a draught—
Young Semele such richness never quaft
In her maternal longing! Happy gloom!
Dark Paradise! where pale becomes the bloom
Of health by due; where silence dreariest
Is most articulate; where hopes infest;   540
Where those eyes are the brightest far that keep
Their lids shut longest in a dreamless sleep.
O happy spirit-home! O wondrous soul!
Pregnant with such a den to save the whole
In thine own depth. Hail, gentle Carian!
For, never since thy griefs and woes began,
Hast thou felt so content: a grievous feud
Hath led thee to this Cave of Quietude.
Aye, his lull'd soul was there, although upborne
With dangerous speed: and so he did not mourn
Because he knew not whither he was going.   551
So happy was he, not the aerial blowing
Of trumpets at clear parley from the east
Could rouse from that fine relish, that high feast.
They stung the feather'd horse: with fierce alarm
He flapp'd towards the sound. Alas, no charm
Could lift Endymion's head, or he had view'd
A skyey mask, a pinion'd multitude,—
And silvery was its passing: voices sweet
Warbling the while as if to lull and greet   560
The wanderer in his path. Thus warbled they,
While past the vision went in bright array.

"Who, who from Dian's feast would be away?
For all the golden bowers of the day
Are empty left? Who, who away would be
From Cynthia's wedding and festivity?
Not Hesperus: lo! upon his silver wings
He leans away for highest heaven and sings,

Snapping his lucid fingers merrily!—
Ah, Zephyrus! art here, and Flora too!   570
Ye tender bibbers of the rain and dew,
Young playmates of the rose and daffodil,
Be careful, ere ye enter in, to fill
        Your baskets high
With fennel green, and balm, and golden pines,
Savory, latter-mint, and columbines,
Cool parsley, basil sweet, and sunny thyme;
Yea, every flower and leaf of every clime,
All gather'd in the dewy morning: hie
        Away! fly, fly!—   580
Crystalline brother of the belt of heaven,
Aquarius! to whom king Jove has given
Two liquid pulse streams 'stead of feather'd wings,
Two fan-like fountains,—thine illuminings
        For Dian play:
Dissolve the frozen purity of air;
Let thy white shoulders silvery and bare
Show cold through watery pinions; make more bright
The Star-Queen's crescent on her marriage night:
        Haste, haste away!—   590
Castor has tamed the planet Lion, see!
And of the Bear has Pollux mastery:
A third is in the race! who is the third
Speeding away swift as the eagle bird?
        The ramping Centaur!
The Lion's mane's on end: the Bear how fierce!
The Centaur's arrow ready seems to pierce
Some enemy: far forth his bow is bent
Into the blue of heaven. He'll be shent,
        Pale unrelentor,   600
When he shall hear the wedding lutes a playing.—
Andromeda! sweet woman! why delaying
So timidly among the stars: come hither!
Join this bright throng, and nimbly follow whither
        They all are going.
Danae's Son, before Jove newly bow'd,
Has wept for thee, calling to Jove aloud.
Thee, gentle lady, did he disenthral:
Ye shall for ever live and love, for all
        Thy tears are flowing.—   610
By Daphne's fright, behold Apollo!—"
                                                    More
Endymion heard not: down his steed him bore,
Prone to the green head of a misty hill.

His first touch of the earth went nigh to kill.
"Alas!" said he, "were I but always borne
Through dangerous winds, had but my footsteps worn
A path in hell, for ever would I bless
Horrors which nourish an uneasiness
For my own sullen conquering: to him
Who lives beyond earth's boundary, grief is dim,
Sorrow is but a shadow: now I see   621
The grass; I feel the solid ground—Ah, me!
It is thy voice—divinest! Where?—who? who
Left thee so quiet on this bed of dew?
Behold upon this happy earth we are;
Let us aye love each other; let us fare
On forest-fruits, and never, never go
Among the abodes of mortals here below,
Or be by phantoms duped. O destiny!
Into a labyrinth now my soul would fly,   630
But with thy beauty will I deaden it.
Where didst thou melt to? By thee will I sit
For ever: let our fate stop here—a kid
I on this spot will offer: Pan will bid
Us live in peace, in love and peace among
His forest wildernesses. I have clung
To nothing, lov'd a nothing, nothing seen
Or felt but a great dream! O I have been
Presumptuous against love, against the sky,
Against all elements, against the tie   640
Of mortals each to each, against the blooms
Of flowers, rush of rivers, and the tombs
Of heroes gone! Against his proper glory
Has my own soul conspired: so my story
Will I to children utter, and repent.
There never liv'd a mortal man, who bent
His appetite beyond his natural sphere,
But starv'd and died. My sweetest Indian, here,
Here will I kneel, for thou redeemed hast
My life from too thin breathing: gone and past   650
Are cloudy phantasms. Caverns lone, farewell!
And air of visions, and the monstrous swell
Of visionary seas! No, never more
Shall airy voices cheat me to the shore
Of tangled wonder, breathless and aghast.
Adieu, my daintiest Dream! although so vast
My love is still for thee. The hour may come
When we shall meet in pure elysium.
On earth I may not love thee; and therefore
Doves will I offer up, and sweetest store   660

All through the teeming year: so thou wilt shine
On me, and on this damsel fair of mine,
And bless our silver lives. My Indian bliss!
My river-lilly bud! one human kiss!
One sign of real breath—one gentle squeeze,
Warm as a dove's nest among summer trees,
And warm with dew at ooze from living blood!
Whither didst melt? Ah, what of that!—all good
We'll talk about—no more of dreaming.—Now,
Where shall our dwelling be? Under the brow   670
Of some steep mossy hill, where ivy dun
Would hide us up, although spring leaves were none;
And where dark yew trees, as we rustle through,
Will drop their scarlet berry cups of dew?
O thou wouldst joy to live in such a place;
Dusk for our loves, yet light enough to grace
Those gentle limbs on mossy bed reclin'd:
For by one step the blue sky shouldst thou find,
And by another, in deep dell below,
See, through the trees, a little river go   680
All in its mid-day gold and glimmering.
Honey from out the gnarled hive I'll bring,
And apples, wan with sweetness, gather thee,—
Cresses that grow where no man may them see,
And sorrel untorn by the dew-claw'd stag:
Pipes will I fashion of the syrinx flag,
That thou mayst always know whither I roam,
When it shall please thee in our quiet home
To listen and think of love. Still let me speak;
Still let me dive into the joy I seek,—   690
For yet the past doth prison me. The rill,
Thou haply mayst delight in, will I fill
With fairy fishes from the mountain tarn,
And thou shalt feed them from the squirrel's barn.
Its bottom will I strew with amber shells,
And pebbles blue from deep enchanted wells.
Its sides I'll plant with dew-sweet eglantine,
And honeysuckles full of clear bee-wine.
I will entice this crystal rill to trace
Love's silver name upon the meadow's face.   700
I'll kneel to Vesta, for a flame of fire;
And to god Phœbus, for a golden lyre;
To Empress Dian, for a hunting spear;
To Vesper, for a taper silver-clear,
That I may see thy beauty through the night;
To Flora, and a nightingale shall light

Tame on thy finger; to the River-gods,
And they shall bring thee taper fishing-rods
Of gold, and lines of Naiads' long bright tress.
Heaven shield thee for thine utter loveliness!   710
Thy mossy footstool shall the altar be
'Fore which I'll bend, bending, dear love, to thee:
Those lips shall be my Delphos, and shall speak
Laws to my footsteps, colour to my cheek,
Trembling or stedfastness to this same voice,
And of three sweetest pleasurings the choice:
And that affectionate light, those diamond things,
Those eyes, those passions, those supreme pearl springs,
Shall be my grief, or twinkle me to pleasure.
Say, is not bliss within our perfect seisure?   720
O that I could not doubt!"
                              The mountaineer
Thus strove by fancies vain and crude to clear
His briar'd path to some tranquillity.
It gave bright gladness to his lady's eye,
And yet the tears she wept were tears of sorrow;
Answering thus, just as the golden morrow
Beam'd upward from the vallies of the east:
"O that the flutter of this heart had ceas'd,
Or the sweet name of love had pass'd away.
Young feather'd tyrant! by a swift decay   730
Wilt thou devote this body to the earth:
And I do think that at my very birth
I lisp'd thy blooming titles inwardly;
For at the first, first dawn and thought of thee,
With uplift hands I blest the stars of heaven.
Art thou not cruel? Ever have I striven
To think thee kind, but ah, it will not do!
When yet a child, I heard that kisses drew
Favour from thee, and so I kisses gave
To the void air, bidding them find out love: 740
But when I came to feel how far above
All fancy, pride, and fickle maidenhood,
All earthly pleasure, all imagin'd good,
Was the warm tremble of a devout kiss,—
Even then, that moment, at the thought of this,
Fainting I fell into a bed of flowers,
And languish'd there three days. Ye milder powers,
Am I not cruelly wrong'd? Believe, believe
Me, dear Endymion, were I to weave
With my own fancies garlands of sweet life,   750
Thou shouldst be one of all. Ah, bitter strife!

I may not be thy love: I am forbidden—
Indeed I am—thwarted, affrighted, chidden,
By things I trembled at, and gorgon wrath.
Twice hast thou ask'd whither I went: henceforth
Ask me no more! I may not utter it,
Nor may I be thy love. We might commit
Ourselves at once to vengeance; we might die;
We might embrace and die: voluptuous thought!
Enlarge not to my hunger, or I'm caught   760
In trammels of perverse deliciousness.
No, no, that shall not be: thee will I bless,
And bid a long adieu."
                         The Carian
No word return'd: both lovelorn, silent, wan,
Into the vallies green together went.
Far wandering, they were perforce content
To sit beneath a fair lone beechen tree;
Nor at each other gaz'd, but heavily
Por'd on its hazle cirque of shedded leaves.

    Endymion! unhappy! it nigh grieves   770
Me to behold thee thus in last extreme:
Ensky'd ere this, but truly that I deem
Truth the best music in a first-born song.
Thy lute-voic'd brother will I sing ere long,
And thou shalt aid—hast thou not aided me?
Yes, moonlight Emperor! felicity
Has been thy meed for many thousand years;
Yet often have I, on the brink of tears,
Mourn'd as if yet thou wert a forester;—
Forgetting the old tale.
                         He did not stir   780
His eyes from the dead leaves, or one small pulse
Of joy he might have felt. The spirit culls
Unfaded amaranth, when wild it strays
Through the old garden-ground of boyish days.
A little onward ran the very stream
By which he took his first soft poppy dream;
And on the very bark 'gainst which he leant
A crescent he had carv'd, and round it spent
His skill in little stars. The teeming tree
Had swollen and green'd the pious character,   790
But not ta'en out. Why, there was not a slope
Up which he had not fear'd the antelope;
And not a tree, beneath whose rooty shade
He had not with his tamed leopards play'd:

Nor could an arrow light, or javelin,
Fly in the air where his had never been—
And yet he knew it not.
                              O treachery!
Why does his lady smile, pleasing her eye
With all his sorrowing? He sees her not.
But who so stares on him? His sister sure!   800
Peona of the woods!—Can she endure—
Impossible—how dearly they embrace!
His lady smiles; delight is in her face;
It is no treachery.
                        "Dear brother mine!
Endymion, weep not so! Why shouldst thou pine
When all great Latmos so exalt will be?
Thank the great gods, and look not bitterly;
And speak not one pale word, and sigh no more.
Sure I will not believe thou hast such store
Of grief, to last thee to my kiss again.   810
Thou surely canst not bear a mind in pain,
Come hand in hand with one so beautiful.
Be happy both of you! for I will pull
The flowers of autumn for your coronals.
Pan's holy priest for young Endymion calls;
And when he is restor'd, thou, fairest dame,
Shalt be our queen. Now, is it not a shame
To see ye thus,—not very, very sad?
Perhaps ye are too happy to be glad:
O feel as if it were a common day;   820
Free-voic'd as one who never was away.
No tongue shall ask, whence come ye? but ye shall
Be gods of your own rest imperial.
Not even I, for one whole month, will pry
Into the hours that have pass'd us by,
Since in my arbour I did sing to thee.
O Hermes! on this very night will be
A hymning up to Cynthia, queen of light;
For the soothsayers old saw yesternight
Good visions in the air,—whence will befal,   830
As say these sages, health perpetual
To shepherds and their flocks; and furthermore,
In Dian's face they read the gentle lore:
Therefore for her these vesper-carols are.
Our friends will all be there from nigh and far.
Many upon thy death have ditties made;
And many, even now, their foreheads shade
With cypress, on a day of sacrifice.
New singing for our maids shalt thou devise,

And pluck the sorrow from our huntsmen's brows.   840
Tell me, my lady-queen, how to espouse
This wayward brother to his rightful joys!
His eyes are on thee bent, as thou didst poize
His fate most goddess-like. Help me, I pray,
To lure—Endymion, dear brother, say
What ails thee?" He could bear no more, and so
Bent his soul fiercely like a spiritual bow,
And twang'd it inwardly, and calmly said:
"I would have thee my only friend, sweet maid!
My only visitor! not ignorant though,   850
That those deceptions which for pleasure go
'Mong men, are pleasures real as real may be:
But there are higher ones I may not see,
If impiously an earthly realm I take.
Since I saw thee, I have been wide awake
Night after night, and day by day, until
Of the empyrean I have drunk my fill.
Let it content thee, Sister, seeing me
More happy than betides mortality.
A hermit young, I'll live in mossy cave,   860
Where thou alone shalt come to me, and lave
Thy spirit in the wonders I shall tell.
Through me the shepherd realm shall prosper well;
For to thy tongue will I all health confide.
And, for my sake, let this young maid abide
With thee as a dear sister. Thou alone,
Peona, mayst return to me. I own
This may sound strangely: but when, dearest girl,
Thou seest it for my happiness, no pearl
Will trespass down those cheeks. Companion fair!   870
Wilt be content to dwell with her, to share
This sister's love with me?" Like one resign'd
And bent by circumstance, and thereby blind
In self-commitment, thus that meek unknown:
"Aye, but a buzzing by my ears has flown,
Of jubilee to Dian:—truth I heard?
Well then, I see there is no little bird,
Tender soever, but is Jove's own care.
Long have I sought for rest, and, unaware,
Behold I find it! so exalted too!   880
So after my own heart! I knew, I knew
There was a place untenanted in it:
In that same void white Chastity shall sit,
And monitor me nightly to lone slumber.
With sanest lips I vow me to the number

Of Dian's sisterhood; and, kind lady,
With thy good help, this very night shall see
My future days to her fane consecrate."

As feels a dreamer what doth most create
His own particular fright, so these three felt: 890
Or like one who, in after ages, knelt
To Lucifer or Baal, when he'd pine
After a little sleep: or when in mine
Far under-ground, a sleeper meets his friends
Who know him not. Each diligently bends
Towards common thoughts and things for very fear;
Striving their ghastly malady to cheer,
By thinking it a thing of yes and no,
That housewives talk of. But the spirit-blow
Was struck, and all were dreamers. At the last   900
Endymion said: "Are not our fates all cast?
Why stand we here? Adieu, ye tender pair!
Adieu!" Whereat those maidens, with wild stare,
Walk'd dizzily away. Pained and hot
His eyes went after them, until they got
Near to a cypress grove, whose deadly maw,
In one swift moment, would what then he saw
Engulph for ever. "Stay!" he cried, "ah, stay!
Turn, damsels! hist! one word I have to say.
Sweet Indian, I would see thee once again.   910
It is a thing I dote on: so I'd fain,
Peona, ye should hand in hand repair
Into those holy groves, that silent are
Behind great Dian's temple. I'll be yon,
At vesper's earliest twinkle—they are gone—
But once, once, once again—" At this he press'd
His hands against his face, and then did rest
His head upon a mossy hillock green,
And so remain'd as he a corpse had been
All the long day; save when he scantly lifted   920
His eyes abroad, to see how shadows shifted
With the slow move of time,—sluggish and weary
Until the poplar tops, in journey dreary,
Had reach'd the river's brim. Then up he rose,
And, slowly as that very river flows,
Walk'd towards the temple grove with this lament:
"Why such a golden eve? The breeze is sent
Careful and soft, that not a leaf may fall
Before the serene father of them all
Bows down his summer head below the west.   930
Now am I of breath, speech, and speed possest,

But at the setting I must bid adieu
To her for the last time. Night will strew
On the damp grass myriads of lingering leaves,
And with them shall I die; nor much it grieves
To die, when summer dies on the cold sward.
Why, I have been a butterfly, a lord
Of flowers, garlands, love-knots, silly posies,
Groves, meadows, melodies, and arbour roses;
My kingdom's at its death, and just it is   940
That I should die with it: so in all this
We miscall grief, bale, sorrow, heartbreak, woe.
What is there to plain of? By Titan's foe
I am but rightly serv'd." So saying, he
Tripp'd lightly on, in sort of deathful glee;
Laughing at the clear stream and setting sun,
As though they jests had been: nor had he done
His laugh at nature's holy countenance,
Until that grove appear'd, as if perchance,
And then his tongue with sober seemlihed   950
Gave utterance as he enter'd: "Ha! I said,
King of the butterflies; but by this gloom,
And by old Rhadamanthus' tongue of doom,
This dusk religion, pomp of solitude,
And the Promethean clay by thief endued,
By old Saturnus' forelock, by his head
Shook with eternal palsy, I did wed
Myself to things of light from infancy;
And thus to be cast out, thus lorn to die,
Is sure enough to make a mortal man   960
Grow impious." So he inwardly began
On things for which no wording can be found;
Deeper and deeper sinking, until drown'd
Beyond the reach of music: for the choir
Of Cynthia he heard not, though rough briar
Nor muffling thicket interpos'd to dull
The vesper hymn, far swollen, soft and full,
Through the dark pillars of those sylvan aisles.
He saw not the two maidens, nor their smiles,
Wan as primroses gather'd at midnight   970
By chilly finger'd spring. "Unhappy wight!
Endymion!" said Peona, "we are here!
What wouldst thou ere we all are laid on bier?"
Then he embrac'd her, and his lady's hand
Press'd, saying: "Sister, I would have command,
If it were heaven's will, on our sad fate."
At which that dark-eyed stranger stood elate

And said, in a new voice, but sweet as love,
To Endymion's amaze: "By Cupid's dove,
And so thou shalt! and by the lilly truth   980
Of my own breast thou shalt, beloved youth!"
And as she spake, into her face there came
Light, as reflected from a silver flame:
Her long black hair swell'd ampler, in display
Full golden; in her eyes a brighter day
Dawn'd blue and full of love. Aye, he beheld
Phœbe, his passion! joyous she upheld
Her lucid bow, continuing thus: "Drear, drear
Has our delaying been; but foolish fear
Withheld me first; and then decrees of fate;   990
And then 'twas fit that from this mortal state
Thou shouldst, my love, by some unlook'd for change
Be spiritualiz'd. Peona, we shall range
These forests, and to thee they safe shall be
As was thy cradle; hither shalt thou flee
To meet us many a time." Next Cynthia bright
Peona kiss'd, and bless'd with fair good night:
Her brother kiss'd her too, and knelt adown
Before his goddess, in a blissful swoon.
She gave her fair hands to him, and behold,   1000
Before three swiftest kisses he had told,
They vanish'd far away!—Peona went
Home through the gloomy wood in wonderment.

THE END

LAMIA,

ISABELLA,

THE EVE OF ST. AGNES,

AND

OTHER POEMS.

1820.

ADVERTISEMENT

IF any apology be thought necessary for the appearance of the unfinished poem of HYPERION, the publishers beg to state that they alone are responsible, as it was printed at their particular request, and contrary to the wish of the author. The poem was intended to have been of equal length with ENDYMION, but the reception given to that work discouraged the author from proceeding.

FLEET STREET, *June* 26, 1820.

LAMIA

PART I

Upon a time, before the faery broods
Drove Nymph and Satyr from the prosperous woods,
Before king Oberon's bright diadem,
Sceptre, and mantle, clasp'd with dewy gem,
Frighted away the Dryads and the Fauns
From rushes green, and brakes, and cowslip'd lawns,
The ever-smitten Hermes empty left
His golden throne, bent warm on amorous theft:
From high Olympus had he stolen light,
On this side of Jove's clouds, to escape the sight   10
Of his great summoner, and made retreat
Into a forest on the shores of Crete.
For somewhere in that sacred island dwelt
A nymph, to whom all hoofed Satyrs knelt;
At whose white feet the languid Tritons poured
Pearls, while on land they wither'd and adored.
Fast by the springs where she to bathe was wont,
And in those meads where sometime she might haunt,
Were strewn rich gifts, unknown to any Muse,
Though Fancy's casket were unlock'd to choose.   20
Ah, what a world of love was at her feet!
So Hermes thought, and a celestial heat
Burnt from his winged heels to either ear,
That from a whiteness, as the lilly clear,
Blush'd into roses 'mid his golden hair,
Fallen in jealous curls about his shoulders bare.

From vale to vale, from wood to wood, he flew,
Breathing upon the flowers his passion new,
And wound with many a river to its head,   29
To find where this sweet nymph prepar'd her secret bed:
In vain; the sweet nymph might nowhere be found,
And so he rested, on the lonely ground,
Pensive, and full of painful jealousies
Of the Wood-Gods, and even the very trees.
There as he stood, he heard a mournful voice,
Such as once heard, in gentle heart, destroys
All pain but pity: thus the lone voice spake:
"When from this wreathed tomb shall I awake!

"When move in a sweet body fit for life,
"And love, and pleasure, and the ruddy strife   40
"Of hearts and lips! Ah, miserable me!"
The God, dove-footed, glided silently
Round bush and tree, soft-brushing, in his speed,
The taller grasses and full-flowering weed,
Until he found a palpitating snake,
Bright, and cirque-couchant in a dusky brake.

She was a gordian shape of dazzling hue,
Vermilion-spotted, golden, green, and blue;
Striped like a zebra, freckled like a pard,
Eyed like a peacock, and all crimson barr'd;   50
And full of silver moons, that, as she breathed,
Dissolv'd, or brighter shone, or interwreathed
Their lustres with the gloomier tapestries—
So rainbow-sided, touch'd with miseries,
She seem'd, at once, some penanced lady elf,
Some demon's mistress, or the demon's self.
Upon her crest she wore a wannish fire
Sprinkled with stars, like Ariadne's tiar:
Her head was serpent, but ah, bitter-sweet!   59
She had a woman's mouth with all its pearls complete:
And for her eyes: what could such eyes do there
But weep, and weep, that they were born so fair?
As Proserpine still weeps for her Sicilian air.
Her throat was serpent, but the words she spake
Came, as through bubbling honey, for Love's sake,
And thus; while Hermes on his pinions lay,
Like a stoop'd falcon ere he takes his prey.

"Fair Hermes, crown'd with feathers, fluttering light,
"I had a splendid dream of thee last night:
"I saw thee sitting, on a throne of gold,   70
"Among the Gods, upon Olympus old,
"The only sad one; for thou didst not hear
"The soft, lute-finger'd Muses chaunting clear,
"Nor even Apollo when he sang alone,
"Deaf to his throbbing throat's long, long melodious moan.
"I dreamt I saw thee, robed in purple flakes,
"Break amorous through the clouds, as morning breaks,
"And, swiftly as a bright Phœbean dart,
"Strike for the Cretan isle; and here thou art!
"Too gentle Hermes, hast thou found the maid?"
Whereat the star of Lethe not delay'd   81
His rosy eloquence, and thus inquired:

"Thou smooth-lipp'd serpent, surely high inspired!
"Thou beauteous wreath, with melancholy eyes,
"Possess whatever bliss thou canst devise,
"Telling me only where my nymph is fled,—
"Where she doth breathe!" "Bright planet, thou hast said,"
Return'd the snake, "but seal with oaths, fair God!"
"I swear," said Hermes, "by my serpent rod,
"And by thine eyes, and by thy starry crown!"   90
Light flew his earnest words, among the blossoms blown.
Then thus again the brilliance feminine:
"Too frail of heart! for this lost nymph of thine,
"Free as the air, invisibly, she strays
"About these thornless wilds; her pleasant days
"She tastes unseen; unseen her nimble feet
"Leave traces in the grass and flowers sweet;
"From weary tendrils, and bow'd branches green,
"She plucks the fruit unseen, she bathes unseen:
"And by my power is her beauty veil'd   100
"To keep it unaffronted, unassail'd
"By the love-glances of unlovely eyes,
"Of Satyrs, Fauns, and blear'd Silenus' sighs.
"Pale grew her immortality, for woe
"Of all these lovers, and she grieved so
"I took compassion on her, bade her steep
"Her hair in weïrd syrops, that would keep
"Her loveliness invisible, yet free
"To wander as she loves, in liberty.
"Thou shalt behold her, Hermes, thou alone,   110
"If thou wilt, as thou swearest, grant my boon!"
Then, once again, the charmed God began
An oath, and through the serpent's ears it ran
Warm, tremulous, devout, psalterian.
Ravish'd, she lifted her Circean head,
Blush'd a live damask, and swift-lisping said,
"I was a woman, let me have once more
"A woman's shape, and charming as before.
"I love a youth of Corinth—O the bliss!
"Give me my woman's form, and place me where he is.
"Stoop, Hermes, let me breathe upon thy brow,   121
"And thou shalt see thy sweet nymph even now."
The God on half-shut feathers sank serene,
She breath'd upon his eyes, and swift was seen
Of both the guarded nymph near-smiling on the green.
It was no dream; or say a dream it was,
Real are the dreams of Gods, and smoothly pass

Their pleasures in a long immortal dream.
One warm, flush'd moment, hovering, it might seem
Dash'd by the wood-nymph's beauty, so he burn'd;   130
Then, lighting on the printless verdure, turn'd
To the swoon'd serpent, and with languid arm,
Delicate, put to proof the lythe Caducean charm.
So done, upon the nymph his eyes he bent
Full of adoring tears and blandishment,
And towards her stept: she, like a moon in wane,
Faded before him, cower'd, nor could restrain
Her fearful sobs, self-folding like a flower
That faints into itself at evening hour:
But the God fostering her chilled hand,   140
She felt the warmth, her eyelids open'd bland,
And, like new flowers at morning song of bees,
Bloom'd, and gave up her honey to the lees.
Into the green-recessed woods they flew;
Nor grew they pale, as mortal lovers do.

    Left to herself, the serpent now began
To change; her elfin blood in madness ran,
Her mouth foam'd and the grass, therewith besprent,
Wither'd at dew so sweet and virulent;
Her eyes in torture fix'd, and anguish drear,   150
Hot, glaz'd, and wide, with lid-lashes all sear,
Flash'd phosphor and sharp sparks, without one cooling tear.
The colours all inflam'd throughout her train,
She writh'd about, convulsed with scarlet pain:
A deep volcanian yellow took the place
Of all her milder-mooned body's grace;
And, as the lava ravishes the mead,
Spoilt all her silver mail, and golden brede;
Made gloom of all her frecklings, streaks and bars,
Eclips'd her crescents, and lick'd up her stars: 160
So that, in moments few, she was undrest
Of all her sapphires, greens, and amethyst,
And rubious-argent: of all these bereft,
Nothing but pain and ugliness were left.
Still shone her crown; that vanish'd, also she
Melted and disappear'd as suddenly;
And in the air, her new voice luting soft,
Cried, "Lycius! gentle Lycius!"—Borne aloft
With the bright mists about the mountains hoar
These words dissolv'd: Crete's forests heard no more.

    Whither fled Lamia, now a lady bright,   171
A full-born beauty new and exquisite?

She fled into that valley they pass o'er
Who go to Corinth from Cenchreas' shore;
And rested at the foot of those wild hills,
The rugged founts of the Peræan rills,
And of that other ridge whose barren back
Stretches, with all its mist and cloudy rack,
South-westward to Cleone. There she stood   180
About a young bird's flutter from a wood,
Fair, on a sloping green of mossy tread,
By a clear pool, wherein she passioned
To see herself escap'd from so sore ills,
While her robes flaunted with the daffodils.

Ah, happy Lycius!—for she was a maid
More beautiful than ever twisted braid,
Or sigh'd, or blush'd, or on spring-flowered lea
Spread a green kirtle to the minstrelsy:
A virgin purest lipp'd, yet in the lore
Of love deep learned to the red heart's core: 190
Not one hour old, yet of sciential brain
To unperplex bliss from its neighbour pain;
Define their pettish limits, and estrange
Their points of contact, and swift counterchange;
Intrigue with the specious chaos, and dispart
Its most ambiguous atoms with sure art;
As though in Cupid's college she had spent
Sweet days a lovely graduate, still unshent,
And kept his rosy terms in idle languishment.

Why this fair creature chose so faerily   200
By the wayside to linger, we shall see;
But first 'tis fit to tell how she could muse
And dream, when in the serpent prison-house,
Of all she list, strange or magnificent:
How, ever, where she will'd, her spirit went;
Whether to faint Elysium, or where
Down through tress-lifting waves the Nereids fair
Wind into Thetis' bower by many a pearly stair;
Or where God Bacchus drains his cups divine,
Stretch'd out, at ease, beneath a glutinous pine;   210
Or where in Pluto's gardens palatine
Mulciber's columns gleam in far piazzian line.
And sometimes into cities she would send
Her dream, with feast and rioting to blend;
And once, while among mortals dreaming thus,
She saw the young Corinthian Lycius
Charioting foremost in the envious race,

Like a young Jove with calm uneager face,
And fell into a swooning love of him.
Now on the moth-time of that evening dim   220
He would return that way, as well she knew,
To Corinth from the shore; for freshly blew
The eastern soft wind, and his galley now
Grated the quaystones with her brazen prow
In port Cenchreas, from Egina isle
Fresh anchor'd; whither he had been awhile
To sacrifice to Jove, whose temple there
Waits with high marble doors for blood and incense rare.
Jove heard his vows, and better'd his desire;
For by some freakful chance he made retire   230
From his companions, and set forth to walk,
Perhaps grown wearied of their Corinth talk:
Over the solitary hills he fared,
Thoughtless at first, but ere eve's star appeared
His phantasy was lost, where reason fades,
In the calm'd twilight of Platonic shades.
Lamia beheld him coming, near, more near—
Close to her passing, in indifference drear,
His silent sandals swept the mossy green;
So neighbour'd to him, and yet so unseen   240
She stood: he pass'd, shut up in mysteries,
His mind wrapp'd like his mantle, while her eyes
Follow'd his steps, and her neck regal white
Turn'd—syllabling thus, "Ah, Lycius bright,
"And will you leave me on the hills alone?
"Lycius, look back! and be some pity shown."
He did; not with cold wonder fearingly,
But Orpheus-like at an Eurydice;
For so delicious were the words she sung,
It seem'd he had lov'd them a whole summer long: 250
And soon his eyes had drunk her beauty up,
Leaving no drop in the bewildering cup,
And still the cup was full,—while he, afraid
Lest she should vanish ere his lip had paid
Due adoration, thus began to adore;
Her soft look growing coy, she saw his chain so sure:
"Leave thee alone! Look back! Ah, Goddess, see
"Whether my eyes can ever turn from thee!
"For pity do not this sad heart belie—
"Even as thou vanishest so shall I die.   260
"Stay! though a Naiad of the rivers, stay!
"To thy far wishes will thy streams obey:
"Stay! though the greenest woods be thy domain,
"Alone they can drink up the morning rain:

"Though a descended Pleiad, will not one
"Of thine harmonious sisters keep in tune
"Thy spheres, and as thy silver proxy shine?
"So sweetly to these ravish'd ears of mine
"Came thy sweet greeting, that if thou shouldst fade
"Thy memory will waste me to a shade:—   270
"For pity do not melt!"—"If I should stay,"
Said Lamia, "here, upon this floor of clay,
"And pain my steps upon these flowers too rough,
"What canst thou say or do of charm enough
"To dull the nice remembrance of my home?
"Thou canst not ask me with thee here to roam
"Over these hills and vales, where no joy is,—
"Empty of immortality and bliss!
"Thou art a scholar, Lycius, and must know
"That finer spirits cannot breathe below   280
"In human climes, and live: Alas! poor youth,
"What taste of purer air hast thou to soothe
"My essence? What serener palaces,
"Where I may all my many senses please,
"And by mysterious sleights a hundred thirsts appease?
"It cannot be—Adieu!" So said, she rose
Tiptoe with white arms spread. He, sick to lose
The amorous promise of her lone complain,
Swoon'd, murmuring of love, and pale with pain.
The cruel lady, without any show   290
Of sorrow for her tender favourite's woe,
But rather, if her eyes could brighter be,
With brighter eyes and slow amenity,
Put her new lips to his, and gave afresh
The life she had so tangled in her mesh:
And as he from one trance was wakening
Into another, she began to sing,
Happy in beauty, life, and love, and every thing,
A song of love, too sweet for earthly lyres,
While, like held breath, the stars drew in their panting fires.
And then she whisper'd in such trembling tone,   301
As those who, safe together met alone
For the first time through many anguish'd days,
Use other speech than looks; bidding him raise
His drooping head, and clear his soul of doubt,
For that she was a woman, and without
Any more subtle fluid in her veins
Than throbbing blood, and that the self-same pains
Inhabited her frail-strung heart as his.
And next she wonder'd how his eyes could miss   310

Her face so long in Corinth, where, she said,
She dwelt but half retir'd, and there had led
Days happy as the gold coin could invent
Without the aid of love; yet in content
Till she saw him, as once she pass'd him by,
Where 'gainst a column he lent thoughtfully
At Venus' temple porch, 'mid baskets heap'd
Of amorous herbs and flowers, newly reap'd
Late on that eve, as 'twas the night before
The Adonian feast; whereof she saw no more,   320
But wept alone those days, for why should she adore?
Lycius from death awoke into amaze,
To see her still, and singing so sweet lays;
Then from amaze into delight he fell
To hear her whisper woman's lore so well;
And every word she spake entic'd him on
To unperplex'd delight and pleasure known.
Let the mad poets say whate'er they please
Of the sweets of Faeries, Peris, Goddesses,
There is not such a treat among them all,   330
Haunters of cavern, lake, and waterfall,
As a real woman, lineal indeed
From Pyrrha's pebbles or old Adam's seed.
Thus gentle Lamia judg'd, and judg'd aright,
That Lycius could not love in half a fright,
So threw the goddess off, and won his heart
More pleasantly by playing woman's part,
With no more awe than what her beauty gave,
That, while it smote, still guaranteed to save.
Lycius to all made eloquent reply,   340
Marrying to every word a twinborn sigh;
And last, pointing to Corinth, ask'd her sweet,
If 'twas too far that night for her soft feet.
The way was short, for Lamia's eagerness
Made, by a spell, the triple league decrease
To a few paces; not at all surmised
By blinded Lycius, so in her comprized.
They pass'd the city gates, he knew not how,
So noiseless, and he never thought to know.

    As men talk in a dream, so Corinth all,   350
Throughout her palaces imperial,
And all her populous streets and temples lewd,
Mutter'd, like tempest in the distance brew'd,
To the wide-spreaded night above her towers.
Men, women, rich and poor, in the cool hours,

Shuffled their sandals o'er the pavement white,
Companion'd or alone; while many a light
Flared, here and there, from wealthy festivals,
And threw their moving shadows on the walls,
Or found them cluster'd in the corniced shade   360
Of some arch'd temple door, or dusky colonnade.

   Muffling his face, of greeting friends in fear,
Her fingers he press'd hard, as one came near
With curl'd gray beard, sharp eyes, and smooth bald crown,
Slow-stepp'd, and robed in philosophic gown:
Lycius shrank closer, as they met and past,
Into his mantle, adding wings to haste,
While hurried Lamia trembled: "Ah," said he,
"Why do you shudder, love, so ruefully?
"Why does your tender palm dissolve in dew?"—
"I'm wearied," said fair Lamia: "tell me who   371
"Is that old man? I cannot bring to mind
"His features:—Lycius! wherefore did you blind
"Yourself from his quick eyes?" Lycius replied,
" 'Tis Apollonius sage, my trusty guide
"And good instructor; but to-night he seems
"The ghost of folly haunting my sweet dreams."

   While yet he spake they had arrived before
A pillar'd porch, with lofty portal door,
Where hung a silver lamp, whose phosphor glow
Reflected in the slabbed steps below,   381
Mild as a star in water; for so new,
And so unsullied was the marble's hue,
So through the crystal polish, liquid fine,
Ran the dark veins, that none but feet divine
Could e'er have touch'd there. Sounds Æolian
Breath'd from the hinges, as the ample span
Of the wide doors disclos'd a place unknown
Some time to any, but these two alone,
And a few Persian mutes, who that same year   390
Were seen about the markets: none knew where
They could inhabit; the most curious
Were foil'd, who watch'd to trace them to their house:
And but the flitter-winged verse must tell,
For truth's sake, what woes afterwards befel,
'Twould humour many a heart to leave them thus,
Shut from the busy world of more incredulous.

PART II

Love in a hut, with water and a crust,
Is—Love, forgive us!—cinders, ashes, dust;
Love in a palace is perhaps at last
More grievous torment than a hermit's fast:—
That is a doubtful tale from faery land,
Hard for the non-elect to understand.
Had Lycius liv'd to hand his story down,
He might have given the moral a fresh frown,
Or clench'd it quite: but too short was their bliss
To breed distrust and hate, that make the soft voice hiss.
Beside, there, nightly, with terrific glare,   11
Love, jealous grown of so complete a pair,
Hover'd and buzz'd his wings, with fearful roar,
Above the lintel of their chamber door,
And down the passage cast a glow upon the floor.

For all this came a ruin: side by side
They were enthroned, in the even tide,
Upon a couch, near to a curtaining
Whose airy texture, from a golden string,
Floated into the room, and let appear   20
Unveil'd the summer heaven, blue and clear,
Betwixt two marble shafts:—there they reposed,
Where use had made it sweet, with eyelids closed,
Saving a tythe which love still open kept,
That they might see each other while they almost slept;
When from the slope side of a suburb hill,
Deafening the swallow's twitter, came a thrill
Of trumpets—Lycius started—the sounds fled,
But left a thought, a buzzing in his head.
For the first time, since first he harbour'd in   30
That purple-lined palace of sweet sin,
His spirit pass'd beyond its golden bourn
Into the noisy world almost forsworn.
The lady, ever watchful, penetrant,
Saw this with pain, so arguing a want
Of something more, more than her empery
Of joys; and she began to moan and sigh
Because he mused beyond her, knowing well
That but a moment's thought is passion's passing bell.
"Why do you sigh, fair creature?" whisper'd he:
"Why do you think?" return'd she tenderly: 41
"You have deserted me;—where am I now?
"Not in your heart while care weighs on your brow:

"No, no, you have dismiss'd me; and I go
"From your breast houseless: aye, it must be so."
He answer'd, bending to her open eyes,
Where he was mirror'd small in paradise,
"My silver planet, both of eve and morn!
"Why will you plead yourself so sad forlorn,
"While I am striving how to fill my heart   50
"With deeper crimson, and a double smart?
"How to entangle, trammel up and snare
"Your soul in mine, and labyrinth you there
"Like the hid scent in an unbudded rose?
"Aye, a sweet kiss—you see your mighty woes.
"My thoughts! shall I unveil them? Listen then!
"What mortal hath a prize, that other men
"May be confounded and abash'd withal,
"But lets it sometimes pace abroad majestical,
"And triumph, as in thee I should rejoice   60
"Amid the hoarse alarm of Corinth's voice.
"Let my foes choke, and my friends shout afar,
"While through the thronged streets your bridal car
"Wheels round its dazzling spokes."—The lady's cheek
Trembled; she nothing said, but, pale and meek,
Arose and knelt before him, wept a rain
Of sorrows at his words; at last with pain
Beseeching him, the while his hand she wrung,
To change his purpose. He thereat was stung,
Perverse, with stronger fancy to reclaim   70
Her wild and timid nature to his aim:
Besides, for all his love, in self despite,
Against his better self, he took delight
Luxurious in her sorrows, soft and new.
His passion, cruel grown, took on a hue
Fierce and sanguineous as 'twas possible
In one whose brow had no dark veins to swell.
Fine was the mitigated fury, like
Apollo's presence when in act to strike
The serpent—Ha, the serpent! certes, she   80
Was none. She burnt, she lov'd the tyranny,
And, all subdued, consented to the hour
When to the bridal he should lead his paramour.
Whispering in midnight silence, said the youth,
"Sure some sweet name thou hast, though, by my truth,
"I have not ask'd it, ever thinking thee
"Not mortal, but of heavenly progeny,
"As still I do. Hast any mortal name,
"Fit appellation for this dazzling frame?

"Or friends or kinsfolk on the citied earth,   90
"To share our marriage feast and nuptial mirth?"
"I have no friends," said Lamia, "no, not one;
"My presence in wide Corinth hardly known:
"My parents' bones are in their dusty urns
"Sepulchred, where no kindled incense burns,
"Seeing all their luckless race are dead, save me,
"And I neglect the holy rite for thee.
"Even as you list invite your many guests;
"But if, as now it seems, your vision rests
"With any pleasure on me, do not bid   100
"Old Apollonius—from him keep me hid."
Lycius, perplex'd at words so blind and blank,
Made close inquiry; from whose touch she shrank,
Feigning a sleep; and he to the dull shade
Of deep sleep in a moment was betray'd.

    It was the custom then to bring away
The bride from home at blushing shut of day,
Veil'd, in a chariot, heralded along
By strewn flowers, torches, and a marriage song,
With other pageants: but this fair unknown   110
Had not a friend. So being left alone,
(Lycius was gone to summon all his kin)
And knowing surely she could never win
His foolish heart from its mad pompousness,
She set herself, high-thoughted, how to dress
The misery in fit magnificence.
She did so, but 'tis doubtful how and whence
Came, and who were her subtle servitors.
About the halls, and to and from the doors,
There was a noise of wings, till in short space   120
The glowing banquet-room shone with wide-arched grace.
A haunting music, sole perhaps and lone
Supportress of the faery-roof, made moan
Throughout, as fearful the whole charm might fade.
Fresh carved cedar, mimicking a glade
Of palm and plantain, met from either side,
High in the midst, in honour of the bride:
Two palms and then two plantains, and so on,
From either side their stems branch'd one to one
All down the aisled place; and beneath all   130
There ran a stream of lamps straight on from wall to wall.
So canopied, lay an untasted feast
Teeming with odours. Lamia, regal drest,
Silently paced about, and as she went,
In pale contented sort of discontent,

Mission'd her viewless servants to enrich
The fretted splendour of each nook and niche.
Between the tree-stems, marbled plain at first,
Came jasper pannels; then, anon, there burst
Forth creeping imagery of slighter trees,   140
And with the larger wove in small intricacies.
Approving all, she faded at self-will,
And shut the chamber up, close, hush'd and still,
Complete and ready for the revels rude,
When dreadful guests would come to spoil her solitude.

    The day appear'd, and all the gossip rout.
O senseless Lycius! Madman! wherefore flout
The silent-blessing fate, warm cloister'd hours,
And show to common eyes these secret bowers?
The herd approach'd; each guest, with busy brain
Arriving at the portal, gaz'd amain,   151
And enter'd marveling: for they knew the street,
Remember'd it from childhood all complete
Without a gap, yet ne'er before had seen
That royal porch, that high-built fair demesne;
So in they hurried all, maz'd, curious and keen:
Save one, who look'd thereon with eye severe,
And with calm-planted steps walk'd in austere;
'Twas Apollonius: something too he laugh'd,
As though some knotty problem, that had daft   160
His patient thought, had now begun to thaw,
And solve and melt:—'twas just as he foresaw.

    He met within the murmurous vestibule
His young disciple. "'Tis no common rule,
Lycius," said he, "for uninvited guest
"To force himself upon you, and infest
"With an unbidden presence the bright throng
"Of younger friends; yet must I do this wrong,
"And you forgive me." Lycius blush'd, and led
The old man through the inner doors broad-spread;
With reconciling words and courteous mien   171
Turning into sweet milk the sophist's spleen.

    Of wealthy lustre was the banquet-room,
Fill'd with pervading brilliance and perfume:
Before each lucid pannel fuming stood
A censer fed with myrrh and spiced wood,
Each by a sacred tripod held aloft,
Whose slender feet wide-swerv'd upon the soft

Wool-woofed carpets: fifty wreaths of smoke
From fifty censers their light voyage took   180
To the high roof, still mimick'd as they rose
Along the mirror'd walls by twin-clouds odorous.
Twelve sphered tables, by silk seats insphered,
High as the level of a man's breast rear'd
On libbard's paws, upheld the heavy gold
Of cups and goblets, and the store thrice told
Of Ceres' horn, and, in huge vessels, wine
Come from the gloomy tun with merry shine.
Thus loaded with a feast the tables stood,
Each shrining in the midst the image of a God.   190

When in an antichamber every guest
Had felt the cold full sponge to pleasure press'd,
By minist'ring slaves, upon his hands and feet,
And fragrant oils with ceremony meet
Pour'd on his hair, they all mov'd to the feast
In white robes, and themselves in order placed
Around the silken couches, wondering
Whence all this mighty cost and blaze of wealth could spring.

Soft went the music the soft air along,
While fluent Greek a vowel'd undersong   200
Kept up among the guests, discoursing low
At first, for scarcely was the wine at flow;
But when the happy vintage touch'd their brains,
Louder they talk, and louder come the strains
Of powerful instruments:—the gorgeous dyes,
The space, the splendour of the draperies,
The roof of awful richness, nectarous cheer,
Beautiful slaves, and Lamia's self, appear,
Now, when the wine has done its rosy deed,
And every soul from human trammels freed,   210
No more so strange; for merry wine, sweet wine,
Will make Elysian shades not too fair, too divine.
Soon was God Bacchus at meridian height;
Flush'd were their cheeks, and bright eyes double bright:
Garlands of every green, and every scent
From vales deflower'd, or forest-trees branch-rent,
In baskets of bright osier'd gold were brought
High as the handles heap'd, to suit the thought
Of every guest; that each, as he did please,
Might fancy-fit his brows, silk-pillow'd at his ease.   220

What wreath for Lamia? What for Lycius?
What for the sage, old Apollonius?

Upon her aching forehead be there hung
The leaves of willow and of adder's tongue;
And for the youth, quick, let us strip for him
The thyrsus, that his watching eyes may swim
Into forgetfulness; and, for the sage,
Let spear-grass and the spiteful thistle wage
War on his temples. Do not all charms fly
At the mere touch of cold philosophy?   230
There was an awful rainbow once in heaven:
We know her woof, her texture; she is given
In the dull catalogue of common things.
Philosophy will clip an Angel's wings,
Conquer all mysteries by rule and line,
Empty the haunted air, and gnomed mine—
Unweave a rainbow, as it erewhile made
The tender-person'd Lamia melt into a shade.

By her glad Lycius sitting, in chief place,
Scarce saw in all the room another face,   240
Till, checking his love trance, a cup he took
Full brimm'd, and opposite sent forth a look
'Cross the broad table, to beseech a glance
From his old teacher's wrinkled countenance,
And pledge him. The bald-head philosopher
Had fix'd his eye, without a twinkle or stir
Full on the alarmed beauty of the bride,
Brow-beating her fair form, and troubling her sweet pride.
Lycius then press'd her hand, with devout touch,
As pale it lay upon the rosy couch: 250
'Twas icy, and the cold ran through his veins;
Then sudden it grew hot, and all the pains
Of an unnatural heat shot to his heart.
"Lamia, what means this? Wherefore dost thou start?
"Know'st thou that man?" Poor Lamia answer'd not.
He gaz'd into her eyes, and not a jot
Own'd they the lovelorn piteous appeal:
More, more he gaz'd: his human senses reel:
Some hungry spell that loveliness absorbs;
There was no recognition in those orbs.   260
"Lamia!" he cried—and no soft-toned reply.
The many heard, and the loud revelry
Grew hush; the stately music no more breathes;
The myrtle sicken'd in a thousand wreaths.
By faint degrees, voice, lute, and pleasure ceased;
A deadly silence step by step increased,
Until it seem'd a horrid presence there,
And not a man but felt the terror in his hair.

"Lamia!" he shriek'd; and nothing but the shriek
With its sad echo did the silence break.   270
"Begone, foul dream!" he cried, gazing again
In the bride's face, where now no azure vein
Wander'd on fair-spaced temples; no soft bloom
Misted the cheek; no passion to illume
The deep-recessed vision:—all was blight;
Lamia, no longer fair, there sat a deadly white.
"Shut, shut those juggling eyes, thou ruthless man!
"Turn them aside, wretch! or the righteous ban
"Of all the Gods, whose dreadful images
"Here represent their shadowy presences,   280
"May pierce them on the sudden with the thorn
"Of painful blindness; leaving thee forlorn,
"In trembling dotage to the feeblest fright
"Of conscience, for their long offended might,
"For all thine impious proud-heart sophistries,
"Unlawful magic, and enticing lies.
"Corinthians! look upon that grey-beard wretch!
"Mark how, possess'd, his lashless eyelids stretch
"Around his demon eyes! Corinthians, see!
"My sweet bride withers at their potency."   290
"Fool!" said the sophist, in an under-tone
Gruff with contempt; which a death-nighing moan
From Lycius answer'd, as heart-struck and lost,
He sank supine beside the aching ghost.
"Fool! Fool!" repeated he, while his eyes still
Relented not, nor mov'd; "from every ill
"Of life have I preserv'd thee to this day,
"And shall I see thee made a serpent's prey?"
Then Lamia breath'd death breath; the sophist's eye,
Like a sharp spear, went through her utterly,   300
Keen, cruel, perceant, stinging: she, as well
As her weak hand could any meaning tell,
Motion'd him to be silent; vainly so,
He look'd and look'd again a level—No!
"A serpent!" echoed he; no sooner said,
Than with a frightful scream she vanished:
And Lycius' arms were empty of delight,
As were his limbs of life, from that same night.
On the high couch he lay!—his friends came round—
Supported him—no pulse, or breath they found,   310
And, in its marriage robe, the heavy body wound.

ISABELLA;

OR

THE POT OF BASIL

A Story from Boccaccio

I

FAIR Isabel, poor simple Isabel!
Lorenzo, a young palmer in Love's eye!
They could not in the self-same mansion dwell
Without some stir of heart, some malady;
They could not sit at meals but feel how well
It soothed each to be the other by;
They could not, sure, beneath the same roof sleep
But to each other dream, and nightly weep.

II

With every morn their love grew tenderer,
With every eve deeper and tenderer still;
He might not in house, field, or garden stir,
But her full shape would all his seeing fill;
And his continual voice was pleasanter
To her, than noise of trees or hidden rill;
Her lute-string gave an echo of his name,
She spoilt her half-done broidery with the same.

III

He knew whose gentle hand was at the latch
Before the door had given her to his eyes;
And from her chamber-window he would catch
Her beauty farther than the falcon spies;
And constant as her vespers would he watch,
Because her face was turn'd to the same skies;
And with sick longing all the night outwear,
To hear her morning-step upon the stair.

IV

A whole long month of May in this sad plight
Made their cheeks paler by the break of June:
"To-morrow will I bow to my delight,
"To-morrow will I ask my lady's boon."—

"O may I never see another night,
  "Lorenzo, if thy lips breathe not love's tune." —
So spake they to their pillows; but, alas,
Honeyless days and days did he let pass;

V

Until sweet Isabella's untouched cheek
  Fell sick within the rose's just domain,
Fell thin as a young mother's, who doth seek
  By every lull to cool her infant's pain:
"How ill she is," said he, "I may not speak,
  "And yet I will, and tell my love all plain:
"If looks speak love-laws, I will drink her tears,
"And at the least 'twill startle off her cares."

VI

So said he one fair morning, and all day
  His heart beat awfully against his side;
And to his heart he inwardly did pray
  For power to speak; but still the ruddy tide
Stifled his voice, and puls'd resolve away—
  Fever'd his high conceit of such a bride,
Yet brought him to the meekness of a child:
Alas! when passion is both meek and wild!

VII

So once more he had wak'd and anguished
  A dreary night of love and misery,
If Isabel's quick eye had not been wed
  To every symbol on his forehead high;
She saw it waxing very pale and dead,
  And straight all flush'd; so, lisped tenderly,
"Lorenzo!"—here she ceas'd her timid quest,
But in her tone and look he read the rest.

VIII

"O Isabella, I can half perceive
  "That I may speak my grief into thine ear;
"If thou didst ever anything believe,
  "Believe how I love thee, believe how near
"My soul is to its doom: I would not grieve
  "Thy hand by unwelcome pressing, would not fear
"Thine eyes by gazing; but I cannot live
"Another night, and not my passion shrive.

IX

"Love! thou art leading me from wintry cold,
  "Lady! thou leadest me to summer clime,
"And I must taste the blossoms that unfold
  "In its ripe warmth this gracious morning time."
So said, his erewhile timid lips grew bold,
  And poesied with hers in dewy rhyme:
Great bliss was with them, and great happiness
Grew, like a lusty flower in June's caress.

X

Parting they seem'd to tread upon the air,
  Twin roses by the zephyr blown apart
Only to meet again more close, and share
  The inward fragrance of each other's heart.
She, to her chamber gone, a ditty fair
  Sang, of delicious love and honey'd dart;
He with light steps went up a western hill,
And bade the sun farewell, and joy'd his fill.

XI

All close they met again, before the dusk
  Had taken from the stars its pleasant veil,
All close they met, all eves, before the dusk
  Had taken from the stars its pleasant veil,
Close in a bower of hyacinth and musk,
  Unknown of any, free from whispering tale.
Ah! better had it been for ever so,
Than idle ears should pleasure in their woe.

XII

Were they unhappy then?—It cannot be—
  Too many tears for lovers have been shed,
Too many sighs give we to them in fee,
  Too much of pity after they are dead,
Too many doleful stories do we see,
  Whose matter in bright gold were best be read;
Except in such a page where Theseus' spouse
Over the pathless waves towards him bows.

XIII

But, for the general award of love,
  The little sweet doth kill much bitterness;
Though Dido silent is in under-grove,
  And Isabella's was a great distress,

Though Young Lorenzo in warm Indian clove
    Was not embalm'd, this truth is not the less—
Even bees, the little almsmen of spring-bowers,
    Know there is richest juice in poison-flowers.

XIV

With her two brothers this fair lady dwelt,
    Enriched from ancestral merchandize,
And for them many a weary hand did swelt
    In torched mines and noisy factories
And many once proud-quiver'd loins did melt
    In blood from stinging whip;—with hollow eyes
Many all day in dazzling river stood,
To take the rich-ored driftings of the flood.

XV

For them the Ceylon diver held his breath,
    And went all naked to the hungry shark;
For them his ears gush'd blood; for them in death
    The seal on the cold ice with piteous bark
Lay full of darts; for them alone did seethe
    A thousand men in troubles wide and dark:
Half-ignorant, they turn'd an easy wheel,
That set sharp racks at work, to pinch and peel.

XVI

Why were they proud? Because their marble founts
    Gush'd with more pride than do a wretch's tears?—
Why were they proud? Because fair orange-mounts
    Were of more soft ascent than lazar stairs?—
Why were they proud? Because red-lin'd accounts
    Were richer than the songs of Grecian years?—
Why were they proud? again we ask aloud,
Why in the name of Glory were they proud?

XVII

Yet were these Florentines as self-retired
    In hungry pride and gainful cowardice,
As two close Hebrews in that land inspired,
    Paled in and vineyarded from beggar-spies;
The hawks of ship-mast forests—the untired
    And pannier'd mules for ducats and old lies—
Quick cat's-paws on the generous stray-away,—
Great wits in Spanish, Tuscan, and Malay.

XVIII

How was it these same ledger-men could spy
  Fair Isabella in her downy nest?
How could they find out in Lorenzo's eye
  A straying from his toil? Hot Egypt's pest
Into their vision covetous and sly!
  How could these money-bags see east and west?—
Yet so they did—and every dealer fair
Must see behind, as doth the hunted hare.

XIX

O eloquent and famed Boccaccio!
  Of thee we now should ask forgiving boon,
And of thy spicy myrtles as they blow,
  And of thy roses amorous of the moon,
And of thy lillies, that do paler grow
  Now they can no more hear thy ghittern's tune,
For venturing syllables that ill beseem
The quiet glooms of such a piteous theme.

XX

Grant thou a pardon here, and then the tale
  Shall move on soberly, as it is meet;
There is no other crime, no mad assail
  To make old prose in modern rhyme more sweet:
But it is done—succeed the verse or fail—
  To honour thee, and thy gone spirit greet;
To stead thee as a verse in English tongue,
An echo of thee in the north-wind sung.

XXI

These brethren having found by many signs
  What love Lorenzo for their sister had,
And how she lov'd him too, each unconfines
  His bitter thoughts to other, well nigh mad
That he, the servant of their trade designs,
  Should in their sister's love be blithe and glad,
When 'twas their plan to coax her by degrees
To some high noble and his olive-trees.

XXII

And many a jealous conference had they,
  And many times they bit their lips alone,
Before they fix'd upon a surest way
  To make the youngster for his crime atone;

And at the last, these men of cruel clay
   Cut Mercy with a sharp knife to the bone;
For they resolved in some forest dim
To kill Lorenzo, and there bury him.

XXIII

So on a pleasant morning, as he leant
   Into the sun-rise, o'er the balustrade
Of the garden-terrace, towards him they bent
   Their footing through the dews; and to him said,
"You seem there in the quiet of content,
   "Lorenzo, and we are most loth to invade
"Calm speculation; but if you are wise,
"Bestride your steed while cold is in the skies.

XXIV

"To-day we purpose, aye, this hour we mount
   "To spur three leagues towards the Apennine;
"Come down, we pray thee, ere the hot sun count
   "His dewy rosary on the eglantine."
Lorenzo, courteously as he was wont,
   Bow'd a fair greeting to these serpents' whine;
And went in haste, to get in readiness,
With belt, and spur, and bracing huntsman's dress.

XXV

And as he to the court-yard pass'd along,
   Each third step did he pause, and listen'd oft
If he could hear his lady's matin-song,
   Or the light whisper of her footstep soft;
And as he thus over his passion hung,
   He heard a laugh full musical aloft;
When, looking up, he saw her features bright
Smile through an in-door lattice, all delight.

XXVI

"Love, Isabel!" said he, "I was in pain
   "Lest I should miss to bid thee a good morrow:
"Ah! what if I should lose thee, when so fain
   "I am to stifle all the heavy sorrow
"Of a poor three hours' absence? but we'll gain
   "Out of the amorous dark what day doth borrow.
"Good bye! I'll soon be back."—"Good bye!" said she:—
And as he went she chanted merrily.

XXVII

So the two brothers and their murder'd man
   Rode past fair Florence, to where Arno's stream
Gurgles through straiten'd banks, and still doth fan
   Itself with dancing bulrush, and the bream
Keeps head against the freshets. Sick and wan
   The brothers' faces in the ford did seem,
Lorenzo's flush with love.—They pass'd the water
Into a forest quiet for the slaughter.

XXVIII

There was Lorenzo slain and buried in,
   There in that forest did his great love cease;
Ah! when a soul doth thus its freedom win,
   It aches in loneliness—is ill at peace
As the break-covert blood-hounds of such sin:
   They dipp'd their swords in the water, and did tease
Their horses homeward, with convulsed spur,
Each richer by his being a murderer.

XXIX

They told their sister how, with sudden speed,
   Lorenzo had ta'en ship for foreign lands,
Because of some great urgency and need
   In their affairs, requiring trusty hands.
Poor Girl! put on thy stifling widow's weed,
   And 'scape at once from Hope's accursed bands;
To-day thou wilt not see him, nor to-morrow,
And the next day will be a day of sorrow.

XXX

She weeps alone for pleasures not to be;
   Sorely she wept until the night came on,
And then, instead of love, O misery!
   She brooded o'er the luxury alone:
His image in the dusk she seem'd to see,
   And to the silence made a gentle moan,
Spreading her perfect arms upon the air,
And on her couch low murmuring "Where? O where?"

XXXI

But Selfishness, Love's cousin, held not long
   Its fiery vigil in her single breast;
She fretted for the golden hour, and hung
   Upon the time with feverish unrest—

Not long—for soon into her heart a throng
  Of higher occupants, a richer zest,
Came tragic; passion not to be subdued,
And sorrow for her love in travels rude.

XXXII

In the mid days of autumn, on their eves
  The breath of Winter comes from far away,
And the sick west continually bereaves
  Of some gold tinge, and plays a roundelay
Of death among the bushes and the leaves,
  To make all bare before he dares to stray
From his north cavern. So sweet Isabel
By gradual decay from beauty fell,

XXXIII

Because Lorenzo came not. Oftentimes
  She ask'd her brothers, with an eye all pale,
Striving to be itself, what dungeon climes
  Could keep him off so long? They spake a tale
Time after time, to quiet her. Their crimes
  Came on them, like a smoke from Hinnom's vale;
And every night in dreams they groan'd aloud,
To see their sister in her snowy shroud.

XXXIV

And she had died in drowsy ignorance,
  But for a thing more deadly dark than all;
It came like a fierce potion, drunk by chance,
  Which saves a sick man from the feather'd pall
For some few gasping moments; like a lance,
  Waking an Indian from his cloudy hall
With cruel pierce, and bringing him again
Sense of the gnawing fire at heart and brain.

XXXV

It was a vision.—In the drowsy gloom,
  The dull of midnight, at her couch's foot
Lorenzo stood, and wept: the forest tomb
  Had marr'd his glossy hair which once could shoot
Lustre into the sun, and put cold doom
  Upon his lips, and taken the soft lute
From his lorn voice, and past his loamed ears
Had made a miry channel for his tears.

XXXVI

Strange sound it was, when the pale shadow spake;
  For there was striving, in its piteous tongue,
To speak as when on earth it was awake,
  And Isabella on its music hung:
Languor there was in it, and tremulous shake,
  As in a palsied Druid's harp unstrung;
And through it moan'd a ghostly under-song,
Like hoarse night-gusts sepulchral briars among.

XXXVII

Its eyes, though wild, were still all dewy bright
  With love, and kept all phantom fear aloof
From the poor girl by magic of their light,
  The while it did unthread the horrid woof
Of the late darken'd time,—the murderous spite
  Of pride and avarice,—the dark pine roof
In the forest,—and the sodden turfed dell,
Where, without any word, from stabs he fell.

XXXVIII

Saying moreover, "Isabel, my sweet!
  "Red whortle-berries droop above my head,
"And a large flint-stone weighs upon my feet;
  "Around me beeches and high chestnuts shed
"Their leaves and prickly nuts; a sheep-fold bleat
  "Comes from beyond the river to my bed:
"Go, shed one tear upon my heather-bloom,
"And it shall comfort me within the tomb.

XXXIX

"I am a shadow now, alas! alas!
  "Upon the skirts of human-nature dwelling
"Alone: I chant alone the holy mass,
  "While little sounds of life are round me knelling,
"And glossy bees at noon do fieldward pass,
  "And many a chapel bell the hour is telling,
"Paining me through: those sounds grow strange to me,
"And thou art distant in Humanity.

XL

"I know what was, I feel full well what is,
  "And I should rage, if spirits could go mad;
"Though I forget the taste of earthly bliss,
  "That paleness warms my grave, as though I had

"A Seraph chosen from the bright abyss
  "To be my spouse: thy paleness makes me glad;
"Thy beauty grows upon me, and I feel
"A greater love through all my essence steal."

XLI

The Spirit mourn'd "Adieu!"—dissolv'd and left
  The atom darkness in a slow turmoil;
As when of healthful midnight sleep bereft,
  Thinking on rugged hours and fruitless toil,
We put our eyes into a pillowy cleft,
  And see the spangly gloom froth up and boil:
It made sad Isabella's eyelids ache,
And in the dawn she started up awake;

XLII

"Ha! ha!" said she, "I knew not this hard life,
  "I thought the worst was simple misery;
"I thought some Fate with pleasure or with strife
  "Portion'd us—happy days, or else to die;
"But there is crime—a brother's bloody knife!
  "Sweet Spirit, thou hast school'd my infancy:
"I'll visit thee for this, and kiss thine eyes,
"And greet thee morn and even in the skies."

XLIII

When the full morning came, she had devised
  How she might secret to the forest hie;
How she might find the clay, so dearly prized,
  And sing to it one latest lullaby;
How her short absence might be unsurmised,
  While she the inmost of the dream would try.
Resolv'd, she took with her an aged nurse,
And went into that dismal forest-hearse.

XLIV

See, as they creep along the river side,
  How she doth whisper to that aged Dame,
And, after looking round the champaign wide,
  Shows her a knife.—"What feverous hectic flame
"Burns in thee, child?—What good can thee betide,
  "That thou should'st smile again?"—The evening came,
And they had found Lorenzo's earthy bed;
The flint was there, the berries at his head.

XLV

Who hath not loiter'd in a green church-yard,
　　And let his spirit, like a demon-mole,
Work through the clayey soil and gravel hard,
　　To see scull, coffin'd bones, and funeral stole;
Pitying each form that hungry Death hath marr'd,
　　And filling it once more with human soul?
Ah! this is holiday to what was felt
When Isabella by Lorenzo knelt.

XLVI

She gaz'd into the fresh-thrown mould, as though
　　One glance did fully all its secrets tell;
Clearly she saw, as other eyes would know
　　Pale limbs at bottom of a crystal well;
Upon the murderous spot she seem'd to grow,
　　Like to a native lilly of the dell:
Then with her knife, all sudden, she began
To dig more fervently than misers can.

XLVII

Soon she turn'd up a soiled glove, whereon
　　Her silk had play'd in purple phantasies,
She kiss'd it with a lip more chill than stone,
　　And put it in her bosom, where it dries
And freezes utterly unto the bone
　　Those dainties made to still an infant's cries:
Then 'gan she work again; nor stay'd her care,
But to throw back at times her veiling hair.

XLVIII

That old nurse stood beside her wondering,
　　Until her heart felt pity to the core
At sight of such a dismal labouring,
　　And so she kneeled, with her locks all hoar,
And put her lean hands to the horrid thing:
　　Three hours they labour'd at this travail sore;
At last they felt the kernel of the grave,
And Isabella did not stamp and rave.

XLIX

Ah! wherefore all this wormy circumstance?
　　Why linger at the yawning tomb so long?
O for the gentleness of old Romance,
　　The simple plaining of a minstrel's song!

Fair reader, at the old tale take a glance,
 For here, in truth, it doth not well belong
To speak:—O turn thee to the very tale,
And taste the music of that vision pale.

L

With duller steel than the Perséan sword
 They cut away no formless monster's head,
But one, whose gentleness did well accord
 With death, as life. The ancient harps have said,
Love never dies, but lives, immortal Lord:
 If Love impersonate was ever dead,
Pale Isabella kiss'd it, and low moan'd.
'Twas love; cold,—dead indeed, but not dethroned.

LI

In anxious secrecy they took it home,
 And then the prize was all for Isabel:
She calm'd its wild hair with a golden comb,
 And all around each eye's sepuchral cell
Pointed each fringed lash; the smeared loam
 With tears, as chilly as a dripping well,
She drench'd away:—and still she comb'd, and kept
Sighing all day—and still she kiss'd, and wept.

LII

Then in a silken scarf,—sweet with the dews
 Of precious flowers pluck'd in Araby,
And divine liquids come with odorous ooze
 Through the cold serpent-pipe refreshfully,—
She wrapp'd it up; and for its tomb did choose
 A garden-pot, wherein she laid it by,
And cover'd it with mould, and o'er it set
Sweet Basil, which her tears kept ever wet.

LIII

And she forgot the stars, the moon, and sun,
 And she forgot the blue above the trees,
And she forgot the dells where waters run,
 And she forgot the chilly autumn breeze;
She had no knowledge when the day was done,
 And the new morn she saw not: but in peace
Hung over her sweet Basil evermore,
And moisten'd it with tears unto the core.

LIV

And so she ever fed it with thin tears,
    Whence thick, and green, and beautiful it grew,
So that it smelt more balmy than its peers
    Of Basil-tufts in Florence; for it drew
Nurture besides, and life, from human fears,
    From the fast mouldering head there shut from view:
So that the jewel, safely casketed,
Came forth, and in perfumed leafits spread.

LV

O Melancholy, linger here awhile!
    O Music, Music, breathe despondingly!
O Echo, Echo, from some sombre isle,
    Unknown, Lethean, sigh to us—O sigh!
Spirits in grief, lift up your heads, and smile;
    Lift up your heads, sweet Spirits, heavily,
And make a pale light in your cypress glooms,
Tinting with silver wan your marble tombs.

LVI

Moan hither, all ye syllables of woe,
    From the deep throat of sad Melpomene!
Through bronzed lyre in tragic order go,
    And touch the strings into a mystery;
Sound mournfully upon the winds and low;
    For simple Isabel is soon to be
Among the dead: She withers, like a palm
Cut by an Indian for its juicy balm.

LVII

O leave the palm to wither by itself;
    Let not quick Winter chill its dying hour!—
It may not be—those Baälites of pelf,
    Her brethren, noted the continual shower
From her dead eyes; and many a curious elf,
    Among her kindred, wonder'd that such dower
Of youth and beauty should be thrown aside
By one mark'd out to be a Noble's bride.

LVIII.

And, furthermore, her brethren wonder'd much
    Why she sat drooping by the Basil green,
And why it flourish'd, as by magic touch;
    Greatly they wonder'd what the thing might mean:

They could not surely give belief, that such
    A very nothing would have power to wean
Her from her own fair youth, and pleasures gay,
And even remembrance of her love's delay.

LIX

Therefore they watch'd a time when they might sift
    This hidden whim; and long they watch'd in vain;
For seldom did she go to chapel-shrift,
    And seldom felt she any hunger-pain;
And when she left, she hurried back, as swift
    As bird on wing to breast its eggs again;
And, patient as a hen-bird, sat her there
Beside her Basil, weeping through her hair.

LX

Yet they contriv'd to steal the Basil-pot,
    And to examine it in secret place;
The thing was vile with green and livid spot,
    And yet they knew it was Lorenzo's face:
The guerdon of their murder they had got,
    And so left Florence in a moment's space,
Never to turn again.—Away they went,
With blood upon their heads, to banishment.

LXI

O Melancholy, turn thine eyes away!
    O Music, Music, breathe despondingly!
O Echo, Echo, on some other day,
    From isles Lethean, sigh to us—O sigh!
Spirits of grief, sing not your "Well-a-way!"
    For Isabel, sweet Isabel, will die;
Will die a death too lone and incomplete,
Now they have ta'en away her Basil sweet.

LXII

Piteous she look'd on dead and senseless things,
    Asking for her lost Basil amorously;
And with melodious chuckle in the strings
    Of her lorn voice, she oftentimes would cry
After the Pilgrim in his wanderings,
    To ask him where her Basil was; and why
'Twas hid from her: "For cruel 'tis," said she,
"To steal my Basil-pot away from me."

LXIII

And so she pined, and so she died forlorn,
  Imploring for her Basil to the last.
No heart was there in Florence but did mourn
  In pity of her love, so overcast.
And a sad ditty of this story born
  From mouth to mouth through all the country pass'd:
Still is the burthen sung—"O cruelty,
"To steal my Basil-pot away from me!"

THE EVE OF ST. AGNES

I

St. Agnes' Eve—Ah, bitter chill it was!
The owl, for all his feathers, was a-cold;
The hare limp'd trembling through the frozen grass,
And silent was the flock in woolly fold:
Numb were the Beadsman's fingers, while he told
His rosary, and while his frosted breath,
Like pious incense from a censer old,
Seem'd taking flight for heaven, without a death,
Past the sweet Virgin's picture, while his prayer he saith.

II

His prayer he saith, this patient, holy man;
Then takes his lamp, and riseth from his knees,
And back returneth, meagre, barefoot, wan,
Along the chapel aisle by slow degrees:
The sculptur'd dead, on each side, seem to freeze,
Emprison'd in black, purgatorial rails:
Knights, ladies, praying in dumb orat'ries,
He passeth by; and his weak spirit fails
To think how they may ache in icy hoods and mails.

III

Northward he turneth through a little door,
And scarce three steps, ere Music's golden tongue
Flatter'd to tears this aged man and poor;
But no—already had his deathbell rung:
The joys of all his life were said and sung:
His was harsh penance on St. Agnes' Eve:
Another way he went, and soon among
Rough ashes sat he for his soul's reprieve,
And all night kept awake, for sinners' sake to grieve.

IV

That ancient Beadsman heard the prelude soft;
And so it chanc'd, for many a door was wide,
From hurry to and fro. Soon, up aloft,
The silver, snarling trumpets 'gan to chide:

The level chambers, ready with their pride,
Were glowing to receive a thousand guests:
The carved angels, ever eager-eyed,
Star'd, where upon their heads the cornice rests,
With hair blown back, and wings put cross-wise on their breasts,

V

At length burst in the argent revelry,
With plume, tiara, and all rich array,
Numerous as shadows haunting faerily
The brain, new stuff'd, in youth, with triumphs gay
Of old romance. These let us wish away,
And turn, sole-thoughted, to one Lady there,
Whose heart had brooded, all that wintry day,
On love, and wing'd St. Agnes' saintly care,
As she had heard old dames full many times declare.

VI

They told her how, upon St. Agnes' Eve,
Young virgins might have visions of delight,
And soft adorings from their loves receive
Upon the honey'd middle of the night,
If ceremonies due they did aright;
As, supperless to bed they must retire,
And couch supine their beauties, lilly white;
Nor look behind, nor sideways, but require
Of Heaven with upward eyes for all that they desire.

VII

Full of this whim was thoughtful Madeline:
The music, yearning like a God in pain,
She scarcely heard: her maiden eyes divine,
Fix'd on the floor, saw many a sweeping train
Pass by—she heeded not at all: in vain
Came many a tiptoe, amorous cavalier,
And back retir'd; not cool'd by high disdain,
But she saw not: her heart was otherwhere:
She sigh'd for Agnes' dreams, the sweetest of the year.

VIII

She danc'd along with vague, regardless eyes,
Anxious her lips, her breathing quick and short:
The hallow'd hour was near at hand: she sighs
Amid the timbrels, and the throng'd resort

Of whisperers in anger, or in sport;
'Mid looks of love, defiance, hate, and scorn,
Hoodwink'd with faery fancy; all amort,
Save to St. Agnes and her lambs unshorn,
And all the bliss to be before to-morrow morn.

                    IX

So, purposing each moment to retire,
She linger'd still. Meantime, across the moors,
Had come young Porphyro, with heart on fire
For Madeline. Beside the portal doors,
Buttress'd from moonlight, stands he, and implores
All saints to give him sight of Madeline,
But for one moment in the tedious hours,
That he might gaze and worship all unseen;
Perchance speak, kneel, touch, kiss—in sooth such things
        have been.

                    X

He ventures in: let no buzz'd whisper tell:
All eyes be muffled, or a hundred swords
Will storm his heart, Love's fev'rous citadel:
For him, those chambers held barbarian hordes,
Hyena foemen, and hot-blooded lords,
Whose very dogs would execrations howl
Against his lineage: not one breast affords
Him any mercy, in that mansion foul,
Save one old beldame, weak in body and in soul.

                    XI

Ah, happy chance! the aged creature came,
Shuffling along with ivory-headed wand,
To where he stood, hid from the torch's flame,
Behind a broad hall-pillar, far beyond
The sound of merriment and chorus bland:
He startled her; but soon she knew his face,
And grasp'd his fingers in her palsied hand,
Saying, "Mercy, Porphyro! hie thee from this place:
"They are all here to-night, the whole blood-thirsty race!

                    XII

"Get hence! get hence! there's dwarfish Hildebrand;
"He had a fever late, and in the fit
"He cursed thee and thine, both house and land:
"Then there's that old Lord Maurice, not a whit

"More tame for his gray hairs—Alas me! flit!
"Flit like a ghost away."—"Ah, Gossip dear,
"We're safe enough; here in this arm-chair sit,
"And tell me how"—"Good Saints! not here, not here;
"Follow me, child, or else these stones will be thy bier."

XIII

He follow'd through a lowly arched way,
Brushing the cobwebs with his lofty plume,
And as she mutter'd "Well-a—well-a-day!"
He found him in a little moonlight room,
Pale, lattic'd, chill, and silent as a tomb.
"Now tell me where is Madeline," said he,
"O tell me, Angela, by the holy loom
"Which none but secret sisterhood may see,
"When they St. Agnes' wool are weaving piously."

XIV

"St. Agnes! Ah! it is St. Agnes' Eve—
"Yet men will murder upon holy days:
"Thou must hold water in a witch's sieve,
"And be liege-lord of all the Elves and Fays,
"To venture so: it fills me with amaze
"To see thee, Porphyro!—St. Agnes' Eve!
"God's help! my lady fair the conjuror plays
"This very night: good angels her deceive!
"But let me laugh awhile, I've mickle time to grieve."

XV

Feebly she laugheth in the languid moon,
While Porphyro upon her face doth look,
Like puzzled urchin on an aged crone
Who keepeth clos'd a wond'rous riddle-book,
As spectacled she sits in chimney nook.
But soon his eyes grew brilliant, when she told
His lady's purpose; and he scarce could brook
Tears, at the thought of those enchantments cold,
And Madeline asleep in lap of legends old.

XVI

Sudden a thought came like a full-blown rose,
Flushing his brow, and in his pained heart
Made purple riot: then doth he propose
A stratagem, that makes the beldame start:

"A cruel man and impious thou art:
"Sweet lady, let her pray, and sleep, and dream
"Alone with her good angels, far apart
"From wicked men like thee. Go, go!—I deem
"Thou canst not surely be the same that thou didst seem."

XVII

"I will not harm her, by all saints I swear,"
Quoth Porphyro: "O may I ne'er find grace
"When my weak voice shall whisper its last prayer,
"If one of her soft ringlets I displace,
"Or look with ruffian passion in her face:
"Good Angela, believe me by these tears;
"Or I will, even in a moment's space,
"Awake, with horrid shout, my foemen's ears,
"And beard them, though they be more fang'd than wolves
    and bears."

XVIII

"Ah! why wilt thou affright a feeble soul?
"A poor, weak, palsy-stricken, churchyard thing,
"Whose passing-bell may ere the midnight toll;
"Whose prayers for thee, each morn and evening,
"Were never miss'd."—Thus plaining, doth she bring
A gentler speech from burning Porphyro;
So woful, and of such deep sorrowing,
That Angela gives promise she will do
Whatever he shall wish, betide her weal or woe.

XIX

Which was, to lead him, in close secrecy,
Even to Madeline's chamber, and there hide
Him in a closet, of such privacy
That he might see her beauty unespied,
And win perhaps that night a peerless bride,
While legion'd faeries pac'd the coverlet,
And pale enchantment held her sleepy-eyed.
Never on such a night have lovers met,
Since Merlin paid his Demon all the monstrous debt.

XX

"It shall be as thou wishest," said the Dame:
"All cates and dainties shall be stored there
"Quickly on this feast-night: by the tambour frame
"Her own lute thou wilt see: no time to spare,

"For I am slow and feeble, and scarce dare
"On such a catering trust my dizzy head.
"Wait here, my child, with patience; kneel in prayer
"The while: Ah! thou must needs the lady wed,
"Or may I never leave my grave among the dead."

XXI

So saying, she hobbled off with busy fear.
The lover's endless minutes slowly pass'd;
The dame return'd, and whisper'd in his ear
To follow her; with aged eyes aghast
From fright of dim espial. Safe at last,
Through many a dusky gallery, they gain
The maiden's chamber, silken, hush'd, and chaste;
Where Porphyro took covert, pleas'd amain.
His poor guide hurried back with agues in her brain.

XXII

Her falt'ring hand upon the balustrade,
Old Angela was feeling for the stair,
When Madeline, St. Agnes' charmed maid,
Rose, like a mission'd spirit, unaware:
With silver taper's light, and pious care,
She turn'd, and down the aged gossip led
To a safe level matting. Now prepare,
Young Porphyro, for gazing on that bed;
She comes, she comes again, like ring-dove fray'd and fled.

XXIII

Out went the taper as she hurried in;
Its little smoke, in pallid moonshine, died:
She clos'd the door, she panted, all akin
To spirits of the air, and visions wide:
No uttered syllable, or, woe betide!
But to her heart, her heart was voluble,
Paining with eloquence her balmy side;
As though a tongueless nightingale should swell
Her throat in vain, and die, heart-stifled, in her dell.

XXIV

A casement high and triple-arch'd there was,
All garlanded with carven imag'ries
Of fruits, and flowers, and bunches of knot-grass,
And diamonded with panes of quaint device,

Innumerable of stains and splendid dyes,
As are the tiger-moth's deep-damask'd wings;
And in the midst, 'mong thousand heraldries,
And twilight saints, and dim emblazonings,
A shielded scutcheon blush'd with blood of queens and kings.

XXV

Full on this casement shone the wintry moon,
And threw warm gules on Madeline's fair breast,
As down she knelt for heaven's grace and boon;
Rose-bloom fell on her hands, together prest,
And on her silver cross soft amethyst,
And on her hair a glory, like a saint:
She seem'd a splendid angel, newly drest,
Save wings, for heaven:—Porphyro grew faint:
She knelt, so pure a thing, so free from mortal taint.

XXVI

Anon his heart revives: her vespers done,
Of all its wreathed pearls her hair she frees;
Unclasps her warmed jewels one by one;
Loosens her fragrant boddice; by degrees
Her rich attire creeps rustling to her knees:
Half-hidden, like a mermaid in sea-weed,
Pensive awhile she dreams awake, and sees,
In fancy, fair St. Agnes in her bed,
But dares not look behind, or all the charm is fled.

XXVII

Soon, trembling in her soft and chilly nest,
In sort of wakeful swoon, perplex'd she lay,
Until the poppied warmth of sleep oppress'd
Her soothed limbs, and soul fatigued away;
Flown, like a thought, until the morrow-day;
Blissfully haven'd both from joy and pain;
Clasp'd like a missal where swart Paynims pray;
Blinded alike from sunshine and from rain,
As though a rose should shut, and be a bud again.

XXVIII

Stol'n to this paradise, and so entranced,
Porphyro gazed upon her empty dress,
And listen'd to her breathing, if it chanced
To wake into a slumberous tenderness;

Which when he heard, that minute did he bless,
And breath'd himself: then from the closet crept,
Noiseless as fear in a wide wilderness,
And over the hush'd carpet, silent, stept,
And 'tween the curtains peep'd, where, lo!—how fast she slept.

XXIX

Then by the bed-side, where the faded moon
Made a dim, silver twilight, soft he set
A table, and, half anguish'd, threw thereon
A cloth of woven crimson, gold, and jet:—
O for some drowsy Morphean amulet!
The boisterous, midnight, festive clarion,
The kettle-drum, and far-heard clarinet,
Affray his ears, though but in dying tone:—
The hall door shuts again, and all the noise is gone.

XXX

And still she slept an azure-lidded sleep,
In blanched linen, smooth, and lavender'd,
While he from forth the closet brought a heap
Of candied apple, quince, and plum, and gourd;
With jellies soother than the creamy curd,
And lucent syrops, tinct with cinnamon;
Manna and dates, in argosy transferr'd
From Fez; and spiced dainties, every one,
From silken Samarcand to cedar'd Lebanon.

XXXI

These delicates he heap'd with glowing hand
On golden dishes and in baskets bright
Of wreathed silver: sumptuous they stand
In the retired quiet of the night,
Filling the chilly room with perfume light.—
"And now, my love, my seraph fair, awake!
"Thou art my heaven, and I thine eremite:
"Open thine eyes, for meek St. Agnes' sake,
"Or I shall drowse beside thee, so my soul doth ache."

XXXII

Thus whispering, his warm, unnerved arm
Sank in her pillow. Shaded was her dream
By the dusk curtains:—'twas a midnight charm
Impossible to melt as iced stream:

The lustrous salvers in the moonlight gleam;
Broad golden fringe upon the carpet lies:
It seem'd he never, never could redeem
From such a stedfast spell his lady's eyes;
So mus'd awhile, entoil'd in woofed phantasies.

XXXIII

Awakening up, he took her hollow lute,—
Tumultuous,—and, in chords that tenderest be,
He play'd an ancient ditty, long since mute,
In Provence call'd, "La belle dame sans mercy:"
Close to her ear touching the melody;—
Wherewith disturb'd, she utter'd a soft moan:
He ceased—she panted quick—and suddenly
Her blue affrayed eyes wide open shone:
Upon his knees he sank, pale as smooth-sculptured stone.

XXXIV

Her eyes were open, but she still beheld,
Now wide awake, the vision of her sleep:
There was a painful change, that nigh expell'd
The blisses of her dream so pure and deep
At which fair Madeline began to weep,
And moan forth witless words with many a sigh;
While still her gaze on Porphyro would keep;
Who knelt, with joined hands and piteous eye,
Fearing to move or speak, she look'd so dreamingly.

XXXV

"Ah, Porphyro!" said she, "but even now
"Thy voice was at sweet tremble in mine ear,
"Made tuneable with every sweetest vow;
"And those sad eyes were spiritual and clear:
"How chang'd thou art! how pallid, chill, and drear!
"Give me that voice again, my Porphyro,
"Those looks immortal, those complainings dear!
"Oh, leave me not in this eternal woe,
"For if thou diest, my Love, I know not where to go."

XXXVI

Beyond a mortal man impassion'd far
At these voluptuous accents, he arose,
Ethereal, flush'd, and like a throbbing star
Seen mid the sapphire heaven's deep repose;

Into her dream he melted, as the rose
Blendeth its odour with the violet,—
Solution sweet: meantime the frost-wind blows
Like Love's alarum pattering the sharp sleet
Against the window-panes; St. Agnes' moon hath set.

XXXVII

'Tis dark: quick pattereth the flaw-blown sleet:
"This is no dream, my bride, my Madeline!"
'Tis dark: the iced gusts still rave and beat:
"No dream, alas! alas! and woe is mine!
"Porphyro will leave me here to fade and pine.—
"Cruel! what traitor could thee hither bring?
"I curse not, for my heart is lost in thine,
"Though thou forsakest a deceived thing;—
"A dove forlorn and lost with sick unpruned wing."

XXXVIII

"My Madeline! sweet dreamer! lovely bride!
"Say, may I be for aye thy vassal blest?
"Thy beauty's shield, heart-shap'd and vermeil dyed?
"Ah, silver shrine, here will I take my rest
"After so many hours of toil and quest,
"A famish'd pilgrim,—sav'd by miracle.
"Though I have found, I will not rob thy nest
"Saving of thy sweet self; if thou think'st well
"To trust, fair Madeline, to no rude infidel.

XXXIX

"Hark! 'tis an elfin-storm from faery land,
"Of haggard seeming; but a boon indeed:
"Arise—arise! the morning is at hand;—
"The bloated wassaillers will never heed:—
"Let us away, my love, with happy speed;
"There are no ears to hear, or eyes to see,—
"Drown'd all in Rhenish and the sleepy mead:
"Awake! arise! my love, and fearless be,
"For o'er the southern moors I have a home for thee."

XL

She hurried at his words, beset with fears,
For there were sleeping dragons all around,
At glaring watch, perhaps, with ready spears—
Down the wide stairs a darkling way they found.—

In all the house was heard no human sound.
A chain-droop'd lamp was flickering by each door;
The arras, rich with horseman, hawk, and hound,
Flutter'd in the besieging wind's uproar;
And the long carpets rose along the gusty floor.

XLI

They glide, like phantoms, into the wide hall;
Like phantoms, to the iron porch, they glide;
Where lay the Porter, in uneasy sprawl,
With a huge empty flaggon by his side:
The wakeful bloodhound rose, and shook his hide,
But his sagacious eye an inmate owns:
By one, and one, the bolts full easy slide;—
The chains lie silent on the footworn stones;—
The key turns, and the door upon its hinges groans.

XLII

And they are gone: aye, ages long ago
These lovers fled away into the storm.
That night the Baron dreamt of many a woe,
And all his warrior-guests, with shade and form
Of witch, and demon, and large coffin-worm,
Were long be-nightmar'd. Angela the old
Died palsy-twitch'd, with meagre face deform;
The Beadsman, after thousand aves told,
For aye unsought-for slept among his ashes cold.

POEMS

ODE TO A NIGHTINGALE

I

My heart aches, and a drowsy numbness pains
　My sense, as though of hemlock I had drunk,
Or emptied some dull opiate to the drains
　One minute past, and Lethe-wards had sunk:
'Tis not through envy of thy happy lot,
　But being too happy in thine happiness,—
　　That thou, light-winged Dryad of the trees,
　　　In some melodious plot
　Of beechen green, and shadows numberless,
　　Singest of summer in full-throated ease.

II

O, for a draught of vintage! that hath been
　Cool'd a long age in the deep-delved earth,
Tasting of Flora and the country green,
　Dance, and Provençal song, and sunburnt mirth!
O for a beaker full of the warm South,
　Full of the true, the blushful Hippocrene,
　　With beaded bubbles winking at the brim,
　　　And purple-stained mouth;
　That I might drink, and leave the world unseen,
　　And with thee fade away into the forest dim:

III

Fade far away, dissolve, and quite forget
　What thou among the leaves hast never known,
The weariness, the fever, and the fret
　Here, where men sit and hear each other groan;
Where palsy shakes a few, sad, last gray hairs,
　Where youth grows pale, and spectre-thin, and dies;
　　Where but to think is to be full of sorrow
　　　And leaden-eyed despairs,
　Where Beauty cannot keep her lustrous eyes,
　　Or new Love pine at them beyond to-morrow.

183

IV

Away! away! for I will fly to thee,
   Not charioted by Bacchus and his pards,
But on the viewless wings of Poesy,
   Though the dull brain perplexes and retards:
Already with thee! tender is the night,
     And haply the Queen-Moon is on her throne,
       Cluster'd around by all her starry Fays;
         But here there is no light,
     Save what from heaven is with the breezes blown
       Through verdurous glooms and winding mossy ways.

V

I cannot see what flowers are at my feet,
   Nor what soft incense hangs upon the boughs,
But, in embalmed darkness, guess each sweet
   Wherewith the seasonable month endows
The grass, the thicket, and the fruit-tree wild;
     White hawthorn, and the pastoral eglantine;
       Fast fading violets cover'd up in leaves;
         And mid-May's eldest child,
     The coming musk-rose, full of dewy wine,
       The murmurous haunt of flies on summer eves.

VI

Darkling I listen; and, for many a time
   I have been half in love with easeful Death,
Call'd him soft names in many a mused rhyme,
   To take into the air my quiet breath;
Now more than ever seems it rich to die,
   To cease upon the midnight with no pain,
     While thou art pouring forth thy soul abroad
       In such an ecstasy!
Still wouldst thou sing, and I have ears in vain—
   To thy high requiem become a sod.

VII

Thou wast not born for death, immortal Bird!
   No hungry generations tread thee down;
The voice I hear this passing night was heard
   In ancient days by emperor and clown:
Perhaps the self-same song that found a path
     Through the sad heart of Ruth, when, sick for home,
       She stood in tears amid the alien corn;
         The same that oft-times hath

Charm'd magic casements, opening on the foam
Of perilous seas, in faery lands forlorn.

VIII

Forlorn! the very word is like a bell
 To toll me back from thee to my sole self!
Adieu! the fancy cannot cheat so well
 As she is fam'd to do, deceiving elf.
Adieu! adieu! thy plaintive anthem fades
 Past the near meadows, over the still stream,
  Up the hill-side; and now 'tis buried deep
   In the next valley-glades:
 Was it a vision, or a waking dream?
 Fled is that music:—Do I wake or sleep?

ODE ON A GRECIAN URN

I

Thou still unravish'd bride of quietness,
 Thou foster-child of silence and slow time,
Sylvan historian, who canst thus express
 A flowery tale more sweetly than our rhyme:
What leaf-fring'd legend haunts about thy shape
 Of deities or mortals, or of both,
  In Tempe or the dales of Arcady?
 What men or gods are these? What maidens loth?
What mad pursuit? What struggle to escape?
  What pipes and timbrels? What wild ecstasy?

II

Heard melodies are sweet, but those unheard
 Are sweeter; therefore, ye soft pipes, play on;
Not to the sensual ear, but, more endear'd,
 Pipe to the spirit ditties of no tone:
Fair youth, beneath the trees, thou canst not leave
 Thy song, nor ever can those trees be bare;
  Bold Lover, never, never canst thou kiss,
Though winning near the goal—yet, do not grieve;
 She cannot fade, though thou hast not thy bliss,
 For ever wilt thou love, and she be fair!

III

Ah, happy, happy boughs! that cannot shed
 Your leaves, nor ever bid the Spring adieu;
And, happy melodist, unwearied,
 For ever piping songs for ever new;

More happy love! more happy, happy love!
  For ever warm and still to be enjoy'd,
    For ever panting, and for ever young;
All breathing human passion far above,
  That leaves a heart high-sorrowful and cloy'd,
    A burning forehead, and a parching tongue.

IV

Who are these coming to the sacrifice?
  To what green altar, O mysterious priest,
Lead'st thou that heifer lowing at the skies,
  And all her silken flanks with garlands drest?
What little town by river or sea shore,
  Or mountain-built with peaceful citadel,
    Is emptied of this folk, this pious morn?
And, little town, thy streets for evermore
  Will silent be; and not a soul to tell
    Why thou art desolate, can e'er return.

V

O Attic shape! Fair attitude! with brede
  Of marble men and maidens overwrought,
With forest branches and the trodden weed;
  Thou, silent form, dost tease us out of thought
As doth eternity: Cold Pastoral!
  When old age shall this generation waste,
    Thou shalt remain, in midst of other woe
Than ours, a friend to man, to whom thou say'st,
  "Beauty is truth, truth beauty,"—that is all
    Ye know on earth, and all ye need to know.

ODE TO PSYCHE

O Goddess! hear these tuneless numbers, wrung
  By sweet enforcement and remembrance dear,
And pardon that thy secrets should be sung
  Even into thine own soft-conched ear:
Surely I dreamt to-day, or did I see
  The winged Psyche with awaken'd eyes?
I wander'd in a forest thoughtlessly,
  And, on the sudden, fainting with surprise,
Saw two fair creatures, couched side by side
  In deepest grass, beneath the whisp'ring roof
  Of leaves and trembled blossoms, where there ran
    A brooklet, scarce espied:

10

'Mid hush'd, cool-rooted flowers, fragrant-eyed,
   Blue, silver-white, and budded Tyrian,
They lay calm-breathing on the bedded grass;
   Their arms embraced, and their pinions too;
   Their lips touch'd not, but had not bade adieu,
As if disjoined by soft-handed slumber,
And ready still past kisses to outnumber
   At tender eye-dawn of aurorean love: 20
      The winged boy I knew;
But who wast thou, O happy, happy dove?
      His Psyche true!

O latest born and loveliest vision far
   Of all Olympus' faded hierarchy!
Fairer than Phœbe's sapphire-region'd star,
   Or Vesper, amorous glow-worm of the sky;
Fairer than these, though temple thou hast none,
     Nor altar heap'd with flowers;
Nor virgin-choir to make delicious moan   30
     Upon the midnight hours;
No voice, no lute, no pipe, no incense sweet
   From chain-swung censer teeming;
No shrine, no grove, no oracle, no heat
   Of pale-mouth'd prophet dreaming.

O brightest! though too late for antique vows,
   Too, too late for the fond believing lyre,
When holy were the haunted forest boughs,
   Holy the air, the water, and the fire;
Yet even in these days so far retir'd   40
   From happy pieties, thy lucent fans,
   Fluttering among the faint Olympians,
I see, and sing, by my own eyes inspir'd.
So let me be thy choir, and make a moan
     Upon the midnight hours;
Thy voice, thy lute, thy pipe, thy incense sweet
   From swinged censer teeming;
Thy shrine, thy grove, thy oracle, thy heat
   Of pale-mouth'd prophet dreaming.

Yes, I will be thy priest, and build a fane   50
   In some untrodden region of my mind,
Where branched thoughts, new grown with pleasant pain,
   Instead of pines shall murmur in the wind:
Far, far around shall those dark-cluster'd trees
   Fledge the wild-ridged mountains steep by steep;

And there by zephyrs, streams, and birds, and bees,
    The moss-lain Dryads shall be lull'd to sleep;
And in the midst of this wide quietness
A rosy sanctury will I dress

With the wreath'd trellis of a working brain,   60
    With buds, and bells, and stars without a name,
With all the gardener Fancy e'er could feign,
    Who breeding flowers, will never breed the same:
And there shall be for thee all soft delight
    That shadowy thought can win,
A bright torch, and a casement ope at night,
    To let the warm Love in!

FANCY

Ever let the fancy roam,
Pleasure never is at home:
At a touch sweet Pleasure melteth,
Like to bubbles when rain pelteth;
Then let winged Fancy wander
Through the thought still spread beyond her:
Open wide the mind's cage-door,
She'll dart forth, and cloudward soar.
O sweet Fancy! let her loose;
Summer's joys are spoilt by use,   10
And the enjoying of the Spring
Fades as does its blossoming;
Autumn's red-lipp'd fruitage too,
Blushing through the mist and dew,
Cloys with tasting: What do then?
Sit thee by the ingle, when
The sear faggot blazes bright,
Spirit of a winter's night;
When the soundless earth is muffled,
And the caked snow is shuffled   20
From the ploughboy's heavy shoon;
When the Night doth meet the Noon
In a dark conspiracy
To banish Even from her sky.
Sit thee there, and send abroad,
With a mind self-overaw'd,
Fancy, high-commission'd:—send her!
She has vassals to attend her:
She will bring, in spite of frost,
Beauties that the earth hath lost;   30

She will bring thee, all together,
All delights of summer weather;
All the buds and bells of May,
From dewy sward or thorny spray;
All the heaped Autumn's wealth,
With a still, mysterious stealth:
She will mix these pleasures up
Like three fit wines in a cup,
And thou shalt quaff it:—thou shalt hear
Distant harvest-carols clear;   40
Rustle of the reaped corn;
Sweet birds antheming the morn:
And, in the same moment—hark!
'Tis the early April lark,
Or the rooks, with busy caw,
Foraging for sticks and straw.
Thou shalt, at one glance, behold
The daisy and the marigold;
White-plum'd lillies, and the first
Hedge-grown primrose that hath burst;   50
Shaded hyacinth, alway
Sapphire queen of the mid-May;
And every leaf, and every flower
Pearled with the self-same shower.
Thou shalt see the field-mouse peep
Meagre from its celled sleep;
And the snake all winter-thin
Cast on sunny bank its skin;
Freckled nest-eggs thou shalt see
Hatching in the hawthorn tree,   60
When the hen-bird's wing doth rest
Quiet on her mossy nest:
Then the hurry and alarm
When the bee-hive casts its swarm;
Acorns ripe down-pattering,
While the autumn breezes sing.

Oh, sweet Fancy! let her loose;
Every thing is spoilt by use:
Where's the cheek that doth not fade,
Too much gaz'd at? Where's the maid   70
Whose lip mature is ever new?
Where's the eye, however blue,
Doth not weary? Where's the face
One would meet in every place?
Where's the voice, however soft,
One would hear so very oft?

At a touch sweet Pleasure melteth
Like to bubbles when rain pelteth.
Let, then, winged Fancy find
Thee a mistress to thy mind: 80
Dulcet-eyed as Ceres' daughter,
Ere the God of Torment taught her
How to frown and how to chide;
With a waist and with a side
White as Hebe's, when her zone
Slipt its golden clasp, and down
Fell her kirtle to her feet,
While she held the goblet sweet,
And Jove grew languid.—Break the mesh
Of the Fancy's silken leash;   90
Quickly break her prison-string
And such joys as these she'll bring.—
Let the winged Fancy roam,
Pleasure never is at home.

ODE

[*Written on the blank page before Beaumont and Fletcher's Tragi-
Comedy "The Fair Maid of the Inn."*]

BARDS of Passion and of Mirth,
Ye have left your souls on earth!
Have ye souls in heaven too,
Double lived in regions new?
Yes, and those of heaven commune
With the spheres of sun and moon;
With the noise of fountains wound'rous,
And the parle of voices thund'rous;
With the whisper of heaven's trees
And one another, in soft ease   10

Seated on Elysian lawns
Brows'd by none but Dian's fawns;
Underneath large blue-bells tented,
Where the daisies are rose-scented,
And the rose herself has got
Perfume which on earth is not;
Where the nightingale doth sing
Not a senseless, tranced thing,
But divine melodious truth;
Philosophic numbers smooth;   20
Tales and golden histories
Of heaven and its mysteries.

Thus ye live on high, and then
On the earth ye live again;
And the souls ye left behind you
Teach us, here, the way to find you,
Where your other souls are joying,
Never slumber'd, never cloying.
Here, your earth-born souls still speak
To mortals, of their little week;   30
Of their sorrows and delights;
Of their passions and their spites;
Of their glory and their shame;
What doth strengthen and what maim.
Thus ye teach us, every day,
Wisdom, though fled far away.

Bards of Passion and of Mirth,
Ye have left your souls on earth!
Ye have souls in heaven too,
Double-lived in regions new!   40

LINES ON THE MERMAID TAVERN

Souls of Poets dead and gone,
What Elysium have ye known,
Happy field or mossy cavern,
Choicer than the Mermaid Tavern?
Have ye tippled drink more fine
Than mine host's Canary wine?
Or are fruits of Paradise
Sweeter than those dainty pies
Of venison? O generous food!
Drest as though bold Robin Hood   10
Would, with his maid Marian,
Sup and bowse from horn and can.

I have heard that on a day
Mine host's sign-board flew away,
Nobody knew whither, till
An astrologer's old quill
To a sheepskin gave the story,
Said he saw you in your glory,
Underneath a new old sign
Sipping beverage divine,   20
And pledging with contented smack
The Mermaid in the Zodiac.

Souls of Poets dead and gone,
What Elysium have ye known,
Happy field or mossy cavern,
Choicer than the Mermaid Tavern?

ROBIN HOOD

TO A FRIEND

No! those days are gone away,
And their hours are old and gray,
And their minutes buried all
Under the down-trodden pall
Of the leaves of many years:
Many times have winter's shears,
Frozen North, and chilling East,
Sounded tempests to the feast
Of the forest's whispering fleeces,
Since men knew nor rent nor leases.   10

  No, the bugle sounds no more,
And the twanging bow no more;
Silent is the ivory shrill
Past the heath and up the hill;
There is no mid-forest laugh,
Where lone Echo gives the half
To some wight, amaz'd to hear
Jesting, deep in forest drear.

  On the fairest time of June
You may go, with sun or moon,   20
Or the seven stars to light you,
Or the polar ray to right you;
But you never may behold
Little John, or Robin bold;
Never one, of all the clan,
Thrumming on an empty can
Some old hunting ditty, while
He doth his green way beguile
To fair hostess Merriment,
Down beside the pasture Trent;   30
For he left the merry tale
Messenger for spicy ale.

Gone, the merry morris din;
Gone, the song of Gamelyn;
Gone, the tough-belted outlaw
Idling in the "grenè shawe";
All are gone away and past!
And if Robin should be cast
Sudden from his turfed grave,
And if Marian should have   40
Once again her forest days,
She would weep, and he would craze:
He would swear, for all his oaks,
Fall'n beneath the dockyard strokes,
Have rotted on the briny seas;
She would weep that her wild bees
Sang not to her—strange! that honey
Can't be got without hard money!

So it is: yet let us sing,
Honour to the old bow-string!   50
Honour to the bugle-horn!
Honour to the woods unshorn!
Honour to the Lincoln green!
Honour to the archer keen!
Honour to tight little John,
And the horse he rode upon!
Honour to bold Robin Hood,
Sleeping in the underwood!
Honour to maid Marian,
And to all the Sherwood-clan!   60
Though their days have hurried by
Let us two a burden try.

TO AUTUMN

I

SEASON of mists and mellow fruitfulness,
    Close bosom-friend of the maturing sun;
Conspiring with him how to load and bless
    With fruit the vines that round the thatch-eves run;
To bend with apples the moss'd cottage-trees,
    And fill all fruit with ripeness to the core;
        To swell the gourd, and plump the hazel shells
    With a sweet kernel; to set budding more,
And still more, later flowers for the bees,
Until they think warm days will never cease,
        For Summer has o'er-brimm'd their clammy cells.

II

Who hath not seen thee oft amid thy store?
　Sometimes whoever seeks abroad may find
Thee sitting careless on a granary floor,
　Thy hair soft-lifted by the winnowing wind;
Or on a half-reap'd furrow sound asleep,
　Drows'd with the fume of poppies, while thy hook
　　Spares the next swath and all its twined flowers:
And sometimes like a gleaner thou dost keep
　Steady thy laden head across a brook;
　Or by a cyder-press, with patient look,
　　Thou watchest the last oozings hours by hours.

III

Where are the songs of Spring? Ay, where are they?
　Think not of them, thou hast thy music too,—
While barred clouds bloom the soft-dying day,
　And touch the stubble-plains with rosy hue;
Then in a wailful choir the small gnats mourn
　Among the river sallows, borne aloft
　　Or sinking as the light wind lives or dies;
And full-grown lambs loud bleat from hilly bourn;
　Hedge-crickets sing; and now with treble soft
　The red-breast whistles from a garden-croft;
　　And gathering swallows twitter in the skies.

ODE ON MELANCHOLY

I

No, no, go not to Lethe, neither twist
　Wolf's bane, tight-rooted, for its poisonous wine;
Nor suffer thy pale forehead to be kiss'd
　By nightshade, ruby grape of Proserpine;
Make not your rosary of yew-berries,
　Nor let the beetle, nor the death-moth be
　　Your mournful Psyche, nor the downy owl
A partner in your sorrow's mysteries;
　For shade to shade will come too drowsily,
　And drown the wakeful anguish of the soul.

II

But when the melancholy fit shall fall
　Sudden from heaven like a weeping cloud,
That fosters the droop-headed flowers all,
　And hides the green hill in an April shroud;

Then glut thy sorrow on a morning rose,
   Or on the rainbow of the salt sand-wave,
   Or on the wealth of globed peonies;
Or if thy mistress some rich anger shows,
   Emprison her soft hand, and let her rave,
    And feed deep, deep upon her peerless eyes.

III

She dwells with Beauty—Beauty that must die;
   And Joy, whose hand is ever at his lips
Bidding adieu; and aching Pleasure nigh,
   Turning to Poison while the bee-mouth sips:
Ay, in the very temple of delight
   Veil'd Melancholy has her sovran shrine,
    Though seen of none save him whose strenuous tongue
   Can burst Joy's grape against his palate fine;
His soul shall taste the sadness of her might,
    And be among her cloudy trophies hung.

HYPERION

A FRAGMENT

BOOK I

DEEP in the shady sadness of a vale
Far sunken from the healthy breath of morn,
Far from the fiery noon, and eve's one star,
Sat gray-hair'd Saturn, quiet as a stone,
Still as the silence round about his lair;
Forest on forest hung about his head
Like cloud on cloud. No stir of air was there,
Not so much life as on a summer's day
Robs not one light seed from the feather'd grass,
But where the dead leaf fell, there did it rest.   10
A stream went voiceless by, still deadened more
By reason of his fallen divinity
Spreading a shade: the Naiad 'mid her reeds
Press'd her cold finger closer to her lips.

Along the margin-sand large foot-marks went,
No further than to where his feet had stray'd,
And slept there since. Upon the sodden ground
His old right hand lay nerveless, listless, dead,
Unsceptred; and his realmless eyes were closed;
While his bow'd head seem'd list'ning to the Earth,
His ancient mother, for some comfort yet.   •   21

It seem'd no force could wake him from his place;
But there came one, who with a kindred hand
Touch'd his wide shoulders, after bending low
With reverence, though to one who knew it not.
She was a Goddess of the infant world;
By her in stature the tall Amazon
Had stood a pigmy's height: she would have ta'en
Achilles by the hair and bent his neck;
Or with a finger stay'd Ixion's wheel.   30
Her face was large as that of Memphian sphinx,
Pedestal'd haply in a palace court,
When sages look'd to Egypt for their lore.

But oh! how unlike marble was that face:
How beautiful, if sorow had not made
Sorrow more beautiful than Beauty's self.
There was a listening fear in her regard,
As if calamity had but begun;
As if the vanward clouds of evil days
Had spent their malice, and the sullen rear   40
Was with its stored thunder labouring up.
One hand she press'd upon that aching spot
Where beats the human heart, as if just there,
Though an immortal, she felt cruel pain:
The other upon Saturn's bended neck
She laid, and to the level of his ear
Leaning with parted lips, some words she spake
In solemn tenour and deep organ tone:
Some mourning words which in our feeble tongue
Would come in these like accents; O how frail   50
To that large utterance of the early Gods!
"Saturn, look up!—though wherefore, poor old King?
"I have no comfort for thee, no not one:
"I cannot say, 'O wherefore sleepest thou?'
"For heaven is parted from thee, and the earth
"Knows thee not, thus afflicted, for a God;
"And ocean too, with all its solemn noise,
"Has from thy sceptre pass'd; and all the air
"Is emptied of thine hoary majesty.
"Thy thunder, conscious of the new command,   60
"Rumbles reluctant o'er our fallen house;
"And thy sharp lightning in unpractis'd hands
"Scorches and burns our once serene domain.
"O aching time! O moments big as years!
"All as ye pass swell out the monstrous truth,
"And press it so upon our weary griefs
"That unbelief has not a space to breathe.
"Saturn, sleep on:—O thoughtless, why did I
"Thus violate thy slumbrous solitude?
"Why should I ope thy melancholy eyes?   70
"Saturn, sleep on! while at thy feet I weep."

    As when, upon a tranced summer-night,
Those green-rob'd senators of mighty woods,
Tall oaks, branch-charmed by the earnest stars,
Dream, and so dream all night without a stir,
Save from one gradual solitary gust
Which comes upon the silence, and dies off,
As if the ebbing air had but one wave;
So came these words and went; the while in tears

She touch'd her fair large forehead to the ground,
Just where her falling hair might be outspread   81
A soft and silken mat for Saturn's feet.
One moon, with alteration slow, had shed
Her silver seasons four upon the night,
And still these two were postured motionless,
Like natural sculpture in cathedral cavern;
The frozen God still couchant on the earth,
And the sad Goddess weeping at his feet:
Until at length old Saturn lifted up
His faded eyes, and saw his kingdom gone,   90
And all the gloom and sorrow of the place,
And that fair kneeling Goddess; and then spake,
As with a palsied tongue, and while his beard
Shook horrid with such aspen-malady:
"O tender spouse of gold Hyperion,
"Thea, I feel thee ere I see thy face;
"Look up, and let me see our doom in it;
"Look up, and tell me if this feeble shape
"Is Saturn's; tell me, if thou hear'st the voice
"Of Saturn; tell me, if this wrinkling brow,   100
"Naked and bare of its great diadem,
"Peers like the front of Saturn. Who had power
"To make me desolate? whence came the strength?
"How was it nurtur'd to such bursting forth,
"While Fate seem'd strangled in my nervous grasp?
"But it is so; and I am smother'd up,
"And buried from all godlike exercise
"Of influence benign on planets pale,
"Of admonitions to the winds and seas,
"Of peaceful sway above man's harvesting,   110
"And all those acts which Deity supreme
"Doth ease its heart of love in.—I am gone
"Away from my own bosom: I have left
"My strong identity, my real self,
"Somewhere between the throne, and where I sit
"Here on this spot of earth. Search, Thea, search!
"Open thine eyes eterne, and sphere them round
"Upon all space: space starr'd, and lorn of light;
"Space, region'd with life-air; and barren void;
"Spaces of fire, and all the yawn of hell.—   120
"Search, Thea, search! and tell me, if thou seest
"A certain shape or shadow, making way
"With wings or chariot fierce to repossess
"A heaven he lost erewhile: it must—it must
"Be of ripe progress—Saturn must be King.
"Yes, there must be a golden victory;

"There must be Gods thrown down, and trumpets blown
"Of triumph calm, and hymns of festival
"Upon the gold clouds metropolitan,
"Voices of soft proclaim, and silver stir   130
"Of strings in hollow shells; and there shall be
"Beautiful things made new, for the surprise
"Of the sky-children; I will give command:
"Thea! Thea! Thea! where is Saturn?"

    This passion lifted him upon his feet,
And made his hands to struggle in the air,
His Druid locks to shake and ooze with sweat,
His eyes to fever out, his voice to cease.
He stood, and heard not Thea's sobbing deep;
A little time, and then again he snatch'd   140
Utterance thus.—"But cannot I create?
"Cannot I form? Cannot I fashion forth
"Another world, another universe,
"To overbear and crumble this to naught?
"Where is another chaos? Where?"—That word
Found way unto Olympus, and made quake
The rebel three.—Thea was startled up,
And in her bearing was a sort of hope,
As thus she quick-voic'd spake, yet full of awe.
"This cheers our fallen house: come to our friends,   150
"O Saturn! come away, and give them heart;
"I know the covert, for thence came I hither."
Thus brief; then with beseeching eyes she went
With backward footing through the shade a space:
He follow'd, and she turn'd to lead the way
Through aged boughs, that yielded like the mist
Which eagles cleave upmounting from their nest.

    Meanwhile in other realms big tears were shed,
More sorrow like to this, and such like woe,
Too huge for mortal tongue or pen of scribe: 160
The Titans fierce, self-hid, or prison-bound,
Groan'd for the old allegiance once more,
And listen'd in sharp pain for Saturn's voice.
But one of the whole mammoth-brood still kept
His sov'reignty, and rule, and majesty;—
Blazing Hyperion on his orbed fire
Still sat, still snuff'd the incense, teeming up
From man to the sun's God; yet unsecure:
For as among us mortals omens drear
Fright and perplex, so also shuddered he—   170
Not at dog's howl, or gloom-bird's hated screech,

Or the familiar visiting of one
Upon the first toll of his passing-bell,
Or prophesyings of the midnight lamp;
But horrors, portion'd to a giant nerve,
Oft made Hyperion ache. His palace bright
Bastion'd with pyramids of glowing gold,
And touch'd with shade of bronzed obelisks,
Glar'd a blood-red through all its thousand courts,
Arches, and domes, and fiery galleries;   180
And all its curtains of Aurorian clouds
Flush'd angerly: while sometimes eagles' wings,
Unseen before by Gods or wondering men,
Darken'd the place; and neighing steeds were heard,
Not heard before by Gods or wondering men.
Also, when he would taste the spicy wreaths
Of incense, breath'd aloft from sacred hills,
Instead of sweets, his ample palate took
Savour of poisonous brass and metal sick:
And so, when harbour'd in the sleepy west,   190
After the full completion of fair day,—
For rest divine upon exalted couch
And slumber in the arms of melody,
He pac'd away the pleasant hours of ease
With stride colossal, on from hall to hall;
While far within each aisle and deep recess,
His winged minions in close clusters stood,
Amaz'd and full of fear; like anxious men
Who on wide plains gather in panting troops,
When earthquakes jar their battlements and towers.   200
Even now, while Saturn, rous'd from icy trance,
Went step for step with Thea through the woods,
Hyperion, leaving twilight in the rear,
Came slope upon the threshold of the west;
Then, as was wont, his palace-door flew ope
In smoothest silence, save what solemn tubes,
Blown by the serious Zephyrs, gave of sweet
And wandering sounds, slow-breathed melodies;
And like a rose in vermeil tint and shape,
In fragrance soft, and coolness to the eye,   210
That inlet to severe magnificence
Stood full blown, for the God to enter in.

He enter'd, but he enter'd full of wrath;
His flaming robes stream'd out beyond his heels,
And gave a roar, as if of earthly fire,
That scar'd away the meek ethereal Hours
And made their dove-wings tremble. On he flared,

From stately nave to nave, from vault to vault,
Through bowers of fragrant and enwreathed light,
And diamond-paved lustrous long arcades,   220
Until he reach'd the great main cupola;
There standing fierce beneath, he stamped his foot,
And from the basements deep to the high towers
Jarr'd his own golden region; and before
The quavering thunder thereupon had ceas'd,
His voice leapt out, despite of godlike curb,
To this result: "O dreams of day and night!
"O monstrous forms! O effigies of pain!
"O spectres busy in a cold, cold gloom!
"O lank-ear'd Phantoms of black-weeded pools!   230
"Why do I know ye? why have I seen ye? why
"Is my eternal essence thus distraught
"To see and to behold these horrors new?
"Saturn is fallen, am I too to fall?
"Am I to leave this haven of my rest,
"This cradle of my glory, this soft clime,
"This calm luxuriance of blissful light,
"These crystalline pavilions, and pure fanes,
"Of all my lucent empire? It is left
"Deserted, void, nor any haunt of mine.   240
"The blaze, the splendour, and the symmetry,
"I cannot see—but darkness, death and darkness.
"Even here, into my centre of repose,
"The shady visions come to domineer,
"Insult, and blind, and stifle up my pomp.—
"Fall!—No, by Tellus and her briny robes!
"Over the fiery frontier of my realms
"I will advance a terrible right arm
"Shall scare that infant thunderer, rebel Jove,
"And bid old Saturn take his throne again."—   250
He spake, and ceas'd, the while a heavier threat
Held struggle with his throat but came not forth;
For as in theatres of crowded men
Hubbub increases more they call out "Hush!"
So at Hyperion's words the Phantoms pale
Bestirr'd themselves, thrice horrible and cold;
And from the mirror'd level where he stood
A mist arose, as from a scummy marsh.
At this, through all his bulk an agony
Crept gradual, from the feet unto the crown,   260
Like a lithe serpent vast and muscular
Making slow way, with head and neck convuls'd
From over-strained might. Releas'd, he fled
To the eastern gates, and full six dewy hours

Before the dawn in season due should blush,
He breath'd fierce breath against the sleepy portals,
Clear'd them of heavy vapours, burst them wide
Suddenly on the ocean's chilly streams.
The planet orb of fire, whereon he rode
Each day from east to west the heavens through,   270
Spun round in sable curtaining of clouds;
Not therefore veiled quite, blindfold, and hid,
But ever and anon the glancing spheres,
Circles, and arcs, and broad-belting colure,
Glow'd through, and wrought upon the muffling dark
Sweet-shaped lightnings from the nadir deep
Up to the zenith,—hieroglyphics old
Which sages and keen-eyed astrologers
Then living on the earth, with labouring thought
Won from the gaze of many centuries: 280
Now lost, save what we find on remnants huge
Of stone, or marble swart; their import gone,
Their wisdom long since fled.—Two wings this orb
Possess'd for glory, two fair argent wings,
Ever exalted at the God's approach:
And now, from forth the gloom their plumes immense
Rose, one by one, till all outspreaded were;
While still the dazzling globe maintain'd eclipse,
Awaiting for Hyperion's command.
Fain would he have commanded, fain took throne   290
And bid the day begin, if but for change.
He might not:—No, though a primeval God:
The sacred seasons might not be disturb'd.
Therefore the operations of the dawn
Stay'd in their birth, even as here 'tis told.
Those silver wings expanded sisterly,
Eager to sail their orb; the porches wide
Open'd upon the dusk demesnes of night;
And the bright Titan, phrenzied with new woes,
Unus'd to bend, by hard compulsion bent   300
His spirit to the sorrow of the time;
And all along a dismal rack of clouds,
Upon the boundaries of day and night,
He stretch'd himself in grief and radiance faint.
There as he lay, the Heaven with its stars
Look'd down on him with pity, and the voice
Of Cœlus, from the universal space,
Thus whisper'd low and solemn in his ear.
"O brightest of my children dear, earth-born
"And sky-engendered, Son of Mysteries   310
"All unrevealed even to the powers

"Which met at thy creating; at whose joys
"And palpitations sweet, and pleasures soft,
"I, Cœlus, wonder, how they came and whence;
"And at the fruits thereof what shapes they be,
"Distinct, and visible; symbols divine,
"Manifestations of that beauteous life
"Diffus'd unseen throughout eternal space:
"Of these new-form'd art thou, oh brightest child!
"Of these, thy brethren and the Goddesses!   320
"There is sad feud among ye, and rebellion
"Of son against his sire. I saw him fall,
"I saw my first-born tumbled from his throne!
"To me his arms were spread, to me his voice
"Found way from forth the thunders round his head!
"Pale wox I, and in vapours hid my face.
"Art thou, too, near such doom? vague fear there is:
"For I have seen my sons most unlike Gods.
"Divine ye were created, and divine
"In sad demeanour, solemn, undisturb'd,   330
"Unruffled, like high Gods, ye liv'd and ruled:
"Now I behold in you fear, hope, and wrath;
"Actions of rage and passion; even as
"I see them, on the mortal world beneath,
"In men who die.—This is the grief, O Son!
"Sad sign of ruin, sudden dismay, and fall!
"Yet do thou strive; as thou art capable,
"As thou canst move about, an evident God;
"And canst oppose to each malignant hour
"Ethereal presence:—I am but a voice;   340
"My life is but the life of winds and tides,
"No more than winds and tides can I avail:—
"But thou canst.—Be thou therefore in the van
"Of circumstance; yea, seize the arrow's barb
"Before the tense string murmur.—To the earth!
"For there thou wilt find Saturn, and his woes.
"Meantime I will keep watch on thy bright sun,
"And of thy seasons be a careful nurse."—
Ere half this region-whisper had come down,
Hyperion arose, and on the stars   350
Lifted his curved lids, and kept them wide
Until it ceased; and still he kept them wide:
And still they were the same bright, patient stars.
Then with a slow incline of his broad breast,
Like to a diver in the pearly seas,
Forward he stoop'd over the airy shore,
And plung'd all noiseless into the deep night.

HYPERION. BOOK II

Just at the self-same beat of Time's wide wings
Hyperion slid into the rustled air,
And Saturn gain'd with Thea that sad place
Where Cybele and the bruised Titans mourn'd.
It was a den where no insulting light
Could glimmer on their tears; where their own groans
They felt, but heard not, for the solid roar
Of thunderous waterfalls and torrents hoarse,
Pouring a constant bulk, uncertain where.
Crag jutting forth to crag, and rocks that seem'd　　　10
Ever as if just rising from a sleep,
Forehead to forehead held their monstrous horns;
And thus in thousand hugest phantasies
Made a fit roofing to this nest of woe.
Instead of thrones, hard flint they sat upon,
Couches of rugged stone, and slaty ridge
Stubborn'd with iron. All were not assembled:
Some chain'd in torture, and some wandering.
Cœus, and Gyges, and Briareüs,
Typhon, and Dolor, and Porphyrion,　　　20
With many more, the brawniest in assault,
Were pent in regions of laborious breath;
Dungeon'd in opaque element, to keep
Their clenched teeth still clench'd, and all their limbs
Lock'd up like veins of metal, crampt and screw'd;
Without a motion, save of their big hearts
Heaving in pain, and horribly convuls'd
With sanguine feverous boiling gurge of pulse,
Mnemosyne was straying in the world;
Far from her moon had Phœbe wandered;　　　30
And many else were free to roam abroad,
But for the main, here found they covert drear.
Scarce images of life, one here, one there,
Lay vast and edgeways; like a dismal cirque
Of Druid stones, upon a forlorn moor,
When the chill rain begins at shut of eve,
In dull November, and their chancel vault,
The Heaven itself, is blinded throughout night.
Each one kept shroud, nor to his neighbour gave
Or word, or look, or action of despair.　　　40
Creüs was one; his ponderous iron mace
Lay by him, and a shatter'd rib of rock
Told of his rage, ere he thus sank and pined.
Iäpetus another; in his grasp,

A serpent's plashy neck; its barbed tongue
Squeez'd from the gorge, and all its uncurl'd length
Dead; and because the creature could not spit
Its poison in the eyes of conquering Jove.
Next Cottus: prone he lay, chin uppermost,
As though in pain; for still upon the flint   50
He ground severe his skull, with open mouth
And eyes at horrid working. Nearest him
Asia, born of most enormous Caf,
Who cost her mother Tellus keener pangs,
Though feminine, than any of her sons:
More thought than woe was in her dusky face,
For she was prophesying of her glory;
And in her wide imagination stood
Palm-shaded temples, and high rival fanes,
By Oxus or in Ganges' sacred isles.   60
Even as Hope upon her anchor leans,
So leant she, not so fair, upon a tusk
Shed from the broadest of her elephants.
Above her, on a crag's uneasy shelve,
Upon his elbow rais'd, all prostrate else,
Shadow'd Enceladus; once tame and mild
As grazing ox unworried in the meads;
Now tiger-passion'd, lion-thoughted, wroth,
He meditated, plotted, and even now
Was hurling mountains in that second war,   70
Not long delay'd, that scar'd the younger Gods
To hide themselves in forms of beast and bird.
Not far hence Atlas; and beside him prone
Phorcus, the sire of Gorgons. Neighbour'd close
Oceanus, and Tethys, in whose lap
Sobb'd Clymene among her tangled hair.
In midst of all lay Themis, at the feet
Of Ops the queen all clouded round from sight;
No shape distinguishable, more than when
Thick night confounds the pine-tops with the clouds:
And many else whose names may not be told.   81
For when the Muse's wings are air-ward spread,
Who shall delay her flight? And she must chaunt
Of Saturn, and his guide, who now had climb'd
With damp and slippery footing from a depth
More horrid still. Above a sombre cliff
Their heads appear'd, and up their stature grew
Till on the level height their steps found ease:
Then Thea spread abroad her trembling arms
Upon the precincts of this nest of pain,   90
And sidelong fix'd her eye on Saturn's face:

There saw she direst strife; the supreme God
At war with all the frailty of grief,
Of rage, of fear, anxiety, revenge,
Remorse, spleen, hope, but most of all despair.
Against these plagues he strove in vain; for Fate
Had pour'd a mortal oil upon his head,
A disanointing poison: so that Thea,
Affrighted, kept her still, and let him pass
First onwards in, among the fallen tribe.   100

    As with us mortal men, the laden heart
Is persecuted more, and fever'd more,
When it is nighing to the mournful house
Where other hearts are sick of the same bruise;
So Saturn, as he walk'd into the midst,
Felt faint, and would have sunk among the rest,
But that he met Enceladus's eye,
Whose mightiness, and awe of him, at once
Came like an inspiration; and he shouted,
"Titans, behold your God!" at which some groan'd;
Some started on their feet; some also shouted;   111
Some wept, some wail'd, all bow'd with reverence:
And Ops, uplifting her black folded veil,
Show'd her pale cheeks, and all her forehead wan,
Her eye-brows thin and jet, and hollow eyes.
There is a roaring in the bleak-grown pines
When Winter lifts his voice; there is a noise
Among immortals when a God gives sign,
With hushing finger, how he means to load
His tongue with the full weight of utterless thought,
With thunder, and with music, and with pomp: 121
Such noise is like the roar of bleak-grown pines:
Which, when it ceases in this mountain'd world,
No other sound succeeds; but ceasing here,
Among these fallen, Saturn's voice therefrom
Grew up like organ, that begins anew
Its strain, when other harmonies, stopt short,
Leave the dinn'd air vibrating silverly.
Thus grew it up—"Not in my own sad breast,
"Which is its own great judge and searcher out,
"Can I find reason why ye should be thus: 131
"Not in the legends of the first of days,
"Studied from that old spirit-leaved book
"Which starry Uranus with finger bright
"Sav'd from the shores of darkness, when the waves
"Low-ebb'd still hid it up in shallow gloom;—
"And the which book ye know I ever kept

"For my firm-based footstool:—Ah, infirm!
"Not there, nor in sign, symbol, or portent
"Of element, earth, water, air, and fire,—   140
"At war, at peace, or inter-quarreling
"One against one, or two, or three, or all
"Each several one against the other three,
"As fire with air loud warring when rain-floods
"Drown both, and press them both against earth's face,
"Where, finding sulphur, a quadruple wrath
"Unhinges the poor world;—not in that strife,
"Wherefrom I take strange lore, and read it deep,
"Can I find reason why ye should be thus:
"No, no-where can unriddle, though I search,   150
"And pore on Nature's universal scroll
"Even to swooning, why ye, Divinities,
"The first-born of all shap'd and palpable Gods,
"Should cower beneath what, in comparison,
"Is untremendous might. Yet ye are here,
"O'erwhelm'd, and spurn'd, and batter'd, ye are here!
"O Titans, shall I say, 'Arise!'—Ye groan:
"Shall I say 'Crouch!'—Ye groan. What can I then?
"O Heaven wide! O unseen parent dear!
"What can I? Tell me, all ye brethren Gods,   160
"How we can war, how engine our great wrath!
"O speak your counsel now, for Saturn's ear
"Is all a-hunger'd. Thou, Oceanus,
"Ponderest high and deep; and in thy face
"I see, astonied, that severe content
"Which comes of thought and musing: give us help!"

   So ended Saturn; and the God of the Sea,
Sophist and sage, from no Athenian grove,
But cogitation in his watery shades,
Arose, with locks not oozy, and began,   170
In murmurs, which his first-endeavouring tongue
Caught infant-like from the far-foamed sands.
"O ye, whom wrath consumes! who, passion-strung,
"Writhe at defeat, and nurse your agonies!
"Shut up your senses, stifle up your ears,
"My voice is not a bellows unto ire.
"Yet listen, ye who will, whilst I bring proof
"How ye, perforce, must be content to stoop:
"And in the proof much comfort will I give,
"If ye will take that comfort in its truth.   180
"We fall by course of Nature's law, not force
"Of thunder, or of Jove. Great Saturn, thou
"Hast sifted well the atom-universe;

"But for this reason, that thou art the King,
"And only blind from sheer supremacy,
"One avenue was shaded from thine eyes,
"Through which I wandered to eternal truth.
"And first, as thou wast not the first of powers,
"So art thou not the last; it cannot be:
"Thou art not the beginning nor the end.   190
"From chaos and parental darkness came
"Light, the first fruits of that intestine broil,
"That sullen ferment, which for wondrous ends
"Was ripening in itself. The ripe hour came,
"And with it light, and light, engendering
"Upon its own producer, forthwith touch'd
"The whole enormous matter into life.
"Upon that very hour, our parentage,
"The Heavens and the Earth, were manifest:
"Then thou first born, and we the giant race,   200
"Found ourselves ruling new and beauteous realms.
"Now comes the pain of truth, to whom 'tis pain;
"O folly! for to bear all naked truths,
"And to envisage circumstance, all calm,
"That is the top of sovereignty. Mark well!
"As Heaven and Earth are fairer, fairer far
"Than Chaos and blank Darkness, though once chiefs;
"And as we show beyond that Heaven and Earth
"In form and shape compact and beautiful,
"In will, in action free, companionship,   210
"And thousand other signs of purer life;
"So on our heels a fresh perfection treads,
"A power more strong in beauty, born of us
"And fated to excel us, as we pass
"In glory that old Darkness: nor are we
"Thereby more conquer'd, than by us the rule
"Of shapeless Chaos. Say, doth the dull soil
"Quarrel with the proud forests it hath fed,
"And feedeth still, more comely than itself?
"Can it deny the chiefdom of green groves?   220
"Or shall the tree be envious of the dove
"Because it cooeth, and hath snowy wings
"To wander wherewithal and find its joys?
"We are such forest-trees, and our fair boughs
"Have bred forth, not pale solitary doves,
"But eagles golden-feather'd, who do tower
"Above us in their beauty, and must reign
"In right thereof; for 'tis the eternal law
"That first in beauty should be first in might:
"Yea, by that law, another race may drive   230

"Our conquerors to mourn as we do now.
"Have ye beheld the young God of the Seas,
"My dispossessor? Have ye seen his face?
"Have ye beheld his chariot, foam'd along
"By noble winged creatures he hath made?
"I saw him on the calmed waters scud,
"With such a glow of beauty in his eyes,
"That it enforc'd me to bid sad farewell
"To all my empire: farewell sad I took,
"And hither came, to see how dolorous fate   240
"Had wrought upon ye; and how I might best
"Give consolation in this woe extreme.
"Receive the truth, and let it be your balm."

   Whether through poz'd conviction, or disdain,
They guarded silence, when Oceanus
Left murmuring, what deepest thought can tell?
But so it was, none answer'd for a space.
Save one whom none regarded, Clymene;
And yet she answer'd not, only complain'd,
With hectic lips, and eyes up-looking mild,   250
Thus wording timidly among the fierce:
"O Father, I am here the simplest voice,
"And all my knowledge is that joy is gone,
"And this thing woe crept in among our hearts,
"There to remain for ever, as I fear:
"I would not bode of evil, if I thought
"So weak a creature could turn off the help
"Which by just right should come of mighty Gods;
"Yet let me tell my sorrow, let me tell
"Of what I heard, and how it made me weep,   260
"And know that we had parted from all hope.
"I stood upon a shore, a pleasant shore,
"Where a sweet clime was breathed from a land
"Of fragrance, quietness, and trees, and flowers.
"Full of calm joy it was, as I of grief;
"Too full of joy and soft delicious warmth;
"So that I felt a movement in my heart
"To chide, and to reproach that solitude
"With songs of misery, music of our woes;
"And sat me down, and took a mouthed shell   270
"And murmur'd into it, and made melody—
"O melody no more! for while I sang,
"And with poor skill let pass into the breeze
"The dull shell's echo, from a bowery strand
"Just opposite, an island of the sea,
"There came enchantment with the shifting wind,

"That did both drown and keep alive my ears.
"I threw my shell away upon the sand,
"And a wave fill'd it, as my sense was fill'd
"With that new blissful golden melody.   280
"A living death was in each gush of sounds,
"Each family of rapturous hurried notes,
"That fell, one after one, yet all at once,
"Like pearl beads dropping sudden from their string:
"And then another, then another strain,
"Each like a dove leaving its olive perch,
"With music wing'd instead of silent plumes,
"To hover round my head, and make me sick
"Of joy and grief at once. Grief overcame,
"And I was stopping up my frantic ears,   290
"When, past all hindrance of my trembling hands,
"A voice came sweeter, sweeter than all tune,
"And still it cried, 'Apollo! young Apollo!
" 'The morning-bright Apollo! young Apollo!'
"I fled, it follow'd me, and cried 'Apollo!'
"O Father, and O Brethren, had ye felt
"Those pains of mine; O Saturn, hadst thou felt,
"Ye would not call this too indulged tongue
"Presumptuous, in thus venturing to be heard."

        So far her voice flow'd on, like timorous brook   300
That, lingering along a pebbled coast,
Doth fear to meet the sea: but sea it met,
And shudder'd; for the overwhelming voice
Of huge Enceladus swallow'd it in wrath:
The ponderous syllables, like sullen waves
In the half-glutted hollows of reef-rocks,
Came booming thus, while still upon his arm
He lean'd; not rising, from supreme contempt.
"Or shall we listen to the over-wise,
"Or to the over-foolish, Giant-Gods?   310
"Not thunderbolt on thunderbolt, till all
"That rebel Jove's whole armoury were spent,
"Not world on world upon these shoulders piled,
"Could agonize me more than baby-words
"In midst of this dethronement horrible.
"Speak! roar! shout! yell! ye sleepy Titans all.
"Do ye forget the blows, the buffets vile?
"Are ye not smitten by a youngling arm?
"Dost thou forget, sham Monarch of the Waves,
"Thy scalding in the seas? What, have I rous'd   320
"Your spleens with so few simple words as these?
"O joy! for now I see ye are not lost:

"O joy! for now I see a thousand eyes
"Wide-glaring for revenge!"—As this he said,
He lifted up his stature vast, and stood,
Still without intermission speaking thus:
"Now ye are flames, I'll tell you how to burn,
"And purge the ether of our enemies;
"How to feed fierce the crooked stings of fire,
"And singe away the swollen clouds of Jove,   330
"Stifling that puny essence in its tent.
"O let him feel the evil he hath done;
"For though I scorn Oceanus's lore,
"Much pain have I for more than loss of realms:
"The days of peace and slumberous calm are fled;
"Those days, all innocent of scathing war,
"When all the fair Existences of heaven
"Came open-eyed to guess what we would speak:—
"That was before our brows were taught to frown,
"Before our lips knew else but solemn sounds;   340
"That was before we knew the winged thing,
"Victory, might be lost, or might be won.
"And be ye mindful that Hyperion,
"Our brightest brother, still is undisgraced—
"Hyperion, lo! his radiance is here!"

    All eyes were on Enceladus's face,
And they beheld, while still Hyperion's name
Flew from his lips up to the vaulted rocks,
A pallid gleam across his features stern:
Not savage, for he saw full many a God   350
Wroth as himself. He look'd upon them all,
And in each face he saw a gleam of light,
But splendider in Saturn's, whose hoar locks
Shone like the bubbling foam about a keel
When the prow sweeps into a midnight cove.
In pale and silver silence they remain'd,
Till suddenly a splendour, like the morn,
Pervaded all the beetling gloomy steeps,
All the sad spaces of oblivion,
And every gulf, and every chasm old,   360
And every height, and every sullen depth,
Voiceless, or hoarse with loud tormented streams:
And all the everlasting cataracts,
And all the headlong torrents far and near,
Mantled before in darkness and huge shade,
Now saw the light and made it terrible.
It was Hyperion:—a granite peak
His bright feet touch'd, and there he stay'd to view

The misery his brilliance had betray'd
To the most hateful seeing of itself.   370
Golden his hair of short Numidian curl,
Regal his shape majestic, a vast shade
In midst of his own brightness, like the bulk
Of Memnon's image at the set of sun
To one who travels from the dusking East:
Sighs, too, as mournful as that Memnon's harp
He utter'd, while his hands contemplative
He press'd together, and in silence stood.
Despondence seiz'd again the fallen Gods
At sight of the dejected King of Day,   380
And many hid their faces from the light:
But fierce Enceladus sent forth his eyes
Among the brotherhood; and, at their glare,
Uprose Iäpetus, and Creüs, too,
And Phorcus, sea-born, and together strode
To where he towered on his eminence.
There those four shouted forth old Saturn's name;
Hyperion from the peak loud answered, "Saturn!"
Saturn sat near the Mother of the Gods,
In whose face was no joy, though all the Gods   390
Gave from their hollow throats the name of "Saturn!"

HYPERION. BOOK III

THUS in alternate uproar and sad peace,
Amazed were those Titans utterly.
O leave them, Muse! O leave them to their woes;
For thou art weak to sing such tumults dire:
A solitary sorrow best befits
Thy lips, and antheming a lonely grief.
Leave them, O Muse! for thou anon wilt find
Many a fallen old Divinity
Wandering in vain about bewildered shores.
Meantime touch piously the Delphic harp,   10
And not a wind of heaven but will breathe
In aid soft warble from the Dorian flute;
For lo! 'tis for the Father of all verse.
Flush every thing that hath a vermeil hue,
Let the rose glow intense and warm the air,
And let the clouds of even and of morn
Float in voluptuous fleeces o'er the hills;
Let the red wine within the goblet boil,
Cold as a bubbling well; let faint-lipp'd shells,
On sands, or in great deeps, vermilion turn   20
Through all their labyrinths; and let the maid

Blush keenly, as with some warm kiss surpris'd.
Chief isle of the embowered Cyclades,
Rejoice, O Delos, with thine olives green,
And poplars, and lawn-shading palms, and beech,
In which the Zephyr breathes the loudest song,
And hazels thick, dark-stemm'd beneath the shade:
Apollo is once more the golden theme!
Where was he, when the Giant of the Sun
Stood bright, amid the sorrow of his peers?   30
Together had he left his mother fair
And his twin-sister sleeping in their bower,
And in the morning twilight wandered forth
Beside the osiers of a rivulet,
Full ankle-deep in lillies of the vale.
The nightingale had ceas'd, and a few stars
Were lingering in the heavens, while the thrush
Began calm-throated. Throughout all the isle
There was no covert, no retired cave
Unhaunted by the murmurous noise of waves,   40
Though scarcely heard in many a green recess.
He listen'd, and he wept, and his bright tears
Went trickling down the golden bow he held.
Thus with half-shut suffused eyes he stood,
While from beneath some cumbrous boughs hard by
With solemn step an awful Goddess came,
And there was purport in her looks for him,
Which he with eager guess began to read
Perplex'd, the while melodiously he said:
"How cam'st thou over the unfooted sea?   50
"Or hath that antique mien and robed form
"Mov'd in these vales invisible till now?
"Sure I have heard those vestments sweeping o'er
"The fallen leaves, when I have sat alone
"In cool mid-forest. Surely I have traced
"The rustle of those ample skirts about
"These grassy solitudes, and seen the flowers
"Lift up their heads, as still the whisper pass'd.
"Goddess! I have beheld those eyes before,
"And their eternal calm, and all that face,   60
"Or I have dream'd."—"Yes," said the supreme shape,
"Thou hast dream'd of me; and awaking up
"Didst find a lyre all golden by thy side,
"Whose strings touch'd by thy fingers, all the vast
"Unwearied ear of the whole universe
"Listen'd in pain and pleasure at the birth
"Of such new tuneful wonder. Is't not strange
"That thou shouldst weep, so gifted? Tell me, youth,

"What sorrow thou canst feel; for I am sad
"When thou dost shed a tear: explain thy griefs
"To one who in this lonely isle hath been   71
"The watcher of thy sleep and hours of life,
"From the young day when first thy infant hand
"Pluck'd witless the weak flowers, till thine arm
"Could bend that bow heroic to all times.
"Show thy heart's secret to an ancient Power
"Who hath forsaken old and sacred thrones
"For prophecies of thee, and for the sake
"Of loveliness new born."—Apollo then,
With sudden scrutiny and gloomless eyes,   80
Thus answer'd, while his white melodious throat
Throbb'd with the syllables.—"Mnemosyne!
"Thy name is on my tongue, I know not how;
"Why should I tell thee what thou so well seest?
"Why should I strive to show what from thy lips
"Would come no mystery? For me, dark, dark,
"And painful vile oblivion seals my eyes:
"I strive to search wherefore I am so sad,
"Until a melancholy numbs my limbs;
"And then upon the grass I sit, and moan,   90
"Like one who once had wings.—O why should I
"Feel curs'd and thwarted, when the liegeless air
"Yields to my step aspirant? why should I
"Spurn the green turf as hateful to my feet?
"Goddess benign, point forth some unknown thing:
"Are there not other regions than this isle?
"What are the stars? There is the sun, the sun!
"And the most patient brilliance of the moon!
"And stars by thousands! Point me out the way
"To any one particular beauteous star,   100
"And I will flit into it with my lyre,
"And make its silvery splendour pant with bliss.
"I have heard the cloudy thunder: Where is power?
"Whose hand, whose essence, what divinity
"Makes this alarum in the elements,
"While I here idle listen on the shores
"In fearless yet in aching ignorance?
"O tell me, lonely Goddess, by thy harp,
"That waileth every morn and eventide,
"Tell me why thus I rave, about these groves!   110
"Mute thou remainest—mute! yet I can read
"A wondrous lesson in thy silent face:
"Knowledge enormous makes a God of me.
"Names, deeds, grey legends, dire events, rebellions,
"Majesties, sovran voices, agonies,

"Creations and destroyings, all at once
"Pour into the wide hollows of my brain,
"And deify me, as if some blithe wine
"Or bright elixir peerless I had drunk,
"And so become immortal."—Thus the God,   120
While his enkindled eyes, with level glance
Beneath his white soft temples, stedfast kept
Trembling with light upon Mnemosyne.
Soon wild commotions shook him, and made flush
All the immortal fairness of his limbs;
Most like the struggle at the gate of death;
Or liker still to one who should take leave
Of pale immortal death, and with a pang
As hot as death's is chill, with fierce convulse
Die into life: so young Apollo anguish'd: 130
His very hair, his golden tresses famed
Kept undulation round his eager neck.
During the pain Mnemosyne upheld
Her arms as one who prophesied.—At length
Apollo shriek'd;—and lo! from all his limbs
Celestial   *   *   *   *   *   *   *,
*   *   *   *   *   *   *   *   *

THE END

POSTHUMOUS

AND

FUGITIVE POEMS

POSTHUMOUS AND FUGITIVE POEMS

ON DEATH

I

Can death be sleep, when life is but a dream,
  And scenes of bliss pass as a phantom by?
The transient pleasures as a vision seem,
  And yet we think the greatest pain's to die.

II

How strange it is that man on earth should roam,
  And lead a life of woe, but not forsake
His rugged path; nor dare he view alone
  His future doom which is but to awake.

WOMEN, WINE, AND SNUFF

Give me women, wine and snuff
Until I cry out "hold, enough!"
You may do so sans objection
Till the day of resurrection;
For bless my beard they aye shall be
My beloved Trinity.

FILL FOR ME A BRIMMING BOWL

Fill for me a brimming bowl
And let me in it drown my soul:
But put therein some drug, designed
To Banish Women from my mind:
For I want not the stream inspiring
That fills the mind with—fond desiring,
But I want as deep a draught
As e'er from Lethe's wave was quaff'd;
From my despairing heart to charm
The Image of the fairest form   10
That e'er my reveling eyes beheld,
That e'er my wandering fancy spell'd.
In vain! away I cannot chace
The melting softness of that face,

The beaminess of those bright eyes,
That breast—earth's only Paradise.
My sight will never more be blest;
For all I see has lost its zest:
Nor with delight can I explore
The Classic page, or Muse's lore.   20
Had she but known how beat my heart,
And with one smile reliev'd its smart
I should have felt a sweet relief,
I should have felt "the joy of grief."
Yet as the Tuscan mid the snow
Of Lapland thinks on sweet Arno,
Even so for ever shall she be
The Halo of my Memory.
        August, 1814.

SONNET

ON PEACE

O PEACE! and dost thou with thy presence bless
    The dwellings of this war-surrounded Isle;
Soothing with placid brow our late distress,
    Making the triple kingdom brightly smile?
Joyful I hail thy presence; and I hail
    The sweet companions that await on thee;
Complete my joy—let not my first wish fail,
    Let the sweet mountain nymph thy favourite be,
With England's happiness proclaim Europa's Liberty.
O Europe! let not sceptred tyrants see   10
    That thou must shelter in thy former state;
Keep thy chains burst, and boldly say thou art free;
    Give thy kings law—leave not uncurbed the great;
    So with the horrors past thou'lt win thy happier fate!

SONNET TO BYRON

BYRON! how sweetly sad thy melody!
    Attuning still the soul to tenderness,
    As if soft Pity, with unusual stress,
Had touch'd her plaintive lute, and thou, being by,
Hadst caught the tones, nor suffer'd them to die.
    O'ershadowing sorrow doth not make thee less
    Delightful: thou thy griefs dost dress
With a bright halo, shining beamily,
As when a cloud the golden moon doth veil,
    Its sides are ting'd with a resplendent glow,   10

Through the dark robe oft amber rays prevail,
And like fair veins in sable marble flow;
Still warble, dying swan! still tell the tale,
The enchanting tale, the tale of pleasing woe.

SONNET TO CHATTERTON

O Chatterton! how very sad thy fate!
Dear child of sorrow—son of misery!
How soon the film of death obscur'd that eye,
Whence Genius mildly flash'd, and high debate.
How soon that voice, majestic and elate,
Melted in dying numbers! Oh! how nigh
Was night to thy fair morning. Thou didst die
A half-blown flow'ret which cold blasts amate.
But this is past: thou art among the stars
Of highest Heaven: to the rolling spheres   10
Thou sweetly singest: naught thy hymning mars,
Above the ingrate world and human fears.
On earth the good man base detraction bars
From thy fair name, and waters it with tears.

SONNET TO SPENSER

Spenser! a jealous honourer of thine,
A forester deep in thy midmost trees,
Did last eve ask my promise to refine
Some English that might strive thine ear to please.
But Elfin Poet 'tis impossible
For an inhabitant of wintry earth
To rise like Phœbus with a golden quill
Fire-wing'd and make a morning in his mirth.
It is impossible to escape from toil
O' the sudden and receive thy spiriting: 10
The flower must drink the nature of the soil
Before it can put forth its blossoming:
Be with me in the summer days and I
Will for thine honour and his pleasure try.

ODE TO APOLLO

In thy western halls of gold
When thou sittest in thy state,
Bards, that erst sublimely told
Heroic deeds, and sang of fate,
With fervour seize their adamantine lyres,
Whose chords are solid rays, and twinkle radiant fires.

Here Homer with his nervous arms
   Strikes the twanging harp of war,
And even the western splendour warms,
   While the trumpets sound afar: **10**
But, what creates the most intense surprise,
His soul looks out through renovated eyes.

Then, through thy Temple wide, melodious swells
   The sweet majestic tone of Maro's lyre:
The soul delighted on each accent dwells,—
   Enraptur'd dwells,—not daring to respire,
The while he tells of grief around a funeral pyre.

'Tis awful silence then again;
   Expectant stand the spheres;
   Breathless the laurel'd peers,   **20**
Nor move, till ends the lofty strain,
Nor move till Milton's tuneful thunders cease,
And leave once more the ravish'd heavens in peace.

Thou biddest Shakspeare wave his hand,
   And quickly forward spring
The Passions—a terrific band—
   And each vibrates the string
That with its tyrant temper best accords,
While from their Master's lips pour forth the inspiring words.

A silver trumpet Spenser blows,   **30**
   And, as its martial notes to silence flee,
From a virgin chorus flows
   A hymn in praise of spotless Chastity.
'Tis still! Wild warblings from the Æolian lyre
Enchantment softly breathe, and tremblingly expire.

Next thy Tasso's ardent numbers
   Float along the pleased air,
Calling youth from idle slumbers,
   Rousing them from Pleasure's lair:—
Then o'er the strings his fingers gently move,
And melt the soul to pity and to love.   **41**

But when *Thou* joinest with the Nine,
And all the powers of song combine,
   We listen here on earth:
The dying tones that fill the air,
And charm the ear of evening fair,
From thee, great God of Bards, receive their heavenly birth.

SONNET

TO A YOUNG LADY WHO SENT ME A LAUREL CROWN

FRESH morning gusts have blown away all fear
  From my glad bosom,—now from gloominess
  I mount for ever—not an atom less
Than the proud laurel shall content my bier.
No! by the eternal stars! or why sit here
  In the Sun's eye, and 'gainst my temples press
  Apollo's very leaves, woven to bless
By thy white fingers and thy spirit clear.   8
Lo! who dares say, "Do this"? Who dares call down
  My will from its high purpose? Who say, "Stand,"
Or "Go"? This mighty moment I would frown
  On abject Cæsars—not the stoutest band
Of mailed heroes should tear off my crown:
  Yet would I kneel and kiss thy gentle hand!

ON RECEIVING A LAUREL CROWN FROM LEIGH HUNT

MINUTES are flying swiftly, and as yet
  Nothing unearthly has enticed my brain
  Into a delphic Labyrinth—I would fain
Catch an unmortal thought to pay the debt
I owe to the kind Poet who has set
  Upon my ambitious head a glorious gain.
  Two bending laurel Sprigs—'tis nearly pain
To be conscious of such a Coronet.
Still time is fleeting, and no dream arises
  Gorgeous as I would have it—only I see   10
A Trampling down of what the world most prizes
  Turbans and Crowns, and blank regality;
And then I run into most wild surmises
  Of all the many glories that may be.

SONNET

TO THE LADIES WHO SAW ME CROWN'D

WHAT is there in the universal Earth
  More lovely than a Wreath from the bay tree?
  Haply a Halo round the Moon—a glee
Circling from three sweet pair of Lips in Mirth;
And haply you will say the dewy birth
  Of morning Roses—ripplings tenderly
  Spread by the Halcyon's breast upon the Sea—

But these Comparisons are nothing worth—
Then is there nothing in the world so fair?
    The silvery tears of April?—Youth of May?   10
Or June that breathes out life for butterflies?
    No—none of these can from my favourite bear
Away the Palm—yet shall it ever pay
    Due Reverence to your most sovereign eyes.

HYMN TO APOLLO

God of the golden bow,
    And of the golden lyre,
And of the golden hair,
    And of the golden fire,
        Charioteer
        Of the patient year,
    Where—where slept thine ire,
When like a blank idiot I put on thy wreath,
    Thy laurel, thy glory,
    The light of thy story,   10
Or was I a worm—too low crawling, for death?
    O Delphic Apollo!

The Thunderer grasp'd and grasp'd,
    The Thunderer frown'd and frown'd;
The eagle's feathery mane
    For wrath became stiffen'd—the sound
        Of breeding thunder
        Went drowsily under,
    Muttering to be unbound.
O why didst thou pity, and for a worm   20
    Why touch thy soft lute
    Till the thunder was mute,
Why was not I crush'd—such a pitiful germ?
    O Delphic Apollo!

The Pleiades were up,
    Watching the silent air;
The seeds and roots in the Earth
    Were swelling for summer fare;
        The Ocean, its neighbour,
        Was at its old labour,   30
    When, who—who did dare
To tie, like a madman, thy plant round his brow,
    And grin and look proudly,
    And blaspheme so loudly,
And live for that honour, to stoop to thee now?
    O Delphic Apollo!

SONNET

As from the darkening gloom a silver dove
  Upsoars, and darts into the Eastern light,
  On pinions that naught moves but pure delight,
So fled thy soul into the realms above,
Regions of peace and everlasting love;
  Where happy spirits, crown'd with circlets bright
  Of starry beam, and gloriously bedight,
Taste the high joy none but the blest can prove.
There thou or joinest the immortal quire
  In melodies that even Heaven fair   **10**
Fill with superiour bliss, or, at desire
  Of the omnipotent Father, cleavest the air
On holy message sent—What pleasures higher?
  Wherefore does any grief our joy impair?

STANZAS TO MISS WYLIE

O COME Georgiana! the rose is full blown,
The riches of Flora are lavishly strown,
The air is all softness, and crystal the streams,
The West is resplendently clothed in beams.
O come! let us haste to the freshening shades,
The quaintly carv'd seats, and the opening glades;
Where the faeries are chanting their evening hymns,
And in the last sun-beam the sylph lightly swims.
And when thou art weary I'll find thee a bed,
Of mosses and flowers to pillow thy head: **10**
And there Georgiana I'll sit at thy feet,
While my story of love I enraptur'd repeat.
So fondly I'll breathe, and so softly I'll sigh,
Thou wilt think that some amorous Zephyr is nigh:
Yet no—as I breathe I will press thy fair knee,
And then thou wilt know that the sigh comes from me.
Ah! why dearest girl should we lose all these blisses?
That mortal's a fool who such happiness misses:
So smile acquiescence, and give me thy hand,
With love-looking eyes, and with voice sweetly bland.   **20**

SONNET

OH! how I love, on a fair summer's eve,
  When streams of light pour down the golden west,
  And on the balmy zephyrs tranquil rest
The silver clouds, far—far away to leave
All meaner thoughts, and take a sweet reprieve.

From little cares; to find, with easy quest,
  A fragrant wild, with Nature's beauty drest,
And there into delight my soul deceive.
There warm my breast with patriotic lore,
  Musing on Milton's fate—on Sydney's bier—   **10**
    Till their stern forms before my mind arise:
Perhaps on wing of Poesy upsoar,
  Full often dropping a delicious tear,
    When some melodious sorrow spells mine eyes.

SONNET

BEFORE he went to feed with owls and bats
  Nebuchadnezzar had an ugly dream,
  Worse than an Hus'if's when she thinks her cream
Made a Naumachia for mice and rats.
So scared, he sent for that "Good King of Cats"
  Young Daniel, who soon did pluck away the beam
  From out his eye, and said he did not deem
The sceptre worth a straw—his Cushions old door-mats.
A horrid nightmare similar somewhat
  Of late has haunted a most motley crew,   **10**
    Most loggerheads and Chapmen—we are told
That any Daniel tho' he be a sot
  Can make the lying lips turn pale of hue
    By belching out "ye are that head of Gold."

SONNET

WRITTEN IN DISGUST OF VULGAR SUPERSTITION

THE church bells toll a melancholy round,
  Calling the people to some other prayers,
  Some other gloominess, more dreadful cares,
More hearkening to the sermon's horrid sound.
Surely the mind of man is closely bound
  In some black spell; seeing that each one tears
  Himself from fireside joys, and Lydian airs,
And converse high of those with glory crown'd.
Still, still they toll, and I should feel a damp,—
  A chill as from a tomb, did I not know   **10**
That they are dying like an outburnt lamp;
  That 'tis their sighing, wailing ere they go
    Into oblivion;—that fresh flowers will grow,
And many glories of immortal stamp.

SONNET

AFTER dark vapours have oppress'd our plains
 For a long dreary season, comes a day
  Born of the gentle South, and clears away
From the sick heavens all unseemly stains.
The anxious month, relieved of its pains,
 Takes as a long-lost right the feel of May;
 The eyelids with the passing coolness play
Like rose leaves with the drip of Summer rains.
The calmest thoughts come round us; as of leaves
 Budding—fruit ripening in stillness—Autumn suns
Smiling at eve upon the quiet sheaves—   11
Sweet Sappho's cheek—a smiling infant's breath—
 The gradual sand that through an hour-glass runs—
A woodland rivulet—a Poet's death.

SONNET

[Written at the end of "The Floure and the Lefe"]

THIS pleasant tale is like a little copse:
 The honied lines do freshly interlace
 To keep the reader in so sweet a place,
So that he here and there full-hearted stops;
And oftentimes he feels the dewy drops
 Come cool and suddenly against his face,
 And by the wandering melody may trace
Which way the tender-legged linnet hops.
Oh! what a power hath white Simplicity!
 What mighty power has this gentle story!   10
 I that for ever feel athirst for glory
Could at this moment be content to lie
 Meekly upon the grass, as those whose sobbings
 Were heard of none beside the mournful robins.

TWO SONNETS

I

TO HAYDON, WITH A SONNET WRITTEN ON SEEING THE ELGIN MARBLES

HAYDON! forgive me that I cannot speak
 Definitively on these mighty things;
  Forgive me that I have not Eagle's wings—
That what I want I know not where to seek:
And think that I would not be over meek

In rolling out upfollow'd thunderings,
  Even to the steep of Heliconian springs,
Were I of ample strength for such a freak—
Think too, that all those numbers should be thine;
  Whose else? In this who touch thy vesture's hem?
For when men star'd at what was most divine   11
  With browless idiotism—o'erwise phlegm—
Thou hadst beheld the Hesperean shine
  Of their star in the East, and gone to worship them.

II

ON SEEING THE ELGIN MARBLES

MY spirit is too weak—mortality
  Weighs heavily on me like unwilling sleep,
  And each imagin'd pinnacle and steep
Of godlike hardship, tells me I must die
Like a sick Eagle looking at the sky.
  Yet 'tis a gentle luxury to weep
  That I have not the cloudy winds to keep,
Fresh for the opening of the morning's eye.
Such dim-conceived glories of the brain
  Bring round the heart an undescribable feud;
So do these wonders a most dizzy pain,   11
  That mingles Grecian grandeur with the rude
Wasting of old Time—with a billowy main—
  A sun—a shadow of a magnitude.

SONNET

ON A PICTURE OF LEANDER

COME hither all sweet maidens soberly,
  Down-looking aye, and with a chasten'd light,
  Hid in the fringes of your eyelids white,
And meekly let your fair hands joined be,
As if so gentle that ye could not see,
  Untouch'd, a victim of your beauty bright,
  Sinking away to his young spirit's night,—
Sinking bewilder'd 'mid the dreary sea:
'Tis young Leander toiling to his death;
  Nigh swooning, he doth purse his weary lips   10
    For Hero's cheek, and smiles against her smile.
  O horrid dream! see how his body dips
    Dead-heavy; arms and shoulders gleam awhile:
He's gone: up bubbles all his amorous breath!

TO ———

THINK not of it, sweet one, so;—
    Give it not a tear;
Sigh thou mayst, and bid it go
    Any, any where.

Do not look so sad, sweet one,—
    Sad and fadingly;
Shed one drop, then it is gone,
    O 'twas born to die.

Still so pale? then dearest weep;
    Weep, I'll count the tears,   10
And each one shall be a bliss
    For thee in after years.

Brighter has it left thine eyes
    Than a sunny rill;
And thy whispering melodies
    Are tenderer still.

Yet—as all things mourn awhile
    At fleeting blisses,
Let us too! but be our dirge
    A dirge of kisses.   20

LINES

I

UNFELT, unheard, unseen,
I've left my little queen,
Her languid arms in silver slumber lying:
    Ah! through their nestling touch,
    Who—who could tell how much
There is for madness—cruel, or complying?

II

Those faery lids how sleek!
Those lips how moist!—they speak,
In ripest quiet, shadows of sweet sounds:
    Into my fancy's ear
    Melting a burden dear,
How "Love doth know no fullness nor no bounds."

III

True!—tender monitors!
I bend unto your laws:
This sweetest day for dalliance was born!
So, without more ado,
I'll feel my heaven anew,
For all the blushing of the hasty morn.

SONNET

ON THE SEA

I⊤ keeps eternal whisperings around
  Desolate shores, and with its mighty swell
  Gluts twice ten thousand Caverns, till the spell
Of Hecate leaves them their old shadowy sound.
Often 'tis in such gentle temper found,
  That scarcely will the very smallest shell
  Be mov'd for days from where it sometime fell,
When last the winds of Heaven were unbound.
Oh ye! who have your eye-balls vex'd and tir'd,
  Feast them upon the wideness of the Sea;   10
    Oh ye! whose ears are dinn'd with uproar rude,
  Or fed too much with cloying melody—
    Sit ye near some old Cavern's Mouth, and brood
Until ye start, as if the sea-nymphs quir'd!

SONNET

ON LEIGH HUNT'S POEM "THE STORY OF RIMINI"

Who loves to peer up at the morning sun,
  With half-shut eyes and comfortable cheek,
  Let him, with this sweet tale, full often seek
For meadows where the little rivers run;
Who loves to linger with that brightest one
  Of Heaven—Hesperus—let him lowly speak
  These numbers to the night, and starlight meek,
Or moon, if that her hunting be begun.
He who knows these delights, and too is prone
  To moralize upon a smile or tear,   10
Will find at once a region of his own,
  A bower for his spirit, and will steer
To alleys where the fir-tree drops its cone,
  Where robins hop, and fallen leaves are sear.

ON OXFORD

A PARODY

I

THE Gothic looks solemn,
The plain Doric column
Supports an old Bishop and Crosier;
The mouldering arch,
Shaded o'er by a larch
Stands next door to Wilson the Hosier.

II

Vice—that is, by turns,—
O'er pale faces mourns
The black tassell'd trencher and common hat;
The Chantry boy sings,
The Steeple-bell rings,
And as for the Chancellor—*dominat.*

III

There are plenty of trees,
And plenty of ease,
And plenty of fat deer for Parsons;
And when it is venison,
Short is the benison,—
Then each on a leg or thigh fastens.

THE POET

A FRAGMENT

WHERE's the Poet? show him! show him,
Muses nine! that I may know him!
'Tis the man who with a man
  Is an equal, be he King,
Or poorest of the beggar-clan,
  Or any other wondrous thing
A man may be 'twixt ape and Plato;
  'Tis the man who with a bird,
Wren or Eagle, finds his way to
  All its instincts; he hath heard   10
The Lion's roaring, and can tell
  What his horny throat expresseth,
And to him the Tiger's yell
  Comes articulate and presseth
On his ear like mother-tongue.

MODERN LOVE

AND what is love? It is a doll dress'd up
For idleness to cosset, nurse, and dandle;
A thing of soft misnomers, so divine
That silly youth doth think to make itself
Divine by loving, and so goes on
Yawning and doting a whole summer long,
Till Miss's comb is made a pearl tiara,
And common Wellingtons turn Romeo boots;
Then Cleopatra lives at number seven,
And Antony resides in Brunswick Square.   10
Fools! if some passions high have warm'd the world,
If Queens and Soldiers have play'd deep for hearts,
It is no reason why such agonies
Should be more common than the growth of weeds.
Fools! make me whole again that weighty pearl
The Queen of Egypt melted, and I'll say
That ye may love in spite of beaver hats.

THE CASTLE BUILDER

FRAGMENTS OF A DIALOGUE

CASTLE BUILDER

*   *   *   *   *   *   *

IN short, convince you that however wise
You may have grown from Convent libraries,
I have, by many yards at least, been carding
A longer skein of wit in Convent garden.

BERNARDINE

A very Eden that same place must be!
Pray what demesne? Whose Lordship's legacy?
What, have you convents in that Gothic Isle?
Pray pardon me, I cannot help but smile.

*   *   *   *   *   *   *

CASTLE BUILDER

Sir, Convent Garden is a monstrous beast
From morning, four o'clock, to twelve at noon,   10
It swallows cabbages without a spoon,
And then, from twelve till two, this Eden made is
A promenade for cooks and ancient ladies;

And then for supper, 'stead of soup and poaches,
It swallows chairmen, damns, and Hackney coaches.
In short, Sir, 'tis a very place for monks,
For it containeth twenty thousand punks,
Which any man may number for his sport,
By following fat elbows up a court.

     *   *   *   *   *   *   *

In such like nonsense would I pass an hour   20
With random Friar, or Rake upon his tour,
Or one of few of that imperial host
Who came unmaimed from the Russian frost

     *   *   *   *   *   *   *

To-night I'll have my friar—let me think
About my room,—I'll have it in the pink;
It should be rich and sombre, and the moon,
Just in its mid-life in the midst of June,
Should look thro' four large windows and display
Clear, but for gold-fish vases in the way,
Their glassy diamonding on Turkish floor;   30
The tapers keep aside, an hour and more,
To see what else the moon alone can show;
While the night-breeze doth softly let us know
My terrace is well bower'd with oranges.
Upon the floor the dullest spirit sees
A guitar-ribband and a lady's glove
Beside a crumple-leaved tale of love;
A tambour-frame, with Venus sleeping there,
All finish'd but some ringlets of her hair;
A viol-bow, strings torn, cross-wise upon   40
A glorious folio of Anacreon;
A skull upon a mat of roses lying,
Ink'd purple with a song concerning dying;
An hour-glass on the turn, amid the trails
Of passion-flower;—just in time there sails
A cloud across the moon,—the lights bring in!
And see what more my phantasy can win.
It is a gorgeous room, but somewhat sad;
The draperies are so, as tho' they had
Been made for Cleopatra's winding-sheet;   50
And opposite the stedfast eye doth meet
A spacious looking-glass, upon whose face,
In letters raven-sombre, you may trace
Old "Mene, Mene, Tekel, Upharsin."
Greek busts and statuary have ever been
Held, by the finest spirits, fitter far
Than vase grotesque and Siamesian jar;

Therefore 'tis sure a want of Attic taste
That I should rather love a Gothic waste
Of eyesight on cinque-coloured potter's clay,   60
Than on the marble fairness of old Greece.
My table-coverlits of Jason's fleece
And black Numidian sheep-wool should be wrought,
Gold, black, and heavy, from the Lama brought.
My ebon sofas should delicious be
With down from Leda's cygnet progeny.
My pictures all Salvator's, save a few
Of Titian's portraiture, and one, though new,
Of Haydon's in its fresh magnificence.
My wine—O good! 'tis here at my desire,   70
And I must sit to supper with my friar.

*   *   *   *   *   *   *

A SONG OF OPPOSITES

"Under the flag
Of each his faction, they to battle bring
Their embryon atoms."—MILTON.

WELCOME joy, and welcome sorrow,
    Lethe's weed and Hermes' feather;
Come to-day, and come to-morrow,
    I do love you both together!
    I love to mark sad faces in fair weather;
And hear a merry laugh amid the thunder;
    Fair and foul I love together.
Meadows sweet where flames are under,
And a giggle at a wonder;
Visage sage at pantomime;   10
Funeral, and steeple-chime;
Infant playing with a skull;
Morning fair, and shipwreck'd hull;
Nightshade with the woodbine kissing;
Serpents in red roses hissing;
Cleopatra regal-dress'd
With the aspic at her breast;
Dancing music, music sad,
Both together, sane and mad;
Muses bright and muses pale;   20
Sombre Saturn, Momus hale;—
Laugh and sigh, and laugh again;
Oh the sweetness of the pain!
Muses bright, and muses pale,
Bare your faces of the veil;

Let me see; and let me write
Of the day, and of the night—
Both together:—let me slake
All my thirst for sweet heart-ache!
Let my bower be of yew,   30
Interwreath'd with myrtles new;
Pines and lime-trees full in bloom,
And my couch a low grass-tomb.

SONNET

TO A CAT

CAT! who hast pass'd thy grand climacteric,
    How many mice and rats hast in thy days
    Destroy'd?—How many tit bits stolen? Gaze
With those bright languid segments green, and prick
Those velvet ears—but pr'ythee do not stick
    Thy latent talons in me—and upraise
    Thy gentle mew—and tell me all thy frays
Of fish and mice, and rats and tender chick.
Nay, look not down, nor lick thy dainty wrists—
    For all the wheezy asthma,—and for all   10
Thy tail's tip is nick'd off—and though the fists
    Of many a maid have given thee many a maul,
Still is that fur as soft as when the lists
    In youth thou enter'dst on glass bottled wall.

LINES ON SEEING A LOCK OF MILTON'S HAIR

CHIEF of organic numbers!
    Old Scholar of the Spheres!
Thy spirit never slumbers,
    But rolls about our ears,
For ever, and for ever!
O what a mad endeavour
        Worketh he,
Who to thy sacred and ennobled hearse
Would offer a burnt sacrifice of verse
        And melody.   10

How heavenward thou soundest,
    Live Temple of sweet noise,
And Discord unconfoundest,
    Giving Delight new joys,
And Pleasure nobler pinions!
O, where are thy dominions?

Lend thine ear
To a young Delian oath,—aye, by thy soul,
By all that from thy mortal lips did roll,
And by the kernel of thine earthly love,   20
Beauty, in things on earth, and things above
I swear!

When every childish fashion
    Has vanish'd from my rhyme,
Will I, grey-gone in passion,
    Leave to an after-time,
        Hymning and harmony
Of thee, and of thy works, and of thy life;
But vain is now the burning and the strife,
Pangs are in vain, until I grow high-rife   30
        With old Philosophy,
And mad with glimpses of futurity!

For many years my offering must be hush'd;
    When I do speak, I'll think upon this hour,
Because I feel my forehead hot and flush'd,
    Even at the simplest vassal of thy power,—
        A lock of thy bright hair,—
        Sudden it came,
And I was startled, when I caught thy name
        Coupled so unaware;   40
Yet, at the moment, temperate was my blood.
I thought I had beheld it from the flood.

SONNET

ON SITTING DOWN TO READ KING LEAR ONCE AGAIN

O GOLDEN tongued Romance, with serene lute!
    Fair plumed Syren, Queen of far-away!
    Leave melodizing on this wintry day,
Shut up thine olden pages, and be mute:
Adieu! for, once again, the fierce dispute
    Betwixt damnation and impassion'd clay
    Must I burn through; once more humbly assay
The bitter-sweet of this Shakespearian fruit:
Chief Poet! and ye clouds of Albion,
    Begetters of our deep eternal theme!   10
When through the old oak Forest I am gone,
    Let me not wander in a barren dream,
But, when I am consumed in the fire,
Give me new Phœnix wings to fly at my desire.

SONNET

WHEN I have fears that I may cease to be
   Before my pen has glean'd my teeming brain,
Before high-piled books, in charactery,
   Hold like rich garners the full ripen'd grain;
When I behold, upon the night's starr'd face,
   Huge cloudy symbols of a high romance,
And think that I may never live to trace
   Their shadows, with the magic hand of chance;
And when I feel, fair creature of an hour,
   That I shall never look upon thee more,   10
Never have relish in the faery power
   Of unreflecting love;—then on the shore
Of the wide world I stand alone, and think
Till love and fame to nothingness do sink.

SHARING EVE'S APPLE

I

O BLUSH not so! O blush not so!
   Or I shall think you knowing;
And if you smile the blushing while,
   Then maidenheads are going.

II

There's a blush for won't, and a blush for shan't,
   And a blush for having done it:
There's a blush for thought and a blush for naught,
   And a blush for just begun it.

III

O sigh not so! O sigh not so!
   For it sounds of Eve's sweet pippin;
By these loosen'd lips you have tasted the pips
   And fought in an amorous nipping.

IV

Will you play once more at nice-cut-core,
   For it only will last our youth out,
And we have the prime of the kissing time,
   We have not one sweet tooth out.

V

There's a sigh for yes, and a sigh for no,
And a sigh for I can't bear it!
O what can be done, shall we stay or run?
O cut the sweet apple and share it!

A DRAUGHT OF SUNSHINE

HENCE Burgundy, Claret, and Port,
    Away with old Hock and Madeira,
Too earthly ye are for my sport;
    There's a beverage brighter and clearer.
Instead of a pitiful rummer,
My wine overbrims a whole summer;
    My bowl is the sky,
    And I drink at my eye,
    Till I feel in the brain
    A Delphian pain—   10
Then follow, my Caius! then follow:
    On the green of the hill
    We will drink our fill
    Of golden sunshine,
    Till our brains intertwine
With the glory and grace of Apollo!
    God of the Meridian,
       And of the East and West,
    To thee my soul is flown,
       And my body is earthward press'd.—   20
It is an awful mission,
A terrible division;
And leaves a gulph austere
To be fill'd with worldly fear.
Aye, when the soul is fled
To high above our head,
Affrighted do we gaze
After its airy maze,
As doth a mother wild,
When her young infant child   30
Is in an eagle's claws—
And is not this the cause
Of madness?—God of Song,
Thou bearest me along
Through sights I scarce can bear:
O let me, let me share

With the hot lyre and thee,
The staid Philosophy.
Temper my lonely hours,
And let me see thy bowers   40
More unalarm'd!

SONNET

TO THE NILE

SON of the old moon-mountains African!
    Chief of the Pyramid and Crocodile!
    We call thee fruitful, and, that very while,
A desert fills our seeing's inward span;
Nurse of swart nations since the world began,
    Art thou so fruitful? or dost thou beguile
    Such men to honour thee, who, worn with toil,
Rest for a space 'twixt Cairo and Decan?
O may dark fancies err! they surely do;
    'Tis ignorance that makes a barren waste   10
Of all beyond itself, thou dost bedew
    Green rushes like our rivers, and dost taste
The pleasant sun-rise, green isles hast thou too,
    And to the sea as happily dost haste.

SONNET

TO A LADY SEEN FOR A FEW MOMENTS AT VAUXHALL

TIME's sea hath been five years at its slow ebb,
    Long hours have to and fro let creep the sand,
Since I was tangled in thy beauty's web,
    And snared by the ungloving of thine hand.
And yet I never look on midnight sky,
    But I behold thine eyes' well memory'd light;
I cannot look upon the rose's dye,
    But to thy cheek my soul doth take its flight.
I cannot look on any budding flower,
    But my fond ear, in fancy at thy lips   10
And hearkening for a love-sound, doth devour
    Its sweets in the wrong sense:—Thou dost eclipse
Every delight with sweet remembering,
And grief unto my darling joys dost bring

SONNET

WRITTEN IN ANSWER TO A SONNET ENDING THUS:—

Dark eyes are dearer far
Than those that mock the hyacinthine bell—
By J. H. REYNOLDS.

BLUE! 'Tis the life of heaven,—the domain
    Of Cynthia,—the wide palace of the sun,—
The tent of Hesperus, and all his train,—
    The bosomer of clouds, gold, grey and dun.
Blue! 'Tis the life of waters:—Ocean
    And all its vassal streams, pools numberless,
May rage, and foam, and fret, but never can
    Subside, if not to dark blue nativeness.
Blue! Gentle cousin of the forest-green,
    Married to green in all the sweetest flowers,—   10
Forget-me-not,—the Blue bell,—and, that Queen
    Of secrecy, the Violet: what strange powers
Hast thou, as a mere shadow! But how great,
When in an Eye thou art, alive with fate!

SONNET

TO JOHN HAMILTON REYNOLDS

O THAT a week could be an age, and we
    Felt parting and warmth meeting every week,
Then one poor year a thousand years would be,
    The flush of welcome ever on the cheek:
So could we live long life in little space,
    So time itself would be annihilate,
So a day's journey in oblivious haze
    To serve our joys would lengthen and dilate.
O to arrive each Monday morn from Ind!
    To land each Tuesday from the rich Levant!   10
In little time a host of joys to bind,
    And keep our souls in one eternal pant!
This morn, my friend, and yester-evening taught
Me how to harbour such a happy thought.

WHAT THE THRUSH SAID

LINES FROM A LETTER TO JOHN HAMILTON REYNOLDS

O THOU whose face hath felt the Winter's wind,
    Whose eye has seen the snow-clouds hung in mist,

And the black elm tops 'mong the freezing stars,
　To thee the spring will be a harvest-time.
O thou, whose only book has been the light
　Of supreme darkness which thou feddest on
　Night after night when Phœbus was away,
　To thee the Spring shall be a triple morn.
O fret not after knowledge—I have none,
　And yet my song comes native with the warmth.
O fret not after knowledge—I have none,   11
　And yet the Evening listens. He who saddens
At thought of idleness cannot be idle,
And he's awake who thinks himself asleep.

SONNET

THE HUMAN SEASONS

FOUR seasons fill the measure of the year;
　There are four seasons in the mind of man:
He has his lusty Spring, when fancy clear
　Takes in all beauty with an easy span:
He has his Summer, when luxuriously
　Spring's honied cud of youthful thought he loves
To ruminate, and by such dreaming nigh
　His nearest unto heaven: quiet coves
His soul has in its Autumn, when his wings
　He furleth close; contented so to look   10
On mists in idleness—to let fair things
　Pass by unheeded as a threshold brook.
He has his Winter too of pale misfeature,
Or else he would forego his mortal nature.

EXTRACTS FROM AN OPERA

O! WERE I one of the Olympian twelve,
Their godships should pass this into a law,—
That when a man doth set himself in toil
After some beauty veiled far away,
Each step he took should make his lady's hand
More soft, more white, and her fair cheek more fair;
And for each briar-berry he might eat,
A kiss should bud upon the tree of love,
And pulp and ripen richer every hour,
To melt away upon the traveller's lips.   10

*　　*　　*　　*　　*　　*

DAISY'S SONG

I

The sun, with his great eye,
Sees not so much as I;
And the moon, all silver-proud,
Might as well be in a cloud.

II

And O the spring—the spring!
I lead the life of a king!
Couch'd in the teeming grass,
I spy each pretty lass.

III

I look where no one dares,
And I stare where no one stares,
And when the night is nigh,
Lambs bleat my lullaby.

*   *   *   *   *   *

FOLLY'S SONG

When wedding fiddles are a-playing,
    Huzza for folly O!
And when maidens go a-maying,
    Huzza, &c.
When a milk-pail is upset,
    Huzza, &c.
And the clothes left in the wet,
    Huzza, &c.
When the barrel's set abroach,
    Huzza, &c.   10
When Kate Eyebrow keeps a coach,
    Huzza, &c.
When the pig is over-roasted,
    Huzza, &c.
And the cheese is over-toasted,
    Huzza, &c.
When Sir Snap is with his lawyer,
    Huzza, &c.
And Miss Chip has kissed the sawyer,
    Huzza, &c.   20

*   *   *   *   *   *

Oh, I am frighten'd with most hateful thoughts!
Perhaps her voice is not a nightingale's,
Perhaps her teeth are not the fairest pearl;
Her eye-lashes may be, for aught I know,
Not longer than the May-fly's small fan-horns;
There may not be one dimple on her hand;
And freckles many; ah! a careless nurse,
In haste to teach the little thing to walk,
May have crumpt up a pair of Dian's legs,
And warpt the ivory of a Juno's neck.

*   *   *   *   *   *   *

SONG

I

The stranger lighted from his steed,
   And ere he spake a word,
He seiz'd my lady's lilly hand,
   And kiss'd it all unheard.

II

The stranger walk'd into the hall,
   And ere he spake a word,
He kissed my lady's cherry lips,
   And kiss'd 'em all unheard.

III

The stranger walk'd into the bower,—
   But my lady first did go,—
Aye hand in hand into the bower,
   Where my lord's roses blow.

IV

My lady's maid had a silken scarf,
   And a golden ring had she,
And a kiss from the stranger, as off he went
   Again on his fair palfrey.

*   *   *   *   *

Asleep! O sleep a little while, white pearl!
And let me kneel, and let me pray to thee,
And let me call Heaven's blessing on thine eyes,
And let me breathe into the happy air,
That doth enfold and touch thee all about,
Vows of my slavery, my giving up,
My sudden adoration, my great love!

FAERY SONGS

I

SHED no tear—O shed no tear!
The flower will bloom another year.
Weep no more—O weep no more!
Young buds sleep in the root's white core.
Dry your eyes—O dry your eyes,
For I was taught in Paradise
To ease my breast of melodies—
       Shed no tear.

Overhead—look overhead
'Mong the blossoms white and red—   10
Look up, look up—I flutter now
On this flush pomegranate bough—
See me—'tis this silvery bill
Ever cures the good man's ill—
Shed no tear—O shed no tear!
The flower will bloom another year.
Adieu—Adieu—I fly, adieu,
I vanish in the heaven's blue—
       Adieu, Adieu!

II

Ah! woe is me! poor silver-wing!
   That I must chant thy lady's dirge,
And death to this fair haunt of spring,
   Of melody, and streams of flowery verge,—
Poor silver-wing! ah! woe is me!
       That I must see
These blossoms snow upon thy lady's pall!
   Go, pretty page! and in her ear
   Whisper that the hour is near!
   Softly tell her not to fear   10
Such calm favonian burial!
   Go, pretty page! and soothly tell,—
   The blossoms hang by a melting spell,
And fall they must, ere a star wink thrice
       Upon her closed eyes,
That now in vain are weeping their last tears,
   At sweet life leaving, and these arbours green,—
Rich dowry from the Spirit of the Spheres,—
       Alas! poor Queen!

SONNET

TO HOMER

STANDING aloof in giant ignorance,
  Of thee I hear and of the Cyclades,
As one who sits ashore and longs perchance
  To visit dolphin-coral in deep seas.
So thou wast blind;—but then the veil was rent,
  For Jove uncurtain'd Heaven to let thee live,
And Neptune made for thee a spumy tent,
  And Pan made sing for thee his forest-hive;
Aye on the shores of darkness there is light,
  And precipices show untrodden green,   10
There is a budding morrow in midnight,
  There is a triple sight in blindness keen;
Such seeing hadst thou, as it once befel
To Dian, Queen of Earth, and Heaven, and Hell.

SONG

[*Written on a blank page in Beaumont and Fletcher's Works, between*
"Cupid's Revenge" and "The Two Noble Kinsmen"]

I

SPIRIT here that reignest!
Spirit here that painest!
Spirit here that burnest!
Spirit here that mournest!
    Spirit, I bow
    My forehead low,
  Enshaded with thy pinions.
    Spirit, I look
    All passion-struck
  Into thy pale dominions.

II

Spirit here that laughest!
Spirit here that quaffest!
Spirit here that dancest!
Noble soul that prancest!
    Spirit, with thee
    I join in the glee
A-nudging the elbow of Momus.
    Spirit, I flush
    With a Bacchanal blush
Just fresh from the Banquet of Comus.

TEIGNMOUTH

"SOME DOGGEREL" SENT IN A LETTER TO B. R. HAYDON

I

HERE all the summer could I stay,
For there's Bishop's teign
And King's teign
And Coomb at the clear teign head—
Where close by the stream
You may have your cream
All spread upon barley bread.

II

There's arch Brook
And there's larch Brook
Both turning many a mill;
And cooling the drouth
Of the salmon's mouth,
And fattening his silver gill.

III

There is Wild wood,
A Mild hood
To the sheep on the lea o' the down,
Where the golden furze,
With its green, thin spurs,
Doth catch at the maiden's gown.

IV

There is Newton marsh
With its spear grass harsh—
A pleasant summer level
Where the maidens sweet
Of the Market Street,
Do meet in the dusk to revel.

V

There's the Barton rich
With dyke and ditch
And hedge for the thrush to live in
And the hollow tree
For the buzzing bee
And a bank for the wasp to hive in.

VI

And O, and O
The daisies blow
And the primroses are waken'd,
And violets white
Sit in silver plight,
And the green bud's as long as the spike end.

VII

Then who would go
Into dark Soho,
And chatter with dack'd hair'd critics,
When he can stay
For the new-mown hay,
And startle the dappled Prickets?

THE DEVON MAID

STANZAS SENT IN A LETTER TO B. R. HAYDON

I

WHERE be ye going, you Devon Maid?
And what have ye there in the Basket?
Ye tight little fairy just fresh from the dairy,
Will ye give me some cream if I ask it?

II

I love your Meads, and I love your flowers,
And I love your junkets mainly,
But 'hind the door I love kissing more,
O look not so disdainly.

III

I love your hills, and I love your dales,
And I love your flocks a-bleating—
But O, on the heather to lie together,
With both our hearts a-beating!

IV

I'll put your Basket all safe in a nook,
Your shawl I hang up on the willow,
And we will sigh in the daisy's eye
And kiss on a grass green pillow.

EPISTLE TO JOHN HAMILTON REYNOLDS

Dear Reynolds! as last night I lay in bed,
There came before my eyes that wonted thread
Of shapes, and shadows, and remembrances,
That every other minute vex and please:
Things all disjointed come from north and south,—
Two Witch's eyes above a Cherub's mouth,
Voltaire with casque and shield and habergeon,
And Alexander with his nightcap on;
Old Socrates a-tying his cravat,
And Hazlitt playing with Miss Edgeworth's cat;   10
And Junius Brutus, pretty well so so,
Making the best of's way towards Soho.

Few are there who escape these visitings,—
Perhaps one or two whose lives have patent wings,
And thro' whose curtains peeps no hellish nose,
No wild-boar tushes, and no Mermaid's toes;
But flowers bursting out with lusty pride,
And young Æolian harps personified;
Some Titian colours touch'd into real life,—
The sacrifice goes on; the pontiff knife   20
Gleams in the Sun, the milk-white heifer lows,
The pipes go shrilly, the libation flows:
A white sail shows above the green-head cliff,
Moves round the point, and throws her anchor stiff;
The mariners join hymn with those on land.

You know the Enchanted Castle,—it doth stand
Upon a rock, on the border of a Lake,
Nested in trees, which all do seem to shake
From some old magic-like Urganda's Sword.
O Phœbus! that I had thy sacred word   30
To show this Castle, in fair dreaming wise,
Unto my friend, while sick and ill he lies!

You know it well enough, where it doth seem
A mossy place, a Merlin's Hall, a dream;
You know the clear Lake, and the little Isles,
The mountains blue, and cold near neighbour rills,
All which elsewhere are but half animate;
There do they look alive to love and hate,
To smiles and frowns; they seem a lifted mound
Above some giant, pulsing underground.   40

Part of the Building was a chosen See,
Built by a banish'd Santon of Chaldee;
The other part, two thousand years from him,
Was built by Cuthbert de Saint Aldebrim;
Then there's a little wing, far from the Sun,
Built by a Lapland Witch turn'd maudlin Nun;
And many other juts of aged stone
Founded with many a mason-devil's groan.

The doors all look as if they op'd themselves,
The windows as if latch'd by Fays and Elves,   50
And from them comes a silver flash of light,
As from the westward of a Summer's night;
Or like a beauteous woman's large blue eyes
Gone mad thro' olden songs and poesies.

See! what is coming from the distance dim!
A golden Galley all in silken trim!
Three rows of oars are lightening, moment whiles,
Into the verd'rous bosoms of those isles;
Towards the shade, under the Castle wall,
It comes in silence,—now 'tis hidden all.   60
The Clarion sounds, and from a Postern-gate
An echo of sweet music doth create
A fear in the poor Herdsman, who doth bring
His beasts to trouble the enchanted spring,—
He tells of the sweet music, and the spot,
To all his friends, and they believe him not.

O that our dreamings all, of sleep or wake,
Would all their colours from the sunset take:
From something of material sublime,
Rather than shadow our own soul's day-time   70
In the dark void of night. For in the world
We jostle,—but my flag is not unfurl'd
On the Admiral-staff,—and so philosophize
I dare not yet! Oh, never will the prize,
High reason, and the love of good and ill,
Be my award! Things cannot to the will
Be settled, but they tease us out of thought;
Or is it that imagination brought
Beyond its proper bound, yet still confin'd,
Lost in a sort of Purgatory blind,   80
Cannot refer to any standard law
Of either earth or heaven? It is a flaw
In happiness, to see beyond our bourn,—
It forces us in summer skies to mourn,
It spoils the singing of the Nightingale.

Dear Reynolds! I have a mysterious tale,
And cannot speak it: the first page I read
Upon a Lampit rock of green sea-weed
Among the breakers; 'twas a quiet eve,
The rocks were silent, the wide sea did weave   90
An untumultuous fringe of silver foam
Along the flat brown sand; I was at home
And should have been most happy,—but I saw
Too far into the sea, where every maw
The greater on the less feeds evermore.—
But I saw too distinct into the core
Of an eternal fierce destruction,
And so from happiness I far was gone.
Still am I sick of it, and tho', to-day,
I've gather'd young spring-leaves, and flowers gay   101
Of periwinkle and wild strawberry,
Still do I that most fierce destruction see,—
The Shark at savage prey,—the Hawk at pounce,—
The gentle Robin, like a Pard or Ounce,
Ravening a worm,—Away, ye horrid moods!
Moods of one's mind! You know I hate them well.
You know I'd sooner be a clapping Bell
To some Kamtschatcan Missionary Church,
Than with these horrid moods be left i' the lurch.

DAWLISH FAIR

Over the Hill and over the Dale,
    And over the Bourne to Dawlish,
Where ginger-bread wives have a scanty sale,
    And ginger-bread nuts are smallish.

FRAGMENT OF AN ODE TO MAIA, WRITTEN ON MAY DAY, 1818

Mother of Hermes! and still youthful Maia!
        May I sing to thee
As thou wast hymned on the shores of Baiæ?
        Or may I woo thee
In earlier Sicilian? or thy smiles
Seek as they once were sought, in Grecian isles,
By bards who died content on pleasant sward,
    Leaving great verse unto a little clan?
O, give me their old vigour, and unheard
    Save of the quiet Primrose, and the span   10

Of heaven and few ears,
Rounded by thee, my song should die away
Content as theirs,
Rich in the simple worship of a day.

ACROSTIC

GEORGIANA AUGUSTA KEATS

GIVE me your patience Sister while I frame
Exact in Capitals your golden name
Or sue the fair Apollo and he will
Rouse from his heavy slumber and instil
Great love in me for thee and Poesy.
Imagine not that greatest mastery
And kingdom over all the Realms of verse
Nears more to Heaven in aught than when we nurse
And surety give to love and Brotherhood.

Anthropophagi in Othello's mood;   10
Ulysses stormed, and his enchanted belt
Glow with the Muse, but they are never felt
Unbosom'd so and so eternal made,
Such tender incense in their Laurel shade,
To all the regent sisters of the Nine
As this poor offering to you, sister mine.

Kind sister! aye, this third name says you are;
Enchanted has it been the Lord knows where.
And may it taste to you like good old wine,
Take you to real happiness and give   20
Sons, daughters and a home like honied hive.

SONNET

ON VISITING THE TOMB OF BURNS

THE town, the churchyard, and the setting sun,
    The clouds, the trees, the rounded hills all seem,
    Though beautiful, cold—strange—as in a dream,
I dreamed long ago, now new begun.
The short-liv'd, paly Summer is but won
    From Winter's ague, for one hour's gleam;
    Though sapphire-warm, their stars do never beam:
All is cold Beauty; pain is never done:

For who has mind to relish, Minos-wise,
  The Real of Beauty, free from that dead hue   10
    Sickly imagination and sick pride
Cast wan upon it! Burns! with honour due
  I oft have honour'd thee. Great shadow, hide
Thy face; I sin against thy native skies.

MEG MERRILIES

I

Old Meg she was a Gipsy,
  And liv'd upon the Moors:
Her bed it was the brown heath turf,
  And her house was out of doors.

II

Her apples were swart blackberries,
  Her currants pods o' broom;
Her wine was dew of the wild white rose,
  Her book a churchyard tomb.

III

Her Brothers were the craggy hills,
  Her Sisters larchen trees—
Alone with her great family
  She liv'd as she did please.

IV

No breakfast had she many a morn,
  No dinner many a noon,
And 'stead of supper she would stare
  Full hard against the Moon.

V

But every morn of woodbine fresh
  She made her garlanding,
And every night the dark glen Yew
  She wove, and she would sing.

VI

And with her fingers old and brown
  She plaited Mats o' Rushes,
And gave them to the Cottagers
  She met among the Bushes.

VII

Old Meg was brave as Margaret Queen
And tall as Amazon:
And old red blanket cloak she wore;
A chip hat had she on.
God rest her aged bones somewhere—
She died full long agone!

A SONG ABOUT MYSELF

FROM A LETTER TO FANNY KEATS

I

THERE was naughty Boy,
A naughty boy was he,
He would not stop at home,
He could not quiet be—
He took
In his Knapsack
A Book
Full of vowels
And a shirt
With some towels—
A slight cap
For night cap—
A hair brush,
Comb ditto,
New Stockings
For old ones
Would split O!
This Knapsack
Tight at's back
He rivetted close
And followed his Nose
To the North,
To the North,
And follow'd his nose
To the North.

II

There was a naughty boy
And a naughty boy was he,
For nothing would he do
But scribble poetry—
He took

An ink stand
In his hand
And a pen
Big as ten
In the other.
And away
In a Pother
He ran
To the mountains
And fountains
And ghostes
And Postes
And witches
And ditches
And wrote
In his coat
When the weather
Was cool,
Fear of gout,
And without
When the weather
Was warm—
Och the charm
When we choose
To follow one's nose
To the north,
To the north,
To follow one's nose
To the north!

III

There was a naughty boy
And a naughty boy was he,
He kept little fishes
In washing tubs three

In spite
Of the might
Of the Maid
Nor afraid
Of his Granny-good—
He often would
Hurly burly
Get up early
And go
By hook or crook
To the brook
And bring home
Miller's thumb,
Tittlebat
Not over fat,
Minnows small
As the stall
Of a glove,
Not above
The size
Of a nice
Little Baby's
Little fingers—
O he made
'Twas his trade
Of Fish a pretty Kettle
A Kettle—
A Kettle

Of Fish a pretty Kettle
A Kettle!

IV

There was a naughty Boy,
And a naughty Boy was he,
He ran away to Scotland
The people for to see—
Then he found
That the ground
Was as hard,
That a yard
Was as long,
That a song
Was as merry,
That a cherry
Was as red—
That lead
Was as weighty,
That fourscore
Was as eighty,
That a door
Was as wooden
As in England—
So he stood in his shoes
And he wonder'd,
He wonder'd,
He stood in his shoes
And he wonder'd.

A GALLOWAY SONG

FROM A LETTER TO TOM KEATS

Ah! ken ye what I met the day
Out oure the Mountains
A coming down by craggi[e]s grey
And mossie fountains—
A [h] goud hair'd Marie yeve I pray
Ane minute's guessing—
For that I met upon the way
Is past expressing.
As I stood where a rocky brig
A torrent crosses
I spied upon a misty rig
A troup o' Horses—

And as they trotted down the glen
I sped to meet them
To see if I might know the Men
To stop and greet them.
First Willie on his sleek mare came
At canting gallop
His long hair rustled like a flame
On board a shallop.   20
Then came his brother Rab and then
Young Peggy's mither
And Peggy too—adown the glen
They went togither—
I saw her wrappit in her hood
Fra wind and raining—
Her cheek was flush wi' timid blood
Twixt growth and waning—
She turn'd her dazed head full oft
For there her Brithers   30
Came riding with her Bridegroom soft
And mony ithers.
Young Tam came up an' eyed me quick
With reddened cheek—
Braw Tam was daffed like a chick—
He coud na speak—
Ah Marie they are all gane hame
Through blustering weather
An' every heart is full on flame
An' light as feather.   40
Ah! Marie they are all gone hame
Fra happy wedding,
Whilst I—Ah is it not a shame?
Sad tears am shedding.

SONNET

TO AILSA ROCK

HEARKEN, thou craggy ocean pyramid!
    Give answer from thy voice, the sea-fowls' screams!
    When were thy shoulders mantled in huge streams?
When, from the sun, was thy broad forehead hid?
How long is't since the mighty power bid
    Thee heave to airy sleep from fathom dreams?
    Sleep in the lap of thunder or sunbeams,
Or when grey clouds are thy cold coverlid.
Thou answer'st not; for thou art dead asleep;
    Thy life is but two dead eternities—   10

The last in air, the former in the deep;
First with the whales, last with the eagle-skies—
Drown'd wast thou till an earthquake made thee steep,
Another cannot wake thy giant size.

SONNET

WRITTEN IN THE COTTAGE WHERE BURNS WAS BORN

THIS mortal body of a thousand days
  Now fills, O Burns, a space in thine own room,
Where thou didst dream alone on budded bays,
  Happy and thoughtless of thy day of doom!
My pulse is warm with thine own Barley-bree,
  My head is light with pledging a great soul,
My eyes are wandering, and I cannot see,
  Fancy is dead and drunken at its goal;
Yet can I stamp my foot upon thy floor,
  Yet can I ope thy window-sash to find   10
The meadow thou hast tramped o'er and o'er,—
  Yet can I think of thee till thought is blind,—
Yet can I gulp a bumper to thy name,—
  O smile among the shades, for this is fame!

LINES WRITTEN IN THE HIGHLANDS AFTER A VISIT TO BURNS'S COUNTRY

THERE is a charm in footing slow across a silent plain,
Where patriot battle has been fought, where glory had the gain;
There is a pleasure on the heath where Druids old have been,
Where mantles grey have rustled by and swept the nettles green;
There is a joy in every spot made known by times of old,
New to the feet, although each tale a hundred times be told;
There is a deeper joy than all, more solemn in the heart,
More parching to the tongue than all, of more divine a smart,
When weary steps forget themselves upon a pleasant turf,
Upon hot sand, or flinty road, or sea-shore iron scurf,   10
Toward the castle or the cot, where long ago was born
One who was great through mortal days, and died of fame unshorn,
Light heather-bells may tremble then, but they are far away;
Wood-lark may sing from sandy fern,—the Sun may hear his lay;
Runnels may kiss the grass on shelves and shallows clear,
But their low voices are not heard, though come on travels drear;
Blood-red the Sun may set behind black mountain peaks;
Blue tides may sluice and drench their time in caves and weedy creeks;
Eagles may seem to sleep wing-wide upon the air;
Ring-doves may fly convuls'd across to some high-cedar'd lair;   20

But the forgotten eye is still fast lidded to the ground,
As Palmer's, that with weariness, mid-desert shrine hath found.
At such a time the soul's a child, in childhood is the brain;
Forgotten is the worldly heart—alone, it beats in vain.—
Aye, if a madman could have leave to pass a healthful day
To tell his forehead's swoon and faint when first began decay,
He might make tremble many a one whose spirit had gone forth
To find a Bard's low cradle-place about the silent North!
Scanty the hour and few the steps beyond the bourn of care,
Beyond the sweet and bitter world,—beyond it unaware!   30
Scanty the hour and few the steps, because a longer stay
Would bar return, and make a man forget his mortal way:
O horrible! to lose the sight of well remember'd face,
Of Brother's eyes, of Sister's brow—constant to every place;
Filling the air, as on we move, with portraiture intense;
More warm than those heroic tints that pain a painter's sense,
When shapes of old come striding by, and visages of old,
Locks shining black, hair scanty grey, and passions manifold.
No, no, that horror cannot be, for at the cable's length
Man feels the gentle anchor pull and gladdens in its strength:—   40
One hour, half-idiot, he stands by mossy waterfall,
But in the very next he reads his soul's memorial:—
He reads it on the mountain's height, where chance he may sit down
Upon rough marble diadem—that hill's eternal crown.
Yet be his anchor e'er so fast, room is there for a prayer
That man may never lose his mind on mountains black and bare;
That he may stray league after league some great birthplace to find
And keep his vision clear from speck, his inward sight unblind.

THE GADFLY

FROM A LETTER TO TOM KEATS

I

ALL gentle folks who owe a grudge
    To any living thing
Open your ears and stay your
        t[r]udge
Whilst I in dudgeon sing.

II

The Gadfly he hath stung me
        sore—
    O may he ne'er sting you!
But we have many a horrid bore
    He may sting black and blue.

III

Has any here an old grey Mare
    With three legs all her store,
O put it to her Buttocks bare
    And straight she'll run on four.

IV

Has any here a Lawyer suit
    Of Seventeen-Forty-Three,
Take Lawyer's nose and put it to't
    And you the end will see.

V

Is there a Man in Parliament
   Dum[b-]founder'd in his
      speech,
O let his neighbour make a rent
   And put one in his breech.

VI

O Lowther how much better thou
   Hadst figur'd t'other day
When to the folks thou mad'st a
      bow
   And hadst no more to say

VII

If lucky Gadfly had but ta'en
   His seat   *   *   *
And put thee to a little pain
   To save thee from a worse.

VIII

Better than Southey it had been,
   Better than Mr. D——,
Better than Wordsworth too, I
      ween,
   Better than Mr. V——.

IX

Forgive me pray good people all
   For deviating so—
In spirit sure I had a call—
   And now I on will go.

X

Has any here a daughter fair
   Too fond of reading novels,
Too apt to fall in love with care
   And charming Mister Lovels,

XI

O put a Gadfly to that thing
   She keeps so white and pert—
I mean the finger for the ring,
   And it will breed a wort.

XII

Has any here a pious spouse
   Who seven times a day
Scolds as King David pray'd, to
      chouse
   And have her holy way—

XIII

O let a Gadfly's little sting
   Persuade her sacred tongue
That noises are a common thing
   But that her bell has rung.

XIV

And as this is the summum bo-
   num of all conquering,
I leave "withouten wordes mo"
   The Gadfly's little sting.

SONNET

ON HEARING THE BAG-PIPE AND SEEING "THE STRANGER" PLAYED AT INVERARY

Of late two dainties were before me plac'd
   Sweet, holy, pure, sacred and innocent,
   From the ninth sphere to me benignly sent
That Gods might know my own particular taste.
First the soft Bag-pipe mourn'd with zealous haste,

The Stranger next with head on bosom bent
Sigh'd; rueful again the piteous Bag-pipe went,
Again the Stranger sighings fresh did waste.
. O Bag-pipe thou didst steal my heart away—
    O Stranger thou my nerves from Pipe didst charm—
O Bag-pipe thou didst re-assert thy sway—   11
    Again thou Stranger gav'st me fresh alarm—
Alas! I could not choose. Ah! my poor heart,
Mum chance art thou with both oblig'd to part.

STAFFA

Not Aladdin magian
Ever such a work began;
Not the wizard of the Dee
Ever such a dream could see;
Not St. John, in Patmos' Isle,
In the passion of his toil,
When he saw the churches seven,
Golden aisl'd, built up in heaven,
Gaz'd at such a rugged wonder.
As I stood its roofing under,   10
Lo! I saw one sleeping there,
On the marble cold and bare.
While the surges wash'd his feet,
And his garments white did beat
Drench'd about the sombre rocks,
On his neck his well-grown locks,
Lifted dry above the main,
Were upon the curl again.
"What is this? and what art thou?"
Whisper'd I, and touch'd his brow;   20
"What art thou? and what is this?"
Whisper'd I, and strove to kiss
The spirit's hand, to wake his eyes;
Up he started in a trice:
"I am Lycidas," said he,
"Fam'd in funeral minstrelsy!
This was architectur'd thus
By the great Oceanus!—
Here his mighty waters play
Hollow organs all the day;   30
Here by turns his dolphins all,
Finny palmers great and small,
Come to pay devotion due—
Each a mouth of pearls must strew.

Many a mortal of these days,
Dares to pass our sacred ways,
Dares to touch audaciously
This Cathedral of the Sea!
I have been the pontiff-priest   40
Where the waters never rest,
Where a fledgy sea-bird choir
Soars for ever; holy fire
I have hid from mortal man;
Proteus is my Sacristan.
But the dulled eye of mortal
Hath pass'd beyond the rocky portal;
So for ever will I leave
Such a taint, and soon unweave
All the magic of the place."

　　　*　　　*　　　*　　　*　　　*

So saying, with a Spirit's glance   50
He dived!

SONNET

WRITTEN UPON THE TOP OF BEN NEVIS

READ me a lesson, Muse, and speak it loud
　　Upon the top of Nevis, blind in mist!
I look into the chasms, and a shroud
　　Vapourous doth hide them,—just so much I wist
Mankind do know of hell; I look o'erhead,
　　And there is sullen mist,—even so much
Mankind can tell of heaven; mist is spread
　　Before the earth, beneath me,—even such,
Even so vague is man's sight of himself!
　　Here are the craggy stones beneath my feet,—   10
Thus much I know that, a poor witless elf,
　　I tread on them,—that all my eye doth meet
Is mist and crag, not only on this height,
But in the world of thought and mental might!

BEN NEVIS

A DIALOGUE

[PERSONS: MRS. CAMERON AND BEN NEVIS]

MRS. C.

UPON my life Sir Nevis I am pique'd
That I have so far panted tugg'd and reek'd
To do an hono[u]r to your old bald pate

And now am sitting on you just to bate,
Without your paying me one compliment.
Alas 'tis so with all, when our intent
Is plain, and in the eye of all Mankind
We fair ones show a preference, too blind!
You Gentle man immediately turn tail—
O let me then my hapless fate bewail!   10
Ungrateful Baldpate, have I not disdain'd
The pleasant Valleys—have I not, madbrain'd,
Deserted all my Pickles and preserves,
My China closet too—with wretched Nerves
To boot—say, wretched ingrate, have I not
Le[f]t my soft cushion chair and caudle pot?
'Tis true I had no corns—no! thank the fates,
My Shoemaker was always Mr. Bates.
And if not Mr. Bates why I'm not old!
Still dumb, ungrateful Nevis—still so cold!   20

Here the Lady took some more w[h]iskey and was putting even
more to her lips when she dashed [it] to the Ground for the
Mountain began to grumble—which continued for a few minutes
before he thus began,

BEN NEVIS

What whining bit of tongue and Mouth thus dares
Disturb my slumber of a thousand years?
Even so long my sleep has been secure—
And to be so awaked I'll not endure.
Oh pain—for since the Eagle's earliest scream
I've had a dam[n]'d confounded ugly dream,
A Nightmare sure. What, Madam, was it you?
It cannot be! My old eyes are not true!
Red-Crag, my Spectacles! Now let me see!
Good Heavens, Lady, how the gemini   30
Did you get here? O I shall split my sides!
I shall earthquake——

MRS. C.

Sweet Nevis, do not quake, for though I love
You[r] honest Countenance all things above,
Truly I should not like to be convey'd
So far into your Bosom—gentle Maid
Loves not too rough a treatment, gentle Sir—
Pray thee be calm and do not quake nor stir,
No not a Stone, or I shall go in fits—

BEN NEVIS

I must—I shall—I meet not such tit bits—　　　　40
I meet not such sweet creatures every day—
By my old night-cap, night-cap night and day,
I must have one sweet Buss—I must and shall!
Red-Crag!—What, Madam, can you then repent
Of all the toil and vigour you have spent
To see Ben Nevis and to touch his nose?
Red-Crag, I say! O I must have them close!
Red-Crag, there lies beneath my farthest toe
A vein of Sulphur—go dear Red-Crag, go—
And rub your flinty back against it—budge!　　　50
Dear Madam, I must kiss you, faith I must!
I must Embrace you with my dearest gust!
Block-head, d'ye hear—Block-head, I'll make her feel—
There lies beneath my east leg's northern heel
A cave of young earth dragons—well, my boy,
Go thither quick and so complete my joy;
Take you a bundle of the largest pines
And when the sun on fiercest Phosphor shines
Fire them and ram them in the Dragon's nest,
Then will the dragons fry and fizz their best　　　60
Until ten thousand now no bigger than
Poor Al[l]igators—poor things of one span—
Will each one swell to twice ten times the size
Of northern whale—then for the tender prize—
The moment then—for then will Red-Crag rub
His flinty back—and I shall kiss and snub
And press my dainty morsel to my breast.
Block-head, make haste!
　　　　　　　　　O Muses weep the rest—
The Lady fainted and he thought her dead
So pulled the clouds again about his head　　　70
And went to sleep again—soon she was rous'd
By her affrighted servants—next day hous'd
Safe on the lowly ground she bless'd her fate
That fainting fit was not delayed too late.

TRANSLATION FROM A SONNET OF RONSARD

NATURE withheld Cassandra in the skies,
　　For more adornment, a full thousand years;
She took their cream of Beauty's fairest dyes,
　　And shap'd and tinted her above all Peers:
Meanwhile Love kept her dearly with his wings,
　　And underneath their shadow fill'd her eyes

With such a richness that the cloudy Kings
Of high Olympus utter'd slavish sighs.
When from the Heavens I saw her first descend,
My heart took fire, and only burning pains,   10
They were my pleasures—they my Life's sad end;
Love pour'd her beauty into my warm veins . . .

    *   *   *   *   *   *   *
  *   *   *   *   *   *   *

A PROPHECY: TO GEORGE KEATS IN AMERICA

'TIS the witching hour of night,
Orbed is the moon and bright,
And the stars they glisten, glisten,
Seeming with bright eyes to listen—
    For what listen they?
For a song and for a charm,
See they glisten in alarm,
And the moon is waxing warm
    To hear what I shall say.
Moon! keep wide thy golden ears—   10
Hearken, stars! and hearken, spheres!—
Hearken, thou eternal sky!
I sing an infant's lullaby,
    A pretty lullaby.
Listen, listen, listen, listen,
Glisten, glisten, glisten, glisten,
    And hear my lullaby!
Though the rushes that will make
Its cradle still are in the lake—
Though the linen that will be   20
Its swathe, is on the cotton tree—
Though the woollen that will keep
It warm, is on the silly sheep—
Listen, starlight, listen, listen,
Glisten, glisten, glisten, glisten,
    And hear my lullaby!
Child, I see thee! Child, I've found thee
Midst of the quiet all around thee!
Child, I see thee! Child, I spy thee!
And thy mother sweet is nigh thee!   30
Child, I know thee! Child no more,
But a Poet evermore!
See, see, the lyre, the lyre,
In a flame of fire,
Upon the little cradle's top

Flaring, flaring, flaring,
Past the eyesight's bearing.
Awake it from its sleep,
And see if it can keep
Its eyes upon the blaze—   40
    Amaze, amaze!
It stares, it stares, it stares,
It dares what no one dares!
It lifts its little hand into the flame
Unharm'd, and on the strings
Paddles a little tune, and sings,
With dumb endeavour sweetly—
Bard art thou completely!
    Little child
    O' th' western wild,   50
Bard art thou completely!
Sweetly with dumb endeavour,
A Poet now or never,
    Little child
    O' th' western wild,
A Poet now or never!

STANZAS

I

In a drear-nighted December,
    Too happy, happy tree,
Thy branches ne'er remember
    Their green felicity:
The north cannot undo them,
With a sleety whistle through them;
Nor frozen thawings glue them
    From budding at the prime.

II

In a drear-nighted December,
    Too happy, happy brook,
Thy bubblings ne'er remember
    Apollo's summer look;
But with a sweet forgetting,
They stay their crystal fretting,
Never, never petting
    About the frozen time.

III

Ah! would 'twere so with many
    A gentle girl and boy!
But were there ever any
    Writh'd not at passed joy?
To know the change and feel it,
When there is none to heal it,
Nor numbed sense to steel it,
    Was never said in rhyme.

SPENSERIAN STANZA

*[Written at the close of Canto II, Book V, of
"The Faerie Queene"]*.

In after-time, a sage of mickle lore
Yclep'd Typographus, the Giant took,
And did refit his limbs as heretofore,
And made him read in many a learned book,
And into many a lively legend look;
Thereby in goodly themes so training him,
That all his brutishness he quite forsook,
When, meeting Artegall and Talus grim,
The one he struck stone-blind, the other's eyes wox dim.

THE EVE OF SAINT MARK

Upon a Sabbath-day it fell:
Twice holy was the Sabbath-bell,
That call'd the folk to evening prayer;
The city streets were clean and fair
From wholesome drench of April rains;
And, on the western window panes,
The chilly sunset faintly told
Of unmatur'd green vallies cold,
Of the green thorny bloomless hedge,
Of rivers new with spring-tide sedge,   10
Of primroses by shelter'd rills,
And daisies on the aguish hills.
Twice holy was the Sabbath-bell:
The silent streets were crowded well
With staid and pious companies,
Warm from their fire-side orat'ries;
And moving, with demurest air,
To even-song, and vesper prayer.
Each arched porch, and entry low,
Was fill'd with patient folk and slow,   20

With whispers hush, and shuffling feet,
While play'd the organ loud and sweet.

The bells had ceas'd, the prayers begun,
And Bertha had not yet half done
A curious volume, patch'd and torn,
That all day long, from earliest morn,
Had taken captive her two eyes,
Among its golden broideries;
Perplex'd her with a thousand things,—
The stars of Heaven, and angels' wings,   30
Martyrs in a fiery blaze,
Azure saints in silver rays,
Moses' breastplate, and the seven
Candlesticks John saw in Heaven,
The winged Lion of Saint Mark,
And the Covenantal Ark,
With its many mysteries,
Cherubim and golden mice.

Bertha was a maiden fair,
Dwelling in the old Minster-square;   40
From her fire-side she could see,
Sidelong, its rich antiquity,
Far as the Bishop's garden-wall;
Where sycamores and elm-trees tall,
Full-leav'd, the forest had outstript,
By no sharp north-wind ever nipt,
So shelter'd by the mighty pile.
Bertha arose, and read awhile,
With forehead 'gainst the window-pane.
Again she try'd, and then again,   50
Until the dusk eve left her dark
Upon the legend of St. Mark.
From plaited lawn-frill, fine and thin,
She lifted up her soft warm chin,
With aching neck and swimming eyes,
And daz'd with saintly imageries.

All was gloom, and silent all,
Save now and then the still foot-fall
Of one returning homewards late,
Past the echoing minster-gate.   60

The clamorous daws, that all the day
Above tree-tops and towers play,
Pair by pair had gone to rest,
Each in its ancient belfry-nest,

Where asleep they fall betimes,
To music of the drowsy chimes.

All was silent, all was gloom,
Abroad and in the homely room:
Down she sat, poor cheated soul!
And struck a lamp from the dismal coal;   70
Lean'd forward, with bright drooping hair
And slant book, full against the glare.
Her shadow, in uneasy guise,
Hover'd about, a giant size,
On ceiling-beam and old oak chair,
The parrot's cage, and panel square;
And the warm angled winter screen,
On which were many monsters seen,
Call'd doves of Siam, Lima mice,
And legless birds of Paradise,   80
Macaw, and tender Avadavat,
And silken-furr'd Angora cat.
Untir'd she read, her shadow still
Glower'd about, as it would fill
The room with wildest forms and shades,
As though some ghostly queen of spades
Had come to mock behind her back,
And dance, and ruffle her garments black.
Untir'd she read the legend page,
Of holy Mark, from youth to age,   90
On land, on sea, in pagan chains,
Rejoicing for his many pains.
Sometimes the learned eremite,
With golden star, or dagger bright,
Referr'd to pious poesies
Written in smallest crow-quill size
Beneath the text; and thus the rhyme
Was parcell'd out from time to time:
——"Als writith he of swevenis,
Men han beforene they wake in bliss,   100
Whanne that hir friendes thinke hem bound
In crimped shroude farre under grounde;
And how a litling child mote be
A saint er its nativitie,
Gif that the modre (God her blesse!)
Kepen in solitarinesse,
And kissen devoute the holy croce.
Of Goddess love, and Sathan's force,—
He writith; and thinges many mo:
Of swiche thinges I may not show.   110

Bot I must tellen verilie
Somdel of Saintè Cicilie,
And chieflie what he auctorethe
Of Saintè Markis life and dethe:"

At length her constant eyelids come
Upon the fervent martyrdom;
Then lastly to his holy shrine,
Exalt amid the tapers' shine
At Venice,—-

ODE TO FANNY

I

PHYSICIAN Nature! let my spirit blood!
   O ease my heart of verse and let me rest;
Throw me upon thy Tripod, till the flood
   Of stifling numbers ebbs from my full breast.
A theme! a theme! great nature! give a theme;
      Let me begin my dream.
I come—I see thee, as thou standest there,
Beckon me not into the wintry air.

II

Ah! dearest love, sweet home of all my fears,
   And hopes, and joys, and panting miseries,—
To-night, if I may guess, thy beauty wears
      A smile of such delight,
      As brilliant and as bright,
   As when with ravished, aching, vassal eyes,
      Lost in soft amaze,
      I gaze, I gaze!

III

Who now, with greedy looks, eats up my feast?
   What stare outfaces now my silver moon!
Ah! keep that hand unravished at the least;
      Let, let, the amorous burn—
      But, pr'ythee, do not turn
   The current of your heart from me so soon.
      O! save, in charity,
      The quickest pulse for me.

IV

Save it for me, sweet love! though music breathe
  Voluptuous visions into the warm air;
Though swimming through the dance's dangerous
        wreath,
      Be like an April day,
      Smiling and cold and gay,
  A temperate lilly, temperate as fair;
      Then, Heaven! there will be
      A warmer June for me.

V

Why, this—you'll say, my Fanny! is not true:
  Put your soft hand upon your snowy side,
Where the heart beats: confess—'tis nothing new—
      Must not a woman be
      A feather on the sea,
  Sway'd to and fro by every wind and tide?
      Of as uncertain speed
      As blow-ball from the mead?

VI

I know it—and to know it is despair
  To one who loves you as I love, sweet Fanny!
Whose heart goes fluttering for you every where,
      Nor, when away you roam,
      Dare keep its wretched home,
  Love, love alone, his pains severe and many.
      Then, loveliest! keep me free,
      From torturing jealousy.

VII

Ah! if you prize my subdued soul above
  The poor, the fading, brief, pride of an hour;
Let none profane my Holy See of love,
      Or with a rude hand break
      The sacramental cake:
  Let none else touch the just new-budded flower;
      If not—may my eyes close,
      Love! on their lost repose.

SONNET

TO SLEEP

O soft embalmer of the still midnight,
　　Shutting, with careful fingers and benign,
Our gloom-pleas'd eyes, embower'd from the light,
　　Enshaded in forgetfulness divine:
O soothest Sleep! if so it please thee, close
　　In midst of this thine hymn my willing eyes,
Or wait the "Amen," ere thy poppy throws
　　Around my bed its lulling charities.
Then save me, or the passed day will shine
Upon my pillow, breeding many woes,—　　　　　　　　　　10
　　Save me from curious Conscience, that still lords
Its strength for darkness, burrowing like a mole;
　　Turn the key deftly in the oiled wards,
And seal the hushed Casket of my Soul.

SONG

I

Hush, hush! tread softly! hush, hush my dear!
　　All the house is asleep, but we know very well
That the jealous, the jealous old bald-pate may hear,
　　Tho' you've padded his night-cap—O sweet Isabel!
　　Tho' your feet are more light than a Fairy's feet,
　　Who dances on bubbles where brooklets meet,—
Hush, hush! soft tiptoe! hush, hush my dear!
For less than a nothing the jealous can hear.

II

No leaf doth tremble, no ripple is there
　　On the river,—all's still, and the night's sleepy eye
Closes up, and forgets all its Lethean care,
　　Charm'd to death by the drone of the humming Mayfly;
　　And the Moon, whether prudish or complaisant,
　　Has fled to her bower, well knowing I want
No light in the dusk, no torch in the gloom,
But my Isabel's eyes, and her lips pulp'd with bloom.

III

Lift the latch! ah gently! ah tenderly—sweet!
　　We are dead if that latchet gives one little clink!
Well done—now those lips, and a flowery seat—
　　The old man may sleep, and the planets may wink;

The shut rose shall dream of our loves, and awake
· Full blown, and such warmth for the morning's take,
The stock-dove shall hatch her soft brace and shall coo,
While I kiss to the melody, aching all through!

SONG

I HAD a dove and the sweet dove died;
   And I have thought it died of grieving:
O, what could it grieve for? Its feet were tied,
   With a silken thread of my own hand's weaving;
Sweet little red feet! why should you die—
Why should you leave me, sweet bird! why?
You liv'd alone in the forest-tree,
Why, pretty thing! would you not live with me?
I kiss'd you oft and gave you white peas;
Why not live sweetly, as in the green trees?   10

ODE ON INDOLENCE

"They toil not, neither do they spin."

I

ONE morn before me were three figures seen,
   With bowed necks, and joined hands, side-faced;
And one behind the other stepp'd serene,
   In placid sandals, and in white robes graced;
They pass'd, like figures on a marble urn,
   When shifted round to see the other side;
     They came again; as when the urn once more
Is shifted round, the first seen shades return;
   And they were strange to me, as may betide
   With vases, to one deep in Phidian lore.

II

How is it, Shadows! that I knew ye not?
   How came ye muffled in so hush a mask?
Was it a silent deep-disguised plot
   To steal away, and leave without a task
My idle days? Ripe was the drowsy hour;
   The blissful cloud of summer-indolence
     Benumb'd my eyes; my pulse grew less and less;
Pain had no sting, and pleasure's wreath no flower:
   O, why did ye not melt, and leave my sense
   Unhaunted quite of all but—nothingness?

III

A third time pass'd they by, and, passing, turn'd
    Each one the face a moment whiles to me;
Then faded, and to follow them I burn'd
    And ach'd for wings because I knew the three;
The first was a fair Maid, and Love her name;
    The second was Ambition, pale of cheek,
        And ever watchful with fatigued eye;
The last, whom I love more, the more of blame
    Is heap'd upon her, maiden most unmeek,—
        I knew to be my demon Poesy.

IV

They faded, and, forsooth! I wanted wings:
    O folly! What is love! and where is it?
And for that poor Ambition! it springs
    From a man's little heart's short fever-fit;
For Poesy!—no,—she has not a joy,—
    At least for me,—so sweet as drowsy noons,
        And evenings steep'd in honied indolence;
O, for an age so shelter'd from annoy,
    That I may never know how change the moons,
        Or hear the voice of busy common-sense!

V

And once more came they by;—alas! wherefore?
    My sleep had been embroider'd with dim dreams;
My soul had been a lawn besprinkled o'er
    With flowers, and stirring shades, and baffled beams:
The morn was clouded, but no shower fell,
    Tho' in her lids hung the sweet tears of May;
        The open casement press'd a new-leav'd vine,
    Let in the budding warmth and throstle's lay;
O Shadows! 'twas a time to bid farewell!
    Upon your skirts had fallen no tears of mine.

VI

So, ye three Ghosts, adieu! Ye cannot raise
    My head cool-bedded in the flowery grass;
For I would not be dieted with praise,
    A pet-lamb in a sentimental farce!
Fade softly from my eyes, and be once more
    In masque-like figures on the dreamy urn;
        Farewell! I yet have visions for the night,
And for the day faint visions there is store;
        Vanish, ye Phantoms! from my idle spright,
    Into the clouds, and never more return!

SONNET

Why did I laugh to-night? No voice will tell:
  No God, no Demon of severe response,
Deigns to reply from heaven or from Hell.
  Then to my human heart I turn at once.
Heart! Thou and I are here sad and alone;
  I say, why did I laugh! O mortal pain!
O Darkness! Darkness! ever must I moan,
  To question Heaven and Hell and Heart in vain.
Why did I laugh? I know this Being's lease,
  My fancy to its utmost blisses spreads;   10
Yet would I on this very midnight cease,
  And the world's gaudy ensigns see in shreds;
Verse, Fame, and Beauty are intense indeed,
But Death intenser—Death is Life's high meed.

SONNET

A DREAM, AFTER READING DANTE'S EPISODE OF PAULO AND FRANCESCA

As Hermes once took to his feathers light,
  When lulled Argus, baffled, swoon'd and slept,
So on a Delphic reed, my idle spright
  So play'd, so charm'd, so conquer'd, so bereft
The dragon-world of all its hundred eyes;
  And, seeing it asleep, so flew away—
Not to pure Ida with its snow-cold skies,
  Nor unto Tempe where Jove griev'd a day;
But to that second circle of sad hell,
  Where 'mid the gust, the whirlwind, and the flaw
Of rain and hail-stones, lovers need not tell   11
  Their sorrows. Pale were the sweet lips I saw,
Pale were the lips I kiss'd, and fair the form
I floated with, about that melancholy storm.

AN EXTEMPORE

FROM A LETTER TO GEORGE KEATS AND HIS WIFE

When they were come into the Faery's Court
They rang—no one at home—all gone to sport
And dance and kiss and love as faeries do
For Fa[e]ries be as humans, lovers true—
Amid the woods they were, so lone and wild,
Where even the Robin feels himself exil'd
And where the very brooks as if afraid
Hurry along to some less magic shade.

"No one at home!" the fretful princess cried
"And all for nothing such a dre[a]ry ride,   10
And all for nothing my new diamond cross,
No one to see my Persian feathers toss,
No one to see my Ape, my Dwarf, my Fool,
Or how I pace my Otaheitan mule.
Ape, Dwarf and Fool, why stand you gaping there?
Burst the door open, quick—or I declare
I'll switch you soundly and in pieces tear."
The Dwarf began to tremble and the 'Ape
Star'd at the Fool, the Fool was all agape,
The Princess grasp'd her switch, but just in time   20
The dwarf with piteous face began to rhyme.
"O mighty Princess did you ne'er hear tell
What your poor servants know but too too well?
Know you the three great crimes in faery land?.
The first, alas! poor Dwarf, I understand—
I made a whipstock of a faery's wand—
The next is snoring in their company—
The next, the last, the direst of the three
Is making free when they are not at home.
I was a Prince—a baby prince—my doom   30
You see, I made a whipstock of a wand—
My top has henceforth slept in faery land.
He was a Prince, the Fool, a grown up Prince,
But he has never been a King's son since
He fell a-snoring at a faery Ball—
Your poor Ape was a prince and he, poor thing,
Picklock'd a faery's boudour—now no king,
But ape—so pray your highness stay awhile;
'Tis sooth indeed, we know it to our sorrow—
Persist and *you* may be an ape tomorrow—   40
While the Dwarf spake the Princess all for spite
Peal'd [*sic*] the brown hazel twig to lilly white,
Clench'd her small teeth, and held her lips apart,
Try'd to look unconcern'd with beating heart.
They saw her highness had made up her mind
And quaver'd like the reeds before the wind,
And they had had it, but, O happy chance!
The Ape for very fear began to dance
And grin'd as all his ugliness did ache—
She staid her vixen fingers for his sake,   50
He was so very ugly: then she took
Her pocket glass mirror and began to look
First at herself and [then] at him and then
She smil'd at her own beauteous face again.

Yet for all this—for all her pretty face
She took it in her head to see the place.
Women gain little from experience
Either in Lovers, husbands or expense.
The more the beauty, the more fortune too,
Beauty before the wide world never knew.   60
So each fair reasons—tho' it oft miscarries.
She thought *her* pretty face would please the fa[e]ries.
"My darling Ape I won't whip you today—
Give me the Picklock, sirrah, and go play."
They all three wept—but counsel was as vain
As crying cup biddy to drops of rain.
Yet lingeringly did the sad Ape forth draw
The Picklock from the Pocket in his Jaw.
The Princess took it and dismounting straight
Trip'd in blue silver'd slippers to the gate   70
And touch'd the wards, the Door full cou[r]teou[s]ly
Opened—she enter'd with her servants three.
Again it clos'd and there was nothing seen
But the Mule grazing on the herbage green.

End of Canto xii

Canto the xiii

The Mule no sooner saw himself alone
Than he prick'd up his Ears—and said "well done!
At least, unhappy Prince, I may be free—
No more a Princess shall side-saddle me.
O King of Otaheitè—tho' a Mule
'Aye every inch a King'—tho' 'Fortune's fool'—   80
Well done—for by what Mr. Dwarfy said
I would not give a sixpence for her head."
Even as he spake he trotted in high glee
To the knotty side of an old Pollard tree
And rub['d] his sides against the mossed bark
Till his Girths burst and left him naked stark
Except his Bridle—how get rid of that,
Buckled and tied with many a twist and plait?
At last it struck him to pretend to sleep
And then the thievish Monkeys down would creep   90
And filch the unpleasant trammels quite away.
No sooner thought of than adown he lay,
Sham'd a good snore—the Monkey-men descended
And whom they thought to injure they befriended.
They hung his Bridle on a topmost bough
And of[f] he went, run, trot, or anyhow —
    Brown is gone to bed—and I am tired of rhyming . . .

SPENSERIAN STANZAS
ON CHARLES ARMITAGE BROWN

I

He is to weet a melancholy carle:
Thin in the waist, with bushy head of hair,
As hath the seeded thistle when in parle
It holds the Zephyr, ere it sendeth fair
Its light balloons into the summer air;
Thereto his beard had not begun to bloom,
No brush had touch'd his chin or razor sheer;
No care had touch'd his cheek with mortal doom,
But new he was and bright as scarf from Persian loom.

II

Ne cared he for wine, or half-and-half
Ne cared he for fish or flesh or fowl,
And sauces held he worthless as the chaff;
He 'sdeigned the swine-head at the wassail-bowl;
Ne with lewd ribbalds sat he cheek by jowl;
Ne with sly Lemans in the scorner's chair;
But after water-brooks this Pilgrim's soul
Panted, and all his food was woodland air
Though he would oft-times feast on gilliflowers rare.

III

The slang of cities in no wise he knew,
Tipping the wink to him was heathen Greek;
He sipp'd no olden Tom or ruin blue,
Or nantz or cherry-brandy drank full meek
By many a damsel hoarse and rouge of cheek;
Nor did he know each aged watchman's beat,
Nor in obscured purlieus would he seek
For curled Jewesses, with ankles neat,
Who as they walk abroad make tinkling with their feet.

TWO OR THREE

FROM A LETTER TO HIS SISTER

Two or three Posies
With two or three simples—
Two or three Noses
With two or three pimples—
Two or three wise men

And two or three ninny's—
Two or three purses
And two or three guineas—
Two or three raps
At two or three doors—   10
Two or three naps
Of two or three hours—
Two or three Cats
And two or three mice—
Two or three sprats
At a very great price—
Two or three sandies
And two or three tabbies—
Two or three dandies
And two Mrs. [Abbeys]   mum!   20
Two or three Smiles
And two or three frowns—
Two or three Miles
To two or three towns—
Two or three pegs
For two or three bonnets—
Two or three dove eggs
To hatch into sonnets.

LA BELLE DAME SANS MERCI

I

Ah, what can ail thee, wretched wight,
    Alone and palely loitering;
The sedge is wither'd from the lake,
    And no birds sing.

II

Ah, what can ail thee, wretched wight,
    So haggard and so woe-begone?
The squirrel's granary is full,
    And the harvest's done.

III

I see a lilly on thy brow,
    With anguish moist and fever dew;
And on thy cheek a fading rose
    Fast withereth too.

IV

I met a lady in the meads
  Full beautiful, a faery's child;
Her hair was long, her foot was light,
  And her eyes were wild.

V

I set her on my pacing steed,
  And nothing else saw all day long;
For sideways would she lean, and sing
  A faery's song.

VI

I made a garland for her head,
  And bracelets too, and fragrant zone;
She look'd at me as she did love,
  And made sweet moan.

VII

She found me roots of relish sweet,
  And honey wild, and manna dew;
And sure in language strange she said,
  I love thee true.

VIII

She took me to her elfin grot,
  And there she gaz'd and sighed deep,
And there I shut her wild sad eyes—
  So kiss'd to sleep.

IX

And there we slumber'd on the moss,
  And there I dream'd, ah woe betide,
The latest dream I ever dream'd
  On the cold hill side.

X

I saw pale kings, and princes too,
  Pale warriors, death-pale were they all;
Who cry'd—"La belle Dame sans merci
  Hath thee in thrall!"

XI

I saw their starv'd lips in the gloam
With horrid warning gaped wide,
And I awoke, and found me here
On the cold hill side.

XII

And this is why I sojourn here
Alone and palely loitering,
Though the sedge is wither'd from the lake,
And no birds sing.

SONG OF FOUR FAERIES,

FIRE, AIR, EARTH, AND WATER,

SALAMANDER, ZEPHYR, DUSKETHA, AND BREAMA

SALAMANDER

HAPPY, happy glowing fire!

ZEPHYR

Fragrant air! delicious light!

DUSKETHA

Let me to my glooms retire!

BREAMA

I to green-weed rivers bright!

SALAMANDER

Happy, happy glowing fire!
Dazzling bowers of soft retire,
Ever let my nourish'd wing,
Like a bat's, still wandering,
Faintless fan your fiery spaces,
Spirit sole in deadly places.   10
In unhaunted roar and blaze,
Open eyes that never daze,
Let me see the myriad shapes
Of men, and beasts, and fish, and apes,
Portray'd in many a fiery den,
And wrought by spumy bitumen.

On the deep intenser roof,
Arched every way aloof,
Let me breathe upon their skies,
And anger their live tapestries;   20
Free from cold, and every care,
Of chilly rain, and shivering air.

ZEPHYR

Spirit of Fire! away! away!
Or your very roundelay
Will sear my plumage newly budded
From its quilled sheath, all studded
With the self-same dews that fell
On the May-grown Asphodel.
Spirit of Fire—away! away!

BREAMA

Spirit of Fire—away! away!   30
Zephyr, blue-eyed Faery, turn,
And see my cool sedge-bury'd urn,
Where it rests its mossy brim
'Mid water-mint and cresses dim;
And the flowers, in sweet troubles,
Lift their eyes above the bubbles,
Like our Queen, when she would please
To sleep, and Oberon *will* teaze.
Love me, blue-eyed Faery, true!
Soothly I am sick for you.   40

ZEPHYR

Gentle Breama! by the first
Violet young nature nurst,
I will bathe myself with thee,
So you sometimes follow me
To my home, far, far, in west,
Beyond the nimble-wheeled quest
Of the golden-browed sun:
Come with me, o'er tops of trees,
To my fragrant palaces,
Where they ever floating are   50
Beneath the cherish of a star
Call'd Vesper, who with silver veil
Ever hides his brilliance pale,
Ever gently-drows'd doth keep
Twilight for the Fayes to sleep.

Fear not that your watery hair
Will thirst in drouthy ringlets there;
Clouds of stored summer rains
Thou shalt taste, before the stains
Of the mountain soil they take,   60
And too unlucent for thee make.
I love thee, crystal Faery, true!
Sooth I am as sick for you!

SALAMANDER

Out, ye aguish Faeries, out!
Chilly lovers, what a rout
Keep ye with your frozen breath,
Colder than the mortal death.
Adder-eyed Dusketha, speak,
Shall we leave these, and go seek
In the earth's wide entrails old   70
Couches warm as their's are cold?
O for a fiery gloom and thee,
Dusketha, so enchantingly
Freckle-wing'd and lizard-sided!

DUSKETHA

By thee, Sprite, will I be guided!
I care not for cold or heat;
Frost and flame, or sparks, or sleet,
To my essence are the same;—
But I honour more the flame.
Sprite of Fire, I follow thee   80
Wheresoever it may be,
To the torrid spouts and fountains,
Underneath earth-quaked mountains;
Or, at thy supreme desire,
Touch the very pulse of fire
With my bare unlidded eyes.

SALAMANDER

Sweet Dusketha! paradise!
Off, ye icy Spirits, fly!
Frosty creatures of the sky!

DUSKETHA

Breathe upon them, fiery sprite!   90

ZEPHYR AND BREAMA

Away! away to our delight!

SALAMANDER

Go, feed on icicles, while we
Bedded in tongue-flames will be.

DUSKETHA

Lead me to those feverous glooms,
Sprite of Fire!

BREAMA

Me to the blooms,
Blue-eyed Zephyr, of those flowers
Far in the west where the May-cloud lowers;
And the beams of still Vesper, when winds are all wist,
Are shed thro' the rain and the milder mist,
And twilight your floating bowers.   100

TWO SONNETS ON FAME

I

FAME, like a wayward Girl, will still be coy
    To those who woo her with too slavish knees,
But makes surrender to some thoughtless Boy,
    And dotes the more upon a heart at ease;
She is a Gipsey, will not speak to those
    Who have not learnt to be content without her;
A Jilt, whose ear was never whisper'd close,
    Who thinks they scandal her who talk about her;
A very Gipsey is she, Nilus-born,
    Sister-in-law to jealous Potiphar;   10
Ye love-sick Bards, repay her scorn for scorn,
    Ye Artists lovelorn, madmen that ye are!
Make your best bow to her and bid adieu,
Then, if she likes it, she will follow you.

II

"You cannot eat your cake and have it too."—*Proverb*.

How fever'd is the man, who cannot look
    Upon his mortal days with temperate blood,
Who vexes all the leaves of his life's book,
    And robs his fair name of its maidenhood;
It is as if the rose should pluck herself,
    Or the ripe plum finger its misty bloom,
As if a Naiad, like a meddling elf,
    Should darken her pure grot with muddy gloom,

But the rose leaves herself upon the briar,
For winds to kiss and grateful bees to feed,   10
And the ripe plum still wears its dim attire,
The undisturbed lake has crystal space,
Why then should man, teasing the world for grace,
Spoil his salvation for a fierce miscreed?

SONNET

ON THE SONNET

IF by dull rhymes our English must be chain'd,
And, like Andromeda, the Sonnet sweet
Fetter'd, in spite of pained loveliness,
Let us find, if we must be constrain'd,
Sandals more interwoven and complete
To fit the naked foot of Poesy:
Let us inspect the Lyre, and weigh the stress
Of every chord, and see what may be gain'd
By ear industrious, and attention meet;
Misers of sound and syllable, no less   10
Than Midas of his coinage, let us be
Jealous of dead leaves in the bay wreath crown;
So, if we may not let the Muse be free,
She will be bound with garlands of her own.

APOLLO AND THE GRACES

WRITTEN TO THE TUNE OF THE AIR IN "DON GIOVANNI"

APOLLO

WHICH of the fairest three
To-day will ride with me?
My steeds are all pawing at the threshold of the morn:
Which of the fairest three
To-day will ride with me
Across the gold Autumn's whole Kingdom of corn?

THE GRACES *all answer*

I will, I— I— I—
O young Apollo let me fly
Along with thee,
I will—I, I, I,   10
The many wonders see
I— I— I— I—
And thy lyre shall never have a slackened string:
I, I, I, I,
Thro' the golden day will sing.

YOU SAY YOU LOVE

I

You say you love; but with a voice
  Chaster than a nun's, who singeth
The soft Vespers to herself
  While the chime-bell ringeth—
    O love me truly!

II

You say you love; but with a smile
  Cold as sunrise in September,
As you were Saint Cupid's nun,
  And kept his weeks of Ember.
    O love me truly!

III

You say you love—but then your lips
  Coral tinted teach no blisses,
More than coral in the sea—
  They never pout for kisses—
    O love me truly!

IV

You say you love; but then your hand
  No soft squeeze for squeeze returneth,
It is like a statue's dead—
  While mine to passion burneth—
    O love me truly!

V

O breathe a word or two of fire!
  Smile, as if those words should burn me,
Squeeze as lovers should—O kiss
  And in thy heart inurn me!
    O love me truly!

OTHO THE GREAT

A TRAGEDY

IN FIVE ACTS

DRAMATIS PERSONÆ

OTHO THE GREAT, *Emperor of Germany.*
LUDOLPH, *his Son.*
CONRAD, *Duke of Franconia.*
ALBERT, *a Knight, favoured by Otho.*
SIGIFRED, *an Officer, friend of Ludolph.*
THEODORE, ⎱ *Officers.*
GONFRED, ⎰
ETHELBERT, *an Abbot.*
GERSA, *Prince of Hungary.*
An Hungarian Captain.
Physician.
Page.
Nobles, Knights, Attendants, and Soldiers.
ERMINIA, *Niece of Otho.*
AURANTHE, *Conrad's Sister.*
Ladies and Attendants.

SCENE. *The Castle of Friedburg, its vicinity, and the Hungarian Camp.*

TIME. *One Day.*

OTHO THE GREAT

ACT I

SCENE I.—*An Apartment in the Castle. Enter* CONRAD.

Conrad. So, I am safe emerged from these broils!
Amid the wreck of thousands I am whole;
For every crime I have a laurel-wreath,
For every lie a lordship. Nor yet has
My ship of fortune furl'd her silken sails,—
Let her glide on! This danger'd neck is saved,
By dexterous policy, from the rebel's axe;
And of my ducal palace not one stone
Is bruised by the Hungarian petards.
Toil hard, ye slaves, and from the miser-earth   10
Bring forth once more my bullion, treasured deep,
With all my jewell'd salvers, silver and gold,
And precious goblets that make rich the wine.
But why do I stand babbling to myself?
Where is Auranthe? I have news for her
Shall—

Enter AURANTHE.

Auranthe. Conrad! what tidings? Good, if I may guess
From your alert eyes and high-lifted brows.
What tidings of the battle? Albert? Ludolph? Otho?
Conrad. You guess aright. And, sister, slurring o'er   20
Our by-gone quarrels, I confess my heart
Is beating with a child's anxiety,
To make our golden fortune known to you.
Auranthe. So serious?
Conrad.   .   Yes, so serious, that before
I utter even the shadow of a hint
Concerning what will make that sin-worn cheek
Blush joyous blood through every lineament,
You must make here a solemn vow to me.
Auranthe. I prythee, Conrad, do not overact
The hypocrite—what vow would you impose?
Conrad. Trust me for once,—that you may be assur'd
'Tis not confiding to a broken reed,   31
A poor Court-bankrupt, outwitted and lost,
Revolve these facts in your acutest mood,

287

In such a mood as now you listen to me:—
A few days since, I was an open rebel
Against the Emperor, had suborn'd his son,
Drawn off his nobles to revolt, and shown
Contented fools causes for discontent
Fresh hatch'd in my ambition's eagle nest—
So thriv'd I as a rebel, and behold   40
Now I am Otho's favourite, his dear friend,
His right hand, his brave Conrad.
    Auranthe.   I confess
You have intrigued with these unsteady times
To admiration; but to be a favourite—
    Conrad. I saw my moment. The Hungarians,
Collected silently in holes and corners,
Appear'd, a sudden host, in the open day.
I should have perish'd in our empire's wreck,
But, calling interest loyalty, swore faith
To most believing Otho; and so help'd   50
His blood-stain'd ensigns to the victory
In yesterday's hard fight, that it has turn'd
The edge of his sharp wrath to eager kindness.
    Auranthe. So far yourself. But what is this to me
More than that I am glad? I gratulate you.
    Conrad. Yes, sister, but it does regard you greatly,
Nearly, momentously,—aye, painfully!
Make me this vow—
    Auranthe.   Concerning whom or what?
    Conrad. Albert!
    Auranthe.   I would inquire somewhat of him:
You had a letter from me touching him?   60
No treason 'gainst his head in deed or word!
Surely you spar'd him at my earnest prayer?
Give me the letter—it should not exist!
    Conrad. At one pernicious charge of the enemy,
I, for a moment-whiles, was prisoner ta'en
And rifled,—stuff! the horses' hoofs have minc'd it!
    Auranthe. He is alive?
    Conrad.   He is! but here make oath
To alienate him from your scheming brain,
Divorce him from your solitary thoughts,
And cloud him in such utter banishment,   70
That when his person meets again your eye,
Your vision shall quite lose its memory,
And wander past him as through vacancy.
    Auranthe. I'll not be perjured.
    Conrad.   No, nor great, nor mighty;
You would not wear a crown, or rule a kingdom.

To you it is indifferent.
    Auranthe.   What means this?
    Conrad. You'll not be perjured! Go to Albert **then,**
That camp-mushroom—dishonour of our house.
Go, page his dusty heels upon a march,
Furbish his jingling baldric while he sleeps,   80
And share his mouldy ration in a siege.
Yet stay,—perhaps a charm may call you back,
And make the widening circlets of your eyes
Sparkle with healthy fevers.—The Emperor
Hath given consent that you should marry Ludolph!
    Auranthe. Can it be, brother? For a golden crown
With a queen's awful lips I doubly thank you!
This is to wake in Paradise! Farewell
Thou clod of yesterday—'twas not myself!
Not till this moment did I ever feel   90
My spirit's faculties! I'll flatter you
For this, and be you ever proud of it;
Thou, Jove-like, struck'dst thy forehead,
And from the teeming marrow of thy brain
I spring complete Minerva! But the prince—
His highness Ludolph—where is he?
    Conrad.   I know **not:**
When, lackeying my counsel at a beck,
The rebel lords, on bended knees, received
The Emperor's pardon, Ludolph kept aloof,
Sole, in a stiff, fool-hardy, sulky pride;   100
Yet, for all this, I never saw a father
In such a sickly longing for his son.
We shall soon see him, for the Emperor
He will be here this morning.
    Auranthe.   That I heard
Among the midnight rumours from the camp.
    Conrad. You give up Albert to me?
    Auranthe.   Harm him **not!**
E'en for his highness Ludolph's sceptry hand,
I would not Albert suffer any wrong.
    Conrad. Have I not laboured, plotted—?
    Auranthe.   See you spare **him:**
Nor be pathetic, my kind benefactor,   110
On all the many bounties of your hand,—
'Twas for yourself you laboured—not for me!
Do you not count, when I am queen, to take
Advantage of your chance discoveries
Of my poor secrets, and so hold a rod
Over my life?

Conrad.   Let not this slave—this villain—
Be cause of feud between us. See! he comes!
Look, woman, look, your Albert is quite safe!
In haste it seems. Now shall I be in the way,
And wish'd with silent curses in my grave,   12C
Or side by side with 'whelmed mariners.

Enter ALBERT.

Albert. Fair on your graces fall this early morrow!
So it is like to do, without my prayers,
For your right noble names, like favourite tunes,
Have fall'n full frequent from our Emperor's lips,
High commented with smiles.
   Auranthe.   Noble Albert!
   Conrad (aside).   Noble!
   Auranthe. Such salutation argues a glad heart
In our prosperity. We thank you, sir.
   Albert. Lady! O, would to Heaven your poor servant
Could do you better service than mere words!   130
But I have other greeting than mine own,
From no less man than Otho, who has sent
This ring as pledge of dearest amity;
'Tis chosen I hear from Hymen's jewel'ry,
And you will prize it, lady, I doubt not,
Beyond all pleasures past, and all to come.
To you great duke—
   Conrad.   To me! What of me, ha?
   Albert. What pleas'd your grace to say?
   Conrad.   Your message, sir!
   Albert. You mean not this to me?
   Conrad.   Sister, this way;
For there shall be no "gentle Alberts" now,   [*Aside.*
No "sweet Auranthes!"   141

                    [*Exeunt* CONRAD *and* AURANTHE.

   Albert (solus). The duke is out of temper; if he knows
More than a brother of a sister ought,
I should not quarrel with his peevishness.
Auranthe—Heaven preserve her always fair!—
Is in the heady, proud, ambitious vein;
I bicker not with her,—bid her farewell!
She has taken flight from me, then let her soar, —
He is a fool who stands at pining gaze!
But for poor Ludolph, he is food for sorrow: 150
No levelling bluster of my licens'd thoughts,
No military swagger of my mind,
Can smother from myself the wrong I've done him,—

Without design, indeed,—yet it is so,—
And opiate for the conscience have I none!   [*Exit.*

SCENE II.—*The Court-yard of the Castle.*

Martial Music. Enter, from the outer gate, OTHO, *Nobles, Knights, and
Attendants. The Soldiers halt at the gate, with Banners in sight.*

 Otho. Where is my noble herald?

 Enter CONRAD, *from the Castle, attended by two Knights and
  Servants.* ALBERT *following.*

          Well, hast told
Auranthe our intent imperial?
Lest our rent banners, too o' the sudden shown,
Should fright her silken casements, and dismay
Her household to our lack of entertainment.
A victory!
 Conrad. God save illustrious Otho!
 Otho. Aye, Conrad, it will pluck out all grey hairs;
It is the best physician for the spleen;
The courtliest inviter to a feast;
The subtlest excuser of small faults;   10
And a nice judge in the age and smack of wine.

 Enter, from the Castle, AURANTHE, *followed by Pages holding
  up her robes, and a train of Women. She kneels.*

Hail my sweet hostess! I do thank the stars,
Or my good soldiers, or their ladies' eyes,
That, after such a merry battle fought,
I can, all safe in body and in soul,
Kiss your fair hand and lady fortune's too.
My ring! now, on my life, it doth rejoice
These lips to feel 't on this soft ivory!
Keep it, my brightest daughter; it may prove
The little prologue to a line of kings.   20
I strove against thee and my hot-blood son,
Dull blockhead that I was to be so blind,
But now my sight is clear; forgive me, lady.
 Auranthe. My lord, I was a vassal to your frown,
And now your favour makes me but more humble;
In wintry winds the simple snow is safe,
But fadeth at the greeting of the sun:
Unto thine anger I might well have spoken,
Taking on me a woman's privilege,
But this so sudden kindness makes me dumb.   30
 Otho. What need of this? Enough, if you will be
A potent tutoress to my wayward boy,
And teach him, what it seems his nurse could not,

To say, for once, I thank you. Sigifred!
    Albert. He has not yet return'd, my gracious liege.
    Otho. What then! No tidings of my friendly Arab?
    Conrad. None, mighty Otho.

                    [*To one of his Knights, who goes out.*

                      Send forth instantly
An hundred horsemen from my honoured gates,
To scour the plains and search the cottages.
Cry a reward, to him who shall first bring   40
News of that vanished Arabian,
A full-heap'd helmet of the purest gold.
    Otho. More thanks, good Conrad; for, except my son's,
There is no face I rather would behold
Than that same quick-eyed pagan's. By the saints,
This coming night of banquets must not light
Her dazzling torches; nor the music breathe
Smooth, without clashing cymbal, tones of peace
And in-door melodies; nor the ruddy wine
Ebb spouting to the lees; if I pledge not,   50
In my first cup, that Arab!
    Albert.   Mighty Monarch,
I wonder not this stranger's victor-deeds
So hang upon your spirit. Twice in the fight
It was my chance to meet his olive brow,
Triumphant in the enemy's shatter'd rhomb;
And, to say truth, in any Christian arm
I never saw such prowess.
    Otho.   Did you ever?
O, 'tis a noble boy!—tut!—what do I say?
I mean a triple Saladin, whose eyes,
When in the glorious scuffle they met mine,   60
Seem'd to say—"Sleep, old man, in safety sleep;
I am the victory!"
    Conrad.   Pity he's not here.
    Otho. And my son too, pity he is not here.
Lady Auranthe, I would not make you blush,
But can you give a guess where Ludolph is?
Know you not of him?
    Auranthe.   Indeed, my liege, no secret—
    Otho. Nay, nay, without more words, dost know of him?
    Auranthe. I would I were so over-fortunate,
Both for his sake and mine, and to make glad
A father's ears with tidings of his son.   70
    Otho. I see 'tis like to be a tedious day.
Were Theodore and Gonfred and the rest
Sent forth with my commands?

Albert.   Aye, my lord.

Otho. And no news! No news! 'Faith! 'tis very strange
He thus avoids us. Lady, is't not strange?
Will he be truant to you too? It is a shame.

    Conrad. Will 't please your highness enter, and accept
The unworthy welcome of your servant's house?
Leaving your cares to one whose diligence
May in few hours make pleasures of them all.   80

    Otho. Not so tedious, Conrad. No, no, no,—
I must see Ludolph or the— What's that shout!

    Voices without. Huzza! huzza! Long live the Emperor!

    Other Voices. Fall back! Away there!

    Otho.   Say, what noise is that?

[ALBERT *advancing from the back of the Stage, whither he had
hastened on hearing the cheers of the soldiery.*

    Albert. It is young Gersa, the Hungarian prince,
Pick'd like a red stag from the fallow herd
Of prisoners. Poor prince, forlorn he steps,
Slow, and demure, and proud in his despair.
If I may judge by his so tragic bearing,
His eye not downcast, and his folded arm,   90
He doth this moment wish himself asleep
Among his fallen captains on yon plains.

Enter GERSA, *in chains, and guarded.*

    Otho. Well said, Sir Albert.

    Gersa.   Not a word of greeting.
No welcome to a princely visitor,
Most mighty Otho? Will not my great host
Vouchsafe a syllable, before he bids
His gentlemen conduct me with all care
To some securest lodgings?—cold perhaps!

    Otho. What mood is this? Hath fortune touch'd thy brain?

    Gersa. O kings and princes of this fev'rous world,
What abject things, what mockeries must ye be,   101
What nerveless minions of safe palaces!
When here, a monarch, whose proud foot is used
To fallen princes' necks, as to his stirrup,
Must needs exclaim that I am mad forsooth,
Because I cannot flatter with bent knees
My conqueror!

    Otho.   Gersa, I think you wrong me:
I think I have a better fame abroad.

    Gersa. I prythee mock me not with gentle speech,
But, as a favour, bid me from thy presence;   110
Let me no longer be the wondering food

Of all these eyes; prythee command me hence!
   Otho. Do not mistake me, Gersa. That you may not,
Come, fair Auranthe, try if your soft hands
Can manage those hard rivets to set free
So brave a prince and soldier.
   Auranthe (sets him free).   Welcome task!
   Gersa. I am wound up in deep astonishment!
Thank you, fair lady. Otho! emperor!
You rob me of myself; my dignity
Is now your infant; I am a weak child.   120
   Otho. Give me your hand, and let this kindly grasp
Live in our memories.
   Gersa.   In mine it will.
I blush to think of my unchasten'd tongue;
But I was haunted by the monstrous ghost
Of all our slain battalions. Sire, reflect,
And pardon you will grant, that, at this hour,
The bruised remnants of our stricken camp
Are huddling undistinguish'd my dear friends,
With common thousands, into shallow graves.
   Otho. Enough, most noble Gersa. You are free
To cheer the brave remainder of your host   131
By your own healing presence, and that too,
Not as their leader merely, but their king;
For, as I hear, the wily enemy,
Who eas'd the crownet from your infant brows,
Bloody Taraxa, is among the dead.
   Gersa. Then I retire, so generous Otho please,
Bearing with me a weight of benefits
Too heavy to be borne.
   Otho.   It is not so;
Still understand me, King of Hungary,   140
Nor judge my open purposes awry.
Though I did hold you high in my esteem
For your self's sake, I do not personate
The stage-play emperor to entrap applause,
To set the silly sort o' the world agape,
And make the politic smile; no, I have heard
How in the Council you condemn'd this war,
Urging the perfidy of broken faith,—
For that I am your friend.
   Gersa.   If ever, sire,
You are mine enemy, I dare here swear   150
'Twill not be Gersa's fault. Otho, farewell!
   Otho. Will you return, Prince, to our banqueting?
   Gersa. As to my father's board I will return.
   Otho. Conrad, with all due ceremony, give

The prince a regal escort to his camp;
Albert, go thou and bear him company.
Gersa, farewell!
   Gersa.   All happiness attend you!
   Otho. Return with what good speed you may; for soon
We must consult upon our terms of peace.

                 [*Exeunt* GERSA *and* ALBERT *with others.*

And thus a marble column do I build   160
To prop my empire's dome. Conrad, in thee
I have another stedfast one, to uphold
The portals of my state; and, for my own
Pre-eminence and safety, I will strive
To keep thy strength upon its pedestal.
For, without thee, this day I might have been
A show-monster about the streets of Prague,
In chains, as just now stood that noble prince:
And then to me no mercy had been shown,
For when the conquer'd lion is once dungeon'd,   170
Who lets him forth again? or dares to give
An old lion sugar-cates of mild reprieve?
Not to thine ear alone I make confession,
But to all here, as, by experience,
I know how the great basement of all power
Is frankness, and a true tongue to the world;
And how intriguing secrecy is proof
Of fear and weakness, and a hollow state.
Conrad, I owe thee much.
   Conrad.   To kiss that hand,
My emperor, is ample recompense,   180
For a mere act of duty.
   Otho.   Thou art wrong;
For what can any man on earth do more?
We will make trial of your house's welcome,
My bright Auranthe!
   Conrad.   How is Friedburg honoured!

        Enter ETHELBERT *and six Monks.*

   Ethelbert. The benison of heaven on your head,
Imperial Otho!
   Otho.   Who stays me? Speak! Quick!
   Ethelbert. Pause but one moment, mighty conqueror
Upon the threshold of this house of joy.
   Otho. Pray, do not prose, good Ethelbert, but speak
What is your purpose.   190
   Ethelbert. The restoration of some captive maids,
Devoted to Heaven's pious ministries,

Who, being driven from their religious cells,
And kept in thraldom by our enemy,
When late this province was a lawless spoil,
Still weep amid the wild Hungarian camp,
Though hemm'd around by thy victorious arms.
    Otho. Demand the holy sisterhood in our name
From Gersa's tents. Farewell, old Ethelbert.   199
    Ethelbert. The saints will bless you for this pious care.
    Otho. Daughter, your hand; Ludolph's would fit it best.
    Conrad. Ho! let the music sound!

    [*Music.* ETHELBERT *raises his hands, as in benediction of* OTHO.
    Exeunt severally. The scene closes on them.

SCENE III.—*The Country, with the Castle in the distance.*

Enter LUDOLPH *and* SIGIFRED.

    Ludolph. You have my secret; let it not be breath'd.
    Sigifred. Still give me leave to wonder that the Prince
Ludolph and the swift Arab are the same;
Still to rejoice that 'twas a German arm
Death doing in a turban'd masquerade.
    Ludolph. The Emperor must not know it, Sigifred.
    Sigifred. I prythee, why? What happier hour of time
Could thy pleas'd star point down upon from heaven
With silver index, bidding thee make peace?
    Ludolph. Still it must not be known, good Sigifred;
The star may point oblique.   11
    Sigifred.   If Otho knew
His son to be that unknown Mussulman
After whose spurring heels he sent me forth,
With one of his well-pleas'd Olympian oaths,
The charters of man's greatness, at this hour
He would be watching round the castle walls,
And, like an anxious warder, strain his sight
For the first glimpse of such a son return'd—
Ludolph, that blast of the Hungarians,
That Saracenic meteor of the fight,   20
That silent fury, whose fell Scymitar
Kept danger all aloof from Otho's head,
And left him space for wonder.
    Ludolph.   Say no more.
Not as a swordsman would I pardon claim,
But as a son. The bronz'd centurion,
Long toil'd in foreign wars, and whose high deeds
Are shaded in a forest of tall spears,
Known only to his troop, hath greater plea

Of favour with my sire than I can have. 29

Sigifred. My lord, forgive me that I cannot see
How this proud temper with clear reason squares.
What made you then, with such an anxious love,
Hover around that life, whose bitter days
You vext with bad revolt? Was 't opium,
Or the mad-fumed wine? Nay, do not frown,
I rather would grieve with you than upbraid.

Ludolph. I do believe you. No, 'twas not to make
A father his son's debtor, or to heal
His deep heart-sickness for a rebel child.
'Twas done in memory of my boyish days, 40
Poor cancel for his kindness to my youth,,
For all his calming of my childish griefs,
And all his smiles upon my merriment.
No, not a thousand foughten fields could sponge
Those days paternal from my memory,
Though now upon my head he heaps disgrace.

Sigifred. My Prince, you think too harshly—
Ludolph. Can I so?
Hath he not gall'd my spirit to the quick?
And with a sullen rigour obstinate
Pour'd out a phial of wrath upon my faults? 50
Hunted me as the Tartar does the boar,
Driven me to the very edge o' the world,
And almost put a price upon my head?

Sigifred. Remember how he spar'd the rebel lords.

Ludolph. Yes, yes, I know he hath a noble nature
That cannot trample on the fallen. But his
Is not the only proud heart in his realm.
He hath wrong'd me, and I have done him wrong;
He hath lov'd me, and I have shown him kindness;
We should be almost equal.

Sigifred. Yet, for all this, 60
I would you had appear'd among those lords,
And ta'en his favour.

Ludolph. Ha! till now I thought
My friend had held poor Ludolph's honour dear.
What! would you have me sue before his throne
And kiss the courtier's missal, its silk steps?
Or hug the golden housings of his steed,
Amid a camp, whose steeled swarms I dar'd
But yesterday? And, at the trumpet sound,
Bow like some unknown mercenary's flag,
And lick the soiled grass? No, no, my friend, 70
I would not, I, be pardon'd in the heap,
And bless indemnity with all that scum,—

Those men I mean, who on my shoulders propp'd
Their weak rebellion, winning me with lies,
And pitying forsooth my many wrongs;
Poor self-deceived wretches, who must think
Each one himself a king in embryo,
Because some dozen vassals cry'd—my lord!
Cowards, who never knew their little hearts,
Till flurried danger held the mirror up,   80
And then they own'd themselves without a blush,
Curling, like spaniels, round my father's feet.
Such things deserted me and are forgiven,
While I, least guilty, am an outcast still,
And will be, for I love such fair disgrace.
   Sigifred. I know the clear truth; so would Otho see,
For he is just and noble. Fain would I
Be pleader for you—
   Ludolph.   He'll hear none of it;
You know his temper, hot, proud, obstinate;
Endanger not yourself so uselessly.   90
I will encounter his thwart spleen myself,
To-day, at the Duke Conrad's, where he keeps
His crowded state after the victory.
There will I be, a most unwelcome guest,
And parley with him, as a son should do,
Who doubly loathes a father's tyranny;
Tell him how feeble is that tyranny;
How the relationship of father and son
Is no more valid than a silken leash
Where lions tug adverse, if love grow not   100
From interchanged love through many years.
Aye, and those turreted Franconian walls,
Like to a jealous casket, hold my pearl—
My fair Auranthe! Yes, I will be there.
   Sigifred. Be not so rash; wait till his wrath shall pass,
Until his royal spirit softly ebbs
Self-influenced; then, in his morning dreams
He will forgive thee, and awake in grief
To have not thy good morrow.
   Ludolph.   Yes, to-day
I must be there, while her young pulses beat   110
Among the new-plum'd minions of the war.
Have you seen her of late? No? Auranthe,
Franconia's fair sister, 'tis I mean.
She should be paler for my troublous days—
And there it is—my father's iron lips
Have sworn divorcement 'twixt me and my right.
   Sigifred (*aside*). Auranthe! I had hop'd this whim had pass'd.

Ludolph. And, Sigifred, with all his love of justice,
When will he take that grandchild in his arms,
That, by my love I swear, shall soon be his?   120
This reconcilement is impossible,
For see—but who are these?
    Sigifred.   They are messengers
From our great emperor; to you, I doubt not,
For couriers are abroad to seek you out.

Enter THEODORE *and* GONFRED.

    Theodore. Seeing so many vigilant eyes explore
The province to invite your highness back
To your high dignities, we are too happy.
    Gonfred. We have no eloquence to colour justly
The emperor's anxious wishes.
    Ludolph.   Go. I follow you.

                 [*Exeunt* THEODORE *and* GONFRED.

I play the prude: it is but venturing—   130
Why should he be so earnest? Come, my friend,
Let us to Friedburg castle.

ACT II

SCENE I.—*An Ante-chamber in the Castle.*

Enter LUDOLPH *and* SIGIFRED.

    Ludolph. No more advices, no more cautioning:
I leave it all to fate—to any thing!
I cannot square my conduct to time, place,
Or circumstances; to me 'tis all a mist!
    Sigifred. I say no more.
    Ludolph.   It seems I am to wait
Here in the ante-room;—that may be a trifle.
You see now how I dance attendance here,
Without that tyrant temper, you so blame,
Snapping the rein. You have medicin'd me
With good advices; and I here remain,   10
In this most honourable ante-room,
Your patient scholar.
    Sigifred.   Do not wrong me, Prince.
By Heavens, I'd rather kiss Duke Conrad's slipper,
When in the morning he doth yawn with pride,
Than see you humbled but a half-degree!
Truth is, the Emperor would fain dismiss
The nobles ere he sees you.

Enter GONFRED *from the Council-room.*

Ludolph.   Well, sir! What?
Gonfred. Great honour to the Prince! The Emperor,
Hearing that his brave son had re-appeared,
Instant dismiss'd the Council from his sight,   20
As Jove fans off the clouds. Even now they pass.

                                                    [*Exit.*

Enter the Nobles from the Council-room. They cross the stage,
     bowing with respect to LUDOLPH, *he frowning on them.*
     CONRAD *follows. Exeunt Nobles.*

Ludolph. Not the discoloured poisons of a fen,
Which he who breathes feels warning of his death,
Could taste so nauseous to the bodily sense,
As these prodigious sycophants disgust
The soul's fine palate.
Conrad.   Princely Ludolph, hail!
Welcome, thou younger sceptre to the realm!
Strength to thy virgin crownet's golden buds,
That they, against the winter of thy sire,
May burst, and swell, and flourish round thy brows,   30
Maturing to a weighty diadem!
Yet be that hour far off; and may he live,
Who waits for thee, as the chapp'd earth for rain.
Set my life's star! I have lived long enough,
Since under my glad roof, propitiously,
Father and son each other re-possess.
Ludolph. Fine wording, Duke! but words could never yet
Forestall the fates; have you not learnt that yet?
Let me look well: your features are the same;
Your gait the same; your hair of the same shade;   40
As one I knew some passed weeks ago,
Who sung far different notes into mine ears.
I have mine own particular comments on 't;
You have your own, perhaps.
Conrad.   My gracious Prince,
All men may err. In truth I was deceived
In your great father's nature, as you were.
Had I known that of him I have since known,
And what you soon will learn, I would have turn'd
My sword to my own throat, rather than held
Its threatening edge against a good King's quiet: 50
Or with one word fever'd you, gentle Prince,
Who seem'd to me, as rugged times then went,
Indeed too much oppress'd. May I be bold

To tell the Emperor you will haste to him?
Ludolph. Your Dukedom's privilege will grant so much.

[*Exit* CONRAD.

He's very close to Otho, a tight leech!
Your hand—I go. Ha! here the thunder comes
Sullen against the wind! If in two angry brows
My safety lies, then Sigifred, I'm safe.

Enter OTHO *and* CONRAD.

Otho. Will you make Titan play the lackey-page   60
To chattering pigmies? I would have you know
That such neglect of our high Majesty
Annuls all feel of kindred. What is son,—
Or friend,—or brother,—or all ties of blood,—
When the whole kingdom, centred in ourself,
Is rudely slighted? Who am I to wait?
By Peter's chair! I have upon my tongue
A word to fright the proudest spirit here!—
Death!—and slow tortures to the hardy fool,
Who dares take such large charter from our smiles!   70
Conrad, we would be private. Sigifred!
Off! And none pass this way on pain of death!

[*Exeunt* CONRAD *and* SIGIFRED.

Ludolph. This was but half expected, my good sire,
Yet I am griev'd at it, to the full height,
As though my hopes of favour had been whole.
Otho. How you indulge yourself! What can you hope for?
Ludolph. Nothing, my liege; I have to hope for nothing.
I come to greet you as a loving son,
And then depart, if I may be so free,
Seeing that blood of yours in my warm veins   80
Has not yet mitigated into milk.
Otho. What would you, sir?
Ludolph.   A lenient banishment;
So please you let me unmolested pass
This Conrad's gates, to the wide air again.
I want no more. A rebel wants no more.
Otho. And shall I let a rebel loose again
To muster kites and eagles 'gainst my head?
No, obstinate boy, you shall be kept cag'd up,
Serv'd with harsh food, with scum for Sunday-drink.
Ludolph. Indeed!
Otho.   And chains too heavy for your life:
I'll choose a gaoler, whose swart monstrous face   91
Shall be a hell to look upon, and she—

Ludolph.   Ha!

Otho. Shall be your fair Auranthe.

Ludolph.   Amaze! Amaze!

Otho. To-day you marry her.

Ludolph.   This is a sharp jest!

Otho. No. None at all. When have I said a lie?

Ludolph. If I sleep not, I am a waking wretch.

Otho. Not a word more. Let me embrace my child.

Ludolph. I dare not. 'Twould pollute so good a father!
O heavy crime! that your son's blinded eyes
Could not see all his parent's love aright,   100
As now I see it. Be not kind to me—
Punish me not with favour.

    Otho.   Are you sure,
Ludolph, you have no saving plea in store?

Ludolph. My father, none!

Otho.   Then you astonish me.

Ludolph. No, I have no plea. Disobedience,
Rebellion, obstinacy, blasphemy,
Are all my counsellors. If they can make
My crooked deeds show good and plausible,
Then grant me loving pardon, but not else,
Good Gods! not else, in any way, my liege!   110

Otho. You are a most perplexing, noble boy.

Ludolph. You not less a perplexing noble father.

Otho. Well, you shall have free passport through the gates.
Farewell!

Ludolph. Farewell! and by these tears believe,
And still remember, I repent in pain
All my misdeeds!

    Otho.   Ludolph, I will! I will!
But, Ludolph, ere you go, I would enquire
If you, in all your wandering, ever met
A certain Arab haunting in these parts.

Ludolph. No, my good lord, I cannot say I did.   120

Otho. Make not your father blind before his time;
Nor let these arms paternal hunger more
For an embrace, to dull the appetite
Of my great love for thee, my supreme child!
Come close, and let me breathe into thine ear.
I knew you through disguise. You are the Arab!
You can't deny it.   [*Embracing him.*

    Ludolph.   Happiest of days!

Otho. We'll make it so.

Ludolph.   'Stead of one fatted calf
Ten hecatombs shall bellow out their last,
Smote 'twixt the horns by the death-stunning mace   130

Of Mars, and all the soldiery shall feast
Nobly as Nimrod's masons, when the towers
Of Nineveh new kiss'd the parted clouds!
  Otho. Large as a God speak out, where all is thine.
  Ludolph. Aye, father, but the fire in my sad breast
Is quench'd with inward tears! I must rejoice
For you, whose wings so shadow over me
In tender victory, but for myself
I still must mourn. The fair Auranthe mine!
Too great a boon! I prythee let me ask   140
What more than I know of could so have changed
Your purpose touching her?
  Otho.   At a word, this:
In no deed did you give me more offense
Than your rejection of Erminia.
To my appalling, I saw too good proof
Of your keen-eyed suspicion,—she is naught!
  Ludolph. You are convinc'd?
  Otho.   Aye, spite of her sweet looks.
O, that my brother's daughter should so fall!
Her fame has pass'd into the grosser lips
Of soldiers in their cups.
  Ludolph.   'Tis very sad.   150
  Otho. No more of her. Auranthe—Ludolph, come!
This marriage be the bond of endless peace!   [*Exeunt.*

SCENE II.—*The Entrance of* GERSA'S *Tent in the Hungarian Camp.*

Enter ERMINIA.

  Erminia. Where! where! where shall I find a messenger?
A trusty soul? A good man in the camp?
Shall I go myself? Monstrous wickedness!
O cursed Conrad! devilish Auranthe!
Here is proof palpable as the bright sun!
O for a voice to reach the Emperor's ears!
                    [*Shouts in the Camp.*

Enter an HUNGARIAN CAPTAIN.

  Captain. Fair prisoner, hear you those joyous shouts?
The king—aye, now our king,—but still your slave,
Young Gersa, from a short captivity
Has just return'd. He bids me say, bright Dame,   10
That even the homage of his ranged chiefs
Cures not his keen impatience to behold
Such beauty once again. What ails you, lady?
  Erminia. Say, is not that a German, yonder? There!
  Captain. Methinks by his stout bearing he should be—

Yes—'tis one Albert; a brave German knight,
And much in the emperor's favour.
    Erminia.   I would fain
Enquire of friends and kinsfolk; how they fared
In these rough times. Brave soldier, as you pass
To royal Gersa with my humble thanks,   20
Will you send yonder knight to me?
    Captain.   I will.   [*Exit.*
    Ermina. Yes, he was ever known to be a man
Frank, open, generous; Albert I may trust.
O proof! proof! proof! Albert's an honest man;
Not Ethelbert the monk, if he were here,
Would I hold more trustworthy. Now!

Enter ALBERT.

    Albert.   Good Gods!
Lady Erminia! are you prisoner
In this beleaguer'd camp? Or are you here
Of your own will? You pleas'd to send for me.
By Venus, 'tis a pity I knew not   30
Your plight before, and, by her Son, I swear
To do you every service you can ask.
What would the fairest—?
    Erminia.   Albert, will you swear?
    Albert. I have. Well?
    Erminia.   Albert, you have fame to lose.
If men, in court and camp, lie not outright,
You should be, from a thousand, chosen forth
To do an honest deed. Shall I confide—?
    Albert. Aye, anything to me, fair creature. Do;
Dictate my task. Sweet woman,—
    Erminia.   Truce with that.
You understand me not; and, in your speech,   40
I see how far the slander is abroad.
Without proof could you think me innocent?
   Albert. Lady, I should rejoice to know you so.
    Erminia. If you have any pity for a maid,
Suffering a daily death from evil tongues;
Any compassion for that Emperor's niece,
Who, for your bright sword and clear honesty,
Lifted you from the crowd of common men
Into the lap of honour;—save me, knight!
    Albert. How? Make it clear; if it be possible,   50
I, by the banner of Saint Maurice, swear
To right you.
    Erminia. Possible!—Easy. O my heart!
This letter's not so soil'd but you may read it;—

Possible! There—that letter! Read—read it.

[Gives him a letter.

Albert (reading). "To the Duke Conrad.—Forget the threat you
made at parting, and I will forget to send the Emperor letters and
papers of your's I have become possessed of. His life is no trifle to
me; his death you shall find none to yourself." (*Speaks to himself:*) 'Tis me—my life that's pleaded for! (*Reads.*) "He, for his
own sake, will be dumb as the grave. Erminia has my shame fix'd
upon her, sure as a wen. We are safe.

AURANTHE."

A she-devil! A dragon! I her imp!
Fire of Hell! Auranthe—lewd demon!
Where got you this? Where? When?
    Erminia. I found it in the tent, among some spoils
Which, being noble, fell to Gersa's lot.
Come in, and see.   *[They go in and return.*
    Albert.   Villainy! Villainy!
Conrad's sword, his corslet, and his helm,   70
And his letter. Caitiff, he shall feel—
    Erminia. I see you are thunderstruck. Haste, haste away!
    Albert. O I am tortured by this villainy.
    Erminia. You needs must be. Carry it swift to Otho;
Tell him, moreover, I am prisoner
Here in this camp, where all the sisterhood,
Forc'd from their quiet cells, are parcell'd out
For slaves among these Huns. Away! Away!
    Albert. I am gone.
    Erminia.   Swift be your steed! Within this hour
The Emperor will see it.
    Albert.   Ere I sleep: 80
That I can swear.   *[Hurries out.*
    Gersa (without). Brave captains! thanks. Enough
Of loyal homage now!

Enter GERSA.

    Erminia.   Hail, royal Hun!
    Gersa. What means this, fair one? Why in such alarm?
Who was it hurried by me so distract?
It seem'd you were in deep discourse together;
Your doctrine has not been so harsh to him
As to my poor deserts. Come, come, be plain.
I am no jealous fool to kill you both,
Or, for such trifles, rob the adorned world
Of such a beauteous vestal.
    Erminia.   I grieve, my Lord,   90
To hear you condescend to ribald phrase.
    Gersa. This is too much! Hearken, my lady pure!

Erminia. Silence! and hear the magic of a name—
Erminia! I am she,—the Emperor's niece!
Prais'd be the Heavens, I now dare own myself!
    Gersa. Erminia! Indeed! I've heard of her.
Prythee, fair lady, what chance brought you here?
    Erminia. Ask your own soldiers.
    Gersa.   And you dare own your name.
For loveliness you may—and for the rest
My vein is not censorious.
    Erminia.   Alas! poor me!   100
'Tis false indeed.
    Gersa.   Indeed you are too fair:
The swan, soft leaning on her fledgy breast,
When to the stream she launches, looks not back
With such a tender grace; nor are her wings
So white as your soul is, if that but be
Twin-picture to your face. Erminia!
To-day, for the first day, I am a king,
Yet would I give my unworn crown away
To know you spotless.
    Erminia.   Trust me one day more,
Generously, without more certain guarantee,   110
Than this poor face you deign to praise so much;
After that, say and do whate'er you please.
If I have any knowledge of you, sir,
I think, nay I am sure, you will grieve much
To hear my story. O be gentle to me,
For I am sick and faint with many wrongs,
Tir'd out, and weary-worn with contumelies.
    Gersa. Poor lady!

Enter ETHELBERT.

    Erminia.   Gentle Prince, 'tis false indeed.
Good morrow, holy father! I have had
Your prayers, though I look'd for you in vain.   120
    Ethelbert. Blessings upon you, daughter! Sure you look
Too cheerful for these foul pernicious days.
Young man, you heard this virgin say 'twas false,
'Tis false, I say. What! can you not employ
Your temper elsewhere, 'mong these burly tents,
But you must taunt this dove, for she hath lost
The Eagle Otho to beat off assault?
Fie! fie! But I will be her guard myself;
In the Emperor's name. I here demand of you
Herself, and all her sisterhood. She false!   130
    Gersa. Peace! peace, old man! I cannot think she is.
    Ethelbert. Whom I have known from her first infancy,

Baptiz'd her in the bosom of the Church,
Watch'd her, as anxious husbandmen the grain,
From the first shoot till the unripe mid-May,
Then to the tender ear of her June days,
Which, lifting sweet abroad its timid green,
Is blighted by the touch of calumny;
You cannot credit such a monstrous tale.
    Gersa. I cannot. Take her. Fair Erminia,   140
I follow you to Friedburg,—is't not so?
    Erminia. Aye, so we purpose.
    Ethelbert.   Daughter, do you so?
How's this? I marvel! Yet you look not mad.
    Erminia. I have good news to tell you, Ethelbert.
    Gersa. Ho! ho, there! Guards!
Your blessing, father! Sweet Erminia,
Believe me, I am well nigh sure—
    Erminia.   Farewell!
Short time will show.   *[Enter Chiefs.*
        Yes, father Ethelbert,
I have news precious as we pass along.
    Ethelbert. Dear daughter, you shall guide me.   149
    Erminia.   To no ill.
    Gersa. Command an escort to the Friedburg lines.
        [Exeunt Chiefs.

Pray let me lead. Fair lady, forget not
Gersa, how he believ'd you innocent.
I follow you to Friedburg with all speed.   *[Exeunt.*

ACT III.

SCENE I.—*The Country.*

Enter ALBERT.

    Albert. O that the earth were empty, as when Cain
Had no perplexity to hide his head!
Or that the sword of some brave enemy
Had put a sudden stop to my hot breath,
And hurl'd me down the illimitable gulph
Of times past, unremember'd! Better so
Than thus fast-limed in a cursed snare,
The white limbs of a wanton. This the end
Of an aspiring life! My boyhood past
In feud with wolves and bears, when no eye saw
The solitary warfare, fought for love   11
Of honour 'mid the growling wilderness.
My sturdier youth, maturing to the sword,
Won by the syren-trumpets, and the ring

Of shields upon the pavement, when bright-mail'd
Henry the Fowler pass'd the streets of Prague.
Was't to this end I louted and became
The menial of Mars, and held a spear
Sway'd by command, as corn is by the wind?
Is it for this, I now am lifted up   20
By Europe's throned Emperor, to see
My honour be my executioner,—
My love of fame, my prided honesty
Put to the torture for confessional?
Then the damn'd crime of blurting to the world
A woman's secret!—Though a fiend she be,
Too tender of my ignominious life;
But then to wrong the generous Emperor
In such a searching point, were to give up
My soul for foot-ball at Hell's holiday!   30
I must confess,—and cut my throat,—to-day?
To-morrow? Ho! some wine!

Enter SIGIFRED.

  Sigifred.   A fine humour—
  Albert. Who goes there? Count Sigifred? Ha! Ha!
  Sigifred. What, man, do you mistake the hollow sky
For a throng'd tavern,—and these stubbed trees
For old serge hangings,—me, your humble friend,
For a poor waiter? Why, man, how you stare!
What gipsies have you been carousing with?
No, no more wine; methinks you've had enough.
  Albert. You well may laugh and banter. What a fool
An injury may make of a staid man!   41
You shall know all anon.
  Sigifred.   Some tavern brawl?
  Albert. 'Twas with some people out of common reach;
Revenge is difficult.
  Sigifred.   I am your friend;
We meet again to-day, and can confer
Upon it. For the present I'm in haste.
  Albert. Whither?
  Sigifred.   To fetch King Gersa to the feast.
The Emperor on this marriage is so hot,
Pray Heaven it end not in apoplexy!
The very porters, as I pass'd the doors,   50
Heard his loud laugh, and answer'd in full choir.
I marvel, Albert, you delay so long
From those bright revelries; go, show yourself,
You may be made a duke.
  Albert.   Aye, very like:

Pray, what day has his Highness fix'd upon?
   Sigifred. For what?
   Albert.   The marriage. What else can I mean?
   Sigifred. To-day! O, I forgot, you could not know;
The news is scarce a minute old with me.
   Albert. Married to-day! To-day! You did not say so?
   Sigifred. Now, while I speak to you, their comely heads   60
Are bow'd before the mitre.
   Albert.   O! Monstrous!
   Sigifred. What is this?
   Albert.   Nothing, Sigifred. Farewell!
We'll meet upon our subject. Farewell, count!
                                            [*Exit.*

   Sigifred. Is this clear-headed Albert? He brain-turn'd!
'Tis as portentous as a meteor.   [*Exit.*

SCENE II.—*An Apartment in the Castle.*

Enter, as from the Marriage, OTHO, LUDOLPH, AURANTHE, CONRAD,
Nobles, Knights, Ladies, &c. Music.

   Otho. Now, Ludolph! Now, Auranthe! Daughter fair!
What can I find to grace your nuptial day
More than my love, and these wide realms in fee?
   Ludolph. I have too much.
   Auranthe.   And I, my liege, by far.
   Ludolph. Auranthe! I have! O, my bride, my love!
Not all the gaze upon us can restrain
My eyes, too long poor exiles from thy face,
From adoration, and my foolish tongue
From uttering soft responses to the love
I see in thy mute beauty beaming forth!   10
Fair creature, bless me with a single word!
All mine!
   Auranthe. Spare, spare me, my Lord! I swoon else.
   Ludolph. Soft beauty! by to-morrow I should die,
Wert thou not mine.   [*They talk apart.*
   First Lady.   How deep she has bewitch'd him!
   First Knight. Ask you for her recipe for love philtres.
   Second Lady. They hold the Emperor in admiration.
   Otho. If ever king was happy, that am I!
What are the cities 'yond the Alps to me,
The provinces about the Danube's mouth,
The promise of fair soil beyond the Rhone;   20
Or routing out of Hyperborean hordes,
To those fair children, stars of a new age?
Unless perchance I might rejoice to win
This little ball of earth, and chuck it them

To play with!
 Auranthe. Nay, my Lord, I do not know.
 Ludolph. Let me not famish.
 Otho (*to Conrad*).   Good Franconia,
You heard what oath I sware, as the sun rose,
That unless Heaven would send me back my son,
My Arab,—no soft music should enrich
The cool wine, kiss'd off with a soldier's smack;   30
Now all my empire, barter'd for one feast,
Seems poverty.
 Conrad.   Upon the neighbour-plain
The heralds have prepar'd a royal lists;
Your knights, found war-proof in the bloody field,
Speed to the game.
 Otho.   Well, Ludolph, what say you?
 Ludolph. My lord!
 Otho.   A tourney?
 Conrad.   Or, if't please you best—
 Ludolph. I want no more!
 First Lady.   He soars!
 Second Lady.   Past all reason.
 Ludolph. Though heaven's choir
Should in a vast circumference descend
And sing for my delight, I'd stop my ears!   40
Though bright Apollo's car stood burning here,
And he put out an arm to bid me mount,
His touch an immortality, not I!
This earth, this palace, this room, Auranthe!
 Otho. This is a little painful; just too much.
Conrad, if he flames longer in this wise,
I shall believe in wizard-woven loves
And old romances; but I'll break the spell.
Ludolph!
 Conrad. He will be calm, anon.
 Ludolph.   You call'd?
Yes, yes, yes, I offend. You must forgive me;   50
Not being quite recover'd from the stun
Of your large bounties. A tourney, is it not?
         [*A senet heard faintly.*
 Conrad. The trumpets reach us.
 Ethelbert (*without*).   On your peril, sirs,
Detain us!
 First Voice (*without*). Let not the abbot pass.
 Second Voice (*without*).   No,
On your lives!
 First Voice (*without*). Holy Father, you must not.
 Ethelbert (*without*). Otho!

Otho.   Who calls on Otho?
Ethelbert (*without*).   Ethelbert!
Otho. Let him come in.

Enter ETHELBERT *leading in* ERMINIA.

Thou cursed abbot, why
Hast brought pollution to our holy rites?
Hast thou no fear of hangman, or the faggot?   59
  Ludolph. What portent—what strange prodigy is this?
  Conrad. Away!
  Ethelbert.   You, Duke?
  Erminia.   Albert has surely fail'd me!
Look at the Emperor's brow upon me bent!
  Ethelbert. A sad delay!
  Conrad.   Away, thou guilty thing!
  Ethelbert. You again, Duke? Justice, most mighty Otho!
You—go to your sister there and plot again,
A quick plot, swift as thought to save your heads;
For lo! the toils are spread around your den,
The word is all agape to see dragg'd forth
Two ugly monsters.
  Ludolph.   What means he, my lord?
  Conrad. I cannot guess.
  Ethelbert.   Best ask your lady sister,   70
Whether the riddle puzzles her beyond
The power of utterance.
  Conrad.   Foul barbarian, cease;
The Princess faints!
  Ludolph.   Stab him! O, sweetest wife!
          [*Attendants bear off* AURANTHE.
  Erminia. Alas!
  Ethelbert.   Your wife?
  Ludolph.   Aye, Satan! does that yerk ye?
  Ethelbert. Wife! so soon!
  Ludolph.   Aye, wife! Oh, impudence!
Thou bitter mischief! Venomous mad priest!
How dar'st thou lift those beetle brows at me?
Me—the prince Ludolph, in this presence here,
Upon my marriage-day, and scandalize
My joys with such opprobrious surprise?   80
Wife! Why dost linger on that syllable,
As if it were some demon's name pronounc'd
To summon harmful lightning, and make roar
The sleepy thunder? Hast no sense of fear?
No ounce of man in thy mortality?
Tremble! for, at my nod, the sharpen'd axe
Will make thy bold tongue quiver to the roots,

Those grey lids wink, and thou not know it more!
 Ethelbert. O, poor deceived Prince! I pity thee!
Great Otho! I claim justice—
 Ludolph.   Thou shalt hav 't!
Thine arms from forth a pulpit of hot fire   91
Shall sprawl distracted! O that that dull cowl
Were some most sensitive portion of thy life,
That I might give it to my hounds to tear!
Thy girdle some fine zealous-pained nerve
To girth my saddle! And those devil's beads
Each one a life, that I might, every day,
Crush one with Vulcan's hammer!
 Otho.   Peace, my son;
You far outstrip my spleen in this affair.
Let us be calm, and hear the abbot's plea   100
For this intrusion.
 Ludolph. I am silent, sire.
 Otho. Conrad, see all depart not wanted here.
       [*Exeunt Knights, Ladies, &c.*
Ludolph, be calm. Ethelbert, peace awhile.
This mystery demands an audience
Of a just judge, and that will Otho be.
 Ludolph. Why has he time to breathe another word?
 Otho. Ludolph, old Ethelbert, be sure, comes not
To beard us for no cause; he's not the man
To cry himself up an ambassador
Without credentials.
 Ludolph. I'll chain up myself.   110
 Otho. Old Abbot, stand here forth. Lady Erminia,
Sit. And now, Abbot! what have you to say?
Our ear is open. First we here denounce
Hard penalties against thee, if't be found
The cause for which you have disturb'd us here,
Making our bright hours muddy, be a thing
Of little moment.
 Ethelbert. See this innocent!
Otho! thou father of the people call'd,
Is her life nothing? Her fair honour nothing?
Her tears from matins until even-song   120
Nothing? Her burst heart nothing? Emperor!
Is this your gentle niece—the simplest flower
Of the world's herbal—this fair lilly blanch'd
Still with the dews of piety, this meek lady
Here sitting like an angel newly-shent,
Who veils its snowy wings and grows all pale,—
Is she nothing?
 Otho. What more to the purpose, abbot?

Ludolph. Whither is he winding?

Conrad.   No clue yet!

Ethelbert. You have heard, my Liege, and so, no
    doubt, all here,
Foul, poisonous, malignant whisperings;   130
Nay open speech, rude mockery grown common,
Against the spotless nature and clear fame
Of the princess Erminia, your niece.
I have intruded here thus suddenly,
Because I hold those base weeds, with tight hand,
Which now disfigure her fair growing stem,
Waiting but for your sign to pull them up
By the dark roots, and leave her palpable,
To all men's sight, a Lady, innocent.
The ignominy of that whisper'd tale   140
About a midnight gallant, seen to climb
A window to her chamber neighbour'd near,
I will from her turn off, and put the load
On the right shoulders; on that wretch's head,
Who, by close stratagems, did save herself,
Chiefly by shifting to this lady's room
A rope-ladder for false witness.

Ludolph.   Most atrocious!

Otho. Ethelbert, proceed.

Ethelbert.   With sad lips I shall:
For in the healing of one wound, I fear
To make a greater. His young highness here   150
To-day was married.

Ludolph.   Good.

Ethelbert.   Would it were good!
Yet why do I delay to spread abroad
The names of those two vipers, from whose jaws
A deadly breath went forth to taint and blast
This guileless lady?

Otho.   Abbot, speak their names.

Ethelbert. A minute first. It cannot be—but may
I ask, great judge, if you to-day have put
A letter by unread?

Otho.   Does 't end in this?

Conrad. Out with their names!

Ethelbert.   Bold sinner, say you so?

Ludolph. Out, tedious monk!

Otho.   Confess, or by the wheel—

Ethelbert. My evidence cannot be far away;   161
And, though it never come, be on my head
The crime of passing an attaint upon
The slanderers of this virgin.

Ludolph.   Speak aloud!
Ethelbert. Auranthe, and her brother there.
Conrad.   Amaze!
Ludolph. Throw them from the windows!
Otho. Do what you will!
    Ludolph.   What shall I do with them?
Something of quick dispatch, for should she hear,
My soft Auranthe, her sweet mercy would
Prevail against my fury. Damned priest!   170
What swift death wilt thou die? As to the lady
I touch her not.
    Ethelbert.   Illustrious Otho, stay!
An ample store of misery thou hast,
Choak not the granary of thy noble mind
With more bad bitter grain, too difficult
A cud for the repentance of a man
Grey-growing. To thee only I appeal,
Not to thy noble son, whose yeasting youth
Will clear itself, and crystal turn again.
A young man's heart, by Heaven's blessing, is   180
A wide world, where a thousand new-born hopes
Empurple fresh the melancholy blood:
But an old man's is narrow, tenantless
Of hopes, and stuff'd with many memories,
Which, being pleasant, ease the heavy pulse—
Painful, clog up and stagnate. Weigh this matter
Even as a miser balances his coin;
And, in the name of mercy, give command
That your knight Albert be brought here before you.
He will expound this riddle; he will show   190
A noon-day proof of bad Auranthe's guilt.
    Otho. Let Albert straight be summon'd.

                           [Exit one of the Nobles.

    Ludolph.   Impossible!
I cannot doubt—I will not—no—to doubt
Is to be ashes!—wither'd up to death!
    Otho. My gentle Ludolph, harbour not a fear;
You do yourself much wrong.
    Ludolph.   O, wretched dolt!
Now, when my foot is almost on thy neck,
Wilt thou infuriate me? Proof! thou fool!
Why wilt thou teaze impossibility
With such a thick-skull'd persevering suit?   200
Fanatic obstinacy! Prodigy!
Monster of folly! Ghost of a turn'd brain!
You puzzle me,—you haunt me,—when I dream

Of you my brain will split! Bald sorcerer!
Juggler! May I come near you? On my soul
I know not whether to pity, curse, or laugh.

Enter ALBERT, *and the Nobleman.*

Here, Albert, this old phantom wants a proof!
Give him his proof! A camel's load of proofs!
   Otho. Albert, I speak to you as to a man
Whose words once utter'd pass like current gold;   210
And therefore fit to calmly put a close
To this brief tempest. Do you stand possess'd
Of any proof against the honourableness
Of Lady Auranthe, our new-spoused daughter?
   Albert. You chill me with astonishment. How's this?
My Liege, what proof should I have 'gainst a fame
Impossible of slur?   [OTHO *rises.*
   Erminia.   O wickedness!
   Ethelbert. Deluded monarch, 'tis a cruel lie.
   Otho. Peace, rebel-priest!
   Conrad.   Insult beyond credence!
   Erminia. Almost a dream!
   Ludolph.   We have awaken'd from   220
A foolish dream that from my brow hath wrung
A wrathful dew. O folly! why did I
So act the lion with this silly gnat?
Let them depart. Lady Erminia!
I ever griev'd for you, as who did not?
But now you have, with such a brazen front,
So most maliciously, so madly striven
To dazzle the soft moon, when tenderest clouds
Should be unloop'd around to curtain her;
I leave you to the desert of the world   230
Almost with pleasure. Let them be set free
For me! I take no personal revenge
More than against a nightmare, which a man
Forgets in the new dawn.

                     [*Exit* LUDOLPH.

   Otho. Still in extremes! No, they must not be loose.
   Ethelbert. Albert, I must suspect thee of a crime
So fiendish—
   Otho.   Fear'st thou not my fury, monk?
Conrad, be they in your sure custody
Till we determine some fit punishment.
It is so mad a deed, I must reflect   240
And question them in private; for perhaps,
By patient scrutiny, we may discover

Whether they merit death, or should be placed
In care of the physicians.

> *[Exeunt* OTHO *and Nobles,* ALBERT *following.*

    Conrad. My guards, ho!
    Erminia.   Albert, wilt thou follow there?
Wilt thou creep dastardly behind his back,
And slink away from a weak woman's eye?
Turn, thou court-Janus! thou forget'st thyself;
Here is the Duke, waiting with open arms,

> *[Enter Guards.*
250

To thank thee; here congratulate each other;
Wring hands; embrace; and swear how lucky 'twas
That I, by happy chance, hit the right man
Of all the world to trust in.
    Albert.   Trust! to me!
    Conrad (aside). He is the sole one in this mystery.
    Erminia. Well, I give up, and save my prayers for Heaven!
You, who could do this deed, would ne'er relent,
Though, at my words, the hollow prison-vaults
Would groan for pity.
    Conrad.   Manacle them both!
    Ethelbert. I know it—it must be—I see it all!
Albert, thou art the minion!
    Erminia.   Ah! too plain—
260
    Conrad. Silence! Gag up their mouths! I cannot bear
More of this brawling. That the Emperor
Had plac'd you in some other custody!
Bring them away.

> *[Exeunt all but* ALBERT.

    Albert. Though my name perish from the book of honour,
Almost before the recent ink is dry,
And be no more remember'd after death,
Than any drummer's in the muster-roll;
Yet shall I season high my sudden fall
With triumph o'er that evil-witted duke!
270
He shall feel what it is to have the hand
Of a man drowning, on his hateful throat.

Enter GERSA *and* SIGIFRED.

    Gersa. What discord is at ferment in this house?
    Sigifred. We are without conjecture; not a soul
We met could answer any certainty.
    Gersa. Young Ludolph, like a fiery arrow, shot
By us.
    Sigifred. The Emperor, with cross'd arms, in thought.
    Gersa. In one room music, in another sadness,
Perplexity every where!

Albert.   A trifle more!
Follow; your presences will much avail   280
To tune our jarred spirits. I'll explain.   [*Exeunt.*

ACT IV.

Scene I.—Auranthe's *Apartment.*

Auranthe *and* Conrad *discovered.*

Conrad. Well, well, I know what ugly jeopardy
We are cag'd in; you need not pester that
Into my ears. Prythee, let me be spared
A foolish tongue, that I may bethink me
Of remedies with some deliberation.
You cannot doubt but 'tis in Albert's power
To crush or save us?
Auranthe.   No, I cannot doubt.
He has, assure yourself, by some strange means,
My secret; which I ever hid from him,
Knowing his mawkish honesty.
Conrad.   Curs'd slave!   10
Auranthe. Ay, I could almost curse him now myself.
Wretched impediment! Evil genius!
A glue upon my wings, that cannot spread,
When they should span the provinces! A snake,
A scorpion, sprawling on the first gold step,
Conducting to the throne, high canopied.
Conrad. You would not hear my council, when his life
Might have been trodden out, all sure and hush'd;
Now the dull animal forsooth must be
Intreated, managed! When can you contrive   20
The interview he demands?
Auranthe.   As speedily
It must be done as my brib'd woman can
Unseen conduct him to me; but I fear
'Twill be impossible, while the broad day
Comes through the panes with persecuting glare.
Methinks, if 't now were night I could intrigue
With darkness, bring the stars to second me,
And settle all this trouble.
Conrad.   Nonsense! Child!
See him immediately; why not now?
Auranthe. Do you forget that even the senseless door-posts   30
Are on the watch and gape through all the house?
How many whispers there are about,
Hungry for evidence to ruin me;
Men I have spurn'd, and women I have taunted?

Besides, the foolish prince sends, minute whiles,
His pages—so they tell me—to enquire
After my health, entreating, if I please,
To see me.
    Conrad.   Well, suppose this Albert here;
What is your power with him?
    Auranthe.   He should be
My echo, my taught parrot! but I fear   **40**
He will be cur enough to bark at me;
Have his own say; read me some silly creed
'Bout shame and pity.
    Conrad.   What will you do then?
    Auranthe. What I shall do, I know not: what I would
Cannot be done; for see, this chamber-floor
Will not yield to the pick-axe and the spade,—
Here is no quiet depth of hollow ground.
    Conrad. Sister, you have grown sensible and wise,
Seconding, ere I speak it, what is now,
I hope, resolv'd between us.
    Auranthe.   Say, what is 't?   **50**
    Conrad. You need not be his sexton too: a man
May carry that with him shall make him die
Elsewhere,—give that to him; pretend the while
You will to-morrow succumb to his wishes,
Be what they may, and send him from the Castle
On some fool's errand; let his latest groan
Frighten the wolves!
    Auranthe.   Alas! he must not die!
    Conrad. Would you were both hears'd up in stifling lead!
Detested—
    Auranthe. Conrad, hold! I would not bear
The little thunder of your fretful tongue,   **60**
Tho' I alone were taken in these toils,
And you could free me; but remember, sir,
You live alone in my security:
So keep your wits at work, for your own·sake,
Not mine, and be more mannerly.
    Conrad.   Thou wasp!
If my domains were emptied of these folk,
And I had thee to starve—
    Auranthe.   O, marvellous!
But Conrad, now be gone; the Host is look'd for;
Cringe to the Emperor, entertain the Lords,
And, do ye mind, above all things, proclaim   **70**
My sickness, with a brother's sadden'd eye,
Condoling with Prince Ludolph. In fit time
Return to me.

Conrad.   I leave you to your thoughts.   [*Exit.*

Auranthe (*sola*). Down, down, proud temper! down,
    Auranthe's pride!
Why do I anger him when I should kneel?
Conrad! Albert! help! help! What can I do?
O wretched woman! lost, wreck'd, swallow'd up,
Accursed, blasted! O, thou golden Crown,
Orbing along the serene firmament
Of a wide empire, like a glowing moon;   80
And thou, bright sceptre! lustrous in my eyes,—
There—as the fabled fair Hesperian tree,
Bearing a fruit more precious! graceful thing,
Delicate, godlike, magic! must I leave
Thee to melt in the visionary air,
Ere, by one grasp, this common hand is made
Imperial? I do not know the time
When I have wept for sorrow; but methinks
I could now sit upon the ground, and shed
Tears, tears of misery. O, the heavy day!   90
How shall I bear my life till Albert comes?
Ludolph! Erminia! Proofs! O heavy day!
Bring me some mourning weeds, that I may 'tire
Myself, as fits one wailing her own death:
Cut off these curls, and brand this lilly hand,
And throw these jewels from my loathing sight,—
Fetch me a missal, and a string of beads,—
A cup of bitter'd water, and a crust,—
I will confess, O holy Abbot—How!
What is this? Auranthe! thou fool, dolt,   100
Whimpering idiot! up! up! act and quell!
I am safe! Coward! why am I in fear?
Albert! he cannot stickle, chew the cud
In such a fine extreme,—impossible!
Who knocks?   [*Goes to the Door, listens, and opens it.*

Enter ALBERT.

Albert, I have been waiting for you here
With such an aching heart, such swooning throbs
On my poor brain, such cruel—cruel sorrow,
That I should claim your pity! Art not well?
    Albert. Yes, lady, well.
    Auranthe.   You look not so, alas!   110
But pale, as if you brought some heavy news.
    Albert. You know full well what makes me look so pale.
    Auranthe. No! Do I? Surely I am still to learn
Some horror; all I know, this present, is
I am near hustled to a dangerous gulph,

Which you can save me from,—and therefore safe,
So trusting in thy love; that should not make
Thee pale, my Albert.
    Albert.   It doth make me freeze.
    Auranthe. Why should it, love?
    Albert.   You should not ask me that,
But make your own heart monitor, and save   120
Me the great pain of telling. You must know.
    Auranthe. Something has vexed you, Albert. There are times
When simplest things put on a sombre cast;
A melancholy mood will haunt a man,
Until most easy matters take the shape
Of unachievable tasks; small rivulets
Then seem impassable.
    Albert.   Do not cheat yourself
With hope that gloss of words, or suppliant action,
Or tears, or ravings, or self-threaten'd death,
Can alter my resolve.
    Auranthe.   You make me tremble;   130
Not so much at your threats, as at your voice,
Untun'd, and harsh, and barren of all love.
    Albert. You suffocate me! Stop this devil's parley,
And listen to me; know me once for all.
    Auranthe. I thought I did. Alas! I am deceiv'd.
    Albert. No, you are not deceiv'd. You took me for
A man detesting all inhuman crime;
And therefore kept from me your demon's plot
Against Erminia. Silent? Be so still;
For ever! Speak no more; but hear my words,
Thy fate. Your safety I have bought to-day   141
By blazoning a lie, which in the dawn
I'll expiate with truth.
    Auranthe.   O cruel traitor!
    Albert. For I would not set eyes upon thy shame;
I would not see thee dragg'd to death by the hair,
Penanc'd, and taunted on a scaffolding!
To-night, upon the skirts of the blind wood
That blackens northward of these horrid towers,
I wait for you with horses. Choose your fate.
Farewell.
    Auranthe. Albert, you jest; I'm sure you must.
You, an ambitious Soldier! I, a Queen,   151
One who could say,—Here, rule these Provinces!
Take tribute from those cities for thyself!
Empty these armouries, these treasuries,
Muster thy warlike thousands at a nod!
Go! conquer Italy!

Albert.   Auranthe, you have made
The whole world chaff to me. Your doom is fix'd.
  Auranthe. Out, villain! dastard!
  Albert.   Look there to the door!
Who is it?
  Auranthe. Conrad, traitor!
  Albert.   Let him in.

Enter CONRAD.

Do not affect amazement, hypocrite,   160
At seeing me in this chamber.
  Conrad.   Auranthe?
  Albert. Talk not with eyes, but speak your curses out
Against me, who would sooner crush and grind
A brace of toads, than league with them to oppress
An innocent lady, gull an Emperor,
More generous to me than autumn's sun
To ripening harvests.
  Auranthe.   No more insult, sir!
  Albert. Aye, clutch your scabbard; but, for prudence sake,
Draw not the sword; 'twould make an uproar, Duke,
You would not hear the end of. At nightfall   170
Your lady sister, if I guess aright,
Will leave this busy castle. You had best
Take farewell too of worldly vanities.
  Conrad. Vassal!
  Albert.   To-morrow, when the Emperor sends
For loving Conrad, see you fawn on him.
Good even!
  Auranthe. You'll be seen!
  Albert.   See the coast clear then.
  Auranthe (*as he goes*). Remorseless Albert! Cruel,
    cruel wretch!
                                    [*She lets him out.*
  Conrad. So, we must lick the dust?
  Auranthe.   I follow him.
  Conrad. How? Where? The plan of your escape?
  Auranthe.   He waits
For me with horses by the forest-side,   180
Northward.
  Conrad. Good, good! he dies. You go, say you?
  Auranthe. Perforce.
  Conrad.   Be speedy, darkness! Till that comes,
Fiends keep you company!   [*Exit.*
  Auranthe.   And you! And you!
And all men! Vanish!
                        [*Retires to an inner Apartment.*

SCENE II.—*An Apartment in the Castle.*

Enter LUDOLPH *and Page.*

Page. Still very sick, my Lord; but now I went
Knowing my duty to so good a Prince;
And there her women in a mournful throng
Stood in the passage whispering: if any
Mov'd 'twas with careful steps and hush'd as death;
They bid me stop.
  Ludolph. Good fellow, once again
Make soft enquiry; prythee be not stay'd
By any hindrance, but with gentlest force
Break through her weeping servants, till thou com'st
E'en to her chamber door, and there, fair boy,   10
If with thy mother's milk thou hast suck'd in
Any diviner eloquence; woo her ears
With plaints for me more tender than the voice
Of dying Echo, echoed.
  Page.   Kindest master!
To know thee sad thus, will unloose my tongue
In mournful syllables. Let but my words reach
Her ears and she shall take them coupled with
Moans from my heart and sighs not counterfeit.
May I speed better!   *[Exit Page.*
  Ludolph. Auranthe! My Life!
Long have I lov'd thee, yet till now not lov'd: 20
Remembering, as I do, hard-hearted times
When I had heard even of thy death perhaps,
And thoughtless, suffered to pass alone
Into Elysium! now I follow thee
A substance or a shadow, wheresoe'er
Thou leadest me,—whether thy white feet press,
With pleasant weight, the amorous-aching earth,
Or thro' the air thou pioneerest me,
A shade! Yet sadly I predestinate!
O unbenignest Love, why wilt thou let   30
Darkness steal out upon the sleepy world
So wearily; as if night's chariot wheels
Were clog'd in some thick cloud. O, changeful Love,
Let not her steeds with drowsy-footed pace
Pass the high stars, before sweet embassage
Comes from the pillow'd beauty of that fair
Completion of all delicate nature's wit.
Pout her faint lips anew with rubious health
And with thine infant fingers lift the fringe
Of her sick eyelids; that those eyes may glow   40

With wooing light upon me, ere the Morn
Peers with disrelish, grey, barren, and cold.

Enter GERSA *and Courtiers.*

Otho calls me his Lion—should I blush
To be so tam'd, so——
 Gersa.   Do me the courtesy
Gentlemen to pass on.
 Courtier.   We are your servants.
        [*Exeunt Courtiers.*
 Ludolph. It seems then, Sir, you have found out the man
You would confer with; me?
 Gersa.   If I break not
Too much upon your thoughtful mood, I will
Claim a brief while your patience.
 Ludolph.   For what cause
Soe'er I shall be honour'd.
 Gersa.   I not less.   50
 Ludolph. What may it be? No trifle can take place
Of such deliberate prologue, serious 'haviour.
But be it what it may I cannot fail
To listen with no common interest—
For though so new your presence is to me,
I have a soldier's friendship for your fame—
Please you explain.
 Gersa. As thus—for, pardon me,
I cannot in plain terms grossly assault
A noble nature; and would faintly sketch
What your quick apprehension will fill up 60
So finely I esteem you.
 Ludolph.   I attend—
 Gersa. Your generous Father, most illustrious Otho,
Sits in the Banquet room among his chiefs—
His wine is bitter, for you are not there—
His eyes are fix'd still on the open doors,
And every passer in he frowns upon
Seeing no Ludolph comes.
 Ludolph.   I do neglect—
 Gersa. And for your absence, may I guess the cause?
 Ludolph. Stay there! no—guess? more princely you must be—
Than to make guesses at me. 'Tis enough, 70
I'm sorry I can hear no more.
 Gersa.   And I
As griev'd to force it on you so abrupt;
Yet one day you must know a grief whose sting
Will sharpen more the longer 'tis conceal'd.
 Ludolph. Say it at once, sir, dead, dead, is she dead?

Gersa. Mine is a cruel task: she is not dead—
And would for your sake she were innocent—
Ludolph. Thou liest! thou amazest me beyond
All scope of thought; convulsest my heart's blood
To deadly churning—Gersa you are young   80
As I am; let me observe you face to face;
Not grey-brow'd like the poisonous Ethelbert,
No rheumed eyes, no furrowing of age,
No wrinkles where all vices nestle in
Like crannied vermin—no, but fresh and young
And hopeful featur'd. Ha! by heaven you weep
Tears, human tears—Do you repent you then
Of a curs'd torturer's office! Why shouldst join—
Tell me, the league of Devils? Confess—confess
The Lie.—
  Gersa. Lie!—but begone all ceremonious points   90
Of honour battailous. I could not turn
My wrath against thee for the orbed world.
  Ludolph. Your wrath, weak boy? Tremble at mine unless
Retraction follow close upon the heels
Of that late stounding insult: why has my sword
Not done already a sheer judgment on thee?
Despair, or eat thy words. Why, thou wast nigh
Whimpering away my reason: hark ye, Sir,
It is no secret;—that Erminia,
Erminia, Sir, was hidden in your tent;   100
O bless'd asylum! comfortable home!
Begone, I pity thee, thou art a Gull—
Erminia's last new puppet—
  Gersa.   Furious fire!
Thou mak'st me boil as hot as thou canst flame!
And in thy teeth I give thee back the lie!
Thou liest! Thou, Auranthe's fool, a wittol——
  Ludolph. Look! look at this bright sword;
There is no part of it to the very hilt
But shall indulge itself about thine heart—
Draw—but remember thou must cower thy plumes,   110
As yesterday the Arab made thee stoop—
  Gersa. Patience! not here, I would not spill thy blood
Here underneath this roof where Otho breathes,
Thy father—almost mine——
  Ludolph.   O faltering coward—

Re-enter PAGE.

Stay, stay, here is one I have half a word with—
Well—What ails thee child?
  Page.   My lord,

Ludolph.   Good fellow!
Page. They are fled!
Ludolph.   They—who?
Page.   When anxiously
I hasten'd back, your grieving messenger,
I found the stairs all dark, the lamps extinct,
And not a foot or whisper to be heard.   120
I thought her dead, and on the lowest step
Sat listening; when presently came by
Two muffled up,—one sighing heavily,
The other cursing low, whose voice I knew
For the Duke Conrad's. Close I follow'd them
Thro' the dark ways they chose to the open air;
And, as I follow'd, heard my lady speak.
   Ludolph. Thy life answers the truth!
   Page.   The chamber's empty!
   Ludolph. As I will be of mercy! So, at last,
This nail is in my temples!
   Gersa.   Be calm in this.   130
   Ludolph. I am.
   Gersa.   And Albert too has disappear'd;
Ere I met you, I sought him everywhere;
You would not hearken.
   Ludolph.   Which way went they, boy?
   Gersa. I'll hunt with you.
   Ludolph.   No, no, no. My senses are
Still whole. I have surviv'd. My arm is strong—
My appetite sharp—for revenge! I'll no sharer
In my feast; my injury is all my own,
And so is my revenge, my lawful chattels!
Terrier, ferret them out! Burn—burn the witch!
Trace me their footsteps! Away!   140
                                        [*Exeunt.*

ACT V.

SCENE I.—*A part of the Forest.*

Enter CONRAD *and* AURANTHE.

   Auranthe. Go no further; not a step more; thou art
A master-plague in the midst of miseries.
Go—I fear thee. I tremble every limb,
Who never shook before. There's moody death
In thy resolved looks—Yes, I could kneel
To pray thee far away. Conrad, go, go—
There! yonder underneath the boughs I see
Our horses!

Conrad.   Aye, and the man.
Auranthe.   Yes, he is there.
Go, go,—no blood, no blood; go, gentle Conrad!
Conrad. Farewell!
Auranthe.   Farewell, for this Heaven pardon you.   10
                                              [*Exit* AURANTHE.
Conrad. If he survive one hour, then may I die
In unimagined tortures—or breathe through
A long life in the foulest sink of the world!
He dies—'tis well she do not advertise
The caitiff of the cold steel at his back.

                                              [*Exit* CONRAD.

Enter LUDOLPH *and* PAGE.

Ludolph. Miss'd the way, boy, say not that on your peril!
Page. Indeed, indeed I cannot trace them further.
Ludolph. Must I stop here? Here solitary die?
Stifled beneath the thick oppressive shade
Of these dull boughs,—this oven of dark thickets,—   20
Silent,—without revenge?—pshaw!—bitter end,—
A bitter death,—a suffocating death,—
A gnawing—silent—deadly, quiet death!
Escap'd?—fled?—vanish'd? melted into air?
She's gone! I cannot clutch her! no revenge!
A muffled death, ensnar'd in horrid silence!
Suck'd to my grave amid a dreamy calm!
O, where is that illustrious noise of war,
To smother up this sound of labouring breath,
This rustle of the trees!
                    [AURANTHE *shrieks at a distance.*
Page.   My Lord, a noise!   30
This way—hark!
Ludolph.   Yes, yes! A hope! A music!
A glorious clamour! How I live again!   [*Exeunt.*

SCENE II.—*Another part of the Forest.*

Enter ALBERT (*wounded*).

Albert. O for enough life to support me on
To Otho's feet—

Enter LUDOLPH.

Ludolph.   Thrice villainous, stay there!
Tell me where that detested woman is
Or this is through thee!
Albert.   My good Prince, with me
The sword has done its worst; not without worst

Done to another—Conrad has it home—
I see you know it all—
   Ludolph.   Where is his sister?

AURANTHE rushes in.

Auranthe. Albert!
  Ludolph. Ha! There! there!—He is the paramour!—
There—hug him—dying! O, thou innocence,
Shrine him and comfort him at his last gasp,   10
Kiss down his eyelids! Was he not thy love?
Wilt thou forsake him at his latest hour?
Keep fearful and aloof from his last gaze,
His most uneasy moments, when cold death
Stands with the door ajar to let him in?
  Albert. O that that door with hollow slam would close
Upon me sudden, for I cannot meet,
In all the unknown chambers of the dead,
Such horrors————
  Ludolph.   Auranthe! what can he mean?
What horrors? Is it not a joyous time?   20
Am I not married to a paragon
"Of personal beauty and untainted soul"?
A blushing fair-eyed Purity! A Sylph,
Whose snowy timid hand has never sin'd
Beyond a flower pluck'd, white as itself?
Albert, you do insult my Bride—your Mistress—
To talk of horrors on our wedding night.
  Albert. Alas! poor Prince, I would you knew my heart.
'Tis not so guilty—
  Ludolph.   Hear you he pleads not guilty—
You are not? or if so what matters it?   30
You have escap'd me,—free as the dusk air—
Hid in the forest—safe from my revenge;
I cannot catch you—You should laugh at me,
Poor cheated Ludolph,—make the forest hiss
With jeers at me—You tremble; faint at once,
You will come to again. O Cockatrice,
I have you. Whither wander those fair eyes
To entice the Devil to your help, that he
May change you to a Spider, so to crawl
Into some cranny to escape my wrath?   40
  Albert. Sometimes the counsel of a dying man
Doth operate quietly when his breath is gone—
Disjoin those hands—part—part, do not destroy
Each other—forget her—our miseries
Are equal shar'd, and mercy is—
  Ludolph.   A boon

When one can compass it. Auranthe, try
Your oratory—your breath is not so hitch'd—
Aye, stare for help—

[ALBERT *groans and dies.*

There goes a spotted soul
Howling in vain along the hollow night—
Hear him—he calls you—Sweet Auranthe, come!   50
  Auranthe. Kill me.
  Ludolph.   No! What? upon our Marriage-night!
The earth would shudder at so foul a deed—
A fair Bride, a sweet Bride, an innocent Bride!
No, we must revel it, as 'tis in use
In times of delicate brilliant ceremony:
Come, let me lead you to our halls again—
Nay, linger not—make no resistance sweet—
Will you—Ah wretch, thou canst not, for I have
The strength of twenty lions 'gainst a lamb—
Now one adieu for Albert—come away.—   60

[*Exeunt.*

SCENE III.—*An inner Court of the Castle.*

Enter SIGIFRED, GONFRED, *and* THEODORE *meeting.*

  Theodore. Was ever such a night?
  Sigifred.   What horrors more?
Things unbeliev'd one hour, so strange they are,
The next hour stamps with credit.
  Theodore.   Your last news?
  Gonfred. After the Page's story of the death
Of Albert and Duke Conrad?
  Sigifred.   And the return
Of Ludolph with the Princess.
  Gonfred.   No more save
Prince Gersa's freeing Abbot Ethelbert,
And the sweet lady, fair Erminia,
From prison.
  Theodore. Where are they now? hast yet heard?
  Gonfred. With the sad Emperor they are closeted;
I saw the three pass slowly up the stairs,   11
The lady weeping, the old Abbot cowl'd.
  Sigifred. What next?
  Thedore.   I ache to think on't.
  Gonfred.   'Tis with fate.
  Theodore. One while these proud towers are hush'd as death.
  Gonfred. The next our poor Prince fills the arched rooms
With ghastly ravings.

Sigifred. I do fear his brain.
Gonfred. I will see more. Bear you so stout a heart?
[*Exeunt into the Castle.*

SCENE IV.—*A Cabinet, opening towards a Terrace.*

OTHO, ERMINIA, ETHELBERT, *and a Physician, discovered.*

Otho. O, my poor Boy! my Son! my Son! My Ludolph!
Have ye no comfort for me, ye Physicians
Of the weak Body and Soul?
Ethelbert. 'Tis not the Medicine
Either of heaven or earth can cure unless
Fit time be chosen to administer—
Otho. A kind forbearance, holy Abbot—come
Erminia, here sit by me, gentle Girl;
Give me thy hand—hast thou forgiven me?
Erminia. Would I were with the saints to pray for you! 9
Otho. Why will ye keep me from my darling child?
Physician. Forgive me, but he must not see thy face—
Otho. Is then a father's countenance a Gorgon?
Hath it not comfort in it? Would it not
Console my poor Boy, cheer him, heal his spirits?
Let me embrace him, let me speak to him—
I will—who hinders me? Who's Emperor?
Physician. You may not, Sire—'twould overwhelm him quite,
He is so full of grief and passionate wrath,
Too heavy a sigh would kill him—or do worse.
He must be sav'd by fine contrivances— 20
And most especially we must keep clear
Out of his sight a Father whom he loves—
His heart is full, it can contain no more,
And do its ruddy office.
Ethelbert. Sage advice;
We must endeavour how to ease and slacken
The tight-wound energies of his despair,
Not make them tenser—
Otho. Enough! I hear, I hear.
Yet you were about to advise more—I listen.
Ethelbert. This learned doctor will agree with me,
That not in the smallest point should he be thwarted
Or gainsaid by one word—his very motions, 31
Nods, becks and hints, should be obey'd with care,
Even on the moment: so his troubled mind
May cure itself—
Physician. There is no other means.
Otho. Open the door: let's hear if all is quiet—
Physician. Beseech you, Sire, forbear.

Erminia.   Do, do.
Otho.   I command!
Open it straight—hush!—quiet—my lost Boy!
My miserable Child!
 Ludolph (*indistinctly without*). Fill, fill my goblet,—
Here's a health!
 Erminia. O, close the door!
 Otho. Let, let me hear his voice; this cannot last—
And fain would I catch up his dying words   41
Though my own knell they be—this cannot last—
O let me catch his voice—for lo! I hear
This silence whisper me that he is dead!
It is so. Gersa?

Enter GERSA.

 Physician. Say, how fares the prince?
 Gersa. More calm—his features are less wild and flush'd—
Once he complain'd of weariness—
 Physician. Indeed!
'Tis good—'tis good—let him but fall asleep,
That saves him.
 Otho. Gersa, watch him like a child— 49
Ward him from harm—and bring me better news—
 Physician. Humour him to the height. I fear to go;
For should he catch a glimpse of my dull garb,
It might affright him—fill him with suspicion
That we believe him sick, which must not be—
 Gersa. I will invent what soothing means I can.
              [*Exit* GERSA.

 Physician. This should cheer up your Highness—weariness
Is a good symptom, and most favourable—
It gives me pleasant hopes. Please you walk forth
Onto the Terrace; the refreshing air
Will blow one half of your sad doubts away.   60
              [*Exeunt*.

SCENE V.—*A Banqueting Hall, brilliantly illuminated, and set forth
with all costly magnificence, with Supper-tables, laden with services
of Gold and Silver. A door in the back scene, guarded by two Soldiers. Lords, Ladies, Knights, Gentlemen, &c., whispering sadly,
and ranging themselves; part entering and part discovered.*

 First Knight. Grievously are we tantaliz'd, one and all—
Sway'd here and there, commanded to and fro
As though we were the shadows of a dream
And link'd to a sleeping fancy. What do we here?
 Gonfred. I am no Seer—you know we must obey

The prince from A to Z—though it should be
To set the place in flames. I pray hast heard
Where the most wicked Princess is?
   First Knight.   There, Sir,
In the next room—have you remark'd those two
Stout soldiers posted at the door?
   Gonfred.   For what?   10
                              [They whisper.

   First Lady. How ghast a train!
   Second Lady. Sure this should be some splendid burial.
   First Lady. What fearful whispering! See, see,—Gersa there.

Enter GERSA.

   Gersa. Put on your brightest looks; smile if you can;
Behave as all were happy; keep your eyes
From the least watch upon him; if he speaks
To any one, answer collectedly,
Without surprise, his questions, howe'er strange.
Do this to the utmost,—though, alas! with me
The remedy grows hopeless! Here he comes,—   20
Observe what I have said,—show no surprise.

Enter LUDOLPH, *followed by* SIGIFRED *and Page.*

   Ludolph. A splendid company! rare beauties here!
I should have Orphean lips, and Plato's fancy,
Amphion's utterance, toned with his lyre,
Or the deep key of Jove's sonorous mouth,
To give fit salutation. Methought I heard,
As I came in, some whispers,—what of that?
'Tis natural men should whisper; at the kiss
Of Psyche given by Love, there was a buzz
Among the gods!—and silence is as natural.   30
These draperies are fine, and, being a mortal,
I should desire no better; yet, in truth,
There must be some superiour costliness,
Some wider-domed high magnificence!
I would have, as a mortal I may not,
Hanging of heaven's clouds, purple and gold,
Slung from the spheres; gauzes of silver mist,
Loop'd up with cords of twisted wreathed light,
And tassell'd round with weeping meteors!
These pendent lamps and chandeliers are bright   40
As earthly fires from dull dross can be cleansed;
Yet could my eyes drink up intenser beams
Undazzled,—this is darkness,—when I close
These lids, I see far fiercer brilliances,—
Skies full of splendid moons, and shooting stars,

And spouting exhalations, diamond fires,
And panting fountains quivering with deep glows!
Yes—this is dark—is it not dark?
    Sigifred.   My Lord,
'Tis late; the lights of festival are ever
Quench'd in the morn.
    Ludolph.   'Tis not to-morrow then?   **50**
    Sigifred. 'Tis early dawn.
    Gersa.   Indeed full time we slept;
Say you so, Prince?
    Ludolph.   I say I quarrell'd with you;
We did not tilt each other,—that's a blessing,—
Good gods! no innocent blood upon my head!
    Sigifred. Retire, Gersa!
    Ludolph.   There should be three more here:
For two of them, they stay away perhaps,
Being gloomy-minded, haters of fair revels,—
They know their own thoughts best.
                         As for the third,
Deep blue eyes—semi-shaded in white lids,
Finish'd with lashes fine for more soft shade,   **60**
Completed by her twin-arch'd ebon brows—
White temples of exactest elegance,
Of even mould felicitous and smooth—
Cheeks fashion'd tenderly on either side,
So perfect, so divine that our poor eyes
Are dazzled with the sweet proportioning,
And wonder that 'tis so,—the magic chance!
Her nostrils, small, fragrant, faery-delicate;
Her lips—I swear no human bones e'er wore
So taking a disguise—you shall behold her!   **70**
We'll have her presently; aye, you shall see her,
And wonder at her, friends, she is so fair—
She is the world's chief Jewel, and by heaven
She's mine by right of marriage—she is mine!
Patience, good people, in fit time I send
A Summoner—she will obey my call,
Being a wife most mild and dutiful.
First I would hear what music is prepared
To herald and receive her—let me hear!
    Sigifred. Bid the musicians soothe him tenderly.   **80**
                         [*A soft strain of Music.*
    Ludolph. Ye have none better—no—I am content;
'Tis a rich sobbing melody, with reliefs
Full and majestic; it is well enough,
And will be sweeter, when ye see her pace
Sweeping into this presence, glisten'd o'er

With emptied caskets, and her train upheld
By ladies, habited in robes of lawn,
Sprinkled with golden crescents; (others bright
In silks, with spangles shower'd,) and bow'd to
By Duchesses and pearled Margravines—   90
Sad, that the fairest creature of the earth—
I pray you mind me not—'tis sad, I say,
That the extremest beauty of the world
Should so entrench herself away from me,
Behind a barrier of engender'd guilt!
   Second Lady. Ah! what a moan!
   First Knight.   Most piteous indeed!
   Ludolph. She shall be brought before this company,
And then—then—
   First Lady.   He muses.
   Gersa.   O, Fortune, where will this end?
   Sigifred. I guess his purpose! Indeed he must not have
That pestilence brought in,—that cannot be,   100
There we must stop him.
   Gersa.   I am lost! Hush, hush!
He is about to rave again.
   Ludolph. A barrier of guilt! I was the fool.
She was the cheater! Who's the cheater now,
And who the fool? The entrapp'd, the caged fool,
The bird-lim'd raven? She shall croak to death
Secure! Methinks I have her in my fist,
To crush her with my heel! Wait, wait! I marvel
My father keeps away: good friend, ah! Sigifred!
Do bring him to me—and Erminia   110
I fain would see before I sleep—and Ethelbert,
That he may bless me, as I know he will
Though I have curs'd him.
   Sigifred.   Rather suffer me
To lead you to them—
   Ludolph.   No, excuse me, no—
The day is not quite done—go bring them hither.
                           [*Exit* SIGIFRED.

Certes, a father's smile should, like sunlight,,
Slant on my sheafed harvest of ripe bliss—
Besides, I thirst to pledge my lovely Bride
In a deep goblet: let me see—what wine?
The strong Iberian juice, or mellow Greek?   120
Or pale Calabrian? Or the Tuscan grape?
Or of old Ætna's pulpy wine presses,
Black stain'd with the fat vintage, as it were
The purple slaughter-house, where Bacchus' self
Prick'd his own swollen veins? Where is my Page?

Page.   Here, here!
Ludolph. Be ready to obey me; anon thou shalt
Bear a soft message for me—for the hour
Draws near when I must make a winding up
Of bridal Mysteries—a fine-spun vengeance!
Carve it on my Tomb, that when I rest beneath   130
Men shall confess—This Prince was gull'd and cheated,
But from the ashes of disgrace he rose
More than a fiery Phœnix—and did burn
His ignominy up in purging fires—
Did I not send, Sir, but a moment past,
For my Father?
     Gersa.   You did.
     Ludolph.   Perhaps 'twould be
Much better he came not.
     Gersa.   He enters now!

Enter OTHO, ERMINIA, ETHELBERT, SIGIFRED, *and Physician.*

     Ludolph. O thou good Man, against whose sacred head
I was a mad conspirator, chiefly too
For the sake of my fair newly wedded wife,   140
Now to be punish'd, do not look so sad!.
Those charitable eyes will thaw my heart,
Those tears will wash away a just resolve,
A verdict ten times sworn! Awake—awake—
Put on a judge's brow, and use a tongue
Made iron-stern by habit! Thou shalt see
A deed to be applauded, 'scribed in gold!
Join a loud voice to mine, and so denounce
What I alone will execute!
     Otho.   Dear son,
What is it? By your father's love, I sue   150
That it be nothing merciless!
     Ludolph.   To that demon?
Not so! No! She is in temple-stall
Being garnish'd for the sacrifice, and I,
The Priest of Justice, will immolate her
Upon the altar of wrath! She stings me through!—
Even as the worm doth feed upon the nut,
So she, a scorpion, preys upon my brain!
I feel her gnawing here! Let her but vanish,
Then, father, I will lead your legions forth,
Compact in steeled squares, and speared files,   160
And bid our trumpets speak a fell rebuke
To nations drows'd in peace!
     Otho.   To-morrow, Son,
Be your word law—forget to-day—

Ludolph.   I will
When I have finish'd it—now! now! I'm pight,
Tight-footed for the deed!
   Erminia.   Alas! Alas!
   Ludolph. What Angel's voice is that? Erminia!
Ah! gentlest creature, whose sweet innocence
Was almost murder'd; I am penitent,
Wilt thou forgive me? And thou, holy Man,
Good Ethelbert, shall I die in peace with you?   170
   Erminia. Die, my lord!
   Ludolph.   I feel it possible.
   Otho.   Physician?
   Physician. I fear me he is past my skill.
   Otho.   Not so!
   Ludolph. I see it, I see it—I have been wandering—
Half-mad—not right here—I forget my purpose.
Bestir, bestir, Auranthe! ha! ha! ha!
Youngster! Page! go bid them drag her to me!
Obey! This shall finish it!   [*Draws a dagger.*
   Otho.   O my Son! my Son!
   Sigifred. This must not be—stop there!
   Ludolph.   Am I obey'd?
A little talk with her—no harm—haste! haste!
                     [*Exit Page.*
                        180
Set her before me—never fear I can strike.
   Several Voices. My Lord! My Lord!
   Gersa.   Good Prince!
   Ludolph. Why do ye trouble me? out—out—out away!
There she is! take that! and that! no, no—
That's not well done—Where is she?
   The doors open. Enter Page. Several women are seen grouped
about AURANTHE *in the inner room.*
   Page. Alas! My Lord, my Lord! they cannot move her!
Her arms are stiff,—her fingers clench'd and cold—
   Ludolph. She's dead!
               [*Staggers and falls into their arms.*
   Ethelbert.   Take away the dagger.
   Gersa.   Softly; so!
   Otho. Thank God for that!
   Sigifred.   I fear it could not harm him.
   Gersa. No!—brief be his anguish!
   Ludolph. She's gone—I am content—Nobles, good night!   190
We are all weary—faint—set ope the doors—
I will to bed!—To-morrow—   [*Dies.*

THE CURTAIN FALLS.

KING STEPHEN

A FRAGMENT OF A TRAGEDY

WRITTEN IN NOVEMBER 1819

KING STEPHEN

A FRAGMENT OF A TRAGEDY

ACT I.

SCENE I.—*Field of Battle.*

Alarum. Enter King STEPHEN, *Knights, and Soldiers.*

Stephen. If shame can on a soldier's vein-swoll'n front
Spread deeper crimson than the battle's toil,
Blush in your casing helmets! for see, see!
Yonder my chivalry, my pride of war,
Wrench'd with an iron hand from firm array,
Are routed loose about the plashy meads,
Of honour forfeit. O that my known voice
Could reach your dastard ears, and fright you more!
Fly, cowards, fly! Glocester is at your backs!
Throw your slack bridles o'er the flurried manes,   10
Ply well the rowel with faint trembling heels,
Scampering to death at last!
   First Knight.   The enemy
Bears his flaunt standard close upon their rear.
   Second Knight. Sure of a bloody prey, seeing the fens
Will swamp them girth-deep.
   Stephen.   Over head and ears,
No matter! 'Tis a gallant enemy;
How like a comet he goes streaming on.
But we must plague him in the flank,—hey, friends?
We are well breathed,—follow!
    Enter Earl BALDWIN *and Soldiers, as defeated.*
   Stephen.   De Redvers!   20
What is the monstrous bugbear that can fright
Baldwin?
   Baldwin. No scare-crow, but the fortunate star
Of boisterous Chester, whose fell truncheon now
Points level to the goal of victory.
This way he comes, and if you would maintain
Your person unaffronted by vile odds,

339

Take horse, my Lord.
  Stephen.   And which way spur for life?
Now I thank Heaven I am in the toils,
That soldiers may bear witness how my arm
Can burst the meshes. Not the eagle more
Loves to beat up against a tyrannous blast,   30
Than I to meet the torrent of my foes.
This is a brag,—be 't so,—but if I fall,
Carve it upon my 'scutcheon'd sepulchre.
On, fellow soldiers! Earl of Redvers, back!
Not twenty Earls of Chester shall brow-beat
The diadem.   [*Exeunt. Alarum.*

SCENE II.—*Another part of the Field.*

Trumpets sounding a Victory. Enter GLOCESTER, *Knights, and Forces.*

  Glocester. Now may we lift our bruised vizors up,
And take the flattering freshness of the air,
While the wide din of battle dies away
Into times past, yet to be echoed sure
In the silent pages of our chroniclers.
  First Knight. Will Stephen's death be mark'd there, my good
    Lord,
Or that we gave him lodging in yon towers?
  Glocester. Fain would I know the great usurper's fate.

Enter two Captains severally.

  First Captain. My Lord!
  Second Captain.   Most noble Earl!
  First Captain.   The King—
  Second Captain. The Empress greets—
  Glocester. What of the King?
  First Captain.   He sole and lone maintains   10
A hopeless bustle mid our swarming arms,
And with a nimble savageness attacks,
Escapes, makes fiercer onset, then anew
Eludes death, giving death to most that dare
Trespass within the circuit of his sword!
He must by this have fallen. Baldwin is taken;
And for the Duke of Bretagne, like a stag
He flies, for the Welsh beagles to hunt down.
God save the Empress!
  Glocester.   Now our dreaded Queen:
What message from her Highness?
  Second Captain.   Royal Maud   20
From the throng'd towers of Lincoln hath look'd down,
Like Pallas from the walls of Ilion,

And seen her enemies havock'd at her feet.
She greets most noble Glocester from her heart,
Intreating him, his captains, and brave knights,
To grace a banquet. The high city gates
Are envious which shall see your triumph pass;
The streets are full of music.

Enter Second Knight.

Glocester. Whence come you?
Second Knight. From Stephen, my good Prince,—Stephen!
Stephen! 29
Glocester. Why do you make such echoing of his name?
Second Knight. Because I think, my lord, he is no man,
But a fierce demon, 'nointed safe from wounds,
And misbaptized with a Christian name.
Glocester. A mighty soldier!—Does he still hold out?
Second Knight. He shames our victory. His valour still
Keeps elbow-room amid our eager swords,
And holds our bladed falchions all aloof—
His gleaming battle-axe being slaughter-sick,
Smote on the morion of a Flemish knight,
Broke short in his hand; upon the which he flung
The heft away with such a vengeful force, 41
It paunch'd the Earl of Chester's horse, who then
Spleen-hearted came in full career at him.
Glocester. Did no one take him at a vantage then?
Second Knight. Three then with tiger leap upon him flew,
Whom, with his sword swift-drawn and nimbly held,
He stung away again, and stood to breathe,
Smiling. Anon upon him rush'd once more
A throng of foes, and in this renew'd strife,
My sword met his and snapp'd off at the hilts. 50
Glocester. Come, lead me to this Mars—and let us move
In silence, not insulting his sad doom
With clamorous trumpets. To the Empress bear
My salutation as befits the time.

[*Exeunt* GLOCESTER *and Forces.*

SCENE III.—*The Field of Battle. Enter* STEPHEN *unarmed.*

Stephen. Another sword! And what if I could seize
One from Bellona's gleaming armoury,
Or choose the fairest of her sheaved spears!
Where are my enemies? Here, close at hand,
Here come the testy brood. O for a sword!
I'm faint—a biting sword! A noble sword!
A hedge-stake—or a ponderous stone to hurl
With brawny vengeance, like the labourer Cain.
Come on! Farewell my kingdom, and all hail

Thou superb, plum'd, and helmeted renown,   **10**
All hail—I would not truck this brilliant day
To rule in Pylos with a Nestor's beard—
Come on!

Enter De Kaims *and Knights, &c.*

 De Kaims. Is 't madness, or a hunger after death,
That makes thee thus unarm'd throw taunts at us?
Yield, Stephen, or my sword's point dip in
 The gloomy current of a traitor's heart.
  Stephen. Do it, De Kaims, I will not budge an inch.
  De Kaims. Yes, of thy madness thou shalt take the meed.
  Stephen. Darest thou?
  De Kaims.   How dare, against a man disarm'd?
  Stephen. What weapons has the lion but himself?
Come not near me, De Kaims, for by the price   **21**
Of all the glory I have won this day,
Being a king, I will not yield alive
To any but the second man of the realm,
Robert of Glocester.
  De Kaims.   Thou shalt vail to me.
  Stephen. Shall I, when I have sworn against it, sir?
Thou think'st it brave to take a breathing king,
That, on a court-day bow'd to haughty Maud,
The awed presence-chamber may be bold
To whisper, there's the man who took alive   **30**
Stephen—me—prisoner. Certes, De Kaims,
The ambition is a noble one.
  De Kaims.   'Tis true,
And, Stephen, I must compass it.
  Stephen.   No, no,
Do not tempt me to throttle you on the gorge,
Or with my gauntlet crush your hollow breast,
Just when your knighthood is grown ripe and full
For lordship.
  A Soldier. Is an honest yeoman's spear
Of no use at a need? Take that.
  Stephen.   Ah, dastard!
  De Kaims. What, you are vulnerable! my prisoner!
  Stephen. No, not yet. I disclaim it, and demand
Death as a sovereign right unto a king
Who 'sdains to yield to any but his peer,
If not in title, yet in noble deeds,
The Earl of Glocester. Stab to the hilts, De Kaims,
For I will never by mean hands be led
From this so famous field. Do ye hear! Be quick!

[*Trumpets. Enter the Earl of* CHESTER *and Knights.*

SCENE IV.—*A Presence Chamber. Queen* MAUD *in a Chair of State, the Earls of* GLOCESTER *and* CHESTER, *Lords, Attendants.*

 Maud. Glocester, no more: I will behold that Boulogne:
Set him before me. Not for the poor sake
Of regal pomp and a vain-glorious hour,
As thou with wary speech, yet near enough,
Hast hinted.
 Glocester. Faithful counsel have I given;
If wary, for your Highness' benefit.
 Maud. The Heavens forbid that I should not think so,
For by thy valour have I won this realm,
Which by thy wisdom I will ever keep.
To sage advisers let me ever bend   10
A meek attentive ear, so that they treat
Of the wide kingdom's rule and government,
Not trenching on our actions personal.
Advis'd, not school'd, I would be; and henceforth
Spoken to in clear, plain, and open terms,
Not side-ways sermon'd at.
 Glocester.   Then, in plain terms,
Once more for the fallen king—
 Maud.   Your pardon, Brother,
I would no more of that; for, as I said,
'Tis not for worldly pomp I wish to see
The rebel, but as dooming judge to give   20
A sentence something worthy of his guilt.
 Glocester. If't must be so, I'll bring him to your presence.
              [*Exit* GLOCESTER.
 Maud. A meaner summoner might do as well—
My Lord of Chester, is 't true what I hear
Of Stephen of Boulogne, our prisoner,
That he, as a fit penance for his crimes,
Eats wholesome, sweet, and palatable food
Off Glocester's golden dishes—drinks pure wine,
Lodgest soft?
 Chester.   More than that, my gracious Queen,
Has anger'd me. The noble Earl, methinks,   30
Full soldier as he is, and without peer
In counsel, dreams too much among his books.
It may read well, but sure 'tis out of date
To play the Alexander with Darius.
 Maud. Truth! I think so. By Heavens it shall not last!
 Chester. It would amaze your Highness now to mark
How Glocester overstrains his courtesy
To that crime-loving rebel, that Boulogne—

Maud. That ingrate!

Chester.   For whose vast ingratitude
To our late sovereign lord, your noble sire,   40
The generous Earl condoles in his mishaps,
And with a sort of lackeying friendliness,
Talks off the mighty frowning from his brow,
Woos him to hold a duet in a smile,
Or, if it please him, play an hour at chess—

Maud. A perjured slave!

Chester.   And for his perjury,
Glocester has fit rewards—nay, I believe,
He sets his bustling household's wits at work
For flatteries to ease this Stephen's hours,
And make a heaven of his purgatory;   50
Adorning bondage with the pleasant gloss
Of feasts and music, and all idle shows
Of indoor pageantry; while syren whispers,
Predestin'd for his ear, 'scape as half-check'd
From lips the courtliest and the rubiest
Of all the realm, admiring of his deeds.

Maud. A frost upon his summer!

Chester.   A queen's nod
Can make his June December. Here he comes.

POEMS

WRITTEN LATE IN 1819

POEMS WRITTEN LATE IN 1819

A PARTY OF LOVERS:

"A few Nonsense Verses" sent in a Letter to George Keats.

PENSIVE they sit, and roll their languid eyes,
Nibble their toast and cool their tea with sighs;
Or else forget the purpose of the night,
Forget their tea, forget their appetite.
See, with cross'd arms they sit—Ah! happy crew,
The fire is going out and no one rings
For coals, and therefore no coals Betty brings.
A fly is in the milk-pot. Must he die
Circled by a humane society?
No, no; there, Mr. Werter takes his spoon,
Inserts it, dips the handle, and lo! soon
The little straggler, sav'd from perils dark,
Across the teaboard draws a long wet mark.

Romeo! Arise, take snuffers by the handle,
There's a large cauliflower in each candle.
A winding sheet—ah, me! I must away
To No. 7, just beyond the circus gay.
Alas, my friend, your coat sits very well;
Where may your Tailor live? I may not tell.
O pardon me. I'm absent now and then.
Where *might* my Tailor live? I say again
I cannot tell, let me no more be teazed;
He lives in Wapping, might live where he pleased.

SONNET

THE day is gone, and all its sweets are gone!
  Sweet voice, sweet lips, soft hand, and softer breast,
Warm breath, light whisper, tender semi-tone,
  Bright eyes, accomplish'd shape, and lang'rous waist!
Faded the flower and all its budded charms,
  Faded the sight of beauty from my eyes,
Faded the shape of beauty from my arms,
  Faded the voice, warmth, whiteness, paradise—

347

Vanish'd unseasonably at shut of eve,
　When the dusk holiday—or holinight 　　　　　10
Of fragrant-curtain'd love begins to weave
　The woof of darkness thick, for hid delight;
But, as I've read love's missal through to-day,
He'll let me sleep, seeing I fast and pray.

LINES TO FANNY

WHAT can I do to drive away
Remembrance from my eyes? for they have seen,
Aye, an hour ago, my brilliant Queen!
Touch has a memory. O say, love, say,
What can I do to kill it and be free
In my old liberty?
When every fair one that I saw was fair,
Enough to catch me in but half a snare,
Not keep me there:
When, howe'er poor or particolour'd things, 　　　　10
My muse had wings,
And ever ready was to take her course
Whither I bent her force,
Unintellectual, yet divine to me;—
Divine, I say!—What sea-bird o'er the sea
Is a philosopher the while he goes
Winging along where the great water throes?

　How shall I do
　To get anew
Those moulted feathers, and so mount once more 　　　　20
　Above, above
　The reach of fluttering Love,
And make him cower lowly while I soar?
Shall I gulp wine? No, that is vulgarism,
A heresy and schism,
　Foisted into the canon law of love;—
No,—wine is only sweet to happy men;
　More dismal cares
　Seize on me unawares,—
Where shall I learn to get my peace again? 　　　　30
To banish thoughts of that most hateful land,
Dungeoner of my friends, that wicked strand
Where they were wreck'd and live a wrecked life;
That monstrous region, whose dull rivers pour,
Ever from their sordid urns unto the shore,
Unown'd of any weedy-haired gods;
Whose winds, all zephyrless, hold scourging rods,

Iced in the great lakes, to afflict mankind;
Whose rank-grown forests, frosted, black, and blind,
Would fright a Dryad; whose harsh herbag'd meads
Make lean and lank the starv'd ox while he feeds;
There bad flowers have no scent, birds no sweet song,
And great unerring Nature once seems wrong.   43

O, for some sunny spell
To dissipate the shadows of this hell!
Say they are gone,—with the new dawning light
Steps forth my lady bright!
O, let me once more rest
My soul upon that dazzling breast!
Let once again these aching arms be plac'd,   50
The tender gaolers of thy waist!
And let me feel that warm breath here and there
To spread a rapture in my very hair,—
O, the sweetness of the pain!
Give me those lips again!
Enough! Enough! it is enough for me
To dream of thee!

SONNET

TO FANNY

I CRY your mercy—pity—love!—aye, love!
   Merciful love that tantalizes not,
One-thoughted, never-wandering, guileless love,
   Unmask'd, and being seen—without a blot!
O! let me have thee whole,—all—all—be mine!
   That shape, that fairness, that sweet minor zest
Of love, your kiss,—those hands, those eyes divine,
   That warm, white, lucent, million-pleasured breast,—
Yourself—your soul—in pity give me all,
   Withhold no atom's atom or I die,   10
Or living on perhaps, your wretched thrall,
   Forget, in the mist of idle misery,
Life's purposes,—the palate of my mind
Losing its gust, and my ambition blind!

THE FALL OF HYPERION

A DREAM

AN ATTEMPT MADE AT THE END OF 1819 TO
RECONSTRUCT THE POEM

THE FALL OF HYPERION

A DREAM

[CANTO I]

FANATICS have their dreams, wherewith they weave
A paradise for a sect; the savage too
From forth the loftiest fashion of his sleep
Guesses at Heaven; pity these have not
Trac'd upon vellum or wild Indian leaf
The shadows of melodious utterance.
But bare of laurel they live, dream, and die;
For Poesy alone can tell her dreams,
With the fine spell of words alone can save
Imagination from the sable chain   10
And dumb enchantment. Who alive can say,
"Thou art no Poet—may'st not tell thy dreams?"
Since every man whose soul is not a clod
Hath visions, and would speak, if he had loved,
And been well nurtured in his mother tongue.
Whether the dream now purpos'd to rehearse
Be poet's or fanatic's will be known
When this warm scribe my hand is in the grave.

Methought I stood where trees of every clime,
Palm, myrtle, oak, and sycamore, and beech,   20
With plantain, and spice-blossoms, made a screen;
In neighbourhood of fountains (by the noise
Soft-showering in my ears), and, (by the touch
Of scent,) not far from roses. Turning round
I saw an arbour with a drooping roof
Of trellis vines, and bells, and larger blooms,
Like floral censers, swinging light in air;
Before its wreathed doorway, on a mound
Of moss, was spread a feast of summer fruits,
Which, nearer seen, seem'd refuse of a meal   30
By angel tasted or our Mother Eve;
For empty shells were scattered on the grass,
And grape-stalks but half bare, and remnants more,
Sweet-smelling, whose pure kinds I could not know.
Still was more plenty than the fabled horn
Thrice emptied could pour forth, at banqueting

For Proserpine return'd to her own fields,
Where the white heifers low. And appetite
More yearning than on Earth I ever felt
Growing within, I ate deliciously;   40
And, after not long, thirsted, for thereby
Stood a cool vessel of transparent juice
Sipp'd by the wander'd bee, the which I took,
And, pledging all the mortals of the world,
And all the dead whose names are in our lips,
Drank. That full draught is parent of my theme.
No Asian poppy nor elixir fine
Of the soon-fading jealous Caliphat;
No poison gender'd in close monkish cell,
To thin the scarlet conclave of old men,   50
Could so have rapt unwilling life away.
Among the fragrant husks and berries crush'd,
Upon the grass I struggled hard against
The domineering potion; but in vain:
The cloudy swoon came on, and down I sank,
Like a Silenus on an antique vase.
How long I slumber'd 'tis a chance to guess.
When sense of life return'd, I started up
As if with wings; but the fair trees were gone,
The mossy mound and arbour were no more: 60
I look'd around upon the carved sides
Of an old sanctuary with roof august,
Builded so high, it seem'd that filmed clouds
Might spread beneath, as o'er the stars of heaven;
So old the place was, I remember'd none
The like upon the Earth: what I had seen
Of grey cathedrals, buttress'd walls, rent towers,
The superannuations of sunk realms,
Or Nature's rocks toil'd hard in waves and winds,
Seem'd but the faulture of decrepit things   70
To that eternal domed Monument.—
Upon the marble at my feet there lay
Store of strange vessels and large draperies,
Which needs had been of dyed asbestos wove,
Or in that place the moth could not corrupt,
So white the linen, so, in some, distinct
Ran imageries from a sombre loom.
All in a mingled heap confus'd there lay
Robes, golden tongs, censer and chafing-dish,
Girdles, and chains, and holy jewelries.   80

     Turning from these with awe, once more I rais'd
My eyes to fathom the space every way;

The embossed roof, the silent massy range
Of columns north and south, ending in mist
Of nothing, then to eastward, where black gates
Were shut against the sunrise evermore.—
Then to the west I look'd, and saw far off
An image, huge of feature as a cloud,
At level of whose feet an altar slept,
To be approach'd on either side by steps,   90
And marble balustrade, and patient travail
To count with toil the innumerable degrees.
Towards the altar sober-paced I went,
Repressing haste, as too unholy there;
And, coming nearer, saw beside the shrine
One minist'ring; and there arose a flame.—
When in mid-way the sickening East wind
Shifts sudden to the south, the small warm rain
Melts out the frozen incense from all flowers,
And fills the air with so much pleasant health   100
That even the dying man forgets his shroud;—
Even so that lofty sacrificial fire,
Sending forth Maian incense, spread around
Forgetfulness of everything but bliss,
And clouded all the altar with soft smoke;
From whose white fragrant curtains thus I heard
Language pronounc'd: "If thou canst not ascend
"These steps, die on that marble where thou art.
"Thy flesh, near cousin to the common dust,
"Will parch for lack of nutriment—thy bones   110
"Will wither in few years, and vanish so
"That not the quickest eye could find a grain
"Of what thou now art on that pavement cold.
"The sands of thy short life are spent this hour,
"And no hand in the universe can turn
"Thy hourglass, if these gummed leaves be burnt
"Ere thou canst mount up these immortal steps."
I heard, I look'd: two senses both at once,
So fine, so subtle, felt the tyranny
Of that fierce threat and the hard task proposed.   120
Prodigious seem'd the toil; the leaves were yet
Burning—when suddenly a palsied chill
Struck from the paved level up my limbs,
And was ascending quick to put cold grasp
Upon those streams that pulse beside the throat:
I shriek'd, and the sharp anguish of my shriek
Stung my own ears—I strove hard to escape
The numbness; strove to gain the lowest step.
Slow, heavy, deadly was my pace: the cold

Grew stifling, suffocating, at the heart;   30
And when I clasp'd my hands I felt them not.
One minute before death, my iced foot touch'd
The lowest stair; and as it touch'd, life seem'd
To pour in at the toes: I mounted up,
As once fair angels on a ladder flew
From the green turf to Heaven—"Holy Power,"
Cried I, approaching near the horned shrine,
"What am I that should so be saved from death?
"What am I that another death come not
"To choke my utterance sacrilegious, here?"   140
Then said the veiled shadow—"Thou hast felt
"What 'tis to die and live again before
"Thy fated hour, that thou hadst power to do so
"Is thy own safety; thou hast dated on
Thy doom."—"High Prophetess," said I, "purge off,
Benign, if so it please thee, my mind's film."—
"None can usurp this height," return'd that shade,
"But those to whom the miseries of the world
"Are misery, and will not let them rest.
"All else who find a haven in the world,   150
"Where they may thoughtless sleep away their days,
"If by a chance into this fane they come,
"Rot on the pavement where thou rottedst half."—
"Are there not thousands in the world," said I,
Encourag'd by the sooth voice of the shade,
"Who love their fellows even to the death,
"Who feel the giant agony of the world,
"And more, like slaves to poor humanity,
"Labour for mortal good? I sure should see
"Other men here; but I am here alone."   160
"Those whom thou spak'st of are no vision'ries,"
Rejoin'd that voice—"They are no dreamers weak,
"They seek no wonder but the human face;
"No music but a happy-noted voice—
"They come not here, they have no thought to come—
"And thou art here, for thou art less than they—
"What benefit canst thou, or all thy tribe,
"To the great world? Thou art a dreaming thing,
"A fever of thyself—think of the Earth;
"What bliss even in hope is there for thee?   170
"What haven? every creature hath its home;
"Every sole man hath days of joy and pain,
"Whether his labours be sublime or low—
"The pain alone; the joy alone; distinct:
"Only the dreamer venoms all his days,
"Bearing more woe than all his sins deserve.

"Therefore, that happiness be somewhat shar'd,
"Such things as thou art are admitted oft
"Into like gardens thou didst pass erewhile,
"And suffer'd in these temples: for that cause   180
"Thou standest safe beneath this statue's knees."
"That I am favour'd for unworthiness,
"By such propitious parley medicin'd
"In sickness not ignoble, I rejoice,
"Aye, and could weep for love of such award."
So answer'd I, continuing, "If it please,
"Majestic shadow, tell me: sure not all
"Those melodies sung into the World's ear
"Are useless: sure a poet is a sage;
"A humanist, physician to all men.   190
"That I am none I feel, as vultures feel
"They are no birds when eagles are abroad.
"What am I then: Thou spakest of my tribe:
"What tribe?" The tall shade veil'd in drooping white
Then spake, so much more earnest, that the breath
Moved the thin linen folds that drooping hung
About a golden censer from the hand
Pendent—"Art thou not of the dreamer tribe?
"The poet and the dreamer are distinct,
"Diverse, sheer opposite, antipodes.   200
"The one pours out a balm upon the World,
"The other vexes it." Then shouted I
Spite of myself, and with a Pythia's spleen
"Apollo! faded! O far flown Apollo!
"Where is thy misty pestilence to creep
"Into the dwellings, through the door crannies
"Of all mock lyrists, large self worshipers
"And careless Hectorers in proud bad verse.
"Though I breathe death with them it will be life
"To see them sprawl before me into graves.   210
"Majestic shadow, tell me where I am,
"Whose altar this; for whom this incense curls;
"What image this whose face I cannot see,
"For the broad marble knees; and who thou art,
"Of accent feminine so courteous?"

Then the tall shade, in drooping linens veil'd
Spoke out, so much more earnest, that her breath
Stirr'd the thin folds of gauze that drooping hung
About a golden censer from her hand
Pendent; and by her voice I knew she shed   220
Long-treasured tears. "This temple, sad and lone,
"Is all spar'd from the thunder of a war

"Foughten long since by giant hierarchy
"Against rebellion: this old image here,
"Whose carved features wrinkled as he fell,
"Is Saturn's; I Moneta, left supreme
"Sole Priestess of this desolation."—
I had no words to answer, for my tongue,
Useless, could find about its roofed home
No syllable of a fit majesty   230
To make rejoinder to Moneta's mourn.
There was a silence, while the altar's blaze
Was fainting for sweet food: I look'd thereon,
And on the paved floor, where nigh were piled
Faggots of cinnamon, and many heaps
Of other crisped spice-wood—then again
I look'd upon the altar, and its horns
Whiten'd with ashes, and its lang'rous flame,
And then upon the offerings again;
And so by turns—till sad Moneta cried,   240
"The sacrifice is done, but not the less
"Will I be kind to thee for thy good will.
"My power, which to me is still a curse,
"Shall be to thee a wonder; for the scenes
"Still swooning vivid through my globed brain,
"With an electral changing misery,
"Thou shalt with these dull mortal eyes behold,
"Free from all pain, if wonder pain thee not."
As near as an immortal's sphered words
Could to a mother's soften, were these last: 250
And yet I had a terror of her robes,
And chiefly of the veils, that from her brow
Hung pale, and curtain'd her in mysteries,
That made my heart too small to hold its blood.
This saw that Goddess, and with sacred hand
Parted the veils. Then saw I a wan face,
Not pin'd by human sorrows, but bright-blanch'd
By an immortal sickness which kills not;
It works a constant change, which happy death
Can put no end to; deathwards progressing   260
To no death was that visage; it had past
The lilly and the snow; and beyond these
I must not think now, though I saw that face—
But for her eyes I should have fled away.
They held me back, with a benignant light,
Soft mitigated by divinest lids
Half-closed, and visionless entire they seem'd
Of all external things;—they saw me not,
But in blank splendour, beam'd like the mild moon,

Who comforts those she sees not, who knows not
What eyes are upward cast. As I had found   271
A grain of gold upon a mountain's side,
· And twing'd with avarice strain'd out my eyes
To search its sullen entrails rich with ore,
So at the view of sad Moneta's brow,
I ask'd to see what things the hollow brain
Behind environed: what high tragedy
In the dark secret chambers of her skull
Was acting, that could give so dread a stress
To her cold lips, and fill with such a light   280
Her planetary eyes; and touch her voice
With such a sorrow—"Shade of Memory!"—
Cried I, with act adorant at her feet,
"By all the gloom hung round thy fallen house,
"By this last temple, by the golden age,
"By great Apollo, thy dear Foster Child,
"And by thyself, forlorn divinity,
"The pale Omega of a withered race,
"Let me behold, according as thou saidst,
"What in thy brain so ferments to and fro!"   290
No sooner had this conjuration pass'd
My devout lips, than side by side we stood
(Like a stunt bramble by a solemn pine)
Deep in the shady sadness of a vale,
Far sunken from the healthy breath of morn,
Far from the fiery noon and eve's one star.
Onward I look'd beneath the gloomy boughs,
And saw, what first I thought an image huge,
Like to the image pedestal'd so high
In Saturn's temple. Then Moneta's voice   300
Came brief upon mine ear—"So Saturn sat
When he had lost his Realms—" whereon there grew
A power within me of enormous ken
To see as a god sees, and take the depth
Of things as nimbly as the outward eye
Can size and shape pervade. The lofty theme
At those few words hung vast before my mind,
With half-unravel'd web. I set myself
Upon an eagle's watch, that I might see,
And seeing ne'er forget. No stir of life   310
·Was in this shrouded vale, not so much air
As in the zoning of a summer's day
Robs not one light seed from the feather'd grass,
But where the dead leaf fell there did it rest:
A stream went voiceless by, still deaden'd more
  ⸰ By reason of the fallen divinity

Spreading more shade; the Naiad 'mid her reeds
Prest her cold finger closer to her lips.

Along the margin-sand large footmarks went
No farther than to where old Saturn's feet   320
Had rested, and there slept, how long a sleep!
Degraded, cold, upon the sodden ground
His old right hand lay nerveless, listless, dead,
Unsceptred; and his realmless eyes were clos'd,
While his bow'd head seem'd listening to the Earth,
His ancient mother, for some comfort yet.

It seem'd no force could wake him from his place;
But there came one who, with a kindred hand
Touch'd his wide shoulders after bending low
With reverence, though to one who knew it not.   330
Then came the griev'd voice of Mnemosyne,
And griev'd I hearken'd. "That divinity
"Whom thou saw'st step from yon forlornest wood,
"And with slow pace approach our fallen King,
"Is Thea, softest-natur'd of our Brood."
I mark'd the Goddess in fair statuary
Surpassing wan Moneta by the head,
And in her sorrow nearer woman's tears.
There was a listening fear in her regard,
As if calamity had but begun;   340
As if the vanward clouds of evil days
Had spent their malice, and the sullen rear
Was with its stored thunder labouring up.
One hand she press'd upon that aching spot
Where beats the human heart, as if just there,
Though an immortal, she felt cruel pain;
The other upon Saturn's bended neck
She laid, and to the level of his hollow ear
Leaning with parted lips, some words she spake
In solemn tenor and deep organ tune;   350
Some mourning words, which in our feeble tongue
Would come in this-like accenting; how frail
To that large utterance of the early Gods!

"Saturn! look up—and for what, poor lost King?
"I have no comfort for thee; no not one;
"I cannot say, wherefore thus sleepest thou?
"For Heaven is parted from thee, and the Earth
"Knows thee not, so afflicted, for a God;
"And Ocean too, with all its solemn noise,
"Has from thy sceptre pass'd, and all the air   360

"Is emptied of thine hoary majesty:
"Thy thunder, captious at the new command,
"Rumbles reluctant o'er our fallen house;
"And thy sharp lightning, in unpracticed hands,
"Scorches and burns our once serene domain,
"With such remorseless speed still come new woes,
"That unbelief has not a space to breathe.
"Saturn! sleep on:—Me thoughtless, why should I
"Thus violate thy slumbrous solitude?
"Why should I ope thy melancholy eyes?   370
"Saturn, sleep on, while at thy feet I weep."

 As when upon a tranced summer-night
Forests, branch-charmed by the earnest stars,
Dream, and so dream all night without a noise,
Save from one gradual solitary gust,
Swelling upon the silence; dying off;
As if the ebbing air had but one wave;
So came these words, and went; the while in tears
She prest her fair large forehead to the earth,   379
Just where her fallen hair might spread in curls,
A soft and silken mat for Saturn's feet.
Long, long these two were postured motionless,
Like sculpture builded-up upon the grave
Of their own power. A long awful time
I look'd upon them: still they were the same;
The frozen God still bending to the earth,
And the sad Goddess weeping at his feet,
Moneta silent. Without stay or prop,
But my own weak mortality, I bore
The load of this eternal quietude,   390
The unchanging gloom, and the three fixed shapes
Ponderous upon my senses, a whole moon.
For by my burning brain I measured sure
Her silver seasons shedded on the night,
And every day by day methought I grew
More gaunt and ghostly.—Oftentimes I pray'd
Intense, that Death would take me from the Vale
And all its burthens—gasping with despair
Of change, hour after hour I curs'd myself;
Until old Saturn rais'd his faded eyes,   400
And look'd around and saw his kingdom gone,
And all the gloom and sorrow of the place,
And that fair kneeling Goddess at his feet.
As the moist scent of flowers, and grass, and leaves,
Fills forest dells with a pervading air,
Known to the woodland nostril, so the words

Of Saturn fill'd the mossy glooms around,
Even to the hollows of time-eaten oaks,
And to the windings of the foxes' hole,
With sad low tones, while thus he spake, and sent
Strange musings to the solitary Pan.
"Moan, brethren, moan; for we are swallow'd up
"And buried from all Godlike exercise
"Of influence benign on planets pale,
"And peaceful sway above man's harvesting,   415
"And all those acts which Deity supreme
"Doth ease its heart of love in. Moan and wail,
"Moan, brethren, moan; for lo, the rebel spheres
"Spin round, the stars their ancient courses keep,
"Clouds still with shadowy moisture haunt the earth,
"Still suck their fill of light from sun and moon;
"Still buds the tree, and still the sea-shores murmur;
"There is no death in all the Universe,   423
"No smell of death—there shall be death—Moan, moan,
"Moan, Cybele, moan; for thy pernicious Babes
"Have changed a god into an aching Palsy.
"Moan, brethren, moan, for I have no strength left,
"Weak as the reed—weak—feeble as my voice—
"O, O, the pain, the pain of feebleness.
"Moan, moan, for still I thaw—or give me help;
"Throw down those imps, and give me victory.   431
"Let me hear other groans, and trumpets blown
"Of triumph calm, and hymns of festival,
"From the gold peaks of Heaven's high-piled clouds;
"Voices of soft proclaim, and silver stir
"Of strings in hollow shells; and there shall be
"Beautiful things made new for the surprise
"Of the sky-children." So he feebly ceas'd,
With such a poor and sickly sounding pause,
Methought I heard some old man of the earth   440
Bewailing earthly loss; nor could my eyes
And ears act with that pleasant unison of sense
Which marries sweet sound with the grace of form.
And dolorous accent from a tragic harp
With large-limb'd visions.—More I scrutinized:
Still fix'd he sat beneath the sable trees,
Whose arms spread straggling in wild serpent forms,
With leaves all hush'd; his awful presence there
(Now all was silent) gave a deadly lie
To what I erewhile heard—only his lips   450
Trembled amid the white curls of his beard.
They told the truth, though, round, the snowy locks
Hung nobly, as upon the face of heaven

A mid-day fleece of clouds. Thea arose,
And stretched her white arm through the hollow dark,
Pointing some whither: whereat he too rose
Like a vast giant, seen by men at sea
To grow pale from the waves at dull midnight.
They melted from my sight into the woods;
Ere I could turn, Moneta cried, "These twain   460
"Are speeding to the families of grief,
"Where roof'd in by black rocks they waste, in pain
"And darkness, for no hope."—And she spake on,
As ye may read who can unwearied pass
Onward from th' Antichamber of this dream,
Where even at the open doors awhile
I must delay, and glean my memory
Of her high phrase:—perhaps no further dare.

END OF CANTO I

CANTO II

"MORTAL, that thou may'st understand aright,
"I humanize my sayings to thine ear,
"Making comparisons of earthly things;
"Or thou might'st better listen to the wind,
"Whose language is to thee a barren noise,
"Though it blows legend-laden thro' the trees.—
"In melancholy realms big tears are shed,
"More sorrow like to this, and such like woe,
"Too huge for mortal tongue, or pen of scribe.
"The Titans fierce, self hid or prison bound,   10
"Groan for the old allegiance once more,
"Listening in their doom for Saturn's voice.
"But one of our whole eagle-brood still keeps
"His sov'reignty, and rule, and majesty;
"Blazing Hyperion on his orbed fire
"Still sits, still snuffs the incense teeming up
"From Man to the Sun's God: yet unsecure.
"For as upon the earth dire prodigies
"Fright and perplex, so also shudders he:
"Nor at dog's howl or gloom-bird's Even screech,   20
"Or the familiar visitings of one
"Upon the first toll of his passing bell:
"But horrors, portioned to a giant nerve,
"Make great Hyperion ache. His palace bright,
"Bastion'd with pyramids of glowing gold,
"And touch'd with shade of bronzed obelisks,
"Glares a blood-red thro' all the thousand courts,

"Arches, and domes, and fiery galleries:
"And all its curtains of Aurorian clouds
"Flush angerly; when he would taste the wreaths   30
"Of incense breathed aloft from sacred hills,
"Instead of sweets, his ample palate takes
"Savour of poisonous brass and metals sick.
"Wherefore when harbour'd in the sleepy West,
"After the full completion of fair day,
"For rest divine upon exalted couch
"And slumber in the arms of melody,
"He paces through the pleasant hours of ease
"With strides colossal, on from hall to hall;
"While far within each aisle and deep recess   40
"His winged minions in close clusters stand
"Amaz'd, and full of fear; like anxious men,
"Who on a wide plain gather in sad troops,
"When earthquakes jar their battlements and towers.
"Even now, while Saturn, roused from icy trance,
"Goes, step for step, with Thea from yon woods,
"Hyperion, leaving twilight in the rear,
"Is sloping to the threshold of the West.—
"Thither we tend."—Now in clear light I stood,
Reliev'd from the dusk vale. Mnemosyne   50
Was sitting on a square-edg'd polish'd stone,
That in its lucid depth reflected pure
Her priestess-garments.—My quick eyes ran on
From stately nave to nave, from vault to vault,
Through bow'rs of fragrant and enwreathed light
And diamond-paved lustrous long arcades.
Anon rush'd by the bright Hyperion;
His flaming robes stream'd out beyond his heels,
And gave a roar, as if of earthly fire,
That scared away the meek ethereal hours,   60
And made their dove-wings tremble. On he flared.

THE CAP AND BELLS

OR THE JEALOUSIES

A FAERY TALE—UNFINISHED

THE CAP AND BELLS

OR THE JEALOUSIES

A FAERY TALE—UNFINISHED

I

In midmost Ind, beside Hydaspes cool,
There stood, or hover'd, tremulous in the air,
A faery city, 'neath the potent rule
Of Emperor Elfinan; fam'd ev'rywhere
For love of mortal women, maidens fair,
Whose lips were solid, whose soft hands were made
Of a fit mould and beauty, ripe and rare,
To pamper his slight wooing, warm yet staid:
He lov'd girls smooth as shades, but hated a mere shade.

II

This was a crime forbidden by the law;
And all the priesthood of his city wept,
For ruin and dismay they well foresaw,
If impious prince no bound or limit kept,
And faery Zendervester overstept;
They wept, he sin'd, and still he would sin on,
They dreamt of sin, and he sin'd while they slept;
In vain the pulpit thunder'd at the throne,
Caricature was vain, and vain the tart lampoon.

III

Which seeing, his high court of parliament
Laid a remonstrance at his Highness' feet,
Praying his royal senses to content
Themselves with what in faery land was sweet,
Befitting best that shade with shade should meet:
Whereat, to calm their fears, he promis'd soon
From mortal tempters all to make retreat,—
Aye, even on the first of the new moon,
An immaterial wife to espouse as heaven's boon.

IV

Meantime he sent a fluttering embassy
To Pigmio, of Imaus sovereign,
To half beg, and half demand, respectfully,
The hand of his fair daughter Bellanaine;
An audience had, and speeching done, they gain
Their point, and bring the weeping bride away;
Whom, with but one attendant, safely lain
Upon their wings, they bore in bright array,
While little harps were touch'd by many a lyric fay.

V

As in old pictures tender cherubim
A child's soul thro' the sapphir'd canvas bear,
So, thro' a real heaven, on they swim
With the sweet princess on her plumag'd lair,
Speed giving to the winds her lustrous hair;
And so she journey'd, sleeping or awake,
Save when, for healthful exercise and air,
She chose to *promener à l'aile*, or take
A pigeon's somerset, for sport or change's sake.

VI

"Dear Princess, do not whisper me so loud,"
Quoth Corallina, nurse and confidant,
"Do not you see there, lurking in a cloud,
Close at your back, that sly old Crafticant?
He hears a whisper plainer than a rant:
Dry up your tears, and do not look so blue;
He's Elfinan's great state-spy militant,
His running, lying, flying foot-man too,—
Dear mistress, let him have no handle against you!

VII

"Show him a mouse's tail, and he will guess,
With metaphysic swiftness, at the mouse;
Show him a garden, and with speed no less,
He'll surmise sagely of a dwelling house,
And plot, in the same minute, how to chouse
The owner out of it; show him a"— "Peace!
Peace! nor contrive thy mistress' ire to rouse!"
Return'd the Princess, "my tongue shall not cease
Till from this hated match I get a free release.

VIII

"Ah, beauteous mortal!" "Hush!" quoth Coralline,
"Really you must not talk of him, indeed."
"You hush!" replied the mistress, with a shine
Of anger in her eyes, enough to breed
In stouter hearts than nurse's fear and dread:
'Twas not the glance itself made nursey flinch,
But of its threat she took the utmost heed;
Not liking in her heart an hour-long pinch,
Or a sharp needle run into her back an inch.

IX

So she was silenc'd, and fair Bellanaine,
Writhing her little body with ennui,
Continued to lament and to complain,
That Fate, cross-purposing, should let her be
Ravish'd away far from her dear countree;
That all her feelings should be set at naught,
In trumping up this match so hastily,
With lowland blood; and lowland blood she thought
Poison, as every staunch true-born Imaian ought.

X

Sorely she griev'd, and wetted three or four
White Provence rose-leaves with her faery tears,
But not for this cause;—alas! she had more
Bad reasons for her sorrow, as appears
In the fam'd memoirs of a thousand years,
Written by Crafticant, and published
By Parpaglion and Co., (those sly compeers
Who rak'd up ev'ry fact against the dead,)
In Scarab Street, Panthea, at the Jubal's Head.

XI

Where, after a long hypercritic howl
Against the vicious manners of the age
He goes on to expose, with heart and soul,
What vice in this or that year was the rage,
Backbiting all the world in every page;
With special strictures on the horrid crime,
(Section'd and subsection'd with learning sage,)
Of faeries stooping on their wings sublime
To kiss a mortal's lips, when such were in their prime.

XII

Turn to the copious index, you will find
Somewhere in the column, headed letter B,
The name of Bellanaine, if you're not blind;
Then pray refer to the text, and you will see
An article made up of calumny
Against this highland princess, rating her
For giving way, so over fashionably,
To this new-fangled vice, which seems a burr
Stuck in his moral throat, no coughing e'er could stir.

XIII

There he says plainly that she lov'd a man!
That she around him flutter'd, flirted, toy'd,
Before her marriage with great Elfinan;
That after marriage too, she never joy'd
In husband's company, but still employ'd
Her wits to 'scape away to Angle-land;
Where liv'd the youth, who worried and annoy'd
Her tender heart, and its warm ardours fann'd
To such a dreadful blaze, her side would scorch her hand.

XIV

But let us leave this idle tittle-tattle
To waiting-maids, and bed-room coteries,
Nor till fit time against her fame wage battle.
Poor Elfinan is very ill at ease,
Let us resume his subject if you please:
For it may comfort and console him much
To rhyme and syllable his miseries;
Poor Elfinan! whose cruel fate was such,
He sat and curs'd a bride he knew he could not touch.

XV

Soon as (according to his promises)
The bridal embassy had taken wing,
And vanish'd, bird-like, o'er the suburb trees,
The Emperor, empierc'd with the sharp sting
Of love, retired, vex'd and murmuring
Like any drone shut from the fair bee-queen,
Into his cabinet, and there did fling
His limbs upon a sofa, full of spleen,
And damn'd his House of Commons, in complete chagrin.

XVI

"I'll trounce some of the members," cried the Prince,
"I'll put a mark against some rebel names,
I'll make the Opposition-benches wince,
I'll show them very soon, to all their shames,
What 'tis to smother up a Prince's flames;
That ministers should join in it, I own,
Surprises me!—they too at these high games!
Am I an Emperor? Do I wear a crown?
Imperial Elfinan, go hang thyself or drown!

XVII

"I'll trounce 'em!—there's the square-cut chancellor,
His son shall never touch that bishopric;
And for the nephew of old Palfior,
I'll show him that his speech has made me sick,
And give the colonelcy to Phalaric;
The tiptoe marquis, moral and gallant,
Shall lodge in shabby taverns upon tick;
And for the Speaker's second cousin's aunt,
She sha'n't be maid of honour,—by heaven that she sha'n't!

XVIII

"I'll shirk the Duke of A.; I'll cut his brother;
I'll give no garter to his eldest son;
I won't speak to his sister or his mother!
The Viscount B. shall live at cut-and-run;
But how in the world can I contrive to stun
That fellow's voice, which plagues me worse than any,
That stubborn fool, that impudent state-dun,
Who sets down ev'ry sovereign as a zany,—
That vulgar commoner, Esquire Biancopany?

XIX

"Monstrous affair! Pshaw! pah! what ugly minx
Will they fetch from Imaus for my bride?
Alas! my wearied heart within me sinks,
To think that I must be so near allied
To a cold dullard fay,—ah, woe betide!
Ah, fairest of all human loveliness!
Sweet Bertha! what crime can it be to glide
About the fragrant pleatings of thy dress,
Or kiss thine eyes, or count thy locks, tress after tress?"

XX

So said, one minute's while his eyes remain'd
Half lidded, piteous, languid, innocent;
But, in a wink, their splendour they regain'd,
Sparkling revenge with amorous fury blent.
Love thwarted in bad temper oft has vent:
He rose, he stampt his foot, he rang the bell,
And order'd some death-warrants to be sent
For signature:—somewhere the tempest fell,
As many a poor felon does not live to tell.

XXI

"At the same time Eban,"—(this was his page,
A fay of colour, slave from top to toe,
Sent as a present, while yet under age,
From the Viceroy of Zanguebar,—wise, slow,
His speech, his only words were "yes" and "no,"
But swift of look, and foot, and wing was he,—)
"At the same time, Eban, this instant go
To Hum the soothsayer, whose name I see
Among the fresh arrivals in our empery.

XXII

"Bring Hum to me! But stay—here, take my ring,
The pledge of favour, that he not suspect
Any foul play, or awkward murdering,
Tho' I have bowstrung many of his sect;
Throw in a hint, that if he should neglect
One hour, the next shall see him in my grasp,
And the next after that shall see him neck'd,
Or swallow'd by my hunger-starved asp,—
And mention ('tis as well) the torture of the wasp."

XXIII

These orders given, the Prince, in half a pet,
Let o'er the silk his propping elbow slide,
Caught up his little legs, and, in a fret,
Fell on the sofa on his royal side.
The slave retreated backwards, humble-eyed,
And with a slave-like silence clos'd the door,
And to old Hum thro' street and alley hied;
He "knew the city," as we say, of yore,
And for short cuts and turns, was nobody knew more.

XXIV

It was the time when wholesale houses close
Their shutters with a moody sense of wealth,
But retail dealers, diligent, let loose
The gas (objected to on score of health),
Convey'd in little solder'd pipes by stealth,
And make it flare in many a brilliant form,
That all the powers of darkness it repell'th,
Which to the oil-trade doth great scaith and harm,
And supersedeth quite the use of the glow-worm.

XXV

Eban, untempted by the pastry-cooks,
(Of pastry he got store within the palace,)
With hasty steps, wrapp'd cloak, and solemn looks,
Incognito upon his errand sallies,
His smelling-bottle ready for the allies;
He pass'd the Hurdy-gurdies with disdain,
Vowing he'd have them sent aboard the gallies;
Just as he made his vow, it 'gan to rain,
Therefore he call'd a coach, and bade it drive amain.

XXVI

"I'll pull the string," said he, and further said,
"Polluted Jarvey! Ah, thou filthy hack!
Whose springs of life are all dried up and dead,
Whose linsey-woolsey lining hangs all slack,
Whose rug is straw, whose wholeness is a crack;
And evermore thy steps go clatter-clitter;
Whose glass once up can never be got back,
Who prov'st, with jolting arguments and bitter,
That 'tis of modern use to travel in a litter.

XXVII

"Thou inconvenience! thou hungry crop
For all corn! thou snail-creeper to and fro,
Who while thou goest ever seem'st to stop,
And fiddle-faddle standest while you go;
I' the morning, freighted with a weight of woe,
Unto some lazar-house thou journeyest,
And in the evening tak'st a double row
Of dowdies, for some dance or party drest,
Besides the goods meanwhile thou movest east and west.

XXVIII

"By thy ungallant bearing and sad mien,
An inch appears the utmost thou couldst budge;
Yet at the slightest nod, or hint, or sign,
Round to the curb-stone patient dost thou trudge,
School'd in a beckon, learned in a nudge,
A dull-eyed Argus watching for a fare;
Quiet and plodding, thou dost bear no grudge
To whisking Tilburies, or Phaetons rare,
Curricles, or Mail-coaches, swift beyond compare."

XXIX

Philosophizing thus, he pull'd the check,
And bade the Coachman wheel to such a street,
Who, turning much his body, more his neck,
Louted full low, and hoarsely did him greet:
"Certes, Monsieur were best take to his feet,
Seeing his servant can no further drive
For press of coaches, that to-night here meet
Many as bees about a straw-capp'd hive,
When first for April honey into faint flowers they dive."

XXX

Eban then paid his fare, and tiptoe went
To Hum's hotel; and, as he on did pass
With head inclin'd, each dusky lineament
Show'd in the pearl-pav'd street, as in a glass;
His purple vest, that ever peeping was
Rich from the fluttering crimson of his cloak,
His silvery trowsers, and his silken sash
Tied in a burnish'd knot, their semblance took
Upon the mirror'd walls, wherever he might look.

XXXI

He smil'd at self, and, smiling, show'd his teeth,
And seeing his white teeth, he smil'd the more;
Lifted his eye-brows, spurn'd the path beneath,
Show'd teeth again, and smil'd as heretofore,
Until he knock'd at the magician's door;
Where, till the porter answer'd, might be seen,
In the clear panel more he could adore,—
His turban wreath'd of gold, and white, and green,
Mustachios, ear-ring, nose-ring, and his sabre keen.

XXXII

"Does not your master give a rout to-night?"
Quoth the dark page. "Oh, no!" return'd the Swiss,
"Next door but one to us, upon the right,
The *Magazin des Modes* now open is
Against the Emperor's wedding;—and, sir, this
My master finds a monstrous horrid bore;
As he retir'd, an hour ago I wis,
With his best beard and brimstone, to explore
And cast a quiet figure in his second floor.

XXXIII

"Gad! he's oblig'd to stick to business!
For chalk, I hear, stands at a pretty price;
And as for aqua vitæ—there's a mess!
The *dentes sapientiæ* of mice,
Our barber tells me too, are on the rise,—
Tinder's a lighter article,—nitre pure
Goes off like lightning,—grains of Paradise
At an enormous figure!—stars not sure!—
Zodiac will not move without a sly douceur!

XXXIV

"Venus won't stir a peg without a fee,
And master is too partial, *entre nous*,
To"— "Hush—hush!" cried Eban, "sure that is he
Coming down stairs,—by St. Bartholomew!
As backwards as he can,—is 't something new?
Or is 't his custom, in the name of fun?"
"He always comes down backward, with one shoe"—
Return'd the porter—"off, and one shoe on,
Like, saving shoe for sock or stocking, my man John!"

XXXV

It was indeed the great Magician,
Feeling, with careful toe, for every stair,
And retrograding careful as he can,
Backwards and downwards from his own two pair:
"Salpietro!" exclaim'd Hum, "is the dog there?
He's always in my way upon the mat!"
"He's in the kitchen, or the Lord knows where,"—
Replied the Swiss,—"the nasty, yelping brat!"
"Don't beat him!" return'd Hum, and on the floor came pat.

XXXVI

Then facing right about, he saw the Page,
And said: "Don't tell me what you want, Eban;
The Emperor is now in a huge rage,—
'Tis nine to one he'll give you the rattan!
Let us away!" Away together ran
The plain-dress'd sage and spangled blackamoor,
Nor rested till they stood to cool, and fan,
And breathe themselves at the Emperor's chamber door,
When Eban thought he heard a soft imperial snore.

XXXVII

"I thought you guess'd, foretold, or prophesied,
That 's Majesty was in a raving fit?"
"He dreams," said Hum, "or I have ever lied,
That he is tearing you, sir, bit by bit."
"He's not asleep, and you have little wit,"
Replied the page: "that little buzzing noise,
Whate'er your palmistry may make of it,
Comes from a play-thing of the Emperor's choice,
From a Man-Tiger-Organ, prettiest of his toys."

XXXVIII

Eban then usher'd in the learned Seer:
Elfinan's back was turn'd, but, ne'ertheless,
Both, prostrate on the carpet, ear by ear,
Crept silently, and waited in distress,
Knowing the Emperor's moody bitterness;
Eban especially, who on the floor 'gan
Tremble and quake to death,—he feared less
A dose of senna-tea or nightmare Gorgon
Than the Emperor when he play'd on his Man-Tiger-Organ.

XXXIX

They kiss'd nine times the carpet's velvet face
Of glossy silk, soft, smooth, and meadow-green,
Where the close eye in deep rich fur might trace
A silver tissue, scantly to be seen,
As daisies lurk'd in June-grass, buds in treen;
Sudden the music ceased, sudden the hand
Of majesty, by dint of passion keen,
Doubled into a common fist, went grand,
And knock'd down three cut glasses, and his best ink-stand.

XL

Then turning round, he saw those trembling two:
"Eban," said he, "as slaves should taste the fruits
Of diligence, I shall remember you
To-morrow, or the next day, as time suits,
In a finger conversation with my mutes,—
Begone!—for you, Chaldean! here remain!
Fear not, quake not, and as good wine recruits
A conjurer's spirits, what cup will you drain?
Sherry in silver, hock in gold, or glass'd champagne?"

XLI

"Commander of the Faithful!" answer'd Hum,
"In preference to these, I'll merely taste
A thimble-full of old Jamaica rum."
"A simple boon!" said Elfinan; "thou may'st
Have Nantz, with which my morning-coffee's lac'd."
"I'll have a glass of Nantz, then," said the Seer,—
"Made racy—(sure my boldness is misplac'd!)—
With the third part—(yet that is drinking dear!)—
Of the least drop of *crème de citron*, crystal clear."

XLII

"I pledge you, Hum! and pledge my dearest love,
My Bertha!" "Bertha! Bertha!" cried the sage,
"I know a many Berthas!" "Mine's above
All Berthas!" sighed the Emperor. "I engage,"
Said Hum, "in duty, and in vassalage,
To mention all the Berthas in the Earth;—
There's Bertha Watson,—and Miss Bertha Page,—
This fam'd for languid eyes, and that for mirth,—
There's Bertha Blount of York,—and Bertha Knox of Perth."

XLIII

"You seem to know"—"I do know," answer'd Hum,
"Your Majesty's in love with some fine girl
Named Bertha; but her surname will not come,
Without a little conjuring." "'Tis Pearl,
'Tis Bertha Pearl that makes my brains so whirl;
And she is softer, fairer than her name!"
"Where does she live?" ask'd Hum. "Her fair locks curl
So brightly, they put all our fays to shame!—
Live?—O! at Canterbury, with her old grand-dame."

XLIV

"Good! good!" cried Hum, "I've known her from a child!
She is a changeling of my management;
She was born at midnight in an Indian wild;
Her mother's screams with the striped tiger's blent,
While the torch-bearing slaves a halloo sent
Into the jungles; and her palanquin,
Rested amid the desert's dreariment,
Shook with her agony, till fair were seen
The little Bertha's eyes oped on the stars serene."

XLV

"I can't say," said the monarch; "that may be
Just as it happen'd, true or else a bam!
Drink up your brandy, and sit down by me,
Feel, feel my pulse, how much in love I am;
And if your science is not all a sham,
Tell me some means to get the lady here."
"Upon my honour!" said the son of Cham,
"She is my dainty changeling, near and dear,
Although her story sounds at first a little queer."

XLVI

"Convey her to me, Hum, or by my crown,
My sceptre, and my cross-surmounted globe,
I'll knock you"—"Does your majesty mean—*down?*
No, no, you never could my feelings probe
To such a depth!" The Emperor took his robe,
And wept upon its purple palatine,
While Hum continued, shamming half a sob,—
"In Canterbury doth your lady shine?
But let me cool your brandy with a little wine."

XLVII

Whereat a narrow Flemish glass he took,
That once belong'd to Admiral de Witt,
Admir'd it with a connoisseuring look,
And with the ripest claret crowned it,
And, ere one lively bead could burst and flit,
He turn'd it quickly, nimbly upside down,
His mouth being held conveniently fit
To catch the treasure: "Best in all the town!"
He said, smack'd his moist lips, and gave a pleasant frown.

XLVIII

"Ah! good my Prince, weep not!" And then again
He fill'd a bumper. "Great Sire, do not weep!
Your pulse is shocking, but I'll ease your pain."
"Fetch me that Ottoman, and prithee keep
Your voice low," said the Emperor; "and steep
Some lady's-fingers nice in Candy wine;
And prithee, Hum, behind the screen do peep
For the rose-water vase, magician mine!
And sponge my forehead,—so my love doth make me pine.

XLIX

"Ah, cursed Bellanaine!" "Don't think of her,"
Rejoin'd the Mago, "but on Bertha muse;
For, by my choicest best barometer,
You shall not throttled be in marriage noose;
I've said it, Sire; you only have to choose
Bertha or Bellanaine." So saying, he drew
From the left pocket of his threadbare hose,
A sampler hoarded slyly, good as new,
Holding it by his thumb and finger full in view.

L

"Sire, this is Bertha Pearl's neat handy-work,
Her *name*, see here, *Midsummer, ninety-one*."
Elfinan snatch'd it with a sudden jerk,
And wept as if he never would have done,
Honouring with royal tears the poor homespun;
Whereon were broider'd tigers with black eyes,
And long-tail'd pheasants, and a rising sun,
Plenty of posies, great stags, butterflies
Bigger than stags,—a moon,—with other mysteries.

LI

The monarch handled o'er and o'er again
These day-school hieroglyphics with a sigh;
Somewhat in sadness, but pleas'd in the main,
Till this oracular couplet met his eye
Astounded—*Cupid I, do thee defy!*
It was too much. He shrunk back in his chair,
Grew pale as death, and fainted—very nigh!
"Pho! nonsense!" exclaim'd Hum, "now don't despair;
She does not mean it really. Cheer up hearty there!

LII

"And listen to my words. You say you won't,
On any terms, marry Miss Bellanaine;
It goes against your conscience—good! Well, don't.
You say you love a mortal. I would fain
Persuade your honour's highness to refrain
From peccadilloes. But, Sire, as I say,
What good would that do? And, to be more plain,
You would do me a mischief some odd day,
Cut off my ears and hands, or head too, by my fay!

LIII

"Besides, manners forbid that I should pass any
Vile strictures on the conduct of a prince
Who should indulge his genius, if he has any,
Not, like a subject, foolish matters mince.
Now I think on 't, perhaps I could convince
Your Majesty there is no crime at all
In loving pretty little Bertha, since
She's very delicate,—not over tall,—
A fairy's hand, and in the waist, why—very small."

LIV

"Ring the repeater, gentle Hum!" " 'Tis five,"
Said gentle Hum; "the nights draw in apace;
The little birds I hear are all alive;
I see the dawning touch'd upon your face;
Shall I put out the candles, please your Grace?"
"Do put them out, and, without more ado,
Tell me how I may that sweet girl embrace,—
How you can bring her to me." "That's for you,
Great Emperor! to adventure, like a lover true."

LV

"I fetch her!"—"Yes, an 't like your Majesty;
And as she would be frighten'd wide awake
To travel such a distance through the sky,
Use of some soft manœuvre you must make,
For your convenience, and her dear nerves' sake;
Nice way would be to bring her in a swoon,
Anon, I'll tell what course were best to take;
You must away this morning." "Hum! so soon?"
"Sire, you must be in Kent by twelve o'clock at noon."

LVI

At this great Cæsar started on his feet,
Lifted his wings and stood attentive-wise.
"Those wings to Canterbury you must beat,
If you hold Bertha as a worthy prize.
Look in the Almanack—*Moore* never lies—
April the twenty-fourth—this coming day,
Now breathing its new bloom upon the skies,
Will end in St. Mark's Eve;—you must away,
For on that eve alone can you the maid convey."

LVII

Then the magician solemnly 'gan frown,
So that his frost-white eyebrows, beetling low,
Shaded his deep-green eyes, and wrinkles brown
Plaited upon his furnace-scorched brow:
Forth from the hood that hung his neck below,
He lifted a bright casket of pure gold,
Touch'd a spring-lock, and there in wool, or snow
Charm'd into ever-freezing, lay an old
And legend-leaved book, mysterious to behold.

LVIII

"Take this same book,—it will not bite you, Sire;
There, put it underneath your royal arm;
Though it's a pretty weight it will not tire,
But rather on your journey keep you warm:
This is the magic, this the potent charm,
That shall drive Bertha to a fainting fit!
When the time comes, don't feel the least alarm,
Uplift her from the ground, and swiftly flit
Back to your palace, where I wait for guerdon fit."

LIX

"What shall I do with this same book?" "Why merely
Lay it on Bertha's table, close beside
Her work-box, and 'twill help your purpose dearly;
I say no more." "Or good or ill betide,
Through the wide air to Kent this morn I glide!"
Exclaim'd the Emperor. "When I return,
Ask what you will,—I'll give you my new bride!
And take some more wine, Hum;—O Heavens! I burn
To be upon the wing! Now, now, that minx I spurn!"

LX

"Leave her to me," rejoin'd the magian:
"But how shall I account, illustrious fay!
For thine imperial absence? Pho! I can
Say you are very sick, and bar the way
To your so loving courtiers for one day;
If either of their two archbishops' graces
Should talk of extreme unction, I shall say
You do not like cold pig with Latin phrases,
Which never should be used but in alarming cases."

LXI

"Open the window, Hum; I'm ready now!"
"Zooks!" exclaim'd Hum, as up the sash he drew,
"Behold, your Majesty, upon the brow
Of yonder hill, what crowds of people!" "Whew!
The monster's always after something new,"
Return'd his Highness, "they are piping hot
To see my pigsny Bellanaine. Hum! do
Tighten my belt a little,—so, so,—not
Too tight,—the book!—my wand!—so, nothing is forgot."

LXII

"Wounds! how they shout!" said Hum, "and there,—see, see!
The Ambassadors return'd from Pigmio!
The morning's very fine,—uncommonly!
See, past the skirts of yon white cloud they go,
Tinging it with soft crimsons! Now below
The sable-pointed heads of firs and pines
They dip, move on, and with them moves a glow
Along the forest side! Now amber lines
Reach the hill top, and now throughout the valley shines."

LXIII

"Why, Hum, you're getting quite poetical!
Those *nows* you managed in a special style."
"If ever you have leisure, Sire, you shall
See scraps of mine will make it worth your while,
Tit-bits for Phœbus!—yes, you well may smile.
Hark! Hah! the bells!" "A little further yet,
Good Hum, and let me view this mighty coil."
Then the great Emperor full graceful set
His elbow for a prop, and snuff'd his mignonnette.

LXIV

The morn is full of holiday; loud bells
With rival clamours ring from every spire;
Cunningly-station'd music dies and swells
In echoing places; when the winds respire,
Light flags stream out like gauzy tongues of fire;
A metropolitan murmur, lifeful, warm,
Comes from the northern suburbs; rich attire
Freckles with red and gold the moving swarm;
While here and there clear trumpets blow a keen alarm.

LXV

And now the fairy escort was seen clear,
Like the old pageant of Aurora's train,
Above a pearl-built minster, hovering near;
First wily Crafticant, the chamberlain,
Balanc'd upon his grey-grown pinions twain,
His slender wand officially reveal'd;
Then black gnomes scattering sixpences like rain;
Then pages three and three; and next, slave-held,
The Imaian 'scutcheon bright,—one mouse in argent field.

LXVI

Gentlemen pensioners next; and after them,
A troop of winged Janizaries flew;
Then Slaves, as presents bearing many a gem;
Then twelve physicians fluttering two and two;
And next a chaplain in a cassock new;
Then Lords in waiting; then (what head not reels
For pleasure?)—the fair Princess in full view,
Borne upon wings,—and very pleas'd she feels
To have such splendour dance attendance at her heels.

LXVII

For there was more magnificence behind:
She wav'd her handkerchief. "Ah, very grand!"
Cried Elfinan, and clos'd the window-blind;
"And, Hum, we must not shilly-shally stand,—
Adieu! adieu! I'm off for Angle-land!
I say, old Hocus, have you such a thing
About you,—feel your pockets, I command,—
I want, this instant, an invisible ring,—
Thank you, old mummy!—now securely I take wing."

LXVIII

Then Elfinan swift vaulted from the floor,
And lighted graceful on the window-sill;
Under one arm the magic book he bore,
The other he could wave about at will;
Pale was his face, he still look'd very ill:
He bow'd at Bellanaine, and said—"Poor Bell!
Farewell! farewell! and if for ever! still
For ever fare thee well!"—and then he fell
A laughing!—snapp'd his fingers!—shame it is to tell!

LXIX

"By'r Lady! he is gone!" cries Hum, "and I—
(I own it)—have made too free with his wine;
Old Crafticant will smoke me. By the bye—
This room is full of jewels as a mine,—
Dear valuable creatures, how ye shine!
Sometime to-day I must contrive a minute,
If Mercury propitiously incline,
To examine his scrutoire, and see what's in it,
For of superfluous diamonds I as well may thin it.

LXX

"The Emperor's horrid bad; yes, that's my cue!"
Some histories say that this was Hum's last speech;
That, being fuddled, he went reeling through
The corridor, and scarce upright could reach
The stair-head; that being glutted as a leech,
And us'd, as we ourselves have just now said,
To manage stairs reversely, like a peach
Too ripe, he fell, being puzzled in his head
With liquor and the staircase: verdict—*found stone dead.*

LXXI

This as a falsehood Crafticanto treats;
And as his style is of strange elegance,
Gentle and tender, full of soft conceits,
(Much like our Boswell's,) we will take a glance
At his sweet prose, and, if we can, make dance
His woven periods into careless rhyme;
O, little faery Pegasus! rear—prance—
Trot round the quarto—ordinary time!
March, little Pegasus, with pawing hoof sublime!

LXXII

Well, let us see,—*tenth book and chapter nine,*—
Thus Crafticant pursues his diary:—
" 'Twas twelve o'clock at night, the weather fine,
Latitude thirty-six; our scouts descry
A flight of starlings making rapidly
Towards Thibet. Mem.:—birds fly in the night;
From twelve to half-past—wings not fit to fly
For a thick fog—the Princess sulky quite
Call'd for an extra shawl, and gave her nurse a bite.

LXXIII

"Five minutes before one—brought down a moth
With my new double-barrel—stew'd the thighs
And made a very tolerable broth—
Princess turn'd dainty;—to our great surprise,
Alter'd her mind, and thought it very nice:
Seeing her pleasant, tried her with a pun,
She frown'd; a monstrous owl across us flies
About this time,—a sad old figure of fun;
Bad omen—this new match can't be a happy one.

LXXIV

"From two till half-past, dusky way we made,
Above the plains of Gobi,—desert, bleak;
Beheld afar off, in the hooded shade
Of darkness, a great mountain (strange to speak),
Spitting, from forth its sulphur-baken peak,
A fan-shap'd burst of blood-red, arrowy fire,
Turban'd with smoke, which still away did reek,
Solid and black from that eternal pyre,
Upon the laden wind that scantly could respire.

LXXV

"Just upon three o'clock a falling star
Created an alarm among our troop,
Kill'd a man-cook, a page, and broke a jar,
A tureen, and three dishes, at one swoop,
Then passing by the Princess, singed her hoop:
Could not conceive what Coralline was at,
She clapp'd her hands three times and cried out 'Whoop!'
Some strange Imaian custom. A large bat
Came sudden 'fore my face, and brush'd against my hat.

LXXVI

"Five minutes thirteen seconds after three,
Far in the west a mighty fire broke out,
Conjectur'd, on the instant, it might be
The city of Balk—'twas Balk beyond all doubt:
A Griffin, wheeling here and there about,
Kept reconnoitring us—doubled our guard—
Lighted our torches, and kept up a shout,
Till he sheer'd off—the Princess very scar'd—
And many on their marrow-bones for death prepar'd.

LXXVII

"At half-past three arose the cheerful moon—
Bivouack'd for four minutes on a cloud—
Where from the earth we heard a lively tune
Of tambourines and pipes, serene and loud,
While on a flowery lawn a brilliant crowd
Cinque-parted danc'd, some half asleep reposed
Beneath the green-fan'd cedars, some did shroud
In silken tents, and 'mid light fragrance dozed,
Or on the open turf their soothed eyelids closed.

LXXVIII

"Dropp'd my gold watch, and kill'd a kettledrum—
It went for apoplexy—foolish folks!—
Left it to pay the piper—a good sum—
(I've got a conscience, maugre people's jokes;)
To scrape a little favour 'gan to coax
Her Highness' pug-dog—got a sharp rebuff—
She wish'd a game at whist—made three revokes—
Turn'd from myself, her partner, in a huff;
His majesty will know her temper time enough.

LXXIX

"She cried for chess—I play'd a game with her—
Castled her king with such a vixen look,
It bodes ill to his Majesty—(refer
To the second chapter of my fortieth book,
And see what hoity-toity airs she took).
At half-past four the morn essay'd to beam—
Saluted, as we pass'd, an early rook—
The Princess fell asleep, and, in her dream,
Talk'd of one Master Hubert, deep in her esteem.

LXXX

"About this time,—making delightful way,—
Shed a quill-feather from my larboard wing—
Wish'd, trusted, hop'd 'twas no sign of decay—
Thank heaven, I'm hearty yet!—'twas no such thing:—
At five the golden light began to spring,
With fiery shudder through the bloomed east;
At six we heard Panthea's churches ring—
The city all her unhiv'd swarms had cast,
To watch our grand approach, and hail us as we pass'd.

LXXXI

"As flowers turn their faces to the sun,
So on our flight with hungry eyes they gaze,
And, as we shap'd our course, this, that way run,
With mad-cap pleasure, or hand-clasp'd amaze;
Sweet in the air a mild-ton'd music plays,
And progresses through its own labyrinth;
Buds gather'd from the green spring's middle-days,
They scatter'd,—daisy, primrose, hyacinth,—
Or round white columns wreath'd from capital to plinth.

LXXXII

"Onward we floated o'er the panting streets,
That seem'd throughout with upheld faces paved;
Look where we will, our bird's-eye vision meets
Legions of holiday; bright standards waved,
And fluttering ensigns emulously craved
Our minute's glance; a busy thunderous roar,
From square to square, among the buildings raved,
As when the sea, at flow, gluts up once more
The craggy hollowness of a wild reefed shore.

LXXXIII

"And 'Bellanaine for ever!' shouted they,
While that fair Princess, from her winged chair,
Bow'd low with high demeanour, and, to pay
Their new-blown loyalty with guerdon fair,
Still emptied, at meet distance, here and there,
A plenty horn of jewels. And here I
(Who wish to give the devil her due) declare
Against that ugly piece of calumny,
Which calls them Highland pebble-stones not worth a fly.

LXXXIV

"Still 'Bellanaine!' they shouted, while we glide
'Slant to a light Ionic portico,
The city's delicacy, and the pride
Of our Imperial Basilic; a row
Of lords and ladies, on each hand, make show
Submissive of knee-bent obeisance,
All down the steps; and, as we enter'd, lo!
The strangest sight—the most unlook'd-for chance—
All things turn'd topsy-turvy in a devil's dance.

LXXXV

" 'Stead of his anxious Majesty and court
At the open doors, with wide saluting eyes,
Congées and scape-graces of every sort,
And all the smooth routine of gallantries,
Was seen, to our immoderate surprise,
A motley crowd thick gather'd in the hall,
Lords, scullions, deputy-scullions, with wild cries
Stunning the vestibule from wall to wall,
Where the Chief Justice on his knees and hands doth crawl.

LXXXVI

"Counts of the palace, and the state purveyor
Of moth's-down, to make soft the royal beds,
The Common Council and my fool Lord Mayor
Marching a-row, each other slipshod treads;
Powder'd bag-wigs and ruffy-tuffy heads
Of cinder wenches meet and soil each other;
Toe crush'd with heel ill-natur'd fighting breeds,
Frill-rumpling elbows brew up many a bother,
And fists in the short ribs keep up the yell and pother.

LXXXVII

"A Poet, mounted on the Court-Clown's back,
Rode to the Princess swift with spurring heels,
And close into her face, with rhyming clack,
Began a Prothalamion;—she reels,
She falls, she faints! while laughter peals
Over her woman's weakness. 'Where!' cried I,
'Where is his Majesty?' No person feels
Inclin'd to answer; wherefore instantly
I plung'd into the crowd to find him or to die.

LXXXVIII

"Jostling my way I gain'd the stairs, and ran
To the first landing, where, incredible!
I met, far gone in liquor, that old man,
That vile impostor Hum,——"
                                So far so well,—
For we have prov'd the Mago never fell
Down stairs on Crafticanto's evidence;
And therefore duly shall proceed to tell,
Plain in our own original mood and tense,
The sequel of this day, though labour 'tis immense!

   *   *   *   *

LINES SUPPOSED TO HAVE BEEN ADDRESSED
TO FANNY BRAWNE

THIS living hand, now warm and capable
Of earnest grasping, would, if it were cold
And in the icy silence of the tomb,
So haunt thy days and chill thy dreaming nights
That thou would[st] wish thine own heart dry of blood
So in my veins red life might stream again,
And thou be conscience-calm'd—see here it is—
I hold it towards you.

SONNET

*Written on a Blank Page in Shakespeare's Poems,
facing "A Lover's Complaint"*

BRIGHT star, would I were stedfast as thou art—
   Not in lone splendour hung aloft the night
And watching, with eternal lids apart,
   Like nature's patient, sleepless Eremite,
The moving waters at their priestlike task
   Of pure ablution round earth's human shores,
Or gazing on the new soft-fallen mask
   Of snow upon the mountains and the moors—
No—yet still stedfast, still unchangeable,
   Pillow'd upon my fair love's ripening breast,
To feel for ever its soft fall and swell,
   Awake for ever in a sweet unrest,
Still, still to hear her tender-taken breath,
And so live ever—or else swoon to death.

10

INDEX OF TITLES

INDEX OF FIRST LINES

THE COMPLETE
POETICAL WORKS OF
PERCY BYSSHE SHELLEY

PREFACE BY MRS. SHELLEY

TO FIRST COLLECTED EDITION, 1839

OBSTACLES have long existed to my presenting the public with a perfect edition of Shelley's Poems. These being at last happily removed, I hasten to fulfil an important duty,—that of giving the productions of a sublime genius to the world, with all the correctness possible, and of, at the same time, detailing the history of those productions, as they sprang, living and warm, from his heart and brain. I abstain from any remark on the occurrences of his private life, except inasmuch as the passions which they engendered inspired his poetry. This is not the time to relate the truth; and I should reject any colouring of the truth. No account of these events has ever been given at all approaching reality in their details, either as regards himself or others; nor shall I further allude to them than to remark that the errors of action committed by a man as noble and generous as Shelley, may, as far as he only is concerned, be fearlessly avowed by those who loved him, in the firm conviction that, were they judged impartially, his character would stand in fairer and brighter light than that of any contemporary. Whatever faults he had ought to find extenuation among his fellows, since they prove him to be human; without them, the exalted nature of his soul would have raised him into something divine.

The qualities that struck any one newly introduced to Shelley were,—First, a gentle and cordial goodness that animated his intercourse with warm affection and helpful sympathy. The other, the eagerness and ardour with which he was attached to the cause of human happiness and improvement; and the fervent eloquence with which he discussed such subjects. His conversation was marked by its happy abundance, and the beautiful language in which he clothed his poetic ideas and philosophical notions. To defecate life of its misery and its evil was the ruling passion of his soul; he dedicated to it every power of his mind, every pulsation of his heart. He looked on political freedom as the direct agent to effect the happiness of mankind; and thus any new-sprung hope of liberty inspired a joy and an exultation more intense and wild than he could have felt for any personal advantage. Those who have never experienced the workings of passion on general and unselfish subjects cannot understand this; and it must be difficult of comprehension to the younger generation rising around, since they cannot remember the scorn and hatred with which the partisans of reform were regarded some few years ago, nor the persecutions to which they were exposed. He had been from youth the victim of the state of feeling inspired by the reaction of the French Revolution; and believing firmly in the justice and excellence of his views, it cannot be wondered that a nature as sensitive, as impetuous, and as generous as his, should put its whole force into the attempt to alleviate for others the evils of those systems from which he had himself suffered. Many advantages

iii

attended his birth; he spurned them all when balanced with what he considered his duties. He was generous to imprudence, devoted to heroism. These characteristics breathe throughout his poetry. The struggle for human weal; the resolution firm to martyrdom; the impetuous pursuit, the glad triumph in good; the determination not to despair;—such were the features that marked those of his works which he regarded with most complacency, as sustained by a lofty subject and useful aim.

In addition to these, his poems may be divided into two classes,—the purely imaginative, and those which sprang from the emotions of his heart. Among the former may be classed the *Witch of Atlas, Adonais*, and his latest composition, left imperfect, the *Triumph of Life*. In the first of these particularly he gave the reins to his fancy, and luxuriated in every idea as it rose; in all there is that sense of mystery which formed an essential portion of his perception of life—a clinging to the subtler inner spirit, rather than to the outward form—a curious and metaphysical anatomy of human passion and perception.

The second class is, of course, the more popular, as appealing at once to emotions common to us all; some of these rest on the passion of love; others on grief and despondency; others on the sentiments inspired by natural objects. Shelley's conception of love was exalted, absorbing, allied to all that is purest and noblest in our nature, and warmed by earnest passion; such it appears when he gave it a voice in verse. Yet he was usually averse to expressing these feelings, except when highly idealized; and many of his more beautiful effusions he had cast aside unfinished, and they were never seen by me till after I had lost him. Others, as for instance *Rosalind and Helen* and *Lines written among the Euganean Hills,* I found among his papers by chance; and with some difficulty urged him to complete them. There are others, such as the *Ode to the Skylark* and *The Cloud,* which, in the opinion of many critics, bear a purer poetical stamp than any other of his productions. They were written as his mind prompted: listening to the carolling of the bird, aloft in the azure sky of Italy; or marking the cloud as it sped across the heavens, while he floated in his boat on the Thames.

No poet was ever warmed by a more genuine and unforced inspiration. His extreme sensibility gave the intensity of passion to his intellectual pursuits; and rendered his mind keenly alive to every perception of outward objects, as well as to his internal sensations. Such a gift is, among the sad vicissitudes of human life, the disappointments we meet, and the galling sense of our own mistakes and errors, fraught with pain; to escape from such, he delivered up his soul to poetry, and felt happy when he sheltered himself, from the influence of human sympathies, in the wildest regions of fancy. His imagination has been termed too brilliant, his thoughts too subtle. He loved to idealize reality; and this is a taste shared by few. We are willing to have our passing whims exalted into passions, for this gratifies our vanity; but few of us understand or sympathize with the endeavour to ally the love of abstract beauty, and adoration of abstract good, the τὸ ἀγαθὸν καὶ τὸ καλόν of the Socratic philosophers, with our sympathies with our kind. In this, Shelley resembled Plato; both taking more delight in the abstract and the ideal than in the special and tangible. This did not result from imitation; for it was not till Shelley resided in Italy that he made Plato his study. He then translated his *Symposium* and his *Ion;* and the English language boasts of no more brilliant composition than Plato's Praise of Love translated by Shelley. To return to his own poetry. The luxury of imagination, which sought nothing beyond itself (as a child burdens itself with spring flowers, thinking of no use beyond the enjoyment of gathering them), often showed itself in his verses: they will be only appreciated by minds which have resemblance to his own; and the mystic subtlety of many of his thoughts will share the same fate. The metaphysical strain that characterizes much of what he has written was, indeed, the portion of his works to which, apart from those whose scope was to awaken mankind to aspirations for what he considered the true and good, he was himself particularly attached. There is much, however, that speaks to the many. When he would consent to dismiss these huntings after the obscure (which, entwined with his nature as they were, he did with difficulty), no poet ever expressed in sweeter, more heart-reaching, or more passionate verse, the gentler or more forcible emotions of the soul.

A wise friend once wrote to Shelley: 'You are still very young, and in certain essential respects you do not yet sufficiently perceive that you are so.' It is seldom that the young know what youth is, till they have got beyond its period; and time was not given him to attain this knowledge. It must be remembered that there is the stamp of such inexperience on all he wrote; he had not completed his nine-and-twentieth year when he died. The calm of middle life did not add the seal of the virtues which adorn maturity to those generated by the vehement spirit of youth. Through life also he was a martyr to ill-health, and constant pain wound up his nerves to a pitch of susceptibility that rendered his views of life different from those of a man in the enjoyment of healthy sensations. Perfectly gentle and forbearing in manner, he suffered a good deal of internal irritability, or rather excitement, and his fortitude to bear was almost always on the stretch; and thus, during a short life, he had gone through more experience of sensation than many whose existence is protracted. 'If I die to-morrow,' he said, on the eve of his unanticipated death, 'I have lived to be older than my father.' The weight of thought and feeling burdened him heavily; you read his sufferings in his attenuated frame, while you perceived the mastery he held over them in his animated countenance and brilliant eyes.

He died, and the world showed no outward sign. But his influence over mankind, though slow in growth, is fast augmenting; and, in the ameliorations that have taken place in the political state of his country, we may trace in part the operation of his arduous struggles. His spirit gathers peace in its new state from the sense that, though late, his exertions were not made in vain, and in the progress of the liberty he so fondly loved.

He died, and his place, among those who knew him intimately, has never been filled up. He walked beside them like a spirit of good to comfort and benefit—to enlighten the darkness of life with irradiations of genius, to cheer it with his sympathy and love. Any one, once attached to Shelley, must feel all other affections, however true and fond, as wasted on barren soil in comparison. It is our best consolation to know that such a pure-minded and exalted being was once among us, and now exists where we hope one day to join him;—although the intolerant, in their blindness, poured down anathemas, the Spirit of Good, who can judge the heart, never rejected him.

In the notes appended to the poems I have endeavoured to narrate the origin and history of each. The loss of nearly all letters and papers which refer to his early life renders the execution more imperfect than it would otherwise have been. I have, however, the liveliest recollection of all that was done and said during the period of my knowing him. Every impression is as clear as if stamped yesterday, and I have no apprehension of any mistake in my statements as far as they go. In other respects I am indeed incompetent: but I feel the importance of the task, and regard it as my most sacred duty. I endeavour to fulfil it in a manner he would himself approve; and hope, in this publication, to lay the first stone of a monument due to Shelley's genius, his sufferings, and his virtues:

> Se al seguir son tarda,
> Forse avverrà che 'l bel nome gentile
> Consacrerò con questa stanca penna.

POSTSCRIPT IN SECOND EDITION OF 1839

In revising this new edition, and carefully consulting Shelley's scattered and confused papers, I found a few fragments which had hitherto escaped me, and was enabled to complete a few poems hitherto left unfinished. What at one time escapes the searching eye, dimmed by its own earnestness, becomes clear at a future period. By the aid of a friend, I also present some poems complete and correct which hitherto have been defaced by various mistakes and omissions. It was suggested that the poem *To the Queen of my Heart* was falsely attributed to Shelley. I certainly find no trace of it among his papers; and, as those of his intimate friends whom I have consulted never heard of it, I omit it.

Two poems are added of some length, *Swellfoot the Tyrant* and *Peter Bell the Third*. I have mentioned the circumstances under which they were written in the notes; and need only add that they are conceived in a very different spirit from Shelley's usual compositions. They are specimens of the burlesque and fanciful; but, although they adopt a familiar style and homely imagery, there shine through the radiance of the poet's imagination the earnest views and opinions of the politician and the moralist.

At my request the publisher has restored the omitted passages of *Queen Mab*. I now present this edition as a complete collection of my husband's poetical works, and I do not foresee that I can hereafter add to or take away a word or line.

Putney, *November* 6, 1839.

PREFACE BY MRS. SHELLEY
TO THE VOLUME OF POSTHUMOUS POEMS
PUBLISHED IN 1824

In nobil sangue vita umile e queta,
Ed in alto intelletto un puro core;
Frutto senile in sul giovenil fiore,
E in aspetto pensoso anima lieta.—PETRARCA.

IT had been my wish, on presenting the public with the Posthumous Poems of Mr. Shelley, to have accompanied them by a biographical notice; as it appeared to me that at this moment a narration of the events of my husband's life would come more gracefully from other hands than mine, I applied to Mr. Leigh Hunt. The distinguished friendship that Mr. Shelley felt for him, and the enthusiastic affection with which Mr. Leigh Hunt clings to his friend's memory, seemed to point him out as the person best calculated for such an undertaking. His absence from this country, which prevented our mutual explanation, has unfortunately rendered my scheme abortive. I do not doubt but that on some other occasion he will pay this tribute to his lost friend, and sincerely regret that the volume which I edit has not been honoured by its insertion.

The comparative solitude in which Mr. Shelley lived was the occasion that he was personally known to few; and his fearless enthusiasm in the cause which he considered the most sacred upon earth, the improvement of the moral and physical state of mankind, was the chief reason why he, like other illustrious reformers, was pursued by hatred and calumny. No man was ever more devoted than he to the endeavour of making those around him happy; no man ever possessed friends more unfeignedly attached to him. The ungrateful world did not feel his loss, and the gap it made seemed to close as quickly over his memory as the murderous sea above his living frame. Hereafter men will lament that his transcendent powers of intellect were extinguished before they had bestowed on them their choicest treasures. To his friends his loss is irremediable: the wise, the brave, the gentle, is gone for ever! He is to them as a bright vision, whose radiant track, left behind in the memory, is worth all the realities that society can afford. Before the critics contradict me, let them appeal to any one who had ever known him. To see him was to love him: and his presence, like Ithuriel's spear, was alone sufficient to disclose the falsehood of the tale which his enemies whispered in the ear of the ignorant world.

His life was spent in the contemplation of Nature, in arduous study, or in acts of kindness and affection. He was an elegant scholar and a profound metaphysician; without possessing much scientific knowledge, he was unrivalled in the justness and extent of his observations on natural objects; he knew every plant by its name, and was familiar with the history and habits of every production of the earth; he could interpret without a fault each appearance in the sky; and the varied phenomena of heaven and earth filled him with deep emotion. He made his study and reading-room of the shadowed copse, the stream, the lake, and the water-fall. Ill health and continual pain preyed upon his powers; and the solitude in which we lived, particularly on our first arrival in Italy, although congenial to his feelings, must frequently have weighed upon his spirits; those beautiful and affecting *Lines written in Dejection near Naples* were composed at such an interval; but, when in health, his spirits were buoyant and youthful to an extraordinary degree.

Such was his love for Nature that every page of his poetry is associated, in the minds of his friends, with the loveliest scenes of the countries which he inhabited. In early life he visited the most beautiful parts of this country and Ireland. Afterwards the Alps of Switzerland became his inspirers. *Prometheus Unbound* was written among the deserted and flower-grown ruins of Rome; and, when he made his home under the Pisan hills, their roofless recesses harboured him as he composed the *Witch of Atlas*, *Adonais*, and *Hellas*. In the wild but beautiful Bay of Spezzia, the winds and waves which he loved became his playmates. His days were chiefly spent on the water; the management of his boat, its alterations and improvements, were his principal occupation. At night, when the unclouded moon shone on the calm sea, he often went alone in his little shallop to the rocky caves that bordered it, and, sitting beneath their shelter, wrote the *Triumph of Life*, the last of his productions. The beauty but strangeness of this lonely place, the refined pleasure which he felt in the companionship of a few selected friends, our entire sequestration from the rest of the world, all contributed to render this period of his life one of continued enjoyment. I am convinced that the two months we passed there were the happiest which he had ever known: his health even rapidly improved, and he was never better than when I last saw him, full of spirits and joy, embark for Leghorn, that he might there welcome Leigh Hunt to Italy. I was to have accompanied him; but illness confined me to my room, and thus put the seal on my misfortune. His vessel bore out of sight with a favouring wind, and I remained awaiting his return by the breakers of that sea which was about to engulf him.

He spent a week at Pisa, employed in kind offices toward his friend, and enjoying with keen delight the renewal of their intercourse. He then embarked with Mr. Williams, the chosen and beloved sharer of his pleasures and of his fate, to return to us. We waited for them in vain; the sea by its restless moaning seemed to desire to inform us of what we would not learn:—but a veil may well be drawn over such misery. The real anguish of those moments transcended all the fictions that the most glowing imagination ever portrayed; our seclusion, the savage nature of the inhabitants of the surrounding villages, and our immediate vicinity to the troubled sea, combined to imbue with strange horror our days of uncertainty. The truth was at last known,—a truth that made our loved and lovely Italy appear a tomb, its sky a pall. Every heart echoed the deep lament, and my only consolation was in the praise and earnest love that each voice bestowed and each countenance demonstrated for him we had lost,—not, I fondly hope, for ever; his unearthly and elevated nature is a pledge of the continuation of his being, although in an altered form. Rome received his ashes; they are deposited beneath its weed-grown wall, and 'the world's sole monument' is enriched by his remains.

I must add a few words concerning the contents of this volume. *Julian and Maddalo*, the *Witch of Atlas*, and most of the *Translations*, were written some years ago; and, with the exception of the *Cyclops*, and the Scenes from the *Magico Prodigioso*, may be considered as having received the author's ultimate corrections. The *Triumph of Life* was his last work, and was left in so unfinished a state that I arranged it in its present form with great difficulty. All his poems which were scattered in periodical works are collected in this volume, and I have added a reprint of *Alastor, or the Spirit of Solitude*: the difficulty with which a copy can be obtained is the cause of its republication. Many of the Miscellaneous Poems, written on the spur of the occasion, and never re-touched, I found among his manuscript books, and have carefully copied. I have subjoined, whenever I have been able, the date of their composition.

I do not know whether the critics will reprehend the insertion of some of the most imperfect among them; but I frankly own that I have been more actuated by the fear lest any monument of his genius should escape me than the wish of presenting nothing but what was complete to the fastidious reader. I feel secure that the lovers of Shelley's poetry (who know how, more than any poet of the present day, every line and word he wrote is instinct with peculiar beauty) will pardon and thank me: I consecrate this volume to them.

The size of this collection has prevented the insertion of any prose pieces. They will hereafter appear in a separate publication.

MARY W. SHELLEY.

London, *June* 1, 1824.

CONTENTS

CONTENTS

CONTENTS

CONTENTS

ALASTOR

OR

THE SPIRIT OF SOLITUDE

PREFACE

THE poem entitled Alastor may be considered as allegorical of one of the most interesting situations of the human mind. It represents a youth of uncorrupted feelings and adventurous genius led forth by an imagination inflamed and purified through familiarity with all that is excellent and majestic, to the contemplation of the universe. He drinks deep of the fountains of knowledge, and is still insatiate. The magnificence and beauty of the external world sinks profoundly into the frame of his conceptions, and affords to their modifications a variety not to be exhausted. So long as it is possible for his desires to point towards objects thus infinite and unmeasured, he is joyous, and tranquil, and self-possessed. But the period arrives when these objects cease to suffice. His mind is at length suddenly awakened and thirsts for intercourse with an intelligence similar to itself. He images to himself the Being whom he loves. Conversant with speculations of the sublimest and most perfect natures, the vision in which he embodies his own imaginations unites all of wonderful, or wise, or beautiful, which the poet, the philosopher, or the lover could depicture. The intellectual faculties, the imagination, the functions of sense, have their respective requisitions on the sympathy of corresponding powers in other human beings. The Poet is represented as uniting these requisitions, and attaching them to a single image. He seeks in vain for a prototype of his conception. Blasted by his disappointment, he descends to an untimely grave.

The picture is not barren of instruction to actual men. The Poet's self-centred seclusion was avenged by the furies of an irresistible passion pursuing him to speedy ruin. But that Power which strikes the luminaries of the world with sudden darkness and extinction, by awakening them to too exquisite a perception of its influences, dooms to a slow and poisonous decay those meaner spirits that dare to abjure its dominion. Their destiny is more abject and inglorious as their delinquency is more contemptible and pernicious. They who, deluded by no generous error, instigated by no sacred thirst of doubtful knowledge, duped by no illustrious superstition, loving nothing on this earth, and cherishing no hopes beyond, yet keep aloof from sympathies with their kind, rejoicing neither in human joy nor mourning with human grief; these, and such as they, have their apportioned curse. They languish, because none feel with them their common nature. They are morally dead. They are neither friends, nor lovers, nor fathers, nor citizens of the world, nor benefactors of their country. Among those who attempt to exist without human sympathy, the pure and tender-hearted perish through the intensity and passion of their search after its communities, when the vacancy of their spirit suddenly makes itself felt. All else, selfish, blind, and torpid, are those unforeseeing multitudes who constitute, together with their own, the lasting misery and loneliness of the world. Those who love not their fellow-beings live unfruitful lives, and prepare for their old age a miserable grave.

> "The good die first,
> And those whose hearts are dry as summer dust,
> Burn to the socket!'

December 14, 1815.

Nondum amabam, et amare amabam, quaerebam quid amarem, amans amare.
The Confessions of St. Augustine.

EARTH, ocean, air, belovèd brotherhood!
If our great Mother has imbued my soul
With aught of natural piety to feel
Your love, and recompense the boon with mine;
If dewy morn, and odorous noon, and even,   5
With sunset and its gorgeous ministers,
And solemn midnight's tingling silentness;
If autumn's hollow sighs in the sere wood,
And winter robing with pure snow and crowns
Of starry ice the grey grass and bare boughs;   10
If spring's voluptuous pantings when she breathes
Her first sweet kisses, have been dear to me;
If no bright bird, insect, or gentle beast
I consciously have injured, but still loved
And cherished these my kindred; then forgive   15
This boast, belovèd brethren, and withdraw
No portion of your wonted favour now!

Mother of this unfathomable world!
Favour my solemn song, for I have loved
Thee ever, and thee only; I have watched   20
Thy shadow, and the darkness of thy steps,
And my heart ever gazes on the depth
Of thy deep mysteries. I have made my bed
In charnels and on coffins, where black death
Keeps record of the trophies won from thee,   25
Hoping to still these obstinate questionings
Of thee and thine, by forcing some lone ghost

Thy messenger, to render up the tale
Of what we are. In lone and silent hours,
When night makes a weird sound of its own stillness,
Like an inspired and desperate alchymist   31
Staking his very life on some dark hope,
Have I mixed awful talk and asking looks
With my most innocent love, until strange tears
Uniting with those breathless kisses, made   35
Such magic as compels the charmèd night
To render up thy charge: . . . and, though ne'er yet
Thou hast unveiled thy inmost sanctuary,
Enough from incommunicable dream,
And twilight phantasms, and deep noon-day thought,   40
Has shone within me, that serenely now
And moveless, as a long-forgotten lyre
Suspended in the solitary dome
Of some mysterious and deserted fane,
I wait thy breath, Great Parent, that my strain   45
May modulate with murmurs of the air,
And motions of the forests and the sea,
And voice of living beings, and woven hymns
Of night and day, and the deep heart of man.

There was a Poet whose untimely tomb   50
No human hands with pious reverence reared,
But the charmed eddies of autumnal winds
Built o'er his mouldering bones a pyramid
Of mouldering leaves in the waste wilderness:—
A lovely youth,—no mourning maiden decked   55
With weeping flowers, or votive cypress wreath,
The lone couch of his everlasting sleep:—
Gentle, and brave, and generous,—no lorn bard
Breathed o'er his dark fate one melodious sigh:
He lived, he died, he sung, in solitude.   60
Strangers have wept to hear his passionate notes,
And virgins, as unknown he passed, have pined
And wasted for fond love of his wild eyes.
The fire of those soft orbs has ceased to burn,
And Silence, too enamoured of that voice,   65
Locks its mute music in her rugged cell.

By solemn vision, and bright silver dream,
His infancy was nurtured. Every sight
And sound from the vast earth and ambient air,
Sent to his heart its choicest impulses.   70
The fountains of divine philosophy
Fled not his thirsting lips, and all of great,

Or good, or lovely, which the sacred past
In truth or fable consecrates, he felt
And knew. When early youth had passed, he left   75
His cold fireside and alienated home
To seek strange truths in undiscovered lands.
Many a wide waste and tangled wilderness
Has lured his fearless steps; and he has bought
With his sweet voice and eyes, from savage men,   80
His rest and food. Nature's most secret steps
He like her shadow has pursued, where'er
The red volcano overcanopies
Its fields of snow and pinnacles of ice
With burning smoke, or where bitumen lakes   85
On black bare pointed islets ever beat
With sluggish surge, or where the secret caves
Rugged and dark, winding among the springs
Of fire and poison, inaccessible
To avarice or pride, their starry domes   90
Of diamond and of gold expand above
Numberless and immeasurable halls,
Frequent with crystal column, and clear shrines
Of pearl, and thrones radiant with chrysolite.
Nor had that scene of ampler majesty   95
Than gems or gold, the varying roof of heaven
And the green earth lost in his heart its claims
To love and wonder; he would linger long
In lonesome vales, making the wild his home,
Until the doves and squirrels would partake   100
From his innocuous hand his bloodless food,
Lured by the gentle meaning of his looks,
And the wild antelope, that starts whene'er
The dry leaf rustles in the brake, suspend
Her timid steps to gaze upon a form   105
More graceful than her own.
                                        His wandering step
Obedient to high thoughts, has visited
The awful ruins of the days of old:
Athens, and Tyre, and Balbec, and the waste
Where stood Jersualem, the fallen towers   110
Of Babylon, the eternal pyramids,
Memphis and Thebes, and whatsoe'er of strange
Sculptured on alabaster obelisk,
Or jasper tomb, or mutilated sphynx,
Dark Æthiopia in her desert hills   115
Conceals. Among the ruined temples there,
Stupendous columns, and wild images
Of more than man, where marble daemons watch

The Zodiac's brazen mystery, and dead men
Hang their mute thoughts on the mute walls around,   120
He lingered, poring on memorials
Of the world's youth, through the long burning day
Gazed on those speechless shapes, nor, when the moon
Filled the mysterious halls with floating shades
Suspended he that task, but ever gazed   125
And gazed, till meaning on his vacant mind
Flashed like strong inspiration, and he saw
The thrilling secrets of the birth of time.

Meanwhile an Arab maiden brought his food,
Her daily portion, from her father's tent,   130
And spread her matting for his couch, and stole
From duties and repose to tend his steps:—
Enamoured, yet not daring for deep awe
To speak her love:—and watched his nightly sleep,
Sleepless herself, to gaze upon his lips   135
Parted in slumber, whence the regular breath
Of innocent dreams arose: then, when red morn
Made paler the pale moon, to her cold home
Wildered, and wan, and panting, she returned.

The Poet wandering on, through Arabie   140
And Persia, and the wild Carmanian waste,
And o'er the aërial mountains which pour down
Indus and Oxus from their icy caves,
In joy and exultation held his way;
Till in the vale of Cashmire, far within   145
Its loneliest dell, where odorous plants entwine
Beneath the hollow rocks a natural bower,
Beside a sparkling rivulet he stretched
His languid limbs. A vision on his sleep
There came, a dream of hopes that never yet   150
Had flushed his cheek. He dreamed a veilèd maid
Sate near him, talking in low solemn tones.
Her voice was like the voice of his own soul
Heard in the calm of thought; its music long,
Like woven sounds of streams and breezes, held   155
His inmost sense suspended in its web
Of many-coloured woof and shifting hues.
Knowledge and truth and virtue were her theme,
And lofty hopes of divine liberty,
Thoughts the most dear to him, and poesy,   160
Herself a poet. Soon the solemn mood
Of her pure mind kindled through all her frame
A permeating fire: wild numbers then

She raised, with voice stifled in tremulous sobs
Subdued by its own pathos: her fair hands   165
Were bare alone, sweeping from some strange harp
Strange symphony, and in their branching veins
The eloquent blood told an ineffable tale.
The beating of her heart was heard to fill
The pauses of her music, and her breath   170
Tumultuously accorded with those fits
Of intermitted song. Sudden she rose,
As if her heart impatiently endured
Its bursting burthen: at the sound he turned,
And saw by the warm light of their own life   175
Her glowing limbs beneath the sinuous veil
Of woven wind, her outspread arms now bare,
Her dark locks floating in the breath of night,
Her beamy bending eyes, her parted lips
Outstretched, and pale, and quivering eagerly.   180
His strong heart sunk and sickened with excess
Of love. He reared his shuddering limbs and quelled
His gasping breath, and spread his arms to meet
Her panting bosom: . . . she drew back a while,
Then, yielding to the irresistible joy,   185
With frantic gesture and short breathless cry
Folded his frame in her dissolving arms.
Now blackness veiled his dizzy eyes, and night
Involved and swallowed up the vision; sleep,
Like a dark flood suspended in its course,   190
Rolled back its impulse on his vacant brain.

  Roused by the shock he started from his trance—
The cold white light of morning, the blue moon
Low in the west, the clear and garish hills,
The distinct valley and the vacant woods,   195
Spread round him where he stood. Whither have fled
The hues of heaven that canopied his bower
Of yesternight? The sounds that soothed his sleep,
The mystery and the majesty of Earth,
The joy, the exultation? His wan eyes   200
Gaze on the empty scene as vacantly
As ocean's moon looks on the moon in heaven.
The spirit of sweet human love has sent
A vision to the sleep of him who spurned
Her choicest gifts. He eagerly pursues   205
Beyond the realms of dream that fleeting shade;
He overleaps the bounds. Alas! Alas!
Were limbs, and breath, and being intertwined
Thus treacherously? Lost, lost, for ever lost,

In the wide pathless desert of dim sleep,   210
That beautiful shape! Does the dark gate of death
Conduct to thy mysterious paradise,
O Sleep? Does the bright arch of rainbow clouds,
And pendent mountains seen in the calm lake,
Lead only to a black and watery depth,   215
While death's blue vault, with loathliest vapours hung,
Where every shade which the foul grave exhales
Hides its dead eye from the detested day,
Conducts, O Sleep, to thy delightful realms?
This doubt with sudden tide flowed on his heart,   220
The insatiate hope which it awakened, stung
His brain even like despair.
                          While daylight held
The sky, the Poet kept mute conference
With his still soul. At night the passion came,
Like the fierce fiend of a distempered dream,   225
And shook him from his rest, and led him forth
Into the darkness.—As an eagle grasped
In folds of the green serpent, feels her breast
Burn with the poison, and precipitates
Through night and day, tempest, and calm, and cloud,
Frantic with dizzying anguish, her blind flight   231
O'er the wide aëry wilderness: thus driven
By the bright shadow of that lovely dream,
Beneath the cold glare of the desolate night,
Through tangled swamps and deep precipitous dells,   235
Startling with careless step the moonlight snake,
He fled. Red morning dawned upon his flight,
Shedding the mockery of its vital hues
Upon his cheek of death. He wandered on
Till vast Aornos seen from Petra's steep   .   240
Hung o'er the low horizon like a cloud;
Through Balk, and where the desolated tombs
Of Parthian kings scatter to every wind
Their wasting dust, wildly he wandered on,
Day after day a weary waste of hours,   245
Bearing within his life the brooding care
That ever fed on its decaying flame.
And now his limbs were lean; his scattered hair
Sered by the autumn of strange suffering
Sung dirges in the wind; his listless hand   250
Hung like dead bone within its withered skin;
Life, and the lustre that consumed it, shone
As in a furnace burning secretly
From his dark eyes alone. The cottagers,
Who ministered with human charity   255

His human wants, beheld with wondering awe
Their fleeting visitant. The mountaineer,
Encountering on some dizzy precipice
That spectral form, deemed that the Spirit of wind
With lightning eyes, and eager breath, and feet   260
Disturbing not the drifted snow, had paused
In its career: the infant would conceal
His troubled visage in his mother's robe
In terror at the glare of those wild eyes,
To remember their strange light in many a dream   265
Of after-times; but youthful maidens, taught
By nature, would interpret half the woe
That wasted him, would call him with false names
Brother, and friend, would press his pallid hand
At parting, and watch, dim through tears, the path   270
Of his departure from their father's door.

    At length upon the lone Chorasmian shore
He paused, a wide and melancholy waste
Of putrid marshes. A strong impulse urged
His steps to the sea-shore. A swan was there,   275
Beside a sluggish stream among the reeds.
It rose as he approached, and with strong wings
Scaling the upward sky, bent its bright course
High over the immeasurable main.
His eyes pursued its flight.—'Thou hast a home,   280
Beautiful bird; thou voyagest to thine home,
Where thy sweet mate will twine her downy neck
With thine, and welcome thy return with eyes
Bright in the lustre of their own fond joy.
And what am I that I should linger here,   285
With voice far sweeter than thy dying notes,
Spirit more vast than thine, frame more attuned
To beauty, wasting these surpassing powers
In the deaf air, to the blind earth, and heaven
That echoes not my thoughts?' A gloomy smile   290
Of desperate hope wrinkled his quivering lips.
For sleep, he knew, kept most relentlessly
Its precious charge, and silent death exposed,
Faithless perhaps as sleep, a shadowy lure,
With doubtful smile mocking its own strange charms.

    Startled by his own thoughts he looked around.   296
There was no fair fiend near him, not a sight
Or sound of awe but in his own deep mind.
A little shallop floating near the shore
Caught the impatient wandering of his gaze.   300

It had been long abandoned, for its sides
Gaped wide with many a rift, and its frail joints
Swayed with the undulations of the tide.
A restless impulse urged him to embark
And meet lone Death on the drear ocean's waste;   305
For well he knew that mighty Shadow loves
The slimy caverns of the populous deep.

The day was fair and sunny, sea and sky.
Drank its inspiring radiance, and the wind
Swept strongly from the shore, blackening the waves.
Following his eager soul, the wanderer   311
Leaped in the boat, he spread his cloak aloft
On the bare mast, and took his lonely seat,
And felt the boat speed o'er the tranquil sea
Like a torn cloud before the hurricane.   315

As one that in a silver vision floats
Obedient to the sweep of odorous winds
Upon resplendent clouds, so rapidly
Along the dark and ruffled waters fled
The straining boat.—A whirlwind swept it on,   320
With fierce gusts and precipitating force,
Through the white ridges of the chafèd sea.
The waves arose. Higher and higher still
Their fierce necks writhed beneath the tempest's scourge
Like serpents struggling in a vulture's grasp.   325
Calm and rejoicing in the fearful war
Of wave ruining on wave, and blast on blast
Descending, and black flood on whirlpool driven
With dark obliterating course, he sate:
As if their genii were the ministers   330
Appointed to conduct him to the light
Of those belovèd eyes the Poet sate
Holding the steady helm. Evening came on,
The beams of sunset hung their rainbow hues
High 'mid the shifting domes of sheeted spray   335
That canopied his path o'er the waste deep;
Twilight, ascending slowly from the east,
Entwined in duskier wreaths her braided locks
O'er the fair front and radiant eyes of day;
Night followed, clad with stars. On every side   340
More horribly the multitudinous streams
Of ocean's mountainous waste to mutual war
Rushed in dark tumult thundering, as to mock
The calm and spangled sky. The little boat
Still fled before the storm; still fled, like foam   345

Down the steep cataract of a wintry river;
Now pausing on the edge of the riven wave;
Now leaving far behind the bursting mass
That fell, convulsing ocean: safely fled—
As if that frail and wasted human form,   350
Had been an elemental god.
                          At midnight
The moon arose: and lo! the ethereal cliffs
Of Caucasus, whose icy summits shone
Among the stars like sunlight, and around
Whose caverned base the whirlpools and the waves   355
Bursting and eddying irresistibly
Rage and resound for ever.—Who shall save?—
The boat fled on,—the boiling torrent drove,—
The crags closed round with black and jagged arms,
The shattered mountain overhung the sea,   360
And faster still, beyond all human speed,
Suspended on the sweep of the smooth wave,
The little boat was driven. A cavern there
Yawned, and amid its slant and winding depths
Ingulfed the rushing sea. The boat fled on   365
With unrelaxing speed.—'Vision and Love!'
The Poet cried aloud, 'I have beheld
The path of thy departure. Sleep and death
Shall not divide us long!'

                          The boat pursued
The windings of the cavern. Daylight shone   370
At length upon that gloomy river's flow;
Now, where the fiercest war among the waves
Is calm, on the unfathomable stream
The boat moved slowly. Where the mountain, riven,
Exposed those black depths to the azure sky,   375
Ere yet the flood's enormous volume fell
Even to the base of Caucasus, with sound
That shook the everlasting rocks, the mass
Filled with one whirlpool all that ample chasm;
Stair above stair the eddying waters rose,   380
Circling immeasurably fast, and laved
With alternating dash the gnarled roots
Of mighty trees, that stretched their giant arms
In darkness over it. I' the midst was left,
Reflecting, yet distorting every cloud,   385
A pool of treacherous and tremendous calm.
Seized by the sway of the ascending stream,
With dizzy swiftness, round, and round, and round,
Ridge after ridge the straining boat arose,

Till on the verge of the extremest curve,   390
Where, through an opening of the rocky bank,
The waters overflow, and a smooth spot
Of glassy quiet mid those battling tides
Is left, the boat paused shuddering.—Shall it sink
Down the abyss? Shall the reverting stress   395
Of that resistless gulf embosom it?
Now shall it fall?—A wandering stream of wind,
Breathed from the west, has caught the expanded sail,
And, lo! with gentle motion, between banks
Of mossy slope, and on a placid stream,   400
Beneath a woven grove it sails, and, hark!
The ghastly torrent mingles its far roar,
With the breeze murmuring in the musical woods.
Where the embowering trees recede, and leave
A little space of green expanse, the cove   405
Is closed by meeting banks, whose yellow flowers
For ever gaze on their own drooping eyes,
Reflected in the crystal calm. The wave
Of the boat's motion marred their pensive task,
Which nought but vagrant bird, or wanton wind,   410
Or falling spear-grass, or their own decay
Had e'er disturbed before. The Poet longed
To deck with their bright hues his withered hair,
But on his heart its solitude returned,
And he forbore. Not the strong impulse hid   415
In those flushed cheeks, bent eyes, and shadowy frame
Had yet performed its ministry: it hung
Upon his life, as lightning in a cloud
Gleams, hovering ere it vanish, ere the floods
Of night close over it.
                 The noonday sun   420
Now shone upon the forest, one vast mass
Of mingling shade, whose brown magnificence
A narrow vale embosoms. There, huge caves,
Scooped in the dark base of their aëry rocks
Mocking its moans, respond and roar for ever.   425
The meeting boughs and implicated leaves
Wove twilight o'er the Poet's path, as led
By love, or dream, or god, or mightier Death,
He sought in Nature's dearest haunt, some bank,
Her cradle, and his sepulchre. More dark   430
And dark the shades accumulate. The oak,
Expanding its immense and knotty arms,
Embraces the light beech. The pyramids
Of the tall cedar overarching, frame
Most solemn domes within, and far-below,   435

Like clouds suspended in an emerald sky,
The ash and the acacia floating hang
Tremulous and pale. Like restless serpents, clothed
In rainbow and in fire, the parasites,
Starred with ten thousand blossoms, flow around   440
The grey trunks, and, as gamesome infants' eyes,
With gentle meanings, and most innocent wiles,
Fold their beams round the hearts of those that love,
These twine their tendrils with the wedded boughs
Uniting their close union; the woven leaves   445
Make net-work of the dark blue light of day,
And the night's noontide clearness, mutable
As shapes in the weird clouds. Soft mossy lawns
Beneath these canopies extend their swells,
Fragrant with perfumed herbs, and eyed with blooms   450
Minute yet beautiful. One darkest glen
Sends from its woods of musk-rose, twined with jasmine,
A soul-dissolving odour, to invite
To some more lovely mystery. Through the dell,
Silence and Twilight here, twin-sisters, keep   455
Their noonday watch, and sail among the shades,
Like vaporous shapes half seen; beyond, a well,
Dark, gleaming, and of most translucent wave,
Images all the woven boughs above,
And each depending leaf, and every speck   460
Of azure sky, darting between their chasms;
Nor aught else in the liquid mirror laves
Its portraiture, but some inconstant star
Between one foliaged lattice twinkling fair,
Or, painted bird, sleeping beneath the moon,   465
Or gorgeous insect floating motionless,
Unconscious of the day, ere yet his wings
Have spread their glories to the gaze of noon.

   Hither the Poet came. His eyes beheld
Their own wan light through the reflected lines   470
Of his thin hair, distinct in the dark depth
Of that still fountain; as the human heart,
Gazing in dreams over the gloomy grave,
Sees its own treacherous likeness there. He heard
The motion of the leaves, the grass that sprung   475
Startled and glanced and trembled even to feel
An unaccustomed presence, and the sound
Of the sweet brook that from the secret springs
Of that dark fountain rose. A Spirit seemed
To stand beside him—clothed in no bright robes   480
Of shadowy silver or enshrining light.

Borrowed from aught the visible world affords
Of grace, or majesty, or mystery;—
But, undulating woods, and silent well,
And leaping rivulet, and evening gloom   485
Now deepening the dark shades, for speech assuming,
Held commune with him, as if he and it
Were all that was,—only . . . when his regard
Was raised by intense pensiveness, . . . two eyes,
Two starry eyes, hung in the gloom of thought,   490
And seemed with their serene and azure smiles
To beckon him.

                Obedient to the light
That shone within his soul, he went, pursuing
The windings of the dell.—The rivulet
Wanton and wild, through many a green ravine   495
Beneath the forest flowed. Sometimes it fell
Among the moss with hollow harmony
Dark and profound. Now on the polished stones
It danced; like childhood laughing as it went:
Then, through the plain in tranquil wanderings crept,   500
Reflecting every herb and drooping bud
That overhung its quietness.—'O stream!
Whose source is inaccessibly profound,
Whither do thy mysterious waters tend?
Thou imagest my life. Thy darksome stillness,   505
Thy dazzling waves, thy loud and hollow gulfs,
Thy searchless fountain, and invisible course
Have each their type in me; and the wide sky,
And measureless ocean may declare as soon
What oozy cavern or what wandering cloud   510
Contains thy waters, as the universe
Tell where these living thoughts reside, when stretched
Upon thy flowers my bloodless limbs shall waste
I' the passing wind!'

                Beside the grassy shore
Of the small stream he went; he did impress   515
On the green moss his tremulous step, that caught
Strong shuddering from his burning limbs. As one
Roused by some joyous madness from the couch
Of fever, he did move; yet, not like him,
Forgetful of the grave, where, when the flame   520
Of his frail exultation shall be spent,
He must descend. With rapid steps he went
Beneath the shade of trees, beside the flow
Of the wild babbling rivulet; and now

The forest's solemn canopies were changed   525
For the uniform and lightsome evening sky.
Grey rocks did peep from the spare moss, and stemmed
The struggling brook: tall spires of windlestrae
Threw their thin shadows down the rugged slope,
And nought but gnarled roots of ancient pines   530
Branchless and blasted, clenched with grasping roots
The unwilling soil. A gradual change was here,
Yet ghastly. For, as fast years flow away,
The smooth brow gathers, and the hair grows thin
And white, and where irradiate dewy eyes   535
Had shone, gleam stony orbs:—so from his steps
Bright flowers departed, and the beautiful shade
Of the green groves, with all their odorous winds
And musical motions. Calm, he still pursued
The stream, that with a larger volume now   540
Rolled through the labyrinthine dell; and there
Fretted a path through its descending curves
With its wintry speed. On every side now rose
Rocks, which, in unimaginable forms,
Lifted their black and barren pinnacles   545
In the light of evening, and, its precipice
Obscuring the ravine, disclosed above,
Mid toppling stones, black gulfs and yawning caves,
Whose windings gave ten thousand various tongues
To the loud stream. Lo! where the pass expands   550
Its stony jaws, the abrupt mountain breaks,
And seems, with its accumulated crags,
To overhang the world: for wide expand
Beneath the wan stars and descending moon
Islanded seas, blue mountains, mighty streams,   555
Dim tracts and vast, robed in the lustrous gloom
Of leaden-coloured even, and fiery hills
Mingling their flames with twilight, on the verge
Of the remote horizon. The near scene,
In naked and severe simplicity,   560
Made contrast with the universe. A pine,
Rock-rooted, stretched athwart the vacancy
Its swinging boughs, to each inconstant blast
Yielding one only response, at each pause
In most familiar cadence, with the howl   565
The thunder and the hiss of homeless streams
Mingling its solemn song, whilst the broad river,
Foaming and hurrying o'er its rugged path,
Fell into that immeasurable void
Scattering its waters to the passing winds.   570

Yet the grey precipice and solemn pine
And torrent, were not all;—one silent nook
Was there. Even on the edge of that vast mountain,
Upheld by knotty roots and fallen rocks,
It overlooked in its serenity   575
The dark earth, and the bending vault of stars.
It was a tranquil spot, that seemed to smile
Even in the lap of horror. Ivy clasped
The fissured stones with its entwining arms,
And did embower with leaves for ever green,   580
And berries dark, the smooth and even space
Of its inviolated floor, and here
The children of the autumnal whirlwind bore,
In wanton sport, those bright leaves, whose decay,
Red, yellow, or ethereally pale,   585
Rivals the pride of summer. 'Tis the haunt
Of every gentle wind, whose breath can teach
The wilds to love tranquillity. One step,
One human step alone, has ever broken
The stillness of its solitude:—one voice   590
Alone inspired its echoes;—even that voice
Which hither came, floating among the winds,
And led the loveliest among human forms
To make their wild haunts the depository
Of all the grace and beauty that endued   595
Its motions, render up its majesty,
Scatter its music on the unfeeling storm,
And to the damp leaves and blue cavern mould,
Nurses of rainbow flowers and branching moss,
Commit the colours of that varying cheek,   600
That snowy breast, those dark and drooping eyes.

The dim and hornèd moon hung low, and poured
A sea of lustre on the horizon's verge
That overflowed its mountains. Yellow mist
Filled the unbounded atmosphere, and drank   605
Wan moonlight even to fulness: not a star
Shone, not a sound was heard; the very winds,
Danger's grim playmates, on that precipice
Slept, clasped in his embrace.—O, storm of death!
Whose sightless speed divides this sullen night: 610
And thou, colossal Skeleton, that, still
Guiding its irresistible career
In thy devastating omnipotence,
Art king of this frail world, from the red field
Of slaughter, from the reeking hospital,   615
The patriot's sacred couch, the snowy bed

Of innocence, the scaffold and the throne,
A mighty voice invokes thee. Ruin calls
His brother Death. A rare and regal prey
He hath prepared, prowling around the world;   620
Glutted with which thou mayst repose, and men
Go to their graves like flowers or creeping worms,
Nor ever more offer at thy dark shrine
The unheeded tribute of a broken heart.

When on the threshold of the green recess   625
The wanderer's footsteps fell, he knew that death
Was on him. Yet a little, ere it fled,
Did he resign his high and holy soul
To images of the majestic past,
That paused within his passive being now,   630
Like winds that bear sweet music, when they breathe
Through some dim latticed chamber. He did place
His pale lean hand upon the rugged trunk
Of the old pine. Upon an ivied stone
Reclined his languid head, his limbs did rest,   635
Diffused and motionless, on the smooth brink
Of that obscurest chasm;—and thus he lay,
Surrendering to their final impulses
The hovering powers of life. Hope and despair,
The torturers, slept; no mortal pain or fear   640
Marred his repose, the influxes of sense,
And his own being unalloyed by pain,
Yet feebler and more feeble, calmly fed
The stream of thought, till he lay breathing there
At peace, and faintly smiling:—his last sight   645
Was the great moon, which o'er the western line
Of the wide world her mighty horn suspended,
With whose dun beams inwoven darkness seemed
To mingle. Now upon the jagged hills
It rests, and still as the divided frame   650
Of the vast meteor sunk, the Poet's blood,
That ever beat in mystic sympathy
With nature's ebb and flow, grew feebler still:
And when two lessening points of light alone
Gleamed through the darkness, the alternate gasp   655
Of his faint respiration scarce did stir
The stagnate night:—till the minutest ray
Was quenched, the pulse yet lingered in his heart.
It paused—it fluttered. But when heaven remained
Utterly black, the murky shades involved   660
An image, silent, cold, and motionless,
As their own voiceless earth and vacant air.

Even as a vapour fed with golden beams
That ministered on sunlight, ere the west
Eclipses it, was now that wondrous frame—   665
No sense, no motion, no divinity—
A fragile lute, on whose harmonious strings
The breath of heaven did wander—a bright stream
Once fed with many-voicèd waves—a dream
Of youth, which night and time have quenched for ever,
Still, dark, and dry, and unremembered now.   671
    O, for Medea's wondrous alchemy,
Which wheresoe'er it fell made the earth gleam
With bright flowers, and the wintry boughs exhale
From vernal blooms fresh fragrance! O, that God,   675
Profuse of poisons, would concede the chalice
Which but one living man has drained, who now,
Vessel of deathless wrath, a slave that feels
No proud exemption in the blighting curse
He bears, over the world wanders for ever,   680
Lone as incarnate death! O, that the dream
Of dark magician in his visioned cave,
Raking the cinders of a crucible
For life and power, even when his feeble hand
Shakes in its last decay, were the true law   685
Of this so lovely world! But thou art fled
Like some frail exhalation; which the dawn
Robes in its golden beams,—ah! thou hast fled!
The brave, the gentle, and the beautiful,
The child of grace and genius. Heartless things   690
Are done and said i' the world, and many worms
And beasts and men live on, and mighty Earth
From sea and mountain, city and wilderness,
In vesper low or joyous orison,
Lifts still its solemn voice:—but thou art fled—   695
Thou canst no longer know or love the shapes
Of this phantasmal scene, who have to thee
Been purest ministers, who are, alas!
Now thou art not. Upon those pallid lips
So sweet even in their silence, on those eyes   700
That image sleep in death, upon that form
Yet safe from the worm's outrage, let no tear
Be shed—not even in thought. Nor, when those hues
Are gone, and those divinest lineaments,
Worn by the senseless wind, shall live alone   705
In the frail pauses of this simple strain,
Let not high verse, mourning the memory
Of that which is no more, or painting's woe
Or sculpture, speak in feeble imagery

Their own cold powers. Art and eloquence,   710
And all the shows o' the world are frail and vain
To weep a loss that turns their lights to shade.
It is a woe too 'deep for tears,' when all
Is reft at once, when some surpassing Spirit,
Whose light adorned the world around it, leaves   715
Those who remain behind, not sobs or groans,
The passionate tumult of a clinging hope;
But pale despair and cold tranquillity,
Nature's vast frame, the web of human things,
Birth and the grave, that are not as they were.   720

NOTE ON ALASTOR, BY MRS. SHELLEY

Alastor is written in a very different tone from *Queen Mab*. In the
latter, Shelley poured out all the cherished speculations of his youth—all
the irrepressible emotions of sympathy, censure, and hope, to which the
present suffering, and what he considers the proper destiny, of his fellow-
creatures, gave birth. *Alastor*, on the contrary, contains an individual
interest only. A very few years, with their attendant events, had checked
the ardour of Shelley's hopes, though he still thought them well grounded,
and that to advance their fulfilment was the noblest task man could
achieve.

This is neither the time nor place to speak of the misfortunes that
chequered his life. It will be sufficient to say that, in all he did, he at the
time of doing it believed himself justified to his own conscience; while
the various ills of poverty and loss of friends brought home to him the
sad realities of life. Physical suffering had also considerable influence in
causing him to turn his eyes inward; inclining him rather to brood over
the thoughts and emotions of his own soul than to glance abroad, and to
make, as in *Queen Mab*, the whole universe the object and subject of his
song. In the Spring of 1815 an eminent physician pronounced that he
was dying rapidly of a consumption; abscesses were formed on his lungs,
and he suffered acute spasms. Suddenly a complete change took place;
and, though through life he was a martyr to pain and debility, every
symptom of pulmonary disease vanished. His nerves, which nature had
formed sensitive to an unexampled degree, were rendered still more
susceptible by the state of his health.

As soon as the peace of 1814 had opened the Continent, he went
abroad. He visited some of the more magnificent scenes of Switzerland,
and returned to England from Lucerne, by the Reuss and the Rhine.
The river-navigation enchanted him. In his favourite poem of *Thalaba*,
his imagination had been excited by a description of such a voyage. In
the summer of 1815, after a tour along the southern coast of Devonshire
and a visit to Clifton, he rented a house on Bishopgate Heath, on the
borders of Windsor Forest, where he enjoyed several months of comparative health and tranquil happiness. The later summer months were

warm and dry. Accompanied by a few friends, he visited the source of the Thames, making a voyage in a wherry from Windsor to Cricklade. His beautiful stanzas in the churchyard of Lechlade were written on that occasion. *Alastor* was composed on his return. He spent his days under the oak-shades of Windsor Great Park; and the magnificent wood land was a fitting study to inspire the various descriptions of forest-scenery we find in the poem.

None of Shelley's poems is more characteristic than this. The solemn spirit that reigns throughout, the worship of the majesty of nature, the broodings of a poet's heart in solitude—the mingling of the exulting joy which the various aspects of the visible universe inspires with the sad and struggling pangs which human passion imparts—give a touching interest to the whole. The death which he had often contemplated during the last months as certain and near he here represented in such colours as had, in his lonely musings, soothed his soul to peace. The versification sustains the solemn spirit which breathes throughout: it is peculiarly melodious. The poem ought rather to be considered didactic than narrative: it was the outpouring of his own emotions, embodied in the purest form he could conceive, painted in the ideal hues which his brilliant imagination inspired, and softened by the recent anticipation of death.

THE DAEMON OF THE WORLD

A FRAGMENT

PART I

Nec tantum prodere vati,
Quantum scire licet. Venit aetas omnis in unam
Congeriem, miserumque premunt tot saecula pectus.
LUCAN, *Phars.* v. 176.

How wonderful is Death,
Death and his brother Sleep!
One pale as yonder wan and hornèd moon,
With lips of lurid blue,
The other glowing like the vital morn,   5
When throned on ocean's wave
It breathes over the world:
Yet both so passing strange and wonderful!

Hath then the iron-sceptred Skeleton,
Whose reign is in the tainted sepulchres,   10
To the hell dogs that couch beneath his throne
Cast that fair prey? Must that divinest form,
Which love and admiration cannot view
Without a beating heart, whose azure veins

Steal like dark streams along a field of snow,   15
Whose outline is as fair as marble clothed
In light of some sublimest mind, decay?
    Nor putrefaction's breath
Leave aught of this pure spectacle
    But loathsomeness and ruin?—   20
    Spare aught but a dark theme,
On which the lightest heart might moralize?
Or is it but that downy-wingèd slumbers
Have charmed their nurse coy Silence near her lids
    To watch their own repose?   25
    Will they, when morning's beam
    Flows through those wells of light,
Seek far from noise and day some western cave,
Where woods and streams with soft and pausing winds
    A lulling murmur weave?—   30
    Ianthe doth not sleep
    The dreamless sleep of death:
Nor in her moonlight chamber silently
Doth Henry hear her regular pulses throb,
    Or mark her delicate cheek   35
With interchange of hues mock the broad moon,
    Outwatching weary night,
    Without assured reward.
    Her dewy eyes are closed;
On their translucent lids, whose texture fine   40
Scarce hides the dark blue orbs that burn below
    With unapparent fire,
    The baby Sleep is pillowed:
    Her golden tresses shade
    The bosom's stainless pride,   45
Twining like tendrils of the parasite
    Around a marble column.

    Hark! whence that rushing sound?
    'Tis like a wondrous strain that sweeps
    Around a lonely ruin   50
When west winds sigh and evening waves respond
    In whispers from the shore:
'Tis wilder than the unmeasured notes
Which from the unseen lyres of dells and groves
    The genii of the breezes sweep.   55
Floating on waves of music and of light,
The chariot of the Daemon of the World
    Descends in silent power:
Its shape reposed within: slight as some cloud
That catches but the palest tinge of day   60

When evening yields to night,
Bright as that fibrous woof when stars indue
    Its transitory robe.
Four shapeless shadows bright and beautiful
Draw that strange car of glory, reins of light   65
Check their unearthly speed; they stop and fold
    Their wings of braided air:
The Daemon leaning from the ethereal car
    Gazed on the slumbering maid.
Human eye hath ne'er beheld   70
A shape so wild, so bright, so beautiful,
As that which o'er the maiden's charmèd sleep
    Waving a starry wand,
    Hung like a mist of light.
Such sounds as breathed around like odorous winds
    Of wakening spring arose,   76
Filling the chamber and the moonlight sky.
Maiden, the world's supremest spirit
    Beneath the shadow of her wings
Folds all thy memory doth inherit   80
    From ruin of divinest things,
        Feelings that lure thee to betray,
        And light of thoughts that pass away.
For thou hast earned a mighty boon,
    The truths which wisest poets see   85
Dimly, thy mind may make its own,
    Rewarding its own majesty,
        Entranced in some diviner mood
        Of self-oblivious solitude.

Custom, and Faith, and Power thou spurnest;   90
    From hate and awe thy heart is free;
Ardent and pure as day thou burnest,
    For dark and cold mortality
        A living light, to cheer it long,
        The watch-fires of the world among.   95

Therefore from nature's inner shrine,
    Where gods and fiends in worship bend,
Majestic spirit, be it thine
    The flame to seize, the veil to rend,
        Where the vast snake Eternity   100
        In charmèd sleep doth ever lie.

All that inspires thy voice of love,
    Or speaks in thy unclosing eyes,
Or through thy frame doth burn or move,
    Or think, or feel, awake, arise!   105

Spirit, leave for mine and me
Earth's unsubstantial mimicry!

It ceased, and from the mute and moveless frame
    A radiant spirit arose,
All beautiful in naked purity.   110
Robed in its human hues it did ascend,
Disparting as it went the silver clouds,
It moved towards the car, and took its seat
    Beside the Daemon shape.

Obedient to the sweep of aëry song,   115
    The mighty ministers
Unfurled their prismy wings.
    The magic car moved on;
The night was fair, innumerable stars
    Studded heaven's dark blue vault;   120
    The eastern wave grew pale
    With the first smile of morn.
    The magic car moved on.
From the swift sweep of wings
The atmosphere in flaming sparkles flew;   125
    And where the burning wheels
Eddied above the mountain's loftiest peak
    Was traced a line of lightning.
Now far above a rock the utmost verge
    Of the wide earth it flew,   130
The rival of the Andes, whose dark brow
    Frowned o'er the silver sea.

Far, far below the chariot's stormy path,
    Calm as a slumbering babe,
    Tremendous ocean lay.   135
Its broad and silent mirror gave to view
    The pale and waning stars,
    The chariot's fiery track,
    And the grey light of morn
    Tingeing those fleecy clouds   140
That cradled in their folds the infant dawn.
    The chariot seemed to fly
Through the abyss of an immense concave,
Radiant with million constellations, tinged
    With shades of infinite colour,   145
    And semicircled with a belt
    Flashing incessant meteors.

    As they approached their goal,
The wingèd shadows seemed to gather speed.
The sea no longer was distinguished; earth   150

Appeared a vast and shadowy sphere, suspended
  In the black concave of heaven
  With the sun's cloudless orb,
  Whose rays of rapid light
Parted around the chariot's swifter course,   155
And fell like ocean's feathery spray
  Dashed from the boiling surge
  Before a vessel's prow.

  The magic car moved on.
  Earth's distant orb appeared   160
The smallest light that twinkles in the heavens,
  Whilst round the chariot's way
Innumerable systems widely rolled,
  And countless spheres diffused
   An ever varying glory.   165
It was a sight of wonder! Some were horned,
And like the moon's argentine crescent hung
In the dark dome of heaven; some did shed
A clear mild beam like Hesperus, while the sea
Yet glows with fading sunlight; others dashed 170
Athwart the night with trains of bickering fire,
Like sphered worlds to death and ruin driven;
Some shone like stars, and as the chariot passed
  Bedimmed all other light.

  Spirit of Nature! here   175
In this interminable wilderness
Of worlds, at whose involved immensity
  Even soaring fancy staggers,
  Here is thy fitting temple.
  Yet not the lightest leaf   180
That quivers to the passing breeze
  Is less instinct with thee,—
  Yet not the meanest worm,
That lurks in graves and fattens on the dead,
  Less shares thy eternal breath.   185
  Spirit of Nature! thou
Imperishable as this glorious scene,
  Here is thy fitting temple.

If solitude hath ever led thy steps
To the shore of the immeasurable sea,   190
  And thou hast lingered there
  Until the sun's broad orb
Seemed resting on the fiery line of ocean,
Thou must have marked the braided webs of gold
  That without motion hang   195

      Over the sinking sphere:
Thou must have marked the billowy mountain clouds,
Edged with intolerable radiancy,
      Towering like rocks of jet
      Above the burning deep: 200
      And yet there is a moment
      When the sun's highest point
Peers like a star o'er ocean's western edge,
When those far clouds of feathery purple gleam
Like fairy lands girt by some heavenly sea: 205
Then has thy rapt imagination soared
Where in the midst of all existing things
The temple of the mightiest Daemon stands.

      Yet not the golden islands
That gleam amid yon flood of purple light,   210
      Nor the feathery curtains
That canopy the sun's resplendent couch,
      Nor the burnished ocean waves
      Paving that gorgeous dome,
      So fair, so wonderful a sight   215
As the eternal temple could afford.
The elements of all that human thought
Can frame of lovely or sublime, did join
To rear the fabric of the fane, nor aught
Of earth may image forth its majesty.   220
Yet likest evening's vault that faëry hall,
As heaven low resting on the wave it spread
      Its floors of flashing light,
      Its vast and azure dome;
And on the verge of that obscure abyss   225
Where crystal battlements o'erhang the gulf
Of the dark world, ten thousand spheres diffuse
Their lustre through its adamantine gates.

      The magic car no longer moved;
      The Daemon and the Spirit   230
      Entered the eternal gates.
      Those clouds of aëry gold
      That slept in glittering billows
      Beneath the azure canopy,
With the ethereal footsteps trembled not;   235
      While slight and odorous mists
Floated to strains of thrilling melody
Through the vast columns and the pearly shrines.

      The Daemon and the Spirit
Approached the overhanging battlement,   240

Below lay stretched the boundless universe!
  There, far as the remotest line
That limits swift imagination's flight,
Unending orbs mingled in mazy motion,
  Immutably fulfilling   245
  Eternal Nature's law.
  Above, below, around,
  The circling systems formed
  A wilderness of harmony,
  Each with undeviating aim   250
In eloquent silence through the depths of space
  Pursued its wondrous way.—

Awhile the Spirit paused in ecstasy.
Yet soon she saw, as the vast spheres swept by,
Strange things within their belted orbs appear.   255
Like animated frenzies, dimly moved
Shadows, and skeletons, and fiendly shapes,
Thronging round human graves, and o'er the dead
Sculpturing records for each memory
In verse, such as malignant gods pronounce,   260
Blasting the hopes of men, when heaven and hell
Confounded burst in ruin o'er the world:
And they did build vast trophies, instruments
Of murder, human bones, barbaric gold,
Skins torn from living men, and towers of skulls 265
With sightless holes gazing on blinder heaven,
Mitres, and crowns, and brazen chariots stained
With blood, and scrolls of mystic wickedness,
The sanguine codes of venerable crime.
The likeness of a thronèd king came by,   270
When these had passed, bearing upon his brow
A threefold crown; his countenance was calm,
His eye severe and cold; but his right hand
Was charged with bloody coin, and he did gnaw
By fits, with secret smiles, a human heart   275
Concealed beneath his robe; and motley shapes,
A multitudinous throng, around him knelt,
With bosoms bare, and bowed heads, and false looks
Of true submission, as the sphere rolled by.
Brooking no eye to witness their foul shame,   280
Which human hearts must feel, while human tongues
Tremble to speak, they did rage horribly,
Breathing in self-contempt fierce blasphemies
Against the Daemon of the World, and high
Hurling their armèd hands where the pure Spirit, 285
Serene and inaccessibly secure,

Stood on an isolated pinnacle,
The flood of ages combating below,
The depth of the unbounded universe
    Above, and all around   290
Necessity's unchanging harmony.

PART II

O HAPPY Earth! reality of Heaven!
To which those restless powers that ceaselessly
Throng through the human universe aspire;
Thou consummation of all mortal hope!   295
Thou glorious prize of blindly-working will!
Whose rays, diffused throughout all space and time,
Verge to one point and blend for ever there:
Of purest spirits thou pure dwelling-place!
Where care and sorrow, impotence and crime,   300
Languor, disease, and ignorance dare not come:
O happy Earth, reality of Heaven!

  Genius has seen thee in her passionate dreams,
And dim forebodings of thy loveliness,
Haunting the human heart, have there entwined   305
Those rooted hopes, that the proud Power of Evil
Shall not for ever on this fairest world
Shake pestilence and war, or that his slaves
With blasphemy for prayer, and human blood
For sacrifice, before his shrine for ever   310
In adoration bend, or Erebus
With all its banded fiends shall not uprise
To overwhelm in envy and revenge
The dauntless and the good, who dare to hurl
Defiance at his throne, girt tho' it be   315
With Death's omnipotence. Thou hast beheld
His empire, o'er the present and the past;
It was a desolate sight—now gaze on mine,
Futurity. Thou hoary giant Time,
Render thou up thy half-devoured babes,—   320
And from the cradles of eternity,
Where millions lie lulled to their portioned sleep
By the deep murmuring stream of passing things,
Tear thou that gloomy shroud.—Spirit, behold
Thy glorious destiny!

        The Spirit saw   325
The vast frame of the renovated world
Smile in the lap of Chaos, and the sense

Of hope thro' her fine texture did suffuse
Such varying glow, as summer evening casts
On undulating clouds and deepening lakes.   330
Like the vague sighings of a wind at even,
That wakes the wavelets of the slumbering sea
And dies on the creation of its breath,
And sinks and rises, fails and swells by fits,
Was the sweet stream of thought that with wild motion
Flowed o'er the Spirit's human sympathies.   336
The mighty tide of thought had paused awhile,
Which from the Daemon now like Ocean's stream
Again began to pour.—

                    To me is given
The wonders of the human world to keep—   340
Space, matter, time and mind—let the sight
Renew and strengthen all thy failing hope.
All things are recreated, and the flame
Of consentaneous love inspires all life:
The fertile bosom of the earth gives suck   345
To myriads, who still grow beneath her care,
Rewarding her with their pure perfectness:
The balmy breathings of the wind inhale
Her virtues, and diffuse them all abroad:
Health floats amid the gentle atmosphere,   350
Glows in the fruits, and mantles on the stream;
No storms deform the beaming brow of heaven,
Nor scatter in the freshness of its pride
The foliage of the undecaying trees;
But fruits are ever ripe, flowers ever fair,   355
And Autumn proudly bears her matron grace,
Kindling a flush on the fair cheek of Spring,
Whose virgin bloom beneath the ruddy fruit
Reflects its tint and blushes into love.

The habitable earth is full of bliss;   360
Those wastes of frozen billows that were hurled
By everlasting snow-storms round the poles,
Where matter dared not vegetate nor live,
But ceaseless frost round the vast solitude
Bound its broad zone of stillness, are unloosed;   365
And fragrant zephyrs there from spicy isles
Ruffle the placid ocean-deep, that rolls
Its broad, bright surges to the sloping sand,
Whose roar is wakened into echoings sweet
To murmur through the heaven-breathing groves   370
And melodise with man's blest nature there.

The vast tract of the parched and sandy waste
Now teems with countless rills and shady woods,
Corn-fields and pastures and white cottages;
And where the startled wilderness did hear   375
A savage conqueror stained in kindred blood,
Hymning his victory, or the milder snake
Crushing the bones of some frail antelope
Within his brazen folds—the dewy lawn,
Offering sweet incense to the sunrise, smiles   380
To see a babe before his mother's door,
Share with the green and golden basilisk
That comes to lick his feet, his morning's meal.

Those trackless deeps, where many a weary sail
Has seen, above the illimitable plain,   385
Morning on night and night on morning rise,
Whilst still no land to greet the wanderer spread
Its shadowy mountains on the sunbright sea,
Where the loud roarings of the tempest-waves
So long have mingled with the gusty wind   390
In melancholy loneliness, and swept
The desert of those ocean solitudes,
But vocal to the sea-bird's harrowing shriek,
The bellowing monster, and the rushing storm,
Now to the sweet and many-mingling sounds   395
Of kindliest human impulses respond:
Those lonely realms bright garden-isles begem,
With lightsome clouds and shining seas between,
And fertile valleys, resonant with bliss,
Whilst green woods overcanopy the wave,   400
Which like a toil-worn labourer leaps to shore,
To meet the kisses of the flowerets there.

Man chief perceives the change, his being notes
The gradual renovation, and defines
Each movement of its progress on his mind.   405
Man, where the gloom of the long polar night
Lowered o'er the snow-clad rocks and frozen soil,
Where scarce the hardiest herb that braves the frost
Basked in the moonlight's ineffectual glow,   409
Shrank with the plants, and darkened with the night;
Nor where the tropics bound the realms of day
With a broad belt of mingling cloud and flame,
Where blue mists through the unmoving atmosphere
Scattered the seeds of pestilence, and fed
Unnatural vegetation, where the land   415
Teemed with all earthquake, tempest and disease,

Was man a nobler being; slavery
Had crushed him to his country's blood-stained dust.

Even where the milder zone afforded man
A seeming shelter, yet contagion there,   420
Blighting his being with unnumbered ills,
Spread like a quenchless fire; nor truth availed
Till late to arrest its progress, or create
That peace which first in bloodless victory waved
Her snowy standard o'er this favoured clime: 425
There man was long the train-bearer of slaves,
The mimic of surrounding misery,
The jackal of ambition's lion-rage,
The bloodhound of religion's hungry zeal.

Here now the human being stands adorning   430
This loveliest earth with taintless body and mind;
Blest from his birth with all bland impulses,
Which gently in his noble bosom wake
All kindly passions and all pure desires.
Him, still from hope to hope the bliss pursuing,   435
Which from the exhaustless lore of human weal
Dawns on the virtuous mind, the thoughts that rise
In time-destroying infiniteness gift
With self-enshrined eternity, that mocks
The unprevailing hoariness of age,   440
And man, once fleeting o'er the transient scene
Swift as an unremembered vision, stands
Immortal upon earth: no longer now
He slays the beast that sports around his dwelling
And horribly devours its mangled flesh,   445
Or drinks its vital blood, which like a stream
Of poison thro' his fevered veins did flow
Feeding a plague that secretly consumed
His feeble frame, and kindling in his mind
Hatred, despair, and fear and vain belief,   450
The germs of misery, death, disease, and crime.
No longer now the wingèd habitants,
That in the woods their sweet lives sing away,
Flee from the form of man; but gather round,
And prune their sunny feathers on the hands   455
Which little children stretch in friendly sport
Towards these dreadless partners of their play.
All things are void of terror: man has lost
His desolating privilege, and stands
An equal amidst equals: happiness   460
And science dawn though late upon the earth;

Peace cheers the mind, health renovates the frame;
Disease and pleasure cease to mingle here,
Reason and passion cease to combat there;
Whilst mind unfettered o'er the earth extends   465
Its all-subduing energies, and wields
The sceptre of a vast dominion there.

Mild is the slow necessity of death:
The tranquil spirit fails beneath its grasp,
Without a groan, almost without a fear,   470
Resigned in peace to the necessity,
Calm as a voyager to some distant land,
And full of wonder, full of hope as he.
The deadly germs of languor and disease
Waste in the human frame, and Nature gifts   475
With choicest boons her human worshippers.
How vigorous now the athletic form of age!
How clear its open and unwrinkled brow!
Where neither avarice, cunning, pride, or care,
Had stamped the seal of grey deformity   480
On all the mingling lineaments of time.
How lovely the intrepid front of youth!
How sweet the smiles of taintless infancy.

Within the massy prison's mouldering courts,
Fearless and free the ruddy children play,   485
Weaving gay chaplets for their innocent brows
With the green ivy and the red wall-flower,
That mock the dungeon's unavailing gloom;
The ponderous chains, and gratings of strong iron,
There rust amid the accumulated ruins   490
Now mingling slowly with their native earth:
There the broad beam of day, which feebly once
Lighted the cheek of lean captivity
With a pale and sickly glare, now freely shines
On the pure smiles of infant playfulness: 495
No more the shuddering voice of hoarse despair
Peals through the echoing vaults, but soothing notes
Of Ivy-fingered winds and gladsome birds
And merriment are resonant around.

The fanes of Fear and Falsehood hear no more   500
The voice that once waked multitudes to war
Thundering thro' all their aisles: but now respond
To the death dirge of the melancholy wind:
It were a sight of awfulness to see
The works of faith and slavery, so vast,   505

So sumptuous, yet withal so perishing!
Even as the corpse that rests beneath their wall.
A thousand mourners deck the pomp of death
To-day, the breathing marble glows above
To decorate its memory, and tongues   510
Are busy of its life: to-morrow, worms
In silence and in darkness seize their prey.
These ruins soon leave not a wreck behind:
Their elements, wide-scattered o'er the globe,
To happier shapes are moulded, and become   515
Ministrant to all blissful impulses:
Thus human things are perfected, and earth,
Even as a child beneath its mother's love,
Is strengthened in all excellence, and grows
Fairer and nobler with each passing year.   520

Now Time his dusky pennons o'er the scene
Closes in steadfast darkness, and the past
Fades from our charmèd sight. My task is done:
Thy lore is learned. Earth's wonders are thine own,
With all the fear and all the hope they bring.   525
My spells are past: the present now recurs.
Ah me! a pathless wilderness remains
Yet unsubdued by man's reclaiming hand.

Yet, human Spirit, bravely hold thy course,
Let virtue teach thee firmly to pursue   530
The gradual paths of an aspiring change:
For birth and life and death, and that strange state
Before the naked powers that thro' the world
Wander like winds have found a human home,
All tend to perfect happiness, and urge   535
The restless wheels of being on their way,
Whose flashing spokes, instinct with infinite life,
Bicker and burn to gain their destined goal:
For birth but wakes the universal mind
Whose mighty streams might else in silence flow   540
Thro' the vast world, to individual sense
Of outward shows, whose unexperienced shape
New modes of passion to its frame may lend;
Life is its state of action, and the store
Of all events is aggregated there   545
That variegate the eternal universe;
Death is a gate of dreariness and gloom,
That leads to azure isles and beaming skies
And happy regions of eternal hope.
Therefore, O Spirit! fearlessly bear on: 550

Though storms may break the primrose on its stalk,
Though frosts may blight the freshness of its bloom,
Yet spring's awakening breath will woo the earth,
To feed with kindliest dews its favourite flower,
That blooms in mossy banks and darksome glens,   555
Lighting the green wood with its sunny smile.

    Fear not then, Spirit, death's disrobing hand,
So welcome when the tyrant is awake,
So welcome when the bigot's hell-torch flares;
'Tis but the voyage of a darksome hour,   560
The transient gulf-dream of a startling sleep.
For what thou art shall perish utterly,
But what is thine may never cease to be;
Death is no foe to virtue: earth has seen
Love's brightest roses on the scaffold bloom,   565
Mingling with freedom's fadeless laurels there,
And presaging the truth of visioned bliss.
Are there not hopes within thee, which this scene
Of linked and gradual being has confirmed?
Hopes that not vainly thou, and living fires   570
Of mind as radiant and as pure as thou,
Have shone upon the paths of men—return,
Surpassing Spirit, to that world, where thou
Art destined an eternal war to wage
With tyranny and falsehood, and uproot   575
The germs of misery from the human heart.
Thine is the hand whose piety would soothe
The thorny pillow of unhappy crime,
Whose impotence an easy pardon gains,
Watching its wanderings as a friend's disease: 580
Thine is the brow whose mildness would defy
Its fiercest rage, and brave its sternest will,
When fenced by power and master of the world.
Thou art sincere and good; of resolute mind,
Free from heart-withering custom's cold control,   585
Of passion lofty, pure and unsubdued.
Earth's pride and meanness could not vanquish thee,
And therefore art thou worthy of the boon
Which thou hast now received: virtue shall keep
Thy footsteps in the path that thou hast trod,   590
And many days of beaming hope shall bless
Thy spotless life of sweet and sacred love.
Go, happy one, and give that bosom joy
    Whose sleepless spirit waits to catch
    Light, life and rapture from thy smile.   595

The Daemon called its wingèd ministers.
Speechless with bliss the Spirit mounts the car,
That rolled beside the crystal battlement,
Bending her beamy eyes in thankfulness.
    The burning wheels inflame   600
The steep descent of Heaven's untrodden way.
    Fast and far the chariot flew:
    The mighty globes that rolled
Around the gate of the Eternal Fane
Lessened by slow degrees, and soon appeared   605
Such tiny twinkles as the planet orbs
That ministering on the solar power
With borrowed light pursued their narrower way.
    Earth floated then below:
    The chariot paused a moment;   610
    The Spirit then descended:
    And from the earth departing
    The shadows with swift wings
Speeded like thought upon the light of Heaven.

    The Body and the Soul united then,   615
A gentle start convulsed Ianthe's frame:
Her veiny eyelids quietly unclosed;
Moveless awhile the dark blue orbs remained:
She looked around in wonder and beheld
Henry, who kneeled in silence by her couch,   620
Watching her sleep with looks of speechless love,
    And the bright beaming stars
    That through the casement shone.

THE REVOLT OF ISLAM

A POEM IN TWELVE CANTOS

*''Οσαις δὲ βροτὸν ἔθνος ἀγλαίαις ἁπτόμεσθα
   περαίνει πρὸς ἔσχατον
πλόον' ναυσὶ δ' οὔτε πεζὸς ἰὼν ἂν εὕροις
ἐς ʿΥπερβορέων ἀγῶνα θαυματὰν ὁδόν.*
              Πινδ. Πυθ. x.

PREFACE

THE Poem which I now present to the world is an attempt from which
I scarcely dare to expect success, and in which a writer of established
fame might fail without disgrace. It is an experiment on the temper of the
public mind, as to how far a thirst for a happier condition of moral and
political society survives, among the enlightened and refined, the tempests

which have shaken the age in which we live. I have sought to enlist the harmony of metrical language, the ethereal combinations of the fancy, the rapid and subtle transitions of human passion, all those elements which essentially compose a Poem, in the cause of a liberal and comprehensive morality; and in the view of kindling within the bosoms of my readers a virtuous enthusiasm for those doctrines of liberty and justice, that faith and hope in something good, which neither violence nor misrepresentation nor prejudice can ever totally extinguish among mankind.

For this purpose I have chosen a story of human passion in its most universal character, diversified with moving and romantic adventures, and appealing, in contempt of all artificial opinions or institutions, to the common sympathies of every human breast. I have made no attempt to recommend the motives which I would substitute for those at present governing mankind, by methodical and systematic argument. I would only awaken the feelings, so that the reader should see the beauty of true virtue, and be incited to those inquiries which have led to my moral and political creed, and that of some of the sublimest intellects in the world. The Poem therefore (with the exception of the first canto, which is purely introductory) is narrative, not didactic. It is a succession of pictures illustrating the growth and progress of individual mind aspiring after excellence, and devoted to the love of mankind; its influence in refining and making pure the most daring and uncommon impulses of the imagination, the understanding, and the senses; its impatience at 'all the oppressions which are done under the sun'; its tendency to awaken public hope, and to enlighten and improve mankind; the rapid effects of the application of that tendency; the awakening of an immense nation from their slavery and degradation to a true sense of moral dignity and freedom; the bloodless dethronement of their oppressors, and the unveiling of the religious frauds by which they had been deluded into submission; the tranquillity of successful patriotism, and the universal toleration and benevolence of true philanthropy; the treachery and barbarity of hired soldiers; vice not the object of punishment and hatred, but kindness and pity; the faithlessness of tyrants; the confederacy of the Rulers of the World, and the restoration of the expelled Dynasty by foreign arms; the massacre and extermination of the Patriots, and the victory of established power; the consequences of legitimate despotism, —civil war, famine, plague, superstition, and an utter extinction of the domestic affections; the judicial murder of the advocates of Liberty; the temporary triumph of oppression, that secure earnest of its final and inevitable fall; the transient nature of ignorance and error, and the eternity of genius and virtue. Such is the series of delineations of which the Poem consists. And, if the lofty passions with which it has been my scope to distinguish this story shall not excite in the reader a generous impulse, an ardent thirst for excellence, an interest profound and strong such as belongs to no meaner desires, let not the failure be imputed to a natural unfitness for human sympathy in these sublime and animating themes. It is the business of the Poet to communicate to others the pleasure and the enthusiasm arising out of those images and feelings in the vivid presence of which within his own mind consists at once his inspiration and his reward.

The panic which, like an epidemic transport, seized upon all classes of men during the excesses consequent upon the French Revolution, is gradually giving place to sanity. It has ceased to be believed that whole generations of mankind ought to consign themselves to a hopeless inheritance of ignorance and misery, because a nation of men who had been dupes and slaves for centuries were incapable of conducting themselves with the wisdom and tranquillity of freemen so soon as some of their fetters were partially loosened. That their conduct could not have been marked by any other characters than ferocity and thoughtlessness is the historical fact from which liberty derives all its recommendations, and falsehood the worst features of its deformity. There is a reflux in the tide of human things which bears the shipwrecked hopes of men into a secure haven after the storms are past. Methinks, those who now live have survived an age of despair.

The French Revolution may be considered as one of those manifestations of a general state of feeling among civilised mankind produced by a defect of correspondence between the knowledge existing in society and the improvement or gradual abolition of political institutions. The year 1788 may be assumed as the epoch of one of the most important crises produced by this feeling. The sympathies connected with that event extended to every bosom. The most generous and amiable natures were those which participated the most extensively in these sympathies. But such a degree of unmingled good was expected as it was impossible to realise. If the Revolution had been in every respect prosperous, then misrule and superstition would lose half their claims to our abhorrence, as fetters which the captive can unlock with the slightest motion of his fingers, and which do not eat with poisonous rust into the soul. The revulsion occasioned by the atrocities of the demagogues, and the re-establishment of successive tyrannies in France, was terrible, and felt in the remotest corner of the civilised world. Could they listen to the plea of reason who had groaned under the calamities of a social state according to the provisions of which one man riots in luxury whilst another famishes for want of bread? Can he who the day before was a trampled slave suddenly become liberal-minded, forbearing, and independent? This is the consequence of the habits of a state of society to be produced by resolute perseverance and indefatigable hope, and long-suffering and long-believing courage, and the systematic efforts of generations of men of intellect and virtue. Such is the lesson which experience teaches now. But, on the first reverses of hope in the progress of French liberty, the sanguine eagerness for good overleaped the solution of these questions, and for a time extinguished itself in the unexpectedness of their result. Thus, many of the most ardent and tender-hearted of the worshippers of public good have been morally ruined by what a partial glimpse of the events they deplored appeared to show as the melancholy desolation of all their cherished hopes. Hence gloom and misanthropy have become the characteristics of the age in which we live, the solace of a disappointment that unconsciously finds relief only in the wilful exaggeration of its own despair. This influence has tainted the literature of the age with the hopelessness of the minds from which it flows. Metaphysics,[1] and inquiries into moral and political science, have become little else than vain attempts to revive exploded superstitions, or sophisms like those [2] of Mr. Malthus, calculated to lull the oppressors of mankind into a security of everlasting triumph. Our works of fiction and poetry have been overshadowed by the same infectious gloom. But mankind appear to me to be emerging from their trance. I am aware, methinks, of a slow, gradual, silent change. In that belief I have composed the following Poem.

I do not presume to enter into competition with our greatest contemporary Poets. Yet I am unwilling to tread in the footsteps of any who have preceded me. I have sought to avoid the imitation of any style of language or versification peculiar to the original minds of which it is the character; designing that, even if what I have produced be worthless, it should still be properly my own. Nor have I permitted any system relating to mere words to divert the attention of the reader, from whatever interest I may have succeeded in creating, to my own ingenuity in contriving to disgust them according to the rules of criticism. I have simply clothed my thoughts in what appeared to me the most obvious and appropriate language. A person familiar with nature, and with the most celebrated productions of the human mind, can scarcely err in following the instinct, with respect to selection of language, produced by that familiarity.

There is an education peculiarly fitted for a Poet, without which genius and sensibility can hardly fill the circle of their capacities. No education, indeed, can entitle to this appellation a dull and unobservant mind, or one, though neither dull nor unobservant, in which the channels of communication between thought and expression have been obstructed or closed. How far it is my fortune to belong to either of the latter classes I cannot know. I aspire to be something better. The circumstances of my accidental education have been favourable to this ambition. I have been familiar from boyhood with mountains and lakes and the sea, and the solitude of forests: Danger, which sports upon the brink of precipices, has been my playmate. I have trodden the glaciers of the Alps, and lived under the eye of Mont Blanc. I have been a wanderer among distant fields. I have sailed down mighty rivers, and seen the sun rise and set, and the stars come forth, whilst I have sailed night and day down a

[1] I ought to except Sir W. Drumond's *Academical Questions;* a volume of very acute and powerful metaphysical criticism.

[2] It is remarkable, as a symptom of the revival of public hope, that Mr. Malthus has assigned, in the later editions of his work, an indefinite dominion to moral restraint over the principle of population. This concession answers all the inferences from his doctrine unfavourable to human improvement, and reduces the *Essay on Population* to a commentary illustrative of the unanswerableness of *Political Justice.*

rapid stream among mountains. I have seen populous cities, and have watched the passions which rise and spread, and sink and change, amongst assembled multitudes of men. I have seen the theatre of the more visible ravages of tyranny and war; cities and villages reduced to scattered groups of black and roofless houses, and the naked inhabitants sitting famished upon their desolated thresholds. I have conversed with living men of genius. The poetry of ancient Greece and Rome, and modern Italy, and our own country, has been to me, like external nature, a passion and an enjoyment. Such are the sources from which the materials for the imagery of my Poem have been drawn. I have considered Poetry in its most comprehensive sense; and have read the Poets and the Historians and the Metaphysicians [1] whose writings have been accessible to me, and have looked upon the beautiful and majestic scenery of the earth, as common sources of those elements which it is the province of the Poet to embody and combine. Yet the experience and the feelings to which I refer do not in themselves constitute men Poets, but only prepares them to be the auditors of those who are. How far I shall be found to possess that more essential attribute of Poetry, the power of awakening in others sensations like those which animate my own bosom, is that which, to speak sincerely, I know not; and which, with an acquiescent and contented spirit, I expect to be taught by the effect which I shall produce upon those whom I now address.

I have avoided, as I have said before, the imitation of any contemporary style. But there must be a resemblance, which does not depend upon their own will, between all the writers of any particular age. They cannot escape from subjection to a common influence which arises out of an infinite combination of circumstances belonging to the times in which they live; though each is in a degree the author of the very influence by which his being is thus pervaded. Thus, the tragic poets of the age of Pericles; the Italian revivers of ancient learning; those mighty intellects of our own country that succeeded the Reformation, the translators of the Bible, Shakespeare, Spenser, the dramatists of the reign of Elizabeth, and Lord Bacon [2]; the colder spirits of the interval that succeeded;—all resemble each other, and differ from every other in their several classes. In this view of things, Ford can no more be called the imitator of Shakespeare than Shakespeare the imitator of Ford. There were perhaps few other points of resemblance between these two men than that which the universal and inevitable influence of their age produced. And this is an influence which neither the meanest scribbler nor the sublimest genius of any era can escape; and which I have not attempted to escape.

I have adopted the stanza of Spenser (a measure inexpressibly beautiful), not because I consider it a finer model of poetical harmony than the

---

[1] In this sense there may be such a thing as perfectibility in works of fiction, notwithstanding the concession often made by the advocates of human improvement, that perfectibility is a term applicable only to science.

[2] Milton stands alone in the age which he illumined.

blank verse of Shakespeare and Milton, but because in the latter there
is no shelter for mediocrity; you must either succeed or fail. This perhaps
an aspiring spirit should desire. But I was enticed also by the brilliancy
and magnificence of sound which a mind that has been nourished upon
musical thoughts can produce by a just and harmonious arrangement of
the pauses of this measure. Yet there will be found some instances where
I have completely failed in this attempt; and one, which I here request
the reader to consider as an erratum, where there is left, most inadvertently, an alexandrine in the middle of a stanza.

But in this as in every other respect I have written fearlessly. It is the
misfortune of this age that its Writers, too thoughtless of immortality,
are exquisitely sensible to temporary praise or blame. They write with
the fear of Reviews before their eyes. This system of criticism sprang up
in that torpid interval when Poetry was not. Poetry, and the art which
professes to regulate and limit its powers, cannot subsist together.
Longinus could not have been the contemporary of Homer, nor Boileau
of Horace. Yet this species of criticism never presumed to assert an understanding of its own: it has always, unlike true science, followed, not
preceded, the opinion of mankind, and would even now bribe with worthless adulation some of our greatest Poets to impose gratuitous fetters on
their own imaginations, and become unconscious accomplices in the daily
murder of all genius either not so aspiring or not so fortunate as their
own. I have sought therefore to write, as I believe that Homer, Shakespeare, and Milton, wrote, with an utter disregard of anonymous censure.
I am certain that calumny and misrepresentation, though it may move
me to compassion, cannot disturb my peace. I shall understand the ex-
pressive silence of those sagacious enemies who dare not trust themselves
to speak. I shall endeavour to extract, from the midst of insult and contempt and maledictions, those admonitions which may tend to correct
whatever imperfections such censurers may discover in this my first
serious appeal to the Public. If certain Critics were as clear-sighted as
they are malignant, how great would be the benefit to be derived from
their virulent writings! As it is, I fear I shall be malicious enough to be
amused with their paltry tricks and lame invectives. Should the Public
judge that my composition is worthless, I shall indeed bow before the
tribunal from which Milton received his crown of immortality; and shall
seek to gather, if I live, strength from that defeat, which may nerve me
to some new enterprise of thought which may *not* be worthless. I cannot
conceive that Lucretius, when he meditated that poem whose doctrines
are yet the basis of our metaphysical knowledge, and whose eloquence
has been the wonder of mankind, wrote in awe of such censure as the
hired sophists of the impure and superstitious noblemen of Rome might
affix to what he should produce. It was at the period when Greece was led
captive, and Asia made tributary to the Republic, fast verging itself to
slavery and ruin, that a multitude of Syrian captives, bigoted to the worship of their obscene Ashtaroth, and the unworthy successors of Socrates
and Zeno, found there a precarious subsistence by administering, under

the name of freedmen, to the vices and vanities of the great. These wretched men were skilled to plead, with a superficial but plausible set of sophisms, in favour of that contempt for virtue which is the portion of slaves, and that faith in portents, the most fatal substitute for benevolence in the imaginations of men, which, arising from the enslaved communities of the East, then first began to overwhelm the western nations in its stream. Were these the kind of men whose disapprobation the wise and lofty-minded Lucretius should have regarded with a salutary awe? The latest and perhaps the meanest of those who follow in his footsteps would disdain to hold life on such conditions.

The Poem now presented to the Public occupied little more than six months in the composition. That period has been devoted to the task with unremitting ardour and enthusiasm. I have exercised a watchful and earnest criticism on my work as it grew under my hands. I would willingly have sent it forth to the world with that perfection which long labour and revision is said to bestow. But I found that, if I should gain something in exactness by this method, I might lose much of the newness and energy of imagery and language as it flowed fresh from my mind. And, although the mere composition occupied no more than six months, the thoughts thus arranged were slowly gathered in as many years.

I trust that the reader will carefully distinguish between those opinions which have a dramatic propriety in reference to the characters which they are designed to elucidate, and such as are properly my own. The erroneous and degrading idea which men have conceived of a Supreme Being, for instance, is spoken against, but not the Supreme Being itself. The belief which some superstitious persons whom I have brought upon the stage entertain of the Deity, as injurious to the character of his benevolence, is widely different from my own. In recommending also a great and important change in the spirit which animates the social institutions of mankind, I have avoided all flattery to those violent and malignant passions of our nature which are ever on the watch to mingle with and to alloy the most beneficial innovations. There is no quarter given to Revenge, or Envy, or Prejudice. Love is celebrated everywhere as the sole law which should govern the moral world.

DEDICATION

> There is no danger to a man, that knows
> What life and death is: there's not any law
> Exceeds his knowledge; neither is it lawful
> That he should stoop to any other law.—CHAPMAN.

TO MARY ———

I

So now my summer task is ended, Mary,
    And I return to thee, mine own heart's home;
As to his Queen some victor Knight of Faëry,
    Earning bright spoils for her enchanted dome;

Nor thou disdain, that ere my fame become
A star among the stars of mortal night,
If it indeed may cleave its natal gloom,
Its doubtful promise thus I would unite
With thy belovèd name, thou Child of love and light.

II

The toil which stole from thee so many an hour, 10
Is ended,—and the fruit is at thy feet!
No longer where the woods to frame a bower
With interlacèd branches mix and meet,
Or where with sound like many voices sweet,
Waterfalls leap among wild islands green, 15
Which framed for my lone boat a lone retreat
Of moss-grown trees and weeds, shall I be seen:
But beside thee, where still my heart has ever been.

III

Thoughts of great deeds were mine, dear Friends, when first
The clouds which wrap this world from youth did pass. 20
I do remember well the hour which burst
My spirit's sleep: a fresh May-dawn it was,
When I walked forth upon the glittering grass,
And wept, I knew not why; until there rose
From the near schoolhouse, voices, that, alas! 25
Were but one echo from a world of woes—
The harsh and grating strife of tyrants and of foes.

IV

And then I clasped my hands and looked around—
—But none was near to mock my streaming eyes,
Which poured their warm drops on the sunny ground— 30
So, without shame, I spake:—'I will be wise,
And just, and free, and mild, if in me lies
Such power, for I grow weary to behold
The selfish and the strong still tyrannise 35
Without reproach or check.' I then controlled
My tears, my heart grew calm, and I was meek and bold.

V

And from that hour did I with earnest thought
Heap knowledge from forbidden mines of lore,
Yet nothing that my tyrants knew or taught
I cared to learn, but from that secret store 40

Wrought linkèd armour for my soul, before
It might walk forth to war among mankind;
    Thus power and hope were strengthened more and more
Within me, till there came upon my mind
A sense of loneliness, a thirst with which I pined.   45

VI

Alas, that love should be a blight and snare
    To those who seek all sympathies in one!—
Such once I sought in vain; then black despair,
    The shadow of a starless night, was thrown
    Over the world in which I moved alone:—   50
Yet never found I one not false to me,
    Hard hearts, and cold, like weights of icy stone
Which crushed and withered mine, that could not be
Aught but a lifeless clod, until revived by thee.

VII

Thou Friend, whose presence on my wintry heart   55
    Fell, like bright Spring upon some herbless plain;
How beautiful and calm and free thou wert
    In thy young wisdom, when the mortal chain
    Of Custom thou didst burst and rend in twain,
And walked as free as light the clouds among,   60
    Which many an envious slave then breathed in vain
From his dim dungeon, and my spirit sprung
To meet thee from the woes which had begirt it long!

VIII

No more alone through the world's wilderness,
    Although I trod the paths of high intent,   65
I journeyed now: no more companionless,
    Where solitude is like despair, I went.—
    There is the wisdom of a stern content
When Poverty can blight the just and good,
    When Infamy dares mock the innocent,   70
And cherished friends turn with the multitude
To trample: this was ours, and we unshaken stood!

IX

Now has descended a serener hour,
    And with inconstant fortune, friends return;
Though suffering leaves the knowledge and the power   75
    Which says:—Let scorn be not repaid with scorn.

And from thy side two gentle babes are born
To fill our home with smiles, and thus are we
    Most fortunate beneath life's beaming morn;
And these delights, and thou, have been to me   80
The parents of the Song I consecrate to thee.

x

Is it, that now my inexperienced fingers
    But strike the prelude of a loftier strain?
Or, must the lyre on which my spirit lingers
    Soon pause in silence, ne'er to sound again,   85
    Though it might shake the Anarch Custom's reign,
And charm the minds of men to Truth's own sway
    Holier than was Amphion's? I would fain
Reply in hope—but I am worn away,
And Death and Love are yet contending for their prey.   90

XI

And what art thou? I know, but dare not speak:
    Time may interpret to his silent years.
Yet in the paleness of thy thoughtful cheek,
    And in the light thine ample forehead wears,
    And in thy sweetest smiles, and in thy tears,   95
And in thy gentle speech, a prophecy
    Is whispered, to subdue my fondest fears:
And through thine eyes, even in thy soul I see
A lamp of vestal fire burning internally.

XII

They say that thou wert lovely from thy birth,   100
    Of glorious parents, thou aspiring Child.
I wonder not—for One then left this earth
    Whose life was like a setting planet mild,
    Which clothed thee in the radiance undefiled
Of its departing glory; still her fame   105
    Shines on thee, through the tempests dark and wild
Which shake these latter days; and thou canst claim
The shelter, from thy Sire, of an immortal name.

XIII

One voice came forth from many a mighty spirit,
    Which was the echo of three thousand years;   110
And the tumultuous world stood mute to hear it,
    As some lone man who in a desert hears

The music of his home:—unwonted fears
Fell on the pale oppressors of our race,
  And Faith, and Custom, and low-thoughted cares,   115
Like thunder-stricken dragons, for a space
Left the torn human heart, their food and dwelling-place.

XIV

Truth's deathless voice pauses among mankind!
  If there must be no response to my cry—
If men must rise and stamp with fury blind   120
On his pure name who loves them,—thou and I,
  Sweet friend! can look from our tranquillity
Like lamps into the world's tempestuous night,—
  Two tranquil stars, while clouds are passing by
Which wrap them from the foundering seaman's sight,   125
That burn from year to year with unextinguished light.

CANTO I

I

When the last hope of trampled France had failed
  Like a brief dream of unremaining glory,
From visions of despair I rose, and scaled
  The peak of an aëreal promontory,   130
  Whose caverned base with the vexed surge was hoary;
And saw the golden dawn break forth, and waken
  Each cloud, and every wave:—but transitory
The calm: for sudden, the firm earth was shaken,
As if by the last wreck its frame were overtaken.   135

II

So as I stood, one blast of muttering thunder
  Burst in far peals along the waveless deep,
When, gathering fast, around, above, and under,
  Long trains of tremulous mist began to creep,
  Until their complicating lines did steep   140
The orient sun in shadow:—not a sound
  Was heard; one horrible repose did keep
The forests and the floods, and all around
Darkness more dread than night was poured upon the ground.

III

Hark! 'tis the rushing of a wind that sweeps   145
  Earth and the ocean. See! the lightnings yawn
Deluging Heaven with fire, and the lashed deeps
  Glitter and boil beneath: it rages on,

One mighty stream, whirlwind and waves upthrown,
  Lightning, and hail, and darkness eddying by.   150
    There is a pause—the sea-birds, that were gone
    Into their caves to shriek, come forth, to spy
What calm has fall'n on earth, what light is in the sky.

IV

For, where the irresistible storm had cloven
    That fearful darkness, the blue sky was seen   155
Fretted with many a fair cloud interwoven
    Most delicately, and the ocean green,
    Beneath that opening spot of blue serene,   .
Quivered like burning emerald: calm was spread
    On all below; but far on high, between   160
Earth and the upper air, the vast clouds fled,
Countless and swift as leaves on autumn's tempest shed.

V

For ever, as the war became more fierce
    Between the whirlwinds and the rack on high,
That spot grew more serene; blue light did pierce   165
    The woof of those white clouds, which seem to lie
    Far, deep, and motionless; while through the sky
The pallid semicircle of the moon
    Passed on, in slow and moving majesty;
Its upper horn arrayed in mists, which soon   170
But slowly fled, like dew beneath the beams of noon.

VI

I could not choose but gaze; a fascination
    Dwelt in that moon, and sky, and clouds, which drew
My fancy thither, and in expectation
    Of what I knew not, I remained:—the hue   175
    Of the white moon, amid that heaven so blue,
Suddenly stained with shadow did appear;
    A speck, a cloud, a shape, approaching grew,
Like a great ship in the sun's sinking sphere
Beheld afar at sea, and swift it came anear.   180

VII

Even like a bark, which from a chasm of mountains,
    Dark, vast, and overhanging, on a river
Which there collects the strength of all its fountains,
    Comes forth, whilst with the speed its frame doth quiver,

Sails, oars, and stream, tending to one endeavour;   185
So, from that chasm of light a wingèd Form
On all the winds of heaven approaching ever
Floated, dilating as it came: the storm
Pursued it with fierce blasts, and lightnings swift and warm.

VIII

A course precipitous, of dizzy speed,   190
   Suspending thought and breath; a monstrous sight!
For in the air do I behold indeed
   An Eagle and a Serpent wreathed in fight:—
   And now relaxing its impetuous flight,
Before the aëreal rock on which I stood,   195
   The Eagle, hovering, wheeled to left and right,
And hung with lingering wings over the flood,
And startled with its yells the wide air's solitude.

IX

A shaft of light upon its wings descended,
   And every golden feather gleamed therein—   200
Feather and scale, inextricably blended.
   The Serpent's mailed and many-coloured skin
   Shone through the plumes its coils were twined within
By many a swoln and knotted fold, and high
   And far, the neck, receding lithe and thin,   205
Sustained a crested head, which warily
Shifted and glanced before the Eagle's steadfast eye.

X

Around, around, in ceaseless circles wheeling
   With clang of wings and scream, the Eagle sailed
Incessantly—sometimes on high concealing   210
   Its lessening orbs, sometimes as if it failed,
   Drooped through the air; and still it shrieked and wailed,
And casting back its eager head, with beak
   And talon unremittingly assailed
The wreathèd Serpent, who did ever seek   215
Upon his enemy's heart a mortal wound to wreak.

XI

What life, what power, was kindled and arose
   Within the sphere of that appalling fray!
For, from the encounter of those wondrous foes,
   A vapour like the sea's suspended spray   220

Hung gathered: in the void air, far away,
Floated the shattered plumes; bright scales did leap,
Where'er the Eagle's talons made their way,
Like sparks into the darkness;—as they sweep,
Blood stains the snowy foam of the tumultuous deep.　　　225

XII

Swift chances in that combat—many a check,
　And many a change, a dark and wild turmoil;
Sometimes the Snake around his enemy's neck
　Locked in stiff rings his adamantine coil,
　Until the Eagle, faint with pain and toil,　　　230
Remitted his strong flight, and near the sea
　Languidly fluttered, hopeless so to foil
His adversary, who then reared on high
His red and burning crest, radiant with victory.

XIII

Then on the white edge of the bursting surge,　　　235
　Where they had sunk together, would the Snake
Relax his suffocating grasp, and scourge
　The wind with his wild writhings; for to break
　That chain of torment, the vast bird would shake
The strength of his unconquerable wings　　　240
　As in despair, and with his sinewy neck,
Dissolve in sudden shock those linkèd rings,
Then soar—as swift as smoke from a volcano springs.

XIV

Wile baffled wile, and strength encountered strength,
　Thus long, but unprevailing:—the event　　　245
Of that portentous fight appeared at length:
　Until the lamp of day was almost spent
　It had endured, when lifeless, stark, and rent,
Hung high that mighty Serpent, and at last
　Fell to the sea, while o'er the continent,　　　250
With clang of wings and scream the Eagle passed,
Heavily borne away on the exhausted blast.

XV

And with it fled the tempest, so that ocean
　And earth and sky shone through the atmosphere—
Only, 'twas strange to see the red commotion　　　255
　Of waves like mountains o'er the sinking sphere

Of sunset sweep, and their fierce roar to hear
Amid the calm: down the steep path I wound
    To the sea-shore—the evening was most clear
And beautiful, and there the sea I found   260
Calm as a cradled child in dreamless slumber bound.

XVI

There was a Woman, beautiful as morning,
    Sitting beneath the rocks, upon the sand
Of the waste sea—fair as one flower adorning
    An icy wilderness—each delicate hand   265
    Lay crossed upon her bosom, and the band
Of her dark hair had fall'n, and so she sate
    Looking upon the waves; on the bare strand
Upon the sea-mark a small boat did wait,
Fair as herself, like Love by Hope left desolate.   270

XVII

It seemed that this fair Shape had looked upon
    That unimaginable fight, and now
That her sweet eyes were weary of the sun,
    As brightly it illustrated her woe;
    For in the tears which silently to flow   275
Paused not, its lustre hung: she watching aye
    The foam-wreaths which the faint tide wove below
Upon the spangled sands, groaned heavily,
And after every groan looked up over the sea.

XVIII

And when she saw the wounded Serpent make   280
    His path between the waves, her lips grew pale,
Parted, and quivered; the tears ceased to break
    From her immovable eyes; no voice of wail
    Escaped her; but she rose, and on the gale
Loosening her star-bright robe and shadowy hair   285
    Poured forth her voice; the caverns of the vale
That opened to the ocean, caught it there,
And filled with silver sounds the overflowing air.

XIX

She spake in language whose strange melody
    Might not belong to earth. I hear, alone,   290
What made its music more melodious be,
    The pity and the love of every tone;

But to the Snake those accents sweet were known
His native tongue and hers; nor did he beat
   The hoar spray idly then, but winding on   295
Through the green shadows of the waves that meet
Near to the shore, did pause beside her snowy feet.

XX

Then on the sands the Woman sate again,
   And wept and clasped her hands, and all between,
Renewed the unintelligble strain   300
   Of her melodious voice and eloquent mien;
   And she unveiled her bosom, and the green
And glancing shadows of the sea did play
   O'er its marmoreal depth:—one moment seen,
For ere the next, the Serpent did obey   305
Her voice, and, coiled in rest in her embrace it lay.

XXI

Then she arose, and smiled on me with eyes
   Serene yet sorrowing, like that planet fair,
While yet the daylight lingereth in the skies
   Which cleaves with arrowy beams the dark-red air,   310
   And said: 'To grieve is wise, but the despair
Was weak and vain which led thee here from sleep:
   This shalt thou know, and more, if thou dost dare
With me and with this Serpent, o'er the deep,
A voyage divine and strange, companionship to keep.'   315

XXII

Her voice was like the wildest, saddest tone,
   Yet sweet, of some loved voice heard long ago.
I wept. 'Shall this fair woman all alone,
   Over the sea with that fierce Serpent go?
   His head is on her heart, and who can know   320
How soon he may devour his feeble prey?'—
   Such were my thoughts, when the tide gan to flow;
And that strange boat like the moon's shade did sway
Amid reflected stars that in the waters lay:—

XXIII

A boat of rare device, which had no sail   325
   But its own curvèd prow of thin moonstone,
Wrought like a web of texture fine and frail,
   To catch those gentlest winds which are not known

To breathe, but by the steady speed alone
With which it cleaves the sparkling sea; and now   330
    We are embarked—the mountains hang and frown
Over the starry deep that gleams below,
A vast and dim expanse, as o'er the waves we go.

XXIV

And as we sailed, a strange and awful tale
    That Woman told, like such mysterious dream   335
As makes the slumberer's cheek with wonder pale!
    'Twas midnight, and around, a shoreless stream,
    Wide ocean rolled, when that majestic theme
Shrined in her heart found utterance, and she bent
    Her looks on mine; those eyes a kindling beam   340
Of love divine into my spirit sent,
And ere her lips could move, made the air eloquent.

XXV

'Speak not to me, but hear! Much shalt thou learn,
    Much must remain unthought, and more untold,
In the dark Future's ever-flowing urn: 345
    Know then, that from the depth of ages old,
    Two Powers o'er mortal things dominion hold
Ruling the world with a divided lot,
    Immortal, all-pervading, manifold,
Twin Genii, equal Gods—when life and thought   350
Sprang forth, they burst the womb of inessential Nought.

XXVI

'The earliest dweller of the world, alone,
    Stood on the verge of chaos. Lo! afar
O'er the wide wild abyss two meteors shone,
    Sprung from the depth of its tempestuous jar: 355
    A blood-red Comet and the Morning Star
Mingling their beams in combat—as he stood,
    All thoughts within his mind waged mutual war,
In dreadful sympathy—when to the flood
That fair Star fell, he turned and shed his brother's blood.

XXVII

'Thus evil triumphed, and the Spirit of evil,   361
    One Power of many shapes which none may know,
One Shape of many names; the Fiend did revel
    In victory, reigning o'er a world of woe,

For the new race of man went to and fro,   365
    Famished and homeless, loathed and loathing, wild,
    And hating good—for his immortal foe,
He changed from starry shape, beauteous and mild,
To a dire Snake, with man and beast unreconciled.

XXVIII

'The darkness lingering o'er the dawn of things,   370
    Was Evil's breath and life; this made him strong
To soar aloft with overshadowing wings;
    And the great Spirit of Good did creep among
    The nations of mankind, and every tongue
Cursed and blasphemed him as he passed; for none   375
    Knew good from evil, though their names were hung
In mockery o'er the fane where many a groan,
As King, and Lord, and God, the conquering Fiend did own,—

XXIX

'The Fiend, whose name was Legion; Death, Decay,
    Earthquake and Blight, and Want, and Madness pale,
Wingèd and wan diseases, an array   381
    Numerous as leaves that strew the autumnal gale;
    Poison, a snake in flowers, beneath the veil
Of food and mirth hiding his mortal head;
    And, without whom all these might nought avail,   385
Fear, Hatred, Faith, and Tyranny, who spread
Those subtle nets which snare the living and the dead.

XXX

'His spirit is their power, and they his slaves
    In air, and light, and thought, and language, dwell;
And keep their state from palaces to graves,   390
    In all resorts of men—invisible,
    But when, in ebon mirror, Nightmare fell
To tyrant or impostor bids them rise,
    Black-wingèd demon forms—whom, from the hell,
His reign and dwelling beneath nether skies,   395
He loosens to their dark and blasting ministries.

XXXI

'In the world's youth his empire was as firm
    As its foundations . . . Soon the Spirit of Good,
Though in the likeness of a loathsome worm,
    Sprang from the billows of the formless flood,   400

Which shrank and fled; and with that Fiend of blood
Renewed the doubtful war . . . Thrones then first shook,
  And earth's immense and trampled multitude
In hope on their own powers began to look,
And Fear, the demon pale, his sanguine shrine forsook.   405

XXXII

'Then Greece arose, and to its bards and sages,
  In dream, the golden-pinioned Genii came,
Even where they slept amid the night of ages,
  Steeping their hearts in the divinest flame
  Which thy breath kindled, Power of holiest name!   410
And oft in cycles since, when darkness gave
  New weapons to thy foe, their sunlike fame
Upon the combat shone—a light to save,
Like Paradise spread forth beyond the shadowy grave.

XXXIII

'Such is this conflict—when mankind doth strive   415
  With its oppressors in a strife of blood,
Or when free thoughts, like lightnings, are alive,
  And in each bosom of the multitude
  Justice and truth with Custom's hydra brood
Wage silent war; when Priests and Kings dissemble   420
  In smiles or frowns their fierce disquietude,
When round pure hearts a host of hopes assemble,
The Snake and Eagle meet—the world's foundations tremble!

XXXIV

'Thou hast beheld that fight—when to thy home
  Thou dost return, steep not its hearth in tears;   425
Though thou may'st hear that earth is now become
  The tyrant's garbage, which to his compeers,
  The vile reward of their dishonoured years,
He will dividing give.—The victor Fiend,
  Omnipotent of yore, now quails, and fears   430
His triumph dearly won, which soon will lend
An impulse swift and sure to his approaching end.

XXXV

'List, stranger, list, mine is an human form,
  Like that thou wearest—touch me—shrink not now!
My hand thou feel'st is not a ghost's, but warm   435
  With human blood.—'Twas many years ago,

Since first my thirsting soul aspired to know
The secrets of this wondrous world, when deep
My heart was pierced with sympathy, for woe
Which could not be mine own—and thought did keep,
In dream, unnatural watch beside an infant's sleep.   441

XXXVI

'Woe could not be mine own, since far from men
I dwelt, a free and happy orphan child,
By the sea-shore, in a deep mountain-glen;
    And near the waves, and through the forests wild,   445
I roamed, to storm and darkness reconciled:
For I was calm while tempest shook the sky:
    But when the breathless heavens in beauty smiled,
I wept, sweet tears, yet too tumultuously
For peace, and clasped my hands aloft in ecstasy.   450

XXXVII

'These were forebodings of my fate—before
A woman's heart beat in my virgin breast,
It had been nurtured in divinest lore:
    A dying poet gave me books, and blessed
With wild but holy talk the sweet unrest   455
In which I watched him as he died away—
    A youth with hoary hair—a fleeting guest
Of our lone mountains: and this lore did sway
My spirit like a storm, contending there alway.

XXXVIII

'Thus the dark tale which history doth unfold   460
I knew, but not, methinks, as others know,
For they weep not; and Wisdom had unrolled
    The clouds which hide the gulf of mortal woe,—
To few can she that warning vision show—
For I loved all things with intense devotion;   465
    So that when Hope's deep source in fullest flow,
Like earthquake did uplift the stagnant ocean
Of human thoughts—mine shook beneath the wide emotion.

XXXIX

'When first the living blood through all these veins
    Kindled a thought in sense, great France sprang forth,
And seized, as if to break, the ponderous chains   471
    Which bind in woe the nations of the earth.

I saw, and started from my cottage-hearth:
And to the clouds and waves in tameless gladness,
  Shrieked, till they caught immeasurable mirth—   475
And laughed in light and music: soon, sweet madness
Was poured upon my heart, a soft and thrilling sadness.

XL

'Deep slumber fell on me:—my dreams were fire—
  Soft and delightful thoughts did rest and hover
Like shadows o'er my brain; and strange desire,   480
  The tempest of a passion, raging over
  My tranquil soul, its depths with light did cover,—
Which passed; and calm, and darkness, sweeter far,
  Came—then I loved; but not a human lover!
For when I rose from sleep, the Morning Star   485
Shone through the woodbine-wreaths which round my casement
    were.

XLI

'Twas like an eye which seemed to smile on me.
  I watched, till by the sun made pale, it sank
Under the billows of the heaving sea;
  But from its beams deep love my spirit drank,   490
  And to my brain the boundless world now shrank
Into one thought—one image—yes, for ever!
  Even like the dayspring, poured on vapours dank,
The beams of that one Star did shoot and quiver
Through my benighted mind—and were extinguished never.

XLII

'The day passed thus: at night, methought in dream   496
  A shape of speechless beauty did appear:
It stood like light on a careering stream
  Of golden clouds which shook the atmosphere;
  A wingèd youth, his radiant brow did wear   500
The Morning Star: a wild dissolving bliss
  Over my frame he breathed, approaching near,
And bent his eyes of kindling tenderness
Near mine, and on my lips impressed a lingering kiss,—

XLIII

'And said: "A Spirit loves thee, mortal maiden,   505
  How wilt thou prove thy worth?" Then joy and sleep
Together fled, my soul was deeply laden,
  And to the shore I went to muse and weep;

But as I moved, over my heart did creep
A joy less soft, but more profound and strong   510
    Than my sweet dream; and it forbade to keep
The path of the sea-shore: that Spirit's tongue
Seemed whispering in my heart, and bore my steps along.

                    XLIV

'How, to that vast and peopled city led,
    Which was a field of holy warfare then,   515
I walked among the dying and the dead,
    And shared in fearless deeds with evil men,
    Calm as an angel in the dragon's den—
How I braved death for liberty and truth,
    And spurned at peace, and power, and fame—and when
Those hopes had lost the glory of their youth,   521
How sadly I returned—might move the hearer's ruth:

                    XLV

'Warm tears throng fast! the tale may not be said—
    Know then, that when this grief had been subdued,
I was not left, like others, cold and dead;   525
    The Spirit whom I loved, in solitude
    Sustained his child: the tempest-shaken wood,
The waves, the fountains, and the hush of night—
    These were his voice, and well I understood
His smile divine, when the calm sea was bright   530
With silent stars, and Heaven was breathless with delight.

                    XLVI

'In lonely glens, amid the roar of rivers,
    When the dim nights were moonless, have I known
Joys which no tongue can tell; my pale lip quivers
    When thought revisits them:—know thou alone,   535
    That after many wondrous years were flown,
I was awakened by a shriek of woe;
    And over me a mystic robe was thrown,
By viewless hands, and a bright Star did glow
Before my steps—the Snake then met his mortal foe.'   540

                    XLVII

'Thou fearest not then the Serpent on thy heart?'
    'Fear it!' she said, with brief and passionate cry,
And spake no more: that silence made me start—
    I looked, and we were sailing pleasantly,

Swift as a cloud between the sea and sky;   545
Beneath the rising moon seen far away,
    Mountains of ice, like sapphire, piled on high,
Hemming the horizon round, in silence lay
On the still waters—these we did approach alway.

XLVIII

And swift and swifter grew the vessel's motion,   550
    So that a dizzy trance fell on my brain—
Wild music woke me: we had passed the ocean
    Which girds the pole, Nature's remotest reign—
    And we glode fast o'er a pellucid plain
Of waters, azure with the noontide day.   555
    Ethereal mountains shone around—a Fane
    Stood in the midst, girt by green isles which lay
On the blue sunny deep, resplendent far away.

XLIX

It was a Temple, such as mortal hand
    Has never built, nor ecstasy, nor dream   560
Reared in the cities of enchanted land:
    'Twas likest Heaven, ere yet day's purple stream
    Ebbs o'er the western forest, while the gleam
Of the unrisen moon among the clouds
    Is gathering—when with many a golden beam   565
The thronging constellations rush in crowds,
Paving with fire the sky and the marmoreal floods.

L

Like what may be conceived of this vast dome,
    When from the depths which thought can seldom pierce
Genius beholds it rise, his native home,   570
    Girt by the deserts of the Universe;
    Yet, nor in painting's light, or mightier verse,
Or sculpture's marble language, can invest
    That shape to mortal sense—such glooms immerse
That incommunicable sight, and rest   575
Upon the labouring brain and overburdened breast.

LI

Winding among the lawny islands fair,
    Whose blosmy forests starred the shadowy deep,
The wingless boat paused where an ivory stair
    Its fretwork in the crystal sea did steep,   580

Encircling that vast Fane's aërial heap:
We disembarked, and through a portal wide
  We passed—whose roof of moonstone carved, did keep
A glimmering o'er the forms on every side,
Sculptures like life and thought; immovable, deep-eyed.   585

LII

We came to a vast hall, whose glorious roof
  Was diamond, which had drank the lightning's sheen
In darkness, and now poured it through the woof
  Of spell-inwoven clouds hung there to screen
  Its blinding splendour—through such veil was seen   590
That work of subtlest power, divine and rare;
  Orb above orb, with starry shapes between,
And hornèd moons, and meteors strange and fair,
On night-black columns poised—one hollow hemisphere!

LIII

Ten thousand columns in that quivering light   595
  Distinct—between whose shafts wound far away
The long and labyrinthine aisles—more bright
  With their own radiance than the Heaven of Day;
  And on the jasper walls around, there lay
Paintings, the poesy of mightiest thought,   600
  Which did the Spirit's history display;
A tale of passionate change, divinely taught,
Which, in their wingèd dance, unconscious Genii wrought.

LIV

Beneath, there sate on many a sapphire throne,
  The Great, who had departed from mankind,   605
A mighty Senate;—some, whose white hair shone
  Like mountain snow, mild, beautiful, and blind;
  Some, female forms, whose gestures beamed with mind;
And ardent youths, and children bright and fair;
  And some had lyres whose strings were intertwined   610
With pale and clinging flames, which ever there
Waked faint yet thrilling sounds that pierced the crystal air.

LV

One seat was vacant in the midst, a throne,
  Reared on a pyramid like sculptured flame,
Distinct with circling steps which rested on   615
  Their own deep fire—soon as the Woman came

Into that hall, she shrieked the Spirit's name
And fell; and vanished slowly from the sight.
Darkness arose from her dissolving frame,
Which gathering, filled that dome of woven light,   620
Blotting its sphered stars with supernatural night.

LVI

Then first, two glittering lights were seen to glide
  In circles on the amethystine floor,
Small serpent eyes trailing from side to side,
  Like meteors on a river's grassy shore,   625
  They round each other rolled, dilating more
And more—then rose, commingling into one,
  One clear and mighty planet hanging o'er
A cloud of deepest shadow, which was thrown
Athwart the glowing steps and the crystalline throne.   630

LVII

The cloud which rested on that cone of flame
  Was cloven; beneath the planet sate a Form,
Fairer than tongue can speak or thought may frame,
  The radiance of whose limbs rose-like and warm
  Flowed forth, and did with softest light inform   635
The shadowy dome, the sculptures, and the state
  Of those assembled shapes—with clinging charm
Sinking upon their hearts and mine. He sate
Majestic, yet most mild—calm, yet compassionate.

LVIII

Wonder and joy a passing faintness threw   640
  Over my brow—a hand supported me,
Whose touch was magic strength: an eye of blue
  Looked into mine, like moonlight, soothingly;
  And a voice said.—'Thou must a listener be
This day—two mighty Spirits now return,   645
  Like birds of calm, from the world's raging sea,
They pour fresh light from Hope's immortal urn;
A tale of human power—despair not—list and learn!'

LIX

I looked, and lo! one stood forth eloquently,
  His eyes were dark and deep, and the clear brow   650
Which shadowed them was like the morning sky,
  The cloudless Heaven of Spring, when in their flow

Through the bright air, the soft winds as they blow
Wake the green world—his gestures did obey
    The oracular mind that made his features glow, 655
And where his curvèd lips half-open lay,
Passion's divinest stream had made impetuous way.

LX

Beneath the darkness of his outspread hair
    He stood thus beautiful: but there was One
Who sate beside him like his shadow there, 660
    And held his hand—far lovelier—she was known
    To be thus fair, by the few lines alone
Which through her floating locks and gathered cloak,
    Glances of soul-dissolving glory, shone:—
None else beheld her eyes—in him they woke 665
Memories which found a tongue as thus he silence broke.

CANTO II

I

THE starlight smile of children, the sweet looks
    Of women, the fair breast from which I fed,
The murmur of the unreposing brooks,
    And the green light which, shifting overhead, 670
    Some tangled bower of vines around me shed,
The shells on the sea-sand, and the wild flowers,
    The lamplight through the rafters cheerly spread,
And on the twining flax—in life's young hours
These sights and sounds did nurse my spirit's folded powers.

II

In Argolis, beside the echoing sea, 676
    Such impulses within my mortal frame
Arose, and they were dear to memory,
    Like tokens of the dead:—but others came
    Soon, in another shape: the wondrous fame 680
Of the past world, the vital words and deeds
    Of minds whom neither time nor change can tame,
Traditions dark and old, whence evil creeds
Start forth, and whose dim shade a stream of poison feeds.

III

I heard, as all have heard, the various story 685
    Of human life, and wept unwilling tears.
Feeble historians of its shame and glory,
    False disputants on all its hopes and fears,

Victims who worshipped ruin,—chroniclers
Of daily scorn, and slaves who loathed their state   690
    Yet, flattering power, had given its ministers
    A throne of judgement in the grave:—'twas fate,
That among such as these my youth should seek its mate.

IV

The land in which I lived, by a fell bane
    Was withered up. Tyrants dwelt side by side,   695
And stabled in our homes,—until the chain
    Stifled the captive's cry, and to abide
    That blasting curse men had no shame—all vied
In evil, slave and despot; fear with lust
    Strange fellowship through mutual hate had tied,   700
Like two dark serpents tangled in the dust,
Which on the paths of men their mingling poison thrust.

V

Earth, our bright home, its mountains and its waters,
    And the ethereal shapes which are suspended
Over its green expanse, and those fair daughters,   705
    The clouds, of Sun and Ocean, who have blended
    The colours of the air since first extended
It cradled the young world, none wandered forth
    To see or feel: a darkness had descended
On every heart: the light which shows its worth,   710
Must among gentle thoughts and fearless take its birth.

VI

This vital world, this home of happy spirits,
    Was as a dungeon to my blasted kind;
All that despair from murdered hope inherits
    They sought, and in their helpless misery blind,   715
    A deeper prison and heavier chains did find,
And stronger tyrants:—a dark gulf before,
    The realm of a stern Ruler, yawned; behind,
Terror and Time conflicting drove, and bore
On their tempestuous flood the shrieking wretch from shore.

VII

Out of that Ocean's wrecks had Guilt and Woe   721
    Framed a dark dwelling for their homeless thought,
And, starting at the ghosts which to and fro
    Glide o'er its dim and gloomy strand, had brought

The worship thence which they each other taught.   725
Well might men loathe their life, well might they turn
Even to the ills again from which they sought
Such refuge after death!—well might they learn
To gaze on this fair world with hopeless unconcern!

VIII

For they all pined in bondage; body and soul,   730
Tyrant and slave, victim and torturer, bent
Before one Power, to which supreme control
Over their will by their own weakness lent,
Made all its many names omnipotent;
All symbols of things evil, all divine;   735
And hymns of blood or mockery, which rent
The air from all its fanes, did intertwine
Imposture's impious toils round each discordant shrine.

IX

I heard, as all have heard, life's various story,
And in no careless heart transcribed the tale;   740
But, from the sneers of men who had grown hoary
In shame and scorn, from groans of crowds made pale
By famine, from a mother's desolate wail
O'er her polluted child, from innocent blood
Poured on the earth, and brows anxious and pale   745
With the heart's warfare; did I gather food
To feed my many thoughts: a tameless multitude!

X

I wandered through the wrecks of days departed
Far by the desolated shore, when even
O'er the still sea and jagged islets darted   750
The light of moonrise; in the northern Heaven,
Among the clouds near the horizon driven,
The mountains lay beneath our planet pale;
Around me, broken tombs and columns riven
Looked vast in twilight, and the sorrowing gale   755
Waked in those ruins gray its everlasting wail!

XI

I knew not who had framed these wonders then,
Nor had I heard the story of their deeds;
But dwellings of a race of mightier men,
And monuments of less ungentle creeds   760

Tell their own tale to him who wisely heeds
The language which they speak; and now, to me
   The moonlight making pale the blooming weeds,
The bright stars shining in the breathless sea,
Interpreted those scrolls of mortal mystery.   765

XII

Such man has been, and such may yet become!
   Ay, wiser, greater, gentler, even than they
Who on the fragments of yon shattered dome
   Have stamped the sign of power—I felt the sway
   Of the vast stream of ages bear away   770
My floating thoughts—my heart beat loud and fast—
   Even as a storm let loose beneath the ray
Of the still moon, my spirit onward past
Beneath truth's steady beams upon its tumult cast.

XIII

It shall be thus no more! too long, too long,   775
   Sons of the glorious dead, have ye lain bound
In darkness and in ruin!—Hope is strong,
   Justice and Truth their wingèd child have found—
   Awake! arise! until the mighty sound
Of your career shall scatter in its gust   780
   The thrones of the oppressor, and the ground
Hide the last altar's unregarded dust,
Whose Idol has so long betrayed your impious trust!

XIV

It must be so—I will arise and waken
   The multitude, and like a sulphurous hill,   785
Which on a sudden from its snows has shaken
   The swoon of ages, it shall burst and fill
   The world with cleansing fire: it must, it will—
It may not be restrained!—and who shall stand
   Amid the rocking earthquake steadfast still,   790
But Laon? on high Freedom's desert land
A tower whose marble walls the leaguèd storms withstand!

XV

One summer night, in commune with the hope
   Thus deeply fed, amid those ruins gray
I watched, beneath the dark sky's starry cope;   795
   And ever from that hour upon me lay

The burden of this hope, and night or day,
In vision or in dream, clove to my breast:
Among mankind, or when gone far away
To the lone shores and mountains, 'twas a guest   800
Which followed where I fled, and watched when I did rest.

XVI

These hopes found words through which my spirit sought
To weave a bondage of such sympathy,
As might create some response to the thought
Which ruled me now—and as the vapours lie   805
Bright in the outspread morning's radiancy,
So were these thoughts invested with the light
Of language: and all bosoms made reply
On which its lustre streamed, whene'er it might
Through darkness wide and deep those trancèd spirits smite.

XVII

Yes, many an eye with dizzy tears was dim,   811
And oft I thought to clasp my own heart's brother,
When I could feel the listener's senses swim,
And hear his breath its own swift gaspings smother
Even as my words evoked them—and another,   815
And yet another, I did fondly deem,
Felt that we all were sons of one great mother;
And the cold truth such sad reverse did seem,
As to awake in grief from some delightful dream.

XVIII

Yes, oft beside the ruined labyrinth   820
Which skirts the hoary caves of the green deep,
Did Laon and his friend, on one gray plinth,
Round whose worn base the wild waves hiss and leap,
Resting at eve, a lofty converse keep:
And that this friend was false, may now be said   825
Calmly—that he like other men could weep
Tears which are lies, and could betray and spread
Snares for that guileless heart which for his own had bled.

XIX

Then, had no great aim recompensed my sorrow,
I must have sought dark respite from its stress   830
In dreamless rest, in sleep that sees no morrow—
For to tread life's dismaying wilderness

Without one smile to cheer, one voice to bless,
Amid the snares and scoffs of human kind,
   Is hard—but I betrayed it not, nor less   835
With love that scorned return, sought to unbind
The interwoven clouds which make its wisdom blind.

XX

With deathless minds which leave where they have passed
   A path of light, my soul communion knew;
Till from that glorious intercourse, at last,   840
   As from a mine of magic store, I drew
   Words which were weapons;—round my heart there grew
The adamantine armour of their power,
   And from my fancy wings of golden hue
Sprang forth—yet not alone from wisdom's tower,   845
A minister of truth, these plumes young Laon bore.

XXI

An orphan with my parents lived, whose eyes
   Were lodestars of delight, which drew me home
When I might wander forth; nor did I prize
   Aught human thing beneath Heaven's mighty dome   850
   Beyond this child: so when sad hours were come,
And baffled hope like ice still clung to me,
   Since kin were cold, and friends had now become
Heartless and false, I turned from all, to be,
Cythna, the only source of tears and smiles to thee.   855

XXII

What wert thou then? A child most infantine,
   Yet wandering far beyond that innocent age
In all but its sweet looks and mien divine:
   Even then, methought, with the world's tyrant rage
   A patient warfare thy young heart did wage,   860
When those soft eyes of scarcely conscious thought
   Some tale, or thine own fancies, would engage
To overflow with tears, or converse fraught
With passion, o'er their depths its fleeting light had wrought.

XXIII

She moved upon this earth a shape of brightness,   865
   A power, that from its objects scarcely drew
One impulse of her being—in her lightness
   Most like some radiant cloud of morning dew,

Which wanders through the waste air's pathless blue,
To nourish some far desert: she did seem   87b
    Beside me, gathering beauty as she grew,
Like the bright shade of some immortal dream
Which walks, when tempest sleeps, the wave of life's dark stream.

XXIV

As mine own shadow was this child to me,
    A second self, far dearer and more fair;   875
Which clothed in undissolving radiancy
    All those steep paths which languor and despair
    Of human things, had made so dark and bare,
But which I trod alone—nor, till bereft
    Of friends, and overcome by lonely care,   880
Knew I what solace for that loss was left,
Though by a bitter wound my trusting heart was cleft.

XXV

Once she was dear, now she was all I had
    To love in human life—this playmate sweet,
This child of twelve years old—so she was made   885
    My sole associate, and her willing feet
    Wandered with mine where earth and ocean meet,
Beyond the aëreal mountains whose vast cells
    The unreposing billows ever beat.
Through forests wide and old, and lawny dells   890
Where boughs of incense droop over the emerald wells.

XXVI

And warm and light I felt her clasping hand
    When twined in mine: she followed where I went,
Through the lone paths of our immortal land.
    It had no waste but some memorial lent   895
    Which strung me to my toil—some monument
Vital with mind: then, Cythna by my side,
    Until the bright and beaming day were spent,
Would rest, with looks entreating to abide,
Too earnest and too sweet ever to be denied.   900

XXVII

And soon I could not have refused her—thus
    For ever, day and night, we two were ne'er
Parted, but when brief sleep divided us:
    And when the pauses of the lulling air

Of noon beside the sea, had made a lair   905
For her soothed senses, in my arms she slept,
  And I kept watch over her slumbers there,
While, as the shifting visions o'er her swept,
Amid her innocent rest by turns she smiled and wept.

XXVIII

And, in the murmur of her dreams was heard   910
  Sometimes the name of Laon:—suddenly
She would arise, and, like the secret bird
  Whom sunset wakens, fill the shore and sky
  With her sweet accents—a wild melody!
Hymns which my soul had woven to Freedom, strong   915
  The source of passion, whence they rose, to be;
Triumphant strains, which, like a spirit's tongue,
To the enchanted waves that child of glory sung—

XXIX

Her white arms lifted through the shadowy stream
  Of her loose hair—oh, excellently great   920
Seemed to me then my purpose, the vast theme
  Of those impassioned songs, when Cythna sate
  Amid the calm which rapture doth create
After its tumult, her heart vibrating,
  Her spirit o'er the ocean's floating state   925
From her deep eyes far wandering, on the wing
Of visions that were mine, beyond its utmost spring.

XXX

For, before Cythna loved it, had my song
  Peopled with thoughts the boundless universe,
A mighty congregation, which were strong   930
  Where'er they trod the darkness to disperse
  The cloud of that unutterable curse
Which clings upon mankind:—all things became
  Slaves to my holy and heroic verse,
Earth, sea and sky, the planets, life and fame   935
And fate, or whate'er else binds the world's wondrous frame.

XXXI

And this beloved child thus felt the sway
  Of my conceptions, gathering like a cloud
The very wind on which it rolls away:
  Hers too were all my thoughts, ere yet, endowed   940

With music and with light, their fountains flowed
In poesy; and her still and earnest face,
　　Pallid with feelings which intensely glowed
Within, was turned on mine with speechless grace,
Watching the hopes which there her heart had learned to trace.

XXXII

In me, communion with this purest being　　946
　　Kindled intenser zeal, and made me wise
In knowledge, which, in hers mine own mind seeing,
　　Left in the human world few mysteries:
　　How without fear of evil or disguise　　950
Was Cythna!—what a spirit strong and mild,
　　Which death, or pain or peril could despise,
Yet melt in tenderness! what genius wild
Yet mighty, was enclosed within one simple child!

XXXIII

New lore was this—old age, with its gray hair,　　955
　　And wrinkled legends of unworthy things,
And icy sneers, is nought: it cannot dare
　　To burst the chains which life for ever flings
　　On the entangled soul's aspiring wings,
So is it cold and cruel, and is made　　960
　　The careless slave of that dark power which brings
Evil, like blight, on man, who, still betrayed,
Laughs o'er the grave in which his living hopes are laid.

XXXIV

Nor are the strong and the severe to keep
　　The empire of the world: thus Cythna taught　　965
Even in the visions of her eloquent sleep,
　　Unconscious of the power through which she wrought
　　The woof of such intelligible thought,
As from the tranquil strength which cradled lay
　　In her smile-peopled rest, my spirit sought　　970
Why the deceiver and the slave has sway
O'er heralds so divine of truth's arising day.

XXXV

Within that fairest form, the female mind
　　Untainted by the poison-clouds which rest
On the dark world, a sacred home did find:　　975
　　But else, from the wide earth's maternal breast,

Victorious Evil, which had dispossessed
All native power, had those fair children torn,
    And made them slaves to soothe his vile unrest,
    And minister to lust its joys forlorn,   980
Till they had learned to breathe the atmosphere of scorn.

XXXVI

This misery was but coldly felt, till she
    Became my only friend, who had endued
My purpose with a wider sympathy;
    Thus, Cythna mourned with me the servitude   985
    In which the half of humankind were mewed
Victims of lust and hate, the slaves of slaves,
    She mourned that grace and power were thrown as food
    To the hyaena lust, who, among graves,
Over his loathèd meal, laughing in agony, raves.   990

XXXVII

And I, still gazing on that glorious child,
    Even as these thoughts flushed o'er her:—'Cythna sweet,
Well with the world art thou unreconciled;
    Never will peace and human nature meet
    Till free and equal man and woman greet   995
Domestic peace; and ere this power can make
    In human hearts its calm and holy seat,
    This slavery must be broken'—as I spake,
From Cythna's eyes a light of exultation brake.

XXXVIII

She replied earnestly:—'It shall be mine,   1000
    This task, mine, Laon!—thou hast much to gain;
Nor wilt thou at poor Cythna's pride repine,
    If she should lead a happy female train
    To meet thee over the rejoicing plain,
When myriads at thy call shall throng around   1005
    The Golden City.'—Then the child did strain
    My arm upon her tremulous heart, and wound
Her own about my neck, till some reply she found.

XXXIX

I smiled, and spake not.—'Wherefore dost thou smile
    At what I say? Laon, I am not weak,   1010
And though my cheek might become pale the while,
    With thee, if thou desirest, will I seek

Through their array of banded slaves to wreak
Ruin upon the tyrants. I had thought
  It was more hard to turn my unpractised cheek   1015
To scorn and shame, and this beloved spot
And thee, O dearest friend, to leave and murmur not.

XL

'Whence came I what I am? Thou, Laon, knowest
  How a young child should thus undaunted be;
Methinks, it is a power which thou bestowest,   1020
  Through which I seek, by most resembling thee,
  So to become most good and great and free,
Yet far beyond this Ocean's utmost roar
  In towers and huts are many like to me,
Who, could they see thine eyes, or feel such lore   1025
As I have learnt from them, like me would fear no more.

XLI

'Think'st thou that I shall speak unskilfully,
  And none will heed me? I remember now,
How once, a slave in tortures doomed to die,
  Was saved, because in accents sweet and low   1030
  He sung a song his Judge loved long ago,
As he was led to death.—All shall relent
  Who hear me—tears, as mine have flowed, shall flow,
Hearts beat as mine now beats, with such intent
As renovates the world; a will omnipotent!   1035

XLII

'Yes, I will tread Pride's golden palaces,
  Through Penury's roofless huts and squalid cells
Will I descend, where'er in abjectness
  Woman with some vile slave her tyrant dwells,
  There with the music of thine own sweet spells   1040
Will disenchant the captives, and will pour
  For the despairing, from the crystal wells
Of thy deep spirit, reason's mighty lore,
And power shall then abound, and hope arise once more.

XLIII

'Can man be free if woman be a slave?   1045
  Chain one who lives, and breathes this boundless air,
To the corruption of a closèd grave!
  Can they whose mates are beasts, condemned to bear

Scorn, heavier far than toil or anguish, dare
To trample their oppressors? in their home   1050
   Among their babes, thou knowest a curse would wear
   The shape of woman—hoary Crime would come
Behind, and Fraud rebuild religion's tottering dome.

XLIV

'I am a child:—I would not yet depart.
   When I go forth alone, bearing the lamp   1055
Aloft which thou hast kindled in my heart,
   Millions of slaves from many a dungeon damp
   Shall leap in joy, as the benumbing cramp
Of ages leaves their limbs—no ill may harm
   Thy Cythna ever—truth its radiant stamp   1060
Has fixed, as an invulnerable charm
Upon her children's brow, dark Falsehood to disarm.

XLV

'Wait yet awhile for the appointed day—
   Thou wilt depart, and I with tears shall stand
Watching thy dim sail skirt the ocean gray;   1065
   Amid the dwellers of this lonely land
   I shall remain alone—and thy command
Shall then dissolve the world's unquiet trance,
   And, multitudinous as the desert sand
Borne on the storm, its millions shall advance,   1070
Thronging round thee, the light of their deliverance.

XLVI

'Then, like the forests of some pathless mountain,
   Which from remotest glens two warring winds
Involve in fire which not the loosened fountain
   Of broadest floods might quench, shall all the kinds
   Of evil, catch from our uniting minds   1076
The spark which must consume them;—Cythna then
   Will have cast off the impotence that binds
Her childhood now, and through the paths of men
Will pass, as the charmed bird that haunts the serpent's den.

XLVII

'We part!—O Laon, I must dare nor tremble   1081
   To meet those looks no more!—Oh, heavy stroke!
Sweet brother of my soul! can I dissemble
   The agony of this thought?'—As thus she spoke

The gathered sobs her quivering accents broke,   1085
And in my arms she hid her beating breast.
I remained still for tears—sudden she woke
As one awakes from sleep, and wildly pressed
My bosom, her whole frame impetuously possessed.

XLVIII

'We part to meet again—but yon blue waste,   1090
   Yon desert wide and deep holds no recess,
Within whose happy silence, thus embraced
   We might survive all ills in one caress:
   Nor doth the grave—I fear 'tis passionless—
Nor yon cold vacant Heaven:—we meet again   1095
   Within the minds of men, whose lips shall bless
Our memory, and whose hopes its light retain
When these dissevered bones are trodden in the plain.'

XLIX

I could not speak, though she had ceased, for now
   The fountains of her feeling, swift and deep,   1100
Seemed to suspend the tumult of their flow;
   So we arose, and by the starlight steep
   Went homeward—neither did we speak nor weep,
But, pale, were calm with passion—thus subdued
   Like evening shades that o'er the mountains creep,   1105
We moved towards our home; where, in this mood,
Each from the other sought refuge in solitude.

CANTO III

I

WHAT thoughts had sway o'er Cythna's lonely slumber
   That night, I know not; but my own did seem
As if they might ten thousand years outnumber   1110
   Of waking life, the visions of a dream
   Which hid in one dim gulf the troubled stream
Of mind; a boundless chaos wild and vast,
   Whose limits yet were never memory's theme:
And I lay struggling as its whirlwinds passed,   1115
Sometimes for rapture sick, sometimes for pain aghast.

II

Two hours, whose mighty circle did embrace
   More time than might make gray the infant world,
Rolled thus, a weary and tumultuous space:
   When the third came, like mist on breezes curled,   1120

From my dim sleep a shadow was unfurled:
Methought, upon the threshold of a cave
I sate with Cythna; drooping briony, pearled
With dew from the wild streamlet's shattered wave,
Hung, where we sate to taste the joys which Nature gave.

III

We lived a day as we were wont to live,   1120
But Nature had a robe of glory on,
And the bright air o'er every shape did weave
Intenser hues, so that the herbless stone,
The leafless bough among the leaves alone,   1130
Had being clearer than its own could be,
And Cythna's pure and radiant self was shown,
In this strange vision, so divine to me,
That, if I loved before, now love was agony.

IV

Morn fled, noon came, evening, then night descended,
And we prolonged calm talk beneath the sphere   1136
Of the calm moon—when suddenly was blended
With our repose a nameless sense of fear;
And from the cave behind I seemed to hear
Sounds gathering upwards!—accents incomplete,   1140
And stifled shrieks,—and now, more near and near,
A tumult and a rush of thronging feet
The cavern's secret depths beneath the earth did beat.

V

The scene was changed, and away, away, away!
Through the air and over the sea we sped,   1145
And Cythna in my sheltering bosom lay,
And the winds bore me—through the darkness spread
Around, the gaping earth then vomited
Legions of foul and ghastly shapes, which hung
Upon my flight; and ever, as we fled,   1150
They plucked at Cythna—soon to me then clung
A sense of actual things those monstrous dreams among.

VI

And I lay struggling in the impotence
Of sleep, while outward life had burst its bound,
Though, still deluded, strove the tortured sense   1155
To its dire wanderings to adapt the sound

Which in the light of morn was poured around
Our dwelling—breathless, pale, and unaware
I rose, and all the cottage crowded found
With armèd men, whose glittering swords were bare,   1160
And whose degraded limbs the tyrant's garb did wear.

VII

And, ere with rapid lips and gathered brow
I could demand the cause—a feeble shriek—
It was a feeble shriek, faint, far and low,
Arrested me—my mien grew calm and meek,   1165
And grasping a small knife, I went to seek
That voice among the crowd—'twas Cythna's cry!
Beneath most calm resolve did agony wreak
Its whirlwind rage:—so I passed quietly
Till I beheld, where bound, that dearest child did lie.   1170

VIII

I started to behold her, for delight
And exultation, and a joyance free,
Solemn, serene and lofty, filled the light
Of the calm smile with which she looked on me:
So that I feared some brainless ecstasy,   1175
Wrought from that bitter woe, had wildered her—
'Farewell! farewell!' she said, as I drew nigh.
'At first my peace was marred by this strange stir,
Now I am calm as truth—its chosen minister.

IX

'Look not so, Laon—say farewell in hope,   1180
These bloody men are but the slaves who bear
Their mistress to her task—it was my scope
The slavery where they drag me now, to share,
And among captives willing chains to wear
Awhile—the rest thou knowest—return, dear friend!   1185
Let our first triumph trample the despair
Which would ensnare us now, for in the end,
In victory or in death our hopes and fears must blend.'

X

These words had fallen on my unheeding ear,
Whilst I had watched the motions of the crew   1190
With seeming-careless glance; not many were
Around her, for their comrades just withdrew

To guard some other victim—so I drew
My knife, and with one impulse, suddenly
    All unaware three of their number slew,   1195
And grasped a fourth by the throat, and with loud cry
My countrymen invoked to death or liberty!

XI

What followed then, I know not—for a stroke
  On my raised arm and naked head, came down,
Filling my eyes with blood—when I awoke,   1200
  I felt that they had bound me in my swoon,
  And up a rock which overhangs the town,
By the steep path were bearing me: below,
  The plain was filled with slaughter,—overthrown
The vineyards and the harvests, and the glow   1205
Of blazing roofs shone far o'er the white Ocean's flow.

XII

Upon that rock a mighty column stood,
  Whose capital seemed sculptured in the sky,
Which to the wanderers o'er the solitude
  Of distant seas, from ages long gone by,   1210
  Had made a landmark; o'er its height to fly
Scarcely the cloud, the vulture, or the blast,
  Has power—and when the shades of evening lie
On Earth and Ocean, its carved summits cast
The sunken daylight far through the aërial waste.   1215

XIII

They bore me to a cavern in the hill
  Beneath that column, and unbound me there:
And one did strip me stark; and one did fill
  A vessel from the putrid pool; one bare
  A lighted torch, and four with friendless care   1220
Guided my steps the cavern-paths along,
  Then up a steep and dark and narrow stair
We wound, until the torch's fiery tongue
Amid the gushing day beamless and pallid hung.

XIV

They raised me to the platform of the pile,   1225
  That column's dizzy height:—the grate of brass
Through which they thrust me, open stood the while,
  As to its ponderous and suspended mass,

With chains which eat into the flesh, alas!
With brazen links, my naked limbs they bound: 1230
The grate, as they departed to repass,
With horrid clangour fell, and the far sound
Of their retiring steps in the dense gloom were drowned.

XV

The noon was calm and bright:—around that column
The overhanging sky and circling sea   1235
Spread forth in silentness profound and solemn
The darkness of brief frenzy cast on me,
So that I knew not my own misery:
The islands and the mountains in the day
Like clouds reposed afar; and I could see   1240
The town among the woods below that lay,
And the dark rocks which bound the bright and glassy bay.

XVI

It was so calm, that scarce the feathery weed
Sown by some eagle on the topmost stone
Swayed in the air:—so bright, that noon did breed   1245
No shadow in the sky beside mine own—
Mine, and the shadow of my chain alone.
Below, the smoke of roofs involved in flame
Rested like night, all else was clearly shown
In that broad glare, yet sound to me none came,   1250
But of the living blood that ran within my frame.

XVII

The peace of madness fled, and ah, too soon!
A ship was lying on the sunny main,
Its sails were flagging in the breathless noon—
Its shadow lay beyond—that sight again   1255
Waked, with its presence, in my trancèd brain
The stings of a known sorrow, keen and cold:
I knew that ship bore Cythna o'er the plain
Of waters, to her blighting slavery sold,
And watched it with such thoughts as must remain untold.

XVIII

I watched, until the shades of evening wrapped   1261
Earth like an exhalation—then the bark
Moved, for that calm was by the sunset snapped.
It moved a speck upon the Ocean dark:

Soon the wan stars came forth, and I could mark
  Its path no more!—I sought to close mine eyes,
    But like the balls, their lids were stiff and stark;
  I would have risen, but ere that I could rise,
My parchèd skin was split with piercing agonies.

XIX

I gnawed my brazen chain, and sought to sever   1270
  Its adamantine links, that I might die:
O Liberty! forgive the base endeavour,
  Forgive me, if, reserved for victory,
    The Champion of thy faith e'er sought to fly.—
That starry night, with its clear silence, sent   1275
  Tameless resolve which laughed at misery
Into my soul—linkèd remembrance lent
To that such power, to me such a severe content.

XX

To breathe, to be, to hope, or to despair
  And die, I questioned not; nor, though the Sun   1280
Its shafts of agony kindling through the air
  Moved over me, nor though in evening dun,
    Or when the stars their visible courses run,
Or morning, the wide universe was spread
  In dreary calmness round me, did I shun   1285
Its presence, nor seek refuge with the dead
From one faint hope whose flower a dropping poison shed.

XXI

Two days thus passed—I neither raved nor died—
  Thirst raged within me, like a scorpion's nest
Built in mine entrails; I had spurned aside   1290
  The water-vessel, while despair possessed
    My thoughts, and now no drop remained! The uprest
Of the third sun brought hunger—but the crust
  Which had been left, was to my craving breast
Fuel, not food. I chewed the bitter dust,   1295
And bit my bloodless arm, and licked the brazen rust.

XXII

My brain began to fail when the fourth morn
  Burst o'er the golden isles—a fearful sleep,
Which through the caverns dreary and forlorn
  Of the riven soul, sent its foul dreams to sweep   1300

With whirlwind swiftness—a fall far and deep,—
A gulf, a void, a sense of senselessness—
These things dwelt in me, even as shadows keep
Their watch in some dim charnel's loneliness,
A shoreless sea, a sky sunless and planetless!   1305

XXIII

The forms which peopled this terrific trance
    I well remember—like a choir of devils,
Around me they involved a giddy dance;
    Legions seemed gathering from the misty levels
    Of Ocean, to supply those ceaseless revels,   1310
Foul, ceaseless shadows:—thought could not divide
    The actual world from these entangling evils,
Which so bemocked themselves, that I descried
All shapes like mine own self, hideously multiplied.

XXIV

The sense of day and night, of false and true,   1315
    Was dead within me. Yet two visions burst
That darkness—one, as since that hour I knew,
    Was not a phantom of the realms accursed,
    Where then my spirit dwelt—but of the first
I know not yet, was it a dream or no.   1320
    But both, though not distincter, were immersed
In hues which, when through memory's waste they flow,
Make their divided streams more bright and rapid now.

XXV

Methought that grate was lifted, and the seven
    Who brought me thither four stiff corpses bare,   1325
And from the frieze to the four winds of Heaven
    Hung them on high by the entangled hair:
    Swarthy were three—the fourth was very fair:
As they retired, the golden moon upsprung,
    And eagerly, out in the giddy air,   1330
Leaning that I might eat, I stretched and clung
Over the shapeless depth in which those corpses hung.

XXVI

A woman's shape, now lank and cold and blue,
    The dwelling of the many-coloured worm,
Hung there; the white and hollow cheek I drew   1335
    To my dry lips—what radiance did inform

Those horny eyes? whose was that withered form?
 Alas, alas! it seemed that Cythna's ghost
  Laughed in those looks, and that the flesh was warm
 Within my teeth!—A whirlwind keen as frost   1340
'Then in its sinking gulfs my sickening spirit tossed.

XXVII

Then seemed it that a tameless hurricane
 Arose, and bore me in its dark career
Beyond the sun, beyond the stars that wane
 On the verge of formless space—it languished there,   1345
 And dying, left a silence lone and drear,
More horrible than famine:—in the deep
 The shape of an old man did then appear,
Stately and beautiful; that dreadful sleep
His heavenly smiles dispersed, and I could wake and weep.

XXVIII

And, when the blinding tears had fallen, I saw   1351
 That column, and those corpses, and the moon,
And felt the poisonous tooth of hunger gnaw
 My vitals, I rejoiced, as if the boon
 Of senseless death would be accorded soon;—   1355
When from that stony gloom a voice arose,
 Solemn and sweet as when low winds attune
The midnight pines; the grate did then unclose,
And on that reverend form the moonlight did repose.

XXIX

He struck my chains, and gently spake and smiled: 1360
 As they were loosened by that Hermit old,
Mine eyes were of their madness half beguiled,
 To answer those kind looks—he did enfold
 His giant arms around me, to uphold
My wretched frame, my scorchèd limbs he wound   1365
 In linen moist and balmy, and as cold
As dew to drooping leaves;—the chain, with sound
Like earthquake, through the chasm of that steep stair did bound,

XXX

As, lifting me, it fell!—What next I heard,
 Were billows leaping on the harbour-bar,   1370
And the shrill sea-wind, whose breath idly stirred
 My hair;—I looked abroad, and saw a star

Shining beside a sail, and distant far
That mountain and its column, the known mark
   Of those who in the wide deep wandering are,   1375
So that I feared some Spirit, fell and dark,
In trance had lain me thus within a fiendish bark.

XXXI

For now indeed, over the salt sea-billow
   I sailed: yet dared not look upon the shape
Of him who ruled the helm, although the pillow   1380
   For my light head was hollowed in his lap,
   And my bare limbs his mantle did enwrap,
Fearing it was a fiend: at last, he bent
   O'er me his aged face, as if to snap
Those dreadful thoughts the gentle grandsire bent,   1385
And to my inmost soul his soothing looks he sent.

XXXII

A soft and healing potion to my lips
   At intervals he raised—now looked on high,
To mark if yet the starry giant dips
   His zone in the dim sea—now cheeringly,   1390
   Though he said little, did he speak to me.
'It is a friend beside thee—take good cheer,
   Poor victim, thou art now at liberty!'
I joyed as those a human tone to hear,
Who in cells deep and lone have languished many a year.

XXXIII

A dim and feeble joy, whose glimpses oft   1396
   Were quenched in a relapse of wildering dreams,
Yet still methought we sailed, until aloft
   The stars of night grew pallid, and the beams
   Of morn descended on the ocean-streams,   1400
And still that aged man, so grand and mild,
   Tended me, even as some sick mother seems
To hang in hope over a dying child,
Till in the azure East darkness again was piled.

XXXIV

And then the night-wind steaming from the shore,   1405
   Sent odours dying sweet across the sea,
And the swift boat the little waves which bore,
   Were cut by its keen keel, though slantingly;

Soon I could hear the leaves sigh, and could see
The myrtle-blossoms starring the dim grove, 1410
As past the pebbly beach the boat did flee
On sidelong wing, into a silent cove,
Where ebon pines a shade under the starlight wove.

CANTO IV

I

THE old man took the oars, and soon the bark
Smote on the beach beside a tower of stone; 1415
It was a crumbling heap, whose portal dark
With blooming ivy-trails was overgrown;
Upon whose floor the spangling sands were strown,
And rarest sea-shells, which the eternal flood,
Slave to the mother of the months, had thrown 1420
Within the walls of that gray tower, which stood
A changeling of man's art, nursed amid Nature's brood.

II

When the old man his boat had anchorèd,
He wound me in his arms with tender care,
And very few, but kindly words he said, 1425
And bore me through the tower adown a stair,
Whose smooth descent some ceaseless step to wear
For many a year had fallen.—We came at last
To a small chamber, which with mosses rare
Was tapestried, where me his soft hands placed 1430
Upon a couch of grass and oak-leaves interlaced.

III

The moon was darting through the lattices
Its yellow light, warm as the beams of day—
So warm, that to admit the dewy breeze,
The old man opened them; the moonlight lay 1435
Upon a lake whose waters wove their play
Even to the threshold of that lonely home:
Within was seen in the dim wavering ray
The antique sculptured roof, and many a tome
Whose lore had made that sage all that he had become.

IV

The rock-built barrier of the sea was past,— 1441
And I was on the margin of a lake,
A lonely lake, amid the forests vast
And snowy mountains:—did my spirit wake

From sleep as many-coloured as the snake   1445
That girds eternity? in life and truth,
   Might not my heart its cravings ever slake?
Was Cythna then a dream, and all my youth,
And all its hopes and fears, and all its joy and ruth?

•

V

Thus madness came again,—a milder madness,   1450
   Which darkened nought but time's unquiet flow
With supernatural shades of clinging sadness;
   That gentle Hermit, in my helpless woe,
   By my sick couch was busy to and fro,
Like a strong spirit ministrant of good: 1455
   When I was healed, he led me forth to show
The wonders of his sylvan solitude,
And we together sate by that isle-fretted flood.

VI

He knew his soothing words to weave with skill
   From all my madness told; like mine own heart,   1460
Of Cythna would he question me, until
   That thrilling name had ceased to make me start,
   From his familiar lips—it was not art,
Of wisdom and of justice when he spoke—
   When mid soft looks of pity, there would dart   1465
A glance as keen as is the lightning's stroke
When it doth rive the knots of some ancestral oak.

VII

Thus slowly from my brain the darkness rolled,
   My thoughts their due array did re-assume
Through the enchantments of that Hermit old;   1470
   Then I bethought me of the glorious doom
   Of those who sternly struggle to relume
The lamp of Hope o'er man's bewildered lot,
   And, sitting by the waters, in the gloom
Of eve, to that friend's heart I told my thought—   1475
That heart which had grown old, but had corrupted not.

VIII

That hoary man had spent his livelong age
   In converse with the dead, who leave the stamp
Of ever-burning thoughts on many a page,
   When they are gone into the senseless damp   1480

Of graves;—his spirit thus became a lamp
Of splendour, like to those on which it fed:
    Through peopled haunts, the City and the Camp,
    Deep thirst for knowledge had his footsteps led,
And all the ways of men among mankind he read.   1485

IX

But custom maketh blind and obdurate
    The loftiest hearts:—he had beheld the woe
In which mankind was bound, but deemed that fate
    Which made them abject, would preserve them so;
    And in such faith, some steadfast joy to know,   1490
He sought this cell: but when fame went abroad,
    That one in Argolis did undergo
Torture for liberty, and that the crowd
High truths from gifted lips had heard and understood;

X

And that the multitude was gathering wide,—   1495
    His spirit leaped within his aged frame,
In lonely peace he could no more abide,
    But to the land on which the victor's flame
    Had fed, my native land, the Hermit came:
Each heart was there a shield, and every tongue   1500
    Was as a sword, of truth—young Laon's name
Rallied their secret hopes, though tyrants sung
Hymns of triumphant joy our scattered tribes among.

XI

He came to the lone column on the rock,
    And with his sweet and mighty eloquence   1505
The hearts of those who watched it did unlock,
    And made them melt in tears of penitence.
    They gave him entrance free to bear me thence.
'Since this,' the old man said, 'seven years are spent,
    While slowly truth on thy benighted sense   1510
Has crept; the hope which wildered it has lent
Meanwhile, to me the power of a sublime intent.

XII

'Yes, from the records of my youthful state,
    And from the lore of bards and sages old,
From whatsoe'er my wakened thoughts create   1515
    Out of the hopes of thine aspirings bold,

Have I collected language to unfold
Truth to my countrymen; from shore to shore
    Doctrines of human power my words have told,
They have been heard, and men aspire to more   1520
Than they have ever gained or ever lost of yore.

                          XIII

'In secret chambers parents read, and weep,
    My writings to their babes, no longer blind;
And young men gather when their tyrants sleep,
    And vows of faith each to the other bind;   1525
    And marriageable maidens, who have pined
With love, till life seemed melting through their look,
    A warmer zeal, a nobler hope now find;
And every bosom thus is rapt and shook,
Like autumn's myriad leaves in one swoln mountain-brook.

                          XIV

'The tyrants of the Golden City tremble   1531
    At voices which are heard about the streets,
The ministers of fraud can scarce dissemble
    The lies of their own heart; but when one meets
    Another at the shrine, he inly weets,   1535
Though he says nothing, that the truth is known;
    Murderers are pale upon the judgement-seats,
And gold grows vile even to the wealthy crone,
And laughter fills the Fane, and curses shake the Throne.

                          XV

'Kind thoughts, and mighty hopes, and gentle deeds   1540
    Abound, for fearless love, and the pure law
Of mild equality and peace, succeeds
    To faiths which long have held the world in awe,
    Bloody and false, and cold:—as whirlpools draw
All wrecks of Ocean to their chasm, the sway   1545
    Of thy strong genius, Laon, which foresaw
This hope, compels all spirits to obey,
Which round thy secret strength now throng in wide array.

                          XVI

'For I have been thy passive instrument'—
    (As thus the old man spake, his countenance   1550
Gleamed on me like a spirit's)—'thou hast lent
    To me, to all, the power to advance

Towards this unforeseen deliverance
From our ancestral chains—ay, thou didst rear
     That lamp of hope on high, which time nor chance   1555
Nor change may not extinguish, and my share
Of good, was o'er the world its gathered beams to bear.

XVII

'But I, alas! am both unknown and old,
     And though the woof of wisdom I know well
To dye in hues of language, I am cold   1560
     In seeming, and the hopes which inly dwell,
     My manners note that I did long repel;
But Laon's name to the tumultuous throng
     Were like the star whose beams the waves compel
And tempests, and his soul-subduing tongue   1565
Were as a lance to quell the maìlèd crest of wrong.

XVIII

'Perchance blood need not flow, if thou at length
     Wouldst rise, perchance the very slaves would spare
Their brethren and themselves; great is the strength
     Of words—for lately did a maiden fair,   1570
     Who from her childhood has been taught to bear
The tyrant's heaviest yoke, arise, and make
     Her sex the law of truth and freedom hear,
And with these quiet words—"For thine own sake
I prithee spare me;"—did with ruth so take   1575

XIX

'All hearts, that even the torturer who had bound
     Her meek calm frame, ere it was yet impaled,
Loosened her, weeping then; nor could be found
     One human hand to harm her—unassailed
     Therefore she walks through the great City, veiled   1580
In virtue's adamantine eloquence,
     'Gainst scorn, and death and pain thus trebly mailed,
And blending, in the smiles of that defence,
The Serpent and the Dove, Wisdom and Innocence.

XX

'The wild-eyed women throng around her path: 1585
     From their luxurious dungeons, from the dust
Of meaner thralls, from the oppressor's wrath,
     Or the caresses of his sated lust

They congregate:—in her they put their trust;
The tyrants send their armèd slaves to quell   1590
    Her power;—they, even like a thunder-gust
Caught by some forest, bend beneath the spell
Of that young maiden's speech, and to their chiefs rebel.

XXI

'Thus she doth equal laws and justice teach
    To woman, outraged and polluted long;   1595
Gathering the sweetest fruit in human reach
    For those fair hands now free, while armèd wrong
    Trembles before her look, though it be strong;
Thousands thus dwell beside her, virgins bright,
    And matrons with their babes, a stately throng!   1600
Lovers renew the vows which they did plight
In early faith, and hearts long parted now unite,

XXII

'And homeless orphans find a home near her,
    And those poor victims of the proud, no less,
Fair wrecks, on whom the smiling world with stir,   1605
    Thrusts the redemption of its wickedness:—
    In squalid huts, and in its palaces
Sits Lust alone, while o'er the land is borne
    Her voice, whose awful sweetness doth repress
All evil, and her foes relenting turn,   1610
And cast the vote of love in hope's abandoned urn.

XXIII

'So in the populous City, a young maiden
    Has baffled Havoc of the prey which he
Marks as his own, whene'er with chains o'erladen
    Men make them arms to hurl down tyranny,—   1615
    False arbiter between the bound and free;
And o'er the land, in hamlets and in towns
    The multitudes collect tumultuously,
And throng in arms; but tyranny disowns
Their claim, and gathers strength around its trembling
                    thrones.   1620

XXIV

'Blood soon, although unwillingly, to shed,
    The free cannot forbear—the Queen of Slaves,
The hoodwinked Angel of the blind and dead,
    Custom, with iron mace points to the graves

Where her own standard desolately waves   1625
Over the dust of Prophets and of Kings.
  Many yet stand in her array—"she paves
Her path with human hearts," and o'er it flings
The wildering gloom of her immeasurable wings.

XXV

'There is a plain beneath the City's wall,   1630
  Bounded by misty mountains, wide and vast,
Millions there lift at Freedom's thrilling call
  Ten thousand standards wide, they load the blast
  Which bears one sound of many voices past,
And startles on his throne their sceptred foe: 1635
  He sits amid his idle pomp aghast,
And that his power hath passed away, doth know—
Why pause the victor swords to seal his overthrow?

XXVI

'The tyrant's guards resistance yet maintain:
  Fearless, and fierce, and hard as beasts of blood,   1640
They stand a speck amid the peopled plain;
  Carnage and ruin have been made their food
  From infancy—ill has become their good,
And for its hateful sake their will has wove
  The chains which eat their hearts—the multitude   1645
Surrounding them, with words of human love,
Seek from their own decay their stubborn minds to move.

XXVII

'Over the land is felt a sudden pause,
  As night and day those ruthless bands around,
The watch of love is kept:—a trance which awes   1650
  The thoughts of men with hope—as, when the sound
  Of whirlwind, whose fierce blasts the waves and clouds con-
      found,
Dies suddenly, the mariner in fear
  Feels silence sink upon his heart—thus bound,
The conquerors pause, and oh! may freemen ne'er   1655
Clasp the relentless knees of Dread the murderer!

XXVIII

'If blood be shed, 'tis but a change and choice
  Of bonds,—from slavery to cowardice
A wretched fall!—Uplift thy charmèd voice!
  Pour on those evil men the love that lies   1660

Hovering within those spirit-soothing eyes—
   Arise, my friend, farewell!'—As thus he spake,
    From the green earth lightly I did arise,
   As one out of dim dreams that doth awake,
And looked upon the depth of that reposing lake.   1665

XXIX

I saw my countenance reflected there;—
   And then my youth fell on me like a wind
Descending on still waters—my thin hair
    Was prematurely gray, my face was lined
    With channels, such as suffering leaves behind,   1670
Not age; my brow was pale, but in my cheek
    And lips a flush of gnawing fire did find
Their food and dwelling; though mine eyes might speak
A subtle mind and strong within a frame thus weak.

XXX

And though their lustre now was spent and faded,   1675
   Yet in my hollow looks and withered mien
The likeness of a shape for which was braided
    The brightest woof of genius, still was seen—
    One who, methought, had gone from the world's scene,
And left it vacant—'twas her lover's face—   1680
    It might resemble her—it once had been
The mirror of her thoughts, and still the grace
Which her mind's shadow cast, left there a lingering trace.

XXXI

What then was I? She slumbered with the dead.
   Glory and joy and peace, had come and gone.   1685
Doth the cloud perish, when the beams are fled
    Which steeped its skirts in gold? or, dark and lone,
    Doth it not through the paths of night unknown,
On outspread wings of its own wind upborne
    Pour rain upon the earth? The stars are shown,   1690
When the cold moon sharpens her silver horn
Under the sea, and make the wide night not forlorn.

XXXII

Strengthened in heart, yet sad, that aged man
   I left, with interchange of looks and tears,
And lingering speech, and to the Camp began   1695
    My way. O'er many a mountain-chain which rears

    Its hundred crests aloft, my spirit bears
My frame: o'er many a dale and many a moor,
    And gaily now meseems serene earth wears
    The blosmy spring's star-bright investiture,   1700
A vision which aught sad from sadness might allure.

                    XXXIII

My powers revived within me, and I went
    As one whom winds waft o'er the bending grass,
Through many a vale of that broad continent.
    At night when I reposed, fair dreams did pass   1705
    Before my pillow;—my own Cythna was,
Not like a child of death, among them ever;
    When I arose from rest, a woful mass
That gentlest sleep seemed from my life to sever,
As if the light of youth were not withdrawn for ever.   1710

                    XXXIV

Aye as I went, that maiden who had reared
    The torch of Truth afar, of whose high deeds
The Hermit in his pilgrimage had heard,
    Haunted my thoughts.—Ah, Hope its sickness feeds
    With whatso'er it finds, or flowers or weeds!   1715
Could she be Cythna?—Was that corpse a shade
    Such as self-torturing thought from madness breeds?
Why was this hope not torture? Yet it made
A light around my steps which would not ever fade.

                   CANTO V
                       I

OVER the utmost hill at length I sped,   1720
    A snowy steep:—the moon was hanging low
Over the Asian mountains, and outspread
    The plain, the City, and the Camp below,
    Skirted the midnight Ocean's glimmering flow;
The City's moonlit spires and myriad lamps,   1725
    Like stars in a sublunar sky did glow,
And fires blazed far amid the scattered camps,
Like springs of flame, which burst where'er swift Earthquake
        stamps.

                       II

All slept but those in watchful arms who stood,
    And those who sate tending the beacon's light,   1730
And the few sounds from that vast multitude
    Made silence more profound.—Oh, what a might

Of human thought was cradled in that night!
How many hearts impenetrably veiled
   Beat underneath its shade, what secret fight   1735
Evil and good, in woven passions mailed,
Waged through that silent throng; a war that never failed!

III

And now the Power of Good held victory,
   So, through the labyrinth of many a tent,
Among the silent millions who did lie   1740
   In innocent sleep, exultingly I went;
   The moon had left Heaven desert now, but lent
From eastern morn the first faint lustre showed
   An armèd youth—over his spear he bent
His downward face.—'A friend!' I cried aloud,   1745
And quickly common hopes made freemen understood.

IV

I sate beside him while the morning beam
   Crept slowly over Heaven, and talked with him
Of those immortal hopes, a glorious theme!
   Which led us forth, until the stars grew dim: 1750
   And all the while, methought, his voice did swim
As if it drownèd in remembrance were
   Of thoughts which make the moist eyes overbrim:
At last, when daylight 'gan to fill the air,
He looked on me, and cried in wonder—'Thou art here!' 1755

V

Then, suddenly, I knew it was the youth
   In whom its earliest hopes my spirit found;
But envious tongues had stained his spotless truth,
   And thoughtless pride his love in silence bound,
   And shame and sorrow mine in toils had wound,   1760
Whilst he was innocent, and I deluded;
   The truth now came upon me, on the ground
Tears of repenting joy, which fast intruded,
Fell fast, and o'er its peace our mingling spirits brooded.

VI

Thus, while with rapid lips and earnest eyes   1765
   We talked, a sound of sweeping conflict spread
As from the earth did suddenly arise;
   From every tent roused by that clamour dread,

Our bands outsprung and seized their arms—we sped
Towards the sound: our tribes were gathering far.   1770
Those sanguine slaves amid ten thousand dead
Stabbed in their sleep, trampled in treacherous war
The gentle hearts whose power their lives had sought to spare.

VII

Like rabid snakes, that sting some gentle child
  Who brings them food, when winter false and fair   1775
Allures them forth with its cold smiles, so wild
  They rage among the camp;—they overbear
  The patriot hosts—confusion, then despair
Descends like night—when 'Laon!' one did cry:
  Like a bright ghost from Heaven that shout did scare
The slaves, and widening through the vaulted sky,   1781
Seemed sent from Earth to Heaven in sign of victory.

VIII

In sudden panic those false murderers fled,
  Like insect tribes before the northern gale:
But swifter still, our hosts encompassèd   1785
  Their shattered ranks, and in a craggy vale,
  Where even their fierce despair might nought avail,
Hemmed them around!—and then revenge and fear
  Made the high virtue of the patriots fail:
One pointed on his foe the mortal spear—   1790
I rushed before its point, and cried, 'Forbear, forbear!'

IX

The spear transfixed my arm that was uplifted
  In swift expostulation, and the blood
Gushed round its point: I smiled, and—'Oh! thou gifted
  With eloquence which shall not be withstood,   1795
  Flow thus!'—I cried in joy, 'thou vital flood,
Until my heart be dry, ere thus the cause
  For which thou wert aught worthy be subdued—
Ah, ye are pale,—ye weep,—your passions pause,—
'Tis well! ye feel the truth of love's benignant laws.   1800

X

'Soldiers, our brethren and our friends are slain.
  Ye murdered them, I think, as they did sleep!
Alas, what have ye done? the slightest pain
  Which ye might suffer, there were eyes to weep,

But ye have quenched them—there were smiles to steep
   Your hearts in balm, but they are lost in woe;   1806
   And those whom love did set his watch to keep
     Around your tents, truth's freedom to bestow,
Ye stabbed as they did sleep—but they forgive ye now.

XI

'Oh wherefore should ill ever flow from ill,   1810
   And pain still keener pain for ever breed?
We all are brethren—even the slaves who kill
   For hire, are men; and to avenge misdeed
   On the misdoer, doth but Misery feed
With her own broken heart! O Earth, O Heaven!   1815
   And thou, dread Nature, which to every deed
And all that lives or is, to be hath given,
Even as to thee have these done ill, and are forgiven!

XII

'Join then your hands and hearts, and let the past
   Be as a grave which gives not up its dead   1820
To evil thoughts.'—A film then overcast
   My sense with dimness, for the wound, which bled
   Freshly, swift shadows o'er mine eyes had shed.
When I awoke, I lay mid friends and foes,
   And earnest countenances on me shed   1825
   The light of questioning looks, whilst one did close
My wound with balmiest herbs, and soothed me to repose;

XIII

And one whose spear had pierced me, leaned beside,
   With quivering lips and humid eyes;—and all
Seemed like some brothers on a journey wide   1830
   Gone forth, whom now strange meeting did befall
   In a strange land, round one whom they might call
Their friend, their chief, their father, for assay
   Of peril, which had saved them from the thrall
Of death, now suffering. Thus the vast array   1835
Of those fraternal bands were reconciled that day.

XIV

Lifting the thunder of their acclamation,
   Towards the City then the multitude,
And I among them, went in joy—a nation
   Made free by love;—a mighty brotherhood   1840

Linked by a jealous interchange of good;
  A glorious pageant, more magnificent
    Than kingly slaves arrayed in gold and blood,
  When they return from carnage, and are sent
In triumph bright beneath the populous battlement.   1845

XV

Afar, the city-walls were thronged on high,
  And myriads on each giddy turret clung,
And to each spire far lessening in the sky
  Bright pennons on the idle winds were hung;
  As we approached, a shout of joyance sprung   1850
At once from all the crowd, as if the vast
  And peopled Earth its boundless skies among
The sudden clamour of delight had cast,
When from before its face some general wreck had passed.

XVI

Our armies through the City's hundred gates   1855
  Were poured, like brooks which to the rocky lair
Of some deep lake, whose silence them awaits,
  Throng from the mountains when the storms are there
  And, as we passed through the calm sunny air
A thousand flower-inwoven crowns were shed,   1860
  The token flowers of truth and freedom fair,
And fairest hands bound them on many a head,
Those angels of love's heaven, that over all was spread.

XVII

I trod as one tranced in some rapturous vision:
  Those bloody bands so lately reconciled,   1865
Were, ever as they went, by the contrition
  Of anger turned to love, from ill beguiled,
  And every one on them more gently smiled,
Because they had done evil:—the sweet awe
  Of such mild looks made their own hearts grow mild,
And did with soft attraction ever draw   1871
Their spirits to the love of freedom's equal law.

XVIII

And they, and all, in one loud symphony
  My name with Liberty commingling, lifted,
'The friend and the preserver of the free!   1875
  The parent of this joy!' and fair eyes gifted

With feelings, caught from one who had uplifted
The light of a great spirit, round me shone;
  And all the shapes of this grand scenery shifted
Like restless clouds before the steadfast sun,—   1880
Where was that Maid? I asked, but it was known of none.

XIX

Laone was the name her love had chosen,
  For she was nameless, and her birth none knew:
Where was Laone now?—The words were frozen
  Within my lips with fear; but to subdue   1885
  Such dreadful hope, to my great task was due,
And when at length one brought reply, that she
  To-morrow would appear, I then withdrew
To judge what need for that great throng might be,
For now the stars came thick over the twilight sea.   1890

XX

Yet need was none for rest or food to care,
  Even though that multitude was passing great,
Since each one for the other did prepare
  All kindly succour—Therefore to the gate
  Of the Imperial House, now desolate,   1895
I passed, and there was found aghast, alone,
  The fallen Tyrant!—Silently he sate
Upon the footstool of his golden throne,
Which, starred with sunny gems, in its own lustre shone.

XXI

Alone, but for one child, who led before him   1900
  A graceful dance: the only living thing
Of all the crowd, which thither to adore him
  Flocked yesterday, who solace sought to bring
  In his abandonment!—She knew the King
Had praised her dance of yore, and now she wove   1905
  Its circles, aye weeping and murmuring
Mid her sad task of unregarded love,
That to no smiles it might his speechless sadness move.

XXII

She fled to him, and wildly clasped his feet
  When human steps were heard:—he moved nor spoke,
Nor changed his hue, nor raised his looks to meet
  The gaze of strangers—our loud entrance woke   1911

The echoes of the hall, which circling broke
The calm of its recesses,—like a tomb
   Its sculptured walls vacantly to the stroke   1915
Of footfalls answered, and the twilight's gloom
Lay like a charnel's mist within the radiant dome.

XXIII

The little child stood up when we came nigh;
   Her lips and cheeks seemed very pale and wan,
But on her forehead, and within her eye   1920
   Lay beauty, which makes hearts that feed thereon
   Sick with excess of sweetness; on the throne
She leaned;—the King, with gathered brow, and lips
   Wreathed by long scorn, did inly sneer and frown
With hue like that when some great painter dips   1925
His pencil in the gloom of earthquake and eclipse.

XXIV

She stood beside him like a rainbow braided
   Within some storm, when scarce its shadows vast
From the blue paths of the swift sun have faded;
   A sweet and solemn smile, like Cythna's cast   1930
   One moment's light, which made my heart beat fast,
O'er that child's parted lips—a gleam of bliss,
   A shade of vanished days,—as the tears passed
Which wrapped it, even as with a father's kiss
I pressed those softest eyes in trembling tenderness.   1935

XXV

The sceptred wretch then from that solitude
   I drew, and, of his change compassionate,
With words of sadness soothed his rugged mood.
   But he, while pride and fear held deep debate,
   With sullen guile of ill-dissembled hate   1940
Glared on me as a toothless snake might glare:
   Pity, not scorn I felt, though desolate
The desolator now, and unaware
The curses which he mocked had caught him by the hair.

XXVI

I led him forth from that which now might seem   1945
   A gorgeous grave: through portals sculptured deep
With imagery beautiful as dream
   We went, and left the shades which tend on sleep

Over its unregarded gold to keep
Their silent watch.—The child trod faintingly,   1950
    And as she went, the tears which she did weep
Glanced in the starlight; wildered seemèd she,
And when I spake, for sobs she could not answer me.

XXVII

At last the tyrant cried, 'She hungers, slave,
    Stab her, or give her bread!'—It was a tone   1955
Such as sick fancies in a new-made grave
    Might hear. I trembled, for the truth was known;
    He with this child had thus been left alone,
And neither had gone forth for food,—but he
    In mingled pride and awe cowered near his throne,
And she a nursling of captivity   1961
Knew nought beyond those walls, nor what such change might be.

XXVIII

And he was troubled at a charm withdrawn
    Thus suddenly; that sceptres ruled no more—
That even from gold the dreadful strength was gone,   1965
    Which once made all things subject to its power—
    Such wonder seized him, as if hour by hour
The past had come again; and the swift fall
    Of one so great and terrible of yore,
To desolateness, in the hearts of all   1970
Like wonder stirred, who saw such awful change befall.

XXIX

A mighty crowd, such as the wide land pours
    Once in a thousand years, now gathered round
The fallen tyrant;—like the rush of showers
    Of hail in spring, pattering along the ground,   1975
    Their many footsteps fell, else came no sound
From the wide multitude: that lonely man
    Then knew the burden of his change, and found,
Concealing in the dust his visage wan,
Refuge from the keen looks which through his bosom ran.

XXX

And he was faint withal: I sate beside him   1981
    Upon the earth, and took that child so fair
From his weak arms, that ill might none betide him
    Or her;—when food was brought to them, her share

To his averted lips the child did bear, 1985
But, when she saw he had enough, she ate
   And wept the while;—the lonely man's despair
Hunger then overcame, and of his state
Forgetful, on the dust as in a trance he sate.

XXXI

Slowly the silence of the multitudes 1990
   Passed, as when far is heard in some lone dell
The gathering of a wind among the woods—
   'And he is fallen!' they cry, 'he who did dwell
   Like famine or the plague, or aught more fell
Among our homes, is fallen! the murderer 1995
   Who slaked his thirsting soul as from a well
Of blood and tears with ruin! he is here!
Sunk in a gulf of scorn from which none may him rear!'

XXXII

Then was heard—'He who judged let him be brought
   To judgement! blood for blood cries from the soil 2000
On which his crimes have deep pollution wrought!
   Shall Othman only unavenged despoil?
   Shall they who by the stress of grinding toil
Wrest from the unwilling earth his luxuries,
   Perish for crime, while his foul blood may boil, 2005
Or creep within his veins at will?—Arise!
And to high justice make her chosen sacrifice.'

XXXIII

'What do ye seek? what fear ye,' then I cried,
   Suddenly starting forth, 'that ye should shed
The blood of Othman?—if your hearts are tried 2010
   In the true love of freedom, cease to dread
   This one poor lonely man—beneath Heaven spread
In purest light above us all, through earth
   Maternal earth, who doth her sweet smiles shed
For all, let him go free; until the worth 2015
Of human nature win from these a second birth.

XXXIV

'What call ye *justice*? Is there one who ne'er
   In secret thought has wished another's ill?—
Are ye all pure? Let those stand forth who hear,
   And tremble not. Shall they insult and kill, 2020

If such they be? their mild eyes can they fill
With the false anger of the hypocrite?
    Alas, such were not pure,—the chastened will
Of virtue sees that justice is the light
Of love, and not revenge, and terror and despite.'   2025

XXXV

The murmur of the people, slowly dying,
    Paused as I spake, then those who near me were,
Cast gentle looks where the lone man was lying
    Shrouding his head, which now that infant fair
    Clasped on her lap in silence;—through the air   2030
Sobs were then heard, and many kissed my feet
    In pity's madness, and to the despair
Of him whom late they cursed, a solace sweet
His very victims brought—soft looks and speeches meet.

XXXVI

Then to a home for his repose assigned,   2035
    Accompanied by the still throng he went
In silence, where, to soothe his rankling mind,
    Some likeness of his ancient state was lent;
    And if his heart could have been innocent
As those who pardoned him, he might have ended   2040
    His days in peace; but his straight lips were bent,
Men said, into a smile which guile portended,
A sight with which that child like hope with fear was blended.

XXXVII

'Twas midnight now, the eve of that great day
    Whereon the many nations at whose call   2045
The chains of earth like mist melted away,
    Decreed to hold a sacred Festival,
    A rite to attest the equality of all
Who live. So to their homes, to dream or wake
    All went. The sleepless silence did recall   2050
Laone to my thoughts, with hopes that make
The flood recede from which their thirst they seek to slake.

XXXVIII

The dawn flowed forth, and from its purple fountains
    I drank those hopes which make the spirit quail,
As to the plain between the misty mountains   2055
    And the great City, with a countenance pale

I went:—it was a sight which might avail
To make men weep exulting tears, for whom
  Now first from human power the reverend veil
Was torn, to see Earth from her general womb   2060
Pour forth her swarming sons to a fraternal doom:

XXXIX

To see, far glancing in the misty morning,
  The signs of that innumerable host,
To hear one sound of many made, the warning
  Of Earth to Heaven from its free children tossed,   2065
  While the eternal hills, and the sea lost
In wavering light, and, starring the blue sky
  The city's myriad spires of gold, almost
With human joy made mute society—
Its witnesses with men who must hereafter be.   2070

XL

To see, like some vast island from the Ocean,
  The Altar of the Federation rear
Its pile i' the midst; a work which the devotion
  Of millions in one night created there,
  Sudden, as when the moonrise makes appear   2075
Strange clouds in the east; a marble pyramid
  Distinct with steps: that mighty shape did wear
The light of genius; its still shadow hid
Far ships: to know its height the morning mists forbid!

XLI

To hear the restless multitudes for ever   2080
  Around the base of that great Altar flow,
As on some mountain-islet burst and shiver
  Atlantic waves; and solemnly and slow
  As the wind bore that tumult to and fro,
To feel the dreamlike music, which did swim   2085
  Like beams through floating clouds on waves below
Falling in pauses, from that Altar dim
As silver-sounding tongues breathed an aëreal hymn.

XLII

To hear, to see, to live, was on that morn
  Lethean joy! so that all those assembled   2090
Cast off their memories of the past outworn;
  Two only bosoms with their own life trembled,

And mine was one,—and we had both dissembled;
  So with a beating heart I went, and one,
    Who having much, covets yet more, resembled;   2095
  A lost and dear possession, which not won,
He walks in lonely gloom beneath the noonday sun.

XLIII

To the great Pyramid I came: its stair
  With female choirs was thronged: the loveliest
Among the free, grouped with its sculptures rare;   2100
  As I approached, the morning's golden mist,
  Which now the wonder-stricken breezes kissed
With their cold lips, fled, and the summit shone
  Like Athos seen from Samothracia, dressed
In earliest light, by vintagers, and one   2105
Sate there, a female Shape upon an ivory throne:

XLIV

A Form most like the imagined habitant
  Of silver exhalations sprung from dawn,
By winds which feed on sunrise woven, to enchant
  The faiths of men: all mortal eyes were drawn,   2110
  As famished mariners through strange seas gone
Gaze on a burning watch-tower, by the light
  Of those divinest lineaments—alone
With thoughts which none could share, from that fair sight
I turned in sickness, for a veil shrouded her countenance bright.

XLV

And, neither did I hear the acclamations,   2116
  Which from brief silence bursting, filled the air
With her strange name and mine, from all the nations
  Which we, they said, in strength had gathered there
  From the sleep of bondage; nor the vision fair   2120
Of that bright pageantry beheld,—but blind
  And silent, as a breathing corpse did fare,
Leaning upon my friend, till like a wind
To fevered cheeks, a voice flowed o'er my troubled mind.

XLVI

Like music of some minstrel heavenly-gifted,   2125
  To one whom fiends enthral, this voice to me;
Scarce did I wish her veil to be uplifted,
  I was so calm and joyous.—I could see

The platform where we stood, the statues three
Which kept their marble watch on that high shrine,   2130
The multitudes, the mountains, and the sea;
As when eclipse hath passed, things sudden shine
To men's astonished eyes most clear and crystalline.

XLVII

At first Laone spoke most tremulously:
But soon her voice the calmness which it shed   2135
Gathered, and—'Thou art whom I sought to see,
And thou art our first votary here,' she said:
'I had a dear friend once, but he is dead!—
And of all those on the wide earth who breathe,
Thou dost resemble him alone—I spread   2140
This veil between us two, that thou beneath
Shouldst image one who may have been long lost in death.

XLVIII

'For this wilt thou not henceforth pardon me?
Yes, but those joys which silence well requite
Forbid reply;—why men have chosen me   2145
To be the Priestess of this holiest rite
I scarcely know, but that the floods of light
Which flow over the world, have borne me hither
To meet thee, long most dear; and now unite
Thine hand with mine, and may all comfort wither   2150
From both the hearts whose pulse in joy now beat together,

XLIX

'If our own will as others' law we bind,
If the foul worship trampled here we fear;
If as ourselves we cease to love our kind!'—
She paused, and pointed upwards—sculptured there   2155
Three shapes around her ivory throne appear;
One was a Giant, like a child asleep
On a loose rock, whose grasp crushed, as it were
In dream, sceptres and crowns; and one did keep
Its watchful eyes in doubt whether to smile or weep;   2160

L

A Woman sitting on the sculptured disk
Of the broad earth, and feeding from one breast
A human babe and a young basilisk;
Her looks were sweet as Heaven's when loveliest

In Autumn eves. The third Image was dressed   2165
In white wings swift as clouds in winter skies;
    Beneath his feet, 'mongst ghastliest forms, repressed
Lay Faith, an obscene worm, who sought to rise,
While calmly on the Sun he turned his diamond eyes.

LI

Beside that Image then I sate, while she   2170
    Stood, mid the throngs which ever ebbed and flowed,
Like light amid the shadows of the sea
    Cast from one cloudless star, and on the crowd
    That touch which none who feels forgets, bestowed;
And whilst the sun returned the steadfast gaze   2175
    Of the great Image, as o'er Heaven it glode.
That rite had place; it ceased when sunset's blaze
Burned o'er the isles. All stood in joy and deep amaze—
    —When in the silence of all spirits there
Laone's voice was felt, and through the air   2180
Her thrilling gestures spoke, most eloquently fair:—

I

'Calm art thou as yon sunset! swift and strong
As new-fledged Eagles, beautiful and young,
That float among the blinding beams of morning;
    And underneath thy feet writhe Faith, and Folly,   2185
    Custom, and Hell, and mortal Melancholy—
Hark! the Earth starts to hear the mighty warning
    Of thy voice sublime and holy;
    Its free spirits here assembled,
        See thee, feel thee, know thee now,—   2190
    To thy voice their hearts have trembled
        Like ten thousand clouds which flow
    With one wide wind as it flies!—
Wisdom! thy irresistible children rise
To hail thee, and the elements they chain   2195
And their own will, to swell the glory of thy train.

2

'O Spirit vast and deep as Night and Heaven!
Mother and soul of all to which is given
The light of life, the loveliness of being,
    Lo! thou dost re-ascend the human heart,   2200
    Thy throne of power, almighty as thou wert
In dreams of Poets old grown pale by seeing
    The shade of thee:—now, millions start

To feel thy lightnings through them burning:
Nature, or God, or Love, or Pleasure,   2205
Or Sympathy the sad tears turning
To mutual smiles, a drainless treasure,
Descends amidst us;—Scorn, and Hate,
Revenge and Selfishness are desolate—
A hundred nations swear that there shall be   2210
Pity and Peace and Love, among the good and free!

3

'Eldest of things, divine Equality!
Wisdom and Love are but the slaves of thee,
The Angels of thy sway, who pour around thee
Treasures from all the cells of human thought,   2215
And from the Stars, and from the Ocean brought,
And the last living heart whose beatings bound thee:
The powerful and the wise had sought
Thy coming, thou in light descending
O'er the wide land which is thine own   2220
Like the Spring whose breath is blending
All blasts of fragrance into one,
Comest upon the paths of men!—
Earth bares her general bosom to thy ken,
And all her children here in glory meet   2225
To feed upon thy smiles, and clasp thy sacred feet.

4

'My brethren, we are free! the plains and mountains,
The gray sea-shore, the forests and the fountains,
Are haunts of happiest dwellers;—man and woman,
Their common bondage burst, may freely borrow   2230
From lawless love a solace for their sorrow;
For oft we still must weep, since we are human.
A stormy night's serenest morrow,
Whose showers are pity's gentle tears,
Whose clouds are smiles of those that die   2235
Like infants without hopes or fears,
And whose beams are joys that lie
In blended hearts, now holds dominion;
The dawn of mind, which upwards on a pinion
Borne, swift as sunrise, far illumines space,   2240
And clasps this barren world in its own bright embrace!

5

'My brethren, we are free! The fruits are glowing
Beneath the stars, and the night winds are flowing

O'er the ripe corn, the birds and beasts are dreaming—
  Never again may blood of bird or beast 2245
    Stain with its venomous stream a human feast,
To the pure skies in accusation steaming;
    Avenging poisons shall have ceased
    To feed disease and fear and madness,
      The dwellers of the earth and air 2250
    Shall throng around our steps in gladness
    Seeking their food or refuge there.
Our toil from thought all glorious forms shall cull,
To make this Earth, our home, more beautiful,
And Science, and her sister Poesy, 2255
Shall clothe in light the fields and cities of the free!

6

'Victory, Victory to the prostrate nations!
Bear witness Night, and ye mute Constellations
Who gaze on us from your crystalline cars!
  Thoughts have gone forth whose powers can sleep no more!
  Victory! Victory! Earth's remotest shore, 2261
Regions which groan beneath the Antarctic stars,
    The green lands cradled in the roar
    Of western waves, and wildernesses
      Peopled and vast, which skirt the oceans 2265
    Where morning dyes her golden tresses,
    Shall soon partake our high emotions:
    Kings shall turn pale! Almighty Fear
The Fiend-God, when our charmèd name he hear,
Shall fade like shadow from his thousand fanes, 2270
While Truth with Joy enthroned o'er his lost empire reigns!'

LII

Ere she had ceased, the mists of night entwining
  Their dim woof, floated o'er the infinite throng;
She, like a spirit through the darkness shining,
  In tones whose sweetness silence did prolong, 2275
  As if to lingering winds they did belong,
Poured forth her inmost soul: a passionate speech
  With wild and thrilling pauses woven among,
Which whoso heard, was mute, for it could teach
To rapture like her own all listening hearts to reach. 2280

LIII

Her voice was as a mountain-stream which sweeps
  The withered leaves of Autumn to the lake,
And in some deep and narrow bay then sleeps
  In the shadow of the shores; as dead leaves wake

Under the wave, in flowers and herbs which make   2285
Those green depths beautiful when skies are blue,
    The multitude so moveless did partake
Such living change, and kindling murmurs flew
As o'er that speechless calm delight and wonder grew.

LIV

Over the plain the throngs were scattered then   2290
    In groups around the fires, which from the sea
Even to the gorge of the first mountain-glen
    Blazed wide and far: the banquet of the free
    Was spread beneath many a dark cypress-tree,
Beneath whose spires, which swayed in the red flame,   2295
    Reclining, as they ate, of Liberty,
And Hope, and Justice, and Laone's name,
Earth's children did a woof of happy converse frame.

LV

Their feast was such as Earth, the general mother,
    Pours from her fairest bosom, when she smiles   2300
In the embrace of Autumn;—to each other
    As when some parent fondly reconciles
    Her warring children, she their wrath beguiles
With her own sustenance; they relenting weep:
    Such was this Festival, which from their isles   2305
And continents, and winds, and oceans deep,
All shapes might throng to share, that fly, or walk, or creep,—

LVI

Might share in peace and innocence, for gore
    Or poison none this festal did pollute,
But piled on high, an overflowing store   2310
    Of pomegranates, and citrons, fairest fruit,
    Melons, and dates, and figs, and many a root
Sweet and sustaining, and bright grapes ere yet
    Accursed fire their mild juice could transmute
Into a mortal bane, and brown corn set   2315
In baskets; with pure streams their thirsting lips they wet.

LVII

Laone had descended from the shrine,
    And every deepest look and holiest mind
Fed on her form, though now those tones divine
    Were silent as she passed; she did unwind   2320

Her veil, as with the crowds of her own kind
She mixed; some impulse made my heart refrain
From seeking her that night, so I reclined
Amidst a group, where on the utmost plain
A festal watchfire burned beside the dusky main.   2325

LVIII

And joyous was our feast; pathetic talk,
And wit, and harmony of choral strains,
While far Orion o'er the waves did walk
That flow among the isles, held us in chains
Of sweet captivity, which none disdains   2330
Who feels: but when his zone grew dim in mist
Which clothes the Ocean's bosom, o'er the plains
The multitudes went homeward, to their rest,
Which that delightful day with its own shadow blessed.

CANTO VI

I

BESIDE the dimness of the glimmering sea,   2335
Weaving swift language from impassioned themes,
With that dear friend I lingered, who to me
So late had been restored, beneath the gleams
Of the silver stars; and ever in soft dreams
Of future love and peace sweet converse lapped   2340
Our willing fancies, till the pallid beams
Of the last watchfire fell, and darkness wrapped
The waves, and each bright chain of floating fire was snapped;

II

And till we came even to the City's wall
And the great gate; then, none knew whence or why,
Disquiet on the multitudes did fall: 2346
And first, one pale and breathless passed us by,
And stared and spoke not;—then with piercing cry
A troop of wild-eyed women, by the shrieks
Of their own terror driven,—tumultuously   2350
Hither and thither hurrying with pale cheeks,
Each one from fear unknown a sudden refuge seeks—

III

Then, rallying cries of treason and of danger
Resounded: and—'They come! to arms! to arms!
The Tyrant is amongst us, and the stranger   2355
Comes to enslave us in his name! to arms!'

In vain: for Panic, the pale fiend who charms
Strength to forswear her right, those millions swept
Like waves before the tempest—these alarms
Came to me, as to know their cause I lept   2360
On the gate's turret, and in rage and grief and scorn I wept!

IV

For to the North I saw the town on fire,
And its red light made morning pallid now,
Which burst over wide Asia;—louder, higher,
The yells of victory and the screams of woe   2365
I heard approach, and saw the throng below
Stream through the gates like foam-wrought waterfalls
Fed from a thousand storms—the fearful glow
Of bombs flares overhead—at intervals
The red artillery's bolt mangling among them falls.   2370

V

And now the horsemen come—and all was done
Swifter than I have spoken—I beheld
Their red swords flash in the unrisen sun.
I rushed among the rout, to have repelled
That miserable flight—one moment quelled   2375
By voice and looks and eloquent despair,
As if reproach from their own hearts withheld
Their steps, they stood; but soon came pouring there
New multitudes, and did those rallied bands o'erbear.

VI

I strove, as, drifted on some cataract   2380
By irresistible streams, some wretch might strive
Who hears its fatal roar:—the files compact
Whelmed me, and from the gate availed to drive
With quickening impulse, as each bolt did rive
Their ranks with bloodier chasm:—into the plain   2385
Disgorged at length the dead and the alive
In one dread mass, were parted, and the stain
Of blood, from mortal steel fell o'er the fields like rain.

VII

For now the despot's bloodhounds with their prey
Unarmed and unaware, were gorging deep   2390
Their gluttony of death; the loose array
Of horsemen o'er the wide fields murdering sweep,

And with loud laughter for their tyrant reap
A harvest sown with other hopes, the while,
Far overhead, ships from Propontis keep   2395
A killing rain of fire:—when the waves smile
As sudden earthquakes light many a volcano-isle,

VIII

Thus sudden, unexpected feast was spread
For the carrion-fowls of Heaven.—I saw the sight—
I moved—I lived—as o'er the heaps of dead,   2400
Whose stony eyes glared in the morning light
I trod;—to me there came no thought of flight,
But with loud cries of scorn which whoso heard
That dreaded death, felt in his veins the might
Of virtuous shame return, the crowd I stirred,   2405
And desperation's hope in many hearts recurred.

IX

A band of brothers gathering round me, made,
Although unarmed, a steadfast front, and still
Retreating, with stern looks beneath the shade
Of gathered eyebrows, did the victors fill   2410
With doubt even in success; deliberate will
Inspired our growing troop, not overthrown
It gained the shelter of a grassy hill,
And ever still our comrades were hewn down,
And their defenceless limbs beneath our footsteps strown.

X

Immovably we stood—in joy I found,   2416
Beside me then, firm as a giant pine
Among the mountain-vapours driven around,
The old man whom I loved—his eyes divine
With a mild look of courage answered mine,   2420
And my young friend was near, and ardently
His hand grasped mine a moment—now the line
Of war extended, to our rallying cry
As myriads flocked in love and brotherhood to die.

XI

For ever while the sun was climbing Heaven   2425
The horseman hewed our unarmed myriads down
Safely, though when by thirst of carnage driven
Too near, those slaves were swiftly overthrown

By hundreds leaping on them:—flesh and bone
Soon made our ghastly ramparts; then the shaft   2430
  Of the artillery from the sea was thrown
More fast and fiery, and the conquerors laughed
In pride to hear the wind our screams of torment waft.

XII

For on one side alone the hill gave shelter,
  So vast that phalanx of unconquered men,   2435
And there the living in the blood did welter
  Of the dead and dying, which, in that green glen,
  Like stifled torrents, made a plashy fen
Under the feet—thus was the butchery waged
  While the sun clomb Heaven's eastern steep—but when
It 'gan to sink—a fiercer combat raged,   2441
For in more doubtful strife the armies were engaged.

XIII

Within a cave upon the hill were found
  A bundle of rude pikes, the instrument
Of those who war but on their native ground   2445
  For natural rights: a shout of joyance sent
  Even from our hearts the wide air pierced and rent,
As those few arms the bravest and the best
  Seized, and each sixth, thus armed, did now present
A line which covered and sustained the rest,   2450
A confident phalanx, which the foe on every side invest.

XIV

That onset turned the foes to flight almost;
  But soon they saw their present strength, and knew
That coming night would to our resolute host
  Bring victory; so dismounting, close they drew   2455
  Their glittering files, and then the combat grew
Unequal but most horrible;—and ever
  Our myriads, whom the swift bolt overthrew,
Or the red sword, failed like a mountain-river
Which rushes forth in foam to sink in sands for ever.   2460

XV

Sorrow and shame, to see with their own kind
  Our human brethren mix, like beasts of blood,
To mutual ruin armed by one behind
  Who sits and scoffs!—That friend so mild and good,

Who like its shadow near my youth had stood,   2465
Was stabbed!—my old preserver's hoary hair
    With the flesh clinging to its roots, was strewed
Under my feet!—I lost all sense or care,
And like the rest I grew desperate and unaware.

XVI

The battle became ghastlier—in the midst   2470
    I paused, and saw, how ugly and how fell
O Hate! thou art, even when thy life thou shedd'st
    For love. The ground in many a little dell
    Was broken, up and down whose steeps befell
Alternate victory and defeat, and there   2475
    The combatants with rage most horrible
Strove, and their eyes started with cracking stare,
And impotent their tongues they lolled into the air,

XVII

Flaccid and foamy, like a mad dog's hanging;
    Want, and Moon-madness, and the pest's swift Bane   2480
When its shafts smite—while yet its bow is twanging—
    Have each their mark and sign—some ghastly stain;
    And this was thine, O War! of hate and pain
Thou loathèd slave. I saw all shapes of death
    And ministered to many, o'er the plain   2485
While carnage in the sunbeam's warmth did seethe,
Till twilight o'er the east wove her serenest wreath.

XVIII

The few who yet survived, resolute and firm
    Around me fought. At the decline of day
Winding above the mountain's snowy term   2490
    New banners shone: they quivered in the ray
    Of the sun's unseen orb—ere night the array
Of fresh troops hemmed us in—of those brave bands
    I soon survived alone—and now I lay
Vanquished and faint, the grasp of bloody hands   2495
I felt, and saw on high the glare of falling brands:

XIX

When on my foes a sudden terror came,
    And they fled, scattering—lo! with reinless speed
A black Tartarian horse of giant frame
    Comes trampling over the dead, the living bleed   2500

Beneath the hoofs of that tremendous steed,
On which, like to an Angel, robed in white,
  Sate one waving a sword;—the hosts recede
And fly, as through their ranks with awful might,
Sweeps in the shadow of eve that Phantom swift and bright;

XX

And its path made a solitude.—I rose   2506
  And marked its coming: it relaxed its course
As it approached me, and the wind that flows
  Through night, bore accents to mine ear whose force
  Might create smiles in death—the Tartar horse   2510
Paused, and I saw the shape its might which swayed,
  And heard her musical pants, like the sweet source
Of waters in the desert, as she said,
'Mount with me, Laon, now!'—I rapidly obeyed.

XXI

Then: 'Away! away!' she cried, and stretched her sword
  As 'twere a scourge over the courser's head,   2516
And lightly shook the reins.—We spake no word,
  But like the vapour of the tempest fled
  Over the plain; her dark hair was dispread
Like the pine's locks upon the lingering blast;   2520
  Over mine eyes its shadowy strings it spread
Fitfully, and the hills and streams fled fast,
As o'er their glimmering forms the steed's broad shadow passed.

XXII

And his hoofs ground the rocks to fire and dust,
  His strong sides made the torrents rise in spray,   2525
And turbulence, as of a whirlwind's gust
  Surrounded us;—and still away! away!
  Through the desert night we sped, while she alway
Gazed on a mountain which we neared, whose crest,
  Crowned with a marble ruin, in the ray   2530
Of the obscure stars gleamed;—its rugged breast
The steed strained up, and then his impulse did arrest.

XXIII

A rocky hill which overhung the Ocean:—
  From that lone ruin, when the steed that panted
Paused, might be heard the murmur of the motion   2535
  Of waters, as in spots for ever haunted

By the choicest winds of Heaven, which are enchanted
To music, by the wand of Solitude,
    That wizard wild, and the far tents implanted
    Upon the plain, be seen by those who stood   2540
Thence marking the dark shore of Ocean's curvèd flood.

XXIV

One moment these were heard and seen—another
    Passed; and the two who stood beneath that night,
Each only heard, or saw, or felt the other;
    As from the lofty steed she did alight,   2545
    Cythna, (for, from the eyes whose deepest light
Of love and sadness made my lips feel pale
    With influence strange of mournfullest delight,
My own sweet Cythna looked), with joy did quail,
And felt her strength in tears of human weakness fail.   2550

XXV

And for a space in my embrace she rested,
    Her head on my unquiet heart reposing,
While my faint arms her languid frame invested:
    At length she looked on me, and half unclosing
    Her tremulous lips, said: 'Friend, thy bands were losing
The battle, as I stood before the King   2556
    In bonds.—I burst them then, and swiftly choosing
The time, did seize a Tartar's sword, and spring
Upon his horse, and, swift as on the whirlwind's wing,

XXVI

'Have thou and I been borne beyond pursuer,   2560
    And we are here.'—Then turning to the steed,
She pressed the white moon on his front with pure
    And rose-like lips, and many a fragrant weed
    From the green ruin plucked, that he might feed;—
But I to a stone seat that Maiden led,   2565
    And kissing her fair eyes, said, 'Thou hast need
Of rest,' and I heaped up the courser's bed
In a green mossy nook, with mountain-flowers dispread.

XXVII

Within that ruin, where a shattered portal
    Looks to the eastern stars, abandoned now   2570
By man, to be the home of things immortal,
    Memories, like awful ghosts which come and go,

And must inherit all he builds below,
When he is gone, a hall stood; o'er whose roof
  Fair clinging weeds with ivy pale did grow,   2575
Clasping its gray rents with a verdurous woof,
A hanging dome of leaves, a canopy moon-proof.

XXVIII

The autumnal winds, as if spell-bound, had made
  A natural couch of leaves in that recess,
Which seasons none disturbed, but, in the shade   2580
  Of flowering parasites, did Spring love to dress
  With their sweet blooms the wintry loneliness
Of those dead leaves, shedding their stars, whene'er
  The wandering wind her nurslings might caress;
Whose intertwining fingers ever there   2585
Made music wild and soft that filled the listening air.

XXIX

We know not where we go, or what sweet dream
  May pilot us through caverns strange and fair
Of far and pathless passion, while the stream
  Of life, our bark doth on its whirlpools bear,   2590
  Spreading swift wings as sails to the dim air;
Nor should we seek to know, so the devotion
  Of love and gentle thoughts be heard still there
Louder and louder from the utmost Ocean
Of universal life, attuning its commotion.   2595

XXX

To the pure all things are pure! Oblivion wrapped
  Our spirits, and the fearful overthrow
Of public hope was from our being snapped,
  Though linkèd years had bound it there; for now
  A power, a thirst, a knowledge, which below   2600
All thoughts, like light beyond the atmosphere,
  Clothing its clouds with grace, doth ever flow,
Came on us, as we sate in silence there,
Beneath the golden stars of the clear azure air:—

XXXI

In silence which doth follow talk that causes   2605
  The baffled heart to speak with sighs and tears,
When wildering passion swalloweth up the pauses
  Of inexpressive speech:—the youthful years

Which we together passed, their hopes and fears,
　　The blood itself which ran within our frames,　　　　2610
　　That likeness of the features which endears
　　The thoughts expressed by them, our very names,
And all the wingèd hours which speechless memory claims,

XXXII

Had found a voice—and ere that voice did pass,
　　The night grew damp and dim, and through a rent　　2615
Of the ruin where we sate, from the morass,
　　A wandering Meteor by some wild wind sent,
　　Hung high in the green dome, to which it lent
A faint and pallid lustre; while the song
　　Of blasts, in which its blue hair quivering bent,　　　2620
Strewed strangest sounds the moving leaves among;
A wondrous light, the sound as of a spirit's tongue.

XXXIII

The Meteor showed the leaves on which we sate,
　　And Cythna's glowing arms, and the thick ties
Of her soft hair, which bent with gathered weight　　　2625
　　My neck near hers, her dark and deepening eyes,
　　Which, as twin phantoms of one star that lies
O'er a dim well, move, though the star reposes,
　　Swam in our mute and liquid ecstasies,
Her marble brow, and eager lips, like roses,　　　　2630
With their own fragrance pale, which Spring but half uncloses.

XXXIV

The Meteor to its far morass returned:
　　The beating of our veins one interval
Made still; and then I felt the blood that burned
　　Within her frame, mingle with mine, and fall　　　2635
　　Around my heart like fire; and over all
A mist was spread, the sickness of a deep
　　And speechless swoon of joy, as might befall
Two disunited spirits when they leap
In union from this earth's obscure and fading sleep.　　2640

XXXV

Was it one moment that confounded thus
　　All thought, all sense, all feeling, into one
Unutterable power, which shielded us
　　Even from our own cold looks, when we had gone

Into a wide and wild oblivion 2645
Of tumult and of tenderness? or now
Had ages, such as make the moon and sun,
The seasons, and mankind their changes know,
Left fear and time unfelt by us alone below?

XXXVI

I know not. What are kisses whose fire clasps 2650
The failing heart in languishment, or limb
Twined within limb? or the quick dying gasps
Of the life meeting, when the faint eyes swim
Through tears of a wide mist boundless and dim,
In one caress? What is the strong control 2655
Which leads the heart that dizzy steep to climb,
Where far over the world those vapours roll,
Which blend two restless frames in one reposing soul?

XXXVII

It is the shadow which doth float unseen,
But not unfelt, o'er blind mortality, 2660
Whose divine darkness fled not, from that green
And lone recess, where lapped in peace did lie
Our linkèd frames till, from the changing sky,
That night and still another day had fled;
And then I saw and felt. The moon was high, 2665
And clouds, as of a coming storm, were spread
Under its orb,—loud winds were gathering overhead.

XXXVIII

Cythna's sweet lips seemed lurid in the moon,
Her fairest limbs with the night wind were chill,
And her dark tresses were all loosely strewn 2670
O'er her pale bosom:—all within was still,
And the sweet peace of joy did almost fill
The depth of her unfathomable look;—
And we sate calmly, though that rocky hill,
The waves contending in its caverns strook, 2675
For they foreknew the storm, and the gray ruin shook.

XXXIX

There we unheeding sate, in the communion
Of interchangèd vows, which, with a rite
Of faith most sweet and sacred, stamped our union.—
Few were the living hearts which could unite 2680

Like ours, or celebrate a bridal-night
With such close sympathies, for they had sprung
From linkèd youth, and from the gentle might
   Of earliest love, delayed and cherished long,
Which common hopes and fears made, like a tempest, strong.

XL

And such is Nature's law divine, that those   2686
   Who grow together cannot choose but love,
If faith or custom do not interpose,
   Or common slavery mar what else might move
   All gentlest thoughts; as in the sacred grove   2690
Which shades the springs of Ethiopian Nile,
   That living tree, which, if the arrowy dove
Strike with her shadow, shrinks in fear awhile,
But its own kindred leaves clasps while the sunbeams smile;

XLI

And clings to them, when darkness may dissever   2695
   The close caresses of all duller plants
Which bloom on the wide earth—thus we for ever
   Were linked, for love had nursed us in the haunts
   Where knowledge, from its secret source enchants
Young hearts with the fresh music of its springing,   2700
   Ere yet its gathered flood feeds human wants,
As the great Nile feeds Egypt; ever flinging
Light on the woven boughs which o'er its waves are swinging.

XLII

The tones of Cythna's voice like echoes were
   Of those far murmuring streams; they rose and fell,
Mixed with mine own in the tempestuous air,—   2706
   And so we sate, until our talk befell
   Of the late ruin, swift and horrible,
And how those seeds of hope might yet be sown,
   Whose fruit is evil's mortal poison: well,   2710
For us, this ruin made a watch-tower lone,
But Cythna's eyes looked faint, and now two days were gone

XLIII

Since she had food:—therefore I did awaken
   The Tartar steed, who, from his ebon mane
Soon as the clinging slumbers he had shaken,   2715
   Bent his thin head to seek the brazen rein,

Following me obediently; with pain
Of heart, so deep and dread, that one caress,
  When lips and heart refuse to part again
Till they have told their fill, could scarce express   2720
The anguish of her mute and fearful tenderness,

XLIV

Cythna beheld me part, as I bestrode
  That willing steed—the tempest and the night,
Which gave my path its safety as I rode
  Down the ravine of rocks, did soon unite   2725
  The darkness and the tumult of their might
Borne on all winds.—Far through the streaming rain
  Floating at intervals the garments white
Of Cythna gleamed, and her voice once again
Came to me on the gust, and soon I reached the plain.   2730

XLV

I dreaded not the tempest, nor did he
  Who bore me, but his eyeballs wide and red
Turned on the lightning's cleft exultingly;
  And when the earth beneath his tameless tread,
  Shook with the sullen thunder, he would spread   2735
His nostrils to the blast, and joyously
  Mock the fierce peal with neighings;—thus we sped
O'er the lit plain, and soon I could descry
Where Death and Fire had gorged the spoil of victory.

XLVI

There was a desolate village in a wood   2740
  Whose bloom-inwoven leaves now scattering fed
The hungry storm; it was a place of blood,
  A heap of heartless walls;—the flames were dead
  Within those dwellings now,—the life had fled
From all those corpses now,—but the wide sky   2745
  Flooded with lightning was ribbed overhead
By the black rafters, and around did lie
Women, and babes, and men, slaughtered confusedly.

XLVII

Beside the fountain in the market-place
  Dismounting, I beheld those corpses stare   2750
With horny eyes upon each other's face,
  And on the earth and on the vacant air,

And upon me, close to the waters where
I stooped to slake my thirst;—I shrank to taste,
    For the salt bitterness of blood was there;   2755
But tied the steed beside, and sought in haste
If any yet survived amid that ghastly waste.

XLVIII

No living thing was there beside one woman,
    Whom I found wandering in the streets, and she
Was withered from a likeness of aught human   2760
    Into a fiend, by some strange misery:
    Soon as she heard my steps she leaped on me,
And glued her burning lips to mine, and laughed
With a loud, long, and frantic laugh of glee,
And cried, 'Now, Mortal, thou hast deeply quaffed   2765
The Plague's blue kisses—soon millions shall pledge the
        draught!

XLIX

'My name is Pestilence—this bosom dry,
    Once fed two babes—a sister and a brother—
When I came home, one in the blood did lie
    Of three death-wounds—the flames had ate the other!
    Since then I have no longer been a mother,   2771
But I am Pestilence;—hither and thither
    I flit about, that I may slay and smother:—
All lips which I have kissed must surely wither,
But Death's—if thou art he, we'll go to work together!   2775

L

'What seek'st thou here? The moonlight comes in flashes,—
    The dew is rising dankly from the dell—
'Twill moisten her! and thou shalt see the gashes
    In my sweet boy, now full of worms—but tell
    First what thou seek'st.'—'I seek for food.'—' 'Tis well,
Thou shalt have food; Famine, my paramour,   2781
    Waits for us at the feast—cruel and fell
Is Famine, but he drives not from his door
Those whom these lips have kissed, alone. No more, no more!'

LI

As thus she spake, she grasped me with the strength   2785
    Of madness, and by many a ruined hearth
She led, and over many a corpse:—at length
    We came to a lone hut where on the earth

Which made its floor, she in her ghastly mirth
Gathering from all those homes now desolate,   2790
  Had piled three heaps of loaves, making a dearth
  Among the dead—round which she set in state
A ring of cold, stiff babes; silent and stark they sate.

LII

She leaped upon a pile, and lifted high
  Her mad looks to the lightning, and cried: 'Eat!   2795
Share the great feast—to-morrow we must die!'
  And then she spurned the loaves with her pale feet,
  Towards her bloodless guests;—that sight to meet,
Mine eyes and my heart ached, and but that she
  Who loved me, did with absent looks defeat   2800
Despair, I might have raved in sympathy;
But now I took the food that woman offered me;

LIII

And vainly having with her madness striven
  If I might win her to return with me,
Departed. In the eastern beams of Heaven   2805
  The lightning now grew pallid—rapidly,
  As by the shore of the tempestuous sea
The dark steed bore me, and the mountain gray
  Soon echoed to his hoofs, and I could see
Cythna among the rocks, where she alway   2810
Had sate, with anxious eyes fixed on the lingering day.

LIV

And joy was ours to meet: she was most pale,
  Famished, and wet and weary, so I cast
My arms around her, lest her steps should fail
  As to our home we went, and thus embraced,   2815
  Her full heart seemed a deeper joy to taste
Than e'er the prosperous know; the steed behind
  Trod peacefully along the mountain waste:
We reached our home ere morning could unbind
Night's latest veil, and on our bridal-couch reclined.   2820

LV

Her chilled heart having cherished in my bosom,
  And sweetest kisses past, we two did share
Our peaceful meal:—as an autumnal blossom
  Which spreads its shrunk leaves in the sunny air,

After cold showers, like rainbows woven there, 2825
Thus in her lips and cheeks the vital spirit
  Mantled, and in her eyes, an atmosphere
Of health, and hope; and sorrow languished near it,
And fear, and all that dark despondence doth inherit.

CANTO VII

I

So we sate joyous as the morning ray 2830
  Which fed upon the wrecks of night and storm
Now lingering on the winds; light airs did play
  Among the dewy weeds, the sun was warm,
  And we sate linked in the inwoven charm
Of converse and caresses sweet and deep, 2835
  Speechless caresses, talk that might disarm
Time, though he wield the darts of death and sleep,
And those thrice mortal barbs in his own poison steep.

II

I told her of my sufferings and my madness,
  And how, awakened from that dreamy mood 2840
By Liberty's uprise, the strength of gladness
  Came to my spirit in my solitude;
  And all that now I was—while tears pursued
Each other down her fair and glistening cheek
  Fast as the thoughts which fed them, like a flood 2845
From sunbright dales; and when I ceased to speak,
Her accents soft and sweet the pausing air did wake.

III

She told me a strange tale of strange endurance,
  Like broken memories of many a heart
Woven into one; to which no firm assurance, 2850
  So wild were they, could her own faith impart.
  She said that not a tear did dare to start
From the swoln brain, and that her thoughts were firm
  When from all mortal hope she did depart,
Borne by those slaves across the Ocean's term, 2855
And that she reached the port without one fear infirm.

IV

One was she among many there, the thralls
  Of the cold Tyrant's cruel lust: and they
Laughed mournfully in those polluted halls;
  But she was calm and sad, musing alway 2860

On loftiest enterprise, till on a day
The Tyrant heard her singing to her lute
A wild, and sad, and spirit-thrilling lay,
Like winds that die in wastes—one moment mute
The evil thoughts it made, which did his breast pollute.   2865

V

Even when he saw her wondrous loveliness,
One moment to great Nature's sacred power
He bent, and was no longer passionless;
But when he bade her to his secret bower
Be borne, a loveless victim, and she tore   2870
Her locks in agony, and her words of flame
And mightier looks availed not; then he bore
Again his load of slavery, and became
A king, a heartless beast, a pageant and a name.

VI

She told me what a loathsome agony   2875
Is that when selfishness mocks love's delight,
Foul as in dream's most fearful imagery
To dally with the mowing dead—that night
All torture, fear, or horror made seem light
Which the soul dreams or knows, and when the day   2880
Shone on her awful frenzy, from the sight
Where like a Spirit in fleshly chains she lay
Struggling, aghast and pale the Tyrant fled away.

VII

Her madness was a beam of light, a power   2884
Which dawned through the rent soul; and words it gave,
Gestures, and looks, such as in whirlwinds bore
Which might not be withstood—whence none could save—
All who approached their sphere,—like some calm wave
Vexed into whirlpools by the chasms beneath;
And sympathy made each attendant slave   2890
Fearless and free, and they began to breathe
Deep curses, like the voice of flames far underneath.

VIII

The King felt pale upon his noonday throne:
At night two slaves he to her chamber sent,—
One was a green and wrinkled eunuch, grown   2895
From human shape into an instrument

Of all things ill—distorted, bowed and bent.
The other was a wretch from infancy
  Made dumb by poison; who nought knew or meant
But to obey: from the fire-isles came he,   2900
A diver lean and strong, of Oman's coral sea.

IX

They bore her to a bark, and the swift stroke
  Of silent rowers clove the blue moonlight seas,
Until upon their path the morning broke;
  They anchored then, where, be there calm or breeze,   2905
  The gloomiest of the drear Symplegades
Shakes with the sleepless surge;—the Ethiop there
  Wound his long arms around her, and with knees
Like iron clasped her feet, and plunged with her
Among the closing waves out of the boundless air.   2910

X

'Swift as an eagle stooping from the plain
  Of morning light, into some shadowy wood,
He plunged through the green silence of the main,
  Through many a cavern which the eternal flood
  Had scooped, as dark lairs for its monster brood;   2915
And among mighty shapes which fled in wonder,
  And among mightier shadows which pursued
His heels, he wound: until the dark rocks under
He touched a golden chain—a sound arose like thunder.

XI

'A stunning clang of massive bolts redoubling   2920
  Beneath the deep—a burst of waters driven
As from the roots of the sea, raging and bubbling:
  And in that roof of crags a space was riven
  Through which there shone the emerald beams of heaven,
Shot through the lines of many waves inwoven,   2925
  Like sunlight through acacia woods at even,
Through which, his way the diver having cloven,
Passed like a spark sent up out of a burning oven.

XII

'And then,' she said, 'he laid me in a cave
  Above the waters, by that chasm of sea,   2930
A fountain round and vast, in which the wave
  Imprisoned, boiled and leaped perpetually,

Down which, one moment resting, he did flee,
Winning the adverse depth; that spacious cell
  Like an hupaithric temple wide and high,   2935
  Whose aëry dome is inaccessible,
Was pierced with one round cleft through which the sunbeams
    fell.

XIII

'Below, the fountain's brink was richly paven
  With the deep's wealth, coral, and pearl, and sand
Like spangling gold, and purple shells engraven   2940
  With mystic legends by no mortal hand,
  Left there, when thronging to the moon's command,
The gathering waves rent the Hesperian gate
  Of mountains, and on such bright floor did stand
Columns, and shapes like statues, and the state   2945
Of kingless thrones, which Earth did in her heart create.

XIV

'The fiend of madness which had made its prey
  Of my poor heart, was lulled to sleep awhile:
There was an interval of many a day,
  And a sea-eagle brought me food the while,   2950
  Whose nest was built in that untrodden isle,
And who, to be the gaoler had been taught
  Of that strange dungeon; as a friend whose smile
Like light and rest at morn and even is sought   2954
That wild bird was to me, till madness misery brought.

XV

'The misery of a madness slow and creeping,
  Which made the earth seem fire, the sea seem air,
And the white clouds of noon which oft were sleeping,
  In the blue heaven so beautiful and fair,
  Like hosts of ghastly shadows hovering there;   2960
And the sea-eagle looked a fiend, who bore
  Thy mangled limbs for food!—Thus all things were
Transformed into the agony which I wore
Even as a poisoned robe around my bosom's core.

XVI

'Again I knew the day and night fast fleeing,   2965
  The eagle, and the fountain, and the air;
Another frenzy came—there seemed a being
  Within me—a strange load my heart did bear.

As if some living thing had made its lair
Even in the fountains of my life:—a long   2970
    And wondrous vision wrought from my despair,
Then grew, like sweet reality among
Dim visionary woes, an unreposing throng.

XVII

'Methought I was about to be a mother—
    Month after month went by, and still I dreamed   2975
That we should soon be all to one another,
    I and my child; and still new pulses seemed
    To beat beside my heart, and still I deemed
There was a babe within—and, when the rain
    Of winter through the rifted cavern streamed,   2980
Methought, after a lapse of lingering pain,
I saw that lovely shape, which near my heart had lain.

XVIII

'It was a babe, beautiful from its birth,—
    It was like thee, dear love, its eyes were thine,
Its brow, its lips, and so upon the earth   2985
    It laid its fingers, as now rest on mine
    Thine own, belovèd!—'twas a dream divine;
Even to remember how it fled, how swift,
    How utterly, might make the heart repine,—
Though 'twas a dream.'—Then Cythna did uplift   2990
Her looks on mine, as if some doubt she sought to shift:

XIX

A doubt which would not flee, a tenderness
    Of questioning grief, a source of thronging tears:
Which having passed, as one whom sobs oppress
    She spoke: 'Yes, in the wilderness of years   2995
    Her memory, aye, like a green home appears;
She sucked her fill even at this breast, sweet love,
    For many month. I had no mortal fears;
Methought I felt her lips and breath approve,—
It was a human thing which to my bosom clove.   3000

XX

'I watched the dawn of her first smiles, and soon
    When zenith-stars were trembling on the wave,
Or when the beams of the invisible moon,
    Or sun, from many a prism within the cave

Their gem-born shadows to the water gave,   3005
Her looks would hunt them, and with outspread hand,
    From the swift lights which might that fountain pave,
She would mark one, and laugh, when that command
Slighting, it lingered there, and could not understand.

XXI

'Methought her looks began to talk with me;   3010
    And no articulate sounds, but something sweet
Her lips would frame,—so sweet it could not be,
    That it was meaningless; her touch would meet
    Mine, and our pulses calmly flow and beat
In response while we slept; and on a day   3015
    When I was happiest in that strange retreat,
With heaps of golden shells we two did play,—
Both infants, weaving wings for time's perpetual way.

XXII

'Ere night, methought, her waning eyes were grown
    Weary with joy, and tired with our delight,
We, on the earth, like sister twins lay down   3020
    On one fair mother's bosom:—from that night
    She fled;—like those illusions clear and bright,
Which dwell in lakes, when the red moon on high
    Pause ere it wakens tempest;—and her flight,   3025
Though 'twas the death of brainless fantasy,
Yet smote my lonesome heart more than all misery.

XXIII

'It seemed that in the dreary night, the diver
    Who brought me thither, came again, and bore
My child away. I saw the waters quiver,   3030
    When he so swiftly sunk, as once before;
    Then morning came—it shone even as of yore,
But I was changed—the very life was gone
    Out of my heart—I wasted more and more,
Day after day, and sitting there alone,   3035
Vexed the inconstant waves with my perpetual moan.

XXIV

'I was no longer mad, and yet methought
    My breasts were swoln and changed:—in every vein
The blood stood still one moment, while that thought
    Was passing—with a gush of sickening pain   3040

It ebbed even to its withered springs again:
When my wan eyes in stern resolve I turned
From that most strange delusion, which would fain
Have waked the dream for which my spirit yearned
With more than human love,—then left it unreturned.   3045

XXV

'So now my reason was restored to me
I struggled with that dream, which, like a beast
Most fierce and beauteous, in my memory
Had made its lair, and on my heart did feast;
But all that cave and all its shapes, possessed   3050
By thoughts which could not fade, renewed each one
Some smile, some look, some gesture which had blessed
Me heretofore: I, sitting there alone,
Vexed the inconstant waves with my perpetual moan.

XXVI

'Time passed, I know not whether months or years;
For day, nor night, nor change of seasons made   3056
Its note, but thoughts and unavailing tears:
And I became at last even as a shade,
A smoke, a cloud on which the winds have preyed,
Till it be thin as air; until, one even,   3060
A Nautilus upon the fountain played,
Spreading his azure sail where breath of Heaven
Descended not, among the waves and whirlpools driven.

XXVII

'And, when the Eagle came, that lovely thing,
Oaring with rosy feet its silver boat,   3065
Fled near me as for shelter; on slow wing,
The Eagle, hovering o'er his prey did float;
But when he saw that I with fear did note
His purpose, proffering my own food to him,
The eager plumes subsided on his throat—   3070
He came where that bright child of sea did swim,
And o'er it cast in peace his shadow broad and dim.

XXVIII

'This wakened me, it gave me human strength;
And hope, I knew not whence or wherefore, rose,
But I resumed my ancient powers at length;   3075
My spirit felt again like one of those

Like thine, whose fate it is to make the woes
Of humankind their prey—what was this cave?
Its deep foundation no firm purpose knows
Immutable, resistless, strong to save,   3080
Like mind while yet it mocks the all-devouring grave.

XXIX

'And where was Laon? might my heart be dead,
While that far dearer heart could move and be?
Or whilst over the earth the pall was spread,
Which I had sworn to rend? I might be free,   3085
Could I but win that friendly bird to me,
To bring me ropes; and long in vain I sought
By intercourse of mutual imagery
Of objects, if such aid he could be taught;
But fruit, and flowers, and boughs, yet never ropes he brought.

XXX

'We live in our own world, and mine was made   3091
From glorious fantasies of hope departed:
Aye we are darkened with their floating shade,
Or cast a lustre on them—time imparted
Such power to me—I became fearless-hearted,   3095
My eye and voice grew firm, calm was my mind,
And piercing, like the morn, now it has darted
Its lustre on all hidden things, behind
Yon dim and fading clouds which load the weary wind.

XXXI

'My mind became the book through which I grew   3100
Wise in all human wisdom, and its cave,
Which like a mine I rifled through and through,
To me the keeping of its secrets gave—
One mind, the type of all, the moveless wave
Whose calm reflects all moving things that are,   3105
Necessity, and love, and life, the grave,
And sympathy, fountains of hope and fear;
Justice, and truth, and time, and the world's natural sphere.

XXXII

'And on the sand would I make signs to range
These woofs, as they were woven, of my thought;   3110
Clear, elemental shapes, whose smallest change
A subtler language within language wrought:

The key of truths which once were dimly taught
In old Crotona;—and sweet melodies
　　Of love, in that lorn solitude I caught　　　　　3115
From mine own voice in dream, when thy dear eyes
Shone through my sleep, and did that utterance harmonize.

XXXIII

'Thy songs were winds whereon I fled at will,
　　As in a wingèd chariot, o'er the plain
Of crystal youth; and thou wert there to fill　　3120
　　My heart with joy, and there we sate again
　　On the gray margin of the glimmering main,
Happy as then but wiser far, for we
　　Smiled on the flowery grave in which were lain
Fear, Faith, and Slavery; and mankind was free,　3125
Equal, and pure, and wise, in Wisdom's prophecy.

XXXIV

'For to my will my fancies were as slaves
　　To do their sweet and subtile ministries;
And oft from that bright fountain's shadowy waves
　　They would make human throngs gather and rise　3130
　　To combat with my overflowing eyes,
And voice made deep with passion—thus I grew
　　Familiar with the shock and the surprise
And war of earthly minds, from which I drew
The power which has been mine to frame their thoughts anew.

XXXV

'And thus my prison was the populous earth—　3136
　　Where I saw—even as misery dreams of morn
Before the east has given its glory birth—
　　Religion's pomp made desolate by the scorn
　　Of Wisdom's faintest smile, and thrones, uptorn,　3140
And dwellings of mild people interspersed
　　With undivided fields of ripening corn,
And love made free,—a hope which we have nursed
Even with our blood and tears,—until its glory burst.

XXXVI

'All is not lost! There is some recompense　　3145
　　For hope whose fountain can be thus profound,
Even thronèd Evil's splendid impotence,
　　Girt by its hell of power, the secret sound

Of hymns to truth and freedom—the dread bound
Of life and death passed fearlessly and well,   315@
   Dungeons wherein the high resolve is found,
Racks which degraded woman's greatness tell,
And what may else be good and irresistible.

XXXVII

'Such are the thoughts which, like the fires that flare
   In storm-encompassed isles, we cherish yet   3155
In this dark ruin—such were mine even there;
   As in its sleep some odorous violet,
   While yet its leaves with nightly dews are wet,
Breathes in prophetic dreams of day's uprise,
   Or, as ere Scythian frost in fear has met   3160
Spring's messengers descending from the skies,
The buds foreknow their life—this hope must ever rise.

XXXVIII

'So years had passed, when sudden earthquake rent
   The depth of ocean, and the cavern cracked
With sound, as if the world's wide continent   316S
   Had fallen in universal ruin wracked:
   And through the cleft streamed in one cataract
The stifling waters—when I woke, the flood
   Whose banded waves that crystal cave had sacked
Was ebbing round me, and my bright abode   3170
Before me yawned—a chasm desert, and bare, and broad.

XXXIX

'Above me was the sky, beneath the sea:
   I stood upon a point of shattered stone,
And heard loose rocks rushing tumultuously
   With splash and shock into the deep—anon   3175
   All ceased, and there was silence wide and lone.
I felt that I was free! The Ocean-spray
   Quivered beneath my feet, the broad Heaven shone
Around, and in my hair the winds did play
Lingering as they pursued their unimpeded way.   3180

XL

'My spirit moved upon the sea like wind
   Which round some thymy cape will lag and hover,
Though it can wake the still cloud, and unbind
   The strength of tempest: day was almost over,

When through the fading light I could discover   3185
A ship approaching—its white sails were fed
With the north wind—its moving shade did cover
The twilight deep;—the Mariners in dread
Cast anchor when they saw new rocks around them spread.

XLI

'And when they saw one sitting on a crag,   3190
They sent a boat to me;—the Sailors rowed
In awe through many a new and fearful jag
Of overhanging rock, through which there flowed
The foam of streams that cannot make abode.
They came and questioned me, but when they heard   3195
My voice, they became silent, and they stood
And moved as men in whom new love had stirred
Deep thoughts: so to the ship we passed without a word.

CANTO VIII

I

'I sate beside the Steersman then, and gazing
Upon the west, cried, "Spread the sails! Behold!   3200
The sinking moon is like a watch-tower blazing
Over the mountains yet;—the City of Gold
Yon Cape alone does from the sight withhold;
The stream is fleet—the north breathes steadily
Beneath the stars, they tremble with the cold!   3205
Yet cannot rest upon the dreary sea!—
Haste, haste to the warm home of happier destiny!"

II

'The Mariners obeyed—the Captain stood
Aloof, and, whispering to the Pilot, said,
"Alas, alas! I fear we are pursued   3210
By wicked ghosts: a Phantom of the Dead,
The night before we sailed, came to my bed
In dream, like that!" The Pilot then replied,
"It cannot be—she is a human Maid—
Her low voice makes you weep—she is some bride,   3215
Or daughter of high birth—she can be nought beside."

III

'We passed the islets, borne by wind and stream,
And as we sailed, the Mariners came near
And thronged around to listen;—in the gleam
Of the pale moon I stood, as one whom fear   3220

May not attaint, and my calm voice did rear;
"Ye all are human—yon broad moon gives light
  To millions who the selfsame likeness wear,
Even while I speak—beneath this very night,   3224
Their thoughts flow on like ours, in sadness or delight.

IV

' "What dream ye? Your own hands have built an home,
  Even for yourselves on a beloved shore:
For some, fond eyes are pining till they come,
  How they will greet him when his toils are o'er, 3229
  And laughing babes rush from the well-known door!
Is 'this your care? ye toil for your own good—
  Ye feel and think—has some immortal power
Such purposes? or in a human mood,
Dream ye some Power thus builds for man in solitude?

V

' "What is that Power? Ye mock yourselves, and give
  A human heart to what ye cannot know: 3236
As if the cause of life could think and live!
  'Twere as if man's own works should feel, and show
  The hopes, and fears, and thoughts from which they flow,
And he be like to them! Lo! Plague is free   3240
  To waste, Blight, Poison, Earthquake, Hail, and Snow,
Disease, and Want, and worse Necessity
Of hate and ill, and Pride, and Fear, and Tyranny!

VI

' "What is that Power? Some moon-struck sophist stood
  Watching the shade from his own soul upthrown   3245
Fill Heaven and darken Earth, and in such mood
  The Form he saw and worshipped was his own,
  His likeness in the world's vast mirror shown;
And 'twere an innocent dream, but that a faith
  Nursed by fear's dew of poison, grows thereon,   3250
And that men say, that Power has chosen Death
On all who scorn its laws, to wreak immortal wrath.

VII

' "Men say that they themselves have heard and seen,
  Or known from others who have known such things,
A Shade, a Form, which Earth and Heaven between   3255
  Wields an invisible rod—that Priests and Kings,

Custom, domestic sway, ay, all that brings
  Man's freeborn soul beneath the oppressor's heel,
  Are his strong ministers, and that the stings
Of death will make the wise his vengeance feel,   3260
Though truth and virtue arm their hearts with tenfold steel.

VIII

" 'And it is said, this Power will punish wrong;
  Yes, add despair to crime, and pain to pain!
And deepest hell, and deathless snakes among,
  Will bind the wretch on whom is fixed a stain,   3265
  Which, like a plague, a burden, and a bane,
Clung to him while he lived;—for love and hate,
  Virtue and vice, they say are difference vain—
The will of strength is right—this human state
Tyrants, that they may rule, with lies thus desolate.   3270

IX

' "Alas, what strength? Opinion is more frail
  Than yon dim cloud now fading on the moon
Even while we gaze, though it awhile avail
  To hide the orb of truth—and every throne
  Of Earth or Heaven, though shadow, rests thereon,   3275
One shape of many names:—for this ye plough
  The barren waves of ocean, hence each one
Is slave or tyrant; all betray and bow,
Command, or kill, or fear, or wreak, or suffer woe.

X

' "Its names are each a sign which maketh holy   .   3280
  All power—ay, the ghost, the dream, the shade
Of power—lust, falsehood, hate, and pride, and folly;
  The pattern whence all fraud and wrong is made,
  A law to which mankind has been betrayed;
And human love, is as the name well known   3285
  Of a dear mother, whom the murderer laid
In bloody grave, and into darkness thrown,
Gathered her wildered babes around him as his own.

XI

' "O Love, who to the hearts of wandering men
  Art as the calm to Ocean's weary waves!   3290
Justice, or Truth, or Joy! those only can
  From slavery and religion's labyrinth caves

Guide us, as one clear star the seaman saves.
To give to all an equal share of good,
    To track the steps of Freedom, though through graves
She pass, to suffer all in patient mood,   3296
To weep for crime, though stained with thy friend's dearest
        blood,—

XII

' "To feel the peace of self-contentment's lot,
    To own all sympathies, and outrage none,
And in the inmost bowers of sense and thought,   3300
    Until life's sunny day is quite gone down,
    To sit and smile with Joy, or, not alone,
To kiss salt tears from the worn cheek of Woe;
    To live, as if to love and live were one,—
This is not faith or law, nor those who bow   3305
To thrones on Heaven or Earth, such destiny may know.

XIII

' "But children near their parents tremble now,
    Because they must obey—one rules another,
And as one Power rules both high and low,
    So man is made the captive of his brother,   3310
    And Hate is throned on high with Fear her mother,
Above the Highest—and those fountain-cells,
    Whence love yet flowed when faith had choked all other,
Are darkened—Woman as the bond-slave dwells
Of man, a slave; and life is poisoned in its wells.   3315

XIV

' "Man seeks for gold in mines, that he may weave
    A lasting chain for his own slavery;—
In fear and restless care that he may live
    He toils for others, who must ever be
    The joyous thralls of like captivity;   3320
He murders, for his chiefs delight in ruin;
    He builds the altar, that its idol's fee
May be his very blood; he is pursuing—
O, blind and willing wretch!—his own obscure undoing.

XV

' "Woman!—she is his slave, she has become   3325
    A thing I weep to speak—the child of scorn,
The outcast of a desolated home;
    Falsehood, and fear, and toil, like waves have worn

Channels upon her cheek, which smiles adorn,
As calm decks the false Ocean:—well ye know   3330
What Woman is, for none of Woman born,
Can choose but drain the bitter dregs of woe,
Which ever from the oppressed to the oppressors flow.

                              XVI

' "This need not be; ye might arise, and will
    That gold should lose its power, and thrones their glory;
That love, which none may bind, be free to fill   3336
    The world, like light; and evil faith, grown hoary
    With crime, be quenched and die.—Yon promontory
Even now eclipses the descending moon!—
    Dungeons and palaces are transitory—   3340
High temples fade like vapour—Man alone
Remains, whose will has power when all beside is gone.

                             XVII

' "Let all be free and equal!—From your hearts
    I feel an echo; through my inmost frame
Like sweetest sound, seeking its mate, it darts—   3345
    Whence come ye, friends? Alas, I cannot name
    All that I read of sorrow, toil, and shame,
On your worn faces; as in legends old
    Which make immortal the disastrous fame
Of conquerors and impostors false and bold,   3350
The discord of your hearts, I in your looks behold.

                            XVIII

' "Whence come ye, friends? from pouring human blood
    Forth on the earth? Or bring ye steel and gold,
That Kings may dupe and slay the multitude?
    Or from the famished poor, pale, weak, and cold,   3355
    Bear ye the earnings of their toil? Unfold!
Speak! Are your hands in slaughter's sanguine hue
    Stained freshly? have your hearts in guile grown old?
Know yourselves thus! ye shall be pure as dew,
And I will be a friend and sister unto you.   3360

                             XIX

' "Disguise it not—we have one human heart—
    All mortal thoughts confess a common home:
Blush not for what may to thyself impart
    Stains of inevitable crime: the doom

Is this, which has, or may, or must become
Thine, and all humankind's. Ye are the spoil
    Which Time thus marks for the devouring tomb,
Thou and thy thoughts and they, and all the toil
Wherewith ye twine the rings of life's perpetual coil.

XX

' "Disguise it not—ye blush for what ye hate,   3370
    And Enmity is sister unto Shame;
Look on your mind—it is the book of fate—
    Ah! it is dark with many a blazoned name
    Of misery—all are mirrors of the same;
But the dark fiend who with his iron pen   3375
    Dipped in scorn's fiery poison, makes his fame
Enduring there, would o'er the heads of men .
Pass harmless, if they scorned to make their hearts his den.

XXI

' "Yes, it is Hate—that shapeless fiendly thing
    Of many names, all evil, some divine,   3380
Whom self-contempt arms with a mortal sting;
    Which, when the heart its snaky folds entwine
    Is wasted quite, and when it doth repine
To gorge such bitter prey, on all beside
    It turns with ninefold rage, as with its twine   3385
When Amphisbæna some fair bird has tied,
Soon o'er the putrid mass he threats on every side.

XXII

' "Reproach not thine own soul, but know thyself,
    Nor hate another's crime, nor loathe thine own.
It is the dark idolatry of self,   3390
    Which, when our thoughts and actions once are gone,
    Demands that man should weep, and bleed, and groan;
O vacant expiation! Be at rest.—
    The past is Death's, the future is thine own;
And love and joy can make the foulest breast   3395
A paradise of flowers, where peace might build her nest.

XXIII

' "Speak thou! whence come ye?"—A Youth made reply:
    "Wearily, wearily o'er the boundless deep
We sail;—thou readest well the misery
    Told in these faded eyes, but much doth sleep   3400

Within, which there the poor heart loves to keep,
    Or dare not write on the dishonoured brow;
    Even from our childhood have we learned to steep
    The bread of slavery in the tears of woe,
And never dreamed of hope or refuge until now.   3405

XXIV

' "Yes—I must speak—my secret should have perished
    Even with the heart it wasted, as a brand
Fades in the dying flame whose life it cherished,
    But that no human bosom can withstand
    Thee, wondrous Lady, and the mild command   3410
Of thy keen eyes:—yes, we are wretched slaves,
    Who from their wonted loves and native land
Are reft, and bear o'er the dividing waves
The unregarded prey of calm and happy graves.

XXV

' "We drag afar from pastoral vales the fairest   3415
    Among the daughters of those mountains lone,
We drag them there, where all things best and rarest
    Are stained and trampled:—years have come and gone
    Since, like the ship which bears me, I have known
No thought;—but now the eyes of one dear Maid   3420
    On mine with light of mutual love have shone—
She is my life,—I am but as the shade
Of her,—a smoke sent up from ashes, soon to fade.

XXVI

' "For she must perish in the Tyrant's hall—
    Alas, alas!"—He ceased, and by the sail   3425
Sate cowering—but his sobs were heard by all,
    And still before the ocean and the gale
    The ship fled fast till the stars 'gan to fail,
And, round me gathered with mute countenance,
    The Seamen gazed, the Pilot, worn and pale   3430
With toil, the Captain with gray locks, whose glance
Met mine in restless awe—they stood as in a trance.

XXVII

' "Recede not! pause not now! Thou art grown old,
    But Hope will make thee young, for Hope and Youth
Are children of one mother, even Love—behold!   3435
    The eternal stars gaze on us! Is the truth

Within your soul? care for your own, or ruth
For others' sufferings? do ye thirst to bear
A heart which not the serpent Custom's tooth
May violate?—Be free! and even here,   3440
Swear to be firm till death!" They cried "We swear! We swear!"

XXVIII

'The very darkness shook, as with a blast
Of subterranean thunder, at the cry;
The hollow shore its thousand echoes cast
Into the night, as if the sea, and sky,   3445
And earth, rejoiced with new-born liberty,
For in that name they swore! Bolts were undrawn,
And on the deck, with unaccustomed eye
The captives gazing stood, and every one   3449
Shrank as the inconstant torch upon her countenance shone.

XXIX

'They were earth's purest children, young and fair,
With eyes the shrines of unawakened thought,
And brows as bright as Spring or Morning, ere
Dark time had there its evil legend wrought
In characters of cloud which wither not.—   3455
The change was like a dream to them; but soon
They knew the glory of their altered lot,
In the bright wisdom of youth's breathless noon,
Sweet talk, and smiles, and sighs, all bosoms did attune.

XXX

'But one was mute, her cheeks and lips most fair,   3460
Changing their hue like lilies newly blown,
Beneath a bright acacia's shadowy hair,
Waved by the wind amid the sunny noon,
Showed that her soul was quivering; and full soon
That Youth arose, and breathlessly did look   3465
On her and me, as for some speechless boon:
I smiled, and both their hands in mine I took,
And felt a soft delight from what their spirits shook.

CANTO IX

I

'THAT night we anchored in a woody bay,
And sleep no more around us dared to hover   3470
Than, when all doubt and fear has passed away,
It shades the couch of some unresting lover,

Whose heart is now at rest: thus night passed over
In mutual joy:—around, a forest grew
 Of poplar and dark oaks, whose shade did cover   3475
The waning stars pranked in the waters blue,
And trembled in the wind which from the morning flew.

II

'The joyous Mariners, and each free Maiden,
 Now brought from the deep forest many a bough,
With woodland spoil most innocently laden;   3480
 Soon wreaths of budding foliage seemed to flow
 Over the mast and sails, the stern and prow
Were canopied with blooming boughs,—the while
 On the slant sun's path o'er the waves we go
Rejoicing, like the dwellers of an isle   3485
Doomed to pursue those waves that cannot cease to smile.

III

'The many ships spotting the dark blue deep
 With snowy sails, fled fast as ours came nigh,
In fear and wonder; and on every steep
 Thousands did gaze, they heard the startling cry,   3490
 Like Earth's own voice lifted unconquerably
To all her children, the unbounded mirth,
 The glorious joy of thy name—Liberty!
They heard!—As o'er the mountains of the earth
From peak to peak leap on the beams of Morning's birth:

IV

'So from that cry over the boundless hills   3496
 Sudden was caught one universal sound,
Like a volcano's voice, whose thunder fills
 Remotest skies,—such glorious madness found
 A path through human hearts with stream which drowned
Its struggling fears and cares, dark Custom's brood;   3501
 They knew not whence it came, but felt around
A wide contagion poured—they called aloud
On Liberty—that name lived on the sunny flood.

V

'We reached the port.—Alas! from many spirits   3505
 The wisdom which had waked that cry, was fled,
Like the brief glory which dark Heaven inherits
 From the false dawn, which fades ere it is spread,

Upon the night's devouring darkness shed:
Yet soon bright day will burst—even like a chasm 3510
Of fire, to burn the shrouds outworn and dead,
Which wrap the world; a wide enthusiasm,
To cleanse the fevered world as with an earthquake's spasm!

VI

'I walked through the great City then, but free
From shame or fear; those toil-worn Mariners 3515
And happy Maidens did encompass me;
And like a subterranean wind that stirs
Some forest among caves, the hopes and fears
From every human soul, a murmur strange
Made as I passed: and many wept, with tears 3520
Of joy and awe, and wingèd thoughts did range,
And half-extinguished words, which prophesied of change.

VII

'For, with strong speech I tore the veil that hid
Nature, and Truth, and Liberty, and Love,—
As one who from some mountain's pyramid 3525
Points to the unrisen sun!—the shades approve
His truth, and flee from every stream and grove.
Thus, gentle thoughts did many a bosom fill,—
Wisdom, the mail of tried affections wove
For many a heart, and tameless scorn of ill, 3530
Thrice steeped in molten steel the unconquerable will.

VIII

'Some said I was a maniac wild and lost;
Some, that I scarce had risen from the grave,
The Prophet's virgin bride, a heavenly ghost:—
Some said, I was a fiend from my weird cave, 3535
Who had stolen human shape, and o'er the wave,
The forest, and the mountain came;—some said
I was the child of God, sent down to save
Women from bonds and death, and on my head
The burden of their sins would frightfully be laid. 3540

IX

'But soon my human words found sympathy
In human hearts: the purest and the best,
As friend with friend, made common cause with me,
And they were few, but resolute;—the rest,

Ere yet success the enterprise had blessed,   3545
Leagued with me in their hearts;—their meals, their slumber,
  Their hourly occupations, were possessed
By hopes which I had armed to overnumber
Those hosts of meaner cares, which life's strong wings encumber.

                                    X

'But chiefly women, whom my voice did waken   3550
  From their cold, careless, willing slavery,
Sought me: one truth their dreary prison has shaken,—
  They looked around, and lo! they became free!
  Their many tyrants sitting desolately
In slave-deserted halls, could none restrain;   3555
  For wrath's red fire had withered in the eye,
Whose lightning once was death,—nor fear, nor gain
Could tempt one captive now to lock another's chain.

                                    XI

'Those who were sent to bind me, wept, and felt
  Their minds outsoar the bonds which clasped them round,
Even as a waxen shape may waste and melt   3561
  In the white furnace; and a visioned swound,
  A pause of hope and awe the City bound,
Which, like the silence of a tempest's birth,
  When in its awful shadow it has wound   3565
The sun, the wind, the ocean, and the earth,
Hung terrible, ere yet the lightnings have leaped forth.

                                    XII

'Like clouds inwoven in the silent sky,
  By winds from distant regions meeting there,
In the high name of truth and liberty,   3570
  Around the City millions gathered were,
  By hopes which sprang from many a hidden lair,—
Words which the lore of truth in hues of flame
  Arrayed, thine own wild songs which in the air
Like homeless odours floated, and the name   3575
Of thee, and many a tongue which thou hadst dipped in flame.

                                    XIII

'The Tyrant knew his power was gone, but Fear,
  The nurse of Vengeance, bade him wait the event—
That perfidy and custom, gold and prayer,
  And whatsoe'er, when force is impotent,   3580

To fraud the sceptre of the world has lent,
Might, as he judged, confirm his failing sway.
   Therefore throughout the streets, the Priests he sent
To curse the rebels.—To their gods did they
For Earthquake, Plague, and Want, kneel in the public way.

XIV

'And grave and hoary men were bribed to tell   3586
   From seats where law is made the slave of wrong,
How glorious Athens in her splendour fell,
   Because her sons were free,—and that among
   Mankind, the many to the few belong,   3590
By Heaven, and Nature, and Necessity.
   They said, that age was truth, and that the young
Marred with wild hopes the peace of slavery,
With which old times and men had quelled the vain and free.

XV

'And with the falsehood of their poisonous lips   3595
   They breathed on the enduring memory
Of sages and of bards a brief eclipse;
   There was one teacher, who necessity
   Had armed with strength and wrong against mankind,
His slave and his avenger aye to be;   3600
   That we were weak and sinful, frail and blind,
And that the will of one was peace, and we
Should seek for nought on earth but toil and misery—

XVI

' "For thus we might avoid the hell hereafter."
   So spake the hypocrites, who cursed and lied;   3605
Alas, their sway was past, and tears and laughter
   Clung to their hoary hair, withering the pride
   Which in their hollow hearts dared still abide;
And yet obscener slaves with smoother brow,
   And sneers on their strait lips, thin, blue and wide,   3610
Said, that the rule of men was over now,
And hence, the subject world to woman's will must bow;

XVII

'And gold was scattered through the streets, and wine
   Flowed at a hundred feasts within the wall.
In vain! the steady towers in Heaven did shine   3615
   As they were wont, nor at the priestly call

Left Plague her banquet in the Ethiop's hall,
Nor Famine from the rich man's portal came,
Where at her ease she ever preys on all
Who throng to kneel for food: nor fear nor shame,   3620
Nor faith, nor discord, dimmed hope's newly kindled flame.

XVIII

'For gold was as a god whose faith began
To fade, so that its worshippers were few,
And Faith itself, which in the heart of man
Gives shape, voice, name, to spectral Terror, knew   3625
Its downfall, as the altars lonelier grew,
Till the Priests stood alone within the fane;
The shafts of falsehood unpolluting flew,
And the cold sneers of calumny were vain,
The union of the free with discord's brand to stain.   3630

XIX

'The rest thou knowest.—Lo! we two are here—
We have survived a ruin wide and deep—
Strange thoughts are mine.—I cannot grieve or fear,
Sitting with thee upon this lonely steep
I smile, though human love should make me weep.   3635
We have survived a joy that knows no sorrow,
And I do feel a mighty calmness creep
Over my heart, which can no longer borrow
Its hues from chance or change, dark children of to-morrow.

XX

'We know not what will come—yet Laon, dearest,   3640
Cythna shall be the prophetess of Love,
Her lips shall rob thee of the grace thou wearest,
To hide thy heart, and clothe the shapes which rove
Within the homeless Future's wintry grove;
For I now, sitting thus beside thee, seem   3645
Even with thy breath and blood to live and move,
And violence and wrong are as a dream
Which rolls from steadfast truth, an unreturning stream.

XXI

'The blasts of Autumn drive the wingèd seeds
Over the earth,—next come the snows, and rain,   3650
And frosts, and storms, which dreary Winter leads
Out of his Scythian cave, a savage train;

Behold! Spring sweeps over the world again,
Shedding soft dews from her ethereal wings;
  Flowers on the mountains, fruits over the plain,   3655
And music, on the waves and woods she flings,
And love on all that lives, and calm on lifeless things.

XXII

'O Spring, of hope, and love, and youth, and gladness
  Wind-wingèd emblem! brightest, best and fairest!
Whence comest thou, when, with dark Winter's sadness   3660
  The tears that fade in sunny smiles thou sharest?
  Sister of joy, thou art the child who wearest
Thy mother's dying smile, tender and sweet;
  Thy mother Autumn, for whose grave thou bearest
Fresh flowers, and beams like flowers, with gentle feet,   3665
Disturbing not the leaves which are her winding-sheet.

XXIII

'Virtue, and Hope, and Love, like light and Heaven,
  Surround the world.—We are their chosen slaves.
Has not the whirlwind of our spirit driven
  Truth's deathless germs to thought's remotest caves?   3670
  Lo, Winter comes!—the grief of many graves,
The frost of death, the tempest of the sword,
  The flood of tyranny, whose sanguine waves
Stagnate like ice at Faith the enchanter's word,
And bind all human hearts in its repose abhorred.   3675

XXIV

'The seeds are sleeping in the soil: meanwhile
  The Tyrant peoples dungeons with his prey,
Pale victims on the guarded scaffold smile
  Because they cannot speak; and, day by day,
  The moon of wasting Science wanes away   3680
Among her stars, and in that darkness vast
  The sons of earth to their foul idols pray,
And gray Priests triumph, and like blight or blast
A shade of selfish care o'er human looks is cast.

XXV

'This is the winter of the world;—and here   3685
  We die, even as the winds of Autumn fade,
Expiring in the frore and foggy air.—
  Behold! Spring comes, though we must pass, who made

The promise of its birth,—even as the shade
Which from our death, as from a mountain, flings　　　3690
The future, a broad sunrise; thus arrayed
As with the plumes of overshadowing wings,
From its dark gulf of chains, Earth like an eagle springs.

XXVI

'O dearest love! we shall be dead and cold
Before this morn may on the world arise;　　　3695
Wouldst thou the glory of its dawn behold?
Alas! gaze not on me, but turn thine eyes
On thine own heart—it is a paradise
Which everlasting Spring has made its own,
And while drear Winter fills the naked skies,　　　3700
Sweet streams of sunny thought, and flowers fresh-blown,
Are there, and weave their sounds and odours into one.

XXVII

'In their own hearts the earnest of the hope
Which made them great, the good will ever find;
And though some envious shades may interlope　　　3705
Between the effect and it, One comes behind,
Who aye the future to the past will bind—
Necessity, whose sightless strength for ever
Evil with evil, good with good must wind
In bands of union, which no power may sever:　　　3710
They must bring forth their kind, and be divided never!

XXVIII

'The good and mighty of departed ages
Are in their graves, the innocent and free,
Heroes, and Poets, and prevailing Sages,
Who leave the vesture of their majesty　　　3715
To adorn and clothe this naked world;—and we
Are like to them—such perish, but they leave
All hope, or love, or truth, or liberty,
Whose forms their mighty spirits could conceive,
To be a rule and law to ages that survive.　　　3720

XXIX

'So be the turf heaped over our remains
Even in our happy youth, and that strange lot,
Whate'er it be, when in these mingling veins
The blood is still, be ours; let sense and thought

Pass from our being, or be numbered not   3725
　Among the things that are; let those who come
　　Behind, for whom our steadfast will has bought
A calm inheritance, a glorious doom,
Insult with careless tread, our undivided tomb.

XXX

'Our many thoughts and deeds, our life and love,   3730
　Our happiness, and all that we have been,
Immortally must live, and burn and move,
　When we shall be no more;—the world has seen
　A type of peace; and—as some most serene
And lovely spot to a poor maniac's eye,   3735
　After long years, some sweet and moving scene
Of youthful hope, returning suddenly,
Quells his long madness—thus man shall remember thee.

XXXI

'And Calumny meanwhile shall feed on us,
　As worms devour the dead, and near the throne   3740
And at the altar, most accepted thus
　Shall sneers and curses be;—what we have done
　None shall dare vouch, though it be truly known;
That record shall remain, when they must pass
　Who built their pride on its oblivion;   3745
And fame, in human hope which sculptured was,
Survive the perished scrolls of unenduring brass.

XXXII

'The while we two, belovèd, must depart,
　And Sense and Reason, those enchanters fair,
Whose wand of power is hope, would bid the heart   3750
　That gazed beyond the wormy grave despair:
　These eyes, these lips, this blood, seems darkly there
To fade in hideous ruin; no calm sleep
　Peopling with golden dreams the stagnant air,
Seems our obscure and rotting eyes to steep   3755
In joy;—but senseless death—a ruin dark and deep!

XXXIII

'These are blind fancies—reason cannot know
　What sense can neither feel, nor thought conceive;
There is delusion in the world—and woe,
　And fear, and pain—we know not whence we live,   3760

Or why, or how, or what mute Power may give
Their being to each plant, and star, and beast,
Or even these thoughts.—Come near me! I do weave
A chain I cannot break—I am possessed
With thoughts too swift and strong for one lone human
    breast.   3765

XXXIV

'Yes, yes—thy kiss is sweet, thy lips are warm—
  O! willingly, belovèd, would these eyes,
Might they no more drink being from thy form,
  Even as to sleep whence we again arise,
  Close their faint orbs in death: I fear nor prize   3770
Aught that can now betide, unshared by thee—
  Yes, Love when Wisdom fails makes Cythna wise:
Darkness and death, if death be true, must be
Dearer than life and hope, if unenjoyed with thee.

XXXV

·Alas, our thoughts flow on with stream, whose waters
  Return not to their fountain—Earth and Heaven,   3776
The Ocean and the Sun, the Clouds their daughters,
  Winter, and Spring, and Morn, and Noon, and Even,
  All that we are or know, is darkly driven
Towards one gulf.—Lo! what a change is come   3780
  Since I first spake—but time shall be forgiven,
Though it change all but thee!'—She ceased—night's gloom
Meanwhile had fallen on earth from the sky's sunless dome.

XXXVI

Though she had ceased, her countenance uplifted
  To Heaven, still spake, with solemn glory bright;   3785
Her dark deep eyes, her lips, whose motions gifted
  The air they breathed with love, her locks undight.
  'Fair star of life and love,' I cried, 'my soul's delight,
Why lookest thou on the crystalline skies?
  O, that my spirit were yon Heaven of night,   3790
Which gazes on thee with its thousand eyes!'
She turned to me and smiled—that smile was Paradise!

CANTO X

I

Was there a human spirit in the steed,
  That thus with his proud voice, ere night was gone,
He broke our linkèd rest? or do indeed   3795
  All living things a common nature own,

And thought erect an universal throne,
Where many shapes one tribute ever bear?
And Earth, their mutual mother, does she groan
To see her sons contend? and makes she bare   3800
Her breast, that all in peace its drainless stores may share?

II

I have heard friendly sounds from many a tongue
Which was not human—the lone nightingale
Has answered me with her most soothing song,
Out of her ivy bower, when I sate pale   3805
With grief, and sighed beneath; from many a dale
The antelopes who flocked for food have spoken
With happy sounds, and motions, that avail
Like man's own speech; and such was now the token   3810
Of waning night, whose calm by that proud neigh was broken.

III

Each night, that mighty steed bore me abroad,
And I returned with food to our retreat,
And dark intelligence; the blood which flowed
Over the fields, had stained the courser's feet;
Soon the dust drinks that bitter dew,—then meet   3815
The vulture, and the wild dog, and the snake,
The wolf, and the hyæna gray, and eat
The dead in horrid truce: their throngs did make
Behind the steed, a chasm like waves in a ship's wake.

IV

For, from the utmost realms of earth, came pouring   3820
The banded slaves whom every despot sent
At that throned traitor's summons; like the roaring
Of fire, whose floods the wild deer circumvent
In the scorched pastures of the South; so bent
The armies of the leaguèd Kings around   3825
Their files of steel and flame;—the continent
Trembled, as with a zone of ruin bound,
Beneath their feet, the sea shook with their Navies' sound.

V

From every nation of the earth they came,
The multitude of moving heartless things,   3830
Whom slaves call men: obediently they came,
Like sheep whom from the fold the shepherd brings

To the stall, red with blood; their many kings
Led them, thus erring, from their native land;
 Tartar and Frank, and millions whom the wings 3835
Of Indian breezes lull, and many a band
The Arctic Anarch sent, and Idumea's sand,

VI

Fertile in prodigies and lies;—so there
 Strange natures made a brotherhood of ill.
The desert savage ceased to grasp in fear 3840
 His Asian shield and bow, when, at the will
 Of Europe's subtler son, the bolt would kill
Some shepherd sitting on a rock secure;
 But smiles of wondering joy his face would fill,
And savage sympathy: those slaves impure, 3845
Each one the other thus from ill to ill did lure.

VII

For traitorously did that foul Tyrant robe
 His countenance in lies,—even at the hour
When he was snatched from death, then o'er the globe,
 With secret signs from many a mountain-tower, 3850
 With smoke by day, and fire by night, the power
Of Kings and Priests, those dark conspirators,
 He called:—they knew his cause their own, and swore
Like wolves and serpents to their mutual wars 3855
Strange truce, with many a rite which Earth and Heaven abhors.

VIII

Myriads had come—millions were on their way;
 The Tyrant passed, surrounded by the steel
Of hired assassins, through the public way,
 Choked with his country's dead:—his footsteps reel
 On the fresh blood—he smiles. 'Ay, now I feel 3860
I am a King in truth!' he said, and took
 His royal seat, and bade the torturing wheel
Be brought, and fire, and pincers, and the hook,
And scorpions; that his soul on its revenge might look.

IX

'But first, go slay the rebels—why return 3865
 The victor bands?' he said, 'millions yet live,
Of whom the weakest with one word might turn
 The scales of victory yet;—let none survive

But those within the walls—each fifth shall give
The expiation for his brethren here.—   3870
    Go forth, and waste and kill!'—'O king, forgive
My speech,' a soldier answered—'but we fear
The spirits of the night, and morn is drawing near;

                              X

'For we were slaying still without remorse,
    And now that dreadful chief beneath my hand   3875
Defenceless lay, when, on a hell-black horse,
    An Angel bright as day, waving a brand
    Which flashed among the stars, passed.'—'Dost thou stand
Parleying with me, thou wretch?' the king replied;
    'Slaves, bind him to the wheel; and of this band,   3880
Whoso will drag that woman to his side
That scared him thus, may burn his dearest foe beside;

                              XI

'And gold and glory shall be his.—Go forth!'
    They rushed into the plain.—Loud was the roar
Of their career: the horsemen shook the earth;   3885
    The wheeled artillery's speed the pavement tore;
    The infantry, file after file, did pour
Their clouds on the utmost hills. Five days they slew
    Among the wasted fields; the sixth saw gore
Stream through the city; on the seventh, the dew   3890
Of slaughter became stiff, and there was peace anew:

                             XII

Peace in the desert fields and villages,
    Between the glutted beasts and mangled dead!
Peace in the silent streets! save when the cries
    Of victims to their fiery judgement led,   3895
    Made pale their voiceless lips who seemed to dread
Even in their dearest kindred, lest some tongue
    Be faithless to the fear yet unbetrayed;
Peace in the Tyrant's palace, where the throng
Waste the triumphal hours in festival and song!   3900

                            XIII

Day after day the burning sun rolled on
    Over the death-polluted land—it came
Out of the east like fire, and fiercely shone
    A lamp of Autumn, ripening with its flame

The few lone ears of corn;—the sky became   3905
Stagnate with heat, so that each cloud and blast
    Languished and died,—the thirsting air did claim
All moisture, and a rotting vapour passed
From the unburied dead, invisible and fast.

XIV.

First Want, then Plague came on the beasts; their food
    Failed, and they drew the breath of its decay.   3911
Millions on millions, whom the scent of blood
    Had lured, or who, from regions far away,
    Had tracked the hosts in festival array,
From their dark deserts; gaunt and wasting now,   3915
    Stalked like fell shades among their perished prey;
In their green eyes a strange disease did glow.
They sank in hideous spasm, or pains severe and slow.

XV

The fish were poisoned in the streams; the birds
    In the green woods perished; the insect race   3920
Was withered up; the scattered flocks and herds
    Who had survived the wild beasts' hungry chase
    Died moaning, each upon the other's face
In helpless agony gazing; round the City
    All night, the lean hyænas their sad case   3925
Like starving infants wailed; a woeful ditty!
And many a mother wept, pierced with unnatural pity.

XVI

Amid the aëreal minarets on high,
    The Ethiopian vultures fluttering fell
From their long line of brethren in the sky,   3930
    Startling the concourse of mankind.—Too well
    These signs the coming mischief did foretell:—
Strange panic first, a deep and sickening dread
    Within each heart, like ice, did sink and dwell,
A voiceless thought of evil, which did spread   3935
With the quick glance of eyes, like withering lightnings shed.

XVII

Day after day, when the year wanes, the frosts
    Strip its green crown of leaves, till all is bare;
So on those strange and congregated hosts
    Came Famine, a swift shadow, and the air   3940

Groaned with the burden of a new despair;
Famine, than whom Misrule no deadlier daughter
  Feeds from her thousand breasts, though sleeping there
With lidless eyes, lie Faith, and Plague, and Slaughter,
A ghastly brood; conceived of Lethe's sullen water.　　3945

XVIII

There was no food, the corn was trampled down,
  The flocks and herds had perished; on the shore
The dead and putrid fish were ever thrown;
  The deeps were foodless, and the winds no more
  Creaked with the weight of birds, but, as before　　3950
Those wingèd things sprang forth, were void of shade;
  The vines and orchards, Autumn's golden store,
Were burned;—so that the meanest food was weighed
With gold, and Avarice died before the god it made.

XIX

There was no corn—in the wide market-place　　3955
  All loathliest things, even human flesh, was sold;
They weighed it in small scales—and many a face
  Was fixed in eager horror then: his gold
  The miser brought; the tender maid, grown bold
Through hunger, bared her scornèd charms in vain;　　3960
  The mother brought her eldest-born, controlled
By instinct blind as love, but turned again
And bade her infant suck, and died in silent pain.

XX

Then fell blue Plague upon the race of man.
  'O, for the sheathèd steel, so late which gave　　3965
Oblivion to the dead, when the streets ran
  With brothers' blood! O, that the earthquake's grave
  Would gape, or Ocean lift its stifling wave!'
Vain cries—throughout the streets, thousands pursued
  Each by his fiery torture howl and rave,　　3970
Or sit, in frenzy's unimagined mood,
Upon fresh heaps of dead; a ghastly multitude.

XXI

It was not hunger now, but thirst. Each well
  Was choked with rotting corpses, and became
A cauldron of green mist made visible　　3975
  At sunrise. Thither still the myriads came,

Seeking to quench the agony of the flame,
Which raged like poison through their bursting veins;
    Naked they were from torture, without shame,
Spotted with nameless scars and lurid blains,   3980
Childhood, and youth, and age, writhing in savage pains.

XXII

It was not thirst but madness! Many saw
    Their own lean image everywhere, it went
A ghastlier self beside them, till the awe
    Of that dread sight to self-destruction sent   3985
    Those shrieking victims; some, ere life was spent,
Sought, with a horrid sympathy, to shed
    Contagion on the sound; and others rent
Their matted hair, and cried aloud, 'We tread
On fire! the avenging Power his hell on earth has spread!'

XXIII

Sometimes the living by the dead were hid.   3991
    Near the great fountain in the public square,
Where corpses made a crumbling pyramid
    Under the sun, was heard one stifled prayer
    For life, in the hot silence of the air;   3995
And strange 'twas, amid that hideous heap to see
    Some shrouded in their long and golden hair,
As if not dead, but slumbering quietly
Like forms which sculptors carve, then love to agony.

XXIV

Famine had spared the palace of the king:—   4000
    He rioted in festival the while,
He and his guards and priests; but Plague did fling
    One shadow upon all. Famine can smile
    On him who brings it food, and pass, with guile
Of thankful falsehood, like a courtier gray,   4005
    The house-dog of the throne; but many a mile
Comes Plague, a wingèd wolf, who loathes alway
The garbage and the scum that strangers make her prey.

XXV

So, near the throne, amid the gorgeous feast,
    Sheathed in resplendent arms, or loosely dight   4010
To luxury, ere the mockery yet had ceased
    That lingered on his lips, the warrior's might

Was loosened, and a new and ghastlier night
In dreams of frenzy lapped his eyes; he fell
    Headlong, or with stiff eyeballs sate upright   4015
Among the guests, or raving mad, did tell
Strange truths; a dying seer of dark oppression's hell.

XXVI

The Princes and the Priests were pale with terror;
    That monstrous faith wherewith they ruled mankind,
Fell, like a shaft loosed by the bowman's error,   4020
    On their own hearts: they sought and they could find
    No refuge—'twas the blind who led the blind!
So, through the desolate streets to the high fane,
    The many-tongued and endless armies wind
In sad procession: each among the train   4025
To his own Idol lifts his supplications vain.

XXVII

'O God!' they cried, 'we know our secret pride
    Has scorned thee, and thy worship, and thy name;
Secure in human power we have defied
    Thy fearful might; we bend in fear and shame   4030
    Before thy presence; with the dust we claim
Kindred; be merciful, O King of Heaven!
    Most justly have we suffered for thy fame
Made dim, but be at length our sins forgiven,
Ere to despair and death thy worshippers be driven.   4035

XXVIII

'O King of Glory! thou alone hast power!
    Who can resist thy will? who can restrain
Thy wrath, when on the guilty thou dost shower
    The shafts of thy revenge, a blistering rain?
    Greatest and best, be merciful again!   4040
Have we not stabbed thine enemies, and made
    The Earth an altar, and the Heavens a fane,
Where thou wert worshipped with their blood, and laid
Those hearts in dust which would thy searchless works have
        weighed?

XXIX

'Well didst thou loosen on this impious City   4045
    Thine angels of revenge: recall them now;
Thy worshippers, abased, here kneel for pity,
    And bind their souls by an immortal vow:

We swear by thee! and to our oath do thou
Give sanction, from thine hell of fiends and flame,   4050
    That we will kill with fire and torments slow,
The last of those who mocked thy holy name,
And scorned the sacred laws thy prophets did proclaim.'

XXX

Thus they with trembling limbs and pallid lips
    Worshipped their own hearts' image, dim and vast,
Scared by the shade wherewith they would eclipse   4056
    The light of other minds;—troubled they passed
    From the great Temple;—fiercely still and fast
The arrows of the plague among them fell,
    And they on one another gazed aghast,   4060
And through the hosts contention wild befell,
As each of his own god the wondrous works did tell.

XXXI

And Oromaze, Joshua, and Mahomet,
    Moses and Buddh, Zerdusht, and Brahm, and Foh,
A tumult of strange names, which never met   4065
    Before, as watchwords of a single woe,
    Arose; each raging votary 'gan to throw
Aloft his armèd hands, and each did howl
    'Our God alone is God!'—and slaughter now
Would have gone forth, when from beneath a cowl   4070
A voice came forth, which pierced like ice through every soul.

XXXII

'Twas an Iberian Priest from whom it came,
    A zealous man, who led the legioned West,
With words which faith and pride had steeped in flame,
    To quell the unbelievers; a dire guest   4075
    Even to his friends was he, for in his breast
Did hate and guile lie watchful, intertwined,
    Twin serpents in one deep and winding nest;
He loathed all faith beside his own, and pined
To wreak his fear of Heaven in vengeance on mankind.

XXXIII

But more he loathed and hated the clear light   4081
    Of wisdom and free thought, and more did fear,
Lest, kindled once, its beams might pierce the night,
    Even where his Idol stood; for, far and near

Did many a heart in Europe leap to hear   4085
That faith and tyranny were trampled down;
    Many a pale victim, doomed for truth to share
The murderer's cell, or see, with helpless groan,
The priests his children drag for slaves to serve their own.

XXXIV

He dared not kill the infidels with fire   4090
    Or steel, in Europe; the slow agonies
Of legal torture mocked his keen desire:
    So he made truce with those who did despise
    The expiation, and the sacrifice,
That, though detested, Islam's kindred creed   4095
    Might crush for him those deadlier enemies;
For fear of God did in his bosom breed
A jealous hate of man, an unreposing need.

XXXV

'Peace! Peace!' he cried, 'when we are dead, the Day
    Of Judgement comes, and all shall surely know   4100
Whose God is God, each fearfully shall pay
    The errors of his faith in endless woe!
    But there is sent a mortal vengeance now
On earth, because an impious race had spurned
    Him whom we all adore,—a subtle foe,   4105
By whom for ye this dread reward was earned,
And kingly thrones, which rest on faith, nigh overturned.

XXXVI

'Think ye, because ye weep, and kneel, and pray,
    That God will lull the pestilence? It rose
Even from beneath his throne, where, many a day,   4110
    His mercy soothed it to a dark repose:
    It walks upon the earth to judge his foes;
And what are thou and I, that he should deign
    To curb his ghastly minister, or close
The gates of death, ere they receive the twain   4115
Who shook with mortal spells his undefended reign?

XXXVII

'Ay, there is famine in the gulf of hell,
    Its giant worms of fire for ever yawn.—
Their lurid eyes are on us! those who fell
    By the swift shafts of pestilence ere dawn,   4120

Are in their jaws! they hunger for the spawn
Of Satan, their own brethren, who were sent
   To make our souls their spoil. See! see! they fawn
Like dogs, and they will sleep with luxury spent,
When those detested hearts their iron fangs have rent!   4125

XXXVIII

'Our God may then lull Pestilence to sleep:—
   Pile high the pyre of expiation now,
A forest's spoil of boughs, and on the heap
   Pour venomous gums, which sullenly and slow,
    When touched by flame, shall burn, and melt, and flow,
A stream of clinging fire,—and fix on high   4131
   A net of iron, and spread forth below
A couch of snakes, and scorpions, and the fry
Of centipedes and worms, earth's hellish progeny!

XXXIX

'Let Laon and Laone on that pyre,   4135
   Linked tight with burning brass, perish!—then pray
That, with this sacrifice, the withering ire
   Of Heaven may be appeased.' He ceased, and they
    A space stood silent, as far, far away
The echoes of his voice among them died;   4140
   And he knelt down upon the dust, alway
Muttering the curses of his speechless pride,
Whilst shame, and fear, and awe, the armies did divide.

XL

His voice was like a blast that burst the portal
   Of fabled hell; and as he spake, each one   4145
Saw gape beneath the chasms of fire immortal,
   And Heaven above seemed cloven, where, on a throne
    Girt round with storms and shadows, sate alone
Their King and Judge—fear killed in every breast
   All natural pity then, a fear unknown   4150
Before, and with an inward fire possessed,
They raged like homeless beasts whom burning woods invest.

XLI

'Twas morn.—At noon the public crier went forth,
   Proclaiming through the living and the dead,
'The Monarch saith, that his great Empire's worth   4155
   Is set on Laon and Laone's head:

He who but one yet living here can lead,
Or who the life from both their hearts can wring,
Shall be the kingdom's heir, a glorious meed!
But he who both alive can hither bring,   4160
The Princess shall espouse, and reign an equal King.'

XLII

Ere night the pyre was piled, the net of iron
Was spread above, the fearful couch below;
It overtopped the towers that did environ
That spacious square; for Fear is never slow   4165
To build the thrones of Hate, her mate and foe,
So, she scourged forth the maniac multitude
To rear this pyramid—tottering and slow,
Plague-stricken, foodless, like lean herds pursued
By gadflies, they have piled the heath, and gums, and wood.

XLIII

Night came, a starless and a moonless gloom.   4171
Until the dawn, those hosts of many a nation
Stood round that pile, as near one lover's tomb
Two gentle sisters mourn their desolation;
And in the silence of that expectation,   4175
Was heard on high the reptiles' hiss and crawl—
It was so deep—save when the devastation
Of the swift pest, with fearful interval,
Marking its path with shrieks, among the crowd would fall.

XLIV

Morn came,—among those sleepless multitudes,   4180
Madness, and Fear, and Plague, and Famine still
Heaped corpse on corpse, as in autumnal woods
The frosts of many a wind with dead leaves fill
Earth's cold and sullen brooks; in silence, still
The pale survivors stood; ere noon, the fear   4185
Of Hell became a panic, which did kill
Like hunger or disease, with whispers drear,
As 'Hush! hark! Come they yet? Just Heaven! thine hour is
near!'

XLV

And Priests rushed through their ranks, some counterfeiting
The rage they did inspire, some mad indeed   4190
With their own lies; they said their god was waiting
To see his enemies writhe, and burn, and bleed,—

And that, till then, the snakes of Hell had need
Of human souls:—three hundred furnaces
Soon blazed through the wide City, where, with speed,
Men brought their infidel kindred to appease   4196
God's wrath, and while they burned, knelt round on quivering
  knees.

XLVI

The noontide sun was darkened with that smoke,
The winds of eve dispersed those ashes gray.
The madness which these rites had lulled, awoke   4200
  Again at sunset.—Who shall dare to say
  The deeds which night and fear brought forth, or weigh
In balance just the good and evil there?
He might man's deep and searchless heart display,
And cast a light on those dim labyrinths, where   4205
Hope, near imagined chasms, is struggling with despair.

XLVII

'Tis said, a mother dragged three children then,
  To those fierce flames which roast the eyes in the head,
And laughed, and died; and that unholy men,
  Feasting like fiends upon the infidel dead,   4210
  Looked from their meal, and saw an Angel tread
The visible floor of Heaven, and it was she!
  And, on that night, one without doubt or dread
Came to the fire, and said, 'Stop, I am he!
Kill me!'—They burned them both with hellish mockery.

XLVIII

And, one by one, that night, young maidens came,   4216
  Beauteous and calm, like shapes of living stone
Clothed in the light of dreams, and by the flame
  Which shrank as overgorged, they laid them down,
  And sung a low sweet song, of which alone   4220
One word was heard, and that was Liberty;
  And that some kissed their marble feet, with moan
Like love, and died; and then that they did die
With happy smiles, which sunk in white tranquillity.

- CANTO XI

I

SHE saw me not—she heard me not— alone   4225
  Upon the mountain's dizzy brink she stood;
She spake not, breathed not, moved not—there was thrown
  Over her look, the shadow of a mood

   Which only clothes the heart in solitude,
A thought of voiceless depth;—she stood alone,   4230
   Above, the Heavens were spread;—below, the flood.
Was murmuring in its caves;—the wind had blown
Her hair apart, through which her eyes and forehead shone.

II

   A cloud was hanging o'er the western mountains;
    Before its blue and moveless depth were flying   4235
   Gray mists poured forth from the unresting fountains
    Of darkness in the North:—the day was dying:—
    Sudden, the sun shone forth, its beams were lying
   Like boiling gold on Ocean, strange to see,
    And on the shattered vapours, which defying   4240
   The power of light in vain, tossed restlessly
In the red Heaven, like wrecks in a tempestuous sea.

III

   It was a stream of living beams, whose bank
    On either side by the cloud's cleft was made;
   And where its chasms that flood of glory drank,   4245
    Its waves gushed forth like fire, and as if swayed
    By some mute tempest, rolled on *her*; the shade
   Of her bright image floated on the river
    Of liquid light, which then did end and fade—
   Her radiant shape upon its verge did shiver;   4250
Aloft, her flowing hair like strings of flame did quiver.

IV

   I stood beside her, but she saw me not—
    She looked upon the sea, and skies, and earth;
   Rapture, and love, and admiration wrought
    A passion deeper far than tears, or mirth,   4255
    Or speech, or gesture, or whate'er has birth
   From common joy; which with the speechless feeling
    That led her there united, and shot forth
   From her far eyes a light of deep revealing,
All but her dearest self from my regard concealing.   4260

V

   Her lips were parted, and the measured breath
    Was now heard there;—her dark and intricate eyes
   Orb within orb, deeper than sleep or death,
    Absorbed the glories of the burning skies,

Which, mingling with her heart's deep ecstasies,   4265
  Burst from her looks and gestures;—and a light
Of liquid tenderness, like love, did rise
From her whole frame, an atmosphere which quite
Arrayed her in its beams, tremulous and soft and bright.

VI

She would have clasped me to her glowing frame;   4270
  Those warm and odorous lips might soon have shed
On mine the fragrance and the invisible flame
  Which now the cold winds stole;—she would have laid
  Upon my languid heart her dearest head;
I might have heard her voice, tender and sweet;   4275
  Her eyes mingling with mine, might soon have fed
My soul with their own joy.—One moment yet
I gazed—we parted then, never again to meet!

VII

Never but once to meet on Earth again!
  She heard me as I fled—her eager tone   4280
Sunk on my heart, and almost wove a chain
  Around my will to link it with her own,
  So that my stern resolve was almost gone.
'I cannot reach thee! whither dost thou fly?
  My steps are faint—Come back, thou dearest one—
Return, ah me! return!'—The wind passed by   4286
On which those accents died, faint, far, and lingeringly.

VIII

Woe! Woe! that moonless midnight!—Want and Pest
  Were horrible, but one more fell doth rear,
As in a hydra's swarming lair, its crest   4290
  Eminent among those victims—even the Fear
  Of Hell: each girt by the hot atmosphere
Of his blind agony, like a scorpion stung
  By his own rage upon his burning bier
Of circling coals of fire; but still there clung   4295
One hope, like a keen sword on starting threads uphung:

IX

Not death—death was no more refuge or rest;
  Not life—it was despair to be!—not sleep,
For fiends and chasms of fire had dispossessed
  All natural dreams: to wake was not to weep,   4300

But to gaze mad and pallid, at the leap
To which the Future, like a snaky scourge,
    Or like some tyrant's eye, which aye doth keep
Its withering beam upon his slaves, did urge
Their steps; they heard the roar of Hell's sulphureous surge.

X

Each of that multitude, alone, and lost   4306
    To sense of outward things, one hope yet knew;
As on a foam-girt crag some seaman tossed
    Stares at the rising tide, or like the crew
    Whilst now the ship is splitting through and through;
Each, if the tramp of a far steed was heard,   4311
    Started from sick despair, or if there flew
One murmur on the wind, or if some word
Which none can gather yet, the distant crowd has stirred.

XI

Why became cheeks, wan with the kiss of death,   4315
    Paler from hope? they had sustained despair.
Why watched those myriads with suspended breath
    Sleepless a second night? they are not here,
    The victims, and hour by hour, a vision drear,
Warm corpses fall upon the clay-cold dead;   4320
    And even in death their lips are wreathed with fear.—
The crowd is mute and moveless—overhead
Silent Arcturus shines—'Ha! hear'st thou not the tread

XII

'Of rushing feet? laughter? the shout, the scream,
    Of triumph not to be contained? See! hark!   4325
They come, they come! give way!' Alas, ye deem
    Falsely—'tis but a crowd of maniacs stark
    Driven, like a troop of spectres, through the dark,
From the choked well, whence a bright death-fire sprung,
    A lurid earth-star, which dropped many a spark   4330
From its blue train, and spreading widely, clung
To their wild hair, like mist the topmost pines among.

XIII

And many, from the crowd collected there,
    Joined that strange dance in fearful sympathies;
There was the silence of a long despair,   4335
    When the last echo of those terrible cries

Came from a distant street, like agonies
Stifled afar.—Before the Tyrant's throne
  All night his aged Senate sate, their eyes
In stony expectation fixed; when one   4340
Sudden before them stood, a Stranger and alone.

XIV

Dark Priests and haughty Warriors gazed on him
  With baffled wonder, for a hermit's vest
Concealed his face; but, when he spake, his tone,
  Ere yet the matter did their thoughts arrest,—   4345
  Earnest, benignant, calm, as from a breast
Void of all hate or terror—made them start;
  For as with gentle accents he addressed
His speech to them, on each unwilling heart
Unusual awe did fall—a spirit-quelling dart.   4350

XV

'Ye Princes of the Earth, ye sit aghast
  Amid the ruin which yourselves have made,
Yes, Desolation heard your trumpet's blast,
  And sprang from sleep!—dark Terror has obeyed
  Your bidding—O, that I whom ye have made   4355
Your foe, could set my dearest enemy free
  From pain and fear! but evil casts a shade,
Which cannot pass so soon, and Hate must be
The nurse and parent still of an ill progeny.

XVI

'Ye turn to Heaven for aid in your distress;   4360
  Alas, that ye, the mighty and the wise,
Who, if ye dared, might not aspire to less
  Than ye conceive of power, should fear the lies
  Which thou, and thou, didst frame for mysteries
To blind your slaves:—consider your own thought,   4365
  An empty and a cruel sacrifice
Ye now prepare, for a vain idol wrought
Out of the fears and hate which vain desires have brought.

XVII

'Ye seek for happiness—alas, the day!
  Ye find it not in luxury nor in gold,   4370
Nor in the fame, nor in the envied sway
  For which, O willing slaves to Custom old,

Severe taskmistress! ye your hearts have sold.
Ye seek for peace, and when ye die, to dream
  No evil dreams: all mortal things are cold   4375
And senseless then; if aught survive, I deem
It must be love and joy, for they immortal seem.

XVIII

'Fear not the future, weep not for the past.
  O, could I win your ears to dare be now
Glorious, and great, and calm! that ye would cast   4380
  Into the dust those symbols of your woe,
  Purple, and gold, and steel! that ye would go
Proclaiming to the nations whence ye came.
  That Want, and Plague, and Fear, from slavery flow;
And that mankind is free, and that the shame   4385
Of royalty and faith is lost in freedom's fame!

XIX

'If thus, 'tis well—if not, I come to say
  That Laon—' while the Stranger spoke, among
The Council sudden tumult and affray
  Arose, for many of those warriors young,   4390
  Had on his eloquent accents fed and hung
Like bees on mountain-flowers; they knew the truth,
  And from their thrones in vindication sprung;
The men of faith and law then without ruth
Drew forth their secret steel, and stabbed each ardent youth.

XX

They stabbed them in the back and sneered—a slave   4396
  Who stood behind the throne, those corpses drew
Each to its bloody, dark, and secret grave;
  And one more daring raised his steel anew
  To pierce the Stranger. 'What hast thou to do   4400
With me, poor wretch?'—Calm, solemn, and severe,
  That voice unstrung his sinews, and he threw
His dagger on the ground, and pale with fear,
Sate silently—his voice then did the Stranger rear.

XXI

'It doth avail not that I weep for ye—   4405
  Ye cannot change, since ye are old and gray,
And ye have chosen your lot—your fame must be
  A book of blood, whence in a milder day

Men shall learn truth, when ye are wrapped in clay:
Now ye shall triumph. I am Laon's friend,   4410
 And him to your revenge will I betray,
So ye concede one easy boon. Attend!
For now I speak of things which ye can apprehend.

XXII

'There is a People mighty in its youth,
 A land beyond the Oceans of the West,   4415
Where, though with rudest rites, Freedom and Truth
 Are worshipped; from a glorious Mother's breast,
 Who, since high Athens fell, among the rest
Sate like the Queen of Nations, but in woe,
 By inbred monsters outraged and oppressed,   4420
Turns to her chainless child for succour now,
It draws the milk of Power in Wisdom's fullest flow.

XXIII

'That land is like an Eagle, whose young gaze
 Feeds on the noontide beam, whose golden plume
Floats moveless on the storm, and in the blaze   4425
 Of sunrise gleams when Earth is wrapped in gloom;
 An epitaph of glory for the tomb
Of murdered Europe may thy fame be made,
 Great People! as the sands shalt thou become;   4429
Thy growth is swift as morn, when night must fade;
The multitudinous Earth shall sleep beneath thy shade.

XXIV

'Yes, in the desert there is built a home
 For Freedom. Genius is made strong to rear
The monuments of man beneath the dome
 Of a new Heaven; myriads assemble there,   4435
 Whom the proud lords of man, in rage or fear,
Drive from their wasted homes: the boon I pray
 Is this—that Cythna shall be convoyed there—
Nay, start not at the name—America!
And then to you this night Laon will I betray.   4440

XXV

'With me do what you will. I am your foe!'
 The light of such a joy as makes the stare
Of hungry snakes like living emeralds glow,
 Shone in a hundred human eyes—'Where, where

Is Laon? Haste! fly! drag him swiftly here!   4445
We grant thy boon.'—'I put no trust in ye,
 Swear by the Power ye dread.'—'We swear, we swear!'
The Stranger threw his vest back suddenly,
And smiled in gentle pride, and said, 'Lo! I am he!'

CANTO XII

I

THE transport of a fierce and monstrous gladness   4450
 Spread through the multitudinous streets, fast flying
Upon the winds of fear; from his dull madness
 The starveling waked, and died in joy; the dying,
 Among the corpses in stark agony lying,
Just heard the happy tidings, and in hope   4455
 Closed their faint eyes; from house to house replying
With loud acclaim, the living shook Heaven's cope,
And filled the startled Earth with echoes: morn did ope

II

Its pale eyes then; and lo! the long array
 Of guards in golden arms, and Priests beside,   4460
Singing their bloody hymns, whose garbs betray
 The blackness of the faith it seems to hide;
 And see, the Tyrant's gem-wrought chariot glide
Among the gloomy cowls and glittering spears—
 A Shape of light is sitting by his side,   4465
A child most beautiful. I' the midst appears
Laon,—exempt alone from mortal hopes and fears.

III

His head and feet are bare, his hands are bound
 Behind and with heavy chains, yet none do wreak
Their scoffs on him, though myriads throng around;   4470
 There are no sneers upon his lip which speak
 That scorn or hate has made him bold; his cheek
Resolve has not turned pale,—his eyes are mild
 And calm, and, like the morn about to break,
Smile on mankind—his heart seems reconciled   4475
To all things and itself, like a reposing child.

IV

Tumult was in the soul of all beside,
 Ill joy, or doubt, or fear; but those who saw
Their tranquil victim pass, felt wonder glide
 Into their brain, and became calm with awe.—   4480

See, the slow pageant near the pile doth draw.
　A thousand torches in the spacious square,
　　Borne by the ready slaves of ruthless law,
　Await the signal round: the morning fair
Is changed to a dim night by that unnatural glare. 　　4485

V

And see! beneath a sun-bright canopy,
　Upon a platform level with the pile,
The anxious Tyrant sit, enthroned on high,
　Girt by the chieftains of the host; all smile
　In expectation, but one child: the while 　　　　　4490
I, Laon, led by mutes, ascend my bier
　Of fire, and look around: each distant isle
Is dark in the bright dawn; towers far and near,
Pierce like reposing flames the tremulous atmosphere.

VI

There was such silence through the host, as when 　　4495
　An earthquake trampling on some populous town,
Has crushed ten thousand with one tread, and men
　Expect the second; all were mute but one,
　That fairest child, who, bold with love, alone
Stood up before the King, without avail, 　　　　　4500
　Pleading for Laon's life—her stifled groan
Was heard—she trembled like one aspen pale
Among the gloomy pines of a Norwegian vale.

VII

What were his thoughts linked in the morning sun,
　Among those reptiles, stingless with delay, 　　　4505
Even like a tyrant's wrath?—The signal-gun
　Roared—hark, again! In that dread pause he lay
　As in a quiet dream—the slaves obey—
A thousand torches drop,—and hark, the last
　Bursts on that awful silence; far away, 　　　　4510
Millions, with hearts that beat both loud and fast,
Watch for the springing flame expectant and aghast.

VIII

They fly—the torches fall—a cry of fear
　Has startled the triumphant!—they recede!
For ere the cannon's roar has died, they hear 　　4515
　The tramp of hoofs like earthquake, and a steed

Dark and gigantic, with the tempest's speed,
Bursts through their ranks: a woman sits thereon,
Fairer, it seems, than aught that earth can breed,
Calm, radiant, like the phantom of the dawn,   4520
A spirit from the caves of daylight wandering gone.

IX

All thought it was God's Angel come to sweep
The lingering guilty to their fiery grave;
The Tyrant from his throne in dread did leap,—
Her innocence his child from fear did save;   4525
Scared by the faith they feigned, each priestly slave
Knelt for his mercy whom they served with blood,
And, like the refluence of a mighty wave
Sucked into the loud sea, the multitude
With crushing panic, fled in terror's altered mood.   4530

X

They pause, they blush, they gaze,—a gathering shout
Bursts like one sound from the ten thousand streams
Of a tempestuous sea:—that sudden rout
One checked, who, never in his mildest dreams
Felt awe from grace or loveliness, the seams   4535
Of his rent heart so hard and cold a creed
Had seared with blistering ice—but he misdeems
That he is wise, whose wounds do only bleed
Inly for self—thus thought the Iberian Priest indeed,

XI

And others too, thought he was wise to see,   4540
In pain, and fear, and hate, something divine;
In love and beauty, no divinity.—
Now with a bitter smile, whose light did shine
Like a fiend's hope upon his lips and eyne,
He said, and the persuasion of that sneer   4545
Rallied his trembling comrades—'Is it mine
To stand alone, when kings and soldiers fear
A woman? Heaven has sent its other victim here.'

XII

'Were it not impious,' said the King, 'to break
Our holy oath?'—'Impious to keep it, say!'   4550
Shrieked the exulting Priest—'Slaves, to the stake
Bind her, and on my head the burden lay

Of her just torments:—at the Judgement Day
  Will I stand up before the golden throne
    Of Heaven, and cry, "To thee did I betray   4555
  An Infidel; but for me she would have known
Another moment's joy! the glory be thine own!"'

XIII

They trembled, but replied not, nor obeyed,
  Pausing in breathless silence. Cythna sprung
From her gigantic steed, who, like a shade   4560
  Chased by the winds, those vacant streets among
  Fled tameless, as the brazen rein she flung
Upon his neck, and kissed his mooned brow.
  A piteous sight, that one so fair and young,
The clasp of such a fearful death should woo   4565
With smiles of tender joy as beamed from Cythna now.

XIV

The warm tears burst in spite of faith and fear
  From many a tremulous eye, but like soft dews
Which feed Spring's earliest buds, hung gathered there,
  Frozen by doubt,—alas! they could not choose   4570
  But weep; for when her faint limbs did refuse
To climb the pyre, upon the mutes she smiled;
  And with her eloquent gestures, and the hues
Of her quick lips, even as a weary child
Wins sleep from some fond nurse with its caresses mild,

XV

She won them, though unwilling, her to bind   4576
  Near me, among the snakes. When there had fled
One soft reproach that was most thrilling kind,
  She smiled on me, and nothing then we said,
  But each upon the other's countenance fed   4580
Looks of insatiate love; the mighty veil
  Which doth divide the living and the dead
Was almost rent, the world grew dim and pale,—
All light in Heaven or Earth beside our love did fail.—

XVI

Yet—yet—one brief relapse, like the last beam   4585
  Of dying flames, the stainless air around
Hung silent and serene—a blood-red gleam
  Burst upwards, hurling fiercely from the ground

The globèd smoke,—I heard the mighty sound
Of its uprise, like a tempestuous ocean;   4590
   And through its chasms I saw, as in a swound,
The tyrant's child fall without life or motion
Before his throne, subdued by some unseen emotion.

XVII

And is this death?—The pyre has disappeared,
   The Pestilence, the Tyrant, and the throng;   4595
The flames grow silent—slowly there is heard
   The music of a breath-suspending song,
   Which, like the kiss of love when life is young,
Steeps the faint eyes in darkness sweet and deep:
   With ever-changing notes it floats along,   4600
Till on my passive soul there seemed to creep
A melody, like waves on wrinkled sands that leap.

XVIII

The warm touch of a soft and tremulous hand
   Wakened me then; lo! Cythna sate reclined
Beside me, on the waved and golden sand   4605
   Of a clear pool, upon a bank o'ertwined
   With strange and star-bright flowers, which to the wind
Breathed divine odour; high above, was spread
   The emerald heaven of trees of unknown kind,
Whose moonlike blooms and bright fruit overhead   4610
A shadow, which was light, upon the waters shed.

XIX

And round about sloped many a lawny mountain
   With incense-bearing forests, and vast caves
Of marble radiance, to that mighty fountain;
   And where the flood its own bright margin laves,   4615
   Their echoes talk with its eternal waves,
Which, from the depths whose jaggèd caverns breed
   Their unreposing strife, it lifts and heaves,—
Till through a chasm of hills they roll, and feed
A river deep, which flies with smooth but arrowy speed.

XX

As we sate gazing in a trance of wonder,   4621
   A boat approached, borne by the musical air
Along the waves which sung and sparkled under
   Its rapid keel—a wingèd shape sate there,

A child with silver-shining wings, so fair,   4625
That as her bark did through the waters glide,
    The shadow of the lingering waves did wear
Light, as from starry beams; from side to side,
While veering to the wind her plumes the bark did guide.

XXI

The boat was one curved shell of hollow pearl,   4630
    Almost translucent with the light divine
Of her within; the prow and stern did curl
    Hornèd on high, like the young moon supine,
    When o'er dim twilight mountains dark with pine,
It floats upon the sunset's sea of beams,   4635
    Whose golden waves in many a purple line
Fade fast, till borne on sunlight's ebbing streams,
Dilating, on earth's verge the sunken meteor gleams.

XXII

Its keel has struck the sands beside our feet;—
    Then Cythna turned to me, and from her eyes   4640
Which swam with unshed tears, a look more sweet
    Than happy love, a wild and glad surprise,
    Glanced as she spake: 'Ay, this is Paradise
And not a dream, and we are all united!
    Lo, that is mine own child, who in the guise   4645
Of madness came, like day to one benighted
In lonesome woods: my heart is now too well requited!'

XXIII

And then she wept aloud, and in her arms
    Clasped that bright Shape, less marvellously fair
Than her own human hues and living charms;   4650
    Which, as she leaned in passion's silence there,
    Breathed warmth on the cold bosom of the air,
Which seemed to blush and tremble with delight;
    The glossy darkness of her streaming hair
Fell o'er that snowy child, and wrapped from sight   4655
The fond and long embrace which did their hearts unite.

XXIV

Then the bright child, the plumèd Seraph came,
    And fixed its blue and beaming eyes on mine,
And said, 'I was disturbed by tremulous shame
    When once we met, yet knew that I was thine   4660

From the same hour in which thy lips divine
Kindled a clinging dream within my brain,
 Which ever waked when I might sleep, to twine
Thine image with *her* memory dear—again
We meet; exempted now from mortal fear or pain.   4665

XXV

'When the consuming flames had wrapped ye round,'
 The hope which I had cherished went away;
I fell in agony on the senseless ground,
 And hid mine eyes in dust, and far astray
 My mind was gone, when bright, like dawning day,
The Spectre of the Plague before me flew,   4671
 And breathed upon my lips, and seemed to say,
"They wait for thee, belovèd!"—then I knew
The death-mark on my breast, and became calm anew.

XXVI

'It was the calm of love—for I was dying.   4675
 I saw the black and half-extinguished pyre
In its own gray and shrunken ashes lying;
 The pitchy smoke of the departed fire
 Still hung in many a hollow dome and spire
Above the towers, like night; beneath whose shade   4680
 Awed by the ending of their own desire
The armies stood; a vacancy was made
In expectation's depth, and so they stood dismayed.

XXVII

'The frightful silence of that altered mood,
 The tortures of the dying clove alone,   4685
Till one uprose among the multitude,
 And said—"The flood of time is rolling on,
 We stand upon its brink, whilst *they* are gone
To glide in peace down death's mysterious stream.   4689
 Have ye done well? They moulder flesh and bone,
Who might have made this life's envenomed dream
A sweeter draught than ye will ever taste, I deem.

XXVIII

' "These perish as the good and great of yore
 Have perished, and their murderers will repent,—
Yes, vain and barren tears shall flow before   4695
 Yon smoke has faded from the firmament

Even for this cause, that ye who must lament
The death of those that made this world so fair,
Cannot recall them now; but there is lent
To man the wisdom of a high despair,   4700
When such can die, and he live on and linger here.

XXIX

' "Ay, ye may fear not now the Pestilence,
From fabled hell as by a charm withdrawn;
All power and faith must pass, since calmly hence
In pain and fire have unbelievers gone;   4705
And ye must sadly turn away, and moan
In secret, to his home each one returning,
And to long ages shall this hour be known;
And slowly shall its memory, ever burning,
Fill this dark night of things with an eternal morning.

XXX

' "For me the world is grown too void and cold,   4711
Since Hope pursues immortal Destiny
With steps thus slow—therefore shall ye behold
How those who love, yet fear not, dare to die;
Tell to your children this!" Then suddenly   4715
He sheathed a dagger in his heart and fell;
My brain grew dark in death, and yet to me
There came a murmur from the crowd, to tell
Of deep and mighty change which suddenly befell.

XXXI

'Then suddenly I stood, a wingèd Thought,   4720
Before the immortal Senate, and the seat
Of that star-shining spirit, whence is wrought
The strength of its dominion, good and great,
The better Genius of this world's estate.
His realm around one mighty Fane is spread,   4725
Elysian islands bright and fortunate,
Calm dwellings of the free and happy dead,
Where I am sent to lead!' These wingèd words she said,

XXXII

And with the silence of her eloquent smile,
Bade us embark in her divine canoe;   4730
Then at the helm we took our seat, the while
Above her head those plumes of dazzling hue

Into the winds' invisible stream she threw,
Sitting beside the prow: like gossamer
On the swift breath of morn, the vessel flew   4735
O'er the bright whirlpools of that fountain fair,
Whose shores receded fast, whilst we seemed lingering there;

XXXIII

Till down that mighty stream, dark, calm, and fleet,
Between a chasm of cedarn mountains riven,
Chased by the thronging winds whose viewless feet   4740
As swift as twinkling beams, had, under Heaven,
From woods and waves wild sounds and odours driven,
The boat fled visibly—three nights and days,
Borne like a cloud through morn, and noon, and even,
We sailed along the winding watery ways   4745
Of the vast stream, a long and labyrinthine maze.

XXXIV

A scene of joy and wonder to behold
That river's shapes and shadows changing ever,
When the broad sunrise filled with deepening gold
Its whirlpools, where all hues did spread and quiver;
And where melodious falls did burst and shiver   4751
Among rocks clad with flowers, the foam and spray
Sparkled like stars upon the sunny river,
Or when the moonlight poured a holier day,
One vast and glittering lake around green islands lay. 4755

XXXV

Morn, noon, and even, that boat of pearl outran
The streams which bore it, like the arrowy cloud
Of tempest, or the speedier thought of man,
Which flieth forth and cannot make abode;
Sometimes through forests, deep like night, we glode,
Between the walls of mighty mountains crowned   4761
With Cyclopean piles, whose turrets proud,
The homes of the departed, dimly frowned
O'er the bright waves which girt their dark foundations round.

XXXVI

Sometimes between the wide and flowering meadows,
Mile after mile we sailed, and 'twas delight   4766
To see far off the sunbeams chase the shadows
Over the grass; sometimes beneath the night

Of wide and vaulted caves, whose roofs were bright
With starry gems, we fled, whilst from their deep   4770
     And dark-green chasms, shades beautiful and white,
     Amid sweet sounds across our path would sweep,
Like swift and lovely dreams that walk the waves of sleep.

XXXVII

And ever as we sailed, our minds were full
     Of love and wisdom, which would overflow   4775
In converse wild, and sweet, and wonderful,
     And in quick smiles whose light would come and go
     Like music o'er wide waves, and in the flow
Of sudden tears, and in the mute caress—
     For a deep shade was cleft, and we did know,   4780
That virtue, though obscured on Earth, not less
Survives all mortal change in lasting loveliness.

XXXVIII

Three days and nights we sailed, as thought and feeling
     Number delightful hours—for through the sky
The spherèd lamps of day and night, revealing   4785
     New changes and new glories, rolled on high,
     Sun, Moon, and moonlike lamps, the progeny
Of a diviner Heaven, serene and fair:
     On the fourth day, wild as a windwrought sea
The stream became, and fast and faster bare   4790
The spirit-wingèd boat, steadily speeding there.

XXXIX

Steady and swift, where the waves rolled like mountains
     Within the vast ravine, whose rifts did pour
Tumultuous floods from their ten thousand fountains,
     The thunder of whose earth-uplifting roar   4795
     Made the air sweep in whirlwinds from the shore,
Calm as a shade, the boat of that fair child
     Securely fled, that rapid stress before,
Amid the topmost spray, and sunbows wild,
Wreathed in the silver mist: in joy and pride we smiled.

XL

The torrent of that wide and raging river   4801
     Is passed, and our aëreal speed suspended.
We look behind; a golden mist did quiver
     Where its wild surges with the lake were blended,—

Our bark hung there, as on a line suspended   4805
Between two heavens,—that windless waveless lake
Which four great cataracts from four vales, attended
By mists, aye feed; from rocks and clouds they break,
And of that azure sea a silent refuge make.

XLI

Motionless resting on the lake awhile,   4810
  I saw its marge of snow-bright mountains rear
Their peaks aloft, I saw each radiant isle,
  And in the midst, afar, even like a sphere
  Hung in one hollow sky, did there appear
The Temple of the Spirit; on the sound   4815
  Which issued thence, drawn nearer and more near,
Like the swift moon this glorious earth around,
The charmèd boat approached, and there its haven found.

NOTE ON THE REVOLT OF ISLAM, BY MRS. SHELLEY

SHELLEY possessed two remarkable qualities of intellect—a brilliant imagination, and a logical exactness of reason. His inclinations led him (he fancied) almost alike to poetry and metaphysical discussions. I say 'he fancied,' because I believe the former to have been paramount, and that it would have gained the mastery even had he struggled against it. However, he said that he deliberated at one time whether he should dedicate himself to poetry or metaphysics; and, resolving on the former, he educated himself for it, discarding in a great measure his philosophical pursuits, and engaging himself in the study of the poets of Greece, Italy, and England. To these may be added a constant perusal of portions of the Old Testament—the Psalms, the Book of Job, the Prophet Isaiah, and others, the sublime poetry of which filled him with delight.

As a poet, his intellect and compositions were powerfully influenced by exterior circumstances, and especially by his place of abode. He was very fond of travelling, and ill-health increased this restlessness. The sufferings occasioned by a cold English winter made him pine, especially when our colder spring arrived, for a more genial climate. In 1816 he again visited Switzerland, and rented a house on the banks of the Lake of Geneva; and many a day, in cloud or sunshine, was passed alone in his boat—sailing as the wind listed, or weltering on the calm waters. The majestic aspect of Nature ministered such thoughts as he afterwards enwove in verse. His lines on the Bridge of the Arve, and his *Hymn to Intellectual Beauty*, were written at this time. Perhaps during this summer his genius was checked by association with another poet whose nature was utterly dissimilar to his own, yet who, in the poem he wrote at that time, gave tokens that he shared for a period the more abstract and etherealised inspiration of Shelley. The saddest events awaited his return to England; but such was his fear to wound the feelings of others that he never expressed the anguish he felt, and seldom gave vent to the indignation roused by the persecutions he underwent; while the course of deep unexpressed passion, and the sense of injury, engendered the desire to embody themselves in forms defecated of all the weakness and evil which cling to real life.

He chose therefore for his hero a youth nourished in dreams of liberty, some of whose actions are in direct opposition to the opinions of the world; but who is animated throughout by an ardent love of virtue, and a resolution to confer the boons of political and intellectual freedom on his fellow-creatures. He created for this youth a woman such as he delighted to imagine—full of enthusiasm for the same objects; and they both, with will unvanquished, and the deepest sense of the justice of their cause, met adversity and death. There exists in this poem a memorial of a friend of his youth. The character of the old man who liberates Laon from his tower-prison, and tends on him in sickness, is founded on that of Doctor Lind, who, when Shelley was at Eton, had often stood by to befriend and support him, and whose name he never mentioned without love and veneration.

During the year 1817 we were established at Marlow in Buckinghamshire. Shelley's choice of abode was fixed chiefly by this town being at no great distance from London, and its neighbourhood to the Thames. The poem was written in his boat, as it floated under the beech-groves of Bisham, or during wanderings in the neighbouring country, which is distinguished for peculiar beauty. The chalk hills break into cliffs that overhang the Thames, or form valleys clothed with beech; the wilder portion of the country is rendered beautiful by exuberant vegetation; and the cultivated part is peculiarly fertile. With all this wealth of Nature which, either in the form of gentlemen's parks or soil dedicated to agriculture, flourishes around, Marlow was inhabited (I hope it is altered now) by a very poor population. The women are lacemakers, and lose their health by sedentary labour, for which they were very ill paid. The Poor-laws ground to the dust not only the paupers, but those who had risen just above that state, and were obliged to pay poor-rates. The changes produced by peace following a long war, and a bad harvest, brought with them the most heart-rending evils to the poor. Shelley afforded what alleviation he could. In the winter, while bringing out his poem, he had a severe attack of ophthalmia, caught while visiting the poor cottages. I mention these things—for this minute and active sympathy with his fellow-creatures gives a thousandfold interest to his speculations, and stamps with reality his pleadings for the human race.

The poem, bold in its opinions and uncompromising in their expression, met with many censurers, not only among those who allow of no virtue but such as supports the cause they espouse, but even among those whose opinions were similar to his own. I extract a portion of a letter written in answer to one of these friends. It best details the impulses of Shelley's mind, and his motives: it was written with entire unreserve; and is therefore a precious monument of his own opinion of his powers, of the purity of his designs, and the ardour with which he clung, in adversity and through the valley of the shadow of death, to views from which he believed the permanent happiness of mankind must eventually spring.

'Marlow, Dec. 11, 1817.

'I have read and considered all that you say about my general powers, and the particular instance of the poem in which I have attempted to develop them. Nothing can be more satisfactory to me than the interest which your admonitions express. But I think you are mistaken in some points with regard to the peculiar nature of my powers, whatever be their amount. I listened with deference and self-suspicion to your censures of *The Revolt of Islam;* but the productions of mine which you commend hold a very low place in my own esteem; and this reassures me, in some degree at least. The poem was produced by a series of thoughts which filled my mind with unbounded and sustained enthusiasm. I felt the precariousness of my life, and I engaged in this task, resolved to leave some record of myself. Much of what the volume contains was written with the same feeling—as real, though not so prophetic—as the communications of a dying man. I never presumed indeed to consider it anything approaching to faultless; but, when I consider contemporary productions of the same apparent pretensions, I own I was filled with confidence. I felt that it was in many respects a genuine picture of my own mind. I felt that the sentiments were true, not assumed. And in this have I long believed that my power consists; in sympathy, and that part of the imagination which relates to sentiment and contemplation. I am formed, if for anything not in common with the herd of mankind, to apprehend minute and remote distinction of feeling, whether relative to external nature or the living beings which surround us, and to communicate the conceptions which result from considering either the moral or the material universe as a whole. Of course, I believe these faculties, which perhaps comprehend all that is sublime in man, to exist very imperfectly in my own mind. But, when you advert to my Chancery-paper, a cold, forced, unimpassioned, insignificant piece of cramped and cautious argument, and to the little scrap about *Mandeville,* which expressed my feelings indeed, but cost scarcely two minutes' thought to express, as specimens of my powers more favourable than that which grew as it were from "the agony and bloody sweat" of intellectual travail; surely I must feel that, in some manner, either I am mistaken in believing that I have any talent at all, or you in the selection of the specimens of it. Yet, after all, I cannot but be conscious, in much of what I write, of an absence of that tranquillity which is the attribute and accompaniment of power. This feeling alone would make your most kind and wise admonitions, on the subject of the economy of intellectual force, valuable to me. And, if I live, or if I see

any trust in coming years, doubt not but that I shall do something, whatever it may be, which a serious and earnest estimate of my powers will
suggest to me, and which will be in every respect accommodated to their
utmost limits.' [Shelley to Godwin.]

PRINCE ATHANASE [1]

A FRAGMENT

PART I

THERE was a youth, who, as with toil and travel,
Had grown quite weak and gray before his time;
Nor any could the restless griefs unravel

Which burned within him, withering up his prime
And goading him, like fiends, from land to land.   5
Not his the load of any secret crime,

For nought of ill his heart could understand,
But pity and wild sorrow for the same;—
Not his the thirst for glory or command,

Baffled with blast of hope-consuming shame;   10
Nor evil joys which fire the vulgar breast,
And quench in speedy smoke its feeble flame,

Had left within his soul their dark unrest:
Nor what religion fables of the grave
Feared he,—Philosophy's accepted guest.   15

For none than he a purer heart could have,
Or that loved good more for itself alone;
Of nought in heaven or earth was he the slave.

What sorrow, strange, and shadowy, and unknown,
Sent him, a hopeless wanderer, through mankind?—   20
If with a human sadness he did groan,

[1] The idea Shelley had formed of Prince Athanase was a good deal modelled
on *Alastor*. In the first sketch of the poem, he named it *Pandemos and Urania*.
Athanase seeks through the world the One whom he may love. He meets, in the
ship in which he is embarked, a lady who appears to him to embody his ideal of
love and beauty. But she proves to be Pandemos, or the earthly and unworthy
Venus; who, after disappointing his cherished dreams and hopes, deserts him.
Athanase, crushed by sorrow, pines and dies. 'On his deathbed, the lady who can
really reply to his soul comes and kisses his lips' (*The Deathbed of Athanase*).
The poet describes her [in the words of the final fragment, p. 185]. This slender
note is all we have to aid our imagination in shaping out the form of the poem,
such as its author imagined. [Mrs. Shelley's Note.]

He had a gentle yet aspiring mind;
Just, innocent, with varied learning fed;
And such a glorious consolation find

In others' joy, when all their own is dead: 25
He loved, and laboured for his kind in grief,
And yet, unlike all others, it is said

That from such toil he never found relief.
Although a child of fortune and of power,
Of an ancestral name the orphan chief,   30

His soul had wedded Wisdom, and her dower
Is love and justice, clothed in which he sate
Apart from men, as in a lonely tower,

Pitying the tumult of their dark estate.—
Yet even in youth did he not e'er abuse   35
The strength of wealth or thought, to consecrate

Those false opinions which the harsh rich use
To blind the world they famish for their pride;
Nor did he hold from any man his dues,

But, like a steward in honest dealings tried,   40
With those who toiled and wept, the poor and wise,
His riches and his cares he did divide.

Fearless he was, and scorning all disguise,
What he dared do or think, though men might start,
He spoke with mild yet unaverted eyes;   45

Liberal he was of soul, and frank of heart,
And to his many friends—all loved him well—
Whate'er he knew or felt he would impart,

If words he found those inmost thoughts to tell;
If not, he smiled or wept; and his weak foes   50
He neither spurned nor hated—though with fell

And mortal hate their thousand voices rose,
They passed like aimless arrows from his ear—
Nor did his heart or mind its portal close

To those, or them, or any, whom life's sphere   55
May comprehend within its wide array.
What sadness made that vernal spirit sere?—

He knew not. Though his life, day after day,
Was failing like an unreplenished stream,
Though in his eyes a cloud and burthen lay,   60

Through which his soul, like Vesper's serene beam
Piercing the chasms of ever rising clouds,
Shone, softly burning; though his lips did seem

Like reeds which quiver in impetuous floods;
And through his sleep, and o'er each waking hour,   65
Thoughts after thoughts, unresting multitudes,

Were driven within him by some secret power,
Which bade them blaze, and live, and roll afar,
Like lights and sounds, from haunted tower to tower

O'er castled mountains borne, when tempest's war   70
Is levied by the night-contending winds,
And the pale dalesmen watch with eager ear;—

Though such were in his spirit, as the fiends
Which wake and feed an everliving woe,—
What was this grief, which ne'er in other minds   75

A mirror found,—he knew not—none could know;
But on whoe'er might question him he turned
The light of his frank eyes, as if to show

He knew not of the grief within that burned,
But asked forbearance with a mournful look;   80
Or spoke in words from which none ever learned

The cause of his disquietude; or shook
With spasms of silent passion; or turned pale:
So that his friends soon rarely undertook

To stir his secret pain without avail;—   85
For all who knew and loved him then perceived
That there was drawn an adamantine veil

Between his heart and mind,—both unrelieved
Wrought in his brain and bosom separate strife.
Some said that he was mad, others believed   90

That memories of an antenatal life
Made this, where now he dwelt, a penal hell;
And others said that such mysterious grief

From God's displeasure, like a darkness, fell
On souls like his, which owned no higher law   95
Than love; love calm, steadfast, invincible

By mortal fear or supernatural awe;
And others,—' 'Tis the shadow of a dream
Which the veiled eye of Memory never saw,

'But through the soul's abyss, like some dark stream   100
Through shattered mines and caverns underground,
Rolls, shaking its foundations; and no beam

'Of joy may rise, but it is quenched and drowned
In the dim whirlpools of this dream obscure;
Soon its exhausted waters will have found   105

'A lair of rest beneath thy spirit pure,
O Athanase!—in one so good and great,
Evil or tumult cannot long endure.'

So spake they: idly of another's state
Babbling vain words and fond philosophy;   110
This was their consolation; such debate

Men held with one another; nor did he,
Like one who labours with a human woe,
Decline this talk: as if its theme might be

Another, not himself, he to and fro   115
Questioned and canvassed it with subtlest wit;
And none but those who loved him best could know

That which he knew not, how it galled and bit
His weary mind, this converse vain and cold;
For like an eyeless nightmare grief did sit   120

Upon his being; a snake which fold by fold
Pressed out the life of life, a clinging fiend
Which clenched him if he stirred with deadlier hold;—
And so his grief remained—let it remain—untold.[1]

---

[1] The Author was pursuing a fuller development of the ideal character of Athanase, when it struck him that in an attempt at extreme refinement and analysis, his conceptions might be betrayed into assuming a morbid character. The reader will judge whether he is a loser or gainer by the difference. [Shelley's Note.]

PART II

FRAGMENT I

PRINCE ATHANASE had one belovèd friend,   125
An old, old man, with hair of silver white,
And lips where heavenly smiles would hang.and blend

With his wise words; and eyes whose arrowy light
Shone like the reflex of a thousand minds.
He was the last whom superstition's blight   130

Had spared in Greece—the blight that cramps and blinds,—
And in his olive bower at Œnoe
Had sate from earliest youth. Like one who finds

A fertile island in the barren sea,
One mariner who has survived his mates   135
Many a drear month in a great ship—so he

With soul-sustaining songs, and sweet debates
Of ancient lore, there fed his lonely being:—
'The mind becomes that which it contemplates.'—

And thus Zonoras, by forever seeing   140
Their bright creations, grew like wisest men;
And when he heard the crash of nations fleeing

A bloodier power than ruled thy ruins then,
O sacred Hellas! many weary years
He wandered, till the path of Laian's glen   145

Was grass-grown—and the unremembered tears
Were dry in Laian for their honoured chief,
Who fell in Byzant, pierced by Moslem spears:—

And as the lady looked with faithful grief
From her high lattice o'er the rugged path,   150
Where she once saw that horseman toil, with brief

And blighting hope, who with the news of death
Struck body and soul as with a mortal blight,
She saw between the chestnuts, far beneath,

An old man toiling up, a weary wight;   155
And soon within her hospitable hall
She saw his white hairs glittering in the light

Of the wood fire, and round his shoulders fall;
And his wan visage and his withered mien,
Yet calm and gentle and majestical.   160

And Athanase, her child, who must have been
Then three years old, sate opposite and gazed
In patient silence.

FRAGMENT II

SUCH was Zonoras; and as daylight finds
One amaranth glittering on the path of frost,   165
When autumn nights have nipped all weaker kinds,

Thus through his age, dark, cold, and tempest-tossed,
Shone truth upon Zonoras; and he filled
From fountains pure, nigh overgrown and lost,

The spirit of Prince Athanase, a child,   170
With soul-sustaining songs of ancient lore
And philosophic wisdom, clear and mild.

And sweet and subtle talk they evermore,
The pupil and the master, shared; until,
Sharing that undiminishable store,   175

The youth, as shadows on a grassy hill
Outrun the winds that chase them, soon outran
His teacher, and did teach with native skill

Strange truths and new to that experienced man;
Still they were friends, as few have ever been   180
Who mark the extremes of life's discordant span.

So in the caverns of the forest green,
Or on the rocks of echoing ocean hoar,
Zonoras and Prince Athanase were seen

By summer woodmen; and when winter's roar   185
Sounded o'er earth and sea its blast of war,
The Balearic fisher, driven from shore,

Hanging upon the peakèd wave afar,
Then saw their lamp from Laian's turret gleam,
Piercing the stormy darkness, like a star   190

Which pours beyond the sea one steadfast beam,
Whilst all the constellations of the sky
Seemed reeling through the storm . . . They did but seem—

For, lo! the wintry clouds are all gone by,
And bright Arcturus through yon pines is glowing,   195
And far o'er southern waves, immovably

Belted Orion hangs—warm light is flowing
From the young moon into the sunset's chasm.—
'O, summer eve! with power divine, bestowing

'On thine own bird the sweet enthusiasm   200
Which overflows in notes of liquid gladness,
Filling the sky like light! How many a spasm

'Of fevered brains, oppressed with grief and madness,
Were lulled by thee, delightful nightingale,—
And these soft waves, murmuring a gentle sadness,—   205

'And the far sighings of yon piny dale
Made vocal by some wind we feel not here.—
I bear alone what nothing may avail

'To lighten—a strange load!'—No human ear
Heard this lament; but o'er the visage wan   210
Of Athanase, a ruffling atmosphere

Of dark emotion, a swift shadow, ran,
Like wind upon some forest-bosomed lake,
Glassy and dark.—And that divine old man

Beheld his mystic friend's whole being shake,   215
Even where its inmost depths were gloomiest—
And with a calm and measured voice he spake,

And, with a soft and equal pressure, pressed
That cold lean hand:—'Dost thou remember yet
When the curved moon then lingering in the west   220

'Paused, in yon waves her mighty horns to wet,
How in those beams we walked, half resting on the sea?
'Tis just one year—sure thou dost not forget—

'Then Plato's words of light in thee and me
Lingered like moonlight in the moonless east,   225
For we had just then read—thy memory

'Is faithful now—the story of the feast;
And Agathon and Diotima seemed
From death and dark forgetfulness released . . . . .'

FRAGMENT III

AND when the old man saw that on the green   230
Leaves of his opening   a blight had lighted
He said: 'My friend, one grief alone can wean

A gentle mind from all that once delighted:—
Thou lovest, and thy secret heart is laden
With feelings which should not be unrequited.'   235

And Athanase . . . then smiled, as one o'erladen
With iron chains might smile to talk (?) of bands
Twined round her lover's neck by some blithe maiden,
And said . . . . .

FRAGMENT IV

'TWAS at the season when the Earth upsprings   240
From slumber, as a spherèd angel's child,
Shadowing its eyes with green and golden wings,

Stands up before its mother bright and mild,
Of whose soft voice the air expectant seems—
So stood before the sun, which shone and smiled   245

To see it rise thus joyous from its dreams,
The fresh and radiant Earth. The hoary grove
Waxed green—and flowers burst forth like starry beams;—

The grass in the warm sun did start and move,
And sea-buds burst under the waves serene:—   250
How many a one, though none be near to love,

Loves then the shade of his own soul, half seen
In any mirror—or the spring's young minions,
The wingèd leaves amid the copses green;—

How many a spirit then puts on the pinions   255
Of fancy, and outstrips the lagging blast,
And his own steps—and over wide dominions

Sweeps in his dream-drawn chariot, far and fast,
More fleet than storms—the wide world shrinks below,
When winter and despondency are past.   260

FRAGMENT V

'TWAS at this season that Prince Athanase
Passed the white Alps—those eagle-baffling mountains
Slept in their shrouds of snow;—beside the ways

The waterfalls were voiceless—for their fountains
Were changed to mines of sunless crystal now,   265
Or by the curdling winds—like brazen wings

Which clanged along the mountain's marble brow—
Warped into adamantine fretwork, hung
And filled with frozen light the chasms below.

Vexed by the blast, the great pines groaned and swung
Under their load of [snow]—   271
    .   .   .   .

    .   .   .   .
Such as the eagle sees, when he dives down
From the gray deserts of wide air, [beheld]   275
[Prince] Athanase; and o'er his mien (?) was thrown

The shadow of that scene, field after field,
Purple and dim and wide . . . . .

FRAGMENT VI

THOU art the wine whose drunkenness is all
We can desire, O Love! and happy souls,   280
Ere from thy vine the leaves of autumn fall,

Catch thee, and feed from their o'erflowing bowls
Thousands who thirst for thine ambrosial dew;—
Thou art the radiance which where ocean rolls

Investeth it; and when the heavens are blue   285
Thou fillest them; and when the earth is fair
The shadow of thy moving wings imbue

Its deserts and its mountains, till they wear
Beauty like some light robe;—thou ever soarest
Among the towers of men, and as soft air   290

In spring, which moves the unawakened forest,
Clothing with leaves its branches bare and bleak,
Thou floatest among men; and aye implorest

That which from thee they should implore:—the weak.
Alone kneel to thee, offering up the hearts   295
The strong have broken—yet where shall any seek

A garment whom thou clothest not? the darts
Of the keen winter storm, barbèd with frost,
Which, from the everlasting snow that parts

The Alps from Heaven, pierce some traveller lost   300
In the wide waved interminable snow
Ungarmented, ...

ANOTHER FRAGMENT (A)

YES, often when the eyes are cold and dry,
And the lips calm, the Spirit weeps within
Tears bitterer than the blood of agony   305

Trembling in drops on the discoloured skin
Of those who love their kind and therefore perish
In ghastly torture—a sweet medicine

Of peace and sleep are tears, and quietly
Them soothe from whose uplifted eyes they fall   310
But . . . . .

ANOTHER FRAGMENT (B)

HER hair was brown, her spherèd eyes were brown,
And in their dark and liquid moisture swam,
Like the dim orb of the eclipsèd moon;

Yet when the spirit flashed beneath, there came   315
The light from them, as when tears of delight
Double the western planet's serene flame.

ROSALIND AND HELEN

A MODERN ECLOGUE

ADVERTISEMENT

THE story of *Rosalind and Helen* is, undoubtedly, not an attempt in the highest style of poetry. It is in no degree calculated to excite profound meditation; and if, by interesting the affections and amusing the imagination, it awakens a certain ideal melancholy favourable to the reception of more important impressions, it will produce in the reader all that the writer experienced in the composition. I resigned myself, as I wrote, to the impulse of the feelings which moulded the conception of the story; and this impulse determined the pauses of a measure, which only pretends to be regular inasmuch as it corresponds with, and expresses, the irregularity of the imaginations which inspired it.

I do not know which of the few scattered poems I left in England will be selected by my bookseller to add to this collection. One,[1] which I sent from Italy, was written after a day's excursion among those lovely mountains which surround what was once the retreat, and where is now the sepulchre, of Petrarch. If any one is inclined to condemn the insertion of the introductory lines, which image forth the sudden relief of a state of deep despondency by the radiant visions disclosed by the sudden burst of an Italian sunrise in autumn on the highest peak of those delightful mountains, I can only offer as my excuse, that they were not erased at the request of a dear friend, with whom added years of intercourse only add to my apprehension of its value, and who would have had more right than any one to complain, that she has not been able to extinguish in me the very power of delineating sadness.

NAPLES, *Dec.* 20, 1818.

ROSALIND, HELEN AND HER CHILD

Scene, the Shore of the Lake of Como

Helen. Come hither, my sweet
    Rosalind.
'Tis long since thou and I have
    met;
And yet methinks it were unkind
Those moments to forget.
Come sit by me. I see thee stand 5
By this lone lake, in this far land,
Thy loose hair in the light wind
    flying,
Thy sweet voice to each tone of
    even
United, and thine eyes replying
To the hues of yon fair heaven. 10
Come, gentle friend: wilt sit by me?
And be as thou wert wont to be
Ere we were disunited?
None doth behold us now: the
    power
That led us forth at this lone hour
Will be but ill requited   16
If thou depart in scorn: oh! come,
And talk of our abandoned home.

Remember, this is Italy,
And we are exiles. Talk with me 20
Of that our land, whose wilds and
    floods,
Barren and dark although they be,
Were dearer than these chestnut
    woods:
Those heathy paths, that inland
    stream,
And the blue mountains, shapes
    which seem 25
Like wrecks of childhood's sunny
    dream:
Which that we have abandoned
    now,
Weighs on the heart like that re-
    morse
Which altered friendship leaves. I
    seek 29
No more our youthful intercourse.
That cannot be! Rosalind, speak.
Speak to me. Leave me not.—When
    morn did come,

[1] 'Lines written among the Euganean Hills.'

When evening fell upon our com-
    mon home,
When for one hour we parted,—
    do not frown:
I would not chide thee, though thy
    faith is broken:
But turn to me. Oh! by this cher-
    ished token,   36
Of woven hair, which thou wilt not
    disown,
Turn, as 'twere but the memory of
    me,
And not my scornèd self who
    prayed to thee.
    Rosalind. Is it a dream, or do I
        see   40
And hear frail Helen? I would flee
Thy tainting touch; but former
    years
Arise, and bring forbidden tears;
And my o'erburthened memory
Seeks yet its lost repose in thee. 45
I share thy crime. I cannot choose
But weep for thee: mine own
    strange grief
But seldom stoops to such relief:
Nor ever did I love thee less,
Though mourning o'er thy wicked-
    ness   50
Even with a sister's woe. I knew
What to the evil world is due,
And therefore sternly did refuse
To link me with the infamy
Of one so lost as Helen. Now   55
Bewildered by my dire despair,
Wondering I blush, and weep that
    thou
Should'st love me still,—thou only!
    —There,
Let us sit on that gray stone,
Till our mournful talk be done. 60
    Helen. Alas! not there; I cannot
        bear
The murmur of this lake to hear.
A sound from there, Rosalind dear,
Which never yet I heard elsewhere
But in our native land, recurs,   65

Even here where now we meet. It
    stirs
Too much of suffocating sorrow!
In the dell of yon dark chestnut
    wood
Is a stone seat, a solitude
Less like our own. The ghost of
    Peace   70
Will not desert this spot. To-
    morrow,
If thy kind feelings should not
    cease,
We may sit here.
    Rosalind. Thou lead, my sweet,
And I will follow.
    Henry.   'Tis Fenici's seat
Where you are going? This is not
    the way,   75
Mamma; it leads behind those
    trees that grow
Close to the little river.
    Helen.   Yes: I know:
I was bewildered. Kiss me, and be
    gay,
Dear boy: why do you sob?
    Henry.   I do not know:
But it might break any one's heart
    to see   80
You and the lady cry so bitterly.
    Helen. It is a gentle child, my
        friend. Go home,
Henry, and play with Lilla till I
    come.
We only cried with joy to see each
    other;
We are quite merry now: Good-
    night.
                The boy   85
Lifted a sudden look upon his
    mother,
And in the gleam of forced and
    hollow joy
Which lightened o'er her face,
    laughed with the glee
Of light and unsuspecting infancy,
And whispered in her ear, 'Bring
    home with you   90

That sweet strange lady-friend.'
   Then off he flew,
But stopped, and beckoned with
   a meaning smile,
Where the road turned. Pale Rosa-
   lind the while,
Hiding her face, stood weeping
   silently.

In silence then they took the way 95
Beneath the forest's solitude.
It was a vast and antique wood,
Thro' which they took their way;
And the gray shades of evening
O'er that green wilderness did
   fling   100
Still deeper solitude.
Pursuing still the path that wound
The vast and knotted trees around
Through which slow shades were
   wandering,
To a deep lawny dell they came,
To a stone seat beside a spring, 106
O'er which the columned wood did
   frame
A roofless temple, like the fane
Where, ere new creeds could faith
   obtain,
Man's early race once knelt be-
   neath   110
The overhanging deity.
O'er this fair fountain hung the sky,
Now spangled with rare stars. The
   snake,
The pale snake, that with eager
   breath
Creeps here his noontide thirst to
   slake,   115
Is beaming with many a mingled
   hue,
Shed from yon dome's eternal blue,
When he floats on that dark and
   lucid flood
In the light of his own loveliness;
And the birds that in the fountain
   dip   120

Their plumes, with fearless fellow-
   ship
Above and round him wheel and
   hover.
The fitful wind is heard to stir
One solitary leaf on high;
The chirping of the grasshopper 125
Fills every pause. There is emotion
In all that dwells at noontide here:
Then, through the intricate wild
   wood,
A maze of life and light and motion
Is woven. But there is stillness
   now: 130
Gloom, and the trance of Nature
   now:
The snake is in his cave asleep;
The birds are on the branches
   dreaming:
Only the shadows creep: 134
Only the glow-worm is gleaming:
Only the owls and the nightingales
Wake in this dell when daylight
   fails,
And gray shades gather in the
   woods:
And the owls have all fled far away
In a merrier glen to hoot and
   play,   140
For the moon is veiled and sleeping
   now.
The accustomed nightingale still
   broods
On her accustomed bough.
But she is mute; for her false mate
Has fled and left her desolate. 145

This silent spot tradition old
Had peopled with the spectral
   dead.
For the roots of the speaker's hair
   felt cold
And stiff, as with tremulous lips he
   told
That a hellish shape at midnight
   led   150

The ghost of a youth with hoary
    hair,
And sate on the seat beside him
    there,
Till a naked child came wandering
    by,
When the fiend would change to a
    lady fair!
A fearful tale! The truth was
    worse: 155
For here a sister and a brother
Had solemnized a monstrous curse,
Meeting in this fair solitude:
For beneath yon very sky,
Had they resigned to one another
Body and soul. The multitude: 161
Tracking them to the secret wood,
Tore limb from limb their innocent
    child,
And stabbed and trampled on its
    mother;
But the youth, for God's most holy
    grace,   165
A priest saved to burn in the
    market-place.

Duly at evening Helen came
To this lone silent spot,
From the wrecks of a tale of wilder
    sorrow
So much of sympathy to borrow 170
As soothed her own dark lot.
Duly each evening from her home,
With her fair child would Helen
    come
To sit upon that antique seat, 174
While the hues of day were pale;
And the bright boy beside her feet
Now lay, lifting at intervals
His broad blue eyes on her;
Now, where some sudden impulse
    calls
Following. He was a gentle boy 180
And in all gentle sports took
    joy;
Oft in a dry leaf for a boat,
With a small feather for a sail,

His fancy on that spring would
    float,   184
If some invisible breeze might stir
Its marble calm: and Helen smiled
Through tears of awe on the gay
    child,
To think that a boy as fair as he,
In years which never more may be,
By that same fount, in that same
    wood,   190
The like sweet fancies had pursued;
And that a mother, lost like her,
Had mournfully sate watching him.
Then all the scene was wont to swim
Through the mist of a burning
    tear.   195

For many months had Helen known
This scene; and now she thither
    turned
Her footsteps, not alone.
The friend whose falsehood she had
    mourned,
Sate with her on that seat of stone.
Silent they sate; for evening, 201
And the power its glimpses bring
Had; with one awful shadow,
    quelled
The passion of their grief. They
    sate
With linkèd hands, for unre-
    pelled   205
Had Helen taken Rosalind's.
Like the autumn wind, when it
    unbinds
The tangled locks of the night-
    shade's hair,
Which is twined in the sultry
    summer air
Round the walls of an outworn
    sepulchre,   210
Did the voice of Helen, sad and
    sweet,
And the sound of her heart that
    ever beat,
As with sighs and words she
    breathed on her,

Unbind the knots of her friend's
    despair,
Till her thoughts were free to float
    and flow;   215
And from her labouring bosom
    now,
Like the bursting of a prisoned
    flame,
The voice of a long pent sorrow
    came.
  Rosalind. I saw the dark earth
    fall upon
The coffin; and I saw the stone 220
Laid over him whom this cold
    breast   ·
Had pillowed to his nightly rest!
Thou knowest not, thou canst not
    know   ·
My agony. Oh! I could not weep:
The sources whence such blessings
    flow   225
Were not to be approached by me!
But I could smile, and I could
    sleep,
Though with a self-accusing heart.
In morning's light, in evening's
    gloom,
I watched,—and would not thence
    depart—   230
My husband's unlamented tomb.
My children knew their sire was
    gone,
But when I told them,—'he is
    dead,'—
They laughed aloud in frantic glee,
They clapped their hands and
    leaped about,   235
Answering each other's ecstasy
With many a prank and merry
    shout.
But I sate silent and alone,
Wrapped in the mock of mourning
    weed.

They laughed, for he was dead:
    but I   240
Sate with a hard and tearless eye,

And with a heart which would
    deny
The secret joy it could not quell,
Low muttering o'er his loathèd
    name;
Till from that self-contention
    came   245
Remorse where sin was none; a hell
Which in pure spirits should not
    dwell.
I'll tell thee truth. He was a man
Hard, selfish, loving only gold,
Yet full of guile: his pale eyes
    ran   250
With tears, which each some false-
    hood told,
And oft his smooth and bridled
    tongue
Would give the lie to his flushing
    cheek:
He was a coward to the strong:
He was a tyrant to the weak,   255
On whom his vengeance he would
    wreak:
For scorn, whose arrows search the
    ' heart,
From many a stranger's eye would
    dart,
And on his memory cling, and fol-
    low
His soul to its home so cold and
    hollow.   260
He was a tyrant to the weak,
And we were such, alas the day!
Oft, when my little ones at play,
Were in youth's natural lightness
    gay,
Or if they listened to some tale 265
Of travellers, or of fairy land,—
When the light from the wood-fire's
    dying brand
Flashed on their faces,—if they
    heard
Or thought they heard upon the
    stair   269
His footstep, the suspended word
Died on my lips: we all grew pale:

The babe at my bosom was hushed
with fear
If it thought it heard its father
near;
And my two wild boys would near
my knee
Cling, cowed and cowering fear-
fully.   275

I'll tell thee truth: I loved another.
His name in my ear was ever
ringing,
His form to my brain was ever
clinging:
Yet if some stranger breathed that
name,
My lips turned white, and my heart
beat fast: 280
My nights were once haunted by
dreams of flame,
My days were dim in the shadow
cast
By the memory of the same!
Day and night, day and night,
He was my breath and life and
light,   285
For three short years, which soon
were passed.
On the fourth, my gentle mother
Led me to the shrine, to be
His sworn bride eternally.
And now we stood on the altar
stair,   290
When my father came from a dis-
tant land,
And with a loud and fearful cry
Rushed between us suddenly.
I saw the stream of his thin gray
hair,
I saw his lean and lifted hand, 295
And heard his words,—and live!
Oh God!
Wherefore do I live?—'Hold,
hold!'
He cried,—'I tell thee 'tis her
brother!
Thy mother, boy, beneath the sod

Of yon churchyard rests in her
shroud so cold: 300
I am now weak, and pale, and old:
We were once dear to one another,
I and that corpse! Thou art our
child!'
Then with a laugh both long and
wild   304
The youth upon the pavement fell:
They found him dead! All looked
on me,
The spasms of my despair to see:
But I was calm. I went away:
I was clammy-cold like clay!   309
I did not weep: I did not speak:
But day by day, week after week,
I walked about like a corpse alive!
Alas! sweet friend, you must be-
lieve
This heart is stone: it did not
break.
My father lived a little while,   315
But all might see that he was dying,
He smiled with such a woeful smile!
When he was in the churchyard
lying
Among the worms, we grew quite
poor,
So that no one would give us
bread: 320
My mother looked at me, and said
Faint words of cheer, which only
meant
That she could die and be content;
So I went forth from the same
church door
To another husband's bed.   325
And this was he who died at last,
When weeks and months and years
had passed,
Through which I firmly did fulfil
My duties, a devoted wife,
With the stern step of vanquished
will,   330
Walking beneath the night of life,
Whose hours extinguished, like
slow rain

Falling for ever, pain by pain,
The very hope of death's dear rest;
Which, since the heart within my
   breast   335
Of natural life was dispossessed,
Its strange sustainer there had been.

Wher flowers were dead, and grass
   was green
Upon my mother's grave,—that
   mother
Whom to outlive, and cheer, and
   make   340
My wan eyes glitter for her sake,
Was my vowed task, the single
   care
Which once gave life to my de-
   spair,—
When she was a thing that did not
   stir
And the crawling worms were
   cradling her   345
To a sleep more deep and so more
   sweet
Than a baby's rocked on its nurse's
   knee,
I lived: a living pulse then beat
Beneath my heart that awakened
   me.
What was this pulse so warm and
   free?   350
Alas! I knew it could not be
My own dull blood: 'twas like a
   thought
Of liquid love, that spread and
   wrought
Under my bosom and in my brain,
And crept with the blood through
   every vein;   355
And hour by hour, day after day,
The wonder could not charm away,
But laid in sleep, my wakeful pain,
Until I knew it was a child,
And then I wept. For long, long
   years   360
These frozen eyes had shed no
   tears:

But now—'twas the season fair and
   mild
When April has wept itself to May:
I sate through the sweet sunny day
By my window bowered round with
   leaves,   365
And down my cheeks the quick
   tears fell
Like twinkling rain-drops from the
   eaves,
When warm spring showers are
   passing o'er:
O Helen, none can ever tell
The joy it was to weep once
   more!   370

I wept to think how hard it were
To kill my babe, and take from it
The sense of light, and the warm
   air,
And my own fond and tender care,
And love and smiles; ere I knew
   yet   375
That these for it might, as for me,
Be the masks of a grinning mock-
   ery.
And haply, I would dream, 'twere
   sweet
To feed it from my faded breast,
Or mark my own heart's restless
   beat   380
Rock it to its untroubled rest,
And watch the growing soul be-
   neath
Dawn in faint smiles; and hear its
   breath,
Half interrupted by calm sighs,
And search the depth of its fair
   eyes   385
For long departed memories!
And so I lived till that sweet load
Was lightened. Darkly forward
   flowed
The stream of years, and on it bore
Two shapes of gladness to my
   sight;   390
Two other babes, delightful more

In my lost soul's abandoned night,
Than their own country ships may
    be
Sailing towards wrecked mariners,
Who cling to the rock of a wintry
    sea.   395
For each, as it came, brought sooth-
    ing tears,
And a loosening warmth, as each
    one lay
Sucking the sullen milk away
About my frozen heart, did play,
And weaned it, oh how pain-
    fully!—   400
As they themselves were weaned
    each one
From that sweet food,—even from
    the thirst
Of death, and nothingness, and
    rest,
Strange inmate of a living breast!
Which all that I had undergone 405
Of grief and shame, since she, who
    first
The gates of that dark refuge
    closed,
Came to my sight, and almost burst
The seal of that Lethean spring;
But these fair shadows inter-
    posed: 410
For all delights are shadows now!
And from my brain to my dull brow
The heavy tears gather and flow:
I cannot speak: Oh let me weep!

The tears which fell from her wan
    eyes   415
Glimmered among the moonlight
    dew:
Her deep hard sobs and heavy sighs
Their echoes in the darkness threw.
When she grew calm, she thus did
    keep
The tenor of her tale:
                He died: 420
I know not how: he was not old,
If age be numbered by its years:

But he was bowed and bent with
    fears,
Pale with the quenchless thirst of
    gold,
Which, like fierce fever, left him
    weak;   425
And his strait lip and bloated cheek
Were warped in spasms by hollow
    sneers;
And selfish cares with barren
    plough,
Not age, had lined his narrow
    brow,
And foul and cruel thoughts, which
    feed   430
Upon the withering life within,
Like vipers on some poisonous
    weed.
Whether his ill were death or sin
None knew, until he died indeed,
And then men owned they were the
    same.   435

Seven days within my chamber lay
That corse, and my babes made
    holiday:
At last, I told them what is death:
The eldest, with a kind of shame,
Came to my knees with silent
    breath,   440
And sate awe-stricken at my feet;
And soon the others left their play,
And sate there too. It is unmeet
To shed on the brief flower of youth
The withering knowledge of the
    grave;   445
From me remorse then wrung that
    truth.
I could not bear the joy which gave
Too just a response to mine own.
In vain. I dared not feign a groan;
And in their artless looks I saw, 450
Between the mists of fear and awe,
That my own thought was theirs;
    and they
Expressed it not in words, but said,
Each in its heart, how every day

Will pass in happy work and play,
Now he is dead and gone away. 456

After the funeral all our kin
Assembled, and the will was read.
My friend, I tell thee, even the dead
Have strength, their putrid shrouds
    within,   460
To blast and torture. Those who
    live
Still fear the living, but a corse
Is merciless, and power doth give
To such pale tyrants half the spoil
He rends from those who groan and
    toil,   465
Because they blush not with re-
    morse
Among their crawling worms. Be-
    hold,
I have no child! my tale grows old
With grief, and staggers: let it
    reach
The limits of my feeble speech, 470
And languidly at length recline
On the brink of its own grave and
    mine.

Thou knowest what a thing is Pov-
    erty
Among the fallen on evil days:
'Tis Crime, and Fear, and In-
    famy,   475
And houseless Want in frozen ways
Wandering ungarmented, and Pain,
And, worse than all, that inward
    stain
Foul Self-contempt, which drowns
    in sneers
Youth's starlight smile, and makes
    its tears   480
First like hot gall, then dry for
    ever!
And well thou knowest a mother
    never
Could doom her children to this ill,
And well he knew the same. The
    will

Imported, that if e'er again   485
I sought my children to behold,
Or in my birthplace did remain
Beyond three days, whose hours
    were told,
They should inherit nought: and
    he,
To whom next came their patri-
    mony,   490
A sallow lawyer, cruel and cold,
Aye watched me, as the will was
    read,
With eyes askance, which sought
    to see
The secrets of my agony;
And with close lips and anxious
    brow   495
Stood canvassing still to and fro
The chance of my resolve, and all
The dead man's caution just did
    call;
For in that killing lie 'twas said—
'She is adulterous, and doth
    hold   500
In secret that the Christian creed
Is false, and therefore is much need
That I should have a care to save
My children from eternal fire.'
Friend, he was sheltered by the
    grave,   505
And therefore dared to be a liar!
In truth, the Indian on the pyre
Of her dead husband, half con-
    sumed,
As well might there be false, as I
To those abhorred embraces
    doomed,   510
Far worse than fire's brief agony.
As to the Christian creed, if true
Or false, I never questioned it:
I took it as the vulgar do:
Nor my vexed soul had leisure
    yet   515
To doubt the things men say, or
    deem
That they are other than they
    seem.

All present who those crimes did
    hear,
In feigned or actual scorn and fear,
Men, women, children, slunk
    away,   520
Whispering with self-contented
    pride,
Which half suspects its own base
    lie.
I spoke to none, nor did abide,
But silently I went my way,
Nor noticed I where joyously 525
Sate my two younger babes at play,
In the court-yard through which I
    passed;
But went with footsteps firm and
    fast
Till I came to the brink of the
    ocean green,
And there, a woman with gray
    hairs,   530
Who had my mother's servant
    been,
Kneeling, with many tears and
    prayers,
Made me accept a purse of gold,
Half of the earnings she had kept
To refuge her when weak and
    old.   535

With woe, which never sleeps or
    slept,
I wander now. 'Tis a vain
    thought—
But on yon alp, whose snowy head
'Mid the azure air is islanded,
(We see it o'er the flood of
    cloud,   540
Which sunrise from its eastern
    caves
Drives, wrinkling into golden
    waves,
Hung with its precipices proud,
From that gray stone where first
    we met)
There—now who knows the dead
    feel nought?—   545

Should be my grave; for he who yet
Is my soul's soul, once said:
    ' 'Twere sweet
'Mid stars and lightnings to abide,
And winds and lulling snows, that
    beat
With their soft flakes the moun-
    tain wide,   550
Where weary meteor lamps repose,
And languid storms their pinions
    close:
And all things strong and bright
    and pure,
And ever during, aye endure:
Who knows, if one were buried
    there,   555
But these things might our spirits
    make,
Amid the all-surrounding air,
Their own eternity partake?'
Then 'twas a wild and playful say-
    ing
At which I laughed, or seemed to
    laugh: 560
They were his words.. now heed
    my praying,
And let them be my epitaph.
Thy memory for a term may be
My monument. Wilt remember
    me?
I know thou wilt, and canst for-
    give   565
Whilst in this erring world to live
My soul disdained not, that I
    thought
Its lying forms were worthy aught
And much less thee.
Helen.   O speak not so,
But come to me and pour thy
    woe   570
Into this heart, full though it be,
Ay, overflowing with its own:
I thought that grief had severed
    me
From all beside who weep and
    groan;
Its likeness upon earth to be, 575

Its express image; but thou art
More wretched. Sweet! we will not
    part
Henceforth, if death be not divi-
    sion;
If so, the dead feel no contrition.
But wilt thou hear since last we
    parted   580
All that has left me broken hearted?
    Rosalind. Yes, speak. The faint-
    est stars are scarcely shorn
Of their thin beams by that delu-
    sive morn
Which sinks again in darkness, like
    the light
Of early love, soon lost in total
    night.   585
    Helen. Alas! Italian winds are
    mild,
But my bosom is cold—wintry
    cold—
When the warm air weaves, among
    the fresh leaves,
Soft music, my poor brain is
    wild,
And I am weak like a nursling
    child,   590
Though my soul with grief is gray
    and old.
    Rosalind. Weep not at thine own
    words, though they must
    make
Me weep. What is thy tale?
    Helen.   I fear 'twill shake
Thy gentle heart with tears. Thou
    well
Rememberest when we met no
    more,   595
And, though I dwelt with Lionel,
That friendless caution pierced me
    sore
With grief; a wound my spirit
    bore
Indignantly, but when he died
With him lay dead both hope and
    pride.   600
Alas! all hope is buried now.

But then men dreamed the agèd
    earth
Was labouring in that mighty birth,
Which many a poet and a sage
Has aye foreseen—the happy
    age   605
When truth and love shall dwell
    below
Among the works and ways of
    men;
Which on this world not power but
    will
Even now is wanting to fulfil.

Among mankind what thence be-
    fell   610
Of strife, how vain, is known too
    well;
When Liberty's dear paean fell
'Mid murderous howls. To Lionel,
Though of great wealth and line-
    age high,
Yet through those dungeon walls
    there came   615
Thy thrilling light, O Liberty!
And as the meteor's midnight
    flame
Startles the dreamer, sun-like truth
Flashed on his visionary youth,
And filled him, not with love, but
    faith,   620
And hope, and courage mute in
    death;
For love and life in him were
    twins,
Born at one birth: in every other
First life then love its course be-
    gins,
Though they be children of one
    mother;   625
And so through this dark world
    they fleet
Divided, till in death they meet:
But he loved all things ever. Then
He passed amid the strife of men,
And stood at the throne of armèd
    power   630

Pleading for a world of woe:
Secure as one on a rock-built tower
O'er the wrecks which the surge
    trails to and fro,
'Mid the passions wild of human
    kind
He stood, like a spirit calming
    them;   635
For, it was said, his words could
    bind
Like music the lulled crowd, and
    stem
That torrent of unquiet dream,
Which mortals truth and reason
    deem,
But is revenge and fear and
    pride.   640
Joyous he was; and hope and peace
On all who heard him did abide,
Raining like dew from his sweet
    talk,
As where the evening star may
    walk   644
Along the brink of the gloomy seas,
Liquid mists of splendour quiver.
His very gestures touched to tears
The unpersuaded tyrant, never
So moved before: his presence
    stung
The torturers with their victim's
    pain,   650
And none knew how; and through
    their ears,
The subtle witchcraft of his tongue
Unlocked the hearts of those who
    keep
Gold, the world's bond of slavery.
Men wondered, and some sneered
    to see   655
One sow what he could never reap:
For he is rich, they said, 'and
    young,
And might drink from the depths
    of luxury.
If he seeks Fame, Fame never
    crowned
The champion of a trampled creed:

If he seeks Power, Power is en-
    throned   661
'Mid ancient rights and wrongs, to
    feed
Which hungry wolves with praise
    and spoil,
Those who would sit near Power
    must toil;
And such, there sitting, all may
    see.   665
What seeks he? All that others seek
He casts away, like a vile weed
Which the sea casts unreturn-
    ingly.
That poor and hungry men should
    break
The laws which wreak them toil
    and scorn,   670
We understand; but Lionel
We know is rich and nobly born.
So wondered they: yet all men
    loved
Young Lionel, though few ap-
    proved;
All but the priests, whose hatred
    fell   675
Like the unseen blight of a smil-
    ing day,
The withering honey dew, which
    clings
Under the bright green buds of
    May,
Whilst they unfold their emerald
    wings:
For he made verses wild and queer
On the strange creeds priests hold
    so dear,   681
Because they bring them land and
    gold.
Of devils and saints and all such
    gear,
He made tales which whoso heard
    or read
Would laugh till he were almost
    dead.   685
So this grew a proverb: 'Don't get
    old

Till Lionel's "Banquet in Hell"
   you hear,
And then you will laugh yourself
   young again.'
So the priests hated him, and he
Repaid their hate with cheerful
   glee.   690

Ah, smiles and joyance quickly
   died,
For public hope grew pale and dim
In an altered time and tide,
And in its wasting withered him,
As a summer flower that blows too
   soon   695
Droops in the smile of the waning
   moon,
When it scatters through an April
   night
The frozen dews of wrinkling
   blight.
None now hoped more. Gray
   Power was seated
Safely on her ancestral throne; 700
And Faith, the Python, undefeated,
Even to its blood-stained steps
   dragged on
Her foul and wounded train, and
   men
Were trampled and deceived again,
And words and shows again could
   bind   705
The wailing tribes of human kind
In scorn and famine. Fire and
   blood
Raged round the raging multitude,
To fields remote by tyrants sent
To be the scornèd instrument 710
With which they drag from mines
   of gore
The chains their slaves yet ever
   wore:
And in the streets men met each
   other,
And by old altars and in halls,
And smiled again at festivals, 715

But each man found in his heart's
   brother
Cold cheer; for all, though half de-
   ceived,
The outworn creeds again believed,
And the same round anew began,
Which the weary world yet ever
   ran.   720
Many then wept, not tears, but
   gall
Within their hearts, like drops
   which fall
Wasting the fountain-stone away.
And in that dark and evil day
Did all desires and thoughts, that
   claim   725
Men's care—ambition, friendship,
   fame,
Love, hope, though hope was now
   despair—
Indue the colours of this change,
As from the all-surrounding air
The earth takes hues obscure and
   strange,   730
When storm and earthquake linger
   there.
And so, my friend, it then befell
To many, most to Lionel,
Whose hope was like the life of
   youth
Within him, and when dead, be-
   came   735
A spirit of unresting flame,
Which goaded him in his distress
Over the world's vast wilderness.
Three years he left his native land,
And on the fourth, when he re-
   turned,   740
None knew him: he was stricken
   deep
With some disease of mind, and
   turned
Into aught unlike Lionel.
On him, on whom, did he pause in
   sleep,   744
Serenest smiles were wont to keep,
And, did he wake, a wingèd band

Of bright persuasions, which had
    fed
On his sweet lips and liquid eyes,
Kept their swift pinions half out-
    spread,
To do on men his least com-
    mand;   750
On him, whom once 'twas paradise
Even to behold, now misery lay:
In his own heart 'twas merciless,
To all things else none may express
Its innocence and tenderness. 755

'Twas said that he had refuge
    sought
In love from his unquiet thought
In distant lands, and been deceived
By some strange show; for there
    were found,   759
Blotted with tears as those relieved
By their own words are wont to do,
These mournful verses on the
    ground,
By all who read them blotted too.

'How am I changed! my hopes
    were once like fire:
I loved, and I believed that life
    was love.   765
How am I lost! on wings of swift
    desire
Among Heaven's winds my spirit
    once did move.
I slept, and silver dreams did aye
    inspire
My liquid sleep: I woke, and did
    approve
All nature to my heart, and thought
    to make   770
A paradise of earth for one sweet
    sake.

'I love, but I believe in love no
    more.
I feel desire, but hope not. O, from
    sleep

Most vainly must my weary brain
    implore
Its long lost flattery now: I wake
    to weep,   775
And sit through the long day gnaw-
    ing the core
Of my bitter heart, and, like a
    miser, keep,
Since none in what I feel take pain
    or pleasure,
To my own soul its self-consuming
    treasure.'
He dwelt beside me near the
    sea: 780
And oft in evening did we meet,
When the waves, beneath the star-
    light, flee
O'er the yellow sands with silver
    feet,
And talked: our talk was sad and
    sweet,
Till slowly from his mien there
    passed   785
The desolation which it spoke;
And smiles,—as when the light-
    ning's blast
Has parched some heaven-delight-
    ing oak,
The next spring shows leaves pale
    and rare,   789
But like flowers delicate and fair,
On its rent boughs,—again arrayed
His countenance in tender light:
His words grew subtile fire, which
    made
The air his hearers breathed de-
    light:
His motions, like the winds, were
    free,   795
Which bend the bright grass grace-
    fully,
Then fade away in circlets faint:
And wingèd Hope, on which up-
    borne
His soul seemed hovering in his
    eyes,   799
Like some bright spirit newly born

Floating amid the sunny skies,
Sprang forth from his rent heart
   anew.
Yet o'er his talk, and looks, and
   mien,
Tempering their loveliness too
   keen,
Past woe its shadow backward
   threw,   805
Till like an exhalation, spread
From flowers half drunk with eve-
   ning dew,
They did become infectious: sweet
And subtile mists of sense and
   thought:
Which wrapped us soon, when we
   might meet,   810
Almost from our own looks and
   aught
The wide world holds. And so, his
   mind
Was healed, while mine grew sick
   with fear:
For ever now his health declined,
Like some frail bark which cannot
   bear   815
The impulse of an altered wind,
Though prosperous: and my heart
   grew full
'Mid its new joy of a new care:
For his cheek became, not pale, but
   fair,
As rose-o'ershadowed lilies are; 820
And soon his deep and sunny hair,
In this alone less beautiful,
Like grass in tombs grew wild and
   rare.
The blood in his translucent veins
Beat, not like animal life, but love
Seemed now its sullen springs to
   move,   826
When life had failed, and all its
   pains:
And sudden sleep would seize him
   oft
Like death, so calm, but that a tear,
His pointed eyelashes between, 830

Would gather in the light serene
Of smiles, whose lustre bright and
   soft
Beneath lay undulating there.
His breath was like inconstant
   flame,
As eagerly it went and came; 835
And I hung o'er him in his sleep,
Till, like an image in the lake
Which rains disturb, my tears
   would break
Then he would bid me not to
   weep,   840
The shadow of that slumber deep:
And say with flattery false, yet
   sweet,
That death and he could never
   meet,
If I would never part with him.
And so we loved, and did unite
All that in us was yet divided: 845
For when he said, that many a rite,
By men to bind but once provided,
Could not be shared by him and
   me,
Or they would kill him in their
   glee,
I shuddered, and then laughing
   said—   850
'We will have rites our faith to
   bind,
But our church shall be the starry
   night,
Our altar the grassy earth out-
   spread,
And our priest the muttering
   wind.'
'Twas sunset as I spoke: one
   star   855
Had scarce burst forth, when from
   afar
The ministers of misrule sent,
Seized upon Lionel, and bore
His chained limbs to a dreary
   tower,
In the midst of a city vast and
   wide

For he, they said, from his mind
    had bent 861
Against their gods keen blasphemy,
For which, though his soul must
    roasted be
In hell's red lakes immortally,
Yet even on earth must he abide 865
The vengeance of their slaves: a
    trial,
I think, men call it. What avail
Are prayers and tears, which chase
    denial
From the fierce savage, nursed in
    hate?
What the knit soul that pleading
    and pale 870
Makes wan the quivering cheek,
    which late
It painted with its own delight?
We were divided. As I could,
I stilled the tingling of my blood,
And followed him in their de-
    spite, 875
As a widow follows, pale and wild,
The murderers and corse of her
    only child;
And when we came to the prison
    door
And I prayed to share his dungeon
    floor
With prayers which rarely have
    been spurned, 880
And when men drove me forth
    and I
Stared with blank frenzy on the
    sky,
A farewell look of love he turned,
Half calming me; then gazed
    awhile,
As if thro' that black and massy
    pile, 885
And thro' the crowd around him
    there,
And thro' the dense and murky air,
And the thronged streets, he did
    espy
What poets know and prophesy;

And said, with voice that made
    them shiver 890
And clung like music in my brain,
And which the mute walls spoke
    again
Prolonging it with deepened
    strain:
'Fear not the tyrants shall rule for
    ever,
Or the priests of the bloody
    faith; 895
They stand on the brink of that
    mighty river,
Whose waves they have tainted
    with death:
It is fed from the depths of a thou-
    sand dells,
Around them it foams, and rages,
    and swells,
And their swords and their scep-
    tres I floating see, 900
Like wrecks in the surge of eter-
    nity.'

I dwelt beside the prison gate,
And the strange crowd that out and
    in
Passed, some, no doubt, with mine
    own fate,
Might have fretted me with its
    ceaseless din, 905
But the fever of care was louder
    within.
Soon, but too late, in penitence
Or fear, his foes released him
    thence:
I saw his thin and languid form,
As leaning on the jailor's arm, 910
Whose hardened eyes grew moist
    the while,
To meet his mute and faded
    smile,
And hear his words of kind fare-
    well,
He tottered forth from his damp
    cell.
Many had never wept before, 915

From whom fast tears then gushed
    and fell:
Many will relent no more,
Who sobbed like infants then: aye,
    all
Who thronged the prison's stony
    hall,
The rulers or the slaves of law, 920
Felt with a new surprise and awe
That they were human, till strong
    shame
Made them again become the same.
The prison blood-hounds, huge
    and grim,
From human looks the infection
    caught,   925
And fondly crouched and fawned
    on him;
And men have heard the prisoners
    say,
Who in their rotting dungeons lay,
That from that hour, throughout
    one day,
The fierce despair and hate which
    kept   930
Their trampled bosoms almost
    slept:
Where, like twin vultures, they
    hung feeding
On each heart's wound, wide torn
    and bleeding,—
Because their jailors' rule, they
    thought,   934
Grew merciful, like a parent's sway.

I know not how, but we were free:
And Lionel sate alone with me,
As the carriage drove thro' the
    streets apace;
And we looked upon each other's
    face;
And the blood in our fingers inter-
    twined   940
Ran like the thoughts of a single
    mind,
As the swift emotions went and
    came

Thro' the veins of each united
    frame.
So thro' the long long streets we
    passed
Of the million-peopled City vast;
Which is that desert, where each
    one   946
Seeks his mate yet is alone,
Beloved and sought and mourned
    of none;
Until the clear blue sky was seen,
And the grassy meadows bright
    and green,   950
And then I sunk in his embrace,
Enclosing there a mighty space
Of love: and so we travelled on
By woods, and fields of yellow
    flowers,
And towns, and villages, and tow-
    ers,
Day after day of happy hours. 956
It was the azure time of June,
When the skies are deep in the
    stainless noon,
And the warm and fitful breezes
    shake
The fresh green leaves of the hedge-
    row briar,   960
And there were odours then to
    make
The very breath we did respire
A liquid element, whereon
Our spirits, like delighted things
That walk the air on subtle wings,
Floated and mingled far away, 966
'Mid the warm winds of the sunny
    day.
And when the evening star came
    forth
Above the curve of the new bent
    moon,
And light and sound ebbed from
    the earth,   970
Like the tide of the full and weary
    sea
To the depths of its tranquillity,
Our natures to its own repose

Did the earth's breathless sleep at-
    tune:
Like flowers, which on each other
    close   975
Their languid leaves when day-
    light's gone,
We lay, till new emotions came,
Which seemed to make each mortal
    frame
One soul of interwoven flame,
A life in life, a second birth   980
In worlds diviner far than earth,
Which, like two strains of harmony
That mingle in the silent sky
Then slowly disunite, passed by
And left the tenderness of tears, 985
A soft oblivion of all fears,
A sweet sleep: so we travelled on
Till we came to the home of Lionel,
Among the mountains wild and
    lone,
Beside the hoary western sea,   990
Which near the verge of the echo-
    ing shore
The massy forest shadowed o'er.

The ancient steward, with hair all
    hoar,
As we alighted, wept to see
His master changed so fearfully;
And the old man's sobs did waken
    me   996
From my dream of unremaining
    gladness;
The truth flashed o'er me like quick
    madness
When I looked, and saw that there
    was death
On Lionel: yet day by day   1000
He lived, till fear grew hope and
    faith,
And in my soul I dared to say,
Nothing so bright can pass away:
Death is dark, and foul, and dull,
But he is—O how beautiful!   1005
Yet day by day he grew more
    weak,

And his sweet voice, when he might
    speak,
Which ne'er was loud, became more
    low;
And the light which flashed through
    his waxen cheek
Grew faint, as the rose-like hues
    which flow   1010
From sunset o'er the Alpine snow:
And death seemed not like death
    in him,
For the spirit of life o'er every limb
Lingered, a mist of sense and
    thought.
When the summer wind faint
    odours brought   1015
From mountain flowers, even as it
    passed
His cheek would change, as the
    noonday sea
Which the dying breeze sweeps fit-
    fully.
If but a cloud the sky o'ercast,
You might see his colour come and
    go,   1020
And the softest strain of music
    made
Sweet smiles, yet sad, arise and
    fade
Amid the dew of his tender eyes;
And the breath, with intermitting
    flow,
Made his pale lips quiver and part.
You might hear the beatings of his
    heart,   1026
Quick, but not strong; and with my
    tresses
When oft he playfully would bind
In the bowers of mossy lonelinesses
His neck, and win me so to mingle
In the sweet depth of woven ca-
    resses,
And our faint limbs were inter-
    twined,   1032
Alas! the unquiet life did tingle
From mine own heart through every
    vein,

Like a captive in dreams of liberty,
Who beats the walls of his stony
   cell.   1036
But his, it seemed already free,
Like the shadow of fire surround-
   ing me!
On my faint eyes and limbs did
   dwell
That spirit as it passed, till soon,
As a frail cloud wandering o'er the
   moon,   1041
Beneath its light invisible,
Is seen when it folds its gray wings
   again
To alight on midnight's dusky
   plain,
I lived and saw, and the gathering
   soul
Passed from beneath that strong
   control,   1046
And I fell on a life which was sick
   with fear
Of all the woe that now I bear.

Amid a bloomless myrtle wood,
On a green and sea-girt promon-
   tory,
Not far from where we dwelt, there
   stood   1051
In record of a sweet sad story,
An altar and a temple bright
Circled by steps, and o'er the gate
Was sculptured, 'To Fidelity;'   1055
And in the shrine an image sate,
All veiled: but there was seen the
   light
Of smiles, which faintly could
   express
A mingled pain and tenderness
Through that ethereal drapery.   1060
The left hand held the head, the
   right—
Beyond the veil, beneath the skin,
You might see the nerves quivering
   within—
Was forcing the point of a barbèd
   dart

Into its side-convulsing heart.   1065
An unskilled hand, yet one in-
   formed
With genius, had the marble
   warmed
With that pathetic life. This tale
It told: A dog had from the sea,
When the tide was raging fearfully,
Dragged Lionel's mother, weak and
   pale,   ' 1071
Then died beside her on the sand,
And she that temple thence had
   planned;
But it was Lionel's own hand
Had wrought the image. Each new
   moon   1075
That lady did, in this lone fane,
The rites of a religion sweet,
Whose god was in her heart and
   brain;
The season's loveliest flowers were
   strewn
On the marble floor beneath her
   feet,
And she brought crowns of sea-
   buds white,   1081
Whose odour is so sweet and faint,
And weeds, like branching chryso-
   lite,
Woven in devices fine and quaint.
And tears from her brown eyes did
   stain   1085
The altar: need but look upon
That dying statue fair and wan,
If tears should cease, to weep again:
And rare Arabian odours came,
Through the myrtle copses steam-
   ing thence   1090
From the hissing frankincense,
Whose smoke, wool-white as ocean
   foam,
Hung in dense flocks beneath the
   dome—
That ivory dome, whose azure night
With golden stars, like heaven, was
   bright—   1095
O'er the split cedar's pointed flame;

And the lady's harp would kindle
    there
The melody of an old air,
Softer than sleep; the villagers
Mixed their religion up with hers,
And as they listened round, shed
    tears.   1101

One eve he led me to this fane:
Daylight on its last purple cloud
Was lingering gray, and soon her
    strain   1104
The nightingale began; now loud,
Climbing in circles the windless sky,
Now dying music; suddenly
'Tis scattered in a thousand notes,
And now to the hushed ear it floats
Like field smells known in in-
    fancy,   1110
Then failing, soothes the air again.
We sate within that temple lone,
Pavilioned round with Parian
    stone:
His mother's harp stood near, and
    oft
I had awakened music soft   1115
Amid its wires: the nightingale
Was pausing in her heaven-taught
    tale:
'Now drain the cup,' said Lionel,
'Which the poet-bird has crowned
    so well
With the wine of her bright and
    liquid song!   1120
Heardst thou not sweet words
    among
That heaven-resounding min-
    strelsy?
Heardst thou not, that those who
    die
Awaken in a world of ecstasy?
That love, when limbs are inter-
    woven,   1125
And sleep, when the night of life
    is cloven,
And thought, to the world's dim
    boundaries clinging,

And music, when one beloved is
    singing,
Is death? Let us drain right joy-
    ously
The cup which the sweet bird fills
    for me.'   1130
He paused, and to my lips he bent
His own: like spirit his words went
Through all my limbs with the
    speed of fire;
And his keen eyes, glittering
    through mine,
Filled me with the flame
    divine,   1135
Which in their orbs was burning
    far,
Like the light of an unmeasured
    star,
In the sky of midnight dark and
    deep:
Yes, 'twas his soul that did inspire
Sounds, which my skill could ne'er
    awaken;   1140
And first, I felt my fingers sweep
The harp, and a long quivering cry
Burst from my lips in symphony:
The dusk and solid air was shaken,
As swift and swifter the notes
    came   1145
From my touch, that wandered like
    quick flame,
And from my bosom, labouring
With some unutterable thing:
The awful sound of my own voice
    made
My faint lips tremble; in some
    mood   1150
Of wordless thought Lionel stood
So pale that even beside his cheek
The snowy column from its shade
Caught whiteness: yet his counte-
    nance
Raised upward, burned with radi-
    ance   1155
Of spirit-piercing joy, whose light,
Like the moon struggling through
    the night

Of whirlwind-rifted clouds, did
 break
With beams that might not be con-
 fined.
I paused, but soon his gestures
 kindled   1160
New power, as by the moving wind
The waves are lifted, and my song
To low soft notes now changed and
 dwindled,
And from the twinkling wires
 among,
My languid fingers drew and flung
Circles of life-dissolving sound, 1166
Yet faint; in aëry rings they bound
My Lionel, who, as every strain
Grew fainter but more sweet, his
 mien
Sunk with the sound relaxed-
 ly;   1170
And slowly now he turned to me,
As slowly faded from his face
That awful joy: with looks serene
He was soon drawn to my embrace,
And my wild song then died away
In murmurs: words I dare not say
We mixed, and on his lips mine fed
Till they methought felt still and
 cold:
'What is it with thee, love?' I said:
No word, no look, no motion! yes,
There was a change, but spare to
 guess,   1181
Nor let that moment's hope be told.
I looked, and knew that he was
 dead,
And fell, as the eagle on the plain
Falls when life deserts her
 brain,   1185
And the mortal lightning is veiled
 again.

O that I were now dead! but such
(Did they not, love, demand too
 much,
Those dying murmurs?) he forbade.

O that I once again were mad! 1190
And yet, dear Rosalind, not so,
For I would live to share thy woe.
Sweet boy, did I forget thee too?
Alas, we know not what we do
When we speak words.
     No memory more   1195
Is in my mind of that sea shore.
Madness came on me, and a troop
Of misty shapes did seem to sit
Beside me, on a vessel's poop,
And the clear north wind was driv-
 ing it.   1200
Then I heard strange tongues, and
 saw strange flowers,
And the stars methought grew un-
 like ours,
And the azure sky and the storm-
 less sea
Made me believe that I had died,
And waked in a world, which was
 to me   1205
Drear hell, though heaven to all
 beside:
Then a dead sleep fell on my mind,
Whilst animal life many long years
Had rescue from a chasm of tears;
And when I woke, I wept to
 find   1210
That the same lady, bright and
 wise,
With silver locks and quick brown
 eyes,
The mother of my Lionel,
Had tended me in my distress,
And died some months before. Nor
 less   1215
Wonder, but far more peace and joy
Brought in that hour my lovely
 boy;
For through that trance my soul
 had well
The impress of thy being kept;
And if I waked, or if I slept, 1220
No doubt, though memory faithless
 be,
Thy image ever dwelt on me;

And thus, O Lionel, like thee
Is our sweet child. 'Tis sure most
   strange
I knew not of so great a
   change,   1225
As that which gave him birth, who
   now
Is all the solace of my woe.

That Lionel great wealth had left
By will to me, and that of all
The ready lies of law bereft   1230
My child and me, might well befall.
But let me think not of the scorn,
Which from the meanest I have
   borne,
When, for my child's belovèd sake,
I mixed with slaves, to vindi-
   cate   1235
The very laws themselves do make:
Let me not say scorn is my fate,
Lest I be proud, suffering the same
With those who live in deathless
   fame.

She ceased.—'Lo, where red morn-
   ing thro' the woods   1240
Is burning o'er the dew;' said
   Rosalind.
And with these words they rose, and
   towards the flood
Of the blue lake, beneath the leaves
   now wind
With equal steps and fingers inter-
   twined:
Thence to a lonely dwelling, where
   the shore   1245
Is shadowed with deep rocks, and
   cypresses
Cleave with their dark green cones
   the silent skies,
And with their shadows the clear
   depths below,
And where a little terrace from its
   bowers,
Of blooming myrtle and faint
   lemon-flowers,   1250

Scatters its sense-dissolving fra-
   grance o'er
The liquid marble of the windless
   lake;
And where the agèd forest's limbs
   look hoar,
Under the leaves which their green
   garments make,
They come: 'tis Helen's home, and
   clean and white,   1255
Like one which tyrants spare on our
   own land
In some such solitude, its casements
   bright
Shone through their vine-leaves in
   the morning sun,
And even within 'twas scarce like
   Italy.
And when she saw how all things
   there were planned,   1260
As in an English home, dim
   memory
Disturbed poor Rosalind: she stood
   as one
Whose mind is where his body can-
   not be,
Till Helen led her where her child
   yet slept,
And said, 'Observe, that brow was
   Lionel's,   1265
Those lips were his, and so he ever
   kept
One arm in sleep, pillowing his head
   with it.
You cannot see his eyes, they are
   two wells
Of liquid love: let us not wake him
   yet.'
But Rosalind could bear no more,
   and wept   1270
A shower of burning tears, which
   fell upon
His face, and so his opening lashes
   shone
With tears unlike his own, as he did
   leap

In sudden wonder from his innocent sleep.

So Rosalind and Helen lived to-
gether
Thenceforth, changed in all else,
yet friends again,   1276
Such as they were, when o'er the
mountain heather
They wandered in their youth,
through sun and rain.
And after many years, for human
things
Change even like the ocean and the
wind,   ,   1280
Her daughter was restored to
Rosalind,
And in their circle thence some
visitings
Of joy 'mid their new calm would
intervene:
A lovely child she was, of looks
serene,
And motions which o'er things in-
different shed   1285
The grace and gentleness from
whence they came.
And Helen's boy grew with her,
and they fed
From the same flowers of thought,
until each mind
Like springs which mingle in one
flood became,
And in their union soon their
parents saw   1290
The shadow of the peace denied to
them.
And Rosalind, for when the living-
stem
Is cankered in its heart, the tree
must fall,
Died ere her time; and with deep
grief and awe
The pale survivors followed her remains   1295
Beyond the region of dissolving
rains,

Up the cold mountain she was wont
to call
Her tomb; and on Chiavenna's
precipice
They raised a pyramid of lasting
ice,
Whose polished sides, ere day had
yet begun,   1300
Caught the first glow of the unrisen
sun,
The last, when it had sunk; and
thro' the night
The charioteers of Arctos wheeled
round
Its glittering point, as seen from
Helen's home,
Whose sad inhabitants each year
would come,   1305
With willing steps climbing that
rugged height,
And hang long locks of hair, and
garlands bound
With amaranth flowers, which, in
the clime's despite,
Filled the frore air with unaccus-
tomed light:
Such flowers, as in the wintry
memory bloom   1310
Of one friend left, adorned that
frozen tomb.

Helen, whose spirit was of softer
mould,
Whose sufferings too were less,
Death slowlier led
Into the peace of his dominion
cold:
She died among her kindred, being
old.   1315
And know, that if love die not in
the dead
As in the living, none of mortal
kind
Are blest, as now Helen and Rosa-
lind.

NOTE BY MRS. SHELLEY

Rosalind and Helen was begun at Marlow, and thrown aside—till I found it; and, at my request, it was completed. Shelley had no care for any of his poems that did not emanate from the depths of his mind and develop some high or abstruse truth. When he does touch on human life and the human heart, no pictures can be more faithful, more delicate, more subtle, or more pathetic. He never mentioned Love but he shed a grace borrowed from his own nature, that scarcely any other poet has bestowed, on that passion. When he spoke of it as the law of life, which inasmuch as we rebel against we err and injure ourselves and others, he promulgated that which he considered an irrefragable truth. In his eyes it was the essence of our being, and all woe and pain arose from the war made against it by selfishness, or insensibility, or mistake. By reverting in his mind to this first principle, he discovered the source of many emotions, and could disclose the secrets of all hearts; and his delineations of passion and emotion touch the finest chords of our nature.

Rosalind and Helen was finished during the summer of 1818, while we were at the baths of Lucca.

JULIAN AND MADDALO

A CONVERSATION

PREFACE

The meadows with fresh streams, the bees with thyme,
The goats with the green leaves of budding Spring,
Are saturated not—nor Love with tears.—VIRGIL's *Gallus*.

COUNT MADDALO is a Venetian nobleman of ancient family and of great fortune, who, without mixing much in the society of his country-men, resides chiefly at his magnificent palace in that city. He is a person of the most consummate genius, and capable, if he would direct his energies to such an end, of becoming the redeemer of his degraded country. But it is his weakness to be proud: he derives, from a comparison of his own extraordinary mind with the dwarfish intellects that surround him, an intense apprehension of the nothingness of human life. His passions and his powers are incomparably greater than those of other men; and, instead of the latter having been employed in curbing the former, they have mutually lent each other strength. His ambition preys upon itself, for want of objects which it can consider worthy of exertion. I say that Maddalo is proud, because I can find no other word to express the concentered and impatient feelings which consume him; but it is on his own hopes and affections only that he seems to trample, for in social life no human being can be more gentle, patient, and unassuming than Maddalo. He is cheerful, frank, and witty. His more serious conversation

is a sort of intoxication; men are held by it as by a spell. He has travelled
much; and there is an inexpressible charm in his relation of his adventures in different countries.

Julian is an Englishman of good family, passionately attached to those
philosophical notions which assert the power of man over his own mind,
and the immense improvements of which, by the extinction of certain
moral superstitions, human society may be yet susceptible. Without concealing the evil in the world, he is for ever speculating how good may be
made superior. He is a complete infidel, and a scoffer at all things reputed
holy; and Maddalo takes a wicked pleasure in drawing out his taunts
against religion. What Maddalo thinks on these matters is not exactly
known. Julian, in spite of his heterodox opinions, is conjectured by his
friends to possess some good qualities. How far this is possible the pious
reader will determine. Julian is rather serious.

Of the Maniac I can give no information. He seems, by his own
account, to have been disappointed in love. He was evidently a very cultivated and amiable person when in his right senses. His story, told at
length, might be like many other stories of the same kind: the unconnected exclamations of his agony will perhaps be found a sufficient
comment for the text of every heart.

        I RODE one evening with Count Maddalo
        Upon the bank of land which breaks the flow
        Of Adria towards Venice: a bare strand
        Of hillocks, heaped from ever-shifting sand,
        Matted with thistles and amphibious weeds,   5
        Such as from earth's embrace the salt ooze breeds,
        Is this; an uninhabited sea-side,
        Which the lone fisher, when his nets are dried,
        Abandons; and no other object breaks
        The waste, but one dwarf tree and some few stakes   10
        Broken and unrepaired, and the tide makes
        A narrow space of level sand thereon,
        Where 'twas our wont to ride while day went down.
        This ride was my delight. I love all waste
        And solitary places; where we taste   15
        The pleasure of believing what we see
        Is boundless, as we wish our souls to be:
        And such was this wide ocean, and this shore
        More barren than its billows; and yet more
        Than all, with a remembered friend I love   20
        To ride as then I rode;—for the winds drove
        The living spray along the sunny air
        Into our faces; the blue heavens were bare,
        Stripped to their depths by the awakening north;
        And, from the waves, sound like delight broke forth   25

Harmonising with solitude, and sent
Into our hearts aëreal merriment.
So, as we rode, we talked; and the swift thought,
Winging itself with laughter, lingered not,
But flew from brain to brain,—such glee was ours,   30
Charged with light memories of remembered hours,
None slow enough for sadness: till we came
Homeward, which always makes the spirit tame.
This day had been cheerful but cold, and now
The sun was sinking, and the wind also.   35
Our talk grew somewhat serious, as may be
Talk interrupted with such raillery
As mocks itself, because it cannot scorn
The thoughts it would extinguish:—'twas forlorn,
Yet pleasing, such as once, so poets tell,   40
The devils held within the dales of Hell
Concerning God, freewill and destiny:
Of all that earth has been or yet may be,
All that vain men imagine or believe,
Or hope can paint or suffering may achieve,   45
We descanted, and I (for ever still
Is it not wise to make the best of ill?)
Argued against despondency, but pride
Made my companion take the darker side.
The sense that he was greater than his kind   50
Had struck, methinks, his eagle spirit blind
By gazing on its own exceeding light.
Meanwhile the sun paused ere it should alight,
Over the horizon of the mountains:—Oh,
How beautiful is sunset, when the glow   55
Of Heaven descends upon a land like thee,
Thou Paradise of exiles, Italy!
Thy mountains, seas, and vineyards, and the towers
Of cities they encircle!—it was ours
To stand on thee, beholding it: and then,   60
Just where we had dismounted, the Count's men
Were waiting for us with the gondola.— ˙
As those who pause on some delightful way
Though bent on pleasant pilgrimage, we stood
Looking upon the evening, and the flood   65
Which lay between the city and the shore,
Paved with the image of the sky . . . the hoar
And aëry Alps towards the North appeared
Through mist, an heaven-sustaining bulwark reared
Between the East and West; and half the sky   70
Was roofed with clouds of rich emblazonry

Dark purple at the zenith, which still grew
Down the steep West into a wondrous hue
Brighter than burning gold, even to the rent
Where the swift sun yet paused in his descent   75
Among the many-folded hills: they were
Those famous Euganean hills, which bear,
As seen from Lido thro' the harbour piles,
The likeness of a clump of peakèd isles—
And then—as if the Earth and Sea had been   80
Dissolved into one lake of fire, were seen
Those mountains towering as from waves of flame
Around the vaporous sun, from which there came
The inmost purple spirit of light, and made,
Their very peaks transparent. 'Ere it fade,'   85
Said my companion, 'I will show you soon
A better station'—so, o'er the lagune
We glided; and from that funereal bark
I leaned, and saw the city, and could mark
How from their many isles, in evening's gleam,   90
Its temples and its palaces did seem
Like fabrics of enchantment piled to Heaven.
I was about to speak, when—'We are even
Now at the point I meant,' said Maddalo,
And bade the gondolieri cease to row.   95
'Look, Julian, on the west, and listen well
If you hear not a deep and heavy bell.'
I looked, and saw between us and the sun
A building on an island; such a one
As age to age might add, for uses vile,   100
A windowless, deformed and dreary pile;
And on the top an open tower, where hung
A bell, which in the radiance swayed and swung;
We could just hear its hoarse and iron tongue:
The broad sun sunk behind it, and it tolled   105
In strong and black relief.—'What we behold
Shall be the madhouse and its belfry tower,'
Said Maddalo, 'and ever at this hour
Those who may cross the water, hear that bell
Which calls the maniacs, each one from his cell,   110
To vespers.'—'As much skill as need to pray
In thanks or hope for their dark lot have they
To their stern maker,' I replied. 'O ho!
You talk as in years past,' said Maddalo.
' 'Tis strange men change not. You were ever still   115
Among Christ's flock a perilous infidel,
A wolf for the meek lambs—if you can't swim
Beware of Providence.' I looked on him,

But the gay smile had faded in his eye.
'And such,'—he cried, 'is our mortality,   120
And this must be the emblem and the sign
Of what should be eternal and divine!—
And like that black and dreary bell, the soul,
Hung in a heaven-illumined tower, must toll
Our thoughts and our desires to meet below   125
Round the rent heart and pray—as madmen do
For what? they know not,—till the night of death
As sunset that strange vision, severeth
Our memory from itself, and us from all
We sought and yet were baffled.' I recall   130
The sense of what he said, although I mar
The force of his expressions. The broad star
Of day meanwhile had sunk behind the hill,
And the black bell became invisible,
And the red tower looked gray, and all between   135
The churches, ships and palaces were seen
Huddled in gloom;—into the purple sea
The orange hues of heaven sunk silently
We hardly spoke, and soon the gondola
Conveyed me to my lodging by the way.   140
     The following morn was rainy, cold and dim:
Ere Maddalo arose, I called on him,
And whilst I waited with his child I played;
A lovelier toy sweet Nature never made,
A serious, subtle, wild, yet gentle being,   145
Graceful without design and unforeseeing,
With eyes—Oh speak not of her eyes!—which seem
Twin mirrors of Italian Heaven, yet gleam
With such deep meaning, as we never see
But in the human countenance: with me   150
She was a special favourite: I had nursed
Her fine and feeble limbs when she came first
To this bleak world; and she yet seemed to know
On second sight her ancient playfellow,
Less changed than she was by six months or so;   155
For after her first shyness was worn out
We sate there, rolling billiard balls about,
When the Count entered. Salutations past—
'The word you spoke last night might well have cast
A darkness on my spirit—if man be   160
The passive thing you say, I should not see
Much harm in the religions and old saws
(Tho' I may never own such leaden laws)
Which break a teachless nature to the yoke:
Mine is another faith'—thus much I spoke   165

And noting he replied not, added: 'See
This lovely child, blithe, innocent and free;
She spends a happy time with little care,
While we to such sick thoughts subjected are
As came on you last night—it is our will   170
That thus enchains us to permitted ill—
We might be otherwise—we might be all
We dream of happy, high, majestical.
Where is the love, beauty, and truth we seek
But in our mind? and if we were not weak   175
Should we be less in deed than in desire?'
'Ay, if we were not weak—and we aspire
How vainly to be strong!' said Maddalo:
'You talk Utopia.' 'It remains to know,'
I then rejoined, 'and those who try may find   180
How strong the chains are which our spirit bind;
Brittle perchance as straw . . . We are assured
Much may be conquered, much may be endured,
Of what degrades and crushes us. We know
That we have power over ourselves to do   185
And suffer—what, we know not till we try;
But something nobler than to live and die—
So taught those kings of old philosophy
Who reigned, before Religion made men blind;
And those who suffer with their suffering kind   190
Yet feel their faith, religion.' 'My dear friend,'
Said Maddalo, 'my judgement will not bend
To your opinion, though I think you might
Make such a system refutation-tight
As far as words go. I knew one like you   195
Who to this city came some months ago,
With whom I argued in this sort, and he
Is now gone mad,—and so he answered me,—
Poor fellow! but if you would like to go
We'll visit him, and his wild talk will show   200
How vain are such aspiring theories.'
'I hope to prove the induction otherwise,
And that a want of that true theory, still,
Which seeks a "soul of goodness" in things ill
Or in himself or others, has thus bowed   205
His being—there are some by nature proud,
Who patient in all else demand but this—
To love and be beloved with gentleness;
And being scorned, what wonder if they die
Some living death? this is not destiny   210
But man's own wilful ill.'
                              As thus I spoke

Servants announced the gondola, and we
Through the fast-falling rain and high-wrought sea
Sailed to the island where the madhouse stands.
We disembarked. The clap of tortured hands,   215
Fierce yells and howlings and lamentings keen,
And laughter where complaint had merrier been,
Moans, shrieks, and curses, and blaspheming prayers
Accosted us. We climbed the oozy stairs
Into an old courtyard. I heard on high,   220
Then, fragments of most touching melody,
But looking up saw not the singer there—
Through the black bars in the tempestuous air
I saw, like weeds on a wrecked palace growing,
Long tangled locks flung wildly forth, and flowing,   225
Of those who on a sudden were beguiled
Into strange silence, and looked forth and smiled
Hearing sweet sounds.—Then I: 'Methinks there were
A cure of these with patience and kind care,
If music can thus move . . . but what is he   230
Whom we seek here?' 'Of his sad history
I know but this,' said Maddalo: 'he came
To Venice a dejected man, and fame
Said he was wealthy, or he had been so;
Some thought the loss of fortune wrought him woe;   235
But he was ever talking in such sort
As you do—far more sadly—he seemed hurt,
Even as a man with his peculiar wrong,
To hear but of the oppression of the strong,
Or those absurd deceits (I think with you   240
In some respects, you know) which carry through
The excellent impostors of this earth
When they outface detection—he had worth,
Poor fellow! but a humorist in his way'—
'Alas, what drove him mad?' 'I cannot say: 245
A lady came with him from France, and· when
She left him and returned, he wandered then
About yon lonely isles of desert sand
Till he grew wild—he had no cash or land
Remaining,—the police had brought him here—   250
Some fancy took him and he would not bear
Removal; so I fitted up for him
Those rooms beside the sea, to please his whim,
And sent him busts and books and urns for flowers,
Which had adorned his life in happier hours,   255
And instruments of music—you may guess
A stranger could do little more or less
For one so gentle and unfortunate:

And those are his sweet strains which charm the weight
From madmen's chains, and make this Hell appear   260
A heaven of sacred silence, hushed to hear.'—
'Nay, this was kind of you—he had no claim,
As the world says'—'None—but the very same
Which I on all mankind were I as he
Fallen to such deep reverse;—his melody   265
Is interrupted—now we hear the din
Of madmen, shriek on shriek, again begin;
Let us now visit him; after this strain
He ever communes with himself again,
And sees nor hears not any.' Having said   270
These words we called the keeper, and he led
To an apartment opening on the sea—
There the poor wretch was sitting mournfully
Near a piano, his pale fingers twined
One with the other, and the ooze and wind   275
Rushed through an open casement, and did sway
His hair, and starred it with the brackish spray;
His head was leaning on a music book,
And he was muttering, and his lean limbs shook;
His lips were pressed against a folded leaf   280
In hue too beautiful for health, and grief
Smiled in their motions as they lay apart—
As one who wrought from his own fervid heart
The eloquence of passion, soon he raised
His sad meek face and eyes lustrous and glazed   285
And spoke—sometimes as one who wrote, and thought
His words might move some heart that heeded not,
If sent to distant lands: and then as one
Reproaching deeds never to be undone
With wondering self-compassion; then his speech   290
Was lost in grief, and then his words came each
Unmodulated, cold, expressionless,—
But that from one jarred accent you might guess
It was despair made them so uniform:
And all the while the loud and gusty storm   295
Hissed through the window, and we stood behind
Stealing his accents from the envious wind
Unseen. I yet remember what he said
Distinctly: such impression his words made.

'Month after month,' he cried, 'to bear this load   300
And as a jade urged by the whip and goad
To drag life on, which like a heavy chain
Lengthens behind with many a link of pain!—
And not to speak my grief—O, not to dare

To give a human voice to my despair,   305
But live and move, and, wretched thing! smile on
As if I never went aside to groan,
And wear this mask of falsehood even to those
Who are most dear—not for my own repose—
Alas! no scorn or pain or hate could be   310
So heavy as that falsehood is to me—
But that I cannot bear more altered faces
Than needs must be, more changed and cold embraces,
More misery, disappointment, and mistrust
To own me for their father . . . Would the dust   315
Were covered in upon my body now!
That the life ceased to toil within my brow!
And then these thoughts would at the least be fled;
Let us not fear such pain can vex the dead.

'What Power delights to torture us? I know   320
That to myself I do not wholly owe
What now I suffer, though in part I may.
Alas! none strewed sweet flowers upon the way
Where wandering heedlessly, I met pale Pain
My shadow, which will leave me not again—   325
If I have erred, there was no joy in error,
But pain and insult and unrest and terror;
I have not as some do, bought penitence
With pleasure, and a dark yet sweet offence,
For them,—if love and tenderness and truth   330
Had overlived hope's momentary youth,
My creed should have redeemed me from repenting;
But loathèd scorn and outrage unrelenting
Met love excited by far other seeming
Until the end was gained . . . as one from dreaming   335
Of sweetest peace, I woke, and found my state
Such as it is.—
                    'O Thou, my spirit's mate
Who, for thou art compassionate and wise,
Wouldst pity me from thy most gentle eyes
If this sad writing thou shouldst ever see—   340
My secret groans must be unheard by thee,
Thou wouldst weep tears bitter as blood to know
Thy lost friend's incommunicable woe.

'Ye few by whom my nature has been weighed
In friendship, let me not that name degrade   345
By placing on your hearts the secret load
Which crushes mine to dust. There is one road
To peace and that is truth, which follow ye!
Love sometimes leads astray to misery.

Yet think not though subdued—and I may well   350
Say that I am subdued—that the full Hell
Within me would infect the untainted breast
Of sacred nature with its own unrest;
As some perverted beings think to find
In scorn or hate a medicine for the mind   355
Which scorn or hate have wounded—O how vain!
The dagger heals not but may rend again . . .
Believe that I am ever still the same
In creed as in resolve, and what may tame
My heart, must leave the understanding free,   360
Or all would sink in this keen agony—
Nor dream that I will join the vulgar cry;
Or with my silence sanction tyranny;
Or seek a moment's shelter from my pain
In any madness which the world calls gain,   365
Ambition or revenge or thoughts as stern
As those which make me what I am; or turn
To avarice or misanthropy or lust . . .
Heap on me soon, O grave, thy welcome dust!
Till then the dungeon may demand its prey,   370
And Poverty and Shame may meet and say—
Halting beside me on the public way—
"That love-devoted youth is ours—let's sit
Beside him—he may live some six months yet."
Or the red scaffold as our country bends,   375
May ask some willing victim, or ye friends
May fall under some sorrow which this heart
Or hand may share or vanquish or avert;
I am prepared—in truth with no proud joy—
To do or suffer aught, as when a boy   380
I did devote to justice and to love
My nature, worthless now! . . .
                                    'I must remove
A veil from my pent mind. 'Tis torn aside!
O, pallid as Death's dedicated bride,
Thou mockery which art sitting by my side,   385
Am I not wan like thee? at the grave's call
I haste, invited to thy wedding-ball
To greet the ghastly paramour, for whom
Thou hast deserted me . . . and made the tomb
Thy bridal bed . . . But I beside your feet   390
Will lie and watch ye from my winding sheet—
Thus . . . wide awake tho' dead . . . yet stay, O stay!
Go not so soon—I know not what I say—
Hear but my reasons . . I am mad, I fear,
My fancy is o'erwrought . . thou art not here . . .   395

Pale art thou, 'tis most true . . but thou art gone,
Thy work is finished . . . I am left alone!—

.   .   .   .

'Nay, was it I who wooed thee to this breast
Which, like a serpent, thou envenomest
As in repayment of the warmth it lent?   400
Didst thou not seek me for thine own content?
Did not thy love awaken mine? I thought
That thou wert she who said, "You kiss me not
Ever, I fear you do not love me now"—
In truth I loved even to my overthrow   405
Her, who would fain forget these words: but they
Cling to her mind, and cannot pass away.

.   .   .   .   .   .

'You say that I am proud—that when I speak
My lip is tortured with the wrongs which break
The spirit it expresses . . . Never one   410
Humbled himself before, as I have done!
Even the instinctive worm on which we tread
Turns, though it wound not—then with prostrate head
Sinks in the dusk and writhes like me—and dies?
No: wears a living death of agonies!   415
As the slow shadows of the pointed grass
Mark the eternal periods, his pangs pass
Slow, ever-moving,—making moments be
As mine seem—each an immortality!

.   .   .   .

'That you had never seen me—never heard   420
My voice, and more than all had ne'er endured
The deep pollution of my loathed embrace—
That your eyes ne'er had lied love in my face—
That, like some maniac monk, I had torn out
The nerves of manhood by their bleeding root   425
With mine own quivering fingers, so that ne'er
Our hearts had for a moment mingled there
To disunite in horror—these were not
With thee, like some suppressed and hideous thought
Which flits athwart our musings, but can find   430
No rest within a pure and gentle mind . . .
Thou sealedst them with many a bare broad word,
And searedst my memory o'er them,—for I heard
And can forget not . . . they were ministered
One after one, those curses. Mix them up   435
Like self-destroying poisons in one cup.

And they will make one blessing which thou ne'er
Didst imprecate for, on me,—death.

    .   .   .   .

                            'It were
A cruel punishment for one most cruel,
If such can love, to make that love the fuel   440
Of the mind's hell; hate, scorn, remorse, despair:
But *me*—whose heart a stranger's tear might wear
As water-drops the sandy fountain-stone,
Who loved and pitied all things, and could moan
For woes which others hear not, and could see   445
The absent with the glance of phantasy,
And with the poor and trampled sit and weep,
Following the captive to his dungeon deep;
Me—who am as a nerve o'er which do creep
The else unfelt oppressions of this earth,   450
And was to thee the flame upon thy hearth,
When all beside was cold—that thou on me
Shouldst rain these plagues of blistering agony—
Such curses are from lips once eloquent
With love's too partial praise—let none relent   455
Who intend deeds too dreadful for a name
Henceforth, if an example for the same
They seek . . . for thou on me lookedst so, and so—
And didst speak thus . . and thus . . . I live to show
How much men bear and die not!   460

    .   .   .   .

                        'Thou wilt tell,
With the grimace of hate, how horrible
It was to meet my love when thine grew less;
Thou wilt admire how I could e'er address
Such features to love's work . . . this taunt, though true,
(For indeed Nature nor in form nor hue   465
Bestowed on me her choicest workmanship)
Shall not be thy defence . . . for since thy lip
Met mine first, years long past, since thine eye kindled
With soft fire under mine, I have not dwindled
Nor changed in mind or body, or in aught   470
But as love changes what it loveth not
After long years and many trials.
                       'How vain
Are words! I thought never to speak again,
Not even in secret,—not to my own heart—
But from my lips the unwilling accents start,   475
And from my pen the words flow as I write,
Dazzling my eyes with scalding tears . . . my sight

Is dim to see that charactered in vain
On this unfeeling leaf which burns the brain
And eats into it . . . blotting all things fair 480
And wise and good which time had written there.

'Those who inflict must suffer, for they see
The work of their own hearts, and this must be
Our chastisement or recompense—O child!
I would that thine were like to be more mild 485
For both our wretched sakes . . . for thine the most
Who feelest already all that thou hast lost
Without the power to wish it thine again;
And as slow years pass, a funereal train
Each with the ghost of some lost hope or friend 490
Following it like its shadow, wilt thou bend
No thought on my dead memory?
   . . . . . .

                          'Alas, love!
Fear me not . . . against thee I would not move
A finger in despite. Do I not live
That thou mayst have less bitter cause to grieve? 495
I give thee tears for scorn and love for hate;
And that thy lot may be less desolate
Than his on whom thou tramplest, I refrain
From that sweet sleep which medicines all pain.
Then, when thou speakest of me, never say 500
"He could forgive not." Here I cast away
All human passions, all revenge, all pride;
I think, speak, act no ill; I do but hide
Under these words, like embers, every spark
Of that which has consumed me—quick and dark 505
The grave is yawning . . . as its roof shall cover
My limbs with dust and worms under and over
So let Oblivion hide this grief . . . the air
Closes upon my accents, as despair
Upon my heart—let death upon despair!' 510

He ceased, and overcome leant back awhile,
Then rising, with a melancholy smile
Went to a sofa, and lay down, and slept
A heavy sleep, and in his dreams he wept
And muttered some familiar name, and we 515
Wept without shame in his society.
I think I never was impressed so much;
The man who were not, must have lacked a touch
Of human nature . . . then we lingered not,
Although our argument was quite forgot, 520

But calling the attendants, went to dine
At Maddalo's; yet neither cheer nor wine
Could give us spirits, for we talked of him
And nothing else, till daylight made stars dim;
And we agreed his was some dreadful ill   525
Wrought on him boldly, yet unspeakable,
By a dear friend; some deadly change in love
Of one vowed deeply which he dreamed not of;
For whose sake he, it seemed, had fixed a blot
Of falsehood on his mind which flourished not   530
But in the light of all-beholding truth;
And having stamped this canker on his youth
She had abandoned him—and how much more
Might be his woe, we guessed not—he had store
Of friends and fortune once, as we could guess   535
From his nice habits and his gentleness;
These were now lost . . . it were a grief indeed
If he had changed one unsustaining reed
For all that such a man might else adorn.
The colours of his mind seemed yet unworn;   540
For the wild language of his grief was high,
Such as in measure were called poetry;
And I remember one remark which then
Maddalo made. He said: 'Most wretched men
Are cradled into poetry by wrong,   545
They learn in suffering what they teach in song.'

    If I had been an unconnected man
I, from this moment, should have formed some plan
Never to leave sweet Venice,—for to me
It was delight to ride by the lone sea;   550
And then, the town is silent—one may write
Or read in gondolas by day or night,
Having the little brazen lamp alight,
Unseen, uninterrupted; books are there,
Pictures, and casts from all those statues fair   555
Which were twin-born with poetry, and all
We seek in towns, with little to recall
Regrets for the green country. I might sit
In Maddalo's great palace, and his wit
And subtle talk would cheer the winter night   560
And make me know myself, and the firelight
Would flash upon our faces, till the day
Might dawn and make me wonder at my stay:
But I had friends in London too: the chief
Attraction here, was that I sought relief   565

From the deep tenderness that maniac wrought
Within me—'twas perhaps an idle thought—
But I imagined that if day by day
I watched him, and but seldom went away,
And studied all the beatings of his heart   570
With zeal, as men study some stubborn art
For their own good, and could by patience find
An entrance to the caverns of his mind,
I might reclaim him from his dark estate:
In friendships I had been most fortunate—   575
Yet never saw I one whom I would call
More willingly my friend; and this was all
Accomplished not; such dreams of baseless good
Oft come and go in crowds or solitude
And leave no trace—but what I now designed   580
Made for long years impression on my mind.
The following morning, urged by my affairs,
I left bright Venice.
                    After many years
And many changes I returned; the name
Of Venice, and its aspect, was the same;   585
But Maddalo was travelling far away
Among the mountains of Armenia.
His dog was dead. His child had now become
A woman; such as it has been my doom
To meet with few,—a wonder of this earth,   590
Where there is little of transcendent worth,—
Like one of Shakespeare's women: kindly she,
And, with a manner beyond courtesy,
Received her father's friend; and when I asked
Of the lorn maniac, she her memory tasked,   595
And told as she had heard the mournful tale:
'That the poor sufferer's health began to fail
Two years from my departure, but that then
The lady who had left him, came again.
Her mien had been imperious, but she now   600
Looked meek—perhaps remorse had brought her low.
Her coming made him better, and they stayed
Together at my father's—for I played,
As I remember, with the lady's shawl—
I might be six years old—but after all   605
She left him' . . . 'Why, her heart must have been tough:
How did it end?' 'And was not this enough?
They met—they parted'—'Child, is there no more?'
'Something within that interval which bore
The stamp of *why* they parted, *how* they met: 610
Yet if thine agèd eyes disdain to wet

Those wrinkled cheeks with youth's remembered tears,
Ask me no more, but let the silent years
Be closed and cered over their memory
As yon mute marble where their corpses lie.'   615
I urged and questioned still, she told me how
All happened—but the cold world shall not know.

CANCELLED FRAGMENTS OF JULIAN AND MADDALO

'What think you the dead are?' 'Why, dust and clay,
What should they be?' ' 'Tis the last hour of day.
Look on the west, how beautiful it is   620
Vaulted with radiant vapours! The deep bliss
Of that unutterable light has made
The edges of that cloud   fade
Into a hue, like some harmonious thought,
Wasting itself on that which it had wrought,   625
Till it dies   and   between
The light hues of the tender, pure, serene,
And infinite tranquillity of heaven.
Ay, beautiful! but when not. . . .'

.   .   .   .   °

'Perhaps the only comfort which remains   630
Is the unheeded clanking of my chains,
The which I make, and call it melody.'

NOTE BY MRS. SHELLEY

FROM the Baths of Lucca, in 1818, Shelley visited Venice; and, circumstances rendering it eligible that we should remain a few weeks in the
neighbourhood of that city, he accepted the offer of Lord Byron, who lent
him the use of a villa he rented near Este; and he sent for his family from
Lucca to join him.

I Capuccini was a villa built on the site of a Capuchin convent, demolished when the French suppressed religious houses; it was situated on the
very overhanging brow of a low hill at the foot of a range of higher ones.
The house was cheerful and pleasant; a vine-trellised walk, a *pergola*,
as it is called in Italian, led from the hall-door to a summer-house at the
end of the garden, which Shelley made his study, and in which he began
the *Prometheus;* and here also, as he mentions in a letter, he wrote *Julian
and Maddalo*. A slight ravine, with a road in its depth, divided the garden
from the hill, on which stood the ruins of the ancient castle of Este, whose
dark massive wall gave forth an echo, and from whose ruined crevices
owls and bats flitted forth at night, as the crescent moon sunk behind the
black and heavy battlements. We looked from the garden over the wide
plain of Lombardy, bounded to the west by the far Apennines, while to
the east the horizon was lost in misty distance. After the picturesque but

limited view of mountain, ravine, and chestnut-wood, at the Baths of Lucca, there was something infinitely gratifying to the eye in the wide range of prospect commanded by our new abode.

Our first misfortune, of the kind from which we soon suffered even more severely, happened here. Our little girl, an infant in whose small features I fancied that I traced great resemblance to her father, showed symptoms of suffering from the heat of the climate. Teething increased her illness and danger. We were at Este, and when we became alarmed, hastened to Venice for the best advice. When we arrived at Fusina, we found that we had forgotten our passport, and the soldiers on duty attempted to prevent our crossing the laguna; but they could not resist Shelley's impetuosity at such a moment. We had scarcely arrived at Venice before life fled from the little sufferer, and we returned to Este to weep her loss.

After a few weeks spent in this retreat, which was interspersed by visits to Venice, we proceeded southward.

PROMETHEUS UNBOUND

A LYRICAL DRAMA

IN FOUR ACTS

AUDISNE HAEC AMPHIARAE, SUB TERRAM ABDITE?

PREFACE

THE Greek tragic writers, in selecting as their subject any portion of their national history or mythology, employed in their treatment of it a certain arbitrary discretion. They by no means conceived themselves bound to adhere to the common interpretation or to imitate in story as in title their rivals and predecessors. Such a system would have amounted to a resignation of those claims to preference over their competitors which incited the composition. The Agamemnonian story was exhibited on the Athenian theatre with as many variations as dramas.

I have presumed to employ a similar licence. The *Prometheus Unbound* of Æschylus supposed the reconciliation of Jupiter with his victim as the price of the disclosure of the danger threatened to his empire by the consummation of his marriage with Thetis. Thetis, according to this view of the subject, was given in marriage to Peleus, and Prometheus, by the permission of Jupiter, delivered from his captivity by Hercules. Had I framed my story on this model, I should have done no more than have attempted to restore the lost drama of Æschylus; an ambition which, if my preference to this mode of treating the subject had incited me to cherish, the recollection of the high comparison such an attempt would challenge might well abate. But, in truth, I was averse from a catastrophe so feeble as that of reconciling the Champion with the Oppressor of mankind. The moral interest of the fable, which is so powerfully sustained by the sufferings and endurance of Prometheus, would be annihilated if we could conceive of him as unsaying his high language and quailing before his successful and perfidious adversary. The only imaginary being resembling in any degree Prometheus, is Satan; and Prometheus is, in my judgement, a more poetical character than Satan, because, in addition to courage, and majesty, and firm and patient opposition to omnipotent force, he is susceptible of being described as exempt from the taints of ambition, envy, revenge, and a desire for personal aggrandisement, which, in the Hero of *Paradise Lost*, interfere with the interest. The character of Satan engenders in the mind a pernicious casuistry which leads us to weigh his faults with his wrongs, and to excuse the former because the latter exceed all measure. In the minds of those who consider that magnificent fiction with a religious feeling it engenders something worse. But Prometheus is, as it were, the type of the highest perfection of moral and intellectual nature, impelled by the purest and the truest motives to the best and noblest ends.

This Poem was chiefly written upon the mountainous ruins of the Baths of Caracalla, among the flowery glades, and thickets of odoriferous blossoming trees, which are extended in ever winding labyrinths upon its immense platforms and dizzy arches suspended in the air. The bright blue sky of Rome, and the effect of the vigorous awakening spring in that divinest climate, and the new life with which it drenches the spirits even to intoxication, were the inspiration of this drama.

The imagery which I have employed will be found, in many instances, to have been drawn from the operations of the human mind, or from those external actions by which they are expressed. This is unusual in modern poetry, although Dante and Shakespeare are full of instances of the same kind. Dante indeed more than any other poet, and with greater success. But the Greek poets, as writers to whom no resource of awakening the sympathy of their contemporaries was unknown, were in the habitual use of this power; and it is the study of their works (since a higher merit would probably be denied me) to which I am willing that my readers should impute this singularity.

One word is due in candour to the degree in which the study of contemporary writings may have tinged my composition, for such has been a topic of censure with regard to poems far more popular, and indeed more deservedly popular, than mine. It is impossible that any one who inhabits the same age with such writers as those who stand in the foremost ranks of our own, can conscientiously assure himself that his language and tone of thought may not have been modified by the study of the productions of those extraordinary intellects. It is true, that, not the spirit of their genius, but the forms in which it has manifested itself, are due less to the peculiarities of their own minds than to the peculiarity of the moral and intellectual condition of the minds among which they have been produced. Thus a number of writers possess the form, whilst they want the spirit of those whom, it is alleged, they imitate; because the former is the endowment of the age in which they live, and the latter must be the uncommunicated lightning of their own mind.

The peculiar style of intense and comprehensive imagery which distinguishes the modern literature of England, has not been, as a general power, the product of the imitation of any particular writer. The mass of capabilities remains at every period materially the same; the circumstances which awaken it to action perpetually change. If England were divided into forty republics, each equal in population and extent to Athens, there is no reason to suppose but that, under institutions not more perfect than those of Athens, each would produce philosophers and poets equal to those who (if we except Shakespeare) have never been surpassed. We owe the great writers of the golden age of our literature to that fervid awakening of the public mind which shook to dust the oldest and most oppressive form of the Christian religion. We owe Milton to the progress and development of the same spirit: the sacred Milton was, let it ever be remembered, a republican, and a bold inquirer into morals and religion. The great writers of our own age are, we have reason to suppose, the companions and forerunners of some unimagined change in our social condition or the opinions which cement it. The cloud of mind is discharging its collected lightning, and the equilibrium between institutions and opinions is now restoring, or is about to be restored.

As to imitation, poetry is a mimetic art. It creates, but it creates by combination and representation. Poetical abstractions are beautiful and new, not because the portions of which they are composed had no previous existence in the mind of man or in nature, but because the whole produced by their combination has some intelligible and beautiful analogy with those sources of emotion and thought, and with the contemporary condition of them: one great poet is a masterpiece of nature which another not only ought to study but must study. He might as wisely and as easily determine that his mind should no longer be the mirror of all that is lovely in the visible universe, as exclude from his contemplation the beautiful which exists in the writings of a great contemporary. The pretence of doing it would be a presumption in any but the greatest; the effect, even in him, would be strained, unnatural, and ineffectual. A poet is the combined product of such internal powers as modify the nature of others; and of such external influences as excite and sustain these powers; he is not one, but both. Every man's mind is, in this respect, modified by all the objects of nature and art; by every word and every suggestion which he ever admitted to act upon his consciousness; it is the mirror upon which all forms are reflected, and in which they compose one form. Poets, not otherwise than philosophers, painters, sculptors, and musicians, are, in one sense, the creators, and, in another, the creations, of their age. From this subjection the loftiest do not escape. There is a similarity between Homer and Hesiod, between Æschylus and Euripides, between Virgil and Horace, between Dante and Petrarch, between Shakespeare and Fletcher, between Dryden and Pope; each has a generic resemblance under which their specific distinctions are arranged. If this similarity be the result of imitation, I am willing to confess that I have imitated.

Let this opportunity be conceded to me of acknowledging that I have, what a Scotch philosopher characteristically terms, 'a passion for reforming the world:' what passion incited him to write and publish his book, he omits to explain. For my part I had rather be damned with Plato and Lord Bacon, than go to Heaven with Paley and Malthus. But it is a mistake to suppose that I dedicate my poetical compositions solely to the direct enforcement of reform, or that I consider them in any degree as containing a reasoned system on the theory of human life. Didactic poetry is my abhorrence; nothing can be equally well expressed in prose that is not tedious and supererogatory in verse. My purpose has hitherto been simply to familiarise the highly refined imagination of the more select classes of poetical readers with beautiful idealisms of moral excellence; aware that until the mind can love, and admire, and trust, and hope, and endure, reasoned principles of moral conduct are seeds cast upon the highway of life which the unconscious passenger tramples into dust, although they would bear the harvest of his happiness. Should I live to accomplish what I purpose, that is, produce a systematical history of what appear to me to be the genuine elements of human society, let not the advocates of injustice and superstition flatter themselves that I should take Æschylus rather than Plato as my model.

The having spoken of myself with unaffected freedom will need little apology with the candid; and let the uncandid consider that they injure me less than their own hearts and minds by misrepresentation. Whatever talents a person may possess to amuse and instruct others, be they ever so inconsiderable, he is yet bound to exert them: if his attempt be ineffectual, let the punishment of an unaccomplished purpose have been sufficient; let none trouble themselves to heap the dust of oblivion upon his efforts; the pile they raise will betray his grave which might otherwise have been unknown.

DRAMATIS PERSONÆ

PROMETHEUS.	APOLLO.	HERCULES.
DEMOGORGON.	MERCURY.	THE PHANTASM OF JUPITER.
JUPITER.	ASIA	THE SPIRIT OF THE EARTH.
THE EARTH.	PANTHEA } Oceanides.	THE SPIRIT OF THE MOON.
OCEAN.	IONE	SPIRITS OF THE HOURS.

SPIRITS. ECHOES. FAUNS. FURIES.

ACT I

SCENE.—*A Ravine of Icy Rocks in the Indian Caucasus.* PROMETHEUS *is discovered bound to the Precipice.* PANTHEA *and* IONE *are seated at his feet. Time, night. During the Scene, morning slowly breaks.*

Prometheus. Monarch of Gods and Dæmons, and all Spirits
But One, who throng those bright and rolling worlds
Which Thou and I alone of living things

Behold with sleepless eyes! regard this Earth
Made multitudinous with thy slaves, whom thou   5
Requitest for knee-worship, prayer, and praise,
And toil, and hecatombs of broken hearts,
With fear and self-contempt and barren hope.
Whilst me, who am thy foe, eyeless in hate,
Hast thou made reign and triumph, to thy scorn,   10
O'er mine own misery and thy vain revenge.
Three thousand years of sleep-unsheltered hours,
And moments aye divided by keen pangs
Till they seemed years, torture and solitude,
Scorn and despair,—these are mine empire:—   15
More glorious far than that which thou surveyest
From thine unenvied throne, O Mighty God!
Almighty, had I deigned to share the shame
Of thine ill tyranny, and hung not here
Nailed to this wall of eagle-baffling mountain,   20
Black, wintry, dead, unmeasured; without herb,
Insect, or beast, or shape or sound of life.
Ah me! alas, pain, pain ever, for ever!

No change, no pause, no hope! Yet I endure.
I ask the Earth, have not the mountains felt?   25
I ask yon Heaven, the all-beholding Sun,
Has it not seen? The Sea, in storm or calm,
Heaven's ever-changing Shadow, spread below,
Have its deaf waves not heard my agony?
Ah me! alas, pain, pain ever, for ever!   30

The crawling glaciers pierce me with the spears
Of their moon-freezing crystals, the bright chains
Eat with their burning cold into my bones.
Heaven's wingèd hound, polluting from thy lips
His beak in poison not his own, tears up   35
My heart; and shapeless sights come wandering by,
The ghastly people of the realm of dream,
Mocking me: and the Earthquake-fiends are charged
To wrench the rivets from my quivering wounds
When the rocks split and close again behind: 40
While from their loud abysses howling throng
The genii of the storm, urging the rage
Of whirlwind, and afflict me with keen hail.
And yet to me welcome is day and night,
Whether one breaks the hoar frost of the morn,   45
Or starry, dim, and slow, the other climbs
The leaden-coloured east; for then they lead
The wingless. crawling hours, one among whom
—As some dark Priest hales the reluctant victim—

Shall drag thee, cruel King, to kiss the blood   50
From these pale feet, which then might trample thee
If they disdained not such a prostrate slave.
Disdain! Ah no! I pity thee. What ruin
Will hunt thee undefended through wide Heaven!
How will thy soul, cloven to its depth with terror,   55
Gape like a hell within! I speak in grief,
Not exultation, for I hate no more,
As then ere misery made me wise. The curse
Once breathed on thee I would recall. Ye Mountains,
Whose many-voicèd Echoes, through the mist   60
Of cataracts, flung the thunder of that spell!
Ye icy Springs, stagnant with wrinkling frost,
Which vibrated to hear me, and then crept
Shuddering through India! Thou serenest Air,
Through which the Sun walks burning without beams!
And ye swift Whirlwinds, who on poisèd wings   66
Hung mute and moveless o'er yon hushed abyss,
As thunder, louder than your own, made rock
The orbèd world! If then my words had power,
Though I am changed so that aught evil wish   70
Is dead within; although no memory be
Of what is hate, let them not lose it now!
What was that curse? for ye all heard me speak.

First Voice (*from the Mountains*).
Thrice three hundred thousand years
   O'er the Earthquake's couch we stood: 75
Oft, as men convulsed with fears,
   We trembled in our multitude.

Second Voice (*from the Springs*).
Thunderbolts had parched our water,
   We had been stained with bitter blood,
And had run mute, 'mid shrieks of slaughter,   80
   Thro' a city and a solitude.

Third Voice (*from the Air*).
I had clothed, since Earth uprose,
   Its wastes in colours not their own,
And oft had my serene repose
   Been cloven by many a rending groan.   85

Fourth Voice (*from the Whirlwinds*).
We had soared beneath these mountains
   Unresting ages; nor had thunder,
Nor yon volcano's flaming fountains,
   Nor any power above or under
   Ever made us mute with wonder.   90

First Voice.

But never bowed our snowy crest
As at the voice of thine unrest.

Second Voice.

Never such a sound before
To the Indian waves we bore.
A pilot asleep on the howling sea   95
Leaped up from the deck in agony,
And heard, and cried, 'Ah, woe is me!'
And died as mad as the wild waves be.

Third Voice.

By such dread words from Earth to Heaven
My still realm was never riven: 100
When its wound was closed, there stood
Darkness o'er the day like blood.

Fourth Voice.

And we shrank back: for dreams of ruin
To frozen caves our flight pursuing
Madé us keep silence—thus—and thus—   105
Though silence is as hell to us.

The Earth. The tongueless Caverns of the craggy hills
Cried, 'Misery!' then; the hollow Heaven replied,
'Misery!' And the Ocean's purple waves,
Climbing the land, howled to the lashing winds,   110
And the pale nations heard it, 'Misery!'
Prometheus. I heard a sound of voices: not the voice
Which I gave forth. Mother, thy sons and thou
Scorn him, without whose all-enduring will
Beneath the fierce omnipotence of Jove,   115
Both they and thou had vanished, like thin mist
Unrolled on the morning wind. Know ye not me,
The Titan? He who made his agony
The barrier to your else all-conquering foe?
Oh, rock-embosomed lawns, and snow-fed streams,   120
Now seen athwart frore vapours, deep below,
Through whose o'ershadowing woods I wandered once
With Asia, drinking life from her loved eyes;
Why scorns the spirit which informs ye, now
To commune with me? me alone, who checked,   125
As one who checks a fiend-drawn charioteer,
The falsehood and the force of him who reigns
Supreme, and with the groans of pining slaves
Fills your dim glens and liquid wildernesses:

Why answer ye not, still? Brethren!

The Earth.   They dare not.   130

  Prometheus. Who dares? for I would hear that curse again.

Ha, what an awful whisper rises up!

'Tis scarce like sound: it tingles through the frame

As lightning tingles, hovering ere it strike.

Speak, Spirit! from thine inorganic voice   135

I only know that thou art moving near

And love. How cursed I him?

    The Earth.   How canst thou hear

Who knowest not the language of the dead?

    Prometheus. Thou art a living spirit, speak as they.

    The Earth. I dare not speak like life, lest Heaven's fell King

Should hear, and link me to some wheel of pain   141

More torturing than the one whereon I roll.

Subtle thou art and good, and though the Gods

Hear not this voice, yet thou art more than God,

Being wise and kind: earnestly hearken now.   145

    Prometheus. Obscurely through my brain, like shadows dim,

Sweep awful thoughts, rapid and thick. I feel

Faint, like one mingled in entwining love;

Yet 'tis not pleasure.

    The Earth.   No, thou canst not hear:

Thou art immortal, and this tongue is known   150

Only to those who die.

    Prometheus.   And what art thou,

O, melancholy Voice?

    The Earth.   I am the Earth,

Thy mother; she within whose stony veins,

To the last fibre of the loftiest tree

Whose thin leaves trembled in the frozen air,   155

Joy ran, as blood within a living frame,

When thou didst from her bosom, like a cloud

Of glory, arise, a spirit of keen joy!

And at thy voice her pining sons uplifted

Their prostrate brows from the polluting dust,   160

And our almighty Tyrant with fierce dread

Grew pale, until his thunder chained thee here.

Then, see those million worlds which burn and roll

Around us: their inhabitants beheld

My spherèd light wane in wide Heaven; the sea   165

Was lifted by strange tempest, and new fire

From earthquake-rifted mountains of bright snow

Shook its portentous hair beneath Heaven's frown;

Lightning and Inundation vexed the plains;

Blue thistles bloomed in cities; foodless toads   170

Within voluptuous chambers panting crawled:

When Plague had fallen on man, and beast, and worm,
And Famine; and black blight on herb and tree;
And in the corn, and vines, and meadow-grass,
Teemed ineradicable poisonous weeds   175
Draining their growth, for my wan breast was dry
With grief; and the thin air, my breath, was stained
With the contagion of a mother's hate
Breathed on her child's destroyer; ay, I heard
Thy curse, the which, if thou rememberest not,   180
Yet my innumerable seas and streams,
Mountains, and caves, and winds, and yon wide air,
And the inarticulate people of the dead,
Preserve, a treasured spell. We meditate
In secret joy and hope those dreadful words,   185
But dare not speak them.
     Prometheus.   Venerable mother!
All else who live and suffer take from thee
Some comfort; flowers, and fruits, and happy sounds,
And love, though fleeting; these may not be mine.
But mine own words, I pray, deny me not.   190
     The Earth. They shall be told. Ere Babylon was dust,
The Magus Zoroaster, my dead child,
Met his own image walking in the garden.
That apparition, sole of men, he saw.
For know there are two worlds of life and death: 195
One that which thou beholdest; but the other
Is underneath the grave, where do inhabit
The shadows of all forms that think and live
Till death unite them and they part no more;
Dreams and the light imaginings of men,   200
And all that faith creates or love desires,
Terrible, strange, sublime and beauteous shapes.
There thou art, and dost hang, a writhing shade,
'Mid whirlwind-peopled mountains; all the gods
Are there, and all the powers of nameless worlds,   205
Vast, sceptred phantoms; heroes, men, and beasts;
And Demogorgon, a tremendous gloom;
And he, the supreme Tyrant, on his throne
Of burning gold. Son, one of these shall utter
The curse which all remember. Call at will   210
Thine own ghost, or the ghost of Jupiter,
Hades or Typhon, or what mightier Gods
From all-prolific Evil, since thy ruin
Have sprung, and trampled on my prostrate sons.
Ask, and they must reply: so the revenge   215
Of the Supreme may sweep through vacant shades,
As rainy wind through the abandoned gate

Of a fallen palace.
  Prometheus.   Mother, let not aught
Of that which may be evil, pass again
My lips, or those of aught resembling me.   220
Phantasm of Jupiter, arise, appear!

Ione.

My wings are folded o'er mine ears:
  My wings are crossèd o'er mine eyes:
Yet through their silver shade appears,
  And through their lulling plumes arise,   225
A Shape, a throng of sounds;
  May it be no ill to thee
O thou of many wounds!
Near whom, for our sweet sister's sake,
Ever thus we watch and wake.   230

Panthea.

The sound is of whirlwind underground.
  Earthquake, and fire, and mountains cloven;
The shape is awful like the sound,
  Clothed in dark purple, star-inwoven.
A sceptre of pale gold   235
  To stay steps proud, o'er the slow cloud
His veinèd hand doth hold.
Cruel he looks, but calm and strong,
Like one who does, not suffers wrong.

Phantasm of Jupiter. Why have the secret powers
  of this strange world   .   240
Driven me, a frail and empty phantom, hither
On direst storms? What unaccustomed sounds
Are hovering on my lips, unlike the voicĕ
With which our pallid race hold ghastly talk
In darkness? And, proud sufferer, who art thou?   245
  Prometheus. Tremendous Image, as thou art must be
He whom thou shadowest forth. I am his foe,
The Titan. Speak the words which I would hear,
Although no thought inform thine empty voice.
  The Earth. Listen! And though your echoes must be mute,
Gray mountains, and old woods, and haunted springs,   251
Prophetic caves, and isle-surrounding streams,
Rejoice to hear what yet ye cannot speak,
  Phantasm. A spirit seizes me and speaks within:
It tears me as fire tears a thunder-cloud.   255
  Panthea. See, how he lifts his mighty looks, the Heaven
Darkens above.

Ione.   He speaks! O shelter me!
Prometheus. I see the curse on gestures proud and cold,
And looks of firm defiance, and calm hate,
And such despair as mocks itself with smiles,   260
Written as on a scroll: yet speak: Oh, speak!

Phantasm.

 Fiend, I defy thee! with a calm, fixed mind,
  All that thou canst inflict I bid thee do;
 Foul Tyrant both of Gods and Human-kind,
  One only being shalt thou not subdue.   265
 Rain then thy plagues upon me here,
 Ghastly disease, and frenzying fear;
 And let alternate frost and fire
 Eat into me, and be thine ire
Lightning, and cutting hail, and legioned forms   270
Of furies, driving by upon the wounding storms.

 Ay, do thy worst. Thou art omnipotent.
  O'er all things but thyself I gave thee power,
 And my own will. Be thy swift mischiefs sent
  To blast mankind, from yon ethereal tower.   275
 Let thy malignant spirit move
 In darkness over those I love:
 On me and mine I imprecate
 The utmost torture of thy hate;
And thus devote to sleepless agony,   280
This undeclining head while thou must reign on high.

 But thou, who art the God and Lord: O, thou,
  Who fillest with thy soul this world of woe,
 To whom all things of Earth and heaven do bow
  In fear and worship: all-prevailing foe!   285
 I curse thee! let a sufferer's curse
 Clasp thee, his torturer, like remorse;
 Till thine Infinity shall be
 A robe of envenomed agony;
And thine Omnipotence a crown of pain,   290
To cling like burning gold round thy dissolving brain.

 Heap on thy soul, by virtue of this Curse,
  Ill deeds, then be thou damned, beholding good;
 Both infinite as is the universe,
  And thou, and thy self-torturing solitude.   295
 An awful image of calm power
 Though now thou sittest, let the hour
 Come, when thou must appear to be
 That which thou art internally;

And after many a false and fruitless crime   300
Scorn track thy lagging fall through boundless space
   and time.

Prometheus. Were these my words, O Parent?
The Earth.   They were thine.
Prometheus. It doth repent me: words are quick and vain;
Grief for awhile is blind, and so was mine.
I wish no living thing to suffer pain.   305

The Earth.

Misery, Oh misery to me,
That Jove at length should vanquish thee.
Wail, howl aloud, Land and Sea,
The Earth's rent heart shall answer ye.
Howl, Spirits of the living and the dead,   310
Your refuge, your defence lies fallen and vanquishèd.

First Echo.

Lies fallen and vanquishèd!

Second Echo.

Fallen and vanquishèd!

Ione.

Fear not: 'tis but some passing spasm,
   The Titan is unvanquished still.   315
But see, where through the azure chasm
   Of yon forked and snowy hill
Trampling the slant winds on high
   With golden-sandalled feet, that glow
Under plumes of purple dye,   320
Like rose-ensanguined ivory,
   A Shape comes now,
Stretching on high from his right hand
A serpent-cinctured wand.
Panthea. 'Tis Jove's world-wandering herald, Mercury.   325

Ione.

And who are those with hydra tresses
   And iron wings that climb the wind,
Whom the frowning God represses
   Like vapours steaming up behind,
Clanging loud, an endless crowd—   330

Panthea.

These are Jove's tempest-walking hounds,
Whom he gluts with groans and blood,

When charioted on sulphurous cloud
He bursts Heaven's bounds.

Ione.

Are they now led, from the thin dead   335
On new pangs to be fed?

Panthea.

The Titan looks as ever, firm, not proud.
First Fury. Ha! I scent life!
Second Fury.   Let me but look into his eyes!
Third Fury. The hope of torturing him smells like a heap
Of corpses, to a death-bird after battle.   340
First Fury. Darest thou delay, O Herald! take cheer, Hounds
Of Hell: what if the Son of Maia soon
Should make us food and sport—who can please long
The Omnipotent?
Mercury.   Back to your towers of iron,
And gnash, beside the streams of fire and wail,   345
Your foodless teeth. Geryon, arise! and Gorgon,
Chimæra, and thou Sphinx, subtlest of fiends
Who ministered to Thebes Heaven's poisoned wine,
Unnatural love, and more unnatural hate:
These shall perform your task.
First Fury.   Oh, mercy! mercy!   350
We die with our desire: drive us not back!
Mercury. Crouch then in silence.
                                        Awful Sufferer!
To thee unwilling, most unwillingly
I come, by the great Father's will driven down,
To execute a doom of new revenge.   355
Alas! I pity thee, and hate myself
That I can do no more: aye from thy sight
Returning, for a season, Heaven seems Hell,
So thy worn form pursues me night and day,
Smiling reproach. Wise art thou, firm and good,   360
But vainly wouldst stand forth alone in strife
Against the Omnipotent; as yon clear lamps
That measure and divide the weary years
From which there is no refuge, long have taught
And long must teach. Even now thy Torturer arms   365
With the strange might of unimagined pains
The powers who scheme slow agonies in Hell,
And my commission is to lead them here,
Or what more subtle, foul, or savage fiends
People the abyss, and leave them to their task.   370
Be it not so! there is a secret known

To thee, and to none else of living things,
Which may transfer the sceptre of wide Heaven,
The fear of which perplexes the Supreme:
Clothe it in words, and bid it clasp his throne   375
In intercession; bend thy soul in prayer,
And like a suppliant in some gorgeous fane,
Let the will kneel within thy haughty heart:
For benefits and meek submission tame
The fiercest and the mightiest.
    Prometheus.   Evil minds   380
Change good to their own nature. I gave all
He has; and in return he chains me here
Years, ages, night and day: whether the Sun
Split my parched skin, or in the moony night
The crystal-wingèd snow cling round my hair: 385
Whilst my belovèd race is trampled down
By his thought-executing ministers.
Such is the tyrant's recompense: 'tis just:
He who is evil can receive no good;
And for a world bestowed, or a friend lost,   390
He can feel hate, fear, shame; not gratitude:
He but requites me for his own misdeed.
Kindness to such is keen reproach, which breaks
With bitter stings the light sleep of Revenge.
Submission, thou dost know I cannot try: 395
For what submission but that fatal word,
The death-seal of mankind's captivity,
Like the Sicilian's hair-suspended sword,
Which trembles o'er his crown, would he accept,
Or could I yield? Which yet I will not yield.   400
Let others flatter Crime, where it sits throned
In brief Omnipotence: secure are they:
For Justice, when triumphant, will weep down
Pity, not punishment, on her own wrongs,
Too much avenged by those who err. I wait,   405
Enduring thus, the retributive hour
Which since we spake is even nearer now.
But hark, the hell-hounds clamour: fear delay:
Behold! Heaven lowers under thy Father's frown.
    Mercury. Oh, that we might be spared: I to inflict   410
And thou to suffer! Once more answer me:
Thou knowest not the period of Jove's power?
    Prometheus. I know but this, that it must come.
    Mercury.   Alas!
Thou canst not count thy years to come of pain?
    Prometheus. They last while Jove must reign: nor
      more, nor less   415

Do I desire or fear.

   Mercury.   Yet pause, and plunge
Into Eternity, where recorded time,
Even all that we imagine, age on age,
Seems but a point, and the reluctant mind
Flags wearily in its unending flight,   420
Till it sink, dizzy, blind, lost, shelterless;
Perchance it has not numbered the slow years
Which thou must spend in torture, unreprieved?

   Prometheus. Perchance no thought can count them, yet
      they pass.

   Mercury. If thou might'st dwell among the Gods the while
Lapped in voluptuous joy?

   Prometheus.   I would not quit   426
This bleak ravine, these unrepentant pains.

   Mercury. Alas! I wonder at, yet pity thee.

   Prometheus. Pity the self-despising slaves of Heaven,
Not me, within whose mind sits peace serene,   430
As light in the sun, throned: how vain is talk!
Call up the fiends.

   Ione.   O, sister, look! White fire
Has cloven to the roots yon huge snow-loaded cedar;
How fearfully God's thunder howls behind!

   Mercury. I must obey his words and thine; alas!   435
Most heavily remorse hangs at my heart!

   Panthea. See where the child of Heaven, with wingèd feet,
Runs down the slanted sunlight of the dawn.

   Ione. Dear sister, close thy plumes over thine eyes
Lest thou behold and die: they come: they come   440
Blackening the birth of day with countless wings,
And hollow underneath, like death.

   First Fury.   Prometheus!

   Second Fury. Immortal Titan!

   Third Fury.   Champion of Heaven's slaves!

   Prometheus. He whom some dreadful voice invokes is here,
Prometheus, the chained Titan. Horrible forms,   445
What and who are ye? Never yet there came
Phantasms so foul through monster-teeming Hell
From the all-miscreative brain of Jove;
Whilst I behold such execrable shapes,
Methinks I grow like what I contemplate,   450
And laugh and stare in loathsome sympathy.

   First Fury. We are the ministers of pain, and fear,
And disappointment, and mistrust, and hate,
And clinging crime; and as lean dogs pursue
Through wood and lake some struck and sobbing fawn,   455
We track all things that weep, and bleed, and live,

When the great King betrays them to our will.
   Prometheus. Oh! many fearful natures in one name,
I know ye; and these lakes and echoes know
The darkness and the clangour of your wings.   460
But why more hideous than your loathèd selves
Gather ye up in legions from the deep?
   Second Fury. We knew not that: Sisters, rejoice, rejoice!
   Prometheus. Can aught exult in its deformity?
   Second Fury. The beauty of delight makes lovers glad,   465
Gazing on one another: so are we.
As from the rose which the pale priestess kneels
To gather for her festal crown of flowers
The aëreal crimson falls, flushing her cheek,
So from our victim's destined agony   470
The shade which is our form invests us round,
Else we are shapeless as our mother Night.
   Prometheus. I laugh your power, and his who sent you here,
To lowest scorn. Pour forth the cup of pain.
   First Fury. Thou thinkest we will rend thee bone from bone,
And nerve from nerve, working like fire within?   476
   Prometheus. Pain is my element, as hate is thine;
Ye rend me now: I care not.
   Second Fury.   Dost imagine
We will but laugh into thy lidless eyes?
   Prometheus. I weigh not what ye do, but what ye suffer,   480
Being evil. Cruel was the power which called
You, or aught else so wretched, into light.
   Third Fury. Thou think'st we will live through thee, one
       by one,
Like animal life, and though we can obscure not
The soul which burns within, that we will dwell   485
Beside it, like a vain loud multitude
Vexing the self-content of wisest men:
That we will be dread thought beneath thy brain,
And foul desire round thine astonished heart,
And blood within thy labyrinthine veins   490
Crawling like agony?
   Prometheus.   Why, we are thus now;
Yet am I king over myself, and rule
The torturing and conflicting throngs within,
As Jove rules you when Hell grows mutinous.   494

Chorus of Furies.

From the ends of the earth, from the ends of the earth,
Where the night has its grave and the morning its birth,
     Come, come, come!
Oh, ye who shake hills with the scream of your mirth,

When cities sink howling in ruin; and ye
Who with wingless footsteps trample the sea,   500
And close upon Shipwreck and Famine's track,
Sit chattering with joy on the foodless wreck;
  Come, come, come!
Leave the bed, low, cold, and red,
Strewed beneath a nation dead;   505
Leave the hatred, as in ashes
 Fire is left for future burning:
It will burst in bloodier flashes
 When ye stir it, soon returning:
Leave the self-contempt implanted   510
In young spirits, sense-enchanted,
 Misery's yet unkindled fuel:
Leave Hell's secrets half unchanted
 To the maniac dreamer; cruel
More than ye can be with hate   515
 Is he with fear.
  Come, come, come!
We are steaming up from Hell's wide gate
And we burthen the blast of the atmosphere,
But vainly we toil till ye come here.   520

Ione. Sister, I hear the thunder of new wings.
Panthea. These solid mountains quiver with the sound
Even as the tremulous air: their shadows make
The space within my plumes more black than night.

    First Fury.

Your call was as a wingèd car   525
Driven on whirlwinds fast and far;
It rapped us from red gulfs of war.

    Second Fury.

From wide cities, famine-wasted;

    Third Fury.

Groans half heard, and blood untasted;

    Fourth Fury.

Kingly conclaves stern and cold,   530
Where blood with gold is bought and sold;

    Fifth Fury.

From the furnace, white and hot,
In which—

A Fury.

Speak not: whisper not:
I know all that ye would tell,
But to speak might break the spell   535
Which must bend the Invincible,
    The stern of thought;
He yet defies the deepest power of Hell.

A Fury.

Tear the veil!

Another Fury.

It is torn.

Chorus.

                    The pale stars of the morn
Shine on a misery, dire to be borne.   540
Dost thou faint, mighty Titan? We laugh thee to scorn.
Dost thou boast the clear knowledge thou waken'dst for man?
Then was kindled within him a thirst which outran
Those perishing waters; a thirst of fierce fever,
Hope, love, doubt, desire, which consume him for ever.   545
    One came forth of gentle worth
    Smiling on the sanguine earth;
    His words outlived him, like swift poison
        Withering up truth, peace, and pity.
    Look! where round the wide horizon   550
    Many a million-peopled city
    Vomits smoke in the bright air.
    Hark that outcry of despair!
    'Tis his mild and gentle ghost
        Wailing for the faith he kindled: 555
    Look again, the flames almost
        To a glow-worm's lamp have dwindled:
    The survivors round the embers
        Gather in dread.
                    Joy, joy, joy!   560
Past ages crowd on thee, but each one remembers,
And the future is dark, and the present is spread
Like a pillow of thorns for thy slumberless head.

Semichorus I.

    Drops of bloody agony flow
    From his white and quivering brow.   565
    Grant a little respite now:
    See a disenchanted nation

Springs like day from desolation;
To Truth its state is dedicate,
And Freedom leads it forth, her mate;   570
A legionèd band of linkèd brothers
Whom Love calls children—

Semichorus II.

'Tis another's:
See how kindred murder kin:
'Tis the vintage-time for death and sin:
Blood, like new wine, bubbles within: 575
Till Despair smothers
The struggling world, which slaves and tyrants win.
[*All the* FURIES *vanish, except one*

Ione. Hark, sister! what a low yet dreadful groan
Quite unsuppressed is tearing up the heart
Of the good Titan, as storms tear the deep,   580
And beasts hear the sea moan in inland caves.
Darest thou observe how the fiends torture him?
Panthea. Alas! I looked forth twice, but will no more.
Ione. What didst thou see?
Panthea.   A woful sight: a youth
With patient looks nailed to a crucifix.   585
Ione. What next?
Panthea.   The heaven around, the earth below
Was peopled with thick shapes of human death,
All horrible, and wrought by human hands,
And some appeared the work of human hearts.
For men were slowly killed by frowns and smiles: 590
And other sights too foul to speak and live
Were wandering by. Let us not tempt worse fear
By looking forth: those groans are grief enough.
Fury. Behold an emblem: those who do endure
Deep wrongs for man, and scorn, and chains, but heap   595
Thousandfold torment on themselves and him.
Prometheus. Remit the anguish of that lighted stare;
Close those wan lips; let that thorn-wounded brow
Stream not with blood; it mingles with thy tears!
Fix, fix those tortured orbs in peace and death,   600
So thy sick throes shake not that crucifix,
So those pale fingers play not with thy gore.
O, horrible! Thy name I will not speak,
It hath become a curse. I see, I see
The wise, the mild, the lofty, and the just,   605
Whom thy slaves hate for being like to thee,
Some hunted by foul lies from their heart's home,
An early-chosen, late-lamented home;

As hooded ounces cling to the driven hind;
Some linked to corpses in unwholesome cells;   610
Some—Hear I not the multitude laugh loud?—
Impaled in lingering fire: and mighty realms
Float by my feet, like sea-uprooted isles,
Whose sons are kneaded down in common blood
By the red light of their own burning homes.   615
    Fury. Blood thou canst see, and fire; and canst hear groans;
Worse things, unheard, unseen, remain behind.
    Prometheus. Worse?
    Fury.   In each human heart terror survives
The ravin it has gorged: the loftiest fear
All that they would disdain to think were true: 620
Hypocrisy and custom make their minds
The fanes of many a worship, now outworn.
They dare not devise good for man's estate,
And yet they know not that they do not dare.
The good want power, but to weep barren tears.   625
The powerful goodness want: worse need for them.
The wise want love; and those who love want wisdom;
And all best things are thus confused to ill.
Many are strong and rich, and would be just,
But live among their suffering fellow-men   630
As if none felt: they know not what they do.
    Prometheus. Thy words are like a cloud of wingèd snakes;
And yet I pity those they torture not.
    Fury. Thou pitiest them? I speak no more!   [*Vanishes.*
    Prometheus.   · ·   Ah woe!
Ah woe! Alas! pain, pain ever, for ever!   635
I close my tearless eyes, but see more clear
Thy works within my woe-illumèd mind,
Thou subtle tyrant! Peace is in the grave.
The grave hides all things beautiful and good:
I am a God and cannot find it there,   640
Nor would I seek it: for, though dread revenge,
This is defeat, fierce king, not victory.
The sights with which thou torturest gird my soul
With new endurance, till the hour arrives
When they shall be no types of things which are.   645
    Panthea. Alas! what sawest thou more?
    Prometheus.   There are two woes:
To speak, and to behold; thou spare me one.
Names are there, Nature's sacred watchwords, they
Were borne aloft in bright emblazonry;
The nations thronged around, and cried aloud,   650
As with one voice, Truth, liberty, and love!
Suddenly fierce confusion fell from heaven

Among them: there was strife, deceit, and fear:
Tyrants rushed in, and did divide the spoil.
This was the shadow of the truth I saw. 655
   The Earth. I felt thy torture, son; with such mixed joy
As pain and virtue give. To cheer thy state
I bid ascend those subtle and fair spirits,
Whose homes are the dim caves of human thought,
And who inhabit, as birds wing the wind, 660
Its world-surrounding aether: they behold
Beyond that twilight realm, as in a glass,
The future: may they speak comfort to thee!
   Panthea. Look, sister, where a troop of spirits gather,
Like flocks of clouds in spring's delightful weather, 665
Thronging in the blue air!
   Ione.   And see! more come,
Like fountain-vapours when the winds are dumb,
That climb up the ravine in scattered lines.
And, hark! is it the music of the pines?
Is it the lake? Is it the waterfall? 670
   Panthea. 'Tis something sadder, sweeter far than all.

Chorus of Spirits.

  From unremembered ages we
  Gentle guides and guardians be
  Of heaven-oppressed mortality;
  And we breathe, and sicken not, 675
  The atmosphere of human thought:
  Be it dim, and dank, and gray, .
  Like a storm-extinguished day,
  Travelled o'er by dying gleams;
    Be it bright as all between 680
  Cloudless skies and windless streams,
    Silent, liquid, and serene;
  As the birds within the wind,
    As the fish within the wave,
  As the thoughts of man's own mind 685
    Float through all above the grave;
  We make there our liquid lair,
  Voyaging cloudlike and unpent
  Through the boundless element:
  Thence we bear the prophecy 690
  Which begins and ends in thee!

   Ione. More yet come, one by one: the air around them
Looks radiant as the air around a star.

First Spirit.

On a battle-trumpet's blast
I fled hither, fast, fast, fast,   695
'Mid the darkness upward cast.
From the dust of creeds outworn,
From the tyrant's banner torn,
Gathering 'round me, onward borne,
There was mingled many a cry—   700
Freedom! Hope! Death! Victory!
Till they faded through the sky;
And one sound, above, around,
One sound beneath, around, above,
Was moving; 'twas the soul of Love;   705
'Twas the hope, the prophecy,
Which begins and ends in thee.

Second Spirit.

A rainbow's arch stood on the sea,
Which rocked beneath, immovably;
And the triumphant storm did flee,   710
Like a conqueror, swift and proud,
Between, with many a captive cloud,
A shapeless, dark and rapid crowd,
Each by lightning riven in half:
I heard the thunder hoarsely laugh: 715
Mighty fleets were strewn like chaff
And spread beneath a hell of death
O'er the white waters. I alit
On a great ship lightning-split,
And speeded hither on the sigh   720
Of one who gave an enemy
His plank, then plunged aside to die.

Third Spirit.

I sate beside a sage's bed,
And the lamp was burning red
Near the book where he had fed,   725
When a Dream with plumes of flame,
To his pillow hovering came,
And I knew it was the same
Which had kindled long ago
Pity, eloquence, and woe;   730
And the world awhile below
Wore the shade, its lustre made.
It has borne me here as fleet
As Desire's lightning feet:

I must ride it back ere morrow,   735
Or the sage will wake in sorrow.

Fourth Spirit.

On a poet's lips I slept
Dreaming like a love-adept
In the sound his breathing kept;
Nor seeks nor finds he mortal blisses,   740
But feeds on the aëreal kisses
Of shapes that haunt thought's wildernesses.
He will watch from dawn to gloom
The lake-reflected sun illume
The yellow bees in the ivy-bloom,   745
Nor heed nor see, what things they be;
But from these create he can
Forms more real than living man,
Nurslings of immortality!
One of these awakened me,   750
And I sped to succour thee.

Ione.

Behold'st thou not two shapes from the east and west
Come, as two doves to one belovèd nest,
Twin nurslings of the all-sustaining air
On swift still wings glide down the atmosphere?   755
And, hark! their sweet, sad voices! 'tis despair
Mingled with love and then dissolved in sound.
Panthea. Canst thou speak, sister? all my words are drowned.
Ione. Their beauty gives me voice. See how they float
On their sustaining wings of skiey grain,   760
Orange and azure deepening into gold:
Their soft smiles light the air like a star's fire.

Chorus of Spirits.

Hast thou beheld the form of Love?

Fifth Spirit.

As over wide dominions
I sped, like some swift cloud that wings the wide air's wilder-
    nesses,
That planet-crested shape swept by on lightning-braided pin-
    ions,
Scattering the liquid joy of life from his ambrosial tresses:
His footsteps paved the world with light; but as I passed 'twas
    fading,   767
And hollow Ruin yawned behind: great sages bound in mad-
    ness,

And headless patriots, and pale youths who perished, unup-
   braiding,
   Gleamed in the night. I wandered o'er, till thou, O King of
     sadness,   770
   Turned by thy smile the worst I saw to recollected gladness.

Sixth Spirit.

Ah, sister! Desolation is a delicate thing:
   It walks not on the earth, it floats not on the air,
But treads with lulling footstep, and fans with silent wing
   The tender hopes which in their hearts the best and gentlest
     bear;   775
Who, soothed to false repose by the fanning plumes above
   And the music-stirring motion of its soft and busy feet,
Dream visions of aëreal joy, and call the monster, Love,
   And wake, and find the shadow Pain, as he whom now we
     greet.

Chorus.

      Though Ruin now Love's shadow be,   780
      Following him, destroyingly,
         On Death's white and wingèd steed,
      Which the fleetest cannot flee,
         Trampling down both flower and weed,
      Man and beast, and foul and fair,   785
      Like a tempest through the air;
      Thou shalt quell this horseman grim,
      Woundless though in heart or limb.

Prometheus. Spirits! how know ye this shall be?

Chorus.

      In the atmosphere we breathe,   790
      As buds grow red when the snow-storms flee,
      From Spring gathering up beneath,
      Whose mild winds shake the elder brake,
      And the wandering herdsmen know
      That the white-thorn soon will blow: 795
        Wisdom, Justice, Love, and Peace,
        When they struggle to increase,
        Are to us as soft winds be
        To shepherd boys, the prophecy
        Which begins and ends in thee.   800
Ione. Where are the Spirits fled?
Panthea.   Only a sense
Remains of them, like the omnipotence
Of music, when the inspired voice and lute
Languish, ere yet the responses are mute,

Which through the deep and labyrinthine soul,   805
Like echoes through long caverns, wind and roll.
   Prometheus. How fair these airborn shapes! and yet I feel
Most vain all hope but love; and thou art far,
Asia! who, when my being overflowed,
Wert like a golden chalice to bright wine   810
Which else had sunk into the thirsty dust.
All things are still: alas! how heavily
This quiet morning weighs upon my heart;
Though I should dream I could even sleep with grief
If slumber were denied not. I would fain   815
Be what it is my destiny to be,
The saviour and the strength of suffering man,
Or sink into the original gulf of things:
There is no agony, and no solace left;
Earth can console, Heaven can torment no more.   820
   Panthea. Hast thou forgotten one who watches thee
The cold dark night, and never sleeps but when
The shadow of thy spirit falls on her?
   Prometheus. I said all hope was vain but love: thou lovest.
   Panthea. Deeply in truth; but the eastern star looks white,
And Asia waits in that far Indian vale,   826
The scene of her sad exile; rugged once
And desolate and frozen, like this ravine;
But now invested with fair flowers and herbs,
And haunted by sweet airs and sounds, which flow   830
Among the woods and waters, from the aether
Of her transforming presence, which would fade
If it were mingled not with thine. Farewell!

END OF THE FIRST ACT.

ACT II

Scene I.—*Morning. A lovely Vale in the Indian Caucasus.* Asia *alone.*

   Asia. From all the blasts of heaven thou hast descended:
Yes, like a spirit, like a thought, which makes
Unwonted tears throng to the horny eyes,
And beatings haunt the desolated heart,
Which should have learnt repose: thou hast descended   5
Cradled in tempests; thou dost wake, O Spring!
O child of many winds! As suddenly
Thou comest as the memory of a dream,
Which now is sad because it hath been sweet;
Like genius, or like joy which riseth up   10
As from the earth, clothing with golden clouds
The desert of our life.

This is the season, this the day, the hour;
At sunrise thou shouldst come, sweet sister mine,
Too long desired, too long delaying, come!   15
How like death-worms the wingless moments crawl!
The point of one white star is quivering still
Deep in the orange light of widening morn
Beyond the purple mountains: through a chasm
Of wind-divided mist the darker lake   20
Reflects it: now it wanes: it gleams again
As the waves fade, and as the burning threads
Of woven cloud unravel in pale air:
'Tis lost! and through yon peaks of cloud-like snow
The roseate sunlight quivers: hear I not   25
The Æolian music of her sea-green plumes
Winnowing the crimson dawn?   [PANTHEA *enters.*
                    I feel, I see
Those eyes which burn through smiles that fade in tears,
Like stars half quenched in mists of silver dew.
Belovèd and most beautiful, who wearest   30
The shadow of that soul by which I live,
How late thou art! the spherèd sun had climbed
The sea; my heart was sick with hope, before
The printless air felt thy belated plumes.
    Panthea. Pardon, great Sister! but my wings were faint
With the delight of a remembered dream,   36
As are the noontide plumes of summer winds
Satiate with sweet flowers. I was wont to sleep
Peacefully, and awake refreshed and calm
Before the sacred Titan's fall, and thy   40
Unhappy love, had made, through use and pity,
Both love and woe familiar to my heart
As they had grown to thine: erewhile I slept
Under the glaucous caverns of old Ocean
Within dim bowers of green and purple moss,   45
Our young Ione's soft and milky arms
Locked then, as now, behind my dark, moist hair,
While my shut eyes and cheek were pressed within
The folded depth of her life-breathing bosom:
But not as now, since I am made the wind   50
Which fails beneath the music that I bear
Of thy most wordless converse; since dissolved
Into the sense with which love talks, my rest
Was troubled and yet sweet; my waking hours
Too full of care and pain.
    Asia.   Lift up thine eyes,   55
And let me read thy dream.
    Panthea.   As I have said

With our sea-sister at his feet I slept.
The mountain mists, condensing at our voice
Under the moon, had spread their snowy flakes,
From the keen ice shielding our linkèd sleep.   60
Then two dreams came. One, I remember not.
But in the other his pale wound-worn limbs
Fell from Prometheus, and the azure night
Grew radiant with the glory of that form
Which lives unchanged within, and his voice fell   65
Like music which makes giddy the dim brain,
Faint with intoxication of keen joy:
'Sister of her whose footsteps pave the world
With loveliness—more fair than aught but her,
Whose shadow thou art—lift thine eyes on me.'   70
I lifted them: the overpowering light
Of that immortal shape was shadowed o'er
By love; which, from his soft and flowing limbs,
And passion-parted lips, and keen, faint eyes,
Steamed forth like vaporous fire; an atmosphere   75
Which wrapped me in its all-dissolving power,
As the warm aether of the morning sun
Wraps ere it drinks some cloud of wandering dew.
I saw not, heard not, moved not, only felt
His presence flow and mingle through my blood   80
Till it became his life, and his grew mine,
And I was thus absorbed, until it passed,
And like the vapours when the sun sinks down,
Gathering again in drops upon the pines,
And tremulous as they, in the deep night   85
My being was condensed; and as the rays
Of thought were slowly gathered, I could hear
His voice, whose accents lingered ere they died
Like footsteps of weak melody: thy name
Among the many sounds alone I heard   90
Of what might be articulate; though still
I listened through the night when sound was none.
Ione wakened then, and said to me:
'Canst thou divine what troubles me to-night?
I always knew what I desired before,   95
Nor ever found delight to wish in vain.
But now I cannot tell thee what I seek;
I know not; something sweet, since it is sweet
Even to desire; it is thy sport, false sister;
Thou hast discovered some enchantment old,   100
Whose spells have stolen my spirit as I slept
And mingled it with thine: for when just now
We kissed, I felt within thy parted lips

The sweet air that sustained me, and the warmth
Of the life-blood, for loss of which I faint,   105
Quivered between our intertwining arms.'
I answered not, for the Eastern star grew pale,
But fled to thee.

    Asia.   — Thou speakest, but thy words
Are as the air: I feel them not: Oh, lift
Thine eyes, that I may read his written soul!   110

    Panthea. I lift them though they droop beneath the load
Of that they would express: what canst thou see
But thine own fairest shadow imaged there?

    Asia. Thine eyes are like the deep, blue, boundless heaven
Contracted to two circles underneath   115
Their long, fine lashes; dark, far, measureless,
Orb within orb, and line through line inwoven.

    Panthea. Why lookest thou as if a spirit passed?

    Asia. There is a change: beyond their inmost depth
I see a shade, a shape: 'tis He, arrayed   120
In the soft light of his own smiles, which spread
Like radiance from the cloud-surrounded moon.
Prometheus, it is thine! depart not yet!
Say not those smiles that we shall meet again
Within that bright pavilion which their beams   125
Shall build o'er the waste world? The dream is told.
What shape is that between us? Its rude hair
Roughens the wind that lifts it, its regard
Is wild and quick, yet 'tis a thing of air,
For through its gray robe gleams the golden dew   130
Whose stars the noon has quenched not.

    Dream.   Follow! Follow!

    Panthea. It is mine other dream.

    Asia.   It disappears.

    Panthea. It passes now into my mind. Methought
As we sate here, the flower-infolding buds
Burst on yon lightning-blasted almond-tree,   135
When swift from the white Scythian wilderness
A wind swept forth wrinkling the Earth with frost:
I looked, and all the blossoms were blown down;
But on each leaf was stamped, as the blue bells
Of Hyacinth tell Apollo's written grief,   140
O, FOLLOW, FOLLOW!

    Asia.   As you speak, your words
Fill, pause by pause, my own forgotten sleep
With shapes. Methought among these lawns together
We wandered, underneath the young gray dawn,
And multitudes of dense white fleecy clouds   145
Were wandering in thick flocks along the mountains

Shepherded by the slow, unwilling wind;
And the white dew on the new-bladed grass,
Just piercing the dark earth, hung silently;
And there was more which I remember not: 150
But on the shadows of the morning clouds,
Athwart the purple mountain slope, was written
FOLLOW, O, FOLLOW! as they vanished by;
And on each herb, from which Heaven's dew had fallen,
The like was stamped, as with a withering fire;   155
A wind arose among the pines; it shook
The clinging music from their boughs, and then
Low, sweet, faint sounds, like the farewell of ghosts,
Were heard: O, FOLLOW, FOLLOW, FOLLOW ME!
And then I said: 'Panthea, look on me.'   160
But in the depth of those belovèd eyes
Still I saw, FOLLOW, FOLLOW!
    Echo.   Follow, follow!
    Panthea. The crags, this clear spring morning, mock
      our voices
As they were spirit-tongued.
    Asia.   It is some being
Around the crags. What fine clear sounds! O, list!   165

       Echoes (unseen).
     Echoes we: listen!
      We cannot stay:
    As dew-stars glisten
     Then fade away—
       Child of Ocean!   170

    Asia. Hark! Spirits speak. The liquid responses
Of their aëreal tongues yet sound.
    Panthea.   I hear.
       Echoes.
     O, follow, follow,
      As our voice recedeth
    Through the caverns hollow,   17.
      Where the forest spreadeth;
       (*More distant.*)
    O, follow, follow!
    Through the caverns hollow,
As the song floats thou pursue,
Where the wild bee never flew,   180
Through the noontide darkness deep,
By the odour-breathing sleep
Of faint night flowers, and the waves
At the fountain-lighted caves,

While our music, wild and sweet,   185
   Mocks thy gently falling feet,
      Child of Ocean!
Asia. Shall we pursue the sound? It grows more faint
And distant.
Panthea.   List! the strain floats nearer now.

           Echoes.

In the world unknown   190
   Sleeps a voice unspoken;
   By thy step alone
     Can its rest be broken;
      Child of Ocean!
Asia. How the notes sink upon the ebbing wind!   195

           Echoes.

   O, follow, follow!
    Through the caverns hollow,
  As the song floats thou pursue,
  By the woodland noontide dew;
  By the forest, lakes, and fountains,   200
  Through the many-folded mountains;
  To the rents, and gulfs, and chasms,
  Where the Earth reposed from spasms,
  On the day when He and thou
  Parted, to commingle now;   205
      Child of Ocean!
Asia. Come, sweet Panthea, link thy hand in mine,
And follow, ere the voices fade away.

SCENE II.—*A Forest, intermingled with Rocks and Caverns.* ASIA *and*
PANTHEA *pass into it. Two young Fauns are sitting on a Rock lis-*
tening.

        Semichorus I. of Spirits.

The path through which that lovely twain
  Have passed, by cedar, pine, and yew,
  And each dark tree that ever grew,
  Is curtained out from Heaven's wide blue;
Nor sun, nor moon, nor wind, nor rain,   5
  Can pierce its interwoven bowers,
  Nor aught, save where some cloud of dew,
Drifted along the earth-creeping breeze,
Between the trunks of the hoar trees,
  Hangs each a pearl in the pale flowers   10
  Of the green laurel, blown anew;
And bends, and then fades silently,
One frail and fair anemone:
Or when some star of many a one

That climbs and wanders through steep night,   15
Has found the cleft through which alone
Beams fall from high those depths upon
Ere it is borne away, away,
By the swift Heavens that cannot stay,
It scatters drops of golden light,   20
Like lines of rain that ne'er unite:
And the gloom divine is all around,
And underneath is the mossy ground.

Semichorus II.

There the voluptuous nightingales,
   Are awake through all the broad noonday.   25
When one with bliss or sadness fails,
    And through the windless ivy-boughs,
   Sick with sweet love, droops dying away
On its mate's music-panting bosom;
Another from the swinging blossom,   30
    Watching to catch the languid close
   Of the last strain, then lifts on high
   The wings of the weak melody,
'Till some new strain of feeling bear
   The song, and all the woods are mute;   35
When there is heard through the dim air
The rush of wings, and rising there
   Like many a lake-surrounded flute,
Sounds overflow the listener's brain
So sweet, that joy is almost pain.   40

Semichorus I.

There those enchanted eddies play
   Of echoes, music-tongued, which draw,
   By Demogorgon's mighty law,
   With melting rapture, or sweet awe,
All spirits on that secret way;   45
   As inland boats are driven to Ocean
Down streams made strong with mountain-thaw:
    And first there comes a gentle sound
    To those in talk or slumber bound,
   And wakes the destined soft emotion,—   50
Attracts, impels them; those who saw
   Say from the breathing earth behind
   There steams a plume-uplifting wind
Which drives them on their path, while they
   Believe their own swift wings and feet   55
The sweet desires within obey:
And so they float upon their way,

Until, still sweet, but loud and strong,
The storm of sound is driven along,
    Sucked up and hurrying: as they fleet   60
    Behind, its gathering billows meet
And to the fatal mountain bear
Like clouds amid the yielding air.

First Faun. Canst thou imagine where those spirits live
Which make such delicate music in the woods?   65
We haunt within the least frequented caves
And closest coverts, and we know these wilds,
Yet never meet them, though we hear them oft:
Where may they hide themselves?

Second Faun.   'Tis hard to tell:
I have heard those more skilled in spirits say,   70
The bubbles, which the enchantment of the sun
Sucks from the pale faint water-flowers that pave
The oozy bottom of clear lakes and pools,
Are the pavilions where such dwell and float
Under the green and golden atmosphere   75
Which noontide kindles through the woven leaves;
And when these burst, and the thin fiery air,
The which they breathed within those lucent domes,
Ascends to flow like meteors through the night,
They ride on them, and rein their headlong speed,   80
And bow their burning crests, and glide in fire
Under the waters of the earth again.

First Faun. If such live thus, have others other lives,
Under pink blossoms or within the bells
Of meadow flowers, or folded violets deep,   85
Or on their dying odours, when they die,
Or in the sunlight of the sphered dew?

Second Faun. Ay, many more which we may well divine.
But, should we stay to speak, noontide would come,
And thwart Silenus find his goats undrawn,   90
And grudge to sing those wise and lovely songs
Of Fate, and Chance, and God, and Chaos old,
And Love, and the chained Titan's woful doom,
And how he shall be loosed, and make the earth
One brotherhood: delightful strains which cheer   95
Our solitary twilights, and which charm
To silence the unenvying nightingales.

SCENE III.—*A Pinnacle of Rock among Mountains.*
ASIA *and* PANTHEA.

Panthea. Hither the sound has borne us—to the realm
Of Demogorgon, and the mighty portal,

Like a volcano's meteor-breathing chasm,
Whence the oracular vapour is hurled up
Which lonely men drink wandering in their youth,   5
And call truth, virtue, love, genius, or joy,
That maddening wine of life, whose dregs they drain
To deep intoxication; and uplift,
Like Mænads who cry loud, Evoe! Evoe!
The voice which is contagion to the world.   10
 Asia. Fit throne for such a Power! Magnificent!
How glorious art thou, Earth! And if thou be
The shadow of some spirit lovelier still,
Though evil stain its work, and it should be
Like its creation, weak yet beautiful,   15
I could fall down and worship that and thee.
Even now my heart adoreth: Wonderful!
Look, sister, ere the vapour dim thy brain:
Beneath is a wide plain of billowy mist,
As a lake, paving in the morning sky,   20
With azure waves which burst in silver light,
Some Indian vale. Behold it, rolling on
Under the curdling winds, and islanding
The peak whereon we stand, midway, around,
Encinctured by the dark and blooming forests,   25
Dim twilight-lawns, and stream-illumèd caves,
And wind-enchanted shapes of wandering mist;
And far on high the keen sky-cleaving mountains
From icy spires of sun-like radiance fling
The dawn, as lifted Ocean's dazzling spray,   30
From some Atlantic islet scattered up,
Spangles the wind with lamp-like water-drops.
The vale is girdled with their walls, a howl
Of cataracts from their thaw-cloven ravines,
Satiates the listening wind, continuous, vast,   35
Awful as silence. Hark! the rushing snow!
The sun-awakened avalanche! whose mass,
Thrice sifted by the storm, had gathered there
Flake after flake, in heaven-defying minds
As thought by thought is piled, till some great truth   40
Is loosened, and the nations echo round,
Shaken to their roots, as do the mountains now.
 Panthea. Look how the gusty sea of mist is breaking
In crimson foam, even at our feet! it rises
As Ocean at the enchantment of the moon   45
Round foodless men wrecked on some oozy isle.
 Asia. The fragments of the clouds are scattered up;
The wind that lifts them disentwines my hair;
Its billows now sweep o'er mine eyes; my brain

Grows dizzy; see'st thou shapes within the mist?   50
    Panthea. A countenance with beckoning smiles: there burns
An azure fire within its golden locks!
Another and another: hark! they speak!

Song of Spirits.

To the deep, to the deep,
                Down, down!   55
Through the shade of sleep,
Through the cloudy strife
Of Death and of Life;
Through the veil and the bar
Of things which seem and are   60
Even to the steps of the remotest throne,
            Down, down!

While the sound whirls around,
            Down, down!
As the fawn draws the hound,   65
As the lightning the vapour,
As a weak moth the taper;
Death, despair; love, sorrow;
Time both; to-day, to-morrow;
As steel obeys the spirit of the stone,   70
            Down, down!

Through the gray, void abysm,
            Down, down!
Where the air is no prism,
And the moon and stars are not,   75
And the cavern-crags wear not
The radiance of Heaven,
Nor the gloom to Earth given,
Where there is One pervading, One alone.
            Down, down!   80

In the depth of the deep,
            Down, down!
Like veiled lightning asleep,
Like the spark nursed in embers,
The last look Love remembers,   85
Like a diamond, which shines
On the dark wealth of mines,
A spell is treasured but for thee alone.
            Down, down!

We have bound thee, we guide thee;   90
            Down, down!

With the bright form beside thee;
Resist not the weakness,
Such strength is in meekness
That the Eternal, the Immortal, 95
Must unloose through life's portal
The snake-like Doom coiled underneath his throne
By that alone.

SCENE IV.—*The Cave of Demogorgon.* ASIA *and* PANTHEA.

Panthea. What veilèd form sits on that ebon throne?
Asia. The veil has fallen.
Panthea.   I see a mighty darkness
Filling the seat of power, and rays of gloom
Dart round, as light from the meridian sun.
—Ungazed upon and shapeless; neither limb, 5
Nor form, nor outline; yet we feel it is
A living Spirit.
Demogorgon. Ask what thou wouldst know.
Asia. What canst thou tell?
Demogorgon.   All things thou dar'st demand.
Asia. Who made the living world?
Demogorgon.   God.
Asia.   Who made all
That it contains? thought, passion, reason, will, 10
Imagination?
Demogorgon. God: Almighty God.
Asia. Who made that sense which, when the winds of Spring
In rarest visitation, or the voice
Of one belovèd heard in youth alone,
Fills the faint eyes with falling tears which dim 15
The radiant looks of unbewailing flowers,
And leaves this peopled earth a solitude
When it returns no more?
Demogorgon.   Merciful God.
Asia. And who made terror, madness, crime, remorse,
Which from the links of the great chain of things, 20
To every thought within the mind of man
Sway and drag heavily, and each one reels
Under the load towards the pit of death;
Abandoned hope, and love that turns to hate;
And self-contempt, bitterer to drink than blood; 25
Pain, whose unheeded and familiar speech
Is howling, and keen shrieks, day after day;
And Hell, or the sharp fear of Hell?
Demogorgon.   He reigns.
Asia. Utter his name: a world pining in pain

Asks but his name: curses shall drag him down.   30
   Demogorgon. He reigns.
   Asia.   I feel, I know it: who?
   Demogorgon.   He reigns.
   Asia. Who reigns? There was the Heaven and Earth at first,
And Light and Love; then Saturn, from whose throne
Time fell, an envious shadow: such the state
Of the earth's primal spirits beneath his sway,   35
As the calm joy of flowers and living leaves
Before the wind or sun has withered them
And semivital worms; but he refused
The birthright of their being, knowledge, power,
The skill which wields the elements, the thought   40
Which pierces this dim universe like light,
Self-empire, and the majesty of love;
For thirst of which they fainted. Then Prometheus
Gave wisdom, which is strength, to Jupiter,
And with this law alone, 'Let man be free,'   45
Clothed him with the dominion of wide Heaven.
To know nor faith, nor love, nor law; to be
Omnipotent but friendless is to reign;
And Jove now reigned; for on the race of man
First famine, and then toil, and then disease,   50
Strife, wounds, and ghastly death unseen before,
Fell; and the unseasonable seasons drove
With alternating shafts of frost and fire,
Their shelterless, pale tribes to mountain caves:
And in their desert hearts fierce wants he sent,   55
And mad disquietude, and shadows idle
Of unreal good, which levied mutual war,
So ruining the lair wherein they raged.
Prometheus saw, and waked the legioned hopes
Which sleep within folded Elysian flowers,   60
Nepenthe, Moly, Amaranth, fadeless blooms,
That they might hide with thin and rainbow wings
The shape of Death; and Love he sent to bind
The disunited tendrils of that vine
Which bears the wine of life, the human heart;   65
And he tamed fire which like some beast of prey,
Most terrible, but lovely, played beneath
The frown of man; and tortured to his will
Iron and gold, the slaves and signs of power,
And gems and poisons, and all subtlest forms   70
Hidden beneath the mountains and the waves.
He gave man speech, and speech created thought,
Which is the measure of the universe;
And Science struck the thrones of earth and heaven,

Which shook, but fell not; and the harmonious mind   75
Poured itself forth in all-prophetic song;
And music lifted up the listening spirit
Until it walked, exempt from mortal care,
Godlike, o'er the clear billows of sweet sound;
And human hands first mimicked and then mocked,   80
With moulded limbs more lovely than its own,
The human form, till marble grew divine;
And mothers, gazing, drank the love men see
Reflected in their race, behold, and perish.
He told the hidden power of herbs and springs,   85
And Disease drank and slept. Death grew like sleep.
He taught the implicated orbits woven
Of the wide-wandering stars; and how the sun
Changes his lair, and by what secret spell
The pale moon is transformed, when her broad eye   90
Gazes not on the interlunar sea:
He taught to rule, as life directs the limbs,
The tempest-wingèd chariots of the Ocean,
And the Celt knew the Indian. Cities then
Were built, and through their snow-like columns flowed
The warm winds, and the azure aether shone,   96
And the blue sea and shadowy hills were seen.
Such, the alleviations of his state,
Prometheus gave to man, for which he hangs
Withering in destined pain: but who rains down   100
Evil, the immedicable plague, which, while
Man looks on his creation like a God
And sees that it is glorious, drives him on,
The wreck of his own will, the scorn of earth,
The outcast, the abandoned, the alone?   105
Not Jove: while yet his frown shook Heaven, ay, when
His adversary from adamantine chains
Cursed him, he trembled like a slave. Declare
Who is his master? Is he too a slave?
   Demogorgon. All spirits are enslaved which serve things evil:
Thou knowest if Jupiter be such or no.   111
   Asia. Whom calledst thou God?
   Demogorgon.   I spoke but as ye speak,
For Jove is the supreme of living things.
   Asia. Who is the master of the slave?
   Demogorgon.   If the abysm
Could vomit forth its secrets. . . . But a voice   115
Is wanting, the deep truth is imageless;
For what would it avail to bid thee gaze
On the revolving world? What to bid speak
Fate, Time, Occasion, Chance, and Change? To these

All things are subject but eternal Love.   120
 Asia. So much I asked before, and my heart gave
The response thou hast given; and of such truths
Each to itself must be the oracle.
One more demand; and do thou answer me
As mine own soul would answer, did it know   125
That which I ask. Prometheus shall arise
Henceforth the sun of this rejoicing world:
When shall the destined hour arrive?
  Demogorgon.   Behold!
 Asia. The rocks are cloven, and through the purple night
I see cars drawn by rainbow-wingèd steeds   130
Which trample the dim winds: in each there stands
A wild-eyed charioteer urging their flight.
Some look behind, as fiends pursued them there,
And yet I see no shapes but the keen stars:
Others, with burning eyes, lean forth, and drink   135
With eager lips the wind of their own speed,
As if the thing they loved fled on before,
And now, even now, they clasped it. Their bright locks
Stream like a comet's flashing hair: they all
Sweep onward.
  Demogorgon. These are the immortal Hours,   140
Of whom thou didst demand. One waits for thee.
 Asia. A spirit with a dreadful countenance
Checks its dark chariot by the craggy gulf.
Unlike thy brethren, ghastly charioteer,
Who art thou? Whither wouldst thou bear me? Speak!   145
 Spirit. I am the shadow of a destiny
More dread than is my aspect: ere yon planet
Has set, the darkness which ascends with me
Shall wrap in lasting night heaven's kingless throne.
 Asia. What meanest thou?
 Panthea.   That terrible shadow floats
Up from its throne, as may the lurid smoke   151
Of earthquake-ruined cities o'er the sea.
Lo! it ascends the car; the coursers fly
Terrified: watch its path among the stars
Blackening the night!
  Asia.   Thus I am answered: strange!   155
 Panthea. See, near the verge, another chariot stays;
An ivory shell inlaid with crimson fire,
Which comes and goes within its sculptured rim
Of delicate strange tracery; the young spirit
That guides it has the dove-like eyes of hope;   160
How its soft smiles attract the soul! as light
Lures wingèd insects through the lampless air.

Spirit.

My coursers are fed with the lightning,
 They drink of the whirlwind's stream,
And when the red morning is bright'ning   165
 They bathe in the fresh sunbeam;
 They have strength for their swiftness I deem,
Then ascend with me, daughter of Ocean.

I desire: and their speed makes night kindle;
 I fear: they outstrip the Typhoon;   170
Ere the cloud piled on Atlas can dwindle
 We encircle the earth and the moon:
 We shall rest from long labours at noon:
Then ascend with me, daughter of Ocean.

SCENE V.—*The Car pauses within a Cloud on the top of a snowy
Mountain.* ASIA, PANTHEA, *and the* SPIRIT OF THE HOUR.

Spirit.

On the brink of the night and the morning
 My coursers are wont to respire;
But the Earth has just whispered a warning
 That their flight must be swifter than fire:
 They shall drink the hot speed of desire!   5

Asia. Thou breathest on their nostrils, but my breath
Would give them swifter speed.
Spirit.   Alas! it could not.
Panthea. Oh Spirit! pause, and tell whence is the light
Which fills this cloud? the sun is yet unrisen.
Spirit. The sun will rise not until noon. Apollo   10
Is held in heaven by wonder; and the light
Which fills this vapour, as the aëreal hue
Of fountain-gazing roses fills the water,
Flows from thy mighty sister.
Panthea.   Yes, I feel—
Asia. What is it with thee, sister? Thou art pale.   15
Panthea. How thou art changed! I dare not look on thee;
I feel but see thee not. I scarce endure
The radiance of thy beauty. Some good change
Is working in the elements, which suffer
Thy presence thus unveiled. The Nereids tell   20
That on the day when the clear hyaline
Was cloven at thine uprise, and thou didst stand
Within a veinèd shell, which floated on
Over the calm floor of the crystal sea,

Among the Ægean isles, and by the shores   25
Which bear thy name; love, like the atmosphere
Of the sun's fire filling the living world,
Burst from thee, and illumined earth and heaven
And the deep ocean and the sunless caves
And all that dwells within them; till grief cast   30
Eclipse upon the soul from which it came:
Such art thou now; nor is it I alone,
Thy sister, thy companion, thine own chosen one,
But the whole world which seeks thy sympathy.
Hearest thou not sounds i' the air which speak the love   35
Of all articulate beings? Feelest thou not
The inanimate winds enamoured of thee? List!   [*Music.*
    Asia. Thy words are sweeter than aught else but his
Whose echoes they are: yet all love is sweet,
Given or returned. Common as light is love,   40
And its familiar voice wearies not ever.
Like the wide heaven, the all-sustaining air,
It makes the reptile equal to the God:
They who inspire it most are fortunate,
As I am now; but those who feel it most   45
Are happier still, after long sufferings,
As I shall soon become.
    Panthea.   List! Spirits speak.

        Voices in the Air, singing.

    Life of Life! thy lips enkindle
      With their love the breath between them;
    And thy smiles before they dwindle   50
      Make the cold air fire; then screen them
    In those looks, where whoso gazes
    Faints, entangled in their mazes.

    Child of Light! thy limbs are burning
      Through the vest which seems to hide them;   55
    As the radiant lines of morning
      Through the clouds ere they divide them;
    And this atmosphere divinest
    Shrouds thee wheresoe'er thou shinest.

    Fair are others; none beholds thee,   60
      But thy voice sounds low and tender
    Like the fairest, for it folds thee
      From the sight, that liquid splendour,
    And all feel, yet see thee never,
    As I feel now, lost for ever!   65

Lamp of Earth! where'er thou movest
  Its dim shapes are clad with brightness,
And the souls of whom thou lovest
  Walk upon the winds with lightness,
Till they fail, as I am failing,   70
Dizzy, lost, yet unbewailing!

Asia.

My soul is an enchanted boat,
  Which, like a sleeping swan, doth float
Upon the silver waves of thy sweet singing;
  And thine doth like an angel sit   75
  Beside a helm conducting it,
Whilst all the winds with melody are ringing.
  It seems to float ever, for ever,
  Upon that many-winding river,
  Between mountains, woods, abysses,   80
A paradise of wildernesses!
Till, like one in slumber bound,
Borne to the ocean, I float down, around,
Into a sea profound, of ever-spreading sound:

  Meanwhile thy spirit lifts its pinions   85
  In music's most serene dominions;
Catching the winds that fan that happy heaven.
  And we sail on, away, afar,
  Without a course, without a star,
But, by the instinct of sweet music driven;   90
  Till through Elysian garden islets
  By thee, most beautiful of pilots,
  Where never mortal pinnace glided,
  The boat of my desire is guided:
Realms where the air we breathe is love,   95
Which in the winds and on the waves doth move,
Harmonizing this earth with what we feel above.

  We have passed Age's icy caves,
  And Manhood's dark and tossing waves,
And Youth's smooth ocean, smiling to betray: 100
  Beyond the glassy gulfs we flee
  Of shadow-peopled Infancy,
Through Death and Birth, to a diviner day;
  A paradise of vaulted bowers,
  Lit by downward-gazing flowers,   105
  And watery paths that wind between
  Wildernesses calm and green.

Peopled by shapes too bright to see,
And rest, having beheld; somewhat like thee;
Which walk upon the sea, and chant melodiously!   110

END OF THE SECOND ACT.

ACT III

SCENE I.—*Heaven.* JUPITER *on his Throne;* THETIS *and the other Deities assembled.*

Jupiter. Ye congregated powers of heaven, who share
The glory and the strength of him ye serve,
Rejoice! henceforth I am omnipotent.
All else had been subdued to me; alone
The soul of man, like unextinguished fire,   5
Yet burns towards heaven with fierce reproach, and doubt,
And lamentation, and reluctant prayer,
Hurling up insurrection, which might make
Our antique empire insecure, though built
On eldest faith, and hell's coeval, fear;   10
And though my curses through the pendulous air,
Like snow on herbless peaks, fall flake by flake,
And cling to it; though under my wrath's night
It climbs the crags of life, step after step,
Which wound it, as ice wounds unsandalled feet,   15
It yet remains supreme o'er misery,
Aspiring, unrepressed, yet soon to fall:
Even now have I begotten a strange wonder,
That fatal child, the terror of the earth,
Who waits but till the destined hour arrive,   20
Bearing from Demogorgon's vacant throne
The dreadful might of ever-living limbs
Which clothed that awful spirit unbeheld,
To redescend, and trample out the spark.
Pour forth heaven's wine, Idæan Ganymede,   25
And let it fill the Dædal cups like fire,
And from the flower-inwoven soil divine
Ye all-triumphant harmonies arise,
As dew from earth under the twilight stars:
Drink! be the nectar circling through your veins   30
The soul of joy, ye ever-living Gods,
Till exultation burst in one wide voice
Like music from Elysian winds.
                       And thou
Ascend beside me, veilèd in the light
Of the desire which makes thee one with me,   35
Thetis, bright image of eternity!

When thou didst cry, 'Insufferable might!
God! Spare me! I sustain not the quick flames,
The penetrating presence; all my being,
Like him whom the Numidian seps did thaw   40
Into a dew with poison, is dissolved,
Sinking through its foundations:' even then
Two mighty spirits, mingling, made a third
Mightier than either, which, unbodied now,
Between us floats, felt, although unbeheld,   45
Waiting the incarnation, which ascends.
(Hear ye the thunder of the fiery wheels
Griding the winds?) from Demogorgon's throne.
Victory! victory! Feel'st thou not, O world,
The earthquake of his chariot thundering up   50
Olympus?

[*The Car of the* HOUR *arrives.* DEMOGORGON *descends,*
and moves towards the Throne of JUPITER.

Awful shape, what art thou? Speak!
Demogorgon. Eternity. Demand no direr name.
Descend, and follow me down the abyss.
I am thy child, as thou wert Saturn's child;
Mightier than thee: and we must dwell together   55
Henceforth in darkness. Lift thy lightnings not.
The tyranny of heaven none may retain,
Or reassume, or hold, succeeding thee:
Yet if thou wilt, as 'tis the destiny
Of trodden worms to writhe till they are dead,   60
Put forth thy might.
    Jupiter.   Detested prodigy!
Even thus beneath the deep Titanian prisons
I trample thee! thou lingerest?
                    Mercy! mercy!
No pity, no release, no respite! Oh,
That thou wouldst make mine enemy my judge,   65
Even where he hangs, seared by my long revenge,
On Caucasus! he would not doom me thus.
Gentle, and just, and dreadless, is he not
The monarch of the world? What then art thou?
No refuge! no appeal!
                    Sink with me then,   70
We two will sink on the wide waves of ruin,
Even as a vulture and a snake outspent
Drop, twisted in inextricable fight,
Into a shoreless sea. Let hell unlock
Its mounded oceans of tempestuous fire,   75
And whelm on them into the bottomless void

This desolated world, and thee, and me,
The conqueror and the conquered, and the wreck
Of that for which they combated.

                         Ai! Ai!

The elements obey me not. I sink   80
Dizzily down, ever, for ever, down.
And, like a cloud, mine enemy above
Darkens my fall with victory! Ai, Ai!

Scene II.—*The Mouth of a great River in the Island Atlantis.* Ocean *is
discovered reclining near the Shore;* Apollo *stands beside him.*

   Ocean. He fell, thou sayest, beneath his conqueror's frown?
   Apollo. Ay, when the strife was ended which made dim
The orb I rule, and shook the solid stars,
The terrors of his eye illumined heaven
With sanguine light, through the thick ragged skirts   5
Of the victorious darkness, as he fell:
Like the last glare of day's red agony,
Which, from a rent among the fiery clouds,
Burns far along the tempest-wrinkled deep.
   Ocean. He sunk to the abyss? To the dark void?   10
   Apollo. An eagle so caught in some bursting cloud
On Caucasus, his thunder-baffled wings
Entangled in the whirlwind, and his eyes
Which gazed on the undazzling sun, now blinded
By the white lightning, while the ponderous hail   15
Beats on his struggling form, which sinks at length
Prone, and the aëreal ice clings over it.
   Ocean. Henceforth the fields of heaven-reflecting sea
Which are my realm, will heave, unstained with blood,
Beneath the uplifting winds, like plains of corn   20
Swayed by the summer air; my streams will flow
Round many-peopled continents, and round
Fortunate isles; and from their glassy thrones
Blue Proteus and his humid nymphs shall mark
The shadow of fair ships, as mortals see   25
The floating bark of the light-laden moon
With that white star, its sightless pilot's crest,
Borne down the rapid sunset's ebbing sea;
Tracking their path no more by blood and groans,
And desolation, and the mingled voice   30
Of slavery and command; but by the light
Of wave-reflected flowers, and floating odours,
And music soft, and mild, free, gentle voices,
And sweetest music, such as spirits love.
   Apollo. And I shall gaze not on the deeds which make   35

My mind obscure with sorrow, as eclipse
Darkens the sphere I guide; but list, I hear
The small, clear, silver lute of the young Spirit
That sits i' the morning star.
    Ocean.   Thou must away;
Thy steeds will pause at even, till when farewell: 40
The loud deep calls me home even now to feed it
With azure calm out of the emerald urns
Which stand for ever full beside my throne.
Behold the Nereids under the green sea,
Their wavering limbs borne on the wind-like stream,   45
Their white arms lifted o'er their streaming hair
With garlands pied and starry sea-flower crowns,
Hastening to grace their mighty sister's joy.
                    [*A sound of waves is heard*.
It is the unpastured sea hungering for calm.
Peace, monster; I come now. Farewell.
    Apollo.   Farewell.   50

SCENE III.—*Caucasus*. PROMETHEUS, HERCULES, IONE, *the* EARTH, SPIRITS, ASIA, *and* PANTHEA, *borne in the Car with the* SPIRIT OF THE HOUR. HERCULES *unbinds* PROMETHEUS, *who descends*.

    Hercules. Most glorious among Spirits, thus doth strength
To wisdom, courage, and long-suffering love,
And thee, who art the form they animate,
Minister like a slave.
    Prometheus.   Thy gentle words
Are sweeter even than freedom long desired   5
And long delayed.
              Asia, thou light of life,
Shadow of beauty unbeheld: and ye,
Fair sister nymphs, who made long years of pain
Sweet to remember, through your love and care:
Henceforth we will not part. There is a cave,   10
All overgrown with trailing odorous plants,
Which curtain out the day with leaves and flowers,
And paved with veinèd emerald, and a fountain
Leaps in the midst with an awakening sound.
From its curved roof the mountain's frozen tears   15
Like snow, or silver, or long diamond spires,
Hang downward, raining forth a doubtful light:
And there is heard the ever-moving air,
Whispering without from tree to tree, and birds,
And bees; and all around are mossy seats,   20
And the rough walls are clothed with long soft grass;
A simple dwelling, which shall be our own;

Where we will sit and talk of time and change,
As the world ebbs and flows, ourselves unchanged.
What can hide man from mutability?   25
And if ye sigh, then I will smile; and thou,
Ione, shalt chant fragments of sea-music,
Until I weep, when ye shall smile away
The tears she brought, which yet were sweet to shed.
We will entangle buds and flowers and beams   30
Which twinkle on the fountain's brim, and make
Strange combinations out of common things,
Like human babes in their brief innocence;
And we will search, with looks and words of love,
For hidden thoughts, each lovelier than the last,   35
Our unexhausted spirits; and like lutes
Touched by the skill of the enamoured wind,
Weave harmonies divine, yet ever new,
From difference sweet where discord cannot be;
And hither come, sped on the charmèd winds,   40
Which meet from all the points of heaven, as bees
From every flower aëreal Enna feeds,
At their known island-homes in Himera,
The echoes of the human world, which tell
Of the low voice of love, almost unheard,   45
And dove-eyed pity's murmured pain, and music,
Itself the echo of the heart, and all
That tempers or improves man's life, now free;
And lovely apparitions,—dim at first,
Then radiant, as the mind, arising bright   50
From the embrace of beauty (whence the forms
Of which these are the phantoms) casts on them
The gathered rays which are reality—
Shall visit us, the progeny immortal
Of Painting, Sculpture, and rapt Poesy,   55
And arts, though unimagined, yet to be.
The wandering voices and the shadows these
Of all that man becomes, the mediators
Of that best worship love, by him and us
Given and returned; swift shapes and sounds, which grow
More fair and soft as man grows wise and kind,   61
And, veil by veil, evil and error fall:
Such virtue has the cave and place around.
                           [*Turning to the* SPIRIT OF THE HOUR.
For thee, fair Spirit, one toil remains. Ione,
Give her that curvèd shell, which Proteus old   65
Made Asia's nuptial boon, breathing within it
A voice to be accomplished, and which thou
Didst hide in grass under the hollow rock.

Ione. Thou most desired Hour, more loved and lovely
Than all thy sisters, this is the mystic shell;   70
See the pale azure fading into silver
Lining it with a soft yet glowing light:
Looks it not like lulled music sleeping there?
    Spirit. It seems in truth the fairest shell of Ocean:
Its sound must be at once both sweet and strange.   75
    Prometheus. Go, borne over the cities of mankind
On whirlwind-footed coursers: once again
Outspeed the sun around the orbèd world;
And as thy chariot cleaves the kindling air,
Thou breathe into the many-folded shell,   80
Loosening its mighty music; it shall be
As thunder mingled with clear echoes: then
Return; and thou shalt dwell beside our cave.
And thou, O, Mother Earth!—
    The Earth.   I hear, I feel;
Thy lips are on me, and their touch runs down   85
Even to the adamantine central gloom
Along these marble nerves; 'tis life, 'tis joy,
And through my withered, old, and icy frame
The warmth of an immortal youth shoots down
Circling. Henceforth the many children fair   90
Folded in my sustaining arms; all plants,
And creeping forms, and insects rainbow-winged,
And birds, and beasts, and fish, and human shapes,
Which drew disease and pain from my wan bosom,
Draining the poison of despair, shall take   95
And interchange sweet nutriment; to me
Shall they become like sister-antelopes
By one fair dam, snow-white and swift as wind,
Nursed among lilies near a brimming stream.
The dew-mists of my sunless sleep shall float   100
Under the stars like balm: night-folded flowers
Shall suck unwithering hues in their repose:
And men and beasts in happy dreams shall gather
Strength for the coming day, and all its joy:
And death shall be the last embrace of her   105
Who takes the life she gave, even as a mother
Folding her child, says, 'Leave me not again.'
    Asia. Oh, mother! wherefore speak the name of death?
Cease they to love, and move, and breathe, and speak,
Who die?
    The Earth. It would avail not to reply: 110
Thou art immortal, and this tongue is known
But to the uncommunicating dead.
Death is the veil which those who live call life:

They sleep, and it is lifted: and meanwhile
In mild variety the seasons mild   115
With rainbow-skirted showers, and odorous winds,
And long blue meteors cleansing the dull night,
And the life-kindling shafts of the keen sun's
All-piercing bow, and the dew-mingled rain
Of the calm moonbeams, a soft influence mild,   120
Shall clothe the forests and the fields, ay, even
The crag-built deserts of the barren deep,
With ever-living leaves, and fruits, and flowers.
And thou! There is a cavern where my spirit
Was panted forth in anguish whilst thy pain   125
Made my heart mad, and those who did inhale it
Became mad too, and built a temple there,
And spoke, and were oracular, and lured
The erring nations round to mutual war,
And faithless faith, such as Jove kept with thee;   130
Which breath now rises, as amongst tall weeds
A violet's exhalation, and it fills
With a serener light and crimson air
Intense, yet soft, the rocks and woods around;
It feeds the quick growth of the serpent vine,   135
And the dark linkèd ivy tangling wild,
And budding, blown, or odour-faded blooms
Which star the winds with points of coloured light,
As they rain through them, and bright golden globes
Of fruit, suspended in their own green heaven,   140
And through their veinèd leaves and amber stems
The flowers whose purple and translucid bowls
Stand ever mantling with aëreal dew,
The drink of spirits: and it circles round,
Like the soft waving wings of noonday dreams,   145
Inspiring calm and happy thoughts, like mine,
Now thou art thus restored. This cave is thine.
Arise! Appear!
                 [A SPIRIT *rises in the likeness of a winged child.*
          This is my torch-bearer;
Who let his lamp out in old time with gazing
On eyes from which he kindled it anew   150
With love, which is as fire, sweet daughter mine,
For such is that within thine own. Run, wayward,
And guide this company beyond the peak
Of Bacchic Nysa, Mænad-haunted mountain,
And beyond Indus and its tribute rivers,   155
Trampling the torrent streams and glassy lakes
With feet unwet, unwearied, undelaying,
And up the green ravine, across the vale,

Beside the windless and crystalline pool,
Where ever lies, on unerasing waves, 160
The image of a temple, built above,
Distinct with column, arch, and architrave,
And palm-like capital, and over-wrought,
And populous with most living imagery,
Praxitelean shapes, whose marble smiles 165
Fill the hushed air with everlasting love.
It is deserted now, but once it bore
Thy name, Prometheus; there the emulous youths
Bore to thy honour through the divine gloom
The lamp which was thine emblem; even as those 170
Who bear the untransmitted torch of hope
Into the grave, across the night of life,
As thou hast borne it most triumphantly
To this far goal of Time. Depart, farewell.
Beside that temple is the destined cave. 175

SCENE IV.—*A Forest. In the Background a Cave.* PROMETHEUS, ASIA,
PANTHEA, IONE, *and the* SPIRIT OF THE EARTH.

Ione. Sister, it is not earthly: how it glides
Under the leaves! how on its head there burns
A light, like a green star, whose emerald beams
Are twined with its fair hair! how, as it moves,
The splendour drops in flakes upon the grass! 5
Knowest thou it?
Panthea.   It is the delicate spirit
That guides the earth through heaven. From afar
The populous constellations call that light
The loveliest of the planets; and sometimes
It floats along the spray of the salt sea, 10
Or makes its chariot of a foggy cloud,
Or walks through fields or cities while men sleep,
Or o'er the mountain tops, or down the rivers,
Or through the green waste wilderness, as now,
Wondering at all it sees. Before Jove reigned 15
It loved our sister Asia, and it came
Each leisure hour to drink the liquid light
Out of her eyes, for which it said it thirsted
As one bit by a dipsas, and with her
It made its childish confidence, and told her 20
All it had known or seen, for it saw much,
Yet idly reasoned what it saw; and called her—
For whence it sprung it knew not, nor do I—
Mother, dear mother.

The Spirit of the Earth (*running to Asia*). Mother, dearest
    mother;
May I then talk with thee as I was wont?   25
May I then hide my eyes in thy soft arms,
After thy looks have made them tired of joy?
May I then play beside thee the long noons,
When work is none in the bright silent air?
   Asia. I love thee, gentlest being, and henceforth   30
Can cherish thee unenvied: speak, I pray:
Thy simple talk once solaced, now delights.
   Spirit of the Earth. Mother, I am grown wiser, though a child
Cannot be wise like thee, within this day;
And happier too; happier and wiser both.   35
Thou knowest that toads, and snakes, and loathly worms,
And venomous and malicious beasts, and boughs
That bore ill berries in the woods, were ever
An hindrance to my walks o'er the green world:
And that, among the haunts of humankind,   40
Hard-featured men, or with proud, angry looks,
Or cold, staid gait, or false and hollow smiles,
Or the dull sneer of self-loved ignorance,
Or other such foul masks, with which ill thoughts
Hide that fair being whom we spirits call man;   45
And women too, ugliest of all things evil,
(Though fair, even in a world where thou art fair,
When good and kind, free and sincere like thee),
When false or frowning made me sick at heart
To pass them, though they slept, and I unseen.   50
Well, my path lately lay through a great city
Into the woody hills surrounding it:
A sentinel was sleeping at the gate:
When there was heard a sound, so loud, it shook
The towers amid the moonlight, yet more sweet   55
Than any voice but thine, sweetest of all;
A long, long sound, as it would never end:
And all the inhabitants leaped suddenly
Out of their rest, and gathered in the streets,
Looking in wonder up to Heaven, while yet   60
The music pealed along. I hid myself
Within a fountain in the public square,
Where I lay like the reflex of the moon
Seen in a wave under green leaves; and soon
Those ugly human shapes and visages   65
Of which I spoke as having wrought me pain,
Passed floating through the air, and fading still
Into the winds that scattered them; and those
From whom they passed seemed mild and lovely forms

After some foul disguise had fallen, and all   70
Were somewhat changed, and after brief surprise
And greetings of delighted wonder, all
Went to their sleep again: and when the dawn
Came, wouldst thou think that toads, and snakes, and efts,
Could e'er be beautiful? yet so they were,   75
And that with little change of shape or hue:
All things had put their evil nature off:
I cannot tell my joy, when o'er a lake
Upon a drooping bough with nightshade twined,
I saw two azure halcyons clinging downward   80
And thinning one bright bunch of amber berries,
With quick long beaks, and in the deep there lay
Those lovely forms imaged as in a sky;
So, with my thoughts full of these happy changes,
We meet again, the happiest change of all.   85
    Asia. And never will we part, till thy chaste sister
Who guides the frozen and inconstant moon
Will look on thy more warm and equal light
Till her heart thaw like flakes of April snow
And love thee.
    Spirit of the Earth. What; as Asia loves Prometheus?   90
    Asia. Peace, wanton, thou art yet not old enough.
Think ye by gazing on each other's eyes
To multiply your lovely selves, and fill
With spherèd fires the interlunar air?
    Spirit of the Earth. Nay, mother, while my sister trims her lamp
'Tis hard I should go darkling.
    Asia.   Listen; look!   96
                    [*The* SPIRIT OF THE HOUR *enters*.
    Prometheus. We feel what thou hast heard and seen: yet speak.
    Spirit of the Hour. Soon as the sound had ceased whose thunder filled
    filled
The abysses of the sky and the wide earth,
There was a change: the impalpable thin air   100
And the all-circling sunlight were transformed,
As if the sense of love dissolved in them
Had folded itself round the spherèd world.
My vision then grew clear, and I could see
Into the mysteries of the universe: 105
Dizzy as with delight I floated down,
Winnowing the lightsome air with languid plumes,
My coursers sought their birthplace in the sun,
Where they henceforth will live exempt from toil,
Pasturing flowers of vegetable fire;   110
And where my moonlike car will stand within
A temple, gazed upon by Phidian forms

Of thee, and Asia, and the Earth, and me,
And you fair nymphs looking the love we feel,—
In memory of the tidings it has borne,—   115
Beneath a dome fretted with graven flowers,
Poised on twelve columns of resplendent stone,
And open to the bright and liquid sky.
Yoked to it by an amphisbaenic snake
The likeness of those wingèd steeds will mock   120
The flight from which they find repose. Alas,
Whither has wandered now my partial tongue
When all remains untold which ye would hear?
As I have said, I floated to the earth:
It was, as it is still, the pain of bliss   125
To move, to breathe, to be; I wandering went
Among the haunts and dwellings of mankind,
And first was disappointed not to see
Such mighty change as I had felt within
Expressed in outward things; but soon I looked,   130
And behold, thrones were kingless, and men walked
One with the other even as spirits do,
None fawned, none trampled; hate, disdain, or fear,
Self-love or self-contempt, on human brows
No more inscribed, as o'er the gate of hell,   135
'All hope abandon ye who enter here;'
None frowned, none trembled, none with eager fear
Gazed on another's eye of cold command,
Until the subject of a tyrant's will
Became, worse fate, the abject of his own,   140
Which spurred him, like an outspent horse, to death.
None wrought his lips in truth-entangling lines
Which smiled the lie his tongue disdained to speak;
None, with firm sneer, trod out in his own heart
The sparks of love and hope till there remained   145
Those bitter ashes, a soul self-consumed,
And the wretch crept a vampire among men,
Infecting all with his own hideous ill;
None talked that common, false, cold, hollow talk
Which makes the heart deny the *yes* it breathes,   150
Yet question that unmeant hypocrisy
With such a self-mistrust as has no name.
And women, too, frank, beautiful, and kind
As the free heaven which rains fresh light and dew
On the wide earth, past; gentle radiant forms,   155
From custom's evil taint exempt and pure;
Speaking the wisdom once they could not think,
Looking emotions once they feared to feel,
And changed to all which once they dared not be,

Yet being now, made earth like heaven; nor pride,   160
Nor jealousy, nor envy, nor ill shame,
The bitterest of those drops of treasured gall,
Spoilt the sweet taste of the nepenthe, love.

Thrones, altars, judgement-seats, and prisons; wherein,
And beside which, by wretched men were borne   165
Sceptres, tiaras, swords, and chains, and tomes
Of reasoned wrong, glozed on by ignorance,
Were like those monstrous and barbaric shapes,
The ghosts of a no-more-remembered fame,
Which, from their unworn obelisks, look forth   170
In triumph o'er the palaces and tombs
Of those who were their conquerors: mouldering round,
These imaged to the pride of kings and priests
A dark yet mighty faith, a power as wide
As is the world it wasted, and are now   175
But an astonishment; even so the tools
And emblems of its last captivity,
Amid the dwellings of the peopled earth,
Stand, not o'erthrown, but unregarded now.
And those foul shapes, abhorred by god and man,—   180
Which, under many a name and many a form
Strange, savage, ghastly, dark and execrable,
Were Jupiter, the tyrant of the world;
And which the nations, panic-stricken, served
With blood, and hearts broken by long hope, and love
Dragged to his altars soiled and garlandless,   186
And slain amid men's unreclaiming tears,
Flattering the thing they feared, which fear was hate,—
Frown, mouldering fast, o'er their abandoned shrines:
The painted veil, by those who were, called life,   190
Which mimicked, as with colours idly spread,
All men believed or hoped, is torn aside;
The loathsome mask has fallen, the man remains
Sceptreless, free, uncircumscribed, but man
Equal, unclassed, tribeless, and nationless,   195
Exempt from awe, worship, degree, the king
Over himself; just, gentle, wise: but man
Passionless?——no, yet free from guilt or pain,
Which were, for his will made or suffered them,
Nor yet exempt, though ruling them like slaves,   200
From chance, and death, and mutability,
The clogs of that which else might oversoar
The loftiest star of unascended heaven,
Pinnacled dim in the intense inane.

END OF THE THIRD ACT.

ACT IV

SCENE.—*A Part of the Forest near the Cave of* PROMETHEUS. PANTHEA
and IONE *are sleeping: they awaken gradually during the first Song.*

Voice of unseen Spirits.

The pale stars are gone!
For the sun, their swift shepherd,   3
To their folds them compelling,
In the depths of the dawn,
Hastes, in meteor-eclipsing array, and they flee   5
Beyond his blue dwelling,
As fawns flee the leopard.
But where are ye?

A Train of dark Forms and Shadows passes by confusedly, singing.
Here, oh, here:
We bear the bier   10
Of the Father of many a cancelled year
Spectres we
Of the dead Hours be,
We bear Time to his tomb in eternity.

                                                                      15
Strew, oh, strew
Hair, not yew!
Wet the dusty pall with tears, not dew!
Be the faded flowers
Of Death's bare bowers
Spread on the corpse of the King of Hours!   20

Haste, oh, haste!
As shades are chased,
Trembling, by day, from heaven's blue waste.
We melt away,
Like dissolving spray,   25
From the children of a diviner day,
With the lullaby
Of winds that die
On the bosom of their own harmony!

Ione.

What dark forms were they?   30

Panthea.

The past Hours weak and gray,
With the spoil which their toil
Raked together
From the conquest but One could foil.

Ione.

Have they passed?

Panthea.

They have passed;   35
They outspeeded the blast,
While 'tis said, they are fled:

Ione.

Whither, oh, whither?

Panthea.

To the dark, to the past, to the dead.

Voice of unseen Spirits.

Bright clouds float in heaven,   40
Dew-stars gleam on earth,
Waves assemble on ocean,
They are gathered and driven
By the storm of delight, by the panic of glee!
They shake with emotion,   45
They dance in their mirth.
    But where are ye?

The pine boughs are singing
Old songs with new gladness,
The billows and fountains
Fresh music are flinging,   50
Like the notes of a spirit from land and from sea;
The storms mock the mountains
With the thunder of gladness.
    But where are ye?   55

Ione. What charioteers are these?
Panthea.   Where are their chariots?

Semichorus of Hours.

The voice of the Spirits of Air and of Earth
    Have drawn back the figured curtain of sleep
Which covered our being and darkened our birth
    In the deep.

A Voice.

In the deep?

Semichorus II.

        Oh, below the deep.   60

Semichorus I.

An hundred ages we had been kept
  Cradled in visions of hate and care,
And each one who waked as his brother slept,
  Found the truth—

Semichorus II.

    Worse than his visions were!

Semichorus I.

We have heard the lute of Hope in sleep;   65
  We have known the voice of Love in dreams;
We have felt the wand of Power, and leap—

Semichorus II.

As the billows leap in the morning beams!

Chorus.

Weave the dance on the floor of the breeze,
  Pierce with song heaven's silent light,   70
Enchant the day that too swiftly flees,
  To check its flight ere the cave of Night.

Once the hungry Hours were hounds
  Which chased the day like a bleeding deer,
And it limped and stumbled with many wounds   75
  Through the nightly dells of the desert year.

But now, oh weave the mystic measure
  Of music, and dance, and shapes of light,
Let the Hours, and the spirits of might and pleasure,
  Like the clouds and sunbeams, unite.

A Voice.

              Unite!   80
Panthea. See, where the Spirits of the human mind
Wrapped in sweet sounds, as in bright veils, approach.

Chorus of Spirits.

We join the throng
  Of the dance and the song,
By the whirlwind of gladness borne along;   85

As the flying-fish leap
From the Indian deep,
And mix with the sea-birds, half asleep.

Chorus of Hours.

Whence come ye, so wild and so fleet,
For sandals of lightning are on your feet,   90
And your wings are soft and swift as thought,
And your eyes are as love which is veilèd not?

Chorus of Spirits.

We come from the mind
Of human kind
Which was late so dusk, and obscene, and blind,   95
Now 'tis an ocean
Of clear emotion,
A heaven of serene and mighty motion.

From that deep abyss
Of wonder and bliss,   100
Whose caverns are crystal palaces;
From those skiey towers
Where Thought's crownèd powers
Sit watching your dance, ye happy Hours!

From the dim recesses   105
Of woven caresses,
Where lovers catch ye by your loose tresses
From the azure isles,
Where sweet Wisdom smiles,
Delaying your ships with her siren wiles.   110

From the temples high
Of Man's ear and eye,
Roofed over Sculpture and Poesy;
From the murmurings
Of the unsealed springs   115
Where Science bedews her Dædal wings.

Years after years,
Through blood, and tears,
And a thick hell of hatreds, and hopes, and fears;
We waded and flew,   120
And the islets were few
Where the bud-blighted flowers of happiness grew.

Our feet now, every palm,
Are sandalled with calm,
And the dew of our wings is a rain of balm;   125

And, beyond our eyes,
The human love lies
Which makes all it gazes on Paradise.

Chorus of Spirits and Hours.

Then weave the web of the mystic measure;
From the depths of the sky and the ends of the earth,
Come, swift Spirits of might and of pleasure,   131
Fill the dance and the music of mirth,
As the waves of a thousand streams rush by
To an ocean of splendour and harmony!.

Chorus of Spirits.

Our spoil is won,   135
Our task is done,
We are free to dive, or soar, or run;
Beyond and around,
Or within the bound
Which clips the world with darkness round.   140

We'll pass the eyes
Of the starry skies
Into the hoar deep to colonize;
Death, Chaos, and Night,
From the sound of our flight,   145
Shall flee, like mist from a tempest's might.

And Earth, Air, and Light,
And the Spirit of Might,
Which drives round the stars in their fiery flight;
And Love, Thought, and Breath,   150
The powers that quell Death,
Wherever we soar shall assemble beneath.

And our singing shall build
In the void's loose field
A world for the Spirit of Wisdom to wield;   155
We will take our plan
From the new world of man,
And our work shall be called the Promethean.

Chorus of Hours.

Break the dance, and scatter the song;
Let some depart, and some remain.   160

Semichorus I.

We, beyond heaven, are driven along:

Semichorus II.

Us the enchantments of earth retain:

Semichorus I.

Ceaseless, and rapid, and fierce, and free,
With the Spirits which build a new earth and sea,
And a heaven where yet heaven could never be.   165

Semichorus II.

Solemn, and slow, and serene, and bright,
Leading the Day and outspeeding the Night,
With the powers of a world of perfect light.

Semichorus I.

We whirl, singing loud, round the gathering sphere,
Till the trees, and the beasts, and the clouds appear   170
From its chaos made calm by love, not fear.

Semichorus II.

We encircle the ocean and mountains of earth,
And the happy forms of its death and birth
Change to the music of our sweet mirth.

Chorus of Hours and Spirits.

Break the dance, and scatter the song,   175
  Let some depart, and some remain,
Wherever we fly we lead along
In leashes, like starbeams, soft yet strong,
  The clouds that are heavy with love's sweet rain.

Panthea. Ha! they are gone!
Ione.   Yet feel you no delight   180
From the past sweetness?
  Panthea.   As the bare green hill
When some soft cloud vanishes into rain,
Laughs with a thousand drops of sunny water
To the unpavilioned sky!
  Ione.   Even whilst we speak
New notes arise. What is that awful sound?   185
  Panthea. 'Tis the deep music of the rolling world
Kindling within the strings of the waved air
Æolian modulation.
  Ione.   Listen too,
How every pause is filled with under-notes,
Clear, silver, icy, keen, awakening tones,   190

Which pierce the sense, and live within the soul,
As the sharp stars pierce winter's crystal air
And gaze upon themselves within the sea.
    Panthea. But see where through two openings in the forest
Which hanging branches overcanopy,   195
And where two runnels of a rivulet,
Between the close moss violet-inwoven,
Have made their path of melody, like sisters
Who part with sighs that they may meet in smiles,
Turning their dear disunion to an isle   200
Of lovely grief, a wood of sweet sad thoughts;
Two visions of strange radiance float upon
The ocean-like enchantment of strong sound,
Which flows intenser, keener, deeper yet
Under the ground and through the windless air.   205
    Ione. I see a chariot like that thinnest boat,
In which the Mother of the Months is borne
By ebbing light into her western cave.
When she upsprings from interlunar dreams;
O'er which is curved an orblike canopy   210
Of gentle darkness, and the hills and woods,
Distinctly seen through that dusk aëry veil,
Regard like shapes in an enchanter's glass;
Its wheels are solid clouds, azure and gold,
Such as the genii of the thunderstorm   215
Pile on the floor of the illumined sea
When the sun rushes under it; they roll
And move and grow as with an inward wind;
Within it sits a wingèd infant, white
Its countenance, like the whiteness of bright snow,   220
Its plumes are as feathers of sunny frost,
Its limbs gleam white, through the wind-flowing folds
Of its white robe, woof of ethereal pearl.
Its hair is white, the brightness of white light
Scattered in strings; yet its two eyes are heavens   225
Of liquid darkness, which the Deity
Within seems pouring, as a storm is poured
From jaggèd clouds, out of their arrowy lashes,
Tempering the cold and radiant air around,
With fire that is not brightness; in its hand   230
It sways a quivering moonbeam, from whose point
A guiding power directs the chariot's prow
Over its wheelèd clouds, which as they roll
Over the grass, and flowers, and waves, wake sounds,
Sweet as a singing rain of silver dew.   235
    Panthea. And from the other opening in the wood
Rushes, with loud and whirlwind harmony,

A sphere, which is as many thousand spheres,
Solid as crystal, yet through all its mass
Flow, as through empty space, music and light: 240
Ten thousand orbs involving and involved,
Purple and azure, white, and green, and golden,
Sphere within sphere; and every space between
Peopled with unimaginable shapes,
Such as ghosts dream dwell in the lampless deep, 245
Yet each inter-transpicuous, and they whirl
Over each other with a thousand motions,
Upon a thousand sightless axles spinning,
And with the force of self-destroying swiftness,
Intensely, slowly, solemnly roll on, 250
Kindling with mingled sounds, and many tones,
Intelligible words and music wild.
With mighty whirl the multitudinous orb
Grinds the bright brook into an azure mist
Of elemental subtlety, like light; 255
And the wild odour of the forest flowers,
The music of the living grass and air,
The emerald light of leaf-entangled beams
Round its intense yet self-conflicting speed,
Seem kneaded into one aëreal mass 260
Which drowns the sense. Within the orb itself,
Pillowed upon its alabaster arms,
Like to a child o'erwearied with sweet toil,
On its own folded wings, and wavy hair,
The Spirit of the Earth is laid asleep, 265
And you can see its little lips are moving,
Amid the changing light of their own smiles,
Like one who talks of what he loves in dream.
   Ione. 'Tis only mocking the orb's harmony.
   Panthea. And from a star upon its forehead, shoot, 270
Like swords of azure fire, or golden spears
With tyrant-quelling myrtle overtwined,
Embleming heaven and earth united now,
Vast beams like spokes of some invisible wheel
Which whirl as the orb whirls, swifter than thought, 275
Filling the abyss with sun-like lightenings,
And perpendicular now, and now transverse,
Pierce the dark soil, and as they pierce and pass,
Make bare the secrets of the earth's deep heart;
Infinite mines of adamant and gold, 280
Valueless stones, and unimagined gems,
And caverns on crystalline columns poised
With vegetable silver overspread;
Wells of unfathomed fire, and water springs

Whence the great sea, even as a child is fed,   285
Whose vapours clothe earth's monarch mountain-tops
With kindly, ermine snow. The beams flash on
And make appear the melancholy ruins
Of cancelled cycles; anchors, beaks of ships;
Planks turned to marble; quivers, helms, and spears,   290
And gorgon-headed targes, and the wheels
Of scythèd chariots, and the emblazonry
Of trophies, standards, and armorial beasts,
Round which death laughed, sepulchred emblems
Of dead destruction, ruin within ruin!   295
The wrecks beside of many a city vast,
Whose population which the earth grew over
Was mortal, but not human; see, they lie,
Their monstrous works, and uncouth skeletons,
Their statues, homes and fanes; prodigious shapes   300
Huddled in gray annihilation, split,
Jammed in the hard, black deep; and over these,
The anatomies of unknown wingèd things,
And fishes which were isles of living scale,
And serpents, body chains, twisted around   305
The iron crags, or within heaps of dust
To which the torture strength of their last pangs
Had crushed the iron crags; and over these
The jaggèd alligator, and the might
Of earth-convulsing behemoth, which once   310
Were monarch beasts, and on the slimy shores,
And weed-overgrown continents of earth,
Increased and multiplied like summer worms
On an abandoned corpse, till the blue globe
Wrapped deluge round it like a cloak, and they   315
Yelled, gasped, and were abolished; or some God
Whose throne was in a comet, passed and cried,
'Be not!' And like my words they were no more.

The Earth.

The joy, the triumph, the delight, the madness!
The boundless, overflowing, bursting gladness,   320
The vaporous exultation not to be confined!
Ha! ha! the animation of delight
Which wraps me, like an atmosphere of light,
And bears me as a cloud is borne by its own wind.

The Moon.

Brother mine, calm wanderer,   325
Happy globe of land and air,
Some Spirit is darted like a beam from thee,

Which penetrates my frozen frame,
And passes with the warmth of flame,
With love, and odour, and deep melody   330
    Through me, through me!

The Earth.

Ha! ha! the caverns of my hollow mountains,
My cloven fire-crags, sound-exulting fountains
Laugh with a vast and inextinguishable laughter.
    The oceans, and the deserts, and the abysses,   335
    And the deep air's unmeasured wildernesses,
Answer from all their clouds and billows, echoing after.

They cry aloud as I do. Sceptred curse,
Who all our green and azure universe
Threatenedst to muffle round with black destruction, sending
    A solid cloud to rain hot thunderstones,   341
    And splinter and knead down my children's bones,
All I bring forth, to one void mass battering and blending,—

Until each crag-like tower, and storied column,
Palace, and obelisk, and temple solemn,   345
My imperial mountains crowned with cloud, and snow, and fire;
    My sea-like forests, every blade and blossom
    Which finds a grave or cradle in my bosom,
Were stamped by thy strong hate into a lifeless mire:

How art thou sunk, withdrawn, covered, drunk up   350
By thirsty nothing, as the brackish cup
Drained by a desert-troop, a little drop for all;
    And from beneath, around, within, above,
    Filling thy void annihilation, love
Burst in like light on caves cloven by the thunder-ball.   355

The Moon.

The snow upon my lifeless mountains
Is loosened into living fountains,
My solid oceans flow, and sing, and shine:
    A spirit from my heart bursts forth,
    It clothes with unexpected birth   360
My cold bare bosom: Oh! it must be thine
    On mine, on mine!

Gazing on thee I feel, I know
Green stalks burst forth, and bright flowers grow,
And living shapes upon my bosom move: 365
    Music is in the sea and air,
    Wingèd clouds soar here and there,

Dark with the rain new buds are dreaming of:
'Tis love, all love!

The Earth.

It interpenetrates my granite mass,   370
Through tangled roots and trodden clay doth pass
Into the utmost leaves and delicatest flowers;
    Upon the winds, among the clouds 'tis spread,
    It wakes a life in the forgotten dead,
They breathe a spirit up from their obscurest bowers.   375

And like a storm bursting its cloudy prison
With thunder, and with whirlwind, has arisen
Out of the lampless caves of unimagined being:
    With earthquake shock and swiftness making shiver
    Thought's stagnant chaos, unremoved for ever,   380
Till hate, and fear, and pain, light-vanquished shadows, fleeing,

Leave Man, who was a many-sided mirror,
Which could distort to many a shape of error,
This true fair world of things, a sea reflecting love;
    Which over all his kind, as the sun's heaven   385
    Gliding o'er ocean, smooth, serene, and even,
Darting from starry depths radiance and life, doth move:

Leave Man, even as a leprous child is left,
Who follows a sick beast to some warm cleft
Of rocks, through which the might of healing springs is poured;
    Then when it wanders home with rosy smile,   391
    Unconscious, and its mother fears awhile
It is a spirit, then, weeps on her child restored.

Man, oh, not men! a chain of linkèd thought,
Of love and might to be divided not,   395
Compelling the elements with adamantine stress;
    As the sun rules, even with a tyrant's gaze,
    The unquiet republic of the maze
Of planets, struggling fierce towards heaven's free wilderness.

Man, one harmonious soul of many a soul,   400
Whose nature is its own divine control,
Where all things flow to all, as rivers to the sea;
    Familiar acts are beautiful through love;
    Labour, and pain, and grief, in life's green grove
Sport like tame beasts, none knew how gentle they could be!

His will, with all mean passions, bad delights,   406
And selfish cares, its trembling satellites,

A spirit ill to guide, but mighty to obey,
Is as a tempest-wingèd ship, whose helm
Love rules, through waves which dare not overwhelm, 410
Forcing life's wildest shores to own its sovereign sway.

All things confess his strength. Through the cold mass
Of marble and of colour his dreams pass;
Bright threads whence mothers weave the robes their children
wear;
Language is a perpetual Orphic song, 415
Which rules with Dædal harmony a throng
Of thoughts and forms, which else senseless and shapeless were.

The lightning is his slave; heaven's utmost deep
Gives up her stars, and like a flock of sheep
They pass before his eye, are numbered, and roll on! 420
The tempest is his steed, he strides the air;
And the abyss shouts from her depth laid bare,
Heaven, hast thou secrets? Man unveils me; I have none.

The Moon.

The shadow of white death has passed
From my path in heaven at last, 425
A clinging shroud of solid frost and sleep;
And through my newly-woven bowers,
Wander happy paramours,
Less mighty, but as mild as those who keep 430
Thy vales more deep.

The Earth.

As the dissolving warmth of dawn may fold
A half unfrozen dew-globe, green, and gold,
And crystalline, till it becomes a wingèd mist,
And wanders up the vault of the blue day,
Outlives the moon, and on the sun's last ray 435
Hangs o'er the sea, a fleece of fire and amethyst.

The Moon.

Thou art folded, thou art lying
In the light which is undying
Of thine own joy, and heaven's smile divine;
All suns and constellations shower 440
On thee a light, a life, a power
Which doth array thy sphere; thou pourest thine
On mine, on mine!

The Earth.

I spin beneath my pyramid of night,
Which points into the heavens dreaming delight, 445

Murmuring victorious joy in my enchanted sleep;
  As a youth lulled in love-dreams faintly sighing,
  Under the shadow of his beauty lying,
Which round his rest a watch of light and warmth doth keep.

The Moon.

  As in the soft and sweet eclipse,   450
  When soul meets soul on lovers' lips,
High hearts are calm, and brightest eyes are dull;
  So when thy shadow falls on me,
  Then am I mute and still, by thee
Covered; of thy love, Orb most beautiful,   455
  Full, oh, too full!

  Thou art speeding round the sun
  Brightest world of many a one;
  Green and azure sphere which shinest
  With a light which is divinest   460
  Among all the lamps of Heaven
  To whom life and light is given;
  I, thy crystal paramour
  Borne beside thee by a power
  Like the polar Paradise,   465
  Magnet-like of lovers' eyes;
  I, a most enamoured maiden
  Whose weak brain is overladen
  With the pleasure of her love,
  Maniac-like around thee move   470
  Gazing, an insatiate bride,
  On thy form from every side
  Like a Mænad, round the cup
  Which Agave lifted up
  In the weird Cadmæan forest.   475
  Brother, wheresoe'er thou soarest
  I must hurry, whirl and follow
  Through the heavens wide and hollow,
  Sheltered by the warm embrace
  Of thy soul from hungry space,   480
  Drinking from thy sense and sight
  Beauty, majesty, and might,
  As a lover or a chameleon
  Grows like what it looks upon,
  As a violet's gentle eye   485
  Gazes on the azure sky
Until its hue grows like what it beholds,
  As a gray and watery mist
  Grows like solid amethyst

Athwart the western mountain it enfolds,   490
   When the sunset sleeps
   Upon its snow—

The Earth.

   And the weak day weeps
     That it should be so.
Oh, gentle Moon, the voice of thy delight   495
Falls on me like thy clear and tender light
Soothing the seaman, borne the summer night,
     Through isles for ever calm;
   Oh, gentle Moon, thy crystal accents pierce
   The caverns of my pride's deep universe,   500
   Charming the tiger joy, whose tramplings fierce
     Made wounds which need thy balm.

Panthea. I rise as from a bath of sparkling water,
A bath of azure light, among dark rocks,
Out of the stream of sound.
   Ione.   Ah me! sweet sister,   505
The stream of sound has ebbed away from us,
And you pretend to rise out of its wave,
Because your words fall like the clear, soft dew
Shaken from a bathing wood-nymph's limbs and hair.
   Panthea. Peace! peace! A mighty Power, which is as
     darkness,   510
Is rising out of Earth, and from the sky
Is showered like night, and from within the air
Bursts, like eclipse which had been gathered up
Into the pores of sunlight: the bright visions,
Wherein the singing spirits rode and shone,   515
Gleam like pale meteors through a watery night.
   Ione. There is a sense of words upon mine ear.
   Panthea. An universal sound like words: Oh, list!

Demogorgon.

Thou, Earth, calm empire of a happy soul,
   Sphere of divinest shapes and harmonies,   520
Beautiful orb! gathering as thou dost roll
   The love which paves thy path along the skies:

The Earth.

I hear: I am as a drop of dew that dies.

Demogorgon.

Thou, Moon, which gazest on the nightly Earth
   With wonder, as it gazes upon thee;   **525**

Whilst each to men, and beasts, and the swift birth
Of birds, is beauty, love, calm, harmony:

The Moon.

I hear: I am a leaf shaken by thee!

Demogorgon.

Ye Kings of suns and stars, Dæmons and Gods,
Aetherial Dominations, who possess   530
Elysian, windless, fortunate abodes
Beyond Heaven's constellated wilderness:

A Voice from above.

Our great Republic hears, we are blest, and bless.

Demogorgon.

Ye happy Dead, whom beams of brightest verse
Are clouds to hide, not colours to portray,   535
Whether your nature is that universe
Which once ye saw and suffered—

A Voice from beneath.

             Or as they
Whom we have left, we change and pass away.

Demogorgon.

Ye elemental Genii, who have homes
From man's high mind even to the central stone   540
Of sullen lead; from heaven's star-fretted domes
To the dull weed some sea-worm battens on:

A confused Voice.

We hear: thy words waken Oblivion.

Demogorgon.

Spirits, whose homes are flesh: ye beasts and birds,
Ye worms, and fish; ye living leaves and buds;   545
Lightning and wind; and ye untameable herds,
Meteors and mists, which throng air's solitudes:—

A Voice.

Thy voice to us is wind among still woods.

Demogorgon.

Man, who wert once a despot and a slave;
A dupe and a deceiver; a decay;   550
A traveller from the cradle to the grave
Through the dim night of this immortal day:

All.

Speak: thy strong words may never pass away.

Demogorgon.

This is the day, which down the void abysm
At the Earth-born's spell yawns for Heaven's despotism,
   And Conquest is dragged captive through the deep: 556
Love, from its awful throne of patient power
In the wise heart, from the last giddy hour
   O dread endurance, from the slippery, steep,
And narrow verge of crag-like agony, springs   560
And folds over the world its healing wings.

Gentleness, Virtue, Wisdom, and Endurance,
These are the seals of that most firm assurance
   Which bars the pit over Destruction's strength;
And if, with infirm hand, Eternity,   565
Mother of many acts and hours, should free
   The serpent that would clasp her with his length;
These are the spells by which to reassume
An empire o'er the disentangled doom.

To suffer woes which Hope thinks infinite;   570
To forgive wrongs darker than death or night;
   To defy Power, which seems omnipotent;
To love, and bear; to hope, till Hope creates
From its own wreck the thing it contemplates;
   Neither to change, nor falter, nor repent;   575
This, like thy glory, Titan, is to be
Good, great and joyous, beautiful and free;
This is alone Life, Joy, Empire, and Victory.

NOTE ON PROMETHEUS UNBOUND, BY MRS. SHELLEY

ON the 12th of March, 1818, Shelley quitted England, never to return.
His principal motive was the hope that his health would be improved by
a milder climate; he suffered very much during the winter previous to his
emigration, and this decided his vacillating purpose. In December, 1817,
he had written from Marlow to a friend, saying:

'My health has been materially worse. My feelings at intervals are of
a deadly and torpid kind, or awakened to such a state of unnatural and
keen excitement that, only to instance the organ of sight, I find the very
blades of grass and the boughs of distant trees present themselves to me
with microscopic distinctness. Towards evening I sink into a state of
lethargy and inanimation, and often remain for hours on the sofa between
sleep and waking, a prey to the most painful irritability of thought. Such,
with little intermission, is my condition. The hours devoted to study are
selected with vigilant caution from among these periods of endurance.

It is not for this that I think of travelling to Italy, even if I knew that Italy would relieve me. But I have experienced a decisive pulmonary attack; and although at present it has passed away without any considerable vestige of its existence, yet this symptom sufficiently shows the true nature of my disease to be consumptive. It is to my advantage that this malady is in its nature slow, and, if one is sufficiently alive to its advances, is susceptible of cure from a warm climate. In the event of its assuming any decided shape, *it would be my duty* to go to Italy without delay. It is not mere health, but life, that I should seek, and that not for my own sake—I feel I am capable of trampling on all such weakness; but for the sake of those to whom my life may be a source of happiness, utility, security, and honour, and to some of whom my death might be all that is the reverse.'

In almost every respect his journey to Italy was advantageous. He left behind friends to whom he was attached; but cares of a thousand kinds, many springing from his lavish generosity, crowded round him in his native country, and, except the society of one or two friends, he had no compensation. The climate caused him to consume half his existence in helpless suffering. His dearest pleasure, the free enjoyment of the scenes of Nature, was marred by the same circumstance.

He went direct to Italy, avoiding even Paris, and did not make any pause till he arrived at Milan. The first aspect of Italy enchanted Shelley; it seemed a garden of delight placed beneath a clearer and brighter heaven than any he had lived under before. He wrote long descriptive letters during the first year of his residence in Italy, which, as compositions, are the most beautiful in the world, and show how truly he appreciated and studied the wonders of Nature and Art in that divine land.

The poetical spirit within him speedily revived with all the power and with more than all the beauty of his first attempts. He meditated three subjects as the groundwork for lyrical dramas. One was the story of Tasso; of this a slight fragment of a song of Tasso remains. The other was one founded on the *Book of Job,* which he never abandoned in idea, but of which no trace remains among his papers. The third was the *Prometheus Unbound*. The Greek tragedians were now his most familiar companions in his wanderings, and the sublime majesty of Æschylus filled him with wonder and delight. The father of Greek tragedy does not possess the pathos of Sophocles, nor the variety and tenderness of Euripides; the interest on which he founds his dramas is often elevated above human vicissitudes into the mighty passions and throes of gods and demi-gods: such fascinated the abstract imagination of Shelley.

We spent a month at Milan, visiting the Lake of Como during that interval. Thence we passed in succession to Pisa, Leghorn, the Baths of Lucca, Venice, Este, Rome, Naples, and back again to Rome, whither we returned early in March, 1819. During all this time Shelley meditated the subject of his drama, and wrote portions of it. Other poems were composed during this interval, and while at the Bagni di Lucca he translated

Plato's *Symposium*. But, though he diversified his studies, his thoughts centred in the *Prometheus*. At last, when at Rome, during a bright and beautiful Spring, he gave up his whole time to the composition. The spot selected for his study was, as he mentions in his preface, the mountainous ruins of the Baths of Caracalla. These are little known to the ordinary visitor at Rome. He describes them in a letter, with that poetry and delicacy and truth of description which render his narrated impressions of scenery of unequalled beauty and interest.

At first he completed the drama in three acts. It was not till several months after, when at Florence, that he conceived that a fourth act, a sort of hymn of rejoicing in the fulfilment of the prophecies with regard to Prometheus, ought to be added to complete the composition.

The prominent feature of Shelley's theory of the destiny of the human species was that evil is not inherent in the system of the creation, but an accident that might be expelled. This also forms a portion of Christianity: God made earth and man perfect, till he, by his fall,

'Brought death into the world and all our woe.'

Shelley believed that mankind had only to will that there should be no evil, and there would be none. It is not my part in these Notes to notice the arguments that have been urged against this opinion, but to mention the fact that he entertained it, and was indeed attached to it with fervent enthusiasm. That man could be so perfectionized as to able to expel evil from his own nature, and from the greater part of the creation, was the cardinal point of his system. And the subject he loved best to dwell on was the image of One warring with the Evil Principle, oppressed not only by it, but by all—even the good, who were deluded into considering evil a necessary portion of humanity; a victim full of fortitude and hope and spirit of triumph emanating from a reliance in the ultimate omnipotence of Good. Such he had depicted in his last poem, when he made Laon the enemy and the victim of tyrants. He now took a more idealized image of the same subject. He followed certain classical authorities in figuring Saturn as the good principle, Jupiter the usurping evil one, and Prometheus as the regenerator, who, unable to bring mankind back to primitive innocence, used knowledge as a weapon to defeat evil, by leading mankind, beyond the state wherein they are sinless through ignorance, to that in which they are virtuous through wisdom. Jupiter punished the temerity of the Titan by chaining him to a rock of Caucasus, and causing a vulture to devour his still-renewed heart. There was a prophecy afloat in heaven portending the fall of Jove, the secret of averting which was known only to Prometheus; and the god offered freedom from torture on condition of its being communicated to him. According to the mythological story, this referred to the offspring of Thetis, who was destined to be greater than his father. Prometheus at last bought pardon for his crime of enriching mankind with his gifts, by revealing the prophecy. Hercules killed the vulture, and set him free; and Thetis was married to Peleus, the father of Achilles.

Shelley adapted the catastrophe of this story to his peculiar views. The son greater than his father, born of the nuptials of Jupiter and Thetis, was to dethrone Evil, and bring back a happier reign than that of Saturn. Prometheus defies the power of his enemy, and endures centuries of torture; till the hour arrives when Jove, blind to the real event, but darkly guessing that some great good to himself will flow, espouses Thetis. At the moment, the Primal Power of the world drives him from his usurped throne, and Strength, in the person of Hercules, liberates Humanity, typified in Prometheus, from the tortures generated by evil done or suffered. Asia, one of the Oceanides, is the wife of Prometheus —she was, according to other mythological interpretations, the same as Venus and Nature. When the benefactor of mankind is liberated, Nature resumes the beauty of her prime, and is united to her husband, the emblem of the human race, in perfect and happy union. In the Fourth Act, the Poet gives further scope to his imagination, and idealizes the forms of creation—such as we know them, instead of such as they appeared to the Greeks. Maternal Earth, the mighty parent, is superseded by the Spirit of the Earth, the guide of our planet through the realms of sky; while his fair and weaker companion and attendant, the Spirit of the Moon, receives bliss from the annihilation of Evil in the superior sphere.

Shelley develops, more particularly in the lyrics of this drama, his abstruse and imaginative theories with regard to the Creation. It requires a mind as subtle and penetrating as his own to understand the mystic meanings scattered throughout the poem. They elude the ordinary reader by their abstraction and delicacy of distinction, but they are far from vague. It was his design to write prose metaphysical essays on the nature of Man, which would have served to explain much of what is obscure in his poetry; a few scattered fragments of observations and remarks alone remain. He considered these philosophical views of Mind and Nature to be instinct with the intensest spirit of poetry.

More popular poets clothe the ideal with familiar and sensible imagery. Shelley loved to idealize the real—to gift the mechanism of the material universe with a soul and a voice, and to bestow such also on the most delicate and abstract emotions and thoughts of the mind. Sophocles was his great master in this species of imagery.

I find in one of his manuscript books some remarks on a line in the *Œdipus Tyrannus*, which show at once the critical subtlety of Shelley's mind, and explain his apprehension of those 'minute and remote distinctions of feeling, whether relative to external nature or the living beings which surround us,' which he pronounces, in the letter quoted in the note to the *Revolt of Islam*, to comprehend all that is sublime in man.

'In the Greek Shakespeare, Sophocles, we find the image,

Πολλὰς δ' ὁδοὺς ἐλθόντα φροντίδος πλάνοις:

a line of almost unfathomable depth of poetry; yet how simple are the images in which it is arrayed!

"Coming to many ways in the wanderings of careful thought."

If the words όδούς and πλάνοις had not been used, the line might have been explained in a metaphorical instead of an absolute sense, as we say *"ways* and means," and "wanderings" for error and confusion. But they meant literally paths or roads, such as we tread with our feet; and wanderings, such as a man makes when he loses himself in a desert, or roams from city to city—as Œdipus, the speaker of this verse, was destined to wander, blind and asking charity. What a picture does this line suggest of the mind as a wilderness of intricate paths, wide as the universe, which is here made its symbol; a world within a world which he who seeks some knowledge with respect to what he ought to do searches throughout, as he would search the external universe for some valued thing which was hidden from him upon its surface.'

In reading Shelley's poetry, we often find similar verses, resembling, but not imitating the Greek in this species of imagery; for, though he adopted the style, he gifted it with that originality of form and colouring which sprung from his own genius.

In the *Prometheus Unbound*, Shelley fulfils the promise quoted from a letter in the Note on the *Revolt of Islam*.[1] The tone of the composition is calmer and more majestic, the poetry more perfect as a whole, and the imagination displayed at once more pleasingly beautiful and more varied and daring. The description of the Hours, as they are seen in the cave of Demogorgon, is an instance of this—it fills the mind as the most charming picture—we long to see an artist at work to bring to our view the

> 'cars drawn by rainbow-wingèd steeds
> Which trample the dim winds: in each there stands
> A wild-eyed charioteer urging their flight.
> Some look behind, as fiends pursued them there,
> And yet I see no shapes but the keen stars:
> Others, with burning eyes, lean forth, and drink
> With eager lips the wind of their own speed,
> As if the thing they loved fled on before,
> And now, even now, they clasped it. Their bright locks
> Stream like a comet's flashing hair: they all
> Sweep onward.'

Through the whole poem there reigns a sort of calm and holy spirit of love; it soothes the tortured, and is hope to the expectant, till the prophecy is fulfilled, and Love, untainted by any evil, becomes the law of the world.

England had been rendered a painful residence to Shelley, as much by the sort of persecution with which in those days all men of liberal opinions

[1] While correcting the proofsheets of that poem, it struck me that the poet had indulged in an exaggerated view of the evils of restored despotism; which, however injurious and degrading, were less openly sanguinary than the triumph of anarchy, such as it appeared in France at the close of the last century. But at this time a book, *Scenes of Spanish Life*, translated by Lieutenant Crawford from the German of Dr. Huber, of Rostock, fell into my hands. The account of the triumph of the priests and the serviles, after the French invasion of Spain in 1823, bears a strong and frightful resemblance to some of the descriptions of the massacre of the patriots in the *Revolt of Islam*.

were visited, and by the injustice he had lately endured in the Court of Chancery, as by the symptoms of disease which made him regard a visit to Italy as necessary to prolong his life. An exile, and strongly impressed with the feeling that the majority of his countrymen regarded him with sentiments of aversion such as his own heart could experience towards none, he sheltered himself from such disgusting and painful thoughts in the calm retreats of poetry, and built up a world of his own—with the more pleasure, since he hoped to induce some one or two to believe that the earth might become such, did mankind themselves consent. The charm of the Roman climate helped to clothe his thoughts in greater beauty than they had ever worn before. And, as he wandered among the ruins made one with Nature in their decay, or gazed on the Praxitelean shapes that throng the Vatican, the Capitol, and the palaces of Rome, his soul imbibed forms of loveliness which became a portion of itself. There are many passages in the *Prometheus* which show the intense delight he received from such studies, and give back the impression with a beauty of poetical description peculiarly his own. He felt this, as a poet must feel when he satisfies himself by the result of his labours; and he wrote from Rome, 'My *Prometheus Unbound* is just finished, and in a month or two I shall send it. It is a drama, with characters and mechanism of a kind yet unattempted; and I think the execution is better than any of my former attempts.'

I may mention, for the information of the more critical reader, that the verbal alterations in this edition of *Prometheus* are made from a list of errata written by Shelley himself.

THE CENCI

A TRAGEDY IN FIVE ACTS

DEDICATION, TO LEIGH HUNT, Esq.

MY DEAR FRIEND—I inscribe with your name, from a distant country, and after an absence whose months have seemed years, this the latest of my literary efforts.

Those writings which I have hitherto published, have been little else than visions which impersonate my own apprehensions of the beautiful and the just. I can also perceive in them the literary defects incidental to youth and impatience; they are dreams of what ought to be, or may be. The drama which I now present to you is a sad reality. I lay aside the presumptuous attitude of an instructor, and am content to paint, with such colours as my own heart furnishes, that which has been.

Had I known a person more highly endowed than yourself with all that it becomes a man to possess, I had solicited for this work the ornament of his name. One more gentle, honourable, innocent and brave; one of more exalted toleration for all who do and think evil, and yet himself more free from evil; one who knows better how to receive, and how to confer a benefit, though he must ever confer far more than he can receive; one of simpler, and, in the highest sense of the word, of purer life and manners I never knew: and I had already been fortunate in friendships when your name was added to the list.

In that patient and irreconcilable enmity with domestic and political tyranny and imposture which the tenor of your life has illustrated, and which, had I health and talents, should illustrate mine, let us, comforting each other in our task, live and die.

All happiness attend you! Your affectionate friend,

PERCY B. SHELLEY.

ROME, *May* 29, 1819.

PREFACE

A MANUSCRIPT was communicated to me during my travels in Italy, which was copied from the archives of the Cenci Palace at Rome, and contains a detailed account of the horrors which ended in the extinction of one of the noblest and richest families of that city during the Pontificate of Clement VIII, in the year 1599. The story is, that an old man having spent his life in debauchery and wickedness, conceived at length an implacable hatred towards his children; which showed itself towards one daughter under the form of an incestuous passion, aggravated by every circumstance of cruelty and violence. This daughter, after long and vain attempts to escape from what she considered a perpetual contamination both of body and mind, at length plotted with her mother-in-law and brother to murder their common tyrant. The young maiden, who was urged to this tremendous deed by an impulse which overpowered its horror, was evidently a most gentle and amiable being, a creature formed to adorn and be admired, and thus violently thwarted from her nature by the necessity of circumstance and opinion. The deed was quickly discovered, and, in spite of the most earnest prayers made to the Pope by the highest persons in Rome, the criminals were put to death. The old man had during his life repeatedly bought his pardon from the Pope for capital crimes of the most enormous and unspeakable kind, at the price of a hundred thousand crowns; the death therefore of his victims can scarcely be accounted for by the love of justice. The Pope, among other motives for severity, probably felt that whoever killed the Count Cenci deprived his treasury of a certain and copious source of revenue.[1] Such a story, if told so as to present to the reader all the feelings of those who once acted it, their hopes and fears, their confidences and misgivings, their various interests, passions, and opinions, acting upon and with each other, yet all conspiring to one tremendous end, would be as

---

[1] The Papal Government formerly took the most extraordinary precautions against the publicity of facts which offer so tragical a demonstration of its own wickedness and weakness; so that the communication of the MS. had become, until very lately, a matter of some difficulty.

a light to make apparent some of the most dark and secret caverns of the human heart.

On my arrival at Rome I found that the story of the Cenci was a subject not to be mentioned in Italian society without awakening a deep and breathless interest; and that the feelings of the company never failed to incline to a romantic pity for the wrongs, and a passionate exculpation of the horrible deed to which they urged her, who has been mingled two centuries with the common dust. All ranks of people knew the outlines of this history, and participated in the overwhelming interest which it seems to have the magic of exciting in the human heart. I had a copy of Guido's picture of Beatrice which is preserved in the Colonna Palace, and my servant instantly recognized it as the portrait of *La Cenci*.

This national and universal interest which the story produces and has produced for two centuries and among all ranks of people in a great City, where the imagination is kept for ever active and awake, first suggested to me the conception of its fitness for a dramatic purpose. In fact it is a tragedy which has already received, from its capacity of awakening and sustaining the sympathy of men, approbation and success. Nothing remained as I imagined, but to clothe it to the apprehensions of my countrymen in such language and action as would bring it home to their hearts. The deepest and the sublimest tragic compositions, *King Lear* and the two plays in which the tale of Œdipus is told, were stories which already existed in tradition, as matters of popular belief and interest, before Shakspeare and Sophocles made them familiar to the sympathy of all succeeding generations of mankind.

This story of the Cenci is indeed eminently fearful and monstrous: anything like a dry exhibition of it on the stage would be insupportable. The person who would treat such a subject must increase the ideal, and diminish the actual horror of the events, so that the pleasure which arises from the poetry which exists in these tempestuous sufferings and crimes may mitigate the pain of the contemplation of the moral deformity from which they spring. There must also be nothing attempted to make the exhibition subservient to what is vulgarly termed a moral purpose. The highest moral purpose aimed at in the highest species of the drama, is the teaching the human heart, through its sympathies and antipathies, the knowledge of itself; in proportion to the possession of which knowledge, every human being is wise, just, sincere, tolerant and kind. If dogmas can do more, it is well: but a drama is no fit place for the enforcement of them. Undoubtedly, no person can be truly dishonoured by the act of another; and the fit return to make to the most enormous injuries is kindness and forbearance, and a resolution to convert the injurer from his dark passions by peace and love. Revenge, retaliation, atonement, are pernicious mistakes. If Beatrice had thought in this manner she would have been wiser and better; but she would never have been a tragic character: the few whom such an exhibition would have interested, could never have been sufficiently interested for a dramatic purpose, from the want of finding sympathy in their interest among the mass who surround them. It is in the restless and anatomizing casuistry with which men seek the justification of Beatrice, yet feel that she has done what needs justification; it is in the superstitious horror with which they contemplate alike her wrongs and their revenge, that the dramatic character of what she did and suffered consists.

I have endeavoured as nearly as possible to represent the characters as they probably were, and have sought to avoid the error of making them actuated by my own conceptions of right or wrong, false or true: thus under a thin veil converting names and actions of the sixteenth century into cold impersonations of my own mind. They are represented as Catholics, and as Catholics deeply tinged with religion. To a Protestant apprehension there will appear something unnatural in the earnest and perpetual sentiment of the relations between God and men which pervade the tragedy of the Cenci. It will especially be startled at the combination of an undoubting persuasion of the truth of the popular religion with a cool and determined perseverance in enormous guilt. But religion in Italy is not, as in Protestant countries, a cloak to be worn on particular days; or a passport which those who do not wish to be railed at carry with them to exhibit; or a gloomy passion for penetrating the impenetrable mysteries of our being, which terrifies its possessor at the darkness of the abyss to the brink of which it has conducted him. Religion coexists, as it were, in the mind of an Italian Catholic, with a faith in that of which all men have the most certain knowledge. It is interwoven with the whole fabric of life. It is adoration, faith, submission, penitence, blind admiration; not a rule for moral conduct. It has no necessary connection with any one virtue. The most atrocious villain may be rigidly devout, and without any shock to established faith, confess himself to be so. Religion pervades intensely the whole frame of society, and is according to the temper of the mind which it inhabits, a passion, a persuasion, an excuse, a refuge; never a check. Cenci himself built a chapel in the court of his Palace, and dedicated it to St. Thomas the Apostle, and established masses for the peace of his soul. Thus in the first scene of the fourth act Lucretia's design in exposing herself to the consequences of an expostulation with Cenci after having administered the opiate, was to induce him by a feigned tale to confess himself before death; this being esteemed by Catholics as essential to salvation; and she only relinquishes her purpose when she perceives that her perseverance would expose Beatrice to new outrages.

I have avoided with great care in writing this play the introduction of what is commonly called mere poetry, and I imagine there will scarcely be found a detached simile or a single isolated description, unless Beatrice's description of the chasm appointed for her father's murder should be judged to be of that nature.[1]

In a dramatic composition the imagery and the passion should inter-

[1] An idea in this speech was suggested by a most sublime passage in *El Purgatorio de San Patricio* of Calderon; the only plagiarism which I have intentionally committed in the whole piece.

penetrate one another, the former being reserved simply for the full development and illustration of the latter. Imagination is as the immortal God which should assume flesh for the redemption of mortal passion. It is thus that the most remote and the most familiar imagery may alike be fit for dramatic purposes when employed in the illustration of strong feeling, which raises what is low, and levels to the apprehension that which is lofty, casting over all the shadow of its own greatness. In other respects, I have written more carelessly; that is, without an over-fastidious and learned choice of words. In this respect I entirely agree with those modern critics who assert that in order to move men to true sympathy we must use the familiar language of men, and that our great ancestors the ancient English poets are the writers, a study of whom might incite us to do that for our own age which they have done for theirs. But it must be the real language of men in general and not that of any particular class to whose society the writer happens to belong. So much for what I have attempted; I need not be assured that success is a very different matter; particularly for one whose attention has but newly been awakened to the study of dramatic literature.

I endeavoured whilst at Rome to observe such monuments of this story as might be accessible to a stranger. The portrait of Beatrice at the Colonna Palace is admirable as a work of art: it was taken by Guido during her confinement in prison. But it is most interesting as a just representation of one of the loveliest specimens of the workmanship of Nature. There is a fixed and pale composure upon the features: she seems sad and stricken down in spirit, yet the despair thus expressed is lightened by the patience of gentleness. Her head is bound with folds of white drapery from which the yellow strings of her golden hair escape, and fall about her neck. The moulding of her face is exquisitely delicate; the eyebrows are distinct and arched: the lips have that permanent meaning of imagination and sensibility which suffering has not repressed and which it seems as if death scarcely could extinguish. Her forehead is large and clear; her eyes, which we are told were remarkable for their vivacity, are swollen with weeping and lustreless, but beautifully tender and serene. In the whole mien there is a simplicity and dignity which, united with her exquisite loveliness and deep sorrow, are inexpressibly pathetic. Beatrice Cenci appears to have been one of those rare persons in whom energy and gentleness dwell together without destroying one another: her nature was simple and profound. The crimes and miseries in which she was an actor and a sufferer are as the mask and the mantle in which circumstances clothed her for her impersonation on the scene of the world.

The Cenci Palace is of great extent; and though in part modernized, there yet remains a vast and gloomy pile of feudal architecture in the same state as during the dreadful scenes which are the subject of this tragedy. The Palace is situated in an obscure corner of Rome, near the quarter of the Jews, and from the upper windows you see the immense ruins of Mount Palatine half hidden under their profuse overgrowth of

trees. There is a court in one part of the Palace (perhaps that in which
Cenci built the Chapel to St. Thomas), supported by granite columns
and adorned with antique friezes of fine workmanship, and built up,
according to the ancient Italian fashion, with balcony over balcony of
open-work. One of the gates of the Palace formed of immense stones and
leading through a passage, dark and lofty and opening into gloomy
subterranean chambers, struck me particularly.

Of the Castle of Petrella, I could obtain no further information than
that which is to be found in the manuscript.

DRAMATIS PERSONÆ

Count Francesco Cenci.
Giacomo, } his Sons.
Bernardo,
Cardinal Camillo.
Orsino, *a Prelate.*

Savella, *the Pope's Legate.*
Olimpio, } *Assassins.*
Marzio,
Andrea, *Servant to Cenci.*
Nobles, Judges, Guards, Servants.

Lucretia, *Wife of* Cenci, *and Step-mother of his children.*
Beatrice, *his Daughter.*

The Scene lies principally in Rome, but changes during the Fourth Act
to Petrella, a castle among the Apulian Apennines.

Time. During the Pontificate of Clement VIII.

ACT I

Scene I.—*An Apartment in the Cenci Palace.*

Enter Count Cenci, *and* Cardinal Camillo.

Camillo. That matter of the murder is hushed up
If you consent to yield his Holiness
Your fief that lies beyond the Pincian gate.—
It needed all my interest in the conclave
To bend him to this point: he said that you
Bought perilous impunity with your gold;
That crimes like yours if once or twice compounded
Enriched the Church, and respited from hell
An erring soul which might repent and live:—
But that the glory and the interest
Of the high throne he fills, little consist
With making it a daily mart of guilt
As manifold and hideous as the deeds

Which you scarce hide from men's revolted eyes.
   Cenci. The third of my possessions—let it go!   15
Ay, I once heard the nephew of the Pope
Had sent his architect to view the ground,
Meaning to build a villa on my vines
The next time I compounded with his uncle:
I little thought he should outwit me so!   20
Henceforth no witness—not the lamp—shall see
That which the vassal threatened to divulge
Whose throat is choked with dust for his reward.
The deed he saw could not have rated higher
Than his most worthless life:—it angers me!   25
Respited me from Hell!—So may the Devil
Respite their souls from Heaven. No doubt Pope Clement,
And his most charitable nephews, pray
That the Apostle Peter and the Saints
Will grant for their sake that I long enjoy   30
Strength, wealth, and pride, and lust, and length of days
Wherein to act the deeds which are the stewards
Of their revenue.—But much yet remains
To which they show no title.
   Camillo.   Oh, Count Cenci!
So much that thou mightst honourably live   35
And reconcile thyself with thine own heart
And with thy God, and with the offended world.
How hideously look deeds of lust and blood
Through those snow white and venerable hairs!—
Your children should be sitting round you now,   40
But that you fear to read upon their looks
The shame and misery you have written there.
Where is your wife? Where is your gentle daughter?
Methinks her sweet looks, which make all things else
Beauteous and glad, might kill the fiend within you.   45
Why is she barred from all society
But her own strange and uncomplaining wrongs?
Talk with me, Count,—you know I mean you well.
I stood beside your dark and fiery youth
Watching its bold and bad career, as men   50
Watch meteors, but it vanished not—I marked
Your desperate and remorseless manhood; now
Do I behold you in dishonoured age
Charged with a thousand unrepented crimes.
Yet I have ever hoped you would amend,   55
And in that hope have saved your life three times.
   Cenci. For which Aldobrandino owes you now
My fief beyond the Pincian.—Cardinal,
One thing, I pray you, recollect henceforth,

And so we shall converse with less restraint.   60
A man you knew spoke of my wife and daughter—
He was accustomed to frequent my house;
So the next day *his* wife and daughter came
And asked if I had seen him; and I smiled:
I think they never saw him any more.   65
    Camillo. Thou execrable man, beware!—
    Cenci.   Of thee?
Nay this is idle:—We should know each other.
As to my character for what men call crime
Seeing I please my senses as I list,
And vindicate that right with force or guile,   70
It is a public matter, and I care not
If I discuss it with you. I may speak
Alike to you and my own conscious heart—
For you give out that you have half reformed me,
Therefore strong vanity will keep you silent   75
If fear should not; both will, I do not doubt.
All men delight in sensual luxury,
All men enjoy revenge; and most exult
Over the tortures they can never feel—
Flattering their secret peace with others' pain.   80
But I delight in nothing else. I love
The sight of agony, and the sense of joy,
When this shall be another's, and that mine.
And I have no remorse and little fear,
Which are, I think, the checks of other men.   85
This mood has grown upon me, until now
Any design my captious fancy makes
The picture of its wish, and it forms none
But such as men like you would start to know,
Is as my natural food and rest debarred   90
Until it be accomplished.
    Camillo.   Art thou not
Most miserable?
    Cenci.   Why, miserable?—
No.—I am what your theologians call
Hardened;—which they must be in impudence,
So to revile a man's peculiar taste.   95
True, I was happier than I am, while yet
Manhood remained to act the thing I thought;
While lust was sweeter than revenge; and now
Invention palls:—Ay, we must all grow old—
And but that there yet remains a deed to act   100
Whose horror might make sharp an appetite
Duller than mine—I'd do—I know not what.
When I was young I thought of nothing else

But pleasure; and I fed on honey sweets:
Men, by St. Thomas! cannot live like bees,   105
And I grew tired:—yet, till I killed a foe,
And heard his groans, and heard his children's groans,
Knew I not what delight was else on earth,
Which now delights me little. I the rather
Look on such pangs as terror ill conceals,   110
The dry fixed eyeball; the pale quivering lip,
Which tell me that the spirit weeps within
Tears bitterer than the bloody sweat of Christ.
I rarely kill the body, which preserves,
Like a strong prison, the soul within my power,   115
Wherein I feed it with the breath of fear
For hourly pain.
    Camillo.   Hell's most abandoned fiend
Did never, in the drunkenness of guilt,
Speak to his heart as now you speak to me;
I thank my God that I believe you not.   120

Enter ANDREA.

    Andrea. My Lord, a gentleman from Salamanca
Would speak with you.
    Cenci.   Bid him attend me in
The grand saloon.   [*Exit* ANDREA.
    Camillo.   Farewell; and I will pray
Almighty God that thy false, impious words
Tempt not his spirit to abandon thee.   [*Exit* CAMILLO.
    Cenci. The third of my possessions! I must use   126
Close husbandry, or gold, the old man's sword,
Falls from my withered hand. But yesterday
There came an order from the Pope to make
Fourfold provision for my cursèd sons;   130
Whom I had sent from Rome to Salamanca,
·Hoping some accident might cut them off;
And meaning if I could to starve them there.
I pray thee, God, send some quick death upon them!
Bernardo and my wife could not be worse   135
If dead and damned:—then, as to Beatrice—
                      [*Looking around him suspiciously.*
I think they cannot hear me at that door;
What if they should? And yet I need not speak
Though the heart triumphs with itself in words.
O, thou most silent air, that shalt not hear   140
What now I think! Thou, pavement, which I tread
Towards her chamber,—let your echoes talk
Of my imperious step scorning surprise,
But not of my intent!—Andrea!

Enter ANDREA.

Andrea.   My lord?
Cenci. Bid Beatrice attend me in her chamber   145
This evening:—no, at midnight and alone.   [*Exeunt.*

SCENE II.—A *Garden of the Cenci Palace. Enter* BEATRICE *and* ORSINO.
as in conversation.

 Beatrice. Pervert not truth,
Orsino. You remember where we held
That conversation;—nay, we see the spot
Even from this cypress;—two long years are past
Since, on an April midnight, underneath   5
The moonlight ruins of mount Palatine,
I did confess to you my secret mind.
 Orsino. You said you loved me then.
 Beatrice.   You are a Priest,
Speak to me not of love.
 Orsino.   I may obtain
The dispensation of the Pope to marry.   10
Because I am a Priest do you believe
Your image, as the hunter some struck deer,
Follows me not whether I wake or sleep?
 Beatrice. As I have said, speak to me not of love.
Had you a dispensation I have not;   15
Nor will I leave this home of misery
Whilst my poor Bernard, and that gentle lady
To whom I owe my life, and these virtuous thoughts,
Must suffer what I still have strength to share.
Alas, Orsino! All the love that once   20
I felt for you, is turned to bitter pain.
Ours was a youthful contract, which you first
Broke, by assuming vows no Pope will loose.
And thus I love you still, but holily,
Even as a sister or a spirit might;   25
And so I swear a cold fidelity.
And it is well perhaps we shall not marry.
You have a sly, equivocating vein
That suits me not.—Ah, wretched that I am!
Where shall I turn? Even now you look on me   30
As you were not my friend, and as if you
Discovered that I thought so, with false smiles
Making my true suspicion seem your wrong.
Ah, no! forgive me; sorrow makes me seem
Sterner than else my nature might have been;   35
I have a weight of melancholy thoughts,
And they forebode,—but what can they forebode
Worse than I now endure?

Orsino.   All will be well.
Is the petition yet prepared? You know
My zeal for all you wish, sweet Beatrice;   40
Doubt not but I will use my utmost skill
So that the Pope attend to your complaint.
    Beatrice. Your zeal for all I wish;—Ah me, you are cold!
Your utmost skill . . . speak but one word . . . (*aside*) Alas!
Weak and deserted creature that I am,   45
Here I stand bickering with my only friend! [*To* ORSINO.
This night my father gives a sumptuous feast,
Orsino; he has heard some happy news
From Salamanca, from my brothers there,
And with this outward show of love he mocks   50
His inward hate. 'Tis bold hypocrisy,
For he would gladlier celebrate their deaths,
Which I have heard him pray for on his knees:
Great God! that such a father should be mine!
But there is mighty preparation made,   55
And all our kin, the Cenci, will be there,
And all the chief nobility of Rome.
And he has bidden me and my pale Mother
Attire ourselves in festival array.
Poor lady! She expects some happy change   60
In his dark spirit from this act; I none.
At supper I will give you the petition:
Till when—farewell.
    Orsino. Farewell. (*Exit* BEATRICE.) I know the Pope
Will ne'er absolve me from my priestly vow
But by absolving me from the revenue   65
Of many a wealthy see; and, Beatrice,
I think to win thee at an easier rate.
Nor shall he read her eloquent petition:
He might bestow her on some poor relation
Of his sixth cousin, as he did her sister,   70
And I should be debarred from all access.
Then as to what she suffers from her father,
In all this there is much exaggeration:—
Old men are testy and will have their way;
A man may stab his enemy, or his vassal,   75
And live a free life as to wine or women,
And with a peevish temper may return
To a dull home, and rate his wife and children;
Daughters and wives call this foul tyranny.
I shall be well content if on my conscience   80
There rest no heavier sin than what they suffer
From the devices of my love—a net
From which she shall escape not. Yet I fear

Her subtle mind, her awe-inspiring gaze,
Whose beams anatomize me nerve by nerve   85
And lay me bare, and make me blush to see
My hidden thoughts.—Ah, no! A friendless girl
Who clings to me, as to her only hope:—
I were a fool, not less than if a panther
Were panic-stricken by the antelope's eye,   90
If she escape me.   *[Exit*

SCENE III.—*A Magnificent Hall in the Cenci Palace. A Banquet. Enter*
    CENCI, LUCRETIA, BEATRICE, ORSINO, CAMILLO, NOBLES.

    Cenci. Welcome, my friends and kinsmen; welcome ye,
Princes and Cardinals, pillars of the church,
Whose presence honours our festivity.
I have too long lived like an anchorite,
And in my absence from your merry meetings   5
An evil word is gone abroad of me;
But I do hope that you, my noble friends,
When you have shared the entertainment here,
And heard the pious cause for which 'tis given,
And we have pledged a health or two together,   10
Will think me flesh and blood as well as you;
Sinful indeed, for Adam made all so,
But tender-hearted, meek and pitiful.
    First Guest. In truth, my Lord, you seem too light of heart,
Too sprightly and companionable a man,   15
To act the deeds that rumour pins on you.
(*To his Companion.*) I never saw such blithe and open cheer
In any eye!
    Second Guest. Some most desired event,
In which we all demand a common joy,
Has brought us hither; let us hear it, Count.   20
    Cenci. It is indeed a most desired event.
If, when a parent from a parent's heart
Lifts from this earth to the great Father of all
A prayer, both when he lays him down to sleep,
And when he rises up from dreaming it;   25
One supplication, one desire, one hope,
That he would grant a wish for his two sons,
Even all that he demands in their regard—
And suddenly beyond his dearest hope
It is accomplished, he should then rejoice,   30
And call his friends and kinsmen to a feast,
And task their love to grace his merriment,—
Then honour me thus far—for I am he.
    Beatrice (*to* LUCRETIA). Great God! How horrible! Some
                dreadful ill

Must have befallen my brothers.

Lucretia.   Fear not, Child,   35

He speaks too frankly.

Beatrice.   Ah! My blood runs cold.

I fear that wicked laughter round his eye,

Which wrinkles up the skin even to the hair.

Cenci. Here are the letters brought from Salamanca;

Beatrice, read them to your mother. God!   40

I thank thee! In one night didst thou perform,

By ways inscrutable, the thing I sought.

My disobedient and rebellious sons

Are dead!—Why, dead!—What means this change of cheer?

You hear me not, I tell you they are dead;   45

And they will need no food or raiment more:

The tapers that did light them the dark way

Are their last cost. The Pope, I think, will not

Expect I should maintain them in their coffins.

Rejoice with me—my heart is wondrous glad.   50

            [LUCRETIA *sinks, half fainting*; BEATRICE *supports her.*

Beatrice. It is not true!—Dear lady, pray look up.

Had it been true, there is a God in Heaven,

He would not live to boast of such a boon.

Unnatural man, thou knowest that it is false.

Cenci. Ay, as the word of God; whom here I call   55

To witness that I speak the sober truth;—

And whose most favouring Providence was shown

Even in the manner of their deaths. For Rocco

Was kneeling at the mass, with sixteen others,

When the church fell and crushed him to a mummy,   60

The rest escaped unhurt. Cristofano

Was stabbed in error by a jealous man.

Whilst she he loved was sleeping with his rival;

All in the self-same hour of the same night;

Which shows that Heaven has special care of me.   65

I beg those friends who love me, that they mark

The day a feast upon their calendars.

It was the twenty-seventh of December:

Ay, read the letters if you doubt my oath.

         [*The Assembly appears confused; several of the guests rise.*

First Guest. Oh, horrible! I will depart—

Second Guest.   And I.—

Third Guest.   No, stay!   70

I do believe it is some jest; though faith!

'Tis mocking us somewhat too solemnly.

I think his son has married the Infanta,

Or found a mine of gold in El Dorado;

'Tis but to season some such news; stay, stay!   75

I see 'tis only raillery by his smile.
    Cenci (*filling a bowl of wine, and lifting it up*). Oh, thou
        bright wine whose purple splendour leaps
And bubbles gaily in this golden bowl
Under the lamplight, as my spirits do,
To hear the death of my accursèd sons!   80
Could I believe thou wert their mingled blood,
Then would I taste thee like a sacrament,
And pledge with thee the mighty Devil in Hell,
Who, if a father's curses, as men say,
Climb with swift wings after their children's souls,   85
And drag them from the very throne of Heaven,
Now triumphs in my triumph!—But thou art
Superfluous; I have drunken deep of joy,
And I will taste no other wine to-night.
Here, Andrea! Bear the bowl around.
    A Guest (*rising*).   Thou wretch!   90
Will none among this noble company
Check the abandoned villain?
    Camillo.   For God's sake
Let me dismiss the guests! You are insane,
Some ill will come of this.
    Second Guest.   Seize, silence him!
    First Guest. I will!
    Third Guest.   And I!
    Cenci (*addressing those who rise with a threatening gesture*).
      Who moves? Who speaks?
                      (*turning to the Company*)
                     'tis nothing,   95
Enjoy yourselves.—Beware! For my revenge
Is as the sealed commission of a king
That kills, and none dare name the murderer.
    [*The Banquet is broken up; several of the Guests are departing.*
    Beatrice. I do entreat you, go not, noble guests;
What, although tyranny and impious hate   100
Stand sheltered by a father's hoary hair?
What, if 'tis he who clothed us in these limbs
Who tortures them, and triumphs? What, if we,
The desolate and the dead, were his own flesh,
His children and his wife, whom he is bound   105
To love and shelter? Shall we therefore find
No refuge in this merciless wide world?
O think what deep wrongs must have blotted out
First love, then reverence in a child's prone mind,
Till it thus vanquish shame and fear! O think!   110
I have borne much, and kissed the sacred hand

Which crushed us to the earth, and thought its stroke
Was perhaps some paternal chastisement!
Have excused much, doubted; and when no doubt
Remained, have sought by patience, love, and tears   115
To soften him, and when this could not be
I have knelt down through the long sleepless nights
And lifted up to God, the Father of all,
Passionate prayers: and when these were not heard
I have still borne,—until I meet you here,   120
Princes and kinsmen, at this hideous feast
Given at my brothers' deaths. Two yet remain,
His wife remains and I, whom if ye save not,
Ye may soon share such merriment again
As fathers make over their children's graves.   125
O Prince Colonna, thou art near kinsman,
Cardinal, thou art the Pope's chamberlain,
Camillo, thou art chief justiciary,
Take us away!

    Cenci. (*He has been conversing with* CAMILLO *during the first*
       part of BEATRICE's *speech; he hears the conclusion, and*
       now advances.) I hope my good friends here   130
Will think of their own daughters—or perhaps
Of their own throats—before they lend an ear
To this wild girl.

    Beatrice (*not noticing the words of Cenci*). Dare no one look
       on me?
None answer? Can one tyrant overbear
The sense of many best and wisest men?
Or is it that I sue not in some form   135
Of scrupulous law, that ye deny my suit?
O God! That I were buried with my brothers!
And that the flowers of this departed spring
Were fading on my grave! And that my father
Were celebrating now one feast for all!   140

    Camillo. A bitter wish for one so young and gentle;
Can we do nothing?

    Colonna.   Nothing that I see.
Count Cenci were a dangerous enemy:
Yet I would second any one.

    A Cardinal.   And I.
    Cenci. Retire to your chamber insolent girl!   145
    Beatrice. Retire thou, impious man! Ay, hide thyself
Where never eye can look upon thee more!
Wouldst thou have honour and obedience
Who art a torturer? Father, never dream
Though thou mayst overbear this company,   150
But ill must come of ill.—Frown not on me!

Haste, hide thyself, lest with avenging looks
My brothers' ghosts should hunt thee from thy seat!
Cover thy face from every living eye,
And start if thou but hear a human step: 155
Seek out some dark and silent corner, there,
Bow thy white head before offended God,
And we will kneel around, and fervently
Pray that he pity both ourselves and thee.
    Cenci. My friends, I do lament this insane girl   160
Has spoilt the mirth of our festivity.
Good night, farewell; I will not make you longer
Spectators of our dull domestic quarrels.
Another time.—   [*Exeunt all but* CENCI *and* BEATRICE.
         My brain is swimming round;
Give me a bowl of wine!   [*To* BEATRICE.
        Thou painted viper!   165
Beast that thou art! Fair and yet terrible!
I know a charm shall make thee meek and tame,
Now get thee from my sight!   [*Exit* BEATRICE.
        Here, Andrea,
Fill up this goblet with Greek wine. I said
I would not drink this evening; but I must;   170
For, strange to say, I feel my spirits fail
With thinking what I have decreed to do.—
        [*Drinking the wine.*
Be thou the resolution of quick youth
Within my veins, and manhood's purpose stern,
And age's firm, cold, subtle villainy;   175
As if thou wert indeed my children's blood
Which I did thirst to drink! The charm works well;
It must be done; it shall be done, I swear!   [*Exit.*
    END OF THE FIRST ACT.

ACT II

SCENE I.—*An Apartment in the Cenci Palace. Enter* LUCRETIA *and*
BERNARDO.

    Lucretia. Weep not, my gentle boy; he struck but me
Who have borne deeper wrongs. In truth, if he
Had killed me, he had done a kinder deed.
O God, Almighty, do Thou look upon us,
We have no other friend but only Thee!   5
Yet weep not; though I love you as my own,
I am not your true mother.
    Bernardo.   O more, more,
Than ever mother was to any child,
That have you been to me! Had he not been

My father, do you think that I should weep!   10
    Lucretia. Alas! Poor boy, what else couldst thou have done?
                Enter BEATRICE.
    Beatrice (*in a hurried voice*). Did he pass this way? Have you
      seen him, brother?
Ah, no! that is his step upon the stairs;
'Tis nearer now; his hand is on the door;
Mother, if I to thee have ever been   15
A duteous child, now save me! Thou, great God,
Whose image upon earth a father is,
Dost Thou indeed abandon me? He comes;
The door is opening now; I see his face;
He frowns on others, but he smiles on me,   20
Even as he did after the feast last night.
                Enter a Servant.
Almighty God, how merciful Thou art!
'Tis but Orsino's servant.—Well, what news?
    Servant. My master bids me say, the Holy Father
Has sent back your petition thus unopened.   [*Giving a paper.*
And he demands at what hour 'twere secure   26
To visit you again?
  Lucretia.   At the Ave Mary.   [*Exit Servant.*
So, daughter, our last hope has failed; Ah me!
How pale you look; you tremble, and you stand
Wrapped in some fixed and fearful meditation,   30
As if one thought were over strong for you:
Your eyes have a chill glare; O, dearest child!
Are you gone mad? If not, pray speak to me.
    Beatrice. You see I am not mad: I speak to you.
    Lucretia. You talked of something that your father did   35
After that dreadful feast? Could it be worse
Than when he smiled, and cried, 'My sons are dead!'
And every one looked in his neighbour's face
To see if others were as white as he?
At the first word he spoke I felt the blood   40
Rush to my heart, and fell into a trance;
And when it passed I sat all weak and wild;
Whilst you alone stood up, and with strong words
Checked his unnatural pride; and I could see
The devil was rebuked that lives in him.   45
Until this hour thus have you ever stood
Between us and your father's moody wrath
Like a protecting presence: your firm mind
Has been our only refuge and defence:
What can have thus subdued it? What can now   50
Have given you that cold melancholy look,
Succeeding to your unaccustomed fear?

Beatrice. What is it that you say? I was just thinking
'Twere better not to struggle any more.
Men, like my father, have been dark and bloody,   55
Yet never—Oh! Before worse comes of it
'Twere wise to die: it ends in that at last.
  Lucretia. Oh, talk not so, dear child! Tell me at once
What did your father do or say to you?
He stayed not after that accursèd feast   60
One moment in your chamber.—Speak to me.
  Bernardo. Oh, sister, sister, prithee, speak to us!
  Beatrice (speaking very slowly with a forced calmness). It was
        one word, Mother, one little word;
One look, one smile. (*Wildly.*) Oh! He has trampled me
Under his feet, and made the blood stream down   65
My pallid cheeks. And he has given us all
Ditch-water, and the fever-stricken flesh
Of buffaloes, and bade us eat or starve,
And we have eaten.—He has made me look
On my beloved Bernardo, when the rust   70
Of heavy chains has gangrened his sweet limbs,
And I have never yet despaired—but now!
What could I say?   [*Recovering herself.*
              Ah, no! 'tis nothing new.
The sufferings we all share have made me wild:
He only struck and cursed me as he passed;   75
He said, he looked, he did;—nothing at all
Beyond his wont, yet it disordered me.
Alas! I am forgetful of my duty,
I should preserve my senses for your sake.   .
  Lucretia. Nay, Beatrice; have courage, my sweet girl,   80
If any one despairs it should be I
Who loved him once, and now must live with him
Till God in pity call for him or me.
For you may, like your sister, find some husband,
And smile, years hence, with children round your knees;   85
Whilst I, then dead, and all this hideous coil
Shall be remembered only as a dream.
  Beatrice. Talk not to me, dear lady, of a husband.
Did you not nurse me when my mother died?
Did you not shield me and that dearest boy?   90
And had we any other friend but you
In infancy, with gentle words and looks,
To win our father not to murder us?
And shall I now desert you? May the ghost
Of my dead Mother plead against my soul   95
If I abandon her who filled the place
She left, with more, even, than a mother's love!

Bernardo. And I am of my sister's mind. Indeed
I would not leave you in this wretchedness,
Even though the Pope should make me free to live   100
In some blithe place, like others of my age,   .
With sports, and delicate food, and the fresh air.
Oh, never think that I will leave you, Mother!
   Lucretia. My dear, dear children!
              Enter CENCI, *suddenly.*
  Cenci.   What, Beatrice here!
Come hither!   [*She shrinks back, and covers her face.*
         Nay, hide not your face, 'tis fair;   105
Look up! Why, yesternight you dared to look
With disobedient insolence upon me,
Bending a stern and an inquiring brow
On what I meant; whilst I then sought to hide
That which I came to tell you—but in vain.   110
   Beatrice (*wildly, staggering towards the door*). O that the earth
      would gape! Hide me, O God!
   Cenci. Then it was I whose inarticulate words
Fell from my lips, and who with tottering steps
Fled from your presence, as you now from mine.
Stay, I command you—from this day and hour   115
Never again, I think, with fearless eye,
And brow superior, and unaltered cheek,
And that lip made for tenderness or scorn,
Shalt thou strike dumb the meanest of mankind;
Me least of all. Now get thee to thy chamber!   120
Thou too, loathed image of thy cursèd mother,

                       [*To* BERNARDO.

Thy milky, meek face makes me sick with hate!
           [*Exeunt* BEATRICE *and* BERNARDO.
   (*Aside.*) So much has passed between us as must make
Me bold, her fearful.—'Tis an awful thing
To touch such mischief as I now conceive: 125
So men sit shivering on the dewy bank,
And try the chill stream with their feet; once in . . .
How the delighted spirit pants for joy!
   Lucretia (*advancing timidly towards him*). O husband! Pray
      forgive poor Beatrice.
She meant not any ill.
   Cenci.   Nor you perhaps?   130
Nor that young imp, whom you have taught by rote
Parricide with his alphabet? Nor Giacomo?
Nor those two most unnatural sons, who stirred
Enmity up against me with the Pope?
Whom in one night merciful God cut off: 135
Innocent lambs! They thought not any ill.

You were not here conspiring? You said nothing
Of how I might be dungeoned as a madman;
Or be condemned to death for some offence,
And you would be the witnesses?—This failing,   140
How just it were to hire assassins, or
Put sudden poison in my evening drink?
Or smother me when overcome by wine?
Seeing we had no other judge but God,
And He had sentenced me, and there were none   145
But you to be the executioners
Of His decree enregistered in Heaven?
Oh, no! You said not this?
   Lucretia.   So help me God,
I never thought the things you charge me with!
   Cenci. If you dare speak that wicked lie again   150
I'll kill you. What! It was not by your counsel
That Beatrice disturbed the feast last night?
You did not hope to stir some enemies
Against me, and escape, and laugh to scorn
What every nerve of you now trembles at?   155
You judged that men were bolder than they are;
Few dare to stand between their grave and me.
   Lucretia. Look not so dreadfully! By my salvation
I knew not aught that Beatrice designed;
Nor do I think she designed any thing   160
Until she heard you talk of her dead brothers.
   Cenci. Blaspheming liar! You are damned for this!
But I will take you where you may persuade
The stones you tread on to deliver you:
For men shall there be none but those who dare   165
All things—not question that which I command.
On Wednesday next I shall set out: you know
That savage rock, the Castle of Petrella:
'Tis safely walled, and moated round about:
Its dungeons underground, and its thick towers   170
Never told tales; though they have heard and seen
What might make dumb things speak.—Why do you linger?
Make speediest preparation for the journey!   [*Exit* Lucretia.
The all-beholding sun yet shines; I hear
A busy stir of men about the streets;   175
I see the bright sky through the window panes:
It is a garish, broad, and peering day;
Loud, light, suspicious, full of eyes and ears,
And every little corner, nook, and hole
Is penetrated with the insolent light.   180
Come darkness! Yet, what is the day to me?
And wherefore should I wish for night, who do

A deed which shall confound both night and day?
'Tis she shall grope through a bewildering mist
Of horror: if there be a sun in heaven   185
She shall not dare to look upon its beams;
Nor feel its warmth. Let her then wish for night;
The act I think shall soon extinguish all
For me: I bear a darker deadlier gloom
Than the earth's shade, or interlunar air,   190
Or constellations quenched in murkiest cloud,
In which I walk secure and unbeheld
Towards my purpose.—Would that it were done!   [*Exit.*

SCENE II.—*A Chamber in the Vatican. Enter* CAMILLO *and* GIACOMO,
in conversation.

  Camillo. There is an obsolete and doubtful law
By which you might obtain a bare provision
Of food and clothing—
    Giacomo.   Nothing more? Alas!
Bare must be the provision which strict law
Awards, and agèd, sullen avarice pays.   5
Why did my father not apprentice me
To some mechanic trade? I should have then
Been trained in no highborn necessities
Which I could meet not by my daily toil.
The eldest son of a rich nobleman   10
Is heir to all his incapacities;
He has wide wants, and narrow powers. If you,
Cardinal Camillo, were reduced at once
From thrice-driven beds of down, and delicate food,
An hundred servants, and six palaces,   15
To that which nature doth indeed require?—
    Camillo. Nay, there is reason in your plea; 'twere hard.
    Giacomo. 'Tis hard for a firm man to bear: but I
Have a dear wife, a lady of high birth,
Whose dowry in ill hour I lent my father   20
Without a bond or witness to the deed:
And children, who inherit her fine senses,
The fairest creatures in this breathing world;
And she and they reproach me not. Cardinal,
Do you not think the Pope would interpose   25
And stretch authority beyond the law?
    Camillo. Though your peculiar case is hard, I know
The Pope will not divert the course of law.
After that impious feast the other night
I spoke with him, and urged him then to check   30
Your father's cruel hand; he frowned and said,
'Children are disobedient, and they sting

Their fathers' hearts to madness and despair,
Requiting years of care with contumely.
I pity the Count Cenci from my heart;   35
His outraged love perhaps awakened hate,
And thus he is exasperated to ill.
In the great war between the old and young
I, who have white hairs and a tottering body,
Will keep at least blameless neutrality.'   40

Enter ORSINO.

You, my good Lord Orsino, heard those words,
   Orsino. What words?
   Giacomo.   Alas, repeat them not again!
There then is no redress for me, at least
None but that which I may achieve myself,
Since I am driven to the brink.—But, say,   45
My innocent sister and my only brother
Are dying underneath my father's eye.
The memorable torturers of this land,
Galeaz Visconti, Borgia, Ezzelin,
Never inflicted on the meanest slave   50
What these endure; shall they have no protection?
   Camillo. Why, if they would petition to the Pope
I see not how he could refuse it—yet
He holds it of most dangerous example
In aught to weaken the paternal power,   55
Being, as 'twere, the shadow of his own.
I pray you now excuse me. I have business
That will not bear delay.   *[Exit* CAMILLO.
   Giacomo.   But you, Orsino,
Have the petition: wherefore not present it?
   Orsino. I have presented it, and backed it with   60
My earnest prayers, and urgent interest;
It was returned unanswered. I doubt not
But that the strange and execrable deeds
Alleged in it—in truth they might well baffle
Any belief—have turned the Pope's displeasure   65
Upon the accusers from the criminal:
So I should guess from what Camillo said.
   Giacomo. My friend, that palace-walking devil Gold
Has whispered silence to his Holiness:
And we are left, as scorpions ringed with fire.   70
What should we do but strike ourselves to death?
For he who is our murderous persecutor
Is shielded by a father's holy name,
Or I would—   *[Stops abruptly.*
   Orsino.   What? Fear not to speak your thought.

Words are but holy as the deeds they cover: 75
A priest who has forsworn the God he serves;
A judge who makes Truth weep at his decree;
A friend who should weave counsel, as I now,
But as the mantle of some selfish guile;
A father who is all a tyrant seems, 80
Were the profaner for his sacred name.
    Giacomo. Ask me not what I think; the unwilling brain
Feigns often what it would not; and we trust
Imagination with such phantasies
As the tongue dares not fashion into words, 85
Which have no words, their horror makes them dim
To the mind's eye.—My heart denies itself
To think what you demand.
    Orsino.   But a friend's bosom
Is as the inmost cave of our own mind
Where we sit shut from the wide gaze of day, 90
And from the all-communicating air.
You look what I suspected—
    Giacomo.   Spare me now!
I am as one lost in a midnight wood,
Who dares not ask some harmless passenger
The path across the wilderness, lest he, 95
As my thoughts are, should be—a murderer.
I know you are my friend, and all I dare
Speak to my soul that will I trust with thee.
But now my heart is heavy, and would take
Lone counsel from a night of sleepless care. 100
Pardon me, that I say farewell—farewell!
I would that to my own suspected self
I could address a word so full of peace.
    Orsino. Farewell!—Be your thoughts better or more bold.
                          [*Exit* GIACOMO.
I had disposed the Cardinal Camillo 105
To feed his hope with cold encouragement:
It fortunately serves my close designs
That 'tis a trick of this same family
To analyse their own and other minds.
Such self-anatomy shall teach the will 110
Dangerous secrets: for it tempts our powers,
Knowing what must be thought, and may be done,
Into the depth of darkest purposes:
So Cenci fell into the pit; even I,
Since Beatrice unveiled me to myself, 115
And made me shrink from what I cannot shun,
Show a poor figure to my own esteem,
To which I grow half reconciled. I'll do

As little mischief as I can; that thought
Shall fee the accuser conscience.
    (*After a pause.*)   Now what harm   120
If Cenci should be murdered?—Yet, if murdered,
Wherefore by me? And what if I could take
The profit, yet omit the sin and peril
In such an action? Of all earthly things
I fear a man whose blows outspeed his words;   125
And such is Cenci: and while Cenci lives
His daughter's dowry were a secret grave
If a priest wins her.—Oh, fair Beatrice!
Would that I loved thee not, or loving thee
Could but despise danger and gold and all   130
That frowns between my wish and its effect,
Or smiles beyond it! There is no escape . . .
Her bright form kneels beside me at the altar,
And follows me to the resort of men,
And fills my slumber with tumultuous dreams,   135
So when I wake my blood seems liquid fire;
And if I strike my damp and dizzy head
My hot palm scorches it: her very name,
But spoken by a stranger, makes my heart
Sicken and pant; and thus unprofitably   140
I clasp the phantom of unfelt delights
Till weak imagination half possesses
The self-created shadow. Yet much longer
Will I not nurse this life of feverous hours:
From the unravelled hopes of Giacomo   145
I must work out my own dear purposes.
I see, as from a tower, the end of all:
Her father dead; her brother bound to me
By a dark secret, surer than the grave;
Her mother scared and unexpostulating   150
From the dread manner of her wish achieved:
And she!—Once more take courage, my faint heart;
What dares a friendless maiden matched with thee?
I have such foresight as assures success:
Some unbeheld divinity doth ever,   155
When dread events are near, stir up men's minds
To black suggestions; and he prospers best,
Not who becomes the instrument of ill,
But who can flatter the dark spirit, that makes
Its empire and its prey of other hearts   160
Till it became his slave . . . as I will do.   [*Exit.*

END OF THE SECOND ACT.

ACT III

SCENE I.—*An Apartment in the Cenci Palace.* LUCRETIA, *to her enter*
BEATRICE.

    Beatrice. (*She enters staggering, and speaks wildly.*) Reach me
      that handkerchief!—My brain is hurt;
My eyes are full of blood; just wipe them for me . . .
I see but indistinctly . . .
    Lucretia.   My sweet child,
You have no wound; 'tis only a cold dew
That starts from your dear brow . . . Alas! Alas!   5
What has befallen?
    Beatrice.   How comes this hair undone?
Its wandering strings must be what blind me so,
And yet I tied it fast.—O, horrible!
The pavement sinks under my feet! The walls
Spin round! I see a woman weeping there,   10
And standing calm and motionless, whilst I
Slide giddily as the world reels. . . . My God!
The beautiful blue heaven is flecked with blood!
The sunshine on the floor is black! The air
Is changed to vapours such as the dead breathe   15
In charnel pits! pah! I am choked! There creeps
A clinging, black, contaminating mist
About me . . . 'tis substantial, heavy, thick,
I cannot pluck it from me, for it glues
My fingers and my limbs to one another,   20
And eats into my sinews, and dissolves
My flesh to a pollution, poisoning
The subtle, pure, and inmost spirit of life!
My God! I never knew what the mad felt
Before; for I am mad beyond all doubt!   25
(*More wildly.*) No, I am dead! These putrefying limbs
Shut round and sepulchre the panting soul
Which would burst forth into the wandering air!   (*A pause.*)
What hideous thought was that I had even now?
'Tis gone; and yet its burthen remains here   30
O'er these dull eyes . . . upon this weary heart!
O, world! O, life! O, day! O, misery!
    Lucretia. What ails thee, my poor child? She answers not:
Her spirit apprehends the sense of pain,
But not its cause; suffering has dried away   35
The source from which it sprung . . .
    Beatrice (*franticly*).   Like Parricide . . .
Misery has killed its father: yet its father
Never like mine . . . O, God! What thing am I?

Lucretia. My dearest child, what has your father done?

Beatrice (*doubtfully*). Who art thou, questioner? I have no
    father.   40

(*Aside.*) She is the madhouse nurse who tends on me,

It is a piteous office.   [*To* LUCRETIA, *in a slow, subdued voice.*

                    Do you know

I thought I was that wretched Beatrice

Men speak of, whom her father sometimes hales

From hall to hall by the entangled hair;   45

At others, pens up naked in damp cells

Where scaly reptiles crawl, and starves her there,

Till she will eat strange flesh. This woful story

So did I overact in my sick dreams,

That I imagined . . . no, it cannot be!   50

Horrible things have been in this wide world,

Prodigious mixtures, and confusions strange

Of good and ill; and worse have been conceived

Than ever there was found a heart to do.

But never fancy imaged such a deed   55

As . . .   [*Pauses, suddenly recollecting herself.*

            Who art thou? Swear to me, ere I die

With fearful expectation, that indeed

Thou art not what thou seemest . . . Mother!

   Lucretia.   Oh!

My sweet child, know you . . .

   Beatrice.   Yet speak it not:

For then if this be truth, that other too   60

Must be a truth, a firm enduring truth,

Linked with each lasting circumstance of life,

Never to change, never to pass away.

Why so it is. This is the Cenci Palace;

Thou art Lucretia; I am Beatrice.   65

I have talked some wild words, but will no more.

Mother, come near me: from this point of time,

I am . . .   [*Her voice dies away faintly.*

   Lucretia. Alas! What has befallen thee, child?

What has thy father done?

   Beatrice.   What have I done?

Am I not innocent? Is it my crime   70

That one with white hair, and imperious brow,

Who tortured me from my forgotten years,

As parents only dare, should call himself

My father, yet should be!—Oh, what am I?

What name, what place, what memory shall be mine?   75

What retrospects, outliving even despair?

   Lucretia. He is a violent tyrant, surely, child:

We know that death alone can make us free;

His death or ours. But what can he have done
Of deadlier outrage or worse injury?   80
Thou art unlike thyself; thine eyes shoot forth
A wandering and strange spirit. Speak to me,
Unlock those pallid hands whose fingers twine
With one another.
  Beatrice.   'Tis the restless life
Tortured within them. If I try to speak   85
I shall go mad. Ay, something must be done;
What, yet I know not ... something which shall make
The thing that I have suffered but a shadow
In the dread lightning which avenges it;
Brief, rapid, irreversible, destroying   90
The consequence of what it cannot cure.
Some such thing is to be endured or done:
When I know what, I shall be still and calm,
And never anything will move me more.
But now!—O blood, which art my father's blood, 95
Circling through these contaminated veins,
If thou, poured forth on the polluted earth,
Could wash away the crime, and punishment
By which I suffer ... no, that cannot be!
Many might doubt there were a God above   100
Who sees and permits evil, and so die:
That faith no agony shall obscure in me.
  Lucretia. It must indeed have been some bitter wrong;
Yet what, I dare not guess. Oh, my lost child,
Hide not in proud impenetrable grief   105
Thy sufferings from my fear.
  Beatrice.   I hide them not.
What are the words which you would have me speak?
I, who can feign no image in my mind
Of that which has transformed me: I, whose thought
Is like a ghost shrouded and folded up   110
In its own formless horror: of all words,
That minister to mortal intercourse,
Which wouldst thou hear? For there is none to tell
My misery: if another ever knew
Aught like to it, she died as I will die,   115
And left it, as I must, without a name.
Death! Death! Our law and our religion call thee
A punishment and a reward . . . Oh, which
Have I deserved?
  Lucretia.   The peace of innocence;
Till in your season you be called to heaven.   120
Whate'er you may have suffered, you have done
No evil. Death must be the punishment

Of crime, or the reward of trampling down
The thorns which God has strewed upon the path
Which leads to immortality.
  Beatrice.   Ay, death . . .   125
The punishment of crime. I pray thee, God,
Let me not be bewildered while I judge.
If I must live day after day, and keep
These limbs, the unworthy temple of Thy spirit,
As a foul den from which what Thou abhorrest   130
May mock Thee, unavenged . . . it shall not be!
Self-murder . . . no, that might be no escape,
For Thy decree yawns like a Hell between
Our will and it:—O! In this mortal world
There is no vindication and no law   135
Which can adjudge and execute the doom
Of that through which I suffer.

     Enter ORSINO.

(*She approaches him solemnly*.) Welcome, Friend!
I have to tell you that, since last we met,
I have endured a wrong so great and strange,
That neither life nor death can give me rest.   140
Ask me not what it is, for there are deeds
Which have no form, sufferings which have no tongue.
  Orsino. And what is he who has thus injured you?
  Beatrice. The man they call my father: a dread name.
  Orsino. It cannot be . . .
  Beatrice.   What it can be, or not, 145
Forbear to think. It is, and it has been;
Advise me how it shall not be again.
I thought to die; but a religious awe
Restrains me, and the dread lest death itself
Might be no refuge from the consciousness   150
Of what is yet unexpiated. Oh, speak!
  Orsino. Accuse him of the deed, and let the law
Avenge thee.
  Beatrice. Oh, ice-hearted counsellor!
If I could find a word that might make known
The crime of my destroyer; and that done,   155
My tongue should like a knife tear out the secret
Which cankers my heart's core; ay, lay all bare
So that my unpolluted fame should be
With vilest gossips a stale mouthèd story;
A mock, a byword, an astonishment:—   160
If this were done, which never shall be done,
Think of the offender's gold, his dreaded hate,
And the strange horror of the accuser's tale,

Baffling belief, and overpowering speech;
Scarce whispered, unimaginable, wrapped   165
In hideous hints . . . Oh, most assured redress!
   Orsino. You will endure it then?
   Beatrice.   Endure?—Orsino,
It seems your counsel is small profit.
           [*Turns from him, and speaks half to herself.*
                 Ay,
All must be suddenly resolved and done.
What is this undistinguishable mist   170
Of thoughts, which rise, like shadow after shadow,
Darkening each other?
   Orsino.   Should the offender live?
Triumph in his misdeed? and make, by use,
His crime, whate'er it is, dreadful no doubt,
Thine element; until thou mayst become   175
Utterly lost; subdued even to the hue
Of that which thou permittest?
   Beatrice (*to herself*).   Mighty death!
Thou double-visaged shadow? Only judge!
Rightfullest arbiter!   [*She retires absorbed in thought.*
   Lucretia.   If the lightning
Of God has e'er descended to avenge . . .   180
   Orsino. Blaspheme not! His high Providence commits
Its glory on this earth, and their own wrongs
Into the hands of men; if they neglect
To punish crime . . .
   Lucretia.   But if one, like this wretch,
Should mock, with gold, opinion, law, and power?   185
If there be no appeal to that which makes
The guiltiest tremble? If because our wrongs,
For that they are unnatural, strange, and monstrous,
Exceed all measure of belief? O God!
If, for the very reasons which should make   190
Redress most swift and sure, our injurer triumphs?
And we, the victims, bear worse punishment
Than that appointed for their torturer?
   Orsino.   Think not
But that there is redress where there is wrong,
So we be bold enough to seize it.
   Lucretia.   How?   195
If there were any way to make all sure,
I know not . . . but I think it might be good
To . . .
   Orsino. Why, his late outrage to Beatrice;
For it is such, as I but faintly guess,
As makes remorse dishonour, and leaves her   200

Only one duty, how she may avenge:
You, but one refuge from ills ill endured;
Me, but one counsel . . .
    Lucretia.   For we cannot hope
That aid, or retribution, or resource
Will arise thence, where every other one   205
Might find them with less need.   [BEATRICE *advances.*
    Orsino.   Then . . .
    Beatrice.   Peace, Orsino!
And, honoured Lady, while I speak, I pray,
That you put off, as garments overworn,
Forbearance and respect, remorse and fear,
And all the fit restraints of daily life,   210
Which have been borne from childhood, but which now
Would be a mockery to my holier plea.
As I have said, I have endured a wrong,
Which, though it be expressionless, is such
As asks atonement; both for what is past,   215
And lest I be reserved, day after day,
To load with crimes an overburthened soul,
And be . . . what ye can dream not. I have prayed
To God, and I have talked with my own heart,
And have unravelled my entangled will,   220
And have at length determined what is right.
Art thou my friend, Orsino? False or true?
Pledge thy salvation ere I speak.
    Orsino.   I swear
To dedicate my cunning, and my strength,
My silence, and whatever else is mine,   225
To thy commands.
    Lucretia.   You think we should devise
His death?
    Beatrice.   And execute what is devised,
And suddenly. We must be brief and bold.
    Orsino. And yet most cautious.
    Lucretia.   For the jealous laws
Would punish us with death and infamy   230
For that which it became themselves to do.
    Beatrice. Be cautious as ye may, but prompt. Orsino,
What are the means?
    Orsino.   I know two dull, fierce outlaws,
Who think man's spirit as a worm's, and they
Would trample out, for any slight caprice,   235
The meanest or the noblest life. This mood
Is marketable here in Rome. They sell
What we now want.

Lucretia.   To-morrow, before dawn,
Cenci will take us to that lonely rock,
Petrella, in the Apulian Apennines.   240
If he arrive there . . .
   Beatrice.   He must not arrive.
   Orsino. Will it be dark before you reach the tower?
   Lucretia. The sun will scarce be set.
   Beatrice.   But I remember
Two miles on this side of the fort, the road
Crosses a deep ravine; 'tis rough and narrow,   245
And winds with short turns down the precipice;
And in its depth there is a mighty rock,
Which has, from unimaginable years,
Sustained itself with terror and with toil
Over a gulf, and with the agony   250
With which it clings seems slowly coming down;
Even as a wretched soul hour after hour,
Clings to the mass of life; yet clinging, leans;
And leaning, makes more dark the dread abyss
In which it fears to fall: beneath this crag   255
Huge as despair, as if in weariness,
The melancholy mountain yawns . . . below,
You hear but see not an impetuous torrent
Raging among the caverns, and a bridge
Crosses the chasm; and high above there grow,   260
With intersecting trunks, from crag to crag,
Cedars, and yews, and pines; whose tangled hair
Is matted in one solid roof of shade
By the dark ivy's twine. At noonday here
'Tis twilight, and at sunset blackest night.   265
   Orsino. Before you reach that bridge make some excuse
For spurring on your mules, or loitering
Until . . .
   Beatrice. What sound is that?
   Lucretia. Hark! No, it cannot be a servant's step
It must be Cenci, unexpectedly   270
Returned . . . Make some excuse for being here.
   Beatrice. (*To* Orsino, *as she goes out.*) That step we hear
     approach must never pass
The bridge of which we spoke.
               [*Exeunt* Lucretia *and* Beatrice.
   Orsino.   What shall I do?
Cenci must find me here, and I must bear
The imperious inquisition of his looks   275
As to what brought me hither: let me mask
Mine own in some inane and vacant smile.

Enter GIACOMO, *in a hurried manner.*

How! Have you ventured hither? Know you then
That Cenci is from home?
 Giacomo.   I sought him here;
And now must wait till he returns.
 Orsino.   Great God!   280
Weigh you the danger of this rashness?
 Giacomo.   Ay!
Does my destroyer know his danger? We
Are now no more, as once, parent and child,
But man to man; the oppressor to the oppressed;
The slanderer to the slandered; foe to foe: 285
He has cast Nature off, which was his shield,
And Nature casts him off, who is her shame;
And I spurn both. Is it a father's throat
Which I will shake, and say, I ask not gold;
I ask not happy years; nor memories   290
Of tranquil childhood; nor home-sheltered love;
Though all these hast thou torn from me, and more;
But only my fair fame; only one hoard
Of peace, which I thought hidden from thy hate,
Under the penury heaped on me by thee,   295
Or I will . . . God can understand and pardon,
Why should I speak with man?
 Orsino.   Be calm, dear friend.
 Giacomo. Well, I will calmly tell you what he did.
This old Francesco Cenci, as you know,
Borrowed the dowry of my wife from me,   300
And then denied the loan; and left me so
In poverty, the which I sought to mend
By holding a poor office in the state.
It had been promised to me, and already
I bought new clothing for my raggèd babes,   305
And my wife smiled; and my heart knew repose.
When Cenci's intercession, as I found,
Conferred this office on a wretch, whom thus
He paid for vilest service. I returned
With this ill news, and we sate sad together   310
Solacing our despondency with tears
Of such affection and unbroken faith
As temper life's worst bitterness; when he,
As he is wont, came to upbraid and curse,
Mocking our poverty, and telling us   315
Such was God's scourge for disobedient sons.
And then, that I might strike him dumb with shame,
I spoke of my wife's dowry; but he coined

A brief yet specious tale, how I had wasted
The sum in secret riot; and he saw   320
My wife was touched, and he went smiling forth.
And when I knew the impression he had made,
And felt my wife insult with silent scorn
My ardent truth, and look averse and cold,
I went forth too: but soon returned again;   325
Yet not so soon but that my wife had taught
My children her harsh thoughts, and they all cried,
'Give us clothes, father! Give us better food!
What you in one night squander were enough
For months!' I looked, and saw that home was hell.   330
And to that hell will I return to more
Until mine enemy has rendered up
Atonement, or, as he gave life to me
I will, reversing Nature's law . . .
    Orsino.   Trust me,
The compensation which thou seekest here   335
Will be denied.
    Giacomo.   Then . . . Are you not my friend?
Did you not hint at the alternative,
Upon the brink of which you see I stand,
The other day when we conversed together?
My wrongs were then less. That word parricide,   340
Although I am resolved, haunts me like fear.
    Orsino. It must be fear itself, for the bare word
Is hollow mockery. Mark, how wisest God
Draws to one point the threads of a just doom,
So sanctifying it: what you devise   345
Is, as it were, accomplished.
    Giacomo.   Is he dead?
    Orsino. His grave is ready. Know that since we met
Cenci has done an outrage to his daughter.
    Giacomo. What outrage?
    Orsino.   That she speaks not, but you may
Conceive such half conjectures as I do,   350
From her fixed paleness, and the lofty grief
Of her stern brow bent on the idle air,
And her severe unmodulated voice,
Drowning both tenderness and dread; and last
From this; that whilst her step-mother and I,   355
Bewildered in our horror, talked together
With obscure hints; both self-misunderstood
And darkly guessing, stumbling, in our talk,
Over the truth, and yet to its revenge,
She interrupted us, and with a look   360
Which told before she spoke it, he must die: . . .

Giacomo. It is enough. My doubts are well appeased;
There is a higher reason for the act
Than mine; there is a holier judge than me,
A more unblamed avenger. Beatrice,   365
Who in the gentleness of thy sweet youth
Hast never trodden on a worm, or bruised
A living flower, but thou hast pitied it
With needless tears! Fair sister, thou in whom
Men wondered how such loveliness and wisdom   370
Did not destroy each other! Is there made
Ravage of thee? O, heart, I ask no more
Justification! Shall I wait, Orsino,
Till he return, and stab him at the door?
Orsino. Not so; some accident might interpose   375
To rescue him from what is now most sure;
And you are unprovided where to fly,
How to excuse or to conceal. Nay, listen:
All is contrived; success is so assured
That . . .

Enter BEATRICE.

Beatrice. 'Tis my brother's voice! You know me not?
Giacomo. My sister, my lost sister!
Beatrice.   Lost indeed!   381
I see Orsino has talked with you, and
That you conjecture things too horrible
To speak, yet far less than the truth. Now, stay not,
He might return: yet kiss me; I shall know   385
That then thou hast consented to his death.
Farewell, farewell! Let piety to God,
Brotherly love, justice and clemency,
And all things that make tender hardest hearts
Make thine hard, brother. Answer not . . . farewell.   390
                                    [*Exeunt severally.*

SCENE II.—*A mean Apartment in* GIACOMO'S *House.* GIACOMO *alone.*

Giacomo. 'Tis midnight, and Orsino comes not yet.
                        [*Thunder, and the sound of a storm.*
What! can the everlasting elements
Feel with a worm like man? If so, the shaft
Of mercy-wingèd lightning would not fall
On stones and trees. My wife and children sleep: 5
They are now living in unmeaning dreams:
But I must wake, still doubting if that deed
Be just which is most necessary. O,
Thou unreplenishing lamp! whose narrow fire
Is shaken by the wind, and on whose edge   10

Devouring darkness hovers! Thou small flame,
Which, as a dying pulse rises and falls,
Still flickerest up and down, how very soon,
Did I not feed thee, wouldst thou fail and be
As thou hadst never been! So wastes and sinks   15
Even now, perhaps, the life that kindled mine:
But that no power can fill with vital oil
That broken lamp of flesh. Ha! 'tis the blood
Which fed these veins that ebbs till all is cold:
It is the form that moulded mine that sinks   20
Into the white and yellow spasms of death:
It is the soul by which mine was arrayed
In God's immortal likeness which now stands
Naked before Heaven's judgement seat!   [*A bell strikes.*
                                                    One! Two!
The hours crawl on; and when my hairs are white,   25
My son will then perhaps be waiting thus,
Tortured between just hate and vain remorse;
Chiding the tardy messenger of news
Like those which I expect. I almost wish
He be not dead, although my wrongs are great;   30
Yet . . . 'tis Orsino's step . . .

                    Enter ORSINO.

                                        Speak!
Orsino.   I am come
To say he has escaped.
        Giacomo.   Escaped!
        Orsino.   And safe
Within Petrella. He passed by the spot
Appointed for the deed an hour too soon.
        Giacomo. Are we the fools of such contingencies?   35
And do we waste in blind misgivings thus
The hours when we should act? Then wind and thunder,
Which seemed to howl his knell, is the loud laughter
With which Heaven mocks our weakness! I henceforth
Will ne'er repent of aught designed or done   40
But my repentance.
        Orsino.   See, the lamp is out.
        Giacomo. If no remorse is ours when the dim air
Has drank this innocent flame, why should we quail
When Cenci's life, that light by which ill spirits
See the worst deeds they prompt, shall sink for ever?   45
No, I am hardened.
        Orsino.   Why, what need of this?
Who feared the pale intrusion of remorse
In a just deed? Although our first plan failed,

Doubt not but he will soon be laid to rest.
But light the lamp; let us not talk i' the dark.   50
    Giacomo (lighting the lamp). And yet once quenched I cannot
      thus relume
My father's life: do you not think his ghost
Might plead that argument with God?
    Orsino.   Once gone
You cannot now recall your sister's peace;
Your own extinguished years of youth and hope;   55
Nor your wife's bitter words; nor all the taunts
Which, from the prosperous, weak misfortune takes;
Nor your dead mother; nor . . .
    Giacomo.   O, speak no more!
I am resolved, although this very hand
Must quench the life that animated it.   60
    Orsino. There is no need of that. Listen: you know
Olimpio, the castellan of Petrella
In old Colonna's time; him whom your father
Degraded from his post? And Marzio,
That desperate wretch, whom he deprived last year   65
Of a reward of blood, well earned and due?
    Giacomo. I knew Olimpio; and they say he hated
Old Cenci so, that in his silent rage
His lips grew white only to see him pass.
Of Marzio I know nothing.
    Orsino.   Marzio's hate   70
Matches Olimpio's. I have sent these men,
But in your name, and as at your request,
To talk with Beatrice and Lucretia.
    Giacomo. Only to talk?
    Orsino.   The moments which even now
Pass onward to to-morrow's midnight hour   75
May memorize their flight with death: ere then
They must have talked, and may perhaps have done,
And made an end . . .
    Giacomo.   Listen! What sound is that?
    Orsino. The house-dog moans, and the beams crack: nought else.
    Giacomo. It is my wife complaining in her sleep: 80
I doubt not she is saying bitter things
Of me, and all my children round her dreaming
That I deny them sustenance.
    Orsino.   Whilst he
Who truly took it from them, and who fills
Their hungry rest with bitterness, now sleeps   85
Lapped in bad pleasures, and triumphantly
Mocks thee in visions of successful hate
Too like the truth of day.

Giacomo.   If e'er he wakes
Again, I will not trust to hireling hands . . .
    Orsino. Why, that were well. I must be gone; good-night.
When next we meet—may all be done!
    Giacomo.   And all   91
Forgotten: Oh, that I had never been!   [*Exeunt.*

END OF THE THIRD ACT.

ACT IV

SCENE I.—*An Apartment in the Castle of Petrella. Enter* CENCI.

    Cenci. She comes not; yet I left her even now
Vanquished and faint. She knows the penalty
Or her delay: yet what if threats are vain?
Am I not now within Petrella's moat?
Or fear I still the eyes and ears of Rome?   5
Might I not drag her by the golden hair?
Stamp on her? Keep her sleepless till her brain
Be overworn? Tame her with chains and famine?
Less would suffice. Yet so to leave undone
What I most seek! No, 'tis her stubborn will   10
Which by its own consent shall stoop as low
As that which drags it down.

                Enter LUCRETIA.

                    Thou loathèd wretch!
Hide thee from my abhorrence: fly, begone!
Yet stay! Bid Beatrice come hither.
    Lucretia.   Oh,
Husband! I pray for thine own wretched sake   15
Heed what thou dost. A man who walks like thee
Through crimes, and through the danger of his crimes,
Each hour may stumble o'er a sudden grave.
And thou art old; thy hairs are hoary gray;
As thou wouldst save thyself from death and hell,   20
Pity thy daughter; give her to some friend
In marriage: so that she may tempt thee not
To hatred, or worse thoughts, if worse there be.
    Cenci. What! like her sister who has found a home
To mock my hate from with prosperity?   25
Strange ruin shall destroy both her and thee
And all that yet remain. My death may be
Rapid, her destiny outspeeds it. Go,
Bid her come hither, and before my mood
Be changed, lest I should drag her by the hair.   30
    Lucretia. She sent me to thee, husband. At thy presence

She fell, as thou dost know, into a trance;
And in that trance she heard a voice which said,
'Cenci must die! Let him confess himself!
Even now the accusing Angel waits to hear   35
If God, to punish his enormous crimes,
Harden his dying heart!'
   Cenci.   Why—such things are . . .
No doubt divine revealings may be made.
'Tis plain I have been favoured from above,   39
For when I cursed my sons they died.—Ay . . . so . . .
As to the right or wrong, that's talk . . . repentance . . .
Repentance is an easy moment's work
And more depends on God than me. Well . . . well . . .
I must give up the greater point, which was
To poison and corrupt her soul.
              [*A pause;* LUCRETIA *approaches anxiously, and
                then shrinks back as he speaks.*
                  One, two;   45
Ay . . . Rocco and Cristofano my curse
Strangled: and Giacomo, I think, will find
Life a worse Hell than that beyond the grave:
Beatrice shall, if there be skill in hate,
Die in despair, blaspheming: to Bernardo,   50
He is so innocent, I will bequeath
The memory of these deeds, and make his youth
The sepulchre of hope, where evil thoughts
Shall grow like weeds on a neglected tomb.
When all is done, out in the wide Campagna,   55
I will pile up my silver and my gold;
My costly robes, paintings and tapestries;
My parchments and all records of my wealth,
And make a bonfire in my joy, and leave
Of my possessions nothing but my name;   60
Which shall be an inheritance to strip
Its wearer bare as infamy. That done,
My soul, which is a scourge, will I resign
Into the hands of him who wielded it;
Be it for its own punishment or theirs,   65
He will not ask it of me till the lash
Be broken in its last and deepest wound;
Until its hate be all inflicted. Yet,
Lest death outspeed my purpose, let me make
Short work and sure . . .   [*Going.*
   Lucretia. (*Stops him.*)   Oh, stay! It was a feint: 70
She had no vision, and she heard no voice.
I said it but to awe thee.
   Cenci.   That is well.

Vile palterer with the sacred truth of God,
Be thy soul choked with that blaspheming lie!
For Beatrice worse terrors are in store   75
To bend her to my will.
    Lucretia.   Oh! to what will?
What cruel sufferings more than she has known
Canst thou inflict?
    Cenci.   Andrea! Go call my daughter,
And if she comes not tell her that I come.
What sufferings? I will drag her, step by step,   80
Through infamies unheard of among men:
She shall stand shelterless in the broad noon
Of public scorn, for acts blazoned abroad,
One among which shall be ... What? Canst thou guess?
She shall become (for what she most abhors   85
Shall have a fascination to entrap
Her loathing will) to her own conscious self
All she appears to others; and when dead,
As she shall die unshrived and unforgiven,
A rebel to her father and her God,   90
Her corpse shall be abandoned to the hounds;
Her name shall be the terror of the earth;
Her spirit shall approach the throne of God
Plague-spotted with my curses. I will make
Body and soul a monstrous lump of ruin.   95

Enter ANDREA.

    Andrea. The Lady Beatrice ...
    Cenci.   Speak, pale slave! What
Said she?
    Andrea. My Lord, 'twas what she looked; she said:
'Go tell my father that I see the gulf
Of Hell between us two, which he may pass,
I will not.'

                     [*Exit* ANDREA.
    Cenci.   Go thou quick, Lucretia,   100
Tell her to come; yet let her understand
Her coming is consent: and say, moreover,
That if she come not I will curse her.

                     [*Exit* LUCRETIA.
               Ha!
With what but with a father's curse doth God
Panic-strike armèd victory, and make pale   105
Cities in their prosperity? The world's Father
Must grant a parent's prayer against his child,
Be he who asks even what men call me.
Will not the deaths of her rebellious brothers

Awe her before I speak? For I on them   110
Did imprecate quick ruin, and it came.

Enter LUCRETIA.

Well; what? Speak, wretch!
　　Lucretia.　　　　　　　She said, 'I cannot come;
Go tell my father that I see a torrent
Of his own blood raging between us.'
　　Cenci (kneeling).　　　　　　God!
Hear me! If this most specious mass of flesh,   115
Which Thou hast made my daughter; this my blood,
This particle of my divided being;
Or rather, this my bane and my disease,
Whose sight infects and poisons me; this devil
Which sprung from me as from a hell, was meant   120
To aught good use; if her bright loveliness
Was kindled to illumine this dark world;
If nursed by Thy selectest dew of love
Such virtues blossom in her as should make
The peace of life, I pray Thee for my sake,   125
As Thou the common God and Father art
Of her, and me, and all; reverse that doom!
Earth, in the name of God, let her food be
Poison, until she be encrusted round
With leprous stains! Heaven, rain upon her head   130
The blistering drops of the Maremma's dew,
Till she be speckled like a toad; parch up
Those love-enkindled lips, warp those fine limbs
To loathèd lameness! All-beholding sun,
Strike in thine envy those life-darting eyes   135
With thine own blinding beams!
　　Lucretia.　　　　　　Peace! Peace!
For thine own sake unsay those dreadful words.
When high God grants He punishes such prayers.
　　Cenci (leaping up, and throwing his right hand towards Heaven).
　　　He does His will, I mine! This in addition,
That if she have a child . . .
　　Lucretia.　　　　　　Horrible thought!   140
　　Cenci. That if she ever have a child; and thou,
Quick Nature! I adjure thee by thy God,
That thou be fruitful in her, and increase
And multiply, fulfilling his command,
And my deep imprecation! May it be   145
A hideous likeness of herself, that as
From a distorting mirror, she may see
Her image mixed with what she most abhors,

Smiling upon her from her nursing breast.
And that the child may from its infancy   150
Grow, day by day, more wicked and deformed,
Turning her mother's love to misery:
And that both she and it may live until
It shall repay her care and pain with hate,
Or what may else be more unnatural.   155
So he may hunt her through the clamorous scoffs
Of the loud world to a dishonoured grave.
Shall I revoke this curse? Go, bid her come,
Before my words are chronicled in Heaven.

                                            [*Exit* LUCRETIA.
I do not feel as if I were a man,   160
But like a fiend appointed to chastise
The offences of some unremembered world.
My blood is running up and down my veins;
A fearful pleasure makes it prick and tingle:
I feel a giddy sickness of strange awe;   165
My heart is beating with an expectation
Of horrid joy.

                        Enter LUCRETIA.

                    What? Speak!
    Lucretia.   She bids thee curse;
And if thy curses, as they cannot do,
Could kill her soul . . .
        Cenci.   She would not come. 'Tis well,
I can do both: first take what I demand,   170
And then extort concession. To thy chamber!
Fly ere I spurn thee: and beware this night
That thou cross not my footsteps. It were safer
To come between the tiger and his prey.   [*Exit* LUCRETIA.
It must be late; mine eyes grow weary dim   175
With unaccustomed heaviness of sleep.
Conscience! Oh, thou most insolent of lies!
They say that sleep, that healing dew of Heaven,
Steeps not in balm the foldings of the brain
Which thinks thee an impostor. I will go   180
First to belie thee with an hour of rest,
Which will be deep and calm, I feel: and then . . .
O, multitudinous Hell, the fiends will shake
Thine arches with the laughter of their joy!
There shall be lamentation heard in Heaven   185
As o'er an angel fallen; and upon Earth
All good shall droop and sicken, and ill things
Shall with a spirit of unnatural life
Stir and be quickened . . . even as I am now.   [*Exit.*

SCENE II.—*Before the Castle of Petrella. Enter* BEATRICE *and* LUCRETIA
above on the Ramparts.

Beatrice. They come not yet.
Lucretia.   'Tis scarce midnight.
Beatrice.   How slow
Behind the course of thought, even sick with speed,
Lags leaden-footed time!
Lucretia.   The minutes pass . . .
If he should wake before the deed is done?
Beatrice. O, mother! He must never wake again.   5
What thou hast said persuades me that our act
Will but dislodge a spirit of deep hell
Out of a human form.
Lucretia.   'Tis true he spoke
Of death and judgement with strange confidence
For one so wicked; as a man believing   10
In God, yet recking not of good or ill.
And yet to die without confession! . . .
Beatrice.   Oh!
Believe that Heaven is merciful and just,
And will not add our dread necessity
To the amount of his offences.

Enter OLIMPIO *and* MARZIO, *below.*   15
Lucretia.   See,
They come.
Beatrice.   All mortal things must hasten thus
To their dark end. Let us go down.
                    [*Exeunt* LUCRETIA *and* BEATRICE *from above*
Olimpio. How feel you to this work?
Marzio.   As one who thinks
A thousand crowns excellent market price
For an old murderer's life. Your cheeks are pale.   20
Olimpio. It is the white reflection of your own,
Which you call pale.
Marzio.   Is that their natural hue?
Olimpio. Or 'tis my hate and the deferred desire
To wreak it, which extinguishes their blood.
Marzio. You are inclined then to this business?
Olimpio.   Ay.   25
If one should bribe me with a thousand crowns
To kill a serpent which had stung my child,
I could not be more willing.

Enter BEATRICE *and* LUCRETIA, *below.*
                    Noble ladies!
Beatrice. Are ye resolved?

Olimpio.   Is he asleep?
Marzio.   Is all
Quiet?
   Lucretia. I mixed an opiate with his drink: 30
He sleeps so soundly . . .
   Beatrice.   That his death will be
But as a change of sin-chastising dreams,
A dark continuance of the Hell within him,
Which God extinguish! But ye are resolved?
Ye know it is a high and holy deed?   35
   Olimpio. We are resolved.
   Marzio.   As to the how this act
Be warranted, it rests with you.
   Beatrice.   Well, follow!
   Olimpio. Hush! Hark! What noise is that?
   Marzio.   Ha! some one comes!
   Beatrice. Ye conscience-stricken cravens, rock to rest
Your baby hearts. It is the iron gate,   40
Which ye left open, swinging to the wind,
That enters whistling as in scorn. Come, follow!
And be your steps like mine, light, quick and bold.   [*Exeunt.*

SCENE III.—*An Apartment in the Castle. Enter* BEATRICE *and* LUCRETIA.

   Lucretia. They are about it now.
   Beatrice.   Nay, it is done.
   Lucretia. I have not heard him groan.
   Beatrice.   He will not groan.
   Lucretia. What sound is that?
   Beatrice.   List! 'tis the tread of feet
About his bed.
   Lucretia.   My God!
If he be now a cold stiff corpse . . .
   Beatrice.   O, fear not   5
What may be done, but what is left undone:
The act seals all.

Enter OLIMPIO *and* MARZIO.

                    Is it accomplished?
   Marzio.   What?
   Olimpio. Did you not call?
   Beatrice.   When?
   Olimpio.   Now.
   Beatrice.   I ask if all is over?
   Olimpio. We dare not kill an old and sleeping man;
His thin gray hair, his stern and reverend brow,   10
His veinèd hands crossed on his heaving breast,
And the calm innocent sleep in which he lay,

Quelled me. Indeed, indeed, I cannot do it.
  Marzio. But I was bolder; for I chid Olimpio,
And bade him bear his wrongs to his own grave   15
And leave me the reward. And now my knife
Touched the loose wrinkled throat, when the old man
Stirred in his sleep, and said, 'God! hear, O, hear,
A father's curse! What, art Thou not our Father?'
And then he laughed. I knew it was the ghost   20
Of my dead father speaking through his lips,
And could not kill him.
  Beatrice.   Miserable slaves!
Where, if ye dare not kill a sleeping man,
Found ye the boldness to return to me
With such a deed undone? Base palterers!   25
Cowards and traitors! Why, the very conscience
Which ye would sell for gold and for revenge
Is an equivocation: it sleeps over
A thousand daily acts disgracing men;
And when a deed where mercy insults Heaven . . .   30
Why do I talk?
              [*Snatching a dagger from one of them and raising it.*
                    Hadst thou a tongue to say,
'She murdered her own father!'—I must do it!
But never dream ye shall outlive him long!
  Olimpio. Stop, for God's sake!
  Marzio.   I will go back and kill him.
  Olimpio. Give me the weapon, we must do thy will.   35
  Beatrice. Take it! Depart! Return!
                      [*Exeunt* OLIMPIO *and* MARZIO.
                      How pale thou art!
We do but that which 'twere a deadly crime
To leave undone.
  Lucretia.   Would it were done!
  Beatrice.   Even whilst
That doubt is passing through your mind, the world
Is conscious of a change. Darkness and Hell   40
Have swallowed up the vapour they sent forth
To blacken the sweet light of life. My breath
Comes, methinks, lighter, and the jellied blood
Runs freely through my veins. Hark!

                Enter OLIMPIO *and* MARZIO.

                      He is . . .
  Olimpio.   Dead!
  Marzio. We strangled him that there might be no blood;   45
And then we threw his heavy corpse i' the garden
Under the balcony; 'twill seem it fell.

Beatrice (*giving them a bag of coin*). Here, take this gold, and
    hasten to your homes.
And, Marzio, because thou wast only awed
By that which made me tremble, wear thou this!   50
                    [*Clothes him in a rich mantle.*
It was the mantle which my grandfather
Wore in his high prosperity, and men
Envied his state: so may they envy thine.
Thou wert a weapon in the hand of God
To a just use. Live long and thrive! And, mark,   55
If thou hast crimes, repent: this deed is none.
                    [*A horn is sounded.*
Lucretia. Hark, 'tis the castle horn; my God! it sounds
Like the last trump.
    Beatrice.   Some tedious guest is coming.
    Lucretia. The drawbridge is let down; there is a tramp
Of horses in the court; fly, hide yourselves!   60
                [*Exeunt* OLIMPIO *and* MARZIO.
    Beatrice. Let us retire to counterfeit deep rest;
I scarcely need to counterfeit it now:
The spirit which doth reign within these limbs
Seems strangely undisturbed. I could even sleep   64
Fearless and calm: all ill is surely past.   [*Exeunt.*

SCENE IV.—*Another Apartment in the Castle. Enter on one side the*
    LEGATE SAVELLA, *introduced by a Servant, and on the other* LUCRE-
TIA *and* BERNARDO.

    Savella. Lady, my duty to his Holiness
Be my excuse that thus unseasonably
I break upon your rest. I must speak with
Count Cenci; doth he sleep?
    Lucretia (*in a hurried and confused manner*). I think he sleeps;
Yet wake him not, I pray, spare me awhile,   5
He is a wicked and wrathful man;
Should he be roused out of his sleep to-night,
Which is, I know, a hell of angry dreams,
It were not well; indeed it were not well.
Wait till day break . . . (*aside*) O, I am deadly sick!   10
    Savella. I grieve thus to distress you, but the Count
Must answer charges of the gravest import,
And suddenly; such my commssion is.
    Lucretia (*with increased agitation*). I dare not rouse him: I
    know none who dare . . .
'Twere perilous; . . . you might as safely waken   15
A serpent; or a corpse in which some fiend
Were laid to sleep.
    Savella.   Lady, my moments here

Are counted. I must rouse him from his sleep,
Since none else dare.
   Lucretia (aside).   O, terror! O, despair!
(*To* BERNARDO.) Bernardo, conduct you the Lord Legate to   20
   Your father's chamber.   [*Exeunt* SAVELLA *and* BERNARDO.

Enter BEATRICE.

   Beatrice.   'Tis a messenger
Come to arrest the culprit who now stands
Before the throne of unappealable God.
Both Earth and Heaven, consenting arbiters,
Acquit our deed.
   Lucretia.   Oh, agony of fear!   25
Would that he yet might live! Even now I heard
The Legate's followers whisper as they passed
They had a warrant for his instant death.
All was prepared by unforbidden means
Which we must pay so dearly, having done.   30
Even now they search the tower, and find the body;
Now they suspect the truth; now they consult
Before they come to tax us with the fact;
O, horrible, 'tis all discovered!
   Beatrice.   Mother,
What is done wisely, is done well. Be bold   35
As thou art just. 'Tis like a truant child
To fear that others know what thou hast done,
Even from thine own strong consciousness, and thus
Write on unsteady eyes and altered cheeks
All thou wouldst hide. Be faithful to thyself,   40
And fear no other witness but thy fear.
For if, as cannot be, some circumstance
Should rise in accusation, we can blind
Suspicion with such cheap astonishment,
Or overbear it with such guiltless pride,   45
As murderers cannot feign. The deed is done,
And what may follow now regards not me.
I am as universal as the light;
Free as the earth-surrounding air; as firm
As the world's centre. Consequence, to me,   50
Is as the wind which strikes the solid rock
But shakes it not.   [*A cry within and tumult.*
   Voices.   Murder! Murder! Murder!

Enter BERNARDO *and* SAVELLA.

   Savella (to his followers). Go search the castle round; sound
   the alarm;
Look to the gates that none escape!

Beatrice.   What now?   54

Bernardo. I know not what to say . . . my father's dead.

Beatrice. How; dead! he only sleeps; you mistake, brother.
His sleep is very calm, very like death;
'Tis wonderful how well a tyrant sleeps.
He is not dead?

Bernardo.   Dead; murdered.

Lucretia (*with extreme agitation*). Oh no, no,
He is not murdered though he may be dead;   60
I have alone the keys of those apartments.

Savella. Ha! Is it so?

Beatrice.   My Lord, I pray excuse us;
We will retire; my mother is not well:
She seems quite overcome with this strange horror.

                          [*Exeunt* LUCRETIA *and* BEATRICE.

Savella. Can you suspect who may have murdered him?   65

Bernardo. I know not what to think.

Savella.   Can you name any
Who had an interest in his death?

Bernardo.   Alas!
I can name none who had not, and those most
Who most lament that such a deed is done;
My mother, and my sister, and myself.   70

Savella. 'Tis strange! There were clear marks of violence.
I found the old man's body in the moonlight
Hanging beneath the window of his chamber,
Among the branches of a pine: he could not
Have fallen there, for all his limbs lay heaped   75
And effortless; 'tis true there was no blood . . .
Favour me, Sir; it much imports your house
That all should be made clear; to tell the ladies
That I request their presence.

                          [*Exit* BERNARDO.

Enter GUARDS *bringing in* MARZIO.

Guard.   We have one.

Officer. My Lord, we found this ruffian and another   80
Lurking among the rocks; there is no doubt
But that they are the murderers of Count Cenci:
Each had a bag of coin; this fellow wore
A gold-inwoven robe, which shining bright
Under the dark rocks to the glimmering moon   85
Betrayed them to our notice: the other fell
Desperately fighting.

Savella.   What does he confess?

Officer. He keeps firm silence; but these lines found on him
May speak.

Savella.   Their language is at least sincere.   [*Reads.*
'To the Lady Beatrice.
'*That the atonement of what my nature sickens to conjecture*
may soon arrive, I send thee, at thy brother's desire, those who will
speak and do more than I dare write . . .
                              '*Thy devoted servant, Orsino.*'

Enter LUCRETIA, BEATRICE, *and* BERNARDO.

Knowest thou this writing, Lady?
          Beatrice.   No.
          Savella.   Nor thou?   95
Lucretia. (*Her conduct throughout the scene is marked by ex-*
          treme agitation.) Where was it found? What is it? It should
          be
Orsino's hand! It speaks of that strange horror
Which never yet found utterance, but which made
Between that hapless child and her dead father
A gulf of obscure hatred.
          Savella.   Is it so?   100
Is it true, Lady, that thy father did
Such outrages as to awaken in thee
Unfilial hate?
          Beatrice.   Not hate, 'twas more than hate:
This is most true, yet wherefore question me?
          Savella. There is a deed demanding question done;   105
Thou hast a secret which will answer not.
          Beatrice. What sayest? My Lord, your words are bold and rash.
          Savella. I do arrest all present in the name
Of the Pope's Holiness. You must to Rome.
          Lucretia. O, not to Rome! Indeed we are not guilty.   110
          Beatrice. Guilty! Who dares talk of guilt? My Lord,
I am more innocent of parricide
Than is a child born fatherless . . . Dear mother,
Your gentleness and patience are no shield
For this keen-judging world, this two-edged lie,   115
Which seems, but is not. What! will human laws,
Rather will ye who are their ministers,
Bar all access to retribution first,
And then, when Heaven doth interpose to do
What ye neglect, arming familiar things   120
To the redress of an unwonted crime,
Make ye the victims who demanded it
Culprits? 'Tis ye are culprits! That poor wretch
Who stands so pale, and trembling, and amazed,
If it be true he murdered Cenci, was   125
A sword in the right hand of justest God.
Wherefore should I have wielded it? Unless

The crimes which mortal tongue dare never name
God therefore scruples to avenge.
    Savella.   You own
That you desired his death?
    Beatrice.   It would have been   130
A crime no less than his, if for one moment
That fierce desire had faded in my heart.
'Tis true I did believe, and hope, and pray,
Ay, I even knew . . . for God is wise and just,
That some strange sudden death hung over him.   135
'Tis true that this did happen, and most true
There was no other rest for me on earth,
No other hope in Heaven . . . now what of this?
    Savella. Strange thoughts beget strange deeds; and here are both:
I judge thee not.
    Beatrice.   And yet, if you arrest me,   140
You are the judge and executioner
Of that which is the life of life: the breath
Of accusation kills an innocent name,
And leaves for lame acquittal the poor life
Which is a mask without it. 'Tis most false   145
That I am guilty of foul parricide;
Although I must rejoice, for justest cause,
That other hands have sent my father's soul
To ask the mercy he denied to me.
Now leave us free; stain not a noble house   150
With vague surmises of rejected crime;
Add to our sufferings and your own neglect
No heavier sum: let them have been enough:
Leave us the wreck we have.
    Savella.   I dare not, Lady.
I pray that you prepare yourselves for Rome: 155
There the Pope's further pleasure will be known.
    Lucretia. O, not to Rome! O, take us not to Rome!
    Beatrice. Why not to Rome, dear mother? There as here
Our innocence is as an armèd heel
To trample accusation. God is there   160
As here, and with His shadow ever clothes
The innocent, the injured and the weak;
And such are we. Cheer up, dear Lady, lean
On me; collect your wandering thoughts. My Lord,
As soon as you have taken some refreshment,   165
And had all such examinations made
Upon the spot, as may be necessary
To the full understanding of this matter,
We shall be ready. Mother; will you come?
    Lucretia. Ha! they will bind us to the rack, and wrest

Self-accusation from our agony!   171
Will Giacomo be there? Orsino? Marzio?
All present; all confronted; all demanding
Each from the other's countenance the thing
Which is in every heart! O, misery!   175
                        [*She faints, and is borne out.*
   Savella. She faints: an ill appearance this.
   Beatrice.   My Lord,
She knows not yet the uses of the world.
She fears that power is as a beast which grasps
And loosens not: a snake whose look transmutes
All things to guilt which is its nutriment.   180
She cannot know how well the supine slaves
Of blind authority read the truth of things
When written on a brow of guilelessness:
She sees not yet triumphant Innocence
Stand at the judgement-seat of mortal man,   185
A judge and an accuser of the wrong
Which drags it there. Prepare yourself, my Lord;
Our suite will join yours in the court below. [*Exeunt.*

END OF THE FOURTH ACT.

ACT V

SCENE I.—*An Apartment in* ORSINO'S *Palace. Enter* ORSINO *and* GIACOMO.

   Giacomo. Do evil deeds thus quickly come to end?
O, that the vain remorse which must chastise
Crimes done, had but as loud a voice to warn
As its keen sting is mortal to avenge!
O, that the hour when present had cast off   5
The mantle of its mystery, and shown
The ghastly form with which it now returns
When its scared game is roused, cheering the hounds
Of conscience to their prey! Alas! Alas!
It was a wicked thought, a piteous deed,   10
To kill an old and hoary-headed father.
   Orsino. It has turned out unluckily, in truth.
   Giacomo. To violate the sacred doors of sleep;
To cheat kind Nature of the placid death
Which she prepares for overwearied age;   15
To drag from Heaven an unrepentant soul
Which might have quenched in reconciling prayers
A life of burning crimes . . .
   Orsino.   You cannot say

I urged you to the deed.

    Giacomo.   O, had I never
Found in thy smooth and ready countenance   20
The mirror of my darkest thoughts; hadst thou
Never with hints and questions made me look
Upon the monster of my thought, until
It grew familiar to desire . . .

    Orsino.   'Tis thus
Men cast the blame of their unprosperous acts   25
Upon the abettors of their own resolve;
Or anything but their weak, guilty selves.
And yet, confess the truth, it is the peril
In which you stand that gives you this pale sickness
Of penitence; confess 'tis fear disguised   30
From its own shame that takes the mantle now
Of thin remorse. What if we yet were safe?

    Giacomo. How can that be? Already Beatrice,
Lucretia and the murderer are in prison.
I doubt not officers are, whilst we speak,   35
Sent to arrest us.

    Orsino.   I have all prepared
For instant flight. We can escape even now,
So we take fleet occasion by the hair.

    Giacomo. Rather expire in tortures, as I may.
What! will you cast by self-accusing flight   40
Assured conviction upon Beatrice?
She, who alone in this unnatural work,
Stands like God's angel ministered upon
By fiends; avenging such a nameless wrong
As turns black parricide to piety;   45
Whilst we for basest ends . . . I fear, Orsino,
While I consider all your words and looks,
Comparing them with your proposal now,
That you must be a villain. For what end
Could you engage in such a perilous crime,   50
Training me on with hints, and signs, and smiles,
Even to this gulf? Thou art no liar? No,
Thou art a lie! Traitor and murderer!
Coward and slave! But, no, defend thyself;   *[Drawing.*
Let the sword speak what the indignant tongue   55
Disdains to brand thee with.

    Orsino.   Put up your weapon.
Is it the desperation of your fear
Makes you thus rash and sudden with a friend,
Now ruined for your sake? If honest anger
Have moved you, know, that what I just proposed   60

Was but to try you. As for me, I think,
Thankless affection led me to this point,
From which, if my firm temper could repent,
I cannot now recede. Even whilst we speak
The ministers of justice wait below: 65
They grant me these brief moments. Now if you
Have any word of melancholy comfort
To speak to your pale wife, 'twere best to pass
Out at the postern, and avoid them so.
   Giacomo. O, generous friend! How canst thou pardon me?
Would that my life could purchase thine!
   Orsino.   That wish   71
Now comes a day too late. Haste; fare thee well!
Hear'st thou not steps along the corridor?

                           [*Exit* GIACOMO.

I'm sorry for it; but the guards are waiting
At his own gate, and such was my contrivance   75
That I might rid me both of him and them
I thought to act a solemn comedy
Upon the painted scene of this new world,
And to attain my own peculiar ends
By some such plot of mingled good and ill   80
As others weave; but there arose a Power
Which grasped and snapped the threads of my device
And turned it to a net of ruin . . . Ha!   [*A shout is heard.*
Is that my name I hear proclaimed abroad?
But I will pass, wrapped in a vile disguise;   85
Rags on my back, and a false innocence
Upon my face, through the misdeeming crowd
Which judges by what seems. 'Tis easy then
For a new name and for a country new,
And a new life, fashioned on old desires,   90
To change the honours of abandoned Rome.
And these must be the masks of that within,
Which must remain unaltered . . . Oh, I fear
That what is past will never let me rest!
Why, when none else is conscious, but myself,   95
Of my misdeeds, should my own heart's contempt
Trouble me? Have I not the power to fly
My own reproaches? Shall I be the slave
Of . . . what? A word? which those of this false world
Employ against each other, not themselves;   100
As men wear daggers not for self-offence.
But if I am mistaken, where shall I
Find the disguise to hide me from myself,
As now I skulk from every other eye?   [*Exit.*

SCENE II.—*A Hall of Justice.* CAMILLO, JUDGES, *&c., are discovered seated;* MARZIO *is led in.*

First Judge. Accused, do you persist in your denial?
I ask you, are you innocent, or guilty?
I demand who were the participators
In your offence? Speak truth and the whole truth.
    Marzio. My God! I did not kill him; I know nothing;   5
Olimpio sold the robe to me from which
You would infer my guilt.
    Second Judge.   Away with him!
    First Judge. Dare you, with lips yet white from the rack's kiss
Speak false? Is it so soft a questioner,
That you would bandy lover's talk with it   10
Till it wind out your life and soul? Away!
    Marzio. Spare me! O, spare! I will confess.
    First Judge.   Then speak.
    Marzio. I strangled him in his sleep.
    First Judge.   Who urged you to it?
    Marzio. His own son Giacomo, and the young prelate
Orsino sent me to Petrella; there   15
The ladies Beatrice and Lucretia
Tempted me with a thousand crowns, and I
And my companion forthwith murdered him.
Now let me die.
    First Judge. This sounds as bad as truth. Guards, there,
Lead forth the prisoner!

       Enter LUCRETIA, BEATRICE, *and* GIACOMO, *guarded.*

               Look upon this man;   20
When did you see him last?
    Beatrice.   We never saw him.
    Marzio. You know me too well, Lady Beatrice.
    Beatrice. I know thee! How? where? when?
    Marzio.   You know 'twas I
Whom you did urge with menaces and bribes
To kill your father. When the thing was done   25
You clothed me in a robe of woven gold
And bade me thrive: how I have thriven, you see.
You, my Lord Giacomo, Lady Lucretia,
You know that what I speak is true.
            [BEATRICE *advances towards him; he covers his*
            face, and shrinks back.
                Oh, dart
The terrible resentment of those eyes   30
On the dead earth! Turn them away from me!
They wound: 'twas torture forced the truth. My Lords,

Having said this let me be led to death.

Beatrice. Poor wretch, I pity thee: yet stay awhile.

Camillo. Guards, lead him not away.

    Beatrice,   Cardinal Camillo,   35
You have a good repute for gentleness
And wisdom: can it be that you sit here
To countenance a wicked farce like this?
When some obscure and trembling slave is dragged
From sufferings which might shake the sternest heart   40
And bade to answer, not as he believes,
But as those may suspect or do desire
Whose questions thence suggest their own reply:
And that in peril of such hideous torments
As merciful God spares even the damned. Speak now   45
The thing you surely know, which is that you,
If your fine frame were stretched upon that wheel,
And you were told: 'Confess that you did poison
Your little nephew; that fair blue-eyed child
Who was the lodestar of your life:'—and though   50
All see, since his most swift and piteous death,
That day and night, and heaven and earth, and time,
And all the things hoped for or done therein
Are changed to you, through your exceeding grief,
Yet you would say, 'I confess anything:'   55
And beg from your tormentors, like that slave,
The refuge of dishonourable death.
I pray thee, Cardinal, that thou assert
My innocence.

    Camillo (*much moved*). What shall we think, my Lords?
Shame on these tears! I thought the heart was frozen   60
Which is their fountain. I would pledge my soul
That she is guiltless.

    Judge.   Yet she must be tortured.

    Camillo. I would as soon have tortured mine own nephew
(If he now lived he would be just her age;
His hair, too, was her colour, and his eyes   65
Like hers in shape, but blue and not so deep)
As that most perfect image of God's love
That ever came sorrowing upon the earth.
She is as pure as speechless infancy!

    Judge. Well, be her purity on your head, my Lord,   70
If you forbid the rack. His Holiness
Enjoined us to pursue this monstrous crime
By the severest forms of law; nay, even
To stretch a point against the criminals.
The prisoners stand accused of parricide   75

Upon such evidence as justifies
Torture.
    Beatrice. What evidence? This man's?
    Judge.   Even so.
    Beatrice (*to* MARZIO). Come near. And who art thou thus chosen
       forth
Out of the multitude of living men
To kill the innocent?
    Marzio.   I am Marzio,   80
Thy father's vassal.
    Beatrice.   Fix thine eyes on mine;
Answer to what I ask.   [*Turning to the* JUDGES.
                  I prithee mark
His countenance: unlike bold calumny
Which sometimes dares not speak the thing it looks,
He dares not look the thing he speaks, but bends   85
His gaze on the blind earth.
(*To* MARZIO.)   .What! wilt thou say
That I did murder my own father?
    Marzio.   Oh!
Spare me! My brain swims round . . . I cannot speak . . .
It was that horrid torture forced the truth.
Take me away! Let her not look on me!   90
I am a guilty miserable wretch;
I have said all I know; now, let me die!
    Beatrice. My Lords, if by my nature I had been
So stern, as to have planned the crime alleged,
Which your suspicions dictate to this slave,   95
And the rack makes him utter, do you think
I should have left this two-edged instrument
Of my misdeed; this man, this bloody knife
With my own name engraven on the heft,
Lying unsheathed amid a world of foes,   100
For my own death? That with such horrible need
For deepest silence, I should have neglected
So trivial a precaution, as the making
His tomb the keeper of a secret written
On a thief's memory? What is his poor life?   105
What are a thousand lives? A parricide
Had trampled them like dust; and, see, he lives!
(*Turning to* MARZIO.) And thou . . .
    Marzio.   Oh, spare me! Speak to me no more!
That stern yet piteous look, those solemn tones,
Wound worse than torture.
    (*To the* JUDGES.)   I have told it all;   110
For pity's sake lead me away to death.
    Camillo. Guards, lead him nearer the Lady Beatrice,

He shrinks from her regard like autumn's leaf
From the keen breath of the serenest north.
   Beatrice. O thou who tremblest on the giddy verge   115
Of life and death, pause ere thou answerest me;
So mayst thou answer God with less dismay:
What evil have we done thee? I, alas!
Have lived but on this earth a few sad years,
And so my lot was ordered, that a father   120
First turned the moments of awakening life
To drops, each poisoning youth's sweet hope; and then
Stabbed with one blow my everlasting soul;
And my untainted fame; and even that peace
Which sleeps within the core of the heart's heart;   125
But the wound was not mortal; so my hate
Became the only worship I could lift
To our great father, who in pity and love,
Armed thee, as thou dost say, to cut him off;
And thus his wrong becomes my accusation;   130
And art thou the accuser? If thou hopest
Mercy in heaven, show justice upon earth:
Worse than a bloody hand is a hard heart.
If thou hast done murders, made thy life's path
Over the trampled laws of God and man,   135
Rush not before thy Judge, and say: 'My maker,
I have done this and more; for there was one
Who was most pure and innocent on earth;
And because she endured what never any
Guilty or innocent endured before: 140
Because her wrongs could not be told, not thought;
Because thy hand at length did rescue her;
I with my words killed her and all her kin.'
Think, I adjure you, what it is to slay
The reverence living in the minds of men   145
Towards our ancient house, and stainless fame!
Think what it is to strangle infant pity,
Cradled in the belief of guileless looks,
Till it become a crime to suffer. Think
What 'tis to blot with infamy and blood   150
All that which shows like innocence, and is,
Hear me, great God! I swear, most innocent,
So that the world lose all discrimination
Between the sly, fierce, wild regard of guilt,
And that which now compels thee to reply   155
To what I ask: Am I or am I not
A parricide?
   Marzio.   Thou art not!
   Judge.   What is this?

Marzio. I here declare those whom I did accuse
Are innocent. 'Tis I alone am guilty.
 Judge. Drag him away to torments; let them be   160
Subtle and long drawn out, to tear the folds '
Of the heart's inmost cell. Unbind him not
Till he confess.
 Marzio. Torture me as ye will:
A keener pang has wrung a higher truth
From my last breath. She is most innocent!   165
Bloodhounds, not men, glut yourselves well with me;
I will not give you that fine piece of nature
To rend and ruin.

         [Exit MARZIO, *guarded.*

 Camillo. What say ye now, my Lords?
 Judge. Let tortures strain the truth till it be white
As snow thrice sifted by the frozen wind.   170
 Camillo. Yet stained with blood.
 Judge (to BEATRICE.) Know you this paper, Lady?
 Beatrice. Entrap me not with questions. Who stands here
As my accuser? Ha! wilt thou be he,
Who art my judge? Accuser, witness, judge,
What, all in one? Here is Orsino's name;   175
Where is Orsino? Let his eye meet mine.
What means this scrawl? Alas! ye know not what,
And therefore on the chance that it may be
Some evil, will ye kill us?

     Enter an Officer.

 Officer.   Marzio's dead.
 Judge. What did he say?
 Officer.   Nothing. As soon as we   180
Had bound him on the wheel, he smiled on us,
As one who baffles a deep adversary;
And holding his breath, died.
 Judge.   There remains nothing
But to apply the question to those prisoners,
Who yet remain stubborn.
 Camillo.   I overrule   185
Further proceedings, and in the behalf
Of these most innocent and noble persons
Will use my interest with the Holy Father.
 Judge. Let the Pope's pleasure then be done. **Meanwhile**
Conduct these culprits each to separate cells;   190
And be the engines ready: for this night
If the Pope's resolution be as grave,
Pious, and just as once, I'll wring the truth
Out of those nerves and sinews, groan by groan. *[Exeunt.*

Scene III.—*The Cell of a Prison.* Beatrice *is discovered asleep on a couch. Enter* Bernardo.

Bernardo. How gently slumber rests upon her face,
Like the last thoughts of some day sweetly spent
Closing in night and dreams, and so prolonged.
After such torments as she bore last night,
How light and soft her breathing comes. Ay me!   5
Methinks that I shall never sleep again.
But I must shake the heavenly dew of rest
From this sweet folded flower, thus . . . wake! awake!
What, sister, canst thou sleep?
    Beatrice (awaking).   I was just dreaming
That we were all in Paradise. Thou knowest   10
This cell seems like a kind of Paradise
After our father's presence.
    Bernardo.   Dear, dear sister.
Would that thy dream were not a dream! O God!
How shall I tell?
    Beatrice.   What wouldst thou tell, sweet brother?
    Bernardo. Look not so calm and happy, or even whilst   15
I stand considering what I have to say
My heart will break.
    Beatrice.   See now, thou mak'st me weep:
How very friendless thou wouldst be, dear child,
If I were dead. Say what thou hast to say.
    Bernardo. They have confessed; they could endure no more
The tortures . . .
    Beatrice.   Ha! What was there to confess?   21
They must have told some weak and wicked lie
To flatter their tormentors. Have they said
That they were guilty? O white innocence,
That thou shouldst wear the mask of guilt to hide   25
Thine awful and serenest countenance
From those who know thee not!

    Enter Judge *with* Lucretia *and* Giacomo, *guarded.*

                   Ignoble hearts!
For some brief spasms of pain, which are at least
As mortal as the limbs through which they pass,
Are centuries of high splendour laid in dust?   30
And that eternal honour which should live
Sunlike, above the reek of mortal fame,
Changed to a mockery and a byword? What!
Will you give up these bodies to be dragged
At horses' heels, so that our hair should sweep   35
The footsteps of the vain and senseless crowd,

Who, that they may make our calamity
Their worship and their spectacle, will leave
The churches and the theatres as void
As their own hearts? Shall the light multitude   40
Fling, at their choice, curses or faded pity,
Sad funeral flowers to deck a living corpse,
Upon us as we pass to pass away,
And leave . . . what memory of our having been?
Infamy, blood, terror, despair? O thou,   45
Who wert a mother to the parentless,
Kill not thy child! Let not her wrongs kill thee!
Brother, lie down with me upon the rack,
And let us each be silent as a corpse;
It soon will be as soft as any grave.   50
'Tis but the falsehood it can wring from fear
Makes the rack cruel.
    Giacomo.   They will tear the truth
Even from thee at last, those cruel pains:
For pity's sake say thou art guilty now.
    Lucretia. Oh, speak the truth! Let us all quickly die;   55
And after death, God is our judge, not they;
He will have mercy on us.
    Bernardo.   If indeed
It can be true, say so, dear sister mine;
And then the Pope will surely pardon you,
And all be well.
    Judge.   Confess, or I will warp   60
Your limbs with such keen tortures . . .
    Beatrice.   Tortures! Turn
The rack henceforth into a spinning-wheel!
Torture your dog, that he may tell when last
He lapped the blood his master shed . . . not me!
My pangs are of the mind, and of the heart,   65
And of the soul; ay, of the inmost soul,
Which weeps within tears as of burning gall
To see, in this ill world where none are true,
My kindred false to their deserted selves.
And with considering all the wretched life   70
Which I have lived, and its now wretched end,
And the small justice shown by Heaven and Earth
To me or mine; and what a tyrant thou art,
And what slaves these; and what a world we make,
The oppressor and the oppressed . . . such pangs compel
My answer. What is it thou wouldst with me?   76
    Judge. Art thou not guilty of thy father's death?
    Beatrice. Or wilt thou rather tax high-judging God
That He permitted such an act as that

Which I have suffered, and which He beheld;   80
Made it unutterable, and took from it
All refuge, all revenge, all consequence,
But that which thou hast called my father's death?
Which is or is not what men call a crime,
Which either I have done, or have not done;   .   85
Say what ye will. I shall deny no more.
If ye desire it thus, thus let it be,
And so an end of all. Now do your will;
No other pains shall force another word.
    Judge. She is convicted, but has not confessed.   90
Be it enough. Until their final sentence
Let none have converse with them. You, young Lord,
Linger not here!
    Beatrice.   Oh, tear him not away!
    Judge. Guards, do your duty.
    Bernardo (*embracing* BEATRICE). Oh! would ye divide
Body from soul?
    Officer.   That is the headsman's business.   95
        [*Exeunt all but* LUCRETIA,. BEATRICE, *and* GIACOMO.
    Giacomo. Have I confessed? Is it all over now?
No hope! No refuge! O weak, wicked tongue
Which hast destroyed me, would that thou hadst been
Cut out and thrown to dogs first! To have killed
My father first, and then betrayed my sister;   100
Ay, thee! the one thing innocent and pure
In this black guilty world, to that which I
So well deserve! My wife! my little ones!
Destitute, helpless, and I . . . Father! God!
Canst Thou forgive even the unforgiving,   105
When their full hearts break thus, thus! . . .
                [*Covers his face and weeps.*
    Lucretia.   O my child!
To what a dreadful end are we all come!
Why did I yield? Why did I not sustain
Those torments? Oh, that I were all dissolved
Into these fast and unavailing tears,   110
Which flow and feel not!
    Beatrice.   What 'twas weak to do,
'Tis weaker to lament, once being done;
Take cheer! The God who knew my wrong, and made
Our speedy act the angel of His wrath,   '
Seems, and but seems, to have abandoned us.   115
Let us not think that we shall die for this.
Brother, sit near me; give me your firm hand,
You had a manly heart. Bear up! Bear up!
O dearest Lady, put your gentle head

Upon my lap, and try to sleep awhile: 120
Your eyes look pale, hollow and overworn,
With heaviness of watching and slow grief.
Come, I will sing you some low, sleepy tune,
Not cheerful, nor yet sad; some dull old thing,
Some outworn and unused monotony,   125
Such as our country gossips sing and spin,
Till they almost forget they live: lie down!
So, that will do. Have I forgot the words?
Faith! They are sadder than I thought they were.

SONG

False friend, wilt thou smile or weep   130
When my life is laid asleep?
Little cares for a smile or a tear,
The clay-cold corpse upon the bier!
        Farewell! Heigho!
        What is this whispers low?   135
There is a snake in thy smile, my dear;
And bitter poison within thy tear.

Sweet sleep, were death like to thee,
Or if thou couldst mortal be,
I would close these eyes of pain;   140
When to wake? Never again.
        O World! Farewell!
        Listen to the passing bell!
It says, thou and I must part,   144
With a light and a heavy heart.   [*The scene closes.*

Scene IV.—*A Hall of the Prison. Enter* Camillo *and* Bernardo.

Camillo. The Pope is stern; not to be moved or bent.
He looked as calm and keen as is the engine
Which tortures and which kills, exempt itself
From aught that it inflicts; a marble form,
A rite, a law, a custom: not a man.   5
He frowned, as if to frown had been the trick
Of his machinery, on the advocates
Presenting the defences, which he tore
And threw behind, muttering with hoarse, harsh voice:
'Which among ye defended their old father   10
Killed in his sleep?' Then to another: 'Thou
Dost this in virtue of thy place; 'tis well.'
He turned to me then, looking deprecation,
And said these three words, coldly: 'They must die.'
    Bernardo. And yet you left him not?

Camillo.   I urged him still;
Pleading, as I could guess, the devilish wrong   16
Which prompted your unnatural parent's death.
And he replied: 'Paolo Santa Croce
Murdered his mother yester evening,
And he is fled. Parricide grows so rife   20
That soon, for some just cause no doubt, the young
Will strangle us all, dozing in our chairs.
Authority, and power, and hoary hair
Are grown crimes capital. You are my nephew,
You come to ask their pardon; stay a moment;   25
Here is their sentence; never see me more
Till, to the letter, it be all fulfilled.'
    Bernardo. O God, not so! I did believe indeed
That all you said was but sad preparation
For happy news. Oh, there are words and looks   30
To bend the sternest purpose! Once I knew them,
Now I forget them at my dearest need.
What think you if I seek him out, and bathe
His feet and robe with hot and bitter tears?
Importune him with prayers, vexing his brain   35
With my perpetual cries, until in rage
He strike me with his pastoral cross, and trample
Upon my prostrate head, so that my blood
May stain the senseless dust on which he treads,
And remorse waken mercy? I will do it!   40
Oh, wait till I return!   [*Rushes out.*
    Camillo.   Alas! poor boy!
A wreck-devoted seaman thus might pray
To the deaf sea.

        Enter LUCRETIA, BEATRICE, *and* GIACOMO, *guarded.*

    Beatrice.   I hardly dare to fear
That thou bring'st other news than a just pardon.
    Camillo. May God in heaven be less inexorable   45
To the Pope's prayers, than he has been to mine.
Here is the sentence and the warrant.
    Beatrice (*wildly*).
My God! Can it be possible I have
To die so suddenly? So young to go
Under the obscure, cold, rotting, wormy ground!   50
To be nailed down into a narrow place;
To see no more sweet sunshine; hear no more
Blithe voice of living thing; muse not again
Upon familiar thoughts, sad, yet thus lost—
How fearful! to be nothing! Or to be . . .   55

What? Oh, where am I? Let me not go mad!
Sweet Heaven, forgive weak thoughts! If there should be
No God, no Heaven, no Earth in the void world;
The wide, gray, lampless, deep, unpeopled world!
If all things then should be . . . my father's spirit,   60
His eye, his voice, his touch surrounding me;
The atmosphere and breath of my dead life!
If sometimes, as a shape more like himself,
Even the form which tortured me on earth,
Masked in gray hairs and wrinkles, he should come   65
And wind me in his hellish arms, and fix
His eyes on mine, and drag me down, down, down!
For was he not alone omnipotent
On Earth, and ever present? Even though dead,
Does not his spirit live in all that breathe,   70
And work for me and mine still the same ruin,
Scorn, pain, despair? Who ever yet returned
To teach the laws of Death's untrodden realm?
Unjust perhaps as those which drive us now,
Oh, whither, whither?
   Lucretia.   Trust in God's sweet love,   75
The tender promises of Christ: ere night,
Think, we shall be in Paradise.
   Beatrice.   'Tis past!
Whatever comes my heart shall sink no more.
And yet, I know not why, your words strike chill:
How tedious, false and cold seem all things. I   80
Have met with much injustice in this world;
No difference has been made by God or man,
Or any power moulding my wretched lot,
'Twixt good or evil, as regarded me.
I am cut off from the only world I know,   85
From light, and life, and love, in youth's sweet prime.
You do well telling me to trust in God,
I hope I do trust in Him. In whom else
Can any trust? And yet my heart is cold.
   [*During the latter speeches* GIACOMO *has retired conversing
         with* CAMILLO, *who now goes out;* GIACOMO *advances.*
   Giacomo. Know you not, Mother . . . Sister, know you not?
Bernardo even now is gone to implore   91
The Pope to grant our pardon.
   Lucretia.   Child, perhaps
It will be granted. We may all then live
To make these woes a tale for distant years:
Oh, what a thought! It gushes to my heart   95
Like the warm blood.

Beatrice.   Yet both will soon be cold.
Oh, trample out that thought! Worse than despair,
Worse than the bitterness of death, is hope:
It is the only ill which can find place
Upon the giddy, sharp and narrow hour   100
Tottering beneath us. Plead with the swift frost
That it should spare the eldest flower of spring:
Plead with awakening earthquake, o'er whose couch
Even now a city stands, strong, fair, and free;
Now stench and blackness yawn, like death. Oh, plead   105
With famine, or wind-walking Pestilence,
Blind lightning, or the deaf sea, not with man!
Cruel, cold, formal man; righteous in words,
In deeds a Cain. No, Mother, we must die:
Since such is the reward of innocent lives;   110
Such the alleviation of worst wrongs.
And whilst our murderers live, and hard, cold men,
Smiling and slow, walk through a world of tears
To death as to life's sleep; 'twere just the grave
Were some strange joy for us. Come, obscure Death,   115
And wind me in thine all-embracing arms!
Like a fond mother hide me in thy bosom,
And rock me to the sleep from which none wake.
Live ye, who live, subject to one another
As we were once, who now . . .

BERNARDO *rushes in.*

Bernardo.   Oh, horrible!   120
That tears, that looks, that hope poured forth in prayer,
Even till the heart is vacant and despairs,
Should all be vain! The ministers of death
Are waiting round the doors. I thought I saw
Blood on the face of one . . . What if 'twere fancy?   125
Soon the heart's blood of all I love on earth
Will sprinkle him, and he will wipe it off
As if 'twere only rain. O life! O world!
Cover me! let me be no more! To see
That perfect mirror of pure innocence   130
Wherein I gazed, and grew happy and good,
Shivered to dust! To see thee, Beatrice,
Who made all lovely thou didst look upon . . .
Thee, light of life . . . dead, dark! while I say, sister,
To hear I have no sister; and thou, Mother,   135
Whose love was as a bond to all our loves . . .
Dead! The sweet bond broken!

Enter CAMILLO *and Guards.*

                              They come! Let me
Kiss those warm lips before their crimson leaves
Are blighted . . . white . . . cold. Say farewell, before
Death chokes that gentle voice! Oh, let me hear   140
You speak!
    Beatrice.   Farewell, my tender brother. Think
Of our sad fate with gentleness, as now:
And let mild, pitying thoughts lighten for thee
Thy sorrow's load. Err not in harsh despair,
But tears and patience. One thing more, my child: 145
For thine own sake be constant to the love
Thou bearest us; and to the faith that I,
Though wrapped in a strange cloud of crime and shame,
Lived ever holy and unstained. And though
Ill tongues shall wound me, and our common name   150
Be as a mark stamped on thine innocent brow
For men to point at as they pass, do thou
Forbear, and never think a thought unkind
Of those, who perhaps love thee in their graves.
So mayest thou die as I do; fear and pain   155
Being subdued. Farewell! Farewell! Farewell!
    Bernardo. I cannot say, farewell!
    Camillo.   Oh, Lady Beatrice!
    Beatrice. Give yourself no unnecessary pain,
My dear Lord Cardinal. Here, Mother, tie
My girdle for me, and bind up this hair   160
In any simple knot; ay, that does well.
And yours I see is coming down. How often
Have we done this for one another; now
We shall not do it any more. My Lord,
We are quite ready. Well, 'tis very well.   165

THE END.

NOTE ON THE CENCI, BY MRS. SHELLEY

THE sort of mistake that Shelley made as to the extent of his own genius and powers, which led him deviously at first, but lastly into the direct track that enabled him fully to develop them, is a curious instance of his modesty of feeling, and of the methods which the human mind uses at once to deceive itself, and yet, in its very delusion, to make its way out of error into the path which Nature has marked out as its right one. He often incited me to attempt the writing a tragedy: he conceived that I possessed some dramatic talent, and he was always most earnest and energetic in his exhortations that I should cultivate any talent I possessed, to the utmost. I entertained a truer estimate of my powers; and above all (though at that time not exactly aware of the fact) I was far too young to have any chance of succeeding, even moderately, in a species of composition that requires a greater scope of experience in, and sympathy with, human passion than could then have fallen to my lot,—or than any perhaps, except Shelley, ever possessed, even at the age of twenty-six, at which he wrote *The Cenci.*

On the other hand, Shelley most erroneously conceived himself to be destitute of this talent. He believed that one of the first requisites was the capacity of forming and following-up a story or plot. He fancied himself to be defective in this portion of imagination: it was that which gave him least pleasure in the writings of others, though he laid great store by it as the proper framework to support the sublimest efforts of poetry. He asserted that he was too metaphysical and abstract, too fond of the theoretical and the ideal, to succeed as a tragedian. It perhaps is not strange that I shared this opinion with himself; for he had hitherto shown no inclination for, nor given any specimen of his powers in framing and supporting the interest of a story, either in prose or verse. Once or twice, when he attempted such, he had speedily thrown it aside, as being even disagreeable to him as an occupation.

The subject he had suggested for a tragedy was Charles I: and he had written to me: 'Remember, remember Charles I. I have been already imagining how you would conduct some scenes. The second volume of *St. Leon* begins with this proud and true sentiment: "There is nothing which the human mind can conceive which it may not execute." Shakespeare was only a human being.' These words were written in 1818, while we were in Lombardy, when he little thought how soon a work of his own would prove a proud comment on the passage he quoted. When in Rome, in 1819, a friend put into our hands the old manuscript account of the story of the Cenci. We visited the Colonna and Doria palaces, where the portraits of Beatrice were to be found; and her beauty cast the reflection of its own grace over her appalling story. Shelley's imagination became strongly excited, and he urged the subject to me as one fitted for a tragedy. More than ever I felt my incompetence; but I entreated him to write it instead; and he began, and proceeded swiftly, urged on by intense sympathy with the sufferings of the human beings whose passions, so long cold in the tomb, he revived, and gifted with poetic language. This tragedy is the only one of his works that he communicated to me during its progress. We talked over the arrangement of the scenes together. I speedily saw the great mistake we had made, and triumphed in the discovery of the new talent brought to light from that mine of wealth (never, alas, through his untimely death, worked to its depths)— his richly gifted mind.

We suffered a severe affliction in Rome by the loss of our eldest child, who was of such beauty and promise as to cause him deservedly to be the idol of our hearts. We left the capital of the world, anxious for a time to escape a spot associated too intimately with his presence and loss.[1] Some friends of ours were residing in the neighbourhood of Leghorn, and we took a small house, Villa Valsovano, about half-way between the town and Monte Nero, where we remained during the summer. Our villa was situated in the midst of a *podere;* the peasants sang as they worked beneath our windows, during the heats of a very hot season, and in the evening the water-wheel creaked as the process of irrigation went on, and the fireflies flashed from among the myrtle hedges: Nature was bright, sunshiny, and cheerful, or diversified by storms of a majestic terror, such as we had never before witnessed.

At the top of the house there was a sort of terrace. There is often such in Italy, generally roofed: this one was very small, yet not only roofed but glazed. This Shelley made his study; it looked out on a wide prospect of fertile country, and commanded a view of the near sea. The storms that sometimes varied our day showed themselves most picturesquely as they were driven across the ocean; sometimes the dark lurid clouds dipped towards the waves, and became waterspouts that churned up the waters beneath, as they were chased onward and scattered by the tempest. At other times the dazzling sunlight and heat made it almost intolerable to every other; but Shelley basked in both, and his health and spirits revived under their influence. In this airy cell he wrote the principal part of *The Cenci.* He was making a study of Calderon at the time, reading his best tragedies with an accomplished lady living near us, to whom his letter from Leghorn was addressed during the following year. He admired Calderon, both for his poetry and his dramatic genius; but it shows his judgement and originality that, though greatly struck by his first acquaintance with the Spanish poet, none of his peculiarities crept into the composition of *The Cenci;* and there is no trace of his new studies, except in that passage to which he himself alludes as suggested by one in *El Purgatorio de San Patricio.*

Shelley wished *The Cenci* to be acted. He was not a playgoer, being of such fastidious taste that he was easily disgusted by the bad filling-up of the inferior parts. While preparing for our departure from England, however, he saw Miss O'Neil several times. She was then in the zenith of her glory; and Shelley was deeply moved by her impersonation of several parts, and by the graceful sweetness, the intense pathos, and sublime vehemence of passion she displayed. She was often in his thoughts as he wrote: and, when he had finished, he became anxious that his tragedy should be acted, and receive the advantage of having this accomplished actress to fill the part of the heroine. With this view he wrote the following letter to a friend in London:

[1] Such feelings haunted him when, in *The Cenci,* he makes Beatrice speak to Cardinal Camillo of

'that fair blue-eyed child
Who was the lodestar of your life:'—

and say—

'All see, since his most swift and piteous death,
That day and night, and heaven and earth, and time,
And all the things hoped for or done therein
Are changed to you, through your exceeding grief.'

'The object of the present letter is to ask a favour of you. I have written a tragedy on a story well known in Italy, and, in my conception, eminently dramatic. I have taken some pains to make my play fit for representation, and those who have already seen it judge favourably. It is written without any of the peculiar feelings and opinions which characterize my other compositions; I have attended simply to the impartial development of such characters as it is probable the persons represented really were, together with the greatest degree of popular effect to be produced by such a development. I send you a translation of the Italian MS. on which my play is founded; the chief circumstance of which I have touched very delicately; for my principal doubt as to whether it would succeed as an acting play hangs entirely on the question as to whether any such a thing as incest in this shape, however treated, would be admitted on the stage. I think, however, it will form no objection; considering, first, that the facts are matter of history, and, secondly, the peculiar delicacy with which I have treated it.[1]

'I am exceedingly interested in the question of whether this attempt of mine will succeed or not. I am strongly inclined to the affirmative at present; founding my hopes on this—that, as a composition, it is certainly not inferior to any of the modern plays that have been acted, with the exception of *Remorse;* that the interest of the plot is incredibly greater and more real; and that there is nothing beyond what the multitude are contented to believe that they can understand, either in imagery, opinion, or sentiment. I wish to preserve a complete incognito, and can trust to you that, whatever else you do, you will at least favour me on this point. Indeed, this is essential, deeply essential, to its success. After it had been acted, and successfully (could I hope for such a thing), I would own it if I pleased, and use the celebrity it might acquire to my own purposes.

'What I want you to do is to procure for me its presentation at Covent Garden. The principal character, Beatrice, is precisely fitted for Miss O'Neil, and it might even seem to have been written for her (God forbid that I should see her play it—it would tear my nerves to pieces); and in all respects it is fitted only for Covent Garden. The chief male character I confess I should be very unwilling that any one but Kean should play. That is impossible, and I must be contented with an inferior actor.'

The play was accordingly sent to Mr. Harris. He pronounced the subject to be so objectionable that he could not even submit the part to Miss O'Neil for perusal, but expressed his desire that the author would write a tragedy on some other subject, which he would gladly accept. Shelley printed a small edition at Leghorn, to ensure its correctness;

[1] In speaking of his mode of treating this main incident, Shelley said that it might be remarked that, in the course of the play, he had never mentioned expressly Cenci's worst crime. Every one knew what it must be, but it was never imaged in words—the nearest allusion to it being that portion of Cenci's curse beginning—
'That, if she have a child,' etc.

as he was much annoyed by the many mistakes that crèpt into his text when distance prevented him from correcting the press.

Universal approbation soon stamped *The Cenci* as the best tragedy of modern times. Writing concerning it, Shelley said: 'I have been cautious to avoid the introducing faults of youthful composition; diffuseness, a profusion of inapplicable imagery, vagueness, generality, and, as Hamlet says, *words, words.*' There is nothing that is not purely dramatic throughout; and the character of Beatrice, proceeding, from vehement struggle, to horror, to deadly resolution, and lastly to the elevated dignity of calm suffering, joined to passionate tenderness and pathos, is touched with hues so vivid and so beautiful that the poet seems to have read intimately the secrets of the noble heart imaged in the lovely countenance of the unfortunate girl. The Fifth Act is a masterpiece. It is the finest thing he ever wrote, and may claim proud comparison not only with any contemporary, but preceding, poet. The varying feelings of Beatrice are expressed with passionate, heart-reaching eloquence. Every character has a voice that echoes truth in its tones. It is curious, to one acquainted with the written story, to mark the success with which the poet has inwoven the real incidents of the tragedy into his scenes, and yet, through the power of poetry, has obliterated all that would otherwise have shown too harsh or too hideous in the picture. His success was a double triumph; and often after he was earnestly entreated to write again in a style that commanded popular favour, while it was not less instinct with truth and genius. But the bent of his mind went the other way; and, even when employed on subjects whose interest depended on character and incident, he would start off in another direction, and leave the delineations of human passion, which he could depict in so able a manner, for fantastic creations of his fancy, or the expression of those opinions and sentiments, with regard to human nature and its destiny, a desire to diffuse which was the master passion of his soul.

THE MASK OF ANARCHY

WRITTEN ON THE OCCASION OF THE MASSACRE AT MANCHESTER

I

As I lay asleep in Italy
There came a voice from over the
    Sea,
And with great power it forth led
    me
To walk in the visions of Poesy.

II

I met Murder on the way—   5
He had a mask like Castlereagh—
Very smooth he looked, yet grim;
Seven blood-hounds followed him:

III

All were fat; and well they might
Be in admirable plight,   10
For one by one, and two by two,
He tossed them human hearts to
    chew
Which from his wide cloak he drew.

IV

Next came Fraud, and he had on,
Like Eldon, an ermined gown;   15
His big tears, for he wept well,
Turned to mill-stones as they fell.

V

And the little children, who
Round his feet played to and fro,
Thinking every tear a gem,   20
Had their brains knocked out by
    them.

VI

Clothed with the Bible, as with
    light,
And the shadows of the night,
Like Sidmouth, next, Hypocrisy
On a crocodile rode by.   25

VII

And many more destructions
    played
In this ghastly masquerade,
All disguised, even to the eyes,
Like Bishops, lawyers, peers, or
    spies.

VIII

Last came Anarchy: he rode   30
On a white horse, splashed with
    blood;
He was pale even to the lips,
Like Death in the Apocalypse.

IX

And he wore a kingly crown;
And in his grasp a sceptre shone; 35
On his brow this mark I saw—
'I AM GOD, AND KING, AND LAW!'

X

With a pace stately and fast,
Over English land he passed,
Trampling to a mire of blood   40
The adoring multitude.

XI

And a mighty troop around,
With their trampling shook the
    ground,
Waving each a bloody sword,
For the service of their Lord.   45

XII

And with glorious triumph, they
Rode through England proud and
    gay,
Drunk as with intoxication
Of the wine of desolation.

XIII

O'er fields and towns, from sea to
    sea,   50
Passed the Pageant swift and free,
Tearing up, and trampling down;
Till they came to London town.

XIV

And each dweller, panic-stricken,
Felt his heart with terror sicken 55
Hearing the tempestuous cry
Of the triumph of Anarchy.

XV

For with pomp to meet him came,
Clothed in arms like blood and
    flame,
The hired murderers, who did
    sing   60
'Thou art God, and Law, and King.

XVI

'We have waited, weak and lone
For thy coming, Mighty One!
Our purses are empty, our swords
    are cold,
Give us glory, and blood, and
    gold.'   65

XVII

Lawyers and priests, a motley
    crowd,
To the earth their pale brows
    bowed;
Like a bad prayer not over loud,
Whispering—'Thou art Law and
    God.'—

XVIII

Then all cried with one accord, 70
'Thou art King, and God, and
    Lord;
Anarchy, to thee we bow,
Be thy name made holy now!'

XIX

And Anarchy, the Skeleton,
Bowed and grinned to every one, 75
As well as if his education
Had cost ten millions to the nation.

XX

For he knew the Palaces
Of our Kings were rightly his;
His the sceptre, crown, and globe,
And the gold-inwoven robe.   81

XXI

So he sent his slaves before
To seize upon the Bank and Tower,
And was proceeding with intent
To meet his pensioned Parlia-
    ment   85

XXII

When one fled past, a maniac maid,
And her name was Hope, she said:
But she looked more like Despair,
And she cried out in the air:

XXIII

'My father Time is weak and
    gray   90
With waiting for a better day;
See how idiot-like he stands,
Fumbling with his palsied hands!

XXIV

'He has had child after child,
And the dust of death is piled   95
Over every one but me—
Misery, oh, Misery!'

XXV

Then she lay down in the street,
Right before the horses' feet,
Expecting, with a patient eye,   100
Murder, Fraud, and Anarchy.

XXVI

When between her and her foes
A mist, a light, an image rose,
Small at first, and weak, and frail
Like the vapour of a vale: 105

XXVII

Till as clouds grow on the blast,
Like tower-crowned giants striding
    fast,
And glare with lightnings as they
    fly,
And speak in thunder to the sky,

XXVIII

It grew,—a Shape arrayed in mail
Brighter than the viper's scale, 111
And upborne on wings whose grain
Was as the light of sunny rain.

XXIX

On its helm, seen far away,
A planet, like the Morning's, lay;
And those plumes its light rained
    through   116
Like a shower of crimson dew.

XXX

With step as soft as wind it passed
O'er the heads of men—so fast
That they knew the presence there,
And looked,—but all was empty
    air.   121

XXXI

As flowers beneath May's footstep
    waken,
As stars from Night's loose hair
    are shaken,
As waves arise when loud winds
    call,
Thoughts sprung where'er that step
    did fall.   125

XXXII

And the prostrate multitude
Looked—and ankle-deep in blood,
Hope, that maiden most serene,
Was walking with a quiet mien:

XXXIII

And Anarchy, the ghastly birth, 130
Lay dead earth upon the earth;
The Horse of Death tameless as
    wind
Fled, and with his hoofs did grind
To dust the murderers thronged
    behind.

XXXIV

A rushing light of clouds and splen-
    dour,   135
A sense awakening and yet tender
Was heard and felt—and at its
    close
These words of joy and fear arose

XXXV

As if their own indignant Earth
Which gave the sons of England
    birth   140
Had felt their blood upon her brow,
And shuddering with a mother's
    throe

XXXVI

Had turnèd every drop of blood
By which her face had been be-
    dewed
To an accent unwithstood,—   145
As if her heart had cried aloud:

XXXVII

'Men of England, heirs of Glory,
Heroes of unwritten story,
Nurslings of one mighty Mother,
Hopes of her, and one another; 150

XXXVIII

'Rise like Lions after slumber
In unvanquishable number,
Shake your chains to earth like dew
Which in sleep had fallen on you—
Ye are many—they are few.   155

XXXIX

'What is Freedom?—ye can tell
That which slavery is, too well—
For its very name has grown
To an echo of your own.

XL

' 'Tis to work and have such
    pay   160
As just keeps life from day to day
In your limbs, as in a cell
For the tyrants' use to dwell,

XLI

'So that ye for them are made
Loom, and plough, and sword, and
    spade,   165
With or without your own will bent
To their defence and nourishment.

XLII

' 'Tis to see your children weak
With their mothers pine and peak,
When the winter winds are bleak,—
They are dying whilst I speak. 171

XLIII

' 'Tis to hunger for such diet
As the rich man in his riot
Casts to the fat dogs that lie
Surfeiting beneath his eye;   175

XLIV

' 'Tis to let the Ghost of Gold
Take from Toil a thousandfold
More than e'er its substance could
In the tyrannies of old.

XLV

'Paper coin—that forgery   180
Of the title-deeds, which ye
Hold to something of the worth
Of the inheritance of Earth.

XLVI

' 'Tis to be a slave in soul
And to hold no strong control   185
Over your own wills, but be
All that others make of ye.

XLVII

'And at length when ye complain
With a murmur weak and vain
'Tis to see the Tyrant's crew   190
Ride over your wives and you—
Blood is on the grass like dew.

XLVIII

'Then it is to feel revenge
Fiercely thirsting to exchange
Blood for blood—and wrong for
         wrong—   195
Do not thus when ye are strong.

XLIX

'Birds find rest, in narrow nest
When weary of their wingèd quest;
Beasts find fare, in woody lair   199
When storm and snow are in the
         air.

L

'Asses, swine, have litter spread
And with fitting food are fed;
All things have a home but one—
Thou, Oh, Englishman, hast none!

LI

'This is Slavery—savage men,   205
Or wild beasts within a den
Would endure not as ye do—
But such ills they never knew.

LII

'What art thou Freedom? O! could
         slaves
Answer from their living graves   210
This demand—tyrants would flee
Like a dream's dim imagery:

LIII

'Thou art not, as impostors say,
A shadow soon to pass away,
A superstition, and a name   215
Echoing from the cave of Fame.

LIV

'For the labourer thou art bread,
And a comely table spread
From his daily labour come
In a neat and happy home.   220

LV

'Thou art clothes, and fire, and
         food
For the trampled multitude—
No—in countries that are free
Such starvation cannot be
As in England now we see.   225

LVI

'To the rich thou art a check,
When his foot is on the neck
Of his victim, thou dost make
That he treads upon a snake.

LVII

'Thou art Justice—ne'er for gold
May thy righteous laws be sold   231
As laws are in England—thou
Shield'st alike the high and low.

LVIII

'Thou art Wisdom—Freemen never
Dream that God will damn for ever
All who think those things untrue
Of which Priests make such ado. 237

LIX

'Thou art Peace—never by thee
Would blood and treasure wasted
    be
As tyrants wasted them, when
    all   240
Leagued to quench thy flame in
    Gaul.

LX

'What if English toil and blood
Was poured forth, even as a flood?
It availed, Oh, Liberty,
To dim, but not extinguish thee.

LXI

'Thou art Love—the rich have
    kissed   246
Thy feet, and like him following
    Christ,
Give their substance to the free
And through the rough world fol-
    low thee,

LXII

'Or turn their wealth to arms, and
    make   250
War for thy belovèd sake
On wealth, and war, and fraud—
    whence they
Drew the power which is their
    prey.

LXIII

'Science, Poetry, and Thought
Are thy lamps; they make the lot
Of the dwellers in a cot   256
So serene, they curse it not.

LXIV

'Spirit, Patience, Gentleness,
All that can adorn and bless
Art thou—let deeds, not words,
    express   260
Thine exceeding loveliness.

LXV

'Let a great Assembly be
Of the fearless and the free
On some spot of English ground
Where the plains stretch wide
    around.   265

LXVI

'Let the blue sky overhead,
The green earth on which ye tread,
All that must eternal be
Witness the solemnity.

LXVII

'From the corners uttermost   270
Of the bounds of English coast;
From every hut, village, and town
Where those who live and suffer
    moan
For others' misery or their own,

LXVIII

'From the workhouse and the
    prison
Where pale as corpses newly risen,
Women, children, young and old 277
Groan for pain, and weep for
    cold—

LXIX

'From the haunts of daily life
Where is waged the daily strife 280
With common wants and common
    cares
Which sows the human heart with
    tares—

LXX

'Lastly from the palaces
Where the murmur of distress
Echoes, like the distant sound 285
Of a wind alive around

LXXI

'Those prison halls of wealth and
    fashion,
Where some few feel such compas-
    sion
For those who groan, and toil, and
    wail
As must make their brethren pale—

LXXII

'Ye who suffer woes untold, 291
Or to feel, or to behold
Your lost country bought and sold
With a price of blood and gold—

LXXIII

'Let a vast assembly be, 295
And with great solemnity
Declare with measured words that
    ye
Are, as God has made ye, free—

LXXIV

'Be your strong and simple words
Keen to wound as sharpened
    swords,
And wide as targes let them be, 301
With their shade to cover ye.

LXXV

'Let the tyrants pour around
With a quick and startling sound,
Like the loosening of a sea, 305
Troops of armed emblazonry.

LXXVI

'Let the charged artillery drive
Till the dead air seems alive
With the clash of clanging wheels,
And the tramp of horses' heels. 310

LXXVII

'Let the fixèd bayonet
Gleam with sharp desire to wet
Its bright point in English blood
Looking keen as one for food.

LXXVIII

'Let the horsemen's scimitars 315
Wheel and flash, like sphereless
    stars
Thirsting to eclipse their burning
In a sea of death and mourning.

LXXIX

'Stand ye calm and resolute,
Like a forest close and mute, 320
With folded arms and looks which
    are
Weapons of unvanquished war,

LXXX

'And let Panic, who outspeeds
The career of armèd steeds
Pass, a disregarded shade 325
Through your phalanx undismayed.

LXXXI

'Let the laws of your own land,
Good or ill, between ye stand
Hand to hand, and foot to foot,
Arbiters of the dispute, 330

LXXXII

'The old laws of England—they
Whose reverend heads with age are
    gray,
Children of a wiser day;
And whose solemn voice must be
Thine own echo—Liberty! 335

LXXXIII

'On those who first should violate
Such sacred heralds in their state
Rest the blood that must ensue,
And it will not rest on you.

LXXXIV

'And if then the tyrants dare   340
Let them ride among you there,
Slash, and stab, and maim, and
    hew,—
What they like, that let them do.

LXXXV

'With folded arms and steady
    eyes,
And little fear, and less surprise,
Look upon them as they slay   346
Till their rage has died away.

LXXXVI

'Then they will return with shame
To the place from which they
    came,
And the blood thus shed will speak
In hot blushes on their cheek.   351

LXXXVII

'Every woman in the land
Will point at them as they stand—
They will hardly dare to greet
Their acquaintance in the street.355

LXXXVIII

'And the bold, true warriors
Who have hugged Danger in wars
Will turn to those who would be
    free,
Ashamed of such base company.

LXXXIX

'And that slaughter to the Nation
Shall steam up like inspiration, 361
Eloquent, oracular;
A volcano heard afar.

XC

'And these words shall then become
Like Oppression's thundered doom
Ringing through each heart and
    brain   366
Heard again—again—again—

XCI

'Rise like Lions after slumber
In unvanquishable number—
Shake your chains to earth like
    dew   370
Which in sleep had fallen on you—
Ye are many—they are few.'

NOTE ON THE MASK OF ANARCHY, BY MRS. SHELLEY

THOUGH Shelley's first eager desire to excite his countrymen to resist openly the oppressions existent during 'the good old times' had faded with early youth, still his warmest sympathies were for the people. He was a republican, and loved a democracy. He looked on all human beings as inheriting an equal right to possess the dearest privileges of our nature; the necessaries of life when fairly earned by labour, and intellectual instruction. His hatred of any despotism that looked upon the people as not to be consulted, or protected from want and ignorance, was intense. He was residing near Leghorn, at Villa Valsovano, writing *The Cenci*, when the news of the Manchester Massacre reached us; it roused in him violent emotions of indignation and compassion. The great truth that the many, if accordant and resolute, could control the few, as was shown some years after, made him long to teach his injured countrymen how to resist. Inspired by these feelings, he wrote the *Mask of Anarchy*, which he sent to his friend Leigh Hunt, to be inserted in the *Examiner*, of which he was then the Editor.

'I did not insert it,' Leigh Hunt writes in his valuable and interesting preface to this poem, when he printed it in 1832, 'because I thought that the public at large had not become sufficiently discerning to do justice to the sincerity and kind-heartedness of the spirit that walked in this flaming robe of verse.' Days of outrage have passed away, and with them the exasperation that would cause such an appeal to the many to be injurious. Without being aware of them, they at one time acted on his suggestions, and gained the day. But they rose when human life was respected by the Minister in power; such was not the case during the Administration which excited Shelley's abhorrence.

The poem was written for the people, and is therefore in a more popular tone than usual: portions strike as abrupt and unpolished, but many stanzas are all his own. I heard him repeat, and admired, those beginning

'My Father Time is old and gray,'

before I knew to what poem they were to belong. But the most touching passage is that which describes the blessed effects of liberty; it might make a patriot of any man whose heart was not wholly closed against his humbler fellow-creatures.

PETER BELL THE THIRD

By MICHING MALLECHO, Esq.

Is it a party in a parlour,
Crammed just as they on earth were
   crammed,
Some sipping punch—some sipping tea;
But, as you by their faces see,
All silent, and all—damned!
    Peter Bell, by W. WORDSWORTH.

OPHELIA.—What means this, my lord?
HAMLET.—Marry, this is Miching Mallecho; it means mischief.
    SHAKESPEARE.

DEDICATION

TO THOMAS BROWN, ESQ., THE YOUNGER, H.F.

DEAR TOM—Allow me to request you to introduce Mr. Peter Bell to the respectable family of the Fudges. Although he may fall short of those very considerable personages in the more active properties which characterize the Rat and the Apostate, I suspect that even you, their historian, will confess that he surpasses them in the more peculiarly legitimate qualification of intolerable dulness.

You know Mr. Examiner Hunt; well—it was he who presented me to two of the Mr. Bells. My intimacy with the younger Mr. Bell naturally sprung from this introduction to his brothers. And in presenting him to you, I have the satisfaction of being able to assure you that he is considerably the dullest of the three.

There is this particular advantage in an acquaintance with any one of the Peter Bells, that if you know one Peter Bell, you know three Peter Bells; they are not one, but three; not three, but one. An awful mystery, which, after having caused torrents of blood, and having been hymned by groans enough to deafen the music of the spheres, is at length illustrated to the satisfaction of all parties in the theological world, by the nature of Mr. Peter Bell.

Peter is a polyhedric Peter, or a Peter with many sides. He changes colours like a chameleon, and his coat like a snake. He is a Proteus of a Peter. He was at first sublime, pathetic, impressive, profound; then dull; then prosy and dull; and now dull—oh so very dull! it is an ultra-legitimate dulness.

You will perceive that it is not necessary to consider Hell and the Devil as supernatural machinery. The whole scene of my epic is in 'this world which is'—so Peter informed us before his conversion to *White Obi*—

> 'The world of all of us, *and where*
> *We find our happiness, or not at all.*'

Let me observe that I have spent six or seven days in composing this sublime piece; the orb of my moonlike genius has made the fourth part of its revolution round the dull earth which you inhabit, driving you mad, while it has retained its calmness and its splendour, and I have been fitting this its last phase 'to occupy a permanent station in the literature of my country.'

Your works, indeed, dear Tom, sell better; but mine are far superior. The public is no judge; posterity sets all to rights.

Allow me to observe that so much has been written of Peter Bell, that the present history can be considered only, like the *Iliad*, as a continuation of that series of cyclic poems, which have already been candidates for bestowing immortality upon, at the same time that they receive it from, his character and adventures. In this point of view I have violated no rule of syntax in beginning my composition with a conjunction; the full stop which closes the poem continued by me being, like the full stops at the end of the *Iliad* and *Odyssey,* a full stop of a very qualified import.

Hoping that the immortality which you have given to the Fudges, you will receive from them; and in the firm expectation, that when London shall be an habitation of bitterns; when St. Paul's and Westminster Abbey shall stand, shapeless and nameless ruins, in the midst of an unpeopled marsh; when the piers of Waterloo Bridge shall become the nuclei of islets of reeds and osiers, and cast the jagged shadows of their broken arches on the solitary stream, some transatlantic commentator will be weighing in the scales of some new and now unimagined system of criticism, the respective merits of the Bells and the Fudges, and their historians. I remain, dear Tom, yours sincerely,

MICHING MALLECHO.

December 1, 1819.

P.S.—Pray excuse the date of place; so soon as the profits of the publication come in, I mean to hire lodgings in a more respectable street.

PROLOGUE

PETER BELLS, one, two and three,
O'er the wide world wandering
    be.—
First, the antenatal Peter,
Wrapped in weeds of the same
    metre,
The so-long-predestined raiment 5
Clothed in which to walk his way
    meant
The second Peter; whose ambition
Is to link the proposition,
As the mean of two extremes—
(This was learned from Aldric's
    themes)   10
Shielding from the guilt of schism
The orthodoxal syllogism;
The First Peter—he who was
Like the shadow in the glass
Of the second, yet unripe,   15
His substantial antitype.—
Then came Peter Bell the Second,
Who henceforward must be reck-
    oned
The body of a double soul,
And that portion of the whole   20
Without which the rest would seem
Ends of a disjointed dream.—
And the Third is he who has
O'er the grave been forced to pass
To the other side, which is,—   25
Go and try else,—just like this.

Peter Bell the First was Peter
Smugger, milder, softer, neater,
Like the soul before it is
Born from *that* world into *this*. 30

The next Peter Bell was he,
Predevote, like you and me,
To good or evil as may come;
His was the severer doom,—
For he was an evil Cotter,   35
And a polygamic Potter.[1]
And the last is Peter Bell,
Damned since our first parents fell,
Damned eternally to Hell—
Surely he deserves it well!   40

PART THE FIRST

DEATH

I

AND Peter Bell, when he had been
    With fresh-imported Hell-fire
        warmed,
Grew serious—from his dress and
        mien
'Twas very plainly to be seen
    Peter was quite reformed.   5

II

His eyes turned up, his mouth
        turned down;
    His accent caught a nasal twang;
He oiled his hair; [2] there might be
        heard
The grace of God in every word
    Which Peter said or sang.   10

III

But Peter now grew old, and had
    An ill no doctor could unravel;

---

[1] The oldest scholiasts read—
        A *dodecagamic* Potter.
This is at once more descriptive and more megalophonous,—but the alliteration of
the text had captivated the vulgar ear of the herd of later commentators.—
[SHELLEY'S NOTE.]

[2] To those who have not duly appreciated the distinction between *Whale*
and *Russia* oil, this attribute might rather seem to belong to the Dandy than the
Evangelic. The effect, when to the windward, is indeed so similar, that it requires
a subtle naturalist to discriminate the animals. They belong, however, to distinct
genera.—[SHELLEY'S NOTE.]

His torments almost drove him
    mad;—
Some said it was a fever bad—
    Some swore it was the gravel. 15

IV

His holy friends then came about,
    And with long preaching and
    persuasion
Convinced the patient that, with-
    out
The smallest shadow of a doubt,
    He was predestined to damna-
    tion. 20

V

They said—'Thy name is Peter
    Bell;
    Thy skin is of a brimstone hue;
Alive or dead—ay, sick or well—
The one God made to rhyme with
    hell;
    The other, I think, rhymes with
    you.' 25

VI

Then Peter set up such a yell!—
    The nurse, who with some water
    gruel
Was climbing up the stairs, as well
As her old legs could climb them—
    fell,
    And broke them both—the fall
    was cruel. 30

VII

The Parson from the casement lept
    Into the lake of Windermere—
And many an eel—though no adept
In God's right reason for it—
    kept 34
    Gnawing his kidneys half a year.

VIII

And all the rest rushed through the
    door,

And tumbled over one another,
And broke their skulls.—Upon the
    floor
Meanwhile sat Peter Bell, and
    swore,
    And cursed his father and his
    mother; 40

IX

And raved of God, and sin, and
    death,
    Blaspheming like an infidel;
And said, that with his clenchèd
    teeth
He'd seize the earth from under-
    neath,
    And drag it with him down to
    hell. 45

X

As he was speaking came a spasm,
    And wrenched his gnashing teeth
    asunder;
Like one who sees a strange phan-
    tasm
He lay,—there was a silent
    chasm 49
    Between his upper jaw and un-
    der.

XI

And yellow death lay on his face;
    And a fixed smile that was not
    human
Told, as I understand the case,
That he was gone to the wrong
    place:—
    I heard all this from the old
    woman. 55

XII

Then there came down from Lang-
    dale Pike
    A cloud, with lightning, wind
    and hail;
It swept over the mountains like
An ocean,—and I heard it strike
    The woods and crags of Gras-
    mere vale. 60

XIII

And I saw the black storm come
  Nearer, minute after minute; 62
Its thunder made the cataracts
    dumb;
With hiss, and clash, and hollow
    hum,
  It neared as if the Devil was
    in it. 65

XIV

The Devil *was* in it:—he had
    bought
  Peter for half-a-crown; and
    when
The storm which bore him van-
    ished, nought
That in the house that storm had
    caught
  Was ever seen again. 70

XV

The gaping neighbours came next
    day—
  They found all vanished from
    the shore:
The Bible, whence he used to pray,
Half scorched under a hen-coop
    lay;
  Smashed glass—and nothing
    more! 75

PART THE SECOND

THE DEVIL

I

THE DEVIL, I safely can aver,
  Has neither hoof, nor tail, nor
    sting;
Nor is he, as some sages swear,
A spirit, neither here nor there,
  In nothing—yet in everything. 80

II

He is—what we are; for sometimes
  The Devil is a gentleman;
At others a bard bartering rhymes
For sack; a statesman spinning
    crimes;
  A swindler, living as he can; 85

III

A thief, who cometh in the night,
  With whole boots and net pan-
    taloons,
Like some one whom it were not
    right
To mention;—or the luckless
    wight
  From whom he steals nine silver
    spoons. 90

IV

But in this case he did appear
  Like a slop-merchant from Wap-
    ping,
And with smug face, and eye se-
    vere,
On every side did perk and peer 94
  Till he saw Peter dead or nap-
    ping.

V

He had on an upper Benjamin
  (For he was of the driving
    schism)
In the which he wrapped his skin
From the storm he travelled in,
  For fear of rheumatism. 100

VI

He called the ghost out of the
    corse;—
  It was exceedingly like Peter,—
Only its voice was hollow and
    hoarse—
It had a queerish look of course—
  Its dress too was a little
    neater. 105

VII

The Devil knew not his name and
  lot;
  Peter knew not that he was
    Bell:
Each had an upper stream of
  thought,
Which made all seem as it was not;
  Fitting itself to all things
    well.   110

VIII

Peter thought he had parents dear,
  Bothers, sisters, cousins, cro-
    nies,
In the fens of Lincolnshire;
He perhaps had found them there
  Had he gone and boldly shown
    his   115

IX

Solemn phiz in his own village;
  Where he thought oft when a
    boy
He'd clomb the orchard walls to
  pillage
The produce of his neighbour's
  tillage,
  With marvellous pride and
    joy.   120

X

And the Devil thought he had,
  'Mid the misery and confusion
Of an unjust war, just made
A fortune by the gainful trade
Of giving soldiers rations bad— 125
  The world is full of strange de-
    lusion—

XI

That he had a mansion planned
  In a square like Grosvenor
    Square,
That he was aping fashion, and

That he now came to Westmoreland   130
  To see what was romantic there.

XII

And all this, though quite ideal,—
  Ready at a breath to vanish,—
Was a state not more unreal
Than the peace he could not
  feel,   135
  Or the care he could not banish.

XIII

After a little conversation,
  The Devil told Peter, if he chose,
He'd bring him to the world of
  fashion
By giving him a situation   140
  In his own service—and new
    clothes.

XIV

And Peter bowed, quite pleased
  and proud,
  And after waiting some few days
For a new livery—dirty yellow
Turned up with black—the wretch-
  ed fellow   145
  Was bowled to Hell in the
    Devil's chaise.

PART THE THIRD

HELL

I

HELL is a city much like London—
  A populous and a smoky city;
There are all sorts of people un-
  done,
And there is little or no fun
  done;   150
  Small justice shown, and still less
    pity.

II

There is a Castles, and a Canning,
  A Cobbett, and a Castlereagh;
All sorts of caitiff corpses planning
All sorts of cozening for trepan-
      ning   155
  Corpses less corrupt than they.

III

There is a * * * , who has lost
  His wits, or sold them, none
      knows which;
He walks about a double ghost,
And though as thin as Fraud al-
      most—   160
  Ever grows more grim and rich.

IV

There is a Chancery Court; a
      King;
  A manufacturing mob; a set
Of thieves who by themselves are
      sent
Similar thieves to represent; 165
  An army; and a public debt.

V

Which last is a scheme of paper
      money,
  And means—being interpret-
      ed—
'Bees, keep your wax—give us the
      honey,
And we will plant, while skies are
      sunny,   170
  Flowers, which in winter serve
      instead.'

VI

There is a great talk of revolu-
      tion—
  And a great chance of despot-
      ism—
German soldiers—camps—confu-
      sion—
Tumults — lotteries — rage — de-
      lusion—   175
  Gin—suicide—and methodism;

VII

Taxes too, on wine and bread,
  And meat, and beer, and tea, and
      cheese,
From which those patriots pure are
      fed,   179
Who gorge before they reel to bed
  The tenfold essence of all these.

VIII

There are mincing women, mew-
      ing,
  (Like cats, who *amant miserè*,[1])
Of their own virtue, and pursuing
Their gentler sisters to that ruin,
  Without which—what were chas-
      tity? [2]   186

IX

Lawyers—judges—old hobnobbers
  Are there — bailiffs — chancel-
      lors—
Bishops—great and little robbers—
Rhymesters—pamphleteers—
      stock-jobbers—   190
  Men of glory in the wars,—

---

[1] One of the attributes in Linnaeus's description of the Cat. To a similar cause the caterwauling of more than one species of this genus is to be referred;—except, indeed, that the poor quadruped is compelled to quarrel with its own pleasures, whilst the biped is supposed only to quarrel with those of others.—[SHELLEY'S NOTE.]

[2] What would this husk and excuse for a virtue be without its kernel prostitution, or the kernel prostitution without this husk of a virtue? I wonder the women of the town do not form an association, like the Society for the Suppression of Vice, for the support of what may be called the 'King, Church, and Constitution' of their order. But this subject is almost too horrible for a joke.—[SHELLEY'S NOTE.]

X

Things whose trade is, over ladies
    To lean, and flirt, and stare, and
      simper,
Till all that is divine in woman
Grows cruel, courteous, smooth, in-
      human,   195
    Crucified 'twixt a smile and
      whimper.

XI

Thrusting, toiling, wailing, moil-
      ing,
    Frowning, preaching—such a
      riot!
Each with never-ceasing labour,
Whilst he thinks he cheats his
      neighbour,   200
    Cheating his own heart of quiet.

XII

And all these meet at levees;—
    Dinners convivial and politi-
      cal;—
Suppers of epic poets;—teas,
    Where small talk dies in agonies;—
    Breakfasts professional and crit-
      ical;   206

XIII

Lunches and snacks so aldermanic
    That one would furnish forth ten
      dinners,
Where reigns a Cretan-tonguèd
      panic,
Lest news Russ, Dutch, or Ale-
      mannic   210
    Should make some losers, and
      some winners;—

XIV

At conversazioni—balls—
    Conventicles—and drawing-
      rooms—

Courts of law—committees—calls
Of a morning—clubs—book-
      stalls—
    Churches—masquerades—and
      tombs.   216

XV

And this is Hell—and in this
      smother
All are damnable and damned;
Each one damning, damns the
      other;
They are damned by one another,
By none other are they damned. 221

XVI

'Tis a lie to say, 'God damns [1]!'
    Where was Heaven's Attorney
      General
When they first gave out such
      flams?
Let there be an end of shams,   225
    They are mines of poisonous
      mineral.

XVII

Statesmen damn themselves to be
    Cursed; and lawyers damn their
      souls
To the auction of a fee;
Churchmen damn themselves to
      see
    God's sweet love in burning coals.

XVIII

The rich are damned, beyond all
      cure,   232
    To taunt, and starve, and tram-
      ple on
The weak and wretched; and the
      poor
Damn their broken hearts to endure
    Stripe on stripe, with groan on
      groan.   236

---

[1] This libel on our national oath, and this accusation of all our countrymen of being in the daily practice of solemnly asseverating the most enormous falsehood, I fear deserves the notice of a more active Attorney General than that here alluded to.—[SHELLEY'S NOTE.]

XIX

Sometimes the poor are damned
    indeed
  To take,—not means for being
    blessed,—
But Cobbett's snuff, revenge; that
    weed
From which the worms that it doth
    feed   240
  Squeeze less than they before
    possessed.

XX

And some few, like we know who,
  Damned—but God alone knows
    why—   243
To believe their minds are given
To make this ugly Hell a Heaven;
  In which faith they live and die.

XXI

Thus, as in a town, plague-stricken,
  Each man be he sound or no
Must indifferently sicken;
As when day begins to thicken, 250
  None knows a pigeon from a
    crow,—

XXII

So good and bad, sane and mad,
  The oppressor and the oppressed;
Those who weep to see what others
Smile to inflict upon their brothers;
  Lovers, haters, worst and best;

XXIII

All are damned—they breathe an
    air,   257
  Thick, infected, joy-dispelling:
Each pursues what seems most fair,
Mining like moles, through mind,
    and there   260
Scoop palace-caverns vast, where
    Care
  In throned state is ever dwelling.

PART THE FOURTH

SIN

I

Lo, Peter in Hell's Grosvenor
    Square,
  A footman in the Devil's service!
And the misjudging world would
    swear   265
That every man in service there
  To virtue would prefer vice.

II

But Peter, though now damned,
    was not
  What Peter was before damna-
    tion.
Men oftentimes prepare a lot   270
Which ere it finds them, is not
    what
  Suits with their genuine station.

III

All things that Peter saw and felt
  Had a peculiar aspect to him;
And when they came within the
    belt   275
Of his own nature, seemed to melt,
  Like cloud to cloud, into him.

IV

And so the outward world uniting
  To that within him, he became
Considerably uninviting   280
To those who, meditation slighting,
  Were moulded in a different
    frame.

V

And he scorned them, and they
    scorned him;
  And he scorned all they did; and
    they
Did all that men of their own trim

Are wont to do to please their
   whim,   286
Drinking, lying, swearing, play.

VI

Such were his fellow-servants; thus
   His virtue, like our own, was
   built
Too much on that indignant fuss 290
Hypocrite Pride stirs up in us
   To bully one another's guilt.

VII

He had a mind which was somehow
   At once circumference and centre
Of all he might or feel or know; 295
Nothing went ever out, although
   Something did ever enter.

VIII

He had as much imagination
   As a pint-pot;—he never could
Fancy another situation,   300
From which to dart his contem-
   plation,
   Than that wherein he stood.

IX

Yet his was individual mind,
   And new created all he saw
In a new manner, and refined   305
Those new creations, and combined
   Them, by a master-spirit's law.

X

Thus—though unimaginative—
   An apprehension clear, intense,
Of his mind's work, had made alive
The things it wrought on; I believe
   Wakening a sort of thought in
     sense.   312

XI

But from the first 'twas Peter's drift
   To be a kind of moral eunuch,
He touched the hem of Nature's
   shift,   315

Felt faint—and never dared uplift
   The closest, all-concealing tunic.

XII

She laughed the while, with an arch
   smile,
   And kissed him with a sister's
   kiss,
And said—'My best Diogenes, 320
I love you well—but, if you please,
   Tempt not again my deepest
   bliss.

XIII

' 'Tis you are cold—for I, not coy,
   Yield love for love, frank, warm,
   and true;
And Burns, a Scottish peasant
   boy—   325
His errors prove it—knew my joy
   More, learnèd friend, than you.

XIV

'Bocca bacciata non perde ventura,
Anzi rinnuova come fa la luna:—
So thought Boccaccio, whose sweet
   words might cure a   330
Male prude, like you, from what
   you now endure, a
   Low-tide in soul, like a stagnant
   laguna.'

XV

Then Peter rubbed his eyes severe,
   And smoothed his spacious fore-
   head down
With his broad palm;—'twixt love
   and fear,   335
He looked, as he no doubt felt,
   queer,
   And in his dream sate down.

XVI

The Devil was no uncommon
   creature;
A leaden-witted thief—just huddled   339

Out of the dross and scum of na-
        ture;
A toad-like lump of limb and fea-
        ture,
    With mind, and heart, and fancy
        muddled.   342

XVII

He was that heavy, dull, cold thing,
    The spirit of evil well may be:
A drone too base to have a sting;
Who gluts, and grimes his lazy
        wing,
    And calls lust, luxury.   347

XVIII

Now he was quite the kind of wight
    Round whom collect, at a fixed
        aera,
Venison, turtle, hock, and claret,—
Good cheer—and those who come
        to share it—   351
    And best East Indian madeira!

XIX

It was his fancy to invite
    Men of science, wit, and learning,
Who came to lend each other light;
He proudly thought that his gold's
        might   356
    Had set those spirits burning.

XX

And men of learning, science, wit,
    Considered him as you and I
Think of some rotten tree, and sit
Lounging and dining under it,   361
    Exposed to the wide sky.

XXI

And all the while, with loose fat
        smile,
    The willing wretch sat winking
        there,   364
Believing 'twas his power that made
That jovial scene—and that all paid
    Homage to his unnoticed chair.

XXII

Though to be sure this place was
        Hell;
    He was the Devil—and all they—
What though the claret circled well,
And wit, like ocean, rose and fell?—
    Were damned eternally.   372

PART THE FIFTH

GRACE

I

Among the guests who often stayed
    Till the Devil's petits-soupers,
A man there came, fair as a
        maid,   375
    And Peter noted what he said,
        Standing behind his master's
        chair.

II

He was a mighty poet—and
    A subtle-souled psychologist;
All things he seemed to understand,
Of old or new—of sea or land— 381
    But his own mind—which was
        a mist.

III

This was a man who might have
        turned
    Hell into Heaven—and so in
        gladness
A Heaven unto himself have
        earned;
But he in shadows undiscerned   386
    Trusted,—and damned himself
        to madness.

IV

He spoke of poetry, and how
    'Divine it was—a light—a love—
A spirit which like wind doth blow
As it listeth, to and fro;   391
    A dew rained down from God
        above;

V

'A power which comes and goes like
    dream,
And which none can ever trace—
Heaven's light on earth—Truth's
    brightest beam.'   395
And when he ceased there lay the
    gleam
Of those words upon his face.

VI

Now Peter, when he heard such
    talk,
Would, heedless of a broken pate,
Stand like a man asleep, or balk 400
Some wishing guest of knife or fork,
    Or drop and break his master's
    plate.

VII

At night he oft would start and
    wake
Like a lover, and began
In a wild measure songs to make 405
On moor, and glen, and rocky lake,
    And on the heart of man—

VIII

And on the universal sky—
    And the wide earth's bosom
    green,—
And the sweet, strange mystery 410
Of what beyond these things may
    lie,
    And yet remain unseen.

IX

For in his thought he visited
    The spots in which, ere dead and
    damned,
He his wayward life had led;   415
Yet knew not whence the thoughts
    were fed
    Which thus his fancy crammed.

X

And these obscure remembrances
    Stirred such harmony in Peter,
That, whensoever he should please,
He could speak of rocks and trees
    In poetic metre.   422

XI

For though it was without a sense
    Of memory, yet he remembered
    well
Many a ditch and quick-set fence;
Of lakes he had intelligence,   426
    He knew something of heath and
    fell.

XII

He had also dim recollections
    Of pedlars tramping on their
    rounds;
Milk-pans and pails; and odd col-
    lections   430
Of saws, and proverbs; and reflec-
    tions
    Old parsons make in burying-
    grounds.

XIII

But Peter's verse was clear, and
    came
    Announcing from the frozen
    hearth
Of a cold age, that none might
    tame   435
The soul of that diviner flame
    It augured to the Earth:

XIV

Like gentle rains, on the dry plains,
    Making that green which late
    was gray,
Or like the sudden moon, that
    stains
Some gloomy chamber's window-
    panes   441
    With a broad light like day.

XV

For language was in Peter's hand
　　Like clay while he was yet a
　　　　potter;
And he made songs for all the
　　　　land,　　　　　445
Sweet both to feel and understand,
　As pipkins late to mountain Cot-
　　　ter.

XVI

And Mr. ——, the bookseller,
　Gave twenty pounds for some;—
　　　then scorning
A footman's yellow coat to wear,
Peter, too proud of heart, I fear, 451
　Instantly gave the Devil warn-
　　　ing.

XVII

Whereat the Devil took offence,
　And swore in his soul a great
　　　oath then,　　　　454
'That for his damned impertinence
He'd bring him to a proper sense
　Of what was due to gentlemen!'

PART THE SIXTH

DAMNATION

I

'O THAT mine enemy had written
　A book!'—cried Job:—a fearful
　　　curse,
If to the Arab, as the Briton,　460
'Twas galling to be critic-bitten:—
　The Devil to Peter wished no
　　　worse.

II

When Peter's next new book found
　　　vent,
　The Devil to all the first Reviews
A copy of it slyly sent,　　　465
With five-pound note as compli-
　　　ment,
　And this short notice—'Pray
　　　abuse.'

III

Then *seriatim,* month and quarter,
　Appeared such mad tirades.—
　　　One said—
'Peter seduced Mrs. Foy's daugh-
　　　ter,
Then drowned the mother in Ulls-
　　　water,　　　　471
　The last thing as he went to bed.'

IV

Another—'Let him shave his head!
　Where's Dr. Willis?—Or is he
　　　joking?
What does the rascal mean or
　　　hope,　　　　475
No longer imitating Pope,
　In that barbarian Shakespeare
　　　poking?'

V

One more, 'Is incest not enough?
　And must there be adultery too?
Grace after meat? Miscreant and
　　　Liar!　　　　480
Thief! Blackguard! Scoundrel!
　　　Fool! Hell-fire
　Is twenty times too good for you.

VI

'By that last book of yours WE
　　　think
　You've double damned yourself
　　　to scorn;
We warned you whilst yet on the
　　　brink　　　　485
You stood. From your black name
　　　will shrink
　The babe that is unborn.'

VII

All these Reviews the Devil made
　Up in a parcel, which he had
Safely to Peter's house con-
　　　veyed.　　　　490
For carriage, tenpence Peter paid—
　Untied them—read them—went
　　　half mad.

VIII

'What!' cried he, 'this is my reward
  For nights of thought, and days
    of toil?
Do poets, but to be abhorred   495
By men of whom they never heard,
  Consume their spirits' oil?

IX

'What have I done to them?—and
  who
  Is Mrs. Foy? 'Tis very cruel
To speak of me and Betty so!   500
Adultery! God defend me! Oh!
  I've half a mind to fight a duel.

X

'Or,' cried he, a grave look collecting,
  'Is it my genius, like the moon,
Sets those who stand her face in-
  specting,   505
That face within their brain reflecting,
Like a crazed bell-chime, out of
  tune?'

XI

For Peter did not know the town,
  But thought, as country readers
    do,
For half a guinea or a crown,   510
He bought oblivion or renown
  From God's own voice [1] in a re-
    view.

XII

All Peter did on this occasion
  Was, writing some sad stuff in
    prose.

It is a dangerous invasion   515
When poets criticize; their station
  Is to delight, not pose.

XIII

The Devil then sent to Leipsic fair
  For Born's translation of Kant's
    book;
A world of words, tail foremost,
  where
Right — wrong — false — true —
  and foul—and fair   521
  As in a lottery-wheel are shook.

XIV

Five thousand crammed octavo
  pages
  Of German psychologics,—he
Who his *furor verborum* as-
  suages   525
Thereon, deserves just seven
  months' wages
  More than will e'er be due to me.

XV

I looked on them nine several days,
  And then I saw that they were
    bad;
A friend, too, spoke in their dis-
  praise,—   530
He never read them;—with amaze
  I found Sir William Drummond
    had.

XVI

When the book came, the Devil
  sent
It to P. Verbovale,[2] Esquire,
With a brief note of compliment,

---

[1] *Vox populi, vox dei.* As Mr. Godwin truly observes of a more famous saying, *of some merit as a popular maxim, but totally destitute of philosophical accuracy.* —[SHELLEY'S NOTE.]

[2] Quasi, *Qui valet verba:—i. e.* all the words which have been, are, or may be expended by, for, against, with, or on him. A sufficient proof of the utility of this history. Peter's progenitor who selected this name seems to have possessed a *pure anticipated cognition* of the nature and modesty of this ornament of his posterity. —·[SHELLEY'S NOTE.]

By that night's Carlisle mail. It
   went,   536
And set his soul on fire.

XVII

Fire, which *ex luce praebens*
   fumum,
Made him beyond the bottom see
Of truth's clear well—when I and
   you, Ma'am,   540
Go, as we shall do, *subter humum,*
   We may know more than he.

XVIII

Now Peter ran to seed in soul
   Into a walking paradox;
For he was neither part nor whole,
Nor good, nor bad—nor knave nor
   fool;   546
   —Among the woods and rocks

XIX

Furious he rode, where late he
   ran,
   Lashing and spurring his tame
     hobby;
Turned to a formal puritan,   550
A solemn and unsexual man,—
   He half believed *White Obi.*

XX

This steed in vision he would ride,
   High trotting over nine-inch
     bridges,   554
With Flibbertigibbet, imp of pride,
Mocking and mowing by his side—
A mad-brained goblin for a guide—
   Over corn-fields, gates, and
     hedges.

XXI

After these ghastly rides, he came
   Home to his heart, and found
     from thence   560
Much stolen of its accustomed
   flame;

His thoughts grew weak, drowsy,
   and lame
   Of their intelligence.

XXII

To Peter's view, all seemed one
   hue;
   He was no Whig, he was no
     Tory;
No Deist and no Christian he;—566
He got so subtle, that to be
   Nothing, was all his glory.

XXIII

One single point in his belief
   From his organization sprung, 570
The heart-enrooted faith, the chief
Ear in his doctrines' blighted sheaf,
   That 'Happiness is wrong';

XXIV

So thought Calvin and Dominic;
   So think their fierce successors,
     who
Even now would neither stint nor
     stick   576
Our flesh from off our bones to pick,
   If they might 'do their do.'

XXV

His morals thus were under-
     mined:—
   The old Peter—the hard, old
     Potter—   580
Was born anew within his mind;
He grew dull, harsh, sly, unrefined,
   As when he tramped beside the
     Otter.[1]

XXVI

In the death hues of agony   584
   Lambently flashing from a fish,
Now Peter felt amused to see
Shades like a rainbow's rise and
   flee,
   Mixed with a certain hungry
     wish.

[1] A famous river in the new Atlantis of the Dynastophylic Pantisocratists.—
[SHELLEY'S NOTE.]

XXVII

So in his Country's dying face
    He looked—and, lovely as she
      lay,
Seeking in vain his last embrace, 591
Wailing her own abandoned case,
    With hardened sneer he turned
      away:

XXVIII

And coolly to his own soul said;—
    'Do you not think that we might
      make   595
A poem on her when she's dead:—
Or no—a thought is in my head—
    Her shroud for a new sheet I'll
      take:

XXIX

'My wife wants one.—Let who will
    bury
    This mangled corpse! And I and
      you,   600
My dearest Soul, will then make
    merry,
As the Prince Regent did with
    Sherry,—'
    'Ay—and at last desert me too.'

XXX

And so his Soul would not be
    gay,
    But moaned within him; like a
      fawn   605
Moaning within a cave, it lay
Wounded and wasting, day by
    day,
    Till all its life of life was gone.

XXXI

As troubled skies stain waters clear,
    The storm in Peter's heart and
      mind
Now made his verses dark and
    queer:
They were the ghosts of what they
    were,   612

Shaking dim grave-clothes in the
    wind.

XXXII

For he now raved enormous folly,
    Of Baptisms, Sunday-schools,
      and Graves,   615
'Twould make George Colman
    melancholy
To have heard him, like a male
    Molly,
    Chanting those stupid staves.

XXXIII

Yet the Reviews, who heaped abuse
    On Peter while he wrote for free-
      dom,   620
So soon as in his song they spy
The folly which soothes tyranny,
    Praise him, for those who feed
      'em.

XXXIV

'He was a man, too great to scan;—
    A planet lost in truth's keen
      rays:—   625
His virtue, awful and prodigious;—
He was the most sublime, religious,
    Pure-minded Poet of these days.'

XXXV

As soon as he read that, cried Peter,
    'Eureka! I have found the way
To make a better thing of metre 631
Than e'er was made by living crea-
    ture
    Up to this blessèd day.'

XXXVI

Then Peter wrote odes to the
    Devil;—
    In one of which he meekly said:
'May Carnage and Slaughter,   636
Thy niece and thy daughter,
May Rapine and Famine,
Thy gorge ever cramming,
    Glut thee with living and dead!

XXXVII

'May Death and Damnation, 641
And Consternation,
Flit up from Hell with pure intent!
Slash them at Manchester,
Glasgow, Leeds, and Chester; 645
Drench all with blood from Avon
   to Trent.

XXXVIII

'Let thy body-guard yeomen
Hew down babes and women,
And laugh with bold triumph till
   Heaven be rent!
When Moloch in Jewry   650
Munched children with fury,
It was thou, Devil, dining with pure
   intent.' ¹

PART THE SEVENTH

DOUBLE DAMNATION

I

THE Devil now knew his proper
   cue.—
Soon as he read the ode, he drove
To his friend Lord MacMurder-
   chouse's,   655
A man of interest in both houses,
   And said:—'For money or for
   love,

II

'Pray find some cure or sinecure;
   To feed from the superfluous
   taxes
A friend of ours—a poet—fewer 660
Have fluttered tamer to the lure
   Than he.' His lordship stands
   and racks his

III

Stupid brains, while one might
   count
   As many beads as he had
   boroughs,—
At length replies; from his mean
   front,   665
Like one who rubs out an account,
   Smoothing away the unmeaning
   furrows:

IV

'It happens fortunately, dear Sir,
   I can. I hope I need require
No pledge from you, that he will
   stir   670
In our affairs;—like Oliver,
   That he'll be worthy of his hire.'

V

These words exchanged, the news
   sent off
   To Peter, home the Devil hied,—
Took to his bed; he had no cough,
No doctor,—meat and drink
   enough,—   676
   Yet that same night he died.

VI

The Devil's corpse was leaded
   down;
   His decent heirs enjoyed his
   pelf,
Mourning-coaches, many a one, 680
Followed his hearse along the
   town:—
   Where was the Devil himself?

VII

When Peter heard of his promotion,
   His eyes grew like two stars for
   bliss:

¹ It is curious to observe how often extremes meet. Cobbett and Peter use the
same language for a different purpose: Peter is indeed a sort of metrical Cobbett.
Cobbett is, however, more mischievous than Peter, because he pollutes a holy and
now unconquerable cause with the principles of legitimate murder; whilst the
other only makes a bad one ridiculous and odious.
   If either Peter or Cobbett should see this note, each will feel more indignation
at being compared to the other than at any censure implied in the moral perver-
sion laid to their charge.—[SHELLEY'S NOTE.]

There was a bow of sleek devotion
Engendering in his back; each mo-
    tion   686
    Seemed a Lord's shoe to kiss.

VIII

He hired a house, bought plate, and
    made
A genteel drive up to his door,
With sifted gravel neatly laid,—690
As if defying all who said,
    Peter was ever poor.

IX

But a disease soon struck into
    The very life and soul of Peter—
He walked about—slept—had the
    hue   695
Of health upon his cheeks—and
    few
    Dug better—none a heartier
    eater.

X

And yet a strange and horrid curse
    Clung upon Peter, night and
    day;
Month after month the thing grew
    worse,   700
And deadlier than in this my verse
    I can find strength to say.

XI

Peter was dull—he was at first
    Dull—oh, so dull—so very dull!
Whether he talked, wrote, or re-
    hearsed—   705
Still with this dulness was he
    cursed—
    Dull—beyond all conception—
    dull.

XII

No one could read his books—no
    mortal,
    But a few natural friends, would
    hear him;

The parson came not near his
    portal;
His state was like that of the im-
    mortal   711
    Described by Swift—no man
    could bear him.

XIII

His sister, wife, and children
    yawned,
    With a long, slow, and drear
    ennui,
All human patience far beyond; 715
Their hopes of Heaven each would
    have pawned,
    Anywhere else to be.

XIV

But in his verse, and in his prose,
    The essence of his dulness was
Concentred and compressed so
    close,
'Twould have made Guatimozin
    doze
    On his red gridiron of brass. 722

XV

A printer's boy, folding those pages,
    Fell slumbrously upon one side;
Like those famed Seven who slept
    three ages.   725
To wakeful frenzy's vigil-rages,
    As opiates, were the same ap-
    plied.

XVI

Even the Reviewers who were hired
    To do the work of his reviewing,
With adamantine nerves, grew
    tired;—   730
Gaping and torpid they retired,
    To dream of what they should be
    doing.

XVII

And worse and worse, the drowsy
    curse

Yawned in him, till it grew a
　　pest—
A wide contagious atmosphere, 735
Creeping ˙like cold through all
　　things near;
　　A power to infect and to infest.

XVIII

His servant-maids and dogs grew
　　dull;
　　His kitten, late a sportive elf;
The woods and lakes, so beautiful,
　　Of dim stupidity were full, 741
　　All grew dull as Peter's self.

XIX

The earth under his feet—the
　　springs,
　　Which lived within it a quick life,
The air, the winds of many wings,
That fan it with new murmurings,
　　Were dead to their harmonious
　　　　strife.   747

XX

The birds and beasts within the
　　wood,
　　The insects, and each creeping
　　　thing,
Were now a silent multitude; 750
Love's work was left unwrought—
　　no brood
　　Near Peter's house took wing.

XXI

And every neighbouring cottager
　　Stupidly yawned upon the other:
No jackass brayed; no little cur 755
Cocked up his ears;—no man
　　would stir
　　To save a dying mother.

XXII

Yet all from that charmed dis-
　　trict went
But some half-idiot and half-
　　knave,
Who rather than pay any rent, 760
Would live with marvellous con-
　　tent,
　　Over his father's grave.

XXIII

No bailiff dared within that space,
　　For fear of the dull charm, to
　　　enter;
A man would bear upon his face, 765
For fifteen months in any case,
　　The yawn of such a venture.

XXIV

Seven   miles   above—below—
　　around—
　　This pest of dulness holds its
　　　sway;
A ghastly life without a sound; 770
To Peter's soul the spell is bound—
　　How should it ever pass away?

NOTE ON PETER BELL THE THIRD, BY MRS. SHELLEY

In this new edition I have added *Peter Bell the Third*. A critique on Wordsworth's *Peter Bell* reached us at Leghorn, which amused Shelley exceedingly, and suggested this poem.

I need scarcely observe that nothing personal to the author of *Peter Bell* is intended in this poem. No man ever admired Wordsworth's poetry more;—he read it perpetually, and taught others to appreciate its beauties. This poem is, like all others written by Shelley, ideal. He conceived the idealism of a poet—a man of lofty and creative genius—quitting the glorious calling of discovering and announcing the beautiful and good, to support and propagate ignorant prejudices and pernicious errors; imparting to the unenlightened, not that ardour for truth and spirit of toleration which Shelley looked on as the sources of the moral improvement and happiness of mankind, but false and injurious opinions, that evil was good, and that ignorance and force were the best allies of purity and virtue. His idea was that a man gifted, even as transcendently as the author of *Peter Bell*, with the highest qualities of genius, must, if he fostered such errors, be infected with dulness. This poem was written as a warning—not as a narration of the reality. He was unacquainted personally with Wordsworth, or with Coleridge (to whom he alludes in the fifth part of the poem), and therefore, I repeat, his poem is purely ideal;—it contains something of criticism on the compositions of those great poets, but nothing injurious to the men themselves.

No poem contains more of Shelley's peculiar views with regard to the errors into which many of the wisest have fallen, and the pernicious effects of certain opinions on society. Much of it is beautifully written: and, though, like the burlesque drama of *Swellfoot*, it must be looked on as a plaything, it has so much merit and poetry—so much of *himself* in it— that it cannot fail to interest greatly, and by right belongs to the world for whose instruction and benefit it was written.

OEDIPUS TYRANNUS

OR

SWELLFOOT THE TYRANT

A TRAGEDY IN TWO ACTS

TRANSLATED FROM THE ORIGINAL DORIC

'Choose Reform or Civil War,
When through thy streets, instead of hare with dogs,
A CONSORT-QUEEN shall hunt a KING with hogs,
Riding on the IONIAN MINOTAUR.'

ADVERTISEMENT

THIS Tragedy is one of a triad, or system of three Plays (an arrangement according to which the Greeks were accustomed to connect their dramatic representations), elucidating the wonderful and appalling fortunes of the SWELLFOOT dynasty. It was evidently written by some *learned Theban*, and, from its characteristic dulness, apparently before the duties on the importation of *Attic salt* had been repealed by the Boeotarchs. The tenderness with which he treats the PIGS proves him to have been a *sus Boeotiae;* possibly *Epicuri de grege porcus;* for, as the poet observes,

'A fellow feeling makes us wondrous kind.'

No liberty has been taken with the translation of this remarkable piece of antiquity, except the suppressing a seditious and blasphemous Chorus of the Pigs and Bulls at the last Act. The word Hoydipouse (or more properly Oedipus) has been rendered literally SWELLFOOT, without its having been conceived necessary to determine whether a swelling of the hind or the fore feet of the Swinish Monarch is particularly indicated.

Should the remaining portions of this Tragedy be found, entitled, *Swellfoot in Angaria,* and *Charité,* the Translator might be tempted to give them to the reading Public.

DRAMATIS PERSONAE

TYRANT SWELLFOOT, *King of Thebes.*
IONA TAURINA, *his Queen.*
MAMMON, *Arch-Priest of Famine.*
PURGANAX ⎫
DAKRY   ⎬ *Wizards, Ministers of*
LAOCTONOS ⎭   SWELLFOOT.

The GADFLY.
The LEECH.
The RAT.
MOSES, *the Sow-gelder.*
SOLOMON, *the Porkman.*
ZEPHANIAH, *Pig-butcher.*

The MINOTAUR.

CHORUS *of the Swinish Multitude.*

GUARDS, ATTENDANTS, PRIESTS, *etc., etc.*

SCENE.—THEBES

ACT I

SCENE I.—*A magnificent Temple, built of thigh-bones and death's-heads, and tiled with scalps. Over the Altar the statue of Famine, veiled; a number of Boars, Sows, and Sucking-Pigs, crowned with thistle, shamrock, and oak, sitting on the steps, and clinging round the Altar of the Temple.*

Enter SWELLFOOT, *in his Royal-robes, without perceiving the* PIGS.

   Swellfoot. Thou supreme Goddess! by whose power divine
These graceful limbs are clothed in proud array
               [*He contemplates himself with satisfaction.*
Of gold and purple, and this kingly paunch
Swells like a sail before a favouring breeze,
And these most sacred nether promontories   5
Lie satisfied with layers of fat; and these
Boeotian cheeks, like Egypt's pyramid,
(Nor with less toil were their foundations laid),[1]
Sustain the cone of my untroubled brain,
That point, the emblem of a pointless nothing!   10
Thou to whom Kings and laurelled Emperors,

---

[1] See Universal History for an account of the number of people who died, and the immense consumption of garlic by the wretched Egyptians, who made a sepulchre for the name as well as the bodies of their tyrants.—[SHELLEY'S NOTE.]

Radical-butchers, Paper-money-millers,
Bishops and Deacons, and the entire army
Of those fat martyrs to the persecution
Of stifling turtle-soup, and brandy-devils,   15
Offer their secret vows! Thou plenteous Ceres
Of their Eleusis, hail!

  The Swine. Eigh! eigh! eigh! eigh!
  Swellfoot.   Ha! what are ye,
Who, crowned with leaves devoted to the Furies,
Cling round this sacred shrine?

  Swine. Aigh! aigh! aigh!
  Swellfoot.   What! ye that are
The very beasts that, offered at her altar   20
With blood and groans, salt-cake, and fat, and inwards,
Ever propitiate her reluctant will
When taxes are withheld?

  Swine. Ugh! ugh! ugh!
  Swellfoot.   What! ye who grub
With filthy snouts my red potatoes up
In Allan's rushy bog? Who eat the oats   25
Up, from my cavalry in the Hebrides?
Who swill the hog-wash soup my cooks digest
From bones, and rags, and scraps of shoe-leather,
Which should be given to cleaner Pigs than you?

    The Swine.—Semichorus I.

    The same, alas! the same;   30
    Though only now the name
     Of Pig remains to me.

     Semichorus II.

    If 'twere your kingly will
    Us wretched Swine to kill,
     What should we yield to thee?   35
Swellfoot. Why, skin and bones, and some few hairs for mortar.

    Chorus of Swine.

  I have heard your Laureate sing,
   That pity was a royal thing;
  Under your mighty ancestors, we Pigs
  Were bless'd as nightingales on myrtle sprigs,   40
  Or grasshoppers that live on noonday dew,
  And sung, old annals tell, as sweetly too;
  But now our sties are fallen in, we catch
   The murrain and the mange, the scab and itch;
  Sometimes your royal dogs tear down our thatch,   45
   And then we seek the shelter of a ditch;

Hog-wash or grains, or ruta-baga, none
Has yet been ours since your reign begun.

First Sow.

My Pigs, 'tis in vain to tug.

Second Sow.

I could almost eat my litter.   50

First Pig.

I suck, but no milk will come from the dug.

Second Pig.

Our skin and our bones would be bitter.

The Boars.

We fight for this rag of greasy rug,
    Though a trough of wash would be fitter.

Semichorus.

Happier Swine were they than we,   55
Drowned in the Gadarean sea—
I wish that pity would drive out the devils,
Which in your royal bosom hold their revels,
And sink us in the waves of thy compassion!
Alas! the Pigs are an unhappy nation!   60
Now if your Majesty would have our bristles
    To bind your mortar with, or fill our colons
With rich blood, or make brawn out of our gristles,
    In policy—ask else your royal Solons—
You ought to give us hog-wash and clean straw,   65
And sties well thatched; besides it is the law!

Swellfoot. This is sedition, and rank blasphemy!
Ho! there, my guards!

Enter a GUARD.

Guard.   Your sacred Majesty.
Swellfoot. Call in the Jews, Solomon the court porkman,
Moses the sow-gelder, and Zephaniah   70
The hog-butcher.
Guard.   They are in waiting, Sire.

Enter SOLOMON, MOSES, *and* ZEPHANIAH.

Swellfoot. Out with your knife, old Moses, and spay those Sows
                    [*The* PIGS *run about in consternation.*
That load the earth with Pigs; cut close and deep.

Moral restraint I see has no effect,
Nor prostitution, nor our own example,   75
Starvation, typhus-fever, war, nor prison—
This was the art which the arch-priest of Famine
Hinted at in his charge to the Theban clergy—
Cut close and deep, good Moses.
    Moses.   Let your Majesty
Keep the Boars quiet, else——
    Swellfoot.   Zephaniah, cut   80
That fat Hog's throat, the brute seems overfed;
Seditious hunks! to whine for want of grains.
    Zephaniah. Your sacred Majesty, he has the dropsy;—
We shall find pints of hydatids in 's liver,
He has not half an inch of wholesome fat   85
Upon his carious ribs——
    Swellfoot.   'Tis all the same,
He'll serve instead of riot money, when
Our murmuring troops bivouac in Thebes' streets;
And January winds, after a day
Of butchering, will make them relish carrion.   90
Now, Solomon, I'll sell you in a lump
The whole kit of them.
    Solomon.   Why, your Majesty,
I could not give——
    Swellfoot.   Kill them out of the way,
That shall be price enough, and let me hear
Their everlasting grunts and whines no more!   95
               [*Exeunt, driving in the* SWINE.

Enter MAMMON, *the Arch-Priest; and* PURGANAX, *Chief of the Council
of Wizards.*

    Purganax. The future looks as black as death, a cloud,
Dark as the frown of Hell, hangs over it—
The troops grow mutinous—the revenue fails—
There's something rotten in us—for the level
Of the State slopes, its very bases topple,   100
The boldest turn their backs upon themselves!
    Mammon. Why what's the matter, my dear fellow, now?
Do the troops mutiny?—decimate some regiments;
Does money fail?—come to my mint—coin paper,
Till gold be at a discount, and ashamed   105
To show his bilious face, go purge himself,
In emulation of her vestal whiteness.
    Purganax. Oh, would that this were all! The oracle!!
    Mammon. Why it was I who spoke that oracle,
And whether I was dead drunk or inspired,   110

I cannot well remember; nor, in truth,
The oracle itself!
    Purganax.   The words went thus:—
'Boeotia, choose reform or civil war!
When through the streets, instead of hare with dogs,
A Consort Queen shall hunt a King with Hogs,   115
Riding on the Ionian Minotaur.'
    Mammon. Now if the oracle had ne'er foretold
This sad alternative, it must arrive,
Or not, and so it must now that it has;
And whether I was urged by grace divine   120
Or Lesbian liquor to declare these words,
Which must, as all words must, be false or true,
It matters not: for the same Power made all,
Oracle, wine, and me and you—or none—
'Tis the same thing. If you knew as much   125
Of oracles as I do——
    Purganax.   You arch-priests
Believe in nothing; if you were to dream
Of a particular number in the Lottery,
You would not buy the ticket?
    Mammon.   Yet our tickets
Are seldom blanks. But what steps have you taken?   .   130
For prophecies, when once they get abroad,
Like liars who tell the truth to serve their ends,
Or hypocrites who, from assuming virtue,
Do the same actions that the virtuous do,
Contrive their own fulfilment. This Iona——   135
Well—you know what the chaste Pasiphae did,
Wife to that most religious King of Crete,
And still how popular the tale is here;
And these dull Swine of Thebes boast their descent
From the free Minotaur. You know they still   140
Call themselves Bulls, though thus degenerate,
And everything relating to a Bull
Is popular and respectable in Thebes.
Their arms are seven Bulls in a field gules;
They think their strength consists in eating beef,—   145
Now there were danger in the precedent
If Queen Iona——
    Purganax.   I have taken good care
That shall not be. I struck the crust o' the earth
With this enchanted rod, and Hell lay bare!
And from a cavern full of ugly shapes   150
I chose a LEECH, a GADFLY, and a RAT.
The Gadfly was the same which Juno sent

To agitate Io,[1] and which Ezekiel [2] mentions
That the Lord whistled for out of the mountains
Of utmost Aethiopia, to torment   155
Mesopotamian Babylon. The beast
Has a loud trumpet like the scarabee,
His crookèd tail is barbed with many stings,
Each able to make a thousand wounds, and each
Immedicable; from his convex eyes   160
He sees fair things in many hideous shapes,
And trumpets all his falsehood to the world.
Like other beetles he is fed on dung—
He has eleven feet with which he crawls,
Trailing a blistering slime, and this foul beast   165
Has tracked Iona from the Theban limits,
From isle to isle, from city unto city,
Urging her flight from the far Chersonese
To fabulous Solyma, and the Aetnean Isle,
Ortygia, Melite, and Calypso's Rock,   170
And the swart tribes of Garamant and Fez,
Aeolia and Elysium, and thy shores,
Parthenope, which now, alas! are free!
And through the fortunate Saturnian land,
Into the darkness of the West.
    Mammon.   But if   175
This Gadfly should drive Iona hither?
    Purganax. Gods, what an *if!* but there is my gray RAT:
So thin with want, he can crawl in and out
Of any narrow chink and filthy hole,
And he shall creep into her dressing-room,   180
And——
    Mammon. My dear friend, where are your wits? as if
She does not always toast a piece of cheese
And bait the trap? and rats, when lean enough
To crawl through *such* chinks——
    Purganax.   But my LEECH—a leech
Fit to suck blood, with lubricous round rings,   185
Capaciously expatiative, which make
His little body like a red balloon,
As full of blood as that of hydrogen,
Sucked from men's hearts; insatiably he sucks
And clings and pulls—a horse-leech, whose deep maw   190
The plethoric King Swellfoot could not fill,
And who, till full, will cling for ever.
    Mammon.   This

---

[1] The *Prometheus Bound* of Aeschylus.—[SHELLEY'S NOTE.]
[2] And the Lord whistled for the gadfly out of Aethiopia, and for the bee of
Egypt, etc.—EZEKIEL.—[SHELLEY'S NOTE.]

For Queen Iona would suffice, and less;
But 'tis the Swinish multitude I fear,
And in that fear I have——
    Purganax.   Done what?
    Mammon.   Disinherited   195
My eldest son Chrysaor, because he
Attended public meetings, and would always
Stand prating there of commerce, public faith,
Economy, and unadulterate coin,
And other topics, ultra-radical;   200
And have entailed my estate, called the Fool's Paradise,
And funds in fairy-money, bonds, and bills,
Upon my accomplished daughter Banknotina,
And married her to the gallows.[1]
    Purganax.   A good match!
    Mammon. A high connexion, Purganax. The bridegroom
Is of a very ancient family,   206
Of Hounslow Heath, Tyburn, and the New Drop,
And has great influence in both Houses;—oh!
He makes the fondest husband; nay, *too* fond,—
New-married people should not kiss in public;   210
But the poor souls love one another so!
And then my little grandchildren, the gibbets,
Promising children as you ever saw,—
The young playing at hanging, the elder learning
How to hold radicals. They are well taught too,   215
For every gibbet says its catechism
And reads a select chapter in the Bible
Before it goes to play.
                       [*A most tremendous humming is heard.*
    Purganax.   Ha! what do I hear?

              Enter the GADFLY.

    Mammon. Your Gadfly, as it seems, is tired of gadding.

                  Gadfly.

            Hum! hum! hum!   220
From the lakes of the Alps, and the cold gray scalps
       Of the mountains, I come!
         Hum! hum! hum!
From Morocco and Fez, and the high palaces
       Of golden Byzantium;   225
From the temples divine of old Palestine,
       From Athens and Rome,
       With a ha! and a hum!
       I come! I come!

---

[1] 'If one should marry a gallows, and beget young gibbets, I never saw one so prone.'—CYMBELINE.—[SHELLEY'S NOTE.]

All inn-doors and windows   230
    Were open to me:
I saw all that sin does,
    Which lamps hardly see
That burn in the night by the curtained bed,—
The impudent lamps! for they blushed not red,   235
    Dinging and singing,
    From slumber I rung her,
Loud as the clank of an ironmonger;
    Hum! hum! hum!

    Far, far, far!   240
With the trump of my lips, and the sting at my hips,
    I drove her—afar!
    Far, far, far!
From city to city, abandoned of pity,
    A ship without needle or star;—   245
Homeless she passed, like a cloud on the blast,
    Seeking peace, finding war;—
    She is here in her car,
    From afar, and afar;—
    Hum! hum!   250

I have stung her and wrung her,
    The venom is working;—
    And if you had hung her
    With canting and quirking,
She could not be deader than she will be soon;—   255
I have driven her close to you, under the moon,
    Night and day, hum! hum! ha!
I have hummed her and drummed her
From place to place, till at last I have dumbed her,
    Hum! hum! hum!   260

    Enter the LEECH *and the* RAT.

           Leech.

    I will suck
    Blood or muck!
The disease of the state is a plethory,
Who so fit to reduce it as I?

           Rat.

I'll slily seize and   265
    Let blood from her weasand,—
Creeping through crevice, and chink, and cranny,
With my snaky tail, and my sides so scranny.

Purganax.

Aroint ye! thou unprofitable worm!   *[To the* LEECH.
And thou, dull beetle, get thee back to hell!   270
            [To the GADFLY.
To sting the ghosts of Babylonian kings,
And the ox-headed Io——

Swine (within).

Ugh, ugh, ugh!
Hail! Iona the divine,
We will be no longer Swine,
But Bulls with horns and dewlaps.

Rat.

        For,   275
You know, my lord, the Minotaur——

Purganax (fiercely).

Be silent! get to hell! or I will call
The cat out of the kitchen. Well, Lord Mammon,
This is a pretty business.   *[Exit the* RAT.

Mammon.

      I will go
And spell some scheme to make it ugly then.—— *[Exit.*

Enter SWELLFOOT.

Swellfoot. She is returned! Taurina is in Thebes, 281
When Swellfoot wishes that she were in hell!
Oh, Hymen, clothed in yellow jealousy,
And waving o'er the couch of wedded kings
The torch of Discord with its fiery hair; 285
This is thy work, thou patron saint of queens!
Swellfoot is wived! though parted by the sea,
The very name of wife had conjugal rights;
Her cursèd image ate, drank, slept with me,
And in the arms of Adiposa oft 290
Her memory has received a husband's——
  [A loud tumult, and cries of 'Iona for ever!—No Swellfoot!'
            Hark!
How the Swine cry Iona Taurina;
I suffer the real presence; Purganax,
Off with her head!
  Purganax.   But I must first impanel
A jury of the Pigs.
  Swellfoot.   Pack them then. 295
  Purganax. Or fattening some few in two separate sties,

And giving them clean straw, tying some bits
Of ribbon round their legs—giving their Sows
Some tawdry lace, and bits of lustre glass,
And their young Boars white and red rags, and tails   300
Of cows, and jay feathers, and sticking cauliflowers
Between the ears of the old ones; and when
They are persuaded, that by the inherent virtue
Of these things, they are all imperial Pigs,
Good Lòrd! they'd rip each other's bellies up,   305
Not to say, help us in destroying her.
    Swellfoot. This plan might be tried too;—where's General
Laoctonos?

Enter LAOCTONOS *and* DAKRY.

           It is my royal pleasure
That you, Lord General, bring the head and body,
If separate it would please me better, hither   310
Of Queen Iona.
    Laoctonos.   That pleasure I well knew,
And made a charge with those battalions bold,
Called, from their dress and grin, the royal apes,
Upon the Swine, who in a hollow square
Enclosed her, and received the first attack   315
Like so many rhinoceroses, and then
Retreating in good order, with bare tusks
And wrinkled snouts presented to the foe,
Bore her in triumph to the public sty.
What is still worse, some Sows upon the ground   320
Have given the ape-guards apples, nuts, and gin,
And they all whisk their tails aloft, and cry,
'Long live Iona! down with Swellfoot!'
    Purganax.   Hark!
    The Swine (*without*). Long live Iona! down with Swellfoot!
    Dakry.   I
Went to the garret of the swineherd's tower,   325
Which overlooks the sty, and made a long
Harangue (all words) to the assembled Swine,
Of delicacy, mercy, judgement, law,
Morals, and precedents, and purity,
Adultery, destitution, and divorce,   330
Piety, faith, and state necessity,
And how I loved the Queen!—and then I wept
With the pathos of my own eloquence,
And every tear turned to a mill-stone, which
Brained many a gaping Pig, and there was made   335
A slough of blood and brains upon the place,
Greased with the pounded bacon; round and round

The mill-stones rolled, ploughing the pavement up,
And hurling Sucking-Pigs into the air,
With dust and stones.——

Enter MAMMON.

Mammon.   I wonder that gray wizards   340
Like you should be so beardless in their schemes;
It had been but a point of policy
To keep Iona and the Swine apart.
Divide and rule! but ye have made a junction
Between two parties who will govern you   345
But for my art.——Behold this BAG! it is
The poison BAG of that Green Spider huge,
On which our spies skulked in ovation through
The streets of Thebes, when they were paved with dead:
A bane so much the deadlier fills it now   350
As calumny is worse than death,—for here
The Gadfly's venom, fifty times distilled,
Is mingled with the vomit of the Leech,
In due proportion, and black ratsbane, which
That very Rat, who, like the Pontic tyrant,   355
Nurtures himself on poison, dare not touch;——
All is sealed up with the broad seal of Fraud,
Who is the Devil's Lord High Chancellor,
And over it the Primate of all Hell
Murmured this pious baptism:—'Be thou called   360
The GREEN BAG; and this power and grace be thine:
That thy contents, on whomsoever poured,
Turn innocence to guilt, and gentlest looks
To savage, foul, and fierce deformity.
Let all baptized by thy infernal dew   365
Be called adulterer, drunkard, liar, wretch!
No name left out which orthodoxy loves,
Court Journal or legitimate Review!——
Be they called tyrant, beast, fool, glutton, lover
Of other wives and husbands than their own——   370
The heaviest sin on this side of the Alps!
Wither they to a ghastly caricature
Of what was human!—let not man or beast
Behold their face with unaverted eyes!
Or hear their names with ears that tingle not   375
With blood of indignation, rage, and shame!'——
This is a perilous liquor;—good my Lords.——
            [SWELLFOOT *approaches to touch the* GREEN BAG.
Beware! for God's sake, beware!—if you should break
The seal, and touch the fatal liquor——
    Purganax.   There,

Give it to me. I have been used to handle 380
All sorts of poisons. His dread Majesty
Only desires to see the colour of it.
   Mammon. Now, with a little common sense, my Lords,
Only undoing all that has been done
(Yet so as it may seem we but confirm it), 385
Our victory is assured. We must entice
Her Majesty from the sty, and make the Pigs
Believe that the contents of the GREEN BAG
Are the true test of guilt or innocence.
And that, if she be guilty, 'twill transform her 390
To manifest deformity like guilt.
If innocent, she will become transfigured
Into an angel, such as they say she is;
And they will see her flying through the air,
So bright that she will dim the noonday sun; 395
Showering down blessings in the shape of comfits.
This, trust a priest, is just the sort of thing
Swine will believe. I'll wager you will see them
Climbing upon the thatch of their low sties,
With pieces of smoked glass, to watch her sail 400
Among the clouds, and some will hold the flaps
Of one another's ears between their teeth,
To catch the coming hail of comfits in.
You, Purganax, who have the gift o' the gab,
Make them a solemn speech to this effect: 405
I go to put in readiness the feast
Kept to the honour of our goddess Famine,
Where, for more glory, let the ceremony
Take place of the uglification of the Queen.
   Dakry (to SWELLFOOT). I, as the keeper of your
          sacred conscience,
Humbly remind your Majesty that the care 411
Of your high office, as Man-milliner
To red Bellona, should not be deferred.
   Purganax. All part, in happier plight to meet again.   *[Exeunt.*

END OF THE FIRST ACT.

ACT II

SCENE I.—*The Public Sty. The* BOARS *in full Assembly.*

Enter PURGANAX.

   Purganax. Grant me your patience, Gentlemen and Boars,
Ye, by whose patience under public burthens
The glorious constitution of these sties
Subsists, and shall subsist. The Lean-Pig rates

Grow with the growing populace of Swine,   5
The taxes, that true source of Piggishness
(How can I find a more appropriate term
To include religion, morals, peace, and plenty,
And all that fit Boeotia as a nation
To teach the other nations how to live?),   10
Increase with Piggishness itself; and still
Does the revenue, that great spring of all
The patronage, and pensions, and by-payments,
Which free-born Pigs regard with jealous eyes,
Diminish, till at length, by glorious steps,   15
All the land's produce will be merged in taxes,
And the revenue will amount to—nothing!
The failure of a foreign market for
Sausages, bristles, and blood-puddings,
And such home manufactures, is but partial;   20
And, that the population of the Pigs,
Instead of hog-wash, has been fed on straw
And water, is a fact which is—you know—
That is—it is a state-necessity—
Temporary, of course. Those impious Pigs,   25
Who, by frequent squeaks, have dared impugn
The settled Swellfoot system, or to make
Irreverent mockery of the genuflexions
Inculcated by the arch-priest, have been whipped
Into a loyal and an orthodox whine.   30
Things being in this happy state, the Queen
Iona——

    [*A loud cry from the* PIGS. 'She is innocent! most innocent!'
  Purganax. That is the very thing that I was saying,
Gentlemen Swine; the Queen Iona being
Most innocent, no doubt, returns to Thebes,   35
And the lean Sows and Boars collect about her,
Wishing to make her think that WE believe
(I mean those more substantial Pigs, who swill
Rich hog-wash, while the others mouth damp straw)
That she is guilty; thus, the Lean-Pig faction   40
Seeks to obtain that hog-wash, which has been
Your immemorial right, and which I will
Maintain you in to the last drop of——
  A Boar (*interrupting him*).   What
Does any one accuse her of?
  Purganax.   Why, no one
Makes *any* positive accusation;—but   45
There were hints dropped, and so the privy wizards
Conceived that it became them to advise
His Majesty to investigate their truth;—

Not for his own sake; he could be content
To let his wife play any pranks she pleased,   50
If, by that suffrance, *he* could please the Pigs;
But then he fears the morals of the Swine,
The Sows especially, and what effect
It might produce upon the purity and
Religion of the rising generation   55
Of Sucking-Pigs, if it could be suspected
That Queen Iona——   [*A pause.*
   First Boar.   Well, go on; we long
To hear what she can possibly have done.
   Purganax. Why, it is hinted, that a certain Bull—
Thus much is *known:*—the milk-white Bulls that feed   60
Beside Clitumnus and the crystal lakes
Of the Cisalpine mountains, in fresh dews
Of lotus-grass and blossoming asphodel
Sleeking their silken hair, and with sweet breath
Loading the morning winds until they faint   65
With living fragrance, are so beautiful!—
Well, *I* say nothing;—but Europa rode
On such a one from Asia into Crete,
And the enamoured sea grew calm beneath
His gliding beauty. And Pasiphae,   70
Iona's grandmother,——but *she* is innocent!
And that both you and I, and all assert.
   First Boar. Most innocent!
   Purganax.   Behold this BAG; a bag——
   Second Boar. Oh! no GREEN BAGS!! Jealousy's eyes are green,
Scorpions are green, and water-snakes, and efts,   75
And verdigris, and——
   Purganax.   Honourable Swine,
In Piggish souls can prepossessions reign?
Allow me to remind you, grass is green—
All flesh is grass;—no bacon but is flesh—
Ye are but bacon. This divining BAG   80
(Which is not green, but only bacon colour)
Is filled with liquor, which if sprinkled o'er
A woman guilty of——we all know what—
Makes her so hideous, till she finds one blind
She never can commit the like again.   85
If innocent, she will turn into an angel,
And rain down blessings in the shape of comfits
As she flies up to heaven. Now, my proposal
Is to convert her sacred Majesty
Into an angel (as I am sure we shall do),   90
By pouring on her head this mystic water.   [*Showing the Bag.*
I know that she is innocent; I wish

Only to prove her so to all the world.

    First Boar. Excellent, just, and noble Purganax.

    Second Boar. How glorious it will be to see her Majesty   95
Flying above our heads, her petticoats
Streaming like—like—like—

    Third Boar.   Anything.

    Purganax.   Oh no!
But like a standard of an admiral's ship,
Or like the banner of a conquering host,
Or like a cloud dyed in the dying day,   100
Unravelled on the blast from a white mountain;
Or like a meteor, or a war-steed's mane,
Or waterfall from a dizzy precipice
Scattered upon the wind.

    First Boar.   Or a cow's tail.

    Second Boar. Or *anything,* as the learned Boar observed.   105

    Purganax. Gentlemen Boars, I move a resolution,
That her most sacred Majesty should be
Invited to attend the feast of Famine,
And to receive upon her chaste white body
Dews of Apotheosis from this BAG.   110

    [*A great confusion is heard of the* PIGS OUT OF DOORS, *which com-
municates itself to those within. During the first Strophe, the
doors of the Sty are staved in, and a number of exceedingly
lean* PIGS *and* SOWS *and* BOARS *rush in.*

Semichorus I.

No! Yes!

Semichorus II.

Yes! No!

Semichorus I.

A law!

Semichorus II.

A flaw!

Semichorus I.

Porkers, we shall lose our wash,   115
    Or must share it with the Lean-Pigs!

First Boar.

Order! order! be not rash!
    Was there ever such a scene, Pigs!

An old Sow (*rushing in*).

I never saw so fine a dash
    Since I first began to wean Pigs.   120

Second Boar (*solemnly*).

The Queen will be an angel time enough.
    I vote, in form of an amendment, that
Purganax rub a little of that stuff
    Upon his face.

Purganax (*his heart is seen to beat through his waistcoat*).

                 Gods! What would ye be at?

Semichorus I.

Purganax has plainly shown a   125
    Cloven foot and jackdaw feather.

Semichorus II.

I vote Swellfoot and Iona
    Try the magic test together;
Whenever royal spouses bicker,
    Both should try the magic liquor.   130

An old Boar (*aside*).

A miserable state is that of Pigs,
    For if their drivers would tear caps and wigs,
The Swine must bite each other's ear therefore.

An old Sow (*aside*).

A wretched lot Jove has assigned to Swine,
    Squabbling makes Pig-herds hungry, and they dine   135
On bacon, and whip Sucking-Pigs the more.

Chorus.

Hog-wash has been ta'en away:
    If the Bull-Queen is divested,
We shall be in every way
    Hunted, stripped, exposed, molested;   140
Let us do whate'er we may,
    That she shall not be arrested.
QUEEN, we entrench you with walls of brawn,
    And palisades of tusks, sharp as a bayonet:
Place your most sacred person here. We pawn   145
    Our lives that none a finger dare to lay on it.

Those who wrong you, wrong us;
Those who hate you, hate us;
Those who sting you, sting us;
Those who bait you, bait us;   150
The *oracle* is now about to be
Fulfilled by circumvolving destiny;
Which says: 'Thebes, choose *reform* or *civil war*,
    When through your streets, instead of hare with dogs,
    A CONSORT QUEEN shall hunt a KING with Hogs,   155
Riding upon the IONIAN MINOTAUR.'

Enter IONA TAURINA.

Iona Taurina (*coming forward*). Gentlemen Swine, and gentle
    Lady-Pigs,
The tender heart of every Boar acquits
Their QUEEN, of any act incongruous
With native Piggishness, and she, reposing   160
With confidence upon the grunting nation,
Has thrown herself, her cause, her life, her all,
Her innocence, into their Hoggish arms;
Nor has the expectation been deceived
Of finding shelter there. Yet know, great Boars,   165
(For such whoever lives among you finds you,
And so do I), the innocent are proud!
I have accepted your protection only
In compliment of your kind love and care,
Not for necessity. The innocent   170
Are safest there, where trials and dangers wait;
Innocent Queens o'er white-hot ploughshares tread
Unsinged, and ladies, Erin's laureate sings it,[1]
Decked with rare gems, and beauty rarer still,
Walked from Killarney to the Giant's Causeway,   175
Through rebels, smugglers, troops of yeomanry,
White-boys and Orange-boys, and constables,
Tithe-proctors, and excise people, uninjured!
Thus I!——
Lord PURGANAX, I do commit myself   180
Into your custody, and am prepared
To stand the test, whatever it may be!
    Purganax. This magnanimity in your sacred Majesty
Must please the Pigs. You cannot fail of being
A heavenly angel. Smoke your bits of glass,   185
Ye loyal Swine, or her transfiguration
Will blind your wondering eyes.
    An old Boar (*aside*).   Take care, my Lord,

[1] 'Rich and rare were the gems she wore.' See Moore's *Irish Melodies.*—[SHEL-
LEY'S NOTE.]

They do not smoke you first.
    Purganax.   At the approaching feast
Of Famine, let the expiation be.
    Swine. Content! content!
    Iona Taurina (aside).   I, most content of all,   190
Know that my foes even thus prepare their fall!   *[Exeunt omnes.*

*Scene II.—The interior of the Temple of Famine. The statue of the
Goddess, a skeleton clothed in parti-coloured rags, seated upon a
heap of skulls and loaves intermingled. A number of exceedingly fat
Priests in black garments arrayed on each side, with marrow-bones
and cleavers in their hands.. [*Solomon, the Court Porkman.*] A
flourish of trumpets.*

Enter Mammon *as arch-priest,* Swellfoot, Dakry, Purganax, Laoctonos, *followed by* Iona Taurina *guarded. On the other side enter
the* Swine.

    Chorus of Priests, *accompanied by the* Court Porkman *on
                marrow-bones and cleavers.*

        Goddess bare, and gaunt, and pale,
        Empress of the world, all hail!
        What though Cretans old called thee
        City-crested Cybele?
            We call thee Famine!   5
    Goddess of fasts and feasts, starving and cramming!
    Through thee, for emperors, kings, and priests and lords,
    Who rule by viziers, sceptres, bank-notes, words,
    The earth pours forth its plenteous fruits,
    Corn, wool, linen, flesh, and roots—   10
Those who consume these fruits through thee grow fat,
    Those who produce these fruits through thee grow lean,
Whatever change takes place, oh, stick to that!
    And let things be as they have ever been;
        At least while we remain thy priests,   15
        And proclaim thy fasts and feasts.
Through thee the sacred Swellfoot dynasty
Is based upon a rock amid that sea
Whose waves are Swine—so let it ever be!

[*Swellfoot, etc., seat themselves at a table magnificently covered
at the upper end of the Temple. Attendants pass over the stage
with hog-wash in pails. A number of* Pigs, *exceedingly lean, follow them licking up the wash.*

    Mammon. I fear your sacred Majesty has lost   20
The appetite which you were used to have.
Allow me now to recommend this dish—

A simple kickshaw by your Persian cook,
Such as is served at the great King's second table.
The price and pains which its ingredients cost   25
Might have maintained some dozen families
A winter or two—not more—so plain a dish
Could scarcely disagree.—
   Swellfoot.   After the trial,
And these fastidious Pigs are gone, perhaps
I may recover my lost appetite,—   30
I feel the gout flying about my stomach—
Give me a glass of Maraschino punch.
   Purganax (*filling his glass, and standing up*). The glorious
      Constitution of the Pigs!
   All. A toast! a toast! stand up, and three times three!
   Dakry. No heel-taps—darken daylights!—
   Laoctonos.   Claret, somehow,   35
Puts me in mind of blood, and blood of claret!
   Swellfoot. Laoctonos is fishing for a compliment,
But 'tis his due. Yes, you have drunk more wine,
And shed more blood, than any man in Thebes.
                      [*To* PURGANAX.
For God's sake stop the grunting of those Pigs!   40
   Purganax. We dare not, Sire, 'tis Famine's privilege.

Chorus of Swine.

Hail to thee, hail to thee, Famine!
   Thy throne is on blood, and thy robe is of rags;
Thou devil which livest on damning;
   Saint of new churches, and cant, and GREEN BAGS,   45
Till in pity and terror thou risest,
Confounding the schemes of the wisest;
When thou liftest thy skeleton form,
   When the loaves and the skulls roll about,
We will greet thee—the voice of a storm   50
   Would be lost in our terrible shout!

Then hail to thee, hail to thee, Famine!
   Hail to thee, Empress of Earth!
When thou risest, dividing possessions;
When thou risest, uprooting oppressions,   55
   In the pride of thy ghastly mirth;
Over palaces, temples, and graves,
We will rush as thy minister-slaves,
Trampling behind in thy train,
Till all be made level again!   60

  Mammon. I hear a crackling of the giant bones
Of the dread image, and in the black pits

Which once were eyes, I see two livid flames.
These prodigies are oracular, and show
The presence of the unseen Deity. 65
Mighty events are hastening to their doom!
    Swellfoot. I only hear the lean and mutinous Swine
Grunting about the temple.
    Dakry.   In a crisis
Of such exceeding delicacy, I think
We ought to put her Majesty, the QUEEN, 70
Upon her trial without delay.
    Mammon.   THE BAG
Is here.
    Purganax. I have rehearsed the entire scene
With an ox-bladder and some ditchwater,
On Lady P——; it cannot fail. (*Taking up the Bag.*) Your
      Majesty   [*To* SWELLFOOT.
In such a filthy business had better 75
Stand on one side, lest it should sprinkle you.
A spot or two on me would do no harm,
Nay, it might hide the blood, which the sad Genius
Of the Green Isle has fixed, as by a spell,
Upon my brow—which would stain all its seas, 80
But which those seas could never wash away!
    Iona Taurina. My Lord, I am ready—nay, I am impatient
To undergo the test.

[*A graceful figure in a semi-transparent veil passes unnoticed
    through the Temple; the word* LIBERTY *is seen through the
    veil, as if it were written in fire upon its forehead. Its words
    are almost drowned in the furious grunting of the* PIGS, *and
    the business of the trial. She kneels on the steps of the Altar,
    and speaks in tones at first faint and low, but which ever be-
    come louder and louder.*

        Mighty Empress! Death's white wife!
        Ghastly mother-in-law of Life! 85
        By the God who made thee such,
        By the magic of thy touch,
        By the starving and the cramming
Of fasts and feasts! by thy dread self, O Famine!
I charge thee! when thou wake the multitude, 90
Thou lead them not upon the paths of blood.
The earth did never mean her foison
For those who crown life's cup with poison
Of fanatic rage and meaningless revenge—
    But for those radiant spirits, who are still 95
The standard-bearers in the van of Change.
    Be they th' appointed stewards, to fill

The lap of Pain, and Toil, and Age!—
Remit, O Queen! thy accustomed rage!
Be what thou art not! In voice faint and low   100
FREEDOM calls *Famine*,—her eternal foe,
To brief alliance, hollow truce.—Rise now!

[*Whilst the Veiled Figure has been chanting this strophe,* MAM-
MON, DAKRY, LAOCTONOS, *and* SWELLFOOT *have surrounded*
IONA TAURINA, *who, with her hands folded on her breast, and
her eyes lifted to Heaven, stands, as with saint-like resignation, to await the issue of the business, in perfect confidence of
her innocence.*

[PURGANAX, *after unsealing the* GREEN BAG, *is gravely about to
pour the liquor upon her head, when suddenly the whole expression of her figure and countenance changes; she snatches
it from his hand with a loud laugh of triumph, and empties it
over* SWELLFOOT *and his whole Court, who are instantly
changed into a number of filthy and ugly animals, and rush
out of the Temple. The image of* FAMINE *then arises with a
tremendous sound, the* PIGS *begin scrambling for the loaves,
and are tripped up by the skulls; all those who* EAT *the loaves
are turned into* BULLS, *and arrange themselves quietly behind
the altar. The image of* FAMINE *sinks through a chasm in the
earth, and a* MINOTAUR *rises.*

Minotaur. I am the Ionian Minotaur, the mightiest
Of all Europa's taurine progeny—
I am the old traditional Man-Bull;   105
And from my ancestors having been Ionian,
I am called Ion, which, by interpretation,
Is JOHN; in plain Theban, that is to say,
My name's JOHN BULL; I am a famous hunter,
And can leap any gate in all Boeotia,   110
Even the palings of the royal park,
Or double ditch about the new enclosures;
And if your Majesty will deign to mount me,
At least till you have hunted down your game,
I will not throw you.   115
    Iona Taurina. (*During this speech she has been putting on
       boots and spurs, and a hunting-cap, buckishly cocked
       on one side, and tucking up her hair, she leaps nimbly
       on his back.*) Hoa! hoa! tallyho! tallyho! ho! ho!
Come, let us hunt these ugly badgers down,
These stinking foxes, these devouring otters,
These hares, these wolves, these anything but men.
Hey, for a whipper-in! my loyal Pigs,
Now let your noses be as keen as beagles',   120
Your steps as swift as greyhounds', and your cries

More dulcet and symphonious than the bells
Of village-towers, on sunshine holiday;
Wake all the dewy woods with jangling music.
Give them no law (are they not beasts of blood?)   125
But such as they gave you. Tallyho! ho!
Through forest, furze, and bog, and den, and desert,
Pursue the ugly beasts! tallyho! ho!

Full Chorus of IONA *and the* SWINE.

Tallyho! tallyho!
Through rain, hail, and snow,   130
Through brake, gorse, and briar,
Through fen, flood, and mire,
We go! we go!

Tallyho! tallyho!
Through pond, ditch, and slough,   135
Wind them, and find them,
Like the Devil behind them,
Tallyho! tallyho!

[*Exeunt, in full cry;* IONA *driving on the* SWINE, *with the empty*
GREEN BAG.

THE END.

NOTE ON OEDIPUS TYRANNUS, BY MRS. SHELLEY

IN the brief journal I kept in those days, I find recorded, in August,
1820, Shelley 'begins *Swellfoot the Tyrant,* suggested by the pigs at the
fair of San Giuliano.' This was the period of Queen Caroline's landing
in England, and the struggles made by George IV to get rid of her claims;
which failing, Lord Castlereagh placed the *'Green Bag'* on the table of
the House of Commons, demanding in the King's name that an inquiry
should be instituted into his wife's conduct. These circumstances were
the theme of all conversation among the English. We were then at the
Baths of San Giuliano. A friend came to visit us on the day when a fair
was held in the square, beneath our windows: Shelley read to us his *Ode
to Liberty;* and was riotously accompanied by the grunting of a quantity
of pigs brought for sale to the fair. He compared it to the 'chorus of
frogs' in the satiric drama of Aristophanes; and, it being an hour of
merriment, and one ludicrous association suggesting another, he imagined
a political-satirical drama on the circumstances of the day, to which the
pigs would serve as chorus—and *Swellfoot* was begun. When finished,
it was transmitted to England, printed, and published anonymously; but
stifled at the very dawn of its existence by the Society for the Suppression
of Vice, who threatened to prosecute it, if not immediately withdrawn.
The friend who had taken the trouble of bringing it out, of course did

not think it worth the annoyance and expense of a contest, and it was laid aside.

Hesitation of whether it would do honour to Shelley prevented my publishing it at first. But I cannot bring myself to keep back anything he ever wrote; for each word is fraught with the peculiar views and sentiments which he believed to be beneficial to the human race, and the bright light of poetry irradiates every thought. The world has a right to the entire compositions of such a man; for it does not live and thrive by the outworn lesson of the dullard or the hypocrite, but by the original free thoughts of men of genius, who aspire to pluck bright truth

> 'from the pale-faced moon;
> Or dive into the bottom of the deep
> Where fathom-line could never touch the ground,
> And pluck up drowned'

truth. Even those who may dissent from his opinions will consider that he was a man of genius, and that the world will take more interest in his slightest word than in the waters of Lethe which are so eagerly prescribed as medicinal for all its wrongs and woe. This drama, however, must not be judged for more than was meant. It is a mere plaything of the imagination; which even may not excite smiles among many, who will not see wit in those combinations of thought which were full of the ridiculous to the author. But, like everything he wrote, it breathes that deep sympathy for the sorrows of humanity, and indignation against its oppressors, which make it worthy of his name.

CHARLES THE FIRST

DRAMATIS PERSONAE

KING CHARLES I.
QUEEN HENRIETTA.
LAUD, *Archbishop of Canterbury*.
WENTWORTH, *Earl of Strafford*.
LORD COTTINGTON.
LORD WESTON.
LORD COVENTRY.
WILLIAMS, *Bishop of Lincoln*.
Secretary LYTTELTON.
JUXON.

ST. JOHN.
ARCHY, *the Court Fool*.
HAMPDEN.
PYM.
CROMWELL.
CROMWELL'S DAUGHTER.
SIR HARRY VANE *the younger*.
LEIGHTON.
BASTWICK.
PRYNNE.

Gentlemen of the Inns of Court, Citizens, Pursuivants, Marshalsmen, Law Students, Judges, Clerk.

SCENE I.—*The Masque of the Inns of Court.*

A Pursuivant. Place, for the Marshal of the Masque!
First Citizen. What thinkest thou of this quaint masque which turns, Like morning from the shadow of the night,

The night to day, and London to a place
Of peace and joy?
   Second Citizen.   And Hell to Heaven.   5
Eight years are gone,
And they seem hours, since in this populous street
I trod on grass made green by summer's rain,
For the red plague kept state within that palace
Where now that vanity reigns. In nine years more   10
The roots will be refreshed with civil blood;
And thank the mercy of insulted Heaven
That sin and wrongs wound, as an orphan's cry,
The patience of the great Avenger's ear.
   A Youth. Yet, father, 'tis a happy sight to see,   15
Beautiful, innocent, and unforbidden
By God or man;—'tis like the bright procession
Of skiey visions in a solemn dream
From which men wake as from a Paradise,
And draw new strength to tread the thorns of life.   20
If God be good, wherefore should this be evil?
And if this be not evil, dost thou not draw
Unseasonable poison from the flowers
Which bloom so rarely in this barren world?
Oh, kill these bitter thoughts which make the present 25
Dark as the future!—

    .   .   .   .   .

When Avarice and Tyranny, vigilant Fear,
And open-eyed Conspiracy lie sleeping
As on Hell's threshold; and all gentle thoughts
Waken to worship Him who giveth joys   30
With His own gift.
   Second Citizen. How young art thou in this old age of time!
How green in this gray world? Canst thou discern
The signs of seasons, yet perceive no hint
Of change in that stage-scene in which thou art   35
Not a spectator but an actor? or
Art thou a puppet moved by [enginery]?
The day that dawns in fire will die in storms,
Even though the noon be calm. My travel's done,—
Before the whirlwind wakes I shall have found   40
My inn of lasting rest; but thou must still
Be journeying on in this inclement air.
Wrap thy old cloak about thy back;
Nor leave the broad and plain and beaten road,
Although no flowers smile on the trodden dust,   45
For the violent paths of pleasure. This Charles the First
Rose like the equinoctial sun, ...

By vapours, through whose threatening ominous veil
Darting his altered influence he has gained
This height of noon—from which he must decline 50
Amid the darkness of conflicting storms,
To dank extinction and to latest night ...
                              There goes
The apostate Strafford; he whose titles
                        whispered aphorisms 55
From Machiavel and Bacon: and, if Judas
Had been as brazen and as bold as he——
  First Citizen.   That
Is the Archbishop.
  Second Citizen. Rather say the Pope:
London will be soon his Rome: he walks
As if he trod upon the heads of men: 60
He looks elate, drunken with blood and gold;—
Beside him moves the Babylonian woman
Invisibly, and with her as with his shadow,
Mitred adulterer! he is joined in sin,
Which turns Heaven's milk of mercy to revenge. 65
  Third Citizen (lifting up his eyes). Good Lord! rain it down upon
      him! ...
Amid her ladies walks the papist queen,
As if her nice feet scorned our English earth.
The Canaanitish Jezebel! I would be
A dog if I might tear her with my teeth! 70
There's old Sir Henry Vane, the Earl of Pembroke,
Lord Essex, and Lord Keeper Coventry,
And others who make base their English breed
By vile participation of their honours
With papists, atheists, tyrants, and apostates. 75
When lawyers masque 'tis time for honest men
To strip the vizor from their purposes.
A seasonable time for masquers this!
When Englishmen and Protestants should sit
                     dust on their dishonoured heads, 80
To avert the wrath of Him whose scourge is felt
For the great sins which have drawn down from Heaven
                       and foreign overthrow.
The remnant of the martyred saints in Rochefort
Have been abandoned by their faithless allies 85
To that idolatrous and adulterous torturer
Lewis of France,—the Palatinate is lost——

Enter LEIGHTON (*who has been branded in the face*) *and* BASTWICK.

Canst thou be—art thou——?
  Leighton.   I *was* Leighton: what

I *am* thou seest. And yet turn thine eyes,
And with thy memory look on thy friend's mind,   90
Which is unchanged, and where is written deep
The sentence of my judge.
          Third Citizen.   Are these the marks with which
Laud thinks to improve the image of his Maker
Stamped on the face of man? Curses upon him,
The impious tyrant!
          Second Citizen.   It is said besides   95
That lewd and papist drunkards may profane
The Sabbath with their
And has permitted that most heathenish custom
Of dancing round a pole dressed up with wreaths
On May-day.   100
A man who thus twice crucifies his God
May well   his brother.—In my mind, friend,
The root of all this ill is prelacy.
I would cut up the root.
          Third Citizen.   And by what means?
          Second Citizen. Smiting each Bishop under the fifth rib.   105
          Third Citizen. You seem to know the vulnerable place
Of these same crocodiles.
          Second Citizen. I learnt it in
Egyptian bondage, sir. Your worm of Nile
Betrays not with its flattering tears like they;
For, when they cannot kill, they whine and weep.   110
Nor is it half so greedy of men's bodies
As they of soul and all; nor does it wallow
In slime as they in simony and lies
And close lusts of the flesh.
          A Marshalsman.   Give place, give place!
You torch-bearers, advance to the great gate,   115
And then attend the Marshal of the Masque
Into the Royal presence.
          A Law Student.   What thinkest thou
Of this quaint show of ours, my agèd friend?
Even now we see the redness of the torches
Inflame the night to the eastward, and the clarions   120
[Gasp?] to us on the wind's wave. It comes!
And their sounds, floating hither round the pageant,
Rouse up the astonished air.
          First Citizen.   I will not think but that our country's wounds
May yet be healed. The king is just and gracious,   125
Though wicked counsels now pervert his will:
These once cast off—
          Second Citizen.   As adders cast their skins
And keep their venom, so kings often change;

Councils and counsellors hang on one another,
Hiding the loathsome   130
Like the base patchwork of a leper's rags.
　　The Youth. Oh, still those dissonant thoughts!—List how the music
Grows on the enchanted air! And see, the torches
Restlessly flashing, and the crowd divided
Like waves before an admiral's prow!
　　A Marshalsman.   Give place   ·   135
To the Marshal of the Masque!
　　A Pursuivant.   Room for the King!
　　The Youth. How glorious! See those thronging chariots
Rolling, like painted clouds before the wind,
Behind their solemn steeds: how some are shaped
Like curved sea-shells dyed by the azure depths   140
Of Indian seas; some like the new-born moon;
And some like cars in which the Romans climbed
(Canopied by Victory's eagle-wings outspread)
The Capitolian—See how gloriously
The mettled horses in the torchlight stir   145
Their gallant riders, while they check their pride,
Like shapes of some diviner element
Than English air, and beings nobler than
The envious and admiring multitude.
　　Second Citizen. Ay, there they are—   150
Nobles, and sons of nobles, patentees,
Monopolists, and stewards of this poor farm,
On whose lean sheep sit the prophetic crows,
Here is the pomp that strips the houseless orphan,
Here is the pride that breaks the desolate heart.   155
These are the lilies glorious as Solomon,
Who toil not, neither do they spin,—unless
It be the webs they catch poor rogues withal.
Here is the surfeit which to them who earn
The niggard wages of the earth, scarce leaves   160
The tithe that will support them till they crawl
Back to her cold hard bosom. Here is health
Followed by grim disease, glory by shame,
Waste by lame famine, wealth by squalid want,
And England's sin by England's punishment.   165
And, as the effect pursues the cause foregone,
Lo, giving substance to my words, behold
At once the sign and the thing signified—
A troop of cripples, beggars, and lean outcasts,
Horsed upon stumbling jades, carted with dung,   170
Dragged for a day from cellars and low cabins
And rotten hiding-holes, to point the moral
Of this presentment, and bring up the rear

Of painted pomp with misery!
   The Youth.   'Tis but
The anti-masque, and serves as discords do   175
In sweetest music. Who would love May flowers
If they succeeded not to Winter's flaw;
Or day unchanged by night; or joy itself
Without the touch of sorrow?
   Second Citizen.   I and thou——
   A Marshalsman. Place, give place!   180

SCENE II.—*A Chamber in Whitehall. Enter the* KING, QUEEN, LAUD, LORD STRAFFORD, LORD COTTINGTON, *and other Lords;* ARCHY; *also* ST. JOHN, *with some Gentlemen of the Inns of Court.*

   King. Thanks, gentlemen. I heartily accept
This token of your service: your gay masque
Was performed gallantly. And it shows well
When subjects twine such flowers of [observance?]
With the sharp thorns that deck the English crown.   5
A gentle heart enjoys what it confers,
Even as it suffers that which it inflicts,
Though Justice guides the stroke.
Accept my hearty thanks.
   Queen.   And gentlemen,
Call your poor Queen your debtor. Your quaint **pageant**   10
Rose on me like the figures of past years,
Treading their still path back to infancy,
More beautiful and mild as they draw nearer
The quiet cradle. I could have almost wept
To think I was in Paris, where these shows   15
Are well devised—such as I was ere yet
My young heart shared a portion of the burthen,
The careful weight of this great monarchy.
There, gentlemen, between the sovereign's pleasure
And that which it regards, no clamour lifts   20
Its proud interposition.
In Paris ribald censurers dare not move
Their poisonous tongues against these sinless sports;
And *his* smile
Warms those who bask in it, as ours would do   25
If . . . Take my heart's thanks: add them, gentlemen,
To those good words which, were he King of France,
My royal lord would turn to golden deeds.
   St. John. Madam, the love of Englishmen can make
The lightest favour of their lawful king   30
Outweigh a despot's.—We humbly take our leaves,
Enriched by smiles which France can never buy.
   [*Exeunt* ST. JOHN *and the Gentlemen of the Inns of Court.*

King. My Lord Archbishop,
Mark you what spirit sits in St. John's eyes?
Methinks it is too saucy for this presence.   35

Archy. Yes, pray your Grace look: for, like an unsophisticated [eye]
sees everything upside down, you who are wise will discern the shadow
of an idiot in lawn sleeves and a rochet setting springes to catch wood-
cocks in haymaking time. Poor Archy, whose owl-eyes are tempered to
the error of his age, and because he is a fool, and by special ordinance of
God forbidden ever to see himself as he is, sees now in that deep eye a
blindfold devil sitting on the ball, and weighing words out between king
and subjects. One scale is full of promises, and the other full of protesta-
tions: and then another devil creeps behind the first out of the dark windings [of a] pregnant lawyer's brain, and takes the bandage from the
other's eyes, and throws a sword into the left-hand scale, for all the world
like my Lord Essex's there.   47

Strafford. A rod in pickle for the Fool's back!

Archy. Ay, and some are now smiling whose tears will make the brine;
for the Fool sees——

Strafford. Insolent! You shall have your coat turned and be whipped
out of the palace for this.   52

Archy. When all the fools are whipped, and all the Protestant writers,
while the knaves are whipping the fools ever since a thief was set to
catch a thief. If all turncoats were whipped out of palaces, poor Archy
would be disgraced in good company. Let the knaves whip the fools, and
all the fools laugh at it. [Let the] wise and godly slit each other's noses
and ears (having no need of any sense of discernment in their craft);
and the knaves, to marshal them, join in a procession to Bedlam, to
entreat the madmen to omit their sublime Platonic contemplations, and
manage the state of England. Let all the honest men who lie [pinched?]
up at the prisons or the pillories, in custody of the pursuivants of the
High-Commission Court, marshal them.   63

Enter Secretary LYTTELTON, *with papers.*

King (*looking over the papers*). These stiff Scots
His Grace of Canterbury must take order
To force under the Church's yoke.—You, Wentworth,
Shall be myself in Ireland, and shall add
Your wisdom, gentleness, and energy,
To what in me were wanting.—My Lord Weston,
Look that those merchants draw not without loss   70
Their bullion from the Tower; and, on the payment
Of shipmoney, take fullest compensation
For violation of our royal forests,
Whose limits, from neglect, have been o'ergrown
With cottages and cornfields. The uttermost   75
Farthing exact from those who claim exemption
From knighthood: that which once was a reward

Shall thus be made a punishment, that subjects
May know how majesty can wear at will
The rugged mood.—My Lord of Coventry,   80
Lay my command upon the Courts below
That bail be not accepted for the prisoners
Under the warrant of the Star Chamber.
The people shall not find the stubbornness
Of Parliament a cheap or easy method   85
Of dealing with their rightful sovereign:
And doubt not this, my Lord of Coventry,
We will find time and place for fit rebuke.—
My Lord of Canterbury.
    Archy.   The fool is here.
    Laud. I crave permission of your Majesty   90
To order that this insolent fellow be
Chastised: he mocks the sacred character,
Scoffs at the state, and—
    King.   What, my Archy?
He mocks and mimics all he sees and hears,
Yet with a quaint and graceful licence—Prithee   95
For this once do not as Prynne would, were he
Primate of England. With your Grace's leave,
He lives in his own world; and, like a parrot
Hung in his gilded prison from the window
Of a queen's bower over the public way,   100
Blasphemes with a bird's mind:—his words, like arrows
Which know no aim beyond the archer's wit,
Strike sometimes what eludes philosophy.—
(*To* ARCHY.) Go, sirrah, and repent of your offence
Ten minutes in the rain; be it your penance   105
To bring news how the world goes there.

                                       [*Exit* ARCHY.

                        Poor Archy!
He weaves about himself a world of mirth
Out of the wreck of ours.
    Laud. I take with patience, as my Master did,
All scoffs permitted from above.
    King.   My lord,   110
Pray overlook these papers. Archy's words
Had wings, but these have talons.
    Queen.   And the lion
That wears them must be tamed. My dearest lord,
I see the new-born courage in your eye
Armed to strike dead the Spirit of the Time,   115
Which spurs to rage the many-headed beast.
Do thou persist: for, faint but in resolve,
And it were better thou hadst still remained

The slave of thine own slaves, who tear like curs   120
The fugitive, and flee from the pursuer;
And Opportunity, that empty wolf,
Flies at his throat who falls. Subdue thy actions
Even to the disposition of thy purpose,
And be that tempered as the Ebro's steel;   125
And banish weak-eyed Mercy to the weak,
Whence she will greet thee with a gift of peace,
And not betray thee with a traitor's kiss,
As when she keeps the company of rebels,
Who think that she is Fear. This do, lest we   130
Should fall as from a glorious pinnacle
In a bright dream, and wake as from a dream
Out of our worshipped state.
   King.   Belovèd friend,
God is my witness that this weight of power,
Which He sets me my earthly task to wield
Under His law, is my delight and pride   135
Only because thou lovest that and me.
For a king bears the office of a God
To all the under world; and to his God
Alone he must deliver up his trust,
Unshorn of its permitted attributes.   140
[It seems] now as the baser elements
Had mutinied against the golden sun
That kindles them to harmony, and quells
Their self-destroying rapine. The wild million
Strike at the eye that guides them; like as humours   145
Of the distempered body that conspire
Against the spirit of life throned in the heart,—
And thus become the prey of one another,
And last of death.
   Strafford.   That which would be ambition in a subject
Is duty in a sovereign; for on him,   150
As on a keystone, hangs the arch of life,
Whose safety is its strength. Degree and form,
And all that makes the age of reasoning man
More memorable than a beast's, depend on this—
That Right should fence itself inviolably   155
With Power; in which respect the state of England
From usurpation by the insolent commons
Cries for reform.
Get treason, and spare treasure. Fee with coin
The loudest murmurers; feed with jealousies   160
Opposing factions,—be thyself of none;
And borrow gold of many, for those who lend
Will serve thee till thou payest them; and thus

Keep the fierce spirit of the hour at bay,
Till time, and its coming generations   165
Of nights and days unborn, bring some one chance,

    .   .   .   .

Or war or pestilence or Nature's self,—
By some distemperature or terrible sign,
Be as an arbiter betwixt themselves.
                    Nor let your Majesty   170
Doubt here the peril of the unseen event.
How did your brother Kirgs, coheritors
In your high interest in the subject earth,
Rise past such troubles to that height of power
Where now they sit, and awfully serene   175
Smile on the trembling world? Such popular storms
Philip the Second of Spain, this Lewis of France,
And late the German head of many bodies,
And every petty lord of Italy,
Quelled or by arts or arms. Is England poorer   180
Or feebler? or art thou who wield'st her power
Tamer than they? or shall this island be—
[Girdled] by its inviolable waters—
To the world present and the world to come
Sole pattern of extinguished monarchy?   185
Not if thou dost as I would have thee do.
    King. Your words shall be my deeds:
You speak the image of my thought. My friend
(If Kings can have a friend, I call thee so),
Beyond the large commission which [belongs]   190
Under the great seal of the realm, take this:
And, for some obvious reasons, let there be
No seal on it, except my kingly word
And honour as I am a gentleman.
Be—as thou art within my heart and mind—   195
Another self, here and in Ireland:
Do what thou judgest well, take amplest licence,
And stick not even at questionable means.
Hear me, Wentworth. My word is as a wall
Between thee and this world thine enemy—   200
That hates thee, for thou lovest me.
    Strafford.   I own
No friend but thee, no enemies but thine:
Thy lightest thought is my eternal law.
How weak, how short, is life to pay——
    King.   Peace, peace.
Thou ow'st me nothing yet.
(*To* LAUD.)   My lord, what say   205
Those papers?

Laud. Your Majesty has ever interposed,
In lenity towards your native soil,
Between the heavy vengeance of the Church
And Scotland. Mark the consequence of warming   210
This brood of northern vipers in your bosom.
The rabble, instructed no doubt
By Loudon, Lindsay, Hume, and false Argyll
(For the waves never menace heaven until
Scourged by the wind's invisible tyranny),   •   215
Have in the very temple of the Lord
Done outrage to His chosen ministers.
They scorn the liturgy of the Holy Church,
Refuse to obey her canons, and deny
The apostolic power with which the Spirit   220
Has filled its elect vessels, even from him
Who held the keys with power to loose and bind,
To him who now pleads in this royal presence.—
Let ample powers and new instructions be
Sent to the High Commissioners in Scotland.   225
To death, imprisonment, and confiscation,
Add torture, add the ruin of the kindred
Of the offender, add the brand of infamy,
Add mutilation: and if this suffice not,
Unleash the sword and fire, that in their thirst   230
They may lick up that scum of schismatics.
I laugh at those weak rebels who, desiring
What we possess, still prate of Christian peace,
As if those dreadful arbitrating messengers
Which play the part of God 'twixt right and wrong,   235
Should be let loose against the innocent sleep
Of templed cities and the smiling fields,
For some poor argument of policy
Which touches our own profit or our pride
(Where it indeed were Christian charity   240
To turn the cheek even to the smiter's hand);
And, when our great Redeemer, when our God,
When He who gave, accepted, and retained
Himself in propitiation of our sins,
Is scorned in His immediate ministry,   245
With hazard of the inestimable loss
Of all the truth and discipline which is
Salvation to the extremest generation
Of men innumerable, they talk of peace!
Such peace as Canaan found, let Scotland now;   250
For, by that Christ who came to bring a sword,
Not peace, upon the earth, and gave command
To His disciples at the Passover

That each should sell his robe and buy a sword,—
Once strip that minister of naked wrath,   255
And it shall never sleep in peace again
Till Scotland bend or break.

    King.   My Lord Archbishop,
Do what thou wilt and what thou canst in this.
Thy earthly even as thy heavenly King
Gives thee large power in his unquiet realm.   260
But we want money, and my mind misgives me
That for so great an enterprise, as yet,
We are unfurnished.

    Strafford.   Yet it may not long
Rest on our wills.

    Cottington.   The expenses
Of gathering shipmoney, and of distraining   265
For every petty rate (for we encounter
A desperate opposition inch by inch
In every warehouse and on every farm),
Have swallowed up the gross sum of the imposts;
So that, though felt as a most grievous scourge   270
Upon the land, they stand us in small stead
As touches the receipt.

    Strafford.   'Tis a conclusion
Most arithmetical: and thence you infer
Perhaps the assembling of a parliament.
Now, if a man should call his dearest enemies   275
To sit in licensed judgement on his life,
His Majesty might wisely take that course.

                              [*Aside to* COTTINGTON.

It is enough to expect from these lean imposts
That they perform the office of a scourge,
Without more profit. (*Aloud*.) Fines and confiscations,   280
And a forced loan from the refractory city,
Will fill our coffers: and the golden love
Of loyal gentlemen and noble friends
For the worshipped father of our common country,
With contributions from the catholics,   285
Will make Rebellion pale in our excess.
Be these the expedients until time and wisdom
Shall frame a settled state of government.

    Laud. And weak expedients they! Have we not drained
All, till the   which seemed   290
A mine exhaustless?

    Strafford.   And the love which *is*,
If loyal hearts could turn their blood to gold.

    Laud. Both now grow barren: and I speak it not
As loving parliaments, which, as they have been

In the right hand of bold bad mighty kings 295
The scourges of the bleeding Church, I hate.
Methinks they scarcely can deserve our fear.
   Strafford. Oh! my dear liege, take back the wealth thou gavest:
With that, take all I held, but as in trust
For thee, of mine inheritance: leave me but 300
This unprovided body for thy service,
And a mind dedicated to no care
Except thy safety:—but assemble not
A parliament. Hundreds will bring, like me,
Their fortunes, as they would their blood, before—— 305
   King. No! thou who judgest them art but one. Alas!
We should be too much out of love with Heaven,
Did this vile world show many such as thee,
Thou perfect, just, and honourable man!
Never shall it be said that Charles of England 310
Stripped those he loved for fear of those he scorns;
Nor will he so much misbecome his throne
As to impoverish those who most adorn
And best defend it. That you urge, dear Strafford,
Inclines me rather—
   Queen.   To a parliament? 315
Is this thy firmness? and thou wilt preside
Over a knot of   censurers,
To the unswearing of thy best resolves,
And choose the worst, when the worst comes too soon?
Plight not the worst before the worst must come. 320
Oh, wilt thou smile whilst our ribald foes,
Dressed in their own usurped authority,
Sharpen their tongues on Henrietta's fame?
It is enough! Thou lovest me no more!   [*Weeps*.
   King. Oh, Henrietta!   [*They talk apart*.
   Cottington (*to* LAUD). Money we have none: 325
And all the expedients of my Lord of Strafford
Will scarcely meet the arrears.
   Laud.   Without delay
An army must be sent into the north;
Followed by a Commission of the Church,
With amplest power to quench in fire and blood, 330
And tears and terror, and the pity of hell,
The intenser wrath of Heresy. God will give
Victory; and victory over Scotland give
The lion England tamed into our hands.
That will lend power, and power bring gold.
   Cottington.   Meanwhile 335
We must begin first where your Grace leaves off.
Gold must give power, or——

Laud. I am not averse
From the assembling of a parliament.
Strong actions and smooth words might teach them soon
The lesson to obey. And are they not 340
A bubble fashioned by the monarch's mouth,
The birth of one light breath? If they serve no purpose,
A word dissolves them.
  Strafford. The engine of parliaments
Might be deferred until I can bring over
The Irish regiments: they will serve to assure 345
The issue of the war against the Scots.
And, this game won—which if lost, all is lost—
Gather these chosen leaders of the rebels,
And call them, if you will, a parliament.
  King. Oh, be our feet still tardy to shed blood, 350
Guilty though it may be! I would still spare
The stubborn country of my birth, and ward
From countenances which I loved in youth
The wrathful Church's lacerating hand.
(*To* LAUD.) Have you o'erlooked the other articles? 355

[Re-enter ARCHY.

  Laud. Hazlerig, Hampden, Pym, young Harry Vane,
Cromwell, and other rebels of less note,
Intend to sail with the next favouring wind
For the Plantations.
  Archy. Where they think to found
A commonwealth like Gonzalo's in the play, 360
Gynaecocoenic and pantisocratic.
  King. What's that, sirrah?
  Archy. New devil's politics.
Hell is the pattern of all commonwealths:
Lucifer was the first republican.
Will you hear Merlin's prophecy, how three [posts?] 365
  'In one brainless skull, when the whitethorn is full,
    Shall sail round the world, and come back again:
  Shall sail round the world in a brainless skull,
  And come back again when the moon is at full:'—
When, in spite of the Church, 370
They will hear homilies of whatever length
Or form they please.
  [*Cottington?*] So please your Majesty to sign this order
For their detention.
  Archy. If your Majesty were tormented night and day by fever, gout,
rheumatism, and stone, and asthma, etc., and you found these diseases
had secretly entered into a conspiracy to abandon you, should you think
it necessary to lay an embargo on the port by which they meant to dis-
people your unquiet kingdom of man? 379

King. If fear were made for kings, the Fool mocks wisely;
But in this case——(*writing*). Here, my lord, take the warrant,
And see it duly executed forthwith.——
That imp of malice and mockery shall be punished.   383

[*Exeunt all but* KING, QUEEN, *and* ARCHY.

Archy. Ay, I am the physician of whom Plato prophesied, who was to
be accused by the confectioner before a jury of children, who found him
guilty without waiting for the summing-up, and hanged him without
benefit of clergy. Thus Baby Charles, and the Twelfth-night Queen of
Hearts, and the overgrown schoolboy Cottington, and that little urchin
Laud—who would reduce a verdict of 'guilty, death,' by famine, if it
were impregnable by composition—all impannelled against poor Archy
for presenting them bitter physic the last day of the holidays.   391

Queen. Is the rain over, sirrah?

King.   When it rains
And the sun shines, 'twill rain again to-morrow:
And therefore never smile till you've done crying.   394

Archy. But 'tis all over now: like the April anger of woman, the gentle
sky has wept itself serene.

Queen. What news abroad? how looks the world this morning?

Archy. Gloriously as a grave covered with virgin flowers.
There's a rainbow in the sky. Let your Majesty look at it, for

'A rainbow in the morning   400
Is the shepherd's warning;'

and the flocks of which you are the pastor are scattered among the
mountain-tops, where every drop of water is a flake of snow, and the
breath of May pierces like a January blast.   404

King. The sheep have mistaken the wolf for their shepherd, my poor
boy; and the shepherd, the wolves for their watchdogs.

Queen. But the rainbow was a good sign, Archy: it says that the waters
of the deluge are gone, and can return no more.

Archy. Ay, the salt-water one: but that of tears and blood must yet
come down, and that of fire follow, if there be any truth in lies.—The
rainbow hung over the city with all its shops, . . . and churches, from
north to south, like a bridge of congregated lightning pieced by the
masonry of heaven—like a balance in which the angel that distributes
the coming hour was weighing that heavy one whose poise is now felt
in the lightest hearts, before it bows the proudest heads under the meanest feet.   416

Queen. Who taught you this trash, sirrah?

Archy. A torn leaf out of an old book trampled in the dirt.—But for
the rainbow. It moved as the sun moved, and . . . until the top of the
Tower . . of a cloud through its left-hand tip, and Lambeth Palace
look as dark as a rock before the other. Methought I saw a crown figured
upon one tip, and a mitre on the other. So, as I had heard treasures were
found where the rainbow quenches its points upon the earth, I set off,

and at the Tower—— But I shall not tell your Majesty what I found
close to the closet-window on which the rainbow had glimmered.   425
    King. Speak: I will make my Fool my conscience.
    Archy. Then conscience is a fool.—I saw there a cat caught in a rat-
trap. I heard the rats squeak behind the wainscots: it seemed to me that
the very mice were consulting on the manner of her death.
    Queen. Archy is shrewd and bitter.
    Archy.   Like the season,   430
So blow the winds.—But at the other end of the rainbow, where the gray
rain was tempered along the grass and leaves by a tender interfusion of
violet and gold in the meadows beyond Lambeth, what think you that
I found instead of a mitre?
    King. Vane's wits perhaps.
    Archy.   Something as vain. I saw   435
a gross vapour hovering in a stinking ditch over the carcass of a dead
ass, some rotten rags, and broken dishes—the wrecks of what once admin-
istered to the stuffing-out and the ornament of a worm of worms. His
Grace of Canterbury expects to enter the New Jerusalem some Palm
Sunday in triumph on the ghost of this ass.   440
    Queen. Enough, enough! Go desire Lady Jane
She place my lute, together with the music
Mari received last week from Italy,
In my boudoir, and——   [*Exit* ARCHY.
    King.   I'll go in.
    Queen.   My beloved lord,
Have you not noted that the Fool of late   445
Has lost his careless mirth, and that his words
Sound like the echoes of our saddest fears?
What can it mean? I should be loth to think
Some factious slave had tutored him.
    King.   Oh, no!
He is but Occasion's pupil. Partly 'tis   450
That our minds piece the vacant intervals
Of his wild words with their own fashioning,—
As in the imagery of summer clouds,
Or coals of the winter fire, idlers find
The perfect shadows of their teeming thoughts: 455
And partly, that the terrors of the time
Are sown by wandering Rumour in all spirits;
And in the lightest and the least, may best
Be seen the current of the coming wind.
    Queen. Your brain is overwrought with these deep thoughts.   460
Come, I will sing to you; let us go try
These airs from Italy; and, as we pass
The gallery, we'll decide where that Correggio
Shall hang—the Virgin Mother

With her child, born the King of heaven and earth, 465
Whose reign is men's salvation. And you shall see
A cradled miniature of yourself asleep,
Stamped on the heart by never-erring love;
Liker than any Vandyke ever made,
A pattern to the unborn age of thee, 470
Over whose sweet beauty I have wept for joy
A thousand times, and now should weep for sorrow
Did I not think that after we were dead
Our fortunes would spring high in him, and that
The cares we waste upon our heavy crown 475
Would make it light and glorious as a wreath
Of Heaven's beams for his dear innocent brow.
    King. Dear Henrietta!

SCENE III.—*The Star Chamber*, LAUD, JUXON, STRAFFORD, *and others,
    as Judges.* PRYNNE *as a Prisoner, and then* BASTWICK.

    Laud. Bring forth the prisoner Bastwick: let the clerk
Recite his sentence.
    Clerk.   'That he pay five thousand
Pounds to the king, lose both his ears, be branded
With red-hot iron on the cheek and forehead,
And be imprisoned within Lancaster Castle 5
During the pleasure of the Court.'
    Laud.   Prisoner,
If you have aught to say wherefore this sentence
Should not be put into effect, now speak.
    Juxon. If you have aught to plead in mitigation,
Speak.
    Bastwick. Thus, my lords. If, like the prelates, I 10
Were an invader of the royal power,
A public scorner of the word of God,
Profane, idolatrous, popish, superstitious,
Impious in heart and in tyrannic act,
Void of wit, honesty, and temperance; 15
If Satan were my lord, as theirs,—our God
Pattern of all I should avoid to do:
Were I an enemy of my God and King
And of good men, as ye are;—I should merit
Your fearful state and gilt prosperity, 20
Which, when ye wake from the last sleep, shall turn
To cowls and robes of everlasting fire.
But, as I am, I bid ye grudge me not
The only earthly favour ye can yield,
Or I think worth acceptance at your hands,— 25
Scorn, mutilation, and imprisonment.
              even as my Master did,

Until Heaven's kingdom shall descend on earth,
Or earth be like a shadow in the light
Of Heaven absorbed—some few tumultuous years   30
Will pass, and leave no wreck of what opposes
His will whose will is power.
    Laud. Officer, take the prisoner from the bar,
And be his tongue slit for his insolence.
    Bastwick. While this hand holds a pen——
    Laud.   Be his hands——
    'uxon.   Stop!   35
Forbear, my lord! The tongue, which now can speak
No terror, would interpret, being dumb,
Heaven's thunder to our harm; . . .
And hands, which now write only their own shame,
With bleeding stumps might sign our blood away.   40
    Laud. Much more such 'mercy' among men would be,
Did all the ministers of Heaven's revenge
Flinch thus from earthly retribution. I
Could suffer what I would inflict.

                         [*Exit* Bastwick *guarded*.
                    Bring up
The Lord Bishop of Lincoln.—
(*To* Strafford.)   Know you not   45
That, in distraining for ten thousand pounds
Upon his books and furniture at Lincoln,
Were found these scandalous and seditious letters
Sent from one Osbaldistone, who is fled?
I speak it not as touching this poor person;   50
But of the office which should make it holy,
Were it as vile as it was ever spotless.
Mark, too, my lord, that this expression strikes
His Majesty, if I misinterpret not.

         Enter Bishop Williams *guarded*.

    Strafford. 'Twere politic and just that Williams taste   55
The bitter fruit of his connection with
The schismatics. But you, my Lord Archbishop,
Who owed your first promotion to his favour,
Who grew beneath his smile——
    Laud.   Would therefore beg
The office of his judge from this High Court,—   60
That it shall seem, even as it is, that I,
In my assumption of this sacred robe,
Have put aside all worldly preference,
All sense of all distinction of all persons,
All thoughts but of the service of the Church.—   65
Bishop of Lincoln!

Williams.   Peace, proud hierarch!
I know my sentence, and I own it just.
Thou wilt repay me less than I deserve,
In stretching to the utmost

.   .   .   .

SCENE IV.—HAMPDEN, PYM, CROMWELL, *his Daughter, and young*
SIR HARRY VANE.

Hampden. England, farewell! thou, who hast been my cradle,
Shalt never be my dungeon or my grave!
I held what I inherited in thee
As pawn for that inheritance of freedom
Which thou hast sold for thy despoiler's smile: 5
How can I call thee England, or my country?—
Does the wind hold?
   Vane.   The vanes sit steady
Upon the Abbey towers. The silver lightnings
Of the evening star, spite of the city's smoke,
Tell that the north wind reigns in the upper air.   10
Mark too that flock of fleecy-wingèd clouds
Sailing athwart St. Margaret's.
   Hampden.   Hail, fleet herald
Of tempest! that rude pilot who shall guide
Hearts free as his, to realms as pure as thee,
Beyond the shot of tyranny,   15
Beyond the webs of that swoln spider . . .
Beyond the curses, calumnies, and [lies?]
Of atheist priests!   And thou
Fair star, whose beam lies on the wide Atlantic,
Athwart its zones of tempest and of calm,   20
Bright as the path to a belovèd home,
Oh, light us to the isles of the evening land!
Like floating Edens cradled in the glimmer
Of sunset, through the distant mist of years
Touched by departing hope, they gleam! lone regions,   25
Where Power's poor dupes and victims yet have never
Propitiated the savage fear of kings
With purest blood of noblest hearts; whose dew
Is yet unstained with tears of those who wake
To weep each day the wrongs on which it dawns;   30
Whose sacred silent air owns yet no echo
Of formal blasphemies; nor impious rites
Wrest man's free worship, from the God who loves,
To the poor worm who envies us His love!
Receive, thou young   of Paradise.   35
These exiles from the old and sinful world!

.   .   .   .

This glorious clime, this firmament, whose lights
Dart mitigated influence through their veil
Of pale blue atmosphere; whose tears keep green
The pavement of this moist all-feeding earth;   40
This vaporous horizon, whose dim round
Is bastioned by the circumfluous sea,
Repelling invasion from the sacred towers,
Presses upon me like a dungeon's grate,
A low dark roof, a damp and narrow wall.   45
The boundless universe
Becomes a cell too narrow for the soul
That owns no master; while the loathliest ward
Of this wide prison, England, is a nest
Of cradling peace built on the mountain tops,—   50
To which the eagle spirits of the free,
Which range through heaven and earth, and scorn the storm
Of time, and gaze upon the light of truth,
Return to brood on thoughts that cannot die
And cannot be repelled.   55
Like eaglets floating in the heaven of time,
They soar above their quarry, and shall stoop
Through palaces and temples thunderproof.

SCENE V

Archy. I'll go live under the ivy that overgrows the terrace, and count
the tears shed on its old [roots?] as the [wind?] plays the song of

    'A widow bird sate mourning
    Upon a wintry bough.'
            [*Sings*]
    'Heigho! the lark and the owl!   5
    One flies the morning, and one lulls the night:—
    Only the nightingale, poor fond soul,
    Sings like the fool through darkness and light.

    'A widow bird sate mourning for her love   10
    Upon a wintry bough;
    The frozen wind crept on above,
    The freezing stream below.

    'There was no leaf upon the forest bare,
    No flower upon the ground,
    And little motion in the air   15
    Except the mill-wheel's sound.'

LETTER TO MARIA GISBORNE

LEGHORN, July 1, 1820.

THE spider spreads her webs, whether she be
In poet's tower, cellar, or barn, or tree;
The silk-worm in the dark green mulberry leaves
His winding sheet and cradle ever weaves;
So I, a thing whom moralists call worm,   5
Sit spinning still round this decaying form,
From the fine threads of rare and subtle thought—
No net of words in garish colours wrought
To catch the idle buzzers of the day—
But a soft cell, where when that fades away,   10
Memory may clothe in wings my living name
And feed it with the asphodels of fame,
Which in those hearts which must remember me
Grow, making love an immortality.

        Whoever should behold me now, I wist,   15
Would think I were a mighty mechanist,
Bent with sublime Archimedean art
To breathe a soul into the iron heart
Of some machine portentous, or strange gin,
Which by the force of figured spells might win   20
Its way over the sea, and sport therein;
For round the walls are hung dread engines, such
As Vulcan never wrought for Jove to clutch
Ixion or the Titan:—or the quick
Wit of that man of God, St. Dominic,   25
To convince Atheist, Turk, or Heretic,
Or those in philanthropic council met,
Who thought to pay some interest for the debt
They owed to Jesus Chirst for their salvation,
By giving a faint foretaste of damnation   30
To Shakespeare, Sidney, Spenser, and the rest
Who made our land an island of the blest.
When lamp-like Spain, who now relumes her fire
On Freedom's hearth, grew dim with Empire:—
With thumbscrews, wheels, with tooth and spike and jag,
Which fishers found under the utmost crag   36
Of Cornwall and the storm-encompassed isles,
Where to the sky the rude sea rarely smiles
Unless in treacherous wrath, as on the morn
When the exulting elements in scorn,   40

Satiated with destroyed destruction, lay
Sleeping in beauty on their mangled prey,
As panthers sleep;—and other strange and dread
Magical forms the brick floor overspread,—
Proteus transformed to metal did not make 45
More figures, or more strange; nor did he take
Such shapes of unintelligible brass,
Or heap himself in such a horrid mass
Of tin and iron not to be understood;
And forms of unimaginable wood, 50
To puzzle Tubal Cain and all his brood:
Great screws, and cones, and wheels, and groovèd blocks,
The elements of what will stand the shocks
Of wave and wind and time.—Upon the table
More knacks and quips there be than I am able 55
To catalogize in this verse of mine:—
A pretty bowl of wood—not full of wine,
But quicksilver; that dew which the gnomes drink
When at their subterranean toil they swink,
Pledging the demons of the earthquake, who 60
Reply to them in lava—cry halloo!
And call out to the cities o'er their head,—
Roofs, towers, and shrines, the dying and the dead,
Crash through the chinks of earth—and then all quaff
Another rouse, and hold their sides and laugh. 65
This quicksilver no gnome has drunk—within
The walnut bowl it lies, veinèd and thin,
In colour like the wake of light that stains
The Tuscan deep, when from the moist moon rains
The inmost shower of its white fire—the breeze 70
Is still—blue Heaven smiles over the pale seas,
And in this bowl of quicksilver—for I
Yield to the impulse of an infancy
Outlasting manhood—I have made to float
A rude idealism of a paper boat:— 75
A hollow screw with cogs—Henry will know
The thing I mean and laugh at me,—if so
He fears not I should do more mischief.—Next
Lie bills and calculations much perplexed,
With steam-boats, frigates, and machinery quaint 80
Traced over them in blue and yellow paint.
Then comes a range of mathematical
Instruments, for plans nautical and statical;
A heap of rosin, a queer broken glass
With ink in it;—a china cup that was 85
What it will never be again, I think,—
A thing from which sweet lips were wont to drink

The liquor doctors rail at—and which I
Will quaff in spite of them—and when we die
We'll toss up who died first of drinking tea,   90
And cry out,—'Heads or tails?' where'er we be.
Near that a dusty paint-box, some odd hooks,
A half-burnt match, an ivory block, three books,
Where conic sections, spherics, logarithms,
To great Laplace, from Saunderson and Sims,   95
Lie heaped in their harmonious disarray
Of figures,—disentangle them who may.
Baron de Tott's Memoirs beside them lie,
And some odd volumes of old chemistry.
Near those a most inexplicable thing,   100
With lead in the middle—I'm conjecturing
How to make Henry understand; but no—
I'll leave, as Spenser says, with many mo,
This secret in the pregnant womb of time,
Too vast a matter for so weak a rhyme.   105

And here like some weird Archimage sit I,
Plotting dark spells, and devilish enginery,
The self-impelling steam-wheels of the mind
Which pump up oaths from clergymen, and grind
The gentle spirit of our meek reviews   110
Into a powdery foam of salt abuse,
Ruffling the ocean of their self-content;—
I sit—and smile or sigh as is my bent,
But not for them—Libeccio rushes round
With an inconstant and an idle sound,   115
I heed him more than them—the thunder-smoke
Is gathering on the mountains, like a cloak
Folded athwart their shoulders broad and bare;
The ripe corn under the undulating air
Undulates like an ocean;—and the vines   120
Are trembling wide in all their trellised lines—
The murmur of the awakening sea doth fill
The empty pauses of the blast;—the hill
Looks hoary through the white electric rain,
And from the glens beyond, in sullen strain,   125
The interrupted thunder howls; above
One chasm of Heaven smiles, like the eye of Love
On the unquiet world;—while such things are,
How could one worth your friendship heed the war
Of worms? the shriek of the world's carrion jays,   130
Their censure, or their wonder, or their praise?

You are not here! the quaint witch Memory sees,
In vacant chairs, your absent images,

And points where once you sat, and now should be
But are not.—I demand if ever we   135
Shall meet as then we met;—and she replies,
Veiling in awe her second-sighted eyes;
'I know the past alone—but summon home
My sister Hope,—she speaks of all to come.'
But I, an old diviner, who knew well   140
Every false verse of that sweet oracle,
Turned to the sad enchantress once again,
And sought a respite from my gentle pain,
In citing every passage o'er and o'er
Of our communion—how on the sea-shore   145
We watched the ocean and the sky together,
Under the roof of blue Italian weather;
How I ran home through last year's thunder-storm,
And felt the transverse lightning linger warm
Upon my cheek—and how we often made   150
Feasts for each other, where good will outweighed
The frugal luxury of our country cheer,
As well it might, were it less firm and clear
Than ours must ever be;—and how we spun
A shroud of talk to hide us from the sun   155
Of this familiar life, which seems to be
But is not:—or is but quaint mockery
Of all we would believe, and sadly blame
The jarring and inexplicable frame
Of this wrong world:—and then anatomize   160
The purposes and thoughts of men whose eyes
Were closed in distant years;—or widely guess
The issue of the earth's great business,
When we shall be as we no longer are—
Like babbling gossips safe, who hear the war   165
Of winds, and sigh, but tremble not;—or how
You listened to some interrupted flow
Of visionary rhyme,—in joy and pain
Struck from the inmost fountains of my brain,
With little skill perhaps;—or how we sought   170
Those deepest wells of passion or of thought
Wrought by wise poets in the waste of years,
Staining their sacred waters with our tears;
Quenching a thirst ever to be renewed!
Or how I, wisest lady! then endued   175
The language of a land which now is free,
And, winged with thoughts of truth and majesty,
Flits round the tyrant's sceptre like a cloud,
And bursts the peopled prisons, and cries aloud,

'My name is Legion!'—that majestic tongue   180
Which Calderon over the desert flung
Of ages and of nations; and which found
An echo in our hearts, and with the sound
Startled oblivion;—thou wert then to me
As is a nurse—when inarticulately   185
A child would talk as its grown parents do.
If living winds the rapid clouds pursue,
If hawks chase doves through the aethereal way,
Huntsmen the innocent deer, and beasts their prey,
Why should not we rouse with the spirit's blast   190
Out of the forest of the pathless past
These recollected pleasures?
                              You are now
In London, that great sea, whose ebb and flow
At once is deaf and loud, and on the shore
Vomits its wrecks, and still howls on for more.   195
Yet in its depth what treasures! You will see
That which was Godwin,—greater none than he
Though fallen—and fallen on evil times—to stand
Among the spirits of our age and land,
Before the dread tribunal of *to come*   200
The foremost,—while Rebuke cowers pale and dumb.
You will see Coleridge—he who sits obscure
In the exceeding lustre and the pure
Intense irradiation of a mind,
Which, with its own internal lightning blind,   205
Flags wearily through darkness and despair—
A cloud-encircled meteor of the air,
A hooded eagle among blinking owls.—
You will see Hunt—one of those happy souls
Which are the salt of the earth, and without whom   210
This world would smell like what it is—a tomb;
Who is, what others seem; his room no doubt
Is still adorned with many a cast from Shout,
With graceful flowers tastefully placed about;
And coronals of bay from ribbons hung,   215
And brighter wreaths in neat disorder flung;
The gifts of the most learned among some dozens
Of female friends, sisters-in-law, and cousins.
And there is he with his eternal puns,
Which beat the dullest brain for smiles, like duns   220
Thundering for money at a poet's door;
Alas! it is no use to say, 'I'm poor!'
Or oft in graver mood, when he will look
Things wiser than were ever read in book,

Except in Shakespeare's wisest tenderness.—   225
You will see Hogg,—and I cannot express
His virtues,—though I know that they are great,
Because he locks, then barricades the gate
Within which they inhabit;—of his wit
And wisdom, you'll cry out when you are bit.   230
He is a pearl within an oyster shell,
One of the richest of the deep;—and there
Is English Peacock, with his mountain Fair,
Turned into a Flamingo;—that shy bird
That gleams i' the Indian air—have you not heard   235
When a man marries, dies, or turns Hindoo,
His best friends hear no more of him?—but you
Will see him, and will like him too, I hope,
With the milk-white Snowdonian Antelope
Matched with this cameleopard—his fine wit   240
Makes such a wound, the knife is lost in it;
A strain too learnèd for a shallow age,
Too wise for selfish bigots; let his page,
Which charms the chosen spirits of the time,
Fold itself up for the serener clime   245
Of years to come, and find its recompense
In that just expectation.—Wit and sense,
Virtue and human knowledge; all that might
Make this dull world a business of delight,
Are all combined in Horace Smith.—And these,   250
With some exceptions, which I need not tease
Your patience by descanting on,—are all
You and I know in London.

                I recall
My thoughts, and bid you look upon the night.
As water does a sponge, so the moonlight   255
Fills the void, hollow, universal air—
What see you?—unpavilioned Heaven is fair,
Whether the moon, into her chamber gone,
Leaves midnight to the golden stars, or wan
Climbs with diminished beams the azure steep;   260
Or whether clouds sail o'er the inverse deep,
Piloted by the many-wandering blast,
And the rare stars rush through them dim and fast:—
All this is beautiful in every land.—
But what see you beside?—a shabby stand   265
Of Hackney coaches—a brick house or wall
Fencing some lonely court, white with the scrawl
Of our unhappy politics;—or worse—
A wretched woman reeling by, whose curse

Mixed with the watchman's, partner of her trade,   270
You must accept in place of serenade—
Or yellow-haired Pollonia murmuring
To Henry, some unutterable thing.
I see a chaos of green leaves and fruit
Built round dark caverns, even to the root   275
Of the living stems that feed them—in whose bowers
There sleep in their dark dew the folded flowers;
Beyond, the surface of the unsickled corn
Trembles not in the slumbering air, and borne
In circles quaint, and ever-changing dance,   280
Like wingèd stars the fire-flies flash and glance,
Pale in the open moonshine, but each one
Under the dark trees seems a little sun,
A meteor tamed; a fixed star gone astray
From the silver regions of the milky way;—   285
Afar the Contadino's song is heard,
Rude, but made sweet by distance—and a bird
Which cannot be the Nightingale, and yet
I know none else that sings so sweet as it
At this late hour;—and then all is still—   290
Now—Italy or London, which you will!

    Next winter you must pass with me; I'll have
My house by that time turned into a grave
Of dead despondence and low-thoughted care,
And all the dreams which our tormentors are;   295
Oh! that Hunt, Hogg, Peacock, and Smith were there,
With everything belonging to them fair!—
We will have books, Spanish, Italian, Greek;
And ask one week to make another week
As like his father, as I'm unlike mine,   300
Which is not his fault, as you may divine.
Though we eat little flesh and drink no wine,
Yet let's be merry: we'll have tea and toast;
Custards for supper, and an endless host
Of syllabubs and jellies and mince-pies,   305
And other such lady-like luxuries,—
Feasting on which we will philosophize!
And we'll have fires out of the Grand Duke's wood,
To thaw the six weeks' winter in our blood.
And then we'll talk;—what shall we talk about?   310
Oh! there are themes enough for many a bout
Of thought-entangled descant;—as to nerves—
With cones and parallelograms and curves
I've sworn to strangle them if once they dare
To bother me—when you are with me there.   315

And they shall never more sip laudanum,
From Helicon or Himeros [1];—well, come,
And in despite of God and of the devil,
We'll make our friendly philosophic revel
Outlast the leafless time; till buds and flowers   320
Warn the obscure inevitable hours,
Sweet meeting by sad parting to renew;—
'To-morrow to fresh woods and pastures new.'

THE WITCH OF ATLAS

TO MARY

(ON HER OBJECTING TO THE FOLLOWING POEM, UPON THE SCORE OF ITS CONTAINING NO HUMAN INTEREST)

I

How, my dear Mary,—are you critic-bitten
    (For vipers kill, though dead) by some review,
That you condemn these verses I have written,
    Because they tell no story, false or true?
What, though no mice are caught by a young kitten,   5
    May it not leap and play as grown cats do,
Till its claws come? Prithee, for this one time,
Content thee with a visionary rhyme.

II

What hand would crush the silken-wingèd fly,
    The youngest of inconstant April's minions,   10
Because it cannot climb the purest sky,
    Where the swan sings, amid the sun's dominions?
Not thine. Thou knowest 'tis its doom to die,
    When Day shall hide within her twilight pinions
The lucent eyes, and the eternal smile,   15
Serene as thine, which lent it life awhile.

III

To thy fair feet a wingèd Vision came,
    Whose date should have been longer than a day,
And o'er thy head did beat its wings for fame,
    And in thy sight its fading plumes display;   20
The watery bow burned in the evening flame,
    But the shower fell, the swift Sun went his way—
And that is dead.—O, let me not believe
That anything of mine is fit to live!

[1] "Ἵμερος, from which the river Himera was named, is, with some slight shade of difference, a synonym of Love.—[SHELLEY'S NOTE.]

IV

Wordsworth informs us he was nineteen years   25
   Considering and retouching Peter Bell;
Watering his laurels with the killing tears
   Of slow, dull care, so that their roots to Hell
Might pierce, and their wide branches blot the spheres
   Of Heaven, with dewy leaves and flowers; this well   30
May be, for Heaven and Earth conspire to foil
The over-busy gardener's blundering toil.

V

My Witch indeed is not so sweet a creature
   As Ruth or Lucy, whom his graceful praise
Clothes for our grandsons—but she matches Peter,   35
   Though he took nineteen years, and she three days
In dressing. Light the vest of flowing metre
   She wears; he, proud as dandy with his stays,
Has hung upon his wiry limbs a dress
Like King Lear's 'looped and windowed raggedness.'   40

VI

If you strip Peter, you will see a fellow
   Scorched by Hell's hyperequatorial climate
Into a kind of a sulphureous yellow:
   A lean mark, hardly fit to fling a rhyme at;
In shape a Scaramouch, in hue Othello.   45
   If you unveil my Witch, no priest nor primate
Can shrive you of that sin,—if sin there be
In love, when it becomes idolatry.

THE WITCH OF ATLAS

I

BEFORE those cruel Twins, whom at one birth
   Incestuous Change bore to her father Time,   50
Error and Truth, had hunted from the Earth
   All those bright natures which adorned its prime,
And left us nothing to believe in, worth
   The pains of putting into learnèd rhyme,
A lady-witch there lived on Atlas' mountain   55
Within a cavern, by a secret fountain.

II

Her mother was one of the Atlantides:
   The all-beholding Sun had ne'er beholden
In his wide voyage o'er continents and seas
   So fair a creature, as she lay enfolden   60

In the warm shadow of her loveliness;—
   He kissed her with his beams, and made all golden
The chamber of gray rock in which she lay—
She, in that dream of joy, dissolved away.

III

'Tis said, she first was changed into a vapour,   65
   And then into a cloud, such clouds as flit,
Like splendour-wingèd moths about a taper,
   Round the red west when the sun dies in it:
And then into a meteor, such as caper
   On hill-tops when the moon is in a fit: 70
Then, into one of those mysterious stars
Which hide themselves between the Earth and Mars.

IV

Ten times the Mother of the Months had bent
   Her bow beside the folding-star, and hidden
With that bright sign the billows to indent   75
   The sea-deserted sand—like children chidden,
At her command they ever came and went—
   Since in that cave a dewy splendour hidden
Took shape and motion: with the living form
Of this embodied Power, the cave grew warm.   80

V

A lovely lady garmented in light
   From her own beauty—deep her eyes, as are
Two openings of unfathomable night
   Seen through a Temple's cloven roof—her hair
Dark—the dim brain whirls dizzy with delight,   85
   Picturing her form; her soft smiles shone afar,
And her low voice was heard like love, and drew
All living things towards this wonder new.

VI

And first the spotted cameleopard came,
   And then the wise and fearless elephant;   90
Then the sly serpent, in the golden flame
   Of his own volumes intervolved;—all gaunt
And sanguine beasts her gentle looks made tame.
   They drank before her at her sacred fount;
And every beast of beating heart grew bold,   95
Such gentleness and power even to behold.

VII

The brinded lioness led forth her young,
  That she might teach them how they should forego
Their inborn thirst of death; the pard unstrung
  His sinews at her feet, and sought to know   100
With looks whose motions spoke without a tongue
  How he might be as gentle as the doe.
The magic circle of her voice and eyes
All savage natures did imparadise.

VIII

And old Silenus, shaking a green stick   105
  Of lilies, and the wood-gods in a crew
Came, blithe, as in the olive copses thick
  Cicadae are, drunk with the noonday dew:
And Dryope and Faunus followed quick,
  Teasing the God to sing them something new;   110
Till in this cave they found the lady lone,
Sitting upon a seat of emerald stone.

IX

And universal Pan, 'tis said, was there,
  And though none saw him,—through the adamant
Of the deep mountains, through the trackless air,   115
  And through those living spirits, like a want,
He passed out of his everlasting lair
  Where the quick heart of the great world doth pant,
And felt that wondrous lady all alone,—
And she felt him, upon her emerald throne.   120

X

And every nymph of stream and spreading tree,
  And every shepherdess of Ocean's flocks,
Who drives her white waves over the green sea,
  And Ocean with the brine on his gray locks,
And quaint Priapus with his company,   125
  All came, much wondering how the enwombèd rocks
Could have brought forth so beautiful a birth;—
Her love subdued their wonder and their mirth.

XI

The herdsmen and the mountain maidens came,
  And the rude kings of pastoral Garamant—   130
Their spirits shook within them, as a flame
  Stirred by the air under a cavern gaunt:

Pigmies, and Polyphemes, by many a name,
  Centaurs, and Satyrs, and such shapes as haunt
Wet clefts,—and lumps neither alive nor dead,   135
Dog-headed, bosom-eyed, and bird-footed.

XII

For she was beautiful—her beauty made
  The bright world dim, and everything beside
Seemed like the fleeting image of a shade:
  No thought of living spirit could abide,   140
Which to her looks had ever been betrayed,
  On any object in the world so wide,
On any hope within the circling skies,
But on her form, and in her inmost eyes.

XIII

Which when the lady knew, she took her spindle   145
  And twined three threads of fleecy mist, and three
Long lines of light, such as the dawn may kindle
  The clouds and waves and mountains with; and she
As many star-beams, ere their lamps could dwindle
  In the belated moon, wound skilfully;   150
And with these threads a subtle veil she wove—
A shadow for the splendour of her love.

XIV

The deep recesses of her odorous dwelling
  Were stored with magic treasures—sounds of air,
Which had the power all spirits of compelling,   155
  Folded in cells of crystal silence there;
Such as we hear in youth, and think the feeling
  Will never die—yet ere we are aware,
The feeling and the sound are fled and gone,
And the regret they leave remains alone.   160

XV

And there lay Visions swift, and sweet, and quaint,
  Each in its thin sheath, like a chrysalis,
Some eager to burst forth, some weak and faint
  With the soft burthen of intensest bliss.
It was its work to bear to many a saint   165
  Whose heart adores the shrine which holiest is,
Even Love's:—and others white, green, gray, and black,
And of all shapes—and each was at her beck.

XVI

And odours in a kind of aviary
   Of ever-blooming Eden-trees she kept,   170
Clipped in a floating net, a love-sick Fairy
   Had woven from dew-beams while the moon yet slept;
As bats at the wired window of a dairy,
   They beat their vans; and each was an adept,
When loosed and missioned, making wings of winds,   175
To stir sweet thoughts or sad, in destined minds.

XVII

And liquors clear and sweet, whose healthful might
   Could medicine the sick soul to happy sleep,
And change eternal death into a night
   Of glorious dreams—or if eyes needs must weep,   180
Could make their tears all wonder and delight,
   She in her crystal vials did closely keep:
If men could drink of those clear vials, 'tis said
The living were not envied of the dead.

XVIII

Her cave was stored with scrolls of strange device,   185
   The works of some Saturnian Archimage,
Which taught the expiations at whose price
   Men from the Gods might win that happy age
Too lightly lost, redeeming native vice;
   And which might quench the Earth-consuming rage   190
Of gold and blood—till men should live and move
Harmonious as the sacred stars above;

XIX

And how all things that seem untameable,
   Not to be checked and not to be confined,
Obey the spells of Wisdom's wizard skill;   195
   Time, earth, and fire—the ocean and the wind,
And all their shapes—and man's imperial will;
   And other scrolls whose writings did unbind
The inmost lore of Love—let the profane
Tremble to ask what secrets they contain.   200

XX

And wondrous works of substances unknown,
   To which the enchantment of her father's power
Had changed those ragged blocks of savage stone,
   Were heaped in the recesses of her bower;

Carved lamps and chalices, and vials which shone   205
   In their own golden beams—each like a flower,
Out of whose depth a fire-fly shakes his light
Under a cypress in a starless night.

XXI

At first she lived alone in this wild home,
   And her own thoughts were each a minister,   210
Clothing themselves, or with the ocean foam,
   Or with the wind, or with the speed of fire,
To work whatever purposes might come
   Into her mind; such power her mighty Sire
Had girt them with, whether to fly or run,   215
Through all the regions which he shines upon.

XXII

The Ocean-nymphs and Hamadryades,
   Oreads and Naiads, with long weedy locks,
Offered to do her bidding through the seas,
   Under the earth, and in the hollow rocks,   220
And far beneath the matted roots of trees,
   And in the gnarlèd heart of stubborn oaks,
So they might live for ever in the light
Of her sweet presence—each a satellite.

XXIII

'This may not be,' the wizard maid replied;   225
   'The fountains where the Naiades bedew
Their shining hair, at length are drained and dried;
   The solid oaks forget their strength, and strew
Their latest leaf upon the mountains wide;
   The boundless ocean like a drop of dew   230
Will be consumed—the stubborn centre must
Be scattered, like a cloud of summer dust.

XXIV

'And ye with them will perish, one by one;—
   If I must sigh to think that this shall be,
If I must weep when the surviving Sun   235
   Shall smile on your decay—oh, ask not me
To love you till your little race is run;
   I cannot die as ye must—over me
Your leaves shall glance—the streams in which ye dwell
Shall be my paths henceforth, and so—farewell!'—   240

XXV

She spoke and wept:—the dark and azure well
  Sparkled beneath the shower of her bright tears,
And every little circlet where they fell
  Flung to the cavern-roof inconstant spheres
And intertangled lines of light:—a knell   245
  Of sobbing voices came upon her ears
From those departing Forms, o'er the serene
Of the white streams and of the forest green.

XXVI

All day the wizard lady sate aloof,
  Spelling out scrolls of dread antiquity,   250
Under the cavern's fountain-lighted roof;
  Or broidering the pictured poesy
Of some high tale upon her growing woof,
  Which the sweet splendour of her smiles could dye
In hues outshining heaven—and ever she   255
Added some grace to the wrought poesy.

XXVII

While on her hearth lay blazing many a piece
  Of sandal wood, rare gums, and cinnamon;
Men scarcely know how beautiful fire is—
  Each flame of it is as a precious stone   260
Dissolved in ever-moving light, and this
  Belongs to each and all who gaze upon.
The Witch beheld it not, for in her hand
She held a woof that dimmed the burning brand.

XXVIII

This lady never slept, but lay in trance   265
  All night within the fountain—as in sleep.
Its emerald crags glowed in her beauty's glance;
  Through the green splendour of the water deep
She saw the constellations reel and dance
  Like fire-flies—and withal did ever keep   270
The tenour of her contemplations calm,
With open eyes, closed feet, and folded palm.

XXIX

And when the whirlwinds and the clouds descended
  From the white pinnacles of that cold hill,
She passed at dewfall to a space extended,   275
  Where in a lawn of flowering asphodel

Amid a wood of pines and cedars blended,
　There yawned an inextinguishable well
Of crimson fire—full even to the brim,
And overflowing all the margin trim.   280

XXX

Within the which she lay when the fierce war
　Of wintry winds shook that innocuous liquor
In many a mimic moon and bearded star
　O'er woods and lawns;—the serpent heard it flicker
In sleep, and dreaming still, he crept afar—   285
　And when the windless snow descended thicker
Than autumn leaves, she watched it as it came
Melt on the surface of the level flame.

XXXI

She had a boat, which some say Vulcan wrought
　For Venus, as the chariot of her star;   290
But it was found too feeble to be fraught
　With all the ardours in that sphere which are,
And so she sold it, and Apollo bought
　And gave it to this daughter: from a car
Changed to the fairest and the lightest boat   295
Which ever upon mortal stream did float.

XXXII

And others say, that, when but three hours old,
　The first-born Love out of his cradle lept,
And clove dun Chaos with his wings of gold,
　And like a horticultural adept,   300
Stole a strange seed, and wrapped it up in mould,
　And sowed it in his mother's star, and kept
Watering it all the summer with sweet dew,
And with his wings fanning it as it grew.

XXXIII

The plant grew strong and green, the snowy flower   305
　Fell, and the long and gourd-like fruit began
To turn the light and dew by inward power
　To its own substance; woven tracery ran
Of light firm texture, ribbed and branching, o'er
　The solid rind, like a leaf's veinèd fan—   310
Of which Love scooped this boat—and with soft motion
Piloted it round the circumfluous ocean.

XXXIV

This boat she moored upon her fount, and lit
   A living spirit within all its frame,
Breathing the soul of swiftness into it.   315
    Couched on the fountain like a panther tame,
One of the twain at Evan's feet that sit—
    Or as on Vesta's sceptre a swift flame—
Or on blind Homer's heart a wingèd thought,—
In joyous expectation lay the boat.   320

XXXV

Then by strange art she kneaded fire and snow
   Together, tempering the repugnant mass
With liquid love—all things together grow
    Through which the harmony of love can pass;
And a fair Shape out of her hands did flow—   325
    A living Image, which did far surpass
In beauty that bright shape of vital stone
Which drew the heart out of Pygmalion.

XXXVI

A sexless thing it was, and in its growth
   It seemed to have developed no defect   330
Of either sex, yet all the grace of both,—
    In gentleness and strength its limbs were decked
The bosom swelled lightly with its full youth,
    The countenance was such as might select
Some artist that his skill should never die,   335
Imaging forth such perfect purity.

XXXVII

From its smooth shoulders hung two rapid wings,
   Fit to have borne it to the seventh sphere,
Tipped with the speed of liquid lightenings,
    Dyed in the ardours of the atmosphere: 340
She led her creature to the boiling springs
    Where the light boat was moored, and said: 'Sit here!'
And pointed to the prow, and took her seat
Beside the rudder, with opposing feet.

XXXVIII

And down the streams which clove those mountains vast,
   Around their inland islets, and amid   346
The panther-peopled forests, whose shade cast
    Darkness and odours, and a pleasure hid

In melancholy gloom, the pinnace passed;
　By many a star-surrounded pyramid　　　350
Of icy crag cleaving the purple sky,
And caverns yawning round unfathomably.

XXXIX

The silver noon into that winding dell,
　With slanted gleam athwart the forest tops,
Tempered like golden evening, feebly fell;　　355
　A green and glowing light, like that which drops
From folded lilies in which glow-worms dwell,
　When Earth over her face Night's mantle wraps;
Between the severed mountains lay on high,
Over the stream, a narrow rift of sky.　　360

XL

And ever as she went, the Image lay
　With folded wings and unawakened eyes;
And o'er its gentle countenance did play
　The busy dreams, as thick as summer flies,
Chasing the rapid smiles that would not stay,　　365
　And drinking the warm tears, and the sweet sighs
Inhaling, which, with busy murmur vain,
They had aroused from that full heart and brain.

XLI

And ever down the prone vale, like a cloud
　Upon a stream of wind, the pinnace went:　　370
Now lingering on the pools, in which abode
　The calm and darkness of the deep content
In which they paused; now o'er the shallow road
　Of white and dancing waters, all besprent
With sand and polished pebbles:—mortal boat　　375
In such a shallow rapid could not float.

XLII

And down the earthquaking cataracts which shiver
　Their snow-like waters into golden air,
Or under chasms unfathomable ever
　Sepulchre them, till in their rage they tear　　380
A subterranean portal for the river,
　It fled—the circling sunbows did upbear
Its fall down the hoar precipice of spray,
Lighting it far upon its lampless way.

XLIII

And when the wizard lady would ascend   385
    The labyrinths of some many-winding vale,
Which to the inmost mountain upward tend—
    She called 'Hermaphroditus!'—and the pale
And heavy hue which slumber could extend
    Over its lips and eyes, as on the gale   390
A rapid shadow from a slope of grass,
Into the darkness of the stream did pass.

XLIV

And it unfurled its heaven-coloured pinions,
    With stars of fire spotting the stream below;
And from above into the Sun's dominions   395
    Flinging a glory, like the golden glow
In which Spring clothes her emerald-wingèd minions,
    All interwoven with fine feathery snow
And moonlight splendour of intensest rime,
With which frost paints the pines in winter time.   400

XLV

And then it winnowed the Elysian air
    Which ever hung about that lady bright,
With its aethereal vans—and speeding there,
    Like a star up the torrent of the night,
Or a swift eagle in the morning glare   405
    Breasting the whirlwind with impetuous flight,
The pinnace, oared by those enchanted wings,
Clove the fierce streams towards their upper springs.

XLVI

The water flashed, like sunlight by the prow
    Of a noon-wandering meteor flung to Heaven;   410
The still air seemed as if its waves did flow
    In tempest down the mountains; loosely driven
The lady's radiant hair streamed to and fro:
    Beneath, the billows having vainly striven
Indignant and impetuous, roared to feel   415
The swift and steady motion of the keel.

XLVII

Or, when the weary moon was in the wane,
    Or in the noon of interlunar night,
The lady-witch in visions could not chain
    Her spirit; but sailed forth under the light   420

Of shooting stars, and bade extend amain
  Its storm-outspeeding wings, the Hermaphrodite;
She to the Austral waters took her way,
Beyond the fabulous Thamondocana,—

XLVIII

Where, like a meadow which no scythe has shaven,   425
  Which rain could never bend, or whirl-blast shake,
With the Antarctic constellations paven,
  Canopus and his crew, lay the Austral lake—
There she would build herself a windless haven
  Out of the clouds whose moving turrets make   430
The bastions of the storm, when through the sky
The spirits of the tempest thundered by:

XLIX

A haven beneath whose translucent floor
  The tremulous stars sparkled unfathomably,
And around which the solid vapours hoar,   435
  Based on the level waters, to the sky
Lifted their dreadful crags, and like a shore
  Of wintry mountains, inaccessibly
Hemmed in with rifts and precipices gray,
And hanging crags, many a cove and bay.   440

L

And whilst the outer lake beneath the lash
  Of the wind's scourge, foamed like a wounded thing,
And the incessant hail with stony clash
  Ploughed up the waters, and the flagging wing
Of the housed cormorant in the lightning flash   445
  Looked like the wreck of some wind-wandering
Fragment of inky thunder-smoke—this haven
Was as a gem to copy Heaven engraven,—

LI

On which that lady played her many pranks,
  Circling the image of a shooting star,   450
Even as a tiger on Hydaspes' banks
  Outspeeds the antelopes which speediest are,
In her light boat; and many quips and cranks
  She played upon the water, till the car
Of the late moon, like a sick matron wan,   455
To journey from the misty east began.

LII

And then she called out of the hollow turrets
   Of those high clouds, white, golden and vermilion,
The armies of her ministering spirits—
   In mighty legions, million after million,   460
They came, each troop emblazoning its merits
   On meteor flags; and many a proud pavilion
Of the intertexture of the atmosphere
They pitched upon the plain of the calm mere.

LIII

They framed the imperial tent of their great Queen   465
   Of woven exhalations, underlaid
With lambent lightning-fire, as may be seen
   A dome of thin and open ivory inlaid
With crimson silk—cressets from the serene
   Hung there, and on the water for her tread   470
A tapestry of fleece-like mist was strewn,
Dyed in the beams of the ascending moon.

LIV

And on a throne o'erlaid with starlight, caught
   Upon those wandering isles of aëry dew,
Which highest shoals of mountain shipwreck not,   475
   She sate, and heard all that had happened new
Between the earth and moon, since they had brought
   The last intelligence—and now she grew
Pale as that moon, lost in the watery night—
And now she wept, and now she laughed outright.   480

LV

These were tame pleasures; she would often climb
   The steepest ladder of the crudded rack
Up to some beakèd cape of cloud sublime,
   And like Arion on the dolphin's back
Ride singing through the shoreless air;—oft-time   485
   Following the serpent lightning's winding track,
She ran upon the platforms of the wind,
And laughed to hear the fire-balls roar behind.

LVI

And sometimes to those streams of upper air
   Which whirl the earth in its diurnal round,   490
She would ascend, and win the spirits there
   To let her join their chorus. Mortals found

That on those days the sky was calm and fair,
  And mystic snatches of harmonious sound
Wandered upon the earth where'er she passed,   495
And happy thoughts of hope, too sweet to last.

LVII .

But her choice sport was, in the hours of sleep,
  To glide adown old Nilus, where he threads
Egypt and Aethiopia, from the steep
  Of utmost Axumè, until he spreads,   500
Like a calm flock of silver-fleecèd sheep,
  His waters on the plain: and crested heads
Of cities and proud temples gleam amid,
And many a vapour-belted pyramid.

LVIII

By Moeris and the Mareotid lakes,   505
  Strewn with faint blooms like bridal chamber floors,
Where naked boys bridling tame water-snakes,
  Or charioteering ghastly alligators,
Had left on the sweet waters mighty wakes
  Of those huge forms—within the brazen doors   510
Of the great Labyrinth slept both boy and beast,
Tired with the pomp of their Osirian feast.

LIX

And where within the surface of the river
  The shadows of the massy temples lie,
And never are erased—but tremble ever   515
  Like things which every cloud can doom to die,
Through lotus-paven canals, and wheresoever
  The works of man pierced that serenest sky
With tombs, and towers, and fanes, 'twas her delight
To wander in the shadow of the night.   520

LX

With motion like the spirit of that wind
  Whose soft step deepens slumber, her light feet
Passed through the peopled haunts of humankind,
  Scattering sweet visions from her presence sweet,
Through fane, and palace-court, and labyrinth mined   525
  With many a dark and subterranean street
Under the Nile, through chambers high and deep
She passed, observing mortals in their sleep.

LXI

A pleasure sweet doubtless it was to see
   Mortals subdued in all the shapes of sleep.   530
Here lay two sister twins in infancy;
   There, a lone youth who in his dreams did weep;
Within, two lovers linkèd innocently
   In their loose locks which over both did creep
Like ivy from one stem;—and there lay calm   535
Old age with snow-bright hair and folded palm.

LXII

But other troubled forms of sleep she saw,
   Not to be mirrored in a holy song—
Distortions foul of supernatural awe,
   And pale imaginings of visioned wrong;   540
And all the code of Custom's lawless law
   Written upon the brows of old and young:
'This,' said the wizard maiden, 'is the strife
Which stirs the liquid surface of man's life.'

LXIII

And little did the sight disturb her soul,—   545
   We, the weak mariners of that wide lake
Where'er its shores extend or billows roll,
   Our course unpiloted and starless make
O'er its wild surface to an unknown goal:—
   But she in the calm depths her way could take,   550
Where in bright bowers immortal forms abide
Beneath the weltering of the restless tide.

LXIV

And she saw princes couched under the glow
   Of sunlike gems; and round each temple-court
In dormitories ranged, row after row,   555
   She saw the priests asleep—all of one sort—
For all were educated to be so.—
   The peasants in their huts, and in the port
The sailors she saw cradled on the waves,
And the dead lulled within their dreamless graves.   560

LXV

And all the forms in which those spirits lay
   Were to her sight like the diaphanous
Veils, in which those sweet ladies oft array
   Their delicate limbs, who would conceal from us

Only their scorn of all concealment: they
  Move in the light of their own beauty thus.
But these and all now lay with sleep upon them,
And little thought a Witch was looking on them.

LXVI

She, all those human figures breathing there,
  Beheld as living spirits—to her eyes   570
The naked beauty of the soul lay bare,
  And often through a rude and worn disguise
She saw the inner form most bright and fair—
  And then she had a charm of strange device,
Which, murmured on mute lips with tender tone, 575
Could make that spirit mingle with her own.

LXVII

Alas! Aurora, what wouldst thou have given
  For such a charm when Tithon became gray?
Or how much, Venus, of thy silver heaven
  Wouldst thou have yielded, ere Proserpina   580
Had half (oh! why not all?) the debt forgiven
  Which dear Adonis had been doomed to pay,
To any witch who would have taught you it?
The Heliad doth not know its value yet.

LXVIII

'Tis said in after times her spirit free   585
  Knew what love was, and felt itself alone—
But holy Dian could not chaster be
  Before she stooped to kiss Endymion,
Than now this lady—like a sexless bee
  Tasting all blossoms, and confined to none, 590
Among those mortal forms, the wizard-maiden
Passed with an eye serene and heart unladen.

LXIX

To those she saw most beautiful, she gave
  Strange panacea in a crystal bowl:—
They drank in their deep sleep of that sweet wave, 595
  And lived thenceforward as if some control,
Mightier than life, were in them; and the grave
  Of such, when death oppressed the weary soul,
Was as a green and overarching bower
Lit by the gems of many a starry flower.   600

LXX

For on the night when they were buried, she
   Restored the embalmers' ruining, and shook
The light out of the funeral lamps, to be
   A mimic day within that deathy nook;
And she unwound the woven imagery   605
   Of second childhood's swaddling bands, and took
The coffin, its last cradle, from its niche,
And threw it with contempt into a ditch.

LXXI

And there the body lay, age after age,
   Mute, breathing, beating, warm, and undecaying,   610
Like one asleep in a green hermitage,
   With gentle smiles about its eyelids playing,
And living in its dreams beyond the rage
   Of death or life; while they were still arraying
In liveries ever new, the rapid, blind   615
And fleeting generations of mankind.

LXXII

And she would write strange dreams upon the brain
   Of those who were less beautiful, and make
All harsh and crooked purposes more vain
   Than in the desert is the serpent's wake   620
Which the sand covers—all his evil gain
   The miser in such dreams would rise and shake
Into a beggar's lap;—the lying scribe
Would his own lies betray without a bribe.

LXXIII

The priests would write an explanation full,   625
   Translating hieroglyphics into Greek,
How the God Apis really was a bull,
   And nothing more; and bid the herald stick
The same against the temple doors, and pull
   The old cant down; they licensed all to speak   630
Whate'er they thought of hawks, and cats, and geese,
By pastoral letters to each diocese.

LXXIV

The king would dress an ape up in his crown
   And robes, and seat him on his glorious seat,
And on the right hand of the sunlike throne   635
   Would place a gaudy mock-bird to repeat

The chatterings of the monkey.—Every one
    Of the prone courtiers crawled to kiss the feet
Of their great Emperor, when the morning came,
And kissed—alas, how many kiss the same!   640

LXXV

The soldiers dreamed that they were blacksmiths, and
    Walked out of quarters in somnambulism;
Round the red anvils you might see them stand
    Like Cyclopses in Vulcan's sooty abysm,
Beating their swords to ploughshares;—in a band   645
    The gaolers sent those of the liberal schism
Free through the streets of Memphis, much, I wis,
To the annoyance of king Amasis.

LXXVI

And timid lovers who had been so coy,
    They hardly knew whether they loved or not,   650
Would rise out of their rest, and take sweet joy,
    To the fulfilment of their inmost thought;
And when next day the maiden and the boy
    Met one another, both, like sinners caught,
Blushed at the thing which each believed was done   655
Only in fancy—till the tenth moon shone;

LXXVII

And then the Witch would let them take no ill:
    Of many thousand schemes which lovers find,
The Witch found one,—and so they took their fill
    Of happiness in marriage warm and kind.   660
Friends who, by practice of some envious skill,
    Were torn apart—a wide wound, mind from mind!—
She did unite again with visions clear
Of deep affection and of truth sincere.

LXXVIII

These were the pranks she played among the cities   665
    Of mortal men, and what she did to Sprites
And Gods, entangling them in her sweet ditties
    To do her will, and show their subtle sleights,
I will declare another time; for it is
    A tale more fit for the weird winter nights   670
Than for these garish summer days, when we
Scarcely believe much more than we can see.

·

NOTE ON THE WITCH OF ATLAS, BY MRS. SHELLEY

WE spent the summer of 1820 at the Baths of San Giuliano, four miles from Pisa. These baths were of great use to Shelley in soothing his nervous irritability. We made several excursions in the neighbourhood. The country around is fertile, and diversified and rendered picturesque by ranges of near hills and more distant mountains. The peasantry are a handsome intelligent race; and there was a gladsome sunny heaven spread over us, that rendered home and every scene we visited cheerful and bright. During some of the hottest days of August, Shelley made a solitary journey on foot to the summit of Monte San Pellegrino—a mountain of some height, on the top of which there is a chapel, the object, during certain days of the year, of many pilgrimages. The excursion delighted him while it lasted; though he exerted himself too much, and the effect was considerable lassitude and weakness on his return. During the expedition he conceived the idea, and wrote, in the three days immediately succeeding to his return, the *Witch of Atlas*. This poem is peculiarly characteristic of his tastes—wildly fanciful, full of brilliant imagery, and discarding human interest and passion, to revel in the fantastic ideas that his imagination suggested.

The surpassing excellence of *The Cenci* had made me greatly desire that Shelley should increase his popularity by adopting subjects that would more suit the popular taste than a poem conceived in the abstract and dreamy spirit of the *Witch of Atlas*. It was not only that I wished him to acquire popularity as redounding to his fame; but I believed that he would obtain a greater mastery over his own powers, and greater happiness in his mind, if public applause crowned his endeavours. The few stanzas that precede the poem were addressed to me on my representing these ideas to him. Even now I believe that I was in the right. Shelley did not expect sympathy and approbation from the public; but the want of it took away a portion of the ardour that ought to have sustained him while writing. He was thrown on his own resources, and on the inspiration of his own soul; and wrote because his mind overflowed, without the hope of being appreciated. I had not the most distant wish that he should truckle in opinion, or submit his lofty aspirations for the human race to the low ambition and pride of the many; but I felt sure that, if his poems were more addressed to the common feelings of men, his proper rank among the writers of the day would be acknowledged, and that popularity as a poet would enable his countrymen to do justice to his character and virtues, which in those days it was the mode to attack with the most flagitious calumnies and insulting abuse. That he felt these things deeply cannot be doubted, though he armed himself with the consciousness of acting from a lofty and heroic sense of right. The truth burst from his heart sometimes in solitude, and he would write a few unfinished verses that showed that he felt the sting; among such I find the following:—

'Alas! this is not what I thought Life was.
  I knew that there were crimes and evil men,
Misery and hate; nor did I hope to pass
  Untouched by suffering through the rugged glen.
In mine own heart I saw as in a glass
  The hearts of others.... And, when
I went among my kind, with triple brass
  Of calm endurance my weak breast I armed,
To bear scorn, fear, and hate—a woful mass!'

I believed that all this morbid feeling would vanish if the chord of sympathy between him and his countrymen were touched. But my persuasions were vain, the mind could not be bent from its natural inclination. Shelley shrunk instinctively from portraying human passion, with its mixture of good and evil, of disappointment and disquiet. Such opened again the wounds of his own heart; and he loved to shelter himself rather in the airiest flights of fancy, forgetting love and hate, and regret and lost hope, in such imaginations as borrow their hues from sunrise or sunset, from the yellow moonshine or paly twilight, from the aspect of the far ocean or the shadows of the woods,—which celebrated the singing of the winds among the pines, the flow of a murmuring stream, and the thousand harmonious sounds which Nature creates in her solitudes. These are the materials which form the *Witch of Atlas:* it is a brilliant congregation of ideas such as his senses gathered, and his fancy coloured, during his rambles in the sunny land he so much loved.

EPIPSYCHIDION

VERSES ADDRESSED TO THE NOBLE AND UNFORTUNATE LADY, EMILIA V——,

NOW IMPRISONED IN THE CONVENT OF ——

L' anima amante si slancia fuori del creato, e si crea nell' infinito un Mondo tutto per essa, diverso assai da questo oscuro e pauroso baratro. HER OWN WORDS.

ADVERTISEMENT

THE Writer of the following lines died at Florence, as he was preparing for a voyage to one of the wildest of the Sporades, which he had bought, and where he had fitted up the ruins of an old building, and where it was his hope to have realised a scheme of life, suited perhaps to that happier and better world of which he is now an inhabitant, but hardly practicable in this. His life was singular; less on account of the romantic vicissitudes which diversified it, than the ideal tinge which it received from his own character and feelings. The present Poem, like the *Vita Nuova* of Dante, is sufficiently intelligible to a certain class of readers without a matter-of-fact history of the circumstances to which it relates; and to a certain other class it must ever remain incomprehensible, from a defect of a common organ of perception for the ideas of which it treats. Not but that *gran vergogna sarebbe a colui, che rimasse cosa sotto veste di figura, o di colore rettorico: e domandato non sapesse denudare le sue parole da cotal veste, in guisa che avessero verace intendimento.*

The present poem appears to have been intended by the Writer as the dedication to some longer one. The stanza on the opposite page is almost a literal translation from Dante's famous Canzone

Voi, ch' intendendo, il terzo ciel movete, etc.

The presumptuous application of the concluding lines to his own composition will raise a smile at the expense of my unfortunate friend: be it a smile not of contempt, but pity.   S.

> My Song, I fear that thou wilt find but few
> Who fitly shall conceive thy reasoning,
> Of such hard matter dost thou entertain;
> Whence, if by misadventure, chance should bring
> Thee to base company (as chance may do),   5
> Quite unaware of what thou dost contain,
> I prithee, comfort thy sweet self again,
> My last delight! tell them that they are dull,
> And bid them own that thou art beautiful.

EPIPSYCHIDION

> Sweet Spirit! Sister of that orphan one,
> Whose empire is the name thou weepest on,
> In my heart's temple I suspend to thee
> These votive wreaths of withered memory.
>
> Poor captive bird! who, from thy narrow cage,   5
> Pourest such music, that it might assuage
> The ruggèd hearts of those who prisoned thee,
> Were they not deaf to all sweet melody;
> This song shall be thy rose: its petals pale
> Are dead, indeed, my adored Nightingale!   10
> But soft and fragrant is the faded blossom,
> And it has no thorn left to wound thy bosom.
>
> High, spirit-wingèd Heart! who dost for ever
> Beat thine unfeeling bars with vain endeavour,
> Till those bright plumes of thought, in which arrayed 15
> It over-soared this low and worldly shade,
> Lie shattered; and thy panting, wounded breast
> Stains with dear blood its unmaternal nest!
> I weep vain tears: blood would less bitter be,
> Yet poured forth gladlier, could it profit thee.   20

Seraph of Heaven! too gentle to be human,
Veiling beneath that radiant form of Woman
All that is insupportable in thee
Of light, and love, and immortality!
Sweet Benediction in the eternal Curse!　　　　25
Veilèd Glory of this lampless Universe!
Thou Moon beyond the clouds! Thou living Form
Among the Dead! Thou Star above the Storm!
Thou Wonder, and thou Beauty, and thou Terror!
Thou Harmony of Nature's art! Thou Mirror　　　30
In whom, as in the splendour of the Sun,
All shapes look glorious which thou gazest on!
Ay, even the dim words which obscure thee now
Flash, lightning-like, with unaccustomed glow;
I pray thee that thou blot from this sad song　　35
All of its much mortality and wrong,
With those clear drops, which start like sacred dew
From the twin lights thy sweet soul darkens through,
Weeping, till sorrow becomes ecstasy:
Then smile on it, so that it may not die.　　　　40

I never thought before my death to see
Youth's vision thus made perfect. Emily,
I love thee; though the world by no thin name
Will hide that love from its unvalued shame.
Would we two had been twins of the same mother!　45
Or, that the name my heart lent to another
Could be a sister's bond for her and thee,
Blending two beams of one eternity!
Yet were one lawful and the other true,
These names, though dear, could paint not, as is due,　50
How beyond refuge I am thine. Ah me!
I am not thine: I am a part of *thee*.

Sweet Lamp! my moth-like Muse has burned its wings
Or, like a dying swan who soars and sings,
Young Love should teach Time, in his own gray style,　55
All that thou art. Art thou not void of guile,
A lovely soul formed to be blessed and bless?
A well of sealed and secret happiness,
Whose waters like blithe light and music are,
Vanquishing dissonance and gloom? A Star　　　　60
Which moves not in the moving heavens, alone?
A Smile amid dark frowns? a gentle tone
Amid rude voices? a belovèd light?
A Solitude, a Refuge, a Delight?
A Lute, which those whom Love has taught to play　65
Make music on, to soothe the roughest day

And lull fond Grief asleep? a buried treasure?
A cradle of young thoughts of wingless pleasure?
A violet-shrouded grave of Woe?—I measure
The world of fancies, seeking one like thee,   70
And find—alas! mine own infirmity.

    She met me, Stranger, upon life's rough way,
And lured me towards sweet Death; as Night by Day,
Winter by Spring, or Sorrow by swift Hope,
Led into light, life, peace. An antelope,   75
In the suspended impulse of its lightness,
Were less aethereally light: the brightness
Of her divinest presence trembles through
Her limbs, as underneath a cloud of dew
Embodied in the windless heaven of June   80
Amid the splendour-wingèd stars, the Moon
Burns, inextinguishably beautiful:
And from her lips, as from a hyacinth full
Of honey-dew, a liquid murmur drops,
Killing the sense with passion; sweet as stops   85
Of planetary music heard in trance.
In her mild lights the starry spirits dance,
The sunbeams of those wells which ever leap
Under the lightnings of the soul—too deep
For the brief fathom-line of thought or sense.   90
The glory of her being, issuing thence,
Stains the dead, blank, cold air with a warm shade
Of unentangled intermixture, made
By Love, of light and motion: one intense
Diffusion, one serene Omnipresence,   95
Whose flowing outlines mingle in their flowing,
Around her cheeks and utmost fingers glowing
With the unintermitted blood, which there
Quivers, (as in a fleece of snow-like air
The crimson pulse of living morning quiver,)   100
Continuously prolonged, and ending never,
Till they are lost, and in that Beauty furled
Which penetrates and clasps and fills the world;
Scarce visible from extreme loveliness.
Warm fragrance seems to fall from her light dress   105
And her loose hair; and where some heavy tress
The air of her own speed has disentwined,
The sweetness seems to satiate the faint wind;
And in the soul a wild odour is felt,
Beyond the sense, like fiery dews that melt   110
Into the bosom of a frozen bud.—
See where she stands! a mortal shape indued

With love and life and light and deity,
And motion which may change but cannot die;
An image of some bright Eternity;   115
A shadow of some golden dream; a Splendour
Leaving the third sphere pilotless; a tender
Reflection of the eternal Moon of Love
Under whose motions life's dull billows move;
A Metaphor of Spring and Youth and Morning;   120
A Vision like incarnate April, warning,
With smiles and tears, Frost the Anatomy
Into his summer grave.
      Ah, woe is me!
What have I dared? where am I lifted? how
Shall I descend, and perish not? I know   125
That Love makes all things equal: I have heard
By mine own heart this joyous truth averred:
The spirit of the worm beneath the sod
In love and worship, blends itself with God.

 Spouse! Sister! Angel! Pilot of the Fate   130
Whose course has been so starless! O too late
Belovèd! O too soon adored, by me!
For in the fields of Immortality
My spirit should at first have worshipped thine,
A divine presence in a place divine;   135
Or should have moved beside it on this earth,
A shadow of that substance, from its birth;
But not as now:—I love thee; yes, I feel
That on the fountain of my heart a seal
Is set, to keep its waters pure and bright   140
For thee, since in those *tears* thou hast delight.
We—are we not formed, as notes of music are,
For one another, though dissimilar;
Such difference without discord, as can make
Those sweetest sounds, in which all spirits shake   145
As trembling leaves in a continuous air?

 Thy wisdom speaks in me, and bids me dare
Beacon the rocks on which high hearts are wrecked.
I never was attached to that great sect,
Whose doctrine is, that each one should select   150
Out of the crowd a mistress or a friend,
And all the rest, though fair and wise, commend
To cold oblivion, though it is in the code
Of modern morals, and the beaten road
Which those poor slaves with weary footsteps tread,   155
Who travel to their home among the dead

By the broad highway of the world, and so
With one chained friend, perhaps a jealous foe,
The dreariest and the longest journey go.

True Love in this differs from gold and clay,   160
That to divide is not to take away.
Love is like understanding, that grows bright,
Gazing on many truths; 'tis like thy light,
Imagination! which from earth and sky,
And from the depths of human fantasy,   165
As from a thousand prisms and mirrors, fills
The Universe with glorious beams, and kills
Error, the worm, with many a sun-like arrow
Of its reverberated lightning. Narrow
The heart that loves, the brain that contemplates,   170
The life that wears, the spirit that creates
One object, and one form, and builds thereby
A sepulchre for its eternity.

Mind from its object differs most in this:
Evil from good; misery from happiness;   175
The baser from the nobler; the impure
And frail, from what is clear and must endure.
If you divide suffering and dross, you may
Diminish till it is consumed away;
If you divide pleasure and love and thought,   180
Each part exceeds the whole; and we know not
How much, while any yet remains unshared,
Of pleasure may be gained, of sorrow spared:
This truth is that deep well, whence sages draw
The unenvied light of hope; the eternal law   185
By which those live, to whom this world of life
Is as a garden ravaged, and whose strife
Tills for the promise of a later birth
The wilderness of this Elysian earth.

There was a Being whom my spirit oft   190
Met on its visioned wanderings, far aloft,
In the clear golden prime of my youth's dawn,
Upon the fairy isles of sunny lawn,
Amid the enchanted mountains, and the caves
Of divine sleep, and on the air-like waves   195
Of wonder-level dream, whose tremulous floor
Paved her light steps;—on an imagined shore,
Under the gray beak of some promontory
She met me, robed in such exceeding glory,
That I beheld her not. In solitudes   200
Her voice came to me through the whispering woods.

And from the fountains, and the odours deep
Of flowers, which, like lips murmuring in their sleep
Of the sweet kisses which had lulled them there,
Breathed but of *her* to the enamoured air;   205
And from the breezes whether low or loud,
And from the rain of every passing cloud,
And from the singing of the summer-birds,
And from all sounds, all silence. In the words
Of antique verse and high romance,—in form,   210
Sound, colour—in whatever checks that Storm
Which with the shattered present chokes the past;
And in that best philosophy, whose taste
Makes this cold common hell, our life, a doom
As glorious as a fiery martyrdom;   215
Her Spirit was the harmony of truth.—

    Then, from the caverns of my dreamy youth
I sprang, as one sandalled with plumes of fire,
And towards the lodestar of my one desire,
I flitted, like a dizzy moth, whose flight   220
Is as a dead leaf's in the owlet light,
When it would seek in Hesper's setting sphere
A radiant death, a fiery sepulchre,
As if it were a lamp of earthly flame.—
But She, whom prayers or tears then could not tame,   225
Passed, like a God throned on a wingèd planet,
Whose burning plumes to tenfold swiftness fan it,
Into the dreary cone of our life's shade;
And as a man with mighty loss dismayed,
I would have followed, though the grave between   230
Yawned like a gulf whose spectres are unseen:
When a voice said:—'O thou of hearts the weakest,
The phantom is beside thee whom thou seekest.'
Then I—'Where?'—the world's echo answered 'where?'
And in that silence, and in my despair,   235
I questioned every tongueless wind that flew
Over my tower of mourning, if it knew
Whither 'twas fled, this soul out of my soul;
And murmured names and spells which have control
Over the sightless tyrants of our fate;   240
But neither prayer nor verse could dissipate
The night which closed on her; nor uncreate
That world within this Chaos, mine and me,
Of which she was the veiled Divinity,
The world I say of thoughts that worshipped her: 245
And therefore I went forth, with hope and fear

And every gentle passion sick to death,
Feeding my course with expectation's breath,
Into the wintry forest of our life;
And struggling through its error with vain strife,   250
And stumbling in my weakness and my haste,
And half bewildered by new forms, I passed,
Seeking among those untaught foresters
If I could find one form resembling hers,
In which she might have masked herself from me,   255
There,—One, whose voice was venomed melody
Sate by a well, under blue nightshade bowers;
The breath of her false mouth was like faint flowers,
Her touch was as electric poison,—flame
Out of her looks into my vitals came,   260
And from her living cheeks and bosom flew
A killing air, which pierced like honey-dew
Into the core of my green heart, and lay
Upon its leaves; until, as hair grown gray
O'er a young brow, they hid its unblown prime   265
With ruins of unseasonable time.

   In many mortal forms I rashly sought
The shadow of that idol of my thought.
And some were fair—but beauty dies away:
Others were wise—but honeyed words betray: 270
And One was true—oh! why not true to me?
Then, as hunted deer that could not flee,
I turned upon my thoughts, and stood at bay,
Wounded and weak and panting; the cold day
Trembled, for pity of my strife and pain.   275
When, like a noonday dawn, there shone again
Deliverance. One stood on my path who seemed
As like the glorious shape which I had dreamed
As is the Moon, whose changes ever run
Into themselves, to the eternal Sun;   280
The cold chaste Moon, the Queen of Heaven's bright isles,
Who makes all beautiful on which she smiles,
That wandering shrine of soft yet icy flame
Which ever is transformed, yet still the same,
And warms not but illumines. Young and fair   285
As the descended Spirit of that sphere,
She hid me, as the Moon may hide the night
From its own darkness, until all was bright
Between the Heaven and Earth of my calm mind,
And, as a cloud charioted by the wind,   290
She led me to a cave in that wild place,
And sate beside me, with her downward face

Illumining my slumbers, like the Moon
Waxing and waning o'er Endymion.
And I was laid asleep, spirit and limb,   295
And all my being became bright or dim
As the Moon's image in a summer sea,
According as she smiled or frowned on me;
And there I lay, within a chaste cold bed:
Alas, I then was nor alive nor dead:—   300
For at her silver voice came Death and Life,
Unmindful each of their accustomed strife,
Masked like twin babes, a sister and a brother,
The wandering hopes of one abandoned mother,
And through the cavern without wings they flew,   305
And cried 'Away, he is not of our crew.'
I wept, and though it be a dream, I weep.

What storms then shook the ocean of my sleep,
Blotting that Moon, whose pale and waning lips
Then shrank as in the sickness of eclipse;—   310
And how my soul was as a lampless sea,
And who was then its Tempest; and when She,
The Planet of that hour, was quenched, what frost
Crept o'er those waters, till from coast to coast
The moving billows of my being fell   315
Into a death of ice, immovable;—
And then—what earthquakes made it gape and split,
The white Moon smiling all the while on it,
These words conceal:—If not, each word would be
The key of staunchless tears. Weep not for me!   320

At length, into the obscure Forest came
The Vision I had sought through grief and shame.
Athwart that wintry wilderness of thorns
Flashed from her motion splendour like the Morn's,
And from her presence life was radiated   325
Through the gray earth and branches bare and dead;
So that her way was paved, and roofed above
With flowers as soft as thoughts of budding love;
And music from her respiration spread
Like light,—all other sounds were penetrated   330
By the small, still, sweet spirit of that sound,
So that the savage winds hung mute around;
And odours warm and fresh fell from her hair
Dissolving the dull cold in the frore air:
Soft as an Incarnation of the Sun,   335
When light is changed to love, this glorious One
Floated into the cavern where I lay,
And called my Spirit, and the dreaming clay

Was lifted by the thing that dreamed below
As smoke by fire, and in her beauty's glow   340
I stood, and felt the dawn of my long night
Was penetrating me with living light:
I knew it was the Vision veiled from me
So many years—that it was Emily.

   Twin Spheres of light who rule this passive Earth,   345
This world of love, this *me;* and into birth
Awaken all its fruits and flowers, and dart
Magnetic might into its central heart;
And lift its billows and its mists, and guide
By everlasting laws, each wind and tide   350
To its fit cloud, and its appointed cave;
And lull its storms, each in the craggy grave
Which was its cradle, luring to faint bowers
The armies of the rainbow-wingèd showers;
And, as those married lights, which from the towers   355
Of Heaven look forth and fold the wandering globe
In liquid sleep and splendour, as a robe;
And all their many-mingled influence blend,
If equal, yet unlike, to one sweet end;—
So ye, bright regents, with alternate sway   360
Govern my sphere of being, night and day!
Thou, not disdaining even a borrowed might;
Thou, not eclipsing a remoter light;
And, through the shadow of the seasons three,
From Spring to Autumn's sere maturity,   365
Light it into the Winter of the tomb,
Where it may ripen to a brighter bloom.
Thou too, O Comet beautiful and fierce,
Who drew the heart of this frail Universe
Towards thine own; till, wrecked in that convulsion,   370
Alternating attraction and repulsion,
Thine went astray and that was rent in twain;
Oh, float into our azure heaven again!
Be there Love's folding-star at thy return;
The living Sun will feed thee from its urn   375
Of golden fire; the Moon will veil her horn
In thy last smiles; adoring Even and Morn
Will worship thee with incense of calm breath
And lights and shadows; as the star of Death
And Birth is worshipped by those sisters wild   380
Called Hope and Fear—upon the heart are piled
Their offerings,—of this sacrifice divine
A World shall be the altar.
                    Lady mine,

Scorn not these flowers of thought, the fading birth
Which from its heart of hearts that plant puts forth   385
Whose fruit, made perfect by thy sunny eyes,
Will be as of the trees of Paradise.

   The day is come, and thou wilt fly with me.
To whatsoe'er of dull mortality
Is mine, remain a vestal sister still;   390
To the intense, the deep, the imperishable,
Not mine but me, henceforth be thou united
Even as a bride, delighting and delighted.
The hour is come:—the destined Star has risen
Which shall descend upon a vacant prison.   395
The walls are high, the gates are strong, thick set
The sentinels—but true Love never yet
Was thus constrained: it overleaps all fence:
Like lightning, with invisible violence
Piercing its continents; like Heaven's free breath,   400
Which he who grasps can hold not; liker Death,
Who rides upon a thought, and makes his way
Through temple, tower, and palace, and the array
Of arms: more strength has Love than he or they;
For it can burst his charnel, and make free   405
The limbs in chains, the heart in agony,
The soul in dust and chaos.
                Emily,
A ship is floating in the harbour now,
A wind is hovering o'er the mountain's brow;
There is a path on the sea's azure floor,   410
No keel has ever ploughed that path before;
The halcyons brood around the foamless isles;
The treacherous Ocean has forsworn its wiles;
The merry mariners are bold and free:
Say, my heart's sister, wilt thou sail with me?   415
Our bark is as an albatross, whose nest
Is a far Eden of the purple East;
And we between her wings will sit, while Night,
And Day, and Storm, and Calm, pursue their flight,
Our ministers, along the boundless Sea,   420
Treading each other's heels, unheededly.
It is an isle under Ionian skies,
Beautiful as a wreck of Paradise,
And, for the harbours are not safe and good,
This land would have remained a solitude   425
But for some pastoral people native there,
Who from the Elysian, clear, and golden air

Draw the last spirit of the age of gold,
Simple and spirited; innocent and bold.
The blue Aegean girds this chosen home,   430
With ever-changing sound and light and foam,
Kissing the sifted sands, and caverns hoar;
And all the winds wandering along the shore
Undulate with the undulating tide:
There are thick woods where sylvan forms abide;   435
And many a fountain, rivulet, and pond,
As clear as elemental diamond,
Or serene morning air; and far beyond,
The mossy tracks made by the goats and deer
(Which the rough shepherd treads but once a year)   440
Pierce into glades, caverns, and bowers, and halls
Built round with ivy, which the waterfalls
Illumining, with sound that never fails
Accompany the noonday nightingales;
And all the place is peopled with sweet airs;   445
The light clear element which the isle wears
Is heavy with the scent of lemon-flowers,
Which floats like mist laden with unseen showers,
And falls upon the eyelids like faint sleep;
And from the moss violets and jonquils peep,   450
And dart their arrowy odour through the brain
Till you might faint with that delicious pain.
And every motion, odour, beam, and tone,
With that deep music is in unison:
Which is a soul within the soul—they seem   455
Like echoes of an antenatal dream.—
It is an isle 'twixt Heaven, Air, Earth, and Sea,
Cradled, and hung in clear tranquillity;
Bright as that wandering Eden Lucifer,
Washed by the soft blue Oceans of young air.   460
It is a favoured place. Famine or Blight,
Pestilence, War and Earthquake, never light
Upon its mountain-peaks; blind vultures, they
Sail onward far upon their fatal way:
The wingèd storms, chanting their thunder-psalm   465
To other lands, leave azure chasms of calm
Over this isle, or weep themselves in dew,
From which its fields and woods ever renew
Their green and golden immortality.
And from the sea there rise, and from the sky   470
There fall, clear exhalations, soft and bright,
Veil after veil, each hiding some delight,
Which Sun or Moon or zephyr draw aside,
Till the isle's beauty, like a naked bride

Glowing at once with love and loveliness,   475
Blushes and trembles at its own excess:
Yet, like a buried lamp, a Soul no less
Burns in the heart of this delicious isle,
An atom of th' Eternal, whose own smile
Unfolds itself, and may be felt, not seen   480
O'er the gray rocks, blue waves, and forests green,
Filling their bare and void interstices.—
But the chief marvel of the wilderness
Is a lone dwelling, built by whom or how
None of the rustic island-people know: 485
'Tis not a tower of strength, though with its height
It overtops the woods; but, for delight,
Some wise and tender Ocean-King, ere crime
Had been invented, in the world's young prime,
Reared it, a wonder of that simple time,   490
An envy of the isles, a pleasure-house
Made sacred to his sister and his spouse.
It scarce seems now a wreck of human art,
But, as it were Titanic; in the heart
Of Earth having assumed its form, then grown   495
Out of the mountains, from the living stone,
Lifting itself in caverns light and high:
For all the antique and learnèd imagery
Has been erased, and in the place of it
The ivy and the wild-vine interknit   500
The volumes of their many-twining stems;
Parasite flowers illume with dewy gems
The lampless halls, and when they fade, the sky
Peeps through their winter-woof of tracery
With moonlight patches, or star atoms keen,   505
Or fragments of the day's intense serene;—
Working mosaic on their Parian floors.
And, day and night, aloof, from the high towers
And terraces, the Earth and Ocean seem
To sleep in one another's arms, and dream   510
Of waves, flowers, clouds, woods, rocks, and all that we
Read in their smiles, and call reality.

This isle and house are mine, and I have vowed
Thee to be lady of the solitude.—
And I have fitted up some chambers there   515
Looking towards the golden Eastern air,
And level with the living winds, which flow
Like waves above the living-waves below.—
I have sent books and music there, and all
Those instruments with which high Spirits call   520

The future from its cradle, and the past
Out of its grave, and make the present last
In thoughts and joys which sleep, but cannot die,
Folded within their own eternity.
Our simple life wants little, and true taste　　　　525
Hires not the pale drudge Luxury, to waste
The scene it would adorn, and therefore still,
Nature with all her children haunts the hill.
The ring-dove, in the embowering ivy, yet
Keeps up her love-lament, and the owls flit　　　　530
Round the evening tower, and the young stars glance
Between the quick bats in their twilight dance;
The spotted deer bask in the fresh moonlight
Before our gate, and the slow, silent night
Is measured by the pants of their calm sleep.　　　535
Be this our home in Life, and when years heap
Their withered hours, like leaves, on our decay,
Let us become the overhanging day,
The living soul of this Elysian isle,
Conscious, inseparable, one. Meanwhile　　　　　540
We two will rise, and sit, and walk together,
Under the roof of blue Ionian weather,
And wander in the meadows, or ascend
The mossy mountains, where the blue heavens bend
With lightest winds, to touch their paramour;　　　545
Or linger, where the pebble-paven shore,
Under the quick, faint kisses of the sea
Trembles and sparkles as with ecstasy,—
Possessing and possessed by all that is
Within that calm circumference of bliss,　　　　550
And by each other, till to love and live
Be one:—or, at the noontide hour, arrive
Where some old cavern hoar seems yet to keep
The moonlight of the expired night asleep,
Through which the awakened day can never peep;　555
A veil for our seclusion, close as night's,
Where secure sleep may kill thine innocent lights;
Sleep, the fresh dew of languid love, the rain
Whose drops quench kisses till they burn again.
And we will talk, until thought's melody　　　　560
Become too sweet for utterance, and it die
In words, to live again in looks, which dart
With thrilling tone into the voiceless heart,
Harmonizing silence without a sound.
Our breath shall intermix, our bosoms bound,　　　565
And our veins beat together; and our lips
With other eloquence than words, eclipse

The soul that burns between them, and the wells
Which boil under our being's inmost cells,
The fountains of our deepest life, shall be   570
Confused in Passion's golden purity,
As mountain-springs under the morning sun.
We shall become the same, we shall be one
Spirit within two frames, oh! wherefore two?
One passion in twin-hearts, which grows and grew,   575
Till like two meteors of expanding flame,
Those spheres instinct with it become the same,
Touch, mingle, are transfigured; ever still
Burning, yet ever inconsumable:
In one another's substance finding food,   580
Like flames too pure and light and unimbued
To nourish their bright lives with baser prey,
Which point to Heaven and cannot pass away:
One hope within two wills, one will beneath
Two overshadowing minds, one life, one death,   585
One Heaven, one Hell, one immortality,
And one annihilation. Woe is me!
The wingèd words on which my soul would pierce
Into the height of Love's rare Universe,
Are chains of lead around its flight of fire—   590
I pant, I sink, I tremble, I expire!

Weak Verses, go, kneel at your Sovereign's feet,
And say:—'We are the masters of thy slave;
What wouldest thou with us and ours and thine?'
Then call your sisters from Oblivion's cave,   595
All singing loud: 'Love's very pain is sweet,
But its reward is in the world divine
Which, if not here, it builds beyond the grave.'
So shall ye live when I am there. Then haste
Over the hearts of men, until ye meet   600
Marina, Vanna, Primus, and the rest,
And bid them love each other and be blessed:
And leave the troop which errs, and which reproves,
And come and be my guest,—for I am Love's.

FRAGMENTS CONNECTED WITH EPIPSYCHIDION

THREE EARLY DRAFTS OF THE PREFACE
(ADVERTISEMENT)

PREFACE I

THE following Poem was found amongst other papers in the Portfolio
of a young Englishman with whom the Editor had contracted an intimacy
at Florence, brief indeed, but sufficiently long to render the Catastrophe

by which it terminated one of the most painful events of his life.

The literary merit of the Poem in question may not be considerable; but worse verses are printed every day, &

He was an accomplished & amiable person but his error was, θνητος ὢν μη θνητα φϱονειν,—his fate is an additional proof that 'The tree of Knowledge is not that of Life.'—He had framed to himself certain opinions, founded no doubt upon the truth of things, but built up to a Babel height; they fell by their own weight, & the thoughts that were his architects, became unintelligible one to the other, as men upon whom confusion of tongues has fallen.

[These] verses seem to have been written as a sort of dedication of some work to have been presented to the person whom they address: but his papers afford no trace of such a work—The circumstances to which [they] the poem allude, may easily be understood by those to whom [the] spirit of the poem itself is [un]intelligible: a detail of facts, sufficiently romantic in [themselves but] their combinations

The melancholy [task] charge of consigning the body of my poor friend to the grave, was committed to me by his desolated family. I caused him to be buried in a spot selected by himself.

PREFACE II

[Epips]   T. E. V. Epipsych
          Lines addressed to
          the Noble Lady
          [Emilia] [E. V.]
          Emilia

[The following Poem was found in the PF. of a young Englishman, who died on his passage from Leghorn to the Levant. He had bought one of the Sporades] He was accompanied by a lady [who might have been] supposed to be his wife, & an effeminate looking youth, to whom he shewed an [attachment] so [singular] excessive an attachment as to give rise to the suspicion, that she was a woman—at his death this suspicion was confirmed;   object speedily found a refuge both from the taunts of the brute multitude, and from the   of her grief in the same grave that contained her lover.—He had bought one of the Sporades, & fitted up a Saracenic castle which accident had preserved in some repair with simple elegance, & it was his intention to dedicate the remainder of his life to undisturbed intercourse with his companions

These verses apparently were intended as a dedication of a longer poem or series of poems

PREFACE III

The writer of these lines died at Florence in [January 1820] while he was preparing * * for one wildest of the of the Sporades, where he bought & fitted up the ruins of some old building—His life was singular, less on account of the romantic vicissitudes which diversified it, than the ideal tinge which they received from his own character & feelings—

The verses were apparently intended by the writer to accompany some
longer poem or collection of poems, of which there* [are no remnants
in his] * ** remains [in his] portfolio.—

The editor is induced to

The present poem, like the vita Nova of Dante, is sufficiently intelligible to a certain class of readers without a matter of fact history of
the circumstances to which it relate, & to a certain other class, it must
& ought ever to remain incomprehensible—It was evidently intended to
be prefixed to a longer poem or series of poems—but among his papers
there are no traces of such a collection.

PASSAGES OF THE POEM, OR CONNECTED THEREWITH

HERE, my dear friend, is a new book for you;
I have already dedicated two
To other friends, one female and one male,—
What you are, is a thing that I must veil;
What can this be to those who praise or rail?   5
I never was attached to that great sect
Whose doctrine is that each one should select
Out of the world a mistress or a friend,
And all the rest, though fair and wise, commend
To cold oblivion—though 'tis in the code   10
Of modern morals, and the beaten road
Which those poor slaves with weary footsteps tread
Who travel to their home among the dead
By the broad highway of the world—and so
With one sad friend, and many a jealous foe,   15
The dreariest and the longest journey go.

Free love has this, different from gold and clay,
That to divide is not to take away.
Like ocean, which the general north wind breaks
Into ten thousand waves, and each one makes   20
A mirror of the moon—like some great glass,
Which did distort whatever form might pass,
Dashed into fragments by a playful child,
Which then reflects its eyes and forehead mild;
Giving for one, which it could ne'er express,   25
A thousand images of loveliness.

If I were one whom the loud world held wise,
I should disdain to quote authorities
In commendation of this kind of love:—
Why there is first the God in heaven above,   30
Who wrote a book called Nature, 'tis to be
Reviewed, I hear, in the next Quarterly;

And Socrates, the Jesus Christ of Greece,
And Jesus Christ Himself, did never cease
To urge all living things to love each other,   35
And to forgive their mutual faults, and smother
The Devil of disunion in their souls.

　　　·　　·　　·　　·　　·　　·　　·

I love you!—Listen, O embodied Ray
Of the great Brightness; I must pass away
While you remain, and these light words must be   40
Tokens by which you may remember me.
Start not—the thing you are is unbetrayed,
If you are human, and if but the shade
Of some sublimer spirit . . . .

　　　·　　·　　·　　·　　·　　·　　·

And as to friend or mistress, 'tis a form;   45
Perhaps I wish you were one. Some declare
You a familiar spirit, as you are;
Others with a   more inhuman
Hint that, though not my wife, you are a woman;
What is the colour of your eyes and hair?   50
Why, if you were a lady, it were fair
The world should know—but, as I am afraid,
The Quarterly would bait you if betrayed;
And if, as it will be sport to see them stumble
Over all sorts of scandals, hear them mumble   55
Their litany of curses—some guess right,
And others swear you're a Hermaphrodite;
Like that sweet marble monster of both sexes,
Which looks so sweet and gentle that it vexes
The very soul that the soul is gone   60
Which lifted from her limbs the veil of stone.

　　　·　　·　　·　　·　　·　　·　　·

It is a sweet thing, friendship, a dear balm,
A happy and auspicious bird of calm,
Which rides o'er life's ever tumultuous Ocean;
A God that broods o'er chaos in commotion;   65
A flower which fresh as Lapland roses are,
Lifts its bold head into the world's frore air,
And blooms most radiantly when others die,
Health, hope, and youth, and brief prosperity;
And with the light and odour of its bloom,   70
Shining within the dungeon and the tomb;

Whose coming is as light and music are
'Mid dissonance and gloom—a star
Which moves not 'mid the moving heavens alone—
A smile among dark frowns—a gentle tone   75
Among rude voices, a belovèd light,
A solitude, a refuge, a delight.
If I had but a friend! Why, I have three
Even by my own confession; there may be
Some more, for what I know, for 'tis my mind   80
To call my friends all who are wise and kind,—
And these, Heaven knows, at best are very few;
But none can ever be more dear than you.
Why should they be? My muse has lost her wings,
Or like a dying swan who soars and sings,   85
I should describe you in heroic style,
But as it is, are you not void of guile?
A lovely soul, formed to be blessed and bless:
A well of sealed and secret happiness;
A lute which those whom Love has taught to play   90
Make music on to cheer the roughest day,
And enchant sadness till it sleeps? . . . .

   .   .   .   .

To the oblivion whither I and thou,
All loving and all lovely, hasten now
With steps, ah, too unequal! may we meet   95
In one Elysium or one winding-sheet!

   If any should be curious to discover
Whether to you I am a friend or lover,
Let them read Shakespeare's sonnets, taking thence
A whetstone for their dull intelligence   100
That tears and will not cut, or let them guess
How Diotima, the wise prophetess,
Instructed the instructor, and why he
Rebuked the infant spirit of melody
On Agathon's sweet lips, which as he spoke   105
Was as the lovely star when morn has broke
The roof of darkness, in the golden dawn,
Half-hidden, and yet beautiful.
                      I'll pawn
My hopes of Heaven—you know what they are worth—
That the presumptuous pedagogues of Earth,   110
If they could tell the riddle offered here
Would scorn to be, or being to appear
What now they seem and are—but let them chide,
They have few pleasures in the world beside;

Perhaps we should be dull were we not chidden,   115
Paradise fruits are sweetest when forbidden.
Folly can season Wisdom, Hatred Love.

    .   .   .   .   .   .

Farewell, if it can be to say farewell
To those who

    .   .   .   .   .   .

   I will not, as most dedicators do,   120
Assure myself and all the world and you,
That you are faultless—would to God they were
Who taunt me with your love! I then should wear
These heavy chains of life with a light spirit,
And would to God I were, or even as near it   125
As you, dear heart. Alas! what are we? Clouds
Driven by the wind in warring multitudes,
Which rain into the bosom of the earth,
And rise again, and in our death and birth,
And through our restless life, take as from heaven   130
Hues which are not our own, but which are given,
And then withdrawn, and with inconstant glance
Flash from the spirit to the countenance.
There is a Power, a Love, a Joy, a God
Which makes in mortal hearts its brief abode,   135
A Pythian exhalation, which inspires
Love, only love—a wind which o'er the wires
Of the soul's giant harp
There is a mood which language faints beneath;
You feel it striding, as Almighty Death   140
His bloodless steed . . . .

    .   .   .   .   .   .

And what is that most brief and bright delight
Which rushes through the touch and through the sight,
And stands before the spirit's inmost throne,
A naked Seraph? None hath ever known.   145
Its birth is darkness, and its growth desire;
Untameable and fleet and fierce as fire,
Not to be touched but to be felt alone,
It fills the world with glory—and is gone.

    .   .   .   .   .   .

It floats with rainbow pinions o'er the stream   150
Of life, which flows, like a   dream
Into the light of morning, to the grave
As to an ocean . . . .

What is that joy which serene infancy
Perceives not, as the hours content them by,   155
Each in a chain of blossoms, yet enjoys
The shapes of this new world, in giant toys
Wrought by the busy   ever new?
Remembrance borrows Fancy's glass, to show
These forms more   sincere   160
Than now they are, than then, perhaps, they were.
When everything familiar seemed to be
Wonderful, and the immortality
Of this great world, which all things must inherit,
Was felt as one with the awakening spirit,   165
Unconscious of itself, and of the strange
Distinctions which in its proceeding change
It feels and knows, and mourns as if each were
A desolation . . . .

   .   .   .   .   .   .

Were it not a sweet refuge, Emily,   170
For all those exiles from the dull insane
Who vex this pleasant world with pride and pain,
For all that band of sister-spirits known
To one another by a voiceless tone?

   .   .   .   .   .

If day should part us night will mend division   175
And if sleep parts us—we will meet in vision
And if life parts us—we will mix in death
Yielding our mite [?] of unreluctant breath
Death cannot part us—we must meet again
In all in nothing in delight in pain: 180
How, why or when or where—it matters not
So that we share an undivided lot. . . . .

   .   .   .   .   .   .

And we will move possessing and possessed
Wherever beauty on the earth's bare [?] breast
Lies like the shadow of thy soul—till we   185
Become one being with the world we see. . . .

ADONAIS

AN ELEGY ON THE DEATH OF JOHN KEATS, AUTHOR OF ENDYMION, HYPERION, Etc.

'Αστὴρ πρὶν μὲν ἔλαμπες ἐνὶ ζωοῖσιν 'Εῷος·
νῦν δὲ θανὼν λάμπεις "Εσπερος ἐν φθιμένοις.—PLATO.

PREFACE

Φάρμακον ἦλθε, Βίων, ποτὶ σὸν στόμα, φάρμακον εἶδες.
πῶς τευ τοῖς χείλεσσι ποτέδραμε, κοὐκ ἐγλυκάνθη;
τίς δὲ βροτὸς τοσσοῦτον ἀνάμερος, ἦ κεράσαι τοι,
ἦ δοῦναι λαλέοντι τὸ φάρμακον; ἔκφυγεν ὠδάν.
                    —MOSCHUS, EPITAPH. BION.

It is my intention to subjoin to the London edition of this poem a criticism upon the claims of its lamented object to be classed among the writers of the highest genius who have adorned our age. My known repugnance to the narrow principles of taste on which several of his earlier compositions were modelled prove at least that I am an impartial judge. I consider the fragment of *Hyperion* as second to nothing that was ever produced by a writer of the same years.

John Keats died at Rome of a consumption, in his twenty-fourth year, on the —— of —— 1821; and was buried in the romantic and lonely cemetery of the Protestants in that city, under the pyramid which is the tomb of Cestius, and the massy walls and towers, now mouldering and desolate, which formed the circuit of ancient Rome. The cemetery is an open space among the ruins, covered in winter with violets and daisies. It might make one in love with death, to think that one should be buried in so sweet a place.

The genius of the lamented person to whose memory I have dedicated these unworthy verses was not less delicate and fragile than it was beautiful; and where cankerworms abound, what wonder if its young flower was blighted in the bud? The savage criticism on his *Endymion*, which appeared in the *Quarterly Review*, produced the most violent effect on his susceptible mind; the agitation thus originated ended in the rupture of a blood-vessel in the lungs; a rapid consumption ensued, and the succeeding acknowledgements from more candid critics of the true greatness of his powers were ineffectual to heal the wound thus wantonly inflicted.

It may be well said that these wretched men know not what they do. They scatter their insults and their slanders without heed as to whether the poisoned shaft lights on a heart made callous by many blows or one like Keats's composed of more penetrable stuff. One of their associates is, to my knowledge, a most base and unprincipled calumniator. As to

Endymion, was it a poem, whatever might be its defects, to be treated
contemptuously by those who had celebrated, with various degrees of
complacency and panegyric, *Paris,* and *Woman,* and a *Syrian Tale,* and
Mrs. Lefanu, and Mr. Barrett, and Mr. Howard Payne, and a long list of
the illustrious obscure? Are these the men who in their venal good nature
presumed to draw a parallel between the Rev. Mr. Milman and Lord
Byron? What gnat did they strain at here, after having swallowed all
those camels? Against what woman taken in adultery dares the foremost
of these literary prostitutes to cast his opprobrious stone? Miserable man!
you, one of the meanest, have wantonly defaced one of the noblest specimens of the workmanship of God. Nor shall it be your excuse, that,
murderer as you are, you have spoken daggers, but used none.

The circumstances of the closing scene of poor Keats's life were not
made known to me until the *Elegy* was ready for the press. I am given
to understand that the wound which his sensitive spirit had received from
the criticism of *Endymion* was exasperated by the bitter sense of unrequited benefits; the poor fellow seems to have been hooted from the
stage of life, no less by those on whom he had wasted the promise of his
genius, than those on whom he had lavished his fortune and his care.
He was accompanied to Rome, and attended in his last illness by Mr.
Severn, a young artist of the highest promise, who, I have been informed,
'almost risked his own life, and sacrificed every prospect to unwearied attendance upon his dying friend.' Had I known these circumstances before
the completion of my poem, I should have been tempted to add my feeble
tribute of applause to the more solid recompense which the virtuous man
finds in the recollection of his own motives. Mr. Severn can dispense with
a reward from 'such stuff as dreams are made of.' His conduct is a golden
augury of the success of his future career—may the unextinguished
Spirit of his illustrious friend animate the creations of his pencil, and
plead against Oblivion for his name!

I

I WEEP for Adonais—he is dead!
O, weep for Adonais! though our tears
Thaw not the frost which binds so dear a head!
And thou, sad Hour, selected from all years
To mourn our loss, rouse thy obscure compeers,   5
And teach them thine own sorrow, say: 'With me
Died Adonais; till the Future dares
Forget the Past, his fate and fame shall be
An echo and a light unto eternity!'

II

Where wert thou, mighty Mother, when he lay,   10
When thy Son lay, pierced by the shaft which flies
In darkness? where was lorn Urania
When Adonais died? With veilèd eyes,

'Mid listening Echoes, in her Paradise
She sate, while one, with soft enamoured breath,   15
Rekindled all the fading melodies,
With which, like flowers that mock the corse beneath,
He had adorned and hid the coming bulk of Death.

III

Oh, weep for Adonais—he is dead!
Wake, melancholy Mother, wake and weep!   20
Yet wherefore? Quench within their burning bed
Thy fiery tears, and let thy loud heart keep
Like his, a mute and uncomplaining sleep;
For he is gone, where all things wise and fair
Descend;—oh, dream not that the amorous Deep   25
Will yet restore him to the vital air;
Death feeds on his mute voice, and laughs at our despair.

IV

Most musical of mourners, weep again!
Lament anew, Urania!—He died,
Who was the Sire of an immortal strain,   30
Blind, old, and lonely, when his country's pride,
The priest, the slave, and the liberticide,
Trampled and mocked with many a loathèd rite
Of lust and blood; he went, unterrified,
Into the gulf of death; but his clear Sprite   35
Yet reigns o'er earth; the third among the sons of light.

V

Most musical of mourners, weep anew!
Not all to that bright station dared to climb;
And happier they their happiness who knew,
Whose tapers yet burn through that night of time   40
In which suns perished; others more sublime,
Struck by the envious wrath of man or god,
Have sunk, extinct in their refulgent prime;
And some yet live, treading the thorny road,
Which leads, through toil and hate, to Fame's serene abode.   45

VI

But now, thy youngest, dearest one, has perished—
The nursling of thy widowhood, who grew,
Like a pale flower by some sad maiden cherished,
And fed with true-love tears, instead of dew;
Most musical of mourners, weep anew!   50

Thy extreme hope, the loveliest and the last,
The bloom, whose petals nipped before they blew
Died on the promise of the fruit, is waste;
The broken lily lies—the storm is overpast.

VII

To that high Capital, where kingly Death   55
Keeps his pale court in beauty and decay,
He came; and bought, with price of purest **breath,**
A grave among the eternal.—Come away!
Haste, while the vault of blue Italian day
Is yet his fitting charnel-roof! while still   60
He lies, as if in dewy sleep he lay;
Awake him not! surely he takes his fill
Of deep and liquid rest, forgetful of all ill.

VIII

He will awake no more, oh, never more!—
Within the twilight chamber spreads apace   65
The shadow of white Death, and at the door
Invisible Corruption waits to trace
His extreme way to her dim dwelling-place;
The eternal Hunger sits, but pity and awe
Soothe her pale rage, nor dares she to deface   70
So fair a prey, till darkness, and the law
Of change, shall o'er his sleep the mortal curtain **draw.**

IX

Oh, weep for Adonais!—The quick Dreams,
The passion-wingèd Ministers of thought,
Who were his flocks, whom near the living streams   75
Of his young spirit he fed, and whom he taught
The love which was its music, wander not,—
Wander no more, from kindling brain to brain,
But droop there, whence they sprung; and mourn **their lot**
Round the cold heart, where, after their sweet **pain,**   8(
They ne'er will gather strength, or find a home again.

X

And one with trembling hands clasps his cold **head,**
And fans him with her moonlight wings, and cries;
'Our love, our hope, our sorrow, is not dead;
See, on the silken fringe of his faint eyes,   85
Like dew upon a sleeping flower, there lies
A tear some Dream has loosened from his brain.'
Lost Angel of a ruined Paradise!

She knew not 'twas her own; as with no stain
She faded, like a cloud which had outwept its rain.   90

XI

One from a lucid urn of starry dew
Washed his light limbs as if embalming them;
Another clipped her profuse locks, and threw
The wreath upon him, like an anadem,
Which frozen tears instead of pearls begem;   95
Another in her wilful grief would break
Her bow and wingèd reeds, as if to stem
A greater loss with one which was more weak;
And dull the barbèd fire against his frozen cheek.

XII

Another Splendour on his mouth alit,   100
That mouth, whence it was wont to draw the breath
Which gave it strength to pierce the guarded wit,
And pass into the panting heart beneath
With lightning and with music: the damp death
Quenched its caress upon his icy lips;   105
And, as a dying meteor stains a wreath
Of moonlight vapour, which the cold night clips,
It flushed through his pale limbs, and passed to its eclipse.

XIII

And others came . . . Desires and Adorations,
Wingèd Persuasions and veiled Destinies,   110
Splendours, and Glooms, and glimmering Incarnations
Of hopes and fears, and twilight Phantasies;
And Sorrow, with her family of Sighs,
And Pleasure, blind with tears, led by the gleam
Of her own dying smile instead of eyes,   115
Came in slow pomp;—the moving pomp might seem
Like pageantry of mist on an autumnal stream.

XIV

All he had loved, and moulded into thought,
From shape, and hue, and odour, and sweet sound,
Lamented Adonais. Morning sought   120
Her eastern watch-tower, and her hair unbound,
Wet with the tears which should adorn the ground,
Dimmed the aëreal eyes that kindle day;
Afar the melancholy thunder moaned,
Pale Ocean in unquiet slumber lay,   125
And the wild Winds flew round, sobbing in their dismay.

XV

Lost Echo sits amid the voiceless mountains,
And feeds her grief with his remembered lay,
And will no more reply to winds or fountains,
Or amorous birds perched on the young green spray,   130
Or herdsman's horn, or bell at closing day;
Since she can mimic not his lips, more dear
Than those for whose disdain she pined away
Into a shadow of all sounds:—a drear
Murmur, between their songs, is all the woodmen hear.   135

XVI

Grief made the young Spring wild, and she threw down
Her kindling buds, as if she Autumn were,
Or they dead leaves; since her delight is flown,
For whom should she have waked the sullen year?
To Phoebus was not Hyacinth so dear   140
Nor to himself Narcissus, as to both
Thou, Adonais: wan they stand and sere
Amid the faint companions of their youth,
With dew all turned to tears; odour, to sighing ruth.

XVII

Thy spirit's sister, the lorn nightingale   145
Mourns not her mate with such melodious pain;
Not so the eagle, who like thee could scale
Heaven, and could nourish in the sun's domain
Her mighty youth with mourning, doth complain,
Soaring and screaming round her empty nest,   150
As Albion wails for thee: the curse of Cain
Light on his head who pierced thy innocent breast,
And scared the angel soul that was its earthly guest!

XVIII

Ah, woe is me! Winter is come and gone,
But grief returns with the revolving year;   155
The airs and streams renew their joyous tone;
The ants, the bees, the swallows reappear;
Fresh leaves and flowers deck the dead Seasons' bier;
The amorous birds now pair in every brake,
And build their mossy homes in field and brere;   160
And the green lizard, and the golden snake,
Like unimprisoned flames, out of their trance awake.

XIX

Through wood and stream and field and hill and Ocean
A quickening life from the Earth's heart has burst
As it has ever done, with change and motion,   165
From the great morning of the world when first
God dawned on Chaos; in its stream immersed,
The lamps of Heaven flash with a softer light;
All baser things pant with life's sacred thirst;
Diffuse themselves; and spend in love's delight,   170
The beauty and the joy of their renewèd might.

XX

The leprous corpse, touched by this spirit tender,
Exhales itself in flowers of gentle breath;
Like incarnations of the stars, when splendour
Is changed to fragrance, they illumine death   175
And mock the merry worm that wakes beneath;
Nought we know, dies. Shall that alone which knows
Be as a sword consumed before the sheath
By sightless lightning?—the intense atom glows
A moment, then is quenched in a most cold repose.   180

XXI

Alas! that all we loved of him should be,
But for our grief, as if it had not been,
And grief itself be mortal! Woe is me!
Whence are we, and why are we? of what scene
The actors or spectators? Great and mean   185
Meet massed in death, who lends what life must borrow.
As long as skies are blue, and fields are green,
Evening must usher night, night urge the morrow,
Month follow month with woe, and year wake year to sorrow.

XXII

He will awake no more, oh, never more!   190
'Wake thou,' cried Misery, 'childless Mother, rise
Out of thy sleep, and slake, in thy heart's core,
A wound more fierce than his, with tears and sighs.'
And all the Dreams that watched Urania's eyes,
And all the Echoes whom their sister's song   195
Had held in holy silence, cried: 'Arise!'
Swift as a Thought by the snake Memory stung,
From her ambrosial rest the fading Splendour sprung.

XXIII

She rose like an autumnal Night, that springs
Out of the East, and follows wild and drear   200
The golden Day, which, on eternal wings,
Even as a ghost abandoning a bier,
Had left the Earth a corpse. Sorrow and fear
So struck, so roused, so rapped Urania;
So saddened round her like an atmosphere   205
Of stormy mist; so swept her on her way
Even to the mournful place where Adonais lay.

XXIV

Out of her secret Paradise she sped,
Through camps and cities rough with stone, and steel,
And human hearts, which to her aery tread   210
Yielding not, wounded the invisible
Palms of her tender feet where'er they fell:
And barbèd tongues, and thoughts more sharp than they,
Rent the soft Form they never could repel,
Whose sacred blood, like the young tears of May,   215
Paved with eternal flowers that undeserving way.

XXV

In the death-chamber for a moment Death,
Shamed by the presence of that living Might,
Blushed to annihilation, and the breath
Revisited those lips, and Life's pale light   220
Flashed through those limbs, so late her dear delight.
'Leave me not wild and drear and comfortless,
As silent lightning leaves the starless night!
Leave me not!' cried Urania: her distress
Roused Death: Death rose and smiled, and met her vain caress.

XXVI

'Stay yet awhile! speak to me once again;   226
Kiss me, so long but as a kiss may live;
And in my heartless breast and burning brain
That word, that kiss, shall all thoughts else survive,
With food of saddest memory kept alive,   230
Now thou art dead, as if it were a part
Of thee, my Adonais! I would give
All that I am to be as thou now art!
But I am chained to Time, and cannot thence depart!

XXVII

'O gentle child, beautiful as thou wert,   235
Why didst thou leave the trodden paths of men
Too soon, and with weak hands though mighty heart
Dare the unpastured dragon in his den?
Defenceless as thou wert, oh, where was then
Wisdom the mirrored shield, or scorn the spear?   240
Or hadst thou waited the full cycle, when
Thy spirit should have filled its crescent sphere,
The monsters of life's waste had fled from thee like deer.

XXVIII

'The herded wolves, bold only to pursue;
The obscene ravens, clamorous o'er the dead;   245
The vultures to the conqueror's banner true
Who feed where Desolation first has fed,
And whose wings rain contagion;—how they fled,
When, like Apollo, from his golden bow
The Pythian of the age one arrow sped   250
And smiled!—The spoilers tempt no second blow,
They fawn on the proud feet that spurn them lying low.

XXIX

'The sun comes forth, and many reptiles spawn;
He sets, and each ephemeral insect then
Is gathered into death without a dawn,   255
And the immortal stars awake again;
So is it in the world of living men:
A godlike mind soars forth, in its delight
Making earth bare and veiling heaven, and when
It sinks, the swarms that dimmed or shared its light   260
Leave to its kindred lamps the spirit's awful night.'

XXX

Thus ceased she: and the mountain shepherds came,
Their garlands sere, their magic mantles rent;
The Pilgrim of Eternity, whose fame
Over his living head like Heaven is bent,   265
An early but enduring monument,
Came, veiling all the lightnings of his song
In sorrow; from her wilds Ierne sent
The sweetest lyrist of her saddest wrong,
And Love taught Grief to fall like music from his tongue.   270

XXXI

Midst others of less note, came one frail Form,
A phantom among men; companionless
As the last cloud of an expiring storm
Whose thunder is its knell; he, as I guess,
Had gazed on Nature's naked loveliness,   275
Actaeon-like, and now he fled astray
With feeble steps o'er the world's wilderness,
And his own thoughts, along that rugged way,
Pursued, like raging hounds, their father and their prey.

XXXII

A pardlike Spirit beautiful and swift—   280
A Love in desolation masked;—a Power
Girt round with weakness;—it can scarce uplift
The weight of the superincumbent hour;
It is a dying lamp, a falling shower,
A breaking billow;—even whilst we speak   .   285
Is it not broken? On the withering flower
The killing sun smiles brightly: on a cheek
The life can burn in blood, even while the heart may break.

XXXIII

His head was bound with pansies overblown,
And faded violets, white, and pied, and blue;   290
And a light spear topped with a cypress cone,
Round whose rude shaft dark ivy-tresses grew
Yet dripping with the forest's noonday dew,
Vibrated, as the ever-beating heart
Shook the weak hand that grasped it; of that crew   295
He came the last, neglected and apart;
A herd-abandoned deer struck by the hunter's dart.

XXXIV

All stood aloof, and at his partial moan
Smiled through their tears; well knew that gentle band
Who in another's fate now wept his own,   300
As in the accents of an unknown land
He sung new sorrow; sad Urania scanned
The Stranger's mien, and murmured: 'Who art thou?'
He answered not, but with a sudden hand
Made bare his branded and ensanguined brow,   305
Which was like Cain's or Christ's—oh! that it should be so!

XXXV

What softer voice is hushed over the dead?
Athwart what brow is that dark mantle thrown?
What form leans sadly o'er the white death-bed,
In mockery of monumental stone,   310
The heavy heart heaving without a moan?
If it be He, who, gentlest of the wise,
Taught, soothed, loved, honoured the departed one,
Let me not vex, with inharmonious sighs,
The silence of that heart's accepted sacrifice.   315

XXXVI

Our Adonais has drunk poison—oh!
What deaf and viperous murderer could crown
Life's early cup with such a draught of woe?
The nameless worm would now itself disown:
It felt, yet could escape, the magic tone   320
Whose prelude held all envy, hate, and wrong,
But what was howling in one breast alone,   ·
Silent with expectation of the song,
Whose master's hand is cold, whose silver lyre unstrung.

XXXVII

Live thou, whose infamy is not thy fame!   325
Live! fear no heavier chastisement from me,
Thou noteless blot on a remembered name!
But be thyself, and know thyself to be!
And ever at thy season be thou free
To spill the venom when thy fangs o'erflow;   330
Remorse and Self-contempt shall cling to thee;
Hot Shame shall burn upon thy secret brow,
And like a beaten hound tremble thou shalt—as now.

XXXVIII

Nor let us weep that our delight is fled
Far from these carrion kites that scream below;   335
He wakes or sleeps with the enduring dead;
Thou canst not soar where he is sitting now—
Dust to the dust! but the pure spirit shall flow
Back to the burning fountain whence it came,
A portion of the Eternal, which must glow   340
Through time and change, unquenchably the same,
Whilst thy cold embers choke the sordid hearth of shame.

XXXIX

Peace, peace! he is not dead, he doth not sleep—
He hath awakened from the dream of life—
'Tis we, who lost in stormy visions, keep   345
With phantoms an unprofitable strife,
And in mad trance, strike with our spirit's knife
Invulnerable nothings.—*We* decay
Like corpses in a charnel; fear and grief
Convulse us and consume us day by day,   350
And cold hopes swarm like worms within our living clay.

XL

He has outsoared the shadow of our night;
Envy and calumny and hate and pain,
And that unrest which men miscall delight,
Can touch him not and torture not again;   355
From the contagion of the world's slow stain
He is secure, and now can never mourn
A heart grown cold, a head grown gray in vain;
Nor, when the spirit's self has ceased to burn,
With sparkless ashes load an unlamented urn.   360

XLI

He lives, he wakes—'tis Death is dead, not he;
Mourn not for Adonais.—Thou young Dawn,
Turn all thy dew to splendour, for from thee
The spirit thou lamentest is not gone;
Ye caverns and ye forests, cease to moan!   365
Cease, ye faint flowers and fountains, and thou Air,
Which like a mourning veil thy scarf hadst thrown
O'er the abandoned Earth, now leave it bare
Even to the joyous stars which smile on its despair!

XLII

He is made one with Nature: there is heard   370
His voice in all her music, from the moan
Of thunder, to the song of night's sweet bird;
He is a presence to be felt and known
In darkness and in light, from herb and stone,
Spreading itself where'er that Power may move   375
Which has withdrawn his being to its own;
Which wields the world with never-wearied love,
Sustains it from beneath, and kindles it above.

XLIII

He is a portion of the loveliness
Which once he made more lovely: he doth bear 380
His part, while the one Spirit's plastic stress
Sweeps through the dull dense world, compelling there,
All new successions to the forms they wear;
Torturing th' unwilling dross that checks its flight
To its own likeness, as each mass may bear; 385
And bursting in its beauty and its might
From trees and beasts and men into the Heaven's light.

XLIV

The splendours of the firmament of time
May be eclipsed, but are extinguished not;
Like stars to their appointed height they climb, 390
And death is a low mist which cannot blot
The brightness it may veil. When lofty thought
Lifts a young heart above its mortal lair,
And love and life contend in it, for what
Shall be its earthly doom, the dead live there 395
And move like winds of light on dark and stormy air.

XLV

The inheritors of unfulfilled renown
Rose from their thrones, built beyond mortal thought,
Far in the Unapparent. Chatterton
Rose pale,—his solemn agony had not 400
Yet faded from him; Sidney, as he fought
And as he fell and as he lived and loved
Sublimely mild, a Spirit without spot,
Arose; and Lucan, by his death approved:
Oblivion as they rose shrank like a thing reproved. 405

XLVI

And many more, whose names on Earth are dark,
But whose transmitted effluence cannot die
So long as fire outlives the parent spark,
Rose, robed in dazzling immortality.
'Thou art become as one of us,' they cry, 410
'It was for thee yon kingless sphere has long
Swung blind in unascended majesty,
Silent alone amid an Heaven of Song.
Assume thy wingèd throne, thou Vesper of our throng!'

XLVII

Who mourns for Adonais? Oh, come forth,   415
Fond wretch! and know thyself and him aright.
Clasp with thy panting soul the pendulous Earth;
As from a centre, dart thy spirit's light
Beyond all worlds, until its spacious might
Satiate the void circumference: then shrink   420
Even to a point within our day and night;
And keep thy heart light lest it make thee sink
When, hope has kindled hope, and lured thee to the brink.

XLVIII

Or go to Rome, which is the sepulchre,
Oh, not of him, but of our joy: 'tis nought   425
That ages, empires, and religions there
Lie buried in the ravage they have wrought;
For such as he can lend,—they borrow not
Glory from those who made the world their prey;
And he is gathered to the kings of thought   430
Who waged contention with their time's decay,
And of the past are all that cannot pass away.

XLIX

Go thou to Rome,—at once the Paradise,
The grave, the city, and the wilderness;
And where its wrecks like shattered mountains rise,   435
And flowering weeds, and fragrant copses dress
The bones of Desolation's nakedness
Pass, till the spirit of the spot shall lead
Thy footsteps to a slope of green access
Where, like an infant's smile, over the dead   440
A light of laughing flowers along the grass is spread;

L

And gray walls moulder round, on which dull Time
Feeds, like slow fire upon a hoary brand;
And one keen pyramid with wedge sublime,
Pavilioning the dust of him who planned   445
This refuge for his memory, doth stand
Like flame transformed to marble; and beneath,
A field is spread, on which a newer band
Have pitched in Heaven's smile their camp of death,
Welcoming him we lose with scarce extinguished breath. 450

LI

Here pause: these graves are all too young as yet
To have outgrown the sorrow which consigned
Its charge to each; and if the seal is set,
Here, on one fountain of a mourning mind,
Break it not thou! too surely shalt thou find   455
Thine own well full, if thou returnest home,
Of tears and gall. From the world's bitter wind
Seek shelter in the shadow of the tomb.
What Adonais is, why fear we to become?

LII

The One remains, the many change and pass;   460
Heaven's light forever shines, Earth's shadows fly;
Life, like a dome of many-coloured glass,
Stains the white radiance of Eternity,
Until Death tramples it to fragments.—Die,
If thou wouldst be with that which thou dost seek!   465
Follow where all is fled!—Rome's azure sky,
Flowers, ruins, statues, music, words, are weak
The glory they transfuse with fitting truth to speak.

LIII

Why linger, why turn back, why shrink, my Heart?
Thy hopes are gone before: from all things here   470
They have departed; thou shouldst now depart!
A light is passed from the revolving year,
And man, and woman; and what still is dear
Attracts to crush, repels to make thee wither.
The soft sky smiles,—the low wind whispers near: 475
'Tis Adonais calls! oh, hasten thither,
No more let Life divide what Death can join together.

LIV

That Light whose smile kindles the Universe,
That Beauty in which all things work and move,
That Benediction which the eclipsing Curse   480
Of birth can quench not, that sustaining Love
Which through the web of being blindly wove
By man and beast and earth and air and sea,
Burns bright or dim, as each are mirrors of
The fire for which all thirst; now beams on me,   485
Consuming the last clouds of cold mortality.

LV

The breath whose might I have invoked in song
Descends on me; my spirit's bark is driven,
Far from the shore, far from the trembling throng
Whose sails were never to the tempest given;   490
The massy earth and spherèd skies are riven!
I am borne darkly, fearfully, afar;
Whilst, burning through the inmost veil of Heaven,
The soul of Adonais, like a star,
Beacons from the abode where the Eternal are.   495

Cancelled Passages of the Poem

And ever as he went he swept a lyre
Of unaccustomed shape, and   strings
Now like the   of impetuous fire,
Which shakes the forest with its murmurings,
Now like the rush of the aëreal wings   5
Of the enamoured wind among the treen,
Whispering unimaginable things,
And dying on the streams of dew serene,
Which feed the unmown meads with ever-during green.

   .   .   .   .

And the green Paradise which western waves   10
Embosom in their ever-wailing sweep,
Talking of freedom to their tongueless caves,
Or to the spirits which within them keep
A record of the wrongs which, though they sleep,
Die not, but dream of retribution, heard   15
His hymns, and echoing them from steep to steep,
Kept——

   .   .   .   .

And then came one of sweet and earnest looks,
Whose soft smiles to his dark and night-like eyes
Were as the clear and ever-living brooks   20
Are to the obscure fountains whence they rise,
Showing how pure they are: a Paradise
Of happy truth upon his forehead low
Lay, making wisdom lovely, in the guise
Of earth-awakening morn upon the brow   25
Of star-deserted heaven, while ocean gleams below.

His song, though very sweet, was low and faint,
A simple strain——

.   .   .   .   .   .

A mighty Phantasm, half concealed
In darkness of his own exceeding light,   30
Which clothed his awful presence unrevealed,
Charioted on the   night
Of thunder-smoke, whose skirts were chrysolite.

And like a sudden meteor, which outstrips
The splendour-wingèd chariot of the sun,   35
                eclipse
The armies of the golden stars, each one
Pavilioned in its tent of light—all strewn
Over the chasms of blue night——

HELLAS

A LYRICAL DRAMA

ΜΑΝΤΙΣ 'ΕΙΜ' 'ΕΣΘΛΩΝ 'ΑΓΩΝΩΝ.—Oedip. Colon.

TO HIS EXCELLENCY

PRINCE ALEXANDER MAVROCORDATO
LATE SECRETARY FOR FOREIGN AFFAIRS TO THE HOSPODAR OF WALLACHIA

THE DRAMA OF HELLAS IS INSCRIBED AS AN
IMPERFECT TOKEN OF THE ADMIRATION,
SYMPATHY, AND FRIENDSHIP OF
THE AUTHOR

Pisa, *November* 1, 1821.

PREFACE

The poem of *Hellas,* written at the suggestion of the events of the moment, is a mere improvise, and derives its interest (should it be found to possess any) solely from the intense sympathy which the Author feels with the cause he would celebrate.

The subject, in its present state, is insusceptible of being treated otherwise than lyrically, and if I have called this poem a drama from the circumstance of its being composed in dialogue, the licence is not greater than that which has been assumed by other poets who have called their productions epics, only because they have been divided into twelve or twenty-four books.

The *Persae* of Aeschylus afforded me the first model of my conception, although the decision of the glorious contest now waging in Greece being yet suspended forbids a catastrophe parallel to the return of Xerxes and the desolation of the Persians. I have, therefore, contented myself with exhibiting a series of lyric pictures, and with having wrought upon the curtain of futurity, which falls upon the unfinished scene, such figures of indistinct and visionary delineation as suggest the final triumph of the Greek cause as a portion of the cause of civilisation and social improvement.

The drama (if drama it must be called) is, however, so inartificial that I doubt whether, if recited on the Thespian waggon to an Athenian village at the Dionysiaca, it would have obtained the prize of the goat. I shall bear with equanimity any punishment, greater than the loss of such a reward, which the Aristarchi of the hour may think fit to inflict.

The only *goat-song* which I have yet attempted has, I confess, in spite of the unfavourable nature of the subject, received a greater and a more valuable portion of applause than I expected or than it deserved.

Common fame is the only authority which I can allege for the details which form the basis of the poem, and I must trespass upon the forgiveness of my readers for the display of newspaper erudition to which I have been reduced. Undoubtedly, until the conclusion of the war, it will be impossible to obtain an account of it sufficiently authentic for historical materials; but poets have their privilege, and it is unquestionable that actions of the most exalted courage have been performed by the Greeks—that they have gained more than one naval victory, and that their defeat in Wallachia was signalized by circumstances of heroism more glorious even than victory.

The apathy of the rulers of the civilised world to the astonishing circumstance of the descendants of that nation to which they owe their civilisation, rising as it were from the ashes of their ruin, is something perfectly inexplicable to a mere spectator of the shows of this mortal scene. We are all Greeks. Our laws, our literature, our religion, our arts have their root in Greece. But for Greece—Rome, the instructor, the conqueror, or the metropolis of our ancestors, would have spread no illumination with her arms, and we might still have been savages and idolaters; or, what is worse, might have arrived at such a stagnant and miserable state of social institution as China and Japan possess.

The human form and the human mind attained to a perfection in Greece which has impressed its image on those faultless productions, whose very fragments are the despair of modern art, and has propagated impulses which cannot cease, through a thousand channels of manifest or imperceptible operation, to ennoble and delight mankind until the extinction of the race.

The modern Greek is the descendant of those glorious beings whom the imagination almost refuses to figure to itself as belonging to our kind, and he inherits much of their sensibility, their rapidity of conception, their enthusiasm, and their courage. If in many instances he is degraded by moral and political slavery to the practice of the basest vices it engenders—and that below the level of ordinary degradation—let us reflect that the corruption of the best produces the worst, and that habits which subsist only in relation to a peculiar state of social institution may be expected to cease as soon as that relation is dissolved. In fact, the Greeks, since the admirable novel of *Anastasius* could have been a faithful picture of their manners, have undergone most important changes; the flower of their youth, returning to their country from the universities of Italy, Germany, and France, have communicated to their fellow-citizens the latest results of that social perfection of which their ancestors were the original source. The University of Chios contained before the breaking out of the revolution eight hundred students, and among them several Germans and Americans. The munificence and energy of many of the Greek princes and merchants, directed to the renovation of their country with a spirit and a wisdom which has few examples, is above all praise.

The English permit their own oppressors to act according to their natural sympathy with the Turkish tyrant, and to brand upon their name the indelible blot of an alliance with the enemies of domestic happiness, of Christianity and civilisation.

Russia desires to possess, not to liberate Greece; and is contented to see the Turks, its natural enemies, and the Greeks, its intended slaves, enfeeble each other until one or both fall into its net. The wise and generous policy of England would have consisted in establishing the independence of Greece, and in maintaining it both against Russia and the Turk;—but when was the oppressor generous or just?

Should the English people ever become free, they will reflect upon the part which those who presume to represent their will have played in the great drama of the revival of liberty, with feelings which it would become them to anticipate. This is the age of the war of the oppressed against the oppressors, and every one of those ringleaders of the privileged gangs of murderers and swindlers, called Sovereigns, look to each other for aid against the common enemy, and suspend their mutual jealousies in the presence of a mightier fear. Of this holy alliance all the despots of the earth are virtual members. But a new race has arisen throughout Europe, nursed in the abhorrence of the opinions which are its chains, and she will continue to produce fresh generations to accomplish that destiny which tyrants foresee and dread.

The Spanish Peninsula is already free. France is tranquil in the enjoyment of a partial exemption from the abuses which its unnatural and feeble government are vainly attempting to revive. The seed of blood and misery has been sown in Italy, and a more vigorous race is arising to go forth to the harvest. The world waits only the news of a revolution of Germany to see the tyrants who have pinnacled themselves on its supineness precipitated into the ruin from which they shall never arise. Well do these destroyers of mankind know their enemy, when they impute the insurrection in Greece to the same spirit before which they tremble throughout the rest of Europe, and that enemy well knows the

power and the cunning of its opponents, and watches the moment of their
approaching weakness and inevitable division to wrest the bloody sceptres
from their grasp.

PROLOGUE TO HELLAS

Herald of Eternity. It is the day when all the sons of God
Wait in the roofless senate-house, whose floor
Is Chaos, and the immovable abyss
Frozen by His steadfast word to hyaline
.   .   .   .
The shadow of God, and delegate   5
Of that before whose breath the universe
Is as a print of dew.
                    Hierarchs and kings
Who from your thrones pinnacled on the past
Sway the reluctant present, ye who sit
Pavilioned on the radiance or the gloom   10
Of mortal thought, which like an exhalation
Steaming from earth, conceals the   of heaven
Which gave it birth,   assemble here
Before your Father's throne; the swift decree
Yet hovers, and the fiery incarnation   15
Is yet withheld, clothèd in which it shall
                    annul
The fairest of those wandering isles that gem
The sapphire space of interstellar air,
That green and azure sphere, that earth enwrapped   20
Less in the beauty of its tender light
Than in an atmosphere of living spirit
Which interpenetrating all the . . .
                    it rolls from realm to realm
And age to age, and in its ebb and flow   25
Impels the generations
To their appointed place,
Whilst the high Arbiter
Beholds the strife, and at the appointed time
Sends His decrees veiled in eternal . . .   30

Within the circuit of this pendent orb
There lies an antique region, on which fell
The dews of thought in the world's golden dawn
Earliest and most benign, and from it sprung
Temples and cities and immortal forms   35
And harmonies of wisdom and of song,
And thoughts, and deeds worthy of thoughts so fair.
And when the sun of its dominion failed,
And when the winter of its glory came,

The winds that stripped it bare blew on and swept   40
That dew into the utmost wildernesses
In wandering clouds of sunny rain that thawed
The unmaternal bosom of the North.
Haste, sons of God,   for ye beheld,
Reluctant, or consenting, or astonished,   45
The stern decrees go forth, which heaped on Greece
Ruin and degradation and despair.
A fourth now waits: assemble, sons of God,
To speed or to prevent or to suspend,
If, as ye dream, such power be not withheld,   50
The unaccomplished destiny.

    .   .   .   .   .   .

Chorus.

  The curtain of the Universe
    Is rent and shattered,
  The splendour-wingèd worlds disperse
    Like wild doves scattered.   55

    Space is roofless and bare,
  And in the midst a cloudy shrine,
    Dark amid thrones of light.
  In the blue glow of hyaline
  Golden worlds revolve and shine.   60
    In   flight
    From every point of the Infinite,
    Like a thousand dawns on a single night
  The splendours rise and spread;
  And through thunder and darkness dread   65
  Light and music are radiated,
  And in their pavilioned chariots led
  By living wings high overhead
    The giant Powers move,
  Gloomy or bright as the thrones they fill.   70

    .   .   .   .   .

  A chaos of light and motion
  Upon that glassy ocean.

    .   .   .   .   .

  The senate of the Gods is met,
  Each in his rank and station set;
    There is silence in the spaces—   75
  Lo! Satan, Christ, and Mahomet
    Start from their places!

Christ.   Almighty Father!
Low-kneeling at the feet of Destiny

    .   .   .   .   .

There are two fountains in which spirits weep   80
When mortals err, Discord and Slavery named,
And with their bitter dew two Destinies
Filled each their irrevocable urns; the third,
Fiercest and mightiest, mingled both, and added
Chaos and Death, and slow Oblivion's lymph,   85
And hate and terror, and the poisoned rain

.   .   .   .

The Aurora of the nations. By this brow
Whose pores wept tears of blood, by these wide wounds,
By this imperial crown of agony,
By infamy and solitude and death,   90
For this I underwent, and by the pain
Of pity for those who would   for me
The unremembered joy of a revenge,
For this I felt—by Plato's sacred light,
Of which my spirit was a burning morrow—   95
By Greece and all she cannot cease to be.
Her quenchless words, sparks of immortal truth,
Stars of all night—her harmonies and forms,
Echoes and shadows of what Love adores
In thee, I do compel thee, send forth Fate,   100
Thy irrevocable child: let her descend,
A seraph-wingèd Victory [arrayed]
In tempest of the omnipotence of God
Which sweeps through all things.

From hollow leagues, from Tyranny which arms   105
Adverse miscreeds and emulous anarchies
To stamp, as on a wingèd serpent's seed,
Upon the name of Freedom; from the storm
Of faction, which like earthquake shakes and sickens
The solid heart of enterprise; from all   110
By which the holiest dreams of highest spirits
Are stars beneath the dawn . . .
                              She shall arise
Victorious as the world arose from Chaos!
And as the Heavens and the Earth arrayed
Their presence in the beauty and the light   115
Of Thy first smile, O Father,—as they gather
The spirit of Thy love which paves for them
Their path o'er the abyss, till every sphere
Shall be one living Spirit,—so shall Greece—

    Satan. Be as all things beneath the empyrean,   120
Mine! Art thou eyeless like old Destiny,
Thou mockery-king, crowned with a wreath of thorns?

Whose sceptre is a reed, the broken reed
Which pierces thee! whose throne a chair of scorn;
For seest thou not beneath this crystal floor   125
The innumerable worlds of golden light
Which are my empire, and the least of them
          which thou wouldst redeem from me?
Know'st thou not them my portion?
Or wouldst rekindle the   strife   130
Which our great Father then did arbitrate
Which he assigned to his competing sons
Each his apportioned realm?
                Thou Destiny,
Thou who art mailed in the omnipotence
Of Him who sends thee forth, whate'er thy task,   135
Speed, spare not to accomplish, and be mine
Thy trophies, whether Greece again become
The fountain in the desert whence the earth
Shall drink of freedom, which shall give it strength
To suffer, or a gulf of hollow death   140
To swallow all delight, all life, all hope.
Go, thou Vicegerent of my will, no less
Than of the Father's; but lest thou shouldst faint,
The wingèd hounds, Famine and Pestilence,
Shall wait on thee, the hundred-forkèd snake   145
Insatiate Superstition still shall . . .
The earth behind thy steps, and War shall hover
Above, and Fraud shall gape below, and Change
Shall flit before thee on her dragon wings,
Convulsing and consuming, and I add   150
Three vials of the tears which daemons weep
When virtuous spirits through the gate of Death
Pass triumphing over the thorns of life,
Sceptres and crowns, mitres and swords and snares,
Trampling in scorn, like Him and Socrates.   155
The first is Anarchy; when Power and Pleasure,
Glory and science and security,
On Freedom hang like fruit on the green tree,
Then pour it forth, and men shall gather ashes.
The second Tyranny—
   Christer.   Obdurate spirit!   160
Thou seest but the Past in the To-come.
Pride is thy error and thy punishment.
Boast not thine empire, dream not that thy worlds
Are more than furnace-sparks or rainbow-drops
Before the Power that wields and kindles them.   165
True greatness asks not space, true excellence

Lives in the Spirit of all things that live,
Which lends it to the worlds thou callest thine.

.   .   .   .

Mahomet. . . . Haste thou and fill the waning crescent
With beams as keen as those which pierced the shadow   170
Of Christian night rolled back upon the West,
When the orient moon of Islam rode in triumph
From Tmolus to the Acroceraunian snow.

.   .   .   .

Wake, thou Word
Of God, and from the throne of Destiny   175
Even to the utmost limit of thy way
May Triumph

.   .   .   .

Be thou a curse on them whose creed
Divides and multiplies the most high God.

HELLAS

DRAMATIS PERSONAE

MAHMUD. | DAOOD.
HASSAN. | AHASUERUS, *a Jew.*
CHORUS *of Greek Captive Women.* [*The Phantom of Mahomet II.*]
Messengers, Slaves, and Attendants.

SCENE, *Constantinople.*   TIME, *Sunset.*

SCENE.—*A Terrace on the Seraglio.* MAHMUD *sleeping, an
Indian Slave sitting beside his Couch.*

Chorus of Greek Captive Women.

WE strew these opiate flowers
    On thy restless pillow,—
They were stripped from Orient bowers,
    By the Indian billow.
        Be thy sleep   5
        Calm and deep,
Like theirs who fell—not ours who weep!

Indian.

Away, unlovely dreams!
    Away, false shapes of sleep!
Be his, as Heaven seems,   10
    Clear, and bright, and deep!
Soft as love, and calm as death,
Sweet as a summer night without a breath.

Chorus.

Sleep, sleep! our song is laden
   With the soul of slumber;   15
It was sung by a Samian maiden,
   Whose lover was of the number
     Who now keep
     That calm sleep
Whence none may wake, where none shall weep.   20

Indian.

I touch thy temples pale!
   I breathe my soul on thee!
And could my prayers avail,
   All my joy should be
Dead, and I would live to weep,   25
So thou mightst win one hour of quiet sleep.

Chorus.

Breathe low, low
The spell of the mighty mistress now!
When Conscience lulls her sated snake,
And Tyrants sleep, let Freedom wake.   30
   Breathe low—low
The words which, like secret fire, shall flow
Through the veins of the frozen earth—low, low!

Semichorus I.

Life may change, but it may fly not;
Hope may vanish, but can die not;   35
Truth be veiled, but still it burneth;
Love repulsed,—but it returneth!

Semichorus II.

Yet were life a charnel where
Hope lay coffined with Despair;
Yet were truth a sacred lie,   40
Love were lust—

Semichorus I.

     If Liberty
Lent not life its soul of light,
Hope its iris of delight,
Truth its prophet's robe to wear,
Love its power to give and bear.   45

Chorus.

In the great morning of the world,
The Spirit of God with might unfurled
The flag of Freedom over Chaos,
  And all its banded anarchs fled,
Like vultures frighted from Imaus,   50
  Before an earthquake's tread.—
So from Time's tempestuous dawn
Freedom's splendour burst and shone:—
Thermopylae and Marathon
Caught, like mountains beacon-lighted,   55
  The springing Fire.—The wingèd glory
On Philippi half-alighted,
  Like an eagle on a promontory.
Its unwearied wings could fan
The quenchless ashes of Milan.   60
From age to age, from man to man,
  It lived; and lit from land to land
  Florence, Albion, Switzerland.

Then night fell; and, as from night,
Reassuming fiery flight,   65
From the West swift Freedom came,
  Against the course of Heaven and doom,
A second sun arrayed in flame,
  To burn, to kindle, to illume.
From far Atlantis its young beams   70
Chased the shadows and the dreams.
France, with all her sanguine steams,
  Hid, but quenched it not: again
  Through clouds its shafts of glory rain
From utmost Germany to Spain.   75

As an eagle fed with morning
Scorns the embattled tempest's warning,
When she seeks her aerie hanging
  In the mountain-cedar's hair,
And her brood expect the clanging   80
  Of her wings through the wild air,
Sick with famine:—Freedom, so
To what of Greece remaineth now
Returns; her hoary ruins glow
Like Orient mountains lost in day;   85
  Beneath the safety of her wings
Her renovated nurslings prey,
  And in the naked lightenings
Of truth they purge their dazzled eyes.

Let Freedom leave—where'er she flies,   90
A Desert, or a Paradise:
   Let the beautiful and the brave
   Share her glory, or a grave.

Semichorus I.

   With the gifts of gladness
     Greece did thy cradle strew;   95

Semichorus II.

   With the tears of sadness
     Greece did thy shroud bedew!

Semichorus I.

   With an orphan's affection
     She followed thy bier through Time;

Semichorus II.

   And at thy resurrection   100
     Reappeareth, like thou, sublime!

Semichorus I.

   If Heaven should resume thee,
     To Heaven shall her spirit ascend;

Semichorus II.

   If Hell should entomb thee,
     To Hell shall her high hearts bend.   105

Semichorus I.

   If Annihilation——

Semichorus II.

   Dust let her glories be!
   And a name and a nation
     Be forgotten, Freedom, with thee!

Indian.

His brow grows darker—breathe not—move not!   110
He starts—he shudders—ye that love not,
   With your panting loud and fast,
   Have awakened him at last.

Mahmud (*starting from his sleep*). Man the Seraglio-guard!
   make fast the gate!
What! from a cannonade of three short hours?   115
'Tis false! that breach towards the Bosphorus

Cannot be practicable yet—who stirs?
Stand to the match; that when the foe prevails
One spark may mix in reconciling ruin
The conqueror and the conquered! Heave the tower   120
Into the gap—wrench off the roof!
    (*Enter* HASSAN.)   Ha! what!
The truth of day lightens upon my dream
And I am Mahmud still.
    Hassan.   Your Sublime Highness
Is strangely moved.
    Mahmud.   The times do cast strange shadows
On those who watch and who must rule their course,   125
Lest they, being first in peril as in glory,
Be whelmed in the fierce ebb:—and these are of them.
Thrice has a gloomy vision hunted me
As thus from sleep into the troubled day;
It shakes me as the tempest shakes the sea,   130
Leaving no figure upon memory's glass.
Would that——no matter. Thou didst say thou knewest
A Jew, whose spirit is a chronicle
Of strange and secret and forgotten things.
I bade thee summon him:—'tis said his tribe   135
Dream, and are wise interpreters of dreams.
    Hassan. The Jew of whom I spake is old,—so old
He seems to have outlived a world's decay;
The hoary mountains and the wrinkled ocean
Seem younger still than he;—his hair and beard   140
Are whiter than the tempest-sifted snow;
His cold pale limbs and pulseless arteries
Are like the fibres of a cloud instinct
With light, and to the soul that quickens them
Are as the atoms of the mountain-drift   145
To the winter wind:—but from his eye looks forth
A life of unconsumèd thought which pierces
The Present, and the Past, and the To-come.
Some say that this is he whom the great prophet
Jesus, the son of Joseph, for his mockery,   150
Mocked with the curse of immortality.
Some feign that he is Enoch: others dream
He was pre-adamite and has survived
Cycles of generation and of ruin.
The sage, in truth, by dreadful abstinence   155
And conquering penance of the mutinous flesh,
Deep contemplation, and unwearied study,
In years outstretched beyond the date of man,
May have attained to sovereignty and science
Over those strong and secret things and thoughts   160

Which others fear and know not.
   Mahmud.   I would talk
With this old Jew.
   Hassan.   Thy will is even now
Made known to him, where he dwells in a sea-cavern
'Mid the Demonesi, less accessible
Than thou or God! He who would question him   165
Must sail alone at sunset, where the stream
Of Ocean sleeps around those foamless isles,
When the young moon is westering as now,
And evening airs wander upon the wave;
And when the pines of that bee-pasturing isle,   170
Green Erebinthus, quench the fiery shadow
Of his gilt prow within the sapphire water,
Then must the lonely helmsman cry aloud
'Ahasuerus!' and the caverns round
Will answer 'Ahasuerus!' If his prayer   175
Be granted, a faint meteor will arise
Lighting him over Marmora, and a wind
Will rush out of the sighing pine-forest,
And with the wind a storm of harmony
Unutterably sweet, and pilot him   180
Through the soft twilight to the Bosphorus:
Thence at the hour and place and circumstance
Fit for the matter of their conference
The Jew appears. Few dare, and few who dare
Win the desired communion—but that shout   185
Bodes——   [*A shout within*.
   Mahmud. Evil, doubtless; like all human sounds.
Let me converse with spirits.
   Hassan.   That shout again.
   Mahmud. This Jew whom thou hast summoned—
   Hassan.   Will be here—
   Mahmud. When the omnipotent hour to which are yoked
He, I, and all things shall compel—enough!   190
Silence those mutineers—that drunken crew,
That crowd about the pilot in the storm.
Ay! strike the foremost shorter by a head!
They weary me, and I have need of rest.
Kings are like stars—they rise and set, they have 195
The worship of the world, but no repose.   [*Exeunt severally*.

Chorus.

   Worlds on worlds are rolling ever
      From creation to decay,
   Like the bubbles on a river
      Sparkling, bursting, borne away.   200

But they are still immortal
Who, through birth's orient portal
And death's dark chasm hurrying to and fro,
    Clothe their unceasing flight
    In the brief dust and light   205
Gathered around their chariots as they go;
    New shapes they still may weave,
    New gods, new laws receive,
Bright or dim are they as the robes they last
    On Death's bare ribs had cast.   210

A power from the unknown God,
    A Promethean conqueror, came;
Like a triumphal path he trod
    The thorns of death and shame.
    A mortal shape to him   215
    Was like the vapour dim
Which the orient planet animates with light;
    Hell, Sin, and Slavery came,
    Like bloodhounds mild and tame,
Nor preyed, until their Lord had taken flight;   220
    The moon of Mahomet
    Arose, and it shall set:
While blazoned as on Heaven's immortal noon
    The cross leads generations on.

Swift as the radiant shapes of sleep   225
    From one whose dreams are Paradise
Fly, when the fond wretch wakes to weep,
    And Day peers forth with her blank eyes;
    So fleet, so faint, so fair,
    The Powers of earth and air   230
Fled from the folding-star of Bethlehem:
    Apollo, Pan, and Love,
    And even Olympian Jove
Grew weak, for killing Truth had glared on them;
    Our hills and seas and streams,   235
    Dispeopled of their dreams,
Their waters turned to blood, their dew to tears,
    Wailed for the golden years.

Enter MAHMUD, HASSAN, DAOOD, *and others.*

Mahmud. More gold? our ancestors bought gold with victory,
And shall I sell it for defeat?
    Daood.   The Janizars   240
Clamour for pay.
    Mahmud.   Go! bid them pay themselves

With Christian blood! Are there no Grecian virgins
Whose shrieks and spasms and tears they may enjoy?
No infidel children to impale on spears?
No hoary priests after that Patriarch   245
Who bent the curse against his country's heart,
Which clove his own at last? Go! bid them kill,
Blood is the seed of gold.
  Daood.   It has been sown,
And yet the harvest to the sicklemen
Is as a grain to each.
  Mahmud.   Then, take this signet,   250
Unlock the seventh chamber in which lie
The treasures of victorious Solyman,—
An empire's spoil stored for a day of ruin.
O spirit of my sires! is it not come?
The prey-birds and the wolves are gorged and sleep;   255
But these, who spread their feast on the red earth,
Hunger for gold, which fills not.—See them fed;
Then, lead them to the rivers of fresh death. [*Exit* DAOOD.
O miserable dawn, after a night
More glorious than the day which it usurped!   260
O faith in God! O power on earth! O word
Of the great prophet, whose o'ershadowing wings
Darkened the thrones and idols of the West,
Now bright!—For thy sake cursèd be the hour,
Even as a father by an evil child,   265
When the orient moon of Islam rolled in triumph
From Caucasus to White Ceraunia!
Ruin above, and anarchy below;
Terror without, and treachery within;
The Chalice of destruction full, and all   270
Thirsting to drink; and who among us dares
To dash it from his lips? and where is Hope?
  Hassan. The lamp of our dominion still rides high;
One God is God—Mahomet is His prophet.
Four hundred thousand Moslems, from the limits   275
Of utmost Asia, irresistibly
Throng, like full clouds at the Sirocco's cry;
But not like them to weep their strength in tears:
They bear destroying lightning, and their step
Wakes earthquake to consume and overwhelm,   280
And reign in ruin. Phrygian Olympus,
Tmolus, and Latmos, and Mycale, roughen
With horrent arms; and lofty ships even now,
Like vapours anchored to a mountain's edge,
Freighted with fire and whirlwind, wait at Scala   285
The convoy of the ever-veering wind.

Samos is drunk with blood;—the Greek has paid
Brief victory with swift loss and long despair.
The false Moldavian serfs fled fast and far,
When the fierce shout of 'Allah-illa-Allah!'   290
Rose like the war-cry of the northern wind
Which kills the sluggish clouds, and leaves a flock
Of wild swans struggling with the naked storm.
So were the lost Greeks on the Danube's day!
If night is mute, yet the returning sun   295
Kindles the voices of the morning birds;
Nor at thy bidding less exultingly
Than birds rejoicing in the golden day,
The Anarchies of Africa unleash
Their tempest-wingèd cities of the sea,   300
To speak in thunder to the rebel world.
Like sulphurous clouds, half-shattered by the storm,
They sweep the pale Aegean, while the Queen
Of Ocean, bound upon her island-throne,
Far in the West, sits mourning that her sons   305
Who frown on Freedom spare a smile for thee:
Russia still hovers, as an eagle might
Within a cloud, near which a kite and crane
Hang tangled in inextricable fight,
To stoop upon the victor;—for she fears   310
The name of Freedom, even as she hates thine.
But recreant Austria loves thee as the Grave
Loves Pestilence, and her slow dogs of war
Fleshed with the chase, come up from Italy,
And howl upon their limits; for they see   315
The panther, Freedom, fled to her old cover,
Amid seas and mountains, and a mightier brood
Crouch round. What Anarch wears a crown or mitre,
Or bears the sword, or grasps the key of gold,
Whose friends are not thy friends, whose foes thy foes?   320
Our arsenals and our armouries are full;
Our forts defy assault; ten thousand cannon
Lie ranged upon the beach, and hour by hour
Their earth-convulsing wheels affright the city;
The galloping of fiery steeds makes pale   325
The Christian merchant; and the yellow Jew
Hides his hoard deeper in the faithless earth.
Like clouds, and like the shadows of the clouds,
Over the hills of Anatolia,
Swift in wide troops the Tartar chivalry   330
Sweep;—the far flashing of their starry lances
Reverberates the dying light of day.
We have one God, one King, one Hope, one Law;

But many-headed Insurrection stands
Divided in itself, and soon must fall.   335
    Mahmud. Proud words, when deeds come short, are seasonable:
Look, Hassan, on yon crescent moon, emblazoned
Upon that shattered flag of fiery cloud
Which leads the rear of the departing day;
Wan emblem of an empire fading now!   340
See how it trembles in the blood-red air,
And like a mighty lamp whose oil is spent
Shrinks on the horizon's edge, while, from above,
One star with insolent and victorious light
Hovers above its fall, and with keen beams,   345
Like arrows through a fainting antelope,
Strikes its weak form to death.
    Hassan.   Even as that moon
Renews itself——
    Mahmud.   Shall we be not renewed!
Far other bark than ours were needed now
To stem the torrent of descending time: 350
The Spirit that lifts the slave before his lord
Stalks through the capitals of armèd kings,
And spreads his ensign in the wilderness:
Exults in chains; and, when the rebel falls,
Cries like the blood of Abel from the dust;   355
And the inheritors of the earth, like beasts
When earthquake is unleashed, with idiot fear
Cower in their kingly dens—as I do now.
What were Defeat when Victory must appal?
Or Danger, when Security looks pale?—   360
How said the messenger—who, from the fort
Islanded in the Danube, saw the battle
Of Bucharest?—that—
    Hassan.   Ibrahim's scimitar
Drew with its gleam swift victory from Heaven,
To burn before him in the night of battle—   365
A light and a destruction.
    Mahmud.   Ay! the day
Was ours: but how?——
    Hassan.   The light Wallachians,
The Arnaut, Servian, and Albanian allies
Fled from the glance of our artillery
Almost before the thunderstone alit.   370
One half the Grecian army made a bridge
Of safe and slow retreat, with Moslem dead;
The other—
    Mahmud. Speak—tremble not.—
    Hassan.   Islanded

By victor myriads, formed in hollow square
With rough and steadfast front, and thrice flung back   375
The deluge of our foaming cavalry;
Thrice their keen wedge of battle pierced our lines,
Our baffled army trembled like one man
Before a host, and gave them space; but soon,
From the surrounding hills, the batteries blazed,   380
Kneading them down with fire and iron rain:
Yet none approached; till, like a field of corn
Under the hook of the swart sickleman,
The band, intrenched in mounds of Turkish dead,
Grew weak and few.—Then said the Pacha, 'Slaves,   385
Render yourselves—they have abandoned you—
What hope of refuge, or retreat, or aid?
We grant your lives.' 'Grant that which is thine own!'
Cried one, and fell upon his sword and died!
Another—'God, and man, and hope abandon me;   390
But I to them, and to myself, remain
Constant:'—he bowed his head, and his heart burst.
A third exclaimed, 'There is a refuge, tyrant,
Where thou darest not pursue, and canst not harm
Shouldst thou pursue; there we shall meet again.'   395
Then held his breath, and, after a brief spasm,
The indignant spirit cast its mortal garment
Among the slain—dead earth upon the earth!
So these survivors, each by different ways,
Some strange, all sudden, none dishonourable,   400
Met in triumphant death; and when our army
Closed in, while yet wonder, and awe, and shame
Held back the base hyaenas of the battle
That feed upon the dead and fly the living,
One rose out of the chaos of the slain: 405
And if it were a corpse which some dread spirit
Of the old saviours of the land we rule
Had lifted in its anger, wandering by;—
Or if there burned within the dying man
Unquenchable disdain of death, and faith   410
Creating what it feigned;—I cannot tell—
But he cried, 'Phantoms of the free, we come!
Armies of the Eternal, ye who strike
To dust the citadels of sanguine kings,
And shake the souls throned on their stony hearts,   415
And thaw their frostwork diadems like dew;—
O ye who float around this clime, and weave
The garment of the glory which it wears,
Whose fame, though earth betray the dust it clasped,
Lies sepulchred in monumental thought;—   420

Progenitors of all that yet is great,
Ascribe to your bright senate, O accept
In your high ministrations, us, your sons—
Us first, and the more glorious yet to come!
And ye, weak conquerors! giants who look pale   425
When the crushed worm rebels beneath your tread,
The vultures and the dogs, your pensioners tame,
Are overgorged; but, like oppressors, still
They crave the relic of Destruction's feast.
The exhalations and the thirsty winds   430
Are sick with blood; the dew is foul with death;
Heaven's light is quenched in slaughter: thus, where'er
Upon your camps, cities, or towers, or fleets,
The obscene birds the reeking remnants cast
Of these dead limbs,—upon your streams and mountains, 435
Upon your fields, your gardens, and your housetops,
Where'er the winds shall creep, or the clouds fly,
Or the dews fall, or the angry sun look down
With poisoned light—Famine, and Pestilence,
And Panic, shall wage war upon our side!   440
Nature from all her boundaries is moved
Against ye: Time has found ye light as foam.
The Earth rebels; and Good and Evil stake
Their empire o'er the unborn world of men
On this one cast;—but ere the die be thrown,   445
The renovated genius of our race,
Proud umpire of the impious game, descends,
A seraph-wingèd Victory, bestriding
The tempest of the Omnipotence of God,
Which sweeps all things to their appointed doom,   450
And you to oblivion!'—More he would have said,
But—
    Mahmud. Died—as thou shouldst ere thy lips had painted
Their ruin in the hues of our success.
A rebel's crime, gilt with a rebel's tongue!
Your heart is Greek, Hassan.
    Hassan.   It may be so: 455
A spirit not my own wrenched me within,
And I have spoken words I fear and hate;
Yet would I die for—
    Mahmud.   Live! oh live! outlive
Me and this sinking empire. But the fleet—
    Hassan. Alas!——
    Mahmud.   The fleet which, like a flock of clouds 460
Chased by the wind, flies the insurgent banner!
Our wingèd castles from their merchant ships!
Our myriads before their weak pirate bands!

Our arms before their chains! our years of empire
Before their centuries of servile fear!   465
Death is awake! Repulse is on the waters!
They own no more the thunder-bearing banner
Of Mahmud; but, like hounds of a base breed,
Gorge from a stranger's hand, and rend their master.
    Hassan. Latmos, and Ampelos, and Phanae saw   470
The wreck——
    Mahmud.   The caves of the Icarian isles
Told each to the other in loud mockery,
And with the tongue as of a thousand echoes,
First of the sea-convulsing fight—and, then,—
Thou darest to speak—senseless are the mountains: 475
Interpret thou their voice!
    Hassan.   My presence bore
A part in that day's shame. The Grecian fleet
Bore down at daybreak from the North, and hung
As multitudinous on the ocean line,
As cranes upon the cloudless Thracian wind.   480
Our squadron, convoying ten thousand men,
Was stretching towards Nauplia when the battle
Was kindled.—
First through the hail of our artillery
The agile Hydriote barks with press of sail   485
Dashed:—ship to ship, cannon to cannon, man
To man were grappled in the embrace of war,
Inextricable but by death or victory.
The tempest of the raging fight convulsed
To its crystalline depths that stainless sea,   490
And shook Heaven's roof of golden morning clouds,
Poised on an hundred azure mountain-isles.
In the brief trances of the artillery
One cry from the destroyed and the destroyer
Rose, and a cloud of desolation wrapped   495
The unforeseen event, till the north wind
Sprung from the sea, lifting the heavy veil
Of battle-smoke—then victory—victory!
For, as we thought, three frigates from Algiers
Bore down from Naxos to our aid, but soon   500
The abhorrèd cross glimmered behind, before,
Among, around us; and that fatal sign
Dried with its beams the strength in Moslem hearts,
As the sun drinks the dew.—What more? We fled!—
Our noonday path over the sanguine foam   505
Was beaconed,—and the glare struck the sun pale,—
By our consuming transports; the fierce light
Made all the shadows of our sails blood-red,

And every countenance blank. Some ships lay feeding
The ravening fire, even to the water's level;   510
Some were blown up; some, settling heavily,
Sunk; and the shrieks of our companions died
Upon the wind, that bore us fast and far,
Even after they were dead. Nine thousand perished!
We met the vultures legioned in the air   515
Stemming the torrent of the tainted wind;
They, screaming from their cloudy mountain-peaks,
Stooped through the sulphurous battle-smoke and perched
Each on the weltering carcase that we loved,
Like its ill angel or its damnèd soul,   520
Riding upon the bosom of the sea.
We saw the dog-fish hastening to their feast.
Joy waked the voiceless people of the sea,
And ravening Famine left his ocean cave
To dwell with War, with us, and with Despair.   525
We met night three hours to the west of Patmos,
And with night, tempest——
    Mahmud.   Cease!

Enter a Messenger.

    Messenger.   Your Sublime Highness,
That Christian hound, the Muscovite Ambassador,
Has left the city.—If the rebel fleet
Had anchored in the port, had victory   530
Crowned the Greek legions in the Hippodrome,
Panic were tamer.—Obedience and Mutiny,
Like giants in contention planet-struck,
Stand gazing on each other.—There is peace
In Stamboul.—
    Mahmud.   Is the grave not calmer still?   535
Its ruins shall be mine.
    Hassan.   Fear not the Russian:
The tiger leagues not with the stag at bay
Against the hunter.—Cunning, base, and cruel,
He crouches, watching till the spoil be won,
And must be paid for his reserve in blood.   540
After the war is fought, yield the sleek Russian
That which thou canst not keep, his deserved portion
Of blood, which shall not flow through streets and fields,
Rivers and seas, like that which we may win,
But stagnate in the veins of Christian slaves!   545

Enter second Messenger.

    Second Messenger. Nauplia, Tripolizza, Mothon, Athens,
Navarin, Artas, Monembasia,

Corinth, and Thebes are carried by assault,
And every Islamite who made his dogs
Fat with the flesh of Galilean slaves   550
Passed at the edge of the sword: the lust of blood,
Which made our warriors drunk, is quenched in death;
But like a fiery plague breaks out anew
In deeds which make the Christian cause look pale
In its own light. The garrison of Patras   555
Has store but for ten days, nor is there hope
But from the Briton: at once slave and tyrant,
His wishes still are weaker than his fears,
Or he would sell what faith may yet remain
From the oaths broke in Genoa and in Norway;   560
And if you buy him not, your treasury
Is empty even of promises—his own coin.
The freedman of a western poet-chief
Holds Attica with seven thousand rebels,
And has beat back the Pacha of Negropont: 565
The agèd Ali sits in Yanina
A crownless metaphor of empire:
His name, that shadow of his withered might,
Holds our besieging army like a spell
In prey to famine, pest, and mutiny;   570
He, bastioned in his citadel, looks forth
Joyless upon the sapphire lake that mirrors
The ruins of the city where he reigned
Childless and sceptreless. The Greek has reaped
The costly harvest his own blood matured,   575
Not the sower, Ali—who has bought a truce
From Ypsilanti with ten camel-loads
Of Indian gold.

                    Enter a third Messenger.

  Mahmud. What more?
  Third Messenger.   The Christian tribes
Of Lebanon and the Syrian wilderness
Are in revolt;—Damascus, Hems, Aleppo   580
Tremble;—the Arab menaces Medina,
The Aethiop has intrenched himself in Sennaar,
And keeps the Egyptian rebel well employed,
Who denies homage, claims investiture
As price of tardy aid. Persia demands   585
The cities on the Tigris, and the Georgians
Refuse their living tribute. Crete and Cyprus,
Like mountain-twins that from each other's veins
Catch the volcano-fire and earthquake-spasm,
Shake in the general fever. Through the city,   590

Like birds before a storm, the Santons shriek,
And prophesyings horrible and new
Are heard among the crowd: that sea of men
Sleeps on the wrecks it made, breathless and still.
A Dervise, learnèd in the Koran, preaches   595
That it is written how the sins of Islam
Must raise up a destroyer even now.
The Greeks expect a Saviour from the West,
Who shall not come, men say, in clouds and glory,
But in the omnipresence of that Spirit   600
In which all live and are. Ominous signs
Are blazoned broadly on the noonday sky:
One saw a red cross stamped upon the sun;
It has rained blood; and monstrous births declare
The secret wrath of Nature and her Lord.   605
The army encamped upon the Cydaris
Was roused last night by the alarm of battle,
And saw two hosts conflicting in the air,
The shadows doubtless of the unborn time
Cast on the mirror of the night. While yet   610
The fight hung balanced, there arose a storm
Which swept the phantoms from among the stars.
At the third watch the Spirit of the Plague
Was heard abroad flapping among the tents;
Those who relieved watch found the sentinels dead.   615
The last news from the camp is, that a thousand
Have sickened, and——

                   Enter a Fourth Messenger.

   Mahmud.   And thou, pale ghost, dim shadow
Of some untimely rumour, speak!
   Fourth Messenger.   One comes
Fainting with toil, covered with foam and blood:
He stood, he says, on Chelonites'   620
Promontory, which o'erlooks the isles that groan
Under the Briton's frown, and all their waters
Then trembling in the splendour of the moon,
When as the wandering clouds unveiled or hid
Her boundless light, he saw two adverse fleets   625
Stalk through the night in the horizon's glimmer,
Mingling fierce thunders and sulphureous gleams,
And smoke which strangled every infant wind
That soothed the silver clouds through the deep air.
At length the battle slept, but the Sirocco   630
Awoke, and drove his flock of thunder-clouds
Over the sea-horizon, blotting out
All objects—save that in the faint moon-glimpse

He saw, or dreamed he saw, the Turkish admiral
And two the loftiest of our ships of war,   635
With the bright image of that Queen of Heaven,
Who hid, perhaps, her face for grief, reversed;
And the abhorrèd cross—

Enter an Attendant.

Attendant.   Your Sublime Highness,
The Jew, who——
    Mahmud.   Could not come more seasonably:
Bid him attend. I'll hear no more! too long   640
We gaze on danger through the mist of fear,
And multiply upon our shattered hopes
The images of ruin. Come what will!
To-morrow and to-morrow are as lamps
Set in our path to light us to the edge   645
Through rough and smooth, nor can we suffer aught
Which He inflicts not in whose hand we are.   [*Exeunt.*

Semichorus I.

    Would I were the wingèd cloud
    Of a tempest swift and loud!
        I would scorn   650
        The smile of morn
    And the wave where the moonrise is born!
        I would leave
        The spirits of eve
    A shroud for the corpse of the day to weave   655
From other threads than mine!
Bask in the deep blue noon divine.
        Who would? Not I.

Semichorus II.

        Whither to fly?

Semichorus I.

    Where the rocks that gird th' Aegean   660
    Echo to the battle paean
        Of the free—
        I would flee
    A tempestuous herald of victory!
        My golden rain   665
        For the Grecian slain
    Should mingle in tears with the bloody main,
        And my solemn thunder-knell
        Should ring to the world the passing-bell
            Of Tyranny!   670

Semichorus II.

Ah king! wilt thou chain
The rack and the rain?
Wilt thou fetter the lightning and hurricane?
The storms are free,
But we—   675

Chorus.

O Slavery! thou frost of the world's prime,
  Killing its flowers and leaving its thorns bare!
Thy touch has stamped these limbs with crime,
  These brows thy branding garland bear,
    But the free heart, the impassive soul   680
      Scorn thy control!

Semichorus I.

Let there be light! said Liberty,
And like sunrise from the sea,
Athens arose!—Around her born,
Shone like mountains in the morn   685
Glorious states;—and are they now
Ashes, wrecks, oblivion?

Semichorus II.

      Go,
Where Thermae and Asopus swallowed
  Persia, as the sand does foam;
Deluge upon deluge followed,   690
  Discord, Macedon, and Rome:
And lastly thou!

Semichorus I.

      Temples and towers,
  Citadels and marts, and they
Who live and die there, have been ours,
  And may be thine, and must decay;   695
But Greece and her foundations are
Built below the tide of war,
Based on the crystàlline sea
Of thought and its eternity;
Her citizens, imperial spirits,   700
  Rule the present from the past,
On all this world of men inherits
  Their seal is set.

Semichorus II.

      Hear ye the blast,
Whose Orphic thunder thrilling calls

From ruin her Titanian walls?
Whose spirit shakes the sapless bones
    Of Slavery? Argos, Corinth, Crete
Hear, and from their mountain thrones
    The daemons and the nymphs repeat
The harmony.

Semichorus I.

I hear! I hear!   710

Semichorus II.

The world's eyeless charioteer,
        Destiny, is hurrying by!
What faith is crushed, what empire bleeds
Beneath her earthquake-footed steeds?
What eagle-wingèd victory sits   715
At her right hand? what shadow flits
    Before? what splendour rolls behind?
        Ruin and renovation cry
'Who but We?'

Semichorus I.

        I hear! I hear!
    The hiss as of a rushing wind,   720
The roar as of an ocean foaming,
The thunder as of earthquake coming
        I hear! I hear!
The crash as of an empire falling,
The shrieks as of a people calling   725
'Mercy! mercy!'—How they thrill!
Then a shout of 'kill! kill! kill!'
And then a small still voice, thus—

Semichorus II.

                            For
Revenge and Wrong bring forth their kind,
    The foul cubs like their parents are,   730
Their den is in the guilty mind,
    And Conscience feeds them with despair.

Semichorus I.

In sacred Athens, near the fane
    Of Wisdom, Pity's altar stood:
Serve not the unknown God in vain,   735
But pay that broken shrine again,
    Love for hate and tears for blood.

Enter MAHMUD *and* AHASUERUS.

Mahmud. Thou art a man, thou sayest, even as we.
Ahasuerus. No more!
Mahmud.   But raised above thy fellow-men
By thought, as I by power.
   Ahasuerus.   Thou sayest so.   740
   Mahmud. Thou art an adept in the difficult lore
Of Greek and Frank philosophy; thou numberest
The flowers, and thou measurest the stars;
Thou severest element from element;
Thy spirit is present in the Past, and sees   745
The birth of this old world through all its cycles
Of desolation and of loveliness,
And when man was not, and how man became
The monarch and the slave of this low sphere,
And all its narrow circles—it is much—   750
I honour thee, and would be what thou art
Were I not what I am; but the unborn hour,
Cradled in fear and hope, conflicting storms,
Who shall unveil? Nor thou, nor I, nor any
Mighty or wise. I apprehended not   755
What thou hast taught me, but I now perceive
That thou art no interpreter of dreams;
Thou dost not own that art, device, or God,
Can make the Future present—let it come!
Moreover thou disdainest us and ours;   760
Thou art as God, whom thou contemplatest.
   Ahasuerus. Disdain thee?—not the worm beneath thy feet!
The Fathomless has care for meaner things
Than thou canst dream, and has made pride for those
Who would be what they may not, or would seem   765
That which they are not. Sultan! talk no more
Of thee and me, the Future and the Past;
But look on that which cannot change—the One,
The unborn and the undying. Earth and ocean,
Space, and the isles of life or light that gem   770
The sapphire floods of interstellar air,
This firmament pavilioned upon chaos,
With all its cressets of immortal fire,
Whose outwall, bastioned impregnably
Against the escape of boldest thoughts, repels them   775
As Calpe the Atlantic clouds—this Whole
Of suns, and worlds, and men, and beasts, and flowers,
With all the silent or tempestuous workings
By which they have been, are, or cease to be,
Is but a vision;—all that it inherits   780
Are motes of a sick eye, bubbles and dreams;

Thought is its cradle and its grave, nor less
The Future and the Past are idle shadows
Of thought's eternal flight—they have no being:
Nought is but that which feels itself to be.   785
    Mahmud. What meanest thou? Thy words stream like a tempest
Of dazzling mist within my brain—they shake
The earth on which I stand, and hang like night
On Heaven above me. What can they avail?
They cast on all things surest, brightest, best,   790
Doubt, insecurity, astonishment.
    Ahasuerus.   Mistake me not! All is contained in each.
Dodona's forest to an acorn's cup
Is that which has been, or will be, to that
Which is—the absent to the present. Thought   795
Alone, and its quick elements, Will, Passion,
Reason, Imagination, cannot die;
They are, what that which they regard appears,
The stuff whence mutability can weave
All that it hath dominion o'er, worlds, worms,   800
Empires, and superstitions. What has thought
To do with time, or place, or circumstance?
Wouldst thou behold the Future?—ask and have!
Knock and it shall be opened—look, and lo!
The coming age is shadowed on the Past   805
As on a glass.
    Mahmud.   Wild, wilder thoughts convulse
My spirit—Did not Mahomet the Second
Win Stamboul?
    Ahasuerus.   Thou wouldst ask that giant spirit
The written fortunes of thy house and faith.
Thou wouldst cite one out of the grave to tell   810
How what was born in blood must die.
    Mahmud.   Thy words
Have power on me! I see——
    Ahasuerus.   What hearest thou?
    Mahmul. A far whisper——
Terrible silence.
    Ahasuerus.   What succeeds?
    Mahmud.   The sound
As of the assault of an imperial city,   815
The hiss of inextinguishable fire,
The roar of giant cannon; the earthquaking
Fall of vast bastions and precipitous towers,
The shock of crags shot from strange enginery,
The clash of wheels, and clang of armèd hoofs,   820
And crash of brazen mail as of the wreck
Of adamantine mountains—the mad blast

Of trumpets, and the neigh of raging steeds,
The shrieks of women whose thrill jars the blood,
And one sweet laugh, most horrible to hear,   825
As of a joyous infant waked and playing
With its dead mother's breast, and now more loud
The mingled battle-cry,—ha! hear I not
''Εν τούτω νίκη!' 'Allah-illa-Allah!'?
    Ahasuerus. The sulphurous mist is raised—thou seest—
    Mahmud.   A chasm,   830
As of two mountains, in the wall of Stamboul;
And in that ghastly breach the Islamites,
Like giants on the ruins of a world,
Stand in the light of sunrise. In the dust
Glimmers a kingless diadem, and one   835
Of regal port has cast himself beneath
The stream of war. Another proudly clad
In golden arms spurs a Tartarian barb
Into the gap, and with his iron mace
Directs the torrent of that tide of men,   840
And seems—he is—Mahomet!
    Ahasuerus.   What thou seest
Is but the ghost of thy forgotten dream.
A dream itself, yet less, perhaps, than that
Thou call'st reality. Thou mayest behold
How cities, on which Empire sleeps enthroned,   845
Bow their towered crests to mutability.
Poised by the flood, e'en on the height thou holdest,
Thou mayst now learn how the full tide of power
Ebbs to its depths.—Inheritor of glory,
Conceived in darkness, born in blood, and nourished   850
With tears and toil, thou seest the mortal throes
Of that whose birth was but the same. The Past
Now stands before thee like an Incarnation
Of the To-come; yet wouldst thou commune with
That portion of thyself which was ere thou   855
Didst start for this brief race whose crown is death,
Dissolve with that strong faith and fervent passion
Which called it from the uncreated deep,
Yon cloud of war, with its tempestuous phantoms
Of raging death; and draw with mighty will   860
The imperial shade hither.   [*Exit* AHASUERUS. *The*
                Phantom of MAHOMET THE SECOND *appears.*
    Mahmud.   Approach!
    Phantom.   I come
Thence whither thou must go! The grave is fitter
To take the living than give up the dead;
Yet has thy faith prevailed, and I am here.

The heavy fragments of the power which fell 865
When I arose, like shapeless crags and clouds,
Hang round my throne on the abyss, and voices
Of strange lament soothe my supreme repose,
Wailing for glory never to return.—
    A later Empire nods in its decay: 870
The autumn of a greener faith is come,
And wolfish change, like winter, howls to strip
The foliage in which Fame, the eagle, built
Her aerie, while Dominion whelped below.
The storm is in its branches, and the frost 875
Is on its leaves, and the blank deep expects
Oblivion on oblivion, spoil on spoil,
Ruin on ruin:—Thou art slow, my son;
The Anarchs of the world of darkness keep
A throne for thee, round which thine empire lies 880
Boundless and mute; and for thy subjects thou,
Like us, shalt rule the ghosts of murdered life,
The phantoms of the powers who rule thee now—
Mutinous passions, and conflicting fears,
And hopes that sate themselves on dust, and die!— 885
Stripped of their mortal strength, as thou of thine.
Islam must fall, but we will reign together
Over its ruins in the world of death:—
And if the trunk be dry, yet shall the seed
Unfold itself even in the shape of that 890
Which gathers birth in its decay. Woe! woe!
To the weak people tangled in the grasp
Of its last spasms.
    Mahmud.   Spirit, woe to all!
Woe to the wronged and the avenger! Woe
To the destroyer, woe to the destroyed! 895
Woe to the dupe, and woe to the deceiver!
Woe to the oppressed, and woe to the oppressor!
Woe both to those that suffer and inflict;
Those who are born and those who die! but say,
Imperial shadow of the thing I am, 900
When, how, by whom, Destruction must accomplish
Her consummation!
    Phantom.   Ask the cold pale Hour,
Rich in reversion of impending death,
When *he* shall fall upon whose ripe gray hairs
Sit Care, and Sorrow, and Infirmity— 905
The weight which Crime, whose wings are plumed with years,
Leaves in his flight from ravaged heart to heart
Over the heads of men, under which burthen
They bow themselves unto the grave: fond wretch!

He leans upon his crutch, and talks of years   910
To come, and how in hours of youth renewed
He will renew lost joys, and——
   Voice without.   Victory! Victory!
                        [*The Phantom vanishes.*
   Mahmud. What sound of the importunate earth has broken
My mighty trance?
   Voice without.   Victory! Victory!
   Mahmud. Weak lightning before darkness! poor faint smile
Of dying Islam! Voice which art the response   916
Of hollow weakness! Do I wake and live?
Were there such things, or may the unquiet brain,
Vexed by the wise mad talk of the old Jew,
Have shaped itself these shadows of its fear?   920
It matters not!—for nought we see or dream,
Possess, or lose, or grasp at, can be worth
More than it gives or teaches. Come what may,
The Future must become the Past, and I
As they were to whom once this present hour,   925
This gloomy crag of time to which I cling,
Seemed an Elysian isle of peace and joy
Never to be attained.—I must rebuke
This drunkenness of triumph ere it die,
And dying, bring despair. Victory! poor slaves!   930
                        [*Exit* MAHMUD.
   Voice without. Shout in the jubilee of death! The Greeks
Are as a brood of lions in the net
Round which the kingly hunters of the earth
Stand smiling. Anarchs, ye whose daily food
Are curses, groans, and gold, the fruit of death,   935
From Thule to the girdle of the world,
Come, feast! the board groans with the flesh of men;
The cup is foaming with a nation's blood,
Famine and Thirst await! eat, drink, and die!

Semichorus I.

   Victorious Wrong, with vulture scream,   940
  Salutes the rising sun, pursues the flying day!
   I saw her, ghastly as a tyrant's dream,
 Perch on the trembling pyramid of night,
 Beneath which earth and all her realms pavilioned lay
In visions of the dawning undelight.   945
     · Who shall impede her flight?
     Who rob her of her prey?

   Voice without. Victory! Victory! Russia's famished eagles
Dare not to prey beneath the crescent's light.

Impale the remnant of the Greeks! despoil!
Violate! make their flesh cheaper than dust!

Semichorus II.

Thou voice which art
The herald of the ill in splendour hid!
Thou echo of the hollow heart
Of monarchy, bear me to thine abode   955
When desolation flashes o'er a world destroyed:
Oh, bear me to those isles of jaggèd cloud
Which float like mountains on the earthquake, mid
The momentary oceans of the lightning,
Or to some toppling promontory proud   960
Of solid tempest whose black pyramid,
Riven, overhangs the founts intensely bright'ning
Of those dawn-tinted deluges of fire
Before their waves expire,
When heaven and earth are light, and only light   965
In the thunder-night!

Voice without. Victory! Victory! Austria, Russia, England,
And that tame serpent, that poor shadow, France,
Cry peace, and that means death when monarchs speak.
Ho, there! bring torches, sharpen those red stakes,   970
These chains are light, fitter for slaves and poisoners
Than Greeks. Kill! plunder! burn! let none remain.

Semichorus I.

Alas! for Liberty!
If numbers, wealth, or unfulfilling years,
Or fate, can quell the free!   975
Alas! for Virtue, when
Torments, or contumely, or the sneers
Of erring judging men
Can break the heart where it abides.
Alas! if Love, whose smile makes this obscure world splendid,
Can change with its false times and tides,   981
Like hope and terror,—
Alas for Love!
And Truth, who wanderest lone and unbefriended,
If thou canst veil thy lie-consuming mirror   985
Before the dazzled eyes of Error,
Alas for thee! Image of the Above.

Semichorus II.

Repulse, with plumes from conquest torn,
Led the ten thousand from the limits of the morn

Through many an hostile Anarchy!   990
At length they wept aloud, and cried, 'The Sea! the Sea!'
     Through exile, persecution, and despair,
       Rome was, and young Atlantis shall become
       The wonder, or the terror, or the tomb
Of all whose step wakes Power lulled in her savage lair: 995
     But Greece was as a hermit-child,
       Whose fairest thoughts and limbs were built
     To woman's growth, by dreams so mild,
       She knew not pain or guilt;
And now, O Victory, blush! and Empire, tremble   1000
       When ye desert the free—
       If Greece must be
A wreck, yet shall its fragments reassemble,
And build themselves again impregnably
       In a diviner clime,   1005
To Amphionic music on some Cape sublime,
Which frowns above the idle foam of Time.

Semichorus I.

Let the tyrants rule the desert they have made;
     Let the free possess the Paradise they claim;
Be the fortune of our fierce oppressors weighed   1010
     With our ruin, our resistance, and our name!

Semichorus II.

Our dead shall be the seed of their decay,
     Our survivors be the shadow of their pride,
Our adversity a dream to pass away—
     Their dishonour a remembrance to abide!   1015

Voice without. Victory! Victory! The bought Briton sends
The keys of ocean to the Islamite.—
Now shall the blazon of the cross be veiled,
And British skill directing Othman might,
Thunder-strike rebel victory. Oh, keep holy   1020
This jubilee of unrevengèd blood!
Kill! crush! despoil! Let not a Greek escape!

Semichorus I.

     Darkness has dawned in the East
       On the noon of time:
     The death-birds descend to their feast   1025
       From the hungry clime.
     Let Freedom and Peace flee far
       To a sunnier strand,
     And follow Love's folding-star
       To the Evening land!   1030

Semichorus II.

The young moon has fed
Her exhausted horn
With the sunset's fire:
The weak day is dead,
But the night is not born;   1035
And, like loveliness panting with wild desire
While it trembles with fear and delight,
Hesperus flies from awakening night,
And pants in its beauty and speed with light
Fast-flashing, soft, and bright.   1040
Thou beacon of love! thou lamp of the free!
Guide us far, far away,
To climes where now veiled by the ardour of day
Thou art hidden
From waves on which weary Noon   1045
Faints in her summer swoon,
Between kingless continents sinless as Eden,
Around mountains and islands inviolably
Pranked on the sapphire sea.

Semichorus I.

Through the sunset of hope,   1050
Like the shapes of a dream,
What Paradise islands of glory gleam!
Beneath Heaven's cope,
Their shadows more clear float by—
The sound of their oceans, the light of their sky,   1055
The music and fragrance their solitudes breathe
Burst, like morning on dream, or like Heaven on death,
Through the walls of our prison;
And Greece, which was dead, is arisen!

Chorus.

The world's great age begins anew,   1060
The golden years return,
The earth doth like a snake renew
Her winter weeds outworn:
Heaven smiles, and faiths and empires gleam,
Like wrecks of a dissolving dream.   1065

A brighter Hellas rears its mountains
From waves serener far;
A new Peneus rolls his fountains
Against the morning star.
Where fairer Tempes bloom, there sleep   1070
Young Cyclads on a sunnier deep.

A loftier Argo cleaves the main,
    Fraught with a later prize;
Another Orpheus sings again,
    And loves, and weeps, and dies.   1075
A new Ulysses leaves once more
Calypso for his native shore.

Oh, write no more the tale of Troy,
    If earth Death's scroll must be!
Nor mix with Laian rage the joy   1080
    Which dawns upon the free:
Although a subtler Sphinx renew
Riddles of death Thebes never knew.

Another Athens shall arise,
    And to remoter time   1085
Bequeath, like sunset to the skies,
    The splendour of its prime;
And leave, if nought so bright may live,
All earth can take or Heaven can give.

Saturn and Love their long repose   1090
    Shall burst, more bright and good
Than all who fell, than One who rose,
    Than many unsubdued:
Not gold, not blood, their altar dowers,
But votive tears and symbol flowers.   1095

Oh, cease! must hate and death return?
    Cease! must men kill and die?
Cease! drain not to its dregs the urn
    Of bitter prophecy.
The world is weary of the past,   1100
Oh, might it die or rest at last!

NOTES

(1) *The quenchless ashes of Milan* [l. 60, p. 509].

MILAN was the centre of the resistance of the Lombard league against the Austrian tyrant. Frederic Barbarossa burnt the city to the ground, but liberty lived in its ashes, and it rose like an exhalation from its ruin. See Sismondi's *Histoire des Républiques Italiennes*, a book which has done much towards awakening the Italians to an imitation of their great ancestors.

(2) *The Chorus* [p. 512].

The popular notions of Christianity are represented in this chorus as true in their relation to the worship they superseded, and that which in all probability they will supersede, without considering their merits in a relation more universal. The first stanza contrasts the immortality of the living and thinking beings which inhabit the planets, and to use a common and inadequate phrase, *clothe themselves in matter,* with the transience of the noblest manifestations of the external world.

The concluding verses indicate a progressive state of more or less exalted existence, according to the degree of perfection which every distinct intelligence may have attained. Let it not be supposed that I mean to dogmatise upon a subject, concerning which all men are equally ignorant, or that I think the Gordian knot of the origin of evil can be disentangled by that or any similar assertions. The received hypothesis of a Being resembling men in the moral attributes of His nature, having called us out of non-existence, and after inflicting on us the misery of the commission of error, should superadd that of the punishment and the privations consequent upon it, still would remain inexplicable and incredible. That there is a true solution of the riddle, and that in our present state that solution is unattainable by us, are propositions which may be regarded as equally certain: meanwhile, as it is the province of the poet to attach himself to those ideas which exalt and ennoble humanity, let him be permitted to have conjectured the condition of that futurity towards which we are all impelled by an inextinguishable thirst for immortality. Until better arguments can be produced than sophisms which disgrace the cause, this desire itself must remain the strongest and the only presumption that eternity is the inheritance of every thinking being.

(3) *No hoary priests after that Patriarch* [1. 245, p. 514].

The Greek Patriarch, after having been compelled to fulminate an anathema against the insurgents, was put to death by the Turks.

Fortunately the Greeks have been taught that they cannot buy security by degradation, and the Turks, though equally cruel, are less cunning than the smooth-faced tyrants of Europe. As to the anathema, his Holiness might as well have thrown his mitre at Mount Athos for any effect that it produced. The chiefs of the Greeks are almost all men of comprehension and enlightened views on religion and politics.

(4) *The freedman of a western poet-chief* [1. 563, p. 521].

A Greek who had been Lord Byron's servant commands the insurgents in Attica. This Greek, Lord Byron informs me, though a poet and an enthusiastic patriot, gave him rather the idea of a timid and unenterprising person. It appears that circumstances make men what they are, and that we all contain the germ of a degree of degradation or of greatness whose connection with our character is determined by events.

(5) *The Greeks expect a Saviour from the West* [1. 598, p. 522].

It is reported that this Messiah had arrived at a seaport near Lacedaemon in an American brig. The association of names and ideas is irresistibly ludicrous, but the prevalence of such a rumour strongly marks the state of popular enthusiasm in Greece.

(6) *The sound as of the assault of an imperial city* [ll. 814-15, p. 527].

For the vision of Mahmud of the taking of Constantinople in 1453, see Gibbon's *Decline and Fall of the Roman Empire,* vol. xii, p. 223.

The manner of the invocation of the spirit of Mahomet the Second will be censured as over subtle. I could easily have made the Jew a regular conjuror, and the Phantom an ordinary ghost. I have preferred to represent the Jew as disclaiming all pretension, or even belief, in supernatural agency, and as tempting Mahmud to that state of mind in which ideas may be supposed to assume the force of sensations through the confusion of thought with the objects of thought, and the excess of passion animating the creations of imagination.

It is a sort of natural magic, susceptible of being exercised in a degree by any one who should have made himself master of the secret associations of another's thoughts.

(7) *The Chorus* [p. 533].

The final chorus is indistinct and obscure, as the event of the living drama whose arrival it foretells. Prophecies of wars, and rumours of wars, etc., may safely be made by poet or prophet in any age, but to anticipate however darkly a period of regeneration and happiness is a more hazardous exercise of the faculty which bards possess or feign. It will remind the reader 'magno *nec* proximus intervallo' of Isaiah and Virgil, whose ardent spirits overleaping the actual reign of evil which we endure and bewail, already saw the possible and perhaps approaching state of society in which the *'lion shall lie down with the lamb,'* and 'omnis feret omnia tellus.' Let these great names be my authority and my excuse.

(8) *Saturn and Love their long repose shall burst* [l. 1090, p. 534].

Saturn and Love were among the deities of a real or imaginary state of innocence and happiness. *All* those *who fell,* or the Gods of Greece, Asia, and Egypt; the *One who rose,* or Jesus Christ, at whose appearance the idols of the Pagan World were amerced of their worship; and *the many unsubdued,* or the monstrous objects of the idolatry of China, India, the Antarctic islands, and the native tribes of America, certainly have reigned over the understandings of men in conjunction or in succession during periods in which all we know of evil has been in a state of portentous, and, until the revival of learning and the arts, perpetually increasing, activity. The Grecian gods seem indeed to have been personally more innocent, although it cannot be said, that as far as temperance and chastity are concerned, they gave so edifying an example as their successor. The sublime human character of Jesus Christ was deformed by an imputed identification with a Power, who tempted, betrayed, and punished the innocent beings who were called into existence by His sole will; and for the period of a thousand years, the spirit of this most just, wise, and benevolent of men has been propitiated with myriads of hecatombs of those who approached the nearest to His innocence and wisdom, sacrificed under every aggravation of atrocity and variety of torture. The horrors of the Mexican, the Peruvian, and the Indian superstitions are well known.

NOTE ON HELLAS, BY MRS. SHELLEY

The South of Europe was in a state of great political excitement at the beginning of the year 1821. The Spanish Revolution had been a signal to Italy; secret societies were formed; and, when Naples rose to declare the Constitution, the call was responded to from Brundusium to the foot of the Alps. To crush these attempts to obtain liberty, early in 1821 the Austrians poured their armies into the Peninsula: at first their coming rather seemed to add energy and resolution to a people long enslaved. The Piedmontese asserted their freedom; Genoa threw off the yoke of the King of Sardinia; and, as if in playful imitation, the people of the little state of Massa and Carrara gave the *congé* to their sovereign, and set up a republic.

Tuscany alone was perfectly tranquil. It was said that the Austrian minister presented a list of sixty Carbonari to the Grand Duke, urging their imprisonment; and the Grand Duke replied, 'I do not know whether these sixty men are Carbonari, but I know, if I imprison them, I shall directly have sixty thousand start up.' But, though the Tuscans had no desire to disturb the paternal government beneath whose shelter they slumbered, they regarded the progress of the various Italian revolutions with intense interest, and hatred for the Austrians was warm in every bosom. But they had slender hopes; they knew that the Neapolitans would offer no fit resistance to the regular German troops, and that the overthrow of the constitution in Naples would act as a decisive blow against all struggles for liberty in Italy.

We have seen the rise and progress of reform. But the Holy Alliance was alive and active in those days, and few could dream of the peaceful triumph of liberty. It seemed then that the armed assertion of freedom in the South of Europe was the only hope of the liberals, as, if it prevailed, the nations of the north would imitate the example. Happily the reverse has proved the fact. The countries accustomed to the exercise of the privileges of freemen, to a limited extent, have extended, and are extending, these limits. Freedom and knowledge have now a chance of proceeding hand in hand; and, if it continue thus, we may hope for the durability of both. Then, as I have said—in 1821—Shelley, as well as every other lover of liberty, looked upon the struggles in Spain and Italy as decisive of the destinies of the world, probably for centuries to come. The interest he took in the progress of affairs was intense. When Genoa declared itself free, his hopes were at their highest. Day after day he read the bulletins of the Austrian army, and sought eagerly to gather tokens of its defeat. He heard of the revolt of Genoa with emotions of transport. His whole heart and soul were in the triumph of the cause. We were living at Pisa at that time; and several well-informed Italians, at the head of whom we may place the celebrated Vaccà, were accustomed to seek for sympathy in their hopes from Shelley: they did not find such for the despair they too generally experienced, founded on contempt for their southern countrymen.

While the fate of the progress of the Austrian armies then invading Naples was yet in suspense, the news of another revolution filled him with exultation. We had formed the acquaintance at Pisa of several Constantinopolitan Greeks, of the family of Prince Caradja, formerly Hospodar of Wallachia; who, hearing that the bowstring, the accustomed finale of his viceroyalty, was on the road to him, escaped with his treasures, and took up his abode in Tuscany. Among these was the gentleman to whom the drama of *Hellas* is dedicated. Prince Mavrocordato was warmed by those aspirations for the independence of his country which filled the hearts of many of his countrymen. He often intimated the possibility of an insurrection in Greece; but we had no idea of its being so near at hand, when, on the 1st of April 1821, he called on Shelley, bringing the proclamation of his cousin, Prince Ypsilanti, and, radiant with exultation and delight, declared that henceforth Greece would be free.

Shelley had hymned the dawn of liberty in Spain and Naples, in two odes dictated by the warmest enthusiasm; he felt himself naturally impelled to decorate with poetry the uprise of the descendants of that people whose works he regarded with deep admiration, and to adopt the vaticinatory character in prophesying their success. *Hellas* was written in a moment of enthusiasm. It is curious to remark how well he overcomes the difficulty of forming a drama out of such scant materials. His prophecies, indeed, came true in their general, not their particular, purport. He did not foresee the death of Lord Londonderry, which was to be the epoch of a change in English politics, particularly as regarded foreign affairs; nor that the navy of his country would fight for instead of against the Greeks, and by the battle of Navarino secure their enfranchisement from the Turks. Almost against reason, as it appeared to him, he resolved to believe that Greece would prove triumphant; and in this spirit, auguring ultimate good, yet grieving over the vicissitudes to be endured in the interval, he composed his drama.

Hellas was among the last of his compositions, and is among the most beautiful. The choruses are singularly imaginative, and melodious in their versification. There are some stanzas that beautifully exemplify Shelley's peculiar style; as, for instance, the assertion of the intellectual empire which must be for ever the inheritance of the country of Homer, Sophocles, and Plato:—

'But Greece and her foundations are
Built below the tide of war,
Based on the crystàlline sea
Of thought and its eternity.'

And again, that philosophical truth felicitously imaged forth—

> 'Revenge and Wrong bring forth their kind,
> The foul cubs like their parents are,
> Their den is in the guilty mind,
> And Conscience feeds them with despair.'

The conclusion of the last chorus is among the most beautiful of his lyrics. The imagery is distinct and majestic; the prophecy, such as poets love to dwell upon, the Regeneration of Mankind—and that regeneration reflecting back splendour on the foregone time, from which it inherits so much of intellectual wealth, and memory of past virtuous deeds, as must render the possession of happiness and peace of tenfold value.

FRAGMENTS OF AN UNFINISHED DRAMA

THE following fragments are part of a Drama undertaken for the amusement of the individuals who composed our intimate society, but left unfinished. I have preserved a sketch of the story as far as it had been shadowed in the poet's mind.

An Enchantress, living in one of the islands of the Indian Archipelago, saves the life of a Pirate, a man of savage but noble nature. She becomes enamoured of him; and he, inconstant to his mortal love, for a while returns her passion; but at length, recalling the memory of her whom he left, and who laments his loss, he escapes from the Enchanted Island, and returns to his lady. His mode of life makes him again go to sea, and the Enchantress seizes the opportunity to bring him, by a spirit-brewed tempest, back to her Island.—[MRS. SHELLEY'S NOTE, 1839.]

SCENE.—*Before the Cavern of the Indian Enchantress.*

The ENCHANTRESS *comes forth.*

Enchantress.

HE came like a dream in the dawn of life,
    He fled like a shadow before its noon;
He is gone, and my peace is turned to strife,
    And I wander and wane like the weary moon.
        O, sweet Echo, wake,   5
        And for my sake
Make answer the while my heart shall break!

But my heart has a music which Echo's lips,
    Though tender and true, yet can answer not,
And the shadow that moves in the soul's eclipse   10
    Can return not the kiss by his now forgot;
        Sweet lips! he who hath
        On my desolate path
Cast the darkness of absence, worse than death!

The ENCHANTRESS *makes her spell: she is answered by a Spirit.*

Spirit. Within the silent centre of the earth   15
My mansion is; where I have lived insphered
From the beginning, and around my sleep
Have woven all the wondrous imagery
Of this dim spot, which mortals call the world;
Infinite depths of unknown elements   20
Massed into one impenetrable mask;
Sheets of immeasurable fire, and veins
Of gold and stone, and adamantine iron.
And as a veil in which I walk through Heaven
I have wrought mountains, seas, and waves, and clouds,
And lastly light, whose interfusion dawns   26
In the dark space of interstellar air.

A good Spirit, who watches over the Pirate's fate, leads, in a mysterious manner, the lady of his love to the Enchanted Isle. She is accompanied by a Youth, who loves the lady, but whose passion she returns only
with a sisterly affection. The ensuing scene takes place between them
on their arrival at the Isle. [MRS. SHELLEY'S NOTE, 1839.]

ANOTHER SCENE

INDIAN YOUTH *and* LADY.

Indian. And, if my grief should still be dearer to me
Than all the pleasures in the world beside,
Why would you lighten it?—
      Lady.   I offer only   30
That which I seek, some human sympathy
In this mysterious island.
      Indian.   Oh! my friend,
My sister, my beloved!—What do I say?
My brain is dizzy, and I scarce know whether
I speak to thee or her.
      Lady.   Peace, perturbed heart!   35
I am to thee only as thou to mine,
The passing wind which heals the brow at noon,
And may strike cold into the breast at night,
Yet cannot linger where it soothes the most,
Or long soothe could it linger.
      Indian.   But you said   40
You also loved?
      Lady.   Loved! Oh, I love. Methinks
This word of love is fit for all the world,
And that for gentle hearts another name
Would speak of gentler thoughts than the world owns.
I have loved.

Indian.   And thou lovest not? if so,   45
Young as thou art thou canst afford to weep.
 Lady. Oh! would that I could claim exemption
From all the bitterness of that sweet name.
I loved, I love, and when I love no more
Let joys and grief perish, and leave despair   50
To ring the knell of youth. He stood beside me,
The embodied vision of the brightest dream,
Which like a dawn heralds the day of life;
The shadow of his presence made my world
A Paradise. All familiar things he touched,   55
All common words he spoke, became to me
Like forms and sounds of a diviner world.
He was as is the sun in his fierce youth,
As terrible and lovely as a tempest;
He came, and went, and left me what I am.   60
Alas! Why must I think how oft we two
Have sate together near the river springs,
Under the green pavilion which the willow
Spreads on the floor of the unbroken fountain,
Strewn, by the nurslings that linger there,   65
Over that islet paved with flowers and moss,
While the musk-rose leaves, like flakes of crimson snow,
Showered on us, and the dove mourned in the pine,
Sad prophetess of sorrows not her own?
The crane returned to her unfrozen haunt,,   70
And the false cuckoo bade the spray good morn;
And on a wintry bough the widowed bird,
Hid in the deepest night of ivy-leaves,
Renewed the vigils of a sleepless sorrow.
I, left like her, and leaving one like her,   75
Alike abandoned and abandoning
(Oh! unlike her in this!) the gentlest youth,
Whose love had made my sorrows dear to him,
Even as my sorrow made his love to me!
 Indian. One curse of Nature stamps in the same mould
The features of the wretched; and they are   81
As like as violet to violet,
When memory, the ghost, their odours keeps
Mid the cold relics of abandoned joy.—
Proceed.
 Lady. He was a simple innocent boy.   85
I loved him well, but not as he desired;
Yet even thus he was content to be:—
A short content, for I was——
 Indian [*aside*].   God of Heaven!
From such an islet, such a river-spring——!

I dare not ask her if there stood upon it   90
A pleasure-dome surmounted by a crescent,
With steps to the blue water. [*Aloud.*] It may be
That Nature masks in life several copies
Of the same lot, so that the sufferers
May feel another's sorrow as their own,   95
And find in friendship what they lost in love.
That cannot be; yet it is strange that we,
From the same scene, by the same path to this
Realm of abandonment—— But speak! your breath—
Your breath is like soft music, your words are   100
The echoes of a voice which on my heart
Sleeps like a melody of early days.
But as you said——
    Lady.   He was so awful, yet
So beautiful in mystery and terror,
Calming me as the loveliness of heaven   105
Soothes the unquiet sea:—and yet not so,
For he seemed stormy, and would often seem
A quenchless sun masked in portentous clouds;
For such his thoughts, and even his actions were;
But he was not of them, nor they of him,   110
But as they hid his splendour from the earth.
Some said he was a man of blood and peril,
And steeped in bitter infamy to the lips.
More need was there I should be innocent,
More need that I should be most true and kind,   115
And much more need that there should be found one
To share remorse and scorn and solitude,
And all the ills that wait on those who do
The tasks of ruin in the world of life.
He fled, and I have followed him.
    Indian.   Such a one   120
Is he who was the winter of my peace.
But, fairest stranger, when didst thou depart
From the far hills where rise the springs of India?
How didst thou pass the intervening sea?
    Lady. If I be sure I am not dreaming now,   125
I should not doubt to say it was a dream.
Methought a star came down from heaven,
And rested mid the plants of India,
Which I had given a shelter from the frost
Within my chamber. There the meteor lay,   130
Panting forth light among the leaves and flowers,
As if it lived, and was outworn with speed;
Or that it loved, and passion made the pulse
Of its bright life throb like an anxious heart,

Till it diffused itself, and all the chamber 135
And walls seemed melted into emerald fire
That burned not; in the midst of which appeared
A spirit like a child, and laughed aloud
A thrilling peal of such sweet merriment
As made the blood tingle in my warm feet: 140
Then bent over a vase, and murmuring
Low, unintelligible melodies,
Placed something in the mould like melon-seeds,
And slowly faded, and in place of it
A soft hand issued from the veil of fire, 145
Holding a cup like a magnolia flower,
And poured upon the earth within the vase
The element with which it overflowed,
Brighter than morning light, and purer than
The water of the springs of Himalah. 150
   Indian. You waked not?
   Lady.   Not until my dream became
Like a child's legend on the tideless sand,
Which the first foam erases half, and half
Leaves legible. At length I rose, and went,
Visiting my flowers from pot to pot, and thought 155
To set new cuttings in the empty urns,
And when I came to that beside the lattice,
I saw two little dark-green leaves
Lifting the light mould at their birth, and then
I half-remembered my forgotten dream. 160
And day by day, green as a gourd in June,
The plant grew fresh and thick, yet no one knew
What plant it was; its stem and tendrils seemed
Like emerald snakes, mottled and diamonded
With azure mail and streaks of woven silver; 165
And all the sheaths that folded the dark buds
Rose like the crest of cobra-di-capel,
Until the golden eye of the bright flower,
Through the dark lashes of those veinèd lids,
. . . disencumbered of their silent sleep, 170
Gazed like a star into the morning light.
Its leaves were delicate, you almost saw
The pulses
With which the purple velvet flower was fed
To overflow, and like a poet's heart 175
Changing bright fancy to sweet sentiment,
Changed half the light to fragrance. It soon fell,
And to a green and dewy embryo-fruit
Left all its treasured beauty. Day by day
I nursed the plant, and on the double flute 180

Played to it on the sunny winter days
Soft melodies, as sweet as April rain
On silent leaves, and sang those words in which
Passion makes Echo taunt the sleeping strings;
And I would send tales of forgotten love   185
Late into the lone night, and sing wild songs
Of maids deserted in the olden time,
And weep like a soft cloud in April's bosom
Upon the sleeping eyelids of the plant,
So that perhaps it dreamed that Spring was come,   190
And crept abroad into the moonlight air,
And loosened all its limbs, as, noon by noon,
The sun averted less his oblique beam.
  Indian. And the plant died not in the frost?
  Lady.   It grew;
And went out of the lattice which I left   195
Half open for it, trailing its quaint spires
Along the garden and across the lawn,
And down the slope of moss and through the tufts
Of wild-flower roots, and stumps of trees o'ergrown
With simple lichens, and old hoary stones,   200
On to the margin of the glassy pool,
Even to a nook of unblown violets
And lilies-of-the-valley yet unborn,
Under a pine with ivy overgrown.
And there its fruit lay like a sleeping lizard   205
Under the shadows; but when Spring indeed
Came to unswathe her infants, and the lilies
Peeped from their bright green masks to wonder at
This shape of autumn couched in their recess,
Then it dilated, and it grew until   210
One half lay floating on the fountain wave,
Whose pulse, elapsed in unlike sympathies,
Kept time
Among the snowy water-lily buds.
Its shape was such as summer melody   215
Of the south wind in spicy vales might give
To some light cloud bound from the golden dawn
To fairy isles of evening, and it seemed
In hue and form that it had been a mirror
Of all the hues and forms around it and   220
Upon it pictured by the sunny beams
Which, from the bright vibrations of the pool,
Were thrown upon the rafters and the roof
Of boughs and leaves, and on the pillared stems
Of the dark sylvan temple, and reflections   225
Of every infant flower and star of moss

And veined leaf in the azure odorous air.
And thus it lay in the Elysian calm
Of its own beauty, floating on the line
Which, like a film in purest space, divided   230
The heaven beneath the water from the heaven
Above the clouds; and every day I went
Watching its growth and wondering;
And as the day grew hot, methought I saw
A glassy vapour dancing on the pool,   235
And on it little quaint and filmy shapes,
With dizzy motion, wheel and rise and fall,
Like clouds of gnats with perfect lineaments.

.   .   .   .

O friend, sleep was a veil uplift from Heaven—
As if Heaven dawned upon the world of dream—   240
When darkness rose on the extinguished day
Out of the eastern wilderness.
   Indian.   I too
Have found a moment's paradise in sleep
Half compensate a hell of waking sorrow.

THE TRIUMPH OF LIFE

SWIFT as a spirit hastening to his task
Of glory and of good, the Sun sprang forth
Rejoicing in his splendour, and the mask

Of darkness fell from the awakened Earth—
The smokeless altars of the mountain snows   5
Flamed above crimson clouds, and at the birth

Of light, the Ocean's orison arose,
To which the birds tempered their matin lay.
All flowers in field or forest which unclose

Their trembling eyelids to the kiss of day,   10
Swinging their censers in the element,
With orient incense lit by the new ray

Burned slow and inconsumably, and sent
Their odorous sighs up to the smiling air;
And, in succession due, did continent,   15

Isle, ocean, and all things that in them wear
The form and character of mortal mould,
Rise as the Sun their father rose, to bear

Their portion of the toil, which he of old
Took as his own, and then imposed on them: 20
But I, whom thoughts which must remain untold

Had kept as wakeful as the stars that gem
The cone of night, now they were laid asleep
Stretched my faint limbs beneath the hoary stem

Which an old chestnut flung athwart the steep   25
Of a green Apennine: before me fled
The night; behind me rose the day; the deep

Was at my feet, and Heaven above my head,—
When a strange trance over my fancy grew
Which was not slumber, for the shade it spread   30

Was so transparent, that the scene came through
As clear as when a veil of light is drawn
O'er evening hills they glimmer; and I knew

That I had felt the freshness of that dawn
Bathe in the same cold dew my brow and hair,   35
And sate as thus upon that slope of lawn

Under the self-same bough, and heard as there
The birds, the fountains and the ocean hold
Sweet talk in music through the enamoured air,
And then a vision on my brain was rolled.   40

As in that trance of wondrous thought I lay,
This was the tenour of my waking dream:—
Methought I sate beside a public way

Thick strewn with summer dust, and a great stream
Of people there was hurrying to and fro,   45
Numerous as gnats upon the evening gleam,

All hastening onward, yet none seemed to know
Whither he went, or whence he came, or why
He made one of the multitude, and so

Was borne amid the crowd, as through the sky   50
One of the million leaves of summer's bier;
Old age and youth, manhood and infancy,

Mixed in one mighty torrent did appear,
Some flying from the thing they feared, and some
Seeking the object of another's fear;   55

And others, as with steps towards the tomb,
Pored on the trodden worms that crawled beneath,
And others mournfully within the gloom

Of their own shadow walked, and called it death;
And some fled from it as it were a ghost,   60
Half fainting in the affliction of vain breath:

But more, with motions which each other crossed,
Pursued or shunned the shadows the clouds threw,
Or birds within the noonday aether lost,

Upon that path where flowers never grew,—   65
And, weary with vain toil and faint for thirst,
Heard not the fountains, whose melodious dew

Out of their mossy cells forever burst;
Nor felt the breeze which from the forest told
Of grassy paths and wood-lawns interspersed   70

With overarching elms and caverns cold,
And violet banks where sweet dreams brood, but they
Pursued their serious folly as of old.

And as I gazed, methought that in the way
The throng grew wilder, as the woods of June   75
When the south wind shakes the extinguished day,

And a cold glare, intenser than the noon,
But icy cold, obscured with blinding light
The sun, as he the stars. Like the young moon—

When on the sunlit limits of the night   80
Her white shell trembles amid crimson air,
And whilst the sleeping tempest gathers might—

Doth, as the herald of its coming, bear
The ghost of its dead mother, whose dim form
Bends in dark aether from her infant's chair,—   85

So came a chariot on the silent storm
Of its own rushing splendour, and a Shape
So sate within, as one whom years deform,

Beneath a dusky hood and double cape,
Crouching within the shadow of a tomb;   90
And o'er what seemed the head a cloud-like crape

Was bent, a dun and faint aethereal gloom
Tempering the light. Upon the chariot-beam
A Janus-visaged Shadow did assume

The guidance of that wonder-wingèd team;   95
The shapes which drew it in thick lightenings
Were lost:—I heard alone on the air's soft stream

The music of their ever-moving wings.
All the four faces of that Charioteer
Had their eyes banded; little profit brings   .   100

Speed in the van and blindness in the rear,
Nor then avail the beams that quench the sun,—
Or that with banded eyes could pierce the sphere

Of all that is, has been or will be done;
So ill was the car guided—but it passed   105
With solemn speed majestically on.

The crowd gave way, and I arose aghast,
Or seemed to rise, so mighty was the trance,
And saw, like clouds upon the thunder-blast,

The million with fierce song and maniac dance   110
Raging around—such seemed the jubilee
As when to greet some conqueror's advance

Imperial Rome poured forth her living sea
From senate-house, and forum, and theatre,
When   upon the free   115

Had bound a yoke, which soon they stooped to bear.
Nor wanted here the just similitude
Of a triumphal pageant, for where'er

The chariot rolled, a captive multitude
Was driven;—all those who had grown old in power   120
Or misery,—all who had their age subdued

By action or by suffering, and whose hour
Was drained to its last sand in weal or woe,
So that the trunk survived both fruit and flower;—

All those whose fame or infamy must grow   125
Till the great winter lay the form and name
Of this green earth with them for ever low;—

All but the sacred few who could not tame
Their spirits to the conquerors—but as soon
As they had touched the world with living flame,   130

Fled back like eagles to their native noon,
Or those who put aside the diadem
Of earthly thrones or gems . . .

Were there, of Athens or Jerusalem,
Were neither mid the mighty captives seen, 135
Nor mid the ribald crowd that followed them,

Nor those who went before fierce and obscene.
The wild dance maddens in the van, and those
Who lead it—fleet as shadows on the green,

Outspeed the chariot, and without repose 140
Mix with each other in tempestuous measure
To savage music, wilder as it grows,

They, tortured by their agonizing pleasure,
Convulsed and on the rapid whirlwinds spun
Of that fierce Spirit, whose unholy leisure 145

Was soothed by mischief since the world begun,
Throw back their heads and loose their streaming hair;
And in their dance round her who dims the sun,

Maidens and youths fling their wild arms in air
As their feet twinkle; they recede, and now 150
Bending within each other's atmosphere,

Kindle invisibly—and as they glow,
Like moths by light attracted and repelled,
Oft to their bright destruction come and go,

Till like two clouds into one vale impelled, 155
That shake the mountains when their lightnings mingle
And die in rain—the fiery band which held

Their natures, snaps—while the shock still may tingle;
One falls and then another in the path
Senseless—nor is the desolation single, 160

Yet ere I can say *where*—the chariot hath
Passed over them—nor other trace I find
But as of foam after the ocean's wrath

Is spent upon the desert shore;—behind,
Old men and women foully disarrayed, 165
Shake their gray hairs in the insulting wind,

And follow in the dance, with limbs decayed,
Seeking to reach the light which leaves them still
Farther behind and deeper in the shade.

But not the less with impotence of will   170
They wheel, though ghastly shadows interpose
Round them and round each other, and fulfil

Their work, and in the dust from whence they rose
Sink, and corruption veils them as they lie,
And past in these performs what   in those.   175

Struck to the heart by this sad pageantry,
Half to myself I said—'And what is this?
Whose shape is that within the car? And why—'

I would have added—'is all here amiss?—'
But a voice answered—'Life!'—I turned, and knew   180
(O Heaven, have mercy on such wretchedness!)

That what I thought was an old root which grew
To strange distortion out of the hill side,
Was indeed one of those deluded crew,

And that the grass, which methought hung so wide   185
And white, was but his thin discoloured hair,
And that the holes he vainly sought to hide,

Were or had been eyes:—'If thou canst, forbear
To join the dance, which I had well forborne!'
Said the grim Feature (of my thought aware).   190

'I will unfold that which to this deep scorn
Led me and my companions, and relate
The progress of the pageant since the morn;

'If thirst of knowledge shall not then abate,
Follow it thou even to the night, but I   195
Am weary.'—Then like one who with the weight

Of his own words is staggered, wearily
He paused; and ere he could resume, I cried:
'First, who art thou?'—'Before thy memory,

'I feared, loved, hated, suffered, did and died,   200
And if the spark with which Heaven lit my spirit
Had been with purer nutriment supplied,

'Corruption would not now thus much inherit
Of what was once Rousseau,—nor this disguise
Stain that which ought to have disdained to wear it;   205

'If I have been extinguished, yet there rise
A thousand beacons from the spark I bore'—
'And who are those chained to the car?'—'The wise,

'The great, the unforgotten,—they who wore
Mitres and helms and crowns, or wreaths of light, 210
Signs of thought's empire over thought—their lore

'Taught them not this, to know themselves; their might
Could not repress the mystery within,
And for the morn of truth they feigned, deep night

'Caught them ere evening.'—'Who is he with chin 215
Upon his breast, and hands crossed on his chain?'—
'The child of a fierce hour; he sought to win

'The world, and lost all that it did contain
Of greatness, in its hope destroyed; and more
Of fame and peace than virtue's self can gain 220

'Without the opportunity which bore
Him on its eagle pinions to the peak
From which a thousand climbers have before

'Fallen, as Napoleon fell '—I felt my cheek
Alter, to see the shadow pass away, 225
Whose grasp had left the giant world so weak

That every pigmy kicked it as it lay;
And much I grieved to think how power and will
In opposition rule our mortal day,

And why God made irreconcilable 230
Good and the means of good; and for despair
I half disdained mine eyes' desire to fill

With the spent vision of the times that were
And scarce have ceased to be.—'Dost thou behold,'
Said my guide, 'those spoilers spoiled, Voltaire, 235

'Frederick, and Paul, Catherine, and Leopold,
And hoary anarchs, demagogues, and sage—
    names which the world thinks always old,

'For in the battle Life and they did wage,
She remained conqueror. I was overcome 240
By my own heart alone, which neither age,

'Nor tears, nor infamy, nor now the tomb
Could temper to its object.'—'Let them pass,'
I cried, 'the world and its mysterious doom

'Is not so much more glorious than it was, 245
That I desire to worship those who drew
New figures on its false and fragile glass

'As the old faded.'—'Figures ever new
Rise on the bubble, paint them as you may;
We have but thrown, as those before us threw,   250

'Our shadows on it as it passed away.
But mark how chained to the triumphal chair
The mighty phantoms of an elder day;

'All that is mortal of great Plato there
Expiates the joy and woe his master knew not;   255
The star that ruled his doom was far too fair.

'And life, where long that flower of Heaven grew not,
Conquered that heart by love, which gold, or pain,
Or age, or sloth, or slavery could subdue not.

'And near him walk the   twain,   260
The tutor and his pupil, whom Dominion
Followed as tame as vulture in a chain.

'The world was darkened beneath either pinion
Of him whom from the flock of conquerors
Fame singled out for her thunder-bearing minion;   265

'The other long outlived both woes and wars,
Throned in the thoughts of men, and still had kept
The jealous key of Truth's eternal doors,

'If Bacon's eagle spirit had not lept
Like lightning out of darkness—he compelled   270
The Proteus shape of Nature, as it slept

'To wake, and lead him to the caves that held
The treasure of the secrets of its reign.
See the great bards of elder time, who quelled

'The passions which they sung, as by their strain   275
May well be known: their living melody
Tempers its own contagion to the vein

'Of those who are infected with it—I
Have suffered what I wrote, or viler pain!
And so my words have seeds of misery—   280

'Even as the deeds of others, not as theirs.'
And then he pointed to a company,

'Midst whom I quickly recognized the heirs
Of Caesar's crime, from him to Constantine;
The anarch chiefs, whose force and murderous snares   285

Had founded many a sceptre-bearing line,
And spread the plague of gold and blood abroad:
And Gregory and John, and men divine,

Who rose like shadows between man and God;
Till that eclipse, still hanging over heaven,   290
Was worshipped by the world o'er which they strode,

For the true sun it quenched—'Their power was given
But to destroy,' replied the leader:—'I
Am one of those who have created, even

'If it be but a world of agony.'—   295
'Whence camest thou? and whither goest thou?
How did thy course begin?' I said, 'and why?

'Mine eyes are sick of this perpetual flow
Of people, and my heart sick of one sad thought—
Speak!'—'Whence I am, I partly seem to know,   300

'And how and by what paths I have been brought
To this dread pass, methinks even thou mayst guess;—
Why this should be, my mind can compass not;

'Whither the conqueror hurries me, still less;—
But follow thou, and from spectator turn   305
Actor or victim in this wretchedness,

'And what thou wouldst be taught I then may learn
From thee. Now listen:—In the April prime,
When all the forest-tips began to burn

'With kindling green, touched by the azure clime   310
Of the young season, I was laid asleep
Under a mountain, which from unknown time

'Had yawned into a cavern, high and deep;
And from it came a gentle rivulet,
Whose water, like clear air, in its calm sweep   315

'Bent the soft grass, and kept for ever wet
The stems of the sweet flowers, and filled the grove
With sounds, which whoso hears must needs forget

'All pleasure and all pain, all hate and love,
Which they had known before that hour of rest;   320
A sleeping mother then would dream not of

'Her only child who died upon the breast
At eventide—a king would mourn no more
The crown of which his brows were dispossessed

'When the sun lingered o'er his ocean floor   325
To gild his rival's new prosperity.
Thou wouldst forget thus vainly to deplore

'Ills, which if ills can find no cure from thee,
The thought of which no other sleep will quell,
Nor other music blot from memory,   330

'So sweet and deep is the oblivious spell;
And whether life had been before that sleep
The Heaven which I imagine, or a Hell

'Like this harsh world in which I wake to weep,
I know not. I arose, and for a space   335
The scene of woods and waters seemed to keep,

'Though it was now broad day, a gentle trace
Of light diviner than the common sun
Sheds on the common earth, and all the place

'Was filled with magic sounds woven into one   340
Oblivious melody, confusing sense
Amid the gliding waves and shadows dun;

'And, as I looked, the bright omnipresence
Of morning through the orient cavern flowed,
And the sun's image radiantly intense   345

'Burned on the waters of the well that glowed
Like gold, and threaded all the forest's maze
With winding paths of emerald fire; there stood

'Amid the sun, as he amid the blaze
Of his own glory, on the vibrating   350
Floor of the fountain, paved with flashing rays,

'A Shape all light, which with one hand did fling
Dew on the earth, as if she were the dawn,
And the invisible rain did ever sing

'A silver music on the mossy lawn;   355
And still before me on the dusky grass,
Iris her many-coloured scarf had drawn:

'In her right hand she bore a crystal glass,
Mantling with bright Nepenthe; the fierce splendour
Fell from her as she moved under the mass   360

'Of the deep cavern, and with palms so tender,
Their tread broke not the mirror of its billow,
Glided along the river, and did bend her

'Head under the dark boughs, till like a willow
Her fair hair swept the bosom of the stream   365
That whispered with delight to be its pillow.

'As one enamoured is upborne in dream
O'er lily-paven lakes, mid silver mist,
To wondrous music, so this shape might seem

'Partly to tread the waves with feet which kissed   370
The dancing foam; partly to glide along
The air which roughened the moist amethyst,

'Or the faint morning beams that fell among
The trees or the soft shadows of the trees;
And her feet, ever to the ceaseless song   375

'Of leaves, and winds, and waves, and birds, and bees,
And falling drops, moved in a measure new
Yet sweet, as on the summer evening breeze,

'Up from the lake a shape of golden dew
Between two rocks, athwart the rising moon,   380
Dances i' the wind, where never eagle flew;

'And still her feet, no less than the sweet tune
To which they moved, seemed as they moved to blot
The thoughts of him who gazed on them; and soon

'All that was, seemed as if it had been not;   385
And all the gazer's mind was strewn beneath
Her feet like embers; and she, thought by thought,

'Trampled its sparks into the dust of death;
As day upon the threshold of the east
Treads out the lamps of night, until the breath   390

'Of darkness re-illumine even the least
Of heaven's living eyes—like day she came,
Making the night a dream; and ere she ceased

'To move, as one between desire and shame
Suspended, I said—If, as it doth seem,   395
Thou comest from the realm without a name

'Into this valley of perpetual dream,
Show whence I came, and where I am, and why—
Pass not away upon the passing stream.

'Arise and quench thy thirst, was her reply.   400
And as a shut lily stricken by the wand
Of dewy morning's vital alchemy,

'I rose; and, bending at her sweet command,
Touched with faint lips the cup she raised,
And suddenly my brain became as sand   405

'Where the first wave had more than half erased
The track of deer on desert Labrador;
Whilst the wolf, from which they fled amazed,

'Leaves his stamp visibly upon the shore,
Until the second bursts;—so on my sight   410
Burst a new vision, never seen before,

'And the fair shape waned in the coming light,
As veil by veil the silent splendour drops
From Lucifer, amid the chrysolite

'Of sunrise, ere it tinge the mountain-tops;   415
And as the presence of that fairest planet,
Although unseen, is felt by one who hopes

'That his day's path may end as he began it,
In that star's smile, whose light is like the scent
Of a jonquil when evening breezes fan it,   420

'Or the soft note in which his dear lament
The Brescian [1] shepherd breathes, or the caress
That turned his weary slumber to content;

'So knew I in that light's severe excess
The presence of that Shape which on the stream   425
Moved, as I moved along the wilderness,

'More dimly than a day-appearing dream,
The ghost of a forgotten form of sleep;
A light of heaven, whose half-extinguished beam

'Through the sick day in which we wake to weep   430
Glimmers, for ever sought, for ever lost;
So did that shape its obscure tenour keep

'Beside my path, as silent as a ghost;
But the new Vision, and the cold bright car,
With solemn speed and stunning music, crossed   435

'The forest, and as if from some dread war
Triumphantly returning, the loud million
Fiercely extolled the fortune of her star.

'A moving arch of victory, the vermilion
And green and azure plumes of Iris had   440
Built high over her wind-wingèd pavilion,

---

[1] The favourite song, *Stanco di pascolar le pecorelle*, is a Brescian national air.
—[MRS. SHELLEY'S NOTE.]

'And underneath aethereal glory clad
The wilderness, and far before her flew
The tempest of the splendour, which forbade

'Shadow to fall from leaf and stone; the crew   445
Seemed in that light, like atomies to dance
Within a sunbeam;—some upon the new

'Embroidery of flowers, that did enhance
The grassy vesture of the desert, played,
Forgetful of the chariot's swift advance;   450

'Others stood gazing, till within the shade
Of the great mountain its light left them dim;
Others outspeeded it; and others made

'Circles around it, like the clouds that swim
Round the high moon in a bright sea of air;   455
And more did follow, with exulting hymn,

'The chariot and the captives fettered there:—
But all like bubbles on an eddying flood
Fell into the same track at last, and were

'Borne onward.—I among the multitude   460
Was swept—me, sweetest flowers delayed not long;
Me, not the shadow nor the solitude;

'Me, not that falling stream's Lethean song;
Me, not the phantom of that early Form
Which moved upon its motion—but among   465

'The thickest billows of that living storm
I plunged, and bared my bosom to the clime
Of that cold light, whose airs too soon deform.

'Before the chariot had begun to climb
The opposing steep of that mysterious dell,   470
Behold a wonder worthy of the rhyme

'Of him who from the lowest depths of hell,
Through every paradise and through all glory,
Love led serene, and who returned to tell

'The words of hate and awe; the wondrous story   475
How all things are transfigured except Love;
For deaf as is a sea, which wrath makes hoary,

'The world can hear not the sweet notes that move
The sphere whose light is melody to lovers—
A wonder worthy of his rhyme.—The grove   480

'Grew dense with shadows to its inmost covers,
The earth was gray with phantoms, and the air
Was peopled with dim forms, as when there hovers

'A flock of vampire-bats before the glare
Of the tropic sun, bringing, ere evening,   485
Strange night upon some Indian isle;—thus were

'Phantoms diffused around; and some did fling
Shadows of shadows, yet unlike themselves,
Behind them; some like eaglets on the wing

'Were lost in the white day; others like elves   490
Danced in a thousand unimagined shapes
Upon the sunny streams and grassy shelves;

'And others sate chattering like restless apes
On vulgar hands, . . .
Some made a cradle of the ermined capes   495

'Of kingly mantles; some across the tiar
Of pontiffs sate like vultures; others played
Under the crown which girt with empire

'A baby's or an idiot's brow, and made
Their nests in it. The old anatomies   500
Sate hatching their bare broods under the shade

'Of daemon wings, and laughed from their dead eyes
To reassume the delegated power,
Arrayed in which those worms did monarchize,

'Who made this earth their charnel. Others more   505
Humble, like falcons, sate upon the fist
Of common men, and round their heads did soar;

'Or like small gnats and flies, as thick as mist
On evening marshes, thronged about the brow
Of lawyers, statesmen, priest and theorist;—   510

'And others, like discoloured flakes of snow
On fairest bosoms and the sunniest hair,
Fell, and were melted by the youthful glow

'Which they extinguished; and, like tears, they were
A veil to those from whose faint lids they rained   515
In drops of sorrow. I became aware

'Of whence those forms proceeded which thus stained
The track in which we moved. After brief space,
From every form the beauty slowly waned;

'From every firmest limb and fairest face
The strength and freshness fell like dust, and left
The action and the shape without the grace

'Of life. The marble brow of youth was cleft
With care; and in those eyes where once hope shone,
Desire, like a lioness bereft   525

'Of her last cub, glared ere it died; each one
Of that great crowd sent forth incessantly
These shadows, numerous as the dead leaves blown

'In autumn evening from a poplar tree.
Each like himself and like each other were   530
At first; but some distorted seemed to be

'Obscure clouds, moulded by the casual air;
And of this stuff the car's creative ray
Wrought all the busy phantoms that were there,

'As the sun shapes the clouds; thus on the way   535
Mask after mask fell from the countenance
And form of all; and long before the day

'Was old, the joy which waked like heaven's glance
The sleepers in the oblivious valley, died;
And some grew weary of the ghastly dance,   540

'And fell, as I have fallen, by the wayside;—
Those soonest from whose forms most shadows passed,
And least of strength and beauty did abide.

'Then, what is life? I cried.'—

EARLY POEMS [1814, 1815]

STANZA, WRITTEN AT BRACKNELL

THY dewy looks sink in my breast;
  Thy gentle words stir poison
    there;
Thou hast disturbed the only rest
  That was the portion of despair!
Subdued to Duty's hard control, 5
I could have borne my wayward
    lot:
The chains that bind this ruined
    soul
Had cankered then—but crushed
    it not.

STANZAS.—APRIL, 1814

AWAY! the moor is dark beneath the moon.
  Rapid clouds have drank the last pale beam of even:
Away the gathering winds will call the darkness soon.
  And profoundest midnight shroud the serene lights of heaven.

Pause not! the time is past! Every voice cries, Away!   5
   Tempt not with one last tear thy friend's ungentle mood:
Thy lover's eye, so glazed and cold, dares not entreat thy stay:
   Duty and dereliction guide thee back to solitude.

Away, away! to thy sad and silent home;
   Pour bitter tears on its desolated hearth;   10
Watch the dim shades as like ghosts they go and come,
   And complicate strange webs of melancholy mirth.

The leaves of wasted autumn woods shall float around thine head:
   The blooms of dewy spring shall gleam beneath thy feet:
But thy soul or this world must fade in the frost that binds the dead,
   Ere midnight's frown and morning's smile, ere thou and peace may
     meet.

The cloud shadows of midnight possess their own repose,   17
   For the weary winds are silent, or the moon is in the deep:
Some respite to its turbulence unresting ocean knows;
   Whatever moves, or toils, or grieves, hath its appointed sleep.   20

Thou in the grave shalt rest—yet till the phantoms flee
   Which that house and heath and garden made dear to thee erewhile,
Thy remembrance, and repentance, and deep musings are not free
   From the music of two voices and the light of one sweet smile.

TO HARRIET

Thy look of love has power to calm
   The stormiest passion of my soul;
Thy gentle words are drops of balm
   In life's too bitter bowl;
No grief is mine, but that alone 5
These choicest blessings I have known.

Harriet! if all who long to live
   In the warm sunshine of thine eye,
That price beyond all pain must give,—
   Beneath thy scorn to die;   10

Then hear thy chosen own too late
His heart most worthy of thy hate.

Be thou, then, one among mankind
   Whose heart is harder not for state,
Thou only virtuous, gentle, kind, 15
   Amid a world of hate;
And by a slight endurance seal
A fellow-being's lasting weal.

For pale with anguish is his cheek,
   His breath comes fast, his eyes are dim,   20
Thy name is struggling ere he speak,
   Weak is each trembling limb;

In mercy let him not endure
The misery of a fatal cure.

Oh, trust for once no erring
    guide! 25

Bid the remorseless feeling flee;
'Tis malice, 'tis revenge, 'tis pride,
    'Tis anything but thee;
Oh, deign a nobler pride to prove,
And pity if thou canst not love. 30

TO MARY WOLLSTONECRAFT GODWIN

I

MINE eyes were dim with tears un-
    shed;
    Yes, I was firm—thus wert not
        thou;—
My baffled looks did fear yet
    dread
    To meet thy looks—I could not
        know
How anxiously they sought to
    shine 5
With soothing pity upon mine.

II

To sit and curb the soul's mute
    rage
    Which preys upon itself alone;
To curse the life which is the cage
    Of fettered grief that dares not
        groan, 10
Hiding from many a careless eye
The scornèd load of agony.

III

Whilst thou alone, then not re-
    garded,
    The   thou alone should be,
To spend years thus, and be re-
    warded, 15
    As thou, sweet love, requited me
When none were near—Oh! I did
    wake

From torture for that moment's
    sake.

IV

Upon my heart thy accents sweet
    Of peace and pity fell like dew 20
On flowers half dead;—thy lips did
    meet
    Mine tremblingly; thy dark eyes
        threw
Their soft persuasion on my brain,
Charming away its dream of pain.

V

We are not happy, sweet! our state
    Is strange and full of doubt and
        fear; 26
More need of words that ills
    abate;—
    Reserve or censure come not
        near
Our sacred friendship, lest there be
No solace left for thee and me. 30

VI

Gentle and good and mild thou art,
    Nor can I live if thou appear
Aught but thyself, or turn thine
    heart
    Away from me, or stoop to wear
The mask of scorn, although it
    be 35
To hide the love thou feel'st for me.

TO ———

YET look on me—take not thine eyes away,
    Which feed upon the love within mine own,
Which is indeed but the reflected ray
    Of thine own beauty from my spirit thrown.

Yet speak to me—thy voice is as the tone   5
Of my heart's echo, and I think I hear
That thou yet lovest me; yet thou alone
Like one before a mirror, without care
Of aught but thine own features, imaged there;
And yet I wear out life in watching thee;   10
A toil so sweet at times, and thou indeed
Art kind when I am sick, and pity me.

MUTABILITY

We are as clouds that veil the midnight moon;
How restlessly they speed, and gleam, and quiver,
Streaking the darkness radiantly!—yet soon
Night closes round, and they are lost for ever:

Or like forgotten lyres, whose dissonant strings   5
Give various response to each varying blast,
To whose frail frame no second motion brings
One mood or modulation like the last.

We rest.—A dream has power to poison sleep;
We rise.—One wandering thought pollutes the day;   10
We feel, conceive or reason, laugh or weep;
Embrace fond woe, or cast our cares away:

It is the same!—For, be it joy or sorrow,
The path of its departure still is free:
Man's yesterday may ne'er be like his morrow;   15
Nought may endure but Mutability.

ON DEATH

There is no work, nor device, nor knowledge, nor wisdom, in the grave, whither thou goest.—*Ecclesiastes.*

The pale, the cold, and the moony smile
Which the meteor beam of a starless night
Sheds on a lonely and sea-girt isle,
Ere the dawning of morn's undoubted light,
Is the flame of life so fickle and wan   5
That flits round our steps till their strength is gone.

O man! hold thee on in courage of soul
Through the stormy shades of thy worldly way,
And the billows of cloud that around thee roll
Shall sleep in the light of a wondrous day,   10

Where Hell and Heaven shall leave thee free
To the universe of destiny.

This world is the nurse of all we know,
   This world is the mother of all we feel,
And the coming of death is a fearful blow   15
   To a brain unencompassed with nerves of steel;
When all that we know, or feel, or see,
Shall pass like an unreal mystery.

The secret things of the grave are there,
   Where all but this frame must surely be,   20
Though the fine-wrought eye and the wondrous ear
   No longer will live to hear or to see
All that is great and all that is strange
In the boundless realm of unending change.

Who telleth a tale of unspeaking death?   25
   Who lifteth the veil of what is to come?
Who painteth the shadows that are beneath
   The wide-winding caves of the peopled tomb?
Or uniteth the hopes of what shall be
With the fears and the love for that which we see?   30

A SUMMER EVENING CHURCHYARD

Lechlade, Gloucestershire

The wind has swept from the wide atmosphere
Each vapour that obscured the sunset's ray;
And pallid Evening twines its beaming hair
In duskier braids around the languid eyes of Day:
Silence and Twilight, unbeloved of men,   5
Creep hand in hand from yon obscurest glen.

They breathe their spells towards the departing day,
Encompassing the earth, air, stars, and sea;
Light, sound, and motion own the potent sway,
Responding to the charm with its own mystery.   10
The winds are still, or the dry church-tower grass
Knows not their gentle motions as they pass.

Thou too, aëreal Pile! whose pinnacles
Point from one shrine like pyramids of fire,
Obeyest in silence their sweet solemn spells,   15
Clothing in hues of heaven thy dim and distant spire,
Around whose lessening and invisible height
Gather among the stars the clouds of night.

The dead are sleeping in their sepulchres:
And, mouldering as they sleep, a thrilling sound,   20
Half sense, half thought, among the darkness stirs,
Breathed from their wormy beds all living things around,
And mingling with the still night and mute sky
Its awful hush is felt inaudibly.

Thus solemnized and softened, death is mild   25
And terrorless as this serenest night:
Here could I hope, like some inquiring child
Sporting on graves, that death did hide from human sight
Sweet secrets, or beside its breathless sleep
That loveliest dreams perpetual watch did keep.   30

TO ——

ΔΑΚΡΥΣΙ ΔΙΟΙΣΩ ΠΟΤΜΟΝ 'ΑΠΟΤΜΟΝ.

Oh! there are spirits of the air,
    And genii of the evening breeze,
And gentle ghosts, with eyes as fair
    As star-beams among twilight trees:—
Such lovely ministers to meet   5
Oft hast thou turned from men thy lonely feet.

With mountain winds, and babbling springs,
    And moonlight seas, that are the voice
Of these inexplicable things,
    Thou didst hold commune, and rejoice   10
When they did answer thee; but they
Cast, like a worthless boon, thy love away.

And thou hast sought in starry eyes
    Beams that were never meant for thine,
Another's wealth:—tame sacrifice   15
    To a fond faith! still dost thou pine?
Still dost thou hope that greeting hands,
Voice, looks, or lips, may answer thy demands?

Ah! wherefore didst thou build thine hope
    On the false earth's inconstancy?   20
Did thine own mind afford no scope
    Of love, or moving thoughts to thee?
That natural scenes or human smiles
Could steal the power to wind thee in their wiles?

Yes, all the faithless smiles are fled
    Whose falsehood left thee broken-hearted;
The glory of the moon is dead;   25
    Night's ghosts and dreams have now departed;

Thine own soul still is true to thee,
But changed to a foul fiend through misery. 30

This fiend, whose ghastly presence ever
  Beside thee like thy shadow hangs,
Dream not to chase;—the mad endeavour
  Would scourge thee to severer pangs.
Be as thou art. Thy settled fate, 35
Dark as it is, all change would aggravate.

TO WORDSWORTH

POET of Nature, thou hast wept to know
That things depart which never may return:
Childhood and youth, friendship and love's first glow,
Have fled like sweet dreams, leaving thee to mourn.
These common woes I feel. One loss is mine 5
Which thou too feel'st, yet I alone deplore.
Thou wert as a lone star, whose light did shine
On some frail bark in winter's midnight roar:
Thou hast like to a rock-built refuge stood
Above the blind and battling multitude: 10
In honoured poverty thy voice did weave
Songs consecrate to truth and liberty,—
Deserting these, thou leavest me to grieve,
Thus having been, that thou shouldst cease to be.

FEELINGS OF A REPUBLICAN ON THE FALL OF BONAPARTE

I HATED thee, fallen tyrant! I did groan
To think that a most unambitious slave,
Like thou, shouldst dance and revel on the grave
Of Liberty. Thou mightst have built thy throne
Where it had stood even now: thou didst prefer 5
A frail and bloody pomp which Time has swept
In fragments towards Oblivion. Massacre,
For this I prayed, would on thy sleep have crept,
Treason and Slavery, Rapine, Fear, and Lust,
And stifled thee, their minister. I know 10
Too late, since thou and France are in the dust,
That Virtue owns a more eternal foe
Than Force or Fraud: old Custom, legal Crime,
And bloody Faith the foulest birth of Time.

LINES

I

THE cold earth slept below,
  Above the cold sky shone;
And all around, with a chilling
    sound,
  From caves of ice and fields of
    snow,
  The breath of night like death
    did flow   5
  Beneath the sinking moon.

II

The wintry hedge was black,
  The green grass was not seen,
The birds did rest on the bare
    thorn's breast,
  Whose roots, beside the pathway
    track,   10
  Had bound their folds o'er many
    a crack
  Which the frost had made be-
    tween.

III

Thine eyes glowed in the glare
  Of the moon's dying light;
As a fen-fire's beam on a sluggish
    stream   15
  Gleams dimly, so the moon shone
    there,
  And it yellowed the strings of thy
    raven hair,
  That shook in the wind of
    night.

IV

The moon made thy lips pale,
    beloved—
  The wind made thy bosom
    chill—
The night did shed on thy dear
    head   21
  Its frozen dew, and thou didst
    lie
  Where the bitter breath of the
    naked sky
  Might visit thee at will.

NOTE ON THE EARLY POEMS, BY MRS. SHELLEY

THE remainder of Shelley's Poems will be arranged in the order in which they were written. Of course, mistakes will occur in placing some of the shorter ones; for, as I have said, many of these were thrown aside, and I never saw them till I had the misery of looking over his writings after the hand that traced them was dust; and some were in the hands of others, and I never saw them till now. The subjects of the poems are often to me an unerring guide; but on other occasions I can only guess, by finding them in the pages of the same manuscript book that contains poems with the date of whose composition I am fully conversant. In the present arrangement all his poetical translations will be placed together at the end.

The loss of his early papers prevents my being able to give any of the poetry of his boyhood. Of the few I give as *Early Poems*, the greater part were published with *Alastor;* some of them were written previously, some at the same period. The poem beginning 'Oh, there are spirits in the air' was addressed in idea to Coleridge, whom he never knew; and at whose character he could only guess imperfectly, through his writings, and accounts he heard of him from some who knew him well. He regarded his change of opinions as rather an act of will than conviction, and believed that in his inner heart he would be haunted by what Shelley considered the better and holier aspirations of his youth. The summer evening that suggested to him the poem written in the churchyard of Lechlade occurred during his voyage up the Thames in 1815. He had been advised by a physician to live as much as possible in the open air; and a fortnight of a bright warm July was spent in tracing the Thames to its source. He never spent a season more tranquilly than the summer of 1815. He had just recovered from a severe pulmonary attack; the weather was warm and pleasant. He lived near Windsor Forest; and his life was spent under its shade or on the water, meditating subjects for verse. Hitherto, he had chiefly aimed at extending his political doctrines, and attempted so to do by appeals in prose essays to the people, exhorting them to claim their rights; but he had now begun to feel that the time for action was not ripe in England, and that the pen was the only instrument wherewith to prepare the way for better things.

In the scanty journals kept during those years I find a record of the books that Shelley read during several years. During the years of 1814 and 1815 the list is extensive. It includes, in Greek, Homer, Hesiod, Theocritus, the histories of Thucydides and Herodotus, and Diogenes Laertius. In Latin, Petronius, Suetonius, some of the works of Cicero, a large proportion of those of Seneca and Livy. In English, Milton's poems, Wordsworth's *Excursion,* Southey's *Madoc* and *Thalaba,* Locke *On the Human Understanding,* Bacon's *Novum Organum.* In Italian, Ariosto, Tasso, and Alfieri. In French, the *Rêveries d'un Solitaire* of Rousseau. To these may be added several modern books of travel. He read few novels.

POEMS WRITTEN IN 1816

THE SUNSET

THERE late was One whose subtle being,
As light and wind within some delicate cloud
That fades amid the blue noon's burning sky,
Genius and death contended. None may know
The sweetness of the joy which made his breath   5
Fail, like the trances of the summer air,
When, with the Lady of his love, who then
First knew the unreserve of mingled being,
He walked along the pathway of a field
Which to the east a hoar wood shadowed o'er,   10
But to the west was open to the sky.
There now the sun had sunk, but lines of gold
Hung on the ashen clouds, and on the points
Of the far level grass and nodding flowers
And the old dandelion's hoary beard,   15
And, mingled with the shades of twilight, lay
On the brown massy woods—and in the east
The broad and burning moon lingeringly rose
Between the black trunks of the crowded trees,
While the faint stars were gathering overhead.—   20
'Is it not strange, Isabel,' said the youth,
'I never saw the sun? We will walk here
To-morrow; thou shalt look on it with me.'

That night the youth and lady mingled lay
In love and sleep—but when the morning came   25
The lady found her lover dead and cold.
Let none believe that God in mercy gave
That stroke. The lady died not, nor grew wild,
But year by year lived on—in truth I think
Her gentleness and patience and sad smiles,   30
And that she did not die, but lived to tend
Her agèd father, were a kind of madness,
If madness 'tis to be unlike the world.
For but to see her were to read the tale
Woven by some subtlest bard, to make hard hearts   35
Dissolve away in wisdom-working grief;—
Her eyes were black and lustreless and wan:
Her eyelashes were worn away with tears,
Her lips and cheeks were like things dead—so pale;
Her hands were thin, and through their wandering veins   40
And weak articulations might be seen

Day's ruddy light. The tomb of thy dead self
Which one vexed ghost inhabits, night and day,
Is all, lost child, that now remains of thee!

'Inheritor of more than earth can give,   45
Passionless calm and silence unreproved,
Whether the dead find, oh, not sleep! but rest,
And are the uncomplaining things they seem,
Or live, or drop in the deep sea of Love;
Oh, that like thine, mine epitaph were—Peace!'   50
This was the only moan she ever made.

HYMN TO INTELLECTUAL BEAUTY

I

THE awful shadow of some unseen Power
  Floats though unseen among us,—visiting
  This various world with as inconstant wing
As summer winds that creep from flower to flower,—
Like moonbeams that behind some piny mountain shower, 5
    It visits with inconstant glance
    Each human heart and countenance;
Like hues and harmonies of evening,—
    Like clouds in starlight widely spread,—
    Like memory of music fled,—   10
    Like aught that for its grace may be
Dear, and yet dearer for its mystery.

II

Spirit of BEAUTY, that dost consecrate
  With thine own hues all thou dost shine upon
  Of human thought or form,—where art thou gone?   15
Why dost thou pass away and leave our state,
This dim vast vale of tears, vacant and desolate?
    Ask why the sunlight not for ever
    Weaves rainbows o'er yon mountain-river,
Why aught should fail and fade that once is shown,   20
    Why fear and dream and death and birth
    Cast on the daylight of this earth
    Such gloom,—why man has such a scope
For love and hate, despondency and hope?

III

No voice from some sublimer world hath ever   25
  To sage or poet these responses given—
  Therefore the names of Demon, Ghost, and Heaven,
Remain the records of their vain endeavour,

Frail spells—whose uttered charm might not avail to sever,
    From all we hear and all we see,   30
    Doubt, chance, and mutability.
Thy light alone—like mist o'er mountains driven,
    Or music by the night-wind sent
    Through strings of some still instrument,
    Or moonlight on a midnight stream,   35
Gives grace and truth to life's unquiet dream.

IV

Love, Hope, and Self-esteem, like clouds depart
    And come, for some uncertain moments lent.
    Man were immortal, and omnipotent,
Didst thou, unknown and awful as thou art,   40
Keep with thy glorious train firm state within his heart.
    Thou messenger of sympathies,
    That wax and wane in lovers' eyes—
Thou—that to human thought art nourishment,
    Like darkness to a dying flame!   45
    Depart not as thy shadow came,
    Depart not—lest the grave should be,
Like life and fear, a dark reality.

V

While yet a boy I sought for ghosts, and sped
    Through many a listening chamber, cave and ruin,   50
    And starlight wood, with fearful steps pursuing
Hopes of high talk with the departed dead.
I called on poisonous names with which our youth is fed;
    I was not heard—I saw them not—
    When musing deeply on the lot   55
Of life, at that sweet time when winds are wooing
    All vital things that wake to bring
    News of birds and blossoming,—
    Sudden, thy shadow fell on me;
I shrieked, and clasped my hands in ecstasy!   60

VI

I vowed that I would dedicate my powers
    To thee and thine—have I not kept the vow?
    With beating heart and streaming eyes, even now
I call the phantoms of a thousand hours
Each from his voiceless grave: they have in visioned bowers   65
    Of studious zeal or love's delight
    Outwatched with me the envious night—
They know that never joy illumed my brow

Unlinked with hope that thou wouldst free
This world from its dark slavery,   70
That thou—O awful LOVELINESS,
Wouldst give whate'er these words cannot express.

VII

The day becomes more solemn and serene
    When noon is past—there is a harmony
    In autumn, and a lustre in its sky,   75
Which through the summer is not heard or seen,
As if it could not be, as if it had not been!
        Thus let thy power, which like the truth
        Of nature on my passive youth
    Descended, to my onward life supply   80
        Its calm—to one who worships thee,
        And every form containing thee,
        Whom, SPIRIT fair, thy spells did bind
To fear himself, and love all human kind.

MONT BLANC

LINES WRITTEN IN THE VALE OF CHAMOUNI

I

THE everlasting universe of things
Flows through the mind, and rolls its rapid waves,
Now dark—now glittering—now reflecting gloom—
Now lending splendour, where from secret springs
The source of human thought its tribute brings   5
Of waters,—with a sound but half its own,
Such as a feeble brook will oft assume
In the wild woods, among the mountains lone,
Where waterfalls around it leap for ever,
Where woods and winds contend, and a vast river   10
Over its rocks ceaselessly bursts and raves.

II

Thus thou, Ravine of Arve—dark, deep Ravine—
Thou many-coloured, many-voicèd vale,
Over whose pines, and crags, and caverns sail
Fast cloud-shadows and sunbeams: awful scene,   15
Where Power in likeness of the Arve comes down
From the ice-gulfs that gird his secret throne,
Bursting through these dark mountains like the flame
Of lightning through the tempest;—thou dost lie,
Thy giant brood of pines around thee clinging,   20

Children of elder time, in whose devotion
The chainless winds still come and ever came
To drink their odours, and their mighty swinging
To hear—an old and solemn harmony;
Thine earthly rainbows stretched across the sweep　25
Of the aethereal waterfall, whose veil
Robes some unsculptured image; the strange sleep
Which when the voices of the desert fail
Wraps all in its own deep eternity;—
Thy caverns echoing to the Arve's commotion,　30
A loud, lone sound no other sound can tame;
Thou art pervaded with that ceaseless motion,
Thou art the path of that unresting sound—
Dizzy Ravine! and when I gaze on thee
I seem as in a trance sublime and strange　35
To muse on my own separate fantasy,
My own, my human mind, which passively
Now renders and receives fast influencings,
Holding an unremitting interchange
With the clear universe of things around;　40
One legion of wild thoughts, whose wandering wings
Now float above thy darkness, and now rest
Where that or thou art no unbidden guest,
In the still cave of the witch Poesy,
Seeking among the shadows that pass by　45
Ghosts of all things that are, some shade of thee,
Some phantom, some faint image; till the breast
From which they fled recalls them, thou art there!

III

Some say that gleams of a remoter world
Visit the soul in sleep,—that death is slumber,　50
And that its shapes the busy thoughts outnumber
Of those who wake and live.—I look on high;
Has some unknown omnipotence unfurled
The veil of life and death? or do I lie
In dream, and does the mightier world of sleep　55
Spread far around and inaccessibly
Its circles? For the very spirit fails,
Driven like a homeless cloud from steep to steep
That vanishes among the viewless gales!
Far, far above, piercing the infinite sky,　60
Mont Blanc appears,—still, snowy, and serene—
Its subject mountains their unearthly forms
Pile around it, ice and rock; broad vales between
Of frozen floods, unfathomable deeps,
Blue as the overhanging heaven, that spread　65

And wind among the accumulated steeps;
A desert peopled by the storms alone,
Save when the eagle brings some hunter's bone,
And the wolf tracks her there—how hideously
Its shapes are heaped around! rude, bare, and high, 7 \
Ghastly, and scarred, and riven.—Is this the scene
Where the old Earthquake-daemon taught her young
Ruin? Were these their toys? or did a sea
Of fire envelop once this silent snow?
None can reply—all seems eternal now. 7£
The wilderness has a mysterious tongue
Which teaches awful doubt, or faith so mild,
So solemn, so serene, that man may be,
But for such faith, with nature reconciled;
Thou hast a voice, great Mountain, to repeal 80
Large codes of fraud and woe; not understood
By all, but which the wise, and great, and good
Interpret, or make felt, or deeply feel.

IV

The fields, the lakes, the forests, and the streams,
Ocean, and all the living things that dwell 85
Within the daedal earth; lightning, and rain,
Earthquake, and fiery flood, and hurricane,
The torpor of the year when feeble dreams
Visit the hidden buds, or dreamless sleep
Holds every future leaf and flower;—the bound 90
With which from that detested trance they leap;
The works and ways of man, their death and birth,
And that of him and all that his may be;
All things that move and breathe with toil and sound
Are born and die; revolve, subside, and swell. 9£
Power dwells apart in 'ts tranquillity,
Remote, serene, and inaccessible:
And *this*, the naked countenance of earth,
On which I gaze, even these primaeval mountains
Teach the adverting mind. The glaciers creep 100
Like snakes that watch their prey, from their far fountains,
Slow rolling on; there, many a precipice,
Frost and the Sun in scorn of mortal power
Have piled: dome, pyramid, and pinnacle,
A city of death, distinct with many a tower 105
And wall impregnable of beaming ice.
Yet not a city, but a flood of ruin
Is there, that from the boundaries of the sky
Rolls its perpetual stream; vast pines are strewing
Its destined path, or in the mangled soil 110

Branchless and shattered stand; the rocks, drawn down
From yon remotest waste, have overthrown
The limits of the dead and living world,
Never to be reclaimed. The dwelling-place
Of insects, beasts, and birds, becomes its spoil   115
Their food and their retreat for ever gone,
So much of life and joy is lost. The race
Of man flies far in dread; his work and dwelling
Vanish, like smoke before the tempest's stream,
And their place is not known. Below, vast caves   120
Shine in the rushing torrents' restless gleam,
Which from those secret chasms in tumult welling
Meet in the vale, and one majestic River,
The breath and blood of distant lands, for ever
Rolls its loud waters to the ocean-waves,   125
Breathes its swift vapours to the circling air.

                        v

Mont Blanc yet gleams on high:—the power is there,
The still and solemn power of many sights,
And many sounds, and much of life and death.
In the calm darkness of the moonless nights,   130
In the lone glare of day, the snows descend
Upon that Mountain; none beholds them there,
Nor when the flakes burn in the sinking sun,
Or the star-beams dart through them:—Winds contend
Silently there, and heap the snow with breath   135
Rapid and strong, but silently! Its home
The voiceless lightning in these solitudes
Keeps innocently, and like vapour broods
Over the snow. The secret Strength of things
Which governs thought, and to the infinite dome   140
Of Heaven is as a law, inhabits thee!
And what were thou, and earth, and stars, and sea,
If to the human mind's imaginings
Silence and solitude were vacancy?

    July 23, 1816.

        FRAGMENT: HOME

DEAR home, thou scene of earliest hopes and joys,
The least of which wronged Memory ever makes
Bitterer than all thine unremembered tears.

FRAGMENT OF A GHOST STORY

A SHOVEL of his ashes took
From the hearth's obscurest nook,
Muttering mysteries as she went.
Helen and Henry knew that Granny
Was as much afraid of Ghosts as any,　　　　　5
　　And so they followed hard—
But Helen clung to her brother's arm,
And her own spasm made her shake.

NOTE ON POEMS OF 1816, BY MRS. SHELLEY

SHELLEY wrote little during this year. The poem entitled *The Sunset* was written in the spring of the year, while still residing at Bishopsgate. He spent the summer on the shores of the Lake of Geneva. The *Hymn to Intellectual Beauty* was conceived during his voyage round the lake with Lord Byron. He occupied himself during this voyage by reading the *Nouvelle Héloïse* for the first time. The reading it on the very spot where the scenes are laid added to the interest; and he was at once surprised and charmed by the passionate eloquence and earnest enthralling interest that pervade this work. There was something in the character of Saint-Preux, in his abnegation of self, and in the worship he paid to Love, that coincided with Shelley's own disposition; and, though differing in many of the views and shocked by others, yet the effect of the whole was fascinating and delightful.

Mont Blanc was inspired by a view of that mountain and its surrounding peaks and valleys, as he lingered on the Bridge of Arve on his way through the Valley of Chamouni. Shelley makes the following mention of this poem in his publication of the *History of a Six Weeks' Tour, and Letters from Switzerland*: 'The poem entitled *Mont Blanc* is written by the author of the two letters from Chamouni and Vevai. It was composed under the immediate impression of the deep and powerful feelings excited by the objects which it attempts to describe; and, as an undisciplined overflowing of the soul, rests its claim to approbation on an attempt to imitate the untamable wildness and inaccessible solemnity from which those feelings sprang.'

This was an eventful year, and less time was given to study than usual. In the list of his reading I find, in Greek, Theocritus, the *Prometheus* of Aeschylus, several of Plutarch's *Lives*, and the works of Lucian. In Latin, Lucretius, Pliny's *Letters*, the *Annals* and *Germany* of Tacitus. In French, the *History of the French Revolution* by Lacretelle. He read for the first time, this year, Montaigne's *Essays*, and regarded them ever after as one of the most delightful and instructive books in the world. The list is scanty in English works: Locke's *Essay, Political Justice,* and Coleridge's *Lay Sermon*, form nearly the whole. It was his frequent habit to read aloud to me in the evening; in this way we read, this year, the New Testament, *Paradise Lost,* Spenser's *Faery Queen,* and *Don Quixote*.

POEMS WRITTEN IN 1817

MARIANNE'S DREAM

I

A PALE Dream came to a Lady fair,
  And said, A boon, a boon, I pray!
I know the secrets of the air,
  And things are lost in the glare
    of day,
Which I can make the sleeping
  see,   5
If they will put their trust in me.

II

And thou shalt know of things un-
  known,
  If thou wilt let me rest between
The veiny lids, whose fringe is
  thrown
    Over thine eyes so dark and
      sheen: 10
And half in hope, and half in fright,
The Lady closed her eyes so bright.

III

At first all deadly shapes were
  driven
  Tumultuously across her sleep,
And o'er the vast cope of bending
  heaven   15
    All ghastly-visaged clouds did
    sweep;
And the Lady ever looked to spy
If the golden sun shone forth on
  high.

IV

And as towards the east she turned,
  She saw aloft in the morning air,
Which now with hues of sunrise
  burned,   21
    A great black Anchor rising
    there;

And wherever the Lady turned her
  eyes,
It hung before her in the skies.

V

The sky was blue as the summer
  sea,
  The depths were cloudless over-
  head,   26
The air was calm as it could be,
  There was no sight or sound of
    dread,
But that black Anchor floating still
Over the piny eastern hill.   30

VI

The Lady grew sick with a weight
  of fear
  To see that Anchor ever hanging,
And veiled her eyes; she then did
  hear
    The sound as of a dim low clang-
    ing,
And looked abroad if she might
  know   35
Was it aught else, or but the flow
Of the blood in her own veins, to
  and fro.

VII

There was a mist in the sunless air,
  Which shook as it were with an
    earthquake's shock,
But the very weeds that blossomed
  there   40
    Were moveless, and each mighty
    rock
Stood on its basis steadfastly;
The Anchor was seen no more on
  high.

VIII

But piled around, with summits
     hid
   In lines of cloud at intervals, 45
Stood many a mountain pyramid
   Among whose everlasting walls
Two mighty cities shone, and ever
Through the red mist their domes
     did quiver.

IX

On two dread mountains, from
     whose crest,   50
   Might seem, the eagle, for her
     brood,
Would ne'er have hung her dizzy
     nest,
   Those tower-encircled cities
     stood.
A vision strange such towers to see,
Sculptured and wrought so gor-
     geously   55
Where human art could never be.

X

And columns framed of marble
     white,
   And giant fanes, dome over dome
Piled, and triumphant gates, all
   bright
   With workmanship, which could
     not come   60
From touch of mortal instrument,
Shot o'er the vales, or lustre lent
From its own shapes magnificent.

XI

But still the Lady heard that clang
   Filling the wide air far away; 65
And still the mist whose light did
     hang
   Among the mountains shook
     alway,
So that the Lady's heart beat fast,
As half in joy, and half aghast,
On those high domes her look she
     cast.   70

XII

Sudden, from out that city sprung
   A light that made the earth grow
     red;
Two flames that each with quiver-
     ing tongue
   Licked its high domes, and over-
     head
Among those mighty towers and
     fanes   75
Dropped fire, as a volcano rains
Its sulphurous ruin on the plains.

XIII

And hark! a rush as if the deep
   Had burst its bonds; she looked
     behind
And saw over the western steep 80
   A raging flood descend, and wind
Through that wide vale; she felt
     no fear,
But said within herself, 'Tis clear
These towers are Nature's own, and
     she   84
To save them has sent forth the
     sea.

XIV

And now those raging billows came
   Where that fair Lady sate, and
     she
Was borne towards the showering
     flame
   By the wild waves heaped tumul-
     tuously,
And, on a little plank, the flow 90
Of the whirlpool bore her to and
     fro.

XV

The flames were fiercely vomited
   From every tower and every
     dome,
And dreary light did widely shed
   O'er that vast flood's suspended
     foam,   95

Beneath the smoke which hung its
    night
On the stained cope of heaven's
    light.

XVI

The plank whereon that Lady sate
    Was driven through the chasms,
        about and about,
Between the peaks so desolate   100
    Of the drowning mountains, in
        and out,
As the thistle-beard on a whirlwind
        sails—
While the flood was filling those
    hollow vales.

XVII

At last her plank an eddy crossed,
    And bore her to the city's wall,
Which now the flood had reached
        almost;   106
    It might the stoutest heart appal
To hear the fire roar and hiss
Through the domes of those mighty
    palaces.

XVIII

The eddy whirled her round and
        round   110
    Before a gorgeous gate, which
        stood
Piercing the clouds of smoke which
        bound
    Its aëry arch with light like
        blood;
She looked on that gate of marble
        clear,
With wonder that extinguished
    fear.

XIX

For it was filled with sculptures
        rarest,   116
    Of forms most beautiful and
        strange,
Like nothing human, but the fairest

Of wingèd shapes, whose legions
        range
Throughout the sleep of those that
        are,   120
Like this same Lady, good and fair.

XX

And as she looked, still lovelier
        grew
    Those marble forms;—the sculp-
        tor sure
Was a strong spirit, and the hue
    Of his own mind did there en-
        dure
After the touch, whose power had
        braided   126
Such grace, was in some sad change
    faded.

XXI

She looked, the flames were dim,
        the flood
    Grew tranquil as a woodland
        river
Winding through hills in solitude;
    Those marble shapes then seemed
        to quiver,   131
And their fair limbs to float in
        motion,
Like weeds unfolding in the ocean.

XXII

And their lips moved; one seemed
        to speak,
    When suddenly the mountains
        cracked,   135
And through the chasm the flood
        did break
    With an earth-uplifting cataract:
The statues gave a joyous scream,
And on its wings the pale thin
        Dream
Lifted the Lady from the stream.

XXIII

The dizzy flight of that phantom
        pale   141

Waked the fair Lady from her
    sleep,
And she arose, while from the veil
    Of her dark eyes the Dream did
    creep,

And she walked about as one who
    knew   145
That sleep has sights as clear and
    true
As any waking eyes can view.

TO CONSTANTIA, SINGING

I

Thus to be lost and thus to sink and die,
    Perchance were death indeed!—Constantia, turn!
In thy dark eyes a power like light doth lie,
    Even though the sounds which were thy voice, which burn
Between thy lips, are laid to sleep;   5
    Within thy breath, and on thy hair, like odour, it is yet,
And from thy touch like fire doth leap.
    Even while I write, my burning cheeks are wet,
    Alas, that the torn heart can bleed, but not forget!

II

A breathless awe, like the swift change   10
    Unseen, but felt in youthful slumbers,
Wild, sweet, but uncommunicably strange,
    Thou breathest now in fast ascending numbers.
The cope of heaven seems rent and cloven
    By the enchantment of thy strain,   15
And on my shoulders wings are woven,
    To follow its sublime career
Beyond the mighty moons that wane
    Upon the verge of Nature's utmost sphere,
    Till the world's shadowy walls are past and disappear.   20

III

Her voice is hovering o'er my soul—it lingers
    O'ershadowing it with soft and lulling wings,
The blood and life within those snowy fingers
    Teach witchcraft to the instrumental strings.
My brain is wild, my breath comes quick—   25
    The blood is listening in my frame,
And thronging shadows, fast and thick,
    Fall on my overflowing eyes;
My heart is quivering like a flame;
    As morning dew, that in the sunbeam dies,   30
    I am dissolved in these consuming ecstasies.

IV

I have no life, Constantia, now, but thee,
  Whilst, like the world-surrounding air, thy song
Flows on, and fills all things with melody.—
  Now is thy voice a tempest swift and strong,   35
On which, like one in trance upborne,
  Secure o'er rocks and waves I sweep,
Rejoicing like a cloud of morn.
  Now 'tis the breath of summer night,
Which when the starry waters sleep,
  Round western isles, with incense-blossoms bright,   40
  Lingering, suspends my soul in its voluptuous flight.

TO CONSTANTIA

I

THE rose that drinks the fountain dew
  In the pleasant air of noon,
Grows pale and blue with altered hue—
  In the gaze of the nightly moon;
For the planet of frost, so cold and bright,   5
Makes it wan with her borrowed light.

II

Such is my heart—roses are fair,
  And that at best a withered blossom;
But thy false care did idly wear
  Its withered leaves in a faithless bosom;   10
And fed with love, like air and dew,
Its growth——

FRAGMENT: TO ONE SINGING

MY spirit like a charmèd bark doth swim
  Upon the liquid waves of thy sweet singing,
Far far away into the regions dim

  Of rapture—as a boat, with swift sails winging
Its way adown some many-winding river,   5
Speeds through dark forests o'er the waters swinging . . .

A FRAGMENT: TO MUSIC

SILVER key of the fountain of tears,
  Where the spirit drinks till the brain is wild;
Softest grave of a thousand fears,
  Where their mother, Care, like a drowsy child,
  Is laid asleep in flowers.   5

ANOTHER FRAGMENT TO MUSIC

No, Music, thou art not the 'food of Love,'
Unless Love feeds upon its own sweet self,
Till it becomes all Music murmurs of.

'MIGHTY EAGLE'

SUPPOSED TO BE ADDRESSED TO WILLIAM GODWIN

MIGHTY eagle! thou that soarest
O'er the misty mountain forest,
   And amid the light of morning
Like a cloud of glory hiest,
And when night descends defiest   5
   The embattled tempests' warning!

TO THE LORD CHANCELLOR

I

THY country's curse is on thee, darkest crest
Of that foul, knotted, many-headed worm
Which rends our Mother's bosom—Priestly Pest!
Masked Resurrection of a buried Form!

II

Thy country's curse is on thee! Justice sold,   5
   Truth trampled, Nature's landmarks overthrown,
And heaps of fraud-accumulated gold,
   Plead, loud as thunder, at Destruction's throne.

III

And, whilst that sure slow Angel which aye stands
   Watching the beck of Mutability   10
Delays to execute her high commands,
   And, though a nation weeps, spares thine and thee.

IV

Oh, let a father's curse be on thy soul,
   And let a daughter's hope be on thy tomb;
Be both, on thy gray head, a leaden cowl   15
   To weigh thee down to thine approaching doom!

V

I curse thee by a parent's outraged love,
   By hopes long cherished and too lately lost,
By gentle feelings thou couldst never prove,
   By griefs which thy stern nature never crossed;   20

VI

By those infantine smiles of happy light,
    Which were a fire within a stranger's hearth,
Quenched even when kindled, in untimely night
    Hiding the promise of a lovely birth:

VII

By those unpractised accents of young speech,   25
    Which he who is a father thought to frame
To gentlest lore, such as the wisest teach—
    Thou strike the lyre of mind!—oh, grief and shame!

VIII

By all the happy see in children's growth—
    That undeveloped flower of budding years—   30
Sweetness and sadness interwoven both,
    Source of the sweetest hopes and saddest fears—

IX

By all the days, under an hireling's care,
    Of dull constraint and bitter heaviness,—
O wretched ye if ever any were,—   35
    Sadder than orphans, yet not fatherless!

X

By the false cant which on their innocent lips
    Must hang like poison on an opening bloom,
By the dark creeds which cover with eclipse
    Their pathway from the cradle to the tomb—   40

XI

By thy most impious Hell, and all its terror;
    By all the grief, the madness, and the guilt
Of thine impostures, which must be their error—
    That sand on which thy crumbling power is built—

XII

By thy complicity with lust and hate—   45
    Thy thirst for tears—thy hunger after gold—
The ready frauds which ever on thee wait—
    The servile arts in which thou hast grown old—

XIII

By thy most killing sneer, and by thy smile—
    By all the arts and snares of thy black den,   50
And—for thou canst outweep the crocodile—
    By thy false tears—those millstones braining men—

XIV

By all the hate which checks a father's love—
  By all the scorn which kills a father's care—
By those most impious hands which dared remove   55
  Nature's high bounds—by thee—and by despair—

XV

Yes, the despair which bids a father groan,
  And cry, 'My children are no longer mine—
The blood within those veins may be mine own,
  But—Tyrant—their polluted souls are thine;'—   60

XVI

I curse thee—though I hate thee not.—O slave!
  If thou couldst quench the earth-consuming Hell
Of which thou art a daemon, on thy grave
  This curse should be a blessing. Fare thee well!

TO WILLIAM SHELLEY

I

THE billows on the beach are leaping around it,
  The bark is weak and frail,
The sea looks black, and the clouds that bound it
  Darkly strew the gale.
Come with me, thou delightful child,   5
Come with me, though the wave is wild,
And the winds are loose, we must not stay,
Or the slaves of the law may rend thee away.

II

They have taken thy brother and sister dear,
  They have made them unfit for thee;   10
They have withered the smile and dried the tear
  Which should have been sacred to me.
To a blighting faith and a cause of crime
They have bound them slaves in youthly prime,
And they will curse my name and thee   15
Because we fearless are and free.

III

Come thou, belovèd as thou art;
  Another sleepeth still
Near thy sweet mother's anxious heart,
  Which thou with joy shalt fill.   20

With fairest smiles of wonder thrown
On that which is indeed our own,
And which in distant lands will be
The dearest playmate unto thee.

IV

Fear not the tyrants will rule for ever,   25
  Or the priests of the evil faith;
They stand on the brink of that raging river,
  Whose waves they have tainted with death.
It is fed from the depth of a thousand dells,
Around them it foams and rages and swells;   30
And their swords and their sceptres I floating see,
Like wrecks on the surge of eternity.

V

Rest, rest, and shriek not, thou gentle child!
  The rocking of the boat thou fearest,
And the cold spray and the clamour wild?—   35
  There, sit between us two, thou dearest—
Me and thy mother—well we know
The storm at which thou tremblest so,
With all its dark and hungry graves,
Less cruel than the savage slaves   40
Who hunt us o'er these sheltering waves.

VI

This hour will in thy memory
  Be a dream of days forgotten long.
We soon shall dwell by the azure sea
Of serene and golden Italy,   45
Or Greece, the Mother of the free;
  And I will teach thine infant tongue
To call upon those heroes old
In their own language, and will mould
Thy growing spirit in the flame
Of Grecian lore, that by such name   50
A patriot's birthright thou mayst claim!

FROM THE ORIGINAL DRAFT OF THE POEM
TO WILLIAM SHELLEY

I

THE world is now our dwelling-place;
Where'er the earth one fading trace
  Of what was great and free does keep,
That is our home! . . .

Mild thoughts of man's ungentle race   5
  Shall our contented exile reap;
For who that in some happy place
His own free thoughts can freely chase
By woods and waves can clothe his face
  In cynic smiles? Child! we shall weep.   10

II

This lament,
  The memory of thy grievous wrong
Will fade ...
But genius is omnipotent
To hallow ...   15

ON FANNY GODWIN

HER voice did quiver as we parted,
  Yet knew I not that heart was broken
From which it came, and I departed
  Heeding not the words then spoken.
    Misery—O Misery,   5
    This world is all too wide for thee.

LINES

I

THAT time is dead for ever,
    child!
Drowned, frozen, dead for ever!
  We look on the past
  And stare aghast
At the spectres wailing, pale and
    ghast,   5
Of hopes which thou and I be-
    guiled
  To death on life's dark river.

II

The stream we gazed on then rolled
    by;
Its waves are unreturning;
  But we yet stand   10
  In a lone land,
Like tombs to mark the memory
Of hopes and fears, which fade and
    flee
  In the light of life's dim morn-
    ing.

DEATH

I

THEY die—the dead return not—Misery
  Sits near an open grave and calls them over,
A Youth with hoary hair and haggard eye—
  They are the names of kindred, friend and lover,
Which he so feebly calls—they all are gone—   5
Fond wretch, all dead! those vacant names alone,
  This most familiar scene, my pain—
  These tombs—alone remain.

II

Misery, my sweetest friend—oh, weep no more!
   Thou wilt not be consoled—I wonder not!   10
For I have seen thee from thy dwelling's door
   Watch the calm sunset with them, and this spot
Was even as bright and calm, but transitory,
And now thy hopes are gone, thy hair is hoary;
   This most familiar scene, my pain—   15
   These tombs—alone remain.

OTHO

I

Thou wert not, Cassius, and thou couldst not be,
   Last of the Romans, though thy memory claim
From Brutus his own glory—and on thee
   Rests the full splendour of his sacred fame:
Nor he who dared make the foul tyrant quail   5
   Amid his cowering senate with thy name,
Though thou and he were great—it will avail
To thine own fame that Otho's should not fail.

II

'Twill wrong thee not—thou wouldst, if thou couldst feel,
   Abjure such envious fame—great Otho died   10
Like thee—he sanctified his country's steel,
   At once the tyrant and tyrannicide,
In his own blood—a deed it was to bring
   Tears from all men—though full of gentle pride,
Such pride as from impetuous love may spring,   15
   That will not be refused its offering.

FRAGMENTS SUPPOSED TO BE PARTS OF OTHO

I

Those whom nor power, nor lying faith, nor toil,
   Nor custom, queen of many slaves, makes blind,
Have ever grieved that man should be the spoil
   Of his own weakness, and with earnest mind
Fed hopes of its redemption; these recur   5
   Chastened by deathful victory now, and find
Foundations in this foulest age, and stir
Me whom they cheer to be their minister.

II

Dark is the realm of grief: but human things
Those may not know who cannot weep for them.   10

III

                        Once more descend
The shadows of my soul upon mankind,
For to those hearts with which they never blend,
    Thoughts are but shadows which the flashing mind
From the swift clouds which track its flight of fire,   15
    Casts on the gloomy world it leaves behind.

·   ·   ·   ·   ·   ·

'O THAT A CHARIOT OF CLOUD WERE MINE'

O THAT a chariot of cloud were mine!
    Of cloud which the wild tempest weaves in air,
When the moon over the ocean's line
    Is spreading the locks of her bright gray hair.
O that a chariot of cloud were mine!   5
    I would sail on the waves of the billowy wind
To the mountain peak and the rocky lake,
And the . . .

FRAGMENT: TO A FRIEND RELEASED FROM PRISON

FOR me, my friend, if not that tears did tremble
    In my faint eyes, and that my heart beat fast
With feelings which make rapture pain resemble,
    Yet, from thy voice that falsehood starts aghast,
        I thank thee—let the tyrant keep   5
        His chains and tears, yea, let him weep
        With rage to see thee freshly risen,
        Like strength from slumber, from the prison,
In which he vainly hoped the soul to bind
Which on the chains must prey that fetter humankind.   10

FRAGMENT: SATAN BROKEN LOOSE

A GOLDEN-WINGED Angel stood
    Before the Eternal Judgement-seat:
His looks were wild, and Devil's blood
    Stained his dainty hands and feet.
The Father and the Son   5
Knew that strife was now begun.
They knew that Satan had broken his chain,
And with millions of daemons in his train,
Was ranging over the world again.
Before the Angel had told his tale,   10
    A sweet and a creeping sound
    Like the rushing of wings was heard around;

And suddenly the lamps grew pale—
The lamps, before the Archangels seven,
That burn continually in Heaven.   15

FRAGMENT: *IGNICULUS DESIDERII*

To thirst and find no fill—to wail and wander
With short unsteady steps—to pause and ponder—
To feel the blood run through the veins and tingle
Where busy thought and blind sensation mingle;
To nurse the image of unfelt caresses   5
Till dim imagination just possesses
The half-created shadow, then all the night
Sick . . .

FRAGMENT: *AMOR AETERNUS*

WEALTH and dominion fade into the mass
Of the great sea of human right and wrong,
When once from our possession they must pass;
But love, though misdirected, is among
The things which are immortal, and surpass   5
All that frail stuff which will be—or which was.

FRAGMENT: THOUGHTS COME AND GO IN SOLITUDE

MY thoughts arise and fade in solitude,
The verse that would invest them melts away
Like moonlight in the heaven of spreading day:
How beautiful they were, how firm they stood,
Flecking the starry sky like woven pearl!   5

A HATE-SONG

A HATER he came and sat by a ditch,
And he took an old cracked lute;
And he sang a song that was more of a screech
'Gainst a woman that was a brute.

LINES TO A CRITIC

I

HONEY from silkworms who can gather,
Or silk from the yellow bee?
The grass may grow in winter weather
As soon as hate in me.

II

Hate men who cant, and men who pray,   5
And men who rail like thee;
An equal passion to repay
They are not coy like me.

III

Or seek some slave of power and
    gold
  To be thy dear heart's mate; 10
Thy love will move that bigot
    cold
Sooner than me, thy hate.

IV

A passion like the one I prove
  Cannot divided be;
I hate thy want of truth and
    love,
  How should I then hate thee? 16

OZYMANDIAS

I MET a traveller from an antique land
Who said: Two vast and trunkless legs of stone
Stand in the desert . . . Near them, on the sand,
Half sunk, a shattered visage lies, whose frown,
And wrinkled lip, and sneer of cold command,   5
Tell that its sculptor well those passions read
Which yet survive, stamped on these lifeless things,
The hand that mocked them, and the heart that fed:
And on the pedestal these words appear:
'My name is Ozymandias, king of kings: 10
Look on my works, ye Mighty, and despair!'
Nothing beside remains. Round the decay
Of that colossal wreck, boundless and bare
The lone and level sands stretch far away.

NOTE ON POEMS OF 1817, BY MRS. SHELLEY

THE very illness that oppressed, and the aspect of death which had
approached so near Shelley, appear to have kindled to yet keener life
the Spirit of Poetry in his heart. The restless thoughts kept awake by
pain clothed themselves in verse. Much was composed during this year.
The *Revolt of Islam,* written and printed, was a great effort—*Rosalind
and Helen* was begun—and the fragments and poems I can trace to the
same period show how full of passion and reflection were his solitary
hours.

In addition to such poems as have an intelligible aim and shape, many
a stray idea and transitory emotion found imperfect and abrupt expression, and then again lost themselves in silence. As he never wandered without a book and without implements of writing, I find many
such, in his manuscript books, that scarcely bear record; while some of
them, broken and vague as they are, will appear valuable to those who
love Shelley's mind, and desire to trace its workings.

He projected also translating the *Hymns* of Homer; his version of
several of the shorter ones remains, as well as that to Mercury already
published in the *Posthumous Poems.* His readings this year were chiefly
Greek. Besides the *Hymns* of Homer and the *Iliad,* he read the dramas

of Aeschylus and Sophocles, the *Symposium* of Plato, and Arrian's *Historia Indica*. In Latin, Apuleius alone is named. In English, the Bible was his constant study; he read a great portion of it aloud in the evening. Among these evening readings I find also mentioned the *Faerie Queen;* and other modern works, the production of his contemporaries, Coleridge, Wordsworth, Moore, and Byron.

His life was now spent more in thought than action—he had lost the eager spirit which believed it could achieve what it projected for the benefit of mankind. And yet in the converse of daily life Shelley was far from being a melancholy man. He was eloquent when philosophy or politics or taste were the subjects of conversation. He was playful; and indulged in the wild spirit that mocked itself and others—not in bitterness, but in sport. The author of *Nightmare Abbey* seized on some points of his character and some habits of his life when he painted Scythrop. He was not addicted to 'port or madeira,' but in youth he had read of 'Illuminati and Eleutherarchs,' and believed that he possessed the power of operating an immediate change in the minds of men and the state of society. These wild dreams had faded; sorrow and adversity had struck home; but he struggled with despondency as he did with physical pain. There are few who remember him sailing paper boats, and watching the navigation of his tiny craft with eagerness—or repeating with wild energy *The Ancient Mariner*, and Southey's *Old Woman of Berkeley;* but those who do will recollect that it was in such, and in the creations of his own fancy when that was most daring and ideal, that he sheltered himself from the storms and disappointments, the pain and sorrow, that beset his life.

No words can express the anguish he felt when his elder children were torn from him. In his first resentment against the Chancellor, on the passing of the decree, he had written a curse, in which there breathes, besides haughty indignation, all the tenderness of a father's love, which could imagine and fondly dwell upon its loss and the consequences.

At one time, while the question was still pending, the Chancellor had said some words that seemed to intimate that Shelley should not be permitted the care of any of his children, and for a moment he feared that our infant son would be torn from us. He did not hesitate to resolve, if such were menaced, to abandon country, fortune, everything, and to escape with his child; and I find some unfinished stanzas addressed to this son, whom afterwards we lost at Rome, written under the idea that we might suddenly be forced to cross the sea, so to preserve him. This poem, as well as the one previously quoted, were not written to exhibit the pangs of distress to the public; they were the spontaneous outbursts of a man who brooded over his wrongs and woes, and was impelled to shed the grace of his genius over the uncontrollable emotions of his heart. I ought to observe that the fourth verse of this effusion is introduced in *Rosalind and Helen*. When afterwards this child died at Rome, he wrote, *à propos* of the English burying-ground in that city: 'This spot is the repository of a sacred loss, of which the yearnings of a parent's heart are now prophetic; he is rendered immortal by love, as his memory is by death. My beloved child lies buried here. I envy death the body far less than the oppressors the minds of those whom they have torn from me. The one can only kill the body, the other crushes the affections.'

POEMS WRITTEN IN 1818

TO THE NILE

MONTH after month the gathered rains descend
Drenching yon secret Aethiopian dells,
And from the desert's ice-girt pinnacles
Where Frost and Heat in strange embraces blend
On Atlas, fields of moist snow half depend.   5
Girt there with blasts and meteors Tempest dwells
By Nile's aëreal urn, with rapid spells
Urging those waters to their mighty end.
O'er Egypt's land of Memory floods are level
And they are thine, O Nile—and well thou knowest   10
That soul-sustaining airs and blasts of evil
And fruits and poisons spring where'er thou flowest.
Beware, O Man—for knowledge must to thee,
Like the great flood to Egypt, ever be.

PASSAGE OF THE APENNINES

LISTEN, listen, Mary mine,
To the whisper of the Apennine,
It bursts on the roof like the thunder's roar,
Or like the sea on a northern shore,
Heard in its raging ebb and flow   5
By the captives pent in the cave below.
The Apennine in the light of day
Is a mighty mountain dim and gray,
Which between the earth and sky doth lay;
But when night comes, a chaos dread   10
On the dim starlight then is spread,
And the Apennine walks abroad with the storm,
Shrouding . . .

THE PAST

I

WILT thou forget the happy hours
Which we buried in Love's sweet bowers,
Heaping over their corpses cold
Blossoms and leaves, instead of mould?
Blossoms which were the joys that fell,   5
And leaves, the hopes that yet remain.

II

Forget the dead, the past? Oh, yet
There are ghosts that may take revenge for it,
Memories that make the heart a tomb,
Regrets which glide through the spirit's gloom,   10
      And with ghastly whispers tell
      That joy, once lost, is pain.

TO MARY ————

O MARY dear, that you were here
With your brown eyes bright and
      clear,
And your sweet voice, like a bird
Singing love to its lone mate
In the ivy bower disconsolate;   5
Voice the sweetest ever heard!
And your brow more ....
Than the   sky

Of this azure Italy.
Mary dear, come to me soon,   10
I am not well whilst thou art far;
As sunset to the spherèd moon,
As twilight to the western star,
Thou, belovèd, art to me.
O Mary dear, that you were
      here: 15
The Castle echo whispers 'Here!'

ON A FADED VIOLET

I

THE odour from the flower is gone
      Which like thy kisses breathed on me;
The colour from the flower is flown
      Which glowed of thee and only thee!

II

A shrivelled, lifeless, vacant form,   5
      It lies on my abandoned breast,
And mocks the heart which yet is warm,
      With cold and silent rest.

III

I weep,—my tears revive it not!
      I sigh,—it breathes no more on me;   10
Its mute and uncomplaining lot
      Is such as mine should be.

LINES WRITTEN AMONG THE EUGANEAN HILLS
OCTOBER, 1818.

MANY a green isle needs must be
In the deep wide sea of Misery,
Or the mariner, worn and wan,
Never thus could voyage on—

Day and night, and night and day,
Drifting on his dreary way,   6
With the solid darkness black
Closing round his vessel's track;

Whilst above the sunless sky,
Big with clouds, hangs heavily,   10
And behind the tempest fleet
Hurries on with lightning feet,
Riving sail, and cord, and plank,
Till the ship has almost drank   14
Death from the o'er-brimming
    deep;
And sinks down, down, like that
    sleep
When the dreamer seems to be
Weltering through eternity;
And the dim low line before
Of a dark and distant shore   20
Still recedes, as ever still
Longing with divided will,
But no power to seek or shun,
He is ever drifted on
O'er the unreposing wave   25
To the haven of the grave.
What, if there no friends will
    greet;
What, if there no heart will meet
His with love's impatient beat;
Wander wheresoe'er he may.   30
Can he dream before that day
To find refuge from distress
In friendship's smile, in love's
    caress?
Then 'twill wreak him little woe
Whether such there be or no: 35
Senseless is the breast, and cold,
Which relenting love would fold;
Bloodless are the veins and chill
Which the pulse of pain did fill;
Every little living nerve   40
That from bitter words did swerve
Round the tortured lips and brow,
Are like sapless leaflets now
Frozen upon December's bough.

On the beach of a northern sea   45
Which tempests shake eternally,
As once the wretch there lay to
    sleep,
Lies a solitary heap,

One white skull and seven dry
    bones,
On the margin of the stones,   50
Where a few gray rushes stand,
Boundaries of the sea and land:
Nor is heard one voice of wail
But the sea-mews, as they sail
O'er the billows of the gale;   55
Or the whirlwind up and down
Howling, like a slaughtered town,
When a king in glory rides
Through the pomp of fratri-
    cides:
Those unburied bones around   60
There is many a mournful sound;
There is no lament for him,
Like a sunless vapour, dim,
Who once clothed with life and
    thought
What now moves nor murmurs not.

Ay, many flowering islands lie   66
In the waters of wide Agony:
To such a one this morn was led,
My bark by soft winds piloted:
'Mid the mountains Euganean   70
I stood listening to the paean
With which the legioned rooks did
    hail
The sun's uprise majestical;
Gathering round with wings all
    hoar,
Through the dewy mist they soar 75
Like gray shades, *till the eastern
    heaven
Bursts, and then, as clouds of even,
Flecked with fire and azure, lie
In the unfathomable sky,
So their plumes of purple grain,   80
Starred with drops of golden rain,
Gleam above the sunlight woods,
As in silent multitudes
On the morning's fitful gale   84
Through the broken mist they sail,
And the vapours cloven and gleam-
    ing

Follow down the dark steep streaming,
Till all is bright, and clear, and still,
Round the solitary hill.

Beneath is spread like a green sea   90
The waveless plain of Lombardy,
Bounded by the vaporous air,
Islanded by cities fair;
Underneath Day's azure eyes
Ocean's nursling, Venice lies,   95
A peopled labyrinth of walls,
Amphitrite's destined halls,
Which her hoary sire now paves
With his blue and beaming waves.
Lo! the sun upsprings behind,   100
Broad, red, radiant, half-reclined
On the level quivering line
Of the waters crystalline;
And before that chasm of light,
As within a furnace bright,   105
Column, tower, and dome, and spire,
Shine like obelisks of fire,
Pointing with inconstant motion
From the altar of dark ocean
To the sapphire-tinted skies;   110
As the flames of sacrifice
From the marble shrines did rise,
As to pierce the dome of gold
Where Apollo spoke of old.

Sun-girt City, thou hast been   115
Ocean's child, and then his queen;
Now is come a darker day,
And thou soon must be his prey,
If the power that raised thee here
Hallow so thy watery bier.   120
A less drear ruin then than now,
With thy conquest-branded brow
Stooping to the slave of slaves
From thy throne, among the waves
Wilt thou be, when the sea-mew   125
Flies, as once before it flew,
O'er thine isles depopulate,

And all is in its ancient state,
Save where many a palace gate
With green sea-flowers overgrown
Like a rock of Ocean's own,   131
Topples o'er the abandoned sea
As the tides change sullenly.
The fisher on his watery way,
Wandering at the close of day,   135
Will spread his sail and seize his oar
Till he pass the gloomy shore,
Lest thy dead should, from their sleep
Bursting o'er the starlight deep,
Lead a rapid masque of death   140
O'er the waters of his path.

Those who alone thy towers behold
Quivering through aëreal gold,
As I now behold them here,
Would imagine not they were   145
Sepulchres, where human forms,
Like pollution-nourished worms,
To the corpse of greatness cling,
Murdered, and now mouldering:
But if Freedom should awake   150
In her omnipotence, and shake
From the Celtic Anarch's hold
All the keys of dungeons cold,
Where a hundred cities lie
Chained like thee, ingloriously,   155
Thou and all thy sister band
Might adorn this sunny land,
Twining memories of old time
With new virtues more sublime;
If not, perish thou and they!—   160
Clouds which stain truth's rising day
By her sun consumed away—
Earth can spare ye: while like flowers,
In the waste of years and hours,
From your dust new nations spring
With more kindly blossoming.   166

Perish—let there only be
Floating o'er thy heartless sea

As the garment of thy sky
Clothes the world immortally,   170
One remembrance, more sublime
Than the tattered pall of time,
Which scarce hides thy visage
   wan;—
That a tempest-cleaving Swan
Of the songs of Albion,   175
Driven from his ancestral streams
By the might of evil dreams,
Found a nest in thee; and Ocean
Welcomed him with such emotion
That its joy grew his, and sprung
From his lips like music flung   181
O'er a mighty thunder-fit,
Chastening terror:—what though
   yet
Poesy's unfailing River,
Which through Albion winds for-
   ever
Lashing with melodious wave   186
Many a sacred Poet's grave,
Mourn its latest nursling fled?
What though thou with all thy dead
Scarce can for this fame repay   190
Aught thine own? oh, rather say
Though thy sins and slaveries foul
Overcloud a sunlike soul?
As the ghost of Homer clings
Round Scamander's wasting
   springs;   195
As divinest Shakespeare's might
Fills Avon and the world with light
Like omniscient power which he
Imaged 'mid mortality;
As the love from Petrarch's urn, 200
Yet amid yon hills doth burn,
A quenchless lamp by which the
   heart
Sees things unearthly;—so thou
   art,
Mighty spirit—so shall be
The City that did refuge thee. 205

Lo, the sun floats up the sky
Like thought-wingèd Liberty,

Till the universal light
Seems to level plain and height;
From the sea a mist has spread, 210
And the beams of morn lie dead
On the towers of Venice now,
Like its glory long ago.
By the skirts of that gray cloud
Many-domèd Padua proud   215
Stands, a peopled solitude,
'Mid the harvest-shining plain,
Where the peasant heaps his grain
In the garner of his foe,
And the milk-white oxen slow 220
With the purple vintage strain,
Heaped upon the creaking wain,
That the brutal Celt may swill
Drunken sleep with savage will;
And the sickle to the sword   225
Lies unchanged, though many a
   lord,
Like a weed whose shade is poison,
Overgrows this region's foison,
Sheaves of whom are ripe to come
To destruction's harvest-home: 230
Men must reap the things they
   sow,
Force from force must ever flow,
Or worse; but 'tis a bitter woe
That love or reason cannot change
The despot's rage, the slave's re-
   venge.
Padua, thou within whose walls
Those mute guests at festivals,
Son and Mother, Death and Sin,
Played at dice for Ezzelin,   239
Till Death cried, "I win, I win!"
And Sin cursed to lose the wager,
But Death promised, to assuage
   her,
That he would petition for
Her to be made Vice-Emperor,
When the destined years were o'er,
Over all between the Po   246
And the eastern Alpine snow,
Under the mighty Austrian.
Sin smiled so as Sin only can,

And since that time, ay, long be-
    fore,   250
Both have ruled from shore to
    shore,—
That incestuous pair, who follow
Tyrants as the sun the swallow,
As Repentance follows Crime,
And as changes follow Time.   255

In thine halls the lamp of learning,
Padua, now no more is burning;
Like a meteor, whose wild way
Is lost over the grave of day,
It gleams betrayed and to betray:
Once remotest nations came   261
To adore that sacred flame,
When it lit not many a hearth
On this cold and gloomy earth:
Now new fires from antique light
Spring beneath the wide world's
    might;   266
But their spark lies dead in thee,
Trampled out by Tyranny.
As the Norway woodman quells,
In the depth of piny dells,   270
One light flame among the brakes,
While the boundless forest shakes,
And its mighty trunks are torn
By the fire thus lowly born:
The spark beneath his feet is dead,
He starts to see the flames it fed 276
Howling through the darkened sky
With a myriad tongues victoriously,
And sinks down in fear: so thou,
O Tyranny, beholdest now   280
Light around thee, and thou hearest
The loud flames ascend, and fear-
    est:
Grovel on the earth; ay, hide
In the dust thy purple pride!

Noon descends around me now: 285
'Tis the noon of autumn's glow,
When a soft and purple mist
Like a vaporous amethyst,
Or an air-dissolvèd star
Mingling light and fragrance,
    far   290

From the curved horizon's bound
To the point of Heaven's profound,
Fills the overflowing sky;
And the plains that silent lie
Underneath, the leaves unsod-
    den   295
Where the infant Frost has trodden
With his morning-wingèd feet,
Whose bright print is gleaming yet;
And the red and golden vines,
Piercing with their trellised lines 300
The rough, dark-skirted wilderness;
The dun and bladed grass no less,
Pointing from this hoary tower
In the windless air; the flower
Glimmering at my feet; the line 305
Of the olive-sandalled Apennine
In the south dimly islanded;
And the Alps, whose snows are
    spread
High between the clouds and sun;
And of living things each one; 310
And my spirit which so long
Darkened this swift stream of
    song,—
Interpenetrated lie
By the glory of the sky:
Be it love, light, harmony,   315
Odour, or the soul of all
Which from Heaven like dew doth
    fall,
Or the mind which feeds this verse
Peopling the lone universe.

Noon descends, and after noon 320
Autumn's evening meets me soon,
Leading the infantine moon,
And that one star, which to her
Almost seems to minister
Half the crimson light she brings 325
From the sunset's radiant springs:
And the soft dreams of the morn
(Which like wingèd winds had
    borne
To that silent isle, which lies
Mid remembered agonies,   330
The frail bark of this lone being)
Pass, to other sufferers fleeing,

And its ancient pilot, Pain,
Sits beside the helm again.

Other flowering isles must be   335
In the sea of Life and Agony:
Other spirits float and flee
O'er that gulf: even now, perhaps,
On some rock the wild wave wraps,
With folded wings they waiting sit
For my bark, to pilot it   341
To some calm and blooming cove,
Where for me, and those I love,
May a windless bower be built,
Far from passion, pain, and guilt,
In a dell mid lawny hills,   346
Which the wild-sea murmur fills,
And soft sunshine, and the sound
Of old forests echoing round,
And the light and smell divine   350
Of all flowers that breathe and
     shine:
We may live so happy there,
That the Spirits of the Air,

Envying us, may even entice
To our healing Paradise   355
The polluting multitude;
But their rage would be subdued
By that clime divine and calm,
And the winds whose wings rain
     balm
On the uplifted soul, and leaves 360
Under which the bright sea
     heaves;
While each breathless interval
In their whisperings musical
The inspired soul supplies
With its own deep melodies,   365
And the love which heals all strife
Circling, like the breath of life,
All things in that sweet abode
With its own mild brotherhood:
They, not it, would change; and
     soon   370
Every sprite beneath the moon
Would repent its envy vain,
And the earth grow young again.

SCENE FROM 'TASSO'

MADDÁLO, *a Courtier.*   PIGNA, *a Minister.*
MALPIGLIO, *a Poet.*   ALBANO, *an Usher.*

Maddalo. No access to the Duke! You have not said
That the Count Maddalo would speak with him?
Pigna. Did you inform his Grace that Signor Pigna
Waits with state papers for his signature?
Malpiglio. The Lady Leonora cannot know   5
That I have written a sonnet to her fame,
In which I   Venus and Adonis.
You should not take my gold and serve me not.
Albano. In truth I told her, and she smiled and said,
'If I am Venus, thou, coy Poesy,   10
Art the Adonis whom I love, and he
The Erymanthian boar that wounded him.'
O trust to me, Signor Malpiglio,
Those nods and smiles were favours worth the zechin.
Malpiglio. The words are twisted in some double sense   15
That I reach not: the smiles fell not on me.
Pigna. How are the Duke and Duchess occupied?
Albano. Buried in some strange talk. The Duke was leaning,
His finger on his brow, his lips unclosed

The Princess sate within the window-seat,
And so her face was hid; but on her knee
Her hands were clasped, veinèd, and pale as snow,
And quivering—young Tasso, too, was there.
    Maddalo. Thou seest on whom from thine own worshipped
        heaven
Thou drawest down smiles—they did not rain on thee.   25
    Malpiglio. Would they were parching lightnings for his sake
On whom they fell!

SONG FOR 'TASSO'

I

I LOVED—alas! our life is love;
But when we cease to breathe and move
I do suppose love ceases too.
I thought, but not as now I do,
Keen thoughts and bright of linkèd lore,   5
Of all that men had thought before,
And all that Nature shows. and more.

II

And still I love and still I think,
But strangely, for my heart can drink
The dregs of such despair, and live,   10
And love; . . .
And if I think, my thoughts come fast,
I mix the present with the past,
And each seems uglier than the last.

III

Sometimes I see before me flee   15
A silver spirit's form, like thee,
O Leonora, and I sit
. . . still watching it,
Till by the grated casement's ledge
It fades, with such a sigh, as sedge   20
Breathes o'er the breezy streamlet's edge.

INVOCATION TO MISERY

I

COME, be happy!—sit near me,
Shadow-vested Misery:
Coy, unwilling, silent bride,
Mourning in thy robe of pride,
Desolation—deified!   5

II

Come, be happy!—sit near me:
Sad as I may seem to thee,
I am happier far than thou,
Lady, whose imperial brow
Is endiademed with woe.   10

III

Misery! we have known each other,
Like a sister and a brother
Living in the same lone home,
Many years—we must live some
Hours or ages yet to come.   15

IV

'Tis an evil lot, and yet
Let us make the best of it;
If love can live when pleasure dies,
We two will love, till in our eyes
This heart's Hell seem Paradise. 20

V

Come, be happy!—lie thee down
On the fresh grass newly mown,
Where the Grasshopper doth sing
Merrily—one joyous thing
In a world of sorrowing!   25

VI

There our tent shall be the willow,
And mine arm shall be thy pillow;
Sounds and odours, sorrowful
Because they once were sweet, shall
    lull
Us to slumber, deep and dull.   30

VII

Ha! thy frozen pulses flutter
With a love thou darest not utter.
Thou art murmuring—thou art
    weeping—
Is thine icy bosom leaping
While my burning heart lies sleep-
    ing?   35

VIII

Kiss me;—oh! thy lips are cold:
Round my neck thine arms en-
    fold—

They are soft, but chill and dead;
And thy tears upon my head
Burn like points of frozen lead.   40

IX

Hasten to the bridal bed—
Underneath the grave 'tis spread:
In darkness may our love be hid,
Oblivion be our coverlid—
We may rest, and none forbid.   45

X

Clasp me till our hearts be grown
Like two shadows into one;
Till this dreadful transport may
Like a vapour fade away,
In the sleep that lasts alway.   50

XI

We may dream, in that long sleep,
That we are not those who weep;
E'en as Pleasure dreams of thee,
Life-deserting Misery,
Thou mayst dream of her with
    me.   55

XII

Let us laugh, and make our mirth,
At the shadows of the earth,
As dogs bay the moonlight clouds,
Which, like spectres wrapped in
    shrouds,
Pass o'er night in multitudes.   60

XIII

All the wide world, beside us,
Show like multitudinous
Puppets passing from a scene;
What but mockery can they mean,
Where I am—where thou hast
    been?   65

STANZAS

WRITTEN IN DEJECTION, NEAR NAPLES

I

THE sun is warm, the sky is clear,
   The waves are dancing fast and bright,
Blue isles and snowy mountains wear
   The purple noon's transparent might,
   The breath of the moist earth is light,   5
Around its unexpanded buds;
   Like many a voice of one delight,
The winds, the birds, the ocean floods,
The City's voice itself, is soft like Solitude's.

II

I see the Deep's untrampled floor   10
   With green and purple seaweeds strown;
I see the waves upon the shore,
   Like light dissolved in star-showers, thrown:
   I sit upon the sands alone,—
The lightning of the noontide ocean   15
   Is flashing round me, and a tone
Arises from its measured motion,
How sweet! did any heart now share in my emotion.

III

Alas! I have nor hope nor health,
   Nor peace within nor calm around,   20
Nor that content surpassing wealth
   The sage in meditation found,
   And walked with inward glory crowned—
Nor fame, nor power, nor love, nor leisure.
   Others I see whom these surround—   25
Smiling they live, and call life pleasure;—
To me that cup has been dealt in another measure.

IV

Yet now despair itself is mild,
   Even as the winds and waters are;
I could lie down like a tired child,   30
   And weep away the life of care
   Which I have borne and yet must bear,
Till death like sleep might steal on me,
   And I might feel in the warm air
My cheek grow cold, and hear the sea   35
Breathe o'er my dying brain its last monotony.

V

Some might lament that I were cold,
  As I, when this sweet day is gone,
Which my lost heart, too soon grown old,
  Insults with this untimely moan;   40
  They might lament—for I am one
Whom men love not,—and yet regret,
  Unlike this day, which, when the sun
Shall on its stainless glory set,
Will linger, though enjoyed, like joy in memory yet.   45

THE WOODMAN AND THE NIGHTINGALE

A WOODMAN whose rough heart was out of tune
(I think such hearts yet never came to good)
Hated to hear, under the stars or moon,

One nightingale in an interfluous wood
Satiate the hungry dark with melody;—   5
And as a vale is watered by a flood,

Or as the moonlight fills the open sky
Struggling with darkness—as a tuberose
Peoples some Indian dell with scents which lie

Like clouds above the flower from which they rose,   10
The singing of that happy nightingale
In this sweet forest, from the golden close

Of evening till the star of dawn may fail,
Was interfused upon the silentness;
The folded roses and the violets pale   15

Heard her within their slumbers, the abyss
Of heaven with all its planets; the dull ear
Of the night-cradled earth; the loneliness

Of the circumfluous waters,—every sphere
And every flower and beam and cloud and wave,   20
And every wind of the mute atmosphere,

And every beast stretched in its ruggèd cave,
And every bird lulled on its mossy bough,
And every silver moth fresh from the grave

Which is its cradle—ever from below   25
Aspiring like one who loves too fair, too far,
To be consumed within the purest glow

Of one serene and unapproachèd star,
As if it were a lamp of earthly light,
Unconscious, as some human lovers are,   30

Itself how low, how high beyond all height
The heaven where it would perish!—and every form
That worshipped in the temple of the night

Was awed into delight, and by the charm
Girt as with an interminable zone,   35
Whilst that sweet bird, whose music was a storm

Of sound, shook forth the dull oblivion
Out of their dreams; harmony became love
In every soul but one.

And so this man returned with axe and saw   40
At evening close from killing the tall treen,
The soul of whom by Nature's gentle law

Was each a wood-nymph, and kept ever green
The pavement and the roof of the wild copse,
Chequering the sunlight of the blue serene   45

With jaggèd leaves,—and from the forest tops
Singing the winds to sleep—or weeping oft
Fast showers of aëreal water-drops

Into their mother's bosom, sweet and soft,
Nature's pure tears which have no bitterness;—   50
Around the cradles of the birds aloft

They spread themselves into the loveliness
Of fan-like leaves, and over pallid flowers
Hang like moist clouds:—or, where high branches kiss,

Make a green space among the silent bowers,   55
Like a vast fane in a metropolis,
Surrounded by the columns and the towers

All overwrought with branch-like traceries
In which there is religion—and the mute
Persuasion of unkindled melodies,   60

Odours and gleams and murmurs, which the lute
Of the blind pilot-spirit of the blast
Stirs as it sails, now grave and now acute,

Wakening the leaves and waves, ere it has passed
To such brief unison as on the brain   65
One tone, which never can recur, has cast,
One accent never to return again.

.   .   .   .

The world is full of Woodmen who expel
Love's gentle Dryads from the haunts of life,
And vex the nightingales in every dell.   70

MARENGHI [1]

I

Let those who pine in pride or in revenge,
   Or think that ill for ill should be repaid,
Who barter wrong for wrong, until the exchange
   Ruins the merchants of such thriftless trade,
Visit the tower of Vado, and unlearn   5
Such bitter faith beside Marenghi's urn.

II

A massy tower yet overhangs the town,
   A scattered group of ruined dwellings now . . . .

.   .   .   .   .

III

Another scene ere wise Etruria knew
   Its second ruin through internal strife,   10
And tyrants through the breach of discord threw
   The chain which binds and kills. As death to life,
As winter to fair flowers (though some be poison)
So Monarchy succeeds to Freedom's foison.

IV

In Pisa's church a cup of sculptured gold   15
   Was brimming with the blood of feuds forsworn:
A Sacrament more holy ne'er of old
   Etrurians mingled mid the shades forlorn
Of moon-illumined forests, when . . . .

V

And reconciling factions wet their lips   20
   With that dread wine, and swear to keep each spirit
Undarkened by their country's last eclipse . . . .

.   .   .   .   .

[1] This fragment refers to an event told in Sismondi's *Histoire des Républiques Italiennes*, which occurred during the war when Florence finally subdued Pisa, and reduced it to a province.—[Mrs. Shelley's Note, 1824.]

VI

Was Florence the liberticide? that band
   Of free and glorious brothers who had planted,
Like a green isle mid Aethiopian sand,   25
   A nation amid slaveries, disenchanted
Of many impious faiths—wise, just—do they,
   Does Florence, gorge the sated tyrants' prey?

VII

O foster-nurse of man's abandoned glory,
   Since Athens, its great mother, sunk in splendour;   30
Thou shadowest forth that mighty shape in story,
   As ocean its wrecked fanes, severe yet tender:—
The light-invested angel Poesy
Was drawn from the dim world to welcome thee.

VIII

And thou in painting didst transcribe all taught   35
   By loftiest meditations; marble knew
The sculptor's fearless soul—and as he wrought,
   The grace of his own power and freedom grew.
And more than all, heroic, just, sublime,
Thou wert among the false . . . was this thy crime?   40

IX

Yes; and on Pisa's marble walls the twine
   Of direst weeds hangs garlanded—the snake
Inhabits its wrecked palaces;—in thine
   A beast of subtler venom now doth make
Its lair, and sits amid their glories overthrown,   45
And thus thy victim's fate is as thine own.

X

The sweetest flowers are ever frail and rare,
   And love and freedom blossom but to wither;
And good and ill like vines entangled are,
   So that their grapes may oft be plucked together;—   50
Divide the vintage ere thou drink, then make
Thy heart rejoice for dead Marenghi's sake.

x a

[Albert] Marenghi was a Florentine;
   If he had wealth, or children, or a wife
Or friends, [or farm] or cherished thoughts which twine   55
   The sights and sounds of home with life's own life
Of these he was despoiled and Florence sent . . . .

    .   .   .   .   .   .

XI

No record of his crime remains in story,
    But if the morning bright as evening shone,
It was some high and holy deed, by glory   60
    Pursued into forgetfulness, which won
From the blind crowd he made secure and free
The patriot's meed, toil, death, and infamy

XII

For when by sound of trumpet was declared
    A price upon his life, and there was set   65
A penalty of blood on all who shared
    So much of water with him as might wet
His lips, which speech divided not—he went
Alone, as you may guess, to banishment.

XIII

Amid the mountains, like a hunted beast,   70
    He hid himself, and hunger, toil, and cold,
Month after month endured; it was a feast
    Whene'er he found those globes of deep-red gold
Which in the woods the strawberry-tree doth bear,
Suspended in their emerald atmosphere.   75

XIV

And in the roofless huts of vast morasses,
    Deserted by the fever-stricken serf,
All overgrown with reeds and long rank grasses,
    And hillocks heaped of moss-inwoven turf,
And where the huge and speckled aloe made,   80
Rooted in stones, a broad and pointed shade,—

XV

He housed himself. There is a point of strand
    Near Vado's tower and town; and on one side
The treacherous marsh divides it from the land,
    Shadowed by pine and ilex forests wide,   85
And on the other, creeps eternally,
Through muddy weeds, the shallow sullen sea.

XVI

Here the earth's breath is pestilence, and few
    But things whose nature is at war with life—
Snakes and ill worms—endure its mortal dew.   90
    The trophies of the clime's victorious strife—
And ringed horns which the buffalo did wear,
And the wolf's dark gray scalp who tracked him there.

XVII

And at the utmost point . . . stood there
   The relics of a reed-inwoven cot,   95
Thatched with broad flags. An outlawed murderer
   Had lived seven days there: the pursuit was hot
When he was cold. The birds that were his grave
Fell dead after their feast in Vado's wave.

XVIII

There must have burned within Marenghi's breast   100
   That fire, more warm and bright than life and hope,
(Which to the martyr makes his dungeon . . . .
   More joyous than free heaven's majestic cope
To his oppressor), warring with decay,—
Or he could ne'er have lived years, day by day.   105

XIX

Nor was his state so lone as you might think.
   He had tamed every newt and snake and toad,
And every seagull which sailed down to drink
   Those freshes ere the death-mist went abroad.
And each one, with peculiar talk and play,   110
Wiled, not untaught, his silent time away.

XX

And the marsh-meteors, like tame beasts, at night
   Came licking with blue tongues his veinèd feet;
And he would watch them, as, like spirits bright,
   In many entangled figures quaint and sweet   115
To some enchanted music they would dance—
Until they vanished at the first moon-glance.

XXI

He mocked the stars by grouping on each weed
   The summer dew-globes in the golden dawn;
And, ere the hoar-frost languished, he could read   120
   Its pictured path, as on bare spots of lawn
Its delicate brief touch in silver weaves
The likeness of the wood's remembered leaves.

XXII

And many a fresh Spring morn would he awaken—
   While yet the unrisen sun made glow, like iron   125
Quivering in crimson fire, the peaks unshaken
   Of mountains and blue isles which did environ
With air-clad crags that plain of land and sea,—
And feel   liberty.

XXIII

And in the moonless nights, when the dun ocean   130
    Heaved underneath wide heaven, star-impearled,
Starting from dreams . . .
    Communed with the immeasurable world;
And felt his life beyond his limbs dilated,
Till his mind grew like that it contemplated.   135

XXIV

His food was the wild fig and strawberry;
    The milky pine-nuts which the autumn-blast
Shakes into the tall grass; or such small fry
    As from the sea by winter-storms are cast;
And the coarse bulbs of iris-flowers he found   140
Knotted in clumps under the spongy ground.

XXV

And so were kindled powers and thoughts which made
    His solitude less dark. When memory came
(For years gone by leave each a deepening shade),
    His spirit basked in its internal flame,—   145
As, when the black storm hurries round at night,
The fisher basks beside his red firelight.

XXVI

Yet human hopes and cares and faiths and errors,
    Like billows unawakened by the wind,
Slept in Marenghi still; but that all terrors,   150
    Weakness, and doubt, had withered in his mind.
His couch . . .

    .   .   .   .

XXVII

And, when he saw beneath the sunset's planet
    A black ship walk over the crimson ocean,—
Its pennon streaming on the blasts that fan it,   155
    Its sails and ropes all tense and without motion,
Like the dark ghost of the unburied even
Striding athwart the orange-coloured heaven,—

XXVIII

The thought of his own kind who made the soul
    Which sped that wingèd shape through night and day,— 160
The thought of his own country . . .

    .   .   .   .   .

SONNET

Lift not the painted veil which those who live
Call Life: though unreal shapes be pictured there,
And it but mimic all we would believe
With colours idly spread,—behind, lurk Fear
And Hope, twin Destinies; who ever weave　　　　5
Their shadows, o'er the chasm, sightless and drear.
I knew one who had lifted it—he sought,
For his lost heart was tender, things to love,
But found them not, alas! nor was there aught
The world contains, the which he could approve.　　10
Through the unheeding many he did move,
A splendour among shadows, a bright blot
Upon this gloomy scene, a Spirit that strove
For truth, and like the Preacher found it not.

FRAGMENT: TO BYRON

O mighty mind, in whose deep stream this age
Shakes like a reed in the unheeding storm,
Why dost thou curb not thine own sacred rage?

FRAGMENT: APOSTROPHE TO SILENCE

Silence! Oh, well are Death and Sleep and Thou
Three brethren named, the guardians gloomy-winged
Of one abyss, where life, and truth, and joy
Are swallowed up—yet spare me, Spirit, pity me,
Until the sounds I hear become my soul,　　　　5
And it has left these faint and weary limbs,
To track along the lapses of the air
This wandering melody until it rests
Among lone mountains in some . . .

FRAGMENT: THE LAKE'S MARGIN

The fierce beasts of the woods and wildernesses
Track not the steps of him who drinks of it;
For the light breezes, which for ever fleet
Around its margin, heap the sand thereon.

FRAGMENT: 'MY HEAD IS WILD WITH WEEPING'

My head is wild with weeping for a grief
　　Which is the shadow of a gentle mind.
I walk into the air (but no relief
　　To seek,—or haply, if I sought, to find;
It came unsought);—to wonder that a chief　　5
　　Among men's spirits should be cold and blind.

FRAGMENT: THE VINE-SHROUD

FLOURISHING vine, whose kindling clusters glow
Beneath the autumnal sun, none taste of thee;
For thou dost shroud a ruin, and below
The rotting bones of dead antiquity.

NOTE ON POEMS OF 1818, BY MRS. SHELLEY

WE often hear of persons disappointed by a first visit to Italy. This was not Shelley's case. The aspect of its nature, its sunny sky, its majestic storms, of the luxuriant vegetation of the country, and the noble marble-built cities, enchanted him. The sight of the works of art was full enjoyment and wonder. He had not studied pictures or statues before; he now did so with the eye of taste, that referred not to the rules of schools, but to those of Nature and truth. The first entrance to Rome opened to him a scene of remains of antique grandeur that far surpassed his expectations; and the unspeakable beauty of Naples and its environs added to the impression he received of the transcendent and glorious beauty of Italy.

Our winter was spent at Naples. Here he wrote the fragments of *Marenghi* and *The Woodman and the Nightingale,* which he afterwards threw aside. At this time, Shelley suffered greatly in health. He put himself under the care of a medical man, who promised great things, and made him endure severe bodily pain, without any good results. Constant and poignant physical suffering exhausted him; and though he preserved the appearance of cheerfulness, and often greatly enjoyed our wanderings in the environs of Naples, and our excursions on its sunny sea, yet many hours were passed when his thoughts, shadowed by illness, became gloomy,—and then he escaped to solitude, and in verses, which he hid from fear of wounding me, poured forth morbid but too natural bursts of discontent and sadness. One looks back with unspeakable regret and gnawing remorse to such periods; fancying that, had one been more alive to the nature of his feelings, and more attentive to soothe them, such would not have existed. And yet, enjoying as he appeared to do every sight or influence of earth or sky, it was difficult to imagine that any melancholy he showed was aught but the effect of the constant pain to which he was a martyr.

We lived in utter solitude. And such is often not the nurse of cheerfulness; for then, at least with those who have been exposed to adversity, the mind broods over its sorrows too intently; while the society of the enlightened, the witty, and the wise, enables us to forget ourselves by making us the sharers of the thoughts of others, which is a portion of the philosophy of happiness. Shelley never liked society in numbers,—it harassed and wearied him; but neither did he like loneliness, and usually, when alone, sheltered himself against memory and reflection in a book. But, with one or two whom he loved, he gave way to wild and joyous spirits, or in more serious conversation expounded his opinions with vivacity and eloquence. If an argument arose, no man ever argued better. He was clear, logical, and earnest, in supporting his own views; attentive, patient, and impartial, while listening to those on the adverse side. Had not a wall of prejudice been raised at this time between him and his countrymen, how many would have sought the acquaintance of one whom to know was to love and to revere! How many of the more enlightened of his contemporaries have since regretted that they did not seek him! how very few knew his worth while he lived! and, of those few, several were withheld by timidity or envy from declaring their sense of it. But no man was ever more enthusiastically loved—more looked up to, as one superior to his fellows in intellectual endowments and moral worth, by the few who knew him well, and had sufficient nobleness of soul to appreciate his superiority. His excellence is now acknowledged; but, even while admitted, not duly appreciated. For who, except those who were acquainted with him, can imagine his unwearied benevolence, his generosity, his systematic forbearance? And still less is his vast superiority in intellectual attainments sufficiently understood—his sagacity, his clear understanding, his learning, his prodigious memory. All these, as displayed in conversation, were known to few while he lived, and are now silent in the tomb:

> 'Ahi orbo mondo ingrato!
> Gran cagion hai di dever pianger meco;
> Chè quel ben ch' era in te, perdut' hai seco.'

POEMS WRITTEN IN 1819

LINES WRITTEN DURING THE CASTLEREAGH ADMINISTRATION

I

Corpses are cold in the tomb;
Stones on the pavement are dumb;
Abortions are dead in the womb,
And their mothers look pale—like the death-white shore
    Of Albion, free no more.   5

II

Her sons are as stones in the way—
They are masses of senseless clay—
They are trodden, and move not away,—
The abortion with which *she* travaileth
    Is Liberty, smitten to death.   10

III

Then trample and dance, thou Oppressor!
For thy victim is no redresser;
Thou art sole lord and possessor
Of her corpses, and clods, and abortions—they pave
    Thy path to the grave.   15

IV

Hearest thou the festival din
Of Death, and Destruction, and Sin,
And Wealth crying *Havoc!* within?
'Tis the bacchanal triumph that makes Truth dumb,
Thine Epithalamium. 20

V

Ay, marry thy ghastly wife!
Let Fear and Disquiet and Strife
Spread thy couch in the chamber of Life!
Marry Ruin, thou Tyrant! and Hell be thy guide
To the bed of the bride! 25

SONG TO THE MEN OF ENGLAND

I

MEN of England, wherefore plough
For the lords who lay ye low?
Wherefore weave with toil and care
The rich robes your tyrants wear?

II

Wherefore feed, and clothe, and
save, 5
From the cradle to the grave,
Those ungrateful drones who would
Drain your sweat—nay, drink your
blood?

III

Wherefore, Bees of England, forge
Many a weapon, chain, and scourge,
That these stingless drones may
spoil 11
The forced produce of your toil?

IV

Have ye leisure, comfort, calm,
Shelter, food, love's gentle balm?
Or what is it ye buy so dear 15
With your pain and with your fear?

V

The seed ye sow, another reaps;
The wealth ye find, another keeps;
The robes ye weave, another wears;
The arms ye forge, another bears. 20

VI

Sow seed,—but let no tyrant reap;
Find wealth,—let no impostor
heap;
Weave robes,—let not the idle
wear;
Forge arms,—in your defence to
bear.

VII

Shrink to your cellars, holes, and
cells; 25
In halls ye deck another dwells.
Why shake the chains ye wrought?
Ye see
The steel ye tempered glance on ye.

VIII

With plough and spade, and hoe
and loom,
Trace your grave, and build your
tomb, 30
And weave your winding-sheet, till
fair
England be your sepulchre.

SIMILES FOR TWO POLITICAL CHARACTERS OF 1819

I

As from an ancestral oak
  Two empty ravens sound their
    clarion,
Yell by yell, and croak by croak,
When they scent the noonday
    smoke
  Of fresh human carrion:— 5

II

As two gibbering night-birds flit
  From their bowers of deadly
    yew
Through the night to frighten it,
When the moon is in a fit,
  And the stars are none, or
    few:—

III

As a shark and dog-fish wait   11
  Under an Atlantic isle,
For the negro-ship, whose freight
Is the theme of their debate,
  Wrinkling their red gills the
    while—   15

IV

Are ye, two vultures sick for battle,
  Two scorpions under one wet
    stone,
Two bloodless wolves whose dry
    throats rattle,
Two crows perched on the mur-
    rained cattle,
  Two vipers tangled into one. 20

FRAGMENT: TO THE PEOPLE OF ENGLAND

PEOPLE of England, ye who toil and groan,
Who reap the harvests which are not your own,
Who weave the clothes which your oppressors wear,
And for your own take the inclement air;
Who build warm houses . . .   5
And are like gods who give them all they have,
And nurse them from the cradle to the grave . . .

.   .   .   .

FRAGMENT: 'WHAT MEN GAIN FAIRLY'

WHAT men gain fairly—that they should possess,
And children may inherit idleness,
From him who earns it—This is understood;
Private injustice may be general good.
But he who gains by base and armèd wrong,   5
Or guilty fraud, or base compliances,
May be despoiled; even as a stolen dress
Is stripped from a convicted thief, and he
Left in the nakedness of infamy.

A NEW NATIONAL ANTHEM

I

GOD prosper, speed, and save,
God raise from England's grave
   Her murdered Queen!
Pave with swift victory
The steps of Liberty,   5
Whom Britons own to be
   Immortal Queen.

II

See, she comes throned on high,
On swift Eternity!
   God save the Queen!   10
Millions on millions wait,
Firm, rapid, and elate,
On her majestic state!
   God save the Queen!

III

She is Thine own pure soul   15
Moulding the mighty whole,—
   God save the Queen!
She is Thine own deep love
Rained down from Heaven above,—
Wherever she rest or move,   20
   God save our Queen!

IV

'Wilder her enemies
In their own dark disguise,—
   God save our Queen!
All earthly things that dare   25
Her sacred name to bear,
Strip them, as kings are, bare;
   God save the Queen!

V

Be her eternal throne
Built in our hearts alone—   30
   God save the Queen!
Let the oppressor hold
Canopied seats of gold;
She sits enthroned of old
   O'er our hearts Queen.   35

VI

Lips touched by seraphim
Breathe out the choral hymn
   'God save the Queen!'
Sweet as if angels sang,
Loud as that trumpet's clang   40
Wakening the world's dead gang,—
   God save the Queen!

SONNET: ENGLAND IN 1819

AN old, mad, blind, despised, and dying king,—
Princes, the dregs of their dull race, who flow
Through public scorn,—mud from a muddy spring,—
Rulers who neither see, nor feel, nor know,
But leech-like to their fainting country cling,   5
Till they drop, blind in blood, without a blow,—
A people starved and stabbed in the untilled field,—
An army, which liberticide and prey
Makes as a two-edged sword to all who wield,—
Golden and sanguine laws which tempt and slay;   10
Religion Christless, Godless—a book sealed;
A Senate,—Time's worst statute unrepealed,—
Are graves, from which a glorious Phantom may
Burst, to illumine our tempestuous day.

AN ODE

WRITTEN OCTOBER, 1819, BEFORE THE SPANIARDS HAD RECOVERED THEIR LIBERTY

ARISE, arise, arise!
There is blood on the earth that denies ye bread;
    Be your wounds like eyes
To weep for the dead, the dead, the dead.
What other grief were it just to pay?   5
Your sons, your wives, your brethren, were they;
Who said they were slain on the battle day?

    Awaken, awaken, awaken!
The slave and the tyrant are twin-born foes;
    Be the cold chains shaken   10
To the dust where your kindred repose, repose:
Their bones in the grave will start and move,
When they hear the voices of those they love,
Most loud in the holy combat above.

    Wave, wave high the banner!   15
When Freedom is riding to conquest by:
    Though the slaves that fan her
Be Famine and Toil, giving sigh for sigh.
And ye who attend her imperial car,
Lift not your hands in the banded war,   20
But in her defence whose children ye are.

    Glory, glory, glory,
To those who have greatly suffered and done!
    Never name in story
Was greater than that which ye shall have won.   25
Conquerors have conquered their foes alone,
Whose revenge, pride, and power they have overthrown:
Ride ye, more victorious, over your own.

    Bind, bind every brow
With crownals of violet, ivy, and pine: 30
    Hide the blood-stains now
With hues which sweet Nature has made divine:
Green strength, azure hope, and eternity:
But let not the pansy among them be;
Ye were injured, and that means memory.   35

CANCELLED STANZA

GATHER, O gather,
Foeman and friend in love and peace!
    Waves sleep together
When the blasts that called them to battle, cease.

For fangless Power grown tame and mild   5
Is at play with Freedom's fearless child—
The dove and the serpent reconciled!

ODE TO HEAVEN

CHORUS OF SPIRITS

First Spirit.

PALACE-ROOF of cloudless nights!
Paradise of golden lights!
  Deep, immeasurable, vast,
Which art now, and which wert
    then
  Of the Present and the Past,   5
Of the eternal Where and When,
  Presence-chamber, temple, home,
  Ever-canopying dome,
  Of acts and ages yet to come!

Glorious shapes have life in thee,   10
Earth, and all earth's company;
  Living globes which ever throng
Thy deep chasms and wildernesses;
  And green worlds that glide
    along;
And swift stars with flashing tresses;
  And icy moons most cold and
    bright,   16
  And mighty suns beyond the
    night,
  Atoms of intensest light.

Even thy name is as a god,
Heaven! for thou art the abode   20
  Of that Power which is the glass
Wherein man his nature sees.
  Generations as they pass
Worship thee with bended knees.
  Their unremaining gods and they
  Like a river roll away: 26
  Thou remainest such—alway!—

Second Spirit.

Thou art but the mind's first
  chamber,

Round which its young fancies
  clamber,
  Like weak insects in a cave,   30
Lighted up by stalactites;
  But the portal of the grave,
Where a world of new delights
  Will make thy best glories seem
  But a dim and noonday gleam   35
  From the shadow of a dream!

Third Spirit.

Peace! the abyss is wreathed with
  scorn
At your presumption, atom-born!
  What is Heaven? and what are
    ye
Who its brief expanse inherit?   40
  What are suns and spheres which
    flee
  With the instinct of that Spirit
  Of which ye are but a part?
  Drops which Nature's mighty
    heart
  Drives through thinnest veins!
    Depart!   45

What is Heaven? a globe of dew,
Filling in the morning new
  Some eyed flower whose young
    leaves waken
On an unimagined world:
  Constellated suns unshaken,   50
Orbits measureless, are furled
  In that frail and fading sphere,
  With ten millions gathered
    there,
  To tremble, gleam, and dis
    appear.

CANCELLED FRAGMENTS OF THE ODE TO HEAVEN

THE [living frame which sustains
    my soul]
Is [sinking beneath the fierce con-
    trol]
    Down through the lampless deep
      of song
    I am drawn and driven along—

When a Nation screams aloud 5
Like an eagle from the cloud

When a . . .

. . . . .

When the night . . .

. . . . .

    Watch the look askance and
      old—   9
    See neglect, and falsehood fold. . .

ODE TO THE WEST WIND [1]

I

O WILD West Wind, thou breath of Autumn's being,
Thou, from whose unseen presence the leaves dead
Are driven, like ghosts from an enchanter fleeing,

Yellow, and black, and pale, and hectic red,
Pestilence-stricken multitudes: O thou,   5
Who chariotest to their dark wintry bed

The wingèd seeds, where they lie cold and low,
Each like a corpse within its grave, until
Thine azure sister of the Spring shall blow

Her clarion o'er the dreaming earth, and fill   10
(Driving sweet buds like flocks to feed in air)
With living hues and odours plain and hill:

Wild Spirit, which art moving everywhere;
Destroyer and preserver; hear, oh, hear!

II

Thou on whose stream, mid the steep sky's commotion, 15
Loose clouds like earth's decaying leaves are shed,
Shook from the tangled boughs of Heaven and Ocean,

[1] This poem was conceived and chiefly written in a wood that skirts the Arno, near Florence, and on a day when that tempestuous wind, whose temperature is at once mild and animating, was collecting the vapours which pour down the autumnal rains. They began, as I foresaw, at sunset with a violent tempest of hail and rain, attended by that magnificent thunder and lightning peculiar to the Cisalpine regions.

The phenomenon alluded to at the conclusion of the third stanza is well known to naturalists. The vegetation at the bottom of the sea, of rivers, and of lakes, sympathizes with that of the land in the change of seasons, and is consequently influenced by the winds which announce it.—[SHELLEY'S NOTE.]

Angels of rain and lightning: there are spread
On the blue surface of thine aëry surge,
Like the bright hair uplifted from the head   20

Of some fierce Maenad, even from the dim verge
Of the horizon to the zenith's height,
The locks of the approaching storm. Thou dirge

Of the dying year, to which this closing night
Will be the dome of a vast sepulchre,   25
Vaulted with all thy congregated might

Of vapours, from whose solid atmosphere
Black rain, and fire, and hail will burst: oh, hear!

III

Thou who didst waken from his summer dreams
The blue Mediterranean, where he lay,   30
Lulled by the coil of his crystàlline streams,

Beside a pumice isle in Baiae's bay,
And saw in sleep old palaces and towers
Quivering within the wave's intenser day,

All overgrown with azure moss and flowers   35
So sweet, the sense faints picturing them! Thou
For whose path the Atlantic's level powers

Cleave themselves into chasms, while far below
The sea-blooms and the oozy woods which wear
The sapless foliage of the ocean, know   40

Thy voice, and suddenly grow gray with fear,
And tremble and despoil themselves: oh, hear!

IV

If I were a dead leaf thou mightest bear;
If I were a swift cloud to fly with thee;
A wave to pant beneath thy power, and share   45

The impulse of thy strength, only less free
Than thou, O uncontrollable! If even
I were as in my boyhood, and could be

The comrade of thy wanderings over Heaven,
As then, when to outstrip thy skiey speed   50
Scarce seemed a vision; I would ne'er have striven

As thus with thee in prayer in my sore need.
Oh, lift me as a wave, a leaf, a cloud!
I fall upon the thorns of life! I bleed!

A heavy weight of hours has chained and bowed   55
One too like thee: tameless, and swift, and proud.

V

Make me thy lyre, even as the forest is:
What if my leaves are falling like its own!
The tumult of thy mighty harmonies

Will take from both a deep, autumnal tone,   60
Sweet though in sadness. Be thou, Spirit fierce,
My spirit! Be thou me, impetuous one!

Drive my dead thoughts over the universe
Like withered leaves to quicken a new birth!
And, by the incantation of this verse,   65

Scatter, as from an unextinguished hearth
Ashes and sparks, my words among mankind!
Be through my lips to unawakened earth

The trumpet of a prophecy! O, Wind,
If Winter comes, can Spring be far behind?   70

AN EXHORTATION

CHAMELEONS feed on light and air:
   Poets' food is love and fame:
If in this wide world of care
   Poets could but find the same
With as little toil as they,   5
   Would they ever change their hue
   As the light chameleons do,
Suiting it to every ray
   Twenty times a day?

Poets are on this cold earth,   10
   As chameleons might be,
Hidden from their early birth
   In a cave beneath the sea;
Where light is, chameleons change:
Where love is not, poets do: 15
   Fame is love disguised: if few
Find either, never think it strange
   That poets range.

Yet dare not stain with wealth or
       power   19
   A poet's free and heavenly mind:
If bright chameleons should devour
   Any food but beams and wind,
They would grow as earthly soon
   As their brother lizards are.
Children of a sunnier star,   25
Spirits from beyond the moon,
   Oh, refuse the boon!

THE INDIAN SERENADE

I

I ARISE from dreams of thee
In the first sweet sleep of night,
When the winds are breathing low,
And the stars are shining bright:
I arise from dreams of thee,   5
And a spirit in my feet
Hath led me—who knows how?
To thy chamber window, Sweet!

II

The wandering airs they faint
On the dark, the silent stream— 10

The Champak odours fail
Like sweet thoughts in a dream;
The nightingale's complaint,
It dies upon her heart;—
As I must on thine,   15
Oh, belovèd as thou art!

III

Oh lift me from the grass!
I die! I faint! I fail!

Let thy love in kisses rain
On my lips and eyelids pale.   20
My cheek is cold and white, alas!
My heart beats loud and fast;—
Oh! press it to thine own again,
Where it will break at last.

CANCELLED PASSAGE

O PILLOW cold and wet with tears!
Thou breathest sleep no more!

TO SOPHIA [MISS STACEY]

I

THOU art fair, and few are fairer
    Of the Nymphs of earth or ocean;
They are robes that fit the wearer—
    Those soft limbs of thine, whose motion
Ever falls and shifts and glances   5
As the life within them dances.

II

Thy deep eyes, a double Planet,
    Gaze the wisest into madness
With soft clear fire,—the winds that fan it
    Are those thoughts of tender gladness   10
Which, like zephyrs on the billow,
Make thy gentle soul their pillow.

III

If, whatever face thou paintest
    In those eyes, grows pale with pleasure,
If the fainting soul is faintest   15
    When it hears thy harp's wild measure,
Wonder not that when thou speakest
Of the weak my heart is weakest.

IV

As dew beneath the wind of morning,
    As the sea which whirlwinds waken,
As the birds at thunder's warning,
    As aught mute yet deeply shaken,
As one who feels an unseen spirit
Is my heart when thine is near it.

TO WILLIAM SHELLEY

(With what truth may I say—
Roma! Roma! Roma!
Non è più come era prima!)

I

My lost William, thou in whom
Some bright spirit lived, and did
That decaying robe consume
Which its lustre faintly hid,—
Here its ashes find a tomb,   5
But beneath this pyramid
Thou art not—if a thing divine
Like thee can die, thy funeral shrine
Is thy mother's grief and mine.

II

Where art thou, my gentle child? 10
Let me think thy spirit feeds,
With its life intense and mild,
The love of living leaves and weeds
Among these tombs and ruins wild;—
Let me think that through low seeds   15
Of sweet flowers and sunny grass
Into their hues and scents may pass
A portion——

TO WILLIAM SHELLEY

Thy little footsteps on the sands
Of a remote and lonely shore;
The twinkling of thine infant hands,
Where now the worm will feed no more;
Thy mingled look of love and glee   5
When we returned to gaze on thee—

TO MARY SHELLEY

My dearest Mary, wherefore hast thou gone,
And left me in this dreary world alone?
Thy form is here indeed,—a lovely one—
But thou art fled, gone down the dreary road,
That leads to Sorrow's most obscure abode;   5
Thou sittest on the hearth of pale despair,

Where

For thine own sake I cannot follow thee.

TO MARY SHELLEY

The world is dreary,
And I'm weary
Of wandering on without thee, Mary;
A joy was erewhile
In thy voice and thy smile,   5
And 'tis gone, when I should be gone too, Mary.

ON THE MEDUSA OF LEONARDO DA VINCI IN THE FLORENTINE GALLERY

I

It lieth, gazing on the midnight sky,
  Upon the cloudy mountain-peak supine;
Below, far lands are seen tremblingly;
  Its horror and its beauty are divine.
Upon its lips and eyelids seems to lie   5
  Loveliness like a shadow, from which shine,
Fiery and lurid, struggling underneath,
The agonies of anguish and of death.

II

Yet it is less the horror than the grace
  Which turns the gazer's spirit into stone,   10
Whereon the lineaments of that dead face
  Are graven, till the characters be grown
Into itself, and thought no more can trace;
  'Tis the melodious hue of beauty thrown   15
Athwart the darkness and the glare of pain,
Which humanize and harmonize the strain.

III

And from its head as from one body grow,
  As   grass out of a watery rock,
Hairs which are vipers, and they curl and flow
  And their long tangles in each other lock,   20
And with unending involutions show
  Their mailèd radiance, as it were to mock
The torture and the death within, and saw
The solid air with many a raggèd jaw.

IV

And, from a stone beside, a poisonous eft   25
  Peeps idly into those Gorgonian eyes;
Whilst in the air a ghastly bat, bereft
  Of sense, has flitted with a mad surprise
Out of the cave this hideous light had cleft,
  And he comes hastening like a moth that hies   30
After a taper; and the midnight sky
Flares, a light more dread than obscurity.

V

'Tis the tempestuous loveliness of terror;
  For from the serpents gleams a brazen glare
Kindled by that inextricable error,   35
  Which makes a thrilling vapour of the air
Become a   and ever-shifting mirror
  Of all the beauty and the terror there—
A woman's countenance, with serpent-locks,
Gazing in death on Heaven from those wet rocks.   40

LOVE'S PHILOSOPHY

I

THE fountains mingle with the
    river
And the rivers with the Ocean,
The winds of Heaven mix for ever
  With a sweet emotion;
Nothing in the world is single;   5
  All things by a law divine
In one spirit meet and mingle.
  Why not I with thine?—

II

See the mountains kiss high Heaven
  And the waves clasp one another;
No sister-flower would be for-
    given   11
  If it disdained its brother;
And the sunlight clasps the earth
  And the moonbeams kiss the sea:
What is all this sweet work worth
  If thou kiss not me?   16

FRAGMENT: 'FOLLOW TO THE DEEP WOOD'S WEEDS'

FOLLOW to the deep wood's weeds,
Follow to the wild-briar dingle,
Where we seek to intermingle,
And the violet tells her tale

To the odour-scented gale,   5
For they two have enough to
    do
Of such work as I and you.

THE BIRTH OF PLEASURE

AT the creation of the Earth
Pleasure, that divinest birth,
From the soil of Heaven did rise,
Wrapped in sweet wild melodies—
Like an exhalation wreathing   5
To the sound of air low-breathing
Through Aeolian pines, which make
A shade and shelter to the lake

Whence it rises soft and slow;
Her life-breathing [limbs] did
    flow   10
In the harmony divine
Of an ever-lengthening line
Which enwrapped her perfect form
With a beauty clear and warm.

FRAGMENT: LOVE THE UNIVERSE TO-DAY

AND who feels discord now or sorrow?
Love is the universe to-day—
These are the slaves of dim to-morrow,
Darkening Life's labyrinthine way.

FRAGMENT: 'A GENTLE STORY OF TWO LOVERS YOUNG'

A GENTLE story of two lovers young,
  Who met in innocence and died in sorrow,
And of one selfish heart, whose rancour clung
  Like curses on them; are ye slow to borrow
    The lore of truth from such a tale?   5
    Or in this world's deserted vale,
    Do ye not see a star of gladness
    Pierce the shadows of its sadness,—
  When ye are cold, that love is a light sent
From Heaven, which none shall quench, to cheer the innocent? 10

FRAGMENT: LOVE'S TENDER ATMOSPHERE

THERE is a warm and gentle atmosphere
  About the form of one we love, and thus
As in a tender mist our spirits are
    Wrapped in the   of that which is to us
The health of life's own life—   5

FRAGMENT: WEDDED SOULS

        I AM as a spirit who has dwelt
Within his heart of hearts, and I have felt
His feelings, and have thought his thoughts, and known
The inmost converse of his soul, the tone
Unheard but in the silence of his blood,   5
When all the pulses in their multitude
Image the trembling calm of summer seas.
I have unlocked the golden melodies
Of his deep soul, as with a master-key,
And loosened them and bathed myself therein—   10
Even as an eagle in a thunder-mist
Clothing his wings with lightning.

FRAGMENT: 'IS IT THAT IN SOME BRIGHTER SPHERE'

Is it that in some brighter sphere
We part from friends we meet with
  here?
Or do we see the Future pass
Over the Present's dusky glass?

Or what is that that makes us
  seem   5
To patch up fragments of a dream,
Part of which comes true, and part
Beats and trembles in the heart?

FRAGMENT: SUFFICIENT UNTO THE DAY

Is not to-day enough? Why do I peer
  Into the darkness of the day to come?
Is not to-morrow even as yesterday?
  And will the day that follows change thy doom?

Few flowers grow upon thy wintry way;   5
And who waits for thee in that cheerless home
Whence thou hast fled, whither thou must return
Charged with the load that makes thee faint and mourn?

FRAGMENT: 'YE GENTLE VISITATIONS OF CALM THOUGHT'

YE gentle visitations of calm thought—
    Moods like the memories of happier earth,
    Which come arrayed in thoughts of little worth,
Like stars in clouds by the weak winds enwrought,—
    But that the clouds depart and stars remain,   5
While they remain, and ye, alas, depart!

FRAGMENT: MUSIC AND SWEET POETRY

How sweet it is to sit and read the tales
    Of mighty poets and to hear the while
Sweet music, which when the attention fails
    Fills the dim pause——

FRAGMENT: THE SEPULCHRE OF MEMORY

AND where is truth? On tombs? for such to thee
Has been my heart—and thy dead memory
Has lain from childhood, many a changeful year,
Unchangingly preserved and buried there.

FRAGMENT: 'WHEN A LOVER CLASPS HIS FAIREST'

I

WHEN a lover clasps his fairest,
Then be our dread sport the rarest.
Their caresses were like the chaff
In the tempest, and be our laugh
His despair—her epitaph!   5

II

When a mother clasps her child,
Watch till dusty Death has piled
His cold ashes on the clay;
She has loved it many a day—
She remains,—it fades away.   10

FRAGMENT: 'WAKE THE SERPENT NOT'

WAKE the serpent not—lest he
Should not know the way to go,—
Let him crawl which yet lies sleeping
Through the deep grass of the meadow!
Not a bee shall hear him creeping,   5
Not a may-fly shall awaken
From its cradling blue-bell shaken,
Not the starlight as he's sliding
Through the grass with silent gliding.

FRAGMENT: RAIN

THE fitful alternations of the rain,
When the chill wind, languid as with pain
Of its own heavy moisture, here and there
Drives through the gray and beamless atmosphere.

FRAGMENT: A TALE UNTOLD

ONE sung of thee who left the tale untold,
  Like the false dawns which perish in the bursting;
Like empty cups of wrought and daedal gold,
  Which mock the lips with air, when they are thirsting.

FRAGMENT: TO ITALY

As the sunrise to the night,
  As the north wind to the clouds,
As the earthquake's fiery flight,
  Ruining mountain solitudes,
Everlasting Italy,   5
Be those hopes and fears on thee.

FRAGMENT: WINE OF THE FAIRIES

I AM drunk with the honey wine
Of the moon-unfolded eglantine,
Which fairies catch in hyacinth bowls.
The bats, the dormice, and the moles
Sleep in the walls or under the sward   5
Of the desolate castle yard;
And when 'tis split on the summer earth
  Or its fumes arise among the dew,
Their jocund dreams are full of mirth,
  They gibber their joy in sleep; for few   10
Of the fairies bear those bowls so new!

FRAGMENT: A ROMAN'S CHAMBER

I

In the cave which wild weeds cover
Wait for thine aethereal lover;
For the pallid moon is waning,
  O'er the spiral cypress hanging
And the moon no cloud is staining.   5

II

It was once a Roman's chamber,
  Where he kept his darkest revels,
And the wild weeds twine and clamber;
  It was then a chasm for devils.

FRAGMENT: ROME AND NATURE

ROME has fallen, ye see it lying
Heaped in undistinguished ruin:
Nature is alone undying.

VARIATION OF THE SONG OF THE MOON

(*Pometheus Unbound*, ACT IV.)

As a violet's gentle eye
Gazes on the azure sky
Until its hue grows like what it
    beholds;

As a gray and empty mist
Lies like solid amethyst   5
Over the western mountain it en-
    folds,

When the sunset sleeps
    Upon its snow;
As a strain of sweetest sound
Wraps itself the wind around   10

Until the voiceless wind be music
    too;
As aught dark, vain, and dull,
Basking in what is beautiful,
Is full of light and love—

CANCELLED STANZA OF THE MASK OF ANARCHY

(FOR WHICH STANZAS LXVIII, LXIX HAVE BEEN SUBSTITUTED.)

FROM the cities where from caves,
Like the dead from putrid graves,
Troops of starvelings gliding come,
Living Tenants of a tomb.

NOTE BY MRS. SHELLEY

SHELLEY loved the People; and respected them as often more virtuous, as always more suffering, and therefore more deserving of sympathy, than the great. He believed that a clash between the two classes of society was inevitable, and he eagerly ranged himself on the people's side. He had an idea of publishing a series of poems adapted expressly to commemorate their circumstances and wrongs. He wrote a few; but, in those days of prosecution for libel, they could not be printed. They are not among the best of his productions, a writer being always shackled when he endeavours to write down to the comprehension of those who could not understand or feel a highly imaginative style; but they show his earnestness, and with what heartfelt compassion he went home to the direct point of injury—that oppression is detestable as being the parent of starvation, nakedness, and ignorance. Besides these outpourings of compassion and indignation, he had meant to adorn the cause he loved with loftier poetry of glory and triumph: such is the scope of the *Ode to the Assertors of Liberty*. He sketched also a new version of our national anthem, as addressed to Liberty.

POEMS WRITTEN IN 1820

THE SENSITIVE PLANT

PART FIRST

A SENSITIVE Plant in a garden grew,
And the young winds fed it with silver dew,
And it opened its fan-like leaves to the light,
And closed them beneath the kisses of Night.

And the Spring arose on the garden fair,   5
Like the Spirit of Love felt everywhere;
And each flower and herb on Earth's dark breast
Rose from the dreams of its wintry rest.

But none ever trembled and panted with bliss
In the garden, the field, or the wilderness,   10
Like a doe in the noontide with love's sweet want.
As the companionless Sensitive Plant.

The snowdrop, and then the violet,
Arose from the ground with warm rain wet,
And their breath was mixed with fresh odour, sent   15
From the turf, like the voice and the instrument.

Then the pied wind-flowers and the tulip tall,
And narcissi, the fairest among them all,
Who gaze on their eyes in the stream's recess,
Till they die of their own dear loveliness;   20

And the Naiad-like lily of the vale,
Whom youth makes so fair and passion so pale
That the light of its tremulous bells is seen
Through their pavilions of tender green;

And the hyacinth purple, and white, and blue,   25
Which flung from its bells a sweet peal anew
Of music so delicate, soft, and intense,
It was felt like an odour within the sense;

And the rose like a nymph to the bath addressed,
Which unveiled the depth of her glowing breast,   30
Till, fold after fold, to the fainting air
The soul of her beauty and love lay bare:

And the wand-like lily, which lifted up,
As a Maenad its moonlight-coloured cup,
Till the fiery star, which is its eye,   35
Gazed through clear dew on the tender sky;

And the jessamine faint, and the sweet tuberose,
The sweetest flower for scent that blows;
And all rare blossoms from every clime
Grew in that garden in perfect prime.   40

And on the stream whose inconstant bosom
Was pranked, under boughs of embowering blossom,
With golden and green light, slanting through
Their heaven of many a tangled hue,

Broad water-lilies lay tremulously,   45
And starry river-buds glimmered by,
And around them the soft stream did glide and dance
With a motion of sweet sound and radiance.

And the sinuous paths of lawn and of moss,
Which led through the garden along and across,   50
Some open at once to the sun and the breeze,
Some lost among bowers of blossoming trees,

Were all paved with daisies and delicate bells
As fair as the fabulous asphodels,
And flow'rets which, drooping as day drooped too,   55
Fell into pavilions, white, purple, and blue,
To roof the glow-worm from the evening dew.

And from this undefilèd Paradise
The flowers (as an infant's awakening eyes
Smile on its mother, whose singing sweet   60
Can first lull, and at last must awaken it),

When Heaven's blithe winds had unfolded them,
As mine-lamps enkindle a hidden gem,
Shone smiling to Heaven, and every one
Shared joy in the light of the gentle sun;   65

For each one was interpenetrated
With the light and the odour its neighbour shed,
Like young lovers whom youth and love make dear
Wrapped and filled by their mutual atmosphere.

But the Sensitive Plant which could give small fruit   70
Of the love which it felt from the leaf to the root,
Received more than all, it loved more than ever,
Where none wanted but it, could belong to the giver,—

For the Sensitive Plant has no bright flower;
Radiance and odour are not its dower;   75
It loves, even like Love, its deep heart is full,
It desires what it has not, the Beautiful!

The light winds which from unsustaining wings
Shed the music of many murmurings;
The beams which dart from many a star   80
Of the flowers whose hues they bear afar;

The plumèd insects swift and free,
Like golden boats on a sunny sea,
Laden with light and odour, which pass
Over the gleam of the living grass;   85

The unseen clouds of the dew, which lie
Like fire in the flowers till the sun rides high,
Then wander like spirits among the spheres,
Each cloud faint with the fragrance it bears;

The quivering vapours of dim noontide,   90
Which like a sea o'er the warm earth glide,
In which every sound, and odour, and beam,
Move, as reeds in a single stream;

Each and all like ministering angels were
For the Sensitive Plant sweet joy to bear,   95
Whilst the lagging hours of the day went by
Like windless clouds o'er a tender sky.

And when evening descended from Heaven above,
And the Earth was all rest, and the air was all love,
And delight, though less bright, was far more deep,   100
And the day's veil fell from the world of sleep,

And the beasts, and the birds, and the insects were drowned
In an ocean of dreams without a sound;
Whose waves never mark, though they ever impress
The light sand which paves it, consciousness;   105

(Only overhead the sweet nightingale
Ever sang more sweet as the day might fail,
And snatches of its Elysian chant
Were mixed with the dreams of the Sensitive Plant);—

The Sensitive Plant was the earliest   110
Upgathered into the bosom of rest;
A sweet child weary of its delight,
The feeblest and yet the favourite,
Cradled within the embrace of Night.

Part Second

There was a Power in this sweet place,
An Eve in this Eden; a ruling Grace
Which to the flowers, did they waken or dream,
Was as God is to the starry scheme.

A Lady, the wonder of her kind,   5
Whose form was upborne by a lovely mind
Which, dilating, had moulded her mien and motion
Like a sea-flower unfolded beneath the ocean,

Tended the garden from morn to even:
And the meteors of that sublunar Heaven,   10
Like the lamps of the air when Night walks forth,
Laughed round her footsteps up from the Earth!

She had no companion of mortal race,
But her tremulous breath and her flushing face
Told, whilst the morn kissed the sleep from her eyes,   15
That her dreams were less slumber than Paradise:

As if some bright Spirit for her sweet sake
Had deserted Heaven while the stars were awake,
As if yet around her he lingering were,
Though the veil of daylight concealed him from her.   20

Her step seemed to pity the grass it pressed;
You might hear by the heaving of her breast,
That the coming and going of the wind
Brought pleasure there and left passion behind.

And wherever her aëry footstep trod,   25
Her trailing hair from the grassy sod
Erased its light vestige, with shadowy sweep,
Like a sunny storm o'er the dark green deep.

I doubt not the flowers of that garden sweet
Rejoiced in the sound of her gentle feet;   30
I doubt not they felt the spirit that came
From her glowing fingers through all their frame.

She sprinkled bright water from the stream
On those that were faint with the sunny beam;
And out of the cups of the heavy flowers   35
She emptied the rain of the thunder-showers.

She lifted their heads with her tender hands,
And sustained them with rods and osier-bands;
If the flowers had been her own infants, she
Could never have nursed them more tenderly.   40

And all killing insects and gnawing worms,
And things of obscene and unlovely forms,
She bore, in a basket of Indian woof,
Into the rough woods far aloof,—

In a basket, of grasses and wild-flowers full,   45
The freshest her gentle hands could pull
For the poor banished insects, whose intent,
Although they did ill, was innocent.

But the bee and the beamlike ephemeris
Whose path is the lightning's, and soft moths that kiss   50
The sweet lips of the flowers, and harm not, did she
Make her attendant angels be.

And many an antenatal tomb,
Where butterflies dream of the life to come,
She left clinging round the smooth and dark   55
Edge of the odorous cedar bark.

This fairest creature from earliest Spring
Thus moved through the garden ministering
All the sweet season of Summertide,
And ere the first leaf looked brown—she died!   60

PART THIRD

Three days the flowers of the garden fair,
Like stars when the moon is awakened, were,
Or the waves of Baiae, ere luminous
She floats up through the smoke of Vesuvius.

And on the fourth, the Sensitive Plant   5
Felt the sound of the funeral chant,
And the steps of the bearers, heavy and slow,
And the sobs of the mourners, deep and low;

The weary sound and the heavy breath,
And the silent motions of passing death,   10
And the smell, cold, oppressive, and dank,
Sent through the pores of the coffin-plank;

The dark grass, and the flowers among the grass,
Were bright with tears as the crowd did pass;
From their sighs the wind caught a mournful tone,   15
And sate in the pines, and gave groan for groan.

The garden, once fair, became cold and foul,
Like the corpse of her who had been its soul,
Which at first was lovely as if in sleep,
Then slowly changed, till it grew a heap   20
To make men tremble who never weep.

Swift Summer into the Autumn flowed,
And frost in the mist of the morning rode,
Though the noonday sun looked clear and bright,
Mocking the spoil of the secret night.   25

The rose-leaves, like flakes of crimson snow,
Paved the turf and the moss below.
The lilies were drooping, and white, and wan,
Like the head and the skin of a dying man.

And Indian plants, of scent and hue   30
The sweetest that ever were fed on dew,
Leaf by leaf, day after day,
Were massed into the common clay.

And the leaves, brown, yellow, and gray, and red,
And white with the whiteness of what is dead,   35
Like troops of ghosts on the dry wind passed;
Their whistling noise made the birds aghast.

And the gusty winds waked the wingèd seeds,
Out of their birthplace of ugly weeds,
Till they clung round many a sweet flower's stem,   40
Which rotted into the earth with them.

The water-blooms under the rivulet
Fell from the stalks on which they were set;
And the eddies drove them here and there,
As the winds did those of the upper air.   45

Then the rain came down, and the broken stalks
Were bent and tangled across the walks;
And the leafless network of parasite bowers
Massed into ruin; and all sweet flowers.

Between the time of the wind and the snow   50
All loathliest weeds began to grow,
Whose coarse leaves were splashed with many a speck,
Like the water-snake's belly and the toad's back.

And thistles, and nettles, and darnels rank,
And the dock, and henbane, and hemlock dank,   55
Stretched out its long and hollow shank,
And stifled the air till the dead wind stank.

And plants, at whose names the verse feels loath,
Filled the place with a monstrous undergrowth,
Prickly, and pulpous, and blistering, and blue,   60
Livid, and starred with a lurid dew.

And agarics, and fungi, with mildew and mould
Started like mist from the wet ground cold;
Pale, fleshy, as if the decaying dead
With a spirit of growth had been animated! 65

Spawn, weeds, and filth, a leprous scum,
Made the running rivulet thick and dumb,
And at its outlet flags huge as stakes
Dammed it up with roots knotted like water-snakes.

And hour by hour, when the air was still, 70
The vapours arose which have strength to kill,
At morn they were seen, at noon they were felt,
At night they were darkness no star could melt.

And unctuous meteors from spray to spray
Crept and flitted in broad noonday 75
Unseen; every branch on which they alit
By a venomous blight was burned and bit.

The Sensitive Plant, like one forbid,
Wept, and the tears within each lid
Of its folded leaves, which together grew, 80
Were changed to a blight of frozen glue.

For the leaves soon fell, and the branches soon
By the heavy axe of the blast were hewn;
The sap shrank to the root through every pore
As blood to a heart that will beat no more. 85

For Winter came: the wind was his whip:
One choppy finger was on his lip:
He had torn the cataracts from the hills
And they clanked at his girdle like manacles;

His breath was a chain which without a sound 90
The earth, and the air, and the water bound;
He came, fiercely driven, in his chariot-throne
By the tenfold blasts of the Arctic zone.

Then the weeds which were forms of living death
Fled from the frost to the earth beneath. 95
Their decay and sudden flight from frost
Was but like the vanishing of a ghost!

And under the roots of the Sensitive Plant
The moles and the dormice died for want:
The birds dropped stiff from the frozen air 100
And were caught in the branches naked and bare.

First there came down a thawing rain
And its dull drops froze on the boughs again;
Then there steamed up a freezing dew
Which to the drops of the thaw-rain grew;   105

And a northern whirlwind, wandering about
Like a wolf that had smelt a dead child out,
Shook the boughs thus laden, and heavy, and stiff,
And snapped them off with his rigid griff.

When Winter had gone and Spring came back   110
The Sensitive Plant was a leafless wreck;
But the mandrakes, and toadstools, and docks, and darnels,
Rose like the dead from their ruined charnels.

CONCLUSION

Whether the Sensitive Plant, or that
Which within its boughs like a Spirit sat,   115
Ere its outward form had known decay,
Now felt this change, I cannot say.

Whether that Lady's gentle mind,
No longer with the form combined
Which scattered love, as stars do light,   120
Found sadness, where it left delight,

I dare not guess; but in this life
Of error, ignorance, and strife,
Where nothing is, but all things seem,
And we the shadows of the dream,   125

It is a modest creed, and yet
Pleasant if one considers it,
To own that death itself must be,
Like all the rest, a mockery.

That garden sweet, that lady fair,   130
And all sweet shapes and odours there,
In truth have never passed away:
'Tis we, 'tis ours, are changed; not they.

For love, and beauty, and delight,
There is no death nor change: their might   135
Exceeds our organs, which endure
No light, being themselves obscure.

A VISION OF THE SEA

'Tis the terror of tempest. The rags of the sail
Are flickering in ribbons within the fierce gale:
From the stark night of vapours the dim rain is driven,
And when lightning is loosed, like a deluge from Heaven,

She sees the black trunks of the waterspouts spin   5
And bend, as if Heaven was ruining in,
Which they seemed to sustain with their terrible mass
As if ocean had sunk from beneath them: they pass
To their graves in the deep with an earthquake of sound,
And the waves and the thunders, made silent around,   10
Leave the wind to its echo. The vessel, now tossed
Through the low-trailing rack of the tempest, is lost
In the skirts of the thunder-cloud: now down the sweep
Of the wind-cloven wave to the chasm of the deep
It sinks, and the walls of the watery vale   15
Whose depths of dread calm are unmoved by the gale,
Dim mirrors of ruin, hang gleaming about;
While the surf, like a chaos of stars, like a rout
Of death-flames, like whirlpools of fire-flowing iron,
With splendour and terror the black ship environ,   20
Or like sulphur-flakes hurled from a mine of pale fire
In fountains spout o'er it. In many a spire
The pyramid-billows with white points of brine
In the cope of the lightning inconstantly shine,
As piercing the sky from the floor of the sea.   25
The great ship seems splitting! it cracks as a tree,
While an earthquake is splintering its root, ere the blast
Of the whirlwind that stripped it of branches has passed.
The intense thunder-balls which are raining from Heaven
Have shattered its mast, and it stands black and riven.   30
The chinks suck destruction. The heavy dead hulk
On the living sea rolls an inanimate bulk,
Like a corpse on the clay which is hungering to fold
Its corruption around it. Meanwhile, from the hold,
One deck is burst up by the waters below,   35
And it splits like the ice when the thaw-breezes blow
O'er the lakes of the desert! Who sit on the other?
Is that all the crew that lie burying each other,
Like the dead in a breach, round the foremast? Are those
Twin tigers, who burst, when the waters arose,   40
In the agony of terror, their chains in the hold;
(What now makes them tame, is what then made them bold;)
Who crouch, side by side, and have driven, like a crank,
The deep grip of their claws through the vibrating plank:—
Are these all? Nine weeks the tall vessel had lain   45
On the windless expanse of the watery plain,
Where the death-darting sun cast no shadow at noon,
And there seemed to be fire in the beams of the moon,
Till a lead-coloured fog gathered up from the deep,
Whose breath was quick pestilence; then, the cold sleep   50

Crept, like blight through the ears of a thick field of corn,
O'er the populous vessel. And even and morn,
With their hammocks for coffins the seamen aghast
Like dead men the dead limbs of their comrades cast
Down the deep, which closed on them above and around,   55
And the sharks and the dogfish their grave-clothes unbound,
And were glutted like Jews with this manna rained down
From God on their wilderness. One after one
The mariners died; on the eve of this day,
When the tempest was gathering in cloudy array,   60
But seven remained. Six the thunder has smitten,
And they lie black as mummies on which Time has written
His scorn of the embalmer; the seventh, from the deck
An oak-splinter pierced through his breast and his back,
And hung out to the tempest, a wreck on the wreck.   65
No more? At the helm sits a woman more fair
Than Heaven, when, unbinding its star-braided hair,
It sinks with the sun on the earth and the sea.
She clasps a bright child on her upgathered knee;
It laughs at the lightning, it mocks the mixed thunder   70
Of the air and the sea, with desire and with wonder
It is beckoning the tigers to rise and come near,
It would play with those eyes where the radiance of fear
Is outshining the meteors; its bosom beats high,
The heart-fire of pleasure has kindled its eye,   75
While its mother's is lustreless. 'Smile not, my child,
But sleep deeply and sweetly, and so be beguiled
Of the pang that awaits us, whatever that be,
So dreadful since thou must divide it with me!
Dream, sleep! This pale bosom, thy cradle and bed,   80
Will it rock thee not, infant? 'Tis beating with dread!
Alas! what is life, what is death, what are we,
That when the ship sinks we no longer may be?
What! to see thee no more, and to feel thee no more?
To be after life what we have been before?   85
Not to touch those sweet hands? Not to look on those eyes,
Those lips, and that hair,—all the smiling disguise
Thou yet wearest, sweet Spirit, which I, day by day,
Have so long called my child, but which now fades away
Like a rainbow, and I the fallen shower?'—Lo! the ship   90
Is settling, it topples, the leeward ports dip;
The tigers leap up when they feel the slow brine
Crawling inch by inch on them; hair, ears, limbs, and eyne,
Stand rigid with horror; a loud, long, hoarse cry
Bursts at once from their vitals tremendously,   95
And 'tis borne down the mountainous vale of the wave,
Rebounding, like thunder, from crag to cave,

Mixed with the clash of the lashing rain,
Hurried on by the might of the hurricane:
The hurricane came from the west, and passed on   100
By the path of the gate of the eastern sun,
Transversely dividing the stream of the storm;
As an arrowy serpent, pursuing the form
Of an elephant, bursts through the brakes of the waste.
Black as a cormorant the screaming blast,   105
Between Ocean and Heaven, like an ocean, passed,
Till it came to the clouds on the verge of the world
Which, based on the sea and to Heaven upcurled,
Like columns and walls did surround and sustain
The dome of the tempest; it rent them in twain,   110
As a flood rends its barriers of mountainous crag:
And the dense clouds in many a ruin and rag,
Like the stones of a temple ere earthquake has passed,
Like the dust of its fall, on the whirlwind are cast;
They are scattered like foam on the torrent; and where 115
The wind has burst out through the chasm, from the air
Of clear morning the beams of the sunrise flow in,
Unimpeded, keen, golden, and crystalline,
Banded armies of light and of air, at one gate
They encounter, but interpenetrate.   120
And that breach in the tempest is widening away,
And the caverns of cloud are torn up by the day,
And the fierce winds are sinking with weary wings,
Lulled by the motion and murmurings
And the long glassy heave of the rocking sea,   125
And overhead glorious, but dreadful to see,
The wrecks of the tempest, like vapours of gold,
Are consuming in sunrise. The heaped waves behold
The deep calm of blue Heaven dilating above,
And, like passions made still by the presence of Love, 130
Beneath the clear surface reflecting it slide
Tremulous with soft influence; extending its tide
From the Andes to Atlas, round mountain and isle,
Round sea-birds and wrecks, paved with Heaven's azure smile,
The wide world of waters is vibrating. Where   135
Is the ship? On the verge of the wave where it lay
One tiger is mingled in ghastly affray
With a sea-snake. The foam and the smoke of the battle
Stain the clear air with sunbows: the jar, and the rattle
Of solid bones crushed by the infinite stress   140
Of the snake's adamantine voluminousness;
And the hum of the hot blood that spouts and rains
Where the gripe of the tiger has wounded the veins
Swollen with rage, strength, and effort; the whirl and the splash

As of some hideous engine whose brazen teeth smash   145
The thin winds and soft waves into thunder; the screams
And hissings crawl fast o'er the smooth ocean-streams,
Each sound like a centipede. Near this commotion,
A blue shark is hanging within the blue ocean,
The fin-wingèd tomb of the victor. The other   150
Is winning his way from the fate of his brother
To his own with the speed of despair. Lo! a boat
Advances: twelve rowers with the impulse of thought
Urge on the keen keel,—the brine foams. At the stern
Three marksmen stand levelling. Hot bullets burn   155
In the breast of the tiger, which yet bears him on
To his refuge and ruin. One fragment alone,—
'Tis dwindling and sinking, 'tis now almost gone,—
Of the wreck of the vessel peers out of the sea.
With her left hand she grasps it impetuously.   160
With her right she sustains her fair infant. Death, Fear,
Love, Beauty, are mixed in the atmosphere,
Which trembles and burns with the fervour of dread
Around her wild eyes, her bright hand, and her head,
Like a meteor of light o'er the waters! her child   165
Is yet smiling, and playing, and murmuring; so smiled
The false deep ere the storm. Like a sister and brother
The child and the ocean still smile on each other,
Whilst——

THE CLOUD

I BRING fresh showers for the thirsting flowers,
     From the seas and the streams;
I bear light shade for the leaves when laid
     In their noonday dreams.
From my wings are shaken the dews that waken   5
     The sweet buds every one,
When rocked to rest on their mother's breast,
     As she dances about the sun.
I wield the flail of the lashing hail,
     And whiten the green plains under,   10
And then again I dissolve it in rain,
     And laugh as I pass in thunder.

I sift the snow on the mountains below,
     And their great pines groan aghast;
And all the night 'tis my pillow white,   15
     While I sleep in the arms of the blast.
Sublime on the towers of my skiey bowers,
     Lightning my pilot sits;
In a cavern under is fettered the thunder,
     It struggles and howls at fits;   20

Over earth and ocean, with gentle motion,
    This pilot is guiding me,
Lured by the love of the genii that move
    In the depths of the purple sea;
Over the rills, and the crags, and the hills,   25
    Over the lakes and the plains,
Wherever he dream, under mountain or stream,
    The Spirit he loves remains;
And I all the while bask in Heaven's blue smile,
    Whilst he is dissolving in rains.   30

The sanguine Sunrise, with his meteor eyes,
    And his burning plumes outspread,
Leaps on the back of my sailing rack,
    When the morning star shines dead;
As on the jag of a mountain crag,   35
    Which an earthquake rocks and swings,
An eagle alit one moment may sit
    In the light of its golden wings.
And when Sunset may breathe, from the lit sea beneath,
    Its ardours of rest and of love,   40
And the crimson pall of eve may fall
    From the depth of Heaven above,
With wings folded I rest, on mine aëry nest,
    As still as a brooding dove.

That orbèd maiden with white fire laden,   45
    Whom mortals call the Moon,
Glides glimmering o'er my fleece-like floor,
    By the midnight breezes strewn;
And wherever the beat of her unseen feet,
    Which only the angels hear,   50
May have broken the woof of my tent's thin roof,
    The stars peep behind her and peer;
And I laugh to see them whirl and flee,
    Like a swarm of golden bees,
When I widen the rent in my wind-built tent,   55
    Till the calm rivers, lakes, and seas,
Like strips of the sky fallen through me on high,
    Are each paved with the moon and these.

I bind the Sun's throne with a burning zone,
    And the Moon's with a girdle of pearl;   60
The volcanoes are dim, and the stars reel and swim,
    When the whirlwinds my banner unfurl.
From cape to cape, with a bridge-like shape,
    Over a torrent sea,
Sunbeam-proof, I hang like a roof,—   65
    The mountains its columns be.

The triumphal arch through which I march
    With hurricane, fire, and snow,
When the Powers of the air are chained to my chair,
    Is the million-coloured bow;   70
The sphere-fire above its soft colours wove,
    While the moist Earth was laughing below.

I am the daughter of Earth and Water,
    And the nursling of the Sky;
I pass through the pores of the ocean and shores;   75
    I change, but I cannot die.
For after the rain when with never a stain
    The pavilion of Heaven is bare,
And the winds and sunbeams with their convex gleams
    Build up the blue dome of air,   80
I silently laugh at my own cenotaph,
    And out of the caverns of rain,
Like a child from the womb, like a ghost from the tomb,
    I arise and unbuild it again.

TO A SKYLARK

HAIL to thee, blithe Spirit!
    Bird thou never wert,
That from Heaven, or near it,
    Pourest thy full heart
In profuse strains of unpremedi-
      tated art.   5

Higher still and higher
    From the earth thou springest
Like a cloud of fire;
    The blue deep thou wingest,
And singing still dost soar, and
      soaring ever singest.   10

In the golden lightning
    Of the sunken sun,
O'er which clouds are bright-
      'ning,
Thou dost float and run;
Like an unbodied joy whose race is
      just begun.   15

The pale purple even
    Melts around thy flight;
Like a star of Heaven,
    In the broad daylight
Thou art unseen, but yet I hear thy
      shrill delight,   20

Keen as are the arrows
    Of that silver sphere,
Whose intense lamp narrows
    In the white dawn clear
Until we hardly see—we feel that
      it is there.   25

All the earth and air
    With thy voice is loud,
As, when night is bare,
    From one lonely cloud
The moon rains out her beams, and
      Heaven is overflowed.   30

What thou art we know not;
    What is most like thee?
From rainbow clouds there flow
      not
    Drops so bright to see
As from thy presence showers a
      rain of melody.   35

Like a Poet hidden
    In the light of thought,
Singing hymns unbidden,
    Till the world is wrought
To sympathy with hopes and fears
      it heeded not: 40

Like a high-born maiden
In a palace-tower,
Soothing her love-laden
Soul in secret hour
With music sweet as love, which
    overflows her bower: 45

Like a glow-worm golden
In a dell of dew,
Scattering unbeholden
Its aëreal hue
Among the flowers and grass, which
    screen it from the view! 50

Like a rose embowered
In its own green leaves,
By warm winds deflowered,
Till the scent it gives
Makes faint with too much sweet
    those heavy-wingèd
    thieves:

Sound of vernal showers   56
On the twinkling grass,
Rain-awakened flowers,
All that ever was
Joyous, and clear, and fresh, thy
    music doth surpass: 60

Teach us, Sprite or Bird,
What sweet thoughts are
    thine:
I have never heard
Praise of love or wine
That panted forth a flood of rap-
    ture so divine.   65

Chorus Hymeneal,
Or triumphal chant,
Matched with thine would be all
But an empty vaunt,
A thing wherein we feel there is
    some hidden want.   70

What objects are the fountains
Of thy happy strain?

What fields, or waves, or moun-
    tains?
What shapes of sky or plain?
What love of thine own kind? what
    ignorance of pain?   75

With thy clear keen joyance
Languor cannot be:
Shadow of annoyance
Never came near thee:
Thou lovest—but ne'er knew love's
    sad satiety.   80

Waking or asleep,
Thou of death must deem
Things more true and deep
Than we mortals dream,
Or how could thy notes flow in such
    a crystal stream?   85

We look before and after,
And pine for what is not:
Our sincerest laughter
With some pain is fraught;
Our sweetest songs are those that
    tell of saddest thought.   90

Yet if we could scorn
Hate, and pride, and fear;
If we were things born
Not to shed a tear,
I know not how thy joy we ever
    should come near.   95

Better than all measures
Of delightful sound,
Better than all treasures
That in books are found,
Thy skill to poet were, thou scorner
    of the ground!   100

Teach me half the gladness
That thy brain must know,
Such harmonious madness
From my lips would flow
The world should listen then—as
    I am listening now.   105

ODE TO LIBERTY

Yet, Freedom, yet, thy banner, torn but flying,
Streams like a thunder-storm against the wind.—Byron.

I

A glorious people vibrated again
  The lightning of the nations: Liberty
From heart to heart, from tower to tower, o'er Spain,
  Scattering contagious fire into the sky,
Gleamed. My soul spurned the chains of its dismay,   5
    And in the rapid plumes of song
    Clothed itself, sublime and strong,
(As a young eagle soars the morning clouds among,)
  Hovering in verse o'er its accustomed prey;
    Till from its station in the Heaven of fame   10
  The Spirit's whirlwind rapped it, and the ray
  Of the remotest sphere of living flame
Which paves the void was from behind it flung,
  As foam from a ship's swiftness, when there came
A voice out of the deep: I will record the same.   15

II

The Sun and the serenest Moon sprang forth:
  The burning stars of the abyss were hurled
Into the depths of Heaven. The daedal earth,
  That island in the ocean of the world,
Hung in its cloud of all-sustaining air: 20
    But this divinest universe
    Was yet a chaos and a curse,
For thou wert not: but, power from worst producing worse,
  The spirit of the beasts was kindled there,
    And of the birds, and of the watery forms,   25
  And there was war among them, and despair
    Within them, raging without truce or terms:
The bosom of their violated nurse
  Groaned, for beasts warred on beasts, and worms on worms,
And men on men; each heart was as a hell of storms.   30

III

Man, the imperial shape, then multiplied
  His generations under the pavilion
Of the Sun's throne: palace and pyramid,
  Temple and prison, to many a swarming million
Were, as to mountain-wolves their ragged caves.   35
    This human living multitude
    Was savage, cunning, blind, and rude,
For thou wert not; but o'er the populous solitude,

Like one fierce cloud over a waste of waves,
　　Hung Tyranny; beneath, sate deified   40
The sister-pest, congregator of slaves;
　　Into the shadow of her pinions wide
Anarchs and priests, who feed on gold and blood
　　Till with the stain their inmost souls are dyed,
　　Drove the astonished herds of men from every side.   45

IV

The nodding promontories, and blue isles,
　　And cloud-like mountains, and dividuous waves
Of Greece, basked glorious in the open smiles
　　Of favouring Heaven: from their enchanted caves
Prophetic echoes flung dim melody.   50
　　　　On the unapprehensive wild
　　　　The vine, the corn, the olive mild,
Grew savage yet, to human use unreconciled;
　　And, like unfolded flowers beneath the sea,
　　　　Like the man's thought dark in the infant's brain,   55
　　Like aught that is which wraps what is to be,
　　　　Art's deathless dreams lay veiled by many a vein
Of Parian stone; and, yet a speechless child,
　　Verse murmured, and Philosophy did strain
　　Her lidless eyes for thee; when o'er the Aegean main   60

V

Athens arose: a city such as vision
　　Builds from the purple crags and silver towers
Of battlemented cloud, as in derision
　　Of kingliest masonry: the ocean-floors
Pave it; the evening sky pavilions it;   65
　　　　Its portals are inhabited
　　　　By thunder-zonèd winds, each head
Within its cloudy wings with sun-fire garlanded,—
　　A divine work! Athens, diviner yet,
　　　　Gleamed with its crest of columns, on the will   70
　　Of man, as on a mount of diamond, set;
　　　　For thou wert, and thine all-creative skill
Peopled, with forms that mock the eternal dead
　　In marble immortality, that hill
　　Which was thine earliest throne and latest oracle.   75

VI

Within the surface of Time's fleeting river
　　Its wrinkled image lies, as then it lay
Immovably unquiet, and for ever
　　It trembles, but it cannot pass away!

The voices of thy bards and sages thunder   80
    With an earth-awakening blast
    Through the caverns of the past:
(Religion veils her eyes; Oppression shrinks aghast:)
    A wingèd sound of joy, and love, and wonder,
      Which soars where Expectation never flew,   85
    Rending the veil of space and time asunder!
      One ocean feeds the clouds, and streams, and dew;
One Sun illumines Heaven; one Spirit vast
    With life and love makes chaos ever new,
    As Athens doth the world with thy delight renew.   90

VII

Then Rome was, and from thy deep bosom fairest,
  · Like a wolf-cub from a Cadmaean Maenad,[1]
She drew the milk of greatness, though thy dearest
    From that Elysian food was yet unweanèd;
And many a deed of terrible uprightness   95
    By thy sweet love was sanctified;
    And in thy smile, and by thy side,
Saintly Camillus lived, and firm Atilius died.
    But when tears stained thy robe of vestal whiteness,
      And gold profaned thy Capitolian throne,   100
    Thou didst desert, with spirit-wingèd lightness,
      The senate of the tyrants: they sunk prone
Slaves of one tyrant: Palatinus sighed
    Faint echoes of Ionian song; that tone
    Thou didst delay to hear, lamenting to disown.   105

VIII

From what Hyrcanian glen or frozen hill,
    Or piny promontory of the Arctic main,
Or utmost islet inaccessible,
    Didst thou lament the ruin of thy reign,
Teaching the woods and waves, and desert rocks,   110
    And every Naiad's ice-cold urn,
    To talk in echoes sad and stern
Of that sublimest lore which man had dared unlearn?
    For neither didst thou watch the wizard flocks
      Of the Scald's dreams, nor haunt the Druid's sleep. 115
What if the tears rained through thy shattered locks
    Were quickly dried? for thou didst groan, not weep,
When from its sea of death, to kill and burn,
    The Galilean serpent forth did creep,
    And made thy world an undistinguishable heap.   120

---

[1] See the *Bacchae* of Euripides.—[SHELLEY'S NOTE.]

IX

A thousand years the Earth cried, 'Where art thou?'
  And then the shadow of thy coming fell
On Saxon Alfred's olive-cinctured brow:
  And many a warrior-peopled citadel,
Like rocks which fire lifts out of the flat deep,   125
     Arose in sacred Italy,
     Frowning o'er the tempestuous sea
Of kings, and priests, and slaves, in tower-crowned majesty;
  That multitudinous anarchy did sweep
     And burst around their walls, like idle foam,   130
  Whilst from the human spirit's deepest deep
     Strange melody with love and awe struck dumb
Dissonant arms; and Art, which cannot die,
  With divine wand traced on our earthly home
  Fit imagery to pave Heaven's everlasting dome.   135

X

Thou huntress swifter than the Moon! thou terror
  Of the world's wolves! thou bearer of the quiver,
Whose sunlike shafts pierce tempest-wingèd Error,
  As light may pierce the clouds when they dissever
In the calm regions of the orient day!   140
     Luther caught thy wakening glance;
     Like lightning, from his leaden lance
Reflected, it dissolved the visions of the trance
  In which, as in a tomb, the nations lay;
     And England's prophets hailed thee as their queen,   145
  In songs whose music cannot pass away,
     Though it must flow forever: not unseen
Before the spirit-sighted countenance
  Of Milton didst thou pass, from the sad scene
  Beyond whose night he saw, with a dejected mien.   150

XI

The eager hours and unreluctant years
  As on a dawn-illumined mountain stood,
Trampling to silence their loud hopes and fears,
  Darkening each other with their multitude,
And cried aloud, 'Liberty!' Indignation   155
     Answered Pity from her cave;
     Death grew pale within the grave,
And Desolation howled to the destroyer, Save!
  When like Heaven's Sun girt by the exhalation
     Of its own glorious light, thou didst arise,   160
  Chasing thy foes from nation unto nation

    Like shadows: as if day had cloven the skies
At dreaming midnight o'er the western wave,
    Men started, staggering with a glad surprise,
    Under the lightnings of thine unfamiliar eyes.   165

XII

Thou Heaven of earth! what spells could pall thee then
    In ominous eclipse? a thousand years
Bred from the slime of deep Oppression's den,
    Dyed all thy liquid light with blood and tears,
Till thy sweet stars could weep the stain away;   170
        How like Bacchanals of blood
          Round France, the ghastly vintage, stood
Destruction's sceptred slaves, and Folly's mitred brood!
    When one, like them, but mightier far than they,
        The Anarch of thine own bewildered powers,   175
    Rose: armies mingled in obscure array,
        Like clouds with clouds, darkening the sacred bowers
Of serene Heaven. He, by the past pursued,
    Rests with those dead, but unforgotten hours,
    Whose ghosts scare victor kings in their ancestral towers.   180

XIII

England yet sleeps: was she not called of old?
    Spain calls her now, as with its thrilling thunder
Vesuvius wakens Aetna, and the cold
    Snow-crags by its reply are cloven in sunder:
O'er the lit waves every Aeolian isle   185
        From Pithecusa to Pelorus
          Howls, and leaps, and glares in chorus:
They cry, 'Be dim; ye lamps of Heaven suspended o'er us!'
    Her chains are threads of gold, she need but smile
        And they dissolve; but Spain's were links of steel,   190
    Till bit to dust by virtue's keenest file.
        Twins of a single destiny! appeal
To the eternal years enthroned before us
    In the dim West; impress us from a seal,
    All ye have thought and done! Time cannot dare conceal.   195

XIV

Tomb of Arminius! render up thy dead
    Till, like a standard from a watch-tower's staff,
His soul may stream over the tyrant's head;
    Thy victory shall be his epitaph,
Wild Bacchanal of truth's mysterious wine,   200
        King-deluded Germany,
        His dead spirit lives in thee.

Why do we fear or hope? thou art already free!
  And thou, lost Paradise of this divine
    And glorious world! thou flowery wilderness!   205
  Thou island of eternity! thou shrine
    Where Desolation, clothed with loveliness,
Worships the thing thou wert! O Italy,
  Gather thy blood into thy heart; repress
  The beasts who make their dens thy sacred palaces.   210

XV

Oh, that the free would stamp the impious name
  Of KING into the dust! or write it there,
So that this blot upon the page of fame
  Were as a serpent's path, which the light air
Erases, and the flat sands close behind!   215
    Ye the oracle have heard:
    Lift the victory-flashing sword,
And cut the snaky knots of this foul gordian word,
  Which, weak itself as stubble, yet can bind
    Into a mass, irrefragably firm,   220
  The axes and the rods which awe mankind;
    The sound has poison in it, 'tis the sperm
Of what makes life foul, cankerous, and abhorred;
  Disdain not thou, at thine appointed term,
  To set thine armèd heel on this reluctant worm.   225

XVI

Oh, that the wise from their bright minds would kindle
  Such lamps within the dome of this dim world,
That the pale name of PRIEST might shrink and dwindle
  Into the hell from which it first was hurled,
A scoff of impious pride from fiends impure;   230
    Till human thoughts might kneel alone,
    Each before the judgment-throne
Of its own aweless soul, or of the Power unknown!
  Oh, that the words which make the thoughts obscure
    From which they spring, as clouds of glimmering dew   235
From a white lake blot Heaven's blue portraiture,
  Were stripped of their thin masks and various hue
And frowns and smiles and splendours not their own,
  Till in the nakedness of false and true
  They stand before their Lord, each to receive its due!   240

XVII

He who taught man to vanquish whatsoever
  Can be between the cradle and the grave
Crowned him the King of Life. Oh, vain endeavour!
  If on his own high will, a willing slave,

He has enthroned the oppression and the oppressor.   245
     What if earth can clothe and feed
     Amplest millions at their need,
And power in thought be as the tree within the seed?
     Or what if Art, an ardent intercessor,
        Driving on fiery wings to Nature's throne,   250
     Checks the great mother stooping to caress her,
        And cries: 'Give me, thy child, dominion
Over all height and depth'? if Life can breed
     New wants, and wealth from those who toil and groan,
     Rend of thy gifts and hers a thousandfold for one!   255

XVIII

Come thou, but lead out of the inmost cave
Of man's deep spirit, as the morning-star
Beckons the Sun from the Eoan wave,
     Wisdom. I hear the pennons of her car
Self-moving, like cloud charioted by flame;   ·   260
        Comes she not, and come ye not,
        Rulers of eternal thought,
To judge, with solemn truth, life's ill-apportioned lot?
     Blind Love, and equal Justice, and the Fame
        Of what has been, the Hope of what will be?   265
     O Liberty! if such could be thy name
     Wert thou disjoined from these, or they from thee:
If thine or theirs were treasures to be bought
     By blood or tears, have not the wise and free
     Wept tears, and blood like tears?—The solemn harmony   270

XIX

Paused, and the Spirit of that mighty singing
     To its abyss was suddenly withdrawn;
Then, as a wild swan, when sublimely winging
     Its path athwart the thunder-smoke of dawn,
Sinks headlong through the aëreal golden light   275
        On the heavy-sounding plain,
        When the bolt has pierced its brain;
As summer clouds dissolve, unburthened of their rain;
     As a far taper fades with fading night,
        As a brief insect dies with dying day,—   280
     My song, its pinions disarrayed of might,
        Drooped; o'er it closed the echoes far away
Of the great voice which did its flight sustain,
     As waves which lately paved his watery way
     Hiss round a drowner's head in their tempestuous play.   285

TO ———

I

I FEAR thy kisses, gentle maiden,
   Thou needest not fear mine;
My spirit is too deeply laden
   Ever to burthen thine.

II

I fear thy mien, thy tones, thy motion,   5
   Thou needest not fear mine;
Innocent is the heart's devotion
   With which I worship thine.

ARETHUSA

I

ARETHUSA arose
   From her couch of snows
In the Acroceraunian mountains,—
   From cloud and from crag,
   With many a jag,   5
Shepherding her bright fountains.
   She leapt down the rocks,
   With her rainbow locks
Streaming among the streams;—
   Her steps paved with green   10
   The downward ravine
Which slopes to the western gleams;
   And gliding and springing
   She went, ever singing,
In murmurs as soft as sleep;   15
   The Earth seemed to love her,
   And Heaven smiled above her,
As she lingered towards the deep.

II

Then Alpheus bold
   On his glacier cold,   20
With his trident the mountains strook;
   And opened a chasm
   In the rocks—with the spasm
All Erymanthus shook.
   And the black south wind   25
   It unsealed behind
The urns of the silent snow,

And earthquake and thunder
   Did rend in sunder
The bars of the springs below.   30
   And the beard and the hair
   Of the River-god were
Seen through the torrent's sweep,
   As he followed the light
   Of the fleet nymph's flight   35
To the brink of the Dorian deep.

III

'Oh, save me! Oh, guide me!
   And bid the deep hide me,
For he grasps me now by the hair!'
   The loud Ocean heard,   40
   To its blue depth stirred,
And divided at her prayer;
   And under the water
   The earth's white daughter
Fled like a sunny beam;   45
   Behind her descended
   Her billows, unblended
With the brackish Dorian stream:—
   Like a gloomy stain
   On the emerald main   50
Alpheus rushed behind,—
   As an eagle pursuing
   A dove to its ruin
Down the streams of the cloudy wind.

IV

Under the bowers   55
Where the Ocean Powers
Sit on their pearlèd thrones;
    Through the coral woods,
    Of the weltering floods,
Over heaps of unvalued stones; 60
    Through the dim beams
    Which amid the streams
Weave a network of coloured
        light;
    And under the caves,
    Where the shadowy waves   65
Are as green as the forest's night:—
    Outspeeding the shark,
    And the sword-fish dark,
Under the Ocean's foam,
    And up through the rifts   70
    Of the mountain clifts
They passed to their Dorian home.

V

And now from their fountains
    In Enna's mountains,
Down one vale where the morning
        basks,   75
    Like friends once parted
    Grown single-hearted,
They ply their watery tasks.
    At sunrise they leap
    From their cradles steep   80
In the cave of the shelving hill;
    At noontide they flow
    Through the woods below
And the meadows of asphodel;
    And at night they sleep   85
    In the rocking deep
Beneath the Ortygian shore;—
    Like spirits that lie
    In the azure sky
When they love but live no more. 90

SONG OF PROSERPINE

WHILE GATHERING FLOWERS ON THE PLAIN OF ENNA

I

SACRED Goddess, Mother Earth,
    Thou from whose immortal bosom
Gods, and men, and beasts have birth,
    Leaf and blade, and bud and blossom,
Breathe thine influence most divine   5
On thine own child, Proserpine.

II

If with mists of evening dew
    Thou dost nourish these young flowers
Till they grow, in scent and hue,
    Fairest children of the Hours,
Breathe thine influence most divine   10
On thine own child, Proserpine.

HYMN OF APOLLO

I

THE sleepless Hours who watch me as I lie,
    Curtained with star-inwoven tapestries
From the broad moonlight of the sky,
    Fanning the busy dreams from my dim eyes,—

Waken me when their Mother, the gray Dawn,   5
Tells them that dreams and that the moon is gone.

II

Then I arise, and climbing Heaven's blue dome,
   I walk over the mountains and the waves,
Leaving my robe upon the ocean foam;
   My footsteps pave the clouds with fire; the caves   .   10
Are filled with my bright presence, and the air
Leaves the green Earth to my embraces bare.

III

The sunbeams are my shafts, with which I kill
   Deceit, that loves the night and fears the day;
All men who do or even imagine ill   15
   Fly me, and from the glory of my ray
Good minds and open actions take new might,
Until diminished by the reign of Night.   .

IV

I feed the clouds, the rainbows and the flowers
   With their aethereal colours; the moon's globe   20
And the pure stars in their eternal bowers
   Are cinctured with my power as with a robe;
Whatever lamps on Earth or Heaven may shine
Are portions of one power, which is mine.

V

I stand at noon upon the peak of Heaven,   25
   Then with unwilling steps I wander down
Into the clouds of the Atlantic even;
   For grief that I depart they weep and frown:
What look is more delightful than the smile
With which I soothe them from the western isle?   30

VI

I am the eye with which the Universe
   Beholds itself and knows itself divine;
All harmony of instrument or verse,
   All prophecy, all medicine is mine,
All light of art or nature;—to my song   35
Victory and praise in its own right belong.

HYMN OF PAN

I

FROM the forests and highlands
  We come, we come;
From the river-girt islands,
  Where loud waves are dumb
    Listening to my sweet pipings.
The wind in the reeds and the
  rushes,   6
  The bees on the bells of thyme,
The birds on the myrtle bushes,
  The cicale above in the lime,
And the lizards below in the grass,
Were as silent as ever old Timolus
  was,   11
    Listening to my sweet pipings.

II

Liquid Peneus was flowing,
  And all dark Tempe lay
In Pelion's shadow, outgrowing   15
  The light of the dying day,
    Speeded by my sweet pipings.
The Sileni, and Sylvans, and
  Fauns,
  And the Nymphs of the woods
    and the waves,
To the edge of the moist river-
  lawns,   20
And the brink of the dewy caves,

And all that did then attend and
  follow,
Were silent with love, as you now,
  Apollo,
    With envy of my sweet pip-
      ings.

III

I sang of the dancing stars,   25
  I sang of the daedal Earth,
And of Heaven—and the giant
  wars,
  And Love, and Death, and
    Birth,—
    And then I changed my pip-
      ings,—
Singing how down the vale of Mae-
  nalus   30
  I pursued a maiden and clasped
    a reed.
Gods and men, we are all deluded
  thus!
  It breaks in our bosom and then
    we bleed:
All wept, as I think both ye now
  would,
If envy or age had not frozen your
  blood,
    At the sorrow of my sweet
      pipings.

THE QUESTION

I

I DREAMED that, as I wandered by the way,
  Bare Winter suddenly was changed to Spring,
And gentle odours led my steps astray,
  Mixed with a sound of waters murmuring
Along a shelving bank of turf, which lay   5
  Under a copse, and hardly dared to fling
Its green arms round the bosom of the stream,
But kissed it and then fled, as thou mightest in dream.

II

There grew pied wind-flowers and violets,
    Daisies, those pearled Arcturi of the earth,   10
The constellated flower that never sets;
    Faint oxslips; tender bluebells, at whose birth
The sod scarce heaved; and that tall flower that wets —
    Like a child, half in tenderness and mirth—
Its mother's face with Heaven's collected tears,   15
When the low wind, its playmate's voice, it hears.

III

And in the warm hedge grew lush eglantine,
    Green cowbind and the moonlight-coloured may,
And cherry-blossoms, and white cups, whose wine
    Was the bright dew, yet drained not by the day;   20
And wild roses, and ivy serpentine,
    With its dark buds and leaves, wandering astray;
And flowers azure, black, and streaked with gold,
Fairer than any wakened eyes behold.

IV

And nearer to the river's trembling edge   25
    There grew broad flag-flowers, purple pranked with white,
And starry river buds among the sedge,
    And floating water-lilies, broad and bright,
Which lit the oak that overhung the hedge
    With moonlight beams of their own watery light;   30
And bulrushes, and reeds of such deep green
As soothed the dazzled eye with sober sheen.

V

Methought that of these visionary flowers
    I made a nosegay, bound in such a way
That the same hues, which in their natural bowers   35
    Were mingled or opposed, the like array
Kept these imprisoned children of the Hours
    Within my hand,—and then, elate and gay,
I hastened to the spot whence I had come,
That I might there present it!—Oh! to whom?   40

THE TWO SPIRITS: AN ALLEGORY

First Spirit.

O THOU, who plumed with strong desire
    Wouldst float above the earth, beware!
A Shadow tracks thy flight of fire—
    Night is coming!

Bright are the regions of the air,
And among the winds and beams
It were delight to wander there—
    Night is coming!

Second Spirit.

The deathless stars are bright above;
    If I would cross the shade of night,   10
Within my heart is the lamp of love,
    And that is day!
And the moon will smile with gentle light
On my golden plumes where'er they move;
    The meteors will linger round my flight,   15
    And make night day.

First Spirit.

But if the whirlwinds of darkness waken
    Hail, and lightning, and stormy rain;
See, the bounds of the air are shaken—
    Night is coming!   20
The red swift clouds of the hurricane
Yon declining sun have overtaken,
    The clash of the hail sweeps over the plain—
    Night is coming!

Second Spirit.

I see the light, and I hear the sound;   25
    I'll sail on the flood of the tempest dark,
With the calm within and the light around
    Which makes night day:
And thou, when the gloom is deep and stark,
Look from thy dull earth, slumber-bound,   30
    My moon-like flight thou then mayst mark
    On high, far away.

Some say there is a precipice
    Where one vast pine is frozen to ruin
O'er piles of snow and chasms of ice   35
    Mid Alpine mountains;
And that the languid storm pursuing
That wingèd shape, for ever flies
    Round those hoar branches, aye renewing
    Its aëry fountains.   40

Some say when nights are dry and clear,
    And the death-dews sleep on the morass,
Sweet whispers are heard by the traveller,

Which make night day:
And a silver shape like his early love doth pass   45
Upborne by her wild and glittering hair,
And when he awakes on the fragrant grass,
He finds night day.

ODE TO NAPLES [1]

EPODE I α

I STOOD within the City disinterred; [2]
And heard the autumnal leaves like light footfalls
Of spirits passing through the streets; and heard
The Mountain's slumberous voice at intervals
Thrill through those roofless halls;   5
The oracular thunder penetrating shook
The listening soul in my suspended blood;
I felt that Earth out of her deep heart spoke—
I felt, but heard not:—through white columns glowed
The isle-sustaining ocean-flood,   10
A plane of light between two heavens of azure!
Around me gleamed many a bright sepulchre
Of whose pure beauty, Time, as if his pleasure
Were to spare Death, had never made erasure;
But every living lineament was clear   15
As in the sculptor's thought; and there
The wreaths of stony myrtle, ivy, and pine,
Like winter leaves o'ergrown by moulded snow,
Seemed only not to move and grow
Because the crystal silence of the air   20
Weighed on their life; even as the Power divine
Which then lulled all things, brooded upon mine.

EPODE II α

Then gentle winds arose
With many a mingled close
Of wild Aeolian sound, and mountain-odours keen;   25
And where the Baian ocean
Welters with airlike motion,
Within, above, around its bowers of starry green,
Moving the sea-flowers in those purple caves,
Even as the ever stormless atmosphere   30

[1] The Author has connected many recollections of his visit to Pompeii and Baiae with the enthusiasm excited by the intelligence of the proclamation of a Constitutional Government at Naples. This has given a tinge of picturesque and descriptive imagery to the introductory Epodes which depicture these scenes, and some of the majestic feelings permanently connected with the scene of this animating event.—[SHELLEY'S NOTE.]

[2] Pompeii.—[SHELLEY'S NOTE.]

Floats o'er the Elysian realm.
It bore me, like an Angel, o'er the waves
  Of sunlight, whose swift pinnace of dewy air
  No storm can overwhelm.
  I sailed, where ever flows   35
  Under the calm Serene
  A spirit of deep emotion
  From the unknown graves
  Of the dead Kings of Melody.[1]
Shadowy Aornos darkened o'er the helm   40
The horizontal aether; Heaven stripped bare
Its depth over Elysium, where the prow
Made the invisible water white as snow;
From that Typhaean mount, Inarime,
  There streamed a sunbright vapour, like the standard   45
    Of some aethereal host;
    Whilst from all the coast,
  Louder and louder, gathering round, there wandered
Over the oracular woods and divine sea
Prophesyings which grew articulate—   50
They seize me—I must speak them!—be they fate!

STROPHE I

Naples! thou Heart of men which ever pantest
  Naked, beneath the lidless eye of Heaven!
Elysian City, which to calm enchantest
  The mutinous air and sea! they round thee, even   55
  As sleep round Love, are driven!
Metropolis of a ruined Paradise
  Long lost, late won, and yet but half regained!
Bright Altar of the bloodless sacrifice,
  Which armèd Victory offers up unstained   60
  To Love, the flower-enchained!
Thou which wert once, and then didst cease to be,
Now art, and henceforth ever shalt be, free,
  If Hope, and Truth, and Justice can avail,
    Hail, hail, all hail!   65

STROPHE II

Thou youngest giant birth
Which from the groaning earth
Leap'st, clothed in armour of impenetrable scale!
  Last of the Intercessors!
  Who 'gainst the Crowned Transgressors   70
Pleadest before God's love! Arrayed in Wisdom's mail,
  Wave thy lightning lance in mirth

[1] Homer and Virgil.—[SHELLEY'S NOTE.]

Nor let thy high heart fail,
Though from their hundred gates the leagued Oppressors
    With hurried legions move!   75
    Hail, hail, all hail!

ANTISTROPHE I α

What though Cimmerian Anarchs dare blaspheme
    Freedom and thee? thy shield is as a mirror
To make their blind slaves see, and with fierce gleam
    To turn his hungry sword upon the wearer;   80
    A new Actæon's error
Shall theirs have been—devoured by their own hounds!
    Be thou like the imperial Basilisk
Killing thy foe with unapparent wounds!
    Gaze on Oppression, till at that dread risk   85
    Aghast she pass from the Earth's disk:
Fear not, but gaze—for freemen mightier grow,
And slaves more feeble, gazing on their foe:—
    If Hope, and Truth, and Justice may avail,
    Thou shalt be great—All hail!   90

ANTISTROPHE II α

    From Freedom's form divine,
    From Nature's inmost shrine,
Strip every impious gawd, rend Error veil by veil;
    O'er Ruin desolate,
    O'er Falsehood's fallen state,   95
Sit thou sublime, unawed; be the Destroyer pale!
    And equal laws be thine,
    And wingèd words let sail,
Freighted with truth even from the throne of God:
    That wealth, surviving fate,   100
    Be thine.—All hail!

ANTISTROPHE I β

Didst thou not start to hear Spain's thrilling paean
    From land to land re-echoed solemnly,
Till silence became music? From the Aeaean [1]
    To the cold Alps, eternal Italy   105
    Starts to hear thine! The Sea
Which paves the desert streets of Venice laughs
    In light and music; widowed Genoa wan
By moonlight spells ancestral epitaphs,
    Murmuring, 'Where is Doria?' fair Milan,   110
    Within whose veins long ran

[1] Aeaea, the island of Circe.—[Shelley's Note.]

The viper's [1] palsying venom, lifts her heel
To bruise his head. The signal and the seal
  (If Hope and Truth and Justice can avail)
  Art thou of all these hopes.—O hail!   115

ANTISTROPHE II β

    Florence! beneath the sun,
    Of cities fairest one,
Blushes within her bower for Freedom's expectation:
    From eyes of quenchless hope
    Rome tears the priestly cope,   120
As ruling once by power, so now by admiration,—
    An athlete stripped to run
    From a remoter station
For the high prize lost on Philippi's shore:—
  As then Hope, Truth, and Justice did avail,   125
  So now may Fraud and Wrong! O hail!

EPODE I β

Hear ye the march as of the Earth-born Forms
  Arrayed against the ever-living Gods?
The crash and darkness of a thousand storms
    Bursting their inaccessible abodes   130
    Of crags and thunder-clouds?
See ye the banners blazoned to the day,
    Inwrought with emblems of barbaric pride?
Dissonant threats kill Silence far away,
    The serene Heaven which wraps our Eden wide   135
    With iron light is dyed;
The Anarchs of the North lead forth their legions
    Like Chaos o'er creation, uncreating;
An hundred tribes nourished on strange religions
And lawless slaveries,—down the aëreal regions   140
    Of the white Alps, desolating,
    Famished wolves that bide no waiting,
Blotting the glowing footsteps of old glory,
Trampling our columned cities into dust,
    Their dull and savage lust   145
    On Beauty's corse to sickness satiating—
They come! The fields they tread look black and hoary
With fire—from their red feet the streams run gory!

EPODE II β

    Great Spirit, deepest Love!
    Which rulest and dost move   150

[1] The viper was the armorial device of the Visconti, tyrants of Milan.—[SHELLEY'S NOTE.]

All things which live and are, within the Italian shore;
 Who spreadest Heaven around it,
 Whose woods, rocks, waves, surround it;
Who sittest in thy star, o'er Ocean's western floor;
Spirit of beauty! at whose soft command   155
 The sunbeams and the showers distil its foison
  From the Earth's bosom chill;
Oh, bid those beams be each a blinding brand
 Of lightning! bid those showers be dews of poison!
  Bid the Earth's plenty kill!   160
  Bid thy bright Heaven above,
  Whilst light and darkness bound it,
  Be their tomb who planned
  To make it ours and thine!
Or, with thine harmonizing ardours fill   165
And raise thy sons, as o'er the prone horizon
Thy lamp feeds every twilight wave with fire—
Be man's high hope and unextinct desire
The instrument to work thy will divine!
 Then clouds from sunbeams, antelopes from leopards, 170
  And frowns and fears from thee,
  Would not more swiftly flee
Than Celtic wolves from the Ausonian shepherds.—
Whatever, Spirit, from thy starry shrine
 Thou yieldest or withholdest, oh, let be   175
 This city of thy worship ever free!

AUTUMN: A DIRGE

I

THE warm sun is failing, the bleak wind is wailing,
The bare boughs are sighing, the pale flowers are dying,
   And the Year
On the earth her death-bed, in a shroud of leaves dead,
   Is lying.   5
   Come, Months, come away,
   From November to May,
   In your saddest array;
   Follow the bier
   Of the dead cold Year,   10
And like dim shadows watch by her sepulchre.

II

The chill rain is falling, the nipped worm is crawling,
The rivers are swelling, the thunder is knelling
   For the Year;
The blithe swallows are flown, and the lizards each gone 15

To his dwelling;
Come, Months, come away;
Put on white, black, and gray;
Let your light sisters play—
Ye, follow the bier   20
Of the dead cold Year,
And make her grave green with tear on tear.

THE WANING MOON

AND like a dying lady, lean and pale,
Who totters forth, wrapped in a gauzy veil,
Out of her chamber, led by the insane
And feeble wanderings of her fading brain,
The moon arose up in the murky East,   5
A white and shapeless mass—

TO THE MOON

I

ART thou pale for weariness
Of climbing heaven and gazing on the earth,
Wandering companionless
Among the stars that have a different birth,—
And ever changing, like a joyless eye   5
That finds no object worth its constancy?

II

Thou chosen sister of the Spirit,
That gazes on thee till in thee it pities . . .

DEATH

I

DEATH is here and death is there,
Death is busy everywhere,
All around, within, beneath,
Above is death—and we are death.

II

Death has set his mark and
    seal   5
On all we are and all we feel,
On all we know and all we fear,

            .   .   .

III

First our pleasures die—and then
Our hopes, and then our fears—
    and when
These are dead, the debt is due, 10
Dust claims dust—and we die too.

IV

All things that we love and cherish,
Like ourselves must fade and per-
    ish;
Such is our rude mortal lot—
Love itself would, did they not. 15

LIBERTY

I

THE fiery mountains answer each other;
  Their thunderings are echoed from zone to zone;
The tempestuous oceans awake one another,
  And the ice-rocks are shaken round Winter's throne,
    When the clarion of the Typhoon is blown.   5

II

From a single cloud the lightening flashes,
  Whilst a thousand isles are illumined around,
Earthquake is trampling one city to ashes,
  An hundred are shuddering and tottering; the sound
    Is bellowing underground.   10

III

But keener thy gaze than the lightening's glare,
  And swifter thy step than the earthquake's tramp;
Thou deafenest the rage of the ocean; thy stare
  Makes blind the volcanoes; the sun's bright lamp
    To thine is a fen-fire damp.   15

IV

From billow and mountain and exhalation
  The sunlight is darted through vapour and blast;
From spirit to spirit, from nation to nation,
  From city to hamlet thy dawning is cast,—
And tyrants and slaves are like shadows of night   20
  In the van of the morning light.

SUMMER AND WINTER

IT was a bright and cheerful afternoon,
Towards the end of the sunny month of June,
When the north wind congregates in crowds
The floating mountains of the silver clouds
From the horizon—and the stainless sky   5
Opens beyond them like eternity.
All things rejoiced beneath the sun; the weeds,
The river, and the corn-fields, and the reeds;
The willow leaves that glanced in the light breeze,
And the firm foliage of the larger trees.   10

It was a winter such as when birds die
In the deep forests; and the fishes lie

Stiffened in the translucent ice, which makes
Even the mud and slime of the warm lakes
A wrinkled clod as hard as brick; and when, 15
Among their children, comfortable men
Gather about great fires, and yet feel cold:
Alas, then, for the homeless beggar old!

THE TOWER OF FAMINE

AMID the desolation of a city,
Which was the cradle, and is now the grave
Of an extinguished people,—so that Pity

Weeps o'er the shipwrecks of Oblivion's wave,
There stands the Tower of Famine. It is built 5
Upon some prison-homes, whose dwellers rave

For bread, and gold, and blood: Pain, linked to Guilt,
Agitates the light flame of their hours,
Until its vital oil is spent or spilt.

There stands the pile, a tower amid the towers 10
And sacred domes; each marble-ribbèd roof,
The brazen-gated temples, and the bowers

Of solitary wealth,—the tempest-proof
Pavilions of the dark Italian air,—
Are by its presence dimmed—they stand aloof, 15

And are withdrawn—so that the world is bare;
As if a spectre wrapped in shapeless terror
Amid a company of ladies fair

Should glide and glow, till it became a mirror
Of all their beauty, and their hair and hue, 20
The life of their sweet eyes, with all its error,
Should be absorbed, till they to marble grew.

AN ALLEGORY

I

A PORTAL as of shadowy adamant
    Stands yawning on the highway of the life
Which we all tread, a cavern huge and gaunt;
    Around it rages an unceasing strife
Of shadows, like the restless clouds that haunt 5
The gap of some cleft mountain, lifted high
Into the whirlwinds of the upper sky.

II

And many pass it by with careless tread,
   Not knowing that a shadowy . . .
Tracks every traveller even to where the dead   10
   Wait peacefully for their companion new;
But others, by more curious humour led,
   Pause to examine;—these are very few,
And they learn little there, except to know
That shadows follow them where'er they go.   15

THE WORLD'S WANDERERS

I

Tell me, thou Star, whose wings of light
Speed thee in thy fiery flight,
In what cavern of the night
      Will thy pinions close now?

II

Tell me, Moon, thou pale and gray   5
Pilgrim of Heaven's homeless way,
In what depth of night or day
      Seekest thou repose now?

III

Weary Wind, who wanderest
Like the world's rejected guest,   10
Hast thou still some secret nest
      On the tree or billow?

SONNET

Ye hasten to the grave! What seek ye there,
Ye restless thoughts and busy purposes
Of the idle brain, which the world's livery wear?
O thou quick heart, which pantest to possess
All that pale Expectation feigneth fair!   5
Thou vainly curious mind which wouldest guess
Whence thou didst come, and whither thou must go,
And all that never yet was known would know—
Oh, whither hasten ye, that thus ye press,
With such swift feet life's green and pleasant path,   10
Seeking, alike from happiness and woe,
A refuge in the cavern of gray death?
O heart, and mind, and thoughts! what thing do you
Hope to inherit in the grave below?

LINES TO A REVIEWER

ALAS, good friend, what profit can you see
In hating such a hateless thing as me?
There is no sport in hate where all the rage
Is on one side: in vain would you assuage
Your frowns upon an unresisting smile,   5
In which not even contempt lurks to beguile
Your heart, by some fain sympathy of hate.
Oh, conquer what you cannot satiate!
For to your passion I am far more coy
Than ever yet was coldest maid or boy   10
In winter noon. Of your antipathy
If I am the Narcissus, you are free
To pine into a sound with hating me.

FRAGMENT OF A SATIRE ON SATIRE

IF gibbets, axes, confiscations, chains,
And racks of subtle torture, if the pains
Of shame, of fiery Hell's tempestuous wave,
Seen through the caverns of the shadowy grave,
Hurling the damned into the murky air   5
While the meek blest sit smiling; if Despair
And Hate, the rapid bloodhounds with which Terror
Hunts through the world the homeless steps of Error,
Are the true secrets of the commonweal
To make men wise and just; ...   10
And not the sophisms of revenge and fear,
Bloodier than is revenge ...
Then send the priests to every hearth and home
To preach the burning wrath which is to come,
In words like flakes of sulphur, such as thaw   15
The frozen tears ...
If Satire's scourge could wake the slumbering hounds
Of Conscience, or erase the deeper wounds,
The leprous scars of callous Infamy;
If it could make the present not to be,   20
Or charm the dark past never to have been,
Or turn regret to hope; who that has seen
What Southey is and was, would not exclaim,
'Lash on!'   be the keen verse dipped in flame;
Follow his flight with wingèd words, and urge   25
The strokes of the inexorable scourge
Until the heart be naked, till his soul
See the contagion's spots   foul;
And from the mirror of Truth's sunlike shield,

From which his Parthian arrow...   30
Flash on his sight the spectres of the past,
Until his mind's eye paint thereon—
Let scorn like   yawn below,
And rain on him like flakes of fiery snow.
This cannot be, it ought not, evil still—   35
Suffering makes suffering, ill must follow ill.
Rough words beget sad thoughts,   and, beside,
Men take a sullen and a stupid pride
In being all they hate in others' shame,
By a perverse antipathy of fame.   40
'Tis not worth while to prove, as I could, how
From the sweet fountains of our Nature flow
These bitter waters; I will only say,
If any friend would take Southey some day,
And tell him, in a country walk alone,   45
Softening harsh words with friendship's gentle tone,
How incorrect his public conduct is,
And what men think of it, 'twere not amiss.
Far better than to make innocent ink—

GOOD-NIGHT

I

Good-night? ah! no; the hour is ill
    Which severs those it should unite;
Let us remain together still,
    Then it will be *good* night.

II

How can I call the lone night good,   5
    Though thy sweet wishes wing its flight?
Be it not said, thought, understood—
    Then it will be—*good* night.

III

To hearts which near each other move
    From evening close to morning light,   10
The night is good; because, my love,
    They never *say* good-night.

BUONA NOTTE

I

'Buona notte, buona notte!'—Come mai
    La notte sarà buona senza te?
Non dirmi buona notte,—chè tu sai,
    La notte sà star buona da per sè.

II

Solinga, scura, cupa, senza speme,   5
    La notte quando Lilla m'abbandona;
Pei cuori chi si batton insieme
    Ogni notte, senza dirla, sarà buona.

III

Come male buona notte si suona
    Con sospiri e parole interrotte!—   10
Il modo di aver la notte buona
    E mai non di dir la buona notte.

ORPHEUS

A.   Not far from hence. From yonder pointed hill,
Crowned with a ring of oaks, you may behold
A dark and barren field, through which there flows,
Sluggish and black, a deep but narrow stream,
Which the wind ripples not, and the fair moon   5
Gazes in vain, and finds no mirror there.
Follow the herbless banks of that strange brook
Until you pause beside a darksome pond,
The fountain of this rivulet, whose gush
Cannot be seen, hid by a rayless night   10
That lives beneath the overhanging rock
That shades the pool—an endless spring of gloom,
Upon whose edge hovers the tender light,
Trembling to mingle with its paramour,—
But, as Syrinx fled Pan, so night flies day,   15
Or, with most sullen and regardless hate,
Refuses stern her heaven-born embrace.
On one side of this jagged and shapeless hill
There is a cave, from which there eddies up
A pale mist, like aëreal gossamer,   20
Whose breath destroys all life—awhile it veils
The rock—then, scattered by the wind, it flies
Along the stream, or lingers on the clefts,
Killing the sleepy worms, if aught bide there.
Upon the beetling edge of that dark rock   25
There stands a group of cypresses; not such
As, with a graceful spire and stirring life,
Pierce the pure heaven of your native vale,
Whose branches the air plays among, but not
Disturbs, fearing to spoil their solemn grace;   30
But blasted and all wearily they stand,
One to another clinging; their weak boughs
Sigh as the wind buffets them, and they shake

Beneath its blasts—a weatherbeaten crew!

Chorus. What wondrous sound is that, mournful and faint,   35
But more melodious than the murmuring wind
Which through the columns of a temple glides?

A. It is the wandering voice of Orpheus' lyre,
Borne by the winds, who sigh that their rude king
Hurries them fast from these air-feeding notes;   40
But in their speed they bear along with them
The waning sound, scattering it like dew
Upon the startled sense.

Chorus.   Does he still sing?
Methought he rashly cast away his harp
When he had lost Eurydice.

A.   Ah, no!   45
Awhile he paused. As a poor hunted stag
A moment shudders on the fearful brink
Of a swift stream—the cruel hounds press on
With deafening yell, the arrows glance and wound,—
He plunges in: so Orpheus, seized and torn   50
By the sharp fangs of an insatiate grief,
Maenad-like waved his lyre in the bright air,
And wildly shrieked 'Where she is, it is dark!'
And then he struck from forth the strings a sound
Of deep and fearful melody. Alas!   55
In times long past, when fair Eurydice
With her bright eyes sat listening by his side,
He gently sang of high and heavenly themes.
As in a brook, fretted with little waves
By the light airs of spring—each riplet makes   60
A many-sided mirror for the sun,
While it flows musically through green banks,
Ceaseless and pauseless, ever clear and fresh,
So flowed his song, reflecting the deep joy
And tender love that fed those sweetest notes,   65
The heavenly offspring of ambrosial food.
But that is past. Returning from drear Hell,
He chose a lonely seat of unhewn stone,
Blackened with lichens, a herbless plain.
Then from the deep and overflowing spring   70
Of his eternal ever-moving grief
There rose to Heaven a sound of angry song.
'Tis a mighty cataract that parts
Two sister rocks with waters swift and strong,
And casts itself with horrid roar and din   75
Adown a steep; from a perennial source
It ever flows and falls, and breaks the air
With loud and fierce, but most harmonious roar,

And as it falls casts up a vaporous spray
Which the sun clothes in hues of Iris light.   80
Thus the tempestuous torrent of his grief
Is clothed in sweetest sounds and varying words
Of poesy. Unlike all human works,
It never slackens, and through every change
Wisdom and beauty and the power divine   85
Of mighty poesy together dwell,
Mingling in sweet accord. As I have seen
A fierce south blast tear through the darkened sky,
Driving along a rack of wingèd clouds,
Which may not pause, but ever hurry on,   90
As their wild shepherd wills them, while the stars,
Twinkling and dim, peep from between the plumes.
Anon the sky is cleared, and the high dome
Of serene Heaven, starred with fiery flowers,
Shuts in the shaken earth; or the still moon   95
Swiftly, yet gracefully, begins her walk,
Rising all bright behind the eastern hills.
I talk of moon, and wind, and stars, and not
Of song; but, would I echo his high song,
Nature must lend me words ne'er used before,   100
Or I must borrow from her perfect works,
To picture forth his perfect attributes.
He does no longer sit upon his throne
Of rock upon a desert herbless plain,
For the evergreen and knotted ilexes,   105
And cypresses that seldom wave their boughs,
And sea-green olives with their grateful fruit,
And elms dragging along the twisted vines,
Which drop their berries as they follow fast,
And blackthorn bushes with their infant race   110
Of blushing rose-blooms; beeches, to lovers dear,
And weeping willow trees; all swift or slow,
As their huge boughs or lighter dress permit,
Have circled in his throne, and Earth herself
Has sent from her maternal breast a growth   115
Of starlike flowers and herbs of odour sweet,
To pave the temple that his poesy
Has framed, while near his feet grim lions couch,
And kids, fearless from love, creep near his lair.
Even the blind worms seem to feel the sound.   120
The birds are silent, hanging down their heads,
Perched on the lowest branches of the trees;
Not even the nightingale intrudes a note
In rivalry, but all entranced she listens.

FIORDISPINA

THE season was the childhood of sweet June,
Whose sunny hours from morning until noon
Went creeping through the day with silent feet,
Each with its load of pleasure; slow yet sweet;
Like the long years of blest Eternity   5
Never to be developed. Joy to thee,
Fiordispina and thy Cosimo,
For thou the wonders of the depth canst know
Of this unfathomable flood of hours,
Sparkling beneath the heaven which embowers—   10

.   .   .   .

They were two cousins, almost like to twins,
Except that from the catalogue of sins
Nature had rased their love—which could not be
But by dissevering their nativity.
And so they grew together like two flowers   15
Upon one stem, which the same beams and showers
Lull or awaken in their purple prime,
Which the same hand will gather—the same clime
Shake with decay. This fair day smiles to see
All those who love—and who e'er loved like thee,   20
Fiordispina? Scarcely Cosimo,
Within whose bosom and whose brain now glow
The ardours of a vision which obscure
The very idol of its portraiture.
He faints, dissolved into a sea of love;   25
But thou art as a planet sphered above;
But thou art Love itself—ruling the motion
Of his subjected spirit: such emotion
Must end in sin and sorrow, if sweet May
Had not brought forth this morn—your wedding-day.   30

.   .   .   .

'Lie there; sleep awhile in your own dew,
Ye faint-eyed children of the   Hours,'
Fiordispina said, and threw the flowers
Which she had from the breathing—

.   .   .   .

A table near of polished porphyry.   35
They seemed to wear a beauty from the eye
That looked on them—a fragrance from the touch
Whose warmth   checked their life; a light such
As sleepers wear, lulled by the voice they love,
                         which did reprove   40

The childish pity that she felt for them,
And a   remorse that from their stem
She had divided such fair shapes   made
A feeling in the   which was a shade
Of gentle beauty on the flowers: there lay   45
All gems that make the earth's dark bosom gay.
          rods of myrtle-buds and lemon-blooms,
And that leaf tinted lightly which assumes
The livery of unremembered snow—
Violets whose eyes have drunk—   50

   ·   ·   ·   ·   ·   ·   ·

Fiordispina and her nurse are now
Upon the steps of the high portico;
Under the withered arm of Media
She flings her glowing arm

   ·   ·   ·   ·   ·   ·   ·

          step by step and stair by stair,   55
That withered woman, gray and white and brown—
More like a trunk by lichens overgrown
Than anything which once could have been human.
And ever as she goes the palsied woman

   ·   ·   ·   ·   ·   ·   ·

'How slow and painfully you seem to walk,   60
Poor Media! you tire yourself with talk.'
          'And well it may,
Fiordispina, dearest—well-a-day!
You are hastening to a marriage-bed;
I to the grave!'—'And if my love were dead,   65
Unless my heart deceives me, I would lie
Beside him in my shroud as willingly
As now in the gay night-dress Lilla wrought.'
'Fie, child! Let that unseasonable thought
Not be remembered till it snows in June;   70
Such fancies are a music out of tune
With the sweet dance your heart must keep to-night.
What! would you take all beauty and delight
Back to the Paradise from which you sprung,
And leave to grosser mortals?——   75
And say, sweet lamb, would you not learn the sweet
And subtle mystery by which spirits meet?
Who knows whether the loving game is played,
When, once of mortal [vesture] disarrayed,
The naked soul goes wandering here and there   80
Through the wide deserts of Elysian air?
The violet dies not till it'——

TIME LONG PAST

I

LIKE the ghost of a dear friend
        dead
                Is Time long past.
A tone which is now forever fled,
A hope which is now forever past,
A love so sweet it could not last, 5
                Was time long past.

II

There were sweet dreams in the
        night
                Of Time long past:
And, was it sadness or delight,
Each day a shadow onward cast 10
Which made us wish it yet might
        last—
                That Time long past.

III

There is regret, almost remorse,
                For Time long past.
'Tis like a child's belovèd corse 15
A father watches, till at last
Beauty is like remembrance, cast
                From Time long past.

FRAGMENT: THE DESERTS OF DIM SLEEP

I WENT into the deserts of dim sleep—
        That world which, like an unknown wilderness,
Bounds this with its recesses wide and deep—

FRAGMENT: 'THE VIEWLESS AND INVISIBLE CONSEQUENCE'

THE viewless and invisible Consequence
Watches thy goings-out, and comings-in,
And . . . hovers o'er thy guilty sleep,
Unveiling every new-born deed, and thoughts
More ghastly than those deeds—   5

FRAGMENT: A SERPENT-FACE

HIS face was like a snake's—wrinkled and loose
And withered—

FRAGMENT: DEATH IN LIFE

My head is heavy, my limbs are weary,
And it is not life that makes me move.

FRAGMENT: 'SUCH HOPE, AS IS THE SICK DESPAIR OF GOOD'

SUCH hope, as is the sick despair of good,
Such fear, as is the certainty of ill,
Such doubt, as is pale Expectation's food
Turned while she tastes to poison, when the will
Is powerless, and the spirit . . .   5

FRAGMENT: 'ALAS! THIS IS NOT WHAT I THOUGHT LIFE WAS'

ALAS! this is not what I thought life was.
I knew that there were crimes and evil men,
Misery and hate; nor did I hope to pass
Untouched by suffering, through the rugged glen.
In mine own heart I saw as in a glass   5
The hearts of others   And when
I went among my kind, with triple brass
Of calm endurance my weak breast I armed,
To bear scorn, fear, and hate, a woful mass!

FRAGMENT: MILTON'S SPIRIT

I DREAMED that Milton's spirit rose, and took
   From life's green tree his Uranian lute;
And from his touch sweet thunder flowed, and shook
All human things built in contempt of man,—
And sanguine thrones and impious altars quaked,   5
Prisons and citadels . . .

FRAGMENT: 'UNRISEN SPLENDOUR OF THE BRIGHTEST SUN'

UNRISEN splendour of the brightest sun,
To rise upon our darkness, if the star
Now beckoning thee out of thy misty throne
Could thaw the clouds which wage an obscure war
With thy young brightness!   5

FRAGMENT: *PATER OMNIPOTENS*

SERENE in his unconquerable might
Endued[,] the Almighty King, his steadfast throne
Encompassed unapproachably with power
And darkness and deep solitude and awe
Stood like a black cloud on some aëry cliff   5
Embosoming its lightning—in his sight
Unnumbered glorious spirits trembling stood
Like slaves before their Lord—prostrate around
Heaven's multitudes hymned everlasting praise.

FRAGMENT: TO THE MIND OF MAN

THOU living light that in thy rainbow hues
   Clothest this naked world; and over Sea
   And Earth and air, and all the shapes that be
      In peopled darkness of this wondrous world

The Spirit of thy glory dost diffuse   5
         truth   thou Vital Flame
   Mysterious thought that in this mortal frame
Of things, with unextinguished lustre burnest
       Now pale and faint now high to Heaven upcurled
That eer as thou dost languish still returnest   10
   And ever

Before the   before the Pyramids

   So soon as from the Earth formless and rude
   One living step had chased drear Solitude
Thou wert, Thought; thy brightness charmed the lids   15
   Of the vast snake Eternity, who kept
   The tree of good and evil.—

NOTE ON POEMS OF 1820, BY MRS. SHELLEY

WE spent the latter part of the year 1819 in Florence, where Shelley passed several hours daily in the Gallery, and made various notes on its ancient works of art. His thoughts were a good deal taken up also by the project of a steamboat, undertaken by a friend, an engineer, to ply between Leghorn and Marseilles, for which he supplied a sum of money. This was a sort of plan to delight Shelley, and he was greatly disappointed when it was thrown aside.

There was something in Florence that disagreed excessively with his health, and he suffered far more pain than usual; so much so that we left it sooner than we intended, and removed to Pisa, where we had some friends, and, above all, where we could consult the celebrated Vaccà as to the cause of Shelley's sufferings. He, like every other medical man, could only guess at that, and gave little hope of immediate relief; he enjoined him to abstain from all physicians and medicine, and to leave his complaint to Nature. As he had vainly consulted medical men of the highest repute in England, he was easily persuaded to adopt this advice. Pain and ill-health followed him to the end; but the residence at Pisa agreed with him better than any other, and there in consequence we remained.

In the Spring we spent a week or two near Leghorn, borrowing the house of some friends who were absent on a journey to England. It was on a beautiful summer evening, while wandering among the lanes whose myrtle-hedges were the bowers of the fire-flies, that we heard the carolling of the skylark which inspired one of the most beautiful of his poems. He addressed the letter to Mrs. Gisborne from this house, which was hers: he had made his study of the workshop of her son, who was an engineer. Mrs. Gisborne had been a friend of my father in her younger days. She was a lady of great accomplishments, and charming from her frank and affectionate nature. She had the most intense love of knowledge, a delicate and trembling sensibility, and preserved freshness of mind after a life of considerable adversity. As a favourite friend of my father, we had sought her with eagerness; and the most open and cordial friendship was established between us.

Our stay at the Baths of San Giuliano was shortened by an accident. At the foot of our garden ran the canal that communicated between the Serchio and the Arno. The Serchio overflowed its banks, and, breaking its bounds, this canal also overflowed; all this part of the country is below the level of its rivers, and the consequence was that it was speedily flooded. The rising waters filled the Square of the Baths, in the lower part of which our house was situated. The canal overflowed in the garden behind; the rising waters on either side at last burst open the doors, and, meeting in the house, rose to the height of six feet. It was a picturesque sight at night to see the peasants driving the cattle from the plains below to the hills above the Baths. A fire was kept up to guide them across the ford; and the forms of the men and the animals showed in dark relief against the red glare of the flame, which was reflected again in the waters that filled the Square.

We then removed to Pisa, and took up our abode there for the winter. The extreme mildness of the climate suited Shelley, and his solitude was enlivened by an intercourse with several intimate friends. Chance cast us strangely enough on this quiet half-unpeopled town; but its very peace suited Shelley. Its river, the near mountains, and not distant sea, added to its attractions, and were the objects of many delightful excursions. We feared the south of Italy, and a hotter climate, on account of our child; our former bereavement inspiring us with terror. We seemed to take root here, and moved little afterwards; often, indeed, entertaining projects for visiting other parts of Italy, but still delaying. But for our fears on account of our child, I believe we should have wandered over the world, both being passionately fond of travelling. But human life, besides its great unalterable necessities, is ruled by a thousand lilliputian ties that shackle at the time, although it is difficult to account afterwards for their influence over our destiny.

POEMS WRITTEN IN 1821

DIRGE FOR THE YEAR

I

Orphan Hours, the Year is dead,
    Come and sigh, come and weep!
Merry Hours, smile instead,
    For the Year is but asleep.
See, it smiles as it is sleeping,   5
Mocking your untimely weep-
    ing.

II

As an earthquake rocks a corse
    In its coffin in the clay,
So White Winter, that rough nurse,
    Rocks the death-cold Year to-
        day;   10
Solemn Hours! wail aloud
For your mother in her shroud.

III

As the wild air stirs and sways
  The tree-swung cradle of a
    child,
So the breath of these rude days 15
  Rocks the Year:—be calm and
    mild,
Trembling Hours, she will arise
With new love within her eyes.

IV

January gray is here,
  Like a sexton by her grave;   20
February bears the bier,
  March with grief doth howl and
    rave,
And April weeps—but, O ye
    Hours!
Follow with May's fairest flowers.

TO NIGHT

I

SWIFTLY walk o'er the western
    wave,
      Spirit of Night!
Out of the misty eastern cave,
Where, all the long and lone day-
    light,
Thou wovest dreams of joy and
    fear,   5
Which make thee terrible and
    dear,—
      Swift be thy flight!

II

Wrap thy form in a mantle gray,
      Star-inwrought!
Blind with thine hair the eyes of
    Day;   10
Kiss her until she be wearied out,
Then wander o'er city, and sea, and
    land,
Touching all with thine opiate
    wand—
      Come, long-sought!

III

When I arose and saw the dawn, 15
  I sighed for thee;

When light rode high, and the dew
    was gone,
And noon lay heavy on flower and
    tree,
And the weary Day turned to his
    rest,
Lingering like an unloved guest, 20
  I sighed for thee.

IV

Thy brother Death came, and cried,
      Wouldst thou me?
Thy sweet child Sleep, the filmy-
    eyed,
Murmured like a noontide bee,   25
Shall I nestle near thy side?
Wouldst thou me?—And I replied,
      No, not thee!

V

Death will come when thou art
    dead,
      Soon, too soon—   30
Sleep will come when thou art
    fled;
Of neither would I ask the boon
I ask of thee, belovèd Night—
Swift be thine approaching flight,
      Come soon, soon!   35

TIME

UNFATHOMABLE Sea! whose waves are years,
  Ocean of Time, whose waters of deep woe
Are brackish with the salt of human tears!
  Thou shoreless flood, which in thy ebb and flow

Claspest the limits of mortality,   5
And sick of prey, yet howling on for more,
Vomitest thy wrecks on its inhospitable shore;
Treacherous in calm, and terrible in storm,
        Who shall put forth on thee,
        Unfathomable Sea?   10

LINES

I

FAR, far away, O ye
Halcyons of Memory,
Seek some far calmer nest
Than this abandoned breast!
No news of your false spring   5
To my heart's winter bring,
Once having gone, in vain
        Ye come again.

II

Vultures, who build your bowers
High in the Future's towers,   10
Withered hopes on hopes are
        spread!
Dying joys, choked by the dead,
Will serve your beaks for prey
        Many a day.

FROM THE ARABIC: AN IMITATION

I

My faint spirit was sitting in the light
        Of thy looks, my love;
It panted for thee like the hind at noon
        For the brooks, my love.
Thy barb whose hoofs outspeed the tempest's flight   5
        Bore thee far from me;
My heart, for my weak feet were weary soon,
        Did companion thee.

II

Ah! fleeter far than fleetest storm or steed,
        Or the death they bear,   10
The heart which tender thought clothes like a dove
        With the wings of care;
In the battle, in the darkness, in the need,
        Shall mine cling to thee,
Nor claim one smile for all the comfort, love,   15
        It may bring to thee.

TO EMILIA VIVIANI

I

MADONNA, wherefore hast thou sent to me
        Sweet-basil and mignonette?
Embleming love and health, which never yet
In the same wreath might be.

  Alas, and they are wet!   5
Is it with thy kisses or thy tears?
  For never rain or dew
  Such fragrance drew
From plant or flower—the very doubt endears
  My sadness ever new,   10
The sighs I breathe, the tears I shed for thee.

     II

Send the stars light, but send not love to me,
  In whom love ever made
Health like a heap of embers soon to fade—

THE FUGITIVES

I

THE waters are flashing,
The white hail is dashing,
The lightnings are glancing,
The hoar-spray is dancing—
  Away!   5

The whirlwind is rolling,
The thunder is tolling,
The forest is swinging,
The minster bells ringing—
  Come away!   10

The Earth is like Ocean,
Wreck-strewn and in motion:
Bird, beast, man and worm
Have crept out of the storm—
  Come away!   15

II

'Our boat has one sail,
And the helmsman is pale;—
A bold pilot I trow,
Who should follow us now,'—
  Shouted he—   20

And she cried: 'Ply the oar!
Put off gaily from shore!'—
As she spoke, bolts of death
Mixed with hail, specked their path
  O'er the sea.   25

And from isle, tower and rock,
The blue beacon-cloud broke,
And though dumb in the blast,
The red cannon flashed fast
  From the lee.   30

III

And 'Fear'st thou?' and 'Fear'st
  thou?'
And 'Seest thou?' and 'Hear'st
  thou?'
And 'Drive we not free
O'er the terrible sea,
  I and thou?'   35

One boat-cloak did cover
The loved and the lover—
Their blood beats one measure,
They murmur proud pleasure
  Soft and low;—   40

While around the lashed Ocean,
Like mountains in motion,
Is withdrawn and uplifted,
Sunk, shattered and shifted
  To and fro.   45

IV

In the court of the fortress
Beside the pale portress,
Like a bloodhound well beaten
The bridegroom stands, eaten
  By shame;   50

On the topmost watch-turret,
As a death-boding spirit,
Stands the gray tyrant father,
To his voice the mad weather
    Seems tame;   55

And with curses as wild
As e'er clung to child,
He devotes to the blast,
The best, loveliest and last
    Of his name!   60

TO ——

Music, when soft voices die,
Vibrates in the memory—
Odours, when sweet violets sicken,
Live within the sense they quicken.

Rose leaves, when the rose is dead,   5
Are heaped for the belovèd bed;
And so thy thoughts, when thou art gone,
Love itself shall slumber on.

SONG

I

Rarely, rarely, comest thou,
  Spirit of Delight!
Wherefore hast thou left me now
  Many a day and night?
Many a weary night and day   5
'Tis since thou art fled away.

II

How shall ever one like me
  Win thee back again?
With the joyous and the free
  Thou wilt scoff at pain.   10
Spirit false! thou hast forgot
  All but those who need thee not.

III

As a lizard with the shade
  Of a trembling leaf,
Thou with sorrow art dismayed;   15
  Even the sighs of grief
Reproach thee, that thou art not
    near,
And reproach thou wilt not hear.

IV

Let me set my mournful ditty
  To a merry measure;   20
Thou wilt never come for pity,
  Thou wilt come for pleasure;

Pity then will cut away
Those cruel wings, and thou wilt
    stay.

V

I love all that thou lovest,   25
  Spirit of Delight!
The fresh Earth in new leaves
    dressed,
  And the starry night;
Autumn evening, and the morn
When the golden mists are born. 30

VI

I love snow, and all the forms
  Of the radiant frost;
I love waves, and winds, and
    storms,
  Everything almost
Which is Nature's, and may be   35
Untainted by man's misery.

VII

I love tranquil solitude,
  And such society
As is quiet, wise, and good;
  Between thee and me   40
What difference? but thou dost
    possess
  The things I seek, not love them
    less.

VIII

I love Love—though he has wings,
   And like light can flee,
But above all other things,   45

Spirit, I love thee—
Thou art love and life! Oh, come,
Make once more my heart thy
   home.

MUTABILITY

I

THE flower that smiles to-day
   To-morrow dies;
All that we wish to stay
   Tempts and then flies.
What is this world's delight?   5
Lightning that mocks the night,
   Brief even as bright.

II

Virtue, how frail it is!
   Friendship how rare!
Love, how it sells poor bliss   10

   For proud despair!
But we, though soon they fall,
Survive their joy, and all
   Which ours we call.

III

Whilst skies are blue and bright, 15
   Whilst flowers are gay,
Whilst eyes that change ere night
   Make glad the day;
Whilst yet the calm hours creep,
Dream thou—and from thy sleep 20
   Then wake to weep.

LINES WRITTEN ON HEARING THE NEWS OF THE DEATH OF NAPOLEON

   WHAT! alive and so bold, O Earth?
      Art thou not overbold?
      What! leapest thou forth as of old
In the light of thy morning mirth,
The last of the flock of the starry fold?   5
Ha! leapest thou forth as of old?
Are not the limbs still when the ghost is fled,
And canst thou move, Napoleon being dead?

How! is not thy quick heart cold?
      What spark is alive on thy hearth?   10
How! is not *his* death-knell knolled?
      And livest *thou* still, Mother Earth?
Thou wert warming thy fingers old
O'er the embers covered and cold
Of that most fiery spirit, when it fled—   15
What, Mother, do you laugh now he is dead?

'Who has known me of old,' replied Earth,
   'Or who has my story told?
   It is thou who art overbold.'
And the lightning of scorn laughed forth   20
As she sung, 'To my bosom I fold
All my sons when their knell is knolled
And so with living motion all are fed,
And the quick spring like weeds out of the dead.

'Still alive and still bold,' shouted Earth,   25
  'I grow bolder and still more bold.
The dead fill me ten thousandfold
Fuller of speed, and splendour, and mirth.
I was cloudy, and sullen, and cold,
Like a frozen chaos uprolled,   30
Till by the spirit of the mighty dead
My heart grew warm. I feed on whom I fed.

'Ay, alive and still bold,' muttered Earth,
  'Napoleon's fierce spirit rolled,
    In terror and blood and gold,   35
A torrent of ruin to death from his birth.
Leave the millions who follow to mould
The metal before it be cold;
And weave into his shame, which like the dead
Shrouds me, the hopes that from his glory fled.   40

SONNET: POLITICAL GREATNESS

Nor happiness, nor majesty, nor fame,
Nor peace, nor strength, nor skill in arms or arts,
Shepherd those herds whom tyranny makes tame;
Verse echoes not one beating of their hearts,
History is but the shadow of their shame,   5
Art veils her glass, or from the pageant starts
As to oblivion their blind millions fleet,
Staining that Heaven with obscene imagery
Of their own likeness. What are numbers knit
By force or custom? Man who man would be,   10
Must rule the empire of himself; in it
Must be supreme, establishing his throne
On vanquished will, quelling the anarchy
Of hopes and fears, being himself alone.

THE AZIOLA

I

'Do you not hear the Aziola cry?
  Methinks she must be nigh,'
    Said Mary, as we sate
In dusk, ere stars were lit, or candles brought;
  And I, who thought   5
This Aziola was some tedious woman,
  Asked, 'Who is Aziola?' How elate
I felt to know that it was nothing human,
  No mockery of myself to fear or hate:
    And Mary saw my soul,   10
And laughed, and said, 'Disquiet yourself not;
    'Tis nothing but a little downy owl.'

II

Sad Aziola! many an eventide
    Thy music I had heard
By wood and stream, meadow and mountain-side,   15
    And fields and marshes wide,—
Such as nor voice, nor lute, nor wind, nor bird,
    The soul ever stirred;
Unlike and far sweeter than them all.
Sad Aziola! from that moment I   20
    Loved thee and thy sad cry.

A LAMENT

I

O WORLD! O life! O time!
On whose last steps I climb,
    Trembling at that where I had stood before;
When will return the glory of your prime?
        No more—Oh, never more!   5

II

Out of the day and night
A joy has taken flight;
    Fresh spring, and summer, and winter hoar,
Move my faint heart with grief, but with delight
        No more—Oh, never more!   1C

REMEMBRANCE

I

SWIFTER far than summer's flight—
Swifter far than youth's delight—
Swifter far than happy night,
    Art thou come and gone—
As the earth when leaves are
        dead,   5
As the night when sleep is sped,
As the heart when joy is fled,
    I am left lone, alone.

II

The swallow summer comes
        again—
The owlet night resumes her
        reign—
But the wild-swan youth is fain 11
To fly with thee, false as
        thou.—
My heart each day desires the mor-
        row;
Sleep itself is turned to sorrow;
Vainly would my winter borrow 15
    Sunny leaves from any bough.

II

Lilies for a bridal bed—
Roses for a matron's head—
Violets for a maiden dead—
    Pansies let *my* flowers be: 20
On the living grave I bear
Scatter them without a tear—
Let no friend, however dear,
    Waste one hope, one fear for
        me.

TO EDWARD WILLIAMS

I

THE serpent is shut out from Paradise.
    The wounded deer must seek the herb no more
      In which its heart-cure lies:
    The widowed dove must cease to haunt a bower
Like that from which its mate with feignèd sighs   5
      Fled in the April hour.
    I too must seldom seek again
Near happy friends a mitigated pain.

II

Of hatred I am proud,—with scorn content;
    Indifference, that once hurt me, now is grown   10
      Itself indifferent;
    But, not to speak of love, pity alone
Can break a spirit already more than bent.
      The miserable one
    Turns the mind's poison into food,—   15
Its medicine is tears,—its evil good.

III

Therefore, if now ɪ see you seldomer,
    Dear friends, dear *friend!* know that I only fly
      Your looks, because they stir
    Griefs that should sleep, and hopes that cannot die: 20
The very comfort that they minister
      I scarce can bear, yet I,
    So deeply is the arrow gone,
Should quickly perish if it were withdrawn.

IV

When I return to my cold home, you ask   25
    Why I am not as I have ever been.
      You spoil me for the task
    Of acting a forced part in life's dull scene,—
Of wearing on my brow the idle mask
      Of author, great or mean,   30
    In the world's carnival. I sought
Peace thus, and but in you I found it not.

V

Full half an hour, to-day, I tried my lot
    With various flowers, and every one still said,
      'She loves me—loves me not.'   35
    And if this meant a vision long since fled—
If it meant fortune, fame, or peace of thought—
      If it meant,—but I dread

To speak what you may know too well:
Still there was truth in the sad oracle.   40

VI

The crane o'er seas and forests seeks her home;
    No bird so wild but has its quiet nest,
        When it no more would roam;
    The sleepless billows on the ocean's breast
Break like a bursting heart, and die in foam,   45
        And thus at length find rest:
    Doubtless there is a place of peace
Where *my* weak heart and all its throbs will cease.

VII

I asked her, yesterday, if she believed
    That I had resolution. One who *had*   50
        Would ne'er have thus relieved
    His heart with words,—but what his judgement bade
Would do, and leave the scorner unrelieved.
        These verses are too sad
    To send to you, but that I know,   55
Happy yourself, you feel another's woe.

TO ———

I

ONE word is too often profaned
    For me to profane it,
One feeling too falsely disdained
    For thee to disdain it;
One hope is too like despair   5
    For prudence to smother,
And pity from thee more dear
    Than that from another.

II

I can give not what men call love,
    But wilt thou accept not   10
The worship the heart lifts above
    And the Heavens reject not,—
The desire of the moth for the star,
    Of the night for the morrow,
The devotion to something afar   15
    From the sphere of our sor-
        row?

TO ———

I

WHEN passion's trance is overpast,
If tenderness and truth could last,
Or live, whilst all wild feelings keep
Some mortal slumber, dark and
    deep,
I should not weep, I should not
    weep!   5

II

It were enough to feel, to see,
Thy soft eyes gazing tenderly,

And dream the rest—and burn
    and be
The secret food of fires unseen,
Couldst thou but be as thou hast
    been.   10

III

After the slumber of the year
The woodland violets reappear;
All things revive in field or grove,
And sky and sea, but two, which
    move
And form all others, life and love. 15

A BRIDAL· SONG

I

THE golden gates of Sleep unbar
  Where Strength and Beauty, met
    together,
Kindle their image like a star
  In a sea of glassy weather!
Night, with all thy stars look
    down,—   5
  Darkness, weep thy holiest
    dew,—
Never smiled the inconstant moon
  On a pair so true.

Let eyes not see their own de-
    light;—   9
Haste, swift Hour, and thy flight
    Oft renew.

II

Fairies, sprites, and angels, keep
    her!
  Holy stars, permit no wrong!
And return to wake the sleeper,
    Dawn,—ere it be long! 15
O joy! O fear! what will be done
In the absence of the sun!
    Come along!

EPITHALAMIUM

ANOTHER VERSION OF THE PRECEDING

NIGHT, with all thine eyes look
    down!
  Darkness shed its holiest dew!
When ever smiled the inconstant
    moon
  On a pair so true?
Hence, coy hour! and quench thy
    light,   5
Lest eyes see their own delight!
Hence, swift hour! and thy loved
    flight
    Oft renew.

Boys.

O joy! O fear! what may be done
In the absence of the sun?   10
    Come along!
The golden gates of sleep unbar!
  When strength and beauty meet
    together,
Kindles their image like a star
  In a sea of glassy weather. 15
Hence, coy hour! and quench thy
    light,
Lest eyes see their own delight!

Hence, swift hour! and thy loved
    flight
    Oft renew.

Girls.

O joy! O fear! what may be done
In the absence of the sun?   21
    Come along!
Fairies! sprites! and angels, keep
    her!
  Holiest powers, permit no
    wrong!
And return, to wake the sleeper, 25
  Dawn, ere it be long.
Hence, swift hour! and quench thy
    light,
Lest eyes see their own delight!
Hence, coy hour! and thy loved
    flight
    Oft renew!   30

Boys and Girls.

O joy! O·fear! what will be done
In the absence of the sun?
    Come along!

ANOTHER VERSION OF THE SAME

Boys Sing.

NIGHT! with all thine eyes look
  down!
Darkness! weep thy holiest dew!
Never smiled the inconstant moon
  On a pair so true.
Haste, coy hour! and quench all
  light,   5
Lest eyes see their own delight!
Haste, swift hour! and thy loved
  flight
    Oft renew!

Girls Sing.

Fairies, sprites, and angels, keep
  her!
  Holy stars! permit no wrong!   10
And return, to wake the sleeper,
  Dawn, ere it be long!
O joy! O fear! there is not one
Of us can guess what may be done
In the absence of the sun:—   15
    Come along!

Boys.

Oh! linger long, thou envious eastern lamp

In the damp
  Caves of the deep!

Girls.

Nay, return, Vesper! urge thy lazy
  car!   20
Swift unbar
  The gates of Sleep!

Chorus.

The golden gate of Sleep unbar,
  When Strength and Beauty, met
    together,
Kindle their image, like a star   25
  In a sea of glassy weather.
May the purple mist of love
Round them rise, and with them
  move,
Nourishing each tender gem
Which, like flowers, will burst from
  them.   30
As the fruit is to the tree
May their children ever be!

LOVE, HOPE, DESIRE, AND FEAR

.   .   .   .
AND many there were hurt by that
  strong boy,
  His name, they said, was Pleas-
    ure,
And near him stood, glorious be-
  yond measure,
Four Ladies who possess all empery
  In earth and air and sea,   5
Nothing that lives from their award
  is free.
  Their names will I declare to
    thee,
  Love, Hope, Desire, and Fear,
  And they the regents are

Of the four elements that frame
    the heart,   10
And each diversely exercised her art
  By force or circumstance or
    sleight
    To prove her dreadful might
    Upon that poor domain.
Desire presented her [false] glass,
    and then   15
    The spirit dwelling there
Was spellbound to embrace what
    seemed so fair
    Within that magic mirror,
    And dazed by that bright
      error,

It would have scorned the [shafts]
   of the avenger,　　20
And death, and penitence, and
   danger,
   Had not then silent Fear
   Touched with her palsying
     spear,
So that as if a frozen torrent
The blood was curdled in its cur-
   rent;　　25
It dared not speak, even in look or
   motion,
But chained within itself its proud
   devotion.
   Between Desire and Fear thou
     wert
   A wretched thing, poor heart!
Sad was his life who bore thee in
   his breast,　　30
   Wild bird for that weak nest.
Till Love even from fierce Desire
   it bought,
And from the very wound of tender
   thought
Drew solace, and the pity of sweet
   eyes
Gave strength to bear those gentle
   agonies,　　35

Surmount the loss, the terror, and
   the sorrow.
Then Hope approached, she who
   can borrow
For poor to-day, from rich to-
   morrow,
And Fear withdrew, as night
   when day
Descends upon the orient ray, 40
And after long and vain endur-
   ance
The poor heart woke to her as-
   surance.
—At one birth these four were
   born
With the world's forgotten morn,
And from Pleasure still they hold
All it circles, as of old.　　46
When, as summer lures the
   swallow,
Pleasure lures the heart to fol-
   low—
O weak heart of little wit!
The fair hand that wounded it, 50
Seeking, like a panting hare,
Refuge in the lynx's lair,
Love, Desire, Hope, and Fear,
   Ever will be near.

FRAGMENTS WRITTEN FOR HELLAS

I

FAIREST of the Destinies,
Disarray thy dazzling eyes:
Keener far thy lightnings are
   Than the wingèd [bolts] thou
     bearest,
   And the smile thou wearest　5
Wraps thee as a star
   Is wrapped in light.

II

Could Arethuse to her forsaken urn
From Alpheus and the bitter Doris
   run,
   Or could the morning shafts of
     purest light　　10

Again into the quivers of the Sun
   Be gathered—could one thought
     from its wild flight
Return into the temple of the brain
   Without a change, without a
     stain,—
   Could aught that is, ever
     again　　15
   Be what it once has ceased to
     be.
     Greece might again be
     free!

III

A star has fallen upon the earth
Mid the benighted nations,

A quenchless atom of immortal
   light,   20
A living spark of Night,
A cresset shaken from the constel-
   lations.
Swifter than the thunder fell
To the heart of Earth, the well
Where its pulses flow and beat, 25
And unextinct in that cold source
Burns, and on   course
Guides the sphere which is its
   prison,

Like an angelic spirit pent
   In a form of mortal birth, 30
Till, as a spirit half-arisen
   Shatters its charnel, it has
      rent,
In the rapture of its mirth,
The thin and painted garment of
   the Earth,   34
Ruining its chaos—a fierce breath
Consuming all its forms of living
   death.

FRAGMENT: 'I WOULD NOT BE A KING'

I WOULD not be a king—enough
   Of woe it is to love;
The path to power is steep and
   rough,
And tempests reign above.
I would not climb the imperial
   throne;   5

'Tis built on ice which fortune's sun
   Thaws in the height of noon.
Then farewell, king, yet were I
   one,
Care would not come so soon.
Would he and I were far away 10
Keeping flocks on Himalay!

GINEVRA

WILD, pale, and wonder-stricken, even as one
Who staggers forth into the air and sun
From the dark chamber of a mortal fever,
Bewildered, and incapable, and ever
Fancying strange comments in her dizzy brain   5
Of usual shapes, till the familiar train
Of objects and of persons passed like things
Strange as a dreamer's mad imaginings,
Ginevra from the nuptial altar went;
The vows to which her lips had sworn assent   10
Rung in her brain still with a jarring din,
Deafening the lost intelligence within.

And so she moved under the bridal veil,
Which made the paleness of her cheek more pale,
And deepened the faint crimson of her mouth,
And darkened her dark locks, as moonlight doth,—   15
And of the gold and jewels glittering there
She scarce felt conscious,—but the weary glare
Lay like a chaos of unwelcome light,
Vexing the sense with gorgeous undelight,   20
A moonbeam in the shadow of a cloud
Was less heavenly fair—her face was bowed,

And as she passed, the diamonds in her hair
Were mirrored in the polished marble stair
Which led from the cathedral to the street;   25
And ever as she went her light fair feet
Erased these images.

The bride-maidens who round her thronging came,
Some with a sense of self-rebuke and shame,
Envying the unenviable; and others   30
Making the joy which should have been another's
Their own by gentle sympathy; and some
Sighing to think of an unhappy home:
Some few admiring what can ever lure
Maidens to leave the heaven serene and pure   35
Of parents' smiles for life's great cheat; a thing
Bitter to taste, sweet in imagining.

But they are all dispersed—and, lo! she stands
Looking in idle grief on her white hands,
Alone within the garden now her own;   40
And through the sunny air, with jangling tone,
The music of the merry marriage-bells,
Killing the azure silence, sinks and swells;—
Absorbed like one within a dream who dreams
That he is dreaming, until slumber seems   45
A mockery of itself—when suddenly
Antonio stood before her, pale as she.
With agony, with sorrow, and with pride,
He lifted his wan eyes upon the bride,
And said—'Is this thy faith?' and then as one   50
Whose sleeping face is stricken by the sun
With light like a harsh voice, which bids him rise
And look upon his day of life with eyes
Which weep in vain that they can dream no more,
Ginevra saw her lover, and forbore   55
To shriek or faint, and checked the stifling blood
Rushing upon her heart, and unsubdued
Said—'Friend, if earthly violence or ill,
Suspicion, doubt, or the tyrannic will
Of parents, chance or custom, time or change,   60
Or circumstance, or terror, or revenge,
Or wildered looks, or words, or evil speech,
With all their stings and venom can impeach
Our love,—we love not:—if the grave which hides
The victim from the tyrant, and divides   65
The cheek that whitens from the eyes that dart
Imperious inquisition to the heart

That is another's, could dissever ours,
We love not.'—'What! do not the silent hours
Beckon thee to Gherardi's bridal bed?   70
Is not that ring'—a pledge, he would have said,
Of broken vows, but she with patient look
The golden circle from her finger took,
And said—'Accept this token of my faith,
The pledge of vows to be absolved by death;   75
And I am dead or shall be soon—my knell
Will mix its music with that merry bell,
Does it not sound as if they sweetly said
"We toll a corpse out of the marriage-bed"?
The flowers upon my bridal chamber strewn   80
Will serve unfaded for my bier—so soon
That even the dying violet will not die
Before Ginevra.' The strong fantasy
Had made her accents weaker and more weak,
And quenched the crimson life upon her cheek,   85
And glazed her eyes, and spread an atmosphere
Round her, which chilled the burning noon with fear,
Making her but an image of the thought
Which, like a prophet or a shadow, brought
News of the terrors of the coming time.   90
Like an accuser branded with the crime
He would have cast on a belovèd friend,
Whose dying eyes reproach not to the end
The pale betrayer—he then with vain repentance
Would share, he cannot now avert, the sentence—   95
Antonio stood and would have spoken, when
The compound voice of women and of men
Was heard approaching; he retired, while she
Was led amid the admiring company
Back to the palace,—and her maidens soon   100
Changed her attire for the afternoon,
And left her at her own request to keep
An hour of quiet and rest:—like one asleep
With open eyes and folded hands she lay,
Pale in the light of the declining day.   105

    Meanwhile the day sinks fast, the sun is set,
And in the lighted hall the guests are met;
The beautiful looked lovelier in the light
Of love, and admiration, and delight
Reflected from a thousand hearts and eyes,   110
Kindling a momentary Paradise.
This crowd is safer than the silent wood,
Where love's own doubts disturb the solitude;

On frozen hearts the fiery rain of wine
Falls, and the dew of music more divine   115
Tempers the deep emotions of the time
To spirits cradled in a sunny clime:—
How many meet, who never yet have met,
To part too soon, but never to forget.
How many saw the beauty, power and wit   120
Of looks and words which ne'er enchanted yet;
But life's familiar veil was now withdrawn,
As the world leaps before an earthquake's dawn,
And unprophetic of the coming hours,
The matin winds from the expanded flowers   125
Scatter their hoarded incense, and awaken
The earth, until the dewy sleep is shaken
From every living heart which it possesses,
Through seas and winds, cities and wildernesses,
As if the future and the past were all   130
Treasured i' the instant;—so Gherardi's hall
Laughed in the mirth of its lord's festival,
Till some one asked—'Where is the Bride?' And then
A bridesmaid went,—and ere she came again
A silence fell upon the guests—a pause   135
Of expectation, as when beauty awes
All hearts with its approach, though unbeheld,
Then wonder, and then fear that wonder quelled;—
For whispers passed from mouth to ear which drew
The colour from the hearer's cheeks, and flew   140
Louder and swifter round the company;
And then Gherardi entered with an eye
Of ostentatious trouble, and a crowd
Surrounded him, and some were weeping loud.

They found Ginevra dead! if it be death   145
To lie without motion, or pulse, or breath,
With waxen cheeks, and limbs cold, stiff, and white,
And open eyes, whose fixed and glassy light
Mocked at the speculation they had owned.
If it be death, when there is felt around   150
A smell of clay, a pale and icy glare,
And silence, and a sense that lifts the hair
From the scalp to the ankles, as it were
Corruption from the spirit passing forth,
And giving all it shrouded to the earth,   155
And leaving as swift lightning in its flight
Ashes, and smoke, and darkness: in our night
Of thought we know thus much of death,—no more
Than the unborn dream of our life before

Their barks are wrecked on its inhospitable shore.   160
The marriage feast and its solemnity
Was turned to funeral pomp—the company,
With heavy hearts and looks, broke up; nor they
Who loved the dead went weeping on their way
Alone, but sorrow mixed with sad surprise   165
Loosened the springs of pity in all eyes,
On which that form, whose fate they weep in vain,
Will never, thought they, kindle smiles again.
The lamps which, half extinguished in their haste,
Gleamed few and faint o'er the abandoned feast,   170
Showed as it were within the vaulted room
A cloud of sorrow hanging, as if gloom
Had passed out of men's minds into the air.
Some few yet stood around Gherardi there,
Friends and relations of the dead,—and he,   175
A loveless man, accepted torpidly
The consolation that he wanted not;
Awe in the place of grief within him wrought.
Their whispers made the solemn silence seem
More still—some wept, . . .   180
Some melted into tears without a sob,
And some with hearts that might be heard to throb
Leaned on the table, and at intervals
Shuddered to hear through the deserted halls
And corridors the thrilling shrieks which came   185
Upon the breeze of night, that shook the flame
Of every torch and taper as it swept
From out the chamber where the women kept;—
Their tears fell on the dear companion cold
Of pleasures now departed; then was knolled   190
The bell of death, and soon the priests arrived,
And finding Death their penitent had shrived,
Returned like ravens from a corpse whereon
A vulture has just feasted to the bone.
And then the mourning women came.—   195

    .   .   .   .

THE DIRGE

Old winter was gone
In his weakness back to the mountains hoar,
And the spring came down
From the planet that hovers upon the shore
Where the sea of sunlight encroaches   200
On the limits of wintry night;—
If the land. and the air, and the sea,

                Rejoice not when spring approaches,
                We did not rejoice in thee,
                        Ginevra!   205

                    She is still, she is cold
                            On the bridal couch,
                    One step to the white deathbed,
                            And one to the bier,
                    And one to the charnel—and one, oh where?   210
                            The dark arrow fled
                            In the noon.

                    Ere the sun through heaven once more has rolled,
                    The rats in her heart
                    Will have made their nest,   215
                    And the worms be alive in her golden hair,
                    While the Spirit that guides the sun,
                    Sits throned in his flaming chair,
                            She shall sleep.

EVENING: PONTE AL MARE, PISA

I

THE sun is set; the swallows are asleep;
    The bats are flitting fast in the gray air;
The slow soft toads out of damp corners creep,
    And evening's breath, wandering here and there
Over the quivering surface of the stream,   5
Wakes not one ripple from its summer dream.

II

There is no dew on the dry grass to-night,
    Nor damp within the shadow of the trees;
The wind is intermitting, dry, and light;
    And in the inconstant motion of the breeze   10
The dust and straws are driven up and down,
And whirled about the pavement of the town.

III

Within the surface of the fleeting river
    The wrinkled image of the city lay,
Immovably unquiet, and forever   15
    It trembles, but it never fades away;
Go to the . . .
You, being changed, will find it then as now.

IV

The chasm in which the sun has sunk is shut
  By darkest barriers of cinereous cloud,   20
Like mountain over mountain huddled—but
  Growing and moving upwards in a crowd,
And over it a space of watery blue,
Which the keen evening star is shining through.

THE BOAT ON THE SERCHIO

Our boat is asleep on Serchio's stream,
Its sails are folded like thoughts in a dream,
The helm sways idly, hither and thither;
  Dominic, the boatman, has brought the mast,
  And the oars, and the sails; but 'tis sleeping fast,   5
Like a beast, unconscious of its tether.

The stars burnt out in the pale blue air,
And the thin white moon lay withering there;
To tower, and cavern, and rift, and tree,
The owl and the bat fled drowsily.   10
Day had kindled the dewy woods,
  And the rocks above and the stream below,
And the vapours in their multitudes,
  And the Apennine's shroud of summer snow,
And clothed with light of aëry gold   15
The mists in their eastern caves uprolled.

Day had awakened all things that be,
The lark and the thrush and the swallow free,
  And the milkmaid's song and the mower's scythe,
And the matin-bell and the mountain bee: 20
Fireflies were quenched on the dewy corn,
  Glow-worms went out on the river's brim,
  Like lamps which a student forgets to trim:
The beetle forgot to wind his horn,
  The crickets were still in the meadow and hill: 25
Like a flock of rooks at a farmer's gun
Night's dreams and terrors, every one,
Fled from the brains which are their prey
From the lamp's death to the morning ray.

All rose to do the task He set to each,   30
  Who shaped us to His ends and not our own;
The million rose to learn, and one to teach
  What none yet ever knew or can be known.
    And many rose

Whose woe was such that fear became desire;—   35
Melchior and Lionel were not among those;
They from the throng of men had stepped aside,
And made their home under the green hill-side.
It was that hill, whose intervening brow
    Screens Lucca from the Pisan's envious eye,   40
Which the circumfluous plain waving below,
    Like a wide lake of green fertility,
With streams and fields and marshes bare,
    Divides from the far Apennines—which lie
Islanded in the immeasurable air.   45

'What think you, as she lies in her green cove,
Our little sleeping boat is dreaming of?'
'If morning dreams are true, why I should guess
That she was dreaming of our idleness,
And of the miles of watery way   50
We should have led her by this time of day.'—

    'Never mind,' said Lionel,
    'Give care to the winds, they can bear it well
About yon poplar-tops; and see
The white clouds are driving merrily,   55
And the stars we miss this morn will light
More willingly our return to-night.—
How it whistles, Dominic's long black hair!
List, my dear fellow; the breeze blows fair:
Hear how it sings into the air—'   60

—'Of us and of our lazy motions,'
    Impatiently said Melchior,
'If I can guess a boat's emotions;
    And how we ought, two hours before,
To have been the devil knows where.'   65
And then, in such transalpine Tuscan
As would have killed a Della-Cruscan,

.   .   .   .

So, Lionel according to his art
    Weaving his idle words, Melchior said:
'She dreams that we are not yet out of bed;   70
We'll put a soul into her, and a heart
Which like a dove chased by a dove shall beat.'

.   .   .   .

    'Ay, heave the ballast overboard,
    And stow the eatables in the aft locker.'
'Would not this keg be best a little lowered?'   75
'No, now all's right.' 'Those bottles of warm tea—

(Give me some straw)—must be stowed tenderly;
Such as we used, in summer after six,
To cram in greatcoat pockets, and to mix
Hard eggs and radishes and rolls at Eton,   80
And, couched on stolen hay in those green harbours
Farmers called gaps, and we schoolboys called arbours,
Would feast till eight.'

   With a bottle in one hand,
As if his very soul were at a stand,   85
Lionel stood—when Melchior brought him steady:—
'Sit at the helm—fasten this sheet—all ready!'

  The chain is loosed, the sails are spread,
   The living breath is fresh behind,
  As, with dews and sunrise fed,   90
   Comes the laughing morning wind;—
The sails are full, the boat makes head
Against the Serchio's torrent fierce,
Then flags with intermitting course,
   And hangs upon the wave, and stems   95
  The tempest of the . . .
Which fervid from its mountain source
Shallow, smooth and strong doth come,—
  Swift as fire, tempestuously
It sweeps into the affrighted sea   100
In morning's smile its eddies coil,
Its billows sparkle, toss and boil,
Torturing all its quiet light
Into columns fierce and bright.

   The Serchio, twisting forth   105
Between the marble barriers which it clove
  At Ripafratta, leads through the dread chasm
The wave that died the death which lovers love,
  Living in what it sought; as if this spasm
Had not yet passed, the toppling mountains cling,   110
  But the clear stream in full enthusiasm
Pours itself on the plain, then wandering
  Down one clear path of effluence crystalline
Sends its superfluous waves, that they may fling
  At Arno's feet tribute of corn and wine;   115
Then, through the pestilential deserts wild
  Of tangled marsh and woods of stunted pine,
It rushes to the Ocean.

MUSIC

I

I PANT for the music which is divine,
  My heart in its thirst is a dying flower;
Pour forth the sound like enchanted wine,
  Loosen the notes in a silver shower;
Like a herbless plain, for the gentle rain,   5
I gasp, I faint, till they wake again.

II

Let me drink of the spirit of that sweet sound,
  More, oh more,—I am thirsting yet;
It loosens the serpent which care has bound
  Upon my heart to stifle it;   10
The dissolving strain, through every vein,
  Passes into my heart and brain.

III

As the scent of a violet withered up,
  Which grew by the brink of a silver lake,
When the hot noon has drained its dewy cup,   15
  And mist there was none its thirst to slake—
And the violet lay dead while the odour flew
On the wings of the wind o'er the waters blue—

IV

As one who drinks from a charmèd cup
  Of foaming, and sparkling, and murmuring wine,   20
Whom, a mighty Enchantress filling up,
  Invites to love with her kiss divine . . .

SONNET TO BYRON

[I AM afraid these verses will not please you, but]
If I esteemed you less, Envy would kill
Pleasure, and leave to Wonder and Despair
The ministration of the thoughts that fill
The mind which, like a worm whose life may share
A portion of the unapproachable,   5
Marks your creations rise as fast and fair
As perfect worlds at the Creator's will.
But such is my regard that nor your power
To soar above the heights where others [climb],
Nor fame, that shadow of the unborn hour   10
Cast from the envious future on the time,
Move one regret for his unhonoured name
Who dares these words:—the worm beneath the sod
May lift itself in homage of the God.

FRAGMENT ON KEATS

WHO DESIRED THAT ON HIS TOMB SHOULD BE INSCRIBED—

'HERE lieth One whose name was writ on water.'
  But, ere the breath that could erase it blew,
Death, in remorse for that fell slaughter,
  Death, the immortalizing winter, flew
  Athwart the stream,—and time's printless torrent grew   5
A scroll of crystal, blazoning the name
  Of Adonais!

FRAGMENT: 'METHOUGHT I WAS A BILLOW IN THE CROWD'

METHOUGHT I was a billow in the crowd
  Of common men, that stream without a shore,
That ocean which at once is deaf and loud;
  That I, a man, stood amid many more
  By a wayside . . . , which the aspect bore   5
Of some imperial metropolis,
  Where mighty shapes—pyramid, dome, and tower—
Gleamed like a pile of crags—

TO-MORROW

WHERE art thou, beloved To-morrow?
  When young and old, and strong and weak,
Rich and poor, through joy and sorrow,
  Thy sweet smiles we ever seek,—
In thy place—ah! well-a-day!   5
We find the thing we fled—To-day.

STANZA

IF I walk in Autumn's even
  While the dead leaves pass,
If I look on Spring's soft heaven,—
  Something is not there which was.
Winter's wondrous frost and snow,   5
Summer's clouds, where are they now?

FRAGMENT: A WANDERER

HE wanders, like a day-appearing dream,
  Through the dim wildernesses of the mind;
Through desert woods and tracts, which seem
  Like ocean, homeless, boundless, unconfined.

FRAGMENT: LIFE ROUNDED WITH SLEEP

THE babe is at peace within the womb;
The corpse is at rest within the tomb:
We begin in what we end.

FRAGMENT: 'I FAINT, I PERISH WITH MY LOVE!'

I FAINT, I perish with my love! I grow
Frail as a cloud whose [splendours] pale
Under the evening's ever-changing glow:
I die like mist upon the gale,
And like a wave under the calm I fail.   5

FRAGMENT: THE LADY OF THE SOUTH

FAINT with love, the Lady of the South
Lay in the paradise of Lebanon
Under a heaven of cedar boughs: the drouth
Of love was on her lips; the light was gone
Out of her eyes—   5

FRAGMENT: ZEPHYRUS THE AWAKENER

COME, thou awakener of the spirit's ocean,
Zephyr, whom to thy cloud or cave
No thought can trace! speed with thy gentle motion!

FRAGMENT: RAIN

THE gentleness of rain was in the wind.

FRAGMENT: 'WHEN SOFT WINDS AND SUNNY SKIES'

WHEN soft winds and sunny skies
With the green earth harmonize,
And the young and dewy dawn,
Bold as an unhunted fawn,
Up the windless heaven is gone,—   5
Laugh—for ambushed in the day,—
Clouds and whirlwinds watch their prey.

FRAGMENT: 'AND THAT I WALK THUS PROUDLY CROWNED'

AND that I walk thus proudly crowned withal
Is that 'tis my distinction; if I fall,
I shall not weep out of the vital day,
To-morrow dust, nor wear a dull decay.

FRAGMENT: 'THE RUDE WIND IS SINGING'

THE rude wind is singing
 The dirge of the music dead;
The cold worms are clinging
 Where kisses were lately fed.

FRAGMENT: 'GREAT SPIRIT'

GREAT Spirit whom the sea of boundless thought
Nurtures within its unimagined caves,
In which thou sittest sole, as in my mind,
Giving a voice to its mysterious waves—

FRAGMENT: 'O THOU IMMORTAL DEITY'

O THOU immortal deity
Whose throne is in the depth of human thought,
 I do adjure thy power and thee
By all that man may be, by all that he is not,
 By all that he has been and yet must be!   5

FRAGMENT: THE FALSE LAUREL AND THE TRUE

'WHAT art thou, Presumptuous, who profanest
 The wreath to mighty poets only due,
Even whilst like a forgotten moon thou wanest?
 Touch not those leaves which for the eternal few
Who wander o'er the Paradise of fame,   5
 In sacred dedication ever grew:
One of the crowd thou art without a name.'
 'Ah, friend, 'tis the false laurel that I wear;
Bright though it seem, it is not the same
 As that which bound Milton's immortal hair; 10
Its dew is poison; and the hopes that quicken
 Under its chilling shade, though seeming fair,
Are flowers which die almost before they sicken.'

FRAGMENT: MAY THE LIMNER

WHEN May is painting with her colours gay
The landscape sketched by April her sweet twin . . .

FRAGMENT: BEAUTY'S HALO

THY beauty hangs around thee like
 Splendour around the moon—
Thy voice, as silver bells that strike
 Upon

FRAGMENT: 'THE DEATH KNELL IS RINGING'

THE death knell is ringing
The raven is singing
The earth worm is creeping
The mourners are weeping
Ding dong, bell— 5

FRAGMENT: 'I STOOD UPON A HEAVEN-CLEAVING TURRET'

I STOOD upon a heaven-cleaving turret
  Which overlooked a wide Metropolis—
And in the temple of my heart my Spirit
  Lay prostrate, and with parted lips did kiss
The dust of Desolations [altar] hearth— 5
And with a voice too faint to falter
It shook that trembling fane with its weak prayer
'Twas noon,—the sleeping skies were blue
  The city

NOTE ON POEMS OF 1821, BY MRS. SHELLEY

My task becomes inexpressibly painful as the year draws near that which sealed our earthly fate, and each poem, and each event it records, has a real or mysterious connexion with the fatal catastrophe. I feel that I am incapable of putting on paper the history of those times. The heart of the man, abhorred of the poet, who could

'peep and botanize
Upon his mother's grave,'

does not appear to me more inexplicably framed than that of one who can dissect and probe past woes, and repeat to the public ear the groans drawn from them in the throes of their agony.

The year 1821 was spent in Pisa, or at the Baths of San Giuliano. We were not, as our wont had been, alone; friends had gathered round us. Nearly all are dead, and, when Memory recurs to the past, she wanders among tombs. The genius, with all his blighting errors and mighty powers; the companion of Shelley's ocean-wanderings, and the sharer of his fate, than whom no man ever existed more gentle, generous, and fearless; and others, who found in Shelley's society, and in his great knowledge and warm sympathy, delight, instruction, and solace; have joined him beyond the grave. A few survive who have felt life a desert since he left it. What misfortune can equal death? Change can convert every other into a blessing, or heal its sting—death alone has no cure. It shakes the foundations of the earth on which we tread; it destroys its beauty; it casts down our shelter; it exposes us bare to desolation. When those we love have passed into eternity, 'life is the desert and the solitude' in which we are forced to linger—but never find comfort more.

There is much in the *Adonais* which seems now more applicable to Shelley himself than to the young and gifted poet whom he mourned. The poetic view he takes of death, and the lofty scorn he displays towards his calumniators, are as a prophecy on his own destiny when received among immortal names, and the poisonous breath of critics has vanished into emptiness before the fame he inherits.

Shelley's favourite taste was boating; when living near the Thames or by the Lake of Geneva, much of his life was spent on the water. On the shore of every lake or stream or sea near which he dwelt, he had a boat moored. He had latterly enjoyed this pleasure again. There are no pleasure-boats on the Arno; and the shallowness of its waters (except in winter-time, when the stream is too turbid and impetuous for boating) rendered it difficult to get any skiff light enough to float. Shelley, however, overcame the difficulty; he, together with a friend, contrived a boat such as the huntsmen carry about with them in the Maremma, to cross the sluggish but deep streams that intersect the forests,—a boat of laths and pitched canvas. It held three persons; and he was often seen on the Arno in it, to the horror of the Italians, who remonstrated on the danger and could not understand how any one could take pleasure in an exercise that risked life. 'Ma va per la vita!' they exclaimed. I little thought how true their words would prove. He once ventured, with a friend, on the glassy sea of a calm day, down the Arno and round the coast to Leghorn, which, by keeping close in shore, was very practicable. They returned to Pisa by the canal, when, missing the direct cut, they got entangled among weeds, and the boat upset; a wetting was all the harm done, except that the intense cold of his drenched clothes made Shelley faint. Once I went down with him to the mouth of the Arno, where the stream, then high and swift, met the tideless sea, and disturbed its sluggish waters. It was a waste and dreary scene; the desert sand stretched into a point surrounded by waves that broke idly though perpetually around; it was a scene very similar to Lido, of which he had said—

> 'I love all waste
> And solitary places; where we taste
> The pleasure of believing what we see
> Is boundless, as we wish our souls to be:
> And such was this wide ocean, and this shore
> More barren than its billows.'

Our little boat was of greater use, unaccompanied by any danger, when we removed to the Baths. Some friends lived at the village of Pugnano, four miles off, and we went to and fro to see them, in our boat, by the canal; which, fed by the Serchio, was, though an artificial, a full and picturesque stream, making its way under verdant banks, sheltered by trees that dipped their boughs into the murmuring waters. By day, multitudes of ephemera darted to and fro on the surface; at night, the fireflies came out among the shrubs on the banks; the cicale at noon-day kept up their hum; the aziola cooed in the quiet evening. It was a pleasant summer, bright in all but Shelley's health and inconstant spirits; yet he enjoyed himself greatly, and became more and more attached to the part of the country where chance appeared to cast us. Sometimes he projected taking a farm situated on the height of one of the near hills, surrounded by chestnut and pine woods, and overlooking a wide extent of country: or settling still farther in the maritime Apennines, at Massa. Several of his slighter and unfinished poems were inspired by these scenes, and by the companions around us. It is the nature of that poetry, however, which overflows from the soul oftener to express sorrow and regret than joy; for it is when oppressed by the weight of life, and away from those he loves, that the poet has recourse to the solace of expression in verse.

Still, Shelley's passion was the ocean; and he wished that our summers, instead of being passed among the hills near Pisa, should be spent on the shores of the sea. It was very difficult to find a spot. We shrank from Naples from a fear that the heats would disagree with Percy: Leghorn had lost its only attraction, since our friends who had resided there were returned to England; and, Monte Nero being the resort of many English, we did not wish to find ourselves in the midst of a colony of chance travellers. No one then thought it possible to reside at Via Reggio, which latterly has become a summer resort. The low lands and bad air of Maremma stretch the whole length of the western shores of the Mediterranean, till broken by the rocks and hills of Spezia. It was a vague idea, but Shelley suggested an excursion to Spezia, to see whether it would be feasible to spend a summer there. The beauty of the bay enchanted him. We saw no house to suit us; but the notion took root, and many circumstances, enchained as by fatality, occurred to urge him to execute it.

He looked forward this autumn with great pleasure to the prospect of a visit from Leigh Hunt. When Shelley visited Lord Byron at Ravenna, the latter had suggested his coming out, together with the plan of a periodical work in which they should all join. Shelley saw a prospect of good for the fortunes of his friend, and pleasure in his society; and instantly exerted himself to have the plan executed. He did not intend himself joining in the work: partly from pride, not wishing to have the air of acquiring readers for his poetry by associating it with the compositions of more popular writers; and also because he might feel shackled in the free expression of his opinions, if any friends were to be compromised. By those opinions, carried even to their utmost extent, he wished to live and die, as being in his conviction not only true, but such as alone would conduce to the moral improvement and happiness of mankind. The sale of the work might meanwhile, either really or supposedly, be injured by the free expression of his thoughts; and this evil he resolved to avoid.

POEMS WRITTEN IN 1822
THE ZUCCA

I

SUMMER was dead and Autumn was expiring,
  And infant Winter laughed upon the land
All cloudlessly and cold;—when I, desiring
  More in this world than any understand,
Wept o'er the beauty, which, like sea retiring,   5
  Had left the earth bare as the wave-worn sand
Of my lorn heart, and o'er the grass and flowers
Pale for the falsehood of the flattering Hours.

II

Summer was dead, but I yet lived to weep
  The instability of all but weeping;   10
And on the Earth lulled in her winter sleep
  I woke, and envied her as she was sleeping.
Too happy Earth! over thy face shall creep
  The wakening vernal airs, until thou, leaping
From unremembered dreams, shalt   see   15
No death divide thy immortality.

III

I loved—oh, no, I mean not one of ye,
  Or any earthly one, though ye are dear
As human heart to human heart may be;—
  I loved, I know not what—but this low sphere   20
And all that it contains, contains not thee,
  Thou, whom, seen nowhere, I feel everywhere.
From Heaven and Earth, and all that in them are,
Veiled art thou, like a   star.

IV

By Heaven and Earth, from all whose shapes thou flowest,   25
  Neither to be contained, delayed, nor hidden;
Making divine the loftiest and the lowest,
  When for a moment thou art not forbidden
To live within the life which thou bestowest;
  And leaving noblest things vacant and chidden,   30
Cold as a corpse after the spirit's flight,
Blank as the sun after the birth of night.

V

In winds, and trees, and streams, and all things common,
   In music and the sweet unconscious tone
Of animals, and voices which are human,   35
   Meant to express some feelings of their own;
In the soft motions and rare smile of woman,
   In flowers and leaves, and in the grass, fresh-shown,
Or dying in the autumn, I the most
Adore thee present or lament thee lost.   40

VI

And thus I went lamenting, when I saw
   A plant upon the river's margin lie,
Like one who loved beyond his nature's law,
   And in despair had cast him down to die;
Its leaves, which had outlived the frost, the thaw   45
   Had blighted; like a heart which hatred's eye
Can blast not, but which pity kills; the dew
Lay on its spotted leaves like tears too true.

VII

The Heavens had wept upon it, but the Earth
   Had crushed it on her unmaternal breast   50

  .   .   .   .

VIII

I bore it to my chamber, and I planted
   It in a vase full of the lightest mould;
The winter beams which out of Heaven slanted
   Fell through the window-panes, disrobed of cold,
Upon its leaves and flowers; the stars which panted   55
   In evening for the Day, whose car has rolled
Over the horizon's wave, with looks of light
Smiled on it from the threshold of the night.

IX

The mitigated influences of air
   And light revived the plant, and from it grew   60
Strong leaves and tendrils, and its flowers fair,
   Full as a cup with the vine's burning dew,
O'erflowed with golden colours; an atmosphere
   Of vital warmth enfolded it anew,
And every impulse sent to every part   65
The unbeheld pulsations of its heart

X

Well might the plant grow beautiful and strong,
  Even if the air and sun had smiled not on it;
For one wept o'er it all the winter long
  Tears pure as Heaven's rain, which fell upon it   70
Hour after hour; for sounds of softest song
  Mixed with the stringèd melodies that won it
To leave the gentle lips on which it slept,
Had loosed the heart of him who sat and wept.

XI

Had loosed his heart, and shook the leaves and flowers   75
  On which he wept, the while the savage storm
Waked by the darkest of December's hours
  Was raving round the chamber hushed and warm;
The birds were shivering in their leafless bowers,
  The fish were frozen in the pools, the form   80
Of every summer plant was dead . . .
Whilst this . . .

.   .   .   .

THE MAGNETIC LADY TO HER PATIENT

I

'SLEEP, sleep on! forget thy pain;
  My hand is on thy brow,
My spirit on thy brain;
My pity on thy heart, poor friend;
  And from my fingers flow   5
The powers of life, and like a sign,
  Seal thee from thine hour of woe;
And brood on thee, but may not
    blend
  With thine.

II

'Sleep, sleep on! I love thee not;   10
  But when I think that he
Who made and makes my lot
As full of flowers as thine of weeds,
  Might have been lost like thee;
And that a hand which was not
    mine   15
  Might then have charmed his
    agony
As I another's—my heart bleeds
  For thine.

III

'Sleep, sleep, and with the slumber
    of
  The dead and the unborn   20
Forget thy life and love;
Forget that thou must wake for-
    ever;
  Forget the world's dull scorn;
Forget lost health, and the divine
  Feelings which died in youth's
    brief morn;   25
And forget me, for I can never
  Be thine.

IV

'Like a cloud big with a May
    shower,
  My soul weeps healing rain
On thee, thou withered flower!   30
It breathes mute music on thy
    sleep;
  Its odour calms thy brain!
Its light within thy gloomy breast

Spreads like a second youth
  again.
By mine thy being is to its deep 35
  Possessed.

V

'The spell is done. How feel you
  now?'
  'Better—Quite well,' replied
The sleeper.—'What would do 39

You good when suffering and
  awake?
What cure your head and
  side?—'
'What would cure, that would kill
  me, Jane:
And as I must on earth abide
Awhile, yet tempt me not to break
  My chain.'   45

LINES: 'WHEN THE LAMP IS SHATTERED'

I

WHEN the lamp is shattered
The light in the dust lies dead—
When the cloud is scattered
The rainbow's glory is shed.
  When the lute is broken,   5
Sweet tones are remembered not;
  When the lips have spoken,
Loved accents are soon forgot.

II

  As music and splendour
Survive not the lamp and the
  lute,   10
  The heart's echoes render
No song when the spirit is mute:—
  No song but sad dirges,
Like the wind through a ruined
  cell,
  Or the mournful surges   15
That ring the dead seaman's knell.

III

When hearts have once mingled
Love first leaves the well-built nest;
  The weak one is singled
To endure what it once pos-
  sessed.   20
  O Love! who bewailest
The frailty of all things here,
  Why choose you the frailest
For your cradle, your home, and
  your bier?

IV

  Its passions will rock thee 25
As the storms rock the ravens on
  high;
  Bright reason will mock thee,
Like the sun from a wintry sky.
  From thy nest every rafter
Will rot, and thine eagle home 30
  Leave thee naked to laughter,
When leaves fall and cold winds
  come.

TO JANE: THE INVITATION

BEST and brightest, come away!
Fairer far than this fair Day,
Which, like thee to those in sorrow,
Comes to bid a sweet good-morrow
To the rough Year just awake 5
In its cradle on the brake.
The brightest hour of unborn
  Spring,
Through the winter wandering,

Found, it seems, the halcyon Morn
To hoar February born.   10
Bending from Heaven, in azure
  mirth,
It kissed the forehead of the
  Earth,
And smiled upon the silent sea,
And bade the frozen streams be
  free,

And waked to music all their foun-
   tains,   15
And breathed upon the frozen
   mountains,
And like a prophetess of May
Strewed flowers upon the barren
   way,
Making the wintry world appear
Like one on whom thou smilest,
   dear.   20

Away, away, from men and towns,
To the wild wood and the downs—
To the silent wilderness
Where the soul need not repress
Its music lest it should not find   25
An echo in another's mind,
While the touch of Nature's art
Harmonizes heart to heart.
I leave this notice on my door
For each accustomed visitor:—   30
'I am gone into the fields
To take what this sweet hour
   yields,—
Reflection, you may come to-mor-
   row,
Sit by the fireside with Sorrow.—
You with the unpaid bill, De-
   spair,—
You, tiresome verse-reciter,
   Care,—   35
I will pay you in the grave,—
Death will listen to your stave.
Expectation too, be off!

To-day is for itself enough;   40
Hope, in pity mock not Woe
With smiles, nor follow where I go;
Long having lived on thy sweet
   food,
At length I find one moment's good
After long pain—with all your love,
This you never told me of.'   46

Radiant Sister of the Day,
Awake! arise! and come away!
To the wild woods and the plains,
And the pools where winter rains 50
Image all their roof of leaves,
Where the pine its garland weaves
Of sapless green and ivy dun
Round stems that never kiss the
   sun;
Where the lawns and pastures be, 55
And the sandhills of the sea;—
Where the melting hoar-frost wets
The daisy-star that never sets,
And wind-flowers, and violets,
Which yet join not scent to hue, 60
Crown the pale year weak and new;
When the night is left behind,
In the deep east, dun and blind,
And the blue noon is over us,
And the multitudinous   65
Billows murmur at our feet,
Where the earth and ocean meet,
And all things seem only one
In the universal sun.

TO JANE: THE RECOLLECTION

I

Now the last day of many days,
   All beautiful and bright as thou,
   The loveliest and the last, is
     dead,
Rise, Memory, and write its praise!
   Up,—to thy wonted work! come,
     trace   5
   The epitaph of glory fled,—

For now the Earth has changed its
     face,
   A frown is on the Heaven's brow.

II

We wandered to the Pine Forest
   That skirts the Ocean's foam, 10
The lightest wind was in its nest,
   The tempest in its home.

The whispering waves were half
    asleep,
The clouds were gone to play,
And on the bosom of the deep   15
The smile of Heaven lay;
It seemed as if the hour were one
Sent from beyond the skies,
Which scattered from above the
    sun
A light of Paradise.   20

III

We paused amid the pines that
    stood
The giants of the waste,
Tortured by storms to shapes as
    rude
As serpents interlaced,
And soothed by every azure breath,
That under Heaven is blown,   26
To harmonies and hues beneath, •
As tender as its own;
Now all the tree-tops lay asleep,
Like green waves on the sea,   30
As still as in the silent deep
The ocean woods may be.

IV

How calm it was!—the silence
    there
By such a chain was bound
That even the busy woodpecker   35
Made stiller by her sound
The inviolable quietness;
The breath of peace we drew
With its soft motion made not less
The calm that round us grew.   40
There seemed from the remotest
    seat
Of the white mountain waste,
To the soft flower beneath our feet,
A magic circle traced,—
A spirit interfused around,   45
A thrilling, silent life.—
To momentary peace it bound
Our mortal nature's strife;
And still I felt the centre of

The magic circle there   50
Was one fair form that filled with
    love
The lifeless atmosphere.

V

We paused beside the pools that lie
Under the forest bough.—
Each seemed as 'twere a little sky 55
Gulfed in a world below;
A firmament of purple light
Which in the dark earth lay,
More boundless than the depth of
    night,
And purer than the day—   60
In which the lovely forests grew,
As in the upper air,
More perfect both in shape and hue
Than any spreading there.
There lay the glade and neighbour-
    ing lawn,   65
And through the dark green wood
The white sun twinkling like the
    dawn
Out of a speckled cloud.
Sweet views which in our world
    above
Can never well be seen,   70
Were imaged by the water's love
Of that fair forest green.
And all was interfused beneath
With an Elysian glow,
An atmosphere without a breath, 75
A softer day below.
Like one beloved the scene had lent
To the dark water's breast,
Its every leaf and lineament
With more than truth expressed;
Until an envious wind crept by, 81
Like an unwelcome thought,
Which from the mind's too faithful
    eye
Blots one dear image out.
Though thou art ever fair and kind,
The forests ever green,   86
Less oft is peace in Shelley's mind,
Than calm in waters, seen.

THE PINE FOREST OF THE CASCINE NEAR PISA

DEAREST, best and brightest,
 Come away,
To the woods and to the fields!
Dearer than this fairest day
Which, like thee to those in sor-
  row,   5
Comes to bid a sweet good-morrow
To the rough Year just awake
In its cradle in the brake.
The eldest of the Hours of Spring,
Into the Winter wandering, 10
Looks upon the leafless wood,
And the banks all bare and rude;
Found, it seems, this halcyon Morn
In February's bosom born,
Bending from Heaven, in azure
  mirth,   15
Kissed the cold forehead of the
  Earth,
And smiled upon the silent sea,
And bade the frozen streams be
  free;
And waked to music all the foun-
  tains,
And breathed upon the rigid moun-
  tains,   20
And made the wintry world appear
Like one on whom thou smilest,
  Dear.

Radiant Sister of the Day,
Awake! arise! and come away!
To the wild woods and the plains, 25
To the pools where winter rains
Image all the roof of leaves,
Where the pine its garland weaves
Sapless, gray, and ivy dun
Round stems that never kiss the
  sun—   30
To the sandhills of the sea,
Where the earliest violets be.

Now the last day of many days,
All beautiful and bright as thou,
The loveliest and the last, is
  dead,   35

Rise, Memory, and write its praise!
And do thy wonted work and trace
The epitaph of glory fled;
For now the Earth has changed its
  face,
A frown is on the Heaven's brow. 40

We wandered to the Pine Forest
 That skirts the Ocean's foam,
The lightest wind was in its nest,
 The tempest in its home.

The whispering waves were half
  asleep,   45
 The clouds were gone to play,
And on the woods, and on the deep
 The smile of Heaven lay.

It seemed as if the day were one
 Sent from beyond the skies, 50
Which shed to earth above the sun
 A light of Paradise.

We paused amid the pines that
  stood,
 The giants of the waste,
Tortured by storms to shapes as
  rude   55
 With stems like serpents interlaced.

How calm it was—the silence there
 By such a chain was bound,
That even the busy woodpecker
 Made stiller by her sound 60

The inviolable quietness;
 The breath of peace we drew
With its soft motion made not less
 The calm that round us grew.

It seemed that from the remotest
  seat   65
 Of the white mountain's waste
To the bright flower beneath our
  feet,
 A magic circle traced;—

A spirit interfused around,
  A thinking, silent life;   70
To momentary peace it bound
  Our mortal nature's strife;—

And still, it seemed, the centre of
  The magic circle there,
Was one whose being filled with
    love
  The breathless atmosphere.   76

Were not the crocuses that grew
  Under that ilex-tree
As beautiful in scent and hue
  As ever fed the bee?   80

We stood beneath the pools that lie
  Under the forest bough,
And each seemed like a sky
  Gulfed in a world below;

A purple firmament of light   85
  Which in the dark earth lay,
More boundless than the depth of
    night,
  And clearer than the day—

In which the massy forests grew
  As in the upper air,   90
More perfect both in shape and hue
  Than any waving there.

Like one beloved the scene had lent
  To the dark water's breast

Its every leaf and lineament   95
  With that clear truth expressed;

There lay far glades and neighbour-
    ing lawn,
  And through the dark green
    crowd
The white sun twinkling like the
    dawn
  Under a speckled cloud.   100

Sweet views, which in our world
    above
  Can never well be seen,
Were imaged by the water's love
  Of that fair forest green.

And all was interfused beneath 103
  With an Elysian air,
An atmosphere without a breath,
  A silence sleeping there.

Until a wandering wind crept by,
  Like an unwelcome thought, 110
Which from my mind's too faithful
    eye
  Blots thy bright image out.

For thou art good and dear and
    kind,
  The forest ever green,
But less of peace in S——'s mind,
  Than calm in waters, seen.   116

WITH A GUITAR, TO JANE

Ariel to Miranda:—Take
This slave of Music, for the sake
Of him who is the slave of thee,
And teach it all the harmony
In which thou canst, and only thou,
Make the delighted spirit glow, 6
Till joy denies itself again,
And, too intense, is turned to pain;
For by permission and command
Of thine own Prince Ferdinand, 10
Poor Ariel sends this silent token
Of more than ever can be spoken;
Your guardian spirit, Ariel, who,
From life to life, must still pursue

Your happiness;—for thus alone 15
Can Ariel ever find his own.
From Prospero's enchanted cell,
As the mighty verses tell,
To the throne of Naples, he
Lit you o'er the trackless sea, 20
Flitting on, your prow before,
Like a living meteor.
When you die, the silent Moon,
In her interlunar swoon,
Is not sadder in her cell   25
Than deserted Ariel.
When you live again on earth,
Like an unseen star of birth,

Ariel guides you o'er the sea
Of life from your nativity.   30
Many changes have been run
Since Ferdinand and you begun
Your course of love, and Ariel still
Has tracked your steps, and served
    your will;
Now, in humbler, happier lot,   35
This is all remembered not;
And now, alas! the poor sprite is
Imprisoned, for some fault of his,
In a body like a grave;—
From you he only dares to crave,   40
For his service and his sorrow,
A smile to-day, a song to-morrow.

The artist who this idol wrought,
To echo all harmonious thought,
Felled a tree, while on the steep   45
The woods were in their winter
    sleep,
Rocked in that repose divine
On the wind-swept Apennine;
And dreaming, some of Autumn
    past,
And some of Spring approaching
    fast,   50
And some of April buds and show-
    ers,
And some of songs in July bowers,
And all of love; and so this tree,—
O that such our death may be!—
Died in sleep, and felt no pain,   55
To live in happier form again:
From which, beneath Heaven's fair-
    est star,

The artist wrought this loved
    Guitar,
And taught it justly to reply,
To all who question skilfully,   60
In language gentle as thine own;
Whispering in enamoured tone
Sweet oracles of woods and dells,
And summer winds in sylvan cells;
For it had learned all harmonies 65
Of the plains and of the skies,
Of the forests and the mountains,
And the many-voicèd fountains;
The clearest echoes of the hills,
The softest notes of falling rills, 70
The melodies of birds and bees,
The murmuring of summer seas,
And pattering rain, and breathing
    dew,
And airs of evening; and it knew
That seldom-heard mysterious
    sound,   75
Which, driven on its diurnal round,
As it floats through boundless day,
Our world enkindles on its way.—
All this it knows, but will not tell
To those who cannot question well
The Spirit that inhabits it;   81
It talks according to the wit
Of its companions; and no more
Is heard than has been felt before,
By those who tempt it to betray 85
These secrets of an elder day:
But, sweetly as its answers will
Flatter hands of perfect skill,
It keeps its highest, holiest tone
For our belovèd Jane alone.   90

TO JANE: 'THE KEEN STARS WERE TWINKLING'

I

THE keen stars were twinkling,
And the fair moon was rising among
    them,
    Dear Jane!
The guitar was tinkling,

But the notes were not sweet till
    you sung them   5
    Again.

II

As the moon's soft splendour
O'er the faint cold starlight of
    Heaven

Is thrown,
So your voice most tender   10
To the strings without soul had
    then given
Its own.

III

The stars will awaken,
Though the moon sleep a full hour
    later,
    To-night;   15
No leaf will be shaken

Whilst the dews of your melody
    scatter
    Delight.

IV

Though the sound overpowers,
Sing again, with your dear voice
    revealing   20
   A tone
Of some world far from ours,
Where music and moonlight and
    feeling
    Are one.

A DIRGE

Rough wind, that moanest loud
    Grief too sad for song;
Wild wind, when sullen cloud
    Knells all the night long;

Sad storm, whose tears are vain,   5
Bare woods, whose branches strain,
Deep caves and dreary main,—
    Wail, for the world's wrong!

LINES WRITTEN IN THE BAY OF LERICI

She left me at the silent time
When the moon had ceased to climb
The azure path of Heaven's steep,
And like an albatross asleep,
Balanced on her wings of light,   5
Hovered in the purple night,
Ere she sought her ocean nest
In the chambers of the West.
She left me, and I stayed alone
Thinking over every tone   10
Which, though silent to the ear,
The enchanted heart could hear,
Like notes which die when born, but
    still
Haunt the echoes of the hill;
And feeling ever—oh, too much!—
The soft vibration of her touch,   16
As if her gentle hand, even now,
Lightly trembled on my brow;
And thus, although she absent were,
Memory gave me all of her   20
That even Fancy dares to claim:—
Her presence had made weak and
    tame
All passions, and I lived alone
In the time which is our own;

The past and future were forgot, 25
As they had been, and would be,
    not.
But soon, the guardian angel gone,
The daemon reassumed his throne
In my faint heart. I dare not speak
My thoughts, but thus disturbed
    and weak   30
I sat and saw the vessels glide
Over the ocean bright and wide,
Like spirit-wingèd chariots sent
O'er some serenest element
For ministrations strange and
    far;   35
As if to some Elysian star
Sailed for drink to medicine
Such sweet and bitter pain as mine.
And the wind that winged their
    flight
From the land came fresh and light,
And the scent of wingèd flowers, 41
And the coolness of the hours
Of dew, and sweet warmth left by
    day.
Were scattered o'er the twinkling
    day,

And the fisher with his lamp   45
And spear about the low rocks
    damp
Crept, and struck the fish which
    came
To worship the delusive flame.

Too happy they, whose pleasure
    sought
Extinguishes all sense and thought
Of the regret that pleasure leaves, 51
Destroying life alone, not peace!

LINES: 'WE MEET NOT AS WE PARTED'

I

WE meet not as we parted,
    We feel more than all may see;
My bosom is heavy-hearted,
    And thine full of doubt for me:—
    One moment has bound the
        free.   5

II

That moment is gone for ever,
    Like lightning that flashed and
        died—
Like a snowflake upon the river—
    Like a sunbeam upon the tide,
    Which the dark shadows hide. 10

III

That moment from time was singled
    As the first of a life of pain;
The cup of its joy was mingled

    —Delusion too sweet though
        vain!
Too sweet to be mine again.   15

IV

Sweet lips, could my heart have
    hidden
    That its life was crushed by you,
Ye would not have then forbidden
    The death which a heart so true
    Sought in your briny dew.   20

V

.   .   .   .   .

.   .   .   .   .

.   .   .   .   .

Methinks too little cost
    For a moment so found, so
        lost!   25

THE ISLE

THERE was a little lawny islet
By anemone and violet,
    Like mosaic, paven:
And its roof was flowers and leaves
Which the summer's breath en-
    weaves,   5
Where nor sun nor showers nor
    breeze

Pierce the pines and tallest trees,
    Each a gem engraven;—
Girt by many an azure wave
With which the clouds and moun-
    tains pave   10
    A lake's blue chasm.

FRAGMENT: TO THE MOON

BRIGHT wanderer, fair coquette of
    Heaven,
To whom alone it has been given
To change and be adored for ever,

Envy not this dim world, for
    never
But once within its shadow grew 5
One fair as ——

EPITAPH

THESE are two friends whose lives were undivided;
So let their memory be, now they have glided

Under the grave; let not their bones be parted,
For their two hearts in life were single-hearted.

NOTE ON POEMS OF 1822, BY MRS. SHELLEY

THIS morn thy gallant bark
  Sailed on a sunny sea:
'Tis noon, and tempests dark
  Have wrecked it on the lee.
    Ah woe! ah woe!
By Spirits of the deep
  Thou'rt cradled on the billow
To thy eternal sleep.
Thou sleep'st upon the shore
  Beside the knelling surge,
And Sea-nymphs evermore
  Shall sadly chant thy dirge.
    They come, they come,
The Spirits of the deep,—
  While near thy seaweed pillow
My lonely watch I keep.
From far across the sea
  I hear a loud lament,
By Echo's voice for thee
  From Ocean's caverns sent.
    O list! O list!
The Spirits of the deep!
  They raise a wail of sorrow,
While I forever weep.

WITH this last year of the life of Shelley these Notes end. They are not what I intended them to be. I began with energy, and a burning desire to impart to the world, in worthy language, the sense I have of the virtues and genius of the beloved and the lost; my strength has failed under the task. Recurrence to the past, full of its own deep and unforgotten joys and sorrows, contrasted with succeeding years of painful and solitary struggle, has shaken my health. Days of great suffering have followed my attempts to write, and these again produced a weakness and languor that spread their sinister influence over these notes. I dislike speaking of myself, but cannot help apologizing to the dead, and to the public, for not having executed in the manner I desired the history I engaged to give of Shelley's writings.[1]

---

[1] I at one time feared that the correction of the press might be less exact through my illness; but I believe that it is nearly free from error. Some asterisks occur in a few pages, as they did in the volume of *Posthumous Poems*, either because they refer to private concerns, or because the original manuscript was left imperfect. Did any one see the papers from which I drew that volume, the wonder would be how any eyes or patience were capable of extracting it from so confused a mass, interlined and broken into fragments, so that the sense could only be deciphered and joined by guesses which might seem rather intuitive than founded on reasoning. Yet I believe no mistake was made.

The winter of 1822 was passed in Pisa, if we might call that season winter in which autumn merged into spring after the interval of but few days of bleaker weather. Spring sprang up early, and with extreme beauty. Shelley had conceived the idea of writing a tragedy on the subject of Charles I. It was one that he believed adapted for a drama; full of intense interest, contrasted character, and busy passion. He had recommended it long before, when he encouraged me to attempt a play. Whether the subject proved more difficult than he anticipated, or whether in fact he could not bend his mind away from the broodings and wanderings of thought, divested from human interest, which he best loved, I cannot tell; but he proceeded slowly, and threw it aside for one of the most mystical of his poems, the *Triumph of Life*, on which he was employed at the last.

His passion for boating was fostered at this time by having among our friends several sailors. His favourite companion, Edward Ellerker Williams, of the 8th Light Dragoons, had begun his life in the navy, and had afterwards entered the army; he had spent several years in India, and his love for adventure and manly exercises accorded with Shelley's taste. It was their favourite plan to build a boat such as they could manage themselves, and, living on the sea-coast, to enjoy at every hour and season the pleasure they loved best. Captain Roberts, R.N., undertook to build the boat at Genoa, where he was also occupied in building the *Bolivar* for Lord Byron. Ours was to be an open boat, on a model taken from one of the royal dockyards. I have since heard that there was a defect in this model, and that it was never seaworthy. In the month of February, Shelley and his friend went to Spezia to seek for houses for us. Only one was to be found at all suitable; however, a trifle such as not finding a house could not stop Shelley; the one found was to serve for all. It was unfurnished; we sent our furniture by sea, and with a good deal of precipitation, arising from his impatience, made our removal. We left Pisa on the 26th of April.

The Bay of Spezia is of considerable extent, and divided by a rocky promontory into a larger and smaller one. The town of Lerici is situated on the eastern point, and in the depth of the smaller bay, which bears the name of this town, is the village of San Terenzo. Our house, Casa Magni, was close to this village; the sea came up to the door, a steep hill sheltered it behind. The proprietor of the estate on which it was situated was insane; he had begun to erect a large house at the summit of the hill behind, but his malady prevented its being finished, and it was falling into ruin. He had (and this to the Italians had seemed a glaring symptom of very decided madness) rooted up the olives on the hillside, and planted forest trees. These were mostly young, but the plantation was more in English taste than I ever elsewhere saw in Italy; some fine walnut and ilex trees intermingled their dark massy foliage, and formed groups which still haunt my memory, as then they satiated the eye with a sense of loveliness. The scene was indeed of unimaginable beauty. The blue extent of waters, the almost landlocked bay, the near castle of Lerici shutting it in to the east, and distant Porto Venere to the west; the varied forms of the precipitous rocks that bound in the beach, over which there was only a winding rugged footpath towards Lerici, and none on the other side; the tideless sea leaving no sands nor shingle, formed a picture such as one sees in Salvator Rosa's landscapes only. Sometimes the sunshine vanished when the sirocco raged—the 'ponente' the wind was called on that shore. The gales and squalls that hailed our first arrival surrounded the bay with foam; the howling wind swept round our exposed house, and the sea roared unremittingly, so that we almost fancied ourselves on board ship. At other times sunshine and calm invested sea and sky, and the rich tints of Italian heaven bathed the scene in bright and ever-varying tints.

The natives were wilder than the place. Our near neighbours of San Terenzo were more like savages than any people I ever before lived among. Many a night they passed on the beach, singing, or rather howling; the women dancing about among the waves that broke at their feet, the men leaning against the rocks and joining in their loud wild chorus. We could get no provisions nearer than Sarzana, at a distance of three miles and a half off, with the torrent of the Magra between; and even there the supply was very deficient. Had we been wrecked on an island of the South Seas, we could scarcely have felt ourselves farther from civilization and comfort; but, where the sun shines, the latter becomes an unnecessary luxury, and we had enough society among ourselves. Yet I confess housekeeping became rather a toilsome task, especially as I was suffering in my health, and could not exert myself actively.

At first the fatal boat had not arrived, and was expected with great impatience. On Monday, 12th May, it came. Williams records the long-wished-for fact in his journal: 'Cloudy and threatening weather. M. Maglian called; and after dinner, and while walking with him on the terrace, we discovered a strange sail coming round the point of Porto Venere, which proved at length to be Shelley's boat. She had left Genoa on Thursday last, but had been driven back by the prevailing bad winds. A Mr. Heslop and two English seamen brought her round, and they speak most highly of her performances. She does indeed excite my surprise and admiration. Shelley and I walked to Lerici, and made a stretch off the land to try her: and I find she fetches whatever she looks at. In short, we have now a perfect plaything for the summer.'— It was thus that short-sighted mortals welcomed Death, he having disguised his grim form in a pleasing mask! The time of the friends was now spent on the sea; the weather became fine, and our whole party often passed the evenings on the water when the wind promised pleasant sailing. Shelley and Williams made longer excursions; they sailed several times to Massa. They had engaged one of the seamen who brought her round, a boy, by name Charles Vivian; and they had not the slightest apprehension of danger. When the weather was unfavourable, they employed themselves with alterations in the rigging, and by building a boat of canvas and reeds, as light as possible, to have on board the other for the convenience of landing in waters too shallow for the larger vessel. When Shelley was on board, he had his papers with him; and much of the *Triumph of Life* was written as he sailed or weltered on that sea which was soon to engulf him.

The heats set in in the middle of June; the days became excessively hot. But the sea-breeze cooled the air at noon, and extreme heat always put Shelley in spirits. A long drought had preceded the heat; and prayers for rain were being put up in the churches, and processions of relics for the same effect took place in every town. At this time we received letters announcing the arrival of Leigh Hunt at Genoa. Shelley was very eager to see him. I was confined to my room by severe illness, and could not move; it was agreed that Shelley and Williams should go to Leghorn in the boat. Strange that no fear of danger crossed our minds! Living on the sea-shore, the ocean became as a plaything: as a child may sport with a lighted stick, till a spark inflames a forest, and spreads destruction over all, so did we fearlessly and blindly tamper with danger, and make a game of the terrors of the ocean. Our Italian neighbours, even, trusted themselves as far as Massa in the skiff; and the running down the line of coast to Leghorn gave no more notion of peril than a fair-weather inland navigation would have done to those who had never seen the sea. Once, some months before, Trelawny had raised a warning voice as to the difference of our calm bay and the open sea beyond; but Shelley and his friend, with their one sailor-boy, thought themselves a match for the storms of the Mediterranean, in a boat which they looked upon as equal to all it was put to do.

On the 1st of July they left us. If ever shadow of future ill darkened the present hour, such was over my mind when they went. During the whole of our stay at Lerici, an intense presentiment of coming evil brooded over my mind, and covered this beautiful place and genial summer with the shadow of coming misery. I had vainly struggled with these emotions—they seemed accounted for by my illness; but at this hour of separation they recurred with renewed violence. I did not anticipate danger for them, but a vague expectation of evil shook me to agony, and I could scarcely bring myself to let them go. The day was calm and clear; and, a fine breeze rising at twelve, they weighed for Leghorn. They made the run of about fifty miles in seven hours and a half. The *Bolivar* was in port; and, the regulations of the Health-office not permitting them to go on shore after sunset, they borrowed cushions from the larger vessel, and slept on board their boat.

They spent a week at Pisa and Leghorn. The want of rain was severely felt in the country. The weather continued sultry and fine. I have heard that Shelley all this time was in brilliant spirits. Not long before, talking of presentiment, he had said the only one that he ever found infallible was the certain advent of some evil fortune when he felt peculiarly joyous. Yet, if ever fate whispered of coming disaster, such inaudible but not unfelt prognostics hovered around us. The beauty of the place seemed unearthly in its excess; the distance we were at from all signs of civilization, the sea at our feet, its murmurs or its roaring for ever in our ears,—all these things led the mind to brood over strange thoughts, and, lifting it from everyday life, caused it to be familiar with the unreal. A sort of spell surrounded us; and each day, as the voyagers did not return, we grew restless and disquieted, and yet, strange to say, we were not fearful of the most apparent danger.

The spell snapped; it was all over; an interval of agonizing doubt— of days passed in miserable journeys to gain tidings, of hopes that took firmer root even as they were more baseless—was changed to the certainty of the death that eclipsed all happiness for the survivors for evermore.

There was something in our fate peculiarly harrowing. The remains of those we lost were cast on shore; but, by the quarantine-laws of the coast, we were not permitted to have possession of them—the law with respect to everything cast on land by the sea being that such should be burned, to prevent the possibility of any remnant bringing the plague into Italy; and no representation could alter the law. At length, through the kind and unwearied exertions of Mr. Dawkins, our Chargé d'Affaires at Florence, we gained permission to receive the ashes after the bodies were consumed. Nothing could equal the zeal of Trelawny in carrying our wishes into effect. He was indefatigable in his exertions, and full of forethought and sagacity in his arrangements. It was a fearful task; he stood before us at last, his hands scorched and blistered by the flames of the funeral-pyre, and by touching the burnt relics as he placed them in the receptacle prepared for the purpose. And there, in compass of that small case, was gathered all that remained on earth of him whose genius and virtue were a crown of glory to the world—whose love had been the source of happiness, peace, and good,—to be buried with him!

The concluding stanzas of the *Adonais* pointed out where the remains ought to be deposited; in addition to which our beloved child lay buried in the cemetery at Rome. Thither Shelley's ashes were conveyed; and they rest beneath one of the antique weed-grown towers that recur at intervals in the circuit of the massy ancient wall of Rome. He selected the hallowed place himself; there is

> 'the sepulchre,
> Oh, not of him, but of our joy!—
> .   .   .   .
> And gray walls moulder round, on which dull Time
> Feeds, like slow fire upon a hoary brand;
> And one keen pyramid with wedge sublime,
> Pavilioning the dust of him who planned
> This refuge for his memory, doth stand
> Like flame transformed to marble; and beneath,
> A field is spread, on which a newer band
> Have pitched in Heaven's smile their camp of death,
> Welcoming him we lose with scarce extinguished breath.'

Could sorrow for the lost, and shuddering anguish at the vacancy left behind, be soothed by poetic imaginations, there was something in Shelley's fate to mitigate pangs which yet, alas! could not be so mitigated; for hard reality brings too miserably home to the mourner all that is lost of happiness, all of lonely unsolaced struggle that remains. Still, though dreams and hues of poetry cannot blunt grief, it invests his fate with a sublime fitness, which those less nearly allied may regard with complacency. A year before he had poured into verse all such ideas about death as give it a glory of its own. He had, as it now seems, almost anticipated his own destiny; and, when the mind figures his skiff wrapped from sight by the thunder-storm, as it was last seen upon the purple sea, and then, as the cloud of the tempest passed away, no sign remained of where it had been [1]—who but will regard as a prophecy the last stanza of the *Adonais?*

> 'The breath whose might I have invoked in song
> Descends on me; my spirit's bark is driven,
> Far from the shore, far from the trembling throng
> Whose sails were never to the tempest given;
> The massy earth and sphered skies are riven!
> I am borne darkly, fearfully, afar;
> Whilst burning through the inmost veil of Heaven,
> The soul of Adonais, like a star,
> Beacons from the abode where the Eternal are.'

PUTNEY, *May* 1, 1839.

TRANSLATIONS

HYMN TO MERCURY

TRANSLATED FROM THE GREEK OF HOMER

I

SING, Muse, the son of Maia and of Jove,
  The Herald-child, king of Arcadia
And all its pastoral hills, whom in sweet love
  Having been interwoven, modest May
Bore Heaven's dread Supreme. An antique grove   5
  Shadowed the cavern where the lovers lay
In the deep night, unseen by Gods or Men,
And white-armed Juno slumbered sweetly then.

---

[1] Captain Roberts watched the vessel with his glass from the top of the lighthouse of Leghorn, on its homeward track. They were off Via Reggio, at some distance from shore, when a storm was driven over the sea. It enveloped them and several larger vessels in darkness. When the cloud passed onwards, Roberts looked again, and saw every other vessel sailing on the ocean except their little schooner, which had vanished. From that time he could scarcely doubt the fatal truth; yet we fancied that they might have been driven towards Elba or Corsica, and so be saved. The observation made as to the spot where the boat disappeared caused it to be found, through the exertions of Trelawny for that effect. It had gone down in ten fathom water; it had not capsized, and, except such things as had floated from her, everything was found on board exactly as it had been placed when they sailed. The boat itself was uninjured. Roberts possessed himself of her, and decked her; but she proved not seaworthy, and her shattered planks now lie rotting on the shore of one of the Ionian islands, on which she was wrecked.

II

Now, when the joy of Jove had its fulfilling,
  And Heaven's tenth moon chronicled her relief,   10
She gave to light a babe all babes excelling,
  A schemer subtle beyond all belief;
A shepherd of thin dreams, a cow-stealing,
  A night-watching, and door-waylaying thief,
Who 'mongst the Gods was soon about to thieve,   15
And other glorious actions to achieve.

III

The babe was born at the first peep of day;
  He began playing on the lyre at noon,
And the same evening did he steal away
  Apollo's herds;—the fourth day of the moon   20
On which him bore the venerable May,
  From her immortal limbs he leaped full soon,
Nor long could in the sacred cradle keep,
But out to seek Apollo's herds would creep.

IV

Out of the lofty cavern wandering   25
  He found a tortoise, and cried out—'A treasure!'
(For Mercury first made the tortoise sing)
  The beast before the portal at his leisure
The flowery herbage was depasturing,
  Moving his feet in a deliberate measure   30
Over the turf. Jove's profitable son
Eying him laughed, and laughing thus begun:—

V

'A useful godsend are you to me now,
  King of the dance, companion of the feast,
Lovely in all your nature! Welcome, you   35
  Excellent plaything! Where, sweet mountain-beast,
Got you that speckled shell? Thus much I know,
  You must come home with me and be my guest;
You will give joy to me, and I will do
All that is in my power to honour you.   40

VI

'Better to be at home than out of door,
  So come with me; and though it has been said
That you alive defend from magic power,
  I know you will sing sweetly when you're dead.'

Thus having spoken, the quaint infant bore,   45
  Lifting it from the grass on which it fed
And grasping it in his delighted hold,
His treasured prize into the cavern old.

VII

Then scooping with a chisel of gray steel,
  He bored the life and soul out of the beast.——   50
Not swifter a swift thought of woe or weal
  Darts through the tumult of a human breast
Which thronging cares annoy—not swifter wheel
  The flashes of its torture and unrest
Out of the dizzy eyes—than Maia's son   55
All that he did devise hath featly done.

VIII

  .   .   .   .
  And through the tortoise's hard stony skin
At proper distances small holes he made,
  And fastened the cut stems of reeds within,
And with a piece of leather overlaid   60
  The open space and fixed the cubits in,
Fitting the bridge to both, and stretched o'er all
Symphonious cords of sheep-gut rhythmical.

IX

When he had wrought the lovely instrument,
  He tried the chords, and made division meet,   65
Preluding with the plectrum, and there went
  Up from beneath his hand a tumult sweet
Of mighty sounds, and from his lips he sent
  A strain of unpremeditated wit
Joyous and wild and wanton—such you may   70
Hear among revellers on a holiday.

X

He sung how Jove and May of the bright sandal
  Dallied in love not quite legitimate;
And his own birth, still scoffing at the scandal,
  And naming his own name, did celebrate;   75
His mother's cave and servant maids he planned all
  In plastic verse, her household stuff and state,
Perennial pot, trippet, and brazen pan,—
But singing, he conceived another plan.

XI

. . . .
Seized with a sudden fancy for fresh meat,   80
He in his sacred crib deposited
   The hollow lyre, and from the cavern sweet
Rushed with great leaps up to the mountain's head,
   Revolving in his mind some subtle feat
Of thievish craft, such as a swindler might   85
Devise in the lone season of dun night.

XII

Lo! the great Sun under the ocean's bed has
   Driven steeds and chariot—the child meanwhile strode
O'er the Pierian mountains clothed in shadows,
   Where the immortal oxen of the God   90
Are pastured in the flowering unmown meadows,
   And safely stalled in a remote abode.—
The archer Argicide, elate and proud,
Drove fifty from the herd, lowing aloud.

XIII

He drove them wandering o'er the sandy way,   95
   But, being ever mindful of his craft,
Backward and forward drove he them astray,
   So that the tracks which seemed before, were aft;
His sandals then he threw to the ocean spray,
   And for each foot he wrought a kind of raft   100
Of tamarisk, and tamarisk-like sprigs,
And bound them in a lump with withy twigs.

XIV

And on his feet he tied these sandals light,
The trail of whose wide leaves might not betray
   His track; and then, a self-sufficing wight,   105
Like a man hastening on some distant way,
   He from Pieria's mountain bent his flight;
But an old man perceived the infant pass
Down green Onchestus heaped like beds with grass.

XV

The old man stood dressing his sunny vine: 110
   'Halloo! old fellow with the crooked shoulder!
You grub those stumps? before they will bear wine
   Methinks even you must grow a little older:

Attend, I pray, to this advice of mine,
  As you would 'scape what might appal a bolder—   115
Seeing, see not—and hearing, hear not—and—
If you have understanding—understand.'

XVI

So saying, Hermes roused the oxen vast;
  O'er shadowy mountain and resounding dell,
And flower-paven plains, great Hermes passed;   120
  Till the black night divine, which favouring fell
Around his steps, grew gray, and morning fast
  Wakened the world to work, and from her cell
Sea-strewn, the Pallantean Moon sublime
Into her watch-tower just began to climb.   125

XVII

Now to Alpheus he had driven all
  The broad-foreheaded oxen of the Sun;
They came unwearied to the lofty stall
  And to the water-troughs which ever run
Through the fresh fields—and when with rushgrass tall,   130
  Lotus and all sweet herbage, every one
Had pastured been, the great God made them move
Towards the stall in a collected drove.

XVIII

A mighty pile of wood the God then heaped,
  And having soon conceived the mystery   135
Of fire, from two smooth laurel branches stripped
  The bark, and rubbed them in his palms;—on high
Suddenly forth the burning vapour leaped
  And the divine child saw delightedly.—
Mercury first found out for human weal   140
Tinder-box, matches, fire-irons, flint and steel.

XIX

And fine dry logs and roots innumerous
  He gathered in a delve upon the ground—
And kindled them—and instantaneous
  The strength of the fierce flame was breathed around: 145
And whilst the might of glorious Vulcan thus
  Wrapped the great pile with glare and roaring sound,
Hermes dragged forth two heifers, lowing loud,
Close to the fire—such might was in the God.

XX

And on the earth upon their backs he threw   150
    The panting beasts, and rolled them o'er and o'er,
And bored their lives out. Without more ado
    He cut fat and flesh, and down before
The fire, on spits of wood he placed the two,
    Toasting their flesh and ribs, and all the gore   155
Pursed in the bowels; and while this was done
He stretched their hides over a craggy stone.

XXI

We mortals let an ox grow old, and then
    Cut it up after long consideration,—
But joyous-minded Hermes from the glen   160
    Drew the fat spoils to the more open station
Of a flat smooth space, and portioned them; and when
    He had by lot assigned to each a ration
Of the twelve Gods, his mind became aware
Of all the joys which in religion are.   165

XXII

For the sweet savour of the roasted meat
    Tempted him though immortal. Natheless
He checked his haughty will and did not eat,
    Though what it cost him words can scarce express,
And every wish to put such morsels sweet   170
    Down his most sacred throat, he did repress;
But soon within the lofty portalled stall
He placed the fat and flesh and bones and all.

XXIII

And every trace of the fresh butchery
    And cooking, the God soon made disappear,   175
As if it all had vanished through the sky;
    He burned the hoofs and horns and head and hair,—
The insatiate fire devoured them hungrily;—
    And when he saw that everything was clear,
He quenched the coal, and trampled the black dust,   180
And in the stream his bloody sandals tossed.

XXIV

All night he worked in the serene moonshine—
    But when the light of day was spread abroad
He sought his natal mountain-peaks divine.
    On his long wandering neither Man nor God   185

Had met him, since he killed Apollo's kine,
   Nor house-dog had barked at him on his road;
Now he obliquely through the keyhole passed,
Like a thin mist, or an autumnal blast.

XXV

Right through the temple of the spacious cave   190
   He went with soft light feet—as if his tread
Fell not on earth; no sound their falling gave;
   Then to his cradle he crept quick, and spread
The swaddling-clothes about him; and the knave
   Lay playing with the covering of the bed   195
With his left hand about his knees—the right
Held his belovèd tortoise-lyre tight.

XXVI

There he lay innocent as a new-born child,
   As gossips say; but though he was a God,
The Goddess, his fair mother, unbeguiled,   200
   Knew all that he had done being abroad:
'Whence come you, and from what adventure wild,
   You cunning rogue, and where have you abode
All the long night, clothed in your impudence?
What have you done since you departed hence?   205

XXVII

'Apollo soon will pass within this gate
   And bind your tender body in a chain
Inextricably tight, and fast as fate,
   Unless you can delude the God again,
Even when within his arms—ah, runagate!   210
   A pretty torment both for Gods and Men
Your father made when he made you!'—'Dear mother,'
Replied sly Hermes, 'wherefore scold and bother?

XXVIII

'As if I were like other babes as old,
   And understood nothing of what is what;   215
And cared at all to hear my mother scold.
   I in my subtle brain a scheme have got,
Which whilst the sacred stars round Heaven are rolled
   Will profit you and me—nor shall our lot
Be as you counsel, without gifts or food,   220
To spend our lives in this obscure abode.

XXIX

'But we will leave this shadow-peopled cave
   And live among the Gods, and pass each day
In high communion, sharing what they have
   Of profuse wealth and unexhausted prey;   225
And from the portion which my father gave
   To Phoebus, I will snatch my share away,
Which if my father will not—natheless I,
Who am the king of robbers, can but try.

XXX

'And, if Latona's son should find me out,   230
   I'll countermine him by a deeper plan;
I'll pierce the Pythian temple-walls, though stout,
   And sack the fane of everything I can—
Caldrons and tripods of great worth no doubt,
   Each golden cup and polished brazen pan,   235
All the wrought tapestries and garments gay.'—
So they together talked;—meanwhile the Day

XXXI

Aethereal born arose out of the flood
   Of flowing Ocean, bearing light to men.
Apollo passed toward the sacred wood,   240
   Which from the inmost depths of its green glen
Echoes the voice of Neptune,—and there stood
   On the same spot in green Onchestus then
That same old animal, the vine-dresser,
Who was employed hedging his vineyard there.   245

XXXII

Latona's glorious Son began:—'I pray
   Tell, ancient hedger of Onchestus green,
Whether a drove of kine has passed this way,
   All heifers with crooked horns? for they have been
Stolen from the herd in high Pieria,   250
   Where a black bull was fed apart, between
Two woody mountains in a neighbouring glen,
And four fierce dogs watched there, unanimous as men.

XXXIII

'And what is strange, the author of this theft
   Has stolen the fatted heifers every one,   255
But the four dogs and the black bull are left:—
   Stolen they were last night at set of sun.

Of their soft beds and their sweet food bereft.—
   Now tell me, man born ere the world begun,
Have you seen any one pass with the cows?'—   260
To whom the man of overhanging brows:

XXXIV

'My friend, it would require no common skill
   Justly to speak of everything I see:
On various purposes of good or ill
   Many pass by my vineyard,—and to me   265
'Tis difficult to know the invisible
   Thoughts, which in all those many minds may be:—
Thus much alone I certainly can say,
I tilled these vines till the decline of day,

XXXV

'And then I thought I saw, but dare not speak   270
   With certainty of such a wondrous thing,
A child, who could not have been born a week,
   Those fair-horned cattle closely following,
And in his hand he held a polished stick:
   And, as on purpose, he walked wavering   275
From one side to the other of the road,
And with his face opposed the steps he trod.'

XXXVI

Apollo hearing this, passed quickly on—
   No wingèd omen could have shown more clear
That the deceiver was his father's son.   280
   So the God wraps a purple atmosphere
Around his shoulders, and like fire is gone
   To famous Pylos, seeking his kine there,
And found their track and his, yet hardly cold,
And cried—'What wonder do mine eyes behold!   285

XXXVII

'Here are the footsteps of the hornèd herd
   Turned back towards their fields of asphodel;—
But *these* are not the tracks of beast or bird,
   Gray wolf, or bear, or lion of the dell,
Or manèd Centaur—sand was never stirred   290
   By man or woman thus! Inexplicable!
Who with unwearied feet could e'er impress
The sand with such enormous vestiges?

XXXVIII

'That was most strange—but this is stranger still!'
    Thus having said, Phoebus impetuously   295
Sought high Cyllene's forest-cinctured hill,
    And the deep cavern where dark shadows lie,
And where the ambrosial nymph with happy will
    Bore the Saturnian's love-child, Mercury—
And a delightful odour from the dew   300
Of the hill pastures, at his coming, flew.

XXXIX

And Phoebus stooped under the craggy roof
    Arched over the dark cavern:—Maia's child
Perceived that he came angry, far aloof,
    About the cows of which he had been beguiled;   305
And over him the fine and fragrant woof
    Of his ambrosial swaddling-clothes he piled—
As among fire-brands lies a burning spark
Covered, beneath the ashes cold and dark.

XL

There, like an infant who had sucked his fill   310
    And now was newly washed and put to bed,
Awake, but courting sleep with weary will,
    And gathered in a lump, hands, feet, and head,
He lay, and his belovèd tortoise still
    He grasped and held under his shoulder-blade.   315
Phoebus the lovely mountain-goddess knew,
Not less her subtle, swindling baby, who

XLI

Lay swathed in his sly wiles. Round every crook
    Of the ample cavern, for his kine, Apollo
Looked sharp; and when he saw them not, he took   320
    The glittering key, and opened three great hollow
Recesses in the rock—where many a nook
    Was filled with the sweet food immortals swallow,
And mighty heaps of silver and of gold
Were piled within—a wonder to behold!   325

XLII

And white and silver robes, all overwrought
    With cunning workmanship of tracery sweet—
Except among the Gods there can be nought
    In the wide world to be compared with it.

Latona's offspring, after having sought 330
  His herds in every corner, thus did greet
Great Hermes:—'Little cradled rogue, declare
Of my illustrious heifers, where they are!

XLIII

'Speak quickly! or a quarrel between us
  Must rise, and the event will be, that I 335
Shall hurl you into dismal Tartarus,
  In fiery gloom to dwell eternally;
Nor shall your father nor your mother loose
  The bars of that black dungeon—utterly
You shall be cast out from the light of day, 340
To rule the ghosts of men, unblessed as they.'

XLIV

To whom thus Hermes slily answered:—'Son
  Of great Latona, what a speech is this!
Why come you here to ask me what is done
  With the wild oxen which it seems you miss? 345
I have not seen them, nor from any one
  Have heard a word of the whole business;
If you should promise an immense reward,
I could not tell more than you now have heard.

XLV

'An ox-stealer should be both tall and strong, 350
  And I am but a little new-born thing,
Who, yet at least, can think of nothing wrong:—
  My business is to suck, and sleep, and fling
The cradle-clothes about me all day long,—
  Or half asleep, hear my sweet mother sing, 355
And to be washed in water clean and warm,
And hushed and kissed and kept secure from harm.

XLVI

'O, let not e'er this quarrel be averred!
  The astounded Gods would laugh at you, if e'er
You should allege a story so absurd 360
  As that a new-born infant forth could fare
Out of his home after a savage herd.
  I was born yesterday—my small feet are
Too tender for the roads so hard and rough:—
And if you think that this is not enough, 365

XLVII

'I swear a great oath, by my father's head,
   That I stole not your cows, and that I know
Of no one else, who might, or could, or did.—
   Whatever things cows are, I do not know,
For I have only heard the name.'—This said,   370
   He winked as fast as could be, and his brow
Was wrinkled, and a whistle loud gave he,
Like one who hears some strange absurdity.

XLVIII

Apollo gently smiled and said:—'Ay, ay,—   375
   You cunning little rascal, you will bore
Many a rich man's house, and your array
   Of thieves will lay their siege before his door,
Silent as night, in night; and many a day
   In the wild glens rough shepherds will deplore   380
That you or yours, having an appetite,
Met with their cattle, comrade of the night!

XLIX

'And this among the Gods shall be your gift,
   To be considered as the lord of those
Who swindle, house-break, sheep-steal, and shop-lift;—
   But now if you would not your last sleep doze;   385
Crawl out!'—Thus saying, Phoebus did uplift
   The subtle infant in his swaddling clothes,
And in his arms, according to his wont,
A scheme devised, the illustrious Argiphont.

L

.   .   .   .   .   .
   .   .   .   .
And sneezed and shuddered—Phoebus on the grass   390
   Him threw, and whilst all that he had designed
He did perform—eager although to pass,
   Apollo darted from his mighty mind
Towards the subtle babe the following scoff:—
'Do not imagine this will get you off,   395

LI

'You little swaddled child of Jove and May!'
   And seized him:—'By this omen I shall trace
My noble herds, and you shall lead the way.'—
   Cyllenian Hermes from the grassy place,

Like one in earnest haste to get away, 400
   Rose, and with hands lifted towards his face
Round both his ears up from his shoulders drew
His swaddling clothes, and—'What mean you to do

LII

'With me, you unkind God?'—said Mercury:
   'Is it about these cows you tease me so? 405
I wish the race of cows were perished!—I
   Stole not your cows—I do not even know
What things cows are. Alas! I well may sigh
   That, since I came into this world of woe,
I should have ever heard the name of one— 410
But I appeal to the Saturnian's throne.'

LIII

Thus Phoebus and the vagrant Mercury
   Talked without coming to an explanation,
With adverse purpose. As for Phoebus, he
   Sought not revenge, but only information, 415
And Hermes tried with lies and roguery
   To cheat Apollo.—But when no evasion
Served—for the cunning one his match had found—
He paced on first over the sandy ground.

LIV

He of the Silver Bow the child of Jove 420
Followed behind, till to their heavenly Sire
   Came both his children, beautiful as Love,
And from his equal balance did require
   A judgement in the cause wherein they strove.
O'er odorous Olympus and its snows 425
A murmuring tumult as they came arose,—

LV

And from the folded depths of the great Hill,
   While Hermes and Apollo reverent stood
Before Jove's throne, the indestructible
   Immortals rushed in mighty multitude; 430
And whilst their seats in order due they fill,
   The lofty Thunderer in a careless mood
To Phoebus said:—'Whence drive you this sweet prey,
This herald-baby, born but yesterday?—

LVI

'A most important subject, trifler, this   435
    To lay before the Gods!'—'Nay, Father, nay,
When you have understood the business,
    Say not that I alone am fond of prey.
I found this little boy in a recess
    Under Cyllene's mountains far away—   440
A manifest and most apparent thief,
A scandalmonger beyond all belief.

LVII

'I never saw his like either in Heaven
    Or upon earth for knavery or craft:—
Out of the field my cattle yester-even,   445
    By the low shore on which the loud sea laughed,
He right down to the river-ford had driven;
    And mere astonishment would make you daft
To see the double kind of footsteps strange
He has impressed wherever he did range.   450

LVIII

'The cattle's track on the black dust, full well
    Is evident, as if they went towards
The place from which they came—that asphodel
    Meadow, in which I feed my many herds,—
His steps were most incomprehensible—   455
    I know not how I can describe in words
Those tracks—he could have gone along the sands
Neither upon his feet nor on his hands;—

LIX

'He must have had some other stranger mode
    Of moving on: those vestiges immense,   460
Far as I traced them on the sandy road,
    Seemed like the trail of oak-toppings:—but thence
No mark nor track denoting where they trod
    The hard ground gave:—but, working at his fence,
A mortal hedger saw him as he passed   465
To Pylos, with the cows, in fiery haste.

LX

'I found that in the dark he quietly
    Had sacrificed some cows, and before light
Had thrown the ashes all dispersedly
    About the road—then, still as gloomy night,   470

Had crept into his cradle, either eye
  Rubbing, and cogitating some new sleight,
No eagle could have seen him as he lay
Hid in his cavern from the peering day.

LXI

'I taxed him with the fact, when he averred   475
  Most solemnly that he did neither see
Nor even had in any manner heard
  Of my lost cows, whatever things cows be;
Nor could he tell, though offered a reward,
  Not even who could tell of them to me.'   480
So speaking, Phoebus sate; and Hermes then
Addressed the Supreme Lord of Gods and Men:—

LXII

'Great Father, you know clearly beforehand
  That all which I shall say to you is sooth;
I am a most veracious person, and   485
  Totally unacquainted with untruth.
At sunrise Phoebus came, but with no band
  Of Gods to bear him witness, in great wrath,
To my abode, seeking his heifers there,
And saying that I must show him where they are,   490

LXIII

'Or he would hurl me down the dark abyss.
  I know that every Apollonian limb
Is clothed with speed and might and manliness,
  As a green bank with flowers—but unlike him
I was born yesterday, and you may guess   495
  He well knew this when he indulged the whim
Of bullying a poor little new-born thing
That slept, and never thought of cow-driving.

LXIV

'Am I like a strong fellow who steals kine?
  Believe me, dearest Father—such you are—   500
This driving of the herds is none of mine;
  Across my threshold did I wander ne'er,
So may I thrive! I reverence the divine
  Sun and the Gods, and I love you, and care
Even for this hard accuser—who must know   505
I am as innocent as they or you.

LXV

'I swear by these most gloriously-wrought portals
   (It is, you will allow, an oath of might)
Through which the multitude of the Immortals
   Pass and repass forever, day and night,   510
Devising schemes for the affairs of mortals—
   That I am guiltless; and I will requite,
Although mine enemy be great and strong,
His cruel threat—do thou defend the young!'

LXVI

So speaking, the Cyllenian Argiphont   515
   Winked, as if now his adversary was fitted:—
And Jupiter, according to his wont,
   Laughed heartily to hear the subtle-witted
Infant give such a plausible account,
   And every word a lie. But he remitted   520
Judgement at present—and his exhortation
Was, to compose the affair by arbitration.

LXVII

And they by mighty Jupiter were bidden
   To go forth with a single purpose both,
Neither the other chiding nor yet chidden: 525
   And Mercury with innocence and truth
To lead the way, and show where he had hidden
   The mighty heifers.—Hermes, nothing loth,
Obeyed the Aegis-bearer's will—for he
Is able to persuade all easily.   530

LXVIII

These lovely children of Heaven's highest Lord
   Hastened to Pylos and the pastures wide
And lofty stalls by the Alphean ford,
   Where wealth in the mute night is multiplied
With silent growth. Whilst Hermes drove the herd   535
   Out of the stony cavern, Phoebus spied
The hides of those the little babe had slain,
Stretched on the precipice above the plain.

LXIX

'How was it possible,' then Phoebus said,
   'That you, a little child, born yesterday,   540
A thing on mother's milk and kisses fed,
   Could two prodigious heifers ever flay?

Even I myself may well hereafter dread
   Your prowess, offspring of Cyllenian May,
When you grow strong and tall.'—He spoke, and bound   545
Stiff withy bands the infant's wrists around,

LXX

He might as well have bound the oxen wild;
   The withy bands, though starkly interknit,
Fell at the feet of the immortal child,
   Loosened by some device of his quick wit.   550
Phoebus perceived himself again beguiled,
   And stared—while Hermes sought some hole or pit,
Looking askance and winking fast as thought,
Where he might hide himself and not be caught.

LXXI

Sudden he changed his plan, and with strange skill   555
   Subdued the strong Latonian, by the might
Of winning music, to his mightier will;
   His left hand held the lyre, and in his right
The plectrum struck the chords—unconquerable
   Up from beneath his hand in circling flight   560
The gathering music rose—and sweet as Love
The penetrating notes did live and move

LXXII

Within the heart of great Apollo—he
   Listened with all his soul, and laughed for pleasure.
Close to his side stood harping fearlessly   565
   The unabashèd boy; and to the measure
Of the sweet lyre, there followed loud and free
   His joyous voice; for he unlocked the treasure
Of his deep song, illustrating the birth
Of the bright Gods, and the dark desert Earth: 570

LXXIII

And how to the Immortals every one
   A portion was assigned of all that is;
But chief Mnemosyne did Maia's son
   Clothe in the light of his loud melodies;—
And, as each God was born or had begun,   575
   He in their order due and fit degrees
Sung of his birth and being—and did move
Apollo to unutterable love.

LXXIV

These words were wingèd with his swift delight:
  'You heifer-stealing schemer, well do you   580
Deserve that fifty oxen should requite
  Such minstrelsies as I have heard even now.
Comrade of feasts, little contriving wight,
  One of your secrets I would gladly know,
Whether the glorious power you now show forth   585
Was folded up within you at your birth,

LXXV

'Or whether mortal taught or God inspired
  The power of unpremeditated song?
Many divinest sounds have I admired,
  The Olympian Gods and mortal men among;   590
But such a strain of wondrous, strange, untired,
  And soul-awakening music, sweet and strong,
Yet did I never hear except from thee,
Offspring of May, impostor Mercury!

LXXVI

'What Muse, what skill, what unimagined use,   595
  What exercise of subtlest art, has given
Thy songs such power?—for those who hear may choose
  From three, the choicest of the gifts of Heaven,
Delight, and love, and sleep,—sweet sleep, whose dews
  Are sweeter than the balmy tears of even:—   600
And I, who speak this praise, am that Apollo
Whom the Olympian Muses ever follow:

LXXVII

'And their delight is dance, and the blithe noise
  Of song and overflowing poesy;
And sweet, even as desire, the liquid voice   605
  Of pipes, that fills the clear air thrillingly;
But never did my inmost soul rejoice
  In this dear work of youthful revelry
As now. I wonder at thee, son of Jove;
Thy harpings and thy song are soft as love.   610

LXXVIII

'Now since thou hast, although so very small,
  Science of arts so glorious, thus I swear,—
And let this cornel javelin, keen and tall,
  Witness between us what I promise here,—

That I will lead thee to the Olympian Hall,
    Honoured and mighty, with thy mother dear,
And many glorious gifts in joy will give thee,
And even at the end will ne'er deceive thee.'

LXXIX

To whom thus Mercury with prudent speech:—
    'Wisely hast thou inquirèd of my skill: 620
I envy thee no thing I know to teach
    Even this day:—for both in word and will
I would be gentle with thee; thou canst reach
    All things in thy wise spirit, and thy sill
Is highest in Heaven among the sons of Jove,   625
Who loves thee in the fulness of his love.

LXXX

'The Counsellor Supreme has given to thee
    Divinest gifts, out of the amplitude
Of his profuse exhaustless treasury;
    By thee, 'tis said, the depths are understood   630
Of his far voice; by thee the mystery
    Of all oracular fates,—and the dread mood
Of the diviner is breathed up; even I—
A child—perceive thy might and majesty.

LXXXI

'Thou canst seek out and compass all that wit   635
    Can find or teach;—yet since thou wilt, come take
The lyre—be mine the glory giving it—
    Strike the sweet chords, and sing aloud, and wake
Thy joyous pleasure out of many a fit
    Of trancèd sound—and with fleet fingers make   640
Thy liquid-voicèd comrade talk with thee,—
It can talk measured music eloquently.

LXXXII

'Then bear it boldly to the revel loud,
    Love-wakening dance, or feast of solemn state,
A joy by night or day—for those endowed   645
    With art and wisdom who interrogate
It teaches, babbling in delightful mood
    All things which make the spirit most elate,
Soothing the mind with sweet familiar play,
Chasing the heavy shadows of dismay.   650

LXXXIII

'To those who are unskilled in its sweet tongue,
  Though they should question most impetuously
Its hidden soul, it gossips something wrong—
  Some senseless and impertinent reply.
But thou who art as wise as thou art strong   655
  Canst compass all that thou desirest. I
Present thee with this music-flowing shell,
Knowing thou canst interrogate it well.

LXXXIV

'And let us two henceforth together feed,
  On this green mountain-slope and pastoral plain,   660
The herds in litigation—they will breed
  Quickly enough to recompense our pain,
If to the bulls and cows we take good heed;—
  And thou, though somewhat over fond of gain,
Grudge me not half the profit.'—Having spoke,   665
The shell he proffered, and Apollo took;

LXXXV

And gave him in return the glittering lash,
  Installing him as herdsman;—from the look
Of Mercury then laughed a joyous flash.
  And then Apollo with the plectrum strook   670
The chords, and from beneath his hands a crash
  Of mighty sounds rushed up, whose music shook
The soul with sweetness, and like an adept
His sweeter voice a just accordance kept.

LXXXVI

The herd went wandering o'er the divine mead,   675
  Whilst these most beautiful Sons of Jupiter
Won their swift way up to the snowy head
  Of white Olympus, with the joyous lyre
Soothing their journey; and their father dread
  Gathered them both into familiar   680
Affection sweet,—and then, and now, and ever,
Hermes must love Him of the Golden Quiver,

LXXXVII

To whom he gave the lyre that sweetly sounded,
  Which skilfully he held and played thereon.
He piped the while, and far and wide rebounded   685
  The echo of his pipings; every one

Of the Olympians sat with joy astounded;
  While he conceived another piece of fun,
One of his old tricks—which the God of Day
Perceiving, said:—'I fear thee, Son of May;—   690

LXXXVIII

'I fear thee and thy sly chameleon spirit,
  Lest thou should steal my lyre and crookèd bow;
This glory and power thou dost from Jove inherit,
  To teach all craft upon the earth below;
Thieves love and worship thee—it is thy merit   695
  To make all mortal business ebb and flow
By roguery:—now, Hermes, if you dare
By sacred Styx a mighty oath to swear

LXXXIX

'That you will never rob me, you will do
  A thing extremely pleasing to my heart.'   700
Then Mercury sware by the Stygian dew,
  That he would never steal his bow or dart,
Or lay his hands on what to him was due,
  Or ever would employ his powerful art
Against his Pythian fane. Then Phoebus swore   705
There was no God or Man whom he loved more.

XC

'And I will give thee as a good-will token,
  The beautiful wand of wealth and happiness;
A perfect three-leaved rod of gold unbroken,
  Whose magic will thy footsteps ever bless;   710
And whatsoever by Jove's voice is spoken
  Of earthly or divine from its recess,
It, like a loving soul, to thee will speak,
And more than this, do thou forbear to seek.

XCI

'For, dearest child, the divinations high   715
  Which thou requirest, 'tis unlawful ever
That thou, or any other deity
  Should understand—and vain were the endeavour;
For they are hidden in Jove's mind, and I,
  In trust of them, have sworn that I would never   720
Betray the counsels of Jove's inmost will
To any God—the oath was terrible.

XCII

'Then, golden-wanded brother, ask me not
    To speak the fates by Jupiter designed;
But be it mine to tell their various lot   725
    To the unnumbered tribes of human-kind.
Let good to these, and ill to those be wrought
    As I dispense—but he who comes consigned
By voice and wings of perfect augury
To my great shrine, shall find avail in me.   730

XCIII

'Him will I not deceive, but will assist;
    But he who comes relying on such birds
As chatter vainly, who would strain and twist
    The purpose of the Gods with idle words,
And deems their knowledge light, he shall have missed   735
    His road—whilst I among my other hoards
His gifts deposit. Yet, O son of May,
I have another wondrous thing to say.

XCIV

'There are three Fates, three virgin Sisters, who
    Rejoicing in their wind-outspeeding wings,   740
Their heads with flour snowed over white and new,
    Sit in a vale round which Parnassus flings
Its circling skirts—from these I have learned true
    Vaticinations of remotest things.
My father cared not. Whilst they search out dooms,   745
They sit apart and feed on honeycombs.

XCV

'They, having eaten the fresh honey, grow
    Drunk with divine enthusiasm, and utter
With earnest willingness the truth they know;
    But if deprived of that sweet food, they mutter   750
All plausible delusions;—these to you
    I give;—if you inquire, they will not stutter;
Delight your own soul with them:—any man
You would instruct may profit if he can.

XCVI

'Take these and the fierce oxen, Maia's child—   755
    O'er many a horse and toil-enduring mule,
O'er jaggèd-jawèd lions, and the wild
    White-tuskèd boars, o'er all, by field or pool,

Of cattle which the mighty Mother mild
  Nourishes in her bosom, thou shalt rule—   760
Thou dost alone the veil from death uplift—
Thou givest not—yet this is a great gift.'

XCVII

Thus King Apollo loved the child of May
  In truth, and Jove covered their love with joy.
Hermes with Gods and Men even from that day   765
  Mingled, and wrought the latter much annoy,
And little profit, going far astray
  Through the dun night. Farewell, delightful Boy,
Of Jove and Maia sprung,—never by me,
Nor thou, nor other songs, shall unremembered be.   770

HOMER'S HYMN TO CASTOR AND POLLUX

YE wild-eyed Muses, sing the Twins of Jove,
Whom the fair-ankled Leda, mixed in love
With mighty Saturn's Heaven-obscuring Child,
On Taygetus, that lofty mountain wild,
Brought forth in joy: mild Pollux, void of blame,   5
And steed-subduing Castor, heirs of fame.
These are the Powers who earth-born mortals save
And ships, whose flight is swift along the wave.
When wintry tempests o'er the savage sea
Are raging, and the sailors tremblingly   10
Call on the Twins of Jove with prayer and vow,
Gathered in fear upon the lofty prow,
And sacrifice with snow-white lambs,—the wind
And the huge billow bursting close behind,
Even then beneath the weltering waters bear   15
The staggering ship—they suddenly appear,
On yellow wings rushing athwart the sky,
And lull the blasts in mute tranquillity,
And strew the waves on the white Ocean's bed,
Fair omen of the voyage; from toil and dread   20
The sailors rest, rejoicing in the sight,
And plough the quiet sea in safe delight.

HOMER'S HYMN TO THE MOON

DAUGHTERS of Jove, whose voice is melody,
Muses, who know and rule all minstrelsy,
Sing the wide-wingèd Moon! Around the earth,
From her immortal head in Heaven shot forth,
Far light is scattered—boundless glory springs;   5
Where'er she spreads her many-beaming wings
The lampless air glows round her golden crown.

But when the Moon divine from Heaven is gone
Under the sea, her beams within abide,
Till, bathing her bright limbs in Ocean's tide,   10
Clothing her form in garments glittering far,
And having yoked to her immortal car
The beam-invested steeds whose necks on high
Curve back, she drives to a remoter sky
A western Crescent, borne impetuously.   15
Then is made full the circle of her light,
And as she grows, her beams more bright and bright
Are poured from Heaven, where she is hovering then,
A wonder and a sign to mortal men.

The Son of Saturn with this glorious Power   20
Mingled in love and sleep—to whom she bore
Pandeia, a bright maid of beauty rare
Among the Gods, whose lives eternal are.

Hail Queen, great Moon, white-armed Divinity,
Fair-haired and favourable! thus with thee   25
My song beginning, by its music sweet
Shall make immortal many a glorious feat
Of demigods, with lovely lips, so well
Which minstrels, servants of the Muses, tell.

HOMER'S HYMN TO THE SUN

OFFSPRING of Jove, Calliope, once more
To the bright Sun, thy hymn of music pour;
Whom to the child of star-clad Heaven and Earth
Euryphaëssa, large-eyed nymph, brought forth;
Euryphaëssa, the famed sister fair   5
Of great Hyperion, who to him did bear
A race of loveliest children; the young Morn,
Whose arms are like twin roses newly born,
The fair-haired Moon, and the immortal Sun,
Who borne by heavenly steeds his race doth run   10
Unconquerably, illuming the abodes
Of mortal Men and the eternal Gods.

Fiercely look forth his awe-inspiring eyes,
Beneath his golden helmet, whence arise
And are shot forth afar, clear beams of light;   15
His countenance, with radiant glory bright,
Beneath his graceful locks far shines around,
And the light vest with which his limbs are bound,
Of woof aethereal delicately twined,
Glows in the stream of the uplifting wind.   20

His rapid steeds soon bear him to the West;
Where their steep flight his hands divine arrest,
And the fleet car with yoke of gold, which he
Sends from bright Heaven beneath the shadowy sea.

HOMER'S HYMN TO THE EARTH: MOTHER OF ALL

O UNIVERSAL Mother, who dost keep
From everlasting thy foundations deep,
Eldest of things, Great Earth, I sing of thee!
All shapes that have their dwelling in the sea,
All things that fly, or on the ground divine 5
Live, move, and there are nourished—these are thine;
These from thy wealth thou dost sustain; from thee
Fair babes are born, and fruits on every tree
Hang ripe and large, revered Divinity!

The life of mortal men beneath thy sway 10
Is held; thy power both gives and takes away!
Happy are they whom thy mild favours nourish;
All things unstinted round them grow and flourish.
For them, endures the life-sustaining field
Its load of harvest, and their cattle yield 15
Large increase, and their house with wealth is filled.
Such honoured dwell in cities fair and free,
The homes of lovely women, prosperously;
Their sons exult in youth's new budding gladness,
And their fresh daughters free from care or sadness, 20
With bloom-inwoven dance and happy song,
On the soft flowers the meadow-grass among,
Leap round them sporting—such delights by thee
Are given, rich Power, revered Divinity.

Mother of gods, thou Wife of starry Heaven, 25
Farewell! be thou propitious, and be given
A happy life for this brief melody,
Nor thou nor other songs shall unremembered be.

HOMER'S HYMN TO MINERVA

I SING the glorious Power with azure eyes,
Athenian Pallas! tameless, chaste, and wise,
Tritogenia, town-preserving Maid,
Revered and mighty; from his awful head
Whom Jove brought forth, in warlike armour dressed, 5
Golden, all radiant! wonder strange possessed
The everlasting Gods that Shape to see,
Shaking a javelin keen, impetuously

Rush from the crest of Aegis-bearing Jove;
Fearfully Heaven was shaken, and did move   10
Beneath the might of the Cerulean-eyed;
Earth dreadfully resounded, far and wide;
And, lifted from its depths, the sea swelled high
In purple billows, the tide suddenly
Stood still, and great Hyperion's son long time   15
Checked his swift steeds, till where she stood sublime,
Pallas from her immortal shoulders threw
The arms divine; wise Jove rejoiced to view.
Child of the Aegis-bearer, hail to thee,
Nor thine nor others' praise shall unremembered be. 20

HOMER'S HYMN TO VENUS

[Vv. 1-55, with some omissions.]

MUSE, sing the deeds of golden Aphrodite,
Who wakens with her smile the lulled delight
Of sweet desire, taming the eternal kings
Of Heaven, and men, and all the living things
That fleet along the air, or whom the sea,   5
Or earth, with her maternal ministry,
Nourish innumerable, thy delight
All seek   O crownèd Aphrodite!
Three spirits canst thou not deceive or quell:—
Minerva, child of Jove, who loves too well   10
Fierce war and mingling combat, and the fame
Of glorious deeds, to heed thy gentle flame.
Diana   golden-shafted queen,
Is tamed not by thy smiles; the shadows green
Of the wild woods, the bow, the . . .   15
And piercing cries amid the swift pursuit
Of beasts among waste mountains,—such delight
Is hers, and men who know and do the right.
Nor Saturn's first-born daughter, Vesta chaste,
Whom Neptune and Apollo wooed the last,   20
Such was the will of aegis-bearing Jove;
But sternly she refused the ills of Love,
And by her mighty Father's head she swore
An oath not unperformed, that evermore
A virgin she would live mid deities   25
Divine: her father, for such gentle ties
Renounced, gave glorious gifts—thus in his hall
She sits and feeds luxuriously. O'er all
In every fane, her honours first arise
From men—the eldest of Divinities.   30

These spirits she persuades not, nor deceives,
But none beside escape, so well she weaves
Her unseen toils; nor mortal men, nor gods
Who live secure in their unseen abodes.
She won the soul of him whose fierce delight   35
Is thunder—first in glory and in might.
And, as she willed, his mighty mind deceiving,
With mortal limbs his deathless limbs inweaving,
Concealed him from his spouse and sister fair,
Whom to wise Saturn ancient Rhea bare.   40
     but in return,
In Venus Jove did soft desire awaken,
That by her own enchantments overtaken,
She might, no more from human union free,
Burn for a nursling of mortality.   45
For once, amid the assembled Deities,
The laughter-loving Venus from her eyes
Shot forth the light of a soft starlight smile,
And boasting said, that she, secure the while,
Could bring at will to the assembled Gods   50
The mortal tenants of earth's dark abodes,
And mortal offspring from a deathless stem
She could produce in scorn and spite of them.
Therefore he poured desire into her breast
Of young Anchises,   55
Feeding his herds among the mossy fountains
Of the wide Ida's many-folded mountains,—
Whom Venus saw, and loved, and the love clung
Like wasting fire her senses wild among.

THE CYCLOPS

A SATYRIC DRAMA

TRANSLATED FROM THE GREEK OF EURIPIDES

Silenus.	Ulysses.
Chorus of Satyrs.	The Cyclops.

Silenus. O Bacchus, what a world of toil, both now
And ere these limbs were overworn with age,
Have I endured for thee! First, when thou fled'st
The mountain-nymphs who nursed thee, driven afar
By the strange madness Juno sent upon thee;   5
Then in the battle of the sons of Earth,
When I stood foot by foot close to thy side,
No unpropitious fellow-combatant,
And, driving through his shield my wingèd spear,
Slew vast Enceladus. Consider now,   10

Is it a dream of which I speak to thee?
By Jove, it is not, for you have the trophies!
And now I suffer more than all before.
For when I heard that Juno had devised
A tedious voyage for you, I put to sea   15
With all my children quaint in search of you,
And I myself stood on the beakèd prow
And fixed the naked mast; and all my boys
Leaning upon their oars, with splash and strain
Made white with foam the green and purple sea,—   20
And so we sought you, king. We were sailing
Near Malea, when an eastern wind arose,
And drove us to this waste Aetnean rock;
The one-eyed children of the Ocean God,
The man-destroying Cyclopses, inhabit,   25
On this wild shore, their solitary caves,
And one of these, named Polypheme, has caught us
To be his slaves; and so, for all delight
Of Bacchic sports, sweet dance and melody,
We keep this lawless giant's wandering flocks.   30
My sons indeed, on far declivities,
Young things themselves, tend on the youngling sheep,
But I remain to fill the water-casks,
Or sweeping the hard floor, or ministering
Some impious and abominable meal   35
To the fell Cyclops. I am wearied of it!
And now I must scrape up the littered floor
With this great iron rake, so to receive
My absent master and his evening sheep
In a cave neat and clean. Even now I see   40
My children tending the flocks hitherward.
Ha! what is this? are your Sicinnian measures
Even now the same, as when with dance and song
You brought young Bacchus to Althaea's halls?

Chorus of Satyrs.

STROPHE

Where has he of race divine   45
   Wandered in the winding rocks?
Here the air is calm and fine
   For the father of the flocks;—
Here the grass is soft and sweet,
And the river-eddies meet   50
In the trough beside the cave,
Bright as in their fountain wave.—
Neither here, nor on the dew

Of the lawny uplands feeding?
Oh, you come!—a stone at you   55
   Will I throw to mend your breeding;—
Get along, you hornèd thing,
Wild, seditious, rambling!

EPODE

An Iacchic melody
   To the golden Aphrodite   60
Will I lift, as erst did I
   Seeking her and her delight
With the Maenads, whose white feet
To the music glance and fleet.
Bacchus, O belovèd, where,   65
Shaking wide thy yellow hair,
Wanderest thou alone, afar?
   To the one-eyed Cyclops, we,
Who by right thy servants are,
   Minister in misery,   70
In these wretched goat-skins clad,
   Far from thy delights and thee.

Silenus. Be silent, sons; command the slaves to drive
The gathered flocks into the rock-roofed cave.
   Chorus. Go! But what needs this serious haste, O father?
   Silenus. I see a Grecian vessel on the coast,   76
And thence the rowers with some general
Approaching to this cave.—About their necks
Hang empty vessels, as they wanted food,
And water-flasks.—Oh, miserable strangers!   80
Whence come they, that they know not what and who
My master is, approaching in ill hour
The inhospitable roof of Polypheme,
And the Cyclopian jaw-bone, man-destroying?
Be silent, Satyrs, while I ask and hear   85
Whence coming, they arrive the Aetnean hill.
   Ulysses. Friends, can you show me some clear water-spring,
The remedy of our thirst? Will any one
Furnish with food seamen in want of it?
Ha! what is this? We seem to be arrived   90
At the blithe court of Bacchus. I observe
This sportive band of Satyrs near the caves.
First let me greet the elder.—Hail!
   Silenus.   Hail thou,
O Stranger! tell thy country and thy race.
   Ulysses. The Ithacan Ulysses and the king   95
Of Cephalonia.

Silenus.   Oh! I know the man,
Wordy and shrewd, the son of Sisyphus.

Ulysses. I am the same, but do not rail upon me.—

Silenus. Whence sailing do you come to Sicily?

Ulysses. From Ilion, and from the Trojan toils.   10(

Silenus. How, touched you not at your paternal shore?

Ulysses. The strength of tempests bore me here by force.

Silenus. The self-same accident occurred to me.

Ulysses. Were you then driven here by stress of weather?

Silenus. Following the Pirates who had kidnapped Bacchus.

Ulysses. What land is this, and who inhabit it?—   106

Silenus. Aetna, the loftiest peak in Sicily.

Ulysses. And are there walls, and tower-surrounded towns?

Silenus. There are not.—These lone rocks are bare of men.

Ulysses. And who possess the land? the race of beasts?

Silenus. Cyclops, who live in caverns, not in houses.   111

Ulysses. Obeying whom? Or is the state popular?

Silenus. Shepherds: no one obeys any in aught.

Ulysses. How live they? do they sow the corn of Ceres?

Silenus. On milk and cheese, and on the flesh of sheep.   115

Ulysses. Have they the Bromian drink from the vine's stream?

Silenus. Ah! no; they live in an ungracious land.

Ulysses. And are they just to strangers?—hospitable?

Silenus. They think the sweetest thing a stranger brings
Is his own flesh.

Ulysses.   What! do they eat man's flesh?   120

Silenus. No one comes here who is not eaten up.

Ulysses. The Cyclops now—where is he? Not at home?

Silenus. Absent on Aetna, hunting with his dogs.

Ulysses. Know'st thou what thou must do to aid us hence?

Silenus. I know not: we will help you all we can.   125

Ulysses. Provide us food, of which we are in want.

Silenus. Here is not anything, as I said, but meat.

Ulysses. But meat is a sweet remedy for hunger.

Silenus. Cow's milk there is, and store of curdled cheese.

Ulysses. Bring out:—I would see all before I bargain.   130

Silenus. But how much gold will you engage to give?

Ulysses. I bring no gold, but Bacchic juice.

Silenus.   Oh, joy!
'Tis long since these dry lips were wet with wine.

Ulysses. Maron, the son of the God, gave it me.

Silenus. Whom I have nursed a baby in my arms.   135

Ulysses. The son of Bacchus, for your clearer knowledge.

Silenus. Have you it now?—or is it in the ship?

Ulysses. Old man, this skin contains it, which you see.

Silenus. Why, this would hardly be a mouthful for me.

Ulysses. Nay, twice as much as you can draw from thence.   140

Silenus. You speak of a fair fountain, sweet to me.
Ulysses. Would you first taste of the unmingled wine?
Silenus. 'Tis just—tasting invites the purchaser.
Ulysses. Here is the cup, together with the skin.
Silenus. Pour: that the draught may fillip my remembrance.
Ulysses. See!
Silenus.　　　　Papaiapax! what a sweet smell it has!　　146
Ulysses. You see it then?—
Silenus.　　　　　　　By Jove, no! but I smell it.
Ulysses. Taste, that you may not praise it in words only.
Silenus. Babai! Great Bacchus calls me forth to dance!
Joy! joy!
Ulysses. Did it flow sweetly down your throat?　　150
Silenus. So that it tingled to my very nails.
Ulysses. And in addition I will give you gold.
Silenus. Let gold alone! only unlock the cask.
Ulysses. Bring out some cheeses now, or a young goat.
Silenus. That will I do, despising any master.　　155
Yes, let me drink one cup, and I will give
All that the Cyclops feed upon their mountains.

.　　　　.　　　.　　　.　　　.　　　.　　.

Chorus. Ye have taken Troy and laid your hands on Helen?
Ulysses. And utterly destroyed the race of Priam.

.　　　.　　　.　　　.　　　.　　.

Silenus. The wanton wretch! she was bewitched to see　　160
The many-coloured anklets and the chain
Of woven gold which girt the neck of Paris,
And so she left that good man Menelaus.
There should be no more women in the world
But such as are reserved for me alone.—　　165
See, here are sheep, and here are goats, Ulysses,
Here are unsparing cheeses of pressed milk;
Take them; depart with what good speed ye may;
First leaving my reward, the Bacchic dew
Of joy-inspiring grapes.
Ulysses.　　　　Ah me! Alas!　　170
What shall we do? the Cyclops is at hand!
Old man, we perish! whither can we fly?
Silenus. Hide yourselves quick within that hollow rock.
Ulysses. 'Twere perilous to fly into the net.
Silenus. The cavern has recesses numberless;　　175
Hide yourselves quick.
Ulysses.　　　　That will I never do!
The mighty Troy would be indeed disgraced
If I should fly one man. How many times
Have I withstood, with shield immovable,

Ten thousand Phrygians!—if I needs must die,   180
Yet will I die with glory;—if I live,
The praise which I have gained will yet remain.
    Silenus. What, ho! assistance, comrades, haste, assistance!

     The CYCLOPS, SILENUS, ULYSSES; CHORUS.
    Cyclops. What is this tumult? Bacchus is not here,
Nor tympanies nor brazen castanets.   185
How are my young lambs in the cavern? Milking
Their dams or playing by their sides? And is
The new cheese pressed into the bulrush baskets?
Speak! I'll beat some of you till you rain tears—
Look up, not downwards when I speak to you.   190
    Silenus. See! I now gape at Jupiter himself;
I stare upon Orion and the stars.
    Cyclops. Well, is the dinner fitly cooked and laid?
    Silenus. All ready, if your throat is ready too.
    Cyclops. Are the bowls full of milk besides?
    Silenus.   O'er-brimming;
So you may drink a tunful if you will.   196
    Cyclops. Is it ewe's milk or cow's milk, or both mixed?—
    Silenus. Both, either; only pray don't swallow me.
    Cyclops. By no means.——

   .   .   .   .

What is this crowd I see beside the stalls?   200
Outlaws or thieves? for near my cavern-home
I see my young lambs coupled two by two
With willow bands; mixed with my cheeses lie
Their implements; and this old fellow here
Has his bald head broken with stripes.
    Silenus.   Ah me!   205
I have been beaten till I burn with fever.
    Cyclops. By whom? Who laid his fist upon your head?
    Silenus. Those men, because I would not suffer them
To steal your goods.
    Cyclops.   Did not the rascals know
I am a God, sprung from the race of Heaven?   210
    Silenus. I told them so, but they bore off your things,
And ate the cheese in spite of all I said,
And carried out the lambs—and said, moreover,
They'd pin you down with a three-cubit collar,
And pull your vitals out through your one eye,   215
Furrow your back with stripes, then, binding you,
Throw you as ballast into the ship's hold,
And then deliver you, a slave, to move
Enormous rocks, or found a vestibule.
    Cyclops. In truth? Nay, haste, and place in order quickly

The cooking-knives, and heap upon the hearth, 221
And kindle it, a great faggot of wood.—
As soon as they are slaughtered, they shall fill
My belly, broiling warm from the live coals,
Or boiled and seethed within the bubbling caldron. 225
I am quite sick of the wild mountain game;
Of stags and lions I have gorged enough,
And I grow hungry for the flesh of men.
    Silenus. Nay, master, something new is very pleasant
After one thing forever, and of late 230
Very few strangers have approached our cave.
    Ulysses. Hear, Cyclops, a plain tale on the other side.
We, wanting to buy food, came from our ship
Into the neighbourhood of your cave, and here
This old Silenus gave us in exchange 235
These lambs for wine, the which he took and drank,
And all by mutual compact, without force.
There is no word of truth in what he says,
For slyly he was selling all your store.
    Silenus. I? May you perish, wretch—
    Ulysses.   If I speak false!
    Silenus. Cyclops, I swear by Neptune who begot thee, 241
By mighty Triton and by Nereus old,
Calypso and the glaucous Ocean Nymphs,
The sacred waves and all the race of fishes—
Be these the witnesses, my dear sweet master, 245
My darling little Cyclops, that I never
Gave any of your stores to these false strangers;—
If I speak false may those whom most I love,
My children, perish wretchedly!
    Chorus.   There stop!
I saw him giving these things to the strangers. 250
If I speak false, then may my father perish,
But do not thou wrong hospitality.
    Cyclops. You lie! I swear that he is juster far
Than Rhadamanthus—I trust more in him.
But let me ask, whence have ye sailed, O strangers? 255
Who are you? And what city nourished ye?
    Ulysses. Our race is Ithacan—having destroyed
The town of Troy, the tempests of the sea
Have driven us on thy land, O Polypheme.
    Cyclops. What, have ye shared in the unenvied spoil 260
Of the false Helen, near Scamander's stream?
    Ulysses. The same, having endured a woful toil.
    Cyclops. Oh, basest expedition! sailed ye not
From Greece to Phrygia for one woman's sake?
    Ulysses. 'Twas the Gods' work—no mortal was in fault. 265

But, O great Offspring of the Ocean-King,
We pray thee and admonish thee with freedom,
That thou dost spare thy friends who visit thee,
And place no impious food within thy jaws.
For in the depths of Greece we have upreared   270
Temples to thy great Father, which are all
His homes. The sacred bay of Taenarus
Remains inviolate, and each dim recess
Scooped high on the Malean promontory,
And aëry Sunium's silver veinèd crag,   275
Which divine Pallas keeps unprofaned ever,
The Gerastian asylums, and whate'er
Within wide Greece our enterprise has kept
From Phrygian contumely; and in which
You have a common care, for you inhabit   280
The skirts of Grecian land, under the roots
Of Aetna and its crags, spotted with fire.
Turn then to converse under human laws,
Receive us shipwrecked suppliants, and provide
Food, clothes, and fire, and hospitable gifts;   285
Nor fixing upon oxen-piercing spits
Our limbs, so fill your belly and your jaws.
Priam's wide land has widowed Greece enough;
And weapon-wingèd murder heaped together
Enough of dead, and wives are husbandless,   290
And ancient women and gray fathers wail
Their childless age;—if you should roast the rest—
And 'tis a bitter feast that you prepare—
Where then would any turn? Yet be persuaded;
Forgo the lust of your jaw-bone; prefer   295
Pious humanity to wicked will:
Many have bought too dear their evil joys.
 Silenus. Let me advise you, do not spare a morsel
Of all his flesh. If you should eat his tongue
You would become most eloquent, O Cyclops. 300
 Cyclops. Wealth, my good fellow, is the wise man's God,
All other things are a pretence and boast.
What are my father's ocean promontories,
The sacred rocks whereon he dwells, to me?
Stranger, I laugh to scorn Jove's thunderbolt, 305
I know not that his strength is more than mine.
As to the rest I care not.—When he pours
Rain from above, I have a close pavilion
Under this rock, in which I lie supine,
Feasting on a roast calf or some wild beast,   310
And drinking pans of milk, and gloriously
Emulating the thunder of high Heaven.

And when the Thracian wind pours down the snow,
I wrap my body in the skins of beasts,
Kindle a fire, and bid the snow swirl on.   315
The earth, by force, whether it will or no,
Bringing forth grass, fattens my flocks and herds,
Which, to what other God but to myself
And this great belly, first of deities,
Should I be bound to sacrifice? I well know   320
The wise man's only Jupiter is this,
To eat and drink during his little day,
And give himself no care. And as for those
Who complicate with laws the life of man,
I freely give them tears for their reward.   325
I will not cheat my soul of its delight,
Or hesitate in dining upon you:—
And that I may be quit of all demands,
These are my hospitable gifts;—fierce fire
And yon ancestral caldron, which o'er-bubbling   330
Shall finely cook your miserable flesh.
Creep in!—

    .   .   .   .   .   .

    Ulysses. Ai! ai! I have escaped the Trojan toils,
I have escaped the sea, and now I fall
Under the cruel grasp of one impious man.   335
O Pallas, Mistress, Goddess, sprung from Jove,
Now, now, assist me! Mightier toils than Troy
Are these;—I totter on the chasms of peril;—
And thou who inhabitest the thrones
Of the bright stars, look, hospitable Jove,   340
Upon this outrage of thy deity,
Otherwise be considered as no God!

          Chorus (*alone*).
For your gaping gulf and your gullet wide,
The ravin is ready on every side,
The limbs of the strangers are cooked and done;   345
    There is boiled meat, and roast meat, and meat from the coal,
You may chop it, and tear it, and gnash it for fun,
    An hairy goat's-skin contains the whole.
Let me but escape, and ferry me o'er
The stream of your wrath to a safer shore.   350
The Cyclops Aetnean is cruel and bold,
      He murders the strangers
        That sit on his hearth,
      And dreads no avengers
        To rise from the earth.   355
He roasts the men before they are cold,

He snatches them broiling from the coal,
And from the caldron pulls them whole,
And minces their flesh and gnaws their bone
With his cursèd teeth, till all be gone.   360
    Farewell, foul pavilion:
        Farewell, rites of dread!
    The Cyclops vermilion,
        With slaughter uncloying,
      Now feasts on the dead,   365
        In the flesh of strangers joying!
    Ulysses. O Jupiter! I saw within the cave
Horrible things; deeds to be feigned in words,
But not to be believed as being done.
    Chorus. What! sawest thou the impious Polypheme   370
Feasting upon your loved companions now?
    Ulysses. Selecting two, the plumpest of the crowd,
He grasped them in his hands.—
    Chorus.   Unhappy man!

   .   .   .   .

    Ulysses. Soon as we came into this craggy place,
Kindling a fire, he cast on the broad hearth   375
The knotty limbs of an enormous oak,
Three waggon-loads at least, and then he strewed
Upon the ground, beside the red firelight,
His couch of pine-leaves; and he milked the cows,
And pouring forth the white milk, filled a bowl   380
Three cubits wide and four in depth, as much
As would contain ten amphorae, and bound it
With ivy wreaths; then placed upon the fire
A brazen pot to boil, and made red hot
The points of spits, not sharpened with the sickle,   385
But with a fruit tree bough, and with the jaws
Of axes for Aetnean slaughterings.[1]
And when this God-abandoned Cook of Hell
Had made all ready, he seized two of us
And killed them in a kind of measured manner;   390
For he flung one against the brazen rivets
Of the huge caldron, and seized the other
By the foot's tendon, and knocked out his brains
Upon the sharp edge of the craggy stone:
Then peeled his flesh with a great cooking-knife   395
And put him down to roast. The other's limbs
He chopped into the caldron to be boiled.
And I, with the tears raining from my eyes
Stood near the Cyclops, ministering to him;

[1] I confess I do not understand this.—[SHELLEY'S NOTE.]

The rest, in the recesses of the cave,   400
Clung to the rock like bats, bloodless with fear.
When he was filled with my companions' flesh,
He threw himself upon the ground and sent
A loathsome exhalation from his maw.
Then a divine thought came to me. I filled   405
The cup of Maron, and I offered him
To taste, and said:—'Child of the Ocean God,
Behold what drink the vines of Greece produce,
The exultation and the joy of Bacchus.'
He, satiated with his unnatural food,   410
Received it, and at one draught drank it off,
And taking my hand, praised me:—'Thou hast given
A sweet draught after a sweet meal, dear guest.'
And I, perceiving that it pleased him, filled
Another cup, well knowing that the wine   415
Would wound him soon and take a sure revenge.
And the charm fascinated him, and I
Plied him cup after cup, until the drink
Had warmed his entrails, and he sang aloud
In concert with my wailing fellow-seamen   420
A hideous discord—and the cavern rung.
I have stolen out, so that if you will
You may achieve my safety and your own.
But say, do you desire, or not, to fly
This uncompanionable man, and dwell   425
As was your wont among the Grecian Nymphs
Within the fanes of your belovèd God?
Your father there within agrees to it,
But he is weak and overcome with wine,
And caught as if with bird-lime by the cup,   430
He claps his wings and crows in doting joy.
You who are young escape with me, and find
Bacchus your ancient friend; unsuited he
To this rude Cyclops.
   Chorus.   Oh my dearest friend,
That I could see that day, and leave for ever   435
The impious Cyclops.

.   .   .   .

   Ulysses. Listen then what a punishment I have
For this fell monster, how secure a flight
From your hard servitude.
   Chorus.   O sweeter far
Than is the music of an Asian lyre   440
Would be the news of Polypheme destroyed.
   Ulysses. Delighted with the Bacchic drink he goes
To call his brother Cyclops—who inhabit

A village upon Aetna not far off.
   Chorus. I understand, catching him when alone   445
You think by some measure to dispatch him,
Or thrust him from the precipice.
   Ulysses.   Oh no;
Nothing of that kind; my device is subtle.
   Chorus. How then? I heard of old that thou wert wise.
   Ulysses. I will dissuade him from this plan, by saying   450
It were unwise to give the Cyclopses
This precious drink, which if enjoyed alone
Would make life sweeter for a longer time.
When, vanquished by the Bacchic power, he sleeps,
There is a trunk of olive wood within,   455
Whose point having made sharp with this good sword
I will conceal in fire, and when I see
It is alight, will fix it, burning yet,
Within the socket of the Cyclops' eye
And melt it out with fire—as when a man   460
Turns by its handle a great auger round,
Fitting the framework of a ship with beams,
So will I, in the Cyclops' fiery eye
Turn round the brand and dry the pupil up.
   Chorus. Joy! I am mad with joy at your device.   465
   Ulysses. And then with you, my friends, and the old man,
We'll load the hollow depth of our black ship,
And row with double strokes from this dread shore.
   Chorus. May I, as in libations to a God,
Share in the blinding him with the red brand?   470
I would have some communion in his death.
   Ulysses. Doubtless: the brand is a great brand to hold.
   Chorus. Oh! I would lift an hundred waggon-loads,
If like a wasp's nest I could scoop the eye out
Of the detested Cyclops.
   Ulysses.   Silence now!   475
Ye know the close device—and when I call,
Look ye obey the masters of the craft.
I will not save myself and leave behind
My comrades in the cave: I might escape,
Having got clear from that obscure recess,   480
But 'twere unjust to leave in jeopardy
The dear companions who sailed here with me.

Chorus.

Come! who is first, that with his hand
Will urge down the burning brand
Through the lids, and quench and pierce   485
The Cyclops' eye so fiery fierce?

Semichorus I. (Song within.)

Listen! listen! he is coming,
A most hideous discord humming.
Drunken, museless, awkward, yelling,
Far along his rocky dwelling; 490
Let us with some comic spell
Teach the yet unteachable.
By all means he must be blinded,
If my counsel be but minded.

Semichorus II.

Happy thou made odorous 495
 With the dew which sweet grapes weep,
To the village hastening thus,
 Seek the vines that soothe to sleep;
Having first embraced thy friend,
Thou in luxury without end, 500
With the strings of yellow hair,
Of thy voluptuous leman fair,
Shalt sit playing on a bed!—
Speak! what door is openèd?

Cyclops.

Ha! ha! ha! I'm full of wine, 505
Heavy with the joy divine,
With the young feast oversated;
Like a merchant's vessel freighted
To the water's edge, my crop
Is laden to the gullet's top. 510
The fresh meadow grass of spring
Tempts me forth thus wandering
 To my brothers on the mountains,
 Who shall share the wine's sweet fountains.
Bring the cask, O stranger, bring! 515

Chorus.

One with eyes the fairest
 Cometh from his dwelling;
Some one loves thee, rarest,
 Bright beyond my telling.
In thy grace thou shinest 520
Like some nymph divinest
In her caverns dewy:—
All delights pursue thee,
Soon pied flowers, sweet-breathing,
Shall thy head be wreathing. 525

Ulysses. Listen, O Cyclops, for I am well skilled
In Bacchus, whom I gave thee of to drink.
  Cyclops. What sort of God is Bacchus then accounted?
  Ulysses. The greatest among men for joy of life.
  Cyclops. I gulped him down with very great delight.   530
  Ulysses. This is a God who never injures men.
  Cyclops. How does the God like living in a skin?
  Ulysses. He is content wherever he is put.
  Cyclops. Gods should not have their body in a skin.
  Ulysses. If he gives joy, what is his skin to you?   535
  Cyclops. I hate the skin, but love the wine within.
  Ulysses. Stay here now: drink, and make your spirit glad.
  Cyclops. Should I not share this liquor with my brothers?
  Ulysses. Keep it yourself, and be more honoured so.
  Cyclops. I were more useful, giving to my friends.   540
  Ulysses. But village mirth breeds contests, broils, and blows.
  Cyclops. When I am drunk none shall lay hands on me.—
  Ulysses. A drunken man is better within doors.
  Cyclops. He is a fool, who drinking, loves not mirth.
  Ulysses. But he is wise, who drunk, remains at home.   545
  Cyclops. What shall I do, Silenus? Shall I stay?
  Silenus. Stay—for what need have you of pot companions?
  Cyclops. Indeed this place is closely carpeted
With flowers and grass.
  Silenus.   And in the sun-warm noon
'Tis sweet to drink. Lie down beside me now,   550
Placing your mighty sides upon the ground.
  Cyclops. What do you put the cup behind me for?
  Silenus. That no one here may touch it.
  Cyclops.   Thievish one!
You want to drink;—here place it in the midst.
And thou, O stranger, tell how art thou called?   555
  Ulysses. My name is Nobody. What favour now
Shall I receive to praise you at your hands?
  Cyclops. I'll feast on you the last of your companions.
  Ulysses. You grant your guest a fair reward, O Cyclops.
  Cyclops. Ha! what is this? Stealing the wine, you rogue!
  Silenus. It was this stranger kissing me because   561
I looked so beautiful.
  Cyclops.   You shall repent
For kissing the coy wine that loves you not.
  Silenus. By Jupiter! you said that I am fair.
  Cyclops. Pour out, and only give me the cup full.   565
  Silenus. How is it mixed? let me observe.
  Cyclops.   Curse you!
Give it me so.
  Silenus.   Not till I see you wear

That coronal, and taste the cup to you.
   Cyclops. Thou wily traitor!
   Silenus.   But the wine is sweet.
Ay, you will roar if you are caught in drinking.   570
   Cyclops. See now, my lip is clean and all my beard.
   Silenus. Now put your elbow right and drink again.
As you see me drink— . . .
   Cyclops. How now?
   Silenus.   Ye Gods, what a delicious gulp!
   Cyclops. Guest, take it;—you pour out the wine for me.   575
   Ulysses. The wine is well accustomed to my hand.
   Cyclops. Pour out the wine!
   Ulysses.   I pour; only be silent.
   Cyclops. Silence is a hard task to him who drinks.
   Ulysses. Take it and drink it off; leave not a dreg.
Oh, that the drinker died with his own draught!   580
   Cyclops. Papai! the vine must be a sapient plant.
   Ulysses. If you drink much after a mighty feast,
Moistening your thirsty maw, you will sleep well;
If you leave aught, Bacchus will dry you up.
   Cyclops. Ho! ho! I can scarce rise. What pure delight!
The heavens and earth appear to whirl about   586
Confusedly. I see the throne of Jove
And the clear congregation of the Gods.
Now if the Graces tempted me to kiss
I would not—for the loveliest of them all   590
I would not leave this Ganymede.
   Silenus.   Polypheme,
I am the Ganymede of Jupiter.
   Cyclops. By Jove, you are; I bore you off from Dardanus.
.   .   .   .

ULYSSES *and the* CHORUS

   Ulysses. Come, boys of Bacchus, children of high race,
This man within is folded up in sleep,   595
And soon will vomit flesh from his fell maw;
The brand under the shed thrusts out its smoke,
No preparation needs, but to burn out
The monster's eye;—but bear yourselves like men.
   Chorus. We will have courage like the adamant rock,   600
All things are ready for you here; go in,
Before our father shall perceive the noise.
   Ulysses. Vulcan, Aetnean king! burn out with fire
The shining eye of this thy neighbouring monster!
And thou, O Sleep, nursling of gloomy Night,   605
Descend unmixed on this God-hated beast,
And suffer not Ulysses and his comrades,
Returning from their famous Trojan toils,

To perish by this man, who cares not either
For God or mortal; or I needs must think   610
That Chance is a supreme divinity,
And things divine are subject to her power.

Chorus.

Soon a crab the throat will seize
    Of him who feeds upon his guest,
Fire will burn his lamp-like eyes   615
    In revenge of such a feast!
A great oak stump now is lying
    In the ashes yet undying.
        Come, Maron, come!
Raging let him fix the doom,   620
Let him tear the eyelid up
Of the Cyclops—that his cup
        May be evil!
Oh! I long to dance and revel
With sweet Bromian, long desired,   625
In loved ivy wreaths attired;
Leaving this abandoned home,—
Will the moment ever come?

Ulysses. Be silent, ye wild things! Nay, hold your peace,
And keep your lips quite close; dare not to breathe,   630
Or spit, or e'en wink, lest ye wake the monster,
Until his eye be tortured out with fire.
    Chorus. Nay, we are silent, and we chaw the air.
    Ulysses. Come now, and lend a hand to the great stake
Within—it is delightfully red hot.   635
    Chorus. You then command who first should seize the stake
To burn the Cyclops' eye, that all may share
In the great enterprise.
    Semichorus I.   We are too far;
We cannot at this distance from the door
Thrust fire into his eye.
    Semichorus II.   And we just now   640
Have become lame! cannot move hand or foot.
    Chorus. The same thing has occurred to us,—our ankles
Are sprained with standing here, I know not how.
    Ulysses. What, sprained with standing still?
    Chorus.   And there is dust
Or ashes in our eyes, I know not whence.   645
    Ulysses. Cowardly dogs! ye will not aid me then?
    Chorus. With pitying my own back and my back-bone,
And with not wishing all my teeth knocked out,
This cowardice comes of itself—but stay,

I know a famous Orphic incantation 650
To make the brand stick of its own accord
Into the skull of this one-eyed son of Earth.
    Ulysses. Of old I knew ye thus by nature; now
I know ye better.—I will use the aid
Of my own comrades. Yet though weak of hand 655
Speak cheerfully, that so ye may awaken
The courage of my friends with your blithe words.
    Chorus. This I will do with peril of my life,
And blind you with my exhortations, Cyclops.
          Hasten and thrust, 660
          And parch up to dust,
          The eye of the beast
          Who feeds on his guest.
          Burn and blind
          The Aetnean hind! 665
          Scoop and draw,
          But beware lest he claw
          Your limbs near his maw.
    Cyclops. Ah me! my eyesight is parched up to cinders.
    Chorus. What a sweet paean; sing me that again! 670
    Cyclops. Ah me! indeed, what woe has fallen upon me!
But, wretched nothings, think ye not to flee
Out of this rock; I, standing at the outlet,
Will bar the way and catch you as you pass.
    Chorus. What are you roaring out, Cyclops?
    Cyclops.   I perish! 675
    Chorus. For you are wicked.
    Cyclops.   And besides miserable.
    Chorus. What, did you fall into the fire when drunk?
    Cyclops. 'Twas Nobody destroyed me.
    Chorus.   Why then no one
Can be to blame.
    Cyclops.   I say 'twas Nobody
Who blinded me.
    Chorus.   Why then you are not blind. 680
    Cyclops. I wish you were as blind as I am.
    Chorus.   Nay,
It cannot be that no one made you blind.
    Cyclops. You jeer me; where, I ask, is Nobody?
    Chorus. Nowhere, O Cyclops.
    Cyclops. It was that stranger ruined me:—the wretch 685
First gave me wine and then burned out my eye,
For wine is strong and hard to struggle with.
Have they escaped, or are they yet within?
    Chorus. They stand under the darkness of the rock
And cling to it.

Cyclops.   At my right hand or left?   690
Chorus. Close on your right.
Cyclops.   Where?
Chorus.   Near the rock itself.
You have them.
    Cyclops.   Oh, misfortune on misfortune!
I've cracked my skull.
    Chorus.   Now they escape you—there.
Cyclops. Not there, although you say so.
Chorus.   Not on that side.
Cyclops. Where then?
Chorus.   They creep about you on your left. 695
Cyclops. Ah! I am mocked! They jeer me in my ills.
Chorus. Not there! he is a little there beyond you.
Cyclops. Detested wretch! where are you?
Ulysses.   Far from you
I keep with care this body of Ulysses.
    Cyclops. What do you say? You proffer a new name.   700
    Ulysses. My father named me so; and I have taken
A full revenge for your unnatural feast;
I should have done ill to have burned down Troy
And not revenged the murder of my comrades.
    Cyclops. Ai! ai! the ancient oracle is accomplished;   705
It said that I should have my eye sight blinded
By your coming from Troy, yet it foretold
That you should pay the penalty for this
By wandering long over the homeless sea.
    Ulysses. I bid thee weep—consider what I say;   710
I go towards the shore to drive my ship
To mine own land, o'er the Sicilian wave.
    Cyclops. Not so, if whelming you with this huge stone,
I can crush you and all your men together;
I will descend upon the shore, though blind,   715
Groping my way adown the steep ravine.
    Chorus. And we, the shipmates of Ulysses now,
Will serve our Bacchus all our happy lives.

EPIGRAMS

I.—TO STELLA

FROM THE GREEK OF PLATO

Thou wert the morning star among the living,
    Ere thy fair light had fled;
Now, having died, thou art as Hesperus, giving
    New splendour to the dead.

II.—KISSING HELENA

FROM THE GREEK OF PLATO

KISSING Helena, together
  With my kiss, my soul beside it
    Came to my lips, and there I kept it,—
For the poor thing had wandered thither,
  To follow where the kiss should guide it,   5
    Oh, cruel I, to intercept it!

III.—SPIRT OF PLATO

FROM THE GREEK

EAGLE! why soarest thou above that tomb?
To what sublime and starry-paven home
  Floatest thou?—
I am the image of swift Plato's spirit,
Ascending heaven; Athens doth inherit   5
  His corpse below.

IV.—CIRCUMSTANCE

FROM THE GREEK

A MAN who was about to hang himself,
  Finding a purse, then threw away his rope;
The owner, coming to reclaim his pelf,
  The halter found, and used it. So is Hope
Changed for Despair—one laid upon the shelf,   5
  We take the other. Under Heaven's high cope
Fortune is God—all you endure and do
Depends on circumstance as much as you.

FRAGMENT OF THE ELEGY ON THE DEATH OF ADONIS

FROM THE GREEK OF BION

I MOURN Adonis dead—loveliest Adonis—
Dead, dead Adonis—and the Loves lament.
Sleep no more, Venus, wrapped in purple woof—
  Wake violet-stolèd queen, and weave the crown
Of Death,—'tis Misery calls,—for he is dead.   5

  The lovely one lies wounded in the mountains,
His white thigh struck with the white tooth; he scarce
Yet breathes; and Venus hangs in agony there.
The dark blood wanders o'er his snowy limbs,
His eyes beneath their lids are lustreless,   10
The rose has fled from his wan lips, and there
That kiss is dead, which Venus gathers yet.

A deep, deep wound Adonis . . .
A deeper Venus bears upon her heart.
See, his belovèd dogs are gathering round—   15
The Oread nymphs are weeping—Aphrodite
With hair unbound is wandering through the woods,
'Wildered, ungirt, unsandalled—the thorns pierce
Her hastening feet and drink her sacred blood.
Bitterly screaming out, she is driven on   20
Through the long vales; and her Assyrian boy,
Her love, her husband, calls—the purple blood
    From his struck thigh stains her white navel now,
Her bosom, and her neck before like snow.

    Alas for Cytherea—the Loves mourn—   25
The lovely, the beloved is gone!—and now
Her sacred beauty vanishes away.
For Venus whilst Adonis lived was fair—
Alas! her loveliness is dead with him.
The oaks and mountains cry, Ai! ai! Adonis!   30
The springs their waters change to tears and weep—
The flowers are withered up with grief . . .

    Ai! ai!   Adonis is dead
Echo resounds   Adonis dead.
Who will weep not thy dreadful woe, O Venus?   35
Soon as she saw and knew the mortal wound
Of her Adonis—saw the life-blood flow
From his fair thigh, now wasting,—wailing loud
She clasped him, and cried   'Stay, Adonis!
Stay, dearest one, . . .
                        and mix my lips with thine—   40
Wake yet a while, Adonis—oh, but once,
That I may kiss thee now for the last time—
But for as long as one short kiss may live—
Oh, let thy breath flow from thy dying soul   45
Even to my mouth and heart, that I may suck
That . . .'

FRAGMENT OF THE ELEGY ON THE DEATH OF BION

FROM THE GREEK OF MOSCHUS

Ye Dorian woods and waves, lament aloud,—
Augment your tide, O streams, with fruitless tears,
For the belovèd Bion is no more.
Let every tender herb and plant and flower,
From each dejected bud and drooping bloom,   5
Shed dews of liquid sorrow, and with breath
Of melancholy sweetness on the wind

Diffuse its languid love; let roses blush,
Anemones grow paler for the loss
Their dells have known; and thou, O hyacinth,   10
Utter thy legend now—yet more, dumb flower,
Than 'Ah! alas!'—thine is no common grief—
Bion the [sweetest singer] is no more.

FROM THE GREEK OF MOSCHUS

Τὰν ἄλα τὰν γλαυκὰν ὅταν ὤνεμος ἀτρέμα βάλλῃ—κ.τ.λ.

WHEN winds that move not its calm surface sweep
The azure sea, I love the land no more;
The smiles of the serene and tranquil deep
Tempt my unquiet mind.—But when the roar
Of Ocean's gray abyss resounds, and foam   5
Gathers upon the sea, and vast waves burst,
I turn from the drear aspect to the home
Of Earth and its deep woods, where, interspersed,
When winds blow loud, pines make sweet melody.
Whose house is some lone bark, whose toil the sea,   10
Whose prey the wandering fish, an evil lot
Has chosen.—But I my languid limbs will fling
Beneath the plane, where the brook's murmuring
Moves the calm spirit, but disturbs it not.

PAN, ECHO, AND THE SATYR

FROM THE GREEK OF MOSCHUS

PAN loved his neighbour Echo—but that child
    Of Earth and Air pined for the Satyr leaping;
The Satyr loved with wasting madness wild
    The bright nymph Lyda,—and so three went weeping.
As Pan loved Echo, Echo loved the Satyr,   5
    The Satyr, Lyda; and so love consumed them.—
And thus to each—which was a woful matter—
    To bear what they inflicted Justice doomed them;
For, inasmuch as each might hate the lover,
    Each, loving, so was hated.—Ye that love not   10
Be warned—in thought turn this example over,
    That when ye love, the like return ye prove not.

FROM VERGIL'S TENTH ECLOGUE

[Vv. 1-26]

MELODIOUS Arethusa, o'er my verse
    Shed thou once more the spirit of thy stream:
Who denies verse to Gallus? So, when thou

Glidest beneath the green and purple gleam
Of Syracusan waters, mayst thou flow · 5
    Unmingled with the bitter Doric dew!
Begin, and, whilst the goats are browsing now
    The soft leaves, in our way let us pursue
The melancholy loves of Gallus. List!
    We sing not to the dead: the wild woods knew 10
His sufferings, and their echoes . . .
    Young Naiads, . . . in what far woodlands wild
Wandered ye when unworthy love possessed
    Your Gallus? Not where Pindus is up-piled,
Nor where Parnassus' sacred mount, nor where 15
    Aonian Aganippe expands . . .
The laurels and the myrtle-copses dim.
    The pine-encircled mountain, Maenalus,
The cold crags of Lycaeus, weep for him;
    And Sylvan, crowned with rustic coronals, 20
Came shaking in his speed the budding wands
    And heavy lilies which he bore: we knew
Pan the Arcadian.

. . . .

'What madness is this, Gallus? Thy heart's care
With willing steps pursues another there.' 25

FROM VERGIL'S FOURTH GEORGIC

[Vv. 360 et seq.]

AND the cloven waters like a chasm of mountains
Stood, and received him in its mighty portal
And let him through the deep's untrampled fountains

He went in wonder through the path immortal
Of his great Mother and her humid reign 5
And groves profaned not by the step of mortal

Which sounded as he passed, and lakes which rain
Replenished not girt round by marble caves
'Wildered by the watery motion of the main

Half 'wildered he beheld the bursting waves 10
Of every stream beneath the mighty earth
Phasis and Lycus which the   sand paves,

[And] the chasm where old Enipeus has its birth
And father Tyber and Anienas[?] glow
And whence Caicus, Mysian stream, comes forth 15

And rock-resounding Hypanis, and thou
Eridanus who bearest like empire's sign
Two golden horns upon thy taurine brow

Thou than whom none of the streams divine
Through garden-fields and meads with fiercer power,   20
Burst in their tumult on the purple brine.

SONNET

FROM THE ITALIAN OF DANTE

Dante Alighieri to Guido Cavalcanti

GUIDO, I would that Lapo, thou, and I,
Led by some strong enchantment, might ascend
A magic ship, whose charmèd sails should fly
With winds at will where'er our thoughts might wend,
So that no change, nor any evil chance   5
Should mar our joyous voyage; but it might be,
That even satiety should still enhance
Between our hearts their strict community:
And that the bounteous wizard then would place
Vanna and Bice and my gentle love,   10
Companions of our wandering, and would grace
With passionate talk, wherever we might rove,
Our time, and each were as content and free
As I believe that thou and I should be.

THE FIRST CANZONE OF THE CONVITO

FROM THE ITALIAN OF DANTE

I

YE who intelligent the Third Heaven move,
Hear the discourse which is within my heart,
    Which cannot be declared, it seems so new.
The Heaven whose course follows your power and art,
    Oh, gentle creatures that ye are! me drew,   5
    And therefore may I dare to speak to you,
Even of the life which now I live—and yet
    I pray that ye will hear me when I cry,
    And tell of mine own heart this novelty;
How the lamenting Spirit moans in it,   10
And how a voice there murmurs against her
Who came on the refulgence of your sphere.

II

A sweet Thought, which was once the life within
    This heavy heart, many a time and oft
        Went up before our Father's feet, and there   15
    It saw a glorious Lady throned aloft;
And its sweet talk of her my soul did win,

So that I said, 'Thither I too will fare.'
That Thought is fled, and one doth now appear
Which tyrannizes me with such fierce stress,   20
   That my heart trembles—ye may see it leap—
   And on another Lady bids me keep
Mine eyes, and says—Who would have blessedness
Let him but look upon that Lady's eyes,
Let him not fear the agony of sighs.   25

III

This lowly Thought, which once would talk with me
Of a bright seraph sitting crowned on high,
   Found such a cruel foe it died, and so
   My Spirit wept, the grief is hot even now—
And said, Alas for me! how swift could flee   30
That piteous Thought which did my life console!
   And the afflicted one   questioning
     Mine eyes, if such a Lady saw they never,
   And why they would . . .
     I said: 'Beneath those eyes might stand for ever   35
He whom   regards must kill with . . .
To have known their power stood me in little stead,
Those eyes have looked on me, and I am dead.'

IV

'Thou art not dead, but thou hast wandered,
   Thou Soul of ours, who thyself dost fret,'   40
A Spirit of gentle Love beside me said;
   For that fair Lady, whom thou dost regret,
Hath so transformed the life which thou hast led,
Thou scornest it, so worthless art thou made.
And see how meek, how pitiful, how staid,   45
Yet courteous, in her majesty she is.
   And still call thou her Woman in thy thought;
   Her whom, if thou thyself deceivest not,
Thou wilt behold decked with such loveliness,
That thou wilt cry [Love] only Lord, lo! here   50
Thy handmaiden, do what thou wilt with her.

V

My song, I fear that thou wilt find but few
   Who fitly shall conceive thy reasoning
     Of such hard matter dost thou entertain.
Whence, if by misadventure chance should bring   55
Thee to base company, as chance may do,
     Quite unaware of what thou dost contain,
   I prithee comfort thy sweet self again,

My last delight; tell them that they are dull,
And bid them own that thou art beautiful.   60

MATILDA GATHERING FLOWERS

FROM THE PURGATORIO OF DANTE, CANTO XXVIII, ll. 1-51

AND earnest to explore within—around—
The divine wood, whose thick green living woof
Tempered the young day to the sight—I wound

Up the green slope, beneath the forest's roof,
With slow, soft steps leaving the mountain's steep,   5
And sought those inmost labyrinths, motion-proof

Against the air, that in that stillness deep
And solemn, struck upon my forehead bare,
The slow, soft stroke of a continuous . . .

In which the   leaves tremblingly were   10
All bent towards that part where earliest
The sacred hill obscures the morning air.

Yet were they not so shaken from the rest,
But that the birds, perched on the utmost spray,
Incessantly renewing their blithe quest,   15

With perfect joy received the early day,
Singing within the glancing leaves, whose sound
Kept a low burden to their roundelay,

Such as from bough to bough gathers around
The pine forest on bleak Chiassi's shore,   20
When Aeolus Sirocco has unbound.

My slow steps had already borne me o'er
Such space within the antique wood, that I
Perceived not where I entered any more,—

When, lo! a stream whose little waves went by,   25
Bending towards the left through grass that grew
Upon its bank, impeded suddenly

My going on. Water of purest hue
On earth, would appear turbid and impure
Compared with this, whose unconcealing dew,   30

Dark, dark, yet clear, moved under the obscure
Eternal shades, whose interwoven looms
The rays of moon or sunlight ne'er endure.

I moved not with my feet, but mid the glooms
Pierced with my charmèd eye, contemplating   35
The mighty multitude of fresh May blooms

Which starred that night, when, even as a thing
That suddenly, for blank astonishment,
Charms every sense, and makes all thought take wing,—

A solitary woman! and she went   40
Singing and gathering flower after flower,
With which her way was painted and besprent.

'Bright lady, who, if looks had ever power
To bear true witness of the heart within,
Dost bask under the beams of love, come lower   45

Towards this bank. I prithee let me win
This much of thee, to come, that I may hear
Thy song: like Proserpine, in Enna's glen,

Thou seemest to my fancy, singing here
And gathering flowers, as that fair maiden when   50
She lost the Spring, and Ceres her, more dear.'

FRAGMENT

ADAPTED FROM THE VITA NUOVA OF DANTE

WHAT Mary is when she a little smiles
I cannot even tell or call to mind,
It is a miracle so new, so rare.

UGOLINO

INFERNO xxxiii. 22-75

Now had the loophole of that dungeon, still
Which bears the name of Famine's Tower from me,
And where 'tis fit that many another will

Be doomed to linger in captivity,
Shown through its narrow opening in my cell   5
Moon after moon slow waning, when a sleep,

*That of the future burst the veil, in dream
Visited me. It was a slumber deep
And evil; for I saw, or I did seem*

To see, *that* tyrant Lord his revels keep,   10
The leader of the cruel hunt to them,
Chasing the wolf and wolf-cubs up the steep

Ascent, that from *the Pisan is the screen
Of Lucca;* with him Gualandi came,
Sismondi, and Lanfranchi, *bloodhounds lean,*   15

*Trained to the sport and eager for the game
Wide ranging in his front;* but soon were seen
Though by so short a course, with *spirits tame,*

The father and *his whelps* to flag at once,
And then the sharp fangs gored their bosoms deep   20
Ere morn I roused myself, and heard my sons,

For they were with me, moaning in their sleep,
And begging bread. Ah, for those darling ones!
Right cruel art thou, if thou dost not weep

In thinking of my soul's sad augury;   25
And if thou weepest not now, weep never more!
They were already waked, as wont drew nigh

The allotted hour for food, and in that hour
Each drew a presage from his dream. When I
Heard locked beneath me of that horrible tower   30

The outlet; then into their eyes alone
I looked to read myself, without a sign
Or word. I wept not—turned within to stone.

They wept aloud, and little Anselm mine,
Said—'twas my youngest, dearest little one,—   35
'What ails thee, father? Why look so at thine?'

In all that day, and all the following night,
I wept not, nor replied; but when to shine
Upon the world, not us, came forth the light

Of the new sun, and thwart my prison thrown   40
Gleamed through its narrow chink, a doleful sight,
Three faces, each the reflex of my own,

Were imaged by its faint and ghastly ray;
Then I, of either hand unto the bone,
Gnawed, in my agony; and thinking they   45

'Twas done from sudden pangs, in their excess,
All of a sudden raise themselves, and say,
'Father! our woes, so great, were yet the less

Would you but eat of us,—'twas *you who clad*
Our bodies in these weeds of wretchedness;   50
Despoil them.' Not to make their hearts more sad,

I *hushed* myself. That day is at its close,—
Another—still we were all mute. Oh, had
The obdurate earth opened to end our woes!

The fourth day dawned, and when the new sun shone,   55
Outstretched himself before me as it rose
My Gaddo, saying, 'Help, father! hast thou none

For thine own child—is there no help from thee?'
He died—there at my feet—and one by one,
I saw them fall, plainly as you see me.   60

Between the fifth and sixth day, ere 'twas dawn,
I found *myself blind-groping o'er the three.*
Three days I called them after they were gone.

Famine of grief can get the mastery.

SONNET

FROM THE ITALIAN OF CAVALCANTI

GUIDO CAVALCANTI TO DANTE ALIGHIERI

RETURNING from its daily quest, my Spirit
Changed thoughts and vile in thee doth weep to find:
It grieves me that thy mild and gentle mind
Those ample virtues which it did inherit
Has lost. Once thou didst loathe the multitude   5
Of blind and madding men—I then loved thee—
I loved thy lofty songs and that sweet mood
When thou wert faithful to thyself and me.
I dare not now through thy degraded state
Own the delight thy strains inspire—in vain   10
I seek what once thou wert—we cannot meet
And we were wont. Again and yet again
Ponder my words: so the false Spirit shall fly
And leave to thee thy true integrity.

SCENES FROM THE MAGICO PRODIGIOSO

FROM THE SPANISH OF CALDERON

SCENE I.—*Enter* CYPRIAN, *dressed as a Student;* CLARIN *and* MOSCON *as poor Scholars, with books.*

  Cyprian. In the sweet solitude of this calm place,
This intricate wild wilderness of trees
And flowers and undergrowth of odorous plants,
Leave me; the books you brought out of the house
To me are ever best society.   5
And while with glorious festival and song,
Antioch now celebrates the consecration
Of a proud temple to great Jupiter,
And bears his image in loud jubilee
To its new shrine, I would consume what still   10
Lives of the dying day in studious thought,
Far from the throng and turmoil. You, my friends,
Go, and enjoy the festival; it will

Be worth your pains. You may return for me
When the sun seeks its grave among the billows   15
Which, among dim gray clouds on the horizon,
Dance like white plumes upon a hearse;—and here
I shall expect you.
    Moscon.   I cannot bring my mind,
Great as my haste to see the festival
Certainly is, to leave you, Sir, without   20
Just saying some three or four thousand words.
How is it possible that on a day
Of such festivity, you can be content
To come forth to a solitary country
With three or four old books, and turn your back   25
On all this mirth?
    Clarin.   My master's in the right;
There is not anything more tiresome
Than a procession day, with troops, and priests,
And dances, and all that.
    Moscon.   From first to last,
Clarin, you are a temporizing flatterer;   30
You praise not what you feel but what he does;—
Toadeater!
    Clarin.   You lie—under a mistake—
For this is the most civil sort of lie
That can be given to a man's face. I now
Say what I think.
    Cyprian.   Enough, you foolish fellows!   35
Puffed up with your own doting ignorance,
You always take the two sides of one question.
Now go; and as I said, return for me
When night falls, veiling in its shadows wide
This glorious fabric of the universe.   40
    Moscon. How happens it, although you can maintain
The folly of enjoying festivals,
That yet you go there?
    Clarin.   Nay, the consequence
Is clear:—who ever did what he advises
Others to do?—
    Moscon.   Would that my feet were wings,   45
So would I fly to Livia.   [*Exit.*
    Clarin.   To speak truth,
Livia is she who has surprised my heart;
But he is more than half-way there.—Soho!
Livia, I come; good sport, Livia, soho!   [*Exit.*
    Cyprian. Now, since I am alone, let me examine   50
The question which has long disturbed my mind
With doubt, since first I read in Plinius

The words of mystic import and deep sense
In which he defines God. My intellect
Can find no God with whom these marks and signs   55
Fitly agree. It is a hidden truth
Which I must fathom.

[CYPRIAN *reads; the* DAEMON, *dressed in a Court dress, enters.*

Daemon.   Search even as thou wilt,
But thou shalt never find what I can hide.
Cyprian. What noise is that among the boughs? Who moves?
What art thou?—
Daemon.   'Tis a foreign gentleman.   60
Even from this morning I have lost my way
In this wild place; and my poor horse at last,
Quite overcome, has stretched himself upon
The enamelled tapestry of this mossy mountain,
And feeds and rests at the same time. I was   65
Upon my way to Antioch upon business
Of some importance, but wrapped up in cares
(Who is exempt from this inheritance?)
I parted from my company, and lost
My way, and lost my servants and my comrades.   70
Cyprian. 'Tis singular that even within the sight
Of the high towers of Antioch you could lose
Your way. Of all the avenues and green paths
Of this wild wood there is not one but leads,
As to its centre, to the walls of Antioch;   75
Take which you will, you cannot miss your road.
Daemon. And such is ignorance! Even in the sight
Of knowledge, it can draw no profit from it.
But as it still is early, and as I
Have no acquaintances in Antioch,   80
Being a stranger there, I will even wait
The few surviving hours of the day,
Until the night shall conquer it. I see
Both by your dress and by the books in which
You find delight and company, that you   85
Are a great student;—for my part, I feel
Much sympathy in such pursuits.
Cyprian.   Have you
Studied much?
Daemon.   No,—and yet I know enough
Not to be wholly ignorant.
Cyprian.   Pray, Sir,
What science may you know?—
Daemon.   Many.
Cyprian.   Alas!   90

Much pains must we expend on one alone,
And even then attain it not;—but you
Have the presumption to assert that you
Know many without study.
   Daemon.   And with truth.
For in the country whence I come the sciences   95
Require no learning,—they are known.
   Cyprian.   Oh, would
I were of that bright country! for in this
The more we study, we the more discover
Our ignorance.
   Daemon.   It is so true, that I
Had so much arrogance as to oppose   100
The chair of the most high Professorship,
And obtained many votes, and, though I lost,
The attempt was still more glorious, than the failure
Could be dishonourable. If you believe not,
Let us refer it to dispute respecting   105
That which you know the best, and although I
Know not the opinion you maintain, and though
It be the true one, I will take the contrary.
   Cyprian. The offer gives me pleasure. I am now
Debating with myself upon a passage   110
Of Plinius, and my mind is racked with doubt
To understand and know who is the God
Of whom he speaks.
   Daemon.   It is a passage, if
I recollect it right, couched in these words:
'God is one supreme goodness, one pure essence,   115
One substance, and one sense, all sight, all hands.'
   Cyprian. 'Tis true.
   Daemon.   What difficulty find you here?
   Cyprian. I do not recognize among the Gods
The God defined by Plinius; if he must
Be supreme goodness, even Jupiter   120
Is not supremely good; because we see
His deeds are evil, and his attributes
Tainted with mortal weakness; in what manner
Can supreme goodness be consistent with
The passions of humanity?
   Daemon.   The wisdom   125
Of the old world masked with the names of Gods
The attributes of Nature and of Man;
A sort of popular philosophy.
   Cyprian. This reply will not satisfy me, for
Such awe is due to the high name of God   130
That ill should never be imputed. Then,

Examining the question with more care,
It follows, that the Gods would always will
That which is best, were they supremely good.
How then does one will one thing, one another?   135
And that you may not say that I allege
Poetical or philosophic learning:—
Consider the ambiguous responses
Of their oracular statues; from two shrines
Two armies shall obtain the assurance of   140
One victory. Is it not indisputable
That two contending wills can never lead
To the same end? And, being opposite,
If one be good, is not the other evil?
Evil in God is inconceivable;   145
But supreme goodness fails among the Gods
Without their union.
  Daemon.   I deny your major.
These responses are means towards some end
Unfathomed by our intellectual beam.
They are the work of Providence, and more   150
The battle's loss may profit those who lose,
Than victory advantage those who win.
  Cyprian. That I admit; and yet that God should not
(Falsehood is incompatible with deity)
Assure the victory; it would be enough   155
To have permitted the defeat. If God
Be all sight,—God, who had beheld the truth,
Would not have given assurance of an end
Never to be accomplished: thus, although
The Deity may according to his attributes   160
Be well distinguished into persons, yet
Even in the minutest circumstance
His essence must be one.
  Daemon.   To attain the end
The affections of the actors in the scene
Must have been thus influenced by his voice.   165
  Cyprian. But for a purpose thus subordinate
He might have employed Genii, good or evil,—
A sort of spirits called so by the learned,
Who roam about inspiring good or evil,
And from whose influence and existence we   170
May well infer our immortality.
Thus God might easily, without descent
To a gross falsehood in his proper person,
Have moved the affections by this mediation
To the just point.
  Daemon.   These trifling contradictions   175

Do not suffice to impugn the unity
Of the high Gods; in things of great importance
They still appear unanimous; consider
That glorious fabric, man,—his workmanship
Is stamped with one conception.
    Cyprian.   Who made man   180
Must have, methinks, the advantage of the others.
If they are equal, might they not have risen
In opposition to the work, and being
All hands, according to our author here,
Have still destroyed even as the other made?   185
If equal in their power, unequal only
In opportunity, which of the two
Will remain conqueror?
    Daemon.   On impossible
And false hypothesis there can be built
No argument. Say, what do you infer   190
From this?
    Cyprian.   That there must be a mighty God
Of supreme goodness and of highest grace,
All sight, all hands, all truth, infallible,
Without an equal and without a rival,
The cause of all things and the effect of nothing,   195
One power, one will, one substance, and one essence.
And, in whatever persons, one or two,
His attributes may be distinguished, one
Sovereign power, one solitary essence,
One cause of all cause.   *[They rise.*
    Daemon.   How can I impugn   200
So clear a consequence?
    Cyprian.   Do you regret
My victory?
    Daemon.   Who but regrets a check
In rivalry of wit? I could reply
And urge new difficulties, but will now
Depart, for I hear steps of men approaching,   205
And it is time that I should now pursue
My journey to the city.
    Cyprian.   Go in peace!
    Daemon. Remain in peace!—Since thus it profits him
To study, I will wrap his senses up
In sweet oblivion of all thought but of   210
A piece of excellent beauty; and, as I
Have power given me to wage enmity
Against Justina's soul, I will extract
From one effect two vengeances.   *[Aside and exit.*
    Cyprian.   I never

Met a more learnèd person. Let me now   215
Revolve this doubt again with careful mind.   [*He reads.*

FLORO *and* LELIO *enter.*

Lelio. Here stop. These toppling rocks and tangled boughs,
Impenetrable by the noonday beam,
Shall be sole witnesses of what we——
Floro.   Draw!
If there were words, here is the place for deeds.   220
Lelio. Thou needest not instruct me; well I know
That in the field, the silent tongue of steel
Speaks thus,—   [*They fight.*
Cyprian.   Ha! what is this? Lelio,—Floro,
Be it enough that Cyprian stands between you,
Although unarmed.
Lelio.   Whence comest thou, to stand   225
Between me and my vengeance?
Floro.   From what rocks
And desert cells?

Enter MOSCON *and* CLARIN.

Moscon.   Run! run! for where we left
My master, I now hear the clash of swords.
Clarin. I never run to approach things of this sort,
But only to avoid them. Sir! Cyprian! sir!   230
Cyprian. Be silent, fellows! What! two friends who are
In blood and fame the eyes and hope of Antioch,
One of the noble race of the Colalti,
The other son o' the Governor, adventure
And cast away, on some slight cause no doubt,   235
Two lives, the honour of their country?
Lelio.   Cyprian!
Although my high respect towards your person
Holds now my sword suspended, thou canst not
Restore it to the slumber of the scabbard:
Thou knowest more of science than the duel;   240
For when two men of honour take the field,
No counsel nor respect can make them friends
But one must die in the dispute.
Floro.   I pray
That you depart hence with your people, and
Leave us to finish what we have begun   245
Without advantage.—
Cyprian.   Though you may imagine
That I know little of the laws of duel,
Which vanity and valour instituted,
You are in error. By my birth I am
Held no less than yourselves to know the limits   250

Of honour and of infamy, nor has study
Quenched the free spirit which first ordered them;
And thus to me, as one well experienced
In the false quicksands of the sea of honour,
You may refer the merits of the case;   255
And if I should perceive in your relation
That either has the right to satisfaction
From the other, I give you my word of honour
To leave you.
  Lelio. Under this condition then
I will relate the cause, and you will cede   260
And must confess the impossibility
Of compromise; for the same lady is
Beloved by Floro and myself.
  Floro.   It seems
Much to me that the light of day should look
Upon that idol of my heart—but he——   265
Leave us to fight, according to thy word.
  Cyprian. Permit one question further: is the lady
Impossible to hope or not?
  Lelio.   She is
So excellent, that if the light of day
Should excite Floro's jealousy, it were   270
Without just cause, for even the light of day
Trembles to gaze on her.
  Cyprian. Would you for your
Part, marry her?
  Floro. Such is my confidence.
  Cyprian. And you?
  Lelio.   Oh! would that I could lift my hope
So high, for though she is extremely poor,   275
Her virtue is her dowry.
  Cyprian.   And if you both
Would marry her, is it not weak and vain,
Culpable and unworthy, thus beforehand
To slur her honour? What would the world say
If one should slay the other, and if she   280
Should afterwards espouse the murderer?

 [*The rivals agree to refer their quarrel to* Cyprian; *who in
consequence visits* Justina, *and becomes enamoured of her;
she disdains him, and he retires to a solitary sea-shore.*

Scene II

Cyprian.

O memory! permit it not
That the tyrant of my thought

Be another soul that still
Holds dominion o'er the will,
That would refuse, but can no more,   5
To bend, to tremble, and adore.
Vain idolatry!—I saw,
    And gazing, became blind with error;
Weak ambition, which the awe
    Of her presence bound to terror!   10
So beautiful she was—and I,
Between my love and jealousy,
Am so convulsed with hope and fear,
Unworthy as it may appear;—
So bitter is the life I live,   15
That, hear me, Hell! I now would give
To thy most detested spirit
My soul, for ever to inherit,
To suffer punishment and pine,
So this woman may be mine.   20
Hear'st thou, Hell! dost thou reject it?
My soul is offered!
        Daemon (unseen).   I accept it.
            [*Tempest, with thunder and lightning.*

                    Cyprian.

What is this? ye heavens for ever pure,
At once intensely radiant and obscure!
    Athwart the aethereal halls   25
The lightning's arrow and the thunder-balls
        The day affright,
        As from the horizon round,
        Burst with earthquake sound,
In mighty torrents the electric fountains;—   30
    Clouds quench the sun, and thunder-smoke
Strangles the air, and fire eclipses Heaven.
    Philosophy, thou canst not even
Compel their causes underneath thy yoke:
From yonder clouds even to the waves below   35
The fragments of a single ruin choke
        Imagination's flight;
    For, on flakes of surge, like feathers light,
The ashes of the desolation, cast
        Upon the gloomy blast,   40
    Tell of the footsteps of the storm;
And nearer, see, the melancholy form
Of a great ship, the outcast of the sea,
        Drives miserably!
And it must fly the pity of the port,   45

Or perish, and its last and sole resort
  Is its own raging enemy.
  The terror of the thrilling cry
  Was a fatal prophecy
  Of coming death, who hovers now   50
    Upon that shattered prow,
That they who die not may be dying still.
And not alone the insane elements
    Are populous with wild portents,
But that sad ship is as a miracle   55
  Of sudden ruin, for it drives so fast
It seems as if it had arrayed its form
    With the headlong storm.
  It strikes—I almost feel the shock,—
  It stumbles on a jaggèd rock,—   60
Sparkles of blood on the white foam are cast.

                                    [A tempest.

All exclaim (within). We are all lost!
  Daemon (within).   Now from this plank will I
Pass to the land and thus fulfil my scheme.

                Cyprian.

As in contempt of the elemental rage
  A man comes forth in safety, while the ship's   65
  Great form is in a watery eclipse
Obliterated from the Ocean's page,
And round its wreck the huge sea-monsters sit,
A horrid conclave, and the whistling wave
Is heaped over its carcase, like a grave.   70

   The DAEMON *enters, as escaped from the sea.*

  Daemon (aside). It was essential to my purposes
To wake a tumult on the sapphire ocean,
That in this unknown form I might at length
Wipe out the blot of the discomfiture
Sustained upon the mountain, and assail   75
With a new war the soul of Cyprian,
Forging the instruments of his destruction
Even from his love and from his wisdom.—O
Belovèd earth, dear mother, in thy bosom
I seek a refuge from the monster who   80
Precipitates itself upon me.
  Cyprian.   Friend,
Collect thyself; and be the memory
Of thy late suffering, and thy greatest sorrow
But as a shadow of the past,—for nothing
Beneath the circle of the moon, but flows   85

And changes, and can never know repose.
Daemon.   And who art thou, before whose feet my fate
has prostrated me?
     Cyprian.   One who, moved with pity,
Would soothe its stings.
     Daemon.   Oh, that can never be!
No solace can my lasting sorrows find.   90
     Cyprian.   Wherefore?
     Daemon.   Because my happiness is lost.
Yet I lament what has long ceased to be
The object of desire or memory,
And my life is not life.
     Cyprian.   Now, since the fury
Of this earthquaking hurricane is still,   95
And the crystàlline Heaven has reassumed
Its windless calm so quickly, that it seems
As if its heavy wrath had been awakened
Only to overwhelm that vessel,—speak,
Who art thou, and whence comest thou?
     Daemon.   Far more   100
My coming hither cost, than thou hast seen
Or I can tell. Among my misadventures
This shipwreck is the least. Wilt thou hear?
     Cyprian.   Speak.
     Daemon.   Since thou desirest, I will then unveil
Myself to thee;—for in myself I am   105
A world of happiness and misery;
This I have lost, and that I must lament
Forever. In my attributes I stood
So high and so heroically great,
In lineage so supreme, and with a genius   110
Which penetrated with a glance the world
Beneath my feet, that, won by my high merit,
A king—whom I may call the King of kings,
Because all others tremble in their pride
Before the terrors of His countenance,   115
In His high palace roofed with brightest gems
Of living light—call them the stars of Heaven—
Named me His counsellor. But the high praise
Stung me with pride and envy, and I rose
In mighty competition, to ascend   120
His seat and place my foot triumphantly
Upon His subject thrones. Chastised, I know
The depth to which ambition falls; too mad
Was the attempt, and yet more mad were now
Repentance of the irrevocable deed:—   125
Therefore I chose this ruin, with the glory

Of not to be subdued, before the shame
Of reconciling me with Him who reigns
By coward cession.—Nor was I alone,
Nor am I now, nor shall I be alone;   130
And there was hope, and there may still be hope,
For many suffrages among His vassals
Hailed me their lord and king, and many still
Are mine, and many more, perchance shall be.
Thus vanquished, though in fact victorious,   135
I left His seat of empire, from mine eye
Shooting forth poisonous lightning, while my words
With inauspicious thunderings shook Heaven,
Proclaiming vengeance, public as my wrong,
And imprecating on His prostrate slaves   140
Rapine, and death, and outrage. Then I sailed
Over the mighty fabric of the world,—
A pirate ambushed in its pathless sands,
A lynx crouched watchfully among its caves
And craggy shores; and I have wandered over   145
The expanse of these wide wildernesses
In this great ship, whose bulk is now dissolved
In the light breathings of the invisible wind,
And which the sea has made a dustless ruin,
Seeking ever a mountain, through whose forests   150
I seek a man, whom I must now compel
To keep his word with me. I came arrayed
In tempest, and although my power could well
Bridle the forest winds in their career,
For other causes I forbore to soothe   155
Their fury to Favonian gentleness;
I could and would not; (thus I wake in him   [*Aside.*
A love of magic art). Let not this tempest,
Nor the succeeding calm excite thy wonder;
For by my art the sun would turn as pale   160
As his weak sister with unwonted fear;
And in my wisdom are the orbs of Heaven
Written as in a record; I have pierced
The flaming circles of their wondrous spheres
And know them as thou knowest every corner   165
Of this dim spot. Let it not seem to thee
That I boast vainly; wouldst thou that I work
A charm over this waste and savage wood,
This Babylon of crags and agèd trees,
Filling its leafy coverts with a horror   170
Thrilling and strange? I am the friendless guest
Of these wild oaks and pines—and as from thee
I have received the hospitality

Of this rude place, I offer thee the fruit
Of years of toil in recompense; whate'er   175
Thy wildest dream presented to thy thought
As object of desire, that shall be thine.

    .   .   .   .

And thenceforth shall so firm an amity
'Twixt thee and me be, that neither Fortune,
The monstrous phantom which pursues success,   180
That careful miser, that free prodigal,
Who ever alternates, with changeful hand,
Evil and good, reproach and fame; nor Time,
That lodestar of the ages, to whose beam
The wingèd years speed o'er the intervals   185
Of their unequal revolutions; nor
Heaven itself, whose beautiful bright stars
Rule and adorn the world, can ever make
The least division between thee and me,
Since now I find a refuge in thy favour.   190

SCENE III.—*The* DAEMON *tempts* JUSTINA, *who is a Christian.*

Daemon.

Abyss of Hell! I call on thee,
Thou wild misrule of thine own anarchy!
    From thy prison-house set free
    The spirits of voluptuous death,
        That with their mighty breath   5
They may destroy a world of virgin thoughts;
Let her chaste mind with fancies thick as motes
    Be peopled from thy shadowy deep,
    Till her guiltless fantasy
    Full to overflowing be!   10
    And with sweetest harmony,
Let birds, and flowers, and leaves, and all things move
    To love, only to love.
    Let nothing meet her eyes
But signs of Love's soft victories;   15
    Let nothing meet her ear
    But sounds of Love's sweet sorrow,
So that from faith no succour she may borrow,
    But, guided by my spirit blind
    And in a magic snare entwined,   20
    She may now seek Cyprian.
    Begin, while I in silence bind
My voice, when thy sweet song thou hast began.

A Voice (within).

What is the glory far above
All else in human life?

All.

> Love! love!   25

[*While these words are sung, the* DAEMON *goes out at one door, and* JUSTINA *enters at another.*

The First Voice.

There is no form in which the fire
    Of love its traces has impressed not.
Man lives far more in love's desire
    Than by life's breath, soon possessed not.
If all that lives must love or die,   30
All shapes on earth, or sea, or sky,
With one consent to Heaven cry
That the glory far above
All else in life is—

All.

> Love! oh, Love!

Justina.

Thou melancholy Thought which art   35
So flattering and so sweet, to thee
When did I give the liberty
    Thus to afflict my heart?
What is the cause of this new Power
    Which doth my fevered being move,   40
Momently raging more and more?
What subtle Pain is kindled now
Which from my heart doth overflow
    Into my senses?—

All.

> Love! oh, Love!

Justina.

'Tis that enamoured Nightingale   45
    Who gives me the reply;
He ever tells the same soft tale
    Of passion and of constancy
To his mate, who rapt and fond,
Listening sits, a bough beyond.   50

Be silent, Nightingale—no more
Make me think, in hearing thee
Thus tenderly thy love deplore,
If a bird can feel his so,
What a man would feel for me.   55
And, voluptuous Vine, O thou
Who seekest most when least pursuing,—
To the trunk thou interlacest
Art the verdure which embracest,
And the weight which is its ruin,—   60
No more, with green embraces, Vine,
Make me think on what thou lovest,—
For whilst thus thy boughs entwine,
I fear lest thou shouldst teach me, sophist,
How arms might be entangled too.   65

Light-enchanted Sunflower, thou
Who gazest ever true and tender
On the sun's revolving splendour!
Follow not his faithless glance
With thy faded countenance,   70
Nor teach my beating heart to fear,
If leaves can mourn without a tear,
How eyes must weep! O Nightingale,
Cease from thy enamoured tale,—
Leafy Vine, unwreathe thy bower,   75
Restless Sunflower, cease to move,—
Or tell me all, what poisonous Power
Ye use against me—

All.

Love! Love! Love!
Justina. It cannot be!—Whom have I ever loved?
Trophies of my oblivion and disdain,   80
Floro and Lelio did I not reject?
And Cyprian?—   [*She becomes troubled at the name of Cyprian.*
Did I not requite him
With such severity, that he has fled
Where none has ever heard of him again?—
Alas! I now begin to fear that this   85
May be the occasion whence desire grows bold,
As if there were no danger. From the moment
That I pronounced to my own listening heart,
'Cyprian is absent!'—O me miserable!
I know not what I feel! [*More calmly.*] It must be pity   90
To think that such a man, whom all the world
Admired, should be forgot by all the world,

And I the cause.   [*She again becomes troubled.*

And yet if it were pity,
Floro and Lelio might have equal share,
For they are both imprisoned for my sake.   95
(*Calmly.*) Alas! what reasonings are these? it is
Enough I pity him, and that, in vain,
Without this ceremonious subtlety.
And, woe is me! I know not where to find him now,
Even should I seek him through this wide world.   100

Enter DAEMON.

Daemon. Follow, and I will lead thee where he is.
Justina. And who art thou, who hast found entrance hither,
Into my chamber through the doors and locks?
Art thou a monstrous shadow which my madness
·Has formed in the idle air?
Daemon.   No. I am one   105
Called by the Thought which tyrannizes thee
From his eternal dwelling; who this day
Is pledged to bear thee unto Cyprian.
Justina. So shall thy promise fail. This agony
Of passion which afflicts my heart and soul   110
May sweep imagination in its storm;
The will is firm.
Daemon.   Already half is done
In the imagination of an act.
The sin incurred, the pleasure then remains;
Let not the will stop half-way on the road.   115
Justina. I will not be discouraged, nor despair,
Although I thought it, and although 'tis true
That thought is but a prelude to the deed:—
Thought is not in my power, but action is:
I will not move my foot to follow thee.   120
Daemon. But a far mightier wisdom than thine own
Exerts itself within thee, with such power
Compelling thee to that which it inclines
That it shall force thy step; how wilt thou then
Resist, Justina?
Justina.   By my free-will.
Daemon.   I   125
Must force thy will.
Justina.   It is invincible;
It were not free if thou hadst power upon it.
                    [*He draws, but cannot move her.*
Daemon. Come, where a pleasure waits thee.
Justina.   It were bought
Too dear.

Daemon. 'Twill soothe thy heart to softest peace.
Justina. 'Tis dread captivity.
Daemon.   'Tis joy, 'tis glory.   130
Justina. 'Tis shame, 'tis torment, 'tis despair.
Daemon.   But how
Canst thou defend thyself from that or me,
If my power drags thee onward?
Justina.   My defence
Consists in God.

       [*He vainly endeavours to force her, and at last releases her.*

Daemon.   Woman, thou hast subdued me,
Only by not owning thyself subdued.   135
But since thou thus findest defence in God,
I will assume a feignèd form, and thus
Make thee a victim of my baffled rage.
For I will mask a spirit in thy form
Who will betray thy name to infamy,   140
And doubly shall I triumph in thy loss,
First by dishonouring thee, and then by turning
False pleasure to true ignominy.   [*Exit.*
Justina.   I
Appeal to Heaven against thee; so that Heaven
May scatter thy delusions, and the blot   145
Upon my fame vanish in idle thought,
Even as flame dies in the envious air,
And as the floweret wanes at morning frost;
And thou shouldst never—But, alas! to whom
Do I still speak?—Did not a man but now   150
Stand here before me?—No, I am alone,
And yet I saw him. Is he gone so quickly?
Or can the heated mind engender shapes
From its own fear? Some terrible and strange
Peril is near. Lisander! father! lord!   155
Livia!—

          Enter LISANDER *and* LIVIA.

Lisander. Oh, my daughter! What?
Livia.   What!
Justina.   Saw you
A man go forth from my apartment now?—
I scarce contain myself!
Lisander.   A man here!
Justina. Have you not seen him?
Livia.   No, Lady.
Justina. I saw him.
Lisander.   'Tis impossible; the doors   160
Which led to this apartment were all locked.

Livia (*aside*). I daresay it was Moscon whom she saw,
For he was locked up in my room.
    Lisander.   It must
Have been some image of thy fantasy.
Such melancholy as thou feedest is   165
Skilful in forming such in the vain air
Out of the motes and atoms of the day.
    Livia. My master's in the right.
    Justina.   Oh, would it were
Delusion; but I fear some greater ill.
I feel as if out of my bleeding bosom   170
My heart was torn in fragments; ay,
Some mortal spell is wrought against my frame;
So potent was the charm that, had not God
Shielded my humble innocence from wrong,
I should have sought my sorrow and my shame   175
With willing steps.—Livia, quick, bring my cloak,
For I must seek refuge from these extremes
Even in the temple of the highest God
Where secretly the faithful worship.
    Livia.   Here.
    Justina (*putting on her cloak*). In this, as in a shroud of snow, may I
Quench the consuming fire in which I burn,   181
Wasting away!
    Lisander.   And I will go with thee.
    Livia. When I once see them safe out of the house
I shall breathe freely.
    Justina.   So do I confide
In thy just favour, Heaven!
    Lisander.   Let us go.   **185**
    Justina. Thine is the cause, great God! turn for my sake,
And for Thine own, mercifully to me!

STANZAS FROM CALDERON'S CISMA DE INGLATERRA

I

HAST thou not seen, officious with delight,
    Move through the illumined air about the flower
The Bee, that fears to drink its purple light,
    Lest danger lurk within that Rose's bower?
Hast thou not marked the moth's enamoured flight   **5**
    About the Taper's flame at evening hour,
Till kindle in that monumental fire
His sunflower wings their own funereal pyre?

II

My heart, its wishes trembling to unfold,
　Thus round the Rose and Taper hovering came,　　10
And Passion's slave, Distrust, in ashes cold,
　Smothered awhile, but could not quench the flame,—
Till Love, that grows by disappointment bold,
　And Opportunity, had conquered Shame;
And like the Bee and Moth, in act to close,　　15
I burned my wings, and settled on the Rose.

SCENES FROM THE FAUST OF GOETHE

SCENE I.—PROLOGUE IN HEAVEN. *The* LORD *and the* HOST *of* HEAVEN.

Enter three ARCHANGELS.

Raphael.

THE sun makes music as of old
　Amid the rival spheres of Heaven,
On its predestined circle rolled
　With thunder speed: the Angels even
Draw strength from gazing on its glance,　　5
　Though none its meaning fathom may:—
The world's unwithered countenance
　Is bright as at Creation's day.

Gabriel.

And swift and swift, with rapid lightness,
　The adornèd Earth spins silently,　　10
Alternating Elysian brightness
　With deep and dreadful night; the sea
Foams in broad billows from the deep
　Up to the rocks, and rocks and Ocean,
Onward, with spheres which never sleep,　　15
　Are hurried in eternal motion.

Michael.

And tempests in contention roar
　From land to sea, from sea to land;
And, raging, weave a chain of power,
　Which girds the earth, as with a band.—　　20
A flashing desolation there,
　Flames before the thunder's way;
But Thy servants, Lord, revere
　The gentle changes of Thy day.

Chorus of the Three.

The Angels draw strength from Thy glance,   25
   Though no one comprehend Thee may;—
Thy world's unwithered countenance
Is bright as on Creation's day.[1]

Enter MEPHISTOPHELES.

Mephistopheles. As thou, O Lord, once more art kind enough
To interest Thyself in our affairs,   30
And ask, 'How goes it with you there below?'
And as indulgently at other times
Thou tookest not my visits in ill part,
Thou seest me here once more among Thy household.
Though I should scandalize this company,   35
You will excuse me if I do not talk
In the high style which they think fashionable;
My pathos certainly would make You laugh too,
Had You not long since given over laughing.
Nothing know I to say of suns and worlds;   40
I observe only how men plague themselves;—

[1] *Raphael.* The sun sounds, according to ancient custom,
In the song of emulation of his brother-spheres.
And its fore-written circle
Fulfils with a step of thunder.
Its countenance gives the Angels strength
Though no one can fathom it.
The incredible high works
Are excellent as at the first day.
   Gabriel. And swift, and inconceivably swift
The adornment of earth winds itself round,
And exchanges Paradise-clearness
With deep dreadful night.
The sea foams in broad waves
From its deep bottom, up to the rocks,
And rocks and sea are torn on together
In the eternal swift course of the spheres.
   Michael. And storms roar in emulation
From sea to land, from land to sea,
And make, raging, a chain
Of deepest operation round about.
There flames a flashing destruction
Before the path of the thunderbolt.
But Thy servants, Lord, revere
The gentle alternations of Thy day.
   Chorus. Thy countenance gives the Angels strength,
Though none can comprehend Thee:
And all Thy lofty works
Are excellent as at the first day.

Such is a literal translation of this astonishing chorus; it is impossible to represent in another language the melody of the versification; even the volatile strength and delicacy of the ideas escape in the crucible of translation, and the reader is surprisd to find a *caput mortuum.*—[SHELLEY'S NOTE.]

The little god o' the world keeps the same stamp,
As wonderful as on creation's day:—
A little better would he live, hadst Thou
Not given him a glimpse of Heaven's light   45
Which he calls reason, and employs it only
To live more beastlily than any beast.
With reverence to Your Lordship be it spoken,
He's like one of those long-legged grasshoppers,
Who flits and jumps about, and sings for ever   50
The same old song i' the grass. There let him lie,
Burying his nose in every heap of dung.
    The Lord. Have you no more to say? Do you come here
Always to scold, and cavil, and complain?
Seems nothing ever right to you on earth?   55
    Mephistopheles. No, Lord! I find all there, as ever, bad at best.
Even I am sorry for man's days of sorrow;
I could myself almost give up the pleasure
Of plaguing the poor things.
    The Lord.   Knowest thou Faust?
    Mephistopheles. The Doctor?
    The Lord.   Ay; My servant Faust.
    Mephistopheles.   In truth   60
He serves You in a fashion quite his own;
And the fool's meat and drink are not of earth.
His aspirations bear him on so far
That he is half aware of his own folly,
For he demands from Heaven its fairest star,   65
And from the earth the highest joy it bears,
Yet all things far, and all things near, are vain
To calm the deep emotions of his breast.
    The Lord. Though he now serves Me in a cloud of error,
I will soon lead him forth to the clear day.   70
When trees look green, full well the gardener knows
That fruits and blooms will deck the coming year.
    Mephistopheles. What will You bet?—now I am sure of winning—
Only, observe You give me full permission
To lead him softly on my path.
    The Lord.   As long   75
As he shall live upon the earth, so long
Is nothing unto thee forbidden—Man
Must err till he has ceased to struggle.
    Mephistopheles.   Thanks.
And that is all I ask; for willingly
I never make acquaintance with the dead.   80
The full fresh cheeks of youth are food for me,
And if a corpse knocks, I am not at home.
For I am like a cat—I like to play

A little with the mouse before I eat it.

The Lord. Well, well! it is permitted thee. Draw thou   85
His spirit from its springs; as thou find'st power,
Seize him and lead him on thy downward path;
And stand ashamed when failure teaches thee
That a good man, even in his darkest longings,
Is well aware of the right way.

    Mephistopheles.   Well and good.   90
I am not in much doubt about my bet,
And if I lose, then 'tis Your turn to crow;
Enjoy Your triumph then with a full breast.
Ay; dust shall he devour, and that with pleasure,
Like my old paramour, the famous Snake.   95

    The Lord. Pray come here when it suits you; for I never
Had much dislike for people of your sort.
And, among all the Spirits who rebelled,
The knave was ever the least tedious to Me.
The active spirit of man soon sleeps, and soon   100
He seeks unbroken quiet; therefore I
Have given him the Devil for a companion,
Who may provoke him to some sort of work,
And must create forever.—But ye, pure
Children of God, enjoy eternal beauty;—   105
Let that which ever operates and lives
Clasp you within the limits of its love;
And seize with sweet and melancholy thoughts
The floating phantoms of its loveliness.

                   [Heaven closes; the Archangels exeunt.

    Mephistopheles. From time to time I visit the old fellow,
And I take care to keep on good terms with Him.   111
Civil enough is the same God Almighty,
To talk so freely with the Devil himself.

    SCENE II.—MAY-DAY NIGHT. *The Hartz Mountain, a desolate
          Country.* FAUST, MEPHISTOPHELES.

    Mephistopheles. Would you not like a broomstick? As for me
I wish I had a good stout ram to ride;
For we are still far from the appointed place.

    Faust. This knotted staff is help enough for me,
Whilst I feel fresh upon my legs. What good   5
Is there in making short a pleasant way?
To creep along the labyrinths of the vales,
And climb those rocks, where ever-babbling springs,
Precipitate themselves in waterfalls,
Is the true sport that seasons such a path.   10
Already Spring kindles the birchen spray,
And the hoar pines already feel her breath:

Shall she not work also within our limbs?
Mephistopheles. Nothing of such an influence do I feel.
My body is all wintry, and I wish　　　　　　　　　15
The flowers upon our path were frost and snow.
But see how melancholy rises now,
Dimly uplifting her belated beam,
The blank unwelcome round of the red moon,
And gives so bad a light, that every step　　　　　20
One stumbles 'gainst some crag. With your permission,
I'll call an Ignis-fatuus to our aid:
I see one yonder burning jollily.
Halloo, my friend! may I request that you
Would favour us with your bright company?　　　25
Why should you blaze away there to no purpose?
Pray be so good as light us up this way.
　　Ignis-fatuus. With reverence be it spoken, I will try
To overcome the lightness of my nature;
Our course, you know, is generally zigzag.　　　30
　　Mephistopheles. Ha, ha! your worship thinks you have to deal
With men. Go straight on, in the Devil's name,
Or I shall puff your flickering life out.
　　Ignis-fatuus.　　　　　　　　　Well,
I see you are the master of the house;
I will accommodate myself to you.　　　　　　　35
Only consider that to-night this mountain
Is all enchanted, and if Jack-a-lantern
Shows you his way, though you should miss your own,
You ought not to be too exact with him.

FAUST, MEPHISTOPHELES, *and* IGNIS-FATUUS, *in alternate Chorus.*

　　The limits of the sphere of dream,　　　　　　40
　　　　The bounds of true and false, are past.
　　Lead us on, thou wandering Gleam,
　　　　Lead us onward, far and fast,
　　　　To the wide, the desert waste.

　　But see, how swift advance and shift　　　　　45
　　　　Trees behind trees, row by row,—
　　How, clift by clift, rocks bend and lift
　　　　Their frowning foreheads as we go.
　　　　The giant-snouted crags, ho! ho!
　　　　How they snort, and how they blow!　　　50

　　Through the mossy sods and stones,
　　　　Stream and streamlet hurry down—
　　　　A rushing throng! A sound of song
　　　　Beneath the vault of Heaven is blown!
　　Sweet notes of love, the speaking tones　　　55

Of this bright day, sent down to say
That Paradise on Earth is known,
Resound around, beneath, above.
All we hope and all we love
Finds a voice in this blithe strain,   60
  Which wakens hill and wood and rill,
  And vibrates far o'er field and vale,
  And which Echo, like the tale
Of old times, repeats again.

To-whoo! to-whoo! near, nearer now   65
The sound of song, the rushing throng!
Are the screech, the lapwing, and the jay,
All awake as if 'twere day?
See, with long legs and belly wide,
  A salamander in the brake!   70
  Every root is like a snake,
And along the loose hillside,
With strange contortions through the night,
Curls, to seize or to affright;
And, animated, strong, and many,   75
They dart forth polypus-antennae,
To blister with their poison spume
The wanderer. Through the dazzling gloom
The many-coloured mice, that thread
The dewy turf beneath our tread,   80
In troops each other's motions cross,
Through the heath and through the moss;
And, in legions intertangled,
  The fire-flies flit, and swarm, and throng,
Till all the mountain depths are spangled.   85

Tell me, shall we go or stay?
  Shall we onward? Come along!
  Everything around is swept
Forward, onward, far away!
Trees and masses intercept   90
The sight, and wisps on every side
Are puffed up and multiplied.

Mephistopheles. Now vigorously seize my skirt, and gain
This pinnacle of isolated crag.
One may observe with wonder from this point,   95
How Mammon glows among the mountains.
  Faust.   Ay—
And strangely through the solid depth below
A melancholy light, like the red dawn,
Shoots from the lowest gorge of the abyss
Of mountains, lightning hitherward: there rise   100

Pillars of smoke, here clouds float gently by;
Here the light burns soft as the enkindled air,
Or the illumined dust of golden flowers;
And now it glides like tender colours spreading;
And now bursts forth in fountains from the earth;   105
And now it winds, one torrent of broad light,
Through the far valley with a hundred veins;
And now once more within that narrow corner
Masses itself into intensest splendour.
And near us, see, sparks spring out of the ground,   110
Like golden sand scattered upon the darkness;
The pinnacles of that black wall of mountains
That hems us in are kindled.
    Mephistopheles.   Rare: in faith!
Does not Sir Mammon gloriously illuminate
His palace for this festival?—it is   115
A pleasure whch you had not known before.
I spy the boisterous guests already.
    Faust.   How
The children of the wind rage in the air!
With what fierce strokes they fall upon my neck!

        Mephistopheles.

Cling tightly to the old ribs of the crag.   120
    Beware! for if with them thou warrest
  In their fierce flight towards the wilderness,
Their breath will sweep thee into dust, and drag
    Thy body to a grave in the abyss.
A cloud thickens the night.   125
    Hark! how the tempest crashes through the forest!
    The owls fly out in strange affright;
The columns of the evergreen palaces
    Are split and shattered;
    The roots creak, and stretch, and groan;   130
    And ruinously overthrown,
    The trunks are crushed and shattered
By the fierce blast's unconquerable stress.
Over each other crack and crash they all
In terrible and intertangled fall;   135
And through the ruins of the shaken mountain
    The airs hiss and howl—
It is not the voice of the fountain,
    Nor the wolf in his midnight prowl.
    Dost thou not hear?   140
      Strange accents are ringing
    Aloft, afar, anear?
      The witches are singing!

The torrent of a raging wizard song
Streams the whole mountain along. 145

Chorus of Witches.

The stubble is yellow, the corn is green,
Now to the Brocken the witches go;
The mighty multitude here may be seen
Gathering, wizard and witch, below.
Sir Urian is sitting aloft in the air; 150
Hey over stock! and hey over stone!
'Twixt witches and incubi, what shall be done?
Tell it who dare! tell it who dare!

A Voice.

Upon a sow-swine, whose farrows were nine,
Old Baubo rideth alone. 155

Chorus.

Honour her, to whom honour is due,
Old mother Baubo, honour to you!
An able sow, with old Baubo upon her,
Is worthy of glory, and worthy of honour!
The legion of witches is coming behind, 160
Darkening the night, and outspeeding the wind—

A Voice.

Which way comest thou?

A Voice.

Over Ilsenstein;
The owl was awake in the white moonshine;
I saw her at rest in her downy nest,
And she stared at me with her broad, bright eyne. 165

Voices.

And you may now as well take your course on to Hell,
Since you ride by so fast on the headlong blast.

A Voice.

She dropped poison upon me as I passed.
Here are the wounds——

Chorus of Witches.

Come away! come along!
The way is wide, the way is long, 170
But what is that for a Bedlam throng?
Stick with the prong, and scratch with the broom.

The child in the cradle lies strangled at home,
And the mother is clapping her hands.—

Semichorus of Wizards I.

We glide in
  Like snails when the women are all away;   175
And from a house once given over to sin
  Woman has a thousand steps to stray.

Semichorus II.

A thousand steps must a woman take,
Where a man but a single spring will make.

Voices above.

Come with us, come with us, from Felsensee.   180

Voices below.

  With what joy would we fly through the upper sky!
We are washed, we are 'nointed, stark naked are we;
  But our toil and our pain are forever in vain.

Both Choruses.

The wind is still, the stars are fled,
The melancholy moon is dead;   185
The magic notes, like spark on spark,
Drizzle, whistling through the dark.
    Come away!

Voices below.

Stay, Oh, stay!

Voices above.

Out of the crannies of the rocks   190
Who calls?

Voices below.

    Oh, let me join your flocks!
I, three hundred years have striven
To catch your skirt and mount to Heaven,—
And still in vain. Oh, might I be
With company akin to me!   195

Both Choruses.

Some on a ram and some on a prong,
On poles and on broomsticks we flutter along;
  Forlorn is the wight who can rise not to-night.

A Half-Witch below.

I have been tripping this many an hour:
Are the others already so far before?   200
No quiet at home, and no peace abroad!
And less methinks is found by the road.

Chorus of Witches.

Come onward, away! aroint thee, aroint!
A witch to be strong must anoint—anoint—
Then every trough will be boat enough;   205
With a rag for a sail we can sweep through the sky,
Who flies not to-night, when means he to fly?

Both Choruses.

We cling to the skirt, and we strike on the ground;
Witch-legions thicken around and around;
Wizard-swarms cover the heath all over.   [*They descend.*

Mephistopheles.

What thronging, dashing, raging, rustling;   211
What whispering, babbling, hissing, bustling;
What glimmering, spurting, stinking, burning,
As Heaven and Earth were overturning.
There is a true witch element about us;   215
Take hold on me, or we shall be divided:—
Where are you?
　　Faust (from a distance). Here!
　　Mephistopheles.   What!
I must exert my authority in the house.
Place for young Voland! pray make way, good people.
Take hold on me, doctor, and with one step   220
Let us escape from this unpleasant crowd:
They are too mad for people of my sort.
Just there shines a peculiar kind of light—
Something attracts me in those bushes. Come
This way: we shall slip down there in a minute.   225
　　Faust. Spirit of Contradiction! Well, lead on—
'Twere a wise feat indeed to wander out
Into the Brocken upon May-day night,
And then to isolate oneself in scorn,
Disgusted with the humours of the time.   230
　　Mephistopheles. See yonder, round a many-coloured flame
A merry club is huddled altogether:
Even with such little people as sit there
One would not be alone.
　　Faust.   Would that I were

Up yonder in the glow and whirling smoke,   235
Where the blind million rush impetuously
To meet the evil ones; there might I solve
Many a riddle that torments me!
    Mephistopheles.   Yet
Many a riddle there is tied anew
Inextricably. Let the great world rage!   240
We will stay here safe in the quiet dwellings.
'Tis an old custom. Men have ever built
Their own small world in the great world of all.
I see young witches naked there, and old ones
Wisely attired with greater decency.   245
Be guided now by me, and you shall buy
A pound of pleasure with a dram of trouble.
I hear them tune their instruments—one must
Get used to this damned scraping. Come, I'll lead you
Among them; and what there you do and see,   250
As a fresh compact 'twixt us two shall be.
How say you now? this space is wide enough—
Look forth, you cannot see the end of it—
An hundred bonfires burn in rows, and they
Who throng around them seem innumerable: 255
Dancing and drinking, jabbering, making love,
And cooking, are at work. Now tell me, friend,
What is there better in the world than this?
    Faust. In introducing us, do you assume
The character of Wizard or of Devil?   260
    Mephistopheles. In truth, I generally go about
In strict incognito; and yet one likes
To wear one's orders upon gala days.
I have no ribbon at my knee; but here
At home, the cloven foot is honourable.   265
See you that snail there?—she comes creeping up,
And with her feeling eyes hath smelt out something.
I could not, if I would, mask myself here.
Come now, we'll go about from fire to fire:
I'll be the Pimp, and you shall be the Lover.   270
[*To some old Women, who are sitting round a heap of glimmering coals.*
Old gentlewomen, what do you do out here?
You ought to be with the young rioters
Right in the thickest of the revelry—
But every one is best content at home.

General.

Who dare confide in right or a just claim?   275
    So much as I had done for them! and now—
With women and the people 'tis the same,

Youth will stand foremost ever,—age may go
To the dark grave unhonoured.

Minister.

Nowadays
People assert their rights: they go too far;   280
But as for me, the good old times I praise;
      Then we were all in all—'twas something worth
One's while to be in place and wear a star;
      That was indeed the golden age on earth.

Parvenu.

We too are active, and we did and do   28
What we ought not, perhaps; and yet we now
Will seize, whilst all things are whirled round and round,
A spoke of Fortune's wheel, and keep our ground.

Author.

Who now can taste a treatise of deep sense
And ponderous volume? 'tis impertinence   290
To write what none will read, therefore will I
To please the young and thoughtless people try.
    Mephistopheles (*who at once appears to have grown very old*). I
      find the people ripe for the last day,
Since I last came up to the wizard mountain;
And as my little cask runs turbid now,   295
So is the world drained to the dregs.
    Pedlar-witch.   Look here,
Gentlemen; do not hurry on so fast;
And lose the chance of a good pennyworth.
I have a pack full of the choicest wares
Of every sort, and yet in all my bundle   300
Is nothing like what may be found on earth;
Nothing that in a moment will make rich
Men and the world with fine malicious mischief—
There is no dagger drunk with blood; no bowl
From which consuming poison may be drained   305
By innocent and healthy lips; no jewel,
The price of an abandoned maiden's shame;
No sword which cuts the bond it cannot loose,
Or stabs the wearer's enemy in the back;
No——
    Mephistopheles. Gossip, you know little of these times.   310
What has been, has been; what is done, is past,
They shape themselves into the innovations
They breed, and innovation drags us with it.
The torrent of the crowd sweeps over us:
You think to impel, and are yourself impelled.   315

Faust. What is that yonder?
Mephistopheles. Mark her well. It is
Lilith.
Faust. Who?
Mephistopheles. Lilith, the first wife of Adam.
Beware of her fair hair, for she excels
All women in the magic of her locks;
And when she winds them round a young man's neck, 320
She will not ever set him free again.

Faust.

There sit a girl and an old woman—they
Seem to be tired with pleasure and with play.

Mephistopheles.

There is no rest to-night for any one:
When one dance ends another is begun; 325
Come, let us to it. We shall have rare fun.
[FAUST *dances and sings with a girl, and* MEPHISTOPHELES *with an old
Woman.*

Faust.

I had once a lovely dream
In which I saw an apple-tree,
Where two fair apples with their gleam
To climb and taste attracted me. 330

The Girl.

She with apples you desired
From Paradise came long ago:
With you I feel that if required,
Such still within my garden grow.
. . . .

Procto-Phantasmist. What is this cursèd multitude about?
Have we not long since proved to demonstration 336
That ghosts move not on ordinary feet?
But these are dancing just like men and women.
The Girl. What does he want then at our ball?
Faust. Oh! he
Is far above us all in his conceit: 340
Whilst we enjoy, he reasons of enjoyment;
And any step which in our dance we tread,
If it be left out of his reckoning,
Is not to be considered as a step.
There are few things that scandalize him not: 345
And when you whirl round in the circle now,
As he went round the wheel in his old mill,
He says that you go wrong in all respects,
Especially if you congratulate him

Upon the strength of the resemblance.
    Procto-Phantasmist.   Fly!   350
Vanish! Unheard-of impudence! What, still there!
In this enlightened age too, since you have been
Proved not to exist!—But this infernal brood
Will hear no reason and endure no rule.
Are we so wise, and is the *pond* still haunted?   355
How long have I been sweeping out this rubbish
Of superstition, and the world will not
Come clean with all my pains!—it is a case
Unheard of!
    The Girl. Then leave off teasing us so.
    Procto-Phantasmist. I tell you, spirits, to your faces now,   360
That I should not regret this despotism
Of spirits, but that mine can wield it not.
To-night I shall make poor work of it,
Yet I will take a round with you, and hope
Before my last step in the living dance   365
To beat the poet and the devil together.
    Mephistopheles. At last he will sit down in some foul puddle;
That is his way of solacing himself;
Until some leech, diverted with his gravity,
Cures him of spirits and the spirit together.   370
                        [To FAUST, *who has seceded from the dance.*
Why do you let that fair girl pass from you,
Who sung so sweetly to you in the dance?
    Faust. A red mouse in the middle of her singing
Sprung from her mouth.
    Mephistopheles.   That was all right, my friend:
Be it enough that the mouse was not gray.   375
Do not disturb your hour of happiness
With close consideration of such trifles.
    Faust. Then saw I——
    Mephistopheles.   What?
    Faust.   Seest thou not a pale,
Fair girl, standing alone, far, far away?
She drags herself now forward with slow steps,   380
And seems as if she moved with shackled feet:
I cannot overcome the thought that she
Is like poor Margaret.
    Mephistopheles.   Let it be—pass on—
No good can come of it—it is not well
To meet it—it is an enchanted phantom,   385
A lifeless idol; with its numbing look,
It freezes up the blood of man; and they
Who meet its ghastly stare are turned to stone,
Like those who saw Medusa.

Faust.   Oh, too true!
Her eyes are like the eyes of a fresh corpse   390
Which no belovèd hand has closed, alas!
That is the breast which Margaret yielded to me—
Those are the lovely limbs which I enjoyed!
   Mephistopheles. It is all magic, poor deluded fool!
She looks to every one like his first love.   395
   Faust. Oh, what delight! what woe! I cannot turn
My looks from her sweet piteous countenance.
How strangely does a single blood-red line,
Not broader than the sharp edge of a knife,
Adorn her lovely neck!
   Mephistopheles.   Ay, she can carry   400
Her head under her arm upon occasion;
Perseus has cut it off for her. These pleasures
End in delusion.—Gain this rising ground,
It is as airy here as in a . . .
And if I am not mightily deceived,   405
I see a theatre.—What may this mean?
   Attendant. Quite a new piece, the last of seven, for 'tis
The custom now to represent that number.
'Tis written by a Dilettante, and
The actors who perform are Dilettanti;   410
Excuse me, gentlemen; but I must vanish.
I am a Dilettante curtain-lifter.

JUVENILIA

QUEEN MAB

A PHILOSOPHICAL POEM, WITH NOTES

ECRASEZ L'INFAME!—*Correspondance de Voltaire.*
Avia Pieridum poragro loca, nullius ante
Trita solo; juvat integros accedere fonteis;
Atque haurire: juvatque novos decerpere flores.

   .   .   .   .   .   .

Unde prius nulli velarint tempora musae.
Primum quod magnis doceo de rebus; et arctis
Religionum animos nodis exsolvere pergo.—*Lucret.* lib. iv.
Δος που στω, και κοσμον κινησω.—*Archimedes.*

TO HARRIET * * * * *

WHOSE is the love that gleaming through the world,	Virtue's most sweet reward?
Wards off the poisonous arrow of its scorn?	Beneath whose looks did my reviving soul 5
Whose is the warm and partial praise,	Riper in truth and virtuous daring grow?

Whose eyes have I gazed fondly
on,
And loved mankind the more?

HARRIET! on thine:—thou wert
my purer mind;
Thou wert the inspiration of my
song; 10
Thine are these early wilding
flowers,
Though garlanded by me.

Then press into thy breast this
pledge of love;
And know, though time may change
and years may roll,
Each floweret gathered in my
heart 15
It consecrates to thine.

QUEEN MAB

I

How wonderful is Death,
Death and his brother Sleep!
One, pale as yonder waning
moon
With lips of lurid blue;
The other, rosy as the morn 5
When throned on ocean's wave
It blushes o'er the world:
Yet both so passing wonderful!

Hath then the gloomy Power
Whose reign is in the tainted sepul-
chres 10
Seized on her sinless soul?
Must then that peerless form
Which love and admiration cannot
view
Without a beating heart, those
azure veins
Which steal like streams along a
field of snow, 15
That lovely outline, which is fair
As breathing marble, perish?
Must putrefaction's breath
Leave nothing of this heavenly
sight

But loathsomeness and ruin?
Spare nothing but a gloomy
theme, 21
On which the lightest heart might
moralize?
Or is it only a sweet slumber
Stealing o'er sensation,
Which the breath of roseate
morning 25
Chaseth into darkness?
Will Ianthe wake again,
And give that faithful bosom joy
Whose sleepless spirit waits to
catch
Light, life and rapture from her
smile? 30

Yes! she will wake again,
Although her glowing limbs are
motionless,
And silent those sweet lips,
Once breathing eloquence,
That might have soothed a
tiger's rage, 35
Or thawed the cold heart of a
conqueror.
Her dewy eyes are closed,
And on their lids, whose texture
fine
Scarce hides the dark blue orbs
beneath,
The baby Sleep is pillowed: 40
Her golden tresses shade
The bosom's stainless pride,
Curling like tendrils of the para-
site
Around a marble column.

Hark! whence that rushing
sound?
'Tis like the wondrous strain 46
That round a lonely ruin swells,
Which, wandering on the echo-
ing shore,
The enthusiast hears at eve-
ning:
'Tis softer than the west wind's
sigh; 50

'Tis wilder than the unmeasured
   notes
Of that strange lyre whose strings
The genii of the breezes sweep:
Those lines of rainbow light
Are like the moonbeams when
   they fall   55
Through some cathedral window,
   but the tints
Are such as may not find
Comparison on earth.

Behold the chariot of the Fairy
   Queen!
Celestial coursers paw the unyield-
   ing air;   60
Their filmy pennons at her word
   they furl,
And stop obedient to the reins of
   light:
These the Queen of Spells drew
   in,
She spread a charm around the
   spot,
And leaning graceful from the
   aethereal car,   65
Long did she gaze, and silently,
Upon the slumbering maid.

Oh! not the visioned poet in his
   dreams,
When silvery clouds float through
   the 'wildered brain,
When every sight of lovely, wild
   and grand   70
Astonishes, enraptures, elevates,
When fancy at a glance com-
   bines
The wondrous and the beauti-
   ful,—
So bright, so fair, so wild a
   shape
Hath ever yet beheld,   75
As that which reined the coursers
   of the air,
And poured the magic of her
   gaze

Upon the maiden's sleep.

The broad and yellow moon
Shone dimly through her
   form—   80
That form of faultless sym-
   metry;
The pearly and pellucid car
Moved not the moonlight's
   line:
'Twas not an earthly pageant:
Those who had looked upon the
   sight,   85
Passing all human glory,
Saw not the yellow moon,
Saw not the mortal scene,
Heard not the night-wind's
   rush,
Heard not an earthly sound,   90
Saw but the fairy pageant,
Heard but the heavenly
   strains
That filled the lonely dwelling

The Fairy's frame was slight,
   yon fibrous cloud,
That catches but the palest
   tinge of even,   95
And which the straining eye can
   hardly seize
When melting into eastern twi-
   light's shadow,
Were scarce so thin, so slight;
   but the fair star
That gems the glittering coronet
   of morn,
Sheds not a light so mild, so pow-
   erful,   100
As that which, bursting from the
   Fairy's form,
Spread a purpureal halo round
   the scene,
Yet with an undulating mo-
   tion,
Swayed to her outline grace-
   fully.

From her celestial car   105
The Fairy Queen descended,
And thrice she waved her
   wand

Circled with wreaths of amaranth:
Her thin and misty form 109
Moved with the moving air,
And the clear silver tones,
As thus she spoke, were such
As are unheard by all but gifted ear.

Fairy.

'Stars! your balmiest influence shed! 114
Elements! your wrath suspend!
Sleep, Ocean, in the rocky bounds
That circle thy domain!
Let not a breath be seen to stir
Around yon grass-grown ruin's height, 119
Let even the restless gossamer
Sleep on the moveless air!
Soul of Ianthe! thou,
Judged alone worthy of the envied boon,
That waits the good and the sincere; that waits
Those who have struggled, and with resolute will 125
Vanquished earth's pride and meanness, burst the chains,
The icy chains of custom, and have shone
The day-stars of their age;—Soul of Ianthe!
Awake! arise!'

Sudden arose 130
Ianthe's Soul; it stood
All beautiful in naked purity,
The perfect semblance of its bodily frame.
Instinct with inexpressible beauty and grace,
Each stain of earthliness 135
Had passed away, it reassumed
Its native dignity, and stood
Immortal amid ruin.

Upon the couch the body lay
Wrapped in the depth of slumber: 140
Its features were fixed and meaningless,
Yet animal life was there,
And every organ yet performed
Its natural functions: 'twas a sight
Of wonder to behold the body and soul. 145
The self-same lineaments, the same
Marks of identity were there:
Yet, oh, how different! One aspires to Heaven,
Pants for its sempiternal heritage,
And ever-changing, ever-rising still,
Wantons in endless being. 151
The other, for a time the unwilling sport
Of circumstance and passion, struggles on;
Fleets through its sad duration rapidly:
Then, like an useless and worn-out machine, 155
Rots, perishes, and passes.

Fairy.

'Spirit! who hast dived so deep;
Spirit! who hast soared so high;
Thou the fearless, thou the mild,
Accept the boon thy worth hath earned, 160
Ascend the car with me.'

Spirit.

'Do I dream? Is this new feeling
But a visioned ghost of slumber?
If indeed I am a soul,
A free, a disembodied soul, 165
Speak again to me.'

Fairy.

'I am the Fairy MAB: to me 'tis given

The wonders of the human world
    to keep:
The secrets of the immeasurable
    past,
In the unfailing consciences of
    men,
Those stern, unflattering chron-
    iclers, I find: 171
The future, from the causes which
    arise
In each event, I gather: not the
    sting
Which retributive memory im-
    plants
In the hard bosom of the selfish
    man;
Nor that ecstatic and exulting
    throb
Which virtue's votary feels when
    he sums up   177
The thoughts and actions of a well-
    spent day,
Are unforeseen, unregistered by me:
And it is yet permitted me, to
    rend   180
The veil of mortal frailty, that the
    spirit,
Clothed in its changeless purity,
    may know
How soonest to accomplish the
    great end
For which it hath its being, and
    may taste
That peace, which in the end all
    life will share.   185
This is the meed of virtue; happy
    Soul,
    Ascend the car with me!'

The chains of earth's immure-
    ment
Fell from Ianthe's spirit;
They shrank and brake like ban-
    dages of straw   190
  Beneath a wakened giant's
    strength.
  She knew her glorious change,

And felt in apprehension uncon-
    trolled   193
New raptures opening round:
Each day-dream of her mortal
    life,
Each frenzied vision of the slum-
    bers
  That closed each well-spent
    day,
  Seemed now to meet reality.

The Fairy and the Soul pro-
    ceeded;
  The silver clouds disparted;
And as the car of magic they as-
    cended,   201
Again the speechless music
    swelled,
Again the coursers of the air
Unfurled their azure pennons, and
    the Queen
  Shaking the beamy reins 205
  Bade them pursue their way.

The magic car moved on.
The night was fair, and countless
    stars
Studded Heaven's dark blue
    vault,—
  Just o'er the eastern wave 210
Peeped the first faint smile of
    morn:—
  The magic car moved on—
  From the celestial hoofs
The atmosphere in flaming sparkles
    flew,
  And where the burning wheels
Eddied above the mountain's lofti-
    est peak,   216
Was traced a line of lightning.
Now it flew far above a rock,
  The utmost verge of earth,
The rival of the Andes, whose
    dark brow   220
  Lowered o'er the silver sea.

Far, far below the chariot's path,
  Calm as a slumbering babe,
  Tremendous Ocean lay.

The mirror of its stillness showed
The pale and waning stars, 226
The chariot's fiery track,
And the gray light of morn
Tinging those fleecy clouds
That canopied the dawn. 230
Seemed it, that the chariot's way
Lay through the midst of an im-
mense concave,
Radiant with million constella-
tions, tinged
With shades of infinite colour,
And semicircled with a belt 235
Flashing incessant meteors.

The magic car moved on.
As they approached their goal
The coursers seemed to gather
speed;
The sea no longer was distin-
guished; earth 240
Appeared a vast and shadowy
sphere;
The sun's unclouded orb
Rolled through the black con-
cave;
Its rays of rapid light
Parted around the chariot's swifter
course, 245
And fell, like ocean's feathery
spray
Dashed from the boiling surge
Before a vessel's prow.

The magic car moved on.
Earth's distant orb appeared
The smallest light that twinkles in
the heaven; 251
Whilst round the chariot's way
Innumerable systems rolled,
And countless spheres diffused
An ever-varying glory. 255
It was a sight of wonder: some
Were hornèd like the crescent
moon;
Some shed a mild and silver
beam

Like Hesperus o'er the western
sea;
Some dashed athwart with trains
of flame, 260
Like worlds to death and ruin
driven;
Some shone like suns, and, as the
chariot passed,
Eclipsed all other light.

Spirit of Nature! here!
In this interminable wilderness 265
Of worlds, at whose immensity
Even soaring fancy staggers,
Here is thy fitting temple.
Yet not the lightest leaf
That quivers to the passing breeze
Is less instinct with thee: 271
Yet not the meanest worm
That lurks in graves and fattens on
the dead
Less shares thy eternal breath.
Spirit of Nature! thou! 275
Imperishable as this scene,
Here is thy fitting temple.

II

IF solitude hath ever led thy steps
To the wild Ocean's echoing
shore,
And thou hast lingered there,
Until the sun's broad orb
Seemed resting on the burnished
wave, 5
Thou must have marked the
lines
Of purple gold, that motionless
Hung o'er the sinking sphere:
Thou must have marked the bil-
lowy clouds
Edged with intolerable radiancy
Towering like rocks of jet 11
Crowned with a diamond
wreath.
And yet there is a moment,
When the sun's highest point

Peeps like a star o'er Ocean's west-
  ern edge,   15
When those far clouds of feathery
  gold,
Shaded with deepest purple,
  gleam
Like islands on a dark blue sea;
Then has thy fancy soared above
  the earth,
And furled its wearied wing 20
Within the Fairy's fane.

Yet not the golden islands
Gleaming in yon flood of light,
Nor the feathery curtains
Stretching o'er the sun's bright
  couch,   25
Nor the burnished Ocean
  waves
Paving that gorgeous dome,
So fair, so wonderful a sight
As Mab's aethereal palace could
  afford.
Yet likest evening's vault, that
  faery Hall!   30
As Heaven, low resting on the
  wave, it spread
Its floors of flashing light,
Its vast and azure dome,
Its fertile golden islands
Floating on a silver sea; 35
Whilst suns their mingling beam-
  ings darted
Through clouds of circumambient
  darkness,
And pearly battlements around
Looked o'er the immense of
  Heaven.

The magic car no longer
  moved.
The Fairy and the Spirit 41
Entered the Hall of Spells:
Those golden clouds
That rolled in glittering bil-
  lows
Beneath the azure canopy 45

With the aethereal footsteps trem-
  bled not:
The light and crimson mists,
Floating to strains of thrilling mel-
  ody
Through that unearthly dwell-
  ing,
Yielded to every movement of the
  will.
Upon their passive swell the Spirit
  leaned,   51
And, for the varied bliss that
  pressed around,
Used not the glorious privilege
Of virtue and of wisdom.

'Spirit!' the Fairy said, 55
And pointed to the gorgeous
  dome,
'This is a wondrous sight
And mocks all human gran-
  deur;
But, were it virtue's only meed, to
  dwell
In a celestial palace, all resigned 60
To pleasurable impulses, immured
Within the prison of itself, the will
Of changeless Nature would be un-
  fulfilled.
Learn to make others happy. Spirit,
  come!
This is thine high reward:—the
  past shall rise;   65
Thou shalt behold the present; I
  will teach
The secrets of the future.'

The Fairy and the Spirit
Approached the overhanging bat-
  tlement.—
Below lay stretched the uni-
  verse!
There, far as the remotest line
That bounds imagination's
  flight,   72
Countless and unending
  orbs

In mazy motion intermingled,
Yet still fulfilled immutably
   Eternal Nature's law. 76
   Above, below, around,
   The circling systems
     formed
A wilderness of harmony;
Each with undeviating aim,
In eloquent silence, through the
   depths of space   81
Pursued its wondrous way.

There was a little light
That twinkled in the misty dis-
   tance:
   None but a spirit's eye   85
Might ken that rolling orb;
None but a spirit's eye
And in no other place
But that celestial dwelling, might
   behold
Each action of this earth's in-
   habitants.   90
   But matter, space and time
In those aëreal mansions cease to
   act;
And all-prevailing wisdom, when
   it reaps
The harvest of its excellence, o'er-
   bounds
Those obstacles, of which an
   earthly soul   95
Fears to attempt the conquest.

The Fairy pointed to the earth.
The Spirit's intellectual eye
Its kindred beings recognized.
The thronging thousands, to a pass-
   ing view,   100
Seemed like an ant-hill's citi-
   zens.
How wonderful! that even
The passions, prejudices, interests,
That sway the meanest being, the
   weak touch
That moves the finest nerve,
And in one human brain 106

Causes the faintest thought, becomes a link
   In the great chain of Nature.

'Behold,' the Fairy cried,
'Palmyra's ruined palaces!— 110
   Behold! where grandeur
     frowned;
   Behold! where pleasure
     smiled;
What now remains?—the mem-
   ory
   Of senselessness and
     shame—
What is immortal there? 115
Nothing—it stands to tell
A melancholy tale, to give
An awful warning: soon
Oblivion will steal silently
   The remnant of its fame. 120
Monarchs and conquerors
   there
Proud o'er prostrate millions
   trod—
The earthquakes of the human
   race;
Like them, forgotten when the
   ruin
   That marks their shock is
     past.

'Beside the eternal Nile, 126
   The Pyramids have risen.
Nile shall pursue his changeless
   way:
   Those Pyramids shall fall;
Yea! not a stone shall stand to
   tell   130
   The spot whereon they stood!
Their very site shall be for-
   gotten,   132
   As is their builder's name!

'Behold yon sterile spot;
Where now the wandering Arab's
   tent   135
   Flaps in the desert-blast.

There once old Salem's haughty
    fane
Reared high to Heaven its thou-
    sand golden domes,
And in the blushing face of day
    Exposed its shameful glory.
Oh! many a widow, many an
    orphan cursed   141
The building of that fane; and
    many a father,
Worn out with toil and slavery,
    implored
The poor man's God to speed it
    from the earth,
And spare his children the detested
    task   145
Of piling stone on stone, and poi-
    soning
    The choicest days of life,
    To soothe a dotard's vanity.
There an inhuman and uncultured
    race
Howled hideous praises to their
    Demon-God;   150
They rushed to war, tore from the
    mother's womb
The unborn child,—old age and
    infancy,
Promiscuous perished; their vic-
    torious arms
Left not a soul to breathe. Oh! they
    were fiends:
But what was he who taught them
    that the God   155
Of nature and benevolence hath
    given
A special sanction to the trade of
    blood?
His name and theirs are fading, and
    the tales
Of this barbarian nation, which im-
    posture
Recites till terror credits, are pur-
    suing   160
    Itself into forgetfulness.

'Where Athens, Rome, and
    Sparta stood,

There is a moral desert now:
    The mean and miserable huts,
The yet more wretched pal-
    aces,   165
Contrasted with those ancient
    fanes,
Now crumbling to oblivion;
The long and lonely colonnades,
Through which the ghost of
    Freedom stalks,
    Seem like a well-known
    tune,
Which in some dear scene we have
    loved to hear,   171
    Remembered now in sad-
    ness.
    But, oh! how much more
    changed,
    How gloomier is the con-
    trast
    Of human nature there! 175
Where Socrates expired, a tyrant's
    slave,
A coward and a fool, spreads death
    around—
    Then, shuddering, meets his
    own.
Where Cicero and Antoninus
    lived,
    A cowled and hypocritical
    monk   180
    Prays, curses and deceives.

'Spirit, ten thousand years
    Have scarcely passed away,
Since, in the waste where now the
    savage drinks
His enemy's blood, and aping Eu-
    rope's sons,   185
    Wakes the unholy song of war,
    Arose a stately city,
Metropolis of the western conti-
    nent:
    There, now, the mossy column-
    stone,   189
Indented by Time's unrelaxing
    grasp,

Which once appeared to brave
All, save its country's ruin;
There the wide forest scene,
Rude in the uncultivated loveliness
Of gardens long run wild,
Seems, to the unwilling sojourner,
whose steps 196
Chance in that desert has delayed,
Thus to have stood since earth was what it is.
.Yet once it was the busiest haunt,
Whither, as to a common centre, flocked 200
Strangers, and ships, and merchandise:
Once peace and freedom blessed
The cultivated plain:
But wealth, that curse of man,
Blighted the bud of its prosperity:
Virtue and wisdom, truth and liberty, 206
Fled, to return not, until man shall know
That they alone can give the bliss
Worthy a soul that claims
Its kindred with eternity. 210

'There's not one atom of yon earth
But once was living man;
Nor the minutest drop of rain,
That hangeth in its thinnest cloud, 214
But flowed in human veins:
And from the burning plains
Where Libyan monsters yell,
From the most gloomy glens

Of Greenland's sunless clime, 219
To where the golden fields
Of fertile England spread
Their harvest to the day,
Thou canst not find one spot
Whereon no city stood. 224

'How strange is human pride!
I tell thee that those living things,
To whom the fragile blade of grass,
That springeth in the morn
And perisheth ere noon,
Is an unbounded world; 230
I tell thee that those viewless beings,
Whose mansion is the smallest particle
Of the impassive atmosphere,
Think, feel and live like man;
That their affections and antipathies,
Like his, produce the laws 236
Ruling their moral state;
And the minutest throb
That through their frame diffuses
The slightest, faintest motion,
Is fixed and indispensable 241
As the majestic laws
That rule yon rolling orbs.'

The Fairy paused. The Spirit,
In ecstasy of admiration, felt 245
All knowledge of the past revived; the events
Of old and wondrous times,
Which dim tradition interruptedly
Teaches the credulous vulgar, were unfolded
In just perspective to the view;
Yet dim from their infinitude.251
The Spirit seemed to stand
High on an isolated pinnacle;
The flood of ages combating below,
The depth of the unbounded universe

Above, and all around   256
Nature's unchanging harmony.

III

'FAIRY!' the Spirit said,
And on the Queen of Spells
Fixed her aethereal eyes,
'I thank thee. Thou hast
     given
A boon which I will not resign,
     and taught   5
A lesson not to be unlearned. I
     know
The past, and thence I will essay
     to glean
A warning for the future, so that
     man
May profit by his errors, and derive
     Experience from his folly: 10
For, when the power of imparting
     joy
Is equal to the will, the human soul
     Requires no other Heaven.'

Mab.

'Turn thee, surpassing Spirit!
Much yet remains unscanned.
Thou knowest how great is
     man,   16
Thou knowest his imbecility:
Yet learn thou what he is:
Yet learn the lofty destiny
Which restless time prepares
For every living soul.   21

'Behold a gorgeous palace, that,
     amid
Yon populous city rears its thou-
     sand towers
And seems itself a city. Gloomy
     troops
Of sentinels, in stern and silent
     ranks,
Encompass it around: the dweller
     there   26
Cannot be free and happy; hearest
     thou not

The curses of the fatherless, the
     groans
Of those who have no friend? He
     passes on:
The King, the wearer of a gilded
     chain
That binds his soul to abjectness,
     the fool   31
Whom courtiers nickname mon-
     arch, whilst a slave
Even to the basest appetites—that
     man
Heeds not the shriek of penury; he
     smiles
At the deep curses which the desti-
     tute   35
Mutter in secret, and a sullen joy
Pervades his bloodless heart when
     thousands groan
But for those morsels which his
     wantonness
Wastes in unjoyous revelry, to save
All that they love from famine:
     when he hears   40
The tale of horror, to some ready-
     made face
Of hypocritical assent he turns,
Smothering the glow of shame,
     that, spite of him,
Flushes his bloated cheek.
           Now to the meal
Of silence, grandeur, and excess,
     he drags   45
His palled unwilling appetite. If
     gold,
Gleaming around, and numerous
     viands culled
From every clime, could force the
     loathing sense
To overcome satiety,—if wealth
The spring it draws from poisons
     not,—or vice,   50
Unfeeling, stubborn vice, convert-
     eth not
Its food to deadliest venom; then
     that king

Is happy; and the peasant who
    fulfils
His unforced task, when he returns
    at even,
And by the blazing faggot meets
    again
Her welcome for whom all his toil
    is sped,   56
Tastes not a sweeter meal.
                Behold him now
Streched on the gorgeous couch;
    his fevered brain
Reels dizzily awhile: but ah! too
    soon
The slumber of intemperance sub-
    sides,   60
And conscience, that undying ser-
    pent, calls
Her venomous brood to their noc-
    turnal task.
Listen! he speaks! oh! mark that
    frenzied eye—
Oh! mark that deadly visage.'

    King.
            'No cessation!
Oh! must this last for ever? Awful
    Death,   65
I wish, yet fear to clasp thee!—Not
    one moment
Of dreamless sleep! O dear and
    blessèd peace!
Why dost thou shroud thy vestal
    purity
In penury and dungeons? where-
    fore lurkest
With danger, death, and solitude;
    yet shunn'st   70
The palace I have built thee?
    Sacred peace!
Oh visit me but once, but pitying
    shed
One drop of balm upon my withered
    soul.'

    The Fairy.
'Vain man! that palace is the vir-
    tuous heart,

And Peace defileth not her snowy
    robes
In such a shed as thine. Hark! yet
    he mutters;   76
His slumbers are but varied ago-
    nies,
They prey like scorpions on the
    springs of life.
There needeth not the hell that
    bigots frame
To punish those who err: earth in
    itself   80
Contains at once the evil and the
    cure;
And all-sufficing Nature can chas-
    tise
Those who transgress her law,—
    she only knows
How justly to proportion to the
    fault
The punishment it merits.
                Is it strange 85
That this poor wretch should pride
    him in his woe?
Take pleasure in his abjectness,
    and hug
The scorpion that consumes him?
    Is it strange
That, placed on a conspicuous
    throne of thorns,
Grasping an iron sceptre, and im-
    mured   90
Within a splendid prison, whose
    stern bounds
Shut him from all that's good or
    dear on earth,
His soul asserts not its humanity?
That man's mild nature rises not
    in war
Against a king's employ? No—'tis
    not strange.   95
He, like the vulgar, thinks, feels,
    acts and lives
Just as his father did; the uncon-
    quered powers
Of precedent and custom inter-
    pose

Between a *king* and virtue. Stran-
    ger yet,
To those who know not Nature, nor
    deduce   100
The future from the present, it may
    seem,
That not one slave, who suffers
    from the crimes
Of this unnatural being; not one
    wretch,
Whose children famish, and whose
    nuptial bed
Is earth's unpitying bosom, rears
    an arm
To dash him from his throne!
          Those gilded flies 106
That, basking in the sunshine of a
    court,
Fatten on its corruption!—what
    are they?
—The drones of the community;
    they feed
On the mechanic's labour: the
    starved hind   110
For them compels the stubborn
    glebe to yield
Its unshared harvest; and yon
    squalid form,
Leaner than fleshless misery, that
    wastes
A sunless life in the unwholesome
    mine,
Drags out in labour a protracted
    death,
To glut their grandeur; many
    faint with toil,   116
That few may know the cares and
    woe of sloth.

'Whence, think'st thou, kings and
    parasites arose?
Whence that unnatural line of
    drones, who heap
Toil and unvanquishable penury
On those who build their palaces,
    and bring   121
Their daily bread?—From vice,
    black loathsome vice;

From rapine, madness, treachery,
    and wrong;
From all that 'genders misery, and
    makes
Of earth this thorny wilderness;
    from lust,   125
Revenge, and murder. . . . And
    when Reason's voice,
Loud as the voice of Nature, shall
    have waked
The nations; and mankind per-
    ceive that vice
Is discord, war, and misery; that
    virtue
Is peace, and happiness and har-
    mony;   130
When man's maturer nature shall
    disdain
The playthings of its childhood;—
    kingly glare
Will lose its power to dazzle; its
    authority
Will silently pass by; the gorgeous
    throne
Shall stand unnoticed in the regal
    hall,   135
Fast falling to decay; whilst false-
    hood's trade
Shall be as hateful and unprofitable
As that of truth is now.
          Where is the fame
Which the vainglorious mighty of
    the earth
Seek to eternize? Oh! the faintest
    sound   140
From Time's light footfall, the mi-
    nutest wave
That swells the flood of ages,
    whelms in nothing
The unsubstantial bubble. Ay! to-
    day
Stern is the tyrant's mandate, red
    the gaze
That flashes desolation, strong the
    arm   145
That scatters multitudes. To-mor-
    row comes!

That mandate is a thunder-peal
    that died
In ages past; that gaze, a transient
    flash
On which the midnight closed, and
    on that arm
The worm has made his meal.
       The virtuous man, 150
Who, great in his humility, as kings
Are little in their grandeur; he
    who leads
Invincibly a life of resolute good,
And stands amid the silent dun-
    geon-depths
More free and fearless than the
    trembling judge,   155
Who, clothed in venal power,
    vainly strove
To bind the impassive spirit;—
    when he falls,
His mild eye beams benevolence
    no more:
Withered the hand outstretched
    but to relieve;
Sunk Reason's simple eloquence,
    that rolled   160
But to appal the guilty. Yes! the
    grave
Hath quenched that eye, and
    Death's relentless frost
Withered that arm: but the unfad-
    ing fame
Which Virtue hangs upon its vo-
    tary's tomb;
The deathless memory of that man,
    whom kings   165
Call to their mind and tremble;
    the remembrance
With which the happy spirit con-
    templates
Its well-spent pilgrimage on earth,
Shall never pass away.

'Nature rejects the monarch, not
    the man;   170
The subject, not the citizen: for
    kings

And subjects, mutual foes, forever
    play
A losing game into each other's
    hands,
Whose stakes are vice and misery.
    The man
Of virtuous soul commands not,
    nor obeys.   175
Power, like a desolating pestilence,
Pollutes whate'er it touches; and
    obedience,
Bane of all genius, virtue, freedom,
    truth,
Makes slaves of men, and, of the
    human frame,
A mechanized automaton.
         When Nero, 180
High over flaming Rome, with sav-
    age joy
Lowered like a fiend, drank with
    enraptured ear
The shrieks of agonizing death, be-
    held
The frightful desolation spread,
    and felt
A new-created sense within his
    soul
Thrill to the sight, and vibrate to
    the sound;   186
Think'st thou his grandeur had not
    overcome
The force of human kindness? and,
    when Rome,
With one stern blow, hurled not
    the tyrant down,
Crushed not the arm red with her
    dearest blood,   190
Had not submissive abjectness de-
    stroyed
Nature's suggestions?
        Look on yonder earth:
The golden harvests spring; the
    unfailing sun
Sheds light and life; the fruits, the
    flowers, the trees,
Arise in due succession; all things
    speak   195

Peace, harmony, and love. The universe,
In Nature's silent eloquence, declares
That all fulfil the works of love and joy,—
All but the outcast, Man. He fabricates
The sword which stabs his peace; he cherisheth   200
The snakes that gnaw his heart; he raiseth up
The tyrant, whose delight is in his woe,
Whose sport is in his agony. Yon sun,
Lights it the great alone? Yon silver beams,
Sleep they less sweetly on the cottage thatch   205
Than on the dome of kings? Is mother Earth
A step-dame to her numerous sons, who earn
Her unshared gifts with unremitting toil;
A mother only to those puling babes
Who, nursed in ease and luxury, make men   210
The playthings of their babyhood, and mar,
In self-important childishness, that peace
Which men alone appreciate?

'Spirit of Nature! no.
The pure diffusion of thy essence throbs   215
Alike in every human heart.
Thou, aye, erectest there
Thy throne of power unappealable:
Thou art the judge beneath whose nod
Man's brief and frail authority   220
Is powerless as the wind
That passeth idly by.

Thine the tribunal which surpasseth
The show of human justice,
As God surpasses man.   225

'Spirit of Nature; thou
Life of interminable multitudes;
Soul of those mighty spheres
Whose changeless paths through Heaven's deep silence lie;
Soul of that smallest being,   230
The dwelling of whose life
Is one faint April sungleam;—
Man, like these passive things,
Thy will unconsciously fulfilleth:
Like theirs, his age of endless peace,   235
Which time is fast maturing,
Will swiftly, surely come;
And the unbounded frame, which thou pervadest,
Will be without a flaw
Marring its perfect symmetry.   240

IV

'How beautiful this night! the balmiest sigh,
Which vernal zephyrs breathe in evening's ear,
Were discord to the speaking quietude
That wraps this moveless scene. Heaven's ebon vault,
Studded with stars unutterably bright,   5
Through which the moon's unclouded grandeur rolls,
Seems like a canopy which love had spread
To curtain her sleeping world. Yon gentle hills,
Robed in a garment of untrodden snow;

Yon darksome rocks, whence icicles
    depend,   10
So stainless, that their white and
    glittering spires
Tinge not the moon's pure beam;
    yon castled steep,
Whose banner hangeth o'er the
    time-worn tower
So idly, that rapt fancy deemeth
    it
A metaphor of peace;—all form a
    scene
Where musing Solitude might love
    to lift   16
Her soul above this sphere of earth-
    liness;
Where Silence undisturbed might
    watch alone,
So cold, so bright, so still.
                The orb of day,
In southern climes, o'er ocean's
    waveless field   20
Sinks sweetly smiling: not the
    faintest breath
Steals o'er the unruffled deep; the
    clouds of eve
Reflect unmoved the lingering
    beam of day;
And vesper's image on the western
    main
Is beautifully still. To-morrow
    comes:
Cloud upon cloud, in dark and
    deepening mass,   26
Roll o'er the blackened waters;
    the deep roar
Of distant thunder mutters aw-
    fully;
Tempest unfolds its pinion o'er the
    gloom
That shrouds the boiling surge; the
    pitiless fiend,   30
With all his winds and lightnings,
    tracks his prey;
The torn deep yawns,—the vessel
    finds a grave

Beneath its jaggèd gulf.
             Ah! whence yon glare
That fires the arch of Heaven?—
    that dark red smoke
Blotting the silver moon? The stars
    are quenched   35
In darkness, and the pure and
    spangling snow
Gleams faintly through the gloom
    that gathers round!
Hark to that roar, whose swift and
    deaf'ning peals
In countless echoes through the
    mountains ring,
Startling pale Midnight on her
    starry throne!   40
Now swells the intermingling din;
    the jar
Frequent and frightful of the burst-
    ing bomb;
The falling beam, the shriek, the
    groan, the shout,
The ceaseless clangour, and the
    rush of men
Inebriate with rage:—loud, and
    more loud   45
The discord grows; till pale Death
    shuts the scene,
And o'er the conqueror and the
    conquered draws
His cold and bloody shroud.—Of
    all the men
Whom day's departing beam saw
    blooming there,
In proud and vigorous health; of
    all the hearts   50
That beat with anxious life at sun-
    set there;
How few survive, how few are
    beating now!
All is deep silence, like the fearful
    calm
That slumbers in the storm's por-
    tentous pause;
Save when the frantic wail of
    widowed love   55

Comes shuddering on the blast, or
    the faint moan
With which some soul bursts from
    the frame of clay
Wrapped round its struggling pow-
    ers.   The gray morn
Dawns on the mournful scene; the
    sulphurous smoke
Before the icy wind slow rolls
    away,
And the bright beams of frosty
    morning dance   61
Along the spangling snow. There
    tracks of blood
Even to the forest's depth, and
    scattered arms,
And lifeless warriors, whose hard
    lineaments
Death's self could change not,
    mark the dreadful path 65
Of the outsallying victors: far be-
    hind,
Black ashes note where their proud
    city stood.
Within yon forest is a gloomy
    glen—
Each tree which guards its dark-
    ness from the day,
Waves o'er a warrior's tomb.
        I see thee shrink, 70
Surpassing Spirit!—wert thou hu-
    man else?
I see a shade of doubt and horror
    fleet
Across thy stainless features: yet
    fear not;
This is no unconnected misery,
Nor stands uncaused and irretriev-
    able.   75
Man's evil nature, that apology
Which kings who rule, and cowards
    who crouch, set up
For their unnumbered crimes,
    sheds not the blood
Which desolates the discord-wasted
    land.

From kings, and priests, and states-
    men, war arose,   80
Whose safety is man's deep unbet-
    tered woe,
Whose grandeur his debasement.
    Let the axe
Strike at the root, the poison-tree
    will fall;
And where its venomed exhalations
    spread
Ruin, and death, and woe, where
    millions lay   85
Quenching the serpent's famine,
    and their bones
Bleaching unburied in the putrid
    blast,
A garden shall arise, in loveliness
Surpassing fabled Eden.
        Hath Nature's soul,
That formed this world so beauti-
    ful, that spread   90
Earth's lap with plenty, and life's
    smallest chord
Strung to unchanging unison, that
    gave
The happy birds their dwelling in
    the grove,
That yielded to the wanderers of
    the deep
The lovely silence of the unfath-
    omed main,   95
And filled the meanest worm that
    crawls in dust
With spirit, thought, and love; on
    Man alone,
Partial in causeless malice, wan-
    tonly
Heaped ruin, vice, and slavery; his
    soul
Blasted with withering curses;
    placed afar   100
The meteor-happiness, that shuns
    his grasp,
But serving on the frightful gulf to
    glare,
Rent wide beneath his footsteps?
        Nature!—no!

Kings, priests, and statesmen, blast
   the human flower
Even in its tender bud; their influence darts   105
Like subtle poison through the
   bloodless veins
Of desolate society. The child,
Ere he can lisp his mother's sacred
   name,
Swells with the unnatural pride of
   crime, and lifts
His baby-sword even in a hero's
   mood.   110
This infant-arm becomes the blood-
   iest scourge
Of devastated earth; whilst spe-
   cious names,
Learned in soft childhood's unsus-
   pecting hour,
Serve as the sophisms with which
   manhood dims
Bright Reason's ray, and sanctifies
   the sword   115
Upraised to shed a brother's inno-
   cent blood.
Let priest-led slaves cease to pro-
   claim that man
Inherits vice and misery, when
   Force
And Falsehood hang even o'er the
   cradled babe,
Stifling with rudest grasp all natu-
   ral good.   120
Ah! to the stranger-soul, when
   first it peeps
From its new tenement, and looks
   abroad
For happiness and sympathy, how
   stern
And desolate a tract is this wide
   world!
How withered all the buds of natu-
   ral good!   125
No shade, no shelter from the
   sweeping storms
Of pitiless power! On its wretched
   frame,

Poisoned, perchance, by the disease
   and woe
Heaped on the wretched parent
   whence it sprung
By morals, law, and custom, the
   pure winds   130
Of Heaven, that renovate the insect tribes,
May breathe not. The untainting
   light of day
May visit not its longings. It is
   bound
Ere it has life: yea, all the chains
   are forged
Long ere its being: all liberty and
   love   135
And peace is torn from its defence-
   lessness;
Cursed from its birth, even from
   its cradle doomed
To abjectness and bondage!

'Throughout this varied and eternal
   world
Soul is the only element: the
   block   140
That for uncounted ages has remained
The moveless pillar of a mountain's
   weight
Is active, living spirit. Every grain
Is sentient both in unity and
   part,
And the minutest atom compre-
   hends   145
A world of loves and hatreds; these
   beget
Evil and good: hence truth and
   falsehood spring;
Hence will and thought and action,
   all the germs
Of pain or pleasure, sympathy or
   hate,
That variegate the eternal universe.   150
Soul is not more polluted than the
   beams

Of Heaven's pure orb, ere round
　　their rapid lines
The taint of earth-born atmos-
　　pheres arise.
'Man is of soul and body, formed
　　for deeds
Of high resolve, on fancy's boldest
　　wing　　　　155
To soar unwearied, fearlessly to
　　turn
The keenest pangs to peacefulness,
　　and taste
The joys which mingled sense and
　　spirit yield.
Or he is formed for abjectness and
　　woe,
To grovel on the dunghill of his
　　fears,　　　　160
To shrink at every sound, to quench
　　the flame
Of natural love in sensualism, to
　　know
That hour as blessed when on his
　　worthless days
The frozen hand of Death shall set
　　its seal,
Yet fear the cure, though hating the
　　disease.　　　　165
The one is man that shall hereafter
　　be;
The other, man as vice has made
　　him now.

'War is the statesman's game, the
　　priest's delight,
The lawyer's jest, the hired assas-
　　sin's trade,
And, to those royal murderers,
　　whose mean thrones　170
Are bought by crimes of treachery
　　and gore,
The bread they eat, the staff on
　　which they lean.
Guards, garbed in blood-red livery,
　　surround
Their palaces, participate the
　　crimes

That force defends, and from a na-
　　tion's rage　　　　175
Secure the crown, which all the
　　curses reach
That famine, frenzy, woe and
　　penury breathe.
These are the hired bravos who de-
　　fend
The tyrant's throne—the bullies of
　　his fear:
These are the sinks and channels
　　of worst vice,　　　180
The refuse of society, the dregs
Of all that is most vile: their cold
　　hearts blend
Deceit with sternness, ignorance
　　with pride,
All that is mean and villanous, with
　　rage
Which hopelessness of good, and
　　self-contempt,　　　185
Alone might kindle; they are
　　decked in wealth,
Honour and power, then are sent
　　abroad
To do their work. The pestilence
　　that stalks
In gloomy triumph through some
　　eastern land
Is less destroying. They cajole with
　　gold,　　　　190
And promises of fame, the thought-
　　less youth
Already crushed with servitude: he
　　knows
His wretchedness too late, and
　　cherishes
Repentance for his ruin, when his
　　doom
Is sealed in gold and blood!　　195
Those too the tyrant serve, who,
　　skilled to snare
The feet of Justice in the toils of
　　law,
Stand, ready to oppress the weaker
　　still;

And right or wrong will vindicate
for gold,
Sneering at public virtue, which
beneath 200
Their pitiless tread lies torn and
trampled, where
Honour sits smiling at the sale of
truth.

Then grave and hoary-headed
hypocrites,
Without a hope, a passion, or a
love,
Who, through a life of luxury and
lies, 205
Have crept by flattery to the seats
of power,
Support the system whence their
honours flow. . . .
They have three words:—well ty-
rants know their use,
Well pay them for the loan, with
usury
Torn from a bleeding world!—God,
Hell, and Heaven. 210
A vengeful, pitiless, and almighty
fiend,
Whose mercy is a nickname for the
rage
Of tameless tigers hungering for
blood.
Hell, a red gulf of everlasting fire,
Where poisonous and undying
worms prolong 215
Eternal misery to those hapless
slaves
Whose life has been a penance for
its crimes.
And Heaven, a meed for those who
dare belie
Their human nature, quake, be-
lieve, and cringe
Before the mockeries of earthly
power 220

'These tools the tyrant tempers to
his work,
Wields in his wrath, and as he wills
destroys,
Omnipotent in wickedness: the
while
Youth springs, age moulders, manhood tamely does
His bidding, bribed by short-lived
joys to lend 225
Force to the weakness of his trembling arm.

'They rise, they fall; one generation
comes
Yielding its harvest to destruction's
scythe.
It fades, another blossoms: yet behold!
Red glows the tyrant's stamp-mark
on its bloom, 230
Withering and cankering deep its
passive prime.
He has invented lying words and
modes,
Empty and vain as his own coreless
heart;
Evasive meanings, nothings of
much sound,
To lure the heedless victim to the
toils 235
Spread round the valley of its paradise.

'Look to thyself, priest, conqueror,
or prince!
Whether thy trade is falsehood, and
thy lusts
Deep wallow in the earnings of the
poor,
With whom thy Master was:—or
thou delight'st 240
In numbering o'er the myriads of
thy slain,
All misery weighing nothing in the
scale
Against thy short-lived fame: or
thou dost load

With cowardice and crime the
    groaning land,
A pomp-fed king. Look to thy
    wretched self!   245
Ay, art thou not the veriest slave
    that e'er
Crawled on the loathing earth?
    Are not thy days
Days of unsatisfying listless-
    ness?
Dost thou not cry, ere night's long
    rack is o'er,
"When will the morning come?" Is
    not thy youth   250
A vain and feverish dream of sen-
    sualism?
Thy manhood blighted with unripe
    disease?
Are not thy views of unregretted
    death
Drear, comfortless, and horrible?
    Thy mind,
Is it not morbid as thy nerveless
    frame,   255
Incapable of judgment, hope, or
    love?
And dost thou wish the errors to
    survive
That bar thee from all sympathies
    of good,
After the miserable interest
Thou hold'st in their protraction?
    When the grave   260
Has swallowed up thy memory and
    thyself,
Dost thou desire the bane that
    poisons earth
To twine its roots around thy
    coffined clay,
Spring from thy bones, and blossom
    on thy tomb,
That of its fruit thy babes may
    eat and die?   265

V

'Thus do the generations of the
    earth

Go to the grave, and issue from the
    womb,
Surviving still the imperishable
    change
That renovates the world; even as
    the leaves
Which the keen frost-wind of the
    waning year   5
Has scattered on the forest soil,
    and heaped
For many reasons there—though
    long they choke,
Loading with loathsome rottenness
    the land,
All germs of promise, yet when the
    tall trees
From which they fell, shorn of their
    lovely shapes,   10
Lie level with the earth to moulder
    there,
They fertilize the land they long
    deformed,
Till from the breathing lawn a for-
    est springs
Of youth, integrity, and loveliness,
Like that which gave it life, to
    spring and die,   15
Thus suicidal selfishness, that
    blights
The fairest feelings of the opening
    heart,
Is destined to decay, whilst from
    the soil
Shall spring all virtue, all delight,
    all love,
And judgment cease to wage un-
    natural war   20
With passion's unsubduable array.
Twin-sister of religion, selfishness!
Rival in crime and falsehood, aping
    all
The wanton horrors of her bloody
    play;
Yet frozen, unimpassioned, spirit-
    less,   25
Shunning the light, and owning not
    its name,

Compelled, by its deformity, to
    screen
With flimsy veil of justice and of
    right,
Its unattractive lineaments, that
    scare
All, save the brood of ignorance: at
    once   30
The cause and the effect of ty-
    ranny;
Unblushing, hardened, sensual, and
    vile;
Dead to all love but of its abject-
    ness,
With heart impassive by more
    noble powers
Than unshared pleasure, sordid
    gain, or fame;   35
Despising its own miserable
    being,
Which still it longs, yet fears to dis-
    enthrall.

'Hence commerce springs, the venal
    interchange
Of all that human art or nature
    yield;
Which wealth should purchase not,
    but want demand,   40
And natural kindness hasten to sup-
    ply
From the full fountain of its bound-
    less love,
For ever stifled, drained, and
    tainted now.
Commerce! beneath whose poison-
    breathing shade
No solitary virtue dares to
    spring,   45
But Poverty and Wealth with
    equal hand
Scatter their withering curses, and
    unfold
The doors of premature and vio-
    lent death,
To pining famine and full-fed
    disease,

To all that shares the lot of human
    life,   50
Which poisoned, body and soul,
    scarce drags the chain,
That lengthens as it goes and
    clanks behind.

'Commerce has set the mark of sel-
    fishness,
The signet of its all-enslaving
    power
Upon a shining ore, and called it
    gold: 55
Before whose image bow the vulgar
    great,
The vainly rich, the miserable
    proud,
The mob of peasants, nobles,
    priests, and kings,
And with blind feelings reverence
    the power
That grinds them to the dust of
    misery.   60
But in the temple of their hireling
    hearts
Gold is a living god, and rules in
    scorn
All earthly things but virtue.

'Since tyrants, by the sale of hu-
    man life,
Heap luxuries to their sensualism,
    and fame   65
To their wide-wasting and insatiate
    pride,
Success has sanctioned to a credu-
    lous world
The ruin, the disgrace, the woe of
    war.
His hosts of blind and unresisting
    dupes
The despot numbers; from his
    cabinet   70
These puppets of his schemes he
    moves at will,
Even as the slaves by force or
    famine driven,

Beneath a vulgar master, to perform
A task of cold and brutal drudg-
 . ery;—
Hardened to hope, insensible to
 fear, 75
Scarce living pulleys of a dead
 machine,
Mere wheels of work and articles of
 trade,
That grace the proud and noisy
 pomp of wealth!

'The harmony and happiness of
 man
Yields to the wealth of nations;
 that which lifts 80
His nature to the heaven of its
 pride,
Is bartered for the poison of his
 soul;
The weight that drags to earth his
 towering hopes,
Blighting all prospect but of selfish
 gain,
Withering all passion but of slavish
 fear, 85
Extinguishing all free and generous
 love
Of enterprise and daring, even the
 pulse
That fancy kindles in the beating
 heart
To mingle with sensation, it de-
 stroys,—
Leaves nothing but the sordid lust
 of self, 90
The grovelling hope of interest and
 gold,
Unqualified, unmingled, unre-
 deemed
Even by hypocrisy.
   And statesmen boast
Of wealth! The wordy eloquence,
 that lives
After the ruin of their hearts, can
 gild 95

The bitter poison of a nation's
 woe,
Can turn the worship of the servile
 mob
To their corrupt and glaring idol,
 Fame,
From Virtue, trampled by its iron
 tread,
Although its dazzling pedestal be
 raised 100
Amid the horrors of a limb-strewn
 field,
With desolated dwellings smoking
 round.
The man of ease, who, by his warm
 fireside,
To deeds of charitable intercourse,
And bare fulfilment of the common
 laws 105
Of decency and prejudice, con-
 fines
The struggling nature of his human
 heart,
Is duped by their cold sophistry;
 he sheds
A passing tear perchance upon the
 wreck
Of earthly peace, when near his
 dwelling's door 110
The frightful waves are driven,—
 when his son
Is murdered by the tyrant, or religion
Drives his wife raving mad. But the
 poor man,
Whose life is misery, and fear, and
 care;
Whom the morn wakens but to
 fruitless toil; 115
Who ever hears his famished offspring's scream,
Whom their pale mother's uncomplaining gaze
For ever meets, and the proud rich
 man's eye
Flashing command, and the heart-
 breaking scene

Of thousands like himself;—he
little heeds 120
The rhetoric of tyranny; his hate
Is quenchless as his wrongs; he
laughs to scorn
The vain and bitter mockery of
words,
Feeling the horror of the tyrant's
deeds,
And unrestrained but by the arm of
power, 125
That knows and dreads his enmity.

'The iron rod of Penury still com-
pels
Her wretched slave to bow the knee
to wealth,
And poison, with unprofitable toil,
A life too void of solace to con-
firm 130
The very chains that bind him to
his doom.
'Nature, impartial in munificence,
Has gifted man with all-subduing
will.
Matter, with all its transitory
shapes,
Lies subjected and plastic at his
feet, 135
That, weak from bondage, tremble
as they tread.
How many a rustic Milton has
passed by,
Stifling the speechless longings of
his heart,
In unremitting drudgery and
care!
How many a vulgar Cato has com-
pelled 140
His energies, no longer tameless
then,
To mould a pin, or fabricate a nail!
How many a Newton, to whose pas-
sive ken
Those mighty spheres that gem in-
finity

Were only specks of tinsel, fixed in
Heaven 145
To light the midnights of his native
town!

'Yet every heart contains perfec-
tion's germ:
The wisest of the sages of the earth,
That ever from the stores of reason
drew
Science and truth, and virtue's
dreadless tone, 150
Were but a weak and inexperienced
boy,
Proud, sensual, unimpassioned, un-
imbued
With pure desire and universal love,
Compared to that high being, of
cloudless brain,
Untainted passion, elevated will, 155
Which Death (who even would
linger long in awe
Within his noble presence, and be-
neath
His changeless eyebeam) might
alone subdue.
Him, every slave now dragging
through the filth
Of some corrupted city his sad
life, 160
Pining with famine, swoln with
luxury,
Blunting the keenness of his spir-
itual sense
With narrow schemings and un-
worthy cares,
Or madly rushing through all vio-
lent crime,
To move the deep stagnation of his
soul,— 165
Might imitate and equal.
But mean lust
Has bound its chains so tight
around the earth,
That all within it but the virtuous
man

Is venal: gold or fame will surely
   reach
The price prefixed by selfishness,
   to all   170
But him of resolute and unchanging
   will;
Whom, nor the plaudits of a servile
   crowd,
Nor the vile joys of tainting luxury,
Can bribe to yield his elevated
   soul
To Tyranny or Falsehood, though
   they wield   175
With blood-red hand the sceptre of
   the world.

'All things are sold: the very light
   of Heaven
Is venal; earth's unsparing gifts of
   love,
The smallest and most despicable
   things
That lurk in the abysses of the
   deep,   180
All objects of our life, even life
   itself,
And the poor pittance which the
   laws allow
Of liberty, the fellowship of man,
Those duties which his heart of human love
Should urge him to perform instinctively,   185
Are bought and sold as in a public
   mart
Of undisguising selfishness, that
   sets
On each its price, the stamp-mark
   of her reign.
Even love is sold; the solace of all
   woe
Is turned to deadliest agony, old
   age   190
Shivers in selfish beauty's loathing
   arms,
And youth's corrupted impulses
   prepare

A life of horror from the blighting
   bane
Of commerce; whilst the pestilence
   that springs
From unenjoying sensualism, has
   filled   195
All human life with hydra-headed
   woes.

'Falsehood demands but gold to
   pay the pangs
Of outraged conscience; for the
   slavish priest
Sets no great value on his hireling
   faith:
A little passing pomp, some servile
   souls,   200
Whom cowardice itself might safely
   chain,
Or the spare mite of avarice could
   bribe
To deck the triumph of their languid zeal,
Can make him minister to tyranny.
More daring crime requires a loftier
   meed: 205
Without a shudder, the slave-
   soldier lends
His arm to murderous deeds, and
   steels his heart,
When the dread eloquence of dying
   men,
Low mingling on the lonely field
   of fame,
Assails that nature, whose applause
   he sells   210
For the gross blessings of a patriot
   mob,
For the vile gratitude of heartless
   kings,
And for a cold world's good word,
   —viler still!

'There is a nobler glory, which survives
Until our being fades, and, solacing   215

All human care, accompanies its
    change;
Deserts not virtue in the dungeon's
    gloom,
And, in the precincts of the palace,
    guides
Its footsteps through that labyrinth
    of crime;
Imbues his lineaments with daunt-
    lessness, 220
Even when, from Power's avenging
    hand, he takes
Its sweetest, last and noblest title
    —death;
—The consciousness of good, which
    neither gold,
Nor sordid fame, nor hope of heav-
    enly bliss
Can purchase; but a life of resolute
    good, 225
Unalterable will, quenches desire
Of universal happiness, the heart
That beats with it in unison, the
    brain,
Whose ever wakeful wisdom toils to
    change
Reason's rich stores for its eternal
    weal. 230

'This commerce of sincerest virtue
    needs
No mediative signs of selfish-
    ness,
No jealous intercourse of wretched
    gain,
No balancings of prudence, cold
    and long;
In just and equal measure all is
    weighed, 235
One scale contains the sum of hu-
    man weal,
And one, the good man's heart.
              How vainly seek
The selfish for that happiness de-
    nied
To aught but virtue! Blind and
    hardened, they,

Who hope for peace amid the
    storms of care, 240
Who covet power they know not
    how to use,
And sigh for pleasure they refuse
    to give,—
Madly they frustrate still their own
    designs;
And, where they hope that quiet to
    enjoy
Which virtue pictures, bitterness of
    soul, 245
Pining regrets, and vain repent-
    ances,
Disease, disgust, and lassitude, per-
    vade
Their valueless and miserable lives.

'But hoary-headed Selfishness has
    felt
Its death-blow, and is tottering to
    the grave: 250
A brighter morn awaits the human
    day,
When every transfer of earth's
    natural gifts
Shall be a commerce of good words
    and works;
When poverty and wealth, the
    thirst of fame,
The fear of infamy, disease and
    woe, 255
War with its million horrors, and
    fierce hell
Shall live but in the memory of
    Time,
Who, like a penitent libertine, shall
    start,
Look back, and shudder at his
    younger years.'

VI

ALL touch, all eye, all ear,
The Spirit felt the Fairy's burning
    speech.
O'er the thin texture of its frame,
The varying periods painted chang-
    ing glows,

As on a summer even,   5
When soul-enfolding music floats
      around,
The stainless mirror of the lake
Re-images the eastern gloom,
Mingling convulsively its purple
      hues
With   sunset's   burnished
      gold.   10

Then thus the Spirit spoke:
'It is a wild and miserable world!
Thorny, and full of care,
Which every fiend can make his
      prey at will.
O Fairy! in the lapse of years, 15
Is there no hope in store?
Will yon vast suns roll on
Interminably, still illuming
The night of so many wretched
      souls,
And   see   no   hope   for
      them?   20
Will not the universal Spirit e'er
Revivify this withered limb of
      Heaven?'

The Fairy calmly smiled
In comfort, and a kindling gleam
      of hope
Suffused the Spirit's linea-
      ments.   25
'Oh! rest thee tranquil; chase those
      fearful doubts,
Which ne'er could rack an ever-
      lasting soul,
That sees the chains which bind it
      to its doom.
Yes! crime and misery are in yon-
      der earth,
Falsehood,   mistake,   and
      lust;   30
But the eternal world
Contains at once the evil and the
      cure.
Some eminent in virtue shall start
      up,
Even in perversest time:

The truths of their pure lips, that
      never die,   35
Shall bind the scorpion falsehood
      with a wreath
Of ever-living flame,
Until the monster sting itself to
      death.

'How sweet a scene will earth be-
      come!
Of purest spirits a pure dwelling-
      place,   40
Symphonious with the planetary
      spheres;
When man, with changeless Nature
      coalescing,
Will   undertake   regeneration's
      work,
When its ungenial poles no longer
      point
To the red and baleful sun 45
That faintly twinkles there.

'Spirit! on yonder earth,
Falsehood now triumphs; deadly
      power
Has fixed its seal upon the lip of
      truth!
Madness and misery are there! 50
The happiest is most wretched! Yet
      confide,
Until pure health-drops, from the
      cup of joy,
Fall like a dew of balm upon the
      world.
Now, to the scene I show, in silence
      turn,
And read the blood-stained charter
      of all woe,   55
Which Nature soon, with re-creat-
      ing hand,
Will blot in mercy from the book
      of earth.
How bold the flight of Passion's
      wandering wing,
How swift the step of Reason's
      firmer tread,

How calm and sweet the victories
    of life, 60
How terrorless the triumph of the
    grave!
How powerless were the mightiest
    monarch's arm,
Vain his loud threat, and impotent
    his frown!
How ludicrous the priest's dog-
    matic roar!
The weight of his exterminating
    curse 65
How light! and his affected char-
    ity,
To suit the pressure of the changing
    times,
What palpable deceit!—but for thy
    aid,
Religion! but for thee, prolific
    fiend,
Who peoplest earth with demons,
    Hell with men, 70
And Heaven with slaves!

'Thou taintest all thou look'st
    upon!—the stars,
Which on thy cradle beamed so
    brightly sweet,
Were gods to the distempered play-
    fulness
Of thy untutored infancy: the
    trees, 75
The grass, the clouds, the moun-
    tains, and the sea,
All living things that walk, swim,
    creep, or fly,
Were gods: the sun had homage,
    and the moon
Her worshipper. Then thou be-
    cam'st, a boy,
More daring in thy frenzies: every
    shape, 80
Monstrous or vast, or beautifully
    wild,
Which, from sensation's relics,
    fancy culls;

The spirits of the air, the shudder-
    ing ghost,
The genii of the elements, the pow-
    ers
That give a shape to Nature's
    varied works, 85
Had life and place in the corrupt
    belief
Of thy blind heart: yet still thy
    youthful hands
Were pure of human blood. Then
    manhood gave
Its strength and ardour to thy
    frenzied brain;
Thine eager gaze scanned the stu-
    pendous scene, 90
Whose wonders mocked the knowl-
    edge of thy pride:
Their everlasting and unchanging
    laws
Reproached thine ignorance.
    Awhile thou stoodst
Baffled and gloomy; then thou
    didst sum up
The elements of all that thou didst
    know; 95
The changing seasons, winter's
    leafless reign,
The budding of the Heaven-breath-
    ing trees,
The eternal orbs that beautify the
    night,
The sunrise, and the setting of the
    moon,
Earthquakes and wars, and poisons
    and disease, 100
And all their causes, to an abstract
    point
Converging, thou didst bend and
    called it God!
The self-sufficing, the omnipo-
    tent,
The merciful, and the avenging
    God!
Who, prototype of human misrule,
    sits 105

High in Heaven's realm, upon a
    golden throne,
Even like an earthly king; and
    whose dread work,
Hell, gapes for ever for the un-
    happy slaves
Of fate, whom He created, in his
    sport,
To triumph in their torments when
    they fell!   110
Earth heard the name; Earth trem-
    bled, as the smoke
Of His revenge ascended up to
    Heaven,
Blotting the constellations; and
    the cries
Of millions, butchered in sweet
    confidence
And unsuspecting peace, even
    when the bonds   115
Of safety were confirmed by·wordy
    oaths
Sworn in His dreadful name, rung
    through the land;
Whilst innocent babes writhed on
    thy stubborn spear,
And thou didst laugh to hear the
    mother's shriek
Of maniac gladness, as the sacred
    steel   120
Felt cold in her torn entrails!

'Religion! thou wert then in man-
    hood's prime:
But age crept on: one God would
    not suffice
For senile puerility; thou framedst
A tale to suit thy dotage, and to
    glut   125
Thy misery-thirsting soul, that the
    mad fiend
Thy wickedness had pictured might
    afford
A plea for sating the unnatural
    thirst
For murder, rapine, violence, and
    crime,

That still consumed thy being, even
    when   130
Thou heardst the step of Fate;—
    that flames might light
Thy funeral scene, and the shrill
    horrent shrieks
Of parents dying on the pile that
    burned
To light their children to thy paths,
    the roar
Of the encircling flames, the ex-
    ulting cries   135
Of thine apostles, loud commingling
    there,
Might sate thine hungry ear
Even on the bed of death!

'But now contempt is mocking thy
    gray hairs;
Thou art descending to the dark-
    some grave,   140
Unhonoured and unpitied, but by
    those
Whose pride is passing by like
    thine, and sheds,
Like thine, a glare that fades be-
    fore the sun
Of truth, and shines but in the
    dreadful night
That long has lowered above the
    ruined world.   145

'Throughout these infinite orbs of
    mingling light,
Of which yon earth is one, is wide
    diffused
A Spirit of activity and life,
That knows no terms, cessation, or
    decay;
That fades not when the lamp of
    earthly life,   150
Extinguished in the dampness of the
    grave,
Awhile there slumbers, more than
    when the babe
In the dim newness of its being feels
The impulses of sublunary things,

And all is wonder to unpractised
    sense: 155
But, active, steadfast, and eternal,
    still
Guides the fierce whirlwind, in the
    tempest roars,
Cheers in the day, breathes in the
    balmy groves,
Strengthens in health, and poisons
    in disease;
And in the storm of change, that
    ceaselessly   160
Rolls round the eternal universe,
    and shakes
Its undecaying battlement, pre-
    sides,
Apportioning with irresistible law
The place each spring of its ma-
    chine shall fill;
So that when waves on waves tu-
    multuous heap   165
Confusion to the clouds, and
    fiercely driven
Heaven's lightnings scorch the up-
    rooted ocean-fords,
Whilst, to the eye of shipwrecked
    mariner,
Lone sitting on the bare and shud-
    dering rock,
All seems unlinked contingency and
    chance: 170
No atom of this turbulence fulfils
A vague and unnecessitated task,
Or acts but as it must and ought to
    act.
Even the minutest molecule of light,
That in an April sunbeam's fleet-
    ing glow   175
Fulfils its destined, though invisi-
    ble work,
The universal Spirit guides; nor
    less,
When merciless ambition, or mad
    zeal,
Has led two hosts of dupes to bat-
    tle-field,

That, blind, they there may dig
    each other's graves,   180
And call the sad work glory, does it
    rule
All passions: not a thought, a will,
    an act,
No working of the tyrant's moody
    mind,
Nor one misgiving of the slaves who
    boast
Their servitude, to hide the shame
    they feel,   185
Nor the events enchaining every
    will,
That from the depths of unre-
    corded time
Have drawn all-influencing virtue,
    pass
Unrecognized, or unforeseen by
    thee,
Soul of the Universe! eternal
    spring   190
Of life and death, of happiness and
    woe,
Of all that chequers the phantas-
    mal scene
That floats before our eyes in
    wavering light,
Which gleams but on the darkness
    of our prison,
    Whose chains and massy
        walls   195
    We feel, but cannot see.

'Spirit of Nature! all-sufficing
    Power,
Necessity! thou mother of the
    world!
Unlike the God of human error,
    thou
Requir'st no prayers or praises;
    the caprice   200
Of man's weak will belongs no
    more to thee
Than do the changeful passions of
    his breast
To thy unvarying harmony: the
    slave,

Whose horrible lusts spread misery
    o'er the world,
And the good man, who lifts, with
    virtuous pride,   205
His being, in the sight of happiness,
That springs from his own works;
    the poison-tree,
Beneath whose shade all life is
    withered up,
And the fair oak, whose leafy
    dome affords
A temple where the vows of happy
    love   210
Are registered, are equal in thy
    sight:
No love, no hate thou cherishest:
    revenge
And favouritism, and worst desire
    of fame
Thou know'st not: all that the wide
    world contains
Are but thy passive instruments,
    and thou   215
Regard'st them all with an impar-
    tial eye,
Whose joy or pain thy nature can-
    not feel,
    Because thou hast not human
        sense,
    Because thou art not human
        mind.

'Yes! when the sweeping storm
    of time   220
Has sung its death-dirge o'er the
    ruined fanes
And broken altars of the almighty
    Fiend
Whose name usurps thy honours,
    and the blood
Through centuries clotted there, has
    floated down
The tainted flood of ages, shalt
    thou live   225
Unchangeable! A shrine is raised
    to thee,
    Which, nor the tempest-breath
    of time,

Nor the interminable flood,
Over earth's slight pageant
    rolling,
    Availeth to destroy,—   230
The sensitive extension of the
    world.
That wondrous and eternal
    fane,
Where pain and pleasure, good and
    evil join,
To do the will of strong necessity,
And life, in multitudinous shapes,
Still pressing forward where no
    term can be,   236
Like hungry and unresting
    flame
Curls round the eternal columns of
    its strength.'

VII

Spirit.

'I was an infant when my mother
    went
To see an atheist burned. She took
    me there:
The dark-robed priests were met
    around the pile;
The multitude was gazing silently;
And as the culprit passed with
    dauntless mien,   5
Tempered disdain in his unaltering
    eye,
Mixed with a quiet smile, shone
    calmly forth:
The thirsty fire crept round his
    manly limbs;
His resolute eyes were scorched to
    blindness soon;
His death-pang rent my heart! the
    insensate mob   10
Uttered a cry of triumph, and I
    wept.
"Weep not, child!" cried my
    mother, "for that man
Has said, There is no God."'

Fairy.

'There is no God!
Nature confirms the faith his death-
    groan sealed:
Let heaven and earth, let man's
    revolving race,   15
His ceaseless generations tell their
    tale;
Let every part depending on the
    chain
That links it to the whole, point to
    the hand
That grasps its term! let every seed
    that falls
In silent eloquence unfold its
    store   20
Of argument; infinity within,
Infinity without, belie creation;
The exterminable spirit it contains
Is nature's only God; but human
    pride   24
Is skilful to invent most serious
    names
To hide its ignorance.
        The name of God
Has fenced about all crime with
    holiness,
Himself the creature of His wor-
    shippers,
Whose names and attributes and
    passions change,
Seeva, Buddh, Foh, Jehovah, God,
    or Lord,   30
Even with the human dupes who
    build His shrines,
Still serving o'er the war-polluted
    world
For desolation's watchword;
    whether hosts
Stain His death-blushing chariot-
    wheels, as on
Triumphantly they roll, whilst
    Brahmins raise   35
A sacred hymn to mingle with the
    groans;
Or countless partners of His power
    divide

His tyranny to weakness; or the
    smoke
Of burning towns, the cries of fe-
    male helplessness,
Unarmed old age, and youth, and
    infancy,   40
Horribly massacred, ascend to
    Heaven
In honour of His name; or, last and
    worst,
Earth groans beneath religion's iron
    age,
And priests dare babble of a God
    of peace,
Even whilst their hands are red
    with guiltless blood,   45
Murdering the while, uprooting
    every germ
Of truth, exterminating, spoiling
    all,
Making the earth a slaughter-
    house!

'O Spirit! through the sense
By which thy inner nature was ap-
    prised   50
Of outward shows, vague dreams
    have rolled,
And varied reminiscences have
    waked
    Tablets that never fade;
All things have been imprinted
    there,
The stars, the sea, the earth, the
    sky,   55
Even the unshapeliest lineaments
Of wild and fleeting visions
Have left a record there
To testify of earth.

'These are my empire, for to me is
    given   60
The wonders of the human world
    to keep,
And Fancy's thin creations to
    endow
With manner, being, and reality;

Therefore a wondrous phantom,
from the dreams
Of human error's dense and purblind faith,   65
I will evoke, to meet thy questioning.
Ahasuerus, rise!'

A strange and woe-worn
wight
Arose beside the battlement,
And stood unmoving
there.   70
His inessential figure cast no shade
Upon the golden floor;
His port and mien bore mark of
many years,
And chronicles of untold ancient-
ness
Were legible within his beamless
eye: 75
Yet his cheek bore the mark of
youth;
Freshness and vigour knit his
manly frame;
The wisdom of old age was min-
gled there
With youth's primaeval daunt-
lessness;
And inexpressible woe,   80
Chastened by fearless resignation,
gave
An awful grace to his all-speaking
brow.

Spirit.

'Is there a God?'

Ahasuerus.

'Is there a God!—ay, an almighty
God,
And vengeful as almighty! Once
His voice   85
Was heard on earth; earth shud-
dered at the sound;
The fiery-visaged firmament ex-
pressed

Abhorrence, and the grave of
Nature yawned
To swallow all the dauntless and
the good
That dared to hurl defiance at His
throne,   90
Girt as it was with power. None but
slaves
Survived, — cold-blooded slaves,
who did the work
Of tyrannous omnipotence; whose
souls
No honest indignation ever urged
To elevated daring, to one deed 95
Which gross and sensual self did
not pollute.
These slaves built temples for the
omnipotent Fiend,
Gorgeous and vast: the costly
altars smoked
With human blood, and hideous
paeans rung
Through all the long-drawn aisles.
A murderer heard   100
His voice in Egypt, one whose gifts
and arts
Had raised him to his eminence in
power,
Accomplice of omnipotence in
crime,
And confidant of the all-knowing
one.
These were Jehovah's words:—

'From an eternity of idleness   106
I, God, awoke; in seven days' toil
made earth
From nothing; rested, and created
man:
I placed him in a Paradise, and
there
Planted the tree of evil, so that he
Might eat and perish, and My soul
procure   111
Wherewith to sate its malice, and
to turn,
Even like a heartless conqueror of
the earth,

All misery to My fame. The race
of men
Chosen to My honour, with impunity   115
May sate the lusts I planted in
their heart.
Here I command thee hence to
lead them on,
Until, with hardened feet, their conquering troops
Wade on the promised soil through
woman's blood,
And make My name be dreaded
through the land.   120
Yet ever-burning flame and ceaseless woe
Shall be the doom of their eternal
souls,
With every soul on this ungrateful
earth,
Virtuous or vicious, weak or strong,
—even all
Shall perish, to fulfil the blind revenge   125
(Which you, to men, call justice)
of their God.'

       The murderer's brow
Quivered with horror.
          'God omnipotent,
Is there no mercy? must our pun-
ishment
Be endless? will long ages roll
away   130
And see no term? Oh! wherefore
hast Thou made
In mockery and wrath this evil
earth?
Mercy becomes the powerful—be
but just:
O God! repent and save.'

       'One way remains:
I will beget a Son, and He shall
bear   135
The sins of all the world; He shall
arise

In an unnoticed corner of the
earth,
And there shall die upon a cross,
and purge
The universal crime; so that the
few
On whom My grace descends,
those who are marked 140
As vessels to the honour of their
God,
May credit this strange sacrifice,
and save
Their souls alive: millions shall live
and die,
Who ne'er shall call upon their
Saviour's name,
But, unredeemed, go to the gaping
grave.   145
Thousands shall deem it an old
woman's tale,
Such as the nurses frighten babes
withal:
These in a gulf of anguish and of
flame
Shall curse their reprobation end-
lessly,
Yet tenfold pangs shall force them
to avow,   150
Even on their beds of torment,
where they howl,
My honour, and the justice of their
doom.
What then avail their virtuous
deeds, their thoughts
Of purity, with radiant genius
bright,
Or lit with human reason's earthly
ray?   155
Many are called, but few will I
elect.
Do thou My bidding, Moses!'
       Even the murderer's cheek
Was blanched with horror, and his
quivering lips
Scarce faintly uttered — 'O al-
mighty One,
I tremble and obey!'   160

'O Spirit! centuries have set their
    seal
On this heart of many wounds, and
    loaded brain,
Since the Incarnate came: humbly
    He came,
Veiling His horrible Godhead in
    the shape
Of man, scorned by the world, His
    name unheard,   165
Save by the rabble of His native
    town,
Even as a parish demagogue. He
    led
The crowd; He taught them jus-
    tice, truth, and peace,
In semblance; but He lit within
    their souls
The quenchless flames of zeal, and
    blessed the sword   170
He brought on earth to satiate with
    the blood
Of truth and freedom His malig-
    nant soul.
At length His mortal frame was led
    to death.
I stood beside Him: on the tortur-
    ing cross
No pain assailed His unterrestrial
    sense;   175
And yet He groaned. Indignantly I
    summed
The massacres and miseries which
    His name
Had sanctioned in my country, and
    I cried,
"Go! Go!" in mockery.
A smile of godlike malice reillumed
His fading lineaments.—"I go,"
    He cried,   181
"But thou shalt wander o'er the
    unquiet earth
Eternally."—The dampness of the
    grave
Bathed my imperishable front. I
    fell,

And long lay tranced upon the
    charmèd soil.   185
When I awoke Hell burned within
    my brain,
Which staggered on its seat; for all
    around
The mouldering relics of my kin-
    dred lay,
Even as the Almighty's ire arrested
    them,
And in their various attitudes of
    death   190
My murdered children's mute and
    eyeless skulls
Glared ghastlily upno me.
                   But my soul,
From sight and sense of the pollut-
    ing woe
Of tyranny, had long learned to
    prefer
Hell's freedom to the servitude of
    Heaven.   195
Therefore I rose, and dauntlessly
    began
My lonely and unending pil-
    grimage,
Resolved to wage unweariable war
With my almighty Tyrant, and to
    hurl
Defiance at His impotence to harm
Beyond the curse I bore. The very
    hand   201
That barred my passage to the
    peaceful grave
Has crushed the earth to misery,
    and given
Its empire to the chosen of His
    slaves.
These have I seen, even from the
    earliest dawn   205
Of weak, unstable and precarious
    power,
Then preaching peace, as now they
    practise war;
So, when they turned but from the
    massacre

Of unoffending infidels, to quench
Their thirst for ruin in the very
    blood 210
That flowed in their own veins,
    and pitiless zeal
Froze every human feeling, as the
    wife
Sheathed in her husband's heart
    the sacred steel,
Even whilst its hopes were dream-
    ing of her love;
And friends to friends, brothers to
    brothers stood 215
Opposed in bloodiest battle-field,
    and war,
Scarce satiable by fate's last death-
    draught, waged,
Drunk from the winepress of the
    Almighty's wrath;
Whilst the red cross, in mockery of
    peace,
Pointed to victory! When the fray
    was done, 220
No remnant of the exterminated
    faith
Survived to tell its ruin, but the
    flesh,
With putrid smoke poisoning the
    atmosphere,
That rotted on the half-extin-
    guished pile.

'Yes! I have seen God's worship-
    pers unsheathe 225
The sword of His revenge, when
    grace descended,
Confirming all unnatural impulses,
To sanctify their desolating deeds;
And frantic priests waved the ill-
    omened cross
O'er the unhappy earth: then shone
    the sun 230
On showers of gore from the up-
    flashing steel
Of safe assassination, and all crime
Made stingless by the Spirits of the
    Lord,

And blood-red rainbows canopied
    the land.

'Spirit, no year of my eventful be-
    ing 235
Has passed unstained by crime and
    misery,
Which flows from God's own faith.
    I've marked His slaves
With tongues whose lies are venom-
    ous, beguile
The insensate mob, and, whilst one
    hand was red
With murder, feign to stretch the
    other out 240
For brotherhood and peace; and
    that they now
Babble of love and mercy, whilst
    their deeds
Are marked with all the narrow-
    ness and crime
That Freedom's young arm dare
    not yet chastise,
Reason may claim our gratitude,
    who now 245
Establishing the imperishable
    throne
Of truth, and stubborn virtue,
    maketh vain
The unprevailing malice of my Foe,
Whose bootless rage heaps tor-
    ments for the brave,
Adds impotent eternities to pain,
Whilst keenest disappointment
    racks His breast 251
To see the smiles of peace around
    them play,
To frustrate or to sanctify their
    doom.

'Thus have I stood,—through a
    wild waste of years
Struggling with whirlwinds of mad
    agony, 255
Yet peaceful, and serene, and self-
    enshrined,
Mocking my powerless Tyrant's
    horrible curse

With stubborn and unalterable will,
Even as a giant oak, which Heav-
　　en's fierce flame
Had scathèd in the wilderness, to
　　stand　　　　　260
A monument of fadeless ruin there;
Yet peacefully and movelessly it
　　braves
The midnight conflict of the win-
　　try storm,
　　As in the sunlight's calm it
　　spreads
　　Its worn and withered arms on
　　high　　　　　265
To meet the quiet of a summer's
　　noon.'
　　The Fairy waved her wand:
Ahasuerus fled
Fast as the shapes of mingled shade
　　and mist,
That lurk in the glens of a twilight
　　grove,　　　　270
　　Flee from the morning
　　beam:
The matter of which dreams are
　　made
Not more endowed with actual
　　life
Than this phantasmal portrai-
　　ture
Of wandering human thought. 275

VIII

The Fairy.

'THE Present and the Past thou
　　hast beheld:
It was a desolate sight. Now,
　　Spirit, learn
The secrets of the Future.—
　　Time!
Unfold the brooding pinion of thy
　　gloom,
Render thou up thy half-devoured
　　babes,　　　　5
And from the cradles of eternity,
Where millions lie lulled to their
　　portioned sleep

By the deep murmuring stream of
　　passing things,
Tear thou that gloomy shroud.—
　　Spirit, behold
　　Thy glorious destiny!'　10

Joy to the Spirit came.
Through the wide rent in Time's
　　eternal veil,
Hope was seen beaming through
　　the mists of fear:
　　Earth was no longer Hell;
　　Love, freedom, health, had
　　given　　　　　15
Their ripeness to the manhood of
　　its prime,
　　And all its pulses beat
Symphonious to the planetary
　　spheres:
　　Then dulcet music swelled
Concordant with the life-strings of
　　the soul;　　　20
It throbbed in sweet and languid
　　beatings there,
Catching new life from transitory
　　death,—
Like the vague sighings of a wind
　　at even,
That wakes the wavelets of the
　　slumbering sea
And dies on the creation of its
　　breath,　　　　25
And sinks and rises, fails and
　　swells by fits:
　　Was the pure stream of feel-
　　ing
　　That sprung from these
　　sweet notes,
And o'er the Spirit's human sym-
　　pathies
With mild and gentle motion
　　calmly flowed.　　30

Joy to the Spirit came,—
Such joy as when a lover sees
The chosen of his soul in happiness,
And witnesses her peace

Whose woe to him were bitterer
    than death,   35
    Sees her unfaded cheek
Glow mantling in first luxury of
    health,
    Thrills with her lovely eyes,
Which like two stars amid the
    heaving main
    Sparkle through liquid bliss.

Then in her triumph spoke the
    Fairy Queen: 41
'I will not call the ghost of ages
    gone
To unfold the frightful secrets of
    its lore;
    The present now is past,
And those events that desolate the
    earth   45
Have faded from the memory of
    Time,
Who dares not give reality to that
Whose being I annul. To me is
    given
The wonders of the human world
    to keep,
Space, matter, time, and mind.
    Futurity   50
Exposes now its treasure; let the
    sight
Renew and strengthen all thy fail-
    ing hope.
O human Spirit! spur thee to the
    goal
Where virtue fixes universal peace,
And midst the ebb and flow of hu-
    man things,   55
Show somewhat stable, somewhat
    certain still,
A lighthouse o'er the wild of dreary
    waves.

'The habitable earth is full of bliss;
Those wastes of frozen billows
    that were hurled
By everlasting snowstorms round
    the poles,   60

Where matter dared not vegetate
    or live,
But ceaseless frost round the vast
    solitude
Bound its broad zone of stillness,
    are unloosed;
And fragrant zephyrs there from
    spicy isles
Ruffle the placid ocean-deep, that
    rolls   65
Its broad, bright surges to the
    sloping sand,
Whose roar is wakened into echo-
    ings sweet
To murmur through the Heaven-
    breathing groves
And melodize with man's blest na-
    ture there.

'Those deserts of immeasurable
    sand,   70
Whose age - collected fervours
    scarce allowed
A bird to live, a blade of grass to
    spring,
Where the shrill chirp of the green
    lizard's love
Broke on the sultry silentness
    alone,
Now teem with countless rills and
    shady woods,   75
Cornfields and pastures and white
    cottages;
And where the startled wilderness
    beheld
A savage conqueror stained in kin-
    dred blood,
A tigress sating with the flesh of
    lambs
The unnatural famine of her tooth-
    less cubs,   80
Whilst shouts and howlings through
    the desert rang,
Sloping and smooth the daisy-
    spangled lawn,
Offering sweet incense to the sun-
    rise, smiles

To see a babe before his mother's
    door,
Sharing his morning's meal 85
With the green and golden bas-
    ilisk
That comes to lick his feet.

'Those trackless deeps, where many
    a weary sail
Has seen above the illimitable
    plain,
Morning on night, and night on
    morning rise,   90
Whilst still no land to greet the
    wanderer spread
Its shadowy mountains on the sun-
    bright sea,
Where the loud roarings of the
    tempest-waves
So long have mingled with the
    gusty wind
In melancholy loneliness, and
    swept   95
The desert of those ocean soli-
    tudes,
But vocal to the sea-bird's harrow-
    ing shriek,
The bellowing monster, and the
    rushing storm,
Now to the sweet and many-min-
    gling sounds
Of kindliest human impulses re-
    spond.   100
Those lonely realms bright garden-
    isles begem,
With lightsome clouds and shining
    seas between,
And fertile valleys, resonant with
    bliss,
Whilst green woods overcanopy the
    wave,
Which like a toil-worn labourer
    leaps to shore,   105
To meet the kisses of the flow'rets
    there.

'All things are recreated, and the
    flame

Of consentaneous love inspires all
    life:
The fertile bosom of the earth gives
    suck
To myriads, who still grow be-
    neath her care,   110
Rewarding her with their pure per-
    fectness:
The balmy breathings of the wind
    inhale
Her virtues, and diffuse them all
    abroad:
Health floats amid the gentle at-
    mosphere,
Glows in the fruits, and mantles on
    the stream: 115
No storms deform the beaming
    brow of Heaven,
Nor scatter in the freshness of its
    pride
The foliage of the ever-verdant
    trees;
But fruits are ever ripe, flowers
    ever fair,
And Autumn proudly bears her
    matron grace,   120
Kindling a flush on the fair cheek
    of Spring,
Whose virgin bloom beneath the
    ruddy fruit
Reflects its tint, and blushes into
    love.

'The lion now forgets to thirst for
    blood:
There might you see him sporting
    in the sun   125
Beside the dreadless kid; his claws
    are sheathed,
His teeth are harmless, custom's
    force has made
His nature as the nature of a lamb.
Like passion's fruit, the night-
    shade's tempting bane
Poisons no more the pleasure it be-
    stows: 130
All bitterness is past; the cup of
    joy

Unmingled mantles to the goblet's
   brim,
And courts the thirsty lips it fled
   before.

'But chief, ambiguous Man, he
   that can know
More misery, and dream more joy
   than all;   135
Whose keen sensations thrill within
   his breast
To mingle with a loftier instinct
   there,
Lending their power to pleasure
   and to pain,
Yet raising, sharpening, and refining each;
Who stands amid the ever-varying
   world,   140
The burthen or the glory of the
   earth;
He chief perceives the change, his
   being notes
The gradual renovation, and defines
Each movement of its progress on
   his mind.

'Man, where the gloom of the long
   polar night   145
Lowers o'er the snow-clad rocks
   and frozen soil,
Where scarce the hardiest herb that
   braves the frost
Basks in the moonlight's ineffectual
   glow,
Shrank with the plants, and darkened with the night;
His chilled and narrow energies,
   his heart,   150
Insensible to courage, truth, or
   love,
His stunted stature and imbecile
   frame,
Marked him for some abortion of
   the earth,
Fit compeer of the bears that
   roamed around,

Whose habits and enjoyments were
   his own: 155
His life a feverish dream of stagnant woe,
Whose meagre wants, but scantily
   fulfilled,
Apprised him ever of the joyless
   length
Which his short being's wretchedness had reached;
His death a pang which famine,
   cold and toil   160
Long on the mind, whilst yet the
   vital spark
Clung to the body stubbornly, had
   brought:
All was inflicted here that Earth's
   revenge
Could wreak on the infringers of
   her law;
One curse alone was spared—the
   name of God.   165

'Nor where the tropics bound the
   realms of day
With a broad belt of mingling cloud
   and flame,
Where blue mists through the unmoving atmosphere
Scattered the seeds of pestilence,
   and fed
Unnatural vegetation, where the
   land
Teemed with all earthquake, tempest and disease,   171
Was Man a nobler being; slavery
Had crushed him to his country's
   blood-stained dust;
Or he was bartered for the fame of
   power,
Which all internal impulses destroying,
Makes human will an article of
   trade;
Or he was changed with Christians
   for their gold,   177
And dragged to distant isles, where
   to the sound

Of the flesh-mangling scourge, he
    does the work
Of all-polluting luxury and wealth,
Which doubly visits on the ty-
    rants' heads   181
The long-protracted fulness of
    their woe;
Or he was led to legal butchery,
To turn to worms beneath that
    burning sun,
Where kings first leagued against
    the rights of men,   185
And priests first traded with the
    name of God.

'Even where the milder zone af-
    forded Man
A seeming shelter, yet contagion
    there,
Blighting his being with unnum-
    bered ills,
Spread like a quenchless fire; nor
    truth till late   190
Availed to arrest its progress, or
    create
That peace which first in bloodless
    victory waved
Her snowy standard o'er this fa-
    voured clime:
There man was long the train-
    bearer of slaves,   194
The mimic of surrounding misery,
The jackal of ambition's lion-rage,
The bloodhound of religion's hun-
    gry zeal.

'Here now the human being stands
    adorning
This loveliest earth with taintless
    body and mind;
Blessed from his birth with all
    bland impulses,   200
Which gently in his noble bosom
    wake
All kindly passions and all pure de-
    sires.
Him, still from hope to hope the
    bliss pursuing

Which from the exhaustless lore of
    human weal
Dawns on the virtuous mind, the
    thoughts that rise   205
In time-destroying infiniteness, gift
With self-enshrined eternity, that
    mocks
The unprevailing hoariness of age,
And man, once fleeting o'er the
    transient scene
Swift as an unremembered vision,
    stands   210
Immortal upon earth: no longer
    now
He slays the lamb that looks him
    in the face,
And horribly devours his mangled
    flesh,
Which, still avenging Nature's
    broken law,
Kindled all putrid humours in his
    frame,   215
All evil passions, and all vain belief,
Hatred, despair, and loathing in
    his mind,
The germs of misery, death, dis-
    ease, and crime.
No longer now the wingèd habi-
    tants,
That in the woods their sweet lives
    sing away,   220
Flee from the form of man; but
    gather round,
And prune their sunny feathers on
    the hands
Which little children stretch in
    friendly sport
Towards these dreadless partners
    of their play.
All things are void of terror: Man
    has lost   225
His terrible prerogative, and stands
An equal amidst equals: happiness
And science dawn though late upon
    the earth;
Peace cheers the mind, health reno-
    vates the frame;

Disease and pleasure cease to
   mingle here,   230
Reason and passion cease to combat there;
Whilst each unfettered o'er the
   earth extend
Their all-subduing energies, and
   wield
The sceptre of a vast dominion
   there;
Whilst every shape and mode of
   matter lends   235
Its force to the omnipotence of
   mind,
Which from its dark mine drags the
   gem of truth
To decorate its Paradise of peace.'

IX

'O HAPPY Earth! reality of
   Heaven!
To which those restless souls that
   ceaselessly
Throng through the human uni-
   verse, aspire;
Thou consummation of all mortal
   hope!
Thou glorious prize of blindly-
   working will!   5
Whose rays, diffused throughout
   all space and time,
Verge to one point and blend for
   ever there:
Of purest spirits thou pure dwell-
   ing place!
Where care and sorrow, impotence
   and crime,
Languor, disease, and ignorance
   dare not come: 10
O happy Earth, reality of Heaven!

'Genius has seen thee in her passionate dreams,
And dim forebodings of thy loveliness
Haunting the human heart, have
   there entwined

Those rooted hopes of some sweet
   place of bliss   15
Where friends and lovers meet to
   part no more.
Thou art the end of all desire and
   will,
The product of all action; and
   the souls
That by the paths of an aspiring
   change
Have reached thy haven of perpetual peace,   20
There rest from the eternity of toil
That framed the fabric of thy perfectness.

'Even Time, the conqueror, fled
   thee in his fear;
That hoary giant, who, in lonely
   pride,
So long had ruled the world, that
   nations fell,   25
Beneath his silent footstep. Pyra-
   mids,
That for millenniums had withstood the tide
Of human things, his storm-breath
   drove in sand
Across that desert where their
   stones survived
The name of him whose pride had
   heaped them there.   30
Yon monarch, in his solitary pomp,
Was but the mushroom of a summer day,
That his light-wingèd footstep
   pressed to dust:
Time was the king of earth: all
   things gave way
Before him, but the fixed and virtuous will,   35
The sacred sympathies of soul and
   sense,
That mocked his fury and prepared his fall.

'Yet slow and gradual dawned the
   morn of love;

Long lay the clouds of darkness
o'er the scene,
Till from its native Heaven they
rolled away: 40
First, Crime triumphant o'er all
hope careered
Unblushing, undisguising, bold and
strong;
Whilst Falsehood, tricked in Vir-
tue's attributes,
Long sanctified all deeds of vice
and woe,
Till done by her own venomous
sting to death,   45
She left the moral world without
a law,
No longer fettering Passion's fear-
less wing,
Nor searing Reason with the brand
of God.
Then steadily the happy ferment
worked;
Reason was free; and wild though
Passion went   50
Through tangled glens and wood-
embosomed meads,
Gathering a garland of the strang-
est flowers,
Yet like the bee returning to her
queen,
She bound the sweetest on her
sister's brow,
Who meek and sober kissed the
sportive child,   55
No longer trembling at the broken
rod.

'Mild was the slow necessity of
death:
The tranquil spirit failed beneath
its grasp,
Without a groan, almost without
a fear,
Calm as a voyager to some distant
land,   60
And full of wonder, full of hope as
he.

The deadly germs of languor and
disease
Died in the human frame, and
Purity
Blessed with all gifts her earthly
worshippers.
How vigorous then the athletic
form of age!   65
How clear its open and unwrinkled
brow!
Where neither avarice, cunning,
pride, nor care,
Had stamped the seal of gray de-
formity
On all the mingling lineaments of
time.
How lovely the intrepid front of
youth!   70
Which meek-eyed courage decked
with freshest grace;
Courage of soul, that dreaded not
a name,
And elevated will, that journeyed
on
Through life's phantasmal scene in
fearlessness,
With virtue, love, and pleasure,
hand in hand.   75

'Then, that sweet bondage which
is Freedom's self,
And rivets with sensation's softest
tie
The kindred sympathies of human
souls,
Needed no fetters of tyrannic
law: 79
Those delicate and timid impulses
In Nature's primal modesty arose,
And with undoubted confidence
disclosed
The growing longings of its dawn-
ing love,
Unchecked by dull and selfish
chastity,
That virtue of the cheaply vir-
tuous,   85

Who pride themselves in senselessness and frost.
No longer prostitution's venomed
 bane
Poisoned the springs of happiness
 and life;
Woman and man, in confidence and
 love,
Equal and free and pure together
 trod   90
The mountain-paths of virtue,
 which no more
Were stained with blood from
 many a pilgrim's feet.

'Then, where, through distant
 ages, long in pride
The palace of the monarch-slave
 had mocked
Famine's faint groan, and Penury's
 silent tear,   95
A heap of crumbling ruins stood,
 and threw
Year after year their stones upon
 the field,
Wakening a lonely echo; and the
 leaves
Of the old thorn, that on the top-
 most tower
Usurped the royal ensign's gran-
 deur, shook   100
In the stern storm that swayed
 the topmost tower
And whispered strange tales in the
 Whirlwind's ear.

'Low through the lone cathedral's
 roofless aisles
The melancholy winds a death-
 dirge sung: 104
It were a sight of awfulness to see
The works of faith and slavery, so
 vast,
So sumptuous, yet so perishing
 withal!
Even as the corpse that rests beneath its wall.

A thousand mourners deck the
 pomp of death
To-day, the breathing marble glows
 above   110
To decorate its memory, and
 tongues
Are busy of its life: to-morrow,
 worms
In silence and in darkness seize
 their prey.

'Within the massy prison's mouldering courts,
Fearless and free the ruddy children played,   115
Weaving gay chaplets for their innocent brows
With the green ivy and the red
 wall-flower,
That mock the dungeon's unavailing gloom;
The ponderous chains, and gratings of strong iron,
There rusted amid heaps of broken
 stone   120
That mingled slowly with their
 native earth:
There the broad beam of day,
 which feebly once
Lighted the cheek of lean Captivity
With a pale and sickly glare, then
 freely shone
On the pure smiles of infant playfulness: 125
No more the shuddering voice of
 hoarse Despair
Pealed through the echoing vaults,
 but soothing notes
Of ivy-fingered winds and gladsome birds
And merriment were resonant
 around.

'These ruins soon left not a wreck
 behind: 130
Their elements, wide scattered o'er
 the globe,

To happier shapes were moulded,
　　and became
Ministrant to all blissful impulses:
Thus human things were perfected,
　　and earth,
Even as a child beneath its mother's
　　love,　　　　　　　135
Was strengthened in all excellence,
　　and grew
Fairer and nobler with each pass-
　　ing year.

'Now Time his dusky pennons o'er
　　the scene
Closes in steadfast darkness, and
　　the past
Fades from our charmèd sight. My
　　task is done:　　　140
Thy lore is learned. Earth's won-
　　ders are thine own,
With all the fear and all the hope
　　they bring.
My spells are passed: the present
　　now recurs.
Ah me! a pathless wilderness re-
　　mains
Yet unsubdued by man's reclaim-
　　ing hand.　　　　145

'Yet, human Spirit, bravely hold
　　thy course,
Let virtue teach thee firmly to
　　pursue
The gradual paths of an aspiring
　　change:
For birth and life and death, and
　　that strange state
Before the naked soul has found its
　　home,　　　　　150
All tend to perfect happiness, and
　　urge
The restless wheels of being on their
　　way,
Whose flashing spokes, instinct
　　with infinite life,
Bicker and burn to gain their
　　destined goal:

For birth but wakes the spirit to
　　the sense　　　　155
Of outward shows, whose unexpe-
　　rienced shape
New modes of passion to its frame
　　may lend;
Life is its state of action, and the
　　store
Of all events is aggregated there
That variegate the eternal uni-
　　verse;　　　　　160
Death is a gate of dreariness and
　　gloom,
That leads to azure isles and beam-
　　ing skies
And happy regions of eternal hope.
Therefore, O Spirit! fearlessly bear
　　on:
Though storms may break the
　　primrose on its stalk, 165
Though frosts may blight the
　　freshness of its bloom,
Yet Spring's awakening breath will
　　woo the earth,
To feed with kindliest dews its
　　favourite flower,
That blooms in mossy banks and
　　darksome glens,
Lighting the greenwood with its
　　sunny smile.　　　170

'Fear not then, Spirit, Death's dis-
　　robing hand,
So welcome when the tyrant is
　　awake
So welcome when the bigot's hell-
　　torch burns;
'Tis but the voyage of a darksome
　　hour,
The transient gulf-dream of a
　　startling sleep.　　175
Death is no foe to Virtue: earth
　　has seen
Love's brightest roses on the scaf-
　　fold bloom,
Mingling with Freedom's fadeless
　　laurels there,

And presaging the truth of vi-
    sioned bliss.
Are there not hopes within thee,
    which this scene   180
Of linked and gradual being has
    confirmed?
Whose stingings bade thy heart
    look further still,
When, to the moonlight walk by
    Henry led,
Sweetly and sadly thou didst talk
    of death?
And wilt thou rudely tear them
    from thy breast,   185
Listening supinely to a bigot's
    creed,
Or tamely crouching to the tyrant's
    rod,
Whose iron thongs are red with
    human gore?
Never: but bravely bearing on, thy
    will
Is destined an eternal war to wage
With tyranny and falsehood, and
    uproot   191
The germs of misery from the hu-
    man heart.
Thine is the hand whose piety
    would soothe
The thorny pillow of unhappy
    crime,
Whose impotence an easy pardon
    gains,   195
Watching its wanderings as a
    friend's disease:
Thine is the brow whose mildness
    would defy
Its fiercest rage, and brave its
    sternest will,
When fenced by power and master
    of the world.
Thou art sincere and good; of reso-
    lute mind,   200
Free from heart-withering custom's
    cold control,
Of passon lofty, pure and unsub-
    dued.

Earth's pride and meanness could
    not vanquish thee,
And therefore art thou worthy of
    the boon
Which thou hast now received:
    Virtue shall keep   205
Thy footsteps in the path that
    thou hast trod,
And many days of beaming hope
    shall bless
Thy spotless life of sweet and
    sacred love.
Go, happy one, and give that
    bosom joy
Whose sleepless spirit waits to
    catch   210
Light, life and rapture from thy
    smile.'

The Fairy waves her wand of
    charm.
Speechless with bliss the Spirit
    mounts the car,
That rolled beside the battle-
    ment,
Bending her beamy eyes in thank-
    fulness.   215
Again the enchanted steeds were
    yoked,
Again the burning wheels inflame
The steep descent of Heaven's un-
    trodden way.
Fast and far the chariot flew:
The vast and fiery globes that
    rolled   220
Around the Fairy's palace-gate
Lessened by slow degrees and soon
    appeared
Such tiny twinklers as the planet
    orbs
That there attendant on the solar
    power
With borrowed light pursued their
    narrower way.   225

Earth floated then below:
The chariot paused a moment
    there;

The Spirit then descended:
The restless coursers pawed the
  ungenial soil,
Snuffed the gross air, and then,
  their errand done,   230
Unfurled their pinions to the winds
  of Heaven.

The Body and the Soul united
  then,
A gentle start convulsed Ianthe's
  frame:

Her veiny eyelids quietly unclosed;
Moveless awhile the dark blue orbs
  remained: 235
She looked around in wonder and
  beheld
Henry, who kneeled in silence by
  her couch,
Watching her sleep with looks of
  speechless love,
And the bright beaming stars
That through the casement
  shone.   240

NOTE ON QUEEN MAB, BY MRS. SHELLEY

SHELLEY was eighteen when he wrote *Queen Mab;* he never published it. When it was written, he had come to the decision that he was too young to be a 'judge of controversies'; and he was desirous of acquiring 'that sobriety of spirit which is the characteristic of true heroism.' But he never doubted the truth or utility of his opinions; and, in printing and privately distributing *Queen Mab,* he believed that he should further their dissemination, without occasioning the mischief either to others or himself that might arise from publication. It is doubtful whether he would himself have admitted it into a collection of his works. His severe classical taste, refined by the constant study of the Greek poets, might have discovered defects that escape the ordinary reader; and the change his opinions underwent in many points would have prevented him from putting forth the speculations of his boyish days. But the poem is too beautiful in itself, and far too remarkable as the production of a boy of eighteen, to allow of its being passed over: besides that, having been frequently reprinted, the omission would be vain. In the former edition certain portions were left out, as shocking the general reader from the violence of their attack on religion. I myself had a painful feeling that such erasures might be looked upon as a mark of disrespect towards the author, and am glad to have the opportunity of restoring them.

A series of articles was published in the *New Monthly Magazine* during the autumn of the year 1832, written by a man of great talent, a fellow-collegian and warm friend of Shelley: they describe admirably the state of his mind during his collegiate life. Inspired with ardour for the acquisition of knowledge, endowed with the keenest sensibility and with the fortitude of a martyr, Shelley came among his fellow-creatures, congregated for the purposes of education, like a spirit from another sphere; too delicately organized for the rough treatment man uses towards man, especially in the season of youth, and too resolute in carrying out his own sense of good and justice, not to become a victim. To a devoted attachment to those he loved he added a determined resistance to oppression. Refusing to fag at Eton, he was treated with revolting cruelty by masters and boys: this roused instead of taming his spirit, and he rejected the duty of obedience when it was enforced by menaces and punishment. To aversion to the society of his fellow-creatures, such as he found them when collected together in societies, where one egged-on the other to acts of tyranny, was joined the deepest sympathy and compassion; while the attachment he felt for individuals, and the admiration with which he regarded their powers and their virtues, led him to entertain a high opinion of the perfectibility of human nature; and he believed that all could reach the highest grade of moral improvement, did not the customs and prejudices of society foster evil passions and excuse evil actions.

The oppression which, trembling at every nerve yet resolute to heroism, it was his ill-fortune to encounter at school and at college, led him to dissent in all things from those whose arguments were blows, whose faith appeared to engender blame and hatred. 'During my existence,' he wrote to a friend in 1812, 'I have incessantly speculated, thought, and read.' His readings were not always well chosen; among them were the works of the French philosophers: as far as metaphysical argument went, he temporarily became a convert. At the same time, it was the cardinal article of his faith that, if men were but taught and induced to treat their fellows with love, charity, and equal rights, this earth would realize paradise. He looked upon religion, as it is professed, and above all practised, as hostile instead of friendly to the cultivation of those virtues which would make men brothers.

Can this be wondered at? At the age of seventeen, fragile in health and frame, of the purest habits in morals, full of devoted generosity and universal kindness, glowing with ardour to attain wisdom, resolved at every personal sacrifice to do right, burning with a desire for affection and sympathy,—he was treated as a reprobate, cast forth as a criminal.

The cause was that he was sincere; that he believed the opinions which he entertained to be true. And he loved truth with a martyr's love; he was ready to sacrifice station and fortune, and his dearest affections, at its shrine. The sacrifice was demanded from, and made by, a youth of seventeen. It is a singular fact in the history of society in the civilized nations of modern times that no false step is so irretrievable as one made in early youth. Older men, it is true, when they oppose their fellows and transgress ordinary rules, carry a certain prudence or hypocrisy as a shield along with them. But youth is rash; nor can it imagine, while asserting what it believes to be true, and doing what it believes to be right, that it should be denounced as vicious, and pursued as a criminal.

Shelley possessed a quality of mind which experience has shown me to be of the rarest occurrence among human beings: this was his *unworld-liness*. The usual motives that rule men, prospects of present or future advantage, the rank and fortune of those around, the taunts and censures, or the praise, of those who were hostile to him, had no influence whatever over his actions, and apparently none over his thoughts. It is difficult even to express the simplicity and directness of purpose that adorned him. Some few might be found in the history of mankind, and some one at least among his own friends, equally disinterested and scornful, even to severe personal sacrifices, of every baser motive. But no one, I believe, ever joined this noble but passive virtue to equal active endeavours for the benefit of his friends and mankind in general, and to equal power to produce the advantages he desired. The world's brightest gauds and its most solid advantages were of no worth in his eyes, when compared to the cause of what he considered truth, and the good of his fellow-creatures. Born in a position which, to his inexperienced mind, afforded the greatest facilities to practise the tenets he espoused, he boldly declared the use he would make of fortune and station, and enjoyed the belief that he should materially benefit his fellow-creatures by his actions; while, conscious of surpassing powers of reason and imagination, it is not strange that he should, even while so young, have believed that his written thoughts would tend to disseminate opinions which he believed conducive to the happiness of the human race.

If man were a creature devoid of passion, he might have said and done all this with quietness. But he was too enthusiastic, and too full of hatred of all the ills he witnessed, not to scorn danger. Various disappointments tortured, but could not tame, his soul. The more enmity he met, the more earnestly he became attached to his peculiar views, and hostile to those of the men who persecuted him.

He was animated to greater zeal by compassion for his fellow-creatures. His sympathy was excited by the misery with which the world is burning. He witnessed the sufferings of the poor, and was aware of the evils of ignorance. He desired to induce every rich man to despoil himself of superfluity, and to create a brotherhood of property and service, and was ready to be the first to lay down the advantages of his birth. He was of too uncompromising a disposition to join any party. He did not in his youth look forward to gradual improvement: nay, in those days of intolerance, now almost forgotten, it seemed as easy to look forward to the sort of millennium of freedom and brotherhood which he thought the proper state of mankind as to the present reign of moderation and improvement. Ill-health made him believe that his race would soon be run; that a year or two was all he had of life. He desired that these years should be useful and illustrious. He saw, in a fervent call on his fellow-creatures to share alike the blessings of the creation, to love and serve each other, the noblest work that life and time permitted him. In this spirit he composed *Queen Mab*.

He was a lover of the wonderful and wild in literature, but had not fostered these tastes at their genuine sources—the romances and chivalry of the middle ages—but in the perusal of such German works as were current in those days. Under the influence of these he, at the age of fifteen, wrote two short prose romances of slender merit. The sentiments and language were exaggerated, the composition imitative and poor. He wrote also a poem on the subject of Ahasuerus—being led to it by a German fragment he picked up, dirty and torn, in Lincoln's Inn Fields. This fell afterwards into other hands, and was considerably altered before it was printed. Our earlier English poetry was almost unknown to him. The love and knowledge of Nature developed by Wordsworth —the lofty melody and mysterious beauty of Coleridge's poetry—and the wild fantastic machinery and gorgeous scenery adopted by Southey —composed his favourite reading; the rhythm of *Queen Mab* was founded on that of *Thalaba,* and the first few lines bear a striking resemblance in spirit, though not in idea, to the opening of that poem. His fertile imagination, and ear tuned to the finest sense of harmony, preserved him from imitation. Another of his favourite books was the poem of *Gebir* by Walter Savage Landor. From his boyhood he had a wonderful facility of versification, which he carried into another language; and his Latin school-verses were composed with an ease and correctness that procured for him prizes, and caused him to be resorted to by all his friends for help. He was, at the period of writing *Queen Mab,* a great traveller within the limits of England, Scotland, and Ireland. His time was spent among the loveliest scenes of these countries. Mountain and lake and forest were his home; the phenomena of Nature were his favourite study. He loved to inquire into their causes, and was addicted to pursuits of natural philosophy and chemistry, as far as they could be carried on as an amusement. These tastes gave truth and vivacity to his descriptions, and warmed his soul with that deep admiration for the wonders of Nature which constant association with her inspired.

He never intended to publish *Queen Mab* as it stands; but a few years after, when printing *Alastor,* he extracted a small portion which he entitled *The Daemon of the World.* In this he changed somewhat the versification, and made other alterations scarcely to be called improvements.

Some years after, when in Italy, a bookseller published an edition of *Queen Mab* as it originally stood. Shelley was hastily written to by his friends, under the idea that, deeply injurious as the mere distribution of the poem had proved, the publication might awaken fresh persecutions. At the suggestion of these friends he wrote a letter on the subject, printed in the *Examiner* newspaper—with which I close this history of his earliest work.

To the Editor of the 'Examiner.'

'Sir,

'Having heard that a poem entitled *Queen Mab* has been surreptitiously published in London, and that legal proceedings have been instituted against the publisher, I request the favour of your insertion of the following explanation of the affair, as it relates to me.

'A poem entitled *Queen Mab* was written by me at the age of eighteen,

I daresay in a sufficiently intemperate spirit—but even then was not intended for publication, and a few copies only were struck off, to be distributed among my personal friends. I have not seen this production for several years. I doubt not but that it is perfectly worthless in point of literary composition; and that, in all that concerns moral and political speculation, as well as in the subtler discriminations of metaphysical and religious doctrine, it is still more crude and immature. I am a devoted enemy to religious, political, and domestic oppression; and I regret this publication, not so much from literary vanity, as because I fear it is better fitted to injure than to serve the sacred cause of freedom. I have directed my solicitor to apply to Chancery for an injunction to restrain the sale; but, after the precedent of Mr. Southey's *Wat Tyler* (a poem written, I believe, at the same age, and with the same unreflecting enthusiasm), with little hope of success.

'Whilst I exonerate myself from all share in having divulged opinions hostile to existing sanctions, under the form, whatever it may be, which they assume in this poem, it is scarcely necessary for me to protest against the system of inculcating the truth of Christianity or the excellence of Monarchy, however true or however excellent they may be, by such equivocal arguments as confiscation and imprisonment, and invective and slander, and the insolent violation of the most sacred ties of Nature and society.

'SIR,

'I am your obliged and obedient servant,

'*Pisa, June 22, 1821.*'   'PERCY B. SHELLEY.

VERSES ON A CAT

I

A CAT in distress,
Nothing more, nor less;
Good folks, I must faithfully tell ye,
As I am a sinner,
It waits for some dinner   5
To stuff out its own little belly.

II

You would not easily guess
All the modes of distress
Which torture the tenants of earth;
And the various evils,   10
Which like so many devils,
Attend the poor souls from their
          birth.

III

Some a living require,
And others desire

An old fellow out of the way;   15
And which is the best
I leave to be guessed,
For I cannot pretend to say.

IV

One wants society,
Another variety,   20
Others a tranquil life;
Some want food,
Others, as good,
Only want a wife.

V

But this poor little cat   25
Only wanted a rat,
To stuff out its own little maw;
And it were as good
Some people had such food,
To make them *hold their jaw!*   30

FRAGMENT: OMENS

Hark! the owlet flaps his wings
  In the pathless dell beneath;
Hark! 'tis the night-raven sings
  Tidings of approaching death.

● EPITAPHIUM

[Latin Version of the Epitaph
in Gray's Elegy.]

I

Hic sinu fessum caput hospitali
Cespitis dormit juvenis, nec illi
Fata ridebant, popularis ille
        Nescius aurae.

II

Musa non vultu genus arroganti 5
Rustica natum grege despicata,
Et suum tristis puerum notavit
        Sollicitudo.

III

Indoles illi bene larga, pectus
Veritas sedem sibi vindicavit,   10
Et pari tantis meritis beavit
        Munere coelum.

IV

Omne quod moestis habuit miserto
Corde largivit lacrimam, recepit
Omne quod coelo voluit, fidelis 15
        Pectus amici.

V

Longius sed tu fuge curiosus
Caeteras laudes fuge suspicari,
Caeteras culpas fuge velle tractas
        Sede tremenda.   20

VI

Spe tremescentes recubant in illa
Sede virtutes pariterque culpae,
In sui Patris gremio, tremenda
        Sede Deique.

IN HOROLOGIUM

Inter marmoreas Leonorae pen-
  dula colles

Fortunata nimis Machina dicit
    horas.
Quas *manibus* premit illa duas
  insensa papillas.
Cur mihi sit *digito* tangere, amata,
  nefas?

A DIALOGUE

Death.

For my dagger is bathed in the
  blood of the brave,
I come, care-worn tenant of life,
  from the grave,
Where Innocence sleeps 'neath the
  peace-giving sod,
And the good cease to tremble at
  Tyranny's nod;
I offer a calm habitation to thee,—
Say, victim of grief, wilt thou slum-
    ber with me?   6
My mansion is damp, cold silence
  is there,
But it lulls in oblivion the fiends of
  despair;
Not a groan of regret, not a sigh,
  not a breath,
Dares dispute with grim Silence the
  empire of Death.   10
I offer a calm habitation to thee,—
Say, victim of grief, wilt thou slum-
    ber with me?

Mortal.

Mine eyelids are heavy; my soul
  seeks repose,
It longs in thy cells to embosom its
  woes,
It longs in thy cells to deposit its
  load,   15
Where no longer the scorpions of
  Perfidy goad,—
Where the phantoms of Prejudice
  vanish away,
And Bigotry's bloodhounds lose
  scent of their prey.
Yet tell me, dark Death, when
  thine empire is o'er,

What awaits on Futurity's mist-
covered shore?   20

Death.

Cease, cease, wayward Mortal! I
dare not unveil
The shadows that float o'er Eternity's vale;
Nought waits for the good but a
spirit of Love,
That will hail their blest advent to
regions above.
For Love, Mortal, gleams through
the gloom of my sway,   25
And the shades which surround me
fly fast at its ray.
Hast thou loved?—Then depart
from these regions of hate,
And in slumber with me blunt the
arrows of fate.
I offer a calm habitation to
thee,—
Say, victim of grief, wilt thou slumber with me?   30

Mortal.

Oh! sweet is thy slumber! oh!
sweet is the ray
Which after thy night introduces
the day;
How concealed, how persuasive,
self-interest's breath,
Though it floats to mine ear from
the bosom of Death!
I hoped that I quite was forgotten
by all,   35
Yet a lingering friend might be
grieved at my fall,
And duty forbids, though I languish to die,
When departure might heave Virtue's breast with a sigh.
O Death! O my friend! snatch this
form to thy shrine,
And I fear, dear destroyer, I shall
not repine.   40

TO THE MOONBEAM

I

Moonbeam, leave the shadowy
vale,
To bathe this burning brow.
Moonbeam, why art thou so pale,
As thou walkest o'er the dewy
dale,
Where humble wild-flowers
grow?   5
Is it to mimic me?
But that can never be;
For thine orb is bright,
And the clouds are light,
That at intervals shadow the star-
studded night.   10

II

Now all is deathly still on earth;
Nature's tired frame reposes;
And, ere the golden morning's
birth
Its radiant hues discloses,
Flies forth its balmy
breath.   15
But mine is the midnight
of Death,
And Nature's morn
To my bosom forlorn
Brings but a gloomier night, im-
plants a deadlier thorn.

III

Wretch! Suppress the glare of
madness   20
Struggling in thine haggard
eye,
For the keenest throb of sadness,
Pale Despair's most sickening
sigh,
Is but to mimic me;
And this must ever be, 25
When the twilight of care,
And the night of despair,
Seem in my breast but joys to the
pangs that rankle there.

THE SOLITARY

I

Dar'st thou amid the varied multi-
tude
To live alone, an isolated thing?
To see the busy beings round
thee spring,
And care for none; in thy calm
solitude,
A flower that scarce breathes in the
desert rude   5
To Zephyr's passing wing?

II

Not the swart Pariah in some Indian grove,
Lone, lean, and hunted by his
brother's hate,
Hath drunk so deep the cup of
bitter fate
As that poor wretch who cannot,
cannot love: 10
He bears a load which nothing can
remove,
A killing, withering weight.

III

He smiles—'tis sorrow's deadliest
mockery;
He speaks—the cold words flow
not from his soul;
He acts like others, drains the
genial bowl,—   15
Yet, yet he longs—although he
fears—to die;
He pants to reach what yet he
seems to fly,
Dull life's extremest goal.

TO DEATH

Death! where is thy victory?
To triumph whilst I die,
To triumph whilst thine ebon
wing
Enfolds my shuddering soul?
O Death! where is thy sting? 5
Not when the tides of murder
roll,
When nations groan, that kings
may bask in bliss,

Death! canst thou boast a victory
such as this—
When in his hour of pomp and
power
His blow the mightiest mur-
derer gave,   10
Mid Nature's cries the sacrifice
Of millions to glut the grave;
When sunk the Tyrant Desolation's
slave;
Or Freedom's life-blood streamed
upon thy shrine;
Stern Tyrant, couldst thou boast a
victory such as mine? 15

To know in dissolution's void
That mortals' baubles sunk
decay;
That everything, but Love, de-
stroyed
Must perish with its kindred
clay,—
Perish Ambition's crown, 20
Perish her sceptred sway;
From Death's pale front fades
Pride's fastidious frown.
In Death's damp vault the lurid
fires decay,
That Envy lights at heaven-born
Virtue's beam—
That all the cares subside, 25
Which lurk beneath the tide
Of life's unquiet stream;—
Yes! this is victory!
And on yon rock, whose dark form
glooms the sky,
To stretch these pale limbs, when
the soul is fled;   30
To baffle the lean passions of
their prey,
To sleep within the palace of the
dead!
Oh! not the King, around whose
dazzling throne
His countless courtiers mock the
words they say,
Triumphs amid the bud of glory
blown,   35

As I in this cold bed, and faint
    expiring groan!

Tremble, ye proud, whose grandeur
    mocks the woe
Which props the column of un-
    .natural state!
You the plainings, faint and
    low,
From Misery's tortured soul
    that flow,   40
Shall usher to your fate.
Tremble, ye conquerors, at whose
    fell command
The war-fiend riots o'er a peaceful
    land!
You Desolation's gory throng
Shall bear from Victory
    along   45
To that mysterious strand.

. . . . . .

LOVE'S ROSE

I

HOPES, that swell in youthful
    breasts,
Live not through the waste of
    time!
Love's rose a host of thorns invests;
    Cold, ungenial is the clime,
    Where its honours blow.   5
Youth says, 'The purple flowers are
    mine,'
Which die the while they glow.

II

Dear the boon to Fancy given,
    Retracted whilst it's granted:

Sweet the rose which lives in
    Heaven,   10
Although on earth 'tis planted,
    Where its honours blow,
While by earth's slaves the leaves
    are riven
Which die the while they glow.

III

Age cannot Love destroy,   15
    But perfidy can blast the flower,
    Even when in most unwary hour
    It blooms in Fancy's bower.
Age cannot Love destroy,
But perfidy can rend the shrine   20
In which its vermeil splendours
    shine.

EYES: A FRAGMENT

How eloquent are eyes!
Not the rapt poet's frenzied lay
When the soul's wildest feelings
    stray
    Can speak so well as they.
How eloquent are eyes!   5
Not music's most impassioned note
On which Love's warmest fervours
    float
    Like them bids rapture rise.
    Love, look thus again,—
That your look may light a waste
    of years,   10
Darting the beam that conquers
    cares
    Through the cold shower of
    tears.
Love, look thus again!

. . . . . .

ORIGINAL POETRY
BY VICTOR AND CAZIRE

*A Person complained that whenever he began to write, he never could
arrange his ideas in grammatical order. Which occasion suggested the
idea of the following lines:*

I

HERE I sit with my paper, my pen
    and my ink,

First of this thing, and that thing,
    and t'other thing think;
Then my thoughts come so pell-
    mell all into my mind,

That the sense or the subject I
  never can find:
This word is wrong placed,—no
  regard to the sense,   5
The present and future, instead of
  past tense,
Then my grammar I want; O dear!
  what a bore,
I think I shall never attempt to
  write more,
With patience I then my thoughts
  must arraign,
Have them all in due order like
  mutes in a train,   10
Like them too must wait in due
  patience and thought,
Or else my fine works will all come
  to nought.
My wit too's so copious, it flows
  like a river,
But disperses its waters on black
  and white never;
Like smoke it appears independent
  and free,   15
But ah luckless smoke! it all passes
  like thee—
Then at length all my patience entirely lost,
My paper and pens in the fire are
  tossed;
But come, try again—you must
  never despair,
Our Murray's or Entick's are not
  all so rare,   20
Implore their assistance—they'll
  come to your aid,
Perform all your business without
  being paid,
They'll tell you the present tense,
  future and past,
Which should come first, and which
  should come last,
This Murray will do—-then to Entick repair,   25
To find out the meaning of any
  word rare.

This they friendly will tell, and
  ne'er make you blush,
With a jeering look, taunt, or an
  O fie! tush!
Then straight all your thoughts in
  black and white put,
Not minding the if's, the be's, and
  the but,   30
Then read it all over, see how it
  will run,
How answers the wit, the retort,
  and the pun,
Your writings may then with old
  Socrates vie,
May on the same shelf with Demos-
  thenes lie,
May as Junius be sharp, or as Plato
  be sage,   35
The pattern or satire to all of the
  age;
But stop—a mad author I mean not
  to turn,
Nor with thirst of applause does my
  heated brain burn,
Sufficient that sense, wit, and gram-
  mar combined,
My letters may make some slight
  food for the mind;   40
That my thoughts to my friends I
  may freely impart,
In all the warm language that flows
  from the heart.
Hark! futurity calls! it loudly
  complains,
It bids me step forward and just
  hold the reins,
My excuse shall be humble, and
  faithful, and true,   45
Such as I fear can be made but by
  few—
Of writers this age has abundance
  and plenty,
Three score and a thousand, two
  millions and twenty,
Three score of them wits who all
  sharply vie,

To try what odd creature they best
   can belie,   50
A thousand are prudes who for
   Charity write,
And fill up their sheets with spleen,
   envy, and spite[,]
One million are bards, who to
   Heaven aspire,
And stuff their works full of bom-
   bast, rant, and fire,
T'other million are wags who in
   Grub-street attend,   55
And just like a cobbler the old writ-
   ings mend,
The twenty are those who for pul-
   pits indite,
And pore over sermons all Saturday
   night.
And now my good friends—who
   come after I mean,
As I ne'er wore a cassock, or dined
   with a dean,   60
Or like cobblers at mending I never
   did try,
Nor with poets in lyrics attempted
   to vie;
As for prudes these good souls I
   both hate and detest,
So here I believe the matter must
   rest.—
I've heard your complaint—my
   answer I've made,   65
And since to your calls all the
   tribute I've paid,
Adieu my good friend; pray never
   despair,
But grammar and sense and everything dare,
Attempt but to write dashing, easy,
   and free,
Then take out your grammar and
   pay him his fee,   70
Be not a coward, shrink not to a
   tense,
But read it all over and make it
   out sense.

What a tiresome girl!—pray soon
   make an end,
Else my limited patience you'll
   quickly expend.
Well adieu, I no longer your patience will try—   75
So swift to the post now the letter
   shall fly.

JANUARY, 1810.

II

To Miss —— [HARRIET GROVE]
   FROM MISS —— [ELIZABETH
      SHELLEY]

FOR your letter, dear —— [Hattie],
   accept my best thanks,
Rendered long and amusing by
   virtue of franks,
Though concise they would please,
   yet the longer the better,
The more news that's crammed in,
   more amusing the letter,
All excuses of etiquette nonsense I
   hate,   5
Which only are fit for the tardy and
   late,
As when converse grows flat, of the
   weather they talk,
How fair the sun shines—a fine day
   for a walk,
Then to politics turn, of Burdett's
   reformation,
One declares it would hurt, t'other
   better the nation,   10
Will ministers keep? sure they've
   acted quite wrong,
The burden this is of each morning-
   call song.
So —— is going to —— you say,
I hope that success her great efforts
   will pay [——]
That [the Colonel] will see her, be
   dazzled outright,   15
And declare he can't bear to be out
   of her sight.
Write flaming epistles with love's
   pointed dart,

Whose sharp little arrow struck
   right on his heart,
Scold poor innocent Cupid for mischievous ways,
He knows not how much to laud
   forth her praise,   20
That he neither eats, drinks or
   sleeps for her sake,
And hopes her hard heart some
   compassion will take,
A refusal would kill him, so desperate his flame,
But he fears, for he knows she is
   not common game,
Then praises her sense, wit, discernment and grace,   25
He's not one that's caught by a sly
   looking face,
Yet that's *too* divine—such a black
   sparkling eye,
At the bare glance of which near a
   thousand will die;
Thus runs he on meaning but one
   word in ten,
More than is meant by most such
   kind of men,   30
For they're all alike, take them one
   with another,
Begging pardon—with the excep-
   tion of my brother.
Of the drawings you mention much
   praise I have heard,
Most opinion 's the same, with the
   difference of word,
Some get a good name by the voice
   of the crowd,   35
Whilst to poor humble merit small
   praise is allowed,
As in parliament votes, so in pic-
   tures a name,
Oft determines a fate at the altar
   of fame.—
So on Friday this City's gay vortex
   you quit,
And no longer with Doctors and
   Johnny cats sit—   40

Now your parcel 's arrived ——
   [Bysshe's] letter shall go,
I hope all your joy mayn't be
   turned into woe,
Experience will tell you that pleas-
   ure is vain,
When it promises sunshine how
   often comes rain.
So when to fond hope every bless-
   ing is nigh,   45
How oft when we smile it is
   checked with a sigh,
When Hope, gay deceiver, in pleas-
   ure is dressed,
How oft comes a stroke that may
   rob us of rest.
When we think ourselves safe, and
   the goal near at hand,
Like a vessel just landing, we're
   wrecked near the strand, 50
And though memory forever the
   sharp pang must feel,
'Tis our duty to bear, and our hardship to steel—
May misfortunes dear Girl, ne'er
   thy happiness cloy,
May the days glide in peace, love,
   comfort and joy,
May thy tears with soft pity for
   other woes flow,   55
Woes, which thy tender heart
   never may know,
For hardships our own, God has
   taught us to bear,
Though sympathy's soul to a friend
   drops a tear.
Oh dear! what sentimental stuff
   have I written,
Only fit to tear up and play with a
   kitten.   60
What sober reflections in the midst
   of this letter!
Jocularity sure would have suited
   much better;
But there are exceptions to all common rules,

For this is a truth by all boys
learned at schools.
Now adieu my dear —— [Hattie]
I'm sure I must tire,   65
For if I do, you may throw it into
the fire,
So accept the best love of your cou-
sin and friend,
Which brings this nonsensical
rhyme to an end.
April 30, 1810.

III. SONG

COLD, cold is the blast when December is howling,
Cold are the damps on a dying
man's brow,—
Stern are the seas when the wild
waves are rolling,
And sad is the grave where a
loved one lies low;
But colder is scorn from the being
who loved thee,   5
More stern is the sneer from the
friend who has proved thee,
More sad are the tears when their
sorrows have moved thee,
Which mixed with groans, anguish and wild madness
flow—
And ah! poor —— has felt all this
horror,
Full long the fallen victim contended with fate: 10
'Till a destitute outcast abandoned
to sorrow,
She sought her babe's food at her
ruiner's gate—
Another had charmed the remorseless betrayer,
He turned laughing aside from her
moans and her prayer,
She said nothing, but wringing the
wet from her hair,   15
Crossed the dark mountain side,
though the hour it was late.
'Twas on the wild height of the
dark Penmanmawr,

That the form of the wasted ——
reclined;
She shrieked to the ravens that
croaked from afar,
And she sighed to the gusts of
the wild sweeping wind.—
'I call not yon rocks where the
thunder peals rattle,   21
I call not yon clouds where the
elements battle,
But thee, cruel —— I call thee
unkind!'—

Then she wreathed in her hair the
wild flowers of the moun-
tain,
And deliriously laughing, a garland entwined,   25
She bedewed it with tears, then she
hung o'er the fountain,
And leaving it, cast it a prey
to the wind.
'Ah! go,' she exclaimed, 'when the
tempest is yelling,
'Tis unkind to be cast on the sea
that is swelling,
But I left, a pitiless outcast, my
dwelling,   30
My garments are torn, so they
say is my mind—'
Not long lived ——, but over her
grave
Waved the desolate form of a
storm-blasted yew,
Around it no demons or ghosts dare
to rave,
But spirits of peace steep her
slumbers in dew.   35
Then stay thy swift steps mid the
dark mountain heather,
Though chill blow the wind and
severe is the weather,
For perfidy, traveller! cannot be-
reave her,
Of the tears, to the tombs of the
innocent due.—
JULY, 1810.

IV. SONG

Come [Harriet]! sweet is the hour,
 Soft Zephyrs breathe gently
  around,
The anemone's night-boding flower,
 Has sunk its pale head on the
  ground.

'Tis thus the world's keenness hath
  torn.   5
 Some mild heart that expands
  to its blast,
'Tis thus that the wretched forlorn,
 Sinks poor and neglected at
  last.—

The world with its keenness and
  woe,
 Has no charms or attraction for
  me,   10
Its unkindness with grief has laid
  low,
 The heart which is faithful to
  thee.

The high trees that wave past the
  moon,
 As I walk in their umbrage with
  you,
All declare I must part with you
  soon,   15
 All bid you a tender adieu!—

Then [Harriet]! dearest farewell,
 You and I love, may ne'er meet
  again;
These woods and these meadows
  can tell
 How soft and how sweet was the
  strain.—   20
      April, 1810.

V. SONG

DESPAIR

Ask not the pallid stranger's woe,
 With beating heart and throb-
  bing breast,
Whose step is faltering, weak, and
  slow,
 As though the body needed
  rest.—
Whose 'wildered eye no object
  meets,   5
 Nor cares to ken a friendly
  glance,
With silent grief his bosom beats,—
 Now fixed, as in a deathlike
  trance.

Who looks around with fearful eye,
 And shuns all converse with
  mankind,   10
As though some one his griefs
  might spy,
 And soothe them with a kindred
  mind.

A friend or foe to him the same,
 He looks on each with equal eye;
The difference lies but in the
  name,   15
 To none for comfort can he fly.—
'Twas deep despair, and sorrow's
  trace,
 To him too keenly given,
Whose memory, time could not ef-
  face—
 His peace was lodged in
  Heaven.—   20

He looks on all this world be-
  stows,
 The pride and pomp of power,
As trifles best for pageant shows
 Which vanish in an hour.
When torn is dear affection's tie,
 Sinks the soft heart full low; 26
It leaves without a parting sigh,
 All that these realms bestow.
      June, 1810.

VI. SONG

SORROW

To me this world's a dreary blank,
 All hopes in life are gone and
  fled,

My high strung energies are sank,
 And all my blissful hopes lie
 dead.—

The world once smiling to my
 view,   5
 Showed scenes of endless bliss
 and joy;
The world I then but little knew,
 Ah! little knew how pleasures
 cloy;

All then was jocund, all was gay,
 No thought beyond the present
 hour,   10
I danced in pleasure's fading ray,
 Fading alas! as drooping flower.

Nor do the heedless in the throng,
 One thought beyond the morrow
 give[,]
They court the feast, the dance,
 the song,   15
 Nor think how short their time
 to live.

The heart that bears deep sorrow's
 trace,
 What earthly comfort can console,
It drags a dull and lengthened
 pace,
 'Till friendly death its woes en-
 roll.—   20

The sunken cheek, the humid eyes,
 E'en better than the tongue can
 tell;
In whose sad breast deep sorrow
 lies,
 Where memory's rankling traces
 dwell.—

The rising tear, the stifled sigh, 25
 A mind but ill at ease display,
Like blackening clouds in stormy
 sky,
 Where fiercely vivid lightnings
 play.

Thus when souls' energy is dead,
 When sorrow dims each earthly
 view,   30
When every fairy hope is fled,
 We bid ungrateful world adieu.
                          AUGUST, 1810.

VII. SONG

HOPE

AND said I that all hope was fled,
 That sorrow and despair were
 mine,
That each enthusiast wish was
 dead,
 Had sank beneath pale Misery's
 shrine.—

Seest thou the sunbeam's yellow
 glow,   5
 That robes with liquid streams
 of light;
Yon distant Mountain's craggy
 brow.
 And shows the rocks so fair,—
 so bright ——

Tis thus sweet expectation's ray,
 In softer view shows distant
 hours,   10
And portrays each succeeding day,
 As dressed in fairer, brighter
 flowers,—

The vermeil tinted flowers that
 blossom;
 Are frozen but to bud anew,
Then sweet deceiver calm my
 bosom,   15
 Although thy visions be not
 true,—

Yet true they are,—and I'll believe,
 Thy whisperings soft of love and
 peace,
God never made thee to deceive,
 'Tis sin that bade thy empire
 cease.   20

Yet though despair my life should
    gloom,
Though horror should around me
    close,
With those I love, beyond the
    tomb,
Hope shows a balm for all my
    woes.

AUGUST, 1810.

VIII. SONG

TRANSLATED FROM THE ITALIAN

OH! what is the gain of restless
    care,
And what is ambitious treasure?
And what are the joys that the
    modish share,
In their sickly haunts of pleas-
    sure?

My husband's repast with delight
    I spread,   5
What though 'tis but rustic fare,
May each guardian angel protect
    his shed,
May contentment and quiet be
    there.

And may I support my husband's
    years,
May I soothe his dying pain, 10
And then may I dry my fast fall-
    ing tears,
And meet him in Heaven again.

JULY, 1810.

IX. SONG

TRANSLATED FROM THE GERMAN

AH! grasp the dire dagger and
    couch the fell spear,
If vengeance and death to thy
    bosom be dear,
The dastard shall perish, death's
    torment shall prove,
For fate and revenge are decreed
    from above.

Ah! where is the hero, whose
    nerves strung by youth,   5
Will defend the firm cause of jus-
    tice and truth;
With insatiate desire whose bosom
    shall swell,
To give up the oppressor to judge-
    ment and Hell—

For him shall the fair one twine
    chaplets of bays,
To him shall each warrior give
    merited praise,   10
And triumphant returned from the
    clangour of arms,
He shall find his reward in his
    loved maiden's charms.

In ecstatic confusion the warrior
    shall sip,
The kisses that glow on his love's
    dewy lip,
And mutual, eternal, embraces shall
    prove,   15
The rewards of the brave are the
    transports of love.

OCTOBER, 1809.

X

THE IRISHMAN'S SONG

THE stars may dissolve, and the
    fountain of light
May sink into ne'er ending chaos
    and night,
Our mansions must fall, and earth
    vanish away,
But thy courage O Erin! may
    never decay.

See! the wide wasting ruin extends
    all around,   5
Our ancestors' dwellings lie sunk
    on the ground,
Our foes ride in triumph through-
    out our domains,
And our mightiest heroes lie
    stretched on the plains.

Ah! dead is the harp which was
    wont to give pleasure,
Ah! sunk is our sweet country's
    rapturous measure,   10
But the war note is waked, and the
    clangour of spears,
The dread yell of Sloghan yet
    sounds in our ears.

Ah! where are the heroes! tri-
    umphant in death,
Convulsed they recline on the
    blood sprinkled heath,
Or the yelling ghosts ride on the
    blast that sweeps by,   15
And 'my countrymen! vengeance!'
    incessantly cry.
            OCTOBER, 1809.

XI. SONG

FIERCE roars the midnight
    storm
O'er the wild mountain,
Dark clouds the night deform,
Swift rolls the fountain—

See! o'er yon rocky height,   5
    Dim mists are flying—
See by the moon's pale light,
    Poor Laura's dying!

Shame and remorse shall howl,
    By her false pillow—   10
Fiercer than storms that roll,
    O'er the white billow;

No hand her eyes to close,
    When life is flying,
But she will find repose,   15
    For Laura's dying!

Then will I seek my love,
    Then will I cheer her,
Then my esteem will prove.
    When no friend is near her. 20

On her grave I will lie,
    When life is parted,
On her grave I will die,
    For the false hearted.
            DECEMBER, 1809.

XII. SONG

To ———— [HARRIET]

AH! sweet is the moonbeam that
    sleeps on yon fountain,
And sweet the mild rush of the
    soft-sighing breeze,
And sweet is the glimpse of yon
    dimly-seen mountain,
'Neath the verdant arcades of
    yon shadowy trees.

But sweeter than all was thy tone
    of affection,   5
Which scarce seemed to break on
    the stillness of eve,
Though the time it is past!—yet
    the dear recollection,
For aye in the heart of thy
    [Percy] must live.

Yet he hears thy dear voice in the
    summer winds sighing,
Mild accents of happiness lisp
    in his ear,   10
When the hope-wingèd moments
    athwart him are flying,
And he thinks of the friend to
    his bosom so dear.—

And thou dearest friend in his
    bosom for ever
Must reign unalloyed by the fast
    rolling year,
He loves thee, and dearest one
    never, Oh! never   15
Canst thou cease to be loved by
    a heart so sincere.
            AUGUST, 1810.

XIII. SONG

To ———— [HARRIET]

STERN, stern is the voice of fate's
    fearful command,
When accents of horror it
    breathes in our ear,
Or compels us for aye bid adieu to
    the land.

Where exists that loved friend to
    our bosom so dear,
'Tis sterner than death o'er the
    shuddering wretch bending,
And in skeleton grasp his fell
    sceptre extending,   6
Like the heart-stricken deer to that
    loved covert wending,
Which never again to his eyes
    may appear—
And ah! he may envy the heart-
    stricken quarry,
Who bids to the friend of affec-
    tion farewell,   10
He may envy the bosom so bleed-
    ing and gory,
He may envy the sound of the
    drear passing knell,
Not so deep is his grief on his
    death couch reposing,
When on the last vision his dim
    eyes are closing!
As the outcast whose love-raptured
    senses are losing,   15
The last tones of thy voice on the
    wild breeze that swell!

Those tones were so soft, and so
    sad, that ah! never,
Can the sound cease to vibrate
    on Memory's ear,
In the stern wreck of Nature for
    ever and ever,
The remembrance must live of a
    friend so sincere.   20
            AUGUST, 1810.

XIV

SAINT EDMOND'S EVE

OH! did you observe the Black
    Canon pass,
    And did you observe his frown?
He goeth to say the midnight mass,
    In holy St. Edmond's town.

He goeth to sing the burial chaunt,
    And to lay the wandering sprite,

Whose shadowy, restless form doth
    haunt,   7
The Abbey's drear aisle this
    night.

It saith it will not its wailing cease,
    'Till that holy man come near, 10
'Till he pour o'er its grave the
    prayer of peace,
And sprinkle the hallowed tear.

The Canon's horse is stout and
    strong
    The road is plain and fair,
But the Canon slowly wends along,
    And his brow is gloomed with
    care.   16

Who is it thus late at the Abbey-
    gate?
    Sullen echoes the portal bell,
It sounds like the whispering voice
    of fate,
    It sounds like a funeral knell. 20

The Canon his faltering knee thrice
    bowed,
    And his frame was convulsed
    with fear,
When a voice was heard distinct
    and loud,
    'Prepare! for thy hour is near.'

He crosses his breast, he mutters a
    prayer,   25
    To Heaven he lifts his eye,
He heeds not the Abbot's gazing
    stare,
    Nor the dark Monks who mur-
    mured by.

Bare-headed he worships the sculp-
    tured saints
    That frown on the sacred walls,
His face it grows pale,—he trem-
    bles, he faints,   31
    At the Abbot's feet he falls.

And straight the father's robe he
    kissed,

Who cried, 'Grace dwells with
thee,
The spirit will fade like the morning mist,   35
At your benedicite.

'Now haste within! the board is
spread,
Keen blows the air, and cold,
The spectre sleeps in its earthy bed,
'Till St. Edmond's bell hath
tolled,—   40

'Yet rest your wearied limbs to-
night,
You've journeyed many a mile,
To-morrow lay the wailing sprite,
That shrieks in the moonlight
aisle.

'Oh! faint are my limbs and my
bosom is cold,   45
Yet to-night must the sprite be
laid,
Yet to-night when the hour of horror's told,
Must I meet the wandering
shade.

'Nor food, nor rest may now de-
lay,—
For hark! the echoing pile,   50
A bell loud shakes!—Oh haste
away,
O lead to the haunted aisle.'

The torches slowly move before,
The cross is raised on high,
A smile of peace the Canon wore, 55
But horror dimmed his eye—

And now they climb the footworn
stair,
The chapel gates unclose,
Now each breathed low a fervent
prayer,   59
And fear each bosom froze——

Now paused awhile the doubtful
band

And viewed the solemn scene,—
Full dark the clustered columns
stand,
The moon gleams pale be-
tween—

'Say father, say, what cloisters'
gloom   65
Conceals the unquiet shade,
Within what dark unhallowed
tomb,
The corse unblessed was laid.'

'Through yonder drear aisle alone
it walks,
And murmurs a mournful plaint,
Of thee! Black Canon, it wildly
talks,   71
And call on thy patron saint—

'The pilgrim this night with wondering eyes,
As he prayed at St. Edmond's
shrine,
From a black marble tomb hath
seen it rise,   75
And under yon arch recline.'—

'Oh! say upon that black marble
tomb,
What memorial sad appears.'—
'Undistinguished it lies in the chan-
cel's gloom,
No memorial sad it bears'—   80

The Canon his paternoster reads,
His rosary hung by his side,
Now swift to the chancel doors he
leads,
And untouched they open wide,

Resistless, strange sounds his steps
impel,   85
To approach to the black marble
tomb,
'Oh! enter, Black Canon,' a whisper fell,
'Oh! enter, thy hour is come.'

He paused, told his beads, and the
threshold passed,

Oh! horror, the chancel doors
  close,   90
A loud yell was borne on the rising
  blast,
. And a deep, dying groan arose.

The Monks in amazement shud-
  dering stand,
  They burst through the chan-
    cel's gloom,
From St. Edmond's shrine, lo! a
  skeleton's hand,   95
Points to the black marble tomb.

Lo! deeply engraved, an inscription
  blood red,
  In characters fresh and clear—
'The guilty Black Canon of Elm-
  ham's dead,   99
  And his wife lies buried here!'

In Elmham's tower he wedded a
  Nun,
  To St. Edmond's his bride he
    bore,
On this eve her noviciate here was
  begun,
  And a Monk's gray weeds she
    wore;—

O! deep was her conscience dyed
  with guilt,   105
  Remorse she full oft revealed,
Her blood by the ruthless Black
  Canon was spilt,
  And in death her lips he sealed;

Her spirit to penance this night was
  doomed,
  'Till the Canon atoned the deed,
Here together they now shall rest
  entombed,   111
  'Till their bodies from dust are
    freed—

Hark! a loud peal of thunder
  shakes the roof,
  Round the altar bright light-
    nings play,
Speechless with horror the Monks
  stand aloof,   115

And the storm dies sudden
  away—

The inscription was gone! a cross
  on the ground,
  And a rosary shone through the
    gloom,
But never again was the Canon
  there found,
  Or the Ghost on the black mar-
    ble tomb.   120

XV. REVENGE

'Ah! quit me not yet, for the wind
  whistles shrill,
Its blast wanders mournfully over
  the hill,
The thunder's wild voice rattles
  madly above,
You will not then, cannot then,
  leave me my love.—'

I must dearest Agnes, the night is
  far gone—   5
I must wander this evening to
  Strasburg alone,
I must seek the drear tomb of my
  ancestors' bones,
And must dig their remains from
  beneath the cold stones.

'For the spirit of Conrad there
  meets me this night,
And we quit not the tomb 'till dawn
  of the light,   10
And Conrad's been dead just a
  month and a day!
So farewell dearest Agnes for I
  must away,—

'He bid me bring with me what
  most I held dear,
Or a month from that time should
  I lie on my bier,
And I'd sooner resign this false
  fluttering breath,   15
Than my Agnes should dread either
  danger or death,

'And I love you to madness my
    Agnes I love,
My constant affection this night
    will I prove,
This night will I go to the sepul-
    chre's jaw,
Alone will I glut its all conquering
    maw'—   20

'No! no loved Adolphus thy Agnes
    will share,
In the tomb all the dangers that
    wait for you there,
I fear not the spirit,—I fear not the
    grave,
My dearest Adolphus I'd perish to
    save'—

'Nay seek not to say that thy love
    shall not go,   25
But spare me those ages of horror
    and woe,
For I swear to thee here that I'll
    perish ere day,
If you go unattended by Agnes
    away'—

The night it was bleak the fierce
    storm raged around,
The lightning's blue fire-light
    flashed on the ground, 30
Strange forms seemed to flit,—and
    howl tidings of fate,
As Agnes advanced to the sepul-
    chre gate.—

The youth struck the portal,—the
    echoing sound
Was fearfully rolled midst the
    tombstones around,
The blue lightning gleamed o'er the
    dark chapel spire,   35
And tinged were the storm clouds
    with sulphurous fire.

Still they gazed on the tombstone
    where Conrad reclined,
Yet they shrank at the cold chill-
    ing blast of the wind,

When a strange silver brilliance
    pervaded the scene,
And a figure advanced—tall in
    form—fierce in mien.   40

A mantle encircled his shadowy
    form,
As light as a gossamer borne on
    the storm,
Celestial terror sat throned in his
    gaze,
Like the midnight pestiferous me-
    teor's blaze.—

Spirit.

Thy father, Adolphus! was false,
    false as hell,   45
And Conrad has cause to remember
    it well,
He ruined my Mother, despised me
    his son,
I quitted the world ere my venge-
    ance was done.

I was nearly expiring—'twas close
    of the day,—
A demon advanced to the bed
    where I lay,   50
He gave me the power from whence
    I was hurled,
To return to revenge, to return to
    the world,—

Now Adolphus I'll seize thy best
    loved in my arms,
I'll drag her to Hades all blooming
    in charms,
On the black whirlwind's thunder-
    ing pinion I'll ride,   55
And fierce yelling fiends shall exult
    o'er thy bride—

He spoke, and extending his
    ghastly arms wide,
Majestic advanced with a swift
    noiseless stride,
He clasped the fair Agnes—he
    raised her on high,

And cleaving the roof sped his way
   to the sky—   60

All was now silent,—and over the
   tomb,
Thicker, deeper, was swiftly extended a gloom,
Adolphus in horror sank down on
   the stone,
And his fleeting soul fled with a
   harrowing groan.
            DECEMBER, 1809.

XVI. GHASTA

OR, THE AVENGING DEMON!!!

*The idea of the following tale
was taken from a few unconnected
German Stanzas.—The principal
Character is evidently the Wandering Jew, and although not mentioned by name, the burning Cross
on his forehead undoubtedly alludes to that superstition, so preva-
lent in the part of Germany called
the Black Forest, where this scene
is supposed to lie.*

HARK! the owlet flaps her wing,
   In the pathless dell beneath,
Hark! night ravens loudly sing,
   Tidings of despair and death.—

Horror covers all the sky,   5
   Clouds of darkness blot the
      moon,
Prepare! for mortal thou must die,
   Prepare to yield thy soul up
      soon—

Fierce the tempest raves around,
   Fierce the volleyed lightnings
      fly,   10
Crashing thunder shakes the
      ground,
   Fire and tumult fill the sky.—

Hark! the tolling village bell,
   Tells the hour of midnight come,
Now can blast the powers of Hell,

Fiend-like goblins now can
   roam—   16

See! his crest all stained with rain,
   A warrior hastening speeds his
      way,
He starts, looks round him, starts
      again,
   And sighs for the approach of
      day.   20

See! his frantic steed he reins,
   See! he lifts his hands on high,
Implores a respite to his pains,
   From the powers of the sky.—

He seeks an Inn, for faint from
      toil,   25
   Fatigue had bent his lofty form,
To rest his wearied limbs awhile,
   Fatigued with wandering and the
      storm.

   . . . .

Slow the door is opened wide—
   With trackless tread a stranger
      came,   30
His form Majestic, slow his stride,
   He sate, nor spake,—nor told his
      name—

Terror blanched the warrior's
      cheek,
   Cold sweat from his forehead
      ran,
In vain his tongue essayed to
      speak,—   35
   At last the stranger thus be-
      gan:

'Mortal! thou that saw'st the sprite,
   Tell me what I wish to know,
Or come with me before 'tis light,
   Where cypress trees and man-
      drakes grow.   40

'Fierce the avenging Demon's ire,
   Fiercer than the wintry blast,
Fiercer than the lightning's fire,
   When the hour of twilight's
      past'—

The warrior raised his sunken
   eye,   45
It met the stranger's sullen scowl,
'Mortal! Mortal! thou must die,'
   In burning letters chilled his soul.

Warrior.

Stranger! whoso'er you are,
   I feel impelled my tale to tell— 50
Horrors stranger shalt thou hear,
   Horrors drear as those of Hell.

O'er my Castle silence reigned,
   Late the night and drear the
      hour,
When on the terrace I observed, 55
   A fleeting shadowy mist to
      lower.—

Light the cloud as summer fog,
   Which transient shuns the morn-
      ing beam;
Fleeting as the cloud on bog,
   That hangs or on the mountain
      stream.—   60

Horror seized my shuddering brain,
   Horror dimmed my starting eye,
In vain I tried to speak,—In vain
   My limbs essayed the spot to
      fly—

At last the thin and shadowy
   form,   65
   With noiseless, trackless foot-
      steps came,—
Its light robe floated on the storm,
   Its head was bound with lambent
      flame.

In chilling voice drear as the breeze
   Which sweeps along th' autum-
      nal ground,   70
Which wanders through the leafless
      trees,
   Or the mandrake's groan which
      floats around.

'Thou art mine and I am thine,
   'Till the sinking of the world,

I am thine and thou art mine,   75
   'Till in ruin death is hurled——

'Strong the power and dire the fate,
   Which drags me from the depths
      of Hell,
Breaks the tomb's eternal gate,
   Where fiendish shapes and dead
      men yell,   80

'Haply I might ne'er have shrank
   From flames that rack the guilty
      dead,
Haply I might ne'er have sank
   On pleasure's flow'ry, thorny
      bed—

—'But stay! no more I dare dis-
      close,   85
   Of the tale I wish to tell,
On Earth relentless were my woes,
   But fiercer are my pangs in
      Hell—

'Now I claim thee as my love,
   Lay aside all chilling fear,   90
My affection will I prove
   Where sheeted ghosts and spec-
      tres are!

'For thou art mine, and I am thine,
   'Till the dreaded judgement day,
I am thine, and thou art mine— 95
   Night is past— I must away.'

Still I gazed, and still the form
   Pressed upon my aching sight,
Still I braved the howling storm,
   When the ghost dissolved in
      night.—

Restless, sleepless fled the night, 101
   Sleepless as a sick man's bed,
When he sighs for morning light,
   When he turns his aching
      head,—

Slow and painful passed the day,105
   Melancholy seized my brain,
Lingering fled the hours away,
   Lingering to a wretch in pain.—

At last came night, ah! horrid hour,
　Ah! chilling time that wakes the
　　dead,　　　　　　　　　110
When demons ride the clouds that
　　lower,
　—The phantom sat upon my
　　bed.

In hollow voice, low as the sound
　Which in some charnel makes its
　　moan,
What floats along the burying
　　ground,　　　　　　　　115
　The phantom claimed me as her
　　own.

Her chilling finger on my head,
　With coldest touch congealed my
　　soul—
Cold as the finger of the dead,
　Or damps which round a tomb-
　　stone roll—　　　　　　120

Months are passed in lingering
　　round,
　Every night the spectre comes,
With thrilling step it shakes the
　　ground,
　With thrilling step it round me
　　roams—

Stranger! I have told to thee,　125
　All the tale I have to tell—
Stranger! canst thou tell to me,
　How to 'scape the powers of
　　Hell?—

Stranger.

Warrior! I can ease thy woes,
　Wilt thou, wilt thou, come with
　　me—　　　　　　　　130
Warrior! I can all disclose,
　Follow, follow, follow me.

Yet the tempest's duskiest wing,
　Its mantle stretches o'er the sky,
Yet the midnight ravens sing,　135
　'Mortal! Mortal! thou must die.'

At last they saw a river clear,
　That crossed the heathy path
　　they trod,
The Stranger's look was wild and
　　drear,
　The firm Earth shook beneath
　　his nod—　　　　　　　140

He raised a wand above his head,
　He traced a circle on the plain,
In a wild verse he called the dead,
　The dead with silent footsteps
　　came.

A burning brilliance on his head, 145
　Flaming filled the stormy air,
In a wild verse he called the dead,
　The dead in motley crowd were
　　there.—

'Ghasta! Ghasta! come along,
　Bring thy fiendish crowd with
　　thee,
Quickly raise th' avenging Song, 151
　Ghasta! Ghasta! come to me.'

Horrid shapes in mantles gray,
　Flit athwart the stormy night,
'Ghasta! Ghasta! come away,　155
　Come away before 'tis light.'

See! the sheeted Ghost they bring,
　Yelling dreadful o'er the heath,
Hark! the deadly verse they sing,
　Tidings of despair and death! 160

The yelling Ghost before him
　　stands,
　See! she rolls her eyes around,
Now she lifts her bony hands,
　Now her footsteps shake the
　　ground.

Stranger.

Phantom of Theresa say,　　165
　Why to earth again you came,
Quickly speak, I must away!
　Or you must bleach for aye in
　　flame,—

Phantom.

Mighty one I know thee now,
    Mightiest power of the sky,   170
Know thee by thy flaming brow,
    Know thee by thy sparkling eye.

That fire is scorching! Oh! I came,
    From the caverned depth of Hell,
My fleeting false Rodolph to claim,
    Mighty one! I know thee
        well.—   176

Stranger.

Ghasta! seize yon wandering sprite,
    Drag her to the depth beneath,
Take her swift, before 'tis light,
    Take her to the cells of death! 180

Thou that heardst the trackless
        dead,
    In the mouldering tomb must lie,
Mortal! look upon my head,
    Mortal! Mortal! thou must die.

Of glowing flame a cross was there
    Which threw a light around his
        form,   186
Whilst his lank and raven hair,
    Floated wild upon the storm.—

The warrior upwards turned his
        eyes,
    Gazed upon the cross of fire, 190
There sat horror and surprise,
    There sat God's eternal ire.—

A shivering through the Warrior
        flew,
    Colder than the nightly blast,
Colder than the evening dew,   195
    When the hour of twilight 's
        past.—

Thunder shakes th' expansive sky,
    Shakes the bosom of the heath,
'Mortal! Mortal! thou must die'—
    The warrior sank convulsed in
        death.   200
                    JANUARY, 1810.

XVII. FRAGMENT,

OR THE TRIUMPH OF
CONSCIENCE

'TWAS dead of the night when I
    sate in my dwelling,
One glimmering lamp was ex-
    piring and low,—
Around the dark tide of the tem-
    pest was swelling,
Along the wild mountains night-
    ravens were yelling,
    They bodingly presaged destruc-
        tion and woe!   5

'Twas then that I started, the wild
    storm was howling,
Nought was seen, save the light-
    ning that danced on the sky,
Above me the crash of the thunder
    was rolling,
And low, chilling murmurs the
    blast wafted by.—

My heart sank within me, unheeded
    the jar   10
Of the battling clouds on the
    mountain-tops broke,
Unheeded the thunder-peal crashed
    in mine ear,
This heart hard as iron was stran-
    ger to fear,
    But conscience in low noiseless
        whispering spoke.

'Twas then that her form on the
    whirlwind uprearing,   15
The dark ghost of the murdered
    Victoria strode,
Her right hand a blood reeking dag-
    ger was bearing,
    She swiftly advanced to my lone-
        some abode.—
I wildly then called on the tempest
    to bear me!

.   .   .   .

.   .   .   .

POEMS FROM ST. IRVYNE, OR, THE ROSICRUCIAN

I.—VICTORIA

[Another version of *The Triumph of Conscience* immediately preceding.]

I

'TWAS dead of the night, when I
    sat in my dwelling;
One glimmering lamp was expir-
    ing and low;
Around, the dark tide of the tem-
    pest was swelling,
Along the wild mountains night-
    ravens were yelling,—
They bodingly presaged destruc-
    tion and woe.   5

II

'Twas then that I started!—the
    wild storm was howling,
Nought was seen, save the light-
    ning, which danced in the
    sky;
Above me, the crash of the thunder
    was rolling,
And low, chilling murmurs, the
    blast wafted by.

III

My heart sank within me—un-
    heeded the war   10
Of the battling clouds, on the
    mountain-tops, broke;—
Unheeded the thunder-peal crashed
    in mine ear—
This heart, hard as iron, is stranger
    to fear;
But conscience in low, noiseless
    whispering spoke.

IV

'Twas then that her form on the
    whirlwind upholding,   15

The ghost of the murdered Vic-
    toria strode;
In her right hand, a shadowy
    shroud she was holding,
She swiftly advanced to my lone-
    some abode.

V

I wildly then called on the tempest
    to bear me—
· · · · · ·

II.—'ON THE DARK HEIGHT OF JURA'

I

GHOSTS of the dead! have I not
    heard your yelling
Rise on the night-rolling breath
    of the blast,
When o'er the dark aether the tem-
    pest is swelling,
And on eddying whirlwind the
    thunder-peal passed?

II

For oft have I stood on the dark
    height of Jura,   5
Which frowns on the valley that
    opens beneath;
Oft have I braved the chill night-
    tempest's fury,
Whilst around me, I thought,
    echoed murmurs of death.

III

And now, whilst the winds of the
    mountain are howling,
O father! thy voice seems to
    strike on mine ear;   10
In air whilst the tide of the night-
    storm is rolling,
It breaks on the pause of the ele-
    ments' jar.

IV

On the wing of the whirlwind which
    roars o'er the mountain
Perhaps rides the ghost of my
    sire who is dead:
On the mist of the tempest which
    hangs o'er the fountain,   15
Whilst a wreath of dark vapour
    encircles his head.

III.—Sister Rosa: A Ballad

I

The death-bell beats!—
    The mountain repeats
The echoing sound of the knell;
    And the dark Monk now
Wraps the cowl round his brow, 5
As he sits in his lonely cell.

II

And the cold hand of death
Chills his shuddering breath,
As he lists to the fearful lay
    Which the ghosts of the sky,   10
    As they sweep wildly by,
Sing to departed day.
    And they sing of the hour
    When the stern fates had power
To resolve Rosa's form to its
    clay.   15

III

But that hour is past;
And that hour was the last
Of peace to the dark Monk's brain.
    Bitter tears, from his eyes,
    gushed silent and fast;
And he strove to suppress them in
    vain.

IV

Then his fair cross of gold he
    dashed on the floor,   21
When the death-knell struck on his
    ear.—
'Delight is in store

For her evermore;
But for me is fate, horror, and
    fear.'   25

V

Then his eyes wildly rolled,
When the death-bell tolled,
And he raged in terrific woe.
    And he stamped on the ground,—
    But when ceased the sound,   30
Tears again began to flow.

VI

And the ice of despair
Chilled the wild throb of care,
And he sate in mute agony still;
    Till the night-stars shone
        through the cloudless air, 35
And the pale moonbeam slept on
    the hill.

VII

Then he knelt in his cell:—
And the horrors of hell
Were delights to his agonized pain,
And he prayed to God to dissolve
    the spell,   40
Which else must for ever remain.

VIII

And in fervent pray'r he knelt on
    the ground,
Till the abbey bell struck One:
His feverish blood ran chill at the
    sound:
A voice hollow and horrible mur-
    mured around—   45
'The term of thy penance is
    done!'

IX

Grew dark the night;
The moonbeam bright
Waxed faint on the mountain high;
    And, from the black hill,   50
    Went a voice cold and still,—
'Monk! thou art free to die.'

X

Then he rose on his feet,
And his heart loud did beat,
And his limbs they were palsied
　　with dread;　　　　　　　55
Whilst the grave's clammy dew
O'er his pale forehead grew;
And he shuddered to sleep with the
　　dead.

XI

And the wild midnight storm
Raved around his tall form,　60
As he sought the chapel's gloom:
And the sunk grass did sigh
To the wind, bleak and high,
As he searched for the new-made
　　tomb.

XII

And forms, dark and high,　　65
Seemed around him to fly,
And mingle their yells with the
　　blast:
And on the dark wall
Half-seen shadows did fall,
As enhorrored he onward passed. 70

XIII

And the storm-fiends wild rave
O'er the new-made grave,
And dread shadows linger around.
The Monk called on God his soul
　　to save,
And, in horror, sank on the
　　ground.　　　　　　　75

XIV

Then despair nerved his arm
To dispel the charm,
And he burst Rosa's coffin asunder.
And the fierce storm did swell
More terrific and fell,　　　80
And louder pealed the thunder.

XV

And laughed, in joy, the fiendish
　　throng,

Mixed with ghosts of the mould-
　　ering dead:
And their grisly wings, as they
　　floated along,
Whistled in murmurs dread.　85

XVI

And her skeleton form the dead
　　Nun reared
Which dripped with the chill dew
　　of hell.
In her half-eaten eyeballs two pale
　　flames appeared,
And triumphant their gleam on the
　　dark Monk glared,
As he stood within the cell.　90

XVII

And her lank hand lay on his shud-
　　dering brain;
But each power was nerved by
　　fear.—
'I never henceforth, may breathe
　　again;
Death now ends mine anguished
　　pain.—
The grave yawns,—we meet
　　there.'　　　　　　　95

XVIII

And her skeleton lungs did utter the
　　sound,
So deadly, so lone, and so fell,
That in long vibrations shuddered
　　the ground;
And as the stern notes floated
　　around,
A deep groan was answered from
　　hell.　　　　　　　100

IV.—ST. IRVYNE'S TOWER

I

How swiftly through Heaven's wide
　　expanse
Bright day's resplendent colours
　　fade!

How sweetly does the monbeam's
    glance
With silver tint St. Irvyne's
    glade!

II

No cloud along the spangled air, 5
    Is borne upon the evening
    breeze;
How solemn is the scene! how fair
    The moonbeams rest upon the
    trees!

III

Yon dark gray turret glimmers
    white,
Upon it sits the mournful owl;
Along the stillness of the night, 11
    Her melancholy shriekings roll.

IV

But not alone on Irvyne's tower,
    The silver moonbeam pours her
    ray;
It gleams upon the ivied bower, 15
    It dances in the cascade's spray.

V

'Ah! why do dark'ning shades con-
    ceal
    The hour, when man must cease
    to be?
Why may not human minds unveil
    The dim mists of futurity?   20

VI

'The keenness of the world hath
    torn
    The heart which opens to its
    blast;
Despised, neglected, and forlorn,
    Sinks the wretch in death at
    last.'

V.—BEREAVEMENT

I

How stern are the woes of the
    desolate mourner,

As he bends in still grief o'er
    the hallowèd bier,
As enanguished he turns from the
    laugh of the scorner,
And drops, to Perfection's re-
    membrance, a tear;
When floods of despair down his
    pale cheek are streaming, 5
When no blissful hope on his bosom
    is beaming,
Or, if lulled for awhile, soon he
    starts from his dreaming,
And finds torn the soft ties to
    affection so dear.

II

Ah! when shall day dawn on the
    night of the grave,
Or summer succeed to the winter
    of death?   10
Rest awhile, hapless victim, and
    Heaven will save
    The spirit, that faded away with
    the breath.
Eternity points in its amaranth
    bower,
Where no clouds of fate o'er the
    sweet prospect lower,
Unspeakable pleasure, of goodness
    the dower,   15
When woe fades away like the
    mist of the heath.

VI.—THE DROWNED LOVER

I

AH! faint are her limbs, and her
    footstep is weary,
    Yet far must the desolate wan-
    derer roam;
Though the tempest is stern, and
    the mountain is dreary,
    She must quit at deep midnight
    her pitiless home.
I see her swift foot dash the dew
    from the whortle,   5
As she rapidly hastes to the green
    grove of myrtle;

And I hear, as she wraps round
    her figure the kirtle,
'Stay thy boat on the lake,—
    dearest Henry, I come.'

II

High swelled in her bosom the
    throb of affection,
As lightly her form bounded over
    the lea,   10
And arose in her mind every dear
    recollection;
'I come, dearest Henry, and wait
    but for thee.'
How sad, when dear hope every
    sorrow is soothing,
When sympathy's swell the soft
    bosom is moving,
And the mind the mild joys of af-
    fection is proving,   15

Is the stern voice of fate that
    bids happiness flee!

III

Oh! dark lowered the clouds on
    that horrible eve,
And the moon dimly gleamed
    through the tempested air;
Oh! how could fond visions such
    softness deceive?
Oh! how could false hope rend
    a bosom so fair?   20
Thy love's pallid corse the wild
    surges are laving,
O'er his form the fierce swell of
    the tempest is raving;
But, fear not, parting spirit; thy
    goodness is saving,
In eternity's bowers, a seat for
    thee there.

POSTHUMOUS FRAGMENTS
OF MARGARET NICHOLSON

Being Poems found amongst the Papers of that noted Female who
attempted the life of the King in 1786. Edited by John Fitzvictor.

ADVERTISEMENT

THE energy and native genius of these Fragments must be the only
apology which the Editor can make for thus intruding them on the public
notice. The first I found with no title, and have left it so. It is intimately
connected with the dearest interests of universal happiness; and much
as we may deplore the fatal and enthusiastic tendency which the ideas
of this poor female had acquired, we cannot fail to pay the tribute of
unequivocal regret to the departed memory of genius, which, had it
been rightly organized, would have made that intellect, which has since
become the victim of frenzy and despair, a most brilliant ornament to
society.

In case the sale of these Fragments evinces that the public have any
curiosity to be presented with a more copious collection of my unfortunate Aunt's poems, I have other papers in my possession which shall,
in that case, be subjected to their notice. It may be supposed they
require much arrangement; but I send the following to the press in the
same state in which they came into my possession.   J. F.

WAR

AMBITION, power, and avarice, now
    have hurled
Death, fate, and ruin, on a bleed-
    ing world.
See! on yon heath what countless
    victims lie,
Hark! what loud shrieks ascend
    through yonder sky;
Tell then the cause, 'tis sure the
    avenger's rage   5
Has swept these myriads from
    life's crowded stage:
Hark to that groan, an anguished
    hero dies,
He shudders in death's latest
    agonies;
Yet does a fleeting hectic flush his
    cheek,
Yet does his parting breath essay
    to speak—   10
'Oh God! my wife, my children—
    Monarch thou
For whose support this fainting
    frame lies low;
For whose support in distant lands
    I bleed,
Let his friends' welfare be the war-
    rior's meed.
He hears me not—ah! no—kings
    cannot hear,   15
For passion's voice has dulled their
    listless ear.
To thee, then, mighty God, I lift
    my moan,
Thou wilt not scorn a suppliant's
    anguished groan.
Oh! now I die—but still is death's
    fierce pain—
God hears my prayer—we meet,
    we meet again,'   20
He spake, reclined him on death's
    bloody bed,
And with a parting groan his spirit
    fled.

Oppressors of mankind to *you*
    we owe
The baleful streams from whence
    these miseries flow;
For you how many a mother weeps
    her son,   25
Snatched from life's course ere
    half his race was run!
For you how many a widow drops
    a tear,
In silent anguish, on her husband's
    bier!
'Is it then Thine, Almighty
    Power,' she cries,
'Whence tears of endless sorrow
    dim these eyes?   30
Is this the system which Thy
    powerful sway,
Which else in shapeless chaos sleep-
    ing lay,
Formed and approved?—it cannot
    be—but oh!
Forgive me, Heaven, my brain is
    warped by woe.'
'Tis not—He never bade the war-
    note swell,   35
He never triumphed in the work of
    hell—
Monarchs of earth! thine is the
    baleful deed,
Thine are the crimes for which thy
    subjects bleed.
Ah! when will come the sacred
    fated time,
When man unsullied by his leaders'
    crime,   40
Despising wealth, ambition, pomp,
    and pride,
Will stretch him fearless by his foe-
    men's side?
Ah! when will come the time, when
    o'er the plain
No more shall death and desolation
    reign?
When will the sun smile on the
    bloodless field,   45

And the stern warrior's arm the
    sickle wield?
Not whilst some King, in cold am-
    bition's dreams,
Plans for the field of death his
    plodding schemes;
Not whilst for private pique the
    public fall,
And one frail mortal's mandate
    governs all.   50
Swelled with command and mad
    with dizzying sway;
Who sees unmoved his myriads
    fade away.
Careless who lives or dies—so that
    he gains
Some trivial point for which he
    took the pains.
What then are Kings?—I see the
    trembling crowd,   55
I hear their fulsome clamours
    echoed loud;
Their stern oppressor pleased ap-
    pears awhile,
But April's sunshine is a Mon-
    arch's smile—
Kings are but dust—the last event-
    ful day
Will level all and make them lose
    their sway;   60
Will dash the sceptre from the
    Monarch's hand,
And from the warrior's grasp wrest
    the ensanguined brand.
    Oh! Peace, soft Peace, art thou
    for ever gone,
Is thy fair form indeed for ever
    flown?
And love and concord hast thou
    swept away,   65
As if incongruous with thy parted
    sway?
Alas, I fear thou hast, for none
    appear.
Now o'er the palsied earth stalks
    giant Fear,

With War, and Woe, and Terror in
    his train;
List'ning he pauses on the embat-
    tled plain,   70
Then speeding swiftly o'er the en-
    sanguined heath,
Has left the frightful work to Hell
    and Death.
See! gory Ruin yokes his blood-
    stained car,
He scents the battle's carnage from
    afar;
Hell and Destruction mark his mad
    career,   75
He tracks the rapid step of hurry-
    ing Fear;
Whilst ruined towns and smoking
    cities tell,
That thy work, Monarch, is the
    work of Hell.
'It is thy work!' I hear a voice
    repeat,
Shakes the broad basis of thy
    blood-stained seat;   80
And at the orphan's sigh, the
    widow's moan,
Totters the fabric of thy guilt-
    stained throne—
'It is thy work, O Monarch;' now
    the sound
Fainter and fainter, yet is borne
    around,
Yet to enthusiast ears the murmurs
    tell   85
That Heaven, indignant at the
    work of Hell,
Will soon the cause, the hated cause
    remove,
Which tears from earth peace, in-
    nocence, and love.

FRAGMENT

SUPPOSED TO BE AN EPITHALAMIUM
OF FRANCIS RAVAILLAC AND
CHARLOTTE CORDAY

'TIS midnight now—athwart the
    murky air,

Dank lurid meteors shoot a livid
gleam;
From the dark storm-clouds flashes
a fearful glare,
It shows the bending oak, the
roaring stream.

I pondered on the woes of lost mankind, 5
I pondered on the ceaseless rage
of Kings;
My rapt soul dwelt upon the ties
that bind
The mazy volume of commingling things,
When fell and wild misrule to man
stern sorrow brings.

I heard a yell—it was not the knell,
When the blasts on the wild lake
sleep, 11
That floats on the pause of the summer gale's swell,
O'er the breast of the waveless
deep.

I thought it had been death's accents cold
That bade me recline on the
shore; 15
I laid mine hot head on the surge-
beaten mould,
And thought to breathe no more.

But a heavenly sleep
That did suddenly steep
In balm my bosom's pain, 20
Pervaded my soul,
And free from control,
Did mine intellect range
again.

Methought enthroned upon a silvery cloud,
Which floated mid a strange and
brilliant light; 25
My form upborne by viewless
aether rode,
And spurned the lessening realms
of earthly night.

What heavenly notes burst on my
ravished ears,
What beauteous spirits met my
dazzled eye!
Hark! louder swells the music of
the spheres, 30
More clear the forms of speechless bliss float by,
And heavenly gestures suit aethereal melody.

But fairer than the spirits of the air,
More graceful than the Sylph of
symmetry,
Than the enthusiast's fancied love
more fair, 35
Were the bright forms that swept
the azure sky.
Enthroned in roseate light, a heavenly band
Strewed flowers of bliss that
never fade away;
They welcome virtue to its native
land,
And songs of triumph greet the
joyous day 40
When endless bliss the woes of fleeting life repay.

Congenial minds will seek their
kindred soul,
E'en though the tide of time has
rolled between;
They mock weak matter's impotent
control,
And seek of endless life the eternal scene. 45
At death's vain summons *this* will
never die,
In Nature's chaos *this* will not
decay—
These are the bands which closely,
warmly, tie
Thy soul, O Charlotte, 'yond this
chain of clay,
To him who thine must be till time
shall fade away. 50

Yes, Francis! thine was the dear
    knife that tore
A tyrant's heart-strings from his
    guilty breast,
Thine was the daring at a tyrant's
    gore,
To smile in triumph, to contemn
    the rest;
And thine, loved glory of thy sex!
    to tear   55
From its base shrine a despot's
    haughty soul,
To laugh at sorrow in secure de-
    spair,
To mock, with smiles, life's lin-
    gering control,
And triumph mid the griefs that
    round thy fate did roll.

Yes! the fierce spirits of the aveng-
    ing deep   60
With endless tortures goad their
    guilty shades.
I see the lank and ghastly spectres
    sweep
Along the burning length of yon
    arcades;
And I see Satan stalk athwart the
    plain;
He hastes along the burning soil
    of Hell.   65
'Welcome, ye despots, to my dark
    domain,
With maddening joy mine an-
    guished senses swell
To welcome to their home the
    friends I love so well.'

Hark! to those notes, how sweet,
    how thrilling sweet
They echo to the sound of angels'
    feet.   70

Oh haste to the bower where roses
    are spread,
For there is prepared thy nuptial
    bed.

Oh haste—hark! hark!—they're
    gone.

Chorus of Spirits.

Stay, ye days of contentment and
    joy,   74
Whilst love every care is erasing,
Stay ye pleasures that never can
    cloy,
And ye spirits that can never
    cease pleasing.

And if any soft passion be near,
    Which mortals, frail mortals, can
    know,
Let love shed on the bosom a tear,
    And dissolve the chill ice-drop of
    woe.   81

SYMPHONY.

Francis.

'SOFT, my dearest angel, stay,
Oh! you suck my soul away;
Suck on, suck on, I glow, I glow!
Tides of maddening passion roll, 85
And streams of rapture drown my
    soul.
Now give me one more billing kiss,
Let your lips now repeat the bliss,
Endless kisses steal my breath,
No life can equal such a death.' 90

Charlotte.

'Oh! yes I will kiss thine eyes so
    fair,
And I will clasp thy form;
Serene is the breath of the balmy
    air,
But I think, love, thou feelest me
    warm
And I will recline on thy marble
    neck   95
Till I mingle into thee;
And I will kiss the rose on thy
    cheek,
And thou shalt give kisses to me.

For here is no morn to flout our de-
  light,
Oh! dost thou not joy at this? 100
And here we may lie an endless
  night,
  A long, long night of bliss.'

Spirits! when raptures move,
Say what it is to love,
When passion's tear stands on the
  cheek,   105
  When bursts the unconscious
    sigh;
And the tremulous lips dare not
  speak
What is told by the soul-felt eye.
But what is sweeter to revenge's ear
  Than the fell tyrant's last expir-
    ing yell?   110
Yes! than love's sweetest blisses 'tis
  more dear
  To drink the floatings of a des-
    pot's knell.
I wake—'tis done—'tis over.

.   .   .   .   .

DESPAIR

AND canst thou mock mine agony,
  thus calm
  In cloudless radiance, Queen of
    silver night?
Can you, ye flow'rets, spread your
  perfumed balm
  Mid pearly gems of dew that
    shine so bright?
And you wild winds, thus can you
  sleep so still   5
  Whilst throbs the tempest of my
    breast so high?
Can the fierce night-fiends rest on
  yonder hill,
  And, in the eternal mansions of
    the sky,
Can the directors of the storm in
  powerless silence lie?

Hark! I hear music on the zephyr's
  wing,   10

Louder it floats along the un-
  ruffled sky;
Some fairy sure has touched the
  viewless string—
  Now faint in distant air the mur-
    murs die.
Awhile it stills the tide of agony.
  Now—now it loftier swells—
    again stern woe   15
Arises with the awakening melody.
Again fierce torments, such as
  demons know,
In bitterer, feller tide, on this torn
  bosom flow.

Arise ye sightless spirits of the
  storm,
  Ye unseen minstrels of the aëreal
    song,   20
Pour the fierce tide around this
  lonely form,
  And roll the tempest's wildest
    swell along.
Dart the red lightning, wing the
  forkèd flash,
  Pour from thy cloud-formed hills
    the thunder's roar;
Arouse the whirlwind—and let
  ocean dash   25
  In fiercest tumult on the rocking
    shore,—
Destroy this life or let earth's fab-
  ric be no more.

Yes! every tie that links me here is
  dead;
  Mysterious Fate, thy mandate I
    obey,
Since hope and peace, and joy, for
  aye are fled,   30
  I come, terrific power, I come
    away.
Then o'er this ruined soul let spirits
  of Hell,
  In triumph, laughing wildly,
    mock its pain;
And though with direst pangs mine
  heart-strings swell,

I'll echo back their deadly yells
again,   35
Cursing the power that ne'er made
aught in vain.

FRAGMENT

YES! all is past—swift time has
fled away,
Yet its swell pauses on my sickening mind;
How long will horror nerve this
frame of clay?
I'm dead, and lingers yet my soul
behind.
Oh! powerful Fate, revoke thy
deadly spell,   5
And yet that may not ever, ever
be,
Heaven will not smile upon the
work of Hell;
Ah! no, for Heaven cannot smile
on me;
Fate, envious Fate, has sealed my
wayward destiny.

I sought the cold brink of the midnight surge,   10
I sighed beneath its wave to hide
my woes,
The rising tempest sung a funeral
dirge,
And on the blast a frightful yell
arose.
Wild flew the meteors o'er the maddened main,
Wilder did grief athwart my
bosom glare;   15
Stilled was the unearthly howling,
and a strain,
Swelled mid the tumult of the
battling air,
'Twas like a spirit's song, but yet
more soft and fair.

I met a maniac—like he was to me,
I said—'Poor victim, wherefore
dost thou roam?   20
And canst thou not contend with
agony.

That thus at midnight thou dost
quit thine home?'
'Ah there she sleeps: cold in her
bloodless form,
And I will go to slumber in her
grave;
And then our ghosts, whilst raves
the maddened storm,   25
Will sweep at midnight o'er the
wildered wave;
Wilt thou our lowly beds with tears
of pity lave?'

'Ah! no, I cannot shed the pitying
tear,
This breast is cold, this heart can
feel no more;
But I can rest me on thy chilling
bier,   30
Can shriek in horror to the tempest's roar.'

.   .   .   .   .

THE SPECTRAL
HORSEMAN

WHAT was the shriek that struck
Fancy's ear
As it sate on the ruins of time that
is past?
Hark! it floats on the fitful blast of
the wind,
And breathes to the pale moon a
funeral sigh.
It is the Benshie's moan on the
storm,   5
Or a shivering fiend that thirsting
for sin,
Seeks murder and guilt when virtue
sleeps,
Winged with the power of some
ruthless king,
And sweeps o'er the breast of the
prostrate plain.
It was not a fiend from the regions
of Hell   10
That poured its low moan on the
stillness of night:

It was not a ghost of the guilty
    dead,
Nor a yelling vampire reeking with
    gore;
But aye at the close of seven years'
    end,
That voice is mixed with the swell
    of the storm,   15
And aye at the close of seven
    years' end,
A shapeless shadow that sleeps on
    the hill
Awakens and floats on the mist of
    the heath.
It is not the shade of a murdered
    man,
Who has rushed uncalled to the
    throne of his God,   20
And howls in the pause of the eddy-
    ing storm.
This voice is low, cold, hollow, and
    chill,
'Tis not heard by the ear, but is felt
    in the soul.
'Tis more frightful far than the
    death-daemon's scream,
Or the laughter of fiends when they
    howl o'er the corpse   25
Of a man who has sold his soul to
    Hell.
It tells the approach of a mystic
    form,
A white courser bears the shadowy
    sprite;
More thin they are than the mists
    of the mountain,
When the clear moonlight sleeps on
    the waveless lake.   30
More pale *his* cheek than the snows
    of Nithona,
When winter rides on the northern
    blast,
And howls in the midst of the leaf-
    less wood.
Yet when the fierce swell of the
    tempest is raving,

And the whirlwinds howl in the
    caves of Inisfallen,   35
Still secure mid the wildest war of
    the sky,
The phantom courser scours the
    waste,
And his rider howls in the thunder's
    roar.
O'er him the fierce bolts of avenging
    Heaven
Pause, as in fear, to strike his
    head.   40
The meteors of midnight recoil
    from his figure,
Yet the 'wildered peasant, that oft
    passes by,
With wonder beholds the blue flesh
    through his form:
And his voice, though faint as the
    sighs of the dead,
The startled passenger shudders to
    hear,   45
More distinct than the thunder's
    wildest roar.
Then does the dragon, who, chained
    in the caverns
To eternity, curses the champion
    of Erin,
Moan and yell loud at the lone
    hour of midnight,
And twine his vast wreaths round
    the forms of the daemons;
Then in agony roll his death-swim-
    ming eyeballs,   51
Though 'wildered by death, yet
    never to die!
Then he shakes from his skeleton
    folds the nightmares,
Who, shrieking in agony, seek the
    couch
Of some fevered wretch who courts
    sleep in vain;   55
Then the tombless ghosts of the
    guilty dead
In horror pause on the fitful gale.
They float on the swell of the eddy-
    ing tempest,

And scared seek the caves of gigantic ...
Where their thin forms pour unearthly sounds   - 60
On the blast that sweeps the breast
of the lake,
And mingles its swell with the
moonlight air.

MELODY TO A SCENE OF FORMER TIMES

ART thou indeed forever gone,
Forever, ever, lost to me?
Must this poor bosom beat alone,
Or beat at all, if not for thee?
Ah! why was love to mortals
given,   5
To lift them to the height of
Heaven,
Or dash them to the depths of Hell?
Yet I do not reproach thee, dear!
Ah, no! the agonies that swell
This panting breast, this fren-
zied brain,   10
Might wake my ——'s slum-
b'ring tear.
Oh! Heaven is witness I did love,
And Heaven does know I love thee
still,
Does know the fruitless sick'ning
thrill,
When reason's judgment vainly
strove   15
To blot thee from my memory;
But which might never, never be.
Oh! I appeal to that blest day
When passion's wildest ecstasy
Was coldness to the joys I knew, 20
When every sorrow sunk away.
Oh! I had never lived before,
But now those blisses are no more.
And now I cease to live again,
I do not blame thee, love; ah,
no!   25
The breast that feels this anguished
woe

Throbs for thy happiness alone.
Two years of speechless 'bliss are
gone,
I thank thee, dearest, for the dream.
'Tis night—what faint and distant
scream   30
Comes on the wild and fitful blast?
It moans for pleasures that are past,
It moans for days that are gone by.
Oh! lagging hours, how slow you
fly!
I see a dark and lengthened
vale,   35
The black view closes with the
tomb;
But darker is the lowering gloom
That shades the intervening
dale.
In visioned slumber for awhile
I seem again to share thy smile, 40
I seem to hang upon thy tone.
Again you say, 'Confide in me,
For I am thine, and thine alone,
And thine must ever, ever be.'
But oh! awak'ning still anew,   45
Athwart my enanguished senses
flew
A fiercer, deadlier agony!
[End of *Posthumous Fragments
of Margaret Nicholson*.]

STANZA FROM A TRANSLA-TION OF THE MARSEIL-LAISE HYMN

TREMBLE, Kings despised of man!
Ye traitors to your Country,
Tremble! Your parricidal plan
At length shall meet its des-
tiny ...
We all are soldiers fit to fight,   5
But if we sink in glory's night
Our mother Earth will give ye new
The brilliant pathway to pursue
Which leads to Death or Vic-
tory ...

BIGOTRY'S VICTIM

I

DARES the lama, most fleet of the
    sons of the wind,
The lion to rouse from his skull-
    covered lair?
When the tiger approaches can the
    fast-fleeting hind
Repose trust in his footsteps of
    air?
No! Abandoned he sinks in a trance
    of despair,   5
    The monster transfixes his
      prey,
    On the sand flows his life-
      blood away;
Whilst India's rocks to his death-
    yells reply,
Protracting the horrible harmony.

II

Yet the fowl of the desert, when
    danger encroaches,   10
    Dares fearless to perish defend-
      ing her brood,
Though the fiercest of cloud-pierc-
    ing tyrants approaches
Thirsting—ay, thirsting for
    blood;
And demands, like mankind, his
    brother for food;
    Yet more lenient, more gen-
      tle than they;   15
    For hunger, not glory, the
      prey
Must perish. Revenge does not howl
    in the dead.
Nor ambition with fame crown the
    murderer's head.

III

Though weak as the lama that
    bounds on the mountains,
And endued not with fast-fleet-
    ing footsteps of air,   20

Yet, yet will I draw from the purest
    of fountains,
    Though a fiercer than tiger is
      there.
Though, more dreadful than death,
    it scatters despair,
    Though its shadow eclipses
      the day,
    And the darkness of deepest
      dismay   25
Spreads the influence of soul-chill-
    ing terror around,
And lowers on the corpses, that rot
    on the ground.

IV

They came to the fountain to draw
    from its stream
    Waves too pure, too celestial, for
      mortals to see;
They bathed for awhile in its sil-
    very beam,   30
    Then perished, and perished like
      me.
For in vain from the grasp of the
    Bigot I flee;
    The most tenderly loved of
      my soul
    Are slaves to his hated con-
      trol.
He pursues me, he blasts me! 'Tis
    in vain that I fly: 35
What remains, but to curse him,—
    to curse him and die?

ON AN ICICLE THAT CLUNG
TO THE GRASS OF A GRAVE

I

OH! take the pure gem to where
    southerly breezes,
    Waft repose to some bosom as
    faithful as fair,
In which the warm current of love
    never freezes,
    As it rises unmingled with selfish-
    ness there,

Which, untainted by pride, un-
    polluted by care,   5
Might dissolve the dim icedrop,
    might bid it arise,
Too pure for these regions, to gleam
    in the skies.

II

Or where the stern warrior, his
    country defending,
    Dares fearless the dark-rolling
      battle to pour,
ʃOr o'er the fell corpse of a dread
    tyrant bending,   10
    Where patriotism red with his
      guilt-reeking gore   –
    Plants Liberty's flag on the slave-
      peopled shore,
With victory's cry, with the shout
    of the free,
Let it fly, taintless Spirit, to mingle
    with thee.

III

For I found the pure gem, when
    the daybeam returning, 15
    Ineffectual gleams on the snow-
      covered plain,
When to others the wished-for ar-
    rival of morning
    Brings relief to long visions of
      soul-racking pain;
But regret is an insult—to grieve
    is in vain:
And why should we grieve that a
    spirit so fair   20
Seeks Heaven to mix with its own
    kindred there?

IV

But still 'twas some Spirit of kind-
    ness descending
    To share in the load of mortal-
    ity's woe,
Who over thy lowly-built•sepulchre
    bending

Bade sympathy's tenderest tear-
    drop to flow.   25
Not for *thee* soft compassion
    celestials did know,
But if *angels* can weep, sure *man*
    may repine,
May weep in mute grief o'er thy
    low-laid shrine.

V

And did I then say, for the altar of
    glory,
    That the earliest, the loveliest of
      flowers I'd entwine,   30
Though with millions of blood-
    reeking victims 'twas gory,
    Though the tears of the widow
      polluted its shrine,
    Though around it the orphans,
      the fatherless pine?
Oh! Fame, all thy glories I'd yield
    for a tear
To shed on the grave of a heart so
    sincere.   35

LOVE

WHY is it said thou canst not live
    In a youthful breast and fair,
Since thou eternal life canst give,
    Canst bloom for ever there?
Since withering pain no power pos-
    sessed,   5
    Nor age, to blanch thy vermeil
    hue,
Nor time's dread victor, death, con-
    fessed,
    Though bathed with his poison
    dew,
Still thou retain'st unchanging
    bloom,
Fixed tranquil, even in the tomb. 10
And oh! when on the blest, reviv-
    ing,
    The day-star dawns of love,
Each energy of soul surviving
    More vivid, soars above,

Hast thou ne'er felt a rapturous
    thrill,   15
  Like June's warm breath,
    athwart thee fly,
O'er each idea then to steal,
  When other passions die?
Felt it in some wild noonday dream,
When sitting by the lonely stream,
Where Silence says, 'Mine is the
    dell';   21
  And not a murmur from the
    plain,
And not an echo from the fell,
  Disputes her silent reign.

ON A FETE AT CARLTON HOUSE: FRAGMENT

      By the mossy brink,
With me the Prince shall sit and
    think;
Shall muse in visioned Regency,
Rapt in bright dreams of dawning
    Royalty.

TO A STAR

Sweet star, which gleaming o'er
  the darksome scene
Through fleecy clouds of silvery
  radiance fliest,
Spanglet of light on evening's
  shadowy veil,
Which shrouds the day-beam from
  the waveless lake,
Lighting the hour of sacred love;
  more sweet   5
Than the expiring morn-star's paly
  fires:—
Sweet star! When wearied Nature
  sinks to sleep,
And all is hushed,—all, save the
  voice of Love,
Whose broken murmurings swell
  the balmy blast
Of soft Favonius, which at intervals   10
Sighs in the ear of stillness, art
  thou aught but

Lulling the slaves of interest to re-
  pose
With that mild, pitying gaze? Oh,
  I would look
In thy dear beam till every bond of
  sense
Became enamoured——   15

TO MARY, WHO DIED IN THIS OPINION

I

Maiden, quench the glare of sor-
  row
  Struggling in thine haggard eye:
Firmness dare to borrow
  From the wreck of destiny;
For the ray morn's bloom reveal-
  ing   5
Can never boast so bright an hue
  As that which mocks concealing,
And sheds its loveliest light on you.

II

  Yet is the tie departed
Which bound thy lovely soul to
  bliss?   10
  Has it left thee broken-hearted
In a world so cold as this?
  Yet, though, fainting fair one,
Sorrow's self thy cup has given,
  Dream thou'lt meet thy dear
    one,   15
Never more to part, in Heaven.

III

  Existence would I barter
  For a dream so dear as thine,
  And smile to die a martyr
On affection's bloodless shrine. 20
  Nor would I change for pleas-
    ure
That withered hand and ashy
  cheek,
  If my heart enshrined a treasure
Such as forces thine to break.

A TALE OF SOCIETY AS IT IS: FROM FACTS, 1811

I

SHE was an agèd woman; and the years
Which she had numbered on her
    toilsome way
Had bowed her natural powers
    to decay.
She was an agèd woman; yet the
    ray
Which faintly glimmered through
    her starting tears,   5
Pressed into light by silent
    misery,
Hath soul's imperishable energy.
    She was a cripple, and in-
    capable
To add one mite to gold-fed
    luxury:
    And therefore did her spirit
    dimly feel   10
    That poverty, the crime of
    tainting stain,
Would merge her in its depths,
    never to rise again.

II

One only son's love had sup-
    ported her.
    She long had struggled with
    infirmity,
    Lingering to human life-
    scenes; for to die,   15
When fate has spared to rend
    some mental tie,
Would many wish, and surely
    fewer dare.
But, when the tyrant's blood-
    hounds forced the child
For his cursed power unhallowed
    arms to wield—
    Bend to another's will—be-
    come a thing   20
More senseless than the sword of
    battlefield—

Then did she feel keen sor-
    row's keenest sting;
And many years had passed ere
    comfort they would bring.

III

For seven years did this poor
    woman live
    In unparticipated solitude. 25
    Thou mightst have seen her
    in the forest rude
    Picking the scattered rem-
    nants of its wood.
If human, thou mightst then
    have learned to grieve.
The gleanings of precarious
    charity
Her scantiness of food did scarce
    supply.   30
    The proofs of an unspeaking
    sorrow dwelt
Within her ghastly hollowness of
    eye:
    Each arrow of the season's
    change she felt.
Yet still she groans, ere yet her
    race were run,
One only hope: it was—once more
    to see her son.   35

IV

It was an eve of June, when
    every star
    Spoke peace from Heaven to
    those on earth that live.
    She rested on the moor. 'Twas
    such an eve
    When first her soul began in-
    deed to grieve:
Then he was here; now he is very
    far.   40
The sweetness of the balmy eve-
    ning
A sorrow o'er her agèd soul did
    fling,
    Yet not devoid of rapture's
    mingled tear:

A balm was in the poison of the
    sting.
This agèd sufferer for many a
    year   45
Had never felt such comfort. She
    suppressed
A sigh—and turning round, clasped
    William to her breast!

V

And, though his form was wasted
    by the woe
Which tyrants on their victims
    love to wreak,
Though his sunk eyeballs and
    his faded cheek   50
Of slavery's violence and scorn
    did speak,
Yet did the agèd woman's bosom
    glow.
The vital fire seemed re-illumed
    within
By this sweet unexpected wel-
    coming.
Oh, consummation of the fond-
    est hope   55
That ever soared on Fancy's
    wildest wing!
Oh, tenderness that foundst so
    sweet a scope!
Prince who dost pride thee on
    thy mighty sway,
When *thou* canst feel such love,
    thou shalt be great as they!

VI

Her son, compelled, the country's
    foes had fought,   60
    Had bled in battle; and the
    stern control
Which ruled his sinews and
    coerced his soul
Utterly poisoned life's unmin-
    gled bowl,
And unsubduable evils on him
    brought.

He was the shadow of the lusty
    child   65
Who, when the time of summer
    season smiled,
Did earn for her a meal of
    honesty,
And with affectionate discourse
    beguiled
The keen attacks of pain and
    poverty;
Till Power, as envying her this
    only joy,   70
From her maternal bosom tore the
    unhappy boy.

VII

And now cold charity's unwel-
    come dole
Was insufficient to support the
    pair;
And they would perish rather
    than would bear
The law's stern slavery, and
    the insolent stare   75
With which law loves to rend the
    poor man's soul—
The bitter scorn, the spirit-sink-
    ing noise
Of heartless mirth which women,
    men, and boys
Wake in this scene of legal
    misery.

.   .   .   .   .

TO THE REPUBLICANS OF NORTH AMERICA

I

BROTHERS! between you and me
    Whirlwinds sweep and billows
    roar:
Yet in spirit oft I see
    On thy wild and winding shore
Freedom's bloodless banners
    wave,—   5
Feel the pulses of the brave

Unextinguished in the grave,—
  See them drenched in sacred
    gore,—
Catch the warrior's gasping breath
Murmuring 'Liberty or death!'   10

II

Shout aloud! Let every slave,
  Crouching at Corruption's
    throne,
Start into a man, and brave
  Racks and chains without a
    groan;
And the castle's heartless glow,   15
And the hovel's vice and woe,
Fade like gaudy flowers that
    blow—
  Weeds that peep, and then are
    gone
Whilst, from misery's ashes risen,
Love shall burst the captive's
    prison.   20

III

Cotopaxi! bid the sound
  Through thy sister mountains
    ring,
Till each valley smile around
  At the blissful welcoming!
And, O thou stern Ocean deep,   25
Thou whose foamy billows sweep
Shores where thousands wake to
    weep
  Whilst they curse a villain king,
On the winds that fan thy breast
Bear thou news of Freedom's rest!

IV

Can the daystar dawn of love,   31
  Where the flag of war unfurled
Floats with crimson stain above
  The fabric of a ruined world?
Never but to vengeance driven   35
When the patriot's spirit shriven
Seeks in death its native Heaven!
  There, to desolation hurled,
Widowed love may watch thy bier,
Balm thee with its dying tear?   40

TO IRELAND

I

BEAR witness, Erin! when thine in-
    jured isle
Sees summer on its verdant pas-
    tures smile,
Its cornfields waving in the winds
    that sweep
The billowy surface of thy circling
    deep!
Thou tree whose shadow o'er the
    Atlantic gave   5
Peace, wealth and beauty, to its
    friendly wave,
      Its blossoms fade,
And blighted are the leaves that
    cast its shade;
Whilst the cold hand gathers its
    scanty fruit,
Whose chillness struck a canker to
    its root.   10

II

      I could stand
Upon thy shores, O Erin, and could
    count
The billows that, in their unceasing
    swell,
Dash on thy beach, and every wave
    might seem
An instrument in Time the giant's
    grasp,   15
To burst the barriers of Eternity.
Proceed, thou giant, conquering and
    to conquer;
March on thy lonely way! The
    nations fall
Beneath thy noiseless footstep;
    pyramids
That for millenniums have defied
    the blast,   20
And laughed at lightnings, thou
    dost crush to nought.
Yon monarch, in his solitary pomp,
Is but the fungus of a winter day
That thy light footstep presses into
    dust.

Thou art a conqueror, Time; all
    things give way   25
Before thee but the 'fixed and vir-
    tuous will';
The sacred sympathy of soul which
    was
When thou wert not, which shall be
    when thou perishest.

.   .   .   .   .

ON ROBERT EMMET'S GRAVE

.   .   .   .   .

VI

No trump tells thy virtues—the
    grave where they rest
  With thy dust shall remain un-
    polluted by fame,
Till thy foes, by the world and by
    fortune caressed,
  Shall pass like a mist from the
    light of thy name.

VII

When the storm-cloud that lowers
    o'er the day-beam is gone, 5
  Unchanged, unextinguished its
    life-spring will shine;
When Erin has ceased with their
    memory to groan,
  She will smile through the tears
    of revival on thine.

THE RETROSPECT: CWM ELAN, 1812

A scene, which 'wildered fancy
    viewed
In the soul's coldest solitude,
With that same scene when peace-
    ful love
Flings rapture's colour o'er the
    grove,
When mountain, meadow, wood
    and stream   5
With unalloying glory gleam,
And to the spirit's ear and eye
Are unison and harmony.

The moonlight was my dearer day;
Then would I wander far away, 10
And, lingering on the wild brook's
    shore
To hear its unremitting roar,
Would lose in the ideal flow
All sense of overwhelming woe;
Or at the noiseless noon of night 15
Would climb some heathy moun-
    tain's height,
And listen to the mystic sound
That stole in fitful gasps around.
I joyed to see the streaks of day
Above the purple peaks decay, 20
And watch the latest line of light
Just mingling with the shades of
    night;
For day with me was time of woe
When even tears refused to flow;
Then would I stretch my languid
    frame   25
Beneath the wild woods' gloomiest
    shade,
And try to quench the ceaseless
    flame
That on my withered vitals preyed;
Would close mine eyes and dream I
    were
On some remote and friendless
    plain,   30
And long to leave existence there,
If with it I might leave the pain
That with a finger cold and lean
Wrote madness on my withering
    mien.

It was not unrequited love   35
That bade my 'wildered spirit rove;
'Twas not the pride disdaining life,
That with this mortal world at
    strife
Would yield to the soul's inward
    sense,
Then groan in human impotence, 40
And weep because it is not given
To taste on Earth the peace of
    Heaven.
'Twas not that in the narrow sphere

Where Nature fixed my wayward
    fate
There was no friend or kindred dear
Formed to become that spirit's
    mate,   46
Which, searching on tired pinion,
    found
Barren and cold repulse around;
Oh, no! yet each one sorrow gave
New graces to the narrow grave. 50
For broken vows had early quelled
The stainless spirit's vestal flame;
Yes! whilst the faithful bosom
    swelled,
Then the envenomed arrow came,
And Apathy's unaltering eye   55
Beamed coldness on the misery;
And early I had learned to scorn
The chains of clay that bound a
    soul
Panting to seize the wings of morn,
And where its vital fires were born
To soar, and spur the cold control
Which the vile slaves of earthly
    night   62
Would twine around its struggling
    flight.

Oh, many were the friends whom
    fame
Had linked with the unmeaning
    name,   65
Whose magic marked among man-
    kind
The casket of my unknown mind,
Which hidden from the vulgar glare
Imbibed no fleeting radiance there.
My darksome spirit sought — it
    found   70
A friendless solitude around.
For who that might undaunted
    stand,
The saviour of a sinking land,
Would crawl, its ruthless tyrant's
    slave,
And fatten upon Freedom's grave,
Though doomed with her to perish,
    where   76

The captive clasps abhorred de-
    spair.

They could not share the bosom's
    feeling,
Which, passion's every throb re-
    vealing,
Dared force on the world's notice
    cold   80
Thoughts of unprofitable mould,
Who bask in Custom's fickle ray,
Fit sunshine of such wintry day!
They could not in a twilight walk
Weave an impassioned web of talk,
Till mysteries the spirits press   86
In wild yet tender awfulness,
Then feel within our narrow sphere
How little yet how great we are!
But they might shine in courtly
    glare,   90
Attract the rabble's cheapest stare,
And might command where'er they
    move
A thing that bears the name of
    love;
They might be learnèd, witty, gay,
Foremost in fashion's gilt array, 95
On Fame's emblazoned pages
    shine,
Be princes' friends, but never
    mine!

Ye jagged peaks that frown sub-
    lime,
Mocking the blunted scythe of
    Time,
Whence I would watch its lustre
    pale   100
Steal from the moon o'er yonder
    vale
Thou rock, whose bosom black and
    vast,
Bared to the stream's unceasing
    flow,
Ever its giant shade doth cast
On the tumultuous surge below: 105
Woods, to whose depths retires to
    die

The wounded Echo's melody,
And whither this lone spirit bent
The footstep of a wild intent:
Meadows! whose green and span-
 gled breast   110
These fevered limbs have often
 pressed,
Until the watchful fiend Despair
Slept in the soothing coolness there!
Have not your varied beauties seen
The sunken eye, the withering
 mien,   115
Sad traces of the unuttered pain
That froze my heart and burned my
 brain.
How changed since Nature's sum-
 mer form
Had last the power my grief to
 charm,
Since last ye soothed my spirit's
 sadness,   120
Strange chaos of a mingled mad-
 ness!
Changed!—not the loathsome
 worm that fed
In the dark mansions of the dead,
Now soaring through the fields of
 air,
And gathering purest nectar there,
A butterfly, whose million hues 126
The dazzled eye of wonder views,
Long lingering on a work so strange,
Has undergone so bright a change.
How do I feel my happiness? 130
I cannot tell, but they may guess
Whose every gloomy feeling, gone,
Friendship and passion feel alone;
Who see mortality's dull clouds
Before affection's murmur fly, 135
Whilst the mild glances of her eye
Pierce the thin veil of flesh that
 shrouds
The spirit's inmost sanctuary.
O thou! whose virtues latest
 known,
First in this heart yet claim'st a
 throne;   140

Whose downy sceptre still shall
 share
The gentle sway with virtue there;
Thou fair in form, and pure in
 mind,
Whose ardent friendship rivets
 fast
The flowery band our fates that
 bind,   145
Which incorruptible shall last
When duty's hard and cold control
Has thawed around the burning
 soul,—
The gloomiest retrospects that
 bind
With crowns of thorn the bleeding
 mind,   150
The prospects of most doubtful
 hue
That rise on Fancy's shuddering
 view,—
Are gilt by the reviving ray
Which thou hast flung upon my
 day.

FRAGMENT OF A SONNET

TO HARRIET

EVER as now with Love and Virtue's glow
May thy unwithering soul not
 cease to burn,
Still may thine heart with those
 pure thoughts o'erflow
Which force from mine such quick
 and warm return.

TO HARRIET

IT is not blasphemy to hope that
 Heaven
More perfectly will give those
 nameless joys
Which throb within the pulses of
 the blood
And sweeten all that bitterness
 which Earth

Infuses in the heaven-born soul. O
thou 5
Whose dear love gleamed upon the
gloomy path
Which this lone spirit travelled,
drear and cold,
Yet swiftly leading to those awful
limits
Which mark the bounds of Time
and of the space
When Time shall be no more; wilt
thou not turn 10
Those spirit-beaming eyes and look
on me,
Until I be assured that Earth is
Heaven,
And Heaven is Earth?—will not
thy glowing cheek,
Glowing with soft suffusion, rest
on mine,
And breathe magnetic sweetness
through the frame 15
Of my corporeal nature, through
the soul
Now knit with these fine fibres?
I would give
The longest and the happiest day
that fate
Has marked on my existence but
to feel
One soul-reviving kiss ... O thou
most dear, 20
'Tis an assurance that this Earth
is Heaven,
And Heaven the flower of that un-
tainted seed
Which springeth here beneath such
love as ours.
Harriet! let death all mortal ties
dissolve,
But ours shall not be mortal! The
cold hand 25
Of Time may chill the love of
earthly minds
Half frozen now; the frigid inter-
course

Of common souls lives but a sum-
mer's day;
It dies, where it arose, upon this
earth.
But ours! oh, 'tis the stretch of
Fancy's hope 30
To portray its continuance as now,
Warm, tranquil, spirit-healing;
nor when age
Has tempered these wild ecstasies,
and given
A soberer tinge to the luxurious
glow
Which blazing on devotion's pin-
nacle 35
Makes virtuous passion supersede
the power
Of reason; nor when life's aestival
sun
To deeper manhood shall have
ripened me;
Nor when some years have added
judgement's store
To all thy woman sweetness, all
the fire 40
Which throbs in thine enthusiast
heart; not then
Shall holy friendship (for what
other name
May love like ours assume?), not
even then
Shall Custom so corrupt, or the
cold forms
Of this desolate world so harden
us, 45
As when we think of the dear
love that binds
Our souls in soft communion, while
we know
Each other's thoughts and feelings,
can we say
Unblushingly a heartless compliment,
Praise, hate, or love with the unthinking world, 50
Or dare to cut the unrelaxing nerve

That knits our love to virtue. Can
 those eyes,
Beaming with mildest radiance on
 my heart
To purify its purity, e'er bend
To soothe its vice or consecrate 'its
 fears?   55
Never, thou second Self! Is con-
 fidence
So vain in virtue that I learn to
 doubt
The mirror even of Truth? Dark
 flood of Time,
Roll as it listeth thee; I measure
 not
By month or moments thy ambiguous course.   60
Another may stand by me on thy
 brink,
And watch the bubble whirled be-
 yond his ken,
Which pauses at my feet. The sense
 of love,
The thirst for action, and the im-
 passioned thought
Prolong my being; if I wake no
 more,   65
My life more actual living will contain
Than some gray veteran's of the
 world's cold school,
Whose listless hours unprofitably
 roll
By one enthusiast feeling unredeemed,
Virtue and Love! unbending Fortitude,   70
Freedom, Devotedness and Purity!
That life my Spirit consecrates to
 you.

SONNET

TO A BALLOON LADEN WITH KNOWLEDGE

Bright ball of flame that through
 the gloom of even

Silently takest thine aethereal
 way,
And with surpassing glory
 dimm'st each ray
Twinkling amid the dark blue
 depths of Heaven,—
Unlike the fire thou bearest, soon
 shalt thou   5
Fade like a meteor in surround-
 ing gloom,
Whilst that, unquenchable, is
 doomed to glow
A watch-light by the patriot's
 lonely tomb;
A ray of courage to the oppressed
 and poor;
A spark, though gleaming on the
 hovel's hearth,   10
Which through the tyrant's gilded
 domes shall roar;
A beacon in the darkness of the
 Earth;
A sun which, o'er the renovated
 scene,
Shall dart like Truth where False-
 hood yet has been.

SONNET

ON LAUNCHING SOME BOTTLES FILLED WITH KNOWLEDGE INTO THE BRISTOL CHANNEL

Vessels of heavenly medicine! may
 the breeze
Auspicious waft your dark green
 forms to shore;
Safe may ye stem the wide surrounding roar
Of the wild whirlwinds and the raging seas;
And oh! if Liberty e'er deigned to
 stoop   5
From yonder lowly throne her
 crownless brow,
Sure she will breathe around your
 emerald group

The fairest breezes of her West
that blow.
Yes! she will waft ye to some free-
born soul
Whose eye-beam, kindling as it
meets your freight, 10
Her heaven-born flame in suffering Earth will light,
Until its radiance gleams from pole
to pole,
And tyrant-hearts with powerless envy burst
To see their night of ignorance
dispersed.

THE DEVIL'S WALK

A BALLAD

I

ONCE, early in the morning,
Beelzebub arose,
With care his sweet person adorn-
ing,
He put on his Sunday clothes.

II

He drew on a boot to hide his
hoof, 5
He drew on a glove to hide his
claw,
His horns were concealed by a *Bras
Chapeau,*
And the Devil went forth as natty
a *Beau*
As Bond-street ever saw.

III

He sate him down, in London
town, 10
Before earth's morning ray;
With a favourite imp he began to
chat,
On religion, and scandal, this and
that,
Until the dawn of day.

IV

And then to St. James's Court he
went, 15
And St. Paul's Church he took on
his way;
He was mighty thick with every
Saint,
Though they were formal and he
was gay.

V

The Devil was an agriculturist,
And as bad weeds quickly
grow, 20
In looking over his farm, I wist,
He wouldn't find cause for
woe.

VI

He peeped in each hole, to each
chamber stole,
His promising live-stock to
view;
Grinning applause, he just showed
them his claws, 25
And they shrunk with affright from
his ugly sight,
Whose work they delighted to
do.

VII

Satan poked his red nose into
crannies so small
One would think that the inno-
cents fair,
Poor lambkins! were just doing
nothing at all 30
But settling some dress or arrang-
ing some ball,
But the Devil saw deeper
there.

VIII

A Priest, at whose elbow the Devil
during prayer
Sate familiarly, side by side,

Declared that, if the Tempter were
    there,   35
       His presence he would not
       abide.
Ah! ah! thought Old Nick, that's a
    very stale trick,
For without the Devil, O favourite
    of Evil,
       In your carriage you would
       not ride.

IX

Satan next saw a brainless King, 40
       Whose house was as hot as his
       own;
Many Imps in attendance were
    there on the wing,
They flapped the pennon and
    twisted the sting,
       Close by the very Throne.

X

Ah! ah! thought Satan, the pasture
    is good,   45
       My Cattle will here thrive better
       than others;
They dine on news of human blood,
They sup on the groans of the dy-
    ing and dead,
And supperless never will go to
    bed;
       Which will make them fat as
       their brothers.   50

XI

Fat as the Fiends that feed on
    blood,
       Fresh and warm from the fields
       of Spain,
       Where Ruin ploughs her gory
       way,
Where the shoots of earth are
    nipped in the bud,
       Where Hell is the Victor's
       prey,   55
Its glory the meed of the slain.

XII

Fat—as the Death-birds on Erin's
    shore,
That glutted themselves in her
    dearest gore,
       And flitted round Castlereagh,
When they snatched the Patriot's
    heart, that *his* grasp   60
Had torn from its widow's maniac
    clasp,
       And fled at the dawn of day.

XIII

Fat—as the Reptiles of the tomb,
    That riot in corruption's spoil,
That fret their little hour in
    gloom,   65
       And creep, and live the while.

XIV

Fat as that Prince's maudlin brain,
    Which, addled by some gilded
    toy,
Tired, gives his sweetmeat, and
    again
       Cries for it, like a humoured
       boy.   70

XV

For he is fat,—his waistcoat gay,
When strained upon a levee day,
    Scarce meets across his princely
    paunch;
And pantaloons are like half-moons
    Upon each brawny haunch. 75

XVI

How vast his stock of calf! when
    plenty
    Had filled his empty head and
    heart,
Enough to satiate foplings twenty,
    Could make his pantaloon seams
    start.

XVII

The Devil (who sometimes is called
  Nature),   80
  For men of power provides thus
    well,
Whilst every change and every fea-
  ture,
  Their great original can tell.

XVIII

Satan saw a lawyer a viper slay,
  That crawled up the leg of his
    table,   85
It reminded him most marvellously
  Of the story of Cain and Abel.

XIX

The wealthy yeoman, as he wan-
  ders
  His fertile fields among,
And on his thriving cattle pon-
  ders,   90
  Counts his sure gains, and hums
    a song;
Thus did the Devil, through earth
  walking,
  Hum low a hellish song.

XX

For they thrive well whose garb of
  gore
  Is Satan's choicest livery,   95
And they thrive well who from the
  poor
  Have snatched the bread of
    penury,
And heap the houseless wanderer's
  store
  On the rank pile of luxury.

XXI

The Bishops thrive, though they
  are big;   100
  The Lawyers thrive, though they
    are thin;

For every gown, and every wig,
  Hides the safe thrift of Hell
    within.

XXII

Thus pigs were never counted
  clean,
  Although they dine on finest
    corn;   105
And cormorants are sin-like lean,
  Although they eat from night to
    morn.

XXIII

Oh! why is the Father of Hell in
  such glee,
  As he grins from ear to ear?
Why does he doff his clothes joy-
  fully,   110
  As he skips, and prances, and
    flaps his wing,
As he sidles, leers, and twirls his
  sting,
  And dares, as he is, to appear?

XXIV

A statesman passed—alone to him,
  The Devil dare his whole shape
    uncover,   115
To show each feature, every limb,
  Secure of an unchanging lover.

XXV

At this known sign, a welcome
  sight,
  The watchful demons sought
    their King,
And every Fiend of the Stygian
  night,   120
  Was in an instant on the wing.

XXVI

Pale Loyalty, his guilt-steeled
  brow,
  With wreaths of gory laurel
    crowned:

The hell-hounds, Murder, Want
    and Woe,
    Forever hungering, flocked
      around;   125
From Spain had Satan sought their
    food,
'Twas human woe and human
    blood!

XXVII

Hark! the earthquake's crash I
    hear,—
    Kings turn pale, and Conquerors
      start,
Ruffians tremble in their fear,   130
    For their Satan doth depart.

XVIII

This day Fiends give to revelry
    To celebrate their King's return,
And with delight its Sire to see
    Hell's adamantine limits burn.

XXIX

But were the Devil's sight as keen
    As Reason's penetrating eye, 137
His sulphurous Majesty I ween,
    Would find but little cause for
      joy.

XXX

For the sons of Reason see   140
    That, ere fate consume the Pole,
The false Tyrant's cheek shall be
    Bloodless as his coward soul.

FRAGMENT OF A SONNET

FAREWELL TO NORTH DEVON

Where man's profane and tainting
    hand
Nature's primaeval loveliness has
    marred,
And some few souls of the high
    bliss debarred

Which else obey her powerful com-
    mand;
    . . . mountain piles   5
That load in grandeur Cambria's
    emerald vales.

ON LEAVING LONDON FOR WALES

HAIL to thee, Cambria; for the
    unfettered wind
Which from thy wilds even now
    methinks I feel,
Chasing the clouds that roll in
    wrath behind,
And tightening the soul's laxest
    nerves to steel;
True mountain Liberty alone
    may heal   5
The pain which Custom's obdur-
    acies bring,
And he who dares in fancy even
    to steal
One draught from Snowdon's
    ever sacred spring
Blots out the unholiest rede of
    worldly witnessing.

And shall that soul, to selfish
    peace resigned,   10
So soon forget the woe its fellows
    share?
Can Snowdon's Lethe from the
    free-born mind
So soon the page of injured pen-
    ury tear?
Does this fine mass of human
    passion dare
To sleep, unhonouring the patri-
    ot's fall,   15
Or life's sweet load in quietude
    to bear
While millions famish even in
    Luxury's hall,
And Tyranny, high raised, stern
    lowers on all?

No, Cambria! never may thy
    matchless vales

A heart so false to hope and vir-
  tue shield;   20
Nor ever may thy spirit-breath-
  ing gales –
Waft freshness to the slaves who
  dare to yield.
For me! . . . the weapon that I
  burn to wield
I seek amid thy rocks to ruin
  hurled,
That Reason's flag may over
  Freedom's field,   25
Symbol of bloodless victory,
  wave unfurled,
A meteor-sign of love effulgent o'er
  the world.

.   .   .   .   .

Do thou, wild Cambria, calm
  each struggling thought;
Cast thy sweet veil of rocks and
  woods between,
That by the soul to indignation
  wrought   30
Mountains and dells be mingled
  with the scene;
Let me forever be what I have
  been,
But not forever at my needy door
Let Misery linger speechless, pale
  and lean;
I am the friend of the unfriended
  poor,—   35
Let me not madly stain their
  righteous cause in gore.

THE WANDERING JEW'S SOLILOQUY

Is it the Eternal Triune, is it He
Who dares arrest the wheels of
  destiny
And plunge me in the lowest Hell
  of Hells?
Will not the lightning's blast destroy my frame?
Will not steel drink the blood-life
  where it swells?   5

No—let me hie where dark Destruction dwells,
To rouse her from her deeply caverned lair,
And, taunting her cursed sluggish-
  ness to ire,
Light long Oblivion's death-torch
  at its flame
And calmly mount Annihilation's
  pyre.   10
Tyrant of Earth! pale Misery's
  jackal Thou!
Are there no stores of vengeful vio-
  lent fate
Within the magazines of Thy fierce
  hate?
No poison in the clouds to bathe
  a brow
That lowers on Thee with desperate
  contempt?   15
Where is the noonday Pestilence
  that slew
The myriad sons of Israel's fa-
  voured nation?
Where the destroying Minister that
  flew
Pouring the fiery tide of desolation
Upon the leagued Assyrian's at-
  tempt?   20
Where the dark Earthquake-
  daemon who engorged
At the dread word Korah's uncon-
  scious crew?
Or the Angel's two-edged sword of
  fire that urged
Our primal parents from their
  bower of bliss
(Reared by Thine hand) for errors
  not their own   25
By Thine omniscient mind fore-
  doomed, foreknown?
Yes! I would court a ruin such as
  this,
Almighty Tyrant! and give thanks
  to Thee—
Drink deeply—drain the cup of
  hate: remit this—I may die.

EVENING

TO HARRIET

O THOU bright Sun! beneath the
    dark blue line
Of western distance that sublime
    descendest,
And, gleaming lovelier as thy
    beams decline,
Thy million hues to every vapour
    lendest,
And, over cobweb lawn and grove
    and stream   5
    Sheddest the liquid magic of thy
      light,
    Till calm Earth, with the parting
      splendour bright,
    Shows like the vision of a
      beauteous dream;
What gazer now with astronomic
    eye
    Could coldly count the spots
      within thy sphere?   10
    Such were thy lover, Harriet,
      could he fly
The thoughts of all that makes his
    passion dear,
    And, turning senseless from thy
      warm caress,
    Pick flaws in our close-woven
      happiness.

TO IANTHE

I LOVE thee, Baby! for thine own
    sweet sake;
    Those azure eyes, that faintly
      dimpled cheek,
    Thy tender frame, so eloquently
      weak,
Love in the sternest heart of hate
    might wake;
But more when o'er thy fitful slum-
    ber bending   5
    Thy mother folds thee to her
      wakeful heart,
    Whilst love and pity, in her
      glances blending,

All that thy passive eyes can feel
    impart:
More, when some feeble lineaments
    of her,
    Who bore thy weight beneath her
      spotless bosom,   10
    As with deep love I read thy
      face, recur,—
More dear art thou, O fair and
    fragile blossom;
    Dearest when most thy tender
      traits express
The image of thy mother's love-
    liness.

SONG FROM
THE WANDERING JEW

SEE yon opening flower
    Spreads its fragrance to the
      blast;
It fades within an hour,
    Its decay is pale—is fast.
Paler is yon maiden;   5
    Faster is her heart's decay;
Deep with sorrow laden,
    She sinks in death away.

FRAGMENT FROM THE
WANDERING JEW

THE Elements respect their Mak-
    er's seal!
    Still like the scathèd pine tree's
      height,
    Braving the tempests of the
      night
Have I 'scaped the flickering flame.
Like the scathed pine, which a
    monument stands   5
Of faded grandeur, which the
    brands
    Of the tempest-shaken air
Have riven on the desolate heath;
Yet it stands majestic even in
    death,
    And rears its wild form there. 10

TO THE QUEEN OF MY HEART

I

SHALL we roam, my love,
To the twilight grove,
When the moon is rising bright;
Oh, I'll whisper there,
In the cool night-air,　　5
What I dare not in broad daylight!

II

I'll tell thee a part
Of the thoughts that start
To being when thou art nigh;
And thy beauty, more bright　10
Than the stars' soft light,
Shall seem as a weft from the sky.

III

When the pale moonbeam
On tower and stream
Sheds a flood of silver sheen,　　15
How I love to gaze
As the cold ray strays
O'er thy face, my heart's throned
queen!

IV

Wilt thou roam with me
To the restless sea,　　20
And linger upon the steep,
And list to the flow
Of the waves below
How they toss and roar and leap?

V

Those boiling waves,　　25
And the storm that raves
At night o'er their foaming crest,
Resemble the strife
That, from earliest life,
The passions have waged in my
breast.　　30

VI

Oh, come, then, and rove
To the sea or the grove,
When the moon is rising bright;
And I'll whisper there,
In the cool night-air,　　35
What I dare not in broad day-
light.

INDEX OF FIRST LINES

A WORD FROM OUR SPONSOR

The Trust for Architectural Easements is committed to the preservation of America's architectural heritage. We strive to ensure that individual properties and entire neighborhoods are preserved for future generations. Since the campaign to save George Washington's Mount Vernon in the 19th century, preservation of America's historic places has been accepted as a cultural endeavor that helps us remember our identity as Americans. Urban landscapes nurture public history because historic places, built and natural, are "storehouses for...social memories...that frame the lives of many people and often outlast lifetimes."[1]

Following a national trend spurred by often destructive urban renewal projects, residents of Fort Greene and Clinton Hill began to advocate for the creation of historic districts to protect the character of their neighborhoods during the 1970s. Together the neighborhoods comprise one of the largest intact 19th century urban areas in New York State. In 1978, the Fort Greene Landmarks Preservation Committee—now the Fort Greene Association—was successful in designating the neighborhood as a historic district. Three years later, in 1981, the Society for Clinton Hill achieved the same goal. Fort Greene was listed in the National Register of Historic Places in 1983; National Register listing for Clinton Hill followed in 1985.

Although the cultural value of preservation remains critical, the 21st century offers another reason to preserve historic buildings: sustainable development. Constructing and operating buildings consumes 35 percent of the energy and 40 percent of the material resources, generates 25 percent of the solid waste, and emits 35 percent of the greenhouse gases in the United States.[2] Retaining and making existing buildings more energy efficient is an incredibly effective form of recycling. It saves the energy embodied in the building's construction, keeps its materials out of landfills, and negates the need for material- and energy-consumptive new construction. From an environmental standpoint, adapting a historic building to a new use is preferable to tearing it down and building anew, even when new is "green." As Richard Moe, president emeritus of the National Trust for Historic Preservation, has said, "we can't build our way out of the global warming crisis. We have to conserve our way out."[3]

[1] Dolores Hayden, *The Power of Place: Urban Landscapes as Public History* (Cambridge: The MIT Press, 1995), 9.

[2] Carl Elefante, "Valuing What We Have" *Urban Land Green*, Spring 2008, 45.

[3] Richard Moe, "Sustainable Stewardship: Historic Preservation's Essential Role in Fighting Climate Change" Remarks on the Occasion of Receiving the Vincent Scully Prize, 13 December 2007.

The Fort Greene/Clinton Hill Neighborhood & Architectural History Guide is the eighth in the Brooklyn Historical Society's *Neighborhood History Guide* series. Each volume has been a little more ambitious than the one that came before—longer, denser, with a greater amount of original research and analysis. Still, each volume can only tell a small and necessarily very selective part of a neighborhood's history. This may be especially so in the case of the large and diverse Fort Greene/Clinton Hill area, which is really a collection of neighborhoods and other distinct places. In acknowledgment of this, the guide does not attempt an integrated history of the entire area, but breaks it up into five sections. The first chapter is "North of Myrtle," which covers the history of the area bounded by Myrtle Avenue on the south, Flushing Avenue on the north, Prince Street (roughly) on the west, and Classon Avenue on the east. The second chapter, "Fort Greene Park," deals exclusively with the park bounded by Myrtle Avenue on the north, St. Edward's Street and the line of Fort Greene Place on the west, Washington Park (as the two blocks of Cumberland Street between DeKalb and Myrtle avenues are named) on the east, and DeKalb Avenue on the south. The third chapter, "Fort Greene," covers the area bounded by Flatbush Avenue on the west, Myrtle Avenue on the north, Vanderbilt Avenue on the east, and Atlantic Avenue on the south, excepting Fort Greene Park. The fourth chapter, "Clinton Hill," covers the area bounded by Vanderbilt Avenue on the west, Myrtle Avenue on the north, Classon Avenue on the east, and Fulton Street on the south. The fifth chapter, "The Brooklyn Academy of Music and Some Other Institutions," deals with the histories of four institutions near the western edge of Fort Greene: the Brooklyn Academy of Music, Brooklyn Technical High School, Brooklyn Hospital, and Long Island University.

The area as a whole offers a city in microcosm: institutions, industries, parks, churches, grand 19th-century architecture, one of the oldest African American communities in New York, the arts, urban renewal, and gentrification. It's a story that perhaps cannot be done justice at less than book length. But I offer what I hope are a few tantalizing glimpses of a rich history and suggestions for avenues of further research.

I would like to thank Etienne Frossard for his superb contemporary photographs, David Lee and 40 Acres and a Mule Filmworks for their generously allowing us to use several of Mr. Lee's wonderful photographs from the 1980s, Liz McEnaney for her research assistance, and the Trust for Architectural Easements for their generosity and patience.

FRANCIS MORRONE

I moved into Fort Greene on Brooklyn Day 1985. It was a beautiful, brisk, and sunny day. I remember it well. I'd been living in Jamaica, Queens since graduating from St. John's University in 1979. But I was born and raised in Brooklyn, growing up in Crown Heights, Brownsville, and East New York, so this was a kind of a return. The difference was instead of living in a poor area where the elevated subway was the most interesting architectural landmark, I'd moved into an area with a big, roomy park and fantastic, sturdy brownstones.

I'd moved into a duplex apartment on the corner of Willoughby and Carlton, just a block from Fort Greene Park. I knew little about the area. I had never had any friends who lived there. I had never dated any girls from the area. All I really knew was that Fort Greene was just east of downtown Brooklyn, where I'd spent my childhood going shopping at Abraham & Strauss, watching movies at the Albee Theater, and having cheesecake at Junior's.

Streets such as DeKalb, St. Felix, and Carlton were as foreign to me as avenues in Staten Island. I did know that the Fort Greene projects had produced the basketball greats Bernard and Albert King. I'd also been warned that the area had long been a hotbed of gang activity—first in the seventies with the Tomahawks and in the eighties with the Decepticons.

But Fort Greene, and my place, were easy to love. In contrast to Brownsville and my post-college life in Queens, Fort Greene was close to Manhattan. On almost every major subway line the neighborhood was no more than two or three stops into Brooklyn, so going out, especially anywhere below Fourteenth Street, was very convenient.

The apartment itself was a marvel. Wood floors, twenty foot high ceilings, a large kitchen, exposed brick walls, and a large backyard. You could have slid the project apartment I grew up in right into my new living room.

Some twenty-five years later I still live in Fort Greene, though not in that building, but actually not far away. There are skyscrapers ringing the area now. Fast food franchises are slowly edging into our space. Real estate brokerage store fronts now rival bodegas on Fulton Street. Change is happening, with lots more about to come.

Still, that core beauty that caught me when I first moved here remains the same. Whether it's snowing or spring, whether it's sunny or overcast, there is a magic in the area. Walt Whitman was inspired by it. So were Richard Wright, Spike Lee, and legions of artists over the decades. You can walk Fort Greene and Clinton Hill's streets any time of the year and feel connected to beauty, history, and some intangible form of inspiration, one that has filled with me with joy ever since that day in 1985.

NELSON GEORGE

Today we don't think of Fort Greene and Clinton Hill as waterfront communities. But at least those parts of the area to the north of Myrtle Avenue owe much of their development to the opportunities for waterfront work at Wallabout Bay and the East River.

Between 1636 and 1638 European settlers employed by the Dutch West India Company (established in 1621) made the earliest purchases (at least so far as the settlers were concerned) of land in what is now Brooklyn. One was near Gowanus; one was near Jamaica Bay; and the one that concerns us was on Wallabout Bay. The Wallabout land was purchased by Joris Jansen de Rapalje, a Walloon. The Walloons, who were numerous among the Dutch West India Company, were French-speaking Protestants from present-day Belgium. Rapalje purchased his land from the native Lenape. *Wallabout*, we believe, comes from the Dutch for *Walloon curve* or *Walloon bend*, a reference to the shape of the bay that is today situated right in the middle of the waterfront between the Williamsburg Bridge and the Manhattan Bridge. Rapalje is remembered in the name of today's Rapelye Street, a short street in Carroll Gardens.

The Wallabout area thereafter remained for many years a sleepy agricultural settlement, like most of the rest of Kings County. The area was dominated by such farms as those of the Ryersons, the Spaders, the Cowenhovens, and the Jacksons. The Ryersons, a major landowner, are remembered today in the name of Ryerson Street, which runs for two blocks between Flushing and Myrtle avenues (and continues as Ryerson Walk through the Pratt Institute campus). Martin and Annetje Ryerszens came to Brooklyn in the 17th century from their native Netherlands.

Wallabout Bay entered American history in a major way in 1776, following the British defeat of Continental troops in the Battle of Brooklyn. The British held prisoners of war on ships docked in Wallabout Bay. According to the historians Edwin G. Burrows and Mike Wallace (*Gotham* [1999]):

> The conditions on board were atrocious—hundreds of men packed together in squalid, reeking holds without adequate food or water and brutalized by their guards....Dysentery was rampant, said Christopher Hawkins, and because only two prisoners at a time were allowed to relieve themselves on the upper deck, he and the others below spent many nights smeared with "bloody and loathsome filth." Every morning the ships awakened to the call "Prisoners turn out your dead!"

Dead prisoners were buried or just left on the shore. By war's end, an estimated 11,500 patriots had perished on the prison ships. The prisoners' remains were later reinterred on land owned by John Jackson a bit farther inland, on Hudson Avenue in today's Vinegar Hill. That project was undertaken by an organization called the Society of St. Tammany. Founded in Manhattan as a national organization to honor and care for the descendants of common soldiers who died in the Revolutionary War (unlike the Society of the Cincinnati, which honored officers), it evolved into New York's powerful Tammany Hall Democratic political machine. The Hudson Avenue site, unfortunately, was, following the death of John Jackson, perceived to be imperiled by development, and in 1855 a Martyrs' Memorial Association proposed the relocation of the remains to the recently established Washington Park. When the park was redesigned by Calvert Vaux and Frederick Law Olmsted in 1867, they incorporated a vault for the patriot remains, and planned a hilltop monument. The bones of the deceased were relocated to Washington Park (renamed Fort Greene Park in 1897), though the monument did not come until 1908 when architect Stanford White's 149-foot-high Prison Ship Martyrs Monument was dedicated by President-elect William Howard Taft.

John Jackson had purchased a half-mile-long tract along the bay in 1781. (The Rapalje or Rapelye family lost its area landholdings when they picked the wrong side in the Revolution and were forced after the war to flee abroad.) Jackson and his brothers established a shipyard and in 1798 built the 28-gun frigate *John Adams* for the United States Navy. In 1801, Jackson sold his shipyard to the U.S. Navy for $40,000, whereupon the Brooklyn Navy Yard began its illustrious 165-year history. Shortly after the purchase, the Navy erected the beautiful Commandant's House, built in 1805–06, which still stands in the westernmost part of the Navy Yard site, visible through a fence from Little Street, off Water Street, in Vinegar Hill, and still used as a private residence. Most of the Navy Yard site is used today as a 300-acre city-owned industrial park managed by the Brooklyn Navy Yard Development Corporation. (The city purchased the site from the federal government in 1969 for $24 million.) The Navy Yard site (expanded over the years) today stretches from the East River inland to Flushing Avenue, and from Kent Avenue, in Williamsburg, on the east, to Navy Street (and its northward continuations), in Vinegar Hill, on the west. To the south lay Fort Greene and the neighborhood called Wallabout. (The story of the Navy Yard is beyond the scope of this guide. But its presence, as well as that of other nearby waterfront industry, helped shape the neighborhood. The neighborhood name "Wallabout" has been promoted by DK Holland and Rogen Brown, respectively the publisher and onetime editor of *The Hill*, the indispensable twice-yearly publication, founded in 1983, that covers all aspects of the past and present of Clinton Hill, Wallabout, and Fort Greene.)

Fort Greene and Wallabout, like Fort Greene and Clinton Hill to the south of Myrtle Avenue, are not historically distinct neighborhoods. They became distinct when the Fort Greene Houses were built to the west of Carlton Avenue in the 1940s. To the east of Carlton, the west of Classon Avenue (roughly on the line of the eastern border of the Navy Yard site), the south of Flushing Avenue, and the north of Myrtle is the area proposed as a Wallabout Historic District; a *Wallabout Cultural Resources Survey* was prepared in 2005 for the Myrtle Avenue Revitalization Project Local Development Corporation (founded in 1999) by the architectural historian Andrew S. Dolkart. This area retains much of the 19th-century fabric that was once also found to the west of Carlton Avenue.

The working-class and industrial character of the area north of Myrtle Avenue is strikingly different from the areas to the south and east of Fort Greene Park. Wallabout contains a mix of pre-Civil War wooden houses, late 19th-century single-family masonry houses and tenements, and late 19th- and early 20th-century industrial properties. Though it has always been a neighborhood of people of varied nationalities, for many decades it bore a strong Irish identity. Sacred Heart Roman Catholic Church, on Clermont Avenue between Park and Flushing avenues, held its first Mass in 1871, at which time the parish was predominately Irish. (The current edifice was built between 1874 and 1877.)

On February 24, 1858, the *New York Times* ran a long, sensational, and often-cited article entitled "Homes of the Poor: Jackson's Hollow and the People Who Live in It."

The *Times* defined the poor area as "extending from Flushing-avenue southward to DeKalb-avenue, and bounded by Classon-avenue on the east, and Ryerson-street on the west." The name "Jackson's Hollow" comes from the John Jackson farm, and the area included the present site of Pratt Institute. The *Times* called this area the "city of shanties."

Around 1850,

> There was an extensive colony of Irish people who had settled on the vacant lots around Fort Green [sic], which, from their style of architecture, and the number of pigs and dogs there, was known as "Young Dublin."

The residents of Young Dublin defied city ordinances prohibiting the keeping of pigs in the city. "At length a general and concerted attack was made upon pigdom," reported the *Times*, "by the Police; the pens were all demolished and the pigs ran about the streets. Their main stay thus removed a general hegira of the inhabitants soon occurred; their shanties were pulled down and, gathering up their household gods [*sic*], they moved out of town, where it was supposed the advancing tide of civilization would never overtake them."

This hegira took the Irish from "the vacant lots around Fort Green to Jackson's Hollow." Though the *Times* article does not note this, the timing of the hegira corresponds with the establishment of Washington Park. We may presume that the vacant lots included ones incorporated into the park. Ryerson Street, the western boundary of Jackson's Hollow, is nine blocks to the east of the park.

These Irish, who had been tenant farmers in Ireland, were now tenants on the Jackson farm, paying an annual ground rent of $10 to $15. "[T]his remarkable little colony is now hemmed in," said the *Times*, "on all sides by a desirable class of houses," as Fort Greene and Clinton Hill were beginning to take shape as Brooklyn's newest middle- and upper-class suburban areas.

> [O]ut of this Constantinople multitudes of poor women issue daily, heading for City Hall, in pursuit of coal, and, on election days, whole regiments of Democratic voters find their way thence to the polls.

The one-story (and usually one-room) shanties included side sheds where cows or goats were kept; poultry and dogs were also common—though not pigs, who had had war declared on them by the authorities.

> Around the walls are hung, in every house, pictures of the Virgin, of Christ, of the Apostles, or of Archbishop Hughes.

(At the time the article was written, 1858, Brooklyn had been its own Diocese of the Roman Catholic Church for six years, with its own Irish bishop, John Loughlin. It is interesting that Archbishop John Hughes, of the Archdiocese of New York, formed in 1850, still commanded the veneration of these Brooklyn Irish.)

"Upon Grand-avenue, north of Myrtle-avenue, there are 44 shanties, having 230 inmates; on Steuben-street, 57, with 268 inmates; between Myrtle and DeKalb avenues 94, with 230 inmates; between DeKalb and Lafayette avenues 20 shanties, having 90 inmates; and south of Lafayette-avenue an estimated number of 125 shanties, which, at the average of the others, contain an aggregate population of 500—making a total of 340 shanties and 1,427 inhabitants in the Hollow."

A man of sober appearance, who said he was a blacksmith by trade, had a wife and three children, but no fire or provisions in his house. He traveled every day from Greenpoint to Gowanus after work, but could find none, and his children were in a state of starvation.

The blocks of Jackson's Hollow north of Myrtle Avenue are today fairly nondescript, although at the very time, at its western edge, on Ryerson Street, lived Walt Whitman.

In the June 12, 1995 *New Yorker*, the writer Paul Berman told the story of how Elias Wilentz, the retired owner of Manhattan's legendary Eighth Street Bookshop, had become obsessed, following the demolition of the Cranberry Street building in which Whitman had set the type in the Rome brothers' print shop for the first edition of *Leaves of Grass*, with finding out if any of the buildings in which Whitman had once lived in Brooklyn still stood. With hints provided by books on Whitman, Wilentz, his son (the distinguished American historian Sean Wilentz), and Berman set out for Ryerson Street. Unable to determine which of the street's row houses was once Whitman's home, they embarked upon research in city records and directories and concluded it was 99 Ryerson Street, between Myrtle and Park avenues.

Walt Whitman as he appeared c. 1855, when he lived at 99 Ryerson Street.

Three events are known to have taken place in that most distinguished of houses. The Whitmans moved there in May, 1855. The poet, having given up carpentry and newspaper editing for the moment, used to sleep late, get up and work on his writings, and then make his way over to the Rome brothers' printshop. And in the early summer of 1855 he finally brought home the first printed copies of "Leaves of Grass." The house where Walt Whitman lived while he was putting the finishing touches on that book…is in fact the place on Ryerson.

Whitman lived in the house with his mother, Louisa (who was the recorded owner); his father, Walter; and his brothers. The second major event to take place in that house was the death of Walter Whitman Sr. on July 11, 1855. The third event occurred after Whitman sent a copy of *Leaves of Grass* to one of his idols, Ralph Waldo Emerson, "who replied by mailing to Whitman the single most celebrated appreciation in this history of American literature," saying "I find it the most extraordinary piece of wit and wisdom that America has yet contributed." Emerson said he wished to visit Whitman in New York. Before he could do so, however, his friend Moncure Conway set out for Brooklyn, and Ryerson Street. Conway wrote to Emerson, on September 17, 1855:

I found by the directory that one Walter Whitman lived fearfully far (out of Brooklyn, nearly), on Ryerton [sic] Street a short way from Myrtle Avenue. The way to reach the house is to go down to Fulton Street Ferry, after crossing take the Fulton and Myrtle Avenue car, and get out at Ryerton Street. It is one of a row of small wooden houses with porches, which all seem occupied by mechanics.

When Emerson at last went to visit Whitman in Brooklyn, in December 1855, the Whitman family had probably moved one month earlier from 99 Ryerson Street. (Whitman's biographer Justin Kaplan wrote that Emerson visited Whitman on Ryerson Street, but that is probably incorrect.) They were there for only six or seven months—but they were extremely significant months in Whitman's life and career.

99 Ryerson Street (the taller house) where Walt Whitman lived with his mother in 1855 when he self-published the first edition of *Leaves of Grass*.

Berman wrote:

There's still life in "Leaves of Grass," its political and labor poems included; and it may be that in Brooklyn something of the real-life past that created the poet similarly clings to life, ineradicable, like a weed in the pavement. And, by God, here is the proof: his own house, his mother's house, the birthplace of "Leaves of Grass." Rickety, but standing. Not as a museum, either, but as a working person's house on an ordinary block filled with Xerox technicians, art students from Pratt Institute, old-time workers left over from the days before the Brooklyn Navy Yard closed in the nineteen-sixties, newcomers from Mexico and Nicaragua and the West Indies.

When Berman rang the doorbell of 99 Ryerson, he encountered Clifford Richardson, an immigrant from St. Kitts. He was a highly trained electrician and, on the side, a reggae singer. A mechanic and an artist—a Whitmanian combination.

A few years earlier, on August 16, 1847, Whitman took us on a tour of Myrtle Avenue in the *Brooklyn Daily Eagle*:

This wide and extended thoroughfare seems likely to become one of the most business places in the city of Brooklyn—answering somewhat here to what the Bowery is to N. York. And when the new ferry gets in operation at the foot of Montague street it is probable that the passage through the avenue will be still greater. To the east it stretches in a straight line some three miles from Fulton street. It is regulated, paved, lighted and pumped, to the "head of the pavements," two or three blocks beyond its intersection with Bedford avenue—beyond which it assumes more the appearance of a country road.

He continued:

On each side, (still coming westward), lie immense tracts of land, all properly laid out on the city map, and the proper grade fixed, but still unoccupied by houses....Off on the streets which are still unregulated, the owners are glad to sell, at moderate prices, in order to save the future assessments, which run up alarmingly against the large properties. Many a mechanic who pays $100 or $150 a year rent, *would do far better to go out here and buy a lot, or a couple of lots, if possible, and build himself a little cottage. The place is healthier, and the whole arrangement would be cheaper.*

The unregulated streets to which he refers, one may presume, would include those of Jackson's Hollow, west of Bedford Avenue, neatly bisected by Myrtle Avenue. And this would of course also include 99 Ryerson Street, to which he would move eight years later.

Clinton avenue, which intersects Myrtle at a distance of two miles from the Fulton ferry, is the finest street of its kind in Brooklyn. It runs from the water, at the Wallabout, to the old Bedford turnpike. Ample in width, and lined on each side by thrifty shade trees—to which ornament, all along, we are glad to see the East Brooklynites devote considerable pains and expense. Clinton avenue may be said to promise, in the future, as it already is, a charming spot for residence or promenade.

And on his sojourn he came upon Young Dublin, not yet removed to Jackson's Hollow:

Descending Fort Greene one comes amid a colony of squatters, whose chubby children, and the good-natured brightness of the eyes of many an Irishwoman, tell plainly enough that you are wending your way among the shanties of the Emeralders. They are permitted by the owners here, until the ground shall be wanted, to live rent free, as far as the land is concerned.

Remarkably, the shanties of Young Dublin were but a stone's throw from a clamoring commercial thoroughfare:

From Raymond to Fulton street, all is the clattering din of traffic, turmoil, passage, and business.—The street floor of nearly every building is occupied as a retail shop; and the inhabitants of the neighborhood can buy every article for human comfort or luxury about as well as the dweller in any part of the great city over the river.

In 1800 one in four residents of Kings County was black; most of them enslaved. Enslaved people had helped build Fort Putnam and Fort Greene. In 1827, New York State abolished slavery. In 1860, by which time the population had increased from 5,740 to 279,122, only one in fifty Kings residents was black. The largest number of black Brooklynites had settled in what is now Fort Greene, with the greatest concentration north of Myrtle Avenue. In 1870, more than one half of all the African Americans in Brooklyn lived in Fort Greene (broadly defined), where blacks made up about ten percent of the population. By that time, the streets to the south and east of Washington Park were becoming the newly fashionable *faubourgs* for middle- and upper-class Brooklynites, and it would remain fashionable until well into the 20th century. But the streets north of Myrtle were never fashionable in that way. In this working-class district lived the mechanics and artisans celebrated by Whitman. Many of them worked at waterfront jobs, and among these were many African Americans.

In 1827, the year New York State abolished slavery, the First African Wesleyan Methodist Episcopal Church (founded in 1818 and located on High Street between Bridge and Jay streets) established a school for black children. (The school was under the direction of First A.W.M.E. Church trustee Henry C. Thompson, who in 1838 sold to James Weeks the tract of land, in present-day Crown Heights, that would grow into the Weeksville community.) The school was located on Nassau Street between Bridge and Jay streets. In 1845 the school was incorporated into the Brooklyn public school system and designated as Colored School No. 1. In 1863

Colored School No. 1 moved to Willoughby Street at Raymond Street (now Ashland Place). Fifteen years later, the school moved to North Elliot Place at Park Avenue in Fort Greene. In 1887, Colored School No. 1 became Public School 67, but in spite of the name change remained exclusively black. As Craig Steven Wilder notes in *A Covenant with Color: Race and Social Power in Brooklyn* (2000), although in the early 1890s, when the prominent black attorney and intellectual leader T. McCants Stewart served on the Brooklyn Board of Education, steps were taken to integrate the city's public schools, and in 1901, under Governor Theodore Roosevelt, the state mandated public school desegregation, P.S. 67 remained predominately black. In 1923 (*New York Times*, 9/11/1923, "City Schools Open; Ten New Buildings") P.S. 67 moved to its present location at 51 St. Edwards Street, between Auburn Place and Park Avenue, in the 1940s being engulfed by the Fort Greene Houses. In 1977 the school was named for Charles A. Dorsey, who was its principal from 1863 to 1897 and oversaw its transition from Colored School No. 1 to P.S. 67. Dorsey died in 1907 at his home at 81 Adelphi Street between Myrtle and Park avenues, only three blocks from the school that would later bear his name. (The house still stands.)

Dorsey's onetime assistant principal, Maritcha Remond Lyons, was born in 1848 in Manhattan and died in 1929 in Bedford-Stuyvesant. Her father was a prosperous merchant and Maritcha grew up in material comfort that was unusual at the time for New York African Americans. Maritcha's father, Albro Lyons, was an agent for the Underground Railroad. He said he believed he and his wife, Mary, had helped a thousand fugitives. Maritcha's godfather, and the best man at her parents' wedding, was Dr. James McCune Smith, who in 1837 had been the first African American to earn an M.D.—though he had to go to the University of Glasgow in Scotland to do it. Smith was also a leader of New York's black intellectual elite. The Lyonses were part of a highly educated, cultured, intellectual, and financially successful New York African American middle class. Nonetheless, the Lyonses left New York following the July 1863 draft riots, during which their home on Vandewater Street (since demapped, near the present Police Plaza) was destroyed by rioters. They moved to Providence, Rhode Island, where Maritcha became the first black graduate of Providence Public High School. She returned to New York and in 1869 began teaching at Colored School No. 1. She was a writer (she contributed several essays to Hallie Q. Brown's 1926 *Homespun Heroines and Other Women of Distinction*, an important source on notable African American women) and an outspoken advocate of women's rights and of racial integration. Clarence Taylor, in *The Black Churches of Brooklyn* (1996), quotes her,

> *The abuses that exist are the outcome of unscientific, unscrupulous propaganda on the part of those who have abrogated to themselves the right to obstruct the path of the colored Americans. These obstacles, illogical assertions, preconceived notions, false premises, specious reasoning—must be cut down or dug up by the keen blade of unprejudiced opinion; must be burned away by the ardent glow of an unquenchable reverence for humanity.*

Maritcha Lyons, who never married, and Mr. and Mrs. Charles A. Dorsey were leading members of St. Augustine Episcopal Church on Canton Street (now St. Edwards Street) at Park Avenue, one block from the North Elliot Place home of P.S. 67. The congregation occupied a chapel owned by Brooklyn Heights' Church of the Holy Trinity. (St. Augustine Church, which moved to Canton Street in 1889, moved in 1924 to Lafayette and Marcy avenues in Bedford-Stuyvesant, and is now on Avenue D at East 43rd Street in East Flatbush. It is the oldest black Episcopal congregation in Brooklyn, formed in 1875.) They were also members, along with

Fort Greene resident Dr. Susan Smith McKinney and many other prominent black Brooklynites (including several members, of whom Charles A. Dorsey was one, of what was identified as Brooklyn's "Negro 400," or black social elite), of the Brooklyn Literary Union. Albro and Mary Lyons, by the way, later moved to Fort Greene, to 51 St. Felix Street between DeKalb Avenue and Fulton Street.

Another onetime assistant principal of Charles A. Dorsey's at Colored School No. 1, and a woman whose biography Maritcha Lyons contributed to *Homespun Heroines and Other Women of Distinction*, was Georgiana Putnam. She was born in 1832 in Boston and, like Maritcha Lyons, came from a highly educated free black family. Georgiana's father was a successful hairdresser and part of the abolitionist circle that formed around William Lloyd Garrison. In 1852 Georgiana moved to Williamsburgh (as it was then spelled), not yet part of the City of Brooklyn, to teach in its African American school. There she was a colleague of Sarah Smith Tompkins Garnet, the famous educator, suffragist, and sister of Fort Greene's Dr. Susan Smith McKinney. In 1863 Georgiana became assistant principal of Fort Greene's Colored School No. 1, in the year Charles A. Dorsey became its principal. Between 1869 and 1896 she lived at 37 Fort Greene Place, between DeKalb and Lafayette avenues, on the present site of Brooklyn Technical High School.

In her biographical sketch of Georgiana Putnam, Maritcha Lyons wrote that at the time Georgiana Putnam came to Brooklyn,

> The number of colored people in the locality was then comparatively small. Slavery in the state had long been abolished and none living there had any practical knowledge of it, nor were any of its after effects especially apparent. Being an epoch before the large influx of immigrants, the strenuous life was unknown, habits were simple and restrained, desires were limited and there was work enough for every worker. Tasks were undertaken leisurely and all were contented with small gains. Gradually as the population increased, the era of hustling and competition was launched, an economic revolution ensued in which old ways were swamped and the weaker worker as usual went to the wall....While it lasted many colored men and women acquired property in lands and houses, were able to accumulate savings and invest them judiciously. Their material prosperity was genuine if not extensive....Our women in New York included not a few engaged in widely differing trades and professions, each of whom was an ornament to her sex.

Edwin G. Burrows and Mike Wallace wrote, in *Gotham* (p. 972),

> Brooklyn was indeed something of a paradise for the African-American middle-class. Though the vast majority of black Brooklynites consisted of manual laborers, the city was also home to a small elite of professionals (doctors, lawyers, journalists, ministers, and teachers) and businesspeople (dressmakers, undertakers, carpenters, barbers, tailors). Some were affluent enough to invest in real estate during the 1870s, via the Excelsior Land Association of Brooklyn, and some owned substantial middle-class dwellings, complete with pianos, libraries, and pictures of Lincoln, John Brown, and AME Bishop Richard Allen.

Beginning in 1884 the city established Wallabout Market, a wholesale produce market, on a site leased from the U.S. Navy that eventually extended north from Flushing Avenue to Wallabout Channel and from Washington Avenue east to Ryerson Street. This was only about a block from where Walt Whitman had lived at 99 Ryerson Street in 1855. Between 1894 and 1896 the city built the remarkable market buildings designed by William B. Tubby. These distinctive, picturesque structures, with their stepped Dutch gables, were ordered by Alfred Tredway

White, who had recently (1890) built the Riverside Buildings model tenements in the Willowtown section of Brooklyn Heights and who was serving as Commissioner of City Works in the reform administration of Mayor Charles Adolph Schieren, a Clinton Hill resident. The Wallabout Market buildings are gone, but Tubby's work can be studied at length in nearby Clinton Hill, where he designed the mansion at 241 Clinton Avenue for Charles Millard Pratt (the eldest son of Charles Pratt), as well as several of the original buildings of the Pratt Institute campus. By the turn of the century Wallabout Market was one of the largest wholesale food markets in the world, and, thanks to Schieren and White, possibly the best equipped.

In the wee small hours of the morning, market wagons and stalls overflowed with farm-fresh vegetables and fruits, as well as meats, seafood, and dairy products. A central administration building

The fanciful buildings of the Wallabout Market, Brooklyn's wholesale produce market. The market, on Flushing Avenue, was established in 1884; the distinctive buildings by William Tubby were erected in 1894–96. The market moved to Canarsie in 1941 when the adjacent Brooklyn Navy Yard was expanded for wartime operations.

and clocktower were personally paid for by Alfred Tredway White. Soon after the market buildings were erected, the market was hooked into the waterfront rail network—the Eastern District Terminal—that served Williamsburg industry to the north and that connected to other railroads all up and down Brooklyn's East River shore. In the first decade of the 20th century extensive pier facilities were built to accommodate the carfloat operations of all the major area railroads, including the Pennsylvania, the New York Central, the Baltimore & Ohio, the New Jersey Central, the Lehigh Valley, and the Erie. In 1913 the *New York Times* reported that 45,325 farmers' wagons occupied the market. Wallabout Market flourished until World War II, when the federal government desperately required the market's land for an emergency expansion of the Navy Yard.

On June 14, 1941, the *New York Times* reported: "The closing chapter to the story of the century-old Wallabout Market in Brooklyn will be written today at ceremonies at Washington and

Flushing Avenues, Brooklyn. Captain Harold V. McKittrick, commandant of the navy yard, will join officers of the Department of Markets and former tenants in the observance. The ceremonies will include a parade of 500 trucks and automobiles to the site of the new Brooklyn Terminal Market at Remsen Avenue and East Eighty-seventh Street in Canarsie." At the ceremony, a Navy Yard bugler played *Taps*.

In 1888, shortly after the market opened, the Brooklyn Elevated Railroad Company opened the Myrtle Avenue line between Adams Street in downtown Brooklyn and Grand Avenue in Clinton Hill, including stations at Navy Street, Vanderbilt Avenue, and Washington Avenue. The El was dismantled in 1969. It both served Fort Greene and Clinton Hill residents who commuted to jobs in downtown Brooklyn and Manhattan, and also facilitated the movement of workers employed at the Brooklyn Navy Yard, Wallabout Market, and the various other industrial enterprises that, in the late 19th and early 20th centuries, emerged in the blocks between Park and Flushing avenues.

The tracks of the Myrtle Avenue elevated railroad after the blizzard of March 1888, a few weeks before the opening of the elevated line that operated until 1969.

Those blocks were at first residential but became an integral part of Brooklyn's great waterfront chain of industry, running down from Greenpoint through Williamsburg, Wallabout, Vinegar Hill, and DUMBO, down into Red Hook and Sunset Park. This was one of the mightiest concentrations of manufacturing and related waterfront enterprise in America. Major Wallabout factories included the vast complexes of the Mergenthaler Linotype Company, the Drake Brothers Bakery, and the Rockwood Chocolate Company. None of these businesses is any longer active in Wallabout, but their imposing buildings still stand, mute testimony to Brooklyn's onetime status as a world-renowned manufacturing powerhouse.

The Rockwood Chocolate Factory, built at Waverly and Park avenues in 1910, was one of the country's largest chocolate factories and until it closed in 1967 imparted its delicious aroma to this part of Brooklyn.

On the east side of Waverly Avenue and the west side of Washington Avenue between Park and Flushing avenues, and on Park Avenue between Waverly and Washington avenues, the U.S. Department of the Interior's National Register of Historic Places in 1984 designated a 17-building Rockwood Chocolate Factory Historic District. In this district are buildings Rockwood built in the 1910s and 1920s, as well as earlier buildings Rockwood purchased and refitted. At the northeast corner of Park and Washington avenues stands an 1891 wholesale grocery warehouse that was later taken over by Rockwood. It is the oldest building in the complex. (In a sign of the times, this handsome building has been converted into the Chocolate Factory loft apartments.) Rockwood Building No. 4, at 47–53 Waverly Avenue, was designed by the prominent Brooklyn architects the Parfitt brothers, with a ground-floor design by the renowned Ernest Flagg (who had recently designed Manhattan's Singer Tower, then the tallest building in the world). It was built in 1910 as the first of the Rockwood-built structures in the complex. Rockwood was founded in Manhattan in 1886. In 1904 the company moved to Wallabout, and there grew into America's second-largest chocolate manufacturer, after Hershey of Pennsylvania. The location was not accidental: Rockwood was one of many food-related concerns that set up near Wallabout Market, which was right across Flushing Avenue. Like the adjoining Navy Yard, Rockwood made a World War II contribution: Their chocolate was included in U.S. soldiers' K-rations. In 1957 Rockwood closed the Wallabout plant, which was then operated for the next ten years by Sweets Corporation

The Mergenthaler Linotype Building, designed by the famous industrial architect Albert Kahn and built in 1907 on Park Avenue between Hall and Ryerson streets, was part of one of the largest industrial complexes ever built in New York.

of America. For decades the factory filled the neighborhood with the aroma of chocolate. (Sources: National Register of Historic Places Rockwood Chocolate Factory Historic District Nomination [1984]; *Wallabout Cultural Resources Survey* [2005])

Another manufacturing concern of note in the district was the Mergenthaler Linotype Company, whose campus of buildings can be found on Hall and Ryerson streets and Grand Avenue between Park and Flushing avenues. The campus took shape through the first half of the 20th century. Ottmar Mergenthaler (1854–99) was born in Germany and migrated to Baltimore, Maryland, in 1872. In 1884 he invented the linotype machine. This was a major innovation in printing, introducing hot-metal typesetting in which a "slug," or piece of type metal, of an entire line of type is set by machine, replacing the laborious hand-setting of a single character at a time. This produced an exponentially speeded-up typesetting process that allowed for the rapid assembly of printed materials, including books, newspapers, and magazines. The *New York Tribune,* beginning in 1886, was the world's first newspaper to make use of the linotype technology, which remained in wide use until the 1970s and 1980s when phototypesetting took over (followed by computerized typesetting). The Mergenthaler Linotype Company manufactured the machines used for "linecasting," as the typesetting process was known. The company was formed in Baltimore but in 1890 moved its manufacturing operations to Brooklyn. Mergenthaler Linotype was soon one of the largest employers in Brooklyn, and in 1920 moved even its corporate offices to Ryerson Street. The earliest of the company's buildings, on Ryerson Street, no longer stands; the oldest still standing, on the east side of Hall Street, was built in 1905. In 1907 the company began to build its factory buildings of reinforced concrete, and they are among the pioneer examples of Brooklyn's rich heritage of reinforced-concrete industrial architecture. Of special note is that the 1907 building at the northwest corner of Ryerson Street and Park Avenue was designed by Albert Kahn, one of America's most important industrial architects, known especially for his automobile assembly plants in Detroit. The last of the Mergenthaler Linotype campus was completed in 1942 when the federal government's Defense Plant Corporation erected the striking Modernist building on Park Avenue between Ryerson Street and Grand Avenue. This was then leased to the Mergenthaler Linotype Company, which used it for manufacturing precision instruments for the U.S. military. By this year, the *Brooklyn Daily Eagle* reported that the company employed 2,872 workers.

Mergenthaler Linotype left Brooklyn in 1959, two years after Rockwood Chocolate closed up shop. Such industrial departures or closings were as damaging to Brooklyn's self-identity as the defection in 1958 of the Dodgers, or the shuttering in 1955 of the *Brooklyn Eagle.* Among the most devastating closings was that in 1966 of the Brooklyn Navy Yard, after 165 years in operation. The Navy Yard had attained its peak productivity during World War II, at a time when New York was a major national center of military production. During the war, Wallabout was a hive of activity. But as soon as the war ended (the Japanese signed the peace treaty aboard the U.S.S. *Missouri,* which had been built at the Brooklyn Navy Yard), activity slowed dramatically. Wallabout became an isolated, largely forgotten place. The area, as with so many inner city neighborhoods, suffered from disinvestment and deterioration.

By the 1930s, an area near P.S. 67 had acquired the sobriquet "The Jungle." "This area," said the *New York Times* in 1934, "is a particularly virulent source of delinquency, and the refuge of criminal characters." It was an area of substandard housing, poverty, and crime, and beginning in 1941 most of the physical fabric between St. Edwards Street on the west, Myrtle Avenue on the south, Carlton Avenue on the east, and Park Avenue on the north was razed for the construction of a housing development that was one of the most ambitious building projects that had ever been undertaken by local government in the United States, and that was heralded with high idealism.

Fort Greene Houses, the development that took shape on that site, was conceived as state- and city-subsidized housing for low-income New Yorkers. The *New York Times* said in 1941 that Fort Greene Houses "seemed destined to breathe new life, color and usefulness into a part of the city that had become dingy and rundown." Ground was broken on May 6, 1941. In attendance were Governor Herbert H.

Lehman and Mayor Fiorello La Guardia, the latter of whom called Fort Greene Houses "the largest low-rent housing unit ever attempted in this or any other country." The governor added that the development was "the first State-aided public housing project anywhere in this great nation of ours." The groundbreaking ceremonies took place at Park and Carlton avenues, in the midst of a desolate area where only weeks before had stood more than 700 buildings.

The first 816 units of the 3,501-unit project opened in October 1942. It was completed in 1944, and covered 38 acres. About three quarters of the acreage was open space. This type of housing project came to be called "towers in a park." The idea was that low-income residents, used to living on treeless, tenement-crammed streets, would benefit, physically and psychologically, from the landscaped, park-like grounds, and that the many children's playgrounds would help keep kids out of trouble. At the time Fort Greene Houses was built, such housing was considered by most experts and civic reformers to be a necessary solution to the problems of the slums. Only later did such housing reveal itself to be flawed in its own ways, and did a generation, led by the urbanist and activist Jane Jacobs, rise up against the continuing construction of such housing. This generation suggested that traditional city streets and neighborhoods, even when crammed with tenements, had special virtues and only needed to be reformed, not destroyed. But that was not how most urban experts saw things in 1941.

There are basketball courts throughout the projects. I have great memories of playing basketball in the rain and in the winter, we shoveled the snow away to play. It was a way of life back then. Our entertainment was basketball, everyone just gathering around the court and watching everyone play. You win, you stay on the court, you lose, you get on line for the next game. It was very competitive, sometimes it was a little bit too competitive, and we'd have a little fight now and then. Everyone wanted to fulfill that dream of playing professional basketball. Living in the inner city, of course you're poor, you don't have a lot, and you're watching TV and seeing Kareem Abdul-Jabbar, Wilt Chamberlain, Walt Frazier, all these professional players. And then when you're on the court you become someone; I became Dr. J. We're playing skins and shirts on the pavement, but maybe one day we'll be able to play at Madison Square Garden.

ALBERT KING
Grew up in Fort Greene Houses and played
forward in the NBA from 1981 to 1992

Thirty-five brick buildings were built, ranging from six to fifteen stories, and housing more than 13,000 people. A few structures left standing remind us of the neighborhood before the houses were built. The strikingly picturesque Roman Catholic Church of St. Michael and St. Edward (originally the Church of St. Edward), on St. Edwards Street between Myrtle and Park avenues, opposite Auburn Place, was built in 1902. Across the street from the church, on the northeast corner of St. Edwards Street and Auburn Place, stands the Walt Whitman Branch of the Brooklyn Public Library. When it was built in 1908, the library was called the City

The vast Fort Greene Houses complex, north of Fort Greene Park, was built between 1941 and 1944. The 35 buildings originally housed wartime workers including service personnel. Later the project transitioned to subsidized low-income tenancy; the houses were later renamed the Walt Whitman Houses (to the east) and the Raymond V. Ingersoll Houses (to the west).

Park Branch (as it was still called in 1938 when Richard Wright used the library), and was renamed for Whitman in 1943. P.S. 67 also remained.

The development was conceived before the demolition of Wallabout Market and expansion of the Navy Yard and the need to provide housing for a massive influx of wartime workers. It was, essentially, commandeered by the federal government for military purposes. Because of emergency wartime needs and the wartime shortage of building materials, the idealistically conceived development was hurried, corners were cut, and the end result did not meet the original quality projections. The new housing served military personnel and other wartime workers, and not until after the war did Fort Greene Houses revert to its original intended use as housing for low-income New Yorkers. By the 1950s, the towers had begun to exhibit serious physical decay. As the newspapers reported on sometimes horrific crimes that took place there, Fort Greene Houses earned a fearsome reputation, and emerged as a poster child for the ills of inadequately conceived, poorly built, and over-hyped solutions to the problems of the slums. Public housing was viewed as one of the principal breeding grounds of that 1950s epidemic known as "juvenile delinquency."

Within the grounds of the former Fort Greene Houses stands the Roman Catholic Church of St. Michael and St. Edward (St. Edwards Street opposite Auburn Place), built in 1902.

When I was drafted by the Nets, the neighborhood response was incredible. They would have loved for me to play for the Knicks, but being with the Nets was a thrill for everyone. What was even more exciting, was when we went to college. Not a lot of people in the neighborhood had the opportunity to go away to college.

ALBERT KING

In 1957 the New York City Housing Authority announced a thorough renovation of Fort Greene Houses, noting that because the development had been built during wartime, substandard materials were used. "Leaky walls, chipped plaster, rusted elevator mechanisms and other physical shortcomings of Fort Greene Houses in Brooklyn are being remedied in the biggest home fix-it job undertaken by the City Housing Authority," said the *Times* in February 1958.

In 1957 and 1958 the towers were renovated and divided into two separately managed housing developments, the Raymond V. Ingersoll Houses (20 buildings with 1,802 apartments housing more than 4,500 residents) to the west of St. Edwards Street, and the Walt Whitman Houses (15 buildings with 1,636 apartments housing more than 4,200 residents) to the east of St. Edwards Street. But it was too little, too late. Public housing was coming in for stinging criticism. On July 27, 1959, for example, *Newsweek* magazine, in a sensational article entitled "Metropolis in a Mess," ran a scathing indictment of public housing projects. Fort Greene Houses, said *Newsweek*, was "one of the starkest examples" of how public housing had "become million-dollar barracks, in which no one develops a sense of responsibility, or of belonging, or wanting to belong." From a distance, Fort Greene Houses "has the look of a fine development. Closer inspection reveals windows broken as in an abandoned factory; walls cracking; light fixtures inoperative; doors unhinged; elevators that clearly are used as toilets."

My parents were very strict. My mother and father have been married for over 58 years. We went to church every Sunday. We had to do our homework. A lot of families in Fort Greene had two parents, but the majority didn't. Maybe they lived with one parent, or grandparents, or lived with relatives. In that case, you're out on the street more; you're not at home, you're not doing what you need to do. So, we grew up in a more stable environment. When we went to other areas of Brooklyn we were able to handle it. Of course, we were still Fort Greene, and will always be Fort Greene.

ALBERT KING

A year earlier, on March 26, 1958, Harrison E. Salisbury, a celebrated journalist, wrote in the *New York Times*:

> *Most visitors to the Fort Greene Houses in Brooklyn prefer to walk up three or four flights instead of taking the elevator. They choose the steep, cold staircases rather than face the stench of stale urine that pervades the elevators.*

Nowhere this side of Moscow are you likely to find public housing so closely duplicating the squalor it was designed to supplant.

The Fort Greene project houses more than 3,400 families. It is described as the world's largest public housing project. It is also described as a $20,000,000 slum. The epithet is a fitting one.

This was in a series of articles Salisbury wrote that later formed his 1958 book *The Shook-Up Generation*. This was about the generation of New Yorkers "shook up" by, among other things, the constant tearing down and building up of the city in the age of "urban renewal." People—both the poor and the middle class—were, in the postwar years, moved around like so many pawns on a chess board as the city—during a time when it was perhaps the wealthiest and most powerful in the history of the world—sought to remedy its problems by the most heavy-handed, top-down means possible. Whole established neighborhoods vanished in the blink of an eye. In their place typically rose "projects" based on radical ideas of urban form that had gestated in avant-garde circles of post-World War I Europe. And these ideas were implemented at the very moment that industry began to abandon Brooklyn and African American and Puerto Rican migrants had come to form a demographically transformational influx.

My whole life growing up is Fort Greene: It's the Korean store right across from Fort Greene Park where we used to always go to get pumpkin seeds, peanuts, soda; it's Cumberland Hospital; it's the monkey bars, the swings; it's playing ringolevio....it's being outside, just running....People say there's crime, it's not clean, all these things. But it was home. The twelfth floor, the three-bedroom apartment, with four brothers in one room, your parents in another, your sister and your other little brother in another, cramped, living in a place where the elevator works every couple days and the other days you have to run up the steps, or you've got to take the shopping cart and push it up the steps for twelve flights. In the summertime, not having any air conditioning, people have to have the windows open, the Brooklyn-Queens Expressway keeping you up all night because it's right across the street. In the wintertime, freezing cold, four or five blankets. But I think the big thing is: I would do it all over again. It's where I will always, always call home. I've lost touch with most of my friends from there. There was a lot of despair, a lot of crime. But there was a lot of togetherness. The older people living in that area took care of each other, took care of the kids. Growing up, you did something wrong, they must have had some type of mental telepathy—your parents knew about it before you got home. It was like they sent a signal from one building to the next. Everyone wants money, everyone wants to live in a nice place, everyone wants to drive a nice car and dress in nice clothes and all. But to experience Fort Greene, to experience Brooklyn, there's nothing like it. Brooklyn has changed. Brooklyn is the new Manhattan, we all know that. But back then, there was a togetherness.

ALBERT KING

When planning began for Fort Greene Park in the 1840s, the area had not yet taken on the solidly middle-class and upper-middle-class character it soon would. When the park was redesigned by Calvert Vaux and Frederick Law Olmsted in 1867, however, the neighborhood to the east and south of the park had filled with prosperous residents.

Fort Greene Park, view to the north from the top of the hill toward the former Fort Greene Houses and lower Manhattan.

When Walt Whitman, as editor of the *Brooklyn Daily Eagle* between 1846 and 1848, advocated for the creation of a public park in East Brooklyn, it was, he said, to benefit the humble "mechanics and artificers of our city."

In 1776 the Continental army built Fort Putnam on the present site of Fort Greene Park. Fort Putnam was named for a military engineer named Rufus Putnam. The site recommended itself because of its high elevation; the present hill in Fort Greene Park was formed by the receding Wisconsin ice sheet. Following the retreat across the East River of the troops under General Washington, the British destroyed the Continental fortifications, including Fort Putnam.

During the Revolutionary War, New York took in Continental prisoners of war whom the British eventually held on transport ships docked in Wallabout Bay, near the site of Fort Putnam. The crowding and lack of sanitary facilities bred disease and an estimated 11,500 patriots died on the ships over a six-year period. (The book to read is Edwin G. Burrows, *Forgotten Patriots: The Untold Story of American Prisoners During the Revolutionary War* [2008].) Dead prisoners were ferried from the ships to the Brooklyn shore and buried near the present site of the Brooklyn Navy Yard.

When the War of 1812 broke out, many feared the British would attack New York, and in 1814 the site of Fort Putnam became home to a brand-new fortification called Fort Greene, named for the late General Nathanael Greene, who had overseen construction of the earlier fort. The British, however, never attacked New York (though they did attack Washington, D.C.).

The Town of Brooklyn became the City of Brooklyn in 1834, and in 1839 the city established its street plan. The site of the disused Fort Greene was first proposed as a city park in 1845; the site was chosen because, with its hill, it was not attractive to real-estate developers. (The 1839 plan had actually envisioned a "square," bounded by Atlantic Avenue, Ashland Place, Fort Greene Place, and Fulton Street, but soon this land was considered too valuable for a park.) Still, the usual squabbling (over such things as the boundaries of the assessment area) took place. On June 11, 1846, Walt Whitman wrote in the *Brooklyn Daily Eagle*:

> *Very sorry indeed shall we be, if the present effort to have the ground known as Fort Green [sic] reserved for a Public Park, be an unsuccessful effort—if the small objections and jealousies which seem to be arrayed against it, be allowed to defeat the establishment of the most noble and desirable convenience for the present and future health and recreation of the citizens of Brooklyn....*

Fort Green Park, Brooklyn, N. Y.

Postcard photo of Fort Greene Park before the construction of the Prison Ship Martyrs Monument, c. 1900.

Any one who walks down Myrtle avenue, and sees the rapid manner in which buildings are crowding on, up the hill at the farther extremity, and across on the intersecting streets, needs no argument to prove the unavoidable certainty that twelve years from this time will see a city of itself, in size and traffic, to the east of Bridge street. There, too, the mechanics and artificers of our city, most do congregate. There you will see row upon row of their neat plain wooden houses, with unpretensive appearance—and without the ornamental attractions (except the plentiful children thereabout, may be called so), which are characteristic of the Heights. We have a desire that these, and the generations after them, should have such a place of recreation as Washington Park, where, of hot summer evenings, and Sundays, they can spend a few grateful hours in the enjoyment of wholesome rest and fresh air.

In early 1848 the Brooklyn Common Council adopted an assessment plan and allocated $90,000 for the construction of the park. The park opened in 1850. It was designed in the naturalistic style promoted by the popular and influential landscape gardener Andrew Jackson Downing. It was called Washington Park.

Washington Park was in fact the second park established in the City of Brooklyn. City Park, at St. Edwards Street and Park Avenue, was created on swampy land in 1836 after the efforts of Hezekiah Beers Pierrepont to create an elegant park on Brooklyn Heights failed due to landowners' objections. Situated in a rough area, City Park soon developed a bad reputation. In 1871 the *Brooklyn Daily Eagle* called it "the resort of the idle, the dissolute and the depraved, and a nuisance to respectable citizens, and it can never, whatever pains and expense may be bestowed upon it, be made sacred to any better uses." The ten-acre park was renamed Commodore Barry Park in 1951.

In 1867 Frederick Law Olmsted and Calvert Vaux, who had designed Prospect Park, were hired to redesign Washington Park. In its 17 years the park had been so intensively used (that heavy use was one of the reasons the city decided to build Prospect Park) that it was in a degraded condition and in need of a thorough overhaul. It is good to bear in mind that parks require constant upkeep. During those inevitable times when city coffers are stretched, park maintenance may fall below the "state of good repair," and as soon as that happens spiraling decay sets in. We find that all city parks go through their own boom and bust cycles. Thus, in 1867, Washington Park was considered in need of rebuilding. Another such time was 1937, during the Great Depression. On June 30 of that year, the *New York Times* reported:

The restored and rehabilitated Fort Greene Park in Brooklyn, which in the last few years had become so scarred by vandals and unkempt from lack of proper maintenance as to present a dilapidated appearance, was opened officially to the public yesterday at exercises in the park presided over by Park Commissioner Moses.

That was not the first and not the last time that Fort Greene Park had come to "present a dilapidated appearance."

Calvert Vaux and Frederick Law Olmsted submitted their plans for Washington Park to Brooklyn's park commissioners on September 9, 1867. They worked on Washington Park just after working on Prospect Park and Central Park, and the challenges were altogether different. Unlike the other parks, Washington Park already existed; their job was to remake it, not create a park where there had not been one. And it was much smaller—30 acres compared to Prospect Park's 585. They also had to work with a dominating natural topographical feature in the form of the great hill. Most of the topography of Prospect Park and Central Park is man-made. Vaux and Olmsted were also charged with creating a new site for the remains of the patriot martyrs. Finally, the neighborhood surrounding the park was already developed and densely populated, unlike the areas bordering Prospect Park. Vaux and Olmsted sought to create, within a fairly small compass, a combination of a contemplative park and a recreational park; to incorporate an area for public gatherings and military drills (which was the purpose of the Parade Grounds abutting the south end of Prospect Park); and to create a suitable setting for a monument to the prison ship martyrs. The designers intended that the main entrance to the park be in its northwest corner, at Myrtle Avenue and St. Edwards Street. Here they placed a large circular area capable of accommodating a gathering of 30,000 people. Any meetings or gatherings in that space, the designers believed, would be inspired to solemnity and seriousness by the proximity of the martyrs monument. This space was also suited to the precision military drills that were a major public

entertainment of the time. This included drills staged by the 23rd Regiment of the National Guard, whose Clermont Avenue Armory, three blocks to the east of the park, between Willoughby and Myrtle avenues, was built between 1871 and 1873. (Designed by William A. Mundell, the armory featured a notably large clear-span drill hall that remained intact after the armory façade was altered in 1911. The building remained an armory until 1964, and between 1964 and 1986 was a city storage facility. Between 1986 and 2000 the building was vacant, and during that time was stripped of all its valuable fittings. In 2000 the building was renovated into 110 moderate-income apartments under the New York City Housing Development Corporation's New Housing Opportunities Program.)

A Fort Greene Park outing of children (possibly kindergarteners) and their adult minders from Emmanuel House, 131 Steuben Street, the settlement house operated by Emmanuel Baptist Church; photo taken c. 1910–14.

This was also the corner of the park that led directly up to the top of the hill where Vaux and Olmsted planned a monument. Throughout the park Vaux and Olmsted placed the curving, looping walkways and bobbing terrain that were hallmarks of their park designs. Though the park was altered in the first decade of the 20th century by McKim, Mead & White, most of Vaux and Olmsted's plan remained. The loop of green in the southeast corner of the park, in from the northwest corner of DeKalb Avenue and Washington Park, was originally a girls' playground, while the loop to its west, just in from DeKalb Avenue between South Portland Avenue and South Elliott Place, where the tennis courts now are, was originally a boys' playground. Not all of Vaux and Olmsted's walkways are still in place, but the basic configuration of loops and of park entrances is intact, as is the basic layout of the approach to the monument from the northwest. In the renovation completed in 1937 under the direction of Park Commissioner Robert Moses, Vaux and Olmsted's walkway network and planting scheme were simplified by the landscape architect Gilmore D. Clarke. Thus, while the park is still recognizably a Vaux and Olmsted creation, the names of McKim, Mead & White and of Gilmore D. Clarke must also be credited by those who use and enjoy the park today.

Fort Greene Park, view to the east with the houses of Washington Park visible.

The remains of the prisoners who died on the British ships in Wallabout Bay had been transferred by the Society of St. Tammany (which had originated as a national organization to honor the common soldiers who had fought in the Revolutionary War) to a site on Hudson Avenue (in today's Vinegar Hill) donated by the landowner John Jackson. That site, however, was not considered safe from possible development, and in 1855 a Martyrs' Memorial Association proposed that a permanent vault for the remains be constructed in Washington Park. Vaux and Olmsted incorporated a vault in the hill of the park, and proposed a hilltop monument. The redesigned park was opened in stages in 1869 and 1870, though the monument that Vaux designed in 1873 was left unbuilt. In 1897 the park's name was changed to Fort Greene Park, in recognition of Brooklynites' never having ceased to refer to the site as Fort Greene.

One Fort Greene resident who made use of the park in the 1880s and 1890s was Juliette Paxton Atkinson. A physician's daughter, she and her sister Kathleen taught themselves how to play lawn tennis in Fort Greene Park. "They carried their own net, poles, rackets, and balls, erecting and dismantling their court each trip" (Frank V. Phelps, *American National Biography Online*). Both became competitive tennis players and in 1895 the 5-foot-tall Juliette won the U.S. women's singles championship and did so again in 1897. Juliette and Kathleen were national doubles champions in 1897 and 1898, and in the latter year Juliette again won the singles championship. Juliette went on to further tennis glory and also excelled in swimming, golf, basketball, cycling, and bowling—and opera singing. Wallis Merrihew, longtime editor of *American Lawn Tennis* magazine, judged Juliette to be the greatest American female tennis player of the 19th century. She was elected to the International Tennis Hall of Fame in 1974. (And to think Walt Whitman had something to do with it!)

A monument finally rose at the crest of the hill in 1908. Stanford White of McKim, Mead & White designed a 149-foot-high Doric column surmounted by a bronze lantern. The lantern was designed by the sculptor Adolph Alexander Weinman (1871–1952), who often worked for McKim, Mead & White. (Weinman designed "Civic Fame" atop the firm's

Children playing in Fort Greene Park, with the Prison Ship Martyrs Monument visible through the trees.

Municipal Building in Manhattan and created the bronze eagles that ornamented the firm's original Pennsylvania Station. He had also once worked for Olin Levi Warner, the sculptor of the portrait busts on the exterior of the Brooklyn Historical Society.) The bronze lantern was cast in Brooklyn at the Whale Creek Iron Works in Greenpoint. On November 14, 1908, the monument was dedicated by President-elect William Howard Taft. (Just weeks before, then candidate Taft held a rousing rally in the newly opened Brooklyn Academy of Music on Lafayette Avenue.) The McKim, Mead & White-designed plaza surrounding the monument is where Richard Wright sat in the early mornings of 1938 to write *Native Son,* and features prominently in Spike Lee's 1986 film *She's Gotta Have It.* McKim, Mead & White also designed the comfort station that now serves as the park's Visitors' Center just to the east of the monument.

The monument, like the park itself, has seen better and worse days. The monument decayed from lack of routine maintenance, and was vandalized and scarred by graffiti. Through the splendid efforts of the Fort Greene Park Conservancy (founded 1998), however, funds were raised for a restoration and rededication of the monument in November 2008, the centennial of the original

The Prison Ship Martyrs Monument in Fort Greene Park.

dedication. A highlight was the relighting of the lantern's "eternal flame," which had last shone in 1921. At the rededication ceremony, New York City Parks & Recreation Commissioner Adrian Benepe said, "The Prison Ship Martyrs Monument...may be 100 years old but it has never looked better."

The Prison Ship Martyrs Monument and the grand stairway leading up to it in Fort Greene Park. The doorway set in the steps leads to the crypt containing the remains of the patriots who perished on British prison ships docked at Wallabout Bay in the Revolutionary War.

Neither Vaux, who died in 1895, nor Olmsted, who died in 1903, lived to see Stanford White's renovations to the park. (Nor did White himself, who had been shot and killed by Harry Thaw in 1906.) But Olmsted had previously worked with White, and despaired over the triumph of the City Beautiful movement, which White represented, over the *rus in urbe* (or country-in-the-city) philosophy that Olmsted promoted. In his biography of Vaux, *Country, Park & City* (1998), the historian Francis R. Kowsky wrote:

> The new men, disciples of the Ecole des Beaux-Arts, saw the role of landscape design, said Olmsted, as "an intensification and aggrandizement of urban art rather than a means of recreation from the town; any broad rural effect being considered out of place and anachronistic." Olmsted chiefly singled out Stanford White...as the black beast of this position. White, he said, "has been trying to establish the rule of those motives that are at war with those that ruled in the original laying out of the Brooklyn park." In Olmsted's view, White detested the older style and wished to see it replaced by "efforts approaching the ruling Versailles character....They have struck down Vaux," he lamented, "and are doing their best to kill him in the name of the Lord of France."

But it must be mentioned that White respected Vaux and Olmsted's plan for the park. And since then a whole host of other enemies of civic art—one need look only at the large modern institutional buildings to the immediate west of the park—have sprung up, such that today we view Vaux and White more as allies than as each other's nemeses.

A park of 30 acres is too small to be a major metropolitan park (Central Park is 843 acres, Prospect Park is 585) and too large to be a residential square (Carroll Park, in Carroll Gardens, is 1.8 acres, Washington Square in Manhattan is just under 10 acres). Yet Fort Greene Park works as both. It packs a great deal within its borders, and with its hill, affording some of the most dramatic views in New York City, and beautiful monument, it certainly is a metropolitan attraction as well as a neighborhood square. But it also divides the neighborhood into two parts that have had distinct histories and distinct fates.

For us, I will say that living in Fort Greene has been the best thing that could happen. And now it has changed a lot, tremendous. We can't even recognize it now. When we went to the park, you didn't go over there by yourself. We went as a group. We played soccer there every Saturday, and it was men, women, children, everybody— but we were always a group. And now I go there by myself, even in the evening....We cleaned up the park— no Parks Department was there cleaning up.

MARIANNE ENGBERG
Photographer and Fort Greene resident since 1972

People and dogs enjoying the leaf-strewn verdant expanses of beautiful Fort Greene Park, the Prison Ship Martyrs Monument towering nearby, on a bright day.

View east along
Lafayette Avenue;
visible at the top just
right of center are the
Masonic Temple and
Our Lady Queen of All
Saints Church and
School.

From its earliest European settlement in the 17th century through
the first half of the 19th century, present-day Fort Greene was
dominated by farms. The farms tended to be long, linear affairs,
extending south from Wallabout Bay like fingers. These farms'
subdivisions for residential development in the mid-19th century
spawned the Fort Greene neighborhood. The Dutch Ryerson
(originally Ryerszens) family, for example, began building up its
landholdings in present-day Clinton Hill, where there is a Ryerson
Street, and in Fort Greene in the 17th century. In the 1840s the
widow of Jacob Ryerson began selling off the family's farmland for
residential development, such as that along Carlton Avenue and
Adelphi Street to the east of present-day Fort Greene Park (which
opened in 1850 and was originally called Washington Park). The
Greek Revival houses at 237 and 239 Carlton Avenue (according
to the Landmarks Preservation Commission, these are the oldest
masonry houses in the Fort Greene Historic District), between
DeKalb and Willoughby avenues, were built in the mid-1840s,
among the earliest structures erected on the recently subdivided
Ryerson farmland. Other major area farms were subdivided
between the 1840s and 1860s.

In recent times the term "urban sprawl" (or "suburban sprawl")
has become quite common. It refers to metropolitan regions that
spread (or sprawl) outward, usurping countrysides as farms and
other rural areas are subdivided and sold for residential
development. But sprawl is not a recent phenomenon. Kings
County, established under British colonial rule in 1683, originally
comprised six towns: Flatbush, Flatlands, Bushwick, New Utrecht,
Gravesend, and Brooklyn. Though these were called towns, they
were at first sparsely settled rural areas dominated by farms. In
1800, about one in four residents of Kings County was black—and
most likely slaves. (New York State did not abolish slavery until
1827.) In 1800 the population of Kings County was 5,740. Of
these, 1,477 were slaves, and 332 were free blacks. Between 1800

and 1820, the population of Kings County roughly doubled, then between 1820 and 1840 quadrupled. By 1850, when Washington Park opened and Fort Greene had begun to take shape as an urban neighborhood, the population was 138,882.

In fact, most of the population growth occurred in only one of the six towns: Brooklyn. The town of Brooklyn had grown sufficiently that in 1834 it was incorporated by New York State as the City of Brooklyn. Even most of Brooklyn was sparsely settled. Though what is now Park Slope, for example, was within the boundaries of the City of Brooklyn, it did not experience significant population growth until the 1860s. The center of Brooklyn's population was Brooklyn Heights and the area to its immediate north (Fulton Ferry and today's DUMBO). These were the waterfront areas served by the swift steam-powered ferryboats that had begun to cross the East River between Long Island and Manhattan in 1814. The steam ferries made it possible and desirable to live on Brooklyn Heights and to commute to work in lower Manhattan. Brooklyn Heights is thus sometimes referred to as New York's first suburb.

As additional ferries were established, and as land transportation improved—from horse-drawn omnibuses to horse-drawn streetcars that ran on iron rails to steam-powered surface and elevated railroads—Brooklyn "sprawled" to the south and east. To the south, the neighborhoods that are today known by the names Cobble Hill, Boerum Hill, Carroll Gardens, and Park Slope took form between the 1840s and the 1870s. By the 1870s, horse-drawn streetcars had made it possible—and Prospect Park had it made it desirable—for well-to-do professionals and businesspeople to commute to Manhattan jobs from Park Slope. These neighborhoods were then known—and are still often referred to as—South Brooklyn. Today they are not in the southern part of Brooklyn at all; but before New Utrecht and Gravesend became part of Brooklyn in 1894, "South Brooklyn" really was southern Brooklyn.

ARMORY. TWENTY THIRD REGIMENT.

Brooklyn's population sprawled eastward, too, to what was in the 19th century called East Brooklyn: the places now known as Fort Greene, Clinton Hill, and Bedford-Stuyvesant.

Between 1850 and 1860 the population of Kings County more than doubled, to 279,122. The population of Brooklyn alone in 1860 was 266,661. Five years earlier, Brooklyn had annexed the only other Kings County town, Bushwick, that had experienced appreciable population growth. Between 1851 and 1855 a part of Bushwick became the short-lived City of Williamsburgh, which in 1850 had actually been the 23rd largest city (or, more accurately, "urban place") in America. By 1860, Brooklyn was the third largest city in the United States, with a comfortable lead over fourth-

The 23rd Regiment Armory on Clermont Avenue between Myrtle and Willoughby avenues in 1873, the year the armory, designed by William A. Mundell, opened.

place Baltimore (though well behind second-place Philadelphia, let alone first-place New York).

It is against this background of the phenomenal growth of the City of Brooklyn that Fort Greene grew from a handful of finger-like farms to a densely populated urban neighborhood.

The City of Brooklyn conceived its street plan in 1839. But historic real-estate maps show that in the early 1840s, though what is now Fort Greene had been platted, development generally pulled up well to the west of Raymond Street (now Ashland Place). But that would soon change. Washington Park was opened in 1850 at a time when town houses—such as the mid-1840s Greek Revival houses at 237 and 239 Carlton Avenue, one block to the east of the park—had only just begun to sprout up. It's tempting to think that the park was a lure to development. But the population growth—in 1850, Brooklyn was the seventh largest city in America—was such that the development of Fort Greene would likely have occurred whether the park was there or not. When Walt Whitman, as editor of the *Brooklyn Daily Eagle,* advocated the creation of the park, he felt it was necessary for the health and well-being of the "mechanics and artificers of our city." In other words, the earliest population growth in Fort Greene occurred north of Myrtle Avenue, nearer the waterfront and near the Brooklyn Navy Yard, which had been in operation, when Washington Park opened, for 49 years. The shanties of Young Dublin in the 1840s were right in the vicinity of the future park, on farmland that had not yet been subdivided and where the city streets had, for the most part, not yet been cut through. By the time Washington Park was redesigned by Calvert Vaux and Frederick Law Olmsted in 1867, the neighborhood to the east and south of the park had become the fashionable new section of burgeoning Brooklyn.

BROOKLYN'S ELITE

In 1867 the street running along the east side of the park was still called Cumberland Street, named after Cumberland Terrace in London's Regent's Park. But the two blocks of Cumberland Street running along the park came to be called Washington Park—an indication that there was prestige in living right on the park ("I live on Washington Park"). It may have been less confusing if it had been named "Washington Park East," but it wasn't. The two blocks of Washington Park housed, for many years, several of the most elite families of Brooklyn.

The brownstone house at 175 Washington Park, between Willoughby and Myrtle avenues, was built, together with the three houses at 173, 174, and 176, around 1868, one year after the redesign of the park. This was the home of Abner C. Keeney. Keeney was born in 1830 on a farm in Pennsylvania. As a young man he became a schoolteacher, then, wishing to make more money, took up engineering. He made his name and fortune as a contractor of public works, first on his own and then in partnership with William C. Kingsley. Keeney moved to Brooklyn in 1856 and soon formed Kingsley & Keeney with another recent arrival to the fast-growing city. Together they built the Nassau Water Works, and the Kent Avenue sewer, the largest in the city, and the Atlantic Avenue water main running from East New York to Clinton Street, and the Hudson Avenue sewer. After the completion of the famous storage reservoir at Hempstead, Keeney pretty much ceased his active role in the firm, and though he was one of the original incorporators of the Brooklyn Bridge Company, he watched the bridge's progress from the sidelines. He lived at 175 Washington Park for 17 years, until his death in 1884 at the age of 54. His funeral was held at 175 Washington Park, and he was, as most prominent Brooklynites were, interred in Green-Wood Cemetery. (Green-Wood Cemetery, opened in 1839 at the farthest edge of the then new City of Brooklyn, was throughout the 19th century the most fashionable place for both Brooklynites and Manhattanites to be buried. Located in present-day Sunset Park, the 478-acre cemetery, with breathtaking harbor views from Brooklyn's highest elevation, is both beautiful and extraordinarily rich in historical associations.)

For 18 years, No. 176 was the home of Keeney's better-known partner, William C. Kingsley. When he died in 1885, the *Brooklyn Daily Eagle* ran the headline: "The Builder of the Brooklyn Bridge Crosses the Dark River."

The stately brownstones of Washington Park, along the east side of Fort Greene Park.

Kingsley was born in 1833 in Franklin County, in northernmost New York. He was born, like Keeney, on a farm, and, like Keeney, was a Pennsylvania schoolteacher before embarking on an engineering career. He achieved success building canals in Pennsylvania and railroads in the Midwest before he moved to Brooklyn in 1857. He soon entered into the partnership with Keeney, who was also an owner of the *Brooklyn Daily Eagle*. Kingsley & Keeney was one of the most successful firms of its kind. In addition to their sewers and water mains and reservoirs, the firm built most of Prospect Park. They built the handsome stone walls surrounding Central Park, Prospect Park, and Washington Park. In 1868 Kingsley began his involvement with the Brooklyn Bridge—building it, promoting it, and managing it. Kingsley and Keeney invested $160,000 in the Brooklyn Bridge Company, the largest private subscription. They later bought out other investors. As the *New York Times* put it, "Mr. Kingsley was made one of the Board of Trustees, and when Col. John A. Roebling, the General Superintendent of the work, met with his melancholy death, Mr. Kingsley was appointed to fill his place." David McCullough wrote, in *The Great Bridge* (1972), that "Kingsley would have more at stake in the venture ahead than any other man, with the single, notable exception of Washington Roebling."

The story of the Brooklyn Bridge is that Kingsley's enthusiasm for the project inspired Henry Cruse Murphy, the powerful Brooklyn Democrat and in many ways Brooklyn's first citizen, to back it. On the bitterly cold night of December 21, 1866, during the legendary winter when the East River froze over so solidly that, it is said, one could get to Manhattan faster from Albany than from Brooklyn, Kingsley trekked four miles to Murphy's villa, at the present site of Owl's Head Park in Bay Ridge. Murphy, so the story goes, had up to then been skeptical about bridging the East River, but on that night Kingsley was so persuasive that thereafter Murphy was fully in support of the bridge, and due to his status and influence the bridge went from dream to (slow-moving) reality. David McCullough describes Kingsley in 1867 as

> *Hard, resourceful, ambitious....he was Brooklyn's most prosperous contractor. He had paved streets, put down sewers, built the big storage reservoir at Hempstead, built much of Prospect Park, some of Central Park, branched out into the lumber business, the granite business, bought up real estate, and became "identified" with Brooklyn's gas company and banking interests. Just ten years after stepping off the Fulton Ferry, a total stranger, and with no money to speak of, he was worth close to a million dollars and was one of the best-known men in Brooklyn.*

The residence, known as The Abbey, of Edward Macomber, Fulton Street between DeKalb and Hudson avenues. Macomber later developed his land and for some years the triangle formed by Fulton, DeKalb, and Flatbush avenues was known as Macomber's Square. Picture from early 19th century.

Kingsley, almost as soon as he arrived in Brooklyn in 1857, became extremely close to Brooklyn's Democratic Party boss, Hugh McLaughlin. (According to David McCullough, McLaughlin was the first political leader ever to be honored with the title of "boss.") Kingsley was for nearly a quarter of a century a major force in Democratic politics in Brooklyn, though he never sought elective office. His and Keeney's contracting firm profited handsomely—and controversially—from political connections. Kingsley also became Keeney's partner in running the *Brooklyn Daily Eagle*, a Democratic organ, and following Keeney's death in 1884, Kingsley ran the paper (which had been founded by Henry Murphy) by himself. In 1882, when Murphy died, Kingsley replaced him as the president of the Brooklyn Bridge Company, and served in that capacity when the bridge triumphantly opened in 1883. The next year Kingsley resigned, and the year following that died, at the age of 52, in his home at 176 Washington Park. The *New York Times* reported: "The flags on all the public buildings in Brooklyn and on the bridge towers were at half mast yesterday

in respect to the memory of the late William C. Kingsley." His funeral was held at 176 Washington Park. As the *Times* reported, "Probably 300 persons walked past the coffin, which rested, half buried in flowers, near the archway dividing the ceilings of the two parlors." Before he was taken to be buried at Green-Wood, a service was led by the Reverend Henry Ward Beecher, of Plymouth Church, and by the Reverend Theodore Ledyard Cuyler, of Lafayette Avenue Presbyterian Church.

THEODORE LEDYARD CUYLER AND LAFAYETTE AVENUE PRESBYTERIAN CHURCH

Theodore Ledyard Cuyler was born in 1822 in Aurora, in Cayuga County in western New York, of Dutch and Huguenot ancestry, and in 1841 graduated from Princeton University. After graduating he traveled abroad and in England met Charles Dickens, Thomas Carlyle, and William Wordsworth, meetings Cuyler vividly recalls in his 1902 autobiography *Recollections of a Long Life*. (Cuyler loved Dickens, but could not bear that he failed to denounce alcohol. The often-repeated story that Dickens lectured at Lafayette Avenue Presbyterian Church, by the way, is false.) In 1846 Cuyler graduated from Princeton Theological Seminary. After serving as a pastor in New Jersey, he became, in 1853, pastor of the Market Street Reformed Church, which is still standing on Henry and Market streets in the Lower East Side of Manhattan. (Protestant ministers often moved from one denomination to another. Interestingly, six years after Cuyler left Market Street it became a Presbyterian church, known as the Sea and Land Church. It is now called the First Chinese Presbyterian Church. Built between 1817 and 1819, it is a designated New York City landmark.) He was renowned for his preaching and for his mission work among the poor in his church's neighborhood, which had become among the poorest in New York. In 1860 Brooklyn's Park Presbyterian Church, then building a new church on Lafayette Avenue in Fort Greene, invited the already celebrated Cuyler to be its pastor. When the church was completed in 1862, the congregation changed its name to Lafayette Avenue Presbyterian Church. There Cuyler spent the next 30 years. In 1860, when he became pastor, the congregation numbered 140 people; when he left, in 1890, it had grown to 2,330, and was the third largest Presbyterian congregation in America. He wrote 22 books and more than 4,000 articles (according to *American National Biography Online*). Cuyler and Henry Ward Beecher, the famous pastor of Plymouth Church in Brooklyn Heights, were wary friends, and sometimes shared a podium—as, for example, when they both spoke at the funeral service for William C. Kingsley. In 1872, Cuyler invited the Quaker leader Sarah Smiley to address his congregation. He was criticized by the Presbytery of Brooklyn for inviting a woman to address a mixed-sex assembly (or, as it was charmingly called, a "promiscuous audience"). Cuyler barely escaped formal censure.

Cuyler's vociferous opposition to slavery is a large part of what commended him to Park Presbyterian Church, which was founded by abolitionists. In 1856, while still in Manhattan, Cuyler openly supported the first Republican presidential candidate, John C. Frémont. "On the Sunday when fire was opened on Fort Sumter," said the *Brooklyn Daily Eagle*, "the American flag was raised on the steeple of the Lafayette Avenue Church and it stayed there until after Lee surrendered and the confederacy collapsed." "During the Civil War riots in this city," wrote the *New York Tribune*, "his church, with that of Henry Ward Beecher's, was closely guarded by the authorities." As Lafayette's current pastor, the Reverend David Dyson, points out, the church was established too late to have served as "a full-blown Underground Railroad" station, though it may have been an emergency backup when full-time stations were being too closely monitored by Pinkerton agents.

Three blocks from the church is a small park called Cuyler Gore, bounded by Fulton Street and Greene and Carlton avenues. It was named in 1901, while Cuyler was still alive. He consented to the naming, but insisted that no statue of him be placed there.

He died on February 26, 1909, in his home at 176 South Oxford Street, between Atlantic Avenue and Hanson Place, in Fort Greene. (The house is no longer standing.) The *New York Times* said: "He had not the rare gifts or oratory that Mr. Beecher possessed, or the scholarship of Dr. Storrs, to mention two men

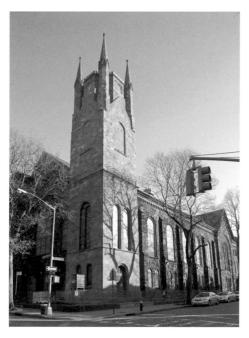

of high reputation in the same calling in his own city, nor did he cultivate his literary faculty to a marked degree. But he was a man of exalted ideals applied with childlike simplicity to all the activities of a long and laborious life. He had sympathies at once keen and broad with his fellow-men, an unflagging interest in their every-day existence, inexhaustible kindness, and a sturdy, unfailing, unaffected faith in the sufficiency of the common virtues." "Dr. Cuyler was, perhaps," said the *New York Tribune*, "the most conspicuous figure among the ministers of Brooklyn." (This was some years after the death of Henry Ward Beecher.) Two thousand persons crammed into Lafayette Presbyterian Church for Cuyler's funeral on March 1, 1909. His coffin was carried by six pallbearers (one of whom was the Clinton Hill typewriter king John Thomas Underwood) for two blocks from 176 South Oxford Street to the church. Among the ministers who led the congregation in prayer was Samuel Parkes Cadman of Central Congregational Church on Hancock Street and Franklin Avenue in Bedford-Stuyvesant; Cadman would succeed Cuyler as Brooklyn's most famous clergyman. Cuyler is also buried in Green-Wood Cemetery.

The architecture of the church, which opened on March 12, 1862, is noteworthy. It is one of the finest examples of early Romanesque Revival church architecture in New York. (That mode had been inaugurated in the 1840s by the architect Richard Upjohn at the Congregational Church of the Pilgrims on Remsen and Henry streets in Brooklyn Heights.) The simplicity and, some would say, primitivism of the Romanesque style commended itself to dissenting Protestant sects that objected to the Gothic style embraced by high Episcopalian and Roman Catholic congregations for whom sacramental ritual rather than preaching was the main point of the worship service. Lafayette Avenue Presbyterian Church adopted a semi-circular, "theatrical" seating plan, influenced by that of Henry Ward Beecher's Plymouth Church (1849), which was felt better to serve congregants who wished to hang on the every word of a gifted preacher.

In 1976, under the Reverend George Litch Knight, who was Lafayette's pastor for 33 years, the church interior was significantly altered by the incorporation of murals, "Mighty Cloud of Witnesses," painted by Hank Prussing, who was then 27 years old and a graduate of nearby Pratt Institute. Prussing was then working on his well-known, four-story mural "The Spirit of East Harlem," at 104th Street and Lexington Avenue in Manhattan. For the Lafayette Avenue commission, he took 500 photographs of neighborhood scenes and residents as preparation for a mural sequence that depicts vividly observed vignettes of neighborhood life and characters. It's a startling thing to see when you enter the church, but the murals proved popular with many congregants, who even recognized local faces among Prussing's subjects. In 1982 Hank Prussing got married to Susan Pearson in Lafayette Avenue Presbyterian Church, amid his murals. He went on to create murals at Third Avenue and 149th Street in the Bronx, and, for Bronx-Lebanon Hospital Center, on the Grand Concourse at Mount Eden Parkway, and, in a different vein, at the Palladium discotheque on East 14th Street in Manhattan, and the "Frog and Turtle Barn," in Hartland, Connecticut.

> I remember when Hank Prussing did the "Cloud of Witnesses" mural, I thought that was the most wonderful thing. Hank said to me, "Irene, I put these all up because it's just so the church can always be full of people."
>
> IRENE LEVY
> Member of Lafayette Avenue Presbyterian Church

Prussing arranged and colored his mural—which the Reverend Dyson said in a 2008 interview in the *Brooklyn Daily Eagle* can, with its unmistakably seventies look, seem like "Jackson Five meets Brady Bunch at high noon"—in harmony with the church's treasured opalescent stained-glass windows—produced by Tiffany Studios, Benjamin Sellers, Alex S. Locke, and Joseph Lauber—that were installed beginning in the 1890s under the Reverend David Gregg, who succeeded Cuyler as Lafayette's pastor.

In 1996 the *New York Times* reported, "Lafayette…has emerged, without much fanfare, as a center of political activism and cultural life—a more intimate version of Manhattan's Riverside Church." The Reverend David Dyson became pastor in 1992. A former union organizer, he had spent two years at Riverside. He had worked for the United Farm Workers and then the Amalgamated Clothing and Textile Workers Union. He led the successful—Labor Secretary Robert Reich called it a "watershed"—campaign to get clothing giant The Gap to improve labor conditions in its factories in Central America.

IRONDALE CENTER

In 2008, Lafayette's Sunday school space, abutting the church on South Oxford Street between Lafayette and DeKalb avenues, was renovated into the home of the Irondale Ensemble Project. Called the Irondale Center for Theater, Education, and Outreach, the space serves the acclaimed experimental theater company as a performance venue for itself and for visiting companies, and as a place for educational and outreach programs among area children, teens, and senior citizens, as well as collaborative programs with other arts organizations in the neighborhood. The Irondale Ensemble Project was founded in 1983 by Jim Niesen, Terry Greiss, and Barbara Mackenzie-Wood to further the experimental methods they had developed in the late 1970s when they were involved with New Haven's Long Wharf Theatre. In addition to producing a number of major off-Broadway shows, the company has also all along been involved in outreach programs, working in city schools and even among inmates at Riker's Island. *Harper's* magazine editor Lewis Lapham is quoted on Irondale's Web site: "The Irondale Ensemble Project is as close as we come these days to the Elizabethan acting companies that once presented Shakespeare's plays to the Earl of Leicester, Sir Francis Drake and the Virgin Queen of England." Irondale represents a significant new chapter in the history of Lafayette Avenue Presbyterian Church, and an important addition to the cultural district that has taken root and flourished in recent years in Fort Greene.

Fort Greene has always had a significant black population. In 1870 as many as half of Brooklyn's blacks lived in Fort Greene, where they formed roughly ten percent of the population. Most of Fort Greene's African Americans lived north of Myrtle Avenue. But some also lived south of Myrtle, in the heart of the fashionable neighborhood. The longtime principal of Colored School No. 1, Charles A. Dorsey, long located on North Elliot Place and Park Avenue, lived north of Myrtle; but his assistant principal, Georgiana Putnam, lived in a row house on Fort Greene Place, where Brooklyn Technical High School now stands, south of DeKalb Avenue.

SUSAN SMITH MCKINNEY STEWARD

Susan Maria Smith was born in Brooklyn in 1847, the daughter of Sylvanus Smith, a pork merchant, and Ann Springstead. As a teenager she was an accomplished organist. She studied under John Zundel, the famous organist of Henry Ward Beecher's Plymouth Church, and Henry Eyre Brown, the organist of the Brooklyn Tabernacle. In 1870, at the age of 23, she earned an M.D. from the New York Medical College for Women, which had been formed in 1863. She was her class valedictorian, and the first African American woman to be granted a medical degree in New York State, and the third in America. In her postgraduate studies at Long Island College Hospital, she was the only woman in her class. She married the Reverend William McKinney in 1874, and practiced medicine under the name Susan Smith McKinney. She lived and practiced medicine in the 1880s at 178 Ryerson Street between Myrtle and Park avenues, and in the 1890s at 205 DeKalb Avenue between Carlton Avenue and Adelphi Street. The Ryerson house no longer stands, but the DeKalb house, built in the 1860s, is still standing in the Fort Greene Historic District. The practice was located in the heart of the fashionable, affluent, and white part of Fort Greene, and she served both white and black patients. She was at this time also the organist of the Bridge Street African Methodist Episcopal

Church, on Bridge Street between Myrtle Avenue and Johnson Street; the church building is still standing, though now it is engulfed by the campus of MetroTech Center. In the 19th century, before the construction of the Manhattan Bridge (let alone that of MetroTech Center), the neighborhood of Bridge Street Church would not have been thought of as a separate neighborhood from what we now call Fort Greene. The church is about twelve blocks from 205 DeKalb Avenue.

Dr. Susan Smith McKinney Steward (1846–1918).

Between 1881 and 1896 Dr. McKinney served as staff physician of the Brooklyn Women's Homeopathic Hospital and Dispensary, which provided care for women and of which she was a co-founder. Later named the Memorial Hospital for Women and Children, the hospital occupied several successive locations in Dr. McKinney's time, including 1318 Fulton Street, between Nostrand and New York avenues, in Bedford-Stuyvesant; then 811 Bedford Avenue, between Myrtle and Park avenues, also in Bedford-Stuyvesant, about nine blocks from where Dr. McKinney lived at 178 Ryerson Street. In the year Dr. McKinney left Brooklyn the hospital relocated to Classon and St. Mark's avenues, in Crown Heights. (In 1903 the hospital was sold for debt.) In 1896, following the death of the Reverend McKinney, Susan Smith McKinney married the Reverend Theophilus Steward, an Army chaplain. With the Reverend Steward she left Brooklyn, first on tours of duty in western military bases and then for Ohio, where the couple settled when she became a professor and resident physician at Wilberforce University, which was affiliated with the African Methodist Episcopal Church. She served in both capacities until her death in 1918. (The Reverend Steward also became a professor at Wilberforce.)

Junior High School 265, on Park Avenue between North Portland Avenue and North Oxford Street, was renamed the Susan S. McKinney Junior High School in 1974.

THE CASE OF HIRAM S. THOMAS

While it is true that some prominent African Americans, such as Georgiana Putnam and Susan McKinney, lived in the predominately white area of Fort Greene in the 1890s, pockets of the neighborhood resisted black residents. The case of Hiram S. Thomas drew considerable publicity, with several *New York Times* and *Brooklyn Daily Eagle* articles reporting on white residents' indignation when Thomas purchased a house at 131 Fort Greene Place, between Hanson Place and Lafayette Avenue, in 1894.

Thomas was, according to the *Daily Eagle*, the proprietor of "one of the most famous road houses in the United States," in Saratoga Springs, New York. He was a chef and restaurateur of high repute. The *New York Times* even reported, in his obituary in 1907, that he "originated Saratoga chips," or modern potato chips, though the claim has also been made on behalf of others. On October 1, 1894, the *Times* ran the headline "They Want No Colored Neighbor." According to the *Times*, Fort Greene Place resident Dr. Emma Onderdonk led the protest against Thomas, saying his presence would depreciate property values. The paper said neighbors had tried to purchase the house from Thomas, but his asking price was too high—giving rise to the accusation that he had tried to "blackmail" the residents of Fort Greene Place. In reading through the press reports, it is hard to ascertain how much of the "stir among the neighbors" was real, and how much an exaggeration by the newspapers. Thomas vehemently denied any blackmail intent. He told a reporter that he had long wanted to purchase a house in Brooklyn for himself and his four children for those times of year he was not away managing his resorts at Saratoga and at Lakewood, in New Jersey. He said that when an agent showed him 131 Fort Greene Place, he "immediately purchased it, not dreaming at the time that there would be the slightest objection made by the people in the neighborhood." Thomas said "that he did not like so much notoriety and that altogether too much had been published about what he considered to be nothing." He moved into the house on October 22, 1894.

At least one neighbor felt differently from Dr. Onderdonk. The Reverend S.B. Halliday had been Henry Ward Beecher's assistant pastor at Plymouth Church. Halliday said: "I have supposed that the residents of Fort Greene Place were so eminently respectable that they could not have feared that their respectability could ever be called in question by the coming of half a dozen respectable families of color settling around them, much less by a single family. What a pretty story it is to get abroad over the country that a black man cannot move into a respectable neighborhood without stirring up a rebellion."

The house at 131 Fort Greene Place still stands, and is included in the Brooklyn Academy of Music Historic District established in 1978. It was part of a row of nine built in 1857.

MARIANNE MOORE OF CUMBERLAND STREET

"Lafayette Avenue Church is my true and fruitful church home," said the poet Marianne Moore, "where I go for healthful spiritual food."

Longtime Lafayette parishioner Marianne Moore lived for 36 years in an apartment on the fifth floor of 260 Cumberland Street, a 6-story apartment house built in 1912 between Lafayette and DeKalb avenues.

Marianne Moore was born on November 15, 1887, outside of St. Louis, Missouri. She never knew her father, who had suffered a nervous breakdown and left the family before she was born. When she was seven she moved with her mother and brother to Carlisle, Pennsylvania. She graduated from Bryn Mawr College in 1909, then taught secretarial courses at Carlisle Indian School, where one of her students was the famous Native American athlete Jim Thorpe. During this time her first poems appeared in several important literary magazines.

In 1916 she and her mother moved from Carlisle to Chatham, New Jersey, to keep house for her brother, who had graduated from Yale and become, like his maternal grandfather, a Presbyterian minister. He joined the Navy in 1918, which is when Marianne and her mother moved to Manhattan. They occupied a basement apartment at 14 St. Luke's Place in Greenwich Village. (At one point,

Moore, Theodore Dreiser, and Sherwood Anderson all lived on the one-block-long St. Luke's Place at the same time.) Marianne, because of her writing, had an instant social circle in New York. She counted among her friends the poets Wallace Stevens and William Carlos Williams. Admirers of her work included T.S. Eliot and Ezra Pound. In London in 1921, the poet and editor Hilda Doolittle (who had been Marianne's classmate at Bryn Mawr) published a book of 24 of Marianne's poems. Between 1921 and 1925 Marianne worked as a part-time assistant librarian at the Hudson Park Branch of the New York Public Library, conveniently located directly across the street from her home. In 1924 she expanded the London book to 53 poems for publication in America as *Observations*.

The apartment building at 260 Cumberland Street where the poet Marianne Moore resided between 1929 and 1965; the building was erected in 1912. A handsome reddish brown plaque to the right of the front entrance tells of Moore's residency in the building.

Marianne Moore (1887–1972) of 260 Cumberland Street.

In 1925 Moore became editor of the *Dial*, presiding over the distinguished publication until its demise in 1929. From then onward, she made her living as a freelance writer, often with the aid of grants and awards.

In 1929 Moore and her mother moved from St. Luke's Place, where they had lived for eleven years, to 260 Cumberland Street in Fort Greene (which Marianne always referred to as Clinton Hill). The reason was to be nearer Marianne's brother, who was now the chaplain at the Brooklyn Navy Yard.

From the 1930s onward she was immensely successful as a poet, appearing in all the best publications and winning all the major awards. Her works appeared in *Kenyon Review* and the *Nation*. In 1935 her *Selected Poems* featured an introduction by T.S. Eliot. From the 1930s to the 1960s she published several acclaimed volumes of verse. She won fellowships, awards, and prizes. She spent the better part of a decade translating the *Fables* of Jean de La Fontaine. Her 1951 *Collected Poems* won both the National Book Award and the Pulitzer Prize. In 1953 she was awarded the prestigious Bollingen Prize. (*New York Times* headline: "Brooklyn Woman Wins Bollingen Poetry Prize.") The translation of the *Fables* appeared in 1954. The critical reception was mixed, but the French government knighted her for her effort. (Living just seven blocks apart, Marianne Moore and typewriter baron John Thomas

Underwood were both Lafayette Avenue Presbyterian Church parishioners—and both knights of France. Moore was honored for her translation of La Fontaine; Underwood for his contributions to war relief efforts after World War I.)

It was really during the 1950s that Moore's public persona became more famous than her poetry. She became one of the most identifiable public figures in New York, typically appearing in a black cape and a tricorn hat. She went everywhere in the city, and was a fixture at concerts, and openings, and not least in the stands at Ebbets Field where she was one of the Dodgers' most ardent and best-known fans. She was profiled in magazines and newspapers. The Ford Motor Company asked her to help them name a new car they were developing. (Two of her best suggestions were "Mongoose Civique" and "Andante con Moto.") In the end, Ford rejected her suggestions and came up with its own name: Edsel. In 1966 she attended Truman Capote's legendary "Black and White Ball" at the Plaza Hotel, and in 1968 threw out the ceremonial first ball on opening day at Yankee Stadium.

Witty and unpretentious, she was an exponent of precise observation, epigram-matic appreciation, and plain syntax. As one critic put it, "Her 'predilection'—a favorite word with her and more likely to appear than 'passion'—is for grace and neatness." These qualities brought her legions of adoring fans—an unusual thing for a difficult Modernist poet. The critic Randall Jarrell wrote in 1945, "Miss Moore is reviewed not as a poet but as an institution...one reviewer calls Miss Moore the greatest living poet...ending with the demand that she be placed in Fort Knox for the duration. Certainly she writes better poetry than any other woman alive; but I have used up my small share of superlative in previous reviews of her—this time let me look through Miss Moore and see neither lies nor Beauty, but some trees. (Whoever you are, I like her as much as you; so don't complain.)"

In 1964, Moore gave directions to her building to *Paris Review* editor George Plimpton, who was coming to visit her: "am on right, middle of the block, with what look like mothballs on iron stands flanking the entrance."

Of her Fort Greene apartment, Alden Whitman wrote in the *New York Times*: "It was crammed with books and bric-a-brac—porcelain and ivory animals, a walrus tusk, prints and paintings, shells and feathers, old coins." In the introduction to his *Paris Review* interview with her, in 1960, the poet Donald Hall wrote: "To visit Marianne Moore at her home in Brooklyn, you had to cross the Brooklyn Bridge, turn left on Myrtle Avenue, follow the elevated for a mile or two, and then turn right onto her street. It was pleasantly lined with trees, and Miss Moore's apartment was conveniently near a grocery store and the Presbyterian church that she attended." How reminiscent this is of Emerson's friend Moncure Conway's description of a visit to the home of Walt Whitman more than a hundred years before: "The way to reach the house is to go down to Fulton Street Ferry, after crossing take the Fulton and Myrtle Avenue car, and get out at Ryerton [*sic*] Street."

Moore's service to Brooklyn included campaigns she helped lead to save the Camperdown elm in Prospect Park, as well as to save the park's Boathouse.

In 1960 her essay, "Brooklyn from Clinton Hill," appeared in *Vogue*.

> *Decorum marked life on Clinton Hill in the autumn of 1929 when my mother and I came to Brooklyn to live. An atmosphere of privacy with a touch of diffidence prevailed, as when a neighbor in a furred jacket, veil, and gloves would emerge from a four-story house to*

shop at grocer's or meat market. Anonymity, without social or professional duties after a
life of pressure in New York, we found congenial.

It was not unusual in those days, towards teatime, to catch a glimpse of a maid with
starched cap and apron, adjusting accessories on a silver tray, in a certain particularly
correct house of which the parlor windows were screened by a Gauguin-green miscellany of
glossy leaves—elephant-ear-sharp and rounder—amid ferns and tiny palms from the sill
up, more than ever a grateful sight by contrast with starker windows.

She wrote of her admiration of the Brooklyn Academy of Music, where every year
for 30 years she had attended dozens of concerts, lectures, readings, and classes.
"In the structure of the building itself certain materials intrinsically seem to me a
feature: the interlacing Italian-Irish designs on the ground-floor concourse—
related in period to the ground-floor mosaics in the Plaza Hotel in Manhattan.
Then, for some stonemason, a triumph: the unpieced aspect of the staircase—satin-
smooth oyster-gray marble with massive hand-rail—a deeply-grooved extension of
the wall, with which it is continuous." In this essay she trained her precise
observation and epigrammatic praise on the small wonders of Brooklyn—the
Brooklyn Museum, Prospect Park, the Brooklyn Botanic Garden, and McDonough
and Company, the "eminent stationer" on Montague Street.

Someone should delineate the Hill, the Heights, the center—doing justice to landmarks
and losses. I like living here. Brooklyn has given me pleasure, has helped to educate me;
has afforded me, in fact, the kind of tame excitement on which I thrive.

That last sentence appears on a plaque placed by the New York Landmarks
Conservancy on the outside of 260 Cumberland Street. Marianne Moore died on
February 2, 1972.

The Reverend Dr. George Litch Knight presided over Miss Moore's funeral at
Lafayette Avenue Presbyterian Church, her church for 34 years, on February 8,
1972. During her membership in the church, she punctually attended services
every Wednesday evening and every Sunday morning. Once, when it was arranged
for her to meet President and Mrs. Lyndon B. Johnson in Manhattan, she had to
cut the meeting short lest she be late for her Wednesday evening service on
Lafayette Avenue. The *New York Times* reported:

A disparate throng of about 200 mourners sat in the long, curved pews of the sanctuary,
reflecting the catholicity of Miss Moore's friendships. The mourners included blacks and
whites, the very elderly and the young, relatives, long-time friends, educators, literary
persons, booksellers and, of course, baseball personalities, including Michael Burke,
president of the New York Yankees....

The ethnically mixed Brooklyn district...has a few remnants of its old society and several
august survivors came in and hung their canes over the backs of pews.

Also among those in attendance were Maurice Sendak and Elizabeth Bishop. The
closing prayer at her funeral service was one she herself had written for the funeral,
in the same church, of her mother, in 1947:

One by one Thou dost gather us out of earthly light into heavenly glory, from the
distractions of time to the peace of eternity. We thank Thee for the labors and joys of these
mortal years. We thank Thee for our deepening sense of the mysteries that lie behind our
dust, and for the eye of faith which Thou hast opened for all who believe in Thy Son, to
behold through the darkness the shining future.

Her body was taken from the church to Green-Wood Cemetery for cremation, thence to be buried in the Moore family plot in Gettysburg, Pennsylvania.

BROOKLYN LOSES MARIANNE MOORE

By the time she died, she had not lived in Fort Greene for six years.

On January 20, 1966, the *New York Times* ran a headline, "Brooklyn Loses Marianne Moore." The sub-head was "Frightened Poet, 78, Reluctantly Moves to the 'Village.'"

Marianne Moore put a $17 burglarproof lock on her door. She had a peephole installed. She kept a bag of pepper on a table in the hall. And she had a tear-gas cylinder to repel attackers.

At the turn of the century the area near Fort Greene Park was one of the city's most elegant, its brownstone townhouses and Victorian mansions housing the wealthy and the fashionable.

Today it is a mixture of deterioration, preservation and government-aided attempts at renewal.

The brownstones nearest the historic park...have largely been converted to rooming houses or subdivided into one-room and two-room apartments. They are tenanted mainly by Negro and Puerto Rican families, and many are badly run down.

But she still did not feel safe in her fifth-floor apartment.

Several of her neighborhood friends had been victims of break-ins or muggings. But it was not until she felt her own building to be under siege that she finally decided to leave. The building never had a doorman. She said that at three in the morning her buzzer would ring and someone outside would ask to come up to use her phone. Junkies began to hang out in the inside entry vestibule of her building at night.

"Me," she said, "who never was afraid of anything. But it wears on you a great deal. I just had to move."

She moved to an apartment building—a very nice one—at 35 West 9th Street, between Fifth and Sixth avenues, in November 1965. Her living room that is so charmingly on display in the Rosenbach Museum & Library in Philadelphia is from the West 9th Street apartment.

RICHARD WRIGHT OF CARLTON AVENUE

Richard Wright was born in 1908 in rural Mississippi, and had a difficult boyhood, recounted in his 1945 autobiography *Black Boy*. His sharecropper father left the family when Richard was five, and his mother became very ill. Richard then lived in the home of his strict Seventh-Day Adventist grandparents in Jackson, Mississippi. He was an excellent student, and published his first short story when he was 16. But at 17 he dropped out of high school and moved to Memphis, Tennessee, where he worked odd jobs and read books, coming particularly under the spell of H.L. Mencken. In 1927, when he was 19, he moved to Chicago. He spent ten years there, working at a variety of jobs, joining the John Reed Club, and becoming involved with the Federal Writers' Project during the Great Depression. In 1937 he moved to New York City. The following year he moved to 175 Carlton Avenue, between

Willoughby and Myrtle avenues in Fort Greene, no more than three blocks from where Marianne Moore had been living for the last eight years, though there is no indication that they ever knew each other. In 1937 he had just published his first collection of short stories, *Uncle Tom's Children*, and had been living in a boarding house on West 143rd Street in Harlem. He became engaged to the landlady's daughter, Marion Sawyer, and invitations were sent out for the wedding, which was to take place in May 1938. But when the couple received their Board of Health blood test results, it turned out Marion had syphilis, and they were denied a marriage license. Wright then moved in with his Communist Party friends Jane and Herbert Newton and their three children on Carlton Avenue.

He lived in a large room in the back of the house. While living on Carlton Avenue, Wright wrote his novel *Native Son*. He liked to rise early—6:00 AM or earlier—and walk to the top of the hill in Fort Greene Park (one block away), where he would sit on a bench—now suitably bearing a commemorative plaque—near the Prison Ship Martyrs Monument and compose—with a fountain pen and a yellow legal pad—the manuscript of his novel. He would return to the Newtons' house around 10:00 for breakfast and his endless discussions with Jane Newton about his progress on the novel. Later he would go to his room to type up what he had written that day. Wright would spend the rest of the day reading, often at the Brooklyn Public Library's nearby City Park branch, on St. Edwards Street and Auburn Place, just north of Fort Greene Park, where the Fort Greene Houses would soon be built. He would then join the Newtons for dinner. In October 1938 he sent the manuscript to his publisher, Harper & Brothers, who gave him a $250 advance. That month, the Newtons were forced to move from 175 Carlton Avenue. Their landlord had become ill and he could not keep up his house payments. Herbert Newton and Wright did the house hunting: Since Herbert was black and Jane was white, they feared that if they went looking for a home together they would inevitably be rejected. They found an apartment at 552 Gates Avenue, between Tompkins and Throop avenues, in Bedford-Stuyvesant. Not happy with the place, they all soon moved to 101 Lefferts Place, between Grand and Classon avenues, near where Clinton Hill, Bedford-Stuyvesant, and Crown Heights blend into one another. Wright lived on Carlton Avenue a mere six months. But it was arguably the most crucial six months in his life as a writer— and among the most crucial six months in the history of black American literature.

Native Son was published in 1940. It was the first national bestseller—and the first Book-of-the-Month Club selection—ever by an African American writer. *Native Son* is a brute, uncompromising book about Bigger Thomas, a black man from Chicago who murders two women, one of them white, the other black, and the society that both created him and that does not know how to deal with him. Wright later wrote that after *Uncle Tom's Children*, "I found that I had written a book which even bankers' daughters could read and weep over and feel good about. I swore to myself that if I ever wrote another book, no one would weep over it; that it would be so hard and deep that they would have to face it without the consolation of tears." *Native Son*, which upset many older African American writers who preached uplift, set black American literature on a new course of gritty realism and social analysis. Communist characters in *Native Son* do not come off as any better than anyone else, so it should be no surprise that Wright in 1942 left the Communist Party and later wrote of his disillusionment with it. After a brief failed marriage to a Russian-Jewish ballet dancer, Wright in 1941 married Ellen Poplar, a white woman he had come to know through the Communist Party. In 1942 Richard, Ellen, and their child lived at 7 Middagh Street (only about 14 blocks from 175 Carlton Avenue), in Brooklyn Heights, in the same house as the poet W.H. Auden and the novelist Carson McCullers. According to Sherill Tippins, in *February House* (2005), "While their neighbors had appeared remarkably tolerant of the wild goings-on at the house in previous years, occupancy by a black man, his white wife, and their baby daughter was another matter. Stones were thrown at the windows, and the coal deliverer, himself African American, resigned rather than serve someone of his own race." In 1947, the Wrights left New York for Paris. As a mixed-race couple they had grown tired of the prejudice they faced even in New York. They faced no such discrimination in Paris, and it was there that Richard Wright lived out his years, dying in 1960 at the age of 52.

I lived in the neighborhood for years before I knew that Richard Wright had written the majority of *Native Son* in Fort Greene Park. *Native Son* was one of the most important books to me growing up. I actually have two first editions of *Native Son*....He was one of the two black authors that was basically taught in school, James Baldwin and Richard Wright.... When I did a column for the *Village Voice* in the early nineties I named it "Native Son." When I went to Paris for the first time I went on a pilgrimage and found both where he lived in Paris, most of his life he lived there in a building on Monsieur le Prince Street on the Left Bank from '48 to '60. And his ashes are buried in a cemetery in Paris and I went there. So I have these connections. He's really, really special to me. And I love that that bench is in the park dedicated to him, and I always felt like for someone who wanted to be a writer, who moved to Fort Greene to really fulfill the dream of a writer, to have this legacy of this person who not only wrote books that—literally I lived around the corner from where he lived on Carlton, I lived on Willoughby and Carlton and I had no idea he lived around the corner there and wrote *Native Son* there.

NELSON GEORGE
Author, filmmaker, television producer, cultural critic,
and resident of Fort Greene since 1985

DISINVESTMENT AND RENEWAL

Marianne Moore's move from Fort Greene prompted a series of *New York Times* articles on Fort Greene's declining fortunes.

"In one spacious brownstone" on Washington Park, said the *Times*, "heavy oaken doors with carved heraldic designs still greet the visitor, and the walls of the 15-foot-high entry still have their floral patterns in bas-relief." But, the *Times* added, "a thick coat of grit now covers the protruding patterns and carvings, and on the wall are 20 bells with 20 names."

On that same February 6, 1966, the *Times* ran a photo essay headlined "Ft. Greene: Twilight of a Neighborhood."

The *Times* noted that some Fort Greene residents were angered by the publicity surrounding Miss Moore's departure. The paper quoted the Reverend Richard Johnson of Emmanuel Baptist Church, on Lafayette Avenue at St. James Place: "Of course crime has always been greater than we'd like it to be, but basically this is a solid community." He added, "On the whole, this is a very heterogeneous neighborhood in housing, income level and racial composition. It is unfair and misleading to portray it as one big slum."

Fort Greene, though, had changed, and was fighting for its life.

Fort Greene south of Myrtle Avenue had, in the days of William C. Kingsley and Theodore Ledyard Cuyler, been a fashionable neighborhood where some of the wealthiest and most prominent of Brooklynites resided. By the time Marianne Moore moved to Cumberland Street, in 1929, the neighborhood still was genteel, with pockets of wealth, although it was no longer fashionable. The children of the Kingsley and Cuyler years had moved away. The Great Depression dealt a blow to many inner-city neighborhoods. Financial constraints led to the chopping up of stately town houses into apartments and rooming houses, as well as to "deferred maintenance" that left many places looking droopy, dingy, and ill-kempt, and to outright abandonment of properties. It could take but a decade for a neatly groomed neighborhood to begin to appear derelict. The war years exacerbated this trend, though in Fort Greene with results more tragic than in many other neighborhoods. The proximity of Fort Greene to the Brooklyn Navy Yard and to waterfront industrial plants that were involved in wartime production meant a vast temporary influx of Armed Services personnel and private-sector workers. The Fort Greene Houses, north of Myrtle Avenue, had been conceived as government-planned housing for low-income New Yorkers, but were pressed into emergency service as housing for wartime workers. The desperate need for housing accelerated the already existing trend of carving up Fort Greene's row houses into multiple units, the worst of which were not classifiable as apartment houses but as rooming houses. From there the story takes on an all-too-familiar form. Government housing aid to war veterans favored newly constructed suburban homes, while lending institutions followed government guidelines and ceased providing mortgage or home-maintenance loans in inner-city neighborhoods with aging housing stock—and with growing black populations.

In his 2006 study of the effects of gentrification, *There Goes the 'Hood*, Columbia University sociologist Lance Freeman wrote: "With the great migrations of blacks from the South to Northern cities…the complexion of Brooklyn changed dramatically. Although the first wave of blacks from the South and the Caribbean targeted Harlem, the second wave during the middle decades of the twentieth century increasingly made Brooklyn their choice. They settled mostly along the axis of Fulton Street and Atlantic Avenue stretching from the downtown and Fort Greene areas through Bedford and Stuyvesant and into Brownsville and East New York. Blacks rarely penetrated beyond these major thoroughfares and the immediately adjoining streets."

In 1941 the *Times* described the years 1936–41 as "the period in which many Negroes, forced out of Harlem by the overcrowding and high rents there, have migrated along the route of the new Eighth Avenue subway to settle in the old brownstone houses of the Bedford-Stuyvesant section, formerly occupied by substantial middle-class families."

In 1936, the A line of the IND subway had opened stations under Fulton Street. Stations opened at Lafayette and South Portland avenues and at Fulton and Vanderbilt avenues, with further stops in Bedford-Stuyvesant at Franklin Avenue, Nostrand Avenue, Kingston Avenue, Utica Avenue, and Ralph Avenue. African Americans settled in the vicinity of the A train along Fulton Street.

THE CATHEDRAL THAT NEVER WAS

In 1860, just as Fort Greene was booming, the Roman Catholic Diocese of Brooklyn, which had been established only in 1852, purchased the site bounded by Lafayette, Vanderbilt, Greene, and Clermont avenues for the purpose of building the diocese's cathedral—the seat of the Bishop of Brooklyn, John Loughlin. It was to be called the Cathedral of the Immaculate Conception, and Bishop Loughlin hired Patrick Charles Keely, Brooklyn resident and America's most prolific architect of Roman Catholic churches, to design it. Forty thousand people attended the laying of the cornerstone on June 21, 1868. The cathedral was projected to be the second largest in the country, after St. Patrick's Cathedral, then under construction on Fifth Avenue in Manhattan. The Brooklyn cathedral was to have twin 350-foot-high towers, higher than those eventually added to St. Patrick's Cathedral. The Brooklyn towers would, in fact, have been the highest structures in New York City or Brooklyn. Construction began, but when the walls had risen ten to twenty feet, funds ran out, and the project was put on hold. Brooklyn has a strange history of beginning grand building projects that then get put on hold. Brooklyn's City Hall, for example, was begun in 1835 and then, as a result of the Panic of 1837, construction ceased until 1845; the structure (now called Borough Hall) was not completed until 1848. The Brooklyn Public Library, at Grand Army Plaza, was partly built when in 1913 construction was suspended, not resuming until 1938; the library opened in 1941. And the Brooklyn Museum, on Eastern Parkway, was begun in the 1890s and only completed to about one quarter the size originally projected. On December 28, 1878, the *Brooklyn Daily Eagle* reported: "It is now some ten years since the Cathedral was commenced, and the consecration of the chapel is an earnest that the great work is steadily, although slowly, progressing. The hardness of the times has no doubt retarded the work, but when Cardinal Archbishop Manning was speaking to the Catholics of London, about the grand cathedral which is to be built there...he reminded them that Noah was one hundred and twenty years in building the ark. The sacred edifice which is to crown the diocese of Brooklyn and the Episcopate of Bishop Loughlin, will not be so imposing in external appearance as St. Patrick's Cathedral in New York, but as a model of pure Gothic architecture it will have few if any equals in this country." The cathedral—save for a single completed chapel—remained mostly a hole in the ground when, in 1898, two years after Keely's death, Bishop Charles Edward McDonnell hired the British architect John Francis Bentley, designer of London's Westminster Roman Catholic Cathedral, then under construction, to resume work on the long-delayed Brooklyn edifice. But Bentley died in 1902 and progress sputtered. Decades passed and in 1931 the diocese chose to pull down the partly built walls as well as the completed Chapel of St. John and to occupy the site with Bishop Loughlin Memorial High School. Brooklyn's Catholics never got their grand cathedral.

The high school opened in 1933. Long the jewel in the crown of Roman Catholic secondary education in Brooklyn, the school remained all-male until 1973. Its most famous alumnus is former New York mayor Rudolph W. Giuliani, class of

Elevation drawing of Our Lady Queen of All Saints Roman Catholic church and school complex on Lafayette Avenue, northwest corner of Vanderbilt Avenue, from the office of Reiley & Steinback, Architects, 1914.

1961. Today, Bishop Loughlin Memorial High School enrolls students without regard to religious background, and its diverse student body reflects the diversity of the surrounding community.

Patrick Keely designed the Roman Catholic Bishop's residence at 367 Clermont Avenue, at Greene Avenue, erected between 1883 and 1887. It remained the bishop's home until 1938, when the residence was relocated to the former Charles Millard Pratt mansion at 241 Clinton Avenue. Brooklyn's first three Roman Catholic bishops—John Loughlin, Charles Edward McDonnell, and Thomas Edmund Molloy—all resided at 367 Clermont, which has served since 2006 as Bishop Loughlin Boarding School. Though the Cathedral of the Immaculate Conception was never completed, the cathedral-esque Roman Catholic complex of Our Lady Queen of All Saints, seamlessly combining a church and a school in a single grand structure, rose between 1910 and 1915, during the episcopacy of Bishop George Mundelein, across the street from the cathedral site, at the northwest corner of Lafayette and Vanderbilt avenues. The church, though not yet completed, was dedicated in 1913, at which time the *Brooklyn Daily Eagle* said: "It is one of the two or three most beautiful specimens of church architecture in the United States."

Distinctive mid-19th-century brownstone row houses on South Portland Avenue between DeKalb and Lafayette avenues; the "Italianate" style is identifiable by, among other features, the elaborately carved brackets on either side of the wide front doorways. Such houses when they were new were—as they are again today—the height of fashion.

In Depression-era Fort Greene and Clinton Hill there were tensions, sometimes escalating to violence, between black and Italian youth gangs, often corresponding to gangs formed at parochial schools and gangs formed at public schools.

In 1937, the *New York Times* described South Portland Avenue in Fort Greene as "a tree-lined street of old brownstone dwellings now mostly rooming houses," and said that recently "Fort Greene Park has been the scene of numerous hold-ups."

A few months before *Newsweek's* July 1959 exposé on the Fort Greene Houses, the *New York Times* (November 19, 1958) reported that Brooklyn District Attorney Edward S. Silver had toured some of the borough's slums along with staff members and reporters. "The inspection was cut short after one hour because the prosecutor and many of the staff members and newspapermen accompanying him feared they would become sick if they continued," Silver said. "These conditions are as bad as anything I ever saw in this city."

> *The worst conditions among three locations observed were at Lafayette Avenue and Cumberland Street in the Fort Greene section. There the hulks of four red-brick, three-story dwellings leaned against one another. Fifty years ago, this row at 123 to 129 Lafayette Avenue had been proper, private, one-family homes with the high stoops and English basements of the period.*

*Today the mortar is crumbling from the outside walls and the plaster
on the interior is in large part destroyed. Nearly every window is
broken, the frames being boarded over with scrap wood or cardboard.
The entry to No. 125 was half-blocked yesterday with piles of garbage
and whisky bottles. The residents said the refuse had not been collected
for five days.*

*At least nineteen persons, twelve of them small children, live in No.
125....There is one bathroom on each floor. But the toilets have ceased
to work, and the floors and bathtubs were covered with filth.*

Corinne Green lived with four children in one and a half rooms
at 125 Lafayette Avenue. Their only heat came from an oven that
was missing its door. The five of them slept on two mattresses
without bedding.

Silver told the *Times*, "I do know you cannot cure overcrowding in
slums by waving a magic wand."

Lafayette Avenue, between South Oxford and Cumberland streets,
was, by 1958, being called a slum.

The houses, built in the 1860s, are still standing, and are
included in the Fort Greene Historic District, though all their
original Italianate detail has been removed.

This was on the corner of Marianne Moore's block, six lots away
from 260 Cumberland Street.

In a *New York Times* article, "Historic Area Seeks to Survive," on
February 6, 1966, Joseph P. Fried wrote, "When the poet
Marianne Moore recently moved out of her Brooklyn apartment
after 36 years, she drew
attention to a neighborhood
that had sharply departed
from its silk-stocking past."

By the 1960s it had
appeared that Fort Greene
and Clinton Hill had been
caught up in the outward-
spreading physical blight of
Bedford-Stuyvesant to the
east, where the tolls of
disinvestment ("redlining")
had been felt earlier and
more comprehensively than
in its neighboring communities. Where a century earlier Fort
Greene had been roughly 90 percent white and 10 percent black,
the numbers were now nearly reversed.

View north along Fort
Greene Place toward
Fort Greene Park, the
East River, and
Manhattan; the
prominent building
near the center is
Brooklyn Technical
High School.

But by 1971, even as social problems—drugs, crime, deteriorating
housing—intensified, there were unmistakable signs of change.
A July 11, 1971, article in the *New York Times* referred to Fort
Greene as "Brownstoneurbia." The article profiled several Fort

Greene homeowners, including one middle-class black family, the Adamses, who had bought a house on South Elliot Place between DeKalb and Lafayette avenues in 1969, and one middle-class white family, the O'Donnells, who had bought a house on the same block in 1968. "Prices have tripled since we came here," said William O'Donnell, an advertising copywriter, whose family had been renting an apartment in Brooklyn Heights before buying in Fort Greene. The paper noted that a house such as the O'Donnells', at 29 South Elliot Place, cost about $18,000 in 1968 (a little more than $106,000 in 2007 dollars). But there were tensions. An attempted South Elliot Place block association failed. One 14-year resident of the block, a black woman named Annie Clay, accused white newcomers of prejudice against blacks. William O'Donnell admitted that the block association meetings had not gone well, but suggested the battle-lines were not between whites and blacks, but between newcomers, who were both white and black, and older residents, who were mostly black. "Those who aren't able to get in on the ground floor when things start developing," said O'Donnell, "find themselves on the outside."

> The neighborhood was very, very different when we moved in. People said, "You can't move to Fort Greene. It's dangerous." But coming from Denmark we didn't really think about what they were saying about dangers. Perhaps we were naïve, but we moved over. Friends helped us move. And a man from the block, Larry, came down and he said "Welcome to the neighborhood." Nobody said, "Welcome to the neighborhood" when we moved to Brooklyn Heights.
>
> MARIANNE ENGBERG

Four months later, in a *Times* article on November 24, 1971, the architectural historian Charles Lockwood wrote:

> *In the last few years, Fort Greene has improved with startling swiftness. Even a casual Sunday afternoon visitor to the area now sees such unmistakable signs of neighborhood renaissance as small trees recently planted along streets lined with brownstones and energetic young couples stripping layers of brown paint from mahogany front doors.*

Lockwood wrote that around 1870 a fine large brownstone in Fort Greene may have cost $35,000 (a little more than $567,000 in 2007 dollars); it cost about the same 100 years later (almost $185,000 in 2007 dollars). In a century, a Fort Greene brownstone had lost about two thirds of its value.

> *During World War II, most brownstones in Fort Greene were converted into rooming houses for Navy officers at the bustling Brooklyn Navy Yard nearby....After the war, activity at the Navy Yard subsided and Navy officers and workers left the neighborhood. The proud brownstones declined into less and less desirable rooming houses. In the troubled nineteen-fifties and sixties, old mattresses thrown in the middle of tree-lined South Portland Avenue in the daytime impeded traffic down the street. On South Oxford Street, workmen spent three days carrying mahogany and rosewood paneling and crystal chandeliers from the once-elegant Healy-Todd mansion before its conversion into 17 small apartments.*

The "Healy-Todd mansion" is 26 South Oxford Street, two houses combined in 1893 by Montrose Morris into one for leather merchant Frank Healy.

Lockwood continued:

> In Fort Greene, the mortgage and renovation money available from the Bedford-Stuyvesant Restoration Corporation enables brownstone owners to undertake unusually thorough and swift renovations. In mid-1968, major New York banks and insurance companies committed nearly $65-million for the purchase and refinancing of one-family to four-family dwellings within the area bounded by Eastern Parkway, Flatbush Avenue, Flushing Avenue, and Broadway, an area which includes all of Fort Greene.

According to Lockwood, between 1968 and 1971 hundreds of brownstones in the Restoration Corporation area had been renovated with Corporation assistance.

In 1973 Herbert Scott-Gibson founded the Fort Greene Landmarks Preservation Committee to advocate for the protection of the neighborhood's distinctive—indeed breathtaking—19th-century architectural fabric. Scott-Gibson had worked in development and education for the Bedford-Stuyvesant Restoration Corporation (where he served as director of the Billie Holiday Theatre), the Brooklyn Academy of Music, and the Metropolitan Museum of Art, and had also been a professional opera singer who had performed with the New York City Opera. He was also a trustee of the Brooklyn Museum and of Brooklyn Hospital. This is a startlingly ample résumé for someone who died at the young age of 52, in 1980. He and his wife, Evelyn, a dancer, moved to Washington Park in 1967—one year after Marianne Moore moved out. One of his most important accomplishments was leading the fight to have Fort Greene designated by the New York City Landmarks Preservation Commission as a historic district, a fight won on September 26, 1978, when the commission designated the Fort Greene Historic District and the Brooklyn Academy of Music Historic District. Scott-Gibson and other community volunteers teamed with Long Island University's Urban Studies Program to conduct research at the Buildings Department and at the Brooklyn Historical Society and in 1973 presented their building-by-building survey to the Landmarks Preservation Commission. In 1993, the Fort Greene Landmarks Preservation Committee became the Fort Greene Association, which to this day addresses all aspects of neighborhood improvement.

When we had the blackout, we are Danish and we always have candles, so we sat on the stoop and I went around and gave the whole block candles. We stayed up all night. The kids were sleeping upstairs. And you saw people coming from downtown, and they were stealing and breaking in. But nobody came into our block, because we were lit up with all the candles. So we did this amazing thing to see how people stick together.

MARIANNE ENGBERG

Historic district recognition certainly increased the neighborhood's citywide profile. Social problems did not ease. In the 1980s New York as a whole endured a record wave of homicides, many of them related to the traffic in illegal drugs, particularly the form of cocaine known as crack. Fort Greene was not immune. At the same time, however, the neighborhood's popularity among young families seeking city homes reached the red-hot level. Not since the 19th century had Fort Greene been such a desirable address. Indeed, for many longtime community residents, a new problem had overtaken the blight and crime of previous decades: gentrification. The term *gentrification* was coined in 1964 by a British sociologist, Ruth Glass, to describe a process occurring in a London district called Islington, where professional-class homebuyers were seen to be inflating property values and pushing longtime working-class residents out of the area. Not until the late 1970s did the term begin to be used in connection with New York, and especially with Brooklyn's brownstone neighborhoods, including Park Slope, Boerum Hill, Fort Greene, and Clinton Hill. But though the term may not have been coined, the phenomenon of gentrification had been going on for some time in New York. The first gentrified pockets of New York sprung up in Greenwich Village and Gramercy Park in the early 20th century. Before that time, affluent residents of the city had tended to move ever farther uptown in Manhattan, or, in Brooklyn, ever farther east and south of Brooklyn Heights. As they did so, the neighborhoods left behind came to be populated by less-affluent social classes. For example, Greenwich Village had been an affluent neighborhood in the 19th century, but by the turn of the 20th century had lost most of its "gentry" to newer uptown neighborhoods such as Murray Hill and Gramercy Park. Much of the Village came to be populated by new, poor immigrants. As elegant houses yielded to new tenements, and the houses that remained deteriorated, property values fell. This attracted artists and "bohemians" lured by cheap rents and quaint streets and mews. The cachet the newcomers lent to the neighborhood lured other, more affluent residents, especially as Manhattan came to be fully developed and there no longer was any "uptown" left to it. Around 1910 the "doubling back" of the well-to-do led to the gentrification of places such as Greenwich Village.

In Brooklyn, much the same phenomenon occurred. Brooklyn Heights had lost much of its old upper class, but in time its new artistic ambience and beautiful, affordable houses lured young professional families. By the 1960s Brooklyn Heights had reemerged as a high-rent district. By the end of the sixties, a family such as the O'Donnells, cited above, who were renters in Brooklyn Heights, found they could not afford to buy a house there, and set their sights on other nearby row-house neighborhoods, settling on Fort Greene in 1968. (In an excellent essay, "Rich Man, Poor Man: A History of Fort Greene," in the December 2005–January 2006 issue of the *Brooklyn Rail*, writer Carl Hancock Rux wrote of how remarkably the recent controversial gentrification of Fort Greene recapitulated the neighborhood's earliest history.) Families such as the O'Donnells were in the vanguard of what in the 1980s became a mass movement, as Fort Greene real estate shot up in value and one house after another was rehabilitated to something like its former glory.

When we came to Brooklyn Heights in '63 you had Atlantic Avenue, and you didn't go over on the other side of Atlantic Avenue. You can go down to Sahadi's but you stay on this side. It was really like that. Strangely enough, when you walked down to [what is now] the Fulton Street Mall, that was nice. Really nice. You put nice clothes on when you went out shopping. It was beautiful. You had Gage & Tollner restaurant there, you had nice stores there—it was amazing. That changed to the other way. Now you don't walk down there....And none of us, not any of us, had seen all that was over here in Fort Greene. If you take this block here, all the people of my age we have all lived in Brooklyn Heights.

MARIANNE ENGBERG

Gentrification is problematic for neighborhoods in some of the same ways postwar urban renewal was. People are displaced, established social networks are disrupted. Some social scientists suggest that neighborhoods with large rooming-house populations are inherently unstable, and that gentrification, far from being a destabilizing influence, actually increases neighborhood cohesion. It is far from the purpose of this guide to interpret these phenomena, but rather to report that gentrification is controversial, and that while rising property values are, in an abstract sense, indicative of urban success, they may also be the opposite, in that inner city neighborhoods exist in part to shelter economically diverse populations including the poor who seek to enjoy the benefits and exploit the opportunities of urban living.

That said, gentrification in Fort Greene and Clinton Hill has drawn a lot of attention among sociologists because, unlike in many other places, it has not dramatically altered the racial profile of the community. As many of Fort Greene's gentrifiers are black as are white. And, in the process, Fort Greene became a mecca for the black creative class.

CAPITAL OF THE BLACK CREATIVE CLASS

In a 1998 essay in *Cityscape: A Journal of Policy Development and Research*, Long Island University sociologist Jan Rosenberg wrote:

> By the mid-1980s, Fort Greene was moving beyond stabilization. Some of its brownstone blocks were taking on considerable cachet, particularly for artistic members of the Black middle class. The area is home to filmmaker Spike Lee's production company and, until

1998, two small retail outlets as well as his personal residence. Numerous well-known jazz musicians, including Cecil Taylor and Branford Marsalis, and other accomplished, prominent Black artists live in Fort Greene. Comparisons with the Harlem Renaissance and other artistic centers were unavoidable.

In fact, Fort Greene had long been a place for the black creative class, though the fact tended to go unnoticed by the mainstream press until the 1980s. Jazz musicians in particular were drawn to the neighborhood in the postwar years. In Fort Greene they could find suitable, affordable housing and an easy commute to the lower Manhattan jazz clubs where they made their living. Longtime Fort Greene resident Lillie Mae Jones was born in Flint, Michigan, in 1929. She sang in a Detroit church choir and studied piano. At 16 she sat in with Charlie Parker when he came to perform in Detroit. Between 1948 and 1951 she became famous for her scat singing with the Lionel Hampton big band (which at the time also included Charles Mingus and Wes Montgomery). She'd been using the stage name Lorraine Carter. Then Hampton nicknamed her "Betty Bebop," and she became Betty Carter. It was while she was with the Hampton band that she moved to New York. She performed with Dizzy Gillespie, Miles Davis, and Sonny Rollins. Her 1961 duet with Ray Charles on "Baby, It's Cold Outside" topped the R&B chart. Still, she struggled through the 1950s and 1960s because she was a pure jazz singer who did not wish to adapt to cabaret or pop, which would have gotten her more work. By the late 1960s she seemed to lack a marketable niche, being uninterested in moving either in the avant-garde or the pop directions. So, with entrepreneurial zeal, she set about to create her own niche, and in 1971 formed her own record label, Bet-Car Productions, which gave her complete control over production and arrangement, and in a way can be seen as a template for the independent entrepreneurial spirit that would mark black creative enterprise in Fort Greene in the decades to come. Unfettered by the expectations of a marketplace she could not control, in a sense Betty Carter created her own marketplace. She drew in a new generation of fans that conventional wisdom had said did not exist. She also mentored and nurtured young musicians, including Mulgrew Miller, Kenny Washington, and Cyrus Chestnut. Her reputation skyrocketed in the 1980s when she was universally acknowledged as one of the small handful of the most important jazz vocalists of all time. She was renowned as a small-group arranger at a time when few singers did their own arrangements. Verve Records reissued her Bet-Car releases on CD. Her album "Look What I Got!" won a Grammy Award (Best Female Jazz Vocalist) in 1988; she performed at the White House in 1994; and in 1997 President Bill Clinton awarded her the National Medal of Arts. She died the following year, of pancreatic cancer, at the age of 69, in her home in Fort Greene. The *New York Times* referred to her and the young musicians who surrounded her as "Betty Carter U." In 1999 she was a posthumous inductee into *Down Beat* magazine's Jazz Hall of Fame. Between 1993 and her death in 1998 she ran the Jazz Ahead series at the Brooklyn Academy of Music, showcasing up-and-coming talents, a short walk from her home.

Cecil Percival Taylor was born in the same year as Betty Carter—1929. But his background and music were quite different. A native New Yorker, he had a Classical training and attended the New England Conservatory of Music. His first recording was *Jazz Advance*, made with saxophonist Steve Lacy in 1956. Taylor evolved a unique, demanding style of performance that, in a way very different from that of Betty Carter, had trouble finding its commercial niche. He was the pioneering pianist of the "free jazz" movement in the late 1950s. Betty Carter said in a 1970s interview, "Coltrane came along, so everybody starts to play free. They didn't realize that is not black culture. The moment they did that, they alienated blacks. Whites began to absorb that free stuff, because they're classically trained. They know about dissonance. That's their culture. Blacks run from it, because none of our music would swing anymore." The jazz culture of Fort Greene was never monolithic. In the 1980s two Fort Greene trumpeters, Lester Bowie and Wynton Marsalis, would carry forward the debate about the avant-garde vs. tradition. And yet Betty Carter and Cecil Taylor were friends. Taylor is devoted to the art of jazz vocalists and holds Carter in particular esteem (along with Billie Holiday, Lena Horne, Bessie Smith, Ethel Waters, Ivie Anderson, Frank Sinatra, and Ella Fitzgerald). (But there has been no love lost between Taylor and Wynton Marsalis, to say the least.) In any event, Cecil Taylor by the 1970s had made a big name for himself in the world of avant-garde jazz just at the time when such jazz had achieved its largest audience. Taylor performed at the White House for President Jimmy Carter, and in 1991 won a MacArthur Fellowship (the "genius grant"). In 1983 Cecil Taylor moved to Fort Greene, where he has lived on Fort Greene Place, between Lafayette Avenue and Hanson Place (the same block as Hiram S. Thomas) in a house that at least as early as the 1940s had been a rooming house.

Locksley Wellington Hampton was born in 1932, three years after Betty Carter and Cecil Taylor. Born in western Pennsylvania, his parents and nine siblings all played musical instruments and toured as a family band. His father bought Locksley, or "Slide" as he would come to be known, a trombone when he was a boy. In the early 1950s Slide played with the Lionel Hampton big band, not long after Betty Carter had left. Slide played and arranged with Maynard Ferguson, Art Blakey, Tadd Dameron, Thad Jones and Mel Lewis, Max Roach, and Woody Herman. His Slide Hampton Octet, formed in 1962, included trumpeters Booker Little and Freddie Hubbard and saxophonist George Coleman. He also worked for Motown and was a musical director for Stevie Wonder and the Four Tops.

Slide Hampton lived at 245 Carlton Avenue (built c. 1867), between DeKalb and Willoughby avenues, in the 1960s. He made his house into a kind of boarding house for jazz musicians, and an improbably high number of jazz greats resided under the roof of 245 at one time or other. In fact, Eric Dolphy, who once lived there, recorded a number titled "245." Freddie Hubbard, Wes Montgomery, and Wayne Shorter all lived there at one time, and John Coltrane was a visitor (his cousin Mary lived there). Slide Hampton notes that 245 was right around the corner from the home of bassist Bill Lee. (In 2010 a 2-bedroom, 800-square-foot co-op in 245 sold for $575,000 with a monthly maintenance of $607.) Hampton left the house in 1968 when he went to live in Europe, where he remained until 1976. He now lives in northern New Jersey.

By the 1980s a new generation of black creative people had emerged in Fort Greene. Nelson George wrote, in a 1990 *Village Voice* essay reprinted in his book *Buppies, B-Boys, Baps & Bohos: Notes on Post-Soul Black Culture* (2001), "Through the '60s and '70s, jazz musicians were attracted to Fort Greene's beautiful and relatively inexpensive brownstones, the artistic ambience created by Pratt Institute, the short subway ride to work in the Village….But since the mid-'80s, a slew of sub-30 achievers has ventured into the Fort: Branford (and for a minute Wynton) Marsalis, Living Colour's Vernon Reid, actress/singer Alva Rogers, saxophonist/bandleader

Steve Coleman and other members of the jazz collective M-Base, Public Enemy executive producer Bill Stephney, cinematographer Ernest Dickerson, actress Sandye Wilson of Sidewalk Stories, and Stretsasonic's Daddy-O are a few of the more visible Fort Greeners. Less celebrated but crucial to the community's mix is an ever-growing list of creative professionals—the publicists, video producers, entertainment attorneys, record promoters, literary agents, graphic artists, clothing designers, cartoonists, sound engineers, and jingle singers who daily parade up and down DeKalb Avenue, eating Italian food at Cino's, buying groceries at Perry's, or, to satisfy a late-night craving, venturing up to Junior's."

I made some money in 1984, I did a book on Michael Jackson, and it's the first time I actually had any money, real cash of any kind. I was 26 or 27. A woman who worked with me, doing publicity and helping me with all kinds of stuff, said her boyfriend owned a building in this area called Fort Greene. There was an empty apartment, a duplex with a fireplace, exposed brick walls, backyard access, and I could get it for, I forget the exact rent I paid, somewhere between $900 and $1000—it was a lot of space for relatively little money. And so I moved in in 1985....I'd lived in Queens for 4 or 5 years out of college....So I moved into this place on the corner of Willoughby and Carlton, 19 Willoughby Avenue.... The first or second day I lived in here I was actually sitting in my little den-office in the downstairs back room. I was sitting there looking out the window, thinking "Oh my God, I've got a backyard, that's fantastic," when a guy jumps over the fence with a TV, which he has stolen from someone else on the block. And I'm like, wow, what the hell. And he's kind of taking the TV across my yard to try to take it over the next fence. And two policemen hop over the fence, and arrest him in my backyard. Then they took him out through my space.

NELSON GEORGE

But the scene did not involve a lot of the kind of socializing that characterized older New York bohemias, famous for their artistic hangouts like the Cedar Tavern in Greenwich Village. "One reason," wrote George, "quite simply, is that folks be busy. Fort Greeners are always 'in the studio,' 'on the road,' or 'on the Coast.'" While the Harlem Renaissance of the 1920s and other New York creative flourishings centered around painters, poets, and musicians, the Fort Greene scene was far more varied, and included filmmakers, graphic artists, fashion designers, and jazz and hip-hop musicians. Fort Greene is bohemia with "technology and marketing acumen....overriding it all is the idea of businessperson/artist." The creative people of Fort Greene, wrote George, "aren't simply bottom-line-oriented buppies, though some fit that description— they're astute enough to know that art without finance is a nuisance....right now the genius of the Fort Greene posse is more entrepreneurial than artistic."

> If you were young and hip and black and artistic in that period, you don't want to go to Harlem, you wanted to be in Brooklyn....I've always found the neighborhood to be very magical. It's one thing if you talk to people who move here, and even younger people today, they speak to this sense of possibility in the neighborhood, the sense that things can happen here, and you can have a good life, and yet also get a chance to be creative.
>
> NELSON GEORGE

A driving force and symbol of the new Fort Greene was filmmaker Spike Lee.

Shelton Jackson Lee was born on March 20, 1957, in Atlanta to a family with deep roots in the venerable black educational institutions of the South. His great-grandfather graduated from Tuskegee Institute in Alabama, his grandfather and father from Morehouse College in Atlanta, and his mother and grandmother from Spelman College in Atlanta. Spike's father, the jazz bassist, composer, and arranger Bill Lee, moved the family to Brooklyn in 1961. At first they settled not in Fort Greene but in Cobble Hill, where the Lees were the only black family on their block and Spike's schoolmates and friends were Italian-Americans. In 1969 the Lees bought a brownstone in Fort Greene. Marianne Moore may have moved out in 1966, but Herbert Scott-Gibson arrived in the following year, and the Lees two years after that. In brownstone Brooklyn, "decline" and "rebirth" often occur simultaneously.

Spike, as his mother nicknamed him when he was a baby, attended John Dewey High School, near Coney Island, and then followed in his father's and grandfather's footsteps by attending Morehouse College. It was while he was in college that his mother, Jacquelyn Shelton Lee, a teacher at the prestigious Saint

40 Acres and a Mule Filmworks, director Spike Lee's production company, is located at 75 South Elliott Place, between DeKalb and Lafayette avenues.

Cinematographer (and Fort Greene resident) Ernest Dickerson with director Spike Lee and crew members. *Courtesy of 40 Acres and a Mule Filmworks, photo taken by David Lee.*

Director and actor Spike Lee.
Courtesy of 40 Acres and a Mule Filmworks, photo taken by David Lee.

Bill Lee with actress Tracy Camilla Johns on a Fort Greene row house stoop.
Courtesy of 40 Acres and a Mule Filmworks, photo taken by David Lee.

Actress Raye Dowell sitting on a Fort Greene brownstone stoop.
Courtesy of 40 Acres and a Mule Filmworks, photo taken by David Lee.

Actors Tracy Camilla Johns and Tommy Redmond Hicks on a bench in Fort Greene Park in *She's Gotta Have It.*
Courtesy of 40 Acres and a Mule Filmworks, photo taken by David Lee.

Ann's School in Brooklyn Heights, died. It was also while he was in college that he took film courses and developed an interest in becoming a filmmaker. He graduated from Morehouse in 1979 and in the fall entered the M.F.A. filmmaking program at New York University. During that time he rented an apartment in Fort Greene. His 1982 thesis film, *Joe's Bed-Stuy Barbershop: We Cut Heads*, received an Oscar for best student film. He spent the next four years scraping together the money to produce his first feature film, *She's Gotta Have It,* released in 1986. The film's success, both at the box office and with critics, spread the word about Fort Greene. That's because much of the film was shot in Fort Greene, and also because Lee established his own studio, 40 Acres and a Mule Filmworks, in Fort Greene.

Lee shot *She's Gotta Have It* in the summer of 1985 at a cost of $175,000. The musical score was composed by Bill Lee. The film is about Nola Darling (played by Tracy Camilla Johns), a young black woman (who in the film actually lives in a loft in DUMBO, not in Fort Greene) juggling three lovers, each of whom is a black man representing a different facet of Fort Greene life: Jamie Overstreet (played by Tommy Redmond Hicks) is serious, sensitive, intellectual, and possessive; Greer Childs (John Canada Terrell) is a narcissistic male model; and loquacious, immature, quick-witted Mars Blackmon (played by Spike Lee himself). The Mars Blackmon character, as portrayed by Lee, became a kind of pop culture icon of the late 1980s, far out of proportion to the film's actual scale of distribution, appearing, for example, in TV commercials (which Lee also directed) with Michael Jordan. The film was shot in black and white, with the exception of a single dazzling modern dance sequence filmed in color on the steps of the Prison Ship Martyrs Monument in Fort Greene Park. The cinematographer, Ernest Dickerson, a Fort Greene resident, began collaborating with Lee when they were students together at NYU film school. Dickerson shot such Lee films as *School Daze* (1988), *Do the Right Thing* (1989), *Mo' Better Blues* (1990), *Jungle*

Courtesy of 40 Acres and a Mule Filmworks, photo taken by David Lee.

Courtesy of 40 Acres and a Mule Filmworks, photo taken by David Lee.

Fever (1991), and *Malcolm X* (1992). He then turned to directing with *Juice* (1992) and several episodes of the acclaimed HBO series *The Wire.*

Another Lee film, the semi-autobiographical *Crooklyn* (1994), though set in Bedford-Stuyvesant, contains a jazz concert scene featuring Delroy Lindo, who plays a jazz pianist, loosely based on Spike Lee's father, shot in Fort Greene Park. Lee co-wrote the film with his sister Joie and brother Cinqué, and the music was composed by trumpeter and onetime Fort Greene resident Terence Blanchard.

Between 1990 and 1999, after he had achieved success with *She's Gotta Have It* (1986) and *Do the Right Thing* (1989), Lee lived in the French Second Empire-style brownstone house at 180 Washington Park, just south of Willoughby Avenue. (It was built in c. 1866 as part of the seven-house row from No. 179 to No. 185. It was at one time the home of the Reverend Charles Carroll Albertson [1865–1959], who between 1913 and 1928 was pastor of Lafayette Avenue Presbyterian Church.) In 1999, Spike Lee and his wife Tonya moved out of Fort Greene to the Upper East Side of Manhattan. He lived in the neighborhood—with time off for college—for thirty years.

In recent years, many restaurants and cafés, such as Café Lafayette at 99 South Portland Avenue, have opened in Fort Greene, some with outdoor seating that enhances the charm of the streets.

Courtesy of 40 Acres and a Mule
Filmworks, photo taken by David Lee.

Courtesy of 40 Acres and a Mule
Filmworks, photo taken by David Lee.

Courtesy of 40 Acres and a Mule
Filmworks, photo taken by David Lee.

Spike Lee founded 40 Acres and a Mule Filmworks in 1986 in a converted firehouse at 124 DeKalb Avenue, between Fort Greene Place and St. Felix Street. The company remained at that location until 2008 when it moved its Fort Greene operations to 75 South Elliott Place, between DeKalb and Lafayette avenues. Lee told reporters he did not own the DeKalb building and left it after 22 years when faced with a steep rent increase. He moved 40 Acres and a Mule to a nearby building he owns that is right around the corner from the site of his former retail store, Spike's Joint.

But when *She's Gotta Have It* came out in 1986...it's kind of a Valentine to Fort Greene, it was shot in the park, and some of the brownstones and all of that stuff. That really became like a magnet, and that put the neighborhood on the map as a cool place for young black artists to come to. And then the thing that really confirmed that was that Spike rented (everyone thought he owned it, but he actually rented) this firehouse right across from Brooklyn Tech. And that building was really a mecca, because it confirmed Spike wasn't leaving to go off to Manhattan, he was staying in Brooklyn, and what happened was that began drawing people to move here like Ernest Dickerson....When [Spike Lee] was shooting movies, he was shooting a lot of things in Brooklyn like *Do the Right Thing* or *Crooklyn*, artists would come and stay in the neighborhood. You would see Halle Berry walking down DeKalb Avenue to Spike's office—which was quite a sight for a lot of men there....Plus he was doing commercials. Michael Jordan came to hang out at the firehouse.

NELSON GEORGE

The company name, 40 Acres and a Mule, refers to a post–Civil War field order issued by General William Tecumseh Sherman that would compensate freed slaves by giving them 40 acres of land and a mule. President Andrew Johnson later revoked the order.

The company has produced all of Lee's films, including his television work, such as the acclaimed *When the Levees Broke* (2006), which was co-produced by Home Box Office. 40 Acres and a Mule was also conceived as an organization that would aid the entry of young African Americans into the film industry by offering classes at nearby Long Island University and an "intern boot camp," and that would develop projects by other filmmakers, including Gina Prince-Blythewood's *Love & Basketball* (2000) and Ernest Dickerson's *Good Fences* (2003). It would sponsor teams in local sports leagues, donate food and toys to shelters, organize summer basketball camps, and provide SAT prep classes to local students. The Spike's Joint stores in Fort Greene and Los Angeles and 40 Acres and a Mule Musicworks were offshoots.

In 1990 Spike Lee opened a retail store, Spike's Joint, at 1 South Elliot Place, at DeKalb Avenue, in a brownstone house (with added storefront) built in c. 1872 as part of a six-house row extending south on South Elliot Place from DeKalb Avenue. At first the store, which sold clothing and memorabilia related to Spike Lee's films, was a huge success with both New Yorkers and tourists. It closed in 1997 after its novelty wore off and the kind of "urban wear" it offered became more widely available, including on the Internet.

> In two stops or one stop you are in Manhattan. It's different living in Fort Greene from living in Manhattan. You feel you're a little bit out in fresh air, out in the country. It's a different pace, too. So when you came home from work—and I ran a commercial photography studio, which is a very tough thing to run—and you come home here, you're home and you can go play tennis. It was like in the countryside....I can see why all the European people are falling for this neighborhood.
>
> MARIANNE ENGBERG

The end of the 1980s and beginning of the 1990s witnessed a major deflation of real estate values in New York. In just a few years many town houses in brownstone Brooklyn lost 30 to 40 percent of their value. The frenetic pace of gentrification in the 1980s had ebbed. In 1991 the *New York Times* reported, "In some corners of the city, the experts say, gentrification may be remembered, along with junk bonds, stretch limousines and television evangelism, as just another grand excess of the 1980's." Some brownstone Brooklyn neighborhoods, such as Park Slope, had already experienced such a significant degree of gentrification that they were no longer counted as "gentrifying" but as "gentrified." The real estate market slammed on the brakes as Fort Greene was still gentrifying. As a result, Fort Greene entered the 1990s, so far as the pace of gentrification was concerned, in a sort of state of suspended animation, with much of its economic and, especially, racial mix intact. And also a certain edginess. The jazz saxophonist Branford Marsalis moved to Fort Greene in 1988. He later recalled an experience in Fort Greene Park. "I was walking along holding my son's hand when a crackhead came up and, bold as day, told me exactly what she would do for $10 to score some rocks. I was in shock. The next day Spike [Lee] called and asked how I was doing. I said, 'I'm outta here, man!' I didn't want my kid dealing with that crap." Branford Marsalis left in 1991. "If I was single, I'd still be in Fort Greene," Marsalis told Entertainment Weekly in 1992. "I loved it. I didn't just live there, I hung out. I played basketball in the park, ate at places like the Greene Avenue Grill and Cino's." (That year Marsalis achieved national fame as the bandleader on the Tonight Show with Jay Leno, leaving in 1995.)

But the black creative efflorescence continued through the 1990s. In a 2009 essay in the *New York Times*, Nelson George, who had helped to finance *She's Gotta Have It*, wrote, "I walk past a bodega where the 'clockers' used to sell drugs by the pay phones. My friends and I used to joke that the presence of these crack dealers on select corners 'protected' us from real-estate speculators and home-hungry Manhattanites." But a revived real estate market and a significant reduction in crime sent Fort Greene right back into gentrification overdrive. It turned out that the gentrification of brownstone Brooklyn wasn't "just another grand excess of the 1980s." In fact, by the first decade of the 21st century, gentrification began to outpace the 1980s. George wrote, "Once the aura of danger left Fort Greene, its many charms could no longer be hidden. When Corcoran opened a real estate office on Lafayette Avenue several years ago, it was clear to me that my Fort Greene was history." Nelson George, who had grown up in the tough Brooklyn neighborhoods of Brownsville and East New York, came to Fort Greene in 1985. At the time the neighborhood mix included working-class blacks who had lived there for some years, white homeowners in the brownstone blocks south of Fort Greene Park, and black creative people. In 2009 he wrote, "I've stayed anchored to the area, still inspired by the creative energy I felt when I moved here as a young man. It's as if so much good work has been conceived in Fort Greene that it has seeped into the neighborhood's DNA. Yet I fear that this new Fort Greene of high-rises, planned sports arenas and traffic jams won't be a very congenial place for a middle-aged black author. Thing is, I'm not sure who I'd be somewhere else."

For me, having lived here now close to 25 years, it's been interesting to live through it. I grew up in a Brooklyn where basically we spent our whole life watching white people leave Brooklyn. I grew up during white flight. So this is the first time in my life that I've seen a return of white people to Brooklyn. But what's interesting to me is they're very different from the people who left. The people who left were Irish, Italian, Jewish, very ethnic New Yorkers, real New Yorkers from that '40s, '50s, '60s kind of New York. I grew up eating knishes and going to Italian restaurants....My white friends at school, there weren't any WASPs....So they all kind of left, they left East New York, East Flatbush, Flatbush, Canarsie, and so on....Now it feels much more college-educated, it feels much more white collar,...the dynamic and the energy is different.

NELSON GEORGE

The October 12–18, 2006 issue of the weekly *Time Out New York* featured a cover story on the "best blocks in New York City." Such a piece is inevitably highly subjective, but the *Time Out* feature was carefully and intelligently conceived and written, and cast a very wide net, including streets in all five boroughs, with many surprises. One of the biggest surprises was that the magazine's choice for the number one best block in New York City was in Fort Greene: South Portland Avenue between DeKalb and Lafayette avenues.

The king of all New York blocks seems straight out of Sesame Street, not only for the unbroken rows of brownstones and brick townhouses, but also because it's still home to the diverse crowd for which Fort Greene has become known: The old guard of the black middle class shares the street with transplants from far and near; kids and senior citizens roost on stoops. Slate sidewalks and a canopy of London Plane trees, plus proximity to the C and G trains and the nearby cluster of great bars and restaurants, make this block a standout. And that's not mentioning Fort Greene Park, which begins right where South Portland meets DeKalb.

The black cast-iron railings of the brownstone stoops (as seen on South Portland Avenue) have a powerful visual rhythm that, combined with the carved brownstone details, street trees, and bluestone sidewalks, create Fort Greene streets of beguiling beauty.

When I was a kid, I so vividly and fondly recall my father saying to me, "You're going to laugh at what I'm telling you, but someday this neighborhood is going to be worth a lot of money." I said, "If it's going to be worth a lot of money, why don't you buy some buildings?" And he said: "Well where am I getting the money from?" He said that eventually people will not be able to afford Manhattan....Somebody's going to live here because look at what's here.

HAL GLICKSMAN

Hopefully, Fort Greene will always be Fort Greene.

MARIANNE ENGBERG

Clinton Hill experienced a pattern of growth unique among Brooklyn neighborhoods. In the 1830s and 1840s the high ground emerged as a suburban retreat as
property owners erected "villas" well removed from the hubbub of city life. Then,
as one would expect, as the city sprawled eastward it devoured the suburban idyll as
row houses went up by the hundreds, infilling the lawns and grounds of the old
villas. But then something unexpected occurred. While many of the row houses
were posh residences of the upper middle class, in the late 19th century several
stupendous mansions—the equal of anything in New York—replaced earlier
houses, particularly on Clinton Avenue. One of the exciting things about Clinton
Hill today is that notable traces of each of these periods of development remain.

For a taste of the early suburban villa era, go to 136 Clinton Avenue, between
Myrtle and Park avenues. From its period, this clapboarded Greek Revival house
is very likely Brooklyn's last remaining one bearing a full temple front, with
four freestanding two-story columns supporting an entablature and a broad
triangular pediment with raking cornices. As is typical of New York's Greek Revival
buildings, of which Brooklyn Borough Hall (1845–48) is another example, the
pediment is left bare rather than filled, as the ancient Greeks would have done,
with figure sculpture. (In part this is because our Greek Revival was based perhaps
less on the way the Greeks actually built than on a melancholy cult of ruins, and in
part because in the 1830s we simply lacked the requisite affordable craftsmen.)
The house is a grand thing, set back behind a broad lawn enclosed by an iron
fence. The record, such as we are able to reconstruct it (often a daunting task
when it comes to pre-Civil War buildings in Brooklyn), indicates a construction
date of between 1836 and 1840. In 1834, according to the excellent research of
the Landmarks Preservation Commission, George Washington Pine, the
Manhattan auctioneer who laid out Clinton Avenue on the farmland of John
Spader, sold the lot to a man named Henry Ryer, who a year later sold it to a
Richard White. White, a carver with a shop on Fulton Street, built a modest house
on the site. But only a year later he sold it to the brothers-in-law Rem Lefferts and
John Laidlaw. They decided to move White's modest house to the rear of the lot
and incorporate it as a service wing in a grander edifice, which is the columned
house that fronts on Clinton Avenue today. The original occupant of the house
appears to have been Rem Lefferts's sister-in-law, Amelia Lefferts. What's curious is
that Amelia was by then separated from her husband, Rem's brother Leffert
Lefferts Jr., a prominent Kings County property owner. It appears that amid that
marital discord Rem sided not with his brother but with his sister-in-law. In any
event, Amelia moved into the house with the three youngest of her five children.
One of these, Marshall Lefferts (1821–76), became a surveyor and worked
with David B. Douglass on the laying out of Green-Wood Cemetery in the late
1830s, very near the time his family moved into 136 Clinton Avenue. He later, years
after moving from this house, achieved great prominence in the telegraph business
and, in 1851, joined the Seventh Regiment of the New York National Guard. He
began as a private but by the beginning of the Civil War had become a colonel.
At war's outbreak he led the Seventh Regiment in defense of Washington, D.C.,
was promoted to general, and in 1863 led the regiment in helping to put down
the draft riots in Manhattan. Between 1866 and 1881 the house was owned
by a German immigrant family named Mannheim. In 1935 it was divided
into a two-family residence, and in 1948 sold to Anthony and Yolanda Ingenito

(by then there were many Italians in the neighborhood), who occupied one of the two apartments until they sold the house in 1960. Sometime during the 1940s or 1950s the house's columns were replaced by square piers, and the house was refaced in asphalt shingles and synthetic brick siding. But in the late 1970s and early 1980s the house was restored by owners Allen Handelman and Richard Arnow. In 2001 the Landmarks Preservation Commission designated the house as a landmark. (It falls a block or so outside of the Clinton Hill Historic District that was designated in 1981.)

136 Clinton Avenue, between Myrtle and Park avenues, known as the Laidlaw-Lefferts house, was built c. 1836–40 and is a fine surviving example of a Greek Revival villa.

Two blocks south, at 284 Clinton Avenue, between Willoughby and DeKalb avenues, stands another of the first generation of Clinton Hill houses, this one a Gothic Revival suburban villa of the type popularized by the enormously influential pre-Civil War landscape gardener and arbiter of taste Andrew Jackson Downing. (By the way, we distinguish a "villa" from a "cottage" by the former's greater size and scale, more elaborate massing, and greater pretension.) Downing, who may be said to be the inventor of the American front lawn, was also, at around the same time he was an influence on 284 Clinton Avenue, the main influence on the landscaping of the original Washington Park, opened in 1850. (The park was redesigned in 1867 by two Downing protégés, Calvert Vaux and Frederick Law Olmsted.) The house was built, according to the Landmarks Preservation Commission, in c. 1854. Today the house is faced in wood shingles but probably originally was faced in board and

Charles Pratt, a partner in the Standard Oil Trust and one of the richest men ever to live in Brooklyn, built this Victorian villa as his home in 1874, at 232 Clinton Avenue. It is now owned by St. Joseph's College.

batten; the present shingling would have made the house a bit more stylish by the standards of the later 19th century. The house, which has a very rural appearance, was built by a man named William W. Crane, of whom we know little beyond that, according to directories, he was a "fancy goods dealer." We also know he was, as we would expect of a devotee of Downing, the vice president of the Brooklyn Horticultural Society. In 1854, Crane, Henry Crossman, and several other Clinton Avenue homeowners placed a notice in the *New York Times* objecting to the proposed new Clinton Avenue Congregational Church on the southwest corner of Clinton and Lafayette avenues. "A strong feeling exists in the minds of the majority of the residents on the avenue against the proposed location of the…church, both on account of the injury which will result to the value of property in the neighborhood, from its near approach to the line of the street, as well as to the finances of the church itself from the falling off of subscriptions, which will follow from the same cause, owing to the dissatisfaction which many feel at the site which has been now chosen for its front." In other words, the church was not to be sufficiently set back behind the broad lawn that was considered *de rigueur* on early Clinton Avenue. The present church on the site (now called Cadman Memorial Church), by the way, was built in 1922, replacing the 1855 edifice designed by James Renwick Jr., who would soon design St. Patrick's Cathedral on Fifth Avenue in Manhattan. Crane was also, with all his neighbors, opposed to the construction of the Myrtle Avenue elevated railroad. The Crane house's lawn originally extended to DeKalb Avenue; in c. 1871 much of the lawn was filled in by the three brownstones that are there today. At that time the Crane family still owned 284, but by then their desire to make a quick buck off their land won out over their Downingesque aesthetics.

Both of these houses are protected by law. The Lefferts-Laidlaw house, as 136 Clinton Avenue is known, is a New York City landmark designated in 2001. The Crane house, at 284 Clinton Avenue, is protected by its inclusion in the Clinton Hill Historic District, designated by the city's Landmarks Preservation Commission in 1981. The historic district has irregular boundaries: on the west, Vanderbilt and Clinton avenues; on the north, Willoughby Avenue; on the east, Hall and Downing streets and Grand Avenue; and on the south, the blocks between Gates Avenue and Fulton Street. The district contains nothing to the north of Willoughby Avenue, a situation local groups, such as the Myrtle Avenue Revitalization Project Local Development Corporation, which was founded in 1999 and which sponsored the *Wallabout Cultural Resources Survey* of 2005, are trying to rectify. The Society for Clinton Hill was formed in 1973. According to the *New York Times*, the group "was instrumental in gaining landmark status for the area. Its members did research on the neighborhood and lobbied government officials"—thus playing a role analogous to the one played by the Fort Greene Landmarks Preservation Committee (now Fort Greene Association) in promoting the 1978 designations of the Fort Greene and Brooklyn Academy of Music historic districts. And like the Fort Greene Association, the Society for Clinton Hill also concerns itself with neighborhood livability issues of all kinds.

A bit to the north of 284 Clinton Avenue, in the Clinton Hill Historic District, stands 232 Clinton Avenue, built in 1874 and either the last of the suburban villas or the first of the splendiferous mansions. The style is Italianate, which succeeded the Greek Revival and the Gothic Revival in popularity, and, unlike with the slightly earlier 136 and 284, we can identify an architect: Ebenezer L. Roberts. Roberts was a prominent Brooklyn practitioner much favored by the house's owner, Charles Pratt. (Roberts died in 1890 from what the *Daily Eagle* called "nervous prostration, brought on by over work.") Pratt's grounds originally exended westward to Vanderbilt Avenue; in 1899, Pratt's widow built a great glass greenhouse where the Dillon Child Study Center of St. Joseph's College now stands. The Pratt mansion is now owned by St. Joseph's College.

Charles Pratt was born on October 2, 1830, in Watertown, Massachusetts. Forced to go to work at an early age, he attended school when he could, and by 19 was a clerk in a paint and oil store in Boston. He furthered his education by membership in that city's Mercantile Library, which taught him the importance of libraries and would lead him many years later to create the Pratt Free Library in Brooklyn. Two years later he moved to New York and, in 1854, formed, with two colleagues, a paint and oil business called Raynolds, Devoe & Pratt. On August 27, 1859, Edwin Drake struck oil 69 feet below ground in Titusville, in northwestern Pennsylvania. This was the world's first successful oil well. And while the automobile—which would make petroleum into the most precious commodity on earth—was still some decades in the future, the Pennsylvania crude nonetheless had an immediate economic impact. And Charles Pratt decided to go into oil refining, in 1867 forming Charles Pratt & Company, refining crude oil at a plant on the East River waterfront at the border of Williamsburg and Greenpoint, Brooklyn. One of Pratt's products, Astral Oil, a high-quality illuminating kerosene, was especially famous and profitable. Pratt's success aroused the interest of John Davison Rockefeller, who was putting together the biggest vertically integrated petroleum company in the world and who in 1874 made a deal with Pratt to acquire his refining company. As part of the deal, Pratt became one of the nine immensely powerful board members of Rockefeller's Standard Oil Company. Pratt built his villa on Clinton Avenue in the year he merged his company with Standard Oil.

Pratt always felt frustrated by the desultory nature of his own formal schooling, and throughout his life placed a high value on education. As a rich man, he sought to aid educational institutions. He made large donations to Amherst College and to the University of Rochester, and was a benefactor of Clinton Hill's Adelphi Academy. In 1887 he founded Pratt Institute on Clinton Hill.

Pratt died in 1891, having fathered eight children by two wives. (His first wife died.) The *Brooklyn Daily Eagle* reported Pratt's death on May 5, 1891.

Charles Pratt, Brooklyn's wealthiest man and greatest philanthropist, died suddenly in his office in the Standard oil company building, 26 Broadway, New York, at 7 o'clock last evening. Mr. Pratt left his home in Clinton avenue about 10 o'clock yesterday morning, in good health and spirits. He stopped at the Pratt institute, on Ryerson street, on his way to New York, and spent something over an hour discussing contemplated improvements and additions to that institution. He arrived at his office a little before noon and attended to his usual duties. At 3:30 a friend called upon him and requested him to make a contribution to the Brooklyn bureau of charities. Mr. Pratt immediately signed a check for $5,000, and in handing it to his friend remarked that he was more than glad to be able to assist such a noble charity. It was his last gift.

His funeral was held at the church he had built, Emmanuel Baptist Church (1886–87, Francis H. Kimball, architect), on Lafayette Avenue at St. James Place. Among the many speakers was the Reverend Theodore Ledyard Cuyler, pastor of Lafayette Avenue Presbyterian Church, as well as Emmanuel's pastor, the Reverend John Humpstone. Present at the funeral were Standard Oil partners Henry Flagler and Benjamin Brewster (but not John or William Rockefeller), Pratt's longtime right-hand man and Standard Oil vice president Henry Rogers, and Pratt's Clinton Avenue neighbors John Arbuckle (No. 315) and Cornelius Hoagland (No. 410). Pratt is buried in Green-Wood Cemetery.

Pratt's house is large and in its way splendid, but it still says "villa" not "mansion." Not so with the homes of his sons, which were built between 1890 and 1906 on the other side of Clinton Avenue.

The first of these was 241 Clinton Avenue, between Willoughby and DeKalb avenues, built between 1890 and 1893, and therefore under construction when Charles Pratt died in 1891. This was the home of his eldest son, Charles Millard

Pratt. It was a wedding gift from Pratt père and Mrs. Pratt, an outstanding "Richardsonian Romanesque" mansion with a dramatic arched port-cochère that puts some people in mind of Frank Lloyd Wright (who was influenced by this kind of architecture). The architect of 241 Clinton Avenue was William B. Tubby, who had worked for Ebenezer L. Roberts, the architect of the elder Pratt's house at No. 232. Roberts had also designed Standard Oil's headquarters at 26 Broadway in Manhattan, and at the time he died in 1890 was designing a house for William Rockefeller in Tarrytown, New York. A year before hiring Tubby to design 241 Clinton Avenue, Pratt had hired him to design the Pratt Free Library. Another outstanding example of Tubby's work could once be seen nearby: Tubby designed Wallabout Market's wonderfully picturesque buildings, with their distinctive stepped gables, built between 1894 and 1896 north of Flushing Avenue between Washington Avenue and Ryerson Street. The market buildings were demolished in 1941 for an emergency wartime expansion of the Brooklyn Navy Yard.

At 241 Clinton Avenue stands the remarkable Romanesque Revival mansion of Charles Millard Pratt, the eldest son of Charles Pratt; designed by William Tubby, the house—now the residence of the Roman Catholic Bishop of Brooklyn—was built between 1890 and 1893.

Charles Millard Pratt was the eldest of the six sons of Charles Pratt. He was born in Brooklyn in 1855 and graduated from Adelphi Academy and Amherst College. He became a partner in Charles Pratt & Co. and served as president of Pratt Institute. He was also for 25 years a trustee of Vassar College, to which he gave nearly a million dollars. He was vice president of the Long Island Railroad, and, between 1899 and 1911, director, secretary, and treasurer of Standard Oil. His wife, Mary Seymour Morris, was the daughter of onetime Connecticut governor Luzon Morris. Charles Millard Pratt died in 1935 at his country house in Glen Cove, Long Island. His wife Mary was left the house at 241 Clinton Avenue. In 1923 he had been found by the courts to be mentally incompetent to manage his own business affairs. He left an estate worth more than $20 million.

The house became the Catholic Bishop's residence in 1938. The first occupant was Bishop Thomas Edmund Molloy, who served for 34 years as Brooklyn's third bishop. He lived there until his death in 1956. Bishop Molloy had previously resided, as had Brooklyn's first two bishops, at 367 Clermont Avenue, at the northeast corner of Greene Avenue, in Fort Greene. The Clinton Avenue house is currently occupied by Nicholas Anthony DiMarzio, who in 2003 became the seventh Bishop of the Diocese of Brooklyn.

The Frederic Bayley Pratt mansion at 229 Clinton Avenue was designed by Babb, Cook & Willard and built in 1895. It is now owned by Pratt Institute.

Frederic Bayley Pratt, the second and last surviving son of Charles Pratt, lived in the splendid Georgian Revival mansion at 229 Clinton Avenue, between Willoughby and DeKalb avenues. The house was designed by the prominent firm of Babb, Cook & Willard and was built in 1895.

BROOKLYN BACK IN THE DAY

Miss Mary Caroline Pratt made her début yesterday at a tea given for her by her mother, Mrs. Frederick [*sic*] B. Pratt, at her home, 229 Clinton Avenue, Brooklyn. Miss Pratt had her cousin, Miss Lydia Pratt Babbott, receiving with her....Mrs. Pratt and Frank L. Babbott are to give a dance together on Dec. 20 at the Heights Casino for their débutante daughters. Miss Babbott, who is at Vassar, is to make her début at the dance.

New York Times, November 24, 1915

The second son of Charles Pratt, Frederic was born in 1865 and died in 1945, in Glen Cove, Long Island. He attended Adelphi Academy and Amherst College. At the time of his death, he still resided for part of the year at 229 Clinton Avenue. He became secretary to the board of trustees of Pratt Institute in 1887. In 1923 he became its president, serving in that capacity until 1937. He and his friend Alfred Tredway White together donated the first chunk of land for the establishment of Marine Park in Brooklyn. He was a founder and between 1928 and 1935 was the head of the New York Museum of Science and Industry that once was in Rockefeller Center (and that was a great favorite of Fort Greene's Marianne Moore), and he was a trustee of the American Academy in Rome. He was a member of the New York City Art Commission and of the Committee on Regional Planning of New York and Its Environs. The house is now the Caroline Ladd Pratt House of Pratt Institute.

Frederic Pratt's house replaced the large wooden house of Henry Crossman (1805–81). He was "a manufacturer of umbrellas and parasols." He settled on Clinton Avenue in 1846. He was a director of the New-York Ferry Company, the United States Warehouse Company, the New-York and Dry Dock Railroad Company, and the Brooklyn and Coney Island Railroad Company. In 1881 the *New York Times* said "his death leaves only two of the original settlers of that fashionable thoroughfare alive." He was one of the first subscribers to the Brooklyn Academy of Music. The *Brooklyn Daily Eagle* wrote: "Of the original settlers on Clinton avenue, the most beautiful thoroughfare, probably, on this continent, his death leaves only two survivors." He was, said the *Daily Eagle,* "one of Brooklyn's most prominent, wealthy and worthy citizens."

Babb, Cook & Willard, known as the architects of, among much else, the Manhattan mansion of Andrew Carnegie, built between 1899 and 1903 on 91st Street at Fifth Avenue, which is now the Cooper-Hewitt National Design Museum, also designed the beautiful Georgian Revival mansion of another of Charles Pratt's sons, George Dupont Pratt, at 245 Clinton Avenue between Willoughby and DeKalb avenues. This was built in 1901 and since 1918 has been the main building of St. Joseph's College, founded (as St. Joseph's College for Women) in 1916.

George Dupont Pratt died in 1935, the same year as his brother Charles. By then, however, he resided in a town house at 580 Park Avenue in Manhattan. He was born in Brooklyn in 1869 and attended— you guessed it—Adelphi Academy and Amherst College. He then went to work for the Long Island Railroad, later leaving to become treasurer of Chelsea Fibre Mills and treasurer and vice president of Pratt Institute. He was known as a big game hunter and an art collector, especially of "primitive art," and was a trustee of the Metropolitan Museum of Art.

Brooklyn Daily Eagle postcard of the gardens of the Convent of the Sisters of Mercy on Willoughby Avenue between Classon Avenue and Taaffe Place, c. 1910. The "Walking Sisters," known for helping the poor, came to Clinton Hill in 1862 and remained until 2009, when the costs of maintaining the facilities became too much for the sisters to bear.

ST. JOSEPH'S COLLEGE

St. Joseph's College for Women was founded in 1916 as a private liberal arts college for women. Although founded by the Sisters of St. Joseph of Brentwood, the college was open to students of all faiths. (The Sisters of St. Joseph were established in France in 1650 and came to America—to teach the deaf in Missouri—in 1836. In 1856 the sisters were invited to Brooklyn by Bishop John Loughlin, and they took up residence in Brentwood, in Suffolk County. Nassau and Suffolk counties were part of the Diocese of Brooklyn before the 1957 creation of the Diocese of Rockville Centre.) The first freshman class admitted twelve students (dubbed the "Twelve Apostles") and classes were held at St. Angela Hall, which the Sisters of St. Joseph had maintained at 286 Washington Avenue, between Willoughby and DeKalb avenues, since 1906. When the college needed more space two years later, it purchased the recently vacated former mansion of George Dupont Pratt at 245 Clinton Avenue. The first class graduated in 1920, with the ceremony taking place at the Brooklyn Academy of Music on Lafayette Avenue.

The Reverend William T. Dillon, dean of the College from 1927 to 1945 and president from 1945 to 1956, oversaw the expansion of the college during its early years. In 1928 St. Joseph's demolished the two mansions to the immediate south of 245 Clinton Avenue and built a new building, connected to No. 245, to house administrative offices, classrooms, science laboratories, a gymnasium, and an auditorium. (One of the demolished structures, 249 Clinton Avenue, had been the home of Frederick A. Schroeder, a onetime mayor of Brooklyn.)

Despite the Depression, the college continued to expand and in 1936 purchased the Charles Pratt villa at 232 Clinton Avenue. During this time a pioneering program in pre-school child development was created, out of which grew the Dillon Child Study Center, which was founded in 1934 and has since 1968 been located in a building on part of the garden of the Pratt villa, on Vanderbilt Avenue between Willoughby and DeKalb avenues. A library building, McEntegart Hall, named for Bryan Joseph McEntegart, the fourth Bishop of the Diocese of Brooklyn, was opened in 1965 at the southwest corner of Clinton and Willoughby avenues.

Men were admitted to the College for the first time in 1970, at which point the "for Women" was dropped from the school name. A year later the college expanded to suburban Long Island, moving in 1979 to a 25-acre campus in Patchogue. The Clinton Hill campus expanded again in 2001 with the purchase of St. Angela Hall Academy, which was built in c. 1929 on the site of St. Angela Hall on Washington Avenue.

PRATT INSTITUTE

Charles Pratt dreamed of founding a school similar to Cooper Union, which was established by the great industrialist and philanthropist Peter Cooper on East 8th Street and Third Avenue in Manhattan in 1859. Cooper's purpose was to provide technical training to working people who had few other opportunities for the advanced training that would allow them to build fulfilling and prosperous careers for themselves, and to offer this training to people without regard to their sex, race, or religion. Pratt realized his dream when on October 17, 1887, Pratt Institute opened in Clinton Hill, only six blocks from Pratt's mansion on Clinton Avenue.

A few months before Pratt Institute opened, the *Daily Eagle* reported (February 17, 1887) that the school "will undertake to educate both sexes in the ordinary branches of education, but its special aim will be to afford its students opportunities to become acquainted with manufactured materials, fabrics, wares and arts, so as to educate the eye and the hand in the practical use of tools and machinery....Household economy will also be taught and the preparation of clothing and of food, and there likewise will be instruction in sanitary laws."

On the opening day the *Daily Eagle* reported: "Pratt Institute was opened to-day, but owing to the fact that work on the building has not progressed so rapidly as was expected, only one department, drawing, begins its sessions...The tuition fee is $10 per year, payable quarterly in advance. This fee, while not large enough to keep anybody away, is yet sufficient to deprive any supersensitive person of the idea that he is receiving charity....The only other requisite for admission is a good moral character."

Postcard showing the Main Building and South Hall of Pratt Institute, on Ryerson Street. Dated February 28, 1907, the handwriting on the card says: "Mama and Geo. Are both sick in bed with grippe and Sue has laryngitis. I think I'll fill out an application for nurse. M + G feel lots better than they did last night. Expect they'll get up tomorrow. Don't stew about us."

Such acts of benevolence no doubt stemmed in large part from pure charitable motives such as Pratt's Baptist faith inspired in him, but it should also be pointed out that such philanthropic largess took place against a background of labor strife and fears of social unrest. For example, Chicago's Haymarket riot had taken place only in 1886, and it and related issues were very much of concern to captains of industry. The *Daily Eagle* noted as much when on January 22, 1888, the paper editorialized that

> Against the dark background of the present struggle between capital and labor, such acts of wise benevolence stand forth with a significance that can neither be overlooked nor misunderstood....It would be impossible to imagine such scenes as those of which we have daily accounts from the Pennsylvania mining regions, in a world made up of George Peabodys, Peter Coopers and Charles Pratts.

As Charles Pratt had been inspired by Peter Cooper, so, in turn, other titans of the business world copied Pratt: Financier Anthony J. Drexel founded Drexel Institute (now Drexel University) in 1891 in Philadelphia, and meatpacking baron Philip D. Armour established the Armour Institute (now Illinois Institute of Technology) in 1893 in Chicago.

Pratt died only four years after his school opened, and so never had the chance to see his school become a world-famous institution of higher learning. But it remained very much a family concern. His sons Charles Millard Pratt and Frederic Bayley Pratt took over

Art Nouveau-style postcard of Pratt Institute, 1910. "You were good to write. I thought of you all week, because I knew I ought to write and yesterday your letter arrived. Did you say busy? If only you knew."

and guided the school for many years. The elder Pratt intended that the school train young people in manual arts. The *New York Times* reported on December 22, 1888, that

> *Scholars attending the evening classes of the Pratt Institute, Ryerson-street, near De Kalb-avenue, Brooklyn, were found hard at work last night by the bands of visitors who made tours of inspection through the school. All kinds of work was going on. Boys in tight-fitting jackets were laying brick, building walls, and making fire-places. Young girls were embroidering and making dresses, young men were hammering away at iron work, others were rapping into shape windows in miniature and embryo doors….[I]n the art department…young girls and boys were busy with free-hand sketching in charcoal from plaster cast and in mechanical and architectural drawing.*

While today bricklaying and typewriting are absent from Pratt's course offerings, the school also from the earliest focused on subjects for which it is now, and has long been, best known: art, architecture, and design.

In 1890 the Institute opened one of the country's first library schools, with the Pratt Free Library as its laboratory. The *Daily Eagle* reported on January 20, 1895: "Pratt Institute's new library

Art installation on the campus of Pratt Institute. The Pratt Free Library is the building on the left.

building…is gradually nearing completion. When ready for occupancy it will be one of the most imposing structures in this big city." The Pratt library had earlier been located in the Main Building and opened to the public in 1888 as the first free public library in Brooklyn—not limited to Pratt students. Excessive demand for its services—it was, said the *Daily Eagle* in 1895, "thronged with students, literary workers, and bibliomaniacs every afternoon"—led to the construction of a separate library building, dedicated on May 26, 1896. At the dedication, Pratt President Frederic Bayley Pratt presided; the Reverend John Humpstone, pastor of Emmanuel Baptist Church, said a prayer; and the famous Dannreuther Quartet performed Mendelssohn's overture to *Athalie*, Anton Rubinstein's *Music of the Spheres*, and "Walther's Prize Song" from Wagner's *Die Meistersinger*. And then New York State Librarian Melvil Dewey (of decimal system fame) addressed the assembly, followed by a prayer from the Reverend Samuel McConnell, pastor of the Church of the Holy Trinity on Montague Street. It was a grand event.

Architect William B. Tubby's Romanesque Revival building housed reference and circulating collections, including a children's collection, as well as an exhibition room, and classrooms for the library school. (In 1982 architect Giorgio

Cavaglieri added the south terrace with views down onto new stacks.) Until 1940 the library was open to all Brooklyn residents. After 1940, with the opening of the new Central Library at Grand Army Plaza, Pratt's library was no longer the much-needed municipal resource it had been for 52 years, and was restricted to Institute students. That must have been hard for Fort Greene poet Marianne Moore, who in the 1930s made extensive use of the library, once checking out fourteen books when she was at work on an essay about Emily Dickinson.

In June of 1938 Pratt, in commencement exercises at the Brooklyn Academy of Music, awarded its first bachelor's degrees—in architecture, teacher training, mechanical engineering, electrical engineering, and chemical engineering. Pratt was once as renowned for engineering as for art, architecture, and design, but in an effort to make optimal use of its resources and to focus its mission, Pratt closed its engineering school in 1993.

The campus today is a superblock with DeKalb Avenue on the south, Classon Avenue on the east (the unofficial border between Clinton Hill and Bedford-Stuyvesant), Willoughby Avenue on the north, and Hall Street on the west. There are 22 buildings in the superblock. The buildings originally fronted on city streets that were demapped in the 1960s to allow Pratt to create a superblock campus. About 3,800 students attend Pratt.

The Pratt Institute Library was designed by William Tubby and built in 1896. Between 1896 and 1940 the library was open to any Brooklynite over the age of 14. After the new Central Library opened at Grand Army Plaza, Pratt restricted access to its own library to Pratt students.

At the start of the 1970s, at a time of increasing crime and physical deterioration in Clinton Hill, some feared that Pratt— which was also experiencing its fair share of the student unrest that was a feature of the era—might uproot itself from Brooklyn and move out of the city. But under Richardson Pratt Jr., president of the Institute from 1972 to 1990, a series of new building projects loudly signaled Pratt Institute's commitment to Brooklyn. (Richardson Pratt Jr. was the grandson of Charles Pratt's eldest son, Charles Millard Pratt, and was the fifth Pratt family member to serve as the Institute's president.) Since 1993 Pratt's president has been Thomas F. Schutte. Notable Pratt alumni include cartoonist Jules Feiffer, fashion designer Betsey Johnson, photographer Robert Mapplethorpe, sculptor Eva Hesse, actor Robert Redford (who studied painting at Pratt), Pritzker Prize-winning architect Peter Zumthor, painter Ellsworth Kelly, Arnold Lobel (who wrote and illustrated the classic *Frog and Toad* children's books), graphic designer Paul Rand, architect William

Van Alen (of Chrysler Building fame), and many other leading 20th-century artists, designers, and architects.

Pratt Institute has also played a major role in the community, especially through the Pratt Center for Community Development. The Center began, with the help of a Rockefeller Brothers grant, in 1963 when George Raymond, the chair of Pratt's Department of City and Regional Planning, teamed with one of his students, Ron Shiffman, and a group of local ministers on a study of Bedford-Stuyvesant. The idea was to bring to local communities the ideas of urban planning and the resources of Pratt's esteemed planning department to confront the urban scourges of the day, such as poverty and disinvestment. In 1971 Ron Shiffman (by then a Pratt planning professor) told the *New York Times*: "We work in the communities providing the technical assistance and guidance for the gamut of urban problems that the people face every day—education, housing, health, pollution....The community is not used as a laboratory. The students must respond to the community by going into the streets and making real contributions in terms of community needs." In 1983 the *Village Voice*'s Jack Newfield wrote of the Center that "They have been the voice of the voiceless inside the closed, elitist world of developers, bankers, lawyers, planners, and politicians." Shiffman went on to chair, between 1991 and 1999, Pratt's Department of City and Regional Planning as well as to one of the most distinguished urban planning careers of the last five decades, including a stint (between 1990 and 1996) as a New York City Planning Commissioner. He has been involved in seemingly every significant community planning initiative in New York in that time, from a major role in the formation of the Bedford-Stuyvesant Restoration Corporation in the 1960s, to his role, in the wake of the September 11 attacks, as co-convener of the Civic Alliance to Rebuild Downtown New York. More recently, Brad Lander directed the Center form 2003 to 2009, when he was elected New York City Council Member for the 39th District. Today the Center is called the Pratt Center for Community Development, and can be found at http://prattcenter.net.

Pratt Institute, together with Fort Greene's Long Island University, Clinton Hill's St. Joseph's College, and the nearby City University of New York College of Technology and New York University Polytechnic Institute, have been a stabilizing influence on the community in times of crisis and give to Fort Greene and Clinton Hill a very large student population that adds life to the community.

View northeast from the roof of the Pratt Institute library. At the far right is Pratt's Memorial Hall, fronting on Ryerson Street. In the center rises the frame of one of the Willoughby Walk apartment towers constructed in the late 1950s with federal Title I housing funds.

This view east across the Pratt Institute campus shows, from left to right, the Main Building (1885–87, Lamb & Rich, architects), South Hall (1889–91, William Tubby, architect), and the Library (1896, William Tubby, architect).

Adelphi Academy was founded in 1863 by Aaron Chadwick and Edward S. Bunker, two teachers from Brooklyn Polytechnic Institute, and was soon after taken over by John Lockwood, a Quaker educator and abolitionist who believed that education should encourage the development of both body and mind. (Lockwood was one of the "Fighting Quakers" who, though Quakers were known for their pacifism, was so opposed to slavery he joined the Union Army.) The school was unique in requiring of its students a course in calisthenics developed by Truman Ellinwood, a disciple of Dio Lewis, a then famous temperance advocate and promoter of homeopathic medicine. (Ellinwood lived in the brownstone, built c. 1872, at 130 St. James Place between Greene and Gates avenues.)

The preparatory school opened at 412 Adelphi Street (hence the school's name), between Greene Avenue and Fulton Street, in Fort Greene, admitting eleven boys. When girls were admitted four years later, Adelphi became the first private co-educational school in Brooklyn. By 1867 enrollment had grown to 308 students and the following year the school relocated to a new building at the southeast corner of Lafayette Avenue and St. James Place.

The Reverend Henry Ward Beecher laid the cornerstone of the new edifice, and used his address to remark on the importance of educating women: "It seems that no man can give any reason why a woman should not be educated as well as, and in the same respect which, a man is educated." The Romanesque Revival building was designed by Mundell & Teckritz, and enlarged—apparently in keeping with Mundell & Teckritz's original plans—in 1870 (mansard roof), 1873 (west wing), and 1880 (east wing, funded in part by Charles Pratt). William A. Mundell, one of Brooklyn's most underrated architects, designed, either on his own or as a partner in Mundell & Teckritz, several notable buildings in Clinton Hill and Fort Greene. These include the notorious Raymond Street Jail (Willoughby Street and Ashland Place, opened 1880, demolished 1963), the lovely Simpson Methodist Episcopal Church (Clermont and Willoughby avenues, 1863, now Eglise Baptiste d'Expression Française), and the 23rd Regiment Armory (Clermont Avenue between Willoughby and Myrtle avenues, 1872–73).

The prestigious Adelphi Academy (where Adelphi University was born) occupied two buildings designed in slightly different variants of the Romanesque Revival style 21 years apart. On the left the building was designed by Mundell & Teckritz and built in 1867; on the right by Charles C. Haight and built in 1888. After Adelphi Academy moved to Bay Ridge, the buildings, on St. James Place between Lafayette Avenue and Clifton Place, became part of Pratt Institute.

In 1888 Adelphi opened its south building, donated by Charles Pratt and designed by the prominent New York architect Charles Coolidge Haight. With the new building, Adelphi Academy became the first school in Brooklyn equipped with a gymnasium. Pratt also established a scholarship fund and prizes for academic excellence at the school.

Under the leadership of the progressive educator Dr. Charles Herbert Levermore, Adelphi College (now Adelphi University) was founded in 1896 as a degree-granting, co-educational liberal arts college. Between 1896 and 1909 Levermore served as both headmaster of Adelphi Academy and president of Adelphi College, and both the academy and the college were administered by a single board of trustees until 1925. In 1929 Adelphi College moved from Clinton Hill to Garden City, Long Island. Since 1963 it has been known as Adelphi University.

In 1891 Adelphi Academy's enrollment peaked at 1,291. When Adelphi was founded, the Hill was one of the most affluent sections of Brooklyn, and it remained so until well into the 20th century. It was for many years exactly the sort of place where a prestigious private preparatory school might flourish. But after World War II, economic and demographic changes altered the character of the district, which became distinctly poorer. By 1965 Adelphi's enrollment had fallen to 300. In that year Adelphi Academy left the Hill after 102 years and moved to Ridge Boulevard, between 85th and 86th streets, in Bay Ridge, Brooklyn, where the school continues in operation today.

At 315 Clinton Avenue (house on right) between Lafayette and DeKalb avenues stands the Romanesque Revival mansion of John Arbuckle, one of Brooklyn's most innovative and successful 19th-century entrepreneurs; designed by Montrose Morris, the house was built in 1887-88.

CLINTON HILL NOTABLES

JOHN ARBUCKLE

At 315 Clinton Avenue, between Lafayette and DeKalb avenues, stands a "Richardsonian Romanesque" town house designed by the prominent Brooklyn architect Montrose W. Morris and built in 1887–88. This was originally the home of John Arbuckle.

John Arbuckle was born in 1838 in Scotland and came to America as a young boy when his family moved to the Pittsburgh area, where his father ran a cotton mill. The Arbuckles were, said the *New York Tribune,* part of "the great Scotch immigration in that city," which also included Andrew Carnegie, who was only three years John's senior. John had a strong technical bent and dropped out of Washington & Jefferson College, in western Pennsylvania, to go into the coffee roasting business with his younger brother Charles. In 1870 they relocated their business to Brooklyn. John invented the machinery that filled, vacuum-sealed, and labeled packages of coffee, which were then shipped all over the country. "One machine," said the *New York*

Times, "would do the work of 500 girls." The Arbuckles were among the earliest businessmen to make extensive and profitable use of the recently established transcontinental railroad, becoming the dominant coffee provider to America's Western frontier. (In any Hollywood Western where cowboys sit around the chuck wagon drinking coffee from tin cups, it's Arbuckle coffee, from Brooklyn, that they're drinking.) The Arbuckles' coffee was even once nicknamed "cowboy coffee." Arbuckle Brothers became the world's largest importer of coffee beans, and one of the largest owners of ships in America. (An Arbuckle seasonal blend was called Yuletide Banquet. The shortened version of its name, Yuban, persists as a brand-name on supermarket shelves today.) The Arbuckles figured they could sell sugar in the same way, but this put them into nearly ruinous competition with the Havemeyer interests, which dominated the American sugar market from their base in Williamsburg, Brooklyn. It is said that the wrangling between the Arbuckles and the Havemeyers cost the two sides a combined $25 million.

John Arbuckle died, age 74, on March 27, 1912, in his home at 315 Clinton Avenue, "from," according to the *New York Times,* "a general breakdown due to old age." Less than a week before his death he "continued to go to the offices of Arbuckle Brothers at the foot of Jay Street," in what is now called DUMBO. He survived his wife by five years, and had no children. He survived his brother Charles by 20 years. His philanthropies were numerous, including the Deep Sea Hotel, a yacht, docked at 23rd Street and the Hudson River, outfitted as low-cost housing for working men and women; and a "colony farm" in New Paltz, New York, where city wage earners could go to breathe country air. He also funded the children's magazine *Sunshine,* and became the leading figure in the raising of wrecked ships, being the first to use compressed air for the purpose. His funeral was held in his Clinton Street home; the service was led by the Reverend Dwight Hillis of Plymouth Church. He was buried in Pittsburgh. His fortune at the time of his death was estimated to be between $20 and $30 million. He was nearly as rich as Charles Pratt.

CHARLES PFIZER AND CHARLES ERHART

Charles Pfizer lived in a mansion at 295 Washington Avenue, between Willoughby and DeKalb avenues; in 1925 Pfizer's house was replaced by the present 6-story apartment building on the site. Pfizer and his cousin, Charles Erhart, co-founded Charles Pfizer & Co. Erhart lived across the street from Pfizer, at 270 Washington Avenue. Erhart's mansion and carriage house were replaced in 1928 by the present 6-story apartment building. Many articles and blog posts cite 280 Washington Avenue, a fine 1887 brownstone still standing, as the "Pfizer mansion." The *New York Times* even once went so far as to give specifics of Charles Pfizer's residency in the house. However, Pfizer never lived there. The confusion apparently stems from the fact that Pfizer's business partner and cousin Erhart, according to the research of the Landmarks Preservation Commission, built the house, and its neighbor at 282, as a speculative development. People naturally want to believe that Pfizer's mansion still stands, and so the story got confused and No. 280 became the "Pfizer mansion."

Pfizer and Erhart founded their pharmaceutical company in 1849 in Williamsburg, Brooklyn, at the intersection of Bartlett Street and Harrison Avenue, close to Clinton Hill. The company expanded at this site and manufactured chemicals there until 2005—156 years. (The Pfizer company was thus in Brooklyn for almost as long as the Brooklyn Navy Yard.) Erhart came to America from Ludwigsburg, near

Stuttgart, in southwestern Germany. He was a skilled confectioner, which helped in the flavoring of medications to make them more palatable. In fact, the company's first big success was with a palatable version of the otherwise bitter anthelminthic called Santonin, used to combat the intestinal worms that were an unfortunately common feature of 19th-century life. Erhart made it taste like almond toffee. (Yum.) In 1856 Erhart became Charles Pfizer's brother-in-law as well as cousin. Erhart was instrumental in the company's move into the manufacture of food-processing ingredients in the 1860s and 1870s. He died, at the age of 70, in 1891. His funeral was held at St. Luke's Evangelical Lutheran Church, which at that time was located at Carlton and Myrtle avenues; three years later the church moved to the very block of Washington Avenue on which Erhart had lived.

Charles Pfizer, a chemist, also came to America from Ludwigsburg, and served as president of Charles Pfizer & Co. from 1849 to 1900. He died in 1906 in his house in Newport, Rhode Island. He was 83. His funeral service was held in the house at 295 Washington Avenue. The company prospered during the Civil War with the production of tartaric acid and cream of tartar, both of which Pfizer was the first company to produce in America, as well as iodine, morphine, chloroform, and other compounds needed on the bloody battlefields and military hospitals. In 1880 Pfizer began production of citric acid, and became thereafter the country's biggest producer of an essential ingredient of the carbonated soft drinks (such as Coca-Cola) then soaring in popularity. During World War II, Pfizer contracted with the federal government to produce penicillin, which had only been discovered in 1928. Pfizer's name practically became synonymous with penicillin, one of the most important inventions of the 20th century. In 1998 Pfizer introduced Viagra.

On September 6, 1904, the *New York Times* ran a headline "Brooklyn Girl a Baroness." Miss Alice Pfizer, daughter of Mr. and Mrs. Charles Pfizer, had just married Baron Reinhart Bachofen von Echt of Austria. She was an 1899 graduate of Adelphi College, then still in Clinton Hill. Between 1904 and 1940 she resided in Vienna, Austria. Alice died in 1959 at the age of 82 in her home at 300 East 57th Street in Manhattan. But her funeral was held at St. Luke's Evangelical Lutheran Church (built 1894), still standing at 259 Washington Avenue between DeKalb and Willoughby avenues, on the block where she grew up, and she was buried in Green-Wood Cemetery—proof that you can't take the girl out of Brooklyn. Her sister, Helen, married Sir William Duncan and became Lady Helen Duncan; she died in Montreux, Switzerland, in 1953. Alice and Helen's brother, Charles Pfizer Jr., "well known as a master of hounds of the Essex County Hunt," died in 1929, at the age of 68, in Bernardsville, New Jersey. Another brother, Emile Pfizer, died in 1941 at the age of 77 at Roosevelt Hospital in Manhattan. Emile served as president of Charles Pfizer & Co. from 1906 to 1941, taking over after the company's board asked Emile's older brother, Charles, to step down after six years as president. (Charles had more interest in hounds than in business.) Emile's funeral, too, was held at St. Luke's Evangelical Lutheran Church on Washington Avenue. He never married, and left an estate of $3 million. All the children grew up on Washington Avenue.

CHARLES ADOLPH SCHIEREN

Charles Adolph Schieren died on March 10, 1915, in his home at 405 Clinton Avenue, between Greene and Gates avenues. For days the newspapers reported that he and his wife both lay dying from pneumonia, in adjoining rooms, unbeknownst to each other. Mrs. Louisa Bramm Schieren died approximately 24 hours after her husband, and a double funeral was held, seven months shy of their golden anniversary. They had four surviving children. Charles was born near Düsseldorf, Germany, in 1842, and came to America with his family, settling in Brooklyn, in 1856. Charles worked in a tobacco store, operated by the brothers of his future wife, at 35 Atlantic Avenue, and then for a leather manufacturer in Manhattan's "Swamp" district—today's South Street Seaport. He attended night school at Cooper Union, and saved his money to form his own leather manufacturing firm, Charles A. Schieren & Co., which became one of the largest such firms in the country. He was an active member of the Lutheran Church of the Redeemer at Bedford Avenue and Hewes Street in Williamsburg, just north of Clinton Hill. He was involved in numerous charitable activities, ranging from the Young Men's Christian Association to his serving as vice president of the Brooklyn Institute of Arts and Sciences. He was a Republican (and Union League Club member) and was elected Brooklyn mayor as a reformer in 1893, allied with William J. Gaynor who in that year was elected a Justice of the Supreme Court. Schieren served his three-year mayoral term and chose not to run for a second term. He is the mayor who named Alfred Tredway White as Commissioner of City Works; it was under White that William B. Tubby designed the picturesque market buildings for Wallabout Market. The Schierens' double funeral was held in the house on Clinton Avenue, and they were both buried in Green-Wood Cemetery. On March 21, a public memorial service was held for the Schierens at the Brooklyn Academy of Music on Lafayette Avenue; 1800 people attended. The Borough of Brooklyn was represented at the memorial by Borough President Lewis Pounds, who was also noteworthy as the developer of Ditmas Park in Flatbush. Alfred Tredway White presided over the memorial service. Another of the speakers was the Reverend Samuel Parkes Cadman, pastor of Central Congregational Church in Bedford-Stuyvesant.

Schieren's mayoralty was notable. He presided over the consolidation, not of Brooklyn and New York, which took place two years after his term in office, but of the City of Brooklyn with the towns of New Utrecht, Gravesend, Flatbush, and Flatlands, which took place between 1894 and 1896. The presence of Lewis Pounds was symbolic, as Fort Greene and Clinton Hill, and the rest of "brownstone Brooklyn," were just ceasing to be the fashionable Brooklyn neighborhoods, yielding to new developments in Flatbush, such as Prospect Park South, Ditmas Park, and Midwood.

JOHN THOMAS UNDERWOOD

John Thomas Underwood was born in 1857 in London, England. He came to America with his father, a chemist who manufactured paper and ink, settling in New Jersey in 1873. At that time the typewriter was becoming popular (the first commercially successful typewriter had only come out in 1867), and the Underwoods began making typewriter supplies such as ribbons and carbon paper. In 1883, a year after his father's death, the 26-year-old John Underwood moved the business to Brooklyn. There Underwood became interested in producing typewriters themselves. The market was dominated by the Remington company in Herkimer County in central New York. In 1895, having bought the rights to a German-designed front-stroke typewriting machine that was a vast improvement over the awkwardly designed Remington models (which made it hard to see what you were typing), Underwood began manufacturing "visible typewriting machines" in a factory in lower Manhattan. In 1898 the factory moved to Bayonne, New Jersey. The company moved to Hartford, Connecticut, in 1901. By 1915 the Underwood Typewriter Company—with 7,500 employees producing 500 typewriters a day—was the world's largest manufacturer of typewriters. Underwood produced Chinese, Japanese, and Hebrew typewriters, the last with a reverse carriage. In 1959, twenty-two years after John Underwood's death, the company was taken over by the Italian typewriter giant Olivetti.

Underwood, his wife, and his daughter lived for many years at 336 Washington Avenue, between Lafayette and DeKalb avenues, in Clinton Hill, and he was a parishioner and trustee of Lafayette Avenue Presbyterian Church, eight blocks away. He was a notable philanthropist, supporting missionary work, giving aid to the poor, and supporting the Brooklyn Academy of Music and the Brooklyn Institute of Arts and Sciences. The French government, to honor him for his support of relief efforts during and after World War I, made him a chevalier of the Legion of Honor. He died in 1937 at his summer home on Cape Cod. His funeral was held on July 4, 1937, at Lafayette Avenue Presbyterian Church, with 350 people attending the service led by Lafayette's pastor, the Reverend Dr. Alvin Magary. Underwood was buried in Green-Wood Cemetery.

Between 1951 and 1953 John Underwood's widow, Grace Underwood Barton, and daughter, Gladys Underwood James, donated 336 Washington Avenue to the city with the intention that the house be razed and the site be made a park. It is said that Underwood's widow and daughter saw that Clinton Hill was deteriorating, and preferred to see their house torn down rather than to witness its decline. Underwood Park opened in 1956. The 1.187-acre park's present appearance dates from a 1997 renovation.

Clinton Hill endured the same postwar hardships as Fort Greene. During World War II, when tens of thousands labored round the clock at the nearby Brooklyn Navy Yard, grand houses were carved up into multiple units to accommodate the temporary influx of workers. On February 2, 1942, the *New York Times* ran an article headlined "Old Brooklyn Mansions in Neighborhood Chosen for a New Apartment Project."

The work of razing some of these sturdy houses already has started, to clear the site for a vast housing project sponsored by the Equitable Life Assurance Society of the United States. In this former social center will be provided at least 1,200 apartments for occupancy by the families of defense workers, overlooking the bustling Brooklyn Navy Yard where many of them are employed. After the war the new structures will be returned to their normal role of accommodating civilian families of moderate income.

Remember that in 1942 "after the war" was about as uncertain a phrase as there was. No one had any idea when that would be, or if we would win the war, or if we did not what the impact on New York would be.

One of the mansions to go was the one that had been built for Herbert L. Pratt, a son of Charles Pratt, on Willoughby Avenue between Clinton and Waverly avenues. It was built in 1906 and designed by John Brite. It included two pipe organs and an art gallery. But Herbert Pratt moved to Manhattan in 1914. In 1916 the house was bought by the legendary film producer J. Stuart Blackton, who was active at the Vitagraph Studios in Midwood. Blackton owned the house for only a few years before he suffered financial setbacks, and for many years the house stood vacant. Blackton and later vandals stripped the house of many of its expensive fittings. At

On left, frame cottage at 341 Clinton Avenue, southeast corner of Lafayette Avenue, and, on right, 345 Clinton Avenue, the Alfred J. Pouch mansion, built in 1887 and designed by William A. Mundell. Both houses were razed in 1942 for the construction of Equitable Life Assurance Society's high-rise Clinton Hill Apartments.

the time of the *New York Times* article, Frederic Bayley Pratt still lived at 229 Clinton Avenue; he was then the president of Pratt Institute. The Charles Pratt house was a convent; the Charles Millard Pratt house was by then the residence of Bishop Molloy; and the George Dupont Pratt house was owned by St. Joseph's College. Other houses demolished for the Equitable project included those built by Edward T. Bedford and Frederick T. Bedford of the Thompson & Bedford oil company that became a part of Standard Oil, and by Alfred J. Pouch of the J.A. Bostwick Oil Company, which also merged with Standard Oil. (If the 1980s TV drama *Dallas* had been set around 1900, it would have been called *Clinton Avenue*.) The Equitable development was designed by Harrison, Fouilhoux & Abramovitz, a major architectural firm, with landscaping by Gilmore D. Clarke, who had recently re-landscaped Fort Greene Park. The development comprised five 14-story brick-clad apartment buildings occupying most of the square block bounded by Clinton, Myrtle, Waverly, and Willoughby avenues, a 13-story building on the north side of Willoughby Avenue between Clinton and Vanderbilt avenues, four 14-story buildings occupying the whole square block bounded by Clinton, Lafayette, Waverly, and Greene avenues, and a 14-story building on the north side of Lafayette Avenue between Clinton and Waverly avenues. Not only were several noteworthy houses destroyed, but the scale, style, and intended use of the new high rises—whatever the quality of their Modernist design or of their landscaping—signified the end of any pretense that the mansion days of Clinton Hill—still seemingly thriving not much more than a decade earlier—had any life left in them.

In 1964, the Reverned Paul Valentiner, pastor of St. Luke's Evangelical Lutheran Church—the Pfizers' church—on Washington Avenue told a reporter "I've had to cut out all night activities at the church because no one will come." In response to the deterioration of housing stock that resulted from rooming-house conversions and the complete absence of institutional sources of mortgage and property-maintenance funds, and to the growing fear of crime, the Pratt Area Community Council (PACC) was founded in 1964. Still going strong, PACC served as an umbrella organization for area PTAs, block associations, tenant groups, churches, and so on, to advocate for affordable housing, tenants' rights, and improved city services. In the 1960s PACC was particularly concerned with increasing the police presence in the neighborhood. Later, PACC focused on improving housing conditions, eventually leading to the council's purchasing, renovating, and managing residential properties. But where once the council's and other groups' efforts were about halting the tide of blight, by the 1970s concerns switched to preserving affordable housing amid a new tide, that of gentrification.

CHRISTOPHER WALLACE

The rapper known as the Notorious B.I.G. was born Christopher Wallace in 1972 and grew up at 226 St. James Place, between Gates Avenue and Fulton Street, in a 7-room apartment with his mother, a Jamaican immigrant named Voletta Wallace. She taught pre-school while earning her master's degree and attended Jehovah's Witnesses services in the evenings. He attended middle school at Queen of All Saints on Vanderbilt Avenue between DeKalb and Lafayette avenues in Fort Greene. He went on to George Westinghouse High School on Johnson Street between Bridge and Lawrence streets in downtown Brooklyn, just on the other side of Flatbush Avenue Extension from Fort Greene. At Westinghouse he overlapped with Shawn Carter and Trevor Smith Jr., who also won great fame as rappers—as, respectively, Jay-Z and Busta Rhymes. The school is only a block away from the former Bridge Street African Wesleyan Methodist Episcopal Church where Fort Greene's Dr. Susan Smith McKinney played the organ at Sunday services in the 19th century. At the age of 17 Christopher Wallace dropped out of high school. (Richard Wright had dropped out of high school at the same age; both had also been, in spite of their decision to drop out, good students.) Wallace was lured from the straight and narrow by the money to be made in the crack trade that flourished on Fulton Street in the 1980s.

A Sunday school class from Emmanuel House, the settlement house, operated by Emmanuel Baptist Church, at 131 Steuben Street between DeKalb and Willoughby avenues, on what is now part of the Pratt Institute campus. The photo is from c. 1910–14.

He always told people he grew up in Bedford-Stuyvesant, though the family lived in the Clinton Hill Historic District (designated 1981). The building was one of nine eight-family apartment buildings designed by Axel Hedman, a prolific Brooklyn architect, and built in 1905, and, in a sign of the times, has in recent years been converted to condominiums. In the 1980s Wallace rapped for fun on the streets of Clinton Hill. He enthralled locals with the fluency and verve of his verbal inventions. Indeed, some said that in the 15-or-so-year history of rap they'd never before encountered

Wallace's endurance, his endless ability to improvise and rhyme. He made tapes of himself, he said, just for the fun of hearing his own voice. He had no designs on stardom when one of his tapes made its way to the rap magazine *The Source*, which then asked him to take part in a recording of the best unsigned talent they had come across. He rapped under the names Biggie Smalls and Notorious B.I.G. (He was 6 feet 3 inches tall and weighed more than 300 pounds.) He then began to appear on other artists' albums, including one by Mary J. Blige. He was signed by Sean Combs to his Bad Boy Records. His 1994 album *Ready to Die* went platinum and in 1995 he was named Billboard's rap artist of the year. Wallace married the singer Faith Evans in 1994. Their son, Christopher Wallace Jr., was born in 1996. (He also had a daughter from a previous relationship.) In 1995 Wallace formed Junior M.A.F.I.A., known as a "protégé group," consisting of his friends, and the group released the album *Conspiracy*. One Junior M.A.F.I.A. member was Bedford-Stuyvesant's Kimberly Jones, who went on to a solo career as Lil' Kim. Also in 1995, Wallace worked on Michael Jackson's album *HIStory*. Christopher Wallace, 24 years old, had attained the pinnacle of pop music stardom when he was tragically killed in a drive-by shooting in Beverly Hills in 1997. The 2009 film *Notorious* told his story.

THE BROOKLYN ACADEMY OF MUSIC AND SOME OTHER INSTITUTIONS

BROOKLYN ACADEMY OF MUSIC

The Brooklyn Academy of Music (BAM), on Lafayette Avenue between Ashland Place and St. Felix Street, was built between 1906 and 1908. It was the second BAM. The original opened in 1861 on Montague Street between Clinton and Court streets, in Brooklyn Heights. It was an impressive structure designed by Leopold Eidlitz, and hosted many of the world's top performers as well as the larger events of many of Brooklyn's leading institutions, from the early lectures presented by the Long Island Historical Society, to the first graduation ceremony of St. Joseph's College for Women. It burned down in 1903. The trustees decided that rather than rebuild on the same site, a new location, nearer where, by the first decade of the 20th century, BAM's audiences were likely to live, made more sense. The Lafayette Avenue location was equally convenient to the residents of Park Slope, Brooklyn Heights, Fort Greene, and Bedford-Stuyvesant. New York's leading theater designers, Henry Beaumont Herts and Hugh Tallant, whose credits included Manhattan's Lyceum and New Amsterdam theaters, designed what was the city's most complex performing arts facility until Lincoln Center was built in the 1960s. The new BAM included an opera house with more than 2,000 seats; a music hall with more than 1,000 seats; and a ballroom/banquet hall space that could accommodate some 600 people.

The new BAM opened in the fall of 1908 with a series of events. These included an organ concert, on the afternoon of September 16, in the Music Hall, and, on the evening of the same day, a concert, in the Opera House, of the 23rd Regiment Band, from Fort Greene; an October 8 performance, in the Opera House, of Haydn's "Creation," by the Brooklyn Oratorio Society; the 95th convention of the American Board of Foreign Missions, opening on October 13 in the Music Hall; a speech on October 26, in the Opera House, by presidential candidate William Howard Taft, who would be president-elect when only a couple of weeks later he would be present at the dedication of the Prison Ship Martyrs Monument in Fort

Greene Park; and a November 11 "kirmess" for the Church Charity Foundation of Long Island, in the ballroom, among other events. And then, climactically, on November 14, the Metropolitan Opera Company staged a production of Charles François Gounod's *Faust*, starring Enrico Caruso and Geraldine Farrar.

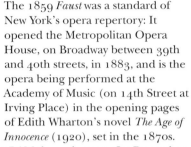

The 1859 *Faust* was a standard of New York's opera repertory: It opened the Metropolitan Opera House, on Broadway between 39th and 40th streets, in 1883, and is the opera being performed at the Academy of Music (on 14th Street at Irving Place) in the opening pages of Edith Wharton's novel *The Age of Innocence* (1920), set in the 1870s.

The Brooklyn Academy of Music on Lafayette Avenue.

The Met conducted seasons at BAM through 1921. On December 11, 1920, Caruso suffered a throat hemorrhage while singing in Gaetano Donizetti's *L'Elisir d'Amore* at BAM. In the first act he began to cough up blood, but finished the act. According to the *New York Times* of December 12, 1920,

> Back-stage the whole company had been thrilled and excited as perhaps never before during a performance, as they watched and assisted as best they might, while Caruso, visibly bleeding, struggled on, his voice clear as a bell save when now and then the exudate choked him....He threw up his head with a touch of defiance, swallowed hard and went ahead singing as usual....using handkerchief after handkerchief and coughing and expectorating in the wings, whenever he could find opportunity, he fought bravely to the end of the first act.

The audience of 3,000 sat stunned as the curtain failed to rise for the second act. Caruso sang again only three more times and died eight months later, at the age of 48.

At the Brooklyn Academy of Music in those days was mostly older-line families of Brooklyn who would come to the Boston Symphony concerts that they performed at the Academy three times a year. And you could see that this was old money. You could see from the cloth of the clothing they wore that this was old money. These were people that didn't have to work for it. Those people have either moved out of New York or they just didn't come downtown during the difficult times of the fifties when the neighborhood went through all these changes. They felt it wasn't safe because of the crime, the muggings that went on in those days. It was tough for [BAM].

HAL GLICKSMAN

Before 1970, BAM was part of the Brooklyn Institute of Arts and Sciences. So many non-musical events, such as courses and lectures, took place at BAM that people often called it the "Brooklyn Institute." The Brooklyn Institute of Arts and Sciences had its roots in the Apprentices' Library founded by Brooklyn business leaders in 1823 to provide education and uplift to young business "apprentices." The Apprentices' Library changed its name to Brooklyn Institute in 1843, thence to Brooklyn Institute of Arts and Sciences in 1890. The Institute founded the Brooklyn Museum in 1897, the Brooklyn Children's Museum in 1899, and the Brooklyn Botanic Garden in 1910.

BAM was quite vigorous through the Depression, offering a dizzying number and variety of recitals, lectures, classes, and workshops. Marianne Moore, after moving to Cumberland Street in 1929, attended so many events at BAM—sometimes one in the afternoon and another in the evening of the same day—that her mother joked that Marianne had taken up residence there. But after World War II, as Brooklyn experienced major demographic changes, BAM's traditionally white, middle-class audiences dwindled. The Brooklyn Institute of Arts and Sciences took to renting out the building for any kind of activity that would generate a bit of income, including martial arts classes and use as a boys' school. There was talk of just shutting the place down and maybe even getting rid of the building. But that all changed when Harvey Lichtenstein came on the scene, two years after Marianne Moore left Brooklyn.

Harvey Lichtenstein ran BAM from 1967 to 1999. He was a native Brooklynite (and Brooklyn College graduate) and a former dancer who had performed with Martha Graham. Before coming to BAM, he had worked in audience development for the New York City Ballet and the New York City Opera. In 1967, most of the population of Fort Greene had never set foot inside the academy. Lichtenstein immediately stressed the need for community outreach and attracting minority audiences. For example, in 1968 the three-year-old Chelsea Theater Center, which had begun at the Church of the Holy Apostles on Ninth Avenue in Manhattan, moved to BAM; the nonprofit group's purpose was to develop new playwrights and present works to new, diverse audiences. Lichtenstein also wished to raise BAM's profile as a cutting-edge center of modern dance and, also in 1968, lured the Merce Cunningham Dance Company, the Alvin Ailey American Dance Theater, and Eliot Feld's company to be BAM's resident dance troupes, and inaugurated an annual Festival of Dance. Alvin Ailey took charge of providing dance classes to disadvantaged children from nearby neighborhoods. In 1969 the *New York Times* wrote: "In the past six months, the crusty 110-year-old Academy has stripped itself of its 19th-century image and, with unaccustomed abandon, embraced the avant-garde." The *Times* noted that BAM "presented the far-out plays of Julian Beck and Judith Malina's Living Theater. In one gorgeous leap, the old place became the mecca for almost every hippie in the metropolitan area." By November 1968, *New York Times* dance critic Clive Barnes proclaimed BAM to be "the dance center of the entire world." (He also said of BAM's Opera House that "this house really is one of the finest in the world to watch dancing in.") Lichtenstein had taken over an ailing institution and in a series of deft moves made it, in two years, more central to the cultural life of New York than it had, in fact, ever been.

In 1971 the *Times* wrote, "Not since those memorable baseball games between the Brooklyn Dodgers and the New York Giants have so many Manhattanites been venturing across the East River for an evening's enjoyment." In 1972 Woody Allen and Beverly Sills, among others, performed at a "Back to Brooklyn" concert at

BAM. In 1976, Brendan Gill called BAM "a veritable Vesuvius of incessant cultural activity, lighting up the sky over Flatbush Avenue in a fashion readily visible even from myopic Manhattan." The old upstairs ballroom was converted into a performance hall called the Lepercq Space; James Stewart Polshek renovated the Music Hall into a fully outfitted modern theater.

When I was eight years old my father and I went to the Brooklyn Academy of Music to do some glass work. When we were through my father gave his bill to the house manager who said, "Thanks very much, we'll see that you get a check. Is there anything else I can do for you?" I said, "I understand that Jascha Heifetz is going to be performing here tonight. My father and I would love to have the opportunity to see this great violinist." He said, "That's not a problem." He walks right over to th e box office and says, "Give me two seats in the house manager's box." So we got home and my father says, "You're not going to believe what your son did today." My mother said, "What did he do now?" My father said, "He's got two tickets for him and me to go see Jascha Heifetz tonight." And my mother said, "Two tickets? What am I, chopped liver?" That was 63 years ago, and I can remember it like it was a minute ago, that's how clear and vivid it is in my mind. Because we sat twelve feet from where Jascha Heifetz performed with the Boston Symphony Orchestra. And to this day I have heard many great violinists, and there was Jascha Heifetz and there was everybody else. And I got to see and hear him when he was at the height of his career, from the box of the house manager of the Brooklyn Academy of Music, for nothing.

HAL GLICKSMAN

Lichtenstein inaugurated the Next Wave Festival in 1983 as a kind of concentrated showcase for the avant-garde composers and choreographers he had been presenting at BAM since 1969. In 1985 the *Times* enthused that regular patrons of BAM's performances included such glittering celebrities as Richard Gere, Bianca Jagger, Diane Keaton, Calvin Klein, and Andy Warhol. By then, the Fort Greene and Brooklyn Academy of Music historic districts had been established by the city's Landmarks Preservation Commission, and Fort Greene real estate was riding the crest of the decade's ferocious wave of gentrification. Restaurants were opening nearby, and Manhattanites had become less skittish about taking the subway to Atlantic Avenue. (In the 1970s, Manhattanites traveled to BAM by taxi cab or special shuttle buses.) BAM, dependent in part on city funds, had survived the fiscal meltdown of the 1970s, and also survived the soaring crime that was associated in part with the crack epidemic. (Indeed, nearby Fulton Street was in the 1980s a market for crack sales.) And more and more Brooklynites themselves were going to BAM. At the same time, BAM had become internationally renowned, so much so that for vast numbers of cultured foreigners the first thing to come to mind upon hearing "Brooklyn" was "BAM." In fact, concern arose in the arts community that BAM had become all-powerful in the avant-garde scene, that, as John Rockwell of the *Times* put it, BAM's "prominence has stunted growth elsewhere."

And yet such naysaying only underscored the improbable and phenomenal success of Harvey Lichtenstein in remaking Brooklyn's venerable performing arts institution.

BAM featured Philip Glass's "Satyagraha" (1981), Laurie Anderson's "United States: Parts I–IV" (1983), Philip Glass and Robert Wilson's "Einstein on the Beach" (1984), John Adams's "Nixon in China" (1987), and many other of the defining avant-garde musical and theatrical works of the late 20th century.

The Brooklyn Academy of Music on Lafayette Avenue, in the evening.

BAMcafé opened in the third-floor Lepercq Space in 1997, and BAM Rose Cinemas, with four screens, opened in 1998. Lichtenstein founded the BAM Local Development Corporation in 1998, and the next year he yielded as BAM's head to Karen Brooks Hopkins.

The Local Development Corporation took Lichtenstein's vision for BAM to the next logical stage: promoting the BAM neighborhood as a center of the arts, the Brooklyn Academy of Music Cultural District. Since then BAM has helped to house numerous arts groups in nearby buildings both old and new. Combined with the creative flowering of Fort Greene in the 1980s and 1990s, this part of Brooklyn has become a cultural haven on a par with any in New York. The very notion would have appeared laughable not so long ago.

At the northeast corner of Lafayette Avenue and Rockwell Place is the Mark Morris Dance Center. The center, designed by the prestigious Beyer Blinder Belle, was built between 1999 and 2001. The *New York Times* called it "the most lavish dance center in New York." The Mark Morris Dance Group, which makes its home in the center, is now 24 years old. Its first performance was in 1980 at the Merce Cunningham Studio in Manhattan. It first performed at BAM's Next Wave Festival in 1984. Between 1988 and 1991 the company was based in Brussels, Belgium. Today the company is one of the most important dance ensembles in the world. Remarkably, it seems only fitting that it should be headquartered in Fort Greene.

80 Hanson Place, at South Portland Avenue, had once been the clubhouse of the Brooklyn Bicycle Club, one of the country's leading cycling clubs in the 1890s when cycling was the hot pastime of the urban upper class. It was later a drug testing center and in 2001 the 8-story building was sold by the state to the BAM Local Development Corporation. In 2003 it was named the James E. Davis Arts Building, after the slain City Council member. Today the building houses numerous cultural organizations including *BOMB* Magazine (the major art magazine founded in 1981 and especially renowned for its in-depth artists' interviews), Cool Culture (founded by Edwina Meyers and Gail Velez in 1999 to promote the participation of low-income families in the programs of the city's cultural institutions), StoryCorps (founded in 2003 with the opening of the StoryBooth in Grand Central Terminal), Franklin Furnace (a hugely important avant-garde arts organization founded in 1976 by Martha Wilson), and MoCADA, the Museum of Contemporary African Diasporan Arts. MoCADA was founded by Laurie A. Cumbo in 1999 and moved to 80 Hanson in 2006.

The area surrounding BAM is technically in Fort Greene but has always seemed like its own little slice of Brooklyn. Along Atlantic Avenue, which separates Fort Greene from Prospect Heights, is an open railroad cut serving trains of the Long Island Railroad, which uses the Flatbush Avenue Terminal. A new terminal was unveiled in 2010, a replacement for a historic structure built between 1902 and 1906. At its height, in 1919, the old terminal handled 70 percent as many passengers as Grand Central Terminal. It was sadly demolished in 1988. The new terminal abuts the Atlantic Terminal shopping center, opened in 2003 and bounded by Hanson Place, Fort Greene Place, Atlantic Avenue, and Flatbush Avenue. It was built by Forest City Ratner. For many years the Fort Greene Meat Market, Brooklyn's main wholesale outlet for meat, established in 1892, was located adjacent. It was removed in the late 1970s as part of the city's envisioned Atlantic Terminal Urban Renewal Area (first proposed in 1962), a site bounded by Hanson Place on the north, Vanderbilt Avenue on the east, Atlantic Avenue on the south, and Flatbush Avenue on the west, which has seen fitful development over four decades.

At first the city announced the meat market was to be relocated to a waterfront site between the Manhattan and Brooklyn bridges. This move was vigorously opposed by civic organizations including the Municipal Art Society and the Long Island Historical Society; the site became Empire-Fulton Ferry State Park and is now (in the summer of 2010 as this guide goes to press) under redevelopment as part of the ambitious Brooklyn Bridge Park. Instead, the market was moved to a waterfront site between 54th and 57th streets at the border of Sunset Park and Bay Ridge. When the Brooklyn Dodgers announced that they could no longer play in antiquated Ebbets Field in Crown Heights, Brooklyn Borough President John Cashmore proposed, in 1955, a site, at the northwest corner of Atlantic Avenue and South Elliott Place, adjacent to the rail cut, for a new 50,000-seat stadium. (The proposed site soon shifted to the triangle bounded by Flatbush, Atlantic, Fourth and Fifth avenues, and Warren Street.) The new stadium did not happen, and the Dodgers, in 1958, left Brooklyn for Los Angeles. The original site proposed by Cashmore is now occupied by the Atlantic Center shopping mall, opened in 1996 and bounded by Hanson Place, Fort Greene Place, Atlantic Avenue, and South Elliott Place and South Portland Avenue. The mall was built by Forest City Ratner, builders of nearby MetroTech Center. Forest City Ratner has proposed decking over the rail cut and constructing a vast project, called Atlantic Yards, the centerpiece of which will be a new arena for the National Basketball Association team now known as the New Jersey Nets. This proposed development, while backed by many city and state officials, has been enormously controversial owing to its size, a planning process that some have claimed is less than transparent, and, especially, to its need to invoke eminent domain in order to prepare the way for a private commercial development. The area's City Council member, Letitia "Tish" James, is adamantly opposed to the development. (Ms. James's City Council District 35 comprises Fort Greene and Clinton Hill as well as parts of Crown Heights, Prospect Heights, and Bedford-Stuyvesant.) Supporters of the project cite the Community Benefits Agreement between Forest City Ratner and a coalition of

View of Fort Greene Meat Market, c. 1900, intersection of Atlantic Avenue, Fifth Avenue, and Fort Greene Place.

local organizations as a model for how big developments such as this can be done while ensuring that benefits—affordable housing, jobs, financial contributions to local social welfare organizations, etc.—accrue to the community. For a variety of reasons, other proposals for the site have fallen by the wayside, including the construction of a new campus for the City University's Baruch College; that one was nipped in the bud by the city's fiscal crisis of the 1970s. A large mixed-use project planned by the developer Rose Associates was killed by the severe real-estate recession of the late 1980s and early 1990s. A housing component of that project, devised by the renowned urban planner Peter Calthorpe, did morph into the government-subsidized Atlantic Commons row housing development that was eventually built, to the designs of Swanke Hayden Connell, by Forest City Ratner. The site was also once coveted by Long Island University, which has long been a fixture in Fort Greene.

> The Fort Greene Meat Market is gone. So all of that filth and degradation and congestion has been removed, and now you've got Atlantic Mall....It's like a different borough today, as opposed to what it was fifty years ago. There are a few things that are still left. On Flatbush Avenue, Triangle Sporting Goods store is still there. I bought my first baseball glove there, maybe sixty years ago, for four dollars and ninety-five cents.
>
> HAL GLICKSMAN

LONG ISLAND UNIVERSITY

Long Island University (LIU) was founded in 1926 as a private, nonsectarian, co-educational liberal arts college with the purpose of providing an affordable higher education to, in the words of the *New York Times*, the "two-thirds of the young men and women of Brooklyn and Long Island who might be expected to attend college or professional school" and who "are either not doing so or are obliged to seek admission elsewhere because adequate provision is not made at home." The university opened in September 1927 on the fifteenth floor of the brand-new Brooklyn Chamber of Commerce Building on Livingston and Court streets. (The Chamber of Commerce was an early financial supporter of the university.) The first student to register was New York State Assemblyman Joseph Ricca whose goal was to take law-school preparatory courses. In its first year LIU enrolled 500 students. In 1928 the Brooklyn College of Pharmacy, founded in 1886, became formally affiliated with LIU. At the time the College of Pharmacy was located at Nostrand and Lafayette avenues in Bedford-Stuyvesant. The merger allowed the College of Pharmacy to be able to award the Bachelor of Science degree, which it had not previously done. Today it is the Arnold & Marie Schwartz College of Pharmacy and Health Sciences and is one of the top programs of its kind in the country, graduating countless of the pharmacists who work in area hospitals and drugstores. Also in 1928 LIU moved into its new building at 300 Pearl Street, at Tillary Street.

Long Island University was a product of the go-go euphoria of the late 1920s. In fact, just before the stock market crashed in 1929, the president of LIU's trustees,

Ralph Jonas, announced plans to build a 75-story hotel—it would have been the second-tallest building in New York—on Clinton and Montague streets. It of course fell victim to the new financial realities. All universities struggled through the Depression, but for a university that was just getting off the ground before the financial calamity struck, the 1930s were especially difficult. On June 9, 1932, the *Times* reported that LIU faculty had not been paid since April 1, and were calling for the ouster of Dean George Hardie, who was accused of, among other things, financial mismanagement. An oil painting of Dean Hardie was mutilated, the head ripped from the canvas that hung in LIU's Pearl Street building. And as if that would not send a message, a group of seniors burned the dean in effigy—a reminder that campus unrest did not begin in the 1960s. Three days after the *Times* report, Dean Hardie resigned. (At the time, incidentally, the also recently formed Brooklyn College, which had not yet built its Midwood campus, operated out of nine floors of a nearby building at 80 Willoughby Street.)

The Brooklyn Paramount Theater Building was erected at DeKalb Avenue and Flatbush Avenue Extension in 1928 and contained what was until 1962 one of the most sumptuous movie theaters in New York. Since 1950 the building has been owned by Long Island University, founded in Brooklyn in 1926.

In 1943 LIU, its student body down to 260, filed for bankruptcy reorganization. The following year LIU sold 300 Pearl Street. The university then shared space in 375 Pearl Street, the Brooklyn Law School (now Brooklyn Friends School) building a block away, and later set up shop across the street in the Brooklyn Edison Building. But LIU miraculously held on to prosper from the postwar boom in higher education. In 1947 the courts approved a new LIU financial structure, and by then, partly through the GI Bill of Rights, the enrollment astonishingly exceeded 3,000.

In 1947 LIU purchased the estate of Marjorie Merriweather Post and established the C.W. Post Campus in Brookville, in Nassau County, Long Island. Beginning in 1963 LIU also maintained a campus in Southampton, in Suffolk County, Long Island, but closed the campus and merged its programs with C.W. Post in 2005.

The Brooklyn Campus of LIU established a permanent presence in Fort Greene in 1950 when it purchased the 12-story Brooklyn Paramount Theater Building (built 1927, now Metcalfe Hall) on Flatbush Avenue Extension and DeKalb Avenue. The building housed one of the most sumptuous movie palaces in New York. The 4,188-seat theater continued to operate until 1962 while LIU occupied the office floors above it. (When it purchased the Paramount Building, LIU had already made inroads into Fort

Greene: The university's athletic department operated out of the Young Men's Christian Association building at 55 Hanson Place, between Fort Greene and South Elliott places.) At the June 1953 commencement ceremony held in the theater, Board of Trustees President William Zeckendorf—the fabled real-estate tycoon—announced that LIU had been granted permission to purchase seven adjoining acres in what had been declared a slum-clearance district.

Construction of the Zeckendorf Campus began in 1958 and included the construction of a 16-story residence hall, a tree-lined mall and athletic fields, and the renovation of the Paramount Theater to house a gymnasium, lecture halls, and a student cafeteria. In 1964 LIU purchased three 15-story apartment buildings, known as University Towers, that had been built with federal Title I urban renewal funds in 1957 and 1958. The towers are bounded by Willoughby Street, Fleet Place, Myrtle Avenue, and Ashland Place. They are adjacent to the Kingsview cooperative housing project, bounded by Myrtle Avenue, St. Edwards Street, Willoughby Street, and Ashland Place, five buildings of 14 and 15 stories built in 1955 and 1956, also with Title I funds. These middle-income housing developments, together with LIU, are credited by many with having had a stabilizing influence on this corner of Fort Greene—abutting the low-income housing projects to the north of Fort Greene Park—and helping to curb the spread of postwar blight.

LIU continued to expand in the 1970s with the construction of a new library, but it was another 20 years until the next new building was built—the William Zeckendorf Health Sciences Center at DeKalb and Hudson avenues, topped with a distinctive bell tower with an electronic clock that chimes the hours and marks the entrance to the campus. A 3,000-seat athletic arena was constructed in 2005, so the LIU Blackbirds NCAA Division I basketball team no longer plays, as it did for 42 years, beneath the rococo fountains and statues of the Paramount Theater. In the 1990s the Blackbirds were one of the nation's top teams, and it was briefly almost as fashionable to attend their games—as Spike Lee did—at the old Paramount Theater as it was to go to BAM.

Today LIU enrolls more than 11,000 students at its Brooklyn Campus.

Other nearby institutions that have long defined this corner of Fort Greene include Brooklyn Hospital and Brooklyn Technical High School.

BROOKLYN HOSPITAL

The Brooklyn City Hospital was officially incorporated in 1845. The trustees purchased a private two-story wooden house on what is now Hudson Avenue, and that was the hospital's first home. The first patient was admitted on December 10, 1847. In 1852 the first hospital building was built on Raymond Street (now Ashland Place), adjoining the then new Washington (now Fort Greene) Park. It was a state-of-the-art modern hospital with 160 beds, and was built in large part through the generosity of Augustus Graham (1776–1851), the wealthy distiller who was one of early Brooklyn's most public-spirited citizens. When the new facility was announced, the *Brooklyn Daily Eagle* in 1850 wrote: "Brooklyn is at last to have a hospital. The stain that has so long rested on the escutcheon of the 'City of Churches' is to be wiped away."

During the Civil War the hospital cared for wounded soldiers. In 1880 the hospital established the first nursing school in Brooklyn, and the second in New York State.

The hospital changed its name to Brooklyn Hospital in 1883, dropping the word *City*, which (according to a report of the time, quoted on Brooklyn Hospital Center's Web site) "conveyed the erroneous idea that [the hospital] was a municipal corporation and supported by the city proper." The hospital's ambulance service, begun in 1890, covered downtown Brooklyn, Fort Greene, the Brooklyn Navy Yard, and Bedford-Stuyvesant.

The 20th century saw mergers and modernizations that increased the size and capabilities of Brooklyn Hospital. Between 1969 and 1980 a sweeping reconstruction of facilities took place in accordance with a master plan.

Brooklyn Hospital, DeKalb Avenue at Raymond Street (now Ashland Place), c. 1900.

In 1976 a 20-story staff residence, Maynard Center, was erected on the site of the old Raymond Street Jail at DeKalb Avenue and Ashland Place. (Maynard Center's architects, Walker O. Cain & Associates, were technically the successor firm of McKim, Mead & White, designers of the Prison Ship Martyrs Monument across the street in Fort Greene Park.)

In 1998, the Brooklyn Hospital Center (its official name since 1990) became part of the New York-Presbyterian Healthcare System, and between 1997 and 2001 undertook another major renovation and rebuilding project. Today the hospital has 440 beds.

BROOKLYN TECH

Brooklyn Technical High School—"Brooklyn Tech"—was the idea of Albert Colston, a math teacher at Manual Training (now John Jay) High School in Park Slope. After World War I he felt the nation needed to improve the training of young people in math, engineering, and science. He first undertook his program at Manual Training in 1919, and the new Brooklyn Technical High School opened in 1922 on Flatbush Avenue Extension and Concord Street, in what can be argued is the northwesternmost corner of Fort Greene, four blocks from the Brooklyn Navy Yard. The school enrolled 2,400 students in its first year.

On September 17, 1930, Mayor Jimmy Walker broke ground for a new building for Brooklyn Tech at 29 Fort Greene Place, at DeKalb Avenue. The first classes were held in the new eleven-story, "modern Gothic" building (which, said the *New York Times*, "rises above the surrounding tenements and stores like a cathedral") in 1933. With a capacity of 5,500 students, the new Brooklyn Tech was the largest and, at $5.5 million, most expensive public school ever built in New York. Courses in such subjects as aeronautics and radio broadcasting gave the school a cutting-edge aura. The building housed 165 classrooms and laboratories, as well as a swimming pool, a gymnasium, and a 3,000-seat auditorium. The tower of the building also contained living quarters for Dr. Colston.

From 1938 Brooklyn Tech hosted the Board of Education radio station, WNYE. The 304-foot radio antenna still rises above Fort Greene today. Another distinguishing feature of the building is the WPA mural *The History of Mankind in Terms of Mental and Physical Labor*, located in the foyer. The work of Maxwell Starr, the mural traces the development of mankind through the 1930s and includes depictions of scientists and inventors. It was restored in 1997 through the Adopt-a-Mural program of the Municipal Art Society of New York.

During World War II, Brooklyn Tech provided war job training programs for unemployed men in courses such as aircraft mechanics, radio operation, and ship carpentry.

Females were first admitted to the school in 1970 and renovations were made shortly thereafter to provide adequate toilet, shower, and locker facilities for these new students.

Brooklyn Technical High School, its 304-foot-high antenna (the highest structure in Brooklyn) visible on the upper left, on DeKalb Avenue.

With the help of its active alumni foundation, and through partnerships with corporations, city government, and the Department of Education, Brooklyn Tech opened a pre-engineering lab in 2005 and a $600,000 Con Edison Environmental Science and Engineering Laboratory the following year. Notable alumni include Congressman Gary Ackerman, songwriter Gerry Goffin, folk singer Richard Fariña, longtime BAM president Harvey Lichtenstein, Living Colour guitarist Vernon Reid, Congressman Anthony Weiner, science fiction author Frederick Pohl, Nobel Prize-winning biologist George Wald, and Barnes & Noble chairman Leonard Riggio.

The Brooklyn Flea in the glorious former banking room of One Hanson Place.

CODA

Clinton Hill resident Jonathan Butler founded the Brownstoner blog in 2004. The blog rapidly became the principal forum for news and discussion of brownstone Brooklyn real estate, architecture, and preservation. In 2007 the Web site Outside.in, which tracks and indexes blogs around the nation that concern themselves with discussion of local issues, conducted a study to determine the "bloggiest neighborhood in America." The winner? Clinton Hill—and the Brownstoner blog had more than a little to do with that. Not content simply to be the king of Brooklyn bloggers, Butler teamed with Eric Demby to create the Brooklyn Flea in April 2008. The Brooklyn Flea is New York's classiest "flea market," a carefully culled collection of all manner of local dealers in antiques and fine craft items—and local foods—representing the creative entrepreneurial spirit of many Brooklynites in the early 21st century. The Brooklyn Flea originated in the schoolyard of Bishop Loughlin Memorial High School, on Lafayette Avenue between Clermont and Vanderbilt avenues—the site of the Roman Catholic cathedral that never was. As this guide goes to press in the summer of 2010, the Flea operates there on Saturday afternoons, and, on Sundays, in the glorious former banking room of One Hanson Place, the onetime Williamsburgh Savings Bank Building.

The 512-foot-high Williamsburgh Savings Bank Building, designed by Halsey, McCormack & Helmer, is a proud symbol of Brooklyn. Erected in 1929 just south of the Brooklyn Academy of Music, it represented the continued movement south of the Brooklyn central business district—a movement halted first by the Great Depression and then by economic and demographic changes of the postwar years. The building, long the tallest in Brooklyn, has stood in splendid isolation for years. Its banking room—a lofty space rich with marbles and mosaics—ranks as one of New York's most magnificent interior spaces. The presence in that space of the wildly successful Brooklyn Flea brings together old and new visions of Fort Greene, and of Brooklyn,

The interior of the BAM Harvey Theater, 651 Fulton Street at Rockwell Place, is a "preserved ruin" for which architects Hardy Holzman Pfeiffer took their cue from director Peter Brook's Théâtre des Bouffes du Nord in Paris. The Majestic Theater opened in 1903 but had fallen on hard times when it was renovated by the Brooklyn Academy of Music in 1987. The new venue opened with Brook's production of *The Mahabharata*. The theater was renamed in 1999 for BAM president Harvey Lichtenstein.

and serves as a potent reminder that there is no foreordained future for Brooklyn neighborhoods, but only the uncertain course of history, of failures and successes, of urban character lost and urban character found—or invented on the background of past glories and upsets. Fort Greene and Clinton Hill, for all their rich uniqueness, are also microcosms of urban America, and are in all their vicissitudes never less than enthralling.

You can follow Francis Morrone on walking tours of Fort Greene and Clinton Hill, and listen to long-time residents reflect on their neighborhood. This audio is available for download to an mp3 player from our website *www.brooklynhistory.org* or you can visit us at the iTunes store by searching for the Brooklyn Historical Society's free podcast.

Produced by Sady Sullivan, Director of Oral History, Brooklyn Historical Society. Interviews recorded by Alexis Taines Coe; Ann Heppermann; Selma Jackson, 2008–2009 Revson Fellow and Lafayette Avenue Presbyterian Church member; and Sady Sullivan.

FORT GREENE

🎧 ① Fort Greene Park—Bounded by DeKalb Avenue on the south, Washington Park on the east, Myrtle Avenue on the north, and Fort Greene Place on the west.

🎧 ② Prison Ship Martyrs Monument—At the crest of the hill in Fort Greene Park.

🎧 ③ Fort Greene Houses (Ingersoll and Whitman Houses)— Bounded by Myrtle Avenue, St. Edward's Street, the Brooklyn-Queens Expressway, and Carlton Avenue. Within the houses' boundaries, on St. Edward's Street opposite Auburn Place, stands the Church of St. Michael and St. Edward, designed by John J. Deery and built in 1902. Its distinctive design features twin high round towers ringed by spiky finials. Inside, a new altar and cross were added in 1972, making use of salvaged bits of the Myrtle Avenue elevated railway that once ran past the church and that was dismantled in 1969.

🎧 ④ Washington Park—Between Myrtle and DeKalb avenues. The two blocks of Cumberland Street facing Fort Greene Park are called Washington Park, which was the original name of Fort

Greene Park. The AIA Guide to New York City says, "These two blocks of brownstones were once the equal in social stature of any in Brooklyn." The 51 houses range in date between 1866 and 1884. The majority of the houses are Italianate brownstones. William C. Kingsley, an early promoter of the Brooklyn Bridge and later the president of the Brooklyn Bridge Company, lived at No. 176. Abner Keeney, who with his neighbor Kingsley was the contractor who built Prospect Park, lived next door at No. 175. Kingsley and Keeney were also once owners of the *Brooklyn Daily Eagle*.

5 Brooklyn Technical High School—Southeast corner Fort Greene Place and DeKalb Avenue. Brooklyn Tech's skyline-dominating 465-foot-high antenna, rising from the roof 132 feet high, is the tallest structure in Brooklyn.

6 175 Carlton Avenue (house)—Between Willoughby and Myrtle avenues. Richard Wright lived at this address in 1938 when he wrote his novel *Native Son* (published in 1940). At the time he lived here, he had just published his short story collection *Uncle Tom's Children*. Wright worked on the manuscript of *Native Son* in the early mornings while sitting on the top of the hill in Fort Greene Park, near the Prison Ship Martyrs Monument. At the time, he was employed by the Federal Writers Project and was one of the authors of their New York City Guide published in 1939.

7 Simpson Methodist Episcopal Church— Now Eglise Baptiste d'Expression Française (formerly the Jewish Center of Fort Greene)—Southeast corner of Willoughby and Clermont avenues. Designed by Brooklyn architect William A. Mundell and built in 1869, this is one of the loveliest early Romanesque Revival churches in New York City.

8 Cathedral of the Immaculate Conception (proposed site)/Bishop Loughlin Memorial High School—Bounded by Lafayette, Vanderbilt, Greene, and Clermont avenues. Bishop Loughlin Memorial High School, a Roman Catholic high school whose alumni include former New York City mayor Rudolph Giuliani, and its schoolyard occupy the site that had been designated for Brooklyn's Roman Catholic cathedral. The Bishop Loughlin schoolyard is the site of the Brooklyn Flea, a highly popular outdoor market, founded in 2008, that takes place on Saturday afternoons. Nearby, at 367 Clermont Avenue (northeast corner of Greene Avenue) is a distinctive Victorian house built in 1883–87 as the Roman Catholic bishop's residence. Designed by Patrick C. Keely, architect of the ill-fated cathedral, the house now serves Bishop Loughlin Boarding School. The bishop now resides at 241 Clinton Avenue.

The former Simpson Methodist Episcopal Church (now Eglise Baptiste d'Expression Française) is one of Brooklyn's finest early Romanesque Revival churches, built in 1869 at Willoughby and Clermont avenues.

9 Our Lady Queen of All Saints—Lafayette Avenue northwest corner of Vanderbilt Avenue. The Roman Catholic cathedral may never have been built across Lafayette Avenue, but this very distinctive Roman Catholic church and school, designed by Gustave Steinback and built in 1910–15, seems almost cathedral-like. The stained-glass windows by the Locke Decorative Company are notable.

10 Masonic Temple—317 Clermont Avenue northeast corner of Lafayette Avenue. Built in 1906, the Masonic Temple was designed by Lord & Hewlett and Pell & Corbett, and its use of colorful ornamental glazed terra-cotta is notable. Architect J. Monroe Hewlett was the father-in-law of engineer and visionary R. Buckminster Fuller.

11 200 Lafayette Avenue—Southeast corner of Vanderbilt Avenue. The pitched roof and octagonal cupola are Italian villa-like flourishes on this otherwise Greek Revival frame house built around 1850. This house dates from right around the time of the opening of Washington Park.

12 260 Cumberland Street between DeKalb and Lafayette avenues. The poet Marianne Moore resided in this apartment building between 1929 and 1965. The building was erected in 1912.

13 Lafayette Avenue Presbyterian Church—Lafayette Avenue southeast corner of South Oxford Street. The Romanesque Revival church was built in 1860–62. This is where the poet Marianne Moore worshipped regularly and where her funeral was held in 1972. The church's Sunday school annex at 85 South Oxford Street has since 2008 been home to the celebrated Irondale Ensemble Project, a theatrical company founded in 1983.

14 South Portland Avenue between Lafayette and DeKalb avenues—In the "50 Best Blocks in New York" feature in the October 12–18, 2006, issue of *Time Out New York*, the block of South Portland Avenue between Lafayette and DeKalb avenues was ranked No. 1. It's easy to see why. Most of the many Italianate brownstones are in superb condition, including the intricately carved floral brackets on either side of the parlor-floor doorways. At the end of the block is Fort Greene Park, and the block's residents are only a short walk from popular cafés and restaurants and from public transportation.

15 Mark Morris Dance Center—Lafayette Avenue northeast corner of Rockwell Place. The *New York Times* calls the center, designed by Beyer Blinder Belle and built in 1999–2001, "the most lavish dance center in New York." It is the headquarters of the world-famous Mark Morris Dance Group, founded in 1980.

🎧 16 Brooklyn Academy of Music—30 Lafayette Avenue between Ashland Place and St. Felix Street. The 1905–08 building designed by Herts & Tallant was recently restored.

The Central Methodist Church was built together with One Hanson Place next door and designed by the same architects, Halsey McCormack & Helmer; oddly, the church was built with commercial storefronts but the adjacent bank tower was not.

17 Central Methodist Church— Hanson Place northwest corner of St. Felix Street. Built in 1929–31, this distinctive church, unusually designed to include commercial storefronts, was designed by Halsey, McCormack & Helmer at the same time as their adjacent Williamsburgh Savings Bank Building. Interestingly, the adjacent bank building contains no commercial storefronts.

18 One Hanson Place—Former Williamsburgh Savings Bank Building—1 Hanson Place northeast corner of Ashland Place. At 512 feet, this was for seventy years the tallest building in Brooklyn. Designed by Halsey, McCormack & Helmer and built in 1929, this is one of New York City's classic skyscrapers, topped by a distinctive dome and four-faced clock. The dramatically lofty former banking room, with its variety of marbles, mosaics, and elaborate ironwork, is one of the outstanding spaces of its kind in New York. Before its recent conversion to residential use, this building is said to have housed more dentist offices than any other single building in America. The *New York Times* reports

(February 2, 2003) that the corner of Hanson and Ashland places just outside the building has an unusual "microclimate" that may make it the coldest and windiest spot in New York City.

(left) The majestic One Hanson Place was built in 1929 as the headquarters of the Williamsburgh Savings Bank and was for many years the tallest building in Brooklyn.

(right) The magnificent banking hall of the former Williamsburgh Savings Bank Building at One Hanson Place features some of the finest mosaics in New York.

19 Hanson Place Seventh Day Adventist Church—Before 1963 the Hanson Place Baptist Church. Hanson Place southeast corner of South Portland Avenue. Built in 1857–60, this Italianate church attains grandeur by including a tetrastyle Corinthian portico. Inside, it has the kind of semicircular, "theatrical" seating plan that had recently been pioneered by Henry Ward Beecher's Plymouth Church (1849) in Brooklyn Heights.

20 40 Acres and a Mule Filmworks—75 South Elliott Place between DeKalb and Lafayette avenues.

21 Long Island University—Brooklyn Center—Campus bounded by DeKalb Avenue on the south, Flatbush Avenue Extension on the west, Willoughby Street on the north, and Ashland Place on the east.

22 Brooklyn Hospital Center—DeKalb Avenue between Ashland Place and Fort Greene Place. Originally called Brooklyn City Hospital, Brooklyn Hospital Center was founded in 1845 and admitted its first patient two years later. It has been at its present location since 1852. The hospital today has 440 beds.

23 James E. Davis Arts Building—80 Hanson Place between South Portland Avenue and South Elliott Place. 80 Hanson Place—the James E. Davis Arts Building—was developed in 2003 by the Brooklyn Academy of Music Local Development Corporation as part of its vision of a BAM Cultural District. It is home to the Museum of Contemporary African Diasporan Arts, *BOMB* Magazine, StoryCorps, Franklin Furnace, and other creative tenants.

24 Brooklyn Paramount Theater—Northeast corner of Flatbush Avenue Extension and DeKalb Avenue. One of America's great movie palaces, the Brooklyn Paramount opened on Nov. 23, 1928, with *Manhattan Cocktail* starring Nancy Carroll. It closed on Aug. 21, 1962, with a showing of *Hatari* starring John Wayne. Designed by renowned movie palace architects Rapp & Rapp of Chicago, the Paramount was as famous for stage performances as for movies. Bing Crosby and Buddy Holly are two performers strongly associated with the Brooklyn Paramount, which was also the location in 1955 of disc jockey Alan Freed's first rock-and-roll stage shows. In 1962 the theater was converted into the athletic center of Long Island University.

25 BAM Harvey Theater—651 Fulton Street between Rockwell and Ashland places. Originally called the Majestic Theater, it was built in 1903. Empty since 1968, in 1987 it was renovated by the Brooklyn Academy of Music (BAM) and architects Hardy Holzman Pfeiffer into a BAM annex. The initial production was *The Mahabharata* staged by Peter Brook, and the theater renovation was modeled on the "functional ruin" aesthetic of Brook's Théâtre des Bouffes du Nord in Paris. In 1999 the Majestic was renamed for BAM impresario Harvey Lichtenstein.

26 Brooklyn Music School—122–128 St. Felix Street between Lafayette Avenue and Hanson Place. The Brooklyn Music School (below left) was founded in 1912, and moved to its present complex (comprising four former row houses) on St. Felix Street in 1920. Founded as a musical settlement house offering training to poor inner-city children, the school offers on-site music and dance instruction to 400 students, as well as public school outreach programs. The school has a faculty of 32 and the building contains a 266-seat theater.

The Brooklyn Music School was founded in 1912 and eight years later moved to its present location, comprising several former town houses, on St. Felix Street behind the Brooklyn Academy of Music.

27 Strand Theater—Fulton Street northeast corner of Rockwell Place. The Strand Theater was built in 1918 and had 4,000 seats. Today it is home to the world-famous Urban Glass and to BRIC (Brooklyn Information and Culture). Urban Glass, founded in 1977, is the largest public art-glass facility in the world, offering studio space for glass artists, classes (including ones in conjunction with New York University and Long Island University), open houses, a shop, and the Robert Lehman Gallery.

On Fulton Street and Rockwell Place, next to the BAM Harvey Theatre, stands another former movie theater, the Strand, which today houses the world-renowned Urban Glass, the largest public art-glass facility in the world.

CLINTON HILL

🎧 ① Charles Pratt house—232 Clinton Avenue between Willoughby and DeKalb avenues. The house, an Italianate suburban villa, was designed by Ebenezer Roberts and built in 1874. It is now part of the campus of St. Joseph's College.

② Frederic B. Pratt house—229 Clinton Avenue between Willoughby and DeKalb avenues. Now the Caroline Ladd Pratt House, a residence for foreign students at Pratt Institute, this house was designed by Babb, Cook & Willard and built in 1895 for Frederic Bayley Pratt, a son of Charles Pratt.

3 Charles Millard Pratt house—241 Clinton Avenue between Willoughby and DeKalb avenues. Charles Pratt, who lived across the street, built this house in 1890–93 as a wedding gift for his eldest son Charles Millard Pratt. In their book *New York 1880*, Robert A.M. Stern, Thomas Mellins, and David Fishman call it "the climax of the impact of the Richardsonian Romanesque on urban villa building." Designed by prominent Brooklyn architect William B. Tubby, it is now the residence of the Roman Catholic Bishop of Brooklyn.

4 George Dupont Pratt house—245 Clinton Avenue. This Georgian Revival mansion was designed by Babb, Cook & Willard and built in 1901 for a son of Charles Pratt. It is now part of St. Joseph's College.

5 John Arbuckle house—315 Clinton Avenue between Lafayette Avenue and DeKalb Street. John Arbuckle, who with his brother co-founded the Arbuckle Coffee Company, built this Romanesque Revival mansion in 1887–88; the architect was Montrose W. Morris.

The last of the surviving mansions of the sons of Charles Pratt—George Dupont Pratt's house at 245 Clinton Avenue— was designed by Babb, Cook & Willard and erected in 1901. It is now owned by St. Joseph's College.

6 Underwood Park—Lafayette Avenue between Washington and Waverly avenues. The small park is the site of the home of John Thomas Underwood (1857–1937), a pioneer of the typewriter industry. His widow and daughter donated the house to the City of New York so that it could be demolished to make way for a park, which opened in 1956. (It is said the widow and daughter saw that Clinton Hill was entering a period of physical deterioration and they did not want their family house to be a part of that.) Note the adjacent former Graham Home for Old Ladies on Washington Avenue. Built in 1851, the lovely Italianate building has been converted to apartments.

Emmanuel Baptist Church, on Lafayette Avenue at St. James Place, was built by Charles Pratt. Designed by Francis H. Kimball, the church was erected in 1886-87.

7 Emmanuel Baptist Church—Lafayette Avenue northwest corner of St. James Place. Charles Pratt funded the construction of this impressive Baptist church designed by Francis H. Kimball (architect of Park Slope's Montauk Club) and built in 1886–87. It is an original mix of 12th-century French Romanesque, 13th-century French Gothic, and 14th-century French Gothic.

8 Adelphi Academy—St. James Place between Lafayette Avenue and Clifton Place. The northern building was built in 1867 and designed by Mundell & Teckritz; the southern building was added in 1888 and designed by Charles C. Haight.

9 St. Luke's Church (Episcopal)—520 Clinton Avenue between Fulton Street and Atlantic Avenue. This grand and original Romanesque Revival church was designed by John W. Welch and built in 1888–91.

10 Charles Adolph Schieren house—485 Clinton Avenue between Gates and Greene avenues. Brooklyn mayor Charles Adolph Schieren built this house in 1889. It was designed by the prominent Brooklyn architect William B. Tubby in a distinctive hybrid Romanesque/Renaissance style.

Cornelius Hoagland, founder of Royal Baking Powder and benefactor of Long Island College Hospital, built his house at 410 Clinton Avenue in 1882; the Parfitt brothers were the architects.

11 Cornelius N. Hoagland house—410 Clinton Avenue between Gates and Greene avenues. Cornelius N. Hoagland, founder of Royal Baking Powder and benefactor of the Hoagland Laboratory for bacteriological research at Long Island College Hospital, built this Queen Anne-style house in 1882; the Parfitt Brothers were the architects.

12 Pratt Institute—Superblock bounded by DeKalb Avenue on the south, Classon Avenue on the east, Willoughby Avenue on the north, and Hall Street on the west.

Memorial Hall, designed by John Mead Howells, was built on the Pratt Institute campus in 1926-27.

Main Building—Ryerson Walk between DeKalb and Willoughby avenues. This was designed by Lamb & Rich and built in 1885–87 in a utilitarian Romanesque Revival style not unlike many industrial buildings of the time. In fact, Charles Pratt wanted Pratt Institute's first building to be designed in such a way that, if Pratt Institute failed, it could be easily converted into a factory. The distinctive porch was added by architect William B. Tubby in 1894.

South Hall—Built in 1889–91, South Hall was designed by William B. Tubby and, like the Main Building, evokes the industrial architecture of the Romanesque Revival.

Memorial Hall—Pratt Institute added this in 1926–27; designed by John Mead Howells (son of novelist William Dean Howells), its Romanesque Revival style is more like that of a synagogue than a factory.

Machine Shop Building (also called East Building)—Built in 1887 and one of the two original buildings of the Pratt Institute campus, it can be accessed via the gate between the Main Building and

South Hall. This was Pratt Institute's original mechanical plant and contains three steam engines installed in 1900; remarkably, they continue to provide some of the power to the campus. Meticulously maintained, the steam engines, intended to be teaching tools as well as to provide power to the campus, can be viewed in action today. Together with a collection of architectural and industrial odds and ends, they make the East Building into a museum of industrial archaeology.

Pratt Institute's East Building was built in 1887 and is one of the two original buildings of the Pratt campus.

Library—Hall Street between DeKalb and Willoughby avenues, east side. Pratt Institue's library was conceived not only as a laboratory for the institute's renowned library school, but also served as Brooklyn's first free public library. Between 1896 and 1940 it was open to all Brooklynites over the age of 14. Today it is open only to Pratt Institute students. The original part of the building, in a Romanesque Revival style, was designed by William B. Tubby and built in 1896. The north porch was added in 1936 by architect John Mead Howells. A major renovation in 1982 expanded the library underground and created the south terrace with windows looking down onto the subterranean stacks.

The Thrift—Northeast corner of Ryerson Walk and DeKalb Avenue. In 1889 Charles Pratt founded a savings-and-loan to help working people obtain mortgages. In 1916 it moved from its original location, on the site of Memorial Hall, to the present neo-Georgian building. The Thrift ceased business in the 1940s.

13 99 Ryerson Street between Myrtle Avenue and Park Avenue— This modest row house is the only known surviving residence of Walt Whitman. The poet lived in this house in 1855 when he published *Leaves of Grass*. Today the house has vinyl siding.

14 178 Ryerson Street between Myrtle and Willoughby avenues— Site of the home and office of Dr. Susan Smith McKinney Steward.

15 St. Mary's Church (Episcopal)—230 Classon Avenue northwest corner of Willoughby Avenue. This beautiful Gothic Revival church, designed by Richard T. Auchmuty, was built in 1858–59.

16 Lefferts-Laidlaw house—136 Clinton Avenue between Myrtle and Park avenues. This imposing Greek Revival house, with a four-columned temple front, was built in c. 1836–40. It was designated as a New York City landmark in 2001.

17 Drake Brothers Bakery—77 Clinton Avenue between Myrtle and Park avenues. By the time this reinforced-concrete factory

building was built in 1913–14 (Dodge & Morrison, architects), Drake was one of the leading commercial bakers in the country. In 1914, this bakery produced fifteen tons of pound cake a day. Products that emerged with imperfect shapes were given out for free to neighborhood children.

The Drake Brothers Bakery was built on Clinton Avenue between Myrtle and Park avenues in 1913-14.

18 Sacred Heart Roman Catholic Church—Clermont Avenue between Park and Flushing avenues. This large Roman Catholic church was erected in 1874–77 to serve the neighborhood's working-class Irish population. It was designed in the Gothic style by the major Brooklyn church architect Thomas F. Houghton, the son-in-law of Patrick C. Keely, architect of the ill-fated cathedral in Fort Greene.

19 Mergenthaler Linotype Building—Park Avenue between Hall and Ryerson streets. The building on the northwest corner of Park Avenue and Ryerson Street was a pioneering reinforced-concrete factory designed by America's preeminent industrial architect Albert Kahn (famous for his Detroit automobile plants) and built in 1907. Kahn extended the factory to the west in 1912. Other buildings of Mergenthaler Linotype were built near here up to 1942. The Mergenthaler company manufactured the machines that once dominated the printing of magazines, newspapers, and books. This was one of the largest factory complexes in New York City.

20 Site of Wallabout Market—North of Flushing Avenue between Washington and Ryerson streets. Brooklyn's large produce market (once the second largest such market in the world) was established here in the 1880s. In the 1890s new market buildings with romantic Dutch gables, designed by William B. Tubby and ordered by Brooklyn building commissioner Alfred Tredway White, were erected. The market was razed during World War II when the federal government felt the need of expanding the adjacent Brooklyn Navy Yard.

21 Rockwood Chocolate Factory—Northwest corner of Waverly Avenue and Park Avenue. This handsome brick-and-limestone-faced reinforced-concrete factory building was erected in 1910 by the largest chocolate maker and cocoa processor in New York State (and at one time second in the country only to Hershey). The factory, designed by Brooklyn's Parfitt Brothers with a first floor and showroom by the great American architect Ernest Flagg, operated here until 1967. Rockwood actually operated a campus of factories on Waverly and Washington avenues between Park and Flushing avenues that is now a National Register historic district, though not (yet) a New York City landmark, which provides much greater protection.